# Oxford Encyclopedia of Chess Games

Edited by David Levy & Kevin O'Connell

# Oxford Encyclopedia of Chess Games

## David N. L. Levy
## and
## Kevin J. O'Connell



**Originally printed in 1981 as "*Oxford Encyclopedia of Chess Games: Volume 1: 1485-1866*". Volume 2 was never published, so the title has been shortened to "*Oxford Encyclopedia of Chess Games*".**

**Current Printing March, 2009 by
Ishi Press in New York and Tokyo**



**ISBN 0-923891-54-4
978-0-923891-54-1**

**Ishi Press International
1664 Davidson Avenue, Suite 1B
Bronx NY 10453
USA
1-917-507-7226**

**Printed in the United States of America**

To Philidor

# Contents

## INTRODUCTION

In this encyclopedia we set out to publish all the important games of chess which have been played since the modern laws came into force in the late 1400s. We have chosen to include all the recorded games played up to 1800, every game played in all major tournaments and matches from 1801, and every traceable game of each player who was at one time one of the best two players in the world.

The games are arranged chronologically. Within each year the tournaments are presented first, followed by the matches, and then the miscellaneous games. Each game is allotted a unique code number which locates it in the book. Thus, **1849-LON-3** is the third game played in the tournament London 1849. All tournaments are identified by date and place. We use the year in which the tournament started for events played in December–January. The complete list of places and codes is on page xviii.

Matches are indicated by the symbol ⚔ and the initial letters of the players, so that the second game of the Lewis–Wilson match of 1819 is **1819-⚔LW-2**. Miscellaneous games are shown by ★, as in **1841-★PS-1**; for further information see the complete list of symbols.

At the top of each game appears the date on which it was played, the place (for miscellaneous games) and, if the game has analysis, the name of the annotator. At the end of the game appears the bibliographic reference which explains (through the full bibliography on pages 455–6) where the game was found.

The computer-generated indexes are the most detailed ever produced for a chess book, and present a mine of information and statistical analysis. The 'player index' gives, for each player in the book, a complete list of opponents, with the result and code number for each game, and for every major player a complete tournament and match record. The 'openings index' lists every opening variation which appears in the book, and the code number for every game played with each. The 'endgame index' refers the reader to all those games in which particular endgames occur.

These games were buried deep in the chess libraries of the world. Our principal sources have been the British Library (whose system of Cyrillic transliteration we have employed), the Bodleian Library at Oxford, the Bibliotheca van der Linde-Niemeijeriana, Koninklijke Bibliotheek, 's-Gravenhage, and the John G. White Collection, Cleveland Public Library, Cleveland, Ohio. Of the many friends, acquaintances, and scholars who have helped us in our search we should particularly like to thank Mr Jeremy Gaige, Miss K. M. E. Murray (for permission to use the H. J. R. Murray collection at the Bodleian Library), Mr David Lawson, Mr Craig Pritchett, Mr Ken Whyld, and Mr Baruch H. Wood.

## INLEIDING

De bedoeling van deze encyclopedie is de publikatie van alle belangrijke schaakpartijen die gespeeld zijn sinds de huidige regels aan het eind van de vijftiende eeuw geldig werden. Wij besloten alle genoteerde partijen op te nemen die vóór het jaar 1800 gespeeld werden, voorts iedere partij van de belangrijke toernooien en matches vanaf 1801 en tenslotte elke te achterhalen partij van alle spelers die op een gegeven moment één van de beste twee spelers ter wereld waren.

De partijen zijn chronologisch per jaar opgenomen. Voor ieder jaar zijn eerst de toernooipartijen afgedrukt, daarna de partijen uit matches en vervolgens de afzonderlijke partijen. Iedere partij heeft een eigen codenummer die hem zijn plaats in het boek geeft. Bijvoorbeeld: **1849-LON-3** betekent de derde partij in het toernooi van Londen in 1849. Alle toernooien zijn aangegeven met datum en plaats. Voor toernooien die in december–januari gehouden werden, hebben wij het jaar aangehouden waarin het toernooi is begonnen. De volledige lijst van plaatsnamen en codes vindt men op de pagina xviii.

Tweekampen worden aangeduid door het symbool ✕ en de beginletters van de namen van de spelers. Zo betekent **1819-✕ LW-2** de tweede partij van de match Lewis–Wilson in 1819. Op zichzelf staande partijen worden met ★ aangegeven, zoals bijvoorbeeld in **1941-★PS-1**. Voor verdere informatie verwijzen wij naar de volledige lijst van de symbolen.

Boven iedere partij staan vermeld de datum, de plaats (voor op zichzelf staande partijen) en, in geval van een analyse, de naam van de commentator. Aan het slot van de partij volgt vermelding van de bibliografische bron die, via de volledige bibliografie op de pagina's 455–6, de herkomst van de partij aangeeft.

De door een computer samengestelde registers zijn meer gedetailleerd dan in welke schaakuitgave tot dusvez dan ook en zij bieden een schat aan inlichtingen en mogelijkheden tot statistiche analyse. Het register op spelers bevat, voor iedere in het boek voorkomende speler, een volledige lijst van tegenstanders, met resultaat en codenummer van iedere partij en tevens van de belangrijker spelers een volledig toernooi- en tweekampenoverzicht. Het openingenregister vermeldt iedere openingsvariant met de codenummers van de partijen waarin deze varianten zijn gespeeld. Het eindspelregister verwijst de gebruiker naar alle partijen waarin bijzondere eindspelen voorkomen.

Zeer veel partijen lagen diep begraven in de schaakbibliotheken over degehele wereld. Onze voornaamste bronnen zijn geweest het British Museum in London (wij hebben het cyrillische transcriptiesysteem van het museum overgenomen), de Bodleian Library in Oxford, de Bibliotheca Van der Linde-Niemeijeriana in de Koninklijke Bibliotheek te's Gravenhage en de John G. White Collection van de Cleveland Public Library, Cleveland, Ohio. Van de vele vrienden, relaties en wetenschapsmensen die ons bij het speurwerk hebben geholpen willen wij vooral dank zeggen aan mevrouw K. M. E. Murray (voor haar toestemming gebruik te mogen maken van de H. J. R. Murray-verzameling in de Bodleian Library) en de heren Jeremy Gaige, David Lawson, Craig Pritchett Ken Whyld en Baruch H. Wood.

## INTRODUCTION

Dans cette encyclopédie, notre but est de publier l'histoire de toutes les parties d'échecs importantes jouées depuis l'entrée en viguer des règles modernes vers la fin du quinzième siècle. Nous avons décidé d'y inclure toutes les parties répertoriées jouées avant 1800, toutes les parties jouées dans tous les principaux tournois et concours depuis 1801, et toutes les parties connues de chaque joueur d'échecs considéré à son époque comme l'un des meilleurs joueurs du monde.

Les parties sont classées par ordre chronologique. Pour chaque année nous avons présenté tout d'abord les tournois, suivis des matches, et enfin des diverses parties. Un chiffre codifié attribué à chaque partie facilite l'orientation du lecteur. Ansi, **1849-LON-3** signifie la troisième partie du tournoi ayante eu lieu à Londres en 1849. La date et le lieu sont indiqués pour chaque tournoi. Dans le cas des tournois débutant en décembre et se poursuivant en janvier, l'année mentionnée est celle du début de tournoi. Une liste complète des lieux des tournois et des codes se trouve page xviii.

L'emblème ⚔ et les initiales des joueurs dénotent les matches; ainsi la deuxième partie du match Lewis–Wilson en 1819 est: **1819-⚔LW-2**. Les diverses parties sont indiquées par ★: par exemple **1841-★PS-1**. Pour d'autres détails, se reporter à la liste complète des symboles.

Au début de commentaire de chaque partie nous indiquons la date, le lieu (pour les parties diverses) et, en cas d'analyse de la partie, le nom de l'annotateur. En fin de commentaire se trouve la référence bibliographique qui indique (au moyen de la bibliographie complète page 544–6) où la partie a été trouvée.

Les index, dressés par ordinateur, sont les plus détaillés qui aient été publiés dans un livre d'échecs, et sont une mine d'information et d'analyse statistique. L'index des joueurs donne, pour chaque joueur cité, une liste complète de ses adversaires, avec le résultat et le chiffre codifié de chaque partie; et pour chaque joueur célèbre un dossier complet des tournois et des matches. L'index des débuts de parties indique chaque début différent cité dans l'ouvrage, et le chiffre codifié de chaque partie où le début est différent. L'index des fins de parties renvoie le lecteur à toutes les parties ayant des fins particulières.

L'histoire de ces parties d'échecs était enfouie dans les bibliothèques d'échecs du monde. Nos sources principales ont été le British Museum (dont nous avons employé le système cyrillique de translitération), la Bibliothèque Bodléienne à Oxford, Bibliotheca van der Linde-Niemeijeriana, Koninklijke Bibliotheek, 'z Gravenhage, et la Collection de John G. White à la Bibliothèque de Cleveland, Ohio. Parmi tous les amis, personnes de notre connaissance et experts qui nous ont aidés, nous voudrions remercier particulièrement Monsieur Jeremy Gaige, Miss K. M. E. Murray (qui nous a donné la permission de nous servir de la Collection de H. J. R. Murray à la Bibliothèque Bodléienne), Monsieur David Lawson, Monsieur Craig Pritchett, Monsieur Ken Whyld, et Monsieur Baruch Wood.

## EINLEITUNG

Das Vorhaben dieser Enzyklopädie ist es, alle bedeutenden Schachpartien zu veröffentlichen, die seit der Einführung der modernen Regeln gegen Ende des 15. Jahrhunderts gespielt worden sind. Wir haben uns entschieden, alle belegten Partien bis zum Jahre 1800 aufzunehmen, ebenso alle bei bedeutenden Turnieren und Wettkämpfen seit 1801 gespielten Partien, sowie jede auffindbare Partie aller Spieler, die einmal zu den zwei besten Spielern der Welt gehört haben.

Die Spiele sind chronologisch nach Jahreszahlen angeordnet. Innerhalb der einzelnen Jahre sind die Turniere zuerst aufgeführt, darauf folgen die Zweikämpfe und dann die vermischten Partien. Jeder Partie wurde eine eigene Kennziffer gegeben, anhand deren sie im Buch auffindbar ist. So bedeutet beispielsweise **1849-LON-3**, daß es sich um die dritte Partie beim Turnier London 1849 handelt. Bei allen Turnieren sind Zeitpunkt und Ort angegeben. Für Begegnungen, die in den Monaten Dezember–Januar stattfanden, ist das Jahr des Turnierbeginns ausschlaggebend. Ein vollständiges Verzeichnis der Austragungsorte und Kennziffern befindet sich auf der Seite xviii.

Wettkämpfe sind durch das Symbol ⚔ und die Anfangsbuchstaben der Spieler gekennzeichnet, **1819-⚔LW-2** ist also die zweite Partie in dem Match Lewis–Wilson aus dem Jahre 1819. Vermischte Partien sind durch ★ gekennzeichnet, wie z.B. **1841-★PS-1**. Weitere Hinweise sind der vollständigen Liste der Symbole zu entnehmen.

Vorangestellt ist jeder Partie der Austragungszeitpunkt und (bei vermischten Partien) der Ort, sowie bei analysierten Partien der Name des Kommentators. Am Schluß der Partie erscheint der bibliographische Verweis, der (mittels der ausführlichen Bibliographie auf den Seiten 455–6) erläutert, wo das Spiel gefunden wurde.

Die durch Computereinsatz erstellten Register sind die bislang für ein Schachbuch ausführlichsten und erweisen sich als Fundgrube von Informationen und statistischen Auswertungen. Das *Spieler-Register* gibt für jeden im Buch erwähnten Spieler eine vollständige Liste der Gegner, einschließlich der Resultate und Kennziffern für alle Partien. Fur jeden bedeutenderen Spieler sind vollständige Turnier- und Meisterschaftsberichte aufgeführt. Das *Eröffnungs–Register* verzeichnet alle Eröffnungsvarianten, die in dem Buch vorkommen, dazu Kennziffer für die jeweiligen Partien mit allen Eröffnungen. Das *Endspiel–Register* verweist den Leser auf alle Partien, in denen besondere Endspiele vorkommen.

Diese Partien waren tief in den Schachbibliotheken der Welt vergraben. Unser Material entstammt in erster Linie folgenden Bibliotheken: dem Britischen Museum (dessen kyrillisches Transliterationssystem wir benutzt haben), der Bodleian Library in Oxford, der Bibliotheca van der Linde-Niemeijeriana, Koninklijke Bibliotheek, 's-Gravenhage, und der John G. White Collection, Cleveland Public Library, Cleveland, Ohio. Von den vielen Freunden, Bekannten und Gelehrten, die bei unserer Suche behilflich waren, möchten wir ganz besonders Mr Jeremy Gaige, Miss K. M. E. Murray (für die Erlaubnis, die Sammlung H. J. R. Murray in der Bodleian Library zu benutzen), Mr David Lawson, Mr Craig Pritchett, Mr Ken Whyld, und Mr Baruch H. Wood danken.

# ПРЕДИСЛОВИЕ

Нашей задачей в этой энциклопедии является публикация всех значительных шахматных партий, которые имели место со времени введения современных правил в конце XV века. Мы включили все записанные партии, сыгранные до 1800 года, все партии важнейших турниров и матчей с 1801 года, и все известные партии каждого шахматиста, который был когда-либо одним из двух лучших шахматистов мира.

Партии расположены в хронологическом порядке. В каждом году сначала представлены турниры, за ними следуют матчи, потом разнообразные партии. Каждая игра наделена уникальным кодовым числом, которое указывает её место в книге. Так, **1849-LON-3** есть третья партия турнира в Лондоне 1849 года. Все турниры опознаются по датам и месту, где они проходили. Турниры, проходившие в декабре – январе, отнесены к году их начала. Полный список мест и кодов находится на странице xviii.

Матчи означены символом ⨯ и инициалами шахматистов. Таким образом, вторая партия Люиса–Вилсона матча 1819 года обозначается: **1819-⨯LW-2**. Разнообразные партии показаны значком ★, например, **1841-★PS-1**. Для дополнительной информации смотрите полный список символов.

Над каждой партией есть указание, когда она проходила и (для разнообразных партий), где она проходила; если игра анализируется, то даётся фамилия аннотатора. В конце партии дается библиографическая ссылка, которая объясняет (посредством полной библиографии на страницах 455–6) где эта партия была найдена.

Указатели, составленные вычислительной машиной, являются самыми подробными, которые когда-либо были приведены в шахматной книге, и представляют собой богатый источник информации и статистического анализа. ‘Указатель шахматистов’ приводит для каждого шахматиста в книге полный список его противников с результатом и кодовым номером каждой партии, а для каждого значительного шахматиста – данные всего турнира или матча. В ‘Указателе дебютов’ даётся каждый вступительный вариант, который приведен в книге, и кодовый номер каждой партии, сыгранной с каждым. ‘Указатель эндшпилей’ отсылает читателя ко всем тем партиям, в которых имеется та или иная завершающая часть партии.

Эти партии были далеко укрыты в шахматных библиотеках мира. Нашими главными источниками были: Британский музей (чью систему транслитерации кириллицы мы применили), Бодлеанская библиотека в Оксфорде, библиотека ван дер Линде-Нимейериана, Конинклейке библиотека, ’с-Гравенхаге и собрание Джона Д. Вайта, Кливлендская публичная библиотека в Кливленде, Огайо. Мы благодарны многим друзьям, знакомым и учёным, которые нам помогли в наших поисках и особенно господину Джереми Гейджу и госпоже К.М.Е. Марри (за разрешение пользоваться коллекцией Х.Д.Р. Марри в Бодлеанской библиотеке), господину Крэгу Причету, господину Кену Уайлду, господину Дэвиду Лоусону и господину Б. Вуду.

## PREDGOVOR

Postavili smo sebi za cilj da u ovoj enciklopediji prikažemo sve važne šahovske partije koje su odigrane otkad su savremena pravila uvedena krajem petnaestog veka. Odlučili smo da uključimo sve zabeležene partije odigrane do 1800 godine, svaku partiju odigranu na svim glavnim turnirima i takmičenjima od 1801 godine, kao i svaku zabeleženu partiju svakog pojedinog šahiste koji je svojevremeno bio jedan od dvojice najboljih šahista na svetu.

Partije su prikazane hronološki po godinama. U okviru svake godine prvo su prikazani turniri, zatim takmičenja a na kraju pojedinačne partije. Svaka utakmica je obeležena specifičnom oznakom pomoću koje se može naći u knjizi. Tako, na primer, **1849-LON-3** označava treću partiju koja je odigrana na turniru London 1849. Svi su turniri identifikovani pomoću datuma i mesta. Turniri koji se odigravaju u mesecima decembar i januar su označeni godinom u kojoj je turnir započeo. Potpun spisak mesta i oznaka se nalazi na strani xviii.

Takmičenja su označena simbolom ✕ i početnim slovima imena šahista, tako da, na primer, druga partija u takmičenju Lewis-a i Wilson-a u 1819 godini nosi oznaku **1819-✕LW-2**. Partije van takmičenja su označene sa ★, kao na primer **1841-★PS-1**; dalja obaveštenja se mogu naći na spisku oznaka.

Iznad svake partije nalazi se datum kada je odigrana, mesto (za pojedinačne partije) i, ukoliko je partija analizirana, ime komentatora. Pri kraju se nalazi bibliografska beleška o tome gde je opis partije pronadjen (potpune bibliografske beleške nalaze se na strani 455–6).

Na računaru zasnovani registri su najdetaljniji što su ikada sastavljeni za knjigu o šahu i pretstavljaju obilje obaveštenja i statističke analize. *Registar šahista* daje za svakog igrača u knjizi potpun spisak protivnika sa ishodom i oznakom za svaku partiju, a o svakom poznatijem šahisti potpuna obaveštenja u pogledu turnira i takmičenja. *Registar početnih poteza* sadržava svaku varijantu otvaranja koja je zabeležena u knjizi kao i broj oznake svake partije u kojoj je ono upotrebljeno. *Registar završnih poteza* se odnosi na sve partije gde su ti završni potezi odigrani.

Prikazi ovih partija bili su zatrpani po svetskim bibliotekama šaha. Naši glavni izvori su bili Britanski Muzej (čiji smo sistem ćirilične transkripcije upotrebili), Bodleanska Biblioteka u Oksfordu, zatim Bibliotheca van der Linde-Niemeijeriana, Koninklijke Bibliotheek, 's-Gravenhage, zbirka John G. White-a u javnoj biblioteci Cleveland-a u američkoj državi Ohio. Medju mnogim prijateljima, poznanicima i naučnicima koji su nas pomogli u našem istraživanju, našu naročitu zahvalnost zaslužuju gospodin Jeremy Gaige, gospodjica K. M. E. Murray (što nam je dozvolila da upotrebimo zbirku H. J. R. Murray-a u Bodleanskoj Biblioteci) kao i gospoda David Lawson, Craig Pritchett, Ken Whyld, i Baruch H. Wood.

## INLEDNING

I denna encyklopedi publiceras alla berömda schackpartier som spelats sedan de moderna spelreglerna trädde i kraft i slutet av 1400 talet. Vi har valt att ta med de upptecknade partier som spelats fram till år 1800, alla de partier som spelats i samtliga större turneringar och matcher sedan 1801 och de partier som har kunnat spåras för de spelare som vid något tillfälle var en utav världens två bästa.

Partierna är kronologiskt ordnade, år för år. För varje år presenteras turneringarna först, följda av matcher och olika partier. Varje parti har tilldelat ett kodnummer så att man lätt kan finna det i boken. **1849-LON-3** är alltså det tredje partiet som spelades i Londonturneringen 1849. Alla turneringar identifieras med datum och spelplats. I det fall en turnering pågått från december till januari hänvisas till det år turneringen börjat. En fullständig lista över plaster och koder finns pa šidan xviii.

Matcher betecknas med symbolen ⚔ och spelarnas initialer. Lewis och Wilsons andra parti i deras match 1819 betecknas alltså **1819-⚔LW-2**. De olika partierna betecknas med ★, t. ex. **1841-★PS-1**; ytterligare information slår man upp i den fullständiga symbolförteckningen.

Före varje parti anges speldatum och spelplats (for olika partier) och, om partiet analyserats, namnet på den som skrivit kommentaren. Efter varje parti finner man en bibliografihänvisning med en redogörelse över var partiet anträffats (med hjälp av den fullständiga bibliografin på sidorna 455–6).

Innehållsförteckningarna är dataframställda och de mest detaljerade någonsin i en schackbok. De är utomordentliga informations- och statistikkällor. *Förteckningen över spelare* är försedd med en fullständig lista över motståndare med resultat och kodnummer för varje parti. För samtliga stora spelare finns en fullständig förteckning över deras turneringar och matcher. *Förteckningen över öppningar* upptar alla de öppningsvariationer som finns i boken, med kodnummer för varje parti som spelats med dessa. *Förteckningen över slutpartier* hänvisar läsaren till partier där speciella slutpartier förekommit.

Dessa schackpartier har legat djupt begravna i schackbibliotek runtom i världen. Våra främsta källor har varit British Museum (vars Cyrilliska transkription vi har använt), Universitetsbiblioteket i Oxford (the Bodleian Library), Bibliotheca van der Linde-Niemeijeriana, Koninklijke Bibliotheek, 's-Gravenhage och John G. White samlingen vid Cleveland Public Library i Cleveland, Ohio. Av de många vänner, bekanta och lärda som hjälpt oss i vårt sökande skulle vi speciellt vilja framföra vårt tack till Mr Jeremy Gaige, Miss K. M. E. Murray (för hennes tillstånd att använda H. J. R. Murray samlingen vid universitetsbiblioteket i Oxford), Mr David Lawson, Mr Craig Pritchett, Mr Ken Whyld, och Mr B. H. Wood.

| | SYMBOLS | SYMBOLEN | SYMBOLES |
|---|---|---|---|
| ✕ | Match | Match | Match |
| ⊠ | Correspondence, adjourned | Correspondentie, uitgesteld | Par correspondance, ajourne |
| ★ | Miscellaneous game | Vrije partij | Partie amicale |
| ●○ | White blindfold | Wit blind | Les blancs sans voir |
| ○● | Black blindfold | Zwart blind | Les noirs sans voir |
| ●● | White and black blindfold | Blindpartij | Les blancs et les noirs sans voir |
| ϟ | Blitz chess | Snelschaak | Partie blitz |
| ⌂ | Simultaneous exhibition | Simultaan | Séance simultanée |
| ⌛ | Tele-chess | Tele-schaak | Par télécommunication |
| ⏱ | Time limit | Tijdslimiet | Délai |
| □ | White | Wit | Les blancs |
| ■ | Black | Zwart | Les noirs |
| O | Consulting team | Secondanten | Équipe consultante |
| + | White won | Wit wint | Les blancs gagnent |
| = | Drawn | Remise | Partie nulle |
| − | Black won | Zwart wint | Les noirs gagnent |
| ⊕ | White won by default | Wit won door niet opkomen van zwart | Les blancs gagnent par défaut |
| ○ | Both sides defaulted | Beide spelers kwamen niet op | Les deux camps font défaut |
| ⊖ | Black won by default | Zwart won door niet opkomen van wit | Les noirs gagnent par défaut |
| Φ | Game unfinished | Partij niet beëindigd | Partie inachavée |
| ˙ | Uncertainty | Onzekerheid | Incertitude |
| ℘ | Information not available | Geen informatie beschikbaar | Pas d'information |
| + | Check | Schaak | Échec |
| # | Mate | Mat | Mat |
| ◇ | Stalemate | Pat | Pat |
| △ | Idea or threat | Plan/dreiging | Idée ou menace |
| ⌓ | Better is | Beter is | Mieux vaut |
| ~ | Any move | Iedere willekeurige zet | Tout coup |
| ! | Good move | Goede zet | Bon coup |
| !! | Brilliant move | Zeer goede zet | Très bon coup |
| !? | Interesting move | Interessante zet | Coup intéressant |
| ?! | Doubtful move | Dubieuze zet | Coup douteux |
| ? | Bad move | Slechte zet | Mauvais coup |
| ?? | Blunder | Blunder | Gaffe |
| ⩲ | White has a small advantage | Licht voordeel voor wit | Les blancs ont un léger avantage |
| ± | White has a large advantage | Groot voordeel voor wit | Les blancs ont un avantage marqué |
| +− | White is winning | Wit wint | Les blancs ont un avantage décisif |
| ⩱ | Black has a small advantage | Licht voordeel voor zwart | Les noirs ont un léger avantage |
| ∓ | Black has a large advantage | Groot voordeel voor zwart | Les noirs ont un avantage marqué |
| −+ | Black is winning | Zwart wint | Les noirs ont un avantage décisif |
| ∞ | The position is unclear | Onduidelijke stelling | Le jeu est incertain |

| | ZEICHENERKLÄRUNG | УСЛОВНЫЕ ОБОЗНАЧЕНИЯ | SISTEM ZNAKOVA | SYMBOLER |
|---|---|---|---|---|
| ✕ | Match | Матч | Mač | Match |
| ⊠ | Fernpartie, vertagt | Игра по переписке, партия отложена | Dopisna partija, prekinuta partija | Korrespondens, uppskjutet parti |
| ★ | Freundschaftspartie | Игра ради удовольствия | Mešovita partija | Blandat parti |
| ●○ | Blindspiel von Weiß | Игра белых вслепую | Beli naslepo | Vitt blindparti |
| ○● | Blindspiel von Schwarz | Игра черных вслепую | Crni naslepo | Svart blindparti |
| ●● | Blindspiel von beiden Spielern | Игра белых и черных вслепую | Beli i crni naslepo | Vitt och svart blindparti |
| ϟ | Blitzschach | Молниеносная игра, блиц | Brzopotezna partija | Blixtschack |
| ○ | Simultanschachspiel | Сеанс одновременной игры | Istovremeno izlaganje | Simultanuppvisning |
| ☎ | Teleschach | Игра по телевидению | Tele-šah | Tele-schack |
| ⏱ | Frist | Лимит времени | Vremensko ograničenje | Tidsbegränsning |
| □ | Weiß | Белые | Beli | Vit |
| ■ | Schwarz | Черные | Crni | Svart |
| ○ | Beratungsmannschaft | Консультирующаяся группа | Savetodavci | Rådgivande lag |
| + | Weiß gewinnt | Белые выиграли | Beli pobedio | Vit vann |
| = | Remis | Ничья | Remi | Oavgjort |
| − | Schwarz gewinnt | Черные выиграли | Crni pobedio | Svart vann |
| ⊕ | Weiß gewinnt durch Nichtantreten von Schwarz | Выигрыш белых вследствие отсутствия черных | Beli pobedio propustom | Vit vann genom frånvaro |
| O | Beide Spieler nicht erschienen | Обе стороны отсутствовали | Propust oba igrača | Båda sidor frånvarande |
| ⊖ | Schwarz gewinnt durch Nichtantreten von Weiss | Выигрыш черных вследствие отсутствия белых | Crni pobedio propustom | Svart vann genom frånvaro |
| Φ | Spiel unentschieden | Игра незакончена | Partija nedovršena | Oavslutat parti |
| - | Ungewißheit | Неопределенность, неуверенность | Neizvesno | Osäkerhet |
| ? | Keine Auskunft vorhanden | Информации нет в наличии | Bez podataka | Ingen tillgång på uppgifter |
| + | Schach | Шах | Kralj u šahu | Schack |
| # | Schachmatt | Мат | Mat | Matt |
| ◇ | Patt | Пат | Pat | Pattställning |
| Δ | Idee oder Gefahr | Замысел или угроза | Zamisao ili pretnja | Plan eller hot |
| ⌂ | Besser ist | Лучше | Bolje je | Bättre vore |
| ~ | Jeder Zug | Любой ход | Bilo koji potez | Vilket drag som helst |
| ! | Guter Zug | Сильный ход | Dobar potez | Bra drag |
| !! | Glänzender Zug | Очень сильный ход | Sjajan potez | Strålande drag |
| !? | Interessanter Zug | Интересный ход | Interesantan potez | Intressant drag |
| ?! | Fraglicher Zug | Сомнительный ход | Sumnjiv potez | Tveksamt drag |
| ? | Fehler | Слабый ход | Slab potez | Dåligt drag |
| ?? | Großer Fehler | Грубая ошибка | Greška | Feldrag |
| ⩲ | Kleiner Vorteil Weiß | Белые имеют небольшое преимущество | Beli ima malu premoć | Vit har ett litet försprång |
| ± | Großer Vorteil Weiß | Белые имеют большое преимущество | Beli ima veliku premoć | Vit har ett stort försprång |
| +− | Weiß gewinnt | Белые выигрывают | Beli dobija | Vit vinner |
| ⩱ | Kleiner Vorteil Schwarz | Черные имеют небольшое преимущество | Crni ima malu premoć | Svart har ett litet försprång |
| ∓ | Großer Vorteil Schwarz | Черные имеют большое преимущество | Crni ima veliku premoć | Svart har ett stort försprång |
| −+ | Schwarz gewinnt | Черные выигрывают | Crni dobija | Svart vinner |
| ∞ | Lage ungewiß | Положение неясно | Igra je neizvesna | Ställningen är oklar |

## PLACE CODES

| | |
|---|---|
| AMS | Amsterdam |
| BAC | Dublin |
| BIR | Birmingham |
| BRI | Bristol |
| BRL | Berlin |
| CMB | Cambridge |
| DUS | Düsseldorf |
| ELB | Elberfeld |
| LON | London |
| LPZ | Leipzig |
| NMC | Manchester |
| NYC | New York City |

| | |
|---|---|
| Amsterdam | AMS |
| Berlin | BRL |
| Birmingham | BIR |
| Bristol | BRI |
| Cambridge | CMB |
| Dublin | BAC |
| Düsseldorf | DUS |
| Elberfeld | ELB |
| Leipzig | LPZ |
| London | LON |
| Manchester | MNC |
| New York City | NYC |

**14??-★CV-1**
**Castellvi+ Viñoles**
1 e4 d5 2 exd5 ♕xd5 3 ♘c3 ♕d8 4 ♗c4 ♘f6 5 ♘f3 ♗g4 6 h3 ♗xf3 7 ♕xf3 e6 8 ♕xb7 ♘bd7 9 ♘b5 ♖c8 10 ♘xa7 ♘b6 11 ♘xc8 ♘xc8 12 d4 ♘d6 13 ♗b5+ ♘xb5 14 ♕xb5+ ♘d7 15 d5 exd5 16 ♗e3 ♗d6 17 ♖d1 ♕f6 18 ♖xd5 ♕g6 19 ♗f4 ♗xf4 20 ♕xd7+ ♔f8 21 ♕d8# **1-0** +1

**15??-★??-1**
**?+?**
1 e4 e5 2 ♘f3 ♕f6 3 c3 ♗c5 4 d4 ♗b6 5 ♗e3 d6 6 dxe5 dxe5 7 ♗g5 ♕g6 8 ♕d8# **1-0** +1

**1560-★LL-1**
**Lopez+ Leonardo**
Roma
1 e4 e5 2 ♘f3 f6 3 ♘xe5 fxe5 4 ♕h5+ g6 5 ♕xe5+ ♕e7 6 ♕xh8 ♘f6 7 d4 ♔f7 8 ♗c4+ d5 9 ♗xd5+ ♘xd5 ...? **1-0** +1

**Leonardo✕Lopez** Madrid
[1575-✕LL]

| | | | |
|---|---|---|---|
| Leonardo | 1̂ | 1̂ | 2 |
| Lopez | 0̂ | 0̂ | 0 |

**1575-✕LL-1̂**
**Leonardo+Lopez**
Madrid
1 e4 e5 2 ♘f3 d6 3 ♗c4 f5 4 d3 ♗e7 5 ♕e2 c6 6 h3 f4 7 g3 fxg3 8 fxg3 ♔c7 [sic] 9 ♘c3 ♘f6 10 b4 ...? **1-0** +1

**1575-✕LL-2̂**
**Leonardo+Lopez**
Madrid
1 e4 e5 2 ♘f3 ♘c6 3 ♗c4 ♗c5 4 c3 ♕e7 5 b4 ♗b6 6 a4 a6 7 ♗a3 d6 8 d3 ♘f6 9 ♕e2 ♗g4 10 ♘bd2

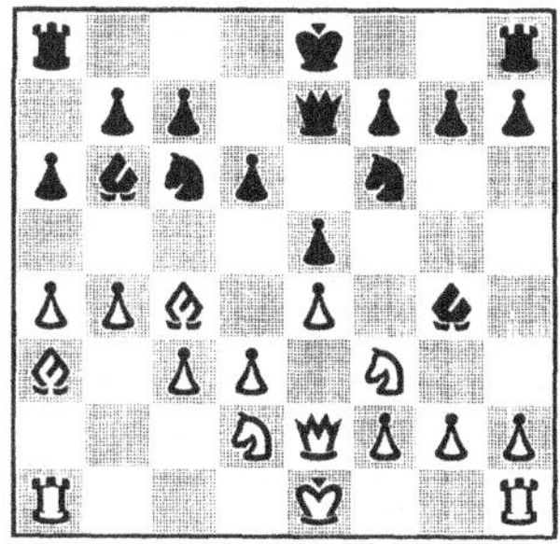

...? **1-0** +1

**1575-★BS-1**
**Scovara+ Boi**
Madrid
1 e4 e5 2 ♗c4 ♗c5 3 ♘f3 ♘c6 4 c3 ♕e7 5 d4 exd4 6 cxd4 ♕xe4+ 7 ♗e3 ♗b4+ 8 ♘c3 d5 9 ♗d3 ♕e7 10 h3 ♘f6 11 ♔g1 [sic] 11 ... ♖f8 12 g4 ♔g8 [sic] 13 ♖h2 ♗d6 14 ♖g2 ...? **1-0** +1

**1575-★CP-1**
**Castiglio− Polerio**
Madrid
1 e4 e5 2 ♗c4 ♗c5 3 ♘f3 ♘c6 4 c3 ♕e7 5 d4 exd4 6 cxd4 ♕xe4+ 7 ♔d2 ♗b4+ 8 ♘c3 ♕g6 9 ♖e1+ ♔d8 ...? **0-1** +1

**157?-★LP-1**
**Polerio+ Lorenzo**
Sora?
1 e4 e5 2 ♘f3 ♘c6 3 ♗c4 ♗c5 4 c3 ♕e7 5 0-0 d6 6 d4 ♗b6 7 ♗g5 ♘f6 8 a4 a6 9 ♗d5 ♘b8 10 ♘bd2 c6 11 ♗a2 ♗g4 12 ♕b3 ♗a7 13 ♕d1 g6 14 dxe5 dxe5 15 ♗xf7+ ♔d8 16 ♘xe5 ♕xe5 17 ♗xf6+ ♔c8 18 ♕xg4+ ♘d7 19 ♗xh8 ♕xh8 20 ♗e6 ♕e8 21 ♘c4 ♔c7 22 ♕f4+ ♔d8 23 ♕d6 ♗b8 24 ♕xd7+ ♕xd7 25 ♗xd7 ♔xd7 26 ♘b6+ ♔d6 27 ♘xa8 ♗a7 28 ♖fd1+ ♔c5 29 ♖d4 a5 30 ♖ad1 b5 31 b4+ axb4 32 cxb4# **1-0** +1

**1590-★BP-1**
**Polerio○ Busnardo**
[Polerio]
1 e4 e5 2 f4 exf4 3 ♗c4 ♕h4+ 4 ♔f1 g5 5 ♘f3 ♕h5 6 d4 d6 7 h4 g4 8 ♘g5 ♘h6 9 ♗xf4 f6 10 ♘e6 ♗xe6 11 ♗xe6±/± ...? +1

**1590-★BP-2**
**Busnardo○ Polerio**
Roma [Polerio]
1 e4 e5 2 ♘f3 ♘c6 3 ♗c4 ♗c5 4 c3 ♕e7 5 0-0 d6 6 d4 ♗b6 7 ♗g5 ♘f6 8 ♗d5 ♘d8 9 ♘bd2 c6 10 ♗b3 ♘e6 [Δ 11 ... 0-0∓/∓] ...? +1

**1590-★BS-1**
**Benavides○ Saduleto**
[Polerio]
1 e4 e5 2 f4 exf4 3 ♘f3 g5 4 ♗c4 g4 5 ♘e5 ♕h4+ 6 ♔f1 ♘h6 7 d4 d6 8 ♘d3 f3 9 g3 ♕e7 10 ♔f2 ♗g7 11 ♘f4 [Δ 12 ♖e1±/±] ...? +1

**1590-★BS-2**
**Saduleto○ Benavides**
[Polerio]
1 d4 d5 2 c4 dxc4 3 e4 b5 4 a4 c6 5 axb5 cxb5 6 b3 a5 7 bxc4 b4 8 f4±/± ...? +1

**1590-★B?-1**
**Busnardo+?**
Roma
1 e4 e5 2 ♘f3 ♘c6 3 ♗c4 ♗c5 4 c3 ♕e7 5 0-0 d6 6 d4 ♗b6 7 ♗g5 f6 8 ♗h4 g5 9 ♘xg5 fxg5 10 ♕h5+ ♔d7 11 ♗xg5 ♕g7 12 ♗e6+ ♔xe6 13 ♕e8+ ∼ 14 d5# **1-0** +1

**1590-★PS-1**
**Saduleto− Polerio**
Roma
1 e4 e5 2 ♘f3 ♘c6 3 ♗c4 ♗c5 4 c3 ♕e7 5 0-0 d6 6 d4 ♗b6 7 ♗g5 ♘f6 8 d5 ♘b8 9 ♘bd2 ♗g4 10 ♕c2 h6 11 ♗h4 g5 12 ♗g3 a6 13 b4 ♘bd7 14 a4 ♘f8 15 a5 ♗a7 16 b5 ♘g6 17 bxa6 bxa6 18 ♗xa6 ♗xf2+ 19 ♖xf2 ♖xa6 20 ♕d3 ♖a8 21 ♕b5+ ♔f8 22 ♕b7 ♔g7 23 a6 ♖hb8 24 ♕c6 ♖a7

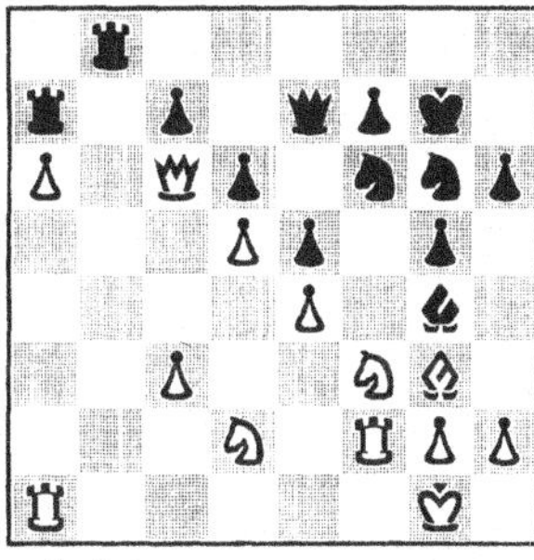

...? **0-1** +1

**1590-★PS-2**
**Saduleto○ Polerio**
Roma
1 e4 e5 2 ♘f3 ♘c6 3 ♗c4 ♗c5 4 c3 ♕e7 5 0-0 d6 6 d4 ♗b6 7 h3 h6 8 ♗e3 ♘f6 9 ♘bd2 0-0 10 ♖e1 ♘a5 11 ♗d3 a6 12 ♘f1 ♗a7 13 ♘g3 ...? +1

**1604-✕AS-1̂**
**Arminio○ Salvio**
1 e4 e5 2 f4 exf4 3 d4 ♕h4+ 4 g3 fxg3 5 ♔g2 [sic] 5 ... gxh2 6 ♖xh2 ♕xe4+ 7 ♘f3 ...? +1

**162Ô-★G?-1**
**Greco, G.?+?**
[Greco]
1 e4 e5 2 ♘f3 ♘c6 3 ♗c4 ♗c5 4 c3 ♘f6 5 d4 exd4 6 cxd4 ♗b4+ 7 ♘c3 ♘xe4 8 0-0 ♘xc3 9 bxc3 ♗xc3 10 ♕b3 ♗xa1 11 ♗xf7+ ♔f8 12 ♗g5 ♘e7 [12 ... ♘xd4 13 ♕a3+ ♔xf7 14 ♗xd8 ♖xd8 15 ♖xa1 ♘c2 16 ♕b3+ ♔f8 17 ♕xc2+−] 13 ♘e5 ♗xd4 [13 ... d5 14 ♕f3 ♗f5 15 ♗e6 g6 16 ♗h6+ ♔e8 17 ♗f7#] 14 ♗g6 d5 15 ♕f3+ ♗f5 16 ♗xf5 ♗xe5 17 ♗e6+ ♗f6 18 ♗xf6 gxf6 19 ♕xf6+ ♔e8 20 ♕f7# **1-0**
L/N398

### 1620-★G?-2
**Greco, G.?+?**

[Greco]

1 e4 e5 2 ♘f3 ♘c6 3 ♗c4 ♗c5 4 c3 ♘f6 5 d4 exd4 6 cxd4 ♗b4+ 7 ♘c3 ♘xe4 8 0-0 ♘xc3 9 bxc3 ♗xc3 10 ♕b3 ♗xd4 11 ♗xf7+ ♔f8 12 ♗g5 ♗f6 13 ♖ae1 ♘e7 14 ♗h5

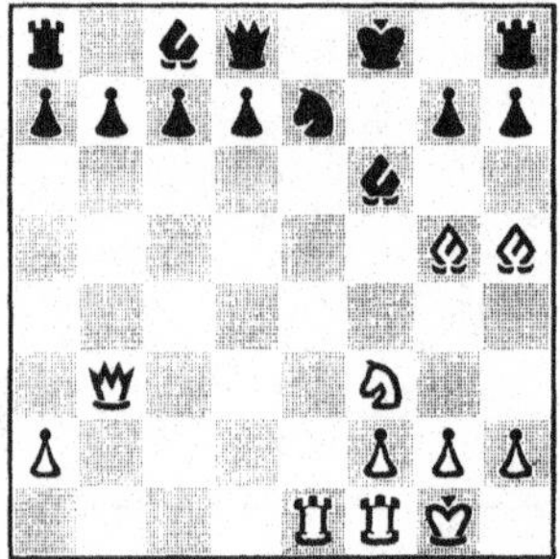

14 ... ♘g6 [14 ... d5 15 ♖xe7 ♔xe7 16 ♖e1+ ♔f8 17 ♕b4+ ♔g8 18 ♖e8+ ♕xe8 19 ♗xe8+-; 14 ... d5 15 ♖xe7 ♔xe7 16 ♖e1+ ♔d6 17 ♗f4+ ♔c6 18 ♖c1+ ♔d7 19 ♕xd5+ ♔e7 20 ♕f7#; 14 ... d5 15 ♖xe7 ♕xe7 16 ♖e1 ♕d7 17 ♕b4+ ♔g8 18 ♖e8+ ♕xe8 19 ♗xe8+-; 14 ... d5 15 ♖xe7 ♕xe7 16 ♖e1 ♗e6 17 ♘d4 ♗xg5 18 ♘xe6+ ♔g8 19 ♕xd5 c6 20 ♕b3 ♕f6 21 ♘xg5+ ♔f8 22 ♕b4+ ♔g8 23 ♗f7+ ♕xf7 24 ♘xf7+-] 15 ♘e5 ♘xe5 16 ♖xe5 g6 17 ♗h6+ ♗g7 18 ♖f5+ gxf5 19 ♕f7# **1-0** L/N398

### 1620-★G?-3
**Greco, G.?+?**

1 e4 e5 2 ♘f3 ♘c6 3 ♗c4 ♗c5 4 c3 ♘f6 5 d4 exd4 6 cxd4 ♗b4+ 7 ♗d2 ♘xe4 8 ♗xb4 ♘xb4 9 ♗xf7+ ♔xf7 10 ♕b3+ d5 11 ♘e5+ ♔g8 12 ♕xb4 ♕f6 13 0-0 c5 14 ♕b5 b6 15 ♕e8+ ♕f8 16 ♕c6 ♗a6 17 ♕xd5+ ♕f7 18 ♕xf7# **1-0** L/N398

### 1620-★G?-4
**Greco, G.?+?**

[Greco]

1 e4 e5 2 ♘f3 ♘c6 3 ♗c4 ♗c5 4 c3 ♘f6 5 d4 exd4 6 cxd4 ♗b6 7 e5 ♘g8 8 d5 ♘ce7 9 d6 ♘c6 [9 ... cxd6 10 exd6 ♘c6 11 ♕d5 ♕f6 12 0-0 ♘h6 13 ♖e1+ ♔f8 14 ♗g5 ♕xb2 (14 ... ♕f5 15 ♕d2 ♗a5 16 ♘c3 b6 17 ♗xh6 gxh6 18 ♕xh6+ ♔g8 19 ♖e8#) 15 ♗xh6 ♗xf2+ 16 ♔f1 ♕f6 17 ♗g5 ♕g6 18 ♔xf2 a6 19 ♘h4 ♕h5 20 ♗e7+ ♔g8 21 ♕xh5 g6 22 ♕h6+-] 10 ♕d5 ♘h6 11 ♗xh6 ♖f8 12 ♗xg7 ♘b4 13 ♕d2 ♖g8 14 ♗f6 ...? **1-0** L/N398

### 1620-★G?-5
**Greco, G.?+?**

1 e4 e5 2 ♘f3 ♘c6 3 ♗c4 ♗c5 4 c3 ♘f6 5 d4 ♗b6 6 dxe5 ♘xe4 7 ♕d5 ...? **1-0** L/N398

### 1620-★G?-6
**Greco, G.?+?**

1 e4 e5 2 ♘f3 ♘c6 3 ♗c4 ♗c5 4 c3 ♘f6 5 ♘g5 0-0 6 d3 h6 7 h4 hxg5 8 hxg5 ♘h7 9 ♕h5 ...? **1-0** L/N398

### 1620-★G?-7
**Greco, G.?+?**

[Greco]

1 e4 e5 2 ♘f3 ♘c6 3 ♗c4 ♗c5 4 c3 ♕e7 5 0-0 d6 6 d4 ♗b6 7 ♗g5 f6 8 ♗h4 g5 9 ♘xg5 fxg5 10 ♕h5+ ♔d7 11 ♗xg5 ♕g7 [11 ... ♕f8 12 ♗f7 ♘ce7 (12 ... exd4 13 ♕g4#) 13 dxe5 dxe5 14 ♖d1+ ♔c6 15 ♗e8+ ♔c5 16 ♗e3+ ♔c4 17 b3#] 12 ♗e6+ ♔xe6 13 ♕e8+ ♘ce7 [13 ... ♘ge7 14 d5#] 14 d5# **1-0** L/N398

### 1620-★G?-8
**Greco, G.?+?**

[Greco]

1 e4 e5 2 ♘f3 ♘c6 3 ♗c4 ♗c5 4 c3 ♕e7 5 0-0 d6 6 d4 ♗b6 7 ♗g5 f6 8 ♗h4 g5 9 ♘xg5 fxg5 10 ♕h5+ ♔d7 11 ♗xg5 ♕f8 12 ♗f7 ♘ce7 13 dxe5 h6 14 ♗h4 ♖h7 15 e6+

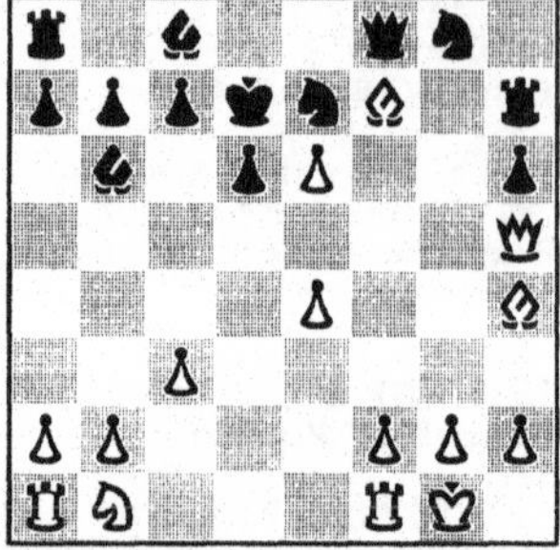

15 ... ♔c6 [15 ... ♔d8 16 e5 d5 17 ♕f3 c6 18 c4 ♔c7 19 ♕a3 c5 (19 ... ♔b8 20 ♗xg8 ♕xg8 21 ♗xe7+-) 20 cxd5 ♘f5 (20 ... ♘xd5 21 ♕d3 ♖xf7 22 ♕xd5 ♖f5 23 e7 ♘xe7 24 ♕d6#) 21 ♗g3 ♘xg3 22 ♕xg3 ♖g7 23 ♕b3 h5 24 e7 ♘xe7 (24 ... ♕xf7 25 d6+ ♔d7 26 ♕b5+ ♔e6 27 e8♕+ ♕xe8 28 ♕xe8++-) 25 d6+ ♔d7 26 ♕e6+ ♔d8 27 dxe7+ ♕xe7 28 ♖d1+ ♗d7 29 ♕xe7+ ♔xe7 30 ♗xh5 ♖ag8 31 ♗f3 ♗c6 32 ♗xc6 bxc6 33 g3 ♖g5 34 f4+-] 16 ♗e8+ ♕xe8 17 ♕xe8+ ...? **1-0** L/N398

### 1620-★G?-9
**Greco, G.?+?**

[Greco]

1 e4 e5 2 ♘f3 ♘c6 3 ♗c4 ♗c5 4 c3 ♕e7 5 0-0 d6 6 d4 ♗b6 7 ♗g5 f6 8 ♗h4 g5 9 ♘xg5 fxg5 10 ♕h5+ ♔d8 11 ♗xg5 ♘f6 12 ♕h6 ♖f8 13 f4 exd4 14 e5 dxc3+ 15 ♔h1 cxb2 16 exf6 bxa1♕ [16 ... ♖xf6 17 ♕xf6 bxa1♕ 18 ♕xa1 ♗d4 19 ♗xe7+ ♔xe7 20 ♘c3+-] 17 fxe7+ ♘xe7 18 ♕xf8+ ♔d7 19 ♗b5+ ♘c6 20 ♕e7# **1-0** L/N398

### 1620-★G?-10
**Greco, G.?+?**

[Greco]

1 e4 e5 2 ♘f3 ♘c6 3 ♗c4 ♗c5 4 c3 ♕e7 5 0-0 d6 6 d4 ♗b6 7 ♗g5 f6 8 ♗h4 g5 9 ♘xg5 fxg5 10 ♕h5+ ♔f8 11 ♗xg5 ♕e8 12 ♕f3+ ♔g7 13 ♗xg8 ♖xg8 [13 ... ♕xg8 14 d5 ♘e7 15 ♗f6 ♕f7 16 ♘d2 h6 17 ♗xh8 ♕xf3 18 ♘xf3 ♔xh8 19 h3 ♗d7 20 c4 ♗d4 21 ♘xd4 exd4 22 ♖ad1 c5 23 f4 ♖f8 24 e5 dxe5 25 fxe5 ♖xf1+ 26 ♖xf1 ♔g7 27 e6 ♗e8 28 d6 ♘c6 29 d7 ♗g6 30 e7 ♘xe7 31 d8♕+-] 14 ♕f6# **1-0** L/N398

### 1620-★G?-11
**Greco, G.?+?**

[Greco]

1 e4 e5 2 ♘f3 ♘c6 3 ♗c4 ♗c5 4 c3 d6 5 d4 exd4 6 cxd4 ♗b4+ 7 ♘c3 ♘f6 8 0-0 ♗xc3 9 bxc3 ♘xe4 10 ♖e1 d5 11 ♖xe4+ dxe4 12 ♘g5 0-0 13 ♕h5 h6 14 ♘xf7 ♕f6 [14 ... ♖xf7 15 ♗xf7+ ♔h8 (15 ... ♔f8 16 ♗a3+ ♘e7 17 ♗b3 ♕e8 18 ♕d5 c5 19 ♗xc5 a6 20 ♕g8#; 15 ... ♔h7 16 ♗xh6 gxh6 17 ♕g6+ ♔h8 18 ♕xh6#) 16 ♗xh6 ♗g4 17 ♗xg7+ ♔xg7 18 ♕g6+ ♔f8 19 ♗b3 ♕e8 20 ♕g8+ ♔e7 21 ♕xg4 ♔d8 22 ♖e1 e3 23 ♖xe3+-] 15 ♘xh6+ ♔h8 16 ♘f7+ ♔g8 17 ♕h8# **1-0** L/N398

### 1620-★G?-12
**?– Greco, G.?**

[Greco]

1 e4 e5 2 ♘f3 ♘c6 3 ♗c4 ♗c5 4 0-0 ♘f6 5 ♖e1 0-0 6 c3 ♕e7 7 d4 exd4 8 e5 ♘g4 9 cxd4 ♘xd4 10 ♘xd4 ♕h4 11 ♘f3 [11 h3 ♘xf2 12 ♕~ ♗xd4-+; 11 ♗e3 ♕xh2+ 12 ♔f1 ♕h1+ 13 ♔e2 ♕xg2 14 ♖g1 ♘xe3 15 ♔xe3 ♗xd4+ 16 ♔xd4 ♕xf2+ 17 ♔c3 ♕e3+ 18 ♗d3 ♕xe5+-+] 11 ... ♕xf2+ 12 ♔h1 ♕g1+ 13 ♘xg1 [13 ♖xg1 ♘f2#] 13 ... ♘f2# **0-1** L/N398

### 1620-★G?-13
**?– Greco, G.?**

[Greco]

1 e4 e5 2 ♘f3 ♘c6 3 ♗c4 ♗c5 4 0-0 ♘f6 5 ♖e1 0-0 6 c3 ♖e8 7 d4 exd4 8 e5 ♘g4 9 ♗g5 ♗xf2 10 ♗xd8 [10 ♔xf2 dxc3+ 11 ♔f1 cxb2 12 ♘c3 bxa1♕ 13 ♕xa1 ♗e7-+; 10 ♕b3 dxc3 11 ♗xd8 cxb2 12 ♕xb2 ♘d3+ 13 ♔f1 ♘xb2 14 ♗xc7 ♘xc4-+] 10 ... ♘xd1 11 ♖xd1 dxc3+ 12 ♔f1 cxb2 13 ♘bd2 bxa1♕ 14 ♖xa1 ♘xd8 ...? **0-1** L/N398

**162̂0̂-★G?-14**
**?– Greco, G.?**

[Greco]

1 e4 e5 2 ♘f3 ♘c6 3 ♗c4 ♗c5 4 0-0 ♘f6 5 ♖e1 0-0 6 c3 ♖e8 7 d4 exd4 8 e5 ♘g4 9 ♗g5

9 ... ♘xf2 10 ♕b3 dxc3 11 ♗xd8 [11 ♘xc3 ♘h3+ 12 ♔h1 ♘f2+ 13 ♔g1 ♘h3+ 14 ♔f1 ♘xg5 15 ♘xg5 ♕xg5 16 ♗xf7+ ♔f8 17 ♗xe8 ♕f4+ 18 ♔e2 ♘d4+ 19 ♔d1 ♘xb3 20 axb3 ♔xe8−+] 11 ... cxb2 12 ♘c3 ♘d1+ 13 ♔f1 bxa1♕ 14 ♖xd1 ♕xd1+ 15 ♘xd1 ♘xd8 ...? **0-1** L/N398

**162̂0̂-★G?-15**
**Greco, G.?+?**

1 e4 e5 2 ♘f3 ♘f6 3 ♘xe5 ♘xe4 4 ♕e2 ♕e7 5 ♕xe4 d6 6 d4 f6 7 f4 ♘d7 8 ♘c3 dxe5 9 ♘d5 ♕d6 10 dxe5 fxe5 11 fxe5 ♕c6 12 ♗b5 ♕c5 13 ♗e3 ♕xb5 14 ♘xc7+ ♔d8 15 ♘xb5 ...? **1-0** L/N398

**162̂0̂-★G?-16**
**Greco, G.?+?**

1 e4 e5 2 ♘f3 d6 3 ♗c4 ♗g4 4 h3 ♗h5 5 c3 ♘f6 6 d3 ♗e7 7 ♗e3 0-0 8 g4 ♗g6 9 ♘h4 c6 10 ♘xg6 hxg6 11 h4 b5 12 ♗b3 a5 13 a4 b4 14 h5 gxh5 15 g5 ♘g4 16 ♖xh5 ♘xe3 17 ♖h8+ ♔xh8 18 ♕h5+ ♔g8 19 g6 ♖e8 20 ♕h7+ ♔f8 21 ♕h8# **1-0** L/N398

**162̂0̂-★G?-17**
**Greco, G.?+?**

1 e4 e5 2 ♘f3 d6 3 ♗c4 ♗g4 4 h3 ♗xf3 5 ♕xf3 ♘f6 6 ♕b3 ♘xe4 7 ♗xf7+ ♔d7 8 ♕xb7 ♘g5 9 ♗d5 ♘a6 10 ♕c6+ ♔e7 11 ♕xa8 ...? **1-0** L/N398

**162̂0̂-★G?-18**
**Greco, G.?+?**

[Greco]

1 e4 e5 2 ♘f3 d6 3 ♗c4 ♗g4 4 h3 ♗xf3 5 ♕xf3 ♕f6 6 ♕b3 b6 7 ♘c3 c6 [7 ... ♘e7 8 ♘b5 ♘a6 9 ♕a4 ♘c5 10 ♘xd6+ ♔d8 11 ♕e8#] 8 ♘d5 ♕d8 9 ♘xb6 ♕xb6 10 ♗xf7+ ♔d7 11 ♗xg8 d5 12 exd5 ♕xb3 13 dxc6+ ♘xc6 14 ♗xb3 ...? **1-0** L/N398

**162̂0̂-★G?-19**
**Greco, G.?+?**

[Greco]

1 e4 e5 2 ♘f3 d6 3 h3 ♘f6 4 c3 ♘xe4 [4 ... ♘c6 5 d4 ♘xe4 6 d5 ♘e7 7 ♕a4+ c6 8 dxc6 ♘c5 9 cxb7+ ♘xa4 10 bxa8♕] 5 ♕a4+ c6 6 ♕xe4 ...? **1-0** L/N398

**162̂0̂-★G?-20**
**Greco, G.?+?**

[Greco]

1 e4 e5 2 ♘f3 ♘c6 3 ♗c4 ♘f6 4 ♘g5 d5 5 exd5 ♘xd5 6 ♘xf7 ♔xf7 7 ♕f3+ ♔e6 8 ♘c3 ♘e7 9 0-0 c6 10 ♖e1 ♗d7 11 d4 ♔d6 12 ♖xe5 ♘g6 13 ♘xd5 ♘xe5 [13 ... cxd5 14 ♖xd5+ ♔c7 15 ♗f4+ ♘xf4 16 ♕xf4+ ♔c8 17 ♗b5 ♕c7 18 ♕xc7+ ♔xc7 19 ♖xd7++−] 14 dxe5+

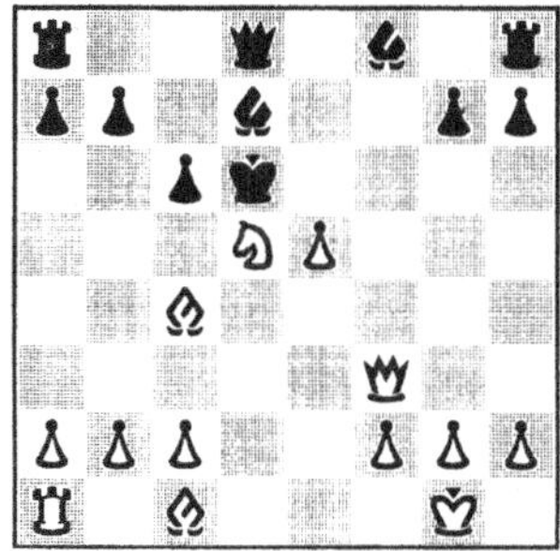

14 ... ♔c5 [14 ... ♔xe5 15 ♕f4+ ♔e6 16 ♘c7+ ♔e7 17 ♕g5+ ♔d6 18 ♗f4#; 14 ... ♔e6 15 ♘c7+ ♔xe5 16 ♕f4#] 15 ♕a3+ ♔xc4 16 ♕d3+ ♔c5 17 b4# **1-0** L/N398

**162̂0̂-★G?-21**
**Greco, G.?+?**

[Greco]

1 e4 e5 2 ♘f3 ♕f6 3 ♗c4 ♕g6 4 0-0 ♕xe4 5 ♗xf7+ ♔xf7 [5 ... ♔d8 6 ♘xe5 ♘f6 (6 ... ♕xe5 7 ♖e1 ♕f6 8 ♖e8#) 7 ♖e1 ♕f5 8 ♗g6 ♕e6 (8 ... hxg6 9 ♘f7#) 9 ♘f7+ ♔e8 10 ♘xh8+ hxg6 11 ♖xe6+ dxe6 12 ♘xg6+−] 6 ♘g5+ ♔e8 7 ♘xe4 ...? **1-0** L/N398

**162̂0̂-★G?-22**
**Greco, G.?+?**

[Greco]

1 e4 e5 2 ♘f3 ♕f6 3 ♗c4 ♕g6 4 0-0 ♕xe4 5 ♗xf7+ ♔e7 6 ♖e1 ♕f4 7 ♖xe5+ ♔xf7 8 d4 ♕f6 9 ♘g5+ ♔g6 10 ♕d3+ ♔h6 [10 ... ♔h5 11 ♘f7+ ♔g4 (11 ... g5 12 ♖xg5++−) 12 h3+ ♔h4 13 ♕g3#] 11 ♘f7# **1-0** L/N398

**162̂0̂-★G?-23**
**Greco, G.?+?**

[Greco]

1 e4 e5 2 ♘f3 ♕f6 3 ♗c4 ♕g6 4 0-0 ♕xe4 5 ♗xf7+ ♔e7 6 ♖e1 ♕f4 7 ♖xe5+ ♔d8 [7 ... ♔f6 8 d4 ♕g4 9 ♗h5+−; 7 ... ♔d6 8 ♖d5+ ♔e7 9 ♕e1+ ♔xf7 10 d4 ♕f6 11 ♘g5+ ♔g6 12 ♕e8+ ♔h6 13 ♘f7+ ♔g6 14 ♘xh8#] 8 ♖e8# **1-0** L/N398

**162̂0̂-★G?-24**
**Greco, G.?+?**

[Greco]

1 e4 e5 2 ♘f3 f6 3 ♘xe5 fxe5 4 ♕h5+ ♔e7 5 ♕xe5+ ♔f7 6 ♗c4+

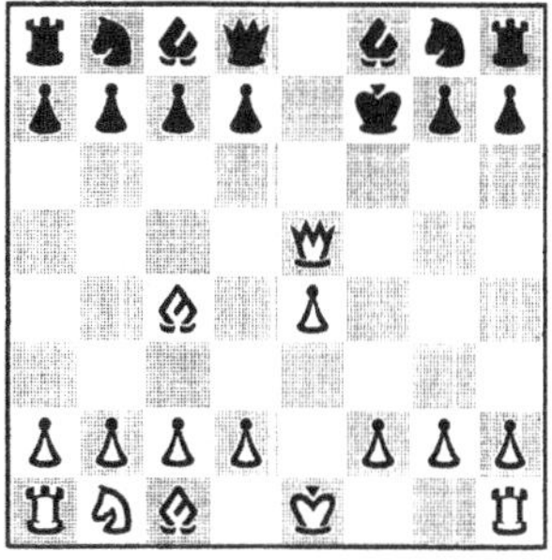

6 ... ♔g6 [6 ... d5 7 ♗xd5+ ♔g6 8 h4 h6 9 ♗xb7 ♗xb7 10 ♕f5#; 6 ... d5 7 ♗xd5+ ♔g6 8 h4 h5 9 ♗xb7 ♗xb7 10 ♕f5+ ♔h6 11 d4+ g5 12 ♗xg5+ ♕xg5 13 hxg5+ ♔g7 14 ♕e5+ ♔f7 15 ♕xh8+−; 6 ... d5 7 ♗xd5+ ♔g6 8 h4 ♕f6 9 ♕e8+ ♔h6 10 d4+ g5 11 hxg5+ ♔g7 12 gxf6+ ♘xf6 13 ♕f7#; 6 ... d5 7 ♗xd5+ ♔g6 8 h4 ♗d6 9 h5+ ♔h6 10 d4+ g5 11 ♕xh8 c6 12 ♗xg8 ♕e7 13 ♗xh7 ♕xh7 14 ♕f6+ ♕g6 15 ♕xg6#] 7 ♕f5+ ♔h6 8 d4+ g5 9 h4 ♔g7 10 ♕f7+ ♔h6 11 hxg5# **1-0** L/N398

**162̂0̂-★G?-25**
**Greco, G.?+?**

[Greco]

1 e4 e6 2 d4 ♘f6 3 ♗d3 ♘c6 4 ♘f3 ♗e7 5 h4 0-0 6 e5 ♘d5 7 ♗xh7+ ♔xh7 8 ♘g5+ ♗xg5 [8 ... ♔g6 9 h5+ ♔h6 (9 ... ♔f5 10 g4#) 10 ♘xf7+ ♔h7 11 ♘xd8+−] 9 hxg5+ ♔g8 [9 ... ♔g6 10 ♕h5+ ♔f5 11 ♕h7+ g6 12 ♕h3+ ♔e4 13 ♕d3#] 10 ♕h5 f5 11 g6 ♖e8 12 ♕h8# **1-0** L/N398

**162̂0̂-★G?-26**
**Greco, G.?+?**

1 e4 e6 2 d4 d5 3 e5 c5 4 c3 cxd4 5 cxd4 ♗b4+ 6 ♘c3 ♗xc3+ 7 bxc3 ♘c6 8 ♗d3 ♘ge7 9 f4 ♘f5 10 ♘f3 0-0 11 g4 ♘h4 12 0-0 ♘xf3+ 13 ♕xf3 ♗d7 14 ♕h3 g6 15 f5 exf5 16 gxf5 gxf5 17 ♖xf5 ♗xf5 18 ♗xf5 ...? **1-0** L/N398

**1620-★G?-27**
**?– Greco, G.?**
1 e4 e6 2 d4 d5 3 e5 c5 4 c3 ♘c6 5 ♘f3 ♗d7 6 ♗e3 c4 7 b3 b5 8 a4 a6 9 axb5 axb5 10 ♖xa8 ♕xa8 11 bxc4 dxc4 12 ♗e2 ♘ge7 13 0-0 ♘d5 14 ♗d2 ♗e7 15 ♘g5 ♗xg5 16 ♗xg5 0-0 17 ♗f3 ♘a5 18 ♗xd5 ♕xd5 19 f4 ♗c6 20 ♕d2 ♘b3 21 ♕c2

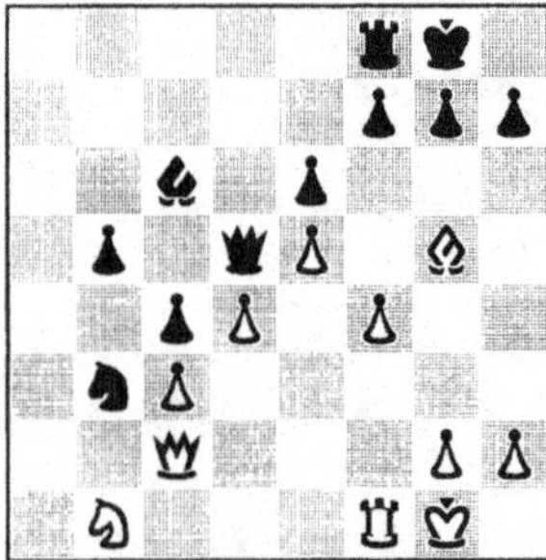

21 ... ♘xd4 22 cxd4 ♕xd4+ 23 ♔h1 ♗e4 24 ♕c3 ♕c5 25 ♘d2 ♗d3 26 ♖c1 ♖c8 27 ♘b3 cxb3 28 ♕xc5 ♖xc5 29 ♖xc5 h6 30 ♖c3 b2 31 ♖b3 b1♕+ 32 ♖xb1 ♗xb1 33 ♗e7 ♔h7 34 g4 ♗e4+ 35 ♔g1 ♗f3 36 h3 h5 37 g5 ♔g6 38 ♔f2 ♗d5 39 ♔e3 h4 40 ♔f2 ♔f5 41 ♔e3 ♗g2 42 ♗f8 g6 43 ♗b4 ♗xh3 44 ♗e1 ♔g4 45 ♗d2 ♗g2 46 ♔f2 h3 47 ♗c1 ♗d5 48 ♔g1 ♔g3 49 ♗e3 h2+ 50 ♔f1 h1♕+ ...? **0-1** L/N398

**1620-★G?-28**
**Greco, G.?+?**
[Greco]
1 e4 b6 2 d4 ♗b7 3 ♗d3 ♘c6 4 ♗e3 g6 5 f4 ♗g7 6 ♘f3 ♘f6 7 c4 0-0 8 ♘c3± ...? **1-0** L/N398

**1620-★G?-29**
**Greco, G.?+?**
1 e4 b6 2 d4 ♗b7 3 ♗d3 f5 4 exf5 ♗xg2 5 ♕h5+ g6 6 fxg6 ♘f6 7 gxh7+ ♘xh5 8 ♗g6# **1-0** L/N398

**1620-★G?-30**
**Greco, G.?+?**
1 e4 b6 2 d4 ♗b7 3 ♗d3 g6 4 f4 ♗g7 5 ♗e3 ♘c6 6 ♘f3 ♘f6 7 c4 0-0 8 ♘c3 e6 9 e5 ♘e8 10 g4 d5 11 cxd5 exd5 12 h4 a6 13 h5 b5 14 hxg6 hxg6 15 ♕e2 b4 16 ♕h2 bxc3 17 ♕h7# **1-0** L/N398

**1620-★G?-31**
**Greco, G.?+?**
1 e4 c5 2 b4 cxb4 3 d4 e6 4 a3 bxa3 5 c4 ♗b4+ 6 ♗d2 ♗xd2+ 7 ♕xd2 d5 8 e5 dxc4 9 ♗xc4 ♘c6 10 ♘e2 ♘ge7 11 ♖xa3 0-0 12 0-0 ♘f5 13 ♖d3 a6 14 f4 b5 15 ♗b3 a5 16 g4 ♘h6 17 h3 a4 18 ♗c2 b4 19 f5 exf5 20 g5 b3 21 ♗d1 ♕a5 22 ♕f4 ♕b5 23 ♖g3 ♗d7 24 gxh6 g6 25 ♕g5 f6 26 exf6 ♖f7 27 ♘f4 ♘xd4 28 ♘xg6 ♘e6 29 ♘e7+ ♔h8 30 ♕g7+ ♘xg7 31 fxg7+ ♖xg7 32 hxg7# **1-0** L/N398

**1620-★G?-32**
**Greco, G.?+?**
1 e4 c5 2 b4 cxb4 3 d4 e6 4 a3 bxa3 5 ♗xa3 ♗xa3 6 ♖xa3 ♘c6 7 c4 ♘f6 8 e5 ♘g8 9 f4 ♘h6 10 ♘f3 0-0 11 d5 exd5 12 cxd5 ♘e7 13 d6 ♘g6 14 ♕d2 ♕b6 15 ♘c3 ♘f5 16 ♘d5 ♕b1+ 17 ♔f2 b6 18 ♖g1 ♕e4 19 ♘c7 ♖b8 20 ♗d3 ...? **1-0** L/N398

**1620-★G?-33**
**?– Greco, G.?**
1 e4 c5 2 f4 ♘c6 3 ♘f3 d6 4 ♗c4 ♘h6 5 0-0 ♗g4 6 c3 e6 7 h3 ♗xf3 8 ♕xf3 ♕d7 9 d3 0-0-0 10 f5 ♘e5 11 ♕e2 ♘xc4 12 ♗xh6 ♘a5 13 b4 ♘c6 14 ♗d2 exf5 15 exf5 f6 16 b5 ♘e7 17 ♕e6 ♕xe6 18 fxe6 ♘g6 19 d4 d5 20 ♗e3 c4 21 ♗c1 ♖e8 22 ♖e1 ♗d6 23 a4 ♘f8 24 ♘d2 ♘xe6 25 ♘f3 g5 26 ♘h2 h5 27 a5 ♖hg8 28 a6 b6 29 ♘f1 f5 30 ♘e3 ♘c7 31 ♖f1 f4 32 ♘d1 ♘e6 33 ♖a2 g4 34 ♘f2 f3 35 hxg4 hxg4 36 ♘h1 ...? **0-1** L/N398

**1620-★G?-34**
**Greco, G.?○?**
1 e4 c5 2 f4 e6 3 ♘f3 ♘c6 4 c3 d5 5 e5 ♗e7 6 d4 c4 7 ♗e2 ♗h4+ 8 g3 ♗e7 9 ♗e3 ♗d7 10 ♘bd2 ♘h6 11 b3 b5 12 a4 a6 13 axb5 axb5 14 b4 0-0 15 0-0 ♘f5 16 ♗f2 ♖xa1 17 ♕xa1 ♘xb4 18 cxb4 ♗xb4 19 ♕b1 ♕a5 20 ♕c2 ♗c3 21 h3 ...? L/N398

**1620-★G?-35**
**Greco, G.?+?**
1 f4 e5 2 fxe5 ♕h4+ 3 g3 ♕e4 4 ♘f3 ♘c6 5 ♘c3 ♕f5 6 e4 ♕e6 7 d4 ♕e7 8 ♗g5 ♕b4 9 a3 ♕xb2 10 ♘a4 ...? **1-0** L/N398

**1620-★G?-36**
**?– Greco, G.?**
[Greco]
1 e4 e5 2 ♗c4 ♗c5 3 ♕h5 ♕e7 4 ♘c3 c6 5 ♘f3 ♘f6 6 ♕xe5 ♗xf2+ 7 ♔xf2 [7 ♔f1 ♕xe5 8 ♘xe5 ♗d4 9 ♘xf7 d5 10 ♘xh8 dxc4 ∆ 11 ... ♔f8→] 7 ... ♘g4+ 8 ♔f1 ♘xe5 ...? **0-1** L/N398

**1620-★G?-37**
**?– Greco, G.?**
[Greco]
1 e4 e5 2 ♗c4 ♘f6 3 ♘c3 c6 4 ♕f3 b5 5 ♗b3 b4 6 ♘a4 d5 7 d3 [7 exd5 cxd5 8 ♘e2 ♕a5 9 ♘g3 ♗g4 10 ♕e3 d4 11 ♕d3 ♗d7→] 7 ... h6 8 ♘e2 d4 9 ♘g3 ♗g4 ...? **0-1** L/N398

**1620-★G?-38**
**Greco, G.?+?**
1 e4 e5 2 ♗c4 ♘f6 3 f4 ♘xe4 4 ♘f3 exf4 5 0-0 ♗c5+ 6 d4 ♗b6 7 ♖e1 f5 8 ♘c3 ♕e7 9 ♗d5 c6 10 ♗xe4 ♕f6 11 ♗xf5+ ♔d8 12 ♘e4 ♕h6 13 g3 ♘a6 14 ♘d6 ♕xd6 15 ♘e5 ♕f6 16 ♕h5 g6 17 ♗xg6 hxg6 18 ♕xh8+ ♕xh8 19 ♘f7+ ♔c7 20 ♗xf4+ d6 21 ♗xd6+ ♔d7 22 ♖e7# **1-0** L/N398

**1620-★G?-39**
**Greco, G.?+?**
[Greco]
1 e4 e5 2 ♗c4 ♗c5 3 ♕e2 d6 4 c3 ♘c6 5 f4 exf4 6 ♘f3 g5 7 h4 g4 8 ♘g5 ♘h6 9 d4 ♗b6 10 ♗xf4 ♕e7 11 ♖f1 f6 12 ♘d2 fxg5 13 ♗xg5 ♕g7 14 ♕e3 ♘g8 15 ♗f7+

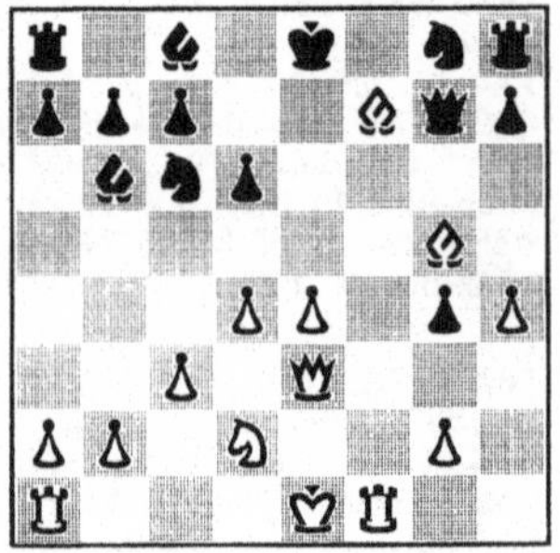

15 ... ♔d7 [15 ... ♔f8 16 ♗h5+ ♘f6 17 ♗h6 ♕xh6 18 ♕xh6++−; 15 ... ♕xf7 16 ♖xf7 ♔xf7 17 ♕f4+ ♔g7 18 0-0-0 ♗d7 19 ♖f1 ♗e8 20 ♕f8+ ♔g6 21 ♖f6+ ♔h5 22 ♖h6+ ♘xh6 23 ♕xh6#] 16 ♕f4 ♘ge7 17 ♕xg4+ ♔d8 18 ♗xe7+ ♘xe7 19 ♕xg7 ...? **1-0** L/N398

**1620-★G?-40**
**Greco, G.?+?**
1 e4 e5 2 ♗c4 ♗c5 3 ♕e2 ♕e7 4 f4 ♗xg1 5 ♖xg1 exf4 6 d4 ♕h4+ 7 g3 fxg3 8 ♖xg3 ♘f6 9 ♘c3 ♘h5 10 ♗xf7+ ♔xf7 11 ♗g5 ♘xg3 12 ♕f3+ ♔g6 13 ♗xh4 ♘h5 14 ♕f5+ ♔h6 15 ♕g5# **1-0** L/N398

**1620-★G?-41**
**Greco, G.?+?**
1 e4 e5 2 ♗c4 ♗c5 3 ♕e2 ♕e7 4 f4 exf4 5 ♘f3 g5 6 h4 f6 7 hxg5 fxg5 8 ♘c3 c6 9 d4 g4 10 ♘h4 ♗xd4 11 ♘f5 ♗xc3+ 12 bxc3 ♕f6 13 ♗xf4

♕xc3+ 14 ♔f2 b5 15 ♗b3 a5 16 ♘d6+ ♔d8 17 ♕xg4 ♘e7 18 ♘f7+ ♔e8 19 ♕h5 ♕d4+ 20 ♔f3 ♕c3+ 21 ♔e2 ♖f8 22 ♘d6+ ♔d8 23 ♕e8+ ♖xe8 24 ♘f7# **1-0** L/N398

**1620-★G?-42**
**Greco, G.?+?**

[Greco]

1 e4 e5 2 ♗c4 ♗c5 3 ♕e2 ♕e7 4 f4 exf4 5 ♘f3 g5 6 d4 ♗b4+ 7 c3 ♗a5 8 h4 f6 [8 ... g4 9 ♘g5 ♘h6 10 ♗xf4 f6 11 0-0 fxg5 12 ♗xg5 ♕g7 13 ♕e3 ♘g8 14 ♖f7 ♕g6 15 ♕f4 d6 16 ♖f8+ ♔d7 17 ♗f7 ♕g7 18 ♗e8+ ♔e6 19 d5#] 9 hxg5 fxg5 10 g3 g4 11 ♘e5 f3 12 ♕e3 ♘f6 13 ♘g6 ♕g7 14 ♘xh8 ♕xh8 15 e5 ♘g8 16 ♕g5 ♘e7 17 ♕h5+ ♔d8 18 ♕xh7 ♕xh7 19 ♖xh7 d6 20 e6 d5 21 ♖h8+ ♘g8 22 ♗g5+ ♔e8 23 ♖xg8# **1-0** L/N398

**1620-★G?-43**
**Greco, G.?+?**

[Greco]

1 e4 e5 2 ♗c4 ♗c5 3 ♕e2 ♕e7 4 f4 exf4 5 ♘f3 ♘f6 6 d4 ♗b4+ 7 c3 ♗a5 8 e5 ♘h5 9 0-0 0-0 10 ♘e1 ♕h4 11 ♘d3 g5 12 ♘d2 c6 13 ♘e4

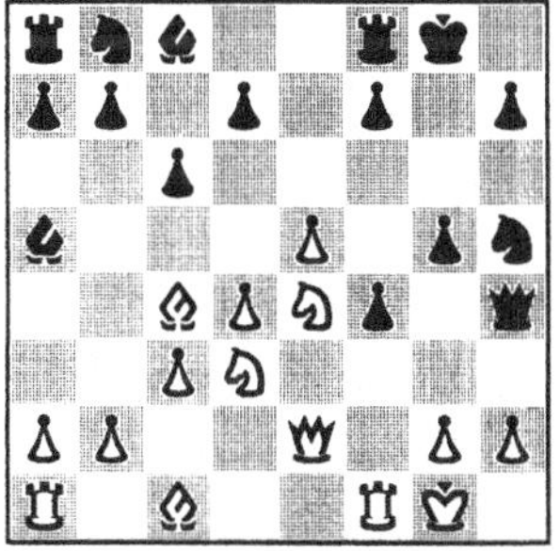

13 ... ♔h8 [13 ... b5 14 ♗b3 ♗c7 15 ♕xh5 ♕xh5 16 ♘f6+ ♔g7 17 ♘xh5++-; 13 ... ♘g7 14 ♘xf4 gxf4 15 ♖xf4 ♕e7 16 ♘f6+ ♔h8 17 ♕e4+-] 14 ♘d6 ♘a6 15 ♘f5 ...? **1-0** L/N398

**1620-★G?-44**
**Greco, G.?+?**

[Greco]

1 e4 e5 2 f4 exf4 3 ♘f3 g5 4 ♗c4 ♗g7 5 d4 d6 6 ♘c3 c6 7 h4 h6 8 hxg5 hxg5 9 ♖xh8 ♗xh8 10 ♘e5 dxe5 11 ♕h5 ♕f6 12 dxe5 ♕g7 13 e6 ♘f6 14 exf7+

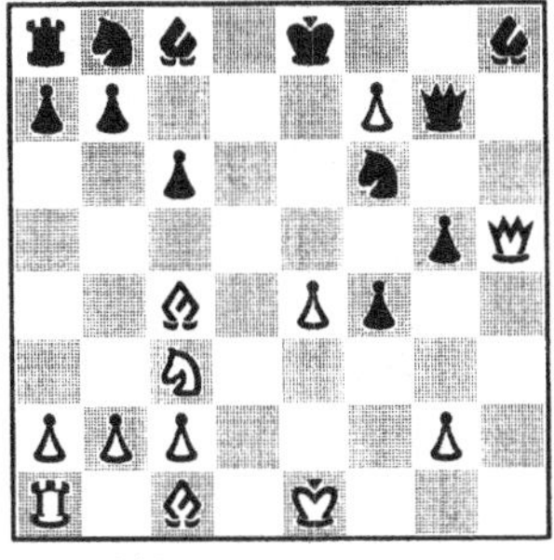

14 ... ♔f8 [14 ... ♔e7 15 ♕e2 ♗e6 16 ♗xe6 ♔xe6 17 ♕c4+ ♔e7 18 ♕b4+ ♔xf7 19 ♕xb7+ ♘bd7 20 ♕xa8+-; 14 ... ♔d8 15 ♕xg5 ♕xg5 16 f8♕+ ♔d7 17 ♕xh8 ♕xg2 18 ♕xf6 f3 19 ♕f7+ ♔d6 20 ♗f4+ ♔c5 21 ♘a4+ ♔b4 (21 ... ♔d4 22 c3+ ♔xe4 23 ♘c5#) 22 ♗d2+ ♔xa4 23 b3+ ♔a3 24 ♕e7+ ♔b2 25 ♕e5+ ♔a3 (25 ... ♔xc2 26 ♖c1#) 26 ♗c1+ ♔b4 27 c3#] 15 ♗xf4 ♘xh5 16 ♗d6# **1-0** L/N398

**1620-★G?-45**
**Greco, G.?+?**

[Greco]

1 e4 e5 2 f4 exf4 3 ♘f3 g5 4 ♗c4 ♗g7 5 h4 g4 6 ♘g5 ♘h6 7 d4 d6 8 ♗xf4 ♕e7 9 0-0 f6 10 c3 fxg5 11 ♗xg5 ♕d7 12 ♕d2 ♘g8 13 ♗f7+ ♔f8 [13 ... ♕xf7 14 ♖xf7 ♔xf7 15 ♘a3 ♘e7 16 ♖f1+ ♔e8 17 ♗xe7 ♔xe7 18 ♕g5+ ♔e6 (18 ... ♔e8 19 ♕xg7+-) 19 d5+ ♔d7 20 ♖f7+ ♔e8 21 ♕e7#] 14 ♗e6+ ♔e8 15 ♗xd7+ ...? **1-0** L/N398

**1620-★G?-46**
**Greco, G.?+?**

[Greco]

1 e4 e5 2 f4 exf4 3 ♘f3 g5 4 ♗c4 g4 5 ♘e5 ♕h4+ 6 ♔f1 ♘h6 7 d4 d6 8 ♘d3 f3 9 g3 ♕h3+

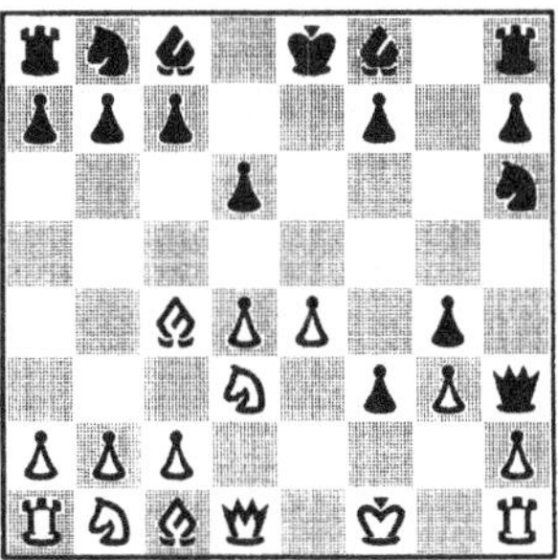

10 ♔f2 [10 ♔e1 ♕h5 (10 ... ♕g2 11 ♘f2 ♘c6 12 ♗f1+-) 11 ♘f4 ♕a5+ 12 ♗d2 ♕a4 (12 ... ♕b6 13 ♘d5 ♕xd4 14 ♗d3 ♕c5 15 ♗e3 ♕a5+ 16 b4 ♕a4 17 ♗b5+ ♕xb5 18 ♘xc7+ ♔d7 19 ♘xb5+-) 13 ♘a3 c6 (13 ... ♕d7 14 ♘d5 ♗g7 15 ♗xh6 ♗xh6 16 ♘f6+ ♔f8 17 ♘xd7++-) 14 ♘d5 b5 15 b3 ♕xa3 16 ♗b4 ♕b2 17 ♖b1 ♕xa2 18 ♖a1 ♕b2 19 ♗c3 ♕xa1 20 ♕xa1 cxd5 21 ♗xd5 ♘d7 22 ♗xa8+-] 10 ... ♕g2+ 11 ♔e3 ♘g8 12 ♘f4 ♗h6 13 ♗f1 ♕xh1 14 ♗b5+ c6 15 ♗xc6+ bxc6 16 ♕xh1 ...? **1-0** L/N398

**1620-★G?-47**
**Greco, G.?+?**

[Greco]

1 e4 e5 2 f4 exf4 3 ♘f3 g5 4 ♗c4 g4 5 ♘e5 ♕h4+ 6 ♔f1 ♘f6 7 ♗xf7+ [7 ♘xf7 d5 8 ♗xd5 ♘xd5 9 ♘xh8 ♘f6 10 e5 ♘e4 11 ♕e2 ♘g3+ 12 hxg3 ♕xh1+ 13 ♔f2 ♗c5+-+] 7 ... ♔d8 8 d4 [8 ♗b3 ♘h5 9 ♘f7+ ♔e8 10 ♘xh8 ♘g3+ 11 hxg3 (11 ♔g1 ♗c5+ 12 d4 ♗xd4+ 13 ♕xd4 ♘e2+ 14 ♔f1 ♘xd4-+) 11 ... ♕xh1+ 12 ♔e2 f3+ 13 gxf3 gxf3+ 14 ♔f2 ♕xd1-+] 8 ... ♘xe4 9 ♕e2 ♘g3+ 10 hxg3 ♕xh1+ 11 ♔f2 fxg3+ 12 ♔xg3 ♕xc1 13 ♘c6+ ♘xc6 14 ♕e8# **1-0** L/N398

**1620-★G?-48**
**?– Greco, G.?**

[Greco]

1 e4 e5 2 f4 exf4 3 ♘f3 g5 4 ♗c4 g4 5 ♘e5 ♘h6 6 ♘xg4 ♕h4+ 7 ♘f2 d5 8 ♗xd5 [8 exd5 f3 9 ♗b5+ c6 10 dxc6 ♕e7+ 11 ♔f1 fxg2+ 12 ♔xg2 ♕g5+ 13 ♔f1 ♕xb5+ 14 d3 ♘xc6-+] 8 ... ♗g4 ...? **0-1** L/N398

**1620-★G?-49**
**?– Greco, G.?**

1 e4 e5 2 f4 exf4 3 ♘f3 g5 4 ♗c4 g4 5 ♘e5 ♘h6 6 ♘xg4 ♘xg4 7 ♕xg4 d5 8 ♕xf4 dxc4 9 ♕e5+ ♗e6 10 ♕xh8 ♕h4+ 11 ♔f1 ♕f4+ 12 ♔g1 ♕xe4 13 h3 ♗d5 14 ♕g8 f5 15 ♕g3 f4 16 ♕f3 ♕e1+ 17 ♕f1 ♗c5+ 18 ♔h2 ♕g3# **0-1** L/N398

**1620-★G?-50**
**Greco, G.?+?**

1 e4 e5 2 f4 exf4 3 ♘f3 g5 4 h4 g4 5 ♘e5 h5 6 ♗c4 ♘h6 7 d4 ♗e7 8 ♗xf4 ♗xh4+ 9 g3 ♗g5 10 ♖xh5 ♗xf4 11 gxf4 d6 12 ♘xg4 ♗xg4 13 ♕xg4 ♘xg4 14 ♖xh8+ ♔e7 15 ♖xd8 ♔xd8 16 ♗xf7 ♘c6 17 c3 ♔e7 18 ♗b3 ♘e3 19 ♔f2 ♘g4+ 20 ♔f3 ...? **1-0** L/N398

**1620-★G?-51**
**Greco, G.?+?**

[Greco]

1 e4 e5 2 f4 exf4 3 ♘f3 h6 4 ♗c4 g5 5 h4 f6 [5 ... g4 6 ♘e5 ♖h7 7 d4 d6 8 ♘d3 f3 9 g3 ♕e7 10 ♘f4 ♕xe4+ 11 ♔f1 ♕c6 12 ♕d3 ♖g7 13 ♗b5+-] 6 ♘xg5 fxg5 [6 ... ♕e7 7 ♕h5+ ♔d8 8 ♘f7+ ♔e8 9 ♘xh8+ ♔d8 10 ♘f7+ ♔e8 11 ♘xh6+ ♔d8 12 ♘xg8+-] 7 ♕h5+ ♔e7 8 ♕f7+ ♔d6 9 ♕d5+ ♔e7 10 ♕e5# **1-0** L/N398

**1620-★G?-52**
**Greco, G.?+?**

[Greco]

1 e4 e5 2 f4 exf4 3 ♘f3 ♘e7 4 h4 h5 5 ♗c4 ♘g6 6 ♘g5 ♘e5 7 ♗b3 f6 8 ♘h3 ♘g6 [8 ... g5 9 hxg5 fxg5 10 d4 ♘f7 11 g3 fxg3 12 ♗xf7+ ♔xf7 13 ♘xg5+ ♔g6 14 ♕f3 ♕f6 15 ♕xg3 d6 16 ♘e6+ ♔h7 (16 ... ♔f7 17 ♖f1+–) 17 ♖xh5+ ♗h6 18 ♖xh6+ ♕xh6 19 ♗xh6+–] 9 d4 ♘xh4 10 ♘xf4 g5 11 ♖xh4 gxh4 12 ♘g6 ♖h7 13 ♗g8 ♖g7 14 ♕xh5 ♖xg8 15 ♘e5+ ♔e7 16 ♕f7+ ♔d6 17 ♘c4+ ♔c6 18 ♕d5# **1-0** L/N398

**1620-★G?-53**
**Greco, G.?+?**

[Greco]

1 e4 e5 2 f4 exf4 3 ♘f3 ♘e7 4 h4 h5 5 ♗c4 ♘g6 6 ♘g5 ♘e5 7 ♗b3 f6 8 ♘h3 g5 9 hxg5 fxg5 10 d4 ♘f7 11 g3 fxg3 12 ♗xf7+ ♔xf7 13 ♘xg5+ ♔e8 14 ♖xh5 ♖xh5 [14 ... ♖g8 15 ♖h7 ♕f6 16 ♕h5+ ♕g6 17 ♗f4 ♕xh5 18 ♖xh5 ♗e7 19 ♘d2 ♘c6 20 c3 d6 21 ♘h3 ♗g4 22 ♖h7 ♗xh3 23 ♖xh3 g2 24 ♔f2 ♔d7 25 ♖g1 ♖af8 26 ♖f3 ♗h4+ 27 ♔e2 ♔d8 28 ♗e3 ♖xf3 29 ♘xf3 ♗f6 30 ♔f2 ♖e8 31 ♘d2 ♖g8 32 ♖xg2 ♖xg2+ 33 ♔xg2+–] 15 ♕xh5+ ♔e7 16 ♕f7+ ♔d6 17 ♕d5+ ♔e7 18 ♕e5# **1-0** L/N398

**1620-★G?-54**
**Greco, G.?+?**

1 e4 e5 2 f4 exf4 3 ♘f3 ♘e7 4 h4 h5 5 ♗c4 ♘g6 6 ♘g5 ♘e5 7 ♗b3 f6 8 ♘h3 g5 9 hxg5 fxg5 10 d4 ♘g6 11 g3 fxg3 12 ♘xg5 g2 13 ♗f7+ ♔e7 14 ♖g1 ♘h4 15 ♗xh5 ♗g7 16 ♕g4 ♗xd4 17 ♕xh4 ♖xh5 18 ♕xh5 ♗xg1 19 ♕f7+ ♔d6 20 ♕d5+ ♔e7 21 ♕e5+ ♔f8 22 ♕h8+ ♔e7 23 ♕g7+ ♔d6 24 ♘f7+ ...? **1-0** L/N398

**1620-★G?-55**
**Greco, G.?+?**

1 e4 e5 2 f4 exf4 3 ♘f3 g5 4 ♗c4 f6 5 ♘xg5 fxg5 6 ♕h5+ ♔e7 7 ♕xg5+ ♔e8 8 ♕h5+ ♔e7 9 ♕e5# **1-0** L/N398

**1620-★G?-56**
**Greco, G.?+?**

1 e4 e5 2 f4 exf4 3 ♘f3 g5 4 ♗c4 g4 5 ♗xf7+ ♔xf7 6 ♘e5+ ♔e6 7 ♕xg4+ ♔xe5 8 ♕f5+ ♔d6 9 d4 ♗g7 10 ♗xf4+ ♔e7 11 ♗g5+ ♗f6 12 e5 ♗xg5 13 ♕xg5+ ♔e8 14 ♕h5+ ♔e7 15 0-0 ♕e8 16 ♕g5+ ♔e6 17 ♖f6+ ♘xf6 18 ♕xf6+ ♔d5 19 ♘c3+ ♔xd4 20 ♕f4+ ♔c5

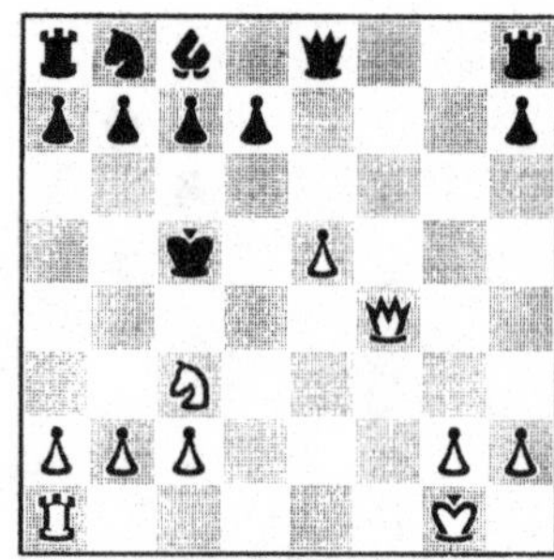

21 b4+ ♔c6 22 ♕c4+ ♔b6 23 ♘a4# **1-0** L/N398

**1620-★G?-57**
**Greco, G.?+?**

[Greco]

1 e4 e5 2 f4 exf4 3 ♗c4 ♕h4+ 4 ♔f1 ♗c5 5 d4 ♗b6 6 ♘f3 ♕g4 7 ♗xf7+ ♔xf7 [7 ... ♔f8 8 h3 ♕g3 9 ♘c3 ♔xf7 10 ♘e2 ♕g6 11 ♘e5+ ♔f8 12 ♘xg6++–] 8 ♘e5+ ♔f8 9 ♘xg4 ...? **1-0** L/N398

**1620-★G?-58**
**Greco, G.?+?**

[Greco]

1 e4 e5 2 f4 exf4 3 ♗c4 ♕h4+ 4 ♔f1 ♗c5 5 d4 ♗b6 6 ♘f3 ♕h6 [6 ... ♕f6 7 e5 ♕f5 8 ♗d3 ♕g4 9 h3 ♕g3 10 ♗d2 ♘c6 11 ♗e1+–] 7 g3 [7 ♘e5 d5 8 ♗xd5 ♗e6 9 ♗xb7+–] 7 ... ♕h3+ 8 ♔f2 fxg3+ 9 hxg3 ♕g4 10 ♗xf7+ ♔f8 11 ♖h4 ...? **1-0** L/N398

**1620-★G?-59**
**Greco, G.?+?**

[Greco]

1 e4 e5 2 f4 exf4 3 ♗c4 ♕h4+ 4 ♔f1 ♗c5 5 d4 ♗b6 6 ♘f3 ♕e7 7 ♗xf4 ♕xe4 8 ♗xf7+ ♔f8 9 ♗g3 ♘h6 10 ♘c3 ♕e7 11 ♗b3 c6 12 ♕d3 d5 13 ♖e1 ♕f7 14 ♗d6+ ♔g8 15 ♖e7 ♕f6 16 ♘xd5 ♕xd6 [16 ... cxd5 17 ♗xd5+ ♔f8 (17 ... ♘f7 18 ♖e8#) 18 ♖f7+ ♔e8 19 ♖xf6 gxf6 20 ♕e3+ ♔d8 21 ♕e7#] 17 ♘f6+ ♔f8 18 ♖e8# **1-0** L/N398

**1620-★G?-60**
**Greco, G.?+?**

[Greco]

1 e4 e5 2 f4 exf4 3 ♗c4 ♕h4+ 4 ♔f1 ♗c5 5 d4 ♗b6 6 ♘f3 ♕e7 7 ♗xf4 ♕xe4 8 ♗xf7+ ♔f8 9 ♗g3 ♘h6 10 ♘c3 ♕e7 11 ♗b3 c6 12 ♕d3 d5 13 ♖e1 ♕f6 14 ♗h4 ♕g6 15 ♗e7+ ♔g8 16 ♕xg6 hxg6 17 ♘xd5 cxd5 18 ♗xd5+ ♔h7 [18 ... ♘f7 19 ♘g5 ♖h5 20 ♗xf7+ ♔h8 21 ♗xg6 ♖h4 22 ♘f7+ ♔g8 23 ♗xh4+–] 19 ♘g5# **1-0** L/N398

**1620-★G?-61**
**Greco, G.?+?**

[Greco]

1 e4 e5 2 f4 exf4 3 ♗c4 ♕h4+ 4 ♔f1 d6 5 ♘f3 ♗g4 6 d4 ♕h6 7 g3 ♕h3+ 8 ♔f2 fxg3+ 9 hxg3 ♗xf3 10 ♗xf7+ ♔d8 11 ♕xf3 ♕d7 12 ♖xh7 ♖xh7 13 ♗xg8 ♖h2+ 14 ♔g1

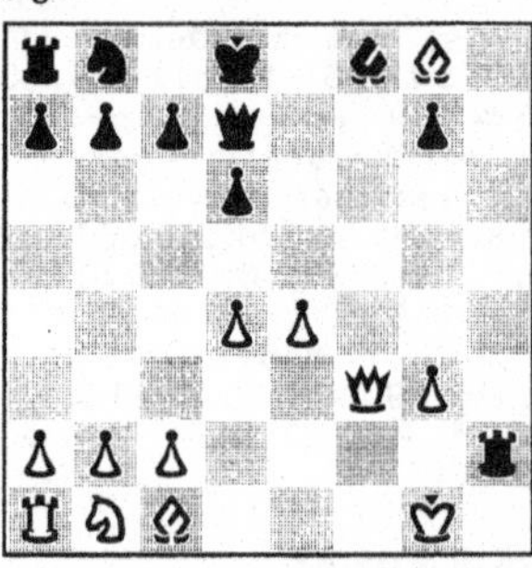

14 ... ♖xc2 [14 ... ♖h8 15 ♕xf8+ ♕e8 16 ♗g5+ ♔d7 17 ♕xg7+ ♔c6 18 ♕xh8 ♘d7 19 ♗d5+ ♔b6 20 ♕xe8 ♖xe8 21 ♘d2+–;14 ... ♕h3 15 ♕xf8+ ♔d7 16 ♕f7+ ♔c6 17 ♕c4+ ♔d7 18 ♗e6+ ♕xe6 19 ♕xe6+ ♔xe6 20 ♔xh2+–] 15 ♕xf8+ ♕e8 16 ♗g5+ ♔d7 17 ♗e6+ ♕xe6 18 ♕d8+ ♔c6 19 d5+ ♕xd5 20 exd5+ ♔xd5 21 ♘c3+ ♔e5 22 ♕e8+ ♔d4 23 ♕e4+ ♔c5 24 ♗e3# **1-0** L/N398

**1620-★G?-62**
**Greco, G.?+?**

[Greco]

1 e4 e5 2 f4 exf4 3 ♗c4 ♕h4+ 4 ♔f1 d6 5 ♘f3 ♗g4 6 d4 ♕f6 7 e5 ♕h6 [7 ... dxe5 8 dxe5 ♕xe5 (8 ... ♗xf3 9 ♕xf3 ♕xe5 10 ♕xb7+–) 9 ♘xe5 ♗xd1 10 ♘xf7 ♘h6 11 ♘xh8 g6 12 ♗xf4 ♗g7 13 c3 ♘f5 14 ♘f7+–] 8 g3 ♕h3+ 9 ♔f2 fxg3+ 10 hxg3 ♗xf3 11 ♕xf3 ♕d7 12 ♕xb7 ♕c6 13 ♗b5 ...? **1-0** L/N398

**1620-★G?-63**
**Greco, G.?+?**

[Greco]

1 e4 e5 2 f4 exf4 3 ♗c4 ♕h4+ 4 ♔f1 d6 5 ♘f3 ♗g4 6 d4 ♕h6 7 g3 g5 8 h4 f6 9 e5 dxe5 10 dxe5 fxe5 11 ♕d5 ♗xf3 12 ♕xf3 c6 13 hxg5 ♕xg5 14 gxf4 exf4 15 ♗xf4 ♕f6 16 ♘c3 ♗h6 17 ♖e1+ ♔f8 [17 ... ♔d8 18 ♖xh6 ♘xh6 19 ♗c7+ ♔xc7 20 ♕xf6+–;17 ... ♔d7 18 ♕d3+ ♔c8 19 ♖e8+ ♕d8 20 ♕xd8#] 18 ♗xh6+ ♘xh6 19 ♕xf6+ ♘f7 20 ♕xf7# **1-0** L/N398

**1620-★G?-64**
**Greco, G.?+?**

[Greco]

1 e4 e5 2 f4 exf4 3 ♗c4 ♕h4+ 4 ♔f1 d6 5 ♘f3 ♗g4 6 d4 ♕h6 7 g3

g5 8 h4 f6 9 e5 d×e5 10 d×e5 f×e5 11 ♕d5 ♗×f3 12 ♕×f3 c6 13 h×g5 ♕×g5 14 g×f4 e×f4 15 ♗×f4 ♕f6 16 ♘c3 ♗d6 17 ♖e1+

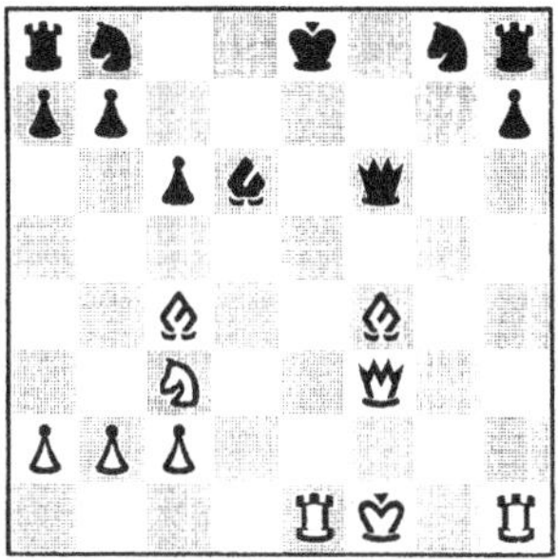

17 ... ♔d8 [17 ... ♘e7 18 ♘e4 ♕×f4 19 ♘×d6+ ♕×d6 20 ♖h6 ♕d7 (20 ... ♕×h6 21 ♕f7+ ♔d8 22 ♕×e7+ ♔c8 23 ♗e6+ ♘d7 24 ♕×d7+ ♔b8 25 ♕d6#) 21 ♕h5+ ♔d8 22 ♖d1 ♘d5 23 ♗×d5 ♖f8+ 24 ♔g1 ♕g7+ 25 ♗g2+ ♔c8 26 ♕h3+ ♘d7 27 ♖×h7 ♕×b2 28 ♕×d7+ ♔b8 29 ♕c7#; 17 ... ♗e7 18 ♘e4 ♕×b2 19 ♘d6+ ♔d7 (19 ... ♔f8 20 ♗h6#) 20 ♕g4+ ♔c7 (20 ... ♔d8 21 ♕c8#) 21 ♘c8+ ♔d8 22 ♖d1+ ♔e8 23 ♕h5+ ♔f8 24 ♕f7#] 18 ♖d1 ...? **1-0** L/N398

**162̂0̂-★G?-65**
**Greco, G.?+?**
1 e4 e5 2 f4 e×f4 3 ♗c4 ♗e7 4 d4 ♗h4+ 5 ♔f1 g5 6 g3 f×g3 7 h×g3 ♗×g3 8 ♕h5 ♕f6+ 9 ♘f3 d6 10 ♗×g5 ♕g6 11 ♕×g6 f×g6 12 ♗×g8 ♖×g8 13 ♔g2 ...? **1-0** L/N398

**162̂0̂-★G?-66**
**Greco, G?+?**
1 e4 e5 2 f4 e×f4 3 ♗c4 ♘e7 4 ♕f3 ♘g6 5 d4 ♕h4+ 6 g3 f×g3 7 ♗×f7+ ♔d8 8 h×g3 ♕f6 9 ♕×f6+ g×f6 10 ♗×g6 ...? **1-0** L/N398

**162̂0̂-★G?-67**
**Greco, G.?+?**
[Greco]
1 e4 e5 2 f4 ♘f6 3 ♘c3 e×f4 4 d4 ♗b4 5 ♗d3 ♕e7 6 ♕e2 ♘c6 7 e5 ♘×d4 [7 ... ♘d5 8 ♗d2 ♘×d4 9 ♘×d5 ♕h4+ 10 g3 f×g3 11 ♕g2 g×h2+ 12 ♔f1 h×g1♕+ 13 ♕×g1 ♕d8 14 ♕×g7 ♖f8 15 ♘f6+ ♔e7 16 ♗×b4+ d6 17 e×d6+ c×d6 18 ♘d5+ ♔e8 19 ♕×d4 ♗e6 20 ♗b5+ ♗d7 21 ♕e4+ ♕e7 22 ♕×e7#] 8 e×f6 ♘×e2 9 f×e7 ♘×c3 10 a3 ♗a5 11 ♗d2 ...? **1-0** L/N398

**162̂0̂-★G?-68**
**Greco, G?+?**
1 e4 e5 2 f4 d5 3 e×d5 ♕×d5 4 ♘c3 ♕e6 5 ♘f3 e×f4+ 6 ♔f2 ♗c5+ 7 d4 ♗d6 8 ♗b5+ ♔f8 9 ♖e1 ♕f5 10 ♖e8# **1-0** L/N398

**162̂0̂-★G?-69**
**Greco, G.?+?**
1 e4 e5 2 f4 ♗c5 3 ♘f3 d6 4 c3 ♕e7 5 d4 e×d4 6 c×d4 ♕×e4+ 7 ♔f2 ♗b4 8 a3 ♗a5 9 b4 ♗b6 10 ♗b5+ ♔f8 11 ♖e1 ♕f5 12 ♖e8# **1-0** L/N398

**162̂0̂-★G?-70**
**?– Greco, G.?**
[Greco]
1 e4 e5 2 ♘f3 f5 3 ♘×e5 ♕e7 4 ♕h5+ g6 5 ♘×g6 ♕×e4+ 6 ♔d1 [6 ♗e2 ♘f6 7 ♕h3 (7 ♕h4 ♕×g2 8 ♘×h8 ♕×h1+ 9 ♗f1 ♕e4+ 10 ♕×e4 f×e4 11 ♗c4 d5 12 ♗b5+ c6 13 ♗e2 ♗g7→) 7 ... h×g6 8 ♕×h8 ♕×g2 9 ♖f1 ♔f7 10 ♗c4+ d5 11 ♗e2 ♘c6 12 c3 ♗d7 13 d4 ♘×d4 14 c×d4 ♗b4+ 15 ♗d2 ♗×d2+ 16 ♘×d2 ♖×h8→] 6 ... ♘f6 7 ♕h3 h×g6 8 ♕×h8 ♘g4 9 ♕h4 ♘e3+ 10 d×e3 ♕×h4 ...? **0-1** L/N398

**162̂0̂-★G?-71**
**?– Greco, G.?**
[Greco]
1 e4 e5 2 ♘f3 f5 3 ♘×e5 ♕e7 4 ♕h5+ g6 5 ♘×g6 ♕×e4+ 6 ♔d1 ♘f6 7 ♕h3 h×g6 8 ♕×h8 ♘g4 9 d3 ♘×f2+ 10 ♔d2 ♕g4 11 ♗e2 [11 ♖g1 ♕d1+ 12 ♔e3 ♘g4+ 13 ♔d4 ♕×c1→; 11 ♕e5+ ♔f7 12 ♕d5+ ♔g7 13 ♕e5+ ♔h7 14 ♖g1 ♕d1+ 15 ♔e3 ♘g4+→] 11 ... ♕f4+ 12 ♔c3 [12 ♔e1 ♕×c1+ 13 ♔×f2 ♕×h1→] 12 ... ♕b4# **0-1** L/N398

**162̂0̂-★G?-72**
**?– Greco, G.?**
1 e4 e5 2 ♘f3 f5 3 e×f5 e4 4 ♘e5 ♘f6 5 g4 d6 6 ♘c4 h6 7 ♗g2 d5 8 ♘e3 d4 9 ♘c4 b5 10 ♘ca3 a6 11 d3 ♗b7 12 d×e4 ♘×e4 13 ♘d2 ♗b4 14 c3 d×c3 15 ♘×e4 c×b2+ 16 ♗d2 ♗×d2+ 17 ♘×d2 ♗×g2 18 ♖g1 b×a1♕ 19 ♕×a1 0-0 20 ♖×g2 ♕e7+ 21 ♔f1 ♕×a3 ...? **0-1** L/N398

**162̂0̂-★G?-73**
**?– Greco, G.?**
1 e4 e5 2 ♗c4 f5 3 ♗×g8 ♖×g8 4 ♕h5+ g6 5 ♕×h7 ♖g7 6 ♕h8 ♕g5 7 ♕h3 f×e4 8 ♘c3 ♕f5 9 ♕e3 ♖f7 10 ♘h3 d5 11 ♘×d5 ♘c6 12 c3 ♗e6 13 c4 ♘d4 14 ♕c3 ♕g4 15 0-0 ♘e2+ ...? **0-1** L/N398

**162̂0̂-★G?-74**
**?– Greco, G.?**
1 e4 e5 2 f4 f5 3 e×f5 ♕h4+ 4 g3 ♕e7 5 ♕h5+ ♔d8 6 f×e5 ♕×e5+ 7 ♗e2 ♘f6 8 ♕f3 d5 9 g4 h5 10 h3 h×g4 11 h×g4 ♖×h1 12 ♕×h1 ♕g3+ 13 ♔d1 ♘×g4 14 ♕×d5+ ♗d7 15 ♘f3 ♘f2+ 16 ♔e1 ♘d3+ 17 ♔d1 ♕e1+ 18 ♘×e1 ♘f2#

**0-1** L/N398

**162̂0̂-★G?-75**
**Greco, G.?+?**
1 d4 d5 2 c4 d×c4 3 e3 b5 4 a4 c6 5 a×b5 c×b5 6 ♕f3 ...? **1-0** L/N398

**162̂0̂-★G?-76**
**Greco, G.?+?**
1 d4 d5 2 c4 d×c4 3 e4 b5 4 a4 c6 5 a×b5 c×b5 6 b3 a5 7 b×c4 b4 8 d5 e6 9 ♘d2 e×d5 10 e×d5 ♗c5 11 ♘b3 ♗b6 12 c5 ♕e7+ 13 ♕e2 ♕×e2+ 14 ♗×e2 ♗d8 15 ♗b5+ ♔f8 16 c6 ♗b6 17 ♗e3 ♗×e3 18 f×e3 ♘f6 19 d6 g6 20 d7 ♗×d7 21 c×d7 ♘b×d7 22 ♗×d7 ♘×d7 23 ♖×a5 ...? **1-0** L/N398

**162̂0̂-★G?-77**
**Greco, G.?+?**
1 d4 d5 2 c4 c5 3 d×c5 ♕a5+ 4 ♕d2 ♕×d2+ 5 ♘×d2 d×c4 6 ♘×c4 e6 7 ♘d6+ ♗×d6 8 c×d6 ♘f6 9 f3 0-0 10 e4 e5 11 b3 ♖d8 12 ♗a3 ♘e8 13 ♖d1 ♗e6 14 ♗c4 ♗d7 15 g3 b5 16 ♗d5 ♗c6 17 ♗c5 ♗×d5 18 ♖×d5 ♘d7 19 b4 a5 20 a3 a×b4 21 a×b4 ♖a1+ 22 ♔f2 ♖c1 23 ♔g2 ♘×c5 24 b×c5 b4 25 ♘e2 ♖c2 26 ♔f2 b3 27 ♖b1 b2 28 ♔e1 f6 29 ♔d1 ♖c4 30 ♖×b2 ♔f7 31 ♖b7+ ♔e6 32 ♖e7# **1-0** L/N398

**1634-★C?-1**
**Cascio+?**
Napoli?
1 e4 e5 2 f4 e×f4 3 ♘f3 g5 4 ♗c4 g4 5 0-0 [♔h1, ♖f1] 5 ... g×f3 6 ♕×f3 ♕e7 7 ♕×f4 ♘h6 8 ♕×c7 ♘c6 9 ♘c3 ♕d6 10 ♘d5 ...? **1-0** +1

**1634-★LS-1**
**Leonardis○Salvio**
1 e4 e5 2 d3 ♗c5 3 ♗e2 ♘f6 4 f4 e×f4 5 ♗×f4 c6 6 ♘f3 ♕b6 7 ?c1 ♘g4 ...? +1

**1634-★MN-1**
**Nicodemo○Mancino**
Napoli [Salvio]
1 e4 e5 2 ♗c4 ♗c5 3 ♘f3 ♘c6 4 0-0 [♔g1, ♖e1] 4 ... ♘f6 5 c3 ♘g4 6 d4

**203** Salvio, A. JGW.CPL

exd4 7 ♗xf7+ ♔xf7 8 ♘g5+ ♔g8 9 ♕xg4 d6 10 ♕f3 ♕f6= …⚲ +1

**1680-★AA-1**
**Abbé de Lionne & Morant+ Auzout & Maubisson**
Paris
1 e4 e5 2 f4 exf4 3 ♘f3 g5 4 h4 g4 5 ♘e5 h5 6 ♗c4 ♖h7 7 d4 d6 8 ♘d3 f3 9 g3 ♘c6 10 c3 ♘ce7 11 ♔f2 c6 12 ♘f4 ♕c7 13 ♕b3 b5 14 ♗d3 ♖h8 15 ♖e1 ♘g6 16 ♘xg6 fxg6 17 e5 ♘e7 18 ♗xg6+ ♔d8 19 ♕f7 ♘xg6 20 ♕xg6 ♕g7 21 ♗g5+ ♔c7 22 exd6+ ♔b6 23 ♗d8+ ♔a6 24 ♕xg7 ♗xg7 25 ♗c7 ♗f6 26 a4 b4 27 ♘d2 ♗f5 28 ♘b3 ♔b7 29 ♘a5+ ♔a6 30 ♘xc6 ♖ae8 31 ♘xb4+ ♔b7 32 ♘d5 ♗d8 33 ♗xd8 ♖xd8 34 ♖e7+ ♔c6 35 c4 ♔xd6 36 ♖xa7 ♗d3 37 ♖a6+ ♔d7 38 b3 ♖b8 39 ♖b6 ♖xb6 40 ♘xb6+ …⚲ **1-0** +1

**1680-★AA-2**
**Abbé de Lionne & Morant+ Auzout & Maubisson**
Paris
1 e4 e5 2 f4 exf4 3 ♗c4 ♕h4+ 4 ♔f1 g5 5 ♕f3 ♗c5 6 g3 ♕h6 7 ♘e2 ♘c6 8 gxf4 ♕f6 9 ♕b3 d6 10 d3 ♗b6 11 ♘bc3 ♗h3+ 12 ♔e1 ♘d4 13 ♘xd4 ♕xd4 14 ♘d1 0-0-0 15 ♗e3 ♕f6 16 ♗xb6 cxb6 17 f5 ♘h6 18 ♘c3 ♖he8 19 ♔d2 ♕d4 20 ♖ae1 ♘g4 21 ♔c1 f6 22 ♕a4 a6 23 ♗e6+ ♖xe6 24 ♕xd4 **1-0** +1

**1680-★AA-3**
**Abbé de Lionne & Morant– Auzout & Maubisson**
Paris
1 e4 e5 2 f4 exf4 3 h4 ♗e7 4 ♕g4 d5 5 ♕xf4 dxe4 6 ♕xe4 ♘f6 7 ♕a4+ c6 8 d3 0-0 9 ♗f4 ♖e8 10 ♗e2 ♘a6 11 c4 ♗b4+ 12 ♔f1 ♕d4 13 ♗d2 ♗c5 14 ♗e1 ♗g4 15 ♘c3 ♖e5 16 ♘f3 ♗xf3 17 gxf3 ♖ae8 18 ♕d1 ♘h5 19 ♘e4 ♗b6 20 ♗c3 ♘g3+ 21 ♔g2 ♕e3 22 ♔xg3

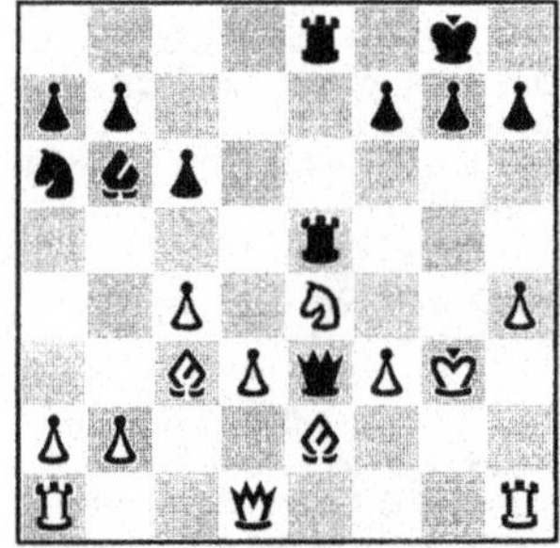

22 … ♖xe4 23 dxe4 ♖xe4 24 ♕d3 ♕f2+ 25 ♔h3 ♖xh4# **0-1** +1

**1680-★AJ-1**
**Jannisson & Maubisson+ Abbé de Lionne & Morant**
Paris
1 e4 e5 2 f4 exf4 3 ♘f3 g5 4 h4 h5 5 ♗c4 g4 6 ♘e5 ♖h7 7 d4 d6 8 ♘d3 f3 9 g3 ♘c6 10 c3 ♘ge7 11 ♘f4 a6 12 a4 ♗g7 13 ♕b3 ♗h8 14 ♘xh5 ♔f8 15 ♘f4 ♘a5 16 ♕a2 ♘xc4 17 ♕xc4 c6 18 ♘d2 d5 19 exd5 cxd5 20 ♕b4 ♗f6 21 ♘f1 ♔g7 22 h5 ♘c6 23 ♕c5 ♗e6 24 ♕a3 ♕d7 25 b3 ♖e8 26 ♗e3 ♘e7 27 0-0-0 ♘f5 28 ♗d2 ♖eh8 29 ♔b1 ♔g8 30 ♕c1 ♗g5 31 ♘xe6 ♗xd2 32 ♕xd2 ♕xe6 33 ♖e1 ♕b6 34 ♖e8+ ♔g7 35 ♕g5+ ♕g6 36 hxg6 …⚲ **1-0** +1

**1680-★AL-1**
**Abbé de Lionne & Morant+ Lafon le jeune & Roussereau**
Paris
1 e4 e5 2 f4 exf4 3 ♘f3 g5 4 h4 g4 5 ♘e5 ♕e7 6 d4 d6 7 ♘xg4 ♕xe4+ 8 ♕e2 ♕xe2+ 9 ♗xe2 h5 10 ♘f2 ♘c6 11 c3 ♗f5 12 ♗xf4 0-0-0 13 ♗d3 ♖e8+ 14 ♔d2 ♗g6 15 ♘a3 d5 16 ♘c2 a6 17 ♖ae1 ♖xe1 18 ♖xe1 ♗h6 19 ♗xh6 ♘xh6 20 ♘e3 ♘e7 21 a4 c6 22 b4 ♗xd3 23 ♘xd3 ♘ef5 24 ♘xf5 ♘xf5 25 ♖h1 ♖g8 26 ♘f4 ♖g4 27 ♘xh5 ♖xg2+ 28 ♔d3 ♖g4 29 ♖f1 ♘d6 30 ♖f4 f5 31 ♔e3 ♘e4 32 ♖xg4 fxg4 33 c4 ♔d7 34 cxd5 cxd5 35 ♘f4 ♔d6 36 h5 ♘f6 37 h6 ♔e7 38 ♔f2 ♔f7 39 ♔g3 ♔g8 40 ♘e6 ♔h7 41 ♘c5 ♔xh6 42 ♘xb7 ♔g5 43 ♘c5 ♘h5+ 44 ♔g2 ♔h4 45 ♘d3 ♘g7 46 b5 axb5 47 axb5 …⚲ **1-0** +1

**1680-★AM-1**
**Maubisson & Morant– Abbé de Lionne & Auzout**
Paris
1 e4 e5 2 f4 exf4 3 ♗c4 ♕h4+ 4 ♔f1 g5 5 ♘f3 ♕h5 6 h4 ♗g7 7 d4 h6 8 ♔f2 ♕g6 9 ♕d3 d6 10 ♘c3 c6 11 d5 ♘d7 12 b4 ♘e5 13 ♘xe5 ♗xe5 14 ♗d2 ♘f6 15 ♖ae1 g4 16 dxc6 bxc6 17 b5 g3+ 18 ♔g1 c5 19 ♘d5 ♘xd5 20 ♕xd5 ♖b8 21 h5 ♕f6 22 ♗a5 ♗d4+ 23 ♔f1 0-0 24 ♗c7 ♗e6 25 e5 ♗xd5 26 exf6 ♗xc4+ 27 ♖e2 ♖be8 28 ♗xd6 ♖xe2 29 ♗xf8 ♖e4# **0-1** +1

**1680-★AM-2**
**Morant+ Abbé de Feuquières**
Paris
1 e4 e5 2 f4 exf4 3 ♘f3 ♘e7 4 d4 g5 5 ♘xg5 ♘g6 6 h4 ♗g7 7 ♗c4 0-0 8 ♕h5 h6 9 ♕xg6 hxg5 10 hxg5 ♖e8 11 ♕xf7# **1-0** +1

**1680-★AR-1**
**Abbé de Lionne○ Roussereau**
Paris [Caze]
1 e4 e5 2 f4 exf4 3 ♗c4 f5 4 ♕e2 ♘f6 5 e5 ♘e4 6 ♘f3 d5 7 ♗b3 g5 8 d3 ♘c5 9 h4 ♗e7 10 hxg5 ♗xg5 11 ♘xg5 ♕xg5 12 ♗xd5 c6 13 ♗b3 ♘xb3 14 axb3 h5 15 ♕f3 ♕g3+ 16 ♔f1 ♗e6 17 ♗xf4 ♕xf3+ 18 gxf3 ♘a6 19 ♘d2 ♘b4 20 ♖c1 0-0-0 21 ♗e3 a6 22 ♗c5 ♘d5 23 c4 ♘f4 24 d4 ♘d3 25 ♖b1 ♘xc5∓ …⚲ +1

**1680-★DJ-1**
**Jannisson & Morant– De Pennautier & Maubisson**
Paris
1 e4 e5 2 f4 exf4 3 ♗c4 ♕h4+ 4 ♔f1 g5 5 d4 d6 6 ♘f3 ♕h5 7 ♘c3 ♘e7 8 e5 ♘f5 9 ♘d5 ♗e7 10 ♔g1 ♗d8 11 ♕e1 0-0 12 exd6 ♘xd6 13 ♗e2 ♗g4 14 b3 ♗xf3 15 ♗xf3 g4 16 ♗e4 ♗h4 17 ♕e2 ♘c6 18 ♗xf4 ♘xe4 19 ♕xe4 ♖ae8 20 ♗e5 ♘xe5 21 dxe5 ♖xe5 **0-1** +1

**1680-★DL-1**
**Lafon le jeune & Morant– De Pennautier & Jannisson**
Paris
1 e4 e5 2 f4 exf4 3 ♗c4 ♕h4+ 4 ♔f1 ♗d6 5 d4 g5 6 e5 ♗e7 7 c3 ♘h6 8 ♘d2 ♘f5 9 ♘e4 d6 10 ♕e2 dxe5 11 ♘f3 ♕h5 12 ♘xe5 ♕xe2+ 13 ♔xe2 ♗e6 14 d5 ♗d7

15 d6 ♘xd6 16 ♘xd6+ cxd6 17 ♘xf7 ♖f8 18 ♘h6 ♘c6 19 h3 ♘e5 20 ♗d5 0-0-0 21 b3 ♗f6 22 h4 ♖de8 23 ♔d1 ♘g4 24 ♘xg4 ♗xg4+ 25 ♔c2 ♖e2+ ...♀ **0-1**
+1

**1680̂-★DM-1**
**De Villette Murcey+ Maubisson**
Paris
1 e4 e5 2 f4 exf4 3 ♘f3 g5 4 ♗c4 g4 5 ♗xf7+ ♔xf7 6 ♘e5+ ♔e8 7 ♕xg4 ♘f6 8 ♕xf4 d6 9 ♘c4 ♕e7 10 ♘c3 ♘c6 11 0-0 ♗g7 12 d3 ♖f8 13 ♕g5 ♗e6 14 ♘e3 ♔d7 15 ♗d2 ♖ae8 16 ♘cd5 ♗xd5 17 exd5 ♘e5 18 ♘f5 ♕f7 19 ♘xg7 ♖e7 20 ♕f5+ ♔d8 21 ♘e6+ ♔e8 22 ♘xf8 ♔xf8 23 ♕xf6 ...♀ **1-0**
+1

**1680̂-★DM-2**
**De Villette Murcey+ Maubisson**
Paris [Caze♀]
1 e4 e5 2 f4 exf4 3 ♘f3 g5 4 d4 ♗g7 5 ♘c3 h6 6 ♗c4 ♘e7 7 ♕d3 d6 8 ♗d2 f5 9 e5 d5 10 ♗b3 c6 11 h4 g4 12 ♘g1 ♘g6 13 h5 ♘h4? 14 ♕e2 ♘xg2+? 15 ♕xg2 ...♀ **1-0**
+1

**1680̂-★LM-1**
**Lafon l'aisné– Maubisson**
Paris
1 e4 e5 2 f4 exf4 3 ♘f3 g5 4 ♗c4 g4 5 0-0 gxf3 6 ♕xf3 ♕f6 7 c3 ♘c6 8 d4 ♘xd4 9 ♕d3 ♘e6 10 ♘d2 ♗d6 11 ♘f3 ♘e7 12 ♗d2 b6 13 ♖ae1 ♗e5 14 ♗xe6 fxe6 15 ♘xe5 ♕xe5 16 ♗xf4 ♕g7 17 ♗xc7 ♖g8 18 ♕h3 ♗a6 19 ♖f3 ♕g5 20 ♖ee3 ♕c5 21 ♗g3 ♗e2 22 ♗f2 ♗xf3 23 ♖xf3 ♕d6 24 ♖d3 ♕f4 25 ♕h5+ ♘g6 26 ♗e3 ♕xe4 27 ♕b5 ♘e5 **0-1**
+1

**1680̂-★LM-2**
**Lafon l'aisné– Maubisson**
Paris
1 e4 e5 2 f4 exf4 3 ♘f3 g5 4 ♗c4 ♗g7 5 h4 h6 6 hxg5 hxg5 7 ♖xh8 ♗xh8 8 d4 ♕e7 9 ♕d3 ♘c6 10 c3 d6 11 ♗b5 ♗d7 12 ♗xc6 ♗xc6 13 d5 ♗d7 14 ♘d4 ♗xd4 15 ♕xd4 f5 16 ♘d2 ♘f6 17 ♔f1 fxe4 ...♀ **0-1**
+1

**1680̂-★LM-3**
**Lafon L'aisné+ Maubisson**
Paris
1 e4 e5 2 f4 exf4 3 ♘f3 ♘c6 4 h4 d5 5 e5 ♗g4 6 d4 ♗xf3 7 gxf3 ♗e7 8 c3 ♗xh4+ 9 ♔d2 ♕g5 10 ♔c2 ♗g3 11 ♗d3 h6 12 ♘d2 ♘ge7 13 ♘f1 ♘f5 14 ♔b1 a6 15 a3 ♘a5 16 ♕a4+ ♘c6 17 ♔a2 0-0 18 ♖g1 ♘ce7 19 ♗d2 c6 20 ♕c2 h5 21 ♕c1 h4 22 ♘xg3 ♘xg3 23 ♗xf4 ♕h5 24 ♗xg3 hxg3 25 ♖xg3 ♘f5 26 ♖g1 ♕xf3 27 ♗c2 ♘e3 28 ♗b3 a5 29 a4 b5 30 ♕d2 b4 31 ♖ae1 ♘c4 32 ♕g5 g6 33 e6 ♕f2 34 exf7+ ♖xf7 35 ♕xg6+ **1-0**
+1

**1680̂-★LR-1**
**Lafon le jeune+ Roussereau**
Paris
1 e4 e5 2 f4 exf4 3 ♘f3 g5 4 h4 g4 5 ♘e5 h5 6 ♗c4 ♘h6 7 d4 d6 8 ♘d3 ♕e7 9 ♘c3 ♘f5 10 ♗xf4 ♘xh4 11 ♕d2 ♘g6 12 0-0-0 c6 13 ♖hf1 ♗e6 14 ♗g5

14 ... ♕xg5 15 ♕xg5 ♗h6 16 ♕xh6 ♖xh6 17 ♗xe6 fxe6 18 ♖f6 ♔d7 19 ♘f4 ♘xf4 20 ♖xh6 **1-0**
+1

**1680̂-★R♀-1**
**Roussereau+ ♀**
Paris
1 e4 e5 2 f4 exf4 3 ♘f3 g5 4 ♗c4 g4 5 ♘e5 ♕h4+ 6 ♔f1 ♘h6 7 d4 d6 8 ♘d3 f3 9 g3 ♕h3+ 10 ♔f2 ♕h5 11 ♘f4 ♕g5 12 ♘e6 ♕e7 13 ♗g5 f6 14 ♗xh6 ♗xh6 15 d5 ♗xe6 16 dxe6 ♘c6 17 h3 ♘a5 18 ♗b5+ c6 19 hxg4 cxb5 20 ♖xh6 ♕xe6 21 ♕xf3 ...♀ **1-0**
+1

**1723̂-★S♀-1**
**♀– Severino, A.**
Napoli
1 e4 c5 2 ♘c3 e5 3 ♘f3 ♘c6 4 ♘d5 d6 5 c3 f5 6 exf5 ♗xf5 7 ♗b5 ♕d7 8 d4 cxd4 9 cxd4 0-0-0 [... ♔b8, ... ♖e8] 10 dxe5 ♘xe5

11 ♗xd7 ♘xf3+ 12 ♔f1 ♗d3+ 13 ♕xd3 ♖e1# **0-1**
+1

**1750̂-★♀♀-1**
**♀=♀**
1 e4 e5 2 ♘f3 ♘c6 3 ♗c4 ♗c5 4 0-0 [♔h1, ♖f1] 4 ... ♘f6 5 ♘c3 ♘g4 6 d3 0-0 [♔h8, ♖f8] 7 ♘g5 d6 8 h3 h6 9 ♘xf7+ ♖xf7 10 ♗xf7 ♕h4 11 ♕f3 ♘xf2+ 12 ♖xf2 ♗xf2 13 ♘d5 ♘d4 14 ♘e7 ♘xf3 15 ♘g6+ ♔h7 **½-½**
+1

**192** Philidor, F.A.D. M58 BL

**1780-★BP-1**
**Carlier & Bernard+ Philidor, F.A.D.**
[Bourdonnais]
⟨♙f7⟩ 1 e4 e6 2 d4 d5 3 exd5 exd5 4 ♕h5+ g6 5 ♕e5+ ♕e7 6 ♗f4 c6 7 ♗e2 ♗g7 8 ♕xe7+ ♘xe7 9 ♘f3 0-0 10 ♗e5 ♘d7 11 0-0 ♘xe5 12 ♘xe5 ♗xe5 13 dxe5 ♖f4 [△ ... ♖e4] 14 ♗d3 ♗f5 15 ♗xf5 ♘xf5 16 g3 ♖e4 17 f4 ♖e2 18 ♘a3 ♘e3 19 ♖f2 ♖xf2 20 ♔xf2 ♘g4+ 21 ♔g2 ♖d8 22 h3 ♘h6 23 g4 a6 24 ♖d1 ♘f7 25 h4 c5 26 c3 b5 27 ♘c2 a5 28 ♘e3 d4 29 cxd4 cxd4 30 ♘c2 d3 31 ♘e1 d2 32 ♘f3 **1-0**
L/N6013-1836

**1783-★BP-1** ○●○ 8 v 83
**Bowdler= Philidor, F.A.D.**
London [Staunton]
1 e4 c5 2 ♗c4 e6 3 ♕e2 ♘c6 4 c3 a6 5 a4 b6 6 f4 d6 7 ♘f3 ♘ge7 8

♗a2 g6 9 d3 ♗g7 10 ♗e3 d5 11 ♘bd2 0-0 12 0-0 f5 13 e5 h6 14 d4 c4 15 b4 b5 16 ♗b1 ♗d7 17 ♗c2 ♕c7 18 h3 ♔h7 19 ♔h2 ♘a7 20 g4 bxa4 21 ♗xa4 ♘b5 22 ♗xb5 ♗xb5 23 ♖g1 ♖g8 24 ♖g3 a5 25 bxa5 ♖xa5 26 ♖gg1 ♖ga8 27 ♖xa5 ♕xa5 28 ♖c1 ♕a3 29 ♘f1 ♕b3 30 ♕d1 ♖a2+ 31 ♗d2 ♕xd1 32 ♖xd1 ♗a4 33 ♖b1 ♗b3 34 ♔g3 ♘c6 35 ♘e3 ♗f8 36 ♗c1 ♗a3 37 h4 ♗xc1 38 ♖xc1 ♘e7 39 h5 ♖e2 40 ♖e1 ♖xe1 41 ♘xe1 fxg4 42 ♔xg4 ♘f5 43 ♘xf5 gxf5+ 44 ♔g3 ♗d1 45 ♘f3 ♗xf3 [⌓ 45 ... ♔g7 46 ♔f2 ♔f7−+] 46 ♔xf3 ♔g7 47 ♔e3 ♔f7 48 ♔d2 ♔e7 49 ♔c2 ♔d7 50 ♔b2 ♔c6 51 ♔a3 ♔b5 **½-½**

L/N6123-1843

**1783-★BP-2 ○●○** 8 v 83
**Brühl, J.M.– Philidor, F.A.D.**
London [Staunton]

1 e4 e5 2 ♗c4 c6 3 ♕e2 d6 4 c3 f5 5 d3 ♘f6 6 exf5? ♗xf5 7 d4 e4 8 ♗g5 d5 9 ♗b3 ♗d6 10 ♘d2 ♘bd7 11 h3 h6 12 ♗e3 ♕e7 13 f4 h5 14 c4 a6 15 cxd5 cxd5 16 ♕f2 0-0 17 ♘e2 b5 18 0-0 ♘b6 19 ♘g3 g6 20 ♖ac1 ♘c4 21 ♘xf5 gxf5 22 ♕g3+ ♕g7 23 ♕xg7+ ♔xg7 24 ♗xc4 bxc4 25 g3 ♖ab8 26 b3 ♗a3 27 ♖c2 cxb3 28 axb3 ♖fc8 29 ♖xc8 ♖xc8 30 ♖a1 ♗b4 31 ♖xa6 ♖c3 32 ♔f2 ♖d3 33 ♖a2 ♗xd2 34 ♖xd2 ♖xb3 35 ♖c2 h4 36 ♖c7+ ♔g6 37 gxh4 ♘h5 38 ♖d7 [⌓ 38 ♖c6+=] 38 ... ♘xf4 39 ♗xf4 ♖f3+ 40 ♔g2 ♖xf4 41 ♖xd5 ♖f3 42 ♖d8 ♖d3 43 d5 f4 44 d6 ♖d2+ 45 ♔f1 ♔f7 46 h5 e3 47 h6 f3 **0-1**

L/N6123-1843

**1783-★MP-1 ○●○** 8 v 83
**Maseres– Philidor, F.A.D.**
London

⟨△f7⟩ 1 e4 ♘h6 2 d4 ♘f7 3 ♗d3 e6 4 ♘f3 d5 5 e5 c5 6 c3 ♘c6 7 ♗e3 b6 8 ♗b5 ♗d7 9 a4 a6 10 ♗d3 g6 11 0-0 ♕c7 12 ♕e2 c4 13 ♗c2 ♖b8 14 ♘a3 ♗e7 15 h3 0-0 16 ♘h2 b5 17 axb5 axb5 18 ♕g4 ♔g7 19 f4 ♘h6 20 ♕g3 ♘f5 21 ♗xf5 ♖xf5 22 ♕f3 b4 23 cxb4 ♘xb4 24 g4 ♖ff8 25 ♕g2 ♘d3 26 ♗c1 ♕b6 27 ♘c2 ♘xc1 28 ♖axc1 ♕xb2 29 ♘e3 ♕xg2+ 30 ♔xg2 ♖b3 31 ♖f3 ♖d3 32 ♖d1 ♗a4 33 ♖xd3 cxd3 34 ♘hf1 ♗b4 35 ♖f2 ♗c3 36 ♖a2 ♗b3 37 ♖f2 ♗xd4 38 ♖d2 ♖xf4 39 ♖xd3 ♗c4 40 ♘xc4 dxc4 41 ♖f3 ♖xf3 42 ♔xf3 ♗xe5 43 ♔e4 ♗f6 44 ♘e3 c3 45 ♔d3 ♔f7 46 ♘d1 ♔e7 47 ♘xc3 ♗xc3 48 ♔xc3 ♔d6 49 ♔d4 e5+ 50 ♔e4 ♔e6 51 h4 h6 52 ♔e3 ♔d5 53 ♔d3 e4+ 54 ♔e3 ♔e5 55 g5 h5 56 ♔e2 ♔f4 57 ♔f2 ♔g4 58 ♔e3 ♔xh4 59 ♔xe4 ♔xg5 **0-1**

L/N6123-1843

**1787-★BC-1** v87
**Beaurevoir, de– Conway, H.S.**
London

⟨△f2⟩ 1 c4 f5 2 d4 ♘f6 3 ♗g5 e6 4 ♗xf6 ♕xf6 5 ♘c3 a6 6 a3 ♗e7 7 ♘f3 0-0 8 e3 c5 9 d5 d6 10 ♗e2 ♘d7 11 e4 ♘e5 12 0-0 ♗d7 13 ♘d2 ♕h6 14 ♔h1 ♗f6

15 ♗f3 ♘xf3 16 ♕xf3 ♗e5 17 g3 ♕xd2 18 dxe6 ♗xe6 19 exf5 ♗xc3 20 bxc3 ♗xf5 21 ♖ad1 ♕g5 22 h4 ♕g4 **0-1** +1

**1787-★BP-1** 6 v 87
**Brühl, J.M.= Philidor, F.A.D.**
London

1 e4 e5 2 ♗c4 c6 3 ♕e2 ♘f6 4 d3 ♗c5 5 ♗e3 ♗xe3 6 fxe3 d6 7 c3 ♗e6 8 ♗xe6 fxe6 9 ♘h3 ♘bd7 10 0-0 ♕e7 11 ♘d2 0-0 12 ♔h1 d5 13 exd5 exd5 14 e4 dxe4 15 ♘xe4 ♘xe4 16 ♕xe4 ♖xf1+ 17 ♖xf1 ♘f6 18 ♕c4+ ♔h8 19 ♕h4 h6 20 d4 exd4 21 ♖e1 ♕f7 22 cxd4 ♕h5 23 ♕xh5 ♘xh5 24 ♖e5 g5 25 ♖e6 ♔g7 26 ♖e7+ ♔g6 27 ♖xb7 g4 28 ♘g1 ♖d8 29 ♖xa7 ♖xd4 30 ♖c7 ♖b4 31 a4 ♖xa4 32 ♖xc6+ ♔g5 33 ♖c5+ ♔g6 34 ♖b5 ♖a1 35 g3 ♖d1 36 b4 ♖d2 37 ♖b6+ ♘f6 38 b5 ♖b2 39 ♖b8 ♘e4 40 b6 ♘g5 41 b7 ♔h5 42 ♖f8 ♖xb7 43 ♖f2 ♖b1 44 ♔g2 **½-½** +1

**1788-★BB-1**
**Beaurevoir, de○Bowdler**
London♀

1 e4 e5 2 ♘f3 ♘c6 3 ♗c4 ♗c5 4 c3 d6 5 d4 ♗b6 6 a4 a5 7 ♗b5 ♗d7 ...♀ +1

**1788-★BB-2**
**Bowdler= Beaurevoir, de**
London♀ [Atwood]

1 e4 e5 2 f4 exf4 3 ♘f3 g5 4 d4 ♕e7 [⌓ 4 ... g4] 5 ♗d3 d5 6 0-0 dxe4 7 ♗xe4 c6 8 ♖e1 ♗e6 9 c4 ♘a6 10 d5 0-0-0 11 ♕d4 ♕c5 12 ♗d2 ♕xd4+ 13 ♘xd4 cxd5 14 cxd5 ♗xd5 ...♀ **½-½** +1

**1788-★BC-1**
**Bowdler+ Conway, H.S.**
London♀

1 e4 e5 2 ♗c4 ♗c5 3 d3 c6 4 ♕e2 d6 5 f4 exf4 6 ♗xf4 ♕b6 7 ♕f3 ♕xb2 8 ♗xf7+ ♔d7 9 ♘e2 ♕xa1 10 ♔d2 ♗b4+ 11 ♘bc3 ♗xc3+ 12 ♘xc3 ♕xh1 13 ♕g4+ ♔c7 14 ♕xg7 ♘d7 15 ♕g3 b6 16 ♘b5+ cxb5 17 ♗xd6+ ♔b7 18 ♗d5+ ♔a6 19 d4 b4 20 ♗xb4 ♔b5 21 c4+ ♔xb4 22 ♕b3+ ♔a5 23 ♕b5# **1-0** +1

**1788-★BC-2**
**Conway, H.S.+ Brühl, J.M.**
London♀

1 e4 e5 2 ♗c4 ♘f6 3 ♘c3 c6 4 ♘ge2 d5 5 exd5 cxd5 6 ♗b3 ♘c6 7 d4 e4 8 0-0 ♗e6 9 a3 h6 10 ♘f4 g5 11 ♘xe6 fxe6 12 ♗e3 ♘e7 13 f3 ♘f5 14 ♕e2 ♗d6 15 fxe4 ♘xe3 16 ♕xe3 ♗xh2+ 17 ♔h1 ♗c7 18 exd5 0-0 19 dxe6 ♕e7 20 d5 ♕d6 21 ♕h3 ♘g4 22 ♘b5 ♕e5 23 ♘xc7 ♖xf1+ 24 ♖xf1 ♘f2+ 25 ♖xf2 ♕e1+ 26 ♔h2 ♕xf2 27 d6 ♕d4 28 d7 ♕d6+ 29 ♕g3 ♕e7 30 ♘d5 ♕d8 31 e7 **1-0** +1

**1788-★BC-3**
**Brühl, J.M.+ Conway, H.S.**
London♀

1 e4 e5 2 ♗c4 b6 3 d3 ♘f6 4 f4 exf4 5 ♗xf4 d5 6 exd5 ♘xd5 7 ♕e2+ ♗e7 8 ♗xd5 ♕xd5 9 ♗xc7 ♘c6 10 ♘f3 ♕c5 11 ♗g3 0-0 12 ♗f2 ♕a5+ 13 c3 ♗b7 14 0-0 ♖fe8 15 ♕c2 ♕h5 16 ♘bd2 ♖ad8 17 ♘e4 ♕g6 18 ♖ad1 ♔h8 19 ♕b1 f5 20 ♘g3 ♗f6 21 d4 ♘e7 22 ♕c1 ♗xf3 23 gxf3 ♘d5 24 ♕c2 f4 25 ♕xg6 hxg6 26 ♘e4 ♖e6 27 ♘xf6 gxf6 28 ♖fe1 ♘e3 29 ♗xe3 fxe3 30 ♖d3 ♖de8 31 ♔g2 f5 32 f4 ♔g7 33 ♖e2 g5 34 fxg5 ♔g6 35 ♔f3 f4 36 h4 ♖e4 37 d5 ♖4e7 38 ♖d4 ♖d7 39 ♖xf4 **1-0** +1

**1788-★BC-4**
**Conway, H.S.+ Brühl, J.M.**
London♀

1 e4 e5 2 ♗c4 c6 3 ♗b3 d5 4 exd5 cxd5 5 ♘e2 f5 6 0-0 ♘c6 7 c3 ♘f6 8 d4 e4 9 ♗g5 ♗e6 10 ♘f4 ♗f7 11 ♗xf6 gxf6 12 f3 ♗h6 13 fxe4 ♗xf4 14 ♖xf4 fxe4 15 ♕f1 0-0 16 ♖xf6 ♘e7 17 ♘a3 ♕d7 18 ♕f4 ♘g6 19 ♕g3 ♖ad8 20 ♖af1 a6 21 ♘c2 ♔h8 22 ♘e3 ♕e7 23 h4 ♗g8 24 ♖xf8 ♖xf8 25 ♖xf8 ♕xf8 26 ♕g5 ♕f4 27 ♕xf4 ♘xf4 28 g3 ♘d3 29

♗xd5 ♗xd5 30 ♘xd5 ♘xb2 31 ♔f1 ♔g7 32 ♔e2 ♘c4 33 ♘e3 ♘d6 34 g4 b5 35 a3 ♔f7 36 ♔f2 ♔e6 37 ♔g3 ♘c4 38 ♘xc4 bxc4 39 ♔f4 ♔d5 40 ♔e3 h6 41 g5 **1-0**

+1

**1788-★BC-5**
**Brühl, J.M.= Cotter**
London?
1 e4 e5 2 ♘f3 d6 3 d4 exd4 4 ♘xd4 a6 5 c4 ♗e7 6 ♗d3 ♘f6 7 ♘c3 ♗d7 8 0-0 0-0 9 f4 ♘c6 10 ♘xc6 ♗xc6 11 ♕c2 h6 12 b3 ♕d7 13 ♗b2 ♖ae8 14 ♖ad1 ♗d8 15 e5 dxe5 16 ♗h7+ ♘xh7 17 ♖xd7 ♗xd7 18 fxe5 ♖xe5 19 ♘d5 ♖g5 20 ♖e1 c6 21 ♘e7+ ♗xe7 22 ♖xe7 ♗h3 23 g3 ♖f5 24 ♖e1 ♘g5 25 ♕c3 f6 26 ♖d1 ♖e8 27 ♕d3 ♖fe5 28 ♗xe5 ♖xe5 29 ♕g6 ♘f7 30 ♕d3 h5 31 ♕d2 ♖g5 32 ♕f4 ♖e5 33 ♔f2 ♖f5 34 ♕xf5 ♗xf5 35 ♔e3 ♔f8 36 ♔d4 ♔e7 37 ♔c5 ♗d7 38 ♔b6 ♘d8 39 ♔c7 ♘e6+ 40 ♔xb7 a5 41 ♔b6 g5 42 ♔xa5 f5 43 ♔b6 h4 44 a4 hxg3 45 hxg3 f4 46 gxf4 gxf4 47 a5 ♔d8 48 a6 ♔c8 49 a7 ♘c7 50 ♖a1 ♘a8+ 51 ♔a6 ♘c7+ **½-½**

–1

**1788-★BC-6**
**Cotter+ Brühl, J.M.**
London?
1 e4 e5 2 f4 exf4 3 ♘f3 g5 4 h4 g4 5 ♘g5 h6 6 ♘xf7 ♔xf7 7 ♕xg4 ♘f6 8 ♕xf4 d6 9 ♗c4+ ♗e6 10 ♗xe6+ ♔xe6 11 0-0 ♘bd7 12 d4 ♔e7 13 e5 dxe5 14 dxe5 ♗g7 15 exf6+ ♘xf6 16 ♘c3 a5 17 ♗e3 ♖e8 18 ♘b5 ♔f7 19 ♘xc7 ♖xe3 20 ♘xa8 ♖e7 21 ♕c4+ ♔g6 22 ♕d3+ ♕xd3 23 cxd3 ♘d5 24 ♖ac1 ♗xb2 25 ♖ab1 ♗d4+ 26 ♔h1 ♖e8 27 ♖b5 ♖d8 28 ♖xa5 ♘e3 29 h5+ ♔g7 30 ♖c1 ♘g4 31 ♘c7 ♘f2+ 32 ♔h2 ♘g4+ 33 ♔g3 ♗f2+ **1-0**

+1

**1788-★BC-7**
**Brühl, J.M.+ Cotter**
London?
1 e4 e5 2 ♗c4 c6 3 ♕e2 ♗c5 4 ♗xf7+ ♔xf7 5 ♕c4+ ♔e8 6 ♕xc5 d6 7 ♕e3 ♘f6 8 h3 ♖f8 9 d3 ♔f7 10 ♘c3 ♔g8 11 ♗d2 ♘h5 12 ♕e2 ♘f6 13 f4 exf4 14 ♗xf4 ♘a6 15 0-0-0 ♘d7 16 ♗xd6 ♖f7 17 ♘f3 h6 18 ♖hf1 ♘b6 19 ♗g3 ♗e6 20 a3 ♘c5 21 ♘e5 ♖xf1 22 ♖xf1 ♘ba4 23 ♘xa4 ♘xa4 24 c3 ♕g5+ 25 ♗f4 ♕e7 26 ♗e3 ♕d6 27 ♘g6 ♗f7 28 ♘h4 ♕e6

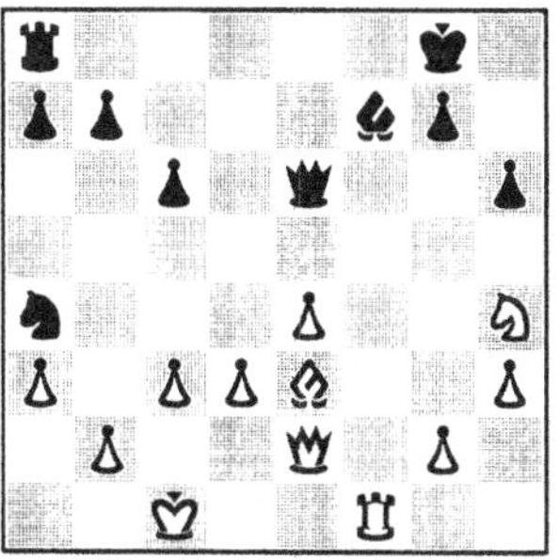

29 c4 ♕e7 30 ♘f5 ♕e6 31 ♕g4 ♗g6 32 ♘xh6+ gxh6 33 ♕xe6+ **1-0**

+1

**1788-★BC-8**
**Cotter○ Brühl, J.M.**
London?
1 e4 e5 2 f4 exf4 3 ♘f3 g5 4 h4 g4 5 ♘g5 h5 6 d4 f6 7 ♗xf4 fxg5 8 hxg5 d5 9 e5 ♗f5 10 ♗d3 ♘e7 11 0-0 ♗g7 12 ♗g3 ♖f8 13 ♗h4 ♕d7 14 ♘c3 a6 15 ♕e2 ♘bc6 16 ♗f2 0-0-0 17 ♘a4 ♗xd3 18 ♕xd3 ♘xe5 19 ♕b3 b5 20 dxe5 bxa4 21 ♕c3 d4 22 ♕d3 ♕b5 23 ♕a3 ♘g6 24 b3 ♗xe5 25 bxa4 ♕c6 26 ♖ab1 ...?

+1

**1788-★BH-1**
**Harrowby– Bowdler**
London?
1 e4 e5 2 ♗c4 ♗c5 3 d3 ♘c6 4 c3 ♕e7 5 ♕e2 d6 6 f4 ♗xg1 7 ♖xg1 exf4 8 ♗xf4 ♘e5 9 ♗xe5 ♕xe5 10 g3 ♘f6 11 ♘d2 ♗g4 12 ♕g2 d5 13 ♗b3 dxe4 14 dxe4 0-0-0 15 h3 ♖xd2 16 ♔xd2 ♘xe4+ 17 ♔c2 ♗f5 18 ♖ae1 ♖d8 19 ♔c1 ♗g6 20 h4 ♕c5 21 ♖gf1 ♘xc3 22 ♗c2 ♘xa2+ 23 ♔b1 ♘b4 24 ♗xg6 fxg6 25 ♕e4 ♕a5 26 ♕e6+ ♔b8 27 ♕f7 ♕a4 28 ♖c1 ♘c6 29 ♖f4 ♕b5 30 ♖f3 a5 31 ♕xg7 ♕d5 32 ♖fc3 ♖d7 33 ♕f8+ ♔a7 34 ♕f2+ ♕d4 35 ♕f3 ♕d5 36 ♕f4 ♕f5+ 37 ♕xf5 gxf5 38 ♖c5 ♖d3 39 ♖1c3 ♖d1+ 40 ♔c2 ♖f1 41 ♔b3 h5 42 ♖d5 ♔b6 43 ♖d7 f4 44 ♖f7 ♘d4+ 45 ♔a2 ♘e2 46 ♖b3+ ♔c6 47 gxf4 ♘c1+ 48 ♔a3 ♘xb3 49 ♔xb3 ♖h1 50 ♖f5 ♖xh4 51 ♔c4 b5+ 52 ♔d4 ♔b6 53 ♔e5 ♖h2 54 ♔f6 a4 **0-1**

+1

**1788-★BH-2** 11 v 88
**Brühl, J.M.+ Harrowby**
London
1 e4 e5 2 ♗c4 c6 3 c3 d5 4 exd5 cxd5 5 ♗b3 ♘c6 6 d4 e4 7 ♗e3 b5 8 ♘e2 ♗e6 9 ♘d2 ♗d6 10 ♘xe4 dxe4 11 d5 ♗d7 12 dxc6 ♗xc6 13 ♘d4 ♗d7 14 ♕h5 ♕e7 15 ♘xb5 ♘f6 16 ♘xd6+ ♕xd6 17 ♕xf7+ ♔d8 18 ♖d1 ♕e7 19 ♕xe7+ ♔xe7 20 ♗c5+ ♔d8 21 ♖d6 ♖e8 22 0-0 ♖e5 23 ♗a3 ♔c7 24 ♖fd1 h5 25 ♖xf6 gxf6 26 ♗d6+ **1-0**

+1

**1788-★BP-1** 24 ii 88
**Beaurevoir, de= Philidor, F.A.D.**
London
⟨♙f7⟩ 1 e4 ... 2 d4 e6 3 c4 g6 4 f4 d5 5 cxd5 exd5 6 e5 c5 7 ♗b5+ ♘c6 8 ♘f3 ♕b6 9 ♘c3 cxd4 10 ♘xd4 ♗b4 11 ♗e3 ♘ge7 12 a3 ♗c5 13 b4 ♗xd4 14 ♗xd4 ♕c7 15 ♗c5 ♗e6 16 ♗xe7 ♕xe7 17 ♘xd5 ♕d8 18 ♘f6+ ♔f7 19 ♕f3 ♕b6 20 ♗xc6 bxc6 21 ♘e4 ♗d5 22 ♘d6+ ♔g7 23 ♕f2 ♖hf8 24 ♖f1 ♖ad8 25 ♕xb6 axb6 26 g3 h5 27 h4 b5 28 ♔f2 ♖xd6 29 exd6 ♖d8 30 ♖fe1 ♖xd6 31 ♖e5 ♗e6 32 ♖ae1 ♔f6 ...? **½-½**

+1

**1788-★BP-2** 31 iii 88
**Beaurevoir, de– Philidor, F.A.D.**
London
⟨♙f7⟩ 1 e4 ... 2 d4 e6 3 f4 d5 4 e5 c5 5 c3 ♘c6 6 ♘f3 ♕b6 7 a3 a5 8 a4 ♘h6 9 ♗d3 ♗d7 10 ♘a3 0-0-0 11 ♘b5 ♘f7 12 ♗e3 c4 13 ♗c2 ♘b8 14 ♘a3 ♕xb2 15 ♘b5 ♗xb5 16 axb5 ♕xb5 17 ♗a4 ♕a6 18 ♖b1 ♗e7 19 0-0 ♕a7 20 ♕c2 g6 21 ♖b5 ♖d7 22 ♖fb1 ♘d8 23 ♖b6 ♘dc6 24 g4 ♖f8 25 h4 ♖c7 26 ♔g2 ♘b4 27 ♖6xb4 axb4 28 cxb4 b5 29 ♗xb5 ♖b7 30 ♗xc4 ♖c7 31 ♘d2 dxc4 32 ♘xc4 ♕b7+ 33 ♔g3 ♘a6 34 ♕e2 ♘xb4 35 ♘d6+ ♗xd6 36 exd6 ♖c3 37 ♔h2 ♖c2 38 ♗d2 ♖xf4 39 ♕xe6+ ♔d8 40 ♕g8+ ♔d7 41 ♕xh7+ ♔c8 42 ♕xb7+ ♔xb7 43 ♖xb4+ ♔c6 44 ♔g3 ♖f1 45 d5+ ♔xd6 46 ♖d4 ♔e5 47 ♖d3 ♔e4 48 ♖e3+ ♔xd5 49 ♖d3+ ♔e4 50 ♖e3+ ♔d4 51 ♖e2 ♔d3 52 ♖e6 ♔xd2 53 ♖xg6 ♖c3+ 54 ♔g2 ♖ff3 55 h5 ♖ce3 56 h6 ♔e2 **0-1**

+1

**1788-★BP-3** 31 iii 88
**Beaurevoir, de– Philidor, F.A.D.**
London
⟨♙f7⟩ 1 d4 ... 2 c4 e6 3 e4 g6 4 f4 d5 5 cxd5 exd5 6 e5 c5 7 ♗b5+ ♘c6 8 ♘c3 a6 9 ♗xc6+ bxc6 10 ♗e3 cxd4 11 ♕xd4 ♘h6 12 ♕b6 ♕xb6 13 ♗xb6 ♖b8 14 ♘a4 ♗b4+ 15 ♔e2 0-0 16 a3 ♗e7 17 g3 c5 18 ♖b1 ♗f5 19 ♖d1 ♗e4 20 ♘f3 ♗c2 21 ♗xc5 ♗xd1+ 22 ♖xd1 ♗xc5 23 ♘xc5 ♖xb2+ 24 ♔f1 ♘f5 25 ♖d3 ♖c8 26 ♘b3 ♖cc2 27 ♘fd2 d4 28 ♔e2 ♖a2 29 ♘xd4 ♘xd4+

30 ♖xd4 ♖xa3 31 g4 ♖h3 32 f5 ♖xh2+ 33 ♔d1 ♖cxd2+ 34 ♖xd2 ♖xd2+ 35 ♔xd2 gxf5 36 gxf5 h5 37 e6 a5 38 ♔d3 a4 39 ♔e4 a3 **0-1** +1

**1788-★BP-4** iv88
**Bowdler− Philidor, F.A.D.**
London
⟨♙f7⟩ 1 e4 ... 2 f4 e6 3 d4 d5 4 e5 c5 5 ♘f3 ♘c6 6 ♗b5 ♕b6 7 ♗xc6+ bxc6 8 c3 cxd4 9 ♘xd4 c5 10 ♘f3 ♗a6 11 ♕b3 ♗e7 12 g4 h5 13 gxh5 ♖xh5 14 ♘g5 ♗xg5 15 fxg5 ♘e7 16 ♕xb6 axb6 17 ♘d2 ♘g6 18 ♘f3 ♗d3 19 ♔f2 ♗e4 20 ♖e1 ♖h3 21 ♖xe4 dxe4 22 ♘g1 ♖d3 23 ♘e2 ♘xe5 24 ♘f4 ♘g4+ 25 ♔g2 c4 26 ♘xe6 ♔e7 27 ♘d4 ♖f8 28 ♔g1 ♖d1+ 29 ♔g2 ♖f2+ 30 ♔g3 ♖g1+ 31 ♔h4 ♖xh2# **0-1** +1

**1788-★BP-5** iv88
**Bowdler− Philidor, F.A.D.**
London
⟨♙f7⟩ 1 e4 ... 2 f4 e6 3 d4 d5 4 e5 c5 5 c3 ♘c6 6 ♘f3 ♕b6 7 ♕b3 ♘h6 8 ♘g5 ♗e7 9 ♕xb6 axb6 10 ♗b5 ♗d7 11 ♗xc6 bxc6 12 h4 cxd4 13 cxd4 ♗xg5 14 hxg5 ♘f5 15 ♔e2 ♘xd4+ 16 ♔d3 c5 17 ♘c3

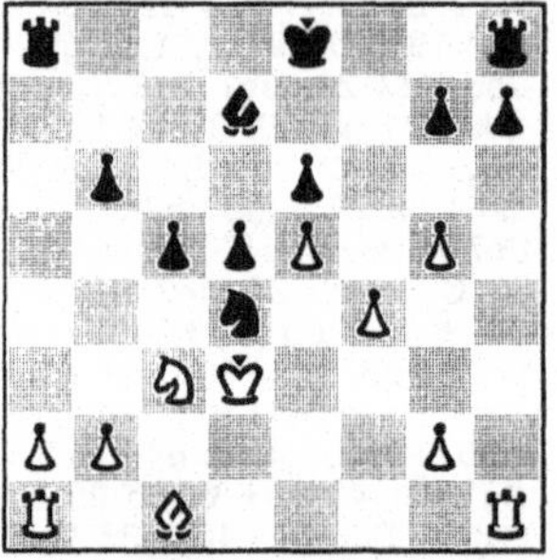

17 ... ♘b3 18 ♖b1 c4+ 19 ♔e2 ♘d4+ 20 ♔e3 ♘f5+ 21 ♔f3 d4 22 ♘e4 ♗c6 23 g4 ♗xe4+ 24 ♔xe4 ♘g3+ 25 ♔xd4 ♘xh1 26 ♗e3 ♘g3 27 ♔xc4 h5 28 gxh5 ♖xh5 29 ♗xb6 ♖h4 30 ♗e3 ♘h5 31 ♖f1 ♖h2 32 b4 ♖e2 33 ♗d4 ♘g3 34 ♔d3 ♖a3+ **0-1** +1

**1788-★BP-6** iv88
**Bowdler+ Philidor, F.A.D.**
London
⟨♙f7⟩ 1 e4 ... 2 f4 e6 3 d4 d5 4 e5 c5 5 c3 ♘c6 6 ♘f3 ♕b6 7 ♕b3 ♘h6 8 ♗d3 c4 9 ♕xb6 axb6 10 ♗c2 b5 11 ♘g5 g6 12 ♘xh7 ♖xh7 13 ♗xg6+ ♖f7 14 ♗xf7+ ♔xf7 15 ♘a3 b4 16 ♘b5 ♖a5 17 a4 b3 18 h3 ♗d7 19 g4

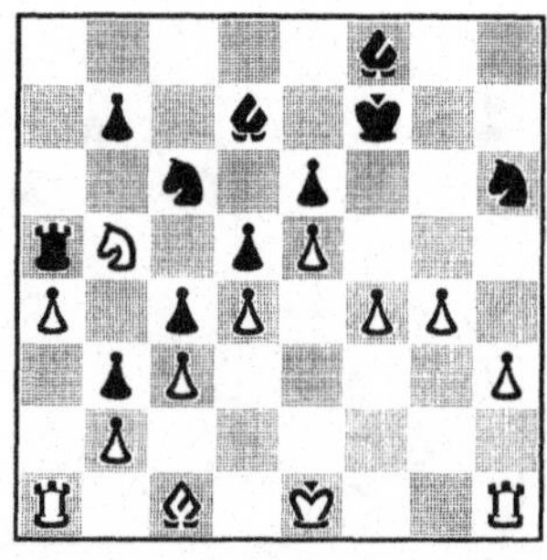

19 ... ♘xe5 20 fxe5 ♗xb5 21 ♖f1+ ♔e8 22 ♖xf8+ ♔xf8 23 ♗xh6+ ♔f7 24 ♔d2 ♔g6 25 ♗f8 ♖xa4 26 ♗a3 ♗e8 27 h4 ♔g7 28 ♖f1 ♗g6 29 ♔c1 b5 30 ♖f6 ♖a6 31 h5 ♗e4 32 g5 ♗f5 33 g6 ♖a7 34 ♗f8+ ♔g8 35 ♗h6 ♖a8 36 g7 ♔h7 37 ♖f8 ♔xh6 38 g8♕ **1-0** +1

**1788-★BP-7**
**Bowdler= Philidor, F.A.D.**
[Bourdonnais]
⟨♙f7⟩ 1 e4 ... 2 f4 e6 3 d4 d5 4 e5 c5 5 c3 ♘c6 6 ♘f3 ♘h6 7 ♗d3 ♕b6 8 ♕b3 c4 9 ♕xb6 axb6 10 ♗c2 b5 11 b4 ♗xb4? 12 cxb4 ♘xb4 13 ♔d2 0-0 14 g3 ♗d7 15 ♗a3? [□ 15 ♗b2] 15 ... ♘xc2 16 ♔xc2 ♖xa3 17 ♘xa3 b4 18 ♖hb1? ♗a4+ 19 ♔d2 bxa3 20 ♖xb7 ♘g4 21 ♖a7 ♗e8 22 ♖b1 ♗g6 23 ♖bb7 ♔h8 24 ♖xg7 ♘f2 25 ♖xg6 hxg6 26 ♘g5 ♖b8 27 ♖xa3 ♖b2+ 28 ♔e3 ♘g4+ 29 ♔f3 ♘xh2+ ½-½
L/N6013-1837

**1788-★BP-8**
**Bowdler= Philidor, F.A.D.**
[Bourdonnais]
⟨♙f7⟩ 1 e4 ... 2 f4 e6 3 ♘f3 d5 4 e5 c5 5 d4 ♘c6 6 c3 ♕b6 7 ♕b3 ♘h6 8 ♗d3 c4 9 ♕xb6 axb6 10 ♗c2 g6 11 ♘g5 ♗d6 12 ♘xh7 ♖xh7 13 ♗xg6+ ♖f7 14 ♗xf7+ ♔xf7 15 h3 ♘f5 16 g4 ♘g3 17 ♖g1 ♘e4 18 ♘d2 ♘xd2 19 ♗xd2 b5 20 ♗e3 b4 21 h4 b5 22 h5 b3 23 a3 b4 24 ♗c1 bxc3 25 bxc3 ♘xd4! 26 cxd4 c3 27 ♖b1 ♗xa3 28 ♖xb3 ♗xc1 29 ♖xc3 ♗xf4 30 ♖f3 ♖a1+ 31 ♔f2 ♖a2+ 32 ♔e1 ♖a1+ ½-½
L/N6013-1837

**1788-★BP-9** 7v88
**Philidor, F.A.D.○Brühl, J.M.**
London
⟨♖a1,♙f7⟩ 1 e4 e6 2 f4 d5 3 e5 c5 4 c3 ♘c6 5 d4 ♗d7 6 ♘f3 ♗e7 7 g4 ♘h6 8 h3 cxd4 9 cxd4 ♕a5+ 10 ♘c3 a6 11 ♔f2 b5 12 ♗d3 g6 13 f5 b4 14 ♘e2 ♘xf5 15 gxf5 gxf5 16 ♗b1 ♖g8 17 ♘f4 0-0-0 18 ♗e3 ♔b7 19 ♕b3 ♔a8 20 ♗d3 ♗c8 21 a3 bxa3 22 bxa3 ♘a7 23 ♖b1 ♕c7 24 ♕b6 ♕b7 25 ♗xa6 ♕xb6 26 ♖xb6 ♗xa3 27 ♘xe6 ♗xe6 28 ♗b7+ ♔b8 29 ♗xd5+ ♔c7 30 ♖b7+ ♔c8 31 ♖xa7 ♗xd5 32 ♖xa3 ♔b7 33 ♖a5 ♔b6 34 ♖c5 ♖g7 35 ♗g5 ♖dd7 36 ♗f6 ♖g8 37 ♘g5 h6 38 e6 ♖d6 39 ♘f7 ♖g2+ 40 ♔f1 ♖xe6 41 ♗d8+ ♔b7 42 ♖xd5 ♖b2 43 ♖xf5 ♖c6 44 ♗h4 ♖c1+ 45 ♗e1 ♖h2 46 ♖e5 ♖xh3 47 ♔g2 ♖d3 48 ♘d6+ ♔c6 49 ♘f5 ♖c2+ ...? +1

**149** Brühl, J.M JGW.CPL

**1788-★BP-10** v88
**Philidor, F.A.D.= Brühl, J.M.**
London
⟨♖a1,♙f7⟩ 1 e4 e6 2 f4 d5 3 e5 ♘h6 4 ♘f3 ♗e7 5 c3 ♗d7 6 ♗d3 c5 7 ♗c2 ♘c6 8 d3 ♕b6 9 ♕e2 0-0-0 10 ♘bd2 ♗e8 11 ♘f1 ♗h5 12 h3 ♗xf3 13 ♕xf3 ♖df8 14 ♕e2 ♖f7 15 a3 a5 16 b3 ♖hf8 17 g3 g5 18 fxg5 ♖f2 19 ♕d1 ♘g8 20 ♗e3 ♖2f3 21 d4 cxd4 22 cxd4 ♗xa3 23 ♗xh7 ♔d7 24 ♗xg8 ♗b4+ 25 ♔e2 ♕b5+ 26 ♕d3 ♕xd3+ 27 ♔xd3 ♖xf1 28 ♖xf1 ♖xf1 29 h4 ♘e7 30 ♗h7 ♖f8 31 g4 ♖h8 32 g6 ♘xg6 33 ♗xg6 ♖xh4 34 g5 ♗e7 35 ♗f7 ♗f8 36 g6 ♖h3 37 ♔e2 ♖xe3+ 38 ♔xe3 b5 39 ♔d3 a4 40 bxa4 bxa4 41 ♔c3 ½-½ +1

**1788-★BP-11** v88
**Philidor, F.A.D.= Brühl, J.M.**
London
⟨♖a1,♙f7⟩ 1 e4 c5 2 ♕h5+ g6 3 ♕xc5 d6 4 ♕e3 ♘c6 5 f4 e5 6 g3 exf4 7 gxf4 ♕h4+ 8 ♕g3 ♕xg3+ 9 hxg3 ♘f6 10 d3 ♗g4 11 ♘h3 ♘d4 12 c3 ♖c8 13 ♔f2 ♗g7 14 ♗g2 ♘c6 15 d4 ♗xh3 16 ♗xh3 ♘xe4+ 17 ♔f3 ♘xg3 18 ♖e1+ ♔d8 19 ♗xc8 ♔xc8 20 ♔xg3 ♔d7 21 ♘d2 ♘e7 22 ♘f3 ♖f8 23 a3 ♘f5+ 24 ♔f2 h6 25 d5 ♖f7 26 ♖g1 ♖f6 27 ♗e3 b6 28 ♘d4 ♘xd4 29 ♗xd4 ♖xf4+ 30 ♔e3 ♗xd4+ 31 cxd4 ♖f6 32 b4 g5 33 a4 ♖f5 34 ♖h1 ♖f6 35 ♖g1 ♖f5 ½-½ +1

**1788-★BP-12** v 88
**Philidor, F.A.D.– Brühl, J.M.**
London
⟨♖a1,♙f7⟩ 1 e4 c5 2 ♕h5+ g6 3 ♕xc5 d6 4 ♕e3 ♘c6 5 c3 e5 6 ♗c4 ♗h6 7 ♕e2 ♘f6 8 ♘f3 ♗g4 9 h3 ♗xf3 10 ♕xf3 ♖f8 11 0-0 ♕e7 12 b4 ♘h5 13 ♕e2 0-0-0 14 a4 ♖f6 15 ♘a3 ♘f4 16 ♕g4+ ♔b8 17 d3 ♕d7 18 ♔h2 ♕xg4 19 hxg4 g5 20 ♖e1 d5 21 g3 dxc4 22 gxf4 gxf4 23 dxc4

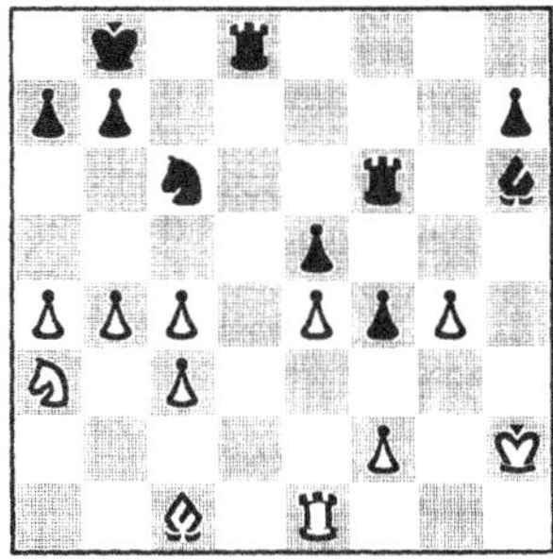

23 ... ♖d3 24 c5 ♗g5 25 ♗b2 ♖h6+ 26 ♔g1 ♖dh3 27 ♔g2 f3+ 28 ♔f1 ♖h1# **0-1** +1

**1788-★BP-13** v 88
**Philidor, F.A.D.– Brühl, J.M.**
London
⟨♖a1,♙f7⟩ 1 e4 e6 2 f4 d5 3 e5 ♘h6 4 ♘f3 ♘f7 5 d3 ♗e7 6 g4 g5 7 h4 gxh4 8 g5 c5 9 ♖xh4 h6 10 ♕d2 hxg5 11 ♖xh8+ ♘xh8 12 fxg5 ♘g6 13 ♕h2 ♔d7 14 ♕h6 ♕g8 15 c4 d4 16 ♘bd2 ♘c6 17 ♕h2 ♕h8 18 ♕xh8 ♘xh8 19 ♘e4 ♘g6 20 ♘f6+ ♔c7 ...? **0-1** +1

**1788-★BP-14** v 88
**Philidor, F.A.D.+ Brühl, J.M.**
London
⟨♖a1,♙f7⟩ 1 e4 e6 2 f4 d5 3 e5 ♘h6 4 c3 c5 5 ♘f3 ♗e7 6 d4 ♘f7 7 ♗e3 ♕b6 8 ♕d2 ♘c6 9 a3 a5 10 a4 ♗d7 11 ♗b5 0-0-0 12 0-0 ♘a7 13 dxc5 ♗xc5 14 ♗xc5 ♕xc5+ 15 ♕d4 ♕xd4+ 16 ♘xd4 ♗xb5 17 axb5 b6 18 ♘xe6 ♖d7 19 ♘d4 ♖c7 20 ♘a3 ♖e8 21 h3 ♘d8 22 ♘f5 ♘b7 23 ♖d1 g6 24 ♘e3 ♖c5 25 ♘xd5 ♘xb5 26 ♘xb6+ ♔c7 27 ♘a4 ♘xa3 28 ♘xc5 ♘xc5 29 bxa3 ♖d8 30 ♖b1 a4 31 ♖b5 ♔c6 32 ♖b1 ♖d2 33 g4 ♔d5 34 ♖b4 ♖c2 35 ♖d4+ ♔e6 36 ♖d6+ ♔e7 37 f5 ♖xc3 38 ♔g2 ♖xa3 39 fxg6 ♖g3+ 40 ♔xg3 ♘e4+ 41 ♔f4 **1-0** +1

**1788-★BP-15** 20 v 88
**Philidor, F.A.D.+ Brühl, J.M.**
London
⟨♘b1,♙f7⟩ 1 e4 e6 2 f4 ♘h6 3 ♘f3 d5 4 e5 c5 5 c3 ♘c6 6 ♗d3 ♘e7 7 0-0 ♘ef5 8 ♗c2 ♗e7 9 ♕e1 ♗d7 10 d4 ♖f8 11 g3 c4 12 h3 g6 13 g4 ♘h4 14 ♘g5 ♗xg5 15 fxg5 ♘f3+ 16 ♖xf3 ♖xf3 17 ♔g2 ♖f7 18 gxh6 ♕e7 19 h4 ♕f8 20 ♗g5 ♗c6 21 a3 b5 22 ♕e2 a5 23 ♔g3 ♔d7 24 ♕e3 b4 25 axb4 axb4 26 ♖xa8 ♕xa8 27 ♕d2 b3 28 ♗d1 ♕a1 29 h5 ♕b1 30 ♗f6 ♗b7 31 hxg6 hxg6 32 g5 ♕e4 33 ♗g4 ♕c2 34 ♕g2 ♕e4 35 ♕h3 ♕d3+ 36 ♔h4 ♕xh3+ 37 ♔xh3 ♗c8 38 ♔h4 ♔e8

39 ♗h5 ♖h7 40 ♗g7 gxh5 41 g6 ♖xh6 42 ♗xh6 ♔e7 43 ♗g7 ♗d7 44 ♔xh5 ♗e8 45 ♔g5 ♗f7 46 gxf7 ♔xf7 47 ♗f8 ♔xf8 48 ♔f6 **1-0** +1

**1788-★BP-16** 10 v 88
**Brühl, J.M.– Philidor, F.A.D.**
London
1 e4 e5 2 f4 exf4 3 ♘f3 g5 4 ♗c4 ♗g7 5 h4 h6 6 hxg5 hxg5 7 ♖xh8 ♗xh8 8 d4 g4 9 ♗xf4 gxf3 10 ♕xf3 ♕e7 11 c3 ♘f6 12 ♘d2 d5 13 ♗d3 dxe4 14 ♘xe4 ♘xe4 15 ♕xe4 ♕xe4+ 16 ♗xe4 c6 17 ♔d2 ♗e6 18 b3 ♘d7 19 ♖h1 ♗f6 20 ♔c2 0-0-0 21 ♗d6 ♘b6 22 ♗c5 ♔c7 23 ♖h7 ♖h8 24 c4 ♖xh7 25 ♗xh7 ♘d7 26 ♔d3 ♘xc5+ 27 dxc5 ♗e7 28 b4 a6 29 a3 f5 30 ♗g6 ♔d7 31 ♗h5 ♗g5 32 ♗d1 ♗c1 33 ♗a4 ♗xa3 34 ♔c3 ♗c1 35 ♗d1 ♗f4 36 ♔d4 ♔e7 37 b5 ♔f6 38 ♗f3 ♗d7 39 b6 ♗g3 40 ♗d1 ♗h4 41 ♔e3 ♔e5 42 ♗f3 ♗f2+ 43 ♔d3 ♗xc5 44 ♔c3 ♗xb6 **0-1** +1

**1788-★CP-1** 6 iv 88
**Philidor, F.A.D.– Conway, H.S.**
London
⟨♘b1⟩ 1 e4 ... 2 f4 d5 3 e5 f6 4 d4 ♘h6 5 ♘f3 ♘f7 6 ♗d3 ♗g4 7 h3 ♗xf3 8 ♕xf3 e6 9 ♗e3 ♘d7 10 c3 c5 11 0-0 f5 12 ♗xf5 exf5 13 ♕xd5 ♘b6 14 ♕e6+ ♗e7 15 ♕xf5 0-0 16 ♖ad1 cxd4 17 ♗xd4 ♕c7 18 ♕e4 ♗c5 19 b4 ♗xd4+ 20 cxd4 ♖ad8 21 d5 ♘xe5 22 fxe5 ♖xf1+ 23 ♔xf1 ♕f7+ 24 ♔g1 ♖xd5 25 ♖f1 ♕e6 26 ♕f3 ♘d7 27 ♕c3 ♘xe5 28 ♕c7 ♕b6+ **0-1** +1

**1788-★CP-2** 6 iv 88
**Philidor, F.A.D.+ Conway, H.S.**
London
⟨♘b1⟩ 1 e4 ... 2 f4 d5 3 e5 d4 4 ♗c4 c5 5 d3 e6 6 c3 ♘c6 7 a4 ♗e7 8 ♘f3 ♘h6 9 0-0 0-0 10 ♗d2 ♔h8 11 h3 ♘f5 12 g4 ♘e3 13 ♗xe3 dxe3 14 ♕e2 ♘a5 15 ♗a2 c4 16 d4 ♘b3 17 ♖ad1 ♕a5 18 ♕xc4 ♘d2 19 ♘xd2 exd2 20 ♖xd2 a6 21 ♗b1 f5 22 b3 b5 23 axb5 ♕xb5 24 ♗d3 ♕xc4 25 bxc4 ♗b7 26 c5 ♖ad8 27 ♔h2 ♗e4 28 ♗xe4 fxe4 29 ♖e2 a5 30 ♔g3 ♗xc5 31 ♖xe4 ♗e7 32 ♖a1 ♖a8 33 h4 ♖fc8 34 ♖e3 a4 35 f5 a3 36 fxe6 a2 37 d5 ♗c5 38 ♖f3 ♔g8 39 d6 ♖f8 40 e7 ♖xf3+ 41 ♔xf3 ♔f7 42 ♔e4 ♔e8 43 ♔d5 ♗xd6 44 exd6 **1-0** +1

**1788-★CP-3** 24 iv 88
**Philidor, F.A.D.– Conway, H.S.**
London
⟨♘b1⟩ 1 e4 ... 2 f4 d6 3 ♘f3 b6 4 d4 ♗b7 5 ♗d3 f6 6 c3 ♘h6 7 ♗e3 ♘f7 8 g3 ♘d7 9 b4 e5 10 d5 ♕e7 11 ♔f2 f5 12 ♖e1 fxe4 13 ♗xe4 ♘f6 14 ♕d3 ♘xe4+ 15 ♕xe4 g6 16 ♗d4 ♗g7 17 fxe5 dxe5 18 ♗xe5 ♗xe5 19 ♘xe5 0-0 20 ♔g2 ♖ae8 21 ♘xf7 ♕xe4+ 22 ♖xe4 ♖xe4 **0-1** +1

**1788-★CP-4** iv 88
**Philidor, F.A.D.+ Conway, H.S.**
London
⟨♘b1⟩ 1 e4 ... 2 f4 d6 3 d4 f6 4 ♗d3 ♘h6 5 ♘f3 ♘f7 6 c3 ♗g4 7 f5 ♘d7 8 h3 ♗xf3 9 ♕xf3 c5 10 0-0 cxd4 11 cxd4 ♕b6 12 ♕f2 ♖c8 13 ♗e3 ♕d8 14 ♖ac1 g5 15 ♖xc8 ♕xc8 16 ♖c1 ♕b8 17 ♗c4 ♗g7 18 ♗e6 ♘d8 19 ♕e2 ♘xe6 20 fxe6 ♘b6 21 ♕b5+ ♔f8 22 d5 ♗h6 23 ♗xb6 axb6 24 ♕xb6 ♔g7 25 ♖c7 ♖e8 26 g4 ♔f8 27 ♕xb7 ♕xb7 28 ♖xb7 ♗g7 29 ♔f2 ♖c8 30 ♔e3 h5 31 ♔d3 hxg4 32 hxg4 f5 33 a4 f4 34 b4 ♖a8 35 a5 ♗f6 36 ♔c4 ♔e8 37 ♖d7 ♖a6 38 ♔b5 ♖a8 39 a6 ♖b8+ 40 ♔a5 **1-0** +1

**1788-★CP-5** iv 88
**Philidor, F.A.D.+ Conway, H.S.**
London
⟨♘b1⟩ 1 e4 ... 2 f4 d6 3 d4 f5 4 e5 e6 5 ♘f3 ♗e7 6 c3 ♘h6 7 ♗d3 ♘f7 8 ♗e3 0-0 9 ♗c2 a6 10 a4 ♘d7 11 0-0 c5 12 exd6 ♗xd6 13 dxc5

♘xc5 14 c4 ♗e7 15 a5 ♕c7 16 ♕e2 ♗d7 17 ♕f2 ♖ac8 18 ♖fd1 ♗c6 19 ♘d4 ♗d7 20 ♘b3 ♘h6 21 h3 ♗c6 22 ♖d2 ♘a4 23 c5 ♗f6 24 ♖ad1 ♔h8 25 ♖d6 ♖fe8 26 ♗d4 ♘f7 27 ♗xf6 gxf6 28 ♕h4 ♕e7 29 ♔h2 ♖g8 30 g4 ♖g6 31 ♕f2 ♖h6 32 gxf5 ♘xd6 33 cxd6 ♕f7 34 fxe6 ♕xe6 35 ♖d3 ♗e4 36 ♘d4 ♕xd6 37 ♘f5 ...? **1-0** +1

**1788-★LP-1** 29 iii 88

**Leycester– Philidor, F.A.D.**

London

⟨♘b8⟩ 1 e4 b6 2 d4 ♗b7 3 ♗d3 g6 4 f3 ♗g7 5 ♘e2 e6 6 c3 h6 7 ♗e3 a6 8 ♕c2 f5 9 exf5 gxf5 10 ♘d2 ♕h4+ 11 g3 ♕f6 12 ♖g1 h5 13 h4 ♘e7 14 ♗g5 ♕f7 15 ♗xe7 ♕xe7 16 0-0-0 ♗h6 17 f4 ♖g8 18 ♕b3 0-0-0 19 ♖de1 d6 20 ♘c4 ♗d5 21 ♕a4 ♔b7 22 ♘e3 b5 23 ♘xd5 exd5 24 ♕b3 ♕f7 25 a4 c5

26 a5 cxd4 27 ♘xd4 ♖xg3 28 ♖xg3 ♗xf4+ 29 ♔b1 ♗xg3 ...? **0-1** +1

**1788-★LP-2** 30 iii 88

**Leycester+ Philidor, F.A.D.**

London

⟨♘b8⟩ 1 e4 e6 2 ♗c4 g6 3 c3 b6 4 a3 ♗b7 5 d3 ♗g7 6 ♕e2 h6 7 f4 d6 8 f5 gxf5 9 exf5 ♕h4+ 10 ♔f1 ♕f6 11 ♘f3 ♕xf5 12 ♔f2 a6 13 ♖e1 e5 14 ♔g1 ♘e7 15 ♖f1 d5 16 ♗b3 ♕e6 17 d4 e4 18 ♘e1 b5 19 ♘c2 f5 20 ♗f4 ♔d7 21 ♘e3 c6 22 a4 ♕g6 23 ♘d2 h5 24 ♕f2 ♖hf8 25 ♕g3 ♕xg3 26 hxg3 ♔e6 27 axb5 axb5 28 ♖xa8 ♖xa8 29 ♗g5 ♗f6 30 ♘xe4 ♗xg5 31 ♘xg5+ ♔f6 32 ♘f3 ♗c8 33 ♘h4 ♔g5 34 ♗c2 ♖a2 35 ♘hxf5 ♗xf5 36 ♘xf5 ♖xb2 37 ♘xe7 ♖xc2 38 ♘xc6 ♖xc3 39 ♘e5 b4 40 ♖b1 b3 41 ♔h2 ♔f5 42 ♔h3 ♔e4 43 ♘f3 ♔d3 44 ♖b2 ♔c4 45 ♘d2+ ♔b4 46 ♔h4 ♔a3 **1-0** +1

**1788-★LP-3** 30 iii 88

**Leycester= Philidor, F.A.D.**

London

⟨♘b8⟩ 1 e4 e6 2 f4 ♗c5 3 d4 ♗b6 4 ♘f3 c6 5 ♕e2 d6 6 e5 d5 7 g3 h6 8 h4 h5 9 ♗h3 ♕e7 10 c3 f6 11 exf6 gxf6 12 ♗e3 ♗d7 13 ♘bd2 0-0-0 14 0-0-0 ♘h6 15 ♖de1 ♖de8 16 ♗f2 ♖hg8 17 ♘h2 ♕f7 18 ♕f3 ♕g6 19 ♘hf1 ♘g4 20 ♖g1 e5 21 fxe5 fxe5 22 ♗xg4 ♗xg4 23 ♕g2 e4 24 ♘e3 ♖gf8 25 ♖gf1 ♗f3 26 ♕h3+ ♕e6 27 ♕xe6+ ♖xe6 28 ♘d1 ♖ef6 29 ♘xf3 ♖xf3 30 ♖e3 ♖3f6 31 ♖ee1 ♗c7 32 ♖e3 ♖f3 33 ♖xf3 ♖xf3 34 ♔d2 ♗xg3 35 ♔e2 ♗d6 36 ♗e1 ♖h3 37 ♖f5 ♖h2+ 38 ♗f2 ♔d7 39 ♖xh5 ♔e6 40 ♖g5 ♗f4 41 ♖g7 b5 42 ♖g6+ ♔d7 43 ♖g7+ ♔e6 44 ♖xa7 ♗g3 45 h5 ♗xf2 46 ♘xf2 ♖xh5 47 ♖c7 ♔d6 48 ♖f7 ♖g5 49 ♖f4 ♖g1 50 ♘d1 ♖h1 51 ♖f2 ♖g1 52 a3 ♖h1 53 ♖f6+ ♔d7 54 ♔d2 ♖h2+ 55 ♖f2 ♖h1 56 ♔c2 ♔e6 57 ♘e3 ♖e1 58 ♘g4 ♖g1 59 ♘e5 c5 60 ♖e2 c4 61 ♔d2 ♖f1 62 ♖h2 ♖b1 63 ♔e3 ♖e1+ 64 ♖e2 ♖f1 65 ♔d2 ♖b1 66 ♔c2 ♖f1 67 b3 ♔f5 68 bxc4 bxc4 69 ♔b2 ♔f4 70 a4 e3 71 ♔a3 ♖f2 72 ♖xe3 ♔xe3 73 ♘g4+ ♔d2 74 ♘xf2 ♔xc3 75 a5 ♔d2 76 a6 c3 77 a7 c2 78 a8♕ c1♕+ **½-½** +1

**1788-★LP-4** 3 v 88

**Leycester+ Philidor, F.A.D.**

London

⟨♘b8⟩ 1 e4 e5 2 ♗c4 f5 3 ♗xg8 ♖xg8 4 exf5 d5 5 ♕h5+ g6 6 fxg6 ♖xg6 7 g3 ♕f6 8 ♕f3 ♕d6 9 h3 ♗d7 10 d3 0-0-0 11 ♘d2 ♗c6 12 ♕e2 ♗g7 13 c3 ♗b5 14 c4 ♗a6 15 ♘gf3 c6 16 ♘h4 ♖f6 17 ♕g4+ ♕d7 18 ♕xd7+ ♖xd7 19 0-0 b5 20 b3 bxc4 21 dxc4 ♗h6 22 ♘df3 ♗xc1 23 ♖axc1 e4 24 ♘e5 ♖e7 25 ♘g4 ♖fe6 26 cxd5 ♗xf1 27 dxe6 ♗xh3 28 ♖xc6+ ♔b7 29 ♘e5 ♗xe6 30 ♖c3 ♗d5 31 ♘g4 ♗c6 32 ♘e3 ♖f7 33 ♘hf5 ♖f6 34 ♘d4 ♗e8 35 ♖c5 ♖d6 36 ♘df5 ♖a6 37 a4 ♗g6 38 ♖e5 ♖f6 39 ♘e7 ♖d6 40 ♘7f5 ♗xf5 41 ♘xf5 ♖d1+ 42 ♔g2 ♖d3 **1-0** +1

**1788-★LP-5** v 88

**Leycester– Philidor, F.A.D.**

London

⟨♘b8⟩ 1 e4 e5 2 ♗c4 f5 3 ♗xg8 ♖xg8 4 exf5 d5 5 ♕h5+ g6 6 fxg6 ♖xg6 7 ♕xh7 ♕f6 8 g3 ♗c5 9 f3 ♗d7 10 ♕h4 ♕xh4 11 gxh4 ♖xg1+ 12 ♖xg1 ♗xg1 13 d3 ♗xh2 14 ♗g5 ♗g3+ 15 ♔d1 ♔f7 16 ♘d2 c6 17 ♔e2 ♖h8 18 ♖h1 ♗f5 19 h5 ♖g8 20 ♗e3 d4 21 ♗f2 ♗f4 22 h6 ♖h8 23 ♘c4 b5 24 ♖h5 ♔g6 25 ♖xf5 ♔xf5 26 ♘d2 ♗xd2 27 ♔xd2 ♖xh6 28 ♔e2 ♖h2 29 ♔f1 ♔f4 30 ♔g1 ♔xf3 31 ♔xh2 ♔xf2 32 ♔h3 ♔f3 33 b3 c5 34 a3 e4 35 dxe4 ♔xe4 **0-1** +1

**1788-★LP-6** v 88

**Leycester– Philidor, F.A.D.**

London

⟨♘b8⟩ 1 e4 e5 2 ♗c4 f5 3 ♗xg8 ♖xg8 4 exf5 d5 5 ♕h5+ g6 6 fxg6 ♖xg6 7 g3 ♗c5 8 ♕e2 ♕e7 9 ♘c3 c6 10 d3 ♗d7 11 ♘a4 ♗b4+ 12 ♗d2 0-0-0 13 0-0-0 ♗d6 14 ♘c3 ♖f8 15 ♖f1 b5 16 ♘d1 ♕e6 17 ♔b1 d4 18 f3 ♗d5 19 ♘f2 ♕f7 20 ♘e4 ♗xa2+ 21 ♔c1 ♕e7 22 f4 ♕e6 23 ♖f2 ♗g4 24 ♕e1 ♕a2 25 c4 bxc4 26 dxc4 ♕xc4+ 27 ♘c3 dxc3 28 ♗xc3 ♗f6 29 ♕f1 ♕c5 30 ♘h3 exf4 31 ♘xf4 ♗xc3 32 bxc3 ♕xc3+ 33 ♖c2 ♕a1+ 34 ♔d2 ♖d8+ 35 ♔e3 ♕d4# **0-1** +1

**1788-★LP-7** 10 v 88

**Leycester– Philidor, F.A.D.**

London

⟨♙f7⟩ 1 e4 c5 2 ♕h5+ g6 3 ♕xc5 ♘c6 4 c3 e5 5 ♕e3 ♘f6 6 h3 d5 7 exd5 ♘xd5 8 ♕e2 ♘f4 9 ♕f3 ♗h6 10 ♗b5 0-0 11 ♕e4 ♗f5 12 ♕c4+ ♔h8 13 ♕f1 ♗d3 14 ♗xd3 ♘xd3+ 15 ♔e2 ♖xf2+ 16 ♕xf2 ♘xf2 17 ♔xf2 ♕d3 18 ♘e2 ♖f8+ 19 ♔e1 e4 20 ♖f1 ♖xf1+ 21 ♔xf1 ♕c2 22 ♔e1 ♘e5 23 ♘a3 ♘d3+ 24 ♔f1 ♕d1# **0-1** +1

**1788-★NP-1** 10 v 88

**Nowell– Philidor, F.A.D.**

London

⟨♙f7⟩ 1 e4 ♘h6 2 ♗c4 e6 3 d3 ♘f7 4 f4 d5 5 ♗b3 ♗c5 6 ♘f3 0-0 7 e5 c6 8 d4 ♗b6 9 a3 ♕e7 10 0-0 c5 11 c3 ♘c6 12 ♗e3 ♗d7 13 ♕e2 g6 14 ♗c2 ♘h6 15 ♘bd2 ♘f5 16 ♖f2 ♘xe3 17 ♕xe3 ♖ac8 18 ♘b3 cxd4 19 ♘bxd4 ♘xd4 20 ♘xd4 ♖c4 21 ♖d1 ♖cc8 22 h3 ♖f7 23 ♔h2 ♖cf8 24 ♕g3 ♗d8 25 ♖df1 b5 26 ♕e3 a5 27 ♖f3 ♖g7 28 ♕d2 ♗c7 29 ♗d3 ♖b8 30 ♔h1 g5 31 ♖g3 gxf4 32 ♖xg7+ ♕xg7 33 ♖xf4 ♕xe5 34 ♖g4+ ♔h8 35 ♘f3 ♕f6 36 ♖h4 ♔g8 37 ♗xh7+ ♔g7 38 ♗d3 ♖h8 39 ♖g4+ ♔f8 40 ♕e3 ♔e8 41 ♖g6 ♕f4 42 ♕c5 ♔d8 43 ♖g7 ♕d6 44 ♕e3 ♖f8 45 ♕g5+ ♔c8 46 ♕d2 e5 47 ♖g6 ♗e6 48 ♕h6 ♖e8 49 ♗xb5 ♖e7 50 ♕h8+ ♔b7 51 ♖g5 e4 52 ♘e5 ♔b6 53 a4 e3 54 ♘f3

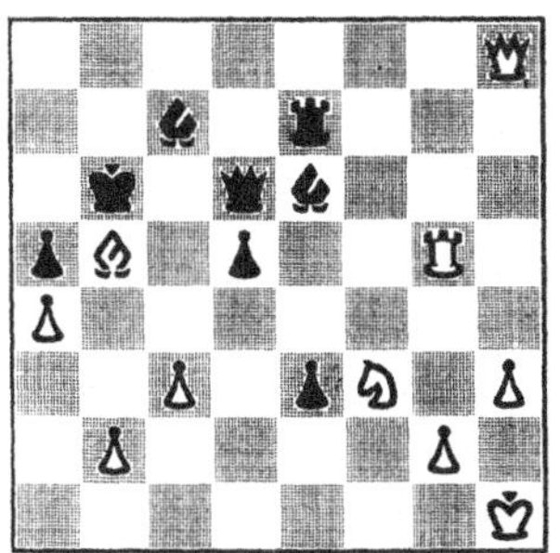

54 ... ♗d7 55 ♕d4+ ♕c5 56 ♕xc5+ ♔xc5 57 ♗xd7 e2 58 ♘e1 ♖xd7 59 ♔g1 ♖f7 60 ♘f3 ♖xf3 **0-1** +1

**1789-★BP-1**
**Bowdler– Philidor, F.A.D.**
London [Bourdonnais]
⟨♙f7⟩ 1 e4 ♘h6?! 2 ♗c4 e6 3 ♘c3 ♘f7 4 f4 c6 5 ♕e2 ♗c5 6 ♘f3 0-0 7 d4 ♗e7 8 ♗d3 d5 9 e5 ♘d7 10 ♗e3 g6 11 h4 [△ 12 h5] 11 ... ♘h6 12 h5 ♘f5 13 ♕f2 ♔g7 14 g4 ♘xe3 15 ♕xe3 ♖h8 16 ♔d2 [□ 16 0-0-0] 16 ... c5 17 hxg6 hxg6 18 g5 c4 19 ♗e2 a6 20 ♖xh8 ♕xh8 21 ♕g1 b5 22 ♕h1 ♕xh1 23 ♖xh1 ♘b6 24 ♖h6 b4 25 ♘d1 ♗d7 26 ♘h4 ♗e8 27 ♗g4 ♗f7 28 ♘e3 ♖h8 29 ♖xh8 ♔xh8 30 ♘xg6+ ♗xg6 31 ♗xe6 ♗e4 32 ♘g4 c3+ 33 bxc3 ♘c4+ 34 ♔e2 bxc3 35 ♘f6 ♗xf6 36 exf6 ♘d6 37 ♔d1 ♘b5 38 f5 ♘xd4 39 g6 ♘xe6 40 g7+ ♘xg7 **0-1**
L/N6013-1837

**1789-★BP-2** 14 i 89
**Philidor, F.A.D.– Brühl, J.M.**
London
⟨♘b1,♙f7⟩ 1 e4 d5 2 e5 ♗f5 3 g4 ♗g6 4 e6 ♕d6 5 ♕e2 ♘f6 6 d3 ♘c6 7 g5 ♘d4 8 ♕d2 ♕xe6+ 9 ♔d1 ♘d7 10 c3 ♕g4+ 11 f3 ♘xf3 12 ♗e2 ♘de5 13 ♘xf3 ♘xf3 14 ♕e3 ♗h5 15 ♖f1 ♕g2 16 ♖xf3 ♗xf3 17 ♗xf3 ♕f1+ 18 ♔c2 c6 19 ♖b1 ♕h3 20 ♕f4 ♕d7 21 ♗d2 ♕d6 22 ♕f5 g6 23 ♕h3 ♗g7 24 ♖e1 e5 25 ♕g3 0-0-0 26 d4 ♖de8 27 dxe5 ♗xe5 28 ♖xe5 ♕xe5 29 ♗g4+ ♔d8 30 ♗f4 ♕e4+ 31 ♔d2 ♖e7 32 ♗d6 ♖f7 33 ♗e5 ♖e8 34 ♗f6+ ♖xf6 35 ♕b8+ ♔e7 36 ♕c7+ ♔f8 37 gxf6 ♕e1+ 38 ♔d3 ♕e3+ 39 ♔c2 ♕f2+ **0-1** +1

**1789-★BP-3** 23 i 89
**Philidor, F.A.D.– Brühl, J.M.**
London
⟨♘b1,♙f7⟩ 1 e4 d5 2 e5 ♗f5 3 d4 c5 4 dxc5 ♕a5+ 5 c3 ♕xc5 6 ♗e3 ♕c6 7 a4 a6 8 g4 ♗g6 9 ♗g2 e6 10 ♘e2 ♘d7 11 f4 ♗c5 12 ♗d4 ♗f7 13 ♕d2 ♘e7 14 b4 ♗xd4 15 ♘xd4 ♕c7 16 h4 ♖c8 17 ♖c1 ♘b6 18 a5 ♘c4 19 ♕e2 0-0 20 h5 ♘c6 21 ♘f3 b5 22 ♕d3 ♕a7 23 ♔e2 ♔h8 24 ♘h4 ♗e8 25 ♘g6+ ♗xg6 26 hxg6 ♖xf4 27 ♖xh7+ ♔g8 28 ♗xd5 ♕f2+ 29 ♔d1 ♘b2# **0-1** +1

**1789-★BP-4** 26 i 89
**Philidor, F.A.D.– Brühl, J.M.**
London
⟨♘b1,♙f7⟩ 1 e4 d5 2 e5 ♗f5 3 g4 ♗g6 4 b4 e6 5 c3 a5 6 b5 c5 7 d4 cxd4 8 cxd4 ♗b4+ 9 ♗d2 ♗xd2+ 10 ♕xd2 ♕b6 11 ♘h3 ♘h6 12 ♖g1 ♘d7 13 ♘f4 ♗e4 14 ♖g3 0-0 15 f3 ♗g6 16 h4 ♖ac8 17 h5 ♗c2 18 a4 ♖c7 19 ♗d3 ♗xd3 20 ♘xd3 ♕xd4 **0-1** +1

**1789-★BP-5** 26 i 89
**Philidor, F.A.D.+ Brühl, J.M**
London
⟨♘b1,♙f7⟩ 1 e4 d5 2 e5 ♗f5 3 g4 ♗g6 4 h4 c5 5 h5 ♗f7 6 c3 e6 7 f4 ♘c6 8 d4 cxd4 9 cxd4 ♗b4+ 10 ♔f2 ♘ge7 11 ♘f3 a6 12 a3 ♗a5 13 b4 ♗b6 14 ♗e3 0-0 15 ♗d3 ♔h8 16 ♔g3 ♕d7 17 ♖a2 ♗g8 18 ♗b1 ♘d8 19 ♘h4 ♘f7

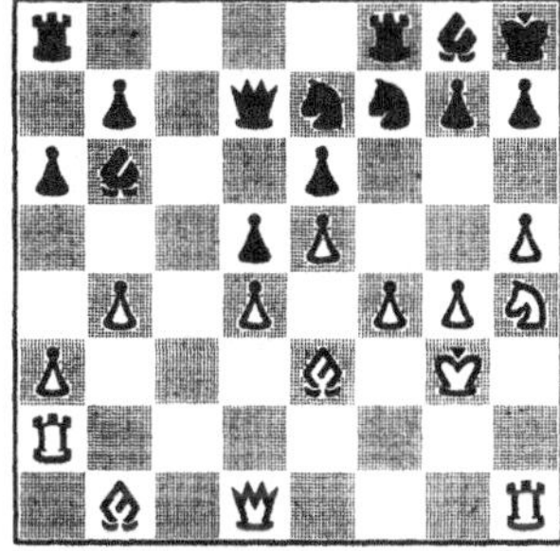

20 ♘g6+ ♘xg6 21 hxg6 ♘h6 22 ♖ah2 hxg6 23 ♗xg6 ♗h7 24 ♕b1 ♖ae8 25 ♗xh7 ♖e7 26 ♗g6 ♔g8 27 g5 ♘f5+ **1-0** +1

**1789-★BP-6** 26 i 89
**Philidor, F.A.D.+ Brühl, J.M.**
London
⟨♘b1,♙f7⟩ 1 e4 d5 2 e5 ♗f5 3 g4 ♗g6 4 h4 h5 5 ♘h3 ♕d7 6 ♘f4 ♗f7 7 g5 g6 8 ♗d3 e6 9 ♘xg6 ♗g7 ...⚲ **1-0** +1

**1789-★BP-7** 26 i 89
**Philidor, F.A.D.+ Brühl, J.M.**
London
⟨♘b1,♙f7⟩ 1 e4 d5 2 e5 ♗f5 3 g4 ♗g6 4 h4 h5 5 ♘h3 ♕d7 6 ♘f4 ♗f7 7 g5 ♕f5 8 d4 ♕e4+ 9 ♕e2 ♕xh1 10 g6 e6 11 ♕b5+ ♘d7 12 gxf7+ ♔d8 13 fxg8♕ ♖xg8 14 ♘xe6+ ♔c8 15 ♗e3 ♕xh4 16 ♕xd5 ♗e7 17 ♗a6 ♖b8 18 ♕c4 ♗d8 19 ♗g5

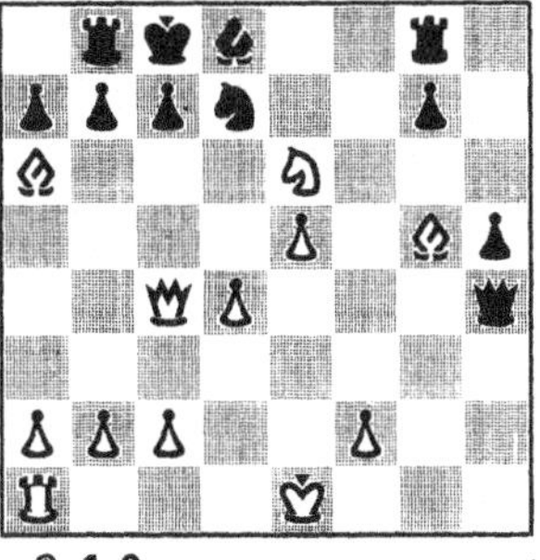

...⚲ **1-0** +1

**1789-★BP-8**
**Brühl, J.M.○ Philidor, F.A.D.**
London
⟨♙f7⟩ 1 e4 e6 2 ♗c4 g6 3 ♕e2 c5 4 d3 ♘c6 5 ♗e3 ♘f6 6 f4 d5 7 exd5 exd5 8 ♗xc5+ ♔f7 9 ♗xf8 ♖xf8 10 ♗xd5+ ♕xd5 11 ♘c3 ♕d4 12 0-0-0 ♕xf4+ 13 ♔b1 ♗g4 14 ♘f3 ♗xf3 15 gxf3 ♘d4 16 ♕g2 ♕xf3 17 ♕xf3 ♘xf3 ...⚲ +1

**1789-★CP-1** 11 i 89
**Philidor, F.A.D.+ Cotter**
London
⟨♖a1⟩ 1 e4 e5 2 f4 d5 3 ♘f3 exf4 4 exd5 ♕xd5 5 ♘c3 ♕e6+ 6 ♔f2 ♗e7 7 d4 ♘f6 8 ♗xf4 ♘e4+ 9 ♘xe4 ♕xe4 10 ♗xc7 ♘c6 11 ♗d3 ♕e6 12 ♖e1 ♕xa2 13 ♗b5 ♗d7 14 d5 ♕xb2 15 dxc6 bxc6

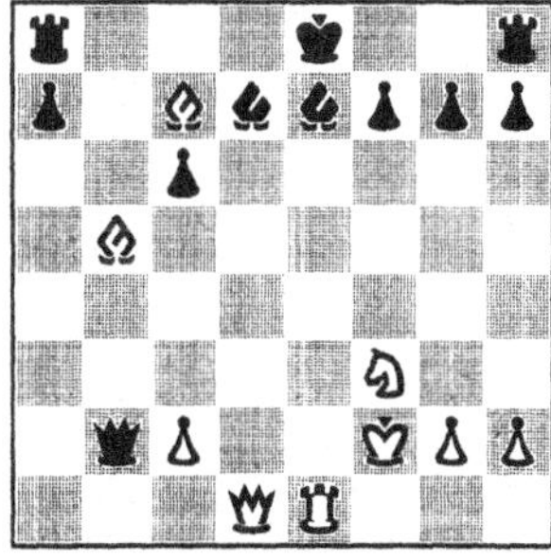

16 ♗xc6 ♗xc6 17 ♖xe7+ ♔xe7 18 ♕d6+ ♔e8 19 ♕xc6+ ♔e7 20 ♗d6+ ♔d8 21 ♕c7+ ♔e8 22 ♕e7# **1-0** +1

**1789-★PW-1**
**Philidor, F.A.D.+ Wilson, J.**
London
⟨♘b1,♙f7⟩ 1 e4 ♘h6 2 d4 ♘f7 3 f4 e6 4 ♗d3 c5 5 c3 cxd4 6 cxd4 ♘c6 7 ♘f3 ♗b4+ 8 ♔e2 ♕c7 9 a3 ♗e7 10 ♗e3 d6 11 b4 ♗d7 12 ♖c1 ♕d8 13 h3 ♖c8 14 g4 ♘b8 15 ♕d2 ♖xc1 16 ♖xc1 d5 17 e5 a6 18 f5 h6 19 fxe6 ♗xe6 20 ♗f5 ♗xf5 21 gxf5 ♗g5 22 e6 ♗xe3 23 exf7+

♔xf7 24 ♕xe3 ♖e8 25 ♘e5+ ♔g8 26 ♕f4 ♕f6 27 ♔f3 ♖f8 28 ♘g6 ♖e8 29 ♕e5 ♕xe5 30 dxe5 ♘c6 31 ♔f4 ♔f7 32 ♖d1 d4 33 h4 ♖d8 34 ♔e4 b5 35 h5 a5 36 ♖c1 d3 37 ♖xc6 d2 38 ♖c7+ ♔g8 39 f6 gxf6 40 exf6 ♖d4+ 41 ♔e5 ♖d5+ 42 ♔f4 ♖d4+ 43 ♔g3 ♖g4+ 44 ♔h3 ♖xg6 45 hxg6 **1-0** +1

**1789-★PW-2**
**Philidor, F.A.D.+Wilson, J.**
London
⟨♘b1,♙f7⟩ 1 e4 ♘h6 2 f4 ♘f7 3 ♗c4 e6 4 ♗b3 c5 5 ♕e2 ♘c6 6 c3 ♕e7 7 ♘f3 d6 8 d4 b6 9 e5 d5 10 f5 c4 11 fxe6 ♗xe6 12 ♗c2 0-0-0 13 0-0 h6 14 b3 g5 15 bxc4 dxc4 16 ♘d2 ♘a5 17 a4 h5 18 ♗e4 g4 19 ♖b1 ♗h6 20 ♖b5 ♗xd2 21 ♗xd2 ♕d7 22 d5 ♘xe5 23 dxe6 ♕xd2 24 ♕xd2 ♖xd2 25 ♖xe5 ♘b3 26 e7 **1-0** +1

**1790-★BP-1 σ●⌂**
**Brühl, J.M.= Philidor, F.A.D.**
London [Morphy]
⟨♙f7⟩ 1 e4 e6 2 d4 d5 3 e5 c5 4 ♗b5+? [□ 4 ♗d3] 4 ... ♘c6 5 ♘e2 cxd4 6 ♗xc6+ bxc6 7 ♕xd4 ♕b6 [□ 7 ... c5] 8 0-0 ♗c5 9 ♕g4 g6 10 c3 a5 11 ♘d4 ♔f7 12 b3 ♗d7 13 ♘a3 h5 14 ♕d1 ♘e7 15 ♘ac2 ♘f5 16 ♘xf5 gxf5 17 ♗e3 ♗xe3 18 fxe3 ♖af8 19 ♘d4 c5 20 ♘xf5? exf5 21 ♕xd5+ ♗e6 22 ♖xf5+ ♔e7? [□ 22 ... ♔g6 23 ♖xf8 ♗xd5 24 ♖xh8 ♕e6-+] 23 ♕d6+ ♕xd6 24 exd6+ ♔xd6 25 ♖d1+ ♔c6 26 ♖e5 ♖e8 27 c4 ♖h7 28 e4 ♖d7? [□ 28 ... ♖he7] 29 ♖dd5! ♖d6 30 ♖xh5 [□ 30 ♖xc5+] 30 ... ♗d7 31 ♖xd6+ [□ 31 ♖xc5+] 31 ... ♔xd6 32 ♖d5+ ♔c6 33 e5 ♗f5 34 h3 ♗b1 35 ♖d6+ ♔c7 36 ♖a6 ♖xe5 37 ♖xa5 ♔b6 38 b4 ♖e1+ 39 ♔f2 ♖c1 40 ♖b5+ ♔a6 41 ♖xc5 ♖c2+ 42 ♔g3 ♗xa2 43 ♖c6+? [□ 43 h4+-] 43 ... ♔b7 44 ♖c5 ♗xc4 45 h4 ♖c3+ 46 ♔f4 ♖c1 47 g4 ♖f1+ 48 ♔e5? [□ 48 ♔g5] 48 ... ♗e2 49 g5 ♗h5 50 ♔d6 ♖f4 51 b5 ♔b6 52 ♔e5 ♖b4 53 g6 ♗xg6 **½-½** L/N6389-1860

**1790-★BP-2 σ●**
**Brühl, J.M.= Philidor, F.A.D.**
London [Morphy]
⟨♙f7⟩ 1 e4 ♘h6 2 d4 ♘f7 3 ♗c4 e6 4 ♗b3 d5 5 e5 c5 6 c3 ♘c6 7 ♘e2 [□ 7 f4] 7 ... ♕b6 8 ♗a4? ♗d7 9 ♗xc6 bxc6 10 0-0 cxd4 11 cxd4 c5 12 ♗e3 cxd4 13 ♗xd4 ♗c5 14 f4 0-0 15 ♗xc5 ♕xc5+ 16 ♕d4 ♕xd4+ 17 ♘xd4 g5 18 g3 gxf4 19 gxf4 ♖ab8 20 ♖f2 ♘h8 21 f5 [□ 21 ♘c3, 22 f5] 21 ... exf5 22 ♘c3 ♖be8 23 ♖e1 ♗e6 24 ♘xe6 ♖xe6 25 ♘xd5 ♘g6 26 ♖g2 ♔h8 27 ♖ge2 f4 28 ♘f6 ♔g7 29 ♔f2 ♖f7 30 h4 ♖fe7 31 ♘d5 ♖d7 32 ♘f6 ♖de7 **½-½** L/N6389-1860

**1790-★BP-3 σ●⌂**
**Brühl, J.M.– Philidor, F.A.D.**
London [Morphy]
⟨♙f7⟩ 1 e4 ♘h6 2 d4 ♘f7 3 ♗c4 e6 4 ♗b3 [□ 4 ♕e2] 4 ... d5 5 e5 c5 6 c3 ♘c6 7 f4 ♕b6 8 ♘f3 ♗e7 9 ♗c2 ♗d7 10 b3 cxd4 11 cxd4 ♗b4+ 12 ♔f2 g5! [Δ 13 fxg5 ♘fxe5∓] 13 ♗e3? [□ 13 g3] 13 ... gxf4 14 ♗xf4 ♖f8 [Δ 15 ... ♘xe5] 15 ♗e3 h6 16 h4 0-0-0 17 a3 ♗e7 18 ♕d3 ♖g8 19 ♘bd2 ♖df8 20 ♕c3 ♔b8 [□ 20 ... ♘fxe5] 21 ♖h3? ♘fxe5

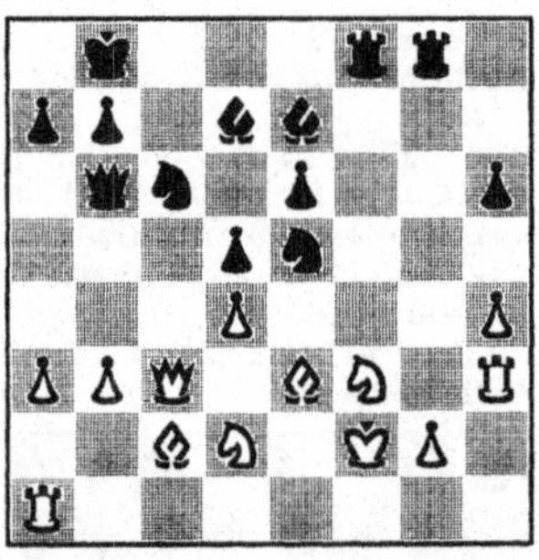

22 dxe5 d4 23 ♘c4 dxe3+ 24 ♘xe3 [24 ♕xe3 ♕xe3+ 25 ♔xe3 ♘xe5; 25 ... ♖xg2] 24 ... ♗c5 25 b4?? [□ 25 ♖e1] 25 ... ♗xe3+ 26 ♕xe3 ♖xg2+ 27 ♔xg2 ♕xe3 28 ♖e1 ♕f4 29 ♖e4 ♕c1 30 ♘e1 ♘e7 31 ♖c4 ♕xe1 32 ♗d3 ♖f2+ 33 ♔g3 ♕g1# **0-1** L/N6389-1860

**1790-★CP-1 σ●** 13 iii 90
**Conway, H.S.– Philidor, F.A.D.**
London
1 e4 e5 2 ♗c4 c6 3 ♘c3 ♗d6 4 d3 ♗c7 5 ♕f3 ♕e7 6 ♗g5 ♘f6 7 ♘ge2 d6 8 h3 ♗e6 9 ♗b3 b5 10 0-0-0 h6 11 ♗xf6 ♕xf6 12 ♕xf6 gxf6 13 d4 a5 14 f4 exd4 15 ♖xd4 a4 16 ♗xe6 fxe6 17 ♖hd1 ♔e7 18 ♘g1 ♘d7 19 ♘f3 h5 20 e5 fxe5 21 ♘xe5 ♘xe5 22 fxe5 d5 23 ♖e1 ♖af8 24 ♖d3 ♖f5 25 b3 axb3 26 axb3 ♖xe5 27 ♖f1 ♖g5 28 g3 ♖hg8 29 ♘e2 e5 30 ♖df3 ♖8g7 31 ♖f6 ♗d6 32 ♖h6 ♖7g6 33 ♖xg6 ♖xg6 34 ♖f5 e4 35 ♖xh5 ♗xg3 36 ♘xg3 ♖xg3 37 ♔d2 ♔d6 38 ♖h8 ♔c5 39 c3 b4 40 cxb4+ ♔d4 41 ♖h6 ♖g2+ 42 ♔c1 e3 43 ♖xc6 ♖g1+ 44 ♔b2 e2 45 ♖e6 e1♕ 46 ♖xe1 ♖xe1 **0-1** +1

**1790-★JP-1 σ●**
**Jennings– Philidor, F.A.D.**
London [Morphy]
⟨♙f7⟩ 1 e4 c5 2 ♕h5+ g6 3 ♕xc5 ♘c6 4 ♕c3 [□ 4 ♕c4] 4 ... e5 5 a3 ♘f6 6 f3 a5 7 ♗c4 [7 d3 ♗b4!] 7 ... d5 8 ♗b5 ♕b6 9 ♕xe5+ ♔f7 10 ♗xc6 bxc6 11 d4 ♗g7 12 ♘e2 ♖e8 13 ♕g5 dxe4 14 ♘bc3 [□ 14 f4] 14 ... exf3 15 gxf3 ♕xd4 16 ♘e4 ♘xe4 17 fxe4 ♕xe4 18 0-0+ ♔g8 19 ♖f2 [19 ♘∼? ♗d4-+] 19 ... ♗a6 20 ♘g3 ♕e1+ 21 ♔g2 ♗d4 22 ♖f3 ♕g1+ 23 ♔h3 ♗c8+ 24 ♘f5 ♕xg5 25 ♗xg5 ♗xf5+ 26 ♔h4 ♖e4+ 27 ♗f4 ♗e5 28 ♖af1 h6 29 ♔g3 ♖xf4 30 ♖xf4 g5 **0-1** L/N6389-1860

**1790-★JP-2 σ●⌂**
**Jennings– Philidor, F.A.D.**
London [Morphy]
⟨♙f7⟩ 1 e4 c5?! 2 ♕h5+ g6 3 ♕xc5 ♘c6 4 ♕e3 [□ 4 ♕c4] 4 ... e5 5 ♗c4 ♘f6 6 ♘c3? [□ 6 c3] 6 ... ♘d4 7 ♗b3 ♗c5 8 ♕g5 d6 9 d3 ♗e6 10 ♗e3? [□ 10 ♗xe6] 10 ... ♗xb3 11 ♗xd4 exd4 12 axb3 dxc3 13 bxc3 ♗xf2+ 14 ♔e2 ♗b6 15 ♘h3 0-0 16 ♖hf1 ♕e7 17 ♘f4 ♖ae8 18 h4 ♕e5 19 ♘h3 ♕xc3 20 ♖ac1 d5 21 h5 dxe4 22 hxg6 exd3+ 23 ♔d1 ♗e3 24 gxh7+ ♔h8 25 ♕g8+ ♘xg8 26 hxg8♕+ ♔xg8 27 ♖xf8+ ♔xf8 28 cxd3 ♕d2# **0-1** L/N6389-1860

**1790-★JP-3 σ●**
**Jennings+ Philidor, F.A.D.**
London [Morphy]
⟨♙f7⟩ 1 e4 ♘h6 2 d4 ♘f7 3 ♗d3 d6 [□ 3 ... e6; 3 ... e5] 4 ♘f3 e5 5 d5 c5 [□ 5 ... ♗e7 Δ 6 ... 0-0, 7 ... c6] 6 0-0 ♗e7 7 ♗e3 0-0 8 ♘bd2 a6 9 a4 ♗g4 10 ♗e2 [□ 10 h3] 10 ... ♘d7 11 c4 b6 12 ♔h1 ♗xf3 13 ♘xf3 g5 14 g4 ♔g7 15 ♕d2 h6 16 ♘g1 ♖h8 17 ♖a3 ♘f8 18 h3 ♘g6 19 ♕c3 [Δ 20 f4] 19 ... ♗f6 20 ♗d2 ♘f4 21 ♕g3 ♖h7 22 ♖f3 ♘h8 23 ♗c3 ♘hg6 24 ♖e3 ♕e7 25 ♗d1 ♖ah8 26 ♕h2 h5 27 gxh5 ♘xh5 28 ♗g4 ♘gf4 29 ♖a1 a5 30 ♖a3 ♔f8 31 ♗d2 ♕g7 32 ♖ab3 ♗d8 33 ♖f3 ♘f6 34 ♕g3 ♘xg4? [□ 34 ... ♘xe4-+] 35 ♕xg4 ♖h4 36 ♕c8 ♕e7 37 ♖xb6 g4 38 ♖b7 ♕xb7 [38 ... gxf3 39 ♖xe7 ♖xh3+ 40 ♘xh3 ♖xh3+ 41 ♕xh3 ♘xh3-+] 39 ♖xf4+ exf4 40 ♕xb7 ♔e8 41 ♗xf4 gxh3 42 ♕c6+ ♔f8 43 ♗xd6+ ♗e7 44 ♕c8+ ♔f7 45 ♕e6+ **1-0** L/N6389-1860

**1790-★PS-1** 13 iii 90
**Sheldon– Philidor, F.A.D.**
London
1 e4 e5 2 ♗c4 c6 3 ♘f3 d5 4 exd5 cxd5 5 ♗b3 ♘c6 6 d4 e4 7 ♘e5

♗e6 8 0-0 f6 9 ♘xc6 bxc6 10 f3 f5 11 ♗e3 ♘f6 12 ♘d2 ♗d6 13 c4 0-0 14 ♗a4 ♕c7 15 f4 ♘g4 16 ♕e2 ♘xe3 17 ♕xe3 c5 18 ♘b3 dxc4 19 ♘xc5 ♗xc5 20 dxc5 ♖ac8 21 c6 ♖fd8 22 ♖fd1 ♖d3 23 ♖xd3 cxd3 24 ♗b3 ♗xb3 25 axb3 ♕b6 26 ♔f2 ♕xe3+ 27 ♔xe3 ♖xc6 28 ♖xa7 ♖d6 29 ♔d2 e3+ 30 ♔xe3 d2 31 ♖a1 d1♕ **0-1** +1

**1790-★PS-2** 13 iii 90
**Smith– Philidor, F.A.D.**
London

1 e4 e5 2 ♗c4 ♘f6 3 d3 c6 4 ♗g5 h6 5 ♗xf6 ♕xf6 6 ♘c3 b5 7 ♗b3 a5 8 a3 ♗c5 9 ♘f3 d6 10 ♕d2 ♗e6 11 ♗xe6 fxe6 12 0-0 g5 13 h3 ♘d7 14 ♘h2 h5 15 g3 ♔e7 16 ♔g2 d5 17 f3 ♘f8 18 ♘e2 ♘g6 19 c3 ♖ag8 20 d4 ♗b6 21 dxe5 ♕xe5 22 ♘d4 ♔d7 23 ♖ae1 h4 24 ♕f2 ♗c7 25 ♘e2

25 ... hxg3 26 ♕xg3 ♕xg3+ 27 ♘xg3 ♘f4+ 28 ♔h1 ♖xh3 29 ♖g1 ♖xh2+ 30 ♔xh2 ♖h8+ 31 ♘h5 ♖xh5+ 32 ♔g3 ♘h3+ 33 ♔g4 ♖h4# **0-1** +1

**1794-★AP-1** 22 iii 94
**Atwood, G.– Philidor, F.A.D.**
London

1 e4 c5 2 f4 e6 3 ♘f3 ♘c6 4 c3 d5 5 e5 f5 6 d4 ♘h6 7 a3 ♘f7 8 ♗e3 ♕b6 9 ♕d2 ♗d7 10 ♕f2 c4 11 ♗xc4 dxc4 12 d5 ♕c7 13 dxc6 ♗xc6 14 ♗xa7 ♗xf3 15 gxf3 g5 16 ♗e3 gxf4 17 ♗xf4 ♘xe5 18 ♗xe5 ♕xe5+ 19 ♕e2 ♕xe2+ 20 ♔xe2 h5 21 ♘d2 ♖c8 22 ♖hg1 ♔f7 23 ♖g2 ♗e7 24 ♖ag1 ♗f6 25 ♘f1 e5 26 ♘e3 ♔e6 27 ♖d1 ♖hg8 28 ♖xg8 ♖xg8 29 ♘xc4 ♖g2+ 30 ♔d3 ♖xh2 31 ♖d2 ♖h3 32 ♔e2 b5 33 ♘e3 ♖h2+ 34 ♔e1 ♖xd2 35 ♔xd2 ♗g5 36 ♔e2 ♗xe3 37 ♔xe3 h4 38 ♔f2 e4 39 ♔g2 e3 40 ♔h3 e2 **0-1** +1

**1794-★AP-2** iii 94
**Atwood, G.+ Philidor, F.A.D.**
London

1 e4 c5 2 f4 ♘c6 3 ♘f3 e6 4 c3 d5 5 e5 f5 6 d4 ♘h6 7 h3 ♕b6 8 b3 ♗d7 9 ♗e3 ♘f7 10 ♕d2 0-0-0 11 ♕f2 cxd4 12 ♘xd4 ♘xd4 13 ♗xd4 ♕c6 14 ♘d2 b6 15 a4 ♗c5 16 ♗b5 ♗xd4 17 ♕xd4 ♕c5

18 ♘f3 ♗xb5 19 ♕xc5+ bxc5 20 axb5 ♔b7 21 ♔e2 ♖a8 22 ♖a6 ♖he8 23 ♖d1 ♘d8 24 ♘e1 c4 25 bxc4 dxc4 26 ♖d7+ ♔c8 27 ♖xg7 ♖b8 28 ♖axa7 ♖xb5 29 ♖ac7+ ♔b8 30 ♖xc4 ♖b7 31 ♖b4 ♖xb4 32 cxb4 ♘c6 33 ♘d3 ♖e7 34 ♖xe7 ♘xe7 35 ♘c5 ♘g6 36 ♘xe6 ♔c8 37 ♔e3 ♔d7 38 ♘d4 ♘e7 39 g4 ♔e8 40 g5 **1-0** +1

**1794-★AP-3** iii 94
**Atwood, G.= Philidor, F.A.D.**
London

1 d4 d5 2 c4 dxc4 3 e3 e5 4 d5 c6 5 ♗xc4 b5 6 ♗b3 c5 7 a4 c4 8 ♗c2 ♗b7 9 e4 a6 10 ♗d2 ♗c5 11 ♕e2 ♘e7 12 ♘f3 f6 13 axb5 axb5 14 ♖xa8 ♗xa8 15 0-0 ♕b6 16 ♘c3 ♗b4 17 b3 cxb3 18 ♗xb3 0-0 19 d6+ ♔h8 20 dxe7 ♗xe7 21 ♖b1 b4 22 ♘d5 ♗xd5 23 ♗xd5 f5 24 ♘e1 fxe4 25 ♗xe4 ♘a6 26 ♘d3 b3 27 ♗d5 b2 28 ♖xb2 ♕d4 29 ♗b7 ♘c5 30 ♗e3 ♕xd3 31 ♗xc5 ♕xe2 32 ♖xe2 ♗xc5 33 ♖c2 ♗d4 34 ♔f1 g6 35 ♖c8 ♖xc8 36 ♗xc8 ♔g7 37 h4 h5 38 ♔e2 ♔f6 39 ♔f3 ♔g7 40 ♔e4 ½-½ +1

**1795-★AC-1** 8 ii 95
**Cotter– Atwood, G.**
London

1 e4 e5 2 ♗c4 c6 3 ♕f3 ♘f6 4 ♘c3 a6 5 a4 ♗b4 6 ♘ge2 d5 7 exd5 ♗g4 8 ♕e3 0-0 9 f3 ♗f5 10 ♘a2 cxd5 11 ♘xb4 dxc4 12 c3 a5 13 ♘a2 ♘d5 14 ♕c5 ♗d3 15 ♔f2 f5 16 b3 b6 17 ♕b5 ♕c7 18 ♕xd5+ ♔h8 19 ♕xa8 ♕c5+ 20 ♔f1 ♘c6 21 ♕b7 e4 22 ♗b2 exf3 23 gxf3 ♖e8 24 ♘c1 ♕d5 25 ♔g2 ♗xe2 26 ♘xe2 ♖xe2+ 27 ♔g1 ♕c5+ 28 ♔f1 ♕f2# **0-1** +1

**202** Philidor, F.A.D. Brühl, J.M., Wilson, J. London, 23 ii 1794 SM.BL

**1795-★AC-2**
**Atwood, G.– Cotter**
London
1 e4 e5 2 ♗c4 c6 3 ♘f3 d5 4 exd5 cxd5 5 ♗b5+ ♗d7 6 ♗xd7+ ♘xd7 7 0-0 ♗d6 8 d3 ♘e7 9 ♘c3 0-0 10 ♘g5 h6 11 ♘f3 f5 12 h3 g5 13 ♘xg5 hxg5 14 ♗xg5 ♖f7 15 ♘xd5 ♕f8 16 ♕f3 ♕g7 17 ♘xe7+ ♗xe7 18 ♗xe7 ♖xe7 19 ♕xf5 ♖f8 20 ♕e4 ♘f6 21 ♕e2 ♘d5 22 ♖ae1 ♖f6 23 ♔h2 ♖g6 24 ♕e4 ♘f4 25 g3 ♘e6 26 a3 ♘d4 27 f4 ♖xg3 28 ♕d5+ ♔h8 29 ♖xe5 ♘f3+ 30 ♖xf3 ♖g2+ 31 ♔h1 ♖g1+ 32 ♔h2 ♕g2# **0-1** +1

**1795-★AD-1** 26 vi 95
**Douglass, G.– Atwood, G.**
London
⟨♙f7⟩ 1 e4 e6 2 d4 d5 3 e5 c5 4 c3 ♘c6 5 f4 ♘h6 6 ♗e3 ♘f5 7 ♗f2 h5 8 ♘f3 ♕b6 9 b3 cxd4 10 cxd4 ♗b4+ 11 ♘bd2 ♘fxd4 12 ♘xd4 ♘xd4 13 ♗e2 g6 14 0-0 ♗c5 15 ♖c1 ♘xe2+ 16 ♕xe2 ♗xf2+ 17 ♕xf2 ♕xf2+ 18 ♖xf2 ♖h7 19 ♘f3 ♖e7 20 ♖fc2 ♗d7 21 ♖c7 ♗c6 22 ♖xe7+ ♔xe7 23 ♔f2 ♖f8 24 g3 ♖d8 25 ♘d4 ♖c8 26 h4 ♔f7 ...♀ **0-1** +1

**1795-★AH-1** 2 ii 95
**Atwood, G.○ Harrowby**
London
1 e4 e5 2 f4 exf4 3 ♘f3 g5 4 ♗c4 g4 5 d4 gxf3 6 ♕xf3 ♕f6 7 e5 ♕c6 8 ♗d5 ♕xc2 9 ♗xb7 ♗b4+ 10 ♔f1 ♕c4+ 11 ♔f2 ♕xd4+ 12 ♔f1 ♕c4+ 13 ♔f2 ♗c5+ 14 ♔e1 ...♀ +1

**1795-★AM-1**
**Maseres ♀○ Atwood, G.**
London
1 e4 c5 2 c4 d6 3 ♘c3 f5 4 d3 ♘c6 5 b3 g6 6 ♗b2 ♗g7 ...♀ +1

**1795-★AP-1** 14 i 95
**Philidor, F.A.D.○ Atwood, G.**
London
1 e4 e5 2 f4 exf4 3 ♘f3 g5 4 ♗c4 g4 5 c3 gxf3 6 ♕xf3 ♗h6 7 g3 ...♀ +1

**1795-★AP-2** 2 i 95
**Philidor, F.A.D.○ Atwood, G.**
London
1 e4 e5 2 ♗c4 c6 3 ♕e2 ♘f6 4 f4 ♕c7 5 f5 ♘xe4 6 ♕xe4 d5 7 ♗xd5 cxd5 8 ♕xd5 ♗xf5 ...♀ +1

**1795-★AP-3** 8 ii 95
**Atwood, G.○ Philidor, F.A.D.**
London
1 e4 e5 2 f4 exf4 3 ♘f3 g5 4 ♗c4 g4 5 d4 gxf3 6 ♕xf3 ♘c6 7 c3 ♗h6 8 ♗xf4 ♕f6 9 ♗xc7 ♕xf3 10 gxf3 ♘f6 ...♀ +1

**1795-★AP-4** 7 ii 95
**Philidor, F.A.D.+ Atwood, G.**
London
⟨♘b1⟩ 1 e4 e5 2 f4 exf4 3 ♘f3 g5 4 ♗c4 ♗g7 5 c3 ♕e7 6 d4 d6 7 0-0 h5 8 h4 g4 9 ♘g5 ♘h6 10 ♗xf4 0-0 11 ♕b3 ♘c6 12 ♗d2 ♘d8 13 ♕c2 ♔h8 14 ♖ae1 ♘e6 15 e5 ♘xg5 16 hxg5 ♘g8 17 exd6 ♕xd6 18 ♗xf7 ♕c6 19 d5 ♕d7 20 ♕g6 ♘e7 21 ♕xh5+ ♗h6 22 ♕xh6# **1-0** +1

**1795-★AP-5** 9 ii 95
**Atwood, G.○ Philidor, F.A.D.**
London
1 e4 e5 2 f4 exf4 3 ♘f3 g5 4 ♗c4 g4 5 d4 gxf3 6 ♕xf3 ♘c6 7 c3 ♕f6 8 e5 ♕xe5+ 9 ♔d1 ♕f6 10 ♖e1+ ♗e7 11 ♗xf4 d6 12 ♕e3 ...♀ +1

**1795-★AP-6** 12 ii 95
**Philidor, F.A.D.+ Atwood, G.**
London
⟨♘b1⟩ 1 e4 e5 2 f4 ♘c6 3 ♘f3 ♗c5 4 c3 f6 5 ♗c4 ♘ge7 6 ♕e2 d6 7 f5 ♗d7 8 b4 ♗b6 9 a4 a6 10 d3 g6 11 g4 h5 12 g5 gxf5 13 gxf6 ♘g6 14 ♗g5 ♕c8 15 0-0-0 f4 16 ♗b3 ♔f8 17 d4 ♗g4

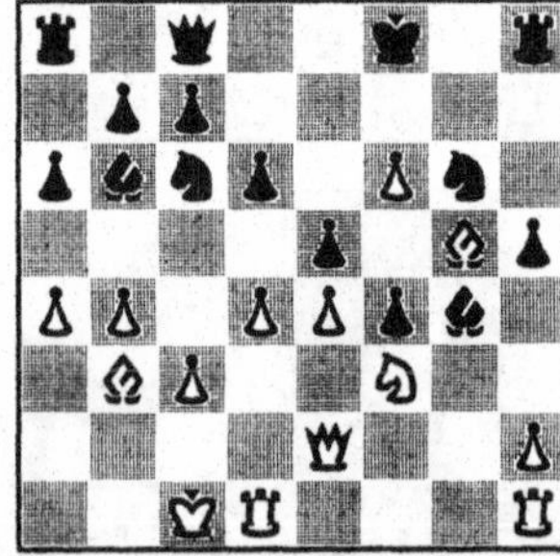

18 ♕c4 ♘d8 19 dxe5 ♗e6 20 ♖d5 ♗e3+ 21 ♔b2 c6 22 ♕e2 cxd5 23 exd5 dxe5 24 dxe6 ♘xe6 25 ♕d3 ♕e8 26 ♗xe6 ♕xe6 27 ♕xg6 **1-0** +1

**1795-★AP-7** 13 ii 95
**Philidor, F.A.D.– Atwood, G.**
London
⟨♘b1⟩ 1 e4 e5 2 f4 ♘c6 3 ♘f3 ♗c5 4 c3 f6 5 d4 ♗b6 6 d5 ♘b8 7 f5 d6 8 ♗d3 c6 9 c4 ♗a5+ 10 ♗d2 b5 11 cxb5 cxd5 12 exd5 ♘e7 13 ♘h4 ♗b7 14 ♕a4 ♗b6 15 ♗e4 ♘xd5 16 ♗b4 ♘d7 17 ♗xd6 ♗c5 18 ♖d1 ♘7b6 **0-1** +1

**1795-★AP-8** 13 ii 95
**Philidor, F.A.D.– Atwood, G.**
London
⟨♘b1⟩ 1 e4 e5 2 f4 ♘c6 3 ♘f3 ♗c5 4 ♗c4 d6 5 ♘g5 exf4 6 ♕h5 ♕e7 7 ♘xf7 ♘f6 8 ♘xd6+ ♔d8 9 ♘f7+ ♔e8 10 ♕f3 ♘d4 11 ♕xf4 ♘xc2+ 12 ♔f1 ♖f8 13 ♖b1 ♘xe4 14 ♗d3 ♖xf7 **0-1** +1

**1795-★AP-9** 21 vi 95
**Philidor, F.A.D.– Atwood, G.**
London
⟨♖a1,♙f7⟩ 1 e4 e6 2 f4 d5 3 e5 c5 4 ♗d3 g6 5 c3 ♘c6 6 h4 ♗e7 7 h5 g5 8 g3 gxf4 9 gxf4 ♗h4+ 10 ♔f1 ♘h6 11 ♗c2 ♘f5 12 ♗xf5 exf5 13 d4 b6 14 ♘f3 ♗e7 15 ♗e3 cxd4 16 cxd4 ♗a6+ 17 ♔f2 ♖g8 18 ♘c3 ♕d7 19 ♕a4 ♘b4 20 ♕xd7+ ♔xd7 21 ♘e1 ♘d3+ 22 ♘xd3 ♗xd3 23 ♘xd5 ♗e4 24 ♘xe7 ♔xe7 25 ♖h2 ♖ac8 26 ♔e1 ♖g2 27 ♖xg2 ♗xg2 **0-1** +1

**1795-★AP-10** 24 vi 95
**Philidor, F.A.D.– Atwood, G.**
London
⟨♖a1,♙f7⟩ 1 e4 e6 2 d4 d5 3 e5 c5 4 c3 cxd4 5 cxd4 ♗b4+ 6 ♔e2 b6 7 ♕a4+ ♘d7 8 ♕xb4 ♗a6+ 9 ♔e1 ♗xf1 10 ♔xf1 ♖c8 11 ♘c3 ♕h4 12 g3 ♕h5 13 ♗e3 ♘e7 14 ♘b5 ♘f5 15 ♘d6+ ♘xd6 16 ♕xd6 ♕g6 17 ♘f3 h6 18 ♘h4 ♕f7 19 ♔g2 g5 20 ♘f3 ♖f8 21 ♘e1 g4 22 ♖f1 h5 23 ♗h6 ♖h8 24 ♗f4 h4 25 f3 gxf3+ 26 ♖xf3 hxg3 27 ♗xg3 ♕g6 28 ♘d3 ♖c2+ 29 ♘f2 ♖xb2 30 ♖f4 ♖xa2 31 h4 ♖g8 32 ♖f3 ♖c2 33 h5 ♕g4 34 h6 ♖xf2+ 35 ♔xf2 ♕xd4+ 36 ♔g2 ♕d2+ 37 ♖f2 ♕xh6 38 ♖f6 ♘xf6 39 ♕xe6+ ♔f8 40 exf6 ♕d2+ 41 ♔h3 ♖h8+ **0-1** +1

**1795-★AP-11** 25 vi 95
**Philidor, F.A.D.– Atwood, G.**
London
⟨♖a1,♙c7⟩ 1 e4 e5 2 f4 d6 3 ♘f3 ♗g4 4 ♗c4 ♘c6 5 c3 ♘f6 6 d3 exf4 7 ♗xf4 ♕b6 8 ♗xf7+ ♔e7 9 ♗b3 ♘a5 10 ♘bd2 ♖e8 11 ♕e2 ♔d8 12 h3 ♗xf3 13 ♕xf3 ♗e7 14 0-0-0 [sic;♔c1] 14 ... ♖hf8 15 ♗e3 ♕c7 16 ♗a4 ♘d7 17 ♕e2 a6 18 b4 ♘c6 19 ♔b2 ♗f6 20 d4 ♔c8 21 ♗c2 b5 22 a4 ♕b7 23 ♗d3 ♔c7 24 ♖a1 ♖b8 25 ♔c2 bxa4 26 ♗xa6 ♘xb4+ 27 cxb4 ♕xb4 28 ♖b1 ♕a3 29 ♕c4+ ♔d8 30 ♖xb8+ ♘xb8 31 ♕c8+ ♔e7 32 ♕c7+ ♘d7 33 ♗b5 ♖d8 34 ♗f2 ♗g5 35 ♕c3 ♕xc3+ 36 ♔xc3 ♗xd2+ 37 ♔xd2 ♖a8 38 ♗h4+

Ke8 39 Kc2 h6 40 Be1 Ke7 41 e5 d5 42 Bb4+ Ke6 43 Kb2 Nxe5 44 dxe5 Rb8 45 Ka3 Rxb5 46 Kxa4 Rxb4+ 47 Kxb4 Kxe5 **0-1** +1

**1795-★AP-12** 27 vi 95
**Atwood, G.– Philidor, F.A.D.**
London
⟨Δf7⟩ 1 e4 ... 2 d4 e6 3 f4 d5 4 e5 c5 5 c3 Nc6 6 Nf3 Nh6 7 Bd3 Nf7 8 Qc2 c4 9 Be2 b5 10 Be3 Qa5 11 Nbd2 Bd7 12 b4 Qa3 13 Kf2 Nh6 14 h3 Nf5 15 Nb1 Qa6 16 Nbd2 Qa3 17 Nb1 Qa6 18 a4 bxa4 19 Rxa4 Qb6 20 Bd2 a5 21 g4

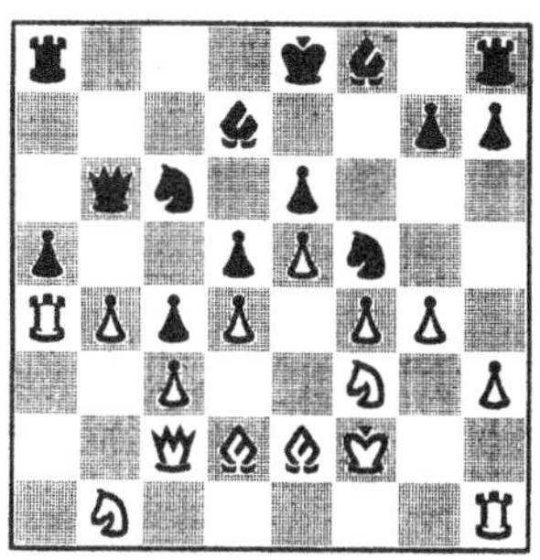

21 ... Nfxd4 22 Nxd4 Nxd4 23 cxd4 g5 24 f5 exf5 25 gxf5 Qxd4+ 26 Be3 Qxe5 **0-1** +1

**1795-★AP-13** 27 vi 95
**Atwood, G.– Philidor, F.A.D.**
London
⟨Δf7⟩ 1 e4 ... 2 d4 e6 3 f4 d5 4 e5 c5 5 c3 Nc6 6 Nf3 Nh6 7 Bd3 Qb6 8 Qb3 c4 9 Qxb6 axb6 10 Bc2 b5 11 Ng5 g6 12 Nxh7 Rxh7 13 Bxg6+ Rf7 14 Na3 b4 15 Nb5 Kd8 16 Bxf7 Nxf7 17 g4 Bd7 18 0-0 Nb8 19 Nd6 Nxd6 20 exd6 Bxd6 21 f5 exf5 22 gxf5 b5 23 Bg5+ Ke8 24 h4 Nc6 25 Rf2 bxc3 **0-1** +1

**1795-★AP-14** 27 vi 95
**Atwood, G.+ Philidor, F.A.D.**
London
⟨Δf7⟩ 1 e4 ... 2 d4 e6 3 f4 d5 4 e5 c5 5 c3 Nc6 6 Nf3 Qb6 7 Bd3 Nh6 8 Qb3 c4 9 Qxb6 axb6 10 Bc2 b5 11 Na3 b4 12 Nb5 Kd8 13 b3 Ra5 14 a4 Bd7 15 Bd2 Nxe5 16 Nxe5 Bxb5 17 f5 bxc3 18 Bxh6 gxh6 19 Nf7+ Ke7 20 Nxh8 Bg7 21 fxe6 Bxh8 22 b4 Ra8 23 Ke2 Be8 24 Bf5 Bg6 25 g4 Bxd4 26 Rhd1 Be5 27 Rxd5 Bxf5 28 gxf5 Kf6 29 e7 Re8 30 Rd7 Rxe7 31 Rxe7 Kxe7 32 a5 c2 33 Rc1 **1-0** +1

**1795-★AP-15** 28 vi 95
**Atwood, G.+ Philidor, F.A.D.**
London
⟨Δf7⟩ 1 e4 ... 2 d4 e6 3 f4 d5 4 e5 c5 5 c3 Nc6 6 Nf3 Qb6 7 Bd3 Nh6 8 Qb3 c4 9 Qxb6 axb6 10 Bc2 b5 11 Ng5 g6 12 Nxh7 Rxh7 13 Bxg6+ Rf7 14 Be3 b4 15 h3 b3 16 a3 b5 17 g4 Ke7 18 Bxf7 Kxf7 19 Rf1 b4 20 Rf2 Be7 21 f5 Nxf5 22 gxf5 exf5 23 Rg2 Be6 24 Kf1 bxa3 25 bxa3 Rh8 26 Rg3 Bh4 27 Rg2 f4 28 Bxf4 Bxh3 29 Kg1 Bxg2 30 Kxg2 b2 31 Ra2 Rb8 32 e6+ Kxe6 33 Bxb8 Nxb8 34 Rxb2 Nc6 35 Rb6 Kd6 36 a4 Bd8 37 Rb7 Ba5 38 Kf3 **1-0** +1

**1795-★AP-16** 29 vi 95
**Atwood, G.– Philidor, F.A.D.**
London
⟨Δf7⟩ 1 e4 ... 2 d4 e6 3 f4 d5 4 e5 c5 5 c3 Nc6 6 Nf3 Qb6 7 Bd3 Nh6 8 Qb3 c4 9 Qxb6 axb6 10 Bc2 b5 11 b4 Bxb4 12 cxb4 Nxb4 13 Kd2 Nxc2 14 Kxc2 b4 15 Bd2 Ra4 16 h3 Rf8 17 g4 Nf7 18 Ng5 Nxg5 19 fxg5 Rf2 20 h4 b5 21 h5 b3+ 22 Kb2 b4 23 g6 hxg6 24 hxg6 Ba6 25 Rh8+ Kd7 ...⚲ **0-1** +1

**1795-★AP-17** 29 vi 95
**Atwood, G.– Philidor, F.A.D.**
London
⟨Δf7⟩ 1 e4 ... 2 d4 e6 3 f4 d5 4 e5 c5 5 c3 Nc6 6 Nf3 Qb6 7 Bd3 Nh6 8 Qb3 c4 9 Qxb6 axb6 10 Bc2 b5 11 Na3 b4 12 Nb5 Ra5 13 a4 Bd7 14 b3 Nb8 15 Bb2 Be7 16 0-0 Bxb5 17 axb5 Rxb5 18 Ra8 0-0 19 bxc4 dxc4 20 Be4 Nd7 21 Rxf8+ Bxf8 22 Ng5 bxc3 23 Bxc3 Rb3 24 Rc1 Ba3 25 Rc2 Ng4 26 Nxe6 Rb1+ **0-1** +1

**1795-★AP-18** 29 vi 95
**Atwood, G.– Philidor, F.A.D.**
London
⟨Δf7⟩ 1 e4 ... 2 d4 e6 3 f4 d5 4 e5 c5 5 c3 Nc6 6 Nf3 Qb6 7 Bd3 Nh6 8 Qb3 c4 9 Qxb6 axb6 10 Bc2 b5 11 Na3 b4 12 Nb5 Ra5 13 a4 b3 14 Bb1 Bd7 15 Ng5 g6 16 Nxh7 Rxh7 17 Bxg6+ Rf7 18 f5 Nxf5 19 0-0 Nce7 20 Bxf7+ Kxf7 ...⚲ **0-1** +1

**1795-★AP-19** 5 vii 95
**Atwood, G.+ Philidor, F.A.D.**
London
⟨Δf7⟩ 1 e4 ... 2 d4 e6 3 f4 d5 4 e5 c5 5 c3 Nc6 6 Nf3 Qb6 7 Bd3 Nh6 8 Qb3 c4 9 Qxb6 axb6 10 Bc2 b5 11 b3 b4 12 bxc4 dxc4 13 Bb2 Bd7 ...⚲ **1-0** +1

**1795-★AP-20**
**Philidor, F.A.D.+ Atwood, G.**
London
⟨Ra1, Δf7⟩ 1 e4 e6 2 d4 d5 3 e5 c5 4 c3 cxd4 5 cxd4 Bb4+ 6 Nc3 Nc6 7 f4 Qa5 8 Ne2 b6 9 Be3 Ba6 10 Qc1 Bxe2 11 Bxe2 Qxa2 12 Bd3 Nh6 13 h3 Nf5 14 Bc2 h5 15 Rg1 Qa5 16 g4 hxg4 17 hxg4 Nfe7 18 f5 Kd7 19 f6 gxf6 20 exf6 Rh2 21 g5 Rah8 22 Kf1 Nc8 23 g6 Rh1 24 g7 Rxg1+ 25 Bxg1 ...⚲ **1-0** +1

**1795-★AV-1**
**Verdoni– Atwood, G.**
London
⟨Nb1⟩ 1 e4 ... 2 Bc4 e5 3 Nf3 Nc6 4 c3 Bc5 5 b4 Bb6 6 d4 exd4 7 cxd4 Qe7 8 0-0 Qxb4 9 Qd3 Bxd4 10 Nxd4 Ne5 11 Bxf7+ Kxf7 12 Qe3 Nf6 13 Ba3 Qa4 14 Bc1 Nfg4 15 Qf4+ Ke8 16 Nf5 d6 17 Nxg7+ Ke7 18 h3 Rg8 19 Nf5+ Bxf5 20 Qxf5 Nf6 21 Bg5 Nf3+ 22 gxf3 Rxg5+ 23 Qxg5 Rg8 24 Qg3 Rxg3+ 25 fxg3 Qd4+ 26 Kg2 Qb2+ 27 Kg1 Nh5 28 Rab1 Qd4+ 29 Kg2 Qe5 **0-1** +1

**1795-★AW-1** 18 i 95
**Wilson, J.○ Atwood, G.**
London
1 e4 e5 2 f4 exf4 3 Nf3 g5 4 Bc4 g4 5 d4 gxf3 6 Qxf3 Bb4+ 7 c3 Qh4+ 8 g3 fxg3 9 Qxf7+ Kd8 10 hxg3 ...⚲ +1

**1795-★AW-2** i 95
**Wilson, J.+ Atwood, G.**
London
1 e4 e5 2 f4 exf4 3 Nf3 g5 4 Bc4 g4 5 0-0 gxf3 6 Qxf3 Qf6 7 c3 Nc6 8 d4 Nxd4 9 Bxf7+ Qxf7 10 cxd4 Bh6 11 Nc3 Ne7 12 e5 c6 13 Ne4 d5 14 Nd6+ **1-0** +1

**1795-★AW-3** ii 95
**Wilson, J.○ Atwood, G.**
London
1 e4 e5 2 f4 exf4 3 Nf3 g5 4 Bc4 g4 5 d4 gxf3 6 0-0 Bh6 7 Qxf3 Qf6 8 e5 Qg7 9 Bxf4 Bxf4 10 Qxf4 Nh6 ...⚲ +1

**1795-★AW-4** 21 vii 95
**Wilson, J.+ Atwood, G.**
London
1 d4 d5 2 c4 dxc4 3 e3 e5 4 dxe5 Qxd1+ 5 Kxd1 Nc6 6 f4 Bg4+ 7 Be2 0-0-0+ 8 Bd2 f5 9 Bxg4 fxg4 10 Ne2 Nb4 11 a3 Nd3 12 Kc2 Bc5 13 Rf1 Nh6 14 Ng3 Rhf8 15 Nc3 a6 16 Nce4 Ba7

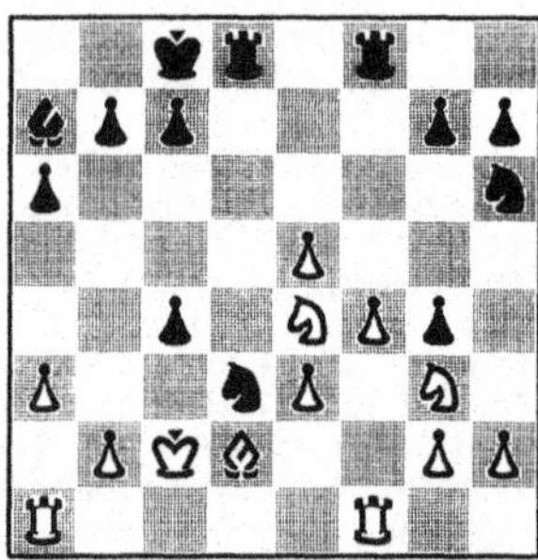

17 ♘g5 ♖fe8 18 ♘xh7 ♘f7 19 ♘e4 ♖h8 20 ♘hg5 ♘xg5 21 ♘xg5 ♖xh2 22 e6 ♘xb2 23 e7 ♖xd2+ 24 ♔xd2 ♖xg2+ 25 ♔c3 ♔d7 26 ♖ab1 ♘a4+ 27 ♔xc4 b5+ 28 ♔d3 c5 29 ♖bd1 ♔xe7 30 ♔e4 ♘c3+ 31 ♔f5 ♘xd1 32 ♖xd1 ♖e2 33 e4 g3 34 e5 g2 35 e6 ♖d2 36 ♖xd2 g1♕ 37 ♖d7+ ♔e8 38 ♖xg7 ♕b1+ 39 ♘e4 ♕d3 40 ♖g8+ ♔e7 41 ♖g7+ ♔d8 42 ♖d7+ ♕xd7 43 exd7 ♔xd7 44 ♔g6 ♔e7 45 f5 c4 46 f6+ ♔f8 47 f7 c3 48 ♘g5 **1-0** +1

**1795-★AW-5** 11 ii 95
**Atwood, G.+Wilson, J.**
London
1 e4 e5 2 ♘f3 d6 3 d4 ♗g4 4 dxe5 ♗xf3 5 ♕xf3 dxe5 6 ♗c4 ♕d7 7 ♕b3 c6 8 a4 ♗d6 9 0-0 ♘f6 10 ♘c3 0-0 11 ♗e3 ♔h8 12 ♖ad1 ♘h5 13 ♖xd6 ♕xd6 14 ♕xb7 ♘d7 15 ♖d1 ♕b8 16 ♖xd7 ♕xb7 17 ♖xb7 f5 18 ♖xa7 ♖ab8 19 h3 ♖xb2 20 ♗c5 ♖g8 21 ♗d3 g5 22 ♗d6 **1-0** +1

**1795-★AW-6**
**Atwood, G.○Wilson, J.**
London
1 e4 e5 2 f4 exf4 3 ♘f3 g5 4 h4 g4 5 ♘g5 d5 6 exd5 ♕xd5 7 d4 h6 8 c4 ♕d8 9 ♘e4 f5 10 ♘f2 ♗g7 11 d5 ♗e5 12 ♘d3 ♗f6 13 ♘xf4 ♗xh4+ 14 ♔e2 ♕d6 15 ♗e3 ♗g5 16 ♕d4 ♗f6 17 ♕d2 ♔f7 18 ♘c3 ♗d7 19 ♔f2 ...♀ +1

**1795-★BV-1** 12 vi 95
**Brühl, J.M.–Verdoni**
London
1 e4 ... 2 f4 c5 3 ♘f3 b6 4 c4 ♘c6 5 ♘a3 e6 6 ♘c2 ♗b7 7 d3 ♘ge7 8 ♗e2 f5 9 e5 ♘g6 10 ♗d2 ♗e7 11 a3 0-0 12 0-0 h6 13 h3 ♘h8 14 ♕c1 ♘f7 15 g4 g6 16 ♔h2 ♔h7 17 b4 a6 18 ♖b1 ♖b8 19 ♕e1 g5 20 gxf5 exf5 21 d4 cxd4 22 ♘cxd4 ♘xd4 23 ♘xd4 ♗e4 24 ♖b3 gxf4 25 ♗xf4 ♗h4 26 ♗g3 ♗xg3+ 27 ♖xg3 ♘xe5 28 ♖fg1 ♕f6 29 ♖g7+ ♔h8 30 ♕f2 ♘g4+ 31 ♖7xg4 fxg4 32 ♕xf6+ ♖xf6 33 ♗xg4 ♖g8 34 ♖e1 d5 35 cxd5 ♗xd5 36 ♖e5 ♗a8 37 ♖h5 ♔h7 38 ♔g3 ♖g5 39 ♖xg5 hxg5 40 ♗f5+ ♔h6 41 ♔g4 ♗d5 42 ♘c2 ♗e6 43 ♘d4 ♖xf5 44 ♘xe6 ♖f1 45 ♘c7 a5 46 bxa5 bxa5 47 ♘e8 ♖f4+ 48 ♔g3 ♖a4 49 ♘d6 ♖xa3+ 50 ♔g4 ♖a4+ 51 ♔g3 ♖f4 52 h4 ♖xh4 53 ♘f5+ ♔h5 54 ♘xh4 gxh4+ **0-1** +1

**1795-★BV-2** 14 vi 95
**Brühl, J.M.–Verdoni**
London
1 e4 ... 2 ♗c4 c5 3 c3 e6 4 ♕e2 ♘c6 5 f4 ♘ge7 6 d3 f5 7 ♗b3 b6 8 ♘f3 g6 9 ♘a3 ♗g7 10 ♘b5 0-0 11 ♘d6 ♕c7 12 e5 a5 13 a4 ♗a6 14 0-0 h6 15 h3 ♔h7 16 ♘b5 ♗xb5 17 axb5 ♘d8 18 c4 ♘f7 19 ♗c2 ♖g8 20 ♔h2 g5 21 b3 gxf4 22 ♗xf4 ♘g6 23 g3 ♘fxe5 24 ♘xe5 ♗xe5 25 ♗xe5 ♕xe5 26 ♕xe5 ♘xe5 27 ♖ae1 d6 28 ♖f4 ♖g5 29 ♖e3 ♖ag8 30 ♖f2 ♔h8 31 ♖d2 ♖h5 32 ♗d1 ♖hg5 33 d4 cxd4 34 ♖xd4 ♘f7 35 ♖xe6 ♖xg3 36 ♖d2 f4 37 ♗h5 ♖xh3+ 38 ♔xh3 ♘g5+ 39 ♔h4 ♘xe6 40 ♖xd6 ♘c5 41 ♖xh6+ ♔g7 42 ♖g6+ ♔f8 43 ♖f6+ ♔e7 44 ♖xf4 ♘xb3 45 ♗d1 ♘c5 46 ♖f1 a4 47 ♗h5 ♖a8 48 ♖e1+ ♔d6 49 ♗g6 a3 50 ♗c2 a2 51 ♖a1 ♔e5 52 ♔g4 ♔d4 **0-1** +1

**1795-★BV-3** 17 vii 95
**Brühl, J.M.+Verdoni**
London
⟨♙f7⟩ 1 e4 e6 2 f4 ♘e7 3 ♗c4 d5 4 exd5 exd5 5 ♗b3 ♗e6 6 ♘f3 h6 7 d4 ♘d7 8 ♘e5 ♘xe5 9 fxe5 ♕d7 10 0-0 0-0-0 11 ♗e3 ♘f5 12 ♗f2 ♗e7 13 ♘d2 g5 14 c3 ♖dg8 15 ♗c2 h5 16 ♘b3 g4 17 ♗xf5 ♗xf5 18 ♕e2 h4 19 ♗e3 ♗e6 20 ♗f4 g3 21 h3 ♗xh3 22 gxh3 ♕xh3 23 ♖f3 ♖h7 24 ♘d2 ♕g4 25 ♕e3 ♕h3 26 ♘f1 ♖f7 27 e6 ♖f5 28 c4 ♖gf8 29 cxd5 ♕g4 30 d6 cxd6 31 ♕c3+ ♔b8 32 ♖c1 a6 33 ♕c7+ ♔a7 34 ♖b3 ♖b5 35 ♖xb5 ♕f3 36 ♗e3 ♗g5 37 ♕xb7+ ♕xb7 38 ♖xb7+ ♔xb7 39 ♗xg5 g2 40 ♗xh4 gxf1♕+ 41 ♖xf1 ♖e8 ...♀ **1-0** +1

**1795-★BV-4** 9 vii 95
**Brühl, J.M.+Verdoni**
London
⟨♙f7⟩ 1 e4 ♘h6 2 d4 ♘f7 3 ♗c4 e6 4 ♕e2 ♗e7 5 e5 0-0 6 f4 b6 7 ♘f3 ♗b7 8 ♘bd2 ♘c6 9 c3 ♘h6 10 ♘b3 a6 11 0-0 b5 12 ♗d3 g6 13 ♗e3 ♘f5 14 ♘bd2 d5 15 g4 ♘g7 16 ♗c2 ♕e8 17 ♕d3 ♘d8 18 h4 ♘f7 19 h5 ♘h6 20 ♘h2 ♘xh5 21 gxh5 ♘f5 22 ♔h1 gxh5 23 ♖g1+ ♔h8 24 ♘df3 h6 25 ♗f2 ♕f7 26 ♘f1 h4 27 ♖g4 c5 28 ♘xh4 ♕h5 29 ♕f3 ♗xh4 30 ♖g8+ ♔xg8 31 ♕xh5 ♗xf2 32 ♕g6+ ♔h8 33 ♗xf5 exf5 34 ♕xh6+ ♔g8 35 ♔g2 cxd4 36 ♘g3 ♗xg3 37 ♖h1 ♔f7 38 ♕f6+ ♔e8 39 ♕e6+ ♔d8 40 ♖h7 **1-0** +1

**1795-★BV-5** 11 vii 95
**Brühl, J.M.–Verdoni**
London
⟨♙f7⟩ 1 e4 e6 2 d4 ♘e7 3 ♗d3 d5 4 e5 c5 5 c3 cxd4 6 cxd4 ♘bc6 7 ♗c2 ♗d7 8 a3 ♕b6 9 ♘e2 g6 10 0-0 ♗g7 11 ♔h1 0-0 12 b3

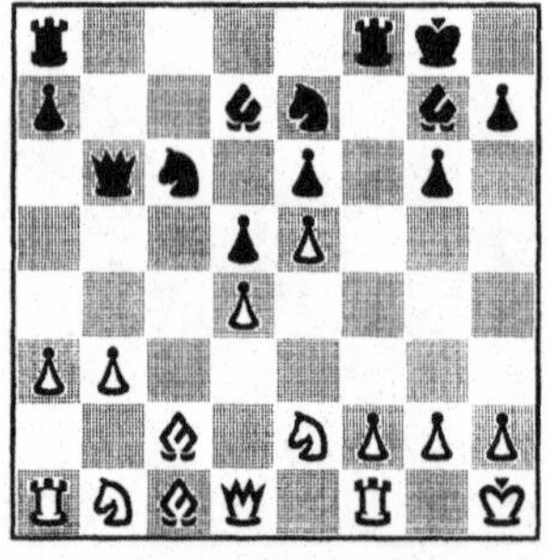

12 ... ♘xe5 13 dxe5 ♗xe5 14 ♖a2 ♖xf2 15 ♗b2 ♗xb2 16 ♖xb2 ♖af8 17 ♘g3 ♕e3 18 ♖e1 ♕f4 19 ♘c3 ♕f6 20 ♕d3 ♗c6 21 ♖bb1 e5 22 ♘h5 ♕g5 23 ♘g3 ♖d2 24 ♕e3 ♕xe3 25 ♖xe3 ♖xc2 26 ♖f1 ♖xf1+ 27 ♘xf1 d4 28 ♖xe5 dxc3 29 ♖xe7 ♖xg2 **0-1** +1

**1795-★PW-1** 13 vi 95
**Philidor, F.A.D.=Wilson, J.**
London
⟨♖a1,♙f7⟩ 1 e4 ♘h6 2 d4 ♘f7 3 f4 e6 4 ♗e3 d5 5 e5 b6 6 c3 c5 7 ♗d3 g6 8 ♘f3 cxd4 9 cxd4 ♘c6 10 ♘c3 ♗d7 11 g4 ♕c7 12 h4 0-0-0 13 h5 gxh5 14 ♖xh5 h6 15 ♗g6 ♗e8 16 ♗d3 ♔b7 17 ♕e2 ♘b4 18 ♗b1 ♖c8 19 a3 ♘a6 20 ♗d3 ♘b8 21 ♗d2 a6 22 ♖h2 b5 23 f5 ♗d7 24 f6 ♖g8 25 ♘h4 b4 26 axb4 ♗xb4 27 ♗g6 ♗e8 28 ♗h7 ♖h8 29 ♗d3 ♕b6 30 ♘f3 a5 31 ♔f2 ♘c6 32 ♘a4 ♕a7 33 ♗e3 ♘cd8 34 ♗b5 ♔a8 35 ♗xe8 ♖xe8 36 ♕b5 ♘b7 37 ♘b6+ ♔b8 38 ♘xc8 ♖xc8 39 ♕d7 ♖c2+ 40 ♔g3 ♖xh2 41 ♔xh2 ♘bd8 42 ♕xa7+ ♔xa7 43 ♔g3 ♔b6 44 ♔h4 ♔b5 45 b3 ♗c3 46 ♔h5 ♔b4 47 ♗xh6 ♔xb3 48 g5 ♘xg5 49 ♘xg5 a4 50 ♗f8 ♗b4 51 ♗e7 a3 52 ♗xd8 a2 53 ♘xe6 a1♕ 54 ♗e7 ♕a7 55 ♗xb4 ♕f7+ 56 ♔g5 ♕xe6 57 ♗c5 ♔c4 58 ♔g6 ♕g8+ 59 ♔f5 ♔b5 60 e6 ♕h7+ 61 ♔g5 ♕g8+ 62 ♔f5 **½-½** +1

**1795-★W♀-1** 12 i 95
**Wilson, J.–♀**
London
1 e4 e5 2 f4 exf4 3 ♘f3 g5 4 ♗c4 g4 5 c3 gxf3 6 ♕xf3 ♗h6 7 d4 ♕h4+ 8 g3 fxg3 9 ♕xf7+ ♔d8 10 ♗xh6 g2+ 11 ♔e2 ♘xh6 **0-1** +1

**1795-★W♀-2** i 95
**Wilson, J.–♀**
London
1 e4 e5 2 f4 exf4 3 ♘f3 g5 4 ♗c4 g4 5 0-0 gxf3 6 ♕xf3 ♕f6 7 c3 ♘c6 8 ♕f2 ♘e5 9 ♗e2 f3 10 ♗d1 ♘h6 11 h3 ♖g8 12 g4 ♘hxg4 13 hxg4 ♖xg4+ 14 ♔h1 ♖h4+ **0-1** +1

**1795-★W♀-3** i 95
**♀○Wilson, J.**
London
1 e4 e5 2 ♗c4 c6 3 d4 ♘f6 4 c3 ♘xe4 5 dxe5 d5 6 exd6 ♗xd6 7 ♕e2 0-0 ...♀ +1

**1796-★AB-1** vii 96
**Atwood, G.♀Brühl, J.M.**
London
1 e4 c5 2 f4 e5 3 ♗c4 exf4 4 ♘f3 g5 5 d3 g4 6 ♘e5 ♕h4+ 7 ♔f1 f3 8 ♘xf7 ...♀ +1

**1796-★AB-2**
**Atwood, G.–Brühl, J.M.**
London
1 e4 e5 2 ♘f3 d6 3 d4 f5 4 dxe5 fxe4 5 ♘g5 d5 6 e6 ♘h6 7 g3 c6 8 ♗h3 ♘a6 9 0-0 ♘c7 10 f4 ♗c5+ 11 ♔g2 0-0 12 f5 ♕f6 13 c3 ♔h8 14 g4 ♘g8 15 ♗f4 ♘e8 16 ♘f7+ ♖xf7 17 exf7 ♕xf7 18 ♗e5 ♗d7 19 g5 ♕e7 20 ♗f4 ♘d6 21 ♗c1 ♖f8 22 f6 ♗xh3+ 23 ♔xh3 gxf6 24 gxf6 ♕e6+ 25 ♔g2 ♖xf6 26 ♗f4 ♖g6+ 27 ♗g3 ♘f5 28 ♕e1 ♘xg3 29 hxg3 ♗d6 **0-1** +1

**1796-★AV-1** 21 i 96
**Atwood, G.=Verdoni**
London
⟨♙f7⟩ 1 e4 ... 2 d4 e6 3 ♗d3 c5 4 d5 d6 5 c4 e5 6 f4 ♘d7 7 f5 ♘gf6 8 g4 h6 9 h4 ♗e7 10 g5 hxg5 11 ♗xg5 ♘xd5 12 ♗xe7 ♘xe7 13 ♕g4 ♔f8 14 ♘f3 ♘f6 15 ♕g5 ♖h5 16 ♕g2 ♔g8 17 ♘c3 ♗d7 18 ♘d5 ♘exd5 19 cxd5 ♕e7 20 a4

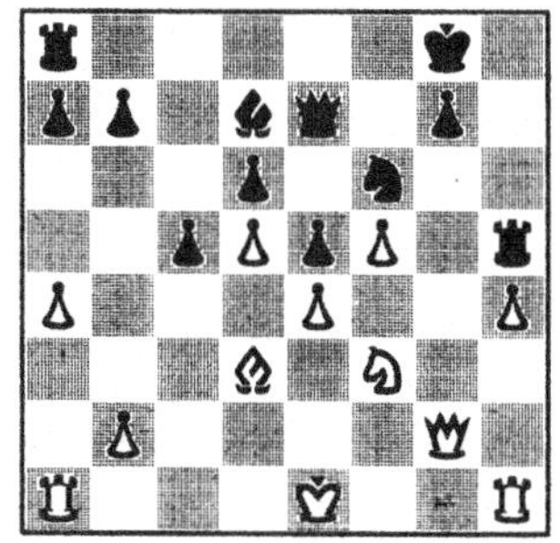

20 ... ♗xf5 21 exf5 e4 22 ♘g5 exd3+ 23 ♘e6 ♖xf5 24 ♔d2 ♖e5 25 ♖ae1 ♔h8 26 ♔xd3 ♖g8 27 ♕g5 ½-½ +1

**1796-★AV-2** 23 i 96
**Atwood, G.–Verdoni**
London
⟨♙f7⟩ 1 e4 ... 2 d4 e6 3 ♗d3 c5 4 d5 d6 5 c4 e5 6 f4 exf4 7 ♗xf4 ♕f6 8 ♕d2 ♗g4 9 h3 ♗h5 10 ♘c3 h6 11 ♘ce2 g5 12 ♗e3 ♗g7 13 ♖b1 ♘d7 14 g4 ♗g6 15 ♘g3 ♘e5 16 ♕e2 ♘e7 17 ♘f5 ♗xf5 18 exf5 0-0-0 19 b4 b6 20 bxc5 dxc5 21 ♘f3 ♖hf8 22 ♔f2 ♘7c6 23 ♘xe5 ♘xe5 24 ♕c2 ♖d7 25 ♖he1 ♖e7 26 ♕b3 ♕d6 27 ♗f1 ♘xg4+ 28 hxg4 ♖xe3 29 ♖xe3 ♗d4 30 ♖be1 ♕f4+ 31 ♔g2 ♗xe3 32 ♔h1 **0-1** +1

**1796-★AW-1** 4 i 96
**Wilson, J.○Atwood, G.**
London [Atwood]
1 e4 c5 2 f4 b6 3 ♗c4 e6 4 ♘f3 ♗b7 5 d3 ♘e7 6 0-0 d5 7 ♗b5+ ♘ec6 8 e5 a6 9 ♗xc6+ ♘xc6 10 g4 g6 11 c3 d4 12 ♗d2 dxc3 13 ♗xc3 ♕d5 14 d4 0-0-0 15 ♘bd2 cxd4 16 ♖c1 dxc3 17 ♖xc3 ♗c5+ 18 ♔h1 ♘d4 19 ♖d3 a5 20 ♘b3

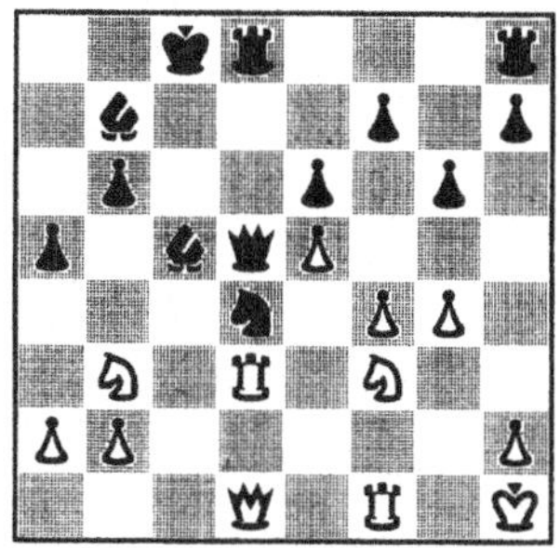

20 ... a4 [20 ... ♕xf3+-+] 21 ♘xd4 ♗xd4 22 ♕xa4 ♕a5 23 ♖xd4 ♕xa4 24 ♖xa4 ♖d3 25 ♔g2 ♖d2+ 26 ♖f2 ♖hd8 27 ♖c4+ ♔b8 28 ♖c2 ♖xc2 29 ♖xc2 ♖d4 30 ♖f2 ♗d5 31 b3 ...♀ +1

**1796-★AW-2** 29 xii 96
**Wilson, J.–Atwood, G.**
London
1 e4 c5 2 f4 ♘c6 3 ♘f3 e6 4 c3 d5 5 e5 ♗e7 6 d4 ♘h6 7 ♗e3 b6 8 ♘bd2 ♗h4+ 9 ♗f2 ♗xf2+ 10 ♔xf2 0-0 11 ♗d3 f6 12 g3 fxe5 13 dxe5 ♗b7 14 ♕c2 g6 15 ♗xg6 ♕e7 16 ♗h5 d4 17 ♘e4 ♘f5 18 ♘f6+ ♔h8 19 g4 ♘e3 20 ♕d2 ♘c4 21 ♕c2 ♘6xe5 22 fxe5 ♘xe5 23 g5 ♖xf6

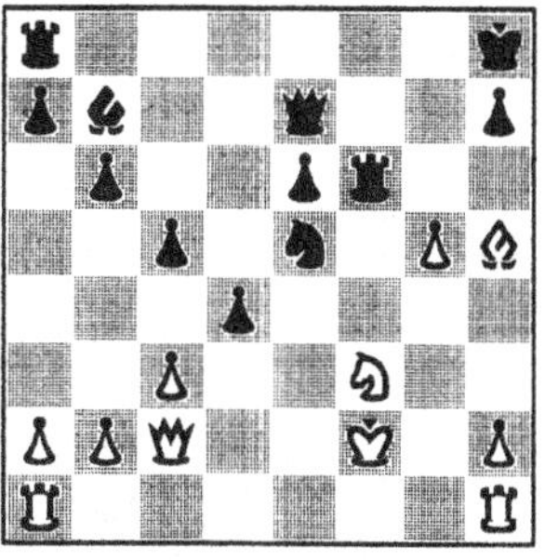

24 gxf6 ♕xf6 25 ♕e2 ♖f8 26 ♖ae1 ♕h4+ 27 ♔f1 ♘xf3 28 ♗xf3 ♖xf3+ 29 ♔g1 ♖g3+ 30 hxg3 ♕xh1+ 31 ♔f2 ♕g2# **0-1** +1

**1796-★AW-3**
**Atwood, G.+Wilson, J.**
London
1 e4 e5 2 ♘f3 ♘c6 3 ♗c4 ♗c5 4 c3 d6 5 b4 ♗b6 6 a4 a6 7 ♕b3 ♕f6 8 0-0 ♗e6 9 ♗xe6 fxe6 10 ♗b2 ♘ge7 11 ♘a3 0-0 12 ♖ad1 g5 13 d4 g4 14 dxe5 dxe5 15 ♘e1 h5 16 ♘d3 h4 17 c4 ♘d4 18 ♕a2 ♘g6 19 ♖d2 g3 20 c5 gxh2+ 21 ♔h1 ♗a7 22 ♘xe5 ♕xe5 23 ♖xd4 ♘f4 24 ♖d7 ♕xe4 25 ♖g7+ ♔h8 26 ♖g4+ ♔h7 27 ♖xh4+ ♔g6 28 ♀ e5 29 f3 ♕e2 30 ♖xf4 ♔g7 31 ♕c4 ♕xb2 32 ♖xf8 ♖xf8 33 ♘c2 ♖f4 34 ♕d3 ♖f7 35 ♖d1 ♔f6 36 ♕d8+ ♔g7 **1-0** +1

**1797-★AW-1** 6 i 97
**Atwood, G.+Wilson, J.**
London
1 e4 e5 2 ♘f3 ♘c6 3 ♗c4 ♗c5 4 c3 ♘f6 5 0-0 d6 6 d4 ♗b6 7 dxe5 ♘xe4 8 ♕d5 ♗e6 9 ♕xe4 d5 10 ♗xd5 ♗xd5 11 ♕g4 g6 12 ♗g5 ♗xf3 13 gxf3 ♕d7 14 ♗f6 ♖g8 15 ♘a3 h5 16 ♕g3 ♕f5 17 ♖ad1 g5 18 h4 g4 19 f4 ♘e7 20 ♖d3 c5 21 ♘c4 ♕e6 22 ♘d6+ ♔f8 23 ♗xe7+ ♔xe7 24 ♖fd1 ♕xa2 25 ♖3d2 ♖ad8 26 ♕e1 ♕b3 27 f5 a5 28 e6 f6 29 ♘c8+ ♖xc8 30 ♕d6+ ♔e8 31 ♕d7+ ♔f8 32 ♕f7# **1-0** +1

**1798-★AC-1** 30 xi 98
**Atwood, G.+ Campbell**
London
1 e4 e5 2 ♘f3 d6 3 d4 exd4 4 ♘xd4 ♗e6 5 ♘xe6 fxe6 6 ♕h5+ ♔d7 7 ♕b5+ ♔c8 8 ♗c4 ♕e7 9 ♕b3 d5 10 exd5 exd5+ 11 ♗e2 c6 12 ♘c3 ♘f6 13 ♗g5 ♘bd7 14 0-0-0 ♘c5 15 ♕a3 ♕e5 16 ♗xf6 ♕xf6 17 ♔b1 ♕xf2 18 ♖hf1 ♕xg2 19 ♖xf8+ ♖xf8 20 ♕xc5 ♔c7 21 ♘b5+ ♔d7 22 ♕d6+ ♔e8 23 ♘c7+ ♔f7 24 ♕e6# **1-0** +1

**1798-★AV-1** 14 iv 98
**Atwood, G.+ Verdoni**
⟨♙f7⟩ 1 e4 ... 2 d4 e6 3 ♗d3 c5 4 d5 d6 5 c4 e5 6 f4 exf4 7 ♗xf4 ♘d7 8 e5 dxe5 9 ♕h5+ ♔e7 10 ♗g5+ ♘gf6 11 ♘c3 a6 12 ♘h3 ♕b6 13 0-0 ♕xb2 14 ♘e4 ♕d4+ 15 ♘hf2 b6 16 ♖ad1 a5 17 d6+ ♔d8 18 ♗b1 ♕xc4 19 ♘g4 h6 20 ♗xf6+ ♘xf6 21 ♘gxf6 gxf6 22 ♘xf6 ♕e6 23 d7 ♗xd7 24 ♖xd7+ ♕xd7 25 ♘xd7 ♔xd7 26 ♗e4 ♖e8 27 ♗c6+ ♔xc6 28 ♕xe8+ **1-0** +1

**1798-★AV-2** 14 iv 98
**Atwood, G.+ Verdoni**
⟨♙f7⟩ 1 e4 ... 2 d4 e6 3 ♗d3 c5 4 d5 d6 5 c4 e5 6 f4 exf4 7 ♗xf4 ♕f6 8 ♕d2 ♗g4 9 h3 ♗h5 10 ♘a3 a6 11 ♖h2 ♗e7 12 g4 ♕h4+ 13 ♔f1 ♗g6 14 ♘f3 ♕f6 15 ♖f2 h6 16 ♗g3 ♘d7 17 ♘e5 ♕xe5 18 ♗xe5 ♘xe5 19 ♘c2 ♗h4 20 ♘e3 ♗xf2 21 ♔xf2 ♘f6 22 ♘f5 0-0 23 ♔g3 ♗xf5 24 exf5 ♘xc4 25 ♕f4 ♘e5 26 ♗e2 g5 27 fxg6 ♘h5+ 28 gxh5 ♖xf4 29 ♔xf4 ♖f8+ 30 ♔e3 ♔g7 31 a3 b5 32 b4 c4 33 a4 ♖c8 34 axb5 axb5 35 ♖a7+ ♔f6 36 ♖a6 ♖d8 37 ♖b6 ♔f5 38 ♖xb5 ♖e8 39 ♔d2 ♔e4 40 ♔c3 ♔e3 41 ♗g4 ♘xg4 42 hxg4 ♔f4 43 ♖b6 ♖d8 44 ♔d4 ♔xg4 45 g7 ♔xh5 46 ♖xd6 ♖g8 47 ♖d7 ♔g5 48 ♖a7 h5 49 d6 h4 50 d7 h3 51 ♖a2 ♔g4 52 ♔xc4 ♔g3 53 ♔c5 h2 54 ♖xh2 **1-0** +1

**1798-★AW-1** 4 viii 98
**Atwood, G.+ Wilson, J.**
London
1 e4 e5 2 ♘f3 d6 3 d4 f5 4 dxe5 fxe4 5 ♘g5 d5 6 e6 ♘h6 7 ♘c3 c6 8 ♘gxe4 dxe4 9 ♕h5+ g6 10 ♕e5 ♖g8 11 ♗xh6 ♗xh6 12 ♖d1 ♕e7 13 ♗c4 b5 14 ♗b3 a5 15 a4 ♗g7 16 ♕xe4 ♗xc3+ 17 bxc3 bxa4 18 ♗a2 ♗b7 19 0-0 c5 20 ♕c4 ♗c6 21 ♖fe1 ♖a7 22 ♕f4 ♘a6

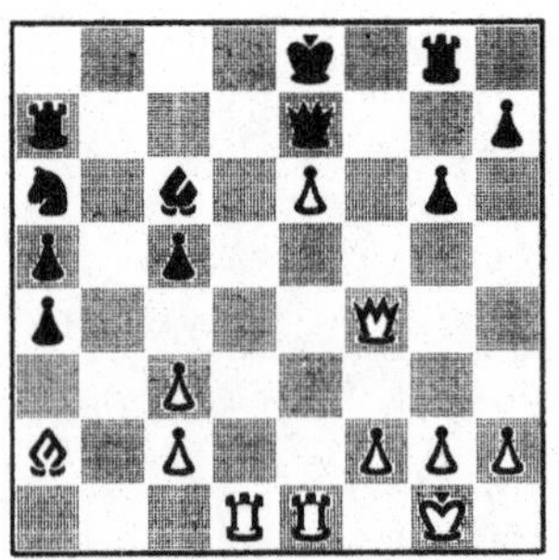

23 ♕f7+ ♕xf7 24 exf7+ ♔f8 25 fxg8♕# **1-0** +1

**1798-★AW-2**
**Wilson, J.– Atwood, G.**
London
1 e4 e5 2 f4 exf4 3 ♘f3 g5 4 ♗c4 g4 5 ♘e5 ♘h6 6 0-0 d6 7 ♗xf7+ ♘xf7 8 ♘xf7 ♔xf7 9 ♖xf4+ ♔g8 10 d4 h5 11 ♘c3 c6 12 ♕d3 ♗h6 13 ♖f2 ♗xc1 14 ♖xc1 ♕e8 15 ♖cf1 ♘d7 16 ♕e3 ♔g7 17 ♖f7+ ♔g6 18 ♖7f5 ♔h7 19 ♕g5 ♖f8 20 ? ♖xf5 21 ♖xf5 ♘f8 22 ♖f6 ♘g6 23 ♖xd6 ♗d7 24 ♕xh5+ ♔g7 25 e5 ♕f7 26 ♘e4 ♕f5 27 ♘g5 ♖h8 28 ♖xd7+ ♕xd7 29 ♘e6+ ♕xe6 30 ♕g5 ♖f8 31 ♕d2 ♕f5 32 ♕e2 ♘f4 33 ♕d2 ♘h3+ **0-1** +1

**1798-★AW-3**
**Atwood, G.+ Wilson, J.**
London
1 e4 e5 2 ♘f3 d6 3 d4 f5 4 dxe5 fxe4 5 ♘g5 d5 6 e6 ♘h6 7 ♘c3 c6 8 ♘gxe4 dxe4 9 ♕h5+ g6 10 ♕e5 ♖g8 11 ♗xh6 ♗xh6 12 ♖d1 ♕e7 13 ♗c4 a6 14 0-0 ♗g7 15 ♕xe4 ♗xc3 16 bxc3 ♖f8 17 ♖fe1 ♕f6 18 e7 ♗d7 19 exf8♕+ ♔xf8 20 ♖xd7 ♘xd7 21 ♖e3 ♘c5 22 ♕f3 ♕xf3 23 ♖xf3+ ♔g7 ... ? **1-0** +1

**179̂8̂-★A?-1**
**?– Atwood, G.**
London?
1 e4 e5 2 f4 exf4 3 ♘f3 g5 4 ♗c4 g4 5 ♘e5 ♘h6 6 d4 d6 7 ♘d3 ♕h4+ 8 ♔f1 f3 9 g3 ♕h3+ 10 ♔f2 ♕g2+ 11 ♔e3 ♘f5+ 12 exf5 ♗h6+ 13 ♘f4 ♗xf5 14 ♗d3 ♗xf4+ 15 ♔xf4 ♗xd3 16 cxd3 ♘c6 17 ♕f1 ♕c2 18 ♕d1 ♕f2 19 ♖e1+ ♔d7 20 ♖e4 ♘xd4 21 ♗e3 ♘e2+ 22 ♔xg4 ♖hg8+ 23 ♗g5 ♕xh2 **0-1** +1

**179̂?-★AV-1**
**Atwood, G.+ Verdoni**
London
⟨♙f7⟩ 1 e4 ... 2 d4 e6 3 ♗d3 c5 4 d5 d6 5 c4 e5 6 f4 exf4 7 ♗xf4 ♘d7 8 ♘f3 ♕c7 9 ♘c3 a6 10 0-0 ♗e7 11 ♘g5 ♗xg5 12 ♗xg5 ♘gf6 13 e5 dxe5 14 d6 ♕xd6 15 ♗g6+ ♔e7 16 ♘d5+ ♔d8 17 ♗xf6+ gxf6 18 ♕h5 b5 19 ♖ad1 ♖a7 20 ♘xf6 ♕e6 21 ♗f5 ♕xf6 22 ♗xd7 ♕e7 23 ♗e6+ ♗d7 24 ♕xe5 **1-0** +1

**179̂?-★AW-1**
**Atwood, G.+ Wilson, J.**
London
1 e4 e5 2 ♘f3 d6 3 d4 f5 4 dxe5 fxe4 5 ♘g5 d5 6 e6 ♘h6 7 ♘c3 c6 8 ♘gxe4 dxe4 9 ♕h5+ g6 10 ♕e5 ♖g8 11 ♗xh6 ♗xh6 12 ♖d1 ♕e7 13 ♗c4 ♗g7 14 ♕xe4 ♖f8 15 ♘b5 cxb5 16 ♗xb5+ ♘c6 17 ♗xc6+ bxc6 18 ♕xc6+ ♗d7 19 ♕xa8+ ♕d8 20 exd7+ ♔e7 21 ♕e4+ **1-0** +1

**179̂?-★AW-2**
**Atwood, G.+ Wilson, J.**
London
1 e4 e5 2 ♘f3 d6 3 d4 f5 4 dxe5 fxe4 5 ♘g5 d5 6 e6 ♘h6 7 ♘c3 c6 8 ♘gxe4 dxe4 9 ♕h5+ g6 10 ♕e5 ♖g8 11 ♗xh6 ♗xh6 12 ♖d1 ♕e7 13 ♗c4 b5 14 ♗b3 a5 15 ♘xe4 a4 16 ♘f6+ ♔f8 17 ♘xg8 ♔xg8 18 ♖d8+ ♕xd8 19 e7+ **1-0** +1

**179̂?-★AW-3**
**Atwood, G.+ Wilson, J.**
London
1 e4 e5 2 ♘f3 d6 3 d4 f5 4 dxe5 fxe4 5 ♘g5 d5 6 e6 ♘h6 7 ♘c3 c6 8 ♘gxe4 dxe4 9 ♕h5+ g6 10 ♕e5 ♖g8 11 ♗xh6 ♗xh6 12 ♖d1 ♕e7 13 ♗c4 ♗g7 14 ♕xe4 ♗xc3+ 15 bxc3 ♖f8 16 0-0 ♖f6 17 ♖fe1 ♕c5 18 ♖d7 ♕xf2+ 19 ♔h1 ♖f4 20 ♕e5 **1-0** +1

**17??-★L?-1**
**Légal, de K.S.+ ?**
⟨♖a1⟩ 1 e4 e5 2 ♗c4 d6 3 ♘f3 ♘c6 4 ♘c3 ♗g4 5 ♘xe5 ♗xd1 6 ♗xf7+ ♔e7 7 ♘d5#

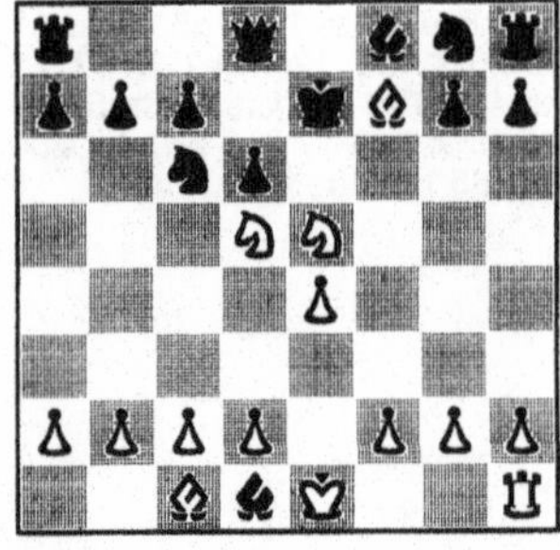

**1-0** +1

**17̂??-★??-1**
**?+?**
1 e4 e5 2 ♗c4 ♗c5 3 d4 ♗xd4 4 ♘f3 c5 5 c3 ♕a5 6 0-0 b5 7 ♗d5 ♘c6 8 ♗xc6 dxc6 9 cxd4 exd4 10 ♕c2 ♕b6 11 ♘bd2 c4 12 b4 a5 13 bxa5 ♖xa5 14 ♖b1 ♗e6 15 ♘e5 d3 16 ♕c3 ♖xa2 17 ♘dxc4 ♕c5 18 ♗e3 ♕e7 19 ♕xd3 ♖a8 20 ♘d6+ ♔f8 21 ♗c5 ♖d8 22 ♘xc6 ♕d7 23 ♘xd8 ♕xd8 **1-0** +1

**1800-★AV-1** 16 ii 00
**Atwood, G.+Verdoni**
London
⟨♙f7⟩ 1 e4 ... 2 d4 e6 3 ♗d3 c5 4 d5 d6 5 c4 e5 6 f4 exf4 7 ♗xf4 ♘f6 8 e5 dxe5 9 ♗xe5 ♘bd7 10 ♗c3 ♗e7 11 ♘f3 0-0 12 ♗f5 ♘b6 13 ♗xc8 ♖xc8 14 b3 ♘bd7 15 ♘bd2 ♗d6 16 0-0 a6 17 ♘g5 ♖e8 18 ♘e6 ♕e7 19 ♘f3 ♕f7 20 ♕d2 ♕g6 21 ♖ae1 ♕h5 22 ♕e3 ♕h6 23 ♗d2 ♕h5 24 ♖e2 ♖e7 25 ♖fe1 ♖ce8 26 ♗c3 ♘g4 27 g3 ♘gf6 28 ♗e5 ♘xe5 29 ♘xe5 ♘g4 30 ♘xg4 ♕xg4 31 ♖f2 b6 32 ♖ef1 ♖a7 33 ♖f5 h6 34 ♔g2 ♖xe6 35 dxe6 ♕d4 **1-0** +1

**1800-★??-1** i 00
**?○?**
London
1 e4 c5 2 f4 ♘c6 3 ♘f3 e6 4 c3 ♘ge7 5 d4 cxd4 6 cxd4 d5 7 e5 ♕b6 8 ♘c3 ♘f5 9 ♘e2 ♗b4+ 10 ♗d2 ♘e3 11 ♕c1 ♗d7 12 ♗xb4 ♘xb4 ...? +1

**1804-☒M?-1**
**Mauvillon, F.W. von?+?**
1 e4 e5 2 d3 d6 3 f4 h5 4 ♘f3 f5 5 fxe5 fxe4 6 dxe4 dxe5 7 ♗c4 ♕xd1+ 8 ♔xd1 ♘f6 9 ♘c3 ♘g4 10 ♔e2 ♗c5 11 h3 ♘f2 12 ♖f1 ♘c6 13 ♗e3 ♗xe3 14 ♔xe3 ♘xh3 15 gxh3 ♗xh3 16 ♖f2 ♖f8 17 ♘b5 0-0-0 18 c3 ♘a5 19 b3 a6 20 ♘a3 b5 21 ♗e2 ♘c6 22 ♘g5 ♗d7 23 ♖xf8 ♖xf8 24 ♗xh5 b4 25 ♘b1 ♖f4 26 ♗f3 bxc3 27 ♘xc3 ♘d4 28 ♖h1 ♖f8 29 ♗e2 ♔b7 30 ♘f3 ♘c6 31 ♖h7 ♖g8 32 ♗c4 ♖f8 33 ♖xg7 ♗e8 34 ♗d5 ♗h5 35 ♘xe5 ♖f6 36 ♗xc6+ ♖xc6 37 ♘xc6 ♔xc6 38 e5 ♗e8 39 ♔d4 ♔b6 40 a3 c5+ 41 ♔c4 ♗b5+ 42 ♘xb5 axb5+ 43 ♔d5 ♔a6 44 e6 c4 45 e7 **1-0** +1

**1804-☒M?-2**
**?– Mauvillon, F.W. von?**
1 e4 e5 2 ♗c4 ♗c5 3 d3 ♘f6 4 ♕f3 ♘c6 5 c3 d6 6 h3 a6 7 b4 ♗b6 8 g4 ♗e6 9 g5 ♗xc4 10 dxc4 ♘g8 11 h4 ♕d7 12 a4 ♗a7 13 a5 b6 14 b5 ♘xa5 15 bxa6 ♘xc4 16 ♘e2 ♘e7 17 ♘g3 g6 18 h5 ♘c6 19 ♕f6 0-0-0 20 h6 d5 21 ♘d2 dxe4 22 ♘gxe4 ♘4a5 23 ♕f3 ♕f5 24 c4 ♕xf3 25 ♘xf3 ♘xc4 26 ♘c3 ♖d3 27 ♘xe5 ♘4xe5 28 ♘b5 ♖d5 29 ♘xa7+ ♘xa7 30 ♔e2 ♖e8 31 ♗e3 ♘c4 32 ♖hc1 ♘xe3 33 fxe3 ♖xg5 34 ♖ab1 ♖e6 35 ♖f1 f6 36 ♖h1 ♖a5 37 ♖a1 f5 38 ♔f3 g5 39 ♖xa5 bxa5 40 ♖h5 ♖g6 41 e4 fxe4+ 42 ♔xe4 ♖xa6 43 ♔f5 ♖g6 44 ♖xg5 ♖xh6 45 ♔e4 ♖a6 46 ♔d3 a4 47 ♔c2 a3 48 ♔b1 a2+ 49 ♔a1 **0-1** +1

**1804-☒M?-3**
**Mauvillon, F.W. von?+?**
1 e4 e5 2 d4 ♕f6 3 d5 ♗c5 4 ♘h3 d6 5 f3 ♗xh3 6 gxh3 c6 7 c4 a5 8 ♘c3 ♘a6 9 a3 h6 10 ♕d3 ♗d4 11 ♘a4 ♘e7 12 ♗d2 ♘c5 13 ♘xc5 ♗xc5 14 ♗e3 ♗xe3 15 ♕xe3 c5 16 ♕b3 0-0 17 ♕e3 ♘g6 18 ♖g1 ♘f4 19 0-0-0 ♘g6 20 ♖d2 ♕f4 21 ♕f2 h5 22 ♔b1 ♘h4 23 ♕g3 g6 24 ♖d3 a4 25 ♗e2 ♔h7 26 ♔a2 ♖fb8 27 ♖b1 b5 28 cxb5 ♖xb5 29 ♗d1 ♖b6 30 b3 axb3+ 31 ♖bxb3 ♖ab8 32 ♕xf4 exf4 33 ♗c2 ♘g2 34 ♖dc3 ♖xb3 35 ♖xb3 ♖xb3 36 ♔xb3 ♘e1 37 ♗d1 ♘d3 38 h4 ♔g7 39 ♔c3 ♘e5 40 a4 ♘d7 41 a5 ♘b8 42 ♔c4 ♘a6 43 ♔b5 ♘b4 44 e5 ♘xd5 45 exd6 ♘c3+ 46 ♔xc5 ♘xd1 47 d7 **1-0** +1

**1810-★SW-1** 12 xi 10
**Wood, J.– Samuda, A.**
1 e4 e5 2 f4 exf4 3 ♘f3 g5 4 ♗c4 ♕e7 5 ♕e2 f5 6 e5 c6 7 d4 d5 8 ♗b3 g4 9 ♗xf4 gxf3 10 ♕xf3 ♗e6 11 h4 ♗h6 12 ♘c3 ♗xf4 13 ♕xf4 ♕g7 14 0-0-0 ♕h6 15 ♘e2 ♘a6 16 ♔b1 ♕xf4 17 ♘xf4 ♘c7 18 ♖hf1 ♘e7 19 ♘xe6 ♘xe6 20 c4 ♘c7 21 cxd5 ♘cxd5 22 ♖c1 ♖f8 23 ♗c4 0-0-0 24 ♖f3 ♔c7 25 ♗xd5 ♘xd5 26 ♖cf1 ♘e7 27 ♖f4 ♖g8 28 ♖1f2 h5 29 ♔c2 ♖g4 30 ♖xg4 hxg4 31 ♔d3 c5 32 ♖c2 ♖xd4+ 33 ♔e3 ♖e4+ 34 ♔d3 ♖xe5 35 b4 ♔c6 36 h5 f4 37 ♖xc5+ ♖xc5 38 bxc5 ♔d5 39 h6 f3 40 gxf3 gxf3 41 ♔e3 ♘f5+ 42 ♔xf3 **0-1** +1

**181Ô-★S?-1**
**?– Sarratt, J.H.**
1 e4 e5 2 f4 exf4 3 ♘f3 g5 4 ♗c4 g4 5 0-0 gxf3 6 ♕xf3 ♗h6 7 e5 ♘c6 8 c3 ♕e7 9 ♕d5 ♘xe5 10 ♗b3 ♘f6 11 ♕b5 c6 12 ♕e2 f3 13 gxf3 ♖g8+ 14 ♔h1 d5 15 ♘a3 ♘g6 16 ♕f2 ♘f4 17 ♖e1 ♗e6 18 ♕d4 ♘h3 19 ♕h4 ♗g5 20 ♕a4 ♗xd2 21 ♖f1 ♕c5 22 ♕d4 ♕xd4 23 cxd4 ♗xc1 24 ♖axc1 ♔d7 25 f4 ♗g4 26 ♖c3 ♘e4 27 ♖g3 ♗e2 28 ♖e1 ♗f3+ 29 ♖xf3 ♘hf2+

30 ♖xf2 ♘xf2# **0-1** +1

**181Ô-★S?-2**
**Sarratt, J.H.–?**
1 e4 e5 2 f4 exf4 3 ♘f3 g5 4 ♗c4 g4 5 0-0 gxf3 6 ♕xf3 ♗h6 7 c3 ♘c6 8 d4 ♕e7 9 e5 ♘xe5 10 dxe5 ♕c5+ 11 ♔h1 ♕xc4 12 ♘a3 ♕c6 13 ♕h5 ♕g6 14 ♕f3 ♘e7 15 ♘b5 ♔d8 16 ♗xf4 ♗xf4 17 ♕xf4 ♖g8 18 ♖f2 a6 19 ♘d4 b6 20 g3 ♗b7+ 21 ♔g1 ♖g7 22 ♕f6 ♔e8 23 ♖af1 ♗d5 24 b3 c5 25 c4 cxd4 26 cxd5 ♘xd5 27 ♕f3 ♕c6 28 e6 dxe6 29 ♖e1 ♖c8 30 ♖e5 ♘e3 31 ♖xe3 ♕c1+ 32 ♔g2 dxe3 33 ♖f1 ♕d2+ 34 ♔h3 e2 35 ♖f2 ♕h6+ 36 ♔g2 e1♘+ 37 ♔h1 ♘xf3 **0-1** +1

**181Ô-★S?-3**
**?– Sarratt, J.H.**
1 e4 e5 2 f4 exf4 3 ♘f3 g5 4 ♗c4 g4 5 0-0 gxf3 6 ♕xf3 ♕e7 7 d4 ♘c6 8 c3 ♘e5 9 dxe5 ♕c5+ 10 ♔h1 ♕xc4 11 ♗xf4 ♗h6 12 ♘d2 ♕e6 13 ♘b3 d6 14 ♘d4 ♕g4 15 exd6 ♕xf3 16 ♖xf3 ♗xf4 17 ♖xf4 cxd6 18 ♘b5 ♔e7 19 ♖d1 ♗e6 20 ♘xd6 ♖d8 21 e5 ♘h6 22 c4 b6 23 b4 ♖hg8 24 c5 ♖g5 25 ♖e1 ♘f5 26 h3 ♘g3+ 27 ♔h2 ♗d5 28 ♖f2 ♖dg8 29 c6 ♘f5 30 ♘xf5+ ♖xf5 31 ♖ee2 ♖xf2 32 ♖xf2 ♗xg2 **0-1** +1

**18** Lewis, W. L/N3087.BL

**1813-★LP-1** vi 13
**Lewis, W.+ Parkinson, J.**
1 e4 e5 2 f4 exf4 3 ♘f3 g5 4 ♗c4 ♗g7 5 h4 g4 6 ♘g5 ♘h6 7 d4 f6 8 ♗xf4 d5 9 exd5 fxg5 10 ♗xg5

♔d6 11 ♕e2+ ♔d7 12 ♗xh6 ♖e8 13 ♕xe8+

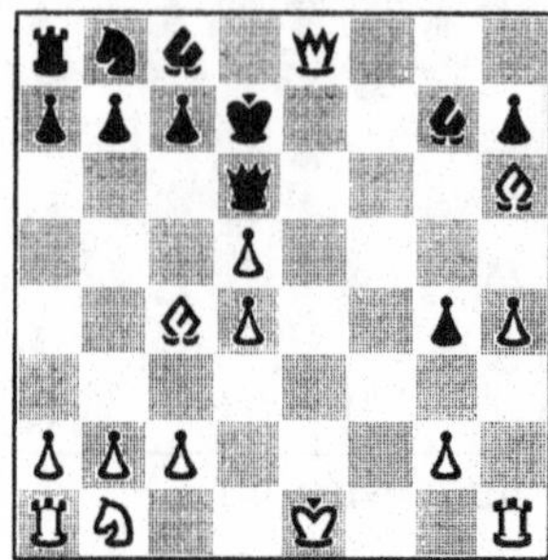

13 ... ♔xe8 14 ♗xg7 ♕g3+ 15 ♔d1 ♕xg2 16 ♖f1 g3 17 ♖f8+ ♔e7 18 d6+ cxd6 19 ♖f7+ ♔e8 20 ♖f8+ ♔d7 21 ♖f7+ ♔c6 22 d5+ ♔c5 23 ♖f4 ♗g4+ 24 ♖xg4 ♕f3+ 25 ♗e2 ♕xd5+ 26 ♘d2 ♕h1+ 27 ♗f1 ♘c6 28 c3 ♘e5 29 ♗xe5 dxe5 30 ♖xg3 ♕xh4 31 ♖h3 ♕f4 32 ♔c2 ♖d8 33 ♖d3 ♖e8 34 ♗g2 h5 35 ♖f1 ♕g4 36 ♖d5+ ♔b6 37 ♖f6+ ♔c7 38 ♗e4 ♖e7 39 ♖c5+ ♔d8 40 ♗f5 ♕a4+ 41 ♘b3 ♖g7 42 ♖c8+ ♔e7 43 ♖e6+ ♔f7 44 ♖c7+ ♔f8 45 ♖f6+ ♔e8 46 ♖xg7 ♕h4 47 ♗g6+ ♔d8 48 ♖f8# **1-0** +1

**1813-★LP-2** vi 13
**Lewis, W.+ Parkinson, J.**
1 e4 e5 2 f4 exf4 3 ♘f3 g5 4 ♗c4 ♗g7 5 h4 g4 6 ♘g5 ♘h6 7 d4 ♘c6 8 c3 ♘a5 9 ♗b3 ♘xb3 10 ♕xb3 f6 11 ♗xf4 ♔e7 12 e5 f5 13 d5 ♕e8 14 0-0 ♕h5 15 d6+ cxd6 16 exd6+ ♔d8 17 g3 ♕g6 18 ♘a3 ♖f8 19 ♘b5 ♘g8 20 ♘xa7 ♘f6 21 ♕b6+ ♔e8 22 ♘b5 ♖a4 23 ♘c7+ ♔d8 24 ♘ce6+ ♔e8 25 ♕d8# **1-0** +1

**1815-★LW-1** x 15
**Wood, J.= Lewis, W.**
1 e4 e5 2 f4 exf4 3 ♘f3 g5 4 ♗c4 g4 5 0-0 gxf3 6 ♕xf3 ♕f6 7 d3 ♗h6 8 ♗d2 ♘c6 9 ♗c3 ♘e5 10 ♕h5 d6 11 g3 ♗g4 12 ♗xe5 ♗xh5 13 ♗xf6 ♘xf6 14 gxf4 ♖g8+ 15 ♔h1 ♘g4 16 ♘a3 ♘e3 17 ♖f2 0-0-0 18 h3 ♘xc4 19 ♘xc4 c6 20 ♘e3 f6 21 ♖af1 ♗g6 22 c4 ♖ge8 23 h4 f5 24 h5 fxe4 25 hxg6 exd3 26 ♘g4 ♗g7 27 gxh7 ♖e2 28 f5 ♖h8 29 f6 ♖xh7+ 30 ♔g2 ♗f8 31 ♖xe2 dxe2 32 ♖e1 ♖h5 33 ♖xe2 ♔d7 34 ♔g3 ♖f5 35 b4 b6 36 ♖e4 d5 37 cxd5 ♗d6+ 38 ♔h4 ♖xd5 39 a3 ♖f5 40 ♖e2 a6 41 ♖f2 ♖xf2 42 ♘xf2 ♔e6 43 ♔g5 ♗e5 44 ♘e4 ♗xf6+ ½-½ +1

**1816-★LP-1** 8 vi 16
**Lewis, W.= Parkinson, J.**
1 e4 e5 2 f4 exf4 3 ♘f3 g5 4 ♗c4 g4 5 0-0 gxf3 6 ♕xf3 ♗h6 7 d4 ♕e7 8 ♗xf4 ♘c6 9 ♗xh6 ♘xh6 10 ♕h5 ♕f8 11 ♖f6 ♕g7 12 ♕xh6 ♕xh6 13 ♖xh6 ♘xd4 14 ♘a3 c6 15 ♖d6 ♘e6 16 ♖ad1 ♖g8 17 ♗xe6 fxe6 18 ♘c4 ♖g5 19 ♔f2 ♔e7 20 ♘e3 a5 21 ♔f3 b5 22 ♘g4 ♖a7 23 ♔f4 ♖c5 24 c3 b4 25 cxb4 axb4 26 ♘e5 ♖c2 27 a4 ♖xb2 28 ♖xc6 ♖f2+ 29 ♔e3 ♖f8 30 ♖dc1 ♗a6 31 ♖c7 ♖xc7 32 ♖xc7 ♔d6 33 ♖a7 ♔xe5 34 ♖xa6 ♖b8 35 ♖a5+ d5 36 exd5 exd5 37 ♔d3 ♖c8 38 ♖b5 ♖c3+ 39 ♔d2 ♖c4 40 a5 ♖f4 41 a6 ♖f2+ 42 ♔e3 ♖a2 43 ♖xb4 ♖xa6 ½-½ +1

**1816-★LS-1** 14 vii 16
**Sarratt, J.H.○ Lewis W.**
1 e4 e5 2 f4 exf4 3 ♘f3 g5 4 ♗c4 g4 5 0-0 gxf3 6 ♕xf3 ♕f6 7 d3 ♗h6 8 ♘c3 ♘e7 9 ♗d2 ♘bc6 10 ♘b5 ♘e5 11 ♕f2 ♔d8 12 ♗c3 ♘7c6 13 ♗b3 d6 14 d4 ♘g4 15 ♕e1 ♕g6 16 ♗d2 a6 17 d5 ♘ce5 18 ♘d4 ♘e3 19 ♗xe3 fxe3 20 ♖d1 ♘g4 ...? +1

**1816-★LS-2** 28 vii 16
**Sarratt, J.H.○ Lewis, W.**
1 e4 e5 2 f4 exf4 3 ♘f3 g5 4 ♗c4 g4 5 0-0 gxf3 6 ♕xf3 ♕f6 7 e5 ♕xe5 8 d3 ♗h6 9 ♗d2 ♘e7 10 ♗c3 ♕c5+ 11 ♔h1 ♖g8 12 ♘d2 d5 13 ♕h5 ♕d6 14 ♗b3 ♗g4 15 ♕h4 ♘bc6 16 ♖ae1 0-0-0 ...? +1

**1816-★LS-3** 28 vii 16
**Sarratt, J.H.○ Lewis, W**
1 e4 e5 2 f4 exf4 3 ♘f3 g5 4 ♗c4 g4 5 0-0 gxf3 6 ♕xf3 ♕f6 7 e5 ♕xe5 8 d3 ♗h6 9 ♗d2 ♘e7 10 ♘c3 c6 11 ♘e4 d5 12 ♗c3 dxe4 13 ♗xe5 exf3 14 ♗xh8 fxg2 15 ♔xg2 ♗e6 16 ♖ae1 ♗xc4 17 dxc4 ♘d7 18 ♗e5 ♘xe5 19 ♖xe5 ♔f8 ...? +1

**1816-★LS-4** 28 vii 16
**Sarratt, J.H.○ Lewis, W.**
[Lewis]
1 e4 e5 2 f4 exf4 3 ♘f3 g5 4 ♗c4 g4 5 0-0 gxf3 6 ♕xf3 ♕f6 7 e5 ♕xe5 8 d3 ♗h6 9 ♘c3 ♘e7 10 ♘e2 d5 11 ♗b3 ♖g8 12 ♘xf4 ♗g4 13 ♕f2 c6 14 ♘xd5 cxd5 15 ♕xf7+ ♔d7 16 ♗xh6 ♗h3 17 ♖f2 ♘bc6 18 ♗f4 ♕g7 [18 ... ♕e6!] 19 ♗xd5 ♕xf7 20 ♗xf7 ♖g7 ...? +1

**1816-★LS-5** 28 vii 16
**Sarratt, J.H.= Lewis, W.**
1 e4 e5 2 f4 exf4 3 ♘f3 g5 4 ♗c4 g4 5 ♘e5 ♕h4+ 6 ♔f1 f3 7 g3 ♕h3+ 8 ♔f2 ♕g2+ 9 ♔e3 ♗h6+ 10 ♔d3 d5 11 ♗xd5 c6 12 ♗xf7+ ♔e7 13 ♕f1 ♔f6 14 ♗xg8 ♔xe5 15 ♗b3 ♖d8+ 16 ♔c3 ♗g7 17 d3 ♔d6+ 18 d4 ♔c7 19 ♗f4+ ♔b6 20 e5 a5 21 ♘d2 ♔a7 22 ♕xg2 fxg2 23 ♖hg1 b5 24 ♘e4 ♗f5 25 ♖ae1 ♘a6 26 a3 c5 27 ♘xc5 ♖ac8 28 ♗f7 ♘xc5 29 dxc5 ♖xc5+ 30 ♔b3 ♖xc2 31 ♖c1 ♖dc8 32 ♖xc2 ♖xc2 33 ♗d5 ♖e2 34 ♖xg2 ♖e1 ½-½ +1

**1816-★LS-6** 4 viii 16
**Sarratt, J.H.= Lewis, W.**
1 e4 e5 2 f4 exf4 3 ♘f3 g5 4 ♗c4 g4 5 0-0 gxf3 6 d4 d5 7 exd5 ♗g4 8 ♖f2 ♗d6 9 ♘d2 ♘f6 10 ♘xf3 ♘e4 11 ♕e1 f5 12 ♘d2 ♕e7 13 ♘xe4 fxe4 14 ♗xf4 ♘d7 15 ♕d2 h6 16 ♖af1 0-0-0

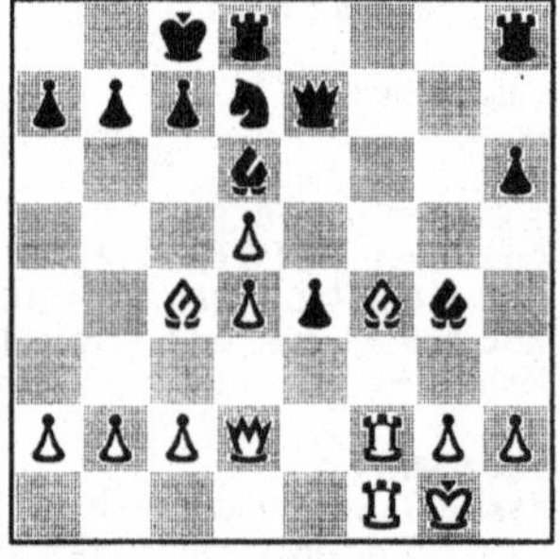

17 ♕a5 ♔b8 18 ♗e3 ♗b4 19 d6 ♕xd6 20 ♕a4 ♘b6 21 ♕b3 ♖hf8 22 ♗f7 ♕e7 23 c4 ♗d6 24 c5 ♗xc5 25 dxc5 ♖d3 26 ♕c2 ♖xe3 27 cxb6 axb6 28 ♕d2 ♖d3 29 ♕c2 ♖fd8 30 ♗c4 ♗d1 31 ♕c1 e3 32 ♖f7 ♕c5 33 b4 ♕d4 34 ♗xd3 e2+ 35 ♔h1 exf1♕+ 36 ♗xf1 c6 37 a3 ♗b3 38 ♕f4+ ♕xf4 39 ♖xf4 ♖d1 40 ♖f2 ♗c4 41 ♔g1 ♖xf1+ ½-½ +1

**1816-★LS-7** 11 viii 16
**Sarratt, J.H.○ Lewis, W.**
1 e4 e5 2 f4 exf4 3 ♘f3 g5 4 ♗c4 g4 5 0-0 gxf3 6 ♕xf3 ♕f6 7 d3 ♗h6 8 ♗d2 ♘c6 9 ♗c3 ♘e5 10 ♗xe5 ♕xe5 11 ♘c3 ♘e7 12 ♘b5 ♕c5+ 13 ♔h1 d6 14 ♘c3 a5 15 ♖ae1 ♕g5 16 e5 dxe5 17 ♘e4 ♕g7 18 ♕h5 ♖f8 19 d4 ♗d7 20 dxe5 0-0-0 21 ♘f6 ♗e6 22 ♗d3 ♘d5 23 ♘xd5 ♖xd5 24 ♖f2 ♖g8 25 ♕e2 ♗g5 ...? +1

**1816-★LS-8** ●○ 11 viii 16
**Sarratt, J.H.○Lewis, W.**
1 e4 e5 2 f4 exf4 3 ♘f3 g5 4 ♗c4 g4 5 0-0 gxf3 6 d4 d5 7 exd5 ♗g4 8 ♖f2 ♗d6 9 ♘d2 ♘f6 10 ♘xf3 ♘e4 11 ♕e1 ♕e7 12 ♖e2 f5 13 ♗d3 ♕g7 14 ♗xe4 fxe4 15 ♖xe4+ ♔d8 16 ♕h4+ ♔c8 17 ♘e5 ♗d7 18 ♗xf4 b6 19 ♕h5 ♖g8 20 ♖ae1 ♗e8 21 ♕h3+ ...? +1

**1816-★LS-9** ●○ 11 viii 16
**Sarratt, J.H.○Lewis, W.**
1 e4 e5 2 f4 exf4 3 ♘f3 g5 4 ♗c4 g4 5 0-0 gxf3 6 ♕xf3 ♕f6 7 d3 ♗h6 8 ♘c3 ♘e7 9 ♗d2 ♘bc6 10 ♕h5 ♕g6 11 ♕xg6 ♘xg6 12 ♘d5 ♔d8 13 ♗c3 ♘ce5 14 ♘f6 d6 15 ♘h5 ♗e6 16 ♖f2 ...? +1

**1816-★LS-10** ●○ 3 xii 16
**Lewis, W.+Sarratt, J.H.**
⟨♙f7⟩ 1 e4 ... 2 d4 ♘c6 3 d5 ♘e5 4 f4 ♘f7 5 e5 e6 6 c4 ♗c5 7 ♘f3 d6 8 ♗d3 ♘e7 9 ♘c3 0-0 10 ♕c2 h6 11 ♗d2 exd5 12 cxd5 dxe5 13 fxe5 ♘xd5 14 ♘xd5 ♕xd5 15 ♗c4 ♕c6 16 0-0-0 ♔h8 17 e6 ♘d6 18 ♘e5 **1-0** +1

**Keen⚔Lewis** [1817-⚔KL]

| | | | | | | | |
|---|---|---|---|---|---|---|---|
| B. Keen | 0 | Ô | 0 | 0 | 0 | ½ | ½ |
| W. Lewis | 1 | Ô | 1 | 1 | 1 | ½ | 4½ |

**1817-⚔KL-1** 20 viii 17
**Lewis, W.+Keen, B.**
⟨♘g1⟩1 e4 c5 2 ♗c4 e6 3 ♘c3 ♘c6 4 d3 a6 5 a4 ♘ge7 6 0-0 ♘g6 7 f4 ♗e7 8 e5 f5 9 exf6 ♗xf6 10 ♕h5 ♗d4+ 11 ♔h1 0-0 12 ♗d2 d5 13 ♗a2 ♖f5 14 ♕e2 ♗xc3 15 bxc3 ♕c7 16 ♕f2 ♘ce5 17 ♕g3 ♕f7 18 ♗e3 b6 19 ♖f2 ♘d7 20 ♕h3 ♘xf4 21 ♗xf4 e5 22 ♗xd5 ♕xd5 23 ♕xf5 ♘f6 24 ♕xe5 ♕xe5 25 ♗xe5 ♘g4 26 ♖e2 ♘xe5 27 ♖xe5 ♗d7 28 a5 b5 29 ♖xc5 ♖f8 30 ♔g1 h6 31 ♖e1 ♖f6 32 ♖c7 ♗c6 33 ♖ee7 ♖g6 34 g3 ♗f3 35 c4 bxc4 36 ♖xc4 h5 37 ♔f2 ♖f6 38 ♖f4 ♖xf4 39 gxf4 ♗c6 40 ♖e6 ♗b5 41 c4 ♗d7 42 ♖xa6 **1-0** +1

**1817-⚔KL-2** ix 17
**Lewis, W.○Keen, B.**
⟨♖a1⟩1 e4 c5 2 f4 ♘c6 3 ♘c3 e6 4 ♘f3 d5 5 ♗b5 ♘ge7 6 f5 a6 7 ♗xc6+ ♘xc6 8 exd5 exd5 9 0-0 ♗xf5 10 d3 ♗e7 11 ♘h4 ♗e6 12 ♘f5 ♗f6 13 ♕e1 0-0 14 ♕g3 ♕d7 15 ♘e3 ♘d4 16 ♖xf6 ♘f5 17 ♘xf5 ♗xf5 18 ♖d6 ♕e7 19 ♘xd5 ♕e2 20 h3 ♖ae8 21 ♘f6+ ♔h8 22 ♘xe8 ♖xe8 23 ♗f4 ♕xc2 24 ♔h2 ♕xb2 ...? +1

**1817-⚔KL-3** ix 17
**Lewis, W.+Keen, B.**
⟨♘b1⟩1 e4 c5 2 c3 ♘c6 3 d4 e6 4 d5 exd5 5 exd5 ♘e5 6 f4 ♘g6 7 ♗b5 a6 8 ♗a4 b5 9 ♗c2 ♕h4+ 10 ♔f1 c4 11 d6 ♕f6 12 f5 ♗xd6 13 ♕f3 ♖b8 14 fxg6 fxg6 15 ♗e4 ♕xf3+ 16 ♗xf3 ♘f6 17 ♗e3 ♗c7 18 ♗a7 d5 19 ♖e1+ ♔f7 20 ♗xb8 ♗xb8 21 ♘e2 ♗a7 22 ♘d4 ♗d7 23 ♔e2 h5 24 ♖hf1 ♗xd4 25 cxd4 ♗f5 26 ♔d2 ♖c8 27 ♔c3 a5 28 a3 ♗e6 29 ♖e3 g5 30 ♗xh5+ g6 31 ♖ef3 ♔g7 32 ♖xf6 **1-0** +1

**1817-⚔KL-4** ix 17
**Lewis, W.+Keen, B.**
⟨♖a1⟩1 e4 e5 2 ♘f3 ♘c6 3 ♗c4 ♗c5 4 c3 d6 5 0-0 ♘f6 6 d4 exd4 7 cxd4 ♗b6 8 h3 ♘xe4 9 ♖e1 d5 10 ♗xd5 ♕xd5 11 ♘c3 ♕d8 12 ♖xe4+ ♘e7 13 ♕e2 ♗e6 14 ♗g5 ♕d6 15 ♗xe7 ♔xe7 16 d5 ♖hd8 17 ♘g5 c6 18 ♘xe6 fxe6 19 ♖xe6+ ♕xe6 20 ♕xe6+ ♔f8 21 d6 ♖e8 22 ♕f5+ ♔g8 23 ♘e4 ♖f8 24 ♕e6+ ♔h8 25 ♘g5 ♗xf2+ 26 ♔h2 ♖ae8 27 ♘f7+ ♔g8 28 ♘h6+ ♔h8

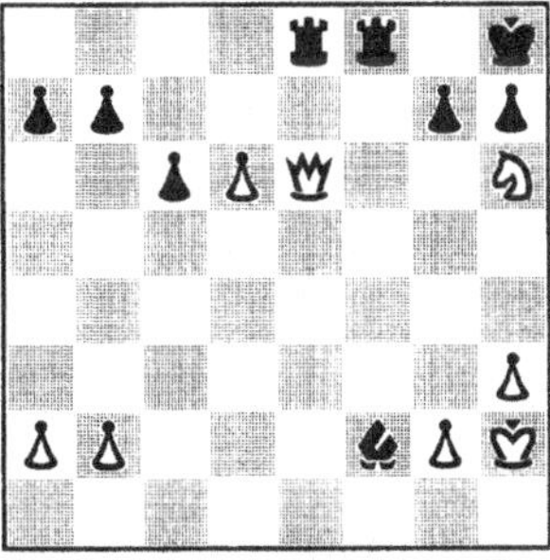

29 ♕g8+ ♖xg8 30 ♘f7# **1-0** +1

**1817-⚔KL-5** ix 17
**Lewis, W.+Keen, B.**
⟨♘g1⟩ 1 e4 c5 2 c3 e6 3 d4 d5 4 exd5 exd5 5 ♗e3 cxd4 6 ♗xd4 ♘c6 7 ♗b5 a6 8 ♗xc6+ bxc6 9 0-0 c5 10 ♗e5 ♗e6 11 f4 ♘h6 12 ♖e1 ♕b6 13 ♘d2 ♘g4 14 ♗xg7 ♗xg7 15 ♕xg4 ♖g8 16 ♕f3 0-0-0 17 ♔h1 ♕xb2 18 ♘b3 ♕xc3 19 ♖e3 ♕b4 20 ♖c1 ♗d4 21 ♖d3 ♗g4 22 ♕f1 ♔b7 23 ♘xc5+ ♔a7 24 ♖xd4 ♕b5 25 ♕f2 ♕e2 26 ♕xe2 ♗xe2 27 ♖e1 ♖ge8 28 ♔g1 ♔b6 29 ♘a4+ ♔c6 30 ♖c1+ ♔b5 31 ♖c5# **1-0** +1

**1817-⚔KL-6** ix 17
**Lewis, W.=Keen, B.**
⟨♖a1⟩1 e4 c5 2 f4 e6 3 ♘f3 ♗e7 4 ♘c3 d5 5 exd5 exd5 6 ♗b5+ ♘c6 7 0-0 ♘f6 8 ♘e5 0-0 9 ♗xc6 bxc6 10 ♘xc6 ♕c7 11 ♘e5 ♖b8 12 g4 d4 13 ♘b1 ♗d6 14 d3 ♗xe5 15 fxe5 ♘xg4 16 ♗f4 ♕c6 17 ♖f3 ♗b7 18 ♘d2 ♕g6 19 ♖g3 ♕h5 20 ♖xg4 ♔h8 21 ♔f2 ♗c8 22 ♖g1 ♕xd1 23 ♖xd1 ♖xb2 24 ♖c1 ♗e6 25 ♘e4 ♖c8 26 ♘d6 ♖c6 27 ♔g3 ♗xa2 28 c4 dxc3 29 ♖xc3 ♔g8 30 ♘f5 ♔f8 31 ♗e3 c4 32 ♘d4 ♖c5 33 ♘e6+ fxe6 34 ♗xc5+ ♔f7 35 dxc4 ♖b3 36 ♖xb3 ♗xb3 37 ♗xa7 ♗xc4 38 ♔f4 ♔g6 39 ♗c5 ♔h5 40 ♗e7 h6 41 h4 **½-½** +1

**Lewis⚔Pratt** [1817-⚔LP]

| | | | | | |
|---|---|---|---|---|---|
| W. Lewis | 0 | 1 | 0 | 1 | 2 |
| P. Pratt | 1 | 0 | 1 | 0 | 2 |

**1817-⚔LP-1** viii 17
**Lewis, W.–Pratt, P.**
⟨♘b1⟩1 e4 d5 2 e5 ♗f5 3 d4 c5 4 c3 cxd4 5 cxd4 f6 6 f4 fxe5 7 fxe5 e6 8 ♘f3 ♗b4+ 9 ♔f2 ♘c6 10 ♗b5 ♘ge7 11 ♖f1 0-0 12 ♔g1 ♕b6 13 ♗e2 ♗e4 14 ♗e3 ♗xf3 15 ♗xf3 ♘xe5 16 ♗e2 ♘f5 17 ♗f2 ♘c6 18 ♗g4 ♘cxd4 19 ♗xf5 ♖xf5 20 ♕xd4 ♕xd4 21 ♗xd4 ♖xf1+ 22 ♖xf1 b6 23 ♖c1 ♖e8 24 ♗e5 ♗c5+ 25 ♔h1 ♖f8 26 g4 a5 27 a3 h5 28 h3 hxg4 29 hxg4 ♖f2 30 b4 axb4 31 axb4 ♗xb4 32 ♖c7 ♗f8 33 ♗d4 ♖h2+ 34 ♔g1 ♖h4 35 ♗xb6 ♖xg4+ 36 ♔f2 e5 37 ♖d7 d4 38 ♗c7 ♖f4+ 39 ♔e2 ♖e4+ 40 ♔f3 ♖e3+ 41 ♔f2 g5 42 ♗d8 g4 43 ♗g5 ♖f3+ 44 ♔e2 ♖f7 45 ♖d8 g3 46 ♗h4 g2 47 ♗f2 ♔g7 48 ♖d5 ♗e7 49 ♖xe5 d3+ 50 ♔e3 d2 51 ♖d5 ♗c5+ 52 ♔e4 ♗xf2 **0-1** +1

**1817-⚔LP-2** 28 viii 17
**Lewis, W.+Pratt, P.**
⟨♘g1⟩1 e4 e5 2 ♗c4 c6 3 d4 f6 4 dxe5 ♕a5+ 5 c3 ♕xe5 6 0-0 ♗d6 7 g3 h5 8 ♗xg8 g5 9 ♕b3 ♕e7 10 ♗e3 h4 11 ♘d2 ♘a6 12 ♗c4 hxg3 13 fxg3 ♕h7 14 ♘f3 ♗xg3 15 hxg3 ♕h1+ 16 ♔f2 ♕h7 17 ♖h1 ♕xh1 18 ♖xh1 ♖xh1 19 ♗xa6 bxa6 20 ♕g8+ ♔e7 21 ♗c5+ d6 22 ♕g7+ ♔d8 23 ♗xd6 **1-0** +1

**1817-⚔LP-3** 28 viii 17
**Lewis, W.–Pratt, P.**
⟨♘g1⟩1 e4 e5 2 ♗c4 c6 3 d4 f6 4 dxe5 ♕a5+ 5 c3 ♕xe5 6 0-0 ♗d6 7 g3 ♘e7 8 ♗f4 ♕c5 9 ♗xd6 ♕xc4 10 ♘a3 ♕f7 11 f4 0-0 12 ♘c2 ♖e8 13 ♕d4 b6 14 ♘e3 c5 15 ♕d2 ♗b7 16 e5 ♘c8 17 ♖ae1 ♘xd6 18 exd6 f5 19 b3 ♘a6 20 ♕d3 ♖e4 21 ♘c4 ♖xe1 22 ♖xe1 ♕d5 23 ♕xd5+ ♗xd5 24 ♘e5 ♖e8 25 ♔f2 ♗e6 26 a3 ♗xb3 27 ♘xd7 ♖xe1 28 ♔xe1 ♔f7 29 ♘e5+ ♔e6 30 d7 ♔e7 31 ♔d2 ♘b8 32 ♔e3 ♘xd7 33 ♘c6+ ♔d6 34 ♘xa7 ♗a4 35 ♘c8+ ♔e6

36 h3 g6 37 ♔d3 b5 38 ♘a7 ♔d5 39 ♘c8 c4+ 40 ♔e3 ♔c5 41 ♘e7 ♘f6 42 h4 ♘d5+ 43 ♘xd5 ♔xd5 **0-1** +1

**1817-⚔LP-4** 28 viii 17
**Lewis, W.+Pratt, P.**
⟨♘g1⟩1 e4 e5 2 ♗c4 c6 3 d4 f6 4 0-0 d6 5 dxe5 dxe5 6 ♕e2 ♕e7 7 ♗xg8 ♖xg8 8 f4 b6 9 ♗e3 ♗a6 10 c4 ♘d7 11 ♘d2 g5 12 fxg5 fxg5 13 ♕h5+ ♖g6 14 ♖f5 ♘f6 15 ♕e2 ♗c8 16 ♖xg5 ♗g4 17 ♕f2 ♗h6 18 ♖xg6 ♗xe3 19 ♕xe3 hxg6 20 ♖f1 0-0-0 21 ♕g5 ♗h5 22 ♖xf6 ♖xd2 23 ♖xc6+ ♔d8 24 ♖c8+ ♔xc8 25 ♕xe7 ♖xb2 26 ♕e6+ ♔b7 27 g4 ♖b1+ 28 ♔g2 ♖b2+ 29 ♔g3 ♗xg4 30 ♕xg4 ♖b1 31 ♕d7+ ♔a6 32 ♕c8+ ♔a5 33 ♕b8 a6 34 ♕xe5+ b5 35 c5 ♖g1+ 36 ♔f2 **1-0** +1

**1817-★LS-1** 13 xi 17
**Sarratt, J.H.○Lewis, W.**
1 e4 e5 2 f4 exf4 3 ♘f3 g5 4 ♗c4 g4 5 0-0 gxf3 6 d4 d5 7 ♗xd5 ♗g4 8 ♖f2 ♗h6 9 ♘d2 ♕d6 10 ♘xf3 ♘e7 11 ♕e1 ♗xf3 12 ♖xf3 ♘d7 13 ♗d2 c5 14 c3 0-0 15 ♖h3 ♖fe8 16 ♕h4 ♘f5 17 ♕g4+ ♕g6 18 ♕xg6+ hxg6 19 g3 fxg3 20 ♗xh6 gxh2+ 21 ♖xh2 ♘xh6 22 ♖xh6 ...♀ +1

**1817-★PS-1** 25 xi 17
**Parkinson, J+Scrimgour, W.**
⟨♘b1⟩ 1 e4 e5 2 f4 exf4 3 ♗c4 ♗c5 4 d4 ♗e7 5 ♘f3 ♗h4+ 6 g3 fxg3 7 0-0 gxh2+ 8 ♔h1 ♗e7 9 ♗xf7+ ♔xf7 10 ♘e5+ ♔e8 11 ♕h5+ g6 12 ♘xg6 ♘f6 13 ♖xf6 ♗xf6 14 ♘xh8+ ♔e7 15 ♕f7+ ♔d6 16 ♗f4+ ♔c6 17 ♕d5+ ♔b6 18 ♕c5+ ♔a6 19 ♗xc7 **1-0** +1

**1817-★♀♀-1**
**♀+♀**
1 e4 e5 2 f4 exf4 3 ♘f3 g5 4 ♗c4 g4 5 0-0 gxf3 6 ♕xf3 ♕e7 7 d4 ♗g7 8 ♗xf4 ♗xd4+ 9 ♔h1 ♗xb2 10 ♘c3 ♗xa1 11 ♘d5 ♕c5

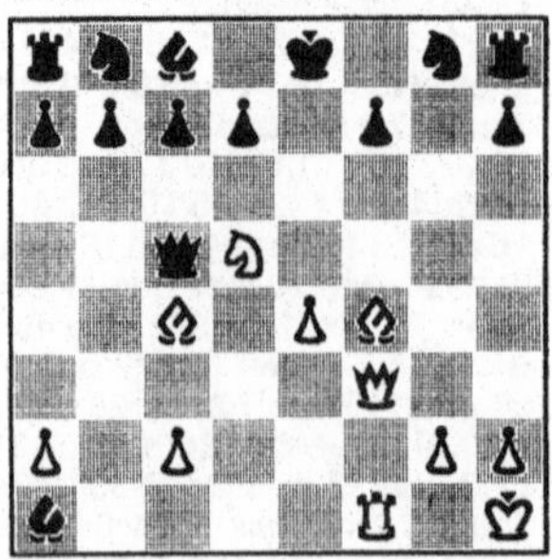

12 ♗d6 ♕xd6 13 ♕xf7+ ♔d8 14 ♕f8+ ♕xf8 15 ♖xf8# **1-0** +1

**1818-★L♀-1** 31 xii
**Lewis, W.+♀**
London
1 e4 e5 2 f4 exf4 3 ♗c4 ♕h4+ 4 ♔f1 d6 5 c3 ♘c6 6 d4 ♕e7 7 ♘f3 ♘f6 8 ♗xf4 ♘xe4 9 ♘bd2 ♗f5 10 ♘xe4 ♗xe4 11 ♕b3 ♘d8 12 ♖e1 f5 13 ♘g5 b6 14 ♗d5 c6 15 ♗xe4 fxe4 16 ♖xe4 ♕xe4 17 ♘xe4 ♗e7 18 ♘xd6+ ♔d7 19 ♕d1 h5 20 ♘f5 g6 21 ♘xe7 ♔xe7 22 ♗g5+ ♔d7 23 d5 c5 24 g3 b5 25 ♕d3 c4 26 ♕xg6 ♖f8+ 27 ♔g2 ♔c7 28 ♕g7+ ♘f7 29 ♖f1 ♔b6 30 ♖xf7 ♖xf7 31 ♕xf7 h4 **1-0** +1

**1818-★CH-1**
**Cazenove, J.+Hull, T.**
1 e4 e5 2 ♗c4 c6 3 ♕e2 ♘f6 4 c3 d6 5 d4 ♗e7 6 dxe5 dxe5 7 ♗g5 h6 8 ♗xf6 ♗xf6 9 ♘d2 0-0 10 ♗b3 ♗g5 11 ♘df3 ♗g4 12 ♖d1 ♕e7 13 ♗c2 ♘d7 14 h3 ♗h5 15 g4 ♗g6 16 ♘xg5 hxg5 17 ♘f3 ♖ad8 18 h4 gxh4 19 ♘xh4 ♖de8 20 ♘xg6 fxg6 21 ♗b3+ ♖f7 22 f3 ♖ef8 23 ♕h2 **1-0** +1

**1818-★CT-1**
**Cazenove, J.+Tomalin, D.**
1 e4 e5 2 f4 exf4 3 ♘f3 g5 4 ♗c4 ♗g7 5 d4 ♕e7 6 0-0 h6 7 ♘c3 c6 8 e5 ♕b4 9 ♘e4 ♗f8 10 ♕e2 g4 11 ♘d6+ ♗xd6 12 exd6+ ♔d8 13 ♘e5 ♖h7 14 c3 f3 15 ♕e4 ♘f6 16 ♕xh7 ♘xh7

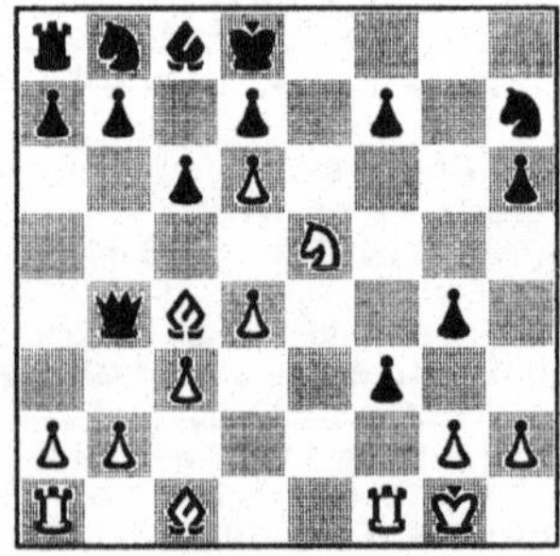

**1-0** +1

**1818-★HL-1**
**Lewis, W.+Hull, T.**
⟨♘b1⟩ 1 e4 e5 2 f4 exf4 3 ♗c4 ♕e7 4 d3 ♘c6 5 ♗xf4 d6 6 ♘f3 ♗g4 7 0-0 ♘d4 8 c3 ♗xf3 9 ♕a4+ ♕d7 10 ♗xf7+ ♔e7 11 ♗g5+ ♘f6 12 ♕xd4 c5 13 ♕d5 ♗g4 14 ♖xf6 gxf6 15 ♗xf6+ ♔xf6 16 ♖f1+ ♔g7 ♕g5# **1-0** +1

**1818-★LS-1**
**Lewis, W.+Scrimgour, W.**
⟨♘b1⟩ 1 e4 e5 2 f4 exf4 3 ♗c4 ♕h4+ 4 ♔f1 g5 5 d4 d6 6 ♘f3 ♕h5 7 h4 g4 8 ♘g5 ♘h6 9 c3 f6 10 ♗e6 ♗xe6 11 ♘xe6 ♔d7 12 ♘xf4 ♕b5+ 13 ♔g1 ♘c6 14 ♘d5 f5 15 a4 ♕a6 16 exf5 ♘e7 17 ♘f6+ ♔c8 18 ♗xh6 ♗xh6 19 ♕xg4 ♕d3 20 ♖e1 ♗e3+ 21 ♔h2 ♘xf5 22 ♖xe3 ♕xe3 23 ♕xf5+ ♔b8 24 ♘d7+ ♔c8 25 ♘b6+ ♔b8

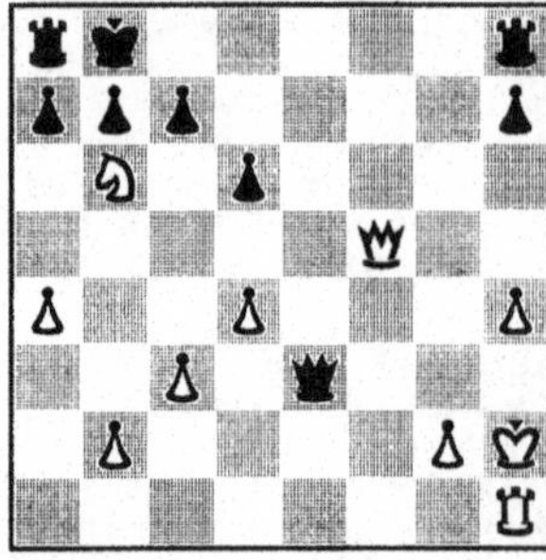

26 ♕c8+ ♖xc8 27 ♘d7# **1-0** +1

**1818-★ST-1** iii 18
**Thierré−Sarratt, J.H.**
⟨♘b8⟩ 1 e4 e5 2 c3 f5 3 exf5 ♘f6 4 d4 e4 5 ♗g5 d5 6 ♘d2 ♗xf5 7 ♕a4+ c6 8 0-0-0 ♗d6 9 ♕b3 ♕e7 10 c4 0-0 11 ♗xf6 ♖xf6 12 cxd5 cxd5 13 ♕xd5+ ♗e6 14 ♕xe4 ♖c8+ 15 ♗c4 b5 16 d5 ♗f7 17 ♕xe7 ♗xe7 18 b3 bxc4 19 ♘e4 ♖f4 20 f3 cxb3+ 21 ♔b2 bxa2 22 ♔xa2 ♖c2+ 23 ♔b3 ♖xg2 **0-1** +1

**1818-★S♀-1**
**Sarratt, J.H.+♀**
1 e4 e5 2 f4 exf4 3 ♘f3 g5 4 ♗c4 ♗g7 5 h4 h6 6 d4 d6 7 c3 c6 8 ♕b3 ♕e7 9 0-0 b5 10 ♗d3 ♗b7 11 a4 a6 12 axb5 axb5 13 ♖xa8 ♗xa8 14 ♕a3 ♗b7 15 ♕a7 ♘a6 16 hxg5 hxg5 17 ♘xg5 ♕xg5 18 ♕xb7 ♕h4 19 ♕xc6+ ♔e7 20 ♗xf4 ♕h1+ 21 ♔f2 ♕h4+ 22 g3 ♕h2+ 23 ♔e1 ♕xb2 24 ♗xd6+ ♔d8 25 ♕b6+ ♔d7 26 ♗xb5+ ♔e6 27 d5# **1-0** +1

**1818-★S♀-2**
**Sarratt, J.H.+♀**
1 e4 e5 2 f4 exf4 3 ♘f3 g5 4 ♗c4 ♗g7 5 h4 h6 6 d4 d6 7 c3 c6 8 ♕b3 ♕e7 9 0-0 b5 10 ♗d3 g4 11 ♘h2 ♕xh4 12 ♖xf4 ♘f6 13 e5 ♘d5 14 ♖f1 g3 15 ♘f3 ♕h5 16 exd6 ♗g4 17 ♖e1+ ♔d7 18 ♘bd2 ♖e8 19 ♖xe8 ♔xe8 20 ♕d1 ♘d7 21 ♕e1+ ♔f8 22 ♕xg3 ♖e8 23 ♘e4 ♗xf3 24 ♕xf3 ♕xf3 25 gxf3 f5 26 ♘c5 **1-0** +1

**1818̂-★S♀-3**
**Sarratt, J.H.+♀**
1 d4 d5 2 ♗f4 ♗f5 3 ♘c3 ♘c6 4 f3 ♘b4 5 e4 dxe4 6 fxe4 ♗g6 7 a3 ♘c6 8 ♗b5 a6 9 d5 axb5 10 ♘xb5 ♘a5 11 ♘xc7+ ♔d7 12 ♕g4+ e6 13 dxe6+ ♔e7 14 ♕g5+ f6 15 ♕c5+ ♕d6 16 ♕xd6# **1-0** +1

**1818̂-★S♀-4**
**Sarratt, J.H.+♀**
1 e4 e5 2 f4 exf4 3 ♘f3 g5 4 ♗c4 ♗g7 5 h4 g4 6 ♘g5 ♘h6 7 d4 f6 8 ♗xf4 fxg5 9 hxg5 ♘g8 10 ♕xg4 d5 11 ♕h5+ ♔f8 12 ♗xd5 ♕e7 13 0-0 ♗xd4+ 14 ♗e3+ ♗f6 15 gxf6 ♘xf6 16 ♗h6+ ♕g7 17 ♕f7# **1-0** +1

**1818̂-★S♀-5**
**Sarratt, J.H.+♀**
1 e4 e5 2 f4 exf4 3 ♘f3 g5 4 ♗c4 ♗g7 5 h4 h6 6 d4 d6 7 c3 c6 8 ♕b3 ♕e7 9 0-0 ♘d7 10 hxg5 hxg5 11 ♘xg5 ♕xg5 12 ♗xf7+ ♔f8 13 ♗xf4 ♕h4 14 ♗xd6+ ♘e7 15 ♗g6+ ♘f6 16 ♕f7# **1-0** +1

**1818̂-★S♀-6**
**Sarratt, J.H.+♀**
1 e4 e5 2 f4 exf4 3 ♘f3 g5 4 ♗c4 ♗g7 5 h4 h6 6 d4 d6 7 c3 ♗g4 8 ♕b3 ♗xf3 9 ♗xf7+ ♔f8 10 gxf3 b6 11 hxg5 hxg5 12 ♖xh8 ♗xh8 13 ♗xg8 **1-0** +1

**1818̂-★S♀-7**
**Sarratt, J.H.+♀**
1 d4 d5 2 c4 dxc4 3 e3 b5 4 a4 ♗d7 5 axb5 ♗xb5 6 ♘c3 ♗a6 7 ♕f3 c6 8 ♖xa6 ♘xa6 9 ♕xc6+ ♕d7 10 ♕xa8+ ♕d8 11 ♕c6+ ♕d7 12 ♕xa6 **1-0** +1

**1818̂-★S♀-8**
**Sarratt, J.H.+♀**
1 e4 e5 2 ♘f3 ♘c6 3 ♗c4 ♗c5 4 d4 exd4 5 ♘g5 ♘e5 6 ♘xf7 ♘xf7 7 ♗xf7+ ♔xf7 8 ♕h5+ g6 9 ♕xc5 **1-0** +1

**Lewis✕Wilson** [1819-✕LW]

| | | | |
|---|---|---|---|
| W. Lewis | 1̂ | 1̂ | 2 |
| H. Wilson | 0̂ | 0̂ | 0 |

**1819-✕LW-1̂** ii 19
**Lewis, W.+Wilson, H.**
London
⟨♘b1⟩ 1 e4 c5 2 f4 e6 3 ♘f3 d5 4 ♗b5+ ♘c6 5 e5 a6 6 ♗xc6+ bxc6 7 0-0 ♗e7 8 c3 a5 9 d3 ♘h6 10 ♘e1 a4 11 g4 ♗h4 12 f5 exf5 13 ♗xh6 gxh6 14 gxf5 c4 15 ♕f3 ♕g5+ 16 ♔h1 ♗xe1 17 ♖axe1 cxd3 18 e6 ♗a6 19 ♖g1 ♕f6 20 exf7+ ♔xf7 21 ♕h5+ ♔f8 22 ♖e6 ♕xe6 23 fxe6 ♔e7 24 ♕e5 ♖hg8 25 ♖f1 ♖af8 26 ♕c7+ ♔xe6 27 ♕xc6+ ♔e7 28 ♖e1+ ♔f7 29 ♕e6+ ♔g7 30 ♖g1+ ♔h8 31 ♕e5+ **1-0** +1

**1819-✕LW-2̂**
**Lewis, W.+Wilson, H.**
London
⟨♘b1⟩ 1 e4 e6 2 f4 d5 3 e5 c5 4 ♗b5+ ♘c6 5 ♘f3 ♗d7 6 ♕e2 ♗e7 7 c3 a6 8 ♗a4 d4 9 ♗c2 ♘h6 10 0-0 0-0 11 ♕e4 g6 12 d3 ♘f5 13 ♗d2 ♕b6 14 ♖ab1 ♘d8 15 ♕e1 ♗c6 16 g4 ♘e3 17 ♗xe3 dxe3 18 ♕xe3 ♗xf3 19 ♖xf3 ♕c7 20 f5 exf5 21 gxf5 f6 22 ♗b3+ ♘f7 23 fxg6 c4 24 gxf7+ ♔xf7 25 ♗xc4+ ♔g7 26 ♖g3+ ♔h8 27 ♕h6 ♖g8 28 ♗xg8 ♖xg8 29 ♖xg8+ ♔xg8 30 exf6 ♕b6+ 31 d4 ♕e6 32 ♕g7# **1-0** +1

**1819̂-★AL-1**
**Lewis, W.+Allen, G.**
⟨♖a1⟩ 1 e4 e5 2 ♘f3 ♘c6 3 ♗c4 ♗c5 4 0-0 d6 5 c3 a6 6 d4 exd4 7 cxd4 ♗a7 8 ♗g5 ♘ge7 9 ♗e3 ♗g4 10 ♗xf7+ ♔f8 11 ♗c4 d5 12 exd5 ♘xd5 13 ♘bd2 b5 14 ♗b3

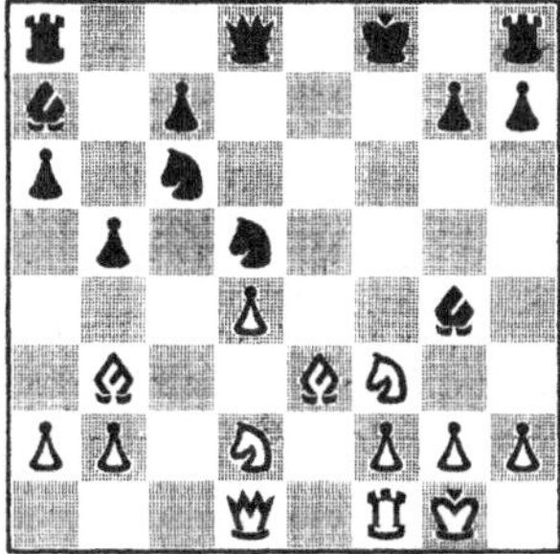

14 ... ♗xd4 15 ♘xd4 ♗xd1 16 ♘e6+ ♔e8 17 ♘xd8 ♗xb3 18 ♘xc6 ♗xa2 19 b3 a5 20 ♖a1 ♘b4 21 ♘d4 c6 22 ♘e6 ♔f7 23 ♘g5+ ♔g6 24 ♘ge4 ♖ad8 25 ♘c3 a4 26 bxa4 ♗f7 27 ♘f3 ♔h5 28 g4+ ♔g6 29 ♘e4 h6 30 ♘e5+ ♔h7 31 ♘xf7 ♖a8 32 g5 ♘c2 33 ♖c1 ♘xe3 34 fxe3 ♖xa4 35 ♖xc6 ♖xe4 36 g6+ ♔g8 37 ♖c8+ **1-0** +1

**1819̂-★C♀-1**
**Cazenove, J.+♀**
1 e4 e5 2 f4 exf4 3 ♗c4 ♗c5 4 d4 ♗e7 5 ♘f3 ♗h4+ 6 g3 fxg3 7 0-0 gxh2+ 8 ♔h1 ♗e7 9 ♗xf7+ ♔xf7 10 ♘e5+ ♔e8 11 ♕h5+ g6 12 ♘xg6 ♘f6 13 ♖xf6 ♗xf6 14 ♘xh8+ ♔e7 15 ♕f7+ ♔d6 16 ♗f4+ ♔c6 17 ♕d5+ ♔b6 18 ♕c5+ ♔a6 19 ♗xc7 ♕xc7 20 ♕xc7 ♘c6 21 ♘f7 **1-0** +1

**1819̂-★LS-1**
**Lewis, W.+Samson, H.**
⟨♖a1⟩ 1 e4 e5 2 ♘f3 ♘c6 3 ♗c4 ♗c5 4 c3 ♗b6 5 0-0 ♘f6 6 d4 exd4 7 e5 ♘g8 8 ♗g5 ♘ge7 9 ♗d5 ♘a5 10 ♘h4 c6 11 ♘f5 cxd5 12 ♘d6+ ♔f8 13 ♕f3 **1-0** +1

**1819̂-★LW-1**
**Lewis, W.+Williams, P.W.**
London
1 e4 e5 2 f4 exf4 3 ♘f3 g5 4 ♗c4 ♗g7 5 d4 d6 6 c3 c6 7 0-0 ♕e7 8 ♘e1 h5 9 h4 f6 10 ♗xg8 ♖xg8 11 ♕xh5+ ♔d8 12 hxg5 fxg5 13 ♘f3 ♗f6 14 e5 dxe5 15 ♘xe5 ♗xe5 16 dxe5 ♕xe5 17 ♗xf4 ♕c5+ 18 ♖f2 ♘d7 19 ♗g3 ♘f6 20 ♕d1+ ♗d7 21 b4 ♕b6 22 ♕d4 ♕xd4 23 cxd4 ♘e4 24 ♖f3 ♘xg3 25 ♖xg3 a5 26 ♖a3 a4 27 ♘d2 ♗e6 28 ♘e4 b5 29 ♘c5 ♗d5 30 ♖f1 ♔e7 31 ♖e3+ ♔d8 32 a3 ♖a7 33 ♖f2 ♖e7 34 ♖xe7 ♔xe7 35 ♖d2 ♗c4 36 ♔f2 ♖f8+ 37 ♔g3 ♖f5 38 ♘e4 ♔e6 39 ♘c3 ♔d6 40 ♖d1 ♖f4 41 ♖d2 ♖f1 42 ♘e4+ ♔d5 43 ♘c3+ ♔e6 44 ♘d1 ♗b3 45 ♖e2+ ♔f6 46 ♖f2+ ♖xf2 47 ♘xf2 ♔e6 48 ♔f3 ♗d5+ 49 ♘e4 ♔f5 50 g4+ ♔e6 51 ♔e3 ♗a2 52 ♘xg5+ ♔d5 53 ♔d3 ♗b1+ 54 ♔c3 ♗g6 55 ♘f3 ♔e6 56 ♘e5 ♗e8 57 g5 ♔f5 58 g6 ♔f6 59 ♔d3 ♗xg6+ 60 ♘xg6 ♔xg6 61 d5 ♔f6 62 ♔d4 ♔e7 63 dxc6 ♔d6 64 c7 ♔xc7 65 ♔c5 **1-0** +1

**1819̂-★LW-2**
**Lewis, W.+Wilson, H.**
London
1 e4 c5 2 f4 e6 3 ♘f3 d5 4 ♗b5+ ♘c6 5 e5 a6 6 ♗xc6+ bxc6 7 d3 ♗e7 8 c3 ♘h6 9 0-0 a5 10 d4 a4 11 ♗e3 ♘f5 12 ♕e2 c4 13 ♕f2 ♖b8 14 ♗c1 ♖b5 15 ♘bd2 c5 16 ♖e1 h6 17 ♘f1 cxd4 18 cxd4 g6 19 ♘e3 ♖g8 20 ♘xf5 gxf5 21 ♕c2 ♗d7 22 ♗d2 ♗b4 23 ♗c3 ♖g4 24 ♕d2 ♕e7 25 h3 ♖g7 26 ♕f2 a3 27 ♗xb4 ♕xb4 28 bxa3 ♕xa3 29 ♖ab1 ♕c3 30 ♖xb5 ♗xb5 31 ♖b1 ♔d7 32 ♖xb5 ♕c1+ 33 ♘e1 c3 34 ♔h2 h5 35 ♘d3 ♕d1 36 ♘b4 ♕d2 37 ♕f1 ♕xd4 38 ♖b7+ ♔c8 39 ♖b8+ ♔c7 40 ♘a6+ ♔d7 41 ♕b5+ ♔e7 42 ♕b7# **1-0** +1

**1819̂-★LW-3**
**Lewis, W.+Wilson, H.**
London
1 e4 c5 2 f4 e6 3 ♘f3 d5 4 ♗b5+ ♗d7 5 ♗xd7+ ♘xd7 6 e5 ♘h6 7 c3 ♗e7 8 d4 c4 9 0-0 b5 10 ♗e3 ♘f5 11 ♕e2 ♘xe3 12 ♕xe3 h6 13 ♘bd2 a5 14 h3 ♘f8 15 ♘h2 ♘h7 16 ♕e2 g5 17 f5 exf5 18 ♖xf5 0-0 19 ♕h5 ♖a6 20 ♘g4 ♕b6 21 ♖af1

♕e6 22 ♖1f3 b4 23 ♘f1 bxc3 24 bxc3 ♕g6 25 ♘g3 ♔g7 26 ♘e3 ♕e6 27 ♘g4 ♕g6 28 ♕xg6+ fxg6 29 ♖xf8 ♘xf8 30 ♘e3 ♘e6 31 ♘xd5 ♗a3 32 ♖f6 ♗c1 33 ♘e4 ♘c7 34 ♘xc7 ♖a7 35 ♘d6 ♔h7 36 ♘de8 ♗e3+ 37 ♔f1 ♗d2 38 ♖f7+ ♔g8 39 e6 ♗xc3 40 ♘f6+ ♔h8 41 ♖h7# **1-0** +1

**1820-★BM-1**
**Brand= Mouret, J–F.**
⟨♙f7⟩ 1 e4 e6 2 d4 c6 3 ♗d3 g6 4 f4 d5 5 e5 c5 6 c3 ♘c6 7 ♘f3 ♕b6 8 ♕b3 ♕c7 9 ♗b5 ♗d7 10 ♗xc6 bxc6 11 0-0 cxd4 12 cxd4 c5 13 ♗e3 ♘h6 14 ♕c3 ♘g4 15 ♗f2 ♗b5 16 ♖e1 ♘xf2 17 ♔xf2 ♗e7 18 b3 c4 19 a4 ♗d7 20 b4 a5 21 ♖e3 ♖b8 22 b5 0-0 23 g3 g5 24 fxg5 ♗xg5 25 ♖e2 ♗e8 26 ♔g2 ♗h5 27 ♖f2 ♗e7 28 ♕e3 ♖f7 29 ♘c3 ♖bf8 30 ♖af1 ♗b4 31 ♘g5 ♖xf2+ 32 ♖xf2 ♖xf2+ 33 ♔xf2 ♕e7 34 ♘h3 ♕f7+ 35 ♘f4 ♕f5 36 b6 ♕c2+ 37 ♘fe2 ♗xc3 38 ♕g5+ ♗g6 39 ♕d8+ **½-½** +1

**1820-★BM-2**
**Brand– Mouret, J–F.**
⟨♙f7⟩ 1 e4 e6 2 d4 c6 3 ♗d3 g6 4 ♘f3 d5 5 e5 c5 6 c3 ♘c6 7 0-0 cxd4 8 cxd4 ♘h6 9 ♘g5 ♕e7 10 ♗e3 ♗d7 11 ♕b3 ♖b8 12 f4 ♘g4 13 ♕c2 ♘xe3 14 ♗xg6+ ♔d8 15 ♘f7+ ♕xf7 16 ♕e2 ♕xg6 17 ♕xe3 ♕e4 **0-1** +1

**1820-★BM-3**
**Brand+ Mouret, J–F.**
1 e4 e5 2 ♘f3 ♘c6 3 d4 exd4 4 ♗c4 ♕f6 5 0-0 d6 6 ♘g5 ♘h6 7 f4 ♗e7 8 e5 ♕g6 9 exd6 cxd6 10 c3 dxc3 11 ♘xc3 0-0 12 ♘d5 ♗d7 13 ♖f3 ♗g4 14 ♗d3 ♗xf3 15 ♕xf3 f5 16 ♗c4 ♔h8 17 ♘xe7 ♘xe7 18 ♕xb7 ♕f6 19 ♗e3 ♖fb8 20 ♕d7 ♖d8 21 ♕b7 d5 22 ♗b3 ♘c6 23 ♗xd5 ♘d4 24 ♖d1 ♘e2+ 25 ♔f1 ♖ab8 26 ♕xa7 ♖xb2 27 ♘e6 ♕xe6 28 ♗xe6 ♖xd1+ 29 ♔f2 **1-0** +1

**1820-★CL-1** 15iii20
**Lewis, W.+ Cochrane, J.**
⟨♘b1⟩ 1 e4 e5 2 ♘f3 ♘c6 3 d4 exd4 4 ♗c4 h6 5 0-0 d6 6 h3 ♘e5 7 ♘xe5 dxe5 8 f4 d3 9 cxd3 ♗c5+ 10 ♔h1 ♕h4 11 ♕f3 exf4 12 ♗xf4 ♕f6 13 e5 ♕e7 14 ♗b5+ ♔f8 15 ♖ad1 a6 16 ♗a4 ♗d4 17 ♕e4 c5 18 b4 f5 19 exf6 ♕xe4 20 ♗d6+ ♔f7 21 fxg7+ ♔xg7 22 dxe4 ♗e6 23 bxc5 ♗c3 24 ♖d3 ♗f6 25 ♖g3+ ♔h7 26 e5 ♗e7 27 ♗c2+ ♗f5 28 ♗xf5# **1-0** +1

**1820-★CM-1**
**Cochrane, J.– Mouret, J–F.**
⟨♙f7⟩ 1 e4 e6 2 d4 c6 3 f4 d5 4 e5 c5 5 c3 ♘c6 6 ♗b5 ♕b6 7 ♗xc6+ bxc6 8 ♘f3 ♗a6 9 ♔f2 cxd4 10 ♘xd4 c5 11 ♘f3 ♘h6 12 h3 ♗e7 13 g4 0-0 14 ♕b3 ♕c6 15 ♔g3 ♖ae8 16 ♕d1 ♘f7 17 h4 ♗d8 18 ♕c2 ♗b7 19 ♘g5 ♗xg5 20 hxg5 g6 21 ♕h2 h6 22 gxh6 ♔h7 23 ♕g2 ♕c7 24 ♕e2 d4 25 ♖f1 ♕c6 26 cxd4 cxd4 27 ♖f2 ♕xc1 **0-1** +1

**1820-★MM-1**
**Mercier= Mouret, J–F.**
⟨♙f7⟩ 1 e4 e6 2 d4 c6 3 f4 d5 4 e5 c5 5 c3 ♘c6 6 ♘f3 ♕b6 7 ♕b3 ♕c7 8 ♗b5 ♗d7 9 ♗e3 cxd4 10 cxd4 ♘h6 11 0-0 ♘g4 12 ♘bd2 ♘xe3 13 ♕xe3 ♗e7 14 ♖ac1 0-0 15 ♗d3 g6 16 a3 ♕b6 17 b4 a5 18 b5 ♘d8 19 a4 ♘f7 20 ♘b3 ♘h6 21 h3 ♘f5 22 ♗xf5 gxf5 23 ♘c5 ♗e8 24 ♕f2 ♔h8 25 h4 h6 26 ♖c2 ♖g8 27 ♖fc1 ♖g4 28 g3 ♗h5 29 ♔h2 ♖ag8 30 ♖g1 ♖4g6 31 ♖cc1 ♔h7 32 ♘d2 ♕a7 33 b6 ♕xb6 34 ♖b1 ♕c6 35 ♖xb7 ♖6g7 36 ♘db3 ♗xc5 37 ♖xg7+ ♖xg7 38 ♘xc5 ♕b6 39 ♕d2 ♗f3 40 ♕c3 ♗e4 41 ♕b3 ♕xb3 42 ♘xb3 ♖b7 43 ♘c5 ♖b2+ 44 ♔h3 ♗f3 45 g4 ♗xg4+ 46 ♖xg4 fxg4+ 47 ♔xg4 ♔g6 48 ♘xe6 h5+ 49 ♔g3 ♖b3+ 50 ♔h2 ♔f5 51 ♘c5 ♖e3 52 ♘b7 ♔xf4 53 ♘xa5 ♖e2+ 54 ♔h3 ♖e3+ 55 ♔h2 ♔g4 56 ♘c6 ♖e2+ 57 ♔g1 ♔xh4 58 a5 ♖c2 59 ♘b4 ♖d2 60 a6 ♔g3 61 ♔f1 ♖xd4 62 a7 ♖f4+ 63 ♔e2 ♖f8 64 ♘xd5 ♖a8 65 e6 ♖xa7 66 e7 ♖a8 67 ♘f6 h4 68 e8♕ ♖xe8+ 69 ♘xe8 ♔g2 70 ♘f6 h3 71 ♘g4 **½-½** +1

**1820-★MM-2**
**Mercier– Mouret, J–F.**
⟨♙f7⟩ 1 e4 e6 2 ♗c4 c6 3 ♘f3 d5 4 exd5 exd5 5 ♗b3 ♘f6 6 0-0 ♗e7 7 d3 0-0 8 c4 ♗g4 9 h3 ♗h5 10 ♕e2 ♕d7 11 ♘c3 ♗b4 12 ♗d2 ♗xc3 13 ♗xc3 ♘a6 14 ♗d1 d4 15 ♗d2 ♖ae8 16 ♗e3 dxe3 17 fxe3 ♘c5 18 d4 ♘ce4 19 ♕e1 ♗xf3 20 ♖xf3 ♘g5 21 ♖f1 ♘fe4 22 ♗g4 ♕e7 23 c5 ♘f6 24 ♗d1 ♕xe3+ 25 ♕xe3 ♖xe3 **0-1** +1

**1820-★MR-1**
**Rawdon– Mouret, J–F.**
⟨♙f7⟩ 1 e4 e6 2 d4 c6 3 c4 d6 4 ♘c3 g6 5 ♗d3 ♗g7 6 ♗e3 ♘e7 7 ♕b3 b6 8 ♘ge2 c5 9 d5 e5 10 0-0-0 0-0 11 ♖df1 ♘d7 12 f4 exf4 13 ♗xf4 ♘e5 14 ♗xe5 ♗xe5 15 ♔b1 ♗d7 16 ♕d1 a6 17 ♖xf8+ ♕xf8 18 ♖f1 ♕g7 19 g3 ♖b8 20 ♔c1 b5 21 ♕d2 ♘c8 22 ♕g5 ♘b6 23 ♕d2 bxc4 24 ♗c2 a5 25 a4 ♘a8 26 ♖f2 ♘c7 27 ♗d1 ♘a6 28 ♘g1 ♘b4 29 ♘f3 ♘d3+ 30 ♔b1 ♖xb2+ 31 ♕xb2 ♘xb2 32 ♖xb2 ♗xc3 33 ♖b8+ ♔f7 **0-1** +1

**1820-★MS-1**
**Scrivener– Mouret, J–F.**
⟨♙f7⟩ 1 e4 e6 2 ♗c4 c6 3 d3 d5 4 ♗b3 ♗d6 5 f4 ♘e7 6 ♘f3 ♕b6 7 e5 ♗c7 8 d4 c5 9 c3 ♘b6 10 ♗a4 ♗d7 11 ♗xc6 bxc6 12 ♕e2 cxd4 13 cxd4 ♘f5 14 ♘bd2 ♘xd4 15 ♘xd4 ♕xd4 16 ♘b3 ♕a4 17 0-0 ♗b6+ 18 ♔h1 c5 19 ♕f3 0-0 20 ♗e3 d4 21 ♗d2 ♗c6 22 ♕g3 ♖f5 23 ♘c1 ♕c2 24 ♕d3 ♕xd3 25 ♘xd3 ♖b8 26 b3 ♖bf8 27 h3 g5 28 ♔h2 ♗b5 29 ♖f3 ♗xd3 30 ♖xd3 gxf4 31 ♖e1 ♗c7 32 ♖e4 ♖xe5 33 ♖xe5 ♗xe5 34 ♖f3 ♗c7 **0-1** +1

**1820-★M?-1**
**?– Mouret, J–F.**
⟨♙f7⟩ 1 e4 e6 2 d4 c6 3 ♕f3 d5 4 ♗d3 g6 5 ♘h3 dxe4 6 ♗xe4 ♕xd4 7 0-0 ♘f6 8 ♘g5 ♗g7 9 ♖d1 ♕b6 10 ♕h3 0-0 11 ♘xh7 ♘xh7 12 ♗xg6 ♕xf2+ 13 ♔h1 ♕f1+ 14 ♖xf1 ♖xf1# **0-1** +1

**182̂0̂-★??-1**
**?+?**
⟨♘b1⟩ 1 e4 c5 2 f4 ♘c6 3 ♘f3 d5 4 e5 ♗g4 5 c3 e6 6 ♗e2 ♗e7 7 0-0 h6 8 d4 cxd4 9 cxd4 ♕b6 10 ♗e3 ♘f6 11 exf6 ♗xf6 12 ♘e5 ♗xe2 13 ♕xe2 ♗xe5 14 fxe5 ♖d8 15 ♕g4 g5 16 ♖f3 ♖d7 17 ♖d1 ♕xb2 18 ♕h5 ♕c2 19 ♖f6 a5 20 ♗xg5 ♖g8 21 ♖xe6+ ♘e7 22 ♗d2 ♕xd1+ 23 ♕xd1 fxe6 24 ♗xh6 b5 25 ♕h5+ ♖g6 26 ♗g5 ♔f7 27 ♗f6 ♘f5 28 ♕h7+ ♘g7 29 h4 ♖c7 30 h5 ♖g4 31 h6 ♖c8 32 ♔h2 ♖c2 33 ♕xc2 **1-0** +1

**182̂0̂-★??-2**
**?+?**
⟨♘b1⟩ 1 e4 c5 2 f4 ♘c6 3 ♘f3 d5 4 e5 ♗g4 5 c3 e6 6 ♗e2 c4 7 0-0 ♗c5+ 8 ♔h1 ♘ge7 9 d4 cxd3 10 ♗xd3 h6 11 ♕c2 ♗xf3 12 ♖xf3 d4 13 ♗d2 a5 14 ♖e1 dxc3 15 bxc3 0-0 16 ♖d1 ♕d7 17 ♗e3 ♕c7 18 ♗xc5 ♘xe5 19 ♗d6 ♕xd6 20 ♗h7+ ♔h8 21 ♖xd6 ♘xf3 22 gxf3 g6 23 ♖d7 ♘f5 24 ♗xg6 fxg6 25 ♕e4 ♖f6 26 ♕xb7 ♖af8 27 c4 ♔g8 28 c5 ♖8f7 29 c6 ♘h4 30 ♖xf7 ♖xf7

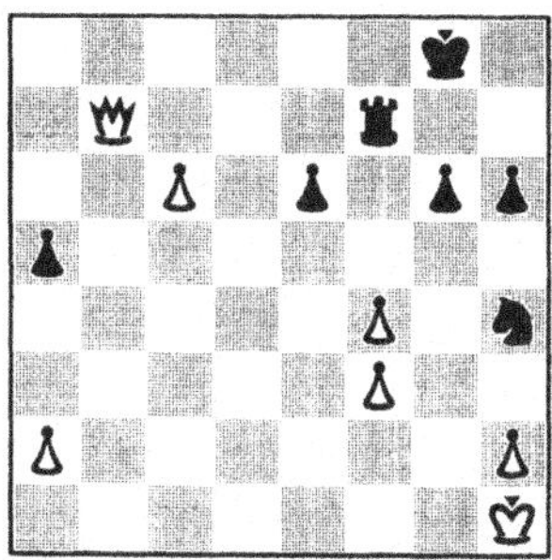

31 ♕xf7+ ♔xf7 32 c7 **1-0** +1

### 1820̂-★??-3
?+?

⟨♘b1⟩ 1 e4 c5 2 f4 ♘c6 3 ♘f3 d5 4 e5 ♗g4 5 c3 e6 6 ♗b5 ♕b6 7 ♗a4 ♗e7 8 d4 c4 9 0-0 ♘h6 10 h3 ♗f5 11 ♘g5 0-0 12 ♗c2 ♗xc2 13 ♕xc2 ♗xg5 14 fxg5 ♘f5 15 ♕f2 ♘cxd4 16 cxd4 ♕xd4 17 ♗f4 ♕xf2+ 18 ♖xf2 d4 19 g4 ♘e7 20 ♗d2 ♖fd8 21 ♖af1 ♘c6 22 ♖xf7 ♘xe5 23 ♖xb7 ♘g6 24 ♖ff7 ♘f8 25 ♖xg7+ ♔h8 26 ♗f4 ♖d5 27 ♗d2 d3 28 ♖gc7 ♖ad8 29 ♖xc4 e5 30 ♖cc7 ♖8d7 31 ♖xd7 ♘xd7 32 ♖xa7 ♔g8 33 ♔f2 ♘c5 34 ♖a5 e4 35 b4 e3+ 36 ♔xe3 ♖e5+ 37 ♔d4 **1-0** +1

### 1820̂-★??-4
?–?

1 e4 e5 2 ♘f3 ♘c6 3 ♗c4 ♗c5 4 c3 d5 5 exd5 ♘a5 6 d3 ♗g4 7 b4 ♘xc4 8 dxc4 ♗e7 9 ♕a4+ ♗d7 10 b5 ♘f6 11 ♘xe5 0-0 12 ♕c2 g6 13 0-0 ♗f5 14 ♕e2 ♖e8 15 ♗f4 ♘h5 16 ♕f3 ♗g5 17 g3 f6 18 ♗xg5 ♖xe5 19 g4 ♗e4 20 ♕h3 ♖xg5 21 ♘d2 ♘f4 22 ♕xh7+ ♔xh7 23 ♘xe4 ♖xg4+ 24 ♘g3 c6 25 ♖ae1 cxd5 26 ♖d1 b6 27 ♖xd5 ♕c7 28 ♖e1 ♖d8 29 ♖d4 ♖xd4 30 cxd4 ♕xc4 31 ♔h1 ♘h3 32 ♔g2 ♕xd4 33 ♔xh3 ♕xf2 34 ♖e7+ ♔h6 35 ♖e6 ♔g5 36 ♘e4+ ♖xe4 37 ♖xe4 ♕f3# **0-1** +1

### 1820̂-★??-5
?–?

1 e4 e6 2 d4 d5 3 e5 c5 4 ♘f3 ♘c6 5 ♗b5 ♕b6 6 ♗a4 ♗d7 7 0-0 ♘xe5 8 ♘xe5 ♗xa4 9 ♘c3 ♗b5 10 ♖e1 cxd4 11 ♘xd5 ♕d6 12 ♕xd4 f6 13 ♘c4 ♗xc4 14 ♖xe6+ ♕xe6 15 ♘c7+ ♔f7 16 ♘xe6 ♗xe6 17 c4 b6 18 ♕e4 ♖d8 19 ♗f4 f5 20 ♕e2 ♖d4 21 ♕f3 ♖e4 22 g4 ♘f6 23 g5 ♘d7 24 ♖d1 ♗c5 25 h4 ♗d4 26 b3 ♘e5 27 ♕g3 ♘g4 28 ♗e3 ♗e5 29 ♕f3 ♘h2 30 ♕h3 ♖g4+ 31 ♔h1 ♗c8 32 f3 ♘xf3 33 ♕xf3 ♖xh4+ 34 ♔g2 ♖e4 35 ♖d5 ♔e6 36 ♗d4 ♖g4+ 37 ♕xg4 fxg4 38 ♖xe5+ ♔f7 39 ♔g3 ♖d8 40 ♖e4 ♔g6 41 ♔h4 ♗f5 42 ♖f4 h6 43 gxh6 gxh6 44 c5 bxc5 45 ♗xc5 ♖d3 46 ♖xf5 ♔xf5 **0-1** +1

## Deschappelles⚔Lewis
[1821-⚔DL]

| | | | | |
|---|---|---|---|---|
| A. Deschappelles | ½ | ½ | 0 | 1 |
| W. Lewis | ½ | ½ | 1 | 2 |

### 1821-⚔DL-1 iv 21
**Lewis, W.= Deschappelles, A.L.H.L.**

[Staunton]

⟨♙f7⟩ 1 e4 ♘c6 2 d4 e5 3 d5 ♘ce7 4 ♗g5 d6 5 ♗xe7 ♕xe7 6 ♗d3 g6 7 ♘e2 [□ 7 h4] 7 ... ♗h6 8 ♘d2 ♘f6 9 ♘f3 0-0 10 ♘g3 ♗g4 11 h3 ♗xf3 12 gxf3 ♗f4 13 ♕e2 ♖f7 14 ♕f1?! ♖af8 15 ♕g2 ♔h8 16 h4 ♕d7 17 ♕h3 ♕a4 [□ 17 ... ♗xg3] 18 c3 ♕a5 [□ 18 ... ♗xg3] 19 ♔e2 ♕b6 20 ♖ab1 c6 21 h5 ♗xg3 22 fxg3 gxh5 23 ♕h2 ♖e7 [□ 23 ... ♘g4 24 fxg4 (24 ♔d1 ♕g1+±) 24 ... ♖f2+∓] 24 ♔d2 ♖ef7 25 ♔c2 ♕e3 [□ 25 ... ♘g4] 26 ♖f1 ♕b6 27 dxc6 bxc6 28 ♕e6 ♕c7 29 ♖hh1 ♖e8 30 ♕f5 d5 31 ♖h2 ♕d6 32 ♔b1 ♖ef8 33 exd5 ♘xd5 34 ♕xh5 ♘xc3+ 35 ♔c2 ♖d8 36 ♕g6 ♕xg6 [□ 36 ... e4] 37 ♗xg6 ♖g7 38 ♗xh7 ♖xh7 39 ♖xh7+ ♔xh7 40 ♔xc3 ♔g6 41 ♖e1 ♔f5 42 ♖e4 ♖d7 43 ♖h4 ♔e6 44 ♖h5 ♖f7 **½-½**

L/N6123-1842

### 1821-⚔DL-1 iv 21
**Lewis, W.= Deschappelles, A.L.H.L.**

[Staunton]

⟨♙f7⟩ 1 e4 ♘c6 2 d4 e5 3 d5 ♘ce7 4 ♗g5 ♘f6 5 ♗xf6 gxf6 6 ♕h5+ ♘g6 7 ♘f3 ♗c5 8 ♘h4 ♔f7 9 d6 ♕f8 10 ♗c4+ ♔e8 11 ♘xg6 hxg6 12 ♕xg6+ ♔d8 13 dxc7+ ♔xc7 14 0-0 ♖h6 15 ♕g3 [□ 15 ♕g8] 15 ... d6 16 ♘c3 ♗d7 17 ♘d5+ ♔d8 18 b4 ♗b6 19 ♘xb6 axb6 20 ♕g8?! ♕xg8 21 ♗xg8 ♖g6 22 ♗d5 [□ 22 ♗f7] 22 ... ♗h3 23 g3 ♗xf1 24 ♔xf1 ♔c7 25 a4 ♖f8 26 ♔e2 f5 27 ♖a3 ♖h6 28 h4 f4 29 ♖f3 ♖ff6 30 b5 ♔b8 31 ♔e1 ♖h7 32 ♔e2 ♖c7 33 ♔d2 ♖g7 34 ♔e2 ♖c7 35 ♔d2 **½-½**

L/N6123-1842

### 1821-⚔DL-3 iv 21
**Lewis, W.+ Deschappelles, A.L.H.L.**

[Staunton]

⟨♙f7⟩ 1 e4 ♘c6 2 d4 e5 3 d5 ♘ce7 4 ♗g5 ♘f6 5 ♗xf6 gxf6 6 ♕h5+ ♘g6 7 ♘f3 ♕e7 8 d6 ♕xd6 9 ♘h4 ♗g7 10 ♘xg6 hxg6 11 ♕xg6+ ♔f8 12 ♗c4 ♕e7 13 0-0 ♖h6 14 ♕g3 c6 15 ♘c3 d6 16 ♖ad1 f5 17 f4 d5 18 ♗b3 [18 exd5 ♕c5+] 18 ... dxe4 19 ♘xe4! fxe4

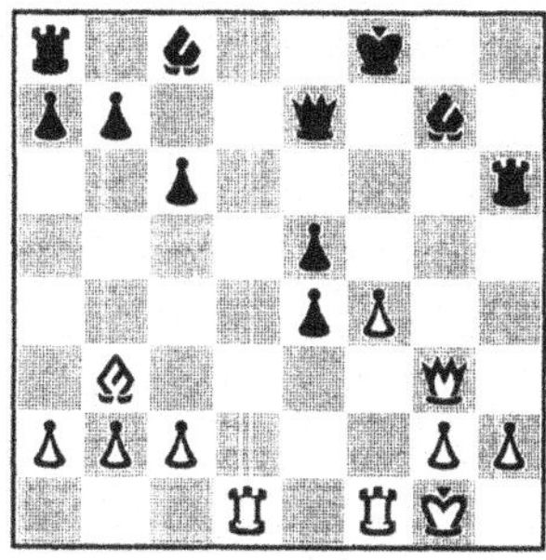

20 fxe5+ ♔e8 21 ♗f7+ ♕xf7 22 ♖xf7 ♔xf7 23 ♕b3+ ♔e7 24 ♕g8 ♗f8 25 ♕g5+ ♔f7 26 ♖f1+ ♔e8 27 ♕g8 **1-0**

L/N6123-1842

**194** Cochrane, J. M58.BL

### 1821-★CD-1
**Cochrane, J.– Deschapelles, A.L.H.L.**

Paris [Saint-Amant]

⟨♙f7⟩ 1 e4 ... 2 d4 ♘c6 3 f4?! d5 4 e5 ♗f5 5 c3?! e6 6 ♗d3 ♘h6 7 ♘e2 [□ 7 ♘f3] 7 ... ♕h4+ 8 g3 [□ 8 ♘g3] 8 ... ♕h3 9 ♔d2? ♗xd3 10 ♔xd3 ♕f5+ 11 ♔d2 ♘g4 12 ♔e1 ♕e4 13 ♖g1 ♘xh2∓ 14 ♘d2 ♕d3 15 ♔f2 ♘g4+ 16 ♔e1 ♕e3 [16 ... ♘e3 △ 17 ... ♘c2+→]

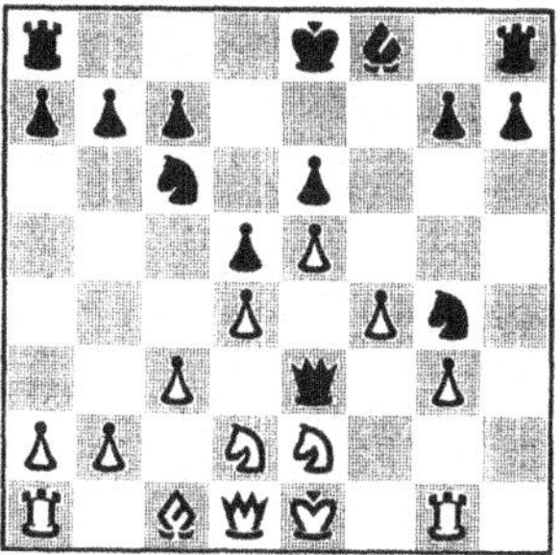

17 ♘f1 ♕f2+ 18 ♔d2 ♕f3 19 ♔c2 ♘f2 20 ♕d2 ♕e4+ 21 ♔b3 ♘a5+ 22 ♔a4 ♘c4 23 ♕e1 ♕c2+ 24 b3

♘b6+ 25 ♔b5 c6+ **0-1**
L/N6013-1844

**1821-★CD-2**
**Cochrane, J.– Deschapelles, A.L.H.L.**
Paris [Saint-Amant]
⟨♙f7⟩ 1 e4 ... 2 d4 e6 3 f4?! d5 4 e5 c5 5 c3 ♘c6 6 ♘f3 cxd4 7 cxd4 ♕b6 8 ♘c3 ♗d7 9 a3 [◻ 9 ♗e3; 9 ♕e2] 9 ... ♘h6 10 h3 ♘f5 11 ♘e2 ♗e7 12 g4 ♗h4+ 13 ♘xh4 ♘xh4 14 ♔f2 0-0 15 ♔g3 ♘g6 16 b4 a5 17 ♗d2 axb4 18 ♗xb4 ♘xb4 19 axb4 ♕xb4 20 ♖b1 ♖a3+ 21 ♔h2 ♕e7! 22 ♖xb7 ♕h4 23 ♖xd7 ♕f2+ 24 ♗g2 ♖xh3+! 25 ♔xh3 ♕h4# **0-1** L/N6013-1844

**1821-★CD-3**
**Cochrane, J.+ Deschapelles, A.L.H.L.**
Paris [Saint-Amant]
1 e4 e5 2 ♘f3 ♘c6 3 d4 exd4 4 ♗c4 ♗c5 [4 ... ♗b4+?] 5 ♘g5 ♘e5 [◻ 5 ... ♘h6] 6 ♗xf7+ ♘xf7 7 ♘xf7 ♗b4+? 8 c3 dxc3 9 bxc3 ♗xc3+ 10 ♘xc3 ♔xf7 11 ♕d5+ ♔f8 12 ♗a3+ d6 13 e5! ♕g5 14 exd6 ♕xd5 15 dxc7+ ♔f7 16 ♘xd5 ♗d7 17 0-0 ♖c8 18 ♗d6 ♔e6 19 ♗g3 ♗c6 [19 ... ♔xd5?] 20 ♖ad1 ♗xd5 21 ♖fe1+ ♔f6 22 ♖xd5 ♘h6 23 ♖a5 ♘f5 24 ♖c5 ♘xg3 25 hxg3 ♔f7 26 ♖d1 ♖he8 27 ♖d6 ♖e7 28 ♖f5+ ♔e8? [◻ 28 ... ♔g8] 29 ♖d8+ ♖xd8 30 ♖f8+ ♔xf8 31 cxd8♕+ **1-0** L/N6013-1844

**1821̂-★CL-1̂**
**Cochrane, J.+ Lewis, W.**
⟨♙f7⟩ 1 e4 ... 2 d4 ♘c6 3 c4 e5 4 d5 ♘ce7 5 ♗g5 ♘f6 6 ♗xf6 gxf6 7 ♕h5+ ♘g6 8 ♘f3 ♗b4+ 9 ♘c3 ♕e7 10 a3 ♗xc3+ 11 bxc3 d6 12 ♘h4 ♕f7 13 ♘xg6 ♕xg6 14 ♕e2 b6 15 ♕e3 ♗d7 16 g3 ♔e7 17 ♗d3 ♖hf8 18 ♔d2 ♖ae8 19 f4 f5 20 c5 ♔d8 21 c6 ♗c8 22 ♖hf1 exf4 23 ♕xf4 ♕h5 24 ♖ae1 ♕xh2+ 25 ♖f2 ♕h5 26 e5 dxe5 27 ♖xe5 ♖xe5 28 ♕xe5 ♕g5+ 29 ♔c2 ♕e7 30 ♕f4 ♕xa3 31 ♖e2 ♗a6 32 ♗xa6 ♕xa6 33 ♕g5+ ♔c8

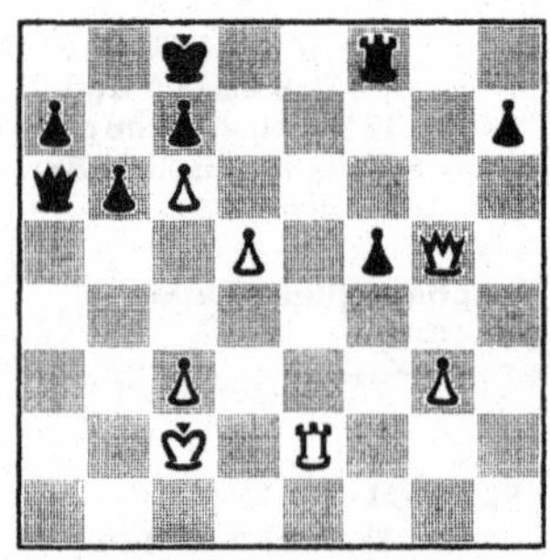

34 ♕xf5+ ♖xf5 35 ♖e8# **1-0** +1

**1821̂-★CL-2̂**
**Cochrane, J.– Lewis, W.**
⟨♙f7⟩ 1 e4 ... 2 d4 ♘c6 3 c4 e5 4 d5 ♘ce7 5 ♗g5 ♘f6 6 ♗xf6 gxf6 7 ♕h5+ ♘g6 8 ♘f3 ♗b4+ 9 ♘c3 ♗xc3+ 10 bxc3 ♕e7 11 ♘h4 ♕f7 12 ♘xg6 ♕xg6 13 ♕xg6+ hxg6 14 ♗d3 d6 15 ♔d2 b6 16 ♖af1 g5 17 f3 ♔e7 18 h3 ♗d7 19 ♖f2 ♖h5 20 ♗e2 ♖h6 21 g3 ♖ah8 22 ♗f1 a5 23 ♖fh2 ♖6h7 24 ♔e3 ♔f7 25 f4 exf4+ 26 gxf4 gxf4+ 27 ♔xf4 ♖h4+ 28 ♔e3 ♖e8 29 ♗d3 ♗f5 30 ♖e1 ♗xe4 31 ♔d2 ♗xd3 32 ♖xe8 ♔xe8 33 ♔xd3 ♔f7 34 a4 f5 35 ♖h1 ♔f6 36 ♖h2 f4 37 ♖f2 ♖xh3+ 38 ♔e4 ♖e3+ 39 ♔xf4 ♖xc3 40 ♔e4+ ♔e7 41 ♔d4 ♖a3 42 ♖e2+ ♔d7 43 ♖h2 ♖xa4 44 ♔c3 ♖a3+ 45 ♔d4 ♖g3 46 ♖h8 ♖a3 47 ♖b8 ♖b3 48 ♖a8 ♖f3 49 ♖a7 ♖f8 50 ♔c3 ♖e8 51 ♖a6 ♖g8 52 ♖a7 ♖g3+ 53 ♔d4 ♔c8 54 ♖a8+ ♔b7 55 ♖f8 a4 56 ♖f2 ♔a6 57 ♖b2 ♖b3 58 ♖xb3 axb3 59 ♔c3 b2 60 ♔xb2 b5 61 ♔c3 bxc4 62 ♔xc4 ♔a5 **0-1** +1

**1821̂-★CL-3̂**
**Cochrane, J.– Lewis, W.**
⟨♙f7⟩ 1 e4 ... 2 d4 ♘c6 3 ♗d3 e5 4 dxe5 ♘xe5 5 ♕h5+ ♘f7 6 ♗c4 ♕e7 7 ♘c3 ♘f6 8 ♗xf7+ ♕xf7 9 ♕xf7+ ♔xf7 10 e5 ♘g4 11 ♘f3 ♗b4 12 h3 ♗xc3+ 13 bxc3 ♘h6 14 ♗xh6 gxh6 15 ♔d2 b6 16 ♖ae1 ♗b7 17 ♘h4 ♗d5 18 a3 ♖hg8 19 ♖hg1 ♖ad8 20 f4 d6 21 ♘f5 ♖xg2+ 22 ♖xg2 ♗xg2 23 e6+ ♔f6 24 e7 ♖e8 25 ♘xh6 ♗xh3 26 f5 ♔g5 27 ♘g8 ♔xf5 28 ♖e3 ♗g4 29 ♖e4 ♗h5 30 ♔e3 ♖xg8 31 ♖f4+ ♔e6 32 ♖f8 ♖g3+ 33 ♔f2 ♔xe7 **0-1**

**1821̂-★♀♀-1**
**♀+♀**
⟨♖a1⟩ 1 e4 e5 2 f4 exf4 3 ♘f3 g5 4 ♗c4 ♗g7 5 h4 h6 6 d4 d6 7 c3 ♗g4 8 ♕b3 ♗xf3 9 ♗xf7+ ♔f8 10 ♗g6 ♕e7 11 ♕xb7 ♗g4 12 ♕xa8 ♕d8 13 0-0 ♘f6 14 e5 ♘fd7 15 ♗xf4 gxf4 16 ♖xf4+ ♔g8 17 ♕d5+ ♗e6 18 ♕xe6# **1-0** +1

**1822̂-★C♀-1**
**Cochrane, J.+♀**
1 e4 e5 2 ♘f3 ♘c6 3 ♗c4 ♗c5 4 c3 ♘f6 5 d4 exd4 6 e5 ♘g4 7 ♗d5 ♘xf2 8 ♗xf7+ ♔xf7 9 ♘g5+ ♔g8 10 ♕b3+ d5 11 exd6+ ♗e6 12 ♕xe6+ ♔f8 13 ♕f7# **1-0** +1

**1822̂-★C♀-2**
**Cochrane, J.+♀**
1 e4 e5 2 ♗c4 ♗c5 3 c3 ♕e7 4 ♘f3 d6 5 0-0 ♘f6 6 d4 ♗b6 7 ♗g5 ♗g4 8 ♘bd2 exd4 9 cxd4 ♗xd4 10 ♕b3 ♗b6 11 e5 dxe5 12 ♘xe5 ♗e6 13 ♖ae1 0-0 14 ♘e4 ♖e8 15 ♘xf7 ♔f8 16 ♘xf6 gxf6 17 ♖xe6 ♕xf7 18 ♗h6+ ♔g8 19 ♖xe8# **1-0** +1

**1822̂-★C♀-3**
**Cochrane, J.+♀**
⟨♘b1⟩ 1 e4 e5 2 ♘f3 d6 3 c3 ♗e6 4 d4 exd4 5 cxd4 c6 6 ♗d3 ♘d7 7 0-0 f6 8 ♘h4 ♗f7 9 f4 g5 10 fxg5 fxg5 11 ♖xf7 ♔xf7 12 ♕h5+ ♔e7 13 ♘f5+ ♔e6 14 ♗c4+ d5 15 exd5+ cxd5 16 ♗xd5+ ♔xd5 17 ♕f3+ ♔e6 18 d5+ ♔f6 19 ♘d6+ ♔g7 20 ♕f7+ ♔h6 21 ♘f5# **1-0** +1

**1822̂-★C♀-4**
**Cochrane, J.+♀**
1 e4 e5 2 ♘f3 ♘c6 3 ♗c4 ♗c5 4 c3 ♕e7 5 0-0 d6 6 a4 a5 7 ♔h1 ♘f6 8 d3 0-0 9 ♗e3 ♗a7 10 ♗xa7 ♖xa7 11 ♘g1 ♘g4 12 h3 ♕h4 13 ♕f3 ♔h8 14 ♘e2 f5 15 exf5 ♗xf5 16 ♘g3 ♘e7 17 ♘xf5 ♘xf5 18 ♕xg4 ♘g3+ 19 ♔g1 ♕xg4 20 hxg4 ♘xf1 21 ♔xf1 c6 22 ♘d2 d5 23 ♗b3 ♖f6 24 ♖e1 ♖e6 25 f4 **1-0** +1

**1822̂-★C♀-5**
**Cochrane, J.+♀**
1 e4 e5 2 ♘f3 ♘c6 3 ♗c4 ♗c5 4 c3 ♕e7 5 0-0 d6 6 ♔h1 ♘f6 7 d4 ♗b6 8 ♗g5 ♗g4 9 h3 ♗xf3 10 ♕xf3 exd4 11 ♗d5 ♘e5 12 ♗xf6 gxf6 13 ♕f5 c6 14 ♗b3 ♘d3 15 ♘d2 dxc3 16 bxc3 ♘c5 17 ♘c4 ♘xb3 18 axb3 ♗c7 19 f4 ♕e6 20 ♕h5 ♔d7

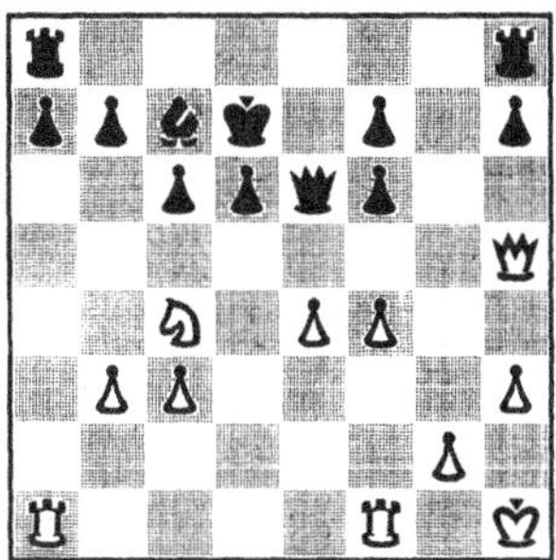

21 e5 d5 22 f5 ♕e8 23 e6+ fxe6 24 fxe6+ ♕xe6 25 ♖ae1 ♗e5 26 ♘xe5+ fxe5 27 ♖xe5 ♖af8 28 ♖xe6 ♖xf1+ 29 ♔h2 ♔xe6 30 ♕e2+ **1-0** +1

**1822̂-★C♀-6**
**♀– Cochrane, J.**

1 e4 e5 2 ♘f3 ♘c6 3 ♗c4 ♗c5 4 c3 ♕e7 5 0-0 d6 6 d3 ♗g4 7 ♗e3 ♗b6 8 h3 ♗h5 9 ♘bd2 ♘f6 10 ♕e1 0-0 11 ♘h2 ♔h8 12 f4 ♗xe3+ 13 ♕xe3 exf4 14 ♖xf4 d5 15 ♗b3 dxe4 16 ♘xe4 ♘xe4 17 ♖xe4 ♕d7 18 d4 ♖ae8 19 ♖e1 ♖xe4 20 ♕xe4 ♗g6 21 ♕f4 ♘a5 22 ♘f3 ♘xb3 23 axb3 f6 24 ♘h4 ♗f7 25 ♕e3 ♗xb3 26 ♕e7 ♕xe7 27 ♖xe7 ♖c8 28 ♘f5 g6 29 ♘e3 b5 30 ♘g4 ♖f8 31 ♖xc7 a5 32 ♘e3 f5 33 ♖a7 f4 34 ♘g4 f3 35 gxf3 ♖xf3 36 ♖xa5 b4 37 ♔g2 bxc3 38 ♔xf3 cxb2 **0-1** +1

**1822̂-★♀♀-1**
**♀+♀**

1 e4 e5 2 f4 exf4 3 ♗c4 ♕h4+ 4 ♔f1 g5 5 ♘f3 ♕g4 6 ♗xf7+ ♔d8 7 ♘c3 c6 8 h3 ♕g3 9 ♘e2 ♕xf3+ 10 gxf3 **1-0** +1

**1822̂-★♀♀-2**
**♀+♀**

1 e4 e5 2 ♗c4 ♗c5 3 c3 ♘f6 4 d4 exd4 5 e5 ♘e4 6 cxd4 ♗b4+ 7 ♔f1 0-0 8 ♗d5 ♘g5 9 f4 c6 10 ♗c4 ♘e6 11 f5 ♘c7 12 ♕g4 d5 13 ♗g5 ♗e7 14 h4 ♗xg5 15 hxg5 dxc4 16 ♖xh7 ♖e8 17 ♕h5 ♔f8 18 f6 **1-0** +1

**1822̂-★♀♀-3**
**♀+♀**

⟨♖a1⟩ 1 e4 e5 2 ♗c4 ♗c5 3 c3 ♕e7 4 ♘f3 c6 5 0-0 d5 6 exd5 e4 7 dxc6 exf3 8 ♖e1 ♗e6 9 ♗xe6 fxe6 10 d4 ♗d6 11 ♕b3 ♕h4 12 g3 ♕h3 13 ♕xe6+ ♕xe6 14 ♖xe6+ ♔f7 15 cxb7 ♔xe6 16 bxa8♕ ♘f6 17 ♗e3 ♘d5 18 c4 ♘xe3 19 fxe3 ♖f8 20 ♔f2 **1-0** +1

**1822̂-★♀♀-4**
**♀+♀**

1 e4 e5 2 f4 exf4 3 ♘f3 g5 4 ♗c4 ♗g7 5 d4 d6 6 c3 ♘c6 7 ♕b3 ♕e7 8 ♘xg5 ♕xg5 9 ♗xf7+ ♔f8 10 ♗xg8 ♖xg8 11 ♗xf4 ♕xg2 12 ♖f1 ♔e7 13 ♗g5+ ♕xg5 14 ♕f7+ ♔d8 15 ♕xg8+ ♔d7 16 ♖f7+ ♘e7 17 ♕xg7 ♕c1+ 18 ♔e2 ♕xb2+ 19 ♘d2 ♕xa1 20 d5 **1-0** +1

## EDINBURGH⚔LONDON ⊠
[1824-⚔EL]

| | | | | | | |
|---|---|---|---|---|---|---|
| Edinburgh | 1 | ½ | ½ | 1 | 1 | 4 |
| London | 0 | ½ | ½ | 0 | 0 | 1 |

**1824-⚔EL-1 ⊠** iv 24-ii 25
**London– Edinburgh**

[Lewis]

1 e4 e5 2 ♘f3 ♘c6 3 d4 exd4 4 ♗c4 ♗c5 5 c3 [5 ♘g5] 5 … ♕e7?! [◻ 5 … d3] 6 0-0 dxc3 [◻ 6 … d3] 7 ♘xc3 d6 8 ♘d5 ♕d7 [8 … ♕d8 9 b4 ♗xb4 (9 … ♘xb4?+–) 10 ♘xb4 ♘xb4 11 ♕b3 ♘c6 12 ♗b2 ♘a5 13 ♕a4+ (13 ♕c3) 13 … c6 14 ♗xg7 b5 15 ♗xb5 cxb5 16 ♕xb5+ ♗d7 17 ♕~, 18 ♗xh8+–; 12 … ♘e5 13 ♘xe5 dxe5 14 ♗xf7+ ♔e7 (14 … ♔f8 15 ♗xg8 ♖xg8 16 ♗a3+ ♔e8 17 ♕xg8++–) 15 ♗a3+ ♔f6 16 ♕f3+ ♔g5 17 h4+ ♔~ 18 ♕h5#; 12 … ♘f6 13 ♗xf7+ ♔f8 (13 … ♔e7 14 e5 d5 15 ♘g5 h6 16 ♗a3+ ♔d7 17 ♘e6+–; 14 … dxe5 15 ♗a3++–; 14 … ♘xe5 15 ♘xe5 dxe5 16 ♗a3++–; 14 … ♘f~ 15 exd6++–) 14 e5 dxe5 15 ♗a3+ ♘e7 16 ♖ad1 ♗d7 17 ♘xe5 ♕c8 18 ♗g6 ♗e6 19 ♖d8+ ♕xd8 20 ♕xe6+–; 14 … ♘xe5 15 ♘xe5 ♕e7 16 ♗g6 ♗e6 (16 … dxe5 17 ♗a3+–; 16 … ♕e6 17 ♕a3 c5 18 ♘f7 ♖g8 19 ♘g5 ♕g4 20 ♕d3+–) 17 ♕xb7 ♗d5 18 ♘c6 ♗xc6 19 ♕xc6 ♖~ 20 ♗d3+–; 14 … ♘d7 15 exd6 ♘c5 16 ♕c3+–; 14 … ♘g8 15 exd6 cxd6 16 ♖fe1 ♗d7 (16 … ♘ge7 17 ♕c3; 16 … ♘ce7 17 ♘g5) 17 ♗xg8 ♖xg8 18 ♘e5 ♘xe5 (18 … dxe5 19 ♗a3+ ♘e7 20 ♖xe5+–; 18 … ♗e8 19 ♕f3++–) 19 ♖xe5 ♖h8 (19 … fxe5 20 ♗a3+) 20 ♕f3+ ♔g8 (20 … ♕f6 21 ♖e8+) 21 ♕d5+ ♔f8 22 ♕xd6++–] 9 b4 ♘xb4 [9 … ♗xb4 10 ♗b2 ♔f8 (10 … ♘f6 11 ♗xf6; 10 … f6 11 ♘xb4 ♘xb4 12 ♗xg8 ♖xg8 13 ♕b3+–) 11 ♘xb4 ♘xb4 12 ♘g5 ♘h6 13 ♕d4 f6 14 ♘e6+ ♔e8 15 ♕d2 ♕e7 (15 … ♘c6 16 ♗xf6) 16 ♘xc7+ ♕xc7 17 ♕xb4±] 10 ♘xb4 ♗xb4 11 ♘g5 ♘h6 12 ♗b2 ♔f8 [12 … 0-0 13 ♕d4+–; 12 … f6 13 ♗xf6 gxf6 14 ♕h5+ ♔d8 (14 … ♔e7 15 ♕xh6 fxg5 16 ♕g7+ ♔d8 17 ♕xh8++–; 14 … ♘f7 15 ♘xf7 ♕g4 16 ♕b5+ ♗d7 17 ♕xb4+–) 15 ♘e6+ ♔e7 16 ♕xh6 ♔e8 17 ♕h5+ ♔e7 18 ♘xc7 ♕xc7 19 ♕f7+ ♔d8 20 ♕xf6+ ♕e7 21 ♕xh8++–] 13 ♕b3 ♕e7 [13 … ♗c5 14 ♕c3 (14 ♗xg7+ ♔xg7 15 ♕b2+ ♔g8 16 ♕f6 d5 17 ♗xd5 ♗f8) 14 … f6 (14 … ♖g8 15 ♘xh7+) 15 ♘e6+ ♔e8 16 ♕g3 ♖g8 17 ♘xc5 dxc5 18 ♗xg8 ♘xg8±; 13 … ♗a5 (13 … c5) 14 ♗xg7+ ♔xg7 15 ♕b2+ ♔g8 16 ♕f6 ♗c3 (16 … ♘g4 17 ♗xf7+, 18 ♕xh8+) 17 ♕xh6! ♗g7 18 ♕h5 ♗xa1 19 ♖xa1 ♔f8 (19 … ♔g7 20 ♘xf7+–; 19 … h6 20 ♘xf7+–; 19 … ♕e7 20 ♕h6+–) 20 ♕h6+ ♔e7 (20 … ♔e8 21 ♗xf7+ ♔e7 22 ♕g7 ♕d8 23 ♗e8+ ♔xe8 24 ♕f7#) 21 ♕g7 ♕e8 (21 … ♖f8 22 ♘xh7 ♕e8 23 ♕f6+ ♔d7 24 ♘xf8+ ♕xf8 25 ♗xf7±) 22 e5 ♕f8 23 ♕f6+ ♔d7 24 ♘xf7 ♖g8 25 e6+ ♔c6 26 ♕f3++–; 15 … f6 16 ♘e6+ ♔g6 17 ♘f4+ ♔g7 18 ♘h5+ ♔f8 (18 … ♔g6 19 ♕xf6+ ♔xh5 20 ♖ad1+–) 19 ♕xf6+ ♘f7 20 ♕g7+ ♔e7 21 ♕xf7+ ♔d8 22 ♕f6++–; 17 … ♔g5 18 h4+ ♔xf4 19 ♕c1+ ♔xe4 (19 … ♔g4 20 ♗e2+ ♔xh4 21 ♕xh6#; 19 … ♔e5 20 f4+ ♔d4 21 ♖d1+ ♔xe4 22 ♗d3+ ♔d4 23 ♕c4+ ♔e3 24 ♕e4#) 20 ♕e3+ ♔f5 21 ♗d3+ ♔g4 22 ♕f3+ ♔xh4 23 g3+ ♔g5 24 ♕f4+ ♔h5 25 ♕h4#] 14 ♘xf7 ♘xf7 15 ♕xb4 ♘e5 [15 … ♕xe4 16 ♖ae1, 17 ♖e3, 18 ♖f3; 18 ♖g3] 16 f4 ♘xc4 17 ♕xc4 ♕f7 18 ♕c3 ♗e6 19 f5 [19 e5] 19 … ♗c4 [19 … ♗xa2+–] 20 ♖f4 [△ 21 e5] 20 … b5 [20 … ♗a6 21 e5 (△ 22 e6) 21 … dxe5 22 ♕xe5 b6 (22 … ♖e8 23 ♕c5+ ♔g8 24 ♖g4+–; 23 … ♖e7 24 f6; 23 … ♕e7 24 ♗xg7+ ♔xg7 25 f6++–; 24 … ♔g8 25 ♕xe7 ♖xe7 26 ♗xh8+–; 22 … ♕f6 23 ♕xf6 gxf6 24 ♗xf6+–; 22 … ♕e7 23 ♗a3! ♕xa3 24 f6 g6 25 f7+–; 24 … gxf6 25 ♖xf6 ♔g8 26 ♕g5#; 24 … g5 25 ♕xg5 ♖g8 26 ♕h6+ ♔f7 27 ♕xh7+ ♔e6 28 ♖e1+ ♔d5 29 ♕f5++–) 23 f6 g6 24 ♖e1 ♔g8 (24 … ♖d8 25 ♕e7+ ♕xe7 26 fxe7++–; 24 … ♖c8 25 ♗a3+ c5 26 ♕d6+, 27 ♖e7; 25 … ♔g8 26 ♕e7 ♕xe7 27 fxe7 ♖e8 28 ♖f8+ ♔g7 29 ♗b2++–) 25 ♕e7 ♖f8 (25 … ♕xe7 26 fxe7, 27 ♖f8+; 25 … ♗c4 26 ♖xc4+–; 25 … h5 26 ♕xf7+ ♔xf7 27 ♖e7+ ♔f8 28 ♖xc7+–) 26 ♕xf7+ ♖xf7 (26 … ♔xf7 27 ♖e7+ ♔g8 28 ♖g7#) 27 ♖e8+ ♖f8 27 f7#] 21 e5 [21 f6] 21 … dxe5 22 ♕xe5 h6 [22 … ♕e7 23 ♗a3 ♕xa3 (23 … b4 24 ♗xb4, 25 f6) 24 f6 g5 25 ♕xg5 ♖g8 26 ♕h6+ ♔f7 (26 … ♔e8 27 f7+ ♗xf7 28 ♕c6+ ♔f8 29 ♖af1 ♖g7 30 ♕xa8++–) 27 ♕xh7+ ♔e6 28 ♖e1+ ♔d5 29 ♕e4+ ♔d6 (29 … ♔c5 30 ♕e7++–) 30 ♕e7++–; 22 … ♕f6 23 ♕xf6 gxf6 24 ♗xf6 ♖g8 25 g4 (25 ♖h4) 25 … ♔f7 26 g5 ♖ge8 27 ♖d1 ♔g8 28 ♖d7 ♖e2 (28 … ♗f7 29 g6) 29 ♖g7+ ♔f8 30 ♖xh7 ♖ae8 31 ♗c3 ♗d5 32 g6 ♖c2 33 f6 ♖xc3 34 ♖h8+ ♗g8 35 ♖xg8+ ♔xg8 36 f7+ ♔f8 37 g7+ ♔xg7 38 fxe8♕+–; 25 … ♖e8 26 g5 h6 27 g6 ♖e2 28 ♖d1 ♗xa2 29 ♖d8+ ♖e8 30 ♖d7 ♖b8 31 g7+ ♔e8 32 ♖e7+ ♔d8 33 ♖e2++–; 25 … c6 26 a4 (26 ♖d1 ♗d5) 26 … a6 27 axb5 ♗xb5 (27 … cxb5 28 ♖d1) 28 g5 a5 29 ♖e4 ♖a7 30 ♖d1 c5 (30 … a4 31 ♖d8+ ♔f7 32 ♖xg8 ♔xg8 33 ♖e8+ ♔f7 34 ♖h8 ♖d7 35 ♖xh7+ ♔e8 36 g6+–) 31 ♖d8+ ♔f7 32 ♖h4 ♖xd8 33 ♖xh7 ♔g8 34 ♖xa7 ♖d1+ 35 ♔g2 ♗d3 36 g6 ♗e4+ 37 ♔g3 ♖d6 38 ♗e5 ♖d8 39 ♖h7+–; 29 … ♗d3 30 ♖e7 ♗xf5 (30 … ♖e8 31 ♖xe8+ ♔xe8 32 ♖xa5) 31 ♖f1 ♗g6 32 ♖b7 a4 33 ♗d4+ ♔e8 34 ♖e1+ ♔d8 35 ♗f6+ ♔c8 36 ♖ee7+–] 23 ♖e1 ♖h7 24 f6 [24 ♕c5+ ♔g8 25 ♖e7 ♕d5 ♖xc4 ♕d1+ (26 … ♕xc4 27 ♕e5 ♕g4+–; 27 … ♖f8+–; 27 … ♕c6+–) 27 ♔f2 bxc4 28 ♕xc4+ ♔h8 29 ♕f7 ♕d2+ (29 … ♕c2+ 30 ♔g3 ♕d3+ 31 ♔h4 ♖g8 32 ♖e8 ♕d8+ 33

♖xd8 ♖xd8 34 ♕g6 ♖b8 35 f6+-) 30 ♔g3 ♕d6+ (30 ... ♕xb2 31 ♖e8++-) 31 ♔h3 ♕d3+ 32 ♔h4+-; 25 ... ♕h5 26 g4 ♕g5 27 ♖xc4 bxc4 28 ♕d5++-; 25 ... ♕f8 26 ♖xc4 bxc4 27 ♕d5+ ♔h8 28 f6 g6 (28 ... gxf6 29 ♗xf6+ ♕xf6 30 ♕xa8++-; 28 ... g5 29 ♖xh7+ ♔xh7 30 ♕f5+ ♔g8 31 ♕g6+ ♔h8 32 f7+-) 29 f7+ ♖g7 30 ♕xa8 ♕xa8 31 ♖e8+ ♔h7 32 ♖xa8 ♖xf7 33 ♖h8#] 24 ... g5 25 ♖f5 a5 26 ♕c5+?! [26 ♗d4] 26 ... ♔g8 27 ♖xg5+ hxg5 28 ♕xg5+ ♔f8 [28 ... ♔h8 29 ♖e7 ♖h5 (29 ... ♕~ 30 f7; 29 ... ♖g8 30 ♖xf7 ♖xg5 31 ♖f8+ ♖g8 32 f7+ ♖g7 33 ♖xg8+ ♔h7 34 ♖xg7++-) 30 ♕xh5+ ♕xh5+ 31 f7+ ♔h7 32 f8♕++-; 28 ... ♖g7 29 fxg7 ♗d3 30 ♕h4 ♗h7 31 ♖f1 ♕c4 (31 ... ♕e6 32 ♖f8+ ♖xf8 33 ♕xh7+ ♔f7 34 g8♕++-; 33 ... ♔xh7 34 gxf8♘+, 35 ♘xe6+-) 32 ♕e7+-; 29 ... ♖e8 30 ♗e5 ♕d5 (30 ... ♕e6 31 ♕h5 a4 32 ♖e4 ♗xa2 33 ♖f4+-) 31 ♕h5 ♖d8 32 ♕h8+ ♔f7 33 g8♕+ ♖xg8 34 ♕f6+ ♔e8 35 ♗d6+ ♔d7 36 ♕e7+ ♔~ 37 ♕xc7#] 29 ♗d4 ♗e6 [29 ... ♖a6 (29 ... ♖d8) 30 ♗c5+ ♖d6 31 ♕f5 ♕d7 (31 ... ♔g8 32 ♗xd6+-; 31 ... ♗e6 32 ♖xe6+-) 32 ♕e4 (△ 33 ♕a8+) 32 ... ♗e6 (32 ... c6 33 ♗xd6++-; 32 ... ♔g8 33 ♗xd6+-) 33 ♗xd6+ cxd6 34 ♕xe6 ♕xe6 35 ♖xe6 ♖d7 36 ♖e2 d5 (36 ... ♔f7 37 ♖f2 ♖c7 38 g4 ♖c5 39 h4 ♖c4 40 g5 ♖xh4 41 g6+ ♔f8 42 g7+ ♔f7 43 ♖g2 ♔g8 44 f7++-; 37 ... ♔g6 38 g4 ♖f7 39 ♖f5 ♖xf6 40 ♖xb5 ♖f4 41 h3 ♖f3 42 ♔g2 ♖a3 43 ♖d5 ♖xa2+ 44 ♔g3 a4 45 ♖xd6+ ♔g7 46 ♔h4+-; 41 ... ♖a4 42 ♖b2 ♔g5 43 ♔g2 ♔h4 44 ♔f3 ♔xh3 45 g5 ♖a3+ 46 ♔f4 ♖a4+ 47 ♔f5 ♔g3 48 ♖b3+ ♔h4 49 g6 ♖g4 50 ♔f6 a4 51 ♖d3 ♖f4+ 52 ♔g7 ♖f2 53 a3 ♔g5 54 ♖d5+ ♔h4 55 ♔h7+-) 37 g4 d4 38 ♖d2 d3 39 ♔f2 ♔f7 40 ♔e3 (40 g5 ♔g6 41 h4 ♖d4 42 ♔g3 b4) 40 ... ♔xf6 41 ♖xd3 ♖c7 (41 ... ♖xd3+ 42 ♔xd3+-) 42 h4 ♖c2 43 ♖d2 ♖c4 44 ♔f3 ♖c3+ 45 ♔e4 ♖c4+ 46 ♖d4 ♖c2 47 ♖d6+ ♔e7 48 ♖d5 ♖xa2 49 ♖xb5 a4 50 ♔f5 a3 51 ♔g6 ♖g2 52 g5 a2 53 ♖a5 ♔f8 54 ♔h6+-] 30 ♕c5+ ♔g8 31 ♕g5+ ♔f8 32 ♗c5+ ♔e8 33 ♕d5 ♖a6 34 ♕b7 ♕h5 35 f7+ [35 ♕xa6=] 35 ... ♔xf7 36 ♖f1+ ♔g6 37 ♕e4+ ♗f5 38 ♕e8+ ♖f7 39 ♕g8+ ♔f6 [39 ... ♖g7 40 ♕e8+ ♔h6 41 ♗e3+ ♖g5 42 ♕xb5 ♗c8 (42 ... ♖g6 43 ♕xf5; 42 ... ♖f6 43 ♖xf5) 43 ♕e5 ♖e6 44 ♕h8+ ♔g6 45 ♕g8+ ♔h6 46 ♕xc8+-] 40 g4 ♖a8 41 ♕xa8 ♕xg4+ 42 ♔h1 ♖d7 43 ♗a3 ♔f7 44 ♕c6 ♖d1 45 ♕xb5 ♕e4+ 46 ♔g1 ♔g6 47 ♕b2 ♕g4+ 48 ♕g2 ♖xg2+ 49 ♔xg2 ♗h3+ 50 ♔xh3 ♖xf1 51 ♗e7 a4 52 a3 ♖f5 **0-1** L/N3371

**1824-✕EL-2☒** iv 24-xii 24
**Edinburgh= London**

[Lewis]

1 e4 e5 2 ♗c4 ♗c5 3 c3 ♕e7 4 ♘f3 d6 5 d3 ♘f6 6 ♕e2 [□6 0-0] 6 ... 0-0 7 ♗g5 h6 [□7 ... ♘c6] 8 ♗h4 ♗e6 9 ♗b3 ♗xb3 10 axb3 ♘c6 11 ♘bd2 ♕e6 12 b4 ♗b6 13 ♗xf6 ♕xf6 14 ♘c4 ♕e6 [□14 ... ♘e7 △ 15 ... ♘g6; 15 ... ♕e6] 15 ♘h4 ♘e7 16 g4 ♘g6 [□16 ... d5] 17 ♘xg6 [□17 ♘g2] 17 ... fxg6 18 0-0 ♖f4 19 h3 ♖af8 20 ♘xb6 axb6 21 f3 ♕f6 22 ♔g2 c6 23 ♖f2 b5 24 ♕e3 h5 25 ♔g3 ♕g5 26 ♖e1 ♔h7 27 ♕e2 ♖h8 28 ♕e3 ♔g8 29 ♖h2 hxg4 30 hxg4 [30 fxg4 ♕h4+, 31 ... ♖xg4-+] 30 ... ♖xf3+ 31 ♔xf3 [31 ♕xf3-+] 31 ... ♕xe3+ 32 ♔xe3 [32 ♖xe3-+] 32 ... ♖xh2 33 ♖a1 [33 ♖e2 ♖h3+] 33 ... ♖h3+ [33 ... ♖xb2=] 34 ♔e2 ♖h2+ [34 ... ♖g3, 35 ... ♖xg4=] 35 ♔e3 ♖h3+ **½-½** L/N3371

**1824-✕EL-3☒** xii 24-iii 28
**Edinburgh= London**

[Lewis]

1 e4 e5 2 ♘f3 ♘c6 3 d4 exd4 4 ♗c4 ♗b4+ 5 c3 dxc3 6 0-0 d6 7 a3 ♗c5 8 b4 ♗b6 9 ♕b3 ♕f6 10 ♘xc3 ♗e6 11 ♘d5 ♗xd5 12 ♗xd5 [12 exd5 ♘e5 13 ♗b5+ ♔f8 (13 ... c6 14 dxc6±; 13 ... ♘d7 14 ♖e1++-) 14 ♘xe5 ♕xe5=] 12 ... ♘ge7 13 ♗g5 [13 ♗b2 ♕g6 14 ♘h4 ♕h5 15 ♗xg7 (□ 15 ♗xc6+ ♘xc6 16 ♘f5 0-0-0 17 ♘xg7±; 15 ... bxc6 16 ♗xg7 ♖g8 17 ♗f6±) 15 ... ♖g8 16 ♗f6 ♗d4 17 ♗xc6+ ♘xc6 18 ♗xd4 ♘xd4 19 ♕c4 (19 ♕d3 ♘e6 20 ♘f5 ♖xg2+=) 19 ... ♘e6 20 ♘f5 ♖xg2+ 21 ♔xg2 ♘f4+ 22 ♔g3 (22 ♔h1-+; 22 ♔g1 ♕g4+ 23 ♘g3 ♕f3-+) 22 ... ♘e2+ 23 ♔g2 ♕g4+ 24 ♘g3 ♘f4+ 25 ♔g1 ♕f3-+] 13 ... ♕g6 14 ♗xe7 ♔xe7 15 a4 a5 16 b5 ♖ab8 17 ♘h4 [17 bxc6 bxc6 △ 18 ... ♗xf2+] 17 ... ♕f6 18 ♘f5+ ♔f8 19 ♖ac1 [19 bxc6 bxc6 20 ♖ab1 cxd5 (20 ... ♗xf2+ 21 ♖xf2 ♖xb3 22 ♖xb3 ♕d8 23 ♖fb2 cxd5 24 ♖b8 ♕e8 25 ♖xe8 ♔xe8 26 ♖b8++-; 23 ... ♔e8 24 ♗xc6+; 25 ♖b8+-) 21 ♕xd5 g6 22 ♘e3 ♔g7±] 19 ... ♘e5 20 ♔h1 h5 21 g3 g6 22 ♘h4 ♘g4 23 h3 g5 24 ♘f3 [24 hxg4 hxg4 25 ♔g2 gxh4 26 gxh4 ♕xh4 27 ♕g3 ♕h3+ 28 ♕xh3 gxh3+ 29 ♔h2+-] 24 ... c6 25 ♗c4 ♖h7 26 ♔g2 ♔g7 27 ♗e2 [27 hxg4 hxg4 28 ♘d2 ♖h2+ 29 ♔xh2 (29 ♔g1 ♖bh8-+) 29 ... ♕h6+ 30 ♔g2 ♕h3+; 31 ... ♖h8-+; 27 ♗xf7 ♕xf7 (27 ... ♖f8 28 ♗e6 ♘e5 29 ♘xe5 ♕xe5 30 ♗f5 ♖h6 31 bxc6+-) 28 ♕xf7+ ♔xf7 29 hxg4 ♔g6 30 gxh5+ ♖xh5 31 bxc6 bxc6 32 ♖xc6±] 27 ... ♘e5 28 ♘xg5 ♕xg5 29 f4 ♕g6 30 fxe5 ♕xe4+ 31 ♗f3 ♕e3 32 ♕b1 ♔h8 [32 ... h4 33 ♖ce1 ♕c3 34 ♕f5 dxe5 35 ♗e4 (35 gxh4 ♕d2+ 36 ♖e2 ♕f4 37 ♕g5+ ♔h8 38 ♗e4 ♕xh4 39 ♕xh4 ♖xh4 40 ♖xf7 ♖g8+∓) 35 ... ♖h6 (35 ... ♕xg3+ 36 ♔h1+-) 36 ♕g5+ ♖g6 37 ♗xg6 fxg6 38 ♕f6+ ♔h7 39 ♕xh4++-] 33 ♖ce1 ♕g5 34 h4 ♕g7 35 ♗e4 ♖h6 36 ♖f5 dxe5 37 ♖g5 ♕f8 38 ♕c1 ♗d8 [38 ... ♕c5 39 ♖g8+ ♔xg8 40 ♕xh6 ♕f2+ 41 ♔h3 ♗c7 (41 ... ♕xe1 42 ♗h7++-) 42 ♗h7+ ♔h8 43 ♗d3+ ♔g8 44 ♖f1+-] 39 ♖xe5 ♗f6 40 ♖f5 ♖e8 41 bxc6 bxc6 42 ♖xa5 ♔g7 43 ♖c5 ♖e6 44 ♕c4 ♕e7 45 ♖e3 [45 a5 ♗xh4 46 gxh4 (46 a6 ♗xg3) 46 ... ♕xh4 47 ♕c3+ (47 ♖e2 ♖hg6+ 48 ♗xg6 ♖xg6+ 49 ♔f1 ♕h1+ 50 ♔f2 ♕g1+ 51 ♔f3 ♖g3+ 52 ♔e4 ♖g4+-+; 47 ♖e3 ♖hg6+ 48 ♗xg6 ♖xg6+ 49 ♔f1 ♖f6+ 50 ♔e2 ♕f2+∓; 47 ♖e3 ♖hg6+ 48 ♔f3 ♖g3+=; 48 ♔f1 ♖ef6+=) 47 ... ♔g8 48 ♖c4 ♖hg6+ 49 ♗xg6 (49 ♔f1 ♖gf6+) 49 ... ♖xg6+ 50 ♔f1 ♕h1+ 51 ♔e2 ♖e6+ 52 ♔d1 ♖xe1+ 53 ♕xe1 ♕d5+=] 45 ... ♕a7 46 ♖e2 ♖d6 47 a5 ♖d1 [47 ... ♖d4 48 ♕c1 ♖a4 (48 ... ♖d1 49 ♕e3) 49 ♖g5+ ♗xg5 (49 ... ♔h8 50 ♖g8+ ♔xg8 51 ♕xh6+-) 50 ♕xg5+ ♖g6 51 ♗xg6+-] 48 ♗f3 [48 ♖xc6 (48 a6 ♖d4) 48 ... ♕g1+ 49 ♔h3 ♗e5 50 ♖g2 ♕h1+ 51 ♖h2 ♖g1 52 ♗xh1 ♖xg3#; 52 ♖xh1 ♖xg3+=; 50 ♗g2 ♖d4 51 ♕c1 (51 ♕b3 ♖xc6-+) 51 ... ♖xh4+ 52 ♔xh4 ♕h2+ 53 ♔g5 ♖xc6 54 ♗xc6 (54 ♕xc6 ♕xg3+ 55 ♔xh5 ♕h2+ 56 ♔~ ♕f4+ 57 ♔h5 ♗f6-+) 54 ... ♕xe2 55 ♗d7 (55 ♔f5 f6-+) 55 ... f6+ 56 ♔h4 ♕h2+ 52 ♗h3 ♕xg3+-+] 48 ... ♗d4 [48 ... ♖a1 49 ♗xh5 ♖xh5 (49 ... ♖xa5 50 ♖xa5+-) 50 ♕g4++- (50 ♖xh5 ♕g1+ 51 ♔h3 ♕f1+ 52 ♔g4 ♖a4 53 ♖g5+ ♗xg5 54 ♕xa4 ♕xe2+ 55 ♔xg5 f6+ 56 ♔f5 ♕e5+ 57 ♔g4 ♕e2+ 58 ♔f4 ♕f2+ 59 ♔e4 ♕xg3=)] 49 ♖g5+ ♖g6 50 ♕xc6 ♗f6 [50 ... ♗e3 51 ♖xg6+ fxg6 52 ♗e4 ♕f7 (52 ... ♕xa5 53 ♕xg6+ ♔f8 54 ♕f6+ ♔g8 55 ♔h3+-; 55 ♗g6? ♕d5+ 56 ♔h3 ♖h1+ 57 ♖h2 ♖xh2+ 58 ♔xh2 ♗g1+ 59 ♔xg1 ♕g2+ 60 ♔xg2◇) 53 ♕xg6+ ♕xg6 54 ♗xg6 ♗c5 (54 ... ♔xg6 55 ♖xe3+-) 55 ♖e6 (55 ♗xh5 ♖a1) 55 ... ♖a1 56 a6+-] 51 ♖xg6+ [□51 ♕b6 ♕xb6 (51 ... ♖d7 52 ♖xg6+ fxg6 53 ♖e6 ♖d2+ 54 ♔h1 ♕f7 55 ♗e4) 52 ♖xg6+ fxg6 53 axb6 ♖b1 (53 ... ♖d8 54 b7 ♔f7 55 ♗d5+ ♔f8 56 ♖e6 ♔g7 57 ♗e4 ♔f7 58 ♖c6+-) 54 b7 ♗d4 (54 ... ♗d8 55 ♖e8 ♗c7 ♖e7++-; 54 ... ♔f8 55 ♖e6 ♔f7 56 ♗d5 ♔g7 57 ♖e8+-) 55 ♖e8 ♗a7 56 ♖a8+-] 51 ... fxg6 52 ♕b6 [52 ♖f2 ♖h1 53 ♔xh1 (53 ♕b6 ♕xb6 54 axb6 ♖b1 55 b7 ♗e5=; 53 ♕b7+ ♕xb7 54 ♗xb7 ♖a1 55 a6 ♗d4=) 53 ... ♕xf2; 54 ... ♗d4=] 52 ... ♕f7 [52 ... ♕xb6 53 axb6±] 53 ♖c2 ♖d7 54 ♗c6 ♕e6 55 ♔h2 ♖d4 56 ♕a7+ [56 ♕b7+ ♔h6 57 ♗f3 ♕e5 58 a6 ♗xh4 59 ♖g2 ♖d2 60 a7 (60 ♖xd2 ♕xg3+ 61 ♔h1 ♕e1+ 62 ♔h2 ♕xd2+ 63 ♔h3 ♕f4 64 ♔g2 ♕g3+ 65 ♔h1 ♕e1+ 66 ♔h2 ♕f2+ 67 ♗g2 ♕g3+ 68 ♔g1 ♕e1+ 69 ♔h2 ♗g3+-+; 69 ♗f1 ♕f2+ 70 ♔h1 ♕xf1+ 71 ♔h2 ♕f2+ 72 ♕g2 ♗g3+ 73 ♔h1 ♕xg2+ 74 ♔xg2 ♗b8-+; 63 ♗g2 ♕f4+ 64 ♔h1=; 64 ♔g1 ♕e3+ 65 ♔h2 ♕g3+ 66 ♔g1 ♕e1+-+) 60 ... ♕xg3+ 61 ♔h1 ♖xg2 62 ♗xg2 ♕e1+ 63 ♔h2 ♗g3+ 64 ♔h3 ♗d6 65 ♕b3 g5 66 ♗d5 (66 ♗e4 ♕xe4 67 ♕d1 g4+ 68 ♕xg4 ♕xg4#) 66 ... ♕f2-+] 56 ... ♔h6 57 ♗f3 ♕e3 58 ♕f7 ♖d2+ 59 ♖xd2 ♕xd2+ 60 ♔h3 ♕f2 61 ♗g2 ♗d4 62 ♕f4+ ♔g7 63 ♗e4 ♗a7 64 ♗d3 ♗d4 65 ♗c4 ♔h7 66 a6 ♔g7 67 ♕e4 ♕f6 68 ♕f4 ♗b6 69 ♔g2 ♗d4 70 ♗d3 ♗a7 71 ♔h2 ♕b2+ 72 ♔h3 ♕f6 73 ♕e4 ♗d4 74 ♕d5 ♗a7 75 ♗c4 ♗d4 76 ♕g8+ ♔h6 77 ♗d3 ♗a7 78 ♗e4

♗d4 79 ♕c8 ♔g7 80 ♕d7+ ♔h6 81 ♗g2 ♕f2 82 ♕b5 ♔g7 83 ♗e4 ♕f6 84 ♕d3 ♕e6+ 85 ♔h2 ♕a2+ 86 ♗g2 ♕f2 87 ♔h3 ♕f6 88 ♗f3 ♕e6+ 89 ♔h2 ♕e3 90 ♕d1 ♕f2+ 91 ♗g2 ♗e5 92 ♕d3 ♕d4 93 ♕e4 ♕xe4 94 ♗xe4 ♗b8 95 ♔g2 ♔f6 96 ♔f3 ♗a7 97 ♗c6 ♗b6 98 ♗e8 ♗a7 99 ♔e4 ♗b6 **½-½** L/N3371

**1824-✕EL-4☒** ii 25 - ix 26
**Edinburgh+London**
[Lewis]

1 e4 e5 2 ♗c4 ♗c5 3 c3 ♕e7 4 d3 d6 5 ♘f3 ♗b6 6 0-0 ♗g4 7 ♗e3 ♘d7 8 ♘bd2 ♘gf6 9 h3 ♗h5 10 ♕c2 ♗xf3 11 ♘xf3 ♘h5 12 a4 a5 13 ♗a2 h6 14 ♗xb6 ♘xb6 15 ♔h2 g5 16 g3 ♘d7 17 ♘g1 ♕f6 18 d4 ♕g6 19 ♘f3 ♘hf6 20 ♘d2 h5 21 ♔g2 b6 22 ♕d3 0-0 23 ♔h2 ♔h8 24 ♖ae1 d5 25 ♗b1 ♖ae8 26 ♕b5 c6 27 ♕b3 dxe4 28 dxe5 ♘xe5 29 f4? gxf4 30 ♖xf4 ♖d8! 31 ♘f1 [31 ♖d1 ♘d3 32 ♗xd3 (32 ♖ff1 e3) 32 ... ♖xd3 33 ♘f1 e3 34 ♖xd3 (34 ♕c2 ♖e8 35 ♖xd3 e2) 34 ... ♕xd3 35 ♘xe3 ♕xe3 36 ♖f6 ♖g8 37 g4 ♕e5+→; 31 ♖e2 (31 ♖f2 ♖xd2 32 ♖xd2 ♘f3+) 31 ... ♖g8 32 ♘f1 ♘f3+ 33 ♖xf3 (33 ♔g2 ♕g5) 33 ... exf3 34 ♗xg6 fxe2→] 31 ... ♖d3 32 ♕xb6 [32 ♗xd3 ♘xd3 33 ♖e3 ♘xf4 34 gxf4 ♕f5 35 ♕d1 ♕xf4+ 36 ♔h1 ♖g8→; 32 ♖e3 ♖xe3 33 ♘xe3 ♖g8 34 ♘f1 (34 ♘f5 ♘d5→) 34 ... ♕g5 35 h4 (35 ♗xe4 ♘xe4 36 ♖xe4 ♕f5→) 35 ... ♕xf4 36 gxf4 ♘f3+ 37 ♔h3 ♘d5→; 32 ♔g2 ♘f3 33 ♖e2 ♘d4 34 ♕a3 ♘xe2 35 ♕xf8+ ♔h7 36 ♖f2 ♘xg3→; 32 ♔h1 ♖xg3 33 ♘xg3 ♕xg3 34 ♖ef1 ♘f3 35 ♖~xf3 exf3→] 32 ... ♘f3+ 33 ♖xf3 ♖xf3 34 ♕d4 ♔h7 35 ♔g2 [35 ♖xe4 ♖xf1 36 ♖e1 ♖xe1 37 ♗xg6 fxg6 38 g4 ♘e4→] 35 ... ♖e8 36 ♕g1 h4 37 g4 ♘d5 38 ♕d4 ♘f4+ 39 ♔h1 ♘xh3 40 ♘h2 [40 ♗xe4 ♖xe4 41 ♖xe4 ♖d3 (41 ... ♘f2+; 42 ... ♘xe4±; 41 ... ♖xf1+±) 42 ♕c4 (42 ♕e5 ♘f2+) 42 ... ♕f6→] 40 ... ♘f2+ 41 ♔g1 [41 ♔g2 h3+ 42 ♔g1 ♘xg4 43 ♘xf3 (43 ♖xe4 ♘xh2+ 44 ♖g4 ♕xb1+→; 43 ♗xe4 ♖xe4 44 ♕xe4 ♖g3+ 45 ♔f1 ♘xh2+→] 41 ... h3 42 ♔f1 [42 ♘xf3 ♕xg4+ 43 ♔f1 ♘d3→; 42 ♖e2 ♘xg4 43 ♘xf3 ♘e5+ 44 ♔h1 (44 ♔f1 ♘xf3 45 ♗xe4 ♖xe4 46 ♕xe4 ♘d2+→; 44 ♔f2 ♕g2+ 45 ♔e3 ♕xf3+ 46 ♔d2 ♕f4+ 47 ♔d1 ♕f1+ 48 ♖e1 ♕xe1+ 49 ♔xe1 ♘f3+→) 44 ... ♘xf3 45 ♗xe4 (45 ♕e3 f5 46 ♗a2 ♖e7→) 45 ... f5 46 ♕d7+ ♔h8 47 ♕xe8+ ♕xe8 48 ♗xf3 ♕g6 49 ♔h2 (49 ♖h2 ♕g3→) 49 ... f4 50 ♗e4 ♕g3+ 51 ♔h1 f3 52 ♖c2 ♕e1+→] 42 ... ♘d3+ 43 ♔e2 c5! [43 ... ♖f2+ 44 ♔d1 ♖xh2 45 ♗xd3 (46 ♖xe4→) 45 ... ♕xg4+ 46 ♗e2 ♖xe2 47 ♖xe2 h2→; 46 ♖e2 exd3 47 ♕xd3+ (47 ♕xg4 dxe2→) 47 ... ♔g7→; 46 ♔c1 exd3 47 ♖xe8 (47 ♕xd3+ ♔g7 48 ♖xe8 ♖h1+ 49 ♔c2 ♕xa4+ 50 ♔d2 ♖d1+→) 47 ... ♖h1+ 48 ♔d2 ♖d1+ 49 ♔e3 ♕g3+ 50 ♔e4 ♖e1+→] 44 ♕g1 [44 ♕c4 (44 ♕d5 ♘f4+) 44 ... ♖f2+ 45 ♔d1 ♘xb2+ 46 ♔c1 ♕g5+ 47 ♖e3 ♕xe3♯] 44 ... ♖f2+ 45 ♕xf2 ♘xf2 46 ♔xf2 ♕d6 47 ♘f3 ♕f4 48 ♖xe4 [48 ♗xe4+ ♔g7] 48 ... ♖xe4 49 ♗xe4+ ♔g7 50 ♗c6 [◻ 50 ♗b7] 50 ... h2 51 ♔g2 ♕h6 52 ♘xh2 ♕xc6+ 53 ♘f3 ♕xa4 54 ♔g3 ♕b3 55 ♘d4 cxd4 **0-1** L/N3371

**1824-✕EL-5** x 26 - vii 28
**Edinburgh+London**
[Lewis]

1 e4 e5 2 ♘f3 ♘c6 3 d4 ♘xd4 4 ♘xd4 [4 ♘xe5] 4 ... exd4 5 ♕xd4 ♘e7 6 ♗c4 ♘c6 7 ♕d5 ♕f6 8 ♘c3? [◻ 8 0-0] 8 ... ♗b4 9 ♗d2 d6 10 ♗b5 ♗d7 11 ♕c4 ♗c5 12 0-0 0-0 13 ♕d3 [13 ♘d5 ♕h4 14 ♘xc7 (14 ♗xc6 ♗xc6 15 ♘xc7 ♖ac8 16 ♘d5 a6) 14 ... ♖ac8 15 ♘d5 (15 ♗xc6 ♖xc7!) 15 ... ♘e5 16 ♕e2 (16 ♕b3 ♘g4 17 ♗f4 ♗xf2+ 18 ♔h1 ♗xb5 19 ♕xb5 ♘xh2→) 16 ... ♗g4 17 ♕e1 ♘f3+ 18 gxf3 ♗xf3→] 13 ... ♘e5 14 ♕g3 ♗xb5 15 ♘xb5 c6 16 ♘c3 ♘c4 17 ♗g5 ♕g6 18 b3 f6 19 ♗c1 ♕xg3 20 hxg3 ♗d4 21 bxc4 ♗xc3 22 ♖b1 b6 23 ♖d1 ♖ae8 24 ♖b3 ♗a5 25 f3 f5 26 exf5 ♖e2?! [◻ 26 ... ♖xf5] 27 g4 ♖xc2 28 ♗f4 ♖xc4 29 ♗xd6 ♖e8 30 ♖a3 h6 31 ♗c7 ♖e7 32 ♖d8+ ♔h7 33 ♖c8 ♖c1+ [33 ... ♗b4 34 ♖xa7 (34 ♖d3 ♖d4 35 ♖xd4 ♗c5=) 34 ... ♗d6 35 ♖aa8 (35 ♗xd6 ♖xa7; 35 f4 ♗xf4; 35 g3 ♖c2) 35 ... ♖c1+ 36 ♔f2 ♖c2+=] 34 ♔h2 ♖ee1 35 ♔h3 ♖h1+ 36 ♗h2 ♗c3 [36 ... ♗d2 37 f4 (37 ♖a4 ♗e3 38 ♖e4 ♗g1 39 ♖ee8+-; 37 ♖xa7 ♗f4 38 g3 ♖c2 39 g5 ♖cxh2+ 40 ♔g4 hxg5 41 f6 ♔g6 42 ♖xg7+ ♔xf6 43 ♖8c7 ♖h4+ 44 gxh4 ♖xh4♯) 37 ... ♗xf4 38 g3 ♖c2 39 gxf4 ♖cxh2+ 40 ♔g3 ♖h3+ 41 ♔g2 ♖xa3 42 ♔xh1 ♖g3∓] 37 f4 [37 ♖xa7 ♗e5 38 f4 (38 g3 ♖c2) 38 ... ♖c3+ (38 ... ♗xf4=) 39 g3 ♖c2 40 g5 ♖hxh2+ 41 ♔g4 h5+ 42 ♔f3 ♖c3+ 43 ♔e4 ♖e2♯] 37 ... ♗d2 [37 ... ♗d4 38 g5 (38 ♖xa7 ♗g1 39 g5 ♖c3+ 40 ♔g4 h5+ 41 ♔xh5 ♖xh2+ 42 ♔g4 ♖xg2+ 43 ♔h4 ♗f2+ 44 ♔h5 ♖h3♯) 38 ... hxg5 39 fxg5 ♗e5 (39 ... ♗g1 40 ♔g4+-) 40 g3 ♖c2 (40 ... ♖hf1 41 ♔g4 ♖c4+ 42 ♔h5 ♖xf5 43 g4 g6+ 44 ♔h4 a5 45 ♖e3 ♗g7 46 ♖e7+-) 41 ♖a4 ♖xh2+ 42 ♔g4+-] 38 g3 ♗a5 [38 ... ♖c2 39 g5+-] 39 ♖e3! ♖c2 40 g5 ♖hxh2+ 41 ♔g4 h5+ 42 ♔f3 ♖hf2+ 43 ♔e4 g6 44 ♖c7+ ♔g8 45 ♔e5 ♖c5+ [45 ... ♗c3+ 46 ♖xc3; 47 ♔f6+-] 46 ♔f6 ♖xf5+ 47 ♔xg6 ♖f8 48 ♖g7+ ♔h8 49 ♔h6 ♗b4 [49 ... ♖d8 (49 ... ♖d2 50 ♖e6 ♖fd8 51 ♖h7+ ♔g8 52 ♖g6+ ♔f8 53 ♖gg7+-) 50 ♖ee7 ♗c3 (50 ... ♖d6+ 51 g6) 51 ♖g6+-] 50 ♖e6 ♖f5 51 ♖h7+ ♔g8 52 ♖g6+

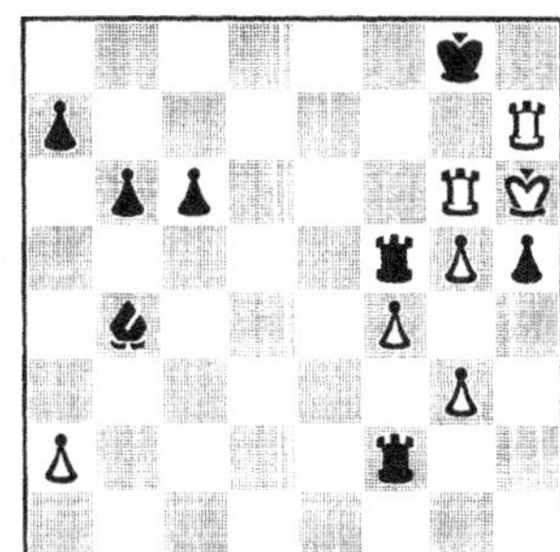

[52 g6 ♗f8+ (52 ... ♖g2 53 g7 ♖xg3 54 ♖g6 ♖xg6+ 55 ♔xg6 ♖f6+ 56 ♔xf6 ♔xh7 57 ♔f7+-; 53 ... ♔f7 54 ♖g6 ♗f8 55 ♖xc6 ♗e7 56 g8♕+ ♔xg8 57 ♖g7+ ♔h8 58 ♖xe7+-) 53 g7 ♗xg7+ 54 ♖xg7+ ♔f8 55 ♖ee7 ♖f6+ 56 ♔h7 ♖d2 57 ♖xa7 ♔e8 58 ♖a8+ ♖d8 59 ♖g8+ ♖f8 60 ♖xf8+ ♔xf8 61 ♖xd8++-; 55 ... h4 56 ♔g6+-] 52 ... ♔f8 53 ♖xc6 ♖c5 54 ♖f6+ ♔e8 55 g6 ♖c3 56 g4 ♗f8+ 57 ♖xf8+ ♔xf8 58 g7+ [58 ♖h8+ ♔e7 59 g7 ♖c6+ 60 ♔g5 (60 ♔h7 ♖xf4 61 ♖e8+ ♔xe8 62 g8♕+ ♔e7=; 60 ♔xh5 ♔f6 61 ♖h6+ ♔xg7 62 ♖xc6 ♖xf4 63 ♖c7+ ♖f7=) 60 ... ♖c5+ 61 f5 (61 ♔h4 ♖xf4 62 ♖e8+ ♔xe8 63 g8♕+ ♔e7=) 61 ... hxg4 62 g8♕ ♖cxf5+ 63 ♔h4 (63 ♔xg4=) 63 ... ♖h2+ 64 ♔xg4 ♖xh8=] 58 ... ♔f7 59 ♖h8 ♖c6+ 60 ♔h7 **1-0** L/N3371

**1826-★C♀-1**
**♀– Cochrane, J.**

1 e4 e6 2 ♘f3 d5 3 e5 c5 4 d4 ♘c6 5 ♗b5 ♕b6 6 ♗xc6+ bxc6 7 ♗e3 ♕xb2 8 ♘bd2 ♗a6 9 dxc5 ♕b7 10 ♘b3 ♘e7 11 ♘bd4 ♕c7 12 ♘e2 ♘f5 13 ♕d2 ♗e7 14 0-0 0-0 15 ♖fe1 ♘xe3 16 ♕xe3 ♕a5 17 ♕c3 ♕xc3 18 ♘xc3 ♗xc5 19 ♘a4 ♗b6 20 ♖ab1 ♖ab8 21 ♘xb6 ♖xb6 22 ♖xb6 axb6 23 ♖b1 b5 24 ♘d4 ♖c8 25 f4 ♔f8 26 g4 ♔e7 27 h4 g6 28 ♔f2 ♔d7 29 ♔e3 ♖b8 30 ♘b3 ♔c7 31 ♘c5 ♗c8 32 c3 ♖a8 33 ♖b2 ♖a3 34 ♔d4 b4 35 cxb4 ♖f3 36 ♘d3 ♗a6 37 ♘c5 ♗c4 38 f5 gxf5 39 gxf5 ♖f4+ 40 ♔e3 ♖xf5 41 a4 ♖xe5+ 42 ♔d4 ♖f5 43 ♖g2 e5+ 44 ♔e3 ♖f1 45 ♖g7 d4+ 46 ♔d2 ♔d6 47 ♖xh7 ♔d5 48 a5 e4 49 ♖h5+ f5 50 ♖h7 e3+ 51 ♔c2 d3+ 52 ♔b2 ♖f2+ 53 ♔b1 ♔d4 54 ♖d7+ ♔c3 **0-1** +1

**1826-★EM-1**
**Evans, W.D.+Macdonnell, A.**
London

1 e4 e5 2 ♘f3 ♘c6 3 ♗c4 ♗c5 4 0-0 d6 5 b4 ♗xb4 6 c3 ♗a5 7 d4 ♗g4 8 ♕b3 ♕d7 9 ♘g5 ♘d8 10 dxe5 dxe5 11 ♗a3 ♘h6 12 f3 ♗b6+ 13 ♔h1 ♗h5 14 ♖d1 ♕c8 15 ♖xd8+ ♕xd8 16 ♘xf7 ♕h4 17 ♕b5+ c6

18 ♕xe5+ ♔d7 19 ♕e6+ ♔c7 20 ♗d6# **1-0** L/N6135-1928

**1827-★LW-1**
**Lewis, W.– Walker, G.**
⟨♖a1⟩ 1 e4 e5 2 f4 d5 3 exd5 exf4 4 ♘f3 ♗g4 5 ♗e2 ♗d6 6 0-0 ♗xf3 7 ♗xf3 ♘f6 8 ♖e1+ ♗e7 9 ♕e2 c6 10 ♘c3 g5 11 d4 g4 12 ♗xg4 ♘xg4 13 ♕xg4 ♔f8 14 ♗xf4 h5 15 ♕g3 cxd5 16 ♕e3 ♘c6 17 ♗h6+ ♖xh6 18 ♕xh6+ ♔g8 19 ♖e3 h4 20 ♕h5 ♗g5 21 ♖f3 ♕e7 22 ♕g4 ♘xd4 23 ♖f1 ♘xc2 24 ♘xd5 ♕c5+ 25 ♖f2 ♕xd5 26 ♖xc2 ♖d8 27 ♖c1 ♕d2 28 ♖f1 ♕d4+ **0-1** +1

**1828-★L?-1** 19 vii 28
**Lewis, W.– ?**
⟨♘b1⟩ 1 e4 e5 2 ♘f3 d5 3 ♘xe5 dxe4 4 ♗c4 ♗e6 5 ♗xe6 fxe6 6 ♕h5+ ♔e7 7 ♘g6+ hxg6 8 ♕xh8 ♘h6 9 0-0 ♕d5 10 d3 ♘d7 11 dxe4 ♕xe4 12 ♗xh6 gxh6 13 ♖ae1 ♕h4 14 ♕c3 c5 15 b4 b6 16 bxc5 bxc5 17 ♖e3 e5 18 f4 e4 19 ♕d3 ♘f6 20 ♖d1 ♕xf4 21 h3 ♔f7 22 ♕c4+ ♔g7 23 ♕e2 h5 24 g3 ♕g5 25 h4 ♕g4 26 ♕xg4 hxg4 27 ♖b1 ♗d6 28 ♖b7+ ♔g8 29 c4 ♗e5 30 ♔g2 ♗d4 31 ♖e1 e3 32 ♖c7 ♘e4 33 ♖e7 ♘c3 34 ♖1xe3 ♗xe3 35 ♖xe3 ♘xa2 36 ♖e7 a5 37 ♖c7 a4 38 ♖xc5 ♘c3 39 ♖e5 a3 40 ♖e1 a2 41 ♖a1 ♖b8 42 c5 ♖b1 **0-1**
L/N6123-1845

**1828-★L?-2**
**Lewis, W.– ?**
⟨♘g1⟩ 1 e4 e5 2 ♗c4 ♗c5 3 ♕e2 d6 4 f4 ♕e7 5 c3 ♘f6 6 h3 ♗e6 7 ♗b5+ ♗d7 8 a4 c6 9 ♗d3 exf4 10 b4 ♗b6 11 ♗c2 0-0 12 d4 d5 13 e5 ♘e4 14 ♗xe4 dxe4 15 ♕xe4 ♕h4+ 16 ♔f1 ♗e6 17 ♗xf4 g5 18 g3 ♕h5 19 ♗e3 ♗c4+ 20 ♔g1 ♕d1+ 21 ♔h2 ♕e2+ 22 ♔g1 ♗d5 **0-1** L/N6123-1845

**1828̂-★L?-1**
**Lewis, W.– ?**
[Staunton]
⟨♘g1⟩ 1 e4 e6 2 ♗e2 d5 3 exd5 ♕xd5 4 0-0 ♕d8 5 d4 ♗e7 6 c4 ♘f6 7 ♗e3 ♘bd7 8 f4 c6 9 ♘d2 c5 10 f5 cxd4 11 fxe6 ♘e5 12 exf7+ ♘xf7 13 ♗f4 0-0 14 ♗d3 ♗d6 15 ♕c2 ♗xf4 16 ♖xf4 ♕d6 17 ♖af1 ♗d7 18 ♖xf6 gxf6 19 ♘e4 ♕e7 20 ♘xf6+ ♔h8 21 ♘xh7 ♗c6 22 ♘f6 ♖g8! 23 ♖f2 ♕e3 24 ♗f1 [△ 25 ♕h7#] 24 ... ♘g5 25 ♔h1 ♘e4 26 ♖f3 ♕e1 27 ♖h3+ ♔g7 28 ♘h5+ ♔f7 29 ♖f3+ ♔e7 30 ♘f4 ♖af8 [◻ 30 ... ♘g3+ 31 hxg3 ♖h8+ 32 ♔g1 ♗xf3 ‒+] 31 ♕d3 ♘f2+ 32 ♖xf2 ♕xf2 **0-1**
L/N6123-1845

**1829-★L?-1**
**Lewis, W.+ ?**
[Staunton]
⟨♘g1⟩ 1 e4 e5 2 ♗c4 ♗c5 3 0-0 ♘f6 4 ♕e2 d6 5 h3 ♗e6 6 c3 ♗xc4 7 ♕xc4 c6 8 d4 b5 9 ♕d3 ♗b6 10 ♗g5 ♘bd7 11 f4 a6 12 ♔h1 exf4 13 ♗xf4 ♕c7 14 ♘d2 ♘h5 15 ♗h2 c5 16 ♘f3 0-0-0 17 a4 ♘f8 18 e5 ♘e6 19 exd6 ♖xd6 20 ♕e4 ♔b8 21 axb5 ♘f6 22 ♕e2 a5 23 ♗xd6 ♕xd6 24 ♘e5 ♕c7 25 dxc5 ♘xc5 26 ♖f4 ♖e8 27 ♖e1 ♖xe5 28 ♕xe5 ♕xe5 29 ♖xe5 ♘d3 30 ♖xf6 gxf6 31 ♖e2 f5 32 ♖d2 ♘f2+ 33 ♔h2 ♘e4 34 ♖d7 ♗e3 35 c4 ♗c1 36 c5 ♘xc5 37 ♖d5 ♗xb2?? 38 ♖xc5 ♔b7 [◻ 38 ... a4] 39 ♖c6 a4 40 ♔g3 a3 41 ♖a6 a2 42 ♖xa2 ♗e5+ 43 ♔f3 ♔b6 44 ♖d2 ♔c5 45 ♖d1 f6 46 ♖b1 **1-0** L/N6123-1845

**1829-★L?-2**
**Lewis, W.= ?**
[Staunton]
⟨♘g1⟩ 1 e4 e5 2 ♗c4 c6 3 ♕e2 ♘f6 4 f4 d5 5 exd5 e4 6 dxc6 ♘xc6 7 c3 ♗g4 8 ♕e3 ♕b6 9 d4 ♘a5 10 ♘d2 ♗e7 11 h3 ♗e6 12 ♗e2 ♕c6 13 b3 ♘d5 14 ♕xe4 ♕xc3 15 0-0?! ♕e3+ [◻ 15 ... ♕xa1] 16 ♔h1 0-0 [16 ... f5 △ 17 ♗b5+ ♔f7] 17 f5 ♕xe4 18 ♘xe4 ♗d7 19 ♗d2 ♘c6 20 ♗c4 ♘f6 21 ♘xf6+ ♗xf6 22 d5 ♗xa1 23 dxc6 ♗xc6 24 ♖xa1 b5 25 ♗e2 ♖fe8 26 ♗g4 ♖ad8 27 ♗a5 ♖d3 [△ 28 ... h5] 28 ♔h2 ♗d7 29 ♖c1 h5 30 ♗xh5 ♗xf5 31 ♗f3 a6 32 ♗b7 ♖e2 [△ 33 ... ♖xh3] 33 ♔g1 ♖xa2 34 b4 ♖g3 35 ♗c7 ♖g6 36 ♔h2 ♖c2 37 ♖xc2 ♗xc2 38 ♔g1 ♖e6 39 ♗d5 ♖e7 40 ♗b6 ♗e4 41 ♗b3 ♔h7 42 ♔f2 ♗d3 43 ♗d1 ♔g6 44 g3 ♖e4 45 ♗c5 f5 46 g4 ♔f6 47 gxf5 ♔xf5 48 ♗g4+ ♔e5 49 ♔g3 ♔d5! 50 ♗f3? a5! 51 ♗f8 axb4? [51 ... a4 ‒+] 52 ♗xb4 ♔c4 53 ♗xe4 ♗xe4 54 ♗f8 g6 55 h4 ♗c2 56 ♔f4 ♗d1 57 ♔e3 ♔c3 58 ♗g7+ ♔b3 59 ♔d2 ♗g4 60 ♔c1 **½-½**
L/N6123-1845

**1829-★L?-3**
**Lewis, W.– ?**
[Staunton]
⟨♘g1⟩ 1 e4 e5 2 ♗c4 ♘f6 3 ♕e2 ♘c6 4 c3 ♗e7 5 f4 d6 6 0-0 exf4 7 d4 d5 8 exd5 ♘xd5 9 b4 ♗e6 [9 ... ♘xb4!? △ 10 ... ♕xd4+; 9 ... ♘xc3!? △ 10 ... ♕xd4+] 10 ♗xd5 ♕xd5 11 ♗xf4 ♗f6 [◻ 11 ... ♘xd4] 12 ♔h1 ♖c8 13 ♘a3 0-0 14 ♖ad1 ♕xa2 15 ♕xa2 ♗xa2 16 ♖d2 ♗d5 17 ♘c2 h5 18 ♘e3 ♗e4 19 b5 ♘e7 20 ♘c4 ♘d5 21 ♗e5 ♗xe5 [◻ 21 ... ♗g5] 22 ♘xe5 ♘xc3 23 ♘d7 ♖fe8 24 ♖f4 f5 [24 ... ♗d3; 24 ... ♗c6] 25 h3 ♖cd8 26 ♘c5 ♘xb5 27 ♔h2 g5 28 ♘xe4 gxf4 29 ♘f6+ ♔g7 30 ♘xe8+ ♖xe8 **0-1** L/N6123-1845

**1829-★LM-1** 20 iii 29
**Lavallino+ Macdonnell, A.**
⟨♙f7⟩ 1 e4 ... 2 d4 ♘c6 3 ♗c4 g6 4 h4 e5 5 d5 ♘b8 6 h5 g5 7 h6 ♕f6 8 ♕h5+ ♕g6 9 ♕xg6+ hxg6 10 h7 ♘f6 11 ♗xg5 ♘xe4 12 f4 ♘xg5 13 fxg5 ♗e7 14 ♗d3 ♔f7 15 ♘f3 d6 16 ♘c3 ♔g7 17 0-0-0 ♗g4 18 ♖h6 ♗xg5+ 19 ♘xg5 ♔xh6 20 ♘f7+ ♔xh7 21 ♖h1+ ♔g7 22 ♘xh8 ♗f5 23 ♘xg6 ♗xg6 24 ♗xg6 ♔xg6 25 ♖h8 c6 26 dxc6 bxc6 27 ♘e4 d5 28 ♘c5 a5 29 ♘d7 **1-0**
L/N6123-1844

**1829-★LS-1** 9 v 29
**Lewis, W.– Smart**
[Staunton]
⟨♖a1⟩ 1 e4 e5 2 ♘f3 ♘c6 3 ♗c4 ♗c5 4 b4 ♗xb4 5 0-0 ♘f6 6 c3 ♗c5 7 d4 exd4 8 cxd4 ♗b6 9 e5 ♘g8 10 ♕b3 ♘xd4 11 ♗xf7+ ♔f8 12 ♘xd4 ♗xd4 13 ♗h5 ♕e7 14 ♗a3 [14 ♗g5] 14 ... c5 15 ♘c3 [15 ♕f3+] 15 ... ♕e6 16 ♘d5 ♘e7 17 ♕f3+ ♕f5 18 ♘f4 g5 19 ♗c1 ♗xe5 20 ♖e1 ♗xf4 21 ♗b2 ♖g8 22 g3 d5 [22 ... ♗~ ‒+] 23 gxf4 ♕xf4 24 ♗f6! ♕xf3 25 ♗xe7+ ♔g7 26 ♗xf3 ♗d7 27 ♗xc5 ♗c6 28 ♖e7+ ♔h6 29 ♖f7 ♔g6 30 ♖e7 ♖ge8 31 ♖c7 ♖ac8 32 ♖xc8 ♖xc8 **0-1** L/N6123-1845

**1829-★MW-1** 16 vii 29
**Macdonnell, A.– Walker, G.**
⟨♘b1⟩ 1 e4 e5 2 ♘f3 f5 3 d4 fxe4 4 ♘xe5 ♘f6 5 ♗c4 d5 6 ♗b3 c5 7 c3 cxd4 8 cxd4 ♗b4+ 9 ♗d2 ♗xd2+ 10 ♕xd2 0-0 11 0-0 ♘c6 12 f3 ♕b6 13 ♖ae1 ♗e6 14 ♘xc6 bxc6 15 fxe4 ♘xe4 16 ♖xf8+ ♖xf8 17 ♖xe4 dxe4 18 ♗xe6+ ♔h8 19 h3 ♖d8 20 ♔f2 ♖xd4 21 ♕f4 ♕xb2+ 22 ♔g3 ♕c3+ 23 ♔h2 ♖d8 24 ♕xe4 ♕d4 25 ♕xc6 ♕f4+ 26 g3 ♖d2+ 27 ♔g1 ♕f2+ 28 ♔h1 ♕h2# **0-1** L/N6123-1844

**1829-★MW-2 ○●** 30 v 29
**Worrell+ Macdonnell, A.**
⟨♙f7⟩ 1 e4 ... 2 ♘f3 e6 3 ♘c3 c6 4 e5 d5 5 exd6 ♗xd6 6 d4 ♘f6 7 ♗d3 0-0 8 0-0 ♗c7 9 ♗g5 ♕d6 10 ♗xf6 ♖xf6 11 ♘e4 ♕f8 12 ♘xf6+ ♕xf6 13 ♕e2 ♘d7 14 ♖ae1 ♘f8 15 ♘e5 ♘g6 16 ♗xg6 hxg6 17 ♕g4 ♔h7 18 f4 b6 19 ♘xc6 e5 20 ♕g5 ♕xc6 21 fxe5 ♗f5 22 ♖xf5 gxf5 23 ♕xf5+ ♕g6 24 ♕h3+ ♔g8 25 ♕b3+ ♔h7 26 ♖e3 ♕e8 27 ♖h3+ ♔g6 28 ♕g3+ ♔f5 29 ♕xg7 ♗d8

30 ♖f3+ ♔e6 31 c4 ♗e7 32 ♕g4# **1-0** L/N6123-1844

**Lewis✕Pratt** [182?-✕LP]

| | | | | | | |
|---|---|---|---|---|---|---|
| W. Lewis | 1 | ½ | 1 | 0 | 1 | 3½ |
| P. Pratt | 0 | ½ | 0 | 1 | 0 | 1½ |

**182?-✕LP-1**
**Lewis, W.+Pratt, P.**
⟨♘g1⟩ 1 e4 e5 2 ♗c4 ♗c5 3 ♕e2 ♘f6 4 d3 0-0 5 ♗g5 c6 6 ♗b3 d5 7 ♘d2 a5 8 c3 a4 9 ♗c2 ♘bd7 10 f4 exf4 11 d4 ♗d6 12 e5 ♖e8 13 ♗xf4 ♕b6 14 0-0-0 ♗f8 15 ♕f3 ♖a5 16 exf6 gxf6 17 ♖de1 ♖xe1+ 18 ♖xe1 ♖b5 19 b4 axb3 20 ♘xb3 ♕a7 21 ♕e2 ♕xa2? 22 ♗xh7+ **1-0** +1

**182?-✕LP-2**
**Lewis, W.= Pratt, P.**
⟨♘g1⟩ 1 e4 e5 2 ♗c4 ♗c5 3 ♕e2 ♘f6 4 c3 0-0 5 d3 c6 6 ♗g5 d5 7 ♗b3 a5 8 ♗xf6 gxf6 9 ♘d2 ♔h8 10 ♗c2 ♖g8 11 g3 f5 12 0-0-0 b5 13 exd5 cxd5 14 ♕xe5+ f6 15 ♕e2 b4 16 c4 d4 17 ♖he1 ♘c6 18 ♘f3 a4 19 ♗b1 ♖a7 20 ♘h4 ♖e7 21 ♕d2 ♘e5 22 h3 ♕d6 23 ♖e2 b3 24 a3 ♗xa3 25 bxa3 ♕xa3+ 26 ♕b2 ♕xb2+ 27 ♖xb2 ♗e6 28 ♖e2 a3 29 f4 a2 30 ♗xa2 bxa2 31 ♖xa2 ♘c6 32 ♖a6 ♘b4 33 ♖b6 ♘a2+ 34 ♔b2 ♘c3 35 ♖a1 ♖xg3 36 ♖aa6 ♗d7 37 ♖b8+ ♔g7 38 ♖b7 ♖e2+ 39 ♔b3 ♖xd3 40 ♖xd7+ ♔h6 41 ♘xf5+ ♔g6 42 ♘h4+ ♔h6 43 ♘f5+ ♔g6 ½-½ +1

**182?-✕LP-3**
**Lewis, W.+ Pratt, P.**
⟨♘g1⟩ 1 e4 e5 2 ♗c4 ♗c5 3 ♕e2 ♘f6 4 c3 0-0 5 d3 ♔h8 6 ♗g5 b5 7 ♗xb5 d5 8 exd5 ♕xd5 9 ♗xf6 gxf6 10 ♖g1 ♗a6 11 ♗xa6 ♘xa6 12 ♘d2 ♖g8 13 d4 exd4 14 ♕xa6 ♖ae8+ 15 ♔d1 ♖e6 16 ♕d3 ♕h5+ 17 g4 ♕g5

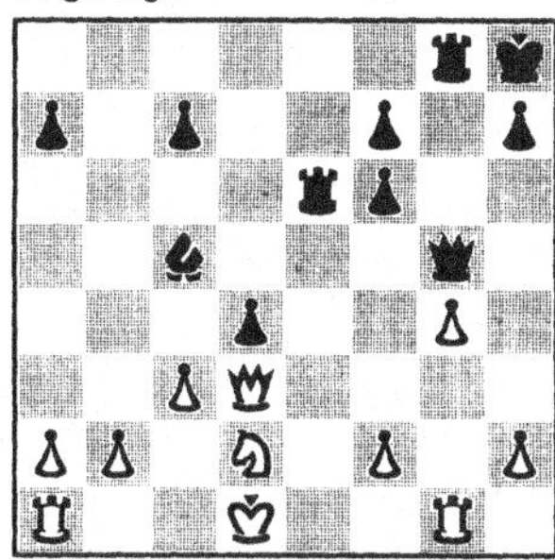

18 ♘e4 ♖xe4 19 ♕xe4 ♖d8 20 c4 d3 21 ♕f5 ♗xf2 22 ♕xg5 fxg5 23 ♖f1 ♗d4 24 ♖xf7 ♗xb2 25 ♖b1 ♗e5 26 ♖f5 ♗f4 27 ♖d5 ♖xd5 28 cxd5 ...? **1-0** +1

**182?-✕LP-4**
**Lewis, W.– Pratt, P.**
⟨♘b1⟩ 1 e4 d5 2 exd5 ♕xd5 3 ♘f3 ♗g4 4 ♗e2 ♗xf3 5 ♗xf3 ♕e5+ 6 ♗e2 ♘c6 7 c3 e6 8 d4 ♕f6 9 0-0 0-0-0 10 b4 ♘xd4 11 cxd4 ♖xd4 12 ♕a4 ♗d6 13 ♕e8+ ♕d8 14 ♕xd8+ ♔xd8 15 ♗b2 ♖d2 16 ♗xg7 ♖xe2 17 ♗xh8 f6 18 ♖fe1 ♖xe1+ 19 ♖xe1 ♔e7 20 a3 ♔f7 21 ♖e4 e5 22 ♖g4 ♗f8 23 ♖h4 h6 24 f4 exf4 25 ♖xf4 ♔g6 26 ♔f2 ♗e7 27 ♖g4+ ♔f7 28 ♗g7 h5 29 ♖g3 ♗d6 30 ♖h3 ♔xg7 31 ♖xh5 ♘h6 32 h3 f5 33 ♖h4 f4 34 ♖h5 b6 35 ♖d5 ♔f6 36 ♖d2 ♘f5 37 ♔f3 ♘g3 38 ♖d1 ♔e5 39 ♖e1+ ♔d5 40 ♖e8 ♔c6 41 h4 ♔b5 42 ♖a8 a5 43 bxa5 bxa5 44 ♔g4 c5 45 h5 ♘xh5 46 ♔xh5 c4 47 ♖e8 ♗xa3 48 ♖e5+ ♔b4 49 ♖e1 ♔c3 50 ♔g4 ♔d2 51 ♖a1 ♗b4 52 ♔xf4 c3 53 ♖f1 ♗f8 54 ♖f2+ ♔c1 55 g4 ♔b1 **0-1** +1

**182?-✕LP-5**
**Lewis, W.+ Pratt, P.**
⟨♘g1⟩ 1 e4 e5 2 ♗c4 ♗c5 3 ♕e2 ♘f6 4 c3 0-0 5 d3 ♔h8 6 ♗g5 b5 7 ♗xb5 d5 8 exd5 ♕xd5 9 ♗xf6 gxf6 10 ♖g1 ♗a6 11 ♗xa6 ♘xa6 12 ♘d2 ♖g8 13 d4 exd4 14 ♕xa6 ♖ae8+ 15 ♔d1 ♖e6 16 ♕d3 ♕h5+ 17 g4 ♕g5 18 ♘e4 ♖xe4 19 ♕xe4 ♖d8 20 c4 d3 21 ♕f5 ♗xf2 22 ♕xg5 fxg5 23 ♖f1 ♗d4 24 ♖xf7 ♗xb2 25 ♖b1 ♗e5 26 ♖f5 ♗f4 27 ♖d5 ♖xd5 28 cxd5 ♔g7 29 ♖b7 a6 30 ♖a7 ♔f6 31 ♖xa6+ ♔e5 32 ♖a3 ♔e4 33 h3 d2 34 ♖b3 ♔xd5 35 a4 ♔c4 36 ♖b7 ♗e5 37 a5 ♔d3 38 a6 c5 39 a7 c4 40 a8♕ **1-0** +1

**182?-★C?-1**
**Cochrane, J.+?**
1 e4 e5 2 f4 exf4 3 ♗c4 ♕h4+ 4 ♔f1 g5 5 ♘c3 ♘c6 6 ♘b5 ♔d8 7 ♗xf7 a6 8 ♘c3 ♗c5 9 ♕e1 ♕xe1+ 10 ♔xe1 ♘d4 11 ♔d1 ♘f6 12 ♘f3 h6 13 d3 ♖f8 14 ♗c4 d6 15 h3 ♘h5 16 ♘xd4 ♗xd4 17 ♘e2 ♘g3 18 ♘xg3 fxg3 19 c3 ♗e5 20 ♗e3 ♗f4 21 ♗xf4 ♖xf4 22 ♔e1 ♔e7 23 ♖f1 ♗e6 24 ♖xf4 gxf4 25 ♗xe6 ♔xe6 26 ♔e2 ♖f8 27 ♔f3 c6 28 ♖e1 h5 29 c4 ♖f7 30 e5 d5 31 b3 ♔f5 32 cxd5 cxd5 33 e6 ♖e7 34 d4 **1-0** +1

**182?-★C?-2**
**Cochrane, J.+?**
1 e4 e5 2 ♘f3 d6 3 d4 f5 4 dxe5 fxe4 5 ♘g5 d5 6 e6 ♘h6 7 ♕h5+ g6 8 ♕h3 ♗g7 9 c4 0-0 10 cxd5 ♕xd5 11 ♘c3 ♕f5 12 ♕h4 ♘c6 13 ♗c4 ♔h8 14 0-0 ♕c5 15 ♗b3 b6 16 ♗e3 ♕e5 17 ♘cxe4 ♘d4 18 ♗xd4 ♕xd4 19 e7 ♖e8 20 ♘f7+ ♘xf7 21 ♗xf7 ♗f5 22 ♗xe8 ♖xe8 23 ♖ad1 ♕xe4 24 ♖d8 ♕c6 25 ♖xe8+ ♕xe8 26 ♖d1 ♗d7 27 ♕e4 ♗f6 28 ♖xd7 ♔g7 29 ♕e6 c5 30 ♖d6 **1-0** +1

**182?-★LM-1**
**Lewis, W.= Macdonnell, A.**
⟨♙f7⟩ 1 e4 ... 2 d4 ♘c6 3 ♘h3 e5 4 d5 ♘ce7 5 f4 exf4 6 ♗xf4 ♘g6 7 e5 ♗c5 8 ♗d3 ♘xf4 9 ♘xf4 ♕g5 10 ♕h5+ ♕xh5 11 ♘xh5 g6 12 ♘f6+ ♘xf6 13 exf6 ♗d4 14 c3 ♗xf6 15 ♘d2 d6 16 0-0-0 0-0 17 ♘e4 ♗e5 18 h3 ♗f5 19 ♘f2 ♗d7 20 ♖hf1 ♗a4 21 b3 ♗d7 22 ♔c2 c6 23 dxc6 bxc6 24 ♘e4 ♖xf1 25 ♖xf1 ♖f8 26 ♖xf8+ ♔xf8 27 ♘g5 ♗f4 28 ♘f3 ♔e7 29 a4 c5 30 a5 d5 31 b4 c4 32 ♗f1 h5 33 h4 ♗e3 34 ♔b2 ♔d6 35 ♗e2 a6 36 ♗d1 ♗g4 37 ♗c2 ♗xf3 38 gxf3 g5 39 hxg5 ♗xg5 40 ♗f5 h4 41 ♗c8 ♗e3 42 ♔c2 ♔e5 43 ♔d1 ♔f4 44 ♔e2 d4 45 cxd4 ♗xd4 46 ♗e6 c3 47 ♔d3 ♔xf3 48 ♗c8 ♔f4 49 ♗xa6 h3 50 ♗b7 ♔e5 51 b5 ♔d6 52 ♗e4 h2 53 b6 ♔d7 ½-½ L/N6123-1842

**182?-★LM-2**
**Macdonnell, A.– Lewis, W.**
⟨♙f7⟩ 1 e4 ... 2 d4 ♘c6 3 ♗d3 e5 4 f4 d6 5 d5 ♘ce7 6 f5 g6 7 ♘h3 c6 8 c4 gxf5 9 ♕h5+ ♔d7 10 exf5 cxd5 11 cxd5 ♕a5+ 12 ♘c3 ♘f6 13 ♕f7 ♘xd5 14 ♗d2 ♘xc3 15 ♕f6 ♖g8 16 ♖c1 ♗g7 17 ♕e6+ ♔e8 18 ♕b3 ♕d5 19 ♖xc3 ♕xb3 20 ♖xb3 ♘xf5 21 ♗xf5 ♗xf5 22 ♖xb7 ♗e4 23 ♖c7 ♗f6 24 ♘f2 ♗h4 25 ♖g1 ♗d8 26 ♖c3 ♖xg2 27 ♖xg2 ♗xg2 28 ♖g3 ♗c6 29 ♖g7 h5 30 ♖h7 ♗f3 31 ♘h3 ♗h4+ 32 ♔f1 ♖c8 33 ♗g5 ♖c4 34 ♖e7+ ♔f8 35 ♖xa7 ♗g4 36 ♗h6+ ♔e8 37 ♖a3 ♖c2 38 ♔g1 ♖xb2 39 ♘g5 ♗xg5 40 ♗xg5 ♔d7 41 h4 ♔c6 42 ♖a6+ ♔d7 43 a4 d5 44 ♗f6 ♖e2 45 a5 d4 46 ♖a8 ♗f3 47 ♖d8+ ♔e6 48 ♗g5 ♖a2 49 ♖f8 e4 50 a6 d3 51 ♖e8+ ♔f5 52 ♖f8+ ♔g4 53 ♗e3 ♖xa6 54 ♖g8+ ♔h3 55 ♗f2 ♗g4 56 ♗e1 ♖a2 57 ♖e8 ♖g2+ 58 ♔h1 ♗f3 59 ♖f8 ♖e2+ **0-1** L/N6123-1842

**182?-★L?-1**
**Lewis, W.+?**
1 e4 e5 2 ♘f3 ♘c6 3 ♗c4 ♗c5 4 c3 ♕e7 5 0-0 d6 6 d3 f5 7 ♗xg8 ♖xg8 8 d4 exd4 9 cxd4 ♗b6 10 e5 d5 11 ♘c3 ♗e6 12 ♗g5 ♕f7 13 ♘a4 h6 14 ♘xb6 axb6 15 ♗c1 g5

16 ♘e1 g4 17 ♗xh6 ♖h8 18 ♗f4 ♘e7 19 f3 0-0-0 20 fxg4 fxg4 21 ♗g3 ♕h7 22 ♖f6 ♕g8 23 ♖c1 ♘f5 24 ♖xf5 ♗xf5 25 e6 c6 26 ♕a4 ♕xe6 27 ♕a8+ ♔d7 28 ♕xb7+ ♔e8 29 ♗e5 g3 30 hxg3 ♕h6 31 ♖c3 ♖h7 32 ♕xb6 ♕d2 33 ♕xc6+ ♖dd7 34 ♘f3 ♕d1+ 35 ♔f2 ♖h1 36 ♕c8+ ♔e7 37 ♗f6+ ♔xf6 38 ♕f8+ ♔g6 39 ♘e5+ ♔g5 40 ♕g8+ ♔h5 41 g4+ ♗xg4 42 ♕g6+ ♔h4 43 ♕h6+ ♗h5 44 ♘g6+ ♔g4 45 ♕f4# **1-0** +1

**182?-★L?-2**
**Lewis, W.?+?**
⟨♖a1⟩ 1 e4 c5 2 ♗c4 ♘c6 3 f4 e6 4 ♘c3 ♘ge7 5 e5 f5 6 ♘f3 a6 7 a3 d5 8 exd6 ♕xd6 9 0-0 ♘g6 10 d3 ♗e7 11 ♗e3 0-0 12 ♕e1 ♘a5 13 ♗a2 b5 14 h4 ♗b7 15 h5 ♗xf3 16 hxg6 ♗b7 17 ♘e2 ♖f6 18 gxh7+ ♔h8 19 ♕xa5 ♕c6 20 ♖f3 ♖g6 21 ♘g3 ♗h4 22 ♗f2 ♖d8 23 ♔f1 ♗xg3 24 ♕xd8+ ♔xh7 25 ♗xg3 ♖h6 26 ♕e7 ♕b6 27 ♗f2 ♖h1+ 28 ♔e2 ♗xf3+ 29 gxf3 e5 30 ♗e6 ♖h5 31 ♕e8 ♔h6 32 ♕h8+ ♔g6 33 ♗f7+ ♔xf7 34 ♕xh5+ **1-0** +1

**182?-★L?-3**
**?– Lewis, W.**
1 e4 e5 2 f4 exf4 3 ♘f3 g5 4 ♗c4 g4 5 ♘e5 ♕h4+ 6 ♔f1 ♘f6 7 ♗xf7+ ♔e7 8 ♗c4 d6 9 ♘d3 f3 10 g3 ♕h3+ 11 ♔f2 ♕g2+ 12 ♔e3 ♗h6+ 13 ♘f4 ♗xf4+ 14 gxf4 f2 15 d3 g3 16 hxg3 ♗g4 17 ♕f1 ♕xg3+ 18 ♔d4 ♘c6+

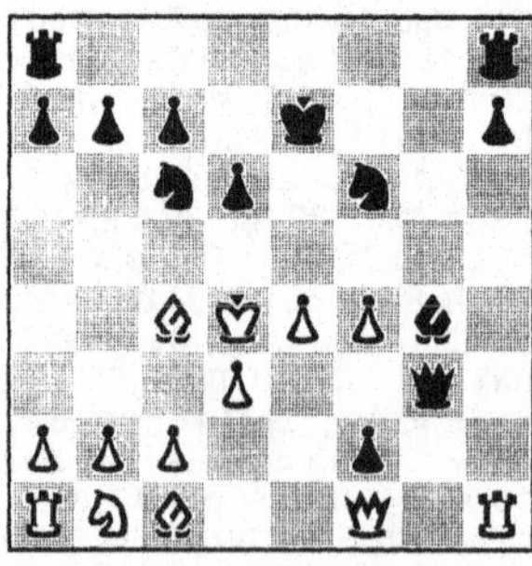

19 ♔c3 ♘xe4+ 20 ♔b3 ♘d4+ 21 ♔a4 ♗d7+ 22 ♔a5 b6+ 23 ♔b4 a5+ 24 ♔a3 ♘xc2+ 25 ♔b3 ♗a4+ 26 ♔xa4 ♘c5+ 27 ♔b5 ♘d4# **0-1** +1

**182?-★L?-4**
**Lewis, W.?+?**
⟨♖a1⟩ 1 e4 e5 2 f4 exf4 3 ♘f3 g5 4 ♗c4 ♗g7 5 d4 d6 6 ♘c3 ♗g4 7 0-0 ♘e7 8 ♗xf7+ ♔f8 9 ♗c4 ♘d7 10 ♘xg5

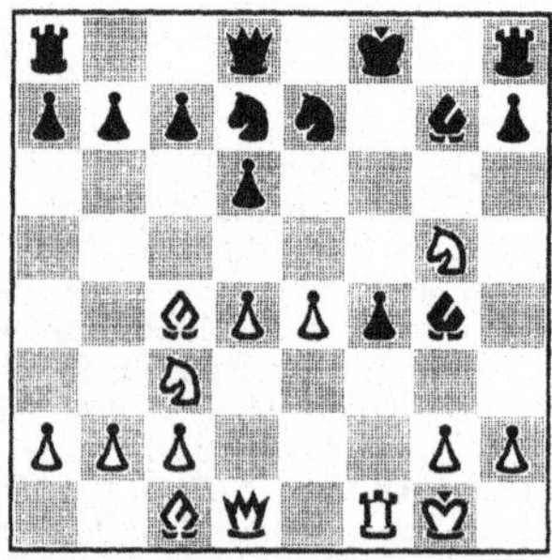

10 ... ♗xd1 11 ♘e6+ ♔f7 12 ♘xd8+ ♔g6 13 ♗f7+ ♔g5 14 ♗xf4+ ♔g4 15 h3+ ♔h4 16 ♔h2 ♘g6 17 ♘e6 ♗f6 18 ♘xd1 b5 19 g3+ ♔h5 20 g4+ ♔h4 21 ♗g3# **1-0** +1

**182?-★L?-5**
**Lewis, W.+?**
1 e4 e5 2 f4 exf4 3 ♘f3 g5 4 ♗c4 g4 5 0-0 gxf3 6 ♕xf3 ♕f6 7 d3 ♘c6 8 ♗xf4 ♗h6 9 ♗xc7 ♕xf3 10 ♖xf3 f6 11 ♘c3 ♘e5 12 ♗xe5 fxe5 13 ♘b5 ♔e7 14 ♖af1 a6 15 ♘c7 ♖b8 16 ♘d5+ ♔d6 17 ♖f6+ ♘xf6 18 ♖xf6+ ♔c5 19 b4+ ♔d4 20 c3# **1-0** +1

**182?-★L?-6**
**Lewis, W.+?**
⟨♖a1⟩ 1 e4 e5 2 f4 exf4 3 ♘f3 g5 4 h4 g4 5 ♘g5 h6 6 ♘xf7 ♔xf7 7 ♕xg4 ♕f6 8 ♗c4+ ♔e7 9 ♘c3 h5 10 ♘d5+ ♔d8

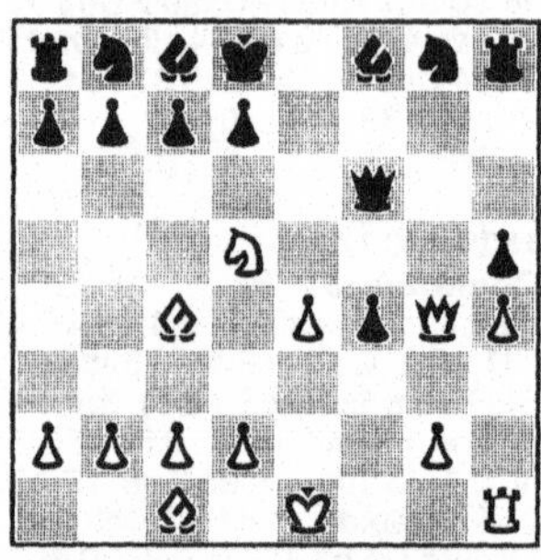

11 ♕f3 ♕d6 12 d4 ♘c6 13 ♗xf4 ♘xd4 14 ♕g3 ♕c5 15 ♗xc7+ ♔e8 16 ♕g6# **1-0** +1

**182?-★L?-7**
**Lewis, W.+?**
⟨♖a1⟩ 1 e4 e5 2 f4 exf4 3 ♘f3 g5 4 h4 g4 5 ♘g5 d5 6 exd5 ♕e7+ 7 ♔f2 h6 8 ♗b5+ ♔d8 9 ♖e1 ♕c5+ 10 d4 ♕xb5 11 ♘xf7+ ♔d7 12 ♕xg4# **1-0** +1

**182?-★??-1**
**?–?**
[Lewis]
1 e4 e5 2 f4 exf4 3 ♗c4 ♕h4+ 4 ♔f1 g5 5 ♘c3 ♗g7 6 ♘f3 ♕h5 7 d4 d6 8 h4 ♗g4 9 ♗e2 h6 10 ♘d5 ♔d7 11 ♔g1 ♕g6 12 hxg5 hxg5 13 ♖xh8 ♗xh8 14 ♕d3? ♗e6 15 ♕b5+ ♘c6 16 ♕xb7 ♖c8 17 c3? ♕xe4 18 ♗a6 ♘ge7 19 ♘xe7 ♔xe7 20 ♕b5 ♖g8 21 ♗d2 ♕d5 22 ♖e1 ♕xb5 23 ♗xb5 ♔d7 24 c4 g4 25 d5 gxf3 26 ♗xc6+ ♔e7 27 dxe6 ♗d4+ 28 ♔f1 fxg2+ 29 ♗xg2 fxe6 30 b3 e5 31 ♖e2? f3 32 ♗e3 fxe2+ 33 ♔xe2 ♖xg2+ 34 ♔f3 ♖xa2 **0-1** +1

**182?-★??-2**
**?+?**
1 e4 e5 2 ♘f3 ♘c6 3 d4 exd4 4 ♗c4 d6 5 ♕d3 ♘e5 6 ♘xe5 dxe5 7 0-0 ♗d6 8 f4 f6 9 fxe5 ♗xe5 10 ♕b3 ♘e7 11 ♗f7+ ♔f8 12 ♗h5 g6 13 ♗e2 ♕d6 14 h3 ♔g7 15 ♘a3 c6 16 ♘c4 ♕e6 17 ♗g4 ♕f7 18 ♗xc8 ♖axc8 19 ♕xb7 ♕xc4 20 ♕xe7+ ♕f7 21 ♗h6+ ♔g8 22 ♕c5 ♕c7 23 ♖ad1 ♔f7 24 ♕c4+ ♔e7 25 ♗g7 ♖hg8 26 ♗xf6+ ♗xf6 27 e5 ♖gf8 28 exf6+ ♖xf6 29 ♖de1+ ♔d7 30 ♕xd4+ ♖d6 31 ♖f7+ ♔d8 32 ♕h8# **1-0** +1

**182?-★??-3**
**?+?**
1 e4 e5 2 ♘f3 ♘c6 3 ♗c4 ♗c5 4 c3 d6 5 0-0 ♕e7 6 h3 ♘d8 7 d4 exd4 8 cxd4 ♗b6 9 ♘c3 c6 10 ♖e1 ♗a5 11 ♗g5 f6 12 e5 ♗e6 13 ♗xe6 ♘xe6 14 exf6 ♘xg5 15 ♖xe7+ ♘xe7 16 ♘xg5 gxf6 17 ♘ce4 fxg5 18 d5 ♘xd5 19 ♕h5+ ♔d7 20 ♕f7+ ♘e7 21 ♘f6+ ♔d8 22 ♕e6 ♔c7 23 ♕xe7+ ♔b6 24 ♕xd6 ♔a6 25 ♕a3 ♔b5 26 ♘d7 ♖ad8 27 ♕d3+ ♔a4 28 ♕b3# **1-0** +1

**182?-★??-4**
**?–?**
1 e4 e5 2 f4 exf4 3 ♘f3 g5 4 ♗c4 g4 5 0-0 gxf3 6 ♕xf3 ♕f6 7 d3 ♗h6 8 ♘c3 ♘e7 9 ♗d2 ♘bc6 10 ♘b5 ♔d8 11 ♗c3 ♘e5 12 ♗xe5 ♕xe5 13 d4 ♕g7 14 ♖ad1 d6 15 ♕b3 a6 16 ♘c3 ♖g8 17 ♖f2 f3 18 ♗xf7 ♗e3 19 ♗xg8 ♕xg2# **0-1** +1

**182?-★??-5**
**?+?**
1 e4 e5 2 ♘f3 ♘c6 3 d4 exd4 4 ♗c4 h6 5 0-0 ♗c5 6 c3 dxc3 7 ♗xf7+ ♔f8 8 ♘xc3 d6 9 ♗b3 ♗g4 10 ♕d5 ♕e7 11 ♘h4 ♘e5 12 ♕xb7 ♕d8 13 ♘d5 ♗b6 14 ♘xb6 axb6

15 f4 ♗e2 16 fxe5+ ♗xf1 17 ♘g6+ ♔e8 18 ♕c6+ **1-0** +1

**182?-★??-6**
**?+?**
⟨♘b1⟩ 1 e4 e5 2 f4 exf4 3 ♗c4 ♗e7 4 ♘f3 ♗h4+ 5 g3 fxg3 6 0-0 gxh2+ 7 ♔h1 d5 8 exd5 ♗f6 9 d4 ♘e7 10 ♘g5 ♗xg5 11 ♗xg5 f6 12 ♗xf6 gxf6 13 ♖xf6 ♖g8 14 ♕h5+ ♖g6 15 ♖e1 ♘d7 16 ♖xg6 hxg6 17 ♕xg6+ ♔f8 18 ♖f1+ **1-0** +1

**182?-★??-7**
**?+?**
1 e4 e5 2 ♘f3 ♘c6 3 d4 exd4 4 ♗c4 d6 5 ♕d3 ♘e5 6 ♘xe5 dxe5 7 0-0 ♗d6 8 ♗d2 ♕f6 9 f4 ♕g6 10 ♕b3 ♘f6 11 fxe5 ♗xe5 12 ♕b5+ **1-0** +1

**1830-★M?-1**
**Macdonnell, A.+?**
⟨♘g1⟩ 1 e4 e5 2 ♗c4 ♗c5 3 b4 ♗xb4 4 c3 ♗c5 5 0-0 d6 6 d4 exd4 7 cxd4 ♗b6 8 f4 ♗e6 9 ♗b5+ c6 10 ♗a4 ♗c4 11 ♖f3 ♘f6 12 ♘c3 ♗a5 13 e5 ♘d5 14 ♘e4 ♗c7 15 ♗a3 dxe5 16 fxe5 b5 17 ♕c2 ♘d7 18 ♖e1 ♘7b6 19 ♘d6+ ♗xd6 20 exd6+ ♔f8 21 d7+ ♘e7 22 ♗xe7+ ♕xe7 23 ♖xe7 **1-0**
L/N6123-1845

**1830-★M?-2**
**Macdonnell, A.–?**
⟨♘b1⟩ 1 e4 e6 2 f4 d5 3 e5 c5 4 c3 ♘c6 5 ♘f3 ♕b6 6 ♗d3 ♘h6 7 ♗c2 ♗d7 8 0-0 ♗e7 9 ♔h1 f5 10 h3 ♘f7 11 d3 h5 12 a3 ♕d8 13 ♕e1 g5 14 fxg5 ♗xg5 15 ♘xg5 ♘xg5 16 ♕g3 ♘f7 17 ♗f4 h4 18 ♕g6 ♕e7 19 b4 0-0-0 20 d4 cxd4 21 cxd4 ♘xd4 22 ♗d1 ♔b8 23 ♖e1 ♖c8 24 ♗h5 ♖xh5 25 ♕xh5 ♘c2 26 ♖ad1 ♘xe1 27 ♖xe1 ♔a8

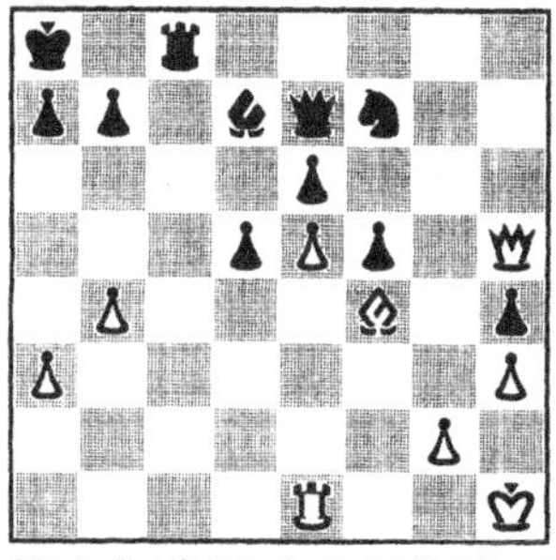

28 ♗e3 b6 29 ♕e2 ♔b7 30 a4 ♕xb4 31 ♖a1 ♗xa4 32 ♕a2 ♖c4 33 ♖b1 ♕c3 34 ♕f2 ♕c2 35 ♕g1 ♘xe5 36 ♗xb6 axb6 37 ♕xb6+ ♔c8 38 ♕xe6+ ♘d7 39 ♕a6+ ♔d8 ...? **0-1** L/N6123-1845

**Fraser✕Macdonnell**
[1831-✕FM]

| | | | | | | |
|---|---|---|---|---|---|---|
| W. Fraser | ½ | 1 | 0 | 0 | 0 | 1½ |
| A. Macdonnell | ½ | 0 | 1 | 1 | 1 | 3½ |

**1831-✕FM-1**
**Macdonnell, A.= Fraser, W.**
1 e4 e6 2 f4 d5 3 e5 c5 4 ♘f3 ♘c6 5 c3 ♗e7 6 ♗d3 ♘h6 7 ♗c2 ♗d7 8 0-0 f5 9 a3 c4 10 h3 ♘f7 11 ♕e1 g6 12 ♔h1 h6 13 d4 ♕b6 14 ♘bd2 ♘a5 15 ♖b1 ♘b3 16 ♗xb3 cxb3 17 c4 dxc4 18 ♘xc4 ♕c7 19 ♘e3 ♗b5 20 ♖g1 ♗d3 21 ♖a1 ♗e4 22 ♗d2 g5 23 ♖c1 ♕d7 24 d5 ♗xd5 25 ♘xd5 ♕xd5 26 ♗b4 ♗xb4 27 ♕xb4 a5 28 ♕b6 0-0 29 ♖gd1 ♖a6 30 ♕c7 ♖c6 31 ♖xd5 ♖xc7 32 ♖xc7 exd5 33 e6 ♘d6 34 ♖d7 ♘e4 35 ♖xd5 gxf4 36 ♔h2 ♘g3 37 ♘d4 a4 38 ♘b5 ♖e8 39 ♘c7 ♖e7 40 ♖d8+ ♔g7 41 ♖d7 ♔f8 42 ♖d8+ ♔g7 43 ♖d7 ♔f8 44 ♖xe7 ♔xe7 45 ♘d5+ ♔xe6 46 ♘xf4+ ♔e5 47 ♔xg3 ♔e4 48 ♘e2 ♔d3 49 ♘c3 ♔c2 50 ♘xa4 b5 51 ♘c3 ♔xb2 52 ♘xb5 ♔a2 53 ♘c3+ ♔xa3 54 ♘d1 ♔a2 55 ♔f3 ♔b1 56 ♔e2 ♔c2 57 g3 h5 58 h4 ♔c1 59 ♘c3 ♔c2 60 ♘a4 ♔c1 61 ♔d3 ♔d1 62 ♘b2+ ♔e1 63 ♔e3 ♔f1 64 ♘d3 ♔g2 65 ♔f4 ♔h2 66 ♔f3 ♔h3 67 ♔f4 ♔g2 68 ♔xf5 ♔xg3 69 ♔g5 ♔f3 70 ♔xh5 ♔e3 71 ♘b2 ♔d4 72 ♔g5 ♔c3 73 ♘d1+ ♔d2 74 ♘b2 ♔c3 **½-½** L/N6123-1843

**1831-✕FM-2**
**Fraser, W.+ Macdonnell, A.**
1 e4 e5 2 ♘f3 ♘c6 3 ♗c4 ♗c5 4 c3 d6 5 0-0 ♘f6 6 d4 exd4 7 cxd4 ♗b6 8 ♘c3 ♗g4 9 d5 ♘e5 10 ♗e2 ♗xf3 11 ♗xf3 0-0 12 ♗g5 h6 13 ♗h4 g5 14 ♗g3 ♘g6 15 ♗e2 ♕e7 16 ♕c2 h5 17 h3 ♖ae8 18 ♖ae1 ♕d7 19 ♕c1 h4 20 ♗h2 g4 21 hxg4 ♘xg4 22 ♕g5 ♘xh2 23 ♔xh2 ♖e5 24 ♕h6 ♗d4 25 f4 ♖ee8 26 f5 ♗g7 27 ♕g5 ♖e5 28 ♕e3 ♘e7 29 f6 ♗h8 30 fxe7 ♕xe7 31 ♗g4 ♖g5 32 ♕f3 ♗e5+ 33 ♔h1 ♔h8 34 ♖e3 ♖fg8 35 ♗h3 f6 36 ♘e2 ♕h7 37 ♖b3 b6 38 ♘f4 ♖g3 39 ♕h5 ♕xh5 40 ♘xh5 ♖xb3 41 axb3 ♖g6 42 ♖f3 ♗xb2 43 ♖f4 ♖h6 44 ♖xh4 ♗c1 45 ♘f4 ♗xf4 46 ♖xf4 a5 47 ♔g1 ♔g8 48 ♗e6+ ♔f8 49 ♖g4 ♖h8 50 ♖g6 ♔e8 51 ♖g7 ♖h4 52 ♗f5 b5 53 ♖xc7 a4 54 bxa4 **1-0** L/N6123-1843

**1831-✕FM-3**
**Macdonnell, A.+ Fraser, W.**
1 e4 e5 2 ♘f3 ♘c6 3 ♗c4 ♗c5 4 c3 ♕e7 5 d4 exd4 6 0-0 d3 7 e5 h6 8 b4 ♗b6 9 ♖e1 ♘d8 10 a4 a5 11 ♕xd3 ♘e6 12 ♗a3 ♕d8 13 bxa5 ♖xa5 14 ♘bd2 ♘e7 15 ♘b3 ♖a8 16 ♘bd4 c5 17 ♘b5 0-0 18 ♘d6 ♖xa4 19 ♖e4 ♖a8 20 ♗b3 c4 21 ♕xc4 ♗c5 22 ♗a4 ♕b6 23 ♗xc5 ♘xc5 24 ♖ee1 ♖xa4 25 ♖xa4 ♘xa4 26 ♕xa4 ♕c6 27 ♕a3 ♘g6 28 ♘d4 ♕d5 29 ♘4f5 b6 30 c4 ♕c6 31 ♕a1 ♗b7 32 ♘xb7 ♕xb7 33 e6 f6 34 e7 ♖e8 35 ♘d6 **1-0**
L/N6013-1836

**1831-✕FM-4**
**Macdonnell, A.+ Fraser, W.**
1 e4 e6 2 f4 d5 3 e5 c5 4 ♘f3 ♘c6 5 c3 ♗e7 6 ♗d3 f5 7 ♗c2 ♘h6 8 0-0 c4 9 ♔h1 ♕b6 10 h3 ♘f7 11 b3 ♕c7 12 bxc4 dxc4 13 ♘a3 ♗xa3 14 ♗xa3 b5 15 ♕e1 ♘e7 16 ♘d4 a6 17 ♕g3 0-0 18 ♗d1 ♖e8 19 ♗f3 ♘d5 20 ♘xf5 exf5 21 ♗xd5 ♗b7 22 ♗d6 ♕b6 23 ♗xf7+ ♔xf7 24 ♖ae1 ♖e6 25 ♕g5 ♖g6 26 ♕xf5+ ♔g8 27 ♖e2 ♖e8 28 ♕d7 ♖d8 29 ♕c7 ♕xc7 30 ♗xc7 ♖d3 31 ♔h2 ♗d5 32 f5 ♖c6 33 ♗d6 a5 34 a3 ♖a6 35 f6 g6 36 e6 ♗xe6 37 ♖xe6 **1-0** L/N6123-1843

**1831-✕FM-5**
**Macdonnell, A.+ Fraser, W.**
1 e4 e5 2 ♘f3 ♘c6 3 ♗c4 ♗c5 4 c3 ♕e7 5 d4 exd4 6 0-0 d3 7 e5 h6 8 b4 ♗b6 9 ♖e1 ♘d8 10 a4 a5 11 ♕xd3 ♘e6 12 ♗a3 ♕d8 13 bxa5 ♖xa5 14 ♘bd2 ♘e7 15 ♘b3 ♖a8 16 ♘bd4 c5 17 ♘b5 0-0 18 ♘d6 ♖xa4 19 ♖e4 ♖a8 20 ♗b3 c4 21 ♕xc4 ♗c5 22 ♗a4 ♕b6 23 ♗xc5 ♘xc5 24 ♖ee1 ♖xa4 25 ♖xa4 ♘xa4 26 ♕xa4 ♕c6 27 ♕a3 ♘g6 28 ♘d4 ♕d5 29 ♘4f5 b6 30 c4 ♕c6 31 ♕a1 ♗b7 32 ♘xb7 ♕xb7 33 e6 f6 34 e7 ♘xe7 35 ♘xe7+ ♔h7 36 ♕b1+ f5 37 ♘xf5 **1-0**
L/N6123-1843

**1833-★M?-1**
**?+ Macdonnell, A.**
London
⟨♙f7⟩ 1 e4 ... 2 d4 ... 3 ♗d3 e6 4 e5 ♕e7 5 ♘f3 d5 6 ♘g5 g6 7 h4 ♗h6 8 f4 ♕g7 9 c4 c6 10 cxd5 cxd5 11 ♘c3 ♘e7 12 g4 ♗xg5 13 hxg5 h6 14 gxh6 ♖xh6 15 ♕f3 ♕h8 16 ♖xh6 ♕xh6 17 ♗e3 ♕h2 18 0-0-0 ♕h7 19 ♖h1 ♕g8 20 ♖h6 ♘d7 21 ♕h3 ♘f8 22 ♘b5 ♔d8 23 ♕h4 ♗d7 24 ♘d6 ♕g7 25 ♘xb7+ ♔c7 26 ♘c5 a5 27 ♘xd7 ♔xd7 28 ♗b5+ ♔c7 29 ♔b1 ♘g8 30 ♖h8 g5 31 ♕h2 ♔b6 32 ♗d3 gxf4 33 ♗xf4 ♖c8 34 g5 ♘e7 35 ♕h6 ♕f7 36 ♕f6 ♕e8 37 ♗e3 ♕a4

38 ♕f3 ♘c6 39 ♗c2 ♕b4 40 a3 ♕e7 41 ♕f6 ♕c7 42 ♖xf8 ♘b4 43 ♕xe6+ ♔b5 44 a4+ ♔c4 45 ♖xc8
**1-0** L/N6123-1844

## BOURDONNAIS ✕ MACDONNELL
[1834 – ✕ BM]

| | L. C. M. De la Bourdonnais | A. Macdonnell |
|---|---|---|
| *1* | ½ | ½ |
| *2* | ½ | ½ |
| *3* | ½ | ½ |
| *4* | 1 | 0 |
| *5* | 0 | 1 |
| *6* | 0 | 1 |
| *7* | 1 | 0 |
| *8* | 1 | 0 |
| *9* | 1 | 0 |
| *10* | 1 | 0 |
| *11* | 1 | 0 |
| *12* | 1 | 0 |
| *13* | ½ | ½ |
| *14* | 1 | 0 |
| *15* | 1 | 0 |
| *16* | 1 | 0 |
| *17* | 1 | 0 |
| *18* | 1 | 0 |
| *19* | 0 | 1 |
| *20* | 1 | 0 |
| *21* | 0 | 1 |
| *22* | 1 | 0 |
| *23* | 0 | 1 |
| *24* | 1 | 0 |
| *25* | 1 | 0 |
| *26* | 0 | 1 |
| *27* | 0 | 1 |
| *28* | 1 | 0 |
| *29* | 0 | 1 |
| *30* | 0 | 1 |
| *31* | 1 | 0 |
| *32* | 1 | 0 |
| *33* | 1 | 0 |
| *34* | 0 | 1 |
| *35* | 0 | 1 |
| *36* | ½ | ½ |
| *37* | 1 | 0 |
| *38* | 0 | 1 |
| *39* | 1 | 0 |
| *40* | 1 | 0 |
| *41* | 1 | 0 |
| *42* | 1 | 0 |
| *43* | 0 | 1 |
| *44* | 0 | 1 |
| *45* | 0 | 1 |
| *46* | 1 | 0 |
| *47* | 1 | 0 |
| *48* | ½ | ½ |
| *49* | ½ | ½ |
| *50* | 0 | 1 |
| *51* | 1 | 0 |
| *52* | ½ | ½ |
| *53* | 1 | 0 |
| *54* | 0 | 1 |
| *55* | ½ | ½ |
| *56* | 1 | 0 |
| *57* | ½ | ½ |
| *58* | 0 | 1 |
| *59* | ½ | ½ |
| *60* | 1 | 0 |
| *61* | ½ | ½ |
| *62* | 1 | 0 |
| *63* | 1 | 0 |
| *64* | 1 | 0 |
| *65* | ½ | ½ |
| *66* | 0 | 1 |
| *67* | 1 | 0 |
| *68* | 0 | 1 |
| *69* | 1 | 0 |
| *70* | 1 | 0 |
| *71* | 1 | 0 |
| *72* | 0 | 1 |
| *73* | 1 | 0 |
| *74* | 1 | 0 |
| *75* | 0 | 1 |
| *76* | 1 | 0 |
| *77* | 0 | 1 |
| *78* | 1 | 0 |
| *79* | 1 | 0 |
| *80* | 1 | 0 |
| *81* | 0 | 1 |
| *82* | 1 | 0 |
| *83* | 0 | 1 |
| *84* | 0 | 1 |
| *85* | 0 | 1 |
| *Total* | 51½ | 33½ |

### 1834-✕BM-1
**Bourdonnais, L.C.M. de la= Macdonnell, A.**

1 e4 e5 2 d4 [⌓ 2 ♘f3 Morphy] 2 … exd4 3 ♘f3 c5 [⌓ 3 … ♗b4+ Staunton] 4 ♗c4 [4 c3 d5 Morphy] 4 … ♘c6 5 c3 ♕f6! 6 0-0 d6 7 cxd4 cxd4 8 ♘g5 [⌓ 8 ♗b5± Morphy] 8 … ♘h6 9 f4 ♗e7 10 e5 ♕g6± 11 exd6 ♕xd6 12 ♘a3 0-0 13 ♗d3 ♗f5 14 ♘c4 ♕g6 15 ♘f3 ♗xd3 16 ♘ce5 ♗c2? [⌓ 16 … ♘xe5 17 ♘xe5 ♕f5∓ Morphy] 17 ♘xg6 ♗xd1 18 ♘xe7+ ♘xe7 19 ♖xd1 ♘hf5 20 g4 [20 ♘xd4?? ♖ad8→ Staunton] 20 … ♘e3 21 ♗xe3 dxe3 22 ♖d7 [⌓ 22 ♖d3 Staunton] 22 … ♖fe8

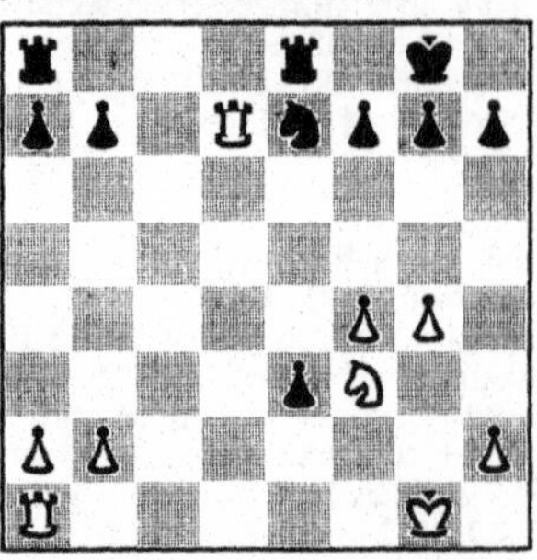

23 ♖e1 ♘g6 24 f5 ♘f4 25 ♖d4 ♘h3+ 26 ♔g2 ♘f2 27 ♖c4 ♖ad8 28 h3 h6 29 ♖e2 b5 30 ♖d4 ♖xd4 31 ♘xd4 a6 32 ♔f3 ♘xh3 33 ♖xe3 ♘g5+ 34 ♔f4 ♖xe3 35 ♔xe3 g6 36 fxg6 fxg6 37 ♘c6 ♘e6 38 ♔e4 ♔f7 39 ♔e5 h5 40 gxh5 gxh5 41 ♔f5 ♘c7 42 b3 ♔e8 43 a4 bxa4 44 bxa4 ♘d5 45 ♔g5 ♘e7 46 ♘b8 [46 ♘xe7= Walker, G.] 46 … a5 47 ♘a6 ♘g6 48 ♔xh5 [48 ♔xg6 h4 49 ♘c5 h3 50 ♘d3 h2 51 ♘f2 ♔e7 52 ♔f5 ♔d6 53 ♔e4 ♔c5= Walker, G.] 48 … ♘f4+ 49 ♔g5 ♘e6+ 50 ♔f5 ♔d7 51 ♔e5 ♘d8 ½-½ L/N6020-1874

### 1834-✕BM-2
**Bourdonnais, L.C.M. de la= Macdonnell, A.**

1 e4 e5 2 ♘f3 ♘c6 3 d4 exd4 4 ♗c4 ♕f6 [4 … ♗b4+ 5 c3 dxc3 6 0-0 ♕f6 Staunton; 4 … ♗c5; 4 … ♘f6 Morphy] 5 c3 d3!? [5 … dxc3 6 ♘xc3 ♗b4 7 ♗d2 ♘ge7 8 ♘b5±; 5 … ♗c5 6 e5 ♕g6 7 cxd4± Morphy] 6 ♕xd3 d6 7 0-0 ♕g6 8 ♗f4 ♗e7 9 ♘bd2 h5?! [⌓ 9 … ♘h6 △ 10 … 0-0 Morphy] 10 ♖fe1 ♗h3 11 ♘h4 ♗xh4 12 ♕xh3 ♗f6 13 e5 dxe5 14 ♗xe5 ♗xe5 15 f4 ♘ge7 16 fxe5 ♕g4 17 ♕xg4 hxg4 18 ♘b3 ♘g6 19 e6! f5 20 ♖ad1 ♘ce5 21 ♗d3 ♖h5 22 ♗c2 ♔e7 23 ♘d4 ♔f6 24 ♖f1 ♘e7 25 b4 [⌓ 25 ♘e2 Morphy] 25 … ♖ah8 26 ♘e2 ♖xh2 27 ♘g3 g6 [⌓ 27 … ♘f3+ 28 gxf3 ♖xc2 Staunton; 27 … ♘f3+ 28 gxf3 ♖xc2 29 fxg4 ♖hh2 30 ♘e4+ ♔xe6 (30 … ♔g6 31

gxf5+ ♘xf5 32 ♖xf5 ♔xf5 33 e7 ♖h8 34 ♖d8 +–) 31 ♘f2 ♖h6 32 ♖fe1+ ♔f7 33 ♖d7 ♖e6 34 ♖xe6 ♔xe6 35 ♖xc7± Morphy] 28 ♗b3 ♔g5 29 ♖de1 ♘d3 30 ♖e3 ♘f4 [30 ... f4 31 ♘e4+! △ 32 ♖xd3 Staunton] 31 ♖f2 ♖2h7 32 ♖d2 ♘h5 33 ♘xh5 ♖xh5 34 ♔f2 f4 35 ♖e5+ ♘f5 36 e7? ♖e8 37 ♖d7 ♖h7 38 ♖xc7 ♖exe7 39 ♖cxe7 ♖xe7 40 ♖xe7 ♘xe7 41 a4 ♔f5 42 a5 ♔e5 43 ♗d1 g3+ 44 ♔f3 ♘d5? [□ 44 ... ♘f5! 45 ♗c2 (45 ♔e2 ♘e3 46 ♗~ ♘xg2–+; 45 ♗e2 ♘h4+ 46 ♔g4 ♘xg2 47 ♗f3 ♘e1 48 ♗xb7 g2 49 ♗xg2 ♘xg2–+) 45 ... ♘h4+ 46 ♔e2 (46 ♔g4 f3 47 ♔xg3 fxg2 48 ♔f2 ♘f3 49 ♔xg2 ♘e1+–+) 46 ... f3+ 47 gxf3 g2 48 ♔f2 ♘xf3 49 ♔xg2 ♘e1+–+ Morphy] 45 ♗c2 g5 46 b5 ♘xc3? [□ 46 ... g4+ 47 ♔e2 ♘xc3+–+ Morphy] 47 b6 axb6 48 axb6 ♘b5? [□ 48 ... ♘d5–+ Morphy] 49 ♔g4 ♘d6 50 ♗d3 ♘e4 51 ♗e2 ♔d4 52 ♗f3 ♔e5 53 ♗e2 ♔f6 54 ♗f3 ♘f2+? [□ 54 ... ♘d6 △ 55 ... ♘c8–+ Lasa] 55 ♔h5 g4 56 ♗xb7 ♔e7 57 ♗c8 ♔d6 58 ♗xg4 ♔c6 ½-½ L/N6020-1874

## 1834-✕BM-3
**Bourdonnais, L.C.M. de la= Macdonnell, A.**

1 e4 e5 2 ♘f3 ♘c6 3 d4 exd4 4 ♗c4 ♕f6 [□ 4 ... ♘f6 Anderssen] 5 0-0 d6 6 c3 d3 7 ♕xd3 ♕g6 8 ♗f4 ♗e7 9 ♘bd2 ♘h6 10 ♖ae1 0-0 11 ♘d4 ♘e5 12 ♗xe5 dxe5 13 ♘4f3 [13 ♘c2 ♖d8 14 ♕e2 ♗h3 15 f3 ♗xg2 16 ♕xg2 ♖xd2–+ Anderssen] 13 ... ♗d6 14 h3 ♔h8 [14 ... ♗xh3 15 ♘h4 ♕g5 16 ♘df3 ♕g4 17 ♔h1± Anderssen; 14 ... ♗xh3 15 ♘h4 ♕g5 16 ♘df3 ♕g4 17 ♔h1 g5 18 ♘xg5 ♗xg2+ △ 19 ... ♕xg5∓ Staunton] 15 ♘h4 ♕h5 16 ♕g3 f5 17 ♘xf5 [17 exf5? e4!–+ Anderssen] 17 ... ♘xf5 18 exf5 ♗xf5 19 ♘e4 ♗xe4 20 ♖xe4 ♖f6 [□ 20 ... ♖f4 Walker, G.] 21 ♖h4 ♕f5 22 ♕e3 [△ 23 ♗d3 Anderssen] 22 ... ♕d7 23 ♗d3 g6 [23 ... h6? 24 ♕e4! Anderssen] 24 ♗e4 ♖af8 25 ♕g3 [25 ♕xa7? b6; 25 ♗xb7? ♕b5 △ 26 ... ♗c5 Anderssen] 25 ... ♕g7 [△ 26 ... ♗c5 Anderssen] 26 b4 a5 27 a3 axb4 28 axb4 c5 29 ♖b1 cxb4 30 cxb4 ♗c7 31 ♔h1 ♖b6 [31 ... ♗b6 32 f3 Anderssen; 31 ... ♖xf2 Staunton] 32 b5 ♗d8 33 ♖g4 g5 [△ 34 ... h5 Anderssen] 34 ♗f3 [□ 34 ♗d3 Anderssen] 34 ... h5 35 ♖e4 g4 36 hxg4? [□ 36 ♗e2 Anderssen] 36 ... hxg4 37 ♕xg4 ♖h6+ 38 ♔g1 ♕h7 39 g3 ♖g8 40 ♕c8 ♗b6 41 ♕c3 ♖xg3+! 42 ♔f1 ♗d4 43 ♕c8+ ♖g8 44 ♕c4 ♖h1+? [□ 44 ... ♖h2–+ Lewis] 45 ♔e2 ♖xb1 46 ♖xd4 ♖b2+ [46 ... exd4 47 ♕xd4+ ♕g7 48 ♕h4+= Morphy] 47 ♖d2 ♖xd2+ 48 ♔xd2 ♖d8+ 49 ♔e2 ♕h6 50 ♕c3 ♕g7 51 ♗e4 ♔g8 52 ♕b3+ ♔f8 53 ♕f3+ ♕f7 54 ♗xb7 ♕xf3+ 55 ♔xf3 ½-½ L/N6020-1874

## 1834-✕BM-4
**Bourdonnais, L.C.M. de la+ Macdonnell, A.**

1 e4 e5 2 ♘f3 ♘c6 3 ♗c4 ♗c5 4 c3 d6 5 d4 exd4 6 cxd4 ♗b6 7 d5 [□ 7 ♘c3 Morphy] 7 ... ♘e5 [□ 7 ... ♘ce7 Staunton] 8 ♘xe5 dxe5 9 ♘c3 ♘f6 10 ♗g5 0-0 11 ♕f3 ♕d6 12 ♗xf6 ♕xf6 13 ♕xf6 gxf6 14 g4 ♔g7 [14 ... ♗xg4?? 15 ♖g1+– Bourdonnais] 15 ♘e2 ♖h8?! 16 ♖g1 ♔f8 17 ♖g2 ♔e7 18 0-0-0 h5 [□ 18 ... ♗d7 △ 19 ... ♖ag8 Morphy] 19 g5 f5 20 ♘c3 ♗c5 21 g6 ♗d6 22 gxf7 ♔xf7 23 f4! exf4 24 ♖dg1 ♔f8 25 ♖g6 f3? 26 exf5 ♗e5 [26 ... ♗xf5 27 ♖f6+– Staunton; □ 26 ... ♗d7 Morphy; □ 26 ... ♗xh2 27 ♖h1 ♗f4+ △ 28 ... h4] 27 d6 cxd6

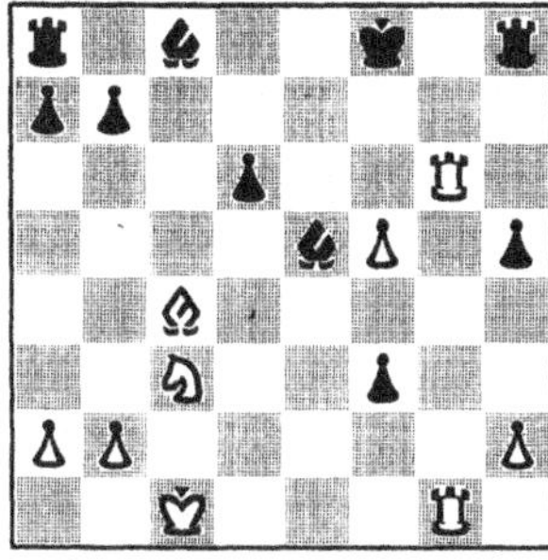

28 ♖g8+ ♖xg8 29 ♖xg8+ ♔e7 30 ♘d5+ ♔d7 31 ♗b5# 1-0 L/N6020-1874

## 1834-✕BM-5
**Macdonnell, A.+ Bourdonnais, L.C.M. de la**

1 e4 c5 2 f4 [□ 2 ♘f3 e6 3 d4 cxd4 4 ♘xd4 ♘c6 5 ♘b5 a6 6 ♘d6+ ♗xd6 7 ♕xd6 ♕e7 8 ♕g3± Anderssen] 2 ... e6 3 ♘f3 d5 4 e5 ♘c6 5 c3 f6 6 ♘a3 ♘h6 7 ♘c2 ♗e7 8 d4 0-0 [□ 8 ... ♕b6 Staunton] 9 ♗d3 c4? [□ 9 ... f5 △ 10 ... ♔h8 Anderssen] 10 ♗e2 ♗d7 11 0-0 b5 12 ♘e3 a5 13 ♔h1 fxe5 14 fxe5 ♘f5 15 g4 ♘xe3 16 ♗xe3 ♗e8 17 ♕d2 [△ 18 ♘g5 Anderssen] 17 ... ♗g6 18 ♘g5 ♗xg5 19 ♗xg5 ♕d7 20 h4 b4 21 ♔h2 bxc3 22 bxc3 a4 23 h5 ♗e4 24 h6 g6 25 ♗f6 ♖ab8 26 ♗g7 ♕e7 [△ 27 ... ♕h4+ 28 ♔g1 ♕h1# Anderssen] 27 ♔g3 [27 ♖f6 Staunton] 27 ... ♖xf1? [□ 27 ... ♖f7 28 ♖xf7 ♔xf7 29 ♖f1+ ♔e8 Anderssen] 28 ♖xf1 a3 29 ♖f6 ♘a5 [29 ... ♖b2 30 ♕f4 ♖b8 31 ♗xc4+– Morphy] 30 ♗d1 ♘b3 31 ♕f2 [31 axb3 cxb3 32 ♗xb3; 31 ♗xb3? cxb3 32 axb3 ♗b1! Anderssen] 31 ... ♘c1 32 ♗a4 [△ 33 ♗d7 Anderssen] 32 ... ♘d3! 33 ♕f1 g5 34 ♗c2 [34 ♗d7 ♘f4 Anderssen] 34 ... ♘c5? [□ 34 ... ♘f4 Bourdonnais] 35 dxc5 ♗xc2 36 c6 ♗a4 37 c7 ♖e8 38 ♕c1! [38 ♖f8+ ♖xf8 39 ♕xf8+ ♕xf8 40 ♗xf8 ♗d7∞ Staunton] 38 ... ♕xc7 39 ♕xg5 ♗c2 40 ♗f8+ ♗g6 41 ♗xa3 ♕d7 42 ♗d6 d4 43 ♕f4 ♕c8 44 ♕xd4 ♕d7 45 ♕f4 ♕c8 46 a4 1-0 L/N6020-1874

## 1834-✕BM-6
**Bourdonnais, L.C.M. de la– Macdonnell, A.**

1 e4 e5 2 ♘f3 ♘c6 3 ♗c4 ♗c5 4 c3 d6 5 d4 exd4 6 cxd4 ♗b6 7 d5 ♘ce7 8 e5 ♗g4 [□ 8 ... dxe5 △ 9 ... ♕d6 Staunton] 9 ♗b5+ [□ 9 ♕a4+ ♗d7 10 ♕b3 △ 11 e6±; 9 ♕a4+ c6 10 dxc6 bxc6 11 ♗xf7+ ♔xf7 11 ♕xg4±; 9 ♕a4+ ♕d7 10 ♗b5 c6 11 e6+–; 9 ♕a4+ ♔f8! 10 ♕b3 ♗xf3 11 ♕xf3 ♘g6= Morphy] 9 ... ♔f8 [□ 9 ... c6; 9 ... ♗d7 Staunton] 10 e6 fxe6 11 dxe6 ♘f6 12 h3 ♗xf3 13 ♕xf3 c6 14 ♗d3 ♕c8 15 ♗f5 [□ 15 ♕e2 Morphy] 15 ... ♔e8 16 0-0 ♖f8 17 ♕d3 ♘xf5 18 ♕xf5 ♔e7 19 ♗g5? [□ 19 ♖e1 ♘d5 20 ♗g5+ ♔e8 21 ♕xh7 ♗xf2+ 22 ♔h2+– Morphy] 19 ... ♕xe6 20 ♕xh7 ♕f7 21 ♘c3 ♔d7 22 ♕f5+ ♔c7 23 ♗f4 ♖ad8 24 ♕c2 [△ 25 ♘b5+ Staunton; □ 24 ♖ad1 Morphy] 24 ... ♔b8 25 a4 ♘h5 26 ♗g5 ♖de8 27 a5 ♗c5 28 ♘a4 ♗d4 29 ♕d2? [□ 29 ♖ad1 Staunton] 29 ... ♘g3! 30 ♖fd1 [30 ♕xd4? ♘e2+–+ Staunton] 30 ... ♗xf2+ 31 ♔h2 ♘e4 32 ♕c1 ♗g3+ 33 ♔g1 ♕f2+ 34 ♔h1 ♗e5 [□ 34 ... ♖h8 Staunton] 35 ♖d3 ♘g3+ 36 ♖xg3 ♕xg3 37 ♕g1 ♕xg5 38 a6 ♕g3 39 axb7 ♖f2 40 ♖a3 ♕f4 [40 ... ♖f1! 41 ♖xg3 ♖xg1+ 42 ♔xg1 ♗xg3 △ 43 ... ♖e1# Morphy] 41 ♘b6 ♖f1 42 ♘d7+ ♔c7 [42 ... ♔xb7? 43 ♖xa7+ ♔c8 44 ♘b6+ ♔b8 (44 ... ♔d8?? 45 ♖d7#) 45 ♘d7+= Morphy] 43 b8♕+ ♖xb8 0-1 L/N6020-1874

## 1834-✕BM-7
**Macdonnell, A.– Bourdonnais, L.C.M. de la**

1 e4 c5 2 f4 e6 3 ♘f3 ♘c6 4 c3 d5 5 e5 [□ 5 exd5 St Amant] 5 ... f6 6 ♗e2 ♗e7 7 ♘a3 ♕b6 8 ♘c2 ♘h6 9 d4 cxd4 10 cxd4 ♗d7 11 ♗d3 ♘b4 12 ♘xb4 ♗xb4+ 13 ♔f2 [□ 13 ♗d2 Staunton] 13 ... 0-0 14 ♖f1 [□ 14 ♔g3 Morphy] 14 ... fxe5 15 fxe5 [15 ♘xe5 ♕xd4+ 16 ♔g3 (16 ♔e2 ♗b5! 17 ♗xb5 ♕e4+ 18 ♗e3 ♗c5–+) 16 ... ♖ad8 17 ♗xh7+ ♔xh7 18 ♕xd4 ♘f5+ 19 ♔ ♘xd4–+ Morphy] 15 ... ♘f5? [□ 15 ... ♕xd4+ Staunton] 16 ♗xf5 ♖xf5 17 ♔g1 ♖c8 18 g4 ♖f7 19 a4 ♖cf8 20 ♗e3 ♗e7 21 ♕e2 ♕b3 22 ♗g5 ♗b4! [22 ... ♖xf3? 23 ♗xe7 Morphy] 23 ♔g2? [□ 23 ♗e3 St Amant] 23 ... ♖xf3! 24 ♖xf3 ♖xf3 25 ♖c1 [25 ♕xf3 ♕xb2+ △ 26 ... ♕xa1–+ Staunton] 25 ... ♖f8 26 ♖c7? ♗c6 27 ♗e3 ♕c4 28 ♕d1 ♗a5 29 ♖e7 ♗xa4 0-1 L/N6020-1874

### 1834-⚔BM-8
**Bourdonnais, L.C.M. de la+ Macdonnell, A.**

1 d4 d5 2 c4 dxc4 3 ♘c3 f5 4 e3 e6 5 ♗xc4 c6 6 ♘f3 ♗d6 7 e4 b5? 8 ♗b3 a5 [□ 8 ... b4 9 ♘e2 fxe4 Staunton] 9 exf5 exf5 10 0-0 a4? 11 ♗xg8 ♖xg8 12 ♗g5 ♕c7 [□ 12 ... ♕b6?] 13 ♕e2+ ♔f8 14 ♖fe1 ♔f7? [□ 14 ... ♗d7?] 15 ♖ac1 [△ 16 ♘xb5 Staunton] 15 ... ♕b7 16 d5 h6? [□ 16 ... ♗d7?] 17 dxc6 ♕a6 18 ♘xb5! hxg5 19 ♘xd6+ ♔g6 20 ♘e5+ ♔f6 21 ♕h5 g6 22 ♕h7 [22 ♘e8+ ♖xe8 23 ♕xg6+ ♔e7 24 ♘d7+ ♔d8 25 c7+ ♔xd7 26 cxb8♘+ ♖xb8 27 ♕xe8+ ♔d6 28 ♖ed1++-] 22 ... ♗e6 23 ♘xg6 [□ 23 ♘g4+ fxg4 24 ♘e4+ ♔f5 25 ♖c5+ ♗d5 26 ♕f7+- Walker, G.]

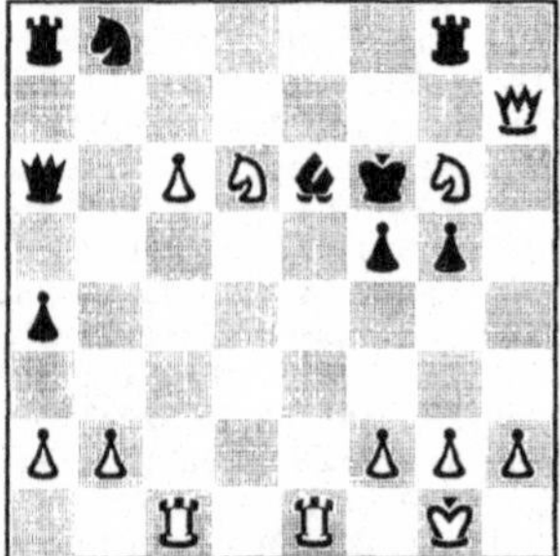

23 ... ♘xc6 [23 ... ♖xg6? 24 ♘e8# Bourdonnais] 24 ♖xc6 ♕d3 [24 ... ♕xc6 25 ♖xe6+ ♔xe6 26 ♕e7+ ♔d5 27 ♕e5# Staunton] 25 ♕e7+ [□ 25 ♕f7+!! ♗xf7 26 ♘e8#; 25 ♖xe6+ ♔xe6 26 ♕f7# Staunton] 25 ... ♔xg6 26 ♖xe6+ ♔h5 27 ♕h7+ ♔g4 28 ♖c4+ f4 29 h3+ ♕xh3 30 ♕xh3# **1-0**

L/N6020-1874

### 1834-⚔BM-9
**Macdonnell, A.– Bourdonnais, L.C.M. de la**

1 e4 e6 2 f4 d5 3 e5 c5 4 ♘f3 ♘c6 5 c3 f6 6 ♘a3 ♘h6 7 ♘c2 ♘f7 8 d4 ♕b6 9 ♘e3 cxd4 10 cxd4 ♗b4+ 11 ♔f2 fxe5 12 fxe5 0-0 13 ♔g3 ♕c7 14 h4 ♘fxe5! 15 dxe5 ♘xe5 16 ♔h3 ♘xf3 17 gxf3 d4 18 ♘g4 [18 ♕xd4?? e5+- Saint-Amant] 18 ... h5 19 ♘f2 ♕e5 20 ♗d3 ♗d6 21 ♘e4 ♗c7 22 ♔g2 ♗d7 23 f4 ♕f5 24 ♘g5 ♗c6+ 25 ♔g1 ♕g4+? 26 ♕xg4 hxg4 27 ♖h2 ♗d5 28 h5 [□ 28 ♖f2 Staunton] 28 ... ♖xf4 29 ♗xf4 ♗xf4 30 ♘e4 ♗e3+! [30 ... ♗xh2+?! 31 ♔xh2± Saint-Amant] 31 ♔g2 ♖f8 32 ♖f1 ♖f5 33 ♖hh1? [□ 33 ♖h4± Staunton] 33 ... ♖e5 34 ♔g3 ♗xe4 35 ♗xe4 ♖xe4 36 ♖h4 e5 37 ♖xg4 ♗f4+ 38 ♔f3 ♖e3+ 39 ♔f2 d3 40 ♖fg1 ♖e2+ 41 ♔f3 ♗h6 42 ♖e4 ♖xb2 43 ♖xe5 ♖xa2 44 ♔g4 d2 45 ♖d5 ♖c2 46 ♖g3 b5 47 ♖gd3 ♖c1 48 ♔f5 ♔h7 49 ♖xd2 ♗xd2 50 ♖xd2 a5 **0-1**

L/N6020-1874

### 1834-⚔BM-10
**Bourdonnais, L.C.M. de la+ Macdonnell, A.**

1 d4 d5 2 c4 dxc4 3 e3 e5 4 dxe5? ♕xd1+ 5 ♔xd1 ♘c6 6 f4 ♗e6 7 ♗d2 ♗c5 8 ♘f3 h6 9 ♘c3 ♖d8 10 ♔e1 ♘ge7 11 ♖c1 ♗b4 12 ♘b5 ♗xd2+ 13 ♘xd2 ♖d7 14 ♗xc4 ♗xc4 15 ♖xc4 0-0 16 ♘f3 ♖fd8 17 ♔e2 ♘d5 18 ♘bd4 ♘xd4+? [□ 18 ... ♘xf4+= Saint-Amant] 19 ♖xd4 [19 ♘xd4? ♘xf4+ Staunton] 19 ... c5 20 ♖d2 ♘b4 21 a3 ♖xd2+ [□ 21 ... ♘d3 △ 22 ... c4 Staunton] 22 ♘xd2 ♘c6 23 ♘c4 b6 24 ♖d1 ♖xd1 25 ♔xd1 ♔f8 26 ♔e2 ♔e7 27 ♔d3 ♔e6 28 ♔e4 ♘e7 29 g4 g6 30 a4 f5+ 31 exf6 ♔xf6 32 ♘e5 ♔e6 33 ♘xg6! ♘c8 [33 ... ♘xg6 34 f5+ ♔f6 35 fxg6+- Staunton] 34 f5+ ♔d6 35 h4 ♔c7 36 ♔e5 ♘d6 37 f6 a6 38 ♔e6 b5 39 axb5 axb5 40 f7 ♘xf7 41 ♔xf7 ♔d6 42 ♘f4 c4 43 g5 hxg5 44 hxg5 b4 45 ♘e2 **1-0**

L/N6020-1874

### 1834-⚔BM-11
**Macdonnell, A.– Bourdonnais, L.C.M. de la**

1 e4 e5 2 f4 exf4 3 ♗c4 ♕h4+ 4 ♔f1 g5 5 ♘c3 ♗g7 6 d4 [6 g3!? Morphy] 6 ... d6 7 ♗e2 [□ 7 ♘f3; 7 e5 Morphy] 7 ... ♘c6 8 e5 ♘ge7 [8 ... dxe5 9 ♘d5 △ 10 dxe5± Dufresne] 9 ♘b5 0-0! 10 ♘xc7 ♖b8 11 ♘f3 ♕h6 12 exd6 ♘f5 13 c3 ♘g3+ 14 hxg3 ♕xh1+ 15 ♔f2 fxg3+ 16 ♔xg3 ♕xd1 17 ♗xd1 h6 18 b3 b5 19 ♗e3 f5 20 d5 f4+ 21 ♔h2 fxe3 22 dxc6 g4! 23 ♘d4 ♗e5+ 24 ♔g1 ♗xd6 25 ♘cxb5 ♗c5 26 b4 [□ 26 ♗e2 Staunton] 26 ... ♗b6 27 ♘d6 ♗xd4 28 cxd4 ♖xb4 29 ♘xc8 ♖xc8 30 d5 ♔f7 31 ♗b3 ♔e7 32 ♔f1 ♖e4 33 ♔e2 ♖f8 34 ♔d3 ♖e5 35 ♖e1 ♔d6 36 ♖xe3 ♖xe3+-+ 37 ♔xe3 h5 38 ♔e4 h4 39 ♗d1 h3 40 gxh3 gxh3 41 ♗f3 h2 42 ♗g2 ♖f1 **0-1**

L/N6020-1874

### 1834-⚔BM-12
**Bourdonnais, L.C.M. de la+ Macdonnell, A.**

1 d4 d5 2 c4 dxc4 3 e3 [3 e4 Staunton] 3 ... e5 4 ♗xc4 exd4 5 exd4 ♘f6 6 ♘f3 ♗d6 7 0-0 0-0 8 ♗g5 h6 9 ♗h4 g5?! 10 ♗g3 ♗g4 11 ♘c3 ♘c6 12 ♕d3 [△ 13 ♕g6+ Staunton] 12 ... ♔g7 [□ 12 ... ♗xf3 13 ♕g6+ ♔h8 14 ♕xh6+ ♘h7 15 gxf3 ♘xd4= Morphy] 13 ♘e5 ♗xe5 [13 ... ♘e7 14 f4 ♗f5 15 ♕d1 g4 16 ♗h4!± Löwenthal] 14 dxe5 ♘h5 15 ♘d5 ♘xg3? [□ 15 ... ♗e6 Löwenthal] 16 ♕xg3 ♗h5 17 f4 ♘a5 18 b3 [□ 18 ♘f6 ♕d4+ (18 ... ♗g6 19 ♖ad1±; 18 ... ♘xc4 19 ♘xh5+ △ 20 ♖ad1±) 19 ♔h1 ♘xc4 20 ♘xh5+ ♔g6 (20 ... ♔h8 21 ♘f6 gxf4 22 ♕h4 ♔g7 23 ♖xf4+-) 21 ♖ad1 ♕c5 22 f5+ ♔h7 23 ♘f6+ ♔h8 24 ♘d7 ♕e3 25 ♖f3 ♕e2 26 ♖e1+- Löwenthal] 18 ... ♘xc4 19 bxc4 c6 20 ♘f6 ♕d4+ 21 ♔h1 ♗g6 22 ♖ad1 ♕xc4? [□ 22 ... gxf4 Bourdonnais] 23 f5 ♗h7 24 ♘d7 ♖fd8 25 e6 f6 [25 ... fxe6 26 ♕e5+ ♔g8 27 ♘f6++- Löwenthal] 26 ♕c7! ♖dc8 27 ♕xb7 ♕b5 28 ♖b1! ♕xb7 29 ♖xb7 ♔h8 30 ♘xf6 ♗g8 31 ♖d1 ♖d8 32 ♖dd7 ♖xd7 33 ♖xd7 c5 34 e7 **1-0**

L/N6020-1874

### 1834-⚔BM-13
**Macdonnell, A.= Bourdonnais, L.C.M. de la**

1 e4 c5 2 f4 e6 3 ♘f3 ♘c6 4 c3 d5 5 e5 f6 6 ♘a3 ♘h6 7 ♘c2 ♕b6 8 d4 cxd4 9 cxd4 ♗b4+ [9 ... ♗d7 10 h4!? ♖c8 11 ♗e2 ♗b4+ 12 ♔f2 0-0 13 ♔g3!? fxe5 14 fxe5 ♘f5+ 15 ♔h3 h5 16 g4 hxg4+ 17 ♔xg4!? Macdonnell] 10 ♘xb4 ♕xb4+ 11 ♔f2 [□ 11 ♕d2 ♕xd2+ △ 12 ... ♘f5∓ Staunton] 11 ... 0-0 12 a3 ♕b6 13 ♔g3? ♘xd4! 14 ♘xd4 ♕xd4 15 ♕xd4 ♘f5+ 16 ♔h3 ♘xd4 17 b4 fxe5 [17 ... ♗d7 △ 18 ... ♖ac8 Saint-Amant] 18 fxe5 ♘c6 19 ♗b2 ♖f7 20 ♖b1 ♗d7 21 ♗d3 ♖af8 22 ♖hf1 a6 23 ♔g3 ♖xf1 24 ♖xf1 ♖xf1 25 ♗xf1 ♘e7 26 ♗d3 ♗e8 27 ♔f4 ♗g6 28 ♗e2 ♗e4 29 g3 ♔f7 30 ♗d1 h6 31 h4 ♘f5 32 h5 ♘e7 33 g4 ♔e8 34 ♗d4 g6 35 hxg6 ♘xg6+ 36 ♔g3 ♗d3 37 ♗a4+ ♔e7 [37 ... b5 Saint-Amant] 38 ♗d1 ♔f7 39 ♗a4 ♘e7 40 ♔h4 b5 41 ♗d1 ♘c6 42 ♗b2 ♔g6 43 ♔g3 a5 44 bxa5 ♘xa5 45 ♔f4 ♘c4 46 ♗c1 ♗b1 47 ♗b3 ♗d3 48 ♗d1 [48 ♗xc4= Saint-Amant] 48 ... ♔f7 49 ♗b3 d4 50 a4 bxa4 51 ♗xa4 ♔e7 52 ♗b3 [□ 52 ♗b5 Saint-Amant] 52 ... ♘a5 53 ♗d1 ♗g6 54 ♗d2 ♘c4 55 ♗b4+ ♔f7 56 ♗a4 d3 57 ♗c3 d2 58 ♗d1 ♔g7 59 ♔f3 h5 60 ♔f4 h4 61 ♗d4 ♗b1 62 ♔f3 ♔g6 63 ♔e2 ♗e4 64 ♗f2 h3? [□ 64 ... ♔g5-+ Saint-Amant] 65 ♗g3 ♔g5 66 ♗h2 ♔xg4 67 ♔f2+ ♔f5 68 ♔e2 ♗d5 69 ♔d3 ♘xe5+ 70 ♔xd2 ♘c6 [70 ... ♘f3+ 71 ♗xf3 ♗xf3= Saint-Amant; □ 70 ... ♘g4! Lewis] 71 ♔e3 e5 72 ♔f2 ♗g2 73 ♔g3 ♔e4 74 ♗g4 ♔e3 75 ♗xh3 ♗xh3 76 ♔xh3 e4 77 ♔g2 ♔e2 78 ♗f4 ♘e7 79 ♗g5 ♘f5 80 ♗f4 ♘e3+ 81 ♔g3 **½-½**

L/N6020-1874

### 1834-⚔BM-14
**Macdonnell, A.– Bourdonnais, L.C.M. de la**

1 e4 c5 2 f4 e6 3 ♘f3 ♘c6 4 c3 d5 5 e5 f6 6 ♘a3 ♘h6 7 ♘c2 ♕b6 8 d4 ♗d7 9 ♘e3 cxd4 10 cxd4 ♗b4+

11 ♔f2 0-0 12 ♔g3 fxe5 13 fxe5 ♗e8 14 ♔h3 ♗h5 15 g4 ♗g6 [15 ... ♖xf3+!?∞ Staunton] 16 ♗g2 ♗e4 17 g5 ♘f5 18 ♘xf5 ♖xf5 19 ♗e3 ♗xf3 20 ♗xf3 ♘xe5 21 ♗g4 ♘xg4 22 ♕xg4 ♖af8 23 ♖ag1 ♗d6 24 ♗c1 ♖f3+ 25 ♔h4? [□ 25 ♖g3∓ Saint-Amant] 25 ... ♖3f4 **0-1** L/N6020-1874

### 1834-✕BM-15
**Bourdonnais, L.C.M. de la+ Macdonnell, A.**

1 d4 d5 2 c4 dxc4 3 e3 e5 4 ♗xc4 exd4 5 exd4 ♘f6 6 ♘c3 ♗e7 7 ♘f3 0-0 [7 ... ♗g4 8 ♗xf7+ ♔xf7 9 ♘e5+± Saint-Amant] 8 h3 c6 9 ♗e3 ♗f5 [9 ... ♗e6 Saint-Amant] 10 g4 ♗g6 [□ 10 ... ♗e4 Saint-Amant] 11 ♘e5 ♘bd7 [□ 11 ... ♗e4 Saint-Amant] 12 ♘xg6 hxg6 13 h4 ♘b6 14 ♗b3 ♘fd5

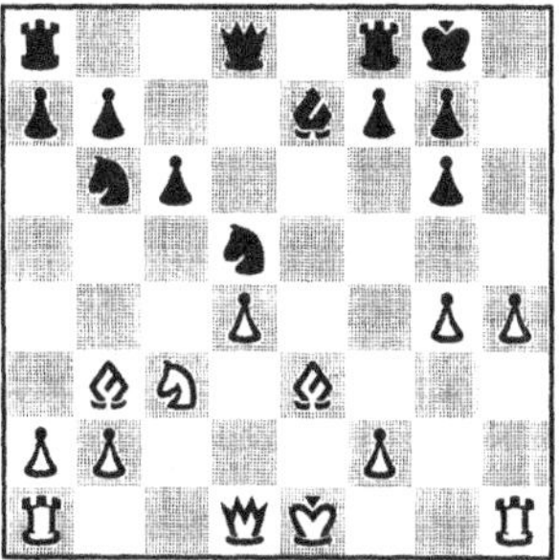

15 h5! ♘xe3 16 fxe3 ♗h4+? [□ 16 ... g5 Morphy] 17 ♔d2 gxh5 18 ♕f3! ♗g5 [∆ 19 ... ♕xd4+; ∆ 19 ... h4 ⁋] 19 ♖af1! ♕xd4+ 20 ♔c2 ♕f6 21 ♖xh5 [∆ 22 ♕h3+- ⁋] 21 ... ♕g6+ [□ 21 ... g6 ∆ 22 ... ♕xf3 Saint-Amant] 22 e4 ♘d5 23 ♖fh1 ♗h6 24 g5 f5 25 ♘xd5 cxd5 26 ♗xd5+ ♔h7 27 ♖xh6+ gxh6 28 ♖xh6+ ♕xh6 29 gxh6 **1-0** L/N6020-1874

### 1834-✕BM-16
**Macdonnell, A.– Bourdonnais, L.C.M. de la**

1 e4 c5 2 f4 ♘c6 [2 ... e6 Saint-Amant] 3 ♘f3 e6 4 c3 [□ 4 ♗b5 a6 5 ♗xc6 bxc6 6 c4 d5 7 e5±; 4 ♗b5 ♕b6 5 c4 ♘ge7 6 ♘c3±; 4 ♗b5 ♘d4 5 ♘xd4 cxd4 6 c4±; 4 ♗b5 ♘ge7 5 d4 cxd4 6 ♘xd4±; 4 ♗b5 ♘ge7 5 c4 Löwenthal] 4 ... d5 5 e5 f6 6 ♘a3 ♘h6 7 ♘c2 ♕b6 8 d4 ♗d7 9 ♘e3 [□ 9 ♗d3 Staunton] 9 ... cxd4 10 cxd4 [□ 10 ♘xd4 Staunton; 10 ♘xd4 ♘xd4 11 cxd4 ♗b4+ Saint-Amant] 10 ... ♗b4+ 11 ♔f2 0-0 12 ♔g3 ♖ac8 13 h4 fxe5 14 fxe5 ♖xf3+!∓ 15 gxf3 [15 ♔xf3? ♕xd4 Morphy] 15 ... ♘xd4 16 ♗d3 ♖f8 17 f4 ♗c5 18 ♖f1 [□ 18 b4 Morphy] 18 ... ♗b5! 19 ♗xb5 ♕xb5 20 ♔h3 ♘e2 21 ♘g2 [□ 21 a4 ♕a6 22 ♘g2 Morphy] 21 ... ♘f5 [∆ 22 ... ♘fg3 23 ♖f3 ♘e4→ Löwenthal] 22 ♔h2 ♘eg3 23 ♖f3 ♘e4 24 ♕f1 ♕e8! 25 b4!? ♗d4 26 ♖b1 ♕h5 27 ♖bb3 ♖c8! 28 ♗e3 ♖c2 29 ♔g1 ♘xe3 30 ♖fxe3 [30 ♘xe3 ♕g4+!→ Bourdonnais] 30 ... ♘d2! 31 ♕d3 ♖c1+ 32 ♔h2 ♘f1+ 33 ♔h3 ♘xe3 34 ♘xe3 ♕f3+ **0-1** L/N6020-1874

### 1834-✕BM-17
**Bourdonnais, L.C.M. de la+ Macdonnell, A.**

1 d4 d5 2 c4 dxc4 3 e3 e5 4 ♗xc4 [4 dxe5? ♕xd1+∓ Bourdonnais] 4 ... exd4 5 exd4 ♘f6 6 ♘c3 ♗e7 [□ 6 ... ♗d6 Bourdonnais] 7 ♘f3 0-0 8 ♗e3 c6 [∆ 9 ... ♘bd7 Bourdonnais; □ 8 ... ♗g4! Saint-Amant] 9 h3! ♘bd7 10 ♗b3 [10 0-0 Saint-Amant] 10 ... ♘b6 11 0-0 ♘fd5 12 a4 a5 13 ♘e5 ♗e6 14 ♗c2 f5 [14 ... f6 15 ♕h5 f5 16 ♕e2 Morphy] 15 ♕e2 [15 f4!? Saint-Amant] 15 ... f4 16 ♗d2 ♕e8 17 ♖ae1! [∆ 18 ♘xc6 Saint-Amant] 17 ... ♗f7 [□ 17 ... ♖f6 Saint-Amant; □ 17 ... ♗d7 Morphy] 18 ♕e4!+- g6 19 ♗xf4 ♘xf4 20 ♕xf4 ♗c4 21 ♕h6 ♗xf1? [□ 21 ... ♗f7± Bourdonnais] 22 ♗xg6! hxg6 23 ♘xg6 ♘c8 [□ 23 ... ♗f6 24 ♖xe8 ♖fxe8 25 ♔xf1 ♗xd4± Morphy] 24 ♕h8+ ♔f7 25 ♕h7+ ♔f6 26 ♘f4 [∆ 27 ♘e4# Bourdonnais] 26 ... ♗d3 27 ♖e6+ ♔g5 28 ♕h6+ ♔f5 29 ♖e5# **1-0** L/N6020-1874

### 1834-✕BM-18
**Macdonnell, A.– Bourdonnais, L.C.M. de la**

1 e4 e5 2 f4 exf4 3 ♗c4 ♕h4+ 4 ♔f1 g5 5 ♘c3 ♗g7 6 d4 ♘c6 7 e5 ♘ge7 8 ♘f3 ♕h5 9 ♘e4 h6 10 ♘f6+ ♗xf6 11 exf6 d5 12 ♗d3 ♘f5 13 ♕e1+ ♔d8 14 ♘e5 [∆ 15 ♗e2 Morphy] 14 ... ♘fxd4 [14 ... ♘g3+? 15 ♔g1 ♘xh1 16 ♘xc6+ ♔d7 17 ♕e7++-; □ 14 ... ♖e8 Morphy] 15 c3 ♘xe5 16 ♕xe5 ♘c6 [16 ... ♕d1+?? 17 ♔f2+- Dufresne] 17 ♕xd5+ ♔e8 18 ♗b5 [□ 18 ♗xf4 Walker] 18 ... ♗e6 19 ♗xc6+ ♔f8 20 ♕c5+ ♔g8 21 ♗f3 ♕g6 22 ♕d4 [□ 22 ♕f2; 22 b3 Morphy] 22 ... c5 23 ♕e5 ♖e8 24 ♗e2? [□ 24 ♕xc5 Staunton; 24 ♕xc5? g4∓; □ 24 ♔f2! ♕c2+ (24 ... ♗d7 25 ♕d6; 24 ... g4 25 ♗e4) 25 ♕e2 Morphy] 24 ... f3!

25 ♔f2 [25 ♗xf3? ♗c4+→; 25 gxf3? ♗h3+→ Staunton] 25 ... fxe2 26 ♗e3 b6 27 h4 ♗d7 28 ♕d5 ♕xf6+ 29 ♔xe2 ♗g4+ 30 ♔d2 ♖d8 **0-1** L/N6020-1874

### 1834-✕BM-19
**Bourdonnais, L.C.M. de la– Macdonnell, A.**

1 e4 e5 2 ♗c4 ♗c5 3 ♕e2!? d6 [3 ... ♘f6; 3 ... ♘c6; 3 ... ♕e7 Morphy] 4 d3 [□ 4 f4 Morphy] 4 ... ♘f6 5 h3 ♘c6 6 c3 ♘e7 7 ♗b3 ♘g6 8 g3 c6 9 f4?! exf4 10 gxf4 ♗xg1 11 ♖xg1 ♗xh3 12 f5 ♘e5 13 ♖g3 ♗g4 14 ♕g2 h5 15 d4 ♘ed7 16 ♗g5 ♕b6 17 ♘d2 0-0 [□ 17 ... 0-0-0 Morphy] 18 ♗f4 [□ 18 ♘c4 ♕c7 19 ♗f4 Staunton; 18 ♘c4? ♕c7 19 ♗f4 ♘xe4! 20 ♖e3 (20 ♕xe4? ♖he8) 20 ... ♘df6 Morphy] 18 ... d5 19 e5 ♖fe8 20 ♗e3? [□ 20 ♖e3 Bourdonnais] 20 ... h4 21 ♖xg4 ♘xg4 22 ♕xg4 ♘xe5 23 dxe5 [□ 23 ♕e2 Staunton] 23 ... ♕xe3+ 24 ♔d1 ♖xe5 25 ♔c2 ♕g3 26 ♕d4 ♕e3 27 ♕xh4 ♕h6 28 ♕xh6 gxh6 29 ♖f1 f6 30 c4 ♔f7 31 cxd5 cxd5 32 ♔d3 [32 ♘e4 Morphy] 32 ... ♖g8 33 ♖f4 ♔e7 34 ♘f3 ♖g3 35 ♔d4 ♔d6 36 ♗d1 b5 37 b4 a6 38 a4 h5 39 axb5 axb5 40 ♗c2 ♖e2 41 ♗d3 ♖b2 42 ♔e3 [42 ♔c3?? ♖f2→ Morphy] 42 ... ♖g4 43 ♘d4 ♖xf4 44 ♔xf4 ♖xb4 45 ♔e3 ♔c5 46 ♘e6+ ♔c6 47 ♘f4 ♖xf4!→ 48 ♔xf4 ♔c5 49 ♗e2 h4 50 ♔g4 b4 51 ♔xh4 ♔d4 52 ♔g3 b3 53 ♗d1 b2 54 ♗c2 ♔e3 **0-1** L/N6020-1874

### 1834-✕BM-20
**Macdonnell, A.– Bourdonnais, L.C.M. de la**

1 e4 e5 2 f4 exf4 3 ♗c4 ♕h4+ 4 ♔f1 d6 [□ 4 ... g5 Löwenthal] 5 d4 [5 ♕f3 g5 6 g3 ♕g4 7 d3 ♗h6 8 ♕xg4 ♗xg4 9 h4 gxh4 10 ♖xh4± Löwenthal] 5 ... ♗g4 6 ♕d3 ♘c6 [□ 6 ... g5 Löwenthal] 7 ♗xf7+?! [7 ♗xf4 Staunton] 7 ... ♔xf7 8 ♕b3+ ♔g6 9 ♕xb7 ♘xd4! 10 ♕xa8 [∆ 11 ♕e8+ Staunton] 10 ... ♘f6 [∆ 11 ... ♘xc2 Löwenthal] 11 ♘a3 f3 12 g3 [12 gxf3 ♗xf3→ Löwenthal] 12 ... ♗h3+ 13 ♔e1 ♕g4 14 ♗e3 d5! [∆ 15 ... ♗b4+→ Bourdonnais; ∆ 15 ... ♗b4+ (15 ... dxe4) Morphy] 15 ♕xa7 ♘c6! 16 ♕xc7 [16 ♕a4 d4 17 ♗f4 ♗b4+ 18 c3 dxc3→ Morphy] 16 ... d4 17 ♗d2?! [□ 17 ♗f2 Bourdonnais; □ 17 ♕xc6 Staunton; 17 ♕xc6 dxe3→; 17 ♗f4 ♗b4+→ Morphy] 17 ... ♕xe4+ 18 ♔d1 f2 19 ♘xh3 ♕f3+ 20 ♔c1 ♕xh1+ **0-1** L/N6020-1874

**1834-⚔BM-21**
**Bourdonnais, L.C.M. de la–Macdonnell, A.**
1 e4 e5 2 ♗c4 ♗c5 3 ♕e2 ♘f6 4 d3 ♘c6 5 c3 ♘e7 [◻ 5 ... d6; 5 ... 0-0 Morphy] 6 f4 exf4?! [◻ 6 ... d6 Löwenthal] 7 d4 ♗b6 8 ♗xf4 d6 [◻ 8 ... d5 Löwenthal] 9 ♗d3 ♘g6 10 ♗e3!? [◻ 10 ♗g5 Löwenthal] 10 ... 0-0 11 h3 ♖e8 12 ♘d2 ♕e7 [△ 13 ... ♘d5 Anderssen] 13 0-0-0 c5 14 ♔b1 cxd4 15 cxd4 a5 [◻ 15 ... ♘d5 Anderssen] 16 ♘gf3 ♗d7 17 g4 h6!? 18 ♖dg1 a4 19 g5 hxg5 20 ♗xg5 a3! 21 b3?! [◻ 21 e5 dxe5 22 ♘e4 ♕b4 (22 ... axb2 23 ♗xf6 ♕a3 24 ♗c4+-; 22 ... ♗e6 23 b3! ♘xe4 24 ♗xe4 ♘f4 25 ♕b5±; 22 ... exd4 23 ♘h4 ♘f4 24 ♘xf6+ ♔h8 25 ♕xe7 ♖xe7 26 ♘xd7 ♖xd7 27 ♗xf4) 23 ♗xf6 gxf6 (23 ... ♕xb2+ 24 ♕xb2 axb2 25 ♗xe5 ♗e6 26 ♘c3±) 24 ♘xf6+ ♔g7 25 ♘xe8+ ♖xe8 26 ♗xg6 fxg6 (26 ... exd4 27 ♗xf7+ ♔xf7 28 ♘g5+ ♔g8 29 ♘e6++-) 27 ♘h4 ♖e6 28 ♘xg6 ♖xg6 Löwenthal] 21 ... ♗c6 22 ♖g4 ♗a5 [△ 23 ... ♗xd2 Anderssen] 23 h4 ♗xd2 24 ♘xd2 ♖a5 25 h5 [◻ 25 ♖hg1 Anderssen] 25 ... ♖xg5! 26 ♖xg5 ♘f4 27 ♕f3 ♘xd3 28 d5 [28 ♕xd3? ♘xe4-+; ◻ 28 ♖hg1 Anderssen] 28 ... ♘xd5!

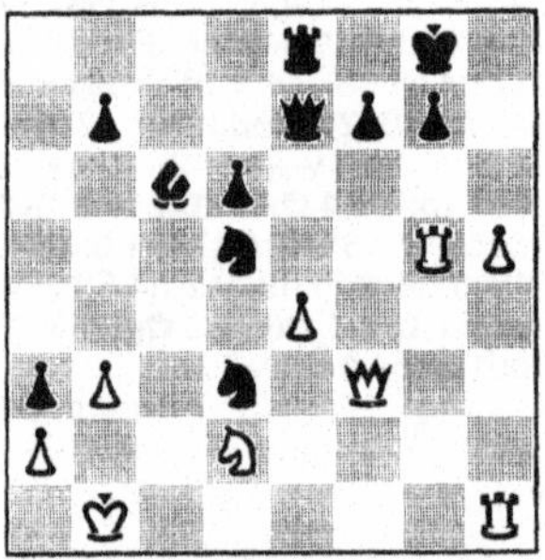

29 ♖hg1! [29 ♖xd5 ♗xd5 30 ♕xd3 (30 exd5 ♕e3 31 ♕xe3 ♖xe3-+) 30 ... ♗xe4 31 ♘xe4 ♕xe4 32 ♕xe4 ♖xe4-+; 29 ♕xd3 ♕xg5 30 exd5 ♕xd5-+; 29 exd5 ♕xg5 30 ♕xd3 ♕xd5-+ Morphy] 29 ... ♘c3+ 30 ♔a1 [◻ 30 ♔c2 Bourdonnais; 30 ♔c2? ♘xe4-+ Löwenthal; 30 ♔c2? ♕xg5 31 ♖xg5 ♘e1+ 32 ♔xc3 ♘xf3 Morphy] 30 ... ♗xe4 31 ♖xg7+ ♔h8 32 ♕g3 [△ 33 ♖h7++- Anderssen] 32 ... ♗g6!? [◻ 32 ... ♕f6 33 ♖g8+! ♔h7 34 ♕g7+ (34 ♖g7+ ♔h6 35 ♕e3+ ♘f4-+) 34 ... ♕xg7 35 ♖8xg7+ (35 ♖1xg7+ ♔h6 36 ♖xe8 ♘b4-+) 35 ... ♔h6 36 ♖xf7 (36 ♘xe4 ♖xe4 37 ♖g8 ♖e1+ 38 ♖xe1 ♘xe1-+) 36 ... ♘b4 37 ♖f6+ ♔xh5 38 ♖c1 ♘c2+-+ Morphy] 33 hxg6 ♕e1+?! 34 ♖xe1? [◻ 34 ♘b1 ♕xg3 35 ♖h7+ ♔g8 36 gxf7+ ♔xh7 37 fxe8♕ ♕xg1 38 ♕f7+ ♔∼ 39 ♕f6+ △ 40 ♕xc3= Anderssen; ◻ 34 ♘b1 ♕xg3 35 ♖h7+ ♔g8 36 gxf7+ ♔xh7 37 ♖h1+! ♔g7 38 fxe8♕+- Staunton] 34 ... ♖xe1+ 35 ♕xe1 ♘xe1 36 ♖h7+ ♔g8 37 gxf7+ ♔xh7 38 f8♕ ♘c2# **0-1** L/N6020-1874

**1834-⚔BM-22**
**Macdonnell, A.–Bourdonnais, L.C.M. de la**
1 e4 e5 2 f4 exf4 3 ♗c4 ♕h4+ 4 ♔f1 g5 5 ♘c3 ♗g7 6 d4 d6 7 ♘d5 [◻ 7 ♘f3; 7 e5 Morphy] 7 ... ♔d8 8 ♗e2? ♘c6 9 e5 ♘ge7 10 ♘c3 ♘f5 11 ♘f3 ♕h6 12 ♘e4 f6 13 exf6 ♗xf6 14 g4? ♘fxd4 15 ♔g2 ♗xg4 16 h4 ♗xf3+ 17 ♗xf3 ♘xf3 18 ♕xf3 ♘e5 19 ♕b3 ♕g6? 20 ♕xb7 ♖c8 21 ♗d2 gxh4+ 22 ♔f1 ♖g8 23 ♘xd6! cxd6 24 ♗a5+ ♔e8 25 ♕xc8+ ♔f7 26 ♕b7+ ♗e7 27 ♕d5+ ♔f8 28 ♖d1 f3 [△ 29 ... ♕g2+-+ Bourdonnais] 29 ♖d2 h3! 30 ♕a8+ ♔f7 31 ♕d5+ ♔f8 32 ♕a8+ ♔g7 [32 ... ♔f7= Bourdonnais] 33 ♕xa7 ♕g2+!-+ 34 ♖xg2+ fxg2+ 35 ♔g1 ♘f3+ 36 ♔f2 gxh1♕ 37 ♕xe7+ ♔h6 38 ♕xd6+ ♔h5 39 ♕d5+ ♖g5 40 ♕f7+ ♔g4 41 ♕c4+ ♘d4! [41 ... ♔h5 42 ♕f7+ Bourdonnais] 42 ♕xd4+ ♔h5 43 ♗b6 ♕h2+ [43 ... ♕g1+ 44 ♔∼ ♕xd4 45 ♗xd4 h2-+ Morphy] 44 ♔e1 ♖e5+ 45 ♔d1 ♕e2+ 46 ♔c1 ♕e1+ 47 ♕d1+ ♕xd1+ 48 ♔xd1 h2 **0-1**
L/N6020-1874

**1834-⚔BM-23**
**Bourdonnais, L.C.M. de la–Macdonnell, A.**
1 d4 d5 2 ♗f4!? c5 3 e3 [3 dxc5?! Saint-Amant] 3 ... ♘c6 4 ♘f3 ♗g4 5 ♗e2 ♗xf3 6 ♗xf3 e6 7 c4 ♘f6 8 ♘c3 cxd4 9 exd4 dxc4 10 0-0 ♗e7 [10 ... ♘d5 11 ♗xd5 exd5 12 ♘b5 ♖c8 13 ♖e1+ ♗e7 14 ♘d6++- Morphy] 11 ♗xc6+ bxc6 12 ♕a4 0-0 13 ♕xc4 ♖c8 14 a3 ♗d6 [◻ 14 ... ♘d5 Morphy] 15 ♗g3 ♗xg3 16 fxg3!? ♘d5 17 ♖ae1 ♕g5?! 18 ♘e4 ♕e7 19 b4 a5 20 ♘c5 [◻ 20 bxa5 Saint-Amant] 20 ... axb4 21 axb4 ♖b8 22 ♘a6 ♖b6 23 b5 ♕a3! [23 ... cxb5 24 ♕xd5 exd5 (24 ... ♖xa6 25 ♕xb5=) 25 ♖xe7 ♖xa6 26 ♖d7= Morphy] 24 ♕c5 ♕xc5 25 ♘xc5 ♖xb5 26 ♘d7 ♖c8 27 ♘e5 ♖b7 28 ♖c1 ♖bc7 29 ♖c5 f6 30 ♘c4 ♔f8 31 ♖a1 ♔e7 32 ♖a6 ♘b4 33 ♖a4 ♖b8 34 ♘a5 ♘d3 [△ 35 ... ♖b1# Staunton] 35 ♔f1 ♘xc5 36 dxc5 ♖b5 **0-1** L/N6020-1875

**1834-⚔BM-24**
**Macdonnell, A.–Bourdonnais, L.C.M. de la**
1 e4 e5 2 ♗c4 ♗c5 3 b4?! ♗xb4 4 f4 d5! [4 ... exf4? Bourdonnais] 5 exd5 e4 6 ♘e2 ♘f6 7 0-0 0-0 8 ♘bc3 c6 9 dxc6 ♘xc6 10 ♔h1 ♗g4 11 ♕e1 e3! 12 dxe3?! ♗xe2 13 ♗xe2 ♘e4 14 ♗b2 ♕a5 15 ♗d3 ♗xc3 16 ♗xc3 ♘xc3 17 ♕h4 f5 18 ♖f3 ♘e4 19 ♖h3 h6 20 ♖f1 ♕c5 21 ♕h5 ♕d6 22 g4 ♖ae8 23 ♗c4+ ♔h7 24 g5 [◻ 24 gxf5 Staunton] 24 ... ♘a5 25 gxh6? [◻ 25 ♗d3; ◻ 25 ♗f7!∞ Staunton] 25 ... g6!-+ 26 ♕e2 ♘xc4 27 ♕xc4 ♘d2 28 ♕c3 ♕c6+ 29 ♕xc6 bxc6 **0-1** L/N6020-1875

**1834-⚔BM-25**
**Bourdonnais, L.C.M. de la+Macdonnell, A.**
1 f4 d5 2 d4?! c5 3 e3 e6 4 ♘f3 ♘c6 5 c4 cxd4? 6 exd4 dxc4 7 ♗xc4 ♘f6 8 ♘c3 ♗e7 9 0-0 0-0 10 ♔h1 a6 11 ♗e3 b5 12 ♗d3 ♗b7 13 ♘e5 ♔h8 14 ♗c2 ♘b4 15 ♗b3 ♘bd5 16 ♘xd5 ♘xd5 17 ♕e2 f6 [◻ 17 ... ♘xe3 Staunton] 18 ♘f3 ♕e8 19 ♖ae1 ♗d6 20 ♗d2 ♘xf4 21 ♗xf4 ♗xf4 22 ♗xe6 ♕h5 23 g4 ♕h6 24 d5 ♖ae8 25 ♕g2 ♖e7 26 ♘d4 g6 27 ♘c6 ♖c7 28 ♖e4 g5 29 ♘d4 ♖d8 30 ♘f5 ♕f8 31 ♖d1 ♖c5 32 ♖ed4 ♗e5 33 ♖4d2 ♖c4 34 ♘e3 ♖c7 35 ♕f3 ♗f4 36 ♖d3 ♕d6 [◻ 36 ... ♕e7 Walker; ◻ 36 ... ♖e7 37 ♗f5 (37 ♕e4 ♖de8 △ 38 ... ♖xe6-+) 37 ... ♗xe3 38 ♖xe3 ♖xd5 39 ♖xd5 ♗xd5 40 ♗e4 ♖xe4 41 ♖xe4 f5 42 gxf5! ♕a8 43 ♔g1 (43 ♖e8+ ♔g7 44 f6+ ♔h6-+) 43 ... ♗xe4 44 ♕c3+ ♔g8 45 ♕f6 ♕a7+ 46 ♔f1 ♗d3+ 47 ♔g1 ♕f7 48 ♕d8+ ♔g7-+ Morphy] 37 ♘f5 ♕xe6?! 38 dxe6 ♗xf3+ 39 ♔g1 ♖xd3 40 ♖xd3 ♖c8 41 e7 ♖e8 42 ♖xf3 ♔g8 43 ♖a3 ♔f7? 44 ♖xa6 ♖c8 45 b3 ♗e5 46 h3 b4 47 ♔g2 ♗f4 48 ♔f3 ♗e5 49 ♔e4 ♗f4 50 ♖a7 ♗e5 51 ♘g7!+- [△ 52 e8♕# Staunton] 51 ... ♖e8 52 ♘xe8 ♔xe8 53 ♔f5 ♔f7 54 ♖b7 h6 55 a4 **1-0**

**1834-⚔BM-26**
**Macdonnell, A.+Bourdonnais, L.C.M. de la**
1 e4 e5 2 ♘f3 ♘c6 3 ♗c4 ♗c5 4 b4 ♗xb4 [4 ... ♘xb4 5 c3 ♘c6 Saint-Amant] 5 c3 ♗a5 6 0-0 d6 [◻ 6 ... ♗b6 Saint-Amant; ◻ 6 ... ♘f6 7 d4 0-0 Morphy] 7 d4 ♗b6 [◻ 7 ... exd4 Staunton] 8 dxe5 ♗g4 9 ♗b5 [9 exd6 cxd6 10 ♕b3± Staunton] 9 ... ♗xf3 10 ♕xf3 dxe5 11 ♕g3 ♕f6 12 ♗g5 [12 ♔h1 △ 13 f4 Staunton] 12 ... ♕e6 13 ♘a3 ♘f6 14 ♗xf6 gxf6 [14 ... ♕xf6 15 ♘c4 0-0 16 ♗xc6 ♕xc6 17 ♘xe5 ♕e6; 17 ... ♕xe4? 18 ♘d7 Morphy] 15 ♖ad1 ♗c5 16 ♕g7 ♔e7? [◻ 16 ... ♖f8 Morphy] 17 ♗c4!+- ♖ag8 18 ♕xg8 ♖xg8 19 ♗xe6 fxe6 20 ♘c2 ♖g4 21 ♖fe1 f5? 22 exf5 exf5 23 ♘e3 ♗xe3 24 ♖xe3 ♔e6 25 ♖h3 ♖g7 26 ♖h6+ ♔e7 27 ♖b1 ♘d8 28 f3 b6 29 ♖d1 ♘f7? [29 ... ♘e6 30 ♖d5+- Morphy] 30 ♖c6 ♖g8 31 ♖xc7+ ♔f6 32 ♖xa7 ♖c8 33 ♖dd7 ♘g5 34 ♖dc7 **1-0**
L/N6020-1875

**1834-✕BM-27**
**Bourdonnais, L.C.M. de la– Macdonnell, A.**

1 f4 d5 2 d4 c5 3 e3 ♘c6 4 ♘f3 ♘f6 5 c4 ♗g4 6 cxd5 ♗xf3 7 ♕xf3 ♕xd5 8 ♕xd5 ♘xd5 9 ♗b5 cxd4 10 exd4 [□ 10 ♗xc6+ Morphy] 10 ... ♘b4 11 ♘a3 0-0-0 12 ♗xc6 ♘xc6 13 ♗e3 ♘xd4 14 0-0-0 e5 [□ 14 ... ♘c6 Morphy] 15 ♘c4? [□ 15 fxe5= Morphy] 15 ... ♗c5 16 ♗xd4? [□ 16 fxe5 Saint-Amant] 16 ... exd4 17 ♖he1 f6 18 ♖e6 ♖he8 19 ♖de1 ♖xe6 20 ♖xe6 ♔d7! 21 f5 ♖e8 22 ♖xe8 ♔xe8

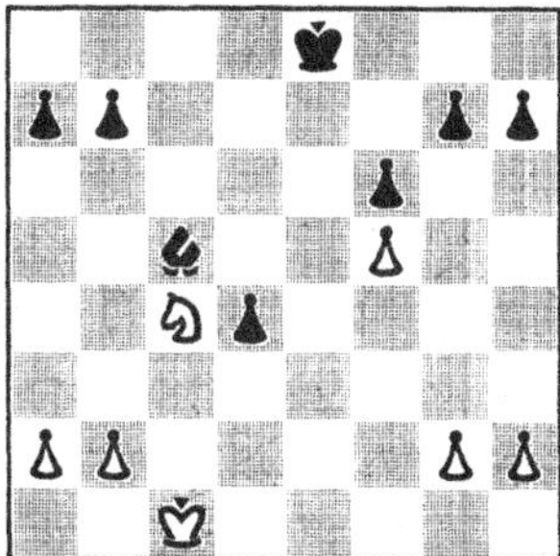

23 ♔c2 ♔d7 24 ♔d3 ♔c6 25 ♔e4 ♔b5 26 ♘d2 ♔b4 27 ♔d3 ♗d6 28 ♘f3 ♗e5 29 h4 [29 ♘xd4 ♗xh2 Staunton] 29 ... ♔c5 30 ♔e4 h5 31 ♘d2 b5 32 ♘b3+ ♔c4 33 ♘a5+ ♔b4 34 ♘c6+ ♔c4 35 ♘a5+ ♔b4 36 ♘c6+ ♔c5 37 ♘a5 [37 ♘xa7?! Saint-Amant] 37 ... b4 38 ♘b3+ ♔c4 39 ♘d2+ ♔b5 40 b3? [□ 40 ♘b3= Saint-Amant] 40 ... a5 41 ♔d5 ♗f4! 42 ♘c4 d3 43 ♘b2 d2 44 ♔e4 ♗e5 45 ♘d1 ♗g3 46 ♔e3 ♗e1 47 ♔e2 ♔c5 48 ♘e3 ♔d4 49 ♘c4 [49 ♘c2+ ♔c3 50 ♘xe1 dxe1♕+ 51 ♔xe1 ♔b2 △ 52 ... ♔xa2→ Staunton] 49 ... ♔c3 50 ♔d1 a4 51 ♘a5 axb3 52 axb3 ♗xh4 53 ♘c4 ♗g5 **0-1** L/N6020-1875

**1834-✕BM-28**
**Macdonnell, A.– Bourdonnais, L.C.M. de la**

1 e4 c5 2 f4 ♘c6 3 ♘f3 e6 4 c3 d5 5 e5 f6 6 ♘a3 ♘h6 7 ♘c2 ♕b6 8 d4 cxd4 9 cxd4 [□ 9 ♘cxd4 Staunton] 9 ... ♗b4+ 10 ♔f2 ♗d7 11 h4? fxe5 12 fxe5 0-0 13 ♔g3 ♘f5+ 14 ♔h3 ♗e7 15 ♗d3 ♕d8 16 g4 [□ 16 ♗g5 Staunton] 16 ... ♘xh4?! [□ 16 ... ♘h6∓ Morphy] 17 ♘xh4 ♗xh4 18 g5! ♗xg5 19 ♕h5 ♗h6 [19 ... h6 20 ♖g1! ♗xc1 21 ♖xg7+ ♔xg7 22 ♕g6+ ♔h8 23 ♕h7# Morphy] 20 ♗xh6? [□ 20 ♖g1! ♔h8 21 ♖xg7! ♔xg7 (21 ... ♖f3+ 22 ♔g2 ♖xd3 23 ♕xh6+–) 22 ♕xh6+ +– Morphy] 20 ... gxh6 21 ♖ag1+ ♔h8 22 ♕xh6? [□ 22 ♗xh7! ♕e7! 23 ♗d3 △ 24 ♕xh6+ +– Morphy] 22 ... ♕e7 23 ♖g3 [□ 23 ♗xh7 ♕xh7 24 ♕xh7+ ♔xh7 25 ♖g3+– Morphy] 23 ... ♖g8 24 ♕f6+? [□ 24 ♗xh7! ♖xg3+ 25 ♔xg3 ♕g7+ 26 ♗g6+ ♕xh6 27 ♖xh6+ ♔g7 28 ♖h7+ ♔xg6 29 ♖xd7+– Saint-Amant] 24 ... ♕xf6 25 exf6 e5+ 26 ♔g2 e4 27 ♗e2 ♖xg3+ 28 ♔xg3 ♖g8+ 29 ♔h4 ♖g2 30 ♖f1 ♔g8 [30 ... ♖xe2?? 31 f7+– Morphy] 31 ♗d1 ♗e6 32 b4 a6 33 a4 ♖h2+ 34 ♔g5 b5 35 axb5 axb5 36 ♗h5?! ♖xc2 37 ♖a1 ♘d8 38 ♖a7 e3 39 ♖g7+ ♔f8 40 ♔h6 ♘f7+ 41 ♗xf7 [41 ♔xh7 ♗f5+ 42 ♖g6 ♖g2 △ 43 ... ♗xg6+→ Saint-Amant] 41 ... ♗xf7 42 ♖g3 ♖h2+ 43 ♔g5 e2 44 ♖e3 ♗h5 **0-1** L/N6020-1875

**1834-✕BM-29**
**Bourdonnais, L.C.M. de la– Macdonnell, A.**

1 e4 e5 2 ♘f3 ♘c6 3 ♗c4 ♗c5 4 c3 d6 5 d3 [□ 5 d4± Morphy] 5 ... ♘f6 6 b4 ♗b6 7 a4 a6 8 b5 ♘e7 9 h3 ♘g6 10 ♕e2 ♗e6 11 ♘a3 0-0 [11 ... ♗xc4= Anderssen] 12 g4 d5 13 ♗a2 dxe4 14 dxe4 ♗xa2 15 ♖xa2 ♘d7 16 ♘c4 ♖e8 [△ 17 ... ♘c5; △ 17 ... ♘f4 Anderssen] 17 h4 ♘c5 18 ♖d2 ♕c8 19 ♖d5 ♘xa4 20 h5 ♘f4! [20 ... ♘xc3 21 ♕d3 ♘xd5 22 hxg6 ♘f6 23 gxf7+ ♔xf7 24 ♕b3+– Morphy] 21 ♗xf4 ♘xc3! 22 ♕d3 ♘xd5 23 ♕xd5 exf4 24 ♘g5 ♖e7 25 h6 g6 26 ♘xb6 cxb6 27 ♕d4 ♕f8 [27 ... f6 28 ♕d5+ (28 ♕xf6 ♕c1+ 29 ♔e2 f3+→) 28 ... ♔h8 29 ♘f7+ ♖xf7 30 ♕xf7 ♕c1+ 31 ♔e2 f3+→ Anderssen] 28 ♕f6 ♖d7 29 ♔e2 ♖ad8 30 e5 ♖d2+ 31 ♔f1 [31 ♔f3 ♕a3+→ Anderssen] 31 ... ♖xf2+!

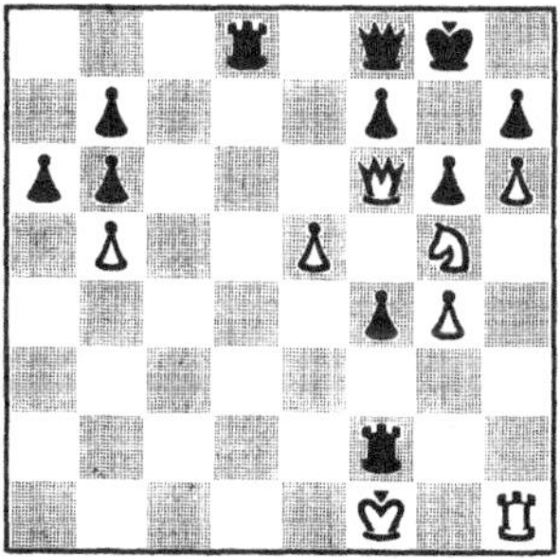

32 ♔xf2 [32 ♔g1 ♖d1+ 33 ♔xf2 ♕c5+→ Anderssen] 32 ... ♕c5+ 33 ♔g2 ♖d2+ 34 ♔h3 ♕e3+ 35 ♘f3 [35 ♔h4 ♕g3# Morphy] 35 ... ♕xf3+ 36 ♔h4 ♕xh1+ 37 ♔g5 ♔f8 [□ 37 ... ♕xh6+! 38 ♔xh6 ♖h2+ 39 ♔g5 h6+ 40 ♔xf4 ♖f2+ 41 ♔~ ♖xf6 42 exf6 a5 Morphy] 38 ♕h8+ ♔e7 39 ♕f6+ ♔e8 40 ♕h8+ ♔d7 41 e6+ fxe6 42 ♕g7+ ♔d6 43 ♕f8+ ♔c7 44 ♕xf4+ ♖d6 45 ♕f7+ ♔c8 46 ♕g8+ ♖d8 47 ♕xh7 ♕d5+ 48 ♔h4 ♕h1+ 49 ♔g5 ♖d5+ 50 ♔f6 ♕f3+ 51 ♔xe6 ♕e4+ 52 ♔f6 ♕e5+ 53 ♔f7 ♖d7+ 54 ♔f8 ♕f6+ **0-1** L/N6020-1875

**1834-✕BM-30**
**Macdonnell, A.+ Bourdonnais, L.C.M. de la**

1 e4 e5 2 ♗c4 ♘f6 3 d4 [3 ♘f3 ♘xe4 4 ♘c3; 3 ♘f3 ♘c6 4 d4; 4 ♘g5 Morphy] 3 ... exd4 4 e5 ♕e7? [□ 4 ... d5 Anderssen] 5 ♕e2 ♘g8 6 ♘f3 ♘c6 7 c3 d6 8 cxd4 ♗g4 9 ♗b5 d5 10 ♘c3 ♕e6 11 h3 ♗xf3 12 ♕xf3 0-0-0? [□ 12 ... ♗b4 Anderssen] 13 ♗xc6 ♕xc6 [□ 13 ... bxc6 Morphy] 14 ♕xf7 ♗b4 15 ♗d2 ♘e7 16 0-0 ♖df8 17 ♕h5 [17 ♕xg7?! Anderssen] 17 ... ♘f5 18 a3 ♗xc3 19 ♗xc3 g6 20 ♕d1 h5 21 ♖c1 ♕e6 22 ♕e1 h4 23 f4 ♖fg8 24 ♖f3 ♔b8 [24 ... g5? 25 fxg5 ♖xg5 26 ♗d2 ♖g7 (26 ... ♘xd4? 27 ♖f6+–) 27 ♕f1 ♖f7 (27 ... ♖hg8 28 g4 ♘xd4 29 ♖f8+) 28 ♕f2± Anderssen] 25 ♕d2 ♖h7 [△ 26 ... ♖hg7 Anderssen] 26 ♕d3 ♖hg7 27 ♗d2 a6 [□ 27 ... ♕b6 Anderssen] 28 b4 ♕b6 29 ♗c3 [□ 29 ♖c5 Morphy] 29 ... ♘g3 30 a4 ♘e4 31 b5 g5 32 f5 g4 33 hxg4 ♖xg4 34 ♖c2 h3 [□ 34 ... ♘g5 Staunton] 35 ♖xh3 ♖g3 36 ♖xg3 ♖xg3 37 a5! ♕h6 [37 ... ♕a7 38 b6+– Anderssen; 37 ... ♖xd3 38 axb6 ♖xc3 (38 ... ♘xc3 39 ♖xc3 ♖xc3 40 f6+–) 39 ♖xc3 ♘xc3 40 e6! ♘e4! 41 e7 ♘f6 42 g4 ♔c8 43 bxa6! (43 g5? cxb6 △ 44 ... ♔d7=) 43 ... bxa6 44 b7+! (44 g5? cxb6 △ 45 ... ♔d7=) 44 ... ♔xb7 45 g5 ♘e8 46 f6+– Morphy] 38 ♗d2 ♕h3 39 ♕f1 ♖g8 40 f6 ♕h4 [△ 41 ... ♘g3] 41 f7 ♖f8 42 e6 ♘g3 43 ♕f3 ♕h1+ 44 ♔f2 ♘e4+ 45 ♔e2 ♕b1 46 e7 ♕xb5+ 47 ♕d3 ♘g3+ 48 ♔d1 **1-0** L/N6020-1875

**1834-✕BM-31**
**Bourdonnais, L.C.M. de la+ Macdonnell, A.**

1 d4 d5 2 c4 dxc4 3 e3 e5! 4 ♗xc4 exd4 5 exd4 ♘f6 6 ♘c3 ♗e7 [□ 6 ... ♗d6 Bourdonnais] 7 ♘f3 0-0 8 0-0 c6 [□ 8 ... ♗g4 Saint-Amant] 9 h3 ♘bd7 10 ♗e3 ♘b6 11 ♗b3 ♘fd5 12 ♕e2 ♔h8? 13 ♖ae1 ♗d6 14 ♗c2 f5 15 ♘e5 f4?! 16 ♕h5! ♘f6 17 ♘g6+ ♔g8 18 ♗b3+ ♘bd5 19 ♘xd5 cxd5 [19 ... ♘xh5?? 20 ♘f6# Morphy] 20 ♗xd5+ ♘xd5 21 ♕xd5+ ♖f7 22 ♘e5 ♗e6 23 ♕xe6 ♗xe5 24 dxe5 fxe3 25 ♖xe3 ♕e8 26 ♕xe8+ ♖xe8 27 f4 ♖c7 28 ♖f2 ♔f7 29 g4 ♖c5 30 ♖fe2 a5 31 ♔f2 b5 32 ♔f3 b4 33 a3 ♖b8 34 axb4 ♖xb4 35 ♖c3 **1-0** L/N6020-1875

**1834-✕BM-32**
**Macdonnell, A.– Bourdonnais, L.C.M. de la**

1 e4 c5 2 f4 e6 3 ♘f3 ♘c6 4 c3 d5 5 e5 f6 6 ♘a3 ♘h6 7 ♘c2 ♕b6 8 d4 ♗d7 9 h4 cxd4 10 cxd4 ♘f5 [□ 10 ... ♗b4+ Morphy] 11 ♔f2 h5 12 g3 0-0-0 13 ♔g2 ♗e7 14 a3 ♗e8 15 b4 ♔b8 16 b5 ♘a5 17 ♘e3 ♗g6 18

♗d3 ♘xe3+ 19 ♗xe3 ♗e4! 20 ♗xe4 dxe4 21 ♘d2 fxe5 22 fxe5 ♕xb5∓ 23 ♕f1 [23 ♘xe4?! Saint-Amant] 23 ... ♕d3 24 ♕xd3 exd3 25 ♖hb1 ♖c8 26 ♔f3 ♖c3 27 ♖b5 ♗d8 28 ♔e4 a6 29 ♖bb1 ♗e7 30 a4? [□ 30 ♖b6 Saint-Amant] 30 ... ♖d8 31 ♖b6 ♖c6 32 ♖ab1 ♔c7 33 ♖xc6+ ♘xc6 34 ♖f1 ♗b4 35 ♖f7+ ♖d7 36 ♖xd7+ ♔xd7 37 ♘f3 ♗e7 38 ♔xd3∓ ♘b4+ 39 ♔e4 [□ 39 ♔c4 Morphy] 39 ... ♘d5 40 ♗d2 b5 41 axb5 axb5 42 ♔d3 ♔e8 43 ♗g5 ♗xg5 44 ♘xg5 ♔d7 45 ♘e4 ♔c6 46 ♘c5 ♘c7 47 ♔e4? [△ 48 ♘xe6; □ 47 ♘e4 Saint-Amant] 47 ... b4 48 ♔d3 [48 ♘xe6 ♘xe6 49 d5+ ♔d7 50 dxe6+ ♔xe6 51 ♔d4 b3 52 ♔c3 ♔xe5 53 ♔xb3 ♔f5→ Morphy] 48 ... ♔d5 49 ♘e4 ♘b5 50 g4? hxg4 51 h5 [51 ♘f6+ gxf6 52 h5 fxe5 53 h6 ♘d6 54 h7 ♘f7→ Morphy] 51 ... ♘xd4 52 h6 gxh6 53 ♘f6+ ♔xe5 54 ♘xg4+ ♔d5 55 ♘xh6 **0-1**

L/N6020-1875

### 1834-⚔BM-33
**Bourdonnais, L.C.M. de la+ Macdonnell, A.**

1 d4 d5 2 c4 dxc4 3 e3 e5 4 ♗xc4 exd4 5 exd4 ♘f6 6 ♘f3 ♗e7 7 0-0 0-0 8 h3 ♘bd7 9 ♘c3 ♘b6 10 ♗b3 c6 11 ♗e3 ♘fd5 12 ♕e2 f5 13 ♖ae1 f4? [□ 13 ... ♔h8; 13 ... ♗b4 Saint-Amant] 14 ♗xf4 ♖xf4 15 ♕xe7 ♕xe7 16 ♖xe7 ♔f8 17 ♖e4 ♖f6 18 ♘xd5 cxd5 19 ♖e3 ♗f5 20 ♘e5 h6 [□ 20 ... ♖c8 Staunton] 21 ♖c1 ♖d8 22 ♖c7 ♗c8 23 ♖g3! ♗d7 24 ♗xd5 ♘xd5 25 ♖xd7 ♖xd7 26 ♘xd7+ **1-0**

L/N6020-1875

### 1834-⚔BM-34
**Macdonnell, A.+ Bourdonnais, L.C.M. de la**

1 e4 c5 2 f4 e6 3 ♘f3 d5 4 e5 ♘c6 5 c3 f6 6 ♘a3 ♘h6 7 ♘c2 ♕b6 8 d4 ♗d7 9 h4 0-0-0 10 a3 ♔b8 11 b4 cxd4 12 cxd4 ♘f5 13 ♔f2 h5 14 ♗d3 ♘h6 [14 ... ♘cxd4? 15 ♘xd4 ♘xd4 16 ♗e3+− Morphy] 15 ♗d2 ♘g4+ 16 ♔g3 ♖c8 17 ♕e2 ♗e7 18 a4 g5 19 a5 ♕c7 20 b5 gxf4+ 21 ♔h3 ♘xd4!? 22 ♘cxd4 fxe5 23 b6 ♕d6 24 ♘xe5 [□ 24 ♖hb1± Morphy] 24 ... ♕xe5 25 ♕xe5+ ♘xe5 26 ♗xf4 ♗d6 27 ♗b5 ♖c3+ 28 g3 ♗c8 29 bxa7+ ♔a8 30 a6 bxa6? [□ 30 ... ♘f7 Morphy] 31 ♗xa6 ♘f7 32 ♗xd6 ♘xd6 33 ♗xc8 ♖hxc8 34 ♘xe6 ♘e4 35 ♖hg1 ♘f2+ [□ 35 ... ♖c2 Bourdonnais] 36 ♔g2 ♘g4 37 ♖gb1 ♖c2+ 38 ♔g1 ♘e5 39 ♖a3 ♖c1+ 40 ♖xc1 ♖xc1+ 41 ♔g2 ♖c2+ 42 ♔f1 ♖c6 43 ♘f4 d4 44 ♔e2 ♖c2+ 45 ♔d1 ♖c4 46 ♘xh5 ♘g4 47 ♘f4 ♘e3+ 48 ♔e2 ♘f5 49 ♘d5 ♘xg3+ 50 ♔f3! ♖c6 51 ♔xg3 **1-0**

L/N6020-1875

### 1834-⚔BM-35
**Macdonnell, A.+ Bourdonnais, L.C.M. de la**

1 e4 e5 2 f4 exf4 3 ♘f3 g5 4 ♗c4 g4 5 ♘c3!? [5 0-0!? Anderssen] 5 ... gxf3 6 ♕xf3 [6 d4 Löwenthal] 6 ... ♕f6? [□ 6 ... d5 7 ♗xd5 c6 Bourdonnais; 6 ... d6 7 ♕xf4 ♗e6 Löwenthal] 7 ♘d5 ♕e5 8 c3 ♗h6 9 d4 ♕d6 10 e5 ♕c6 11 ♗b5 ♕g6 [11 ... ♕xb5?? 12 ♘xc7+ △ 13 ♘xb5 Bourdonnais] 12 ♘xc7+ ♔d8 13 ♘xa8 ♘e7 14 0-0 ♖g8 15 ♗d3 ♕g7 16 b4 ♘g6 17 ♗xg6 ♕xg6 18 b5 [△ 19 b6! Bourdonnais] 18 ... d6 [18 ... b6 19 a4 Anderssen] 19 b6 a6 20 exd6+− ♘c6 [△ 21 ... ♗g4; 20 ... ♗g4 21 ♕xb7 Anderssen] 21 d7 ♗xd7 22 ♘c7 ♗g4 23 ♕d5+ ♔c8

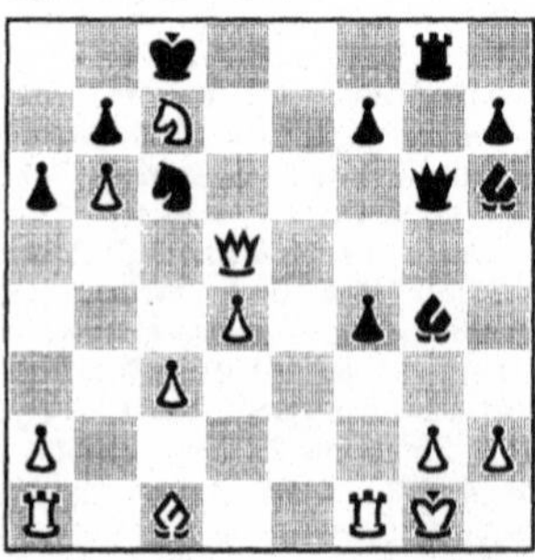

24 ♗xf4? [□ 24 ♖f2 Löwenthal] 24 ... ♗e6 25 ♘xe6 fxe6 26 ♕f3 ♗xf4 27 ♖ae1 e5 28 ♔h1 [△ 29 g3; 28 dxe5 ♗xe5; 28 ... ♘xe5? 29 ♕h3+ △ 30 ♖xf4+− Anderssen] 28 ... ♕h6 [28 ... exd4? 29 ♕h3+ △ 30 ♖xf4+− Anderssen] 29 ♕h3+! ♕xh3 30 gxh3 ♗d2 31 ♖d1 ♗xc3 32 d5 ♘e7 33 ♖f7! [33 ♖c1 ♘xd5 34 ♖xc3+ ♘xc3 35 ♖c1 ♖g6 36 ♖xc3+ ♖c6 37 ♖b3 ♖c1+; 33 ♖c1 ♘xd5 34 ♖fd1 ♘xb6 35 ♖xc3+ ♔b8 36 ♖b3 ♔a7 37 ♖db1 ♖g6 38 a4! a5 39 ♖b5 ♔a6 40 ♖xe5 ♘xa4 Löwenthal] 33 ... ♗b4 34 d6 ♘c6 35 ♖c7+ ♔b8 36 ♖xh7 e4 37 ♖h4 e3 38 ♖e4 ♗c5 39 d7 ♖d8 40 h4 ♗xb6 41 h5 ♔c7 42 h6 e2!? 43 ♖xe2 ♗d4 44 h7 ♔xd7 [44 ... ♖xd7 45 ♖xd4 ♖xh7 46 ♖g4 Löwenthal] 45 ♖g2 [45 ♖xd4+ ♘xd4 46 ♖d2 ♖h8 47 ♖xd4+ ♔e6 48 ♖h4 ♔f6= Löwenthal] 45 ... ♖h8 46 ♖g7+ ♔d6 47 ♖xb7 ♔c5 48 ♔g2 ♘d8 49 ♖d7 ♘e6 50 h4 ♔c6 51 ♖7xd4 ♘xd4 52 ♖xd4 ♖xh7 53 ♔g3 ♔c5 54 ♖d2 a5 55 ♔g4 a4 56 ♖d3 [□ 56 h5 Morphy] 56 ... ♖b7 57 h5 ♖b4+ 58 ♔g3 ♖b1 59 ♖d2 ♖g1+ 60 ♖g2 ♖h1 61 ♖h2 ♖g1+ 62 ♔h4 ♖g8 63 h6 ♔b4 64 ♔h5 ♔a3 65 h7 ♖b8 66 ♔g5 [□ 66 ♖g2 Staunton] 66 ... ♖b5+ 67 ♔f4 ♖b8 68 ♔e4 ♖e8+ 69 ♔d3 ♖d8+ 70 ♔c2 ♖h8 71 ♔b1 ♔b4 72 ♖h4+ ♔c3 73 ♖h3+ ♔c4 74 ♔b2 ♔b4 75 a3+ ♔c4 76 ♖h4+ ♔b5 77 ♔c3 ♖c8+ 78 ♔b2 ♖h8 79 ♖b4+ ♔a5 80 ♖b7 ♔a6 81 ♖g7 ♔a5 82 ♔c3 ♖c8+ 83 ♔d4 ♖h8 84 ♖g5+ ♔b6 85 ♖h5 ♔c6 86 ♔c4 ♔b6 87 ♔b4 ♔c6 88 ♔xa4 ♔b6 89 ♖h6+ ♔c5 90 ♔a5 ♖a8+ 91 ♖a6 ♖b8 92 a4 ♖c8 93 ♖a7 ♖b8 94 ♖c7+ ♔d6 95 ♖c1 ♖a8+ 96 ♔b5 ♖b8+ 97 ♔a6 ♖a8+ 98 ♔b7 ♖h8 99 a5 **1-0**

L/N6020-1875

### 1834-⚔BM-36
**Bourdonnais, L.C.M. de la= Macdonnell, A.**

1 e4 e5 2 ♘f3 ♘c6 3 ♗c4 ♗c5 4 c3 d6 5 d4 exd4 6 cxd4 ♗b6 7 ♘c3 ♘f6 8 d5 ♘e5 [□ 8 ... ♘e7; 8 ... ♘a5 9 ♗d3 △ 10 b4 Dufresne] 9 ♘xe5 dxe5 10 ♗g5 a6 11 ♕f3 ♕d6 12 ♗xf6 ♕xf6 13 ♕xf6 gxf6 14 0-0-0!? ♗xf2 15 ♖hf1 ♗e3+ 16 ♔c2 ♖g8 17 g3 ♖g6 18 d6 c6 19 ♗xf7+ ♔xf7 20 d7 ♗xd7 21 ♖xd7+ ♔e6 22 ♖xh7 ♖h6 23 ♖xh6 ♗xh6 24 ♖d1 b5 25 ♘e2 a5 26 g4 ♖g8 27 h3 c5 28 ♖d3 ♖c8 29 ♘g3 b4 30 ♘f5 ♗f8 31 h4 a4 32 h5 c4 33 ♖h3 b3+ 34 axb3 cxb3+ 35 ♔b1 ♔f7 36 h6 ♔g8 37 h7+ ♔h8 38 ♘e3 a3 39 bxa3 ♗xa3 [39 ... ♖c3 Staunton] 40 ♖h1 b2 [□ 40 ... ♖c3 Lewis] 41 ♘c2 ♗e7 42 ♔xb2 ♖c4 43 ♖e1 ♔xh7 44 ♔b3 ♖c8 45 ♘e3 ♔g6 46 ♖f1 ♖h8 47 ♖f3 ♖c8 48 ♘d5 ♗d8 49 ♖f5 ♖c1 **½-½**

L/N6020-1875

### 1834-⚔BM-37
**Bourdonnais, L.C.M. de la+ Macdonnell, A.**

1 d4 d5 2 c4 dxc4 3 e3 e5 4 ♗xc4 exd4 5 exd4 ♘f6 6 ♘c3 ♗e7 [□ 6 ... ♗d6 Bourdonnais] 7 ♘f3 0-0 8 ♗e3 c6 9 h3 ♘bd7 10 0-0 ♘b6 11 ♗b3 ♘fd5 12 ♕e2 f5 13 ♖ae1 g5?! 14 ♗d2 ♗f6 15 ♘e5 ♕e8 16 f4 g4 17 hxg4 fxg4 18 f5 ♕h5 19 ♗c2 [□ 19 ♘e4!± Staunton] 19 ... ♕h4 20 ♕e4 ♔h8 21 ♘xg4 ♘c4 22 ♘xf6 ♕xf6 23 ♘xd5 cxd5 24 ♕f4 ♘xd2 25 ♕xd2 ♗d7 26 ♖e5 ♖g8 27 ♖fe1 ♕h4 28 ♖1e2 ♗b5 29 ♖f2 ♖g4 30 f6 ♖xd4 31 ♕e3 ♖g4 32 ♖e7 d4 33 ♕e5 ♖g5

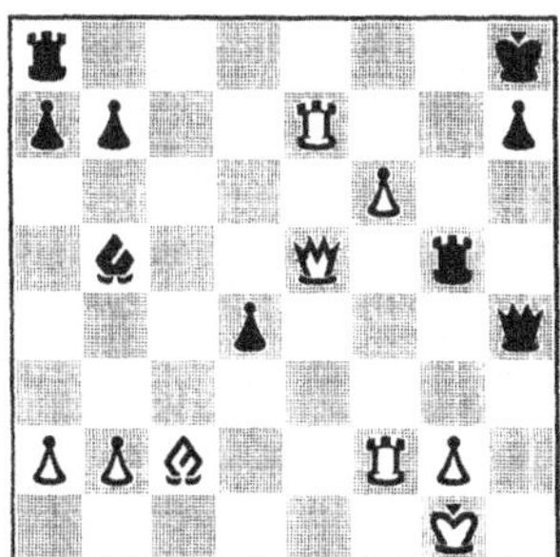

34 f7+! ♖xe5 35 f8♕+ ♖xf8 36 ♖xf8# **1-0** L/N6020-1875

**1834-⚔BM-38**
**Macdonnell, A.+**
**Bourdonnais, L.C.M. de la**

1 d4 e6 2 c4 d5 3 ♘c3 ♘f6 4 ♘f3 c5 5 cxd5 exd5 6 ♗g5 ♗e6 7 e3 ♘c6 8 ♗d3 ♗e7 9 dxc5 ♗xc5 10 0-0 h6 11 ♗xf6 ♕xf6 12 ♖c1 ♗d6 13 ♗b5 0-0 14 ♘xd5 ♕xb2 15 ♖b1 ♕a3 16 e4 ♖ad8 17 ♘d2 a6 18 ♗c4 b5 19 ♗b3 ♘d4 20 ♕h5 ♘xb3 21 ♘xb3 ♕xa2 22 ♘d4 ♕c4 23 ♖fd1 ♗xd5 24 exd5 ♖fe8 25 ♖bc1 ♕a2 26 ♘f5 ♕e2 27 ♕h3 b4 28 g4 a5 [□ 28 ... ♗c5 Staunton] 29 ♖e1 ♕xe1+?! [□ 29 ... ♕d2 St Amant] 30 ♖xe1 ♖xe1+ 31 ♔g2 a4 32 ♕h4 f6 33 ♕h5 ♗f8 [□ 33 ... ♖d7 Staunton] 34 ♕g6 ♔h8 35 ♘xh6 gxh6 36 ♕xf6+ ♔g8 37 ♕xd8 a3 38 ♕a5 ♖d1 39 ♕a4 ♖d2 [39 ... ♖xd5?? 40 ♕b3+- Staunton] 40 d6 ♗xd6 41 ♕e8+ ♔g7 42 ♕d7+ ♔f8 43 ♕f5+ ♔g7 44 g5 ♗e7 45 ♕e5+ ♔g6 46 ♕e4+ ♔f7 47 ♕f4+ ♔g7 48 ♕xd2 hxg5 49 ♕d5 **1-0** L/N6020-1875

**1834-⚔BM-39**
**Bourdonnais, L.C.M. de la+**
**Macdonnell, A.**

1 d4 d5 2 c4 dxc4 3 e3 e5 4 ♗xc4 exd4 5 exd4 ♘f6 6 ♘c3 ♗e7 7 ♘f3 0-0 8 h3 ♘bd7 9 ♗e3 ♘b6 10 ♗b3 c6 11 0-0 ♘fd5 12 ♕e2 f5 13 ♘e5 f4 14 ♗d2 g5?! 15 ♖ae1 ♔g7 16 ♘xd5 ♘xd5 17 ♘xc6! bxc6 18 ♗xd5 ♕xd5 19 ♕xe7+ ♖f7 20 ♕b4 ♗f5 21 ♖e5 ♕d7 22 d5! cxd5 23 ♕d4 ♔h6 24 h4 ♗e6 25 ♖fe1 ♖e8 26 ♖xg5 ♖ef8 27 ♕e5 ♗g4 [27 ... ♗f5 28 ♗xf4+- Saint-Amant] 28 ♖h5+! ♗xh5 29 ♕g5# **1-0** L/N6020-1875

**1834-⚔BM-40**
**Macdonnell, A.–**
**Bourdonnais, L.C.M. de la**

1 e4 e5 2 f4 exf4 3 ♘f3 g5 4 ♗c4 g4 5 ♘c3 gxf3 6 ♕xf3 [6 0-0 fxg2 7 ♗xf7+ Staunton] 6 ... ♘c6 7 d4 ♘xd4 8 ♗xf7+ ♔xf7 9 ♕h5+ ♔g7 10 0-0 ♘e6 11 ♗xf4 ♗c5+ 12 ♔h1 ♘f6 13 ♕h6+ [□ 13 ♗e5 Staunton] 13 ... ♔g8 14 ♖f3 ♗f8 15 ♖g3+ ♔f7 16 ♕h4 ♘xf4 17 ♕xf4 d6 18 ♖f1 ♗e6 19 ♕g5 ♔e8 [19 ... ♗e7? 20 ♕g7++- Staunton] 20 ♖xf6 ♕e7 21 ♖gf3 c6 22 ♘e2 ♖g8 23 ♕h5+ ♔d8 24 ♘d4 ♗g4 25 ♕a5+ [25 ♖xf8++- Staunton] 25 ... ♔c8 [25 ... ♔c7?? 26 ♘e6++- Bourdonnais] 26 ♖f1 [26 ♖f7 Staunton] 26 ... ♗d7 27 ♖f7 ♕e8 28 b4 [□ 28 ♘e6! Staunton] 28 ... b6 29 ♕a6+ ♔c7 30 ♕c4! ♗e7 31 ♘xc6? [□ 31 b5 Lewis; □ 31 ♘e6+; 31 ♖xe7? ♕xe7 32 ♖f7 d5!→ Staunton] 31 ... b5! 32 ♕xb5 ♗xc6 33 ♕a5+ ♔b8 34 ♕f5 ♗d8 35 ♖e1 ♕e5 36 ♕f3 d5 37 b5 ♗b7 38 ♖xb7+ ♔xb7 39 ♕f7+ ♗c7 **0-1** L/N6020-1875

**1834-⚔BM-41**
**Bourdonnais, L.C.M. de la+**
**Macdonnell, A.**

1 d4 d5 2 c4 dxc4 3 e3 e5 4 ♗xc4 exd4 5 exd4 ♘f6 6 ♘c3 ♗d6 7 ♘f3 0-0 [7 ... ♗g4 8 ♕a4+! Saint-Amant] 8 h3 ♖e8+ 9 ♗e3 ♗f4 10 ♕d2 ♕e7 11 0-0! ♗xe3 12 fxe3 ♕xe3+ 13 ♕xe3 ♖xe3 14 ♘e5 ♗e6 15 ♗xe6 fxe6 16 ♔f2 ♖xe5 17 dxe5 ♘fd7 18 ♘b5 ♘a6 19 ♔g3 [19 ♖fe1 Saint-Amant] 19 ... ♘xe5 20 ♖ae1 ♘g6 21 ♖xe6 ♘c5 22 ♖e3 [22 ♘xc7! Staunton] 22 ... c6 23 ♘d6 b6 24 h4 h6 25 h5 ♘f8 26 ♖e7 ♖d8 27 ♘b7 ♖d3+ 28 ♖f3 ♖d5 [□ 28 ... ♖d7 Staunton] 29 ♘xc5 ♖xc5 30 ♖e8 **1-0** L/N6020-1875

**1834-⚔BM-42**
**Macdonnell, A.–**
**Bourdonnais, L.C.M. de la**

1 e4 e5 2 f4 exf4 3 ♘f3 g5 4 ♗c4 ♗g7 5 d4 d6 6 c3 ♘c6 7 ♕b3 ♕e7 8 ♘xg5! ♕xg5 9 ♗xf7+ ♔f8 10 ♗xg8 ♖xg8 11 ♗xf4 ♕g6 12 ♖f1 [12 0-0?? ♗xd4+→ Bourdonnais] 12 ... ♗f6 13 ♘d2 ♕e8 14 0-0-0 ♗e7 15 e5! d5 16 ♕xd5 ♕xg2 17 ♕b3 ♘d8 18 d5 c6 19 d6 ♗e6 20 ♘c4 ♗f8 21 d7+ ♗xd7 22 ♘d6+ ♗xd6 23 exd6 ♖g6 24 ♗g3 ♕h3 25 ♕b4 ♖e6 26 ♕d4 ♘f7 27 ♖f2 ♕h6+ 28 ♔b1 ♕g6+ 29 ♔a1 c5 30 ♕d2 ♖f6 31 ♗f4 ♔f8 32 ♖g2 ♕h5 33 ♖e1 ♖d8 [33 ... ♖e8? 34 ♖xe8+ ♔xe8 (34 ... ♗xe8 35 d7) 35 ♖g8# Bourdonnais] 34 ♕e3 ♗e6 [34 ... ♖e8? 35 ♕e7+ ♖xe7 36 dxe7+ ♔e8 37 ♖g8#; 34 ... ♖e6 35 ♖eg1! Δ 36 ♖g8# Bourdonnais] 35 ♖eg1 ♔e8 36 ♗g5 ♖xd6 37 ♕g3 ♖f3 38 ♕e1 ♖fd3 39 ♗c1 ♖d1 40 ♖g8+ ♔d7 41 ♕e4 ♕d5 42 ♕a4+ ♕c6 43 ♕xa7 ♖xg1 44 ♖xg1 ♕a6 45 ♕xa6 ♖xa6 46 a3 ♗b3 47 ♔b1 ♖f6 48 ♖g2 ♖f1 49 ♖g3 c4 50 ♖g7 ♔e6 51 ♖xh7 ♘e5 52 ♖h6+ ♔d7 53 ♖h7+ ♔c6 54 ♖h6+ ♔b5 55 ♖h5 ♖e1 56 ♖g5 ♔a4 57 ♖g3 ♘d3 58 ♖xd3 cxd3 59 h4 d2 **0-1** L/N6020-1875

**1834-⚔BM-43**
**Bourdonnais, L.C.M. de la–**
**Macdonnell, A.**

1 d4 d5 2 c4 dxc4 3 e3 e5 4 ♗xc4 exd4 5 exd4 ♘f6 6 ♘c3 ♗d6 7 ♘f3 0-0 8 h3 ♖e8+ 9 ♗e3 ♘c6 10 0-0 h6 11 a3 [Δ 12 ♕d3] 11 ... ♗f5 12 g4?! [□ 12 ♕b3! Saint-Amant] 12 ... ♗xg4 [12 ... ♗g6 13 ♘h4 ♗h7 14 ♕b3±; 12 ... ♗e4 13 ♘xe4 Anderssen] 13 hxg4 ♘xg4 14 ♕d3 ♕f6 15 ♔g2 ♘e7 16 ♘e4? [□ 16 ♘d5 Staunton; □ 16 ♖h1 Walker] 16 ... ♕g6 17 ♘g3 ♘xe3+ 18 ♕xe3 ♘f5 19 ♕d3 ♗xg3 [19 ... ♘xg3? 20 ♕xg6 Staunton] 20 fxg3 ♕xg3+ 21 ♔h1 ♘e3 22 ♗xf7+ ♔h8 [22 ... ♔xf7? Staunton] 23 ♕g6 ♘xf1 24 ♖xf1 ♕h3+ 25 ♔g1 ♖e3 26 ♖f2?! [□ 26 ♗d5 Staunton; □ 26 ♕g2 Anderssen] 26 ... ♖xf3 27 ♖g2 ♖xf7 28 ♕xf7 ♕e3+ 29 ♕f2 ♕xf2+ 30 ♖xf2 ♖d8 31 ♖f4 [31 ♖f7 ♖xd4 32 ♖xc7 ♖d1+ 33 ♔f2 ♖d2+ Δ 34 ... ♖xb2 Anderssen] 31 ... ♖d7 32 ♔f2 ♔h7 33 ♔f3 g5 34 ♖f6 ♔g7 35 ♖e6 ♖xd4 36 ♖e7+ ♔g6 37 ♖xc7 ♖d3+ 38 ♔e4 ♖b3 39 ♖c2 h5 40 ♖d2 g4 41 ♔f4 ♖f3+ 42 ♔e5 ♔g5 43 ♖d7 ♖b3 44 ♖d2 g3 45 ♖d8 ♔g4 46 ♖g8+ ♔h3 47 ♔f4 h4 **0-1** L/N6020-1875

**1834-⚔BM-44**
**Bourdonnais, L.C.M. de la–**
**Macdonnell, A.**

1 d4 d5 2 c4 dxc4 3 e3 e5 4 ♗xc4 exd4 5 exd4 ♘f6 6 ♘c3 ♗d6 7 ♘f3 ♘c6 8 0-0 0-0 9 h3 h6 10 a3 ♗f5! 11 g4? ♘xg4 [11 ... ♗xg4 12 hxg4 ♘xg4 Anderssen] 12 hxg4 ♗xg4 13 ♗e2? [□ 13 ♘e4 ♘xd4 (13 ... ♗xf3 14 ♕xf3 ♘xd4 15 ♕g4) 14 ♕xd4 ♗xf3 15 ♘xd6 Staunton] 13 ... ♗xf3 14 ♗xf3 ♕h4 15 ♖e1 ♘xd4 16 ♘e4? [□ 16 ♖e4 Staunton] 16 ... ♗h2+ 17 ♔f1 ♖ad8 18 ♗e3 ♘f5 19 ♕c2 ♕h3+ 20 ♗g2 ♕g4 [Δ 21 ... ♘h4 Anderssen] 21 f3 ♕g6 22 ♗f2 ♘e7 23 ♖ad1 ♘d5 [Δ 24 ... ♘f4 Anderssen] 24 ♗c5? ♕c6 25 ♕b3 ♘f4! 26 ♗xf8 ♕a6+ 27 ♔f2 ♖xd1 28 ♗f1? [□ 28 ♕xd1 ♘d3+ 29 ♔f1 Anderssen] 28 ... ♗g1+! 29 ♔xg1 [29 ♔g3 ♕g6+ Δ 30 ... ♖xe1→ Bourdonnais] 29 ... ♖xe1 30 ♘g3 ♕g6 31 ♔f2 ♖xf1+ 32 ♘xf1 ♔xf8 **0-1** L/N6020-1875

**1834-⚔BM-45**
**Macdonnell, A.+**
**Bourdonnais, L.C.M. de la**

1 e4 e5 2 f4 exf4 3 ♘f3 g5 4 ♗c4 ♗g7 5 d4 d6 6 c3 [Δ 7 ♕b3 Staunton] 6

... h6 7 ♘a3 ♘c6 8 ♗d2 ♕e7 9 0-0 ♗d7 10 b4 0-0-0!? 11 ♗d3 g4 [11 ... ♘f6 12 b5 Δ 13 e5± Anderssen] 12 ♘e1 f3 13 gxf3 ♘f6 [13 ... ♘xb4! 14 cxb4 ♗xd4+ 15 ♔h1 ♗xa1 Staunton] 14 b5 ♘b8 15 ♘ac2 ♖dg8 16 ♔h1 h5 17 ♘e3! [17 a4 h4! Anderssen] 17 ... gxf3 [17 ... h4 18 ♘xg4 ♗xg4 19 fxg4 ♘xe4 20 ♗xe4 ♕xe4+ 21 ♕f3± Anderssen] 18 ♕xf3 ♗g4 19 ♕f4 ♘bd7 20 ♘f5 ♕e6 21 ♘f3 ♗xf3+ 22 ♕xf3 ♘g4 23 a4 ♗h6 24 ♗xh6 ♘xh6 25 a5 ♘xf5? [□ 25 ... ♔b8 Anderssen] 26 exf5 ♕b3 27 a6!

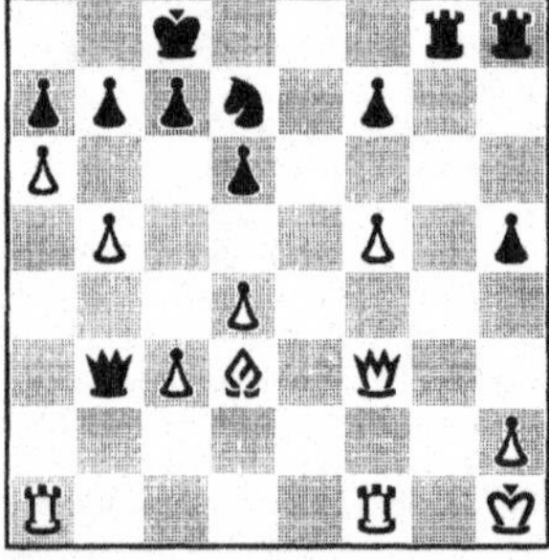

27 ... d5 28 c4 ♘f6 29 axb7+ ♔b8 30 c5 ♘g4 31 b6! axb6 [31 ... cxb6 32 ♕g3+ ♔xb7 33 ♗a6++− Anderssen] 32 c6 **1-0** L/N6020-1875

**1834-✕BM-46**
**Macdonnell, A.–**
**Bourdonnais, L.C.M. de la**

1 e4 e5 2 f4 exf4 3 ♗c4 ♕h4+ 4 ♔f1 g5 5 ♘c3 ♗g7 6 d4 d6 7 ♘d5 ♔d8 8 ♗e2? ♘f6 9 ♘xf6 ♗xf6 10 e5 ♗e7 11 ♕d3 ♘c6 12 c3 ♗d7 13 g3 ♕h6 [13 ... fxg3 14 ♔g2!± Dufresne] 14 exd6 ♗xd6 15 h4 g4! 16 ♗d1 [Δ 17 ♘e2 Bourdonnais] 16 ... ♕f6 17 ♔e1 ♕e7+ 18 ♔f2 ♖e8 [□ 18 ... fxg3+ Bourdonnais] 19 gxf4 ♕e1+ 20 ♔g2 ♕e4+ 21 ♕xe4 ♖xe4 22 ♗c2 ♖e8 23 ♗xh7 ♗e6 24 ♔g3 ♗d5 25 ♖h2 ♖e1 26 ♘e2 ♗c4! 27 d5! ♘e7 28 ♘d4 ♘xd5 29 h5 ♖g1+ [□ 29 ... ♖xc1 30 ♖xc1 ♗xf4+−+ Bourdonnais] 30 ♔f2 ♖f1+ 31 ♔g3 ♘xf4 32 ♔xg4 ♔d7 33 b3 [Δ 34 ♗b2 Bourdonnais] 33 ... ♗e6+ 34 ♘xe6 ♘xe6 35 ♖e2 ♖h8 36 ♗e4 ♖g8+ 37 ♔h4 ♗e7+ [37 ... ♖xc1 38 ♖xc1 ♗g3+ 39 ♔h3 ♘f4#] 38 ♔h3 ♗d6 39 h6 ♖xc1 40 h7 ♖xc3+ 41 ♔h4 ♗e7+ 42 ♔h5 ♖h3# **0-1** L/N6020-1875

**1834-✕BM-47**
**Macdonnell, A.–**
**Bourdonnais, L.C.M. de la**

1 e4 e5 2 ♗c4 ♗c5 3 c3 ♕e7 4 ♘f3 d6 5 0-0 ♗b6 6 d4 ♘f6 7 ♘a3 [□ 7 ♗g5 Staunton] 7 ... ♗g4 8 ♘c2 ♘bd7 [8 ... ♘xe4? 9 ♗d5! Staunton] 9 ♕d3? d5 10 exd5 e4 11 ♕d2 exf3 12 ♖e1 ♘e4 13 ♕f4 f5 14 gxf3 g5 15 ♕e3 ♘e5 16 ♗b5+ c6 17 fxg4 ♘xg4 18 ♕e2 cxb5 19 f3 ♘gf6 20 fxe4 ♘xe4 21 ♕xb5+ ♕d7 22 ♕xd7+ ♔xd7 23 c4 ♖ae8 24 c5 ♗d8 25 d6 f4 26 b4 ♖hf8 27 ♖f1 h5 28 ♘a3 ♗f6 29 ♗b2 g4 [29 ... a5 Staunton] 30 ♘c4 f3 31 ♘e5+ ♗xe5 32 dxe5 h4 33 ♖ad1 f2+ 34 ♔h1 h3 35 ♖d3 ♖g8 36 b5 g3 37 hxg3 ♖xg3 38 ♖d4 ♖eg8 [38 ... ♖xe5 39 c6+ bxc6 40 bxc6+ ♔xc6 41 ♖c4+ ♔xd6 42 ♗xe5+ ♔xe5 Δ 43 ... ♖g2; 38 ... ♖g1+ 39 ♖xg1 ♘g3+ 40 ♔h2 fxg1♕+ 41 ♔xg1 ♘e2+ 42 ♔h2 ♘xd4 43 ♗xd4 ♖f8 44 ♔xh3 ♖f4 45 c6+ bxc6 46 bxc6+ ♔xc6 47 ♗xa7= Walker] 39 e6+ ♔d8 40 ♖dd1 h2 41 e7+ ♔d7 42 c6+ bxc6 43 bxc6+ ♔xc6 44 e8♕+ ♖xe8 45 ♔xh2 ♖e6 46 ♖c1+ ♔b5 47 a4+ ♔b4 48 ♗c3+ ♖xc3 49 ♖xc3 ♔xc3 50 d7 ♖d6 51 ♔g2 ♖xd7 52 ♖c1+ ♔d3 53 ♔f1 ♔e3 **0-1** L/N6020-1875

**1834-✕BM-48**
**Bourdonnais, L.C.M. de la=**
**Macdonnell, A.**

1 d4 d5 2 c4 dxc4 3 e3 e5 4 ♗xc4 exd4 5 exd4 ♘f6 6 ♘c3 ♗d6 7 ♘f3 0-0 8 h3 ♘c6 9 0-0 h6 10 ♕d3 ♘a5 11 ♗b5 a6 12 ♗a4 c5 13 ♗c2 [13 dxc5?? ♗h2+−+ Staunton] 13 ... c4 14 ♕e2 b5 15 ♘e4 ♗b7 16 ♗d2 ♘xe4 17 ♗xe4 ♖e8 18 ♘e5 ♗xe5 19 dxe5 ♗xe4 20 ♗xa5 ♕d5 [□ 20 ... ♗d3 Bourdonnais] 21 f4 ♖e6 [21 ... ♗d3 22 ♕d2 ♕c5+ 23 ♖f2 Staunton] 22 ♖ad1 ♕c6 23 ♖f2 ♖ae8 24 ♗c3 f5 25 ♔h2 ♔h7 26 g4 g6 27 ♕e3 ♗d3 28 ♖g2 ♗e4 29 ♖g3 ♕c7 30 ♖d4 ♖f8 31 ♖d6 ♖fe8 [31 ... ♖xd6? 32 exd6 ♕xd6? 33 ♕a7++− Staunton] 32 ♕d4 ♖8e7 33 h4 ♗d3 34 h5 fxg4 35 hxg6+ ♗xg6 36 ♖xg4 ♗f5 37 ♖g2 ♕b7 38 ♖xe6 ♖xe6 39 ♖d2 ♕f7 40 ♔g1 ♖g6+ 41 ♖g2 ♗h3! 42 ♖xg6 ♕xg6+ 43 ♔f2 ♕g2+ 44 ♔e1 ♕h1+ 45 ♔d2 ♗g4 46 ♔c2 ♕g2+ 47 ♗d2 a5 48 a3 ♗f5+ 49 ♔c3 ♕f3+ 50 ♕e3 ♕d5 51 ♕a7+ ♔g6 52 ♕g1+ ♔f7 53 ♕a7+ ♗d7 54 ♔c2 ♕d3+ 55 ♔c1 a4 56 ♗e1 ♕f5 57 ♕f2 ♕g4 58 ♔d2 h5 59 ♔e3 ♔g6 60 ♕c2+ ♗f5 61 ♕e2 ♕g1+ 62 ♕f2 ♕xf2+ 63 ♔xf2 h4 64 ♔f3 ♔h5 65 ♗d2 ♗e6 66 ♔g2 ♔g4 67 ♗c1 h3+ 68 ♔h2 ♔f3 69 ♗d2 ♔e2 70 ♗c3 ♔d3 71 ♔g3 ♔c2 72 ♔h2 ♔b3 73 ♔g3 b4? [□ 73 ... ♗d7 74 ♔h2 ♗c8 75 ♔g3 b4 76 axb4 a3 77 bxa3 ♔xc3 78 b5 ♔d2 79 b6 c3 80 e6 c2 81 e7 c1♕ 82 e8♕ ♕g1+ 83 ♔f3 ♕g2# Bourdonnais] 74 axb4 a3 75 bxa3 ♔xc3 76 b5 ♔d2 77 b6 ♗d5 78 e6 c3 79 e7 c2 80 e8♕ c1♕ 81 ♔xh3 ♕h1+ 82 ♔g4 ♗f3+ 83 ♔f5 ♕b1+ 84 ♔g5 ♕g1+ 85 ♔f6 ♕xb6+ 86 ♕e6 ♕d8+ 87 ♔g6 ♗d5 88 ♕f6 ♕g8+ 89 ♔h6 ♔e3 90 a4 ♗e4 91 a5 ♕h7+ 92 ♔g5 ♕g8+ 93 ♔h6 **½-½** L/N6020-1875

**1834-✕BM-49**
**Bourdonnais, L.C.M. de la=**
**Macdonnell, A.**

1 e4 e5 2 ♗c4 ♗c5 3 ♘f3 d6 4 c3 ♕e7 5 0-0 ♘f6 6 d4 ♗b6 7 ♗g5 c6 8 ♘bd2 h6 9 ♗h4 g5 10 ♗g3 ♗c7 11 ♗b3 ♗g4 12 ♕e1 ♘bd7 13 ♕e3 ♘h7 14 h3 ♗xf3 15 ♕xf3 ♘hf8 16 ♘c4 h5 17 ♘e3 f6 18 ♘f5 ♕h7 19 h4 ♘g6 20 ♖fd1 0-0-0 21 a4 ♘f4 22 a5 d5 23 ♗c2! ♕f7 24 ♗xf4 g4 25 ♕e2 exf4 26 a6 b6 27 exd5 ♖he8 [27 ... cxd5? 28 ♘e7+ ♔b8 29 ♘c6++− Staunton] 28 ♕c4 ♕xd5 29 ♕xd5 cxd5 30 ♖e1 ♔b8 31 ♘e7 [□ 31 ♗a4! Staunton] 31 ... ♘e5 32 dxe5 ♖xe7 33 exf6 ♖f7 34 ♖e6 ♖d6 35 ♖ae1 ♖xe6 36 ♖xe6 ♗d8 37 ♗g6 [□ 37 ♖d6! Staunton] 37 ... ♖xf6 38 ♖xf6 ♗xf6 39 g3 fxg3 40 fxg3 d4 41 c4 ♔c7 42 ♗xh5 d3 43 b3 ♔d6 44 ♗xg4 ♔c5 45 ♗d1 ♔b4 46 ♔f2 ♔c3 47 ♔e3 ♗d4+ 48 ♔e4 ♗f2 49 ♔f4 [□ 49 h5+− Lewis; 49 h5= Walker] 49 ... ♔d2 50 ♗f3 ♔c3 51 ♗d1 ♔d2 52 ♗g4 ♔c3 53 ♔f3 ♗d4 54 ♗f5 d2 55 ♔e2 ♗f2 56 h5 ♗xg3 57 ♔d1 ♗f4 58 ♗e6 ♗h6 59 ♗f5 ♗g5 **½-½** L/N6020-1875

**1834-✕BM-50**
**Bourdonnais, L.C.M. de la–**
**Macdonnell, A.**

1 d4 d5 2 c4 dxc4 3 e4 [3 e3 Löwenthal] 3 ... e5 4 d5 f5 5 ♘c3 ♘f6 6 ♗xc4 ♗c5 [6 ... fxe4 7 ♘xe4 ♘xe4 8 ♕h5+ g6 9 ♕xe5+ ♕e7 10 ♕xh8 ♕b4+−+ Staunton; 6 ... fxe4 7 ♕e2 ♗f5 8 f3 exf3 9 ♕xe5+ ♕e7 10 ♘xf3 Saint-Amant; 6 ... fxe4 7 ♗g5 ♗f5 8 ♘ge2 Δ 9 ♘g3± Löwenthal] 7 ♘f3 ♕e7 [7 ... fxe4 8 ♘g5 ♗f5 9 ♕e2 ♗g4 10 ♕c2=; 7 ... fxe4 8 ♘xe5? ♕e7 9 ♗f4 ♗d6 10 ♕d4 ♘h5 11 g3 g5 12 ♗e2 ♘g7−+ Anderssen] 8 ♗g5? [□ 8 ♕e2 Staunton] 8 ... ♗xf2+ 9 ♔f1? [□ 9 ♔xf2! ♕c5+ 10 ♔e1 ♕xc4 11 ♘xe5 Δ 12 ♗xf6±; 9 ♔xf2! fxe4 10 d6 cxd6 11 ♘d5± Löwenthal] 9 ... ♗b6 10 ♕e2 [Δ 11 exf5 Löwenthal] 10 ... f4! 11 ♖d1 ♗g4 12 d6 cxd6 13 ♘d5

13 ... ♘xd5!! [13 ... ♕f8 14 ♗xf6 gxf6 15 ♗b5+ ♘c6 (15 ... ♔d8 16 ♕e1 ♘d7 17 ♕h4 ♗e6 18 ♗xd7 ♗xd5 19 ♗b5 △ 20 ♘xe5±; 15 ... ♗d7 16 ♗xd7+ ♘xd7 17 ♘h4 △ 17 ♘f5=; 15 ... ♘d7 16 ♕e1 ♔d8 17 ♕h4±) 16 ♕e1±; 13 ... ♕d8 14 ♗b5+ ♘c6 (14 ... ♘bd7 15 ♗xd7+ ♔xd7 16 ♘xe5+−; 14 ... ♔f8 15 ♕e1 h6 16 ♕h4±) 15 ♕c4 ♖c8 16 ♘xe5± Löwenthal] 14 ♗xe7? [□ 14 ♗xd5 ♗xf3 15 gxf3 ♕xg5 16 ♗xb7± Staunton; 14 ♗xd5 ♗xf3 15 gxf3 (15 ♕xf3 ♕d7) 15 ... ♕d7∓ Löwenthal] 14 ... ♘e3+ 15 ♔e1 [□ 15 ♕xe3 Saint-Amant] 15 ... ♔xe7 16 ♕d3 ♖d8 [16 ... ♘xg2+? 17 ♔e2 ♖d8 18 ♕d5 Anderssen] 17 ♖d2? [□ 17 ♗d5 ♘c6 18 ♗xc6 Anderssen] 17 ... ♘c6 18 b3 [18 a3 ♖ac8 19 b3 ♗a5 20 b4 ♘xb4 21 axb4 ♗xb4→ Anderssen] 18 ... ♗a5 19 a3 [△ 20 b4 Löwenthal; □ 19 ♔f2 Anderssen] 19 ... ♖ac8 20 ♖g1 b5! 21 ♗xb5 [21 ♗d5 Löwenthal] 21 ... ♗xf3 22 gxf3 [22 ♗xc6 ♖xc6 △ 23 ... ♖c2 Anderssen] 22 ... ♘d4 23 ♗c4 ♘xf3+ 24 ♔f2 ♘xd2 25 ♖xg7+ ♔f6 26 ♖f7+ ♔g6 27 ♖b7 ♘dxc4 28 bxc4 ♖xc4 29 ♕b1 [△ 30 ♕g1+ Staunton] 29 ... ♗b6 30 ♔f3 ♖c3 31 ♕a2 ♘c4+ 32 ♔g4 ♖g8 33 ♖xb6 [□ 33 ♖d7 Saint-Amant] 33 ... axb6 34 ♔h4 ♔f6 35 ♕e2 ♖g6 [35 ... ♘e3 Saint-Amant] 36 ♔h5 ♘e3 **0-1**

L/N6020-1875

## 1834-⚔BM-51

**Macdonnell, A.− Bourdonnais, L.C.M. de la**

1 e4 e5 2 ♘f3 ♘c6 3 ♗c4 ♗c5 4 b4 ♗xb4 5 c3 ♗e7 [□ 5 ... ♗a5 Saint-Amant] 6 d4 [□ 6 ♕b3 Staunton] 6 ... d6 7 ♕b3 ♘a5 8 ♕a4+ [□ 8 ♗xf7+ △ 9 ♕a4 Staunton] 8 ... c6 9 ♗d3 b5 10 ♕c2 ♗f6 11 dxe5 dxe5 12 0-0 [12 a4 Staunton] 12 ... ♘e7 13 ♗a3 0-0 14 ♘bd2 ♗e6 15 ♖ad1 ♕c7 16 ♘b3 ♘c4 17 ♗c1 [□ 17 ♗c5 Staunton] 17 ... ♖fd8 18 h3 c5 19 ♘h2 ♘g6 20 ♘g4 ♘d6 21 ♗e2 ♗e7 22 f4 exf4 [22 ... ♗xb3 △ 23 ... c4 Staunton] 23 ♗xf4 ♘xf4 24 ♖xf4 ♘c4 25 ♖f3 ♗xg4 26 hxg4 ♘e5 27 ♖h3 ♖xd1+ 28 ♕xd1 ♖d8 29 ♕f1 c4 30 ♘d4 ♗c5 31 ♕f5 g6 32 ♕f2 ♕e7 33 ♔h1 b4 34 ♕e3 bxc3 35 ♕h6 f6 36 ♘e6? ♕xe6 37 ♕xh7+ ♔f8 38 ♕c7 ♗e7 39 ♖xc3 ♕b6 40 ♕xb6 axb6 41 a4 ♗b4 42 ♖c2 c3 43 ♔h2 ♖d2 **0-1**

L/N6020-1875

## 1834-⚔BM-52

**Bourdonnais, L.C.M. de la= Macdonnell, A.**

1 e4 e5 2 ♘f3 ♘c6 3 ♗c4 ♗c5 4 b4 ♗xb4 5 c3 ♗d6? 6 d4 h6 7 0-0 g5!? 8 ♘xe5 ♗xe5 9 dxe5 ♘xe5 10 ♗b3 [△ 11 f4 Staunton] 10 ... g4 11 ♗f4 ♘g6 12 ♕xg4 d6 13 ♕f3 [□ 13 ♕g3 Saint-Amant] 13 ... ♕f6 14 ♗g3 ♕xf3 15 gxf3 f5 16 f4 [16 exf5 Saint-Amant] 16 ... fxe4 17 ♘d2 ♘f6 18 ♘xe4 ♘xe4 19 ♖fe1 ♗g4 [19 ... ♗f5 20 f3 △ 21 fxe4 Staunton] 20 ♖xe4+ ♔d7 21 ♖ae1 ♖af8 22 ♖b4 b6 23 ♗a4+ c6 24 f5! ♗xf5 25 ♖d4 ♖f6 26 ♖ed1 b5 27 ♖xd6+ ♖xd6 28 ♖xd6+ ♔e7 29 ♗b3 ♖c8 30 h4 ♘xh4 31 ♖xh6 ♘f3+ 32 ♔g2 ♘e1+ 33 ♔f1 ♘d3 34 ♗c2 c5 35 ♖h5 ♗e4 36 f3 [36 ♔g1 Lewis] 36 ... ♖f8 37 ♗xd3 ♖xf3+ 38 ♗f2 ♗xd3+ 39 ♔g2 ♖f5 40 ♗xc5+ ♔f7 41 ♖xf5+ ♗xf5 **½-½**

L/N6020-1875

## 1834-⚔BM-53

**Bourdonnais, L.C.M. de la+ Macdonnell, A.**

1 e4 e5 2 ♘f3 ♘c6 3 ♗c4 ♗c5 4 b4 ♗xb4 5 c3 ♗d6? 6 0-0 h6 7 d4 ♘f6 8 dxe5 ♗xe5 9 ♘xe5 ♘xe5 10 ♗b3 ♕e7 [10 ... ♘xe4? 11 ♖e1+− Staunton] 11 f4 ♕c5+ 12 ♔h1 ♘eg4 13 ♕e2 [□ 13 e5! Staunton] 13 ... ♕h5 14 h3 0-0? [□ 14 ... d6 Saint-Amant] 15 e5 ♖e8 16 ♕f3 ♕h4?! 17 exf6 d6 18 ♘a3 ♖e1 19 ♗d2 ♘f2+ 20 ♔h2 ♗xh3?! 21 ♕xf2 ♕xf2 22 ♖xf2 ♖xa1 23 gxh3 g6 24 ♖g2 ♔f8 25 f5 g5 26 h4 **1-0**

L/N6020-1875

## 1834-⚔BM-54

**Macdonnell, A.+ Bourdonnais, L.C.M. de la**

1 e4 e5 2 f4 exf4 3 ♘f3 g5 4 ♗c4 g4 5 ♘c3 [5 0-0; 5 d4 Staunton] 5 ... gxf3 6 ♕xf3 [6 0-0 Staunton] 6 ... ♗h6? 7 d4 ♘c6 8 0-0 ♘xd4 9 ♗xf7+! ♔xf7 10 ♕h5+ ♔g7 11 ♗xf4 ♗xf4 12 ♖xf4 ♘f6? [□ 12 ... ♘h6 13 ♕e5+ Löwenthal] 13 ♕g5+ ♔f7 14 ♖af1 [14 e5 ♔e8 (14 ... ♕g8 15 ♕xf6+ ♔e8 16 ♘d5+−) 15 exf6 (15 ♖xf6 ♕e7) 15 ... d6 (15 ... ♘e6 16 ♖e1 ♖f8 17 f7+ ♖xf7 18 ♕g8++−) 16 ♕g7 ♖f8 17 ♘b5+− Löwenthal] 14 ... ♔e8 15 ♖xf6 ♕e7 16 ♘d5 ♕c5 17 ♔h1 [17 ♘xc7+ ♕xc7 18 ♕g7 ♘e6 19 ♖xe6+ dxe6 20 ♕xh8+ ♔e7 21 ♖f7+ ♔xf7 22 ♕xh7++− Löwenthal] 17 ... ♘e6 18 ♖xe6+ dxe6 19 ♘f6+ **1-0**

L/N6020-1875

## 1834-⚔BM-55

**Bourdonnais, L.C.M. de la= Macdonnell, A.**

1 e4 e5 2 f4 exf4 3 ♘f3 g5 4 ♗c4 ♗g7 5 d4 d6 6 h4 h6 7 c3 ♘c6 [□ 7 ... g4 Dufresne] 8 hxg5 hxg5 9 ♖xh8 ♗xh8 10 ♕e2 ♕e7∓ 11 ♘a3 ♗g4 12 ♗d2 0-0-0 13 0-0-0 ♘f6 14 ♗d3 ♖e8 15 ♖e1 ♘h5 16 ♕f2 ♗xf3 17 gxf3 a6 18 ♗c2 ♘g3 19 ♗a4 ♗g7? [□ 19 ... ♖∼ Bourdonnais; □ 19 ... b5 Staunton] 20 d5 ♘b8 [20 ... ♘e5? 21 ♕a7!+− Staunton] 21 ♗xe8 ♕xe8 22 ♕g2 ♕h8 23 ♖d1 f5 24 ♗e1 ♗e5 25 exf5 ♕h7 26 ♘c4 ♕xf5 27 ♘xe5 ♕xe5 28 ♗xg3 fxg3 29 ♖g1 ♕xd5 30 ♕xg3 b6 31 ♕g4+ ♘d7 [31 ... ♔b7? 32 ♕e4+− Staunton] 32 ♖d1 [□ 32 ♖e1 Staunton] 32 ... ♕e5 33 ♖g1 ♕e3+ 34 ♔b1 c6 35 ♖h1 ♔c7 36 a3 b5 37 ♔a2 ♕e8 38 ♕f5 ♕e2 39 ♕xg5 ♕xf3 40 ♖h6 ♕e4+− 41 ♕g8 ♕e2 42 ♖h8 ♔b6 43 ♖h7 [43 ♕d8+ ♔c5!= Bourdonnais] 43 ... ♔c7 44 ♕f7 ♔b6 45 ♖g7 ♕e4 46 ♕f2+ ♘c5 47 ♖g1 [47 b4?? ♕c4+→ Staunton] 47 ... ♕c4+ 48 ♔a1 a5 49 ♖d1 ♔c7 50 ♕f6 ♘b7 51 ♖g1 c5 52 ♖g7+ ♔b6 53 ♕f7 [□ 53 ♕f3 Staunton] 53 ... ♕e4 54 ♔a2 a4 55 ♖g8 ♕c6 56 ♕e6 ♕f3 57 ♖c8 ♕h1 58 ♕f7 ♔a7 59 c4? ♕h3 60 ♖c7 ♕b3+ 61 ♔b1 bxc4 [61 ... ♕d1+=] 62 ♕d5 ♕b6 63 ♕c6 ♕xc6 64 ♖xc6 d5 65 ♔c2 d4 66 ♔d1 ♔b8 67 ♖a6 ♔c7 68 ♖xa4 ♘d6 69 ♖a6 ♘e4 70 ♔c2 ♘d6 71 a4 ♘c8 72 a5 ♔b7 73 ♖f6 ♘a7 74 b3 [□ 74 b4 Lewis] 74 ... c3 75 b4 cxb4 76 ♖b6+ ♔c7 77 ♖xb4 ♘c6 78 ♖b5 ♘a7 79 ♖b1 ♔c6 80 a6 ♘c8 81 ♔d3? [□ 81 ♖b7 ♔∼ (81 ... ♘∼ 82 ♖b8+−) 82 a7+− Lewis] 81 ... ♔c7 82 ♔xd4 c2 83 ♖c1 ♔b6 84 ♖xc2 ♘a7 85 ♖a2 ♘b5+ 86 ♔c4 ♘a7 87 ♖a1 ♘c6 88 ♖a3 ♘a7 89 ♔d5? [□ 89 ♖a2 ♘c6 90 ♖a1 ♘a7 91 ♔d5 ♘b5 92 ♔e5 ♔a7 (92 ... ♘a7 93 ♔d6 ♘c8+ 94 ♔d7 ♘a7 95 ♔d8 ♘c6+ 96 ♔c8 ♔a7 97 ♔c7 ♘b8 98 ♖a4 ♘xa6+ 99 ♔c6+−; 92 ... ♘c7 93 a7 ♔b7 94 ♔f6 ♔a8 95 ♔e7 ♘b5 96 ♔d7 ♘xa7 97 ♖b1+−) 93 ♔e6 ♘c7+ 94 ♔d6 ♘xa6 95 ♔c6+− Lewis] 89 ... ♘b5 90 ♖b3 ♔xa6 91 ♔c5 ♘a7 92 ♖b8 ♔a5 **½-½**

L/N6020-1875

## 1834-⚔BM-56

**Bourdonnais, L.C.M. de la+ Macdonnell, A.**

1 e4 e5 2 ♘f3 ♘c6 3 ♗c4 ♗c5 4 b4 ♗xb4 5 c3 ♗a5 6 0-0 d6 7 d4 exd4 8 cxd4 ♗b6 9 ♗b2 ♘f6 10 d5 ♘a5? [□ 10 ... ♘e7 Bourdonnais] 11 ♗d3 [11 e5 Staunton] 11 ... 0-0 12 h3 ♘h5 13 ♕d2 f5 14 ♘c3 [14 e5! Saint-Amant] 14 ... f4 15 ♖fe1 a6 16 e5! ♗f5 [16 ... dxe5 17 ♘xe5 ♗f5 18 ♘a4 ♗xd3 (18 ... ♕xd5?? 19 ♗c4+−; 18 ... c6 19 ♘xb6 ♕xb6

20 ♗c3±) 19 ♘xb6 cxb6 20 ♕xd3± Löwenthal] 17 e6 ♕e7 18 ♘a4 ♗xd3 19 ♕xd3 [19 ♘xb6 ♘c4! Saint-Amant] 19 ... ♗a7 20 ♗c3 b6 21 ♘d4 ♕g5 22 ♘f3 [◻ 22 e7 △ 23 ♘e6 Lewis] 22 ... ♕f5 23 ♕xf5 ♖xf5 24 ♗xa5 bxa5 25 ♖ac1 ♖c8 26 ♖c6! ♖xd5 27 ♖ec1 ♘g3! 28 ♖e1 [28 ♖xc7?? ♖xc7 29 ♖xc7 ♖d1+–+ Staunton] 28 ... ♘f5 29 e7 ♖e8 30 ♖xc7 ♗d4 [30 ... ♗b8 31 ♖c8 ♖xc8 32 e8♕++– Löwenthal] 31 ♘g5 h6? [◻31 ... ♖e5= Saint-Amant]

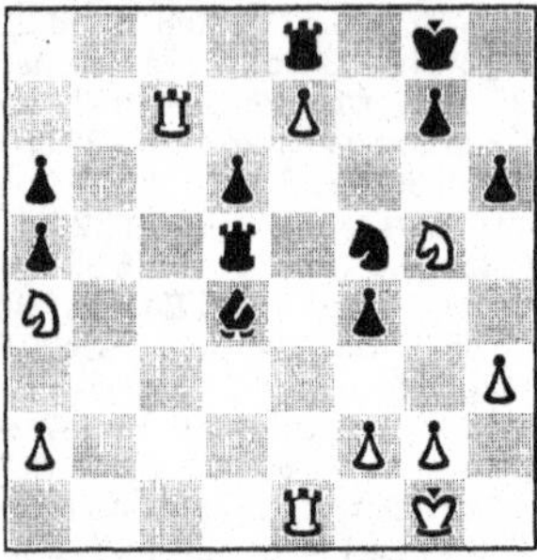

32 ♖c8 hxg5 33 ♖xe8+ ♔h7 34 ♖h8+ ♔xh8 35 e8♕+ ♔h7 36 ♕f7 ♖b5 37 ♕e6 **1-0** L/N6020-1875

### 1834-⚔BM-57
**Macdonnell, A.= Bourdonnais, L.C.M. de la**

1 e4 c5 2 ♘f3 ♘c6 3 d4 cxd4 4 ♘xd4 e5 5 ♘xc6? bxc6 6 ♗c4 ♘f6 [6 ... ♗c5 △ 7 ... h6 Saint-Amant] 7 ♗g5 ♗c5 8 0-0 h6 9 ♗xf6 ♕xf6 10 ♘c3 a5 11 ♔h1 [11 ♘a4 ♗a7 Staunton] 11 ... d6 12 ♕d2 g5 13 ♖ad1 ♔e7 14 ♘a4 ♗d4 15 ♕d3 h5 16 ♕b3 h4 17 f3 h3 18 g3 ♗d7 19 c3 ♖ab8 20 ♕c2 ♗a7 21 ♕d2 ♖hg8 22 b3 ♖bd8 23 ♘b2 ♖g7 24 ♗e2 ♕g6 25 ♘c4 ♗c5 26 ♘xa5 ♖b8 27 b4 ♗b6 28 ♘c4 ♕f6 29 ♘xd6 ♖gg8 30 ♘xf7 ♗e6 31 ♘d6 ♖gd8 32 c4 ♗xc4 33 ♗xc4 ♖xd6 34 ♕xd6+ ♕xd6 35 ♖xd6 ♔xd6 36 ♖b1 ♗d4 37 ♗f1 ♖a8 38 ♗xh3 [◻ 38 ♗c4 Saint-Amant] 38 ... ♖xa2 39 ♗g2 ♖b2± 40 ♖xb2 ♗xb2 41 ♗f1 ♔e6 42 ♔g2 ♔f6 43 ♔h3 ♗c3 44 b5 cxb5 45 ♗xb5 ♗d4 46 ♔g4 ♗e3 47 h4 gxh4 48 ♔xh4 ♗c5= 49 ♔g4 ♗f2 50 f4 ♗d4! [50 ... exf4?± 51 gxf4 Saint-Amant] 51 ♔f3 ♗c3 52 ♔g4 ♗d4 53 ♔h5 ♗f2 54 ♔g4 ♗d4 55 ♗d3 [55 fxe5+= Saint-Amant] 55 ... ♗e3 56 ♔f3 ♗d2 **½-½** L/N6020-1875

### 1834-⚔BM-58
**Macdonnell, A.+ Bourdonnais, L.C.M. de la**

1 e4 c5 2 ♘f3 ♘c6 3 d4 cxd4 4 ♘xd4 ♘xd4 [◻ 4 ... e5 Staunton] 5 ♕xd4 e6 6 ♗c4 ♘e7 7 ♘c3 ♘c6 8 ♕d1 ♗c5 9 0-0 0-0 10 ♔h1 f5? 11 exf5 ♖xf5 12 ♗d3 ♖f8 13 ♕h5 [13 ♗xh7+ ♔xh7 14 ♕h5+± Saint-Amant] 13 ... ♖f5 14 ♗xf5 exf5 15 ♕xf5 d6 16 ♕d5+ ♔h8 17 ♗g5 ♕f8 18 ♘e4 ♘b4 19 ♕b3 ♗f5 20 ♖ae1 ♗d7? 21 a4 **1-0** L/N6020-1875

### 1834-⚔BM-59
**Bourdonnais, L.C.M. de la= Macdonnell, A.**

1 e4 e5 2 ♘f3 ♘c6 3 ♗c4 ♗c5 4 b4 ♗xb4 5 c3 ♗a5 6 0-0 d6 7 d4 exd4 8 cxd4 ♗b6 9 d5 ♘e5 [◻ 9 ... ♘ce7 Staunton] 10 ♘xe5 dxe5 11 ♘d2 [11 ♖e1 △ 12 f4 Staunton] 11 ... ♘e7 12 ♘f3 ♕d6 13 ♗b5+! ♗d7 14 ♗xd7+ ♔xd7 15 ♕a4+ ♔d8 16 ♗a3 ♕f6 17 d6 ♘c6 18 ♖ad1! ♘d4 19 ♘xd4 ♗xd4 20 ♔h1 c5 21 ♖xd4! cxd4 22 f4 exf4 23 ♗c5 d3 24 ♗b6++– axb6 25 ♕xa8+ ♔d7 26 ♕xh8 f3! 27 gxf3? [◻ 27 ♕xh7+– Saint-Amant] 27 ... d2 28 ♕b8 ♕xf3+ 29 ♖xf3 d1♕+ 30 ♔g2 ♕d2+ 31 ♖f2 ♕g5+ 32 ♔f3 ♕f6+ 33 ♔e2 ♕b2+ 34 ♔f1 ♕c1+ 35 ♔e2 ♕b2+ 36 ♔d3 ♕a3+ 37 ♔e2 ♕b2+ 38 ♔f3 ♕f6+ 39 ♔g4 ♕g6+ **½-½** L/N6020-1875

### 1834-⚔BM-60
**Bourdonnais, L.C.M. de la+ Macdonnell, A.**

1 e4 e5 2 ♘f3 ♘c6 3 ♗c4 ♗c5 4 b4 ♗xb4 5 c3 ♗a5 6 0-0 d6 7 d4 exd4 8 cxd4 ♗b6 9 d5 ♘e5 10 ♘xe5 dxe5 11 ♘d2 ♕f6 12 ♘f3 ♘e7 13 ♗b2 ♘g6 14 ♔h1! 0-0? [◻ 14 ... ♗g4 15 ♕a4+ (15 ♗b5+ c6) 15 ... ♗d7 16 ♕~ ♕e7= Saint-Amant] 15 ♘xe5 ♘xe5 16 f4 ♘xc4 17 ♗xf6 gxf6 18 ♖f3 ♔h8 19 ♕d3 ♘d6 20 f5 ♖g8 21 ♖f4 ♗d7 22 ♕c3 ♖g7 23 ♕xf6 ♖ag8 24 ♖h4 ♗e3 25 ♕c3 ♗g5 26 ♖g4 f6 27 h4 h5 28 hxg5! hxg4 29 g6 ♘xe4 30 ♕xc7 ♖e8 31 ♖f1 g3 32 ♕f4 ♔g8 33 ♔g1 ♖e5? [◻ 33 ... ♘c3! △ 34 ... ♘e2+ 35 ♔h1 ♖ee7! Saint-Amant] 34 ♕e3 b6 35 ♕d4 ♘d6 36 ♕h4 ♘e4 37 d6 a5 38 ♖f4 ♘c3 39 ♖f1 ♘e2+ 40 ♔h1 ♗xf5 41 ♖xf5 ♖e8 [41 ... ♖xf5 42 ♕c4+ ♔h8 43 ♕c8+ ♖g8 44 ♕xf5+– Walker] 42 ♕c4+ **1-0** L/N6020-1876

### 1834-⚔BM-61
**Macdonnell, A.= Bourdonnais, L.C.M. de la**

1 e4 c5 2 ♘f3 ♘c6 3 d4 cxd4 4 ♘xd4 e5 5 ♘xc6 bxc6 6 ♗c4 ♘f6 7 ♕e2 ♗e7 8 ♘c3 0-0 9 ♗g5 ♘xe4 10 ♗xe7 ♘xc3 11 ♕xe5! ♖e8! 12 0-0 ♕xe7 13 ♕xc3 d5 14 ♗d3 ♕d6 15 ♖ad1 ♗d7 16 ♕d4 c5 17 ♕h4 g6 18 c3 ♗c6 19 f4 c4 20 ♗b1 ♖e2! 21 ♖f2 ♖ae8 22 f5 ♕e5 23 ♖df1 ♕e3 24 fxg6 fxg6 25 ♕f6 ♖xf2 26 ♕xf2 ♔g7 27 ♕xe3 ♖xe3 28 ♔f2 ♖e5 29 ♖e1 ♖xe1 30 ♔xe1 **½-½** L/N6020-1876

### 1834-⚔BM-62
**Macdonnell, A.– Bourdonnais, L.C.M. de la**

1 e4 c5 2 ♘f3 ♘c6 3 d4 cxd4 4 ♘xd4 [4 ♗c4 Löwenthal] 4 ... e5 5 ♘xc6 [◻ 5 ♘f3 Saint-Amant] 5 ... bxc6 6 ♗c4 ♘f6 7 ♗g5 ♗e7 8 ♕e2 [◻ 8 ♗xf6 △ 9 ♘c3 Löwenthal] 8 ... d5 9 ♗xf6 ♗xf6 10 ♗b3 0-0 11 0-0 a5 [△ 12 ... ♗a6 Bourdonnais] 12 exd5 cxd5 13 ♖d1 d4 14 c4? [◻ 14 c3 Staunton] 14 ... ♕b6 15 ♗c2 ♗b7 [15 ... ♕xb2?? 16 ♗xh7++– Bourdonnais] 16 ♘d2 ♖ae8 [16 ... ♖fe8 Saint-Amant; 16 ... ♕xb2 Löwenthal] 17 ♘e4 ♗d8 18 c5 ♕c6 19 f3 ♗e7 20 ♖ac1 f5 21 ♕c4+ ♔h8! [21 ... ♕d5; 21 ... ♖f7 Löwenthal] 22 ♗a4 ♕h6 23 ♗xe8 fxe4 24 c6 exf3!? 25 ♖c2 [25 cxb7? ♕e3+ 26 ♔h1 fxg2+ 27 ♔xg2 ♖f2+ 28 ♔g1 ♖e2+–+ Löwenthal] 25 ... ♕e3+ 26 ♔h1 ♗c8 27 ♗d7 f2 28 ♖f1 d3 29 ♖c3 ♗xd7 30 cxd7 [30 ♖xd3? ♕e2–+ Löwenthal] 30 ... e4 31 ♕c8 ♗d8 32 ♕c4? [◻ 32 ♖cc1 Bourdonnais] 32 ... ♕e1 33 ♖cc1 d2 34 ♕c5 ♖g8 35 ♖cd1 e3 36 ♕c3 ♕xd1 37 ♖xd1 e2

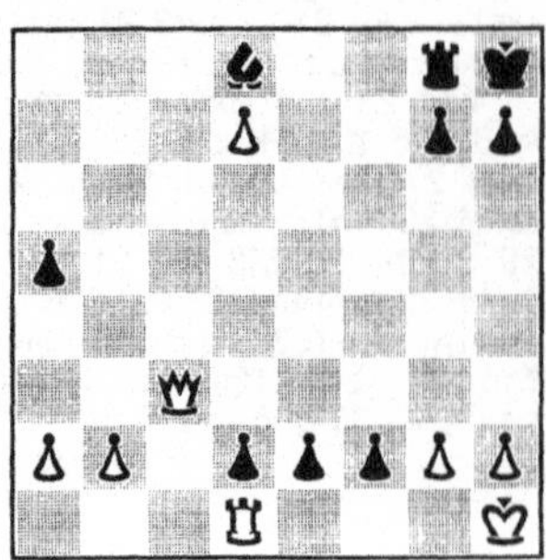

**0-1** L/N6020-1876

### 1834-⚔BM-63
**Bourdonnais, L.C.M. de la+ Macdonnell, A.**

1 e4 e5 2 ♘f3 ♘c6 3 ♗c4 ♗c5 4 b4 ♗xb4 5 c3 ♗a5 6 0-0 d6 7 d4 exd4 8 exd4 ♗b6 9 d5 [9 ♗b2 Saint-Amant] 9 ... ♘a5 [◻ 9 ... ♘ce7; 9 ... ♘e5 Saint-Amant] 10 ♗d3! ♘f6 11 ♘c3 0-0 [11 ... ♗g4 Saint-Amant] 12 h3 ♗d7 [◻ 12 ... h6 Saint-Amant] 13 ♗g5 h6 14 ♗h4 g5?! 15 ♘xg5 hxg5 16 ♗xg5 ♗d4 17 ♘e2! ♗xa1 18 ♕xa1 ♔g7 19 f4 ♕e7 20 ♕c3 [20 e5 Saint-Amant] 20 ... b6 21 ♖f3! ♘c4 22 ♗xf6+ ♕xf6 23 ♖g3+ **1-0** L/N6020-1876

### 1834-⚔BM-64

**Macdonnell, A.–**
**Bourdonnais, L.C.M. de la**

1 e4 c5 2 ♘f3 ♘c6 3 ♗c4 e6 4 ♘c3 ♘f6 [□ 4 ... ♘ge7 Saint-Amant] 5 e5 d5 6 exf6 dxc4 7 fxg7 ♗xg7∓ 8 ♘e4 ♕d5 9 ♘g3 h5 10 h4 e5 11 0-0?! ♗g4 12 ♕e2 f5 [12 ... ♘d4∓ Saint-Amant] 13 ♕e3 ♗xf3 [13 ... f4 14 ♕e4! ♗xf3∓ Saint-Amant] 14 ♕xf3 ♕xf3 15 gxf3 ♘d4 16 ♔g2 ♘xc2 17 ♖b1 ♘d4 18 b3 cxb3 19 axb3 0-0-0 20 d3 ♗f6 21 f4 ♖hg8 22 ♔h3 exf4 23 ♗xf4 ♖g4 24 ♗g5 ♗xg5 25 hxg5 ♘e6 26 ♘xf5 ♖xd3+ 27 ♘e3 ♖xg5 28 b4 ♖d4 29 bxc5 ♖xc5 30 ♖bc1 ♖xc1 31 ♖xc1+ ♔d7 **0-1** L/N6020-1876

### 1834-⚔BM-65

**Macdonnell, A.=**
**Bourdonnais, L.C.M. de la**

1 e4 e5 2 ♘f3 ♘c6 3 ♗c4 ♗c5 4 b4 ♗xb4 5 c3 ♗a5 6 0-0 ♗b6 7 d4 exd4 8 cxd4 d6 9 h3 h6 10 ♘c3 ♘ge7 11 ♗b2 0-0 12 ♘e2 ♘g6 13 ♘g3 ♔h8 14 ♕c2 ♘h4 15 ♘xh4 ♕xh4 16 ♖ad1 ♗d7 17 ♔h2 f5 18 d5 ♘e5 19 ♗xe5 dxe5 20 exf5 ♕f4 21 ♗d3 ♖ae8 22 ♖de1 ♕b4 23 ♖e4 ♕d6 24 ♖g4 ♕xd5 25 ♘h5 ♖e7 26 f6! gxf6 27 ♕c1? [□ 27 ♗c4; 27 ♘xf6 Staunton; □ 27 ♖g6 Saint-Amant] 27 ... ♗xg4 [27 ... ♕xd3? 28 ♕xh6++– Saint-Amant] 28 ♕xh6+ ♔g8 29 ♕g6+ ♔h8 **½-½** L/N6020-1876

### 1834-⚔BM-66

**Macdonnell, A.+**
**Bourdonnais, L.C.M. de la**

1 e4 e5 2 ♘f3 ♘c6 3 ♗c4 ♗c5 4 b4 ♗xb4 5 c3 ♗c5 [□ 5 ... ♗a5 Anderssen] 6 0-0 ♗b6 7 d4 exd4 8 cxd4 d6 9 h3 [□ 9 d5 Anderssen] 9 ... h6 10 ♗b2 ♕e7? [□ 10 ... ♘f6 Staunton] 11 e5 dxe5 12 ♗a3 [□ 12 d5 Lewis] 12 ... ♕f6 13 ♖e1 ♗d7 14 dxe5 ♕f5 [14 ... ♕g6 ∆ 15 ... ♗xh3 Anderssen] 15 ♘c3 0-0-0 16 ♘d5 ♗e6 17 ♗d3! ♖xd5 [17 ... ♕h5? 18 ♘f4! Saint-Amant] 18 ♗xf5 ♖xd1 19 ♗xe6+ fxe6 20 ♖axd1 ♘ge7 21 ♖d3 ♘d5 [∆ 22 ... ♘f4! Anderssen] 22 g3 g5 23 ♔g2 ♖g8 24 ♖e4 a5 25 ♘e1 [∆ 26 ♖f3 Anderssen] 25 ... ♘cb4 26 ♗xb4 axb4 27 a3 bxa3 28 ♖xa3 ♔d7 29 ♖f3 c5 30 ♖f7+ ♔c6 31 ♖h7 ♖g6 32 h4 gxh4 33 ♖xh4 ♗a5 34 ♘f3 ♘c7? [□ 34 ... b5∓ Saint-Amant] 35 ♖7xh6 ♖g7 36 ♔f1 b5 37 ♔e2 ♔d5? [□ 37 ... b4 Staunton] 38 ♖h7 ♖g8 39 ♖d7+ ♔c6 40 ♖d6+ ♔b7 41 ♖h7 b4 42 ♘d2 ♖a8 43 ♖xe6 ♗b6 44 ♘c4 ♖a2+ 45 ♔d3 ♗a7 46 ♖f6 ♖a1 47 e6 ♖e1 48 e7 b3 49 ♘a5+ ♔c8 50 ♖f8+ ♘e8 [50 ... ♔d7 51 e8♕++– Anderssen] 51 ♖xe8+ ♔c7 52 ♘xb3 **1-0**

L/N6020-1876

### 1834-⚔BM-67

**Bourdonnais, L.C.M. de la+**
**Macdonnell, A.**

1 e4 e5 2 ♘f3 ♘c6 3 ♗c4 ♗c5 4 b4 ♗xb4 5 c3 ♗a5 6 0-0 d6 7 d4 exd4 8 cxd4 ♗b6 9 d5 [□ 9 ♗b2 Bourdonnais] 9 ... ♘a5 [□ 9 ... ♘ce7 Bourdonnais] 10 ♗d3 ♘f6 11 ♘c3 0-0 12 h3 h6 13 ♔h2 [∆ 14 ♘d2 Bourdonnais] 13 ... c5 14 ♘d2 ♗d7 15 ♕e1 g5 16 f4 gxf4 17 ♖xf4 c4?! 18 ♗c2 ♗d4 [∆ 19 ... b5 Bourdonnais] 19 ♘f3 ♗xc3? [19 ... ♗e5 Saint-Amant] 20 ♕xc3 ♘h5?! 21 ♖h4 ♘g7 22 ♗xh6 f6 23 ♗xg7 ♔xg7

24 e5! fxe5 25 ♖h7+ ♔g8 26 ♘xe5!+– ♗f5 [26 ... dxe5 27 ♕g3+ Bourdonnais] 27 ♘f7! ♔xh7 28 ♗xf5+ ♔g8 29 ♘h6# **1-0**

L/N6020-1876

### 1834-⚔BM-68

**Macdonnell A.+**
**Bourdonnais, L.C.M. de la**

1 e4 c5 2 f4 ♘c6 3 ♘f3 e6 4 c3 d5 5 e5 f6 6 ♗d3 ♘h6 7 ♗c2 ♗d7 8 0-0 ♕b6 9 d4 0-0-0 [9 ... ♗e7 Saint-Amant] 10 ♔h1 ♘g4 11 a3 ♔b8 12 b4 cxb4 13 cxb4 ♗e7 14 ♘c3 ♖df8 15 ♘a4 ♕c7 16 ♘c5 ♗xc5 17 bxc5 g5 18 h3 h5! 19 ♔g1 [19 hxg4? hxg4+∓ Saint-Amant] 19 ... gxf4 20 hxg4 hxg4∞ 21 ♘e1 fxe5 22 ♗b2 g3 23 dxe5 ♘xe5 24 ♘f3 ♘xf3+ 25 ♖xf3 ♖h4 26 ♕d2 ♕xc5+? [□ 26 ... e5 ∆ 27 ... e4 Saint-Amant] 27 ♗d4 ♕e7 [27 ... ♖fh8 28 ♕xf4+! ♖xf4 29 ♗xc5± Staunton] 28 ♕a5 a6 29 ♖b1 [∆ 30 ♖xb7+ Saint-Amant] 29 ... ♗b5 30 ♖xb5 ♖fh8 31 ♗xh8 ♖h1+ 32 ♔xh1 ♕h4+ 33 ♔g1 ♕h2+ 34 ♔f1 ♕h1+ 35 ♔e2 ♕xg2+ 36 ♔e1 ♕h1+ [36 ... ♕xf3 37 ♕d8+ ♔a7 38 ♕b6++– Saint-Amant] 37 ♔d2 ♕xh8 38 ♕xa6 ♕h2+ 39 ♔c1 **1-0** L/N6020-1876

### 1834-⚔BM-69

**Bourdonnais, L.C.M. de la+**
**Macdonnell, A.**

1 e4 e5 2 ♘f3 ♘c6 3 ♗c4 ♗c5 4 b4 ♗xb4 5 c3 ♗c5 6 0-0 d6 7 d4 exd4 8 cxd4 ♗b6 9 d5 ♘a5 10 ♗d3 ♘f6 11 ♘c3 0-0 12 h3 h6 13 ♔h1 [13 ♔h2 Saint-Amant] 13 ... ♘h7 14 ♕c2 f5?! 15 exf5 c5 16 g4 a6 17 ♗f4 ♗a7 18 a4 c4 19 ♗e4 ♘b3 20 ♖ae1 ♘c5 21 ♘d4 ♘xe4 22 ♖xe4 ♕h4 23 ♔g2 ♘g5 24 ♗xg5 ♕xg5 25 f4 ♕h4 26 ♘e6 ♗xe6 27 dxe6± h5 28 ♕e2 hxg4 29 hxg4 b5 30 ♘d5 ♖fc8 31 e7 ♔f7 32 ♖h1 **1-0** L/N6020-1876

### 1834-⚔BM-70

**Macdonnell, A.–**
**Bourdonnais, L.C.M. de la**

1 e4 c5 2 f4 ♘c6 3 c3 e6 4 ♘f3 d5 5 e5 ♕b6 6 ♗d3 f6 7 ♗c2 ♘h6 8 0-0 ♘f7 9 ♔h1 ♗d7 10 d4 ♗e7 11 a3 a5 12 b3 f5 13 ♗e3 0-0 14 ♘bd2 ♖fc8 15 h3 ♔h8 16 g4 g6 17 ♖g1 cxd4 18 cxd4 g5!? 19 gxf5 exf5 20 fxg5 ♘cxe5 21 ♘xe5 ♘xe5 22 ♖a2 ♘g6 23 ♘f3 ♕e6 24 ♘e5 ♘xe5 25 dxe5 ♖c3 [25 ... ♕xe5?? 26 ♗d4+– Saint-Amant] 26 ♖g3 ♖ac8 [□ 26 ... f4!→ Saint-Amant] 27 ♗b1 ♗e8 [□ 27 ... d4 Saint-Amant] 28 ♖f2 ♗g6 29 b4 axb4 30 axb4 ♖xe3 31 ♖xe3 ♗xg5 32 ♕e1 ♖c1! [32 ... ♗h4 Saint-Amant] 33 ♕xc1 ♗xc1 34 ♖xc1 ♕xe5 35 ♖cf1 d4 36 ♗xf5 ♗xf5 37 ♖xf5 ♕e4+ 38 ♔g1 d3 39 ♖f8+ ♔g7 40 ♖1f6 [∆ 41 ♖8f7+ ♔g8 42 ♖f8+ ♔g7 43 ♖8f7+= Saint-Amant] 40 ... ♕d4+ 41 ♔f1 ♕xf6+ 42 ♖xf6 ♔xf6 43 ♔f2→ ♔e5 44 ♔e3 d2 45 ♔xd2 ♔d4 46 b5 ♔c5 47 ♔c3 ♔xb5 48 ♔b3 h5 **0-1**

L/N6020-1876

### 1834-⚔BM-71

**Bourdonnais, L.C.M. de la+**
**Macdonnell, A.**

1 e4 e5 2 ♘f3 ♘c6 3 ♗c4 ♗c5 4 b4 ♗xb4 5 c3 ♗a5 6 0-0 d6 7 d4 exd4 8 cxd4 ♗b6 9 d5 ♘a5 10 ♗d3 ♘f6 11 h3 0-0 12 ♔h1 c6 13 ♘a3 h6 14 ♗f4 cxd5? 15 exd5 ♗c7? [15 ... ♘xd5 Saint-Amant] 16 ♕d2 ♘h7 17 ♘b5 b6? 18 ♗xh7+ ♔xh7 19 ♕c2+ f5 20 ♕xc7 ♕xc7 21 ♘xc7 **1-0** L/N6020-1876

### 1834-⚔BM-72

**Macdonnell, A.+**
**Bourdonnais, L.C.M. de la**

1 e4 e5 2 ♘f3 ♘c6 3 ♗c4 ♗c5 4 b4 ♗xb4 5 c3 ♗c5 [□ 5 ... ♗a5 Bourdonnais] 6 0-0 d6 7 d4 exd4 8 cxd4 ♗b6 9 h3 h6?! 10 ♗b2 ♕e7? 11 e5 dxe5 12 d5! ♘a5 13 ♘xe5 ♘f6 14 d6! cxd6 15 ♗xf7+ ♔d8

16 ♖e1 ♔c7 17 ♘a3 a6 18 ♖c1+ ♗c5?

19 ♖xc5+! dxc5 20 ♘ec4 ♕d8 21 ♗e5+ ♔c6 22 ♕f3+ ♘d5 23 ♗xd5+ ♔d7 [23 ... ♕xd5 24 ♘xa5++- Bourdonnais] 24 ♕f5+ ♔e8 25 ♕f7# **1-0** L/N6020-1876

**1834-✕BM-73**
**Bourdonnais, L.C.M. de la+ Macdonnell, A.**

1 e4 e5 2 ♘f3 ♘c6 3 ♗c4 ♗c5 4 b4 ♗xb4 5 c3 ♗c5 6 0-0 d6 7 d4 exd4 8 cxd4 ♗b6 9 d5 ♘ce7 10 e5 ♘g6 [10 ... dxe5?± Saint-Amant] 11 ♗b2 dxe5! 12 ♗xe5 ♘f6 13 ♗xf6 ♕xf6 14 ♖e1+ ♔f8? [◻ 14 ... ♘e7 Saint-Amant] 15 ♘bd2 ♗f5 16 ♕b3 h6 17 a4 ♖b8 [17 ... a5? 18 d6! ♕xd6 19 ♗xf7 Dufresne] 18 a5 ♗c5 19 ♗d3 ♘f4 20 ♗xf5 ♕xf5 21 ♘e4 ♕g4 22 g3 ♘h3+ 23 ♔g2 ♗d6 24 ♘xd6 cxd6 25 ♖a4 ♕d7 26 ♖h4 g5 27 ♖xh3 g4 28 ♖h4 gxf3+ 29 ♕xf3 ♕b5 30 ♖he4 [◻ 30 ♕f6! ♕xd5+ 31 ♔g1 ♖h7 (31 ... ♖g8 32 ♕xh6+ ♖g7 33 ♖g4+-) 32 ♖g4 ♖e8 33 ♖g8+ ♔xg8 34 ♖xe8# Staunton] 30 ... ♖h7 31 ♕f5 ♖g7 32 ♖e7 ♕xa5 33 ♖xb7! ♕d8 [33 ... ♖xb7?? 34 ♕c8++- Bourdonnais] 34 ♖xa7 ♕g5 35 ♕xg5 ♖xg5 36 ♖ee7 ♖f5 37 g4 ♖f6 38 ♖e2 ♖b5 39 ♖d2 ♔g7 40 ♖d7 ♖b4 41 h3 ♔g6 42 ♖d3 ♖c4 43 f3 ♖a4 44 ♔g3 ♖b4 45 h4 ♖a4 46 ♖d8 ♔g7 47 ♖e3 ♖a6 48 ♖ee8 ♖g6 49 ♖e7 ♔f6 50 ♖dd7 ♖g7 51 ♖e3 ♖b6 52 f4 ♖h7 53 h5 ♖g7 54 ♔h4 ♖a6 55 ♖f3 ♖b6 56 ♖c3 ♖g8 57 ♖c6 ♖xc6 58 dxc6 ♔e6 59 f5+ ♔e5 60 c7 ♖c8 61 ♖xf7 d5 62 ♖d7 [62 g5 Staunton] 62 ... d4 63 g5 ♔xf5 64 g6 ♔e6 65 ♖xd4 ♖xc7 66 ♖f4 ♖a7 67 ♖f8 ♖a4+ 68 ♔g3 ♖a3+ 69 ♔f4 ♖a4+ 70 ♔e3 ♖a3+ 71 ♔d4 ♖a4+ 72 ♔c3 ♖a3+ 73 ♔c4 ♖a4+ 74 ♔b3 ♖g4 75 ♖h8 ♔f6 76 ♖xh6 ♔g7 77 ♖h7+ ♔g8 78 ♔c3 ♖h4 79 ♔d3 ♖b4 80 ♔e3 ♖a4 81 ♔f3 ♖b4 82 ♔g3 ♖a4 83 ♖f7 ♖b4 84 ♖f4 ♖b1 85 ♔g4 ♖g1+ 86 ♔h4 ♔g7 87 ♖f7+ ♔g8 88 ♖f3 ♔g7 89 ♖g3 ♖a1 90 ♖g4 ♖b1 91 ♖e4 ♖g1 92 ♖e3 ♔h6 93 ♖e7 ♖h1+? [◻ 93 ... ♖g4+!! 94 ♔h3 (94 ♔xg4◇) 94 ... ♖h4+!= Staunton] 94 ♔g4 ♖g1+? [◻ 94 ... ♖h4+!= Saint-Amant] 95 ♔f5 ♖f1+ 96 ♔e6 ♔xh5 97 g7 ♖g1 98 ♔f7 ♖f1+ 99 ♔e8 ♖g1 100 ♔f8 **1-0** L/N6020-1876

**1834-✕BM-74**
**Macdonnell, A.– Bourdonnais, L.C.M. de la**

1 e4 c5 2 f4 ♘c6 3 ♘f3 e6 4 c3 d5 5 e5 f6 6 ♗d3 ♕b6 7 ♗c2 ♗d7 8 0-0 ♘h6 9 ♔h1 ♗e7 10 d4 f5 11 a3 a5 12 h3 0-0 13 g4!? fxg4 14 hxg4 ♗e8! [14 ... ♘xg4!?∞ Saint-Amant] 15 f5 ♘xg4 16 f6 gxf6 17 exf6? [◻ 17 ♖g1 f5 18 ♘h2 h5 19 ♘xg4 hxg4 20 ♖xg4+ ♔f7 (20 ... fxg4 21 ♕xg4++-) 21 ♗h6 ♗d7 (21 ... fxg4 22 ♕xg4+-; 21 ... ♖h8 22 ♖g7+ ♔f8 23 ♖h7+ ♔g8 24 ♕g1++-) 22 ♖g7+ ♔e8 23 ♕h5+ ♔d8 24 ♖xe7 ♗e8 (24 ... ♔xe7 25 ♗g5++-; 24 ... ♘xe7 25 ♗xf8+-) 25 ♕g5 ♘xe7 26 ♗xf8 ♕c7 27 ♕xe7+ Saint-Amant] 17 ... ♗xf6 18 ♖g1 h5 19 ♕d3 ♕c7 20 ♗h6 c4 21 ♕e2 ♗g7 22 ♗xg7 ♖xf3! 23 ♖xg4 hxg4 [23 ... ♖h3+ Saint-Amant] 24 ♕xe6+ ♕f7 25 ♕xf7+ ♗xf7 **0-1** L/N6020-1876

**1834-✕BM-75**
**Bourdonnais, L.C.M. de la– Macdonnell, A.**

1 e4 e5 2 ♘f3 ♘c6 3 ♗c4 ♗c5 4 b4 ♗xb4 5 c3 ♗a5 6 0-0 d6 7 d4 exd4 8 cxd4 ♗b6 9 ♗b2 ♘f6 10 e5 dxe5 11 d5 [◻ 11 ♕b3 Saint-Amant] 11 ... ♘e7 12 ♗xe5 0-0 13 ♗xf6 gxf6 14 ♘c3 f5 15 ♕d2 ♔h8 16 ♖ae1 ♘g6 17 ♕h6 ♕f6 18 ♘e5 ♕g7 19 ♘xg6+ fxg6 20 ♕xg7+? ♔xg7 21 ♖e7+ ♔h6 22 ♘b5 c6 23 dxc6 bxc6 24 ♘d6 ♗c5 25 ♘f7+ ♔g7 26 ♖c7 ♗b6 27 ♖e7 ♔f6 28 ♖fe1 ♗a5 29 ♖1e2 ♖b8 30 h4 ♖b1+ 31 ♔h2 ♗b4 32 ♖c7 ♖c1 33 ♖xc6+ [◻ 33 ♖xa7 Saint-Amant] 33 ... ♔g7 34 ♘g5 ♗d7 35 ♘e6+ ♔h6 36 ♖a6 ♖xc4 37 ♘xf8 ♗xf8 38 ♖xa7 ♖xh4+ 39 ♔g3 f4+ 40 ♔f3 ♗c6+ 41 ♖e4 ♗xe4+ 42 ♔xe4 ♗c5 **0-1** L/N6020-1877

**1834-✕BM-76**
**Macdonnell, A.– Bourdonnais, L.C.M. de la**

1 e4 c5 2 f4 e6 3 ♘f3 d5 4 e5 ♘c6 5 c3 f6 6 ♗d3 ♘h6 7 ♗c2 ♕b6 8 0-0 ♘f7 9 d4 ♗d7 [9 ... cxd4 10 cxd4 ♘xd4 11 ♘xd4 ♗c5 12 ♗e3 ♕xb2 13 ♗a4+ ♗d7 14 ♗xd7+ ♔xd7 15 ♕a4+ b5 (15 ... ♔c8 16 ♘d2 Δ 17 ♖fc1±) 16 ♕a6 ♗xd4 (16 ... ♕xa1? 17 ♕b7++-) 17 ♕b7+ ♔d8! 18 ♗xd4! (18 ♕xa8+?? ♔c7!-+) 18 ... ♕xd4+ 19 ♔h1 ♖c8 (19 ... ♕xa1? 20 ♕xa8++-) 20 ♕xf7 ♖c7± Saint-Amant] 10 ♔h1 ♗e7 11 a3 a5 12 h3 f5 13 b3 h5 14 ♗e3 ♖c8 15 ♘bd2 cxd4 16 cxd4 g5! 17 fxg5 ♘cxe5 18 ♘xe5 ♘xe5 19 ♖e1 ♘g6 20 ♘f3 ♔f7 21 ♖a2 ♗d6 22 ♘e5+ ♗xe5 23 dxe5 ♕c7 24 ♗d4 ♕d8 25 ♕d2 h4 26 b4 a4 27 ♕e3 [Δ 28 ♗xf5 exf5 29 e6+ Staunton] 27 ... ♖e8 28 ♗b1 [◻ 28 ♗d1 Walker; 28 ♗b6 ♕e7 29 ♗c5= Saint-Amant] 28 ... ♕e7 29 ♖f2 ♔g8 30 g4 hxg3 31 ♕xg3 ♖c4 32 ♗c5 ♕h7 33 ♖h2 ♗c6 34 ♔g1 ♕h5 35 ♖d2 ♘h4 36 ♔f2 d4 37 ♖d3 ♖d8 38 g6 ♖d7 39 ♖ed1 ♗e4 40 ♖3d2 ♗xb1 41 ♖xb1 ♖c3 42 ♖d3 ♖c2+ 43 ♔f1 ♖g2 44 ♕e1 ♕g5! 45 ♕xh4 ♕xh4 46 ♔xg2 ♕e4+ 47 ♖f3 ♕xb1 48 h4 ♕e4 49 h5 d3 50 h6 d2 51 h7+ ♔h8 52 ♗f8 ♕xf3+ 53 ♔xf3 d1♕+ **0-1** L/N6020-1877

**1834-✕BM-77**
**Bourdonnais, L.C.M. de la– Macdonnell, A.**

1 e4 e5 2 ♘f3 ♘c6 3 ♗c4 ♗c5 4 b4 ♗xb4 5 c3 ♗a5 6 0-0 d6 7 d4 exd4 8 cxd4 ♗b6 9 ♗b2 ♘f6 10 d5 ♘a5 11 ♗d3 0-0 12 ♘c3 [12 ♘bd2; ◻ 12 h3 Saint-Amant] 12 ... ♗g4 13 h3 ♗h5 14 ♔h1 ♕d7 15 ♔h2 ♖ae8 16 g4? ♘xg4+ 17 hxg4 ♕xg4 18 ♗e2 ♕f4+ 19 ♔h1 ♗xf3+ 20 ♗xf3 f5 21 ♗g2 ♖f6 22 ♕d3 ♖h6+ 23 ♗h3 fxe4 24 ♘xe4 ♖xe4 25 ♗c1

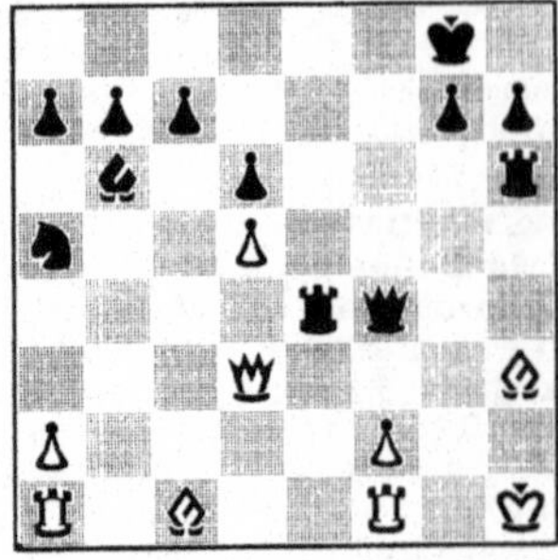

25 ... ♖e3! 26 ♗xe3 ♖xh3+ 27 ♔~ ♕h2# **0-1** L/N6020-1877

**1834-✕BM-78**
**Bourdonnais, L.C.M de la+ Macdonnell, A.**

1 d4 d5 2 c4 dxc4 3 e4 e5 4 d5 f5 5 ♘c3 ♘f6 6 ♗xc4 ♗c5 7 ♘f3 fxe4 8 ♘g5 0-0 9 0-0! [9 d6+!?∞ Staunton] 9 ... ♗d6 10 ♘e6 [◻ 10 ♘gxe4 Lewis] 10 ... ♗xe6 11 dxe6 ♔h8 12 ♗g5 ♘c6 13 ♘xe4 ♕e7 14 ♔h1 ♖ad8 15 ♕a4 a6 16 ♗d5 ♘d4 17 ♗xf6 gxf6 18 ♗xb7 ♕xe6 19 ♖ae1 f5 20 ♘c3 [Δ 21 ♕xd4+- Staunton] 20 ... ♕f6 21 ♕xa6?! [◻ 21 ♖e3 Staunton] 21 ... e4 22 ♕c4 ♗xh2!? [◻ 22 ... ♘f3! Saint-Amant] 23 ♖e3 [23 ♔xh2? ♕h4+ 24 ♔g1 ♘f3+-+ Staunton] 23 ... ♘f3 24 ♖xf3 exf3 25 ♔xh2 ♖d4 26 ♕c5 fxg2 27 ♗xg2 ♖g8 28 f4 ♕g7 29

♖f2 ♖xf4 30 ♖e2 ♖g4 31 ♗h3 ♖f4 32 ♖g2 ♕d4 33 ♕xd4+ ♖xd4 34 ♖f2 f4 35 a4 ♔g7 36 ♗g2 ♖f8 37 a5 ♖d6 38 ♗b7 ♖f5 39 a6 f3 40 ♔g1 ♖g6+? [⌓ 40 ... ♖h6 Lewis] 41 ♔f1 ♖h6 42 ♔e1 ♖h1+ 43 ♔d2 ♖a1 44 ♔d3 ♔f6 45 ♘d5+ ♔g5 46 ♘e3 [⌓ 46 ♘xc7 Lewis] 46 ... ♖f6 47 ♘c4 h5 48 ♘a3 ♖d1+ 49 ♔c2 ♖d8 50 a7+− ♔g4 51 a8♕ ♖xa8 52 ♗xa8 ♔g3 53 ♖f1 ♔g2 54 ♖d1 c6 55 ♗b7 f2 56 ♘c4 ♖e6 57 ♘d2 h4 58 b4 h3 59 b5 h2 60 ♗xc6+ ♔g3 61 ♗h1 ♖b6 62 ♖b1 ♖b8 63 b6 **1-0**

L/N6020-1877

**1834-✕BM-79**
**Bourdonnais, L.C.M. de la+**
**Macdonnell, A.**

1 e4 e5 2 ♘f3 ♘c6 3 ♗c4 ♗c5 4 b4 ♗xb4 5 c3 ♗a5 6 0-0 d6 7 d4 exd4 8 cxd4 ♗b6 9 ♗b2 ♘f6 10 d5 ♘a5 11 ♗d3 0-0 12 h3 ♘h5 13 ♕d2 f5 14 exf5 ♗xf5 15 ♘c3 ♗xh3 16 ♗xh7+ ♔h8 [16 ... ♔xh7? 17 ♘g5+ Saint-Amant] 17 ♗c2 [⌓ 17 ♗d3 Saint-Amant] 17 ... ♖xf3 18 gxf3 ♕h4? [18 ... ♘c4→ Saint-Amant] 19 ♘e2 ♖f8? [⌓ 19 ... ♘g3! Saint-Amant] 20 ♕h6+ ♔g8 21 ♗h7+ [21 ♗xg7 Staunton] 21 ... ♔f7 22 ♗g6+ ♔e7 23 ♕xh5 ♕xh5 24 ♗xh5 ♗xf1 25 ♔xf1+− ♖f5 26 ♗g4 [26 ♖e1 Staunton] 26 ... ♖xd5 27 ♘f4 ♖d2 28 ♖e1+ ♔f8 29 ♖e2 ♖xe2 30 ♔xe2 ♘c4 31 ♘e6+ ♔f7 32 ♗xg7 c5 33 f4 d5 34 f5 ♘d6 35 ♗e5 ♘e8 36 ♗h5+ ♔e7 37 ♗xe8 ♔xe8 38 f6 c4 39 ♘g5 ♗c5 40 f7+ ♔d7 41 ♗g7 **1-0**

L/N6020-1877

**1834-✕BM-80**
**Bourdonnais, L.C.M. de la+**
**Macdonnell, A.**

1 e4 e5 2 ♘f3 ♘c6 3 ♗c4 ♗c5 4 b4 ♗xb4 5 c3 ♗a5 [⌓ 5 ... ♗c5 Saint-Amant] 6 0-0 d6 7 d4 exd4 8 cxd4 ♗b6 9 h3 h6 10 ♗b2 ♘ge7 11 d5 ♘a5 12 ♗d3 0-0 13 ♘c3 ♘g6 14 ♕d2 c5 15 ♘a4 f6 16 ♘xb6 axb6 17 ♖ae1 ♘e5 18 ♘xe5 fxe5 19 f4 exf4 20 ♖xf4 ♖xf4 21 ♕xf4 ♕e7 22 ♖e3 [22 e5! Saint-Amant] 22 ... ♗d7 23 ♖g3 g5 24 h4 ♖f8 25 ♕d2 g4 26 ♕xh6 ♕h7 27 ♕g5+ ♔f7 28 e5 ♕g8 29 e6+ ♔e8 30 ♗g6+ **1-0**

L/N6020-1877

**1834-✕BM-81**
**Macdonnell, A.+**
**Bourdonnais, L.C.M. de la**

1 e4 c5 2 f4 ♘c6 3 c3 e6 4 ♘f3 d5 5 e5 f6 6 ♗d3 ♘h6 7 ♗c2 ♕b6 8 0-0 ♗d7 9 ♔h1 ♗e7 10 d4 f5 11 a3 a5 12 h3 ♘f7 13 b3 h5 14 ♖e1 [△ 14 ♗xf5 exf5 15 e6 Staunton] 14 ... g6 15 ♗e3 ♘h6 16 ♘bd2 cxd4 17 cxd4 ♔f7 18 ♖a2 ♖ac8 19 ♕e2 ♔g7 20 ♘g5 ♘f7 [⌓ 20 ... ♘d8 Staunton] 21 ♘xf7 ♔xf7 22 ♕f2 ♔g7 23 ♘f3 ♘d8 24 ♘h4 ♘f7 25 ♕g3 ♖h6 26 ♗f2 ♗xa3? 27 ♗xf5! exf5 28 ♖xa3 ♗e6 29 ♖ea1 ♕b4 30 ♖a4 ♕c3 31 ♕xc3 ♖xc3 32 ♖xa5 ♖xb3 33 ♘f3 ♖h8 34 ♖a8 ♖c8 35 ♖xc8 ♗xc8 36 ♖c1 ♗e6 37 ♖c7 ♖b6 38 ♘g5 ♔f8 39 ♘xe6+ ♖xe6 40 ♖xb7 ♘d8 41 ♖b8 [⌓ 41 ♖d7+− △ 42 ♖xd5 Saint-Amant] 41 ... ♖e8 42 ♖b5 ♘e6 43 g3 ♖d8 44 ♔g2 h4 45 ♔f3 ♘c7? [⌓ 45 ... g5 Staunton] 46 ♖b6 hxg3 47 ♔xg3 ♔g7 48 h4 ♔f7 ...? **1-0**

L/N6020-1877

**1834-✕BM-82**
**Bourdonnais, L.C.M. de la+**
**Macdonnell, A.**

1 e4 e5 2 ♘f3 ♘c6 3 ♗c4 ♗c5 4 b4 ♗xb4 5 c3 ♗a5 6 0-0 d6 7 d4 exd4 8 cxd4 ♗b6 9 ♗b2 ♘f6 [⌓ 9 ... ♗g4 Saint-Amant] 10 e5 dxe5 11 d5 ♘a5 12 ♗xe5 0-0 [12 ... ♘xc4 13 ♕a4+ △ 14 ♕xc4 Saint-Amant] 13 ♗d3 ♘xd5 14 ♘bd2 ♗g4 15 h3 [⌓ 15 ♕c2 Staunton] 15 ... ♗h5 16 ♕c2 ♗g6 17 ♗xg6 fxg6 18 ♖ad1 ♕e8 19 ♖fe1 ♕c6 20 ♕b2 ♖f7 21 ♗d4 ♘f4 22 ♘e4 ♘xh3+ 23 ♔h2 ♖xf3 24 gxf3 ♘f4 25 ♗xg7 ♘h5 26 ♘f6+ ♘xf6 27 ♕xf6 ♕xf6 28 ♗xf6 ♖f8 29 ♖d8 ♗xf2 30 ♖xf8+ ♔xf8 31 ♖e7 ♗d4! 32 ♗g5 h6 33 ♖e4 ♗g7 34 ♗d8 ♘c6 35 ♗xc7 ♔f7 36 ♔g3 g5 37 a4 h5 38 a5 ♔f6 39 ♖c4 ♔e6 40 ♖c5 ♗f6 41 ♖b5 b6? [⌓ 41 ... ♔d7! Staunton] 42 axb6 axb6 43 ♔g2 ♘e5 44 ♗xb6 ♔f5 45 ♗e3 ♗e7 46 ♔f2 ♗f6 47 ♗d2 ♗e7 48 ♔e3 ♗f6 49 ♗e1 h4 50 ♗c3 ♗g7 51 ♔f2 ♗f6 52 ♔g2 ♗g7 53 ♗d4 ♗f6 54 ♔h3 ♔f4 55 ♔g2 ♔f5 56 ♗g1 ♔g6 57 ♗h2 ♘d3? [⌓ 57 ... ♔f5 Saint-Amant] 58 ♖d5 ♘f4+? 59 ♗xf4 gxf4 60 ♔h3 **1-0**

L/N6020-1872

**1834-✕BM-83**
**Macdonnell, A.+**
**Bourdonnais, L.C.M. de la**

1 e4 e5 2 ♘f3 ♘c6 3 ♗c4 ♗c5 4 b4 ♗xb4 5 c3 ♗a5 6 0-0 ♗b6 7 d4 exd4 8 cxd4 d6 9 h3 ♘f6 10 e5 dxe5 11 ♗a3!? [⌓ 11 d5 Saint-Amant] 11 ... ♗xd4? [⌓ 11 ... ♗e6!∓ Staunton] 12 ♕b3 [△ 13 ♗xf7+ ♔d7 14 ♕e6# Staunton] 12 ... ♕d7 13 ♘g5 ♘d8 14 ♘c3 c5?

15 ♘xf7! ♖f8 [15 ... ♘xf7 16 ♗b5+− Saint-Amant] 16 ♘xe5 ♗xe5 17 ♖fe1 ♘c6 18 ♗xc5 ♕f5 19 ♘b5 ♗d7 20 ♘d6+ **1-0**

L/N6020-1877

**1834-✕BM-84**
**Bourdonnais, L.C.M. de la−**
**Macdonnell, A.**

1 e4 e5 2 ♘f3 ♘c6 3 ♗c4 ♗c5 4 b4 ♗xb4 5 c3 ♗a5 6 0-0 d6 7 d4 exd4 8 cxd4 ♗b6 9 ♘c3 ♘f6 10 ♗g5 h6 11 ♗xf6 ♕xf6 12 e5 dxe5 13 ♘xe5 ♘xe5 14 dxe5 ♕h4 15 ♕e2? [⌓ 15 ♕a4+! Staunton] 15 ... 0-0 16 ♔h1 ♗g4 17 f3 [⌓ 17 ♕e4 Staunton] 17 ... ♗h5 18 ♖ad1 ♖fe8 19 g4 ♗g6 20 f4 c6 21 f5 ♗h7 22 ♖d7 ♖e7 23 ♖xe7 [⌓ 23 ♖fd1 Walker] 23 ... ♕xe7 24 e6? [⌓ 24 f6! gxf6 25 ♖xf6 ♖f8!; 25 ♘e4!± Staunton] 24 ... fxe6 25 ♗xe6+ ♔h8 26 ♖d1 ♖f8 27 ♖d7 ♕c5 28 ♕e1 ♗a5 29 ♘e4 ♕xf5 30 gxf5 ♗xe1 31 ♘d6 ♗g8 32 ♖xb7 ♗f2 33 ♘f7+ ♗xf7 34 ♗xf7 ♗b6 35 ♔g2 ♔h7 36 ♔f3 h5 37 ♗g6+ ♔h6 38 ♖e7 ♖d8 39 ♖e6 ♔g5 40 ♖e7 ♗d4 41 ♖e4 ♗f6 42 ♖c4 ♖c8 43 h4+ ♔h6 44 a4 c5 45 ♗f7 ♗d4 46 ♔f4 [⌓ 46 ♔e4 Walker] 46 ... ♖b8 47 ♖c2 ♖b4 48 ♖c4 ♗f2 49 ♔e5 ♗xh4 50 ♖xc5 ♗f6+ 51 ♔e6 ♖xa4 52 ♖c8 h4 53 ♗e8 ♖e4+ 54 ♔f7 ♔g5 55 ♖c5 ♖e2 56 ♖c7 a5 57 ♗d7 h3 58 ♗e6 h2 59 ♖c1 ♔g4 60 ♗c8 ♔g3 61 ♔g6 a4 62 ♗b7 ♖e3 63 ♖c2 a3 64 ♖g2+ ♔h3 65 ♖d2 ♗b2 66 ♔h5 a2 67 f6 gxf6 **0-1**

L/N6020-1877

**1834-✕BM-85**
**Macdonnell, A.+**
**Bourdonnais, L.C.M. de la**

1 e4 c5 2 f4 e6 3 ♘f3 ♘c6 4 c3 d5 5 e5 f5 [5 ... f6! Saint-Amant] 6 ♗d3 ♗e7 7 ♗c2 ♕b6 8 0-0 ♘h6 9 ♔h1 0-0 10 d4 ♗d7 11 a3 [△ 12 b4 Anderssen] 11 ... a5 [△ 12 ... ♘g4 Anderssen] 12 h3 ♗e8 [12 ... ♖ac8 Saint-Amant; 12 ... a4 Anderssen] 13 b3 cxd4 14 cxd4 ♗h5 15 ♗e3 ♖ac8 16 ♖a2 ♔h8 17 ♕d2 ♕c7 18 ♘h2 ♗h4?! 19 ♖g1 ♗g3 20 ♘f1 ♗h4 21 ♕d3 [△ 22 g4!± Anderssen] 21 ... ♗g6 22 ♘bd2 ♗e7= 23 ♕e2

♕d7 24 g4 ♕e8 25 g5 ♘g8 [⌓25 ... ♗h5 Anderssen] 26 ♗d1 ♗d8 27 h4 ♗f7 28 h5 g6 29 h×g6 ♗×g6 30 ♕h2 ♗b6 31 ♘f3 ♕f7 32 ♘g3 ♘ge7 33 ♖d2 ♔g8 34 ♘h4 ♘×e5? 35 f×e5 f4 36 ♘×g6 ♘×g6 [36 ... h×g6 37 ♖f1 f×g3 38 ♖×f7 g×h2 39 ♖×e7+− Anderssen] 37 ♘h5 f×e3 38 ♘f6+ ♔h8 39 ♖d3 ♖g8 40 ♖g3 ♘f4 41 ♖d×e3 ♖g7 [41 ... ♗×d4? 42 ♘×h7 ♗×e3 43 ♘f6+ ♘h5 44 ♗×h5 ♖c1+ 45 ♗d1+ ♔g7 46 ♕h6# Anderssen] 42 ♖ef3 ♖c1 43 ♕d2 ♖×d1+ 44 ♕×d1 ♘h5 45 ♖h3 ♘×f6 46 ♖×f6 ♕e8 47 ♕f1 ♔g8 48 ♕f4 ♗d8 49 ♕h4! ♗×f6 50 e×f6 ♖c7 51 g6 ♖c1+ 52 ♔h2 ♖c2+ 53 ♔g1 ♖c1+ 54 ♔f2 ♕×g6 55 ♖g3 ♖c2+ 56 ♔e1 ♔f7 57 ♖×g6 ♔×g6 58 f7 ♖c8 59 ♕e7 **1-0**

L/N6020-1877

**1834-★BW-1**
**Bourdonnais, L.C.M. de la+ Walker, G.**
London [Staunton]

⟨♙f2⟩ 1 ... e5 2 ... d5 3 ♘c3 e4 4 d4 h5 5 ♗f4 g5 6 ♗g3 h4 7 ♗f2 ♘f6 8 h3 ♗d6 9 ♕d2 ♗f4 10 e3 ♗d6 11 0-0-0 c6 12 ♘ge2 ♘h5 13 ♖g1 ♘g3 14 ♗×g3 h×g3 15 ♔b1 ♗e6 16 ♘c1 ♘d7 17 ♗e2 ♘f6 18 ♖df1 ♕e7 19 ♘a4 ♘h5 20 ♘b3 ♘g7 21 ♘bc5 b6 22 ♘×e6 ♕×e6 23 c4 f5 24 c×d5 c×d5 25 ♘c3 ♗b4 26 ♕c2 ♗×c3 27 ♕×c3 ♖c8 28 ♕a3 a5 29 ♗a6 ♖a8 30 ♕b3 0-0 31 ♗b7 ♖ad8 32 ♖c1 ♖d6 33 ♖c7 ♖f7 34 ♖gc1 ♖×c7 35 ♖×c7 ♔h7? [⌓35 ... f4] 36 ♕d1 ♔h6 37 h4 g4 38 ♕f1 ♘h5 39 ♗c8 ♕f6 40 ♗×f5 **1-0**

L/N6123-1843̂

**1834-★BW-2**
**Walker, G.W.= Bourdonnais, L.C.M. de la**
London [Staunton]

⟨♙f7⟩1 e4 ... 2 d4 d6 3 c4 e6 4 d5 ♘f6 5 ♘c3 e×d5 6 c×d5 ♗e7 7 f4 0-0 8 ♘f3 ♗g4 9 h3 ♗×f3 10 ♕×f3 c5 11 ♗d3 a6 12 a4 ♘bd7 13 0-0 ♕c7 14 ♗e3 c4 15 ♗c2 ♖ab8 16 ♗a7 ♖a8 17 ♗d4 ♖ab8 18 ♗a7 ♖bc8 19 ♗d4 ♘e8 20 ♕e3 ♗f6 21 ♗×f6 ♘e×f6 22 ♖ae1 ♖ce8 23 g4 ♔h8 24 g5 ♘g8 25 h4 ♘e7 26 h5 b5 27 a×b5 a×b5 28 ♘×b5? ♕b8 29 ♘d4 ♘×d5 30 ♕d2 ♘b4 31 ♗a4 ♕a7 32 ♗×d7 ♕×d7 33 f5! [33 ♕×b4 ♕g4+=] 33 ... ♘d3 34 ♘e6 ♖g8 35 ♘f4 ♘×f4 [35 ... ♘×e1?? 36 ♘g6+ h×g6 37 h×g6+−] 36 ♕×f4 ♕a7+ 37 ♔h1 ♖e5 38 f6 g×f6 39 ♕×f6+ ♕g7 40 ♕×g7+ ♖×g7 41 ♖f8+ ♖g8 42 ♖×g8+ ♔×g8 43 ♖d1 ♖×e4 44 ♖×d6 ♖h4+ 45 ♔g2 ♖×h5 46 ♖c6 ♖×g5+ 47 ♔h3 ♖b5 48 ♖×c4 ♖×b2 **½-½**

L/N6123-1843

**1834-★MP-1**
**Popert, H.W.+ MacDonnell, A.**

⟨♙f7⟩ 1 e4 d6 2 d4 ♘f6 3 ♘c3 ♘c6 4 d5 ♘e5 5 f4 ♘f7 6 ♘f3 e5 7 d×e6 ♗×e6 8 f5 ♗d7 9 ♗c4 ♘e5 10 ♘×e5 d×e5 11 0-0 g6 12 f×g6 h×g6 13 ♗g5 ♗e7 14 ♘d5 ♗c5+ 15 ♔h1 ♘×e4 16 ♘×c7+ ♕×c7 17 ♗f7+ ♔f8 18 ♗×g6+ ♗f5 19 ♕g4 **1-0**

L/N6013-1837

**Fraser✕Saint-Amant**

[1836-✕FS]

| | | | | |
|---|---|---|---|---|
| W. Fraser | ? | ? | 0̂ | ? |
| P.C.F. de Saint-Amant | ? | ? | 1̂ | ? |

**1836-✕FS-3̂** vi 36
**Saint-Amant, P.C.F. de+ Fraser, W.**
[Saint-Amant]

1 f4 f5 2 ♘f3 ♘f6 3 d4 d5 4 c4 c6 5 e3 e6 6 ♘c3 ♘a6? 7 c×d5 c×d5 8 ♗×a6 b×a6 9 0-0 ♗d7 10 a4 ♗b4 11 ♗d2 ♗×c3 12 ♗×c3 0-0 13 b3 ♘e4 14 ♗b2 ♖b8 15 ♘e5 ♗e8 16 ♕d3 ♖f6 17 ♖fc1 ♖h6 18 ♖c2 ♕b6 19 ♖ac1 ♕d8 20 ♕×a6 ♕h4? 21 ♘f3 ♕h5 22 ♖c8 ♖×c8 23 ♖×c8 ♖f6 24 ♕c6 ♖f8 25 ♗a3 h6 26 ♕×e6+ **1-0**

L/N6013-42

**1836-★BB-1**
**Bourdonnais, L.C.M. de la+ Boncourt & Mouret, J-F.**
Paris [Bourdonnais]

1 e4 e5 2 ♘f3 ♘c6 3 ♗c4 ♗c5 4 b4 ♗×b4 5 c3 ♗e7?! [⌓5 ... ♗a5] 6 ♕b3 ♘h6 7 d4 ♘a5 8 ♕a4 ♘×c4 9 ♕×c4 e×d4 10 ♗×h6 g×h6 11 c×d4 ♖g8 12 0-0 d6 13 ♔h1 ♕d7 14 ♘c3 c6 15 d5 ♖×g2!? 16 ♖g1! [16 ♔×g2?? ♕g4+ 17 ♔h1 ♕×f3+ 18 ♔h1 ♗h3 19 ♕g2#] 16 ... ♖×f2 17 ♖g3 c5 18 e5 b6 19 ♖e1 ♔d8 20 e6 f×e6 21 d×e6 ♕e8 22 ♘d5 ♗b7 23 ♖eg1 ♗×d5 24 ♕×d5 ♔c7 25 ♖g7! [25 ♖g8? ♕×g8 26 ♖×g8 ♖×g8] 25 ... ♖c8 26 ♖f7 ♔b8 27 ♖gg7 ♕c6 28 ♕×c6 ♖×c6 29 ♖×e7 ♖×f3 30 ♖b7+ ♔c8 31 ♖×a7 ♔b8 32 ♖ab7+ ♔a8 33 ♖bf7! [33 ... ♖×f7 34 e×f7+−] **1-0**

L/N6013

**1836-★BJ-1**
**Jouy− Bourdonnais, L.C.M. de la**
Paris [Bourdonnais]

1 e4 e5 2 d4 e×d4 3 ♕×d4 ♘c6 4 ♕d3 ♘f6 5 f3 ♗c5 6 ♗e3 ♕e7 7 ♗e2 0-0 8 ♘c3 ♘e5 9 ♕d2 ♗×e3 10 ♕×e3 d6 11 0-0-0 ♗e6 12 b3 a5 13 ♘a4 b5! 14 ♗×b5 ♖fb8 15 c4?? c6 16 ♘b6 c×b5 17 ♘×a8 ♖×a8 18 c×b5 a4 19 ♔b2 a×b3 20 a×b3 d5 21 ♖a1 ♖×a1 22 ♔×a1 ♕a3+ 23 ♔b1 d×e4 24 ♔c2 ♕a2+ 25 ♔d1 ♗×b3+ 26 ♔e1 ♘d3+ 27 ♔f1 ♕b1+ 28 ♔e2 ♕e1# **0-1**

L/N6013-1838

**1836-★BS-1**
**Bourdonnais, L.C.M. de la− Szén, J.**
Paris [Staunton]

⟨♙f2⟩ 1 ... e5 2 ... d5 3 e3 c5 4 ♘c3 ♘f6 5 d4 e4 6 ♗b5+ ♘c6 7 ♘ge2 ♗d6 8 0-0 ♗g4 9 ♕e1 0-0 10 ♕h4 ♗×e2 11 ♘×e2 ♘e7 12 d×c5 ♗×c5 13 ♘d4 h6 14 c3 ♘h7 15 ♗d2 ♗×d4 16 c×d4 ♕d6 17 ♗a4 ♘g6 18 ♕h3 ♘g5 19 ♕h5 ♘e7 20 ♗b3 f5 21 ♗e1 ♖ad8 22 a3 ♕g6 23 ♕×g6 ♘×g6 24 ♖c1 ♘e6 25 ♖c2 b5?! [⌓25 ... f4] 26 ♗b4 ♖f6 27 ♖c6 f4 28 g3 f3 29 h4 h5 30 ♔f2? [⌓30 ♖fc1] 30 ... ♘ef4!! 31 ♖×f6 ♘d3+ 32 ♔g1 g×f6 33 ♖d1 ♔f7 34 ♖d2 ♘×b4 35 a×b4 ♘e7 36 ♔f2 ♔e6 37 ♖c2 ♖c8 38 ♖c5 ♖×c5 39 b×c5 f5 40 ♗c2 ♔d7 41 ♗d1 ♔c6 42 b3 a5 43 ♗c2 ♘g8 **0-1**

L/N6123-1843̂

**1836-★BS-2**
**Szén, J.− Bourdonnais, L.C.M. de la**
Paris [Staunton]

⟨♙f7⟩1 e4 ... 2 d4 e6 3 ♗d3 c5 4 e5 ♕a5+ 5 ♗d2 ♕b6 6 ♕h5+ ♔d8 7 ♕f7 ♘e7 8 ♘c3 c×d4 9 ♘b5 ♕c5 10 ♘f3 ♘bc6 11 0-0 a6 12 ♘d6 ♔c7 13 ♕f4 ♘d5 14 ♕e4 ♗×d6 15 e×d6+ ♕×d6

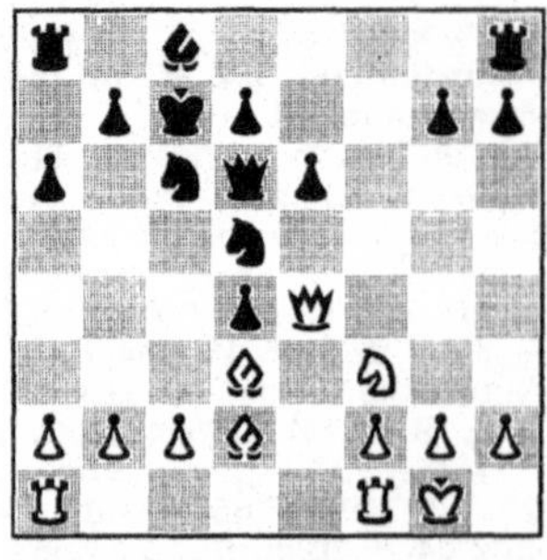

16 ♗g5 e5 17 ♖fe1 ♘f6 18 ♕h4 ♕e6? 19 ♘×e5 ♘×e5 20 f4 [⌓20 ♖×e5!+−] 20 ... ♘f3+ 21 g×f3 ♕c6 22 ♕f2 h6 23 ♗h4 d6 24 ♗×f6 g×f6 25 ♖e7+ ♗d7 26 ♗e4 ♕c5 27 ♖e1 ♖ae8 28 ♗d3 ♖hg8+ 29 ♔h1 ♖×e7 30 ♖×e7 ♔d8 31 ♖e1 ♗c6 32 ♗e4 ♕h5 33 c3?! [⌓33 ♗×c6] 33 ... d5 34 ♗c2 d×c3 35 b×c3 ♔c8 36 ♖e7 ♔b8 37 ♖e6 d4 38 ♗d1 ♗d5 39 ♖×f6 d×c3 40 ♖d6 c2 41 ♖×d5 c1♕ **0-1**

L/N6123-1842

**1836-⊠LP-1**
**London– Paris**

[Bourdonnais]

1 e4 e6 2 d4 d5 3 exd5 exd5 4 ♘f3 ♘f6 5 ♗d3 c5 6 ♕e2+? ♗e7 7 dxc5 0-0 8 ♗e3?! [8 0-0] 8 ... ♖e8 9 ♗b5? ♘c6 10 ♘d4? ♗xc5 11 ♗xc6 [11 ♘xc6 ♕b6] 11 ... bxc6 12 c3 [12 ♘xc6? ♕b6] 12 ... ♗xd4 13 cxd4 c5 14 ♕d3 [⌓ 14 ♕d2] 14 ... ♕b6 15 0-0 ♗a6 16 ♕b3 ♕xb3 17 axb3 ♗xf1 18 ♔xf1 ♘g4 19 dxc5 ♘xe3+ 20 fxe3 ♖xe3 21 ♘d2 ♖ae8 22 b4 ♖d3-+ 23 ♖xa7? ♖xd2 24 b5 ♖xb2 25 b6 d4 26 b7 d3 27 ♖a8 ♔f8 **0-1** L/N6013-1836

**1836̂-★BS-1**
**Szén, J.– Boncourt**

Paris [⚲ Le Palamède]

1 e4 e5 2 ♘f3 ♘c6 3 ♗c4 ♗c5 4 c3 h6 5 d4 exd4 6 cxd4 ♗b4+ 7 ♗d2 ♗xd2+ 8 ♘bxd2 d6 9 0-0 ♘ge7 10 ♕c2 0-0 11 d5 ♘e5 12 ♘xe5 dxe5 13 ♗b3 ♘g6 14 ♖ac1 ♕g5 15 ♘f3 ♕f4 16 ♖fe1 ♗h3 17 gxh3? [17 ♖e3] 17 ... ♕xf3 18 ♖e3 ♕h5 19 ♕d1 ♕g5+ 20 ♕g4 ♕f6 21 ♖g3 ♘f4 22 ♗d1 g6 23 ♖xc7 ♕b6 24 ♖c2 ♕d4 25 ♕f3 ♖ac8 26 ♖c3 ♖xc3 27 bxc3 ♕d2 28 ♔h1 ♖c8 29 ♗b3 ♘e2 30 ♖xg6+ ♔f8 [30 ... fxg6? 31 d6+] 31 ♖g1 ♘xg1 32 ♔xg1 ♖xc3 33 ♕f6 ♕e1+ 34 ♔g2 ♕xe4+ 35 f3 ♕g6+ 36 ♕xg6 fxg6 **0-1** L/N6013-1836

**1836̂-★BS-2**
**Szén, J.– Boncourt**

Paris [⚲ Le Palamède]

1 e4 e6 2 d4 d5 3 exd5 exd5 4 c4 ♘f6 5 ♘c3 ♗b4 6 a3 ♗xc3+ 7 bxc3 ♘e4 8 ♕b3 c6 9 ♗d3 0-0 10 ♘e2 dxc4 11 ♗xc4 b5 12 ♗d3 ♗f5 13 ♕c2 ♖e8 14 0-0 ♗g6 15 ♘f4 ♘d6 16 ♘xg6 hxg6 17 ♗f4 ♘a6 18 ♖fe1 ♕d7 19 a4 ♘c7 20 ♗xd6 ♕xd6 21 ♖xe8+ ♖xe8 22 axb5 cxb5 23 ♖xa7? ♖e1+ 24 ♗f1 ♕c6 25 ♕d2 ♖b1 26 ♕d3 ♖c1 27 ♖a3 ♘d5 28 ♕f3 f6 [28 ... ♘xc3? 29 ♕xc6?-+; 29 ♖a8+-+] 29 ♕d3 ♘f4 30 d5 ♕xd5 31 ♕xd5+ ♘xd5 32 g3 ♘xc3 **0-1** L/N6013-1836

**1836̂-★BS-3**
**Boncourt– Szén, J.**

Paris [⚲ Le Palamède]

1 e4 e5 2 ♗c4 ♗c5 3 ♘f3 ♘c6 4 c3 ♘f6 5 d3 ♗b6 6 b4 a6 7 0-0 d6 8 a4 0-0 9 ♗e3 ♗e6 10 ♘bd2 ♗xe3 11 fxe3 d5 12 exd5 ♘xd5 13 ♗xd5 ♕xd5 14 ♘e4 ♖fd8 15 ♘fg5 ♕xd3?! 16 ♕h5 h6 17 ♘xe6 fxe6 18 ♕g6 ♔h8 19 ♖f7 ♖g8 20 ♖af1 ♖ac8 21 ♖xg7? ♕xe3+ 22 ♔h1 ♖xg7 23 ♕xe6 ♖cg8 24 ♘f6 ♕e2 25 ♖g1 ♘d8 26 ♕h3 ♘f7 27 ♘xg8 ♖xg8 28 ♕e6 ♕f2 29 c4 ♕f4 **0-1** L/N6013-1836

**1836̂-★SS-1**
**Szén, J.= Slous, F.L.**

London [⚲ Le Palemède]

1 e4 e5 2 ♘f3 ♘c6 3 ♗c4 ♗c5 4 b4 ♗xb4 5 c3 ♗a5 6 0-0 d6 7 d4 exd4 8 cxd4 ♗b6 9 d5 ♘ce7 10 ♗b2 f6 11 ♘d4 ♘h6 12 ♕h5+ ♘g6 13 ♘f5 0-0∞ 14 ♘xh6+ gxh6 15 ♕xh6 ♕e7 16 ♘d2 ♕g7 17 ♕xg7+ ♔xg7 18 ♔h1 ♘e5 19 f4 ♘g4 20 h3 ♘e3 21 ♖f3 ♘xc4 22 ♘xc4 ♗c5 23 ♖af1 ♗d7 24 e5 ♗b5 25 ♖c1 ♗xc4 26 exf6+ ♔f7 27 ♖xc4 ♖ae8 28 ♖c2 ♖e1+ 29 ♔h2 ♖fe8 30 ♖d3 ♖1e2 31 ♖dd2 ♖xd2 32 ♖xd2 ♗e3 33 ♖c2 ♗xf4+ 34 g3 ♗e5 35 ♖xc7+ ♔xf6 36 ♖xb7 ♗xb2 37 ♖xb2 ♖e5 [⌓ 37 ... ♖e4] 38 ♖d2 ♖e4 39 ♔g2 ♔e5 40 ♔f3 ♖d4 41 ♖xd4 ♔xd4 42 g4 ♔xd5 43 g5 ♔e5 44 ♔g4 d5 45 h4 d4 46 h5 d3 47 ♔f3 ♔f5 48 g6 ½-½ L/N6013-1837

**1837-★BB-1**
**Bourdonnais, L.C.M. de la= Boncourt**

Paris [Bourdonnais]

1 e4 e5 2 ♘f3 d6 3 ♗c4 f5 4 d3 c6 5 ♘c3 ♗e7 6 0-0 ♘f6 7 ♕e2 b5 8 ♗b3 b4 9 ♘d1 fxe4 10 dxe4 ♗a6 11 ♗c4 ♗xc4 12 ♕xc4 d5 13 exd5 cxd5 14 ♕e2 e4 15 ♘d4 ♕d7 16 ♘e3 ♘c6 17 ♘xc6 ♕xc6 18 ♘f5 ♗f8 19 ♗e3 ♕d7 20 ♘d4 ♗d6 21 f4 0-0 22 h3 h5 23 ♖ad1 ♗c5 24 f5 ♖ae8 25 c4 bxc3 26 bxc3 ♖e5 27 c4 ♗xd4 28 ♗xd4 ♖xf5 29 ♖xf5 ♕xf5 30 ♗xf6 ♕xf6 31 cxd5! ♕e5 32 d6 e3 33 d7 ♖d8 34 ♕c4+ ♔h7 35 ♖d5 ♕a1+ 36 ♔h2 g6 37 ♕c5? [⌓ 37 ♕e4±] 37 ... ♕f6 38 ♕xe3 ♖f8 39 ♖e5 ♕d6 40 g3? [⌓ 40 ♕c5!+-] 40 ... ♖f7 ½-½ L/N6013-1837

**1837-★BB-2**
**Bourdonnais, L.C.M. de la= Bonfil**

Paris [Bourdonnais]

1 ... e5 2 e4 f5 3 exf5 ♗c5 4 ♕h5+ ♔f8 5 g4 ♘f6 6 ♕h4 d5 7 ♗g2 ♘c6 8 ♘e2 h5 9 h3 ♔g8 10 ♕g3 hxg4 11 hxg4 ♖xh1+ 12 ♗xh1 ♘b4 13 ♘a3 d4 14 d3 c6 15 g5 ♘h5 16 ♕h4 ♕e8 17 g6 ♘f6 18 ♘g3 e4 19 ♘xe4? [⌓ 19 ♗xe4] 19 ... ♗xf5 20 ♗g5 ♗xe4 21 ♗xe4 ♕e5 22 ♗xf6 ♕xf6 23 ♕xf6 gxf6 24 ♔d2 ♖e8 25 ♖h1 ♘xa2 26 ♖h7 ♖e7 27 ♖xe7 ♗xe7 28 ♘c4 ♘b4 29 c3 dxc3+ 30 bxc3 ♘d5 31 ♘e3 ♘xe3 32 ♔xe3 a5 33 ♔d2 a4 34 ♔c2 ♔g7 35 f4 ½-½ L/N6013-1837

**1837-★BC-1**
**Chamouillet, M.& Devinck, F.J.& Lécrivain+ Bonfil& Calvi, I.& Saint-Amant, P.C.F. de**

[Bourdonnais & Méry]

⟨Δf7⟩ 1 e4 e6 2 d4 d5 3 exd5 exd5 4 ♕h5+ g6 5 ♕e5+ ♕e7 6 f4 c5 7 ♘f3 ♘c6 8 ♗b5 ♗d7 9 ♗xc6 bxc6 10 0-0 ♕xe5 11 dxe5 ♗f5 12 c3 ♗d3 13 ♖f2 ♘h6 14 h3 c4 15 g4 ♘f7 16 ♗e3 c5 17 ♘bd2 h5 18 g5 ♖b8 19 b3 ♔d7 20 ♘e1 ♔e6 21 bxc4 dxc4 22 ♘xd3 cxd3 [Δ 23 ... c4] 23 c4 ♗e7 24 ♘b3 ♖bc8 25 ♖d2 ♖hd8 26 ♖ad1 ♔f5 27 ♔f2 ♔e4 28 ♘c1 ♘xe5?+- 29 fxe5 ♖f8+ 30 ♔g2 ♔xe3 31 ♖xd3+ ♔f4 32 ♖d7 ♗xg5 33 ♘d3+ ♔e4 34 ♖e1+ ♔f5 35 e6 ♔f6 36 ♖xa7 ...⚲ **1-0** L/N6013-1837

**1837-★BC-2**
**Chamouillet, M.& Devinck, F.J.& Lécrivain= Bonfil & Calvi, I.& Saint-Amant, P.C.F. de**

[Bourdonnais & Méry]

⟨Δf7⟩ 1 e4 ♘h6?! 2 d4 ♘f7 3 c4 e6 4 ♘c3 c5 5 d5 d6 6 f4 ♘a6 7 ♘f3 g6 8 h4 ♗g7 9 h5? e5 10 hxg6 hxg6 11 ♖xh8+ ♗xh8 12 ♗d3 ♕f6 13 fxe5 ♘xe5 [Δ 14 ... ♘xf3+, 15 ... ♕h4+] 14 ♘g5? ♗d7 15 ♗e2 ♗g7 16 ♗e3 ♗h6 17 ♕d2 ♗g4 18 b3 0-0-0 19 ♘h3 ♗xh3 20 ♗xh6 ♕h4+ 21 ♔d1 ♗xg2 22 ♗g5 ♕h1+ 23 ♕e1 ♖h8 24 ♔d2 ♗xe4 25 ♕xh1 ♖xh1 26 ♖xh1 ♗xh1 27 ♘b5 ♔d7 28 ♘xa7 ♗e4 29 a3 ♘c7 30 ♔c3 ♗f5 31 b4 ♘f7 32 ♗e3 b6 33 ♘c6 ♘e8 34 a4 ♘f6 35 b5 g5 36 a5 bxa5 37 ♘xa5 ♔c7 38 ♔d2 ♘e5 39 ♘c6 ♘e4+ 40 ♔e1 ♘g4 41 ♗g1 ♘g3 42 ♘a5 ♘f6 43 ♘b3 ♘xe2 44 ♔xe2 ♘g4

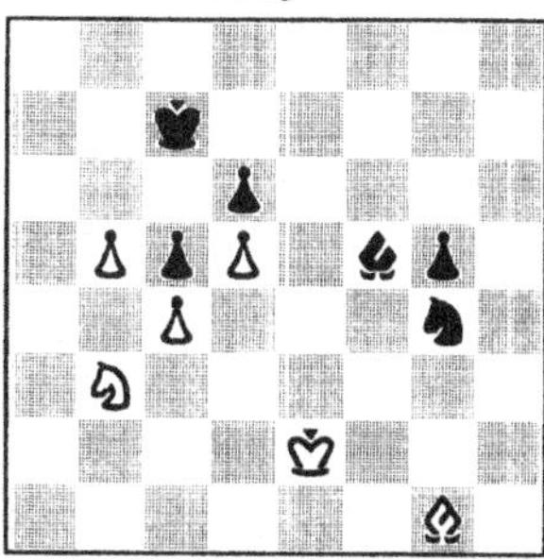

45 ♘xc5! dxc5 46 ♗xc5 ♘e5 47 ♗e3 ♗d3+ 48 ♔d1 ♘f3 49 b6+ ♔c8 50 c5 ♗c4 51 d6 ♗b5 52 ♗f2 ♔b7 53 ♗e3 ♔c6 54 ♗f2 g4 55

♗e3 g3 56 d7 ♔xd7 57 b7 ♔c7 58 ♗f4+ ½-½ L/N6013-1837

**1837-★BC-3**
**Chamouillet, M.& Devinck, F.J.& Lécrivain+ Bonfil& Calvi, I.& Saint-Amant, P.C.F. de**

⟨♙f7⟩ 1 e4 ♘c6 2 d4 d5 3 e5 ♗f5 4 c3 e6 5 ♗d3 ♗xd3 6 ♕xd3 ♘ce7 7 ♘e2 c5 8 0-0 ♘c6 9 ♕h3! ♕d7 10 ♘f4 cxd4 11 ♕xe6+ ♘ge7 12 ♕xd7+ ♔xd7 13 ♘d3 g6 14 ♗g5 ♗g7 15 ♘c5+ ♔c8 16 f4 dxc3 17 ♘xc3 b6 18 ♘e6 ♖g8 19 ♖fd1 d4 20 ♘xd4 ♘xd4 21 ♗xe7 ♘f5 22 ♘d5 ♔b7 23 g4 ♘xe7 24 ♘xe7 ♖gd8 25 ♔g2 ♗f8 26 ♘d5 ♖ac8 27 ♘c3 ♗b4 28 ♖xd8 ♖xd8 29 ♖d1 ♖f8 30 ♔f3 ♔c6 31 ♔e4 h6 32 f5 gxf5+ 33 gxf5 ♖g8 34 e6 ♖g2 35 f6 ♖f2 36 e7 **1-0** L/N6013-1837

**1837-★BD-1**
**Bourdonnais, L.C.M. de la= Delaroche**
Paris [Staunton]

1 e4 e5 2 f4 exf4 3 ♘f3 g5 4 ♗c4 g4 5 ♘c3!? gxf3 6 ♕xf3 [6 0-0!?] 6 ... d5 7 ♗xd5 c6 8 ♗b3 ♗e6 9 ♗xe6 fxe6 10 ♕h5+ ♔d7 11 d4 ♘f6 12 ♕h3 ♕e7 13 ♗xf4 ♗g7 14 0-0 ♘a6 15 ♖ad1 ♖ae8 16 d5 cxd5 17 exd5 ♔c8 18 ♔h1 ♕d7 19 dxe6 ♕xe6 20 ♘b5! ♘d7 [20 ... ♕xh3?? 21 ♘xa7#] 21 ♘xa7+ [□ 21 ♘d6+] 21 ... ♔d8 22 ♗g5+ ♔c7 23 ♕xe6 ♖xe6 24 ♖f7 ♘ab8 25 ♖xg7 ♔b6 26 h3 ♔xa7 27 ♖dxd7 ♘xd7 28 ♖xd7 ♖e2 29 ♗d2 h5 30 g3 ♖g8 31 ♖d3 ♖f8 32 ♔g1 b6 33 ♗e3 ♖e1+ 34 ♔g2 ♖e2+ 35 ♔g1 ♖e1+ ½-½ L/N6123-1843

**1837-★BH-1**
**Bourdonnais, L.C.M. de la= Haxo**
Gilvoisin

1 e4 e5 2 ♘f3 ♘c6 3 d4 exd4 4 ♗c4 ♗c5 5 ♘g5 ♘h6 6 ♘xf7 ♘xf7 7 ♗xf7+ ♔xf7 8 ♕h5+ g6 9 ♕xc5 d6 10 ♕c4+ ♗e6 11 ♕e2 ♘e5 12 f4 ♗c4 13 ♕f2 ♘c6 14 c3 dxc3 15 ♘xc3 ♖e8 16 b3 ♗a6 17 ♗b2 ♘b4 18 0-0-0! ♘d3+ 19 ♖xd3 ♗xd3 20 ♕f3 ♗a6 21 f5 ♕g5+ 22 ♔b1 ♔g8 23 h4 ♕d8 24 fxg6 hxg6 25 h5 ♕g5 26 hxg6 ♕xg6 27 ♘d5 ♕xe4+ 28 ♕xe4 ♖xe4 29 ♘f6+ ♔f7 30 ♘xe4 ♗d3+ 31 ♔c1 ♗xe4 32 ♖g1 ♖g8 33 g3 ½-½ L/N6013-1837

**1837-★BJ-1**
**Bourdonnais, L.C.M. de la+ Jouantho, de**
Gilvoisin [Bourdonnais]

⟨♖a1⟩ 1 e4 e5 2 f4 exf4 3 ♘f3 g5 4 ♗c4 g4 5 d4 gxf3 6 ♕xf3 ♗h6 7 0-0 ♕f6 8 e5 ♕g6 9 ♘c3 c6 10 ♘e4 d5 11 ♘d6+ ♔d8 12 ♗d3 f5 13 ♗xf4 ♔c7? 14 e6 ♗xf4 15 ♕xf4 ♕xe6 16 ♘f7+ ♔b6 17 ♘xh8 ♕f6 18 c4 ♕xh8? [□ 18 ... dxc4] 19 c5+ ♔a5 20 ♕d2+ ♔a4 21 b3+ ♔a3 22 ♕a5+ ♔b2 23 ♖b1# **1-0** L/N6013-1837

**1837̂-★BL-1**
**Bourdonnais, L.C.M. de la+ Lécrivain**
Paris

1 e4 e6 2 f4 d5 3 e5 c5 4 ♘f3 ♘c6 5 c3 ♕b6 6 ♗d3 a6 7 ♗c2 ♗d7 8 d4 cxd4 9 cxd4 ♗b4+ 10 ♘c3 ♘ge7 11 0-0 0-0 12 ♗xh7+ ♔xh7 13 ♘g5+ ♔g8 14 ♕h5 ♖fc8 15 ♕xf7+ ♔h8 16 ♕h5+ ♔g8 17 ♕h7+ ♔f8 18 ♕h8+ ♘g8 19 ♘h7+ ♔f7 20 ♘g5+ ♔f8 21 f5 ♔e7 22 ♕xg7+ ♔d8 23 fxe6 ♘ge7 24 ♖f8+ ♔c7 25 ♘xd5+ ♘xd5 26 ♕xd7+ ♔b8 27 ♕xc8+ ♔a7 28 ♕xa8# **1-0** L/N6013-1837

**1837̂-★BS-1**
**Boncourt– Saint-Amant, P.C.F. de**
[Bourdonnais]

1 e4 e5 2 ♗c4 ♘f6 3 d3 ♗c5 4 ♘f3 ♘c6 5 c3 ♗b6 6 0-0 0-0 7 ♗g5 d6 8 b4 ♗e6 9 ♘bd2 h6 10 ♗h4 ♔h7 11 a4 a6 12 ♔h1 ♖g8! 13 ♕c2 g5 14 ♗g3 h5 15 h3 [□ 15 h4] 15 ... h4 16 ♗h2 ♘h5 17 d4 g4 18 ♗xe6 fxe6 19 hxg4 ♖xg4 20 dxe5 dxe5 21 ♘c4

21 ... ♘g3+ 22 fxg3 hxg3 23 ♖ad1 ♕e7 24 b5 ♖h4 25 ♘xb6 ♖xh2+ 26 ♔g1 ♕c5+ 27 ♖f2 cxb6 28 ♘xh2 axb5 29 axb5 ♖f8 30 ♘f3 ♘a5 31 ♕e2 ♘c4 32 ♘g5+ ♔g6 33 ♘f3 ♖f4 34 ♖d3 gxf2+ 35 ♕xf2 ♕xf2+ 36 ♔xf2 ♖xe4 37 ♖d7 ♖f4 38 ♖xb7 e4 39 ♔g3 exf3 **0-1** L/N6013-1837

**1837̂-★BW-1**
**Bourdonnais, L.C.M. de la+ Wilson, D.**
London [Bourdonnais]

1 e4 e6 2 f4 d5 3 e5 c5 4 ♘f3 ♘c6 5 c3 ♕b6 6 ♗d3 ♗d7 7 ♗c2 f6 8 0-0 ♗e7 9 ♔h1 0-0-0 10 a3 ♘h6 11 d4 fxe5 12 fxe5 ♗e8 13 ♗xh6 gxh6 14 b4 cxd4 15 b5! [15 cxd4?! ♗h5!∓] 15 ... ♕xb5 16 cxd4 ♗h5?! [□ 16 ... ♕b2] 17 ♘c3 ♕b6 18 ♘a4 ♕a5 19 ♖b1 ♖d7 20 ♕d3 ♗g6 21 ♕e2 ♗xc2 22 ♕xc2 ♖c7 23 ♕b3 ♔d7 24 ♖fc1 ♖hc8 25 ♘c5+ ♗xc5 26 ♖xc5 ♘xd4? 27 ♖xc7+ [27 ♕xa5?? ♖c1+–+] 27 ... ♕xc7 28 ♘xd4 ♕xe5 29 ♕xb7+ ♖c7 30 ♕b5+ ♔d6 31 ♘f3 ♕f4 32 ♖e1 h5 33 ♕e8 ♕h6 34 ♘e5 ♕f6 35 ♕b8 ♕f2 36 ♖c1 ♔xe5 37 ♕xc7+ ♔f6 38 ♕xh7 h4 39 ♕h8+ ♔e7 40 ♕g7+ ♔d8 41 ♕c7+ ♔e8 42 ♕b8+ ♔e7 43 ♖c7+ ♔f6 44 ♕f8+ **1-0** L/N6013-1837

**1837̂-★B♀-1**
**Bourdonnais, L.C.M. de la+ ♀**
[Bourdonnais]

1 e4 e5 2 ♘f3 ♘c6 3 d4 ♕f6?! [□ 3 ... exd4] 4 ♘c3 exd4 5 ♘d5 ♕d8 6 ♗c4 ♗c5 7 0-0 h6?! [□ 7 ... ♘f6] 8 b4 ♘xb4 9 ♘xb4 ♗xb4 10 ♕xd4 ♘f6 11 ♗xf7+ ♔xf7 12 ♕xb4 d6 13 ♕b3+ ♗e6 14 ♕xb7 ♕b8 15 ♖b1 ♘xe4 16 ♕xe4 ♕xb1 17 ♗xh6 ♕xa2 18 ♘g5+ ♔e7 19 ♗xg7 ♖hg8 20 ♖e1 ♔d7 21 ♘xe6 ♖ae8 22 c4 ♖xg7 23 ♘c5+ dxc5 24 ♕xe8+ ♔d6 25 ♕e6# **1-0** L/N6013-1837

**1837̂-★B♀-2**
**Bourdonnais, L.C.M. de la= ♀**
[Bourdonnais]

1 e4 e5 2 ♘f3 ♘c6 3 ♗c4 ♗c5 4 b4 ♗xb4 5 c3 ♗a5 6 0-0 ♗b6 7 d4 ♘a5 8 ♗d3 exd4 9 cxd4 ♘e7 10 ♗b2 0-0 11 ♘c3 d6 12 e5 h6 13 exd6 cxd6 14 h3 d5 15 ♗a3 ♖e8 16 ♖e1 ♗e6 17 ♗xe7 ♖xe7 18 ♖c1 ♘c6 19 ♗c2 ♕f8 20 ♕d3 f5 21 ♗b3 ♘b4 22 ♕d2 ♔h8 23 a3 ♘c6 24 ♗xd5? ♗xd5 25 ♘xd5 ♖xe1+ 26 ♖xe1 ♗a5 27 ♘c3 ♕xa3 28 ♖c1 ♖c8 29 ♕e3 ♘xd4 30 ♘xd4 ♖xc3 31 ♖xc3 ♕xc3 32 ♕e8+ ♔h7 33 ♘e6 ♗b4 34 ♔h2 ♕e1?? 35 ♘f8+ ♔g8 36 ♘e6+ ♔h7 37 ♘f8+ ½-½ L/N6013-1837

**1837̂-★DS-1**
**Devinck, F.J.+ Saint-Amant, P.C.F. de**
Paris

⟨♙f7⟩ 1 e4 e6 2 d4 g6 3 ♗d3 d5 4 e5 c5 5 c3 ♘c6 6 ♗e3 ♕b6 7 ♕b3 cxd4? 8 ♕xb6 axb6 9 ♗xd4 ♗g7

10 f4 ♘h6 11 ♘f3 0-0 12 g3 ♘xd4 13 cxd4 ♗d7 14 h3 b5 15 ♘c3 b4 16 ♘b5 ♗xb5 17 ♗xb5 ♘f5 18 ♔f2 g5 19 ♗d7 ♖a6 20 g4 ♘xd4 21 ♘xd4 ♖xf4+ 22 ♔e3 ♖e4+ 23 ♔d3 ♖xe5 24 ♖ae1 ♖xe1 25 ♖xe1 e5 26 ♗e6+ ♔f8 27 ♖f1+ ♔e8 28 ♗f7+ ♔e7 29 ♗xd5 exd4 30 ♖f7+ ♔d6 31 ♗xb7 ♖xa2 32 ♖xg7 ♖xb2 33 ♔xd4 ♖h2 34 ♖xh7 b3 35 ♗e4 b2 36 ♖h5 ♖h1 37 ♔c3 b1♕ 38 ♗xb1 ♖xb1 **1-0** L/N6013

**1837̂-★SW-1**
**Szén, J.=Walker, G.**
1 e4 c5 2 c4 ♘c6 3 f4 e5 4 d3 d6 5 ♗e2 f5 6 ♘c3 ♘f6 7 ♗f3 ♘d4 8 exf5 ♘xf5 9 ♘ge2 ♗e7 10 ♗d5 ♘d4 11 0-0 ♘xd5 12 ♘xd5 ♗g4 13 ♘dc3 0-0 14 h3 ♗xe2 15 ♘xe2 ♘xe2+ 16 ♕xe2 ♗f6 17 ♖b1 ♕d7 18 ♕e4 ♕c6 19 ♕xc6 bxc6 20 fxe5 ♗xe5 21 ♗e3 ♖xf1+ 22 ♔xf1 ♖b8 23 b3 a5 24 a4 ♗d4 25 ♗xd4 cxd4 26 ♔f2 c5 27 ♔f3 ♖e8 28 ♖d1 ♖b8 29 ♖b1 ♖e8 30 ♖d1 ♖e3+ 31 ♔f2 ♔f7 32 ♖d2 g5 33 ♖d1 h5 34 ♖d2 ♔f6 35 ♖d1 ♔f5 36 ♖d2 g4 37 hxg4+ hxg4 38 g3 ♖f3+ 39 ♔g2 **½-½**
L/N6013-1837

**1837̂-★SW-2**
**Walker, G.–Szén, J.**
1 e4 e5 2 f4 exf4 3 ♗c4 ♕h4+ 4 ♔f1 g5 5 ♘c3 ♗g7 6 d4 d6 7 e5 dxe5 8 ♘d5 ♔d8 9 dxe5 ♗d7 10 ♘f3 ♕h5 11 h4 h6 12 ♔g1 ♕g6 13 hxg5 hxg5 14 ♖xh8 ♗xh8 15 ♕e1 ♗g7 16 ♕b4 b6 17 ♗d2 ♘c6 18 ♕c3 ♘ge7 19 ♖e1 ♗e6 20 ♘xe7 ♘xe7 21 ♗b5 ♗d7 22 ♕d4 c6 23 ♗d3 ♘f5 24 ♗xf5 ♕xf5 25 ♖d1 g4 26 ♘g5 ♕xg5 27 ♕xd7+ ♔xd7 28 ♗xf4+ ♔e6 29 ♗xg5 ♗xe5 30 c3 f6 31 ♗e3 ♖h8 32 ♔f2 ♖h7 33 a4 f5 34 a5 f4 35 ♗d4 ♗xd4+ 36 ♖xd4 ♔e5 **0-1**
L/N6013-1837

**1838-⊠JK-1**
**Kieseritsky, L.Φ Jaenisch, C.F.**
1 d4 d5 2 c4 dxc4 3 e4 e5 4 d5 f5 5 ♗xc4 ♘f6 6 ♘c3 ♗c5 7 ♕c2 ♘g4 8 ♘h3 f4 9 g3 g5 10 f3 ♘e3 11 ♗xe3 ♗xe3 12 ♘f2 a6 13 a4 ♕f6 14 g4 ♘d7 15 b3 ♘f8 16 ♖d1 h5 17 gxh5 ♖xh5 18 ♘g4 ♗xg4 19 fxg4 ♖h3 20 ♗f1 ♖h7 L/N6123-1842

**1838-⊠JK-2**
**Kieseritsky, L.Φ Jaenisch, C.F.**
1 e4 e5 2 f4 exf4 3 ♗c4 ♕h4+ 4 ♔f1 c5 5 ♘c3 ♘e7 6 ♘f3 ♕h5 7 ♘b5 d5 8 ♘c7+ ♔d8 9 ♘xd5 ♘xd5 10 ♗xd5 ♔c7 11 d4 g5 12 h4 ♗g4 13 c3 ♔c8 14 ♔f2 ♗xf3 15 gxf3 ♘c6 16 ♕a4 ♘d8 17 ♗d2 ♗d6 18 ♖ag1 gxh4 19 ♖g4 h3 20 e5 ♗c7 21 ♗xf4 a6 22 ♔g3
L/N6123-1842

**1838̂-★BJ-1 ●o⌂**
**Bourdonnais, L.C.M. de la+ Jouy**
Paris [Staunton]
1 e4 e5 2 ♘f3 ♘c6 3 ♗c4 ♗c5 4 b4 ♗xb4 5 c3 ♗a5 6 0-0 ♘f6 7 d4 ♘xe4 8 dxe5 ♘xc3 9 ♘xc3 ♗xc3 10 ♕b3 ♗xa1 11 ♗xf7+ ♔f8 12 ♗g8 ♖xg8 13 ♘g5 ♘xe5 14 f4 [□14 ♘xh7+] 14 ... d5 15 fxe5+ ♔e8 16 ♕d3 ♖f8 17 ♖xf8+ ♔xf8 18 ♕xh7 ♗d4+ 19 ♔h1 ♕e8 20 ♕h8+ ♔e7 21 ♕xg7+ ♔d8 22 ♘f7+ ♔d7 23 ♘d8+!! ♕e7 24 e6+ ♔e8 25 ♕g6+ ♔f8 26 ♗h6+ ♗g7 27 ♕h7 ♗xe6 28 ♕h8+ ♗g8 29 ♗xg7+ ♔e8 [29 ... ♕xg7? 30 ♘e6+−] 30 ♕xg8+ ♔d7 31 ♕xd5+ ♔e8 32 ♘e6 **1-0** L/N6123-1843

**1838̂-★BJ-2**
**Jouy–Bourdonnais, L.C.M. de la**
Paris [Bourdonnais]
1 e4 e5 2 f4 exf4 3 ♘f3 g5 4 ♗c4 g4 5 ♘e5 ♕h4+ 6 ♔f1 f3 7 ♘xf7? [□7 d4] 7 ... ♘c6 8 d4 ♗g7 9 c3 ♘f6 10 ♘xh8 d5 11 exd5 ♘e4 12 ♕e1 g3 13 ♗d3 fxg2+ 14 ♔xg2 ♗h3+ 15 ♔g1 ♘xd4 16 ♕xe4+ ♕xe4 17 ♗xe4 ♘e2# **0-1** L/N6013

**1838̂-⊠CN-1**
**Cambridge–Nottingham**
1 e4 c5 2 f4 e6 3 ♘f3 ♘c6 4 c3 d5 5 exd5 exd5 6 ♗b5 ♗d6 7 d4 ♕b6 8 ♗xc6+ bxc6 9 0-0 ♘e7 10 ♔h1 a5 11 b3 0-0 12 ♗a3 ♖e8 13 ♘e5 ♘f5 14 ♖e1 cxd4 15 ♘c4 ♖xe1+ 16 ♕xe1 ♕d8 17 ♘xd6 ♘xd6 18 ♗xd6 ♕xd6 19 ♕e8+ ♕f8 20 ♕xf8+ ♔xf8 21 cxd4 ♗f5 22 ♘c3 ♖e8 23 ♔g1 ♖e3 24 ♖c1 ♖d3 25 ♘a4 ♖xd4 26 ♘c5 ♖d2 27 a4 ♗c8 28 h3 ♖d4 29 ♔h2 ♔e7 30 ♔g3 ♖b4 31 ♖c3 ♔d6 32 ♔f3 d4 33 ♘e4+ ♔c7 34 ♖d3 ♗a6 **0-1**
L/N6013-1838

**1838̂-⊠CN-2**
**Nottingham+Cambridge**
[† Le Palamède]
1 e4 e5 2 ♘f3 ♘c6 3 d4 exd4 4 ♘xd4 ♘xd4 5 ♕xd4 ♕f6?! 6 e5 ♕g6 7 ♘c3 ♕b6?! 8 ♕xb6 axb6 9 ♘b5 ♔d8 10 ♗f4 c6 11 ♘d6 ♗xd6 12 exd6 ♘f6 13 ♗c4 ♖f8 14 ♗e3 c5 15 f3 ♘e8 16 0-0-0 f5 17 ♗g5+ ♘f6 18 b4 h6 19 ♗e3 ♖a4 20 c3 ♘e8 21 g3 ♖f6 22 ♗f4 cxb4 23 ♗e5 bxc3 24 ♗xf6+ ♘xf6 25 ♗f7 b5 26 ♖he1 b6 27 ♖e7 ♗a6 28 ♗b3 ♖a5 29 ♖xg7 **1-0**
L/N6013-1838

**1838̂-⊠DV-1**
**Valencienne–Douai**
1 e4 e5 2 ♘f3 ♘c6 3 d4 ♘xd4 4 ♘xe5 ♘e6 5 ♗c4 c6 6 ♘c3 ♕c7 7 f4 b5 8 ♗b3 ♗d6 9 ♘xf7 ♔xf7 10 f5 ♘f6 11 fxe6+ dxe6 12 0-0 ♗xh2+ 13 ♔h1 ♔e7 14 ♕d4 ♕e5 15 ♕f2 ♕h5 16 ♕f3 ♕h4 17 ♗g5 ♕xg5 18 ♔xh2 ♘g4+ 19 ♔g1 ♕c5+ 20 ♔h1 ♕h5+ 21 ♕h3 ♕xh3+ 22 gxh3 ♘e5 23 ♖g1 g6 24 ♖g5 ♘f3 25 ♖g2 ♘d4 26 a4 ♘xb3 27 cxb3 ♗b7 28 axb5 cxb5 29 ♖e2 a6 30 ♘d1 ♖hf8 31 ♔g2 ♖ac8 32 ♘f2 ♖fd8 33 h4 ♖d4 34 ♔f3 ♖b4 35 ♖e3 ♖c2 36 ♖ae1 ♖d4 37 ♖1e2 ♖xe2 38 ♔xe2 e5 39 ♔f3 ♖d2 40 ♖e2 ♖xe2 41 ♔xe2 a5 42 ♔e3 b4 43 ♘g4 ♔e6 44 ♔f3 ♗c8 45 ♘h2 ♔d6 46 ♘f1 ♗e6 47 ♘d2 ♔c5 48 ♔e3 h6 49 ♔d3 g5 50 hxg5 hxg5 51 ♘f3 g4 52 ♘xe5 ♔d6 53 ♔d4 g3 54 ♘f3 ♗xb3 55 ♔e3 ♗d1 56 ♘d4 ♔c5 57 ♘f5 g2 58 ♔f2 a4 **0-1** L/N6013-1838

**1838̂-⊠DV-2**
**Douai–Valencienne**
[† Le Palamède]
1 e4 e5 2 ♗c4 ♗c5 3 ♘f3 ♘c6 4 c3 ♘f6 5 d4 exd4 6 cxd4 ♗b4+ 7 ♗d2 ♗xd2+ 8 ♘bxd2 d5 9 exd5 ♘xd5 10 0-0 0-0 11 ♘b3 ♗e6 12 ♖e1 ♘f4 13 ♖c1 ♕f6 14 ♖c3 ♖ad8 15 ♕c1 h5 16 ♗e2? ♘xe2+ 17 ♖xe2 ♗xb3 18 ♖xb3 ♘xd4 19 ♘xd4 ♕xd4 20 ♖e1 ♖fe8 **0-1**
L/N6013-1839

**1839-★HL-1** 28 viii 39
**Lasa, T von H.u.von d.= Hanstein, W.**
[Staunton]
1 e4 e5 2 ♘f3 d6 3 d4 f5 4 dxe5 fxe4 5 ♘g5 d5 6 e6 [6 f4] 6 ... ♘h6 7 c4 [7 ♕h5+; 7 f3; 7 ♘c3; 7 ♘h3] 7 ... ♗b4+ [7 ... c6] 8 ♘c3 d4 9 a3 e3 10 ♕h5+ [10 axb4] 10 ... g6 11 ♕xh6 exf2+ [11 ... dxc3 12 axb4 (12 ♕g7→) 12 ... cxb2→] 12 ♔xf2 ♗f8 13 ♕h3 ♕f6+ 14 ♕f3 ♕xf3+ 15 gxf3 dxc3 16 ♗h3 ♗c5+ 17 ♔g2 ♘c6 18 bxc3 ♘e5 19 ♗f4 ♘xc4 20 ♗xc7 ♘e3+ 21 ♔g3 h5 [∆ 22 ... h4+, 23 ... ♘d5+] 22 f4 b6 [∆ 23 ... ♗b7, 24 ... h4+, 25 ... ♘d5+] 23 ♘e4 h4+ 24 ♔f2 ♘d5+ 25 ♘xc5 bxc5 26 ♗e5 ♖f8 27 ♗g2 ♗xe6 28 c4 ♘xf4 29 ♗xf4 ♖d8 30 ♗c6+ ♔e7 31 ♔e3 ♖d4 32 ♗g5+ ♔d6 33 ♗e4 ♔e5 34 ♗d3 ♗xc4 35 ♗xc4 ♖xc4 36 ♖he1 ♖d4 37 ♖ad1 ♔f5 38 ♗h6 [38 ♖f1+ ♔xg5] 38 ... ♖e8+ 39 ♔f3 ♖xe1 40 ♖xe1

g5 41 ♗g7 g4+ 42 ♔f2 ♖d2+ 43 ♖e2 g3+ 44 hxg3 hxg3+ 45 ♔f1 ♖xe2 ½-½ L/N6123-1859

**1839-★HL-2** 4 ix 39
**Hanstein, W.+ Lasa, T von H u. von d.**
[Staunton]

1 e4 e5 2 ♘f3 d6 3 d4 f5 4 dxe5 fxe4 5 ♘g5 d5 6 e6 ♘h6 7 c4 ♗b4+ 8 ♘c3 d4 9 a3 e3 10 axb4 ♕xg5 11 ♕xd4 exf2+ [11 ... ♘f5 12 ♕e5 exf2+ 13 ♔xf2 ♕h4+ 14 g3 ♕d4+ 15 ♕xd4 ♘xd4 16 e7 Bilguer] 12 ♕xf2 ♕e5+ 13 ♗e2 ♖f8 14 ♕h4 ♘c6 15 ♘b5 [15 ♗xh6] 15 ... ♗xe6 16 ♕h5+ ♕xh5 17 ♗xh5+ ♔d7 18 b3 ♘g4 19 ♗g5 ♘f2 20 ♖f1 ♘d3+ 21 ♔e2 ♖xf1 22 ♖xf1 ♘dxb4 23 ♖d1+ ♔c8 24 ♗f4 ♘a6 25 ♗f3! h6 26 h4 ♘e7 27 ♗e5 ♘f5 28 g4 ♘xh4 29 ♗xg7 ♘xf3 30 ♔xf3 b6 31 ♘d4 ♗d7 32 ♗xh6 ♘c5 33 g5 ♘e6 34 ♘xe6 ♗xe6 35 ♖e1 ♗g8 36 g6 ♔b7 37 ♖e7 b5 38 ♗f4 bxc4?! [38 ... ♖c8] 39 ♖xc7+ ♔b6 40 bxc4 ♖f8 41 c5+ ♔b5 42 ♔e4 a5 43 ♗d6 ♖e8+ 44 ♔d4 a4 45 ♖b7+ ♔c6 46 ♖b6+ ♔d7 47 ♖a6 ♖e6 48 g7 ♖g6 49 c6+ ♔e8 [49 ... ♔xd6 50 c7+-] 50 ♖a8+ ♔f7 51 ♖f8+ ♔xg7 52 ♖xg8+ ♔xg8 53 c7 ♖xd6+ 54 ♔c5 ♖g6 55 c8♕+ ♔h7 56 ♕d7+ ♖g7 57 ♕xa4 ♖g5+ 58 ♔d6 ♖g6+ 59 ♔e5 ♖g5+ 60 ♔f6 ♖g6+ 61 ♔f5 ♖g7 62 ♕e8 **1-0** L/N6123-1859

**1839-★KS-1**
**Saint-Amant, P.C.F. de– Kieseritsky, L.**
Paris? [Bourdonnais & Méry]

1 e4 e5 2 ♘f3 ♘c6 3 ♗c4 ♗c5 4 c3 ♘f6 5 d4 exd4 6 e5 ♘e4 [◻6 ... d5] 7 cxd4 [◻7 ♗d5] 7 ... ♗b4+ 8 ♘bd2 ♘xd2 9 ♗xd2 d5 10 exd6 ♕xd6 11 0-0 ♗xd2 12 ♕xd2 0-0 13 ♖fe1 ♗g4 14 ♘e5 ♘xe5 15 ♖xe5 ♖ad8 16 ♖e4 ♗f5 17 ♖f4 ♗e6 18 b3 f5 19 ♖d1 ♗d5 20 ♖h4 ♖f6 21 f4 ♖g6 22 ♖h3 ♖g4 23 ♖f3 b5 24 h3 ♖g6 25 ♗xd5+ ♕xd5 26 ♖e3 ♖e6 27 ♖e5 ♖xe5 28 fxe5 c5 29 ♕f4 g6 30 ♕h4 cxd4 31 e6 d3 32 ♕e7 ♖f8 33 ♕d7 ♕xd7 34 exd7 ♖d8 35 ♖xd3 ♔f7= ...? **0-1** L/N6013-1839

**1839̂-★BW-1**
**Walker, G.– Boncourt**
Paris [La Bourdonnais]

1 e4 e5 2 ♘f3 ♘c6 3 ♗c4 ♗c5 4 b4 ♗xb4 5 c3 ♗a5 6 0-0 ♘f6? 7 ♘g5! 0-0 8 f4 ♘xe4 9 ♘xf7 ♖xf7 10 fxe5? [10 ♗xf7+ Δ 11 ♕f3] 10 ... ♘xe5 11 ♗xf7+ ♘xf7 12 ♖xf7 ♔xf7 13 ♕h5+ ♔f8 14 ♕xa5 d6 15 ♕h5 ♕f6 16 ♕e2 ♗g4 17 ♕f1 ♕xf1+ 18 ♔xf1 ♔e7-+ 19 d3 ♖f8+ 20 ♔e1 ♘c5 21 ♗g5+ ♔d7 22 d4 ♖e8+ 23 ♔f1 ♘e4 24 ♗h4 g5 25 ♗g3 h5 26 c4 ♘xg3+ 27 hxg3 ♗e2+ 28 ♔f2 ♗xc4 29 ♘c3 g4 30 ♖h1 ♗f7 **0-1**

**1839̂-★BZ-1**
**Boncourt,– Zekeriski**

1 e4 e5 2 ♗c4 ♗c5 3 ♘f3 ♘c6 4 c3 ♘f6 5 d4 exd4 6 e5 d5 7 exf6 dxc4 8 fxg7 ♖g8 9 ♗g5 f6 10 ♕e2+ ♕e7 11 ♗xf6 ♕xe2+ 12 ♔xe2 d3+ 13 ♔d1 ♗g4 14 h3 ♗xf3+ 15 gxf3 ♔f7 16 ♘d2 ♔xf6 17 ♘e4+ ♔xg7 18 ♘xc5 ♘e5 19 f4 ♘f3 20 ♘e6+ ♔f7 21 ♘g5+ ♘xg5 22 hxg5 ♖xg5 23 ♔d2 ♖e8 **0-1** L/N6013-1839

**1839̂-★BZ-2**
**Zekeriski– Boncourt**

1 a3 e5 2 e4 ♗c5 3 ♗c4 ♘f6 4 ♘c3 c6 5 ♘f3 d6 6 d3 0-0 7 ♘e2 d5 8 exd5 cxd5 9 ♗a2 ♘c6 10 b4 ♗d6 11 ♗b2 ♗g4 12 ♕d2 e4 13 ♘fd4 ♖e8 14 0-0 ♗e5 15 ♘xc6 bxc6 16 ♗xe5 ♖xe5 17 d4 ♖h5 18 ♘f4 ♖h6 19 c4 ♕d6 20 h3

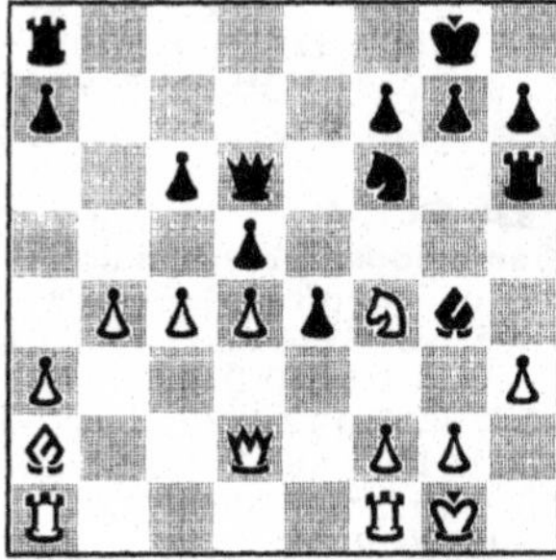

20 ... g5 21 hxg4 ♘xg4 22 f3 e3 23 ♕e1 gxf4 24 fxg4 f3 25 g3 f2+ 26 ♖xf2 exf2+ 27 ♕xf2 ♖h3 28 ♔g2 ♕h6 29 ♕f5 ♖h2+ 30 ♔f3 ♕d2 **0-1** L/N6013-1839

**1839̂-★KS-1**
**Kieseritsky, L.– Saint-Amant, P.C.F. de**
Paris? [Bourdonnais & Méry]

1 e4 e6 2 f4 d5 3 exd5 exd5 4 d4 c5 5 dxc5 ♗xc5 6 ♗b5+ ♘c6 7 ♕e2+ ♘e7 8 ♘f3 ♗e6 9 ♗e3 ♕b6 10 ♗xc5 ♕xc5 11 ♘c3 0-0 12 0-0-0 ♖ad8 13 ♗d3 ♔h8 14 h3 ♗f5 15 g4 ♗xd3 16 ♕xd3 ♘b4 17 ♕d4 ♕a5 18 a3 ♘bc6 19 ♕d3 a6

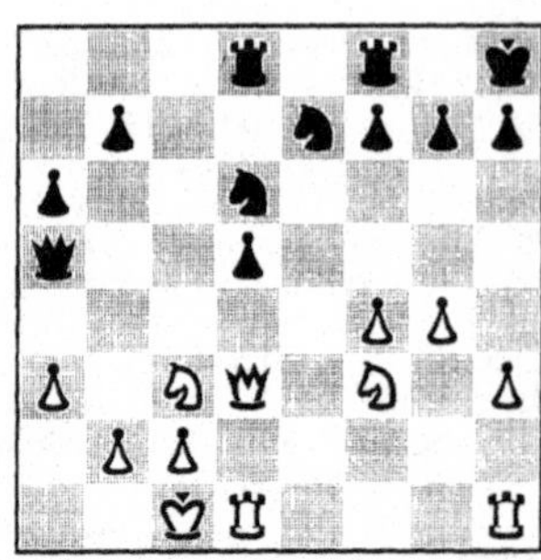

20 ♖he1?∓ [20 ♘g5±] 20 ... b5 21 ♘d4 b4 22 ♘b3 ♕c7 23 ♘e2 bxa3 24 bxa3 ♘a5 25 ♕c3 ♘c4 26 ♕b4 ♖b8 27 ♕a4 ♖fc8 28 f5 ♕e5 29 ♘ed4 ♕d6 30 ♖d3 ♘xa3 31 ♖de3 ♘g8 32 ♖1e2 ♘f6 33 ♘f3 ♘c4 34 ♘g5 ♔g8 35 ♘f3 ♘xe3 36 ♖xe3 ♘e4 **0-1** L/N60131-1839

**1839̂-⊠BP-1**
**Posen– Berlin**
[? Le Palamède]

1 e4 e5 2 ♗c4 ♘f6 3 ♘f3?! ♘xe4 4 ♘xe5 d5 5 ♗b3 ♕g5 6 ♘xf7? ♕xg2 7 ♖f1 ♘c6 8 c3 ♘c5 9 d4 ♘xb3 10 ♘xh8 ♕e4+ 11 ♕e2 ♕xe2+ 12 ♔xe2 ♘xa1 13 ♖g1 ♗f5 14 ♘d2 0-0-0 15 ♘f3 ♖e8+ 16 ♗e3 ♘c2 17 ♘f7 ♘xe3 18 fxe3 g6 19 h4 ♖e7 20 ♘7e5 ♘xe5 21 ♘xe5 ♗g7 22 ♘f3 ♖e4 23 h5 ♗h6 **0-1** L/N6013-1839

**183?-★BP-1**
**Popert, H.W.Φ Bourdonnais, L.C.M. de la**
London [Staunton]

⟨Δf7⟩ 1 e4 ♘h6 2 d4 ♘f7 3 ♗d3 e6 [◻3 ... d5] 4 ♘f3 d5 5 e5?! [◻5 exd5 Δ 6 c4] 5 ... c5 6 c3 ♘c6 7 0-0 ♕b6 8 a4 ♗d7 9 ♗c2 ♗e7 10 ♕d3 0-0-0? 11 dxc5 ♕c7 12 b4 g5 13 ♘a3 ♘cxe5 14 ♘xe5 ♘xe5 15 ♕g3 h5 16 f4 h4 17 ♕e1 ♘g4 18 ♘b5 ♕b8 19 h3 a6 20 ♘d4 e5 21 hxg4 gxf4 [21 ... exd4 22 ♕xe7±] 22 ♘f5 ♖de8 23 c4?! [◻23 ♗xf4!±] 23 ... h3 24 cxd5 hxg2 25 ♔xg2 f3+ 26 ♖xf3 e4 27 ♗xe4 ♕h2+ 28 ♔f1 ♗xc5 29 bxc5 ♕h1+ 30 ♔e2 ♖h2+ 31 ♔d1 ♖xe4 32 ♕xh1 ♖xh1+ 33 ♔c2 ♖xg4 L/N6123-1843̂

**183?-★BS-1**
**Slous, F.L.+ Bourdonnais, L.C.M. de la**
London [Boden]

⟨Δf7⟩ 1 e4 ... 2 d4 d6 3 c4 e6 4 ♗d3 ♘c6 5 d5 ♘ce7 6 ♘f3 e5 7 ♘c3 ♘f6 8 0-0 ♘g6 9 ♘e1 ♘f4 10 ♗xf4 exf4 11 ♘f3 ♘g4 12 h3 ♘e5 13 ♘xe5 dxe5 14 ♕h5+ ♔d7 15 ♕f5+ ♔d6 16 ♘b5+ ♔c5 17 ♕xe5

♔b6 18 ♕xf4 [□ 18 b4!+-] 18 ... a6 19 ♘c3 ♔a7 20 ♕e3+ b6 21 e5 g5 22 ♗e4 ♗c5 23 ♕d2 g4 24 hxg4 ♗xg4 25 ♘a4 ♗f8 26 b4 h5 27 d6 ♖b8 28 c5 cxd6 29 cxd6 h4 30 ♖ac1 ♗c8 31 ♖c7+ ♗b7 32 ♕d4 ♔a8 **1-0** M392-1870

### 183?-★B?-1
**Bourdonnais, L.C.M. de la+?**
London?

⟨♖a1⟩ 1 e4 e5 2 f4 exf4 3 ♗c4 ♕h4+ 4 ♔f1 g5 5 ♘c3 ♗g7 6 d4 d6 7 ♘f3 ♕h5 8 ♘d5 ♔d8 9 h4 c6 10 ♘c3 h6 11 ♔f2 ♗g4 12 hxg5 ♗xf3 13 gxf3 ♕xg5 14 ♘e2 ♘d7 15 ♗xf4 ♕f6 16 ♗e3 ♔c7 17 f4 ♘e7 18 ♘g3 ♖ad8 19 ♘h5 ♕g6 20 ♖g1 ♕xe4 21 ♖xg7 ♘f5 22 ♖g3 ♘xg3 23 ♘xg3 ♕e7 24 d5 ♖de8 25 ♘f5 ♕e4 26 dxc6 bxc6 27 ♕xd6+ ♔d8 28 ♗d3 ♕h1 29 ♕b4 ♖hg8 30 ♕a5+ ♘b6 31 ♗xb6+ axb6 32 ♕xb6+ ♔d7 33 ♕b7+ ♔e6 34 ♕b3+ ♔f6 35 ♕c3+ ♔e6 36 ♕e5+ ♔d7 37 ♕d6+ ♔c8 38 ♗a6# **1-0** L/N6123-1842

### 183?-★B?-2
**?– Bourdonnais, L.C.M. de la**
London [Staunton]

⟨♙f7⟩1 e4 ... 2 d4 d6 3 c4 e6 4 d5 e5 5 ♘c3 ♘f6 6 f4 ♗e7 7 f5 c6 8 ♗e3 ♘a6 9 h3 0-0 10 g4 cxd5 11 cxd5 ♘c5 12 ♗xc5 dxc5 13 ♗d3 ♕b6 14 ♕e2 ♗d7 15 ♘f3 ♖ac8 16 ♘xe5 ♗d6 17 ♘xd7 ♗g3+ 18 ♔f1 ♘xd7 19 ♔g2 ♗h4 20 ♖ad1 c4 21 ♗b1 [21 ♗xc4? ♖xc4-+] 21 ... ♘e5 22 ♖hf1 ♕d6 23 ♘b5 ♕c5 24 ♘d4 ♕d6 25 ♘f3 ♗f6 26 ♘xe5 ♕xe5 27 ♗c2 b5 28 ♕d2 c3! 29 bxc3 ♖xc3 30 ♖f3 ♖fc8 31 ♖xc3 ♖xc3 32 ♕f2 ♗h4! 33 ♕xh4 ♖xc2+ **0-1** L/N6123-1843

### 183?-★DM-1
**Macdonnell, A.+D'Arblay, A.**
[Walker]

⟨♖a1⟩ 1 e4 e5 2 f4 exf4 3 ♘f3 g5 4 ♗c4 g4 5 ♘c3 gxf3 6 0-0 d6 7 ♕xf3 c6 8 d4 ♗h6 9 ♗xf7+ ♔xf7 10 ♕h5+ ♔g7 11 ♗xf4 ♗xf4 12 ♖xf4 ♘f6 13 ♕g5+ ♔f7 14 e5 dxe5 15 fxe5 ♘d7 16 ♘e4 ♖g8 17 ♕h5+ ♔g7 18 exf6+ ♔h8 19 ♖h4 ♘f8 20 ♘g5 ♖xg5 21 ♕xg5 ♘e6 [21 ... ♕d1+ 22 ♔f2 ♕xc2+-+] 22 ♕h5 ♕g8 23 f7 ♕g7 24 ♖g4 ♕f8 25 ♕e5+ ♘g7 26 ♖xg7 ♕xg7 27 f8♕# **1-0** L/N3145

### 183?-★DM-2
**Macdonnell, A.+D'Arblay, A.**
[Walker]

⟨♖a1⟩ 1 e4 e5 2 f4 exf4 3 ♘f3 g5 4 ♗c4 g4 5 ♘c3 gxf3 6 ♕xf3 ♕f6 7 0-0 ♗h6 8 d4 ♘c6 9 ♗xf4 d6 10 ♘d5 ♕xd4+ 11 ♔h1 ♕xc4 12 ♘xc7+ ♔d8 13 ♗xd6 ♘d4 14 ♕d1 ♗g4 15 ♕e1 ♖c8 16 ♘d5 ♗e6 17 b3 ♕e2 18 ♕h4+ ♔d7 19 ♖e1 ♕d2 20 ♗b4 ♕g5 21 ♕f2 ♖xc2 22 ♕g1 ♖c1 23 ♕xd4 ♖xe1+ 24 ♗xe1 ♗xd5 25 exd5 ♗g7 [25 ... ♕c1] 26 ♕a4+ ♔e7 27 ♗h4 ♕xh4 28 ♕xh4+ ♘f6 29 ♕b4+ ♔e8 30 ♕xb7 **1-0** L/N3145

### 183?-★EM-1
**Macdonnell, A.– Evans, W.D.**

⟨♘g1⟩ 1 e4 e5 2 ♗e2 ♘f6 3 d3 ♗c5 4 0-0 0-0 5 ♔h1 d6 6 f4 ♘c6 7 c3 ♕e7 8 f5 ♗d7 9 g4 ♔h8 10 g5 ♘g8 11 h4 f6 12 ♕e1 ♘d8 13 ♕g3 ♘c6 14 b4 ♘xb4 15 a3 ♘c6 16 ♖a2 ♕f7 17 ♖b2 ♕e7 19 ♗d1 a6 18 ♖g2 b5 20 ♘d2 ♖ad8 21 ♘f3 ♗c8 22 g6 h6 23 ♘h2 ♘a5 24 ♘g4 ♖d7 25 d4 exd4 26 ♖fg1 dxc3 27 ♘xh6 gxh6 28 g7+ ♕xg7 29 ♕xc3 ♕e7 30 ♖e1 ♗b7 31 ♕xa5 ♖f7 32 ♖g4 ♖g7 33 ♖f4 d5 34 ♗f3 dxe4 35 ♗xe4 b4 36 ♕a4 ♖d3 37 ♔h2 ♗xe4 38 ♖fxe4 ♕xe4 39 ♖xe4 ♗g1+ 40 ♔h1 ♖h3# **0-1** L/N3145

### 183?-★EM-2
**Macdonnell, A.– Evans, W.D.**

⟨♘b1⟩ 1 e4 e5 2 ♘f3 ♘c6 3 ♗c4 ♗c5 4 b4 ♗xb4 5 c3 ♗c5 6 0-0 d6 7 d4 exd4 8 cxd4 ♗b6 9 d5 ♘e5 10 ♘xe5 dxe5 11 ♗b2 ♕e7 12 ♕d3 f6 13 ♗a3 ♗c5 14 ♗b5+ ♔f8 15 ♗b2 ♗d7 16 ♗c4 ♘h6 17 ♖ac1 ♘f7 18 ♖c3 ♗d6 19 ♕g3 ♘g5 20 ♕d3 a6 21 ♗c1 ♘f7 22 ♕b1 b5 23 ♗e2 g6 24 g3 ♗h3 25 ♖d1 ♔g7 26 g4 ♘g5 27 ♗xg5 fxg5 28 ♖xh3 ♖af8 29 ♖c3 ♗c5 30 ♖f1 ♖f6 31 ♕c1 ♗b6 32 ♔g2 ♖hf8 33 f3 h6 34 a4 b4 35 ♖c2 a5 36 ♕d2 ♖d8 37 ♖fc1 ♕d7 38 ♗b5 ♕f7 39 ♕e2 ♖df8 40 ♖f1 ♗d4 41 ♖c6 ♖xc6 42 ♗xc6 ♕f4 43 ♕b5 ♗b6 44 ♗d7 ♖f7 45 ♗e8 ♕e7 46 ♖d1 ♕f6 47 ♗c6 ♖f7 48 ♖f1 ♖f8 49 ♕e2 h5 50 gxh5 gxh5 51 ♗d7 ♕f4 52 ♗f5 ♕e3 53 ♕b5 ♖f7 54 ♔h1 ♕c5 55 ♕e8 ♕e7 56 ♕c6 ♖f6 57 ♕c1 ♖h6 58 ♖e1 g4 59 f4 exf4 60 ♕xf4 ♖d6 61 ♗e6 ♖d8 62 ♖f1 ♖f8 63 ♕e5+ ♔h6 64 ♖f5 ♖xf5 65 exf5 ♕g7 66 ♕e1 ♕c3 67 ♕f1 ♕f3+ 68 ♕xf3 gxf3 69 d6 cxd6 70 f6 h4 71 f7 ♔g7 72 h3 ♗d8 73 ♔g1 ♗e7 74 ♔f2 ♔f6 75 ♗b3 ♔e5 76 ♔xf3 ♔d4 77 ♔e2 ♔c3 78 ♗e6 b3 79 ♔d1 ♔b2 80 ♔d2 ♗f8 81 ♔d3 ♔a3 82 ♔d2 ♔xa4 83 ♔c1 ♔b4 84 ♔b2 a4 85 ♔b1 a3 86 ♗d5 a2+ 87 ♔a1 ♗g7# **0-1** L/N3145

### 183?-★EM-3
**Macdonnell, A.– Evans, W.D.**

⟨♘b1⟩ 1 e4 e5 2 ♗c4 ♗c5 3 ♕g4 ♕f6 4 d4 ♗xd4 5 ♘f3 ♘c6 6 ♕g3 h6 7 0-0 d6 8 ♘xd4 ♘xd4 9 f4 ♗e6 10 ♗d3 0-0-0 11 fxe5 ♕xe5 12 ♗f4 ♕c5 13 ♗e3 ♕e5 14 ♕f2 ♘c6 15 b4 ♘f6 16 h3 ♘xe4 17 ♗xe4 ♕xe4 18 b5 ♘e5 19 ♗xa7 ♗d5 20 ♗d4 ♘g6 21 ♖ae1 ♕h4 22 ♕d2 ♖he8 23 ♗e3 ♕e4 24 ♗g5 ♕xg2+ 25 ♕xg2 ♗xg2 26 ♗xd8 ♖xe1 27 ♖xe1 ♗xh3 28 ♖e8 ♗d7 29 ♖g8 ♗xb5 30 ♗f6+ ♔d7 31 ♖xg7 ♔e6 32 ♗b2 h5 33 ♖h7 ♗e2 34 ♔f2 ♗g4 35 ♔g3 b5 36 ♖g7 ♘e7 37 ♔f4 ♘d5+ 38 ♔g5 ♘b4 39 ♖g8 ♘xc2 40 ♖e8+ ♔d5 41 ♖e7 f6+ 42 ♗xf6 c5 43 ♖b7 b4 44 ♖b6 ♘e3 45 ♔f4 ♘c4 46 ♖a6 ♗e2 47 ♗e7 ♔e6 48 ♗f8 h4 49 ♖a7 ♗f1 50 ♔e4 ♗g2+ 51 ♔d3 ♘e5+ 52 ♔e2 h3 53 ♔f2 ♘d7 54 ♗h6 c4 55 ♗d2 c3 56 ♗e3 ♘c5 57 ♖c7 ♔d5 58 ♖c8 ♔c4 59 ♔g1 c2 60 ♔h2 ♔d3 61 ♗f4 ♔e2 62 ♖d8 ♘d3 63 ♗g5 d5 64 ♖b8 ♔d1 65 a4 bxa3 66 ♖b3 c1♕ 67 ♖xd3+ ♔e2 68 ♗xc1 ♔xd3 69 ♗xa3 d4 **0-1** L/N3145

### 183?-★FM-1
**Fraser, W.– Macdonnell, A.**
[Walker]

1 e4 e5 2 ♘f3 ♘c6 3 ♗c4 ♗c5 4 c3 d6 5 d3 ♘f6 6 0-0 ♗b6 7 ♗e3 ♘e7 8 ♗xb6 axb6 9 ♘g5 0-0 10 f4 exf4 11 ♖xf4 ♘g6 12 ♖f1 h6 13 ♘f3 c6 14 ♗b3 ♘f4 15 ♘h4 ♗g4 16 ♘f3 ♘6h5 17 ♕d2 ♖a5 18 ♘a3 ♗xf3 19 ♖xf3 ♕g5 20 ♕f2 d5 21 exd5 [21 ♖f1] 21 ... ♖e8 22 dxc6 ♖ae5 23 ♖g3 ♘xg3 24 hxg3 ♘e2+ **0-1** L/N3145

### 183?-★FM-2
**Macdonnell, A.+Finch, J.**

⟨♖a1⟩ 1 e4 e6 2 f4 d5 3 e5 c5 4 ♘f3 a6 5 c3 ♘c6 6 ♗d3 ♗e7 7 ♗c2 ♗d7 8 d4 cxd4 9 cxd4 ♘h6 10 ♘c3 0-0 11 0-0 ♘b4 12 ♗b1 ♘f5 13 g4 ♘h6 14 f5 ♘xg4 15 f6 ♘xf6 16 exf6 ♗xf6 17 ♔h1 ♕b6

18 ♗g5 ♗xg5 19 ♗xh7+ ♔h8 20 ♘xg5 g6 21 ♕g4 ♕d6 22 ♕h4 ♔g7 23 ♗g8 f5 24 ♕h7+ ♔f6 25 ♘ce4+ dxe4 26 ♘xe4# **1-0** L/N3145

**183?-★FM-3**
**Macdonnell, A.+Finch, J.**
⟨♖a1⟩ 1 e4 e5 2 f4 exf4 3 ♘f3 g5 4 ♗c4 ♗g7 5 0-0 ♕e7 6 ♘c3 c6 7 e5 ♕c5+ 8 d4 ♕xc4 9 ♘e4 ♕e6 10 ♘d6+ ♔f8 11 ♘xg5 ♕g6 12 ♘gxf7 ♘e7 13 ♘xh8 ♗xh8 14 ♖xf4+ ♔g8 15 ♖g4 **1-0** L/N3145

**183?-★GM-1**
**Macdonnell, A.+Gamble**
⟨♘b1⟩ 1 e4 e6 2 f4 d5 3 e5 c5 4 c3 ♘c6 5 ♗d3 f5 6 ♗c2 ♘h6 7 ♘f3 ♗e7 8 0-0 0-0 9 d4 cxd4 10 cxd4 b6 11 ♔h1 ♗a6 12 ♖g1 ♘b4 13 ♗b1 ♘g4 14 ♕d2 ♘d3 15 ♗xd3 ♗xd3 16 h3 ♗e4 17 hxg4 fxg4 18 ♘h2 g3 19 ♘f3 ♗xf3 20 gxf3 ♗b4 21 ♕e2 ♕h4+ 22 ♔g2 ♕h2+ 23 ♔f1 ♕h4 24 ♕g2 ♖ac8 25 ♕xg3 ♕xg3 26 ♖xg3 ♖c2 27 a3 ♖fc8 28 ♗e3 ♗d2 29 ♔e2 ♗c3+ 30 ♔d1 ♗xb2 31 ♖b1 ♖h2 32 ♗g1 ♖hc2 33 ♗e3 a5 34 f5 exf5 35 e6 ♗xa3 36 ♖xb6 ♖a2 37 ♖b7 g6 38 ♖h3 ♖a1+ 39 ♔e2 ♖a2+ 40 ♔f1 h5 41 ♖g3 ♖a1+ 42 ♔e2 ♖h1 43 ♖xg6+ ♔h8 44 ♗f4 **1-0** L/N3145

**183?-★GM-2**
**Macdonnell, A.+Gamble**
⟨♘b1⟩ 1 e4 e5 2 ♘f3 ♘c6 3 ♗c4 ♗c5 4 b4 ♗xb4 5 c3 ♗c5 6 0-0 d6 7 d4 exd4 8 cxd4 ♗b6 9 h3 h6 10 ♗b2 f6 11 ♘h4 ♘ge7 12 ♕h5+ ♔d7 13 ♕g4+ ♔e8 14 ♕xg7 ♖f8 15 e5 fxe5 16 dxe5 d5 17 ♘g6 ♖g8 18 ♕h7 ♖xg6 19 ♗e2 ♗e6 20 ♗h5 ♗f7 21 e6 ♖xe6 22 ♕xf7+ ♔d7 23 ♗g4 ♕g8 24 ♗xe6+ **1-0** L/N3145

**183?-★HM-1**
**Macdonnell, A.+Harrison**
⟨♖a1⟩ 1 e4 e5 2 f4 exf4 3 ♗c4 ♕h4+ 4 ♔f1 g5 5 ♘c3 ♗g7 6 d4 d6 7 ♗e2 ♘e7 8 ♘b5 ♔d8 9 ♘c3 ♘bc6 10 g3 fxg3 11 ♔g2 ♕h6 12 hxg3 ♕e6 13 d5 ♕e5 14 ♘f3 ♕f6 15 ♗xg5 ♕g6 16 dxc6 bxc6 17 e5 d5 18 ♘xd5 cxd5 19 ♕xd5+ ♔e8 20 ♕xa8 ♕xc2 21 ♖c1 ♕xe2+ 22 ♔g1 ♗xe5 23 ♖e1 ♕xb2 24 ♖xe5 f6 25 ♗xf6 ♕b1+ 26 ♖e1 ♕b6+ 27 ♗d4 c5 28 ♕xc8+ ♔f7 29 ♘e5+ ♔g7 30 ♕g4+ ♘g6 31 ♘xg6+ cxd4 32 ♘xh8+ ♔xh8 33 ♖e8# **1-0** L/N3145

**183?-★HM-2**
**Macdonnell, A.+Harrison**
⟨♖a1⟩ 1 e4 e5 2 f4 exf4 3 ♘f3 g5 4 h4 g4 5 ♘e5 h5 6 ♗c4 ♖h7 7 d4 d6 8 ♘d3 ♕e7 9 ♘xf4 c6 10 ♘c3 ♘d7 11 g3 ♘b6 12 ♗d3 ♗g7 13 e5 ♖h8 14 0-0 d5 15 ♘g6 ♕c7 16 ♘xh8 ♗xh8 17 ♗g5 ♗e6 18 a4 ♘c8 19 ♘e2 ♘ce7 20 ♘f4 ♕d7 21 ♘xh5 0-0-0 22 b4 b6 23 ♗a6+ ♔b8 24 b5 c5 25 dxc5 bxc5 26 ♗f4 ♔a8 27 a5 d4 28 b6 d3 29 ♗xd3 ♕d4+ 30 ♔h2 ♗xe5 31 ♗e4+ ♘d5 32 b7+ ♔b8 33 ♕xd4 cxd4 34 ♗xe5+ ♔xb7 35 ♗xd4 ♔a6 36 ♖b1 ♖d7 37 ♗d3+ ♔xa5 38 c3 ♘b6 39 ♗xb6+ axb6 40 ♖a1+ ♗a2 41 ♖xa2# **1-0** L/N3145

**183?-★HM-3**
**Macdonnell, A.+Harrison**
⟨♖a1⟩ 1 e4 e5 2 f4 exf4 3 ♘f3 g5 4 h4 g4 5 ♘e5 h5 6 ♗c4 ♖h7 7 d4 d6 8 ♘d3 ♕e7 [8 ... ♗e7] 9 ♘xf4 c6 10 ♘c3 ♘f6 11 0-0 ♘fd7 12 g3 b5

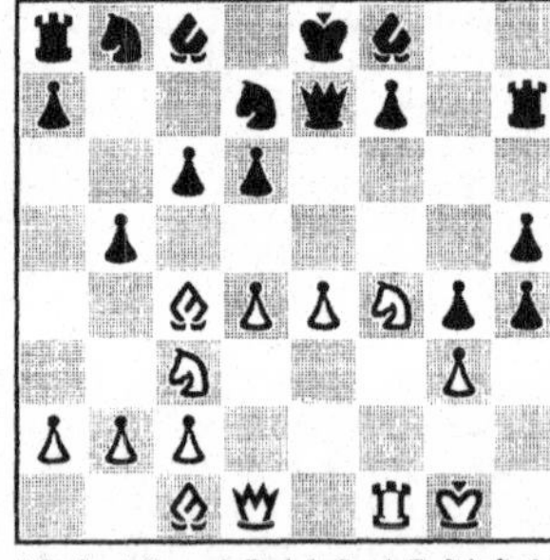

13 ♗xb5 cxb5 14 ♘xb5 ♘b6 15 ♘d5 ♘xd5 16 exd5 ♕d7 17 ♕d3 f5 18 ♖e1+ ♖e7 19 ♖e6 ♖xe6 20 dxe6 ♕h7 21 ♕c4 ♔d8 22 ♗g5+ **1-0** L/N3145

**183?-★HM-4**
**Macdonnell, A.–Harrison**
⟨♖a1⟩ 1 e4 e5 2 f4 exf4 3 ♘f3 g5 4 h4 g4 5 ♘e5 h5 6 ♗c4 ♖h7 7 d4 d6 8 ♘d3 ♘f6 9 ♘c3 ♕e7 10 ♘xf4 ♗e6 11 d5 ♗d7 12 0-0 a6 13 g3 b5 14 ♗d3 ♕e5 15 ♗e3 b4 16 ♘ce2 ♘xe4 17 ♗d4 ♕e7 18 ♘e6 fxe6 19 ♗xe4 ♖h6 20 dxe6 ♗c6 21 ♗f5 ♗f3 22 ♕d3 c5 23 ♗e3 ♖xe6 24 ♗xe6 ♕xe6 25 ♘f4 ♕e4 26 ♕d2 ♔d7 27 ♘xh5 ♔c6 28 ♖e1 ♘d7 29 ♗f2 ♕f5 30 ♘f4 ♗h6 31 ♗e3 ♗xf4 32 ♗xf4 ♕d5 33 ♕f2 ♘f6 34 ♕f1 ♘e4 35 ♔h2 ♔b6 36 a4 ♖f8 **0-1** L/N3145

**183?-★LM-1**
**Lavallino–Macdonnell, A.**
⟨♙f7⟩ 1 e4 ♘c6 2 d4 e5 3 c3 ♘f6 4 ♗g5 ♗e7 5 d5 ♘xe4 6 dxc6 ♘xg5 7 cxd7+ ♗xd7 8 ♕d5 ♗d6 9 h4 ♘e6 10 ♗c4 ♕f6 11 ♕xb7 0-0 12 ♕f3 ♕h6 13 ♕e3 ♗c5 14 ♗xe6+ ♗xe6 15 ♕xh6 ♗xf2+ 16 ♔e2 ♗c4+ 17 ♔d1 gxh6 18 ♘f3 e4 19 ♘e5 ♗e6 20 g4 ♖ad8+ 21 ♔c2 ♗g3 22 ♘c6 ♖f2+ 23 ♔c1 ♗f4+ 24 ♘d2 ♖dxd2 ... ? **0-1** L/N3145

**183?-★LM-2**
**Lavallino–Macdonnell, A.**
⟨♙f7⟩ 1 e4 ♘c6 2 d4 e5 3 d5 ♘ce7 4 ♗g5 ♘f6 5 ♗xf6 gxf6 6 ♕h5+ ♘g6 7 ♘f3 ♕e7 8 d6 ♕f7 9 dxc7 ♗c5 10 ♘bd2 d6 11 ♗b5+ ♗d7 12 ♕f5 a6 13 ♗xd7+ ♕xd7 14 ♕xf6 ♖f8 15 ♕g5 ♕xc7 16 0-0 ♔d7 17 ♕g4+ ♔c6 18 ♘g5 ♖f6 19 ♕e2 ♘f4 20 ♕c4 b5 21 ♕b3 ♕g7 22 g3 ♕xg5 23 ♔h1 ♖g8 24 a4 b4 25 ♕c4 ♔b6 26 c3 ♖h6 27 ♕f7 ♖xh2+ 28 ♔xh2 ♕h6+ 29 ♔g1 ♖xg3# **0-1** L/N3145

**183?-★LM-3**
**Lavallino–Macdonnell, A.**
⟨♙f7⟩ 1 e4 d6 2 d4 ♘f6 3 ♗d3 e5 4 d5 ♗e7 5 f4 exf4 6 ♘f3 0-0 7 0-0 c6 8 c4 ♘g4 9 ♕e2 ♘d7 10 ♘c3 ♘de5 11 ♘xe5 dxe5 12 g3 ♗c5+ 13 ♔h1 f3 14 ♖xf3 ♖xf3 15 ♕xf3 ♘f2+ 16 ♔g1 ♗g4 17 ♕g2 ♘xd3+ **0-1** L/N3145

**183?-★LM-4**
**Lavallino–Macdonnell, A.**
[Walker]
⟨♙f7⟩ 1 e4 ... 2 d4 ♘c6 3 ♗c4 e6 4 ♗b3 g6 5 h4 d5 6 e5 ♘h6 7 ♗g5 ♕d7 8 h5 ♗g7 9 c3 ♘f7 10 ♕d2 ♘xg5 11 ♕xg5 ♕e7 12 ♕e3 ♗d7 13 ♗c2 0-0-0 14 ♘d2 ♗e8 15 h6 ♗f8 16 b4 [16 0-0-0] 16 ... g5 17 a4 ♗g6 18 ♗d3 ♕f7 19 a5 ♗xb4 20 cxb4 ♘xb4 21 ♗xg6 ♕xg6 22 ♖c1 ♘d3+ 23 ♔d1 ♘xc1 24 ♔xc1 ... ? **0-1** L/N3145

**183?-★MM-1**
**Macdonnell, A.–Matthews**
⟨♘b1⟩ 1 e4 e5 2 ♘f3 d6 3 ♗c4 c6 4 c3 d5 5 exd5 cxd5 6 ♗b5+ ♗d7 7 ♗xd7+ ♘xd7 8 0-0 e4 9 ♘e1 ♗d6 10 f4 f5 11 d3 ♘gf6 12 dxe4

♗c5+ 13 ♔h1 dxe4 14 b4 ♗b6 15 c4 ♘g4 16 ♕e2 ♕h4 17 g3 ♕h6 18 ♘c2 0-0 19 c5 ♘xc5 20 bxc5 ♗xc5 21 ♘e3 ♗xe3 22 ♗xe3 ♖fd8 23 ♕c4+ ♔h8 24 ♗g1

♘xh2 25 ♖fd1 ♘g4+ 26 ♔g2 ♕h5 27 ♖ac1 ♖xd1 28 ♖xd1 ♘e3+ 29 ♗xe3 ♕xd1 30 ♕c5 b6 31 ♕c6 ♖d8 32 ♕c7 ♕f3+ 33 ♔h2 ♕e2+ 34 ♔h3 ♕f1+ 35 ♔h2 ♕e2+ 36 ♔h3 ♕h5+ 37 ♔g2 ♕d1 38 a4 h6 39 a5 ♕e2+ 40 ♔h3 ♕g4+ 41 ♔h2 ♖d1 42 ♗g1 ♖d2+ 43 ♔h1 ♕h3+ 44 ♗h2 ♕xh2# **0-1**

L/N3145

### 183?-★MM-2
**Macdonnell, A.– Matthews**

⟨♘b1⟩ 1 e4 e5 2 ♘f3 d6 3 d4 exd4 4 ♘xd4 ♘c6 5 ♘xc6 bxc6 6 f4 ♘f6 7 ♗d3 ♗g4 8 ♕d2 d5 9 e5 ♘e4 10 ♗xe4 dxe4 11 h3 ♕h4+ 12 ♕f2 ♕xf2+ 13 ♔xf2 ♗c5+ 14 ♗e3 ♗xe3+ 15 ♔xe3 ♗f5 16 g4 ♗e6 17 b3 0-0-0 18 f5 ♗d7 19 ♔xe4 ♖he8 20 ♖he1 c5 21 ♔f4 ♗c6 22 ♖e3 ♖d4+ 23 ♔g5 f6+ 24 ♔h5 ♖xe5 25 ♖xe5 fxe5 26 ♖e1 e4 27 ♖e2 ♖d6 28 ♔g5 ♖h6 29 h4 ♔d7 30 ♖h2 ♔e7 31 ♔f4 ♖d6 32 g5 h6 33 c4 hxg5+ 34 hxg5 ♔f7 35 ♔e5 ♖d4 36 ♖h3 ♖d3 37 ♖h8 e3 38 g6+ ♔e7 39 ♖h7 e2 40 f6+ ♔d8 41 ♔e6 e1♕+ 42 ♔f7 ♖d7+ 43 ♔g8 ♕e8# **0-1** L/N3145

### 183?-★MM-3
**Macdonnell, A.– Matthews**

⟨♘b1⟩ 1 e4 e5 2 ♗c4 c6 3 ♕e2 ♗d6 4 f4 ♘e7 5 fxe5 ♗xe5 6 ♘f3 ♗c7 7 ♘g5 d5 8 0-0 0-0 9 exd5 cxd5 10 ♕h5 h6 11 ♗d3 ♗f5 12 ♗xf5 ♘xf5 13 ♖xf5 hxg5 14 ♖xg5 ♕e7 15 ♕h4 ♖e8 16 d4 ♕e1+ 17 ♕xe1 ♖xe1+ 18 ♔f2 ♖h1 19 ♖xd5 ♘c6 20 b3 ♖ae8 21 ♗b2 ♖xh2 22 ♖d7 ♗f4 23 ♖xb7 ♗e3+ 24 ♔g3 ♖h6 25 d5 ♘d4 26 ♗xd4 ♗xd4 27 ♖f1 ♖g6+ 28 ♔h3 ♖e5 29 ♖f4 ♗f2 30 g4 ♗e3 31 ♖f3 ♖f6 32 ♖b8+ ♔h7 33 ♖xf6 gxf6 34 c4 ♗f4 35 ♖b7 ♖e2 36 g5 f5 37 ♖xf7+ ♔g6 39 ♖f6+ ♔xg5 **0-1**

L/N3145

### 183?-★MM-4
**Macdonnell, A.+ Matthews**

⟨♘b1⟩ 1 e4 e5 2 ♗c4 ♘f6 3 d4 exd4 4 e5 ♕e7 5 ♕e2 ♘g8 6 ♘f3 c5 7 0-0 a6 8 ♗g5 f6 9 exf6 gxf6 10 ♕d3 ♕g7 11 ♖ae1+ ♗e7 12 ♗f4 ♘c6 13 ♗d6 ♔d8 14 ♗g3 b5 15 ♗d5 ♗b7 16 ♕e2 ♘a5 17 ♗xb7 ♘xb7 18 ♕e4 ♔c8 19 ♘h4 ♘h6 20 ♕xe7 ♕xe7 21 ♖xe7 ♔d8 22 ♖fe1 ♖ac8 23 ♖g7 ♖c6 24 ♖ee7 **1-0** L/N3145

### 183?-★MM-5
**Macdonnell, A.+ Matthews**

⟨♘b1⟩ 1 e4 e5 2 ♗c4 ♗c5 3 ♕e2 d6 4 f4 exf4 5 ♘f3 ♘f6 6 d4 ♗b6 7 ♗xf4 0-0 8 0-0-0 ♕e7 9 e5 dxe5 10 dxe5 ♘fd7 11 ♖hf1 ♘c5 12 ♗g5 ♕e8 13 ♖d8 ♕a4 14 ♗xf7+ ♔xf7 15 ♘h4+ ♔e6 16 ♖fxf8 ♗d7 17 c4 h5 **1-0** L/N3145

### 183?-★MM-6
**Macdonnell, A.– Matthews**

⟨♘g1⟩ 1 e4 e5 2 ♗e2 d5 3 exd5 ♕xd5 4 0-0 ♗c5 5 ♘c3 ♕d8 6 ♘e4 ♗b6 7 d3 f5 8 ♗g5 ♕d7 9 ♗h5+ g6 10 ♘f6+ ♘xf6 11 ♗xf6 ♖f8 12 ♗xe5 gxh5 13 ♕xh5+ ♔d8 14 ♖ae1 ♗c5 15 ♗g3 ♘c6 16 d4 ♗d6 17 d5 ♘e7 18 ♗h4 b6 19 c4 ♗a6 20 b3 ♕e8 21 ♕h6 ♔c8 22 ♕e6+ ♔b7 23 ♗xe7 ♗xe7 24 ♕xe7 ♕xe7 25 ♖xe7 ♖ad8 26 ♖xh7 ♔b8 27 ♖e1 ♖de8 28 ♖he7 ♖xe7 29 ♖xe7 ♗c8 30 h4 ♖g8 31 g3 f4 32 ♔g2 fxg3 33 fxg3 ♗g4 34 ♖e4 ♗f5 35 ♖f4 ♗g4 36 ♔f2 ♔b7 37 ♔e3 ♔c8 38 b4 ♖e8+ 39 ♔d4 ♖g8 40 c5 ♗e2 41 c6 ♔d8 42 ♔e3 ♗g4 43 ♖f7 a5 44 bxa5 bxa5 45 ♔f4 a4 46 d6 cxd6 47 ♖a7 ♗e6 48 h5 ♖g4+ 49 ♔f3 ♖c4 50 h6 ♗f5 51 ♖d7+ ♔c8 52 ♖xd6 ♖c2 53 g4 ♗h7 54 ♖f6 ♗d3 55 ♔e3 ♖c3 56 ♔d4 ♖a3 57 ♖f3 ♖xa2 58 ♖xd3 ♖h2 59 g5 ♖h5 60 ♖g3 ♔c7 61 ♔e5 ♔xc6 62 ♔f6 ♖h1 63 ♔g7 ♖d1 64 h7 ♖d7+ 65 ♔h6 ♖d6+ 66 ♔h5 ♖d8 67 g6 ♔c5 68 g7 ♖d5+ 69 ♖g5 **1-0** L/N3145

### 183?-★MM-7
**Macdonnell, A.? Matthews**

⟨♘b1⟩ 1 e4 e5 2 ♗c4 ♗c5 3 b4 ♗xb4 4 f4 d5 5 exd5 e4 6 ♘e2 ♗g4 7 0-0 ♘f6 8 ♕e1 ♗c5+ 9 ♔h1 0-0 10 ♘g3 ♘xd5 11 ♕xe4 ♘f6 12 ♕xb7 ♘bd7 13 c3 ♖b8 14 ♕a6 ♖e8 15 d4 ♗b6 16 f5 ♘h5 17 ♗xf7+ ♔xf7 18 ♕c4+ ♔f8 19 ♗a3+ c5 20 dxc5 ♗xc5 21 ♗xc5+ ♘xc5 22 ♕xc5+ ♕e7 23 ♕d4 ♘f6 24 h3 ♗h5 25 ♖ae1 ♕c7 26 ♘xh5 ♘xh5 27 ♖xe8+ ♖xe8 28 ♕b4+ ♔g8 29 ♕b3+ ♔h8 30 ♕b5 ♘g3+ 31 ♔g1 ♕e7 32 ♖f3 ... ? L/N3145

### 183?-★MM-8
**Macdonnell, A.= Matthews**

⟨♘b1⟩ 1 e4 e5 2 ♘f3 ♘c6 3 ♗c4 ♗c5 4 b4 ♗xb4 5 c3 ♗a5 6 0-0 d6 7 h3 ♗b6 8 d4 exd4 9 cxd4 ♘f6 10 e5 dxe5 11 ♗a3 ♗xd4 12 ♖c1 ♗e6 13 ♗b5 ♕d7 14 ♕a4 ♗d5 15 ♘xd4 exd4 16 ♖fe1+ ♔d8 17 ♖e7 ♕f5 18 ♗xc6 bxc6 19 ♕a5 ♘d7 20 ♖xc6 ♖c8 21 ♖d6 ♕b1+ 22 ♖e1 ♕xe1+ 23 ♕xe1 cxd6 24 ♕a5+ ♘b6 25 ♕xa7 ♘c4 26 ♗b4 ♖e8 27 ♗a5+ ♘xa5 28 ♕xa5+ ♔e7 29 ♕xd5 ♖a8 30 ♕xd4 ♔f8 31 ♕xd6+ ♔g8 32 a3 h6 33 ♔h2 ♖ed8 34 ♕b4 ♖db8 35 ♕c3 ♖a7 36 f3 ♖ba8 37 ♕c5 ♖xa3 38 ♕c6 ♖a2 **½-½** L/N3145

### 183?-★MM-9
**Macdonnell, A.? Matthews**

⟨♘b1⟩ 1 e4 e5 2 f4 d5 3 ♕f3 ♘f6 4 exd5 e4 5 ♕b3 ♗d6 6 d4 0-0 7 c4 ♘h5 8 g3 b6 9 ♗g2 ♖e8 10 ♘e2 ♔h8 11 0-0 f5 12 ♗e3 a5 13 c5 ♗e7 14 ♘c3 ♗a6 15 ♖fe1 ♘f6 16 ♖ad1 ♘g4 17 d6 cxd6 18 cxb6 ♘xe3 19 ♖xe3 ♗b7 20 ♗h3 ♖f8 21 ♕e6 ♖a6 22 ♘d5 ♗xd5 23 ♕xd5 g6 24 b7 ♖c6 25 ♖b3 ♕c7 26 ♗f1 ♘d7 27 ♕e6 ♘b6 28 ♗b5 ♖c2 ... ?

L/N3145

### 183?-★MM-10
**Macdonnell, A.– Matthews**

⟨♘b1⟩ 1 e4 e5 2 ♘f3 ♘c6 3 ♗c4 ♗c5 4 b4 ♗xb4 5 c3 ♗a5 6 0-0 d6 7 h3 ♗b6 8 d4 exd4 9 cxd4 ♘f6 10 e5 dxe5 11 ♗a3 ♗xd4 12 ♖c1 ♗e6 13 ♗b5 ♘e4 14 ♖xc6 ♗xf2+ 15 ♔h2 ♗g3+ 16 ♔g1 ♗f2+ 17 ♔h1 ♘g3+ 18 ♔h2 ♘xf1+ 19 ♕xf1 bxc6 20 ♗xc6+ ♗d7 21 ♗xa8 ♕xa8 22 ♕xf2 f6 23 g4 ♕d5 24 ♘h4 ♔f7 25 g5 ♖e8 **0-1**

L/N3145

### 183?-★MM-11
**Macdonnell, A.+ Matthews**

⟨♘b1⟩ 1 e4 e5 2 ♘f3 ♘c6 3 ♗c4 ♗c5 4 b4 ♗xb4 5 c3 ♗a5 6 0-0 d6 7 h3 ♗b6 8 d4 exd4 9 cxd4 ♘f6 10 e5 dxe5 11 ♗a3 ♗xd4 12 ♖c1 ♗e6 13 ♗b5 a6 14 ♗xc6+ bxc6 15 ♖xc6 ♘d5 16 ♕a4 ♗d7 17 ♘xd4 ♘e7 18 ♕c2 exd4 19 ♖e1 ♗xc6 20 ♕xc6+ ♔f8 21 ♖xe7 ♔g8 22 ♕f3 ♕f8 23 ♖xc7 ♕e8 24 ♖xf7 h6 25 ♖e7 ♕f8 26 ♕d5+ ♔h7 27 ♕e4+ ♔g8 28 ♖d7 ♕e8 29 ♖e7 ♕d8 30 ♕e6+ ♔h7 **1-0**

L/N3145

**183?-★MM-12**
**Macdonnell, A.– Matthews**
⟨♘b1⟩ 1 e4 e5 2 ♗c4 ♗c5 3 c3 d5 4 ♗xd5 ♘f6 5 ♗c4 0-0 6 d3 ♘g4 7 ♘h3 ♕h4 8 0-0 ♗e6 9 ♗b5 a6 10 ♗a4 b5 11 ♗c2 ♘c6 12 ♗g5 ♕h5 13 ♕e2 f5 14 d4 exd4 15 exf5 ♗c4 16 ♕e4 ♘ge5 17 cxd4 ♗xd4 18 f6 ♕g6 19 fxg7 ♖f7 20 ♖fe1 ♕xe4 21 ♗xe4 ♗xb2 22 ♖ad1 ♔xg7 23 f4 ♖af8 24 fxe5 ♘xe5 25 ♗e3 ♗c3 26 ♗c5 ♗xe1 27 ♗xf8+ ♖xf8 28 ♖xe1 ♘g6 29 a3 ♖e8 30 ♔f2 ♘e5 31 ♔g3 ♘d3 32 ♖e3 ♘c5 33 ♔f4 ♘xe4 34 ♖xe4 ♖xe4+ 35 ♔xe4 c6 36 ♘f4 ♔f6 37 ♔d4 ♔f5 38 g3 a5 39 ♘g2 ♔g5 40 ♘e3 ♗e2 41 ♔c5 ♗f3 42 ♔d4 h5 43 h4+ ♔g6 44 ♘c2 ♔f6 45 ♘e1 ♗d5 46 ♘d3 ♔f5 47 ♘f2 b4 48 axb4 axb4 49 ♘d3 b3 50 ♔c3 ♗f7 51 ♘f4 ♔g4 52 ♘e2 c5 53 ♔d2 ♔f3 54 ♔d1 ♗g6 55 g4 ♔xg4 56 ♘c3 b2 **0-1**
L/N3145

**183?-★MN-1**
**Newham= Macdonnell, A.**
[Walker]
⟨♙f7⟩ 1 e4 ... 2 d4 ♘c6 3 ♗d3 d5 4 e5 ♗e6 5 c3 g6 6 h4 ♕d7 7 ♘d2 ♘h6 8 ♘b3 b6 9 ♘h3 ♗f5 10 ♘g5 e6 11 ♕c2 a5 12 a4 ♗g7 13 h5 ♔e7 14 ♘f3 ♘f7 15 h6 ♗f8 16 ♖h4 ♗xd3 17 ♕xd3 ♔e8 18 g4 ♗e7 19 g5 ♕d8 20 ♕b5 ♕d7 21 ♗e3 ♖f8 22 ♔e2 ♘h8 23 ♘h2 ♘a7 24 ♕xd7+ ♔xd7 25 ♘g4 b5 26 ♘f6+ ♗xf6 27 exf6 [27 gxf6] 27 ... bxa4 28 ♘c5+ ♔d6 29 ♗f4+ ♔c6 30 ♖xa4 ♘b5 31 ♖h1 ♖fe8 32 ♖ha1 ♘f7 33 ♖xa5 ♖ab8 34 ♖a6+ ♖b6 35 ♖xb6+ cxb6 36 ♘d3 ♔b7 37 ♘e5 ♘fd6 38 ♔d3 ♖c8 39 ♖a4 ♘f5 40 ♗e3 ♘bd6 41 b3 ♘xe3 42 fxe3 ♘e4 43 c4 ♘xg5 44 ♖a1 ♘e4 45 ♖f1 ♘g3 46 f7 ♘xf1 47 ♘d7 ♘g3 48 f8♕ ♖xf8 49 ♘xf8 ♘f5 50 ♘xh7 ♘xh6 51 ♘f8 g5 52 ♘xe6 g4 53 ♔e2 [53 cxd5] 53 ... dxc4 54 bxc4 ♔c6 55 ♔f2 b5 56 cxb5+ ♔xb5 57 d5 ♘f5 58 e4 ♘d6 59 ♘g5 ♔c4 60 ♔g3 ♔d4 61 ♔xg4 ♘xe4 62 ♔xe4 ♔xd5 **½-½**
L/N3145

**183?-★MN-2**
**Newham– Macdonnell, A.**
[Walker]
⟨♙f7⟩ 1 e4 ... 2 d4 ♘c6 3 f4 d5 4 f5 dxe4 5 ♕h5+ ♔d7 6 d5 [6 ♗c4] 6 ... ♘d4 7 ♕d1 c5 8 g4 ♔e8 9 c3 e5 10 h4 ♗e7 11 cxd4 ♗xh4+ 12 ♔e2 cxd4 13 ♕b3 ♗d7 14 ♘d2 ♕g5 15 ♕h3 ♗xf5 16 ♘xe4 ♗xg4+ 17 ♘f3 ♕g6 18 ♘d6+ ♔d7 19 ♕xg4+ ♕xg4 20 ♗h3 ♕xh3 21 ♖xh3 ♔xd6 22 ♖xh4 ♘f6 23 ♗g5 ♔xd5 24 ♗xf6 gxf6

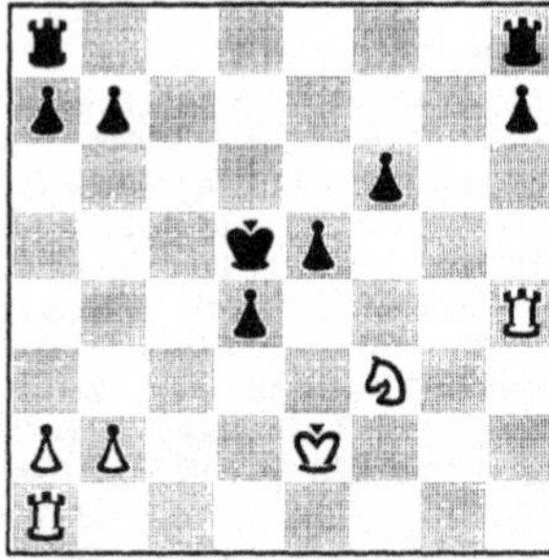

25 ♖ah1 ♖ag8 26 ♔f2 ♖g7 27 ♖h6 ♖c7 28 ♖xf6 ♖c2+ 29 ♔f1 ♖c1+ 30 ♘e1 d3 31 ♖h2 e4 32 ♖ff2 ♖d1 33 ♖d2 ♖f8+ 34 ♖df2 d2 **0-1**
L/N3145

**183?-★MN-3**
**Newham= Macdonnell, A.**
[Walker]
⟨♙f7⟩ 1 e4 ... 2 d4 ♘c6 3 e5 d5 4 c3 e6 5 ♗d3 ♘ge7 6 ♗g5 ♔d7 7 ♘d2 h6 8 ♗e3 g6 9 ♘b3 ♘f5 10 ♕f3 ♕e8 11 h4 ♘d8 12 ♗xf5 gxf5 13 h5 ♘f7 14 ♘h3 c6 15 ♕e2 a5 16 ♘f4 b6 17 ♘g6 ♖g8 18 ♕d2 ♗a6 19 a3 ♔c7 20 ♕c1 c5 21 dxc5 bxc5 22 ♘xf8 ♖xf8 23 ♘xc5 ♔c6 24 ♘xa6 ♖xa6 25 ♗f4 ♕b8 26 ♖h3 ♖g8 27 ♖g3 ♖b6 28 b4 ♖xg3 29 ♗xg3 ♔d7 30 ♕e3 ♖c6 31 ♖d1 ♔e7 32 f4 ♖c4 33 ♖d4 ♖c7 34 ♗h4+ ♔d7 a4 ♕c8 36 ♔d2 ♕g8 37 ♕g3 ♕e8 38 ♕f3 ♔c8 39 ♕d1 axb4 40 ♖xb4 d4 41 ♖xd4 ♕c6 42 ♕f3 ♕a6 43 ♕g3 ♕c6 44 ♕f3 ♕a6 45 ♕d3 ♕c6 [46 ♗f2+–] **½-½**
L/N3145

**183?-★MN-4**
**Newham– Macdonnell, A.**
[Walker]
⟨♙f7⟩ 1 e4 ... 2 d4 ♘c6 3 e5 d5 4 ♘f3 ♗e6 5 ♗d3 ♕d7 6 ♗e3 g6 7 ♘bd2 ♘h6 8 c3 ♗g7 9 ♕c2 ♘f5 10 ♘g5 0-0-0 11 ♘b3 b6 12 ♗a6+ ♔b8 ♘c5 bxc5 14 ♕b3+ ♘b4 15 cxb4 [15 a3+–] 15 ... c4 16 ♕c3 ♘xe3 17 fxe3 ♗h6 18 ♘xe6 ♕xe6 19 b5 [19 ♗b5] 19 ... ♖hf8 20 0-0-0 ♖f2 21 ♖d2 ♖df8 22 b3 ♖f1+ 23 ♖xf1 ♖xf1+ 24 ♔b2 ♕f5 25 ♖c2 ♕e4 26 ♖e2 ♕b1+ 27 ♔a3 e6 28 bxc4 ♖c1 29 ♕b3 ♕a1 30 ♖c2 ♖e1 31 ♖f2 ♕c1+ 32 ♔a4 ♖xe3 33 ♕b4 ♕d1+ 34 ♔a5 ♖a3+ 35 ♕xa3 ♕e1+ 36 ♔a4 ♕xf2 37 cxd5 ♕xd4+ 38 ♕b4 ♕xd5 39 a3 ♕xe5 40 h4 ♕d6 41 ♕xd6 cxd6 42 ♔b3 ♔c7 43 a4 ♗d2 44 g4 h6 45 ♔c4 ♗e1 46 h5 g5 47 ♔d4 ♗f2+ 48 ♔e4 ♗b6 49 ♔d3 d5 50 ♔e2 e5 51 ♔d3 e4+ 52 ♔e2 d4 53 ♔d2 d3 54 ♔c3 ♗a5+ **0-1**
L/N3145

**183?-★MN-5**
**Macdonnell, A.+ Nixon**
⟨♘b1⟩ 1 e4 e5 2 f4 exf4 3 ♘f3 d5 4 e5 ♗f5 5 d4 g5 6 h4 ♗e7 7 hxg5 ♗xg5 8 ♖h5 ♗g4 9 ♖xg5 ♗xf3 10 ♖xg8+ ♖xg8 11 ♕xf3 ♕h4+ 12 ♔d1 ♕g3 13 ♗xf4 ♕xf3+ 14 gxf3 ♘c6 15 c3 ♖g1 16 ♔d2 h5 17 ♖e1 ♔e7 18 ♗e3 ♖g3 19 f4 ♖ag8 20 f5 ♘d8 21 f6+ ♔e8 22 ♗f4 ♖3g4 23 ♗h2 ♖e4 24 ♖xe4 dxe4 25 d5 h4 26 ♗b5+ ♘c6 27 dxc6 b6 28 ♗f4 h3 29 e6 h2 30 ♗xh2 ♖g2+ 31 ♗e2 ♖xh2 32 e7 ♖f2 33 ♔e3 ♖xf6 34 b4 ♖e6 35 ♗c4 ♖xe7 **0-1**
L/N3145

**183?-★MN-6**
**Macdonnell, A.+ Nixon**
⟨♘b1⟩ 1 e4 e5 2 ♗c4 ♗c5 3 b4 ♗xb4 4 f4 exf4 5 ♘f3 g5 6 0-0 d6 7 c3 ♗c5+ 8 d4 ♗b6 9 e5 d5 10 ♗d3 ♗g4 11 a4 a6 12 a5 ♗a7 13 ♗a3 ♗xf3 14 ♕xf3 ♘c6 15 ♖ae1 ♘ge7 16 e6 ♘g6 17 ♕h5 ♕f6 18 ♕h3 ♘ce7 19 exf7+ ♔xf7 20 ♕d7 ♘e5 21 ♕xc7 ♗b8 22 dxe5 ♕e6 23 ♕xb7 ♖a7 24 ♕b1 ♗xe5 25 h4 h6 26 ♕d1 ♕f6 27 ♕h5+ ... ? **1-0**
L/N3145

**183?-★MN-7**
**Macdonnell, A.– Nixon**
⟨♘b1⟩ 1 e4 e5 2 ♗c4 c6 3 ♕e2 ♘f6 4 f4 d5 5 exd5 e4 6 dxc6 ♘xc6 7 c3 ♗e7 8 h3 0-0 9 g4 ♘a5 10 ♗b5 a6 11 ♗a4 ♕d3 12 ♕xd3 exd3 13 ♘f3 b5 14 ♗d1 ♗d6 15 f5 ♗g3+ 16 ♔f1 ♖fe8 17 ♔g2 ♗f4 18 a4 ♗b7 19 ♖hf1 ♘c4 20 ♔g1 ♖e2 21 axb5 axb5 22 ♖xa8+ ♗xa8 23 ♖f2 ♖xf2 24 ♔xf2 ♘e4+ 25 ♔e1 ♗g3+ 26 ♔f1 ♘f2 27 ♔g2 ♘xd1 28 ♔xg3 ♗xf3 29 ♔xf3 ♘dxb2 30 ♔e4 ♔f8 31 ♔d4 ♔e7 32 ♔c5 ♘d1 33 ♔xb5 ♘e5 34 g5 ♘f2 **0-1**
L/N3145

**183?-★MN-8**
**Macdonnell, A.– Nixon**
⟨♘b1⟩ 1 e4 e5 2 f4 exf4 3 ♘f3 d5 4 e5 ♗e6 5 d4 c5 6 c3 ♘c6 7 ♗xf4 h6 8 ♗d3 cxd4 9 cxd4 g5 10 ♗e3 ♗b4+ 11 ♘d2 h5 12 0-0 ♕b6 13 ♘f3 g4 14 ♘g5 ♘xe5 15 ♘xe6 fxe6 16 dxe5 ♕xe3+ 17 ♔h1 0-0-0 18 ♕b3 ♕b6 19 ♖f7 ♘e7 20 a3 ♗c5 21 ♕c2 ♘c6 22 b4 ♗d4 23 ♖c1 ♔b8 24 a4 ♖c8 25 a5 ♘xe5 26 ♖h7 ♕d6 27 a6 ♘d7 28 ♖xh8 ♖xh8 29 axb7 ♔xb7 30 ♕a4 ♗b6 31 ♗a6+ ♔b8 32 ♖c6 ♕e5 33 ♖c1 ♗c7 34 ♕b5+ ♘b6 35 ♖xc7 ♕xc7 36 ♕f1 ♘c4 37 h3 g3 38 b5 ♘e3

39 ♕a1 ♖f8 40 b6 a×b6 41 ♗e2 ♘×g2 42 ♕a3 ♖f2 43 ♗f3 ♘e1 44 ♗g2 ♘×g2 **0-1** L/N3145

### 183?-★MP-1
**Popert, H.W.+Macdonnell, A.**

⟨♙f7⟩ 1 e4 d6 2 d4 ♘f6 3 ♘c3 ♘c6 4 d5 ♘e5 5 f4 ♘f7 6 ♘f3 e5 7 d×e6 ♗×e6 8 f5 ♗d7 9 ♗c4 ♘e5 10 ♘×e5 d×e5 11 0-0 g6 12 f×g6 h×g6 13 ♗g5 ♗e7 14 ♘d5 ♗c5+ 15 ♔h1 ♘×e4 16 ♘×c7+ ♕×c7 17 ♗f7+ ♔f8 18 ♗×g6+ ♗f5 19 ♕g4 ♕f7 20 ♗×f5 ♘f2+ 21 ♖×f2 ♗×f2 22 ♖f1 ♕×a2 23 ♗e6 **1-0** L/N3145

### 183?-★MP-2
**Macdonnell, A.+Popert, H.W.**

⟨♘b1⟩ 1 e4 e5 2 ♘f3 ♘c6 3 ♗c4 ♗c5 4 b4 ♗×b4 5 c3 ♗c5 6 0-0 d6 7 d4 e×d4 8 e×d4 ♗b6 9 h3 h6 10 ♗b2 ♘f6 11 e5 d×e5 12 ♗a3 e4 13 ♕b3 ♕d7 14 ♘e5 ♘×e5 15 d×e5 ♘h5 16 ♖ad1 ♕f5 17 ♗×f7+ ♕×f7 18 ♖d8+ ♔×d8 19 ♕×f7 **1-0** L/N3145

### 183?-★MP-3
**Macdonnell, A.+Pelling**

⟨♘b1⟩ 1 e4 e5 2 ♘f3 ♘c6 3 ♗c4 ♗c5 4 b4 ♗×b4 5 c3 ♗c5 6 0-0 d6 7 d4 e×d4 8 c×d4 ♗b6 9 h3 ♘f6 10 e5 d×e5 11 ♗a3 ♘d5 12 ♕a4 ♘c3 13 ♘×e5 ♗e6 14 ♗×e6 f×e6 15 ♕c4 ♘×d4 16 ♖fe1 ♘cb5 17 ♘g6 ♘×a3 18 ♖×e6+ ♔f7 19 ♖e7+ ♔×g6 20 ♕f7+ ♔h6 21 ♕×g7+ ♔h5 22 g4+ ♔h4 23 ♕h6# **1-0** L/N3145

### 183?-★MP-4
**Macdonnell, A.+Perigal, G.**

⟨♖a1⟩ 1 e4 e5 2 f4 e×f4 3 ♗c4 d6 4 ♘f3 ♗e6 5 ♗×e6 f×e6 6 c3 c6 7 d4 e5 8 d×e5 d×e5 9 ♕b3 ♕e7 10 0-0 ♘f6 11 ♘bd2 ♘a6 ♔h1 ♘c5 13 ♕c4 0-0-0 14 b4 ♖×d2 15 ♘×d2 ♘cd7 16 b5 ♔b8 17 b×c6 ♘c5 18 c×b7 ♕c7 19 ♖e1 ♕b6 20 ♘f3 ♗d6 21 ♘g5 ♘g4 22 ♖f1 h5 23 ♘f7 ♘×e4 24 ♕×e4 ♘f2+ 25 ♖×f2 ♕×f2 26 h3 f3 27 g×f3 ♖f8 28 ♕d5 ♗c7 29 ♗g5 e4 30 ♘e5 e×f3 31 ♘d6# **1-0** L/N3145

### 183?-★MS-1
**Slous, F.L.=Macdonnell, A.**

⟨♙f7⟩ 1 e4 ... 2 d4 ♘c6 3 e5 d5 4 h4 e6 5 g4 ♗b4+ 6 c3 ♗a5 7 ♗d3 ♕e7 8 g5 ♕f7 9 h5 ♘ge7 10 g6 h×g6 11 h×g6 ♕f8 12 ♖h7 ♗d7 13 ♕g4 0-0-0 14 ♘f3 ♖e8 15 ♗e3 ♘f5 16 ♘bd2 ♘ce7 17 0-0-0 c6 18 ♖g1 b5 19 b4 ♗b6 20 ♕h5 ♖g8 21 ♖f1 a5 22 a3 a×b4 23 a×b4 ♔c7 24 ♔b2 ♖a8 25 ♘b3 ♕b8 26 ♖a1 ♖×a1 27 ♘×a1 ♕a7 28 ♖h8 ♕b8 29 ♖×g8 ♕×g8 30 ♘g5 ♗e8 31 ♗×f5 ♘×f5 32 ♘f7 ♕f8 33 ♗g5 ♗×d4 34 c×d4 ♕×b4+ 35 ♘b3 ♘×d4 36 ♕d1 c5 37 ♗d8+ ♔b8 38 ♗a5 ♕a4 39 ♗c3 c4 40 ♗×d4 c×b3 41 ♔b1 b4 42 ♗b2 ♗b5 43 ♕d4 ♕a5 44 ♔c1 ♕c7+ 45 ♔b1 ♔a8 46 ♕d1 ♗a4 47 ♘g5 ♕c6 48 f4 ♕c8 49 ♘f3 ♗e8 50 f5 ♕c4 51 ♘d2 ♕d3+ 52 ♔c1 e×f5 53 ♕×b3 ♕×b3 54 ♘×b3 ♗×g6 55 e6 ♔b7 56 ♗×g7 ♔b6 57 ♔d2 ♔b5 58 ♔e3 **½-½** L/N3145

### 183?-★MS-2
**Macdonnell, A.+Slous, F.L.**

⟨♘b1⟩ 1 e4 e5 2 ♘f3 ♘c6 3 ♗c4 ♗c5 4 b4 ♗×b4 5 c3 ♗c5 6 0-0 d6 7 d4 ♗b6 8 d×e5 ♘×e5 9 ♘×e5 d×e5 10 ♗×f7+ ♔e7 11 ♗a3+ c5 12 ♕b3 ♘f6 13 ♖ad1 ♕c7 14 f4 ♘g4 15 f×e5 ♕×e5 16 g3 ♘e3 17 ♗g8 ♗e6 18 ♖f7+ ♔e8 19 ♕b5+ ♗d7 20 ♕×d7# **1-0** L/N3145

### 183?-★MT-1
**Macdonnell, A.+Taverner, T.**

⟨♘b1⟩ 1 e4 e5 2 ♗c4 ♗c5 3 b4 ♗×b4 4 f4 ♕f6 5 ♘f3 ♘c6 6 0-0 e×f4 7 e5 ♕e7 8 ♔h1 ♘a5 9 ♗e2 d6 10 c3 ♗c5 11 ♕a4+ ♘c6 12 d4 d×e5 13 d×c5 ♗g4 14 ♘×e5 ♗×e2 15 ♘×c6 ♕d7 16 ♕e4+ ♕e6 17 ♕×e6+ f×e6 18 ♖fe1 ♗c4 19 ♘a5 ♗d5 20 c4 b6 21 c×d5 b×a5 22 ♖×e6+ ♔d7 23 c6+ ♔d8 24 ♗b2 ♘f6 25 ♖×f6 ♖b8 26 ♗e5 ♖b5 27 ♖f7 ♖×d5 28 ♗×c7+ ♔e8 29 ♖×g7 ♔f8 30 ♖d7 ♖×d7 31 c×d7 **1-0** L/N3145

### 183?-★MT-2
**Macdonnell, A.+Taverner, T.**

⟨♘b1⟩ 1 e4 e5 2 f4 e×f4 3 ♘f3 g5 4 ♗c4 d6 5 0-0 ♗g7 6 c3 ♗e6 7 ♗×e6 f×e6 8 ♕b3 e5 9 ♘×g5 ♕×g5 10 ♕×b7 ♘f6 11 ♕×a8 ♔d7 12 ♕×a7 ♘c6 13 ♕a4 h5 14 d4 ♘×e4 15 d5 ♘f6 16 d×c6+ ♔e7 17 ♕b3 ♘e8 18 a4 ♕g4 19 ♕d1 ♕e6 20 b4 h4 21 h3 ♗f6 22 ♕g4 ♕c4 23 ♕d7+ ♔f8 24 ♗×f4 e×f4 25 ♖ae1 ♗e5 25 ♖×f4+ ♕×f4 27 ♖f1 ♕×f1+ 28 ♔×f1 ♗×c3 29 b5 ♗a5 30 ♕c8 ♖h5 31 ♕a6 ♗b4 32 a5 ♖c5 33 b6 c×b6 34 a×b6 ♖×c6 35 ♕b5 ♖c1+ 36 ♔e2 ♗c5 37 b7 ♗a7 38 b8♕ ♗×b8 39 ♕×b8 ♖c2+ 40 ♔f1 ♖c1+ 41 ♔f2 ♖c2+ 42 ♔g1 ♖c1+ 43 ♔h2 **1-0** L/N3145

### 183?-★MW-1
**Walker, G.=Macdonnell, A.**

⟨♙f7⟩ 1 e4 ... 2 d4 ♘c6 3 ♗d3 e5 4 d5 ♘ce7 5 f4 e×f4 6 ♗×f4 ♘g6 7 ♗e3 d6 8 ♘f3 ♗g4 9 0-0 ♘f6 10 h3 ♗×f3 11 ♕×f3 ♕d7 12 ♘d2 ♗e7 13 ♘b3 0-0 14 ♕f5 ♕e8 15 ♘d4 ♘h4 16 ♕e6+ ♔h8 17 ♘f5 ♘×f5 18 ♖×f5 ♕f7 19 ♕×f7 ♖×f7 20 ♗d4 c6 21 c4 ♖e8 22 ♖af1 c5 23 ♗c3 ♗d8 24 g4 h6 25 h4 ♖ff8 26 g5 h×g5 27 h×g5 ♘d7 28 ♖f7 ♖×f7 29 ♖×f7 ♖e7 30 g6 ♖×f7 31 g×f7 ♗f6 32 e5 d×e5 33 ♗f5 ♘f8 34 d6 g6 35 d7 g×f5 36 ♗×e5 ♘×d7 37 ♗×f6+ ♔h7 38 ♗e7 ♔g7 39 f8♕+ ♘×f8 40 ♗×c5 b6 41 ♗×f8+ ♔×f8 42 ♔f2 ♔f7 43 ♔e3 ♔f6 44 ♔f4 ♔e6 45 b4 ♔f6 46 c5 b×c5 47 b×c5 ♔e6 48 c6 ♔d6 49 ♔×f5 ♔×c6 50 ♔e4 **½-½** L/N3145

### 183?-★MW-2
**Walker, G.+Macdonnell, A.**

⟨♙f7⟩ 1 e4 ... 2 d4 ♘c6 3 e5 d5 4 h4 ♗e6 5 c3 ♗f7 6 ♗d3 g6 7 ♗e3 e6 8 ♘f3 ♗h6 9 ♘g5 ♕e7 10 ♕f3 ♗g7 11 h5 ♘h6 12 ♘×f7 ♕×f7 13 ♗×h6 ♗×h6 14 h×g6 h×g6 15 ♖h3 ♕×f3 16 ♖×f3 ♗c1 17 ♗×g6+ ♔d7 18 ♘d2 ♗×b2 19 ♖b1 ♖h1+ 20 ♘f1 ♗a3 21 ♖×b7 ♖g8 22 ♖g3 a5 23 ♖b5 ♗c1 24 ♖×d5+ ♔c8 25 ♗f5 ♖f8 26 ♖g8 ♖×g8 27 ♗×e6+ ♔b7 28 ♗×g8 ♔b6 29 a4 **1-0** L/N3145

### 183?-★MW-3
**Walker, G.=Macdonnell, A.**

⟨♙f7⟩ 1 e4 ... 2 d4 d6 3 ♗d3 ♘d7 4 f4 e5 5 c3 ♘gf6 6 ♘f3 e×f4 7 ♗×f4 ♗e7 8 ♘g5 ♘f8 9 ♕b3 d5 10 ♗e5 ♘g6 11 ♗×f6 ♗×f6 12 ♘f3 ♘f4 13 ♕c2 d×e4 14 ♗×e4 0-0 15 ♗×h7+ ♔h8 16 0-0 g6 17 ♕e4 ♕d6 18 ♘e5 ♗×e5 19 d×e5 ♘h3+ 20 g×h3 ♖×f1+ 21 ♔×f1 ♗×h3+ 22 ♔e2 ♕a6+ 23 c4 ♗f5 24 ♕h4 g5 25 ♕d4 ♔×h7 26 ♘d2 ♕h6 27 ♖h1 ♕h5+ 28 ♔e1 ♖f8 29 h4 ♗c2 30 ♘e4 ♔g6 31 ♘×g5 ♖f5 32 ♔d2 ♖×g5 33 h×g5 ♕×h1 34 ♔×c2 ♔×g5 35 e6 ♕g2+ 36 ♕d2+ ♕×d2+ 37 ♔×d2 ♔f6 38 ♔c3 ♔×e6 39 ♔b4 ♔e5 40 ♔c5 ♔e4 41 b4 ♔d3 42 b5 ♔c3 43 ♔d5 ♔b4 44 ♔d4 ♔a3 45 ♔d5 ♔b4 46 ♔d4 a5 47 b×a6 b×a6 48 ♔d5 a5 49 ♔d4 a4 50 ♔d5 a3 51 ♔d4 c6 52 c5 ♔b5 53 ♔c3 ♔×c5 54 ♔b3 ♔d4 55 ♔×a3 ♔c3 56 ♔a4 c5 57 ♔b5 ♔d4 58 a4 c4 59 a5 c3 60 a6 c2 61 a7 c1♕ 62 a8♕ ♕b1+ 63 ♔a6 **½-½** L/N3145

### 183?-★MW-4
**Walker, G.− Macdonnell, A.**

[Walker]

⟨♙f7⟩ 1 e4 ... 2 d4 ♘c6 3 ♗d3 e5 4 d5 ♘ce7 5 ♗g5 ♘f6 6 ♗xf6 gxf6 7 ♕h5+ ♘g6 8 f4 exf4 9 ♘h3 ♕e7 10 ♘xf4 ♕f7 11 ♘xg6 ♕xg6 12 ♕xg6+ hxg6 13 ♘d2 ♗c5 14 c3 d6 15 ♔e2 ♗g4+ 16 ♘f3 ♔f7 17 ♖af1 ♔g7 18 h3 ♗d7 19 ♘d4 ♖ae8 20 ♔d2 c6 21 ♘b3 ♗b6 22 c4 a5 23 ♘c1 ♗d4 24 ♘e2 ♗c5 25 ♘c3 ♗d4 26 ♘e2 ♗e5 27 a3 cxd5 28 cxd5 ♗xb2 29 ♖b1 ♗xa3 30 ♖xb7 ♗b4+ 31 ♔e3 ♖e7 32 ♗b5 ♖d8 33 ♘f4 ♗c5+ 34 ♔d3 ♔f7 35 ♗xd7 ♖dxd7 36 ♖xd7 ♖xd7 37 ♘e6 ♗b4 38 ♖c1 g5 39 ♔e3 ♖a7 40 ♘d8+ ♔g6 41 ♘c6 ♖b7 42 ♘xb4 axb4 43 ♖b1 b3 44 g4 b2 45 ♔d4 ♖b4+ 46 ♔d3 ♔f7 47 ♔c2 ♖xe4 48 ♖xb2 ♖e2+ 49 ♔c1 ♖xb2 50 ♔xb2 f5 51 ♔c3 ♔f6 52 ♔d4 ♔g6 53 ♔e3 f4+ 54 ♔f3 ♔f6 55 h4 gxh4 56 ♔xf4 ♔g6 57 g5 [57 ♔e3=] 57 ... h3 58 ♔g3 ♔xg5 59 ♔xh3 ♔f5 60 ♔g3 ♔e5 61 ♔f3 ♔xd5 **0-1** L/N3145

### 183?-★MW-5
**Walker, G.+ Macdonnell, A.**

⟨♙f7⟩ 1 e4 ... 2 d4 ♘c6 3 e5 d5 4 ♘f3 ♗g4 5 c3 e6 6 ♗d3 g6 7 h3 ♗xf3 8 ♕xf3 ♘h6 9 h4 ♕d7 10 ♗g5 ♗g7 11 ♘d2 ♖f8 12 ♕h3 ♕f7 13 0-0-0 ♘e7 14 ♘f3 ♘hg8 15 h5 0-0-0 16 h6 ♗h8 17 ♕g4 ♖de8 18 ♗e3 ♘f5 19 ♗xf5 gxf5 20 ♕h5 ♕d7 21 ♗f4 ♘e7 22 ♘h4 ♖g8 23 g3 ♘g6 24 ♘xg6 ♖xg6 25 ♕e2 a5 26 ♕d2 ♖g4 27 ♖h5 ♖eg8 28 ♖g5 ♖4xg5 29 ♗xg5 c5 30 ♗f4 c4 31 ♖h1 b5 32 ♖h5 ♔c7 33 ♖xf5 b4 34 cxb4 ♕e7 35 ♗g5 ♕e8 36 ♖f4 ♖xg5 37 bxa5 ♕e7 38 a6 ♔b6

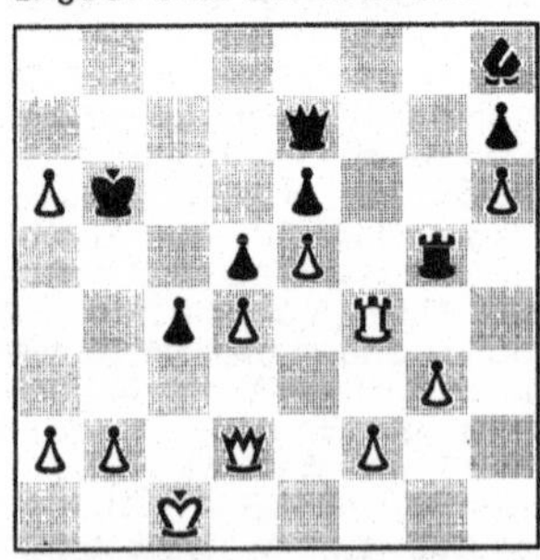

39 ♖f3 ♖g8 40 a7 ♔b7 41 ♕f4 ♔a8 42 ♕f7 ♕g5+ 43 ♔c2 ♕g4 44 ♔c3 ♖c8 45 a4 ♗xe5 46 dxe5 d4+ 47 ♔d2 c3+ 48 bxc3 dxc3+ 49 ♖xc3 ♕d4+ 50 ♖d3 ♕b2+ 51 ♔e3 ♕b6+ 52 ♔e2 ♕b2+ 53 ♔f3 ♕c2 54 ♖e3 ♕c6+ 55 ♔g4 ♕xa4+ 56 ♔h3 **1-0** L/N3145

### 183?-★MW-6
**Walker, G.= Macdonnell, A.**

[Walker]

⟨♙f7⟩ 1 e4 ... 2 d4 ♘c6 3 e5 [3 ♘c3] 3 ... d5 4 c3 ♗f5 5 g4 ♗e4 6 f3 ♗xb1 7 ♖xb1 e6 8 ♗f4 h5 9 ♗d3 hxg4 10 ♗g6+ ♔d7 11 fxg4 ♕h4+ 12 ♗g3 ♕g5 13 ♗d3 ♘h6 14 ♗e2 ♕e3 15 ♔f1 ♗e7 16 ♔g2 ♖af8 17 ♘h3 ♘f7 18 ♕d3 ♕h6 19 ♗f4 ♕h4 20 ♕g3 ♕h7 21 ♗d3 g6 22 ♖af1 ♗h4 23 ♕e3 ♗e7 24 ♖f3 ♕g7 25 g5 ♖h5 26 ♖g3 ♕h7 27 ♖g4 ♗d8 28 ♗b5 a6 29 ♗xc6+ bxc6 30 ♖f1 ♗e7 31 b4 a5 32 a3 axb4 33 cxb4 ♖h8 34 ♖f3 ♘d8 35 ♘f2 ♘f7 36 h4 ♕g8 37 ♗g3 ♖8h7 38 ♘d3 ♕h8 39 ♘c5+ ♗xc5 40 bxc5 ♕a8 41 ♖f6 ♖g7 42 ♖gf4 ♖hh7 43 ♕d3 ♘h8 44 ♖f8 ♕b7 45 ♖f3 ♔e7 46 ♖8f6 ♖g8 47 ♔h3 ♕b2 48 ♕a6 ♕b5 49 ♕a7 ♕b8 50 ♕a5 ♘f7 51 ♔g4 ♕b7 52 ♕a4 ♖a8 53 ♕c2 ♘h8 54 ♖b3 ♕a6 55 ♕b2 ♖g7 56 ♖b8 ♖g8 57 ♖xg8 ♖xg8 58 ♖f3 ♕c8 59 a4 ♕a6 60 ♕c2 ♖a8 61 ♖a3 ♖f8 62 ♖f3 ♖a8 63 ♖a3 ♖f8 64 ♕d3 ♕a5 65 ♕c3 ♕a6 66 ♕d3 ♕a5 67 ♕c3 ♕a6 68 ♕d3 ♕a5 69 ♖a1 ♕b4 70 a5 ♕b2 71 ♖b1 ♕a2 72 ♖f1 ♖f5 73 a6 ♘f7 74 ♖xf5 exf5+ 75 ♔h3 ♕a1 76 ♗f2 ♘d8 77 ♔g2 ♘e6 78 ♗e3 ♕a2+ 79 ♔g3 ♘g7 80 ♔f3 ♔d7 81 ♗f4 ♔c8 82 ♗g3 ♔b8 83 ♕e2 ♕xe2+ 84 ♔xe2 ♔a7 86 ♗f4 ♔xa6 86 ♔e3 ♔b5 87 ♔d3 ♔a4 88 ♔c3 ♘e6 89 ♗e3 ♔a5 90 ♗f2 ♔a6 91 ♔d3 ♔b7 92 ♔e3 ♔c8 93 ♗g3 ♔d7 94 ♗f2 ♘g7 95 ♔f4 ♔e6 96 ♗g3 ♔d7 97 ♔e3 ♔c8 98 ♗f4 ♔d7 99 ♔e2 ♔e6 100 ♗g3 ♔d7 101 ♔f3 ♘h5 102 ♗f2 f4 103 ♗e1 ♔e6 104 ♔g4 ♔e7 105 ♗d2 ♘g7 106 ♗e1 ♘e6 107 ♗f2 ♔e8 108 h5 ♔f7 109 h6 ♔f8 **½-½** L/N3145

### 183?-★MW-7
**Walker, G.+ Macdonnell, A.**

⟨♙f7⟩ 1 e4 ... 2 d4 d6 3 e5 dxe5 4 dxe5 ♕xd1+ 5 ♔xd1 ♘c6 6 f4 ♗g4+ 7 ♗e2 0-0-0+ 8 ♗d2 ♗f5 9 g4 ♗e4 10 ♗f3 ♗xf3+ 11 ♘xf3 e6 12 ♘g5 ♘h6 13 h3 ♖e8 14 ♘c3 ♗c5 15 ♘ce4 ♗b6 16 c4 ♗d4 17 ♔c2 ♖e7 18 ♖ad1 ♘f7 19 ♘xf7 ♖xf7 20 ♘g5 ♖e7 21 b4 ♗f2 22 ♘e4 ♗h4 23 ♗c3 ♖f7 24 ♖hf1 ♖hf8 25 f5 ♘d8 26 f6 gxf6 27 exf6 h6 28 b5 b6 29 a4 ♘b7 30 ♖d3 ♖g8 31 ♔b3 ♖e8 32 a5 bxa5 33 ♔a4 e5 34 ♖d5 **1-0** L/N3145

### 183?-★MW-8
**Walker, G.+ Macdonnell, A.**

[Walker]

⟨♙f7⟩ 1 e4 ... 2 d4 e6 3 c4 ♗b4+ 4 ♘c3 ♕e7 5 ♗d3 c5 6 d5 e5 7 f4 d6 8 fxe5 ♗xc3+ 9 bxc3 ♕xe5 10 ♗d2 ♘f6 11 ♘f3 ♕h5 12 ♗f4 0-0 13 ♗xd6 ♖e8 14 e5 ♘g4 15 ♕e2 ♘xe5 16 ♘xe5 ♗g4 17 ♕e4 ♘d7 18 0-0 ♘xe5 19 ♗xe5 ♖xe5 20 ♕f4 ♖ae8 21 h3 ♗c8 22 g4 ♖g5 23 ♖ae1 h6 24 ♔g2 [24 ♔h2] 24 ... ♖d8 25 ♕e4 g6 26 ♕f4 ♗f5 27 ♖e5 ♖f8 28 ♗xf5 gxf5 29 ♖xf5 ♖gxf5 30 gxf5 ♔h7 31 h4 ♕e2+ 32 ♖f2 ♖g8+ 33 ♔h3 ♕d3+ 34 ♕f3 ♕xc4 35 f6 ♖f8 36 f7 ♕a6 37 ♖g2 ♕d6 28 ♕g4 **1-0** L/N3145

### 183?-★MW-9
**Walker, G.= Macdonnell, A.**

[Walker]

⟨♙f7⟩ 1 e4 ... 2 d4 e6 3 c4 ♗b4+ 4 ♘c3 ♕e7 5 ♗d3 c5 6 d5 e5 7 f4 exf4 8 ♗xf4 ♘f6 9 e5 0-0 10 ♕e2 ♘xd5 11 ♗xh7+ ♔xh7 12 ♕e4+ ♔h8 13 cxd5 ♗xc3+ 14 bxc3 d6 15 ♘f3 [15 e5] 15 ... ♗f5 16 ♕e3 dxe5 17 ♕xe5 ♕f7 18 0-0 ♘d7 19 ♕e1 ♕xd5 20 ♕h4+ ♔g8 21 ♕g5 ♖ae8 22 ♘h4 ♗e6 23 ♕xd5 ♗xd5 24 ♖ad1 ♗c6 25 ♗d6 ♖xf1+ 26 ♔xf1 ♖e3 27 ♖c1 ♖d3 28 ♗f4 ♘f6 29 ♔e2 c4 30 ♘f3 ♗xf3+ 31 gxf3 ♘d5 32 ♗d2 ♔f7 33 ♖b1 b6 34 ♖c1 ♔f6 35 ♖c2 a5 36 a4 g6 37 ♔f2 ♔f5 38 ♔g3 g5 39 h3 ♘f6 40 ♔f2 ♘d5 41 ♔g3 ♘c7 42 ♗e1 ♘d5 43 ♗d2 ♘e7 44 ♔f2 ♘d5 45 ♔g2 ♘f4+ 46 ♔g3 ♔e5 47 ♗xf4+ gxf4+ 48 ♔g4 ♖e3 49 h4 ♖e1 50 h5 ♖g1+ 51 ♔h4 ♔f5 52 ♖h2 ♖g3 53 h6 ♔g6 54 ♖b2 ♖xf3 55 ♖xb6+ ♔h7 56 ♔g5 ♖xc3 57 ♖b7+ ♔h8 58 ♖b8+ ♔h7 **½-½** L/N3145

### 183?-★MW-10
**Walker, G.+ Macdonnell, A.**

[Walker]

⟨♙f7⟩ 1 e4 ... 2 d4 ♘c6 3 e5 d5 4 h4 ♗e6 5 ♘f3 h6 6 ♗d3 ♗f7 7 c3 e6 8 h5 ♕d7 9 ♘h4 0-0-0 110 ♗g6 ♕e8 11 ♗xf7 ♕xf7 12 ♘g6 ♖h7 13 ♕d3 ♕f5 14 ♕xf5 exf5 15 f4 ♘ge7 16 ♘xf8 ♖xf8 17 ♘d2 ♖g8 18 ♘f3 g6 19 hxg6 ♖xg6 20 ♔f2 ♖hg7 21 ♘h4 ♖g4 22 ♗e3 ♘d8 23 ♖ag1 ♖g3 24 ♘f3 ♖7g6 25 ♖h5 ♖3g4 26 ♘h4 ♖b6 27 ♖b1 ♔d7 28 ♘xf5 ♘xf5 29 ♖xf5 ♖bg6 30 ♖g1 ♖h4 31 g3 ♖h2+ 32 ♖g2 ♖h1 33 g4 ♔e7 34 ♔f3 ♖h3+ 35 ♖g3 ♖h2 36 ♗f2 ♖b6 37 ♖h5 ♖xh5 38 gxh5 ♖xb2 39 ♖g7+ ♘f7 40 f5 ♔f8 41 f6 ♘g5+ 42 ♔e3 ♖xa2 43 ♖xc7 ♖b2 44 ♗h4 ♘e6 45 ♖e7 ♖b6 46

♖h7 a5 47 ♖xh6 a4 48 ♖g6 ♔f7 49 ♖g1 ♖b3 50 ♔d2 ♖b2+ 51 ♔e3 ♖h2 [51 ... b5] 52 ♗g3 ♖xh5 53 ♖b1 ♘d8 54 ♖b4 ♖h3 55 ♔f2 b5 56 ♔g2 a3 57 ♖xb5 ♘c6 58 ♖b3 **1-0** L/N3145

**183?-★MW-11**
**Walker, G.– Macdonnell, A.**
⟨♙f7⟩ 1 e4 ... 2 d4 d6 3 ♗d3 e6 4 ♘f3 ♘d7 5 c4 e5 6 d5 ♗e7 7 ♗e3 ♘gf6 8 ♘c3 0-0 9 h4 ♘g4 10 ♕d2 ♘df6 11 ♘e2 ♗d7 12 ♘g3 c6 13 h5 h6 14 c5 cxd5 15 cxd6 ♗xd6 16 exd5 ♕e7 17 0-0 e4 18 ♘h4 ♗xg3 19 d6 ♗h2+ 20 ♔h1 ♕xd6 21 ♗c4+ ♔h7 22 ♘g6 ♕xd2 23 ♘xf8+ ♖xf8 24 ♗xd2 ♘xh5 25 ♗b4 ♖xf2 **0-1** L/N3145

**183?-★MW-12**
**Walker, G.= Macdonnell, A.**
⟨♙f7⟩ 1 e4 ... 2 d4 ♘c6 3 e5 d5 4 h4 ♗e6 5 ♗e3 ♕d7 6 c3 0-0-0 7 ♗d3 g6 8 ♘d2 ♘h6 9 b4 ♘f5 10 ♘b3 ♘xe3 11 fxe3 ♗g4 12 ♘f3 e6 13 b5 ♘b8 14 ♘bd2 ♗h6 15 ♕e2 ♖hf8 16 a4 ♕e7 17 a5 c5 18 bxc6 ♘xc6 19 a6 b6 20 ♘b3 ♖f7 21 ♗b5 ♕c7 22 ♔d2 ♘e7 23 ♗d3 ♘f5 24 ♗xf5 ♖xf5 25 ♖a4 ♖df8 26 ♖f1 ♕f7 27 ♕b5 ♕d7 28 ♕xd7+ ♔xd7 29 ♔e2 ♖c8 30 ♖c1 ♖h5 31 g3 ♗xf3+ 32 ♔xf3 ♖f5+ 33 ♔e2 ♖cf8 34 g4 ♖f2+ 35 ♔d3 ♗xe3 36 ♖c2 ♖2f3 37 ♘d2 ♗xd2+ 38 ♔xd2 ♖f2+ 39 ♔c1 ♖xc2+ 40 ♔xc2 ♖f4 41 h5 ♖xg4 42 hxg6 hxg6 43 ♖a1 g5 44 ♖h1 ♖h4 45 ♖f1 ♔e7 46 ♔b3 ♖f4 47 ♖g1 g4 48 ♔b4 ♔d7 49 ♔b5 ♔e7 50 ♔c6 ♔f8 51 ♔d6 ♔f7 52 ♖g2 b5 53 ♔c5 ♔g6 54 ♔xb5 ♔f5 55 ♔c6 ♖f3 56 ♔b7 ♖xc3 57 ♔xa7 ♖b3 58 ♖f2+ ♔e4 59 ♔a8 g3 60 a7 ♔xd4 61 ♖d2+ ♔c4 62 ♖d4+ ♔c5 63 ♖d2 ♔c4 64 ♖b2 ♖a3 65 ♔b8 ♔d4 66 a8♕ ♖xa8+ 67 ♔xa8 ♔xe5 68 ♖e2+ ♔f4 69 ♖xe6 d4 70 ♖d6 ♔e3 71 ♖g6 ♔f3 72 ♖f6+ ♔e3 73 ♖g6 ♔f2 74 ♖f6+ ½-½ L/N3145

**183?-★MW-13**
**Walker, G.– Macdonnell, A.**
[Walker]
⟨♙f7⟩ 1 e4 ... 2 d4 ♘c6 3 e5 d5 4 c3 ♗f5 5 ♗d3 ♗xd3 6 ♕xd3 e6 7 h4 g6 8 ♘f3 ♘ge7 9 h5 ♕d7 10 h6 0-0-0 11 ♗g5 ♖e8 12 ♘bd2 ♘d8 13 g4 ♘g8 14 ♗xd8 ♕xd8 15 g5 ♘e7 16 ♘f1 ♘f5 17 ♘e3 ♗e7 18 ♘xf5 gxf5 19 ♕e3 ♖hg8 20 ♖g1 [20 ♖h5] 20 ... ♖g6 21 0-0-0 ♖eg8 22 ♖g3 ♗xg5 23 ♘xg5 ♖xg5 24 ♖dg1 ♖xg3 25 ♖xg3 ♕f8 26 ♕f4 ♖xg3 27 fxg3

27 ... ♔d8 28 ♔d2 ♔e7 29 ♕h4+ ♔e8 30 ♔e3 c6 31 ♕h5+ ♕f7 32 ♕g5 ♕f8 33 ♕d8+ ♕e8 34 ♕f6+ ♕f7 35 ♕h8+ ♕g8 36 ♕f6+ ♕f7 37 ♔f4 ♕xf6 38 exf6 ♔f7 [38 ... ♔e8] 39 ♔e5 b6 40 b3 [40 a4+-] 40 ... c5 41 dxc5 bxc5 42 a3 a6 43 a4 a5 44 b4 d4 45 bxa5 dxc3 46 a6 c2 47 a7 c1♕ 48 a8♕ ♕e3+ 49 ♔d6 ♕d4+ 50 ♔c7 c4 51 ♕h8 ♕xf6 52 ♕xh7+ ♔f8 53 ♕d7 ♕xh6 54 ♕d8+ [54 a5] 54 ... ♔f7 55 ♕d7+ ♔g8 56 a5 c3 57 ♔b6 ♕e3+ 58 ♔b5 ♕e2+ 59 ♔b4 c2 60 ♕c8+ ♔f7 61 ♕c7+ ♔f6 62 ♔b3 ♕d2 63 ♕xc2 ♕xa5 64 ♕f2 e5 65 ♔b2 ♕b4+ 66 ♔c2 ♕d4 67 ♕h2 ♕e4+ 68 ♔c3 ♔g5 69 ♔d2 ♔g4 70 ♕h4+ ♔f3 71 ♕h1+ ♔f2 **0-1** L/N3145

**183?-★MW-14 ○●**
**Worrell– Macdonnell, A.**
⟨♙f7⟩ 1 e4 ... 2 ♘f3 e6 3 d4 d5 4 e5 c5 5 ♗b5+ ♘c6 6 ♗xc6+ bxc6 7 0-0 ♗a6 8 ♖e1 ♕b6 9 c3 cxd4 10 cxd4 ♘e7 11 ♘g5 ♗c8 12 a3 ♘f5 13 ♘f3 c5 14 dxc5 ♗xc5 15 b4 ♗xf2+ 16 ♔h1 ♗xe1 17 ♕xe1 0-0 18 a4 ♖b8 19 b5 a6 20 ♘c3 axb5 21 ♘xb5 ♗d7 22 ♗a3 ♖fc8 23 ♘d6 ♘xd6 24 ♗xd6 ♖a8 25 a5 ♕b2 26 ♖b1 ♕c3 27 ♕f1 h6 28 ♘h4 ♕c4 29 ♘g6 ♕xf1+ 30 ♖xf1 ♗b5 31 ♖b1 ♔h7 32 ♘e7 ♖c3 33 h3 ♗d3 34 ♖b6 ♖xa5 35 ♗b4 ♖a1+ 36 ♔h2 ♖c2 37 ♖xe6 ♗e4 38 ♖d6 ♖xg2# **0-1** L/N3145

**183?-★M?-1**
**?– Macdonnell, A.**
Edinburgh
1 e4 e5 2 ♗c4 ♗c5 3 ♘f3 d6 4 0-0 ♘f6 5 d3 ♗g4 6 c3 c6 7 d4 ♗xf3 8 gxf3 ♗b6 9 ♕d3 ♘bd7 10 f4 d5 11 exd5 e4 12 ♕e2 cxd5 13 ♗b3 0-0 14 ♔h1 ♖e8 15 ♖g1 ♘f8 16 ♗e3 ♘g6 17 ♘d2 ♗c7 18 ♕f1 ♗xf4 19 ♕g2 ♗xe3 20 fxe3 ♖e6 21 ♖af1 b5 22 ♗d1 ♕f8 23 ♕g3 b4 24 c4 ♖c8 25 cxd5 ♘xd5 26 ♗g4 ♖cc6 27 ♗xe6 ♖xe6 28 ♖f5 ♘ge7 29 ♖g5 g6 30 ♕h3 ♔h8 31 ♘c4 ♘f5 32 ♖f1 ♕e7 33 ♖fg1 ♕f6 34 ♖1g4 ♖c6 35 b3 ♕e6 36 ♖g1 ♖a6 37 ♘e5 ♘dxe3 38 ♖xg6 fxg6 39 ♘xg6+ ♕xg6 40 ♖xg6 ♖xg6 41 ♕h5 ♔g7 42 ♕e2 ♘g4 43 d5 e3 44 ♔g1 ♘e5+ 45 ♔f1 ♖f6 46 ♔e1 ♘d4 47 ♕h5 ♘ef3+ 48 ♔d1 e2+ 49 ♔c1 e1♕+ 50 ♔b2 ♕c3+ 51 ♔b1 ♕c2+ 52 ♔a1 ♕c1# **0-1** L/N6123-1842

**183?-★M?-2**
**?– Macdonnell, A.**
1 e4 e5 2 ♗c4 ♗c5 3 ♘f3 d6 4 0-0 ♘f6 5 d3 ♗g4 6 c3 c6 7 d4 ♗xf3 8 gxf3 ♗b6 9 ♕d3 ♘bd7 10 f4 d5 11 exd5 e4 12 ♕e2 cxd5 13 ♗b3 0-0 14 ♔h1 ♖e8 15 ♖g1 ♘f8 16 ♗e3 ♘g6 17 ♘d2 ♗c7 18 ♕f1 ♗xf4 19 ♕g2 ♗xe3 20 fxe3 ♖e6 21 ♖af1 b5 22 ♗d1 ♕f8 23 ♕g3 b4 24 c4 ♖c8 25 cxd5 ♘xd5 26 ♗g4 ♖cc6 27 ♗xe6 ♖xe6 28 ♖f5 ♘ge7 29 ♖g5 g6 30 ♕h3 ♔h8 31 ♘c4 ♘f5 32 ♖f1 ♕e7 33 ♖fg1 ♕f6 34 ♖1g4 ♖c6 35 b3 ♕e6 36 ♖g1 ♖a6 37 ♘e5 ♘dxe3 38 ♖xg6 fxg6 39 ♘xg6+ ♕xg6 40 ♖xg6 ♖xg6 41 ♕h5 ♔g7 42 ♕e2 ♘g4 43 d5 e3 44 ♔g1 ♘e5+ 45 ♔f1 ♖f6 46 ♔e1 ♘d4 47 ♕h5 ♘ef3+ 48 ♔d1 e2+ 49 ♔c1 e1♕+ 50 ♔b2 ♕c3+ 51 ♔b1 ♘d2# **0-1** L/N3145

**183?-★M?-3 ●○**
**Macdonnell, A.+?**
[Walker]
1 e4 e5 2 f4 exf4 3 ♘f3 g5 4 ♗c4 ♗g7 5 d4 d6 6 0-0 ♘c6 7 c3 h6 8 ♕a4 ♔f8 9 ♘a3 f6 10 ♗d2 ♗g4 11 g3 fxg3 12 hxg3 ♗h5 13 ♖ae1 ♗e8 14 ♕c2 ♗f7 15 ♗xf7 ♔xf7 16 ♕b3+ ♔g6 18 ♕c2 ♘ge7 18 e5+ f5 19 g4 h5 20 gxf5+ ♘xf5 21 ♘h4+ ♔h7 22 ♕xf5+ ♔g8 23 ♕f7+ ♔h7 24 ♕g6+ [24 ♕f6] 24 ... ♔g8 25 ♖f7 ♖h7 26 ♘f5 ♕e8 27 ♖xg7+ ♔f8 28 ♖g8# **1-0** L/N3145

**183?-★M?-4**
**Macdonnell, A.+?**
⟨♘b1⟩ 1 e4 e5 2 ♘f3 ♘c6 3 ♗c4 ♗c5 4 b4 ♗xb4 5 c3 ♗a5 6 0-0 ♘f6 7 ♕c2 0-0 8 ♗a3 ♖e8 9 d4 d5 10 exd5 ♘xd5 11 dxe5 ♘xc3 12 ♖ad1 ♘xd1 13 ♖xd1 ♗d7

14 ♗xf7+ ♔xf7 15 ♖xd7+ ♕xd7 16 ♘g5+ ♔g8 17 ♕xh7# **1-0** L/N3145

**183?-★M?-5**
**Macdonnell, A.+?**
⟨♘b1⟩ 1 e4 e5 2 ♘f3 f5 3 ♘xe5 ♕e7 4 d4 ♘f6 5 ♗g5 fxe4 6 ♗c4 c6 7 ♗xf6 ♕xf6 8 ♗f7+ ♔d8 9 ♗b3 d5 10 0-0 ♗d6 11 f4 h5 12 ♕e2 ♗e6 13 c4 ♘d7 14 cxd5 ♗xd5 15 ♗xd5 cxd5 16 ♕b5 ♘b6 17 a4 ♗xe5 18 fxe5 ♕c6 19 ♖f7 g5 20 ♕b4 ♕e6 21 ♖af1 ♘d7 22 ♕d2 ♖c8 23 ♕xg5+ ♔c7 24 ♖1f6 ♕e8 25 e6 **1-0** L/N3145

**183?-★M?-6 ◐**
**Macdonnell, A.–?**
⟨♘b1⟩ 1 e4 e5 2 ♘f3 ♘c6 3 ♗c4 ♗c5 4 b4 ♗xb4 5 c3 ♗a5 6 0-0 d6 7 d4 ♗b6 8 ♕b3 ♕e7 9 dxe5 dxe5 10 ♗a3 ♕f6 11 ♘g5 ♘h6 12 h4 ♘a5 13 ♗b5+ c6 14 ♕b4 cxb5 15 ♘xh7 ♕e6 16 ♘f8 ♘c6 17 ♘xe6 ♘xb4 18 ♘xg7+ ♔f8 19 ♘h5 ♗c5 20 cxb4 ♗d4 21 ♖ac1 ♘g4 22 ♘g3 ♖xh4 23 ♖c7 ♘xf2 24 ♖xf2 ♖f4 25 ♖c2 ♗e6 26 ♗b2 ♗xf2+ 27 ♖xf2 ♖xf2 28 ♔xf2 ♗xa2 29 ♗xe5 ... ? **0-1** L/N3145

**183?-★M?-7 ◐**
**Macdonnell, A.+?**
[Walker]
⟨♘b1⟩ 1 e4 e5 2 f4 exf4 3 ♘f3 g5 4 h4 g4 5 ♘e5 h5 6 ♗c4 ♖h7 7 d4 d6 8 ♘d3 ♕e7 9 ♘xf4 ♕xe4+ 10 ♔f2 g3+ 11 ♔xg3 ♗g4 12 ♕d2 ♕c6 13 ♕d3 ♖g7 14 ♔h2 ♕d7 15 ♖e1+ ♗e7 16 ♘d5 ♗e6 17 ♘xe7 ♘xe7 18 d5 ♗g4 19 ♗g5 ♖xg5 20 hxg5 ♕f5 21 ♕e3 ♕d7 22 g6 fxg6 23 ♕h6 ♕f5 24 ♗d3 [24 ♖xe7+-] 24 ... ♕xd5 25 ♗xg6+ ♔d7 26 ♖xe7+ ♔xe7 27 ♖e1+ ♗e6 28 ♕g7+ ♔d8 29 ♕f8+ ♔d7 30 ♕e8# **1-0** L/N3145

**183?-★M?-8**
**Macdonnell, A.+?**
⟨♘b1⟩ 1 e4 e6 2 f4 d5 3 e5 c5 4 c3 f5 5 ♘f3 ♘c6 6 ♗d3 ♘h6 7 ♗c2 ♘f7 8 0-0 ♗e7 9 d3 ♗d7 10 ♔h1 h5 11 ♕e1 g5 12 fxg5 ♗xg5 13 d4 cxd4 14 cxd4 ♗xc1 15 ♖xc1 ♘h6 16 b4 ♕e7 17 b5 ♘b4 18 a4 ♘xc2 19 ♖xc2 ♖c8 20 ♖xc8+ ♗xc8 21 ♕c1 ♔d8 22 ♖f2 b6 23 ♖c2 ♗b7 24 ♘g5 ♘f7

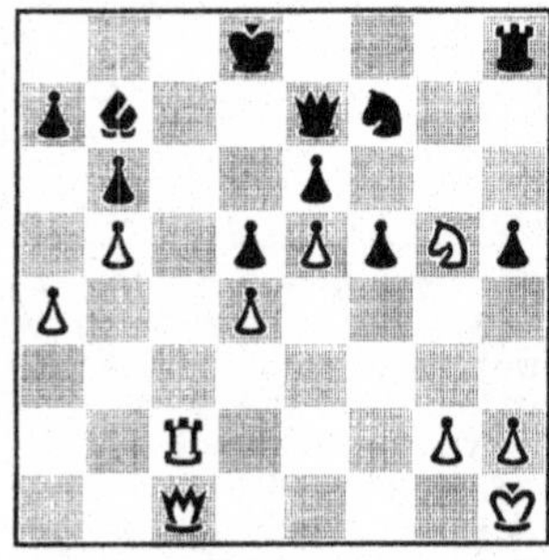

25 ♘xe6+ ♕xe6 26 ♖c7 ♗c8 27 ♖xa7 ♗d7 28 a5 bxa5 29 ♕c7+ ♔e8 30 ♖a8+ **1-0** L/N3145

**183?-★M?-9**
**Macdonnell, A.+?**
[Walker]
⟨♘b1⟩ 1 e4 e5 2 ♗c4 ♘f6 3 d4 ♘c6 4 d5 ♘b8 5 f4 exf4 6 e5 ♘e4 7 ♕f3 ♕h4+ 8 ♔e2 ♘g5 9 ♕xf4 ♕xf4 10 ♗xf4 ♘e4 11 ♖e1 ♗c5 12 ♘h3 d6 13 ♔f3 ♗xh3 14 gxh3 ♘f2 15 exd6+ ♔f8 16 dxc7 ♘d7 17 ♖hf1 ♘xh3 18 ♗d2 h6 19 ♗d3 ♗d6 20 ♗f5 ♘g5+ 21 ♗xg5 hxg5 22 ♗xd7 ♗xc7 23 h3 ♖d8 24 ♗f5 ♖xd5 25 ♔e4 ♖e5+ 26 ♔d4 ♖h4+ 27 ♗g4 ♖xe1 28 ♖xe1 f5 29 ♖f1 ♗f4 [29 ... g6-+] 30 ♗xf5 ... ? **1-0** L/N3145

**183?-★M?-10**
**Macdonnell, A.+?**
⟨♖a1⟩ 1 e4 e5 2 f4 exf4 3 ♗c4 ♕h4+ 4 ♔f1 g5 5 ♘c3 ♗g7 6 ♘d5 ♔d8 7 d4 d6 8 e5 c6 9 ♘c3 d5 10 ♗e2 ♕h6 11 g3 fxg3 12 ♔g2 ♕e6 13 ♗xg5+ ♔c7 14 hxg3 ♘d7 15 ♗g4 ♕e8 16 ♗f4 ♗f8 17 ♕d2 ♘b6 18 e6+ ♔d8 19 exf7 ♕xf7 20 ♗h5 ♕d7 21 ♗e5 ♗g7 22 ♕g5+ ♘e7 23 ♕xg7 ♖g8 24 ♕xh7 ♕f5 25 ♗f7 ♖f8 26 ♕xf5 ♗xf5 27 ♗h5 ♗xc2 28 ♘f3 ♘c4 29 ♗f4 b5 30 ♘g5 ♔c8 31 ♘e6 ♖g8 32 ♘c5 ♘g6 33 ♗g4+ ♔d8 34 ♗g5+ ♔c7 35 ♖h7+ ♔b6 36 ♖b7+ ♔a5 37 a3 ♘xb2 38 ♗d2 ♘c4 39 ♗e1 ♘f4+ 40 gxf4 ♖xg4+ 41 ♔f1 ♖xf4+ 42 ♔e2 ♖e8+ 43 ♘3e4# **1-0** L/N3145

**183?-★M?-11**
**Macdonnell, A.+?**
⟨♖a1⟩ 1 e4 e5 2 f4 exf4 3 ♘f3 g5 4 ♗c4 g4 5 d4 gxf3 6 0-0 d6 7 ♕xf3 ♕f6 8 e5 dxe5 9 dxe5 ♕xe5 10 ♗xf7+ ♔d8 11 ♗xf4 ♕c5+ 12 ♗e3 ♕f5 13 ♕g3 ♕e4 14 ♘c3 ♕g4 15 ♖d1+ ♗d6 16 ♗g5+ ♘e7 17 ♕e3 ♘c6 18 ♗d5 ♖e8 19 h3 ♕b4 20 ♕d3 ♗d7 21 ♕xh7 ♘e5 22 ♘e4 c6 23 ♗b3 ♗c5+ 24 ♔h1 ♔c7 25 ♗f6 ♘d5 26 c3 ♕b6 27 ♗xd5 cxd5 28 ♖xd5 ♖ad8 29 ♘xc5 ♔c8 30 ♗xe5 ♗c6 31 ♕f5+ ♗d7 32 ♘xd7 ♖xd7 33 ♕xd7# **1-0** L/N3145

**183?-★M?-12**
**Macdonnell, A.+?**
⟨♖a1⟩ 1 e4 e5 2 f4 exf4 3 ♘f3 g5 4 h4 ♗e7 5 hxg5 ♗xg5 6 d4 d6 7 ♘c3 c6 8 ♗c4 ♕e7 9 ♔f2 ♗g4 10 e5 d5 11 ♗d3 h5 12 ♕g1 ♘d7 13 ♘xg5 ♕xg5 14 g3 ♕e7 15 ♗xf4 0-0-0 16 ♕c1 ♕b4 17 ♗e3 ♘h6 18 ♗xh6 ♕xd4+ 19 ♗e3 ♕xe5 20 ♗f4 ♕e8 21 ♖e1 ♕g8 22 ♕e3 ♘b6 23 ♕e5 ♖d7 24 ♕b8# **1-0** L/N3145

**183?-★M?-13**
**Macdonnell, A.+?**
⟨♖a1⟩ 1 e4 e5 2 f4 d5 3 exd5 exf4 4 ♘f3 ♗d6 5 c4 ♗g4 6 d4 b6 7 ♗d3 ♕e7+ 8 ♔f2 ♗xf3 9 ♕xf3 ♕h4+ 10 ♔f1 ♘d7 11 ♘c3 ♘gf6 12 ♕e2+ ♗e7 13 ♘b5 0-0 14 ♘xc7 ♖ac8 15 ♘b5 ♖fe8 16 ♕f2 ♕xf2+ 17 ♔xf2 ♘g4+ 18 ♔f3 ♘gf6 19 ♗xf4 ♘h5 20 ♗d2 a6 21 ♘a3 ♖a8 22 ♘c2 ♗d6 23 b4 ♗f8 24 c5 ♘hf6 25 d6 bxc5 26 bxc5 ♘b8 27 ♘a3 ♖a7 28 g4 g6 29 g5 ♘fd7 30 ♖c1 ♗g7 31 ♗e3 ♖c8 32 c6 ♘f8 33 d5 ♖a8 34 ♗e4 ♗e5 35 ♘c4 ♘fd7 36 ♖b1 ♗xh2 37 ♖b7 ♘e5+ 38 ♘xe5 ♗xe5 39 d7 ♘xd7 40 ♖xd7 ♔f8 41 d6 ♖d8 42 c7 **1-0** L/N3145

**183?-★M?-14**
**Macdonnell, A.+?**
⟨♖a1⟩ 1 e4 e5 2 f4 exf4 3 ♗c4 ♕h4+ 4 ♔f1 d6 5 d4 g5 6 ♘c3 ♗g7 7 ♘d5 ♔d8 8 ♗e2 c6 9 g3 ♕h6 10 ♘c3 fxg3 11 ♔g2 ♕f6 12 ♘f3 h6 13 e5 dxe5 14 ♘e4 ♕e7 15 dxe5+ ♗d7 16 ♘d6 ♔c7 17 hxg3 ♗e6 18 ♗d2 ♘d7 19 ♗b4 ♕d8 20 ♕d4 ♘e7 21 ♗a5+ b6 22 ♗a6 ♘c5 23 ♕xc5 ♗xe5 24 ♘b5+ **1-0** L/N3145

**183?-★M?-15**
**Macdonnell, A.+?**
⟨♖a1⟩ 1 e4 e5 2 f4 exf4 3 ♗c4 ♕h4+ 4 ♔f1 g5 5 ♘c3 ♗g7 6 d4 ♘e7 7 g3 fxg3 8 ♔g2 h5 9 hxg3 ♕g4 10 ♗e2 ♕e6 11 ♗xh5 f6 12 ♗xg5+ ♔d8 13 d5 ♕b6 14 ♗f4 d6 15 ♘ge2 f5 16 ♗g5 ♗xc3 17 bxc3 ♖g8 18 ♕d2 ♘d7 19 ♗f7 ♖f8 20 ♖h7 fxe4 21 ♘d4 ♘c5 22 ♗xe7+

♔xe7 23 ♕g5+ ♔d7 **1-0** L/N3145

### 183?-★M?-16
**Macdonnell, A.+?**

⟨♖a1⟩ 1 e4 e5 2 f4 exf4 3 ♗c4 ♕h4+ 4 ♔f1 d6 5 d4 g5 6 ♘c3 ♗g4 7 ♕d3 ♘e7 8 g3 ♗h3+ 9 ♔f2 ♕g4 10 ♕d2 ♗g7 11 ♗e2 ♕e6 12 ♘f3 h6 13 gxf4 gxf4 14 ♕xf4 ♘g6 15 ♕e3 ♗g4 16 ♘d5 ♔d7 17 ♖g1 h5 18 ♘g5 ♕e8 19 e5 ♗xe2 20 ♔xe2 c6 21 ♕h3+ ♔d8 22 ♘xf7+ ♕xf7 23 ♗g5+ ♗f6 24 ♗xf6+ **1-0** L/N3145

### 183?-★M?-17
**Macdonnell, A.=?**

⟨♖a1⟩ 1 e4 e5 2 f4 exf4 3 ♘f3 d6 4 d4 ♘f6 5 ♘c3 ♗g4 6 ♗c4 ♗xf3 7 ♕xf3 c6 8 0-0 ♗e7 9 e5 dxe5 10 dxe5 ♕d4+ 11 ♔h1 ♕xc4 12 exf6 ♗xf6 13 ♖e1+ ♔d7 14 ♕g4+ ♔d8 15 ♖d1+ ♗d4 16 ♗xf4 ♘a6 17 ♘e2 ♕e6 18 ♕xe6 fxe6 19 ♘xd4 e5 20 ♗g5+ ♔e8 21 ♘f5 ♘c5 22 ♘d6+ ♔f8 23 ♖f1+ ♔g8 24 ♗e7 h5 25 ♘f7 ♘e6 26 ♘xh8 ♔xh8 27 ♖f5 ♖e8 28 ♖xh5+ ♔g8 29 ♗b4 ♘f4 30 ♖g5 ♘d5 31 ♗d2 e4 32 ♔g1 e3 33 ♗e1 ♖e6 34 ♖f5 ♖e4 35 g3 e2 36 ♔f2 ♘e3 37 ♔f3 ♖e6 38 ♖c5 ♘d5 39 c4 ♘f6 40 ♖a5 a6 41 ♖a3 b5 42 cxb5 cxb5 43 ♖e3 ♖xe3+ 44 ♔xe3 ♘g4+ 45 ♔xe2 ♘xh2 46 ♔d3 ♔f7 47 ♔e4 ♔e6 48 ♗c3 g6 49 ♔f4 ♘f1 50 g4 ♔f7 51 b3 ♔e6 52 ♗d4 ♘h2 53 ♗e3 ♘f1 54 ♗c1 **½-½** L/N3145

### 183?-★M?-18
**Macdonnell, A.+?**

⟨♖a1⟩ 1 e4 e5 2 f4 exf4 3 ♗c4 c6 4 ♘c3 d5 5 exd5 ♕h4+ 6 ♔f1 f3 7 d4 fxg2+ 8 ♔xg2 ♕g4+ 9 ♕xg4 ♗xg4 10 h3 ♗f5 11 ♘f3 cxd5 12 ♖e1+ ♗e7 13 ♘xd5 ♗e6 14 ♘c7+ ♔d7 15 ♘xe6 fxe6 16 ♗xe6+ ♔d8 17 ♘e5 ♘h6 18 ♗xh6 gxh6 19 ♘f7+ ♔c7 20 ♘xh8 ♘c6 21 d5 ♘d4 22 ♘f7 ♖g8+ 23 ♗g4 ♗h4 24 d6+ ♔b8 25 ♖e4 ♘xc2 26 d7 ♘e1+ 27 ♔h2 ♔c7 28 ♖c4+ ♔b6 29 ♖c8 ♖g7 30 ♘xh6 **1-0** L/N3145

### 183?-★M?-19
**Macdonnell, A.+?**

⟨♖a1⟩ 1 e4 e5 2 f4 d5 3 exd5 exf4 4 ♘f3 ♕xd5 5 ♘c3 ♕d8 6 ♗c4 ♗g4 7 ♗xf7+ ♔xf7 8 ♘e5+ ♔e8 9 ♕xg4 ♘f6 10 ♕e6+ ♕e7 11 ♕c8+ ♕d8 12 ♕xd8+ ♔xd8 13 ♘f7+ ♔e8 14 ♘xh8 ♗c5 15 d4 ♗xd4 16 ♘b5 ♗b6 17 ♗xf4 ♘a6 18 0-0-0 ♘d5 19 ♗e5 ♗e3+ 20 ♔b1 ♗h6 21 c4 ♘e3 22 ♗xc7 ♔d7 23 ♘f7 ♘xc7 24 ♘e5+ ♔c8 25 ♘d6+ ♔d8 26 ♘xb7+ ♔e7 27 ♖e1 ♔f6 28 ♖xe3 ♗xe3 29 ♘g4+ ♔g5 30 ♘xe3 ♖e8 31 ♘c2 ♖e2 32 b4 ♖xg2 33 ♘d6 ♖xh2 34 b5 h5 35 ♘c8 a5 36 b6 ♘a6 37 ♘d6 ♖h1+ 38 ♔b2 ♘b8 39 ♘d4 ♖d1 40 ♔c3 h4 41 ♘e4+ ♔f4 42 ♘f2 ♖xd4 43 ♔xd4 ♔f3 44 ♘h3 ♔g3 45 ♘g5 h3 46 ♘xh3 ♔xh3 47 c5 g5 48 ♔d5 g4 49 c6 ♘xc6 50 ♔xc6 g3 51 b7 g2 52 b8♕ g1♕ 53 ♕h8+ ♔g2 54 ♕g8+ ♔f2 55 ♕xg1+ **1-0** L/N3145

### 183?-★M?-20
**Macdonnell, A.+?**

⟨♖a1⟩ 1 e4 e5 2 f4 exf4 3 ♗c4 ♕h4+ 4 ♔f1 c6 5 ♘c3 ♗b4 6 ♘f3 ♕e7 7 d4 ♗xc3 8 bxc3 ♕xe4 9 ♔f2 ♕f5 10 ♖e1+ ♘e7 11 ♗a3 c5 12 ♗xc5 ♘c6 13 d5 b6 14 ♗a3 ♕f6 15 dxc6 d6 16 ♗xd6 ♗e6 17 ♗e5 ♕g6 18 ♗xe6 0-0 19 ♗d7 ♘xc6 20 ♗xc6 ♕xc6 21 ♘d4 ♕c5 22 ♕g4 g6 23 ♕h4 f5 24 ♕xf4 ♕xc3 25 ♘e6 ♕xc2+ 26 ♖e2 **1-0** L/N3145

### 183?-★M?-21
**Macdonnell, A.+?**

⟨♖a1⟩ 1 e4 e5 2 f4 exf4 3 ♗c4 ♕h4+ 4 ♔f1 d5 5 exd5 f3 6 ♗b5+ c6 7 ♘xf3 ♗g4 8 ♗e2 ♗xf3 9 ♗xf3 ♗d6 10 ♘c3 f5 11 d4 ♘e7 12 dxc6 bxc6 13 ♘b5 ♘c8 14 g3 ♕e7 15 ♔g2 0-0 16 ♖e1 ♕b7 17 c4 a6 18 ♘c3 ♗b4 19 ♕b3 ♖f7 20 c5 h6 21 ♗h5 g6 22 ♗xg6 ♔g7 23 ♗xf7 **1-0** L/N3145

### 183?-★M?-22
**Macdonnell, A.+?**

⟨♖a1⟩ 1 e4 e5 2 f4 exf4 3 ♘f3 g5 4 ♗c4 g4 5 ♘c3 gxf3 6 0-0 c6 7 ♕xf3 ♕f6 8 e5 ♕xe5 9 ♗xf7+ ♔xf7 10 d4 ♕xd4+ 11 ♗e3 ♕g7 12 ♗xf4 ♘f6 13 ♘e4 ♗e7 14 ♗g5 ♖g8 15 ♕h5+ ♕g6 16 ♘d6+ ♔e6 17 ♖e1+ ♔xd6 18 ♗f4# **1-0** L/N3145

### 183?-★M?-23
**Macdonnell, A.+?**

⟨♖a1⟩ 1 e4 e5 2 f4 ♗c5 3 ♘f3 d6 4 ♗c4 ♗g4 5 fxe5 dxe5 6 d4 ♗xd4 7 ♘c3 c6 8 ♗xf7+ ♔e7 9 ♗xg8 ♖xg8 10 ♗g5+ ♔d7 11 ♘xe5+ ♔c7 12 ♗xd8+ ♖xd8 13 ♕xg4 ♗xe5 14 0-0 ♘d7 15 ♖f7 h5 16 ♕e6 ♗xc3 17 bxc3 ♔c8 18 e5 a5 19 ♕d6 ♖a6 20 e6 g5 21 exd7+ **1-0** L/N3145

### 183?-★M?-24
**Macdonnell, A.+?**

⟨♖a1⟩ 1 e4 e5 2 f4 ♗c5 3 ♘f3 exf4 4 d4 ♗b6 5 ♗xf4 d6 6 ♗c4 ♗e6 7 ♗xe6 fxe6 8 0-0 ♘f6 9 ♔h1 ♘bd7 10 e5 ♘g8 11 ♗g5 ♕c8 12 ♕e2 ♘f8 13 ♘c3 ♕d7 14 ♗h4 h6 15 exd6 cxd6 16 ♘b5 a6 17 ♘c3 ♘f6 18 b3 ♗a5 19 b4 ♗xb4 20 ♗xf6 gxf6 21 ♘d5 ♗a5 22 ♘xf6+ **1-0** L/N3145

### 183?-★M?-25
**Macdonnell, A.-?**

⟨♖a1⟩ 1 e4 d5 2 exd5 ♕xd5 3 ♘c3 ♕d8 4 ♗c4 e6 5 ♘f3 c6 6 0-0 ♗e7 7 d4 a5 8 ♗e3 ♘f6 9 ♗d3 a4 10 h3 b5 11 g4 b4 12 ♘e2 ♘d5 13 ♘g3 ♘xe3+ 14 fxe3 ♗a6 15 ♘e5 ♗xd3 16 ♕xd3 f6 17 ♘c4 0-0 18 h4 c5 19 c3 ♘c6 20 h5 ♕c7 21 ♔g2 ♖ad8 22 ♕e4 e5 23 d5 ♘a5 24 ♘d2 a3 25 c4 axb2 26 ♖b1 ♘b7 27 ♖xb2 ♘d6 28 ♕d3 ♘f7 29 ♘f5 ♘g5 30 ♖b1 ♗d6 31 h6 g6 32 ♘g7 ♕d7 33 ♕e2 e4 34 ♖f1 ♕f7 35 ♘b3 ♖a8 36 ♖f2 ♖xg7 37 hxg7 ♔xg7 38 ♔f1 ♕e7 39 ♖g2 ♕e5 40 ♖f2 ♕c3 41 ♔g2 ♘f3 42 ♔f1 ♖a3 43 ♖g2 ♘e5 44 g5 f5 45 ♖h2 ♘f3 46 ♖h1 ♕d3 47 ♕xd3 exd3 48 ♔f2 ♘xg5 **0-1** L/N3145

### 183?-★M?-26
**Macdonnell, A.-?**

⟨♖a1⟩ 1 b3 e5 2 ♗b2 ♘c6 3 g3 ♗c5 4 ♗g2 ♘f6 5 a3 d6 6 h3 ♗e6 7 d3 0-0 8 e3 d5 9 ♘e2 ♘e7 10 ♘d2 ♗d6 11 0-0 c6 12 ♔h2 ♘h5 13 ♘g1 ♘f6 14 f4 ♘f5 15 ♕e1 d4 16 fxe5 ♘xe3 17 exf6 ♘xf1+ 18 ♗xf1 ♕xf6 19 ♘e4 ♕e5 20 ♘f3 ♕h5 21 ♗g2 ♗c7 22 ♘xd4 ♖ae8 23 ♘f3 ♗d5 24 ♕c3 ♕h6 25 ♘fd2 ♗xe4 26 ♘xe4 ♕g6 27 d4 f5 28 ♘c5 f4 29 ♔h1 ♕xg3 30 ♕c4+ ♔h8 31 ♔g1 f3 **0-1** L/N3145

### 183?-★M?-27
**Macdonnell, A.+?**

⟨♖a1⟩ 1 e4 e6 2 f4 d5 3 e5 c5 4 c3 ♘c6 5 ♗d3 ♕b6 6 ♗c2 ♗d7 7 ♘f3 ♗e7 8 0-0 f5 9 ♔h1 ♘h6 10 ♕e1 ♕d8 11 a3 g5 12 fxg5 ♗xg5 13 d4 ♗xc1 14 ♕xc1 ♘f7 15 ♕e1 ♕e7 16 b4 c4 17 a4 a6 18 ♘bd2 b5 19 a5 0-0-0 20 ♖f2 ♘h6 21 h3 f4 22 ♘f1 ♘f5 23 ♗xf5 exf5 24 ♕c1 ♖ag8 25 ♕xf4 h6 26 ♘e3 ♕e6 27 ♘h4 ♘e7 28 ♕f3 ♘g6 29 ♘hxf5 ♔c7 30 ♘xd5+ ♔b8 31 ♘b6 ♔a7 32 ♘d6 ♖b8 33 ♕e3 ♘e7 34 d5 ♘xd5 **1-0** L/N3145

### 183?-★M?-28
**Macdonnell, A.-?**

⟨♖a1⟩ 1 e4 e5 2 f4 exf4 3 ♗c4 ♕h4+ 4 ♔f1 g5 5 ♘c3 ♗g7 6 d4 d6 7 ♗e2 ♘e7 8 g3 fxg3 9 ♔g2 ♕h6 10 hxg3 ♕f6 11 e5 dxe5 12 dxe5 ♕xe5 13 ♘f3 ♕d6 14 ♕e1 h6 15 ♘e4 ♕d8 16 ♗d3 ♗e6 17 ♕f2 ♘bc6 18 ♖d1 ♘f5 19 ♘c5 ♘d6 20 ♘xe6 fxe6 21 ♗g6+ ♔d7 22 c4 ♕f6 23 ♗h5 ♔c8 24 ♕e2 ♖f8 25 c5 ♘f5 26 ♖f1 ♘fd4 27 ♕c4 e5 28 ♗g4+ ♔b8 **0-1** L/N3145

**183?-★M?-29**
**Macdonnell, A.+?**
⟨♖a1⟩ 1 e4 e5 2 f4 exf4 3 ♘f3 g5 4 ♗c4 g4 5 ♘c3 gxf3 6 0-0 fxg2 7 ♖xf4 f6 8 ♕h5+ ♔e7 9 ♕f7+ ♔d6 10 e5+ ♔xe5 11 ♖e4+ ♔d6 12 ♕d5# **1-0** L/N3145

**183?-★M?-30**
**Macdonnell, A.+?**
1 e4 e5 2 f4 exf4 3 ♗c4 ♘f6 4 ♘c3 d6 5 d4 g5 6 h4 gxh4 7 ♗xf4 ♗g4 8 ♘f3 ♗e7 9 ♕d2 h3 10 ♘g5 d5 11 ♘xd5 ♗h5 12 ♘xc7+ ♔f8 13 ♘xf7 ♗xf7 14 ♗h6+ ♔g8 15 ♕g5# **1-0** L/N3145

**183̂?-★AB-1**
**Bourdonnais, L.C.M. de la+ D'Arblay, A.**
⟨♖a1⟩ 1 e4 e5 2 f4 exf4 3 ♘f3 g5 4 h4 g4 5 ♘g5 ♘c6 6 ♗c4 ♘e5 7 ♗b3 h6 8 d4 hxg5 9 dxe5 ♖xh4 10 ♖f1 g3 11 ♘c3 ♗b4 12 ♕d5 ♗xc3+ 13 bxc3 ♕e7 14 ♗a3 d6 15 exd6 ♕e6 16 ♕d4 ♕f6 17 e5 ♕f5 18 dxc7 ♗e6 19 ♗a4+ ♗d7 20 0-0-0 f3 21 ♕c5 ♕f4+ 22 ♔b1 ♗c6 23 ♕xc6+ bxc6 24 ♗xc6# **1-0** L/N3145

**183̂?-★BB-1 ●○**
**Bourdonnais, L.C.M. de la= Bonfil**
1 e4 e5 2 ♘f3 ♘c6 3 ♗c4 ♗c5 4 b4 ♗xb4 5 c3 ♗a5 6 0-0 ♗b6 7 d4 ♘a5 8 ♗d3 exd4 9 cxd4 ♘e7 10 ♗b2 0-0 11 ♘c3 d6 12 e5 h6 13 exd6 cxd6 14 h3 d5 15 ♗a3 ♖e8 16 ♖e1 ♗e6 17 ♗xe7 ♖xe7 18 ♖c1 ♘c6 19 ♗c2 ♕f8 20 ♕d3 f5 21 ♗b3 ♘b4 22 ♕d2 ♔h8 23 a3 ♘c6 24 ♗xd5 ♗xd5 25 ♘xd5 ♖xe1+ 26 ♖xe1 ♗a5 27 ♘c3 ♕xa3 28 ♖c1 ♖c8 29 ♕e3 ♘xd4 30 ♘xd4 ♖xc3 31 ♖xc3 ♕xc3 32 ♕e8+ ♔h7 33 ♘e6 ♗b4 34 ♔h2 ♕e1 35 ♘f8+ ♔g8 36 ♘e6+ ♔h7 37 ♘f8+ **½-½** L/N3145

**183̂?-★BH-1 ●○**
**Bourdonnais, L.C.M. de la+ Haxo**
1 e4 e5 2 ♘f3 ♘c6 3 d4 ♕f6 4 ♘c3 exd4 5 ♘d5 ♕d8 6 ♗c4 ♗c5 7 0-0 h6 8 b4 ♘xb4 9 ♘xb4 ♗xb4 10 ♕xd4 ♘f6 11 ♗xf7+ ♔xf7 12 ♕xb4 d6 13 ♕b3+ ♗e6 14 ♕xb7 ♕b8 15 ♖b1 ♘xe4 16 ♕xe4 ♕xb1 17 ♗xh6 ♕xa2 18 ♘g5+ ♔e7 19 ♗xg7 ♖hg8 20 ♖e1 ♔d7 21 ♘xe6 ♖ae8 22 c4 ♖xg7 **1-0** L/N3145

**183̂?-★BK-1**
**Bourdonnais, L.C.M. de la+ Kieseritsky, L.**
⟨♘b1⟩ 1 e4 d5 2 e5 c5 3 f4 ♘c6 4 ♘f3 ♗g4 5 c3 c4 6 d4 cxd3 7 ♗xd3 e6 8 0-0 ♗f5 9 ♘g5 ♗c5+ 10 ♔h1 ♗xd3 11 ♕xd3 h6 12 ♘f3 ♘ge7 13 ♗d2 ♘f5 14 b4 ♗b6 15 ♖ae1 ♖c8 16 g4 ♘h4 17 b5 ♘a5 18 f5 ♘xf3 19 ♕xf3 ♖c7 20 fxe6 fxe6 21 ♕d3 ♕e7 22 ♕g6+ ♔d8 23 g5 h5 24 ♖f3 ♘c4 25 ♗c1 ♕e8 26 ♕d3 ♖f8 27 g6 ♖xf3 28 ♗g5+ ♖f6 29 exf6 gxf6 30 ♗xf6+ ♔c8 31 g7 ♕g8 32 ♕h3 ♖xg7 33 ♗xg7 ♕xg7 34 ♕xe6+ ♕d7 35 ♕e8+ ♕xe8 36 ♖xe8+ ♔d7 37 ♖h8 ♘d6 38 ♖xh5 ♔e6 39 a4 ♘e4 40 ♔g2 ♗a5 41 ♔f3 ♗xc3 42 ♔e3 ♘c5 43 ♖h6+ ♗f6 44 a5 d4+ 45 ♔f3 d3 46 a6 bxa6 47 ♖h7 d2 48 ♔e2 ♗g5 49 bxa6 ♔d6 50 h4 ♗e3 51 ♖h8 ♘e4 52 ♔xe3 ♔c7 53 ♔e2 **1-0** L/N3145

**183̂?-★BK-2**
**Bourdonnais, L.C.M. de la– Kieseritsky, L.**
⟨♘b1⟩ 1 e4 e5 2 ♘f3 f5 3 ♗c4 ♘f6 4 d3 ♘c6 5 0-0 f4 6 c3 ♘a5 7 ♗b5 c6 8 ♗a4 b5 9 ♗c2 ♕c7 10 a4 b4 11 d4 exd4 12 e5 ♘h5 13 ♘g5 g6 14 ♘xh7 ♖xh7 15 ♗xg6+ ♔d8 16 ♗xh7 ♕xe5 17 ♗g6 bxc3 18 ♗xh5 c2 19 ♕f3 ♗a6 20 ♗xf4 ♕c5 21 ♖fe1 ♔c8 22 ♗d2 ♘c4 23 ♖e8+ ♔b7 24 ♕b3+ ♘b6 25 ♖xa8 ♔xa8 26 ♗f3 ♕c4 27 ♕xc4 ♘xc4 28 ♗e4 ♘xd2 29 ♗xc2 d3 30 ♗d1 ♗g7 31 ♖a2 ♗c4 32 b3 ♘xb3 33 ♖a3 ♘c5 34 a5 ♗b2 35 ♖a4 ♘xa4 36 ♗xa4 ♗b5 37 ♗d1 c5 **0-1** L/N3145

**183̂?-★BL-1**
**Lavallino– Bourdonnais, L.C.M. de la**
⟨♙f7⟩ 1 e4 ... 2 d4 d6 3 c4 e6 4 d5 e5 5 ♘c3 ♘f6 6 f4 ♗e7 7 f5 c6 8 ♗e3 ♘a6 9 h3 0-0 10 g4 cxd5 11 cxd5 ♘c5 12 ♗xc5 dxc5 13 ♗d3 ♕b6 14 ♕e2 ♗d7 15 ♘f3 ♖ac8 16 ♘xe5 ♗d6 17 ♘xd7 ♗g3+ 18 ♔f1 ♘xd7 19 ♔g2 ♗h4 20 ♖ad1 c4 21 ♗b1 ♘e5 22 ♖hf1 ♕d6 23 ♘b5 ♕c5 24 ♘d4 ♕d6 25 ♘f3 ♗f6 26 ♘xe5 ♕xe5 27 ♗c2 b5 28 ♕d2 c3 29 bxc3 ♖xc3 30 ♖f3 ♖fc8 31 ♖xc3 ♖xc3 32 ♕f2 ♗h4 33 ♕xh4 ♖xc2+ **0-1** L/N3145

**183̂?-★BP-1**
**Bourdonnais, L.C.M. de la+ Pelling**
⟨♘b1⟩ 1 e4 e5 2 d4 exd4 3 ♗c4 c5 4 ♘f3 d6 5 c3 dxc3 6 0-0 ♗e6 7 ♗xe6 fxe6 8 ♕b3 ♕d7 9 ♘g5 d5 10 exd5 exd5 11 ♖e1+ ♗e7 12 ♘e6 ♔f7 13 ♕xc3 ♘f6 14 h4 ♖e8 15 ♗f4 ♗d6 16 ♕g3 ♘h5 17 ♕g4 **1-0** L/N3145

**183̂?-★BP-2**
**Perigal, G.– Bourdonnais, L.C.M. de la**
⟨♙f7⟩ 1 e4 ... 2 d4 d6 3 ♗d3 ♗e6 4 f4 ♗f7 5 ♕f3 e6 6 f5 d5 7 e5 c5 8 ♘e2 ♘c6 9 c3 ♕b6 10 fxe6 ♗xe6 11 0-0 ♘h6 12 h3 0-0-0 13 ♗e3 c4 14 ♗xc4 dxc4 15 ♘d2 ♗d5 16 ♕f2 ♗e7 17 ♘f4 ♖hf8 18 ♘xd5 ♖xd5 19 ♘xc4 ♕d8 20 ♕c2 b5 21 ♖xf8 ♗xf8 22 ♗xh6 bxc4 23 ♕f5+ ♔b8 24 ♖f1 gxh6 25 ♕xf8 ♕xf8 26 ♖xf8+ ♔c7 27 ♖f7+ ♖d7 28 e6 ♖e7 29 d5 ♔d6 30 ♔f2 **0-1** L/N3145

**183̂?-★BP-3**
**Perigal, G.+ Bourdonnais, L.C.M. de la**
⟨♙f7⟩ 1 e4 ... 2 d4 ♘c6 3 ♘c3 e6 4 f4 d5 5 exd5 exd5 6 ♕h5+ g6 7 ♕xd5 ♘xd4 8 ♕xd8+ ♔xd8 9 ♗d3 ♗f5 10 ♗e3 c5 11 0-0-0 ♗g7 12 ♗xf5 gxf5 13 ♘b5 ♘e7 14 c3 ♘d5 15 ♘xd4 ♘xe3 16 ♘e6+ ♔e7 17 ♘xg7 ♘xd1 18 ♔xd1 ♖hd8+ 19 ♔c2 ♔f6 20 ♘h5+ ♔g6 21 ♘g3 ♖e8 22 ♘f3 ♖e3 23 ♘h4+ ♔f6 24 ♘hxf5 ♖e6 25 ♘h4 c4 26 ♘f3 b5 27 ♘d4 ♖b6 28 ♖e1 b4 29 ♖e5 bxc3 30 ♔xc3 ♖ab8 31 ♖e2 a5 32 ♘e4+ ♔f7 33 ♘g5+ ♔g6 34 ♖e6+ ♖xe6 35 ♘gxe6 ♔f6 36 g4 h6 37 h4 a4 38 g5+ hxg5 38 hxg5+ ♔f7 40 a3 ♖h8 41 f5 ♖h3+ 42 ♔xc4 ♖h2 43 g6+ ♔f6 44 g7 ♔f7 45 b3 axb3 46 ♔xb3 ♖h1 47 a4 ♖b1+ 48 ♔c4 ♖a1 49 ♔b5 ♖b1+ 50 ♔a6 ♖b8 51 a5 **1-0** L/N3145

**183̂?-★BP-4**
**Perigal, G.– Bourdonnais, L.C.M. de la**
⟨♙f7⟩ 1 e4 ... 2 d4 e6 3 ♗d3 c5 4 d5 d6 5 c4 ♘f6 6 f4 exd5 7 exd5 ♗e7 8 ♘f3 0-0 9 h3 ♘a6 10 ♗d2 b5 11 b3 ♘b8 12 0-0 a5 13 ♗c3 a4 14 ♘g5 h6 15 ♘e4 ♗f5 16 ♘bd2 ♘xe4 17 ♘xe4 axb3 18 axb3 ♖xa1 19 ♗xa1 bxc4 20 bxc4 ♘a6 21 ♗c3 ♘c7 22 ♕f3 ♕e8 23 ♕g3 ♕g6 24 ♕xg6 ♗xg6 25 ♘xc5 ♗xd3 26 ♘xd3 ♖a8 27 ♘b4 ♖a3 28 ♗d4 ♖b3 29 ♘c6 ♗f6 30 ♗xf6 gxf6 31 ♘e7+ ♔f7 32 ♘f5 ♖c3 33 ♖e1 ♘e8 34 ♖e6 ♖xc4 35 ♖e7+

♔g6 36 g4 h5 37 ♖xe8 hxg4 38 hxg4 ♖xf4 39 ♖g8+ ♔h7 40 ♖g7+ ♔h8 41 ♖g6 ♔h7 42 ♔g2 ♔xg6 **0-1** L/N3145

**183̂?-★BP-5**
**Perigal, G.+ Bourdonnais, L.C.M. de la**
⟨♙f7⟩ 1 e4 ... 2 d4 e6 3 ♗d3 c5 4 d5 d6 5 c4 ♘f6 6 f4 exd5 7 exd5 ♗e7 8 ♘f3 b5 9 b3 ♘bd7 10 0-0 ♘b6 11 ♗b2 a5 12 ♘bd2 a4 13 ♕e2 0-0 14 ♘g5 h6 15 ♘e6 ♗xe6 16 ♕xe6+ ♔h8 17 ♕f5 ♕d7 18 ♕g6 ♕e8 19 ♖ae1 ♕xg6 20 ♗xg6 ♖a7 21 ♖e6 axb3 22 axb3 ♖a2 23 ♗c3 b4 24 ♖a1 bxc3 25 cxd2 26 ♖xd2 ♘c8 27 ♖a2 ♖xa2 ♘d7 28 ♖a8 ♘db6 29 ♖b8 ♗d8 30 ♖e8 ♖xe8 31 ♗xe8 ♗c7 32 ♖b7 ♗d8 33 h4 ♔g8 34 ♗f7+ ♔f8 35 ♗e6 ♘e7 36 h5 ♔e8 37 g4 ♘a8 38 ♗d7+ ♔f7 39 ♖b8 ♗b6 40 ♗e6+ ♔f6 41 ♖f8# **1-0** L/N3145

**183̂?-★BP-6**
**Perigal, G.= Bourdonnais, L.C.M. de la**
⟨♙f7⟩ 1 e4 ... 2 d4 e6 3 ♗d3 d5 4 e5 g6 5 h4 c5 6 c3 ♘c6 7 ♘f3 cxd4 8 h5 gxh5 9 ♖xh5 ♗g7 10 cxd4 ♘ge7 11 ♘c3 ♗d7 12 ♘b5 ♘c8 13 ♗g5 ♕a5+ 14 ♕d2 ♕xd2+ 15 ♔xd2 ♔f7 16 ♖xh7 ♖xh7 17 ♗xh7 ♘xe5 18 ♘c7 ♘xf3+ 19 gxf3 ♖b8 20 ♗e3 ♘b6 21 b3 ♖c8 22 ♖c1 ♗c6 23 ♗f4 ♗xd4 24 ♗d6 ♗xf2 25 ♖h1 d4 26 ♗d3 ♗e3+ 27 ♔e2 ♖g8 28 ♖h7+ ♔f6 29 ♗e7+ ♔e5 30 ♖h5+ ♔f4 31 ♘xe6+ ♔g3 32 ♗d6+ ♔g2 33 ♖h2+ ♔g1 34 ♗f5 ♖g2+ 35 ♖xg2+ ♔xg2 36 ♗e4 ♗b5+ 37 ♗d3 ♗c6 38 ♗e4 ♘d5 39 ♗xd5 ♗xd5 40 ♘f4+ ♗xf4 41 ♗xf4 ♗xf3+ 42 ♔d3 **½-½** L/N3145

**183̂?-★BP-7**
**Perigal, G.+ Bourdonnais, L.C.M. de la**
⟨♙f7⟩ 1 e4 e6 2 d4 d5 3 e5 c5 4 ♗d3 ♕a5+ 5 ♗d2 ♕b6 6 ♕h5+ ♔d8 7 ♘c3 ♗d7 8 ♘f3 cxd4 9 ♘ce2 ♘c6 10 ♘fxd4 ♘xd4 11 ♕h4+ ♗e7 12 ♕xd4 ♕xd4 13 ♘xd4 ♗c5 14 c3 ♘e7 15 ♗e3 ♗xd4 16 cxd4 ♘c6 17 a3 ♖c8 18 f4 ♘a5 19 0-0 g6 20 ♖ac1 ♔e7 21 g4 b5 22 f5 gxf5 23 gxf5 exf5 24 ♗xf5 ♖hg8+ 25 ♔h1 ♘c4 26 ♗xd7 ♔xd7 27 ♖f7+ ♔e6 28 ♖f6+ ♔e7 29 ♗h6 ♖g6 30 ♖xg6 hxg6 31 b3 ♘b6 32 ♖xc8 ♘xc8 33 ♔g2 ♔e6 34 ♔f3 ♔f5 35 h3 ♘e7 36 ♗f8 ♘c6 37 ♗c5 a5 38 a4 bxa4 39 bxa4 ♔g5 40 ♔e3 ♔f5 41 h4 ♘d8 42 ♗b6 ♘e6 43 ♔f3 g5 44 hxg5 ♔xg5 45 ♔e3 ♔f5 46 ♗xa5 ♘f8 47 ♗b6 ♔e6 48 a5 ♔d7 49 a6 ♔c6 50 a7 ♔b7 51 ♔d3 ♘d7 52 ♗c5 **1-0** L/N3145

**183̂?-★BP-8**
**Popert, H.W.– Bourdonnais, L.C.M. de la**
⟨♙f7⟩ 1 e4 ... 2 d4 ♘c6 3 ♗d3 d6 4 c3 e5 5 ♗c4 ♘f6 6 ♗g5 ♗e7 7 ♗xf6 ♗xf6 8 ♘e2 ♘a5 9 ♕a4+ c6 10 ♗d3 b5 11 ♕b4 0-0 12 a4 a6 13 ♕a3 ♘c4 14 ♕b3 ♗e6 15 axb5 axb5 16 ♖xa8 ♕xa8 17 0-0 exd4 18 cxd4 ♗f7 19 ♕c2 h6 20 ♘bd2 ♘xd2 21 ♕xd2 ♕a4 22 b4 ♖a8 23 f4 ♕a2 24 ♖d1 ♖a3 25 ♕xa2 ♖xa2 26 ♖c1 ♖d2 27 e5 dxe5 28 dxe5 ♗d8 **0-1** L/N3145

**183̂?-★BP-9**
**Popert, H.W.– Bourdonnais, L.C.M. de la**
⟨♙f7⟩ 1 e4 ... 2 d4 ♘c6 3 ♗d3 e5 4 dxe5 ♘xe5 5 ♕h5+ ♘f7 6 ♗c4 ♕e7 7 ♘c3 ♘f6 8 ♕e2 ♘e5 9 ♗b3 d6 10 f4 ♗g4 11 ♘f3 ♘xf3+ 12 gxf3 ♗e6 13 ♗xe6 ♕xe6 14 ♕b5+ ♔f7 15 ♕xb7 ♗e7 16 ♕xc7 ♖hc8 17 ♕a5 ♖xc3 18 ♕xc3 ♘xe4 19 fxe4 ♕xe4+ 20 ♕e3 ♕xh1+ 21 ♔e2 ♖e8 22 ♕b3+ d5 23 ♗e3 ♕g2+ 24 ♔d3 ♕e4+ 25 ♔e2 ♗c5 **0-1** L/N3145

**183̂?-★BP-10**
**Popert, H.W.+ Bourdonnais, L.C.M. de la**
⟨♙f7⟩ 1 e4 ... 2 d4 ♘c6 3 ♗d3 e5 4 dxe5 ♘xe5 5 ♕h5+ ♘f7 6 f4 ♘f6 7 ♕e2 ♗c5 8 ♘c3 0-0 9 e5 ♖e8 10 ♘f3 d6 11 ♘e4 ♘xe4 12 ♕xe4 g6 13 ♗d2 ♗f5 14 ♕c4 ♗xd3 15 cxd3 b5 16 ♕xb5 ♖b8 17 ♕c4 ♖xb2 18 d4 ♗b6 19 ♘g5 ♕e7 20 ♗c3 ♖xg2 21 0-0-0 dxe5 22 ♖he1 ♖b8 23 ♗b4 ♕f6 24 dxe5 ♕f5 25 ♘xf7 ♕xf7 26 e6 ♕f5 27 e7+ ♔g7 28 e8♘+ **1-0** L/N3145

**183̂?-★BW-1**
**Bourdonnais, L.C.M. de la+ Wyvill, M.**
⟨♖a1⟩ 1 e4 e5 2 f4 exf4 3 ♗c4 ♕h4+ 4 ♔f1 g5 5 ♘c3 ♗g7 6 d4 d6 7 ♘f3 ♕h5 8 ♘d5 ♔d8 9 h4 c6 10 ♘c3 h6 11 ♔f2 ♗g4 12 hxg5 ♗xf3 13 gxf3 ♕xg5 14 ♘e2 ♘d7 15 ♗xf4 ♕f6 16 ♗e3 ♘e7 17 f4 ♔c7 18 ♘g3 ♖ad8 19 ♘h5 ♕g6 20 ♖g1 ♕xe4 21 ♖xg7 ♘f5 22 ♖g3 ♘xg3 23 ♘xg3 ♕e7 24 d5 ♖de8 25 ♘f5 ♕e4 26 dxc6 bxc6 27 ♕xd6+ ♔d8 28 ♗d3 ♕h1 29 ♕b4 ♖hg8 30 ♕a5+ ♘b6 31 ♗xb6+ axb6 32 ♕xb6+ ♔d7 33 ♕b7+ ♔d8 34 ♕b8+ ♔d7 35 ♕d6+ ♔c8 36 ♗a6# **1-0** L/N3145

**183̂?-★BW-2**
**Walker, G.– Bourdonnais, L.C.M. de la**
⟨♙f7⟩ 1 e4 ... 2 d4 ♘c6 3 ♗d3 e5 4 d5 ♘ce7 5 ♗g5 ♘f6 6 ♗xf6 gxf6 7 ♕h5+ ♘g6 8 f4 exf4 9 ♘h3 ♕e7 10 ♘xf4 ♕f7 11 ♘xg6 ♕xg6 12 ♕f3 ♕g5 13 ♘d2 ♗c5 14 0-0-0 d6 15 h4 ♕g7 16 ♖df1 ♗d4 17 ♕h5+ ♔d8 18 ♕e2 ♗g4 19 ♘f3 a5 20 c3 ♗c5 21 ♕d2 c6 22 dxc6 bxc6 23 ♘d4 ♗d7 24 ♘f5 ♗xf5 25 ♖xf5 ♔c7 26 ♕f4 ♔b6 27 g4 ♖hf8 28 ♖hf1 a4 29 g5 fxg5 30 ♕xg5 ♕xg5+ 31 hxg5 ♖xf5 32 ♖xf5 ♖g8 33 ♔d2 ♖g7 34 ♗c2 a3 35 b4 ♗g1 36 ♖a5 ♗h2 37 ♔e3 ♗e5 38 ♖xa3 ♖xg5 39 ♗d1 h5 40 c4 h4 41 ♖b3 ♖g1 42 ♗f3 h3 43 a4 h2 44 ♔e2 h1♕ 45 ♗xh1 ♖xh1 46 ♔f2 ♖h2+ 47 ♔e1 ♖b2 48 ♖xb2 ♗xb2 49 ♔d2 ♗e5 **0-1** L/N3145

**183̂?-★BW-3**
**Walker, G.– Bourdonnais, L.C.M. de la**
⟨♙f7⟩ 1 d4 e6 2 c4 d5 3 ♘c3 ♘f6 4 e3 c6 5 f4 ♗d6 6 ♘f3 0-0 7 ♗d2 c5 8 cxd5 exd5 9 ♗e2 ♘c6 10 ♘b5 cxd4 11 ♘bxd4 ♖e8 12 ♕b3 ♗c5 13 ♘xc6 bxc6 14 ♘e5 ♘e4 15 g3 ♗d7 16 ♕a4 ♖b8 17 b4 ♗b6 18 ♖c1 ♖xe5 19 fxe5 ♕g5 20 e6 ♘xd2 21 exd7 ♕xe3 22 ♖c2 ♘f3+ 23 ♔d1 ♕d4+ 24 ♗d3 ♕xd3+ 25 ♔c1 ♗e3+ 26 ♔b2 ♕d4+ 27 ♔a3 ♗d2 28 b5 ♕e3+ 29 ♔b2 ♘e5 30 ♖d1 ♗e1 31 ♕b3 ♕e4 32 ♖xd5 cxd5 33 ♖c8+ ♔f7 34 d8♕ ♖xc8 35 ♕xc8 ♘c4+ 36 ♕bxc4 dxc4 37 ♕c7+ ♔e6 38 ♕c8+ ♔e5 39 ♕c7+ ♔d4 40 ♕xa7+ ♔d3 41 b6 ♗c3+ 42 ♔a3 ♕d4 43 ♕c7 ♗a5 **0-1** L/N3145

**183̂?-★BW-4**
**Walker, G.= Bourdonnais, L.C.M. de la**
⟨♙f7⟩ 1 e4 ♘c6 2 ♘c3 e6 3 d4 ♗b4 4 ♘f3 ♘ge7 5 d5 exd5 6 exd5 ♗xc3+ 7 bxc3 ♘b8 8 ♗c4 d6 9 ♘d4 ♘g6 10 0-0 0-0 11 f4 ♔h8 12 ♗d3 ♕h4 13 f5 ♘e5 14 ♖f4 ♕e7 15 ♕h5 c5 16 dxc6 ♘bxc6 17 ♗d2 ♘xd3 18 ♖h4 g6 19 fxg6 ♘xd4 20 cxd4 ♗f5 21 ♗g5 ♕g7 22 ♗h6 ♕xg6 23 ♕xg6 ♗xg6 24 ♗xf8 ♖xf8 25 cxd3 ♖c8 26 ♖e1 ♖c3 ...? **½-½** L/N3145

**183̂?-★B?-1**
**?– Bourdonnais, L.C.M. de la**
⟨♙f7⟩ 1 e4 ... 2 d4 ♘c6 3 d5 ♘e5 4 f4 ♘f7 5 e5 e6 6 dxe6 dxe6 7 ♕xd8+ ♘xd8 8 ♗e3 b6 9 ♘f3 ♗b7

10 ♗e2 ♘h6 11 h3 ♗e7 12 ♘bd2 ♘df7 13 0-0 0-0-0 14 ♗c4 ♗d5 15 c3 c5 16 ♗a6+ ♔c7 17 a4 ♖hg8 18 a5 g5 19 axb6+ axb6 20 ♗b5 ♘f5 21 ♗f2 gxf4 22 ♖a7+ ♔b8 23 ♖fa1 ♗b7 24 ♗c4 ♘e3 25 ♗f1 ♘xe5 26 ♘xe5 ♖xd2 27 ♖xb7+ ♔xb7 28 ♗a6+ ♔c7 29 ♗b5 ♖xg2+ 30 ♔h1 ♖dxf2 31 ♖a7+ ♔d6 32 ♘f7+ ♔d5 33 ♖d7+ ♔e4 34 ♗c6+ ♘d5 35 ♗xd5+ exd5 36 ♖xe7+ ♔d3 **0-1** L/N3145

## POPERT✕STAUNTON London

**[1840-✕PS]**

| | | | | | |
|---|---|---|---|---|---|
| H.W. Popert | 0 | 1 | 1 | 0 | 2 |
| H. Staunton | 1 | 0 | 0 | 1 | 2 |

### 1840-✕PS-1̂

**Popert, H.W.– Staunton, H.**

London [Staunton]

1 e4 c5!? 2 f4 [2 ♘f3?!] 2 ... e6 3 ♘f3 ♘c6 4 c3 d5 5 e5 ♘h6 6 ♗d3 ♗e7 7 ♗c2 ♗d7 8 0-0 ♕b6 9 d4 ♖c8 10 ♔h1 0-0 11 a3 a5 12 ♘g5 g6 13 dxc5 ♗xc5 14 ♕e1 ♘g4 15 h3 ♘e3 [15 ... ♘f2+?] 16 ♗xe3 ♗xe3 17 ♘d2 h6? [□ 17 ... ♕xb2] 18 ♘ge4! dxe4 [18 ... ♗xd2? 19 ♘f6++−] 19 ♘c4 ♕b5 20 ♘xe3 h5 21 ♖b1 f5 22 exf6 ♖xf6 23 ♗xe4 ♖cf8 24 ♕g3 ♘e7 25 b4 ♗c6! 26 ♗c2 axb4 27 c4 ♕b6 28 axb4 ♕d4 29 ♖bd1 ♕b6 30 b5 ♗e8± 31 ♖de1? ♕c7 32 ♔h2? ♖xf4 33 ♗e4 ...⚲ **0-1** L/N6122

### 1840-✕PS-2̂

**Staunton, H.– Popert, H.W.**

London [Staunton]

1 e4 e6 2 d4 d5 3 e5 c5 4 c3 ♘c6 5 ♘f3 ♗d7 6 a3 ♖c8 7 b4 cxd4 8 cxd4 ♗e7 9 ♗d3 f6 [□ 9 ... f5] 10 ♗d2 f5 11 ♕e2 ♖c7? 12 0-0 g5? 13 b5 ♘b8 14 ♘xg5 h5 15 ♘h3 h4 16 ♘c3 ♘h6 17 a4 ♔f7 18 ♖ac1 ♕g8 19 f3 ♔e8 20 ♖fe1 ♖c8 21 ♗f4 ♗d8 22 ♘xd5 ♖xc1 23 ♖xc1 exd5 24 e6 ♕xe6 25 ♕xe6+ ♗xe6 26 ♗xb8 [□ 26 ♖e1] 26 ... ♗b6 27 ♗e5 ♖g8 28 ♘f4 ♘f7! 29 ♘xe6? [29 ♗f6+−] 29 ... ♘xe5 30 ♗xf5 ♘xf3+ 31 ♔f2 ♘xd4 32 ♘xd4 ♗xd4+ 33 ♔f3 ♔f7 34 ♖d1 ♗e5 35 ♖xd5 ♗xh2 36 ♖d7+ ♔f6 37 ♗g4 ♖g7 38 ♖d6+?? [38 ♖xg7=] **0-1** L/N6122

### 1840-✕PS-3̂

**Popert, H.W.+ Staunton, H.**

London [Staunton]

1 e4 c5 2 ♘f3 ♘c6 3 d4 cxd4 4 ♘xd4 e5 5 ♘f3 ♘f6 6 ♘c3 ♗b4 7 ♗g5 0-0 8 ♗c4 ♗xc3+ 9 bxc3 ♕a5 10 ♕d3 [10 ♗xf6±] 10 ... d5 11 exd5 e4 12 ♕d2 exf3 13 ♗xf6 ♖e8+ [□ 13 ... fxg2 △ 14 ... ♖e8+ 15 ♔d1∓] 14 ♔f1 gxf6 15 dxc6 ♕h5 16 h3 fxg2+ 17 ♔xg2 ♔h8 18 ♕f4 ♖g8+ 19 ♔f1 ♕g6 20 ♗d3 ♕g2+ 21 ♔e2 ♕xc6 22 ♗xh7± ♕b5+ 23 ♗d3 ♕e5+ 24 ♕xe5 fxe5 25 ♖ab1 f5 26 ♖b5 ♖e8 27 ♗c4 a6? 28 ♖b6 ♗d7 29 ♖h6+ ♔g7 30 ♖d6 ♗b5 31 ♖g1+ ♔h7 32 ♗xb5 axb5 33 ♖dg6 ♖xa2 34 ♖g7+ ♔h6 35 ♖1g6+ ♔h5 36 h4 ♖xc2+ 37 ♔f1 ♖c1+ 38 ♔g2∓ ...⚲ **1-0** L/N6122

### 1840-✕PS-4̂

**Staunton, H.+ Popert, H.W.**

London [Staunton]

1 e4 e5 2 ♗c4 ♗c5 3 c3 d6 4 ♘f3 [□ 4 d4] 4 ... ♘f6 5 d4 exd4 6 cxd4 ♗b4+ 7 ♗d2 ♗xd2+ 8 ♘bxd2 0-0 [□ 8 ... d5] 9 ♗d3 ♘c6 10 a3 ♗g4 11 ♕c2 h6 12 ♖c1 d5 13 e5 ♗xf3 14 ♘xf3 ♘h5 15 g3 g6 16 b4 ♕d7! 17 ♕d2 [17 b5 ♕g4!∓] 17 ... ♔h7 18 0-0 ♖ae8 19 ♖c3 ♘d8 20 ♘h4 c6 21 f4 f5 22 g4 ♘g7 23 gxf5 ♘xf5 24 ♘xf5 gxf5 25 ♔h1 ♖g8 26 ♖cc1 ♕f7 27 ♕c2 ♖ef8 28 ♖g1 ♘e6 29 ♖xg8 ♔xg8 30 ♖g1+ ♔h8 [□ 30 ... ♔h7] 31 ♕f2 ♕h5?+− 32 ♗e2 ♕f7 33 ♕h4 ♕h7 34 ♗h5 ♘xd4 35 ♖g3 b6 36 ♗g6 [□ 36 ♗f7] 36 ... ♕g7 37 ♗f7 ♖xf7 38 ♖xg7 ♔xg7 39 ♔g2 ...⚲ **1-0** L/N6122

### 1840-★BK-1 26 ii 40

**Kieseritsky, L.+ Bourdonnais, L.C.M.de la**

Paris [Kieseritsky & Staunton]

⟨♙f7⟩ 1 e4 ... 2 d4 e6 3 ♗d3 c5 4 dxc5 ♕a5+ 5 ♘c3 ♗xc5 6 ♕h5+ g6 7 ♕f3 ♘e7 8 ♗h6! ♘bc6 9 ♘ge2 d5 10 exd5 exd5 11 0-0 ♗d7 12 a3 ♘d4 13 ♘xd4 ♗xd4 14 ♖fe1 ♕c5?! 15 ♘xd5 ♗c6 16 ♖xe7+ ♕xe7 17 ♘xe7 ♗xf3 18 ♖e1! ♔d7 19 gxf3 a6 [19 ... ♖e8? 20 ♗b5++−] 20 ♘d5 ♖he8 21 ♖e4 ♖xe4 22 fxe4 g5 23 c3 [22 ♗xg5!? ♖g8 23 h4 h6 24 c3 ♗h8 25 f4 hxg5 26 hxg5±] 23 ... ♗a7 24 ♗xg5 ♖f8 25 ♘f6+ ♔e6 26 ♗c4+ ♔d6 27 e5+ ♔c7 28 ♗e3! ♗xe3 29 ♘d5+ ♔c6 30 ♘xe3 b5 31 ♗d3 h6 32 ♗e4+ ♔d7 33 ♗f5+ ♔c6 34 f4 a5 35 b4 ♔b6 36 ♘d5+ ♔c6 37 ♗e4 axb4 38 axb4 ♔d7 39 f5 **1-0** L/N6123-1854

### 1840-★BK-2 13 iii 40

**Kieseritsky, L.= Bourdonnais, L.C.M.de la**

Paris [Kieseritsky & Staunton]

⟨♙f7⟩ 1 e4 ... 2 d4 e6 3 ♗d3 c5 4 dxc5 ♕a5+ 5 ♘c3 ♗xc5 6 ♕h5+ g6 7 ♕f3 [7 ♕e5?? ♗xf2+−+] 7 ... ♘c6 8 ♘ge2 d6 9 a3 ♗d7 10 ♗g5! a6 11 0-0 ♕c7 12 b4 ♗b6 13 ♖fe1 ♘e5 14 ♕g3 ♘f7 15 a4 h6 16 ♗d2 ♘e7 17 a5 ♗a7 18 b5 ♗c5 19 b6 ♕c6 20 ♘a4 0-0-0 21 ♘xc5 ♕xc5 22 ♖ab1 e5 23 ♗e3 ♕c6 [23 ... ♕xa5? 24 ♖a1 ♗a4 (24 ... ♕b4? 25 ♖eb1+−) 25 ♗c4+−] 24 ♖b3 ♔b8 25 ♖a1 d5 26 ♖c3 ♕e6 27 ♘d4! ♕d6 28 ♖c7 g5 [28 ... exd4? 29 ♗f4+−] 29 ♘b5!

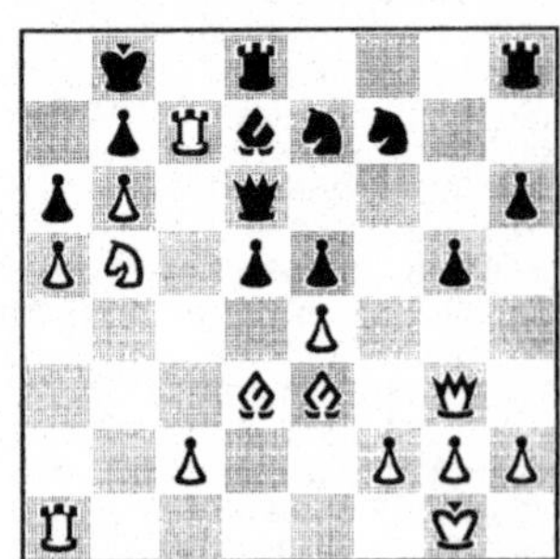

29 ... ♕f6 [29 ... axb5 30 ♗c5 ♕e6 31 a6 ♖c8 32 ♖xb7+ ♔a8 33 ♗xe7 ♕xe7 34 ♗xb5 ♖hd8 (34 ... ♖cd8 35 ♗c6+−) 35 ♖xd7 ♖xd7 36 ♗xd7 ♕xd7 37 b7++−; 31 ... bxa6 32 ♖xa6 ♘d6 (32 ... ♘c8 33 ♗xb5 ♗xb5 34 ♕a3 ♗c6 35 ♖aa7+−) 33 ♗f1 b4 34 ♕b3 d4 35 ♕xb4 ♘ec8 (35 ... ♗c6 36 ♕a5+−) 36 ♗xd6 ♕xd6 37 ♖a8+ ♔xa8 38 ♕a5+ ♔b8 39 ♖xc8+ ♔xc8 40 ♕a6+ ♔b8 41 ♕a7+ ♔c8 42 ♗a6#; 31 ... ♘d6 32 axb7 ♘xb7 33 ♖a8+ ♔xa8 34 ♗xb5 ♘c6 35 ♖xc6 (35 ♗xc6? ♕xc6 36 ♖xc6 ♗xc6 37 ♕a3+ ♔b8 38 ♕a7+ ♔c8 39 exd5 ♖xd5∓) 35 ... ♗xc6 36 ♕a3+ ♔b8 37 ♕a7+ ♔c8 38 ♕a8+ ♔d7 39 ♕xb7+ ♔e8 40 ♗xc6+ ♖d7 41 ♕c8++−] 30 ♗c5 ♘g6 31 ♘c3 ♘f4 32 ♘xd5 ♘xd5 33 exd5 h5 34 ♗e4 h4 35 ♕a3 ♖he8 36 d6 ♗c8 37 ♖d1 ♖d7 38 ♗xb7! ♗xb7 [38 ... ♖xc7 39 bxc7+ ♔xb7 40 ♕b4+ ♔c6 41 ♕e4+ ♔d7 42 ♕a4+ ♔e6 43 ♕xe8+ ♔f5 44 ♕xc8++−] 39 ♖xd7 g4 40 ♖e7 ♖d8 41 d7 g3 42 ♗d6+?! [□ 42 fxg3] 42 ... ♔a8 43 ♕c5 [□ 42 fxg3] 43 ... ♘xd6 44 ♖xe5 gxf2+ 45 ♔f1 ♗xg2+ 46 ♔xg2 ♖g8+? [□ 46 ... f1♕+!−+] 47 ♔f1 ♖g1+ 48 ♔e2 f1♕+ 49 ♖xf1 ♕xf1+ 50 ♔d2 ♖g2+ 51 ♔c3 ♕a1+ 52 ♔b3 ♕b1+ 53 ♔a3 ♘b5+ 54 ♕xb5 ♕a1+ 55 ♔b3 ♕b1+ 56 ♔a3 ♕a1+ **½-½** L/N6123-1854

### 1840-★BW-1

**Walker, G.+ Bourdonnais, L.C.M.de la**

London

⟨♙f7⟩ 1 e4 ♘c6 2 ♘c3 e6 3 d4 d5 4 e5 ♘ce7? 5 ♗g5 ♗d7?! 6 ♗d3 g6 7 h4 c5? 8 ♘b5 ♗xb5 9 ♗xb5+ ♔f7 10 ♕f3+ ♔g7 11 ♗f6+ ♘xf6 12 ♕xf6+ ♔g8 13 ♕xe6+ ♔g7 14 ♕f6+ ♔g8 15 e6 **1-0** L/N6013-1842

**1840-★BW-2** 5 xii 40
**Walker, G.– Bourdonnais, L.C.M.de la**
London [Kieseritsky]
〈♙f7〉 1 d4?! [◻1 e4] 1 ... e6 2 c4 d5 3 ♘c3 ♘f6 4 e3 c6 5 ♗d2 ♗d6 6 f4 0-0 7 ♘f3 c5 8 ♗e2?! [◻8 ♗d3] 8 ... ♘c6 9 cxd5 exd5 10 ♘b5 cxd4 11 ♘bxd4 [11 ♘xd6? dxe3 12 ♘xc8 exd2+ 13 ♕xd2 ♖xc8∓] 11 ... ♖e8! 12 ♕b3 ♗c5 13 ♘xc6 bxc6 14 ♘e5! ♘e4 15 g3 ♗d7 16 ♕a4? ♖b8 17 b4 ♗b6 18 ♖c1 ♖xe5!! 19 fxe5 ♕g5 20 e6? [◻20 ♕b3] 20 ... ♘xd2 21 exd7 ♕xe3 22 ♖c2 ♘f3+ 23 ♔d1 ♕d4+ 24 ♗d3 ♕xd3+ 25 ♔c1 ♗e3+ 26 ♔b2 ♕d4+ 27 ♔a3 ♗d2 28 b5 ♕e3+ 29 ♔b2 ♘e5 30 ♖d1 ♗e1 31 ♕b3 ♕e4 32 ♖xd5! cxd5 33 ♖c8+ ♔f7 34 d8♕ ♖xc8 35 ♕xc8 ♘c4+ 36 ♕bxc4 dxc4 37 ♕c7+ ♔e6 38 ♕c8+ ♔e5 39 ♕c7+ ♔d4 40 ♕xa7+ ♔d3 41 b6 ♕d4+ 42 ♔a3 ♗c3 43 ♕c7 ♗a5 **0-1** L/N6013-1842

**1840̂-★BS-1**
**Bourdonnais, L.C.M.de la– Slous, F.L.**
London
〈♙f2〉 1 ... e5 2 ... d5 3 ♘c3 d4 4 ♘e4 f5 5 ♘f2 ♗d6 6 e4 ♘f6 7 d3 c5 8 ♘f3 ♘c6 9 c3 0-0 10 ♗e2 ♗d7 11 ♗g5 h6 12 ♗xf6 ♖xf6 13 ♕c2 ♕e7 14 ♖g1 ♖af8 15 0-0-0 b5 16 ♕b3+ ♗e6 17 ♕xb5 ♕c7 18 exf5 ♗xf5 19 ♘e4 ♖6f7 20 ♕a4 ♗d7 21 ♕c2 ♗e7 22 g4 ♗e6?! [◻22 ... ♖xf3 23 ♗xf3 ♖xf3∓] 23 ♕a4 ♖b8 24 ♖df1 ♕b6 25 b3 dxc3 26 g5 c4! 27 d4 cxb3 28 g6 b2+ 29 ♔b1 ♘b4 30 gxf7+ ♗xf7 31 ♘xc3 exd4 32 ♘e5 dxc3 33 ♖xg7+ ♔xg7 34 ♖xf7+ ♔g8 35 ♗c4 c2+ 36 ♕xc2 ♘xc2 37 ♖f6+ ♔h8 38 ♖xb6 ♖xb6 39 ♗b3 ♘a3+ 40 ♔xb2 ♗f6 41 ♔xa3 ♖xb3+ **0-1**
L/N6123-1843

**1840-★FM-1**
**Morphy, E.+ Ford, A.P.**
New Orleans [Morphy, E.]
1 e4 e5 2 ♘f3 ♘c6 3 ♗c4 ♗c5 4 b4 ♗xb4 5 c3 ♗a5 6 0-0 ♘ge7? 7 ♘g5 d5 8 exd5 ♘xd5 9 ♘xf7 ♔xf7 10 ♕f3+ ♔e6 11 ♗a3 ♗b6 [△12 ... ♘a5] 12 ♖e1 ♘a5 13 ♖xe5+ ♔xe5 14 d4+ ♔e6 15 g4 g6 16 ♕e4+ ♔f7 17 ♗xd5+ ♔g7 18 ♗e7 ♖e8 [18 ... ♕d7 19 ♕e5+ ♔h6 20 ♗g5#] 19 ♕e5+ ♔h6 20 g5+ ♔h5 21 ♗f3+ ♗g4 22 ♕g3 **1-0** M291

**1841-★BS-1**
**Brown, J.– Staunton, H.**
London [Staunton]
〈♙f7〉 1 e4 ... 2 d4 e6 3 ♗d3 c5 4 e5 g6 5 h4 cxd4 6 h5 ♕a5+ 7 ♔f1 ♕xe5 8 hxg6 h6 9 g7 ♕xg7 10 ♕h5+ ♔d8 11 ♗g5+ ♔c7 12 ♘f3 ♘c6 13 ♘a3 ♗xa3 14 bxa3 ♘f6 15 ♗f4+ [15 ♗xh6 ♘xh5 16 ♗xg7 ♘g3+ 17 fxg3 ♖xh1+] 15 ... d6 16 ♕b5 ♘d5 17 ♗g3 ♖f8 18 ♖h5 a6 19 ♕c5 ♘e3+ 20 ♔g1 [20 fxe3?–+] 20 ... e5

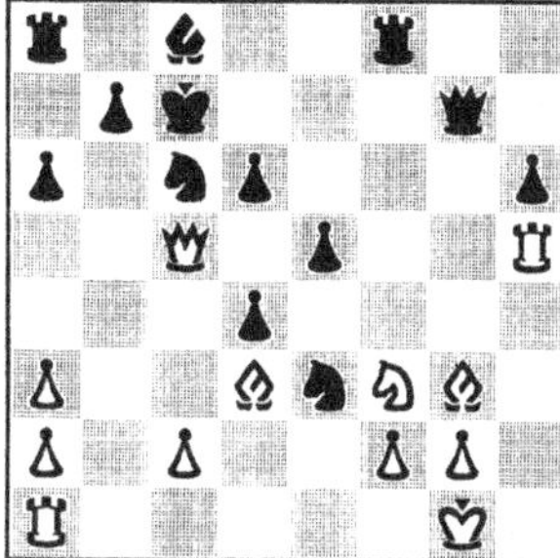

21 ♖xe5! ♖xf3 22 ♖xe3 ♖f6 [22 ... ♖xg3 23 ♖xg3 ♕xg3 24 ♕xc6+ bxc6 25 fxg3] 23 ♖f3 b6 24 ♕d5 ♕f8 25 ♖xf6 [25 ♕xd6+±] 25 ... ♕xf6 26 ♖e1 ♗d7 27 ♖e4 b5 28 f3 [◻28 ♖f4] 28 ... ♖e8 29 ♗f2 ♖xe4 30 ♗xe4 ♕e5 31 ♕g8 ♘d8 32 ♗h4 ♘c6 33 ♔f2 ♕f4 34 ♗g3 ♕e3+ 35 ♔f1 ♕xa3 36 ♗xc6 ♕c1+ 37 ♗e1 ♗xc6 38 ♕g7+ ♔c8 39 ♕xd4 d5 40 ♕h8+ ♔b7 41 ♕h7+ ♔b6 42 ♔e2 ♕f4 43 ♗f2+ ♔a5 44 ♕a7 ♕c4+ 45 ♔d1 b4 46 ♗e1 ♗b5 47 ♕e7 ♕d4+ 48 ♔c1 ♕a1+ 49 ♔d2 ♕xa2 50 ♕c7+ ♔a4 **0-1** L/N6122

**1841-★CS-1**
**Cochrane, J.– Staunton, H.**
London
1 e4 e5 2 ♗c4 ♗c5 3 ♘f3 ♘c6 4 d3 ♘f6 5 0-0 d5 6 exd5 ♘xd5 7 ♗xd5 ♕xd5 8 ♘c3 ♕e6 9 ♘g5 ♕g4 10 ♕xg4 ♗xg4 11 ♗e3 ♗d6 12 ♘ge4 ♗e6 13 ♘xd6+ cxd6 14 f4 f6 15 fxe5 fxe5 16 ♘e4 ♖d8 17 ♘g5 ♗g8 18 ♖f2 h6 19 ♘f3 g5 20 ♖af1 ♖h7 21 ♘d2 ♖f7 22 ♖f6 ♘e7 23 ♘e4 ♘d5 24 ♖xf7 ♗xf7 25 ♘f6+ ♔e7 26 ♘xd5+ ♗xd5 27 h4 gxh4 28 ♗f2 ♖g8 29 ♗xh4+ ♔d7 30 g3 ♖g6 31 a3 b5 32 ♔f2 a5 33 ♔e3 ♗e6 34 ♖f8 ♔c6 35 ♖a8 a4 36 ♖a6+ ♔d5 37 b3 axb3 38 cxb3 ♗d7 39 b4 ♖g4 40 ♖a8 ♔e6 41 ♖f8 ♖g6 42 ♖a8 ♗c6 43 ♖c8 ♔d5 44 ♖f8 ♖g7 45 ♖f6 h5 46 ♖h6 ♗e8 47 ♖h8 ♗g6 48 ♖b8 ♔c6 49 ♗d8 ♖g8 50 ♖b6+ ♔d7 51 ♗h4 ♖a8 52 ♖b7+ ♔c6 53 ♖g7 ♗f5 54 ♖g5 ♗g4 55 ♖g6 ♖xa3 56 ♗e7 ♖xd3+ 57 ♔xd3 ♗f5+ **0-1** L/N6122

**1841-★CS-2**
**Cochrane, J.– Staunton, H.**
London [Staunton]
1 e4 e5 2 ♘f3 ♘c6 3 d4 exd4 4 ♗c4 ♗b4+ 5 c3 dxc3 6 bxc3 ♗a5 7 e5!? h6 [◻7 ... d6] 8 ♕b3 ♕e7 9 ♗a3 d6 10 0-0 ♘xe5 11 ♘xe5 ♕xe5 12 ♗xf7+ ♔f8 13 ♗b2 ♕f6 14 ♗c4 ♗b6 15 ♘d2 ♗f5 16 ♖ae1 ♘e7 17 ♘e4 ♕g6 18 ♘g3 ♗c2 19 ♕b5 c6 20 ♕h5 ♕xh5 21 ♘xh5 d5 22 ♗e2 ♔f7 23 ♗g4 ♗d3 24 ♗e2 ♗xe2 25 ♖xe2 ♖he8 26 ♖fe1 g5 27 ♖e6 ♘g8 28 ♖xe8 ♖xe8 29 ♖xe8 ♔xe8 30 g4 ♔f7 31 ♔g2 ♘f6 32 ♘xf6 ♔xf6 33 ♔f3 ♔e5 34 h4 gxh4 35 ♗c1 ♗a5? 36 ♗xh6 ♔e6 [36 ... ♗xc3?? 37 ♗g7+± 37 ♗g7 ♗c7 38 ♗d4 a5 ... ♀] **0-1** L/N6122

**1841-★CS-3**
**Cochrane, J.Φ Staunton, H.**
London♀ [Staunton]
1 e4 c5 2 c4? e6 3 ♘c3 ♘e7 4 f4 ♘g6 5 d3 ♗e7 6 ♘f3 d6 7 ♗e2 ♘c6 8 0-0 ♗f6 9 ♗e3 ♗d4 10 ♕d2 ♘xf4 11 ♘xd4 cxd4 12 ♗xf4 dxc3 13 bxc3 e5 14 ♗e3 0-0 15 ♖f2 ♕e7 16 ♖af1 b6 17 h4 ♖b8 [17 ... ♕xh4 18 ♗g5+-] 18 h5 f6 19 h6 ♖f7 20 hxg7 ♖xg7 21 ♗h6 ♖g6 22 ♗h5 f5 23 ♗xg6 hxg6 24 exf5 gxf5 25 ♕g5+ ♕xg5 26 ♗xg5 ♖b7 27 g3 ♖g7 28 ♗h4 ♗e6 29 ♖xf5 ♗xf5 30 ♖xf5 ♖g6 31 ♔f2 ♔g7 32 ♔e3+-
L/N6123-1847

**1841-★CS-4**
**Cochrane, J.– Staunton, H.**
London [Staunton]
1 e4 e5 2 ♗c4 ♗c5 3 d4 ♗xd4 4 ♘f3 ♘c6 5 0-0 ♘f6 6 ♘xd4 ♘xd4 7 f4 d6 8 fxe5 dxe5 9 ♗g5 ♗e6 10 ♗xe6 ♘xe6 11 ♕xd8+ ♖xd8 12 ♗xf6 gxf6 13 ♖xf6 ♘f4 14 ♘c3 ♖d2 15 ♖d1? [◻15 g3] 15 ... ♖xg2+ 16 ♔h1 ♖hg8 17 ♖f5 f6 18 ♖xf6 ♘h3 19 ♖ff1

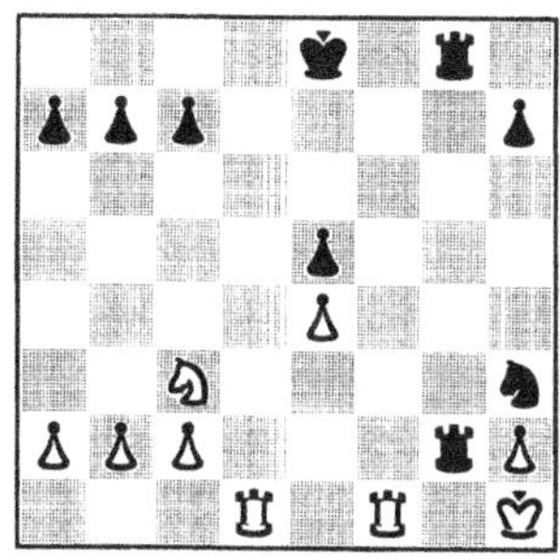

19 ... ♖g1+ 20 ♖xg1 ♘f2# **0-1**
L/N6123-1843

**1841-★CS-5**
**Cochrane, J.– Staunton, H.**
London [Staunton]

1 e4 e5 2 ♘f3 ♘c6 3 ♗c4 ♗c5 4 c3 d6 5 b4 ♗b6 6 a4 a6 7 a5 ♗a7 8 h3 ♘f6 9 d3 h6 10 0-0 0-0 11 ♘h2 ♘e7 12 ♔h1 ♘g6 13 f4 exf4 14 ♗xf4 ♗e6 15 ♘d2? [□ 15 ♘a3] 15 ... ♘xf4 16 ♖xf4 ♗e3 17 ♖f1 ♗xd2 18 ♕xd2 ♗xc4 19 dxc4 ♘xe4 20 ♕e3 f5 21 g4 ♕h4 22 ♔g2 fxg4 23 ♘xg4 [23 ♕xe4?? gxh3+, 24 ... ♕xe4] 23 ... ♘g5 24 ♕d3 h5 25 ♘h2 ♕e4+ 26 ♕xe4 ♘xe4 27 ♖xf8+ ♖xf8 28 ♖e1 ♘xc3 29 ♖e7 ♖f7 30 ♖e8+ ♔h7 31 ♘f3 ♖f4 32 ♖b8 ♖xc4 33 ♖xb7 ♘b5 34 ♘g5+ ♔g6 35 ♘e6 ♔f6 **0-1** L/N6123-1842

**1841-★CS-6**
**Staunton, H.+ Cochrane, J.**
London

1 e4 e5 2 ♘f3 f5 3 ♘xe5 ♕f6 4 d4 d6 5 ♘f3 fxe4 6 ♘g5 ♗f5 7 ♘c3 ♕g6 8 ♗c4 ♘h6 9 0-0 ♗e7 10 ♘gxe4 ♗xe4 11 ♘xe4 ♕xe4 12 ♗xh6 gxh6 13 ♕h5+ ♕g6 14 ♕b5+ ♘d7 15 ♕xb7 ♖b8 16 ♕xc7 d5 17 ♗b3 ♕d6 18 ♕xa7 0-0 19 ♕a5 ♘b6 20 ♖ae1 ♗f6 21 c3 ♖be8 22 ♖xe8 ♖xe8 23 ♕b5 ♖f8 24 a4 ♖b8 25 ♖e1 ♔g7 26 ♕e2 ♕f4 27 g3 ♕g5 28 a5 ♘c4 29 ♗xc4 dxc4 30 ♕xc4 ♖xb2 31 a6 ♕d2 32 ♕c7+ ♔g6 33 ♖f1 ♖a2 34 ♕c6 ♕e2 35 c4 ♕d3 36 d5 ♕a3 37 ♕e8+ ♔g7 38 ♕d7+ ♔g6 39 h4 ♕xa6 40 h5+ ♔xh5 41 ♕f5+ ♗g5 42 ♔g2 ♖a1 43 ♔h3 **1-0** L/N6123

**1841-★CS-7**
**Staunton, H.+ Cochrane, J.**
London

1 e4 e5 2 ♘f3 ♘c6 3 ♗c4 ♗c5 4 b4 ♗xb4 5 c3 ♗a5 6 0-0 ♗b6 7 d4 exd4 8 cxd4 d6 9 ♗b2 ♘f6 10 d5 ♘e7 11 e5 dxe5 12 ♗xe5 0-0 13 ♗xf6 gxf6 14 ♘c3 ♘g6 15 ♘e4 ♗g4 16 ♕b3 ♗xf3 17 ♕xf3 ♔g7 18 ♘g3 ♔h8 19 ♖ad1 ♘e5 20 ♕e4 ♘xc4 21 ♕xc4 ♖g8 22 ♕h4 ♖g6 23 ♖d3 ♕g8 24 ♔h1 ♖g5 25 ♘h5 ♕g6 26 ♖h3 ♗xf2 27 ♕xf2 ♖xh5 28 ♖xh5 ♕xh5 29 ♕xf6+ ♔g8 30 ♖f3 **1-0** L/N6123

**1841-★CS-8**
**Staunton, H.+ Cochrane, J.**
London

1 e4 e5 2 ♘f3 ♘c6 3 d4 exd4 4 ♗c4 ♗c5 5 0-0 ♕f6 6 c3 d6 7 b4 ♗b6 8 ♗g5 ♕g6 9 cxd4 ♘xd4 10 ♘xd4 ♗xd4 11 ♕xd4 ♕xg5 12 f4 ♕g6 13 ♘c3 c6 14 e5 d5 15 ♖ad1 ♘e7 16 ♗d3 ♗f5 17 ♗xf5 ♘xf5 18 ♕c5 b6 19 ♕f2 0-0 20 ♘e2 ♕e6 21 g4 ♘h6 22 h3 c5 23 bxc5 bxc5 24 ♕xc5 ♘xg4 25 hxg4 ♕xg4+ 26 ♔f2 ♕h4+ 27 ♔e3 ♖ac8 28 ♕xd5 ♖fd8 29 ♕b7 ♕h3+ 30 ♖f3 ♕f5 31 ♖xd8+ ♖xd8 32 ♘d4 ♕h5 33 ♕xa7 ♕h1 34 ♘e2 **1-0** L/N6123

**1841-★CS-9**
**Staunton, H.+ Cochrane, J.**
London

1 e4 e5 2 ♗c4 ♗c5 3 ♕e2 ♘f6 4 f4 ♗xg1 5 ♖xg1 exf4 6 d4 0-0 7 ♗xf4 d5 8 ♗xd5 ♘xd5 9 exd5 ♖e8 10 ♗e3 ♕e7 11 ♔d2 ♕b4+ 12 ♘c3 c5 13 dxc5 ♘a6 14 a3 ♕h4 15 g3 ♕f6 16 b4 ♗d7 17 ♖af1 ♕g6 18 ♕d3 ♕h5 19 h4 ♗g4 20 ♖f4 ♖ad8 21 ♖gf1 ♘c7 22 d6 ♘e6 23 ♖4f2 b6 24 ♘d5 bxc5 25 bxc5 f5 26 ♔c1 ♕g6 27 c6 ♖xd6 28 ♘e7+ ♖xe7 29 ♕xd6 ♕f6 30 ♕b8+ ♔f7 31 ♕b2 **1-0** L/N6123

**1841-★CS-10**
**Staunton, H– Cochrane, J.**
London

1 e4 e5 2 ♘f3 ♘c6 3 ♘c3 ♗c5 4 ♗c4 d6 5 ♘a4 ♗g4 6 ♘xc5 dxc5 7 c3 ♕f6 8 ♗e2 0-0-0 9 a4 ♘ge7 10 b3 ♘g6 11 g3 h5 12 d3 ♕e7 13 ♗e3 ♗xf3 14 ♗xf3 h4 15 ♕d2 hxg3 16 fxg3 ♕d7 17 ♖d1 b6 18 ♕e2 ♔b8 19 ♗g4 ♕e7 20 0-0 f6 21 ♖f2 ♘f8 22 ♖df1 ♘e6 23 ♗f5 ♖d6 24 ♖d1 ♖hd8 25 ♗c1 ♕f7 26 ♕g4 ♘f8 27 ♕f3 ♕xb3 28 ♖fd2 c4 29 d4

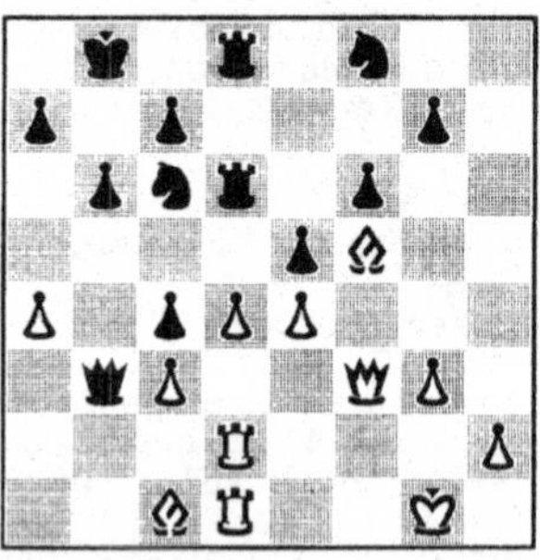

29 ... ♘xd4 **0-1** L/N6123

**1841-★CS-11**
**Staunton, H.+ Cochrane, J.**
London

1 e4 e5 2 ♘f3 ♘c6 3 ♗c4 ♗c5 4 b4 ♗xb4 5 c3 ♗a5 6 0-0 ♗b6 7 d4 exd4 8 cxd4 d6 9 ♗b2 ♘f6 10 e5 dxe5 11 ♗a3 ♗xd4 12 ♕b3 ♕d7 13 ♘g5 ♘d8 14 ♘c3 h6 15 ♘ge4 ♘xe4 16 ♘xe4 b6 17 ♗d5 ♗b7 18 ♗xb7 ♘xb7 19 ♖ad1 0-0-0 20 ♖fe1 f5 21 ♘c3 ♕c6 22 ♘b5 ♔b8 23 ♖dc1 ♘c5 24 ♘xd4 exd4 25 ♗xc5 **1-0** L/N6123

**1841-★CS-12**
**Cochrane, J.– Staunton, H.**
London

1 e4 e5 2 ♗c4 ♗c5 3 ♘f3 ♘c6 4 d3 ♘f6 5 0-0 d5 6 exd5 ♘xd5 7 ♗xd5 ♕xd5 8 ♘c3 ♕e6 9 ♘g5 ♕g4 10 ♕xg4 ♗xg4 11 ♗e3 ♗d6 12 ♘ge4 ♗e6 13 ♘xd6+ cxd6 14 f4 f6 15 fxe5 fxe5 16 ♘e4 ♖d8 17 ♘g5 ♗g8 18 ♖f2 h6 19 ♘f3 g5 20 ♖af1 ♖h7 21 ♘d2 ♖f7 22 ♖f6 ♘e7 23 ♘e4 ♘d5 24 ♖xf7 ♗xf7 25 ♘f6+ ♔e7 26 ♘xd5+ ♗xd5 27 h4 gxh4 28 ♗f2 ♖g8 29 ♗xh4+ ♔d7 30 g3 ♖g6 31 a3 b5 32 ♔f2 a5 33 ♔e3 ♗e6 34 ♖f8 ♔c6 35 ♖a8 a4 36 ♖a6+ ♔d5 37 b3 axb3 38 cxb3 ♗d7 39 b4 ♖g4 40 ♖a8 ♔e6 41 ♖f8 ♖g6 42 ♖a8 ♗c6 43 ♖c8 ♔d5 44 ♖f8 ♖g7 45 ♖f6 h5 46 ♖h6 ♗e8 47 ♖h8 ♗g6 48 ♖b8 ♔c6 49 ♗d8 ♖g8 50 ♖b6+ ♔d7 51 ♗h4 ♖a8 52 ♖b7+ ♔c6 53 ♖g7 ♗f5 54 ♖g5 ♗g4 55 ♖g6 ♖xa3 56 ♗e7

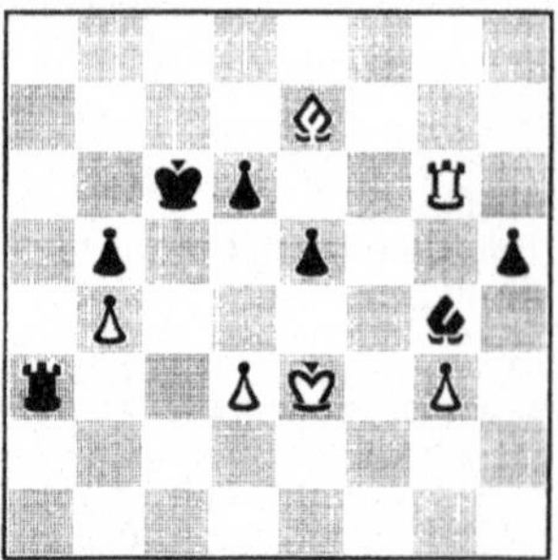

56 ... ♖xd3+ 57 ♔xd3 ♗f5+ **0-1** L/N6123

**1841-★CS-13**
**Cochrane, J.– Staunton, H.**
London

1 e4 e5 2 ♘f3 ♘c6 3 d4 exd4 4 ♗c4 ♗c5 5 0-0 d6 6 c3 ♗g4 7 ♕b3 ♗xf3 8 ♗xf7+ ♔f8 9 gxf3 ♘e5 10 ♗h5 ♕h4 11 cxd4 ♗xd4 12 ♗g4 ♘xg4 13 fxg4 ♕xg4+ 14 ♕g3 ♕xe4 15 ♘c3 ♗xc3 16 bxc3 ♘f6 17 ♗g5 h6 18 ♖ae1 ♕f5 19 ♗xf6 gxf6 20 ♕e3 ♕g5+ 21 ♕g3 ♖g8 **0-1** L/N6123

**1841-★CS-14**
**Cochrane, J.– Staunton, H.**
London

1 e4 e5 2 ♘f3 ♘c6 3 d4 exd4 4 ♘xd4 ♘xd4 5 ♕xd4 ♘e7 6 ♗d3 d6 7 0-0 ♘c6 8 ♕e3 ♗e7 9 ♗d2 ♗f6 10 ♗c3 0-0 11 ♗xf6 ♕xf6 12 ♘c3 ♘e5 13 ♘d5 ♕d8 14 ♗e2 c6 15 ♘f4 f5 16 exf5 ♗xf5 17 ♕b3+ d5 18 ♘d3 ♗xd3 19 ♗xd3 ♕h4 20 ♗e2 ♖ae8 21 ♕g3 ♕f6 22 ♖ae1 ♘g6 23 ♗h5 ♖xe1 24 ♖xe1 ♘f4 ...? **0-1** L/N6123

**1841-★CS-15**
**Cochrane, J.+ Staunton, H.**
London
1 e4 e5 2 ♗c4 ♗c5 3 d4 ♗xd4 4 ♘f3 ♕f6 5 0-0 ♗b6 6 ♘c3 c6 7 ♗g5 ♕g6 8 ♘xe5 ♕xg5 9 ♘xf7 ♕c5 10 ♗b3 d5 11 ♘xh8 ♘f6 12 exd5 cxd5 13 ♘xd5 ♘bd7 14 ♕e2+ ♔f8 15 ♖ae1 a6 16 ♘xf6 ♘xf6 17 ♘f7 ♗d7

18 ♘g5 ♖e8 19 ♕xe8+ ♘xe8 20 ♘xh7# **1-0** L/N6123

**1841-★CS-16**
**Cochrane, J.– Staunton, H.**
London
1 e4 e6 2 d4 d5 3 e5 c5 4 c3 ♘c6 5 f4 ♕b6 6 ♘f3 ♘h6 7 ♗d3 ♗e7 8 ♗c2 0-0 9 0-0 f5 10 ♔h1 ♗d7 11 h3 ♖ac8 12 a3 a5 13 ♖g1 cxd4 14 cxd4 ♕c7 15 ♘c3 ♘a7 16 g4 b5 17 gxf5 b4 18 fxe6 ♗xe6 19 ♘g5 ♗xg5 20 fxg5 ♘f5 21 ♗xf5 ♗xf5 22 ♘e2 ♗e4+ 23 ♔h2 ♕c2 24 ♕e1 ♘b5 25 ♗e3 ♕d3 26 ♖g3 ♖c2 **0-1**
L/N6123

**1841-★DD-1** 21 vi 41
**Demoucheau=**
**Deschapelles, A.L.H.L.**
Paris [Saint-Amant]
⟨♙f7⟩ 1 e4 ... 2 d4 e6 3 ♗d3 ♘c6 4 c3 e5 5 ♘f3 d6 6 h3 ♘f6 7 ♗g5 ♗e7 8 ♗xf6 gxf6 9 ♗c4 ♘a5 10 ♗d3 [◻ 10 ♗b3] 10 ... 0-0 11 g4 d5! 12 dxe5 fxe5 13 exd5 ♖f4 14 ♘xe5 ♗d6 15 ♘f3 ♕e7+ 16 ♔f1 c5 17 ♔g2 ♗d7 18 ♖e1 [◻ 18 ♘bd2] 18 ... ♕g7 19 ♘h2 ♖af8 20 f3 ♕g5 21 ♖e4 h5 22 ♕e1 hxg4 23 hxg4 ♔g7 24 ♘d2 ♕xd5 25 ♖xf4 ♖xf4 26 ♗e4 ♕g5 27 ♖d1! ♕h6 28 ♘df1 ♘c4 29 ♖d5 ♘e5 30 ♕e2 ♘f7 31 ♖h5 ♕f6 32 ♕d3 ♘e5 33 ♕d5 ♗c6 34 ♕b3? c4 35 ♕d1 ♗xe4 36 fxe4 ♘d3 37 ♕a4 ♘e1+ 38 ♔g1 ♕e6 39 ♘e3 ♕xe4 40 ♕d7+ ♗e7 41 ♕d4+ ♕xd4 42 cxd4 ♗f6 43 ♖a5 b5 44 ♘f5+ ♔g6 45 ♖xb5 ♗xd4+ 46 ♘xd4 ♖xd4 47 ♔f2 ♖e4 48 ♘f3 ♘d3+ 49 ♔g3 ♖e2 50 ♘d4 ♖xb2 51 ♖xb2 ♘xb2 ½-½
L/N6013-1842

**81** Devinck, F.J. L/N6396.BL

**1841-★DS-1** 21 xi 41
**Devinck, F.J.= Saint-Amant, P.C.F. de**
⟨♙f7⟩ 1 e4 ♘c6 2 d4 e5 3 d5 ♘ce7 4 ♗g5 g6 5 h4 h6 6 ♗xe7 ♕xe7 7 ♕g4 ♕b4+ 8 ♘d2 ♘e7 9 b3 h5 10 ♕f3 ♗h6 11 c3 ♗xd2+ 12 ♔xd2 ♕a3 13 ♔c2 d6 14 ♗d3 a5 15 ♘e2 ♗g4 16 ♕e3 0-0 17 f3 ♗d7 18 ♖hb1 ♔g7 19 ♕g5 ♘c8 20 ♕e3 b5 21 c4 c5 22 ♘c3 b4 23 ♘b5 ♗xb5 24 cxb5 a4 25 ♗c4 ♘b6 26 ♕d3 axb3+ 27 axb3 ♕xa1 28 ♖xa1 ♖xa1 29 ♕e3 ♖fa8 30 ♕g5 ♖8a2+ 31 ♔d3 ♖d1+ 32 ♔e3 ♖e1+ **½-½** L/N6013-1842

**1841-★HL-1** 13 ix 41
**Lasa, T von H. u. von d.+ Hanstein, W.**
[Staunton]
1 e4 e5 2 ♘f3 ♘c6 3 d4 exd4 4 ♗c4 ♗c5 5 c3 d3 [◻ 5 ... ♘f6] 6 b4 ♗b6 7 a4 [7 b5 Harrwitz - Staunton Match 1846] 7 ... a6 8 ♕b3 ♕e7 9 0-0 d6 10 ♗g5 ♘f6 11 ♘bd2 0-0 12 ♗xd3 ♗e6 13 ♕c2 h6 14 ♗h4 g5 15 ♗g3 ♘h5 16 ♔h1 ♔g7 17 ♖ae1 ♖h8 18 e5 d5 19 ♘b3 ♖ac8 20 a5 ♗a7 21 ♘bd4 ♗xd4 22 ♘xd4 ♘xd4 23 cxd4 ♕xb4 24 f4 ♘xg3+ [◻ 24 ... ♘xf4 25 ♗xf4 gxf4 26 ♕f2 ♕e7 △ 27 ... c5] 25 hxg3

25 ... ♕xd4 [25 ... gxf4 26 gxf4 ♕xd4 27 f5 ♕h4+ 28 ♔g1 ♕d4+ 29 ♖f2 ♗d7 30 e6 ♗e8 31 f6+ ♔f8 (31 ... ♔g8 32 exf7+ ♗xf7 33 ♗f5 ♖e8 34 ♖xe8+ ♗xe8 35 ♗e6+ ♔f8 36 ♕xc7 ♕d1+ 37 ♔h2 ♕h5+ 38 ♗h3 ♕f7 39 ♕d6+ ♔g8 40 ♗e6+–; 33 ... ♖f8 34 ♕xc7 ♕h4 35 ♗g6+–; 32 ... ♔xf7 33 ♕e2+–) 32 e7+ ♔g8 33 ♗f5 ♖a8 34 ♕xc7 ♕h4 35 ♕xb7+–; 30 ... ♗a4 31 f6+ ♔f8 (31 ... ♔g8 32 exf7+ ♔xf7 33 ♗g6++–; 32 ... ♔f8 33 ♗g6+–) 32 e7+ ♔e8 (32 ... ♔g8 33 ♖e3 ♕xe3 34 ♕xa4 ♕e1+ 35 ♖f1 ♕e3+ 36 ♔h1+–; 34 ... ♖c~ 35 ♕g4+ ♕g5 36 ♕d7+–; 33 ... ♕h4 34 ♕xa4 △ 34 ... ♕xa4 35 ♖g3++–) 33 ♕b1 (33 ♕d2?! c5; 33 ♕e2?! ♗d7) 33 ... ♗d7 (33 ... b5 34 ♗f5 ♖a8 35 ♕c1 c5 36 ♕a3 ♖g8 37 ♕h3 b4 38 ♗e6+–; 36 ... ♕b4 37 ♕g3 ♕xe1+ 38 ♔h2+–; 36 ... ♕h4 37 ♕xc5+–; 35 ... ♕c4 36 ♕e3+–; 33 ... b6 34 ♗xa6 ♖b8 35 ♗b5+ c6 36 ♖d1 ♕g4 37 ♖xd5 ♗xb5 38 ♖d6+–; 38 ♖xb5?; 38 ♕xb5? cxb5 39 ♖fd2 ♕c8 40 axb6 ♖g8 41 b7 ♖xg2+) 34 ♗f5 ♗xf5 (34 ... c6 35 ♗xd7+ ♔xd7 36 ♕xb7+ ♖c7 37 ♕xa6 △ 38 ♕e2+–) 35 ♕xf5 ♖b8 36 ♖b1 b5 37 axb6 cxb6 (37 ... ♕e4 38 ♕xe4 △ 39 ♖d2+–) 38 ♖c1+–; 30 ... ♗c6 31 f6+ ♔f8 32 e7+ ♔e8 (32 ... ♔g8 33 ♕xc6+–) 33 ♗f5 ♗d7 (33 ... ♖a8 34 ♗e6 fxe6 35 ♕g6+ ♔d7 36 f7 ♔xe7 37 ♕xe6++–) 34 ♖d1 ♗xf5 (34 ... ♕e5 35 ♗xd7+ ♔xd7 36 ♖f5 ♕e3+ 37 ♔f1 c6 38 ♖fxd5+ ♔c7 39 ♖d7+ ♔b8 40 ♕b2 ♕f4+ 41 ♔g1 ♕e3+ 42 ♕f2 ♕xf2+ 43 ♔xf2+–; 40 ... ♕a7 41 ♕e5+ △ 42 ♖d8+–; 37 ... ♖de8 38 ♖fxd5+ △ 39 ♕f5++–; 34 ... ♕a4 35 ♖xd5+–) 35 ♖xd4 ♗xc2 36 ♖xd5 ♗e4 (36 ... c6 37 ♖xc2; 36 ... ♗b3 37 ♖d3 ♗c4 38 ♖d4 △ 39 ♖fd2+–) 37 ♖d4 ♖g8 (37 ... c6 38 ♖xe4 ♔d7 39 ♖d2+ ♔c7 40 ♖ed4 ♖de8 41 ♖d7+ ♔c8 42 ♔f2 △ ♔b6+–; 38 ... ♖c7 39 ♖d2 ♖d7 40 ♖ed4+–) 38 ♖xe4 c5 39 ♖d2 ♖g6 40 ♖d6 ♖g5 41 ♖e2 ♖g4 42 ♖c2 c4 43 ♖cd2+–; 30 ... ♗b5+–; 30 ... fxe6 31 f6+ ♔g8 (31 ... ♔f7 32 ♗g6+ ♔f8 33 ♗h7 ♗e8 34 ♖xe6 ♕c4 35 f7 ♗d7 36 ♖e8+ ♗xe8 37 fxe8♕+ ♔xe8 38 ♕g6++–) 32 ♗b5 ♖h7 33 ♕g6+ ♔h8 34 ♗d3+–] 26 f5 ♗d7 27 e6 ♗a4 [27 ... fxe6 28 f6+ ♔f8 (28 ... ♔g8 29 ♗b5+–; 28 ... ♔f7 29 ♗g6+ ♔g8 30 ♗h5+–) 29 ♗h7 ♗e8 30 ♖xe6 ♗f7 (30 ... ♕c4 31 ♕f5 ♗d7 32 ♕g6 ♕xf1+ 33 ♔h2+–) 31 ♖e7 ♕c4 32 ♕f5 ♖d8 33 ♖fe1 d4 34 ♗g6 ♗xg6 35 ♕xg6+–] 28 f6+ ♔f8 29 ♕b1 b5 30 ♗f5 ♖b8 31 ♗g6 h5 32 ♗xf7 ♖h6 33 ♗g6 b4 34 e7+ ♔g8 35 f7+ **1-0** L/N6123-1859

**1841-★HL-2** 16 ix 41
**Hanstein, W.+ Lasa, T von H u. von d.**
[Staunton]
1 e4 e5 2 ♘f3 ♘c6 3 d4 exd4 4 ♗c4 ♗c5 5 c3 d3 6 b4 ♗b6 7 a4 a6 8 0-0 d6 9 ♕b3 ♕e7 10 ♗g5 ♘f6 11 ♘bd2 0-0 12 ♗xd3 ♗e6 13 ♕c2 h6 14 ♗h4 ♘e5 15 ♘xe5 dxe5 16 ♔h1 g5 17 ♗g3 ♘d7 18 ♘c4 ♗g4 19 f3 ♗h5 20 ♖ad1 f6 21 a5 ♗a7 22 ♗f2 ♗xf2 23 ♖xf2 ♖ad8 24 ♘e3 ♗g6 25 ♕b3+ ♔g7 26 ♘d5 ♗f7 27 ♕c2 ♗xd5 28 exd5±

♖h8 29 ♗g6 h5 30 ♖fd2 ♕d6 31 ♗f5 ♘f8 32 ♕b1 b5 33 a×b6 c×b6 34 c4 ♘d7 35 ♖a2 ♘b8 36 c5 b×c5 37 b×c5 ♕×c5 38 ♕b7+ ♔h6 39 ♕f7 **1-0** L/N6123-1859

**1841-★HL-3** 21 x 41
**Hanstein, W.= Lasa, T von H u. von d.**
[Staunton]
1 e4 e5 2 ♘f3 ♘c6 3 d4 e×d4 4 ♗c4 ♗c5 5 c3 d3 6 b4 ♗b6 7 a4 a6 8 ♕×d3 d6 9 0-0 ♘ge7 10 ♗f4 0-0 11 ♘bd2 ♘g6 12 ♗g3 ♔h8 13 ♕c2 f5 14 e×f5 ♗×f5 15 ♗d3 ♕d7 16 ♖ae1 ♘f4 17 ♗×f5 ♕×f5 18 ♕×f5 ♖×f5 19 ♘h4 ♖f7 20 ♘e4 ♘e5 21 a5 ♗a7 22 ♘g5 ♖f6 23 ♗×f4 ♖×f4 24 g3 ♖c4 25 ♘e4 ♖f8 [25 ... d5?] 26 ♖e2 h6 27 ♔h1 g5 28 ♘g2 ♘f3 29 ♖d1 ♖e8 30 ♘×d6 ♖×e2 31 ♘×c4 ♖×f2 32 ♘a3 g4 33 ♖a1 ♗e3 34 b5 a×b5 35 ♘×b5 ♗d2 36 ♘×c7 ♗×c3 37 ♖d1 ♗e1 [37 ... ♗×a5−+] 38 ♖×e1 ♘×e1 39 ♘×e1 ♖f1+ 40 ♔g2 ♖×e1 41 a6 b×a6 42 ♘×a6 ♖e2+ [□ 42 ... ♔g7] 43 ♔g1 ♖a2 44 ♘c5 ♖c2 45 ♘d3 ♔h7 46 ♘f4 ♔g7 47 h3 g×h3 48 ♘×h3 ♔g6 49 ♘f2 ♔f5 50 ♔g2 h5 51 ♔f3 ♖c3+ 52 ♔g2 ♔e5 **½-½** L/N6123-1859

**1841-★MS-1**
**Mongredien, A.= Staunton, H.**
London [Staunton]
⟨♙f7⟩ 1 e4 ... 2 d4 e6 3 ♗d3 c5 4 c3 c×d4 5 c×d4 ♗b4+ 6 ♘c3 ♗×c3+ 7 b×c3 ♘e7 8 ♗g5 0-0 9 e5 ♘bc6 10 ♕c2 h6 11 ♗h4 ♕e8 12 g4 b6 13 ♘h3 ♗b7 [△ 14 ... ♘×d4] 14 ♖g1 ♖c8 15 ♕d2 ♘d5 [△ 16 ... ♘×c3 17 ♕×c3 ♘×e5 18 ♕b3 ♘f3+−+] 16 ♖c1 ♖f3 17 ♗g3 ♘×d4!? 18 ♗e4! [18 c×d4 ♖×c1+ △ 19 ... ♖×d3] 18 ... ♖c×c3 19 ♖×c3 ♘×c3! 20 ♗×b7 ♕g6 21 ♔f1 ♕×g4 [21 ... ♖d3?? 22 ♘f4+−] 22 ♗×f3 ♘×f3 23 ♕×c3 ♕×h3+ 24 ♖g2 ♕f5 25 ♔e2 ♕e4+ ...⚲ **½-½** L/N6122

**1841-★MS-2**
**Mongredien, A.= Staunton, H.**
London⚲ [Staunton]
⟨♙f7⟩ 1 e4 ... 2 d4 d6 3 ♗d3 c5 4 c3 [4 d×c5 ♕a5+ △ 5 ... ♕×c5] 4 ... c×d4 5 c×d4 ♘f6 6 f4 [6 e5? d×e5 7 d×e5 ♕a5+∓] 6 ... ♗e6 7 ♘f3 ♘bd7 8 h3 ♗f7 9 0-0 e6 10 e5 ♘d5 11 f5 d×e5 12 f×e6 ♗×e6 13 ♘g5 ♕e7 14 ♕h5+ ♔d8 15 ♘a3 ♘5f6 16 ♘×e6+ ♕×e6 17 ♕e2 ♗×a3 18 b×a3 ♖c8 19 ♗g5 ♕b6 20 ♔h1 e×d4 21 ♖ab1 ♕a5 [△ 22 ... ♕×g5] 22 ♖b5 ♕×a3 23 ♖×b7 ♖c7 24 ♖b3 ♕e7 25 ♕b2! ♖c3! [25 ... ♕e5±; 25 ... ♕d6±; 25 ... ♕c5 26 ♖f5±] 26 ♖×c3 d×c3 27 ♕×c3 ♕c5 28 ♕×c5 ♘×c5 29 ♗f5?! [□ 29 ♗×f6+ g×f6 30 ♖×f6 ♘×d3 31 ♖d6+] 29 ... h6 30 ♗e3 ♘fe4 31 ♖d1+ ♔e7 32 ♗×e4 ♘×e4 33 ♗×a7 ♖a8 34 ♗d4?! [34 ♖e1] 34 ... ♖d8 35 ♔g1 ♔e6 36 ♔f1 g5 37 ♔e2 ♖a8 38 ♖a1 ♔d5 39 ♗g7 ♘g3+ 40 ♔f3 ♘f5 41 ♗b2 ♘h4+ 42 ♔g3 ♘f5+ 43 ♔g4 ♔e4 44 a4 ♘e3+ 45 ♔g3 h5 46 a5 ♖a6 47 ♖a4+ ♔d3 48 ♗c1 h4+ 49 ♔h2 [49 ♔f2−+] 49 ... ♘f1+ 50 ♔g1 ♘d2 51 ♗a3?! [□ 51 ♗×d2 ♔×d2 52 ♖d4+] 51 ... ♖e6 52 ♗b4 ♖e1+ 53 ♔h2 ♘f1+ 54 ♔g1 [54 ♔h1?? ♘g3+ 55 ♔h2 ♖h1#] 54 ... ♘d2+ **½-½** L/N6122

**1841-★PS-1**
**Popert, H.W.+ Staunton, H.**
London⚲ [Staunton]
1 e4 c5 2 c3 e6 3 ♘f3 d5 4 e5 ♘c6 5 d4 ♕b6 6 ♗d3 ♗d7 7 ♗c2 ♖c8 8 0-0 a5 9 a4 g6 10 d×c5 ♗×c5 11 ♘a3 f6 12 e×f6 ♘×f6 13 ♘b5 0-0 14 ♗h6 ♘g4? 15 ♗×f8 ♗×f2+ 16 ♔h1 ♖×f8 17 ♕e2 ♗c5 18 ♘fd4 ♖×f1+ 19 ♖×f1 e5 20 ♕f3! ♘d8 21 ♕×d5+ ♗e6 22 ♘×e6 ♘×e6 23 ♗b3 **1-0** L/N6122

**1841-★PS-2**
**Staunton, H.+ Popert, H.W.**
London⚲
1 e4 e5 2 ♘f3 ♘c6 3 ♗c4 ♗c5 4 c3 ♘f6 5 d3 0-0 6 ♗g5 h6 7 ♗h4 d6 8 0-0 ♗g4 9 ♘bd2 g5 10 ♗g3 ♘h5 11 ♔h1 ♘e7 12 h3 ♗d7 13 d4 e×d4 14 ♘×d4 ♘g7 15 f4 ♘g6 16 f5 ♘e5 17 f6 ♘e6 18 ♗×e5 d×e5 19 ♘4b3 ♗b6 20 ♕h5 ♔h7 21 ♖ad1 ♗e3 22 ♘f3 ♕e8 23 ♘×e5 ♘f4 24 ♖×f4 ♗×f4 25 ♖×d7 **1-0** L/N6122

**1841-★PS-3**
**Staunton, H.= Popert, H.W.**
London [Staunton]
1 e4 e5 2 ♘f3 ♘c6 3 d4 e×d4 4 ♗c4 ♗b4+ 5 c3 d×c3 6 0-0 c2 7 ♕×c2 d6 8 a3 ♗a5 9 b4 ♗b6 10 ♗b2 ♘f6 11 e5 d×e5 12 ♘×e5 ♘×e5 13 ♗×e5 0-0 14 ♘c3 ♘g4 15 ♗g3 ♕g5 16 ♖ae1 ♗f5 17 ♕b3 c6 18 a4 [18 ♗d6 ♘×f2!] 18 ... ♖ad8 19 ♘e2 a6 20 b5 a×b5 21 a×b5 ♗a5 22 ♖a1 c×b5 23 ♕×b5 b6 24 ♖ad1 h6 25 ♖×d8 ♖×d8 26 ♗f4 ♕g6 27 ♘d4 ♗d7 [27 ... ♖×d4 28 ♕e8+ ♔h7 29 ♗×f7+−] 28 ♕b3 ♕f6 29 ♘e2 ♗e6 30 ♗×e6 ♕×e6 31 ♕×e6 f×e6 32 h3 ♘f6 33 ♗e5 ♔f7 34 ♖c1 ♖d7 35 ♖c6 ♘e4 36 ♗d4 b5 37 f3 ♘d2 38 ♗e3 ♘c4 39 ♗c5 ♖d1+ 40 ♔h2 e5 41 h4 ♗d8? 42 ♘c3 ♖d7 43 ♘×b5 ♗×h4 44 ♗d6 ♘×d6 45 ♘×d6+ ♔g8 46 ♘e4 ♗e7 47 ♖e6 ♗d8 48 ♔h3 ♖e7 49 ♖a6 ♗c7 50 ♔g4 ♖f7 51 ♘g3 ♖f4+ 52 ♔h3 ♔h7 53 ♘e4 ♖f5 54 ♔g4 ♖f4+ 55 ♔g3 ♖f8 56 ♔g4 ♗d8 57 ♖e6 ♗f6 58 ♘×f6+ g×f6 59 ♔f5 **½-½** L/N6122

**1841-★PS-4**
**Staunton, H.+ Popert, H.W.**
London [Staunton]
1 e4 e5 2 ♘f3 ♘c6 3 ♗c4 ♗c5 4 c3 ♘f6 5 d3 0-0 6 ♗g5 d6 7 0-0 h6 8 ♗h4 ♗g4 9 ♘bd2 g5 10 ♗g3 d5 11 e×d5 ♘×d5 12 ♘e4 ♗e7 13 b4 a6 14 a4 ♘f4 15 ♖a2 ♔g7 16 ♗×f4 e×f4 17 d4 f5 18 ♘ed2 ♗d6

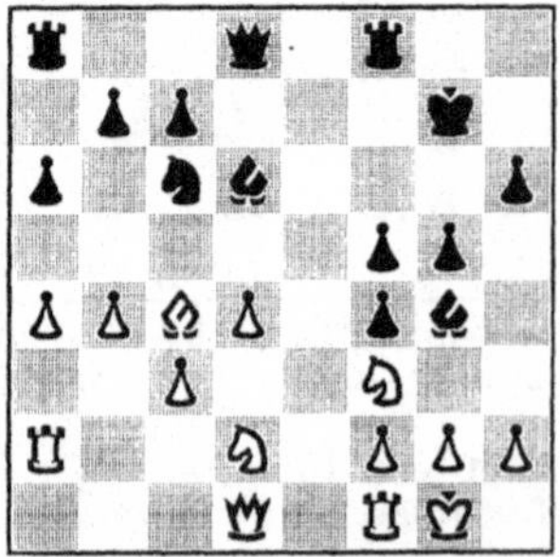

19 ♗e2 ♗×f3 20 g×f3 h5 21 ♔h1 g4 22 f×g4 f×g4 23 ♗×g4 h×g4 24 ♕×g4+ ♔f7 25 ♕h5+ ♔e7 26 ♖e1+ ♗e5 27 ♘f3 ♕d5 28 ♖ae2 ♖f5! 29 ♖×e5+ [29 ♕×f5?? ♕×f3+−+] 29 ... ♘×e5 30 ♖×e5+ ♖×e5 31 ♕×e5+ ♕×e5 32 ♘×e5 ...⚲ **1-0** L/N6122

**1841-★SW-1**
**Williams, E.− Staunton, H.**
London⚲ [Staunton]
⟨♙f7⟩ 1 e4 ... 2 d4 ♘c6 3 ♗d3 e5 [3 ... ♘×d4 4 ♕h5+ g6 5 ♕e5] 4 ♘f3 d6 5 ♗c4 ♗g4 6 h3 ♗×f3 7 ♕×f3 ♕f6 8 ♕b3! 0-0-0 9 ♗×g8 ♘×d4 10 ♕f7 ♘×c2+ 11 ♔d1 ♘×a1 12 ♕×f6 g×f6 13 ♗e6+ ♔b8 14 b3 ♗g7 15 ♗b2 ♖he8 16 ♗c4 ♘×b3 17 a×b3 c6 18 ♘c3 d5 19 e×d5 c×d5 20 ♗b5 [□ 20 ♗×d5 ♖×d5+ 21 ♘×d5 ♖d8] 20 ... ♖e6 21 ♔e2 a6 22 ♗d3 e4 23 ♗b1 f5 24 ♖d1 d4 25 ♘a4 b5 26 ♘c5 ♖c6 27 ♗a3 d3+ 28 ♔f1 a5 29 b4 ♗c3 30 ♘b3 a×b4 31 ♗c1 ♗e5 32 ♗d2 ♖c3! 33 ♘a5 ♔c7 34 ♗a2 ♖a8 35 ♗e6 ♖×a5 36 ♗×f5 ♖c4 37 ♗×h7 ♖a2 [△ 38 ... ♖×d2] 38 f4 ♗d4 39 ♗×e4 ♖×d2 40 ♖×d2 ♖c1+ **0-1** L/N6122

**1841-★SW-2**
**Williams, E.+ Staunton, H.**
London⚲ [Staunton]
⟨♙f7⟩ 1 e4 ... 2 d4 ♘c6 3 d5 ♘e5 4 f4 ♘f7 5 ♗d3 e5 6 f5 ♘f6 7 g4 h6 8 ♗e3 ♘d6? 9 ♕f3 h5? 10 g5 ♘g8 11

♕g3 ♕e7 12 ♘f3 ♘xf5 13 exf5 e4 14 ♔f2 exf3 15 ♕xc7 ♕d6 16 ♕c4 b6 17 ♕e4+ ♘e7 18 c4 ♗b7 19 ♘c3 a6 20 ♗d4 ♔d8 21 b4 ♖c8 22 ♖ae1 h4 23 a3 [△ 24 ♗e5] 23 ... ♘g8 24 ♘a4 ♘e7 25 ♗xb6+ ♔e8 26 f6 g6 27 ♕xg6# **1-0** L/N6122

**1841-★SW-3**
**Williams, E.= Staunton, H.**
[Staunton]

⟨♙f7⟩ 1 e4 ... 2 d4 e6 3 ♗d3 c5 4 e5 g6 5 c3 cxd4 6 cxd4 ♘c6 7 h4 ♘xd4 8 ♗xg6+ hxg6 9 ♕xd4 ♗g7 10 ♕e4 ♕a5+ 11 ♔f1 [11 ♘d2 ♕xe5; 11 ♗d2 ♕xe5] 11 ... ♘e7 12 f4 ♘f5 13 ♘e2 ♖xh4 14 ♖xh4 ♘xh4 15 ♘bc3 ♖b8 16 ♗d2 b6 17 g3 ♗b7 18 ♕d3 ♘f5 19 g4 ♗a6 20 ♕h3 ♘d4 21 ♗e3 ♘xe2 22 ♘xe2 ♔f7 23 ♖d1 ♕b5 24 ♖d2 ♖h8 25 ♕f3 ♔e7 26 ♔g1 ♕c4 27 b3 ♕c7 28 ♕e4 ♔f7 29 ♕a4 ♗c8 30 ♕d4 ♕c6 31 ♘g3 ♕f3 32 ♖g2 ♗f8 [32 ... ♕xg4?] 33 ♘e4 ♔g7 34 f5 ♖h3 35 ♗f2 ♗b7!? 36 ♕xd7+ ♔h8 37 ♕d8 [37 ♕xb7?? ♕d1+ 38 ♗e1 ♕xe1#] 37 ... ♔g8 38 ♘f6+ ♔g7 39 ♘e8+ ♔g8 **½-½** L/N6122

**1841-★SZ-1**
**Zytogorski, A.= Staunton, H.**
London [Staunton]

⟨♙f7⟩ 1 e4 ... 2 d4 e6 3 ♗d3 c6 4 e5 g6 5 h4 c5 6 c3 cxd4 7 h5 g5 8 ♕g4 ♗e7 9 cxd4 ♘h6 10 ♕g3 ♘c6 11 ♘f3 ♘f7 12 h6 d6 13 ♖h5 dxe5 14 ♘xe5 ♘cxe5 15 dxe5 ♕a5+ 16 ♗d2 ♕xe5+ 17 ♕xe5 ♘xe5 18 ♗b5+ ♗d7 [18 ... ♔f7!? △ 19 ♗xg5? ♔g6→] 19 ♗xd7+ ♔xd7 20 ♗xg5 ♘d3+ 21 ♔f1? ♖af8 22 f3 ♖f5 23 ♘c3!? ♘f4 [23 ... ♗xg5? 24 ♖d1] 24 ♖d1+ ♘d5? [□ 21 ... ♔c6] 25 f4 ♖hf8 26 ♔e2 ♗d6 27 ♘xd5 exd5 28 g4 ♖5f7 29 ♖xd5 ♔c6 30 ♖f5 ♖xf5 31 gxf5 ♖xf5 32 ♔f3 ♔d5 33 ♖h2 ♔e6 34 ♔g4 ♖b5 35 a3 ♖b3 36 ♖e2+ ♔f7 37 ♖d2 ♖b6 38 ♗d8 ♖c6 39 ♗g5 ♖b6 40 ♖d3 a6 41 a4 ♔g6 42 b3 ♗f8 43 a5 ♖d6 44 ♖c3 ♖d5 45 ♖c7 ♖b5 46 ♖c8 ♔f7 [46 ... ♗xh6? 47 f5+! ♔xf5 48 ♗xh6] 47 ♖c3 ♔g6 48 ♖c8 ♔f7 49 ♖d8 ♖xb3 50 ♖d7+ ♔g8 51 ♖d8 ♔f7 52 ♖d7+ ♔g8 53 ♔f5 b6 54 axb6 ♖xb6 55 ♖a7 ♖b5+ 56 ♔g4 ♖b6 57 f5 ♗xh6 **½-½** L/N6122

**1841-★SZ-2**
**Zytogorski, A.– Staunton, H.**
London

⟨♙f7⟩ 1 e4 ... 2 d4 e6 3 ♗d3 c5 4 dxc5 ♕a5+ 5 ♘c3 ♕xc5 6 ♗e3 ♕a5 7 ♘e2 ♗d6 8 0-0 ♘f6 9 a3 0-0 10 b4 ♗xh2+ 11 ♔xh2 ♕h5+ 12 ♔g1 ♘g4 **0-1** L/N6122

**1841-★S♀-1**
**Staunton, H.+♀**
London [Staunton]

⟨♘b1⟩ 1 e4 e5 2 ♗c4 ♗c5 3 ♕e2 ♘c6 4 c3 ♘f6 5 f4 ♗xg1 6 ♖xg1 0-0 7 d3 d5 8 ♗b3 dxe4 9 dxe4 exf4 10 ♗c2 ♘g4? [□ 10 ... ♘xe4 △ 11 ... ♖e8] 11 ♗xf4 ♕h4+ 12 ♗g3 ♕h6 13 h3 ♘e3 14 ♗d3 ♗e6 15 ♗f2 ♘xg2+ 16 ♖xg2 ♕xh3 17 ♖g3 ♕h1+ 18 ♖g1 ♕h2 19 0-0-0 ♘e5 20 ♔b1 ♘xd3

21 ♖xg7+ ♔h8 [21 ... ♔xg7 22 ♗d4+ f6 23 ♕xh2+−] 22 ♗d4 ♕xe2 23 ♖xf7+ ♔g8 24 ♖g7+ ♔h8 25 ♖g6+ **1-0** L/N6122

**1841-★S♀-2**
**Staunton, H.+♀**
London♀ [Staunton]

⟨♘g1⟩ 1 e4 e5 2 ♗c4 ♗c5 3 b4 ♗xb4 4 f4 exf4 5 0-0 ♘f6 6 c3 ♗a5 7 d4 0-0 [7 ... ♘xe4?] 8 ♖xf4 d6 9 ♕f3 ♗b6 10 ♗e3 ♘c6 11 ♘d2 ♘a5? 12 ♗d3 c5 13 ♖f1 cxd4 14 cxd4 ♘c6 15 e5 dxe5 16 ♖xf6 ♕xf6 17 ♗xh7+ ♔h8 18 ♕h5 ♕xf1+ [18 ... ♗g4∓] 19 ♘xf1 ♗g4 20 ♕h4 ♗d8 21 ♕xg4 ♔xh7 22 d5 ♘e7 23 ♘g3 ♘g6 [23 ... ♘xd5? 24 ♕e4+] 24 ♘f5 ♖c8 25 h4 ♗f6 26 ♕h5+ ♔g8 27 g4 ♘f4 28 ♗xf4 exf4 29 g5 ♖c1+ 30 ♔g2 ♖c2+ 31 ♔h3 ♗d8 32 d6 ♖e8 33 g6 fxg6 34 ♕xg6 **1-0** L/N6122

**1841-★S♀-3**
**Staunton, H.+♀**
London♀ [Staunton]

1 e4 e5 2 f4 exf4 3 ♘f3 g5 4 ♗c4 g4 5 0-0 gxf3 6 ♕xf3 ♕f6 7 e5 ♕xe5 8 d3 ♗h6 9 ♘c3 c6 10 ♗xf4!? ♕d4+ 11 ♔h1 ♗xf4 12 ♖ae1+ ♘e7 13 ♖e4 ♕g7 14 ♕xf4 d5 15 ♗xd5 cxd5 16 ♖xe7+! ♔xe7 17 ♘xd5+ ♔e6 [17 ... ♔e8 18 ♕d6+−] 18 ♕e4+ ♔d7 [18 ... ♕e5 19 ♖f6++−] 19 ♕e7+ ♔c6 20 ♕c7+ ♔xd5 21 c4+ ♔d4 22 ♕d6+ ♔e3 23 ♕f4+ ♔xd3 [24 ♖d1+ ♔c2 (24 ... ♔e2 25 ♕f3#) 25 ♕d2#] **1-0** L/N6122

**1841-★S♀-4**
**Staunton, H.+♀**
London♀ [Staunton]

1 e4 e5 2 f4 exf4 3 ♘f3 g5 4 ♗c4 g4 5 0-0 gxf3 6 ♕xf3 ♕f6 7 e5 ♕xe5 8 d3 ♗h6 9 ♘c3 c6 10 ♗xf4 ♕xf4 11 ♕h5 ♕d4+ 12 ♔h1 d5 13 ♕xf7+ ♔d8 14 ♖ae1 ♗d7 15 ♗xd5 cxd5 16 ♘xd5 ♕g7! 17 ♕h5 ♕g6 18 ♕h4+ ♔c8 [18 ... ♕g5 19 ♖f8++−; 18 ... ♗g5 19 ♖f8++−] 19 ♖f6! ♕g7 [19 ... ♘xf6 20 ♘e7++−] 20 ♕c4+ ♘c6 21 ♖xc6+ ♗xc6 [□ 21 ... bxc6] 22 ♖e8+ ♔d7 23 ♖xa8 ♕e5 24 ♕g4+ ♔d6 [24 ... ♕e6 25 ♖d8++−] 25 ♖d8+ ♔c5 26 ♕c4# [26 ♕b4#] **1-0** L/N6122

**1841-★S♀-5**
**Staunton, H.+♀**
London

⟨♘b1⟩ 1 e4 e5 2 ♗c4 ♗c5 3 b4 ♗xb4 4 f4 exf4 5 ♘f3 d6 6 c3 ♗c5 7 d4 ♗b6 8 ♗xf4 ♘f6 9 ♕d3 0-0 10 h3 ♘xe4 11 ♕xe4 ♖e8 12 ♗e5 dxe5 13 0-0 exd4

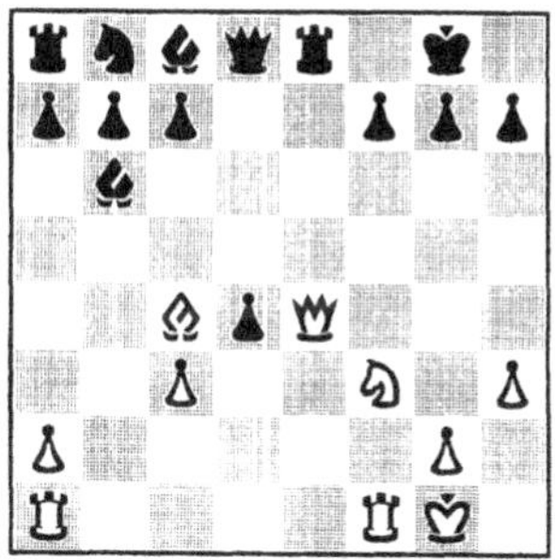

14 ♗xf7+ ♔xf7 15 ♘g5+ ♔g8 16 ♕xh7# **1-0** L/N6122

**1841-★S♀-6**
**Staunton, H.=♀**
London [Staunton]

⟨♘b1⟩ 1 e4 e5 2 ♗c4 ♗c5 3 c3 d6 4 d4 exd4 5 b4 ♗b6 6 cxd4 ♘c6 7 ♘e2 ♘f6 [7 ... ♘xb4?] 8 ♗g5 0-0 9 0-0 ♘xb4 10 f4 h6 11 e5 dxe5 12 fxe5 hxg5 13 exf6 gxf6 14 a3 ♘c6 15 ♕d3 ♘xd4

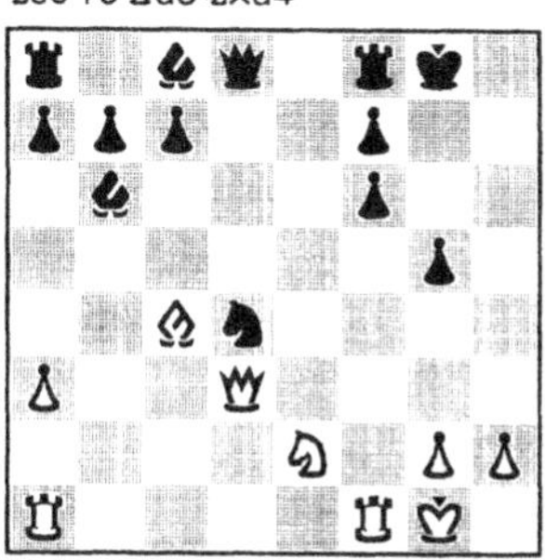

16 ♕g6+ ♔h8 17 ♕h6+ ♔g8 18

♔h1 ♘f5 [18 ... ♘xe2??+-] 19 ♕g6+ ♘g7 20 ♖xf6 ♗e6 21 ♕xg5 ♗xc4 22 ♘g3 ♗d4 23 ♘h5 ♗xf6 24 ♘xf6+ ♕xf6 ...? ½-½ L/N6122

**1841-★S?-7**
**?– Staunton, H.**
London [Staunton]
1 e4 e5 2 f4 ♗c5 3 c3 [3 fxe5 ♕h4+∓] 3 ... ♘c6 4 ♗c4 ♘f6 5 ♕f3 0-0 6 d3 d6 7 f5 ♘a5 8 b4 ♗xg1 9 bxa5 ♗c5 10 ♘d2 c6 11 ♘b3 b5 12 axb6 ♗xb6 13 ♘d2 d5 14 ♗b3 ♗a6 15 ♗a3 ♖e8 16 0-0-0 h6 17 g4 ♘h7 18 h4 ♗a5 19 ♘b1 d4 20 c4 ♖b8 21 ♔c2 f6 22 c5+ ♔h8 23 g5 fxg5 24 hxg5 ♘xg5 25 ♕h5 ♕e7 26 ♖dg1 ♘h7 27 ♖h2 ♗b4 28 ♖hg2 [□ 28 ♗xb4] 28 ... ♕xc5+ 29 ♔d1 ♗xa3 30 ♘xa3 ♕c3 [30 ... ♕xa3+-] 31 ♗c2? [31 ♕g6 ♕xd3+ 32 ♖d2+-] 31 ... ♗xd3 32 ♕g4 ♘g5 33 ♕g3 ♗xc2+ **0-1** L/N6122

**1841-★S?-8**
**Staunton, H.+?**
London [Staunton]
1 e4 e5 2 ♘f3 ♘c6 3 d4 exd4 4 ♗c4 ♘f6 [□ ♗b4+] 5 ♗g5 h6 6 ♗xf6 ♕xf6 7 0-0 ♗c5 8 e5 ♕g6 9 c3 dxc3 10 ♘xc3 0-0 11 ♘d5 ♗b6 12 b4 ♔h8 13 b5 ♘a5 14 ♗d3 ♕e6 15 ♗c2 c6 16 ♘f4 ♕c4 17 g3 ♕xb5 18 ♘g6+ ♔g8 [18 ... fxg6 19 ♕d6±] 19 ♕d6 ♕c5 [□ 19 ... fxg6] 20 ♘e7+ ♔h8 21 ♕d3 g6 22 ♘xg6+ fxg6 23 ♕xg6 ♕e7 24 ♕xh6+ ♔g8 25 ♘g5 ♕g7 26 ♗h7+ ♔h8 27 ♕h5 ♗d8 28 ♗g6+ ♔g8 29 ♘h7 ♗e7 30 ♘xf8 ♗xf8 31 ♖ad1 ♘c4 32 ♖fe1 d5 33 e6 ♗d6 34 ♖d4 ♘e5 35 ♖xe5 ♗xe5 36 ♗f7+ ♔f8 37 ♖g4 ♕f6 38 ♖g6 **1-0** L/N6122

**1841-★S?-9**
**Staunton, H.–?**
London [Staunton]
1 e4 e5 2 ♘f3 ♘c6 3 d4 exd4 4 ♗c4 ♘f6 5 ♗g5 h6 6 ♗xf6 ♕xf6 7 0-0 ♗c5 8 c3 d3 9 e5 ♕f4 10 ♕xd3 0-0 11 b4 ♗b6 12 a4 a5 13 g3 ♕g4 14 b5 ♘e7 15 ♘bd2 ♘g6 16 ♔h1 d5 17 ♗xd5 ♗e6 18 ♗xb7 ♖ad8 19 ♕e4 ♕h5 20 ♕e2 ♗g4 21 ♖ad1 ♖fe8 22 ♘c4 ♖xd1 23 ♖xd1 ♘xe5 24 ♘cxe5 ♖xe5 25 ♕d3 [25 ♕xe5? ♗xf3+-+] 25 ... ♖f5 26 ♘h4 ♖xf2 27 ♕d8+ ♔h7 28 ♗e4+ f5 29 ♗d5 ♗f3+ 30 ♘xf3 ♖xh2+ 31 ♘xh2 ♕xd1+ 32 ♔g2 ♕e2+ 33 ♔h3 ♕h5+ 34 ♕h4 **1-0** L/N6122

**1841-★S?-10**
**?+ Staunton, H.**
London [Staunton]
1 e4 e5 2 f4 exf4 3 ♗c4 d5 4 exd5 ♘f6 5 ♕f3 ♗d6 6 ♘c3 ♗g4 7 ♕f2 c6 8 dxc6 ♘xc6 9 ♘f3 0-0 10 0-0 ♗xf3 11 ♕xf3 ♗c5+ 12 ♔h1 ♘e5 [□ 12 ... ♘d4] 13 ♕e2 ♘fg4 [□ 13 ... ♕d4] 14 ♘e4 ♕h4 15 h3 ♗b6 16 ♖xf4 ♘f2+ 17 ♖xf2 ♗xf2 18 d3! ♕d8 [18 ... ♗b6? 19 ♗g5+-] 19 ♕xf2 ♘xc4 20 dxc4 ♕d1+ 21 ♔h2 f5 22 ♘c3 ♕h5 23 ♗f4 g5 24 ♗d6 ♖f6 25 c5 g4 26 ♘d5 ♖h6 27 ♘e7+ **1-0** L/N6122

**1841-★S?-11**
**Staunton, H.+?**
London [Staunton]
1 e4 e5 2 ♘f3 ♘c6 3 d4 exd4 4 ♘xd4 ♘xd4 5 ♕xd4 ♘e7 6 ♗g5 ♘c6 7 ♕e3 [7 ♗xd8+-] 7 ... ♗e7 8 ♗xe7 ♕xe7 9 ♘d2 d6 10 ♗d3 ♗e6 11 0-0 0-0 12 ♖ae1 ♖ae8 13 f4 f5 14 e5 dxe5 15 fxe5 ♔h8 16 b3 ♗d7 17 ♘f3 f4 18 ♕f2 ♗f5 19 ♗b5 ♕e6 20 ♘h4 ♗g4 21 ♗xc6 ♕xc6 22 c4 ♖e6 23 ♕xa7 b6 24 ♕a3 ♖a8 25 ♖xf4 ♖ee8 26 ♕b2 ♕e6 27 ♕f2 ♔g8 28 ♕g3 ♗h5 29 ♘f5 ♗g6 30 ♘d4 ♕d7 31 a4 ♖a5 32 ♘b5 c6 33 ♖d4 ♕e7 34 ♘d6 ♖xe5 35 ♖xe5 ♕xe5 36 ♕xe5 ♖xe5 37 ♘c8 ♖e3 38 b4 ♖b3 39 ♘e7+ ♔f7 40 ♘xc6 ♔e6 41 ♖d5 ♖b1+ 42 ♔f2 ♗e8 43 ♘d4+ ♔e7 44 b5 ♗f7 45 ♘c6+ ♔f6 46 ♖d6+ ♔f5 47 g4+ ♔e4 48 ♖d4# **1-0** L/N6122

**1841-★S?-12**
**Staunton, H.+?**
London [Staunton]
1 e4 e5 2 ♘f3 ♘c6 3 d4 exd4 4 ♗c4 ♗b4+ 5 c3 dxc3 6 0-0 c2 7 ♕xc2 d6 8 a3 ♗a5 9 b4 ♗b6 10 ♗b2 ♘f6 11 e5 dxe5 12 ♘xe5 ♘xe5 13 ♗xe5 0-0 14 ♘c3 ♘g4 15 ♗g3 ♕g5 16 ♖ae1 ♗f5 17 ♕b3 c6 18 ♗d6 ♘xf2 19 ♗xf8 [19 ♖xf2?] 19 ... ♗h3! 20 ♗xf7+ ♔xf8 21 ♗d5! cxd5 22 ♕xd5 ♕f6 23 gxh3 ♘xh3+ 24 ♔g2 ♘f2 25 ♘e4 ♕g6+ 26 ♕g5 ♕c6 27 ♖xf2+ ♗xf2 28 ♕f5+ ♔g8 29 ♕xf2 **1-0** L/N6122

**1841-★S?-13**
**?– Staunton, H.**
London
1 e4 e5 2 f4 exf4 3 ♗c4 d5 4 exd5 ♘f6 5 ♘c3 c6 6 d3 ♗d6 7 dxc6 ♘xc6 8 ♘f3 0-0 9 0-0 ♗g4 10 ♘e2 ♗xf3 11 gxf3 ♘h5 12 d4 ♕h4 13 c3 ♖ae8 14 ♖f2 ♘e7 15 ♕d3 ♕h3 16 ♖g2 ♘f5 17 ♔h1 ♖xe2 **0-1** L/N6122

## BROWN✕STAUNTON London

**[1841̂-✕PS]**

| | | | |
|---|---|---|---|
| J. Brown | 1̂ | 0 | 1̂ |
| H. Staunton | 0 | 1̂ | 1̂ |

**1841̂-✕BS-1̂** ℵ1̂41̂
**Brown, J.+ Staunton, H.**
London
〈♙f7〉 1 e4 ... 2 d4 e6 3 ♗d3 c5 4 d5 d6 5 c4 ♘f6 6 f4 e5 7 f5 g6 8 g4 gxf5 9 gxf5 h5 10 ♗g5 ♗g7 11 h4 ♘a6 12 ♘f3 ♗h6 13 ♕d2 ♗g7 14 ♘c3 ♕a5 15 ♔e2 ♘g4 16 a3 ♗d7 17 ♖ag1 ♘c7 18 ♘h2 ♘f6 19 ♗xf6 ♗xf6 20 ♖g6 ♔e7 21 ♖xf6 ♔xf6 22 ♕g5+ ♔f7 23 ♕g6+ ♔e7 24 ♕g7+ ♔d8 25 ♕xh8+ **1-0** L/N6123

**1841̂-✕BS-2̂** ℵ1̂41̂
**Brown, J.– Staunton, H.**
London
〈♙f7〉 1 e4 ... 2 d4 e6 3 ♗d3 c5 4 e5 g6 5 c3 ♘c6 6 f4 d5 7 ♘f3 ♘h6 8 0-0 ♗e7 9 b3 0-0 10 ♕c2 ♔g7 11 a3 cxd4 12 cxd4 ♗d7 13 ♘c3 ♖c8 14 ♕d2 ♕b6 15 ♗c2 ♘a5 16 ♖b1 ♕c7 17 ♗b2

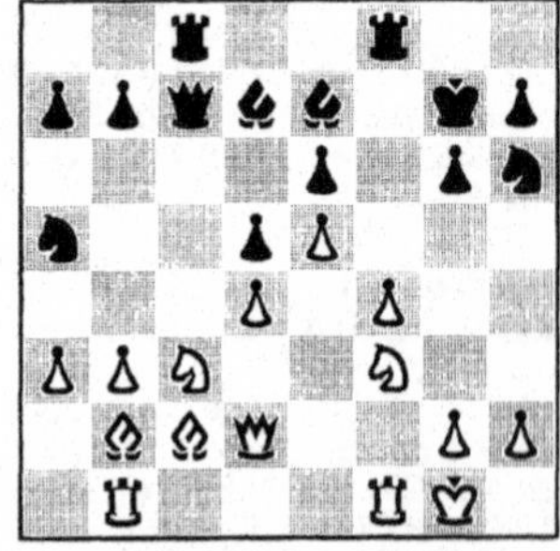

17 ... ♖f7 18 h4 ♗xa3 19 ♗xa3 ♕xc3 20 ♖b2 ♕xd2 21 ♘xd2 ♘g4 22 ♖f3 ♗b5 23 ♗d1 ♘c6 24 ♖c2 ♘h6 25 h5 ♘f5 26 hxg6 hxg6 27 ♗b2 ♖cf8 28 ♗a3 ♖h8 29 ♖h3 ♖xh3 30 gxh3 ♘fxd4 31 ♖c3 ♗e2 **0-1** L/N6123

## STANLEY✕STAUNTON

London

**[1841̂-✕SS]**

| | | | | |
|---|---|---|---|---|
| C.H. Stanley | 1̂ | 1̂ | 0 | 2 |
| H. Staunton | 0 | 0 | 1̂ | 1 |

**1841̂-✕SS-1̂**
**Stanley, C.H.+ Staunton, H.**
London
〈♙f7〉 1 e4 ... 2 d4 ♘c6 3 ♘c3 e5 4 dxe5 ♘xe5 5 f4 ♘f7 6 ♗c4 ♘gh6 7 f5 c6 8 ♗xh6 ♕h4+ 9 g3 ♕xh6 10 ♗xf7+ ♔xf7 11 ♕d4 b6 12 ♕c4+ ♔e8 13 ♘ge2 a5 14 ♕d4 ♗c5 15 ♕e5+ ♔f7 16 ♕f4 ♕xf4 17 ♘xf4 ♖e8 18 0-0-0 b5 19 ♖he1 d6 20 g4 a4 21 ♘d3 b4 22 ♘xc5 dxc5 23 ♘b1 ♖a7 24 ♖d6 ♖c7 25 e5 ♗a6 26 ♘d2 ♗b5 27 e6+ ♔e7 28 ♘e4 ♗c4 29 ♖d7+ ♖xd7 30 exd7 ♔xd7 31 ♘xc5+ ♔d8 32 ♘b7+

**1-0** L/N6123

**1841-✕SS-2**
**Stanley, C.H.+Staunton, H.**
London
⟨♙f7⟩ 1 e4 ... 2 d4 ♘c6 3 ♘c3 d6 4 f4 e6 5 ♘f3 ♘ce7 6 ♗d3 ♘f6 7 e5 dxe5 8 fxe5 ♘fd5 9 ♘h4 g6 10 ♘e4 ♘f5 11 ♘f3 ♗e7 12 c4 ♘b4 13 a3 ♘xd3+ 14 ♕xd3 0-0 15 ♗g5 ♗xg5 16 ♘exg5 c6 17 0-0-0 a6 18 h4 ♘g3 19 h5 ♘xh1 20 ♖xh1 ♖f5 21 ♘e4 b5 22 hxg6 hxg6 23 ♕e3 ♕f8 24 ♘f6+ ♖xf6 25 exf6 ♕xf6 26 ♘e5 g5 27 ♖h5 ♖a7 28 ♕xg5+ ♕xg5+ 29 ♖xg5+ ♖g7 30 ♖xg7+ ♔xg7 31 ♘xc6 ...♀
**1-0** L/N6123

**1841-✕SS-3**
**Stanley, C.H.–Staunton, H.**
London
⟨♙f7⟩ 1 e4 ... 2 d4 ♘c6 3 d5 ♘e5 4 f4 ♘f7 5 ♘f3 d6 6 f5 ♘f6 7 ♗d3 c6 8 c4 ♗d7 9 ♘d4 g6 10 ♘e6 ♗xe6 11 fxe6 ♘e5 12 ♗f4 ♘xd3+ 13 ♕xd3 ♗g7 14 e5 dxe5 15 ♗xe5 0-0 16 ♘c3 b5 17 b3 cxd5 18 ♘xd5 bxc4 19 bxc4 ♘xd5 20 ♗xg7 ♕a5+ 21 ♕d2 ♕xd2+ 22 ♔xd2 ♔xg7 23 cxd5 ♖ad8 24 ♖ae1 ♖xd5+ 25 ♔c1 ♖f2 26 ♖hf1 ♖df5 27 ♖xf2 ♖xf2 28 ♖e3 ♔f6 29 ♖a3 ♖xg2 ...♀ **0-1** L/N6123

**STAUNTON✕ZYTOGORSKI**
London
[1841-✕SZ]

| | | | | |
|---|---|---|---|---|
| H. Staunton | 1 | 1 | 1 | 3 |
| A. Zytogorski | 0 | 0 | 0 | 0 |

**1841-✕SZ-1**
**Zytogorski, A.–Staunton, H.**
London
⟨♙f7⟩ 1 e4 ... 2 d4 e6 3 ♗d3 c5 4 d5 d6 5 e5 ♘e7 6 ♗b5+ ♗d7 7 exd6 ♕a5+ 8 ♗d2 ♕xb5 9 dxe7 ♗xe7 10 a4 ♕b6 11 ♗c3 0-0 12 ♘f3 ♕d6 13 ♗e5 ♕xd5 14 ♕xd5 exd5 15 ♗xb8 ♖axb8 16 0-0 ♗g4 17 ♘e5 ♗f5 18 ♘d2 ♖bd8 19 c3 ♗d6 20 f4 ♗c2 21 g3 c4 22 ♖fc1 ♗f5 23 ♖e1 ♗c5+ 24 ♔g2 a5 25 g4 ♗c2 26 ♔g3 ♖f6 27 ♖ec1?

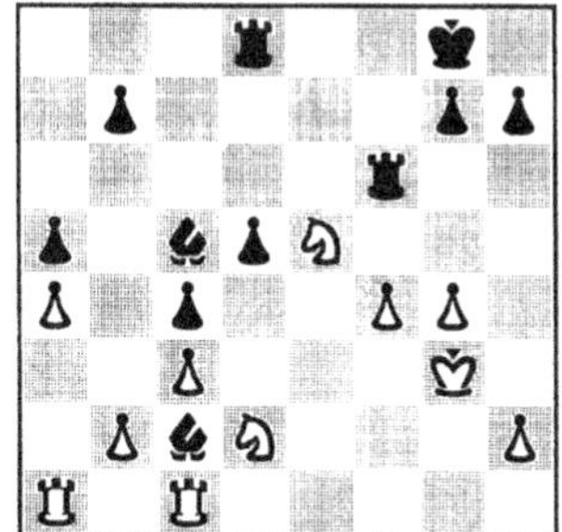

27 ... ♗e3! 28 ♖xc2 ♗xf4+ 29 ♔g2 ♗xe5 30 ♘f3 ♗d6 31 ♖d1 ♗c7 32 ♖cd2 ♖df8 33 ♘d4 g6 34 ♖e2 ♗b6 35 ♘b5 ♖f2+ 36 ♖xf2 ♖xf2+ 37 ♔g3 ♖xb2 38 ♖xd5 ♗f2+ 39 ♔f3 ♗h4 40 ♖c5 ♖xh2 41 ♖xc4 ♖f2+ 42 ♔e3 b6 43 ♘d6 ♖f8 44 ♖c8 ♗f2+ 45 ♔e4 ♖xc8 46 ♘xc8 ♗c5 47 ♘a7 ♔f7 48 ♘c6 ♔f6 49 ♘e5 ♔g5 50 ♔f3 h5 51 gxh5 gxh5 ...♀ **0-1** L/N6123

**1841-✕SZ-2**
**Zytogorski, A.–Staunton, H.**
London
⟨♙f7⟩ 1 e4 ... 2 d4 ♘c6 3 ♘f3 e6 4 c4 ♗b4+ 5 ♘c3 d5 6 e5 ♘ge7 7 ♗g5 0-0 8 a3 ♗xc3+ 9 bxc3 ♕e8 10 ♗e2 ♕h5 11 0-0 dxc4 12 ♗xc4 ♗d7 13 ♗h4 ♘d5 14 ♗g3 ♘xc3 15 ♕b3 ♖xf3 16 gxf3 ♕xf3 17 ♗xe6+ ♔h8 18 ♖ae1 ♘xd4 19 ♕c4 ♗c6 **0-1** L/N6123

**1841-✕SZ-3**
**Zytogorski, A.–Staunton, H.**
London
⟨♙f7⟩ 1 e4 ... 2 d4 ♘c6 3 e5 d6 4 f4 dxe5 5 d5 ♘d4 6 ♕h5+ g6 7 ♕xe5 ♘xc2+ 8 ♔d1 ♘xa1 9 ♕xh8 ♘f6 10 ♘f3 ♕xd5+ 11 ♗d2 ♗g4 12 ♗e2 ♕xa2 13 ♘c3 ♕xb2 14 ♔e1 0-0-0 15 ♔f2 ♗xf3 16 gxf3 ♘b3 17 ♘a4 ♘e4+ **0-1**
L/N6123-1843

**1841-★CS-1**
**Cochrane, J.=Staunton, H.**
London [Staunton]
1 e4 e5 2 ♗c4 ♗c5 3 c3 ♘c6 [□ 3 ... d6] 4 ♘f3 [□ 4 d4 exd4 5 ♗xf7+ ♔xf7 6 ♕h5+ △ 7 ♕xc5±] 4 ... ♘f6 5 d4 exd4 6 e5 d5 7 ♗b5 ♘e4 8 cxd4 ♗b4+ 9 ♗d2 ♗xd2+ 10 ♘bxd2 ♗g4 11 0-0 0-0 12 ♗xc6 bxc6 13 ♕c2 f5 14 ♕xc6 ♖b8 15 b3 [□ 15 ♖ac1] 15 ... ♖b6 16 ♕c2 ♖h6 17 ♖ac1 c6 18 ♕d3 ♕e8 19 b4 ♕g6 20 ♔h1 f4 [△ 21 ... ♘+, 22 ... ♕xd3] 21 ♕c2 ♗f5 22 ♕b3 ♕h5 23 ♘xe4 ♗xe4 24 h3 ♕g4? [□ 24 ... g5→] 25 ♔h2 ♕g6? [□ 25 ... ♖f5] 26 ♖c3 ♖f5 27 b5! ♖fh5 28 ♖xc6

28 ... ♖xh3+ 29 gxh3 ♖xh3+ 30 ♔xh3 ♕h5+ 31 ♘h4 ♗f5+ 32 ♔g2 ♕g4+ 33 ♔h2 ♕xh4+ 34 ♔g1 ♗e4 35 f3 ♕g3+ ½-½
L/N6123-1842

**1841-★CS-2**
**Staunton, H.+Cochrane, J.**
London
1 e4 e5 2 ♗c4 ♗c5 3 ♕e2 ♕e7 4 f4 ♘f6 5 fxe5 ♕xe5 6 ♘f3 ♕xe4 7 ♗xf7+ ♔d8 8 ♕xe4 ♘xe4 9 d4 ♗e7 10 0-0 ♖f8 11 ♗b3 d6 12 ♘bd2 ♘xd2 13 ♗xd2 ♗g4 14 ♘g5 h6 15 ♖xf8+ ♗xf8 16 ♖f1 ♗e7 17 ♗e6 hxg5 18 ♗xg4 ♗f6 19 c3 ♔e7 20 ♗c8 a5 21 ♖e1+ ♔f8 22 ♗xb7 ♖a7 23 ♗c8 c6 24 ♗g4 ♖e7 25 ♖f1 ♔g8 26 ♖f5 ♖b7 27 ♗xg5 d5 28 b3 a4 29 b4 ♗xg5 30 ♖xg5 a3 31 ♔f2 ♖e7 32 ♖e5 ♖xe5 33 dxe5 ♔f7 34 ♔e3 ♘a6 35 ♔d4 ♔e7 36 h4 ♘c7 37 c4 ♘a6 38 cxd5 ♘xb4 39 d6+ **1-0** L/N6123-1842

**1841-★MS-1**
**Mongredien, A.+Staunton, H.**
London
⟨♙f7⟩ 1 e4 ... 2 d4 ♘c6 3 ♗d3 e5 4 d5 ♘ce7 5 f4 d6 6 f5 ♘f6 7 ♗g5 ♘eg8 8 ♗e2 ♗e7 9 ♗h5+ ♔f8 10 ♗f3 ♘xd5 11 ♕xd5 ♗xg5 12 g3 ♗c1 13 ♘d2 ♗xb2 14 ♖b1 ♗c3 15 ♘e2 ♗xd2+ 16 ♕xd2 b6 17 g4 h6 18 ♘g3 ♘f6 19 h4 ♗b7 20 ♔f2 d5 21 g5 ♘xe4+ 22 ♗xe4 dxe4 23 ♕e3 ♕d4 24 g6 ♕xe3+ 25 ♔xe3 ♔e7 26 ♖hf1 ♖ad8 27 ♘h5 ♖hg8 28 ♖f2 ♗d5 29 ♖bf1 c6 30 ♘xg7
**1-0** L/N6123

**1841-★S♀-1**
**♀–Staunton, H.**
London [Staunton]
1 e4 e5 2 f4 exf4 3 ♗c4 d5 4 exd5 ♘f6 5 ♕f3 ♗d6 6 h3 0-0 7 c3 c6 8 dxc6 ♘xc6 9 d4 ♘e4 10 ♗xf4 ♕h4+ 11 g3 ♘xg3 12 ♗xd6 ♘xh1+ 13 ♔f1 ♗e6! 14 ♗d3 ♖fd8 15 ♗h2 ♗d5 16 ♕f4 ♕h5 17 ♘d2 ♘e7 18 c4 ♘g6 19 ♕g4 [19 ♗xg6?] 19 ... ♕h6 20 ♖d1 ♕e3 21 ♕f5 ♗g2+ 22 ♔xg2 ♘h4+ **0-1**
L/N6122

**1841Î-★S?-2**
**Staunton, H.+?**
London
1 e4 e5 2 ♗c4 ♗c5 3 ♕e2 ♘f6 4 f4 ♕e7 5 ♘f3 exf4 6 d4 ♗b6 7 e5 ♘h5 8 ♘c3 c6 9 ♘e4 0-0 10 ♘d6 ♗a5+ 11 c3 b5 12 ♗b3 ♗a6 13 ♕e4 b4 14 ♘f5 ♕d8 15 c4 d5 16 cxd5 ♖e8 17 d6 g6 18 ♘h6+ ♔g7 19 ♘xf7 ♕b6 20 ♗xf4 ♘xf4 21 ♕xf4 ♘d7 22 ♕h6+ **1-0** L/N6122

**1841Î-★S?-3**
**Staunton, H.+?**
London [Staunton]
⟨♘b1⟩ 1 e4 e5 2 ♘f3 ♘c6 3 ♗c4 ♗c5 4 b4 ♗xb4 5 c3 ♗a5 6 0-0 d6 7 d4 ♗xc3 8 ♕b3 ♗xa1 9 ♗xf7+ ♔e7 [9 ... ♔f8?!] 10 ♗g5+ ♘f6 11 ♖xa1 h6 12 ♘h4 ♘xd4 [12 ... hxg5?? 13 ♘g6+ ♔d7 14 ♕e6#] 13 ♘g6+ ♔d7 14 ♕h3+ ♔c6 15 ♖c1+ [15 ♗d5+?] 15 ... ♔b6 16 ♖b1+ ♘b5 17 ♖xb5+ ♔xb5 18 ♕b3+ ♔c6 19 ♕c4+ ♔d7 20 ♘xe5+ ♔e7 21 ♘g6+ ♔d7 22 ♕e6+ ♔c6 23 ♘e5+ ♔b6 24 ♕b3+ **1-0** L/N6123

**65** Chamouillet, M. L/N6396.BL

**1842-★CG-1** 7/8 x 42
**Guinguer & Kieseritsky, L.+ Chamouillet, M., & Devinck, F.J.**
Paris [Saint-Amant]
1 e4 e5 2 f4 exf4 3 ♘f3 g5 4 h4 g4 5 ♘e5 h5 6 ♗c4 ♖h7 7 d4 f3 8 g3 d6 9 ♘d3 ♗e7 10 ♘c3 ♘c6 11 ♘f4 ♗f6 12 ♗e3 ♘ge7 13 ♔f2 ♗d7 14 ♘cd5 ♘xd5 15 ♘xd5 ♗g7 16 ♘f4 [◻ 16 ♗f4, 17 ♕e1] 16 ... f5 17 ♕d3 ♘e7 18 ♕b3 ♗h6 19 ♘xh5 ♗xe3+ 20 ♔xe3 ♘g6 21 e5 [◻ ♗g8±] 21 ... dxe5 22 ♗g8 exd4+ 23 ♔d2 ♖e7 24 ♖ae1 ♔f8 25 ♘f6 ♔g7

26 ♘xd7 ♕xd7 27 ♗e6 ♕d6 28 ♗xf5 ♕xg3 29 ♗xg6 ♕f4+ 30 ♔d1 ♖e3? [◻ 30 ... ♖xe1+ 31 ♖xe1 ♔xg6] 31 ♕xb7 ♖ae8? 32 ♗xe8 f2 33 ♖xe3 dxe3 34 ♗b5 g3 35 ♔e2 ♕e5 36 ♕c6 ♔f8 37 ♖d1 ♕h5+ 38 ♕f3+ ♕xf3+ 39 ♔xf3 **1-0** L/N6013

**1842-★CS-1** 21 vii 42
**Cochrane, J.– Saint-Amant, P.C.F. de**
London [Walker]
1 e4 g6 2 d4 ♗g7 3 c3 e5 4 ♘f3 ♘c6 5 dxe5 ♘xe5 6 ♘xe5 ♗xe5 7 ♗c4 ♘f6 8 0-0 0-0 9 f4 ♗d6 10 e5 ♗c5+ 11 ♔h1 ♘e4 12 ♕f3 d5 13 ♗b3 ♕h4 14 g3 ♕h3 [△ 15 ... ♘xg3+–+; 15 ♘bd2! ♗g4 16 ♕g2; 15 ♘bd2! ♗f5 16 ♗xd5] **0-1** L/N6013-1842

**1842-★CS-2** 22 vii 42
**Saint-Amant, P.C.F. de– Cochrane, J.**
London [Saint-Amant]
1 e4 e5 2 ♘f3 ♘c6 3 ♗c4 ♗c5 4 c3 ♘f6 5 d4 exd4 6 e5 ♘e4? [6 ... d5] 7 cxd4? [7 ♗d5] 7 ... ♗b4+ 8 ♔f1? d5 9 ♗e2 0-0 10 ♘bd2 ♗xd2 11 ♗xd2 f6 12 exf6? ♕xf6 13 ♗e3 ♘e7 14 ♕c2 ♘f5 15 ♗d3 ♘xe3+ 16 fxe3 ♘g5 17 ♗e2 ♗h3! 18 ♕b3 c6 19 e4? ♘xe4 20 ♔g1 ♘d2 21 ♕d3 ♘xf3+ 22 ♗xf3 ♗xg2 23 ♔xg2 ♕g5+ 24 ♔f2 ♖xf3+ 25 ♕xf3 ♖f8 **0-1** L/N6013-1842

**1842-★CS-3** 23 vii 42
**Cochrane, J.= Saint-Amant, P.C.F. de**
London [Saint-Amant]
1 e4 c5 2 c4 ♘c6 3 ♘c3 e5 4 ♗d3 ♕g5 5 ♕f3 ♘f6 6 ♘ge2 ♗d6 7 0-0 0-0= 8 ♕e3 ♕h4 9 ♘d5 ♘d4 10 ♘xf6+ ♕xf6 11 ♘c3 ♕e6 12 ♘e2?∓ f5 13 ♘xd4 exd4 14 ♕h3 f4 [◻ 14 ... fxe4] 15 ♕xe6+ dxe6 16 f3 a6 17 b3= ♗d7 18 ♗b2 g5 19 ♔f2 e5 20 ♖g1 ♔f7 21 g3 ♖g8 22 gxf4 gxf4 23 ♖xg8 ♖xg8 24 ♖g1 ♖xg1 25 ♔xg1 ♔g6 26 ♗f1 ♗e7 27 d3 b6 28 ♗c1 ♗g5 29 ♗d2 a5 30 a3 h6 31 ♗g2 ♗d8 32 ♔f2 ♗h4+ 33 ♔g1 ♗g5 ...? ½-½ L/N6013-1842

**1842-★CS-4**
**Staunton, H.+Cochrane, J.**
London
1 e4 e5 2 ♗c4 ♗c5 3 ♕h5 ♕e7 4 ♘f3 ♘c6 5 d3 d6 6 ♘c3 ♗b4 7 0-0 ♗xc3 8 bxc3 ♘f6 9 ♕h4 ♗g4 10 ♘g5 ♗h5 11 f4 h6 12 ♘h3 0-0-0 13 ♖b1 exf4 14 ♕xf4 ♕e5 15 ♗e3 ♕xf4 16 ♘xf4 ♗g6 17 ♘d5 ♘xd5 18 ♗xd5 ♖hf8 19 ♗xc6 bxc6 20 ♗xa7 ♔d7 21 ♖b7 ♖a8 22 a4 c5 23 a5 ♔c6 24 ♖fb1 c4 25 a6 cxd3 26 cxd3 f5 27 ♗b8 ♖c8 28 a7 **1-0** L/N6123

**21** Jaenisch, C.F. L/N6309.CPL

**1842-★HJ-1** 19 ii 42
**Hanstein, W.+Jaenisch, C.F.**
Berlin
1 e4 e5 2 f4 d5 3 exd5 ♕xd5 4 ♘c3 ♕e6 5 fxe5 ♕xe5+ 6 ♗e2 ♗d6 7 ♘f3 ♕a5 8 d4 ♘f6 9 ♗d2 ♗b4 10 a3 ♗xc3 11 ♗xc3 ♕b6 12 ♗b4 ♘a6 13 c3 ♘xb4 14 axb4 0-0 15 ♖a5 a6 16 0-0 ♗e6 17 ♘e5 ♖ad8 18 ♗d3 ♘d5 19 ♕h5 h6 20 ♖f3 ♘xb4 21 cxb4 ♕xd4+ 22 ♔h1 ♕xb4 23 ♖a1 ♕xb2 24 ♖af1 c5 25 ♘xf7 ♗xf7 26 ♖xf7 ♖xf7 27 ♕xf7+ ♔h8 28 ♕f8+ **1-0** L/N6047-1849

**1842-★HJ-2**
**Hanstein, W.+Jaenisch, C.F.**
Berlin
1 e4 e6 2 d4 d5 3 exd5 exd5 4 ♗e3 ♘f6 5 ♗e2 ♗d6 6 ♘f3 0-0 7 h3 ♕e7 8 c3 ♗e6 9 ♕c2 c5 10 ♘bd2 ♘c6 11 dxc5 ♗xc5 12 ♗xc5 ♕xc5 13 ♘b3 ♕b6 14 0-0 ♖ac8 15 ♕d2 ♖fd8 16 ♖ad1 h6 17 ♗d3 ♖d7 18 ♘bd4 ♖cd8 19 ♖fe1 a6 20 ♖e2 ♖e7 21 ♖de1 ♖de8 22 ♕f4 ♘d8 23 ♗f5 ♕c5 24 ♘e5 ♗xf5 25 ♘xf5

♘e6 26 ♘xe7+ ♖xe7 27 ♕f5 d4 28 ♖c2 d3 29 ♕xd3 ♘f4 30 ♕d4 ♕xd4 31 cxd4 ♘6d5 32 a3 g5 33 ♘f3 ♖xe1+ 34 ♘xe1 ♔g7 35 ♖c5 b6 36 ♖c6 ♘e6 37 ♘c2 ♘df4 38 ♔f1 ♘d3 39 ♖xb6 **1-0**

L/N6047-1849

**1842-★HJ-3**
**Hanstein, W.+Jaenisch, C.F.**
Berlin

1 e4 e6 2 d4 d5 3 exd5 exd5 4 ♘c3 ♘f6 5 ♘f3 c5 6 ♗e3 cxd4 7 ♗xd4 ♘c6 8 ♗b5 ♗b4 9 ♕e2+ ♗e6 10 0-0 0-0 11 ♕d3 ♗xc3 12 ♗xc3 ♘e4 13 ♘d2 f5 14 ♖ae1 ♕b6

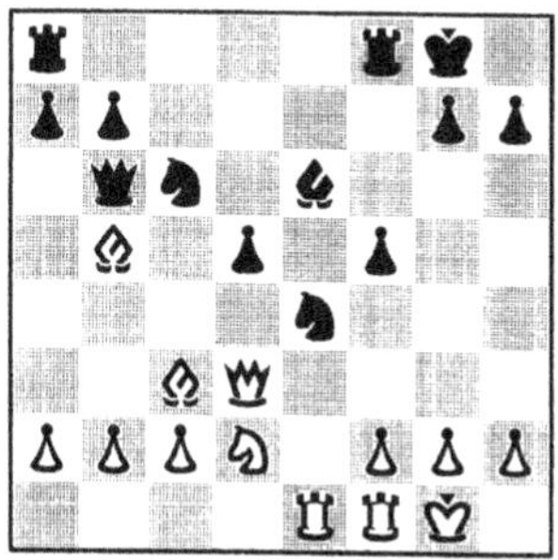

15 ♘b3 ♖ad8 16 ♗xc6 ♕xc6 17 ♘d4 ♕b6 18 ♘xe6 ♕xe6 19 f3 ♕b6+ 20 ♗d4 ♘c5 21 ♕a3 ♖fe8 22 ♗xc5 ♕b5 23 ♕xa7 ♕xb2 24 ♗d4 ♕b5 25 ♖b1 **1-0**

L/N6047-1849

**1842-★HJ-4**
**Hanstein, W.♀+Jaenisch, C.F.♀**
Berlin

1 e4 e5 2 f4 exf4 3 ♘f3 ♗e7 4 ♗c4 ♗h4+ 5 g3 fxg3 6 0-0 gxh2+ 7 ♔h1 ♗f6 8 ♘e5 ♗xe5 9 ♕h5 ♕e7 10 ♖xf7 ♕c5 11 ♖f8+ ♔e7 12 d4 ♕xc4 13 ♕e8+ ♔d6 14 ♕xe5+ ♔c6 15 ♘a3 d6 16 d5+ ♔c5 17 ♗e3+ ♔b4 18 c3+ ♔a4 19 b3+ ♔xa3 20 ♗c1# **1-0** L/N6123-1842

**1842-★JL-1** 16 ii 42
**Jaenisch, C.F.+ Lasa, T. von H. u. von d.**
Berlin♀

1 d4 f5 2 c4 ♘f6 3 ♘c3 e6 4 f3 c5 5 e3 b6 6 ♗d3 ♗b7 7 ♘h3 ♘c6 8 ♗c2 h6 9 a3 g6 10 ♘f2 ♗d6 11 d5 ♘e5 12 b3 a6 13 e4 ♘h5 14 f4 ♘f7 15 e5 ♗b8 16 ♖g1 ♘g7 17 g4 ♔f8 18 gxf5 gxf5 19 ♖g3 ♖h7 20 ♕e2 ♕e8 21 d6 ♗a7 22 ♗e3 ♘h8 23 ♘d3 ♕h5 24 ♕f2

24 ... ♖c8 25 ♔d2 ♕e8 26 ♗d1 h5 27 ♗f3 ♗c6 28 ♗xc6 ♖xc6 29 ♖ag1 h4 30 ♖3g2 ♘f7 31 ♘e1 ♕d8 32 ♘f3 b5 33 ♘xh4 ♕xh4 34 ♕xh4 ♖xh4 35 ♖xg7 ♖xh2+ 36 ♔d1 ♖h8 37 cxb5 axb5 38 ♘xb5 ♗b6 39 ♘c3 ♗d8 40 ♘a4 c4 41 bxc4 ♖xc4 42 ♘c5 ♖c3 43 ♘xd7+ ♔e8 44 ♘c5 ♖f8 45 ♘xe6 ♖xe3 46 ♘xf8 ♗b6 47 ♖1g6 ♘xe5 48 ♖e7+ ♔xf8 49 fxe5 ♗d8 50 ♖f6+ **1-0** L/N6047-1858

**1842-★JL-2** 20 ii 42
**Lasa, T. von H. u. von d.+ Jaenisch, C.F.**
Berlin♀

1 e4 e5 2 f4 exf4 3 ♘f3 g5 4 h4 g4 5 ♘e5 h5 6 ♗c4 ♖h7 7 d4 d6 8 ♘d3 f3 9 g3 ♗h6 10 ♘f4 ♘e7 11 ♘xh5 ♘g6 12 ♗g5 ♗xg5 13 hxg5 ♔f8 14 ♕d2 ♗e6 15 ♘a3 ♗xc4 16 ♘xc4 ♘c6

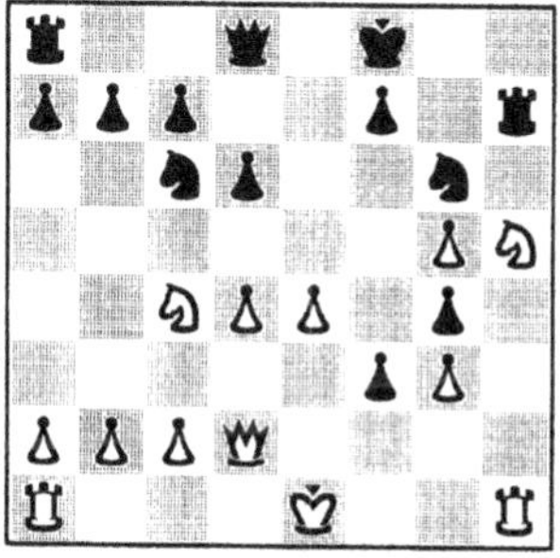

17 d5 ♘ce5 18 ♘xe5 dxe5 19 0-0-0 ♕d6 20 ♘f6 ♖xh1 21 ♖xh1 ♔e7 22 ♘xg4 ♖d8 23 ♖f1 c6 24 ♘f6 ♘f8 25 ♕e3 cxd5 26 ♘xd5+ ♔d7 27 ♖xf3 **1-0** L/N6047-1858

**1842-★JL-3** 29 vii 42
**Jaenisch, C.F.= Lasa, T. von H. u. von d.**
Berlin♀

1 d4 f5 2 c4 ♘f6 3 ♘c3 e6 4 e3 ♗b4 5 ♕b3 ♗xc3+ 6 bxc3 0-0 7 ♗d3 d6 8 ♘f3 ♔h8 9 a4 a5 10 ♗a3 b6 11 0-0 ♗a6 12 ♖ad1 c5 13 d5 exd5 14 cxd5 ♗xd3 15 ♖xd3 ♘e4 16 ♘d2 ♘xd2 17 ♖xd2 ♘d7 18 ♗b2 ♕h4 19 c4 ♖ae8 20 ♖e2 h6 21 ♖fe1 ♔h7 22 f3 ♖f7 23 g3 ♕h5 24 ♔g2 ♖fe7 25 ♕d3 ♕g6 26 e4 fxe4 27 ♖xe4 ♖xe4 28 ♖xe4 ♖xe4 29 ♕xe4 ♕xe4 30 fxe4 g5 31 ♔f3 ♔g6 32 g4 ♘e5+ 33 ♗xe5 dxe5 34 ♔g3 ♔f6 35 h4 ♔f7 **½-½** L/N6047-1858

**1842-★JL-4** 1 ix 42
**Lasa, T. von H. u. von d.+ Jaenisch, C.F.**
Berlin♀

1 e4 e5 2 ♘f3 ♘f6 3 d4 exd4 4 e5 ♘e4 5 ♗d3 d5 6 ♘xd4 c5 7 ♘e2 ♘c6 8 f3 ♘g5 9 f4 ♘e6 10 0-0 ♕b6 11 ♔h1 ♗e7 12 ♘bc3 ♘c7 13 b3 ♘b4 14 ♘g3 ♘xd3 15 ♕xd3 ♕c6 16 f5 g6 17 ♗f4 ♗xf5 18 ♘xf5 gxf5 19 ♕xf5 ♕g6 20 ♗g3 h5 21 ♕xg6 fxg6 22 e6 ♘xe6 23 ♖ae1 ♖f8 24 ♖xf8+ ♘xf8 25 ♘xd5 **1-0**

L/N6047-1857

**1842-★LS-1**
**Löwenthal, J.J.– Szén, J.**
Pesth [Saint-Amant]

1 e4 e5 2 ♘f3 ♘c6 [2 ... d6] 3 ♗c4 ♗c5 4 c3 ♕e7 5 0-0 ♘f6 6 d4 ♗b6 7 ♖e1 d6 8 h3 0-0 9 ♗e3 h6 10 ♘bd2 ♖e8 11 a3 ♗d7 12 ♕c2 ♘h5 13 b4 ♕f6 14 a4?! exd4 15 cxd4 ♗xd4 16 ♘xd4 ♘xd4 17 ♗xd4 ♕xd4 18 ♖a3 ♕e5 19 ♖f3 ♖e7 20 ♗d5 c6 21 ♗b3 ♗e6 22 ♘c4 ♗xc4 23 ♗xc4 g6 24 ♕d2 ♔g7 25 ♖d3 d5 26 ♗xd5? cxd5 27 ♖xd5 ♕f4 28 ♕d4+ ♔h7 29 ♖d6 ♖c8 30 g3 ♘xg3 31 ♖f6 ♕g5 32 fxg3 ♕xg3+ 33 ♔f1 ♖c2 34 ♖f2 ♕xh3+ 35 ♔g1 ♖d7 36 ♕xd7 ♕g3+ 37 ♔h1 ♕h4+ **0-1** L/N6013

**1842-★LS-2**
**Löwenthal, J.J.+ Szeń, J.**
Pesth [Saint-Amant]

1 e4 e5 2 ♘f3 ♘c6 3 ♗c4 ♗c5 4 c3 d6 5 d4 exd4 6 cxd4 ♗b6 7 h3 ♘f6 8 0-0 [◻ 8 ♗g5] 8 ... h6 9 ♘c3 0-0 10 a3 ♘h7 11 ♘e2 ♘e7 12 ♘f4 c6 13 ♗b3 [△ 13 ... d5 14 e5] 13 ... d5 14 e5 ♗c7 15 ♗c2 ♗f5 16 ♗xf5 ♘xf5 17 ♕d3 ♕d7 18 ♗d2 ♘e7 19 ♖ac1 ♖fe8 20 g4 ♘f8 21 ♘h5 ♕e6 22 ♘h4 ♔h8 23 f4 f6 24 f5 ♕f7 25 exf6 gxf6 26 ♗xh6 ♘d7 27 ♗g7+ ♔h7 28 ♕d2 ♘g8 29 ♘g6 ♖e4 30 ♕f2 ♘e7 31 ♕h4 ♔g8 32 ♘xf6+ ♘xg7 33 ♕h7+ ♔xf6 34 g5+ ♔xg5 35 ♕xf7 **1-0** L/N6013

**1842-★SS-1** 15 xii 42
**Saint-Amant, P.C.F. de+ Schulten, J.W.**
Paris [Saint-Amant]

1 e4 e5 2 ♘f3 ♘c6 3 ♗c4 ♗c5 4 0-0 d6 5 c3 ♗e6 6 ♗xe6 fxe6 7 ♕b3

♕d7 8 ♘g5 [8 ♕xb7?!] 8 ... ♘d8± 9 d3 h6 10 ♘f3 g5?! 11 d4 exd4 12 cxd4 ♗b6 [12 ... g4 13 dxc5±] 13 ♗e3 ♘f6 14 ♘c3 ♘g4 15 ♖ad1 ♘c6 16 d5?! ♘a5! 17 dxe6 ♕c6 18 ♕b4 ♘xe3 19 fxe3 ♗xe3+ 20 ♔h1 ♗b6 21 ♘d5 ♕c5 22 ♕xc5 dxc5 23 ♘e5 0-0-0 24 ♘f7 ♖de8 25 ♘f6 ♘c6 26 ♘xh8 ♖xh8 27 ♘d7 ♘d4 28 ♘f8 ♔d8 29 e7+ ♔e8 30 ♘g6 **1-0** L/N6013-1843

**1842-★SS-2** xii 42

**Schulten, J.W.– Saint-Amant, P.C.F. de**

Paris [Saint-Amant]

1 e4 c5 2 c3 e5 3 f4 d6 4 ♘f3 exf4 5 d4 ♘f6 6 ♗d3 ♗e7 7 ♗xf4 0-0 8 ♘bd2± ♘c6 9 0-0 ♗g4 10 e5 dxe5 11 dxe5?? [11 ♗xe5] 11 ... ♘h5 12 ♗xh7+ ♔xh7 13 ♘g5+ ♗xg5 14 ♕xg4 ♘xf4–+ 15 ♘e4 ♘e6 16 ♕h5+ ♔g8 17 ♖ad1 ♕e7 18 ♖d7?! ♕xd7 19 ♘f6+ gxf6 [19 ... ♗xf6] 20 ♖xf6 ♗xf6 **0-1** L/N6013-1842

**19** Walker, G. L/N3087.BL

**1842-★SW-1** 21 vii 42

**Walker, G.– Saint-Amant, P.C.F. de**

London [Saint-Amant]

1 e4 e5 2 ♘f3 ♘f6 3 ♘c3 ♘c6 4 ♗c4 ♗c5 5 d3 h6 6 0-0 d6 7 h3 ♗e6 8 ♗xe6 fxe6 9 ♘a4 ♗b6 10 ♘xb6 axb6 11 c3 0-0 12 ♕e2 ♕e8 13 d4 ♕h5 14 ♖e1 exd4 15 ♘xd4 ♘xd4 16 ♕xh5 ♘xh5∓ 17 cxd4 c5 18 ♗e3 ♘f4 19 dxc5? bxc5 20 ♖ad1 ♖xa2 21 ♖xd6 ♖xb2 22 ♗xc5 b5! 23 ♖a1 e5 24 ♖d7 ♖f6 25 ♔h2 ♖g6 26 g3 ♘e2 27 ♖e7 ♘d4 28 ♔g2 ♖f6 29 ♖f1 ♘f3 30 ♖d1 ♘d4 31 ♖f1 ♘c6 32 ♖d7 b4 33 ♖a1 b3 34 ♖a6 ♖a2 35 ♖b6 ♖c2 36 ♖bb7 ♖xc5? [36 ... ♖g6] 37 ♖xg7+ ♔f8 38 ♖h7 ♔e8 39 ♖h8+ ♖f8 40 ♖xb3?? [40 ♖xf8+ ♔xf8 41 ♖xb3=] 40 ... ♖xh8 **0-1** L/N6013-1842

**1842̂-★CS-1**

**Cochrane, J.⚲ Staunton, H.**

London [Staunton]

1 e4 e5 2 ♘f3 ♘c6 3 d4 ♘xd4 4 ♘xe5 ♘e6 5 ♗e3 c6 [△ 7 ... ♕a5+, 8 ... ♕xe5] 6 f4 ♗c5 7 ♗xc5 ♘xc5 8 ♘xf7 ♕a5+ 9 c3 ♔xf7 10 b4 ♕c7 11 ♕h5+ g6 12 ♕xc5 ♕xf4 13 ♗c4+ ♔g7 14 ♘d2 ♘f6 15 ♖f1 [□ 15 ♕e7+ △ 16 ♖f1] 15 ... ♕xd2+ 16 ♔xd2 ♘xe4+ 17 ♔c2 ♘xc5 ...⚲ L/N6123-1842

**1842̂-★CS-2**

**Cochrane, J.– Staunton, H.**

London [Staunton]

1 d4 d5 2 c4 e6 3 e3 ♘f6 4 ♘f3 ♗b4+ 5 ♘c3 0-0 6 ♗d2 b6 7 ♗e2 ♗xc3 8 bxc3 ♗b7 9 cxd5 ♗xd5 10 0-0 a5 11 h3 ♘c6 12 ♘h2 ♘e7 13 f3 ♗b7 14 e4 ♘g6 15 ♕e1 ♕e7 16 ♗g5 h6 17 ♗xf6 ♕xf6 18 ♕d2 ♘f4 19 ♔h1 ♘xe2 20 ♕xe2 ♗a6 21 ♕e3 ♗xf1 22 ♖xf1 ♕e7 23 g4 c5 24 f4 cxd4 25 cxd4 ♖ad8 26 ♘f3 ♖c8 27 f5 exf5 28 gxf5 ♖c2 29 ♘e1 ♖xa2 30 f6 ♕c7 31 e5 ♕c6+ 32 ♘f3 ♕e6 33 ♘h4 ♕d5+ 34 ♘f3 ♖c8 35 ♖g1 g6 36 e6! ♔h7 [36 ... fxe6??+–; 36 ... ♕xe6??+–] 37 exf7 ♕xf7 38 ♕e4 ♖e8 39 ♕h4 ♖ee2 40 ♕f4 [40 ♘g5+? ♔g8 41 ♘f3! ♖h2+ 42 ♘xh2 ♕d5+–+] 40 ... ♖ac2 41 ♖g4! [△ 42 ♕xh6+ ♔xh6 43 ♖h4#] 41 ... g5 42 ♕f5+ ♔h8 43 d5 ♕c7 **0-1** L/N6123-1844̂

**1842̂-★CS-3**

**Cochrane, J.– Staunton, H.**

London [Staunton]

1 e4 c5 2 d4 cxd4 3 ♕xd4 ♘c6 4 ♕d1 ♘f6 5 ♗d3 e5 6 ♘f3 ♗c5 7 0-0 d6 8 h3 h6 9 ♘c3 0-0 10 ♘h2 ♘d4 11 ♔h1 ♘e6 12 f4 exf4 13 ♗xf4 ♘xf4 14 ♖xf4 ♗e6 15 ♕e2 ♗d4 16 ♖af1 ♗e5 17 ♖4f2 ♖c8 18 a3 ♖c5 19 ♘d1 ♗d4 20 ♖f3 ♖g5 21 c3 ♗e5 22 g4 h5 23 ♕e3 hxg4 24 ♕xg5 gxf3 25 ♖xf3 ♗xh2 26 ♖xf6 [26 ♔xh2?? ♘g4+] 26 ... ♗e5 27 ♖f5 ♗xf5 28 ♕xf5 ♕h4 **0-1** L/N6123-1844̂

**1842̂-★CS-4**

**Cochrane, J.+ Staunton, H.**

London [Staunton]

⟨♙f7⟩ 1 e4 d6 2 f4 ♘f6 3 ♗c4 ♗g4 [3 ... ♘xe4 4 ♕h5+ g6 5 ♕d5] 4 ♗e2 ♗d7 5 d3 ♘c6 6 ♘f3 e5 7 0-0 exf4 8 ♗xf4 ♗e7 9 ♘c3 0-0 10 ♗g5 ♘e5 11 ♘xe5 dxe5 12 ♗xf6 ♗xf6 13 ♗g4 c6 14 ♗xd7 ♕xd7 15 ♕e2 ♖ad8 16 ♖f3 b5 17 ♕e3 ♗e7 18 ♖af1 ♖xf3 19 ♖xf3 a5 20 ♕b6 a4 21 a3 ♗d6 [△ 22 ... ♖b8, 23 ... b4] 22 ♕e3 ♕e7 23 ♔h1 ♗c5 24 ♕e1 ♖d6 25 ♘e2 ♖h6 26 c3 g6 27 h3 [27 ♘g3 ♖xh2+ 28 ♔xh2 ♕h4#] 27 ... ♕e6 ...⚲

**1-0** M954-1849

**1842̂-★CS-5**

**Cochrane, J.= Staunton, H.**

London

1 e4 c5 2 d4 cxd4 3 ♗c4 e5 4 f4 ♘c6 5 ♘f3 ♘f6 6 ♕e2 ♗e7 7 0-0 d6 8 ♘g5 0-0 9 fxe5 dxe5 10 ♕f3 h6 11 ♘xf7? ♖xf7 12 ♕g3 ♘a5 13 ♗xf7+ ♔xf7 14 ♕xe5 ♘c4 15 ♕h5+ ♔g8 16 ♕e2 ♘e5 17 ♗f4 d3 18 ♕d2 ♘xe4 19 ♕e1 ♗c5+ 20 ♔h1 ♕d4 21 ♘c3 ♗f5 22 ♗xe5 ♘f2+ 23 ♖xf2 ♕xf2 24 ♕xf2 ♗xf2 25 cxd3 ♗xd3 26 ♖d1 ♖e8 27 ♖xd3 ♖xe5 **½-½** L/N6123-1844̂

**1842̂-★CS-6**

**Cochrane, J.– Staunton, H.**

London

1 e4 c5 2 d4 cxd4 3 ♕xd4 ♘c6 4 ♕d1 e5 5 ♗c4 ♘f6 6 ♘f3 ♗c5 [6 ... ♘xe4 7 ♗xf7+ △ 8 ♕d5] 7 0-0 0-0 8 ♘c3 h6 9 a3 [△ 10 b4] 9 ... a6 10 ♗d5 d6 11 ♗xc6 bxc6 12 ♘e1 ♘g4 13 h3 ♘f6 14 ♔h1 ♘h7 15 ♘d3 ♗a7 16 f4 ♕h4 17 ♕f3 f5 18 exf5 ♗xf5 19 g4 ♘g5 20 ♕g2 [20 fxg5 ♗e4–+] 20 ... ♘xh3 21 ♕h2 ♕xg4 22 ♕g2 ♕h4 23 ♕h2 e4 24 ♘e1 ♗g1 25 ♖xg1 ♘f2+ 26 ♔g2 ♗h3+

**0-1** L/N6123-1843̂

**1842̂-★CS-7**

**Cochrane, J.+ Staunton, H.**

London [Staunton]

1 e4 e5 2 f4 exf4 3 ♘f3 g5 4 ♗c4 g4 5 d4 gxf3 6 ♕xf3 d5 7 ♗xd5 c6 8 ♗xf7+ ♔xf7 9 0-0 ♗h6 [9 ... ♕xd4+] 10 ♗xf4 ♗xf4 11 ♕xf4+ ♘f6 12 e5 ♖g8 13 ♕h4 ♔e8 14 ♖xf6 ♗g4 15 ♕f2 ♘d7 16 ♖f4 c5 17 ♘c3 ♘b6 18 ♘e4 ♗e6 19 ♘f6+ ♔e7 20 ♕h4 ♖g6 21 d5 ♘xd5 22 ♘xd5+ ♔d7 23 ♕xh7+ ♔c6 24 ♘e7+ ♕xe7 25 ♕xe7 **1-0** L/N6123-1842

**1842̂-★CS-8**
**Cochrane, J.– Staunton, H.**
London [Staunton]
1 e4 c5 2 d4 c×d4 3 ♘f3 e5 4 ♗c4 ♘f6 5 ♘g5 d5 6 e×d5 h6 7 ♘f3 ♗g4 8 h3 ♕c7 9 h×g4 ♕×c4 10 ♘×e5 ♕×d5 11 0-0 ♗d6 12 ♗f4 0-0 13 ♖e1 [□ 13 c4] 13 ... ♖e8 14 c4 ♕a5! 15 ♗d2 ♕c7 16 ♘d3 ♖×e1+ 17 ♗×e1 ♕×c4 18 ♕f3 ♘c6 19 ♗d2 ♖e8 20 g5 [20 ♗×h6 g×h6 21 ♕f6 ♕c1→] 20 ... h×g5 21 ♗×g5 ♘b4 [21 ... ♕×d3 22 ♕×d3 ♖e1+ 23 ♕f1 ♗h2+ 24 ♔×h2 ♖×f1→] 22 ♗f4 ♗×f4 23 ♘×f4 ♕c1+ 24 ♔h2 ♕×b2 **0-1** L/N6123-1843

**1842̂-★CS-9**
**Cochrane, J.– Staunton, H.**
London [Staunton]
1 e4 e6 2 c4 c5 3 ♘c3 ♗e7 4 ♗d3 ♗f6 5 ♘ge2 ♘e7 6 0-0 ♘bc6 7 a3 ♘g6 8 f4 d6 9 ♘g3 ♗d4+ 10 ♔h1 e5 11 ♘d5 e×f4 12 ♘×f4 ♘×f4 13 ♖×f4 ♗e5 14 ♖f1 0-0 [14 ... ♕h4 15 ♕h5 ♗×g3 16 ♕×f7+ ♔d8 17 h3 ♗×h3→] 15 ♕h5 ♘d4 16 ♖b1 ♘e6 17 ♘e2 g6 18 ♕h6 ♗g7 19 ♕e3 ♕h4 20 ♕g3 ♕h5 21 ♕f3 ♕h6 22 ♗c2 ♗e5 23 ♘g3 ♘d4 24 d3 ♕h4 ...⚲ **0-1** L/N6123-1844

**1842̂-★CS-10**
**Cochrane, J.– Staunton, H.**
London [Staunton]
1 e4 e5 2 ♗c4 ♘f6 3 d4 c6 4 ♘f3 ♘×e4 5 d×e5 d5 6 e×d6 ♘×d6 7 ♗e2 [7 ♗d3!?] 7 ... ♗e7 8 0-0 0-0 9 ♗f4 ♗g4 10 ♖e1 ♗e6 11 ♗d3 h6 12 ♘e5 ♘d7 13 ♘g6?! f×g6 14 ♗×d6 ♗×d6 15 ♖×e6 ♗×h2+ 16 ♔×h2 [16 ♔f1 ♖×f2+; 16 ♔h1 ♕h4→] 16 ... ♕h4+ 17 ♔g1 ♕×f2+ 18 ♔h1 ♖f4 19 ♖e4 ♕h4+ 20 ♔g1 ♖×e4 21 ♗×e4 ♕×e4 22 ♕×d7 ♕e3+ 23 ♔h2 ♕e5+ 24 ♔h1 ♕×b2 **0-1** M954-1860

**1842̂-★CS-11**
**Cochrane, J.+ Staunton, H.**
London [Staunton]
1 e4 e5 2 ♗c4 ♗c5 3 ♕e2 d6 [□ 3 ... ♕e7] 4 f4 ♗×g1 5 ♖×g1 ♘c6 6 d3 ♗e6 7 ♗b5 ♗d7 8 ♗×c6 ♗×c6 9 f5 ♕e7 10 ♗e3 d5? [□ 10 ... 0-0-0; 10 ... ♘f6] 11 e×d5 ♗×d5 12 ♘c3 ♗c6?! [12 ... 0-0-0] 13 0-0-0 a6 14 ♕g4 f6 15 d4 0-0-0 16 d×e5 ♘h6 17 ♗×h6 g×h6 18 ♖×d8+ ♖×d8 19 e6 ♔b8 20 ♕f4 ♖g8 21 g4 h5 22 h3 ♕c5 23 ♖d1 h×g4 24 h×g4 ...⚲ **1-0** L/N6123-1843

**1842̂-★CS-12**
**Cochrane, J.+ Staunton, H.**
London [Staunton]
1 e4 e6 2 c4 c5 3 ♘c3 ♗d6 4 ♘f3 ♘c6 5 ♗d3 ♘ge7 6 ♘e2? ♘g6 7 0-0 ♘ge5 8 ♘×e5 ♘×e5 9 ♕c2 ♕h4 10 f4 ♘g4 11 h3 h5 12 e5 ♗c7 13 ♘c3 g5 14 ♘b5 ♗b8 15 ♕c3 ♕g3 16 h×g4 h×g4 17 ♘d6+ ♔f8 [□ 17 ... ♗×d6 △ 18 ... ♕h4] 18 f×g5 f5 19 ♗×f5 ♕h2+ 20 ♔f2 e×f5 [□ 20 ... ♖h3] 21 ♕g3 ♗×d6 22 ♕×h2 ♖×h2 23 e×d6 ...⚲ **1-0** L/N6123-1843

**1842̂-★CS-13**
**Cochrane, J.+ Staunton, H.**
London [Steinitz]
1 e4 e5 2 ♘f3 d5 3 ♘×e5 [□ 3 e×d5] 3 ... ♕e7 4 d4 f6 5 ♘c3!! f×e5 6 ♘×d5 ♕f7 7 ♗c4 ♗e6 8 0-0 c6 9 f4 c×d5 10 f×e5 ♕d7 [□ 10 ... ♕c7; 10 ... d×c4] 11 e×d5 ♗×d5 12 e6

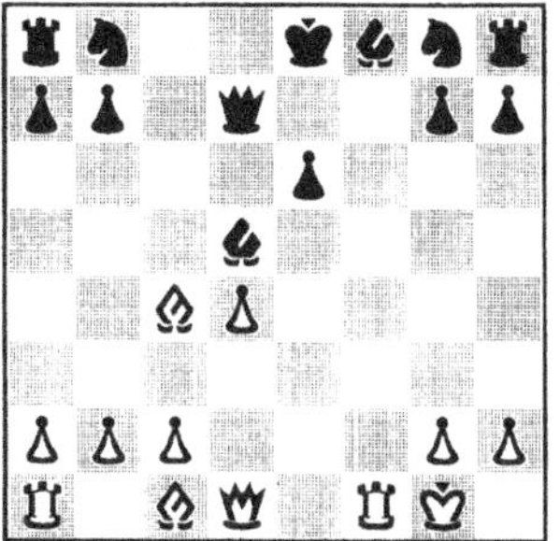

12 ... ♕c6 [12 ... ♕×e6 13 ♖e1 ♗×c4 14 ♖×e6 ♗×e6 15 ♕e2 (△ 16 d5) 15 ... ♔d7 (15 ... ♔f7 16 ♕f3+±) 16 ♕b5 △ 17 ♕×b7; 17 ♕e8+; 17 ♗f4+] 13 ♕h5+ g6 14 ♕×d5 ♘e7 15 ♕e5 ♕×c4 16 ♕×h8 ♘f5 17 ♗h6 ♕b4 18 ♕×f8+ ♕×f8 19 ♗×f8 ♔×f8 20 g4 **1-0** M392-1878

**1842̂-★CS-14**
**Cochrane, J.+ Staunton, H.**
London [Staunton]
1 e4 e5 2 ♘f3 ♘c6 3 d4 ♘×d4 4 ♘×e5 ♘e6 5 ♗c4 c6 6 ♘×f7!? ♔×f7 7 ♗×e6+ ♔×e6 8 0-0 ♔f7 9 ♗e3 ♘e7 10 f4 d5 11 f5 ♔g8? [□ 11 ... ♔e8] 12 c4 b5 13 c×d5 c×d5 14 ♘c3 ♗b7 15 e5 b4 16 f6 g×f6 17 e×f6 ♘g6 18 f7+ ♔g7 19 ♕d4+ **1-0** L/N6123-1843

**1842̂-★CS-15**
**Cochrane, J.+ Staunton, H.**
London
1 e4 e5 2 ♗c4 c6 3 ♕e2 ♘f6 4 f4 d6 5 ♘f3 ♗g4 6 f×e5 ♗×f3 7 ♕×f3 d×e5 8 d3 ♗c5 9 ♘c3 0-0 10 ♗g5 ♘bd7 11 ♘e2 ♕b6 12 0-0-0 a5 13 ♘g3 ♕d8

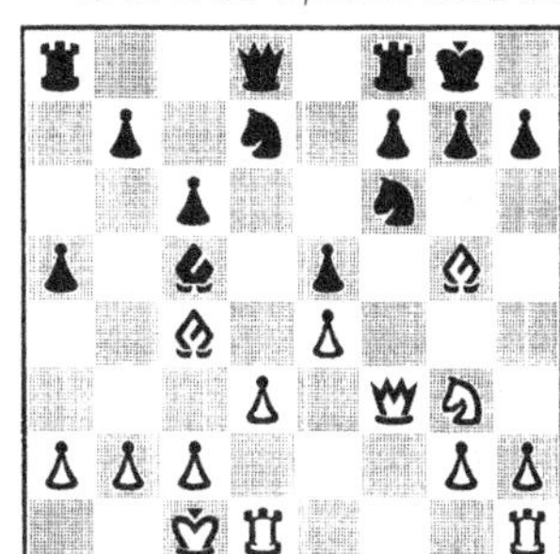

14 a3 b5 15 ♗a2 a4 16 ♘f5 ♗e7 17 ♗h6 ♘e8 18 ♕g3 ♗f6 19 ♖df1 c5 20 ♖f3 b4 21 ♖hf1 b×a3 22 b×a3 ♖b8 23 ♘×g7 ♗×g7 24 ♗×g7 ♘×g7 25 ♖×f7 **1-0** L/N6123

**1842̂-★CS-16**
**Cochrane, J.– Staunton, H.**
London
1 e4 e5 2 ♗c4 ♗c5 3 c3 ♕e7 4 ♕e2 ♘f6 5 ♘f3 ♘c6 6 d4 e×d4 7 e5 ♘g4 8 c×d4 ♗×d4 9 0-0 ♗×e5 10 h3 d5 11 ♗b5 0-0 12 h×g4 ♗×g4 13 ♘c3 ♘d4 14 ♕e3 ♗×f3 15 g×f3 c6 16 ♗e2 ♘c2 17 ♕g5 ♗f6 18 ♕f5 ♘×a1 19 ♗f4 ♗×c3 **0-1** L/N6123

**1842̂-★CS-17**
**Cochrane, J.+ Staunton, H.**
London
1 e4 c5 2 ♗c4 e5 3 f4 ♘c6 4 ♘f3 e×f4 5 0-0 g5 6 d4 c×d4 7 c3 ♗c5 8 c×d4 ♘×d4 9 ♘×d4 ♕b6 10 ♔h1 ♗×d4 11 ♘c3 ♗×c3 12 b×c3 ♘e7 13 g3 d5 14 ♗×d5 ♗h3 15 ♕h5 ♗×f1 16 ♕×f7+ ♔d8 17 ♗a3 ♖e8 18 ♖d1 ♗e2 19 ♗c6+ ♗×d1 **1-0** L/N6123

**1842̂-★CS-18**
**Cochrane, J.– Staunton, H.**
London
1 e4 c5 2 c4 e6 3 ♗d3 ♘e7 4 ♘e2 ♘g6 5 0-0 ♗e7 6 f4 d6 7 ♘bc3 ♘c6 8 a3 ♗f6 9 ♘g3 ♗d4+ 10 ♔h1 0-0 11 ♕h5 e5 12 ♘ce2 e×f4 13 ♘×f4 ♘ce5 14 ♘ge2 ♗g4 **0-1** L/N6123-1845

**1842̂-★CS-19**
**Cochrane, J.– Staunton, H.**
London
1 e4 c5 2 ♗c4 e6 3 ♘f3 ♘c6 4 e5 ♘ge7 5 ♘c3 ♘g6 6 ♕e2 ♘f4 7 ♕e4 g5 8 g3 d5 9 e×d6 f5 **0-1** L/N6123-1843

**1842̂-★CS-20**
**Cochrane, J.– Staunton, H.**
London
1 e4 c5 2 ♗c4 e5 3 f4 ♘c6 4 ♘f3 e×f4 5 0-0 g5 6 d4 c×d4 7 c3 ♗c5 8 c×d4 ♘×d4 9 ♘×d4 ♕b6 10 ♔h1

♗xd4 11 ♘c3 ♗xc3 12 bxc3 ♘e7 13 ♗a3 ♕f6 14 e5 ♕g6 15 e6 fxe6 16 ♕d6 ♘f5 17 ♕c7 ♘e3 18 ♕c5 ♕g7 19 ♗b5 a6 20 ♖ae1 axb5 **0-1** L/N6123

**1842̂-★CS-21**
**Cochrane, J.– Staunton, H.**
London

1 e4 e5 2 ♗c4 ♗c5 3 c3 ♕e7 4 ♘f3 ♘c6 5 0-0 d6 6 h3 h6 7 d4 ♗b6 8 a4 a5 9 d5 ♘d8 10 ♗e3 ♗xe3 11 fxe3 ♘f6 12 ♘bd2 0-0 13 ♕e1 ♗d7 14 ♕h4 c6 15 g4 cxd5 16 exd5 e4 17 ♘d4 ♘xd5 18 ♕xe7 ♘xe7 19 ♘xe4 d5 20 ♘c5 ♗xg4 21 hxg4 dxc4 22 ♘d7 ♖e8 23 ♘b5 ♘d5 ...♀ **0-1** L/N6123

**1842̂-★CS-22**
**Cochrane, J.– Staunton, H.**
London

1 e4 c5 2 c4 e5 3 f4 ♗d6 4 ♘c3 ♘c6 5 ♘f3 exf4 6 d3 ♘ge7 7 ♗e2 ♘g6 8 0-0 0-0 9 ♘d5 ♘ce7 10 b3 ♘xd5 11 exd5 a5 12 ♗b2 ♘h4 13 d4 ♘f5 14 ♕d3 ♘e3 15 ♖fe1 ♖a6 16 dxc5 ♗xc5 17 ♗d4 ♗xd4 18 ♘xd4 ♖g6 19 ♗f3 d6 20 ♖e2 ♕h4 21 ♗e4 f5 22 ♗f3 ♖h6 23 h3 ♕g3 ...♀ **0-1** L/N6123

**1842̂-★CS-23**
**Cochrane, J.– Staunton, H.**
London

1 e4 e5 2 ♗c4 ♗c5 3 ♘f3 d6 4 c3 ♗g4 5 d3 ♘f6 6 0-0 0-0 7 h3 ♗h5 8 ♗e3 ♗b6 9 a4 c6 10 ♘bd2 ♗xe3 11 fxe3 ♕b6 12 ♕e1 ♕xb2 13 ♘b3 d5 14 ♖f2 ♕xf2+ 15 ♕xf2 dxc4 16 dxc4 ♘xe4 17 ♕h4 ♗xf3 18 gxf3 ♘xc3 19 ♔f2 f6 20 ♘c5 ♘a6 21 ♘e6 ♖f7 22 ♖g1 ♖e8 23 ♖c1 ♘xa4 24 c5 ♘b2 25 ♖b1 ♘d3+ 26 ♔e2 ♖xe6 27 ♔xd3 ♘xc5+ 28 ♔e2 b5 29 ♖c1 ♘b7 30 ♕e4 f5 31 ♕b4 a6 32 ♕b3 ♖d6 33 ♕c3 e4 34 f4 h6 35 ♕e5 ♔h7 36 ♖g1 ♖df6 37 h4 h5 38 ♖g5 g6 39 ♖g1 a5 40 ♖d1 b4 41 ♕e8 c5 42 ♖d7 ♔g7 43 ♖d5 c4 44 ♖d7 c3 45 ♖xf7+ ♖xf7 46 ♕e5+ ♔h7 47 ♕d5 ♖g7 48 ♔d1 ♖c7 49 ♕e5 ♖d7+ 50 ♔c1 ♖g7 51 ♕d5 a4 52 ♕b5 b3 53 ♕xa4 ♘c5 **0-1** L/N6123

**1842̂-★CS-24**
**Cochrane, J.+ Staunton, H.**
London

1 e4 e5 2 ♘f3 ♘c6 3 d4 ♘xd4 4 ♘xe5 ♘e6 5 ♗c4 d6 6 ♘f3 ♗e7 7 0-0 ♘f6 8 ♘c3 0-0 9 ♗e3 c6 10 e5 dxe5 11 ♕xd8 ♗xd8 12 ♘xe5 ♗c7 13 ♘d3 ♘g4 14 ♗xe6 fxe6 15 h3 ♘xe3 16 fxe3 ♗d7 17 ♘c5 ♗c8 18 ♖xf8+ ♔xf8 19 ♖d1 b6 20 ♘5e4 h6 21 ♘e2 c5 22 ♖f1+ ♔e7 23 ♘f4 ♗xf4 24 exf4 ♗b7 25 ♖e1 ♗xe4 26 ♖xe4 ♔f6 27 ♔f2 ♖d8 28 ♔f3 ♖d1 29 ♖e2 g5 30 fxg5+ hxg5 31 g3 e5 32 c3 ♖d3+ 33 ♖e3 ♖d2 34 ♖e2 ♖d1 35 ♖f2 ♔e6 36 ♔g4 ♖d3 37 ♖g2 e4 38 ♔xg5 ♔e5 39 h4 e3 40 h5 ♖d2 41 ♖g1 e2 42 ♖e1 ♔e4 43 h6 ♔f3 44 g4 ♔f2 45 ♖xe2+ ♀ **1-0** L/N6123

**1842̂-★CS-25**
**Cochrane, J.+ Staunton, H.**
London

e4 e5 2 ♘f3 ♘c6 3 d4 ♘xd4 4 ♘xd4 exd4 5 ♗c4 ♘f6 6 0-0 d6 7 ♕xd4 ♗e7 8 ♘c3 ♗e6 9 ♗d3 0-0 10 ♗g5 c5 11 ♕e3 ♘g4 12 ♗xe7 ♕xe7 13 ♕g3 ♘e5 14 ♗e2 ♘c6 15 f4 ♘d4 16 f5 ♗xf5 17 ♖xf5 ♘xf5 18 exf5 d5 19 ♖f1 f6 20 ♗f3 d4 21 ♘d5 ♕d7 22 ♘c7 ♖ac8 23 ♘e6 ♖f7 24 h4 ♖e7 25 h5 h6 26 ♘f4 ♖e5 27 ♕g6 c4 28 g4 d3 29 ♘e6 dxc2 30 g5 fxg5 31 f6 ♖xe6 32 ♗d5 ♖cc6 33 ♗xe6+ ♖xe6 34 f7+ ♔f8 35 ♕xg7+ ♔xg7 36 f8♕+ ♔h7 37 ♖f7+ ♕xf7 38 ♕xf7+ ♔h8 39 ♕f8+ ♔h7 40 ♕f5+ **1-0** L/N6123

**1842̂-★CS-26**
**Cochrane, J.+ Staunton, H.**
London

1 e4 e5 2 ♘f3 ♘c6 3 ♗c4 ♗c5 4 c3 ♘f6 5 d4 exd4 6 e5 d5 7 ♗b5 ♘e4 8 ♘xd4 0-0 9 ♗xc6 bxc6 10 0-0 ♕e7 11 ♗e3 ♗b7 12 f3 ♘d6 13 ♗f4 ♘c4 14 ♕e2 ♖fe8 15 ♖e1 ♗a6 16 ♘d2 ♘xd2 17 ♕xd2 ♖ab8 18 ♔h1 ♗xd4 19 cxd4 ♕b4 20 b3 ♖e6 21 ♖ac1 ♕e7 22 ♗g5 ♕b4 23 ♖c5 h6 24 ♗e3 ♕b6 25 f4 f5 26 g4 ♖f8 27 gxf5 ♖xf5 28 ♕c2 g6 29 ♖g1 ♔h7

30 ♖c1 ♗b7 31 b4 ♕xb4 32 ♖b1 ♕a3 33 ♖c3 ♕a6 34 ♕b2 ♗c8 35 ♖a3 ♕c4 36 ♖c1 ♕b5 37 ♕xb5 cxb5 38 ♖xc7+ **1-0** L/N6123

**1842̂-★CS-27**
**Cochrane, J.– Staunton, H.**
London

1 e4 e5 2 ♘f3 ♘c6 3 d4 ♘xd4 4 ♘xd4 exd4 5 ♗c4 ♘f6 6 0-0 d6 7 ♕xd4 ♗e6 8 ♗xe6 fxe6 9 e5 dxe5 10 ♕xe5 ♕d6 11 ♕b5+ ♕c6 12 ♕xc6+ bxc6 13 ♘c3 ♗d6 14 ♖e1 ♔f7 15 ♘e4 h6 16 ♗d2 ♖hd8 17 ♗c3 ♘d5 18 a3 ♖ab8 19 b4 ♘b6 20 ♗b2 ♘c4 21 ♘xd6+ ♖xd6 22 ♗c3 ♖b5 23 ♖e4 ♖bd5 24 g3 ♖d1+ 25 ♖xd1 ♖xd1+ 26 ♔g2 ♘xa3 27 ♖g4 g5 28 h4 ♖d5 29 ♗b2 ♘xc2 30 ♖c4 ♘e1+ 31 ♔f1 ♘d3 32 ♗c3 c5 33 b5 ♖f5 34 ♔e2 ♘xf2 35 g4 ♘xg4 36 ♖xg4 ♔e7 ...♀ **0-1** L/N6123

**1842̂-★CS-28**
**Cochrane, J.+ Staunton, H.**
London

1 e4 e5 2 ♘f3 ♘c6 3 d4 ♘xd4 4 ♘xd4 exd4 5 ♗c4 ♘f6 6 0-0 d6 7 ♕xd4 ♗e7 8 ♘c3 0-0 9 ♘d5 ♗e6 10 ♘xe7+ ♕xe7 11 ♗xe6 ♕xe6 12 ♗g5 c5 13 ♕d3 ♘xe4 14 ♖ae1 ♖fe8 15 f3 ♕g6 16 ♗f4 ♘f6 17 ♕xg6 hxg6 18 ♗xd6 b6 19 ♖xe8+ ♖xe8 20 ♔f2 ♖d8 21 ♗f4 ♖d4 22 ♗e3 ♖d5 23 c4 ♖f5 24 ♔e2 ♘d7 25 ♖d1 ♘e5 26 ♖d8+ ♔h7 27 b3 ♖f6 28 h4 ♖e6 29 ♔f2 a5 30 ♗f4 ♘c6 31 ♖d6 ♖xd6 32 ♗xd6 ♘b4 33 ♗c7 ♘xa2 34 ♗xb6 ♘c1 35 ♗xa5 ♘xb3 36 ♗c3 **1-0** L/N6123

**182** Staunton, H. M1647.BL

**1842̂-★CS-29**
**Cochrane, J.– Staunton, H.**
London

1 e4 c5 2 b3 e5 3 ♗b2 ♘c6 4 ♘f3 d6 5 ♗c4 ♗e6 6 d3 ♗xc4 7 bxc4 ♘ge7 8 ♘c3 ♘g6 9 ♘d5 ♗e7 10 g3 a6 11 a4 ♖b8 12 0-0 ♕d7 13 ♘e3 0-0 14 c3 b5 15 cxb5 axb5 16 axb5 ♖xb5 17 ♗c1 ♖fb8 18 ♘f5 ♗d8 19 h4 ♘ge7 20 ♘xe7+ ♗xe7 21 ♔g2 f5 22 exf5 ♕xf5 23 ♕e2 d5 24 ♖e1 ♗f6 25 ♖a6 ♖5b6 26 ♖xb6 ♖xb6 27 ♗a3 ♖b3 28 ♗b2 e4 29 dxe4 dxe4 30 ♕c4+ ♔f8 31

♕xb3 ♕xf3+ 32 ♔g1 ♗d4 33 ♕c2 ♕xg3+ 34 ♔f1 ♕h3+ 35 ♔g1 ♘e5 **0-1** L/N6123-1843

### 1842̂-★CS-30
**Cochrane, J.– Staunton, H.**
London
1 e4 e5 2 ♗c4 ♘f6 3 d4 c6 4 ♘f3 ♘xe4 5 dxe5 d5 6 exd6 ♗xd6 7 0-0 0-0 8 ♕d4 ♗f5 9 ♗d3 ♗c5 10 ♕e5 ♕d5 11 ♕xd5 cxd5 12 ♗e3 ♘d7 13 ♘d4 ♗g6 14 ♗xe4 dxe4 15 ♘c3 ♖ae8 16 ♖ad1 ♘e5 17 ♘a4 ♗xd4 18 ♗xd4 f5 19 ♗xa7 ♖a8 20 ♗d4 ♖xa4 21 ♗xe5 ♖xa2 22 ♗d6 ♖c8 23 ♗a3 h5 24 c3 ♗f7 25 ♖d7 ♗c4 26 ♖fd1 b5 27 ♖e7 ♗d3 28 f3 ♖c4 29 fxe4 fxe4 30 h3 ♔h7 31 ♔h2 ♖c6 32 ♖f7 ♔h6 33 ♖f8 ♔h7 34 ♖e1 h4 35 g3 ♖xc3 **0-1**
L/N6123

### 1842̂-★CS-31
**Cochrane, J.+ Staunton, H.**
London
1 e4 e5 2 ♘f3 ♘c6 3 d4 ♘xd4 4 ♘xe5 ♘e6 5 ♗c4 ♕f6 6 ♘f3 ♗c5 7 0-0 d6 8 ♘c3 c6 9 e5 dxe5 10 ♘e4 ♕e7 11 ♘xe5 ♘f6 12 ♗xe6 ♗xe6 13 ♗g5 ♗d5 14 ♘xc5 ♕xc5 15 ♗xf6 gxf6 16 ♘d3 ♕d6 17 ♖e1+ ♗e6 18 ♕f3 0-0-0 19 ♕xf6 ♖hg8 20 ♘f4 ♖de8 21 ♖ad1 ♕e7 22 ♕xe7 ♖xe7 23 ♘xe6 fxe6 24 ♖e5 ♖d8 25 ♖xd8+ ♔xd8 26 f4 ♔d7 27 ♔f2 ♔d6 28 ♔e3 c5 29 g4 b5 30 h4 a5 31 b3 a4 32 h5 axb3 33 axb3 h6 34 ♖e4 ♖g7 35 ♔f3 **1-0**
L/N6123-1843

### 1842̂-★CS-32
**Cochrane, J.= Staunton, H.**
London
1 e4 e5 2 ♘f3 ♘c6 3 d4 exd4 4 ♗c4 d6 5 ♘xd4 ♕h4 6 0-0 ♘e5 7 ♘f3 ♘xf3+ 8 ♕xf3 ♘f6 9 ♘c3 ♗e7 10 ♘b5 ♗d8 11 ♗f4 0-0

12 ♗d3 a6 13 ♘c3 ♗d7 14 ♗g3 ♕g5 15 ♗f4 ♕h5 16 ♕g3 ♕g6 17 e5 ♕xg3 18 ♗xg3 dxe5 19 ♗xe5 ♗e6 20 ♗xf6 ♗xf6 21 ♘e4 ♗e7 22 ♖fe1 ♖ad8 23 a3 c5 24 ♖ad1 c4 25 ♗e2 b5 26 c3 h6 27 ♔f1 a5 28 ♖xd8 ♖xd8 29 ♖d1 ♖xd1+ 30 ♗xd1 f5 31 ♘d2 b4 32 axb4 axb4 33 ♗e2 bxc3 34 bxc3 ♗f6 **½-½**
L/N6123

### 1842̂-★CS-33
**Cochrane, J.– Staunton, H.**
London
1 e4 c5 2 d4 cxd4 3 ♕xd4 ♘c6 4 ♕d1 ♘f6 5 ♗d3 e5 6 ♘f3 ♗c5 7 0-0 d6 8 ♗g5 ♗g4 9 ♘c3 ♘d4 10 ♘d5 ♗xf3 11 gxf3 h6 12 ♘xf6+ gxf6 13 ♗h4 ♕d7 14 c3 ♘e6 15 ♗c2 ♔e7 16 b4 ♗b6 17 ♔h1 ♖ac8 18 ♗a4 ♕c7 19 ♖c1 ♖hg8 20 ♗b3 ♘f4 21 ♗g3 ♘h3 22 ♕d5 ♖g7 23 c4 ♖d8 24 ♖cd1 h5 25 ♖d2 ♖dg8 26 f4 exf4 27 c5 dxc5 28 ♕xh5 fxg3 29 fxg3 ♘g5 30 ♖fd1 ♕e5 31 ♖d7+ ♔f8 32 ♗c2 ♖h7 33 ♕e2 ♖gh8 **0-1** L/N6123-1843

### 1842̂-★CS-34
**Cochrane, J.– Staunton, H.**
London
1 d4 d5 2 c4 e6 3 e3 c5 4 cxd5 exd5 5 ♘c3 ♘f6 6 ♘f3 ♘c6 7 dxc5 ♗xc5 8 ♗e2 0-0 9 0-0 ♗e6 10 a3 ♗d6 11 b4 ♘e5 12 ♘b5 ♘xf3+ 13 ♗xf3 ♗e5 14 ♘d4 ♕d6 15 h3 ♕d7 16 ♘xe6 fxe6 17 ♖b1 ♖ac8 18 ♗b2 ♗b8 19 e4 ♕c7 20 e5 ♘d7 21 ♖c1 ♕d8 22 ♖xc8 ♕xc8 23 ♕e2 ♘b6 24 ♗g4 ♖f4 25 ♕d2 ♖c4 26 ♖c1 ♖xc1+ 27 ♕xc1 ♕xc1+ 28 ♗xc1 ♔f7 29 f4 g6 30 ♔f2 ♘c4 31 ♗e2 b5 32 ♗xc4 dxc4 ...? **0-1**
L/N6123-1845

### 1842̂-★CS-35
**Staunton, H.+ Cochrane, J.**
London
1 e4 e5 2 ♗c4 ♗c5 3 ♘f3 d6 4 d4 ♗xd4 5 ♘xd4 exd4 6 ♕xd4 ♕f6 7 ♕e3 ♘e7 8 0-0 ♘bc6 9 f4 0-0 10 ♘c3 a6 11 ♔h1 ♔h8 12 ♗d3 ♕h4 13 ♗d2 f5 14 ♖f3 fxe4 15 ♗xe4 ♗d7 16 ♘e2 ♗g4 17 ♖g3 d5 18 ♗f3 ♗d7 19 ♕b3 ♕f6 20 ♗xd5 ♘xd5 21 ♕xd5 ♗e6 22 ♕c5 ♖f7 23 ♗c3 ♕f5 24 ♕e3 ♕d5 25 ♖g5 ♕d7 26 ♘g3 ♔g8 27 ♖e1 **1-0**
L/N6123-1843

### 1842̂-★CS-36
**Staunton, H.+ Cochrane, J.**
London
1 e4 c5 2 c4 e6 3 f4 ♘c6 4 ♘f3 d6 5 ♗e2 ♗e7 6 0-0 ♗f6 7 ♘c3 b6 8 d3 ♗b7 9 ♗e3 ♗xc3 10 bxc3 ♘ge7 11 h3 h6 12 ♖b1 ♕d7 13 ♔h2 0-0-0 14 d4 ♘a5 15 ♕c2 f5 16 e5 g5 17 exd6 ♕xd6 18 dxc5 bxc5 19 ♘e5 ♖h7 20 ♖b5 ♗e4 21 ♕b2 g4 22 ♗xc5 g3+ 23 ♔g1 ♕c7 24 ♕a3 ♘ec6 25 ♘xc6 **1-0** L/N6123-1843

### 1842̂-★CS-37
**Staunton, H.+ Cochrane, J.**
London
1 e4 e5 2 ♘f3 ♘c6 3 ♗c4 ♗c5 4 c3 ♘f6 5 d4 exd4 6 e5 ♘e4 7 cxd4 ♗b4+ 8 ♗d2 ♗xd2+ 9 ♘bxd2 ♘xd2 10 ♕xd2 d5 11 ♗d3 ♕e7 12 0-0 h6 13 a3 ♗g4 14 ♗e2 ♗xf3 15 ♗xf3 0-0-0 16 b4 ♕h4 17 ♖fd1 ♘e7 18 ♕c2 ♕g5 19 ♖ac1 ♖d7 20 h3 ♕g6 21 ♗g4 ♕xc2 22 ♖xc2 ♔d8 23 ♗xd7 ♔xd7 24 f4 ♘f5 25 ♔f2 **1-0** L/N6123

### 1842̂-★CS-38
**Staunton, H.= Cochrane, J.**
London
1 f4 d5 2 d4 c5 3 c3 ♘c6 4 ♘f3 e6 5 e3 ♘f6 6 ♗d3 ♘e4 7 0-0 f5 8 ♗b5 ♗d7 9 ♘bd2 cxd4 10 ♗xc6 ♗xc6 11 cxd4 ♗e7 12 ♘xe4 fxe4 13 ♘e5 0-0 14 ♗d2 ♗d6 15 ♕g4 ♕e7 16 a3 a5 17 b4 ♗xe5 18 fxe5 b6 19 bxa5 bxa5 20 ♖xf8+ ♔xf8 21 ♖c1 ♕d7 22 ♖c5 a4 23 ♗b4 ♔g8 24 ♖c2 ♗b5 25 ♖f2 ♖c8 26 h4 ♖c1+ 27 ♔h2 ♖f1 28 ♖xf1 ♗xf1 29 ♕f4 ♕f7 **½-½** L/N6123

### 1842̂-★CS-39
**Staunton, H.+ Cochrane, J.**
London
1 e4 e5 2 ♘f3 ♘c6 3 ♗c4 ♗c5 4 c3 ♘f6 5 d4 exd4 6 cxd4 ♗b4+ 7 ♗d2 ♗xd2+ 8 ♘bxd2 d5 9 exd5 ♘xd5 10 0-0 ♗e6 11 ♘e4 0-0 12 ♘eg5 ♗f5 13 ♗d3 ♕f6 14 ♗e4 ♗xe4 15 ♘xe4 ♕f4 16 ♘g3 ♖ad8 17 ♕b3 ♘b6 18 ♕e3 ♘d5 19 ♕b3 b6 20 ♖ad1 ♖d6 21 ♖fe1 ♘f6 22 ♕e3 ♘d5 23 ♕xf4 ♘xf4 24 ♖e4 ♘d5 25 ♘f5 ♖f6 26 ♘e3 ♖f4 27 ♖xf4 ♘xf4 28 g3 ♘g6 29 ♖c1 ♘ge7 30 d5 ♘b4 31 ♖xc7 ♘bxd5 32 ♘xd5 ♘xd5 33 ♖xa7 **1-0**
L/N6123

### 1842̂-★CS-40
**Staunton, H.+ Cochrane, J.**
London
1 d4 d5 2 c4 dxc4 3 e4 e5 4 d5 ♘f6 5 ♗g5 ♗c5 6 ♘c3 0-0 7 ♗xc4 a6 8 h3 b5 9 ♗d3 b4 10 ♘ce2 ♗e7 11 ♗xf6 ♗xf6 12 ♘f3 a5 13 ♖c1 ♕d6 14 ♘g3 g6 15 0-0 ♔h8 16 ♘d2 ♗g5 17 ♖c2 ♗xd2 18 ♕xd2 f5 19 f4 exf4 20 ♖xf4 g5 21 ♖f3 f4 22 ♘e2 ♕e5 23 a3 bxa3 24 bxa3 ♗a6 25 ♗xa6 ♖xa6 26 ♕d4 ♘d7 27 ♖xc7 ♕xd4+ 28 ♘xd4 ♘f6 29 ♘e6 ♖g8 30 ♖b3 ♘xe4 31 ♖3b7 ♘f6 32 ♖f7 **1-0** L/N6123

### 1842̂-★CS-41
**Staunton, H.–Cochrane, J.**
London
1 e4 e5 2 ♘f3 ♘c6 3 d4 exd4 4 ♗c4 d6 5 0-0 ♗g4 6 c3 ♘e5 7 ♗e2 ♗xf3 8 ♗xf3 dxc3 9 ♘xc3 ♘f6 10 ♗e2 ♗e7 11 f4 ♘ed7 12 ♖f3 0-0 13 ♖g3 ♘c5 14 ♗f3 ♔h8 15 ♗e3 ♘fd7 16 f5 ♗f6 17 ♖b1 ♗xc3 18 bxc3 b6 19 ♗d4 ♘e5 20 ♕e2 ♖e8 21 ♖d1 ♕f6 22 ♔h1 ♖ad8 23 ♖h3 ♘cd7 24 g4 c5 25 ♗e3 ♘xf3 26 ♕xf3 ♕e5 27 g5 ♘f8 28 ♕h5 g6 29 ♕h6 ♕g7 30 ♕xg7+ ♔xg7 31 f6+ ♔g8 **0-1** L/N6123

### 1842̂-★CS-42
**Staunton, H.–Cochrane, J.**
London
1 e4 e5 2 ♘f3 ♘c6 3 d4 exd4 4 ♗c4 d6 5 c3 ♘e5 6 cxd4 ♘xc4 7 ♕a4+ c6 8 ♕xc4 d5 9 exd5 ♕xd5 10 ♕e2+ ♗e6 11 0-0 ♗b4 12 a3 ♗a5 13 b4 ♗c7 14 ♘c3 ♕h5 15 ♗g5 ♗xh2+ 16 ♘xh2 ♕xg5 17 f4 ♕f6 18 ♖ad1 0-0-0 19 ♘e4 ♕f5 20 g4 ♕d5 21 f5 ♗d7 22 ♖f3 h5 23 ♘c3 ♕d6 24 g5 f6 25 ♘e4 ♕e7 26 d5 fxg5 27 d6 ♕e5 28 ♕e3 ♔b8 29 ♕xg5 ♘f6 30 ♘c5 ♕e2 31 ♖d2 ♕e1+ 32 ♘f1 ♘e4 33 ♘xe4 ♕xe4 34 ♖f4 ♕e5 35 ♘g3 g6 36 ♖e4 ♕a1+ 37 ♔h2 gxf5 **0-1** L/N6123

### 1842̂-★CS-43
**Staunton, H.+Cochrane, J.**
London
1 e4 e5 2 ♘f3 ♘c6 3 ♗c4 ♗c5 4 c3 ♕e7 5 d4 exd4 6 0-0 d3 7 ♕xd3 d6 8 b4 ♗b6 9 a4 a5 10 b5 ♘e5 11 ♘xe5 ♕xe5 12 ♔h1 ♘f6 13 ♖a2 0-0 14 ♖e2 ♗e6 15 ♗xe6 fxe6 16 f4 ♕h5 17 ♘d2 ♘g4 18 h3 ♖ad8 19 ♘f3 d5 20 e5 ♘h6 21 ♘d4 ♗xd4 22 cxd4 g5 23 ♔h2 ♕h4 24 g3 ♕h5 25 ♖c2 g4 26 h4 ♖f7 27 ♗d2 ♘f5 28 ♗xa5 b6 29 ♗d2 ♔h8 30 ♖fc1 ♖df8 31 ♖xc7 ♘xh4 32 gxh4 ♕xh4+ 33 ♔g2 ♖xc7 34 ♖xc7 g3 35 ♖xh7+ ♕xh7 36 ♕xh7+ ♔xh7 **1-0** L/N6123

### 1842̂-★CS-44
**Staunton, H.–Cochrane, J.**
London
1 e4 e5 2 ♘f3 ♘c6 3 ♗c4 ♗c5 4 c3 ♘f6 5 0-0 ♗b6 6 d4 ♕e7 7 d5 ♘b8 8 ♕d3 d6 9 a4 c6 10 ♗g5 h6 11 ♗xf6 ♕xf6 12 ♘a3 c5 13 b4 cxb4 14 cxb4 ♕e7 15 a5 ♗c7 16 ♘b5 ♗d8 17 h3 a6 18 ♘c3 f5 19 ♘h2 f4 20 ♖a3 ♘d7 21 ♗a2 ♘f6 22 ♘f3 g5 23 ♘a4 ♗d7 24 ♘b2 ♗b5 25 ♘c4 ♔f7 26 g4 ♔g6 27 ♕c3 ♖h7 28 ♔h2 h5 29 gxh5+ ♖xh5 30 ♖g1 ♖c8

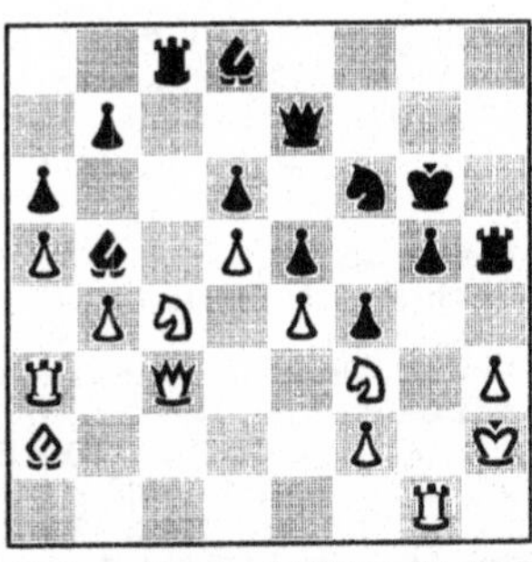

31 ♘cxe5+ dxe5 32 ♘xe5+ ♔h7 33 ♕xc8 ♕xe5 34 ♖f3 ♗e2 35 ♕xd8 ♗xf3 36 ♖c1 **0-1** L/N6123

### 1842̂-★CS-45
**Staunton, H.=Cochrane, J.**
London
1 e4 e5 2 ♗c4 ♗c5 3 ♘f3 d6 4 c3 ♕e7 5 d4 ♗b6 6 0-0 c6 7 a4 h6 8 b3 ♗g4 9 ♗a3 ♗xf3 10 ♕xf3 ♘f6 11 ♖a2 0-0 12 dxe5 ♕xe5 13 ♖e2 ♘bd7 14 ♕h3 a5 15 ♔h1 ♘c5 16 ♘d2 ♖ae8 17 f4 ♕h5 18 ♕xh5 ♘xh5 19 e5 d5 20 ♗xc5 ♗xc5 21 ♗d3 g6 22 f5 gxf5 23 ♗xf5 ♘g7 24 g4 ♖e7 25 ♘f3 ♖fe8 26 ♖fe1 ♔f8 27 h4 ♘e6 28 ♗xe6 fxe6 29 ♔g2 ♔g7 30 ♘d4 ♗xd4 31 cxd4 ♖f7 32 ♖f1 ♖ef8 33 ♖xf7+ ♖xf7 34 ♖f2 ♖xf2+ 35 ♔xf2 **½-½** L/N6123-1843

### 1842̂-★CS-46
**Staunton, H.=Cochrane, J.**
London
1 e4 e5 2 ♘f3 ♘c6 3 ♗c4 ♗c5 4 b4 ♗xb4 5 c3 ♗a5 6 0-0 ♗b6 7 d4 exd4 8 ♘xd4 ♗xd4 9 cxd4 d6 10 f4 ♘f6 11 e5 dxe5 12 fxe5 ♘d5 13 ♗a3 ♗e6 14 ♕d3 ♕g5 15 ♗c1 ♕g4 16 ♗b5 0-0 17 ♗xc6 bxc6 18 a4 ♘b4 19 ♕d2 a5 20 ♖a3 ♖ad8 21 ♖f4 ♕h5 22 ♖g3 c5 23 ♘c3 cxd4 24 ♘e4 ♔h8 25 ♘g5 h6 26 ♘f3 g5 27 ♖xd4 ♖xd4 28 ♕xd4 ♘d5 29 h4 g4 30 ♘d2 c5 31 ♕e4 ♕xh4 32 ♘f1 f5 33 exf6 ♕xf6 34 ♕e2 c4 35 ♘e3 ♘c3 36 ♕c2 ♕f2+ 37 ♕xf2 ♖xf2 38 ♘xg4 ♖c2 39 ♖xc3 ♖xc3 40 ♗b2 ♗xg4 41 ♗xc3+ **½-½** L/N6123

### 1842̂-★CS-47
**Staunton, H.=Cochrane, J.**
London
1 e4 e5 2 ♗c4 ♗c5 3 c3 d5 4 ♗xd5 ♘f6 5 d4 exd4 6 cxd4 ♗b4+ 7 ♗d2 ♗xd2+ 8 ♕xd2 ♘xd5 9 exd5 ♕xd5 10 ♘f3 0-0 11 0-0 ♗g4 12 ♘c3 ♕h5 13 ♘e5 ♗e6 14 f4 f6 15 ♘f3 c6 16 ♖ae1 ♕f7 17 ♖e3 ♘d7 18 ♖fe1 ♖ae8 19 ♘e4 ♗xa2 20 ♘d6 ♖xe3 21 ♘xf7 ♖xe1+ 22 ♕xe1 ♗xf7 23 ♕a5 ♗d5 24 ♕c7 ♖f7 25 ♕c8+ ♘f8 26 ♔f2 ♗xf3 27 ♔xf3 ♖e7 28 g3 ♔f7 29 b4 a6 30 h4 h6 31 g4 ♔g8 32 ♕b8 ♔f7 33 ♕a7 g5 34 ♕c5 ♘h7 35 f5 ♘f8 36 ♕c4+ ♔g7 37 d5 ♘d7 38 ♔g3 ♘b6 39 ♕c5 ♘xd5 **½-5** L/N6123

### 1842̂-★CS-48
**Staunton, H.=Cochrane, J.**
London
1 e4 e5 2 ♘f3 ♘f6 3 ♘c3 ♘c6 4 ♗c4 ♗c5 5 d3 h6 6 ♗e3 ♗b6 7 ♗xb6 axb6 8 ♘e2 d6 9 c3 0-0 10 ♘g3 d5 11 exd5 ♘xd5 12 ♗xd5 ♕xd5 13 c4 ♕d8 14 0-0 ♗g4 15 h3 ♗xf3 16 ♕xf3 ♕d4 17 b3 ♘b4 18 ♖fd1 ♖xa2 19 ♖xa2 ♘xa2 20 ♘f5 ♕f4 21 ♘e7+ ♔h8 22 ♕xb7 ♘c3 23 ♖e1 ♕d2 24 ♖f1 ♘e2+ 25 ♔h1 ♕xd3 26 ♖e1 ♕d2 27 ♖f1 ♕d6 28 ♘d5 c6 29 ♘xb6 ♖b8 30 ♘c8 ♖xb7 31 ♘xd6 ♖d7 32 c5 ♘d4 33 b4 f5 34 ♖d1 ♘b5 35 f3 ♔g8 36 ♔g1 ♘xd6 37 cxd6 ♔f7 38 b5 cxb5 39 ♖d5 ♔e6 40 ♖xb5 ♖xd6 41 ♖b7 g5 42 ♔h2 e4 43 fxe4 fxe4 44 ♔g3 ♔e5 45 ♖b5+ ♖d5 46 ♖b4 h5 47 ♔f2 ♖d2+ 48 ♔e3 ♖xg2 49 ♖b5+ ♔f6 50 ♔xe4 ♖g3 51 ♖b6+ ♔e7 52 ♔f5 **½-½** L/N6123-1843

### 1842̂-★CS-49
**Staunton, H.+Cochrane, J.**
London
1 e4 e5 2 ♘f3 ♘c6 3 d4 exd4 4 ♗c4 d6 5 ♘xd4 ♘xd4 6 ♕xd4 ♗e6 7 ♗d3 c5 8 ♗b5+ ♗d7 9 ♕a4 ♘f6 10 ♗g5 ♗e7 11 ♗xf6 ♗xf6 12 c3 a6 13 ♗xd7+ ♕xd7 14 ♕xd7+ ♔xd7 15 ♘d2 ♖he8 16 0-0 ♔c6 17 g3 h5 18 h4 g5 19 hxg5 ♗xg5 20 f4 ♗f6 21 ♖ad1 b5 22 ♔f2 ♖g8 23 ♖h1 h4 24 gxh4 ♖g4 25 ♔f3 ♖ag8 26 ♘f1 ♗xh4 27 ♖d5 ♖g1 28 ♖xg1 ♖xg1 29 ♘e3 ♗e7 30 ♖f5 ♖g7 31 ♘d5 ♔d7 32 a4 ♗d8 33 axb5 axb5 34 ♘e3 f6 35 ♖d5 ♗e7 36 ♘f5 ♖g1 37 ♘e3 ♖b1 38 ♘d1 ♔e6 39 f5+ ♔d7 40 ♔e2 ♗f8 41 ♖d3 ♗h6 42 ♖h3 ♗g5 43 ♖h7+ ♔c6 44 ♖g7 ♖c1 45 ♘e3 ♖b1 46 ♘d5 ♖xb2+ 47 ♔f3 b4 48 c4 **1-0** L/N6123

### 1842̂-★CS-50
**Staunton, H.–Cochrane, J.**
London
1 e4 e5 2 ♘f3 ♘c6 3 ♗c4 ♗c5 4 c3 ♕e7 5 d4 ♗b6 6 d5 ♘b8 7 0-0 d6 8 a4 a5 9 h3 ♘f6 10 ♕d3 0-0 11 b4 c5 12 ♗e3 ♘bd7 13 b5 ♘db8 14 ♘a3 ♗c7 15 ♖ad1 b6 16 ♘h2 ♘h5 17 f4 exf4 18 ♗xf4 ♘xf4 19 ♖xf4 ♘d7 20 ♘g4 ♘e5 21 ♘xe5 ♕xe5 22 ♖df1 ♗d8 23 ♗b3 ♗g5 24 ♘c4

♕e7 25 ♖4f3 ♖b8 26 ♗c2 g6 27 ♖3f2 ♖b7 28 ♕f3 ♔g7 29 ♔h1 ♗h4 30 ♖e2 ♗f6 31 e5 ♗xe5 32 ♘xe5 dxe5 33 ♕g3 f6 34 h4 ♕d7 35 ♗f5 ♕xd5 36 ♗e4 ♕c4 37 ♕f3 ♖e7 38 h5 f5 39 g4 ♖8f7 40 ♗d5 ♕xd5 41 ♕xd5 ♗b7 42 ♕xb7 ♖xb7 43 ♖xe5 fxg4 44 ♖xf7+ ♔xf7 **0-1** L/N6123

**1842̂-★CS-51**
**Staunton, H.+Cochrane, J.**
London
1 e4 c5 2 c4 e5 3 ♘e2 d6 4 ♘g3 ♘c6 5 ♘c3 ♘ge7 6 ♗e2 ♘d4 7 ♘d5 ♘xd5 8 cxd5 ♕h4 9 d3 ♗e7 10 0-0 0-0 11 f4 f5 12 fxe5 dxe5 13 exf5 ♗xf5 14 ♘xf5 ♘xf5 15 ♗g4 g6 16 ♗d2 h5 17 ♗xf5 gxf5 18 ♗c3 ♗d6 19 ♖f3 ♖f7 20 ♖h3 **1-0**
L/N6123-1843

**1842̂-★CS-52**
**Staunton, H.+Cochrane, J.**
London
1 e4 e5 2 ♘f3 ♘c6 3 ♗c4 ♗c5 4 c3 ♕e7 5 d4 ♗b6 6 0-0 d6 7 a4 a5 8 ♗e3 ♘d8 9 dxe5 dxe5 10 ♗xb6 cxb6 11 ♘a3 ♗d7 12 ♘b5 ♗xb5 13 ♗xb5+ ♘c6 14 ♕d5 **1-0**
L/N6123-1845

**1842̂-★CS-53**
**Staunton, H.−Cochrane, J.**
London
1 e4 e5 2 ♗c4 ♘f6 3 ♘f3 ♘xe4 4 ♘xe5 d5 5 ♕e2 dxc4 6 ♕xe4 ♕e7 7 ♘c3 f6 8 ♘xc4 ♕xe4+ 9 ♘xe4 b5 10 ♘e3 ♗b7 11 ♘c3 a6 12 0-0 ♘d7 13 ♖e1 ♔f7 14 d4 ♘b6 15 ♗d2 g6 16 ♖ad1 ♗d6 17 b3 h5 18 ♘e2 h4 19 h3 ♘d5 20 ♘xd5 ♗xd5 21 ♗f4 g5 22 ♗xd6 cxd6 23 ♘c3 ♗b7 24 d5 ♖ac8 25 ♖d3 f5 26 ♖de3 ♖he8 27 ♖xe8 ♖xe8 28 ♖xe8 ♔xe8 **0-1** L/N6123-1843

**1842̂-★CS-54**
**Staunton, H.+Cochrane, J.**
London
1 e4 e5 2 ♗c4 ♗c5 3 ♘f3 d6 4 d4 exd4 5 ♘xd4 ♗xd4 6 ♕xd4 ♕f6 7 ♕e3 ♘c6 8 ♘c3 ♘ge7 9 ♘b5 ♔d8 10 0-0 a6 11 ♘c3 ♘e5 12 ♗b3 h6 13 f4 ♘g4 14 ♕f3 h5 15 e5 dxe5 16 fxe5 ♕b6+ 17 ♔h1 ♗e6 18 ♗g5 h4 19 ♗xe7+ ♔xe7

20 ♕xg4 ♗xg4 21 ♘d5+ ♔d8 22 ♘xb6 cxb6 23 ♖xf7 **1-0**
L/N6123-1845

**1842̂-★CS-55**
**Cochrane, J.=Staunton, H.**
London
1 d4 e6 2 c4 d5 3 e3 c5 4 dxc5 ♗xc5 5 cxd5 exd5 6 ♘f3 ♘f6 7 ♗d2 0-0 8 ♗c3 ♘c6 9 ♗e2 ♗e6 10 0-0 ♕e7 11 ♘d4 ♘xd4 12 ♗xd4 ♗xd4 13 ♕xd4 a6 14 ♕h4 b5 15 ♗d3 h6 16 ♘c3 ♕d6 17 ♘e2 ♘g4 18 ♕g3 ♕xg3 19 hxg3 ♘e5 20 ♖ad1 ♖ac8 21 ♘d4 ♖c5 22 ♗f5 ♖e8 23 ♖c1 ♖xc1 24 ♖xc1 ♗xf5 25 ♘xf5 ♘d3 26 ♖b1 ♖e5 27 ♘d4 ♖e7 28 a3 ♖c7 29 ♔f1 g6 30 ♔e2 ♘e5 31 ♖d1 ♔g7 32 ♖d2 ♔f6 33 ♘f3 ♘xf3 34 ♔xf3 ♔e5 35 ♔e2 ♖c4 36 f3 f5 37 ♔d3 g5 38 f4+ ♔d6 39 ♖c2 ♖xc2 40 ♔xc2 ♔c5 41 ♔c3 d4+ 42 exd4+ ♔d5 43 ♔d3 a5 44 fxg5 hxg5 45 b3 g4 46 ♔e3 ♔d6 47 ♔f4 ♔d5 48 ♔xf5 ♔xd4 49 ♔xg4 ♔c3 50 ♔f4 ♔xb3 51 g4 ♔xa3 52 g5 b4 53 g6 b3 54 g7 b2 55 g8♕ b1♕ 56 g4 ♕b4+ 57 ♔g3 a4 58 ♔f2 ♔b2 59 ♕g7+ ♔b3 60 g5 a3 61 ♕f7+ ♔b2 62 ♕f6+ ♔c1 63 ♕c6+ ♔b2 64 ♕f6+ ♔b1 65 ♕g6+ ♔a1 66 ♕f5 a2 67 g6 ♕d4+ 68 ♔e2 ...? ½-½
L/N6123-1843

**1842̂-★CS-56**
**Cochrane, J.−Staunton, H.**
London [Staunton]
1 e4 e5 2 ♗c4 c6 3 d4 ♘f6 4 ♘f3 d5 5 exd5 e4 6 ♘e5 cxd5 7 ♗b5+ ♗d7 8 ♗xd7+ ♘bxd7 9 ♘xd7 ♕xd7 10 0-0 ♗d6 11 h3 ♕c7 12 ♘c3 0-0 13 ♘b5 ♕d7 14 ♘xd6 ♕xd6 15 ♗e3 h6 16 ♕e2 ♘h7 17 f3 f5 18 fxe4 fxe4 19 c4 dxc4 20 ♕xc4+ ♔h8 21 d5 ♘f6 22 ♖ad1 ♖ac8 23 ♕d4 ♖fd8? 24 ♖f5? [◻ 24 ♗xh6+−] 24 ... b6 25 b4 ♔h7 26 ♖df1 ♘xd5 27 ♕xe4 ♘c3 28 ♕f3 ♖e8 29 ♖h5 ♕g6 30 ♖h4 ♕e6 31 ♖e1 ♖f8 32 ♕g3 ♖ce8 33 ♔h1 ♘e4 34 ♕g4 ♕xa2 35 ♕d7 ♘g3+ 36 ♔h2 ♖xe3 37 ♖xe3 ♘f1+ **0-1**

L/N6123-1843

**1842̂-★CS-57**
**Cochrane, J.−Staunton, H.**
London [Staunton]
1 e4 e5 2 c4 ♗c5 3 ♘c3 ♘e7 4 ♗d3 ♘bc6 5 ♘f3 d6 6 h3 a6 7 ♘d5 ♘g6 8 g3 ♘d4 9 b4 ♗a7 10 ♗b2 ♘e6 11 h4 c6 12 ♘e3 ♗xe3 13 dxe3 h5 14 ♕d2 a5 15 a3 b6 16 ♖d1 axb4 17 axb4 ♖a7 18 ♗e2 ♖d7 19 ♕c3 ♗b7 20 ♘h2 c5 21 f3 cxb4 22 ♕xb4 ♘c5 23 ♗a3 ♗c6 24 ♖d2 ♖a7 [◻ 24 ... ♘xh4] 25 ♗d1 0-0 26 0-0 ♖a6 27 ♗c2 ♕e7 28 ♖fd1 ♖d8 29 ♕c3 ♘f8 30 ♗xc5 bxc5 31 ♕d3 ♘e6 32 f4 exf4 33 e5 g6 34 exf4? [◻ 34 exd6] 34 ... dxe5 35 ♕e2 ♖xd2 36 ♕xd2 exf4 **0-1**
L/N6123-1844

**1842̂-★CS-58**
**Cochrane, J.−Staunton, H.**
London [Staunton]
1 e4 c5 2 c4 e6 3 ♘c3 ♘e7 4 f4 ♘g6 5 d3 ♗e7 6 ♘f3 d6 7 ♗e2 ♘c6 8 0-0 ♗f6 9 ♗e3 ♗d4 10 ♗xd4 cxd4 11 ♘b1 ♘xf4 12 ♕d2 [12 ♘xd4 ♕b6∓] 12 ... e5 13 b4 ♘xb4 14 ♕xb4 ♘xe2+ 15 ♔h1 0-0 16 ♕d2 ♘f4 17 ♘xd4 ♘xd3 18 ♕xd3 exd4 19 ♕xd4 ♗e6 20 ♘c3 ♖c8 21 ♘d5 b6 22 ♖f3 ♖c5 23 ♖af1 ♗xd5 24 cxd5 ♕g5 [△ 25 ♖f5 ♖c1] 25 ♕a4! ♖c7 26 ♕a3 ♕e5 27 ♕d3 ♖e8 28 ♖e3 f5! 29 g3 [29 exf5?? ♕xe3] 29 ... fxe4 30 ♕b5 h6 31 ♖fe1 ♖c5 32 ♕d7 ♕e7 33 ♕f5 ♕f7 34 ♕xf7+ ♔xf7 35 ♖a3 ♖e7 36 ♖f1+ ♔g6 **0-1** L/N6123-1844

**1842̂-★CS-59**
**Cochrane, J.−Staunton, H.**
London [Staunton]
1 e4 e6 2 c4 c5 3 ♗d3 ♘c6 4 ♘e2 ♘ge7 5 ♘bc3 ♘g6 6 f4 ♘d4 7 0-0 d6 8 b3 ♗e7 9 ♘xd4 cxd4 10 ♘e2 0-0 11 ♗b2 [11 ♘xd4?? ♕b6−+] 11 ... ♗f6 12 ♔h1 e5 13 f5 ♘e7 14 g4 ♘c6 15 a3 ♗h4 16 ♘g1 b6 17 ♘h3 ♗b7 18 ♕f3 h6 19 ♖g1 f6 20 ♖g2 a6 21 b4 ♖c8 22 ♖ag1 ♖c7 23 ♗e2 ♘e7 24 d3 b5 25 cxb5 axb5 26 ♗d1 [◻ 26 ♗c1] 26 ... ♔h8 27 ♗b3 d5 28 ♘f2 ♗g5 29 exd5 ♘xd5 30 ♗xd5 ♗xd5 31 ♘e4 ♕a8 32 ♖e2 ♖fc8 33 ♖gg2 ♕a4 34 h4 ♗xh4 35 ♔h2 ♗g5 36 ♔h3 ♖c2 37 ♖xc2 ♖xc2 38 ♖xc2 ♕xc2 **0-1**
L/N6123-1844

**1842̂-★CS-60**
**Cochrane, J.−Staunton, H.**
London [Staunton]
1 e4 e6 2 c4 c5 3 d3 ♘c6 4 ♘c3 ♗e7 5 f4 b6 6 ♘f3 d6 7 ♗e2 ♗b7 8 0-0 ♗f6 9 ♗e3 ♗d4 10 ♗xd4 cxd4

11 ♘b5 e5 12 f×e5 d×e5 13 ♕e1 a6 14 ♘a3 ♘ge7 15 ♘g5 0-0 16 ♗g4 ♗c8 17 ♗×c8 ♖×c8 18 ♕g3 ♘g6 19 ♖f2 ♖c7 20 ♖af1 ♕d6 21 ♘c2 ♘f4 22 ♘h3 ♘e6 23 ♕h4 h6 24 ♖f3 b5 25 b3 b×c4 26 b×c4 ♖b7 27 a3 ♘e7 28 g3 ♘g6 29 ♕h5 a5 30 ♘f2? ♘g5 31 ♖f5 ♘e7 32 h4 ♘×f5 33 e×f5 ♘h7 [□ 33 ... g6] 34 ♘e4 ♕c6 35 f6 g×f6 36 ♕×h6 ♖b6 37 c5 [□ 37 ♖f5, 38 ♖h5] 37 ... f5 38 ♕d2 f×e4 **0-1** L/N6123-1844

## 1842̂-★CS-61

**Cochrane, J.+Staunton, H.**

London

1 e4 e5 2 ♘f3 ♘c6 3 d4 e×d4 4 ♗c4 d6 5 ♘×d4 ♘e5 6 ♗b3 c5 7 ♘f3 ♗g4 8 ♗a4+ ♘c6 9 ♗×c6+ b×c6 10 h3 ♗h5 11 ♕d3 ♘f6 12 ♕a6 ♕b6 13 ♕e2 ♗e7 14 0-0 0-0 15 ♘c3 ♘d7 16 ♕d3 ♗×f3 17 ♕×f3 ♗f6 18 ♕f5 ♘e5 19 f4 ♘g6 20 e5 d×e5 21 ♘e4 ♗h4 22 ♗e3 ♗e7 23 f×e5 ♕×b2 24 ♖fb1 ♕×e5 25 ♕×e5 ♘×e5 26 ♖b7 ♖fe8 27 ♗×c5 ♗×c5+ 28 ♘×c5 a5 29 ♖ab1 h6 30 ♘e4 ♘c4 31 ♘g3 ♘a3? 32 ♖f1 f6?+− 33 ♘f5 ♘×c2 34 ♖×g7+ ♔h8 35 ♖g6 ♖a7 36 ♖×h6+ ♖h7 37 ♖×f6 ♘e1 38 ♘d6 ♖ee7 39 ♖f8+ ...? **1-0** L/N6123-1843

## 1842̂-★CS-62

**Cochrane, J.−Staunton, H.**

London [Staunton]

1 e4 e5 2 ♘f3 ♘c6 3 ♗c4 ♗c5 4 c3 ♘f6 5 d4 e×d4 6 e5 d5 7 ♗b5 ♘e4 8 c×d4 ♗b4+ 9 ♗d2 ♗×d2+ 10 ♘b×d2 ♗g4 11 0-0 0-0 12 ♗×c6 b×c6 13 ♕c2 ♗×f3 14 ♘×f3 ♖b8 15 ♘d2 f5 16 b3 ♕e8± 17 ♘×e4 d×e4! 18 f4 ♖b6 19 a3 ♕h5 20 ♕c4+ ♔h8 21 b4 g5 22 ♕c5 ♖g8 23 ♕e7 [△ 24 ♕f6+, 25 ♕f8+] 23 ... c5 24 e6! [24 d×c5; 24 b×c5 ♖h6 25 h3 g×f4−+] 24 ... ♕g6 25 ♕f7 c×d4 26 f×g5 ♖×e6 27 ♕×f5 ♕×f5 28 ♖×f5 e3 29 ♖d5 ♖d6 30 ♖×d6 c×d6 31 ♔f1 ♖×g5 32 ♖d1 ♖d5 33 ♔e2 ♔g7 34 ♔d3 ♔f6 35 ♖f1+ ♔e5 36 g3 a5 37 ♖b1 ♖b5 38 ♔c4 ♖b8 39 b5 ♔e4 **0-1** M954-1864

## 1842̂-★CS-63

**Cochrane, J.+Staunton, H.**

London [Staunton]

1 e4 c5 2 d4 c×d4 3 ♕×d4 ♘c6 4 ♕d1 e5 5 ♗c4 ♘f6 6 ♘f3 ♗c5 7 0-0 0-0 8 ♗g5 ♗e7 9 ♘c3 d6 10 ♕e2 ♗g4 11 ♕e3 ♗×f3 12 ♕×f3 ♘d4 13 ♕d3 ♘d7 14 ♗×e7 ♕×e7 15 ♘d5 ♕h4 16 b4 ♘f6 17 ♘×f6+ ♕×f6 18 f4 e×f4 19 ♖ad1 ♘c6 20 ♕×d6 ♕c3 21 ♕c5! ♕f6 22 ♖d6 ♕h4 23 ♖d7 ♖ad8 24 ♖×d8 ♕×d8 25 ♖×f4 ♕d2 26 g3 a6 [26 ... ♘×b4?; 26 ... ♕×b4?] 27 a3 [□ 27 c3] 27 ... g6 28 ♕d5 ♕c1+ 29 ♖f1 ♕e3+ 30 ♔g2 ♘d8 31 e5 ♕×a3 32 e6 ♘×e6 33 ♕×b7 ♘d8 34 ♕e4 ♕a4 35 ♖f6 ♖e8 36 ♕d3 ♕×b4 37 ♗×a6 ♘e6 38 ♗c4 ♖d8 39 ♗d5 ♕b2?? 40 ♖×e6 **1-0** L/N6123-1844

## 1842̂-★CS-64

**Cochrane, J.−Staunton, H.**

London [Staunton]

1 e4 c5 2 c4 e6 3 ♘c3 ♘c6 4 ♘f3 ♗d6 5 ♗d3 ♘ge7 6 ♗c2 ♘g6 7 g3 b6 8 0-0 ♗b7 9 d4 c×d4 10 ♘×d4 ♗c5 11 ♗e3 ♘b4 12 ♘db5 0-0 13 ♗×c5 b×c5 14 ♘d6 ♘×c2 15 ♘×b7 ♕c7 16 ♕×c2 ♕×b7 17 ♘b5 d5 18 e×d5 e×d5 19 f4 ♖ad8 [□ 19 ... d4] 20 ♕g2 ♕b6 21 ♖ae1 f6? 22 ♘c3 d×c4 23 h4 ♕c7 24 h5 ♘e7 25 ♕e4 ♖f7 26 ♕×c4 ♘f5 27 ♖f3 ♕c6 28 ♕e4 ♕×e4 29 ♖×e4 ♖fd7 30 g4 ♘h6 [□ 30 ... ♘d4] 31 g5 ♘f5 32 ♖c4 ♘h4 33 ♖h3 f×g5 34 f×g5 ♘f5 35 ♖×c5 ♘d4 36 ♖e3 ♖f7 37 ♔g2 ♖df8 38 ♘e4 ♘e6 39 ♘f6+ ♖×f6 40 g×f6 ♘×c5 **0-1** L/N6123-1843

## 1842̂-★CS-65

**Cochrane, J.+Staunton, H.**

London [Staunton]

1 e4 c5 2 c4 e6 3 ♘c3 ♘c6 4 ♘f3 ♗d6 5 ♗d3 a6 6 0-0 ♘ge7 7 b3 ♘g6 8 g3 b6 9 ♗b2 ♗b7 10 ♕e2 0-0 11 ♘d1 ♘ge5 12 ♘×e5 ♗×e5 13 ♗×e5 ♘×e5 14 ♘c3 ♘c6 [□ 14 ... ♘×d3∓] 15 f4 ♘d4 16 ♕e3 f5 17 ♘e2 f×e4 18 ♗×e4 ♗×e4 19 ♘×d4 ♗b7 20 ♘f3 ♕f6 21 ♖ae1 ♖ae8 22 ♕d3 d5 23 ♖e5 d×c4 24 b×c4 ♖d8 25 ♕e3 ♖d6 26 ♖e1 [□ 26 ♘g5] 26 ... h6 27 ♔f2 ♗×f3 28 ♔×f3 ♕d8−+ 29 ♕e4 ♖d4 30 ♕c6 ♖d6 31 ♕e4 ♖f6 32 ♖e3 ♖d4 33 ♕c6 ♕f8?+−

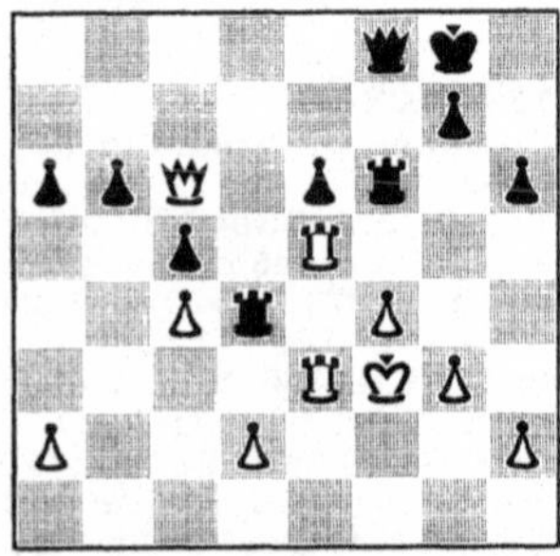

34 ♔e2! ♕f7 35 d3 ♔h7 36 ♕×b6 ♖d7 37 ♕×c5 ♕e8 38 ♖×e6 ♖×e6 39 ♕f5+ ♕g6 40 ♕×e6 ♕h5+ 41 ♔e1 ♕a5+ 42 ♔f2 **1-0** L/N6123-1843

## 1842̂-★CS-66

**Cochrane, J.−Staunton, H.**

London [Staunton]

1 e4 e5 2 ♘f3 ♘c6 3 d4 ♘×d4 4 ♘×e5 ♘e6 5 ♗c4 ♕f6 6 ♘f3 ♗c5 7 0-0 [□ 7 e5!] 7 ... d6 8 ♘c3 ♘e7 9 e5 ♕g6 [9 ... d×e5?? 10 ♘e4+−] 10 e×d6 ♗×d6 11 ♗b5+ ♘c6 12 ♕e2 0-0 13 ♘e4 ♗d7 14 ♘h4 ♘ed4 15 ♘×g6 ♘×e2+ 16 ♗×e2 h×g6 17 ♘×d6 c×d6 18 ♖d1 ♖fe8 19 ♗e3 ♘b4 20 ♖×d6 ♘×c2 21 ♖c1 ♘×e3 22 f×e3 ♖×e3 23 ♗f3 ♗e6 24 b3 ♖b8 25 ♔f2 [□ 25 ♖c7] 25 ... ♖e5 26 ♖c7 ♖a5 27 ♖d2 b6 28 g4 ♔h7 29 h4 ♖c8 30 ♖e7 ♖c1 31 ♖e8 ♖c8 32 ♖e7 g5 33 ♗e4+ ♔g8 34 ♔g3 ♖e5 35 ♖c2! g×h4+ 36 ♔×h4 g5+ 37 ♔g3 ♖×c2 38 ♗×c2 ♖e2 39 ♗f5 a5 40 ♔f3 ♖e5 41 ♔f2 [41 ... ♗d5+, 42 ... ♖×e7] 41 ... ♔f8 42 ♖b7 ♗×f5 43 g×f5 ♖×f5+ **0-1** L/N6123-1843

## 1842̂-★CS-67

**Cochrane, J.+Staunton, H.**

London [Staunton]

1 e4 e5 2 ♗c4 ♘f6 3 d4 c6 4 d×e5 ♕a5+ 5 c3 ♕×e5 6 ♗d3 ♗c5 7 ♘f3 ♕e7 8 0-0 0-0 9 e5 ♘g4 10 ♗×h7+ ♔×h7 11 ♘g5+ ♔g8 12 ♕×g4 ♕×e5 13 ♕h5 ♕f5 14 g4 ♕g6 15 ♕×g6 f×g6 16 ♗e3 ♗×e3 17 f×e3 ♖×f1+ 18 ♔×f1 d5 19 h3 ♘d7 20 ♘d2 ♘e5 21 ♔g2 ♗d7 22 ♘df3 ♘d3 23 ♖d1 ♘×b2 24 ♖b1 ♘c4 25 ♖×b7 ♖d8 26 ♔f2 a5 27 e4 ♘d6 28 ♖c7 ♘b5 29 ♖b7 ♘×c3 30 e5 ♗c8 31 ♖c7 ♘e4+ 32 ♔e3 ♘×g5 33 ♘×g5 d4+ 34 ♔d2 ♗d7 35 ♔d3 ♗e8 36 ♘e6 [36 ♖×g7+ ♔×g7 37 ♘e6+] 36 ... ♖d7 37 ♖×d7 ♗×d7 38 ♘c5! [38 ♔×d4] 38 ... ♗c8 39 ♔×d4 ♔f7 40 ♘e4 ♗a6 41 ♘g5+ ♔e7 42 ♔c5 ♗b5 43 ♔d4 a4 44 a3 ♗f1 45 ♔c5 ♗b5 46 ♘f3 ♔e6 47 ♘d4+ ♔×e5 48 ♘×b5 c×b5 49 ♔×b5 **1-0** L/N6123-1843

## 1842̂-★CS-68

**Cochrane, J.=Staunton, H.**

London [Staunton]

1 e4 e5 2 ♗c4 ♗c5 3 c3 ♕e7 4 ♘f3 ♘c6 5 0-0 d6 6 d4 ♗b6 7 a4 a5 8 ♗b5 ♗d7 9 d5 ♘b8 10 ♗e3 ♗×e3 11 f×e3 ♘f6 12 ♘bd2 0-0 13 ♕e1 c6 14 ♗c4 b5 15 d×c6 b×c4 16 c×d7 ♘b×d7 17 ♕h4 ♘c5 18 ♘×c4 ♘c×e4 19 ♘g5 ♘×g5 20 ♕×g5 ♕e6 21 ♘b6 ♖a6 22 ♖×f6 ♕×f6 23 ♕×f6 g×f6 24 ♘d7 ♖d8 25 ♘×f6+ ♔g7 26 ♘d5 ♖b8 27 b4 ♖c6 [27 ... a×b4?] 28 ♖d1 ♖d8 29 ♖d3 h5 30 e4 ♖c4 31 ♖g3+ ♔f8 32 ♖e3 ♖b8 33 ♔f2 ♖b7 34 ♔e2 a×b4 35 ♔d3 ♖c8 [□ 35 ... b3∓] 36 c×b4 ♖c1 37 a5 ♖a1 38 ♔c4 ♖a2 39 ♔b3 ♖×a5 40 ♖h3 ♖a1 41

♖xh5 ♖e1 42 ♖h4 ♖b1+ 43 ♔c4 ♖d1 44 ♖g4 ♖d4+ 45 ♔c3 f5 46 ♖g6 fxe4 47 ♖xd6 ♖bxb4 48 ♖f6+ ♔g7 49 ♖f5 ♖bc4+ 50 ♔b3 ♖c5? 51 ♘f4 ½-½ L/N6123-1844

## 1842̂-★CS-69

**Cochrane, J.– Staunton, H.**

London [Staunton]

1 e4 c5 2 ♘f3 ♘c6 3 d4 cxd4 4 ♘xd4 e5 5 ♘xc6 bxc6 6 ♗c4 ♘f6 7 ♕d3 d5 8 exd5 cxd5 9 ♗b5+ ♗d7 10 0-0 ♗c5 11 ♗g5 e4 12 ♗xd7+ ♕xd7 13 ♕e2 ♘g4 14 h3 ♘e5 15 ♘c3 f6 16 ♖ad1! fxg5 17 ♖xd5 ♕e7 18 ♕xe4 [◻ 18 ♕b5+] 18 ... ♘d7 19 ♖fd1 ♖d8 20 ♖xg5

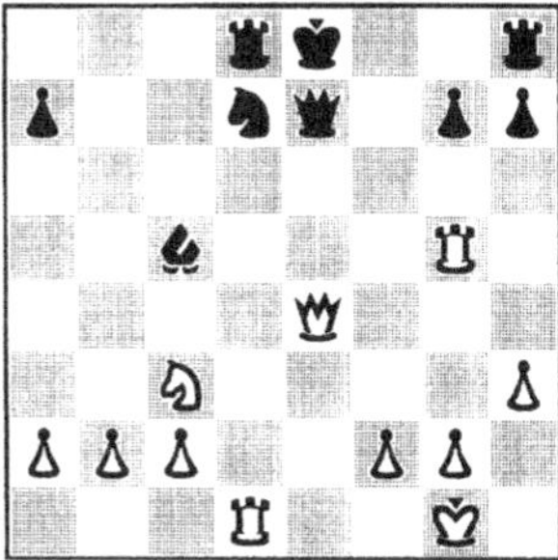

20 ... ♗xf2+ 21 ♔h1 [21 ♔xf2? 0-0+ 22 ♖f5 ♕c4+] 21 ... ♕xe4 22 ♘xe4 ♗b6 23 ♖xg7 ♘c5! 24 ♖xd8+ ♔xd8 25 ♘xc5 ♗xc5 26 b4 ♗b6 27 c4 h5 28 c5 ♗c7 29 ♔g1 h4 30 ♔f2 ♖e8 31 b5 ♖e5 32 ♖g8+ ♔d7 33 ♖g7+ ♔c8 34 ♖g8+ ♔b7 35 c6+ ♔b6 36 a4 a5 37 ♖g4 ♖h5 38 ♔e3 ♗g3 39 ♔d4 ♖f5 40 ♖g7 ♗c7 41 ♖g4 ♖h5 42 ♖g8 ♖f5 [△ 43 ♖a8? ♖f4+, 44 ... ♖xa4] 43 ♖g4 ♖h5 44 ♖g8 ♗e5+ 45 ♔c4 ♔c7 46 ♔d5 ♖h8 47 ♖xh8 ♗xh8 48 ♔c5 ♗c3 49 b6+ ♔c8 50 ♔b5 ♗e1 51 ♔a6 ♗d2 52 ♔b5 ♗e1 53 ♔c4 ♗f2 54 b7+ ♔c7 55 ♔b5 ♗a7 56 ♔a6 ♗b8 57 ♔b5 ♔d6 58 ♔xa5 ♔xc6 59 ♔b4 ♔xb7 60 ♔c4 ♔b6 61 ♔d3 ♔a5 62 g4 ♗f4 **0-1** L/N6123-1843

## 1842̂-★CS-70

**Cochrane, J.+ Staunton, H.**

London [Staunton]

1 e4 e5 2 ♘f3 d5 3 ♘xe5 ♕e7 4 d4 f6 5 ♘c3?! fxe5 6 ♘xd5 ♕d6 7 dxe5 ♕xe5 8 ♗d3 ♗d6 9 f4 ♕e6 10 f5 ♕e5 [◻ 10 ... ♕f7] 11 ♗f4 ♕xb2 12 ♗xd6 cxd6 13 ♘c7+ ♔d8 14 ♘xa8 b6 15 0-0 ♗b7 16 ♗c4 ♕e5 17 ♗d5 ♔c8 18 a4 ♘c6 19 ♖b1 ♗xa8 20 a5 ♔c7 21 ♖b5 ♘d4? [◻ 21 ... ♕d4+, 22 ... ♕xd1–+] 22 axb6+ axb6 23 ♕d3 ♘xb5 24 ♕c4+ ♔b8 25 ♕xb5 ♕d4+ 26 ♔h1 ♗xd5 [◻ 26 ... ♘e7] 27 ♕e8+ ♔c7 28 exd5 ♘f6 29 ♕xh8 ♘g4 30 h3 ♘f2+ 31 ♖xf2 ♕xf2 32 ♕xg7+ **1-0** L/N6123-1844

## 1842̂-★CS-71

**Cochrane, J.– Staunton, H.**

London [Staunton]

1 e4 c5 2 c4 e5 3 ♘c3 ♘c6 4 ♗d3 ♘f6 5 ♘ge2 ♗d6 6 0-0 0-0 7 ♘d5 ♘d4 8 ♘xd4 cxd4 9 a3 b6 10 b4 ♗b7 11 ♕f3 ♗xd5 12 cxd5 ♖c8 13 ♗b2 h6 14 g3 ♘h7 15 ♕h5 ♕e7 16 f4 ♘f6 17 ♕f3 a5 18 b5 ♖fe8 19 ♖fe1 ♘h7 20 ♔g2 ♘f8 21 ♖e2 exf4?+– 22 e5? [◻ 22 gxf4+–] 22 ... ♗c5 23 gxf4 ♘g6 24 ♗xg6 fxg6 25 ♔h1 d6 26 ♕e4 ♕h4 27 ♗xd4 ♗xd4 28 ♕xd4 dxe5 29 ♖xe5 ♖f8 30 d6 ♖xf4 31 d7 ♖c1+! 32 ♖xc1 ♖xd4 **0-1** L/N6123-1843

## 1842̂-★CS-72

**Cochrane, J.– Staunton, H.**

London [Staunton]

1 e4 e5 2 ♗c4 ♗c5 3 ♘f3 d6 4 c3 ♘f6 5 d3 h6 6 0-0 0-0 7 d4 exd4 8 cxd4 ♗b6 9 ♘c3 ♗g4 10 ♗e3 c6 11 ♗d3 ♘bd7 12 ♗e2 ♕e7 13 ♘d2 ♗xe2 14 ♕xe2 ♖ae8 15 ♔h1 ♘h7 16 g4 ♕f6 17 ♘f3 ♘g5 18 ♘xg5 hxg5 19 f4 gxf4 20 ♖xf4 ♕g6 21 ♖f5 ♘f6 22 ♖g5 ♕h7 23 ♕g2 ♘d5 [◻ 23 ... ♘xe4 24 ♖h5 ♕g6 25 ♕h3 f6] 24 ♖h5 ♘xe3 25 ♕h3 ♘xg4 26 ♕xg4 ♕g6 27 ♖g5 [◻ 27 ♕h3] 27 ... ♕f6 28 e5 dxe5 29 ♘e4 ♕h6 30 dxe5 [◻ 30 ♖xg7++–] 30 ... ♗d8 31 ♘f6+ ♗xf6 32 exf6 ♕xf6 33 ♖g1 g6 34 h4 ♖e5 **0-1** L/N6123-1843

## 1842̂-★CS-73

**Cochrane, J.– Staunton, H.**

London [Staunton]

1 d4 d5 2 c4 e6 3 e3 c5 4 dxc5 ♗xc5 5 cxd5 exd5 6 ♘f3 ♘f6 7 ♗e2 ♘c6 8 ♘c3 ♗e6 9 0-0 0-0 10 h3 ♕e7 11 a3 a6 12 b4 ♗d6 13 b5 ♘e5 14 ♘d4 ♖fc8 15 ♗b2 ♘c4 16 ♗xc4 ♖xc4 17 bxa6 bxa6 18 ♘ce2 ♖ac8 19 ♕d3 ♘e4 20 ♘xe6 fxe6 21 ♖ac1 ♕h4 22 ♖xc4 ♖xc4 23 ♘d4 ♘g5 24 e4 [24 ♘xe6? ♘xh3+–+; 24 ... ♘xe6?±] 24 ... ♕f4 25 g3 ♘xh3+ 26 ♔g2 ♕g4 27 ♘xe6 ♕xe6 28 e5 ♗c5 [28 ... ♗xe5?? 29 ♖e1] 29 ♖h1 ♘g5 30 f4 ♘e4 31 f5 ♕xf5 32 ♕xd5+ ♕f7 33 ♕d8+ ♕f8 34 ♕d5+ ♔h8 **0-1** L/N6123-1844

## 1842̂-★CS-74

**Cochrane, J.+ Staunton, H.**

London [Staunton]

1 e4 e5 2 ♗c4 ♘f6 3 d4 c6 4 ♘f3 ♘xe4 5 dxe5 d5 6 exd6 ♘xd6 [◻ 6 ... ♗xd6] 7 ♗d3 ♗e7 8 0-0 0-0 9 ♗f4 ♗g4 10 ♘c3 b5 11 ♖e1 [△ 11 ♖xe7 ♕xe7 12 ♗xd6 ♕xd6?? 13 ♗xh7+] 11 ... ♔h8 12 ♕e2 ♗e6 13 ♗xd6 ♗xd6 14 ♖ad1! [14 ♘xb5 △ 15 ♗e4] 14 ... ♕c7 15 ♗xh7 ♔xh7 16 ♘g5+ [◻ 16 ♕d3+ △ 17 ♕xd6±] 16 ... ♔g8 17 ♘xe6 ♗xh2+ 18 ♔f1 fxe6 19 ♕xe6+ ♖f7 20 ♘e4 ♗f4 21 g3 ♗h6 22 ♘c5 a5 23 ♕e8+ ♔h7 24 ♖d8 ♘a6 25 ♕e4+ g6 26 ♖xa8 ♘xc5 27 ♕d4 ♗g7 28 ♕h4+ ♗h6 29 ♖h8+ ♔xh8 30 ♕xh6+ **1-0** L/N6123-1843

## 1842̂-★CS-75

**Cochrane, J.– Staunton, H.**

London [Staunton]

1 e4 e5 2 ♗c4 ♘f6 3 d4 exd4 4 ♕xd4 ♘c6 5 ♕d1 ♗c5 6 ♘f3 0-0 7 0-0 ♘xe4 8 ♕d5 ♕e7 9 ♗g5 ♘xg5 10 ♘xg5 ♘e5 11 ♖e1 d6 12 h4 h6 13 ♘xf7?? ♗xf2+ 14 ♔xf2 ♕xh4+ 15 g3 ♕h2+ 16 ♔e3 ♕xg3+ **0-1** L/N6123-1842

## 1842̂-★HJ-1

**Jaenisch, C.F.–♀**

Berlin

1 e4 e5 2 ♘f3 ♘c6 3 ♗c4 ♗c5 4 c3 ♗b6 5 d4 ♕e7 6 0-0 d6 7 ♗g5 f6 8 ♗h4 h5 9 h3 g5 10 ♗g3 h4 11 ♗h2 g4 12 hxg4 ♗xg4 13 ♗b5 0-0-0 14 ♗xc6 bxc6 15 a4 a5 16 ♕d3 h3 17 ♘bd2 hxg2 18 ♖fe1 ♕h7 19 b4 exd4 20 cxd4 ♕h5 21 ♔xg2 ♘e7 22 ♔f1 ♕h3+ 23 ♔e2 ♕xh2 24 bxa5 ♗a7 25 ♕a6+ ♔d7 26 ♖h1 ♕f4 27 ♕d3 f5 28 ♖xh8 ♖xh8 29 ♕e3 ♕xe3+ 30 fxe3 fxe4 31 ♘xe4 ♖h2+ 32 ♘f2 c5 33 ♖g1 ♗xf3+ 34 ♔xf3 cxd4 35 exd4 ♖xf2+ 36 ♔xf2 ♗xd4+ **0-1** L/N6123-1842

## 1842̂-★HJ-2

**Hanstein, W.+Jaenisch, C.F.**

Berlin♀

1 e4 e5 2 f4 exf4 3 ♘f3 g5 4 ♗c4 g4 5 0-0 gxf3 6 ♕xf3 ♗h6 7 d4 d5 8 exd5 ♕f6 9 c3 ♘e7 10 ♘d2 ♗f5 11 d6 ♘ec6 12 dxc7 ♘d7 13 ♖e1+ ♔f8 14 b3 ♖c8 15 ♘e4 ♗xe4 16 ♖xe4 ♖e8 17 ♖xe8+ ♔xe8 18 c8♕+ **1-0** L/N6047-1849

## 1842̂-★PS-1

**Staunton, H.= Popert, H.W.**

London

1 e4 e5 2 ♘f3 ♘c6 3 d4 exd4 4 ♗c4 ♗b4+ 5 c3 dxc3 6 bxc3 ♗a5 7 e5 ♘ge7 8 ♗a3 0-0 9 0-0 d5 10 exd6 cxd6 11 ♗xd6 ♗g4 12 ♗e2 ♖e8 13 h3 ♗h5 14 g4 ♗g6 15 ♗b5 h5 16 ♘e5 hxg4 17 hxg4 ♗e4 18 ♖e1 ♗xb1 19 ♖xb1 ♗xc3 20 ♘xf7 ♔xf7 21 ♕b3+ ♔f8 22 ♗xe7+ ♖xe7 23 ♕xc3 ♕d7 24 ♕h3 ♕d5 25 ♗xc6 ♖xe1+ 26 ♖xe1 bxc6 27 ♕h8+ ♕g8 28 ♕xg8+ ♔xg8 29

♖e7 a5 30 ♖c7 ♖a6 31 f4 ½-½ L/N6123-1842

**1842̂-★PS-2**
**Popert, H.W.+Staunton, H.**
London [Staunton]

1 e4 e5 2 ♗c4 ♗c5 3 ♘f3 ♘c6 4 c3 d6 5 0-0 ♗g4 6 d4 exd4 7 ♕b3 ♗xf3 8 ♗xf7+ ♔f8 9 ♗xg8 ♖xg8 10 gxf3 ♘e5 11 f4 ♘g4 12 cxd4 ♗xd4 13 ♕g3 ♘f6 14 e5 g5 15 fxg5 ♗xe5 16 ♕f3 h6 17 h4 hxg5 18 hxg5 ♕d7 19 ♘c3 ♕g4+ 20 ♕xg4 ♘xg4 21 f4 ♗d4+ 22 ♔g2 ♖e8 23 ♗d2 ♗e3 24 ♔g3 ♘h6 25 ♗xe3 ♘f5+ 26 ♔f2 ♘xe3 27 ♖h1 d5 28 ♔f3 ♘c2 29 ♖ad1 c6 30 ♖d2 ♘e3 31 ♖e2 d4 32 ♘e4 ♘d5? [□ 32 ... ♘f5] 33 ♖d2 c5 34 ♘xc5 ♖e3+ 35 ♔g4 1-0 L/N6123-1842

**1842̂-★PS-3**
**Staunton, H.+Popert, H.W.**
London [Staunton]

1 e4 e5 2 ♘f3 ♘c6 3 d4 exd4 4 ♗c4 ♗b4+ 5 c3 dxc3 6 0-0 [□ 6 bxc3] 6 ... c2 7 ♕xc2 d6 8 a3 ♗a5 9 b4 ♗b6 10 ♗b2 ♘f6 11 e5 dxe5 12 ♘xe5 ♘xe5 13 ♗xe5 0-0 14 ♘c3 ♘g4 15 ♗g3 ♕g5 16 ♖ae1 ♗f5 17 ♕b3 ♘f6 18 ♖e7 ♗g6 19 ♗xc7 ♘g4 20 ♘d5 ♗xc7 21 ♖xc7 ♖ae8 22 ♕g3! h6 [□ 22 ... ♖e4] 23 f4 ♕f5 24 ♘e7+ ♖xe7 25 ♖xe7 ♕f6? 26 ♕xg4 ♕xe7 27 ♕xg6 ♕e3+ 28 ♔h1 ♕xa3 29 ♕e4 ♕c3 30 h3 ♖c8 31 ♗d3 ♖d8 32 ♖f3 g6 33 ♗c4 ♖d1+ 34 ♔h2 ♕e1 35 ♕xg6+ ♔h8 36 ♕xh6+ 1-0 L/N6123-1842

**1842̂-★PS-4**
**Popert, H.W.−Staunton, H.**
London [Staunton]

1 e4 c5 2 ♘f3 [□ 2 f4] 2 ... ♘c6 3 c3 e6 4 d4 d5 5 e5 ♗d7 6 ♗d3 ♕b6 7 ♗c2 g6 8 0-0 ♖c8 9 a4 a5 10 ♘a3 cxd4 11 cxd4 ♘b4 12 ♕e2? ♘xc2 13 ♘xc2 ♕b3 14 ♘e3 ♗xa4 15 ♘d2 ♕b4 16 ♕g4 [△ 17 ♘xd5] 16 ... ♗d7 [16 ... h5!?] 17 ♘f3 h5 18 ♕g3 b6 19 ♗d2 ♕e7 [19 ... ♕xb2?!] 20 ♖ac1 ♗c6 21 ♖c2 ♕d7 22 ♖fc1 ♘e7 23 ♘g5 ♗h6 24 h4 0-0 25 ♕f4 [△ 26 g4] 25 ... ♗g7 26 ♘f3 f6 27 ♕g3 fxe5 28 dxe5 ♗b7 [28 ... d4?] 29 ♘d4 ♖xc2 30 ♖xc2 ♖c8 31 ♖xc8+ ♗xc8 32 ♕g5 ♔h7 33 g4 ♗h6 34 ♕f6 ♘g8 35 ♕f3 hxg4 36 ♕xg4 ♕a4 37 ♔g2 ♘e7 38 ♔g3 ♘c6 [□ 38 ... ♘f5+] 39 ♘xc6 ♕xc6 40 h5 ♕e8 41 hxg6+ ♕xg6 42 ♕xg6+ ♔xg6 43 f4 ♗f8 44 f5+! exf5 45 ♘xd5 ♗c5 46 b4 axb4 47 ♗xb4 [47 ♘xb4 ♗b7] 47 ... ♗xb4 48 ♘xb4 ♔g5 49 ♘d5 b5 50 ♔f2 f4 51 ♘b4 ♗b7 52 ♘c2 ♗d5 53 ♔e2 ♔f5 54 e6 [54 ♘d4+ ♔xe5 55 ♘xb5?? ♗c4−+] 54 ... ♔xe6 55 ♔f2 ♔e5 56 ♘e1 ♗e4 57 ♔e2 ♔d4 0-1 L/N6123-1842

**1842̂-★RS-1** 26 viii 42
**Saint-Amant, P.C.F. de—Rousseau, E.**
[Saint-Amant]

1 e4 e5 2 ♘f3 ♘c6 3 d4 exd4 4 ♗c4 ♗b4+ 5 c3 dxc3 6 0-0 d6 7 a3 c2 [7 ... cxb2?] 8 ♕xc2 ♗c5 9 b4 ♗b6 10 ♗b2 f6 11 ♘c3 ♘ge7 12 ♖ad1 [□ 12 h3] 12 ... ♗g4 13 ♘d5 ♘e5 14 ♗xe5 fxe5 15 ♘xe5? ♗xd1 16 ♖xd1 ♘xd5 17 ♗xd5 ♕f6 [17 ... dxe5? 18 ♗xb7] 18 ♕a4+? c6 19 ♗xc6+ [□ 19 ♘xc6] 19 ... ♔e7 20 ♘g4 ♕f4 21 ♗d7 h5 22 g3 ♕f3 23 ♗f5 ♖ad8 24 ♘e3 ♗xe3 25 fxe3 ♕xe3+ 26 ♔g2 h4 27 ♕c2

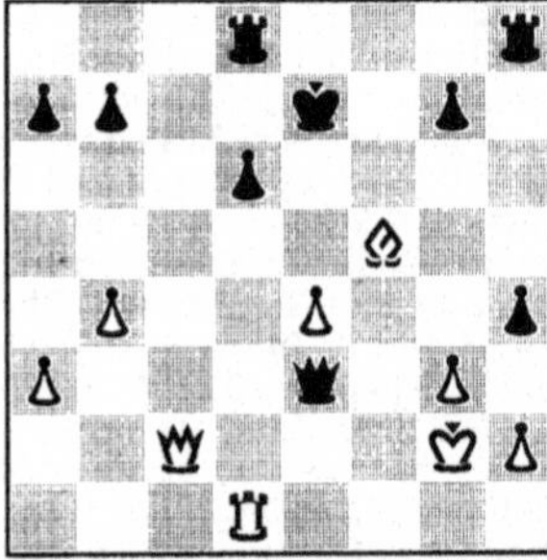

27 ... h3+! 28 ♗xh3 ♕h6 29 ♕c7+ ♔e8 30 ♗f5 ♕xh2+ 31 ♔f3 ♕h5+ 32 ♔e3 g6 [32 ... ♕xd1?? 33 ♗g6+] 33 ♗e6 ♖h7 34 ♕c2 ♕e5−+ 35 ♕c4 ♕xg3+ 36 ♔d4 ♕e5+ 37 ♔e3 ♖h2 [△ 38 ... ♕g3+] 38 ♖g1 g5 39 ♔d3 a6 [△ 39 ... d5] 40 ♕d5 ♕b2! 41 ♖xg5 [41 ♕xb7 ♖d2+; 41 ♕b3 ♖h3+; 41 ♗f7+ ♔f8] 41 ... ♕c2+ 42 ♔e3 ♕d2+ 43 ♔f3 ♕e2+ [43 ... ♕f2+] 44 ♔f4 ♕f2+ 45 ♔g4 ♕xg1+ 0-1 L/N6013-1842

**1842̂-★RS-2** 27 viii 42
**Rousseau, E.− Saint-Amant, P.C.F.de**
[Saint-Amant]

1 e4 c5 2 f4 e6 3 c4?! [3 ♘f3] 3 ... ♘c6 4 ♘f3 d6 5 d3 ♘ge7 6 ♘c3 f5 7 ♗e2 a6 8 0-0 ♕c7 9 b3 g6 10 ♗b2 ♘d4 11 ♕d2 ♗g7 12 ♖ae1 0-0 13 ♗d1 ♘ec6 14 ♘e2 ♘xe2+ 15 ♖xe2 ♗xb2 16 ♕xb2 fxe4 17 ♖xe4 d5 18 ♖ee1 ♕xf4! [18 ... ♖xf4 19 ♘g5] 19 g3 ♕d6∓ 20 cxd5 exd5 21 ♘g5 ♗f5 22 ♖f4 ♘d4 23 b4 ♕f6! 24 ♕g2 [24 ♘? ♘f3+] 24 ... ♖ad8? [24 ... ♕xg5] 25 h4 [□ 25 bxc5] 25 ... h6 26 ♘f3 ♘e6 27 ♘e5 ♘xf4 28 gxf4 ♕xh4−+ 29 ♖f1 ♔h7 30 ♗b3 ♕h3 31 ♕f2 c4 32 ♗d1 ♗xd3 33 ♖e1 [△ 34 ♗g4] 33 ... ♗e4 34 ♘f3 ♖xf4 35 ♖e3 ♖g4+ 0-1 L/N6013-1842

**1842̂-★SS-1**
**Stanley, C.H.=Staunton, H.**
[Staunton]

⟨△f7⟩1 e4 ... 2 d4 e6 3 ♗d3 c5 4 e5 g6 5 c3 ♘c6 6 ♘f3 cxd4 7 cxd4 ♗b4+ 8 ♘c3 ♘ge7 9 ♗g5 d6 10 0-0 ♗xc3 11 bxc3 dxe5 12 dxe5 0-0 13 ♗f6 ♕a5 14 ♕d2 ♘d5 15 ♕h6 ♘xf6 16 exf6 ♖xf6 17 h4 ♘e5 18 ♘g5 ♕c7 19 ♗e2 ♕g7 20 ♕xg7+ ♔xg7 21 ♖ad1 ♘f7 22 ♘xf7 ♖xf7 23 ♖d8 a5 24 ♗c4 ♔f6 25 g4 ♖c7 26 ♗xe6 [□ 26 ♗b5] 26 ... ♔xe6 27 ♖e1+ ♔f7 28 ♖ee8 b6 [□ 28 ... ♖xc3] 29 f4 ½-½ L/N6123-1842

**1842̂-★SS-2**
**Stanley, C.H.+Staunton, H.**
[Staunton]

⟨△f7⟩1 e4 ... 2 d4 ♘c6 3 d5 ♘e5 4 f4 ♘f7 5 ♘f3 e6 6 ♗d3 ♗c5 7 ♘c3 a6 8 a4 ♘e7 9 h4 c6 10 b4 ♗a7 11 d6 ♘xd6 12 ♘g5 h6 13 ♘h3 ♘g6 14 g3 ♘f7 15 ♕g4 ♕f6 16 ♗b2 ♗d4 17 e5 ♘gxe5 18 fxe5 ♘xe5 19 ♕h5+ g6 20 ♘e4 ♕e7

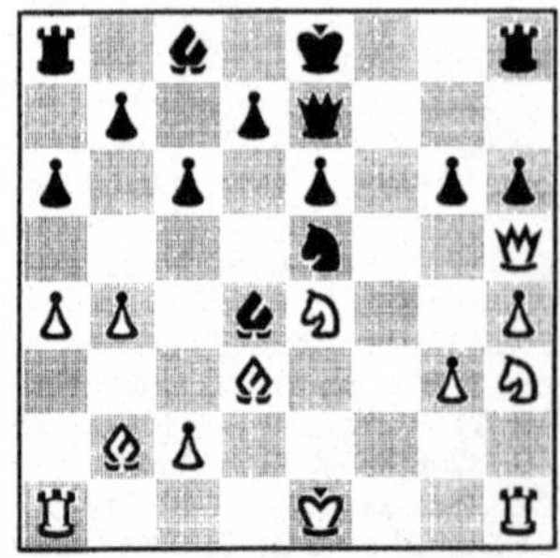

21 ♘d6+! ♕xd6 [21 ... ♔d8 22 ♗xd4! gxh5?? 23 ♗b6#] 22 ♗xg6+ ♔d8 23 0-0-0 c5 24 ♗xd4 cxd4 25 ♖he1 ♘c6 26 ♕f3 [□ 26 ♘g5] 26 ... ♖f8 27 ♕b3 b5 28 ♘f4 a5?? [28 ... e5−+] 29 ♗e4 axb4 30 ♗xc6 ♖xa4?? 31 ♕b2 ♖xf4 32 gxf4 ♕xc6 33 ♖xd4 ♕c3 34 ♕xc3 bxc3 35 ♔b1 d5 36 f5 ♖a6 37 f6 ♖a7 38 ♖g1 ♖f7 39 ♖g8+ ♔d7 40 ♖g7 ♔e8 41 ♖dg4 1-0 L/N6123-1842

**1842̂-★SS-3**
**Stanley, C.H.−Staunton, H.**
[Staunton]

⟨△f7⟩1 e4 ... 2 d4 ♘c6 3 ♗d3 e5 4 d5 ♘ce7 5 ♗g5 d6 6 f4 c6 7 fxe5 dxe5 8 c4 ♕b6 9 ♕e2 ♘g6 10 ♗e3 ♗c5 11 ♗xc5 ♕xc5 12 g3 ♘f6 13 h3 0-0 14 ♘c3 ♘h5! 15 ♕xh5 ♕f2+ 16 ♔d1 ♕xb2 [16 ... ♕g2∓] 17 ♕e2 ♕xa1+ 18 ♔c2 b5 19 cxb5 cxb5 20 ♕g2 b4 21 ♘ge2 ♖f2 22 ♕xf2 ♕xh1 23 ♘b5 ♗a6 24 ♕f5 [△ 25 ♕e6+] 24 ... ♗c8 25 ♕g5 ♗d7 26 ♘c7 ♖f8 27 ♘e6 ♖c8+ 28 ♔d2

♕xh3 29 ♗a6 ♗xe6 30 dxe6 ♕xe6 31 ♗xc8 ♕xc8 32 ♕e3 a5 33 ♕b3+ ♔h8 34 ♕d5 a4 35 ♕a5 [□ 35 ♕b5] 35 ... b3 36 axb3 axb3 37 ♕b4 ♕c2+ 38 ♔e3 h6 **0-1**

L/N6123-1842

**1842̂-★SW-1**
**W♀+ Staunton, H.**

[Staunton]

⟨♙f7⟩1 e4 ... 2 d4 e6 3 c4 ♗b4+ 4 ♘c3 ♘e7 5 ♗g5 0-0 6 ♗d3 ♘bc6 7 ♘e2 ♕e8 8 ♕d2 e5 9 d5 ♘d4 10 f4 d6 11 0-0 ♗g4 12 f5 h6 13 ♗e3 c5 14 ♘g3 ♖c8 15 h3 ♗h5 16 ♖f2 ♔h7 17 ♖af1 ♘g8 18 a3 ♗a5 19 ♔h2 ♘f6 20 ♘xh5 ♕xh5 21 ♕d1 ♕e8 22 g4 a6 23 a4 ♖c7 24 ♖g2 g5 25 fxg6+ ♕xg6 26 ♖gf2 ♖g7 27 ♔h1 ♗d8 28 ♘e2 ♘xg4 29 hxg4 ♕xg4 30 ♘xd4 ♖xf2 31 ♕xg4 ♖xf1+ 32 ♗xf1 ♖xg4 33 ♘e6 ♗a5 34 ♗h3 ♖h4 35 ♔g2 ♔g8 36 ♔g3 ♗e1+ 37 ♔g2 ♖xe4 38 ♗xh6 ♖xc4 39 ♘g5 ♖xa4 40 ♗e6+ ♔h8 41 ♗f8 e4 42 ♗xd6 ♔g7 43 ♗xc5 ♗a5 44 d6 ♔f6 45 ♗b3 ♔xg5 46 ♗xa4 b5 47 ♗c2 ♔f4 48 ♔f2 ♗d8 49 b4 ♔e5 50 ♗b3 a5 51 bxa5 ♗xa5 52 d7 ♗d8 53 ♔e3 ♗g5+ 54 ♔e2 ♗d8 55 ♗f7 ♔f6 56 ♗e8 ♔e6 57 ♔e3 ♔d5 58 ♗a3 ♗g5+ 59 ♔e2 ♗d8 60 ♗f8 ♔c6? 61 ♔e3 ♔d5 62 ♗f7+ ♔c6 [□ 62 ... ♔e5] 63 ♗e6 ♔c7 64 ♔xe4 ♔c6 65 ♔d3 ♗f6 66 ♔c2 ♗d8 67 ♔b3 ♗f6 68 ♔b4 ♗d8 69 ♗f5 ♗f6 **1-0**

L/N6123-1842

**1842̂-★S♀-1**
**♀– Staunton, H.**

⟨♙f7⟩1 e4 ... 2 d4 e6 3 ♗d3 c5 4 d5 d6 5 c4 exd5 6 exd5 ♘f6 7 ♘c3 ♗e7 8 ♘ge2 0-0 9 0-0 ♘bd7 10 f4 ♘g4 11 h3 ♘h6 12 ♘g3 ♘f6 13 ♕c2 ♔h8 14 ♘ge4 a6 15 ♘xf6 ♗xf6 16 ♗xh7 ♗d4+ 17 ♔h1 ♕h4 18 ♘e2 ♗xh3 19 g3 ♕g4 20 ♘xd4 ♗xf1 21 ♔g1 ♕xg3+ 22 ♔xf1 cxd4 23 ♗d3 ♘g4 24 ♗e4 ♖ae8 25 ♕g2 ♖xf4+ 26 ♗xf4 ♕xf4+ 27 ♔g1 ♖xe4 28 ♖f1 ♕e3+ 29 ♔h1 ♘f6 30 ♖f3 ♖h4+ **0-1**

L/N6123-1842

**1842̂-★S♀-2**
**♀– Staunton, H.**

⟨♙f7⟩1 e4 ... 2 d4 e6 3 ♗d3 c5 4 d5 d6 5 c4 exd5 6 exd5 ♘f6 7 ♘c3 ♗e7 8 ♗g5 0-0 9 ♕c2 h6 10 h4 ♘g4 11 ♘f3 ♘d7 12 0-0-0 ♘de5 13 ♘xe5 ♗xg5+ 14 ♔b1 ♘xe5 15 hxg5 ♕xg5 16 ♗h7+ ♔h8 17 ♘e4 ♕e7 18 ♖df1 ♘xc4 19 ♕xc4 ♔xh7 20 ♕c2

20 ... ♕xe4 21 ♕xe4+ ♗f5 **0-1**

L/N6123-1842

**1842̂-★S♀-3**
**♀– Staunton, H.**

London

⟨♙f7⟩1 e4 ... 2 d4 ♘c6 3 ♘c3 e5 4 d5 ♘ce7 5 ♗g5 d6 6 ♘f3 ♗g4 7 h3 ♗d7 8 ♘h4 g6 9 ♗c4 ♗h6 10 ♕d2 ♗g7 11 0-0 ♘f6 12 f4 exf4 13 ♗xf4 0-0 14 e5 ♘h5 15 exd6 cxd6 16 ♗h2 ♕b6+ 17 ♔h1 ♕xb2 18 ♘e4 ♗e5 19 ♖ab1 ♖xf1+ 20 ♖xf1 ♗xh2 21 ♕f2 ♗f4 22 g4 ♕e5 23 ♕f3 ♕xe4 24 ♕xe4 ♘g3+ **0-1**

L/N6123-1842

**1842̂-★S♀-4**
**Staunton, H.+♀**

⟨♖a1⟩1 e4 e5 2 f4 exf4 3 ♘f3 g5 4 ♗c4 g4 5 ♗xf7+ ♔xf7 6 ♘e5+ ♔e8 7 ♕xg4 ♘f6 8 ♕xf4 d6 9 ♘f3 ♘c6 10 d4 ♕e7 11 0-0 ♗d7 12 e5 dxe5 13 dxe5 ♘d5 14 ♕e4 ♗e6 15 ♗g5 ♕c5+ 16 ♔h1 ♘cb4 17 c4 ♘b6 18 b3 ♗e7 19 ♘d4 ♗g8 20 ♗xe7 ♕xe7 21 ♘f5 ♕d7 22 ♕h4 ♖d8 23 ♕f6 **1-0**

L/N6123-1842

**1842̂-★S♀-5**
**Staunton, H.+♀**

⟨♖a1⟩1 e4 e5 2 f4 exf4 3 ♘f3 g5 4 ♗c4 g4 5 d4 gxf3 6 0-0 fxg2 7 ♗xf7+ ♔xf7 8 ♖xf4+ ♘f6 9 e5 ♔g8 10 exf6 d5 11 ♕h5 ♘c6 12 ♖f2 **1-0**

L/N6123-1842

**1842̂-★S♀-6**
**Staunton, H.+♀**

London

⟨♖a1⟩1 e4 e5 2 ♘f3 ♘c6 3 ♗c4 ♗c5 4 b4 ♗xb4 5 c3 ♗a5 6 d4 exd4 7 e5 d6 8 ♕b3 ♕e7 9 0-0 dxe5 10 ♗a3 ♕f6 11 ♘bd2 ♕g6 12 ♘xe5 ♘xe5 13 ♕b5+ ♘c6 14 ♖e1+ ♗e6 15 ♕xb7 ♖d8 16 ♕xc6+ ♖d7 17 ♕a8+ ♖d8 18 ♗b5+ c6 19 ♗xc6# **1-0**

L/N6123-1842

**1842̂-★S♀-7**
**Staunton, H.+♀**

London

⟨♖a1⟩1 e4 e5 2 ♘f3 ♘c6 3 ♗c4 ♗c5 4 b4 ♗xb4 5 c3 ♗a5 6 0-0 d6 7 d4 exd4 8 cxd4 ♗b6 9 ♗b2 ♘f6 10 d5 ♘a5 11 e5 dxe5 12 ♗a3 ♘xc4 13 ♕a4+ ♗d7 14 ♕xc4 e4 15 ♘c3 c5 16 exc6 ♗xc6 17 ♘e5 ♕c7 18 ♘b5 ♗xb5 19 ♕xb5+ ♘d7 20 ♖d1 ♖d8 21 ♘xf7 ♔xf7 22 ♕b3+ ♔f6 23 ♖d6+ ♔g5 24 ♕d5+ ♔f4 25 g3+ ♔g4 26 h3+ **1-0**

L/N6123-1842

**1842̂-★S♀-8**
**Staunton, H.+♀**

London

1 e4 e5 2 ♗c4 ♗c5 3 c3 ♘c6 4 ♘f3 d6 5 d4 exd4 6 cxd4 ♗b6 7 0-0 ♗g4 8 ♕b3 ♗h5 9 e5 dxe5 10 dxe5 ♘ge7 11 e6 0-0 12 exf7+ ♔h8 13 ♘g5 ♘d4 14 ♕h3 ♗g6 15 ♘a3 ♘ef5 16 ♗f4 ♕f6 17 ♖ae1 ♘h6 18 ♘e6 ♗f5 19 ♘xf8

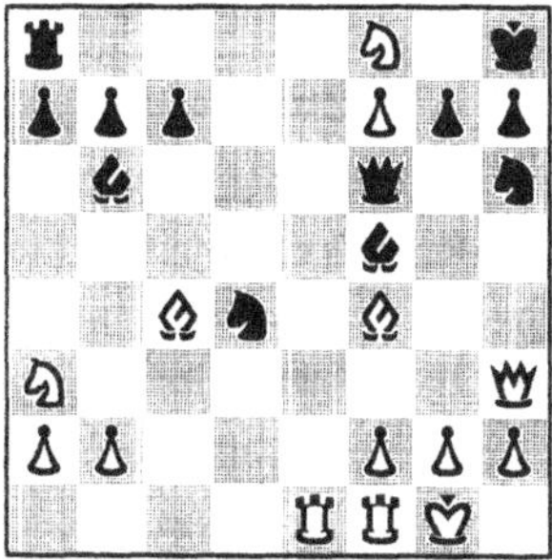

19 ... ♘xf7 20 ♘xh7 ♗xh7 21 ♕d7 ♕xf4 22 ♗xf7 ♗f5 23 ♖e8+ ♖xe8 24 ♕xe8+ ♔h7 25 ♕g8+ ♔h6 26 ♕h8+ ♗h7 27 ♗g8 **1-0**

L/N6123-1842

**1842̂-★S♀-9**
**Staunton, H.+♀**

⟨♘b1⟩1 e4 e5 2 ♗c4 ♘f6 3 d4 d6 4 ♕e2 exd4 5 f4 ♗g4 6 ♘f3 ♘c6 7 0-0 ♗e7 8 e5 dxe5 9 fxe5 ♗xf3 10 ♖xf3 ♘xe5 11 ♕xe5 0-0 12 ♗g5 ♕d7 13 ♖af1 ♖ae8 14 ♕g3 ♘e4 15 ♖xf7 ♔h8 16 ♕e5 ♖xf7 17 ♖xf7 ♗f6 18 ♗xf6 ♘xf6 19 ♕xf6 gxf6 20 ♖xd7 **1-0**

L/N6123-1842

**1842̂-★S♀-10**
**Staunton, H.+♀**

London

⟨♗f1⟩1 d4 d5 2 c4 dxc4 3 ♗f4 ♗f5 4 ♘c3 ♘f6 5 f3 e6 6 e4 ♗g6 7 ♘ge2 ♘c6 8 ♗e3 ♗e7 9 0-0 0-0 10 ♔h1 h6 11 g4 ♘h7 12 f4 f5 13 gxf5 exf5 14 ♖g1 ♗h5 15 d5 ♗xe2 16 ♕xe2 ♘a5 17 ♗d4 ♘f6 18 e5 ♘h7 19 ♖g6 ♔h8 20 ♖ag1 ♖g8 21 e6 ♘f6 22 ♕h5 ♔h7 23 ♕xf5 **1-0**

L/N6123-1842

**1842̂-★S♀-11**
**Staunton, H.+♀**
London
⟨♖a1⟩1 e4 e5 2 ♗c4 ♗c5 3 b4 ♗xb4 4 f4 d5 5 exd5 ♗d6 6 ♘f3 exf4 7 0-0 ♗g4 8 d4 ♘e7 9 ♗d3 0-0 10 ♗xh7+ ♔xh7 11 ♘g5+ ♔g8 12 ♕xg4 ♘g6 13 ♕h5 ♖e8 14 ♘c3 ♕f6 15 ♔h1 ♕xd4 16 ♗b2 ♗e5 17 ♕h7+ ♔f8 18 ♗a3+ ♗d6 19 ♗b2 ♖e5 20 ♘f3 ♕c4 21 ♘d2 ♕b4 22 ♗a1 ♘d7 23 ♘ce4 ♖ae8 24 c3 ♕b6 25 c4 ♕e3 26 h4 ♘f6 27 ♘xf6 gxf6 28 ♘f3 ♔e7 29 ♗xe5 ♗xe5 30 h5 ♘f8 31 ♕f5 ♕e2 32 ♖c1 ♔d6 33 ♖e1 ♕b2 34 ♖b1 ♕xa2 35 ♘xe5 fxe5 36 ♕f6+ ♔c5 37 ♖xb7 ♕a1+ 38 ♔h2 ♕e1 39 ♖b3 ♔xc4 40 ♖h3 ♖b8 41 ♕c6+ ♔b4 42 ♕xc7 ♖b5 43 ♕d6+ ♖c5 44 ♕xf8 f3 45 ♖xf3 ♕h4+ 46 ♔g1 ♕d4+ 47 ♔h2 ♕xd5 48 h6 ♕e4 49 ♕b8+ ♖b5 50 ♖b3+ ♔xb3 51 ♕xb5+ **1-0**
L/N6123-1842

**1842̂-★S♀-12**
**Staunton, H.+♀**
London
⟨♘g1⟩1 d4 d5 2 c4 dxc4 3 e3 e5 4 ♗xc4 cxd4 5 ♕b3 ♕f6 6 0-0 ♘c6 7 ♘d2 ♘e5 8 ♗d5 c6 9 ♗e4 ♗c5 10 ♗c2 ♕e6 11 exd4 ♗xd4 12 ♕a3 ♘f6 13 ♗b3 ♘d5 14 ♘e4 c5 15 ♘g5 ♕d6 16 ♗e3 ♗xe3 17 fxe3 ♗e6 18 ♖ad1 ♘g4 19 ♕a4+ ♔e7 20 g3 ♘gxe3 21 ♕h4 f6 22 ♖fe1 fxg5 23 ♕xg5+ ♔d7 24 ♖xe3 c4 25 ♗xc4 **1-0** L/N6123-1842

**1842̂-★S♀-13**
**Staunton, H.+♀**
⟨♖a1⟩1 e4 e5 2 ♘f3 ♘c6 3 ♗c4 ♗c5 4 b4 ♘xb4 5 c3 ♘c6 6 0-0 d6 7 d4 exd4 8 ♘xd4 ♘xd4 9 cxd4 ♗b6 10 ♕b3 ♕e7 11 e5 dxe5 12 ♗a3 ♕f6 13 dxe5 ♕g6 14 ♗b5+ c6 15 ♕b4 **1-0** L/N6123-1842

**1842̂-★S♀-14**
**Staunton, H.+♀**
London
⟨♖a1⟩1 e4 e5 2 f4 exf4 3 ♗c4 c6 4 ♘c3 d6 5 ♘f3 g5 6 d4 b5 7 ♗b3 ♗g7 8 0-0 h6 9 g3 ♗h3 10 ♖f2 ♗g4 11 gxf4 ♕b6 12 ♘e2 ♗xf3 13 ♖xf3 g4 14 ♖f2 ♘f6 15 ♕d3 d5 16 exd5 cxd5 17 ♘g3 h5 18 ♕e3+ ♕e6 19 ♕d3 0-0 20 ♖e2 ♕d7 21 ♘f5 ♔h8 22 ♖e7 ♕d8 23 ♖e1 ♘c6 24 c3 a6 25 ♗c2 ♘e4 26 ♖xe4 dxe4 27 ♕xe4 ♕f6 28 ♘d6 ♕h6 29 ♗e3 f5 30 ♘xf5 ♖xf5 31 ♕xf5 ♖f8 32 ♕e4 ♔g8 33 d5 ♘d8 34 d6 ♘f7 35 d7 ♘d6 36 ♕d5+ ♔h8 37 ♗c5 ♕xf4 38 ♕xh5+ ♗h6 39 ♗d4+ **1-0** L/N6123-1842

**1842̂-★S♀-15**
**♀Φ Staunton, H.**
1 d4 d5 2 c4 dxc4 3 ♘c3 e5 4 d5 ♘f6 5 e4 ♗d6 6 ♗xc4 0-0 7 h3 c6 8 ♗g5 b5 9 ♗b3 b4 10 ♘ce2 ♗e7 11 ♕c2 ♘xd5 12 ♖d1 ♗xg5 13 ♘f3 ♘e3 14 fxe3 ♕e7 15 ♘xg5 ♕xg5 16 0-0 ♗xh3 17 ♘g3 ♘d7 18 ♖xf7 ♔h8 19 ♘f5 ♖xf7 20 ♗xf7 ♗xf5 21 exf5 ♕xe3+ 22 ♕f2 ♕xf2+ 23 ♔xf2 ♘f6 24 ♔f3 ♖f8 25 ♗e6 a5 26 ♖c1 g6 27 ♖xc6 gxf5 28 ♖a6 e4+ L/N6123-1842

**1842̂-★S♀-16**
**♀– Staunton, H.**
London
1 e4 e5 2 ♘f3 ♘c6 3 d4 ♘xd4 4 ♘xd4 exd4 5 ♕xd4 ♘e7 6 ♗c4 ♘c6 7 ♕d5 ♕f6 8 c3 ♗e7 9 0-0 d6 10 f4 ♗e6 11 ♕d3 0-0 12 ♘d2 ♖ad8 13 ♗xe6 fxe6 14 ♘f3 ♕g6 15 ♕e2 d5 16 e5 d4 17 ♘xd4 ♘xd4 18 cxd4 ♖xd4 19 ♗e3 ♖e4 20 ♕f3 b6 21 ♔h1 ♖xe5 22 ♖ae1 ♖e4 23 g4 ♗d6 24 ♕g3 e5 25 fxe5 ♖xf1+ 26 ♖xf1 ♗xe5 27 ♕f3 ♗d6 28 g5 ♕e6 29 ♗d2 c6 30 a3 ♕d5 31 ♖f2 ♗c5 32 ♖f1 ♗e7 33 ♖f2 ♖e5 34 ♕xd5+ ♖xd5 35 h4 ♖d4 36 ♗f4 ♗d6 37 ♗xd6 ♖xd6 38 ♔g2 h6 39 gxh6 ♖xh6 40 ♔g3 ♖g6+ 41 ♔h3 ♖f6 42 ♖d2 a5 43 ♔g4 ♔h7 44 h5 b5 45 ♔g5 ♖e6 46 ♔f5 ♖e1 47 ♖c2 ♖h1 48 ♔g4 ♖b1 49 ♔f4 a4 50 ♔f5 c5 51 ♔e4 ♔h6 52 ♔f5 b4 53 axb4 cxb4 54 ♖g2 a3 55 bxa3 bxa3 56 ♖a2 ♖b3 57 ♔g4 ♖b4+ 58 ♔f5 ♖b5+ 59 ♔f4 ♖a5 60 ♔g4 ♖a4+ 61 ♔f5 ♔xh5 62 ♖h2+ ♖h4 63 ♖g2 g6+ 64 ♔f6 ♖f4+ **0-1** L/N6123-1842

**1842̂-★S♀-17**
**♀– Staunton, H.**
London
1 e4 e5 2 f4 exf4 3 ♗c4 b5 4 ♗b3 ♕h4+ 5 ♔f1 g5 6 ♘c3 c6 7 ♘f3 ♕h5 8 h4 h6 9 ♔g1 g4 10 ♘h2 d6 11 d4 a5 12 a3 f3 13 gxf3 gxf3 14 ♕xf3 ♕xf3 15 ♘xf3 ♘f6 16 e5 ♘h5 17 exd6 ♗xd6 18 ♘e4 ♗c7 19 ♔f2 f5 20 ♘c5 ♗g3+ 21 ♔g2 ♖a7 22 ♘e5 ♖e7 23 ♘cd3 f4 24 ♔f3 ♗f5 25 ♘xf4 ♗xf4 26 ♗xf4 a4 27 ♗a2 ♗xc2 28 ♖he1 ♖f8 29 ♗f7+ ♖exf7 30 ♘xf7+ ♔xf7 31 ♗xb8 ♖xb8 32 ♖e5 ♘f6 33 ♖c1 ♗b3 34 ♖xc6 ♗d5+ 35 ♖xd5 ♘xd5 36 ♖xh6 ♘f6 37 h5 ♖d8 38 ♔e2 ♖xd4 39 ♖h8 ♔g7 40 ♖b8 ♖d5 41 ♖b7+ ♔h6 42 ♖b6 ♖f5 43 ♔d3 ♔xh5 44 ♔d4 ♔g4 45 ♖b7 ♔f4 46 ♔c3 ♘d5+ 47 ♔d4 ♘e3 48 ♔c3 ♔e4 49 ♔b4 ♘c2+ 50 ♔a5 ♘d4 51 ♔b4 ♘c6+ 52 ♔c3 ♖f3+ 53 ♔c2 ♘d4+ 54 ♔d2 ♖f2+ 55 ♔c3 ♖c2+ 56 ♔b4 ♖xb2+ **0-1**
L/N6123-1842

**1842̂-⊠CK-1**
**Kieseritsky, L.– Chamouillet, M.**
1 e4 e5 2 f4 exf4 3 ♘f3 g5 4 h4 g4 5 ♘e5 h5 6 ♗c4 ♖h7 7 d4 d6 8 ♘d3 f3 9 g3 ♘f6 10 ♘c3 ♘c6 11 ♘f4 ♘e7 12 ♔f2 ♘d7 13 ♕d3 ♘b6 14 ♗b3 ♗g7 15 ♖e1 c6 16 a4 a5 17 ♘d1 ♖h8 18 c4 ♗e6 19 ♗d2 ♔f8 20 ♗c3 d5 21 exd5 ♗f5 22 ♕d2 cxd5 23 cxd5 ♗h6 24 ♖e5 ♕d6 25 ♗xa5 ♗xf4 26 gxf4 ♖xa5 27 ♕xa5 f6 28 ♕c5 ♕xc5 29 dxc5 fxe5 30 cxb6 exf4 31 a5 ♔g7 **0-1** L/N6013

**1842̂-⊠SW-1⊠**
**Staunton, H.+Williams, E. & H♀**
[Staunton]
1 f4 d5 2 ♘f3 c5 3 e3 ♘c6 4 ♗b5 a6 5 ♗xc6+ bxc6 6 0-0 e6 7 c4! ♘h6 [7 ... dxc4 8 ♘e5] 8 ♕e2 ♗d6 9 ♘c3 ♕e7 10 b3 f6 11 d3 [11 d4?! cxd4] 11 ... 0-0 12 e4 dxe4 13 dxe4 e5 14 f5! [14 fxe5 ♗xe5] 14 ... ♘f7 15 ♘h4 ♗d7 16 ♖f3 ♖fd8 [□ 16 ... ♖ad8] 17 ♗e3 ♗e8 18 ♖af1 ♘g5 19 ♖g3 h6 20 ♕g4 ♖d7 21 ♘f3 ♔f8 22 ♘xg5 [22 h4?? h5–+] 22 ... hxg5 23 h4 ♗f7 24 hxg5 ♔e8 25 g6 ♗g8 26 ♖h3 ♔d8 27 ♕e2 ♔c7 28 ♘a4 ♖dd8 29 ♕f2 ♔b7 30 g4 ♕c7 31 ♗xc5 ♗xc5 32 ♘xc5+ ♔c8 33 ♖d3 ♖xd3 34 ♘xd3 ♕d6 35 ♖d1 ♔c7 36 ♖d2 ♕d4 37 ♕xd4 exd4 38 ♔f2 ♖d8 39 ♔f3 **1-0** L/N6123-1842

**1842̂-⊠SW-2⊠**
**Williams, E. & H♀= Staunton, H.**
[Staunton]
1 d4 d5 2 c4 dxc4 3 e3 e5 4 ♗xc4 exd4 5 exd4 ♘f6 6 ♘f3 ♗b4+ 7 ♘c3 0-0 8 0-0 ♗g4 9 ♗e3 ♘c6 10 ♗e2! ♘d5 11 ♕c2! [△ 12 ♘g5] 11 ... ♗h5! 12 a3 ♗a5 13 ♘e5 ♘xc3 14 ♗xh5 ♘xe5 15 dxe5 ♘d5 16 ♗c5 ♖e8 17 f4 c6 18 ♖ad1 ♕h4 19 ♕e2 g6 [19 ... ♘xf4? 20 ♗xf7+!+–] 20 ♗g4 ♗b6! [20 ... h5 21 ♗d7!] 21 ♗xb6 axb6 22 f5? ♖a4! 23 fxg6 hxg6 24 ♗f3 [△ 25 ♗xd5 cxd5 26 ♕f3] 24 ... ♘f4! 25 ♕e3 b5 26 ♖d7 ♕g5 [△ 27 ... ♘h3+] 27 ♔h1 [27 ♕b6 ♖c4 △ 28 ... ♘h3+=] 27 ... ♕xe5 28 ♕xe5 ♖xe5 29 ♖xb7 ♖c4 30 h3 ♘d3 31 ♗d1 ♖f4 32 ♖xf4 ♘xf4 33 ♗f3! [33 ♗b3] 33 ... ♘d5 34 ♔g1 ♔g7 35 ♔f2 ♔f6 36 b3 ♘e7! 37 a4 bxa4 38 bxa4 ♖a5 **½-½** L/N6123-1842

**184̂2̂-★BS-1**
**Brien, R.B.+Staunton, H.**
London [Staunton]

〈♙f7〉1 e4 ... 2 d4 e6 3 ♗d3 c5 4 e5 g6 5 c3 ♘c6 6 h4 cxd4 7 cxd4 ♗g7 8 h5 ♘xd4 9 hxg6 ♕a5+ 10 ♔f1 h6 11 ♕h5 ♕xe5 12 ♘c3 d5 13 ♕d1 ♗d7 14 ♖h5 ♕f6 15 ♘h3 ♖c8 16 ♗f4 ♘e7 17 ♗e5 ♕f8 18 ♗xd4 ♗xd4 19 ♘b5 ♗c5 [◻ 19 ... ♘c6; 19 ... ♘f5] 20 ♖c1 ♕g7 21 ♖xc5! ♖xc5 22 ♘d6+ ♔f8 23 ♕f3+ ♘f5 [◻ 23 ... ♔g8] 24 g4 ♖c1+ 25 ♔g2 ♕xg6 26 ♔h2 ♕g7 27 gxf5 ♕e5+ 28 ♕f4+- ...⚲ **1-0** L/N6123-1842

**184̂2̂-★BS-2**
**Brien, R.B.–Staunton, H.**
London [Staunton]

〈♙f7〉1 e4 ... 2 d4 e6 3 ♗d3 c5 4 d5 d6 5 c4 ♘f6 6 f4 exd5 7 cxd5 ♗g4 8 ♕c2 ♘bd7 9 h3 ♗h5 10 g4 ♗f7 11 ♘c3 a6 12 a4 ♖c8 13 b3 ♗e7 14 ♘f3 0-0 15 ♗e3 ♕a5 16 ♔e2 ♕c7 17 ♘g5 ♘b6 18 e5 dxe5 19 ♗xh7+ ♔h8 20 ♘xf7+ ♖xf7 21 ♗g6 ♖f8 22 ♕f5 ♗d6 23 a5 ♘bd7 24 ♕g5 exf4 25 ♕h4+ ♔g8 26 g5 fxe3 27 ♘e4 ♘e5 28 gxf6 [28 ♘xf6+ gxf6] 28 ... ♘xg6 29 ♕g4 ♘f4+ 30 ♔f3 ♗e5 31 ♖hg1 ♗xf6 32 d6 ♕c6 33 d7 ♖cd8 34 ♖af1 ♗d4 35 ...⚲ **0-1** L/N6123-1842

**184̂2̂-★BS-3**
**Brien, R.B.–Staunton, H.**
London [Staunton]

〈♙f7〉1 e4 ... 2 d4 e6 3 ♗d3 c5 4 d5 d6 5 c4 exd5 6 cxd5 ♘f6 7 ♘c3 ♗g4 8 f3 ♗h5 9 g4 ♗f7 10 ♗f4 a6 11 a4 ♗e7 12 ♘ge2 0-0 13 ♕d2 ♘bd7 14 ♘g3 ♗g6 15 ♘f5 ♘e8 16 ♔e2 ♘e5 17 ♗xe5 dxe5 18 h4 ♘d6 [18 ... ♗xf5 19 gxf5 ♗xh4 ?!] 19 b3 [◻ 19 h5] 19 ... ♖c8 20 ♗c2 ♗xf5 21 gxf5 ♗xh4 22 ♖ag1 ♘f7 23 ♖g4 ♗g5 24 ♕e1 h6 25 ♕g3 c4 26 b4 ♕b6 27 ♖xg5 ♘xg5 28 ♕xe5 ♖ce8 29 ♕g3 ♕xb4 30 f4 ♕b2 31 fxg5 ♕xc2+ 32 ♔f1 ♖xe4 33 ♘xe4 ♕xe4 34 ♖h2 ♖xf5+ 35 ♖f2 ♕b1+ 36 ♔e2 ♕b2+ 37 ...⚲ **0-1** L/N6123-1842

**184̂2̂-★BS-4**
**Brown, J.+Staunton, H.**
London [Staunton]

〈♙f7〉1 e4 ... 2 d4 e6 3 ♗d3 c5 4 c3 cxd4 5 cxd4 ♗b4+ 6 ♘c3 ♘e7 7 a3 ♗a5 8 ♕h5+ g6 9 ♕e5 0-0 10 ♘e2 ♘bc6 11 ♕g3 d5 12 e5 ♘f5 13 ♗xf5 ♖xf5 14 0-0 a6 15 ♗e3 ♗c7 16 f4 b5 17 ♖ac1 ♘a5 18 ♖c2 ♘c4 19 b3 ♘xa3 20 ♖a2 b4 21 ♘a4 a5 22 ♘c5 ♗b6 23 ♖d1 ♖a7 24 ♗c1 ♘b5 25 ♖c2 ♖c7 26 ♕d3 ♘xd4 27 ♕xd4 [27 ♘xd4 ♖xc5∓] 27 ... ♕e7 28 ♗e3 ♗a6 29 ♖dc1 ♗xe2 30 ♖xe2 ♖f8 31 ♖ec2 ♖fc8 32 g3 ♖c6 33 ♔h1 a4 34 ♕xb4 axb3 35 ♖b2 [◻ 35 ♕xb3 ♗xc5 36 ♕b5] 35 ... ♗xc5 36 ♗xc5 ♖xc5 37 ♖xc5 ♕xc5 38 ♕xc5 ♖xc5= 39 ♖xb3 h5 40 ♔g2 ♖c2+ 41 ♔h3 ♔f7 42 ♖b7+ ♔f8 43 ♔h4! ♖xh2+ 44 ♔g5 ♖g2 [◻ 44 ... d4] 45 ♔f6!

45 ... ♔e8 46 ♔xe6 ♔d8 47 ♖b3 d4 48 ♔d6 ♔c8 49 e6 ♖e2 50 e7 ♖e1 51 ♖b5 **1-0** L/N6123-1842

**184̂2̂-★BS-5**
**Brown, J.–Staunton, H.**

〈♙f7〉1 e4 ... 2 d4 e6 3 ♗d3 c5 4 e5 g6 5 c3 ♘c6 6 f4 ♘h6 7 ♘f3 ♗e7 8 0-0 0-0 9 ♘a3 a6 10 ♘c4 b5 11 ♘e3 d5 12 exd6 ♗xd6 13 ♕c2 cxd4 14 ♗xg6 dxe3 15 ♗xh7+ ♔h8 16 ♗xe3 ♗xf4 17 ♗xf4 ♖xf4 18 ♗e4 ♗b7 19 ♗xc6 ♗xc6 20 ♘e5 ♗e4 21 ♕e2 ♕g5 22 ♖xf4 ♕xf4 23 ♖e1 ♕xe5 24 ♕xe4 ♕xe4 25 ♖xe4 ♖e8 26 g4 ♔g7 27 ♔g2 e5 28 ♔f3 ♘f7 29 h4 ♔f6 30 ♖e2 ♘d6 31 b3 ♖c8 32 ♖c2 a5 33 ♔e3 a4 34 ♖f2+ ♔g6 35 ♖c2 a3 36 ♔f3 ♖f8+ 37 ♔e3 ♖f4 38 ♖d2 ♘f7 39 ♖g2 ♘h6 40 g5 ♘f5+ 41 ♔d3 ♘xh4 42 ♖e2 ♔f5 43 c4 ♖f3+ 44 ♔d2 b4 45 ♖e3 ♖f2+ 46 ♖e2 ♖f4 47 c5 ♘f3+ 48 ♔d1 ♖d4+ 49 ♔c1 ♖d5 50 c6 ♘d4 51 ♖g2 ♖c5+ 52 ♔d2 ♖xc6 **0-1** L/N6123-1842

**184̂2̂-★BS-6**
**Brown, J.=Staunton, H.**
London [Staunton]

〈♙f7〉1 e4 ... 2 d4 d6 3 f4 c5 4 d5 [4 dxc5 ♕a5+ △ 5 ... ♕xc5] 4 ... g6 5 c4 ♗g7 6 ♘f3 ♗g4 7 h3 ♗xf3 8 ♕xf3 ♘d7 9 ♘c3 ♘gf6 10 ♗d3 0-0 11 ♗d2 ♘h5 12 ♕g4 ♔h8 13 ♖f1 a6 14 h4 ♗d4 15 ♕h3 ♘df6 16 g4 ♕d7 17 f5 ♘g7 18 h5 gxh5 19 gxh5 ♘gxh5 20 ♗e2 ♘g7 21 ♖h1 ♖f7 22 0-0-0 ♖b8 23 ♗g5 ♘ge8 24 ♗h5 ♖g7 25 ♗g6 b5 26 ♗h6 ♖g8 27 ♗f8! ♖xg6 28 fxg6 ♕xh3 29 ♖xh3 bxc4 30 ♗xe7 ♔g7 31 gxh7 ♘xh7 32 ♖d2 ♘hf6 33 ♗xf6+ ♘xf6 34 ♖e2 ♔f7 35 ♖h4 ♖g8 36 ♔c2 ♘g4 37 ♘d1 ♘e5 38 ♖h7+ ♔f6 39 ♖a7 ♘d3 40 a3 ♖b8 41 ♖xa6 ♔e5 42 ♖a7 ♗xb2 43 ♘e3 ♘f4 44 ♘xc4+ ♔d4 45 ♘xb2 [◻ 45 ♖f2] 45 ... ♘xe2 46 ♖d7 ♔xe4 47 ♖xd6 ♘d4+ 48 ♔c1 ♘e2+ 49 ♔c2 ♘f4 50 ♘a4 ♔d4 51 ♖d7 ♖h8∓ 52 d6 ♖h2+ 53 ♔b3 ♘d5 54 ♘b2 c4+ 55 ♘xc4! ♖h3+ 56 ♔a4 ♔xc4 57 ♖a7 ...⚲ ½-½ L/N6123-1842

**184̂2̂-★BS-7**
**Brown, J.=Staunton, H.**
London [Staunton]

〈♙f7〉1 e4 ... 2 d4 ♘c6 3 d5 ♘e5 4 f4 ♘f7 5 c4 d6 6 ♘c3 g6 7 ♗d3 ♗g7 8 ♘f3 ♗g4 9 h3 ♗xf3 10 ♕xf3 ♘f6 11 ♗d2 0-0 12 ♘e2 ♘d7 13 ♗c3 ♗xc3+ 14 bxc3 ♘c5 15 ♕e3 e6 16 h4 ♕e7 17 ♔d2 ♖ae8 18 ♘g3 c6 19 ♖ae1 exd5 20 cxd5 cxd5 21 exd5 ♕d7 22 ♕d4 ♕g4 23 ♖e3 ♖xe3 24 ♕xe3 ♘h6 25 ♖f1 [◻ 25 h5] 25 ... ♘xd3 26 ♔xd3 ♘f5 27 ♕e6+ ♔g7 28 ♖f3 ♖f6 29 ♘xf5+ ♖xf5 30 ♕e2 ♖xd5+ 31 ♔c2 ♕f5+ 32 ♔c1 ♖b5 33 ♕e7+ ♕f7 34 ♕xd6 ♖d5 35 ♕b4 a5 36 ♕e4 ♕d7 37 ♕e2 ♕a4 38 c4 ♕c6 39 ♖e3 ♖d4 40 ♖e7+ ♔h6 41 ♔b1 ♕c5 [◻ 41 ... ♕xc4] 42 ♖xb7 ♖xc4 43 ♕d2 [△ 44 f5+] 43 ... ♖d4 44 ♕c1 ♕f5+ 45 ♔a1 ♕xf4 46 ♕xf4+ ♖xf4 47 g3 ♖g4 48 ♖b3 a4 49 ♖d3 ♔h5 50 ♔b2 h6 51 ♔c2 ♖c4+ 52 ♔d2 ♔g4 53 ♖a3 ♔h3 54 ♔e2 ♔g2 55 ♔d3 ♖g4 56 ♔e2 h5 57 ♔e1 ♖xg3 58 ♖xa4 ♖g4 59 ♖a6 ♔g3 60 a4 ♔xh4 61 a5 g5 62 ♖a8 ♔g3 63 a6 h4 64 a7 ♖a4 65 ♖g8 ♖a1+ 66 ♔e2 ...⚲ ½-½ L/N6123-1842

**184̂2̂-★CS-1**
**Cochrane, J.–Staunton, H.**
[Staunton]

1 e4 e5 2 ♘f3 ♘c6 3 d4 ♘xd4 4 ♘xd4 exd4 5 ♕xd4 ♘e7 6 ♕d1 [◻ 6 ♗c4] 6 ... ♘g6 7 ♗d3 ♗c5 8 0-0 0-0 9 ♘c3 d6 10 ♔h1 ♕h4 11 ♕f3 c6 12 ♕g3 f5 13 ♕xh4 ♘xh4 14 f3 f4 15 ♘e2 g5 16 ♗d2 ♗d7 17 ♗c4+ ♔g7 18 g3?! fxg3 19 hxg3 ♘xf3 20 ♗c3+ ♘e5 21 ♖xf8 ♖xf8 22 ♔g2 h5 23 ♖d1 [23 ♖f1 ♗h3+] 23 ... ♗g4 24 b4 ♗xb4 [24 ... ♖f2+ 25 ♔g1 ♖xe2+ 26 bxc5] 25 ♗xe5+ dxe5 26 ♖b1 ♗c5 27 ♖xb7+ ♔g6 **0-1** M954-1864

**184̂2̂-★CS-2**
**Cochrane, J.+Staunton, H.**
London [Staunton]

1 e4 e5 2 ♘f3 ♘c6 3 d4 ♘xd4 4 ♘xe5 ♘e6 5 ♗c4 c6 [△ 6 ♗xe6 ♕a5+ 7

~ ♕xe5] 6 0-0 ♘f6 7 ♘c3 [7 ♘xf7 ♔xf7 8 ♗xe6+ ♔xe6 9 e5 ♘d5 10 c4 ♘b6 11 ♔h1 h5 12 f4] 7 ... ♗b4 8 f4 ♕a5 9 ♘xf7 ♔xf7 10 f5 ♕c5+ 11 ♔h1 ♕xc4 12 fxe6+ ♕xe6 13 ♕h5+ g6 14 ♕h4 ♗xc3 15 bxc3 ♖f8 16 ♗h6 ...? **1-0** M954-1864

### 1842-★HJ-1
**H?, von+Jaenisch, C.F.?**

Berlin

1 e4 e5 2 f4 ♗c5 3 ♘f3 d6 4 c3 ♕e7 5 d4 ♗b6 6 ♗d3 ♗g4 7 ♗e3 ♘f6 8 h3 exf4 9 ♗xf4 ♘xe4 10 0-0 ♗f5 11 ♖e1 d5 12 ♘bd2 0-0 13 ♕c2 ♖e8 14 ♘g5 ♕f6 15 ♗xe4 ♗xe4 16 ♘dxe4 dxe4 17 ♖xe4 ♖xe4 18 ♕xe4 ♘c6 19 ♕xh7+ ♔f8 20 ♖e1 g6 21 ♖f1 ♔e7 22 ♘xf7 ♔e6 23 ♘g5+ ♔d5 24 ♕d7+ ♔c4 25 b3+ ♔b5 26 ♕d5+ ♔a6 **1-0** L/N6123-1843

### 1842-★PS-1
**Staunton, H.+Popert, H.W.**

London [Staunton]

1 e4 e5 2 ♘f3 ♘c6 3 d4 exd4 4 ♗c4 ♗b4+ 5 c3 dxc3 6 0-0 c2 7 ♕xc2 d6 8 ♘g5 ♘h6 9 f4 0-0 10 h3 ♗c5+ 11 ♔h1 ♘d4 12 ♕d3 c6 13 b4 ♗b6 14 ♘c3 ♔h8 15 g4 d5 16 exd5 f5 17 ♗e3 ♕f6 18 ♘a4 cxd5 19 ♗xd5 ♘c6 20 ♘xb6 axb6 21 ♗xc6 ♕xc6+ 22 ♔h2 ♗e6 23 ♗d4 ♕d5 24 ♖fc1 ♖xa2+ 25 ♖xa2 ♕xa2+ 26 ♖c2 ♕d5 27 ♖c7 ♘f7 28 ♘xf7+ ♗xf7 29 ♗xg7+ ♔g8 [29 ... ♔xg7? 30 ♕xd5+-] 30 ♕xd5 ♗xd5 31 ♗xf8 **1-0** M954-1864

## GREVILLE✕STAUNTON

London

[1843-✕GS]

| | | | | | | |
|---|---|---|---|---|---|---|
| B. Greville | 0 | 1 | 0 | 0 | 0 | 1 |
| H. Staunton | 1 | 0 | 1 | 1 | 1 | 4 |

### 1843-✕GS-1 vii 43
**Greville, B.–Staunton, H.**

[Staunton]

⟨△f7⟩1 e4 ... 2 d4 e6 3 ♗d3 c5 4 d5 d6 5 c4 g6 6 h4 ♗g7 7 h5 ♘e7 8 ♘c3 e5 9 ♗g5 ♘a6 10 h6 ♗f8 11 ♘h3 [△ 12 ♗f6 ♖g8 13 ♘g5] 11 ... ♖g8 12 ♕d2 ♘b4 13 ♗b1 ♕a5 14 ♘b5 ♕b6 15 a3 ♘a6 16 a4 ♘b4 17 a5 ♕d8 18 ♗f6 ♗xh3 19 ♖xh3 ♕d7 20 ♗g5 ♘c8 21 ♖g3 ♗e7 22 ♗c2 ♗xg5 23 ♖xg5 ♘xc2+ 24 ♕xc2 a6 25 ♘c3 b5 26 axb6 ♘xb6 27 b3 ♖f8 28 ♖g3 ♖f4 29 ♖h3 ♕g4 30 f3 ♕g5 31 ♕d2 ♕e7 32 g4 ♕b7 33 ♕a2 ♔e7 34 ♔e2 ♘d7 35 ♕c2 ♖b8 36 ♖b1 ♖bf8 37 ♔e3 ♕c8 38 ♘e2 ♖4f7 39 g5 ♔e8 [△ 40 ... ♘f6] 40 ♖g3 ♖f4 41 ♖h1 ♘b6 42 ♕c3 ♕b7 43 ♔d2 ♖4f7 44 ♖b1 ♘a4 45 ♕a5 ♘b6 46 ♕c3 ♘a4 47 ♕a5 ♘b6 48 ♕c3 ♘d7 49 ♔c2 ♔e7 50 ♖f1 ♖b8 51 f4 exf4 52 ♖xf4 ♖xf4 53 ♘xf4 ♖f8 54 ♘e6 [54 ♘xg6+? hxg6 55 ♕g7+ ♖f7 56 ♕xg6 ♘f8 57 ♕h5 ♖f2+ 58 ♔~ ♕b4-+] 54 ... ♖f2+ 55 ♔d1 ♘e5 56 ♘xc5 ♕b6 57 ♘d3 ♘xd3 58 ♕xd3 [◻ 58 ♖xd3] 58 ... ♕a5 59 ♕c3 ♕a2-+ ...? **0-1** L/N6123-1844

### 1843-✕GS-2 vii 43
**Greville, B.+Staunton, H.**

[Staunton]

⟨△f7⟩1 e4 ... 2 d4 e6 3 ♗d3 c5 4 d5 d6 5 c4 g6 6 h4 ♗g7 7 f4 ♘h6 8 ♕f3 exd5 9 cxd5 ♗g4 10 ♕g3 ♘d7 11 ♘c3 0-0 12 f5 ♘e5 13 fxg6 hxg6 14 ♘ge2 ♕b6 15 ♖b1 ♗f3 16 ♗c2 [16 gxf3?] 16 ... ♗g4 17 ♗f4 ♖ae8 18 0-0 ♕a6 19 ♕e3 ♘f5 20 exf5 ♘f3+ 21 gxf3 ♖xe3 22 ♗xe3 ♗h3? [22 ... ♗xf5] 23 ♖f2 ♗xf5 24 ♗xf5 ♖xf5 25 ♘f4 ♗d4 26 ♘g2 [26 ♗xd4?? cxd4 27 ♘ce2 d3 28 ♘xg6 dxe2 29 ♘e7+ ♔h7 30 ♘xf5 ♕d3] 26 ... ♔f7 27 ♖d1 ♕c4 28 ♗xd4 cxd4 29 ♘e2 d3 30 ♘c3 g5 31 hxg5 ♖xg5 32 ♔f1 ♕d4 33 ♘e1 ♖e5 34 ♘xd3 ♖e3 35 ♘c1 ♕h8 36 ♘1e2 ♕h3+ 37 ♔g1 ♖e8 38 ♖g2 ♔e7 39 ♖g3 ♕h6 40 f4 ♖h8 41 ♔f2 ♕h2+ 42 ♔e3 ♔d8 43 ♖dg1 ♖e8+ 44 ♔d2 ♕h8 45 ♖g7 ♔c8 46 a4 [46 ♘b5? ♖xe2+ 47 ♔xe2 ♕e8+] 46 ... a6 47 ♔d3 ♔b8 48 ♘e4 ♕h3+ 49 ♖1g3 ♕f5 50 ♘2c3 ♕xf4 51 ♖g8 ♕f1+ 52 ♔d2 ♖xg8 53 ♖xg8+ ♔a7 54 ♔c2 b5 55 axb5 axb5 **1-0** L/N6123-1844

### 1843-★GS-3 vii 43
**Greville, B.–Staunton, H.**

[Staunton]

⟨△f7⟩1 e4 ... 2 d4 e6 3 ♗d3 c5 4 d5 d6 5 c4 g6! [5 ... e5; 5 ... ♘f6] 6 h4 ♗g7 7 h5 e5 8 ♘c3 ♘d7 9 ♘b5 ♘df6 10 hxg6 hxg6 11 ♖xh8 ♗xh8 12 ♕a4 ♗d7 13 ♕b3 [13 ♘xd6+?? ♔e7] 13 ... ♕b6 14 a4 a5 15 ♘f3 ♘e7 16 ♗c2 ♘h5 17 ♕c3 ♗f6 18 ♗g5 ♘g8 19 ♗xf6 ♘gxf6 20 g3 ♔e7 21 ♕e3 ♖g8 22 ♕g5 ♗xb5 23 axb5 ♕d8 24 ♕d2 b6 25 0-0-0 ♕f8 26 ♕g5 ♔d7 27 ♖d2 ♔c7 28 ♕h4 [△ 29 ♘g5] 28 ... ♖h8 29 ♕g5 ♕f7 30 b3 ♘h7 31 ♕e3 ♘5f6 32 ♘g5 ♘xg5 33 ♕xg5 ♖h1+ 34 ♔b2 ♖h2 35 f3 ♘h7 36 ♕e3 ♖xd2 37 ♕xd2 ♕xf3 38 ♕h6 ♕f7 39 g4 ♘f8 40 ♕h8 ♔d7 41 ♔b1 g5 42 ♔b2 ♔e7 43 ♕h6 ♕g6 44 ♕h8 ♕f6 45 ♕h5 ♕f4 46 ♕h6 ♕xg4!? 47 ♕g7+ ♔e8 48 ♕c7 ♕d7 49 ♕xb6 ♕d8 50 ♕xd8+??-+ [50 ♕c6+=∞] 50 ... ♔xd8 51 ♗d1 ♘d7 52 ♗g4 ♘f6 53 ♗f3 g4 54 ♗e2 g3 55 ♗f3 ♘h5 56 ♔c3 ♘f4 ...? **0-1** L/N6123-1844

### 1843-✕GS-4 vii 43
**Greville, B.–Staunton, H.**

[Staunton]

⟨△f7⟩1 e4 ... 2 d4 ♘c6 3 e5 d5 4 ♗d3 ♗e6 5 ♘f3 ♗g4 6 h3 ♗xf3 7 ♕xf3 g6 [7 ... ♘xd4?] 8 ♕g4 ♕d7 9 e6 ♕d6 10 c3 ♘f6 11 ♕e2 ♘d8 12 0-0 ♘xe6 13 ♘a3 a6 14 ♗e3 [△ 15 c4] 14 ... b5 15 ♘c2 ♖b8 16 b4 ♗g7 17 a4 c6 18 ♖fe1 0-0 19 ♗d2 ♘f4 20 ♗xf4 ♕xf4 21 ♕e6+ ♔h8 22 ♕xc6 ♖bc8 23 ♕xa6 ♖xc3 24 ♕xb5 ♘g4 25 hxg4 ♕xf2+ 26 ♔h1 ♖xc2 27 ♕xd5 [27 ♗xc2? ♕h4+ 28 ♔g1 ♗xd4+-+] 27 ... ♖d2! [27 ... ♗xd4 28 ♕xd4+ ♕xd4 29 ♗xc2-+] 28 ♕e4 ♗xd4 29 g5 ♗xa1! [29 ... ♖xd3 30 ♕xd3 ♖f4 31 g3 ♖f3 32 ♕e4] 30 ♖xa1 ♕g3 31 ♖f1 ♖d8 ... 33 **0-1** L/N6123-1844

### 1843-✕GS-5 vii 43
**Greville, B.–Staunton, H.**

[Staunton]

⟨△f7⟩1 e4 ... 2 d4 e6 3 ♗d3 c5 4 dxc5 ♕a5+ 5 ♘c3 ♗xc5 6 ♘h3 d6 7 0-0 ♗d7 8 a3 ♕c7 9 ♔h1 a6 10 f4 ♘e7 11 f5 exf5 12 exf5 ♘bc6 13 ♘g5 ♘e5 [△ 14 ... 0-0-0] 14 ♕h5+ g6 15 fxg6 0-0-0 16 g7 ♖hg8 17 ♕xh7 ♘g4 18 h3 ♘f2+ 19 ♔h2 d5+ 20 g3 ♗d4 21 ♕h4 ♕b6 22 ♘f3 ♗xc3 23 bxc3 ♖xg7 24 ♗g5 ♖e8 25 ♗f6 [△ 26 ♗d4, 26 ♗xg7] 25 ... ♘xd3 26 ♗xg7 ♘f5 27 ♗d4 ♕b2!-+ 28 ♕g5 ♕xc2+ 29 ♕d2 [29 ♔~ ♖e2-+] 29 ... ♖e2+ 30 ♖f2 ♘xf2 31 ♕xc2 ♖xc2 ...? **0-1** L/N6123-1844

## SAINT-AMANT✕STAUNTON [1843-✕SS1]

| | | | | | | | |
|---|---|---|---|---|---|---|---|
| P.C.F. de Saint-Amant | 0 | ½ | 1 | 0 | 1 | 1 | 3½ |
| H. Staunton | 1 | ½ | 0 | 1 | 0 | 0 | 2½ |

### 1843-✕SS1-1 28 iv 43
**Saint-Amant, P.C.F.de–Staunton, H.**

[Saint-Amant & Staunton]

1 e4 c5 2 c4 e6 3 ♘c3 ♘e7 4 d3 ♘bc6 5 ♗e3 ♘g6 6 f4 d6 7 ♘f3 ♗e7 8 a3 ♗f6 9 ♗e2 0-0 10 0-0 ♗d4! 11 ♕d2 ♘xf4 12 ♘xd4 cxd4 [◻ 12 ... ♘h3+! Staunton] 13 ♗xf4 e5! 14 ♘d5 exf4 15 ♕xf4 ♗e6 16 ♕g3 ♗xd5 17 cxd5 ♘e5 18 ♖f2 ♖c8 19 ♗g4 ♖c5! 20 ♖af1 [20 b4? ♖c3∓ Staunton] 20 ... ♕g5 21 h3 ♖c1 [21 ... h5? 22 ♖f5! △ 23 ♖xh5 Staunton] 22 ♔h2 ♖xf1 23 ♖xf1 ♕d2 24 ♖f2 ♕e1 [24 ... ♕xd3? 25 ♕xd3 ♘xd3 26 ♖d2 Staunton] 25 ♖c2 ♕b1 26 ♖d2 g6 27 ♕f2 h5 28 ♗d1 ♕c1 29 g4? hxg4 30

hxg4 [□ 30 ♗xg4 St Amant] 30 ... ♕xd1 31 ♖xd1 ♘xg4+ 32 ♔g3 ♘xf2 33 ♔xf2 ♖c8! 34 ♖d2 ♔g7 35 ♔f3 ♖c1 36 ♖h2 ♔f6 37 ♖h8 ♖d1 38 ♔e2 ♖b1 39 ♔f3 ♖xb2 40 ♖e8 ♖b6 41 e5+! dxe5 42 ♔e4 ♖d6 43 ♖xe5 ♖d7 44 ♔xd4 g5 [□ 44 ... ♖e7 Staunton] 45 ♖e1 g4 46 ♔c5 ♔g5 47 d6 f5 48 ♖e7 ♖d8 49 ♔d5 ♔f4 50 d7 g3 51 ♖g7 ♔f3 52 ♔e5 g2 53 ♔e6 f4 54 d4 ♔f2 55 d5 g1♕ 56 ♖xg1 ♔xg1 57 ♔e7 ♖xd7+ 58 ♔xd7 f3 59 ♔c7 f2 60 d6 f1♕ 61 d7 ♕d3 62 d8♕ ♕xd8+ 63 ♔xd8 b5 64 ♔c7 a5 65 ♔b6 b4 66 a4 b3 67 ♔xa5 b2 68 ♔a6 b1♕ 69 a5 ♕b4 **0-1**

L/N6013,L/N6123

### 1843-⚔SS1-2 — 30 iv 43
**Staunton, H.= Saint-Amant, P.C.F. de**

[Saint-Amant & Staunton]

1 e4 e5 2 ♗c4 ♘f6 3 d4 ♕e7 4 ♘c3 exd4 5 ♕xd4 ♘c6 6 ♕e3 ♘e5 7 ♗b3 c6 8 h3 d6 9 ♘ge2 h6 10 f4 ♘g6 11 0-0 ♗e6!? 12 f5 ♗xb3 13 axb3 ♘ge5 14 ♖xa7 ♖b8 15 ♗d2± ♘ed7 16 ♖fa1 [□ 16 ♖aa1 St Amant] 16 ... ♕d8 17 ♘a4 ♗e7 18 ♘d4 0-0 19 ♗a5 ♕c8 [19 ... ♕e8? 20 ♗c7 ♖~ 21 ♖xb7 St Amant] 20 ♘b6? ♘xb6 21 ♗xb6 c5 22 ♘f3 ♕c6 23 ♗a5 ♘xe4 24 b4 d5 [24 + cxb4? St Amant] 25 c3 ♖fe8 [△ 26 ... b6 Staunton] 26 b5 ♕d6 [□ 26 ... ♕xb5 St Amant] 27 c4 ♗f6 28 ♕d3 b6 29 ♗e1 d4 30 ♘d2! ♘xd2 31 ♗xd2 ♗d8? [△ 32 ... ♗c7; □ 31 ... ♗g5 St Amant] 32 ♖f1 ♗g5 33 ♗xg5 hxg5 34 f6 g6 35 ♕f3 d3 36 ♕g4 ♕e5 37 ♖xf7! ♕e3+ [37 ... ♔xf7 38 ♕d7+ ♖e7 39 fxe7+ ♔g8 40 ♕d8+- Staunton] 38 ♔h1 ♕e2 39 ♖g7+ ♔f8 40 ♖f7+ ♔xf7 41 ♕d7+ ♖e7 42 ♕xe7+ [42 fxe7+?? ♕xf1+ Staunton] 42 ... ♕xe7 43 fxe7+ ♔xe7 44 ♔g1 ♖d8! 45 ♖d1 ♖d4 46 b3 d2 47 ♔f2 ♖d3 48 ♔e2 ♖xb3 49 ♖xd2 [49 ♔xd2 ♖b2+ △ 50 ... ♖xg2 St Amant] 49 ... ♖c3 50 ♖d5 ♖xc4 51 ♖xg5 ♔f6 52 ♖d5 ♔e6 53 ♖g5 ♔f7 54 ♖d5 ♖b4 55 ♖d7+ ♔e6 56 ♖c7 ♔f5 [56 ... ♖xb5 St Amant] 57 ♖f7+ ♔g5 58 ♔d3 ♖xb5 59 ♔c4 ♖b4+ 60 ♔d5 ♖b2 61 g4 ♖b4 62 ♖c7 ♖b3 63 ♖h7 ♖b4 64 ♖c7 c4 65 ♔d4 b5 66 ♖c5+ ♔h4 67 ♖c6 ♔g5 [□ 67 ... c3+! △ 68 ... ♖c4-+; 67 ... c3+! 68 ♔xc3 ♖c4+ 68 ♖xc4 bxc4 69 ♔xc4 ♔xh3-+ St Amant] 68 ♖c5+ ♔h6 69 h4 ♖b3 70 h5 ♖g3 71 hxg6 ♖xg4+ 72 ♔c3 ♖g3+ 73 ♔d4 ♖d3+ 74 ♔e4 ♖b3 75 ♔f5 ♖b1 76 ♔f6 ♖f1+ 77 ♔e6 ♖b1 78 ♔f7 ♖f1+ 79 ♔e6 ♖e1+ 80 ♔f7 ♖f1+ 81 ♔e6 ♔xg6 82 ♖xb5 c3 83 ♖c5 ♖c1 84 ♔d5 c2 85 ♔c6!= ♔f6 86 ♖c4 ♔e5 87 ♔c5 ♔f5 88 ♖c3 ♔e4 89 ♔c4 ½-½

L/N6013,L/N6123

### 1843-⚔SS1-3 — 2 v 43
**Saint-Amant,P.C.F.de+ Staunton, H.**

[Saint-Amant & Staunton]

1 e4 e5 2 ♘f3 ♘c6 3 ♗c4 ♗c5 4 c3 ♘f6 5 b4 ♗b6 6 d3 d6 7 ♗g5 a6 [□ 7 ... ♘e7! Staunton] 8 h3 0-0 9 ♘bd2 ♗e6 10 0-0 ♔h8 11 ♕b3 ♗xc4 12 ♘xc4 ♗a7 13 ♘e3 [△ 14 ♘d5; 14 ♘f5 St Amant] 13 ... ♘e7 14 ♔h2 [14 ♗xf6!? St Amant] 14 ... c6 15 ♘h4 ♘eg8 16 g3 h6 17 ♗xf6 ♘xf6 18 ♖ae1 ♖c8 19 f4 exf4 20 gxf4 ♗xe3 21 ♖xe3 ♘g4+ [□ 21 ... ♘xe4 Staunton] 22 hxg4 ♕xh4+ 23 ♔g2 ♕xg4+ 24 ♖g3 ♕e2+? [□ 24 ... ♕e6 Staunton] 25 ♖f2 ♕h5 26 f5 b5 27 ♕b2 c5 28 ♖f1 ♕h4 29 f6 g6 30 ♕d2 ♔g8 31 ♕f2 [△ 32 ♖xg6+!+- Staunton] 31 ... ♕h5 32 ♖h1 ♕e5 33 ♖xh6 cxb4 34 ♖gh3 ♕g5+ 35 ♔h2 **1-0**

L/N6013,L/N6123

### 1843-⚔SS1-4 — 2 v 43
**Staunton, H.+ Saint-Amant, P.C.F. de**

[Saint-Amant & Staunton]

1 e4 e5 2 ♗c4 ♗c5 3 ♘f3 ♘c6 4 c3 ♕e7 5 d4 exd4 6 0-0 ♘e5 7 ♘xe5 ♕xe5 8 f4 dxc3+ 9 ♔h1 ♕d4 10 ♕b3 ♘h6 11 ♘xc3 0-0 12 h3 c6 13 f5 ♕f6? [□ 13 ... b5; 13 ... d5 St Amant] 14 e5! ♕h4 15 ♗xh6 ♕xh6 16 ♘e4 ♗d4? [□ 16 ... ♗e7 St Amant] 17 ♘d6 ♕h5 18 ♗xf7+ ♖xf7 19 g4! ♗xe5 20 ♖ae1 [20 gxh5 St Amant] 20 ... ♕xh3+ 21 ♕xh3 ♗xd6 22 ♖e8+ ♗f8+- 23 ♖fe1 d5 24 ♖d8 ♖d7 25 ♖ee8 ♖xd8 26 ♖xd8 b6 27 ♕e3 ♗b7 28 ♖xa8 ♗xa8 29 ♕e6+ ♔h8 30 ♕f7 **1-0**

L/N6013,L/N6123

### 1843-⚔SS1-5 — 4 v 43
**Saint-Amant,P.C.F.de+ Staunton, H.**

[Saint-Amant & Staunton]

1 e4 c5 2 c4 e6 3 ♘f3 ♘c6 4 ♘c3 ♘ge7 5 d3 ♘g6 6 ♗e2 ♗e7 7 ♗e3 d6 8 a3 ♗f6 9 ♘d2 0-0 10 0-0 ♘d4 11 ♖b1 a6 12 f4 b5 13 ♔h1 ♖b8 14 ♗h5 ♗d7 15 ♗xd4 ♗xd4 16 ♘e2 ♗e3 17 ♖f3 ♗xd2 18 ♕xd2 bxc4 19 dxc4± ♗c6 20 ♖e3 ♖b7 [□ 20 ... ♖b6 Staunton] 21 ♗f3 ♕c7? [□ 21 ... ♕b8 Staunton] 22 ♖d3 f5 23 exf5 [23 ♖xd6= St Amant] 23 ... ♗xf3 24 gxf3 exf5 25 ♖xd6 ♖b3 26 ♘c3 ♕b8 [△ 27 ... ♖xc3-+ Staunton] 27 ♘e2 ♖xa3 [27 ... ♖xf3? 28 ♕d5++- St Amant] 28 ♕d5+ ♔h8 29 ♖d7 ♖e3 30 ♘g1! ♕xf4 31 ♕xc5 ♖fe8 32 ♖bd1 ♘h4? [□ 32 ... ♖xf3! Staunton] 33 ♖1d4! ♕g5? [□ 33 ... ♕h6 St Amant] 34 ♖g4! ♕h6 35 ♖gxg7 ♖e1 [35 ... ♕xg7 36 ♖xg7 ♔xg7 37 ♕d4++- St Amant] 36 ♖xh7+ [36 ♕d4 St Amant] 36 ... ♕xh7 37 ♕d4+ ♔g8 38 ♖xh7 ♔xh7 [38 ... ♖xg1+! 39 ♕xg1! ♔xh7 St Amant] 39 ♕xh4+ ♔g6 40 ♔g2 ♖d1 41 ♘h3 ♖g8 42 ♘f4+ ♔f7+ 43 ♔h3 ♖dg1 44 ♕h7+ ♔f6 45 ♘h5+ ♔e5 46 ♘g3??

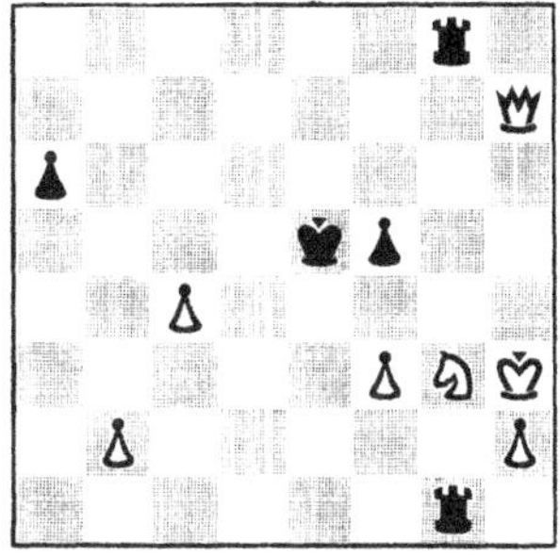

46 ... ♖8xg3+!-+ 47 ♔h4 [47 hxg3 ♖h1+-+ Staunton] 47 ... ♖3g7 48 ♕h8 ♔f6 49 f4 ♖g4+ 50 ♔h5 ♔f7 51 c5 ♖xf4 52 c6 ♖fg4 53 h4 ♖g8 54 ♕h7+ ♔f6 55 c7 ♖4g7 56 ♕h6+ ♔f7 57 b4 ♖c8 58 b5! axb5 59 ♕g6+!= ♔g8?? [59 ... ♖xg6◇ St Amant] 60 ♕e6+ **1-0**

L/N6013,L/N6123

### 1843-⚔SS1-6 — 5+6 v 43
**Staunton, H.- Saint-Amant, P.C.F. de**

[Saint-Amant & Staunton]

1 d4 f5 2 c4 c6 3 ♘c3 e6 4 ♗f4 d5 5 e3 ♘f6 6 ♘f3 ♗e7 [□ 6 ... ♗d6 St Amant] 7 ♗e2 0-0 8 0-0 ♗d6 9 ♘e5 dxc4 10 ♗xc4 ♘d5 11 ♗g3 ♗xe5 12 ♗xe5 ♘d7 13 ♗g3 [13 ♗d6 St Amant] 13 ... ♘7b6 14 ♗b3 h6 15 a3 ♕e7 16 ♖c1 ♗d7 17 ♘xd5 ♘xd5 18 ♗xd5 exd5 [18 ... cxd5? St Amant] 19 ♗e5 ♔h7 20 f4± a6? 21 ♖f3 ♖f7 22 ♖g3 ♖g8 23 ♕h5 ♕e6 [23 ... g6? 24 ♕xh6+!!+- St Amant] 24 ♖f1 ♗e8 [24 ... g6? 25 ♕xh6+!! +- Staunton] 25 ♕h4 ♕e7 26 ♖g5 ♕e6 27 ♖f3 ♖d7 28 ♕h3 ♖f7 29 ♖fg3 b6 30 ♕h5 [30 ♖g6 ♕xg6!=; 30 ♖g6 ♖f6 31 ♖xf6 gxf6 32 ♖xg8 ♕xg8 33 ♕xf5+ ♕g6 34 ♕xf6 ♕xf6 35 ♗xf6 ♗d7∓ St Amant] 30 ... ♖b7 31 ♕h4 ♖f7 32 ♕h3 [□ 32 ♖g6! ♖f6 (32 ... ♕xg6 33 ♖xg6 ♔xg6 34 ♕d8!+-) 33 ♖xf6 gxf6 34 ♖xg8 ♔xg8 (34 ... ♕xg8 35 ♕xf6+-) 35 ♕xh6 +- Staunton] 32 ... c5 33 dxc5 bxc5 34 ♖h5? d4 35 exd4 cxd4 36 ♖hg5 ♕c8∓ 37 ♖f3 ♗b5 38 ♔f2 ♕c2+ 39 ♔g3 ♗e2!-+ 40 ♗xd4 ♗xf3 41 gxf3 g6 42 ♔h4 ♕d2 [42 ... hxg5?? 43 ♔xg5# St Amant] 43 ♗e5 ♕d8 44 ♔g3 ♕d1 45 ♔h4 ♕e1+ 46 ♖g3 ♕d2 47 ♕g2 ♕d8+ 48 ♔h3 ♖d7 49 ♕c2 ♕b6! 50 a4 ♕e6 51 ♖g1 g5 52 ♖c1 g4+ 53 ♔g3! gxf3+ 54 ♔xf3 ♕g6 55

♔e3-+ ♕g4 56 ♖f1 ♖gd8 57 ♗c3 ♖d3+ 58 ♔f2 ♕f3+ **0-1**

## SAINT-AMANT ✕ STAUNTON
[1843 – ✕ SS2]

| | P. C. F. de Saint-Amant | H. Staunton |
|---|---|---|
| *1* | 0 | 1 |
| *2* | 0 | 1 |
| *3* | ½ | ½ |
| *4* | 1 | 0 |
| *5* | 0 | 1 |
| *6* | 0 | 1 |
| *7* | 0 | 1 |
| *8* | 0 | 1 |
| *9* | 1 | 0 |
| *10* | 0 | 1 |
| *11* | 1 | 0 |
| *12* | 0 | 1 |
| *13* | 1 | 0 |
| *14* | ½ | ½ |
| *15* | 0 | 1 |
| *16* | 1 | 0 |
| *17* | ½ | ½ |
| *18* | ½ | ½ |
| *19* | 1 | 0 |
| *20* | 1 | 0 |
| *21* | 0 | 1 |
| *Total* | 8 | 13 |

### 1843-✕SS2-1 14 xi 43
**Saint–Amant, P.C.F.de– Staunton, H.**

[Saint-Amant & Staunton]

1 e4 c5 2 f4 e6 3 ♘f3 ♘c6 4 c3 d5 5 e5 ♘h6 6 ♘a3 ♗e7 7 ♘c2 f5 8 d4 0-0 9 ♗e2 ♗d7 10 0-0 ♖c8∓ 11 ♔h1 [◻ 11 h3 Δ 12 ♔h2 St Amant] 11 ... cxd4 12 cxd4 ♘f7 [Δ 13 ... g5 Staunton] 13 ♖g1 [Δ 14 g4 Staunton] 13 ... ♔h8 14 g4!? fxg4 15 ♖xg4 ♘h6 16 ♖g3 ♗e8 17 ♗d3? [◻ 17 ♖h3 St Amant] 17 ... ♗h5 18 ♕g1 ♗h4 19 ♘xh4 [19 ♖h3 ♗g4-+ Staunton] 19 ... ♕xh4 20 ♘e1 ♘b4!-+ 21 ♗d2 [◻ 21 ♘g2; 21 ♗f1? Staunton] 21 ... ♘xd3 22 ♖xd3 ♗g6 23 ♕g3 ♕h5 24 ♖b3? ♕e2 25 ♕e3? ♕f1+ 26 ♕g1 ♗e4+ 27 ♖f3 ♗xf3+ 28 ♘xf3 ♕xf3+ 29 ♕g2 ♕xg2+ 30 ♔xg2 ♖c2 31 ♖d1 ♖xf4 32 ♔g3 ♖xd4 33 ♗xh6 ♖xd1 **0-1**

L/N6013-1843/4,L/N6123-1844

### 1843-✕SS2-2 16 xi 43
**Staunton, H.+ Saint–Amant, P.C.F. de**

[Saint-Amant & Staunton]

1 d4 c5 2 d5 f5 3 ♘f3 d6 4 ♘c3 ♘f6 5 ♗g5 e5 6 e4 [Δ 7 ♗b5+ St Amant] 6 ... a6? [◻ 6 ... fxe4 Δ 7 ... ♗e7= St Amant] 7 exf5 ♗xf5 8 ♘h4 ♗c8 9 ♗d3± g6 10 0-0 ♗e7 11 f4 c4!? 12 ♗xc4 exf4? [◻ 12 ... ♕b6+ Δ 13 ... ♘g4 Staunton] 13 ♖xf4 ♘bd7 14 ♕d4 ♘e5 15 ♖ae1! ♘fd7 [15 ... 0-0? 16 ♖xe5 dxe5 17 d6+ ♔g7 18 dxe7 ♕xd4 19 ♖xd4 exd4 20 ♗h6+- Staunton] 16 ♗xe7 ♕xe7 17 ♘e4 ♖f8 18 ♖xf8+ ♕xf8 [◻ 18 ... ♔xf8 St Amant] 19 ♘xd6+ ♔d8 20 ♖xe5 ♕xd6 21 ♖e3! ♔c7 22 ♗b3 [Δ 23 c4! Staunton] 22 ... a5 23 ♘f3 ♘f6 24 c4 b6 25 ♘e5 a4 26 ♗c2 a3 27 ♘f7 ♕c5 28 ♕f4+ ♔b7 29 b4!+- ♘h5 30 ♘d8+ ♔a6 31 bxc5 ♘xf4 32 ♖xa3# **1-0**

L/N6013-1843/4L/N6123-1844

### 1843-✕SS2-3 18 xi 43
**Saint–Amant, P.C.F.de= Staunton, H.**

[Saint-Amant & Staunton]

1 e4 c5 2 f4 e6 3 ♘f3 ♘c6 4 c3 d5 5 e5 ♗d7 6 ♘a3 ♘ge7 7 ♘c2 ♘g6 8 d4 ♖c8 9 a3 ♗e7 10 ♗d3 0-0 11 0-0 [11 ♗xg6 St Amant] 11 ... f5 [11 ... f6 St Amant] 12 h3 cxd4 13 ♘cxd4 ♘xd4 14 cxd4 ♕b6 15 g3 ♖c7 16 ♕e2 ♖fc8 17 ♗e3 ♗e8 18 g4 fxg4 19 hxg4 ♘f8 20 ♔g2 g6 21 ♖ac1 [◻ 21 ♖h1 Staunton] 21 ... ♖xc1 22 ♖xc1 ♖xc1 23 ♗xc1 ♕d8 24 ♔h3! [24 f5 exf5 25 gxf5 ♕c8∓ Staunton] 24 ... a6 25 ♕g2 ♗d7 26 ♗e3 [26 f5 exf5 Δ 27 ... ♕c8∓ Staunton] 26 ... ♔h8 27 ♘h2 [Δ 28 g5 Staunton] 27 ... ♕b6 28 ♕c2 ♔g7 29 b4? a5! 30 bxa5 ♕xa5 31 f5 exf5 32 gxf5 gxf5 33 ♗c1 [33 ♗xf5 ♕xa3∓ Staunton] 33 ... ♕e1? [◻ 33 ... ♗xa3 St Amant] 34 ♔g2! ♘g6 35 ♘f3 ♘h4+ 36 ♘xh4 ♕xh4 [◻ 36 ... ♗xh4 St Amant] 37 ♗xf5 ♗xf5 38 ♕xf5 ♕xd4 39 ♗g5!= [39 ♗h6+= Staunton] 39 ... ♕b2+ 40 ♔h1 ♕a1+ 41 ♔g2 ♕a2+ 42 ♔h1 ♕xa3 43 ♗f6+ [43 ♗xe7? St Amant] 43 ... ♗xf6 44 ♕xf6+ ♔g8 45 ♕g5+ ♔f7 46 ♕f6+ ♔e8 47 ♕e6+ ♕e7 48 ♕g8+ ♔d7 49 ♕xd5+ ♔c7 50 ♕c4+ ♔d8 51 ♕g8+ ♔c7 52 ♕c4+ ♔b6 53 ♕b3+ ♔c6 54 ♕c4+ ♕c5 55 ♕e6+ ♔c7 56 ♕f7+ ♔c6 57 ♕e6+ ♔c7 58 ♕f7+ **½-½**

L/N6013-1843/4,L/N6123-1844

### 1843-✕SS2-4 19 xi 43
**Staunton, H.+ Saint–Amant, P.C.F. de**

[Saint-Amant & Staunton]

1 d4 c5 2 d5 f5 3 ♘c3 d6 4 e4 fxe4 5 ♘xe4 e5 6 ♗g5 ♕a5+?! [6 ... ♗e7 7 ♗b5+ ♗d7 8 ♘xd6++- Staunton] 7 c3 ♗f5 8 ♘g3 ♗g6 9 ♗d3 ♗xd3 10 ♕xd3± g6 11 ♘1e2 ♗e7 12 ♘e4 ♕b6 13 0-0 ♘bd7 14 ♗xe7 ♘xe7 15 ♘g5 h6 16 ♘e6 ♘f8 17 ♘xf8 ♖xf8 18 b4 cxb4 19 cxb4 ♔f7!? 20 ♔h1 ♔g7 21 f4 ♖ad8± 22 ♖ad1 h5 23 ♕c3 ♕b5 24 ♕d2 ♖f5? [◻ 24 ... ♖f7; ◻ 24... ♘xd5 St Amant; ◻ 24 ... ♘xd5± Staunton] 25 ♘g3 ♖f6 26 fxe5 ♖xf1+ 27 ♖xf1 dxe5 28 ♕g5+- ♖d7 29 ♕xe5+ ♔h6 30 ♕h8+ ♔g5 31 ♘e4+ ♔h4 32 ♖f4# **1-0**

L/N6013-1843/4,L/N6123-1844

### 1843-✕SS2-5 21 xi 43
**Saint–Amant, P.C.F.de– Staunton, H.**

Saint-Amant & Staunton]

1 e4 c5 2 f4 e6 3 ♘f3 ♘c6 4 c3 d5 5 e5 ♕b6 6 ♗d3 ♗d7 7 ♗c2 ♖c8 8 0-0 ♘h6 9 h3 ♗e7 10 ♔h2 f5 11 a3 a5 12 a4!? ♘f7 13 d4 h6 [Δ 14 ... g5 St Amant] 14 ♖e1 [Δ 15 ♗xf5 Staunton] 14 ... g6 15 ♘a3 cxd4 16 ♘xd4 [16 cxd4? ♘b4! St Amant] 16 ... ♘xd4 17 cxd4 g5 18 ♘b5 ♗xb5 19 axb5 ♖c4?! 20 ♗d3! ♖c8 [20 ... ♖xd4? Staunton] 21 ♗e2 gxf4 22 ♖f1 [◻ 22 ♗xf4 St Amant] 22 ... ♘g5 23 ♗xf4 ♘e4 24 ♖c1 ♖xc1 25 ♕xc1 ♔d7 26 ♕e3 ♗g5 27 ♗d3 ♖g8 28 ♗xe4 dxe4 29 ♗xg5 hxg5 30 ♕b3! g4! 31 ♖d1 [◻ 31 ♖xf5 St Amant] 31 ... gxh3 32 ♕xh3 ♕d8 33 d5 ♔c8 34 ♕c3+ ♔b8 35 d6 f4 36 ♕c5 e3 37 ♕c2 ♕h4+ 38 ♔g1 [Δ 39 ♕c7++- Staunton] 38 ... ♖c8 39 ♕e2? [◻ 39 d7 ♖xc2 40 d8♕+ ♕xd8 41 ♖xd8+ Δ 42 ♖d1 St Amant] 39 ... ♖h8! **0-1**

L/N6013-1843/4,L/N6123-1844

### 1843-✕SS2-6 23 xi 43
**Staunton, H.+ Saint–Amant, P.C.F. de**

[Saint-Amant & Staunton]

1 c4 c5 2 ♘c3 f5 3 e4 d6 4 ♗d3!? e6 [◻ 4 ... ♘h6; 4 ... f4 St Amant] 5 exf5 [5 ♕e2 Staunton] 5 ... exf5 6 ♘h3 ♘f6 7 b3 g6 8 0-0 ♗e7 9 ♗b2 0-0 10 ♘f4 ♘c6 11 ♘cd5 ♘xd5 12 ♘xd5 ♗e6 13 ♘xe7+ ♕xe7 14 ♕e2 ♕f7= 15 ♖ae1 ♖ad8?? [◻ 15 ... ♖ae8 St Amant] 16 ♕xe6 ♕xe6 17 ♖xe6 ♘e5 18 ♗c2? [◻ 18 ♗xe5 St Amant] 18 ... ♔f7 19 ♖xe5 dxe5 20 ♗c3! [20 ♗xe5? St Amant] 20 ... ♖fe8 21 f3 h5 22 ♖e1 ♖e6 23 b4 b6 24 bxc5 bxc5 25 ♔f2 ♖de8 26 g3 ♖8e7 27 h3 ♖e8 28 d3 ♖8e7 29 a4 ♔e8 30 ♖b1 f4 31 a5 ♔f7 32 ♖b5 ♖c7 33 ♗a4 ♖ee7 34 gxf4 exf4 35 ♗d2 ♖e6 36 ♗xf4 ♖ce7 37 ♖b2 ♖a6 38 ♗d2 ♖d6 39 ♗g5 ♖ee6 40 ♖b7+ ♔g8 41 ♗d7!+- ♖xd7 42 ♖xd7 ♖a6 43 ♗d2 ♔f8 44 ♖d5 ♖c6 45 ♖xc5 ♖d6 46 ♗b4 ♖d8 47 ♖c8+ ♔e8 48

♖xd8+ ♔xd8 49 ♔e3 a6 50 d4 ♔d7 51 ♔e4 ♔c6 52 d5+ ♔d7 53 ♔d4 **1-0**

L/N6013-1843/4,L/N6123-1844

**1843-⚔SS2-7** 25 xi 43

**Saint-Amant, P.C.F.de– Staunton, H.**

[Saint-Amant & Staunton]

1 d4 e6 2 c4 d5 3 e3 c5 4 ♘c3 ♘f6 5 ♘f3 ♘c6 6 ♗d3 a6 7 0-0 ♗d6 8 a3 b6 [△ 9 ... ♗b7 Staunton] 9 ♖e1 0-0 10 h3 ♕c7 11 b3 ♘e7 12 ♗d2 ♗b7 13 cxd5 exd5 14 ♔h1?! ♖ae8 15 ♖a2 ♘e4 16 ♗xe4 dxe4 17 ♘g1 cxd4 18 exd4 ♘f5∓ 19 ♘ce2? e3 20 fxe3 ♖xe3 21 ♕c1 [21 ♗xe3? ♘xe3 −+; □ 21 ♖c2 St Amant] 21 ... ♕xc1 22 ♖xc1 ♖xb3−+ 23 ♖c3 ♖xc3 24 ♗xc3 ♘h4 25 ♘f3 [25 ♘c1? ♖c8 St Amant] 25 ... ♘xf3 26 gxf3 ♗xf3+ 27 ♔g1 ♖e8 28 ♔f2 [28 ♘c1? Staunton] 28 ... ♗xe2 29 ♖xe2 ♖xe2+ 30 ♔xe2 ♗xa3 31 ♔d3 f6 32 ♔e4 b5 33 ♔d5 b4 **0-1**

L/N6013-1843/4,L/N6123-1844

**1843-⚔SS2-8** 26 xi 43

**Staunton, H.+ Saint-Amant, P.C.F. de**

[Saint-Amant]

1 e4 c5 2 ♘f3 e6 3 d4 cxd4 4 ♘xd4 ♘c6 5 ♘f3∓ ♗c5 6 ♗d3 ♘ge7 7 ♘c3 a6 8 0-0 ♘g6 9 ♔h1 f6? [□ 9 ... 0-0 St Amant] 10 ♘e1 0-0 11 f4 ♘ce7 12 ♖f3 d6 13 ♖h3 f5 14 exf5 ♘xf5 [14 ... exf5? 15 ♗c4+ St Amant] 15 ♕h5 ♔f7 16 ♘f3 ♖h8? 17 g4 ♘fe7 18 f5 exf5 19 gxf5 ♔f8 20 fxg6 ♗xh3 21 ♕xh3 ♕c8 22 ♕h4 ♕e6 23 ♘g5 ♕e5 24 ♗f4 ♘f5 25 ♗xe5 ♘xh4 26 ♖f1+ ♔e8 27 ♗xg7 ♔d7 28 ♗xh8 ♖xh8 29 ♖f7+ ♔c6 30 ♗e4+ [□ 30 g7 St Amant] 30 ... d5 31 ♗xd5+ ♔d6 32 g7 ♖e8 33 ♖f1 ♗d4 34 g8♕ ♖xg8 35 ♗xg8+− h6 36 ♘ge4+ ♔e5 37 ♗h7 b5 38 ♘e2 ♗e3 39 ♘f6 ♔e6 40 ♘g4 ♗g5 41 ♘g3 ♔d5 42 ♗e4+ ♔c5 43 ♗d3 ♔d5 44 ♘e4 ♗e7 45 ♘xh6 b4 46 ♘f6+ ♔c6 47 ♘hg8 ♗d6 48 ♗xa6 ♔b6 49 ♗d3 b3 50 axb3 ♔a5 51 ♘d5 ♗a3 52 ♖a1 **1-0**

L/N6013-1843/4,L/N6123-1844

**1843-⚔SS2-9** 28 xi 43

**Saint-Amant, P.C.F.de+ Staunton, H.**

[Saint-Amant & Staunton]

1 d4 e6 2 c4 d5 3 ♘c3 ♘f6 4 ♘f3 c5 5 e3 ♘c6 6 a3 b6 7 ♗d3 ♗d6 8 cxd5 exd5 9 ♗b5 ♗b7 10 dxc5 ♗xc5 11 b4 [11 ♘e5?! St Amant] 11 ... ♗d6 12 ♗b2 [12 ♘d4 ♗e5! St Amant; 12 ♘xd5?? Staunton] 12 ... 0-0 13 ♘e2 ♕e7 14 0-0 ♖ad8 15 ♖c1 ♘e5 16 ♘ed4 ♘xf3+ 17 ♕xf3 ♕e5! 18 g3 ♘e4! 19 ♕e2 ♕g5 20 f4 ♕g6 21 ♖c2 ♗c8 [△ 22 ... ♗h3 Staunton] 22 f5 ♕h6 [△ 23 ... ♗xg3 Staunton] 23 ♗d3 ♖fe8 [△ 24 ... ♘xg3!→ Staunton] 24 ♗c1 ♗d7 [△ 25 ... ♗a4 Staunton] 25 ♕f3 ♗a4! 26 ♖g2 ♖c8 27 ♖e1 ♘g5 28 ♕xd5? ♘h3+ 29 ♔f1 [29 ♔h1 ♖xc1 Staunton] 29 ... ♗e5! 30 ♖ge2 ♗xd4 31 ♕xd4 [31 exd4 ♖xc1! (31 ... ♖xe2 32 ♗xh6?? ♖xf2#) Staunton] 31 ... ♖ed8 32 b5!?

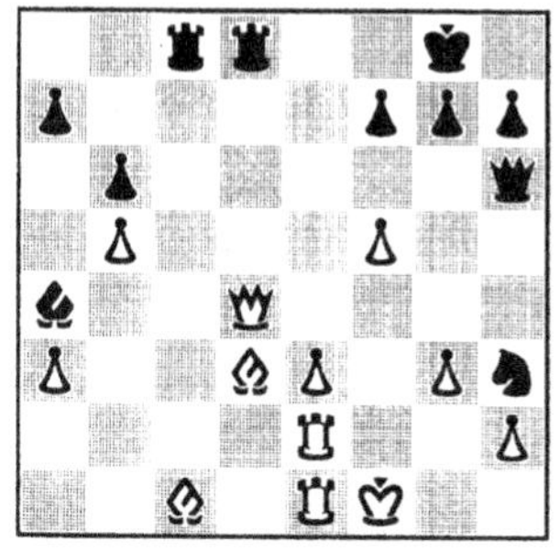

32 ... ♕h5? [□ 32 ... ♗b3; □ 32 ... ♗d1; □ 32 ... ♖xd4 △ 33 ... g5 Staunton; 32 ... Rxd4 33 exd4 g5! 34 fxg6 Rxc1 (34 ... Qxc1 35 gxh7+ Kg7 36 Rxc1 Rxc1+ 37 Kg2 Ng5 38 Re7=) 35 gxf7+ Kxf7! 36 Re7+ Kf6 37 Re6+ Kg5 38 Re5+ Kf6!= St Amant] 33 g4 ♖xd4 34 exd4 f6 35 gxh5 **1-0**

L/N6013-1844,L/N6123-1844

**1843-⚔SS2-10** 30 xi 43

**Staunton, H.+ Saint-Amant, P.C.F. de**

[Saint-Amant & Staunton]

1 e4 c5 2 ♘f3 e6 3 d4 cxd4 4 ♘xd4 ♘c6 5 ♘f3∓ d5 6 exd5 exd5 7 ♗e3 ♘f6 8 ♗e2 ♗e7 9 ♘bd2 ♗e6 10 ♘b3 0-0 11 0-0 ♕c7 12 ♘fd4 ♖ad8 13 f4 ♗c8! 14 c3 a6 15 h3 ♖fe8 16 ♗d3 ♗d6 17 ♕f3 ♘e4 [△ 18 ... f5 Staunton] 18 g4 ♖e7 19 ♗xe4 dxe4 20 ♕f2 f6 21 ♘e2 [△ 22 ♗b6 Staunton] 21 ... ♖de8 22 ♖ad1 f5 23 g5 ♖f7 24 ♔g2 ♗e6 25 ♘bd4 ♘xd4 [25 ... ♗xa2?!± Staunton] 26 ♘xd4 ♗c4 27 ♖h1 ♗d3 [27 ... ♗xa2?? St Amant] 28 h4 [△ 29 h5 Staunton] 28 ... ♖ff8 29 h5 ♕e7 30 ♘b3 ♖c8 31 ♖d2 ♖fe8 32 ♖hd1 ♖ed8 33 ♘c1 ♗c7 34 h6 g6 35 ♗d4 [□ 35 ♘xd3 △ 34 ♗d4 Staunton] 35 ... ♗b5? [□ 35 ... ♖xd4 36 ♕xd4 ♗xf4 37 ♖xd3 ♕xg5+ 38 ♔f1 ♕xh6 39 ♘e2 exd3 40 ♘xf4 ♕h1+ 41 ♔f2 ♕xd1 42 ♕d5+ ♔f8 43 ♕d6+ ♔e8 44 ♕e6+ ♔f8= St Amant] 36 ♗e3 [36 ♗f6?! Staunton] 36 ... ♖xd2 37 ♕xd2 ♖d8 38 ♕c2 ♖xd1 39 ♕xd1 ♕d7± 40 ♕b3+ ♕f7 41 ♕d1 ♕d7 42 ♕c2 ♕d5 [42 ... ♗d3 43 ♕b3+ △ 44 ♕xb7 Staunton] 43 ♔f2 ♔f7? [□ 43 ... ♗d3 St Amant] 44 b3 ♕c6? 45 c4 ♗b6 [□ 45 ... a5 St Amant] 46 ♕c3 ♗xe3+ 47 ♕xe3 ♗xc4 48 bxc4 ♕xc4 49 ♕b3 ♕xb3 50 axb3 ♔e6 51 ♔e3 ♔d5 52 ♘e2 b5 53 ♘d4 ♔c5 54 ♘xf5!+− a5 55 ♘d4 a4 56 bxa4 bxa4 57 f5 gxf5 58 g6 f4+ 59 ♔xe4 f3 60 ♘xf3 a3 61 gxh7 **1-0**

L/N6013-1844,L/N6123-1844

**1843-⚔SS2-11** 2 xii 43

**Saint-Amant, P.C.F.de+ Staunton, H.**

[Saint-Amant & Staunton]

1 d4 e6 2 c4 d5 3 e3 c5 4 ♘c3 ♘f6 5 ♘f3 ♘c6 6 a3 b6? 7 cxd5 exd5 8 ♗b5 ♗b7 [8 ... ♗d7± Staunton; 8 ... ♗d7 9 dxc5 bxc5 10 ♘xd5? ♘xd5 11 ♕xd5 ♕a5+ 12 ♗d2 ♕xb5 13 ♘e5 0-0-0 14 ♘xf7 ♗g4→ St Amant] 9 ♘e5 ♖c8 10 ♕a4 ♕c7 11 ♕xa7! ♗e7 12 ♗xc6+ ♗xc6 13 ♕xc7 ♖xc7 14 ♘xc6 ♖xc6 15 0-0! ♔d7! 16 ♖fd1 c4 17 f3! ♖d8 18 ♗d2 [□ 18 e4 △ 19 ♗g5 Staunton] 18 ... h6 19 ♘a2 g5! 20 ♗b4 ♖e6 21 ♗xe7 ♖xe7 22 ♔f2 g4 23 ♘c3 h5 24 ♖e1 ♖de8 25 ♖e2 h4= 26 ♖ae1 ♖g8 27 e4 g3+ 28 ♔g1 dxe4 29 ♘xe4 ♘xe4 30 fxe4 [30 ♖xe4 St Amant] 30 ... ♖g4! 31 hxg3 hxg3 32 ♖e3! b5 33 ♖1e2 ♖e8 34 ♔f1 ♔d6 35 ♔e1 ♖f4 36 ♔d2 f5 37 ♖xg3 ♖fxe4 38 ♖xe4 ♖xe4 39 ♔c3 ♔d5 40 ♖f3 f4 41 g3? [□ 41 g4!∓ Staunton; □ 41 ♖h3 ♖e3+ 42 ♔d2! St Amant] 41 ... ♖e3+ 42 ♖xe3 fxe3 43 ♔c2

43 ... ♔e4? [□ 43 ... ♔xd4 44 ♔d1 (44 g4 ♔e4 45 g5 ♔f5 46 g6 ♔xg6 ♔c2 47 ♔d1 ♔f5 48 ♔e2 ♔f4→) 44 ... ♔d3 45 g4 e2+ 46 ♔e1 ♔c2 47 g5 ♔xb2 48 g6 c3 49 g7 c2 50 g8♕ c1♕+ 51 ♔xe2 ♕c4+→ Staunton] 44 ♔d1 ♔d3 45 d5 e2+ 46 ♔e1 ♔c2 47 d6 ♔xb2 48 d7 c3 49 d8♕ c2 50 ♕d2 ♔b1 51 ♕b4+ ♔c1 52 ♕c3 ♔b1 53 ♕b3+ ♔c1 54 ♕a2! b4 55 ♕a1# **1-0**

L/N6013-1844,L/N6123-1844

**1843-⚔SS2-12** 5 xii 43

**Staunton, H.+ Saint-Amant, P.C.F. de**

[Saint-Amant & Staunton]

1 c4 c5 2 ♘c3 f5 [2 ... e6 Staunton] 3 e4! d6 4 ♗d3 e6 5 ♘h3 [5 ♕e2 Staunton] 5 ... ♘f6 6 exf5 exf5 7 0-0

♗e7 8 b3 ♘c6 9 ♗b2 0-0 10 ♘f4 ♘g4 [△ 11 ... ♘ge5 Staunton] 11 ♘fd5 ♗f6 12 ♘xf6+ ♘xf6 13 ♘e2 ♘g4 14 f4 b6 15 h3 ♘h6 16 ♖f3 ♕h4?! 17 ♖g3 g6 18 ♕e1 [△ 19 ♖xg6++- Staunton] 18 ... ♕e7 19 ♕f2 ♘b4 20 ♖e1 [◻ 20 ♘d4!! Staunton] 20 ... ♗b7 21 ♗b1 ♖ae8 22 ♖e3 ♕d8 23 ♘g3 ♔f7 24 ♕e2 ♖xe3 25 dxe3?! [◻ 25 ♕xe3= Staunton] 25 ... ♕h4 26 ♘f1 ♘g8 27b ♖d1 ♖d8 28 ♘d2 ♕g3 29 ♘f1 ♕h4 30 ♘h2 h6 31 ♘f3 ♕g3 32 ♘e1 ♖e8! 33 ♕f2 ♕xe3 34 a3 ♘c6 35 ♘f3 [△ 36 ♘e5+ Staunton] 35 ... ♕xf2+ 36 ♔xf2 ♖e6 37 g4 ♘ce7 38 ♘h4 ♗e4 39 ♗xe4 ♖xe4 40 ♖xd6 fxg4 41 hxg4 ♖xf4+ 42 ♔g3 g5 43 ♘f3 ♖e4 44 ♖xh6 ♖e3 [44 ... ♘xh6? 45 ♘xg5++- Staunton; ◻ 44 ... ♖xg4+! St Amant] 45 ♖h7+ ♔e8 46 ♗c1 ♖xb3 47 ♗xg5 ♖xa3± 48 ♔f4 a5 49 ♘e5 [△ 50 ♗xe7 ♘xe7 51 ♖h8++- Staunton] 49 ... ♖a1 50 ♗xe7 ♖f1+ 51 ♔e4 ♘xe7 52 ♖h8+ ♖f8 53 ♖h6 [53 ♖xf8+ ♔xf8 54 ♘d7+ △ 55 ♘xb6= Staunton] 53 ... ♘g8 [53 ... ♘c8?! St Amant] 54 ♖xb6 ♘f6+ 55 ♔e3 ♘d7? 56 ♖e6+ ♔d8 57 ♖d6 ♔e7 58 ♖xd7+ ♔e6 59 ♖d5 ♖f1 60 ♘d3 ♖g1 61 ♘xc5+ ♔f6 62 g5+ ♔g6 63 ♘e4 a4 64 ♖d6+ ♔f5 65 ♖f6+ ♔e5 66 ♖f8 ♖e1+ 67 ♔d3 ♖d1+ 68 ♔c2 ♖g1 69 ♘d2 ♔d6 70 ♖f5 ♔c6 71 ♘e4 ♖g4 72 ♔d3 ♔b6 73 ♖b5+ ♔a6 74 ♘c5+ ♔a7 75 ♘xa4 ♔a6 76 ♘c5+ ♔a7 77 ♘e4 ♖g1 78 ♔d4 ♖c1 79 g6 ♖d1+ 80 ♔e5 ♖g1 81 ♔f6 ♖f1+ 82 ♖f5 ♖d1 83 g7 ♖d8 84 ♔e7 ♖c8 85 ♖f7 ♔b6 86 c5+ ♔c7 87 ♔f6+ ♔c6 88 ♖f8 ♖c7 89 g8♕ **1-0**

L/N6013-1844, L/N6123-1844

## 1843-⚔SS2-13 — 6 xii 43

### Saint-Amant, P.C.F.de+ Staunton, H.

[Saint-Amant & Staunton]

1 d4 e6 2 c4 d5 3 e3 ♘f6 4 ♘c3 c5 5 ♘f3 ♘c6 6 a3 ♗e7 7 ♗d3 0-0 8 0-0= b6 9 b3 ♗b7 10 cxd5 exd5 11 ♗b2 cxd4 12 exd4 ♗d6 13 ♖e1 a6 14 ♖c1 ♖c8 15 ♖c2 ♖c7 16 ♖ce2 ♕c8 17 h3 ♘d8 18 ♕d2 b5 19 b4 ♘e6 20 ♗f5 ♘e4 [20 ... ♗f4 Staunton] 21 ♘xe4 dxe4 22 d5 [22 ♗xe4? ♗xe4 23 ♖xe4 ♖c2-+ Staunton] 22 ... exf3? [◻ 22 ... ♗f4!∓ Staunton; 22 ... ♗xd5? △ 23 ... ♘f4± St Amant] 23 ♖xe6! ♕d8 24 ♗f6!! gxf6 25 ♖xd6! ♔g7 26 ♖xd8 ♖xd8 27 ♗e4 fxg2 28 ♕f4 ♖c4 29 ♕g4+ ♔f8 30 ♕h5 ♔e7 31 d6+ ♔xd6 32 ♗xb7 ♔c7 33 ♗xa6 ♖c3 34 ♕xb5 **1-0**

L/N6013-1844, L/N6123-1844

## 1843-⚔SS2-14 — 7 xii 43

### Staunton, H.= Saint-Amant, P.C.F. de

[Saint-Amant & Staunton]

1 c4 c5 2 ♘c3 ♘c6 3 e3 d6 4 d4 cxd4?! 5 exd4 e6 [5 ... e5; 5 ... ♗f5 St Amant] 6 ♘f3 d5 7 a3 ♘f6 8 c5 ♗e7 9 b4 [◻ 9 ♗d3 Staunton] 9 ... ♘e4 10 ♘e2 a6 11 ♘g3 f5 12 ♗d3 ♗f6 13 ♘h5! 0-0 [13 ... ♘xd4? 14 ♘xf6+ ♕xf6 15 ♘xd4 ♘xf2 (15 ... ♘c3 16 ♕d2 ♕xd4 17 ♗b2+-) 16 ♗b5+ axb5 17 ♔xf2±; 13 ... ♗xd4 14 ♘xd4 ♘xf2 15 ♘xc6 ♕h4 16 g3 ♘xd3+ 17 ♕xd3 ♕xh5 18 ♘e5± Staunton] 14 ♘xf6+ ♕xf6 15 ♗b2 ♗d7 16 0-0 h6 17 ♖a2 ♔h7 18 ♘e1 ♕g5 19 ♗a1 ♗e8 20 ♖e2 [△ 21 f3 Staunton] 20 ... ♗f7 21 f4 [◻ 21 f3 St Amant] 21 ... ♕f6 22 ♖e3 ♖g8 23 ♖h3 ♗g6 24 ♘f3 ♖gf8 25 ♘e5 ♘xe5 26 dxe5 ♕e7 27 ♗d4 ♖f7 28 ♗e2 ♕e8 29 ♖ff3 ♖c7 30 ♖b3 ♕d7 31 ♖he3 ♕e7 32 ♖h3 ♕e8 33 ♕e1 ♕e7 34 ♖h4 ♕e8 35 h3 ♕e7 36 g4 ♖h8 37 ♖d3 ♕d8 38 ♖d1 ♕e7 39 ♔h2 ♖cc8 40 g5 ♔g8 41 gxh6 gxh6 42 ♖b1 ♔h7 43 ♖b2 ♖hg8 44 ♗d3 ♖g7 45 ♗xe4 fxe4 [◻ 45 ... dxe4! St Amant] 46 ♖g4 ♖cg8 47 ♖bg2 ♗h5 48 ♖xg7+ ♖xg7 49 ♖xg7+ ♕xg7 50 a4 ♗e8 51 a5 [51 f5 (△ 52 b5) 51 ... ♕g5∓ Staunton] 51 ... ♗b5 52 ♕h4 ♕f8 53 ♔g3 ♕g7+ 54 ♔f2 ♕f8 55 ♗e3 ♗c6 56 ♔e1 ♗a4 57 ♔f2 ♗b5 58 ♗d4 ♗c6 59 ♔g3 ♕g7+ 60 ♕g4 ♕xg4+ 61 hxg4 ♔g6 62 ♔f2 h5 **½-½**

L/N6103-1844, L/N6123-1844

## 1843-⚔SS2-15 — 9 xii 43

### Saint-Amant, P.C.F.de- Staunton, H.

[Saint-Amant & Staunton]

1 d4 d5 2 c4 e6 3 ♘c3 ♘f6 4 ♘f3 a6 5 c5 ♗e7 6 ♗g5!? 0-0 7 e3 b6 8 b4 ♗b7 9 ♗xf6 ♗xf6 10 ♗d3 a5 11 a3 ♘d7 [△ 12 ... bxc5 13 bxc5 ♘xc5 Staunton] 12 cxb6 [◻ 12 ♖c1!± St Amant] 12 ... cxb6 13 0-0 ♕e7 [13 ... e5 14 dxe5 ♘xe5 15 ♘xe5 ♗xe5 16 ♗xh7+! ♔xh7 17 ♕h5+ ♔g8 18 ♕xe5± Staunton] 14 ♕b3! axb4 15 axb4 ♖fc8 16 ♗b5? ♘f8 17 ♖fc1 ♘g6 18 ♗e2 ♕d8 19 ♘b5 ♗e7 20 ♘e1 ♗a6!∓ 21 f4 ♘h4 22 ♔f2 ♘f5 23 ♘f3 ♗xb5 24 ♖xa8 ♖xa8 25 ♗xb5 ♘d6 26 ♗d3 b5 27 ♘e5 ♘c4! 28 ♘c6 ♕d6 29 ♘xe7+

Staunton, H. ⚔ Saint-Amant, P.C.F. de

SB1.LCL

♕xe7 30 ♗xc4 dxc4! [30 ... bxc4 Staunton] 31 ♕b2 ♖a4 32 ♖b1 ♕a7 33 ♕c2 g6 34 h4 ♕e7 35 ♖h1 ♕xb4 36 ♕e4 ♕b2+ 37 ♔g3 ♖a2 38 ♖f1 b4 39 ♕b7 h5 40 ♔h3 c3 41 ♖g1 ♕f2 42 ♕b8+ ♔h7 43 ♕f8 ♕xe3+ 44 g3 ♖a7 45 ♖a1 ♕xd4 46 ♖xa7 ♕xa7 47 ♕xb4 ♕g1 48 ♕b7 ♔g7 49 ♕e4 ♕c5 50 ♕e1 c2 51 ♕a1+ ♔h7 52 ♕c1 ♕f5+ 53 ♔h2 ♕d3 54 f5 ♕e2+ 55 ♔h3 ♕d1 56 fxg6+ fxg6 **0-1**

L/N6013-1844,L/N6123-1844

**1843-✕SS2-16** 11 xii 43

**Staunton, H.– Saint–Amant, P.C.F. de**

[Saint-Amant & Staunton]

1 c4 c5 2 ♘c3 e5 3 e3 ♘c6 4 a3 f5 5 d3 ♘f6 6 ♘ge2 d6 7 ♘g3 ♗e7 8 ♗e2 0-0 9 0-0 h6 10 ♗f3 ♔h7 11 ♗d5± ♕e8 [11 ... ♘xd5 12 cxd5 ♘b8± Staunton] 12 ♖b1 [△ 13 b4 St Amant] 12 ... a5 13 ♘b5 ♕d8 14 b3 ♘xd5?! 15 cxd5 ♘a7 16 ♘c3! ♗d7 17 f4 ♗f6 18 ♘ce2 g6 19 e4 ♘b5 20 exf5 gxf5 21 ♘h5 ♕e8 22 ♘xf6+ ♖xf6 23 fxe5 ♕xe5∞ 24 a4 ♘d4 25 ♘f4 [△ 26 ♖e1 Staunton] 25 ... ♖ag8! 26 ♗d2 [26 ♔h1 Staunton] 26 ... ♖f7 27 ♖f2 ♖g4? 28 h3 ♖g3 29 ♕h5 ♕f6! 30 ♘e6? [□ 30 ♗xa5 Staunton] 30 ... ♗xe6 31 dxe6 ♕xe6! 32 ♗xh6 ♕g6 33 ♕xg6+ [33 ♕h4 ♖xg2+ 34 ♖xg2 (34 ♔h1 ♕g3∓) 34 ... ♘f3+ 35 ♔h1 ♕xg2+ 36 ♔xg2 ♘xh4+ 37 ♔g3 ♔xh6 38 ♔xh4 ♖e7→ Staunton] 33 ... ♔xg6 34 ♗f4 ♖xd3 35 ♗xd6 ♘xb3 36 ♗f4 ♖e7 37 ♖f3! ♖xf3 38 gxf3 c4 39 ♔f2! ♖e6 40 ♖g1+ ♔f6 [□ 40 ... ♔h7 St Amant] 41 h4 ♘c5 42 ♗d2 ♘xa4 43 h5 c3 44 ♗e3 f4! 45 ♗xf4 ♘b2 46 ♗g5+ ♔f5 47 ♖g4 ♘d3+ 48 ♔g3 ♘e5 49 ♗d8 ♘xg4 50 fxg4+ ♔e5 51 ♗g5 c2 52 h6 ♖c6 53 h7 ♖c8 54 ♗c1 ♔f6 55 ♔f3 ♔g6 56 ♔e2 ♖d8 57 h8♕ ♖xh8 58 ♔d2 ♖c8 **0-1**

L/N6013-1844,L/N6123-1844

**1843-✕SS2-17** 12 xii 43

**Saint–Amant, P.C.F. de,= Staunton, H.**

[Saint-Amant & Staunton]

1 d4 d5 2 c4 e6 3 ♘c3 ♘f6 4 e3 c5 5 ♘f3 ♘c6 6 a3 a6 7 b3 ♗e7 8 ♗e2 b6 9 0-0 0-0 10 ♕d3 ♗b7 11 ♖fd1 cxd4 12 exd4 dxc4 13 bxc4 ♕c7 14 h3 ♖ac8 15 ♗b2 ♖fd8 16 ♖ac1 ♘a5 17 ♘d2 ♕f4! 18 g3 ♕c7 [□ 18 ... ♕h6; 18 ... ♕xd4? 19 ♕xd4 △ 20 ♘d5 Staunton] 19 ♘ce4 ♘xe4 20 ♘xe4 f5 21 ♘d2 ♗f6 22 ♕e3 ♕e7 [□ 22 ... ♔h8 Staunton] 23 ♗c3 ♘c6 24 d5!? ♗xc3 25 ♖xc3 exd5 26 cxd5 ♕xe3 27 fxe3 ♘e5 28 ♖xc8 ♖xc8 29 ♘f3 ♘xf3+ 30 ♗xf3 ♔f8 [30 ... ♖c3? 31 d6 ♗xf3? 32 d7+– Staunton] 31 g4 g6 32 gxf5 gxf5 33 ♔f2 ♔f7 34 ♔g3 ♔f6 35 ♖b1 b5 36 ♖d1 [36 a4 ♖c5 St Amant] 36 ... ♔e5 37 d6 ♗xf3 38 d7 ♖d8 [38 ... ♖g8+?! St Amant] 39 ♔xf3 h5 40 h4 ♔e6 41 ♔f4 ♖xd7 42 ♖xd7 [42 ♖g1!?∞ St Amant] 42 ... ♔xd7 43 ♔xf5= a5 44 ♔e5! ♔c6 [44 ... b4= St Amant] 45 ♔d4 ♔d6 46 e4 b4 47 axb4 axb4 48 ♔c4 ♔e5 49 ♔xb4 ♔xe4 50 ♔c3 ♔e3 51 ♔c2 ♔f2 52 ♔d2 ♔g3 53 ♔e1 ♔xh4 54 ♔f1 **½-½**

L/N6013-1844,L/N6123-1844

**1843-✕SS2-18** 14 xii 43

**Staunton, H.= Saint–Amant, P.C.F. de**

[Saint-Amant & Staunton]

1 c4 d5 2 ♘c3 [2 cxd5!± St Amant] 2 ... e6 3 d4 ♘f6 4 ♘f3 c5 5 e3 ♘c6 6 a3 a6 7 dxc5 ♗xc5 8 b4 ♗e7 9 ♗b2 0-0 10 ♗e2 dxc4 11 ♗xc4 b5 12 ♗d3 ♗b7 13 0-0= ♕c7 14 ♖c1 ♖fd8 15 ♕e2 ♖ac8 16 ♖fd1 ♗d6 17 h3 ♕e7 18 ♗b1 ♘e5 19 ♘xe5 ♗xe5 20 f4 ♖xd1+ 21 ♕xd1 ♗xc3 22 ♗xc3 ♘d5 23 ♗d4 ♖xc1 24 ♕xc1 f5 25 e4 fxe4 26 ♗xe4 ♕d7 [△ 27 ... ♘xf4 Staunton] 27 ♔h2 ♘f6 [27 ... ♘xf4?? 28 ♕xf4 ♕xd4? 29 ♗xh7+ △ 30 ♕xd4+– Staunton] 28 ♗xf6 ♗xe4 [□ 28 ... gxf6 Staunton] 29 ♗e5 ♕c6 30 ♕e1 ♕b7 [30 ... ♗xg2? 31 ♕g3+– St Amant] 31 ♕g3 h6 32 ♕f2 ♔h7 33 h4 ♕d7 34 ♕g3 ♕f7 35 ♕e3 ♕b7 36 ♕d2 ♕c6 37 ♔g1 ♕c2 38 ♕xc2= ♗xc2 39 ♔f2 ♔g6 40 ♔e3 h5 41 ♔d4 ♔f7 [□ 41 ... ♔f5 St Amant] 42 ♔c5 g6 43 ♔b6 ♔e7 44 ♔xa6 ♗a4 45 ♔b6 ♔d7 46 ♔b7 ♔e8 47 g4 ♗d1 48 ♔b6 ♗a4 49 ♔c5 ♔e7 50 ♔c6 ♔e8 51 ♗f6 ♔f7 52 ♗d4 ♔e7 53 ♗c5+ ♔e8 54 ♔d6 ♔f7 55 ♗d4 ♗c2 56 ♗c3 ♗b3 57 ♔d7 ♗c2 **½-½**

L/N6013-1844,L/N6123-1844

**1843-✕SS2-19** 16 xii 43

**Saint–Amant, P.C.F. de+ Staunton, H.**

[Saint-Amant & Staunton]

1 d4 d5 2 c4 dxc4 3 e3 [3 e4 St Amant] 3 ... e5 4 ♗xc4 exd4 5 exd4 ♗d6 6 ♘f3 ♘f6 7 h3 0-0 8 0-0 ♘c6 [□ 8 ... h6 St Amant] 9 ♗g5 ♗e7 10 ♘c3 ♗f5 11 a3 ♘e4 12 ♗e3 ♗f6 13 ♖e1 ♘d6 14 ♗a2 h6 15 ♕a4 ♘e7 16 ♖ad1 ♘g6 17 ♗c1 [△ 18 ♘e5 St Amant] 17 ... c6 [□ 17 ... ♖e8 St Amant] 18 ♘e5 ♕c7 [□ 18 ... ♔h7 Staunton] 19 g4!? b5 20 ♕b4 [20 ♕b3? St Amant] 20 ... ♗c2 21 ♖d2 a5 22 ♕c5 ♗xe5 23 dxe5 ♘b7 24 ♘xb5 ♘xc5 25 ♘xc7 ♘d3 26 ♖xd3 [26 ♘xa8?!; 26 ♖xc2?! St Amant] 26 ... ♗xd3 27 ♘xa8 ♖xa8 28 f4 ♖e8 29 ♖d1 ♗e4 30 ♖d4 ♗d5 31 ♗xd5 cxd5 32 ♔f2? [□ 32 ♖xd5 St Amant] 32 ... ♖c8 33 ♗e3 ♘e7 34 ♔e2 ♖b8 35 ♗c1 ♔f8 36 b4 ♖b5! 37 bxa5 ♘c6 38 ♖a4 ♘xa5 39 ♗d2 ♘c6 40 ♗b4+ ♔e8 41 h4 g5 42 fxg5 hxg5 43 ♖a8+ ♔d7 44 h5 ♘xb4 45 h6 ♘c6 46 h7 ♖b2+ 47 ♔d3 ♖b3+? [□ 47 ... ♘xe5+ Staunton] 48 ♔c2 ♖h3 49 h8♕ ♖xh8 50 ♖xh8 ♘xe5 51 ♔c3 ♘xg4 52 ♔d4 ♘f6 53 ♔e5= ♔e7 54 a4 ♘d7+ 55 ♔f5 d4 56 a5 ♘c5 57 ♔xg5 d3 58 ♔f4 d2 59 ♖h1 ♔d7 60 ♔e3 ♔c6 61 ♖b1 d1♕? 62 ♖xd1 ♔b5 63 ♖d5! ♔c6 64 ♔d4 ♘e6+ 65 ♔c4 ♔b7 66 ♖d7+ ♔a6 67 ♖xf7 ♘d8 68 ♖f5 ♘c6 69 ♖f6 ♔b7 70 ♔b5 ♘a7+ 71 ♔c5 ♘c8 72 ♖h6 ♘a7 73 a6+ ♔b8 74 ♖h7 ♘c8 75 ♖b7+ ♔a8 76 ♔c6 ♘a7+ 77 ♔c7 ♘c6 78 ♔b6 ♘b4 79 ♖d7 **1-0**

L/N6013-1844,L/N6123-1844

**1843-✕SS2-20** 17 xii 43

**Staunton, H.– Saint–Amant, P.C.F. de**

[Saint-Amant & Staunton]

1 c4 e6 2 e4 c6 [△ 3 ... d5 St Amant] 3 d4 d5 4 exd5 exd5 5 ♘c3 ♘f6 6 ♘f3 ♗e7 7 ♗d3 0-0 8 0-0 ♗g4! 9 ♗e3 ♘bd7 10 b3 h6 11 ♔h1!? ♗b4 [11 ... ♗xf3 12 gxf3! St Amant] 12 ♘e2 ♗d6 13 ♗f4 ♗xf4! 14 ♘xf4 ♘h5! 15 ♘xh5 [15 ♘e2? ♗xf3! 16 gxf3∓ St Amant] 15 ... ♗xh5 16 ♗e2 ♖e8 17 ♖e1 ♕c7 18 ♘g1 ♗xe2 19 ♖xe2 ♘f6∓ 20 ♕d3 ♘g4 21 ♘f3 ♖e4! 22 h3 ♖ae8∓ 23 ♘e5? [□ 23 ♖xe4 ♘xf2+ △ 24 ... ♘xe4!∓ St Amant] 23 ... ♘xe5 24 ♖xe4 [24 dxe5 ♕xe5→ St Amant] 24 ... ♘xd3 25 ♖xe8+ ♔h7 26 ♔g1 ♕f4 27 ♖e2 ♕xd4 28 ♖ad1 dxc4 29 ♖ed2 b5 30 a4 a6 **0-1**

L/N6013-1844,L/N6123-1844

**1843-✕SS2-21** 20 xii 43

**Saint–Amant, P.C.F. de– Staunton, H.**

[Saint-Amant & Staunton]

1 d4 d5 2 c4 e6 3 e3 c5 4 ♘c3 ♘f6 5 ♘f3 ♗e7 6 ♗d3 b6 7 0-0 0-0 8 b3 ♗b7 9 cxd5 exd5 10 ♕c2 ♘c6 11 a3 a6 12 ♖d1 cxd4 13 exd4 [△ 14 ♗g5 St Amant] 13 ... h6 14 b4! ♗d6 15 ♖e1 b5 16 h3 ♖c8 17 ♕b3 ♕c7 18 ♗d2 ♕b6 19 ♗e3 ♘e7 20 ♖ac1 ♘h5 21 ♕d1! ♘f6 22 ♘h4!± ♖c7 23 ♕d2 [□ 23 ♕f3 St Amant] 23 ... ♘h7 24 ♕c2 [24 ♗xh6? gxh6 25 ♕xh6?? ♗h2+→ Stauton] 24 ... ♘f6 25 ♘f6 25 ♔h1 ♘e8 26 ♘f5? ♘xf5 27 ♗xf5 a5 28 ♕b3 axb4 29 axb4 ♖c4! 30 ♘a2 ♘f6 31 ♗d3 ♕c6 32 ♕b2 [32 ♗xc4? dxc4→ Stauton] 32 ... ♕d7 33 ♔g1 ♘h5 34 ♕d2 f5 36 f4∓ ♘g3 36 ♗xc4 dxc4 37 ♕b2 ♖f6 38 ♘c3 ♘e4 39 ♖e2 ♖g6 40 ♖cd1? ♘xc3

41 ♕xc3 ♗f3 42 ♖de1 [□ 42 ♖ee1 St Amant; 42 ♖ee1? ♗xd1 43 ♖xd1 ♕e7 44 ♖b1 ♖xg2+! (44 ... ♕e4→; 44 ... ♖g3→) 45 ♔xg2 ♕e4+ △ 46 ... ♕xb1→ Staunton] 42 ... ♗xe2 43 ♖xe2 ♕e7 44 ♕b2 ♖e6 45 ♔f2 ♖e4 [45 ... ♗xb4 St Amant] 46 ♕a2 ♔f7 47 g3 ♕b7 [△ 48 ... ♖~, 49 ... ♕h1!→ Staunton] 48 ♕a3 ♖e8 49 ♕c3 ♕h1! 50 h4 g5 51 ♕e1 ♕h2+ 52 ♔f1 ♕h3+ 53 ♔g1 ♕g4 54 hxg5 ♗xf4! 55 ♗xf4 ♕xe2 56 ♕xe2 ♖xe2 57 gxh6 c3 58 ♔f1 ♖e4 59 ♗c1 ♔g6 60 d5 c2 61 ♗d2 ♖xb4 62 d6 ♖d4 63 ♔e2 ♖xd6 64 ♔e3 ♔xh6 65 ♔e2+ ♔g6 66 ♔e1 b4 **0-1** L/N6013-1844,L/N6123-1844

**1843-★BS-1** 23 vi 43
**Bryan,T.J.+Saint-Amant, P.C.F. de**
[Saint-Amant]

⟨♙f7⟩1 e4 ... 2 d4 ... 3 ♗d3 e6 4 e5 ♕e7! 5 ♘f3 d5 [5 ... d6] 6 ♘g5 g6 7 h4! c5 8 h5 ♗h6 9 ♕g4 c4 10 ♗e2? [10 hxg6!] 10 ... ♗xg5 11 ♕xg5?! ♕xg5 12 ♗xg5 ♔f7 13 hxg6+ ♔xg6 14 f4 h6 15 ♘d2 ♖h7 [△ 16 ... hxg5] 16 ♗h4 ♘c6 17 c3 ♖f7 18 g3 ♘ce7 19 ♗xe7 ♖xe7 20 ♗h5+ ♔g7 21 0-0-0 [21 b3!] 21 ... ♗d7 22 ♖df1 ♖f8 23 ♖f2 ♗e8 24 g4 ♗g6 25 ♗xg6 ♔xg6 26 ♔d1 ♖ef7 27 ♖hf1 ♘e7 28 ♔e2 b5 29 ♖f3 a5 30 ♖1f2 b4 31 ♘f1 bxc3 32 bxc3 ♖b8 33 ♘g3 a4 34 ♘h5 a3 35 ♘f6 ♖ff8 36 f5+ ♔f7 37 ♘d7 ♖b2+ 38 ♔e3 ♖c8 39 fxe6+ ♔g6 [39 ... ♔xe6? 40 ♘f8+] 40 ♖f7 ♘c6 41 ♖2f6+ ♔g5 42 ♖g7+ ♔h4 43 ♖xh6+ ♔g3 44 ♘f6 ♖xa2 45 ♘h5+ ♔g2 46 ♘f4+ ♔g1 47 ♖h3 [□ 47 ♖gh7] 47 ... ♖h2 48 ♖xh2 ♔xh2 49 ♔f2!+- ♖h8 50 e7 ♘xe7 51 ♖xe7 a2 52 ♖a7 ♔h1 53 ♘h5 [53 ♖xa2?? ♖h2+] 53 ... ♖f8+ 54 ♔g3 ♖f1 55 ♖xa2 ♖g1+ 56 ♔h3 ♖c1 57 ♘g3+ ♔g1 58 ♘e2+ [□ 58 ♖g2#] **1-0** L/N6013

**1843-★BS-2** 26 vi 43
**Bryan,T.J.-Saint-Amant, P.C.F. de**
[Saint-Amant]

⟨♙f7⟩1 e4 ... 2 d4 ... 3 ♗d3 e6 4 e5 d5 5 ♕h5+ ♔d7! 6 c4! c6 7 ♘f3 ♕e8 8 ♕h3 ♔c7 9 ♘c3 ♗d7 10 ♘g5 h6 11 f4 g6 12 0-0 ♗g7 13 ♘f3 ♘e7 14 ♘h4 ♘f5 15 ♗xf5 gxf5 16 cxd5? [16 ♗e3 △ 17 ♖ac1] 16 ... cxd5 17 ♗d2 ♘c6 18 ♖fc1 a6 19 a3 ♖c8 20 b4 ♔b8 21 ♕d3 [△ 22 b5] 21 ... ♘a7 22 a4 ♖c4 23 b5 a5 24 ♘e2 ♕h5! 25 ♘f3 ♖hc8? [25 ... ♖xc1+ 26 ♖xc1 b6] 26 ♗xa5 ♗f8 27 ♘d2? ♖xc1+ 28 ♖xc1 ♖xc1+ 29 ♘xc1 ♕d1+ 30 ♕f1 ♕xa4 31 ♘cb3! ♘xb5 32 ♕c1 ♗c6 33 ♗b6 ♗b4 34 ♕b2 ♗c3! 35 ♕b1 ♘xd4 36 ♘c5 ♕a1 37 ♔f2 ♕b2! 38 ♕xb2 ♗xb2 39 ♔e3 ♘c2+ 40 ♔f3 [□ 40 ♔d3] 40 ... d4+ 41 ♔f2 ♗d5 42 ♘d7+ ♔c8 43 ♘f6 ♘e3 44 ♘f3 ♗xf3 45 ♔xf3 ♘c4! 46 ♗c5 b5 47 g4 fxg4+ 48 ♘xg4 ♗c3 49 ♔e2 b4 50 ♔d1 b3 51 ♘f2 b2 52 ♔c2 ♘d2 **0-1** L/N6013

**1843-★BS-3** 28 vi 43
**Bryan,T.J.-Saint-Amant, P.C.F. de**
[Saint-Amant]

⟨♙f7⟩1 e4 ... 2 d4 ... 3 ♗d3 d6 4 ♘c3 c6 5 e5 ♗e6 6 ♘f3 ♗g4 [□ 6 ... ♕d7] 7 h3 ♗h5 8 g4 ♗f7 9 ♘g5 e6 10 ♘xh7 ♗e7 11 g5 g6 12 ♘f6+ ♗xf6 13 exf6+- ♘d7 14 f4 ♕b6 15 ♘e2 0-0-0 16 c3 ♘gxf6 17 gxf6 ♘xf6 18 ♕c2 ♖dg8 19 ♗d2 e5!? 20 0-0-0? ♗xa2 21 b4 ♗d5 22 ♖hg1? e4 23 ♔b2 exd3 24 ♕xd3 ♗e4 25 ♕g3 ♗f5!∓ 26 h4 ♕a6 27 ♘c1 ♖e8 28 ♖de1 ♘e4 29 ♕h2 c5 30 dxc5 dxc5 31 ♘b3 cxb4 [31 ... c4 32 ♘d4] 32 cxb4 ♕f6+ 33 ♔a3 ♖d8 34 ♖c1+ ♔b8 35 ♗e3 ♖d3→ 36 ♕e2 ♕a6+ 37 ♔b2 ♖xb3+ **0-1** L/N6013

**1843-★DS-1** 23 vii 43
**Dumonchau=Saint-Amant, P.C.F. de**
Paris [Saint-Amant]

⟨♙f7⟩1 e4 ♘h6 2 d4 ♘f7 3 f4?! d5 4 e5 c5 5 dxc5 ♗f5 6 ♗e3 e6 7 ♘f3 ♘c6 8 ♗b5 ♘h6 9 0-0 ♗e7 10 h3 0-0 11 c3 [△ 12 b4] 11 ... a5 12 g4 ♗g6 13 ♗d3? ♗xd3 14 ♕xd3 ♕c7 15 ♘bd2 ♖ad8 16 ♕c2 g5!? 17 fxg5 ♘f7 18 ♔g2 [18 g6] 18 ... ♘fxe5 19 ♘d4 ♘xd4 [19 ... ♘g6] 20 cxd4 ♘g6 21 ♘f3 b6 [21 ... ♖xf3?! 22 ♔xf3! △ 23 ♔e2] 22 c6 ♖c8 23 ♖ac1 ♗d8 24 ♕f2! ♕d6 25 ♕g3 ♖xc6 26 h4 ♕xg3+ 27 ♔xg3 ♗c7+ 28 ♔g2 ♖xc1 29 ♖xc1 ♗f4 30 ♖c3 ♗xe3 31 ♖xe3 ♖c8 32 ♖c3! [32 ♖xe6?? ♘f4+] 32 ... ♖c4? 33 ♔g3 [33 ♖xc4 dxc4 34 ♘e5] 33 ... b5 34 h5 ♘e7 35 ♖xc4 dxc4 36 ♔f4 b4 37 ♔e3 ♘c6?+- [37 ... ♘d5+] 38 ♘e5 ♘e7 39 ♘xc4 a4 40 ♘b6 a3 41 bxa3 bxa3 42 ♘c4 ♘d5+ 43 ♔e4 ♔f7 44 ♘xa3 ♘c3+ 45 ♔e5 ♘xa2 46 ♘b5 ♘c1 47 g6+?? [47 ♘c7] 47 ... hxg6 48 hxg6+ ♔xg6 49 ♔xe6 ♘d3 50 ♘d6 ♘f4+ 51 ♔e5 ♔g5= 52 ♘e4+ ♔xg4 **½-½** L/N6013

**1843-★ES-1** 29 vi 43
**Evans, W.D.= Saint-Amant, P.C.F. de**
London [Saint-Amant]

1 e4 e5 2 c3 ♘f6 3 d4 exd4 4 e5 ♕e7 5 ♕e2? [5 cxd4] 5 ... d3! 6 ♕xd3 ♕xe5+ 7 ♗e2 ♗e7 8 ♘f3 ♕e4 9 ♕d1 0-0 10 0-0 ♘c6 11 ♖e1 ♕d5 12 ♗d3 ♕h5 13 h3 d5 14 ♗f4 ♗d6 15 ♗xd6 cxd6 16 ♘bd2 ♘e5? 17 ♘xe5 dxe5 18 ♕xh5 ♘xh5 19 ♖xe5 ♘f4 20 ♗c2 ♗e6 21 ♖ae1 ♖fe8?! 22 ♘f3 f6 23 ♖5e3 ♔f7 24 ♔h2 g6 25 g3± ♘h5 [25 ... ♘xh3?? 26 ♖xe6] 26 ♗a4 ♖e7 27 ♘d4 ♘g7 28 f4 f5 29 g4 a6 30 ♖e5 ♖d8 31 ♗b3 ♖d6 32 ♔g3 ♖ed7 33 ♘f3 h6 34 ♖5e2 fxg4? 35 ♘e5+ ♔g8 36 ♘xd7 ♘h5+ 37 ♔h4 ♗xd7 38 hxg4 ♘xf4 39 ♖d2 g5+ 40 ♔g3 ♔g7 41 ♖e7+ ♔f6 42 ♖h7 ♔e5?! 43 ♖d1 ♗b5 44 ♖e7+ ♔f6 45 ♖de1 h5 46 gxh5 ♘xh5+ 47 ♔g4 ♘f4 48 ♖xb7 ♗d7+ 49 ♔g3 ♘h5+ 50 ♔h2 g4 51 ♖f1+ ♔g5 52 ♖f7 ♗c6 53 ♖bc7 ♖e6 54 ♖xc6 ♖xc6 55 ♗xd5 ♖b6 56 b3 g3+ 57 ♔g1 ♘f4 58 c4 ♖h6 59 ♖g7+ ♔f5 60 ♗f3 ♘d3! 61 ♖xg3 ♔f4 62 ♔g2 ♘e1+ 63 ♔f2 ♘d3+ **½-½** L/N6013

**1843-★KL-1** 1 viii 43
**Laigle, F.C.- Kieseritsky, L.**
Paris [Saint-Amant]

1 f4 d5 2 ♘f3 c5 3 c3 ♘c6 4 e3 e6 5 ♗e2 ♕b6 6 0-0 ♘f6 7 d3 ♗d6 8 ♘bd2 ♗xf4! 9 e4 ♗e3+ 10 ♔h1 ♘g4 11 h3 h5! 12 ♘h2 ♘f2+ 13 ♖xf2 ♗xf2 14 b3 ♗d7 15 ♗b2 c4 16 ♘hf3 cxd3 **0-1** L/N6013

**1843-★KL-2** 1 viii 43
**Kieseritsky, L.+ Laigle, F.C.**
Paris [Saint-Amant]

1 d4 d5 2 c4 e6 3 ♘c3 ♘f6 4 ♗f4 ♗e7 5 ♘b5?! c6 6 ♘c7+ ♔f8 7 ♘xa8 ♘a6 8 e3 b6 9 cxd5 cxd5 10 ♗xa6 ♗xa6 11 ♘c7 [□ 11 ♕a4] 11 ... g6? 12 ♘xa6 ♗b4+? 13 ♘xb4 **1-0** L/N6013

**1843-★PS-1** 26 iv 43
**Perigal,G.+Saint-Amant, P.C.F. de**
London [Saint-Amant]

1 e4 e5 2 ♘f3 ♘f6 3 ♘xe5 d6 4 ♘f3 ♘xe4 5 d3 [□ 5 d4] 5 ... ♘f6 6 ♗g5?! h6 7 ♗h4 ♗e7 8 ♗e2 0-0 9 0-0 ♗e6 10 ♘c3 d5 11 d4 c6? [11 ... c5] 12 ♘e5 ♘bd7 13 f4 ♗f5 14 ♗d3 ♗h7 15 ♗xh7+ ♔xh7 16 ♕d3+ ♔g8 17 ♖ae1 c5 18 ♘xd7 ♕xd7 19 ♗xf6 c4 20 ♖xe7 ♕xe7 21 ♗xe7 cxd3 22 ♗xf8 **1-0** L/N6013

**1843-★PS-2** 26 iv 43
**Saint-Amant,P.C.F.de+ Perigal, G.**
London [Saint-Amant]

1 e4 e5 2 ♘f3 ♘c6 3 ♗c4 ♗c5 4 0-0 d6 5 c3 ♗g4 [5 ... ♗e6] 6 h3 ♗h5 7 b4 ♗b6 8 a4 a6 9 d3 f5 10 ♗e3? [10

♕b3] 10 ... ♗xe3 11 fxe3 fxe4 12 dxe4 ♘f6 13 ♕d3? ♗g6 14 ♘bd2 ♘e7 15 ♗a2 h6 16 ♖ad1 ♕d7 17 ♕c4 ♖f8 18 ♗b1 ♗f7 19 ♕d3 ♕xa4∓ 20 ♘h4 ♕d7 21 ♘f5 ♘xf5 22 exf5 b5 23 ♘e4! ♗c4? 24 ♘xf6+ gxf6 25 ♕e4 d5 26 ♕f3 ♕f7 [26 ... ♗xf1?! 27 ♖xd5] 27 ♖f2 ♖d8 28 ♗c2 e4 29 ♕f4 ♕g7 30 ♖fd2 ♖d6! 31 ♖d4 ♖g8 32 ♖1d2 ♕g3 33 ♕xg3 [33 ♕xh6?!] 33 ... ♖xg3 34 ♔f2 ♖g5 35 g4 a5 [◻ 35 ... h5] 36 bxa5 ♖a6?? 37 ♗xe4! c5! [37 ... dxe4?? 38 ♖d8+-] 38 ♖xd5 ♗xd5 39 ♖xd5 ♖xa5 40 ♖xc5 [△ 41 ♗c6+] 40 ... ♔d7 41 ♔f3! [△ 42 c4] 41 ... ♖g8 42 c4 ♖b8 43 cxb5 ♖a1 [43 ... ♖bxb5? 44 ♗c6+] 44 ♗c6+ ♔c7 45 ♖d5 ♖c8 46 ♖d7+ ♔b6 47 ♖h7+- ... ♀ **1-0** L/N 6013

**1843-★RS-1** 3 ix 43
**Rousseau, E.= Saint-Amant, P.C.F. de**
[Saint-Amant]
1 e4 c5 2 c4?! ♘c6 3 ♘c3 e6 4 f4 d6 5 ♘f3 ♘ge7 6 d3 f5 7 ♗e2 a6 8 a4 g6 9 0-0 ♗g7 10 ♗e3 ♘d4 11 ♗xd4 cxd4 12 ♘a2 ♘c6 13 b4 fxe4∓ 14 dxe4 d3! 15 ♗xd3 ♗xa1 16 ♕xa1 0-0 17 b5 axb5 18 cxb5 ♕b6+ 19 ♔h1 ♕e3 20 ♕c3 ♖xa4 21 bxc6 ♖xa2 22 cxb7 ♗xb7∓ 23 ♕b3 d5 24 ♕xa2 ♕xd3 25 ♖b1 ♖xf4 26 h3 [26 ♖xb7 ♖xf3!] 26 ... ♗c8 27 ♖b8 ♖f8 28 ♕a8 ♕d1+ 29 ♔h2 dxe4 30 ♕xe4! [30 ♖xc8 ♕d6+ △ 31 ... exf3] 30 ... ♕d6+ 31 ♕e5 ♕xe5+? 32 ♘xe5 ♔g7 33 g4 ♖f2+ 34 ♔g3 ♖c2 35 g5! h6 36 h4 hxg5 37 hxg5 ♖c7 38 ♖b6 ♖c5 39 ♔f4 ♖c1 40 ♖c6 ♖xc6 41 ♘xc6 ♗b7 42 ♘d8 ♗d5 43 ♔e5 ♗a2 44 ♘xe6+ ♔f7 [44 ... ♗xe6?? 45 ♔xe6+-] 45 ♘f4 ♗b1 46 ♔d6 ♗f5 47 ♘d5 ♗b1 48 ♘c7 ♗c2 49 ♘e6 ♗b1 50 ♔e5 **½-½** L/N6013

**1843-★ST-1** 5 v 43
**Taverner, T.–Saint-Amant, P.C.F. de**
London [Saint-Amant]
1 e4 e6 2 f4 [5 2 d4] 2 ... c6 3 c4 d5 4 cxd5 cxd5 5 e5? [5 exd5] 5 ... ♘c6∓ 6 ♗b5 a6 7 ♗a4 ♘h6 8 d4 ♗d7 9 ♗xc6 bxc6 10 ♗e3 ♕b6 11 ♕b3 ♖b8! 12 ♕xb6 ♖xb6 13 b3 ♘f5 14 ♗f2 ♗b4+ 15 ♔d1 0-0 16 g4 ♘h6 17 h3 f6 18 ♘e2 fxe5 19 a3 ♗e7 20 dxe5 c5 21 b4 ♗a4+ 22 ♔d2 g5!? 23 ♘bc3 ♗c6 24 ♗xc5 ♗xc5 25 bxc5 ♖b2+ 26 ♔c1 ♖fb8 27 fxg5 ♘f7 28 ♘d4 ♘xe5 29 ♘xc6 ♘xc6 30 ♖d1 ♖h2 31 ♖b1 ♖xb1+ 32 ♔xb1 ♖xh3 33 ♔b2 ♖g3 34 ♖e1 ♔f7 35 ♖h1 ♖g2+ 36 ♔b1 ♔g7 37 ♖h6 ♘d4 38 c6 ♖g1+ 39 ♔b2 ♖g2+ 40 ♔b1 ♖c2 41 ♘b5 axb5 42 ♖xe6 ♖xc6 **0-1** L/N6013

**1843-★S♀-1** 7 ix 43
**♀– Saint-Amant, P.C.F. de**
Orléans [Saint-Amant]
1 e4 e5 2 ♘f3 ♘f6 3 ♘xe5 d6 4 ♘f3 ♘xe4 5 d4 d5 6 h3 [◻ 6 c4] 6 ... c5= 7 c3 ♘c6 8 ♗b5 ♕b6 9 ♗xc6+ bxc6 10 0-0 ♗e7 11 ♘e5?! 0-0 12 ♘d2 f5 [◻ 12 ... f6] 13 ♘b3 ♗a6?! 14 ♘d7 ♕b7 15 ♘xf8 ♗xf1 16 ♘e6 ♗b5 17 ♘bxc5 ♗xc5 18 ♘xc5 ♕e7 19 ♘d3 ♕h4 20 ♗e3 ♗xd3 21 ♕xd3 f4! 22 f3 fxe3 23 fxe4 ♕f2+ 24 ♔h1? [24 ♔h2] 24 ... e2-+ 25 ♕b1 ♖f8 26 ♕g1 ♕f1 27 e5 ♕xa1 **0-1** L/N6013-1845

**1843̂-★BS-1**
**Buckle, H.T.– Staunton, H.**
London
⟨♙f7⟩1 e4 ♘c6 2 d4 d5 3 e5 ♗f5 4 g4 ♗g6 5 h4 e6 6 h5 ♗f7 7 f4 g6 8 hxg6 ♗xg6 9 ♗d3 ♗xd3 10 ♕xd3 ♘h6 11 f5 ♘xg4 12 ♕h3 h5 13 fxe6 ♕e7 14 ♘e2 ♕xe6 15 ♘f4 ♕f5 16 ♘xh5 0-0-0 17 c3 ♕e4+ 18 ♔d1 ♕xh1+ **0-1** L/N6123

**1843̂-★CS-1**
**Saint-Amant, P.C.F. de– Cochrane, J.**
1 e4 e5 2 ♘f3 ♘c6 3 ♗b5 ♗c5 4 ♗xc6 dxc6 5 0-0 ♗g4 6 h3 ♗xf3 7 ♕xf3 ♘e7 8 ♕e2 ♕d6 9 c3 ♘g6 10 b4 ♗b6 11 a4 a5 12 b5 ♘f4 13 ♕g4 h5 14 ♕xg7 0-0-0 15 d4 ♖hg8 16 ♕xe5 ♘xh3+ 17 ♔h2 ♕xe5+ 18 dxe5 ♘xf2 19 bxc6 ♖g4 20 cxb7+ ♔xb7 21 ♘d2 ♖dg8 22 ♖xf2 ♗xf2 23 ♖b1+ ♔c8 **0-1** L/N6123-1843̂

**1843̂-★CS-2**
**Cochrane, J.= Saint-Amant, P.C.F. de♀**
1 e4 c5 2 c4 ♘c6 3 ♘c3 e5 4 ♗d3 ♕g5 5 ♕f3 ♘f6 6 ♘ge2 ♗d6 7 0-0 0-0 8 ♕e3 ♕h4 9 ♘d5 ♘d4 10 ♘xf6+ ♕xf6 11 ♘c3 ♕e6 12 ♘e2 f5 13 ♘xd4 exd4 14 ♕h3 f4 15 ♕xe6+ dxe6 16 f3 a6 17 b3 ♗d7 18 ♗b2 g5 19 ♔f2 e5 20 ♖fg1 ♔f7 21 g3 ♖fg8 22 gxf4 gxf4 23 ♖xg8 ♖xg8 24 ♖g1 ♖xg1 25 ♔xg1 ♔g6 26 ♗f1 ♗e7 27 d3 b6 28 ♗c1 ♗h4 29 ♗d2 a5 30 a4 h5 31 ♗g2 ♗d8 32 ♔f1 ♗h4 33 ♔g1 ♔g5 34 ♔f1 ♔g6 **½-½** L/N6123-1843̂

**1843̂-★CS-3**
**Cochrane, J.– Staunton, H.**
London [Staunton]
⟨♙f7⟩1 e4 d6 2 d4 ♘c6 3 d5 ♘e5 4 f4 ♘f7 5 f5 ♘f6 6 ♗d3 g6 7 ♘c3 c6 8 ♘ge2 cxd5 9 fxg6 hxg6 10 exd5 ♘e5 11 ♗f4 ♘xd3+ 12 ♕xd3 ♗f5 13 ♕d2 ♕b6 14 0-0-0 ♘g4 15 h3 ♘e5 [15 ... ♘f2?? 16 ♗e3] 16 ♗xe5 dxe5 17 g4 0-0-0 18 ♔b1 [18 gxf5?? ♗h6-+] 18 ... ♗d7 19 ♕g5 ♕f6 20 ♕e3 ♔b8 21 ♘e4 ♕h4 22 ♘2g3 ♗h6 23 g5 ♗g7 24 ♕c5 ♖he8 25 d6 ♖c8 26 ♕d5 ♗c6 27 ♕d3 [◻ 27 ♕f7 ♗xe4? 28 ♘xe4 ♕xe4 29 d7 ♕xc2+ 30 ♔a1±] 27 ... ♖ed8 28 ♖he1 exd6 29 ♘xd6 ♗f8 30 ♕a3 ♗a4 **0-1** L/N6123-1844̂

**1843̂-★CS-4**
**Cochrane, J.+ Staunton, H.**
London
⟨♙f7⟩1 e4 d6 2 ♗c4 ♘f6 3 d4 ♗g4 [3 ... ♘xe4??] 4 ♕d3 ♘c6 5 ♘c3 e5 6 ♗b5 exd4 7 ♕xd4 ♗e7 8 ♗e3 0-0 9 ♗xc6 bxc6 10 h3 ♗h5 11 ♕c4+ d5 12 ♕xc6 ♗e8 [12 ... d4 13 ♕c4+ △ 14 ♕xd4] 13 ♕a6 ♗b4 14 ♘e2 ♘xe4 15 0-0 ♗xc3 16 ♘xc3 ♘xc3 17 bxc3 ♖f6 18 ♕e2 ♖g6 19 f4 ♖b8 20 f5 ♗b5 21 ♕f2 ♖c6 22 ♖fe1 ♖xc3 23 ♗xa7 ♖a8 24 ♗d4 ♖c6 25 ♕g3 ♕f8 26 a4 ♗c4 27 f6 g6 28 f7+ ♕xf7 29 ♕e5 **1-0** L/N6123-1844

**1843̂-★CS-5**
**Cochrane, J.– Staunton, H.**
London [Staunton]
⟨♙f7⟩1 e4 ♘c6 2 d4 d5 3 e5 ♗f5 4 c3 e6 5 ♘f3 ♘ge7 6 ♗d3 ♗xd3 7 ♕xd3 ♘g6 8 ♘g5 ♕d7 9 ♕h3 ♘d8 10 0-0 ♗e7 11 ♘xh7 ♘f7 12 ♕h5 ♘h4 [12 ... ♘f8?] 13 g3 g6 14 ♕g4 ♖xh7 15 gxh4 ♗xh4 16 ♕xg6 ♖h8 17 f4 0-0-0 18 ♔h1 ♖dg8 19 ♕c2 ♘h6 20 ♘d2 ♘g4 21 ♘f3 ♗g3 22 ♖g1 ♘f2+ 23 ♔g2 ♗xh2+ 24 ♔xf2 ♗xg1+ 25 ♔f1 ♖h1 26 ♘g5 ♕b5+ 27 c4 dxc4 28 a4 ♗xd4+ 29 ♔g2 ♕d5+ **0-1** L/N6123-1843̂

**1843̂-★GS-1**
**G♀– Staunton, H.**
London
⟨♙f7⟩1 e4 ♘c6 2 d4 e5 3 d5 ♘ce7 4 ♗g5 d6 5 ♗d3 h6 6 ♗xe7 ♘xe7 7 ♘e2 ♘g6 8 0-0 ♗e7 9 f4 ♗g4 10 f5 ♘f4 11 ♘bc3 0-0 12 ♕d2 ♗g5 13 ♘xf4 ♗xf4 14 ♕e1 ♕g5 15 ♗e2 ♗e3+ 16 ♔h1 h5 17 ♖d1 a6 18 ♖d3 ♗a7 19 ♖g3 ♖f6 20 h3 ♖h6 21 ♕d1 ♗e3 22 ♗xg4 ♗f4 23 f6 ♗xg3 24 ♗e6+ ♔h7 25 fxg7 ♔xg7 26 ♖f7+ ♔h8 **0-1** L/N6123-1843̂

**1843̂-★KS-1**
**Kieseritsky, L.= Saint-Amant, P.C.F. de**

1 a3 f5 2 d4 e6 3 c4 c5 4 dxc5 ♗xc5 5 ♘c3 ♘f6 6 b4 ♗b6 7 ♗f4 0-0 8 ♗d6 ♖e8 9 c5 ♗c7 10 ♘b5 ♗xd6 11 ♘xd6 ♖f8 12 ♖c1 ♘c6 13 ♘f3 ♘e4 14 e3 b6 15 ♘xe4 fxe4 16 ♘d4 ♘xd4 17 ♕xd4 bxc5 18 ♖xc5 ♗b7 19 ♗b5 ♗d5 20 0-0 ♕b6 21 ♖d1 d6 22 ♖cxd5 exd5 23 ♕xd5+ ♔h8 24 ♗c6 ♖ac8 25 b5 ♕c5 26 ♕xd6 ♕xd6 27 ♖xd6 ♖fd8 28 ♖d4 ♔g8 29 g3 ♖xd4 30 exd4 ♔f8 31 ♔f1 ♖d8 32 d5 ♔e7 33 ♔e2 ♔d6 34 ♔e3 ♔e5 35 a4 ♖f8 36 a5 ♖f3+ 37 ♔e2 ♖a3 38 a6 g5 39 g4 ♔d6 40 ♔d2 ♔c5 41 ♔c2 ♖f3 42 d6 ♖xf2+ 43 ♔d1 e3 44 d7 ♖d2+ 45 ♔e1 ♔b6 46 h3 ♔c7 47 ♔f1 h6 48 ♔e1 ♖b2 49 ♔f1 ♖f2+ 50 ♔e1 ♖b2 ½-½

L/N6123-1843

**1843̂-★RS-1** 3 ix 43
**Saint-Amant, P.C.F. de+ Rousseau, E.**

[Saint-Amant]

1 e4 e5 2 ♘f3 ♘c6 3 d4 ♘xd4 [5 3 ... exd4] 4 ♘xe5 ♘e6 5 ♗c4 ♕f6 6 ♘f3 d6 7 ♘c3 c6 8 0-0 ♘e7? 9 ♕xd6 ♘d5 10 ♕e5 ♕xe5 11 ♘xe5 ♘xc3± 12 bxc3 f6 13 ♘d3 ♗d6 14 e5! fxe5 15 ♖e1 0-0 16 ♘xe5 ♖e8 17 ♗f4 ♗a3 [Δ 18 ... ♗b2] 18 ♖ab1 ♔f8 19 ♗g3 a6 20 ♖e3 a5? 21 h3 b5 22 ♗d3 ♗c5 23 ♖f3+ ♔g8 24 ♘xc6! ♗b7 25 ♗xb5 ♖ec8 26 ♗c4 ♗xc6 27 ♗xe6+ ♔h8 28 ♗xc8 ♗xf3 29 ♗b7 **1-0** L/N6013-1843

**1843̂-★ST-1**
**Taverner, T.– Staunton, H.**

[Staunton]

⟨♙f7⟩ 1 e4 e6 2 d4 c5 3 ♕h5+ g6 4 ♕e5 ♘f6 5 ♗g5 ♗e7 6 d5 d6 7 ♗b5+ ♔f7 8 ♕f4 e5 9 ♕e3 a6 10 ♗xf6 ♗xf6 11 ♗e2 ♖f8 12 ♘f3 ♔g7 13 h4 ♗g4 14 ♘g5 ♗xg5 15 hxg5 ♗xe2 16 ♔xe2 ♖f4 17 ♘d2 ♕xg5 18 ♘f3 ♕e7 19 g3 ♖g4 20 ♖h6 ♘d7 21 ♖ah1 ♖h8 22 ♖6h4 ♘f6 23 ♕h6+ ♔g8 24 ♘g5 ♕g7 25 ♕xg7+ ♔xg7 26 ♖xg4 ♘xg4 27 ♘e6+ ♔f7 28 f3 ♘f6 29 g4 h5 30 g5 ♘d7 31 ♖h4 ♔e7 32 f4 exf4 33 ♘xf4 ♘e5 34 ♘d3 ♘xd3 35 cxd3 ♖f8 36 a3 b5 37 b4 cxb4 38 axb4 ♔d7 39 d4 ♔c7 40 ♔e3 ♖f1 41 ♖h2 ♖e1+ 42 ♖e2 ♖xe2+ 43 ♔xe2 h4 44 e5 h3 45 ♔f2 h2 46 ♔g2 h1♕+ 47 ♔xh1 a5 48 bxa5 b4 49 a6 b3 50 a7 [□ 50 exd6+] 50 ... ♔b7 51 exd6 b2

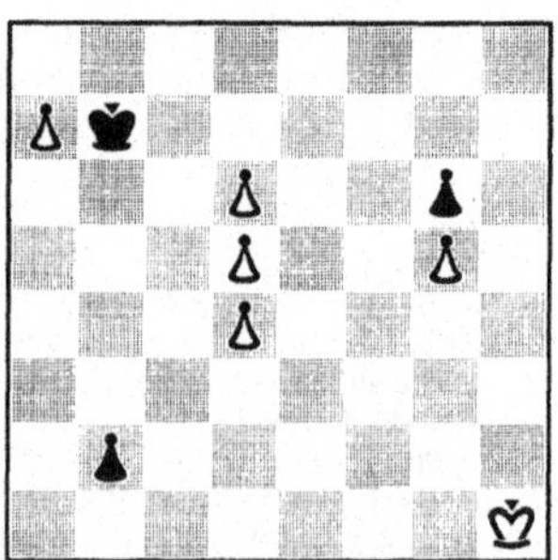

**0-1** L/N6123-1843

**1843̂-★ST-2**
**Taverner, T.+ Staunton, H.**

[Staunton]

⟨♙f7⟩ 1 e4 ♘c6 2 d4 d5 3 e5 ♗f5 4 c3 e6 5 ♗d3 ♘ge7 6 ♗g5 ♕d7 7 ♘e2 h6 8 ♗e3 g5 9 ♘g3 0-0-0 10 ♗xf5 ♘xf5 11 ♘xf5 exf5 12 f4 ♗e7 13 g3 ♖hg8 14 ♖f1 ♖df8 15 ♕d3 gxf4 16 ♗xf4 ♗g5 17 ♘d2 ♘d8 18 ♘b3 b6 19 0-0-0 ♘e6 20 ♖d2 ♔b8 21 ♖df2 ♗xf4+ 22 gxf4 ♖g4 23 ♘a1 c5 24 b3 c4 25 bxc4 dxc4 26 ♕b1! ♕c6 27 ♘c2 ♖g2 28 ♘b4 ♕b7 29 d5 ♖xf2 30 ♖xf2 ♕g7 31 ♕c2 ♘c5 32 ♘c6+ ♔b7 33 ♖g2 ♕f7 34 e6 ♕c7 35 ♘e5 ♖d8 36 ♖d2 ♘e4 37 ♖d4 b5 38 a4 ♖g8 39 ♔b2 ♕c5 40 ♘d7 ♕c7 41 axb5 ♕xf4 42 ♘c5+ ♔b6 43 ♘xe4 fxe4 44 ♖xe4 ♕f1 45 ♖e2 ♖g1 46 ♔a3 **1-0** L/N6123-1843

**1843̂-★ST-3**
**Taverner, T.– Staunton, H.**

[Staunton]

⟨♙f7⟩ 1 e4 e6 2 d4 c5 3 c3 cxd4 4 cxd4 ♗b4+ 5 ♘c3 ♘e7 6 ♗d3 0-0 7 ♘e2 ♘bc6 8 a3 ♗a5 9 ♗e3 a6 10 0-0 b5 11 b4 ♗b6 12 f4 d6 13 ♖f3 e5 14 fxe5 ♖xf3 15 gxf3 dxe5 16 ♗g5 ♘xd4 17 ♔g2 ♕d7 18 ♘xd4 ♗xd4 19 ♖c1 ♘g6 20 ♘d5 h6 21 ♖xc8+ ♖xc8 22 ♕b3 ♔h7 23 ♗d2 ♕f7 24 f4 ♘h4+ 25 ♔g3 ♕h5 [Δ 26 ... ♕f3+; 27 ... ♗f2#] 26 ♗b1 ♖c3+ 27 ♕xc3 ♗xc3 28 ♗xc3 exf4+ 29 ♔f2 ♕d1 **0-1** L/N6123-1843

**1843̂-★ST-4**
**Taverner, T.= Staunton, H.**

⟨♙f7⟩ 1 e4 ♘c6 2 d4 d5 3 e5 ♗f5 4 ♗e3 e6 5 ♗e2 ♘b4 6 ♘a3 ♘c6 7 ♘f3 ♗xa3 8 bxa3 ♕e7 9 ♕c1 ♕d7 10 ♘h4 ♘ge7 11 ♕b2 0-0 12 g4 ♗g6 13 ♘xg6 ♘xg6 14 h4 ♘f4 15 ♗f1 b6 16 h5 ♕f7 17 c3 ♘a5 18 ♕c1 c5 19 dxc5 ♘c6 20 cxb6 axb6 21 ♗xf4 ♕xf4 22 ♕xf4 ♖xf4 23 ♖b1 ♖xa3 24 ♖xb6 ♖xc3 25 ♔d2 ♖c5 26 ♔e3 ♖e4+ 27 ♔d2 ♘xe5 28 ♗e2 ♖a5 29 ♖a1 ♖a3 30 ♖b3 ♖ea4 31 ♖xa3 ♖xa3 ½-½

L/N6123-1843

**1843̂-★ST-5**
**Taverner, T.– Staunton, H.**

[Staunton]

⟨♙f7⟩ 1 e4 ♘c6 2 d4 d5 3 e5 ♗f5 4 c3 e6 5 ♗d3 ♘ge7 6 ♗g5 ♕d7 7 ♘e2 h6 8 ♗e3 ♗h7 9 ♗xh7 ♖xh7 10 ♕d3 g6 11 ♘g3 ♖f7 12 ♘d2 0-0-0 13 b4 ♘f5 14 ♘xf5 gxf5 15 g3 h5 16 f4 ♗e7 17 a4 h4 18 ♗f2 ♖g7 19 a5 ♗xb4 20 cxb4 ♘xb4 21 ♕b3 ♕b5 22 ♖a3 ♕c6 23 ♕c3 [23 ♕xb4? ♕c1+] 23 ... ♘c2+ 24 ♔d1 ♘xa3 25 ♕xa3 ♔b8 26 gxh4 ♖g2 27 ♗g3 ♕b5 28 ♖e1 a6 29 ♖e3 ♖c8 30 ♔c2 ♕c4+ 31 ♕c3 ♕a2+ 32 ♔d3 ♖xd2+ 33 ♕xd2 ♕c4# **0-1** L/N6123-1843

**1843̂-★ST-6**
**Taverner, T.– Staunton, H.**
London

⟨♙f7⟩1 e4 ♘c6 2 d4 d5 3 e5 ♗f5 4 ♘f3 e6 5 ♗e3 ♘b4 6 ♘a3 ♘c6 7 ♗d3 ♗xa3 8 bxa3 ♘ge7 9 ♗g5 0-0 10 ♗xf5 ♖xf5 11 0-0 ♕d7 12 ♗e3 ♖af8 13 ♘h4 ♖5f7 14 ♕d2 b6 15 ♕d3 ♘a5 16 ♖ae1 ♘c4 17 ♗c1 c5 18 c3 ♕a4 19 f4 ♘xa3 20 g4 cxd4 21 cxd4 ♘c2 22 ♖d1 ♘c6 23 ♘f3 ♘2b4 24 ♕b3 ♕xa2 25 ♕xa2 ♘xa2 26 ♗a3 ♘ab4 27 f5 exf5 28 ♘g5 fxg4 29 ♘xf7 ♖xf7 30 ♖xf7 ♔xf7 31 ♔g2

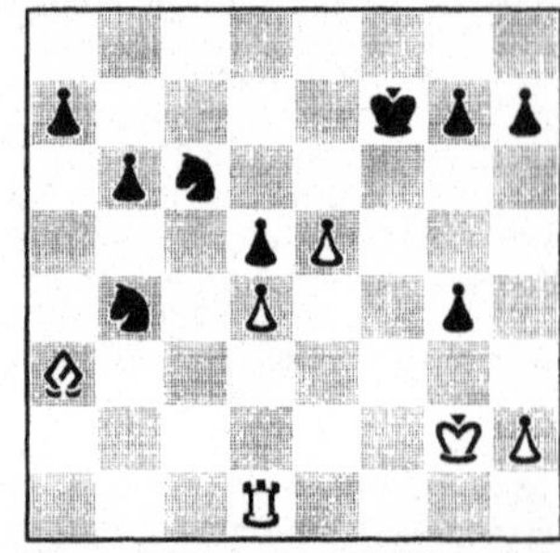

31 ... a5 32 ♔g3 h5 33 ♖f1+ ♔e6 34 ♖f4 ♘d3 35 ♖f1 ♘xd4 36 ♔h4 ♘xe5 37 ♔xh5 b5 38 ♔h4 ♘f5+ 39 ♔g5 g6 40 ♖e1 d4 41 ♗b2 ♔d5 42 ♖a1 a4 43 ♖b1 ♘d3 44 ♗a3 ♔c4 45 ♔xg4 b4 46 ♗xb4 ♘xb4 47 ♔g5 ♘e7 48 ♔f6 ♘bd5+ 49 ♔e6 a3 50 ♖g1 a2 51 h4 d3 52 ♔e5 d2 53 ♔e4 ♔c3 54 ♔f3 ♔c2 **0-1** L/N6123

**1843̂-★ST-7**
**Taverner, T.– Staunton, H.**
London

⟨♙f7⟩1 e4 ♘c6 2 d4 e5 3 dxe5 ♘xe5 4 f4 ♘f7 5 ♗c4 ♘gh6 6 ♘f3 ♗c5 7 ♕d3 c6 8 ♗e3 ♗xe3 9 ♕xe3

0-0 10 ♗b3 d5 11 e5 ♘g4 12 ♕d4 ♘fh6 13 c4 ♘f5 14 ♕d2 d4 15 c5+ ♔h8 16 ♘a3 b6 17 cxb6 axb6 18 0-0-0 c5 19 ♘g5 ♖a7 20 ♘b5 ♖e7 21 h3 ♘ge3 22 ♖de1 c4 23 ♗c2 h6 24 ♘e4 ♗b7 25 g4 ♘xc2 26 gxf5 ♘xe1 27 ♖xe1 ♗xe4 28 ♖xe4 ♕d5 29 ♘d6 d3 30 ♖xc4 ♖d8 31 ♖c3 ♖xd6 32 exd6 ♕h1+ 33 ♕d1 ♖e1 34 ♖xd3 ♕c6+ 35 ♔d2 ♖xd1+ 36 ♔xd1 ♕a4+ 37 b3 ♕e4 38 ♔c2 ♕c6+ 39 ♔d2 ♕d7 40 a4 ♔g8 41 b4 ♔f7 42 a5 bxa5 43 bxa5 ♕xf5 44 d7 ♕xa5+ 45 ♔e3 ♕d8 ...♀ **0-1** L/N6123

**1843̂-★SW-1**
**Walker, G.–Saint-Amant, P.C.F. de**

1 e4 e5 2 ♘f3 ♘f6 3 ♘c3 ♘c6 4 ♗c4 ♗c5 5 d3 h6 6 0-0 d6 7 h3 ♗e6 8 ♗xe6 fxe6 9 ♘a4 ♗b6 10 ♘xb6 axb6 11 c3 0-0 12 ♕e2 ♕e8 13 d4 ♕h5 14 ♖e1 exd4 15 ♘xd4 ♘xd4 16 ♕xh5 ♘xh5 17 cxd4 c5 18 ♗e3 ♘f4 19 dxc5 bxc5 20 ♖ad1 ♖xa2 21 ♖xd6 ♖xb2 22 ♗xc5 b5 23 ♖a1 e5 24 ♖d7 ♖f6 25 ♔h2 ♖g6 26 g3 ♘e2 27 ♖e7 ♘d4 28 ♔g2 ♖f6 29 ♖f1 ♘f3 30 ♖d1 ♘d4 31 ♖f1 ♘c6 32 ♖d7 b4 33 ♖a1 ♘d4 34 ♖f1 ♘c6 35 ♖a1 b3 36 ♖a6 ♖a2 37 ♖b6 ♖c2 38 ♖6b7 ♖xc5 39 ♖xg7+ ♔f8 40 ♖h7 ♔e8 41 ♖h8+ ♖f8 **0-1** L/N6123-1843̂

**1843̂-★SW-2**
**W♀– Staunton, H.**
London

⟨♙f7⟩1 e4 ... 2 d4 e6 3 ♗d3 c5 4 d5 d6 5 ♘c3 ♗e7 6 ♘f3 e5 7 h3 a6 8 a4 ♘f6 9 0-0 0-0 10 ♘h2 b5 11 axb5 ♕b6 12 ♔h1 a5 13 f4 g6 14 fxe5 dxe5 15 ♗c4 ♔h8 16 g4 ♕d8 17 ♗h6 ♖e8 18 ♕f3 ♖a7 19 ♖ad1 ♕d6 20 b3 ♘bd7 21 ♕f2 ♘b6 22 ♗d3 a4 23 ♘xa4 ♘xa4 24 bxa4 ♖xa4 25 c4 ♗d7 26 ♖df1 ♖a3 27 ♕e2 ♖ea8 28 ♘f3

28 ... ♗xg4 29 hxg4 ♘xg4 30 ♖h2 ♘xh2 31 ♘xh2 g5 32 ♘g4 ♕g6 33 ♘xe5 ♕xh6+ 34 ♔g1 ♕h4 35 ♕f3 ♖f8 36 ♘f7+ ♔g8 37 e5 ♕d4+ 38 ♔g2 ♖xd3 39 ♕f5 ♖d2+ **0-1** L/N6123-1843̂

**1843̂-★SW-3**
**Staunton, H.– Worrall, T.H.**

⟨♖a1⟩ 1 e4 e5 2 ♗c4 ♗c5 3 b4 ♗xb4 4 f4 d5 5 ♗xd5 ♘f6 6 c3 ♘xd5 7 exd5 ♗d6 8 ♘f3 exf4 9 0-0 ♗g4 10 d4 0-0 11 c4 c5 12 ♘c3 cxd4 13 ♘e4 f5 14 ♘xd6 ♕xd6 15 ♕xd4 ♗xf3 16 ♖xf3 ♘c6 17 ♕c3 ♕c5+ 18 ♔h1 ♘d4 19 ♗a3 ♕b6 20 ♗b2 ♖ae8 21 h3 ♖e4 22 ♖d3 ♖e1+ 23 ♕xe1 ♕xb2 24 ♕d1 ♘e2 25 ♖d2 ♘g3+ 26 ♔h2 ♕xd2 **0-1** L/N6123-1843

**1843̂-★S♀-1**
**♀– Staunton, H.**
London

⟨♙f7⟩1 e4 ... 2 d4 d6 3 ♘c3 ♘c6 4 ♗c4 e6 5 ♘h3 e5 6 ♘g5 ♘h6 7 ♘e6 ♗xe6 8 ♗xe6 ♘xd4 9 ♗c4 g6 10 h4 ♕d7 11 ♗g5 c6 12 ♕d2 ♘f7 13 ♗f6 ♖g8 14 ♗xf7+ ♕xf7 15 ♗g5 h6 16 ♗e3 ♘e6 17 ♗xh6 ♗xh6 18 ♕xh6 0-0-0 19 ♕e3 ♔b8 20 0-0-0 ♖gf8 21 ♖d2 ♔a8 22 ♖hd1 ♘d4 23 ♔b1 ♕f6 24 ♘e2 ♘xe2 25 ♕xe2 ♕xh4 26 ♖xd6 ♖xd6 27 ♖xd6 ♖xf2

28 ♕d1 a6 29 ♖xg6 ♕xe4 30 ♖g8+ ♔a7 31 g4 ♕c4 **0-1** L/N6123-1843̂

**1843̂-★S♀-2**
**Staunton, H.+♀**

1 e4 e5 2 ♘f3 ♘c6 3 d4 exd4 4 c3 d3 5 ♘d4 ♗c5 6 ♗e3 ♗b6 7 ♗xd3 ♘f6 8 f4 d6 9 h3 0-0 10 0-0 ♕e7 11 ♕f3 ♖e8 12 ♘d2 ♘d5 13 ♗f2 ♘f6 14 ♖ae1 ♘xd4 15 ♗xd4 ♗xd4+ 16 cxd4 c5 17 e5 dxe5 18 fxe5 ♘d7 19 e6 f6 20 d5 ♘e5 21 ♖xe5 **1-0** L/N6123-1843̂

**1843̂-★S♀-3**
**Staunton, H.+♀**
London

1 e4 e5 2 ♘f3 ♘c6 3 ♗c4 ♗c5 4 b4 ♗xb4 5 c3 ♗a5 6 0-0 ♗b6 7 d4 exd4 8 ♘xd4 ♗xd4 9 cxd4 d6 10 f4 ♘f6 11 e5 dxe5 12 fxe5 ♘d5 13 ♗a3 ♗e6 14 ♕d3 ♘ce7 15 ♘d2 0-0 16 ♘e4 h6 17 ♗xd5 ♗xd5 18 ♘f6+ gxf6 19 ♗xe7 ♕xe7 20 ♕g3+ ♔h7 21 exf6 ♖g8 22 fxe7 ♖xg3 23 hxg3 ♖e8 24 ♖ae1 ♗e6 25 ♖e5 **1-0** L/N6123-1843̂

**1843̂-★S♀-4**
**Staunton, H.+♀**

⟨♖a1⟩1 e4 e5 2 ♘f3 ♘c6 3 ♗c4 ♗c5 4 c3 d6 5 d4 exd4 6 b4 ♗b6 7 cxd4 ♘f6 8 ♘c3 h6 9 0-0 0-0 10 b5 ♘e7 11 ♕d3 ♘g6 12 e5 d5 13 ♗b3 ♘h7 14 ♘xd5 c5

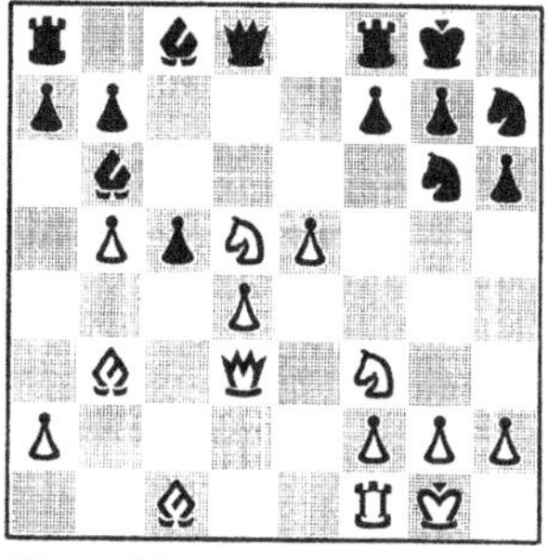

15 ♕xg6 fxg6 16 ♘e7+ **1-0** L/N6123-1843̂

**1843̂-★S♀-5**
**Staunton, H.+♀**

⟨♘b1⟩1 e4 e5 2 ♘f3 ♘c6 3 ♗c4 f5 4 d3 ♗e7 5 c3 ♘f6 6 ♘g5 ♖f8 7 ♘xh7 d5 8 exd5 ♘xh7 9 ♕h5+ g6 10 ♕xg6+ ♖f7 11 dxc6 ♕d6 12 ♕xf7+ **1-0** L/N6123-1843̂

**1843̂-★S♀-6**
**Staunton, H.+♀**

⟨♘b1⟩1 e4 e5 2 ♗c4 ♗c5 3 d4 ♗xd4 4 ♘f3 ♘c6 5 c3 ♗b6 6 ♘g5 ♘h6 7 f4 0-0 8 f5 ♕f6 9 ♕h5 ♘a5 10 ♘xh7 ♔xh7 11 ♗g5 ♕c6 12 ♗d5 ♕c5 13 0-0-0 c6 14 ♗xf7 ♖xf7 15 ♗xh6 ♔g8 16 ♗g5 d5 17 ♖d3 dxe4 18 ♖h3 ♖f8 19 ♕h7+ ♔f7 20 ♕g6+ ♔g8 21 ♖h7 ♖f7 22 ♕h5 **1-0** L/N6123-1843̂

**1843̂-★S♀-7**
**Staunton, H.+♀**

⟨♘b1⟩1 e4 e5 2 ♘f3 ♘c6 3 ♗c4 ♗c5 4 b4 ♗xb4 5 c3 ♗a5 6 0-0 d6 7 d4 exd4 8 cxd4 ♗b6 9 ♗b2 ♘f6 10 d5 ♘a5 11 e5 ♘xc4 12 exf6 ♘xb2 13 fxg7 ♖g8 14 ♖e1+ ♔d7 15 ♕c2 c6 16 ♕xb2 ♔c7 17 a4 ♗c5 18 dxc6 bxc6 19 ♖ab1 ♗a6 20 ♕c3 ♗b6 21 ♘d4 ♗xd4 22 ♕a5+ ♗b6 23 ♕xa6 ♕c8 24 ♖e7+ ♔d8 25 ♕e2 ♕f5 26 ♖e1 **1-0** L/N6123-1843̂

**1843̂-★S♀-8**
**Staunton, H.+♀**
⟨♖a1⟩1 e4 e5 2 ♘f3 ♘c6 3 ♗c4 ♗c5 4 b4 ♗xb4 5 c3 ♗a5 6 0-0 ♗b6 7 d4 exd4 8 e5 d5 9 exd6 ♕xd6 10 ♗a3 ♗c5 11 ♗xf7+ ♔xf7 12 ♘g5+ ♔e8 13 ♖e1+ ♘ge7 14 ♘e4 ♕d5 15 ♗xc5 ♗f5 16 c4 ♕xc4 17 ♘a3 ♕d5 18 ♘b5 ♖c8 19 ♘bc3 ♕d7 20 ♗xe7 ♗xe4 21 ♘xe4 ♘xe7 22 ♕h5+ ♔d8 23 ♘c5 ♕f5 24 ♘xb7+ ♔d7 25 ♖xe7+ ♔xe7 26 ♕xf5 **1-0** L/N6123-1843̂

**1843̂-★S♀-9**
**Staunton, H.+♀**
⟨♘b1⟩1 e4 e5 2 ♗c4 ♗c5 3 d4 ♗xd4 4 f4 ♗xg1 5 ♖xg1 ♕h4+ 6 g3 ♕xh2 7 ♗e3 ♘f6 8 fxe5 ♘xe4 9 ♗xf7+ ♔xf7 10 ♕d5+ ♔e8 11 ♕xe4 ♘c6 12 0-0-0 b6 13 ♕g4 ♘xe5 14 ♕xg7 ♘f7 15 ♖de1 **1-0** L/N6123-1843̂

**1843̂-★S♀-10**
**Staunton, H.+♀**
⟨♘b1⟩1 e4 e5 2 f4 exf4 3 ♘f3 g5 4 ♗c4 g4 5 d4 gxf3 6 0-0 fxg2 7 ♗xf7+ ♔xf7 8 ♖xf4+ ♘f6 9 e5 ♗e7 10 ♕h5+ ♔g8 11 exf6 ♗xf6 12 ♖g4+ ♔f8 13 ♗h6+ ♔e7 14 ♖e1+ **1-0** L/N6123-1843̂

**1843̂-★S♀-11**
**Staunton, H.+♀**
London
⟨♘b1⟩1 e4 e5 2 ♗c4 ♘c6 3 c3 d6 4 ♘f3 ♗g4 5 ♕b3 ♘h6 6 d4 ♘a5 7 ♕a4+ c6 8 ♗e2 b5 9 ♕c2 ♗xf3 10 ♗xf3 exd4 11 cxd4 g6 12 a4 ♘c4 13 axb5 cxb5 14 b3 ♘b6 15 ♕c6+ ♕d7 16 e5 ♖c8 17 ♕xd7+ ♘xd7 18 0-0 dxe5 19 ♖xa7 ♗g7 20 dxe5 ♘xe5 21 ♗xh6 ♘xf3+ 22 gxf3 ♗xh6 23 ♖e1+ ♔f8 24 ♖ee7 ♗g5 25 ♖xf7+ ♔e8 26 f4 ♗d8 27 ♖fb7 h6 28 ♖xb5 g5 29 f5 h5 30 ♔g2 h4 31 ♔f3 ♖g8 32 ♔e4 ♖c2 33 ♖e5+ ♔f8 34 ♔d5 **1-0** L/N6123-1843̂

**1843̂-★S♀-12**
**Staunton, H.+♀**
⟨♘g1⟩1 e4 e5 2 d4 d5 3 f4 exd4 4 e5 ♗b4+ 5 c3 dxc3 6 bxc3 ♗c5 7 ♗d3 ♘e7 8 ♗a3 ♗xa3 9 ♘xa3 c6 10 0-0 ♗f5 11 ♖b1 b5 12 g4 ♗xd3 13 ♕xd3 ♕a5 14 ♘c2 ♕b6+ 15 ♔h1 ♘d7 16 ♖be1 0-0 17 f5 ♘c5 18 ♕h3 ♘e4 19 ♘d4 b4 20 f6 ♘g6 21 ♖xe4 dxe4 22 ♘f5 ♘xe5 23 ♘h6+ ♔h8 24 fxg7+ ♔xg7 25 ♘f5+ ♔f6 26 ♕h4+ ♔e6 27 ♕e7+ ♔d5 28 ♖d1+ ♘d3 29 c4+ ♔xc4 30 ♕xe4+ ♔c5 31 ♕d4+ ♔b5 32 ♕xd3+ ♔a5 33 ♘d6 **1-0** L/N6123-1843̂

**1843̂-★S♀-13**
**♀–Staunton, H.**
⟨♖a8,♙f7⟩1 e4 ... 2 d4 c5 3 d5 d6 4 e5 dxe5 5 ♕h5+ g6 6 ♕xe5 ♘f6 7 c4 ♗g7 8 ♕e3 ♘a6 9 a4 0-0 10 h3 ♗f5 11 g4 ♘b4 12 ♕e2 ♘c2+ 13 ♔d1 ♘d4 14 ♕e3 ♗xg4+ 15 hxg4 ♘xg4 16 ♕g3 ♘xf2+ 17 ♔e1 ♘xh1 18 ♕g2 ♘f2 19 ♗e2 ♘c2+ 20 ♔f1 **0-1** L/N6123-1843̂

**1843̂-★S♀-14**
**♀–Staunton, H.**
London
⟨♙f7⟩ 1 e4 ... 2 d4 e6 3 h4 c5 4 ♘c3 cxd4 5 ♕xd4 ♘c6 6 ♕d1 ♘f6 7 ♘f3 ♗e7 8 ♗d3 0-0 9 ♘g5 h6 10 ♕e2 ♘e5 11 f4 ♘xd3+ 12 cxd3 ♗b4 13 ♗d2 d6 14 e5 ♘h7 15 exd6 ♗xc3 16 bxc3 ♕xd6 17 ♘f3 b6 18 ♘e5 ♗b7 19 0-0 ♖ad8 20 ♖fe1 b5 21 a4 a6 22 axb5 axb5 23 d4 b4 24 ♖a5 ♖fe8 25 ♖b1 bxc3 26 ♗xc3 ♗a8 27 ♕e3 ♘f6 28 ♗b4 ♕b6 29 ♘c4 ♕c6 **0-1** L/N6123-1843

**1843̂-★S♀-15**
**♀+Staunton, H.**
⟨♙f7⟩1 e4 ... 2 d4 ♘c6 3 ♗g5 d6 4 ♗c4 ♘f6 5 ♘c3 e6 6 f4 ♗e7 7 ♘f3 0-0 8 0-0 d5 9 ♗xf6 ♖xf6 10 exd5 ♘a5 11 ♕e2 ♘xc4 12 ♕xc4 ♖xf4 13 dxe6 c6 14 ♖ae1 ♕d6 15 ♘e4 ♕d8 16 ♘eg5 h6 17 ♘h3 ♖f6 18 ♖e5 ♔h8 19 ♕e2 b5 20 ♕e4 ♕e8 21 ♖e1 ♗b7 22 ♕g4 ♖d8 23 ♘f4 c5 24 d5 c4 25 ♖f5 g5 26 ♖xf6 ♗xf6 27 ♘h5 ♕f8 28 ♘xf6 ♕xf6

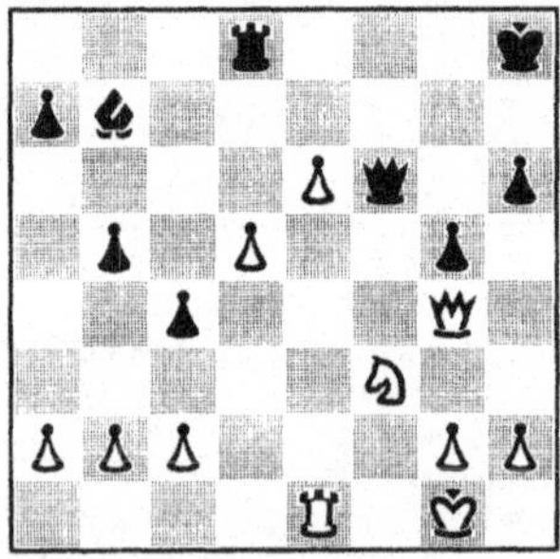

29 e7 ♖e8 30 ♕d7 **1-0** L/N6123-1843̂

## KENNEDY✕STAUNTON

Brighton

[1844-✕KS]

| | | | | | | |
|---|---|---|---|---|---|---|
| H.A. Kennedy | 0 | ½ | 1 | 0 | 0 | 1½ |
| H. Staunton | 1 | ½ | 0 | 1 | 1 | 3½ |

**1844-✕KS-1**
**Kennedy, H.A.–Staunton, H.**
[Staunton]
⟨♙f7⟩1 e4 ... 2 d4 d6 3 ♗d3 ♘d7 4 e5 g6 5 f4 ♗g7 6 ♘f3 ♘f8 7 ♗e3 ♘h6 8 h3 ♗f5 9 g4! ♗xd3 10 ♕xd3 ♕d7 11 ♘c3 d5 12 0-0-0 a6 13 ♔b1! [△ 14 f5 gxf5 15 ♗xh6] 13 ... e6 14 ♘h4 ♕e7 15 ♘f3 [15 f5?] 15 ... ♕d7 16 ♘h4 0-0-0 17 f5 gxf5 18 ♗xh6 ♗xh6 19 gxf5 exf5 20 ♘xf5 ♕e6 [20 ... ♗~?] 21 ♖df1 ♗g5 22 ♘g7 ♕g6 23 ♘f5 ♕e6 24 ♖hg1 ♗e7 25 ♖g7 ♗b4 26 ♘e2 ♘g6 27 ♘f4 ♘xf4 [27 ... ♕b6 28 ♘xg6 hxg6 29 ♖xg6 ♕xg6 30 ♘e7+±] 28 ♖xf4 ♔b8 29 ♘h4 ♖d7 30 ♖xd7 [30 ♕f5?; 30 ♖f6??] 30 ... ♕xd7 31 a3 ♗e7 32 ♖f7 ♕d8 33 ♘f3 h6 34 ♕f5 ♖e8 35 e6 ♕d6 36 ♘e5 ♔a7 37 ♖g7 ♕b6 38 ♕d3 [□ 38 ♘d7 ♕xd4 39 ♖xe7 (39 ♕f7 ♖f8 40 ♘xf8 ♗f6=) 39 ... ♖g8 (39 ... ♖xe7 40 ♕f8+–) 40 ♕d3+–] 38 ... ♗f6 39 ♘d7 ♕xe6 40 ♘xf6 ♕xf6 41 ♖xc7 ♖e4 42 ♕b3 ♕b6 43 ♕xb6+ [43 ♕xd5??] 43 ... ♔xb6 44 ♖h7 ♖h4 45 c3 ♖xh3 46 ♔a2 ♖h2 47 a4 h5 48 a5+ ♔c6 49 ♖f7 h4 50 ♖f6+ ♔c7 51 ♖h6 h3 52 ♔a3 ♖h1 53 b3 h2 54 ♔b4 ♔d7 55 ♔c5 ♖c1 56 ♖h7+ ♔c8 57 ♖h8+ ♔d7 58 ♖h7+ ♔d8 59 ♖h8+ ♔e7?! 60 ♖xh2 ♖xc3+ 61 ♔b4 ♖d3 62 ♖h7+ ♔d6 63 ♖xb7 ♖xd4+ 64 ♔c3 ♖d1 65 ♖b6+ ♔e5 [65 ... ♔c5??] 66 ♖xa6 d4+ 67 ♔c2 ♖a1 68 b4 ♔d5 69 b5 ♔c4 70 b6 d3+ 71 ♔d2 ♖a2+ 72 ♔e3 ♖e2+ 73 ♔f3 ♖e7 74 b7 ♖xb7 75 ♖c6+ ♔d5 76 ♖c1 ♔d4 77 a6 ♖f7+ 78 ♔g3 d2 79 ♖a1 ♔c3 [79 ... ♔d3?=] **0-1** L/N6123

**1844-✕KS-2**
**Kennedy, H.A.=Staunton, H.**
⟨♙f7⟩ 1 e4 ... 2 d4 ♘c6 3 ♘c3 e5 4 dxe5 ♘xe5 5 f4 ♘f7 6 ♗c4 ♘gh6 7 f5 ♗b4 8 ♘e2 ♕h4+ 9 ♘g3 ♘e5 10 ♗xh6 ♕xh6 11 ♗d3 ♕e3+ 12 ♕e2 ♕c5 13 ♔d2 0-0 14 a3 ♗xc3+ 15 bxc3 ♖f6 16 ♕e3 ♕a5 17 ♕d4 ♖d6 18 ♕b4 ♕a6 19 ♕b3+ ♔f8 20 ♕b1 c5 21 f6 g6 22 c4 ♕xc4 23 ♔e2 ♕e6 24 ♔e1 ♘xd3+ 25 cxd3 b6 26 f7 c4 27 ♖f1 ♕e5 28 ♕c1 ♕g7 29 ♖a2 ♗a6 30 dxc4 ♖c8 31 ♖c2 ♖d4 32 ♕b2 ♖cxc4 33 ♖ff2 ♖xc2 34 ♖xc2 ♔xf7 35 ♖d2 ♖xd2 36 ♕xg7+ ♔xg7 37 ♔xd2 ♔f6 38 ♔e3 ♔e5 39 ♘h1 h5 40 ♘f2 ♗b5 41 h4 a5 42 g4 a4 43 gxh5 gxh5 44 ♘h3 ♗c6 45 ♘f4 ♗xe4 46 ♘xh5 d5 47 ♘g3 d4+ 48 ♔d2 ♗h7 49 ♘e2 ♔d5 50 ♔c1 ♔c4 51 ♔b2 b5 52 h5 d3 53 ♘c3 b4 54 ♘d1 b3 55 h6 ♗g6 56 ♔c1 b2+ 57 ♔xb2 d2 58 ♘c3 ♔d3 59 ♘d1 **½-½** L/N6123

**1844-⚔KS-3**
**Kennedy, H.A.+Staunton, H.**
⟨♙f7⟩ 1 e4 ... 2 d4 e6 3 ♗d3 c5 4 e5 g6 5 c3 ♘c6 6 ♘f3 d6 7 h4 dxe5 8 h5 gxh5 9 ♘xe5 ♘xe5 10 dxe5 ♘e7 11 ♕xh5+ ♔d7 12 ♗g5 ♔c7 13 ♗e4 ♗d7 14 ♘d2 ♕e8 15 ♕f3 ♗g7 16 ♗f6 ♕f8 17 0-0-0 ♗c6 18 ♗xe7 ♕xe7 19 ♗xc6 bxc6 20 ♕e4 h5 21 ♘b3 ♖ad8 22 ♘a5 ♖d5 23 c4 ♖d4 24 ♕xc6+ ♔b8 25 ♖xd4 cxd4 26 ♕d6+ ♕xd6 27 exd6 h4 28 c5 ♔c8 29 b4 ♔d7 30 ♔d2 ♗f6 31 ♘c4 ♔c6 32 ♔d3 ♔d5 33 ♘d2 ♖g8 34 ♖g1 ♖g4 35 g3 e5 36 ♘e4 ♖xe4 37 c6 ♖g4 38 c7 e4+ 39 ♔c2 d3+ 40 ♔d1 e3 41 c8♕ ...⚲ **1-0** L/N6123

**1844-⚔KS-4**
**Kennedy, H.A.–Staunton, H.**
[Staunton]
⟨♙f7⟩ 1 e4 ... 2 d4 ♘c6 3 ♘c3 e5 4 dxe5 ♘xe5 5 f4 ♘f7 6 ♗c4 ♘gh6 7 f5 ♗b4 8 ♘f3 ♕e7 9 ♕e2 ♘g4 10 ♗d2 [10 ♗xf7+ ♕xf7 11 ♘g5 ♕f6∓] 10 ... c6 11 0-0-0 ♘fe5 12 ♘xe5 ♘xe5 13 ♗b3 ♘f7 14 a3 ♗a5 15 ♔b1 ♗c7 16 g3 [◻ 16 g4] 16 ... b5 17 ♗xf7+ ♕xf7 18 ♘a2 a5 19 g4 ♗e5 20 ♕e1 b4 21 b3 a4 22 ♗xb4 axb3 23 ♘c3 ♕c4 24 ♕e2 ♕f7 25 cxb3 ♕xb3+ 26 ♕b2 ♕c4 27 ♕a2 ♗a6 28 ♕xc4 ♗xc4 29 ♔c2 ♔d8 30 h3 ♔c7 31 ♘b1 ♖hb8 32 ♘d2 ♖xb4! 33 axb4 ♖a2+ 34 ♔c1 ♗d3 35 ♘f3 ♗f4+ **0-1** L/N6123

**1844-⚔KS-5**
**Kennedy, H.A.–Staunton, H.**
⟨♙f7⟩ 1 e4 ... 2 d4 ♘c6 3 ♘c3 e5 4 dxe5 ♘xe5 5 f4 ♘f7 6 ♗c4 ♘gh6 7 f5 ♗b4 8 ♘f3 ♕e7 9 0-0 ♕c5+ 10 ♕d4 ♘e5 11 ♗e3 ♕xd4 12 ♗xd4 ♘xc4 13 ♘d5 ♗d6 14 ♗xg7 ♘f7 15 ♗xh8 ♘xh8 16 ♘f6+ ♔f7 17 ♘xh7 ♔g7 18 ♘fg5 ♘e5 19 ♖f4 ♘hf7 20 ♘xf7 ♘xf7 21 ♖h4 b6 22 ♖h5 ♗f4 23 g4 ♗b7 24 ♖e1 ♖h8 25 f6+ ♔g6 26 ♖f5 ♗e5 27 h4 ♖xh7 28 h5+ ♔h6 29 ♖e2 d6 30 ♖g2 ♘g5 31 f7 ♖xf7 32 ♖xf7 ♘xf7 ...⚲ **0-1** L/N6123

**STAUNTON⚔TUCKETT**
**[1844-⚔ST]**

| | | | | | | | |
|---|---|---|---|---|---|---|---|
| H. Staunton | 0 | 0 | 1 | 0 | ½ | 0 | 1½ |
| T. Tuckett | 1 | 1 | 0 | 1 | ½ | 1 | 4½ |

**1844-⚔ST-1̂** ix 44
**Tuckett, T.–Staunton, H.**
[Staunton]
⟨♙f7⟩1 e4 ... 2 d4 ♘c6 3 ♘f3 d5 4 exd5 ♕xd5 5 ♘c3 ♕d8 6 d5 ♘b8 7 ♗c4 ♗g4 8 ♗f4 ♘f6 9 h3 ♗h5 10 ♕e2 a6 11 ♖d1 ♘bd7 12 d6 c6 13 dxe7 ♕xe7 14 0-0 ♕xe2 15 ♗xe2 0-0-0 16 ♘g5 ♗xe2 17 ♘xe2 ♖e8 18 ♘d4 h6 19 ♘f7 ♖g8 20 ♘f5 ♘e4 21 f3 ♗c5+ 22 ♔h2 ♖gf8 23 fxe4 ♖xf7 24 ♗d6? g6! 25 ♗xc5 gxf5 26 ♗e3 h5 27 ♖d4 ♘c5 28 ♖d6 ♘xe4 29 ♖h6 ♘g3 30 ♖f3 ♖xe3 31 ♖xg3 [31 ♖xe3?? ♘f1+–+] 31 ... ♖e2 32 ♖xh5 f4 33 ♖g8+ ♔c7 [△ 34 ... f3] 34 ♔g1 ♖xc2 35 a4 ♖xb2 36 a5 ♖b5 37 ♖gg5 b6 38 axb6+ ♔xb6 39 ♔f2 a5 40 ♔e2 a4 41 ♖xb5+ cxb5 42 ♔d2 ♖g7 43 ♔c3 ♖g3+ **0-1** L/N6123

**1844-⚔ST-2̂** ix 44
**Tuckett, T.–Staunton, H.**
[Staunton]
⟨♙f7⟩1 e4 ... 2 d4 e6 3 ♗d3 c5 4 e5 ♘e7 5 c3 cxd4 6 cxd4 ♘bc6 7 ♘f3 ♘b4 8 ♘c3 ♘xd3+ 9 ♕xd3 ♘f5 10 ♕e4 d5 11 exd6 ♗xd6 12 ♘g5 [12 d5] 12 ... ♕f6 13 ♘b5 ♗b4+ 14 ♔d1 0-0 15 g4 h6 16 h4 hxg5 17 hxg5 ♕g6 18 gxf5 ♕xf5 19 ♕xf5 ♖xf5 20 ♘c7 ♖b8 21 f4 ♗d7 22 a4 a6 23 d5 [◻ 23 ♗d2 ♗xd2 24 ♔xd2 △ 25 ♖ac1] 23 ... exd5 24 ♗e3 ♗a5 25 ♖h4 ♗xc7 26 ♔d2 ♗a5+ 27 ♔d3 b5 28 g6 ♖c8 29 ♗d4 ♗d8 30 ♖h7 ♗f6 31 ♖ah1 ♔f8 **0-1** L/N6123

**1844-⚔ST-3̂** ix 44
**Tuckett, T.+Staunton, H.**
[Staunton]
⟨♙f7⟩1 e4 ... 2 d4 d6 3 ♘c3 c6 4 f4 ♗e6 5 f5 ♗f7 6 ♗e2 ♕c7 7 ♕d3 ♘d7 8 ♗e3 e6 9 fxe6 ♗xe6 10 ♘f3 h6 11 ♘h4 ♗f7 12 ♗g4 0-0-0 13 ♗f5 ♘f6 14 ♖f1 g5 [◻ 14 ... ♔b8] 15 ♗xd7+ ♖xd7 16 ♖xf6 gxh4 17 ♕f1 ♗g7 18 ♖f4 ♖f8 19 ♕f3 ♕a5 20 ♖f5 c5 21 ♕g4! ♕b4 22 0-0-0 [22 ♕xg7? ♖g8 23 ♕ ♕xb2] 22 ... ♗xd4 23 ♗xd4 cxd4 24 ♘d5+– ♕a4 [24 ... h5 25 ♖xf7!+–] 25 ♖xf7 ♖xf7 26 ♕g8+ ♖d8 27 ♕xf7 ...⚲ **1-0** L/N6123

**1844-⚔ST-4̂** ix 44
**Tuckett, T.–Staunton, H.**
[Staunton]
⟨♙f7⟩1 e4 ... 2 d4 ♘c6 3 ♘c3 e5 4 dxe5 ♘xe5 5 f4 ♘f7 6 ♗c4 ♘gh6 7 ♕d4! c6 8 ♗e3 b5 9 ♗b3 [9 ♘xb5!? cxb5 10 ♗d5 ♖b8 11 ♕xa7±] 9 ... a5 10 a3 d6 11 f5 ♘e5 12 h3 [12 ♗xh6? ♕h4+] 12 ... ♗d7 [△ 13 ... c5 14 ♕ c4] 13 ♕d2 ♘hf7 14 ♗xf7+ ♔xf7 15 b3 ♗e7 16 ♗f4 ♕e8 17 ♗xe5 dxe5 18 ♘f3 ♗c5 19 ♘e2 ♕e7 20 a4 [20 ♘xe5+? ♕xe5 21 ♕xd7+ ♕e7 22 ♕d1 ♕xe4–+] 20 ... ♖ad8 21 ♕g5 ♕f8 22 ♖d1 bxa4 23 bxa4 ♔g8 24 g4 ♗b6 25 c3 ♗c8 26 ♖xd8 ♖xd8 [△ 27 ... ♕d6] 27 f6 ♕xf6 28 ♕xf6 gxf6 29 ♘c1 [29 g5? ♖d3] 29 ... ♗a6 30 ♖h2 ♗d3 31 ♘d2 ♗e3 32 ♘xd3 ♖xd3 33 c4 ♗f4 34 ♖g2 ♖xh3 35 ♔d1 ♖c3 36 ♔e2 ♗xd2 37 ♔xd2 ♖xc4 38 ♔d3 ♖d4+ 39 ♔e3 ♖xa4 40 ♖c2 ♖a3+ 41 ♔f2 a4 ...⚲ **0-1** L/N6123

**1844-⚔ST-5̂** ix 44
**Tuckett, T.=Staunton, H.**
[Staunton]
⟨♙f7⟩1 e4 ... 2 d4 ♘c6 3 ♘c3 e5 4 d5 ♘ce7 5 ♗g5 d6! [5 ... ♘f6] 6 h4 h6 7 ♗e3 ♘f6 8 ♗e2 c6 9 dxc6 bxc6 10 f4 ♕c7 11 fxe5 [11 f5] 11 ... dxe5 12 h5 ♗e6 13 ♗c5 ♖d8 14 ♗d3 ♘c8 15 ♗xf8 ♖xf8 16 ♕e2 ♗g4 17 ♕e3 ♘xh5 18 ♖h4 ♕d7 19 g3 ♘b6 20 a4 ♕e6 21 a5 ♘c4 22 ♗xc4 ♕xc4 [△ 23 ... ♖f1#] 23 ♘ge2 ♖f3 24 ♕g1 ♘f6 25 a6 ♖d7 26 ♖a4 ♕f7 27 ♖b4 ♖d8 28 ♖b7 ♕c4 29 ♕xa7

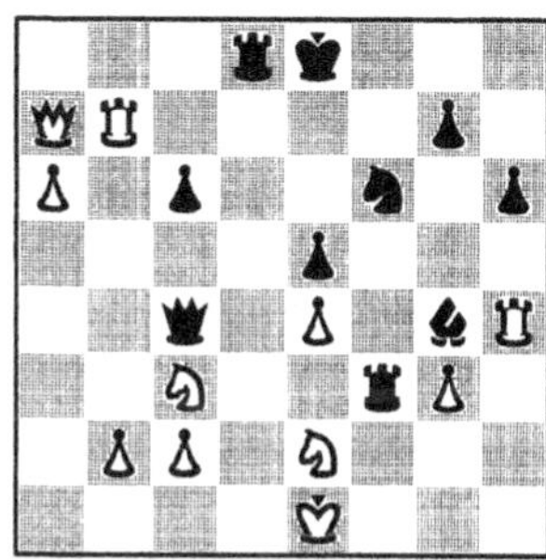

29 ... ♖d1+!? [29 ... ♖xc3! 30 ♘xc3 ♖d1+ 31 ♔f2 ♕f1+ 32 ♔e3 ♕f3#; 29 ... ♖xc3! 30 ♕e7+ ♔f8 31 ♖f7+ ♕xf7 32 ♕xf7+ ♔xf7 33 ♘xc3 ♖a8–+; 29 ... ♖xc3! 30 ♖xg4 ♖xc2–+] 30 ♘xd1 [30 ♔xd1?? ♖f1+ 31 ♔d2 ♘xe4+ 32 ♘xe4 ♖d1+ 33 ♔xd1 ♕xe2+–+] 30 ... ♖f1+ 31 ♔xf1 ♕xe2+ 32 ♔g1 ♕xd1+ **½-½** L/N6123

**1844-⚔ST-6̂** ix 44
**Tuckett, T.–Staunton, H.**
[Staunton]
⟨♙f7⟩1 e4 ... 2 d4 ♘c6 3 ♘c3 e5 4 dxe5 ♘xe5 5 f4 ♘f7 6 ♗c4 ♘gh6 7 ♘f3 ♗b4 8 0-0 c6 9 ♘e2 ♕e7 [△ 10 ... ♕c5+] 10 ♕d3 0-0 11 ♘g3 a5 12 a4 b6 13 ♗e3 ♗c5 14 ♖ae1 ♔h8 15 ♔h1 ♖b8 16 h3 ♘d6 17 ♗a2 ♗xe3 18 ♕xe3 b5 19 axb5 ♖xb5 20 b3 ♖b4 21 c3 ♖b8 22 ♘g5 ♘hf7 23 ♘xf7+ ♕xf7 24 ♖f2 [△ 25 b4] 24 ... ♗a6 25 ♖d1 ♕e7 26 ♕c5 ♕h4 [26 ... ♘xe4? 27 ♕xe7 ♘xf2+ 28 ♔ ♘xd1±] 27 ♖xd6 ♕xg3 28 ♖xd7 ♖bd8 29 ♖fd2 ♗f1 30 ♕e7 ♖de8 31 ♕d6 ♖xf4 32 ♔g1 ♗xg2 33 ♖xg2 ♕e1+ **0-1** L/N6123

**164** Anderssen, A. M1647.BL

**1844-★AS-1** 4 iv 44
**Seligo, H.+Anderssen, A.**
Breslau
1 e4 e5 2 ♗c4 ♘f6 3 ♘c3 ♗c5 4 h3 0-0 5 a3 c6 6 ♘f3 d5 7 exd5 cxd5 8 ♗a2 ♘c6 9 0-0 e4 10 ♘h2 ♕d6 11 d3 ♕g3 12 ♘e2 ♕g6 13 ♔h1 ♘h5 14 d4 ♗d6 15 f4 ♗e6 16 ♕e1 f5 17 b3 ♖f6 18 c4 ♕f7 19 ♗e3 ♖g6 20 ♕h4 ♕f8 21 ♕xh5 ♗e7 22 ♘c3 ♖g4 23 hxg4 g6 24 ♕h3 fxg4 25 ♕g3 h5 26 cxd5 h4 27 ♕e1 ♗f5 28 dxc6 ...? **1-0** L/N3034

**1844-★CD-1** 4 vii 44
**Desloges & Kieseritsky, L.= Calvi, I. & Dumonchau**
Paris
1 e4 e5 2 f4 exf4 3 ♘f3 g5 4 h4 g4 5 ♘e5 ♗e7 6 ♗c4 d5 7 ♗xd5 ♗xh4+ 8 ♔f1 ♘h6 9 g3 fxg3 10 d4 ♕f6+ 11 ♔e2 ♕f2+ 12 ♔d3 g2 13 ♖g1 c6 14 ♗e3 ♕f6 15 ♗b3 ♗g5 16 ♘c3 ♘d7 17 ♘xd7 ♗xd7 18 ♖xg2 ♗xe3 19 ♔xe3 0-0-0 20 ♕f1 ♗f5 21 ♘e2 ♖he8 22 ♖e1 ♕g5+ 23 ♔f2 ♖xe4 24 ♔g1 ♖de8 25 ♗c4 ♖e3 26 ♖d1 ♗e4 27 ♕f4 ♕xf4 28 ♘xf4 ♗xg2 29 ♘xg2 ♖3e7 30 ♗d3 f5 31 ♖f1 ♖f8 32 ♖f4 ♔d7 33 ♔f2 ♔d6 34 ♘e3 g3+ 35 ♔f3 ♖xe3+ 36 ♔xe3 ♖g8 37 ♖f1 ♘g4+ 38 ♔f4 ♘f2 39 ♗xf5 h5 40 ♔f3 h4 41 ♔g2 ♖g5 42 ♗c8 ♔d5 43 c3 ♔c4 44 ♗xb7 h3+ 45 ♔g1 ♔d5 46 ♖e1 h2+ 47 ♔g2 ♖h5 48 ♔xg3 h1♕ 49 ♖xh1 ♘xh1+ 50 ♔g2 ♖h6 51 ♗a6 ♔e4 52 b4 ♔f4 53 b5 cxb5 54 ♗xb5 ♘g3 **0-1** L/N6013

**1844-★HP-1** xi 44
**Hoffmann−Petrov, A.D.**
Warszawa
1 e4 e5 2 ♘f3 ♘c6 3 ♗c4 ♗c5 4 c3 ♘f6 5 d4 exd4 6 e5 ♘e4 7 ♗d5 ♘xf2 8 ♔xf2 dxc3+ 9 ♔g3 cxb2 10 ♗xb2 ♘e7 11 ♘g5 ♘xd5 12 ♘xf7 0-0 13 ♘xd8 **0-1** L/N6047-1849

**1844-★HS-1**
**Henderson−Staunton, H.**
London [Staunton]
⟨♙f7⟩ 1 e4 ... 2 d4 e6 3 ♗d3 c5 4 d5 d6 5 c4 g6 6 ♗d2 ♗g7 7 ♗c3 ♕e7 8 ♗xg7 ♕xg7 9 ♘c3 ♘h6 10 ♘ge2 e5 11 0-0 0-0 12 f4 ♘g4 13 ♕d2 exf4 14 ♖xf4 ♖xf4 15 ♕xf4 ♘e5 16 ♖d1 ♗g4 17 h3 ♗xe2 18 ♗xe2 ♘bd7 19 ♘b5 ♖f8 20 ♕e3 ♘f7 21 b3 ♘de5 22 ♖f1 a6 23 ♘c3 [□ 23 ♘c7] 23 ... ♖e8 24 ♘d1 ♘h6 25 ♕f4 ♘ef7 26 ♗f3 b5 27 ♘e3 ♕d4 [△ 28 ... g5] 28 ♖d1 g5 29 ♕xf7+ ♘xf7 30 ♖xd4 cxd4 31 ♘c2 d3 32 ♘b4 bxc4 33 bxc4 ♘e5→ **0-1** L/N6123

**1844-★HS-2**
**Hampton, T.−Staunton, H.**
London [Staunton]
⟨♙f7⟩ 1 e4 ... 2 d4 e6 3 ♗d3 c5 4 d5 d6 5 c4 g6 6 h4 ♗g7 7 ♘c3 a6 8 ♘ge2 ♘f6 9 ♗g5 e5 10 f4 ♗g4 11 ♕b3 b6 12 0-0-0 ♘bd7 13 ♖df1 exf4 14 ♘xf4 ♘e5 15 ♗c2 [□ 15 ♗e2] 15 ... h6 16 ♗xf6 ♗xf6 17 ♗d1 ♗d7 18 ♘ce2 b5 19 cxb5 c4 20 ♕g3 g5 21 ♘h5 ♘d3+ 22 ♔c2 ♗e5 23 ♕f3 ♕a5 24 ♘c1 ♖c8! 25 ♘g7+ [25 ♘xd3 cxd3+ 26 ♔xd3 (26 ♔b1 ♕d2→) 26 ... ♗xb5+ 27 ♔e3 ♗d4+! 28 ♔xd4 ♕b6#] 25 ... ♔d8 26 ♘e6+ ♗xe6 27 dxe6 ♕xb5 28 e7+ ♔xe7 29 ♘xd3 cxd3+ 30 ♔d2 ♕xb2+ 31 ♔e1 ♗c3# **0-1** L/N6123

**1844-★JP-1** 1 iii 44
**Jaenisch, C.F.= Petrov, A.D.**
Warsawa
⟨♙f7⟩1 e4 ... 2 d4 ♘c6 3 e5 d5 4 ♗d3 ♗e6 5 ♘f3 ♕d7 6 c3 0-0-0 7 b4 ♗g4 8 ♕a4 ♗xf3 9 gxf3 ♘xe5 10 ♕xa7 ♘xd3+ 11 ♔d2 ♕f5 12 ♕a8+ ♔d7 13 ♕xb7 ♘f4 14 ♕b5+ c6 15 ♕b7+ ♔d6 16 ♗a3 ♕d3+ 17 ♔c1 ♕b5 18 ♕a7 ♘f6 19 ♘d2 g6 20 ♔c2 ♗h6 21 ♖he1 ♖d7 22 ♕c5+ ♕xc5 23 bxc5+ ♔c7 24 ♗b4 ♖a8 25 a4 ♔d8 26 a5 ♖da7 27 ♘b3 ♘g2 28 ♖e2 ♘h4 29 ♖e6 ♔d7 30 ♖ae1 ♘e4 31 fxe4 ♔xe6 32 exd5+ ♔d7 33 dxc6+ ♔xc6 34 ♖e6+ ♔d7 35 d5 ♘f5 36 c6+ ♔d8 37 ♗c5 ♗f4 38 ♗b6+ ♗c7 39 ♔d3 ♖a6 40 ♘c5 ♗xb6 41 ♘xa6 ♖xa6 42 axb6 ♖xb6 43 c4 ♖b2 44 ♖e2 ♖xe2 45 ♔xe2 ♔c7 46 ♔d3 ♔d6 47 ♔e4 e6 48 dxe6 ♔xe6 49 c5 ♘e7 50 c7 ♔d7 51 ♔e5 ♔xc7 52 ♔f6 ♘f5 **½-½** L/N6047-1849

**1844-★SS-1**
**Stanley, C.H.+Schulten, J.W.**
1 e4 e5 2 ♗c4 ♗c5 3 c3 d6 4 h3 ♘f6 5 d4 exd4 6 cxd4 ♗b4+ 7 ♗d2 ♗xd2+ 8 ♘xd2 0-0 9 ♗d3 ♘c6 10 ♘gf3 d5 11 e5 ♘e8 12 h4 f5 13 ♘g5 ♕e7 14 ♘b3 ♘f6 15 ♔f1 ♘e4 16 ♗xe4 fxe4 17 ♕e2 a5 18 ♖d1 b6 19 ♔g1 a4 20 ♘a1 ♗a6 21 ♕h5 g6 22 ♕g4 ♖f5 23 ♘c2 ♖af8 24 ♘e3 ♖xf2 25 ♘xd5 ♕e8 26 ♘xe4 ♘xe5 27 ♘ef6+ ♖2xf6 28 ♘xf6+ ♖xf6 29 dxe5 ♕xe5 30 ♖h3 ♗e2 31 ♖d8+ ♔g7 32 ♕g3 ♕xg3 33 ♖xg3 c6 34 ♖e3 ♗c4 35 ♖e7+ ♔h6 36 ♖dd7 ♗g8 37 ♖g7 ♖f8 38 g4 b5 39 ♔h2 c5 40 ♔g3 b4 41 g5+ ♔h5 42 ♖xh7+ **1-0** L/N6013-1844

**1844-★S?-1**
**Staunton, H.+?**
London [Staunton]
⟨♘b1⟩ 1 e4 e5 2 ♘f3 ♘c6 3 ♗c4 ♗c5 4 b4 ♗xb4 5 c3 ♗a5 6 0-0 d6 7 d4 ♗xc3 8 ♕b3 ♗xa1 9 ♗xf7+ ♔e7 [9 ... ♔f8?!] 10 ♗g5+ ♘f6 11 ♖xa1 h6 12 ♘h4 ♘xd4 [12 ... hxg5?? 13 ♘g6+ ♔d7 14 ♕e6#] 13 ♘g6+ ♔d7 14 ♕h3+ ♔c6 15 ♖c1+ [15 ♗d5+?] 15 ... ♔b6 16 ♖b1+ ♘b5 17 ♖xb5+ ♔xb5 18 ♕b3+ ♔c6 19 ♕c4+ ♔d7 20 ♘xe5+ ♔e7 21 ♘g6+ ♔d7 22 ♕e6+ ♔c6 23 ♘e5+ ♔b6 24 ♕b3+ **1-0** L/N6123

**1844̂-★JP-1**
**Jaenisch, C.F.+Petrov, A.D.**
Warszawa
⟨♙f7⟩1 e4 ... 2 d4 ♘c6 3 e5 d5 4 ♗d3 ♗e6 5 ♘f3 ♕d7 6 ♘g5 g6 7 c3 0-0-0 8 b4 h6 9 ♘xe6 ♕xe6 10 0-0 g5 11 a4 ♗g7 12 a5 ♖f8 13 ♕b3 g4 14 b5 ♘b8 15 c4 c6 16 ♘c3 ♖d8 17 ♘a4 ♘d7 18 ♗f4 h5 19 ♖fc1 ♘b8 20 ♖ab1 ♕f7 21 bxc6 e6 22 cxb7+ ♔d7 23 cxd5 exd5 24 ♕b5+ ♔e6 25 ♘c5+ ♔e7 26 ♗g5+ ♗f6 27 exf6+ ♔f8 28 ♗g6 ♕xg6 29 ♘e6+ ♔f7 30 ♘xd8+ ♔f8 31 ♕b4+ **1-0** L/N6123-1844̂

**1844̂-★JP-2**
**Jaenisch, C.F.+Petrov, A.D.**
Warszawa
⟨♙f7⟩1 e4 ... 2 d4 ♘c6 3 e5 d5 4 ♗d3 g6 5 h4 ♘xd4 6 ♗xg6+ hxg6 7 ♕xd4 ♗f5 8 g4 ♗xc2 9 ♘c3 c5 10 ♕d2 d4 11 ♕xc2 dxc3 12 ♕xg6+ ♔d7 13 ♗f4 ♕a5 14 0-0-0+ ♔c7 15 ♕d3 ♕b4 16 ♕d7+ ♔b6 17 ♕e6+ ♔a5 18 bxc3 ♕xc3+ 19 ♔b1 ♕b4+ 20 ♔a1 ♕xf4 21 ♘e2 ♕xf2 22 ♘c3 ♗g7 23 ♕b3 a6 24 ♖b1 b5 25

♘xb5 ♖b8 26 ♕a3+ ♔b6 27 ♘d4+ **1-0** L/N6123-1844

### 1844-★LS-1 27x44
**Saint-Amant,P.C.F.de+Legris**

[Saint-Amant]

⟨♘b1⟩1 e4 e5 2 ♗c4 ♗c5 3 b4 ♗xb4 4 f4 exf4? 5 ♘f3 ♕e7 6 e5! ♘h6 7 c3 ♗a5 8 ♕b3 0-0 9 0-0 ♗b6+ 10 d4 ♘c6 11 ♕c2 g5 [11 ... ♘xe5] 12 h4 ♘xe5 13 ♘xg5 ♘g6 14 ♗xf4 [□ 14 ♘xh7 △ 15 h5] 14 ... d5! 15 ♗d3 [15 ♗xd5 ♗f5!] 15 ... f5 16 ♖ae1 ♕f6 17 ♗c1 ♘xh4 18 ♘h3 ♘g4 19 ♗g5 ♕d6! 20 ♗f4 ♕f6 21 ♗g5 ♕d6 22 ♗f4 ♕d7? 23 ♘g5 ♕g7 24 g3 ♘g6 25 ♗c1 ♗d7 26 ♗xf5 ♗xf5 27 ♖xf5 ♕d7 [27 ... ♖xf5?!] 28 ♘e6? ♖fe8? [28 ... ♖ae8→] 29 ♕e2 c5 30 ♕xg4 ♖xe6?? 31 ♖xe6 cxd4 [31 ... ♕xe6? 32 ♖f8+] 32 ♖xg6+! hxg6 33 ♕xg6+ ♕g7 34 ♕e6+ **1-0** L/N6013-1845

### 1844-★LS-2 27x44
**Saint-Amant,P.C.F.de−Legris**

[Saint-Amant]

⟨♘b1⟩1 e4 e5 2 ♗c4 ♗c5 3 b4 ♗xb4 4 f4!? exf4? [4 ... d5] 5 ♘f3 ♕e7 6 ♕e2 [6 e5; 6 c3] 6 ... d6 7 0-0 ♗g4 8 c3 ♗a5 9 ♗b2 ♘h6 10 d4 0-0 11 a4 ♘d7 12 ♕d3 ♗xf3 13 ♖xf3 c5 14 ♖xf4 ♗c7 15 ♗b3? [15 ♗a2] 15 ... d5 16 e5 c4−+ 17 ♕f3 cxb3 18 ♗a3 ♕e6 19 g4 g5 20 ♖f5 ♘xf5 21 gxf5 ♕c6 22 f6 ♔h8 23 ♖e1 ♕e6 24 ♖e3 ♘b6 25 ♗xf8 ♖xf8 26 ♕h5 b2 **0-1** L/N6013-1845

**20** Mongredien, A. L/N3087.BL

### 1844-★MS-1
**Mongredien,A.−Staunton,H.**

Liverpool [Staunton]

⟨♙f7⟩1 e4 ♘h6 2 d4 ♘f7 3 ♗d3 ♘c6 4 ♗e3 e5 5 d5 ♘e7 6 ♘e2 ♘g6 7 0-0 ♗e7 8 f4 exf4 9 ♘xf4 ♘ge5 10 ♗d4 0-0 11 ♘d2 ♗g5 12 ♘h5 d6 13 ♘g3 ♘g4 14 ♘f3 ♗e3+ 15 ♔h1 ♗xd4 16 ♘xd4 ♘e3! 17 ♕e2 ♘xf1 18 ♖xf1 ♘e5 19 ♘gf5 ♗xf5 20 ♘xf5 ♕g5 21 h4 ♕g4 22 ♕f2 [△ 23 ♘e7++−] 22 ... ♔h8 23 ♕e3 ♘xd3 24 cxd3 ♖ae8 25 ♕d4 [□ 25 ♖f4] 25 ... ♖e5 26 ♕e3 ♖fxf5 27 ♖xf5 ♕xf5 **0-1** L/N6123-1844

### 1844-★MS-2
**Mongredien,A.=Staunton,H.**

Liverpool [Staunton]

⟨♙f7⟩1 e3 ... 2 ♗d3!? ♘h6 [2 ... ♘f6 3 g4!] 3 ♘f3 d6 4 ♘g5 g6 5 ♘xh7 ♖xh7 6 ♗xg6+ ♖f7 7 ♗xf7+ ♘xf7 8 h4 e5 9 g4 ♕f6 10 ♘c3 c6 11 b3 ♗e7 12 ♗b2 ♕g6 13 f3 d5 14 d3 ♕h6! 15 h5 ♕xe3+ 16 ♕e2 ♕f4 17 ♗c1 ♕d4 18 ♗b2 ♗g5 19 ♘a4 ♕b4+ 20 ♗c3 ♕e7 21 ♗d2 b5 22 ♘c3 ♘a6 23 0-0-0 ♕a3+ 24 ♔b1 ♗xd2 25 ♕xd2 d4 26 ♘e2 ♘b4 27 c3 dxc3 28 ♘xc3 a5 29 ♕b2 ♕xb2+ 30 ♔xb2 ♗e6 31 a3 ♘d5 32 ♘e4 0-0-0 33 g5 ♘f4 34 h6 ♗f5 35 ♔c2 ♘h3?

36 h7! ♘f4 37 h8=♕ ♘xh8 38 ♖xh8 ♖xh8 39 ♘d6+ ♔d7 40 ♘xf5 ♖h3 41 d4! ♔e6 42 ♘h6 ♖xf3 43 ♖e1 ♖f2+ 44 ♔d1 ♘g6 45 ♘g4 ♖f5 46 ♘xe5 ♘xe5 47 g6 ♔f6 48 dxe5+ ♔xg6 49 e6 ♖f8 50 e7 ♖e8 51 ♖e6+ ♔f7 52 ♖xc6 ♖xe7 53 ♖c5 ♖b7 54 a4 ♔e6 55 ♔c2 ♔d6 56 ♖h5 ♖c7+ 57 ♔b2 ♖c5 **½-½** L/N6123-1844

### 1844-★MS-3
**Mongredien,A.−Staunton,H.**

Liverpool [Staunton]

⟨♙f7⟩1 e4 ... 2 d4 ♘c6 3 e5 d5 4 ♗d3 ♗e6 5 ♗e3 ♘b4 6 f4 ♘xd3+ 7 ♕xd3 ♕d7 8 ♘e2 ♘h6 9 ♘bc3 ♘f5 10 h3 ♘xe3 11 ♕xe3 g6 12 g4 ♗g7 13 ♘g3 0-0-0 14 0-0-0 h5 15 g5 ♗xh3 16 ♕d3 h4 17 ♘f1 [17 ♕xg6?! hxg3 18 ♕xg7 g2 19 ♖hg1 ♖dg8 20 ♕f7 ♗e6] 17 ... ♗f5 18 ♕d2 h3 19 ♘e3 ♗e6 20 ♘e2 ♖df8 21 ♖df1 ♖h4 22 c4 ♕a4 23 b3 ♕a3+ 24 ♔b1 dxc4 25 d5 ♗f5+ 26 ♘xf5 ♖xf5 27 bxc4 ♕c5 28 ♕c3 [△ 28 ♖xh3] 28 ... c6 29 dxc6 bxc6 30 ♕g3 [30 ♖xh3 ♗xe5!−+] 30 ... ♕b4+ 31 ♕b3 [31 ♔a1 ♖fxf4] 31 ... ♕d2 32 ♖d1! ♕xe2 33 ♕a4 [□ 33 ♖he1!? ♕xe1 (33 ... ♕f2 34 ♖d8+! ♔xd8 35 ♕b8+ ♔d7 36 e6#) 34 ♖xe1∞] 33 ... ♕e4+ 34 ♔a1 ♗xe5+ 35 fxe5 ♕xe5+ 36 ♔b1 ♕e4+ 37 ♔a1 ♕xc4 **0-1** L/N6123-1844

### 1844-★RS-1 26x44
**Saint-Amant,P.C.F.+Rieutord**

[Saint-Amant]

⟨♘b1⟩1 e4 e5 2 ♗c4 ♗c5 3 ♘f3 ♘c6 4 b4 ♗xb4 5 c3 ♗c5 [□ 5 ... ♗a5] 6 0-0 ♘f6 7 d4 exd4 8 cxd4 ♗b6 9 e5 0-0?? [9 ... d5!] 10 exf6 ♕xf6 11 ♗g5 ♕g6 12 ♗d3 f5 13 ♕b3+ ♔h8 14 ♗e3 ♘a5 15 ♕c2 d6 16 ♗d2 ♗e6 17 h3 h6 18 ♖ae1 ♘c6 19 ♘h4 ♕h5 20 ♖xe6 ♕xh4 21 d5 ♘d4 22 ♕c4 ♘f3+ 23 gxf3 ♕g3+ 24 ♔h1 ♕xh3+ 25 ♔g1 ♕g3+ 26 ♔h1 ♗xf2 [□ 26 ... ♕xf3+] 27 ♕f4 ♕h3+ 28 ♕h2 ♕xf3+ 29 ♕g2 ♕xd3 30 ♖xf2 ♖ae8

31 ♖f3!! ♕xd5 [31 ... ♕d4 32 ♖xh6+ gxh6 33 ♗c3+−] 32 ♗xh6 ♕d4 33 ♗xg7+ ♕xg7 34 ♖h3+ ♔g8 35 ♖g6 ♖e1+ 36 ♔h2 ♖f7 37 ♖xg7+ ♖xg7 38 ♕d5+ **1-0** L/N6013-1845

### 1844-★RS-2 26x44
**Saint-Amant,P.C.F.de+Rieutord**

[Saint-Amant]

⟨♘b1⟩1 e4 e5 2 ♗c4 ♗c5 3 ♕g4 ♕f6 4 ♘f3 [4 d4] 4 ... ♘c6 5 ♕g3 d6 6 c3 ♗e6 7 ♗b5 a6 8 ♗a4 b5 9 ♗c2 h6 10 0-0 ♘ge7 11 a4 0-0 12 ♘e1 ♕g6 13 ♕f3 ♕g4 14 d3 ♕xf3 15 ♘xf3 ♗g4 16 ♘d2 f5 17 h3 ♗h5 18 exf5 ♘xf5!? 19 g4 ♘g3 20 gxh5 ♘xf1 21 ♘e4! ♗xf2+ 22 ♘xf2 ♘g3 23 ♗b3+ ♔h8 24 ♗d5 ♘e2+ 25 ♔g2 ♘f4+? 26 ♗xf4 ♖xf4 27 ♗xc6 ♖af8 28 ♘g4 ♖b8 29 axb5 axb5 30 ♖a7 b4 31 c4 [31 cxb4?] 31 ... ♖f7 32 ♘f2 ♖bf8 33 ♘g4 ♖b8

34 c5 ♖f5 35 ♖xc7 dxc5 36 ♗e4 ♖xh5 37 ♖xc5 ♖g5 38 ♖xe5 ♖c8 39 ♗f5 ♖c2+ 40 ♔g3 g6 41 ♖e8+ ♔g7 42 ♗e6 ♖xb2 43 h4 ♖c5 44 ♖g8+ ♔h7 45 ♘f6# **1-0**

L/N6013-1845

### 1844-★RS-3 26 x 44

**Saint-Amant,P.C.F.de-Rieutord**

[Saint-Amant]

⟨♘b1⟩1 e4 e5 [1 ... e6] 2 ♗c4 ♗c5 3 ♕g4 ♕f6 4 ♘f3 [4 d4] 4 ... ♘c6 5 ♕g3 d6 6 0-0 ♘d4 [□6 ... ♗e6] 7 ♘e1 ♗e6 8 ♗d3 ♘e7 9 c3 ♘dc6 10 ♗c2 ♘g6?! 11 d4!? exd4 12 ♘d3? [12 ♗g5 ♕e5 13 f4 dxc3+ 14 ♔h1] 12 ... ♕h4 13 f4 dxc3+? [13 ... ♕xg3] 14 ♘xc5 dxc5 15 f5 [15 ♕xc3 ♘d4!] 15 ... ♕xg3 16 hxg3 ♗c4 17 fxg6 ♗xf1 18 gxf7+ ♔xf7 19 ♔xf1 ♘d4 20 ♗d3 cxb2 21 ♗xb2 ♖hf8 22 ♖c1 ♔g8+ 23 ♔g1 ♖ad8! 24 ♗f1 [24 ♖xc5 ♘f3+] 24 ... b6 25 a4 ♔h8 26 ♖c3 ♖f7 27 ♗c4 ♖fd7 28 e5 ♖e7 29 ♖e3 c6 30 ♖e4 b5 31 axb5 cxb5 32 ♗a2 ♘c6 33 ♖e2 c4 34 ♔h2 ♖e6 35 ♗b1? ♖h6+ 36 ♔g1 ♖d1+ 37 ♔f2 ♖xb1 38 e6 ♘e7 39 g4 b4 40 ♗e5 c3 41 ♗d6 ♖b2 **0-1**

L/N6013-1845

### 1844-★SS-1

**Spreckley,G.S.-Staunton, H.**

Liverpool [Staunton]

⟨♙f7⟩1 e4 ... 2 d4 e6 3 ♗d3 c5 4 e5 ♘e7 5 c3 ♘bc6 6 ♘f3 d6 7 0-0 dxe5 8 dxe5 g6 9 ♗g5 ♗g7 10 ♗b5 ♗d7 11 ♕e2 ♕c7 12 ♗xe7 ♘xe7 13 ♗xd7+ ♕xd7 14 ♘a3 0-0 15 ♖ad1 ♕e8 16 ♘c4 ♘d5 17 ♘d6 ♕e7 18 c4 ♘f4 19 ♕e4 ♖ad8 20 g3 ♘h5 21 h4 ♗xe5 22 ♘xe5 ♖xd6 23 ♖xd6 ♕xd6 24 ♘xg6 hxg6 25 ♕xg6+ ♘g7 26 h5 ♔h8 27 ♕h6+ ♔g8 28 ♕g6 ♔h8 29 h6 ♘f5 30 g4 e5! [31 gxf5 ♖g8+] **0-1**

L/N6123-1844

### 1844-★ST-1

**T♀-Staunton, H.**

London

⟨♙f7⟩1 e4 ... 2 d4 d6 3 f4 ♘f6 4 ♗d3 e5 5 dxe5 dxe5 6 ♘f3 exf4 7 ♗xf4 ♘g4 8 h3 ♕f6 9 ♗xc7 ♕xb2 10 hxg4 ♕xa1 11 ♗xb8 ♗b4+ 12 ♔e2 ♖xb8 13 ♗b5+ ♔e7 14 ♕d5 ♕f6 15 ♖h5 ♗e6 16 e5 ♕g6 17 ♕d4 ♕xg4 18 ♕xg4 ♗xg4 19 ♖g5 ♗xf3+ 20 gxf3 g6 21 ♖g4 ♗a5 22 ♖e4 ♖bd8 23 e6 ♖d5 24 ♗c4 ♖h5 25 ♗b3 ♖d8 26 ♖f4 ♖h2+ 27 ♔e3 ♗d2+ 28 ♔e4 ♖e2# **0-1**

L/N6123-1844

### 1844-★ST-2

**T♀-Staunton, H.**

London

⟨♙f7⟩1 e4 ... 2 d4 d6 3 f4 ♘f6 4 e5 ♘g4 5 f5 ♗xf5 6 h3 ♘h6 7 ♗xh6 gxh6 8 ♗d3 ♗g6 9 ♕g4 ♖g8 10 ♘f3 ♘d7 11 ♘h4 dxe5 12 ♘xg6 ♘f6 13 ♕e6 hxg6 14 dxe5 ♕d5 15 ♕xd5 ♘xd5 16 ♗e4 c6 17 ♘d2 e6 18 c4 ♘e3 19 ♔e2 ♗c5 20 ♖ab1 ♘f5 21 b4 ♗d4 22 ♔f3 ♔e7 23 ♗xf5 gxf5 24 ♔f4 ♖xg2 25 ♘f3 ♖e2 26 ♖he1 ♗e3+ 27 ♔g3 ♖g8+ 28 ♔h4 ♗f2+ 29 ♔h5 ♗xe1 30 ♖xe1 ♖xe1 31 ♘xe1 ♖g3 **0-1**

L/N6123-1844

### 1844-★BS-1

**Buckle, H.T.+Staunton, H.**

London [Staunton]

⟨♙f7⟩1 e4 ♘c6 2 d4 d5 3 e5 ♗e6 4 ♘f3 ♗g4 5 ♗e3 e6 6 ♗d3 ♕e7 7 ♘bd2 g6 8 h3 ♗xf3 9 ♘xf3 ♗h6 10 ♕d2 ♗xe3 11 ♕xe3 ♕b4+ 12 c3 ♕xb2 13 0-0 ♕a3 14 ♘g5 ♕e7 15 ♗e2 ♘h6 16 ♕d2 [16 ♘xe6?] 16 ... ♘f5 17 ♖ab1 b6 18 ♗b5 ♕d7 19 c4 a6 20 cxd5 axb5 21 dxc6 ♕xc6 22 ♕f4 ♖a4 23 ♖fd1 0-0 24 ♘e4, ♔g7 25 ♘f6 ♖c4 26 h4 ♘e7 27 ♕g5 ♘d5 28 ♘g4 ♘f4 29 d5 ♘xd5 [□ 29 ... exd5 30 ♕h6+ ♔g8 31 ♘f6+ ♖xf6 32 exf6 ♕xf6∓] 30 ♕h6+ ♔g8 31 ♘f6+ ♖xf6 32 exf6 ♘xf6 33 ♖d8+ ♘e8 34 ♖bd1 ♖g4 35 g3 ♖c4 36 ♖1d7 **1-0** L/N6123-1844

### 1844-★BS-2

**Buckle, H.T.+Staunton, H.**

London [Staunton]

⟨♙f7⟩1 e4 ♘c6 2 d4 d5 3 e5 ♗e6 4 ♘f3 ♗g4 5 ♗e3 e6 6 ♗d3 ♘ge7 7 c3 ♘f5 8 h3 ♘xe3 9 fxe3 ♗h5 10 ♘bd2 ♗e7 11 0-0 ♗g5 12 ♕e2 0-0 13 ♖ae1 ♗h4 14 ♖d1 ♗g3 15 e4 ♘e7 16 exd5 ♘xd5 17 ♘e4 ♗f4 18 ♘c5 ♕e7 19 ♗c4 c6 20 ♗xd5 cxd5 21 ♘d3 ♗g3 22 ♕e3 ♖f5 23 ♖c1 ♖af8 24 ♘d2 ♗h4 25 ♖xf5 ♖xf5 26 ♖f1 ♗g5 27 ♕e1 ♕f7 28 ♖xf5 ♕xf5 29 ♘f2 ♕c2∓ 30 ♘b3 ♕xb2 31 ♘c5 ♗f7 [□ 31 ... ♕f7] 32 ♘fd3 ♕d2 33 ♔f1 b6 34 ♕xd2 ♗xd2 35 ♘a4 ♗e8 36 ♔e2 ♗g5 37 ♘ab2 ♗b5 38 ♔e1 ♗h4+ 39 ♔d2 ♔f7 40 a4 ♗a6 41 ♘f4 ♗g5 42 g3 ♔e8 43 c4 dxc4 44 ♔c3 ♗xf4 45 gxf4 b5 46 axb5 ♗xb5 47 ♘xc4 ♗xc4 48 ♔xc4 ♔d7 49 ♔c5 ♔c7 50 d5 ...♀ **1-0** L/N6123-1844

## ROUSSEAU ✕ STANLEY

**New Orleans**

[1845-✕RS]

| | E. Rousseau | C. H. Stanley |
|---|---|---|
| *1* | 0 | 1 |
| *2* | 0 | 1 |
| *3* | 0 | 1 |
| *4* | ½ | ½ |
| *5* | 1 | 0 |
| *6* | 1 | 0 |
| *7* | 0 | 1 |
| *8* | 1 | 0 |
| *9* | 0 | 1 |
| *10* | 0 | 1 |
| *11* | 0 | 1 |
| *12* | 0 | 1 |
| *13* | ½ | ½ |
| *14* | ½ | ½ |
| *15* | 0 | 1 |
| *16* | 1 | 0 |
| *17* | 1 | 0 |
| *18* | 0 | 1 |
| *19* | 1 | 0 |
| *20* | ½ | ½ |
| *21* | 1 | 0 |
| *22* | ½ | ½ |
| *23* | ½ | ½ |
| *24* | 0 | 1 |
| *25* | ½ | ½ |
| *26* | 0 | 1 |
| *27* | 1 | 0 |
| *28* | ½ | ½ |
| *29* | 0 | 1 |
| *30* | 0 | 1 |
| *31* | 0 | 1 |
| *Total* | 12 | 19 |

### 1845-✕RS-1

**Stanley, C.H.+Rousseau, E.**

[Stanley]

1 e4 e5 2 ♗c4 ♘f6 3 ♘c3 ♗c5 4 ♘f3 d6 5 h3 0-0 6 d3 ♗e6 7 ♗b3 ♘c6 8 ♘e2 ♕e7 9 ♘g3 ♘d4 10 ♘xd4 ♗xd4 11 c3 ♗b6 12 0-0 d5 13 ♗g5± c6 14 ♘h5 dxe4 15 dxe4 ♗xb3 16 ♕f3!± ♗c4 17 ♗xf6 ♕e6 18 ♘xg7 ♗e2 19 ♘xe6 ♗xf3 20 ♘xf8 **1-0** +6

### 1845-✕RS-2

**Rousseau, E.-Stanley, C.H.**

[Stanley]

1 e4 e5 2 ♘f3 ♘c6 3 d4 exd4 4 ♗c4 d6 5 0-0 ♗g4 6 ♗b5 ♕f6 7 ♗xc6+ bxc6 8 ♕xd4 ♗xf3 9 ♕xf6 ♘xf6 10 gxf3∓ h6 11 ♘c3 g5 12 ♗d2 ♘h5 13 ♖ae1 ♗g7 14 b3 ♗e5 15 ♘e2 ♔d7 16 ♘g3 ♘g7 17 ♘e2 ♘e6 18 ♔h1 ♖af8 19 ♘g3? ♘d4 20 ♔g2 ♘xc2 21 ♖d1 f6 22 ♘f5 c5 23 ♗e3 ♔e6! 24 ♖d2 ♘b4 25 ♖fd1 ♘c6 26 ♘g3 h5 27 ♖e2

♘e7 28 ♗c1 ♘g6 29 ♖d3 ♗f4 30 ♗b2 ♘h4+ 31 ♔h1 g4−+ 32 ♘xh5 ♖xh5 33 fxg4 ♖h7 34 ♖h3 ♖fh8 35 ♖c2 ♘f3 36 ♖xh7 [36 ♖xf3 ♖xh2+,#] 36 ... ♖xh7 37 ♔g2 ♘e1+ **0-1** +6

### 1845-⚔RS-3
**Stanley, C.H.+Rousseau, E.**

[Stanley]

1 e4 e5 2 ♗c4 ♗c5 3 ♘f3 ♘c6 4 d3 ♘f6 5 ♘c3 d6 6 h3 ♗e6 7 ♗b3 h6 8 ♘e2 0-0 9 ♘g3 d5 10 exd5 ♗xd5 11 0-0 ♕d7 12 c3 ♗d6 13 ♘h4 ♗e6 14 ♕f3 ♘h7 15 ♗e3 ♘e7 16 d4 exd4 17 ♗xd4 c5 18 ♗e3 c4 19 ♗c2 f5 20 ♖ad1 ♘g5 [20 ... f4∞] 21 ♗xg5 hxg5

22 ♘hxf5 ♗xf5 23 ♗xf5 ♘xf5 24 ♖xd6 ♕xd6 25 ♘xf5 ♖xf5 26 ♕xf5 ♕d3 27 ♕xg5 [□ 27 ♕xd3] 27 ... ♖e8 28 ♕g4 b5 29 ♖d1 ♕c2 30 ♕h5 ♕e2 31 ♕xe2 ♖xe2 32 ♖b1 ♖c2 33 a4 a6 34 axb5 axb5 35 f3 ♔f7 36 ♔f1 ♔e6? 37 ♖e1+ ♔d5 38 ♖e2 ♖c1+ 39 ♔f2 ♔c5 40 ♔e3 b4 [□ 40 ... ♖b1] 41 cxb4+ ♔xb4 42 ♔d2 ♖f1 43 ♔c2 ♖g1 44 ♖f2 g5 45 ♖e2 ♖f1 46 b3 cxb3+ 47 ♔b2 ♖g1 48 ♖e4+ ♔c5 49 ♖g4 **1-0** +6

### 1845-⚔RS-4
**Rousseau, E.=Stanley, C.H.**

[Stanley]

1 e4 e5 2 ♘f3 ♘c6 3 ♗b5 ♗c5 4 c3 ♕e7 5 0-0 ♘d8?! 6 d4 exd4 7 cxd4 ♗b6 8 e5 c6 9 ♗c4 d5 10 exd6 ♕xd6 11 ♖e1+ ♗e6 12 b3 ♘e7 13 ♗a3 ♕c7 14 ♘c3 ♗a5 15 ♗xe6 ♘xe6 16 b4 ♗b6 17 b5 0-0 18 ♕b3 ♖fe8 19 ♖xe6! fxe6 20 ♕xe6+ ♔h8 21 ♘g5 h6 22 ♘f7+ ♔h7 23 ♘d6 [23 ♘e4] 23 ... ♖f8 24 ♖e1 ♘g6 25 ♖e4 ♖f6 26 ♕g4 ♖xd6 27 ♗xd6 ♕xd6 28 ♖e6 ♕xd4 29 ♕xg6+ ♔h8 30 ♖e8+ ♖xe8 31 ♕xe8+ ♔h7 32 ♕e4+ ♕xe4 33 ♘xe4 cxb5 34 ♘d6 a5? [34 ... b4, ... a5] 35 ♘xb5 ♗c5 36 ♔f1 ♔g6 37 ♔e2 ♔f5 38 f3 h5 39 ♔d3 g5 40 ♘d4+ ♔e5 41 ♘b3 ♗b6 42 a4 g4 43 fxg4 hxg4 44 h3 gxh3 45 gxh3 ♗d8 46 ♔c4 ♔f4 [□ 46 ... ♔d6] 47 ♘c5 ♔g3 48 ♘xb7 ♗c7 49 ♔b5 ♔xh3 50 ♔c6? [50 ♘xa5+−] 50 ... ♗g3 51 ♘xa5 ♗e1 52 ♔b5 ♔g4 53 ♘c6 ♔f5 54 ♘b4 ♔e6 55 a5 ♔d6 56 a6 ♔c7 57 ♘d3 ♗d2 58 ♘c5 ♔b8 59 ♘d7+ ♔a7 60 ♘b6 ♗e3 **½-½** +6

### 1845-⚔RS-5
**Stanley, C.H.−Rousseau, E.**

[Stanley]

1 e4 e5 2 ♘f3 ♘c6 3 ♗c4 ♗c5 4 c3 ♘f6 5 d4 exd4 6 cxd4 ♗b4+ 7 ♗d2 ♗xd2+ 8 ♘bxd2 d5 9 exd5 ♘xd5 10 0-0 0-0 11 ♘e4 ♗g4 12 h3 ♗xf3 13 ♕xf3 ♘xd4 14 ♕g3 c6 15 ♖ad1 ♘f5 16 ♕b3 ♘fe7 17 ♕xb7 ♕b6 18 ♕d7 ♖ad8 19 ♕g4 f5 20 ♕g5 fxe4 21 ♕xe7 ♖fe8 22 ♖xd5 cxd5 [22 ... ♖xe7? 23 ♖xd8#] 23 ♗xd5+ ♔h8 24 ♕b7 e3 25 fxe3 ♕xe3+ 26 ♔h1 ♕e2 27 ♕f7 ♕e7 28 ♕xe7 ♖xe7 29 b3 ♖ed7 30 ♗c4 ♖d1 31 ♖xd1 ♖xd1+ 32 ♔h2 ♖d2 33 a4 a5 34 h4 g6 35 ♔h3 ♔g7 36 g3 ♔f6 37 ♔g4 ♖f2 38 ♔h3 h5 39 ♗g8 ♔e5 40 ♗c4 ♔d4−+ 41 ♗f7?? ♖xf7 **0-1** +6

### 1845-⚔RS-6
**Rousseau, E.+Stanley, C.H.**

[Stanley]

1 e4 e5 2 ♘f3 ♘c6 3 ♗b5 a6 4 ♗a4 b5 5 ♗b3 ♘f6 6 d3 h6 7 ♘c3 ♗c5 8 0-0 d6 9 ♗e3 ♗a7 10 h3 ♘e7 11 a4 b4 12 ♘e2 c5 13 ♘h2 g5! 14 ♘g3 ♘g6 15 ♘h5 ♘f4 16 ♗xf4 gxf4 17 ♘xf6+ ♕xf6 18 ♗d5 ♖b8 19 ♗c6+?! ♔e7 20 ♕h5 ♖g8 21 ♘f3 ♗e6 22 ♔h2 ♖g6 23 ♖g1 c4 24 ♖af1 ♖bg8 25 ♕h4 ♖g5 26 g4 [26 ♘xg5?] 26 ... ♔f8 27 ♖g2 ♗b6 28 ♖d1 ♗d8 29 d4 ♗e7 30 dxe5 dxe5 31 ♗d7 ♗xd7 32 ♖xd7 ♕e6 33 ♖d5 ♔g7 [33 ... ♖xg4? 34 ♖d8+] 34 ♖g1 ♕g6 35 ♖e1 ♖h8 36 ♖d7 ♕e6 37 ♖ed1 ♖e8 38 ♖1d5 ♖g6 39 ♕h5 f6? [39 ... ♖g5=] 40 ♘h4 **1-0** +6

### 1845-⚔RS-7
**Stanley, C.H.+Rousseau, E.**

[Stanley]

1 e4 e5 2 ♘f3 ♘c6 3 ♗c4 ♗c5 4 d3 d6 5 h3 ♘f6 6 ♘c3 ♗e6 7 ♗b3 h6 8 ♘e2 ♘e7 9 ♘g3 ♕d7 10 c3 ♘g6 11 ♗e3 ♗b6 12 ♕d2 0-0 13 0-0 ♖ae8 14 ♗c2 c5 15 a4 ♗c7 16 c4 ♗xh3! 17 gxh3 ♕xh3 18 ♕e2 ♘g4 19 ♖fd1 ♘xe3 20 ♕xe3 ♘f4 21 ♘e1 ♖e6 22 ♕f3 ♖g6 23 ♘g2 f5 24 d4! fxe4 25 ♗xe4 ♘e6 26 ♗f5 ♔h8 [□ 26 ... ♖xf5] 27 ♗xh3 ♖xf3 28 ♘h4 ♖fxg3+ 29 fxg3 ♖xg3+ 30 ♔h2 ♖xh3+ 31 ♔xh3 ♘xd4 32 ♖f1 ♘e6 33 ♔g4 ♘f4 34 ♖xf4 exf4 35 ♘g6+ ♔h7 36 ♔f5 ♗a5 **1-0** +6

### 1845-⚔RS-8
**Rousseau, E.+Stanley, C.H.**

[Stanley]

1 e4 e5 2 ♘f3 ♘c6 3 d4 exd4 4 ♗c4 d6 5 ♘xd4 ♘e5 6 ♗b3 c5 7 ♘f3 ♘xf3+ 8 ♕xf3 ♘f6 9 ♗g5 ♗e7 10 ♘c3 0-0 11 0-0 ♗e6 12 ♘d5 ♗xd5 13 ♗xf6 ♗xe4 14 ♗xe7 ♕xe7 15 ♕e3 ♕e8! 16 ♖fe1 ♗c6 17 ♕g5 h6 18 ♕f4 ♕d7 19 ♖e3 ♖ae8 20 ♖g3 ♔h7 21 ♗c4 f5 22 ♕d2 b5 23 ♗f1 d5 24 ♖d1 ♖e7 25 h3 ♖fe8 26 c3 c4 27 ♖e3 ♖xe3 28 fxe3 ♕e7 29 ♔f2 ♕d6 30 g3 a5 31 ♗g2 b4? 32 ♗xd5 ♖d8 33 ♗g8+ ♔xg8 34 ♕xd6 ♖xd6 35 ♖xd6 ♗e4 36 ♖a6 bxc3 37 bxc3 **1-0** +6

### 1845-⚔RS-9
xii 45

**Stanley, C.H.+Rousseau, E.**

[Stanley]

1 e4 e5 2 ♘f3 ♘c6 3 ♗c4 ♗c5 4 d3 d6 5 h3 ♘f6 6 ♘c3 ♗e6 7 ♗b3 ♕e7 8 ♘e2 h6 9 ♗e3 ♗xe3 10 fxe3 ♖d8 11 ♘g3 d5 12 exd5 ♘xd5 13 ♗xd5 ♖xd5 14 0-0 0-0 15 ♔h1 ♖d7 16 ♘h2 ♘b4? 17 a3 ♘c6 18 ♘g4 ♗xg4 19 ♕xg4 ♕e6 20 ♘f5 g6 21 ♘xh6+ ♔g7 22 ♖xf7+ ♖dxf7 23 ♕xe6 ♔xh6 24 c3 ♖f6 25 ♕g4 g5 26 e4 ♖f4 27 ♕g3 ♘e7 28 d4 ♘g6 29 b3 b6 30 d5 a5 31 c4 ♘e7 32 ♕c3 ♘g6 33 ♕e3 ♔h5 34 b4 axb4 35 axb4 g4 36 hxg4+ ♖xg4 37 c5 ♘f4 38 g3 ♖fg8 39 ♔h2 bxc5 40 bxc5 ♔g6 41 d6! [41 gxf4?∞=] 41 ... cxd6 42 cxd6 ♖h8+ 43 ♔g1 ♖h3 44 ♔f2 ♖h2+?! [□ 44 ... ♖hxg3 45 ♕xg3 ♖xg3 46 ♔xg3] 45 ♔f3 ♔h6 46 ♕a7 ♔g5 47 ♕e7+ ♔g6 ...? **1-0** +6

**69** Stanley, C.H. L/N6396.BL

### 1845-⚔RS-10 xii 45
**Rousseau, E.– Stanley, C.H.**
[Stanley]

1 e4 e5 2 ♘f3 ♘c6 3 d4 exd4 4 ♗c4 d6 5 ♘xd4 ♘e5 6 ♗d3 c5 7 ♘f3 ♗g4 8 ♗b5+ ♘d7 9 ♘c3 ♘f6 10 ♗g5 ♖c8 11 0-0 h6 12 ♗f4 a6 13 ♗xd7+ ♕xd7 14 ♖e1 ♗e7 15 e5 dxe5 16 ♕xd7+ ♗xd7 17 ♘xe5 ♗e6 18 ♘g6 fxg6 19 ♖xe6 ♖c6 20 ♖ae1? [◻ 20 ♖xc6±] 20 ... ♖xe6 21 ♖xe6 ♔d7 22 ♖b6 ♔c8 23 ♔f1 ♖d8 24 ♔e2 g5 25 ♗e5 ♖e8 26 ♖e6 ♔d7 27 ♖b6 ♗d8 28 ♖xb7+ ♔c6 29 ♖xg7 ♖xe5+ 30 ♔d3 ♖e6 31 ♖g6 ♖d6+ 32 ♔e2 ♘e4+ 33 ♖xd6+ ♘xd6 34 ♘d1 ♘f5 35 c3 h5 36 ♔f3 ♘h4+ 37 ♔g3 ♗c7+ 38 ♔h3 ♘g6 39 g3 ♔d5 40 f3 ♔c4 41 ♘f2 ♘e5 42 ♔g2 ♘d3 43 ♘xd3 ♔xd3 44 h4 gxh4 45 g4 hxg4 46 hxg4 ♔c2 47 b4 c4 48 a4 ♔xc3 49 b5 axb5 50 axb5 ♔d4 **0-1** +6

### 1845-⚔RS-11 xii 45
**Stanley, C.H.+ Rousseau, E.**
New Orleans [Stanley]

1 e4 c5 2 f4 e6 3 ♘f3 ♘c6 4 c3 d5 5 exd5 exd5 6 d4 ♘f6 7 ♗d3 ♘e4 8 0-0 f5 9 ♘e5 ♕f6 10 ♗e3 c4 11 ♗xe4 fxe4 12 b3 cxb3 13 axb3 ♗e7 14 c4 ♗e6 15 ♘c3 ♖d8 16 cxd5 ♗xd5 17 ♘xc6 ♗xc6 18 ♖xa7 ♗c5?? 19 ♕h5+ **1-0** +6

### 1845-⚔RS-12 xii 45
**Rousseau, E.– Stanley, C.H.**
[Stanley]

1 e4 e6 2 d4 d5 3 exd5 exd5 4 c4 ♗e6 5 ♕b3 b6 6 ♘f3 ♘e7 7 ♘c3 c6 8 ♗e3 ♘d7 9 ♗d3 ♘f6 10 ♗g5 dxc4 11 ♗xc4 ♘fd5 12 0-0 f6 13 ♖fe1 ♔f7 14 a4! h6 15 ♗d2 ♕d7 16 ♖e2 ♔g8 17 ♖ae1 ♗f7 18 h3 ♖d8 19 ♘h2 ♘f5 20 ♗e3 ♗d6 21 ♘f1 ♗c7 22 ♘xd5 ♗xd5 23 ♗xd5+ ♕xd5 24 ♕xd5+ ♖xd5 25 ♖c2 ♘xd4 26 ♗xd4 ♖xd4 27 ♖e7 ♗e5 28 ♖xa7 c5 29 ♘e3 ♔h7 30 g3 ♖hd8 31 ♘c4 ♖b8 32 f4 ♖d1+ 33 ♔g2 ♗d4 34 ♖e2 b5 35 axb5 ♖xb5 36 ♘d6 ♖xb2 37 ♖xb2 ♗xb2 38 ♘f5 c4 39 ♖xg7+ ♔h8 40 ♖c7 c3 41 ♘e3 ♖d3 42 ♔f2 ♔g8 43 ♘f1 ♔f8 44 ♔e2 ♖d6 45 ♘e3 ♖d2+ 46 ♔f3 ♔e8 47 h4 ♔d8 48 ♖c4 h5 49 g4 hxg4+ 50 ♔xg4 ♔d7 51 h5 ♔d6 52 ♖c8 ♔d7 53 ♖c4 ♔d8 54 f5 ♔d7 55 ♔g3 ♖d3 56 ♔f2 ♗c1 57 ♖e4 ♖d2+ 58 ♔g3 c2 59 ♔g4 ♖h2 60 ♖d4+ ♔e8 61 ♘xc2 ♖xc2 62 ♖d1 ♖c4+ 63 ♔g3 ♗g5 64 ♖h1 ♔f7 65 h6 ♔g8 66 h7+ ♔h8 **0-1** +6

### 1845-⚔RS-13 xii 45
**Stanley, C.H.= Rousseau, E.**

1 e4 c5 2 f4 e6 3 ♘f3 ♘c6 4 c3 d5 5 exd5 exd5 6 d4 ♗e7 7 ♗d3 f6 8 0-0 ♘h6 9 h3 0-0 10 ♕c2 f5 11 ♗e3 b6 12 ♘e5 ♕c7 13 ♘d2 g6 14 ♘df3 ♘f7 15 a3 ♗e6 16 b3 ♖ac8 17 ♖a2 ♕d6 18 ♕f2 cxd4 19 cxd4 ♕d8 20 ♖c1 ♘cxe5 21 dxe5 ♕d7 22 b4 ♖xc1+ 23 ♗xc1 ♖c8 24 ♖c2 ♘d8 25 ♘d4 ♔f7 26 ♗b5 ♖xc2 27 ♕xc2 ♕c8 28 ♗c6 a6 29 ♗xd5 ♕xc2 30 ♗xe6+ ♘xe6 31 ♘xc2 g5 32 g3 gxf4 33 gxf4 ♗f8 34 ♔f2 a5 35 bxa5 bxa5 36 ♗e3 a4 37 ♗d2 ♗c5+ 38 ♔g3 ♘c7 39 ♗b4 ♗g1 40 ♗d6 ♘b5 41 ♔h4 ♔e6 42 ♗b4 ♗h2 43 ♗d2 ♗g1 44 ♔g5 ♗c5 45 ♗c1 ♗f8 46 h4 ♗e7+ 47 ♔h6 ♗xh4 48 ♔xh7 ♗f2 49 ♔g6 ♗c5 50 ♔h5 ♗e7 51 ♗b2 ♗c5 52 ♔h4 ♔d5 53 ♔g5 ♔e6 54 ♗c1 ♗e7+ 55 ♔h5 ♗c5 56 ♔g6 ♗f8 57 ♘e3 ♗xa3 58 ♗xa3 ♘xa3 59 ♘xf5 ♘c2 60 ♘g3 a3 61 ♘e4 a2 62 ♘c5+ ♔d5 63 ♘b3 ♔c4 64 e6 ♔xb3 65 e7 a1♕ 66 e8♕ **½-½** +6

### 1845-⚔RS-14 xii 45
**Rousseau, E.= Stanley, C.H.**

1 e4 e5 2 ♘f3 ♘c6 3 d4 exd4 4 ♗c4 ♘f6 5 ♘g5 ♘a5 6 ♕xd4 ♘xc4 7 ♕xc4 d5 8 exd5 ♕xd5 9 ♕e2+ ♗e6 10 0-0 ♗c5 11 ♘c3 ♕c6 12 ♘xe6 fxe6 13 ♖e1 0-0 14 ♕xe6+ ♕xe6 15 ♖xe6 ♘g4 16 ♗e3 ♘xe3 17 fxe3 ♖ae8 18 ♖xe8 ♖xe8 19 ♖e1 ♖xe3 20 ♖xe3 ♗xe3+ 21 ♔f1 ♗d4 22 ♘d1 ♔f7 23 ♔e2 ♔e6 24 ♔d3 c5 25 ♔e4 b5 26 c3 ♗g1 27 h3 a5 28 b3 b4 29 cxb4 axb4 30 ♘b2 g5 31 g4 h6 32 ♘d3 ♗d4 33 ♘c1 ♗g7 34 ♘d3 ♔d6 35 ♘e1 ♔e6 36 ♘d3 ♗f8 37 ♘f2 ♗g7 38 ♘d3 ♗f8 39 ♘e1 ♗d6 40 ♘g2 ♗e7 41 ♘e3 ♗d6 42 ♘f5 ♗f8 43 h4 gxh4 44 ♘xh4 ♗e7 45 ♘g6 ♗d6 46 ♘f4+ ♗xf4 47 ♔xf4 ♔f6 48 ♔g3 ♔g6 **½-½** +6

### 1845-⚔RS-15 xii 45
**Stanley, C.H.+ Rousseau, E.**
[Stanley]

1 e4 e5 2 ♘f3 ♘c6 3 ♗c4 ♗c5 4 d3 d6 5 ♗e3 ♗xe3 6 fxe3 ♗e6 7 ♗b3 ♘f6 8 0-0 ♕e7 9 ♘c3 0-0 10 ♘e2 d5 11 exd5 ♘xd5 12 ♗xd5 ♗xd5 13 e4 ♗e6 14 ♘g3 f6 15 ♘h4 g6 16 ♔h1 ♕g7 17 ♕d2 ♖f7 18 ♖f2 ♖af8 19 ♖af1 a6 20 h3 ♔h8 21 ♖f3 ♘e7 22 ♕f2 f5 23 exf5 gxf5 24 ♘gxf5? ♗xf5 25 ♘xf5 ♖xf5 26 ♕e3 ♖xf3 27 ♖xf3 ♖xf3 28 ♕xf3 c6 29 c4 ♘g6 30 ♕h5 ♕f6 31 ♔g1 ♔g7 32 ♕g4 ♕f4 33 ♕d7+ ♕f7 34 ♕g4 b5 35 cxb5 axb5 36 b3 ♕a7+ 37 ♔h2 ♕xa2 38 h4 ♕xb3+ 39 h5 ♕xd3 40 hxg6 ♕xg6 41 ♕d7+ ♔h6 42 g3 e4 43 ♕d2+ ♔h5 44 ♔h1 ♔g4?? 45 ♕f4+ **1-0** +6

### 1845-⚔RS-16 xii 45
**Rousseau, E.+ Stanley, C.H.**
[Stanley]

1 e4 e5 2 ♘f3 ♘c6 3 ♗b5 a6 4 ♗a4 b5 5 ♗b3 ♘f6 6 d3 ♗c5 7 0-0 d6 8 ♗e3 ♗a7 9 h3 h6 10 c3 0-0 11 ♕e2 ♘e7 12 ♘bd2 ♘g6 13 ♘h2 ♗e6 14 ♔h1 d5 15 exd5 ♘xd5 16 ♗xd5 ♗xd5 17 ♘df3 e4! 18 dxe4 ♗c4 19 ♕d2 ♗xf1 20 ♘xf1 ♕xd2 21 ♘3xd2 f5 22 ♗xa7 ♖xa7 23 f3 c5 24 exf5 ♖xf5 25 ♘e4 ♖d7 26 ♘e3 ♖e5 27 ♖e1 h5 28 c4 b4 29 ♘d5 ♖d8 30 ♖d1 ♖c8 31 ♔g1 ♘f8 32 ♔f2 ♘h7 33 ♘d6 ♖c6 34 f4 ♖e6 35 ♘f5 ♔f7 36 g4 g6 37 ♘g3 h4 38 ♘f1 ♖e4 39 b3 ♖ce6 40 ♘fe3 ♘f6 41 f5 gxf5 42 ♘xf5 ♖e2+ 43 ♔f3 ♘h7?! 44 ♘xh4 ♘g5+ 45 ♔g3 ♘e4+ 46 ♔f4 ♖f2+ 47 ♘f3 ♘c3 48 ♖d3 ♘e2+ 49 ♔g5 ♔g7 50 ♘h4 ♘d4 51 ♘f4 ♖e5+ 52 ♘f5+ ♔f7 53 ♖xd4! cxd4 54 ♘d3 ♖exf5+ 55 gxf5 a5?? 56 c5?? ♖g2+ 57 ♔f4 ♖xa2 58 c6 ♖c2 59 ♘e5+ ♔e7 60 ♘c4 a4 61 f6+ ♔d8 62 ♔e5 a3 63 ♔d6 a2 64 f7 ♖f2 65 c7+ ♔c8 66 ♘b6+ ♔b7 67 c8♕+ ♔xb6 68 f8♕ ♖xf8 69 ♕xf8 **1-0** +6

### 1845-⚔RS-17 xii 45
**Stanley, C.H.– Rousseau, E.**
[Stanley]

1 e4 e5 2 ♘f3 ♘c6 3 ♗c4 ♗c5 4 d3 ♘f6 5 ♘c3 d6 6 ♗e3 ♗xe3 7 fxe3 ♗e6 8 ♗b3 ♘e7 9 0-0 0-0 10 ♘h4 ♕d7 11 ♘e2 d5 12 exd5 ♘fxd5 13 ♗xd5 ♘xd5 14 ♕d2 f6 15 e4 ♘e7 16 ♘g3 ♖f7 17 ♖f2 ♖af8 18 ♖af1 g6 19 a3 c5 20 c3 a5 21 ♘f3 ♘c6 22 ♘e2 ♖d8 23 ♘c1 c4 24 ♕e3 cxd3 25 ♖d1 ♕c7 26 ♖fd2 ♖fd7 27 ♘xd3 f5 28 exf5 ♗xf5 29 ♘f2 ♖xd2 30 ♖xd2 ♖xd2 31 ♕xd2 ♕d7 32 ♕e3 ♕d5 33 g4 ♗c8! [△ ... ♗b7] 34 ♕e4 ♗e6 35 ♘g5 ♔g7 36 b4 axb4 37 axb4 b5 38 ♘xe6+ ♕xe6 39 ♘d3 h5 40 h3 hxg4 41 hxg4 g5 42 ♔h1 ♕g6 43 ♕d5 e4 44 ♘c5 e3 45 ♘e6+ ♔f6 46 ♕xc6 [46 ♕f3+ ♔e7] 46 ... ♕b1+ 47 ♔g2 ♕a2+ 48 ♔h3 ♕xe6 49 ♕f3+ [49 ♕xe6+→] 49 ... ♔e7 50 ♕b7+ ♔f6 51 ♕f3+ ♔g6 52 ♕e2 ♕e5 53 c4 bxc4→ 54 ♕xc4 e2 55 ♕g8+ ♔h6 **0-1** +6

**1845-⚔RS-18** xii 45
**Rousseau, E.– Stanley, C.H.**
[Stanley]
1 e4 e5 2 ♘f3 ♘c6 3 ♗c4 ♗c5 4 c3 ♕e7 5 0-0 d6 6 d4 ♗b6 7 dxe5 dxe5 8 ♗g5 ♘f6 9 ♘bd2 h6 10 ♗h4 ♗g4 11 ♕c2 ♖d8 12 ♗b5 0-0 13 ♗xc6 bxc6 14 ♗g3 ♘d7 15 h3 ♗h5 16 ♗h2 f6 17 g4?! ♗g6 18 ♘h4 ♗h7 19 ♔h1 ♘c5! 20 ♖g1 [20 f3]

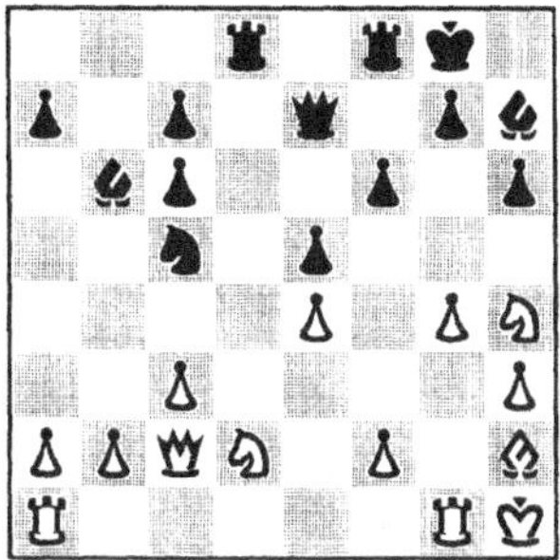

20 ... ♖xd2 21 ♕xd2 ♘xe4 22 ♕e2 ♘xf2+ 23 ♔g2 ♗e4+ 24 ♔g3 f5 25 ♘xf5 ♖xf5 26 ♖gf1 ♕g5 27 ♗g1 ♕f4+ 28 ♔h4 ♖h5+ 29 ♔xh5 ♕g5# **0-1** +6

**1845-⚔RS-19**
**Stanley, C.H.– Rousseau, E.**
1 e4 c5 2 f4 e6 3 ♘f3 ♘c6 4 c3 d5 5 exd5 exd5 6 d4 ♘f6 7 ♗d3 ♗e7 8 0-0 0-0 9 ♘e5 ♕b6 10 ♘xc6 bxc6 11 ♗c2 ♗a6 12 ♖f2 ♖fe8 13 h3 ♖ac8 14 ♗e3 cxd4 15 ♗xd4 c5 16 ♗xf6 ♗xf6 17 ♕xd5?-+ ♖e1+ 18 ♔h2 c4 19 ♕d2 ♖ce8 20 a4 ♗h4 21 g3 ♗xg3+ 22 ♔xg3 ♖8e3+ 23 ♔h2 ♗b7 24 ♘a3

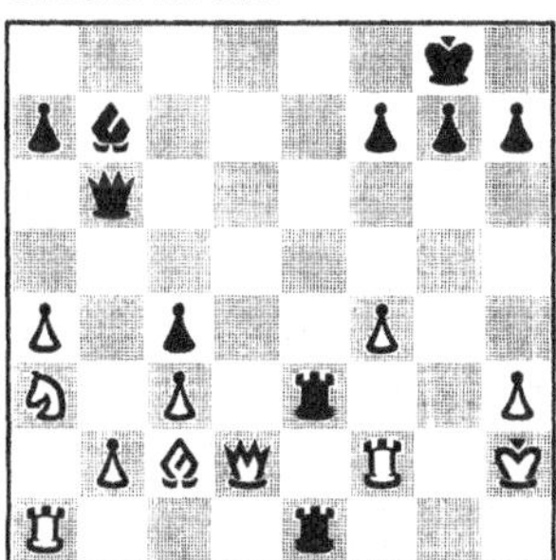

24 ... ♖xh3+! 25 ♔xh3 ♕e3+ 26 ♔g4 [26 ♔h2 ♕h6+,#; 26 ♕xe3 ♕xe3+, 27 ... ♕xf2-+] 26 ... ♗c8+ 27 f5 ♕g6+ 28 ♔h4 ♕g3+ 29 ♔h5 g6+ 30 fxg6 ♕g4+ 31 ♔h6 ♕h4# **0-1** +6

**1845-⚔RS-20**
**Rousseau, E.= Stanley, C.H.**
1 e4 e5 2 ♘f3 ♘c6 3 ♗c4 ♗c5 4 c3 ♕e7 5 0-0 d6 6 d4 ♗b6 7 a4 a6 8 b4 ♗g4 9 a5 ♗a7 10 b5 ♘b8 11 ♗a3± axb5 12 ♗xb5+ c6 13 ♗e2 ♗xf3 14 ♗xf3 c5 15 dxe5 dxe5 16 ♘d2 ♘f6 17 ♘c4 0-0 18 ♕d6! ♕xd6 19 ♘xd6± b6 20 axb6 ♗xb6 21 ♘c4 ♗a5! 22 ♗xc5 ♖c8 23 ♘xa5 ♖xc5 24 ♘b7 ♖xa1 25 ♖xa1 [□ 25 ♘xc5] 25 ... ♖xc3 26 h3 ♖c8 27 ♖a8 ♖f8 28 g4 ♘c6 29 ♖xf8+ ♔xf8 30 ♘d6 ♘d4 31 ♗g2 ♔e7 32 ♘c4 ♘d7 33 f3 g5 34 ♔f2 f6 35 ♗f1 ♘c5 36 ♘e3 ♘ce6 37 ♗c4 ♘f4 38 ♔g3 ♔f8 39 ♘f5 ♘xf5+ 40 exf5 h5 41 h4 gxh4+ 42 ♔xh4 hxg4 43 fxg4 ♘g2+ 44 ♔h5 ♔g7 45 g5 ♘f4+ 46 ♔g4 fxg5 47 ♔xg5 ♘h3+ 48 ♔g4 ♘f2+ 49 ♔f3 ♘d1 50 ♔e4 ♔f6 **½-½** +6

**1845-⚔RS-21** xii 45
**Stanley, C.H.– Rousseau, E.**
[Stanley]
1 d4 d5 2 c4 e6 3 ♘f3 c5 4 e3 ♘f6 5 ♘c3 ♘c6 6 ♗e2 ♗e7 7 0-0 0-0 8 a3 b6 9 cxd5 exd5 10 ♗b5 ♗b7 11 dxc5 bxc5 12 ♖b1 ♖c8 13 ♘e2 ♗d6 14 b4 cxb4 15 ♗xc6 ♗xc6 16 axb4 ♖e8 17 b5 ♗b7 18 ♘ed4 ♘e4 19 ♗b2 ♕d7 20 h3 f5 21 ♘h4 ♖f8 22 ♕h5 g6 23 ♕h6 [23 ♘dxf5 △ 23 ... gxh5 24 ♘h6#; 23 ♘xg6!] 23 ... ♖f6 24 ♘df3 ♖cf8 25 ♖fd1? [□ 25 ♗xf6 △ 26 ♘g5] 25 ... g5 26 ♕h5 gxh4 27 ♘xh4 ♕f7 28 ♕e2 ♖h6 29 ♘f3 ♕g6 30 ♗e5 ♗xe5 31 ♘xe5 ♕g7 32 ♘d3 ♘c3 33 ♕c2 d4 34 ♘f4 ♘xb1 35 ♕xb1 dxe3 36 fxe3 ♔h8 37 ♕a2 ♗e4 38 ♕a5 ♖xh3 39 ♖d8 ♖g3 40 ♖xf8+ ♕xf8 41 ♕c3+ ♔g8 42 ♕c4+ ♕f7 43 ♕c8+ ♔g7 44 ♕c3+ ♔h6 45 ♕e5 ♕g7 46 ♕d6+ ♖g6 47 ♘xg6 ♕xg6 48 ♕h2+ ♔g7 49 ♕e5+ ♕f6 50 ♕c7+ ♕f7 51 ♕e5+ ♔f8 52 ♕b8+ ♕e8 53 ♕xa7 ♕xb5 54 ♕xh7 ...⚲ **0-1** +6

**1845-⚔RS-22** xii 45
**Rousseau, E.= Stanley, C.H.**
[Stanley]
1 e4 e6 2 d4 d5 3 exd5 exd5 4 c4 ♘f6 5 ♘f3 ♗e7 6 ♗e2 dxc4 7 ♗xc4 0-0 8 0-0 ♗g4 9 ♗e3 ♘c6 10 ♗e2 ♕d7 11 ♘bd2 ♖ad8 12 ♖c1 ♗b4 13 a3 ♗xd2 14 ♕xd2 ♖fe8 15 ♖fd1 ♕e7 16 ♖e1 ♕d7 17 h3 ♘e4 18 ♕c2 ♗xh3 19 gxh3 ♕xh3 20 ♗f1?? ♕xf3 21 ♗g2 ♕f5 22 ♖e2 ♖e6 [□ 22 ... ♘d6] 23 ♖ce1 ♖g6 24 ♗c1 ♖xg2+ 25 ♔xg2 ♕g4+ 26 ♔f1 ♕h3+ 27 ♔g1 ♖d6 [□ 27 ... ♘xd4] 28 ♗f4 ♖g6+ 29 ♗g3 f5 30 ♖xe4 fxe4 31 ♕xe4 ♕d7 32 d5 ♘a5 33 b4 ♘b3 34 ♕c4 [□ 34 ♕d3] 34 ... ♘d2 35 ♕d3 ♕h3 36 ♕e3 h5 37 ♕xd2 h4 38 ♖e6 hxg3 39 ♖xg6 ♕h2+ 40 ♔f1 ♕h1+ 41 ♔e2 ♕e4+ 42 ♕e3 ♕c2+ 43 ♔f3 ♕xg6 44 fxg3 ♕f5+ 45 ♔e2 a6 46 ♕f3 ♕xf3+ 47 ♔xf3 ♔f7 48 ♔f4 ♔f6 49 a4 ♔e7 50 ♔e5 ♔d7 51 g4 ♔e7 52 g5 g6 53 a5 b5 [53 ... b6 54 b5+-] 54 axb6 cxb6 55 d6+ ♔d7 56 ♔f6 a5 57 bxa5 bxa5 58 ♔xg6 a4 **½-½** +6

**1845-⚔RS-23** xii 45
**Stanley, C.H.= Rousseau, E.**
[Stanley]
1 e4 c5 2 ♘f3 ♘c6 3 d4 cxd4 4 ♘xd4 e5 5 ♘f3 ♘f6 6 ♗d3 ♗c5 7 0-0 d6 8 h3 ♗e6 9 ♘c3 0-0 10 ♗g5 ♘e7 11 ♗xf6 gxf6 12 ♘h4 ♔h8 13 ♔h2 ♘g6 14 ♘f5 ♖g8 15 g3 ♘e7 16 f4 ♕f8?! 17 ♘xe7 ♕xe7 18 f5 ♗d7 19 ♘d5 ♕d8 20 ♕h5 ♔g7 21 b4 ♗b6 22 a4 ♗c6 23 a5 ♗xd5 24 axb6 ♗c6 25 ♗c4 ♕d7 26 ♖xa7 ♖xa7 27 bxa7 b5 28 ♗xb5 ♖a8 [28 ... ♗xb5 29 ♕g4+ △ 30 ♕xg8+ 31 a8♕++-] 29 ♗xc6 ♕xc6 30 ♕g4+ ♔f8 31 ♖a1 [□ 31 ♕e2] 31 ... ♕xc2+ 32 ♔h1 ♕b2 33 ♕d1 ♕xb4 34 ♕d5 ♖xa7 35 ♖xa7 ♕e1+ 36 ♔g2 ♕e2+ **½-½** +6

**1845-⚔RS-24** xii 45
**Rousseau, E.– Stanley, C.H.**
1 d4 e6 2 c4 d5 3 e3 ♘f6 4 ♘c3 c5 5 ♘f3 ♘c6 6 a3 a5 7 ♗d3 dxc4 8 ♗xc4 cxd4 9 exd4 ♗e7 10 0-0 0-0 11 ♗e3 ♘d5 12 ♕c2 f5 13 ♖ad1 f4 14 ♗c1 ♖b8 15 ♕e4 ♔h8 16 ♗xd5 exd5 17 ♕xd5 ♗g4 18 ♖d3 ♗xf3 19 gxf3 ♗d6 20 ♘e4 ♗c7 21 ♕xd8 ♖bxd8 22 ♖fd1 ♖f5 23 b3 ♖fd5 24 ♗b2 ♗b6 25 ♔f1 h6 26 ♔e2 ♗xd4 27 b4 axb4 28 axb4 b5 29 ♘c5 ♖xc5 30 ♗xd4 ♖e8+ 31 ♔f1 ♖c4 32 ♗a1 ♖e7 33 ♗b2 ♘xb4 34 ♖d7 ♘c6 35 ♖xe7 ♘xe7 36 ♖d7 ♘f5 37 ♖d5 ♖b4 38 ♗c3 ♖b1+ 39 ♔g2 ♘h4+ 40 ♔h3 ♘xf3 41 ♖d7 ♖g1 42 ♖d3 ♘g5+ 43 ♔h4 ♘e4 44 f3 ♘g5 45 ♔h5 ♔h7 46 ♗e5 ♘e6 47 ♖d7 ♖g5+ 48 ♔h4 ♖xe5 49 h3 ♖g5 50 ♖d6 ♖g6 51 ♔h5 ♘f8 52 ♖d8 ♖g5+ 53 ♔h4 ♘g6# **0-1** +6

**1845-⚔RS-25**
**Stanley, C.H.= Rousseau, E.**
[Stanley]
1 e4 c5 2 ♘f3 e6 3 d4 d5 4 exd5 exd5 5 c4 cxd4 6 ♘xd4 ♘c6 7 ♘xc6 bxc6 8 cxd5 ♗b4+ 9 ♗d2 ♗xd2+ 10 ♕xd2 ♘e7 11 dxc6 ♕xd2+ 12 ♘xd2 ♘xc6 13 ♗b5 ♗b7 14 ♖c1 ♖c8 15 0-0 0-0 16 a3 ♘d4 17 ♗c4 ♖c7 18 ♖c3 ♖fc8 19 ♔h1 ♔f8 20 h3 ♖c5 21 ♔h2 ♖g5 22 ♖g3 ♖gc5 23 b3 ♘f5 24 ♖d3 ♖5c6 25 ♖d1 ♖g6 26 ♘f3 ♗xf3 27

♖xf3 ♘d6 28 ♖xd6! ♖xd6 29 ♖xf7+ ♔e8 30 ♖xa7 [⌓ 30 ♖xg7] 30 ... g5 31 ♖xh7 ♖c5 32 ♖h5 ♖d4 33 a4 ♖f5 34 ♔g3 ♔e7 35 h4? gxh4+ 36 ♖xh4 ♖g5+ 37 ♔h3 ♖xh4+ 38 ♔xh4 ♖xg2 39 f4 ♔f6 40 a5 ♔f5 41 ♔h3 ♖a2 42 a6 ♔xf4 43 b4 ♖a3+ 44 ♔h2 ♔e5 45 b5 ♔d6 46 b6 ♔c6 47 b7 ♔c7 48 ♔g2 ♔b8 **½-½** +6

### 1845-⚔RS-26
**Rousseau, E.–Stanley, C.H.**
[Stanley]

1 d4 e6 2 c4 d5 3 e3 ♘f6 4 ♘c3 c5 5 ♘f3 ♘c6 6 a3 a5 7 ♗d3 ♗e7 8 0-0 0-0 9 b3 b6 10 ♗b2 ♗b7 11 ♕c2 h6 12 ♖ad1 ♖c8 13 ♖d2 ♖c7 14 ♖fd1 cxd4 15 exd4 ♔h8 16 ♘b5 ♖c8 17 ♖e2 ♗a6 18 ♕d2 ♗xb5 19 cxb5 ♘b8 20 ♘e5 ♘fd7 21 ♘g4?! ♗d6 22 g3?! ♕g5 23 ♕xg5 hxg5 24 ♔g2 ♖ce8 25 ♖h1 f5 26 ♘e5 ♗xe5 27 dxe5 ♘c5 28 ♗c2 g6 29 f3 ♔g7 30 ♗c1 f4 31 g4 ♖c8 32 ♗b2 ♘e4 33 ♖d1 [33 fxe4?] 33 ... ♘c3 34 ♗xc3 ♖xc3 35 ♖d4 ♖fc8 36 ♗d1 ♘d7 37 ♔f2 ♘c5 38 b4 axb4 39 axb4 ♖d3 40 ♖d2 ♖xd4 41 ♖xd4 ♘d7 42 ♖d3 ♘xe5 43 ♖a3 ♔f6 44 ♖a6 ♖b8 45 ♔e2 ♖h8 46 ♖xb6 ♖xh2+ 47 ♔f1 ♘c4 48 ♖a6 ♖b2 49 ♗e2 ♘e3+ 50 ♔f2 ♖xb4 51 ♔e1 ♖b1+ 52 ♔d2 ♖b2+ 53 ♔d3 ♘c4 54 ♗f1 ♖xb5 55 ♔d4 ♖b3 **0-1** +6

### 1845-⚔RS-27 xii 45
**Stanley, C.H.–Rousseau, E.**

1 e4 e6 2 f4 d5 3 exd5 exd5 4 ♘f3 c5 5 d4 ♘f6 6 ♗d3 ♘c6 7 c3 ♗e7 8 h3 0-0 9 0-0 ♕b6 10 ♔h2 ♖e8 11 a3 ♗d7 12 b4 cxd4 13 cxd4 ♖ac8 14 ♗e3 ♗xb4 15 ♘e5 ♗d6 16 ♘c3 ♘xe5 17 fxe5 ♗xe5+ 18 dxe5 ♕xe3 19 exf6 ♖xc3 20 ♖f3 ♕e5+ 21 ♔h1 ♖e6 22 fxg7 ♖f6 23 ♖b1 ♖xf3 24 ♕xf3 ♖xd3 25 ♕xd3 ♗f5 26 ♕b3 ♗xb1 27 ♕xb1 b6 28 ♕c2 d4 **0-1** +6

### 1845-⚔RS-28 xii 45
**Rousseau, E.=Stanley, C.H**
[Stanley]

1 d4 e6 2 c4 d5 3 e3 c5 4 ♘f3 ♘c6 5 ♘c3 ♘f6 6 a3 ♗e7 7 ♗d3 a6 8 0-0 cxd4 9 exd4 dxc4 10 ♗xc4 0-0 11 ♗e3 b5 12 ♗d3 h6 13 ♕d2 ♘h7 14 ♘xb5! [△ 14 ... axb5 15 ♗xh7+ ♔xh7 16 ♕c2+] 14 ... ♘g5 15 ♘xg5 ♗xg5 16 ♗xg5 ♕xg5 17 ♕xg5 hxg5 18 ♗e4 ♗d7 19 ♗xc6 ♗xc6 20 ♘c3 ♖ad8 21 ♖ad1 ♖d7 22 ♖d2 ♖fd8 23 ♖fd1 ♗d5 24 ♘xd5 ♖xd5 25 ♔f1 e5 26 ♔e2 exd4 27 ♔d3 ♖5d6 28 ♖e1 ♖d5 29 g4 g6 30 ♖c2 ♖b5 31 b4 a5 32 ♖c4 axb4 33 axb4 f5 34 gxf5 gxf5 35 ♖g1 g4 36 h3 ♖db8 37 ♔xd4 ♖xb4 38 ♖xb4 ♖xb4+ 39 ♔e5 ♔f7 40 hxg4 fxg4 41 ♔f5 ♖b2 42 ♖f1 ♖b4 43 ♖a1 ♖b2 44 ♖f1 ♖b4 **½-½** +6

### 1845-⚔RS-29 xii 45
**Stanley, C.H.+Rousseau, E.**
[Stanley]

1 e4 e5 2 ♘f3 ♘c6 3 ♗c4 f5 4 ♗xg8 ♖xg8 5 d4 d6 6 dxe5 dxe5 7 ♕xd8+ ♔xd8 8 ♗g5+ ♗e7 9 ♘c3!± ♗f6 10 0-0-0+ ♗d7 11 exf5 h6 12 ♗xf6+ gxf6 13 ♘e4 ♖f8 14 ♘c5 ♖f7 15 g4 b6 16 ♘e4 ♔e7 17 ♘h4 ♘d4 18 ♘g6+ ♔e8 19 ♖he1 ♘f3 20 ♖e3 ♘xh2

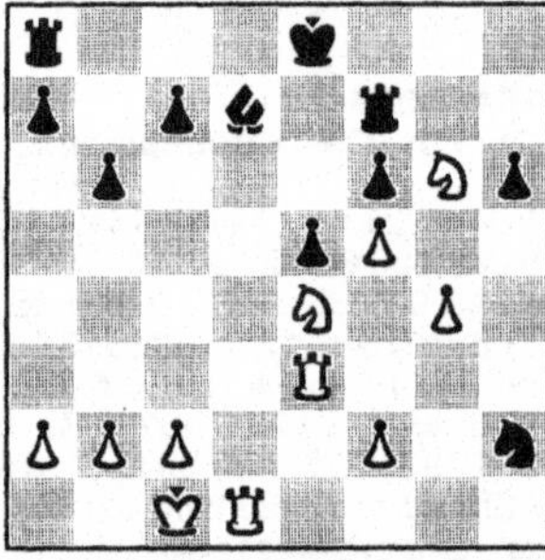

21 ♘xf6+!+− ♖xf6 22 ♘xe5 ♗xf5 23 gxf5 ♖xf5 24 ♘g4+ ♔f8 25 ♘xh2 ♖xf2 26 ♘g4 ♖f4 27 ♘xh6 ♖e8 28 ♖g3 ♖e6 29 ♖g8+ ♔e7 30 ♖g7+ ♔f8 31 ♖xc7 a5 32 ♖h7 ♖h4 33 ♖d8+ ♖e8 34 ♖f7# **1-0** +6

### 1845-⚔RS-30 xii 45
**Rousseau, E.–Stanley, C.H.**
[Stanley]

1 d4 d5 2 c4 e6 3 e3 ♘f6 4 ♘f3 ♘c6 5 ♘c3 ♘e7 6 ♗d3 ♘g6 7 0-0 c6 8 ♖e1 ♗d6 9 a3 0-0 10 c5 ♗c7 11 b4 e5 12 ♗xg6?! fxg6 13 ♘xe5 ♗xe5 14 dxe5 ♘g4 15 f3 ♕h4 16 fxg4 ♕f2+ 17 ♔h1 ♗xg4 18 ♘e2 [⌓ 18 ♖a2] 18 ... ♗xe2 **0-1** +6

### 1845-⚔RS-31 26 xii 45
**Stanley, C.H.+Rousseau, E.**
[Stanley]

1 e4 e5 2 ♗c4 ♗c5 3 ♘f3 d6 4 h3 ♘f6 5 d3 ♗e6 6 ♗b3 h6 7 ♗e3 ♗b6 8 ♘bd2 ♘bd7 9 ♘f1 ♕e7 10 ♘g3 c6 11 ♘h4 g6 12 ♕d2 ♘xe4 13 ♘xe4 d5 14 ♘xg6 fxg6 15 ♘g3 ♗xe3 16 ♕xe3 d4 17 ♕e4 ♖g8 18 0-0 g5! 19 f3 0-0-0 20 ♖fe1 ♖df8 21 ♗xe6 ♕xe6 22 ♕g4 ♖e8 23 ♖e2 ♔c7 24 a3 ♖g6 25 ♖ae1 c5 26 ♕e4 ♕c6 27 ♘f1 ♕xe4 28 ♖xe4 ♔d6 29 ♘d2 ♖ge6 30 c3 ♘f6 31 ♖4e2 b5 32 a4 a6 33 axb5 axb5 34 ♖a1 ♔c7 35 c4 b4 36 ♖a5 ♖c6 37 ♖e1 ♔d6 38 ♖ea1 ♖ec8 39 ♖b5 h5 40 ♘b3 h4 41 ♘a5 ♖6c7 42 ♘b7+ ♔e7 43 ♖aa5 ♘d7 44 ♔f2 ♖g8 45 ♖a7 ♖gc8 46 ♔e2 ♔e6 47 ♖a6+ ♔e7 48 ♔d2 ♖c6 49 ♖a7 ♖8c7??+− 50 ♘a5 ♔d6 51 ♘xc6 ♖xc6 52 ♖bb7 ♘f6 53 ♖f7 [⌓ 53 ♖g7] 53 ... ♔e6 54 ♔e2 ♔f5 55 ♖ac7 ♖xc7 56 ♖xc7 ♘h5 57 ♖xc5 ♘f4+ 58 ♔d2 ♘xg2 59 ♖c8 ♘f4 60 c5 ♘xh3 61 c6 ♘f4 62 ♖f8+ ♔e6 63 c7 **1-0** +6

### 1845-★AL-1 26 iv 45
**Lasa, T. von H. u. von d.+Anderssen, A.**
Breslau

1 e4 e5 2 d4 exd4 3 ♗c4 ♘c6 4 ♘f3 ♕f6 5 0-0 d6 6 c3 d3 7 ♗g5 ♕g6 8 ♗xd3 ♗g4 9 ♘bd2 ♗e7 10 ♗f4 ♘h6 11 ♕b3 ♗xf3 12 ♘xf3 ♖b8 13 ♖ae1 ♕h5 14 ♘d4 0-0 15 ♗xh6 ♕xh6 16 f4 ♗f6 17 ♘f5 ♕h5 18 ♖f3 ♘e7 19 ♖h3 ♕g4 20 ♘h6+ gxh6 21 ♖g3 **1-0** L/N3034

### 1845-★AL-2 26 iv 45
**Anderssen, A.–Lasa, T. von H. u. von d.**
Breslau

1 e4 e5 2 f4 exf4 3 ♘f3 g5 4 ♗c4 ♗g7 5 d4 d6 6 c3 h6 7 ♕b3 ♕e7 8 0-0 ♘d7 9 ♘a3 ♘b6 10 ♗d2 ♗d7 11 ♖ae1 ♗a4 12 ♗b5+ ♗xb5 13 ♕xb5+ c6 14 ♕a5 ♕d7 15 e5 d5 16 e6 fxe6 17 ♖xe6+ ♕xe6 18 ♖e1 ♕xe1+ 19 ♘xe1 ♘f6 20 ♘d3 ♘e4 21 ♗e1 0-0 22 b3 ♖f7 23 ♘c2 g4 24 ♕a3 g3 25 ♕c1 ♖af8 26 ♗d2 f3 27 gxf3 ♖xf3 28 ♘ce1 ♖f1+ 29 ♔g2 ♘xd2 30 ♕xd2 ♖1f2+ 31 ♘xf2 ♖xf2+ 32 ♕xf2 gxf2 ...? **0-1** L/N3034

### 1845-★FS-1 29 x 45
**Saint-Amant, P.C.F. de–Faye**
[Saint-Amant]

⟨♘b1⟩ 1 e4 e5 2 ♗c4 ♗c5 3 ♕g4 ♕f6 4 ♘f3 [4 d4!] 4 ... ♘c6 5 ♕g3 d6 6 c3 ♗e6 7 ♗b5 a6 8 ♗a4 b5 9 ♗c2 h6! 10 d4 [⌓ 10 0-0] 10 ... exd4 11 e5? dxe5 12 ♗e4 ♘ge7 13 ♘xe5 ♗d6 14 cxd4 ♘xd4 15 f4 [15 ♗xa8 ♘c2+] 15 ... 0-0-0 16 ♗e3 ♗b4+ 17 ♔f2 ♘df5 18 ♕f3 ♘xe3 19 ♕xe3 ♖d2+ 20 ♔f3 ♕h4 21 ♕a7 ♕h5+ 22 ♔g3 ♗d5! 23 ♕xa6+ ♔d8 24 ♕xb5 ♘f5+ **0-1** L/N6013-1845

### 1845-★FS-2 29 x 45
**Saint-Amant, P.C.F. de+Faye**
[Saint-Amant]

⟨♘b1⟩ 1 e4 e5 2 ♗c4 ♗c5 3 ♕g4 ♘f6?? [3 ... ♕f6] 4 ♕xg7 ♖f8 5 ♘f3 d6 [□ 5 ... d5; 5 ... ♕e7] 6 d4 exd4 7 ♗g5 ♘bd7 8 0-0-0 c6 9 e5 dxe5 10 ♘xe5 ♘xe5 11 ♗xf6 ♕d6 12 ♖he1+−

12 ... ♗e6 13 ♗xe5 ♕d7 14 ♗xd4 0-0-0 15 ♗xc5 **1-0** L/N6013-1843

**1845-★FS-3** 29 x 45

**Saint-Amant, P.C.F.de− Faye**

[Saint-Amant]

⟨♘b1⟩ 1 e4 e5 2 ♗c4 ♗c5 3 ♘f3 ♘c6 4 b4 ♗xb4 5 0-0 ♘f6 6 c3 ♗a5 7 ♕b3 [7 d4? ♗xc3] 7 ... 0-0 8 d4? ♘xe4 9 ♖e1 ♘f6 [9 ... ♗xc3!] 10 dxe5 d5! 11 ♗d3 ♘e4 12 ♗xe4 dxe4 13 ♖d1 [13 ♖xe4] 13 ... ♕e7 14 ♗a3 ♕e6 15 ♗xf8 ♔xf8 [15 ... exf3] 16 ♘g5 ♕f5 17 ♕a3+ ♔e8 [17 ... ♔g8?!] 18 h4 ♗b6 19 ♖d2 e3! 20 ♖e2 exf2+ 21 ♔f1 ♗e6 22 ♖d1? ♗c4 23 ♕b2 ♘xe5 24 ♖d4 ♗xe2+ 25 ♕xe2 ♗xd4 26 cxd4 ♕d3−+ 27 dxe5 ♕xe2+ 28 ♔xe2 h6 29 ♘e4 ♖d8 30 ♘xf2 ♖d5 31 ♘d3 c5 **0-1** L/N6013-1845

**1845-★GL-1**

**Buckle, H.T.& Evans, W.D.& Perigal, G.& Tuckett, T. & Walker, G.= Kennedy, H.A. & Staunton, H.**

[Staunton]

1 e4 e5 2 ♗c4 ♗c5 3 c3 ♕g5 4 ♕f3 ♕g6 5 d3 ♘c6 6 ♗e3 ♗b6 [□ 6 ... ♗xe3] 7 ♗xb6 axb6 8 ♘a3 ♘a7 9 ♕g3 ♕xg3 [9 ... ♘e7] 10 hxg3 d6 11 f4 ♘h6 12 ♘f3 f6 13 ♔d2 ♗g4 14 d4 0-0-0 15 f5? d5∓ 16 ♗xd5 ♗xf5 17 ♘h4 ♗g4 18 ♘c2 ♖he8 19 ♖ae1 ♘c6 [□ 19 ... f5−+] 20 ♗xc6 bxc6 21 ♔c1 ♗e6 22 ♘f3 ♗g8 [22 ... ♗xa2?!] 23 b3 ♘g4 24 ♖e2 g6 25 ♘e3 h5 26 ♖d1 exd4 27 ♘xg4 d3 28 ♖f2! hxg4 29 ♘d2 f5?! 30 exf5 gxf5 31 ♖xf5 ♖e3 32 ♖f2! b5 [32 ... ♖xg3?!] 33 ♘f1 ♖e2 34 ♖d2 ♖de8 35 ♘h2 ♖2e3 [35 ... ♖e1+] 36 ♘xg4 ♖xg3 37 ♘f6 ♖ee3 38 ♘xg8 ♖xg8 39 ♖f3 ♖g3 40 ♖df2 ♖e2 41 ♖xd3 ♖xg2 42 ♖xe2 ♖xe2 43 ♖d2 ♖e5 ½-½ L/N 6123-1845

**1845-★HK-1** ●● 3 xii 45

**Harrwitz, D.+ Kieseritsy, L.**

Paris [Saint-Amant]

1 e4 c5 2 f4 ♘c6 3 ♘f3 e6 4 ♗c4 d5 5 exd5 exd5 6 ♗b5 ♕b6 7 ♗xc6+ bxc6 8 c3 [□ 8 c4] 8 ... ♘f6 9 d4 cxd4 10 cxd4 ♗b4+ 11 ♘c3 0-0 [□ 11 ... ♗a6] 12 0-0 ♗a6 13 ♖f2 ♘e4∓ 14 ♘xe4 dxe4 15 ♘e5 ♖ad8 16 ♗e3 f6? 17 ♕b3+ ♖d5 18 ♘d7± ♖a5 19 ♘xf8 ♗xf8 20 f5 ♗d3 21 ♖c1 ♕a6 22 ♕b8 ♖b5 23 ♕e8 ♕xa2 24 h3 ♖xb2 25 ♖xc6 ♕b1+ 26 ♔h2 ♖b8 27 ♕e6+ ♔h8 28 ♖f4 ♕e1 29 ♗f2 ♕d2 30 ♗g3 e3 31 ♖h4 ♖b2 32 ♕d5 ♗f1 33 ♖c8 ♕b4 [□ 33 ... ♕xg2+] 34 ♗d6 ♖xg2+ 35 ♔h1 ♖h2+ 36 ♔xh2 ♕d2+ 37 ♔h1 ♗g2+ 38 ♕xg2 ♕e1+ 39 ♔h2 **1-0** L/N6013

**1845̂-★AS-1**

**Staunton, H.+ Avery, T.**

London♀

⟨♘b1⟩ 1 e4 d5 2 e5 ♗f5 3 f4 ♘c6 4 d4 e6 5 ♘f3 h6 6 ♗e2 g5 7 fxg5 hxg5 8 ♘xg5 ♗h6 9 ♘f3 ♕e7 10 c3 a6 11 a4 ♗xc1 12 ♕xc1 ♘h6 13 b4 ♗e4 14 0-0 ♘f5 15 b5 axb5 16 ♗xb5 ♘h4 17 ♘g5 ♖g8 18 ♖f6 ♖g6 19 ♘xe4 dxe4 20 ♖a2 0-0-0 21 ♕f4 ♖h8 22 ♗xc6 ♘f3+ 23 ♔f2 ♖xh2 24 ♗xb7+ ♔xb7 25 ♕xe4+ c6 26 ♔xf3 ♖xf6+ 27 exf6 ♕xf6+ 28 ♕f4 **1-0** L/N6123

**40** Evans, W.D. JGW.CPL

**1845̂-★ES-1**

**Evans, W.D.− Staunton, H.**

[Staunton]

⟨♙f7⟩ 1 e4 ... 2 d4 e6 3 c4 c5 4 d5 d6 5 ♗d3 e5 6 f4 ♘f6 7 fxe5 dxe5 8 ♘f3 ♗g4 9 0-0 ♗e7 10 ♕a4+ ♗d7 11 ♕b3 ♕c7 12 ♘c3 [12 ♘xe5?? △ 13 ♕xb7] 12 ... ♘a6 13 a3 0-0 14 ♘e2 ♘h5 15 ♗d2 ♖ab8 16 ♗c3 ♗d6 17 ♕c2 b5 18 b3 b4 19 axb4 ♘xb4 20 ♗xb4 ♖xb4 21 ♖a6 ♗c8 22 ♖a3 [22 ♖c6? ♕b8 △ 23 ... ♗b7] 22 ... ♗g4 23 ♘c3 ♗xf3 24 gxf3 ♕e7 25 ♔h1 [△ 26 ♘b5 ♖xb5 27 cxb5 c4 28 ♗xc4 ♗xa3?? 29 d6++−] 25 ... ♔h8! 26 ♘b5 ♖xb5 27 cxb5 c4 28 bxc4 ♗xa3 29 ♗e2 ♗c5 30 ♖a1 ♕g5 31 ♕c1 ♘f4 32 ♕f1 ♖f6 **0-1** L/N6123-1845

**1845̂-★ES-2**

**Evans, W.D.− Staunton, H.**

[Staunton]

⟨♙f7⟩ 1 e4 ... 2 d4 e6 3 c4 c5 4 d5 d6 5 ♘c3 ♘e7 6 ♗d3 ♘g6 7 f4 ♗e7 8 ♘f3 [8 dxe6 △ 9 f5] 8 ... 0-0 9 g3 ♘a6 10 0-0 ♘b4 11 ♗b1 exd5 12 exd5 ♗f5 13 a3 ♗xb1 14 axb4 ♗f5 15 bxc5 dxc5 16 ♘e5 a6 17 g4 ♗c8 18 ♘e4 ♗f6 [△ 19 ♘xg6 ♗d4+ 20 ... hxg6] 19 d6! ♗e6 20 ♘xc5 ♕b6 21 ♗e3 ♗xe5 22 fxe5 ♖xf1+ [22 ... ♘xe5? 23 ♕d4] 23 ♔xf1 ♖f8+ 24 ♔g1 ♘xe5 25 ♕c1 [□ 25 b3] 25 ... ♘f3+ 26 ♔h1 ♕xd6 27 ♕c2 ♗xg4 28 ♘xb7 ♕c6 29 ♘a5 ♘e1+ 30 ♘xc6 ♖f1+ 31 ♗g1 ♗f3+ 32 ♕g2 ♗xg2# **0-1** L/N6123-1845

**1845̂-★GS-1**

**G♀= Staunton, H.**

⟨♙f7⟩ 1 e4 ... 2 d4 e6 3 ♗d3 c5 4 d5 d6 5 c4 g6 6 h4 ♗g7 7 f4 exd5 8 cxd5 ♘f6 9 ♘f3 ♗g4 10 ♘c3 a6 11 ♕c2 ♗xf3 12 gxf3 ♘bd7 13 ♗e3 b5 14 a3 ♘h5 15 e5 dxe5 16 ♗xg6+ hxg6 17 ♕xg6+ ♔f8 18 ♘e4 exf4 19 ♗xc5+ ♘xc5 20 ♘xc5 ♕xd5 21 ♘e6+ ♕xe6+ 22 ♕xe6 ♖e8 23 ♕xe8+ ♔xe8 24 0-0-0 ♗f8 25 ♖he1+ ♗e7 26 ♖d6 ♘g3 27 ♖xa6 ♖xh4 28 ♖ae6 ♘f5 29 ♖6e5 ♘e3 30 ♖5xe3 fxe3 31 ♖xe3 ♔d7 32 ♔c2 ♖h2+ 33 ♔b1 ♗f6 34 ♖b3 ♔c6 35 ♔a2 ♔c5 36 ♔b1 ♖h1+ 37 ♔a2 ♖f1 38 ♖e3 ♗d4 39 ♖b3 ♔c6 40 ♖d3 ♗c5 41 ♖b3 ♔b6 42 ♖d3 ♔a5 43 ♖b3 ♖f2 44 ♖d3 ♔a4 45 ♔b1 b4 46 axb4 ♗xb4 ½-½ L/N6123-1845̂

**1845̂-★GS-2**

**G♀− Staunton, H.**

⟨♙f7⟩ 1 e4 ... 2 d4 d6 3 ♗d3 ♘c6 4 c3 e5 5 d5 ♘ce7 6 f4 exf4 7 ♗xf4 ♘g6 8 ♗e3 ♘f6 9 ♘d2 ♗e7 10 ♘gf3 ♘g4 11 ♗d4 0-0 12 ♕c2 ♗g5 13 0-0-0 c5 14 exc6 bxc6 15 h3 ♘4e5 16 ♘xg5 ♕xg5 17 ♔b1 ♗e6 18 ♖de1 ♖ab8 19 ♗e3 ♕g3 20 ♖e2 ♘xd3 21 ♕xd3 ♘f4 22 ♘f1

22 ... ♖xb2+ 23 ♔xb2 ♘xd3+ 24 ♔c2 ♘b4+ 25 cxb4 ♕e5 26 ♘d2 ♕b5 27 ♖f2 ♕a4+ 28 ♔d3 ♕a6+ 29 ♔c3 ♕a3+ 30 ♘b3 ♖b8 31 ♖hf1 ♕xb4+ 32 ♔b2 ♗xb3 **0-1** L/N6123-1845

## 1845̂-★HS-1
**Henderson– Staunton, H.**

[Brien]

⟨♙f7⟩ 1 e4 ... 2 d4 e6 3 ♗d3 c5 4 d5 d6 5 c4 g6 6 ♗d2 ♗g7 7 ♗c3 ♕e7 8 ♗xg7 ♕xg7 9 ♘c3 ♘h6 10 ♘ge2 e5 11 0-0 0-0 12 f4 ♘g4 13 ♕d2 exf4 14 ♖xf4 ♖xf4 15 ♕xf4 ♘e5 16 ♖d1 ♗g4 17 h3 ♗xe2 18 ♗xe2 ♘bd7 19 ♘b5 ♖f8 20 ♕e3 ♘f7 21 b3 ♘de5 22 ♖f1 a6 23 ♘c3 [□ 23 ♘c7] 23 ... ♖e8 24 ♘d1 ♘h6 25 ♕f4 ♘ef7 26 ♗f3 b5 27 ♘e3 ♕d4 [△ 28 ... g5, 29 ... ♕xe3] 28 ♖d1 g5 29 ♕xf7+ ♘xf7 30 ♖xd4 cxd4 31 ♘c2 d3 32 ♘b4 bxc4 33 bxc4 ♘e5 **0-1** L/N6123-1845

## 1845̂-★HS-2
**Staunton, H.– Hannah, J.W.**

Brighton [Staunton]

⟨♘g1⟩ 1 e4 e5 2 ♗c4 ♗c5 3 b4 ♗xb4 4 c3 ♗a5 5 0-0 ♗b6 6 d4 exd4 7 e5 ♘e7 8 ♕h5 0-0 [8 ... ♘g6? 9 ♗g5 f6 10 exf6] 9 ♗g5 ♕e8 10 ♖e1 ♔h8 11 ♘d2 [11 ♗f6!?] 11 ... ♘bc6 12 ♖e4 [12 ♗f6!?] 12 ... f5!–+ 13 exf6 ♕xh5 14 fxe7 ♘xe7 15 ♗xe7 ♖xf2! 16 ♖ae1 dxc3 17 ♘f1 **0-1** L/N6123-1845

## 1845̂-★HS-3
**Staunton, H.+ Hannah, J.W.**

Brighton [Staunton]

⟨♘g1⟩ 1 e4 e5 2 ♗c4 ♘f6 3 d4 d6 4 dxe5 dxe5 5 ♕e2 ♗d6 6 ♗g5 ♘c6 7 c3 ♗e6 8 ♗b5 0-0 9 0-0 a6 10 ♗a4 b5 11 ♗c2 ♗c4 12 ♗d3 ♗xd3 13 ♕xd3 ♗e7 14 ♕e2 ♕d7 15 f4 ♕g4 16 ♕e3 exf4 17 ♗xf4 ♖fe8 [△ 18 ... ♘xe4] 18 ♘d2 ♕e6 19 ♖ae1 ♘h5 20 ♗xc7 ♖ac8 21 ♗b6 ♘e5 22 ♗d4 h6 [△ 23 ... ♗g5] 23 ♕e2 ♘f6 24 h3 ♗d6 25 b4 ♘c4 26 ♗xf6 gxf6 27 ♘f3 ♗g3? 28 ♘d4 ♕e5 29 ♘f5 ♗f4 30 ♕g4+ ♗g5 31 h4 ♕xc3 [31 ... h5+–] 32 ♘xh6+ ♔h7 [32 ... ♔f8 33 ♕xg5] 33 hxg5 **1-0** L/N 6123-1845

## 1845̂-★HS-4
**Hannah, J.W.+ Staunton, H.**

Brighton [Staunton]

⟨♙f7⟩ 1 e4 ... 2 d4 ♘c6 3 ♘c3 e5 4 dxe5 ♘xe5 5 f4 ♘f7 6 ♗c4 ♘gh6 7 f5 ♗b4 8 ♘e2 ♕h4+ 9 ♘g3 c6 10 ♗xh6 ♕xh6 11 0-0 0-0 [11 ... ♗xc3?!] 12 ♖f3 b5 13 ♗xf7+ ♖xf7 14 ♕e2 ♗c5+ 15 ♔h1 a5 16 ♘d1 ♗a6 17 ♘f2 b4 18 ♘d3 ♗d4 19 ♕d1 c5 20 ♘e2 ♗xd3 21 ♖xd3 ♗xb2 22 ♖xd7 ♗xa1 [22 ... ♗e5?] 23 ♖xf7 ♗d4 [23 ... ♗e5+–] 24 ♖d7 ♕h5 25 ♕d3 ♕h4 26 g3 ♕g5 27 ♘xd4 cxd4 28 ♖xd4 **1-0** L/N 6123-1845

## 1845̂-★KS-1 •o
**Kieseritsky, L.– Staunton, H.**

[Staunton]

⟨♖a8⟩ 1 e4 e5 2 ♘f3 ♘c6 3 d4 exd4 4 ♗c4 ♗c5 5 ♘g5 ♘h6 6 ♘xf7 ♘xf7 7 ♗xf7+ ♔xf7 8 ♕h5+ g6 9 ♕xc5 d6 10 ♕g5! ♕d7 11 c3 d3 12 ♗e3 ♖e8 13 f3 ♖e5 14 ♕h6 ♔g8 15 ♗d4 ♖h5 16 ♕e3 ♘e7 17 ♕xd3 b5 18 ♘d2 ♗b7 19 a4 c5 20 ♗e3 c4 21 ♘xc4 [□ 21 ♕c2] 21 ... bxc4 22 ♕xc4+ ♔f8 23 0-0 d5 24 ♕b3 ♗c8 25 exd5 ♕d6 26 h3 ♘xd5 27 ♖ad1

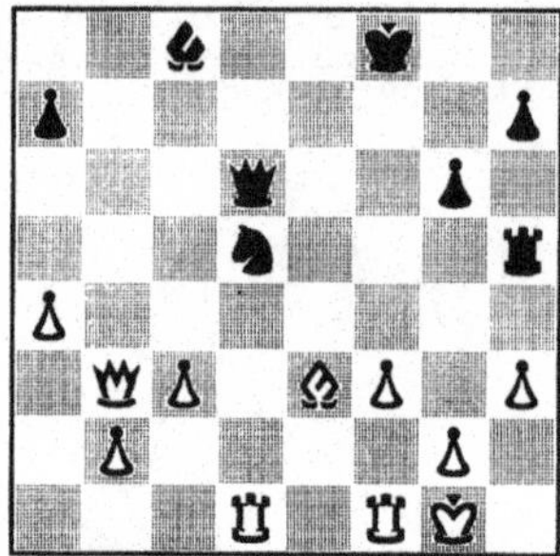

27 ... ♗xh3 28 c4 [□ 28 ♗h6+±; 28 ♖xd5±] 28 ... ♗xg2 29 ♗c5 ♕xc5+ 30 ♖f2 ♖h1+ 31 ♔xg2 ♖xd1 32 cxd5 ♖xd5 **0-1** M954-1845

## 1845̂-★MS-1
**Mongredien, A.– Staunton, H.**

Liverpool [Staunton]

⟨♙f7⟩ 1 e4 ♘c6 2 d4 d5 3 e5 ♗f5 4 g4 ♗g6 5 h4 h5 6 g5 e6 7 ♗h3 ♘b4 8 ♘a3 ♕d7 9 ♗d2 c5 10 ♗xb4 cxb4 11 ♘b1 ♘e7 12 ♘e2 ♖c8 13 c3 ♗e4 14 0-0 ♗f5 15 ♔h2 ♗g4 16 f3 ♗f5 17 ♘f4 ♗xh3 18 ♔xh3 ♘f5 19 ♕d3 ♕f7 [△ 20 ... ♘xh4] 20 ♘e2 a6 21 cxb4 ♗xb4 22 ♘bc3 0-0 23 ♖ac1 ♕g6 [△ 24 ... ♘xh4] 24 ♘f4 ♕e8 25 ♘ce2 ♖xc1 26 ♖xc1 ♘e7 27 ♘xe6??

27 ... ♕d7 28 ♖c7 ♕xe6+ 29 ♔h2 ♘g6 30 ♘g3 ♘xh4 31 ♖xg7+ ♔xg7 32 ♘xh5+ ♔h8 33 ♘f6 ♕f5 **0-1** L/N6123-1845

## 1845̂-★RS-1
**Rhodes, J.+ Saint-Amant, P.C.F. de**

⟨♙f7⟩ 1 e4 ... 2 d4 e6 3 ♗d3 c5 4 dxc5 ♕a5+ 5 ♗d2 ♕xc5 6 ♘c3 d6 7 ♕g4 ♘c6 8 ♗e3 ♕a5 9 f4 ♘f6 10 ♕g3 ♗d7 11 ♘ge2 ♗e7 12 a3 a6 13 0-0 ♕h5 14 ♘d4 ♘g4 15 ♗e2 ♕c5 16 ♗xg4 ♘xd4 17 ♕f2 ♗f6 18 ♖ad1 e5 19 fxe5 dxe5 20 ♗xd7+ ♔xd7 21 ♘e2 ♔c6 22 ♘xd4+ exd4 23 ♗xd4 ♗xd4 24 ♕xd4 ♖hf8 25 ♕xc5+ ♔xc5 26 ♖xf8 ♖xf8 27 ♖d7 ♖g8 28 ♖xb7 ♔d4 29 ♖b4+ ♔e3 30 c3 g5 31 ♖d4 g4 32 e5 h5 33 e6 ♖e8 34 ♖d6 h4 35 c4 ♔e2 36 ♖d4 g3 37 ♖xh4 ♖xe6 38 ♖d4 ♔e3 39 ♖d5 ♖c6 40 b3 ♖b6 41 b4 gxh2+ 42 ♔xh2 ♔f2 43 ♖f5+ **1-0** L/N6046-1846

## 1845̂-★SS-1
**Spreckley, G.S.= Staunton, H.**

[Staunton]

⟨♙f7⟩ 1 e4 ... 2 d4 e6 3 ♗d3 c5 4 e5 ♘e7 5 ♘f3 cxd4 6 0-0 ♘bc6 7 c3 dxc3 8 ♘xc3 ♕a5 9 ♘b5 ♘f5 10 ♗xf5 ♕xb5 11 ♗d3 ♕d5 12 ♕e2 ♘d4 13 ♘xd4 ♕xd4 14 b3 ♕h4 [14 ... ♕xa1 15 ♕h5+ g6 16 ♗xg6+ hxg6 17 ♕xg6+ ♔~ 18 ♗g5++] 15 ♗b2 ♗e7 16 h3 0-0 17 ♔h2 ♕f4+ 18 g3 ♕f7 19 f4 d5 20 exd6 ♗xd6 21 ♗e5 ♗a3 22 ♕e4 g6 23 ♖ae1 a5 24 ♗d4 [△ 25 ♕e5] 24 ... ♗e7 25 ♗c4 ♖fd8 26 a4 [26 ♕e5 ♔f8 27 ♕h8+ ♕g8 28 ♕xg8+ ♔xg8 29 ♗xe6+ ♔f8 30 ♗xc8 ♖axc8 ♗f2 (31 ♗g7+ ♔f7) 31 ... ♖d2 △ 32 ♖cc2∓] 26 ... ♗f8 27 ♖f2 ♕f5 28 ♕e3 h5 29 ♖fe2 ♔h7 [△ 30 ... e5] 30 ♗e5 ♗b4 31 ♕b6! ♕f8 32 ♖f1 ♗c5 33 ♕b5 ♖a6?! 34 ♗c3! ♖a7 35 ♗xe6 [35 ♗xa5?? ♗d7] 35 ... ♗xe6 36 ♖xe6 b6 37 ♖fe1 ♖ad7 38 ♖1e2 h4 39 ♕c4 hxg3+ 40 ♔xg3 ♖d3+ [40 ... ♖d4 41 ♗xd4 ♖xd4 42 ♕c1] 41 ♔g2

♕f5!? [41 ... ♖8d5] 42 ♖e7+ ♗xe7 43 ♖xe7+ ♔h6 44 ♗g7+ ♔h5 [44 ... ♔h7??+-] 45 ♖e5 ♖d2+ 46 ♔f1 ♖d1+ ½-½ L/N6123-1845

### 1845̂-★SS-2
**Spreckley, G.S.+ Staunton, H.**

[Staunton]

⟨♙f7⟩ 1 e4 ... 2 d4 e6 3 ♗d3 c5 4 e5 g6 5 c3 ♘c6 6 ♘f3 d6 7 0-0 dxe5 8 ♘xe5 ♘f6 9 ♗g5 ♗e7 10 ♗b5 ♗d7 11 ♗xc6 ♗xc6 12 ♗xf6 ♗xf6 13 ♘xc6 bxc6 14 dxc5 ♕e7 15 ♕e2 ♖d8 16 ♘d2 ♖d5 17 ♘e4 ♗e5 18 ♖ad1 0-0 19 c4 ♖xd1 20 ♖xd1 ♖f4 21 g3 ♖f5 22 ♘d6 ♖h5 23 f4 ♗g7 24 b4 ♗c3 25 ♔g2! ♗xb4 26 ♖b1 ♖xc5 27 ♖xb4 ♕xd6 28 ♖b2 e5 29 ♖d2 ♕e6 30 ♕d3 ♕e7 31 fxe5 ♖xe5 32 ♕d8+ ♕xd8 33 ♖xd8+ ♔f7 34 ♖d7+ ♖e7 35 ♖xe7+ ♔xe7 36 ♔f3 ♔d6 37 ♔e4 ♔c5 **1-0** L/N6123-1845

### 1845̂-★SS-3
**Spreckley, G.S.– Staunton, H.**

[Staunton]

⟨♙f7⟩ 1 e4 ... 2 d4 ♘c6 3 ♘c3 e5 4 dxe5 ♘xe5 5 f4 ♘f7 6 ♗c4 ♘gh6 7 ♘f3 c6 8 0-0 ♗c5+ 9 ♔h1 d6 10 h3 ♕e7 11 f5 ♗d7 12 a3 a5 13 ♗f4 ♕f6 14 ♗g3 g5 15 ♘a4 ♗e3 16 ♕d3 ♗f4 17 ♗xf4 gxf4 18 ♘b6 ♖d8 19 ♗xf7+ [◻ 19 ♘xd7 ♖xd7 20 ♗e6] 19 ... ♘xf7 20 ♘xd7 ♖xd7 21 ♕d2 ♖g8 22 ♖ad1 ♘g5 23 ♕xf4 ♘xf3 24 ♖xf3 ♕xb2 25 ♖xd6 ♕xc2 26 ♖e6+ ♔f7 27 ♖g3 ♖xg3 28 ♕xg3 ♕c5 [△ 29 ... ♖d1+-+] 29 ♕b3 [◻ 29 ♕f3] 29 ... ♕c1+ 30 ♔h2 ♕f4+ 31 ♕g3 ♕xg3+ 32 ♔xg3 ♖d3+ 33 ♔h4 ♖xa3 34 g4 ♖e3 35 g5 a4 36 ♔g4 a3 37 ♖d6 ♖xe4+ 38 ♔f3 a2 39 ♖d1 ♖a4 **0-1** L/N6123-1845̂

### 1845̂-★SS-4
**Spreckley, G.S.– Staunton, H.**

[Staunton]

⟨♙f7⟩ 1 e4 ... 2 d4 e6 3 ♗d3 c5 4 ♘f3 cxd4 5 ♘xd4 ♘c6 6 ♘f3 ♘f6 7 0-0 ♗e7 8 ♗d2 0-0 9 ♗c3 d6 10 e5 ♘d5 11 exd6 ♗xd6 12 ♗d2 ♗f4 13 ♗xf4 ♘xf4 14 ♘c3 ♗d7 15 ♘e2 ♘xd3 [15 ... ♘h3+ 16 ♔h1] 16 ♕xd3 ♕e7 17 a3 ♖ad8 18 ♘g3 ♗e8 19 ♕e3 ♗g6 20 ♖fe1 ♖f6 21 c3 h6 22 ♖ad1 ♖xd1 23 ♖xd1 a6 24 ♘e5 ♘xe5 25 ♕xe5 ♕f7 26 ♕b8+ ♔h7 27 ♕a7 h5 28 ♕e3 ♖f4 29 f3 h4 30 ♘e4 [◻ 30 ♘e2] 30 ... ♗xe4 31 fxe4 e5 32 ♕d3 ♕g6 33 ♖e1 ♕b6+ 34 ♕e3 ♕xb2 35 ♕e2 ♕xc3 36 ♖d1 g6 37 ♕d3 ♕c5+ 38 ♔h1 ♕c6 39 ♕d8 ♕xe4 40 ♖d7+ ♔h6 41 ♕h8+ ♔g5 42 ♕d8+ ♖f6 43 h3 ♕e1+ 44 ♔h2 ♕g3+ 45 ♔h1 ♕xa3 **0-1** L/N6123-1845

### 1845̂-★ST-1
**T?– Staunton, H.**

⟨♙f7⟩ 1 e4 ... 2 d4 e6 3 ♘c3 g6 4 ♗d3 c5 5 dxc5 ♗xc5 6 h4 ♘c6 7 ♘f3 ♘f6 8 ♘g5 ♕b6 9 ♕e2 0-0 10 f4 ♘h5 11 ♕f3 ♘e5 12 ♕h3 ♖xf4 13 ♗xf4 ♘xf4 14 ♕g3 ♗f2+ **0-1** L/N6123-1845

### 1845̂-★ST-2
**T?– Staunton, H.**

⟨♙f7⟩ 1 e4 ... 2 d4 d6 3 f4 ♘f6 4 ♗d3 e5 5 fxe5 dxe5 6 dxe5 ♘xe4 7 ♕f3 ♘g5 8 ♕h5+ ♘f7 9 ♘f3 g6 10 ♕h4 ♕xh4+ 11 ♘xh4 ♘xe5 12 ♗b5+ ♗d7 13 ♘c3 ♗e7 14 ♘f3 ♘xf3+ 15 gxf3 0-0 **0-1** M954-1845

### 1845̂-★ST-3
**Staunton, H. – Turner, J.**

Brighton [Staunton]

⟨♘b1⟩ 1 e4 e5 2 ♘f3 ♘c6 3 ♗c4 ♗c5 4 b4 ♗xb4 5 c3 ♗a5 6 0-0 d6 7 ♕b3 ♘h6 8 d4 0-0 9 ♗g5 ♕e8 10 ♖ad1 ♗b6 11 ♗xh6 gxh6 12 ♕b1 [△ ♕c1] 12 ... ♗g4 13 ♖d3 ♔h8 14 ♕c1 f5! 15 exf5 e4 16 ♖e1 ♖xf5 17 ♘d2 d5 18 ♖g3 ♘e5 19 ♗xd5 ♘d3 20 ♖xd3 ♖xd5 21 ♖xe4 ♕d7 22 ♖de3 ♗h5! 23 ♖e7 ♕d8 24 ♕e1 c5! 25 ♖3e5 cxd4 26 ♕e4 ♗g6 27 ♕f3 [◻ 27 ♕xd5 ♕xd5 (27 ... dxc3) 28 ♖xd5 dxc3 29 ♘b3 ♖f8∓] 27 ... ♕f8 28 ♕xd5 dxc3 29 ♖e3 [◻ 29 ♘f3-+] 29 ... ♗xe3 30 ♕e5+ ♔g8 31 ♕xe3 cxd2 32 ♖d7 ♕f6 33 ♕xd2 ♕a1+ 34 ♕d1 ♕xd1+ **0-1** L/N6123-1845

### 1845̂-★ST-4
**Turner, J.– Staunton, H.**

Brighton [Staunton]

⟨♙f7⟩ 1 e4 ... 2 d4 e6 3 ♗d3 c5 4 dxc5 ♕a5+ 5 ♘c3 ♗xc5 6 ♗d2 d6 7 ♘d5 ♕d8 8 ♘f4 ♘f6 9 h3 ♘c6 10 ♘f3 0-0 11 ♕e2 a6 12 0-0-0 ♕c7 13 ♗c4 ♖e8 14 ♗c3 d5 15 exd5 ♕xf4+ 16 ♗d2 ♘d4 17 ♗xf4 [17 ♘xd4 ♕xd4 (17 ... ♕d6 18 ♘xe6 ♘xd5 19 ♗f4+-) 18 ♗e3 ♕e5 19 ♗xc5 ♕xe2 20 ♗xe2 exd5] 17 ... ♘xe2+ 18 ♗xe2 exd5 19 ♘e5 ♗xf2 20 ♗f3 ♗f5! 21 ♗xd5+ ♘xd5 22 ♖xd5 ♗e4 23 ♖d7 g5 [23 ... ♗xg2? 24 ♖h2 ♗e3+ 25 ♗xe3 ♖xe5 26 ♖xg2 ♖xe3 27 ♖gxg7++-] 24 ♘g4 [24 ♗xg5?-+; 24 ♗∼?-+] 24 ... gxf4 25 ♘xf2 ♗xg2 26 ♖g1 f3 27 ♘g4 ♖e6 28 h4 ♔h8 [◻ 28 ... ♖ae8; ◻ 28 ... ♖g6] 29 ♖f7 ♖ae8 30 ♖d1 [30 ♘f6 ♖8e7] 30 ... ♖6e7 31 ♖d7? ♖xd7 32 ♖xd7 ♗h3 33 ♖d4 ♗xg4 34 ♖xg4 f2 **0-1** L/N6123-1845

### 1845̂-★ST-5
**Turner, J.– Staunton, H.**

Brighton

⟨♙f7⟩ 1 e4 ... 2 d4 e6 3 c4 c5 4 d5 d6 5 ♗d3 exd5 6 exd5 ♘f6 7 ♗g5 ♗e7 8 ♗xf6 ♗xf6 9 ♘c3 [9 ♕h5+] 9 ... 0-0 10 ♘ge2 ♗e5 11 0-0 ♗g4 12 ♕d2! [△ 13 f4; 12 ♕c2] 12 ... g5 [12 ... ♖f3?; 12 ... ♗f3?] 13 f3 ♗f5 14 ♗xf5 ♖xf5 15 ♘e4 ♕f8 16 g4 [16 ♘xg5? ♗xh2+ △ 17 ... ♕h6+] 16 ... ♕h6 17 ♘2g3 ♖f4 18 ♘h5 [18 ♘f5?!] 18 ... ♘d7! 19 ♘xf4 ♗xf4 20 ♕g2 ♘e5 21 b3 ♖f8 22 ♘g3 ♕f6 23 ♘f5 ♘g6 24 ♖ad1 ♗e5 25 ♔h1

25 ... ♗c3! 26 ♕h3 ♖e8 27 ♕h6 [27 ♘g3? ♘f4] 27 ... ♖e2 28 ♘g3 ♖c2 29 ♘e4 ♕f4 30 ♘xg5? ♘f8! 31 ♖g1 [31 ♕h5 ♗e5] 31 ... ♗g7 [31 ... ♗f6? 32 ♕xf8+ ♔xf8 33 ♘e6+] 32 ♕h5 h6 33 ♕f7+ ♕xf7 34 ♘xf7 ♔xf7 35 ♖g2 ♖c3 36 f4 ♘g6 37 ♖e1 ♖f3 38 ♖ge2 ♘xf4 39 ♖e7+ ♔g6 40 ♖xb7 ♗c3 41 ♖d1 ♖f2 42 ♖xa7 ♘e2 43 ♖e7 ♔g5 44 ♖e6 ♘f4 45 ♖xd6 ♗e5 46 h4+ ♔xg4 47 ♖xh6 ♔h3 **0-1** L/N 6123-1845

### 1845̂-★SW-1
**Williams, E.– Staunton, H.**

⟨♙f7⟩ 1 e4 ... 2 d4 e6 3 ♗d3 c5 4 d5 d6 5 c4 ♗e7 6 ♘e2 ♗f6 7 ♘bc3 ♘e7 8 0-0 0-0 9 f4 exd5 10 cxd5 ♘a6 11 h3 ♘c7 12 ♕e1 a6 13 ♕g3 ♘g6 14 e5 ♗h4 15 ♕h2 dxe5 16 ♗xg6 hxg6 17 fxe5 ♖xf1+ 18 ♔xf1 ♘xd5 19 ♘xd5 ♕xd5 20 ♗e3 ♗d7 21 ♔g1? ♕d3 22 ♕f4 ♕xe2 23 ♗xc5 ♗c6 24 ♕g4 ♕xg4 25 hxg4 **0-1** L/N6123-1845

### 1845̂-★SW-2
**Williams, E.– Staunton, H.**

[Staunton]

⟨♙f7⟩ 1 e4 ... 2 d4 e6 3 ♗d3 c5 4 d5 d6 5 c4 ♗e7 6 e5 g6 7 f4 ♘h6 8 ♘f3 0-0 9 ♘c3 ♘a6 10 a3 ♘c7 11 ♕c2 ♔g7 12 h4 exd5 13 cxd5 ♗g4 14 ♕f2 ♗xf3 15 gxf3 dxe5 16 fxe5 ♘xd5 17 ♗xh6+ ♔xh6 18 0-0-0 ♘xc3 19 ♕d2+ ♔g7 20 ♕xc3 ♖xf3 21 ♖hf1 ♖xf1 22 ♖xf1 ♗xh4 23 ♗c4 ♕d4 24 ♖f7+ ♔h6

25 e6 [⌂ 25 ♕xd4, 26 ♖xb7] 25 ... ♖d8 26 ♔b1 ♕xc3 27 bxc3 b5 28 ♗f1 ♖e8 29 ♗h3 ♖e7 30 ♖f8 ♖b7 31 ♗g2 ♖e7 32 ♗d5 a5 33 ♖a8 b4 34 c4! bxa3 35 ♖xa5 ♗f2 36 ♖xa3 ♗d4 37 ♔c2 ♔g5 38 ♖g3+ ♔f6 39 ♖f3+ ♔g7 40 ♔d3 [⌂ 40 ♖f7+] 40 ... ♗f6 41 ♔e4 h5 42 ♔f4 ♖a7 43 ♔g3 ♖a2 44 e7 ♗e5+ 45 ♔h4 ♔h6 [△#] **0-1** L/N6123-1845

**1845̂-★SW-3**
**Worrall, T.H.– Saint-Amant, P.C.F. de**
[Staunton]
⟨♙f7⟩ 1 e4 ... 2 d4 ♘c6 3 d5 ♘e5 4 f4 ♘f7 5 e5 e6 6 dxe6 dxe6 7 ♗d3 ♗c5 8 ♘f3 ♘gh6 9 h3 0-0 10 g4 ♗d7 11 ♗e4 c6 12 ♕e2 ♕b6 13 ♘c3 ♖ad8 14 a3 a6 15 ♘a4 ♕a5+ 16 b4 ♕xa4 17 bxc5 ♗c8 18 0-0 ♖d4 19 ♖e1 [19 ♘xd4 ♕xd4+ 20 ♗e3 ♕xe4−+] 19 ... ♖c4 20 ♖b1 ♖xc5 21 ♖b4 ♕a5 22 ♕d3 ♖d8 23 ♗xh7+ ♔h8 24 ♕g6 ♖c3 25 ♕e4 ♖xf3 26 ♕xf3 ♔xh7 27 g5 ♘f5 28 ♕h5+ ♔g8 29 g6 ♘7h6 30 ♖ee4 ♕c5+ 31 ♔g2 ♕xc2+ 32 ♖e2 ♕xc1 33 ♕g5 ♖d1 **0-1** L/N6126-1845

**1845-★S♀-1**
**♀– Staunton, H.**
⟨♙f7⟩ 1 e4 ... 2 d4 e6 3 ♗d3 c5 4 dxc5 ♕a5+ 5 ♘c3 ♗xc5 6 ♗d2 ♕b6 7 ♘a4 ♗xf2+ 8 ♔f1 ♕c6 9 ♕h5+ g6 10 ♕e5 ♘f6 11 ♘f3 0-0 12 ♗h6 ♖f7 13 h3 ♕xa4 14 ♔xf2 ♘c6 15 ♕f4 ♘d4 16 b3 ♕a5 17 ♔g1 ♘h5 18 ♕e3 ♘xf3+ 19 gxf3 ♕e5 20 ♔f2 ♕g3+ 21 ♔e2 ♕g2+ 22 ♕f2 ♘g3+ 23 ♔e3 ♕xf2+ 24 ♔xf2 ♘xh1+ 25 ♖xh1 b6 26 ♖g1 ♗b7 27 ♖g3 ♖c8 28 e5 b5 29 ♔e3 a5 30 h4 ♖c3 31 ♔d4 ♖xd3+ 32 cxd3 ♗xf3 33 ♔c5 ♗c6 34 h5 ♖f5 35 hxg6 hxg6 36 d4 ♔f7 37 ♗d2 ♖f2 38 ♗xa5 ♖xa2 39 ♗d8 ♖c2+ 40 ♔d6 ♖f2 41 b4 ♖b2 42 ♗a5 ♔g7 43 ♔c5 ♖c2+ 44 ♔d6 ♖c4 45 ♖g4 ♔h6 46 ♖h4+ ♔g5 47 ♗d8+ ♔f5 **0-1** L/N6123-1845

**1845̂-★S♀-2**
**♀– Staunton, H.**
⟨♙f7⟩ 1 e4 ... 2 d4 ... 3 ♗d3 c5 4 e5 g6 5 d5 ♗g7 6 f4 e6 7 d6 ♘c6 8 c3 c4 9 ♗e4 b5 10 ♘f3 ♗b7 11 ♘g5 ♘h6 12 ♘xh7 ♘xe5 13 ♗xb7 ♘d3+ 14 ♔f1 ♕b6 15 ♕f3 ♖b8 16 ♗e4 ♘xc1 17 ♗xg6+ ♔d8 18 ♘a3 ♘d3 19 ♗xd3 cxd3 20 ♕xd3 ♘f5 21 ♘g5 ♖f8 22 ♖e1 a6 23 ♘e4 ♗e5 24 g3 ♗xd6 25 ♖d1 ♘e3+ 26 ♔e2 ♘d5 27 ♘xd6 ♕xd6 28 ♖he1 ♖xf4 29 ♔d2 ♖f2+ 30 ♔c1 ♕f8 31 ♕d4 b4 32 ♕a7 ♖c8 33 ♖xd5 ♕h6+ 34 ♔b1 ♖xb2+ 35 ♔xb2 bxa3+ 36 ♔a1 exd5 **0-1** L/N6123-1845

**1845̂-★S♀-3**
**♀– Staunton, H.** London
⟨♙f7⟩ 1 e4 ... 2 d4 e6 3 ♗d3 c5 4 dxc5 ♕a5+ 5 ♘c3 ♕xc5 6 ♗e3 ♕a5 7 a3 a6 8 ♘ge2 ♘c6 9 0-0 ♘f6 10 f4 ♘g4 11 ♗f2 ♘xf2 12 ♔xf2 ♗c5+ 13 ♔g3 ♕d8 14 h3 b5 15 b4 ♗a7 16 e5 0-0 17 ♘e4 ♘e7 18 ♘d6 ♘d5 19 ♖f3 ♗e3 20 ♗e4 ♗xf4+ 21 ♘xf4 ♕g5+ 22 ♔h2 ♘xf4 23 ♖g3 ♕xe5 24 ♗xa8 ♘h5 25 ♕d3 ♘xg3 26 ♕xg3 ♕xa1 27 ♗e4 ♖f1 28 ♕g5 ♖f8 29 ♕c5 ♕f6 30 ♗f3 ♕d8 31 ♗e4 g6 32 ♕c3 ♕h4 33 g3 ♕d8 34 h4 a5 35 ♕d3 ♕b6 36 ♔h3 axb4 37 axb4 ♕g1 38 ♔g4 ♕a1 39 c3 ♕c1 40 ♕d4 h5+ 41 ♔h3 ♕f1+ 42 ♗g2 ♕e2 43 ♕c5 ♗a6 44 ♕a7 ♗c8 45 ♕c7 ♕e5 **0-1** L/N6123-1845

**1845̂-★S♀-4**
**Staunton, H.+♀** London
⟨♖a1⟩ 1 e4 e5 2 ♗c4 ♗c5 3 b4 ♗xb4 4 c3 ♗a5 5 ♘f3 ♘c6 6 d4 ♘xd4 7 ♘xe5 ♘e6 8 ♘xf7 ♔xf7 9 ♗xe6+ ♔f8 10 ♗b3 ♗b6 11 e5 ♔e8 12 0-0 ♘e7 13 ♗g5 d6 14 e6 c6 15 ♕f3 ♖f8 16 ♕h5+ g6 17 ♕xh7 ♕c7

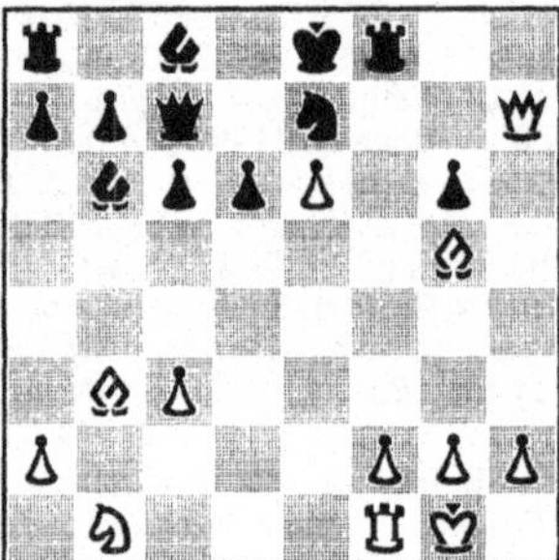

18 ♕f7+ **1-0** L/N6123-1845

**1845̂-★S♀-5**
**♀– Staunton, H.**
[Staunton]
⟨♙f7⟩ 1 e4 ... 2 d4 e6 3 ♗d3 c5 4 dxc5 ♕a5+ 5 ♘c3 ♕xc5 6 ♗e3 ♕a5 7 ♘e2 ♘c6 8 a3 a6 9 0-0 ♘f6 10 h3 ♗e7 11 b4 ♕c7 12 f4 d6 13 b5! axb5 14 ♘xb5 ♕b8 15 ♗b6 [△ 16 ♗c7+−] 15 ... ♗d8 16 ♗xd8 ♘xd8 17 ♘ec3 0-0 18 ♗c4 ♘f7 19 f5 ♖e8 20 ♕d4 ♗d7 21 ♖ad1 ♖a6 22 fxe6 ♗xe6 23 ♘d5 ♗xd5 24 ♗xd5 ♘xd5 25 ♕xd5 ♖e7 26 ♖f3 ♕e8 27 ♖df1 ♖c6 28 ♖xf7 ♖xf7 29 ♘xd6 ♖xd6 30 ♕xd6 ♖xf1+ 31 ♔xf1 ♕xe4 32 ♕d8+ ♔f7 33 ♕d7+ ♔f6 34 ♕d3 ♕e7 35 g4 [△ 36 ♕f5#] 35 ... g6 36 ♔f2 ♕c5+ 37 ♔g2 b5 38 h4 ♔e5 39 ♕g3+ ♔e6 40 ♕b3+ ♔e5 41 ♕g3+ ♔d4 42 ♕d3+ ♔e5 43 ♔f3 ♕c6+ 44 ♔f2 ♕f6+ 45 ♔e2 ♕c6 46 ♕e3+ ♕e4 47 ♕xe4+ ♔xe4 48 c4 [⌂ 48 ♔d2] 48 ... bxc4 49 a4 ♔d4 50 a5 ♔c5 51 a6 ♔b6 **0-1** L/N6123-1845

## HARRWITZ✕HORWITZ

London

[1846-✕HH]

| | | | | | | | | | | | | | |
|---|---|---|---|---|---|---|---|---|---|---|---|---|---|
| D. Harrwitz | 1 | 0 | 1 | 0 | 0 | 0 | 1 | 1 | 1 | 1 | ½ | 0 | 6½ |
| B. Horwitz | 0 | 1 | 0 | 1 | 1 | 1 | 0 | 0 | 0 | 0 | ½ | 1 | 5½ |

**1846-✕HH-1** 12 x 46
**Harrwitz, D.+ Horwitz, B.**
London [Staunton]
1 e4 e5 2 ♘f3 ♘c6 3 c3 d5 [3 ... f5?!] 4 ♗b5 ♗g4? 5 ♕a4 ♗xf3 6 ♗xc6+ bxc6 7 ♕xc6+ ♔e7 8 gxf3+− ♘f6 9 b3 ♕b8? 10 ♗a3+ ♔d8 11 ♖g1 ♘e8 12 ♕xd5+ ♗d6 13 d4 exd4 14 e5 ♘f6 15 exf6 ♖e8+ 16 ♔d1 g6 17 c4 ♖e5 18 ♕xf7 ♕b7 19 ♕g8+ ♖e8 20 ♕d5 ♕xd5 21 cxd5 ♔d7 22 ♗xd6 ♔xd6 23 ♖g5 ♖e5 24 f4 ♖xd5 25 ♘d2 ♖f5 26 ♖xf5 gxf5 27 ♘f3 ♔e6 28 ♘xd4+ ♔xf6 29 ♔c2 ♖g8 30 ♖e1 ♖g2 31 ♖e6+ ♔f7 32 ♖e2 ♔f6 33 f3 ♖g7 34 ♔c3 h5 35 a4 h4 36 ♖e6+ ♔f7 37 ♖h6 **1-0** M954

**1846-✕HH-2** x 46
**Horwitz, B.+ Harrwitz, D.**
London [Staunton]
1 e4 e5 2 ♘f3 ♘c6 3 c3 ♗c5 4 b4 ♗b6 5 b5 ♘a5 6 ♘xe5 ♕e7 7 d4 d6 8 ♗a3! f6 9 ♘f3 [9 ♘g4!] 9 ... ♕xe4+ 10 ♗e2 ♘h6 11 0-0 0-0 12 ♗d3 ♕g4 13 ♗b4 ♕e6 14 ♖e1 [14 ♕a4 ♘c4 15 ♕b3+−; 14 ... a6 15 bxa6 (15 ♗xa5 axb5) 15 ... ♘c6 16 ♘bd2±; 16 ♕c2±; 16 ♗a3±] 14 ... ♕f7 15 d5 [15 ♕a4] 15 ... ♘g4 16 ♖f1 ♘e5 17 ♘xe5 fxe5 18 ♘d2 ♕xd5 19 ♘c4?! [19 ♕c2] 19 ... e4! 20 ♘xb6 axb6 21 ♗c2 ♕xd1 22 ♗xd1 ♗e6? 23 ♗c2 ♖fe8 24 ♗xe4 ♗c4 25 ♖fe1 d5 26 ♗f3 ♗xa2 27 ♖ed1 ♗b3 28 ♗xd5+ ♗xd5 29 ♖xd5 ♘c6 30 ♖c1 [30 ♖xa8 ♖xa8 31 bxc6?? ♖a1+] 30 ... ♘xb4 31 cxb4 ♖a2 32 h3 ♖ee2? [32 ... ♖e7∞=] 33 ♖xc7+− h6 34 ♖d8+ ♔h7 35 ♖dd7 ♖xf2 36 ♖xg7+ ♔h8 37 ♖xb7 ♖fb2 38 ♖g6 h5 39 ♖g5 h4 40 ♖xb6 [40 ♖g4=] 40 ... ♔h7 41 ♖g4 ♖a1+ 42 ♔h2 ♖a4 43 ♖xh4+ ♔g7 44 ♖c4 **1-0** M954

**1846-⚔HH-3** x46
**Harrwitz, D.+Horwitz, B.**
London [Staunton]

1 e4 e5 2 ♘f3 ♘c6 3 c3 d5 4 ♗b5 ♕d6 5 exd5 ♕xd5 6 ♗xc6+ bxc6 7 ♕e2 ♗d6 8 d4 ♗g4 9 ♘bd2 f6 10 0-0 ♘e7?? 11 c4 ♕f7 12 c5+− ♘f5 13 ♕e4 ♗xf3 14 ♘xf3 ♘e7 15 cxd6 cxd6 16 dxe5 fxe5 17 ♘g5 ♕g6 18 f4 0-0 19 ♕xg6 ♘xg6 20 fxe5 ♖xf1+ 21 ♔xf1 ♘xe5 22 b3 ♖f8+ 23 ♔g1 h6 24 ♘e4 d5 25 ♘f2 d4 26 ♗a3 ♖f6 27 ♖d1 ♖g6 28 ♔f1 ♘g4 29 ♘xg4 ♖xg4 30 g3 ♖g5 31 ♖xd4 ♖a5 32 ♖a4 ♖d5 33 ♔e2 ♖e5+ 34 ♔f3 ♖d5 35 ♔e3 ♖e5+ 36 ♔f2 ♖d5 37 ♗c1 ♔h7 38 ♖xa7 ♖c5 39 ♗e3 ♖c2+ 40 ♔g1 c5 41 ♗f2 ♔g6 42 a4 ♔h5 43 ♖xg7 …♀ **1-0** M954

**1846-⚔HH-4** x46
**Horwitz, B.+Harrwitz, D.**
London [Staunton]

1 e4 e5 2 ♘f3 ♘c6 3 c3 ♗c5?! 4 b4 ♗b6 5 b5 ♘b8 6 ♘xe5 ♕e7 7 d4 d6 8 ♗a3 f6 9 ♘f3 ♕xe4+ 10 ♗e2 ♘h6 11 0-0 0-0 12 ♗d3 ♕e7 13 ♗c4+ ♔h8 14 ♖e1 ♕d8 15 ♘bd2± f5 16 ♕c2 ♘d7 17 ♗d3 ♘f6 18 c4 c6 19 c5 dxc5 20 dxc5 ♗c7 21 bxc6 bxc6 22 ♘c4 ♗a6 23 ♖ad1 ♗xc4 24 ♗xc4 ♕b8 25 h3 ♘e4 26 ♗d3 ♗a5 27 ♗xe4 fxe4 [27 … ♗xe1 28 ♗xc6] 28 ♖xe4 ♕c8 29 ♗b2 ♕f5 30 ♖d6 ♖ab8! 31 ♗d4 [31 ♖xh6 ♖xb2] 31 … ♘f7

32 ♗xg7+!+− ♔xg7 33 ♖g4+ ♕xg4 34 hxg4 ♘xd6 35 cxd6 ♗b6 36 ♘g5 ♔h6 37 ♘e4 ♔g7 38 ♕c3+ ♔g6 39 ♕xc6 ♖bc8 40 ♕d5 h6 41 ♕e6+ ♔g7 42 g5 hxg5 43 ♕e7+ ♖f7 44 ♕xg5+ ♔h8 45 ♘f6 **1-0** M954

**1846-⚔HH-5** x46
**Harrwitz, D.−Horwitz, B.**
London [Staunton]

1 e4 e5 2 ♘f3 ♘c6 3 c3 g6 4 ♗c4 d6 5 d4 ♗g7 6 0-0 ♕e7 7 h3 ♘f6 8 d5 ♘d8 9 ♗d3 ♘d7 10 b4 0-0 11 ♕c2 ♘b6 12 c4 f5 13 ♗g5 ♕f7 14 ♘bd2 fxe4 15 ♗xe4 ♗f5 16 ♖ad1 ♗d7 17 ♗xd8 ♖axd8 18 ♘g5 ♕f6 19 ♗xf5 ♕xg5 20 ♗e6+ ♔h8 21 ♘e4 ♕e7 22 c5 dxc5 23 bxc5 ♘f6 24 f3 [24 ♘xf6!?] 24 … c6 25 ♘xf6 ♗xf6 26 ♕c4 cxd5 27 ♗xd5 ♖c8 28 ♖c1 ♗g5 29 ♖c3 ♖fd8?! [29 … ♖xc5; 29 … ♕xc5+] 30 ♖b1 ♖c7 31 ♕b3 ♕d7 32 ♗xb7? ♖xb7 33 ♕xb7 ♕d4+ 34 ♔h1 ♕xc3 35 c6 ♕c2 36 c7?! [36 ♖g1] 36 … ♖d1+ 37 ♖xd1 ♕xd1+ 38 ♔h2 ♗f4+ 39 g3 ♕e2+ 40 ♔h1 ♕f1+ 41 ♔h2 ♕f2+ 42 ♔h1 ♕e1+ 43 ♔g2 ♕xg3+ 44 ♔f1 ♕xh3+ 45 ♔e2 ♕g2+ 46 ♔d3 ♕d2+ 47 ♔c4 ♕c2+= [47 … ♕xa2+=] 48 ♔b5 ♕d3+ 49 ♔c5 ♕c3+ 50 ♔b5 ♕d3+ 51 ♔c5 ♗e3+ 52 ♔c6 ♕c4+ 53 ♔d6?? [53 ♔d7=] 53 … ♗c5+ 54 ♔d7 ♕f7+ **0-1** M954

**1846-⚔HH-6** x46
**Horwitz, B.+Harrwitz, D.**
London [Staunton]

1 e4 e5 2 ♘f3 ♘c6 3 c3 f5 4 exf5 [4 d4!] 4 … d5 5 ♗b5 ♗d6 6 d4 e4 7 ♗g5 ♘e7 8 ♘h4 0-0 9 g4 ♕e8 10 ♘d2 ♗d7 11 ♕e2 ♘c8 12 ♘g2 a6 13 ♗a4 h6 14 ♗e3 ♘6e7 15 ♗xd7 ♕xd7 16 ♘f4 ♗xf4 17 ♗xf4 ♘d6 18 0-0-0 ♕a4 19 ♗xd6 cxd6 20 ♔b1 b5 21 f3 ♘c6 22 fxe4 ♖fe8 [22 … b4!] 23 ♕d3 dxe4 24 ♘xe4 ♖ed8 25 f6 ♖a7 26 fxg7 ♖xg7 27 ♖hf1 b4 28 ♕c4+ ♔h8 29 ♕e6 bxc3 30 ♕xh6+ ♖h7 31 ♖f8+ **1-0** M954

**1846-⚔HH-7** xî46
**Harrwitz, D.+Horwitz, B.**
London [Staunton]

1 e4 e5 2 ♘f3 ♘c6 3 c3 g6 4 ♗c4 d6 5 d4 ♗g7 6 0-0 ♘ge7 7 d5 ♘b8 8 ♘h4 0-0 9 g3 ♗h3 10 ♘g2 f5∓ 11 f3 ♘d7 12 ♗g5 ♘f6 13 ♗xf6 ♖xf6 14 ♘d2 ♕d7 15 ♕b3 b6 16 ♖f2 ♖af8 17 ♖af1 ♗xg2 18 ♔xg2 f4 19 ♗b5 ♕c8 20 ♕a4 fxg3 21 hxg3 a5

22 ♗d7 ♕d8 23 ♗e6+ ♔h8 24 c4 ♗h6 25 ♕d1 ♘c6 26 ♖h1 ♗e3 27 ♖ff1 ♗xd2?? [27 … ♘d4∓] 28 ♕xd2 ♘d4 29 ♖xh7+ ♔xh7 30 ♖h1+ ♔g7 31 ♕h6# **1-0** M954

**1846-⚔HH-8** xî46
**Horwitz, B.−Harrwitz, D.**
London [Staunton]

1 e4 e5 2 ♘f3 ♘c6 3 c3 d5 4 exd5 ♕xd5 5 c4 ♕e4+ 6 ♗e2 ♗e7 7 0-0 ♘h6 8 ♘c3 ♕g6 9 ♘d5 ♗d8 10 d3 0-0 11 ♘e1 f5 12 f4 e4 13 ♘c2 exd3 14 ♗xd3 ♘e7 15 b3 ♘xd5 16 cxd5 ♘g4 17 h3?? ♕b6+ 18 ♔h1 ♘f2+ 19 ♖xf2 ♕xf2 20 ♗e3 ♕h4 21 ♕d2 ♗e7 22 ♖e1 ♗d6 23 ♘d4 a5 24 ♘b5 ♗b4 25 ♘c3 ♗d7 26 ♗d4 c6 27 dxc6 ♗xc6 28 ♔h2 ♖ad8 29 g3 ♕h5 30 ♗c4+ ♔h8 31 ♕f2 ♖xd4 32 ♗e2 [32 ♕xd4 ♕f3] 32 … ♖d2 33 ♕e3 ♗xc3 34 g4 fxg4 35 ♕xc3 ♕d5 36 ♕g3 ♖xe2+ **0-1** M954

**1846-⚔HH-9** xi 46
**Harrwitz, D.+Horwitz, B.**
London [Staunton]

1 e4 e5 2 ♘f3 ♘c6 3 c3 g6 4 ♗c4 ♗g7 5 d4 d6 6 0-0 ♕e7 7 ♘g5 ♘h6 8 d5 ♘d8± 9 f4 0-0 10 fxe5 ♘g4? 11 e6 ♘e5 12 exf7+ ♘dxf7 13 ♘xf7 ♘xc4 14 ♘h6+ ♔h8 15 ♖xf8+ ♗xf8 16 ♕d4+ ♘e5 17 ♘a3 ♕h4 [△ 18 … ♕e1#; 18 … ♗xh6]

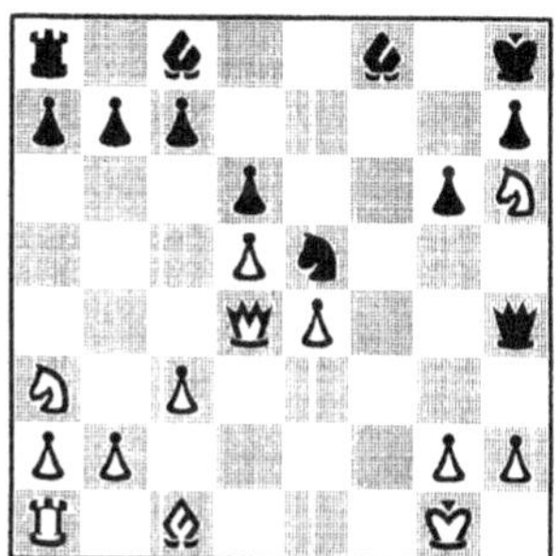

18 ♗g5! ♕h5 19 ♘f7+ ♔g8 20 ♘xe5 ♗g7 21 ♕f2 ♗xe5 22 ♗f4 ♗d7 23 ♗xe5 ♕xe5 24 ♖f1 ♕e7 25 ♕f4 ♖e8 26 c4 c6 27 ♘c2 cxd5 28 exd5 ♗f5 29 ♖e1 ♕f7 30 ♖xe8+ ♕xe8 31 ♘e3 ♕e4 32 ♕xe4 ♗xe4 33 b4 b6 34 ♔f2 ♔f7 35 ♔e2 ♔f6 36 ♔d2 ♔e5 37 ♔c3 h5 38 g3 ♗b1 39 ♘f1 b5 [39 … ♗xa2 40 ♘d2] 40 a3 [40 cxb5 ♗xa2] 40 … bxc4 41 ♘d2 ♗a2 42 ♘xc4+ ♔xd5 43 ♘a5 ♔e4 44 b5 ♔e3 45 a4 d5 46 ♔b2 ♗c4 47 ♘xc4+ dxc4 48 ♔c3 …♀ **1-0** M954

**1846-⚔HH-10** xi 46
**Horwitz, B.−Harrwitz, D.**
London [Staunton]

1 e4 e5 2 ♘f3 ♘c6 3 ♗c4 ♗c5 4 ♘c3 d6 5 d3 ♘f6 6 0-0 ♗e6 7 ♗b5 0-0 8 ♗xc6 bxc6 9 ♗g5 ♖b8 10 ♘a4? [10 b3 △ ♗e2 ♘g3] 10 … ♗b6 11 ♘d2 [△ f4] 11 … h6 12 ♗h4 ♔h7 13 ♔h1 g5∓ 14 ♗g3 h5 15 ♘f3 ♘g4

16 h4 f6 17 ♘c3 ♖g8 18 ♘e2 ♘h6 19 ♘fg1 f5 20 h×g5 ♕×g5 21 ♘f3 ♕g4 22 e×f5 ♘×f5 23 ♘e1 h4 24 ♗h2 h3 25 ♘g3 ♘×g3+ 26 f×g3 h×g2+ 27 ♘×g2 ♕h3 28 ♕f3 ♖g6 29 ♕e4 ♗d5 30 ♕e2 ♖h6 **0-1**
M954

**1846-⚔HH-11** xi 46
**Harrwitz, D.= Horwitz, B.**
London [Staunton]
1 e4 e5 2 ♘f3 ♘c6 3 c3 g6 4 ♗c4 ♗g7 5 d4 d6 6 0-0 a6 7 ♘g5± ♘h6 8 d5 ♘e7 9 f4 0-0 10 f×e5 ♗×e5 11 h3 f5? 12 ♘e6 ♗×e6 13 ♗×h6 ♗d7 14 ♗×f8 ♕×f8 15 e×f5 g×f5 16 ♕h5 ♕g7 17 ♘d2 ♔h8 18 ♖ae1 ♖g8 19 ♖e2 ♕g3∞ 20 ♘f3 ♘g6 21 ♘×e5 ♘×e5 22 ♗b3 f4 23 ♗c2 ♖g7 24 ♗e4 ♗b5 25 ♖fe1 ♗×e2 26 ♖×e2 f3 ... ♀ **½-½** L/N6123-1847

**1846-⚔HH-12** xi 46
**Horwitz, B.+Harrwitz, D.**
London [Staunton]
1 e4 e5 2 ♘f3 ♘c6 3 d4 e×d4 4 ♗c4 ♗b4+ 5 c3 d×c3 6 0-0 d6 7 ♕b3 ♕e7 8 ♗b5 ♗c5 9 ♘×c3 ♗e6 10 ♕a4 ♕d7 11 ♘d5 ♘ge7 12 ♘×e7 ♔×e7 13 ♖d1 [△ 14 ♘e5] 13 ... f6 14 ♗f4 g5 15 ♗g3 h5 [15 ... a6!?] 16 e5 h4 17 e×f6+ ♔×f6 18 ♗e5+ ♔g6 19 ♗×h8 ♖×h8 20 ♘e5+ **1-0** L/N6123-1847

## HORWITZ⚔KIESERITSKY

London

[1846-⚔HK]

| | | | | | | | | | | | | | |
|---|---|---|---|---|---|---|---|---|---|---|---|---|---|
| B. Horwitz | 0 | 0 | 1 | 0 | 0 | 0 | 1 | 1 | 0 | 1 | ½ | 0 | 4½ |
| L. Kieseritsky | 1 | 1 | 0 | 1 | 1 | 1 | 0 | 0 | 1 | 0 | ½ | 1 | 7½ |

**1846-⚔HK-1** 28 vii 46
**Kieseritsky, L.+Horwitz, B.**
London [Staunton]
1 e4 e5 2 ♘f3 ♘c6 3 ♗c4 d6 4 d4 ♗g4 5 c3 e×d4 6 ♕b3 ♕d7 7 ♗×f7+ ♕×f7 8 ♕×b7 ♔d7 9 ♘×d4 [9 ♕×a8 ♗×f3 10 g×f3 ♕×f3 11 ♖f1 d3→] 9 ... ♘×d4 10 c×d4 ♕c4 11 ♘c3 ♕c6→ 12 ♕b3 [△ 13 ♕f7+] 12 ... ♗h5 13 ♗e3 ♘f6 14 0-0 ♗e7 15 e5 ♖ab8 16 ♕c2 ♗g6 17 ♕e2 ♘d5 18 ♕g4+ ♔d8 19 ♕f3 ♘b4 20 d5 ♕a6 21 e×d6 ♗×d6 22 ♗g5+ ♔c8 23 ♕g4+ ♔b7 24 a3 ♘d3 25 b4 ♘e5 26 ♕h3 ♕c4 27 ♘a4 ♕g4 28 ♕×g4 ♘×g4 29 h3 ♘e5 30 ♗e3 ♗e4? 31 ♘c3 ♗g6 32 ♗d4 ♗f5 33 ♖fe1 ♖be8 34 ♖e3 ♘g6 [34 ... ♘c4!?] 35 g4 ♖×e3 36 f×e3 ♗d7 37 ♗×g7 ♖g8 38 ♗h6 ♗e5 39 ♖c1 ♘h4 40 ♘e4 ♔b6 41 ♘c5 ♗c8 42 ♘d3 ♗d6 43 ♔f2 ♗g3+??+– 44 ♔×g3 ♘f5+ 45 ♔f4 ♘×h6 46 ♖c6+ ♔b5 47 ♖×h6 ♖f8+ 48 ♔e4 ♖f7 49 ♔d4 ♔a4 50 ♘e5 ♖g7 51 ♘c4 ♖d7 52 ♖c6 ... ♀ **1-0** M954

**1846-⚔HK-2** vii 46
**Horwitz, B.– Kieseritsky, L.**
London [Staunton]
1 e4 e5 2 ♘f3 ♘c6 3 ♗c4 ♗c5 4 c3 ♘f6 5 d3 d6 6 0-0 0-0 7 b4 ♗b6 8 a4 a5 9 b5 ♘e7 10 ♕b3 ♘g6 11 ♔h1 h6 12 ♖a2 ♗g4 13 ♘g1 ♕d7 14 f4 e×f4 15 ♗×f4 ♘h5 16 ♗c1 ♘e5 17 d4 ♘×c4 18 ♕×c4 ♖ae8∓ 19 ♕d3 f5 20 ♖af2 ♖×e4 21 h3 f4! 22 h×g4 [22 ♕×e4 ♘g3+] 22 ... ♘g3+ 23 ♔h2 ♕×g4 24 ♖×f4 ♘×f1+ 25 ♖×f1 ♖×f1 26 ♕×f1 ♕h4+ 27 ♘h3 ♖e1 28 ♕c4+ ♔f8 29 ♗f4 ♖×b1 30 ♗×d6+ c×d6 31 ♕c8+ ♔e7 32 ♕×b7+ ♔e6 33 ♕c8+? [33 ♕×b6∞] 33 ... ♔f6 34 ♕f8+ ♔g6 35 ♕×d6+ ♕f6 36 ♕g3+ ♔h7 37 ♕d3+ ♕g6 38 ♕×g6+ ♔×g6 ... ♀ **0-1** M954

**1846-⚔HK-3** viii 46
**Kieseritsky, L.– Horwitz, B.**
London
1 e4 e5 2 ♗c4 ♘f6 3 ♘c3 ♗c5 4 d3 ♘c6 5 ♗e3 ♗b4 6 ♘f3 d5 7 e×d5 ♘×d5 8 ♗×d5 ♕×d5 9 0-0 ♗×c3 10 b×c3 ♗g4 11 c4 ♕e6 12 ♘g5 ♕d7 13 ♕b1 b6 14 ♕b2 h6 15 ♘e4 f5 16 ♘c3 f4 17 ♗d2 f3 18 ♖fe1 0-0 19 ♘d5 f×g2 20 ♖e4 ♘d4 21 ♖×e5 ♘f3+ 22 ♔×g2 ♘×d2 23 f4 ♗f3+ 24 ♔f2 ♗×d5 25 ♖g1 ♗b7 26 ♖e6 ♖×f4+ **0-1** M954

**1846-⚔HK-4** viii 46
**Horwitz, B.– Kieseritsky, L.**
[Staunton]
1 e4 e5 2 ♘f3 ♘c6 3 ♗b5 ♗c5 4 ♗×c6 d×c6 5 0-0 ♕d6 6 b4 ♗×b4 7 c3 ♗a5 8 ♗a3 ♕f6 9 d4 e×d4 10 e5 ♕g6 11 ♘×d4 ♗h3 12 ♕f3 ♗g4 13 ♕g3 0-0-0 14 ♘d2? ♖×d4 15 c×d4 ♗×d2 16 f4 ♗f5 17 ♗f8! ♕×g3 18 h×g3 h5 19 ♖f3 ♗e4 20 ♖a3 a5 21 ♖d1 ♗b4 22 ♗×b4 a×b4 23 ♖a8+ ♔d7 24 ♔f2 ♗d5 25 ♖b1 b6! 26 f5 [26 ♖×b4 c5] 26 ... c5 27 ♖b8 ♗e4 28 ♖e1 ♗×f5 29 d×c5 b×c5 30 ♖d1+ ♔c6 31 ♖dd8 ♗e6 32 ♖a8 h4 33 g×h4 ♖×h4 34 ♖×g8 g6 35 a4 b3 36 ♖h8 b2! 37 ♖×h4 b1♕ 38 ♖hh8 ♕b2+ 39 ♔f1 ♗c4+ 40 ♔g1 ♕d4+ 41 ♔h1 ♕a1+ 42 ♔h2 ♕×e5+ 43 ♔g1 ♕e3+ 44 ♔h2 ♕f4+ 45 ♔g1 ♕f1+ 46 ♔h2 ♗d5 47 ♔g3 ♕×g2+ 48 ♔f4 ♕e4+ 49 ♔g5 ♕e3+ 50 ♔f6 ♕d4+ 51 ♔g5 ♕e5+ 52 ♔h6 g5 53 ♔h7 ♕e4+ 54 ♔g7 ♕g6+ 55 ♔f8 f6 **0-1**
M954

**1846-⚔HK-5**
**Kieseritsky, L.+Horwitz, B.**
London [Staunton]
1 d4 d6 2 e4 f5 3 e×f5 ♗×f5 4 ♕f3 ♕c8 5 ♗c4 ♘f6 6 ♗g5 ♗×c2 7 ♘h3 ♕g4 8 ♕×g4 ♘×g4 9 ♗e6 ♘f6 10 ♘a3 ♗e4 11 0-0 ♗d5 12 ♘f4 ♗×e6 13 ♘×e6 ♔d7 14 ♖fe1 ♘a6 15 ♖ac1 c6 16 ♖c3 ♘b4 17 ♖b3 ♘fd5∓ 18 ♘c4 b5 19 ♘×f8+ ♖h×f8 20 ♖×b4 b×c4? [20 ... ♘×b4? 21 ♖×e7++–; 20 ... ♖f5!?∓; 20 ... h6!?∓] 21 ♖×c4 ♖ab8 22 b3 e6 23 ♗d2 ♘b6 24 ♖c3 ♖f5 25 g4 ♖d5 26 ♖e4 ♖f8 27 f4 h6?! [27 ... h5] 28 h4 h5 29 ♔g2 h×g4 30 ♖g3 ♖df5 31 ♖×g4 ♖8f7 32 ♖g5 ♘d5 33 ♖×f5 ♖×f5 34 ♔g3 a5 35 ♖e2 ♘f6 36 ♔f3 c5 37 ♖g2 ♘h5 38 d×c5 ♖×c5 39 ♖g5 ♖×g5 40 h×g5 a4 41 b×a4 g6 42 ♗c3 ♔c6 43 a5 [43 ♔g4! △ 44 f5] 43 ... e5 44 f×e5 ♘g7 45 e×d6 ♘e6 46 a6 ♘×g5+ 47 ♔f4 ♘e6+ 48 ♔e5 ♘c5 49 a7 ♔b7 50 ♗d4 ♘d3+ 51 ♔e6 ♘b4 52 d7 ♘c6 53 ♔d5 ♘e7+ 54 ♔d6 ♘f5+ 55 ♔e6 ♘×d4+ 56 ♔d5 ... ♀ **1-0** M954

**1846-⚔HK-6**
**Horwitz, B.– Kieseritsky, L.**
London [Staunton]
1 e4 e5 2 ♘f3 ♘c6 3 d4 e×d4 4 ♘×d4 ♗c5 5 ♘f5 g6 6 ♘e3 d6 7 ♗d3 ♘f6 8 ♘c3 [8 0-0; 8 h3] 8 ... ♘g4 9 0-0 ♕h4 10 h3 ♘×f2 11 ♖×f2 ♗×e3 12 ♕f3 ♗×f2+ 13 ♕×f2 ♕×f2+ 14 ♔×f2 f5 15 ♘d5 f×e4 16 ♗×e4 0-0+ 17 ♔g3 ♖f7 18 ♗h6 ♗f5 19 ♗f3 ♘d4 20 c3 ♘×f3 21 g×f3 c6 22 ♘e3 ♖e8 23 ♘c4 ♖e6 24 h4 ♖fe7 ... ♀ **0-1** M954

**1846-⚔HK-7**
**Kieseritsky, L.– Horwitz, B.**
London [Staunton]
1 e4 e5 2 ♗c4 ♘f6 3 ♘f3 ♘×e4 4 d3 ♘f6 5 ♘×e5 d5 6 ♕e2 ♗e6 7 ♗b3 ♗d6 8 f4 0-0 9 0-0 ♘bd7 10 ♘c3 ♗c5+ 11 ♔h1 ♘×e5 12 f×e5 ♘g4 13 ♗f4 c6 14 ♘e4? d×e4 15 ♗×e6 ♘f2+ 16 ♖×f2 ♗×f2 17 ♗b3 ♕d4! 18 ♖f1 [18 c3 e×d3] 18 ... e3 19 g3 ♖ad8 20 ♗g5 ♖d7 21 e6 f×e6 22 ♗×e6+ ♔h8 23 ♕×e3 [23 ♗×d7 ♕d5+ 24 ♕f3 ♕×f3#] 23 ... ♕×e3 24 ♗×e3 ♖e7 25 ♗c5 ♖×e6 26 ♗×f8 ♖e2 27 ♔g2 ♗d4+ 28 ♔h3 ♖×c2 29 ♗a3 h6 30 ♔g4 ♗×b2 31 ♗d6 ♗f6 32 h4 ♖×a2 33 ♔f5 ♔h7 34 ♔e6 ♖d2 35 ♖f3 a5 36 ♔d7 ♖c2 37 d4 ♗×d4 **0-1** M954

**1846-⚔HK-8**
**Horwitz, B.+Kieseritsky, L.**
London [Staunton]
1 e4 e5 2 ♘f3 ♘c6 3 c3 ♘f6 4 d4 ♘xe4 5 dxe5 d5 6 ♗b5 ♗c5 7 0-0 0-0 8 ♗xc6 bxc6 9 ♘d4 ♗a6 10 ♖e1 ♕h4 11 ♗e3 ♖ae8 12 ♘f5 ♗xe3 13 ♘xh4 ♗xf2+ 14 ♔h1 ♗xh4 15 ♖xe4 dxe4 16 ♕g4 ♗e7 [16 ... ♗d8!?] 17 ♕xe4 ♗b7 18 ♘d2 ♔h8 19 ♕a4 ♗c5 20 ♖e1 [20 ♘e4 △ 20 ... ♖xe5 21 ♘xc5 △ 22 ♕b4] 20 ... ♖e6 21 ♘f3 ♖fe8 22 ♘g5 ♖6e7 23 ♕c4 **1-0** M954

**1846-⚔HK-9**
**Kieseritsky, L.+Horwitz, B.**
London
1 e4 e5 2 ♗c4 ♘f6 3 ♘f3 ♘xe4 4 d3 ♘f6 5 ♘xe5 d5 6 ♕e2 ♗e6 7 ♗b3 c6 8 f4 ♗e7 9 0-0 g6 10 ♘d2 ♘bd7 11 ♘df3 ♘c5 12 ♗e3 a5 13 c3 ♘xb3 14 axb3 0-0 15 ♖ae1 ♘e8 16 ♘g5 ♗xg5 17 fxg5 ♘g7 18 g4 f5 19 gxf6 ♖xf6 20 ♗h6 ♖xf1+ 21 ♖xf1 ♕b6+ 22 d4 ♖e8 23 ♕f2 ♕d8 24 h4 ♖f8 25 ♕xf8+ ♕xf8 26 ♖xf8+ ♔xf8 27 ♔f2 ♔g8 28 ♗xg7 ♔xg7 29 ♔f3 ♔f6 30 ♘d3 b6 31 ♔f4 h6 32 g5+ hxg5+ 33 hxg5+ ♔g7 34 ♔e5 ♗f5 35 ♘f4 ♗c2 36 ♔d6 ♗xb3 37 ♔xc6 ♔f7 38 ♔xb6 a4 39 ♔c5 ♔e7 40 ♘xg6+ ♔e6 41 ♘e5 **1-0** M954

**1846-⚔HK-10**
**Horwitz, B.+Kieseritsky, L.**
London [Staunton]
1 e4 e5 2 ♘f3 ♘c6 3 ♗c4 ♗c5 4 b4 ♗xb4 5 c3 ♗d6? 6 0-0 ♕e7 7 d4 ♘d8 8 dxe5 ♗xe5 9 ♘xe5 ♕xe5 10 ♕d3 ♘f6 11 f4 ♕xe4 12 ♕xe4+ ♘xe4 13 ♖e1 f5 14 ♘d2 ♘e6 15 ♘xe4 fxe4 16 ♖xe4 g6 17 ♗a3 ♔f7 18 ♖f1 d6 19 g4 ♖g8 20 ♖fe1 **1-0** M954

**1846-⚔HK-11**
**Kieseritsky, L.=Horwitz, B.**
London [Staunton]
1 d4 f5 2 c4 e6 3 ♘c3 ♘f6 4 ♘f3 ♗e7 5 e3 b6 6 ♗d3 ♗b7 7 b3 g6 8 ♗b2 c5 9 d5 exd5 10 ♘xd5 0-0 11 ♗e2 ♘xd5 12 cxd5 d6 13 h4 ♗f6 14 ♗xf6 ♕xf6

15 ♘g5 h6 16 ♘e6 ♖f7 17 ♖c1 ♘a6 18 ♗xa6 ♗xa6 19 ♖h3 ♖e8 20 ♕d2 ♗b7 21 ♖g3 ♖fe7 22 ♕c3 ♔f7 23 ♔f1 ♖g8 24 ♕xf6+ ♔xf6 25 ♖d1 ♔e5! 26 f3 ♗xd5 27 ♘f4 ♗f7 28 ♔f2 d5 29 ♘d3+ ♔d6 30 f4 ♖e4 31 ♘e5 ♖xe5 32 fxe5+ ♔xe5 33 ♖f3 ♗e6 34 ♖h3 ♖c8 35 ♖hh1 b5 36 ♖c1 c4 37 ♖hd1 a5 38 ♖d4 b4 39 ♔e2 a4 40 ♔d2 [40 bxa4 ♖a8] 40 ... axb3 41 axb3 ♖a8 42 ♖c2 ♖a3 43 bxc4 dxc4-+ 44 ♖d8 c3+ 45 ♔d3 ♗b3 46 ♖c1 ♖a2 47 ♖e8+ ♗e6 48 ♖c2 ♖a7 49 ♖b8 ♖a4 50 ♖c1 ♖a2 51 ♖xb4 ♖d2+ 52 ♔xc3 ♖xg2 53 ♖a1 ♖g3± 54 ♖a5+ ♔f6 55 ♔d3 g5 56 ♔e2 ♖h3 57 ♖a6 ♖h2+ 58 ♔f3 ♖h3+ 59 ♔f2 ♖xh4 60 ♖xh4 gxh4 61 ♔f3 h3 62 ♔g3 h5 63 ♖b6 h4+ 64 ♔h2 ♔e5 65 ♖b4 ♗d5 66 ♖xh4 ♗g2 67 ♔g3 ♗f1 **½-½** M954

**1846-⚔HK-12**
**Horwitz, B.−Kieseritsky, L.**
London [Staunton]
1 e4 e5 2 ♘f3 ♘c6 3 ♗c4 ♗c5 4 b4 ♗xb4 5 c3 ♗a5 6 0-0 d6 7 d4 exd4 8 cxd4 ♗b6 9 ♗b2 ♘f6 10 ♘bd2 0-0 11 d5 ♘e7 12 ♗xf6 gxf6 13 ♘h4 ♘g6 14 ♕h5 ♕e7?! 15 ♘f5 ♗xf5 16 exf5 ♘e5 17 ♖ae1 ♖ae8+- 18 ♖e4 ♔g7 19 ♖h4 ♖h8 20 ♕h6+ ♔g8 21 ♖h3!? [21 ♘e4!] 21 ... ♘g4 22 ♕f4?? [22 ♖g3 ♗xf2+ 23 ♖xf2 ♕e1+ 24 ♖f1 ♕xg3-+; 23 ♔h1 ♗xg3-+; 22 ♕h5+-] 22 ... h5-+ 23 ♖g3 ♔f8 24 h3 ♕e5 25 ♕xe5 [25 ♕f3 ♘h2 26 ♔xh2 h4] 25 ... ♘xe5 26 ♗b3 h4 27 ♖c3 ♗a5 28 ♖c2 ♖g8 29 ♔h2 ♗b6 30 f4 ♘d3 31 ♖c3 ♖e2 **0-1** M954

## HAMPPE⚔LÖWENTHAL
[1846-⚔HL]

| | | | | |
|---|---|---|---|---|
| C. Hamppe | 0̂ | 0̂ | 0̂ | 0 |
| J.J. Löwenthal | 1̂ | 1̂ | 1̂ | 3 |

**1846-⚔HL-1̂**
**Löwenthal, J.J.+Hamppe, C.**
[Staunton]
1 e4 e5 2 d4 exd4 3 ♘f3 ♘c6 4 ♗c4 d6 5 c3 d3 6 ♕xd3 ♗e7 7 ♗f4 ♗e6 8 ♘bd2 ♗xc4 9 ♘xc4 ♘f6 10 0-0 d5 11 exd5 ♕xd5 12 ♕e2 0-0-0 13 ♘ce5 ♘xe5 14 ♕xe5 ♗d6 15 ♕xd5 ♘xd5 16 ♗xd6 ♖xd6 17 ♖ad1 ♘b6 18 ♖xd6 cxd6± 19 ♖d1 ♔d7 20 ♘d4 g6 21 b3 a6 22 f4 ♖c8 23 c4 ♖c5 24 ♔f2 ♘c8 25 ♘f3 b5 26 b4!± ♖f5 27 ♔e3 ♘b6 28 c5 ♘c4+ 29 ♔e4 ♖f6 30 ♘e5+ ♔c7 31 ♘xc4 bxc4 32 ♖xd6 c3 33 ♖d3 [33 ♖xf6??-+] 33 ... g5 34 g3 gxf4 35 gxf4 ♖g6 36 ♔f3 ♔c6 37 ♖xc3 ♖g1 38 ♖c2 ♖b1 39 ♖c4 ♖a1 40 ♖d4 ♔b5 41 ♖d2 ♔xb4 42 ♖c2 ♖e1 43 c6 ♖e8 44 ♔g4 ♖c8 45 c7 ♔b5 46 ♔g5 ♔b6 47 ♔f6 **1-0** M954-1852

**1846-⚔HL-2̂**
**Hamppe, C.−Löwenthal, J.J.**
[Staunton]
1 e4 e5 2 ♘c3 ♘f6 3 ♗c4 ♗c5 4 d3 d6 5 ♗g5 ♗e6 6 ♘d5 ♗xd5 7 ♗xd5 c6 8 ♗b3 ♘bd7 9 ♘f3 0-0 10 0-0 h6 11 ♗h4 g5?! 12 ♗g3 ♕e7 13 ♔h1 ♔h8 14 h4 ♘h5 15 ♕d2 [15 ♘xg5? ♘xg3+ 16 fxg3 hxg5 16 ♕h5+ ♔g7!] 15 ... ♖g8 16 hxg5 ♘xg3+ 17 fxg3 hxg5 18 c3 ♖g7 19 d4 ♗b6 20 a4 a5 21 ♔h2? ♘f6 22 ♖h1 ♖h7+ 23 ♔g1 ♖xh1+ 24 ♔xh1 ♘xe4 25 ♕e1 f5 26 g4 ♕h7+ 27 ♔g1 exd4 28 ♘xd4 c5 29 gxf5 cxd4 30 ♕xe4 d3+ **0-1** M954-1852

**1846-⚔HL-3̂**
**Hamppe, C.−Löwenthal, J.J.**
1 e4 e5 2 ♘c3 ♘f6 3 ♗c4 c6 4 d4 ♗b4 5 dxe5 ♘xe4 6 ♗xf7+ ♔xf7 7 ♕f3+ ♘f6 8 exf6 ♖e8+ 9 ♘ge2 ♗xc3+ 10 ♕xc3 ♕xf6 11 ♕xf6+ ♔xf6 12 ♗e3 d5 13 ♔d2 ♗f5 14 h3 ♘d7 15 g4 ♗e4 16 f3 ♗xc2 17 ♘d4 ♗g6 18 h4 h6 19 g5+ hxg5 20 ♗xg5+ ♔f7 21 h5 ♗h7 22 h6 gxh6 23 ♖xh6 ♗g6 24 f4 ♖e4 25 ♘e2 ♖ae8 26 ♖h2 ♘c5 27 f5 ♗xf5 28 ♖f1 ♔g6 29 ♗f4 ♖xe2+ 30 ♖xe2 ♖xe2+ 31 ♔xe2 ♗d3+ 32 ♔f2 ♗xf1 **0-1** M954-1852

## HARRWITZ ⚔ STAUNTON

[1846-⚔HS1]

| | D. Harrwitz | H. Staunton |
|---|---|---|
| *1* | 1 | 0 |
| *2* | 0 | 1 |
| *3* | 1 | 0 |
| *4* | 1 | 0 |
| *5* | 0 | 1 |
| *6* | 0 | 1 |
| *7* | 1 | 0 |
| *8* | 0 | 1 |
| *9* | 1 | 0 |
| *10* | 1 | 0 |
| *11* | 0 | 1 |
| *12* | 0 | 1 |
| *13* | ½ | ½ |
| *14* | 1 | 0 |
| *15* | 0 | 1 |
| *16* | 0 | 1 |
| *17* | 1 | 0 |
| *18* | 0 | 1 |
| *19* | 0 | 1 |
| *20* | 0 | 1 |
| *21* | 0 | 1 |
| *22* | 1 | 0 |
| *Total* | 10½ | 12½ |

### 1846-⚔HS1-1
**Harrwitz, D.+Staunton, H.**

[Staunton]

⟨♙f7⟩ 1 e4 ♘h6? 2 d4 ♘f7 3 ♗c4 e6 4 ♘c3 c6 [△ ... d5] 5 ♕e2 b5 6 ♗d3 b4 7 ♘d1 a5 8 f4 ♗a6 [△ ... ♗xd3] 9 ♘f2 ♗xd3 10 ♘xd3 ♘a6 11 ♘f3 ♗e7 12 0-0 0-0 13 ♗e3 ♘d6 14 ♗f2 ♘c7 15 ♘fe5 ♕e8 16 c3 bxc3? 17 bxc3 ♘cb5 18 ♖ac1 [18 c4?] 18 ... ♘f7 19 a4 [△ ♖b1] 19 ... ♘c7 20 ♖b1 ♘xe5 21 ♘xe5 ♖xf4? 22 ♖b7 ♖c8 23 ♖fb1 d5 24 exd5 cxd5 [24 ... ♘xd5 25 ♘d3 △ ♕xe6+] 25 ♗g3 ♖e4 [25 ... ♖f8] 26 ♕f3 ♗d6 27 ♘c4 ♗xg3 28 hxg3 ♕c6 29 ♖b8 ♘b5? 30 ♖xc8+ ♕xc8 31 ♖xb5 ♖e1+ 32 ♔f2 ♖c1 33 ♘d6 ♖c2+ 34 ♔g1 ♖c1+ 35 ♔h2 ♕f8? [35 ... ♕c7] 36 ♖c5!+− ♕xf3 37 gxf3 g5 38 g4 ♔g7 39 ♘b7 ♔f6 40 ♘xa5 ♖a1 41 c4 ♖xa4 42 ♔g3 h6 43 cxd5 ♖xd4 44 dxe6 ♔xe6 45 ♖c6+ ♖d6 46 ♖xd6+ ♔xd6 47 ♔f2 ♔e5 48 ♔e3 ♔f6 49 ♔e4 ♔g6 50 ♘c4 h5 51 gxh5+ ♔xh5 52 ♔f5 ♔h4 53 ♘e5 ♔h5 54 ♘f7 ♔h4 55 ♘xg5 **1-0** L/N6123

### 1846-⚔HS1-2
**Staunton, H.+Harrwitz, D.**

[Staunton]

1 e4 e5 2 ♘f3 ♘c6 3 d4 exd4 4 ♗c4 ♗c5 5 c3 d3 [5 ... ♘f6] 6 b4 ♗b6 7 b5 ♕e7! [7 ... ♘b8?; 7 ... ♘a5?; 7 ... ♘ce7? 8 ♕b3+−] 8 0-0 ♘d8 9 e5! ♘e6 10 a4 ♗c5 11 ♘bd2 ♘h6 12 ♘e4 ♘f5 13 ♕xd3 d6 14 ♖e1! 0-0 15 exd6 ♗xd6 16 ♘xd6 ♘xd6 17 ♘g5 g6 18 ♗xe6 ♗xe6 19 ♕e3 ♖fe8 20 ♗a3 ♕f6 [20 ... ♘c4+−] 21 ♗xd6 cxd6 22 ♘e4 ♕e7 23 ♕d4 ♖ed8 24 ♘f6+ ♔f8 25 ♘d5 **1-0** L/N6123

### 1846-⚔HS1-3 ix 46
**Harrwitz, D.+Staunton, H.**

[Staunton]

⟨♙f7⟩ 1 e4 ... 2 d4 d6 3 f4 ♘h6 4 ♗c4 ♗g4 5 ♘f3 e6 6 h3 ♗xf3 7 ♕xf3 ♕e7 8 ♕b3 c6 9 ♗xe6 d5 10 exd5 cxd5 11 ♕xd5 ♘c6 12 c3 ♖d8 13 ♕h5+ g6 14 ♕e2 ♕h4+ 15 ♕f2 ♕f6 16 0-0 ♘e7 17 ♕e2 ♖d6 18 ♕b5+ ♘c6? 19 d5 a6 20 ♕a4 ♖xe6? 21 dxe6 ♗c5+ 22 ♔h1 ♘f5 23 ♔h2 ♕h4 24 ♕d1 0-0 25 ♕d5 ♗e7 26 ♕f3 ♕f6 27 ♘d2 ♕xe6 28 ♕e4 ♕d7 29 ♘f3 ♗f6 30 ♗d2 ♖e8 31 ♕c4+ ♔g7 32 ♖ad1 b5 33 ♕c5 ♗e7 34 ♕f2 ♕d5 35 ♗e3 ♕xa2 36 ♘d4 ♘cxd4 37 ♗xd4+ ♔f7 38 ♖a1 ♕e6 39 ♖fe1 ♕c6 40 ♕d2 [◻ 40 b4 ♗h4 41 ♕a2+] 40 ... ♖d8 41 ♕e2 ♗h4 42 ♕e4 ♗g3+∞ 43 ♔g1 ♕d6 44 ♗f2! ♕xf4 45 ♗xg3 ♕xe4 46 ♖xe4 ♘xg3 47 ♖f4+ ♔g7 48 ♖f3 ♘f5 49 ♖xa6 ♖d2 50 b4 ♘h4 51 ♖f2 ♖d1+ 52 ♔h2 ♖d3 53 ♖a7+ ♔h6 54 ♖c7 ♘f5 55 g4 ♘e3 56 ♖ff7 ♔g5 57 ♖c5+ ♖d5 [57 ... ♔h6 58 g5+ ♔h5 59 ♖xh7#] 58 ♖xh7 ♔f4 59 ♖xd5 ♘xd5 60 ♖d7 ♘xc3 61 ♖d4+ ♔e5 62 ♖d3 ♘d5 63 ♔g3 ♔e4 64 ♖f3 ♔d4 65 h4 ♔c4 66 h5 gxh5 67 gxh5 ♔xb4 68 ♖f7 **1-0** L/N6123

### 1846-⚔HS1-4
**Harrwitz, D.+Staunton, H.**

[Staunton]

⟨♙f7⟩ 1 e4 e6 2 d4 d5 3 exd5 exd5 4 ♗d3 ♘f6 5 ♘f3 ♗d6 6 0-0 0-0 7 c4 c6 8 h3 b6 9 ♘c3 ♘a6 10 a3 ♘c7 11 ♗e3 dxc4 12 ♗xc4+ ♘cd5? 13 ♗g5 ♗e6 14 ♘e5 ♖c8? 15 ♘xc6 ♕c7 [15 ... ♖xc6?] 16 ♗xf6 ♕xc6 17 ♗xd5 ♗xd5 18 ♕g4! ♖c7 [△ 18 ... ♖xf6 △ ... ♖g6] 19 ♗e5 ♗xe5 20 dxe5 ♗c4 21 ♖fd1 ♖cf7 22 ♖d2 ♗e6 23 ♕g3 ♖f5 24 ♖e1 ♕c5 25 b4 ♕e7 26 ♘e4 ♔h8 27 ♖ed1 ♗g8 28 ♖d7 ♕xe5 29 ♖xa7∞ ♕xg3 [29 ... ♗d5!? 30 ♖xd5 ♕xg3 31 ♖xf5 ♕b8+−] 30 fxg3 h6 31 ♔h2 ♖e5 32 ♖d4 ♗d5 33 ♘c3 ♗a8 34 ♖dd7 ♖ee8 35 ♖xg7 ♖f2 36 h4 ♖e1 37 ♖ge7! ♖xg2+ 38 ♔h3 ♖xe7 39 ♖xa8+ ♔g7 40 ♔xg2 **1-0** L/N6123

### 1846-⚔HS1-5
**Harrwitz, D.−Staunton, H.**

[Staunton]

1 e4 e5 2 ♘f3 ♘c6 3 ♗c4 ♗c5 4 c3 ♘f6 5 d4 exd4 6 cxd4 ♗b4+ 7 ♘c3 d6 8 h3 h6 9 0-0 0-0 [△ ... ♘xe4] 10 ♗b3 ♘e7 11 ♘h4 ♔h8 12 ♔h2 ♘c6 [△ 13 ... ♘xe4] 13 ♘f3 ♕e7 [△ 14 ... ♘xd4 15 ♘xd4 ♕e5+] 14 d5 ♘e5 15 ♘xe5 dxe5 16 ♕e2 ♗c5! 17 f4 ♘g4+ 18 ♔g3 [18 hxg4?? ; 18 ♔h1→] 18 ... exf4+ 19 ♗xf4 ♘e5 20 ♕h5? ♘g6 [20 ... ♘d3!] 21 e5! [21 ♗xh6?] 21 ... ♖e8 22 d6 cxd6 23 ♘d5 ♘xf4 24 ♖xf4 ♕xe5 25 ♕xe5 dxe5 26 ♖xf7 e4 27 ♘c7 ♗d6+ 28 ♔f2 ♗xc7 29 ♖xc7 ♖b8 30 g4 a5 31 ♔e3 ♗e6 32 ♖f1 ♗xb3 33 axb3 ♖bd8 34 ♖xb7 ♖d3+ 35 ♔e2 ♖xh3 36 ♖ff7 ♖c8 37 ♖xg7 ♖c2+ 38 ♔d1 ♖f2 **0-1** L/N6123

### 1846-⚔HS1-6
**Harrwitz, D.−Staunton, H.**

[Staunton]

⟨♙f7⟩ 1 e4 ... 2 d4 e6 3 ♗d3 c5 4 dxc5 ♕a5+ 5 ♗d2 ♕xc5 6 ♘c3 a6 7 f4 ♘h6 8 ♘h3 ♗e7 9 ♕e2 0-0 10 0-0-0 ♘c6 11 ♗e3 ♕a5 12 ♗c4 b5 13 ♗b3 ♗b4 [13 ... b4? 14 ♘d5 exd5 15 ♖xd5 ♕c7 16 ♖xd7+ (15 ... ♕d8 16 ♖xd7+)] 14 ♘b1 ♕c7 15 g4 ♘a5 16 g5 ♘f7 17 ♘f2 ♗b7 18 ♖hg1 ♘xb3+ 19 axb3 ♘d6 20 ♘c3? ♗xc3 21 bxc3 ♘xe4 [21 ... ♕xc3?] 22 ♘xe4 ♗xe4 23 h4 ♕xc3 24 ♖xd7 ♕a1+ 25 ♔d2 ♕a5+ 26 ♔c1 ♖ad8 27 ♖xd8 ♕a1+ 28 ♔d2 ♖xd8+

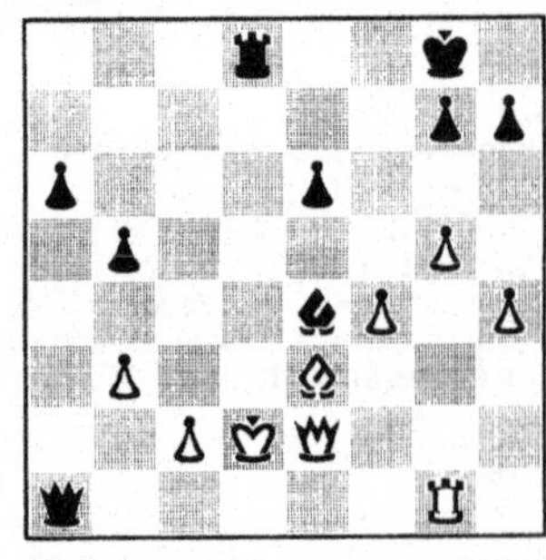

**0-1** L/N6123

### 1846-⚔HS1-7
**Harrwitz, D.+Staunton, H.**

[Staunton]

⟨♙f7⟩ 1 e4 e6 2 d4 d5 3 exd5 exd5 4 c4 ♘f6 5 ♘c3 ♗b4 6 ♘f3 0-0 7 ♕b3 ♗xc3+ 8 bxc3 a5 9 a4

♖e8+ 10 ♗e3 ♘g4 11 ♔d2 ♖a6 12 ♗d3 ♖b6 13 ♕c2 h6 14 ♖ae1 ♖be6 15 h3 ♘xe3 16 fxe3 ♖f6 17 ♖hf1 dxc4 18 ♗xc4+ ♗e6 19 ♗xe6+ ♖exe6 20 ♕d3 ♕e8 21 ♕b5 ♕g6! 22 ♖e2 ♖b6 23 ♕c4+ ♖fe6 24 ♕a2 ♘d7 25 ♕c2 ♕g3 26 ♖b1 c5 27 ♕f5! ♕d6 28 ♔e1 ♕g3+ 29 ♔f1 ♖xb1+? 30 ♕xb1 cxd4 31 cxd4 ♖b6 32 ♕f5 ♕c7 33 ♖c2 ♕d8 34 e4 ♖b1+ 35 ♔f2 ♘f8 36 ♖c8 ♕e7 37 e5 ♖b2+ 38 ♔g1 ♕f7 39 ♕xf7+ ♔xf7 40 d5 ♘g6 41 ♖c7+ ♔f8 42 e6 ♖b6 43 ♖d7 ♔e8 44 ♘d4 ♖b1+ 45 ♔h2 ♘f4 46 ♘f5 **1-0** L/N6123

### 1846-⚔HS1-8
**Staunton, H.+Harrwitz, D.**

[Staunton]

1 e4 e5 2 ♘f3 ♘c6 3 d4 exd4 4 ♗c4 ♗c5 5 c3 ♘f6 6 cxd4 [□ 6 e5] 6 ... ♗b4+ 7 ♗d2 ♗xd2+ 8 ♘bxd2 d5 9 exd5 ♘xd5 10 0-0 0-0 11 h3 ♗f5 12 ♖c1 ♘f4 13 ♘b3 ♕f6! 14 ♔h2 ♕d6 15 ♔h1 ♕h6 16 ♘h2 ♕g6 17 ♖g1 ♖ad8 18 ♕f3 ♘e6 19 ♗xe6 fxe6 20 ♕e3 ♘b4! [△ 21 ... ♘d5] 21 ♘f3 ♘d5 22 ♕e5 ♕h6 23 ♕g3 ♘f4 [△ 24 ... ♘e2] 24 ♖ce1 ♖f6 25 ♘e5 ♖df8 [25 ... ♗xh3?] 26 f3 ♘d3 27 ♘xd3 ♗xd3 28 ♕xc7!? ♖xf3? [□ 28 ... ♖f4 △ ... ♗f5] 29 gxf3 ♕xh3+ 30 ♔h2 ♕xf3+ 31 ♖g2 ♗e4 32 ♘c5 ♗d5 33 ♔g1 ♕xg2+ 34 ♕xg2 ♗xg2 35 ♔xg2 b6 36 ♘xe6 ♖c8 37 ♖f1 h5 38 ♖f2 ♔h7 39 ♖f7 ♔g6 40 ♖xg7+ ♔f6 41 d5 ♖c2+ 42 ♔g3 a5 43 ♖h7 ♖xb2 44 ♖xh5 ♖xa2 45 ♘c7 ♔e7 46 ♘b5 ♖b2 47 ♖h7+ ♔d8 48 ♘d4 a4 49 d6 ♖d2 50 ♘c6+ ♔e8 51 ♖e7+ ♔f8 52 d7 ♖d3+ 53 ♔f4 ♖d4+ 54 ♔e3 ♖d6 55 ♖e8+ **1-0** L/N6123

### 1846-⚔HS1-9
**Harrwitz, D.+Staunton, H.**

[Staunton]

⟨♙f7⟩ 1 e4 ... 2 d4 e6 3 c4 c5 4 d5 d6 5 f4 ♘a6 6 ♘c3 ♘h6 7 a3 ♘c7 8 ♗d3 ♘f7 9 ♘f3 exd5 10 cxd5 ♗g4 11 0-0 ♗xf3 12 ♕xf3 ♕f6! 13 ♗b5+ ♘xb5 14 ♘xb5 ♕e7 15 b4 a6 16 ♘c3 cxb4 17 axb4 g6 18 ♗b2 ♗g7 19 ♖ae1 0-0 20 ♕g3 ♖ac8 21 ♕d3 ♕c7 22 ♘d1 ♗xb2? 23 ♘xb2 ♕b6+ 24 ♕e3 ♕xb4−+ 25 ♘d3 ♕b5 26 ♖b1 ♕d7 27 ♖b6 ♖fe8 28 ♖fb1 ♖c7 29 ♕d4 ♖ec8 30 h3 ♖c4 31 ♕e3 ♕e8?? 32 e5 ♘h6 33 ♖xb7 ♘f5 34 ♕f2 [34 ♕a7? ♖a8] 34 ... ♖c3 35 g4 ♖xd3 36 gxf5 ♕a4 [□ 36 ... gxf5 37 ♕g2+ ♕g6] 37 ♖b8! ♕e8 38 ♕a7! ♖d1+ 39 ♖xd1 ♖xb8 40 f6 ♕f8 41 ♖c1 ♖a8 42 ♕d7 ♖d8 43 ♕e6+ ♔h8 44 ♖c7 dxe5 45 fxe5 ♕b4 [45 ... ♕h6=] 46 ♖xh7+ ♔xh7 47 ♕e7+ ♕xe7 48 fxe7 **1-0** L/N6123

### 1846-⚔HS1-10
**Harrwitz, D.+Staunton, H.**

[Staunton]

⟨♙f7⟩ 1 e4 ♘h6 2 d4 ♘f7 3 f4 e6 4 c4 c6 5 ♘f3 ♗e7 6 ♘c3 ♘a6 7 ♗e3 0-0 8 a3 ♘h6 9 ♗d3 ♘c7 10 0-0 d6 11 h3 ♘f7? 12 ♕c2 h6 13 ♖ad1 ♗d7 14 e5 d5 15 ♔h2 dxc4 16 ♗xc4 ♘d5 17 ♕e4 ♘h8 18 ♗d3 g6 19 ♘e2 ♖f7 20 g4 ♕b6 21 ♖d2 ♖af8 22 ♖g1 ♕d8 23 g5 h5 24 ♘h4 ♖g7 [24 ... ♔g7 25 ♘g3+-] 25 ♘g3 ♘xf4? 26 ♗xf4 ♖xf4 27 ♕xf4 ♗xg5 28 ♕f2 ♗xd2 29 ♘e4!! ♖f7 [29 ... ♗h6 30 ♘f6+ ♔~ 31 ♘xd7+] 30 ♘f6+ ♖xf6 31 exf6 ♕c7+ 32 ♔h1 ♗f4 33 ♗xg6 ♔f8 34 ♗xh5 e5 35 ♕g2 **1-0** L/N6123

### 1846-⚔HS1-11
**Harrwitz, D.−Staunton, H.**

1 e4 e5 2 ♘f3 ♘c6 3 ♗c4 ♗c5 4 c3 ♘f6 5 b4 ♗b6 6 b5 ♘a5 7 ♗d3 d5 8 ♕e2 0-0 9 0-0 ♖e8 10 h3 ♘h5 11 ♕d1 ♘f4 12 ♕c2 f5 13 ♘xe5 ♖xe5 14 exf5 ♕g5 15 g4 ♕h4 **0-1** L/N6123

### 1846-⚔HS1-12
**Harrwitz, D.−Staunton, H.**

[Staunton]

⟨♙f7⟩ 1 e4 ... 2 d4 e6 3 c4 c5 4 d5 d6 5 f4 ♘h6 6 ♘f3 ♘f7 7 ♗d3 ♘a6 8 a3 ♗e7 9 0-0 0-0 10 ♘c3 ♘c7 11 ♕c2 e5 12 fxe5 ♘xe5 13 ♘xe5 ♖xf1+ 14 ♔xf1 dxe5 15 ♗e3 a5 16 ♔g1 ♗d7 [△ 17 ... ♖a6 (16 ... ♖a6 17 ♘a4)] 17 ♖f1 ♖a6 18 h3 ♖g6 19 ♔h2 ♘e8 20 ♘e2 b6 [20 ... ♗h4? 21 ♗xc5] 21 ♘g3 ♗d6 22 ♘f5 ♗b8 [22 ... ♗xf5? 23 ♖xf5] 23 ♕d2 [△ b4] 23 ... ♘d6 24 ♔h1 a4! 25 ♕f2 ♕e8 26 ♕h4 ♗xf5 27 exf5 ♖f6 28 ♗g5 ♖f7 29 f6 g6 30 ♗h6 e4 31 ♗e2 ♕e5 32 ♕f2 ♘e8 [□ 32 ... ♘f5] 33 ♕f4 ♖xf6 34 ♕xe5 ♖xf1+ 35 ♗xf1 ♗xe5 36 ♗c1 ♘d6 37 g4 ♔f7 38 ♔g2 ♔f6 39 ♔f2 g5 40 ♔e1 ♗f4 41 ♗d2 ♔f7 [41 ... ♔e5?? 42 ♗c3#] 42 ♗c3+ ♗e5 43 ♔d2 ♗d4!

44 ♗e2 ♘d6 45 ♔c2 ♔e5 46 ♗e1 [△ 47 ♗g3+] 46 ... ♔f4 47 ♗d2+ e3 48 ♗e1 h6 49 b4 axb3+ 50 ♔xb3 ♘e4 51 ♔c2 ♗e5 52 ♔d3 ♗c7 53 h4 ♗d8 54 hxg5 ♗xg5 55 a4 ♘f2+ 56 ♗xf2 exf2 57 d6 ♔e5 58 d7 ♔f4 59 ♗f1 ♔f3 60 ♗h3 ♔g3 61 ♗f1 ♔xg4 62 ♔e2 ♔g3 63 ♔d3 h5 64 ♔e4 h4 65 ♗e2 h3 **0-1** L/N6123

### 1846-⚔HS1-13
**Harrwitz, D.=Staunton, H.**

[Staunton]

⟨♙f7⟩ 1 e4 ♘c6 2 d4 e5 3 dxe5 ♘xe5 4 f4 ♘f7 5 ♗c4 ♘gh6 6 ♘f3 ♗c5 7 ♘c3 c6 8 h3 b5 9 ♗b3 a5 10 a3 ♕b6 11 ♖f1 a4 12 ♗a2 ♗a6 13 ♘e2 0-0-0! 14 c3 ♖de8 [□ 14 ... ♖he8] 15 ♕c2 ♖hf8 16 g4 g6 17 ♗xf7 ♘xf7 18 ♗d2 ♘d6 19 e5 ♘c4 20 ♘fd4 g5 21 0-0-0 gxf4 22 ♗xf4 ♗e7? 23 ♘f5 ♗c5 24 ♕d3 ♕b7 25 ♕g3 ♘xb2 26 ♔xb2 b4 27 cxb4 ♗xe2 28 ♔a1! ♗e7 29 ♗g5 ♖xf5 30 gxf5 ♕b5 31 ♗xe7 ♗xf1 32 f6 ♗c4 33 ♗d6 ♗e6 [□ 33 ... ♖g8] 34 ♕d3 ♕xd3 35 ♖xd3 ♖g8! 36 ♔b2 ♔d8 37 ♔c3 ♖g2 38 ♔d4 ♔e8 39 ♔c5 ♔f7 40 b5 cxb5! [40 ... ♖c2+??+-] 41 ♔xb5 ♗b3 42 ♗b4 ♔e8 [42 ... ♔e6? 43 ♖d2] 43 ♖c3 ♖g8 44 ♖c7 h5 45 ♔c5 ♗e6 46 ♖a7 ♔f7 47 h4 ♖g4 48 ♖xa4 ♖xh4 49 ♖a8 ♖g4 50 ♖h8 h4 51 a4 ♖e4 52 ♖h7+ ♔g8 53 ♖h5 h3 54 ♔b5 ♖e2 55 ♗d6 ♖b2+ 56 ♔c5 ♖c2+ 57 ♔b6 h2 58 a5 ♗d5 59 e6 [59 ... h1♕+-] 59 ... ♖c6+ 60 ♔b5 ♗xe6 [60 ... ♖xd6 61 f7+- △ 62 ♖h8] 61 ♗xh2 ♔f7 62 ♗e5 ♔g6 63 ♖h8 ♗c4+ 64 ♔b4 ♗e6 65 ♖e8 ♖c4+ 66 ♔a3 ♖c5 67 ♗d4 ♖xa5+ 68 ♔b4 ♖d5 69 ♗c3 ♖d3 70 ♖e7 ♗f7 71 ♗e5 d6 72 ♗c3 ♖f3 73 ♖d7 ♖f4+ 74 ♔a3 ♖c4 75 ♗b2 d5 76 ♗e5 ♖e4 77 ♗c3 ♖e8 78 ♔b2 ♖e2+ 79 ♔a3 ♖h2 80 ♗e5 ♖e2 81 ♗d4 ♖e4 82 ♗c3 ♖e3 83 ♔b2 ♖h3 84 ♗e5 **½-½** L/N6123

### 1846-⚔HS1-14
**Harrwitz, D.+Staunton, H.**

[Staunton]

⟨♙f7⟩ 1 e4 ♘c6 2 d4 e5 3 dxe5 ♘xe5 4 f4 ♘f7 5 ♗c4 ♘gh6 6 ♘f3 ♗c5 7 ♘c3 c6 8 a4 a5 9 ♕e2 ♕b6 10 h3 d6 11 g4 ♖f8 12 ♗b3 ♗d7 13 g5 ♘g8 14 ♗d2 0-0-0 15 0-0-0 g6 16 e5 dxe5 17 fxe5 ♗f5 18 ♘h4 ♘e7 19 ♘xf5 gxf5 [19 ... ♘xf5 20 ♗e6++-] 20 h4 ♔b8 21 h5 ♗d4 22 ♗f4 ♔a8 23 ♖h3 ♗xc3 24 ♖xc3 ♖xd1+ 25 ♕xd1 ♕b4? 26 ♖c4 ♕b6 27 ♖d4 ♖d8 28 ♖xd8+ ♘xd8 29 ♔b1 c5 30 ♕d6 ♘dc6 31 ♗e3 ♕b4 32 ♗xc5 ♕e1+ 33 ♔a2

♔h1 34 ♕d7 **1-0** L/N6123

**1846-⚔HS1-15**
**Staunton, H.+Harrwitz, D.**
[Staunton]

1 e4 e5 2 ♘f3 ♘c6 3 ♗c4 ♗c5 4 0-0 ♘f6 5 d3 d6 6 h3 0-0 7 ♗g5 h6 8 ♗h4 ♗e6 9 ♗b3 ♔h7 10 ♘c3 ♘e7 11 d4 exd4 12 ♘xd4 ♗xb3 13 axb3 g5 14 ♗g3 ♗xd4 15 ♕xd4+− ♘g6 16 ♖xa7 ♖xa7 17 ♕xa7 ♘h5 18 ♕xb7 f5 19 exf5 ♖xf5 20 ♖d1 [Δ 21 ♗xd6; 21 ♖xd6] 20 ... ♘xg3 21 fxg3 ♖f7 22 ♘d5 ♘e5 23 ♕b4 ♕a8 24 ♕a4 ♕b7 25 ♕e4+ ♔g7 26 ♘c3 ♕b6+ 27 ♕d4 ♕c6 28 b4 ♖f5 29 b5 ♕c4 30 b6 ♖f1+ 31 ♔h2 ♖xd1 32 ♕xc4 ♘xc4 33 bxc7 ♖e1 34 c8=♕ ♘e3 35 ♕d7+ ♔g8 36 ♕xd6 ♘f1+ 37 ♔g1 ♘xg3+ 38 ♔f2 **1-0** L/N6123

**1846-⚔HS1-16**
**Harrwitz, D.−Staunton, H.**
[Staunton]

⟨Δf7⟩ 1 e4 ... 2 d4 e6 3 c4 c5 4 d5 d6 5 f4 ♘h6 6 ♘f3 ♘a6 7 ♘c3 ♗e7 8 a3 0-0 9 ♗d3 ♗h4+ 10 g3 ♗e7 11 h3 ♘f7 12 ♗e3 ♘c7 13 ♕c2 e5 14 0-0-0 ♗f6 15 ♖dg1 a6 16 g4 exf4 17 ♗xf4 ♘e5 [17 ... ♗xc3?] 18 ♗xe5 ♗xe5 19 ♘xe5 ♕g5+ 20 ♔b1 ♕xe5 21 h4 ♗d7 22 g5 b5 23 h5 ♖f3 24 ♖g2? ♖b8! [Δ 25 ... bxc4; 25 ... ♕d4] 25 ♘e2 bxc4 26 ♗xc4 ♗a4 27 ♕c1 ♖xa3 [Δ 27 ... ♕xe4+−+] 28 ♘g3 [□ 28 ♖h4−+] 28 ... ♖xg3 29 ♖xg3 ♕xg3 30 g6 h6 31 ♖f1 ♕e5 32 ♗d3 ♘b5 33 ♖f5 ♕d4 34 ♖f3 ♘c3+ 35 ♔a1 ♘d1 **0-1** L/N6123

**1846-⚔HS1-17**
**Harrwitz, D.+Staunton, H.**
[Staunton]

⟨Δf7⟩ 1 e4 ♘c6 2 d4 d5 3 e5 ♗f5 4 ♗e3 e6 5 ♘f3 ♘ge7 6 ♗d3 ♗xd3 7 ♕xd3 ♘b4 8 ♕e2 ♘g6 9 a3 ♘c6 10 c4 ♗e7 11 cxd5 ♕xd5 12 ♘c3 ♕b3 13 0-0 0-0 14 g3 ♖ad8 15 ♖ab1 a6 [15 ... ♗xa3?] 16 ♖fd1 [16 ♖fc1 Δ 17 ♘d2 Δ 18 d5] 16 ... b5 17 ♘d2 ♕c2 18 ♖dc1 ♕f5 19 ♘xb5 ♘cxe5 20 dxe5 axb5 21 f4 [21 ♖xc7??] 21 ... ♕d3 22 ♕xd3 ♖xd3 23 ♘f1 ♖c8 24 ♖c6! ♔f7 25 ♖bc1 ♗d8 26 ♗c5 ♖a8 27 ♗b4 ♘e7 28 ♗xe7 ♔xe7 29 ♔f2 ♖a4 30 ♔e2 ♖b3 31 ♖1c2 ♖e4+ 32 ♔f2 ♖d4 33 ♘d2 ♖bd3 34 ♘f3 ♖d5 35 g4 g6 36 ♔e2 ♔d7 37 ♖a6 ♖b3 38 ♘d2 ♖h3 39 ♘f3 c5 40 ♖d6+! ♖xd6 41 exd6 ♔xd6 42 ♖d2+ ♔c7 43 ♔f2 ♖h6 44 ♔g3 [Δ 45 ♘g5 Δ 46 ♘f7] 44 ... g5 45 fxg5 ♖g6 46 h4 ♔c8?? 47 ♖c2 ♗c7+ 48 ♔h3 ♗b6 49 ♘d4 e5 50 ♘xb5 ♔b7 51 ♖e2 ♔c6 52 ♘c3 ♗c7 53 b3 ♖d6 54 ♖e3 ♖d4 55 ♘e4 ♖d7 56 ♘f6 ♖f7 57 h5 ♗d8 58 ♖xe5 ♗xf6 59 ♖f5 ♖b7 60 gxf6 ♖xb3+ 61 ♔h4 ♖b8 62 f7 ♖f8 63 g5 ♔d6 **1-0** L/N6123

**1846-⚔HS1-18**
**Harrwitz, D.−Staunton, H.**
[Staunton]

1 d4 e6 2 c4 d5 3 e3 c5 4 ♘f3 ♘c6 5 ♘c3 ♘f6 6 cxd5 exd5 7 dxc5 ♗xc5 8 ♗d3 0-0 9 h3 a6 10 0-0 ♕d6 11 b3 ♗a7 [11 ... ♗b6 12 ♘a4 Δ 13 ♗a3] 12 ♘e2 ♗d7 13 ♗b2 ♖ac8 14 ♖c1 ♖fe8! 15 ♘g3 ♗xe3 16 ♘f5 ♗xf5 17 fxe3 [17 ♗xf5?] 17 ... ♗xd3 18 ♕xd3 ♘e4 19 ♘h4 g6! 20 ♖cd1 ♖cd8 21 ♘f3 ♘g3 22 ♖f2 f6 23 a3 ♘f5 24 ♖e1 ♖e6 25 ♘h2 ♕g3 26 ♘g4 ♘e5 27 ♗xe5 fxe5 28 ♖ef1 e4 29 ♕c3 ♕d6 30 ♖xf5 gxf5 31 ♖xf5 d4 32 ♖g5+ [32 ♕c4 b5] 32 ... ♔h8 33 ♕a5 b5 34 ♘e5! ♖f8 35 ♘g4 ♖g6 36 ♖xg6 hxg6 37 exd4 ♕xd4+ 38 ♔h2 ♕d6+ 39 ♔g1 ♖c8 40 ♕e1 ♕c5+ 41 ♔h2 ♕c7+ [Δ 42 ♔~ ♕c1] 42 g3 ♕c2+ 43 ♘f2 ♖c3 44 ♔h1 ♖xg3 45 ♕a1+ ♔h7 **0-1** L/N6123

**1846-⚔HS1-19**
**Harrwitz, D.−Staunton, H.**
[Staunton]

⟨Δf7⟩ 1 e4 ... 2 d4 e6 3 c4 c5 4 d5 d6 5 f4 ♘h6 6 ♘c3 ♘f7 7 ♘f3 ♗e7 8 ♗d3 ♘a6 9 0-0 0-0 10 a3 ♗f6 11 e5!! ♗e7 [11 ... dxe5 12 fxe5 ♗xe5 13 ♘xe5 ♘xe5 14 ♗xh7+ Δ 15 ♕h5] 12 ♕e2 [□ 12 f5] 12 ... ♘h6 13 ♕c2 ♘c7 14 ♗xh7+ ♔h8 15 ♗e4 ♖b8 16 h3 b5 17 cxb5 exd5 18 ♘xd5 ♘xd5 19 ♗xd5 ♖xb5 [19 ... dxe5? 20 ♘xe5 ♗f5 (20 ... ♕xd5 21 ♘g6+ Δ 22 ♘xe7+) 21 ♕c4] 20 g4 ♖b6 21 ♗a2 [Δ ♗b1; □ 21 e6] 21 ... dxe5 22 ♗b1 g6 23 fxe5 ♘g8 24 ♗d2 ♗b7 25 ♗c3 ♗xf3 26 e6+ ♗f6 27 ♖xf3 ♗d4+ 28 ♔g2 ♖xf3 29 ♔xf3 [29 ♕xg6 ♕h4] 29 ... ♖xe6 30 ♗a2 ♕a8+ 31 ♔g3 ♖e3+ 32 ♔h4 g5+ 33 ♔xg5 ♕d8+ **0-1** L/N6123

**1846-⚔HS1-20**
**Harrwitz, D.−Staunton, H.**
[Staunton]

⟨Δf7⟩ 1 e4 e6 2 d4 c5 3 dxc5 ♕a5+ 4 ♘c3 ♗xc5 5 ♗d3 ♘c6 6 ♘f3 ♘ge7 7 0-0 a6 8 ♔h1 ♕c7 9 ♘g5 g6? 10 f4 h6 11 ♘f3 d6 12 ♕e1 ♗d7 13 a3 b5 14 b4 ♗a7 15 ♗b2 ♖f8 [□ 15 ... 0-0] 16 ♘e2 e5 17 ♕g3 exf4 18 ♘xf4 0-0-0 19 ♘xg6 [□ 19 ♗g7] 19 ... ♘xg6 20 ♕xg6 ♗e3 21 c4 ♖g8 22 ♕f6 ♖g4 23 cxb5 axb5 24 ♖fe1 ♕b6 25 ♗xb5 ♖dg8 26 ♗f1 ♖f4 27 ♕c3 ♖xf3 28 gxf3?? [□ 28 ♗c4 ♖xg2 29 ♔xg2 ♖f2+ Δ 30 ... ♗d4] 28 ... ♖g1# **0-1** L/N6123

**1846-⚔HS1-21**
**Staunton, H.+Harrwitz, D.**
[Staunton]

1 e4 e5 2 ♘f3 ♘c6 3 c3 f5? 4 d4 fxe4 5 ♘xe5 ♘f6 6 ♗b5! a6 7 ♗xc6 bxc6 8 ♗g5 [8 ... ♗d6 9 ♘d2+−; 8 ... ♗e7 9 ♗xf6 Δ 10 ♕h5++−] 8 ... ♖b8 9 b4 ♗b7 10 ♕a4 d5 11 0-0 [11 ♘xc6 ♕d7 12 b5 ♖a8! (12 ... axb5 13 ♕a7) 13 ♕d1 axb5; 13 ... ♗xc6±] 11 ... h6 12 ♗h4 ♕d6 13 ♗g3 [Δ 14 ♘f7; 14 ♘g6] 13 ... ♖g8 14 ♘d2 ♖c8 15 ♘b3 ♘d7 16 ♘a5 ♘b6 17 ♕c2 ♗a8 18 f3 [18 ♘exc6?] 18 ... exf3 19 ♖xf3 ♕e6?+− 20 ♖e1 ♗e7 21 ♘exc6 ♕xe1+ 22 ♗xe1 ♗xc6 23 ♕g6+ ♔d8 24 ♘xc6+ **1-0** L/N6123

**1846-⚔HS1-22**
**Harrwitz, D.+Staunton, H.**
[Staunton]

⟨Δf7⟩ 1 e4 ... 2 d4 e6 3 c4 c5 4 d5 d6 5 f4 g6 6 ♘f3 ♗g7 7 ♘c3 ♘e7 8 ♗d3 ♘a6 9 0-0 0-0 10 h3 ♘c7 11 ♕c2 a6 12 a4 ♗d7?! 13 ♗e3 [Δ 14 ♗xc5 dxc5 15 d6] 13 ... ♖c8 14 ♖ad1 exd5 15 cxd5 [Δ e5] 15 ... ♘e8 16 b3 ♕a5 17 ♘e2 b5 [17 ... c4?! 18 bxc4 ♗xa4 19 ♕a2 Δ 20 ♖d] 18 axb5 axb5 19 ♖c1 ♕a3! [Δ ... c4] 20 ♘d2 ♕a5? [□ 20 ... ♘c7−+] 21 ♗f2 ♘c7 22 ♗h4 ♖f7 23 ♗xe7 ♖xe7 24 ♘f3 ♘a6 25 ♔h2 c4?? 26 bxc4 bxc4 27 ♗xc4 ♗b5 28 ♕b3 ♗a4 29 ♕e3 ♗b2 30 ♗xa6! ♗xc1 31 ♖xc1 ♖xc1 32 ♕xc1 ♕xa6 33 ♘g3 ♕b7 34 f5 ♗e8 35 ♕g5 ♖g7 36 f6 ♖d7 37 ♘f5 ♔h8 38 ♘e7 ♕b2 [□ 38 ... ♖xe7 39 fxe7 ♔g7=] 39 e5 dxe5 40 f7 **1-0** L/N6123

119

## HORWITZ ⚔ STAUNTON

[1846 – ⚔ HS2]

| | B. Horwitz | H. Staunton |
|---|---|---|
| *1* | 0 | 1 |
| *2* | 1 | 0 |
| *3* | 0 | 1 |
| *4* | 0 | 1 |
| *5* | 0 | 1 |
| *6* | 0 | 1 |
| *7* | 1 | 0 |
| *8* | 1 | 0 |
| *9* | 0 | 1 |
| *10* | 0 | 1 |
| *11* | 0 | 1 |
| *12* | ½ | ½ |
| *13* | ½ | ½ |
| *14* | 1 | 0 |
| *15* | 0 | 1 |
| *16* | 1 | 0 |
| *17* | 0 | 1 |
| *18* | 0 | 1 |
| *19* | 1 | 0 |
| *20* | 0 | 1 |
| *21* | 0 | 1 |
| *22* | ½ | ½ |
| *23* | 1 | 0 |
| *24* | 0 | 1 |
| *Total* | 8½ | 15½ |

### 1846-⚔HS2-1
**Staunton, H.+Horwitz, B.**

[Staunton]

1 e4 e5 2 ♘f3 ♘c6 3 ♗b5 ♕f6 4 ♘c3 ♗d6?? 5 ♘d5 ♕g6 6 d3 ♘ce7 [6 ... ♕xg2?; 6 ... ♘d4 7 ♘h4 ♕e6 8 ♗c4] 7 ♘h4 ♕e6 8 ♘e3 ♗c5 9 ♗c4 ♕f6 10 ♘f3 d6 11 c3 ♘h6 12 0-0 ♗g4 13 ♘xg4 ♘xg4 14 a4 a5 15 ♗d2 [15 ... 0-0?; 15 ... 0-0-0?] 15 ... ♕g6 16 h3 ♘f6 17 d4 exd4 18 cxd4 ♗b6 19 e5! ♘d7 20 ♕e2 [20 ♘h4? ♕e4] 20 ... d5 21 ♗d3 ♕h5 22 ♔h2 [△ 23 g4] 22 ... f5 23 exf6 ♘xf6 24 ♖ae1 ♘g8 25 ♗g5 ♕f7 26 ♘e5 ♕e6 27 ♕h5+ ♔f8 28 ♘g6+ hxg6 29 ♕xh8 ♕d6+ 30 f4 ♖e8 31 ♖e2 ♗xd4 32 ♖fe1 ♔f7 33 ♕h7!+- ♘f6? 34 ♖xe7+ ♖xe7 35 ♗xg6+ ♔f8 36 ♕h8+ ♘g8 37 ♗xe7+ **1-0**

L/N6123

### 1846-⚔HS2-2
**Horwitz, B.+Staunton, H.**

[Staunton]

1 e4 c5 2 f4 e6 3 ♘f3 ♘c6 4 ♗e2 d6 5 0-0 ♘ge7 6 c4 ♘g6 7 d3 ♗e7 8 ♘c3 ♗f6 9 ♕e1? 0-0 10 ♗e3 ♗d4 11 ♕d2 ♘xf4? [□ 11 ... ♕f6∓] 12 ♗xd4 ♘xe2+ 13 ♘xe2 cxd4 14 ♘exd4 ♕b6 15 ♕f2 ♘b4 [□ 15 ... ♘xd4] 16 ♘e1 ♗d7 17 a3 ♘c6 18 ♘b5! ♕c5?? 19 b4 ♕e5 20 ♘f3 ♕f4 21 g3 ♕h6 22 ♘xd6 b6 23 b5 ♘d8 24 ♘e5+- [24 ... ♗e8 25 ♘xe8 ♖xe8 26 ♘xf7 △ 27 ♘d6] 24 ... ♗c8 25 ♘exf7 ♘xf7 26 ♘xf7 ♕f6 27 ♘h6+ gxh6? [□ 27 ... ♔h8] 28 ♕xf6 ♖xf6 29 ♖xf6 ♔g7 30 ♖af1 a6 31 ♖f7+ ♔g6 32 e5 axb5 [33 ♖1f6+ ♔g5 34 ♖g7+ ♔h5 35 ♖f4 ∼ 36 ♖h4#] **1-0**

L/N6123

### 1846-⚔HS2-3
**Staunton, H.+Horwitz, B.**

[Staunton]

1 d4 f5 2 c4 ♘f6 3 ♘c3 e6 4 ♗g5 ♗e7 5 e3 c5 [△ d5] 6 ♘f3 ♘c6 7 d5 exd5 8 cxd5 ♘xd5 9 ♘xd5 ♗xg5?? 10 ♘xg5 ♕xg5 11 ♘c7+ ♔d8 [11 ... ♔f8 12 ♘xa8+-; 11 ... ♔f7 12 ♘xa8+-; 11 ... ♔e7 12 ♘xa8+-] 12 ♘e6+

**1-0**

L/N6123

### 1846-⚔HS2-4
**Horwitz, B.–Staunton, H.**

[Staunton]

1 e4 c5 2 f4 e6 3 ♘f3 ♘c6 4 c4 d6 5 ♗e2 ♘ge7 6 0-0 ♘g6 7 d3 ♗e7 8 ♘c3 ♗f6 9 ♕e1 a6 10 ♔h1 0-0 11 ♗e3 ♖b8 12 a4 ♘d4 13 ♗d1 ♗d7 [□ 13 ... ♘c6] 14 ♗xd4 cxd4 15 ♘e2 b5 16 cxb5 axb5 17 a5 e5? 18 f5 ♘e7 19 g4 ♘c6 20 ♖g1 ♗g5 21 ♗b3!! ♗e3 22 ♖g2 ♖a8 23 a6 ♘b8 24 g5 ♔h8! 25 ♕h4 ♖xa6 26 ♖f1! [△ 27 ♖g3; 28 ♖h3 (26 ♖xa6 ♘xa6 27 ♖g3 ♗f2)] 26 ... ♘c6 27 ♖g3 ♘b4 28 ♗xf7?? [□ 28 f6!± □ 28 ♖h3±] 28 ... ♖xf7 29 ♕h5 ♕g8 30 ♘h4 d5!!-+ 31 ♖h3 g6! 32 ♕g4 ♘xd3 33 ♕g2 dxe4 34 ♘xg6+ [34 ♕xe4 ♗c6] 34 ... ♖xg6 35 fxg6 ♖xf1+ 36 ♕xf1 ♘f2+ [36 ... ♗xh3?? 37 ♕f6+ ♕g7 38 ♕d8+ ♕g8 39 g7+ ♔xg7 40 ♕f6#!!] 37 ♕xf2 ♗xf2 38 ♖xh7+ ♕xh7 39 gxh7 ♔xh7 40 ♔g2 e3 41 ♔f3 ♗c6+ 42 ♔g4 d3 **0-1**

L/N6123

### 1846-⚔HS2-5
**Staunton, H.+Horwitz, B.**

[Staunton]

1 e4 e5 2 ♘f3 d6 [□ 2 ... ♘c6] 3 d4 exd4 4 ♘xd4 ♘f6 5 ♘c3 ♗e7 6 ♗e2 0-0 7 f4 c5 8 ♘f3 ♘c6 9 0-0 ♗g4 [△ ... ♘d4] 10 ♗e3 a6 11 a3 ♗xf3 12 ♗xf3 ♖c8 13 ♘e2 ♕c7 [△ ... ♘d4, ... ♕xc2] 14 ♘g3 ♖fe8 [14 ... ♘d4?] 15 c3 ♖cd8 16 ♕c2 ♗f8 17 ♖ad1 b6 18 b4 ♘a7 19 c4 cxb4 20 axb4 d5? 21 ♕f2! ♘c8 [21 ... dxe4] 22 cxd5 ♗xb4 23 e5 ♘d7 24 d6 ♕b8 25 ♗c6 g6 [25 ... ♘xd6 26 ♗xd7 ♖xd7 27 ♔h1 (△ 28 exd6) 27 ... ♖de7 28 exd6 ♖xe3 29 d7+-; 26 ♖xd6 ♗xd6 27 exd6 ♕xd6 28 ♗xd7 ♖xd7 29 ♗xb6+-; 26 exd6 ♖xe3 27 ♕xe3 ♗c5 28 ♖d4 ♘f6 29 ♖fd1 ♖xd6 30 ♘f5 ♗xd4 31 ♖xd4+-] 26 ♘e4 ♖e6 27 ♕h4 ♘a7 28 ♗xd7 ♖xd7 29 ♘g5 h5 30 ♘xe6 fxe6 31 f5 a5 32 fxe6 ♖g7 33 e7 **1-0**

L/N6123

### 1846-⚔HS2-6
**Horwitz, B.–Staunton, H.**

[Staunton]

1 e4 e5 2 ♘f3 ♘c6 3 ♗c4 ♗c5 4 c3 ♘f6 5 d4 exd4 6 e5 d5 7 ♗b5 ♘e4 8 cxd4 ♗b6 9 0-0 0-0 10 h3 f6 11 ♘c3 fxe5 12 ♗xc6 bxc6 13 ♘xe5 ♗a6 14 ♘e2 [□ 14 ♘xe4 dxe4 (14 ... ♗xf1? 15 ♘g5) 15 ♕b3+ ♕d5 16 ♕xd5+ cxd5 17 ♖d1∓] 14 ... c5!-+ [14 ... ♗xe2; 14 ... ♘xf2!? 15 ♖xf2 ♖xf2 16 ♔xf2 ♕h4+ 17 ♔f1 ♖f8+ 18 ♘f3 ♗xd4 19 ♕e1 (19 ♕xd4 ♕xd4) 19 ... ♖xf3+ 20 gxf3 ♕xh3#; 17 g3 ♕xh3 18 ♘f3 ♖f8 19 ♘f4 ♗xd4+ 20 ♕xd4 ♕f1+ 21 ♔e3 ♖e8+ 22 ♔d2 (22 ♘e5 ♕g1+) 22 ... ♕xf3-+; 22 ... ♖e4-+; 17 g3 ♕xh3 18 ♘f4 ♗xd4+ 19 ♔f3 (19 ♕xd4 ♕f1+ 20 ♔e3 ♕g1+ 21 ♔∼ ♕xd4; 19 ♗e3 ♕h2+ ... ♗xe5∓) 19 ... ♖f8 20 ♕xd4 ♕h1+ 21 ♔g4 (21 ♔f2 ♕f1+ 22 ♔e3 ♕g1+ 23 ♔∼ ♕xd4; 21 ♔e3 ♕g1+ 22 ♔∼ ♕xd4) 21 ... ♗c8+-+] 15 ♗e3 cxd4 16 ♗xd4-+ [16 ∼-+] 16 ... ♗xe2 17 ♕xe2 ♗xd4 18 ♘c6 ♕f6 19 ♘xd4 ♕xd4 20 ♖ad1 ♕c5 21 ♖c1 ♕b6 22 b3 ♘g3 23 ♕d3 ♘xf1 **0-1**

L/N6123

### 1846-⚔HS2-7
**Staunton, H.–Horwitz, B.**

[Staunton]

1 e4 e5 2 ♘f3 ♘c6 3 d4 exd4 4 ♗c4 ♗b4+ 5 c3 dxc3 6 bxc3 ♗a5 7 0-0 [7 e5 d5!] 7 ... d6 8 e5 ♗e6 9 ♗xe6 fxe6 10 exd6 ♕xd6 11 ♕b3 0-0-0 12 ♘g5 [△ 13 ♘f7] 12 ... ♖d7 13 ♘xe6 ♗b6 [△ 14 ... ♘a5, 15 ... ♕xe6] 14 ♘g5 ♘h6 15 ♘d2 ♘g4 16 ♘df3?? ♘xf2 17 ♖xf2?? ♕d1+ **0-1**

L/N6123

### 1846-⚔HS2-8
**Horwitz, B.+Staunton, H.**

[Staunton]

1 e4 e5 2 ♘f3 ♘c6 3 ♗c4 ♗c5 4 c3 ♘f6 5 d3 d6 6 ♘g5 0-0 7 f4 d5 8 exd5 ♘xd5 9 ♗xd5 ♕xd5 10 ♕f3 ♕d7 11 ♕e4 ♕f5 [11 ... f5??] 12 g4!! ♕xe4+ 13 ♘xe4 ♗b6 14 f5 f6 15 ♘a3 ♘e7 16 ♘c4 ♗d7 17 a4 ♗c6? [□ 17 ... a6; 17 ... a5] 18 a5 ♗xe4 19

dxe4 ♗c5 20 b4 ♗d6 21 ♗e3 a6 22 ♔e2 ♖fd8 23 ♖ad1 ♘c6 24 ♘xd6 cxd6 25 ♗b6 ♖d7 26 ♖d3 ♖c8 [◻ 26 ... ♔f7, 27 ... ♔e7=] 27 ♖hd1 ♘e7 28 ♖xd6 ♖xd6 29 ♖xd6 ♖xc3 30 ♖d8+ ♔f7 31 ♗c5 ♘g6 [31 ... ♘~ 32 ♖f8 +-] 32 fxg6+ ♔xg6 33 ♖d7 ♖c2+ 34 ♔f3 ♖xh2 35 ♗f8 ♖h3+ 36 ♔g2 ♖~ **1-0** L/N6123

**1846-⚔HS2-9**
**Staunton, H.+Horwitz, B.**
[Staunton]

1 e4 e5 2 ♘f3 ♘c6 3 ♗c4 ♗c5 4 c3 d6 5 d3 ♕e7 6 ♗e3 ♗b6 7 ♘bd2 ♘f6 8 b4 ♗e6 9 ♗b5 0-0 10 ♘c4 ♘g4 [△ ... f5] 11 ♗xb6 axb6 12 ♗xc6 [12 h3? ♘a7] 12 ... bxc6 13 ♘cd2 f5 [13 ... ♖xa2?; 13 ... ♗xa2?] 14 a4 fxe4 15 dxe4 [15 ♘xe4?] 15 ... d5 16 ♕e2! b5 [△ 17 0-0 dxe4 18 ♘xe4 (18 ♕xe4) ♗c4] 17 0-0 [17 a5 d4] 17 ... bxa4 18 h3 ♘h6 19 exd5 ♗xd5 20 ♕xe5 ♕xe5 21 ♘xe5 ♘f7 22 ♘ec4 [22 ♘d7? ♖fd8 23 ♘c5 ♗xg2] 22 ... ♖fe8 23 ♘e3 ♘d6 24 ♖fc1 ♗e6 25 ♘f3 ♘c4 26 ♘xc4 ♗xc4 27 ♘d4 ♖a6 28 ♖a3 ♔f7 29 ♖ca1 ♖ea8 30 f4 g6 31 ♔f2 h5 32 g4 hxg4 33 hxg4 ♔f6 34 g5+ ♔e7 35 ♖e1+ ♔d6 36 ♘f3 ♖f8 37 ♔g3 ♗b3 38 ♘d2 ♗c2 39 ♘c4+ ♔d7 40 ♖e2 ♗f5 41 ♖a1 ♔c8 42 ♘a5 ♖h8! 43 ♔g2 ♖h3 44 ♖d1! ♖xa5 45 bxa5 ♖xc3 46 a6 ♔b8 47 ♖d4 ♗c2 48 f5 gxf5 [◻ 48 ... a3! 49 f6 ♗b3 50 a7+! ♔a8! (50 ♖b4+ ♔a7 51 ♖xb3 ♖xb3 52 f7 ♖b8 53 ♖e8 a2 54 ♖xb8 a1♕ 55 f8♕ ♕a2+=) 51 ♖e8+ ♔xa7 52 ♖a4+ ♗xa4 (52 ... ♔b7 53 ♖b4+ ♔a7 54 ♖xb3 ♖xb3 55 f7 ♖b2+ 56 ♔g3 a2 57 f8=♕+-) 53 f7 a2 54 ♖e1+- ; 49 ... a2 50 ♖e1 ♖c5 51 f7 ♖xg5+ 52 ♔h2 ♖f5 53 ♖a1+- ♗b1 (53 ... ♖xf7 54 ♖xa2+-) 54 ♖b4+ ♔a8 (54 ... ♔a7 55 ♖b7+ ♔a8 56 ♖xc7+-; 55 ... ♔xa6 56 ♖bxb1) 55 a7 ♖xf7 56 ♖b8+ ♔xa7 57 ♖bxb1 ♖f2+ 58 ♔g3 ♖c2 59 ♖b3+-] 49 g6 ♔a7 50 g7 ♗b3 51 ♖xa4 ♗d5+ 52 ♔h2 ♖c1 53 ♖g2 ♗g8 54 ♖b2 ♗d5 55 ♖b7+ ♔a8 56 a7 ♖h1+ 57 ♔g3 ♖g1+ 58 ♔f2

**1-0** L/N6123

**1846-⚔HS2-10**
**Horwitz, B.–Staunton, H.**
[Staunton]

1 e4 e5 2 ♘f3 ♘c6 3 ♗c4 ♗c5 4 c3 ♘f6 5 d3 d6 6 ♘g5 0-0 7 f4 d5 8 exd5 ♘xd5 9 ♗xd5 ♕xd5 10 ♕f3 [10 ♕h5 ♗f5∓] 10 ... ♖d8∓ 11 ♕xd5 ♖xd5 12 ♔e2! [12 b4 ♘xb4 13 cxb4 ♗d4] 12 ... ♗g4+ 13 ♘f3 ♖ad8 14 d4! [14 ♖d1??] 14 ... exd4 15 c4 ♖e8+ 16 ♔f2! [△ 16 ... d3+ 17 ♔g3] 16 ... ♖d7 17 ♘bd2 d3+ 18 ♔g3 ♗xf3 19 ♘xf3 ♖e2 20 ♗d2 ♖d6 21 ♖ad1 ♖g6+ 22 ♔h3 [22 ♘g5? △ 23 f5? 23 ... ♗d6+!] 22 ... ♖h6+ 23 ♘h4 ♗e7 24 g3 ♘d4 25 ♗c3 ♘e6 [△ 26 ♖xd3? ♖xh4+ 27 gxh4 ♘xf4+] 26 ♔g4 ♗xh4 27 gxh4 ♖e4 28 ♖hf1 ♖g6+ 29 ♔f5 ♖e3 30 h5 ♖g2 31 h4 ♘c5 [31 ... g6+ 32 hxg6 hxg6+ 33 ♔f6 ♘xf4] 32 ♖fe1 [32 ♗e5 ♘d7] 32 ... g6+ [33 hxg6+ hxg6+ 34 ♔f6 ♘d7#] **0-1** L/N6123

**1846-⚔HS2-11**
**Staunton, H.+Horwitz, B.**
[Staunton]

1 d4 f5 2 e4 fxe4 3 ♘c3 ♘f6 4 ♗g5 c6 5 ♗xf6 exf6 6 ♘xe4 d5 7 ♘g3 ♗d6 8 ♗d3 0-0 9 ♘1e2 f5 10 f4 c5 11 c3 cxd4 12 cxd4 ♗b4+ 13 ♔f2 ♘c6 14 ♖f1 ♗a5 [△ 15 ... ♗b6, 16 ... ♕f6] 15 ♔g1 ♗b6 [△ 16 ... ♕f6] 16 ♗b5 ♕f6 17 ♗xc6 bxc6 [△ 18 ... ♗a6] 18 ♖f3 c5 [△ ... ♗b7] 19 dxc5 ♗xc5+ 20 ♔h1 ♗b7 21 ♖b3 ♗b6 [21 ... ♖f7 22 ♖xb7 ♖xb7 23 ♕xd5+; 21 ... ♖ab8 22 ♖xb7 ♖xb7 23 ♕xd5+] 22 a4 a5 23 ♘xf5 ♕xf5 24 ♖xb6 ♗a6 25 ♘g3 ♕xf4 26 ♕xd5+ ♔h8 27 ♕xa5! ♖ac8! 28 ♕e1! ♖fe8 29 ♕g1 ♗d3 [◻ 29 ... ♗c4] 30 a5 ♗c4 31 a6 [31 ♖b7 ♖e6 32 ♖xg7 ♖h6] 31 ... ♗d5 32 ♖d1 ♕e5 33 ♘f1 ♖c2 34 ♖xd5! [34 ♘e3+-, 35 a7; 34 ♖d2+-] 34 ... ♕xd5 35 ♘e3 ♕d2 [35 ... ♖xe3 36 ♖b8+] 36 ♘xc2 ♕xc2 37 a7 ♕c7 38 ♖e6 ♖a8 39 ♕e3 h6 40 ♖e8+ ♖xe8 41 ♕xe8+ ♔h7 42 ♕e4+ g6 43 ♕e3!+- ♕b7 44 h3 h5 45 b4 h4 46 b5 ♕d5 47 ♕e7+ ♔h6 48 ♕xh4+ ♔g7 49 ♕e7+ ♔h6 50 ♕e3+ g5 51 b6 ♕d1+ 52 ♔h2 ♕d6+ 53 ♕g3 ♕xb6 54 a8♕ ♕f6 55 ♕ab8 ♔g6 56 ♕gd6 **1-0** L/N6123

**1846-⚔HS2-12**
**Horwitz, B.=Staunton, H.**
[Staunton]

1 e4 e5 2 ♘f3 ♘c6 3 ♗c4 ♗c5 4 c3 ♘f6 5 d3 d6 6 b4 ♗b6 7 a4 a5 8 b5 ♘e7 9 ♕b3 0-0 10 ♘g5 ♕e8 11 f4 exf4 12 ♔d1 [12 ♗xf4? d5-+] 12 ... ♘g6 13 ♖f1 ♗g4+ 14 ♔c2 h6 15 ♘f3 ♖d8 16 ♗a3 ♗e3 [16 ... ♗xf3, 17 ... d5-+] 17 ♘bd2 ♘d7 18 d4 ♗e6 [△ 19 d5] 19 h3 ♘b6 20 d5 ♗c8 21 ♗d3 f5 22 ♖fe1 ♕f7 23 c4 fxe4 24 ♘xe4 ♗f5 25 ♗b2 ♗xe4 26 ♗xe4 ♘d7 27 ♕d3∓ ♘ge5 28 ♘xe5 dxe5 29 ♗a3 ♘c5?? 30 ♗xc5 ♗xc5 31 ♗h7+ ♔h8 32 ♖xe5 ♕f6 33 ♖ae1 ♗e3 34 ♖e6 ♕h4 35 ♖e2 ♖d6 36 ♗f5 ♖xe6 37 ♗xe6 b6 38 ♕g6?? ♕f6? [◻ 38 ... f3 39 gxf3 ♕xc4+-+; 39 ♖xe3 ♕xc4+ (39 ... ♕f2+, ... fxg2) 40 ♔d2 fxg2 (40 ... f2-+) 41 ♖g3 (41 ♗f5 ♕xd5+, 42 ... ♕xf5) 41 ... ♖f2+ 42 ♔e3 ♕f4+ 43 ♔d3 ♖d2+ 44 ♔c3 ♕d4+ 45 ♔b3 ♖b2+ 46 ♔a3 ♕b4#] 39 ♕xf6 ♖xf6 40 ♔d3 g5 41 ♗g4 ♔g7 42 ♗h5 ♖f8 43 g3 ♔f6 44 gxf4 gxf4 45 ♖g2 ♔e5 46 ♖g6 ♖f6 47 ♖g7 ♗c5 48 ♗f3 [48 ♖xc7+-] 48 ... ♗d6 **½-½** L/N6123

**1846-⚔HS2-13**
**Staunton, H.=Horwitz, B.**
[Staunton]

1 d4 f5 2 c4 ♘f6 3 ♘c3 e6 4 e3 c6 5 ♗d3 ♘a6 6 a3 ♘c7 7 e4 fxe4 8 ♘xe4 ♗e7 9 ♘xf6+ ♗xf6 10 ♕h5+ g6 11 ♕h6 ♕e7 12 ♘f3 d6 13 0-0 ♗d7 14 b4 0-0-0!? 15 ♖b1 ♕g7 16 ♕e3 d5 17 c5 ♖he8 18 ♘e5 ♗xe5 19 dxe5 a6 20 a4 ♖e7 21 ♗d2 ♗e8 22 ♕d4! [22 ♕g3 △ 23 ♗g5, 24 ♗f6!] 22 ... h6 23 ♖b3 g5 24 b5 cxb5 25 axb5 axb5 26 ♖a1 [26 ♖fb1+-] 26 ... ♗c6 27 ♗a5 ♖ee8 28 ♗xc7 ♕xc7 29 ♗xb5 ♔d7 30 ♖ab1 ♖b8 31 f4 ♖f8 32 fxg5 hxg5 33 ♕e3 [◻ 33 ♕d3] 33 ... ♗xb5 34 ♖xb5 ♖f5 35 c6+ ♕xc6 36 ♕a7 [36 ♖c5 ♕a4 37 ♖c7+ ♔xc7 (37 ... ♔~ 38 ♕c5+-) 38 ♕b6+ ♔d7 39 ♕d6+ ♔e8 40 ♕xe6+ +-; 36 ♖c5 ♕a6 37 ♖bc1 (37 ♕c3 ♕a7 38 ♔h1 b6∓) 37 ... ♖bf8 (△ 38 ... ♖f1+ 39 ♖xf1 ♕xf1#) 38 ♖c7+ ♔e8 39 ♖c8+ ♔f7 40 ♕h3! ♔g7 41 ♖1c7+ ♖5f7 42 ♖xf7+ ♖xf7 43 ♕h8+ ♔g6 44 ♖g8+ ♔f5 45 ♕h3+ ♔xe5 46 ♕g3+ (46 ♖xg5+ ♔d6) 46 ... ♔d4∓; 36 ♖b6 ♕c4 (36 ... ♕a4 37 ♕c5+-) 37 ♖c1 ♖xe5 38 ♖d6+ +-] 36 ... ♖c8! [△ 37 ... ♕c1+ 38 ♖xc1 ♖xc1#] 37 ♖xb7+ ♔e8 38 ♖b8 ♖f7 39 ♖xc8+ ♕xc8 40 ♕a4+ ♔f8 41 ♕a3+ ♔g7 42 ♕e3 ♖f5 43 h3 ♕c7 44 ♖e1 ♕c4 45 ♕a7+ ♔g6 46 ♕b8 ♕c5+ 47 ♔h2 ♕f8 48 ♕b3 ♖f2 49 ♕b6 ♕f5 50 ♕b8 ♕f7 51 ♔g1 ♖f4 52 ♕b1+ ♔h6 53 ♕b8 g4 54 hxg4 ♖xg4 55 ♖f1 ♖f4 56 ♖e1 ♔g5 57 ♕b6 ♔g4 58 ♕e3 ♕f5 59 ♕a7 ♖e4 60 ♕g7+ ♕g5 61 ♖xe4+ dxe4 62 ♕xg5+ ♔xg5 63 ♔f2 ♔f4 64 g3+ ♔xe5 65 ♔e3 ♔d5 66 ♔e2 ♔d4 67 g4 e3 68 g5 ♔e5 69 ♔xe3 ♔f5 70 g6 ♔xg6 71 ♔e4 **½-½** L/N6123

**1846-⚔HS2-14**
**Horwitz, B.+Staunton, H.**
[Staunton]

1 e4 e5 2 ♘f3 ♘c6 3 d4 exd4 4 ♘xd4 ♕h4? [△ 5 ... ♕xe4+] 5 ♘b5! [5

... ♕xe4+ 6 ♗e2 ♗d6 (6 ... ♔d8 7 0-0 a6 8 ♘1c3 ♕e5 9 ♘d5 axb5 10 ♗f4 ♕d4 11 ♗xc7+ ♔e8 12 ♘b6) 7 ♕xd6 ♕xe2+ 8 ♔xe2 cxd6 9 ♘c7++-] 5 ... ♕xe4+? 6 ♗e2 ♕e5??+- 7 f4 ♕c5 8 ♘xc7+ ♔d8 9 ♘xa8 ♘f6 10 ♘c3 ♗e7 11 ♕d2 ♖e8 12 ♘a4 ♕f5 13 0-0 ♘e4 14 ♕d3 ♕e6 15 f5 ♕f6 16 ♗f4 ♗d6 17 ♗xd6 ♘xd6 18 ♖ad1 ♘b4 19 ♕xd6 ♕xd6 20 ♖xd6 ♖xe2 21 c3 ♘c2 22 f6 g6 23 ♖fd1 ♘e3 24 ♖6d2 ♖xg2+ 25 ♖xg2 ♘xd1 26 ♖e2 b6 27 ♖e1 b5 28 ♘c5 ♘xb2 29 ♖e7 d6 30 ♘b7+ ♗xb7 31 ♖xb7 ♘c4 32 ♖xf7 ♘e5 33 ♖xa7 **1-0** L/N6123

**1846-✕HS2-15**
**Staunton, H.+ Horwitz, B.**

[Staunton]

1 e4 e5 2 ♘f3 ♘c6 3 ♗c4 ♗c5 4 c3 d6 5 d4 exd4 6 cxd4 ♗b6 7 ♘c3 ♗g4 8 ♗e3 ♘f6 9 a3 0-0 10 ♗e2 ♖e8 11 d5 ♘e5 12 ♘xe5 ♗xe2 13 ♕xe2 ♖xe5 14 ♗xb6 axb6 15 0-0 ♘xe4 16 ♘xe4 f5 17 f3 fxe4 18 fxe4 ♕e7 19 ♖ae1 ♖e8 20 ♖f4 h6! [20 ... ♖xd5?; 20 ... g5?] 21 ♕f3 ♖xd5 22 ♖f1 [22 ♕b3??] 22 ... ♖e5 23 ♖f7 ♕e6 [23 ... ♕d8 24 ♖xg7+ ♔xg7 25 ♕f7+ ♔h8 26 ♖f6 ♖h5 (26 ... ♖5e6 27 ♖xe6) 27 ♕xh5 ♕xf6 28 ♕xe8+] 24 ♖xc7 ♖xe4 25 ♖xb7 d5 26 h3! [26 ... d4 27 ♕f7+ ♕xf7 28 ♖fxf7+-] 26 ... ♖e1 27 ♖xe1 ♕xe1+ 28 ♕f1 [28 ♔h2?? ♕e5+ 29 ♕g3 ♕xg3+ 30 ♔xg3 ♖e3+ Δ 31 ... ♖b3] 28 ... ♕e3+ 29 ♕f2 ♕c1+ 30 ♔h2 ♖f8 31 ♕d4 ♖f6 32 ♕xd5+ ♔h7 33 ♕e5 ♖g6 [Δ 34 ... ♖xg2+] 34 ♖e7 ♕d2 35 ♕e4 ♕d6+ 36 ♖e5 ♔g8 37 ♕d5+ ♕xd5 38 ♖xd5 ♔f7 39 ♖b5 ♔e7 40 g4 ♔d7 41 ♔g3 ♔c6 42 ♖e5 ♖d6 43 ♖e3 ♔c5 44 h4 g6 45 ♔f4 ♔d4 46 ♖e4+ ♔d5 47 ♖e8 ♖f6+ 48 ♔e3 ♔c4 49 ♖e4+ ♔d5 50 ♖f4 ♖c6 51 ♖b4 ♖e6+ 52 ♔d3 ♖f6 53 ♖b5+ [□ 53 ♔e3] 53 ... ♔c6 54 ♖e5 ♔d6 55 ♖b5 ♔c6 56 ♖b4 ♖f3+ 57 ♔e2 ♖h3 58 ♖f4 ♖xh4 59 ♖f6+ ♔b5 60 ♖xg6 ♖h2+ 61 ♔f3 ♖xb2 62 ♖xh6 ♖b3+ 63 ♔f4 ♖xa3 64 g5 ♖a1 65 ♖h4 ♔c5 66 g6 ♖a7 67 ♔f5 b5 68 ♖g4 b4? [□ 68 ... ♖g7; 68 ... ♖a8] 69 g7 ♖xg7 70 ♖xg7 b3 71 ♔e4 ♔b4 72 ♔d3 **1-0** L/N6123

**1846-✕HS2-16**
**Horwitz, B.+ Staunton, H.**

[Staunton]

1 e4 e5 2 ♘f3 ♘c6 3 d4 exd4 4 ♗c4 ♕f6 5 0-0 d6 6 c3 d3 7 ♗g5 ♕g6 8 ♗xd3 ♗e7 9 e5 ♗f5 10 ♗xf5 ♕xf5 11 ♗xe7 ♘gxe7 12 exd6 0-0-0?? 13 ♘d4 ♘xd4 14 dxe7 ♘c2 15 exd8♕+ ♖xd8 16 ♕c1 ♘xa1 17 ♘a3 g5 18 ♕xa1 h5 19 ♖d1 ♖e8 20 ♕b1 ♕e6 21 ♘b5 a6 22 ♘d4 ♕e7 23 ♘f3 ♕f6 24 ♕d3 ♔b8 25 ♕d7 ♖g8 26 ♖e1 ♕f4 27 ♖e8+ ♔a7 28 g3 ♕c1+ 29 ♔g2 ♖xe8 30 ♕xe8 g4 31 ♕e3+ ♕xe3 32 fxe3 gxf3+ 33 ♔xf3 ♔b6 34 h4 ♔c5 35 g4 ♔d5 36 gxh5 ♔e5 37 ♔g4 ♔f6 38 e4 c5 39 ♔f4 b5 40 e5+ ♔g7 41 ♔g5 a5 42 h6+ ♔h7 43 ♔f6 **1-0** L/N6123

**1846-✕HS2-17**
**Staunton, H.+ Horwitz, B.**

[Staunton]

1 e4 e5 2 ♘f3 ♘c6 3 ♗c4 ♗c5 4 c3 d6 5 d4 exd4 6 cxd4 ♗b6 7 d5 ♘e5 [7 ... ♘e7] 8 ♘xe5 dxe5 9 ♘c3 ♘f6 10 0-0 h6 11 ♕d3 0-0 12 ♕g3 ♗d4 [12 ... ♕d6 13 ♗xh6?? (□ 13 ♘b5 Δ 14 ♗d3+-) 13 ... ♘h5] 13 ♗xh6 ♘h5 14 ♕g5 ♕f6 15 ♕xh5 gxh6 16 ♖ad1 ♔h8 17 ♖d3 ♖g8 18 ♖f3 ♕g6 19 ♕xg6 ♖xg6 20 ♔h1 [20 ♖xf7 ♗h3] 20 ... f6 21 ♘b5 ♗b6 22 d6!? ♗g4 23 ♖g3 c6 24 ♘c3 ♖d8 25 f3 ♗h5 26 ♖h3 ♖g5 27 ♖d1 ♔g7 28 ♗e6 ♗d4 29 d7 ♗f7 30 ♗f5 ♗g6 31 f4 ♗xf5 32 exf5 [32 fxg5∓] 32 ... ♖xf5 33 ♘e2 ♖xd7 34 g4 ♖xf4 35 ♘xf4 exf4 36 ♖hd3 c5 37 ♔g2 ♔g6 38

**118** Horwitz, B. b Staunton, H. M954.BL

♔f3 ♖e7 [38 ... ♔g5? 39 h4+ ♔xh4 40 ♖h1+ ♔g5 41 ♖h5+ ♔g6 42 ♖xc5] 39 b4 b6 40 h4 h5 41 bxc5 hxg4+ 42 ♔xg4 f5+ 43 ♔xf4 ♖e4+ 44 ♔f3 ♗xc5 45 ♖h1 ♔h5 46 ♖d5 ♖xh4 47 ♖xh4+ ♔xh4 48 ♖xf5 a5 49 a4+- ♗g1? [□ 49 ... ♗b4 50 ♖f6? ♔g5 51 ♖xb6=] 50 ♖f8 ♗c5 [50 ... ♔~?] 51 ♖g8 ♔h5 52 ♔e4 ♔h6 53 ♔d5 ♔h7 54 ♖g2 ♗e3 55 ♔c6 **1-0** L/N6123

### 1846-⚔HS2-18
### Horwitz, B.– Staunton, H.

[Staunton]

1 e4 c5 2 f4 e6 3 ♘f3 ♘c6 4 c4 d6 5 ♘c3 ♘h6 6 ♗e2 g6 7 d3 ♗g7! 8 0-0 a6 9 h3 f5! 10 ♗e3 [Δ 10 ... 0-0 11 e5 dxe5 12 ♗xc5] 10 ... b6 11 ♕d2 0-0 12 ♖f2 ♖b8 13 a4 ♗d7 14 ♘g5 ♕e8 15 ♖af1 ♘d4 16 ♗d1 ♗c6 17 b3 b5 18 axb5 axb5 19 ♘e2 bxc4 [□ 19 ... ♘xe2+] 20 ♗xd4 cxd4 21 bxc4 ♘f7 22 ♘xf7 ♖xf7 23 exf5 exf5 24 ♔h2 ♖fb7 25 ♖e1 ♖b2 26 ♗c2 ♕e3 27 ♘g1 ♕xd2 [27 ... ♖xc2 28 ♕xe3 dxe3 29 ♖xc2] 28 ♖xd2 ♖a8 29 ♖de2 ♔f8 30 ♗b1 ♖ab8 31 ♖xb2 [□ 31 ♗a2] 31 ... ♖xb2 32 ♘e2 h6 33 h4 ♗f6 34 ♔h3 ♔f7 [□ 34 ... ♗xg2+ 35 ♔xg2 ♗xh4-+] 35 ♔g3 ♗a8 36 ♔h3 ♗b7 37 ♔g3 ♗d8 38 ♔h3? [□ 38 ♘xd4] 38 ... ♗a5 **0-1** L/N6123

### 1846-⚔HS2-19
### Staunton, H.– Horwitz, B.

[Staunton]

1 e4 e5 2 ♘f3 ♘c6 3 ♗c4 ♗c5 4 c3 ♘f6 5 d3 d6 6 0-0 0-0 7 ♗e3 ♗b6 8 a4 a6 9 ♗xb6 cxb6 10 h3 d5!∓ 11 exd5 ♘xd5 12 ♖e1 ♖e8 13 ♘bd2 ♘f4 14 ♘f1 ♗f5 15 ♖e3 ♕f6 16 ♕e1 ♖ad8 17 d4± e4 [17 ... exd4?] 18 ♘g3?? [□ 18 ♘1h2±; 18 ♘1d2±] 18 ... ♘xg2 19 ♔xg2 exf3+ 20 ♔h2 ♖xe3 21 ♕xe3 ♗d7 22 ♘e4 ♕f5 23 ♘g5 h6 24 ♘xf3 [24 ♗xf7+? ♔h8 25 ♘e6 (25 ♘e6 ♕xg5) 25 ... ♕xf7] 24 ... ♕xh3+ 25 ♔g1 ♕g4+ 26 ♔f1 ♖e8 27 ♘h2 ♖xe3 28 ♘xg4 ♖h3 29 ♔g2 ♗xg4 30 ♖e1 ♔f8 31 d5 ♘e7 32 d6 ♘g6 33 ♖e4 ♘h4+ 34 ♔g1 ♗f3!! **0-1** L/N6123

### 1846-⚔HS2-20
### Horwitz, B.– Staunton, H.

[Staunton]

1 e4 c5 2 f4 e6 3 ♘f3 d5 4 exd5 exd5 5 ♗e2 ♗d6 6 c3 ♘c6 7 d3 ♕c7 8 g3 ♘f6 9 ♘a3 a6 10 ♘c2 0-0 11 d4 ♖e8 12 0-0 ♗d7 13 ♔g2 ♖e7 14 ♖e1 ♖ae8 15 ♗f1 ♕b6 16 ♖xe7 ♖xe7 17 b3 cxd4 18 ♘cxd4 ♗g4 19 ♗d3 ♘e4 20 ♗b2 ♗c5 21 ♕c2 [21 h3?? ♗xh3+ 22 ♔xh3 ♘f2+] 21 ... ♗xd4 22 ♘xd4 ♘xd4 23 cxd4 ♖c7 24 ♕b1 ♗f3+ [24 ♘d2?? 25 ♗xh7+ 26 ♕d3] 25 ♔g1 f5 26 ♕e1 ♖e7 27 ♖c1 ♔f7! [Δ ... g5!, ... ♔g6!] 28 ♗f1 g5 29 fxg5 ♘xg5 30 ♕d2 ♔g6 31 ♖c8 [Δ 32 ♖g8+] 31 ... ♕e6 32 ♖d8 ♗g4 [Δ 33 ... ♘f3+] 33 ♕f4 [Δ ♖d6, ♗d3] 33 ... ♘f3+ [33 ... ♘f7+-; 33 ... ♕e3++-] 34 ♔g2 ♕e1 35 ♖g8+ ♔h5 [36 ♖xg4 ♖e2+ 37 ♗xe2 ♕xe2+ 38 ♔~ ♕xh2#; □ 36 ♖g5+] **0-1** L/N6123

### 1846-⚔HS2-21
### Staunton, H.+Horwitz, B.

[Staunton]

1 d4 f5 2 c4 ♘f6 3 ♘c3 e6 4 e3 ♗b4 5 ♗d3 c5 6 ♘e2 0-0 7 0-0 cxd4 8 exd4 ♘c6 9 ♗f4 ♘h5 10 ♕d2 ♘xf4 11 ♕xf4 ♗a5 12 ♘b5 a6 13 ♘d6 ♗c7 14 c5 ♕e7 [14 ... g5? 15 ♕g3 f4? 16 ♕h3 Δ 17 ♕xh7#] 15 ♕g3 [15 ♘xf5 ♕d8-+] 15 ... ♗xd6 16 cxd6 ♕f6 17 ♕e3 f4 18 ♕e4 g6 19 f3 b5 20 a4 ♗b7∞ 21 axb5 axb5 22 ♗xb5 ♕g5! 23 ♗c4 ♘a5 [23 ... ♖xa1 24 ♖xa1 ♘a5 25 d5 (25 ♖xa5 ♕xa5 Δ ... ♕e1#; 25 ♕d3 ♘xc4 26 ♕xc4 ♗xf3-+; 25 ♗xe6+∓) 25 ... ♘xc4! (25 ... exd5 26 ♖xa5 dxc4 27 ♖xg5 ♗xe4 28 fxe4+-; 25 ... ♗xd5 26 ♖xa5 ♗xe4 27 ♖xg5+-) 26 ♕xc4 ♗xd5! 27 ♕c5 ♕e5 28 ♘c3 ♖b8 29 b4±] 24 ♖xa5 ♕xa5 25 ♕xb7 ♖a7 26 ♕b3 ♖aa8 27 ♘c3 ♖ab8 28 ♕a4 ♕b6 29 ♖d1 ♕xb2 30 ♘e4 ♕b4 31 ♕a2 ♖a8 32 ♕b3 ♕xb3 33 ♗xb3 ♖fb8 34 ♖d3 ♖a1+ 35 ♔f2 ♖b1 36 ♗a4 ♖1b2+ 37 ♖d2 ♖xd2+ 38 ♘xd2 ♖b6 39 ♘c4 [39 ... ♖b4 40 ♗xd7+-] 39 ... ♖b7 40 ♔e2 ♔f8 41 ♔d3 ♔e8 42 ♘e5 ♖a7 43 ♗b5 g5 44 ♔c4 h6 45 d5 exd5+ 46 ♔xd5 ♖a2 47 ♗xd7+ ♔d8 48 ♗h3 ♖d2+ 49 ♔e6 ♖e2 50 ♔f6 g4 51 ♗xg4 ♖xg2 52 ♘f7+ ♔e8 53 d7+ ♔f8 54 d8♕# **1-0** L/N6123

### 1846-⚔HS2-22
### Horwitz, B.= Staunton, H.

[Staunton]

1 e4 c5 2 f4 e6 3 c4 d6 4 ♘f3 ♘h6 5 ♗e2 g6 6 h3 f5 7 e5 ♘c6 8 exd6 ♗xd6 9 d3 ♕c7 10 ♕d2 0-0 11 0-0 ♘f7 12 ♘c3 a6 13 ♔h1 ♖b8 14 b3 b5? [□ 14 ... ♗d7] 15 cxb5 axb5 16 d4 ♘a7 [16 ... cxd4?] 17 dxc5 ♗xc5 18 ♗b2 ♖d8 19 ♕c2??-+ ♗e3 [Δ 20 ... b4] 20 b4 ♗b7 [□ 20 ... ~xf4] 21 ♕b3 ♕xf4 22 ♕xe6 ♖e8 23 ♕f6 [Δ 24 ♘d5+-] 23 ... ♕h6 24 ♘xb5 ♗xf3 [24 ... ♘xb5 25 ♗c4+-] 25 ♖xf3 ♗g5 26 ♕c3 ♘xb5 27 ♗xb5 ♖xb5-+ 28 a4 ♖be5 29 b5 ♗d2 30 ♕c6 ♖5e6 31 ♕c4 ♗a5 32 ♗c3 ♖e4 33 ♕c5 ♗xc3 34 ♕xc3 ♘e5 35 ♕b3+ ♔g7 36 ♕b2 ♕h4 37 a5 ♔h6 38 ♖ff1 ♘g4 39 ♕d2+ ♔h5 40 ♔g1 [Δ 41 hxg4+] 40 ... ♘e3 41 ♖fb1 ♘c4 [□ 41 ... ♘xg2-+ 42 ♕xg2 (42 ♕d1+ ♖e2-+) 42 ... ♖e3-+] 42 ♕f2 ♔g5 43 a6 ♖e2 44 ♕f3+ ♔h6 45 a7 ♘b6 46 a8♕ ♘xa8 47 ♖xa8 ♕xg2+ 48 ♕xg2 ♖xg2+ 49 ♔xg2 ♖xa8 50 ♔f3 ♔g5 51 ♔e3 ♔h4 52 b6 g5 53 b7 ♖b8 54 ♔f3 h5 55 ♔g2 g4 56 hxg4 hxg4 57 ♖b5 f4 58 ♔f2 f3 59 ♖b1 ♔g5 60 ♔g3 ♔f5 61 ♖b4 ♔e5 62 ♖xg4 **½-½** L/N6123

### 1846-⚔HS2-23
### Staunton, H.– Horwitz, B.

[Staunton]

1 e4 e5 2 ♘f3 d6 3 d4 exd4 4 ♘xd4 g6 5 ♗c4 ♗g7 6 c3 ♘f6 7 ♗g5 0-0 8 0-0 h6 9 ♗xf6 ♗xf6 10 f4± ♘d7 11 ♘d2 c6 12 ♕c2 ♘b6 13 ♗b3 d5 14 e5 ♗g7 15 ♖ad1?? c5 16 ♘4f3 c4 17 ♗xc4 [17 ♘xc4 ♘xc4 18 ♗xc4 ♕b6+ Δ 19 ... dxc4; 17 ♗a4 ♗f5] 17 ... dxc4 18 ♘xc4 ♕c7 19 ♘e3 ♘c4 20 ♘d5 ♕c5+ 21 ♔h1 ♘e3??

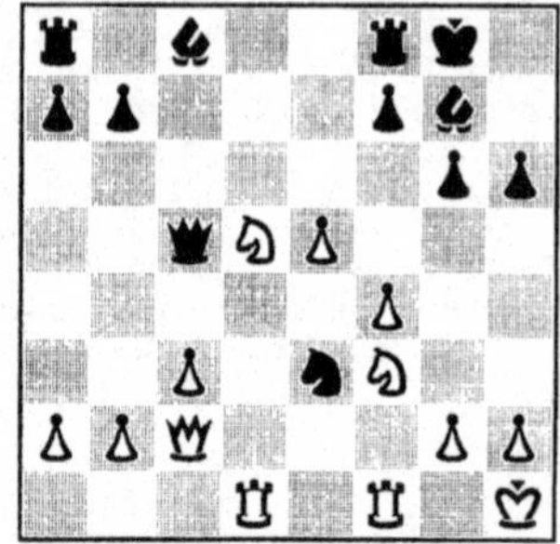

22 ♕f2 ♕xd5 23 ♖xd5 ♘xd5 24 ♘d4 ♘e7 25 h3 h5 26 ♖e1 ♘f5 27 ♔h2?? ♘xd4 28 cxd4 ♗e6 29 b3 ♖ad8 30 ♖d1 ♖d5 31 ♕e3 f6 32 ♖c1 fxe5 33 dxe5 ♖xf4 34 ♕xa7 ♗xe5 35 ♔h1 ♖fd4 36 ♖g1 ♖d7 37 ♕c5 ♖4d5 38 ♕e3 ♔h7 39 ♖e1 ♗f5 40 a4 h4 41 ♕xe5 ♖xe5 42 ♖xe5 ♔g7 43 ♔g1 ♔f6 44 ♖b5 ♗e4 45 ♔f2 ♗c6 46 ♖b6 ♖d2+ 47 ♔f1 ♔f5 48 ♖b4 ♗xg2+ 49 ♔g1 ♗e4 50 a5 ♔f4 51 ♖b5 g5 52 b4 g4 53 hxg4 h3 54 ♖h5 ♔g3 55 ♔f1 ♗f3 **0-1** L/N6123

### 1846-⚔HS2-24
### Horwitz, B.– Staunton, H.

[Staunton]

1 e4 c5 2 ♗c4 e6 3 ♘c3 ♘c6 4 f4 a6 5 a4 g6 6 ♘f3 ♗g7 7 0-0 ♘h6 8 d3 f5 9 ♕e1 0-0 10 ♗e3 b6 11 h3 ♘e7 [Δ ... d5] 12 e5 ♗b7 13 d4 cxd4 14 ♘xd4 ♕c7 15 b3 ♘c6 16 ♕f2 [Δ 17 ♘xc6, 18 ♗xb6] 16 ... ♖ab8 17 ♖ad1 [17 ♘xe6] 17 ... ♘xd4 18 ♗xd4 [Δ 19 ♗xb6] 18 ... ♗c8 [18 ... ♕c6?] 19 ♕e2 [Δ 20 ♗xa6] 19 ... ♕b7 20 ♗f2! [20 ... d5 21 exd6 (□ 21 ♘xd5 exd5 22 ♗xd5++-) 21 ... ♗xc3] 20 ... ♘f7 21 ♖d3 ♖e8 22 ♖fd1 ♗h6! [22 ... ♗f8]

23 g3? ♗f8 24 ♔h2 ♕c6-+ [Δ b5, ... ♗b7] 25 ♖3d2 ♗b4 26 ♗d4 ♗xc3 27 ♗xc3 b5 28 ♖d6! [Δ ♕e5] 28 ... ♘xd6 29 exd6 [Δ ♕e5; ♖d5] 29 ... ♗b7 [29 ... bxc4??+-] 30 axb5 axb5 31 ♗xb5 ♕xc3 32 ♗xd7 ♗f3 33 ♖d3 ♗xe2 34 ♖xc3 ♖ed8 35 ♗xe6+ ♔f8 36 d7 ♗b5 37 h4 ♗xd7 38 ♗c4 ♗b5 39 ♗xb5 ♖xb5 40 ♔h3 h5 41 ♖c6 ♔g7 42 ♖c7+ ♔h6 43 ♖c4 ♖d1 44 b4 ♖bd5 45 ♔g2 ♖5d2+ 46 ♔f3 ♖d4 47 ♖c8 ♖xb4 48 ♔e3 ♖dd4 **0-1** L/N6123

## HANNAH✕STAUNTON

**[1846-✕HS3]**

| | | | | | | |
|---|---|---|---|---|---|---|
| J.W. Hannah | 0 | 1 | 0 | 0 | 0 | 1 |
| H. Staunton | 1 | 0 | 1 | 1 | 1 | 4 |

### 1846-✕HS3-1̂ vi 46
**Staunton, H.+Hannah, J.W.** [Staunton]

⟨♘b1⟩ 1 e4 e5 2 ♘f3 ♘c6 3 c3 ♗c5 4 b4 ♗b6 5 b5 ♘ce7 6 ♘xe5 d6 7 ♘f3 ♗g4 8 a4 c6 [8 ... a6?] 9 d4 ♘f6 10 ♗d3 d5 11 e5 ♘e4 12 ♖a3 [12 ♕c2?? ♘xc3!-+] 12 ... f6 13 ♕c2 fxe5 14 ♘xe5 ♗f5 15 f3 [15 g4] 15 ... ♘d6 16 ♗xf5 ♘exf5 17 bxc6 bxc6 18 ♘xc6 ♕h4+ 19 ♕f2 ♕xf2+ 20 ♔xf2 0-0 21 ♖e1 ♖ac8 22 ♘b4 ♖xc3 23 ♖xc3 ♗xd4+ 24 ♖ce3 ♘c4 25 ♘c2 [25 ♘xd5?] 25 ... ♗c5! 26 ♔f1! [26 g4?!] 26 ... ♘fxe3+ 27 ♗xe3 ♘xe3+ 28 ♘xe3 ♖d8 29 ♘f5 ♔f7 30 ♖d1 ♔f6 31 ♘g3 d4 32 ♔e2 ♔e5 33 ♔d3 ♔d5 34 ♖b1 ♔c6 35 ♘e4 ♗b6 36 ♖c1+ ♔b7 [36 ... ♔d5? 37 a5!+-] 37 ♘c5+ ♗xc5 38 ♖xc5 **1-0** L/N6123

### 1846-✕HS3-2̂ vi 46
**Staunton, H.-Hannah, J.W.** [Staunton]

⟨♘b1⟩ 1 e4 e5 2 f4 exf4 3 ♘f3 g5 4 h4 g4 5 ♘e5 h5 6 ♗c4 ♘h6 7 d4 d6 8 ♘d3 f3 9 g3 ♘c6 10 c3 ♘a5 11 ♗b5+ c6 12 ♗a4 b5 13 ♗c2 ♘g8 14 a4 a6 15 axb5 axb5?? 16 b4 ♗b7 17 bxa5 ♖xa5 18 ♖xa5 ♕xa5 19 ♗d2 ♗h6 20 ♔f2 ♗xd2 21 ♕xd2 ♘f6 22 ♖e1 c5 23 d5 c4 24 ♘b4 ♕b6+ 25 ♔f1 ♘d7 26 ♕g5 ♕d8 27 ♕e3 ♘c5 28 ♖a1 f6 29 e5?? fxe5 30 ♖a7 ♕f6 31 ♘c6 ♕h6 32 ♕e1 ♖f8 33 ♘xe5 f2 34 ♕e2 dxe5 [34 ... ♘e4!-+] 35 ♕xe5+ ♔f7 36 ♖xb7+ ♘xb7 37 ♗f5 ♕c1+ 38 ♔xf2 ♕d2+ 39 ♔g1 ♘d8 40 ♕c7+ ♔f6! 41 ♕d6+ ♔xf5 42 ♕xf8+ ♔e4 ...? **0-1** L/N6123

### 1846-✕HS3-3̂ vi 46
**Staunton, H.+Hannah, J.W.** [Staunton]

⟨♘b1⟩ 1 e4 e5 2 f4 exf4 3 ♘f3 g5 4 ♗c4 d6 5 0-0 ♗g7 6 c3 c6 7 d4 h5 8 h4 g4 9 ♘g5 f6 10 ♗xf4! fxg5 11 ♗xg5 ♕c7 12 ♕d2 d5?? 13 exd5 ♕d6 14 ♖ae1+ ♔d7 **1-0** L/N6123

### 1846-✕HS3-4̂ vi 46
**Staunton, H.+Hannah, J.W.** [Staunton]

⟨♘b1⟩ 1 e4 e5 2 ♗c4 ♗c5 3 ♕e2 d6 4 f4 ♗xg1 5 ♖xg1 ♘c6 6 c3 ♕f6 7 f5 g6 8 g4 gxf5 9 gxf5 ♕h4+ 10 ♖g3 ♘f6 11 d3 ♖g8 [11 ... ♘h5?! 12 ♕g4] 12 ♕g2 ♘h5 13 ♕h3 ♕xh3 14 ♖xh3 ♘f6 15 ♔f2 ♗d7 16 b4 0-0-0? 17 ♗xf7 ♖g7 18 ♗b3 d5! 19 exd5 ♘e7 20 ♖g3 ♖xg3 21 hxg3 ♗xf5 22 ♗g5 ♘fg8 23 ♔e3 ♖d7 24 ♖f1 ♖d6! [24 ... ♗~? 25 ♖f8+ ♖d8 26 ♖xd8+ ♔xd8 27 d6 cxd6 28 ♗xg8] 25 c4 ♖g6 26 ♗h4 ♔d7 27 d4 exd4+ 28 ♔xd4 ♖g4+ 29 ♔c5!? ♘h6 30 ♗a4+ ♔d8 [□ 30 ... ♔c8 31 ♗xe7?? b6+ 32 ♔b5 ♔b7-+] 31 ♗d1 b6+ 32 ♔b5 ♗d7+ 33 ♔a6 ♗c8+? 34 ♔xa7 ♖xc4 35 ♖f8+ ♔d7 36 ♗xe7 ♔xe7 37 ♖xc8 ♘f5 38 ♖h8 ♘xg3 39 ♖xh7+ ♔d6 40 ♖h6+ ♔e5 41 ♖e6+ ♔f5 42 ♗b3 ♖c3 43 ♔b7 c5 44 dxc6 ♖xb3 45 axb3 ♔xe6 46 c7 **1-0** M954

### 1846-✕HS3-5̂ vi 46
**Staunton, H.+Hannah, J.W.** [Staunton]

⟨♘b1⟩ 1 e4 e5 2 ♗c4 ♗c5 3 ♕e2 d6 4 f4 ♗xg1 5 ♖xg1 exf4 6 d3 [6 d4?!] 6 ... ♘c6 7 ♗xf4 ♘d4 8 ♕f2 ♕f6 [Δ 9 ... ♘xc2+] 9 ♖f1 ♘e6 10 ♗xe6 ♗xe6 11 0-0-0 g5 [11 ... ♗xa2? 12 e5!+-] 12 ♗d2 ♕xf2 13 ♖xf2 f6 14 ♖df1 ♔e7 15 d4 [Δ 16 d5 ♗~ 17 ♗xg5] 15 ... h6 16 e5 dxe5 17 dxe5 f5 18 ♖f3 ♖d8 19 ♖h3 [Δ 29 ♗xg5+] 19 ... f4 20 ♖c3 ♖d7 21 g3 fxg3 22 ♖xg3 ♖h7?? 23 ♗b4+! ♖d6 [□ 23 ... c5] 24 ♖d1 ♔d7 25 exd6 c6 26 ♖f1 ♔e8 27 ♖f8+ **1-0** M954

## HARRWITZ✕WILLIAMS

London

**[1846-✕HW]**

| | | | | | | |
|---|---|---|---|---|---|---|
| D. Harrwitz | ½ | 1 | ½ | ½ | 1 | 3½ |
| E. Williams | ½ | 0 | ½ | ½ | 0 | 1½ |

### 1846-✕HW-1
**Williams, E.=Harrwitz, D.**
London [Staunton]

1 d4 d5 2 c4 dxc4 3 e3 e5 4 ♗xc4 exd4 5 exd4 ♘f6 6 ♘c3 ♗d6 7 ♘f3 0-0 8 0-0 ♘bd7 9 ♕d3 ♘b6 10 ♗b3 h6? 11 ♗xh6 gxh6 12 ♕g6+ ♔h8 13 ♕xh6+ ♘h7 14 ♘e4 ♗f5 15 ♘eg5 ♕f6 16 ♕xf6+ ♘xf6 17 ♘xf7+ ♔g7 18 ♘h4 ♗d3 19 ♖fd1 ♗c4 20 ♘xd6 cxd6 21 ♗xc4 ♘xc4 22 b3 ♘b6 23 ♘f5+ ♔g6 24 ♘xd6 ♖ab8 25 f4 ♘bd5 26 f5+ ♔g5 27 ♖d3 ♘f4 28 ♖g3+ ♔h5 29 ♖e1 ♖bd8 30 ♘xb7 ♖xd4 31 ♘c5 ♖d2 32 ♘e6 ♘xe6 33 fxe6 ♖xa2 34 e7 ♖e8 35 ♖e5+ ♔h4 36 ♖e1? [36 ♔f1+-; 36 ♖e6+-] 36 ... ♖c2 37 ♖f3 ♖c6 38 g3+ ♔g5 39 ♖e5+ ♔g6 40 h4 ♖c1+ 41 ♔g2 ♖c2+ 42 ♔h3 ♖h2+! 43 ♔xh2 ♘g4+ 44 ♔h3 ♘xe5 45 h5+ ♔g7 46 ♖c3 ♖xe7 47 g4 ♔h6 48 ♔h4 ♖g7 49 ♖g3 a5 50 ♖g2 ♘f3+ 51 ♔g3 ♘d4 52 ♔h4 ♘f3+ 53 ♔g3 ♘g5 54 ♖a2 ♖a7 55 b4 a4 56 b5 ♘e4+ 57 ♔f4 ♘c3 58 g5+ ♔xh5 59 ♖h2+ ♔g6 60 ♖h6+ ♔g7 61 b6 ♖b7 62 ♖c6 ♘d5+ 63 ♔e5 ♖xb6 64 ♖c4 ♖b5 655 ♔d4 a3 66 ♖c1 [□ 66 ♖a4 ♖b4 67 ♖xb4 ♘xb4 68 ♔c3 a2 69 ♔b2=] 66 ... a2 67 ♖a1 ♘b4 68 ♔c4 ♖b8 69 ♔c3 ♔g6 70 ♔b2 ♔xg5 71 ♖g1+ ♔f4 72 ♔a1 ♖a8 73 ♖c1 ♔e3 74 ♖c4 ♖a4 75 ♖c1 ♔d2 76 ♖c4 ♔d3 [76 ... ♘c2+ 77 ♖xc2+ ♔xc2◇] 77 ♖c3+ ♔d4 78 ♖c1 ♖a3 79 ♖d1+ ♔c5 80 ♖c1+ ♔b5 81 ♖c7 ♘d5 82 ♖c2 ♘c3 83 ♖b2+ ♔c4 84 ♖b3 **½-½** L/N6123-1847

### 1846-✕HW-2
**Williams, E.-Harrwitz, D.**
London [Staunton]

1 d4 d5 2 c4 dxc4 3 e3 e5 4 ♗xc4 exd4 5 exd4 ♘f6 6 ♘c3 ♗d6 7 ♘f3 0-0 8 0-0 ♗g4 9 ♕d3 ♘c6 10 h3 ♗xf3 11 ♕xf3 ♘xd4 12 ♕xb7 ♖b8 13 ♕xa7 ♕d7 14 ♕a4 c6 15 ♕d1 ♗c7 16 f4 ♖fd8 17 b3 ♕f5 18 ♕d3 ♕h5 19 ♕g3 ♕c5 20 ♗e3 ♘d5 21 ♘e4 ♕xc4! 22 bxc4 ♘e2+ 23 ♔f2 ♘xg3 24 ♘xg3 ♖b2+ 25 ♔f3 ♘xe3 26 ♔xe3 ♗b6+ 27 ♔f3 ♖d3+ 28 ♔g4 ♖xg2 29 ♖f3 h5+ 30 ♔xh5 ♖xf3 **0-1** L/N6123-1847

### 1846-✕HW-3
**Harrwitz, D.=Williams, E.**
London [Staunton]

1 e4 e5 2 f4 exf4 3 ♘f3 g5 4 ♗c4 ♗g7 5 d4 d6 6 c3 h6 7 ♕b3 ♕e7 8 0-0 c6 9 a4 ♗e6 10 d5 ♗g4 11 ♗d2 c5 12 ♘a3 a6 13 ♖ae1 ♗xf3 14 ♖xf3 ♗e5 15 ♖f2 ♘f6 16 h3 0-0 17 ♘c2 ♘bd7 18 ♗d3 ♖ab8

19 g3!? fxg3 20 ♖g2 ♘h5 21 ♘e3 ♘f4 22 ♖xg3 ♘xd3 23 ♘f5 ♕f6 24 ♖xd3 b5 25 axb5 axb5 26 ♕d1 ♔h7 27 ♕g4 b4 28 ♘xh6 ♗h2+ 29 ♔xh2 ♘e5 30 ♕h5 ♕xh6 31 ♕xh6+ ♔xh6 32 ♖g3 f6 33 h4 ♔h5 34 hxg5 fxg5 35 ♖xg5+ ♔h4 36 ♖h1! ♖f1 [36 ... ♘f3+ 37 ♔g2+] 37 ♖xf1 bxc3 38 bxc3 ♖b2 39 ♖g2 ♘g4+ 40 ♔g1 ♔h3 41 ♖f3+ ♔h4 42 ♗e1+ ♔h5 43 ♖xb2 **1-0**

L/N6123-1847

**1846-⚔HW-4̂**
**Williams, E.= Harrwitz, D.**
[Staunton]

1 d4 d5 2 c4 dxc4 3 e3 e5 4 ♗xc4 exd4 5 exd4 ♘f6 6 ♘c3 ♗d6 7 ♘f3 0-0 8 h3 ♗f5 9 0-0 ♘bd7 10 ♗g5 h6 11 ♗h4 g5 12 ♗g3 ♗xg3 13 fxg3 ♗g6 14 ♘e5 ♘xe5 15 dxe5 ♕xd1 16 ♖axd1 ♘h5 17 ♔h2 ♖ad8 18 ♘d5 c6 19 ♘e7+ ♔g7 20 ♘xg6 [◻ 20 ♖xd8 ♖xd8 21 ♘xg6 fxg6 22 ♖f7++] 20 ... ♖xd1 21 ♖xd1 ♔xg6 22 ♖d6+ ♔g7 23 ♖d7 [◻ 23 ♗e2+] 23 ... b5 24 ♗b3 [◻ 24 ♗e2] 24 ... a5 25 e6 a4 26 ♗d1 ♘f6 27 ♖c7 ♘d5 28 ♖xc6 fxe6 29 ♖xe6 ♖f2 30 ♖e5 ♖d2 31 ♗f3 ♘b6 32 ♖xb5 ♘c4 33 b3 axb3 34 axb3 ♘e3 35 ♖e5 ♘f1+ 36 ♔g1 ♘xg3 37 b4 ♖b2 38 b5 ♔f6 39 ♖c5 h5 40 ♖c6+ ♔f5 41 b6 h4 42 b7 ♔f4 43 ♖c4+ ♔e3 44 ♖c3+ ♔f4 45 ♖d3 ♖b1+ 46 ♖d1 ♖b2 47 ♔h2 ♔e3 48 ♖d8 ♖b1 49 ♗d1? ♖xb7 50 ♗f3 ♖b1 51 ♖d1 ♖b2 52 ♔g1 ♖a2 53 ♖e1+ ♔f4 54 ♔h2 ♖b2 **½-½**

L/N6123-1847

**1846-⚔HW-5̂**
**Williams, E.– Harrwitz, D.**
[Staunton]

1 e4 e5 2 ♘f3 ♘c6 3 ♗c4 ♗c5 4 d3 d6 5 ♘c3 ♘f6 6 h3 ♗e6 7 ♗b3 ♕d7 8 ♗e3 ♗b6 9 ♕d2 0-0-0 10 a4 ♗xb3 11 cxb3 d5 12 ♗xb6 axb6 13 ♕e2 dxe4 14 dxe4 ♘d4 15 ♘xd4 exd4 16 ♘b5 ♘xe4 17 0-0 ♖he8 18 ♕d3 c6 19 ♘a3 ♘c5 20 ♕g3 f5 21 ♘c4 ♕c7 22 ♕f3 g6 23 b4 ♘e4 24 ♕d3 ♔b8 25 ♖fc1 h5 26 f3 ♘g3 27 ♖c2 ♖e7 28 b5 ♖de8 29 ♔f2 ♘e2 30 bxc6 ♕g3+ 31 ♔f1 ♘f4 32 c7+ ♔a7 33 c8♘+ ♔b8 34 ♕d2 ♖e2 35 ♕xf4+ ♕xf4 36 ♖xe2 ♖xe2 37 ♔xe2 ♔xc8 38 ♘xb6+ ♔d8 39 ♘c4 ♔e7 40 ♖d1 ♔f6 41 b3 ♔g5 42 ♔f2 ♔h4 43 ♔f1 ♔g3 44 ♔g1 d3 45 ♘d2 ♕e3+ 46 ♔h1 ♕e2 47 ♘f1+ ♔f2 **0-1**

L/N6123-1847

**1846-★AL-1** 26 vi 46
**Anderssen, A.+ Lasa, T. von H. u. von d.**
Breslau

1 e4 d5 2 exd5 ♘f6 3 ♘f3 ♗g4 4 ♗e2 ♘xd5 5 0-0 e6 6 d4 c5 7 ♘e5 ♗xe2 8 ♕xe2 cxd4 9 ♖e1 ♗d6 10 ♕b5+ ♘d7 11 ♘c4 ♗c5 12 ♕xb7 0-0 13 ♕b3 ♕c7 14 ♘ba3 ♖ab8 15 ♕h3 e5 16 ♕g3 f6 17 ♗h6 ♖f7 18 ♖ad1 ♗xa3 19 ♘xa3 ♖xb2 20 ♗c1 ♖b8 21 c4 ♘e7 22 ♘b5 ♕c6 23 ♗a3 ♘f5 24 ♕h3 ♕xc4 25 ♕xf5 ♖xb5 26 ♖c1 ♕d5 27 ♖c8+ ♘f8 28 ♖ec1 ♕b7

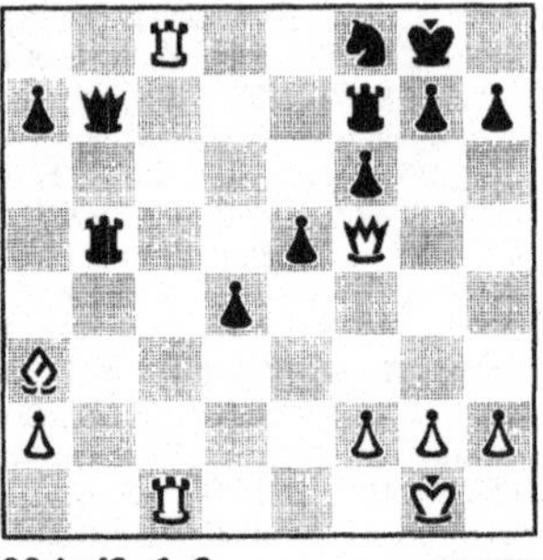

29 ♗xf8 **1-0** L/N3034

**1846-★AL-2** xii 46
**Lasa, T. von H. u. von d. Φ Anderssen, A.**
Breslau

1 e4 e5 2 f4 exf4 3 ♘f3 g5 4 h4 g4 5 ♘e5 h5 6 ♗c4 ♖h7 7 d4 ♕f6 8 ♘c3 ♘e7 9 0-0 ♗h6 10 g3 d6 11 ♘xf7 ♖xf7 12 ♗xf7+ ♕xf7 13 ♗xf4 ♗xf4 14 ♖xf4 ♕g7 15 ♕d3 ♗e6 16 d5 ♗g8 17 ♕b5+ ♘d7 18 ♕xb7 ♕d4+ 19 ♔g2 ♖b8 20 ♕xc7 ♖xb2 21 ♖f2 ♘c5 22 ♖af1 ♘d7 23 ♖e2 ♘e5 24 a4 ♗h7 25 ♖d1 ♕c4 26 ♕xc4 ♘xc4 27 ♘b5 ♘g6 28 ♘xa7 ♖a2 29 ♖b1 ♖xa4 30 ♖b8+ ♔f7 31 ♖b7+ ♔g8 32 ♔f2 ♘ge5 33 ♘c6 ♖a3 34 ♖b8+ ♔g7 35 ♖b7+ ♔h6 36 ♘xe5 dxe5 37 ♖b4 ♘d6 38 ♖b6 ♖f3+ 39 ♔e1 ♖f6 40 c4 ♔g7 41 c5 ♘xe4 42 c6 ♖f7 43 ♖b4 ♘d6 44 ♖xe5 ♗f5 45 ♔e2 ♔f6 46 ♖e3 ♖e7 47 ♖xe7 ♔xe7 48 ♔e3 **1-0** L/N3034

**1846-★AL-3** xii 46
**Lasa, T. von H. u. von d.– Anderssen, A.**
Breslau

1 e4 c5 2 d4 cxd4 3 ♘f3 ♘c6 4 ♗c4 e6 5 ♘xd4 ♗c5 6 ♘f3 ♘ge7 7 ♘c3 0-0 8 a3 ♘g6 9 0-0 f5 10 exf5 ♖xf5 11 ♗d3 ♖h5 12 g4 ♖h3 13 ♔g2 ♖xf3 14 ♔xf3 ♕h4 15 ♔g2 ♘ce5 16 h3 b6 17 ♗xg6 hxg6 18 ♗f4 ♗b7+ 19 f3 ♘xf3 20 ♖xf3

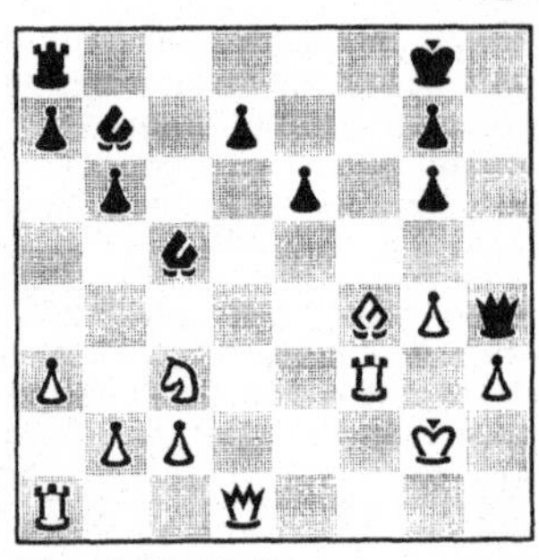

20 ... ♕f2+ **0-1** L/N3034

**1846-★AL-4** xii 46
**Anderssen, A.– Lasa, T. von H. u. von d.**
Breslau

1 e4 e5 2 f4 exf4 3 ♘f3 g5 4 ♗c4 g4 5 0-0 gxf3 6 ♕xf3 ♕f6 7 e5 ♕xe5 8 d3 ♗h6 9 ♗d2 ♘e7 10 ♘c3 c6 11 ♖a1e1 ♕c5+ 12 ♔h1 d5 13 ♕h5 ♕d6 14 ♗xd5 cxd5 15 ♘xd5 ♘bc6 16 ♖xe7+ ♘xe7 17 ♖e1 0-0 18 ♘xe7+ ♔h8 19 ♘d5 ♕g6 20 ♕h4 ♗e6 21 ♗c3+ ♗g7 22 ♘f6 ♖ac8 23 ♘xh7 ♕xh7 24 ♗xg7+ ♔xg7 25 ♕xf4 ♕f5 26 ♕g3+ ♕g4 27 ♕e5+ f6 28 ♕d6 ♖xc2 **0-1**

L/N3034

**1846-★KS-1** vii 46
**Kennedy, H.A.– Staunton, H.**
Brighton [Staunton]

〈♙f7〉 1 e4 ... 2 d4 e6 3 c4 c5 4 d5 d6 5 ♗d3 g6 6 ♗d2 ♗g7 7 ♘c3 e5 8 ♘ge2 ♘h6 9 0-0 0-0 10 f4 exf4 11 ♗xf4 ♘g4 12 ♕d2 ♘e5 13 ♗xe5 ♗xe5 14 ♕h6 ♗g7 15 ♖xf8+ ♕xf8 16 ♕h4? [◻ 16 ♕f4] 16 ... ♗f6 17 ♕f4 ♕e7 18 ♖f1 ♘d7 19 b3 a6 20 ♘d1 ♗g5 21 ♕f2 ♘e5 22 ♗c2 b5! 23 cxb5 axb5 24 ♗b1 ♗d7 25 h3 b4 26 ♘e3 ♗b5 27 ♘g4 ♘xg4 28 hxg4 ♕g7 [△ 29 ... ♕h6] 29 ♕f3 c4 30 bxc4 ♗xc4 31 ♖f2? ♖a3 **0-1**

M954

**1846-★KS-2** vii 46
**Kennedy, H.A.+ Staunton, H.**
Brighton [Staunton]

〈♙f7〉 1 e4 ... 2 d4 ♘c6 3 ♗g5 d5 4 e5 ♗f5 5 ♘c3 ♕d7 6 ♗b5 a6 7 ♗a4 b5 8 ♗b3 e6 9 ♘ce2 ♘a5 10 c3 ♘xb3 11 axb3 c5 12 ♘f3 cxd4 13 ♘fxd4 ♗g6 14 b4 ♘e7 15 0-0 ♘f5 16 ♖a5! ♗e7 17 ♕d2 [17 ♗xe7?] 17 ... 0-0 18 ♗xe7 ♘xe7 19 ♖fa1 ♘c6 20 ♘xc6 ♕xc6 21 ♘d4 ♕b6 22 ♘xb5 ♖f5 23 ♕d4 ♕d8 24 ♘d6 ♖f8 25 ♖xa6 ♖b8 26 b5 ♕g5 27 b6 ♗h5 28 ♕e3 ♕xe3 29 fxe3 ♗e2 30 ♖a7 ♖xb6 31 ♖b7 ♖a6 32 ♖e1 ♖a2 33 h3 [33 ♖xe2?? ♖a1++] 33 ... ♗d3 34 e4 dxe4 35 ♘xe4 h5? 36

♘g5 ♗c4 37 ♖b4! ♖c8 38 ♖d1 [△ 39 ♖xc4+−] 38 … ♖aa8 39 b3 ♗e2 40 ♖e1 ♖a2 41 c4 ♖d8 42 ♖b7 [△ 43 ♖xg7+, 44 ♘xe6+] 42 … g6 43 ♘xe6 ♖dd2 44 ♖g7+ ♔h8 45 ♖xg6 ♗g4 46 ♘f4 [46 hxg4?=] 46 … ♗d1 47 e6 ♗c2 48 ♖g5 ♖d8 49 e7 ♖e8 50 ♘xh5 **1-0** M954

### 1846-★KS-3 vii 46
**Kennedy, H.A.= Staunton, H.**
Brighton [Staunton]

⟨♙f7⟩ 1 e4 … 2 d4 ♘c6 3 ♘f3 e6 4 c4 d5 5 e5 ♗b4+ 6 ♘c3 ♘ge7 7 ♗g5 0-0 8 c5? ♕e8 9 ♗e3 ♕h5 10 ♗d3 b6 11 cxb6 axb6 12 0-0 ♗xc3! 13 bxc3 ♘f5 14 h3 h6 15 a4 [15 g4? ♘xe3∓] 15 … ♗d7 16 ♕e2 ♘xe3 17 fxe3 ♘e7 18 ♗c2 ♘c6? 19 ♕d3 ♕f5 20 ♕xf5 exf5 21 ♘h4 ♘e7 22 ♗d3 g5 23 ♘f3 ♗xa4 24 ♘d2 b5 [25 c4] 25 ♖f2 c5 26 ♖af1 [26 dxc5?] 26 … cxd4 27 cxd4 b4 28 ♗xf5 ♘xf5 29 ♖xf5 ♖xf5 30 ♖xf5 ♖f8 31 ♖xf8+ ♔xf8 32 e4! dxe4 33 ♘xe4 ♗c2 34 ♘d2 ♗d3 [35 ♘c4] 35 ♔f2 ♔e7 36 d5 ♗c2 37 ♘c4 b3 38 ♔e3 h5 39 g3 h4 40 gxh4 gxh4 41 ♔f4 ♗d3 42 ♘b2 ♗f1 43 ♔g4 ♗g2 44 d6+ ♔e6 45 ♔xh4 ♗c6 [45 … ♔xe5??+−] 46 ♘d3 b2 47 ♘xb2 ♔xe5 48 ♘c4+ ♔e6 49 ♔g5 ♗b5 50 ♘a3 ♗d3 **½-½** M954

**197** Harrwitz, D. L/N6395. CPL

### 1846̂-★HS-1
**Harrwitz, D.– Staunton, H.**
London [Staunton]

⟨♙f7⟩ 1 e4 ♘c6 2 d4 e5 3 d5 ♘ce7 4 ♗g5 d6 5 ♗d3 ♕d7 6 ♘c3 ♘g6 7 ♕h5 ♗e7 8 ♘f3 ♕g4 9 ♗b5+ ♔f7 10 ♕xg4 ♗xg4 11 ♗xe7 ♗xf3 12 gxf3 ♔xe7 [12 … ♘1xe7 13 ♗d7] 13 ♘e2 ♖f8 14 ♘g1 ♘h4 15 ♗e2 ♘g2+ 16 ♔f1 ♘h4 17 c4 h6 18 b4 b6 19 ♖c1 ♘f6 20 c5 bxc5 21 bxc5 ♘d7 22 cxd6+ cxd6 23 ♖c7 ♖c8 24 ♖c6 ♖xc6 [◻ 24 … ♘b8] 25 dxc6 ♘b8−+ [◻ 25 … ♖c8−+] 26 c7 ♘d7 27 ♗a6 ♘b6 28 ♔e2 ♔d7 29 f4 ♔xc7 30 fxe5 dxe5 31 ♘f3 ♘xf3 32 ♔xf3 ♖f8+ 33 ♔e3 ♘d7 34 h4 ♖f6 35 ♗c4 ♖c6 36 ♗d5 ♖c3+ 37 ♔d2 ♖f3 38 ♔e2 ♖f4 39 ♖c1+ ♔d8 40 h5 ♘f6 41 f3 ♘xh5 42 ♖c6 ♖f6 43 ♖xf6 ♘xf6 **0-1** M954-1846

### 1846̂-★HS-2
**Saint-Amant, P.C.F.de– Horwitz, B.**
London [Staunton]

1 d4 f5 2 c4 ♘f6 3 ♘c3 e6 4 ♘f3 b6 5 e3 ♗b7 6 ♗e2 ♘e4 7 0-0 ♗e7 8 ♘d2 ♘xc3 9 bxc3 0-0 10 f4 c5 11 ♗f3 ♘c6 12 ♘b3 [◻ 12 d5 ♘ 13 e4] 12 … ♕c7 13 ♗b2? a5 14 a4 ♖f6 15 ♕c2 ♖h6 16 d5 ♘d8 17 ♖ad1 g5 18 g3 gxf4 19 exf4 ♖b8 20 ♖d2 ♘f7 21 ♖fd1 [△ 22 dxe6 dxe6 23 ♖d7] 21 … ♖d8 22 ♗a3 ♘d6 23 ♕d3?−+ ♗a6 24 ♕b1 ♘xc4 25 ♖a2 ♘xa3 26 ♖xa3 c4 27 ♘d4 ♗xa3 28 dxe6 dxe6 29 ♘c6 ♖xd1+ 30 ♕xd1 ♗b7 **0-1** L/N6126-1846; M954

### 1846̂-★HS-3
**Horwitz, B.–Saint-Amant, P.C.F. de**
London [Staunton]

1 e4 c5 2 ♗c4 e6 3 f4 d5 4 exd5 exd5 5 ♗b5+ ♗d7 6 ♗xd7+ ♕xd7 7 ♘f3 ♘c6 8 0-0 f6?! 9 c4 d4 10 ♘a3 a6 11 ♘c2 ♗d6 12 d3 ♘ge7 13 b4? 0-0? [13 … cxb4; 13 … b5] 14 bxc5 ♗xc5 15 ♖b1 ♖fe8 16 ♗d2 ♘f5 17 ♔h1 ♖e7 18 ♘g1 ♖ae8 19 ♕f3 ♘e3 20 ♗xe3 dxe3 21 ♕d5+? ♕xd5 22 cxd5 ♘d4 23 ♘xd4 ♗xd4 24 ♘e2 ♗a7 25 d6 [◻ 25 g3] 25 … ♖d7 26 ♖fc1 b5 27 ♖c6 ♖e6 28 ♖xa6 ♖exd6 29 ♖xd6 ♖xd6 30 ♖b3 ♖c6 31 ♖c3 ♖a6 32 a3

32 … b4! 33 axb4 ♖a2−+ 34 g3 [34 ♘g1 ♖a1 △ 35 … e2] 34 … ♖xe2 35 ♖c8+ ♔f7 36 ♖c7+ ♔e6 37 ♖xa7 ♖d2 38 ♔g1 ♖d1+ 39 ♔g2 e2 …? **0-1** L/N6126-1846 M954

### 1846̂-★KS-1
**Kennedy, H.A.– Staunton, H.**
[Staunton]

⟨♙f7⟩ 1 e4 … 2 d4 e6 3 ♗d3 c5 4 dxc5 ♕a5+ 5 ♘c3 ♕xc5 6 ♗e3 ♕a5 7 ♘ge2 ♘c6 8 0-0 ♘f6 9 ♘g3 ♗e7 10 a3 0-0 11 b4 ♕d8 12 f4 d6 13 b5 ♘b8 14 e5 ♘e8 15 ♕h5 g6 16 ♗xg6 hxg6 17 ♕xg6+ ♘g7 18 ♘h5 ♖f7 19 exd6 ♗f6 [19 … ♗xd6??+−] 20 ♘e4! ♘d7 [20 … ♗xa1?+−] 21 ♘g5 ♗xg5 22 fxg5 ♘e5

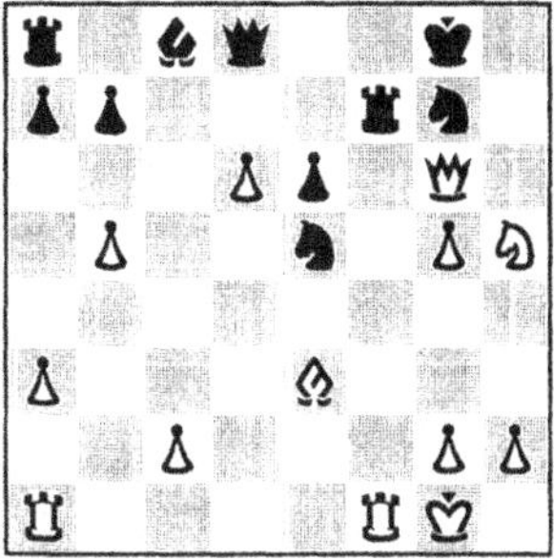

23 ♕e4? [◻ 23 ♖xf7! ♘xg6! 24 ♖xg7+ ♔h8! 25 ♖xg6 e5! 26 ♖h6+ ♔g8 27 ♘f6+ ♔g7 28 ♖h7+ ♔g6 29 h4 ♗g4 30 ♖f1+−] 23 … ♘xh5 24 ♕xe5 ♕d7 25 ♗d4 [25 g6?] 25 … ♘g7 26 ♖f6 ♖xf6 27 gxf6 ♘f5 28 ♖f1 ♕f7 29 ♗c5 ♗d7 30 g4 ♕g6 31 f7+ ♔xf7 32 ♔h1 ♗xb5 33 ♖xf5+ [33 gxf5??−+] 33 … exf5 34 ♕e7+ ♔g8 35 ♕xb7 ♕e8 36 ♕d5+ ♔h7 37 ♕xf5+ ♕g6 38 ♕d5 ♖d8 39 ♕b7+ ♗d7 **0-1** L/N6123-1846

### 1847-★HH-1 12 v 47
**Saint-Amant, P.C.F.de & Horwitz, B.+Staunton, H. & Harrwitz, D.**
Hull

1 e4 e5 2 ♘f3 ♘c6 3 d4 exd4 4 ♗c4 ♗c5 5 0-0 d6 6 c3 dxc3 7 ♘xc3 ♘f6 8 ♗g5 ♗e6 9 ♘d5 ♗xd5 10 exd5 ♘e7 11 ♖e1 0-0 12 ♗xf6 gxf6 13 ♘h4 ♘g6 14 ♕h5 ♔h8 15 ♗d3 ♖g8 16 ♖e4 f5 17 ♘xf5 ♕f6 18 ♖ae1 ♕xb2 19 ♔h1 ♕xf2 20 ♘h6 ♖g7 21 ♖4e2 ♕d4 22 ♘xf7+ ♔g8 23 ♘h6+ ♔h8 24 ♗xg6 **1-0** L/N6047

### 1847̂-★HK-1
**Harrwitz, D.– Kieseritsky, L.**
[Staunton]

1 e4 e5 2 f4 exf4 3 ♗c4 ♕h4+ 4 ♔f1 b5 5 ♗xb5 ♗b7 6 ♘c3 ♗b4 7 d3 ♗xc3 8 bxc3 ♘f6 9 ♘f3 ♕h5 10 ♖b1 g5 11 ♗xd7+ ♘bxd7 12 ♖xb7 0-0 13 ♖b5 c5! 14 d4 ♘xe4 15 dxc5 ♘xc3 16 ♕xd7 ♖ad8 17 ♕f5 ♖d1+ 18 ♔f2 ♖xh1 19 ♗b2 ♘d1+ 20 ♔e2 ♘xb2 21 ♖xb2 ♖xh2 22 ♔f2 g4! 23 ♕xh5 ♖xh5

24 ♘d4 ♖xc5 25 ♖b4 ♖d8 26 ♘e2 ♖xc2 27 ♔f1 ♖d1+ 28 ♔f2 ♖dd2 29 ♖e4 f5 30 ♖e5 h5 31 ♔f1 ♖xe2 32 ♖xe2 ♖xe2 33 ♔xe2 ♔g7 **0-1**

L/N6123-1847

### 1847?-★HK-2

**Harrwitz, D.–Kieseritsky, L.**

[Staunton]

1 e4 e5 2 d4 exd4 3 ♗c4 ♘c6 4 ♘f3 ♗b4+ 5 c3 dxc3 6 bxc3 ♗a5 7 ♘g5 ♘e5 [□ 7 ... ♘h6] 8 ♘xf7 ♘xf7 9 ♗xf7+ ♔xf7 10 ♕h5+ [□ 10 ♕d5+] 10 ... g6 11 ♕xa5 ♘f6 12 0-0 ♖e8 13 e5 b6 14 ♕b5 c6 15 ♕e2 a5! 16 ♗g5 ♗a6 17 c4 d6 18 f4 dxe5 19 fxe5 ♕d4+ 20 ♔h1 ♗xc4

21 ♖xf6+ ♔g8 22 ♕c2 [△ 22 ... ♕xa1 23 ♕xc4+] 22 ... ♖xe5 [△ 23 ... ♖e1+] 23 ♘c3 ♖xg5 24 ♖f3 ♖e8 25 ♖d1 ♗d5 26 h3 ♕h4 27 ♘xd5 cxd5 28 ♖df1 ♖ge5 29 ♕c3 ♕c4 30 ♕d2 ♖e3 31 ♖f7 ♕e4 [△ 31 ... ♖xh3+] 32 ♔h2 ♖e2 33 ♕g5 ♕e5+ 34 ♕xe5 ♖2xe5 35 ♖d7 ♖8e7 36 ♖d8+ ♔g7 37 ♖d1 ♖e2 38 ♖1xd5 ♖xa2 39 ♖b5 ♖ee2 40 ♖g5 a4 41 ♖b8 ♖ab2 42 ♖b7+ ♔f6 43 h4 a3 44 ♖xh7 a2 45 ♖h6 ♖xg2+ 46 ♖xg2 ♖xg2+ 47 ♔xg2 a1♕ **0-1**

L/N6123-1847

### 1847?-★MS-1

**Saint-Amant, P.C.F.de+ Medley, G.W.**

[Staunton]

⟨♘b1⟩ 1 e4 e5 2 ♗c4 ♘f6 3 ♘f3 ♘xe4 4 d3 ♘f6 5 ♘xe5 d5 6 ♗b3 ♗d6 7 d4 ♘c6 8 f4 0-0 9 0-0 ♗f5 10 c3 ♘e7 11 h3 h6 12 ♕e2 c5 13 g4 ♗e4 14 g5 ♘h7 15 dxc5 ♗xc5+ 16 ♔h2 f6? 17 ♕xe4 fxe5 18 ♕xe5 hxg5 19 ♗d2 gxf4 [19 ... ♖f6] 20 ♖g1! ♗xg1+ 21 ♖xg1 ♖f7 22 ♗xf4 ♘c6 23 ♕xd5 ♕xd5 24 ♗xd5 ♔f8 25 ♗d6+ ♔e8 26 ♖e1+ ♔d7 27 ♗xf7 ♔xd6 28 ♖g1 ♘e5 29 ♖xg7 ♘f6 30 ♗b3 b6 31 ♗d1 a5 32 a4 ♖h8 33 ♗e2 ♖h4 34 ♖b7 ♔c6 35 ♖b8 ♖e4 36 ♗f1 ♖e1 37 ♗g2+ ♔c5 38 b4+ axb4 39 cxb4+ ♔c4 40 ♖xb6 ♘fd7 41 ♖b7 ♖b1 42 ♖c7+ ♔b3 [42 ... ♔xb4?? 43 ♖b7+] 43 a5 ♔a4 44 a6 ♘b6 45 a7 ♖b2 46 ♖b7 ♘ec4 47 ♖b8 ♖xb4 48 ♗d5 ♖b2+ 49 ♔g3 ♖b3+ 50 ♔h4 ♖a3 51 ♗xc4 ♔b4

52 ♗a6!! ...? **1-0**

M954-1847

### 1847?-★NS-1

**Newham, S.=Saint-Amant, P.C.F. de**

Yorkshire

1 e4 e5 2 ♘f3 f5 3 ♘xe5 ♕f6 4 d4 d6 5 ♘c4 fxe4 6 ♘c3 c6 7 d5 ♗f5 8 ♘e3 ♘h6 9 g4 ♗g6 10 ♗g2 ♗e7 11 dxc6 0-0 12 0-0 bxc6 13 ♘ed5 cxd5 14 ♕xd5+ ♔h8 15 ♗xh6 ♘d7 16 ♗e3 ♕h4 17 ♘xe4 ♕xg4 18 h3 ♕h4 19 ♘g3 ♖ac8 20 c3 ♘e5 21 ♖ad1 ♗e8 22 ♖d4 ♗c6 23 ♕e6 ♗d7 24 ♕d5 ♗c6 **½-½**

M954-1842

### 1847?-★S?-1

**Staunton, H.+?**

London

⟨♖a1⟩ 1 e4 c5 2 ♘f3 ♘c6 3 c3 e5 4 ♗c4 ♘f6 5 ♘g5 d5 6 exd5 ♘xd5 7 ♘xf7 ♔xf7 8 ♕f3+ ♔e6 9 d4 cxd4 10 0-0 ♗e7 11 ♕e4 ♘a5 12 ♗d3 ♘f6 13 ♕e2 ♘c6 14 ♗c4+ ♔d6 15 f4 e4 16 cxd4 ♗g4 17 ♕e3 ♕b6 18 ♘c3 a6 19 h4 ♗d7 20 ♕g3 ♘h5 **1-0**

M954-1847

## ANDERSSEN⚔HARRWITZ

Breslau

**[1848-⚔AH]**

| | | | | | | | | | | | |
|---|---|---|---|---|---|---|---|---|---|---|---|
| A. Anderssen | 1 | 0 | 0 | 1 | 0 | 1 | 1 | 0 | 0 | 1 | 5 |
| D. Harrwitz | 0 | 1 | 1 | 0 | 1 | 0 | 0 | 1 | 1 | 0 | 5 |

### 1848-⚔AH-1

**Anderssen, A.+Harrwitz, D.**

[Staunton]

1 e4 e5 2 ♘f3 ♘c6 3 d4 exd4 4 ♗c4 ♗c5 5 c3 ♘f6 6 e5 d5 7 ♗b5 ♘e4 8 cxd4 ♗b4+ 9 ♗d2 ♗xd2+ 10 ♘bxd2 0-0 11 ♗xc6 bxc6 12 0-0 f5 13 ♖c1 ♕e8 14 ♕c2 ♖b8 15 ♘b3 ♖b6 16 ♘fd2 ♕h5 17 f3 ♘xd2 18 ♕xd2 f4! 19 ♘c5 ♕g6 [□ 19 ... g5] 20 ♖fe1 ♗e6 21 ♖c3 ♕e8 22 ♖a3 ♗f5 23 b3 [23 ♖xa7 ♕b8!] 23 ... a6 24 ♖xa6 ♖xa6 25 ♘xa6 ♕c8 26 ♘c5 ♗e6? 27 a4 g6 28 a5 ♖e8 29 a6 ♕b8 30 ♖a1 ♕a7 31 ♕b4 ♔f7 32 ♕b7 ♕b6 33 a7 ♕xb7 34 ♘xb7 ♖a8 35 ♘d8+ ♔e7 36 ♘xe6 ♔xe6 37 b4 **1-0**

M954

### 1848-⚔AH-2

1 ii 48

**Harrwitz, D.+Anderssen, A.**

1 e4 e5 2 f4 exf4 3 ♗c4 ♕h4+ 4 ♔f1 ♗c5 5 d4 ♗b6 6 ♘f3 ♕e7 7 ♘c3 ♘f6 8 e5 ♘h5 9 ♘d5 ♕d8 10 g4 fxg3 11 ♗g5 f6 12 exf6 gxf6 13 ♘e5 0-0 14 ♕xh5 fxg5+ 15 ♘f6+ ♔g7 16 ♕xh7+ ♔xf6 17 ♘g4# **1-0**

L/N6047

### 1848-⚔AH-3

1 ii 48

**Anderssen, A.–Harrwitz, D.**

[Staunton]

1 e4 e6 2 d4 d5 3 exd5 exd5 4 c4 ♘f6 5 ♗e2 ♘c6 6 ♘f3 ♗e7 7 0-0 0-0 8 h3 b6 9 ♘c3 ♗e6 10 b3 ♗b4 11 ♗b2 ♗xc3 12 ♗xc3 ♘e4 13 ♖c1 ♖c8 14 ♗a1 ♘e7 15 cxd5? ♗xd5 16 ♗a6 ♖b8 17 ♖e1 ♘g6 18 ♘d2? ♘xd2 19 ♕xd2 b5 20 a4 bxa4? [20 ... ♘h4∓] 21 bxa4 ♘h4 22 ♗f1 ♖b6 23 ♖c3 ♖g6 24 ♖g3 ♖xg3 25 fxg3 ♘f5 26 ♗d3 ♘xg3 27 ♕a5 [27 ♗xh7+ ♔xh7 28 ♕d3+ ♘e4!→] 27 ... c6 28 ♕xa7? ♕g5 29 ♕e7 ♕d2 30 ♗xh7+ ♔h8 [30 ... ♔xh7 31 ♕h4+] 31 ♖e4 ♗xe4 32 ♗xe4 ♕e1+ 33 ♔h2 ♘f1+ 34 ♔g1 ♖g8 35 ♕g5 ♕xe4 36 ♕h5+ ♕h7 37 ♕xh7+ ♔xh7 38 ♔xf1 ♖a8 39 ♗c3 ♖xa4 40 ♔e2 ♔g6 41 g3 ♔f5 42 ♔d3 g6 43 ♗d2 ♖a3+ 44 ♗c3 g5 45 ♔c4 ♔e4 46 ♔b4 ♖a8 47 ♔c5 ♔f3 48 h4 gxh4 49 gxh4 ♔g4 50 ♗e1 ♖e8 51 ♗a5 ♖e6 52 ♗c7 f5 53 ♗d6 f4 54 ♔xc6 f3 55 d5 ♖xd6+ **0-1**

L/N6123

### 1848-⚔AH-4

ii 48

**Harrwitz, D.–Anderssen, A.**

[Schachzeitung]

1 e4 e5 2 f4 exf4 3 ♗c4 ♕h4+ 4 ♔f1 g5 5 ♘c3 ♗g7 6 d4 ♘e7 7 ♘f3 ♕h5 8 e5 g4 9 ♘g1 f3 10 gxf3 gxf3 11 ♕xf3 ♕xf3+ 12 ♘xf3 b6 13 ♖g1 ♗f8 14 ♘g5 ♗a6! 15 ♗xa6 ♘xa6 16 ♘ce4 ♘g8 17 ♘xh7± ♖xh7 18 ♖xg8 0-0-0 19 ♗g5 ♗e7 20 ♖xd8+ ♗xd8 21 ♗xd8 ♔xd8 22 ♔g2 ♖h4 23 ♖e1 ♘b4 24 c3 ♘d3 [24 ... ♘xa2? 24 ♔g3 △ 26 ♖a1±] 25 ♖e2 ♔e7 26 ♔g3 ♖h8 27 h4 [□ 27 ♖d2 △ b3] 27 ... c5 28 ♖d2 c4 29 b3 ♖g8+ 30 ♘g5 b5 31 ♖d1 d6 32 exd6+ ♔xd6 33 ♖f1 b4 34 ♔f3 ♖xg5 35 hxg5 bxc3 36 ♔e3 c2 37 ♔d2 c1♕+ 38 ♖xc1 ♘xc1 39 ♔xc1 cxb3 40 a4 [40 axb3 ♔d5 41 ♔b2 ♔xd4 42 ♔a3=] 40 ... a5 41 ♔b2 ♔d5 42 ♔c3 b2 43 ♔xb2 ♔xd4

44 ♔b3 ♔d3 45 ♔b2 ♔c4 46 ♔c2 ♔b4 47 ♔b2 [47 ♔d3∓] 47 ... ♔xa4 48 ♔c3 ♔b5 49 ♔b3 ♔c5 50 ♔a4 ♔d5 **0-1** L/N6047

### 1848-⚔AH-5 ii 48

**Anderssen, A.– Harrwitz, D.**

[Staunton]

1 d4 d5 2 c4 e6 3 e3 c5 4 ♘c3 ♘f6 5 ♘f3 ♘c6 6 a3 a6 7 b3 b6 8 ♗b2 cxd4 9 exd4 ♗d6 10 ♗d3 ♘e7 11 ♖c1 ♗b7 12 ♘e2 dxc4 13 bxc4 ♗xf3 14 gxf3 0-0 15 h4 ♘h5 16 ♕d2 ♘g6 17 ♔f1 f5 18 ♕e3 ♘gf4 19 ♗b1 ♕e7 20 c5 bxc5 21 dxc5 ♗c7 22 ♘d4 ♔h8

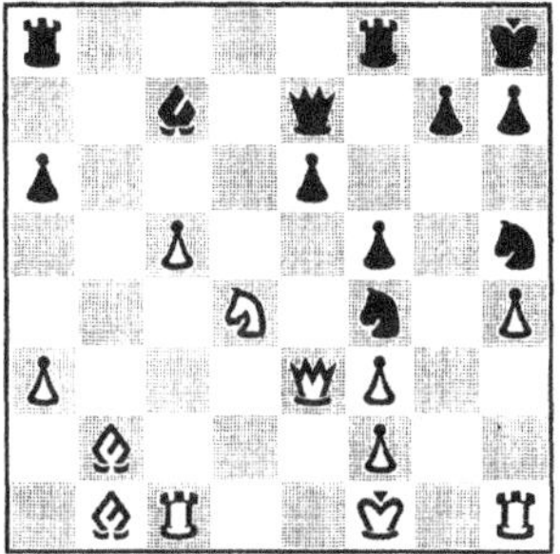

23 ♘xf5? [□ 23 ♗xf5] 23 ... ♖xf5 24 ♗xf5 ♕d7 [△ 25 ... ♕b5∓] 25 ♗xe6 [25 c6 ♕d5; 25 ♗b1 ♕b5+ 26 ♔g1 ♘e2+ 27 ♔g2 ♘hf4+ 28 ♔f1 ♘xc1+→] 25 ... ♕xe6 26 ♕xe6 ♘xe6 27 ♖g1 ♖b8 28 ♖c2 ♘hf4 29 ♖d2 ♗a5 30 ♖c2 h5 31 ♗c1 ♖b1 32 ♖g5 ♘xg5 33 hxg5 ♘d3 34 ♔e2 ♖xc1 **0-1** L/N6123

### 1848-⚔AH-6 ii 48

**Harrwitz, D.– Anderssen, A.**

[Schachzeitung]

1 e4 e5 2 f4 exf4 3 ♗c4 ♕h4+ 4 ♔f1 g5 5 d4 ♗g7 6 ♘c3 ♘e7 7 ♘f3 ♕h5 8 e5 f6 9 ♘e4 ♖f8 10 ♔g1 g4 11 exf6 ♗xf6 12 ♘xf6+ ♖xf6 13 ♘e5 d5 14 ♗e2 f3 15 gxf3 gxf3 16 ♗xf3 ♕h4∓ 17 ♗e3 ♘bc6 18 ♗f2 ♕f4 19 ♗h5+ ♔f8 20 ♘d3 ♕g5+ 21 ♗g3 ♘xd4 22 ♘f2 ♘ef5 23 ♕g4 ♕e3 24 ♗f4 ♘e2+∓ 25 ♕xe2 ♕xf4 26 ♖e1 ♗e6 27 ♕g4 ♕d6 28 ♕g5 ♗f7 29 ♗xf7 ♖xf7 30 ♔f1 ♕a6+ 31 ♘d3 ♕c4 32 ♖g1 ♘h4+ 33 ♔e2 ♕xc2+ 34 ♔e3 ♖f3+ 35 ♔d4 c5+ 36 ♔e5 ♖e8+ **0-1** L/N6047

### 1848-⚔AH-7 ii 48

**Anderssen, A.+ Harrwitz, D.**

[Schachzeitung]

1 e4 c5 2 d4 cxd4 3 ♘f3 e5 4 ♗c4 ♘c6 [4 ... ♕c7] 5 ♘g5 ♘h6 6 f4 d6 7 0-0 ♗g4 8 ♗xf7+ ♔e7 9 ♕e1 ♘xf7 10 fxe5 ♘fxe5∓ 11 c3 d3 12 h3 ♗e6 13 ♗e3 ♔d7 14 ♘d2 ♗e7 15 ♘xe6 ♔xe6 16 ♕d1 ♔d7 17 ♗d4 ♗f6 18 b4 ♘xd4 19 cxd4 ♘c6 20 ♕g4+ ♔c7 21 ♖ac1 ♗xd4+ 22 ♔h1 ♔b8 23 ♘b3 ♗f6 24 ♖xc6 bxc6 25 e5 ♗xe5? [25 ... dxe5! 26 ♘a5 ♕d5 27 ♖c1 ♖c8 28 ♖c5 ♕d6 29 ♕e4 d2→] 26 ♘a5 ♕e8 27 ♕c4 c5 28 ♕d5 **1-0** L/N6047

### 1848-⚔AH-8 ii 48

**Harrwitz, D.+ Anderssen, A.**

[Schachzeitung]

1 e4 e5 2 ♘f3 ♘c6 3 c3 d5 4 ♗b5 dxe4 5 ♘xe5 [□ 5 ♗xc6+ bxc6 6 ♘xe5 ♕g5 7 ♕a4±] 5 ... ♕d5 6 ♕a4 ♘ge7 7 f4 exf3 8 ♘xf3 ♗e6 9 0-0 0-0-0 10 d4 ♕h5 11 c4 ♗g4 12 d5 ♘f5 13 ♗f4 [13 dxc6 ♗c5+∓] 13 ... ♗c5+ 14 ♔h1 ♘ce7 15 b4 ♗d4 16 ♘xd4 ♘xd4 17 ♘c3 ♔b8 18 ♗e3 ♘xb5 19 ♘xb5 a6

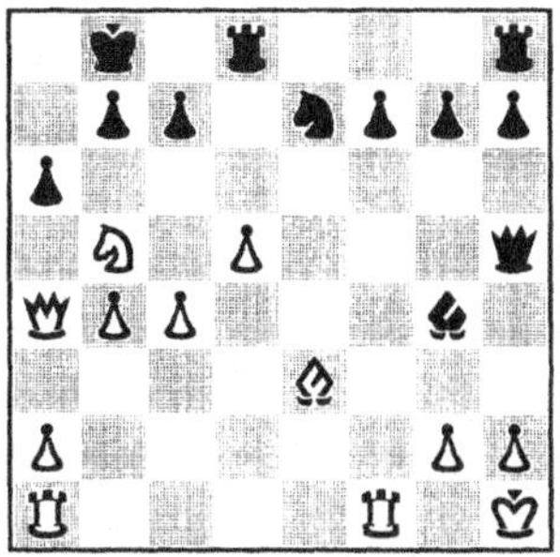

20 ♘xc7! ♔xc7 21 d6+ ♔xd6 22 ♗f4+ ♔e6 23 ♖ae1+ ♗e2 24 ♖f2 ♘f5 25 ♖exe2+ ♔f6 26 ♗e5+ ♔g6 27 g4 ♕xg4 28 ♖g2 h5 29 ♖xg4+ hxg4 30 ♕c2 ♖h3 31 ♕e4 ♔g5 32 ♕f4+ **1-0** L/N6047

### 1848-⚔AH-9 ii 48

**Anderssen, A.– Harrwitz, D.**

[Staunton]

1 e4 c5 2 d4 cxd4 3 ♘f3 e5 4 ♗c4 ♕c7 5 ♗b3 ♗b4+ 6 c3 dxc3 7 0-0 ♘f6 8 ♗xf7+ ♔xf7 9 ♕b3+ d5 10 ♕xb4 dxe4 11 ♘g5+ ♔g6 12 ♘xc3 ♘c6 13 ♕c4 ♗f5 14 f4 h6 15 ♘gxe4 ♘xe4 16 ♘xe4 b5! 17 ♕e2 ♘d4 18 ♕d3 ♕c6 19 ♖e1 [19 ♕g3?] 19 ... ♘c2 20 ♗d2 ♖hd8 21 ♕f3 ♗xe4 22 ♖xe4 ♘xa1 23 fxe5 ♔h7 24 ♗c3 ♕b6+ 25 ♔h1 ♖f8 26 ♕d3 ♖ad8 27 ♕b1 [27 ♖d4+ ♕g6→] 27 ... ♕g6 28 h3 ♖f2 29 ♖e1 ♘c2 30 ♖g1 ♖d3 31 ♔h2 ♕g3+ 32 ♔h1 ♕xh3+ 33 gxh3 ♖xh3# **0-1** L/N6123

### 1848-⚔AH-10 ii 48

**Harrwitz, D.– Anderssen, A.**

[Schachzeitung]

1 e4 e5 2 f4 exf4 3 ♗c4 ♕h4+ 4 ♔f1 g5 5 ♘c3 ♗g7 6 ♘f3 ♕h5 7 ♘d5 ♔d8 8 d4 c6 9 ♘c3 d6 10 h4 h6 11 ♔g1 g4 12 ♘e1 f3 13 ♗e3 f5 14 gxf3 gxf3 15 ♔f2 ♘f6 16 ♕xf3 ♕xf3+ 17 ♔xf3 fxe4+ 18 ♔e2 [18 ♘xe4? d5±] 18 ... d5 19 ♗b3 ♘g4 20 ♘g2 ♘xe3 21 ♔xe3 ♗g4 22 ♖af1 h5 23 ♘f4 ♗h6 24 ♘ce2 ♖f8 25 ♖h2 ♘a6 26 c4 ♘c7 **0-1** L/N6047

### 1848-★MM-1

**Morphy, P.C.+ Morphy, A.**

New Orleans

1 e4 e5 2 f4 exf4 3 ♗c4 ♕h4+ 4 ♔f1 ♗c5 5 d4 ♗b6 6 ♘f3 ♕e7 7 ♘c3 ♘f6 8 ♕d3 c6 9 ♗xf4 d5 10 exd5 0-0 11 d6 ♕d8 12 ♖e1 ♖e8 13 ♘g5 ♖xe1+ 14 ♔xe1 ♕e8+ 15 ♔d2 ♗e6 16 ♖e1 ♘bd7 17 ♘xe6 fxe6 18 ♖xe6 **1-0** +13

### 1848-★MM-2

**Morphy, P.C.+ Morphy, A.**

New Orleans

1 e4 e5 2 ♗c4 f5 3 exf5 ♘f6 4 ♘c3 d5 5 ♘xd5 ♗c5 6 ♘xf6+ ♕xf6 7 d3 ♗xf5 8 ♘f3 ♗g4 9 ♗d5 c6 10 ♗e4 ♘d7 11 0-0 h6 12 c3 0-0-0 13 b4 ♗b6 14 a4 a6 15 ♕b3 ♗xf3 16 ♗xf3 g5 17 ♗e3 g4 18 ♗xg4 ♗c7 19 ♗f3 ♖hg8 20 ♗e4 ♖g4 21 f3 ♖g7 22 b5 axb5 23 axb5 ♘b6 24 bxc6 ♖dg8 25 ♖f2 ♕d8 26 ♖a8+ ♗b8 27 ♗xb6 ♖xg2+ 28 ♖xg2 ♖xg2+ 29 ♔xg2 ♕g5+ 30 ♔h1 ♕c1+ 31 ♗g1 **1-0** +13

### 1848-★M?-1

**Morphy, P.C.+?**

New Orleans

1 e4 e5 2 h3 d5 3 exd5 ♗c5 4 ♗c4 c6 5 ♘c3 ♘f6 6 d3 a5 7 ♗g5 ♘bd7 8 dxc6 bxc6 9 ♘f3 0-0 10 0-0 h6 11 ♗h4 ♕c7 12 d4 exd4 13 ♘xd4 ♗d6 14 ♘f5 ♗h2+ 15 ♔h1 ♘e5 16 ♗b3 ♗a6 17 ♖e1 ♘g6 18 ♗xf6 gxf6 19 ♕h5 **1-0** M1285-1857

### 1848̂-★AK-1

**Angas, S. & Staunton, H.+ Kennedy, H.A. & Kenny, C.**

[Staunton]

1 e4 e5 2 ♘f3 ♘c6 3 d4 exd4 4 ♘xd4 ♘xd4 5 ♕xd4 ♘e7 6 ♗c4 ♘c6 7 ♕e3 ♗b4+ 8 ♗d2 0-0 9 ♘c3 d6 10 ♘e2 ♗xd2+ 11 ♕xd2 ♗e6 12 ♗b3 ♕f6 13 c3 ♕g6 14 ♘g3 ♗xb3 15 axb3 ♖ae8 16 0-0± h5 [△ 16 ... h4] 17 ♕f4 a6 18 ♕h4 ♕g4! 19 ♕xg4 hxg4 20 f4 gxf3 21 gxf3! g6 22 ♔h1 ♖e7 23 ♖g1 ♔h7 24 f4 ♘d8 25 ♖af1 [□ 25 f5] 25 ... f6 26 ♖f3 [△ 27 ♘f5+-] 26 ... ♘f7 27 h4 ♖g8 28 c4 g5 29 fxg5 fxg5 30 ♘h5 ♔g6 31 ♘f4+ ♔h6 [□ 31 ... ♔h7] 32 ♘d5± ♖xe4 33 ♖xf7 ♖xh4+ 34 ♔g2 ♖g4+ 35 ♔f2 ♖xg1 36 ♔xg1 c6 37 ♘e7 ♖e8 38 ♔f2 ♔h5 39 ♔g3 g4 40 ♔f4 [△ 41 ♖h7#] 40 ... ♔h6 41 ♔xg4 b5 42 ♔f5 bxc4 43

bxc4 ♖b8 44 ♔f6 ♔h5 [44 ... ♖xb2 45 ♘f5+ ♔h5 46 ♖g7+-] 45 ♖g7 d5 46 ♘xc6 ♖xb2 47 cxd5 **1-0**

L/N6123-1848

## 1848-★FS-1
**Forth, C.+Staunton, H.**

[Staunton]

⟨♙f7⟩ 1 e4 ... 2 d4 e6 3 ♗d3 c5 4 d5 d6 5 c4 exd5 6 exd5 ♘f6 7 ♘c3 ♗e7 8 ♘f3 0-0 9 0-0 ♗g4 10 h3 ♗h5 11 ♗e2 ♘bd7 12 ♘g5 ♗f7 13 ♘xf7 ♖xf7 14 ♗g4 ♘xg4 15 ♕xg4 ♘e5 16 ♕e2 ♕d7 17 b3 ♖f3 18 ♘e4 [18 gxf3? ♕xh3-+] 18 ... ♖af8 19 ♗b2 ♘g6 20 ♘d2 [20 gxf3? ♕xh3, 21 ... ♘f4; 21 ... ♘h4-+] 20 ... ♖3f5 21 ♖ae1 ♗f6 22 ♗xf6 ♖5xf6 23 ♘e4 ♖f5 24 ♘g3 ♖e5 25 ♕g4 ♕e7 26 ♖xe5 ♘xe5 27 ♕e6+!± ♖f7 28 ♕xe7 ♖xe7 29 ♘f5 ♖d7 30 ♖e1 ♘d3 31 ♖e6 g6 32 ♘xd6 ♘c1 33 ♘e4 ♖d8 34 ♘xc5 ♘xa2 35 ♘xb7 ♖b8 36 ♘a5 ♘c1 37 d6 ♔f8 38 c5 **1-0**

M954-1848

## 1848-★FS-2
**Forth, C.-Staunton, H.**

[Staunton]

⟨♙f7⟩ 1 e4 ... 2 d4 e6 3 ♗d3 c5 4 d5 d6 5 c4 exd5 6 exd5 ♘f6 7 ♘c3 ♗e7 8 ♘f3 0-0 9 0-0 ♗g4 10 h3 ♗h5 11 ♗e2 ♘bd7 12 ♘g5 ♗f7 13 ♘xf7 ♖xf7 14 ♗g4 ♘xg4 15 ♕xg4 ♘e5 16 ♕e2 ♕d7 17 ♘e4 ♖af8 18 ♘xc5?! dxc5 19 ♕xe5 ♗d6 20 ♕e6 ♕d8 21 ♗d2 ♔h8 22 ♖ae1 ♖f6 23 ♕e2 ♖g6 24 ♗c3 ♕g5 25 ♕g4 ♕h6 26 ♕d7 [□ 26 ♕e4] 26 ... ♕f4 27 g3 ♖xg3+ **0-1** M954-1848

## 1848-★HS-1
**Hannah, J.W.-Staunton, H.**

Brighton [Staunton]

⟨♙f7⟩ 1 e4 ... 2 d4 e6 3 ♗d3 c5 4 dxc5 ♕a5+ 5 ♘c3 ♗xc5 6 ♘f3 ♘c6 7 ♗f4 a6 8 0-0 ♘ge7 9 a3 ♗a7 10 ♗d6 ♕h5 11 e5 0-0 12 ♘e4 h6 13 c4 ♖f4 14 ♕d2

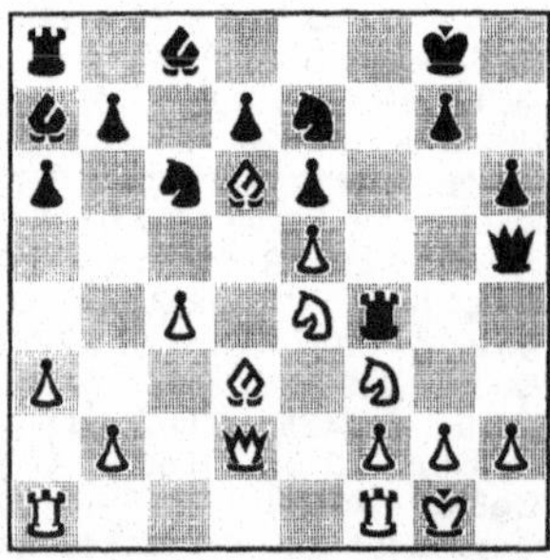

14 ... ♖xf3 15 ♗e2! [15 gxf3?] 15 ... ♘d4 16 ♗xf3 ♘xf3+ 17 gxf3 ♘g6 [17 ... ♘f5? 18 ♘g3] 18 f4 ♕f3 19 ♕d1 ♕xe4 20 ♕g4 [20 ♕h5? ♕g2+ 21 ♔xg2 ♘xf4+] 20 ... ♘xf4 21 ♖ae1 ♕xc4 22 ♔h1 b5! [Δ ... ♘] 23 f3 ♗b7 24 ♖c1 ♕d4 25 ♖g1 g5 26 ♗c5 ♗xc5 27 ♖xc5 ♘d3 [27 ... ♕xc5 28 ♕xf4 ♕xg1+-+] **0-1** M954-1848

## 1848-★ST-1
**Staunton, H.+Turner, J.**

Brighton [Staunton]

⟨♘b1⟩ 1 e4 e5 2 ♘f3 ♘c6 3 ♗c4 ♗c5 4 b4 ♗xb4 5 c3 ♗c5 6 0-0 d6 7 d4 exd4 8 cxd4 ♗b6 9 ♗b2 ♘f6 10 d5 ♘e7 11 ♗xf6 gxf6 12 ♘h4 ♘g6 13 ♕h5 ♘xh4 14 ♕xh4 ♗d7 15 a4 a6 16 ♖fb1 a5 17 ♖a2 ♕e7 18 ♗d3 ♕e5 [Δ 19 ... ♕g5] 19 ♗b5 ♔e7 [□ 19 ... ♗xb5] 20 ♗xd7 ♔xd7 21 ♕h3+ ♔e7 22 ♖c2 ♗c5 23 ♔h1 ♕xe4 24 ♖cc1 ♕xd5 25 ♖e1+ ♔d8 26 ♖bd1 ♕g5 27 ♕b3 ♖g8 28 ♕xb7 ♔d7 29 ♕b5+ ♔c8 30 ♕c6 ♖a7 31 ♖e2 ♕g4 [□ 31 ... ♗b4] 32 ♖de1 ♕xg2+ 33 ♕xg2 ♖xg2 34 ♔xg2 d5 35 ♖d1 d4 36 ♖c2 ♗b6 37 ♖c6 ♔d7 38 ♖xf6 ♔e7 39 ♖h6 ♖a8 40 ♖xh7 ♖g8+ 41 ♔f3 ♖g6 42 ♖e1+ ♔f8 43 ♖h8+ ♔g7 44 ♖ee8 ♖f6+ 45 ♔e2 ♖f4 46 h4 d3+ 47 ♔xd3 ♖f3+ 48 ♔c4 ♖xf2 49 h5 ♖f4+ 50 ♔d5 ♖d4+ 51 ♔e5 f6+ 52 ♔f5 ♖d5+ 53 ♔f4 ♖d4+ 54 ♔f3 ♗c5! 55 h6+ ♔f7 56 ♖c8 ♗d6 57 ♖cg8 ♖xa4 58 ♖g7+ ♔e6 59 ♖e8+ ♔f5 60 h7 **1-0**

M954-1849

# LONDON 1849

## 1849-LON-1
**Smith, C.J.-Buckle, H.T.**

[Staunton]

1 e4 e6 2 c4 c5 3 ♘f3 ♘c6 4 d4 cxd4 5 ♘xd4 ♗c5 6 ♘xc6 bxc6 7 ♕h5? ♕a5+ 8 ♔d1 [8 ♗d2 (8 ♘d2 ♗xf2+-+; 8 ♘c3 ♗xf2+-+) ♗xf2+-+] 8 ... ♘f6 9 ♕h4 0-0 10 e5 ♘e8 11 ♗d3 g6 12 ♗h6 ♘g7 13 ♕f6 [□ 13 ♘d2] 13 ... ♘h5 14 ♕f3 ♖e8 15 g4 ♘g7 16 h4 [□ 16 ♕f6 ♗f8 17 h4±] 16 ... ♗d4 17 ♗xg7 ♔xg7 18 h5 ♕xe5 19 hxg6 fxg6 20 ♖xh7+? [□ 20 ♘d2] 20 ... ♔xh7 21 ♕f7+ ♕g7 22 ♗xg6+ ♔h6 23 g5+ ♔xg5 24 ♘d2 ♕xf7 25 ♗xf7 ♖h8 26 ♔e2 ♔f6 27 ♘f3 c5 28 ♖g1 ♔xf7 29 ♘g5+ ♔e7 **0-1** L/N6123

## 1849-LON-2
**Buckle, H.T.+Smith, C.J.**

[Staunton]

1 e4 e5 2 ♘f3 ♘c6 3 ♗c4 ♗c5 4 ♘c3 ♘f6 5 d3 d6 6 h3 0-0 7 ♗g5 ♗e6 8 ♗b3 ♗b4 9 0-0 ♗xc3 10 bxc3 ♕e7 11 ♘h2 ♘d8 [□ 11 ... h6 12 ♗h4 g5] 12 f4 ♗xb3 [12 ... h6 13 fxe5±] 13 axb3 ♘e6 14 fxe5 dxe5 15 ♗xf6 gxf6 16 g3 ♔h8 17 ♘g4 ♖g8 18 ♔h2 ♖g6 19 ♕f3 ♔g7 20 h4 ♖g8 21 ♘e3 [Δ 22 ♘f5+] 21 ... ♔h8 22 ♘f5 ♕c5 23 ♕f2 ♕f8 24 ♖xa7 ♘g7 25 ♘xg7 ♖8xg7 26 ♖g1 ♕b8 27 ♖ga1 ♖g8 28 ♖a8 ♕xa8 29 ♖xa8 ♖xa8 30 h5! ♖h6 31 g4 ♖g8 32 ♔h3 b6 33 ♕f5 [Δ 34 ♕d7] 33 ... ♖d8 34 ♔h4 ♔g7 35 g5 **1-0**

L/N6123

## 1849-LON-3
**Flower, E.-Williams, E.**

[Staunton]

1 e4 e6 2 d4 d5 3 e5? c5 4 c3 ♘c6 5 ♘f3 ♗d7 6 ♗e2 ♕b6 7 b3? cxd4 8 0-0 [8 cxd4 ♗b4+∓] 8 ... dxc3 9 ♘xc3 ♘ge7 10 ♗f4 ♘g6 11 ♗g3 ♗e7 12 ♗d3 0-0 13 ♖c1 ♖ac8 14 ♗b1 ♗a3 15 ♖c2 ♘b4 16 ♘a4 ♗xa4 17 ♖xc8 ♖xc8 18 bxa4 ♘c6 19 ♕d3 ♗e7 20 h4 ♘b4 21 ♕d2 ♘f8 22 h5 h6 23 ♗h4 ♗xh4 24 ♘xh4 ♘c6 25 ♖c1 ♖e8 26 ♕f4 ♕d4 27 ♕xd4 ♘xd4 28 ♖c7 ♖b8? 29 g4 a6 30 ♗d3 ♘c6 31 f4 ♘b4 32 ♗b1 ♘c6 33 ♗d3 ♘a5 34 f5 ♖d8 35 ♘f3 ♘d7 36 ♔g2 ♘b6 37 fxe6 fxe6 38 ♖e7? [□ 38 ♘d4! (Δ 39 ♖xg7+±) 38 ... ♖d7 (38 ... ♖c8 39 ♖e7 ♘c6 40 ♖xe6 ♘xd4 ♖xb6±) 39 ♖c5 ♘ac4 40 a5 ♘xe5 41 ♗g6+-] 38 ... ♘xa4 39 ♖xe6 ♘c5 40 ♗f5 ♘xe6 41 ♗xe6+ ♔f8 42 ♗f5 d4 43 ♗d3 ♘c6 44 a3 ♔e7 45 ♔f2 ♖f8 46 ♗f5 ♖d8 47 ♔e2 ♖d5 48 ♗e4 ♖d8 49 ♔d3 a5 50 ♗xc6 bxc6 51 ♘d2 ♔e6 52 ♘c4 a4 53 ♘b6 ♔xe5 54 ♘xa4 ♖a8 55 ♘b6 ♖xa3+ 56 ♔d2 ♔e4 57 ♘c4 ♖a2+ 58 ♔d1 ♖g2 59 ♘a5 d3 60 ♘xc6 ♔e3 **0-1** L/N6123

## 1849-LON-4
**Williams, E.+Flower, E.**

1 f4 d5 2 e3 ♘f6 3 h3 ♕d6 4 ♘f3 ♘c6 5 ♗b5 ♗d7 6 0-0 a6 7 ♗xc6 ♗xc6 8 b3 e6 9 ♘e5 d4 10 ♕e2 ♕d5 11 d3 dxe3 12 c4 ♕d8 13 ♗xe3 ♗d6 14 ♘c3 0-0 15 ♘xc6 bxc6 16 ♘e4 c5 17 ♘xc5 ♘d7 18 ♘xd7 ♕xd7 19 d4 c6 20 ♕f3 f5 21 ♖ad1 ♕e7 22 ♕xc6 ♖fc8 23 ♕f3 ♕f6 24 d5 ♖d8 25 dxe6 ♕xe6 26 ♕d5 ♔f7 27 ♗b6 ♕xd5 28 ♖xd5 ♖d7 29 ♖fd1 ♔e6 30 ♖e1+ ♔f6 31 c5 ♖b8 32 ♖ed1 ♔e6 33 ♖xd6+ ♖xd6 34 ♖xd6+ **1-0**

L/N6123

## 1849-LON-5
**Medley, G.W.+Bird, J.H.S.**

[Staunton]

1 c4 f5 [□ 1 ... c5] 2 d4 ♘f6 3 ♘c3 d5 4 cxd5 ♘xd5 5 e3 [□ 5 e4 ♘xc3 6 bxc3 fxe4 7 ♕h5+ g6 8 ♕e5 ♖g8 9 ♕xe4±; 9 ♗c4±] 5 ... e6 6 ♘f3 ♘xc3 7 bxc3 ♗d6 8

♗d3 0-0 9 ♕c2 b6 10 0-0 ♗b7 11 e4 fxe4 12 ♗xe4 ♗xe4 13 ♕xe4 ♘d7 14 ♕xe6+ [□ 14 ♘g5 ♘f6 (14 ... g6 15 ♕xe6+ ♔g7 16 ♕h3+–) 15 ♕xe6+ ♔h8 16 ♘f7++–] 14 ... ♔h8 15 ♘g5 ♕e8 16 ♕h3 ♘f6 17 ♗d2 ♕g6 18 f4 ♘e4 19 ♘xe4 ♕xe4 20 ♖f2 ♖f6 21 ♕f3 ♕xf3 22 ♖xf3 ♖e8 23 ♔f2 ♖e4 24 ♖e1 ♖xe1 25 ♔xe1 g5 26 fxg5 ♖xf3 27 gxf3 ♗xh2 28 f4!+– ♗g3+ 29 ♔e2 ♔g7 30 ♔f3 ♗h4 31 ♔g4 ♗f2 32 ♔h5 a5 33 f5 b5 34 f6+ ♔g8 35 g6 hxg6+ 36 ♔xg6 **1-0** L/N6123

## 1849-LON-6
**Bird, J.H.S.+ Medley, J.R.**

[Staunton]

1 e4 c5 2 d4 cxd4 3 ♘f3 ♘c6 4 ♘xd4 e6 5 ♘c3 ♘f6 6 ♘xc6 bxc6 7 ♗d3 d5 8 0-0 ♗c5 9 ♔h1 [□ 9 e5; □ 9 ♗g5] 9 ... e5 10 f4 ♘g4 11 ♕e1 d4 12 ♘e2 ♗d6 13 h3 ♘f6 14 ♘xd4 exd4 15 e5 0-0 16 ♕h4 h6 17 exf6! ♕xf6 18 ♕xf6 gxf6 19 f5 ♔h7 20 ♗f4 ♗xf4 21 ♖xf4 c5 22 ♖e1 ♗b7 23 ♖e7 ♗d5 24 ♗e4!± ♗xe4 25 ♖fxe4 ♖ab8 26 b3 a5 27 ♖c7 ♖bc8 28 ♖ee7 ♔g8 29 ♖a7 [29 ♖xf7 ♖xf7 30 ♖xc8+ △ 31 ♖xc5+–; 29 ... ♖fe8+–; 29 ... ♖ce8+– (29 ... ♖xc7 30 ♖xc7+–)] 29 ... ♖ce8 30 ♖xe8 ♖xe8 31 ♖xa5 ♖e1+ 32 ♔h2 ♖c1 33 ♖xc5 d3 34 ♖d5 ♖xc2 [34 ... dxc2 35 ♖c5+–] 35 ♖xd3 ♖xa2 36 ♔g3 h5 37 b4 ♖b2 38 ♖d4 ♔g7 39 ♔f3 ♔h6 40 h4 ♔g7 41 g3 ♔f8 42 g4 ♖b3+ 43 ♔f4 ♖h3 44 b5 ♔e7 [44 ... ♖xh4 45 ♔g3 (45 b6 ♖xg4+ 46 ♔e3 ♖g3+ 47 ♔ ♖b3∓) 45 ... ♖h1 46 gxh5 ♖xh5 (46 ... ♖b1 47 h6 ♖xb5 48 ♖d8+ ♔e7 49 h7+–) 47 ♔g4 (47 b6 ♖xf5?? 48 ♖b4+–; □ 47 ... ♔e7 △ 48 ... ♖h8) 47 ... ♖h1 48 ♖b4 ♔e7 49 b6 ♖h8 50 b7 ♖b8=] 45 b6 ♖b3 46 gxh5 ♖xb6 47 h6 ♖b8 48 ♔g4 ♔f8 49 ♖d6 ♔e7 50 ♖a6 ♖h8 51 ♖a7+ ♔d6 52 ♖xf7 ♖xh6 53 ♖g7 ♖h8 54 h5 ♔e5 55 ♖g6 ♖h7 56 h6 ♖h8 57 ♔h5 ♔xf5 58 ♖g7 ♖a8 59 ♖g1 ♔e6 60 h7 ♔f7 61 ♔h6 ♖h8 62 ♖g7+ ♔f8 63 ♖a7 **1-0** L/N6123

## 1849-LON-7
**Medley, G.W.+ Bird, J.H.S.**

[Staunton]

1 e4 e6 2 d4 d5 3 exd5 exd5 4 ♘f3 ♘f6 5 ♗d3 ♗d6 6 0-0 0-0 7 h3 h6 8 ♘c3 a6 9 ♗e3 ♗e6 10 ♕d2 ♘c6 11 ♘h2 ♗xh2+ 12 ♔xh2 ♘e7 13 f4 ♗f5 14 ♖f2 c5 15 g4 ♗xd3 16 ♕xd3 c4 17 ♕e2 ♕d6 18 ♖g1 [△ 19 g5] 18 ... ♖ae8 19 ♕f3 ♘g6 20 ♕g3 ♘e4 21 ♘xe4 ♖xe4 22 f5 ♕xg3+ 23 ♖xg3 ♘h4 24 f6 [24 g5 ♖fe8] 24 ... ♘g6 [□ 24 ... ♖fe8] 25 fxg7 ♔xg7 26 c3 ♖fe8 27 ♗d2 f6 28 ♖gf3 ♖8e6 29 ♔g3 ♖e2 30 ♖f5 ♖xf2 31 ♔xf2 ♖b6 32 ♗c1 ♘e7 33 ♖h5 f5 34 gxf5 ♖f6 35 ♗f4 ♘xf5= 36 ♗e5 ♔g6 37 ♗xf6 ♔xh5 38 ♔f3 ♔g6 39 ♗d8 ♔f7 40 ♔f4 ♔e6 41 ♗c7 b5 42 ♔g4 ♔f6 43 ♔h5 ♔f7 44 ♗e5 a5 45 a3 a4 46 h4 ♔e6 [□ 46 ... ♘e3] 47 ♗f4 ♔f7 48 ♗xh6 ♔g8 49 ♗f4 ♔g7 50 ♔g5 ♘e7 51 h5 ♘g8 52 ♔f5 ♔f7 53 ♗g5 **1-0** L/N6123

## 1849-LON-8
**Simons, A.– Lowe, E.**

[Staunton]

1 e4 c5 2 ♗c4 e6 3 ♘c3 ♘e7 4 f4 d5 5 ♗b5+ ♘bc6 6 d3 d4 7 ♘ce2?? ♕a5+

**0-1** L/N6123

## 1849-LON-9
**Lowe, E.+ Simons, A.**

[Staunton]

1 f4 d5 2 ♘f3 ♘c6 3 d4 e6 4 e3 f6 5 c4 dxc4 6 ♗xc4 ♗d6 7 e4 ♘h6 8 0-0 0-0 9 f5 ♕e7 10 ♗xh6 gxh6 11 fxe6 ♔h8 12 d5 ♘e5 13 ♘bd2 ♘g4 14 ♕e2 ♖g8 15 h3 ♗c5+ 16 ♔h1 ♘e3 17 ♖g1 ♘xc4 18 ♘xc4 ♗xg1 19 ♖xg1 ♕c5 20 ♘e3 c6 21 ♘h4 cxd5 22 exd5 b5 23 ♘hf5 ♗b7 24 d6 ♕e5 25 e7 ♗c8 26 ♘xh6 ♖g7 27 ♕f3 ♗b7?? 28 ♕xb7 ♖ag8 29 ♘xg8 ♖xg8 30 ♕xa7 ♕xd6 31 ♘f5 ♕e6 32 ♕f2 ♖e8 33 ♖e1 **1-0** L/N6123

## 1849-LON-10
**Medley, J.R.+ Finch, J.**

[Staunton]

1 d4 d5 2 c4 c6 3 ♘c3 ♘f6 4 ♗g5 e6 5 e3 ♗e7 6 ♗d3 h6 7 ♗xf6 ♗xf6 8 ♘f3 b6 9 e4! dxe4 10 ♗xe4 ♗b7 11 0-0 0-0 12 ♕d3 ♘d7 13 ♖ad1 ♖b8 14 ♕e2 ♕e7 15 ♖fe1 ♖fd8 16 d5 exd5 17 cxd5 cxd5 18 ♘xd5 ♗xd5 19 ♖xd5 ♘c5 20 ♗h7+! ♔xh7 [□ 20 ... ♔h8] 21 ♕c2+ ♔g8 22 ♖xe7 ♖xd5 23 ♖e1 ♖bd8 24 ♔f1 ♗xb2?? 25 ♕xb2 ♘d3 26 ♕c2 ♘xe1 27 ♘xe1 ♖d1 28 ♔e2 **1-0** L/N6123

## 1849-LON-11
**Finch, J.+ Medley, J.R.**

[Staunton]

1 e4 c5 2 f4 e6 3 c4 g6 4 ♘f3 ♗g7 5 ♘c3 ♘c6 6 d3 ♘ge7 7 ♗e3 b6 8 ♗e2 ♗b7 9 0-0 0-0 10 ♖b1 d5 11 cxd5 exd5 12 exd5 ♘xd5 13 ♘xd5 ♕xd5 14 b3 ♖fe8 15 ♗f2 ♘d4 16 ♗xd4 ♗xd4+∓ 17 ♔h1 ♖e7 18 ♖c1 ♖ae8 19 ♖c2 ♗e3 20 d4??–+ ♗xd4 21 ♗c4 [△ 22 ♘xd4] 21 ... ♕h5! 22 ♗e2 ♕g4 23 ♗b5 ♗xf3?? 24 gxf3 ♕xf4 25 ♗xe8 ♖xe8 26 ♖e2 ♖e6 27 ♖xe6 gxe6 28 ♕e2 ♔f7 29 ♕e4 ♕d2 30 ♖e1 e5 31 ♖f1 ♕e3 32 ♕b7+ ♔f6 33 ♕xh7 ♕e2 34 ♕h4+ ♔f7 35 ♕e1 ♕xe1 36 ♖xe1 ♔f6 37 ♖e4 ♔f5 38 ♔g2 ♗c3 39 ♔f1 a5 40 a4 ♗d2 41 ♔g2 ♗f4 42 h3 ♔g5 43 ♖e1 ♔f5 44 ♖d1 ♔e6 45 ♖d8 c4 46 bxc4 ♗e3 47 ♔g3 g5 48 ♔g4 ♔e7 49 ♖h8 ♔d6 50 ♖c8 ♔d7 51 ♖b8 ♔c6 52 ♔f5 ♗f4 53 ♔e4 ♔c5 54 ♖b7 ♔c6 55 ♖b8 ♔c5 56 ♖c8+ ♔d6 57 ♖e8 ♔c5 58 ♖e6 ♗g3 59 ♔f5 ♗f4 60 ♔g4 ♔xc4 61 ♖xb6 **1-0** L/N6123

## 1849-LON-12
**Medley, J.R.+ Finch, J.**

[Staunton]

1 e4 e6 2 d4 d5 3 exd5 exd5 4 c4 c6 5 ♘c3 ♘f6 6 ♗g5 ♗e7 7 ♗d3 0-0 8 ♗xf6 ♗xf6 9 ♕h5? [□ 9 cxd5] 9 ... g6 10 ♕f3 dxc4 11 ♗xc4 ♕xd4 12 ♖d1 ♕xc4 13 ♕xf6 ♕e6+ 14 ♕xe6 ♗xe6 15 ♘ge2 ♘a6 16 0-0 ♖ad8 17 ♘f4 ♘c7 18 ♘e4 ♔g7 19 ♘c5 ♗xa2 20 ♖a1 ♗c4 21 ♖fe1 ♖fe8 22 ♘xb7 ♖xe1+ 23 ♖xe1 ♖b8 24 ♘d6 ♗e6 25 ♖e2 ♖d8 26 ♖d2 ♘b5??+– 27 ♘f5+ ♗xf5 28 ♖xd8 h5 29 ♔f1 ♔f6 30 ♔e2 g5?? 31 ♘xh5+ ♔e7 32 ♖h8 ♘d4+ 33 ♔d2 ♗g6 34 ♘g3 ♔d7 35 h4 gxh4 36 ♖xh4 ♘b5 37 f4 ♘d4 38 ♔c3 ♘f5 39 ♘xf5 ♗xf5 40 g4 ♗e6 41 f5 ♗d5 42 ♔d4 a5 43 ♔c5 a4 44 g5 ♗b3 45 ♖d4+ ♔e7 46 ♖d6 ♗d5 47 f6+ ♔e8 48 ♖xd5 cxd5 49 ♔xd5 ♔d7 50 ♔e5 ♔e8 51 ♔d6 ♔d8 52 ♔c6 ♔e8 53 ♔d6 ♔d8 54 ♔e5 ♔e8 55 ♔f5 ♔f8 56 g6 fxg6+ 57 ♔xg6 ♔g8 58 ♔f5 ♔f7 59 ♔e5 ♔f8 60 ♔d5 ♔f7 61 ♔c5 ♔xf6 62 ♔b5 ♔e6 63 ♔xa4 ♔d7 64 ♔a5 ♔c7 65 ♔a6 ♔b8 66 b4 ♔a8 67 b5 ♔b8 68 ♔b6 ♔a8 69 ♔c7 **1-0** L/N6123

## 1849-LON-13
**Tuckett, M.J.W.+ Wise, J.G.**

[Staunton]

1 e4 c5 2 d4 cxd4 3 ♘f3 e5 4 ♗c4 ♘f6 [□ 4 ... ♗e7] 5 ♘g5 d5 6 exd5 h6 7 ♘f3 ♗g4 8 h3 ♕c7 9 ♕e2 ♗xf3

**201** Ries' (Simpson's) Divan, London M979. BL

10 gxf3 ♗c5 11 c3 0-0 12 ♖g1 ♔h8 13 ♘d2 ♘h7 14 ♘e4 dxc3 15 ♘xc5 cxb2 16 ♗xb2 ♕xc5 17 ♕xe5 f6 18 ♕c3 ♖e8+ 19 ♔f1 ♘d7 20 ♕b3 ♘b6 21 ♖c1 ♘xc4 22 ♕xc4 ♕e7 23 ♕d3 ♖ad8 24 h4 ♖d7 25 ♖g4 ♘f8 26 ♗a3 ♕f7 27 ♖e4 ♖ed8 28 d6 ♕xa2 29 ♕e3 ♔h7 30 ♖e7 ♕d5 31 ♕e4+ ♕xe4 32 fxe4 ♘g6 33 ♖xd7 ♖xd7 34 ♖c7 ♘f8 35 f4 ♔g6 36 ♔e2 ♔f7 37 ♔d3 b6 38 f5 b5 39 h5 ♔e8 40 ♖c8+ ♖d8 41 ♖c7 ♖d7 42 ♖c8+ ♔f7 43 ♔d4 a6 44 ♔d5 g6 45 ♗c1 ♔g7 46 ♗xh6+ ♔xh6 47 ♖xf8 ♔xh5 48 ♔e6 ♖a7 49 d7 ♖xd7 50 ♔xd7 **1-0** L/N6123

**1849-LON-14**
**Wise, J.G.– Tuckett, M.J.W.**
[Staunton]

1 c4 e6 2 d4 c6 3 e4 d5 4 cxd5 cxd5 5 exd5 ♕xd5 6 ♘f3 ♘c6 7 ♗d3 ♘f6 8 0-0 ♗b4 9 ♘c3 ♗xc3 10 bxc3 0-0 11 c4 ♕d6 12 h3 h6 13 ♖e1 b6 14 a4 ♖d8 15 ♗b2 ♗b7 16 ♕d2 ♖ac8 17 ♖ad1 ♘a5 18 c5 ♕c7 19 cxb6 ♕xb6 20 ♘e5 ♗d5 21 ♗a1 ♘b3 22 ♕f4 ♘xa1 23 ♖xa1 ♖c3 24 a5 ♕d6 25 g4 ♗a8 26 ♖ad1 ♕b4 27 h4 ♕b7 28 f3 ♕e7 29 g5 hxg5 30 hxg5 ♘h5 31 ♕g4 g6 32 ♗xg6

32 ... fxg6 33 ♘xg6 ♕d6 34 ♖xe6 ♕g3+ 35 ♕xg3 ♘xg3 36 ♘h4 ♖c6 37 ♖e7 ♖a6 38 ♖de1 ♗d5 39 g6 ♘h5 40 ♖1e5 ♘f4 41 ♖g5?? ♘h3+ **0-1** L/N6123

**1849-LON-15**
**Buckle, H.T.+Williams, E.**
[Staunton]

1 d4 e6 2 c4 f5 3 ♘f3 ♗b4+ 4 ♗d2 ♗xd2+ 5 ♕xd2 ♘f6 6 ♘c3 b6 7 e3 c5 8 ♗e2 0-0 9 0-0 ♕e7 10 ♖ad1 d6 11 dxc5 dxc5 12 ♘e5 ♗b7 13 ♕d6 ♕xd6 14 ♖xd6 ♖e8 15 ♖fd1 ♘a6 16 f3 ♘c7 17 ♖1d2 ♖e7 [△ ... ♖ae8] 18 ♗d1 ♘ce8 19 ♖6d3 g5 20 ♗a4 g4 21 ♘b5 ♖g7 22 ♔f2 a6? 23 ♘d6 ♘xd6 24 ♖xd6 ♖e7 25 ♖xb6 a5? 26 ♘d7 ♘xd7 27 ♖xb7 ♔f7 28 ♖dxd7 ♖xd7 29 ♖xd7+ ♔g6 30 ♖e7 ♖a6 31 fxg4 fxg4 32 ♗c2+ ♔f6 33 ♖xh7 ♖b6 34 b3 a4 35 ♖a7 ♖d6 36 ♔e2 axb3 37 ♗xb3 ♖d8 38 ♖c7 ♖h8 39 ♖xc5 ♖xh2 40 ♔f2 ♖h1 41 ♔g3 ♖e1 42 ♔f4 ♖g1 43 g3 ♖e1 44 e4 e5+ 45 ♔xg4 ♖xe4+ 46 ♔f3 ♖e1 47 a4 ♖c1 48 ♖b5 ♔f5 49 a5 ♖c3+ 50 ♔g2 ♔g4 51 ♗d1+ ♔f5 52 c5 ♖c1 53 ♗f3 ♖c2+ 54 ♔h3 ♖c3 55 ♗b7 ♖c4 56 a6 e4 57 a7 e3 58 ♖b2 **1-0** L/N6123

**1849-LON-16**
**Williams, E.– Buckle, H.T.**
[Staunton]

1 f4 e6 2 e3 d5 3 ♘f3 ♘f6 4 b3 ♗d6 5 ♗b2 0-0 6 ♗d3 c5 7 ♘g5 h6 8 ♘f3 ♘c6 9 a3 ♕c7? 10 ♗xf6 gxf6 11 ♘h4 f5 12 g4 ♕e7 13 g5 hxg5 14 ♕h5 [14 ♖g1 f6 △ 15 ... ♕g7] 14 ... f6 15 ♘g6 ♕h7 16 ♕xh7+ ♔xh7 17 ♘xf8+ ♗xf8 18 fxg5? fxg5 19 ♖g1 ♘e5 20 ♗e2 ♔g6 21 d4 cxd4 22 exd4 ♘c6 23 c3 ♗g7 [△ 24 ... ♘xd4] 24 ♖a2 ♗d7 25 ♘d2 ♖h8 26 ♗b5 g4 27 ♗xc6 ♗xc6 28 ♘f3 ♖h3 29 ♖f2 ♔h6 30 ♘e5 ♗xe5 31 dxe5 ♖e3+ 32 ♔d2 ♖xe5 33 h3 ♖e4

34 hxg4 fxg4 35 ♖e2 ♖xe2+ 36 ♔xe2 ♔g5 37 ♔e3 e5 38 ♔f2 ♔f4 39 ♖g3 ♗d7 40 ♖d3 ♗e6 41 b4 b5 42 ♖g3 d4! 43 cxd4 exd4 44 ♖d3 ♔e4 45 ♖g3 ♗f5 46 ♔e2 ♔f4 47 ♔f2 ♗e4 48 ♖g1 ♗f3 49 ♖a1 d3 50 ♖a2 g3+ 51 ♔f1 ♔e3 52 a4 d2 53 ♖a3+ ♔f4 **0-1** L/N6123

## 1849-LON-17
**Lowe, E.+Medley, G.W.**

[Staunton]

1 f4 d5 2 ♘f3 c5 3 e3 e6 4 ♗b5+ ♘c6 5 0-0 ♗d6 6 d3 ♘e7 7 e4 0-0 8 ♘c3 a6 9 ♗xc6 bxc6 10 ♘e2 f6 11 ♘h4 [△ 12 f5] 11 ... ♘g6 12 ♘xg6 hxg6 13 ♘g3 f5 14 e5 ♗c7 15 c3 ♔f7?! 16 ♘e2 ♖h8 17 ♖f3 ♗d7 18 ♗e3 ♗b6 19 ♕e1 ♖b8 20 ♕f2 c4 21 d4 ♗a7 22 ♘g3 ♕h4 23 h3 ♖b7 24 ♖d1 ♖hb8 25 ♖d2 a5 26 a3 a4 27 ♖e2 ♖b3 28 ♗c1 ♖3b5 29 ♔h2 c5? [◻ 29 ... ♔f8] 30 ♘xf5! ♕xf2 31 ♘d6+ ♔g8 32 ♖fxf2 ♖b3 33 ♗e3 cxd4 34 ♗xd4 ♗xd4 35 cxd4 c3 36 bxc3 ♖xc3 37 ♖b2 ♖bb3 38 ♖fc2 ♔f8 39 ♖xc3 ♖xc3 [◻ 39 ... ♖xb2] 40 ♖b7? [◻ 40 ♖b8+ ♔e7 41 ♖g8 ♖xa3 42 ♖xg7+ ♔d8 43 ♘b7+ ♔c8 44 ♘c5 ♗e8 45 ♘xe6+-] 40 ... ♔e7 41 ♘b5 ♖b3 42 ♘d6 ♖xb7 [◻ 42 ... ♖xa3] 43 ♘xb7 ♗c6 44 ♘c5 ♔d8 45 ♘xe6+ ♔c8 46 ♘xg7 ♔b7 47 ♘e6 ♔b6 48 ♔g3 ♔b5 49 ♔f3 ♔c4 50 g4 ♔b3 51 ♘d8 ♗e8 52 ♘b7 ♔xa3 53 ♘c5 ♔b4 54 ♘xa4! ♗xa4 55 f5 gxf5 56 gxf5 ♗c2 57 ♔f4 ♔c4 58 e6 ♔xd4 59 f6 **1-0** L/N6123

## 1849-LON-18
**Medley, G.W.+Lowe, E.**

[Staunton]

1 d4 c6? 2 c4 d5 3 ♘c3 ♘f6 4 ♘f3 e6 5 e3 ♗d6 6 ♗d3 0-0 7 0-0 a6 8 ♘e5 c5 9 f4 ♘c6 10 ♗c2 cxd4 11 exd4 dxc4 12 ♘e4 ♗xe5 13 fxe5 ♕xd4+ [◻ 13 ... ♘xe4] 14 ♕xd4 ♘xd4 15 ♘xf6+! gxf6 16 ♗h6! [△ 16 ... ♘xc2 17 ♖f3] 16 ... f5? [◻ 16 ... ♖d8] 17 ♗xf8 ♘xc2 18 ♖ac1 ♘e3 19 ♖f3 ♔xf8 20 ♖xe3 b5 21 ♖h3 ♔g8 22 ♖d1 ♗b7 23 ♖d7 ♗c6 24 ♖d6 ♖c8 25 ♖a3 b4 26 ♖xa6 ♗b5 27 ♖ab6 c3 28 bxc3 bxc3 29 ♖d1 c2 30 ♖c1 ♗d3 31 ♔f2 ♗e4 32 ♖b4 ♖c5 33 a4 ♖xe5?? 34 ♖b5 ♖d5 35 ♖xd5 exd5 36 ♔e3 ♔g7 37 a5 ♔f6 38 ♔d4 f4 39 a6 **1-0** L/N6123

## 1849-LON-19
**Lowe, E.=Medley, G.W.**

[Staunton]

1 f4 d5 2 ♘f3 ♗g4 3 e3 e6 4 ♗e2 ♗d6 5 d3 ♘e7 6 0-0 0-0 7 e4 f5 8 e5 ♗c5+ 9 d4 ♗b6 10 ♗e3 ♗xf3 11 ♖xf3 ♘d7 12 ♘a3 c5 13 c3 a6 14 ♘c2 ♘c6 15 ♖h3 ♖c8 16 ♖c1 ♕e7 17 g4 cxd4 18 cxd4 fxg4 19 ♗xg4 ♕f7 20 ♕d3 g6 21 ♖g3 ♘e7 22 ♖g2 ♘f5 23 ♗xf5 ♕xf5 24 ♕xf5 ♖xf5 25 ♖d1 ♖f7 26 ♘e1 ♗d8 27 ♖c1 ♖xc1 28 ♗xc1 ♘b6 29 ♖c2 ♖c7 30 ♖xc7 ♗xc7 31 ♘d3 ♘d7 32 ♔f2 ♗b6 33 ♗e3 ♘b8 [△ 34 ... ♘c6∓] 34 ♘c5 ♗xc5 35 dxc5 ♘c6 36 a3 g5! 37 ♔f3 ♔f7 38 ♔g4 ♔g6 39 b4 h5+ 40 ♔g3 ♔f5 41 fxg5 ♘xe5 42 a4 ♘c4 [◻ 42 ... ♘g6] 43 ♗c1 e5 [43 ... d4? 44 b5 axb5 45 axb5 d3 46 c6 bxc6 47 bxc6 ♘d6 48 c7] 44 b5 axb5 45 axb5 d4 46 c6 bxc6 47 bxc6 e4 48 c7 ♘d6 49 ♗a3 ♘c8 50 ♗c5 ♔xg5 51 ♗xd4 ♘d6 52 ♗c5 ♘c8 53 ♗e3+ ♔f5 54 ♔h4 ♔g6 55 ♗c5 ♔h6 56 ♔g3 ♔g5 57 ♗e3+ ♔f5 58 ♗c5 ♔g5 59 ♗e3+ ♔f5 60 ♗c5 ♔g5 61 ♗d4 ♔f5 62 h3 ♘d6 63 ♗c5 ♘c8 **½-½** L/N6123

## 1849-LON-20
**Lowe, E.−Medley, G.W.**

[Staunton]

1 f4 f5 2 c4 ♘f6 3 ♘c3 e6 4 d3 ♘c6 5 ♘f3 d5 6 cxd5 ♘xd5 7 e3 ♗e7 8 ♗e2 0-0 9 0-0 ♗f6 10 ♗d2 ♔h8 11 d4 ♘ce7 12 ♗c4 c6 13 ♘e2 ♗d7 14 ♘g3 ♗e8 15 ♖c1 ♗g6 16 ♗b3 ♖g8 17 ♕e2 ♕d6 18 h4 ♖af8 19 a3 h6 20 ♔f2 ♖e8 21 h5 ♗h7 22 ♖h1 ♖ef8 23 ♕d3 g5 24 hxg6 ♖xg6 25 ♘e2 ♖fg8 26 g3 ♖8g7 27 ♖h3 ♘g8 28 ♕c4 h5?! 29 ♖xh5 ♘h6 30 ♘h2 ♗d8 31 ♕c5 ♕xc5 32 dxc5 ♘f6 33 ♗c2?? ♘xh5 34 ♖g1 ♘g4+ 35 ♘xg4 ♖xg4 36 ♗b3 ♖4g6 37 ♗c4 ♔g8 38 b4 ♘xg3−+ 39 ♘xg3 ♖xg3 40 ♗xe6+ ♔f8 41 ♖xg3 ♗h4 42 ♔e2 ♖xg3 43 ♗c3 ♔e7 44 ♗c8 b5 45 cxb6 axb6 46 ♗d4 b5 47 ♗c5+ ♔d8 48 ♗e6 ♗e7 49 ♗b6+ ♔e8 50 ♔d3 ♖g2 51 ♔d4 ♗d6 52 ♔c3 ♔e7 53 ♗c8 ♖a2 54 ♔b3 ♗g8+ 55 ♔c3 ♖xa3+ 56 ♔d4 ♗e6 57 ♗b7 ♔d7 58 ♗c5 ♗xc5+ 59 ♔xc5 ♗d5 60 ♔d4 ♔c7 61 ♔e5 ♗e4 **0-1** L/N6123

## 1849-LON-21
**Medley, J.R.+Tuckett, M.J.W.**

[Staunton]

1 d4 e6 2 e4 d5 3 exd5 exd5 4 ♘f3 ♘c6 5 ♗e3 ♘f6 6 ♗d3 ♗d6 7 ♘c3 0-0 8 0-0 h6 9 h3 ♘e7 10 ♘e5 c6 11 ♕d2 ♘f5 12 ♖ae1 ♕c7 13 g4 ♘h4 14 f4! ♘h7 15 ♕f2 ♗e7 16 g5 hxg5 17 ♗xh7+ ♔xh7 18 fxg5 ♘f5 19 ♕g2 g6 20 h4 ♔g7 21 h5 gxh5 22 g6 f6 23 ♗f4!! ♗d6 24 ♘d3 ♘xd4 25 ♕h2 ♗xf4 26 ♘xf4 ♗g4?? 27 ♘xh5+ ♗xh5 28 ♕xc7+ ♔xg6 29 ♖e7 ♖g8 30 ♕g3+! ♔h6 31 ♖xf6+ ♖g6 32 ♖xg6+ ♗xg6 33 ♕h4+ **1-0** L/N6123

## 1849-LON-22
**Tuckett, M.J.W.−Medley, J.R.**

[Staunton]

1 e4 c5 2 ♘f3 g6 3 d4 ♗g7 4 c3 e6 5 dxc5 ♘e7 6 ♗f4 b6 7 ♗d6 bxc5 8 ♗xc5 0-0 9 ♕d6 ♘ec6 10 ♕g3 ♖e8 11 e5 f6 12 ♗d6 fxe5 13 ♘xe5 ♘xe5 14 ♗xe5 ♗xe5 15 ♕xe5 ♕b6 16 b3 ♖f8 17 ♕g3 ♘a6 18 ♗d3 ♖f6 19 ♘d2 ♘c5 20 ♗c2 ♗a6 21 c4 ♖af8 22 0-0 ♗b7 23 ♖ab1 ♕b4 24 ♕e3 a5 25 ♘e4 ♘xe4 26 ♗xe4 ♗xe4 27 ♕xe4 ♕d2 28 ♕e3 ♕xa2 29 ♖a1 ♖xf2 30 ♕xf2 ♖xf2 31 ♖xa2 ♖xa2 32 h3 ♖b2 33 ♖f3 d5 34 cxd5 exd5 35 ♖d3 d4 36 ♔h2 ♔f7 37 ♔g3 ♔e6 38 ♔f3 ♔d5 39 g4 ♖b1 40 ♔f4 h6 41 ♖f3 ♖e1 42 ♖d3 ♖f1+ 43 ♔g3 ♔e4 44 ♖d2 ♖f3+ 45 ♔h4 ♖xb3 46 ♖a2 ♖b5 47 ♔g3 ♔e3 48 ♖a1 d3 49 ♖e1+ ♔d2 50 ♖e6 ♔d1 51 ♖xg6 d2 52 ♖xh6 ♖c5 53 ♖d6 ♔c1 54 h4 d1♕ **0-1** L/N6123

## 1849-LON-23
**Buckle, H.T.+Medley, J.R.**

[Staunton]

1 d4 e6 2 e4 d5 3 exd5 exd5 4 ♘f3 ♘f6 5 ♘c3 ♗d6 6 ♗d3 0-0 7 0-0 ♗g4 8 h3 ♗xf3 [◻ 8 ... ♗h5] 9 ♕xf3 h6 10 ♘d1 [◻ 10 ♔h1 △ 11 g4] 10 ... ♘c6 11 c3 ♖e8 12 ♘e3 [△ ♘f5] 12 ... ♘e7 13 ♘g4 ♘xg4 14 ♕xg4 ♕c8! 15 ♕h5 ♕e6 16 ♗d2 f5 17 ♖ae1 ♕f7 18 ♕f3 ♘g6?? 19 ♕xf5 ♕xf5 20 ♗xf5 ♘e7 21 ♗d7 ♖f8 22 ♖e6 ♖ad8 23 ♗a4 ♔f7 24 ♖fe1 ♘g8 25 ♗b3 ♘f6 26 c4 c6 27 c5 ♗xc5??+- [◻ 27 ... ♗b8] 28 dxc5 ♖fe8 29 ♖xe8 ♖xe8 30 ♖xe8 ♘xe8 31 ♗c2 ♔e6 32 ♗c3 g5 33 h4! b6 34 hxg5 hxg5 35 b4 ♘f6 36 ♗xf6 ♔xf6 37 ♗a4 b5 38 ♗b3 ♔e5 39 ♔f1 ♔d4 40 a3 a5 41 bxa5 ♔xc5 42 ♔e2 ♔d6 43 a4 b4 44 ♔d3 c5 45 a6 c4+ 46 ♗xc4 dxc4+ 47 ♔xc4 ♔c6 48 a5 ♔c7 49 ♔xb4 ♔b8 50 f3 ♔a7 51 ♔b5 ♔a8 52 g3 ♔a7 53 f4 **1-0** L/N6123

## 1849-LON-24
**Medley, J.R.−Buckle, H.T.**

[Staunton]

1 e4 c5 2 ♘f3 ♘c6 3 d4 cxd4 4 ♘xd4 e5 5 ♘f3 ♘f6 6 ♗c4 ♗c5 [6 ... ♘xe4? 7 ♗xf7+] 7 ♘c3 d6 8 ♗g5 ♗b4 9 ♕d2 ♘xe4?! 10 ♕d5? [◻ 10 ♗xf7+ ♔f8! 11 ♕e3 ♗xc3+ 12 bxc3 ♘xg5 13 ♘xg5 h6 14 ♘e6+ ♗xe6 15 ♗xe6] 10 ... ♗xc3+ 11 bxc3 ♘xg5 12 ♘xg5 ♕xg5 13 ♕xf7+ ♔d8 14 ♖d1 ♕e7 15 ♕h5 ♔c7 16 0-0 g6 17 ♕e2 ♗d7 18 ♗d5 ♖ac8 19 ♖b1 ♔b8 20 ♖b2 ♔a8 21 ♖fb1 ♖c7 22 a4 ♘d8 23 a5 ♗c6 24 ♕e4 ♗xd5 25 ♕xd5 ♕e6 26 ♕b5 ♕c4 27 ♕b4 ♕xb4 28 cxb4 b5 29 axb6 axb6 30 b5 ♘e6 31 ♖a1+ ♖a7 32 ♖d1 ♔b7 33 ♔f1 [33 ♖xd6??] 33 ... ♔c7 34 c3 d5!! 35 g3 [35 ♖xd5?? ♖a1+ 36 ♔e2 ♘f4+] 35 ... d4 36 ♖c2 ♔d6 37 cxd4 ♘xd4 38 ♖c6+ ♔d5 39

♖xb6 ♖f8 40 ♖d2 ♔c5 41 ♖a6 ♖xa6 42 bxa6 ♖a8 43 ♖a2 ♔b6 44 f4 exf4 45 gxf4 ♖xa6 46 ♖b2+ ♔c5 47 ♖b7 h5 48 ♔f2 ♖a2+ 49 ♔g3 ♖a3+ **0-1** L/N6123

**1849-LON-25**
**Medley, G.W.+Medley, J.R.**
[Staunton]

1 e4 c5 2 d4 cxd4 3 ♘f3 e5 4 c3 d3 5 ♗xd3 ♘c6 6 ♗c4 ♗c5? 7 ♗xf7+ ♔xf7 8 ♕d5+ ♔e8 9 ♕xc5 d6 10 ♕e3 ♘f6 11 0-0 h6 12 ♘a3 ♗e6 13 ♕d3 ♕e7 14 ♘h4 ♔f7 15 ♘c4 ♖ad8 16 ♘e3 g6 17 ♘d5 [□ 17 f4] 17 ... ♘xd5 18 exd5 ♕xh4 19 dxe6+ ♔xe6 20 ♕xg6+ ♔d7 21 ♗e3 ♖dg8 [□ 21 ... ♖hg8; 22 ♕xh6 ♖xg2+ 23 ♔xg2 ♕g4+ 24 ♔h1 ♕f3+ 25 ♔g1 ♖g8+ 26 ♗g5 ♕g4+ 27 ♔h1 ♖xg5–+] 22 ♕f7+ ♘e7 23 ♖fd1 ♖g6 24 ♖d2 ♖f6 25 ♕b3 b6 26 ♕b5+ ♘c6 27 a4 ♖b8 28 ♖ad1 ♖g6 29 b4 ♕e4 30 g3 h5 31 ♕d5 ♕f5 32 h4 ♖bg8 33 ♔g2 ♕g4 34 ♗g5 ♖f8 35 b5 ♘a5 36 ♕xe5 ♕f3+ 37 ♔g1 ♘c4 38 ♕e7+ ♔c8 39 ♖e2 ♘e5 40 ♖xd6 ♖xd6 41 ♕xd6 ♕xe2 42 ♕xf8+ ♔d7 43 ♕d8+ ♔e6 44 ♕g8+ ♔d6 45 ♗f4 ♕e1+ 46 ♔g2 ♕e4+ 47 ♔h2 ♔c5 48 ♕c8+ ♔d6 49 ♕b8+ ♔e6 50 ♕xe5+ ♕xe5 51 ♗xe5 ♔xe5 **1-0** L/N6123

**1849-LON-26**
**Medley, J.R.–Medley, G.W.**
[Staunton]

1 e4 e6 2 d4 d5 3 exd5 exd5 4 ♘f3 ♘f6 5 ♘c3 ♗d6 6 ♗d3 0-0 7 0-0 c6 8 ♘e2 ♘e4 9 ♗xe4 dxe4 10 ♘e5 f5 11 c3 h6 [□ 11 ... ♕c7] 12 ♕b3+ ♔h8 13 ♘f7+ ♖xf7 14 ♕xf7 ♘a6 15 ♗f4 ♘c7 16 ♗xd6 ♕xd6 17 ♘g3 ♗e6 18 ♕g6 [□ 18 ♘xf5] 18 ... ♖f8 19 ♘h5 ♕d7 20 f3 e3 21 f4 ♘e8 22 ♖fe1?? ♗f7 23 ♕g3 ♗xh5 24 ♖xe3 ♘f6 25 ♖e5 ♘e4 26 ♕h4 ♗f7 27 g4 ♗d5 28 ♖e1 ♘d2 29 ♖xd5 ♕xd5 30 ♕e7 ♖f6 31 ♕e8+ ♔h7 32 ♖e3 fxg4 33 ♕e5 ♘f3+ 34 ♖xf3 gxf3 35 ♔f2 ♖g6 36 f5 ♖g2+ 37 ♔f1 ♕c4+ 38 ♔e1 ♖e2+ **0-1** L/N6123

**BIRD ✕ MEDLEY** [1849-✕BM]

| | | | | | | | | | |
|---|---|---|---|---|---|---|---|---|---|
| H.E. Bird | 0̂ | ? | 0̂ | 1̂ | 0̂ | 0̂ | ? | 1̂ | ? |
| G.W. Medley | 1̂ | ? | 1̂ | 0̂ | 1̂ | 1̂ | ? | 0̂ | ? |

**1849-✕BM-1̂**
**Medley, G.W.+Bird, H.E.**
[Staunton]

1 d4 d5 2 c4 e6 3 ♘c3 ♘f6 4 e3 c6 5 a3 ♗d6 6 b3 0-0 7 ♗b2 b6 8 ♘f3 ♗a6 9 ♗d3 c5? 10 dxc5 bxc5 11 cxd5 ♗xd3 12 ♕xd3 exd5 13 ♘xd5 ♘xd5 14 ♕xd5 ♘a6 15 ♖d1 [15 0-0? ♗xh2+–+] 15 ... ♗e7 [□ 15 ... ♗c7] 16 ♕e5 ♕xd1+ 17 ♔xd1 ♗f6 18 ♕e4 ♗xb2 19 ♕b7 c4 20 ♕xa6 cxb3 21 ♕a4 [□ 21 ♘d4] 21 ... ♖fc8 22 ♔e2 ♖c2+ 23 ♘d2 ♗c3 24 ♖d1 ♖b8 25 ♕xa7 ♖d8 26 ♕c7 ♗f6 [26 ... ♖dxd2+ 27 ♖xd2 ♖xd2+ 28 ♔f3 ♗f6 29 ♕b8+ ♖d8 30 ♕xb3+–] 27 ♕b6 b2 28 ♕b3 ♖dc8 29 a4 ♖8c3 30 ♕b8+ ♖c8 31 ♕b4 ♗c3 32 ♕b7 ♖cd8 33 ♔f3 ♖c1 34 ♘e4 ♖cxd1 35 ♘xc3 ♖1d2 36 ♘b1 ♖c2 37 ♕b3 ♖dc8 38 a5 g6 39 a6 ♖2c7 40 ♕xb2 ♖a8 41 ♕f6 ♖ca7 42 ♘c3 ♖xa6 43 ♕g5 ♖a5 44 ♕e7 ♖8a7 45 ♕d8+ ♔g7 46 ♘d5 ♖7a6 47 g4 ♖c5 48 g5 ♖e6 49 h4 ♖cc6 50 ♘f6 ♖xf6+ 51 gxf6+ ♖xf6+ 52 ♔g3 **1-0** L/N6123

**1849-✕BM-3̂**
**Medley, G.W.+Bird, H.E.**
[Staunton]

1 d4 d5 2 c4 e6 3 ♘c3 ♘f6 4 e3 c5 5 ♘f3 b6 6 a3 ♗b7 7 b3 ♗d6 8 ♗b2 cxd4 9 exd4 0-0 10 cxd5 exd5 11 ♗d3 ♘c6 12 0-0 ♗c8 13 h3 ♗e6 14 ♖c1 ♘e7 15 ♘e2 ♘g6 16 ♘g3 ♕d7 [□ 16 ... ♘f4] 17 ♘e5 ♕d8 18 f4 ♘e7 19 f5 ♗d7 20 ♘h5 ♘xh5 21 ♕xh5 f6 22 ♖f4!? fxe5 23 f6 e4 24 fxe7 ♕xe7 25 ♕xd5+ ♗e6 26 ♖xf8+ ♖xf8 27 ♕xe4 g6 28 d5 ♗f5 29 ♕xe7 ♗xe7 30 ♗xf5 ♖xf5 31 ♖c8+ ♔f7 32 ♖h8 ♗c5+ 33 ♔h2 ♗d6+ 34 ♔g1 ♖xd5 35 ♖xh7+ ♔e6 36 ♗h8 ♗g3 37 ♔f1 ♖d2 38 ♖g7 ♖f2+ 39 ♔g1 ♔f6 40 ♖xa7+ ♔g5 41 ♖a4 ♖f4 42 ♖xf4 ♗xf4 43 ♗d4 b5 44 a4 bxa4 45 bxa4 ♔f5 46 a5 ♔e4 47 a6 **1-0** L/N6123

**1849-✕BM-4̂**
**Bird, H.E.+Medley, G.W.**
[Staunton]

1 e4 e6 2 f4 d5 3 e5 c5 4 ♘f3 ♘c6 5 ♗b5 ♕b6 6 ♗xc6+ bxc6 7 0-0 ♘h6 8 ♔h1 ♗e7 9 ♘c3 0-0 10 d3 a5 11 b3 f6 12 ♗a3 ♘f5 13 ♕d2 ♗a6 14 exf6 ♖xf6 15 ♘e5 ♕c7 16 ♖ae1 ♖d8 17 ♕f2 ♘d4 18 ♘a4 ♗b5 19 ♗xc5 ♗xa4 20 ♗xd4 ♗b5 [20 ... c5 21 ♘g4 ♖g6 22 ♗e5 ♕b7 23 bxa4 ♖xg4±] 21 ♗b6 **1-0** L/N6123

**1849-✕BM-5̂**
**Medley, G.W.+Bird, H.E.**
[Staunton]

1 c4 e6 2 e3 c5 3 ♘c3 ♘c6 4 ♘f3 ♘f6 5 b3 ♗e7 6 ♗b2 0-0 7 ♗e2 ♘e8 8 0-0 f5 9 d4 f4 10 d5 ♘b8 11 e4 d6 12 dxe6 ♗xe6 13 ♘d5 ♗xd5 14 exd5 ♘d7 15 ♗d3 ♗f6 16 ♖b1 ♗xb2 17 ♖xb2 ♘ef6 [□ 17 ... h6] 18 ♘g5 ♕a5 19 ♘e6 ♖f7 20 ♘xf4 ♘e5 21 ♕d2 ♕c7 22 ♘e6 ♕e7 23 f4 ♘xd3 24 ♕xd3 ♘g4 25 ♘g5 ♕e3+ 26 ♕xe3 ♘xe3 27 ♘xf7 ♘xf1 28 ♘xd6 ♘e3 29 ♘xb7 ♖b8 30 ♖e2 ♘xd5 31 cxd5 ♖xb7 32 d6 ♖d7 33 ♖e8+ ♔f7 34 ♖e7+ ♖xe7 35 dxe7 ♔xe7 36 ♔f2 ♔d6 37 ♔e3 ♔d5 38 ♔d3 h5 39 g3 a6 40 a3 g6 41 h3 a5 42 a4 **1-0**

**1849-✕BM-6̂**
**Bird, H.E.–Medley, G.W.**
[Staunton]

1 e4 e6 2 f4 d5 3 e5 c5 4 ♘f3 ♘c6 5 ♗b5 ♗d7 6 0-0 ♘xe5 7 fxe5 ♗xb5 8 d3 g6 9 ♘c3 ♗c6 10 ♘g5 ♘h6 11 ♕f3 ♕e7 12 ♕h3 ♗g7 13 ♘f3 ♘f5 14 g4 ♘d4 15 ♘g5 f6 16 exf6 ♗xf6 17 ♘f3 ♘xf3+ 18 ♖xf3 0-0 19 ♗h6 ♗d4+ 20 ♗e3 ♖xf3 21 ♕xf3 ♗xe3+ 22 ♕xe3 d4 23 ♕e5 dxc3 24 bxc3 ♖f8 25 ♖e1 ♕f6 26 ♕xe6+ ♕xe6 27 ♖xe6 ♖f4 28 h3 ♖f3 29 ♔h2 ♖f2+ **0-1**

**1849-✕BM-8̂**
**Bird, H.E.+Medley, G.W.**
[Staunton]

1 e4 e6 2 f4 d5 3 e5 c5 4 ♘f3 ♘c6 5 ♗b5 ♗d7 6 ♗xc6 ♗xc6 7 0-0 ♘h6 8 d3 ♗e7 9 ♘c3 0-0 10 ♘e2 f6 11 ♘g3 ♘f7 12 d4 cxd4 13 ♘xd4 fxe5 14 ♘xe6 ♕b6+ 15 ♔h1 ♗b5 16 ♕g4 g6 17 f5! ♗d7 18 ♘xf8 ♖xf8 19 ♕f3 e4 20 ♕b3 ♗b5 21 ♗e3 ♕c6 22 ♖f2 ♗c4 23 ♕c3 ♗f6 24 ♗d4 ♗xd4 25 ♕xd4 ♘h6 26 fxg6 hxg6 27 ♖xf8+ ♔xf8 28 b3 ♗a6 29 c4 dxc4 30 ♖f1+ ♔g8 31 ♕d8+ ♔g7 32 ♕e7+ ♔h8 33 ♖f8+ **1-0**

**HARRWITZ ✕ HORWITZ**
[1849-✕HH]

| | | | | | | | | | | | | | | | |
|---|---|---|---|---|---|---|---|---|---|---|---|---|---|---|---|
| D. Harrwitz | 1 | 1 | 0 | ½ | 0 | 1 | 0 | 1 | 0 | 0 | 1 | ½ | 0 | 1 | 1 | 8 |
| B. Horwitz | 0 | 0 | 1 | ½ | 1 | 0 | 1 | 0 | 1 | 1 | 0 | ½ | 1 | 0 | 0 | 7 |

**1849-✕HH-1** 19 ii 49
**Harrwitz, D.+Horwitz, B.**
[Staunton]

1 e4 e6 2 d4 d5 3 exd5 exd5 4 c4 ♘f6 5 ♘c3 ♗e7 6 cxd5 ♘xd5 7 ♗c4 ♘b6? 8 ♗b3 0-0 9 ♗e3 ♘c6 10 a3 ♗g5 11 ♘f3 ♖e8 12 0-0 ♗f6 13 h3 ♗f5 14 ♗a2 ♗e4? 15 ♘xe4 ♖xe4 16 ♕d3! ♖e8 17 ♖ac1 ♘e5 18 ♘xe5 ♖xe5 19 ♗b1 ♖h5 20 ♖c5

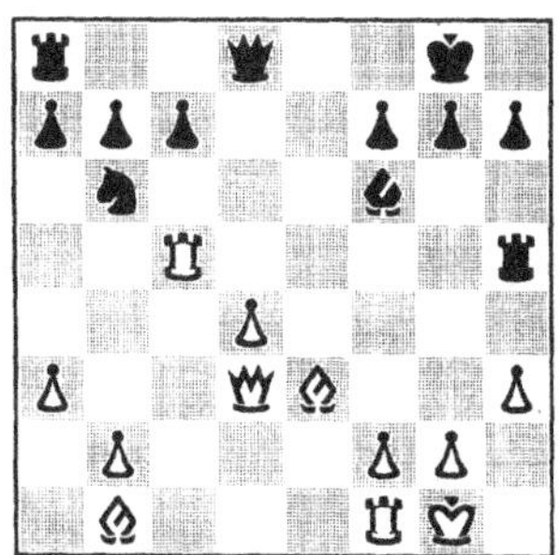

20 ... ♖h4? [20 ... ♘d5 △ ... c6; 20 ... ♖xc5 21 ♕xh7+ ♔f8 22 ♕h8+ (22 dxc5 ♘c4=) 22 ... ♔e7 23 ♕xd8+ ♖xd8 24 dxc5 ♘c4=] 21 g3 ♖xh3 22 ♔g2 ♕d7 23 ♕f5! ♗xd4 24 ♗xd4 ♕xd4 25 ♔xh3 g6 26 ♕c2 h5 27 ♖xc7 ♕g4+ 28 ♔g2 h4 29 ♕e4 h3+ 30 ♔h2 ♕g5 31 ♖xb7 ♖f8 32 ♗a2 ♘c8 33 ♖xf7 **1-0** L/N 6123

**1849-⚔HH-2** 20 ii 49

**Horwitz, B.– Harrwitz, D.**

[Staunton]

1 c4 e5 2 ♘c3 f5 3 e3 c5 4 d3 ♘f6 5 g3 ♘c6 6 ♗g2 d6 7 ♘h3 ♗e7 8 f4 0-0 9 0-0 h6 10 b3 ♔h7 11 ♗b2 ♘g4 12 ♕e2 ♗f6 13 ♘d5 ♖e8 14 ♘xf6+ gxf6 [14 ... ♕xf6?!] 15 ♕d2 exf4 16 ♘xf4! ♘xe3 17 ♖fe1 ♘xg2 18 ♖xe8 ♕xe8 19 ♘d5

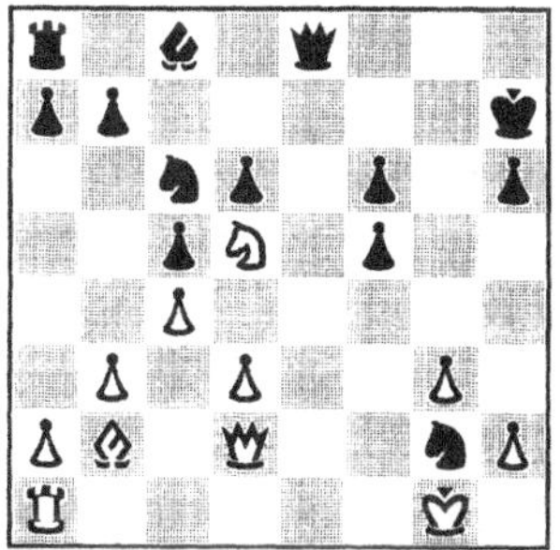

19 ... ♕f7 [19 ... ♘e5 20 ♘xf6+ ♔g6! 21 ♘xe8 ♘f3+ 22 ♔xg2 ♘xd2 23 ♘c7 ♖b8 24 ♖d1 ♗d7 25 ♖xd2+−; 19 ... ♘h4 20 ♘xf6+ ♔g6 21 gxh4 ♕d8 22 h5+ ♔f7 23 ♕xh6+−] 20 ♘xf6+ ♔g6 21 ♕e2??−+ ♘d4 22 ♗xd4 cxd4 23 ♘d5 ♘e3 24 ♘xe3 dxe3 25 ♕xe3 ♕e6 26 ♕f2 ♗d7 27 ♖e1 ♕f6 28 d4 ♖e8 29 ♖xe8 ♗xe8 30 d5 b6 31 h4 ♕e5 32 ♔h2 ♔f6 33 ♕d2 ♔g7 34 ♔g2 ♗h5 35 ♔f2 ♔g6 36 a4 ♕e4 37 ♕e3 ♕xe3+ **0-1** L/N 6123

**1849-⚔HH-3** 21 ii 49

**Harrwitz, D.– Horwitz, B.**

[Staunton]

1 e4 e6 2 d4 d5 3 exd5 exd5 4 c4 ♘f6 5 ♘c3 ♗e7 6 cxd5 ♘xd5 7 ♗c4 ♗e6 8 ♕b3 ♗b4 9 ♘f3 ♘c6 10 0-0 ♗xc3 11 bxc3 0-0 12 ♘g5! ♘a5 13 ♕c2 [△ 14 ♕xh7#] 13 ... g6 14 ♘xe6 fxe6 15 ♗d3 ♘c6 16 ♗h6 ♖f7 [◻ 16 ... ♕h4 △ ... ♘f4] 17 ♗xg6 ♖d7 18 ♗e4 ♕h4! 19 ♗xd5 ♖xd5 20 ♗e3 [◻ 20 ♗d2] 20 ... ♖h5 21 h3 ♔h8 22 ♕b3?!

22 ... ♖g8?+− [22 ... ♕e4! 23 ♔h2 ♖g8 24 g3 (24 ♖g1 ♕f5 25 f3 ♘e5 26 dxe5 ♕xe5+ 27 ♔h1! ♕xe3 28 ♖ae1 ♕xf3 29 ♕xe6! ♕xc3∓) 24 ... ♕g4 25 h4 ♕xh4+−+ (25 ... ♖xh4+−+)] 23 ♕xe6 ♖g6? [23 ... ♘d8!] 24 ♕c8+ ♖g8 25 ♕e6 ♖g6 26 ♕d7 ♖g7 27 ♕c8+ ♖g8 28 ♕e6 ♘d8 29 ♕d7 ♕e4 30 g3 ♘e6 31 ♖fd1 [31 d5!!] 31 ... ♖xh3 32 ♔f1 ♖hxg3 33 fxg3 ♕xe3 34 ♕d5 ♖f8+ 35 ♔g2 ♖f2+ 36 ♔h3 ♘f4+ **0-1** L/N 6123

**1849-⚔HH-4** 22 ii 49

**Horwitz, B.= Harrwitz, D.**

[Staunton]

1 c4 e5 2 ♘c3 f5 3 e3 c5 4 d3 ♘f6 5 g3 ♘c6 6 ♗g2 d6 7 ♘h3 ♗e7 8 f4 0-0 9 0-0 h6 10 b3 ♗d7 11 ♗b2 ♘g4 12 ♕d2 ♗f6 13 ♘d5 ♖e8 14 ♘xf6+ gxf6 15 ♖ae1 ♔h7 16 ♔h1 ♖g8 17 ♘g1 h5 18 ♘f3 ♕e7 19 ♘h4 ♖af8 20 e4 fxe4 21 dxe4 ♘d4 22 f5 ♗e8 23 ♗c1 ♕g7 24 ♗f3 b6 25 h3 ♘h6 26 ♖g1 ♗f7 27 ♗d1 b5! 28 cxb5 d5 29 exd5 ♗xd5+ 30 ♔h2 ♗f7 31 ♗c2 ♖d8 32 ♕f2 ♕f8 33 ♘g6 ♗xg6 34 fxg6+ ♔g7 35 ♗d3 ♖h8! 36 ♖gf1 ♘g4+ 37 hxg4 hxg4+ 38 ♔g2 ♘f3 39 ♖h1 ♘xe1+ 40 ♖xe1 ♖xd3 41 ♗e3 ♕a8+ 42 ♔f1 ♖h1+ [42 ... ♕h1+! 43 ♔e2 ♕e4 44 ♖d1 (44 ♖f1 ♖h2−+) 44 ... ♖h2−+] 43 ♔e2 ♖xe1+ 44 ♔xd3 ♕d5+ 45 ♔c3 ♕d1 46 ♗xc5 ♕c1+ 47 ♔b4 ♖e4+ 48 ♔a5 ♔xg6 49 a4 ♕c3+ 50 b4 f5 51 ♕a2 ♖c4 [△ ... ♖xc5; 52 ... ♖xb4] 52 ♔a6 ♕d3 53 ♔xa7 ♕d7+ 54 ♔a6 ♕c8+ 55 ♔b6 ♕e6+ 56 ♔a5 ♕d5 57 ♕f2 ♕a8+ 58 ♗a7 ♖d4 59 b6 ♕d5+ 60 b5 ♕b3 [◻ 60 ... ♕c4 61 ♕xd4 ♕xd4−+; 61 b7 ♕c7+ 62 ♗b6 ♕c3+−+] 61 ♕xd4 exd4 62 b7 ♕c3+ 63 ♔a6 ♕xg3 64 b8♕ ♕xb8 65 ♗xb8 d3 66 ♗f4 g3 67 b6 g2 68 b7 g1♕ 69 b8♕ ♕g4 70 ♕d6+ ♔f7 71 a5 ♕e2 72 ♔a7 ♕f2+ 73 ♔b8 ♕b2+ 74 ♕b6 ♕h8+ 75 ♔a7 ♕c3 76 a6 d2 77 ♕d6? [77 ♗xd2! ♕xd2 78 ♔b8+−] 77 ... d1♕ 78 ♕xd1 ♕c5+ 79 ♔b7 ♕b4+ 80 ♔c6 ♕c4+ 81 ♔d7 ♕e6+ 82 ♔d8 ♕b6+ 83 ♔d7 ♕e6+ 84 ♔c7 ♕xa6 85 ♕d7+ ♔f6 86 ♕d8+ ♔f7 87 ♕d5+ ♕e6 **½-½** L/N 6123

**1849-⚔HH-5** 23 ii 49

**Harrwitz, D– Horwitz, B.**

[Staunton]

1 e4 c5 2 f4 ♘c6 3 ♘f3 d6 4 b3 ♗g4 5 ♘a3?! [△ 5 ... ♘d4 6 ♘xd4!] 5 ... e6 6 ♗b2 f6 7 h3 ♗xf3 8 ♕xf3 ♘h6 9 ♗c4 ♕d7 10 0-0-0 [10 ♘b5 a6 11 ♗xe6 ♕xe6? 12 ♘c7+; 11 ... ♕e7] 10 ... 0-0-0 11 d4 cxd4 12 ♗xd4 ♘xd4 13 ♖xd4 d5 14 b4 ♗xb4 [14 ... dxe4 15 ♖xe4 ♕d2+ 16 ♔b2 ♕xb4+ 17 ♕b3] 15 exd5 ♕a4 16 ♔b2! exd5 17 ♖xd5 ♔b8 [17 ... ♗xa3+? 18 ♕xa3 ♕xc4 19 ♖c5+; 17 ... ♖xd5 18 ♗xd5 ♗xa3+ 19 ♕xa3 ♕d4+ 20 ♕c3+] 18 ♖hd1 ♖c8! 19 ♖1d4 ♗c5 20 ♕d3 ♗xd4+ 21 ♖xd4 ♕a5 22 g4 ♖cd8 23 ♗d5 ♕b6+ 24 ♔c1 ♖he8 25 c3 ♘g8 26 ♖b4 ♕c7 27 ♔c2 ♘e7 28 ♗xb7 ♖xd3 29 ♗e4+ ♔c8 30 ♗xd3 ♘d5 31 ♖b3 ♕xf4 32 ♗f5+ ♔d8 33 ♖b7 ♘e3+ 34 ♔b3 ♘xf5 **0-1** L/N6123

**1849-⚔HH-6** 26 ii 49

**Horwitz, B.– Harrwitz, D.**

[Staunton]

1 e4 c5 2 f4 e6 3 ♘f3 ♘c6 4 ♗e2 d5 5 e5?∓ f6 6 ♗b5 ♕b6 7 ♗xc6+ bxc6 8 0-0 ♗e7 9 ♘c3 a5 10 ♘a4 ♕b4 11 c3 ♕xf4 12 d4 ♕g4 13 h3 ♕h5 14 ♘b6 ♖b8 15 ♘xc8 ♖xc8 16 ♕a4 cxd4 17 cxd4 ♗d8 18 ♗d2 ♘e7 19 ♗xa5 ♖a8 20 b4 0-0 21 exf6 gxf6 22 ♖ae1 e5 23 dxe5 ♗b6+ 24 ♔h1 fxe5 25 ♖xe5 ♕xe5!! 26 ♘xe5 ♖xf1+ 27 ♔h2 ♗c7 28 g3 ♗xe5 29 ♔g2 ♖8f8 30 ♗b6 d4 31 h4 ♖8f2+ 32 ♔h3 h5! **0-1** L/N6123

**1849-⚔HH-7** 27 ii 49

**Harrwitz, D.– Horwitz, B.**

[Staunton]

1 e4 e5 2 ♘f3 d6 3 d4 exd4 4 ♘xd4 ♘f6 5 ♘c3 ♗e7 6 ♗c4 0-0 7 f4 ♘xe4 8 ♗xf7+ ♖xf7 9 ♘xe4 d5 10 ♘f2 c5 11 ♘f3 ♘c6 12 0-0 b6 13 c3 ♕d6 14 ♖e1 ♗b7! 15 ♘d3 ♗f6 16 ♘de5 ♖e7 17 ♘g4 ♖ae8 18 ♘xf6+ gxf6 19 ♗d2 d4 20 ♕b3+ ♔h8 21 ♖xe7 ♖xe7 22 c4? d3 23 ♔h1 ♖e2 24 ♖e1 ♘a5 25 ♗xa5 ♗xf3 26 gxf3 bxa5 27 ♕d1 ♕xf4! 28 ♖xe2 ♕xf3+ 29 ♔g1 ♕xe2 [29 ... dxe2?] 30 ♕xe2 dxe2 31 ♔f2

♔g7 32 ♔xe2 ♔g6 33 ♔f3 ♔f5 34 b3 ♔e5 35 ♔e3 a4 36 bxa4 a5 37 h3 f5 38 h4 h5 39 a3 f4+ 40 ♔f3 ♔f5 41 ♔f2−+ ♔g4 42 ♔g2 ♔xh4 **0-1** L/N6123

### 1849-⚔HH-8 28 ii 49
**Horwitz, B.− Harrwitz, D.**

[Staunton]

1 e4 c5 2 ♗c4 e6 3 ♘c3 ♘c6 4 ♘f3 ♘8e7 5 ♕e2 a6 6 a3 b5 7 ♗a2 ♘d4 8 ♘xd4 cxd4 9 ♘d1 ♘g6 10 d3 ♗d6 11 0-0 ♕c7 12 f4 f6 13 f5 exf5 [13 ... ♗xh2+? 14 ♔h1 (△ 15 fxg6; 15 ♕h5)] 14 exf5+ ♘e7 15 ♕h5+ ♔d8 16 c4 ♗b7 17 ♘f2 ♕c5 18 ♘e4 ♗xe4 19 b4?! ♕c6 20 dxe4 bxc4 21 ♕e2 d3 22 ♕f3 ♗e5 23 ♖b1 g6 24 ♗h6 gxf5 25 exf5 ♕xf3 26 ♖xf3 d5∓ 27 ♗e3 ♖g8 [27 ... d4?] 28 ♔f2 d4 29 ♗xc4 dxe3+ 30 ♖xe3 ♖g4 31 ♖xd3+ ♖d4 32 ♖xd4+ ♗xd4+ 33 ♔f3 ♗e5 34 ♗e6 ♔c7 35 h3 ♖d8 36 ♖b3 ♘c6 37 ♔g4 ♖d2 38 g3 ♘d4 39 ♖c3+ ♔d6 40 ♗c8 ♘xf5 [△ 41 ... ♗xc3] 41 ♖c5 ♘xg3 42 ♗xa6 f5+ 43 ♔f3 ♘e4 44 ♖a5 ♖h2 45 ♗c8 ♖f2+ 46 ♔e3 ♗f4+ 47 ♔d4 ♖d2+ 48 ♔c4 ♖c2+ 49 ♔d3 ♖c3+ 50 ♔d4 ♗e3# **0-1** L/N6123

### 1849-⚔HH-9 1 ii 49
**Harrwitz, D.− Horwitz, B.**

[Staunton]

1 d4 e6 2 c4 f5 3 ♘c3 ♘f6 4 ♗g5 ♗e7 5 ♘f3 0-0 6 e3 c5 7 d5 ♘e4 8 ♗xe7 ♕xe7 9 ♘xe4 fxe4 10 ♘d2 exd5 11 cxd5 d6 12 ♗c4 ♘d7 13 ♕c2 ♘f6 14 0-0 ♗d7 15 a4 a6 16 a5! [16 ∼ b5, ... xd5] 16 ... ♗f5 17 h3 ♘d7 18 ♖ae1 ♘e5 19 f4 exf3 20 e4 ♗xh3! 21 ♘xf3 [21 gxh3??] 21 ... ♘xf3+ 22 ♖xf3 ♖xf3 23 bxf3 ♕g5+ 24 ♔h1 ♗g2+! 25 ♕xg2 ♕h4+ 26 ♔g1 ♕xe1+ 27 ♔h2 ♖f8 28 ♕g3 ♕e3 29 ♕xd6 ♕f2+ 30 ♔h1 ♕xf3+ 31 ♔h2 ♕f2+ 32 ♔h1 ♕e1+ 33 ♔h2 ♖f2+ 34 ♔h3 ♖f3+ **0-1** L/N6123

### 1849-⚔HH-10 2 iii 49
**Horwitz, B.+ Harrwitz, D.**

[Staunton]

1 e4 c5 2 ♗c4 e6 3 ♘c3 ♘c6 4 ♘f3 a6 5 a3 ♘8e7 6 ♕e2 b5 7 ♗a2 ♘d4 8 ♘xd4 cxd4 9 ♘d1 ♘g6 10 d3 ♗d6 11 0-0 0-0 12 f4 ♕e7 13 ♕h5 ♗b7 14 f5 exf5 15 ♗g5! [15 exf5] 15 ... ♕e8 16 ♖f3 [16 exf5?] 16 ... ♘f4! 17 ♗xf4 ♗xf4 18 ♖xf4 fxe4 19 ♖h4 h6 20 ♕g4? [◻ 20 ♘f2] 20 ... exd3 21 ♘f2 dxc2 22 ♕xd4 ♖c8 23 ♖c1 ♕e7 24 ♖g4 g5 25 h4 ♖fe8 26 ♘d3 ♔h7 27 hxg5 hxg5 28 ♖g3 f5 29 ♗b3 ♕e4 30 ♕f6 [30 ♕xe4] 30 ... g4 31 ♕f7+ ♔h6 32 ♗xc2 ♕d4+ 33 ♘f2 ♖f8 34 ♕e7 ♕xb2 35 ♘xg4+ fxg4 36 ♕h7+ ♔g5 37 ♕g6+ ♔f4 38 ♖xg4+ ♔e5 39 ♖g5+ ♔d4 40 ♕d3# **1-0** L/N6123

### 1849-⚔HH-11 3 iii 49
**Harrwitz, D.+ Horwitz, B.**

[Staunton]

1 d4 e6 2 c4 f5 3 ♘c3 ♘f6 4 ♗g5 ♗e7 5 e3 0-0 6 ♗xf6 ♗xf6 7 f4 c5 8 d5 [8 dxc5 ♗xc3+∓] 8 ... ♗xc3+ 9 bxc3 ♕f6 10 ♕d2 e5 11 fxe5 ♕xe5 12 ♘f3 ♕f6 13 ♗d3 d6 14 0-0 ♘d7 15 ♖f2 ♘e5 16 ♘xe5 ♕xe5 17 ♖1f1 ♗d7 18 ♖f3 ♖f6 19 ♗c2 ♖af8 20 a4 a6 21 ♖b1 ♗c8 22 g3 g6? [◻ 22 ... g5!] 23 h4 g5 24 hxg5 ♖g6 25 e4 ♕g7 26 exf5 ♖xg5 27 ♕f2 ♕f6 28 ♖f1 ♔h8 29 ♕e3 ♖8g8 30 ♔g2 ♕h6 [△ 31 ... ♖xg3+−+] 31 ♕f4! ♕f6 32 ♖h1 ♖8g7 33 ♖h4 ♗d7 34 ♔f2 ♔g8 35 g4 ♗e8 36 ♖e3 ♗f7 37 ♗e4! h5 38 gxh5 ♗xh5 39 ♖3h3 ♖g4 40 ♖xg4 ♖xg4 41 ♕e3 ♖h4 42 ♖g3+ ♔f7 [◻ 42 ... ♔f8] 43 ♗d3 ♖h2+ 44 ♔f1 ♖b2 45 ♖g5 ♗f3 46 ♕e6+ ♕xe6 47 fxe6+ ♔e7 48 ♖g7+ **1-0** L/N6123

### 1849-⚔HH-12 6 iii 49
**Horwitz, B.= Harrwitz, D.**

[Staunton]

1 e4 c5 2 ♗c4 e6 3 ♘c3 ♘c6 4 ♘f3 a6 5 a3 ♘8e7 6 ♕e2 b5 7 ♗a2 ♘d4 8 ♘xd4 cxd4 9 ♘d1 ♗b7 10 d3 d5 11 e5 ♖c8 12 ♗f4 a5 13 0-0 h5 14 ♗g5 ♕c7 15 ♖c1 ♘f5 16 h3 h4 17 c3 ♕d7 18 cxd4 ♖xc1 19 ♗xc1 ♘xd4 20 ♕g4 ♘f5 21 ♘e3 g6 22 ♘xf5 gxf5 23 ♕d4 ♕c7 24 ♗e3 ♗g7 25 ♖c1 ♗c6 [25 ... ♕xe5 26 ♕a7 ♕xb2 27 ♕xb7+−] 26 ♕c5 ♔d7 27 d4 f6 28 exf6 [◻ 28 ♗xd5 exd5 29 e6+ ♔xe6! 30 ♕xc6+ ♕xc6 31 ♖xc6+ ♔d7! 32 ♖a6+−] 28 ... ♗xf6 29 ♗f4 ♕xf4 30 ♕xc6+ ♔e7 31 ♕b7+ ♔e8 32 ♖c8+ ♗d8 33 ♕g7 [33 ♕xb5+?; 33 ♖xd8+?] 33 ... ♕h6 34 ♕c7 ♕g5 35 ♕e5! ♔d7! 36 f4 ♕f6 37 ♖c7+!! ♔e8 38 ♖b7 ♕xe5 39 fxe5 ♖g8 40 ♖xb5 ♖g3 41 ♗b1! ♔d7 42 ♗c2 ♔c6 43 ♗a4 ♔c7 44 ♖c5+ [44 ♖xa5? ♖d3] 44 ... ♔b7 45 ♗d7 ♗b6 46 ♖b5 ♔a6 47 a4 ♖g6 48 ♔f1 ♗xd4 49 ♗c8+ ♔a7 50 ♖xa5+ ♔b8 51 ♗d7 ♔c7 52 ♗e8 ♖g7 53 b4 ♗xe5 54 ♖a7+ ♔d8! [54 ... ♔b8 55 ♖xg7 ♗xg7 56 ♗f7, 57 ♗xe6; 57 ♗xd5] 55 ♗f7 ♗d4 56 ♖b7 ♔c8 57 ♖e7 ♔d8 58 ♖b7 ♗c3 59 a5 ♗xb4 60 a6 ♗c5 61 a7 ♗xa7 62 ♖xa7 d4 63 ♖a8+ ♔e7 64 ♗h5 ♔f6 65 ♗e2 ♖c7 66 ♖h8 ♔g5 67 ♖h5+ ♔f4 68 ♔f2 e5 69 ♖xh4+ ♔g5 70 ♖h5+ ♔g6 71 g4 fxg4 72 hxg4 ♖c2 73 ♔e1 e4 74 ♖e5 d3 75 ♗d1 ♖c4! 76 ♔d2 ♖b4! 77 ♔e3 ♖b1 78 ♗a4 ♖e1+ 79 ♔f4 d2 80 ♖e6+ ♔f7 81 ♖xe4 d1♕ 82 ♗xd1 ♖xd1 83 ♔g5 ♖d6 84 ♖a4 ♖g6+ 85 ♔h5 ♖b6 86 ♖a7+ ♔g8 87 g5 ♖c6 88 g6 ♖c5+ 89 ♔h6 ♖c8 90 ♖g7+ ♔h8 91 ♖f7 ♖b8 92 ♖f6 ♖a8 93 ♖f1 ♖g8 94 ♖e1 **½-½** L/N6123

### 1849-⚔HH-13 7 iii 49
**Harrwitz, D.− Horwitz, B.**

[Staunton]

1 d4 e6 2 c4 c6 3 ♘c3 f5 4 ♘f3 ♘f6 5 ♗g5 ♗e7 6 ♗xf6 ♗xf6 7 e3 ♘a6 [◻ 7 ... c5] 8 c5 b6 9 ♗xa6 ♗xa6 10 ♕a4 ♕c8 11 b4 0-0 12 e4 fxe4 13 ♘xe4 ♗e7 14 ♘e5 ♗b5 15 ♕d1 bxc5 16 bxc5 ♗d8 17 f3 ♗c7 18 a4 ♗a6 19 ♘d3 ♕d8 20 0-0 ♕h4 21 g3 ♕h6 22 ♖e1 ♖ab8 23 ♘3f2 ♗c4 [◻ ... ♗d5!; 23 ... ♗a5 24 ♘g4] 24 ♖a3 ♗d5 25 f4 ♕g6 26 ♕g4 ♕xg4 27 ♘xg4 ♖b4! 28 ♖d3 ♖xa4 29 ♘c3 ♗a5 30 ♘xa4 ♗xe1 31 ♘e5 ♖b8 32 ♘c3 [32 ♘xd7 ♖b1 △ 33 ... ♗xg3+ 34 ♖d1 ♖xd1#] 32 ... ♗xc3 33 ♖xc3 ♖b7 34 ♔f2 ♔f8 35 ♖a3 ♔e7 36 ♖a6 ♔d8 37 ♘f7+ ♔c7 38 ♘d6 ♖b2+ 39 ♔e3 ♔b8 40 h3 ♖b3+ 41 ♔d2 ♖xg3 42 ♖a4 ♖xh3 43 ♖b4+ ♔c7 [43 ... ♔a8=] 44 ♖b7+ ♔d8 45 ♖xa7 ♖g3 46 ♘f7+ ♔e8 47 ♘e5 h5 48 ♖xd7 h4 49 ♖b7 h3 50 ♖b8+ ♔e7 51 ♖b7+ ♔d8 52 ♘f7+ ♔e8 53 ♘d6+ ♔f8 54 f5 ♖g2+ 55 ♔e3 exf5 56 ♔f4 ♔g8 57 ♘xf5 h2 58 ♘e7+ ♔h7 59 ♘xd5 h1♕ 60 ♘f6+ ♔g6 61 ♘e4 ♕h2+ 62 ♔f3 ♕h3+ 63 ♔f4 ♖g4+ 64 ♔e5 ♕h5+ 65 ♔d6 ♕d5+ **0-1** L/N6123

### 1849-⚔HH-14 iii 49
**Horwitz, B.− Harrwitz, D.**

[Staunton]

1 e4 c5 2 ♗c4 e6 3 ♘c3 ♘c6 4 ♘f3 a6 5 a3 ♘8e7 6 d4 cxd4 7 ♘xd4 b5 8 ♗b3 ♘xd4 9 ♕xd4 ♘c6 10 ♕d3 ♗c5 11 ♕g3 0-0 12 ♗g5 f6 [12 ... ♕∼?] 13 ♗h6 ♖f7 14 0-0-0? ♕b6 15 ♖hf1 a5 16 a4 [16 ♘d5!! exd5 17 ♗xd5 g6 18 ♗xf7+ ♔xf7 19 ♕b3+ ♔e7 20 ♕g8+− (20 ... d5 21 ♖xd5±)] 16 ... ♘d4 17 ♖xd4 ♗xd4 18 ♘xb5 ♗a6 19 c4 ♗xb5 20 cxb5 f5! 21 exf5 ♕c5+ 22 ♔b1 [22 ♗c2 ♖c8 23 ♕d3 (23 ♔∼ ♕xc2+) 23 ... gxh6] 22 ... ♕xf5+ 23 ♗c2 ♕c5 24 f3 ♖c8 25 ♗b3 ♕b4 **0-1** L/N6123

### 1849-⚔HH-15 iii 49
**Harrwitz, D.+ Horwitz, B.**

[Staunton]

1 d4 e6 2 c4 c6? 3 e4 f5?! 4 exf5 ♕a5+ 5 ♘c3 ♕xf5 6 ♗d3 ♕f7 7 ♘f3 ♗b4 8 ♘e5 ♕f6 9 0-0! ♗xc3

10 bxc3 ♘e7 11 ♕h5+ g6 12 ♕h6 ♘f5 13 ♗xf5 ♕xf5 14 ♗a3 ♕f6 15 ♖ae1± c5!? 16 ♗xc5 ♘c6 17 ♗d6 ♘e7 18 ♘g4 ♕f7 19 ♕g5 b6 20 ♘f6+ ♔d8 21 ♘d5! ♗a6 [20 ... ♕f8 21 ♕h6+ ♕g7 22 ♕xg7+ (22 ♗xe7+ ♔f7 23 ♕xg7+) 22 ... ♔xg7 23 ♗xe7] 22 ♗xe7+ ♔c8 23 ♕e5 exd5 24 ♕xh8+ ♔b7 25 ♕e5 ♗xc4 26 ♕d6 ♖c8 27 ♗h4 ♖c6 28 ♖e7 ♖xd6 29 ♖xf7 ♔c6 30 ♖e1 ♗xa2 31 ♖a1 ♖e6 32 ♖f6 ♗c4 33 ♖xa7 h6 34 ♖xe6+ dxe6 35 f4 ♗d3 36 ♔f2 ♗f5 37 h3 h5 38 ♔e3 ♗e4 39 g4 ♗g2 40 gxh5 gxh5 41 ♖h7 ♗xh3 42 ♖xh5 ♔b5 43 ♗d8 ♗f5 44 ♖xf5 exf5 45 ♔d3 ♔c6 46 ♔c2 **1-0** L/N6123

## KENNEDY⚔LOWE [1849-⚔KL]

H.A. Kennedy
1̂ ½ 1 1 0 0 0 1 1 0 0 0 1 0 6½
E. Lowe
0̂ ½ 0 0 1 1 1 0 0 1 1 1 0 1 7½

### 1849-⚔KL-1̂
**Kennedy, H.A.+ Lowe, E.**
[Staunton]

1 e4 c5 2 d4 cxd4 3 ♘f3 e5 4 ♗c4 ♕c7 5 ♗b3 ♗e7 [◻ 5 ... ♗b4+] 6 0-0 ♘f6 7 ♕e2 0-0 8 c3 b6 9 ♗c2 [9 cxd4?? ♗a6] 9 ... dxc3 10 ♘xc3 ♗a6 11 ♗d3 ♗xd3 12 ♕xd3 a6 13 ♗g5 ♕d6 14 ♕e3 ♘c6 15 ♖fd1 ♕c5 16 ♕xc5 ♗xc5 17 ♗xf6 gxf6 18 ♖xd7 ♖fd8 19 ♖ad1 ♘d4 20 ♖xd8+ [20 ♘d5] 20 ... ♖xd8 21 ♘xd4 ♗xd4 22 ♔f1 ♖c8 23 ♖d3 ♗xc3 24 bxc3 b5 25 f3 ♖c4 26 ♔e1 ♔f8 27 ♔d1 ♖a4 28 ♖d2 ♖c4 29 ♖c2 ♔e7 30 ♔c1 ♔d6 31 ♖d2+ ♔c6 32 ♔b2 b4 33 axb4 ♖xb4+ 34 ♔c3 ♖b1 35 ♔c2 ♖a1? 36 ♔b2 ♖h1 37 h3 h5 38 ♔c3 ♖g1 39 ♔b4 ♔b6 40 ♖d6+ ♔b7 41 ♖xf6 ♖xg2 42 ♖xf7+ ♔b6 43 ♖f6+ ♔b7 44 a4 ♖g3 45 h4 ♖h3 46 ♖f5 ♖xh4 47 ♖xe5 ♖f4 48 ♖xh5 ♖xf3 49 ♔a5 ♖e3 50 ♖e5 ...♀ **1-0** L/N6123

### 1849-⚔KL-2̂
**Lowe, E.= Kennedy, H.A.**
[Staunton]

1 e4 e5 2 ♘f3 ♘f6 3 ♘xe5 d6 4 ♘f3 ♘xe4 5 d3 [5 d4!] 5 ... ♘f6 6 d4 d5 7 ♗d3 ♗d6 8 0-0 0-0 9 ♘e5 c5 10 c3 ♘c6 11 f4 ♕b6 12 ♘xc6 bxc6 13 ♔h1 ♗g4 14 dxc5 ♗xc5 15 ♕c2 ♖fe8 16 b4 ♗d6 17 h3 ♗d7 18 ♕f2? ♕xf2 19 ♖xf2 ♖e1+ 20 ♖f1 ♖xf1+ 21 ♗xf1 ♘h5 22 ♘a3 ♘xf4 23 ♘c2 a5 24 a4 ♘h5 25 ♗d3 axb4 26 cxb4 ♗e5 27 ♖a3 ♘g3+ 28 ♔g1 ♗f5 29 ♗xf5 ♘xf5 30 a5 f6 31 g4 ♘d4 [◻ 31 ... ♘g3 △ 32 ... ♘e2+] 32 ♘xd4 ♗xd4+ 33 ♗e3 ♗xe3+ 34 ♖xe3 ♔f7 35 ♔f1 ♖b8? [35 ... c5] 36 ♖c3 ♖xb4 37 ♖xc6 ♖a4 38 a6 ♖a2 39 ♖c7+ ♔g6 40 a7 d4 41 ♖d7 d3 42 ♖xd3 ♖xa7 43 ♔g2 h5 44 ♖d5 hxg4 45 hxg4 ...♀ **½-½** L/N6123

### 1849-⚔KL-3
**Lowe, E.– Kennedy, H.A.**
[Staunton]

1 e4 e5 2 ♗c4 ♘f6 3 ♕e2 ♗c5 4 ♘f3 [4 ♗xf7+? ♔xf7 5 ♕c4+ d5 6 ♕xc5 ♘xe4∓] 4 ... d6 5 h3 ♘c6 6 d3 h6 7 ♘c3 0-0 8 ♗e3 ♗b6 9 g4 ♘h7 10 0-0-0 ♗e6 11 ♗b3 ♗xb3 12 axb3 ♘d4 13 ♗xd4 ♗xd4 14 ♘xd4 exd4 15 ♘b5?? ♕g5+ 16 ♕d2 ♕xb5 17 f4 a5 18 ♖dg1 f6 19 h4 a4 20 b4 a3 21 bxa3 ♖xa3 22 ♔d1 ♖a1+ 23 ♔e2 ♖xg1 24 ♖xg1 ♖e8 25 ♔f3 d5 26 ♖c1 dxe4+ 27 dxe4 ♘f8 28 ♕xd4 ♘e6 29 ♕b2 ♕c4 30 ♖d1 ♘xf4! 31 ♕d4 ♕xd4 32 ♖xd4 ♘e6 33 ♖d7 ♔f8 34 c4 ♖d8 35 ♖xd8+ ♘xd8 ...♀ **0-1** L/N6123

### 1849-⚔KL-4
**Kennedy, H.A.+ Lowe, E.**
[Staunton]

1 e4 c5 2 d4 cxd4 3 ♘f3 ♘c6 4 ♗c4 e6 5 ♘xd4 ♗c5 6 ♘xc6 bxc6 7 0-0 d5 8 exd5 cxd5 9 ♗b5+ ♗d7 10 ♗xd7+ ♕xd7 11 ♕g4 ♔f8? [11 ... f5] 12 ♗e3 ♗xe3 [12 ... d4 13 ♖d1] 13 fxe3 f5 14 ♘d2 ♘f6 15 ♕g3 h6 16 c4 ♖c8 17 cxd5 ♕xd5 18 ♘b3 ♘e4 19 ♕f3 [19 ♕g6] 19 ... ♕e5 20 ♕e2 [20 ♘d4 ♘d2 21 ♕b7] 20 ... ♔f7 21 ♖ac1 ♘f6 [△ 22 ... ♘g4] 22 h3 g5 23 ♘d4 ♖xc1 24 ♖xc1 g4 25 hxg4 ♘xg4 26 ♘f3 ♕g3 [26 ... ♕xe3+ 27 ♕xe3 ♘xe3 28 ♖c7+ ♔~ 29 ♖xa7] 27 e4 ♕f4 28 ♖e1! ♖d8 29 exf5 ♕xf5 30 ♘h4 ♕c5+ 31 ♔h1 ♘f2+ 32 ♔h2 ♕d6+ 33 ♔g1 ♘d3 34 ♕h5+ ♔f8 35 ♖f1+ ♘f4 36 ♘g6+ [36 ♖xf4+ ♕xf4 37 ♘g6+] 36 ... ♔g7 37 ♘xf4 e5 38 ♕g4+ ♔h8 39 ♘g6+ ♔h7 40 ♖f7+ ♔g8 41 ♘xe5+ ♔h8 42 ♕g7# **1-0** L/N6123

### 1849-⚔KL-5
**Lowe, E.+ Kennedy, H.A.**
[Staunton]

1 e4 e6 2 d4 d5 3 e5 c5 4 c3 ♘c6 5 ♗d3 ♕b6 6 ♘f3 ♗d7 7 dxc5 ♗xc5∓ 8 0-0 a5 9 a4 ♘ge7 10 ♕c2 ♘g6 11 ♗xg6 hxg6 12 ♗g5 ♖h5 [△ 13 ... ♘xe5] 13 ♖e1 ♖c8 14 ♘bd2?? ♗xf2+ 15 ♔h1 ♗xe1 16 ♖xe1 ♘d4 17 ♘xd4 ♕xd4 18 ♘f3 ♕xa4 19 ♕d2 ♕g4 20 h3

20 ... ♕f5 [20 ... ♖xh3+! 21 gxh3 ♕xf3+–+] 21 ♔g1 f6 22 ♗f4 fxe5? 23 ♗xe5 ♖h8 24 ♗xg7 ♖g8 25 ♖e5 ♕f7 26 ♗h6 ♖c4 27 ♕xd5 ♖c6 28 ♕xa5 b6 29 ♕a8+ ♖c8 30 ♕b7 ♔e7 31 ♕xb6 ♖c6 32 ♕e3 ♖h8 33 ♘d4 ♖c4 34 ♗g5 ♔d6 35 ♗f4 ...♀ **1-0** L/N6123

### 1849-⚔KL-6
**Kennedy, H.A.– Lowe, E.**
[Staunton]

1 d4 d5 2 c4 c6? [2 ... e6] 3 ♘c3 ♘f6 4 f3 e5? 5 dxe5 ♘h5 6 g3? [6 ♗e3; 6 ♕d4! (△ 7 g4) 6 ... c5 7 ♕xd5 ♕h4+ 8 g3 ♘xg3 9 hxg3 ♕xh1 10 ♘b5 ♘a6 11 ♗g5+–] 6 ... d4 7 ♘e4 ♕a5+ 8 ♗d2 ♕xe5 9 ♘h3 f5 10 ♘ef2 ♗d6 11 ♘d3 ♕e7 12 ♕c2 ♘a6 13 0-0-0 ♗e6 14 ♔b1 0-0 15 ♘hf4 ♘xf4 16 ♘xf4 ♗xf4 17 ♗xf4 ♖ad8 18 ♖c1 b5 19 e3? d3! 20 ♕c3 [20 ♗xd3?? ♘b4–+] 20 ... bxc4 21 h4 ♕b4 22 ♗h3 ♕xc3 23 ♖xc3 ♗d5 24 ♗g2 ♘c5 25 ♖d1 ♖f7 26 ♔a1 ♖b7 27 ♖d2 ♖b5 28 e4 fxe4 29 fxe4 ♗xe4 30 ♖xc4 ♗xg2 31 ♖xg2 ♖e8 32 b3 ♖e2 33 ♖xe2 dxe2 34 ♗d2 ♘d3 35 ♖xc6 ♖e5 36 ♖c8+ ♔f7 37 ♔b1 e1♕+ 38 ♗xe1 ♖xe1+ 39 ♔c2 ♖c1+ ...♀ **0-1** L/N6123

### 1849-⚔KL-7
**Lowe, E.+ Kennedy, H.A.**
[Staunton]

1 f4 d5 2 d4 c5 3 ♘f3 f6 4 ♘c3 e6 5 e4 cxd4 6 ♕xd4 ♘c6 7 ♗b5 ♗d7 8 ♗xc6 ♗xc6 9 exd5 exd5 10 0-0 ♕a5 [△ 11 ... ♗c5; 11 ... 0-0-0] 11 ♖e1+ ♔f7 12 ♗e3 ♘h6 13 ♕d3 ♗d6 14 ♘d4 ♖he8 15 ♘b3!± [15 ♕xh7] 15 ... ♕d8 16 ♘xd5 ♔g8 17 c4 ♘g4 18 ♗d2 ♖xe1+ 19 ♖xe1 ♔h8 20 h3 ♘h6 21 ♔h1 ♘g8? 22 ♘d4 ♘e7 23 ♘e6 ♕d7 24 ♖e3 [24 ♘xf6!+–] 24 ... ♘g6 25 ♕d4 ♖e8 26 ♘c5 ♗xc5 27 ♖xe8+ ♕xe8 28 ♕xc5 h6 29 ♕e3 ♕d7 30 ♕e4 f5 31 ♕d3 b5 32 b3 bxc4 33 bxc4 ♗xd5 34 ♕xd5 ♕xd5 35 cxd5 ♔g8 36 ♔g1 ♔f7 37 g3 ♘f8 38 ♔f2 ♘d7 39 ♔e3 g5 40 ♔d4 g4 41 h4 ♔e7 42 ♗b4+ ♔f6 43 a4 a6 44 a5 h5 45 ♗d6 ♔f7

46 ♗c7 ♘f6 47 ♔c5 ♘e4+ 48 ♔c6 ♘f6 49 ♔b6 ...? **1-0** L/N6123

**1849-✕KL-8**
**Kennedy, H.A.+Lowe, E.**
[Staunton]

1 d4 d5 2 c4 e6 3 e3 ♘f6 4 ♘c3 c6? 5 ♘f3 ♗d6 6 b3 ♘bd7 7 ♗b2 h6 8 ♗e2 a6 9 0-0 g5 10 e4! dxe4 11 ♘d2 ♕c7 12 g3 e5 13 c5 ♗e7 14 ♘cxe4 ♘xe4 15 ♘xe4 f5?? 16 ♗h5+ ♔d8

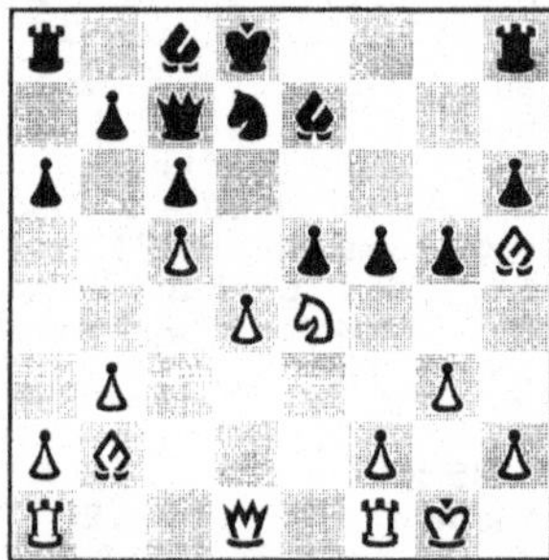

17 dxe5! fxe4 18 e6 ♖f8 19 ♗g4 h5 20 exd7 hxg4 21 dxc8♕+ ♔xc8 22 ♕xg4+ ♔b8 23 ♕xe4 ♗xc5 24 ♗e5 ♗d6 25 ♗xd6 ♕xd6 26 ♖ad1 ♕c5 27 b4! ♕f5 28 ♖d8+ ♔c7? [28 ... ♔a7] 29 ♕xf5 ♖xf5 30 ♖xa8 ...? **1-0** L/N6123

**1849-✕KL-9**
**Lowe, E.–Kennedy, H.A.**
[Staunton]

1 e4 e6 2 c4 c5 3 f4 ♘c6 4 ♘f3 ♘h6 5 ♘c3 f5 6 ♗d3 ♗e7 7 0-0 0-0 8 ♕e2 d6 9 b3 ♗f6 10 ♗b2 [10 e5?? dxe5 11 fxe5 ♘xe5 12 ♘xe5 ♕d4+] 10 ... ♘d4 11 ♘xd4 ♗xd4+ 12 ♔h1 ♘g4 13 ♘d1 ♘xh2!! 14 ♗xd4 ♘xf1 15 ♗f2 ♕f6!→ 16 e5 ♕h6+ 17 ♔g1 ♘h2 18 ♗g3 ♘g4 19 exd6 ♕f6 20 ♖b1 ♕d4+ 21 ♘e3 ♗d7 22 ♔f1 ♕xd6 23 ♘xg4 fxg4 24 ♔g1 ♗c6 25 ♗c2 ♖f6 26 ♖f1 ♕d4+ 27 ♖f2 h5 28 ♔h2 ♖ae8 29 ♕e3 ♕xe3 30 dxe3 e5 31 f5 e4 32 ♗h4 ♖f7 33 f6 gxf6 34 ♖f5 ♖e5 35 ♖xf6 ♖xf6 36 ♗xf6 ♖f5 37 ♗h4 ♖f1 38 b4 cxb4 39 ♗e7 a5 40 ♔g3 ♖c1 41 ♗b3 a4 42 ♗xb4 axb3 ...? **0-1** L/N6123

**1849-✕KL-10**
**Kennedy, H.A.–Lowe, E.**
[Staunton]

1 d4 e6 2 e4 d5 3 exd5 ♕xd5? 4 ♘f3 ♘f6 5 ♗d3 ♗d7 6 0-0 ♗d6 7 c4 ♕h5 8 c5 ♗e7 9 ♗f4 ♘d5 10 ♗g3 0-0 11 ♘c3 f5 12 ♘xd5 exd5 13 ♗xc7 ♘c6 14 ♘e5 ♕xd1 15 ♖axd1 ♗e6 16 ♘xc6 bxc6 17 ♖fe1± ♔f7 18 f4 ♖fe8 19 ♗a6 [△ 20 ♗b7] 19 ... ♗c8 20 ♗d3 ♗d7 21 ♖e3 ♗f6 22 ♗e5 a5 23 ♗c2 ♖a7 24 ♖b3! h5 25 ♔f2 g5 26 fxg5 [26 g3] 26 ... ♗xg5 27 ♖f3 ♔g6 28 h3 h4 29 g4 hxg3+? 30 ♔xg3? [30 ♖xg3 ♔h5 31 h4 ♗xh4 (31 ... ♗d8 32 ♖dg1+–) 32 ♖h1 △ 33 ♗d1++] 30 ... ♖b7 31 b3 ♗f6 32 ♗xf6 ♔xf6 33 ♖df1 ♖g8+ 34 ♔f4 ♖g2 35 ♖1f2 ♖xf2 36 ♖xf2 ♗e6 37 a3 ♖h7 38 ♖f3 ♖g7 39 ♖g3 ♖h7 40 ♖d3 ♖h4+ 41 ♔g3 ♔g5 42 ♔g2 f4 43 ♖f3 ♗f5 44 ♗xf5 ♔xf5 45 ♖d3 ♔e4 46 ♖d1 ♖h7 47 b4 axb4 48 axb4 ♖b7 49 ♖e1+ ♔xd4 50 ♖e6 ♖c7 51 ♔f3 ♔c3 52 ♖e1 d4 53 ♔xf4 d3 54 ♔e5?? ♖e7+ ...? **0-1** L/N6123

**1849-✕KL-11**
**Lowe, E.+Kennedy, H.A.**
[Staunton]

1 f4 c5 2 c4 e6 3 e4 ♘c6 4 ♘f3 d6 5 ♗e2 g6 6 ♘c3 ♗g7 7 d3 ♘h6 8 h3 f5 9 ♗e3 ♘d4 10 ♕d2 ♗d7 11 ♗f2 0-0 12 ♘xd4 ♗xd4 13 ♗f3 ♗c6 14 ♗xd4 cxd4 15 ♘e2 ♕b6 16 b4 fxe4 17 dxe4 d3 18 ♕xd3 ♕xb4+ 19 ♔f2 ♕c5+ 20 ♕d4 ♕xd4+ 21 ♘xd4 ♖xf4 22 ♘xe6 ♖f6 23 ♘c7 ♖c8 24 ♘d5 ♗xd5 25 cxd5 ♖ff8! 26 ♖hc1 ♘f7 27 ♖ab1 b6 28 ♖c6?? ♖xc6 29 dxc6 ♖c8 30 ♖c1 ♖c7 [30 ... ♘e5!] 31 ♗g4 ♘d8?? [30 ... ♘e5–+] 32 ♗d7 ♔g7 33 ♔e3 ♘f7 34 ♔d4 ♘e5 35 ♔d5 ♘xd7 36 ♔xd6+– ♖xc6+ 37 ♖xc6 ♘f6 38 e5 ♘e4+ 39 ♔d7 ♘c5+ 40 ♖xc5 ...? **1-0** L/N6123

**1849-✕KL-12**
**Kennedy, H.A.–Lowe, E.**
[Staunton]

1 d4 c6 2 c4 d6 3 e4 e6 4 ♗d3 e5 5 d5 ♘e7 6 f4 exf4 7 ♗xf4 ♘g6 8 ♗g3 ♗e7 9 ♘f3 ♗f6 10 ♘c3 ♘a6 11 ♕e2 0-0 12 ♖d1 ♗g4 13 a3 ♗e5 14 ♕f2 f6 15 ♗b1 [△ 16 dxc6] 15 ... c5 16 ♖d2 ♗xc3 17 bxc3 ♘e5 18 ♕e2∓ ♕a5 19 ♖c2 ♕xa3 20 0-0 ♕a4 21 ♘xe5 fxe5 22 ♖b2 ♕d7 23 ♕e3 ♗xf3 24 ♖xf3 ♖xf3 25 gxf3 ♖f8 26 ♗d3 b6 27 ♖g2 ♖f4 28 ♖g3 ♘b8 29 ♗f1 ♕a4 30 ♖g4 ♖xg4+ 31 fxg4 ♘d7 32 g5 ♕d1 33 ♕h3 ♘f8 34 ♔f2 ♕d2+ 35 ♗e2 ♕xg5 36 ♗g4 ♕f4+ 37 ♔g1 ♕xe4 38 ♗e6+ ♔h8 39 ♗f5 ♕e1+ 40 ♔g2 ♕d2+ 41 ♔h1 ♕e1+ 42 ♔g2 ♕d2+ 43 ♔f1 g6 44 ♗d3 ♔g7 45 ♗e2 ♕f4+ 46 ♔e1 h5 47 ♕c8 ♕f5 48 ♕d8 ♕f6 49 ♕c8 e4 50 ♕c7+ ♔h6 51 ♕xa7 ♕xc3+ 52 ♔f2 ♕f6+ 53 ♔e3 ♕d4+ 54 ♔f4 g5+ 55 ♔g3 ♕e3+ [55 ... ♕g1+ 56 ♔h3 g4+ 57 ♗xg4 (57 ♔h4 ♘g6#) 57 ... ♕xg4#] 56 ♔g2 ♕xe2+ ...? **0-1** L/N6123

**1849-✕KL-13**
**Lowe, E.–Kennedy, H.A.**
[Staunton]

1 e4 c5 2 ♗c4 e6 3 ♘c3 ♘c6 4 f4 a6 5 a4 ♘ge7 6 ♘f3 d5 7 ♗a2 b5! 8 axb5 axb5 9 ♘xb5?! ♘b4 10 ♘a3 dxe4 11 ♘g5 ♘f5 12 ♕e2

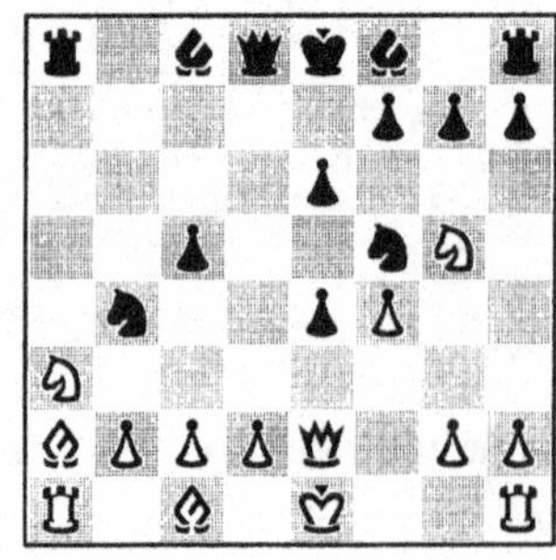

12 ... ♖xa3!! 13 bxa3 ♘xc2+ 14 ♔d1? ♘fe3+ 15 ♕xe3 ♘xe3+ 16 ♔e2 ♕d3+ 17 ♔f2 ♘g4+ 18 ♔e1 ♗a6 **0-1** L/N6123

**1849-✕KL-14**
**Kennedy, H.A.–Lowe, E.**
[Staunton]

1 d4 d6 2 c4 f5 3 e4?! fxe4 4 ♘c3 ♗f5 5 ♕c2 [5 g4 ♗g6 6 ♗g2] 5 ... ♘c6 6 ♗e3 ♘f6 7 f3 e5 8 d5 ♘d4 9 ♗xd4 exd4 10 ♘xe4 ♘xe4 11 fxe4 ♕h4+ 12 ♔d2??–+ ♕f4+ 13 ♔e1 ♗xe4 14 ♗d3?? ♕e3+ 15 ♕e2 ♗xd3 16 ♕xe3+ dxe3 ...? **0-1** L/N6123

**1849-★CM-1**
**Morphy, P.C.+Carpentier, C. le**
New Orleans

⟨♖a1⟩ 1 e4 e5 2 ♘f3 ♘c6 3 d4 exd4 4 ♗c4 ♗b4+ 5 c3 dxc3 6 0-0 cxb2 7 ♗xb2 ♗f8 8 e5 d6 9 ♖e1 dxe5 10 ♘xe5 ♕xd1

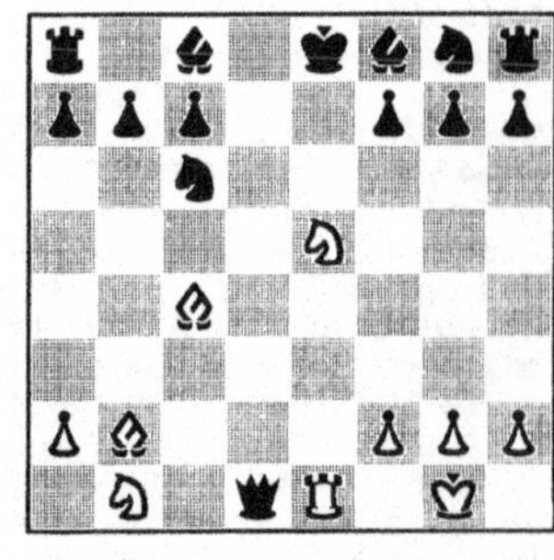

11 ♗xf7+ ♔e7 12 ♘g6+ ♔xf7 13 ♘xh8# **1-0**

**1849-★KS-1** ix 49
**Kennedy, H.A.– Staunton, H.**
[Staunton]

⟨♙f7⟩ 1 e4 ... 2 d4 e6 3 ♘c3 ♗b4 4 ♗d3 ♘c6 5 ♘f3 d6 6 0-0 ♘ge7 7 ♘e2 0-0 8 e5 d5 9 a3 ♗a5 10 b4 ♗b6 11 b5 ♘b8 12 ♘g3 ♕e8 13 c3 c5 14 bxc6 ♘bxc6 15 ♘h4 [∆ 15 ... ♘f5? 16 ♘4xf5] 15 ... ♗d7 16 ♕g4 [∆ 17 ♘h5] 16 ... ♕f7 17 ♘f3 [17 f4? ♘xd4] 17 ... ♘f5! 18 ♘e2 [18 ♘g5 ♕g6] 18 ... ♗d8 19 ♗g5 ♘ce7 20 ♕h3 [∆ 21 g4] 20 ... h6 21 ♗xe7 ♕xe7 [21 ... ♗xe7?? 22 g4+-; 21 ... ♘xe7? 22 ♘g5±] 22 g3 ♖c8 23 ♕h5 ♗e8 24 ♕h3 ♕f7∓ 25 ♗xf5 ♕xf5 26 ♕xf5 ♖xf5 27 ♘d2 ♗b5 28 ♖fe1 ♗xe2! 29 ♖xe2 ♖xc3 30 ♖b1 ♖c2 31 ♔f1 [31 ♖xb7?? ♗a5-+] 31 ... ♗b6 32 ♘b3 ♖c3 33 ♘c5 ♗xc5 34 dxc5 ♖xc5 35 ♖xb7 ♖f7 36 ♖eb2 ♖fc7 37 ♔e2 ♔h7 38 a4 ♔g6 39 ♖xc7 ♖xc7 40 ♖b4 ♔f5 41 f4 g5 42 ♔f3 gxf4 43 gxf4 ♖c4 **0-1** M954

**1849-★KS-2** ix 49
**Kennedy, H.A.+ Staunton, H.**
[Staunton]

1 e4 ... 2 d4 e6 3 ♗d3 c5 4 e5 g6 5 c3 ♘c6 6 ♘f3 d6 7 h4 ♗e7 8 h5 g5 9 exd6 ♕xd6 10 ♗xg5 cxd4 11 ♗xe7 ♔xe7 12 cxd4 ♘xd4 13 ♘c3 ♘f6 14 ♘xd4 ♕xd4 15 ♕e2 ♗d7 16 0-0-0 ♖ac8 17 ♔b1 ♕b6 18 ♔a1 ♖hg8 19 g4! ♕a5 [19 ... ♘xg4?? 20 ♘d5+; 19 ... ♖xg4? 20 ♘d5+] 20 f3 ♖xc3? 21 bxc3 ♘d5 22 ♕e5 ♗a4 23 ♖b1 b6 24 c4 ♘b4 25 ♕xa5 bxa5 26 ♗xh7 ♖d8 27 a3 ♘d3 28 ♖b7+ ♔f6 29 ♖xa7 ♘c5 30 g5+! ♔xg5 31 ♖xa5 ♖c8 32 h6 ♔f6 33 ♖xc5 ♖xc5 34 ♗d3 ♖c8 35 h7 ♔g7 36 h8♕+ ♖xh8 37 ♖xh8 ♔xh8 **1-0** M954

**1849-★MM-1**
**Morphy, P.C.+ Morphy, A.**
New Orleans [Maróczy]

1 e4 e5 2 ♘f3 ♘c6 3 ♗c4 ♗c5 4 b4 ♗xb4 5 c3 ♗c5 6 d4 exd4 7 cxd4 ♗b6 [7 ... ♗b4+ 8 ♔f1! ♕e7 (8 ... d6 9 d5 ∆ 10 ♕a4+) 9 ♗b2 ♕xe4 10 ♘bd2 ♗xd2 11 ♕xd2±] 8 0-0 ♘a5 9 ♗d3 [□ 9 ♘e5! (9 ♗xf7+ ♔xf7 10 ♘e5+ ♔f8 11 ♕h5 ♕f6! 12 ♗g5 ♕e6∓) 9 ... ♘xc4 10 ♘xc4 ♘e7 11 a4 d5 12 exd5 ♕xd5 13 ♘xb6 axb6 14 ♗a3 ♗e6 (14 ... ♘c6 15 ♘c3 ♕xd4 16 ♘b5! ♕d8 17 ♖e1+ ♗e6 18 ♕g4 g6 19 ♖xe6+ fxe6 20 ♕xe6+ ♘e7 21 ♖e1±) 15 ♗xe7 ♔xe7 16 ♘c3 ♕c4 17 d5 ♖hd8 (□ 17 ... ♕xc3) 18 ♕e1 ♖xd5 19 ♘xd5+ ♕xd5 20 ♕c3±] 9 ... ♘e7 10 ♘c3 0-0 11 ♗a3 [11 d5 d6 12 ♘e2 ♘g6 13 ♗b2±] 11 ... d6 12 e5 ♗f5 13 exd6 cxd6 14 ♘e4 d5 [14 ... ♗xe4, f5] 15 ♘f6+ gxf6 16 ♗xe7 ♕xe7 17 ♗xf5 ♘c4 [17 ... ♖fe8, ♕f8] 18 ♖e1 ♕d6 19 ♘e5 [□ 19 ♘h4 ♕f4 20 ♕h5 h6 21 ♘g6±] 19 ... fxe5 20 ♕g4+ [20 ♕h5 ♖e8; 20 ... ♔g7] 20 ... ♔h8 21 ♕h5 ♔g7 22 ♕g5+ [22 ♕xh7+?] 22 ... ♔h8 23 ♕h5 h6 24 ♖xe5 [□ 24 dxe5] 24 ... ♘xe5? [□ 24 ... ♕f6!∓] 25 dxe5 ♕c6 26 e6 ♔g7 27 g4 ♕c3 [27 ... ♖ae8 28 ♖e1 (28 g5 ♖xe6) 28 ... ♕c8!] 28 g5! ♕xa1+ 29 ♔g2 ♕f6 30 gxf6+ ♔xf6 31 exf7 ♖xf7 32 ♕g6+ ♔e7 33 ♕e6+ ♔f8 34 ♕xh6+ ♖g7+ 35 ♗g6 ♔g8! [35 ... ♗d4 36 ♕g5, 37 h4] 36 h4 d4 [□ 36 ... ♖f8! 37 f4 ♗c7! 38 ♕g5 ♗f4 39 ♕xd5+ ♔h8 40 h5 b6=] 37 h5 d3 38 ♕g5 ♖d8 39 h6 d2 40 ♕f6 [□ 40 ♗h7+ ♔f7 41 ♕xg7++-] 40 ... ♖gd7 [40 ... ♖xg6+ (40 ... ♖dd7 41 hxg7 ♖xg7 42 ♕e6+ ♔h8 43 ♕h3+ ∆ 44 ♕c8++-) 41 ♕xg6+ ♔f8 42 ♕g7+ ♔e8 43 h7+-] 41 ♗f5 d1♕ [41 ... ♖f8 (41 ... ♖f7 42 h7++-) 42 ♗e6+ ♔h7! 43 ♕xf8 ♔g6! 44 ♗f5+ ♔g5 45 f4+ ♔h5 46 ♕g8+-] 42 h7+ ♖xh7 43 ♗e6+ ♖f7 44 ♗xf7+ ♔h7 [44 ... ♔f8 45 ♗e6+, ♕f7#] 45 ♕g6+ ♔h8 46 ♕h6# **1-0** L/N3203

**1849-★MM-2**
**Morphy, P.C.+ Morphy, A.**
New Orleans [Maróczy]

1 e4 e5 2 ♘f3 ♘c6 3 ♗c4 ♗c5 4 b4 ♗xb4 5 c3 ♗c5 6 d4 exd4 7 cxd4 ♗b6 8 0-0 ♘a5 9 ♗d3 d5 [□ 9 ... d6; 9 ... ♘e7] 10 exd5 ♕xd5 11 ♗a3 ♗e6 12 ♘c3 ♕d7 13 d5! ♗xd5 [□ 13 ... ♗g4] 14 ♘xd5 ♕xd5 15 ♗b5+ ♕xb5 16 ♖e1+ ♘e7 17 ♖b1 ♕a6 18 ♖xe7+ ♔f8 19 ♕d5 ♕c4 20 ♖xf7+ ♔g8 21 ♖f8# **1-0** L/N3203

**1849-★MM-3** 22 vi 49
**Morphy, P.C.+ Morphy, E.**
New Orleans [Maróczy]

1 e4 e5 2 ♘f3 ♘c6 3 ♗c4 ♗c5 4 c3 d6 5 0-0 ♘f6 [□ 5 ... ♗b6; 5 ... ♕e7; 5 ... ♗g4? 6 ♕b3 ♗xf3 7 ♗xf7+ ♔f8 8 gxf3! (8 ♗xg8 ♖xg8 9 gxf3 g5) 8 ... ♘e5 9 d4! ♗xf7 10 dxc5±] 6 d4 exd4 7 cxd4 ♗b6 8 h3 [8 ♘c3] 8 ... h6 9 ♘c3 0-0 10 ♗e3 [□ 10 ♗b3] 10 ... ♖e8 [□ 10 ... ♘xe4 11 ♘xe4 d5∓] 11 d5 ♗xe3 [□ 11 ... ♘e7] 12 dxc6 ♗b6 13 e5 dxe5 14 ♕b3 ♖e7? [□ 14 ... ♗e6] 15 ♗xf7+ ♖xf7 16 ♘xe5 ♕e8 17 cxb7 ♗xb7 18 ♖ae1 ♗a6 [□ 18 ... ♘e4 19 ♘xf7 ♕xf7 20 ♕xf7 ♔xf7 21 ♘xe4 ♗a6] 19 ♘g6 ♕d8 20 ♖e7 **1-0** L/N3203

**1849-★MM-4**
**Morphy,P.C.+McConnell, L.J.**
New Orleans [Maróczy]

1 e4 e5 2 f4 exf4 3 ♘f3 g5 4 h4 g4 5 ♘e5 h5 [□ 5 ... d5!; 5 ... ♘f6] 6 ♗c4 ♖h7 7 d4 d6 8 ♘d3 f3 9 g3 ♘c6 10 ♘f4 ♗d7 11 ♘c3 ♘f6 12 ♗e3 ♘e7 13 ♔f2 c6 14 ♖e1 ♗g7 15 e5 dxe5 16 dxe5 ♘fd5 17 ♗xd5 cxd5

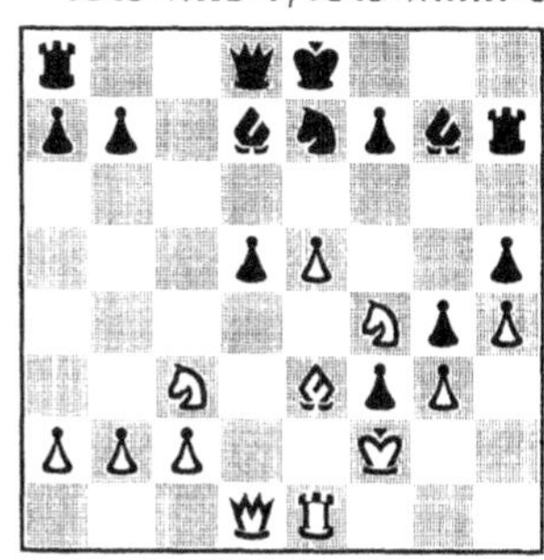

18 ♗c5! ♗c6 19 b4 b6 20 ♗xe7 ♕xe7 21 ♘fxd5 ♕b7 22 ♘f6+ ♗xf6 23 exf6+ ♔f8 24 ♕d6+ ♔g8 25 ♖e7 ♕c8 26 ♖c7 ♕f5 27 ♕xc6 ♕xc2+ 28 ♔e3 ♖d8 29 ♖d1 **1-0** L/N3203

**1849-★MM-5**
**Morphy,P.C.+McConnell, L.J**
New Orleans

1 e4 e5 2 ♘f3 ♕f6 3 ♘c3 c6 4 d4 exd4 5 e5 ♕g6 6 ♗d3 ♕xg2 7 ♖g1 ♕h3 8 ♖g3 ♕h5 9 ♖g5 ♕h3 10 ♗f1 ♕e6 11 ♘xd4 ♕e7 12 ♘e4 h6 13 ♘f5 ♕e6

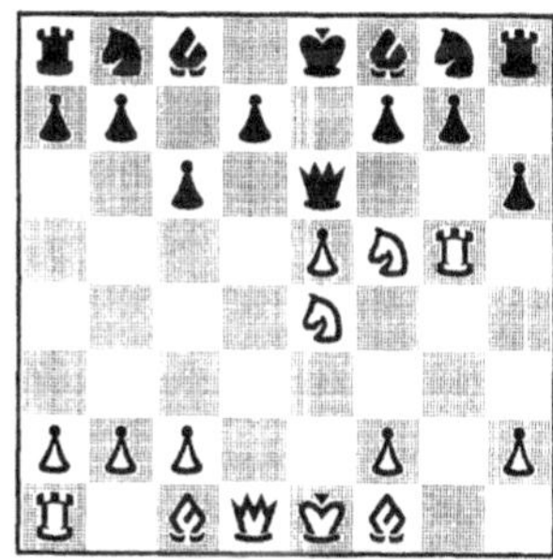

14 ♘fd6+ ♗xd6 15 ♘xd6+ ♔d8 16 ♗c4 ♕e7 17 ♘xf7+ ♔c7 18 ♕d6+ ♕xd6 19 exd6+ ♔b6 20 ♗e3+ c5 21 ♗xc5+ ♔a5 22 ♖g3 b5 23 ♖a3# **1-0** +13

**1849-★MM-6**
**McConnell,L.J.–Morphy, P.C.**
New Orleans

1 e4 e5 2 f4 exf4 3 ♘f3 g5 4 ♗c4 ♗g7 5 d3 h6 6 0-0 ♘f6 7 c3 b5 8 ♗xb5 c6 9 ♗c4 d5 10 exd5 cxd5 11 ♕e2+ ♗e6 12 ♗b3 0-0 13 d4 ♘e4 14 ♗c2 f5 15 ♘bd2 ♘c6 16 c4 ♗xd4+ 17 ♘xd4 ♘xd4 18 ♕d3 ♕b6 19 ♔h1 ♘xc2 20 ♕xc2 ♘f2+ 21 ♔g1 ♘h3+ 22 ♔h1 ♕g1+ 23 ♖xg1 ♘f2# **0-1** +13

**1849-★MM-7**
**Morphy,P.C.+McConnell, L.J.**
New Orleans
1 e4 e5 2 f4 exf4 3 ♘f3 ♗e7 4 ♗c4 ♗h4+ 5 ♔f1 d6 6 d4 ♕f6 7 e5 dxe5 8 dxe5 ♕e7 9 ♗xf4 ♗g4 10 ♘c3 c6 11 ♘e4 ...? **1-0** +13

**1849-★MR-1** 28x49
**Morphy, P.C.+ Rousseau, E.**
New Orleans [Löwenthal]
1 e4 e5 2 ♘f3 ♘c6 3 ♗c4 f5 4 d3 ♘f6 5 0-0 d6 [◻5 ... ♗c5] 6 ♘g5 d5 7 exd5 ♘xd5 8 ♘c3 ♘ce7 9 ♕f3 c6 10 ♘ce4! fxe4 [10 ... h6 11 ♕h5+ g6 12 ♗xd5 fxe4 (12 ... ♕xd5 13 ♘f6+ ♔d8 14 ♘xd5 gxh5 15 ♘xe7 ♔xe7 16 ♘f3 ♔f6 17 ♗d2 ♗d6 18 ♖fe1 ♖d8 19 ♗c3±) 13 ♗f7+ ♔d7 14 ♕g4+ ♔c7 15 ♕xe4 hxg5 16 ♕xe5+±] 11 ♕f7+ ♔d7 12 ♕e6+ ♔c7 13 ♕xe5+ ♕d6 14 ♕xd6+ ♔xd6 15 ♘f7+ ♔e6 16 ♘xh8 exd3 17 cxd3 ♔f6 18 b4 ♗e6 19 ♖e1 ♗g8 20 ♗b2+ ♔g5 21 ♖e5+ ♔h6 22 ♗c1+ g5 23 ♖xg5 **1-0** L/N3161

**1849-★MR-2**
**Morphy, P.C.+ Rousseau, E.**
New Orleans
1 e4 e5 2 f4 exf4 3 ♘f3 g5 4 h4 g4 5 ♘g5 h6 6 ♘xf7 ♔xf7 7 ♕xg4 ♕f6 8 ♗c4+ ♔e7 9 ♘c3 c6 10 e5 ♕xe5+ 11 ♔d1 ♔d8 12 ♖e1 ♕c5 13 ♗xg8 d5 14 ♖e8+ ♔xe8 15 ♕xc8+ ♔e7 16 ♘xd5+ ♔d6 17 ♕c7# **1-0** +13

**1849-★M?-1**
**Morphy, P.C.+?**
New Orleans
1 e4 e5 2 f4 exf4 3 ♘f3 g5 4 h4 g4 5 ♘e5 h5 6 ♗c4 ♘h6 7 d4 d6 8 ♘d3 f3 9 gxf3 ♗e7 10 ♗f4 ♗xh4+ 11 ♔d2 gxf3 12 ♕xf3 ♗g4 13 ♕e3 ♗e7 14 ♘c3 c6 15 ♖af1 f5 16 exf5 ♘xf5 17 ♕e6 ♘xd4 18 ♕xg4 fxg4 19 ♖xh8+ ♔d7 20 ♖xd8+ ...? **1-0** M268-1858

**1849-★RS-1**
**Staunton, H.- Ranken, C.E.**
Oxford [Brien]
⟨♘b1⟩ 1 e4 e5 2 ♘f3 ♘c6 3 ♗c4 ♗c5 4 b4 ♗xb4 5 c3 ♗a5 6 0-0 ♘f6 7 d4 0-0 8 ♕d3 d5 9 exd5 e4 10 ♕c2 exf3 11 dxc6 fxg2 12 ♖e1 ♕d6 13 ♖e3 ♗e6 14 cxb7 ♖ab8 15 ♗d3 ♖xb7 16 ♖g3 g6 17 ♗h6 ♘h5 18 ♗xf8 ♕xf8 19 ♖g5 f5 20 ♖e1 ♘f4 21 ♖e3 ♘xd3 22 ♕xd3 ♕f6 23 ♖gg3 c6 [23 ... f4 24 ♕e4] 24 ♖e1 ♖e7 25 ♖ge3 ♗c7 26 c4 f4 27 ♖3e2 f3 28 ♖e5 ♗xe5 29 dxe5 ♗f7 30 ♕d8+ ♗e8 31 ♖e3 ♕f5 32 ♕d1 ♖xe5 33 ♖xf3 ♕e6 34 ♕d4 ♗d7 35 ♕xa7 ♖e1+ 36 ♔xg2 ♕g4+ 37 ♖g3 ♕e4+ 38 ♖f3 ♗h3+ 39 ♔xh3 ♕xf3+ **0-1** L/N6123-1855

**1849̂-★HS-1**
**Medley,G.W. & Hannah, J.W.+Saint-Amant,P.C.F. de**
[Staunton]
⟨♙f7⟩ 1 e4 e6 2 d4 ♘c6 3 ♘c3 e5? 4 d5 ♘ce7 5 ♗g5 d6 6 ♗d3 ♘f6? [6 ... ♕d7] 7 ♗xf6 gxf6 8 ♕h5+ ♘g6 9 f4 exf4 10 e5 f5 11 e6 ♗g7 [11 ... ♕h4+] 12 ♗xf5 ♗xc3+ 13 bxc3 ♕f6 14 ♘e2 0-0 15 g4! c6 16 0-0 cxd5 17 ♘xf4+– ♕xc3 18 ♗xg6 ♕d4+ 19 ♔h1 ♖xf4 20 ♕xh7+ ♔f8 21 e7# **1-0** M954-1849

**1849̂-★KS-1**
**Kennedy, H.A.- Staunton, H.**
Brighton [Staunton]
⟨♙f7⟩ 1 e4 ... 2 d4 ♘c6 3 ♘f3 e6 4 c4 d6 5 d5 ♘ce7 6 ♗d3 e5 7 ♘h4 ♘g6 8 ♘f5 ♘f6 9 ♗g5? h6 10 ♗xf6 ♕xf6 11 0-0 ♘f4∓ 12 ♗c2 ♕g5 13 g3 g6 14 ♘h4 ♗e7 15 ♔h1 ♘h3 16 ♘d2 0-0 17 ♕e2 ♗d7 18 ♘g2 ♖f7 19 f4 exf4 20 gxf4 ♘xf4 21 ♘xf4 ♖xf4 22 ♖xf4 ♕xf4 23 ♖g1 ♗g5 24 ♘f3 ♗g4 **0-1** L/N6123-1849

**1849̂-★KS-2**
**Kennedy, H.A.- Staunton, H.**
Brighton [Staunton]
⟨♙f7⟩ 1 e4 ... 2 d4 e6 3 ♗d3 c5 4 dxc5 ♕a5+ 5 ♘c3 ♗xc5 6 ♘f3 ♘c6 7 0-0 a6 8 ♗d2 ♕c7 9 ♗g5 ♘ge7 10 ♗h4 0-0 11 ♗g3 d6 12 ♔h1 b5 13 ♘h4 ♗d7 14 ♕h5 ♘b4 15 f4 ♗d4 16 e5 ♘xd3 17 cxd3 dxe5 18 fxe5 ♗xc3 19 ♖fc1 b4 20 a3 bxa3 21 bxc3! [21 bxa3? ♗xa1; 21 ♖xa3? ♗xb2] 21 ... ♕a5 22 ♕e2 ♘d5 23 ♘f3 ♖ab8 24 c4 ♖b2 25 ♕e4 ♘b4 26 ♗e1 [◻26 ♘g5] 26 ... ♕a4 27 ♗xb4 ♕xb4 [27 ... ♗c6? 28 ♗xf8 △ 29 ♗xa3] 28 ♘g5 g6 29 ♕h4 ♕e7 30 ♖f1 ♖xf1+ 31 ♖xf1 a2 32 ♕f4 ♖b1 33 ♘e4 a1♕ **0-1** L/N6123-1849

**1849̂-★KS-3**
**Kennedy, H.A.- Staunton, H.**
[Staunton]
⟨♙f7⟩ 1 e4 ... 2 d4 e6 3 ♗d3 c5 4 dxc5 ♕a5+ 5 ♘c3 ♗xc5 6 ♘f3 ♘c6 7 0-0 a6 8 ♗f4 ♘ge7 9 a3 ♕d8 10 e5 0-0 11 ♗g5 [11 ♗xh7+?!, △ 12 ♘g5+] 11 ... ♕c7 12 b4 ♗a7 13 b5 ♘xe5?! 14 b6! [14 ♘xe5 ♕xe5 15 ♗xe7 ♖f7 16 ♗b4 a5 17 ♗xa5 ♗b8∓] 14 ... ♗xb6 [14 ... ♕xc3?] 15 ♗xe7 ♘xf3+ 16 gxf3 ♖f7 17 ♗xh7+ [17 ♗b4?!] 17 ... ♔xh7 18 ♕d3+ ♖f5 19 ♘e4! [19 ♘d5!] 19 ... ♔g8 20 ♗d6 ♕c6 21 c4 ♗d8 22 ♖fe1 b6 23 f4 ♗b7 24 f3 ♖c8 25 ♖ac1 ♗h4 26 ♖e2 ♖d5 27 cxd5 ♕xc1+ 28 ♔g2 ♗xd5 29 ♗e5 ♕c4 [29 ... ♗c4?+–] 30 ♕d1 ♗e7 31 ♔h3 ♔f7 32 ♔g4 ♗xe4 33 fxe4 d6 34 ♗d4 g6 35 ♖e3 ♕a2 36 ♖e2 ♕xa3 37 ♗b2 ♕c5 38 e5 d5 39 ♗d4 ♕c6 40 ♖e3 ♖h8 41 ♖c3 ♕b7 42 ♕c2 ♗d8 43 h3 ♕e7 44 ♗f2 ♔g7 **0-1** L/N6123-1849

**1849̂-★KS-4**
**Kennedy, H.A.- Staunton, H.**
London [Staunton]
⟨♙f7⟩ 1 e4 ... 2 d4 e6 3 ♗d3 c5 4 dxc5 ♕a5+ 5 ♘c3 ♗xc5 6 ♘ge2 ♘c6 7 0-0 ♘f6 8 ♘g3 0-0 9 a3 ♕d8 10 b4 ♗b6 11 ♗g5 ♗d4 12 ♘ge2 ♗b6 13 ♔h1 ♘e5 14 ♗h4 ♘eg4 15 ♘a4 ♘xe4!–+ 16 ♗xd8 ♘exf2+ 17 ♔g1 [17 ♖xf2–+] 17 ... ♘h3+ 18 ♔h1 ♘gf2+ 19 ♖xf2 ♘xf2+ 20 ♔g1 ♗e3 [20 ... ♘xd1+? 21 ♗xb6 axb6 22 ♘xb6+–] 21 ♕b1 [◻21 ♗g5] **0-1** M954-1849

**1849̂-★KS-5**
**Kennedy, H.A.+ Staunton, H.**
Brighton [Staunton]
⟨♙f7⟩ 1 e4 ... 2 d4 e6 3 ♗d3 c5 4 e5 ♘e7 5 dxc5 ♕a5+ 6 ♗d2 ♕xc5 7 ♘f3 ♘bc6 8 ♗c3 ♘d5 9 0-0! ♘xc3 10 ♘xc3 ♘xe5 11 ♘xe5 ♕xe5 12 ♖e1 ♕a5 13 ♘b5! g6 14 ♕f3 ♗e7 15 ♕g3 ♔d8 16 ♖ad1 ♖f8 17 ♗c4! ♖f6 18 ♖e3 a6 19 ♘d6 ♕b4 20 ♗xe6 ♖xe6 21 ♖xe6 dxe6 22 ♘b5+!+– ♗d7 23 ♕c7+ ♔e8 24 ♕xd7+ ♔f8 25 ♘c7 ♖b8 26 ♘xe6+ ♔f7 27 ♘g5+ ♔g7 28 c3 **1-0** L/N6123

**1849̂-★KS-6**
**Kennedy, H.A.+ Staunton, H.**
[Staunton]
⟨♙f7⟩ 1 e4 ... 2 d4 e6 3 ♗d3 c5 4 dxc5 ♕a5+ 5 ♗d2 ♕xc5 6 ♘c3 a6 7 ♘f3 ♘c6 8 0-0 b5 [9 ♘a4 △ 10 ♗e3] 9 e5! ♘xe5? 10 ♗e3 ♕c7 [10 ... ♘xf3+?±] 11 ♘xe5 ♕xe5 12 ♕f3 ♕b8 [12 ... d5? 13 ♘xd5 exd5 14 ♖fe1+–] 13 ♗e4 d5 [◻13 ... ♖a7] 14 ♘xd5 exd5 15 ♗xd5 ♘f6 16 ♗xa8 ♗d6 17 ♗c6+ ♔f7 18 h3 ♗e6 19 ♗g5 ♖d8 20 ♗xf6 gxf6 21 ♖ad1 ♔g7 22 ♗d5 ♗d7 23 ♕h5 ♔h8 24 ♗e4 f5 25 ♗xf5 ♗xf5 26 ♕xf5 ♖f8 27 ♕h5 ♖g8 28 ♖d5 ♗h2+ 29 ♔h1 ♕f4 30 ♕f5 ♖f8 31 ♕xf4 ♗xf4 32 g3 ♗xg3 33 f3 ♖e8 34 ♖d2 ♗f4 35 ♖d4 ♗c7 36 ♖e4 ♖f8 37 ♖fe1 ♖xf3 38 ♖e8+ ♔g7 39 ♖8e7+ ♖f7 40 ♖xf7+ ♔xf7 **1-0** M954-1849

**1849̂-★MS-1**
**Medley, G.W.- Staunton, H.**
London [Staunton]
⟨♙f7⟩ 1 e4 ... 2 d4 e6 3 ♗d3 c5 4 e5 ♕a5+ 5 ♗d2 ♕b6 6 ♕h5+ ♔d8

7 ♘c3 cxd4 8 ♘e4 ♕xb2 9 ♖d1 g6 10 ♕h3 ♘c6 11 ♘f3 [□ 11 ♘d6] 11 ... ♔c7 12 0-0 b6 13 c3 ♗b7 14 cxd4 ♖ac8 15 ♘c3 [△ 16 ♖b1 ♕a3 17 ♘b5+-] 15 ... ♔b8 16 ♖b1 ♕a3 17 ♖b3 ♕e7 18 ♘b5 [□ 18 d5] 18 ... ♕g7 19 ♗g5 h6 20 ♗f6 ♘xf6 21 exf6 ♕xf6 22 ♕g3+ d6 23 ♘xd6 ♗xd6 24 ♕xd6+ ♔a8 25 ♖e1 ♖hd8! 26 ♕g3 [26 ♕xe6?! ♕xe6 27 ♖xe6 ♘xd4 28 ♘xd4 ♖xd4 29 ♗e4] 26 ... g5 27 ♗e4 ♘xd4 28 ♗xb7+ ♔xb7 29 ♘xd4 ♖xd4 30 ♕f3+ ♕xf3 31 ♖xf3 ♖c2 **0-1** L/N6123-1849

### 1849̂-★MS-2
**Medley, G.W.= Staunton, H.**
London [Staunton]

⟨♙f7⟩ 1 e4 ... 2 d4 e6 3 ♗d3 ♕e7!? 4 ♘f3 d6 5 ♗g5 ♕f7 6 e5 ♗e7 7 h3 ♘c6 8 c3 dxe5 9 dxe5 ♗d7 10 ♘bd2 g6 11 ♘e4 0-0-0 12 ♕e2 ♗xg5 13 ♘exg5 ♕e7 14 a4 ♘h6 15 a5 ♕c5 16 ♘e4 ♕f8 17 a6!? b6 18 ♗c4 ♘f7 19 ♘ed2 [19 ♘f6 ♘fxe5 20 ♘xe5 ♕xf6 21 ♘xc6 ♗xc6 22 ♕xe6+ ♕xe6 23 ♗xe6+ ♔b8∓] 19 ... ♕g7 20 ♘d4 ♕xe5 [20 ... ♘fxe5!?] 21 ♘xc6! ♗xc6 22 ♗xe6+ ♔b8! 23 ♗xf7 ♕f6 24 ♕c4 ♖hf8 25 ♘e4! ♗xe4 26 ♕xe4 c6 27 0-0 ♖xf7 28 ♕e3 ♖fd7 29 ♕g3+ ♔a8 30 ♖fe1 ♖d2 31 ♕e3 [□ 31 ♖a4] 31 ... ♖d8d3 32 ♕e8+ ♖d8 33 ♕e3 ♖d8d3 34 ♕e8+ ♖d8 **½-½** L/N6123-1849

### 1849̂-★MS-3
**Medley, G.W.= Staunton, H.**
London [Staunton]

⟨♙f7⟩ 1 e4 ... 2 d4 e6 3 ♗d3 ♕e7 4 e5 c5!? 5 ♘c3 ♕f7 6 ♘e4 cxd4 7 ♘g5 ♗b4+ 8 c3 [□ 8 ♔f1] 8 ... dxc3 9 ♘xf7 c2+ 10 ♕d2 ♗xd2+ 11 ♗xd2 ♔xf7 12 ♘f3 h6 13 ♘h4 ♘e7 14 ♗b4 ♘bc6 15 ♗d6 b6 16 ♗xc2 ♗a6 17 ♗e4 ♖ac8 18 ♖ad1 ♖hd8 19 f4 ♗c4 20 b3 ♗d5 21 ♗xd5 ♘xd5 22 f5 ♘e3 23 fxe6+ dxe6 [23 ... ♔xe6!?] 24 ♖d3 ♘c2+ 25 ♔d2 ♘2b4 26 ♖f1+ ♔g8 27 ♗xb4 ♖xd3+ 28 ♔xd3 ♘xb4+ 29 ♔e4 ♘xa2 30 ♘g6 ♘c3+ 31 ♔d3 ♘d5 32 h4 ♖c3+ [□ 32 ... h5-+] 33 ♔d2 ♖c2+ 34 ♔d3 ♖xg2!? [34 ... ♖c8] 35 h5 ♖g3+ 36 ♔e2 ♖g2+ 37 ♔e1 ♖xg6 38 hxg6 ♘e7 39 ♖f7 ♘xg6 40 ♖xa7 ♘xe5 [□ 40 ... ♘f4 △ 41 ... ♘d5∓] 41 ♖b7 g5 42 ♖xb6 ♔f7 **½-½** L/N6123-1849

### 1849̂-★MS-4
**Medley, G.W.– Staunton, H.**
London [Staunton]

⟨♙f7⟩ 1 e4 ... 2 d4 e6 3 ♗d3 ♕e7 4 e5 d5 5 ♘f3 ♘c6 6 c3 ♗d7 7 ♗g5 ♕f7 8 0-0 g6 9 ♘h4 ♗h6 10 ♕d2 ♗xg5 11 ♕xg5 ♘ce7 12 f4 0-0-0 13 ♘d2 ♘f5 14 ♗xf5 gxf5 15 a4 ♘e7 16 ♕g3 ♖dg8 17 ♕f2 ♘g6 18 ♘xg6 ♖xg6 19 ♘f3 ♖hg8 20 ♘g5 ♕e7 [20 ... ♕g7 21 h4 h6 22 h5+-] 21 g3 h6 22 ♘f3 ♖g4 23 b4 ♖xf4 24 ♕d2 ♖fg4 25 ♔h1 [25 ♕xh6? f4-+] 25 ... f4 26 gxf4 ♕h7 27 ♕e3 ♕e4 28 ♕xe4 dxe4 29 ♘e1 ♗c6 30 h3 e3+ 31 ♔h2 e2 32 ♖f2 ♖g1 **0-1** L/N6123-1849

### 1849̂-★MS-5
**Medley, G.W.– Staunton, H.**
London [Staunton]

⟨♙f7⟩ 1 e4 ... 2 d4 e6 3 ♗d3 ♕e7 4 ♘f3 d6 5 e5 ♘c6 6 ♘g5?! g6 7 ♘f3 ♗h6 8 ♘c3 ♗d7 9 ♘e4 dxe5 10 dxe5 0-0-0 11 ♗xh6 ♘xh6 12 ♕e2 ♘g4 13 ♘ed2 ♕c5 14 b4! ♕c3 15 0-0 ♘gxe5 16 b5 ♘xf3+ 17 ♘xf3 ♘d4 18 ♘xd4 ♕xd4 19 a4 e5 20 a5 ♖he8 21 b6 cxb6 22 axb6 axb6 23 c3 ♕c5 24 ♗e4 ♔c7 [24 ... ♗b5 25 ♕g4+] 25 ♖fb1 ♖da8 26 ♕b2 ♗c6! 27 ♖e1 b5 28 h3 ♖a4 29 c4 ♖xc4 30 ♗d3 ♖c3 [30 ... ♕d5 31 ♗f1] 31 ♖ec1 b4 32 ♖xc3 bxc3 33 ♕c2 b5 34 ♖c1 b4 35 ♕b3 ♕d5 36 ♕xd5 ♗xd5 **0-1** M954-1849

### 1849̂-★MS-6
**Medley, G.W.– Staunton, H.**
London [Staunton]

⟨♙f7⟩ 1 e4 ... 2 d4 e6 3 ♗d3 ♕e7 4 ♘f3 ♘c6 5 0-0 g6 6 c3 ♗h6 7 d5 ♘d8 8 ♘bd2 d6 9 ♘c4 e5 10 h3 ♘f7 11 ♗e3 ♘f6 12 ♕d2 ♗g7 13 ♘g5 0-0 14 ♘xf7 ♖xf7 15 ♗g5 b5?! 16 ♘a5 ♗d7 17 a4! bxa4 18 ♘c6 ♕e8 19 ♗xf6 ♖xf6 20 ♖xa4 ♔h8! 21 ♖fa1 ♗xc6 22 dxc6 ♕xc6 23 ♖xa7 ♖af8 24 f3 ♖b8 25 ♖a1a6 ♕c5+ 26 ♔h1 d5 27 b4 ♕f8 [27 ... ♖xa6? 28 bxc5 ♖xa7±] 28 ♖xf6 ♕xf6 29 exd5 ♕h4 [29 ... e4!?] 30 ♕e3 [30 ♖xc7?! ♖a8] 30 ... ♕g3 31 ♗e4 ♕h4 32 ♔g1 [32 d6!? ♗h6 33 dxc7; 32 ... cxd6 33 ♖xg7 ♔xg7 34 ♕a7++-] 32 ... ♗h6 33 ♕f2 ♕f4 34 ♕e1??

34 ... ♕e3+ 35 ♕f2 ♕c1+ 36 ♔h2 ♗e3 [□ 36 ... ♗f4+] 37 ♖a1! ♕xc3 38 ♕a2 ♖xb4 39 d6 cxd6! 40 ♕a8+ ♔g7 41 ♗d5 ♗f4+ 42 ♔h1 ♖b8 43 ♕a7+ ♔h6 44 h4 ♗g3 45 h5 ♖c8 46 ♖d1 ♕c2 47 ♖a1 ♕f5 48 ♕e3+ ♗f4 49 ♕b6 ♕xh5+ 50 ♔g1 ♕h2+ 51 ♔f1 ♕h1+ 52 ♕g1 ♕h4 **0-1** L/N6123-1849

### 1849̂-★MS-7
**Medley, G.W.– Staunton, H.**
London [Staunton]

⟨♙f7⟩ 1 e4 ... 2 d4 e6 3 ♗d3 c5 4 dxc5 ♕a5+ 5 ♗d2 ♕xc5 6 ♘c3 ♘f6 7 ♗e3 ♕a5 8 a3 ♘c6 9 f4 [△ 10 b4] 9 ... d6 10 b4 ♕c7 11 ♘b5 ♕d8 12 ♘d4 g6 13 e5 ♘d5 14 ♘xc6 bxc6 15 ♗d4 ♗g7 16 ♕g4 0-0 17 ♘e2 dxe5 18 fxe5 ♘f4 19 0-0 h5! 20 ♕xf4 ♖xf4 21 ♖xf4 ♕g5 22 h4 ♕h6 23 ♖af1 a5 24 ♗e3 ♗xe5 25 ♖f8+ ♕xf8 26 ♖xf8+ ♔xf8 27 ♗xg6 axb4 28 ♗c5+?? [□ 28 axb4] 28 ... ♔g7 29 ♗xh5 bxa3 **0-1** L/N6123-1849

### 1849̂-★MS-8
**Medley, G.W.– Staunton, H.**
London [Staunton]

⟨♙f7⟩ 1 e4 ... 2 d4 ♘c6 3 ♘c3 e5 4 dxe5 ♘xe5 5 f4 ♘f7 6 ♗c4 ♘gh6 7 ♗e3 ♗b4 8 ♘f3 0-0 9 f5 ♔h8 10 0-0 ♗xc3 11 bxc3 ♕e7 12 ♕d3 ♘g4 13 ♗d4 [13 ♗f4 b5!] 13 ... c5 14 ♗e3 d5 15 ♗xd5 ♗xf5 16 exf5 [16 ♗xf7?] 16 ... ♕xe3+ 17 ♕xe3 ♘xe3 18 ♗xb7 ♖ab8 19 ♖fb1 ♘xc2 20 ♗d5 ♘xa1 21 ♖xa1 [21 ♖xb8 ♖xb8 22 ♗xf7] 21 ... ♘h6! 22 ♖e1 ♖xf5 23 ♗e6 ♖f6 24 ♗d5 ♖fb6 25 ♖e7 ♖b1+ 26 ♔f2?? ♖8b2+ **0-1** M954-1849

### 1849̂-★MS-9
**Medley, G.W.+ Staunton, H.**
London [Staunton]

⟨♙f7⟩ 1 e4 ... 2 d4 e6 3 ♗d3 ♕e7 4 ♘f3 d6 5 ♗g5 ♕f7 6 e5 ♘c6 7 c3 d5 8 0-0 ♗e7 9 ♕d2 ♗d7 10 b4 a6 11 a4 ♕h5 12 ♘a3 h6 13 ♗e3 [13 ♕c2!?] 13 ... ♗d8 14 b5 axb5 15 axb5 ♘a5 16 ♕c2 ♘e7 17 c4 0-0 18 ♗e2 c6 19 ♘g5 ♕g6 20 ♗d3 ♘f5 21 ♘h3 ♕g4 22 ♗e2 ♘xe3 23 fxe3 ♖xf1+ 24 ♖xf1 ♕e4 [24 ... ♕h4 25 ♕g6 ♗e7 26 ♗d3+-] 25 ♕xe4 dxe4 26 ♖b1 ♗e7 27 ♘c2 [27 c5 b6] 27 ... cxb5 28 cxb5 ♖c8 29 ♖b2 ♘b3 30 ♔f2 ♘c1 31 ♘f4 g5 32 ♘h5 ♗e8 33 ♘g3 ♗g6 34 ♔e1?! [34 ♘e1 ♗a3 35 ♖d2 ♖f8+ 36 ♔g1 ♗b4 37 ♖d1 ♘xe2+ 38 ♘xe2 ♗h5-+] 34 ... ♘d3+ 35 ♗xd3 exd3 36 ♘b4 ♖c4? [□ 36 ... ♗xb4 37 ♖xb4 ♖c1+ 38 ♔d2 ♖c2+ 39 ♔e1 ♖xg2-+] 37 ♘a2 h5 38 ♘h1 ♗a3 39 ♖d2 ♗b4 40 ♘xb4 ♖xb4 41 ♘f2 ♖b1+ 42 ♖d1 d2+ 43 ♔xd2 ♖b2+ 44 ♔e1 ♖xb5 45 ♘h3 g4 46 ♘f4 ♗f7 47 e4 ♔f8 48 ♔e2 ♖b2+ 49 ♖d2 ♖b4 50 ♔d3 ♔e7 51 d5 b5 52 dxe6 ♗xe6

53 ♘d5+ ♗xd5 54 exd5 ♖b3+ 55 ♔e4 h4 56 d6+ ♔d7 57 e6+ ♔d8 58 d7 **1-0** L/N6123-1849

**184̂9-★SV-1**
**Staunton, H.+ Vitzthum, C.**
London [Staunton]
⟨♙f2⟩ 1 ... e5 2 ... d5 3 e3 ♘f6 4 c4 ♗d6 5 cxd5 ♘xd5 6 ♘c3 ♘xc3 7 bxc3 0-0 8 g3 ♘c6 9 ♗g2 ♗d7 10 ♘e2 f5 11 0-0 ♔h8 12 a4 e4 13 ♗b2 ♘e5 14 ♘f4 ♘c4 15 ♗c1 g5 16 ♘h3 g4 17 ♘f4 ♘e5 18 ♗b2 ♕f6? [□ 18 ... ♘c4] 19 ♕b3 ♖ae8 20 c4 ♕g5 21 ♖ac1 c5 22 ♕xb7 ♖e7 23 ♕d5 ♖f6 24 ♕a8+ ♔g7 25 ♘d5 ♗c6 26 ♕xc6 ♘xc6 27 ♗xf6+ ♕xf6 28 ♘xf6 ♔xf6 29 d3 ♔g5 30 ♖cd1 ♗c7 31 dxe4 fxe4 32 ♖d5+ ♖e5 33 ♗xe4 **1-0** M954-1849

**184̂9-★S?-1**
**Staunton, H.+?**
London
⟨♘b1⟩ 1 e4 e5 2 ♘f3 ♘c6 3 ♗c4 ♗c5 4 c3 ♘f6 5 d4 exd4 6 e5 ♕e7 7 0-0 ♘g4 8 cxd4 ♗b6 9 h3 ♘h6 10 ♗g5 ♕b4 11 b3 ♘f5 12 a3 ♕f8 13 ♗e3 ♘ce7 14 ♘g5 d5 15 ♗d3 ♘xd4 16 ♗xd4 ♗xd4 17 ♗b5+ c6 18 ♕xd4 cxb5 19 ♕c5 a6 20 a4 ♗d7 21 axb5 ♗xb5 22 ♕xb5+ axb5 23 ♖xa8+ ♔d7 24 ♖xf8 ♖xf8 25 ♘xh7 ♖c8 26 ♘g5 f6 27 exf6 gxf6 28 ♘f3 ♖c3 29 ♘d4 ♘c6 30 ♖d1 ♘xd4 31 ♖xd4 ♔d6 32 ♖b4 ♖c5 33 h4 ♔e5 34 h5 d4 35 ♔f1 d3 36 ♔e1 ♖d5 37 ♔d2 **1-0** M954-1849

**184̂9-★JS-1**
**Shumov, I.S.– Jaenisch, C.F.**
1 e4 e5 2 ♘f3 ♘c6 3 ♗b5 a6 4 ♗a4 ♘f6 5 ♕e2 b5 6 ♗b3 ♗c5 7 a4 ♖b8 8 axb5 axb5 9 0-0 0-0 10 d3 d6 11 ♗e3 ♗g4 12 ♘bd2 ♕e7 13 h3 ♗h5 14 g4 ♗g6 15 c3 ♖a8 16 ♘h4 ♘a5 17 ♘xg6 hxg6 18 ♗a2 ♘b7 19 f4 c6 20 f5 gxf5 21 ♗xc5 ♘xc5 22 exf5 d5 23 d4 ♘ce4 24 ♘xe4 ♘xe4 25 ♔g2 exd4 26 cxd4 ♕h4 27 ♕d3 ♖fe8 28 ♖f3 ♖a7 29 ♗xd5 ♖xa1 30 ♗xe4 ♕e1 31 ♖f1 ♕xf1+ 32 ♕xf1 ♖xf1 33 ♗xc6 ♖8e1 34 ♗xb5 ♖f4 **0-1** L/N6047-1849

**184̂9-★JS-2**
**Jaenisch, C.F.– Shumov, I.S.**
1 e4 e5 2 f4 exf4 3 ♗c4 f5 4 ♕e2 fxe4 5 ♗xg8 ♕h4+ 6 ♔d1 ♖xg8 7 ♕xe4+ ♗e7 8 d3 d6 9 ♘f3 ♕g4 10 ♖e1 ♘c6 11 ♘c3 ♗f5 12 ♕xf4 0-0-0 13 ♘d5 ♖de8 14 ♘xe7+ ♖xe7 15 ♖xe7 ♘xe7 16 ♕xg4 ♗xg4 17 ♗g5 ♘c6 18 ♔d2 ♗xf3 19 gxf3 ♘d4 20 ♖f1 ♖f8 21 f4 h6 22 ♗h4 ♘e6 23 f5 g5 24 ♗g3 ♘g7 25 ♔e3 ♘xf5+ 26 ♔d2 ♔d7 27 c3 ♖f6 28 b4 ♔e6 29 ♖e1+ ♔f7 30 ♖e2 ♖e6 31 ♖g2 ♔g6 32 h3 ♘xg3 33 ♖xg3 ♔h5 34 ♖f3 ♔h4 35 c4 ♖e7 36 c5 dxc5 37 bxc5 h5 38 d4 g4 39 hxg4 hxg4 40 ♖f8 ♔h3 41 ♔d3 g3 42 d5 ♔h2 43 ♖h8+ ♔g1 44 ♖d8 g2 45 d6 cxd6 46 cxd6 ♖f7 47 ♔e2 ♖h7 48 ♖e8 ♔h1 49 ♖e7 ♖h8 50 d7 g1♕ 51 ♖h7+ ♖xh7 52 d8♕ ♖h2+ **0-1** L/N6047-1849

**184̂9-★JS-3**
**Shumov, I.S.– Jaenisch, C.F.**
1 e4 e5 2 f4 exf4 3 ♘f3 g5 4 h4 g4 5 ♘e5 h5 6 ♗c4 ♖h7 7 ♗xf7+ ♖xf7 8 ♘xf7 ♔xf7 9 d4 ♗h6 10 ♕d3 f3 11 0-0 ♕xh4 12 ♗xh6 ♘xh6 13 e5 ♔g7 14 ♕e4 d5 15 exd6 ♗f5 16 ♕xb7 g3 17 ♖xf3 ♕h2+ 18 ♔f1 ♕h1+ 19 ♔e2 ♕xg2+ 20 ♔e3 ♕xc2 21 ♖xg3+ ♔f6 22 ♘c3 ♘g4+ 23 ♖xg4 ♕d3+ 24 ♔f2 ♗xg4 25 ♕xa8 ♕xd4+ 26 ♔g2 ♕d2+ 27 ♔h1 ♕d3 28 ♘e4+ ♔g7 29 ♖e1 ♕f3+ 30 ♔h2 ♕f4+ 31 ♔g1 ♘d7 32 ♕xa7 ♘e5 33 ♕d4 ♔g6 34 ♕f2 ♘f3+ 35 ♔h1 cxd6 36 ♖e3 ♕e5 37 ♘c3 ♕f5 38 ♘e4 d5 39 ♘d2 ♘xd2 40 ♕xd2 ♗f3+ 41 ♖xf3 ♕xf3+ 42 ♕g2+ ♕xg2+ 43 ♔xg2 ♔f5 44 a4 ♔e5 45 a5 ♔d6 46 a6 ♔c6 47 b4 ♔b6 48 b5 d4 49 ♔f3 d3 **0-1** L/N6047-1849

**22** Petrov, A.D. L/309. CPL

**184̂9-★P?-1**
**Petrov, A.D.+?**
Warszawa
1 e4 c5 2 d4 cxd4 3 ♘f3 e5 4 ♗c4 ♕c7 5 ♕e2 ♘c6 6 ♘g5 ♘h6 7 f4 ♗e7 8 ♕h5 0-0 9 0-0 d6 10 f5 ♘d8 11 f6 ♗g4 12 ♕h4 ♗xf6 13 ♖xf6 gxf6 14 ♕xh6 fxg5 15 ♕xg5+ ♔h8 16 ♕f6+ ♔g8 17 ♗h6 ♘e6 18 ♗xe6 fxe6 19 ♕g5+ ♔h8 20 ♕xg4 ♖f7 21 ♕xe6 d3 22 ♘c3 ♕b6+ 23 ♔h1 ♕f2 24 ♗e3 ♕f1+ 25 ♖xf1 ♖xf1+ 26 ♗g1 dxc2 27 ♘e2 ♖e1 28 ♕f6+ ♔g8 29 ♘c1 ♖f8 30 ♕g5+ ♔h8 31 h4 ♖ff1 32 h5 ♖xg1+ 33 ♔h2 ♖h1+ 34 ♔g3 ♖xh5 35 ♕xh5 ♖xc1 36 ♕e8+ ♔g7 37 ♕e7+ ♔g6 38 ♕xd6+ ♔f7 39 ♕d2 **1-0** L/N6123-1851

**184̂9-★RS-1**
**Staunton, H.= Rowland**
[Staunton]
⟨♘b1⟩ 1 e4 e5 2 ♘f3 ♘c6 3 d4 exd4 4 ♗c4 ♗c5 5 0-0 d6 6 c3 dxc3 7 bxc3 ♗e6 8 ♗xe6 fxe6 9 ♕b3 ♕c8 10 ♘g5 ♘d8 11 e5 ♘e7 [11 ... dxe5 12 ♕b5+] 12 exd6 cxd6 13 ♕a4+ ♕d7 14 ♕h4 ♘f5 15 ♕h5+ g6 16 ♕h3 ♘f7 17 ♘e4 0-0-0 18 ♖b1 ♕c6 19 ♖fe1 ♘e5 20 ♖e2 ♖df8 21 ♘g5 ♕e8 22 a4 h6 23 ♘e4 ♘c4 24 ♕d3 ♕c6 25 ♘xc5 ♕xc5 26 ♖xe6 ♘e5 27 ♕e4 ♖f7 28 ♗f4 ♘g7 29 ♖b5 ♕c6 30 ♖exe5 dxe5 [□ 30 ... ♖xf4] 31 ♕xe5 ♖c7! 32 ♕xc7+ ♕xc7 33 ♗xc7 ♔xc7 34 ♖b4 ½-½ M954-1850

**184?-★S?-1**
**Staunton, H.+?**
London
⟨♗f1⟩ 1 d4 d5 2 c4 dxc4 3 ♗f4 ♗f5 4 ♘c3 ♘f6 5 f3 e6 6 e4 ♗g6 7 ♘ge2 ♘c6 8 ♗e3 ♗e7 9 0-0 0-0 10 ♔h1 h6 11 g4 ♘h7 12 f4 f5 13 gxf5 exf5 14 ♖g1 ♗h5 15 d5 ♗xe2 16 ♕xe2 ♘a5 17 ♗d4 ♘f6 18 e5 ♘h7 19 ♖g6 ♔h8 20 ♖ag1 ♖g8 21 e6 ♘f6 22 ♕h5 ♔h7 23 ♕xf5 **1-0** M954-1849

**184?-★S?-2**
**Staunton, H.+?**
London
⟨♖a1,♙f7⟩ 1 e4 ♘c6 2 ♘c3 e6 3 d4 ♗b4 4 ♘f3 d5 5 e5 ♘ge7 6 ♗d3 0-0 7 ♗xh7+ ♔xh7 8 ♘g5+ ♔g8 9 ♕h5 ♖f5 10 ♕h7+ ♔f8 11 ♕h8+ ♘g8 12 ♘h7+ ♔f7 13 g4 ♖xe5+ 14 dxe5 ♘xe5 15 ♘g5+ ♔f8 16 f4 ♘xg4 17 ♖g1 e5 18 h3 exf4 19 ♗xf4 ♕e7+ 20 ♔d1 ♘f6 21 ♖e1 ♘e4 22 ♗d2 ♗e6 23 ♘xe6+ ♕xe6 24 ♘xe4 ♗xd2 25 ♖f1+ **1-0** M954-1849

**184?-★S?-3**
**Staunton, H.+?**
1 e4 e5 2 ♘f3 ♘c6 3 ♗c4 ♗c5 4 b4 ♗xb4 5 c3 ♗a5 6 0-0 d6 7 ♕b3 ♕e7 8 d4 exd4 9 e5 dxe5 10 ♗a3 ♕f6 11 cxd4 e4 12 ♘g5 ♘h6 13 ♘xe4 ♕xd4 14 ♘bc3 ♗xc3 15 ♘g5 ♘a5 16 ♗xf7+ ♔d8 17 ♘e6+ ♗xe6 18 ♕xe6 ♘c6 19 ♖ad1 ♗d2 20 ♖fe1 ♘xf7 21 ♕xf7 **1-0** M954-1849

**184?-★S?-4**
**?– Staunton, H.**
⟨♙f7⟩ 1 e4 … 2 d4 … 3 ♗d3 d6 4 e5 g6 5 h4 dxe5 6 h5 ♗g7 7 hxg6 h6 8 dxe5 ♘c6 9 f4 ♘b4 10 ♗e4 ♕xd1+ 11 ♔xd1 ♗g4+ 12 ♘f3 0-0-0+ 13 ♗d2 e6 14 c3 ♘c6 15 ♔c2 ♘ge7 16 ♘d4 ♘b4+ 17 ♔b3 ♘a6 18 ♔a3 ♖d7 19 ♗e3 ♖hd8 20 b4 c5 21 ♘b5 cxb4+ 22 cxb4 ♖d3+ 23 ♗xd3 ♖xd3+ 24 ♘b1c3 ♖xe3 **0-1** M954-1845

**184?★SS-1**
**Stanley, C.H.+Staunton, H.**
London [Staunton]
⟨♙f7⟩ 1 e4 … 2 d4 e6 3 ♗d3 c5 4 e5 g6 5 c3 [5 h4!?] 5 … ♘c6 [5 … cxd4 6 f4] 6 ♘f3 d6 7 h4 cxd4 8 cxd4 dxe5 9 h5 ♗g7 10 hxg6 h6 11 dxe5 ♘xe5 12 ♗b5+ ♘d7 13 0-0 ♘e7 14 ♕e2 ♕b6 15 ♘a3 0-0 16 ♘c4! ♕xb5 17 ♕xe6+ ♔h8 18 ♘d6 ♘e5 19 ♕xe7 ♘xf3+ 20 gxf3 ♕h5 21 ♘f7+ ♖xf7 [21 … ♔g8 22 ♘xh6+] 22 ♕xf7 ♗f5 [22 … ♗h3 23 ♖e1+–]

23 ♗xh6! ♕xh6 [23 … ♗xh6?? 24 ♕h7#] 24 ♕xf5 ♖f8 25 ♕e6 ♖f6 26 ♕c8+ ♗f8 27 ♖fe1 ♖xg6+ 28 ♔f1 ♖g8 29 ♕e6 ♖g6 30 ♕e5+ ♗g7 31 ♕f5! ♖f6 32 ♖e8+ ♗f8 33 ♕g4 ♕h1+ 34 ♕g1 ♕h5 35 ♖ae1 ♖g6 36 ♖xf8+ ♔g7 37 ♕xg6+! ♕xg6 38 ♖f4! ♕d3+ 39 ♔g2 ♕b5 40 ♖g1! ♕h5 41 ♔f1+ ♔h7 42 a4 b5 43 ♖g2 ♕h1+ 44 ♔e2!! bxa4 [44 … ♕xg2 45 ♖h4+! ♔~ 46 ♖g4+ ♕xg4 47 fxg4+–] 45 ♖xa4 a6 46 ♖ag4 ♕h6 47 ♖g7+ ♕xg7 48 ♖xg7+ ♔xg7 **1-0** M954-1855

**184?-★SS-2**
**Stanley, C.H.– Staunton, H.**
London [Staunton]
⟨♙f7⟩ 1 e4 … 2 d4 e6 3 ♗d3 c5 4 e5 g6 5 ♕g4 [□5 h4] 5 … ♘e7 6 ♘f3 cxd4 7 h4 ♘bc6 8 h5 ♘xe5 9 ♕xd4 ♗g7 10 ♘xe5 ♕a5+ 11 ♗d2 ♕xe5+ 12 ♕xe5 ♗xe5 13 hxg6 hxg6 14 ♖xh8+ ♗xh8 15 ♗c3 ♗xc3+ 16 ♘xc3 d5 17 ♘b5 ♔d7 18 c4 a6 19 ♘c3 d4 20 ♘a4 ♔c7 21 0-0-0 b5 22 cxb5 axb5 23 ♗xb5 e5 [23 … ♖a5 24 ♗e8 ♔d8 25 b4 ♖f5 26 g4] 24 b3 ♗f5 25 ♖e1 ♖c8 26 ♗a6 [26 ♖xe5?? ♔d6+] 26 … ♖a8 27 ♗c4 [27 ♖xe5?? ♘c6] 27 … ♔d6 28 f3 ♘c6 29 g4 ♗e6 30 ♗xe6 ♔xe6 31 f4 ♔d6 32 fxe5+ ♘xe5 33 ♖d1 ♖c8+ 34 ♔b2 ♘c6 35 ♘b6 ♖f8 36 ♘c4+ ♔c5 37 a3 ♔d5 38 ♖d2 ♖f4 39 ♖g2 g5 40 ♘d2 ♘e5 41 a4 ♘d3+ 42 ♔a3 ♘e1 43 ♖g1 ♘c2+ 44 ♔b2 ♘e3 45 a5 ♖f2 46 ♔c1 ♔c6 47 b4 ♔b5 48 ♘e4 ♖c2+ 49 ♔b1 ♔xb4 50 a6 ♔b3 51 ♘xg5 ♖b2+ 52 ♔c1 ♖a2 53 ♖g3 ♖xa6 54 ♔d2 ♔c4 **0-1** M954-1855

**184?-★S?-1**
**?– Staunton, H.**
London
1 e4 e5 2 ♘f3 ♘c6 3 d4 exd4 4 ♗c4 ♗c5 5 c3 ♘f6 6 e5 d5 7 ♗b5 ♘e4 8 cxd4 ♗b6 9 h3 0-0 10 ♘c3 f6 11 ♕b3 ♘xc3 12 ♗xc6 bxc6 13 bxc3 fxe5 14 ♘xe5 ♕h4 15 ♗e3 ♗a6 16 ♘xc6 ♗c4 17 ♕c2 ♖ae8 18 0-0-0 ♗b5 19 g3 ♕h5 20 ♘e5 ♖e6 21 f4 ♕e8 22 ♖de1 ♗a4 23 ♕b2 ♗a5 24 ♕a3 ♕b5 25 ♔d2 ♕a6 26 ♘d3 ♕c4 27 ♘c5 ♗xc3+ 28 ♕xc3 ♕xa2+ 29 ♔c1 ♖b8 **0-1** M954-1851

**184?-★S?-2**
**?– Staunton, H.**
⟨♙f7⟩ 1 e4 … 2 d4 … 3 ♗d3 d6 4 e5 g6 5 h4 dxe5 6 h5 ♗g7 7 hxg6 h6 8 dxe5 ♘c6 9 f4 ♕d5 10 ♘f3 ♗g4 11 ♘c3 ♕a5 12 ♗d2 0-0-0 13 ♘e4 ♕b6 14 ♕e2 e6 15 0-0-0 ♘ge7 16 ♗e3 ♕a5 17 ♔b1 ♘d5 18 ♕d2 ♘xe3 19 ♕xe3 ♗xf3 20 ♕xf3 ♖hf8 21 ♕e3 ♘b4 22 a3 ♘d5 **0-1** M954-1879

**STANLEY✕TURNER**
[1850-✕ST]

| | | | | | | | |
|---|---|---|---|---|---|---|---|
| C.H. Stanley | 1 | 0 | 1 | ½ | 1 | 1 | 4½ |
| J.S. Turner | 0 | 1 | 0 | ½ | 0 | 0 | 1½ |

**1850-✕ST-1** ii 50
**Stanley, C.H.+Turner, J.S.**
[Staunton]
1 e4 e5 2 ♗c4 ♘f6 3 ♘c3 ♗c5 4 ♘f3 d6 5 d3 [5 d4] 5 … h6 6 ♘e2 ♘c6 7 ♘g3 ♘e7 8 c3 ♗e6 9 ♗b3 [9 ♗xe6!? fxe6 10 ♕b3] 9 … ♗b6 10 0-0 ♕d7 11 ♕e2 g5 12 ♗e3 ♘g6 13 ♗xe6 fxe6 14 d4 ♘f4 15 ♕d2 ♘g6 16 dxe5 ♘xe5 17 ♘xe5 dxe5 18 ♕xd7+ ♘xd7 19 ♗xb6 ♘xb6 20 ♖ad1 ♔e7 21 f3 ♖ad8 22 b3 ♖d6 23 ♘h1 ♖hd8 24 ♘f2 ♖xd1 25 ♖xd1 ♖xd1+ 26 ♘xd1 ♘d7 27 ♘e3 b5 28 b4 h5 29 ♔f2 c5 30 ♔g3 cxb4 31 cxb4 ♔f6 32 h4 ♘b6 33 hxg5+ ♔xg5 34 ♔f2! ♘c4?? 35 ♘xc4 bxc4 36 g3 **1-0** M954

**1850-✕ST-2** ii 50
**Turner, J.S.+Stanley, C.H.**
[Staunton]
1 e4 e5 2 ♘f3 ♘c6 3 ♗c4 ♗c5 4 c3 ♕e7 5 0-0 [5 d4 ♗b6 (5 … exd4 6 0-0) 6 dxe5 ♘xe5 7 ♘xe5 ♕xe5 8 0-0 d6 9 ♔h1 ♗e6 10 f4±] 5 … d6 6 d4 ♗b6 7 h3 ♘f6 8 ♖e1 0-0 9 ♗g5 ♘d8 10 ♗h4 h6 11 ♘bd2 ♔h8 12 ♗g3 exd4 13 cxd4 ♘h7 14 e5 dxe5 15 ♘xe5 ♕g5 16 ♘df3 ♕f6 17 d5 ♗c5 18 ♘d2 ♗f5 19 ♘e4 ♕b6 20 ♕f3 ♗xe4 21 ♕xe4 ♘f6 22 ♕f5 ♔g8 23 ♗h4± g5 24 ♗g3 [24 ♗d3! (△ 25 ♘d7) 24 … ♔g7 25 ♗xg5 hxg5 26 ♕xg5+ ♔h8 27 ♕h6+ ♔g8 28 ♘d7+–] 24 … ♔g7 25 h4 g4 26 ♘xg4 ♘xg4 27 ♕xg4+ ♕g6 28 ♕f3 c6 29 ♗d3 f5 30 ♗e5+ ♔g8 31 dxc6 ♘xc6 32 ♕d5+ ♔h7 33 ♕xc5 …? **1-0** M954

**1850-✕ST-3** ii 50
**Stanley, C.H.+Turner, J.S.**
[Staunton]
1 e4 e5 2 ♗c4 ♘f6 3 ♘c3 ♗c5 4 ♘f3 d6 5 d3 [5 d4] 5 … h6 6 ♗e3 ♗b6 7 ♘e2 ♗e6 8 ♗b3 c6 9 ♘g3 ♘bd7 10 0-0 0-0 11 ♕e2 [11 ♕d2!] 11 … ♖e8 12 ♖ad1 ♕c7 13 ♘h4! ♘f8 14 ♘hf5± ♘g6 15 ♕d2 ♗xe3 16 fxe3 ♔h7 17 ♕f2 ♖h8?? 18 ♘xg7 ♘g4 19 ♘xe6 fxe6 20 ♕f7++– ♕xf7 21 ♖xf7+ ♔g8 22 ♗xe6 ♖e8 23 ♖e7+ ♔f8 24 ♖xe8+ ♔xe8 25 ♗xg4 …? **1-0** M954

**1850-✕ST-4** ii 50
**Turner, J.S.=Stanley, C.H.**
[Staunton]
1 e4 e5 2 f4 exf4 3 ♘f3 g5 4 ♗c4 ♗g7 5 0-0 d6 6 c3 h6 7 d4 ♘e7 8 g3 g4 9 ♘h4 f3 10 h3! h5 11 ♗g5 f6 12 ♗d2 ♘d7± 13 ♕b3 ♖f8 14 ♘f5 ♘xf5 15 exf5 ♖h8 [□15 … ♘e5] 16 ♗f7+ ♔f8 17 ♗g6 ♕e7 18 ♖e1+– ♘e5 19 dxe5 fxe5 20 h4 ♗f6 21 ♘a3 c6 22 ♘c2 d5 23 ♗e3 ♗xh4! 24 ♗f2 [24 gxh4??→] 24 … ♗f6 25 ♕b4 ♕xb4 26 ♘xb4 e4 27 ♗d4 ♗xd4+ 28 cxd4 ♔g7 29 ♔f2 ♔f6 30 ♖h1 ♔g5 31 ♖h4 ♗xf5 32 ♗xf5 ♔xf5 33 ♖ah1 ♔g5 34 ♘c2 ♖ad8 35 ♘e3 c5 36 ♖d1 ♖h6 37 ♖d2 ♖b6 38 b3 a5 39 ♖h1 a4 40 dxc5 ♖b5 41 ♖hd1 ♖xc5 42 ♖xd5+ ♖cxd5 43 ♖xd5+ ♖xd5 44 ♘xd5 axb3 45 axb3 h4 46 ♘e3 h3??+– 47 ♘f1 ♔f5 48 ♘h2 b5 49 ♔e3 b4 50 ♔d4 f2

51 ♔e3?? [51 ♘f1+−] 51 ... ♔e5 52 ♘xg4+ ♔f5 53 ♘xf2 h2 54 ♘h1 ♔g4 55 ♘f2+ [55 ♔xe4 ♔h3 56 ♔f3◇] 55 ... ♔xg3 ½-½ M954

**1850-⚔ST-5̂** ii 50
**Stanley, C.H.+Turner, J.S.**
[Staunton]
1 e4 e5 2 ♗c4 ♘f6 3 ♘c3 ♗c5 4 d3 d6 5 ♘f3 h6 6 ♗e3 ♗b6 7 ♘e2 ♗e6 8 ♗b3 ♘c6 9 ♘g3 ♕d7 10 c3 ♘e7 11 d4 ♘g6 12 h3 [△ 13 d5] 12 ... ♕e7 13 ♗a4+ ♔f8 [13 ... ♘d7 14 d5+−; 13 ... ♘d7 14 ♘f5±; 13 ... c6 14 d5±] 14 0-0 c6 15 ♗c2 ♖d8 16 ♕d2 ♕d7 17 ♘f5 ♗xf5 18 exf5 e4 19 ♘h2 ♘e7 20 ♘g4 ♘xg4 21 hxg4 d5 22 f3 exf3 23 f6! ♘g6 24 ♗xg6 fxg6 25 ♖xf3 ...? **1-0** M954

**1850-⚔ST-6̂** ii 50
**Turner, J.S.–Stanley, C.H.**
[Staunton]
1 e4 e5 2 f4 exf4 3 ♘f3 g5 4 ♗c4 ♗g7 5 0-0 h6 6 c3 d6 7 d4 ♘e7 8 g3 g4 9 ♘h4 f3 10 h3 h5 11 ♕b3 [11 ♘xf3!±] 11 ... 0-0 12 ♗g5 ♕e8 13 ♗xe7 ♕xe7 14 ♘g6? ♕xe4 15 ♘xf8 d5!!→ 16 ♘d2 [16 ♗xd5 ♕e2→+] 16 ... ♕e3+ 17 ♖f2 dxc4 18 ♘xc4 ♕e4 19 ♘d2 ♕c6 20 d5 ♕b6 21 ♕c2 ♗xf8 22 ♖e1 ♗c5 23 ♖e8+ ♔g7 24 ♘e4 ♗f5 25 ♕d2 ♗e3 **0-1** M954

**1850-★AN-1** vii 50
**Nathan, N.D.–Anderssen, A.**
Berlin [?]
1 e4 e5 2 f4 exf4 3 ♘f3 g5 4 h4 g4 5 ♘e5 h5 6 ♗c4 ♘h6 7 d4 d6 8 ♘d3 f3 9 g3 d5 10 exd5 ♗d6 11 ♔f2 ♘f5 12 ♖e1+ ♔f8 13 ♘e5 f6 14 ♘g6+ ♔g7 15 ♘f4 c5 16 dxc6 ♘xc6 17 c3 ♘e5 18 ♗e6 ♘xg3 19 ♕c2 ♕e8 20 ♗xc8 ♖xc8 21 ♔xg3 ♖h6 22 ♘d2? [□ 22 ♔f2] 22 ... ♘d3 **0-1** L/N6047

**1850-★BP-1**
**Bird, H.E.+Pinkerly, L.**
London [Hoffer]
⟨♖a1⟩ 1 e4 e5 2 ♘f3 ♘c6 3 ♗c4 ♗c5 4 0-0 ♘f6 5 c3 0-0? [5 ... d6] 6 d4 exd4 7 cxd4 ♗b6 8 e5 d5 9 exf6 dxc4 10 ♗g5 g6 [10 ... gxf6 11 ♗h6 ♖e8] 11 d5! ♘b8 12 b3 cxb3 13 ♕xb3 ♗g4 14 ♘bd2 ♗xf3 15 ♘xf3 ♕d7 [□ 15 ... ♘d7] 16 ♗c1! c6 17 ♘e5 ♕c7 [□ 17 ... ♕f5] 18 ♗b2 ♘d7 19 ♘g4 ♘c5 20 ♕e3! ♘e6 21 ♕h6! cxd5 22 ♕g7+! ♘xg7 23 ♘h6+! ♔h8 24 fxg7# **1-0** L/N6138-1889

**1850-★JW-1** 20 v 50
**Wallenrath=Jaenisch, C.F.**
St. Petersburg
1 e4 e5 2 ♗c4 f5 3 exf5 ♘f6 4 g4 d5 5 ♗b3 ♗c5 6 ♕e2 0-0 7 d3 ♘xg4 8 ♕xg4 ♖xf5 9 ♘f3 ♘c6 10 ♖g1 ♖f7 11 ♕g3 ♘d4 12 ♘bd2 ♘xb3 13 ♘xb3 ♗d6 14 ♗g5 ♕e8 15 ♕g2 e4 16 ♘fd4 exd3+ 17 ♔d2 c5 18 ♖ae1 ♕f8 19 ♕xd5 cxd4 20 ♘xd4 ♔h8 21 ♗e3 dxc2 22 ♔xc2 b6 23 ♘e6 ♗b7 24 ♕xb7 ♖xb7 25 ♘xf8 ♖c7+ 26 ♔b1 ♖xf8 27 ♖g2 ♖e7 28 ♗d2 ♖fe8 29 ♖xe7 ♖xe7 30 ♗c3 ♗e5 31 ♗xe5 ♖xe5 32 f3 **½-½** L/N6047-1852

**1850-★JW-2** 21 iv 50
**Wallenrath+Jaenisch, C.F.**
1 e4 e5 2 ♗c4 ♗c5 3 c3 ♕g5 4 ♕f3 ♘f6 5 ♘e2 ♕g6 6 d4 d5 7 exd5 ♗g4 8 ♕e3 ♗xe2 9 ♗xe2 ♗e7 10 0-0 0-0 11 ♕xe5 ♗d6 12 ♕g5 ♕xg5 13 ♗xg5 ♘xd5 14 ♗f3 c6 15 ♗xd5 cxd5 16 ♖e1 ♘c6 17 ♘d2 ♖ae8 18 ♔f1 f6 19 ♗e3 g5 20 g3 ♔f7 21 ♔g2 ♖g8 22 h3 h5 23 f3 f5 24 a3 g4 25 hxg4 hxg4 26 ♗f2 ♘e7 27 ♖h1 f4 28 ♖h7+ ♔f8 29 fxg4 fxg3 30 ♗e3 ♖xg4 31 ♖f1+ ♔g8 32 ♖1f7 ♘f5 33 ♗g1 ♖e2+ 34 ♔f3 ♖xd2 35 ♔xg4 **1-0** L/N6047-1852

**1850-★JW-3** 17 viii 50
**Wallenrath=Jaenisch, C.F.**
St. Petersburg
1 e4 e5 2 ♘f3 ♘c6 3 ♗b5 ♘f6 4 0-0 ♗c5 5 ♗xc6 dxc6 6 ♘xe5 0-0 7 d3 ♗xf2+ 8 ♖xf2 ♘xe4 9 ♕f3 ♘xf2 10 ♕xf2 ♕d6 11 ♗f4 ♕d5 12 c4 ♕a5 13 a3 ♕b6 14 c5 ♕b3 15 ♘d2 ♕d5 16 d4 f6 17 ♘d3 ♕f5 18 ♕g3 ♖f7 19 h3 ♗e6 20 ♘f2 ♕g6 21 ♕xg6 hxg6 22 ♘d3 ♖e7 23 ♖e1 ♔f7 24 ♔f1 g5 25 ♗g3 ♖d8 26 ♗f2 a5 27 b4 axb4 28 axb4 ♖a8 29 ♘b2 ♖a2 30 ♘dc4 ♗d5 31 ♖xe7+ ♔xe7 32 ♗e1 b5 33 cxb6 cxb6 34 b5 cxb5 35 ♘xb6 ♗xg2+ 36 ♔xg2 ♖xb2+ 37 ♔f3 ♖c2 38 ♗g3 f5 39 ♗e5 g6 40 d5 ♖d2 41 ♔e3 ♖d1 42 ♔e2 ♖xd5 43 ♘xd5+ ♔e6 44 ♘c7+ ♔xe5 45 ♘xb5 ♔f4 46 ♔f2 g4 47 hxg4 ♔xg4 48 ♘d4 g5 49 ♘e2 ♔h3 50 ♔f3 ♔h4 51 ♘d4 g4+ 52 ♔f4 g3 53 ♘xf5+ ♔h3 54 ♘xg3 **½-½** L/N6047-1852

**1850-★LM-1** 25 v 50
**Morphy, P.C.+Löwenthal, J.J.**
New Orleans [Löwenthal]
1 e4 c5 2 f4 e6 3 ♘f3 d5 4 exd5 exd5 5 d4 ♗g4 6 ♗e2 ♗xf3 7 ♗xf3 ♘f6 8 0-0 ♗e7 9 ♗e3 cxd4? 10 ♗xd4 0-0 11 ♘c3 ♘c6 12 ♗xf6 ♗xf6 13 ♘xd5 ♗xb2 14 ♖b1 ♗d4+ 15 ♔h1 ♖b8 16 c3 ♗c5 17 f5! ♕h4 [□ 17 ... f6] 18 g3 ♕g5 19 f6 ♘e5 20 exg7 ♖fd8 21 ♗e4 ♕xg7 22 ♕h5! ♖d6 23 ♗xh7+ ♔f8 [23 ... ♕xh7 24 ♘e7+, 25 ♕xe5+−] 24 ♗e4 ♖h6 25 ♕f5 ♕xg3 26 ♖b2 ♖e8 27 ♘f6 ♖e6 28 ♖g2 ♕xg2+ [□ 28 ... ♖exf6] 29 ♗xg2 ♖hxf6 30 ♕xf6 ♖xf6 31 ♖xf6 ♘g4 32 ♖f5 b6 33 ♗d5 ♘h6 34 ♖f6 ♔g7 35 ♖c6 a5 36 ♖c7 ♔g6 37 ♔g2 f6 38 ♔f3 ♘f5 39 ♗e4 ♔g5 40 ♗xf5 ♔xf5 41 h4 ♔g6 42 ♖c6 ♔h5 43 ♔g3 f5 44 ♖f6 f4+ 45 ♔xf4 ♗f2 46 ♔e4 ♗c5 47 ♖f5+ ♔xh4 48 ♖xc5 bxc5 49 ♔d5 **1-0** L/N3161

**1850-★LM-2** 25 v 50
**Morphy, P.C.+Löwenthal, J.J.**
New Orleans
1 e4 e5 2 ♘f3 ♘f6 3 ♘xe5 d6 4 ♘f3 ♘xe4 5 ♕e2 ♕e7 6 d3 ♘f6 7 ♘c3 ♗e6 8 ♗g5 h6 9 ♗xf6 ♕xf6 10 d4 c6 11 0-0-0 d5 12 ♘e5 ♗b4 13 ♘xd5 ♗xd5 14 ♘g6+ ♕e6 15 ♘xh8 ♕xe2 16 ♗xe2 ♔f8 17 a3 ♗d6 18 ♗d3 ♔g8 19 ♘xf7 ♔xf7 20 f3 b5 21 ♗e4 ♘d7 22 ♖de1 ♘f6 23 ♖e2 ♖e8 24 ♗xd5+ cxd5 25 ♖xe8 ♘xe8 26 g3 g5 27 ♔d2 ♘g7 28 ♖a1 a5 29 ♔d3 ♔e6 30 a4 b4 31 c4 ♗c7 32 ♖e1+ ♔d6 33 ♖e5 dxc4+ 34 ♔xc4 ♘e6 35 ♖b5 ♘f8 36 ♖d5+ ♔e6 37 ♖c5 ♔d6 38 d5 ♔d7 39 ♖c6 ♗d6 40 ♖a6 ♘g6 41 ♖xa5 ♘e5+ 42 ♔b5 b3 43 ♖a7+ ♔d8 44 f4 gxf4 45 gxf4 ♘d3 46 ♔c4 ♘xf4 47 ♖h7 ♗e5 48 ♖xh6 ♗xb2 49 ♔xb3 ♗g7 50 ♖h7 ♗e5 51 a5 ♘xd5 52 ♖h5 ♗xh2 53 ♖xd5+ ♔c8 54 ♖b5 ♔c7 55 a6 **1-0** M212-1856

**1850-★MM-1**
**McConnell, L.J.–Morphy, P.C.**
New Orleans [Maróczy]
1 e4 e6 2 d4 d5 3 e5 [□ 3 exd5; 3 ♘c3] 3 ... c5 4 c3 ♘c6 5 f4? [□ 5 ♘f3] 5 ... ♕b6 6 ♘f3 ♗d7 7 a3 ♘h6 8 b4 cxd4 9 cxd4 ♖c8 10 ♗b2 ♘f5 11 ♕d3 ♗xb4+ 12 axb4 ♘xb4 13 ♕d2 ♖c2 14 ♕d1 ♘e3 **0-1** L/N3203

### 1850-★MM-2 20x50

**McConnell,L.J.–Morphy, P.C.**

New Orleans [Maróczy]

1 e4 e5 2 ♘f3 ♘c6 3 ♗c4 ♗c5 4 b4 ♗xb4 5 c3 ♗a5 6 0-0 [6 d4] 6 ... ♘f6 [◻ 6 ... d6!] 7 d4 0-0 8 dxe5! [8 ♘xe5 ♘xe4 9 ♘xf7 ♖xf7 10 ♗xf7+ ♔xf7 11 d5 ♘e7 12 ♕a4 ♗xc3 13 ♘xc3 ♘xc3 14 ♕c4 ♘exd5 15 ♗d2 b5 16 ♕b3 ♕h4 17 ♗xc3 ♕c4 18 ♕d1! (18 ♕xc4?) 18 ... ♗b7 19 ♗b2 ♔g8 20 ♕h5 ♕f4 21 ♖ad1 ♕f7 22 ♕g4 d6∞] 8 ... ♘xe4 9 ♗a3 [◻ 9 ♗d5! ♘c5 (9 ... ♘xc3 10 ♘xc3 ♗xc3 11 ♘g5 ♘xe5 12 ♕c2 ♘g6 13 ♕xc3 ♕f6! 14 ♕xf6 gxf6 15 ♘e4+–; 9 ... ♗xc3 10 ♗xe4 ♗xa1 11 ♗xh7+ ♔xh7 12 ♘g5+ ♔g6 13 ♕d3+=; 13 ♕g4? f5 14 exf6 ♔xf6 15 ♘e4+ ♔f7 16 ♕h5+ g6 17 ♕h7+ ♗g7 18 ♘g5+ ♕xg5!±) 10 ♘g5 ♘xe5 11 f4 c6! 12 ♕h5 h6 13 fxe5 cxd5 14 ♘xf7 ♕e8 15 ♘xh6+ gxh6 16 ♖xf8+ ♕xf8 17 ♗xh6 ♕f7 18 ♕g5+ ♔h7 19 ♘d2 ♕g6∓] 9 ... d6 10 exd6 ♘xd6 11 ♗b3 ♗g4∓ 12 h3 ♗h5 13 ♕d5 ♗g6 14 ♘e5 ♘xe5 15 ♕xa5 ♕g5 [15 ... ♘ec4] 16 ♔h1 [16 ♕xc7 ♗e4 17 f3 ♘xf3+ 18 ♖xf3 ♗xf3–+] 16 ... ♗e4 17 f3 ♗xf3 18 gxf3 ♕g3 19 ♘d2 ♘f5–+ 20 ♖ae1 ♕xh3+ 21 ♔g1 ♖fe8 22 ♖f2 ♕g3+ [22 ... ♘g3 23 ♖h2 ♘xf3+ 24 ♘xf3 ♖xe1+ 25 ♘xe1 ♕f1#] 23 ♔f1 ♘d3 24 ♖xe8+ ♖xe8 25 ♗xf7+ ♔h8 **0-1** L/N3203

### 1850-★MM-3

**McConnell,L.J.–Morphy, P.C.**

New Orleans [Löwenthal]

1 e4 e6 2 d4 d5 3 e5 c5 4 c3 ♘c6 5 f4 ♕b6 6 ♘f3 ♗d7 7 a3 ♘h6 8 b4 cxd4 9 cxd4 ♖c8 10 ♗b2 ♘f5 11 ♕d3 ♗xb4+! 12 axb4 [◻ 12 ♘bd2] 12 ... ♘xb4 13 ♕d2 [13 ♕d1 ♘e3, 13 ... ♘bc2+] 13 ... ♖c2 14 ♕d1 ♘e3 **0-1** L/N3161

### 1850-★MM-4

**Morphy, P.C.+Morphy, E.**

New Orleans

1 e4 e5 2 ♘f3 ♘c6 3 ♗c4 ♗c5 4 0-0 ♘f6 5 b4 ♗xb4 6 c3 ♗d6 7 d4 ♕e7 8 ♗g5 0-0 9 ♖e1 a6 10 ♕c2 h6 11 ♗xf6 ♕xf6 12 ♘bd2 g5 13 dxe5 ♗xe5 14 ♖ac1 g4 15 ♘xe5 ♘xe5 16 ♗b3 h5 17 ♖e3 h4 18 ♖f1 ♔g7 19 f4 ♕b6 20 ♖e1 ♘g6 21 g3 hxg3 22 hxg3 ♖h8 23 ♘c4 ♕c5 24 e5 b5 25 ♘d2 ♖h3 26 ♘e4 ♕b6 27 ♗xf7 ♗b7 28 ♘f2 ♘xf4 29 ♕f5 ♖f8 30 e6 dxe6 31 ♕xg4+ ♔h8 32 ♕xf4 ♕c6 33 ♕f6+ ♔h7 34 ♘e4 ♖xf7 35 ♘g5+ ♔g8 36 ♕xf7+ ♔h8 37 ♕f8# **1-0** M427-1859

### 1850-★MM-5

**Morphy, P.C.+Morphy, E.**

New Orleans [Löwenthal]

1 e4 e5 2 ♘f3 ♘c6 3 ♗c4 ♗c5 4 b4 ♗xb4 5 c3 ♗a5 6 d4 exd4 7 0-0 ♗xc3 8 ♘xc3 dxc3 9 ♗a3 [9 ♘g5 ♘h6 (9 ... ♘e5 10 ♗b3 h6 11 f4 hxg5 12 fxe5 ♘h6 13 ♕h5 g6 14 ♗xf7+ ♘xf7 15 ♕xg6 ♕e7 16 ♗a3 d6 17 exd6 cxd6 18 ♗xd6 ♕d7 19 e5±) 10 e5 ♘xe5 11 ♖e1 ♕e7 12 ♕d4 f6 13 f4 ♖f8 (13 ... ♘f5 14 ♕f2) 14 ♘e4 ♘c6 15 ♕xc3 ♔d8 16 ♗a3±] 9 ... d6 10 ♕b3 [10 e5 ♘a5 (10 ... dxe5 11 ♕b3 ♕f6 12 ♖fe1 ♘ge7 13 ♗xe7 ♔xe7 14 ♘xe5 ♘xe5 15 ♕xc3±) 11 exd6 ♘xc4 12 ♕a4+ ♗d7 13 ♖fe1+ ♘e7 14 ♕xc4 cxd6 15 ♘g5 0-0 16 ♗xd6±] 10 ... ♘h6 11 ♕xc3 ♕f6 12 e5! dxe5 13 ♖fe1 ♗d7 14 ♖ab1 0-0-0 15 ♗a6! ♘a5 [15 ... bxa6 16 ♕b3 ♗e8 (16 ... ♗e6 17 ♕b7+ ♔d7 18 ♖bd1+ ♘d4 19 ♘xe5+ ♔e8 20 ♖xd4 ♖xd4 21 ♕c6+ ♖d7 22 ♘xd7+–) 17 ♕b7+ ♔d7 18 ♘xe5+ ♘xe5 19 ♕d5+ ♔c8 20 ♕a8+ ♔d7 21 ♖bd1+ ♔e6 22 ♖xd8+–] 16 ♖ec1 ♗c6 17 ♕xa5 bxa6 18 ♕xa6+ ♔d7 19 ♖xc6! ♕f5 20 ♖xc7+ ♔e8 21 ♕c6+ ♕d7 22 ♖b8

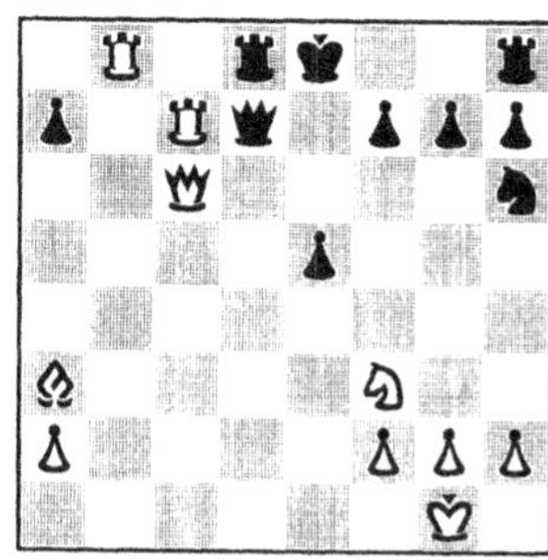

22 ... ♕xc6 23 ♖e7+ ♔f8 24 ♖xd8+ ♕e8 25 ♖7xe8# **1-0** L/N3161

### 1850-★M♀-1

**Morphy, P.C.+♀**

New Orleans

⟨♖a1⟩1 e4 e5 2 ♘f3 ♘c6 3 ♗c4 ♘f6 4 ♘g5 d5 5 exd5 ♘xd5 6 ♘xf7 ♔xf7 7 ♕f3+ ♔e6 8 ♘c3 ♘e7 9 0-0 c6 10 d4 exd4 11 ♖e1+ ♔d7 12 ♘xd5 ♘xd5 13 ♗xd5 cxd5 14 ♕xd5+ ♔c7 15 ♗f4+ ♗d6 16 ♕c5+ ♔b8 17 ♕xd6+ ♕xd6 18 ♗xd6# **1-0** M268-1860

### 1850-★M♀-2

**Morphy, P.C.+♀**

New Orleans

1 e4 e5 2 ♘f3 ♘c6 3 d4 ♘xd4 4 ♘xe5 ♘e6 5 ♗c4 ♘f6 6 ♘xf7 ♔xf7 7 ♗xe6+ ♔e8 8 ♗b3 ♗c5 9 e5 ♕e7 10 0-0 ♘g8 11 ♘c3 c6 12 ♘e4 b5 13 ♘d6+ ♔d8 14 ♗g5 ...♀ **1-0** M268-1859

### 1850-★SS-1 22v50

**Salmon,G.–Saint-Amant, P.C.F. de**

[Staunton]

1 e4 c5 2 ♘f3 ♘c6 3 c4? d6 4 ♘c3 e5 5 h3 f5 6 d3 ♘f6 7 ♗g5 ♗e7 8 ♗xf6 ♗xf6 9 ♗e2 0-0 10 exf5 ♗xf5 11 g4 ♗e6 12 ♕d2 ♘d4 13 ♘xd4 exd4 14 ♘e4 d5!∓ 15 ♘xc5?–+ ♗g5 16 ♕c2 ♕a5+ **0-1** L/N6123-1855

### 185̂0̂-★JS-1

**Jaenisch, C.F.– Shumov, I.S.**

1 e4 c5 2 d4 cxd4 3 ♕xd4 ♘c6 4 ♕d1 e6 5 ♘c3 ♗c5 6 ♘f3 ♘ge7 7 ♗c4 0-0 8 0-0 a6 9 ♗f4 b5 10 ♗b3 d6 11 ♕d3 f5 12 exf5 ♖xf5 13 ♗g5 d5 14 ♖ad1 ♕f8 15 ♗e3 ♗d6 16 ♘g5 h6 17 ♘f3

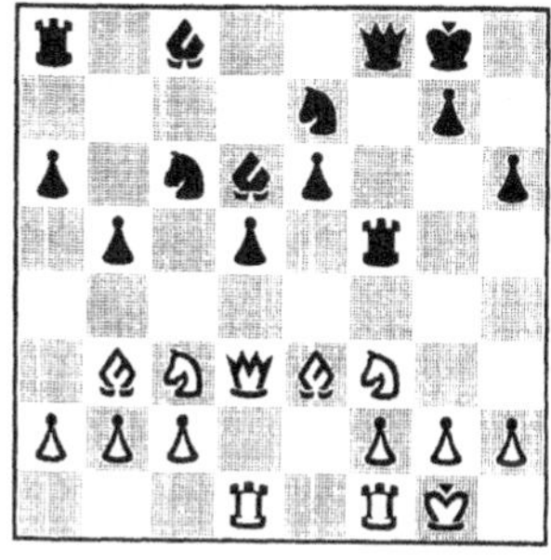

17 ... ♖xf3 18 gxf3 ♘e5 19 ♕e2 ♘xf3+ 20 ♔h1 ♗xh2 21 ♘xd5 exd5 22 ♖xd5 ♗e6 23 ♖xb5 ♗xb3 24 ♖xb3 ♕f5 25 ♗xh6 ♕h3 26 ♕c4+ ♔h8 27 ♗xg7+ ♔xg7 28 ♕d4+ ♗e5# **0-1** L/N6047-1850

### 185̂0̂-★JS-2

**Shumov,I.S.+Jaenisch, C.F.**

1 e4 e5 2 ♘f3 ♘c6 3 d4 exd4 4 ♗c4 ♗c5 5 ♘g5 ♘h6 6 ♘xf7 ♘xf7 7 ♗xf7+ ♔xf7 8 ♕h5+ g6 9 ♕xc5 d6 10 ♕b5 ♖e8 11 0-0 ♖xe4 12 ♕d5+ ♖e6 13 ♗g5 ♕e8 14 f4 ♔g7 15 f5 ♖e5 16 f6+ ♔h8 17 f7 ♔g7 18 fxe8♘+ ♖xe8 19 ♕f7+ ♔h8 20 ♗f6# **1-0** L/N6047-1850

### 185̂0̂-★JS-3

**Shumov, I.S.– Jaenisch, C.F.**

1 e4 e5 2 ♘f3 ♘c6 3 ♗c4 ♗c5 4 c3 ♘f6 5 d4 exd4 6 e5 d5 7 exf6 dxc4 8 ♕e2+ ♗e6 9 fxg7 ♖g8 10 cxd4 ♘xd4 11 ♘xd4 ♗xd4 12 ♕h5 ♕f6 13 0-0 ♖xg7 14 ♕b5+ c6 15 ♕xb7 ♖xg2+ 16 ♔xg2 ♕g6+ 17 ♔h1 ♗d5+ 18 f3 ♗xf3+ 19 ♖xf3 ♕g1# **0-1** L/N6047-1850

### 185Ô-★JS-4
**Jaenisch,C.F.+Shumov, I.S.**

1 e4 c5 2 d4 cxd4 3 ♕xd4 ♘c6 4 ♕d1 e5 5 ♘c3 ♗b4 6 ♗d2 ♘ge7 7 ♘d5 ♗c5 8 ♘f3 d6 9 b4 ♗b6 10 ♗b5 0-0 11 0-0 ♘xd5 12 exd5 ♘e7 13 ♗g5 f6 14 ♗h4 ♗g4 15 ♕d3 g5 16 ♗g3 ♘g6 17 h3 ♗h5 18 ♘d2 f5 19 c4 f4 20 ♗h2 g4 21 hxg4 ♗xg4 22 ♘e4 ♕h4 23 c5 f3 24 cxb6 fxg2 25 ♖fe1 ♗f3

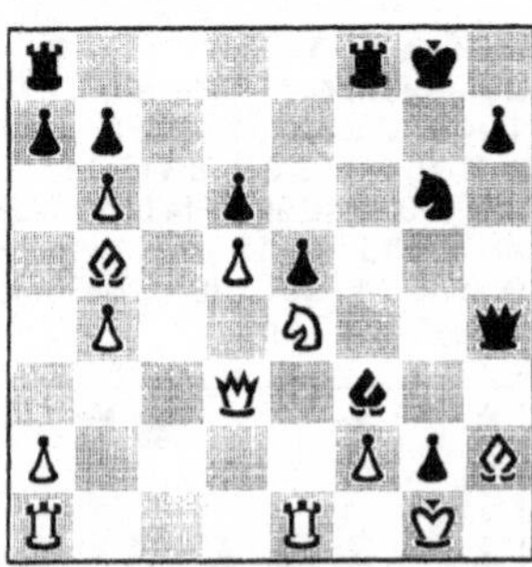

26 ♗d7 ♗xe4 27 ♗e6+ ♔h8 28 ♕g3 ♖f4 29 bxa7 ♕f6 30 ♖ac1 ♖xa7 31 ♖c8+ ♔g7 32 ♖g8+ ♔h6 33 ♕e3 ♖xa2 34 ♗xf4+ ♘xf4 35 ♖g3 ♗g6 36 ♖xg2 ♔g7 37 ♖g3 ♘xe6 38 dxe6 ♕xe6 39 ♖c1 ♕e7 40 f4 ♔f6 41 ♖f1 e4 42 f5 ♗e8 43 ♕g5+ ♔f7 44 ♕g7# **1-0**

L/N6047-1850

### 185Ô-★RS-1
**Staunton, H.= Rowland**

London [Staunton]

〈♘b1〉1 e4 e5 2 ♘f3 ♘c6 3 d4 exd4 4 ♗c4 ♗c5 5 0-0 d6 6 ♘g5 ♘h6 7 f4 d3+ 8 ♔h1 dxc2 9 ♕xc2 ♘d4 10 ♕c3 f6 [10 ... b5 11 ♗xb5 ♘xb5 12 ♕xg7+–] 11 ♗e3 ♘c6 12 ♗xc5 dxc5 13 ♖ad1 ♕e7 14 ♖d5 fxg5 15 fxg5 ♘g4 16 ♖xc5 ♗e6 17 ♗d5 ♘ge5 18 ♗xc6+ ♘xc6 19 ♖xc6 bxc6 20 ♕xc6+ ♕d7 21 ♕xa8+ ♕d8 22 ♕c6+ ♗d7 23 ♕c5 a6 24 ♕e5+ ♕e7 25 ♕xc7 ♗b5 26 ♕c8+ ♕d8 27 ♕e6+ ♕e7 28 ♕c8+ ♕d8 **½-½** M954-1850

### 185Ô-★S♀-1
**Staunton, H.+♀**

London

〈♖a1〉1 e4 e5 2 ♘f3 ♘c6 3 ♗c4 ♗c5 4 b4 ♗xb4 5 c3 ♗a5 6 0-0 ♘f6 7 d4 ♘xe4 8 ♖e1 ♘d6 9 ♗g5 f6 10 dxe5 ♘xc4 11 exf6+ ♔f7 12 ♕d5+ ♔g6 13 ♘h4+ **1-0**

M954-1850

### 185Ô-★S♀-2
**Staunton, H.+♀**

London

〈♖a1〉1 e4 e5 2 ♘f3 ♘c6 3 ♗c4 ♗c5 4 b4 ♗xb4 5 c3 ♗a5 6 0-0 ♗b6 7 d4 exd4 8 e5 d5 9 exd6 ♕xd6 10 ♘g5 ♘h6 11 ♖e1+ ♘e7 12 ♗a3 c5 13 cxd4 0-0 14 ♕b3 ♗c7 15 g3 b6 16 ♘c3 ♗b7 17 ♘b5 ♕c6 18 d5 ♕d7 19 ♗b2 ♘ef5 20 ♘e4 ♖ad8 21 ♕d1 a6 22 ♘xc7 ♕xc7 23 ♕h5 b5 24 ♕g5 bxc4

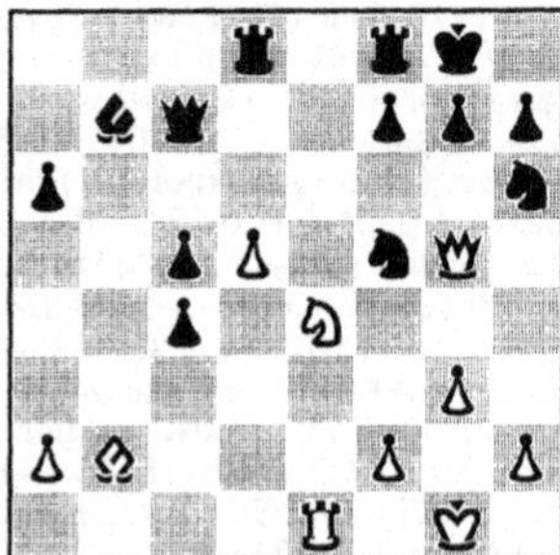

25 ♗xg7 ♘xg7 26 ♘f6+ ♔h8 27 ♕xh6 **1-0** M954-1850

### 185Ô-★S♀-3
**Staunton, H.+♀**

Ryde

〈♖a1, ♘b1〉1 e4 e5 2 f4 d6 3 ♘f3 ♗g4 4 fxe5 dxe5 5 ♗c4 ♕f6 6 0-0 ♗d6 7 c3 ♘h6 8 d4 ♕e7 9 ♕b3 c6 10 ♗g5 f6 11 ♗xh6 gxh6 12 ♘h4 ♕g7 13 ♔h1 ♗c8 14 ♗e6 ♘a6 15 ♘f5 ♕c7 16 ♗xc8 ♖xc8 17 ♕e6+ ♗e7 18 ♘xe7 ♔d8 19 ♘xc8 ♕xc8 20 ♕xf6+ ♔c7 21 ♕xe5+ ♔b6 22 b4 **1-0** M954-1850

### 185Ô-★S♀-4
**Staunton, H.+♀**

Reading

〈♖a1〉1 e4 e5 2 ♗c4 ♗c5 3 b4 ♗xb4 4 f4 exf4 5 ♘f3 ♗e7 6 d4 ♗h4+ 7 g3 fxg3 8 0-0 gxh2+ 9 ♔h1 ♗e7 10 ♗xf7+ ♔xf7 11 ♘e5+ ♔e8 12 ♕h5+ g6 13 ♘xg6 ♘f6 14 ♖xf6 d6 15 ♘f8# **1-0**

M954-1850

## AMSTERDAM

### 1851-AMS-3 vi 51
**Heijmans, F.G.+Mohr, E.**

1 e4 e6 2 d4 d6 3 c4 ♘e7 4 ♘c3 b6 5 ♗e2 ♘d7 6 f4 ♗b7 7 ♘f3 ♘f6 8 ♕c2 a6 9 0-0 g6 10 a4 ♗g7 11 h3 ♘h5 12 ♔h2 ♘c6 13 ♕d1 ♕f6 14 e5 dxe5 15 fxe5 ♘xe5 16 dxe5 ♕e7 17 ♕e1 ♗xf3 18 ♗xf3 ♕c5 19 ♗xh5 ♗xe5+ 20 ♔h1 gxh5 21 ♕e4 ♖d8 22 ♗e3 ♕a5 23 b4 f5 24 ♕c6+ **1-0** L/N5178

### 1851-AMS-4 vi 51
**Mohr, E.– Heijmans, F.G.**

1 e3 d5 2 d3 c5 3 b3 ♘c6 4 ♗b2 ♗f5 5 ♘d2 ♗g6 6 ♗e2 e5 7 a3 ♗d6 8 ♘gf3 a6 9 c4 d4 10 exd4 cxd4 11 ♘e4 ♗xe4 12 dxe4 ♘f6 13 ♗d3 a5 14 0-0 ♘d7 15 ♗c1 0-0 16 ♗g5 f6 17 ♗c1 ♘c5 18 ♘h4 ♘e7 19 g4 ♕d7 20 ♘f5 ♘xf5 21 gxf5 g6 22 ♗h6 ♖f7 23 fxg6 hxg6 24 ♕f3 ♘xd3 25 ♕xd3 ♕g4+ 26 ♕g3 ♕xg3+ 27 fxg3 g5 28 h4 ♗e7 29 ♖f5 ♖a6 30 hxg5 fxg5 31 ♗xg5 ♖xf5 32 exf5 ♗xg5 33 ♖d1 ♖d6 34 c5 ♖d5 35 b4 ♔f7 36 ♔f2 e4 37 ♖h1 ♖xf5+ 38 ♔e2 d3+ 39 ♔d1 e3 40 ♖h7+ ♔e6 41 ♖xb7 e2+ 42 ♔e1 ♖f1# **0-1** L/N5178

### 1851-AMS-12 vi 51
**Calisch, J.M.– Heimann, A.**

1 e4 e5 2 d4 d6 3 d5 ♘f6 4 ♘c3 h6 5 h3 a6 6 ♘f3 b5 7 a3 ♗e7 8 b4 c6 9 ♗b2 cxd5 10 ♘xd5 ♘xe4 11 ♗d3 ♘f6 12 ♘xf6+ ♗xf6 13 ♗e4 ♖a7 14 0-0 ♗e6 15 ♕d2 ♖d7 16 c3 d5 17 ♗c2 e4 18 ♘d4 ♗xd4 19 ♕xd4 ♕g5 20 ♗c1 ♕g6 21 ♕e3 0-0 22 ♗d2 f5 23 ♕g3 ♕f6 24 ♗f4 ♘c6 25 h4 d4 26 cxd4 ♘xd4 27 ♗d1 ♗c4 28 ♖e1 ♘e6 29 ♗e5 ♕f7 30 ♗f4 h5 31 ♗e2 ♗xe2 32 ♖xe2 ♖d3 33 ♖e3 ♖fd8 34 ♖ae1 ♖xe3 35 ♖xe3 ♖d1+ 36 ♔h2 ♘d4 37 f3 exf3 38 gxf3 ♕a2+ **0-1** L/N5178

### 1851-AMS-15 vi 51
**Messemaker, C.+ Neijse**

1 d4 d5 2 c4 c5 3 cxd5 ♕xd5 4 e3 cxd4 5 ♘c3 ♕e5 6 ♘f3 ♕a5 7 ♘xd4 a6 8 ♗d2 ♕c7 9 ♖c1 ♕d8 10 ♗c4 ♘f6 11 0-0 e6 12 ♕f3 ♗e7 13 ♖fd1 0-0 14 ♗e1 ♕c7 15 ♘e4 ♘c6 16 ♗d3 ♗d7 17 ♗c3 ♕d8 18 ♘xf6+ ♗xf6 19 ♘xc6 bxc6 20 ♗e4 ♗xc3 21 ♖xc3 ♖a7 22 ♖xc6 ♕e7 23 ♖cd6 f5 24 ♗c2 ♖c7 25 ♗b3 ♔h8 26 ♖xa6 ♗b5 27 ♖xe6 ♕g5 28 ♖ed6 ♖e7 29 ♖d8 ♖ee8 30 ♖xe8 ♗xe8 31 ♕a8 f4 32 exf4 ♕xf4 33 ♕a7 ♗h5 34 ♖f1 ♗e2 35 ♖a1 ♖c8 36 ♕e3 ♕c7 37 ♕xe2 ♕c1+ 38 ♖xc1 ♖xc1+ 39 ♗d1 **1-0** L/N5178

### 1851-AMS-16 vi 51
**Naret Oliphant, C.+ Wentel, A.**

1 e4 e5 2 f4 exf4 3 ♘f3 ♗e7 4 ♗c4 d6 5 d4 g5 6 ♘c3 ♗g4 7 0-0 ♘c6 8 ♗d5 ♕d7 9 ♗xc6 ♕xc6 10 ♕d3 a6 11 ♘d5 h6 12 c4 f6 13 ♗d2 0-0-0 14 b4 ♗d7 15 a4 b6 16 b5 axb5 17 cxb5 ♕b7 18 ♖fc1 c5 19 bxc6 ♗xc6 20 ♘b4 ♔b8 21 ♘xc6+ ♔a8

22 ♘xd8 ♗xd8 23 a5 b5 24 ♖cb1 f5 25 exf5 ♘e7 26 ♖xb5 ♕a7 27 ♕e4+ d5 28 ♖xd5 ♘xd5 29 ♕xd5+ ♕b7 30 ♕xb7+ ♔xb7 31 ♖b1+ ♔a7 32 ♘e5 ♗c7 33 f6 ♖f8 34 ♖c1 ♗b8 35 ♖c6 ♖d8 36 ♗c3 ♗xe5 37 dxe5 h5 38 ♖d6 ♖c8 39 f7 g4 40 ♗d4+ ♔b7 41 ♖b6+ ♔a8 42 ♖b1 ♖d8 43 e6 **1-0** L/N5178

**1851-AMS-17** vi 51
**Messemaker, C.– Neijse**
1 e4 e6 2 ♗c4 c5 3 d3 d5 4 ♗b5+ ♘c6 5 ♗xc6+ bxc6 6 ♘f3 ♘f6 7 ♕e2 ♗e7 8 c4 d4 9 ♘e5 ♗b7 10 0-0 ♗d6 11 f4 ♕c7 12 ♘g4 ♘xg4 13 ♕xg4 0-0 14 ♔h1 f5 15 exf5 ♖xf5 16 ♗d2 ♖af8 17 ♘a3 e5 18 ♖f2 ♗c8 19 ♕e2 exf4 20 ♖af1 ♗d7 21 ♘c2 ♗e8 22 ♘e1 ♗h5 23 g4 ♖e5 24 ♕d1 ♗g6 25 ♗xf4 ♖xe1 26 ♗xd6 ♖xf1+ 27 ♕xf1 ♖xf2 28 ♕xf2 ♕xd6 29 ♕e2 h6 30 a3 ♔h7 31 ♕f3 ♕e7 32 ♔g2 ♕e3 33 ♕xe3 dxe3 34 ♔f3 ♗xd3 35 ♔xe3 ♗xc4 36 ♔e4 ♗d5+ 37 ♔e5 ♔g6 38 ♔d6 ♔g5 39 ♔xc5 ♔xg4 40 b4 ♔f4 41 b5 ♗e4 42 bxc6 ♔e5 43 a4 ♗f5 44 a5 g5 45 c7 h5 46 ♔c6 ♗c8 47 ♔c5 g4 48 ♔b5 h4 49 a6 g3 50 hxg3 hxg3 **0-1** L/N5178

**1851-AMS-18** vi 51
**Wentel, A.– Naret Oliphant, C.**
1 e4 e6 2 d4 d5 3 ♘c3 c5 4 exd5 exd5 5 dxc5 ♗xc5 6 ♗e2 ♘f6 7 ♘f3 0-0 8 ♗e3 ♕b6 9 ♘a4 ♕a5+ 10 c3 ♗xe3 11 fxe3 ♗d7 12 b3 ♗xa4 13 bxa4 ♕xc3+ 14 ♔f2 ♘e4+ 15 ♔f1 ♕xe3 16 ♕e1 ♘c6 17 ♖d1 ♘b4 18 ♗b5 ♕xe1+ 19 ♘xe1 a6 20 ♖b1 ♘d2+ 21 ♔f2 ♘xb1 22 ♗d3 ♘c3 23 a3 ♘xd3+ 24 ♘xd3 ♖fe8 25 ♖f1 ♖ac8 26 ♘f4 ♖c4 27 ♔g1 ♖xa4 28 ♘h3 f6 29 g3 ♖xa3 30 ♔g2 ♖a2+ 31 ♘f2 ♘e4 **0-1** L/N5178

**1851-AMS-20** vi 51
**Blijdensteijn, W.J.= Kloos, H.**
1 e4 e5 2 ♗c4 ♗c5 3 ♘f3 ♘c6 4 c3 d6 5 d4 exd4 6 cxd4 ♗b6 7 ♗e3 ♘ge7 8 ♘c3 0-0 9 h3 h6 10 0-0 ♘g6 11 ♖e1 ♔h8 12 ♕c2 ♘ce7 13 ♗d3 f5 14 e5 d5 15 b4 a6 16 ♘e2 ♘c6 17 ♕c3 ♘h4 18 ♘xh4 ♕xh4 19 f4 ♗e6 20 ♗c2 ♘a7 21 ♗a4 c6 22 a3 ♖g8 23 ♖f1 g5 24 ♗c2 g4 25 ♗f2 ♕h5 26 h4 ♘b5 27 ♕d3 ♗d8 28 ♘g3 ♕f7 29 ♘xf5 ♗xf5 30 ♕xf5 ♕xf5 31 ♗xf5 g3 32 ♗e3 ♗xh4 33 ♖fc1 ♖ae8 34 a4 ♘d6 35 exd6 ♖xe3 36 ♖e1 ♖ge8 37 ♔f1 ♗f6 38 d7 ♖xe1+ 39 ♖xe1 ♖xe1+ 40 ♔xe1 h5 41 ♔e2 ♔g7 42 ♗e6 ♔f8 43 ♔f3 ♔e7 44 d8♕+ ♔xd8 45 ♔xg3 ♗xd4 46 ♔h4 b5 47 axb5 axb5 48 ♔xh5 ♗c3 49 f5 ♗xb4 50 f6 d4 51 ♔g4 d3 52 ♔f4 d2 53 ♗g4 c5 54 ♔e3 c4 55 ♔d4 c3 56 ♔d3 ♗a5 57 ♗d1 ♔d7 58 ♗b3 ♔e8 59 g4 d1♕+ 60 ♗xd1 ♔f7 61 g5 ♔g6 62 ♗b3 ♔xg5 63 f7 ♗b4 64 f8♕ ♗xf8 **½-½** L/N5178

**1851-AMS-21** vi 51
**De Heer, K.– Messemaker, C.**
1 e4 e6 2 ♗c4 c5 3 c3 a6 4 d4 d5 5 exd5 exd5 6 ♗b3 ♗e6 7 ♕e2 ♗e7 8 h3 h6 9 ♗e3 cxd4 10 cxd4 ♘f6 11 ♘f3 ♘c6 12 a3 ♗d6 13 ♘c3 0-0 14 ♗c2 ♖e8 15 ♕d2 ♗d7 16 0-0 ♘e4 17 ♕d3 ♗f5 18 ♘xd5 ♘g3 19 ♕d2 ♘xf1 20 ♔xf1 ♗xc2 21 ♕xc2 ♗xa3 22 ♘f4 ♗e7 23 ♖d1 ♖c8 24 ♕d2 ♗g5 25 d5 ♘e5 26 ♘xg5 hxg5 27 ♘h5 ♘c4 28 ♕d4 ♘xe3+ 29 fxe3 f6 30 d6 ♖e5 31 ♕d3 ♕d7 32 ♘xf6+ gxf6 33 ♕g6+ ♔f8 34 ♕h6+ ♕g7 35 d7 ♖d8 36 ♕h5 ♖e7 37 ♕g4 ♖exd7 38 ♖xd7 ♕xd7 39 ♕b4+ ♔g7 40 ♕a3 ♕d3+ 41 ♕xd3 ♖xd3 **0-1** L/N5178

**1851-AMS-22** vi 51
**Messemaker, C.– De Heer, K.**
1 d4 d5 2 c4 dxc4 3 e3 b5 4 a4 ♕d7 5 axb5 ♕xb5 6 ♘c3 ♕b3 7 ♕xb3 cxb3 8 ♗c4 ♗d7 9 ♘d5 ♔d8 10 ♗xb3 e6 11 ♘c3 ♘f6 12 ♗d2 ♗b4 13 f3 ♔e7 14 ♘ge2 ♖c8 15 0-0 ♔f8 16 e4 c5 17 d5 c4 18 ♗a4 exd5 19 ♗xd7 ♘bxd7 20 exd5 ♘xd5 21 ♘xd5 ♗xd2 22 ♖fd1 ♗g5 23 ♘ec3 ♘b6 24 ♖a6 ♘xd5 25 ♘xd5 ♖d8 26 ♖c6 ♖ac8 27 ♖xc8 ♖xc8 28 f4 ♗d8 29 ♖c1 ♗b6+ 30 ♔f1 ♗d4 31 ♖c2 ♖c5 32 ♘c3 ♗xc3 33 ♖xc3 ♔e7 34 b3 ♔e6 35 bxc4 ♔f5 36 g3 a5 37 ♔e2 ♔e4 38 ♖e3+ ♔d4 39 ♖e7 a4 40 ♖xf7 ♖a5 41 ♖b7 a3 42 ♖b1 a2 43 ♖a1 ♔xc4 44 ♔d2 ♔b3 45 ♔c1 ♖c5+ 46 ♔d1 ♔b2 47 ♖xa2+ ♔xa2 **0-1** L/N5178

**1851-AMS-23** vi 51
**Heijmans, F.G.= Mohr, E.**
1 e4 e6 2 d4 d6 3 ♗c4 ♘e7 4 f4 ♘d7 5 ♘f3 d5 6 exd5 exd5 7 ♗d3 ♘c6 8 0-0 ♗e7 9 ♗b5 0-0 10 ♘e5 ♘cxe5 11 dxe5 ♗c5+ 12 ♔h1 c6 13 ♗d3 ♕h4 14 ♘d2 ♗e3 15 ♕f3 ♗c5 16 ♕e2 ♖e8 17 c3 ♖e6 18 ♗f5 ♖e8 19 b4 ♗b6 20 ♕d3 ♘f8 21 ♘f3 ♕e7 22 ♗xc8 ♖axc8 23 f5 f6 24 exf6 gxf6 25 ♗h6 ♘d7 26 ♖ae1 ♕f7 27 ♘h4 ♗c7 28 ♗d2 ♕h5 29 ♘f3 ♘e5 30 ♘xe5 ♖xe5 31 ♕g3+ ♔f7 32 ♗f4 ♖g8 33 ♕f2 ♖xf5 34 ♕e3 ♗xf4 35 ♖xf4 ♖xf4 36 ♕xf4 ♔g6 37 h3 ♕g5 38 ♕f2 a6 39 ♖e3 ♔f7 40 ♕e2 ♔g6 41 ♔h2 ♕f4+ 42 g3 ♕f5 43 ♖f3 ♕e4 44 ♖e3 ♕f5 45 ♖e7 ♖g7 46 ♖xg7+ ♔xg7 47 h4 ♕e4 48 ♕d2 h6 49 ♔g1 f5 50 ♕d4+ ♔g6 51 ♕d2 ♕e5 52 ♔g2 ♕e4+ 53 ♔h2 ♕e5 **½-½** L/N5178

**1851-AMS-25** vi 51
**Coopman, M.M.+ Messemaker, C.**
1 e4 e6 2 f4 d5 3 exd5 exd5 4 ♘f3 ♗d6 5 d3 ♘e7 6 ♗e2 ♘g6 7 g3 0-0 8 d4 f6 9 h4 ♘e7 10 c4 c5 11 cxd5 ♘xd5 12 ♗c4 ♕e7+ 13 ♔f2 ♗e6 14 ♖e1 ♕f7 15 ♕e2 ♖e8 16 ♗xd5 ♗xd5 17 ♕xe8+ ♕xe8 18 ♖xe8+ ♔f7 19 ♖e1 ♘c6 20 dxc5 ♗xc5+ 21 ♗e3 ♗xe3+ 22 ♖xe3 ♗xf3 23 ♖xf3 ♘d4 24 ♘c3 ♖c8 25 ♖d3 ♘c6 26 ♖e1 b6 27 ♖d7+ ♔g6 28 g4 h6 29 h5+ ♔h7 30 ♖e6 ♔h8 31 ♘b5 a5 32 ♘d6 ♘d4 33 ♘xc8 ♘xe6 34 f5 ♘c5 35 ♖d4 b5 36 ♘e7 b4 37 ♖d8+ **1-0** L/N5178

**1851-AMS-26** vi 51
**Messemaker, C.= Coopman, M.M.**
1 d4 f5 2 c4 ♘f6 3 ♘c3 e6 4 a3 a5 5 e3 d5 6 ♘f3 c6 7 b3 ♗d6 8 ♗e2 0-0 9 0-0 ♘e4 10 ♗b2 ♔h8 11 ♘e1 ♘d7 12 f4 ♘df6 13 ♘d3 ♘xc3 14 ♗xc3 ♘e4 15 ♗b2 ♖f6 16 ♘e5 ♗xe5 17 dxe5 ♖f8 18 cxd5 cxd5 19 ♗d4 ♗d7 20 a4 ♖c8 21 ♖c1 ♕e7 22 ♕d3 ♕b4 23 ♖xc8 ♖xc8 24 ♖b1 ♘c3 25 ♗xc3 ♖xc3 26 ♕d4 ♖xb3 27 ♖xb3 ♕xb3 28 ♗d1 ♕b4 29 ♕xb4 axb4 30 ♔f2 ♔g8 31 ♔e2 ♔f8 32 ♔d2 ♔e8 33 ♔c1 ♔d8 34 ♔b2 ♔c7 35 ♔b3 ♗c6 36 g3 h6 37 ♔xb4 b6 38 ♗e2 **½-½** L/N5178

**1851-AMS-28** vi 51
**Messemaker, C.– Coopman, M.M.**
1 d4 f5 2 c4 ♘f6 3 ♘c3 e6 4 a3 a5 5 e3 c6 6 ♘f3 ♗e7 7 ♗e2 ♗d6 8 d5 cxd5 9 cxd5 ♕e7 10 ♗c4 e5 11 ♕b3 ♘a6 12 ♗xa6 bxa6 13 ♕b6 a4 14 ♕a5 ♗b7 15 0-0 ♖c8 16 ♖d1 e4 17 ♘d4 ♕e5 18 f4 exf3 19 ♘xf3 ♕e7 20 ♕xa4 0-0 21 ♕b3 ♖b8 22 ♕c4 ♘e4 23 ♕d4 ♖f6 24 ♘xe4 fxe4 25 ♘g5 ♖h6 26 ♘h3 ♖f8

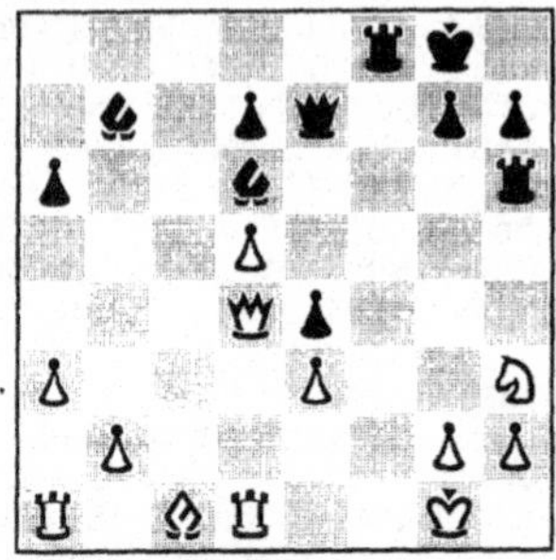

27 ♘f4 ♖xf4 28 exf4 ♗c5 **0-1** /LN5178

**1851-AMS-29** vi 51
**Blijdensteijn, W.J.+ Kloos, H.**
1 e4 e5 2 ♗c4 c6 3 ♘f3 ♗d6 4 c3 ♗c7 5 ♕e2 ♘f6 6 d4 d6 7 ♘g5 0-0 8 ♗xf7+ ♖xf7 9 ♘xf7 ♔xf7 10 dxe5 dxe5 11 ♗g5 ♗e6 12 ♘a3 ♘bd7 13 0-0 h6 14 ♗h4 ♕e7 15 h3 ♘c5 16 ♘c2 ♘cxe4 17 f3 ♕c5+ 18 ♘e3 g5 19 fxe4 gxh4 20 ♕f3 ♕e7 21 ♕h5+ ♔g7 22 ♕xh4 ♖f8 23 ♔h1 ♕f7 24 ♘f5+ ♗xf5 25 ♖xf5 ♕g6 26 ♖af1 a5 27 ♖1f3 ♖d8 28 ♖xf6 ♖d1+ 29 ♔h2 **1-0** L/N5178

**1851-AMS-32** vi 51
**Coopman, M.M.+ Seligmann, J.**
1 e4 e5 2 ♘f3 ♘c6 3 ♗c4 ♗c5 4 0-0 d6 5 c3 ♗g4 6 h3 ♗xf3 7 ♕xf3 ♘f6 8 d3 h6 9 ♗e3 ♗b6 10 a4 0-0 11 b4 a5 12 b5 ♘a7 13 ♗xb6 cxb6 14 ♘d2 ♘c8 15 d4 ♘e7 16 ♖ad1 exd4 17 cxd4 ♘xe4 18 ♘xe4 d5 19 ♗d3 dxe4 20 ♗xe4 ♖b8 21 ♖fe1 ♔h8 22 ♗xb7 ♕d7 23 ♗c6 ♕d6 24 ♕e4 ♘g6 25 ♖d3 f5 26 ♕f3 ♖bd8 27 g3 ♖f6 28 ♖e8+ ♔h7 29 ♖xd8 ♕xd8 30 ♕d5 ♘e7 31 ♕xd8 **1-0** L/N5178

**1851-AMS-33** vi 51
**Kloos, H.–Blijdensteijn, W.J.**
1 e4 e5 2 f4 exf4 3 ♘f3 g5 4 ♗c4 ♗g7 5 d4 d6 6 c3 ♗g4 7 ♗xf7+ ♔xf7 8 ♕b3+ ♔g6 9 ♕xb7 ♘d7 10 ♘xg5 ♔xg5 11 g3 ♘e7 12 0-0 ♗e2 13 ♖xf4 ♔g6 14 ♖f2 ♗g4 15 ♕b5 h6 16 ♕d3 ♖f8 17 ♗f4 ♔h7 18 ♘d2 ♘g6 19 ♗e3 ♖xf2 20 ♗xf2 ♕f6 21 ♗e3 ♗h3 22 ♖e1 c5 23 ♖e2 cxd4 24 ♗xd4 ♘ge5 25 ♗xe5 ♘xe5 26 ♕e3 ♘g4 27 ♕d3 ♔h8 28 ♕d5 ♖f8 29 ♕f5 ♕d8 30 ♕h5 ♕b6+ 31 ♔h1 ♘f2+ 32 ♖xf2 ♕xf2 33 ♕xh3 ♕e1+ 34 ♘f1 ♖xf1+ 35 ♕xf1 ♕xf1# **0-1** L/N5178

**1851-AMS-34** vi 51
**Kloos, H.–Blijdensteijn, W.J.**
1 e4 e5 2 ♘f3 ♘c6 3 ♗c4 h6 4 c3 ♘f6 5 ♕e2 ♗c5 6 d3 0-0 7 h3 d5 8 exd5 ♘xd5 9 0-0 ♖e8 10 ♖e1 ♗f5 11 ♘bd2 ♘f4 12 ♕d1 ♗xd3 13 ♗xd3 ♘xd3 14 ♖e2 e4 15 ♘e1 e3 16 fxe3 ♗xe3+ 17 ♔h1 ♘f2+ 18 ♖xf2 ♗xf2 19 ♘ef3 ♘e5 20 ♕f1 ♘xf3 21 ♘xf3 ♗g3 22 ♗d2 ♕f6 23 b3 ♖e7 24 c4 ♖ae8 25 ♗b4 ♖e2 26 ♗d2 ♖f2 27 ♕g1 ♖ee2 28 ♖f1 ♖xg2 29 ♕xg2 ♖xg2 30 ♔xg2 ♗d6 31 ♗e1 ♕g6+ 32 ♔h1 ♕f5 33 ♔g2 ♗c5 34 ♗f2 ♕c2 35 ♔g1 ♗d6 36 ♗xa7 b6 37 ♗b8 ♕e2 38 a3 ♗c5+ 39 ♔h1 ♕xf1+ **0-1** L/N5178

**1851-AMS-37**
**Heijmans, F.G.+ Van Pruag, J.**
1 e4 e5 2 ♘f3 ♘c6 3 ♗c4 ♗c5 4 c3 ♘f6 5 d3 d5 6 exd5 ♘xd5 7 0-0 0-0 8 ♘g5 f6 9 ♘e4 ♗b6 10 ♔h1 ♘e7 11 a3 a5 12 f4 exf4 13 ♗xf4 ♔h8 14 d4 ♘xf4 15 ♖xf4 c6 16 ♘g3 ♗c7 17 ♖h4 ♗xg3

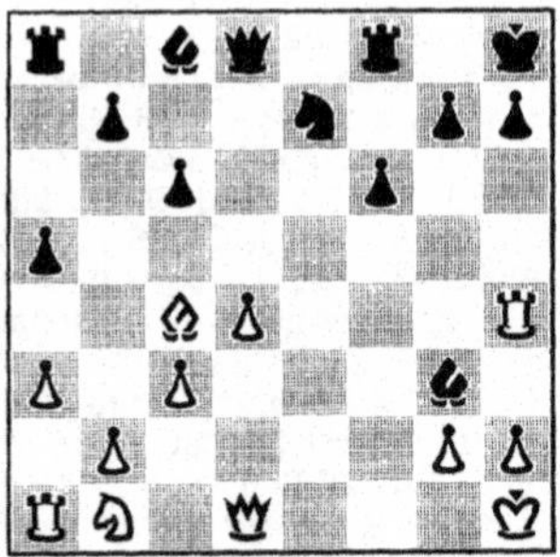

18 ♖xh7+ ♔xh7 19 ♕h5# **1-0** L/N5178

**1851-AMS-60** vi 51
**Heijmans, F.G.–Van't Kruijs, M.**
1 e4 c5 2 ♘f3 ♘c6 3 ♗b5 a6 4 ♗xc6 bxc6 5 b3 d5 6 e5 e6 7 ♗b2 ♘e7 8 0-0 ♘g6 9 c3 ♕c7 10 d4 cxd4 11 cxd4 c5 12 ♕c2 ♕b6 13 ♖c1 cxd4 14 ♗xd4 ♕b7 15 ♗c5 ♗xc5 16 ♕xc5 ♗d7 17 ♘bd2 ♖c8 18 ♕d6 f6 19 h4 ♔f7 20 exf6 gxf6 21 h5 ♘e7 22 ♕f4 ♕b8 23 ♕xb8 ♖xb8 24 ♖c7 ♖hd8 25 g4 h6 26 ♖e1 ♘c6 27 ♖c1 ♖b6 28 a4 ♔e7 29 ♔g2 ♔d6 30 ♖7xc6+ ♖xc6 31 ♖e1 e5 32 ♔h3 ♖g8 33 ♘h2 ♖c3+ 34 ♔h4 e4 35 f4 f5 36 g5 hxg5+ 37 fxg5 f4 **0-1** L/N5178

**1851-AMS-65** vi 51
**Van't Kruijs, M.+ Heijmans, F.G.**
1 d4 f5 2 c4 ♘f6 3 ♘c3 e6 4 e3 ♗b4 5 ♗d3 b6 6 ♘e2 ♗b7 7 0-0 ♗d6 8 f3 0-0 9 e4 fxe4 10 fxe4 ♘g4 11 e5 ♕h4 12 h3 ♖f2 13 ♘e4 ♗xe4 14 ♗xe4 ♘e3 15 ♗xe3 ♖xf1+ 16 ♕xf1 ♕xe4 17 ♕f3 ♕xf3 18 gxf3 ♗e7 19 d5 ♔f7 20 f4 d6 21 ♔g2 exd5 22 cxd5 c6 23 dxc6 ♘xc6 24 ♖c1 ♘b4 25 a3 ♘d3 26 ♖c3 ♘xb2 27 ♗d4 ♘a4 28 ♖c7 dxe5 29 ♗xe5 ♔f8 30 ♘d4 ♗f6 31 ♘e6+ ♔g8 32 ♘xg7 ♗d8 33 ♖c4 b5 34 ♖b4 ♗e7 35 ♖xb5 ♗xa3 36 ♘h5 ♗e7 37 ♖b7 ♔f8 38 f5 ♘c5 39 ♖c7 ♘e4 40 f6 ♘xf6 41 ♘xf6 ♗xf6 42 ♗xf6 a5 43 ♖xh7 ♖a6 44 ♗d4 a4 45 ♖a7 **1-0** L/N5178

**1851-AMS-66** vi 51
**Bruijn, W.=Kloos, H.**
1 e4 e5 2 ♘f3 ♘c6 3 ♗c4 ♘f6 4 d3 d5 5 exd5 ♘xd5 6 a3 ♗e6 7 0-0 ♗d6 8 ♗d2 0-0 9 ♗xd5 ♗xd5 10 ♘c3 ♗e6 11 h3 h6 12 ♘e4 f5 13 ♘xd6 cxd6 14 ♖e1 ♗d5 15 c4 ♗xf3 16 ♕xf3 ♘d4 17 ♕d1 a6 18 ♗c3 ♘e6 19 ♕f3 ♘c5 20 b4 ♘a4 21 ♗d2 ♕d7 22 ♖ab1 ♕c6 23 ♕e2 f4 24 f3 ♕b6+ 25 ♔h1 ♕d4 26 ♕e4 ♕f2 27 ♖e2 ♕b6 28 ♕d5+ ♔h8 29 ♗e1 ♖ac8 30 ♖b3 ♕c6 31 ♕xc6 ♖xc6 32 b5 axb5 33 ♖xb5 ♘c5 34 ♖d2 ♖a8 35 ♗f2 ♖xa3 36 ♗xc5 ♖xc5 37 ♖xb7 ♖c6 38 ♔h2 ♖ca6 39 ♖d7 ♖b6 40 h4 h5 41 d4 ♖a1 42 g3 fxg3+ 43 ♔xg3 ♖g1+ 44 ♔h2 ♖g6 45 dxe5 dxe5 46 c5 ♖bc6 47 ♖d8+ ♔h7 48 ♖8d6 ♖xc5 49 ♖xg6 ♔xg6 50 ♖g2+ ♔f6 51 ♖g5 g6 52 f4 ♖c2+ 53 ♔g3 exf4+ 54 ♔xf4 ♖f2+ 55 ♔g3 ♖f5 56 ♖xf5+ ♔xf5 57 ♔f3 ♔e5 58 ♔e3 ♔f5 59 ♔f3 g5 60 hxg5 ♔xg5 **½-½** L/N5178

**1851-AMS-67** vi 51
**Kloos, H.=Bruijn, W.**
1 e4 e5 2 c3 ♘f6 3 d3 ♗c5 4 h3 0-0 5 ♗g5 h6 6 ♗xf6 ♕xf6 7 ♘f3 ♖e8 8 ♗e2 ♕b6 9 d4 exd4 10 b4 ♗d6 11 ♕xd4 ♕xd4 12 cxd4 ♗xb4+ 13 ♘bd2 ♖xe4 14 a3 ♗xd2+ 15 ♔xd2 d6 16 ♖hc1 c6 17 ♗d3 ♖e8 18 ♖ab1 b6 19 ♘h4 c5 20 dxc5 dxc5 21 ♖c4 ♗a6 22 ♖c3 ♗xd3 23 ♖xd3 ♘c6 24 ♘f5 ♘e7 25 ♘d6 ♖ed8 26 ♖e1 ♘c6 27 ♖e4 ♘d4 28 ♘c4 ♘e6 29 g3 ♖d4 30 ♔e3 ♖xe4+ 31 ♔xe4 ♘g5+ 32 ♔f5 ♘xh3 33 f4 ♘f2 34 ♖d7 ♖e8 35 ♘e5

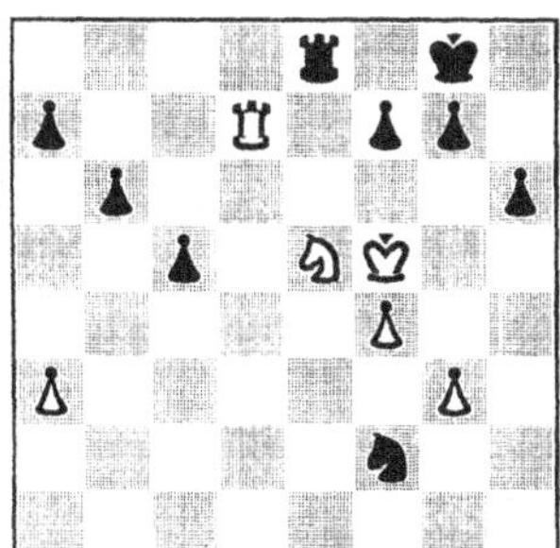

35 ... g6+ 36 ♘xg6 fxg6+ 37 ♔xg6 a6 38 ♖g7+ ½-½ L/N5178

**1851-AMS-68** vi 51
**Bruijn, W.= Kloos, H.**
1 e4 e5 2 ♘f3 ♘c6 3 ♗c4 h6 4 c3 ♘f6 5 d3 d5 6 exd5 ♘xd5 7 0-0 ♕d6 8 ♖e1 ♗e6 9 ♕e2 0-0-0 10 ♘xe5 ♘xe5 11 ♕xe5 ♕xe5 12 ♖xe5 c6 13 ♖e1 ♗d6 14 ♗xd5 ♗xd5 15 c4 ♗e6 16 ♘c3 ♗b4 17 ♖d1 ♗xc3 18 bxc3 ♗xc4 19 ♗e3 ♖xd3 20 ♖xd3 ♗xd3 21 ♗xa7 ♔c7 22 ♗d4 ♖g8 23 ♖e1 ♗c4 24 a4 g6 25 a5 ♔d7 26 h3 ♖e8 27 ♖b1 ♔c8 28 ♗b6 ♖e7 29 ♖b4 ♗e6 30 ♔h2 h5 31 g3 ♖d7 32 ♖e4 ♖d3 33 ♖d4 ♖xd4 34 ♗xd4 ♔d7 35 h4 ♔d6 36 ♔g2 c5 37 ♗f6 ♔d5 38 ♔f3 ♔c4 39 ♔e3 ♗f5 ½-½ L/N5178

**1851-AMS-69** vi 51
**Kloos, H.+ Bruijn, W.**
1 e4 e5 2 f4 exf4 3 ♘f3 ♕e7 4 e5 d6 5 d4 dxe5 6 dxe5 ♘c6 7 ♗xf4 ♕b4+ 8 ♗d2 ♕xb2 9 ♘c3 ♗f5 10 ♖b1 ♕xc2 11 ♕xc2 ♗xc2 12 ♖xb7 ♖c8 13 ♗b5 ♘e7 14 ♘d5 ♔d8 15 ♘xe7 ♘xe7 16 0-0 h6 17 ♖c1 ♗e4 18 ♖xa7 ♗xf3 19 gxf3 ♘f5 20 ♗a5 ♘d4 21 ♗xc7+ ♖xc7 22 ♖a8+ ♔e7 23 ♖xc7+ ♔e6 24 ♖e8+ ♔d5 25 ♗c4# **1-0** L/N5178

**1851-AMS-71** vi 51
**Kloos, H.+ Bruijn, W.**
1 e4 e6 2 d4 d5 3 e5 c5 4 ♗b5+ ♗d7 5 ♗xd7+ ♕xd7 6 c3 ♘c6 7 f4 cxd4 8 cxd4 g6 9 ♘f3 f6 10 0-0 0-0-0 11 ♘c3 a6 12 ♗d2 ♔b8 13 a3 fxe5 14 fxe5 h6 15 b4 b5 16 ♕b3 ♕a7 17 ♘e2 ♗g7 18 ♔h1 g5 19 a4 ♕b7 20 ♘c3 ♘ge7 21 axb5 axb5 22 ♖a2 g4 23 ♘e1 ♘xd4 24 ♕a3 ♘ec6 25 ♗e3 ♗xe5 26 ♗xd4 ♘xd4 27 ♖f7 ♗c7 28 ♘d3 ♖hf8 29 ♘c5 ♖xf7 30 g3 ♕c6 31 ♕a7+ ♔c8 32 ♖a6 ♕xc5 33 ♕xc5 ♘f3 34 ♖a8+ ♔d7 35 ♕xb5+ ♔e7 36 ♖xd8 ♗xd8 37 ♕c5+ ♔f6 38 ♕e3 ♗c7 39 ♘e2 e5 40 ♘c3 ♔e6 41 ♕xh6+ ♖f6 42 ♕h5 ♔d6 43 ♕xg4 ♗d8 44 ♕g8 ♘e1 45 ♕xd8+ ♔e6 46 ♕xd5+ ♔e7 47 ♕xe5+ ♖e6 48 ♘d5+ ♔f7 49 ♕f5+ **1-0** L/N5178

**1851-AMS-72** vi 51
**Blijdensteijn, W.J.+ Naret Oliphant, C.**
1 e4 e6 2 ♗c4 c6 3 a3 d5 4 exd5 cxd5 5 ♗b3 ♘f6 6 h3 ♘c6 7 d3 ♗e7 8 c3 ♗d7 9 ♘f3 ♕c7 10 ♗e3 h6 11 ♗c2 e5 12 0-0 ♗f5 13 ♘bd2 0-0 14 ♘h4 ♗h7 15 ♕e2 e4 16 dxe4 ♘xe4 17 ♘hf3 f5 18 ♘d4 ♘xd4 19 ♗xd4 ♗f6 20 ♗e3 b6 21 ♘f3 ♖ad8 22 ♘d4 ♗xd4 23 ♗xd4 ♔h8 24 ♖ad1 ♖de8 25 ♕f3 ♕b7 26 ♖fe1 ♘g5 27 ♕h5 ♖xe1+ 28 ♖xe1 ♕d7 29 ♕xh6 ♘e4 30 f3 ♘f6 31 ♕h4 ♔g8 32 ♖e5 ♕f7 33 ♗xf5 ♗xf5 34 ♖xf5 ♕g6 35 ♕f4 ♔h7 36 ♖g5 ♕f7 37 ♗xf6 ♕xf6 38 ♕xf6 gxf6 39 ♖xd5 ♖f7 40 g4 ♔g6 41 h4 ♖e7 42 ♔f2 ♔g7 43 h5 ♔h6 44 b4 ♖c7 45 ♖d3 ♖c6 46 ♔g3 a6 47 ♔h4 b5 48 ♔g3 f5 49 ♔f4 fxg4 50 fxg4 ♖c4+ 51 ♔f5 ♖c6 52 ♖e3 ♔g7 53 g5 ♖b6 54 h6+ ♔h7 55 ♖e7+ ♔g8 56 h7+ ♔h8 57 g6 **1-0** L/N5178

**1851-AMS-73** vi 51
**Naret Oliphant, C.— Blijdensteijn, W.J.**
1 e4 e6 2 d4 ♗b4+ 3 c3 ♗a5 4 ♗e2 c6 5 f4 ♗c7 6 ♘f3 b6 7 0-0 ♗a6 8 ♘a3 ♗xe2 9 ♕xe2 b5 10 ♘c2 d6 11 ♘b4 a5 12 ♘d3 h6 13 e5 ♘e7 14 exd6 ♗xd6 15 ♘fe5 ♘d5 16 f5 0-0 17 fxe6 fxe6 18 ♖xf8+ ♕xf8 19 ♗d2 ♗xe5 20 ♘xe5 ♕e8 21 ♖f1 ♖a7 22 ♕f3 ♘e7 23 g4 ♖c7 24 ♕e4 ♘d7 25 ♘xd7 ♕xd7 26 ♗f4 ♖c8 27 ♗e5 ♕e8 28 ♗d6 ♕g6 29 ♕f3 ♘f5 30 ♗g3 ♘xg3 31 ♕xg3 c5 32 dxc5 ♖xc5 33 h3 ♖g5 34 ♔h2 e5 35 ♕f3 e4 36 ♕f4 ♕e6 37 b3 a4 38 ♖f2 axb3 39 axb3 ♕xb3 40 ♕xe4 ♕xc3 41 ♕a8+ ♔h7 42 ♕e4+ ♔g8 43 ♕e6+ ♔h7 44 ♕e4+ ♖g6 45 h4 h5 46 g5 ♕c4 47 ♕f3 ♕xh4+ **0-1** L/N5178

**1851-AMS-74** vi 51
**De Heer, K.+ Kloos, H.**
1 e4 b6 2 ♗c4 ♗b7 3 d3 e6 4 c3 c5 5 ♘f3 ♘e7 6 ♘g5 h6 7 ♘h3 d5 8 exd5 ♘xd5 9 ♗b5+ ♘d7 10 d4 ♘xc3 11 ♗xd7+ ♕xd7 12 bxc3 ♗xg2 13 ♖g1 ♗xh3 14 ♕f3 ♖d8 15 ♕xh3 cxd4 16 ♕d3 g6 17 ♕xd4 ♕xd4 18 cxd4 ♖xd4 19 ♗b2 ♖e4+ 20 ♔f1 ♖g8 21 ♘d2 ♖h4 22 ♖g2 ♗d6 23 ♖d1 ♔e7 24 ♔g1 ♖c8 25 f3 ♖c2 26 ♗f6+ ♔xf6 27 ♘e4+ ♖xe4 28 ♖xc2 ♗c5+ 29 ♖xc5 ♖a4 30 ♖c2 ♔f5 31 ♔g2 h5 32 ♖d7 f6 33 ♖e7 b5 34 ♖ec7 e5 35 ♖7c3 g5 36 a3 a5 37 ♖b2 b4 38 axb4 axb4 39 ♖c4 ♖a8 40 ♖cxb4 ♖g8 41 h3 h4 42 ♖d2 ♖f8 43 ♖d5 ♔g6 44 ♖b6 ♔f5 45 ♖dd6 ♔g6 46 ♖b7 ♔f5 47 ♖bd7 ♔f4 48 ♖d8 ♖f7 49 ♖6d7 ♖xd7 50 ♖xd7 e4 51 ♖d4 f5 52 fxe4 fxe4 53 ♔f2 g4 54 hxg4 h3 55 g5 h2 56 ♔g2 h1=♕+ 57 ♔xh1 ♔f3 58 g6 **1-0** L/N5178

**1851-AMS-75** vi 51
**Van't Kruijs, M.+ De Heer, K.**
1 b3 e5 2 ♗b2 ♘c6 3 g3 d5 4 ♗g2 ♘f6 5 e3 ♗f5 6 d3 ♗c5 7 ♘e2 ♕d6 8 c3 ♖d8 9 0-0 0-0 10 a3 a6 11 d4 exd4 12 cxd4 ♗b6 13 b4 ♘e7 14 ♘bc3 ♗a7 15 f3 ♕e6 16 ♕d2 ♖fe8 17 ♘f4 ♕c6 18 ♔h1 ♘c8 19 ♖fe1 ♘b6 20 ♗f1 ♘c4 21 ♗xc4 dxc4 22 d5 g5 23 e4 ♗g6 24 ♘xg6 hxg6 25 ♕xg5 ♕d6 26 ♘b5 axb5 27 ♗xf6 ♖d7 **1-0** L/N5178

**1851-AMS-77** vi 51
**De Heer, K.– Van't Kruijs, M.**
1 e4 e5 2 ♘f3 d6 3 ♗c4 c6 4 h3 h6 5 d3 a6 6 c3 d5 7 ♗b3 ♕d6 8 0-0 ♗e6 9 ♖e1 f6 10 ♕e2 ♘d7 11 ♘a3 ♘e7 12 ♗e3 g6 13 ♖ad1 ♗g7 14 ♘c2 f5 15 exd5 cxd5 16 c4 0-0 17 cxd5 ♗xd5 18 ♗xd5+ ♘xd5 19 d4 e4 20 ♘h2 f4 21 ♗d2 ♖ae8 22 ♕g4 h5 23 ♕e2 b5 24 f3 e3 25 ♗a5 ♘b8 26 ♘f1 ♘c6 27 ♗c3 b4 28 ♗xb4 ♘cxb4 29 ♘xb4 ♘xb4 30 ♕c4+ ♔h7 31 a3 ♘d5 32 ♖e2 ♖c8 33 ♕d3 ♖f7 34 ♕e4 ♖e7 35 ♕d3 ♖ec7 36 g3 fxg3 37 ♘xe3 ♘f4 38 ♕d2 ♘xe2+ 39 ♕xe2 ♗xd4 40 ♔h1 ♕e5 41 ♕f1 ♕xe3 42 b4 ♖c1 **0-1** L/N5178

## LONDON(1) 1851

**1851-LON1-1**
**Kieseritsky, L.– Anderssen, A.**
[Staunton]
1 e4 c5 2 b3 ♘c6 3 ♗b2 a6 4 a4 e6 5 ♘f3 d6 6 ♘c3 ♘f6 7 ♗e2 ♗e7 8 0-0 0-0 9 d4 cxd4 10 ♘xd4 ♕b6 11 ♘xc6 bxc6 12 a5 ♕c7 13 f4 ♘e8 14 ♗d3 f5 15 exf5 exf5 16 ♕h5 ♘f6 17 ♕h3 ♘g4 18 ♖f3 ♕a7+ 19 ♔f1 ♖f6 [△ 19 ... ♖h6] 20 ♖g3?? ♕f2# **0-1** Staunton(1)

**1851-LON1-2**
**Anderssen, A.=Kieseritsky, L.**
1 e4 e5 2 f4 exf4 3 ♘f3 g5 4 h4 g4 5 ♘e5 h5 6 ♗c4 ♖h7 7 d4 d6 8 ♘d3 f3 9 g3 [□ 9 gxf3 ♗e7 10 ♗e3 (10 ♗f4) 10

... ♗xh4+ 11 ♔d2 gxf3 12 ♕xf3] 9 ... ♗e6 10 d5 ♗c8 11 e5 dxe5 12 ♘xe5 ♗d6 13 ♗f4 ♘e7 14 0-0 ♗f5 15 ♘c3 ♘d7 [□ 15 ... ♗xe5 16 ♗xe5 ♘d7] 16 ♘xd7 ♕xd7 17 ♗b5 c6 18 dxc6 ♗c5+ 19 ♔h2 bxc6 20 ♗d3 ♗xd3 21 cxd3 f5 22 ♖e1 ♖d8 23 ♕a4 f2 [23 ... ♕xd3 24 ♖ad1+-; □ 23 ... ♕b7] 24 ♖e2 ♔f8 25 ♗e3 ♗xe3 26 ♖xe3 ♕d4 27 ♕xd4 ♖xd4 28 ♖f1 f4 29 ♖xf2 ♘f5 30 ♘e2 [∞] 30 ... ♖f7 31 ♖e5 fxg3+ 32 ♘xg3 ♘xg3 33 ♖xf7+ ♔xf7 34 ♔xg3 ♖xd3+ 35 ♔f4 ♖d4+ 36 ♔g3 ♖d5 37 ♖e3 ♔f6 38 ♖c3 c5 39 ♖a3 ♔f5 40 ♖xa7 ♖d3+ 41 ♔f2 ♖d2+ 42 ♔g3 ♖xb2 43 ♖g7 c4 44 ♖g5+ ♔e4 45 ♖xh5 c3 46 ♖c5 ♔d3 47 ♔xg4 ♖b4+ 48 ♔g5 ♖c4 49 ♖d5+ ♔e2 50 ♖e5+ ♔f2 51 ♖b5 ♔g3 [□ 51 ... c2 52 ♖b2! ♔f3 (52 ... ♔g3 53 ♖b3+) 53 ♖xc2 ♖xc2 54 h5! ♖c5+ 55 ♔g6 ♔g4 56 h6 ♖c6+ 57 ♔g7 ♔g5 58 h7 ♖c7+ 59 ♔g8 ♔g6 60 h8♘+! ♔f6 61 a4 (61 ♔f8 ♖b8#) 61 ... ♖d7 62 a5 ♖c7 63 a6 ♖d7 64 a7 ♖xa7→] 52 ♖b1 ♖c5+ 53 ♔f6 ♔f4 54 ♖c1 ♔e4 55 ♖xc3 ½-½ Staunton(1)

## 1851-LON1-3
**Kieseritsky, L.− Anderssen, A.**

[Staunton]

1 e4 c5 2 b3 ♘c6 3 ♗b2 e6 4 ♘f3 d6 5 d4 cxd4 6 ♘xd4 ♗d7 7 ♗d3 ♘f6 8 0-0 ♗e7 9 ♘d2 0-0 10 c4 ♘e5 11 ♕e2 ♘g6 12 f4? [□ 12 g3±] 12 ... e5! 13 fxe5 dxe5 14 ♘c2? [□ 14 ♘f3 ∓] 14 ... ♗c5+ 15 ♔h1 ♗g4! [→] 16 ♘f3 ♘f4 17 ♕d2 ♘xd3 **0-1** Staunton(1)

## 1851-LON1-4
**Szén, J.+ Newham**

[Staunton]

1 e4 c5 2 ♘f3 ♘c6 3 d4 cxd4 4 ♘xd4 e6 5 c3 [5 ♘xc6 △ 6 ♗d3] 5 ... ♘ge7 6 ♗e3 d5 [□ 6 ... ♘g6] 7 exd5 ♘xd5 8 ♘xc6 bxc6 9 ♗d4 ♕c7 10 c4 ♘e7 [□ 10 ... ♕a5+] 11 ♗d3 ♗b7 12 ♗e3 ♘g6 13 0-0 ♗d6 14 ♕h5 0-0-0 [△ 15 ... ♗xh2+] 15 ♗e2 ♘f4 16 ♗xf4 ♗xf4 17 ♘c3 g6 18 ♕h3 f5 19 g3 ♗e5 [△ 20 ... f4] 20 ♕h6 ♗xc3 21 bxc3 ♕e5 22 ♗f3 [22 ♕e3] 22 ... ♕xc3 [□ 22 ... ♖d3] 23 ♗g2 ♖d7 [□ 23 ... ♖d2] 24 ♖fc1 ♕d2 25 ♕h4 ♕d4 26 ♕g5 ♖hd8 27 h4 ♕g7? [□ 27 ... e5] 28 ♕e3 a6 29 ♕xe6 ♕e7 30 ♖e1 ♖e8 31 ♕xe7 ♖dxe7 32 ♖xe7 ♖xe7 33 ♔f1 c5 34 ♗xb7+ ♔xb7 35 ♖d1 ♔c6 36 ♖d8 ♖e4? [□ 36 ... h5 △ ♖e6] 37 ♖c8+ ♔b6 38 ♖h8 ♖xc4 39 ♖xh7 ♖e4 40 ♖h6 c4 41 ♖xg6+ ♔b5 42 ♖g8 c3 43 ♖c8 ♔b4 [43 ... ♖c4?? 44 ♖xc4 ♔xc4 45 ♔e2+-] 44 h5 ♖e6 45 f3 a5 46 g4 fxg4 47 fxg4 ♖h6 48 ♔e2 ♔a3 49 ♖xc3+ ♔xa2 50 ♖c5 a4 51 ♖b5! a3 52 ♔f3 ♔a1 53 ♖a5 a2 54 ♔g3 ♔b2 55 ♔h4 a1♕ 56 ♖xa1 ♔xa1 57 g5 ♖a6 58 h6 ♖a7 59 g6 ♖a4+ 60 ♔g5 ♖a5+ 61 ♔f4 ♖a4+ 62 ♔e5 ♖a5+ 63 ♔d4 ♖a4+ 64 ♔c5 **1-0** Staunton(1)

## 1851-LON1-5
**Newham− Szén, J.**

[Staunton]

1 e4 e6 2 d4 d5 3 exd5 exd5 4 c4 ♗b4+ 5 ♘c3 ♘f6 6 ♗g5 ♕e7+ 7 ♕e2 ♕xe2+ 8 ♗xe2 ♘e4 9 ♗d2 ♘xd2 10 ♔xd2 ♗e6 11 ♗f3!? c6 12 c5 ♘d7 13 a3 ♗a5 14 b4 ♗c7 15 ♘ge2 0-0 16 h3 ♗f5 17 ♗g4 ♗e6 18 ♖ae1 f5 19 ♗f3 ♘f6 20 ♖hf1 ♘e4+ 21 ♔c2 ♖ae8 22 g3 ♘g5 23 ♗g2 f4! 24 gxf4 ♘xh3 25 ♗xh3 ♗xh3 26 ♖h1 ♗g2 27 ♖h4 ♗f3 28 ♔d2 ♗xe2 29 ♖xe2 ♖c8! 30 ♘d1 ♖xf4 31 ♖xf4 ♗xf4+ 32 ♔d3 ♔f7 33 a4 a6 34 b5 axb5 35 axb5 h5 36 f3 ♖a8 37 bxc6 bxc6 38 ♖b2 ♖e8 39 ♖b6 ♖e6 40 ♘c3 h4 41 ♖b7+ ♔f6 42 ♘e4+??! dxe4+ 43 fxe4 h3 **0-1** Staunton(1)

## 1851-LON1-6
**Staunton, H.+ Brodie**

[Staunton]

1 e4 e5 2 ♘f3 ♘c6 3 d4 exd4 4 ♗c4 ♗b4+ 5 c3 dxc3 6 0-0 ♕f6 7 e5 ♕e7 [□ 7 ... ♕g6] 8 a3 cxb2 9 ♗xb2 ♗c5 10 ♘c3 d6 11 ♘d5 ♕d8 12 exd6 ♗xd6 13 ♗xg7 ♗g4 14 ♖e1+ ♘ge7 15 ♘f6# **1-0** Staunton(1)

## 1851-LON1-7
**Brodie− Staunton, H.**

[Staunton]

1 c4 c5 2 d3 e6 3 e3 d5 4 cxd5 exd5 5 ♘f3 ♘c6 6 g3 ♘f6 7 ♗g2 ♗d6 8 ♘c3 a6 9 ♘e2 ♗g4 10 a3 0-0 11 ♕b3 ♔h8 12 ♗d2 b5 13 ♕c2 ♖c8 14 b3 ♖e8 15 0-0 ♕d7 16 ♔h1 ♘e5 17 ♘xe5 ♗xe5 18 ♖ae1 c4 19 d4 ♗xe2 20 ♖xe2 ♗xd4 21 b4 ♗b6 22 ♗c3 ♘e4 23 ♖d1 ♘xc3 24 ♕xc3 d4 25 ♖ee1 d3 26 ♔g1 ♗d8 27 e4 ♗b6 28 ♔f1 ♕g4 29 ♔g1 ♖cd8 30 ♕d2 ♗d4 31 ♔h1 ♗f6 32 f4 c3 33 ♕a2 d2 34 ♖f1 ♕c8 35 ♕c2 ♗d4 36 e5 f5 37 ♗f3 ♗e3 38 ♔g2 ♕c4 39 ♗b7 ♕e2+ 40 ♔h1 ♕d3 41 ♕xd3 ♖xd3 42 ♗xa6 ♖b8 43 a4 c2 44 ♗xb5 ♖xb5 45 axb5 c1♕ 46 ♔g2 ♕c4 47 ♖a1 ♕d5+ 48 ♔h3 g5 49 fxg5 f4 50 ♔g4 d1♕+ 51 ♖fxd1 ♖xd1 52 ♖a6 ♕xe5 **0-1** Staunton(1)

## 1851-LON1-8
**Horwitz, B.= Bird, H.E.**

[Staunton]

1 c4 g6 2 e3 c5 3 f4 ♗g7 4 ♘f3 ♘h6 5 ♗e2 d6 6 0-0 ♘c6 7 ♘a3 0-0 8 ♘c2 ♗f5? [□ 8 ... ♗d7] 9 d3 ♕b6 10 ♕e1 e5 11 fxe5 [□ 11 e4 △ f5] 11 ... ♘xe5 12 ♘xe5 [□ 12 e4] 12 ... dxe5 13 e4 ♗g4 14 ♗xg4 ♘xg4 15 ♕g3 ♘f6 16 ♕xe5 ♘h5 17 ♕g5 ♗xb2 18 ♖b1 ♗d4+ 19 ♗e3 [19 ♘xd4!?] 19 ... ♗xe3+ 20 ♘xe3 ♕d8 21 ♕xd8 ♖axd8 22 ♘d5 b6 23 a4 f5 24 exf5 gxf5 25 ♖be1 [25 ♘e7+∞; 25 ♖xf5∞; 25 a5!] 25 ... ♖f7 26 ♖e5 ♘g7 27 g4 f4 28 ♖f3? [28 ♘xf4 ♖df8 29 ♖e4 ♘e6 30 ♖xe6 ♖xf4 31 ♖xf4 ♖xf4 32 ♖e4+-] 28 ... ♖d6 29 ♖xf4 ♖xd5 30 ♖xf7 ♖xe5 31 ♖xa7 ♖e6 32 ♔f2 ♘e8 33 a5 bxa5 34 ♖xa5 ♖c6 35 ♔f3 ♔f7 36 ♖a7+ ♘c7 37 ♔e4 ♖e6+ 38 ♔f5 ♖c6 [□ 38 ... ♖e7∓] 39 h4 ♔e7 40 g5 ♔f7 41 h5 ♔g7 42 ♖b7 h6 43 g6 ♖f6+ 44 ♔e5 ♖e6+ 45 ♔f4 ♖e7 46 ♔f5 ♘d5 47 ♖b5 [47 ♖xe7+ =] 47 ... ♘b4 48 d4 ♘d3 49 dxc5 ♖e5+ 50 ♔g4 ♖g5+ 51 ♔h4 ♘f2 52 ♖b7+ ♔g8 53 ♖b8+ ♔g7 54 ♖b7+ ½-½ Staunton(1)

## 1851-LON1-9
**Bird, H.E.+ Horwitz, B.**

[Staunton]

1 e4 e5 2 ♘f3 ♘c6 3 ♗b5 ♘f6 4 d4 ♘xd4 5 ♘xd4 exd4 6 e5 ♘d5 7 0-0 [□ 7 ♕xd4] 7 ... ♗c5 8 c3 a6 9 ♗c4 [9 ♗e2 ♕h4] 9 ... ♘b6 10 ♗b3 dxc3 11 ♘xc3 0-0 12 ♘e4 ♕e7 13 ♕h5 d6 [13 ... ♗d4 14 ♘g5 h6 15 ♘xf7 ♖xf7 16 ♗xh6 gxh6 17 ♕g4+ ♔f8 18 ♗xf7 ♕xf7 19 ♕xd4±] 14 ♗g5 ♕xe5 15 ♖ae1 ♘d5!! 16 ♘xc5 ♘f6!? 17 ♕h4 ♕xc5 18 ♗xf6 gxf6 19 ♖e3 ♗f5 20 ♕xf6 ♗g6 21 ♖g3 ♕e5 22 ♕h4 ♕xb2 23 f4 [△ 23 f5] 23 ... ♕d4+ 24 ♔h1 ♖ae8 25 ♕g5 ♕f2 26 ♖gf3 [△ 26 f5] 26 ... ♕d2 27 h4 c6? [△ 28 ... d5; □ 27 ... ♔g7! 28 ♕g3 (28 h5 ♖e5→) 28 ... ♔h8 (△ 29 ... ♖g8) 29 f5 ♗h5∓] 28 h5 ♖e5 29 ♗xf7+! ♖xf7 30 ♕d8+ ♖f8 31 ♕xf8+ ♔xf8 32 fxe5+ ♔g7 [□ 32 ... ♔e7] 33 hxg6 dxe5 34 gxh7 ♔xh7 35 ♔h2 e4 36 ♖h3+ ♔g6 37 ♖g3+ ♔h7 38 ♖f7+ ♔h6 39 ♖f6+ ♔h5 [39 ... ♔h7 40 ♖fg6 (△ 41 ♖6g4 ~ 42 ♖h3#)+-] 40 ♖f8 ♕d4 41 ♖h8+ ♕xh8 42 ♖h3+ ♔g5 43 ♖xh8 ♔f4 44 ♖f8+ ♔e3 45 ♔g3 [□ 45 ♔g1 △ 46 g4] 45 ... c5 46 ♖b8 b5 47 ♖b6 c4 48 ♖xa6 c3 49 ♖c6 ♔d2 50 ♔f4 e3 51 ♖d6+ ♔e2 52 g4 ♔f2 53 ♖h6 e2 54 ♖h2+ ♔f1 55 ♔f3 e1♘+ 56 ♔e3 ♘g2+ 57 ♖xg2 ♔xg2 58 g5 b4 59 ♔d3 **1-0** Staunton(1)

## 1851-LON1-10
**Horwitz, B.+Bird, H.E.**

[Staunton]

1 e4 c5 2 f4 d5 3 exd5 ♕xd5 4 ♘c3 ♕d8 5 ♘f3 ♘f6 6 ♘e5 e6 7 ♗b5+ ♗d7 8 ♕f3 ♕c7 9 ♗xd7+ ♘bxd7 10 0-0 a6 11 d3 ♗d6 12 ♘c4 0-0 13 ♘xd6 ♕xd6 14 f5 ♘e5 15 ♕g3 exf5 16 ♖xf5 ♘fd7 17 ♗f4 f6 18 ♖af1 ♕e6 19 ♗d2 ♖ae8 20 b3 ♘c6 [△ 21 ... ♘d4] 21 ♖5f2 ♘d4 22 ♗h6 ♖f7 23 ♘e4 f5 24 ♘d6 ♕xh6 25 ♘xe8 ♖e7 26 ♕d6 ♕e3 27 ♕d5+ [□ 27 ♘c7 △ 28 ♘d5] 27 ... ♔f8 28 ♘d6 ♘f6 ∓ 29 ♘xf5 ♕xf2+ 30 ♔xf2 ♘xd5 [30 ... ♖e2+? 31 ♔g1 ♘xd5 32 ♘xd4+ ♔~ 33 ♘xe2+-] 31 ♘xe7 ♔xe7 32 ♖e1+ ♔d6 33 ♖c1 ♘c3 [□ 33 ... ♘b4] 34 a3 b5 35 ♔e3 ♔d5 36 ♔d2 b4 37 axb4 ♘a2 38 ♖b1! [39 ♖a1 ♘xb4 40 c3 ♘xb3+-+] 38 ... cxb4 39 ♖a1 ♘c3 40 ♖xa6 ♔e5 41 ♖a7 ♘f5 42 g4 ♘d4 43 ♖xg7 ♘f3+ 44 ♔e3 ♘xh2 45 d4+ ♔f6 46 ♖xh7 ♘xg4+ 47 ♔d3 ♘d5 48 ♔e4 ♔e6 49 ♖a7! ♘gf6+ 50 ♔d3 ♔f5 51 ♔c4 ♔e4 52 ♖a6! ♔e3 53 ♖d6! ♔e4 54 ♔c5!+- ♘e3 55 ♖e6+ **1-0**

Staunton(1)

## 1851-LON1-11
**Bird, H.E.–Horwitz, B.**

[Staunton]

1 e4 c5 2 ♘f3 ♘c6 3 ♗b5 ♕c7 4 0-0 e6 5 ♘c3 a6 6 ♗xc6 bxc6 7 e5 ♘e7 8 d3 ♘g6 9 ♖e1 ♗e7 10 b3 f6 11 ♘e4 fxe5 12 ♗g5 d6 13 ♗xe7 ♕xe7 14 ♘eg5? h6 15 ♘e4 0-0 16 ♖e3 ♘f4 17 g3 ♘d5 18 ♖e1 ♗d7 19 c4 ♘f6 20 ♖e3 ♗e8 21 ♘xf6+ ♕xf6 22 ♕d2 e4!→ 23 ♖ae1 exf3 24 ♖e4 e5 25 ♔h1 ♗d7 26 g4 ♕g5 27 ♕a5 ♗xg4 28 ♖g1 h5 29 ♕c7 ♕d2 30 ♕xd6 ♕xf2 31 ♖xe5 ♕xg1+! 32 ♔xg1 f2+ **0-1**

Staunton(1)

## 1851-LON1-12
**Lowe, E.–Wyvill, M.**

[Staunton]

1 e4 e6 2 c4 c5 3 ♘c3 ♘c6 4 f4 ♘h6 5 ♘f3 g6 6 ♗e2 ♗g7 7 0-0 a6 8 d3 ♖b8 9 h3 d6 10 ♗e3 0-0 11 ♕d2 [△ 11 f5] 11 ... ♕e7? [□ 11 ... ♔h8] 12 f5 ♘xf5 13 exf5 gxf5 14 ♖ae1 b5 15 ♗d1 b4 16 ♘e2 e5 17 ♗h6 f6 18 ♘h4? f4 19 ♗xg7 ♕xg7 20 ♔h2 ♕h6 21 ♘f3 ♔h8 22 ♘eg1 ♖g8 23 ♕f2 ♖b7 24 ♘h4? ♖g3 25 ♗f3 ♖bg7 26 ♗xc6 ♕xh4 27 ♗f3 ♖7g6 28 ♖e4 ♖h6 29 ♘e2

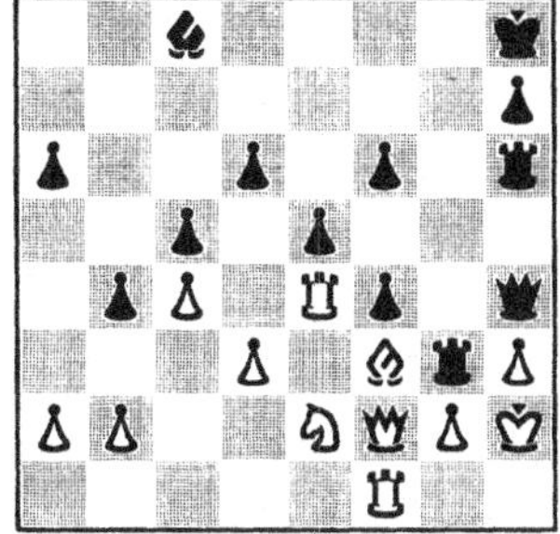

29 ... ♕xh3+ **0-1** Staunton(1)

## 1851-LON1-13
**Wyvill, M.+Lowe, E.**

[Staunton]

1 c4 e5 2 e3 c5 3 ♘c3 ♘c6 4 g3 ♗e7 5 ♗g2 d6 6 d3 ♘f6 7 a3 ♗e6 8 ♘ge2 d5 9 cxd5 ♘xd5 10 0-0 0-0 11 ♕c2 ♘xc3 12 bxc3 ♗d5 13 e4 ♗e6 14 ♗e3 ♕d7 [□ 14 ... f5] 15 f4 f5 16 fxe5 ♘xe5 17 ♘f4 ± ♘g4 18 ♗d2 c4 19 d4 ♗f7? [□ 19 ... fxe4] 20 e5 ♖ab8 21 h3 ♘h6 22 d5 +- ♗c5+ 23 ♔h1 ♕e7 24 ♖ae1 ♕g5? 25 ♘e6! ♕e7 26 ♗g5 ♕e8 27 ♘xc5 ♕b5 28 ♗e7 ♖fe8 29 ♖b1 ♕a5 30 ♗d6 b6 31 ♗xb8 ♕xc5 32 ♗d6 ♕e3 33 e6 ♗g6 34 ♗f4 ♕c5 35 ♕d2 ♔h8 36 ♕d4 ♕xd4 37 cxd4 ♘g8 38 ♖fc1 ♘f6 39 ♖xc4 ♘e4 40 ♖bc1 ♔g8 41 ♖c8 **1-0** Staunton(1)

## 1851-LON1-14
**Mayet, K.–Kennedy, H.A.**

[Staunton]

1 e4 e6 2 f4 d5 3 e5 [□ 3 exd5] 3 ... f6 4 ♘f3 ♘h6 5 d4 c5 6 c3 ♘c6 7 ♗d3 cxd4 [□ 7 ... ♕b6 8 ♗c2 ♗e7 9 b3 cxd4 10 cxd4 ♗b4+ 11 ♔f2 0-0∓] 8 cxd4 ♗b4+ 9 ♘c3 ♕a5 10 ♗d2 0-0 11 a3 ♗xc3 12 ♗xc3 ♕d8 13 0-0 fxe5 14 fxe5 ♗d7 15 ♕c2 ♘f5! 16 ♖ae1 [16 g4 ♘h4 17 ♗xh7+ ♔h8 18 ♘xh4 ♕xh4∓; 16 ... ♘e3 17 ♗xh7+ ♔h8 18 ♕g6 ♗e8 19 ♕d3 ♘xf1∓] 16 ... ♖c8! 17 ♕b1 [17 g4 ♘fxd4∓] 17 ... ♕b6 18 ♔h1 h6 19 ♗xf5 ♖xf5 20 ♕d3 ♖cf8 21 ♖g1 ♗e8! 22 ♘h4 ♖f4 23 g3 ♖f2 24 ♖g2 ♖xg2 25 ♘xg2 ♘e7 26 ♗b4 ♗g6 27 ♕d2 ♖f7 28 ♘f4 ♗e4+ 29 ♔g1 ♘c6 30 ♗c5

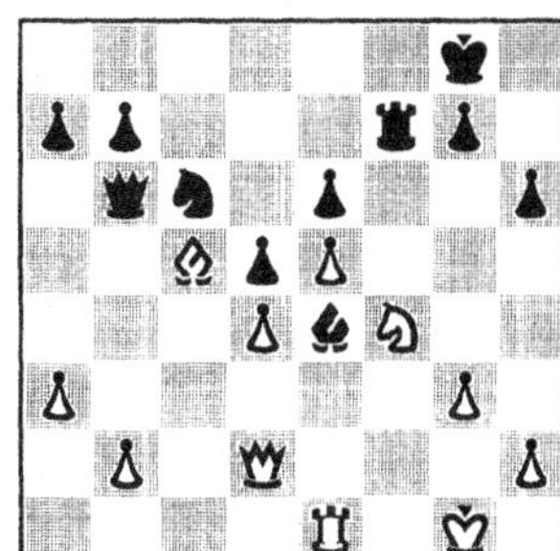

30 ... ♘xe5 31 ♖e3 [31 ♗xb6 ♘f3+] 31 ... ♕c6 32 dxe5 ♕xc5 33 ♘xe6 ♕e7 34 ♘f4 ♕xe5 35 ♕e2 [△ 36 ♘xd5] 35 ... ♕c7 36 ♕d2 ♕b6 37 h4 g5 38 hxg5 hxg5 39 ♘h3 ♖f3 **0-1** Staunton(1)

## 1851-LON1-15
**Kennedy, H.A.+Mayet, K.**

[Staunton]

1 c4 e5 2 ♘c3 f5 3 e3 ♘f6 4 d4 exd4 5 exd4 ♗e7 6 ♗d3 d5 7 ♘f3 c6 8 0-0 [□ 8 ♕c2] 8 ... 0-0 9 ♗g5 [□ 9 ♕c2] 9 ... ♗b4 10 cxd5 ♗xc3 11 bxc3 cxd5 12 ♕c2 ♕d6 13 ♘e5 [13 ♗xf5] 13 ... ♘c6 14 ♗f4 ♘h5 15 ♕d2 ♘xf4 16 ♕xf4 ♗e6 17 ♖fe1 ♖ac8 18 ♖ab1 ♘xe5 19 dxe5 [19 ♕xe5; 19 ♖xe5∞] 19 ... ♕d7 20 ♕d4 b6 21 f4 ♖c5 22 a4 ♖fc8 23 ♖ec1 ♖8c7 24 h3 ♕c8 25 ♖b3 ♔f7 26 g4 ♔g8!? [26 ... fxg4 27 f5! ♗d7 28 e6++-] 27 g5 ♕e8! 28 ♗e2 ♗d7 29 ♖a3 ♖a5 30 ♗d1 [30 ♖ca1 ♕e7 31 ♔f1 ♕c5 32 ♕xc5 ♖axc5 33 ♖c1 d4 34 c4 b5 35 axb5 ♗xb5 36 ♖d1 ♗xc4 37 ♖xd4=] 30 ... ♖c4 31 ♕d2 ♗xa4 32 ♖ca1 ♗c6! 33 ♖xa5 bxa5 34 ♖xa5 ♕d8 35 ♖a6 ♔f8 36 ♗b3 ♖c5 37 ♕d3 [37 ♖xa7?? ♕b6-+] 37 ... ♕d7 38 ♕d4 ♕e7 39 c4! dxc4 40 ♗xc4 ♗e4 41 ♖d6 [41 ♖xa7 ♖xc4!-+ (41 ... ♕xa7?? 42 ♕d8#)] 41 ... ♖c8 42 ♖d7 ♕c5 ...? **1-0** Staunton(1)

## 1851-LON1-16
**Löwenthal, J.J.–Williams, E.**

[Staunton]

1 e4 e6 2 d4 d5 3 exd5 exd5 4 ♘f3 ♘f6 5 ♗d3 ♗d6 6 0-0 0-0 7 h3 h6 8 c4 dxc4 9 ♗xc4 ♘c6 10 ♗e3 ♗f5 11 ♘c3 ♕d7 12 ♘e2 ♖ae8 = 13 ♗f4? ♗e4! ∓ 14 ♗xd6 ♕xd6 15 ♘d2 ♘xd4 16 ♘xe4 ♘xe2+ 17 ♗xe2 ♘xe4 18 ♗f3 ♕b6 19 ♕c2 ♘g5 20 ♗d5 ♘e6 21 ♖fe1 ♘d4 22 ♕c4 ♖xe1+ 23 ♖xe1 ♕xb2 24 ♗xf7+ ♔h8 25 ♕xc7 ♕d2! ∓ 26 ♕e7? ♖xf7 27 ♕xf7 ♕xe1+ 28 ♔h2 ♕e5+ 29 ♔g1 ♘e2+ 30 ♔f1 ♘f4 31 ♔g1 ♕e4 32 f3 ♕e3+ 33 ♔h2 b5 34 ♕f8+ ♔h7 35 ♕f5+

♘g6 36 ♕c2 h5 37 h4 ♕f4+ 38 g3 ♕xf3 39 ♕c5 ♕e2+ 40 ♔g1 ♘e5 41 ♔h1 ♕f1+ 42 ♕g1 ♕h3+ 43 ♕h2 ♕xh2+ 44 ♔xh2 a5 **0-1**
Staunton(1)

**1851-LON1-17**
**Williams,E.–Löwenthal, J.J.**
[Staunton]

1 e4 e5 2 ♘f3 ♘f6 3 ♗c4 ♘xe4 4 d3 [4 ♘c3] 4 ... ♘f6 5 ♘xe5 d5 6 ♗b3 ♗d6 7 d4 0-0 8 0-0 c5 9 c3 ♕c7 10 f4 ♘c6 11 ♗e3 ♕b6 12 ♘xc6 bxc6 13 dxc5 ♗xc5 14 ♗xc5 ♕xc5+ 15 ♕d4 ♕xd4+ 16 cxd4 ♘e4 17 f5 ♖b8! ∓ 18 ♘c3 ♘d2 19 ♖f2 ♘xb3 20 axb3 a6 21 ♖a3 ♖b4 22 ♘e2 ♖e8 23 g4 f6 [23 ... ♖e3] 24 ♔f1 ♖e4 25 ♖g2 h5 26 g5 ♗xf5 27 ♔f2 ♗g4 28 ♘c3 ♖f4+ 29 ♔e3 ♖f3+ 30 ♔e2 ♖xc3+ 31 ♖xg4 ♖cxb3 32 ♖xb3 ♖xb3 33 ♖h4 ♖xb2+ 34 ♔d3 a5 35 g6 a4 36 ♔c3 a3 37 ♖h3 ♖b8 38 ♔c2 ♖a8 39 ♔b1 a2+ 40 ♔a1 ♔f8 41 ♖xh5 ♔e7 42 ♖h7 ♖g8 43 h4 f5 44 ♖h5 ♔f6 45 ♖g5 ♖h8 46 ♖g1 ♖xh4 47 ♖c1 ♔xg6 48 ♖xc6+ ♔g5 49 ♖c7 g6 50 ♖d7 ♖xd4 **0-1** Staunton(1)

**1851-LON1-18**
**Löwenthal,J.J.–Williams, E.**
[Staunton]

1 d4 e6 2 e3 f5 3 c4 ♘f6 4 ♘f3 ♗b4+ 5 ♘c3 ♗xc3+ 6 bxc3 c5 7 ♗d3 [7 dxc5 ♕a5] 7 ... ♕e7 8 0-0 0-0 9 a4 [△ 10 dxc5 ~ 11 ♗a3] 9 ... d6 10 ♕c2 ♘c6 11 ♗a3 b6 12 ♖fe1 ♗a6 13 e4 fxe4 14 ♗xe4 ♗b7 15 ♗xc6 ♗xc6 16 d5! [16 ♘g5 e5] 16 ... ♗b7 17 dxe6 ♗c6 18 ♘g5!? [△ 19 ♘f7] 18 ... h6 19 ♘h3? [⌓ 19 ♘f7] 19 ... ♘g4 20 ♕e2 [⌓ 20 f4] 20 ... ♘e5 21 f4 ♘g6 [△ 21 ... ♘h4] 22 g3?! ♖f6 23 ♕h5? ♖xe6 24 ♖xe6 ♕xe6 25 ♘f2 ♖e8 [△ 26 ... ♕e1+ 27 ♖xe1 ♖xe1#] 26 h3 ♕e3! 27 ♕g4 [27 ♕xg6 ♕f3→] 27 ... ♕xc3 28 ♖f1 ♕xa3 29 ♔h2 ♕f3 30 ♕xf3 ♗xf3 31 f5 ♘e5 32 ♖c1 ♗c6 33 g4 ♖e7 34 ♔g3 ♗xa4 35 ♖c3 ♗c6 36 h4 a5 37 ♘d3 ♘xc4 38 ♖xc4 ♖e3+ 39 ♔f2 ♖xd3 **0-1**
Staunton(1)

**1851-LON1-19**
**Mucklow,J.R.+Kennedy, E.S.**
[Staunton]

1 d4 d5 2 b3 e6 3 e3 ♘f6 4 ♗d3 a6 5 a4 c5 6 ♘e2 ♘c6 7 c3 b6 8 ♗b2 ♗b7 9 ♘d2 ♗d6 10 ♕c2 ♖c8 11 h3 ♘a5 12 dxc5 bxc5 13 0-0 c4 14 bxc4 dxc4 15 ♗e4 ♘xe4 16 ♘xe4 ♗xe4 17 ♕xe4 ♘b3 18 ♖ad1 ♘c5 19 ♕xc4 0-0 20 ♕d4 ♘b7 21 c4 f6 22 ♗c3 ♕c7 23 ♕e4 e5 24 ♖b1 ♘d8 25 ♖fd1 ♘f7 26 ♖b7 ♕c6 27 ♕xc6 ♖xc6 28 ♗b4 ♖fc8 29 ♘g3? [29 ♖xf7+−] 29 ... ♗xb4 30 ♖xb4 ♖xc4 31 ♖db1 ♖xb4 32 ♖xb4 ♔f8 33 ♖b6 ♖a8 34 ♘e4 a5 35 ♘c5 ♖a7 36 ♖b8+ ♔e7 37 ♖b7+ ♖xb7 38 ♘xb7 ♔d7 39 ♘xa5 ♔c7 40 ♔f1 ♔b6 41 ♘b3 ♘d6 42 ♔e2 ♘c4 43 ♔f3 f5 44 e4 f4 45 g3 fxg3 46 ♔xg3 ♘b2 47 a5+ ♔b5 48 f4 exf4+ 49 ♔xf4 ♘c4 50 e5 g6 51 e6 ♔c6 52 a6 ♔d6 53 a7 ♘b6 54 ♘d4 ♔e7 55 ♔e5 h6 56 ♘c6+ ♔e8 57 ♔f6 g5 58 ♘d8 ♘a8 59 ♘f7 ♔f8 60 e7+ ♔e8 61 ♘d6+ ♔d7 62 e8♕+ **1-0** Staunton(1)

**1851-LON1-20**
**Kennedy,E.S.–Mucklow, J.R.**
[Staunton]

1 e4 c5 2 ♘f3 e6 3 d4 cxd4 4 ♘xd4 ♘c6 5 ♘b3 b6 6 ♗c4 ♗b7 7 f4 ♖c8 8 0-0 ♘b4 9 ♗d3 ♕c7 10 c3 ♘c6 11 ♗e3 ♘ge7 12 ♘d4 ♘xd4 13 cxd4 ♕c6 14 ♘c3 a6 15 ♖c1 ♕d6 16 e5 ♕b8 17 ♗e4? ♖xc3 18 ♖xc3 ♗xe4 19 ♕a4 ♘d5 20 ♖b3 ♗c2 21 ♕c4 ♗xb3 22 ♕xb3 ♗e7 23 ♗d2 0-0 24 f5 f6 25 fxe6 dxe6 26 ♕h3 ♕c8 27 ♕g4 ♕d7 28 ♗h6 ♖f7 29 ♖f3 ♗f8 30 ♖g3 ♕e7 31 ♗d2 fxe5 32 ♕e4 exd4 33 ♖h3 g6 34 a3 a5 35 ♖d3 ♗g7 36 h4 ♖f5 37 ♗g5 ♗f6 38 g4 ♖e5 39 ♕xe5 ♗xe5 40 ♗xe7 ♘xe7 41 ♔f2 ♘c6 42 ♔f3 ♗f6 43 h5 ♘e5+ **0-1** Staunton(1)

**1851-LON1-21**
**Anderssen,A.+Szén, J.**
[Staunton]

1 e4 e6 2 d4 d5 3 exd5 exd5 4 c4 ♗b4+ 5 ♘c3 ♕e7+ 6 ♗e3 ♘f6 7 h3 ♗e6 8 ♕b3 dxc4 [⌓ 8 ... 0-0] 9 ♗xc4 ♗xc4 10 ♕xc4 c6 11 ♘f3 ♘bd7 12 0-0 0-0 13 ♖ae1 ♕d6 14 ♘e5 ♗xc3 15 bxc3 ♘d5 16 ♗c1 ♖fe8 17 ♘xd7 ♕xd7 18 ♕b3 [△ 19 c4] 18 ... h6 19 c4 ♘f6 20 ♖d1 ♖ad8 21 ♗b2 b5 22 cxb5 cxb5 23 d5 ♘e4 [23 ... ♘xd5 24 ♕g3 g6 25 ♖xd5 ♕xd5 26 ♕c3 ♔f8 27 ♕g7+ ♔e7 28 ♗f6+=] 24 ♖d4 f6 25 ♖fd1 ♕f5 26 d6+ ♔h8 27 f3 ♘g5 28 ♖d5 ♕f4 29 ♕c2 ♕g3 30 ♔h1 ♖e1+ [30 ... ♘xh3? 31 d7!+− (31 gxh3 ♕xh3+ 32 ♔g1 ♕g3+ 33 ♕g2 ♕xg2+ 34 ♔xg2 ♖e2+∓); 30 ... ♘xf3!∓] 31 ♖xe1 ♕xe1+ 32 ♔h2 ♕e8 33 ♕c7 ♖d7 34 ♕c6 ♕e6 [34 ... ♘xf3+?!] 35 ♕xb5 ♘f7 36 ♗a3 ♔h7 37 ♕d3+ g6 38 f4 f5 39 ♗b2 ♘d8 40 ♕c3 g5 41 ♖xf5 ♕g8 42 ♖e5 **1-0** Staunton(1)

**1851-LON1-22**
**Szén, J.+Anderssen, A.**
[Staunton]

1 e4 c5 2 ♘f3 ♘c6 3 d4 cxd4 4 ♘xd4 e6 5 ♘b5!? d6 6 ♗f4 e5 7 ♗e3 a6 8 ♘b5c3 ♗e6 9 ♘d5 ♗xd5 10 ♕xd5 [⌓ 10 exd5] 10 ... ♘f6 11 ♕b3 d5 12 ♕xb7!? ♘b4 13 ♘a3 ♘xe4 14 c3 ♖b8 15 ♕a7 d4 16 ♗c4! ♘d6 17 cxb4 ♘xc4 [17 ... dxe3 18 0-0! (18 ♕xe3?! ♘xc4 19 ♘xc4 ♗xb4+∞)] 18 ♘xc4 dxe3 19 0-0 e2 20 ♖fe1 ♗xb4 21 ♖xe2 f6? [⌓ 21 ... 0-0] 22 ♕xg7 ♖f8 23 ♕xh7 ♕d5 24 ♕h5+ ♔d8 25 ♖c2 ♔e7 26 ♘e3 ♕e4 27 ♖c7+ ♔e6 28 ♖c4 ♕b7 29 ♖d1 f5 30 g4 f4 31 ♘d5 **1-0**
Staunton(1)

**1851-LON1-23**
**Anderssen, A.–Szén, J.**
[Staunton]

1 d4 d5 2 c4 e6 3 e3 ♘f6 4 ♘c3 c5 5 ♘f3 ♘c6 6 a3 a6 7 b3 b6 8 ♗b2 ♗b7 9 cxd5 exd5 10 ♗d3 cxd4 11 exd4 ♗d6 12 0-0 0-0 13 b4 b5 14 ♖c1 ♖c8 = 15 ♕b3 ♗b8 16 ♖c2 ♖e8 17 ♘e2 ♘e4 18 ♘g3 ♘g5 19 ♘e5 [⌓ 19 ♗f5] 19 ... ♘e6! [19 ... ♘xe5 20 dxe5 ♗xe5 21 ♗xe5 ♖xe5 22 f4+−] 20 ♘e2? [⌓ 20 ♘xc6] 20 ... ♘cxd4! 21 ♖xc8 ♘xe2+ 22 ♗xe2 ♕xc8 23 ♖d1 ♘f4 24 ♗g4 f5! −+ 25 g3 ♗xe5 26 ♗xe5 ♘g6 **0-1** Staunton(1)

**1851-LON1-24**
**Szén, J.–Anderssen, A.**
[Staunton]

1 e4 c5 2 ♘f3 ♘c6 3 ♘c3 e6 4 ♗c4 a6 5 a4 ♘ge7 6 ♕e2 ♘g6 7 d3 ♗e7 8 ♗e3 0-0 9 0-0 f5 10 exf5 ♖xf5 11 ♘b1?! [⌓ 11 d4] 11 ... b6 12 c3 ♗b7 13 ♘bd2 ♕c7 14 d4 ♘f4 15 ♕d1 ♖af8 ∓ 16 dxc5 bxc5 17 ♗xf4 ♕xf4 18 ♖e1? ♘e5 19 ♗e2 ♖g5 ∓ 20 ♔f1 ♘g4 21 h4

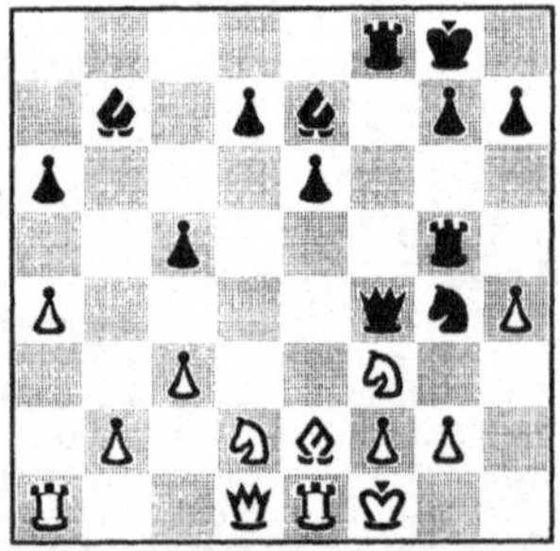

21 ... ♕h2!? [⌓ 21 ... ♘h2+−+] 22 ♗c4 [22 ♘xh2? ♖xf2+ 23 ♔g1 ♖xg2+ 24 ♔h1 ♘f2#] 22 ... ♕h1+ 23 ♔e2 ♕xg2 24 ♘xg5 ♗xg5 25 hxg5 ♕xf2+ 26 ♔d3 ♕f5+ 27 ♔e2 ♕e5+ 28 ♔d3 ♘f2+ 29 ♔c2 ♕f5+ 30 ♔b3 ♘xd1 31 ♖axd1 ♕xg5 32 ♗d3 ♖f2

33 ♘e4 c4+ 34 ♔a2 ♗xe4 35 ♗xe4 ♕a5 36 ♖a1 ♕xc3 **0-1**

Staunton(1)

## 1851-LON1-25
## Anderssen, A.+Szén, J.

[Staunton]

1 e4 c5 2 ♗c4 ♘c6 3 ♘c3 e6 4 d3 ♘ge7 5 ♗f4 ♘g6 6 ♗g3 a6 7 a3 ♗e7 8 ♘ge2 0-0 9 0-0 f5 10 f3 b5 11 ♗a2 ♔h8 12 ♗f2 d6 13 d4 c4 14 d5 ♘a5 [⌓ 14 ... ♘e5] 15 b4 cxb3 16 cxb3 e5 17 ♖c1 ♗d7 18 ♕d3 [△ 19 b4] 18 ... ♗h4 [18 ... ♖c8] 19 g3 ♗g5 20 ♖c2 fxe4 21 ♘xe4 ♗f5 22 b4 ♘b7 23 ♖c6 ♗xe4 24 ♕xe4 ♕d7 25 ♗b1 ♕h3 26 ♖c7 ♘d8 27 f4 exf4 28 ♗d4! ♘f7 29 ♕e6! ♕xe6 30 dxe6 ♘fe5 31 ♗xg6 ♘xg6 [31 ... hxg6? 32 gxf4] 32 ♗xg7+ ♔g8 33 ♗xf8 ♖xf8 34 gxf4 ♗f6 35 f5 ♘e5 36 ♘g3 ♘g4 37 ♘e4 ♗d4+ 38 ♔h1 d5 39 e7 ♖e8 40 ♘d6 **1-0**

Staunton(1)

## 1851-LON1-26
## Szén, J.–Anderssen, A.

[Staunton]

1 e4 c5 2 ♘f3 ♘c6 3 d4 cxd4 4 ♘xd4 e6 5 ♗e3 ♘f6 6 ♗d3 ♗e7 7 0-0 0-0 8 c3 d5 9 ♘xc6 [⌓ 9 exd5] 9 ... bxc6 10 e5 ♘e8 11 f4 f5 12 ♘d2 ♘c7 13 g4! ± g6 14 g5 c5 15 ♘f3 ♗b7 16 ♔f2! ♕d7 17 h4 ♕c6 18 ♗e2? [⌓ 18 ♖g1±] 18 ... ♖fd8 19 ♕c2? [⌓ 19 ♖c1=] d4 20 cxd4 cxd4 21 ♘xd4 [21 ♕xc6?? dxe3+] 21 ... ♕g2+ 22 ♔e1 ♗b4+ 23 ♗d2 ♖xd4 24 ♗xb4 ♖xb4 25 ♕xc7 ♖e4! 26 ♖f2 ♕g1+ 27 ♖f1 ♕g3+ 28 ♔d1 ♖xe2 29 ♔xe2 ♗a6+ 30 ♔d2 ♕d3+ **0-1**

Staunton(1)

## 1851-LON1-27
## Staunton, H.–Horwitz, B.

[Staunton]

1 c4 f5 2 ♘c3 e6 3 e4 fxe4 4 ♘xe4 ♘f6 5 ♘g3 ♘c6 6 a3 ♗c5 7 ♘f3 ♘d4 8 ♗d3 0-0 9 0-0 a5 10 ♖b1 d6 11 ♘xd4 ♗xd4 12 b4 axb4 13 axb4 e5 14 h3= ♗e6 15 ♗b2 ♗a7 16 ♕e2 ♕e7 17 ♖be1 ♕d7 [△ 18 ... ♗xh3] 18 ♔h2 ♖ae8 19 ♖d1 ♗b6 20 f3 ♕f7 21 ♖c1 c6 22 ♗b1 ♗c7 23 b5 ♗b8 24 ♗a1 g6 25 d3 ♕d7 26 ♕b2 c5 27 ♕d2 b6 28 ♕g5 ♗c7 29 ♗b2 ♕g7 30 ♖ce1 ♗c8 31 ♔g1 h6 32 ♕d2 g5 33 ♗c1 ♖e7 34 ♖e2 ♕f7 35 ♕e1 ♖fe8 36 ♘e4 ♘h5 37 h4! ± ♘f4 38 ♖a2 ♗b7 39 hxg5 ♗xe4 40 fxe4 hxg5 41 g3 ♘h3+ 42 ♔h1 ♕h5 43 ♖h2 g4 44 ♖f5 ♕h7 45 ♕e2 ♖g7 46 d4! ♕g6 [46 ... cxd4±] 47 d5 ♖f8 48 ♔g2 ♗d8 49 ♖h1 ♗e7 50 ♗c2 ♖gf7 51 ♖hf1 ♖g7 52 ♗d1 ♕h7 53 ♕a2 ♕g6 54 ♕a6 ♖gf7 55 ♗c2 ♗d8 56 ♕c8! ♔h7 57 ♖xf7+ ♖xf7 58 ♕xd8 ♖xf1 59 ♕h4+ ♔g7 60 ♔xf1 ♕f7+ 61 ♗f4 ♘xf4 62 ♕xg4+? [⌓ 62 gxf4! ♕xf4+ 63 ♕f2+–] 62 ... ♘g6+ 63 ♕f5 ♕xf5+ 64 exf5 ♘e7 65 ♔f2 ♔f6 66 g4 ♔g5 67 ♔e3 ♘g8 68 ♗d1 ♘h6 69 ♔f2 ♔f4 70 ♔g2 e4 71 ♔h3 ♔g5 72 ♔g3 = ♘f7 73 ♗c2 ♘e5 74 f6 ♔xf6 75 ♔f4 e3 76 g5+ ♔f7 77 ♗d1 ♘xc4 78 ♗h5+ ♔g7 79 ♗e2 ♘e5 80 ♔xe3 ♔f7 81 ♗h5+ ♔g7 82 ♔e4 c4 83 ♔f5? [83 ♔d4=] 83 ... c3 84 ♗d1 ♘c4 85 ♔e6 ♔g6 86 ♗e2 ♔xg5 87 ♗d3 ♔f4 88 ♔d7 ♔e5 89 ♔c6 ♔d4 90 ♗xc4 ♔xc4 91 ♔xd6 ♔xb5 92 ♔e7 c2 93 d6 c1♕ 94 d7 ♔c6 **0-1**

Staunton(1)

## 1851-LON1-28
## Horwitz, B.–Staunton, H.

[Staunton]

1 e4 c5 2 f4 ♘c6 3 ♘f3 e6 4 c4 g6 5 ♘c3 ♗g7 6 ♗e2 d6 7 0-0 ♘ge7 8 a3 a6 9 ♖b1 0-0 10 ♕c2 f5 11 d3 ♗d7 12 ♗e3 ♖c8 13 e5 ♘d4 14 ♘xd4 cxd4 15 ♗xd4 ♘c6 16 ♗e3 dxe5 17 fxe5 ♗xe5 18 ♕d2 ♕c7 19 g3 ♗xg3 20 ♗f3 [20 hxg3? ♕xg3+ 21 ♔h1 ♘d4 22 ♗xd4 ♗c6+ 23 ♘e4 fxe4–+] 20 ... ♗d6 21 d4 b6 22 b4 ♗e7 23 c5 bxc5 24 dxc5 ♗f6 25 ♗e2 [±] 25 ... ♘b8 26 ♗f4 ♕b7 27 ♗d6 ♖fd8 28 ♗c4 ♘c6! 29 ♘e4 ♗d4+ 30 ♘f2 ♘e5 31 ♗e2 ♘f3+ [⌓ 31 ... ♕d5!–+] 32 ♗xf3 ♕xf3 33 ♕xd4 ♗c6 34 ♘e4 ♕g4+ 35 ♔f2 ♗xe4 36 ♖b2 ♕f3+ 37 ♔e1 ♕xa3 38 ♖ff2 ♗d5 39 h4 ♕a1+ 40 ♔d2 ♔f7? [⌓ 40 ... ♖xd6! 41 cxd6 ♖c4 42 ♕f6 ♕c1+ 43 ♔e2 ♖e4+–+] 41 h5 ♕h1 42 hxg6+ ♔xg6 43 ♖h2 ♕e4 44 ♕xe4 ♗xe4 45 ♔e3 ♖d7 46 ♖a2 ♖c6 47 ♖a1 ♖7xd6 48 cxd6 ♖xd6 49 ♖g1+ ♔f6 50 ♖xh7 ♔e5 51 ♖c1 f4+ 52 ♔f2 ♗xh7 **0-1**

Staunton(1)

## 1851-LON1-29
## Staunton, H.–Horwitz, B.

[Staunton]

1 c4 f5 2 ♘c3 ♘f6 3 d4 e6 4 g3 ♗e7 5 ♗g2 0-0 6 e3 ♘a6 7 ♘ge2 d6 8 0-0 c6 9 a3 ♘c7 10 f4 d5 11 b3 b6 12 ♗b2 ♗a6 13 ♕c2 ♕d7 14 ♘d1 ♘ce8 15 ♖c1 ♖c8 16 c5? bxc5 17 dxc5 ♗xc5 18 ♕xc5 ♗xe2 19 ♖f2 ♗xd1 20 ♖xd1 ♘d6 21 ♗xf6 ♖xf6 22 ♖c2 ♖ff8 23 ♖d4 ♘e4 24 ♗xe4 fxe4 25 ♖a4 ♖c7 26 b4 ♖fc8 27 ♖a6 ♔f7 28 ♔g2 ♕e7 29 g4 ♕xc5 30 ♖xc5 ♔e7 31 ♖ca5 ♖a8 32 ♔g3 ♔d7 33 ♖c5 ♖b8 34 ♖ca5 ♖bb7 35 h4 ♔c8 36 h5 ♔b8 37 ♖c5 ♖b6 38 ♖a4 ♔b7 39 g5 ♖b5 40 ♔g4 ♔b6 41 ♖aa5? ♖xa5 ∓ 42 ♖xa5 c5 43 ♖xc5 ♖xc5 44 bxc5+ ♔xc5 45 f5 exf5+ 46 ♔xf5 ♔d6 47 a4 a5 48 h6 gxh6 49 gxh6 ♔c6 50 ♔f4 ♔c5 51 ♔f5 ♔c4 52 ♔e5 ♔d3 [⌓ 52 ... d4!–+] 53 ♔f6 ♔xe3 54 ♔g7 d4 55 ♔xh7 d3 56 ♔g6 d2 57 h7 d1♕ 58 h8♕ ♕xa4 59 ♕h3+ ♔d4 60 ♕e6 ♕b5 61 ♕f6+ ♕e5 62 ♕f2+ e3 63 ♕b2+ ♔e4 64 ♕b1+ ♔f3 65 ♕f1+ ♔g4 66 ♕g2+ ♕g3 67 ♕e4+ ♔h3+ 68 ♔h5 ♔h2 69 ♕c2+ ♔h3 70 ♕f5+ ♔g2 71 ♕c2+ ♕f2 72 ♕g6+ ♔h2 73 ♕d6+ ♕g3 74 ♕d3 ♕h3+ 75 ♔g5 e2 76 ♕d2 ♕g2+ 77 ♔h4 e1♕+ 78 ♕xe1 ♕h3+ **0-1**

Staunton(1)

## 1851-LON1-30
## Horwitz, B.–Staunton, H.

[Staunton]

1 e4 c5 2 ♗c4 ♘c6 3 a3 e6 4 ♘c3 g6 5 ♘ge2 ♗g7 6 0-0 a6 7 a4 ♘ge7 8 ♘f4 b6 9 d3 ♗b7 10 ♗e3 ♖c8 11 ♗a2 0-0 12 ♖b1 ♕c7 13 ♘h3 ♘b4 14 ♗b3 d5 15 exd5 exd5 16 d4 ♕c6 17 ♘e2 [17 dxc5?? d4!–+] 17 ... c4 18 c3!? cxb3 19 cxb4 ♕xa4 20 ♖a1 ♕xb4 21 ♖a3 ♖c2 22 ♗c1 ♖fc8 23 ♘hf4 a5 24 ♘d3 ♕c4 25 ♗e3 ♗a6 26 ♘ec1 a4 27 ♖e1 ♘f5 28 ♕g4 ♗xd4 29 ♗xd4 ♘xd4 30 ♕g5 ♖xc1 31 ♘xc1 ♘c2 [31 ... ♕xc1! 32 ♖xc1 ♖xc1+ 33 ♕xc1 ♘e2+–+] 32 ♖d1 ♘xa3 33 bxa3 b2 **0-1**

Staunton(1)

## 1851-LON1-31
## Staunton, H.+Horwitz, B.

[Staunton]

1 c4 f5 2 ♘c3 e6 3 e3 ♘f6 4 g3 ♘a6 5 ♗g2 c6 6 ♘ge2 ♗e7 7 0-0 0-0 8 a3 ♘c7 9 b3 b6 10 ♗b2 ♖b8 11 ♕c2 ♗b7 12 ♖ac1 c5 13 d4 ♗xg2 14 ♔xg2 ♕c8 15 f3 ♕b7 16 a4 cxd4 17 ♘xd4 ♗c5 18 ♕d2 ♖bd8 19 ♘cb5 ♘xb5 20 axb5 ♗xd4 21 ♕xd4 d6 [△ 22 ... e5] 22 ♕f4! ♘g4 23 e4 e5 24 ♕d2 ♘h6 [24 ... fxe4? 25 fxg4 e3+ 26 ♕d5++–] 25 ♕d5+ ♕xd5 26 exd5 ♖f7 27 ♖ca1 ♖c7 28 ♗c1 ♘f7 29 ♖a2 h6 30 ♗e3 ♖dd7 31 f4 e4 32 h3 h5 33 ♖d1 ♘h6 34 ♔f2 ♔f8 35 ♖c2 ♘g8 ...? **1-0**

Staunton(1)

## 1851-LON1-32
## Horwitz, B.+Staunton, H.

[Staunton]

1 f4 c5 2 ♘f3 e6 3 e3 g6 4 c3 ♗g7 5 ♘a3 ♘e7 6 ♗e2 0-0 7 0-0 b6 8 ♘c2 ♗b7 9 ♖b1 ♘bc6 10 b3 e5 11 fxe5 ♘xe5 12 d4 ♘g4 13 h3 ♘f6 14 ♗d3 ♖c8 15 dxc5 ♘fd5 16 ♗d2 bxc5 17 c4 ♘c3 18 ♗xc3 ♗xc3 19 ♘h2 ♕c7 20 ♕e2 ♖ce8 21 ♘e1 d5 22 ♖c1 ♗g7 23 cxd5 ♘xd5 24 e4 ♗d4+ ∓ 25 ♔h1 ♘f4 26 ♕c2 ♘h5 27 ♖f3 ♘g3+ [27 ... ♕g3] 28 ♖xg3

♕xg3 29 ♘ef3 ♖c8 30 ♖f1 h5 31 ♕d2 ♗g7 32 ♕c2 ♔h7 33 ♖f2 ♗d4 34 ♖f1 ♔g7 35 ♕d2 ♖cd8 36 ♕c2 ♖d6 37 ♘xd4 ♖xd4 38 ♘f3 ♖d7 39 ♕c3+ ♔g8 40 ♗c2 [40 ♘e5 ♗xe4!→] 40 ... ♖fd8 41 ♕xc5 ♗a6 42 ♖f2 ♖d4! 43 ♘xd4 [43 ♔g1 ♖d1+→] 43 ... ♕xf2 44 ♘e6 ♕f1+ 45 ♔h2 fxe6 46 ♕g5 ♖d7 47 ♕xg6+ ♔f8 48 ♕xe6 ♕f4+ 49 ♔h1 ♖d6! 50 ♕f5+ ♕xf5 51 exf5 ♗b7 **1-0** Staunton(1)

**1851-LON1-33**
**Staunton, H.+Horwitz, B.**
[Staunton]

1 c4 e6 2 ♘c3 f5 3 g3 ♘f6 4 ♗g2 c6 5 d3 ♘a6 6 a3 ♗e7 7 e3 0-0 8 ♘ge2 ♘c7 9 0-0 d5 10 b3 ♕e8 11 ♗b2 ♕f7 12 ♖c1 ♗d7 13 e4 fxe4 14 dxe4 ♖ad8 15 e5 ♘fe8 16 f4 dxc4 17 bxc4 ♗c5+ 18 ♔h1 ♗e3 19 ♖b1 g6 20 ♕b3 ♗c8 21 ♘e4 ♗b6 22 ♖bd1 ♘a6 23 ♕c3 ♖xd1 24 ♖xd1 [±; △ 25 ♘d6] 24 ... ♘c5 25 ♘d6 ♕c7 [△ 26 ... ♘a4] 26 ♕c2 ♘g7 27 g4 ♕e7 28 ♗d4 ♕c7 29 a4 [△ 30 a5] 29 ... ♘a6 30 c5 ♗a5 31 ♕b3 b6 32 ♘e4 bxc5 33 ♘f6+ ♔h8 34 ♕h3 ← ♘e8 35 ♗a1 ♘xf6 36 exf6 ♔g8 37 ♗e5 ♕b7 38 ♗e4 ♕f7 39 ♘g1!

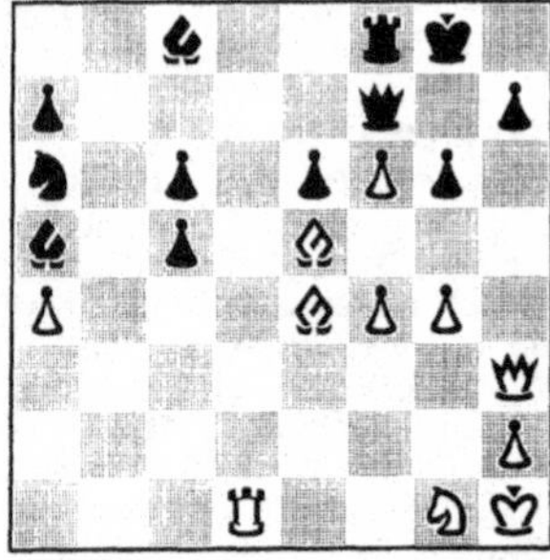

39 ... ♗d8 40 g5 ♗b7 41 ♘f3 ♖e8 42 ♗d6 [△ 43 ♘e5] 42 ... ♗xf6 43 gxf6 ♕xf6 44 ♘g5 ♕g7 45 ♗e5 ♕e7 46 ♗xg6 **1-0** Staunton(1)

**1851-LON1-34**
**Wyvill, M.+Kennedy, H.A.**
[Staunton]

1 c4 e6 2 e3 d5 3 g3 c5 4 ♗g2 ♘c6 [4 ... dxc4 5 ♕a4+] 5 ♘e2 ♘f6 [5 ... dxc4 6 ♗xc6+ bxc6 7 ♕a4] 6 d3 ♗d6 7 ♘bc3 ♗c7 8 0-0 h5!? 9 ♕b3 [△ 10 cxd5] 9 ... ♘a5 10 ♕b5+ ♘c6 11 cxd5 [11 ♕xc5?] 11 ... exd5 12 e4 d4 13 ♘d5 ♘d7 14 ♗g5 f6 15 ♗f4 ± ♗e5 16 ♗h3 ♕a5 17 ♕b3 [17 ♕xa5 ♘xa5 18 ♗xe5 ♘xe5 19 ♘c7+? ♔d8 20 ♘xa8 ♗xh3 21 ♖fd1 ♗g4∓] 17 ... ♘b6 18 ♗xc8 ♖xc8 19 ♖fd1 ♕a4 20 ♕xa4 ♘xa4 21 ♗c1 ♘b6 = 22 ♘ef4 g5 [◻ 22 ... ♗xf4] 23 ♘xb6 axb6 24 ♘d5 g4 [24 ... b5 25 f4] 25 ♘xb6 ♖c7 26 ♗f4 h4 27 ♖ac1 hxg3 28 fxg3 ♖ch7 29 ♖d2 ♗xf4 30 gxf4 g3 31 ♖xc5 gxh2+ 32 ♔h1 ♔d8? [◻ 32 ... ♔f7; ◻ 32 ... ♖h4; ◻ 32 ... ♖h3] 33 ♘d5 ♖h3 34 ♖c1 f5 35 ♖f1 fxe4 36 dxe4 d3 37 ♖ff2 ♘d4 38 ♘b4 ♖e3?

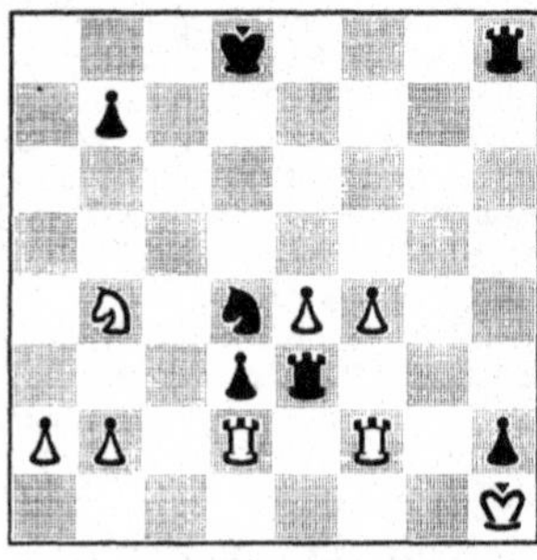

[◻ 38 ... ♖g8 (△ ♖g1#) 39 ♖d1 ♘f3 40 ♖g2 (40 ♖xd3 ♖g1#; 40 ♖xf3 ♖g1+ 41 ♖xg1 hxg1♕+ 42 ♔xg1 ♖xf3→) 40 ... ♖xg2 41 ♔xg2 h1♕+ 42 ♖xh1 ♖xh1 43 ♔xh1 d2→; 39 ♖f1 ♘e2 40 ♖xd3+! ♖xd3 41 ♘xd3 ♘g3+ 42 ♔~ ♘xf1+→; 39 ♖xh2 ♖xh2+ 40 ♖xh2 (40 ♔xh2 ♘f3+) 40 ... ♘f3!→; 39 ♖g2 ♖xg2 40 ♖xg2 ♖e3 41 ♘xd3 (41 ♔xh2 ♘f3+→; 41 ♖xh2 ♖e1+ 42 ♔g2 ♖e2+→) 41 ... ♘f3 42 ♖g8+ ♔c7 43 ♘f2 ♖e1+ 44 ♔g2 ♖g1+ 45 ♔xf3 ♖xg8 46 e5 ♖g1 47 f5 (47 ♔e2 ♖g2+) 47 ... ♖f1+→] 39 ♘xd3 ♖xe4 40 ♖xh2 ♖xh2+ 41 ♖xh2 ♘e2 42 ♖f2 ♔e7 43 ♔g2 ♔f6? 44 ♔f3 ♖a4 45 ♖xe2 ♖xa2 46 ♖e5 ♖a6 47 ♖b5 ♖d6 48 ♘e5 b6 49 ♘c4 ♖d3+ 50 ♔e4 ♖d1 51 ♖xb6+ ♔e7 52 f5 ♖c1 53 f6+ ♔f7 54 ♘e5+ ♔g8 55 f7+ ♔h7 56 ♖h6+ [56 f8♕??◇] 56 ... ♔xh6 57 f8♕+ **1-0** Staunton(1)

**1851-LON1-35**
**Kennedy, H.A.+Wyvill, M.**
[Staunton]

1 f4 d5 2 e3 g6 3 ♘f3 ♗g7 4 c3 e6 5 ♗d3 ♘h6 6 ♗c2 0-0 7 0-0 c5 8 d3 ♘c6 9 ♕e1 b6 10 e4 ♗a6 11 e5 ♘f5 12 g4 ♘h6 13 h3 d4 14 c4 ♘b4 15 ♘a3 ♕c7 16 ♗b1 ♖ae8 17 ♗d2 [◻ 17 ♘xd4! ♕d7 (17 ... ♘xd3 18 ♘xe6!; 17 ... ♖d8 18 ♘db5) 18 ♘db5 ♘xd3 19 ♕d2 ♖d8 20 ♖d1+−] 17 ... ♘c6 18 b4 ♘d8 19 ♗c2 f6? 20 ♗a4 ♖e7 21 bxc5 bxc5 22 exf6 ♗xf6 23 g5 ♘f5 24 gxf6 ♖xf6 25 ♕e5 ♕xe5 26 ♘xe5 ♘g3 27 ♖f2 ♗b7 28 ♗a5 ♘f7 29 ♖b1 ♖xf4 30 ♘xf7 ♖exf7 31 ♖xf4 ♘e2+ 32 ♔h2 ♖xf4 ◻ 32 ... ♘xf4] 33 ♖xb7 ♖f2+ 34 ♔h1 ♘g3+ 35 ♔g1 ♖xa2 36 ♖b8+ ♔g7 37 ♖b7+ ♔h6 38 ♘c2 ♖xa4 39 ♗d2+ g5 40 h4 ♘e2+ 41 ♔f2 ♘f4 42 hxg5+ ♔xg5 43 ♔f3 e5 44 ♗xf4+ exf4 45 ♖b5 ♖a2 46 ♖xc5+ ♔g6 47 ♘xd4 a5 48 ♔xf4 a4 49 ♖c6+ ♔f7 50 ♘b5 ♖a1 51 d4 a3 52 ♖c7+ ♔f6 53 ♘xa3 ♖xa3 54 ♖xh7 ♖c3 55 c5 ♔e6 56 ♔e4 ♖c1 57 ♖h6+ ♔e7 58 ♔d5 ♖g1 59 ♖h7+ ♔d8 60 c6 ♖g5+ 61 ♔c4 ♖g6 62 d5 ♖g4+ 63 ♔c5 ♖g5 64 ♔b6 ♖g6 65 ♔b7 **1-0** Staunton(1)

**1851-LON1-36**
**Wyvill, M.–Kennedy, H.A.**
[Staunton]

1 c4 e6 2 g3 d5 3 ♗g2 dxc4 4 ♕a4+ ♗d7 5 ♕xc4 ♗c6 6 e4 ♘d7 7 ♘e2 ♘e5 8 ♕c2 ♘d3+ 9 ♔f1 ♗c5 10 f4 f5 [◻ 10 ... ♗b5] 11 ♕c4 ♕d7 12 ♘bc3 b5 13 ♕b3 ♘f6 14 ♘d5 fxe4 [14 ... exd5 15 ♕xd3] 15 ♘e3 0-0 16 ♗h3 ♘d5 17 ♘c3 ♘xe3+ 18 dxe3 ♖f6 19 ♗g2 ♗d5 [◻ 19 ... ♘xc1 20 ♖xc1 ♗xe3 21 ♖d1 ♕f7→] 20 ♕xb5? c6 [◻ 20 ... ♕xb5 △ 21 ... ♗c4] 21 ♕a4 ♘xc1 22 ♖xc1 ♗xe3 23 ♖d1 ♕f7 24 ♘xe4 ♗xe4 25 ♕xe4 ♗xf4 26 ♕e2 ♕h5+ 27 ♔d3 ♕b5+ 28 ♔c2 ♗e5 29 b3 ♖f2+ 30 ♖d2 ♕c5+ 31 ♔d1 ♖xd2+ 32 ♔xd2 ♕f2+ 33 ♔c1 ♕b2+ 34 ♔d1 ♖d8+ 35 ♔e1 ♕c3+ **0-1** Staunton(1)

**1851-LON1-37**
**Kennedy, H.A.–Wyvill, M.**
[Staunton]

1 e4 c5 2 ♘f3 ♘c6 3 ♘c3 e6 4 d4 cxd4 5 ♘xd4 d6 6 ♘xc6 bxc6 7 ♗d3 g6 8 0-0 ♗g7 9 ♘e2 ♘e7 10 c3 0-0 11 ♗g5 f6 12 ♗e3 ♔h8 13 f4 ♕c7 14 ♕c2 ♗h6 15 ♖f3 e5 16 ♔h1 ♗g4 17 fxe5 [17 ♖f2±] 17 ... ♗xf3 18 ♗xh6 ♗xe2 19 ♗xe2 [◻ 19 ♕xe2] 19 ... fxe5 [19 ... ♖f7 20 exd6 △ 21 ♗c4; 19 ... ♖d8 20 exf6±] 20 ♗xf8 ♖xf8 21 ♖f1 ♖xf1+ 22 ♗xf1 d5 23 h3 ♔g7 24 b4 dxe4 25 ♕xe4 ♘f5 26 ♔h2 ♔f6 27 g4 ♘d6 28 g5+ ♔e6 29 ♕h4 [◻ 29 ♗c4+] 29 ... e4 30 ♔h1 ♕f7 31 ♗e2 ♔e5 32 c4 ♘f5 ∓ 33 ♕f2 ♕e7 34 c5 ♕xg5 35 ♗g4 ♕c1+ 36 ♔h2 e3 37 ♕g2 ♕d2 38 b5 cxb5 39 ♗e2 b4 40 c6 [△ 41 c7] 40 ... ♔d6 41 ♕f3 ♕xa2 42 ♕f4+ ♔xc6 43 ♕e4+ ♕d5 44 ♕e8+ ♔d6 45 ♕f8+ ♔e5 46 ♕xb4 ♕d6! → 47 ♕g4 ♔f6+ 48 ♔g2 h5 49 ♕a4 ♕g3+ 50 ♔h1 ♕e1+ 51 ♔h2 ♕f2+ 52 ♔h1 ♘g3# **0-1** Staunton(1)

**1851-LON1-38**
**Wyvill, M.=Kennedy, H.A.**
[Staunton]

1 c4 e6 2 ♘c3 d5 3 cxd5 exd5 4 e3 ♘f6 5 g3 ♗d6 6 ♗g2 c6 7 ♘ge2 0-0 8 0-0 ♘a6 9 d4 ♗f5 10 ♔h1 ♕d7 [10 ... ♘b4!?] 11 ♘g1 ♖fe8 12 a3 ♘c7 13 b4 ♘e4 14 ♘ce2 ♘g5 15 f3 ♗h3 16 ♘xh3 ♘xh3 17 f4 g5 18 f5! g4 19 ♘c3 h5 20 ♗xh3 gxh3 21 ♕xh5 f6 22 ♖f3 [◻ 22 e4; 22 ♘e2! △

23 ♘f4] 22 ... ♖e7 23 ♕xh3 a5 24 bxa5 ♖xa5 25 ♕h6? ♘e8 26 ♘e2 ♖h7 27 ♕g6+ ♖g7 28 ♕h5 ♕e7 29 ♘f4 ♖g5 30 ♕h3 ♕e4 31 g4? ♖b5?

[31 ... ♗xf4 32 exf4 ♕e1+ 33 ♔g2 (33 ♖f1 ♕e4+ 34 ♔g1 ♖g7∓) 33 ... ♕e2+ 34 ♔g3 (34 ♔g1 ♕d1+ 35 ♔f2 ♕xd4+ 36 ♗e3 ♕b2+ 37 ♔g3 ♘d6 38 fxg5 ♘e4+ 39 ♔h4 fxg5+→) 34 ... ♕e1+ 35 ♖f2?! (35 ♔g2 ♕e2+=) 35 ... ♘d6 36 fxg5 ♘e4+ 37 ♔h4 ♕xf2+ 38 ♔h5 ♕xd4 39 ♖b1 fxg5 40 ♗xg5 (40 ♖xb7? ♕h8+ 41 ♔g6 ♕f6+ 42 ♔h5 ♖b5+→) 40 ... ♘xg5 41 ♔xg5 ♕g7+ 42 ♔f4 ♕c7+ 43 ♔g5 ♕e7+ 44 ♔f4 (44 f6 d4+) 44 ... ♖xa3 45 ♖b3 ♖a4+ 46 ♔g3 ♕e1+→; 36 ♖a2 ♘e4+ 37 ♔g2 (37 ♔h4 ♖g7→) 37 ... ♘xf2 38 ♖xf2 ♖g7 39 ♗b2 ♕e4+ 40 ♔g3 (40 ♔g1 ♕xf5!→; 40 ♔f1 ♕h1+ △ 41 ... ♕e7+→) ♖b5→] 32 ♕g2 ♘g7 33 h4 ♘xf5! 34 ♘h5! ♖xh5 35 gxh5+ ♘g3+ 36 ♔g1 ♕xh4 37 ♔f2 ♖b3 38 ♖xg3+ ♔f7 39 ♕h3 ♗xg3+ 40 ♕xg3 ♕xh5 41 ♕c7+ ♔e6 42 a4 ♕f5+ 43 ♔e1 ♕f3 44 ♕f4 [◻ 44 ♕h2+−] 44 ... ♕xf4 45 exf4 ♔f5 46 a5 ♔e4 47 a6 [◻ 47 ♖a4] bxa6 48 ♖xa6 ♖c3 49 ♗d2 ♖c4 50 ♖a8 ♖xd4 51 ♔e2 c5 52 ♗e3 ♖c4 53 ♖e8+ ♔f5 54 ♔d3 ♖a4 55 ♖h8 ♖a3+ 56 ♔e2 d4 57 ♗c1 ♖a2+ 58 ♔d3 ♔e6 59 ♖e8+ ♔d5 60 ♖d8+ ♔e6 61 ♖b8 ♔d5 62 ♖d8+ **½-½** Staunton(1)

**1851-LON1-39**
**Kennedy, H.A.+Wyvill, M.**
[Staunton]

1 e4 c5 2 ♘f3 ♘c6 3 ♘c3 e6 4 d4 cxd4 5 ♘xd4 a6 6 ♘xc6 bxc6 7 ♗d3 g6 8 0-0 ♗g7 9 ♔h1 [9 ♘e2] 9 ... ♘e7 10 ♕g4?! 0-0 11 ♕h4 ♖b8 12 f4 d5 13 g4!? f5 14 e5 ♕c7 15 b3 c5 16 ♗e2 ♘c6 17 gxf5 ♖xf5 18 ♗b2 ♘d4 19 ♗g4 ♖f7 20 ♘a4 ♘f5 [◻ 20 ... ♘xc2 21 ♖ac1 ♘e3 22 ♖xc5 ♕b7 23 ♖f3 d4 24 ♗xd4 ♘xg4 25 ♕xg4 ♕e4 △ 26 ... ♗b7∓] 21 ♗xf5 ♖xf5 22 ♗a3 ♗f8 23 h3 ♗e7 24 ♕g3 ♗b7 25 ♔h2 ♖bf8 26 ♖f2 ♔h8 [26 ... ♖xe5? 27 fxe5 ♖xf2+ 28 ♕xf2 ♕xe5+ 29 ♕g3 ♕xa1 30 ♕b8++−] 27 ♖af1 ♖h5 28 ♖e2 d4 29 ♘b2 ♖g5 [◻ 29 ... g5] 30 ♕e1 ♕c6?? 31 fxg5 +− ♖xf1 32 ♕xf1 ♔g7 33 h4 a5 34 ♘c4 h6 35 gxh6+ ♔xh6 36 ♗c1+ ♔g7 37 ♗g5 **1-0** Staunton(1)

**1851-LON1-40**
**Wyvill, M.+Kennedy, H.A.**
[Staunton]

1 c4 e6 2 ♘c3 d5 3 cxd5 exd5 4 d4 ♗b4 5 g3 ♘f6 6 ♗g2 c6 7 e3 0-0 8 ♘ge2 ♗f5 9 ♕b3 a5 10 a3 ♗d6 11 ♕xb7!? ♖a6 12 ♕b3 ♘bd7 13 0-0 ♘e4 14 ♘xd5! ♕g5 [14 ... cxd5 15 ♕xd5 ♗g6 16 ♗xe4 ♘f6 17 ♕c4 ♗xe4 18 ♕xa6 ♗f3 (△ 19 ... ♕d7 20 ~ ♕h3) 19 e4 ♕d7 20 e5!+−; 20 ♕d3? ♗xe4 21 ♕e3 ♕h3 22 f3 ♘g4→] 15 ♘df4 ♕h6 16 f3 ♘g5 17 e4 ♗e6 18 ♘xe6 ♕xe6 19 ♕d3 ♘h3+ 20 ♗xh3 ♕xh3 21 ♗f4 ♘c5 22 ♕c4 ♘xe4 23 ♕xa6 g5!? 24 fxe4 gxf4 25 ♘xf4 ♕d7 26 e5 ♗c7 27 ♕c4 ♗b6 28 ♖ad1 ♖d8 29 ♘e2 [◻ 29 e6 ♗xd4+ 30 ♖xd4 ♕xd4+ 31 ♕xd4 ♖xd4 32 exf7+ ♔xf7 33 ♘e2+−] 29 ... ♖e8 30 ♔g2 ♖e6 31 ♘f4 ♖h6 32 e6 ♕b7 33 exf7+ ♔f8 34 ♘e6+ ♖xe6 35 ♕xe6 c5+ 36 d5 **1-0** Staunton(1)

**1851-LON1-41**
**Kennedy, H.A.–Wyvill, M.**
[Staunton]

1 e4 c5 2 ♘f3 ♘c6 3 d4 cxd4 4 ♘xd4 g6 5 ♘xc6 bxc6 6 ♗d3 ♗g7 7 0-0 e6 8 f4 d5 9 f5!? [◻ 9 e5] 9 ... dxe4 10 fxe6?! [◻ 10 ♗xe4 ♕b6+! 11 ♔h1 exf5 12 ♕f3] 10 ... ♕d4+ 11 ♔h1 ♗xe6 12 ♖f4 ♖d8! 13 ♕e1 f5 14 ♗xe4? [◻ 14 ♘c3] 14 ... fxe4 15 ♘c3 [15 ♖xe4?? ♕xe4!→] 15 ... ♘f6 16 ♗e3 ♕e5 17 ♖h4 0-0 18 ♗xa7 ♗d5 19 ♖d1 ♖d7 20 ♗d4 ♕f5 21 ♕e2 ♘h5 22 ♗e3 ♖df7 23 ♔g1 ♗f6 24 ♖h3 ♗xc3 25 bxc3 ♘f4 26 ♗xf4 ♕xf4 27 c4 ♗e6 28 ♖e3 ♗g4 **0-1** Staunton(1)

**1851-LON1-42**
**Williams, E.+Mucklow, J.R.**
[Staunton]

1 e4 c5 2 f4 e6 3 ♘c3 b6 4 ♘f3 a6 5 ♗e2 ♗b7 6 d3 ♘c6 7 0-0 ♗e7 8 a3 h6 9 ♕e1 d6 10 ♕g3 ♕d7 11 e5 g6 12 ♖b1 h5 13 exd6 ♕xd6 14 ♘e4 ♕d7 15 h3 ♘d4 16 ♘xd4 ♕xd4+ 17 ♗e3 ♕d7 18 ♖bd1 ♗xe4 19 dxe4 ♕a4 20 ♕f2! ♘f6! [20 ... ♕xc2?? ♗b5++; 20 ... ♕xe4?? 21 ♗f3+−] 21 e5 ♘d5 22 c4 ♘xe3 23 ♕xe3 ♖d8 24 ♖xd8+ ♗xd8 25 ♖d1 0-0 26 g4 h4 27 ♖d2 ♕e8 28 g5 ♔g7 29 ♕d3 ♗e7 30 ♕d7 ♕d8 31 ♔f2 ♖e8 32 ♔e3 ♕b8 33 ♗f3 ♔f8 34 ♕b7 ♕xb7 35 ♗xb7 a5 36 ♗f3 ♖b8 37 a4 ♔e8 38 b3 ♖c8 39 ♗b7 ♖c7 40 ♗a6 ♗d8 41 ♖d6 ♖a7 42 ♗b5+ ♔e7 43 ♔f3 ♖b7 44 ♔g4 ♖b8 45 ♔xh4 ♔f8 46 ♔g4 ♔g7 47 h4 ♗e7 48 ♖d7 ♔f8 49 h5 gxh5+ 50 ♔xh5 ♖d8 51 ♖b7 ♖d3 52 ♖xb6 ♖xb3 53 ♖b8+ ♔g7 54 ♖a8 ♖a3 55 ♖xa5 ♗d8 56 ♖a8 ♖d3 57 a5 ♖h3+ 58 ♔g4 ♖d3 59 a6 ♗a5 60 a7 ♗e1 61 ♖g8+ ♔h7 62 ♖h8+ ♔xh8 63 a8♕+ ♔g7 64 ♕g2 [64 f5!+−] 64 ... ♖g3+ 65 ♕xg3 ♗xg3 66 ♔xg3 ♔f8 67 ♔g4 ♔g7 68 ♔h5 ♔h7 69 ♗c6 ♔g7 70 ♗e4 ♔f8 71 ♔h6 ♔g8 72 ♗d3 ♔f8 73 ♗h7 ♔e7 74 ♔g7 ♔e8 75 ♗g8 f5 76 gxf6 ♔d7 77 f7 **1-0** Staunton(1)

**1851-LON1-43**
**Mucklow, J.R.–Williams, E.**
[Staunton]

1 c4 e6 2 e3 f5 3 ♗e2 ♘f6 4 ♗h5+ g6 5 ♗f3 d5 6 cxd5 exd5 7 ♘c3 ♗g7 8 ♘ge2 ♘c6 9 d4 0-0 10 ♕b3 ♘e7 11 h4 h6 12 ♘f4 c6 13 ♗d2 ♔h7 14 ♘ce2 a5 15 a4 ♘e4 16 ♕c2 ♕d6 17 ♗c3 ♗d7 18 h5 g5 19 ♘d3 b6 20 g3 ♘g8 21 b4 ♘xc3 22 ♕xc3 axb4 23 ♘xb4 ♘f6 24 ♘c2 ♘e4 25 ♗xe4 fxe4 26 ♖h2 c5 27 a5 ♖fc8 28 ♕d2 c4 29 axb6 ♖xa1+ 30 ♘xa1 ♕xb6 31 ♘c3 ♗g4 32 ♕a2 ♖b8 33 ♘c2 ♗f8 34 ♘xd5 ♕c6 [◻ 34 ... ♕b3→] 35 ♘f6+ ♕xf6 36 ♕a7+ ♗g7 37 ♕xb8 ♕f3 38 ♔d2 ♕d1+ 39 ♔c3 ♕d3+ 40 ♔b2 c3+ 41 ♔a1 ♕xc2 42 ♕b1 ♕a4+ 43 ♕a2 ♕d1+ 44 ♕b1 c2 **0-1** Staunton(1)

**1851-LON1-44**
**Williams, E.+Mucklow, J.R.**
[Staunton]

1 e4 c5 2 ♘f3 ♘c6 3 ♗b5 e6 4 0-0 ♗e7 5 ♗xc6 bxc6 6 c4 d6 7 d3 e5 8 ♘e1 ♖b8 9 ♘c3 ♘f6 10 h3 0-0 11 ♖b1 ♔h8 12 f4 ♘g8 13 fxe5 dxe5 14 ♘f3 ♕d6 15 ♖f2 ♖b7 16 ♗e3 ♗d8 17 ♕e2 f5 18 exf5 ♗xf5 19 ♘e4 ♗xe4 20 dxe4 ♖d7 21 ♖ff1 ♖df7 22 ♖bd1 ♕e7 23 b3 h6 24 ♕f2 ♗b6 25 ♕g3 ♗c7 26 ♔h2 ♖f6 27 ♕g4 ♖d8 28 ♘h4 ♔h7 29 ♖xd8 ♗xd8 30 ♖d1 ♕f8 31 ♖d7 ♗b6 32 ♘f5 ♖g6 33 ♕h4 ♕f6 34 ♕h5 ♕e6 35 ♖b7 ♔h8 36 ♘h4 ♔h7 37 ♕xg6+ ♕xg6 38 ♘xg6 ♔xg6 ...? **1-0** Staunton(1)

**1851-LON1-45**
**Mucklow, J.R.–Williams, E.**
[Staunton]

1 d4 e6 2 e4 d5 3 e5 c5 4 ♘f3 ♘c6 5 ♗b5 ♕b6 6 ♗xc6+ bxc6 7 0-0 cxd4 8 ♘xd4 c5 9 ♘b3 f6 10 ♖e1 f5 11 a4 a5 12 c3 ♖b8 13 ♘3d2 ♘h6 14 h3 ♘f7 15 ♘f3 ♗e7 16 ♘a3 ♗d7 17 ♘c2 g5 18 ♘e3 h5 19 ♔f1 g4 20 hxg4 hxg4 21 ♘g1 ♗c8 22 g3 ♗a6+ 23 ♔g2 d4 24 cxd4 cxd4 25 ♘c2 d3 26 ♘e3 ♕c6+ 27

f3 ♘xe5 28 ♘xf5 ♘xf3 29 ♘xf3 gxf3+ **0-1** Staunton(1)

**1851-LON1-46**
**Anderssen, A.+Staunton, H.**
[Staunton]

1 e4 c5 2 d4 cxd4 3 ♘f3 e6 4 ♘xd4 ♗c5 5 ♘c3 a6 6 ♗e3 ♗a7 7 ♗d3 ♘e7 8 0-0 0-0 9 ♕h5 ♘g6 10 e5 ♕c7 11 ♖ae1 ± b5 12 f4 ♗b7 13 ♘e4 ♗xe4 14 ♗xe4 ♘c6 15 ♘xc6 dxc6 16 g4 ♖ad8 17 ♔h1 c5 18 ♖f3 ♕a5 19 ♖ef1 ♕a4 20 ♗d3 ♕xa2 21 ♖h3 h6 22 g5 ♖xd3 23 cxd3 ♕d5+ 24 ♖ff3 ♘e7 25 gxh6 g6 26 h7+ ♔h8 27 ♕g5 ♘f5 28 ♕f6+ ♘g7 29 f5 ♕b3 30 ♗h6 ♕d1+ 31 ♔g2 ♕e2+ 32 ♖f2 **1-0** Staunton(1)

**1851-LON1-47**
**Staunton, H.−Anderssen, A.**
[Staunton]

1 e4 e5 2 ♘f3 ♘c6 3 ♗c4 ♗c5 4 d3 d6 5 c3 ♘f6 6 ♗g5 0-0 7 ♘bd2 a6 8 a4 ♗a7 9 b4 ♘e7 10 ♗xf6 gxf6 11 ♘h4 c6 12 ♕f3 d5 13 ♗b3 ♕d6 14 0-0 ♔g7 15 ♖ad1 ♗e6 16 ♗c2 ♘g6 17 ♘f5+ ♗xf5 18 exf5 ♘e7 19 ♕h5 ♔h8 20 ♔h1 ♖ae8 21 f4 ♘g8 [21 ... exf4 22 d4] 22 fxe5? [◻ 22 ♖f3! e4 23 ♖h3 h6 24 ♕g4 (△ 25 ♖g3+−) 24 ... ♗f2 25 dxe4 dxe4 26 ♘xe4+−; 22 ... exf4 23 ♖df1 ♗e3 24 ♖h3 h6 25 ♘f3+−] 22 ... fxe5 23 g4 f6 24 ♖f3 ♖e7 25 h4 ♗b8 26 ♖h3 ♖d8 27 g5 ♖dd7 28 ♖g1 ♖g7 29 ♕e2 ♖de7 30 g6 ♗a7 31 ♖g2 ♕d7 32 ♕h5 ♖e8 33 ♖f3 ♘e7 34 ♘f1! ♘c8 35 ♘h2 e4 36 dxe4 dxe4 37 ♖f1 e3 38 ♗b3? [◻ 38 ♕e2!] 38 ... ♕d3 39 gxh7?? [◻ 39 ♗e6; ◻ 39 ♕e2; ◻ 39 ♕d1] 39 ... ♕e4! 40 ♘f3 e2 41 ♖e1 ♖xg2 42 ♔xg2 ♖e7! 43 ♗e6 [43 ♗f7? ♖xf7 44 ♕xf7 ♕g4+−+] 43 ... ♘d6 44 ♔h3 ♖g7 45 ♘g5 fxg5 46 ♕xe2 ♕xh4+ 47 ♔g2 ♘e4! **0-1** Staunton(1)

**1851-LON1-48**
**Anderssen, A.+Staunton, H.**
[Staunton]

1 e4 e5 2 ♘f3 ♘c6 3 d4 exd4 4 ♗c4 ♗c5 5 0-0 d6 6 c3 ♘f6 7 cxd4 ♗b6 8 ♘c3 ♗g4 9 ♗e3 0-0 10 a3 ♕e7 11 ♕d3 ♗xf3 12 gxf3 ♕d7 13 ♔g2 ♘h5 14 ♘e2 ♘e7 15 ♘g3 ♘xg3 16 hxg3 d5 17 ♗a2 ♖ad8 18 ♖ad1 c6 19 ♖h1 ♘g6 20 ♖h5 dxe4 21 fxe4 ♕g4! 22 ♖dh1 ♖xd4!

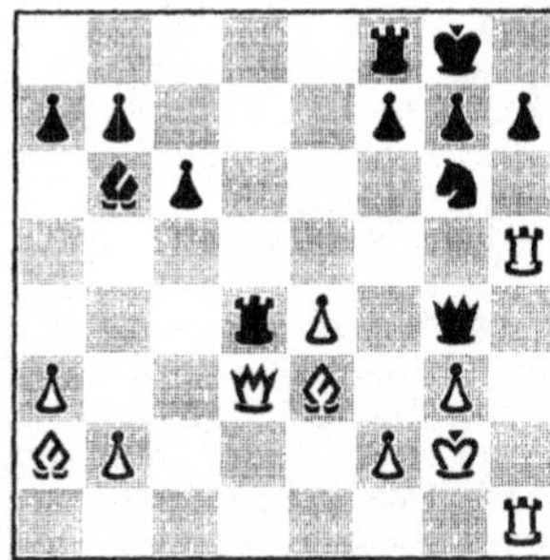

23 ♕c3! ♖xe4 [23 ... ♕xe4+ 24 f3 ♕d3 25 ♗xd4 ♕xd4 26 ♕xd4 ♗xd4 ∞; 25 ... ♕e2+ 26 ♔g1 (26 ♔h3 ♗xd4 27 ♕xd4 ♕xf3−+) 26 ... ♕d1+ 27 ♔g2 ♕xd4 28 ♕xd4 ♗xd4∓] 24 ♖xh7 [△ 25 ♕xg7#] 24 ... ♗d4 25 ♗xd4 ♖xd4? [◻ 25 ... ♘f4+ 26 ♔g1 (26 ♔h2 ♔xh7 27 gxf4 ♖h8−+) 26 ... ♕d1+ 27 ♔h2 ♕xd4 28 ♕xd4 ♖xd4 29 ♖h4 ♘e2−+] 26 ♖1h4! ♘xh4+ 27 ♖xh4 ♕xh4 28 gxh4 ♖xh4 29 ♕g3 ♖h5 30 f4 ♖b5 31 b4 ♖d8 32 ♗c4 ♖d2+ 33 ♔g1 ♖d1+ 34 ♔f2 ♖f5? 35 ♕g4 **1-0** Staunton(1)

**1851-LON1-49**
**Staunton, H.+Anderssen, A.**
[Staunton]

1 e4 e5 2 ♘f3 ♘c6 3 ♗c4 ♗c5 4 c3 ♘f6 5 d4 exd4 6 e5 d5 7 ♗b5 ♘e4 8 cxd4 ♗b4+ 9 ♘bd2 [◻ 9 ♗d2] 9 ... 0-0 10 0-0 ♗g4 11 ♗xc6 bxc6 12 ♕c2 ♗xf3 13 ♘xf3 ♖b8 14 ♕xc6?! ♖b6 15 ♕c2 f5 16 a3 ♗e7 17 b4 f4 18 ♘e1 ♖h6 19 f3 ♘g5 20 ♘d3 ♘e6 21 ♗b2 ♕e8 22 ♖ac1 ♕h5 23 h3 ♖g6 24 ♘f2 ♖g3 25 ♔h2 ♖f5 26 ♕c6?! ♕g6 27 ♖g1 ♖fg5 28 ♘g4 h5 29 ♘f6+ ♔f7? [29 ... ♗xf6∓] 30 ♕e8# **1-0** Staunton(1)

**1851-LON1-50**
**Anderssen, A.+Staunton, H.**
[Staunton]

1 e4 e6 2 d4 g6 3 ♗d3 ♗g7 4 ♗e3 c5 5 c3 cxd4 6 cxd4 ♕b6 7 ♘e2 ♕xb2 8 ♘bc3 ♕b6 9 ♖c1 [9 ♖b1] 9 ... ♘a6 10 ♘b5 [△ 11 d5 ♕∼ 12 ♘d6+] 10 ... ♗f8 11 0-0 d6 12 d5 ♕a5 13 ♗d4 e5 14 ♗c3 ♕d8 15 f4 f6 16 fxe5 fxe5 17 ♕a4 ♗d7 18 ♗b4 ♘h6 19 ♔h1 ♘f7 20 ♕a3 ♘c5? 21 ♘xd6+ ♗xd6 22 ♗xc5 ♗xc5 23 ♕xc5 ♕e7 24 ♕c7 ♘d6 25 ♕a5 h5? 26 ♖c7 ♖f8 27 ♖fc1 a6 28 ♘d4 ♖c8 [28 ... exd4 29 e5 ♕xe5 30 ♗xg6+ (30 ♖e1 ♘e4!) 30 ... ♖f7 (30 ... ♔∼ 31 ♖xd7++−) 31 ♖xd7+−] 29 ♘e6 ♖xc7 30 ♖xc7 ♖f7 31 ♕b6 ♖f6 32 h3 g5 33 ♕b2! ♘b5 34 ♗xb5 axb5 35 ♕xe5 h4 36 ♖xb7 **1-0** Staunton(1)

**1851-LON1-51**
**Williams, E.+Wyvill, M.**
[Staunton]

1 e4 c5 2 f4 e6 3 ♘f3 g6 4 e5 ♘h6 5 b3 ♘c6 6 ♗b5 [△ 7 ♗xc6] 6 ... ♘e7 7 ♘c3 a6 8 ♘e4 [△ 9 ♘d6#; 9 ♘f6#] 8 ... ♗g7? [◻ 8 ... ♘d5 △ 9 ... ♗e7=] 9 ♘d6+ ♔f8 10 ♗e2 ♘hf5 11 ♘e4 b6 12 d3 d5 13 ♘f2 d4 14 g4 ♘h6 15 ♘g5 ± ♘d5 16 ♘fe4 f6 17 exf6 ♗xf6 18 0-0 ♔g7 19 ♘xf6 ♕xf6 20 ♗f3 ♗b7 21 ♕e1 ♖ae8 22 ♗d2 ♖hf8 23 ♕h4 ♖h8 24 ♖ae1 [△ 24 ♘xe6+ ♖xe6 25 g5+−] 24 ... ♘g8 [△ 25 ... h6] 25 ♕g3 h6 26 ♘e4 ♕d8 27 f5 exf5 28 gxf5 g5 29 ♘xg5! hxg5 30 ♗xg5 ♖h3 31 ♗f6+ ♔xf6 32 ♕g6# **1-0** Staunton(1)

**1851-LON1-52**
**Wyvill, M.−Williams, E.**
[Staunton]

1 c4 e6 2 e3 f5 3 ♘h3 ♘f6 4 g3 ♘c6 5 d4 ♗b4+ 6 ♗d2 ♗xd2+ 7 ♘xd2 0-0 8 ♗g2 ♘e7 9 0-0 ♘g6 10 b4 ♕e7 11 ♕b3 d6 12 ♖ae1 e5 13 f4 e4 14 ♔h1 ♗d7 15 ♘f2 [△ 16 g4] 15 ... h5 16 ♕d1 c6 17 h3 d5 18 a3 a5 19 c5 axb4 20 axb4 b5 21 ♘b3 ♖a4 22 ♕d2 h4 23 ♘a5? ♘h5 24 ♖g1 hxg3 25 ♘d1 ♘h4 26 ♖ef1 ♘xg2 27 ♔xg2 ♕h4 28 ♕b2 g5 29 ♘c3 gxf4 30 ♖xf4 ♘xf4+ 31 exf4 ♕xf4 32 ♖f1 ♕h4! 33 ♘xa4? f4 34 ♘c3 ♗xh3+ 35 ♔g1 ♗xf1 **0-1** Staunton(1)

**1851-LON1-53**
**Williams, E.+Wyvill, M.**
[Staunton]

1 e4 c5 2 f4 e6 3 ♘f3 ♘h6 [△ 4 ... g6 5 ∼ ♗g7] 4 b3 a6 5 ♗e2 ♘c6 6 0-0 b5 7 d3 ♗e7 8 c4 ♗f6 9 e5 ♗e7 10 ♘c3 ♖b8 11 ♘e4 ♘f5 12 g4 ♘h6 [◻ 12 ... ♘fd4] 13 h3 f5 14 exf6 ♗xf6 15 ♖b1 ♘d4? 16 ♘d6+ ♔e7 17 ♘e4 ♘xf3+ 18 ♗xf3 ♗d4+ 19 ♔g2 ♕a5 20 ♕e2 bxc4 21 dxc4 ♗b7 22 f5 ♘f7 23 fxe6 dxe6 24 ♗g5+ ♔d7 25 ♗f4 e5 26 ♗g3 ♖hf8 27 ♖bd1 ♗a8 28 h4 ♖be8 29 ♗e1 ♕d8? 30 ♘xc5+ ♔e7 31 ♗b4! ♘d6 32 ♖xd4 ♖xf3 33 ♖xf3 ♗xf3+ 34 ♔xf3 ♖f8+ 35 ♔g2 ♕a8+ 36 ♖d5 **1-0** Staunton(1)

**1851-LON1-54**
**Wyvill, M.+Williams, E.**
[Staunton]

1 c4 e6 2 e3 f5 3 ♘c3 ♘f6 4 f4 ♗b4 5 ♘ce2 d5 6 cxd5 exd5 7 ♘f3 0-0 8 ♘g3 ♘c6 9 ♗b5 ♕e7 10 0-0 ♗d6 11 ♗xc6 bxc6 12 ♘d4 ♘g4 13 h3 ♕h4 14 ♘gxf5 ♗xf5 15 ♘xf5 ♖xf5 16 hxg4 ♖f6 17 g5 ♖g6 18 ♖f3 [△ 19 ♖h3+−] 18 ... ♕h5 19 ♕c2 ♖d8? 20 d3 h6 21 ♖h3 ♕g4 22 d4! ♔f7

23 ♖f3 ♗e7 [23 ... hxg5 24 fxg5+–] 24 ♗d2 hxg5 25 ♗a5! ♗f6 26 ♗xc7 ♖c8 27 ♕xc6 gxf4 28 ♕xd5+ ♕e6 29 ♕xe6+ ♔xe6 30 ♗xf4 ♖c2 31 ♖f2 ♖xf2 32 ♔xf2 ♔d5 33 ♔f3 ♗e7 34 ♗e5 ♗f6 35 ♗xf6 ♖xf6+ 36 ♔e2 ♔e4 37 ♖f1 **1-0**

Staunton(1)

**1851-LON1-55**
**Williams, E.– Wyvill, M.**

[Staunton]

1 e3 c5 2 f4 e6 3 ♘f3 ♘c6 4 b3 f5 5 ♗b2 ♘f6 6 ♗b5 ♗e7 7 ♗xc6 bxc6 8 c4 0-0 9 0-0 ♗a6?! 10 ♕e2 ♕c7 11 ♘c3 ♖ae8 12 d3 d6 13 e4 fxe4 14 dxe4 ♘d7 15 g3 ♗d8 16 ♖fe1 ♘b6 17 ♕e3 ♕c8 18 ♔g2 ♘d7 19 ♕d2 ♕b8 20 ♖ad1 ♗c7 21 ♘a4 [△ 22 ♕c3] 21 ... ♖e7 22 f5? exf5 23 ♕g5 ♗d8! 24 exf5?? ♖e2+ 25 ♖xe2 ♗xg5 26 ♘xg5 ♘f6 27 ♖de1 ♗c8 28 ♖e7 ♗xf5 29 ♗xf6 gxf6 30 ♘f7! ♗g6 31 ♘h6+ ♔h8 32 ♘c3 f5 33 ♘e2 ♖e8 34 ♘f4 ♖xe7 35 ♘xg6+ hxg6 36 ♖xe7 ♕f8! → 37 ♘f7+ ♔g7 38 ♖xa7 ♔f6 [□ 38 ... ♕b8 39 ♖d7 ♕e8 40 ♖a7 ♕e2+ 41 ♔g1 ♔f6 42 h4! f4 43 gxf4 ♕g4+ 44 ♔f2 ♕xf4+ 45 ♔~ ♕xh4–+] 39 h4 d5 [□ 39 ... ♕b8 40 ♖d7 ♕e8 41 ♖a7 ♕e2+ 42 ♔h3 ♕g4+ 43 ♔h2 f4!–+] 40 ♘g5 ♕e8 41 ♔f3 ♔e5 42 ♔e3 ♔d6+ 43 ♔d3 [43 ♔f3 d4 44 ♘f7+ ♔e6 45 ♘g5+ (45 a4 ♕b8 46 ♘g5+ ♔e5 47 ♖e7+ ♔d6–+; 45 g4 fxg4+ 46 ♔xg4 ♔f6–+) 45 ... ♔e5 46 ♘f7+ (46 ♖h7 ♕a8 47 ♘f7+ ♔f6 48 ♘g5 ♕xa2–+) 46 ... ♔f6 47 ♘g5 ♕e3+ 48 ♔g2 ♕e2+ 49 ♔g1 (49 ♔h1 ♕f1+ 50 ♔h2 d3–+) 49 ... ♕d1+ 50 ♔f2 ♕c2+ 51 ♔f1 d3–+] 43 ... f4 44 gxf4 ♕e1 45 ♖h7 ♕d1+ 46 ♔e3 d4+ 47 ♔f2 d3 48 ♔g3 ♕e1+ 49 ♔g4 d2 50 ♘f7+ ♔c7 **0-1**

Staunton(1)

**1851-LON1-56**
**Wyvill, M.+ Williams, E.**

[Staunton]

1 c4 e6 2 e3 f5 3 ♘c3 ♘f6 4 f4 b6 5 ♗e2 ♗b7 6 ♗h5+ ♘xh5 7 ♕xh5+ g6 8 ♕h3 ♘c6 9 ♘f3 ♘b4 10 0-0 ♘d3 11 ♘e5 ♘xe5 12 fxe5 ♗g7 13 d4 d6 14 exd6 cxd6 15 ♖f2 0-0 16 ♗d2 ♕e7 17 ♘e2 ♖ae8 18 ♗b4 e5 19 ♖d1 ♖f7 20 ♘c3 a5 21 ♗a3 ♕e6 22 d5 [22 ♘b5 ♗f8=] 22 ... ♕d7 23 ♖df1 e4 24 ♘e2 ♗e5 25 ♘f4 ♕a4 26 ♖c1 ♗a6 27 ♖fc2 ♖c8 28 ♕h6 b5 29 ♘xg6!

29 ... ♗g7 [29 ... hxg6 30 ♕xg6+ ♖g7 (30 ♔f8 31 ♗xd6++–) 31 ♕e6+ ♖f7 32 ♗xd6 ♗xd6 33 ♕xd6 ♗b7 34 b3 ♕b4 35 c5+–] 30 ♘e7+ ♖xe7 31 ♕xd6 ♖ee8 32 b3 ♗f8 33 ♕g3+ ♔f7 34 ♗xf8 ♖xf8 35 bxa4 bxc4 36 ♕e5 **1-0**

Staunton(1)

**1851-LON1-57**
**Williams, E.– Wyvill, M.**

[Staunton]

1 e4 c5 2 f4 e6 3 ♘f3 ♗e7 4 ♗e2 ♗h4+ 5 g3 ♗e7 6 ♘c3 ♘c6 7 d3 d5 8 e5 ♘h6 9 0-0 0-0 10 ♔g2?! f5 [△ 10 ... d4] 11 ♕e1 b6 12 a3 ♗b7 13 ♘d1 d4 14 ♘f2 ♔h8 15 h4 ♘g4 16 ♘h3 ♕d7 17 ♔g1 ♕d5 [∓] 18 c4 dxc3 19 bxc3 ♘a5 20 c4 ♕c6 21 ♖b1 ♕d7 22 ♗d2 ♘c6 23 ♗c3 ♖ad8 [23 ... ♘e3] 24 ♕d2 ♗a8! 25 ♖bd1 ♕b7 26 ♘hg5 ♗xg5 27 hxg5 g6 28 ♖fe1 ♔g8! 29 ♗f1 ♘cxe5!! 30 ♗xe5 ♕xf3 31 ♕g2 ♕xd1! 32 ♖xd1 ♗xg2 33 ♗xg2 ♘xe5 34 fxe5 ♖d4 35 ♗f3 ♔g7 36 ♔f2 h6 37 gxh6+ ♔xh6 38 ♖h1+ ♔g7 [38 ... ♔g5?!] 39 ♔e3 ♖h8 40 ♖a1 ♖h3 41 ♖g1 g5 42 a4 ♖h2 43 ♗e2 ♔f7 44 a5 f4+ 45 gxf4 gxf4+ 46 ♔f3 ♖h5 47 a6 ♖xe5 48 ♖h1 ♖g5 49 ♖h8 ♖g3+ 50 ♔f2 ♖g7 51 ♖a8 ♖d7 [△ 52 ... ♖g8] 52 ♗f3 ♖g8 53 ♖xg8 ♔xg8 54 ♗e4 ♖d4 55 ♔f3 e5 56 ♗d5+ ♔f8 57 ♔e2 ♖xd5 58 cxd5 ♔e7 59 ♔f3 ♔d6 60 ♔e4 b5 61 d4 cxd4 **0-1**

Staunton(1)

**1851-LON1-58**
**Horwitz, B.– Szén, J.**

[Staunton]

1 e4 c5 2 d4 e6 3 ♘f3 ♕b6 4 d5 d6 5 ♘c3 e5 6 ♗d3 ♘e7 7 ♕e2 ♗g4 8 ♘a4? [8 b3; 8 0-0] 8 ... ♕a5+ 9 ♗d2 ♕c7 10 h3 ♗d7 11 ♘c3 a6 12 a4 ♘g6 13 0-0 ♗e7 14 ♘h2 0-0 15 ♕h5? c4 16 ♗e2 f5 17 ♗g5 ♗xg5 18 ♕xg5 fxe4 19 ♘xe4 ♗f5 20 ♕e3 ♘d7 21 ♘g5 ♘f4 22 ♗f3 h6 23 ♘e6 ♘xe6 24 g4? ♘d4 25 gxf5 ♘xc2 26 ♕e4 ♘xa1 27 ♖xa1 ♘f6 28 ♕h4 c3 29 bxc3 ♕xc3 30 ♖d1 ♖ac8 31 ♔h1 ♖c4 32 ♕g3 e4 33 ♖g1 ♖f7 34 ♗d1 ♕xg3 35 ♖xg3 ♖c1 36 ♖g1 ♖fc7 37 ♘g4 ♘xg4 38 hxg4 ♖7c4 39 ♔g2 ♖d4 40 ♗b3 ♖xg1+ 41 ♔xg1 ♖b4 42 ♗c2 ♖c4 43 ♗b3 ♖c3 **0-1**

Staunton(1)

**1851-LON1-59**
**Szén, J.+ Horwitz, B.**

[Staunton]

1 e4 e5 2 ♘f3 ♘c6 3 ♗b5 ♘f6 4 0-0 ♘xe4 5 ♖e1 ♘f6 6 ♘xe5 ♘xe5 7 ♖xe5+ ♗e7 8 d4 0-0 9 ♕e1! ♗d6 10 ♖e2 c6 11 ♗d3 ♗c7 12 ♗g5? ♗xh2+ 13 ♔h1 ♗c7 14 ♕d2 d5 15 ♘c3 ♕d6 16 g3 ♗g4 ∓ 17 ♖e3 ♗h5 18 ♗xf6 ♕xf6 19 ♔g2 ♕g5? [□ 19 ... ♕h6! 20 ♖h1 ♗f3+!–+; 20 ♖e2? ♗xe2–+] 20 ♖h1 ♗f4? 21 ♖xh5 ♗xe3 22 ♕e2! ♕xh5 23 ♕xh5 g6 24 ♕h4 ♗c1 25 b3 ♖ae8 26 ♘e2 f5?? 27 ♘xc1 f4 28 gxf4 **1-0**

Staunton(1)

**1851-LON1-60**
**Horwitz, B.– Szén, J.**

[Staunton]

1 e4 c5 2 f4 e6 3 ♘f3 d5 4 e5 ♘c6 5 ♗e2 ♘h6 6 0-0 ♗e7 7 b3 0-0 8 c3 ♗d7 9 ♗d3 f6 10 ♗c2 ♖c8 11 ♕e2 ♕c7 12 ♗a3 fxe5 13 fxe5 ♗e8 14 ♕e3? ♘g4 15 ♕e2 ♘gxe5 16 ♘xe5 ♖xf1+ 17 ♔xf1 ♕xe5 18 ♕xe5 ♘xe5 19 d4 ♘g4 20 ♔g1 ♗f8 21 ♗d1 ♘e3 22 ♘d2 cxd4 23 ♗xf8 dxc3 24 ♗a3 cxd2 25 ♔f2 ♘c2 26 ♗xc2 ♖xc2 27 ♔e3 ♗h5 28 ♖f1 h6 **0-1**

Staunton(1)

**1851-LON1-61**
**Szén, J.+ Horwitz, B.**

[Staunton]

1 e4 e5 2 ♘f3 ♘c6 3 ♗b5 ♘f6 4 0-0 ♗e7 5 d4 ♘xd4 6 ♘xd4 exd4 7 e5! ♘d5 8 ♕xd4 ♘b6 9 a4 c6 10 ♗d3 ♘d5 11 ♘c3 [11 c4] 11 ... ♘xc3 12 ♕xc3 0-0 13 ♗f4 f5 [13 ... d5? 14 exd6 ♗xd6 15 ♗xh7+! ♔xh7 18 ♖ad1±] 14 ♖ad1 a5 15 ♗c4+ ♔h8 16 ♖d3 ± ♗b4 17 ♕d4 ♕e7 18 ♖g3 b6? [□ 18 ... ♗c5 △ 19 ... b6] 19 ♕xb6 ♗c5 20 ♕b3 ♗a6 21 ♗xa6 ♖xa6 22 ♕c3 ♗b4 23 ♕c4 ♖aa8 24 c3 ♗c5 25 ♖d1 ♖ab8 26 ♖d2 h6 27 ♖e2 [27 ♗xh6 gxh6 28 ♕f4 ♔h7 29 ♖h3 ♕f6 30 ♕f1 ♖e8∞] 27 ... ♖fe8 28 ♖d2 d5 29 exd6 ♕e1+ 30 ♕f1 g5 31 d7 ♕xf1+ 32 ♔xf1 gxf4 33 dxe8♕+ ♖xe8 34 ♖g6 f3 35 ♖xh6+ ♔g7 36 ♖xc6 ♗e7 37 ♖d7 ♔f8 38 ♖e6 **1-0**

Staunton(1)

**1851-LON1-62**
**Mucklow, J.R.–Kennedy, H.A.**

1 d4 e6 2 b3 c5 3 ♘f3 cxd4 4 ♕xd4 ♘c6 5 ♕b2 ♗e7 6 ♗d2 d5 7 e3 ♗f6 8 c3 e5 9 h3 ♗f5 10 ♘a3 ♘h6 11 ♗e2 0-0 12 ♘c2 ♗e4 13 g4 ♖c8 14 a3 ♗h4 15 ♖f1 ♗xf3 16

♗xf3 e4 17 ♗e2 f5 18 0-0-0 ♘e5 19 gxf5 ♘xf5 20 ♔b1 a5 21 ♗e1 a4 22 f4 ♗xe1 23 ♖fxe1 ♘f7 24 ♗c4 ♖c5 25 ♘b4 ♘e7 26 ♖g1 axb3 27 ♗xb3 ♕c7 28 c4 g6 29 ♘xd5 ♘xd5 30 ♖xd5 ♖xd5 31 cxd5 ♕b6 32 ♕c3 ♘d6 33 h4 ♖c8 34 ♕b2 ♕xe3 35 ♖g4 ♕f3 **0-1** Staunton(1)

**1851-LON1-63**
**Kennedy,H.A.+Mucklow, J.R.**
[Staunton]

1 e4 c5 2 d4 cxd4 3 ♘f3 ♘c6 4 ♗c4 e6 5 ♘xd4 ♘f6 6 ♘xc6 bxc6 7 e5 ♕a5+ 8 ♘c3 ♕xe5+ 9 ♗e2 ♗b4 10 ♗d2 ♗a6 11 f4 ♕a5 12 a3 ♗xe2 13 ♕xe2 ♗xc3 14 ♗xc3 ♕f5 15 0-0 0-0 16 h3 ♘e4 17 ♕c4 ♖ab8 18 ♖ad1 ♖b7 19 ♗e5 h5 20 ♖fe1 d5 21 ♕xc6 ♖b6 22 ♕d7 g5 23 ♗d4 ♖bb8 24 fxg5 ♕xg5 25 ♕xa7 ♖a8 26 ♕d7 ♖ac8 27 c3 ♕g3 28 ♖f1 ♖c4 29 ♖f3 ♕g6 30 ♖df1 f5 31 ♖e1 ♖cc8 32 ♕e7 ♖f7 33 ♕h4 ♖h7 34 ♖xe4 ♔f7 35 ♖ee3 ♕h6 36 ♖g3 ♖e8 37 ♖g5 ♖b8 38 b4 [38 ♖xf5+-] 38 ... ♖a8 39 ♖xh5 ♕xh5 40 ♕f6+ ♔e8 41 ♕xe6+ ♔d8 42 ♗b6+ ♖c7 43 ♕e7+ ♔c8 44 ♕xc7# **1-0** Staunton(1)

**1851-LON1-64**
**Mucklow,J.R.−Kennedy, H.A.**
[Staunton]

1 c4 e6 2 e3 d5 3 cxd5 exd5 4 d3 ♗d6 5 b3 ♘f6 6 ♗e2 0-0 7 ♗b2 c5 8 ♘d2 ♘c6 9 ♘gf3 b6 10 0-0 ♗b7 11 a3 ♖e8 12 ♖a2 ♗c7 13 ♕a1 d4 14 e4 ♘g4 15 ♕e1 ♘ge5 16 ♗c1 ♕d6 17 ♔h1 ♗a6 18 ♕d1 ♘xd3 19 g3 ♘xc1 20 ♗xa6 ♘xa2 **0-1** Staunton(1)

**1851-LON1-65**
**Kennedy,H.A.+Mucklow, J.R.**
[Staunton]

1 d4 d5 2 c4 c6 3 e3 e6 4 ♘c3 g6 5 ♗d3 ♗g7 6 ♘ge2 ♘e7 7 0-0 0-0 8 b3 ♘d7 9 e4 dxc4 10 bxc4 e5 11 d5 cxd5 12 cxd5 a6 13 a4 ♘f6 14 ♗a3 ♖e8 15 ♗c4 ♗g4 16 f3 ♕b6+ 17 ♔h1 ♗d7 18 ♖b1 ♕a7 19 a5 ♘h5 20 ♕b3 b5 21 axb6 ♕b7 22 d6 ♘c6 23 ♗xf7+ ♔h8 24 ♗xe8 ♖xe8 25 ♘a4 ♘a5 26 ♕b4 ♗xa4 27 ♕xa4 ♘c6 28 ♖fc1 ♖c8 29 ♖xc6 ♖xc6 30 ♕xc6 ♕xc6 31 b7 h6 32 b8♕+ ♔h7 33 ♖c1 ♕a4 34 ♕b4 ♕e8 35 ♖c7 ♕d8 36 ♕b7 ♕h4 37 g3 ♕f6 38 ♔g2 g5 39 g4 ♘f4+ 40 ♘xf4 gxf4 41 ♖xg7+ ♕xg7 42 ♕xg7+ ♔xg7 43 d7 **1-0** Staunton(1)

**1851-LON1-66**
**Anderssen, A.+Wyvill, M.**
[Staunton]

1 e4 c5 2 ♗c4 ♘c6 3 ♘c3 e6 4 d3 ♘e5 5 ♗f4 [5 ♗b3] 5 ... ♘xc4 6 dxc4 a6 7 ♕e2 ♘e7 8 0-0-0 ♘g6 9 ♗g3 ♗e7 10 f4 0-0 11 f5 ♗g5+ 12 ♔b1 exf5 13 exf5 ♖e8 14 ♕g4! ♘f8 15 ♘f3 ♗f6 16 ♘e4 b5 17 ♗c7! ♕e7 18 ♘xf6+ ♕xf6 19 ♖d6 ♘e6 20 fxe6 dxe6 21 ♖hd1 ♗b7 22 ♖d7 ♗c6 23 ♗e5 ♗xf3 24 ♕g3! ♕g6 25 ♕xf3 bxc4 26 ♕xa8! **1-0** Staunton(1)

**1851-LON1-67**
**Wyvill, M.=Anderssen, A.**
[Staunton]

1 c4 e6 2 e3 d5 3 d4 ♘f6 4 ♘c3 c5 5 ♘f3 ♘c6 6 a3 a6 7 b3 b6 8 ♗e2 ♗b7 9 0-0 ♖c8 10 ♗b2 cxd4 11 ♘xd4 ♘xd4 12 ♕xd4 [12 exd4] 12 ... ♗e7 13 ♖ad1 dxc4 14 ♕h4! ♕c7 15 ♗xc4 b5 16 ♗d3 ♘e4 17 ♕g4 ♘xc3 18 ♕xg7 ♖f8 19 ♖c1 b4 20 axb4 ♗xb4 21 ♗c4! f6 [21 ... ♘~ 22 ♗b5+-] 22 ♕xc7 ♖xc7 23 ♗xc3 ♖g8 24 g3 ♗xc3 25 ♖xc3 ♔e7 26 ♖a1? [□ 26 ♗xe6! ♖xg3+ 27 hxg3 ♖xc3 28 ♗c4+-] 26 ... ♖d8 27 ♖d3 ♖xd3 28 ♗xd3 ♖c3 29 ♗xa6? [□ 29 ♗c4±] 29 ... ♖xb3 30 ♗f1 ♗f3 31 h4 ♖b2 32 ♗g2 ♗xg2 33 ♔xg2 ♖b7 34 ♖a5? ♔f7 35 ♖h5? [□ 35 ♔~] ♔g6 36 g4 h6 37 ♖a5 ♖c7 38 ♔g3 ♖b7 39 f4 ♖c7 40 ♖a6 ♔f7 41 g5 hxg5 42 hxg5 fxg5 43 fxg5 ♖c4 44 ♔f3 ♔g6 45 ♖a5 ♖h4 46 ♖e5 ♖a4 47 e4 ♖a1 48 ♖b5 ♖a7 49 ♔f4 ♖e7 50 ♖b1 ♖a7 **½-½** Staunton(1)

**1851-LON1-68**
**Anderssen, A.−Wyvill, M.**
[Staunton]

1 e4 c5 2 d4 cxd4 3 ♘f3 ♘c6 4 ♘xd4 e6 5 ♗e3 [5 ♘xc6 △ 6 ♗d3] 5 ... ♘f6 6 ♗d3 ♗e7 7 0-0 0-0 8 ♘d2 d5 9 ♘xc6 bxc6 10 e5 ♘d7 11 f4 f5 12 ♖f3 c5 13 ♖h3 ♖f7 14 b3 g6 15 ♘f3 ♘b6 16 ♗f2 d4! 17 ♗h4 ♘d5 ∓ 18 ♕d2 a5 19 ♗xe7 ♖xe7 20 ♘g5 ♘e3 21 ♕f2 ♗b7 22 ♗f1 ♘g4 23 ♕h4 ♕d7 24 ♖d1 ♖c8 25 ♗e2 h5 26 ♖g3 ♕e8! 27 ♖d2 ♖g7 28 c3 ♘e3

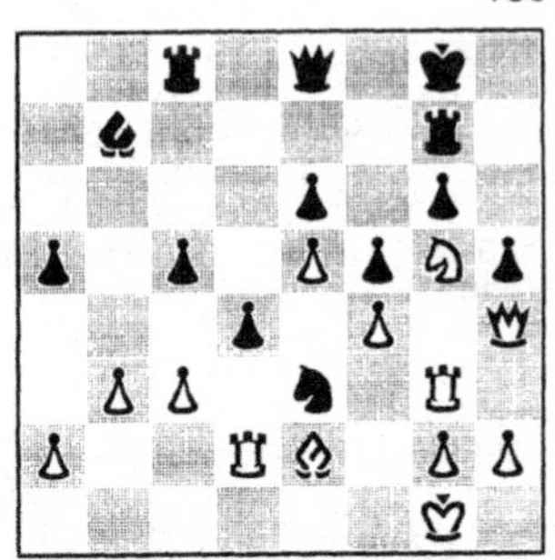

29 cxd4 cxd4 30 ♖xd4 ♖c1+ 31 ♔f2 ♘d5 32 ♖gd3 ♕c6! [32 ... ♖gc7] 33 ♖d2 ♕b6! 34 ♗c4 ♖c2! 35 ♔e1 ♖xd2 36 ♖xd2 ♕g1+ 37 ♗f1 ♖c7 38 ♖d1 ♖c2 [△ 39 ... ♖e2+ 40 ♔xe2 ♕e3#] 39 ♕g3 ♗a6 40 ♕f3 ♗xf1 **0-1** Staunton(1)

**1851-LON1-69**
**Wyvill, M.−Anderssen, A.**
[Staunton]

1 c4 f5 2 e3 ♘f6 3 ♘c3 e6 4 ♗e2 ♗b4 5 ♗h5+?! g6 6 ♗e2 0-0 7 f4 c5 8 ♘f3 ♘c6 9 0-0 ♗xc3 10 bxc3 b6 11 a4? ♗b7 12 ♕c2 ♕c7 13 ♘g5? h6 14 ♘h3 ♖ae8 15 ♗f3 ♖e7 16 d4 ♖g7 17 ♗a3 ♘a5! 18 ♗xb7 ♘xb7 19 ♖ad1 g5 20 g3 ♘d6 21 fxg5 hxg5 22 ♕d3 ♘de4 23 d5 ♕e5 24 ♔g2 ♖h7 25 ♘g1? ♖xh2+ 26 ♔xh2 ♕xg3+ 27 ♔h1 ♔g7 **0-1** Staunton(1)

**1851-LON1-70**
**Anderssen, A.+Wyvill, M.**
[Staunton]

1 e4 c5 2 f4 e6 3 ♘f3 ♘c6 4 ♗b5 ♘ce7 5 c4 f5 6 d3 ♘h6 7 ♘c3 ♘g6 8 0-0 ♗e7 9 ♘g5 0-0 10 ♕h5 b6 ± 11 exf5 exf5 12 ♖f3 ♗b7?! 13 ♖g3 ♕c7 [13 ... ♕e8 14 ♘e6; 13 ... ♔h8 14 ♘e6] 14 ♘xh7 ♘g4 15 ♕xg6 ♖f7 16 ♖h3 ♗f6 17 ♘xf6+ ♖xf6 18 ♕h7+ ♔f7 19 ♗d2 ♘h6 20 ♖e1 [△ 21 ♖xh6 ♖xh6 22 ♖e7++-] 20 ... ♖g8 21 ♘d5! ♗xd5 22 ♖xh6! ♕d6 [22 ... ♖xh6 23 ♕xf5+ △ 24 ♕xd5++-] 23 ♖xf6+ ♕xf6 24 ♗c3 **1-0** Staunton(1)

**1851-LON1-71**
**Wyvill, M.+Anderssen, A.**
[Staunton]

1 c4 f5 2 e3 ♘f6 3 f4 e6 4 ♘f3 ♗e7 5 ♗e2 0-0 6 0-0 d6 7 b3 ♘e4 8 a3 ♗f6 9 ♖a2 a5 10 d3 ♘c5 11 ♘bd2 ♘c6 12 d4 ♘e4 13 ♕c2 d5 14 ♘e5 ♗d7 15 cxd5 exd5 16 ♘xd7 ♕xd7 17 ♗b5 ♗e7 18 ♘xe4 fxe4 19 ♗d2 ♖f6 20 ♖c1 ♖g6 21 ♕d1 ♕c8 22 ♕e1 ♘a7 23 ♗e2 ♘c6 24 h3?? ♕xh3 25 ♕f2 ♗h4 26 ♔f1! ♗xf2 27 gxh3 ♗h4 28 ♗g4! ♔f8 29 ♖c5 ♖d8 30 b4 axb4 31 axb4

♗e7 32 ♖c1 ♗d6 [32 ... ♗xb4∞] 33 ♗e1 ♖h6 34 ♖ac2 ♘e7 35 b5 g6? 36 ♖xc7! ♗xc7 37 ♖xc7 ♘f5 38 ♔e2 ♖a8 39 ♗b4+ ♔e8 40 ♖xb7 ♖a2+ 41 ♗d2 ♘d6 42 ♖b8+ ♔e7 43 ♔e1 ♖b2 44 ♗a5! g5? 45 ♗d8+ ♔f7 46 ♗xg5 ♖g6 47 ♗h5 ♖xb5 48 ♖xb5 ♘xb5 49 f5 **1-0**

Staunton(1)

### 1851-LON1-72
**Anderssen, A.+Wyvill, M.**

[Staunton]

1 e4 c5 2 ♗c4 e6 3 ♘c3 a6 4 a4 ♘c6 5 d3 g6 6 ♘ge2 ♗g7 7 0-0 ♘ge7 8 f4 0-0 9 ♗d2 d5 10 ♗b3 ♘d4 [□ 10 ... d4] 11 ♘xd4 ♗xd4+ 12 ♔h1 ♗d7 13 exd5 ♗xc3 14 ♗xc3 exd5 15 ♗f6 ♗e6 16 f5! ♗xf5 [□ 16 ... ♗d7; 16 ... ♗c8] 17 ♖xf5! gxf5 18 ♕h5! ♕d6 19 ♕h6 ♕xf6 20 ♕xf6 **1-0**

Staunton(1)

### 1851-LON1-73
**Williams, E.+Staunton, H.**

[Staunton]

1 e4 c5 2 f4 ♘c6 3 ♘f3 e6 4 ♗b5 g6 5 ♗xc6 bxc6 6 c4 ♗g7 7 ♕e2 ♕b6 8 e5 ♘h6 9 ♘c3 ♘f5 10 ♘e4 0-0 11 d3 ♖b8 12 0-0 d5 13 ♘c3 [13 exd6 ♗xb2] 13 ... ♗a6? 14 b3 ♕c7? 15 ♗a3 ♖fd8 16 ♗xc5 ♗f8 17 ♗f2 ♕a5 18 ♖ac1 ♖d7 19 g4 ♘g7 20 ♘d1 h5 21 h3 ♕e7 22 ♘e3 d4 23 ♘g2 c5 24 ♘g5 ♗xg5 25 fxg5 ♗b7 26 ♘f4 hxg4 27 hxg4 ♕b6 28 ♗g3 ♕c6 29 ♕h2 ♘e8 30 ♖c2 f5? 31 gxf6 ♖h7 32 ♘xg6! ♘xf6 33 exf6 ♖xh2 34 ♖xh2 ♕e8 **1-0**

Staunton(1)

### 1851-LON1-74
**Staunton, H.+Williams, E.**

[Staunton]

1 e4 e6 2 d4 d5 3 exd5 exd5 4 c4 ♘f6 5 ♘c3 ♗b4 6 ♕b3 ♘c6 7 ♗e3 0-0 8 ♘f3 h6 9 ♗d3 dxc4 10 ♗xc4 ♗d6 11 ♕c2 ♘e7 12 ♘e5 ♗f5 13 ♕b3 ♗xe5 14 dxe5 ♘g4 15 ♖d1 ♕c8 16 ♗c5 ♕e8 17 0-0 ♘xe5 18 ♖fe1 ♘5g6 19 ♘d5 ♗e6 20 ♘xe7+ ♘xe7 21 ♗xe6 fxe6 22 ♖xe6 ♔h8 23 ♖xe7 ♕h5 24 ♗d4 ♖g8 25 ♖de1 ♖ad8 26 ♕c3 ♕g4 27 f4 ♖d6 28 h3 ♕g6 29 f5 ♕g5 30 ♖xc7 b5 31 ♖ee7 ♖gd8 32 ♖xg7 ♕f4 33 ♖g4+ [33 ♖h7+ ♔g8 34 ♖cg7++-] 33 ... ♕xd4+ 34 ♖xd4 **1-0** Staunton(1)

### 1851-LON1-75
**Williams, E.–Staunton, H.**

[Staunton]

1 e4 e5 2 ♘f3 ♘c6 3 ♗b5 ♘f6 4 ♕e2 d6 5 ♗xc6+ bxc6 6 d4 ♗g4 7 dxe5 dxe5 8 0-0 ♗d6 9 ♘c3 h6 10 h3 ♗h5 11 ♕e3 ♕e7 12 ♘h4 ♗g6 13 ♕f3 0-0 14 g4 ♕e6 15 ♘f5 ♖ab8 16 ♖b1 ♖b7 17 h4 h5! ∓ 18 gxh5 ♘xh5 19 ♔h1 ♗b4 20 ♗d2 ♖fb8 [20 ... ♖d8] 21 ♖g1 ♘f6 22 a3 ♗f8 23 ♖g5 ♖xb2 24 ♖bg1 ♖xc2 25 ♗e1 ♖b3 26 h5 ♘xe4 [□ 26 ... ♘xh5 27 ♖xh5 ♗xh5 28 ♕xh5 g6] 27 hxg6? [□ 27 ♕xe4 ♗xf5 28 ♖xf5 ♖bxc3 29 ♗xc3∓] 27 ... ♘xg5 28 ♖xg5 fxg6 29 ♘h4 ♖c1! 30 ♖g1 g5! 31 ♘f5 ♖xa3 32 ♔h2 ♖cxc3 33 ♗xc3 e4 34 ♕h3 ♖xc3 35 ♕xc3 ♕xf5 36 ♕b3+ ♕d5 37 ♕e3 ♗d6+ 38 ♔h3 ♕e6+ 39 ♔g2 [39 ♖g4? ♗f4 40 ♕xa7 ♕h6+ 41 ♔g2 ♕h2+ 42 ♔f1 ♕h3+ 43 ♖g2 ♕d3+ 44 ♔e1 ♗d2+ 45 ♔d1 ♗e3+ 46 ♔e1 ♕d2+ 47 ♔f1 ♕d1#] 39 ... ♗f4 40 ♕xa7 ♕g4+ 41 ♔f1 ♕d1+ 42 ♔g2 ♕f3+ 43 ♔f1 ♕d3+ 44 ♔g2 ♕d5 45 ♔f1 c5 46 ♕a4 ♔f7 47 ♖h1 ♕d3+ 48 ♔g2 ♕f3+ 49 ♔g1 ♕g4+ 50 ♔f1 ♕e6 51 ♖h8 e3 52 ♕d1 ♕c4+ 53 ♔g2 ♕e4+ 54 ♔f1 ♔f6 55 ♕d8+ ♔g6 56 ♕d1 ♕c4+ 57 ♔e2 ♕xe2+ 58 ♔xe2 exf2 59 ♔xf2 c4 60 ♔f3 c3 61 ♖a8 c2 **0-1**

Staunton(1)

### 1851-LON1-76
**Staunton, H.+Williams, E.**

[Staunton]

1 ♘f3 d5 2 d4 e6 3 c4 c5 4 e3 ♘f6 5 ♘c3 ♘c6 6 ♗e2 ♗d6 7 0-0 0-0 8 b3 a6 9 ♗b2 cxd4 10 exd4 ♕c7 11 g3 b6 12 ♖c1 ♗b7 13 ♘h4 ♖ad8 14 cxd5 exd5 15 ♗f3 ♗b4 16 ♘e2 ♕d7 17 ♕d3 ♘e7 18 ♗g2 ♘e4 19 ♘f3 f6 20 ♘f4 [△ 21 ♗h3] 20 ... ♘g6 21 ♘xg6 hxg6 22 ♘h4 g5 23 ♘g6!? ♖f7 24 ♕e2 g4 25 ♖c2 ♕f5 26 ♘f4 ♗d6 27 ♗c1 g5 28 ♘d3 ♔g7 29 f3 gxf3 30 ♗xf3 ♕h7 31 ♗h5 ♖e7 32 ♕f3 ♖h8 33 g4 ♖f8 34 ♘e5 ♖xe5!? 35 dxe5 ♗xe5 [35 ... fxe5 36 ♖c7+ ♔g8 37 ♖xh7 ♖xf3 38 ♖xf3 ♔xh7 39 ♖f7++-] 36 ♗b2 d4 37 ♕d1 ♘c3 38 ♗xc3 ♕e4! 39 ♗b2 ♕h1+ 40 ♔f2 ♕xh2+ 41 ♔e1 ♗g3+ 42 ♖cf2 ♗xf2+ 43 ♖xf2 ♕h1+ 44 ♔d2 ♕d5 45 ♕c2 ♕e5 46 ♔d1 ∞

46 ... ♗e4 47 ♕c4 ♕g3 48 ♕xd4 ♕g1+ 49 ♔e2 ♗c6 50 a4 ♕b1 51 ♔d2 ♖d8?! 52 ♕xd8 ♕xb2+ 53 ♔e1 ♕c1+ 54 ♕d1 ♕e3+ 55 ♖e2 ♕g1+ 56 ♔d2 ♕d4+ 57 ♔c2 ♗e4+ 58 ♖xe4 ♕xe4+ 59 ♕d3 ♕c6+ 60 ♔b2 ♕g2+ 61 ♔a3 ♕f2 62 ♕g6+ ♔h8 63 ♕e8+ ♔g7 64 ♕e7+ ♔h6 65 ♕f8+ ♔h7 66 ♗f7 ♕c5+ 67 ♕xc5 bxc5 68 b4 cxb4+ 69 ♔xb4 f5 70 gxf5 ...? **1-0**

Staunton(1)

### 1851-LON1-77
**Williams, E.+Staunton, H.**

[Staunton]

1 f4 d5 2 e3 c5 3 ♘f3 e6 4 ♗b5+ ♗d7 5 ♗xd7+ ♘xd7 6 0-0 g6 7 c4 d4 8 ♕e2 ♗g7 9 e4 ♘h6 10 d3 0-0 11 h3 f5 12 ♘bd2 a6 13 ♘g5 ♖e8 14 e5 b5 15 b3 ♖b8 16 ♘df3 ♗f8 17 ♕f2 ♖b7 18 ♕h4 ♘b8 19 ♗a3 ♕c7 [19 ... b4] 20 ♘xd4 b4 21 ♘dxe6 ♖xe6 22 ♘xe6 ♕e7 23 ♕xe7 ♖xe7 24 ♘xf8 bxa3 25 ♘xg6 hxg6 26 b4! cxb4? [□ 26 ... ♘c6] 27 d4 ♖c7 28 ♖ac1 ♔f7 29 d5 ♖c5 30 ♔f2 a5 31 ♔e3 a4 32 ♔d4 ♘a6 33 ♖b1 ♖a5 34 ♖fc1 b3 35 c5 [35 axb3? a2-+] 35 ... ♘b4 36 ♔c4! ♘a6 37 c6 ♘g8 38 d6 ♔e6 39 c7 ♘xc7 40 dxc7 ♘e7 41 ♔b4 ♖a8 42 ♔xa3 ♔d7 43 axb3 axb3+ 44 ♔xb3 ♘c6 45 ♖xc6 ♔xc6 46 ♖c1+ **1-0**

Staunton(1)

### 1851-LON1-78
**Staunton, H.–Williams, E.**

[Staunton]

1 c4 e6 2 e3 f5 3 g3 ♘f6 4 ♗g2 ♗e7 5 ♘c3 0-0 6 ♘ge2 ♗b4 7 0-0 d6 8 d4 ♗xc3 9 bxc3 ♕e7 10 ♗a3 c5 11 ♖b1 e5 12 ♖b5 a6 13 ♖b6? ♘bd7 14 ♖b1 e4 15 ♕d2 ♕f7 16 f3? ♕xc4 17 fxe4 fxe4 18 ♗h3 b5 19 ♘f4 ♘b6 20 ♗g2 ♕f7 21 dxc5 ♘c4 22 ♕c1 ♕a7! 23 ♖e1 dxc5 24 ♗b2 g5 25 ♘e2 ♗g4 26 h3 ♗f3 27 ♔h2 ♖ad8 28 ♗a1 ♖d2 29 ♖b2 ♖fd8 30 ♘d4 ♖xb2 31 ♗xb2 cxd4 32 cxd4 ♗xg2 33 ♔xg2 ♘d5 34 ♔h2 ♖f8 35 ♕c2 ♕f7 36 ♖e2 ♕f1 37 ♗c1 ♘b4 **0-1**

Staunton(1)

### 1851-LON1-79
**Williams, E.=Staunton, H.**

[Staunton]

1 e4 e6 2 d4 c5 3 d5 exd5 4 exd5 d6 5 c4 ♗f5 6 ♗d3 ♗xd3 7 ♕xd3 ♘f6 8 ♘c3 ♗e7 9 ♘f3 0-0 10 0-0 ♘bd7 11 ♕f5 a6 12 ♘e2 b5 13 b3 bxc4 14 bxc4 ♖b8 15 ♖b1 ♖xb1 16 ♕xb1 ♕b6 17 ♕c2 ♖b8 18 ♘g3 g6 19 ♖e1 ♗f8 20 ♘d2 ♕b4 21 a3 ♕a5 22 f4 ♗g7 23 ♘f3 ♘g4 [△ 24 ... ♗d4+-+ (25 ♘xd4?? ♕xe1+)] 24 ♖e2 ♕c3 25 ♘e4 [25 ♕xc3 ♗xc3 26 ♘e4 ♖b1!] 25 ... ♕a1 26 ♖e1 ♗d4+ 27 ♔f1! ♖e8! 28 g3 [28 h3!? f5! 29 hxg4 ♖xe4 (29 ... fxe4 30 ♘xd4 ♕xd4 31 ♗b2+-) 30 gxf5 gxf5∓] 28 ... f5 29 ♘xd6 ♖e3!

[29 ... ♖xe1+ 30 ♘xe1±] 30 ♔g2 ♖xe1 31 ♘xe1 ♘e3+ 32 ♗xe3 ♕xe1 33 ♗xd4 [33 ♗f2? ♗xf2 34 ♕xf2 ♕e7 35 ♘~ ♕e4+−+] 33 ... cxd4 34 c5 ♘xc5 35 ♕xc5 ♕e2+ 36 ♔g1 ♕e1+ 37 ♔g2 ♕e2+ ½-½ Staunton(1)

### 1851-LON1-80
### Staunton, H.–Williams, E.

[Staunton]

1 e4 e6 2 d4 d5 3 exd5 exd5 4 ♘f3 ♘f6 5 ♗d3 ♗d6 6 0-0 0-0 7 h3 h6 8 ♗e3 ♘c6 9 a3 ♘e7 10 ♘h4 g5 11 ♕f3 ♔g7 12 ♘c3?? gxh4 13 ♗xh6+ ♔xh6 14 ♕xf6+ ♘g6 15 ♕f3 c6 16 ♖ae1 ♕g5 17 ♘e2 ♘f4 18 ♔h1 ♘xe2 19 ♕xe2 ♗f5 20 f4 ♕g6 21 ♕f2 ♗xd3 22 ♕xh4+ ♔g7 23 cxd3 ♖h8 24 ♕f2 ♖ae8 25 ♕f3 ♖xe1 26 ♖xe1 f5 27 ♕f2 ♕g4 28 ♖f1 ♖h4 29 ♕e3 ♕g6 30 ♖f3 ♕f7 31 ♖f1 ♖h6 32 ♖e1 ♖g6 33 ♖e2 ♖f6 34 ♕g3+ ♕g6 35 ♕e1? ♗xf4 36 ♕h4 ♕g3 37 ♖e7+ ♖f7 38 ♖xf7+ ♔xf7 39 ♕h7+ ♔e6 **0-1**

Staunton(1)

### 1851-LON1-81
### Kennedy, H.A.=Szén, J.

[Staunton]

1 e4 c5 2 ♘f3 e6 3 ♘c3 ♘c6 4 d4 cxd4 5 ♘xd4 ♗b4 6 ♘xc6 bxc6 7 ♗d3 d5 8 0-0 ♘e7 9 ♕g4 ♗xc3 10 bxc3 0-0 11 e5 ♘g6 12 f4 c5 13 ♗e3 c4 14 ♗xg6 fxg6 15 h4 ♕e7 16 h5 gxh5 17 ♕xh5 ♗d7 18 g4! ♕f7 19 ♕xf7+ ♔xf7?! [19 ... ♖xf7] 20 f5 g6 21 ♗c5 ± exf5 [21 ... ♖fc8 22 fxe6+ ♔g8 (22 ... ♔xe6? 23 ♖f6+ ♔xe5 24 ♗d4+ ♔e4 25 ♖e1#) 23 exd7 ♖xc5 24 e6+−] 22 ♗xf8 ♖xf8 23 ♖ab1 ♔e6 24 ♖b7 a5 25 gxf5+ +− gxf5 26 ♖e1 ♖g8+ 27 ♔f2 ♖g6 28 ♖h1 [□ 28 ♔f3] 28 ... ♗a4 29 ♖e1 ♗xc2 30 ♖b6+ ♔e7 31 ♖xg6 hxg6 32 ♔e3 g5 33 ♔d4 ♔e6 34 ♖h1 ♔f7 35 ♖h6 [35 ♔xd5?? ♗e4+−+] 35 ... g4 36 ♔xd5 g3 37 e6+ ♔g7 38 e7 ♗a4 39 ♖h3 f4 40 ♖h4! ♔f7 41 ♖xf4+ ♔xe7 42 ♖xc4? [□ 42 ♖g4!+−] 42 ... ♗d1 43 ♖e4+ ♔f6 44 ♖e3 g2 45 ♖g3 ♔f5

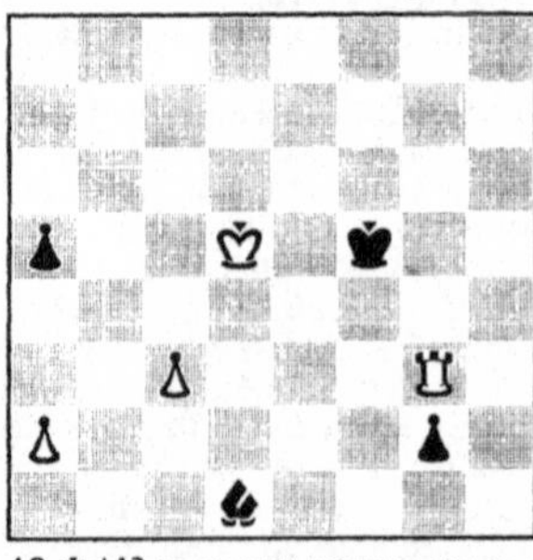

46 ♔d4? [□ 46 ♔d6! ♗f3 47 ♖xf3+ ♔g4 48 ♖f8+−; 46 ... ♔e4 47 ♖xg2 ♔d3 48 ♖g5 a4 49 ♖c5+−] 46 ... ♗f3! 47 ♔e3 [47 ♖xf3+ ♔g4 48 ♖~ g1♕+−+] 47 ... ♗c6 48 c4 a4 49 a3 ♗b7 50 c5 ♗c6 51 ♔f2 ♔e5 52 ♖d3 ♗d5 53 ♖d1 ♔e6 54 ♖d4 ♗b7 55 ♖d6+ ♔e7 56 ♖b6 ♗d5 57 ♖d6 ♗e4 ... ? ½-½

Staunton(1)

### 1851-LON1-82
### Szén, J.+Kennedy, H.A.

[Staunton]

1 e4 c5 2 ♘f3 e6 3 c3 ♘c6 4 d4 d5 5 exd5 exd5 6 ♗d3 ♘f6 7 0-0 ♗e6 8 ♖e1 ♗d6 9 ♗f5 0-0! 10 ♗xe6 fxe6 11 ♖xe6 ♘e4 12 dxc5? [□ 12 ♕b3] 12 ... ♗xc5 13 ♗e3 ♗xe3 14 fxe3 ♔h8? [□ 14 ... ♘c5!−+] 15 b4 ♖f7 [Δ 16 ... ♕d7; 15 ... ♕d7?? 16 ♖xe4+−] 16 h3 ♖c8 [16 ... ♕d7] 17 a4 ♖fc7 18 ♘e5 ♕g5 ∓ 19 ♕xd5 ♕xe3+ 20 ♔h2 ♕g3+ 21 ♔g1 ♕f2+ 22 ♔h2 ♕g3+ 23 ♔g1 ♘f2? [□ 23 ... ♘g5!−+] 24 ♕f3 ♘xh3+ 25 ♔f1 ♕xf3+ 26 ♘xf3 ♖f7 27 ♘bd2 ♘g5 28 ♖e3 ♘b8 29 ♖ae1 ♘xf3 30 ♖e8+ ♖f8 31 ♖xf8+ ♖xf8 32 ♘xf3 h6 33 ♖e7 +− ♘c6 34 ♖xb7 ♘e5 35 ♔e2 ♘xf3 36 gxf3 ♖c8 37 ♖xa7 ♖xc3 38 a5 h5 39 a6 h4 40 ♔f2 ♖c2+ 41 ♔g1 h3 42 ♖b7 ♖g2+ 43 ♔h1 ♔h7 44 ♖b5 ♖c2 45 a7 **1-0**

Staunton(1)

### 1851-LON1-83
### Kennedy, H.A.–Szén, J.

[Staunton]

1 e4 e5 2 ♘f3 ♘c6 3 ♗b5 ♘f6 4 ♕e2 ♗c5? 5 c3 [□ 5 ♗xc6 dxc6 6 ♘xe5 ♕d4 7 ♘d3±] 5 ... d6 6 0-0 ♗g4 7 d3 0-0 8 ♗xc6 bxc6 9 ♗e3 ♗b6 10 a4 a5 11 ♘bd2 ♘d7 12 h3 ♗h5 13 g4 ♗g6 14 h4 h5 15 ♘g5 ♘f6 16 gxh5 ♗xh5 17 f3 ♘h7 18 ♘c4 ♘xg5 19 ♘xb6 ♘xf3+! −+ 20 ♖xf3 cxb6 21 ♗g5 f6 22 ♗e3 ♕d7 23 ♕f2 ♗xf3 24 ♕xf3 f5 25 ♕h3 ♕f7 26 ♗g5 fxe4 27 dxe4 ♕f2+ 28 ♔h1 ♖ae8 29 ♖d1 ♕e2 30 ♖g1 ♕xe4+ **0-1**

Staunton(1)

### 1851-LON1-84
### Szén, J.+Kennedy, H.A.

[Staunton]

1 e4 e6 2 d4 d5 3 exd5 exd5 4 c4 ♘f6 5 ♘c3 ♗b4 6 ♗g5 dxc4?! 7 ♗xc4 0-0 8 ♘ge2 ♗g4 9 0-0 ♗xc3 10 bxc3 ♘bd7 11 f3 ♗f5 12 ♗d3 ♗xd3 13 ♕xd3 c6 14 ♖ab1 b5 15 ♘g3 ♕a5 16 ♖f2 ♘d5 17 c4 bxc4 18 ♕xc4 ♘5b6 19 ♕c1 ♖fe8 20 ♘e4 ♕d5 21 ♕d2 h6 22 ♗f4 f5 23 ♘c3 ♕f7 24 ♕d3 c5? 25 d5 ♖ac8 26 ♖d2 g5 27 ♗g3 f4 28 ♗f2 ♘e5 29 ♕c2 ♘ec4 30 ♖dd1 ♘a3 31 ♕b3 ♘xb1 32 ♕xb1 ♘c4 33 ♘e4 ♕g6 34 d6 ♖ed8 35 ♕b3 ♕f7 36 ♗xc5 ♖d7 [□ 36 ... ♖xc5 37 ♘xc5 ♘xd6] 37 ♖c1 ♘a5? [□ 37 ... ♘e5 38 ♘f6+! ♔f8 39 ♘xd7 ♘xd7∞] 38 ♕c3 ♖xc5 39 ♘xc5 ♖xd6 40 ♕xa5 g4 41 ♘e4 ♖d5 42 ♕xd5 **1-0**

Staunton(1)

### 1851-LON1-85
### Kennedy, H.A.–Szén, J.

[Staunton]

1 e4 e5 2 ♘f3 ♘c6 3 c3 f5 4 d4 d6 5 ♗d3 [□ 5 ♗c4; 5 dxe5] 5 ... fxe4 6 ♗xe4 d5 7 ♗c2 e4 8 ♘e5 ♘f6 9 ♗g5 ♗d6 10 ♗a4 ♗d7 11 ♘xd7 ♕xd7 12 ♘d2 [□ 12 ♗xf6 gxf6 13 ♕h5+] 12 ... 0-0 13 c4 ♕f5 14 ♗e3 ♘g4 15 ♕e2 ♘b4 16 0-0-0 ♘d3+ 17 ♔b1 ♘gxf2 18 ♖df1 ♕g6 19 ♗c2? [19 ♗xf2∓] 19 ... ♘xh1 20 ♗xd3 exd3 21 ♕d1 ♖ae8 22 ♖xf8+ ♗xf8 23 ♕f3 ♕f7 **0-1**

## LONDON(2) 1851
## Provincial Tournament

### 1851-LON2-1
### Angas, S.–Boden, S.S.

[Staunton]

1 c4 c5 2 e3 e6 3 ♘c3 b6 4 ♘f3 ♗e7 5 b3 f5 6 ♗b2 ♘f6 7 ♗e2 0-0 8 d4 cxd4?! 9 ♘xd4 ♗b7 10 ♗f3 ♘e4 11 ♕c2 ♗b4 12 0-0 ♗xc3 13 ♗xc3 ♘a6 14 ♖ad1 ♕e7 15 ♘b5 ♘ac5 16 ♗b4 [□ 16 ♗e5] 16 ... a6 17 ♗xc5 bxc5 18 ♘c3 ♘xc3 19 ♕xc3 [19 ♗xb7? ♘xd1 20 ♗xa8 ♘xe3!] 19 ... ♗xf3 20 gxf3 ♖f6 21 ♕e5 [□ 21 ♔h1] 21 ... ♖g6+ 22 ♔h1 ♕h4 23 ♖xd7? ♕h3 **0-1**

Staunton(1)

### 1851-LON2-2
### Boden, S.S.+Angas, S.

[Staunton]

1 e4 c5 2 ♘f3 ♘c6 [2 ... e6] 3 d4 e6 [□ 3 ... cxd4] 4 d5 exd5 5 exd5 ♕e7+ 6 ♗e2 ♘e5 7 ♘xe5 ♕xe5 8 0-0 ♗d6 9 g3 [9 f4 ♕d4+ Δ 10 ... ♕xd1] 9 ... ♘e7 10 ♘c3 0-0? 11 ♗f4 ♕f6 12 ♘e4 ♕xb2 13 ♗xd6 ♖e8 14 ♗xc5 ♘f5 15 ♘d6 ♘xd6 16 ♗xd6 ♕f6 17 ♗f4 d6 18 ♗g4 ♖e4 19 ♗xc8 ♖xc8 20 ♖e1 ♖ec4 21 ♕e2 h6 22 ♖ac1 ♕g6 [Δ 23 ... ♖xf4; Δ 23 ... ♖xc2] 23 ♕d3 ♕f6 24 ♖e4 ♖c3 25 ♕e2 g5 26 ♗e3 ♕f5 27 ♗d4! +− ♖3c4 28 ♖e8+ ♖xe8 29 ♕xe8+ ♔h7 30 ♕h8+ ♔g6 31 ♕g7+ ♔h5 32 ♕f6 ♕xd5 33 h3! ♕e6 34 g4+ ♔h4 35 ♕f3 **1-0**

Staunton(1)

### 1851-LON2-3
### Trelawny, J.–Brien, R.B.

[Staunton]

1 e4 e5 2 ♘f3 ♘c6 3 ♗b5 ♘f6 4 ♗xc6 dxc6 5 d3 ♗d6 6 ♗g5 h6 7 ♗h4 ♗g4 8 ♘bd2 g5 9 ♗g3 ♕e7 10

c3 ♘h5 11 h3 ♗d7 12 ♗xe5! ♘f6 13 ♗xf6 ♕xf6 14 e5 ♕e6 15 0-0 ♗e7 16 ♕b3 [16 ♖e1; 16 ♘c4; 16 d4] 16 ... 0-0-0 17 ♕xe6 ♗xe6 18 ♘d4?! ♗d7 [18 ... c5! 19 ♘xe6 fxe6 △ 20 ... ♖xd3] 19 g4 h5 20 f3 ♗c5 21 ♔g2 ♗xd4 22 cxd4 ♗e6 23 ♘b3 ♔b8 24 ♘c5 ♗c8 25 ♘b3 b6 26 ♖ac1 ♔b7 27 ♖c3 ♗e6 28 d5 ♗xd5 29 ♖d1 hxg4 30 hxg4 ♖h4 31 ♔f2 ♖h2+ 32 ♔e3 ♖xb2 33 ♘d4 ♖xa2 34 ♖dc1 c5 35 ♘b5 ♖h8 36 d4 ♖hh2 37 dxc5 bxc5 38 ♖xc5 ♖he2+ 39 ♔d4 ♖ad2+ 40 ♔c3 ♔b6 41 ♘d4! ♖a2 42 ♖xd5?? [□ 42 ♖b5+ ♔a6 43 ♖xd5 ♖e3+ 44 ♔b4 ♖ea3 45 ♘b5+−] 42 ... ♖e3+ 43 ♔c4 [43 ♔b4 a5+ 44 ♔c4 ♖a4#] 43 ... ♖a4# **0-1** Staunton(1)

### 1851-LON2-4
**Brien, R.B.+Trelawny, J.**

[Staunton]

1 e4 e6 2 d4 ♗e7 3 ♗d3 d6 4 ♗e3 ♗d7 5 ♘c3 a6 6 ♘f3 c5 7 d5 e5 8 h3 b5 9 b3 ♕a5 10 ♕d2 b4 11 ♘e2 ♗b5 12 0-0 ♘f6 13 a3 ♘bd7? 14 axb4 ♕xb4 15 ♕xb4 cxb4 16 ♗xb5 0-0 17 ♗d3 a5 18 ♘g3 h6 19 ♘f5 ♖fe8 20 ♘3h4 ♗f8 21 g4 ♘h7 22 ♔h2 g5 23 ♘f3 ♘df6 24 ♘d2 h5 25 ♗b5 ♖ed8 26 ♗c6 ♖ac8 27 ♗b6 hxg4 28 ♖xa5 ♖d7 29 ♖fa1 gxh3 30 ♖a8 ♖dc7 31 ♗xc7 ♖xc7 32 ♘xd6 g4 33 ♘2c4 ♔g7 34 ♘b5 g3+ 35 ♔xg3 ♘xe4+ 36 ♔h2 ♖e7 37 ♖g1+ ♘hg5 38 d6 ♖e6 39 ♗xe4 f6 40 d7 **1-0**

Staunton(1)

### 1851-LON2-5
**Ranken, C.E.+Robertson**

[Staunton]

1 e4 e6 2 d4 d5 3 exd5 exd5 4 ♘f3 ♘f6 5 c4 ♗b4+ 6 ♗d2 ♕e7+ 7 ♗e2 0-0 8 0-0 ♗e6 9 ♕b3 ♘c6 10 ♗xb4 ♕xb4 11 ♕xb4 ♘xb4 12 ♘bd2 ♖ad8 13 a3 ♘c6 14 c5! ♘e4 15 ♖ad1 f5 16 ♗b5 ♘e7 17 ♘e5 c6 18 ♗d3 ♗f7 19 f3 ♘g5 20 f4 ♘e4 21 ♘xf7 ♖xf7 22 ♘f3 ♖f6 23 ♘e5 ♘g6 24 ♖f3 ♘f8 25 ♗c2 ♘e6 26 g3 g5 27 fxg5 ♘6xg5 28 ♖b3 ♘f7 29 ♖xb7 ♘xe5 30 dxe5 ♖f7 31 ♖b4 [31 ♖xf7? ♔xf7 △ 32 ... ♔e6 33 ... ♔xe5∓] 31 ... ♘xc5 [31 ... ♖e8] 32 ♖f4 ♖e8 33 ♗xf5 ♖xe5 34 ♖c1 d4?? [□ 34 ... ♖xf5 35 ♖xf5 ♖xf5 36 ♖xc5 ♖f6] 35 ♖xc5! ♖e3 [35 ... ♖xc5 36 ♗e6+−] 36 ♖xc6 **1-0** Staunton(1)

### 1851-LON2-6
**Robertson−Ranken, C.E.**

[Staunton]

1 e4 e5 2 ♘f3 ♘c6 3 ♗c4 ♗c5 4 0-0 ♘f6 5 d3 h6 6 c3 d6 7 d4 exd4 8 cxd4 ♗b6 9 ♘c3 ♗g4 10 ♗b5 0-0 11 ♗xc6 bxc6 12 ♗e3 ♕d7 13 e5 ♘d5 14 ♘e4 ♖ae8 15 ♘ed2 dxe5 16 ♕a4 e4 17 ♘e5 ♖xe5! 18 dxe5 ♘xe3 19 fxe3 ♕xd2 20 ♕xe4 ♗xe3+ [□ 20 ... ♕xe3+] 21 ♔h1 ♗h5 [21 ... ♗e6? 22 ♖fd1! ♗d5 23 ♖xd2 ♗xe4 24 ♖e2+−] 22 e6 ♖e8 23 ♕f5 ♖xe6 [□ 23 ... ♕d5] 24 ♕xh5 ♖g6 25 ♕h3 ♗d4 26 ♖ae1 ♖f6 27 ♖e8+ ♔h7 28 g3 ♗f2 29 ♕g2 ♕xb2 30 ♕e4+ g6 31 ♕e2 [□ 31 ♖b1] 31 ... ♕b6 [31 ... ♕xe2 32 ♖xe2=] 32 ♖d1 ♗d4 33 ♕e4 c5 34 ♕a8 ♖f2 35 ♖b8 ♕e6 **0-1**

Staunton(1)

### 1851-LON2-7
**Gilby−Deacon**

[Staunton]

1 e4 e5 2 ♘f3 ♘c6 3 ♗c4 ♗c5 4 0-0 ♘f6 5 b4 ♗xb4 6 c3 ♗d6 7 d4 ♕e7 8 ♗g5 [□ 8 ♘g5] 8 ... 0-0 9 ♗b5? [□ 9 ♘h4 exd4 10 f4± ♕xe4?? 11 ♖e1+−] 9 ... ♘d8 10 ♖e1 c6 11 dxe5 ♗xe5 12 ♗a4 ♖e8 = 13 ♗b3 d6 14 ♘xe5 ♕xe5 15 f4 ♕c5+ 16 ♔h1 ♘xe4 17 ♕d2 ♗d7 [17 ... ♘f2+?? 18 ♕xf2!+−] 18 ♖xe4 ♖xe4 19 h3 h6 20 ♗c2 ♖e8 21 ♗h4 ♕h5 22 ♕xd6? ♕xh4 23 ♘d2 ♗xh3 24 ♘f3 ♗xg2+ 25 ♔xg2 ♖e2+ 26 ♔g1 ♕f2+ 27 ♔h1 ♕g2# **0-1** Staunton(1)

### 1851-LON2-8
**Deacon−Gilby**

[Staunton]

1 c4 c5 2 ♘c3 e6 3 e3 b6 4 f4 ♗b7 5 ♘f3 ♘a6 6 ♗e2 ♘h6 7 0-0 ♘c7 8 a3 ♗e7 9 ♖b1 ♖b8?! 10 b4 0-0 11 ♕a4 cxb4 12 axb4 ♘a6 13 ♘e5 ♖c8 14 c5 ♘b8?! 15 ♕xa7 d6 16 cxd6 ♕xd6 17 ♕xb7 f6 18 ♘c4 ♕d8 19 ♕xb6 ♕d7 20 ♖a1 ♘c6 21 b5 ♘d8 22 ♖a7 ♕e8 23 ♘e4 ♕g6 24 f5 [24 ♖xe7 ♕xe4 25 ♘d6+−] 24 ... ♘xf5 25 ♖d7 ♖e8 26 ♖f4 h5 27 ♗d3 e5 28 ♘ed6 ♗xd6 29 ♖xf5 [29 ♗xf5 △ 30 ♖f1+−] 29 ... ♖xc4 30 ♗xc4+ ♔h7 31 ♗d3? [□ 31 ♖xd6 ♕xf5 32 ♖xd8 ♖xd8 33 ♕xd8+−] 31 ... e4

32 ♖f4? [□ 32 ♖xd8 ♕xf5 (32 ... ♖xd8 33 ♗xe4+−) 33 ♖xe8 ♗xh2+ 34 ♔xh2 exd3 35 ♕b8+−] 32 ... ♗xf4 33 exf4 exd3 34 ♖xd8 ♖e1+ 35 ♔f2 ♖e2+ 36 ♔∼ ♕xg2# **0-1** Staunton(1)

### 1851-LON2-9
**Gilby−Deacon**

[Staunton]

1 e4 c5 2 f4 e6 3 ♘f3 d5 4 d3 b6 [4 ... dxe4 5 dxe4 ♕xd1+ 6 ♔xd1] 5 exd5 exd5 6 ♗e2 ♗d6 7 d4 ♘c6 8 c3 ♘ge7 9 0-0 ♕c7 10 ♘e5 0-0 11 ♗f3 ♗xe5 12 fxe5 ♗e6 13 ♗g4 ♕d7 14 ♗e2 a6 15 a4 cxd4 16 cxd4 ♘f5 17 ♖f4 ♕c8! 18 ♖a3 [18 ♘c3 ♘cxd4 19 ♖xd4 ♕c5−+; 18 g4 ♘cxd4 19 gxf5 ♘xe2+ 20 ♕xe2 ♕xc1+−+] 18 ... ♘cxd4 19 ♖c3 ♘xe2+ 20 ♕xe2 ♕d7 21 g4 ♘e7 22 ♗e3 ♘g6 23 ♖b4 ♘xe5 24 ♗f4 ♘c4 25 b3?? ♕e7 26 ♗d2?! ♘xd2 27 ♖xb6 ♘xb1 28 ♖d3 ♕c5+ 29 ♕e3 ♕xe3+ 30 ♖xe3 ♖fc8 **0-1**

Staunton(1)

### 1851-LON2-10
**Wellman−Hodges**

[Staunton]

1 e4 c5 2 ♗c4 e6 3 ♘f3 ♘c6 4 c3 a6 5 a3 b5 6 ♗a2 ♗b7 7 d3 a5 8 a4 b4 9 0-0 ♘ge7 10 c4? g6 11 ♘bd2 ♗g7 12 ♖b1 0-0 13 b3? d5 14 ♗b2 d4 15 ♘e1 f5 16 f3 ♕c7 17 ♕e2 ♘e5 18 f4? ♘g4 [△ 19 ... ♘e3] 19 ♖f3 fxe4 20 ♘xe4 ♘f5 21 g3 e5 22 ♗c1 ♖ae8 23 ♖f1? [□ 23 ♘g2] 23 ... ♘ge3 24 ♗xe3 ♘xe3 25 ♖f3 ♗xe4 26 dxe4 exf4 27 gxf4 ♖xf4 28 ♘g2 ♖fxe4 29 ♘xe3 ♖xe3 30 ♖xe3 ♖xe3 31 ♕f2 d3! **0-1**

Staunton(1)

### 1851-LON2-11
**Hodges=Wellman**

[Staunton]

1 d4 d5 2 c4 e6 3 e3 c5 4 ♘f3 ♘c6 5 ♘c3 b6? [□ 5 ... ♘f6] 6 dxc5 ♗xc5 7 cxd5 exd5 8 ♕xd5 ♗b7 9 ♕e4+ [9 ♗a6!?] 9 ... ♘ge7 10 ♗b5 0-0 11 0-0 ♕c7 12 ♘g5 ♘g6 13 ♘d5 ♕e5 14 ♗xc6 ♗xc6 15 ♕xe5 ♘xe5 16 ♘c3 ♖ad8 17 ♘ge4 ♗e7 18 a3 f5 19 ♘g3 ♗d6 20 ♘ge2 ♗b8 21 b3 ♖d6 22 ♘d4 ♗b7 23 a4 ♖g6 24 f3 ♘d3 25 ♗a3 ♘c5 [25 ... ♖c8] 26 ♗xc5 bxc5 27 ♘db5 a6 28 ♘a3 h5 29 ♘c4 h4 30 ♖ad1 ♖f7 31 ♖d3 ♗c7 32 ♔f2?? ♗xh2 33 ♖fd1 ♗g3+ 34 ♔f1 ♔h7 35 ♘d6 [□ 35 f4] 35 ... ♗xd6 36 ♖xd6 ♖xd6 37 ♖xd6 ♖c7 38 ♔f2 ♖c6 39 ♖xc6 ♗xc6 40 ♔e2 ♔g6 41 ♔f2 [41 ♔d3] 41 ... ♔h5 42 g3 hxg3+ 43 ♔xg3 ♔h6 44 ♔f2 ...? **½-½** Staunton(1)

### 1851-LON2-12
**Hodges+Wellman**

[Staunton]

1 e4 e6 2 d4 d5 3 exd5 exd5 4 ♘f3 ♗d6 5 ♗d3 h6? [5 ... ♘f6] 6 0-0 ♘f6 7 ♖e1+ ♗e6 8 ♗f5 ♔d7 9 ♘e5+ ♗xe5 10 dxe5 ♗xf5 11

exf6 ♕xf6 12 ♕xd5+ ♔c8 13 ♗f4 ♖d8 [□ 13 ... ♗xc2] 14 ♕c5 ♘a6 15 ♕a5 ♗xc2 16 ♗e5 ♕g6 17 ♘a3 ♗e4 18 g3 ♗c6 19 ♕c3 ♕f5 [□ 19 ... ♖d3∓] 20 ♖e3 ♕h3 21 f3 f6 22 ♗d4 ♕h5 23 b3 ♖d6 24 ♘c4 ♖d5 25 ♖ae1 b6 26 ♘xb6+! axb6 27 ♕xc6 ♖b8 28 ♖e8+ ♖d8 29 ♖1e7 **1-0** Staunton(1)

**165(50)** Boden, S.S. M960. BL

### 1851-LON2-13
**Boden, S.S.= Brien, R.B.**

[Staunton]

1 e4 e5 2 ♗c4 ♗c5 3 ♘f3 ♘c6 4 0-0 d6 5 h3 ♘f6 6 ♘c3 ♗e6 7 ♗b3 ♕d7 8 ♔h2 0-0 9 d3 h6 10 ♗e3 ♗b6 11 ♘e2 ♘e7 12 ♘g3 ♘g6 13 ♕d2 ♔h7 14 ♖ad1 d5 15 exd5 ♘xd5 16 d4 [16 ♗xb6 △ 17 d4] 16 ... ♘xe3 [16 ... f5!?] 17 fxe3 ♗xb3 18 axb3 ♖ad8 19 c4 exd4 20 exd4 c6 21 ♕c2 ♗c7 22 ♘e5? ♗xe5 23 dxe5 ♕e6 24 ♖de1 ♔g8 25 ♕c3 ♖de8 26 ♘f5 ♘xe5 27 ♕g3 ♕g6 28 ♕c3 f6 29 ♖e3 ♕h7 30 ♖g3 g6 31 ♕d2 ♘f7 32 h4 ♔h8 33 ♘d6 ♘xd6 34 ♕xd6 ♕f7 35 ♕d3 ♔g7 36 ♖ff3 ♖d8 37 ♕e3 ♖fe8 38 ♕xa7 ♖d1 39 ♖e3 ♖xe3 40 ♕xe3 ♖d7 41 ♖f3 ...? **½-½** Staunton(1)

### 1851-LON2-14
**Brien, R.B.+ Boden, S.S.**

[Staunton]

1 e4 e6 2 d4 d5 3 exd5 exd5 4 ♘f3 ♗d6 5 ♗d3 ♘f6 6 0-0 0-0 7 h3 h6 8 ♗e3 ♗e6 9 c3 ♕d7 10 ♘e5 ♘c6?? 11 ♘xd7 **1-0** Staunton(1)

### 1851-LON2-15
**Boden, S.S.+ Brien, R.B.**

[Staunton]

1 e4 e5 2 d4 exd4 3 ♗c4 ♗b4+ [3 ... ♘f6] 4 c3 dxc3 5 bxc3 ♕f6 [5 ... ♗e7?? 6 ♕d5+-; 5 ... ♗a5 6 ♕d5+-; 5 ... ♗c5? 6 ♗xf7+±] 6 cxb4 ♕xa1 7 ♕b3 ♕f6 8 ♗b2 [8 ♘c3] 8 ... ♕g6 9 ♘e2 d5 10 ♗xd5 ♘h6 11 0-0 0-0 12 ♘bc3 c6 13 ♗c4 ♗e6 14 ♘f4 ♗xc4 15 ♕xc4 [15 ♘xg6 ♗xb3 16 ♘xf8 ♗c4-+] 15 ... ♕g4 16 ♘ce2 ♘d7 17 f3 ♕g5 18 ♕c3 f6? 19 ♘e6 ♕b5 20 ♘xf8 ♘xf8 21 ♕b3+ ♔h8 22 ♘d4 ♕b6 23 ♔h1 ♖d8 24 ♕c4 ♕c7 25 ♕e2 [□ 25 f4] 25 ... ♖e8 26 ♗c1 ♕e5 27 ♕f2 ♘f7 28 ♘f5 ♕b5 29 a3 ♖d8 30 ♖e1 [□ 30 ♖g1] 30 ... ♘e5 31 ♕g3 ♘e6 32 ♖g1 ♕e2 33 h4 ♘d3 34 ♔h2 g6 35 ♘h6 ♖d7 36 ♕b8+ ♘d8 [△ 37 ... ♕f2] 37 ♘g4 [37 ♕c8; 37 ♘f7+!?] 37 ... ♘xc1 38 ♖xc1 ♕b2 39 ♕f4 f5? 40 exf5 ♖d2 41 fxg6 ♘e6 42 ♕e5+ [42 ♕f7!+-] 42 ... ♕xe5+ 43 ♘xe5 ♖e2 44 ♘f7+ ♔g7 45 gxh7 ♔xh7 46 ♘g5+ ♘xg5 47 hxg5 **1-0** Staunton(1)

### 1851-LON2-16
**Brien, R.B.– Boden, S.S.**

[Staunton]

1 e4 e5 2 ♘f3 d6 3 d4 exd4 4 ♘xd4 d5 5 ♗d3 [□ 5 ♘f3! dxe4 6 ♕xd8+ ♔xd8 7 ♘g5±; 5 e5 c5] 5 ... c5 6 ♘b5 c4 7 ♗e2 a6 8 ♕xd5!? axb5 [8 ... ♕xd5 9 ♘c7+ △ 10 ♘xd5] 9 ♕xb5+ ♘c6 10 ♗xc4 ♕a5+ 11 ♘c3 ♗d6 12 f4 ♘ge7 13 ♗d2 0-0 14 ♕xa5?! ♘xa5 15 ♗d3 ♘ac6 16 0-0 ♗c5+ 17 ♔h1 ♘b4 18 ♖f3 b6 19 ♘b5 ♘xd3 20 cxd3 ♗d7 21 ♘c3 ♖fd8 22 ♗e3 ♗xe3 23 ♖xe3 ♘c6 24 a3 ♘d4 25 ♖c1 ♖dc8 26 ♔g1 ♘b5 27 ♔f2 ♘xc3 28 bxc3 ♖xa3 29 d4 b5 30 d5 ♔f8 31 e5 ♔e7 32 h3 h5 33 e6? [□ 33 g4] 33 ... fxe6 34 dxe6 ♗c6 35 ♖d1? ♖a2+ 36 ♔g3 ♖xg2+ 37 ♔h4 ♖f8 38 ♖d4 ♖f2 39 ♔g5 h4! [△ 40 ... ♖g2+ 41 ♔xh4 ♖h8#] 40 ♖e5 ♖g2+ 41 ♔xh4 ♗e8! [△ 42 ... ♖h8+ 43 ♖h5 ♖xh5#] **0-1** Staunton(1)

### 1851-LON2-17
**Deacon– Ranken, C.E.**

[Staunton]

1 c4 c5 2 ♘c3 ♘c6 3 e3 e6 4 g3 d5 5 cxd5 exd5 6 ♕b3 ♘f6 7 ♗g2 d4 8 ♘ce2 [□ 8 ♘d5] 8 ... ♕c7 9 exd4 cxd4 10 a3 ♗c5 11 f4 0-0 12 ♕d3 a5 13 b3 ♖e8 14 ♗b2 ♗g4 15 ♘f3 ♕e7 16 h3 ♗f5 ∓ 17 ♕c4 d3 18 ♘e5 ♘xe5 [□ 18 ... dxe2 19 ♘xc6 bxc6 20 ♗xc6 ♖ac8-+] 19 fxe5 ♘d7 20 ♕f4 ♗g6 21 ♘c1 ♘xe5 22 ♔d1 ♗d6 23 ♖e1 ♘c4 24 ♖xe7 ♘xb2+ 25 ♔e1 ♖xe7+ 26 ♔f2 ♗xf4 27 gxf4 ♖ac8 28 b4 a4 29 ♘a2 ♖e2+ 30 ♔g3 ♖xd2 31 ♗xb7 ♖cc2 32 ♖e1 ♖e2 33 ♖f1 ♗e4 34 ♗xe4 ♖xe4 35 ♔f3 ♖ee2 36 ♘c1 ♖f2+ 37 ♖xf2 ♖xf2+ 38 ♔xf2 d2 39 ♘d3 d1♕ 40 ♘xb2 ♕d2+ **0-1** Staunton(1)

### 1851-LON2-18
**Ranken, C.E.+ Deacon**

[Staunton]

1 d4 d5 2 c4 e6 3 ♘c3 ♘f6 4 e3 c5 5 ♘f3 a6 6 ♗d3 dxc4 7 ♗xc4 b5 8 ♗d3 ♗b7 9 0-0 ♘bd7 10 ♕e2 ♘b6 11 ♖d1 ♕c7 12 dxc5 ♗xc5 13 a3 ♖d8 14 h3 0-0 ∓ 15 b4 ♗xf3? 16 ♕xf3 ♕e5 17 ♗b2 ♗d6 18 g3 ♕g5 19 ♗e2 ♘fd5 20 ♘e4 ♕e7 21 ♖ac1 f5 22 ♘xd6 ♕xd6 23 e4 fxe4 24 ♕xe4 ♘d7 25 ♗g4 ♖fe8 26 ♗xe6+! ♖xe6 27 ♕xd5 ♕xd5 28 ♖xd5 ♖e2 29 ♗d4 ♖ee8 30 ♖c7 ♘f6 31 ♖xd8 ♖xd8 32 ♗xf6 gxf6 33 ♖c6 ♖a8 34 ♖xf6 a5 35 ♖b6 axb4 36 axb4 ♔f7 37 ♖xb5 ♔e6 38 ♖b7 ♔d6 39 ♖xh7 ♔c6 40 ♖h4 ♔b5 41 ♖e4 ♖a3 42 ♔g2 ♖b3 43 h4 ♔c6 44 h5 ♔d5 45 ♖f4 ♖a3 46 h6 ♖a8 47 g4 ♖h8 48 ♖f6 ♔e5 49 g5 ♖b8 50 f4+ ♔e4 51 h7 ♖xb4 52 h8♕ ♖b2+ 53 ♔g3 ♖b3+ 54 ♔g4 ♔d3 55 ♕h3+ ♔c2 56 ♖c6+ ♔b2 57 ♕g2+ ♔a3 58 ♕d2 ♔a4 59 ♕a2+ ♔b5 60 ♕a6+ ♔~ 61 ♖c4# **1-0** Staunton(1)

### 1851-LON2-19
**Hodges= Ranken, C.E.**

[Staunton]

1 d4 e6 2 e4 d5 3 exd5 exd5 4 ♘f3 ♘f6 5 ♗d3 ♗d6 6 0-0 0-0 7 ♗g5 ♗e6 8 ♘c3 ♘bd7 9 ♘e2 c5 10 b3 ♕b6 11 ♖b1 ♕c7 12 c4 ♘e4 13 h3 f5 14 ♖c1 ♕b6 15 ♗e3 ♖ae8

16 dxc5 [16 cxd5! ♗xd5 17 ♗xe4 ♗xe4 18 dxc5 ♗xc5! (18 ... ♘xc5? 19 b4 +-) 19 ♕xd7 ♗xe3 20 fxe3 ♕xe3+ 21 ♖f2 ♗xf3 22 ♖c7 (22 gxf3∓) ♕g5 23 ♖xf3 ♖xe2 24 ♕d5+ ♔h8 25 ♖xf5 ♕e3+ 26 ♔h2 ♖g8 27 ♖xb7 ♖e1 28 ♕c5+-] 16 ... ♗xc5 17 ♗xc5 ♘dxc5 18 cxd5 ♗xd5 19 ♗c4 ♗xc4 20 ♖xc4 ♖d8 21 ♖d4 ♘e6 22 ♖xd8 ♖xd8 23 ♕c2 ♕d6 24 ♕c4 ♕d5 25 ♕xd5 ♖xd5 26 ♖c1 ♘d2 27 ♘xd2 ♖xd2 28 ♘c3 ♘f4 29 ♖d1 ♖xd1+ 30 ♘xd1 **½-½** Staunton(1)

### 1851-LON2-20
**Ranken, C.E.+Hodges**

[Staunton]

1 e4 c5 2 ♗c4 ♘c6 3 a3 a6 4 d3 g6 5 ♘c3 e6 6 ♘ge2 ♗g7 7 0-0 ♘ge7 8 ♗f4 d6 9 ♕d2 d5 10 exd5 exd5 11 ♗a2 ♗e6 12 ♖fe1 0-0 13 ♘g3 b5 14 ♗h6 ♗xh6 15 ♕xh6 ♘d4 16 ♕d2 ♕d7 17 ♘ce2 ♘xe2+ 18 ♖xe2 ♖ac8 19 ♖ae1 ♘f5? 20 ♘xf5 ♗xf5 21 c3 ♗e6 22 d4 c4 23 ♗b1 ♕d6 24 ♕h6 ♖c7 [□ 24 ... ♖fe8 △ 25 ... ♕f8] 25 ♖e5 ♖d7 26 h4 ♗g4 27 f3 f6 28 ♖5e2 [□ 28 ♖e8 ♗f5 (28 ... ♗h5 29 ♖xf8+ ♕xf8 30 ♕xf8+ △ 31 g4+-) 29 ♗xf5 gxf5 30 ♖1e6 ♖xe8 31 ♖xe8+ ♔f7 32 ♖h8 ♔e6 (32 ... ♖e7 33 ♕xh7+ ♔e6 34 ♕g8+ ♖f7 35 ♖h7 ♕e7 36 h5+-) 33 ♕e3+ ♔f7 34 ♕e8+ ♔g7 35 h5 ♕e7 36 ♕g8+ ♔h6 37 ♕g6#. 28 ... ♖xe8 29 ♖xe8+ ♔f7 30 ♗xg6+ hxg6 31 ♕h8+-] 28 ... ♗h5 29 ♖e6 ♕c7 [29 ... ♕g3? 30 ♖e7+-] 30 ♖xf6 ♖df7 31 ♖xf7 ♕xf7 32 ♕e3 ♕c7 33 ♕e6+ ♖f7 34 ♖e5 ♔g7 35 ♕xd5 ♕c8 36 ♖e6 h6 37 ♕e5+ ♔h7 38 ♖e8 **1-0**

Staunton(1)

### 1851-LON2-21
**Hodges+Ranken, C.E.**

[Staunton]

1 e4 e5 2 ♘f3 ♘c6 3 ♗c4 ♗c5 4 b4 ♗xb4 5 c3 ♗a5 6 0-0 ♘f6 7 d4 0-0 8 ♗a3 d6 9 dxe5 ♘xe4 10 exd6 ♘xd6 11 ♕b3 ♕f6 12 ♖e1 ♗b6 13 ♗d5 ♗d7 14 ♘bd2 ♖ae8 15 ♘e4 ♕g6 16 ♘eg5 ♖xe1+ 17 ♖xe1 h6 18 ♘e4 ♖e8 19 ♗xd6 cxd6 20 h3 ♘e7 [20 ... ♗xh3?? 21 ♘f6++-] 21 ♘xd6 ♕xd6 22 ♗xf7+ ♔f8 23 ♗xe8 ♗xe8 24 ♖e6 ♕c5 25 ♕c2 ♘c6 26 ♖e4 ♗f7 27 ♖f4 ♔g8 28 ♖f5 ♕c4 29 ♘e5 ♘xe5 30 ♖xe5 ♕xa2?? 31 ♖e8+ ♗xe8 32 ♕xa2+ **1-0**

Staunton(1)

### 1851-LON2-22
**Ranken, C.E.+Hodges**

[Staunton]

1 e4 c5 2 ♗c4 ♘c6 3 d3 e6 4 ♘c3 a6 5 a3 g6 6 ♘f3 ♗g7 7 0-0 ♘ge7 8 ♗f4 0-0 9 ♖b1 d5 10 ♗a2 d4 11 ♘e2 e5 12 ♗g5 ♔h8 13 ♕d2 f5 14 ♗h6 f4 15 ♗xg7+ ♔xg7 16 h3 ♘g8 17 c3 [□ 17 ♗xg8] 17 ... g5 18 cxd4 cxd4 19 ♘h2 h5∓ 20 f3 ♘h6 21 ♔h1 g4 22 fxg4 hxg4 23 ♘g1 g3 24 ♘hf3

24 ... ♖h8 [□ 24 ... ♘g4! 25 hxg4 ♖h8+ 26 ♘h3 ♗xg4 27 ♘fg1 ♖h6 28 ♕c2 ♕f6 29 ♕b3 ♖ah8 30 ♕xb7+ ♘e7 31 ♕c7 ♗xh3 32 gxh3 (32 ♘xh3 f3 33 ♔g1! f2+ 34 ♖xf2 ♖xh3-+) 32 ... ♖c8! (32 ... ♖xh3+? 33 ♘xh3 ♖xh3 34 ♔g2∞; 32 ... f3? 33 ♘xf3 ♖xh3+ 34 ♔g2∞) 33 ♕a5 ♖c2 34 ♘f3 g2+ 35 ♔g1 gxf1♕+ 36 ♔xf1 ♖xh3-+] 25 ♘xe5! ♘xe5 26 ♕xf4 ♘g6 27 ♕xg3 ♕e7 28 ♘e2 ♕e5 29 ♘f4 ♘g4 30 ♔g1 ♖f8 31 ♘h5+ ♕xh5 32 ♕c7+ ♔h6 33 ♖xf8 ♘xf8 34 hxg4 ♗xg4 35 ♖f1 ♘g6 36 ♖f7 ♕e5? [□ 36 ... ♖h8=] 37 ♕c1+ ♘f4 38 ♖xf4 ♔h5 39 ♗f7+ ♔h4 40 ♔f2 **1-0** Staunton(1)

### 1851-LON2-23
**Boden, S.S.–Ranken, C.E.**

[Staunton]

1 e4 e5 2 f4 exf4 3 ♘f3 g5 4 ♗c4 ♗g7 5 0-0 h6 6 d4 d6 7 c3 ♘e7 8 ♘a3 [□ 8 g3] 8 ... ♘g6 9 g3 g4 10 ♘e1 f3 11 ♘xf3!? [8 ♘d3] 11 ... gxf3 12 ♕xf3 0-0 13 ♗xf7+ ♔h7 14 e5 ♖xf7 15 ♕xf7 [△ 16 ♖f6] 15 ... dxe5 16 ♗e3 ♗h3 17 ♖f2 ♕d7 18 dxe5 ♘xe5 19 ♕b3 ♕c6 20 ♕d1 ♘bd7 21 ♗d4 ♖f8 22 ♕c2+ ♔g8 23 ♖xf8+ ♗xf8 24 ♖d1 ♘f3+ 25 ♔f2 ♘de5 26 ♗xe5 ♘xe5 27 ♔e1 ♗e7 28 ♕e2 ♘f3+ 29 ♔f2 ♗c5+ 30 ♖d4 ♘xd4 31 cxd4 ♗xd4+ **0-1**

Staunton(1)

### 1851-LON2-24
**Ranken, C.E.–Boden, S.S.**

[Staunton]

1 e4 e5 2 ♘f3 ♘c6 3 ♗c4 ♗c5 4 c3 ♘f6 5 d4 exd4 6 e5 d5 7 ♗b5 ♘e4 8 cxd4 ♗b6 9 ♗e3 0-0 10 ♘c3 f6 11 ♕b3 ♘xc3 12 ♗xc6 bxc6 13 ♕xc3 ♕e8 14 0-0? [□ 14 exf6 ♖xf6 (14 ... gxf6 15 ♖ac1 ♗d7 16 0-0±) 15 ♘e5 ♗d7 (15 ... ♗a6 16 a4+-; 15 ... ♗b7 16 a4±) 16 0-0±] 14 ... ♗g4 15 exf6 ♗xf3 16 fxg7 ♕g6!!

17 gxf8♕+ ♖xf8 18 g3 ♕g4 19 ♗f4 ♖xf4 20 ♕e3 ♕h3 21 ♕e8+ ♖f8 **0-1** Staunton(1)

### 1851-LON2-25
**Boden, S.S.+Ranken, C.E.**

[Staunton]

1 e4 e5 2 ♗c4 ♗c5 3 c3 ♘c6 4 d4 exd4 5 ♘f3 ♘f6 6 cxd4 ♗b4+ 7 ♗d2 ♗xd2+ 8 ♘bxd2 d5 9 exd5 ♘xd5 10 0-0 [□ 10 ♕b3 ♘ce7] 10 ... 0-0 11 ♘e4 ♘ce7 12 ♕b3 c6 13 ♖ad1 ♘g6 14 ♗xd5 cxd5 15 ♘c3 b6? 16 ♕xd5 ♗g4 17 ♕e4 f5 18 ♕d3 ♘h4 19 ♔h1 [19 ♘e2 ♗xf3 20 gxf3 ♕g5+ 21 ♘g3 f4-+] 19 ... ♘xf3 20 gxf3 ♗h3 21 ♖g1 f4 22 ♘e4 ♕h4 23 ♘g5 ♗f5? [□ 23 ... ♔h8] 24 ♕c4+ ♔h8 25 ♘f7+ ♖xf7 26 ♕xf7 **1-0**

Staunton(1)

### 1851-LON2-26
**Hodges=Brien, R.B.**

[Staunton]

1 d4 d5 2 c4 e6 3 e3 c5 4 ♘f3 ♘c6 5 ♘c3 ♘f6 6 h3 a6 7 a3 ♗d6 8 dxc5 ♗xc5 9 cxd5 exd5 10 ♗d3 0-0 11 0-0 h6 12 b4 ♗d6 13 ♗b2 ♗e6 14 ♘e2 ♘e4 15 ♖c1 ♕d7 16 ♘f4 ♗xf4 17 exf4 f5 18 ♖e1 ♕f7 19 ♖e3 ♔h7 20 ♕e1 ♕h5 21 ♘h2 ♗d7? 22 f3 [□ 22 g4! fxg4 23 hxg4 ♕~ (23 ... ♗xg4 24 ♘xg4 ♕xg4 25 ♖g3+-) 24 f3+-; 22 ... ♕g6 23 f3 d4 24 ♖e2 (24 ♖xe4?) ♘d6 25 ♕f2 ♕f6 26 h4±] 22 ... ♘f6 23 ♖c2 d4 24 ♖ee2 ♘d5 25 ♕g3 ♖ae8 26 ♘g4 ♖xe2 27 ♖xe2 ♖e8 28 ♖xe8 ♕xe8 29 ♘e5 ♘xf4 30 ♘xc6 ♕e3+ 31 ♔h2 ♘xd3 32 ♗xd4 ♕f4 33 ♕xf4 ♘xf4 ½-½ Staunton(1)

### 1851-LON2-27
**Brien, R.B.–Hodges**

[Staunton]

1 e4 c5 2 ♗c4 ♘c6 3 ♘c3 e6 4 d3 g6 5 f4 ♗g7 6 ♘f3 d6 7 0-0 ♘ge7 8 ♗e3 a6 9 d4 cxd4 10 ♘xd4 0-0 11 ♘ce2 b5 12 ♗d3 f5 13 exf5 exf5 14 c3 ♔h8 15 ♘g3 ♘xd4 16 cxd4 ♘d5 17 ♕f3 ♘xe3 [17 ... ♗b7] 18 ♕xe3 ♕b6 19 ♘e2 ♗b7 20 ♔h1 ♖fe8 21 ♕f2 ♖e7 22 ♖ac1 ♖ae8 23 h3 ♖e3! 24 ♖c3 ♗xd4 25 ♘xd4

♕xd4 → 26 ♕h4 ♖xd3 27 ♖c7 ♗xg2+ 28 ♔xg2 ♖e2+ **0-1**
Staunton(1)

**1851-LON2-28**
**Hodges– Brien, R.B.**
[Staunton]
1 d4 d5 2 c4 dxc4 3 e3 e5 4 ♗xc4 exd4 5 exd4 ♘f6 6 ♘f3 ♗d6 7 h3 h6 8 0-0 0-0 9 ♘c3 ♗f5 10 ♗e3 ♕d7 11 ♖e1 ♘c6 12 a3 a6 13 ♗d3 ♘e7 14 ♖c1 ♘g6 15 ♕c2 ♗xh3 16 gxh3 ♕xh3 17 ♗xg6 fxg6 18 ♘e5 ♗xe5 19 dxe5 ♘g4 20 ♕e4 ♖xf2!? [20 ... ♖f3! 21 ♗f4 ♘xf2 22 ♕d5+ ♔h7 23 ♗h2 ♕g4+ 24 ♔f1 ♘d3+→] 21 ♗f4 g5 22 ♕h1 [□ 22 ♘d5 (Δ 23 ♘e7+=) 22 ... ♖xf4∞] 22 ... ♕xh1+ 23 ♔xh1 gxf4 24 ♘d5 ♖xb2 [□ 24 ... f3! 25 ♖ed1 (25 ♘f4 ♖h2+→) 25 ... ♖h2+ 26 ♔g1 ♖g2+ 27 ♔f1 ♘h2+ 28 ♔e1 ♖e2#] 25 ♖xc7 ♘f2+ 26 ♔g1 ♘h3+ 27 ♔h1 f3 28 e6 ♖g2 29 e7 ♘f2# **0-1**
Staunton(1)

**1851-LON2-29**
**Brien, R.B.– Hodges**
[Staunton]
1 d4 d5 2 c4 e6 3 e3 ♘f6 4 ♘c3 c5 5 ♘f3 dxc4 6 ♗xc4 cxd4 7 exd4 ♗d6 8 a3 0-0 9 0-0 h6 10 h3 a6 11 b4 b5 12 ♗d3 ♗b7 13 ♖a2 ♘bd7 14 ♖e1 ♘b6 15 ♕e2 ♖c8 16 ♖c2 ♘c4 [16 ... ♗b8] 17 ♘d2 ♗b8 18 ♘ce4 ♕xd4 19 ♘xf6+ ♕xf6 20 ♘xc4 bxc4 21 ♗xc4 ♕g6 22 f4 ♕g3 23 ♕f2 ♕g6 24 ♗b3 ♗e4 25 ♖ce2 ♗f5 26 ♔h2 ♖c3 27 ♗a2 ♕h5 28 ♖e3 ♗a7 [28 ... ♖fc8] 29 ♕f3 ♕xf3 30 ♖xf3 ♖xf3 31 gxf3 ♖c8 32 ♗b3 ♖c3 33 ♗a4 ♖xf3 34 b5 axb5 35 ♗xb5 ♖xh3+ 36 ♔g2 ♖c3 37 a4 ♖c2+ 38 ♔h1 ♗g4 39 ♗e3 ♗b8 40 ♖c1 ♖xc1+ 41 ♗xc1 ♗f3+ 42 ♔h2 g5 43 a5 ♗a8 44 a6 ♗xf4+ 45 ♗xf4 gxf4 46 ♗d7 [Δ 47 ♗c8 ~ 48 ♗b7] 46 ... ♗d5 47 ♗c8 ♗c4 48 a7? [□ 48 ♗b7] 48 ... ♗d5 49 ♗a6 ♔f8 50 ♔g1 ♔e8 51 ♔f2 ♔d8 52 ♗e2 ♔c7 **0-1**
Staunton(1)

## LONDON 3 1851

**1851-LON3-1**
**Kieseritsky, L.–Anderssen, A.**
[Anderssen & Nathan]
1 e4 c5 2 ♗c4 e6 3 ♘c3 ♘e7 4 ♕e2 ♘bc6 5 ♘f3 a6 6 d3 ♘g6 7 0-0 ♗e7 8 ♗e3 0-0 9 d4 b5 10 dxc5 bxc4 11 ♕xc4 f5 12 ♖fd1 f4 13 ♗d4 ♘xd4 14 ♕xd4 ♕c7 15 b4 ♗f6 16 ♕c4 ♘e5 17 ♘xe5 ♗xe5 18 ♖ab1 ♗xc3 19 ♕xc3 ♗b7 20 f3 ♗c6 21 ♖d6 ♕d8 22 ♕d2 ♕g5 23 c4 ♕e5∓ 24 ♔f1 ♖ab8 25 a4 ♗xa4 26 ♖xa6 ♖a8 27 ♖d6 ♖a7 28 ♖d3 ♖fa8 29 ♖a3 ♗b5 30 ♖c3 ♖a2 31 ♕d3 ♕g5 32 ♖c2 ♖a1 33 ♖cc1 ♖8a2 **0-1**
L/N6047-1852

**1851-LON3-2**
**Anderssen, A.= Horwitz, B.**
[Anderssen & Nathan]
1 e4 e5 2 f4 exf4 3 ♗c4 ♕h4+ 4 ♔f1 d6 5 ♘c3 g5 6 ♘f3 ♕h5 7 ♘d5 ♔d8 8 d4 ♗e6 9 ♕d3 ♘e7 10 ♘xe7 ♗xc4 11 ♕xc4 ♗xe7 12 ♕b5 b6 13 ♗xf4 f5 14 ♘xg5 [□ 14 ♗xg5] 14 ... ♗xg5 15 ♕xf5 h6 16 h4 ♘d7 17 ♔g1 ♖f8 18 ♕d5 c6 19 ♗xg5+ hxg5 20 ♕xd6 gxh4 21 e5 ♕e2 22 ♖h3 ♖g8 23 ♕xc6 ♖c8 24 ♕d5 ♕c4 25 ♕xc4 ♖xc4 26 c3 ♖g4 27 ♖f1 ♖c6 28 ♖f2 ♖cg6 29 ♖hf3 a5 30 ♔h2 ♔e7 31 ♖f7+ ♔e8 32 ♖7f4 ♔e7 **½-½**
L/N6047-1852

**1851-LON3-3**
**Anderssen, A.+ Horwitz, B.**
[Anderssen & Nathan]
1 e4 e5 2 ♘f3 ♘c6 3 d4 exd4 4 ♗c4 ♗c5 5 0-0 d6 6 c3 ♗g4 7 ♕b3 ♗xf3 8 ♗xf7+ ♔f8 9 ♗xg8 ♖xg8 10 gxf3 ♘e5 11 cxd4 ♗xd4 12 f4 ♘g4 13 ♕g3 ♘f6 14 ♕g2 [□ 14 ♕f3] 14 ... d5 15 e5 ♘e4 [Δ g5] 16 ♕f3! ♕h4 17 ♘c3 ♗xc3 18 bxc3 ♖d8 19 c4 c6 20 cxd5 cxd5 21 ♗e3 b6 22 ♖ac1 ♕e7 23 ♖c6 g6 24 ♔h1 ♖g7 25 ♖fc1 ♔g8 26 ♗d4 ♘d2 27 ♕c3 ♘c4 28 e6 ♕b7 29 ♗xg7 ♕xc6 30 ♕f6 ♕c7 31 e7 **1-0**
L/N6047-1852

**1851-LON3-4**
**Anderssen, A.+ Meyerhofer, K.**
[Anderssen & Nathan]
1 e4 e6 2 d4 d5 3 exd5 exd5 4 c4 ♗b4+ 5 ♘c3 ♘e7 6 ♕b3 ♘bc6 7 ♗e3 0-0 8 ♘f3 h6 9 ♗e2 ♔h8 10 0-0 ♗e6 11 cxd5 ♘xd5 12 ♕c2 f5 13 ♖ad1 ♕f6 14 a3 ♗d6 15 ♖fe1 a6 16 ♗c1 ♘ce7 17 ♗c4 c6 18 ♘e5 ♖ad8 19 f4? [□ 19 ♗xd5] 19 ... ♘xf4 20 ♖f1 ♗xe5 21 dxe5 ♕xe5 22 ♖xf4 ♕c5+ 23 ♕f2 ♕xf2+ 24 ♔xf2 ♖xd1 25 ♘xd1 g5 26 ♗xe6 gxf4 27 ♗xf4 ♔g7 28 ♘e3 ♘g6 29 ♔f3 ♔f6 30 ♗b3 [30 ♗xf5?] 30 ... ♖d8 31 ♗c2 [31 ♗xh6 ♖h8] 31 ... ♖d2 32 ♗xh6 ♘e5+ 33 ♔g3 ♘c4 34 ♗xf5 ♘xe3 35 ♗xe3 ♖d5 36 ♗c2 c5 37 ♔f4 c4 38 g4 b5 39 h4 a5 40 g5+ ♔g7 41 h5 b4 42 axb4 axb4 43 h6+ ♔g8 44 g6 b3 45 ♗f5 ♖d8 46 ♗e6+ ♔h8 47 ♗c5 c3 48 ♗e7 **1-0**
L/N6047-1852

**1851-LON3-5**
**Anderssen, A.+ Lowe, E.**
[Anderssen & Nathan]
1 e4 e5 2 ♘f3 ♘c6 3 ♗c4 ♗c5 4 0-0 d6 5 c3 ♘f6 6 d4 exd4 7 cxd4 ♗b6 8 h3

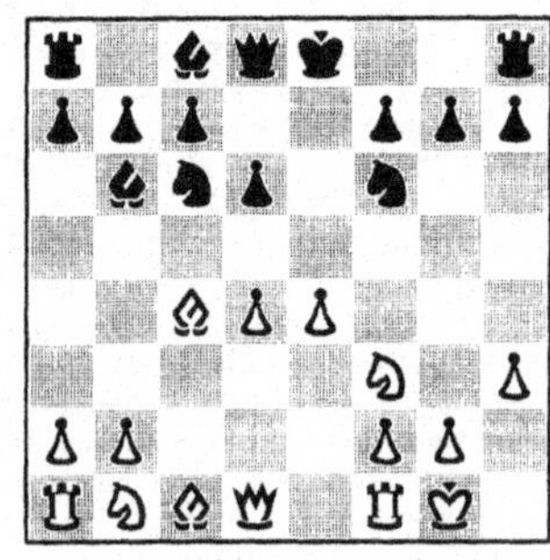

8 ... h6 [8 ... ♘xe4 9 ♖e1 d5 10 ♗xd5 ♕xd5 11 ♘c3 ♕d8 12 ♖xe4+ ♘e7±] 9 ♘c3 0-0 10 ♖e1 ♖e8 11 a3 a6 12 ♕d3 ♗d7 13 e5 ♘xd4?! 14 ♘xd4 dxe5 15 ♘de2 ♗e6 16 ♕xd8 ♖axd8 17 ♗xe6 ♖xe6 18 ♘g3 ♖d3 19 ♗e3 ♗xe3 20 ♖xe3 ♖xe3 21 fxe3 ♖b6 22 ♖b1 ♖b3 23 ♔f2 b5 24 ♔e2 c5 25 ♘ge4 ♘xe4 26 ♘xe4 c4 27 ♘c5 **1-0**
L/N6047-1852

**1851-LON3-6**
**Deacon, F.H.– Anderssen, A.**
[Anderssen & Nathan]
1 f4 f5 2 ♘f3 ♘f6 3 e3 e6 4 ♗e2 ♗e7 5 b3 ♘e4 [Δ 6 ♗b2 ♗f6] 6 ♘a3 b6 7 ♘c4 0-0 8 ♗b2 ♗f6 9 ♖c1 a5 10 d3 ♗xb2 11 ♘xb2 ♘c3 12 ♕d2 ♘xa2 13 ♖a1 ♘b4 14 0-0 d6 15 c3 ♘d5 16 b4 c5 17 bxa5 bxa5 18 ♖a3 ♘c6 19 ♖fa1 ♗a6 20 d4 ♗xe2 21 ♕xe2 cxd4 22 ♘xd4 ♘xd4 23 cxd4 ♖f7 24 ♘c4 ♖fa7 25 ♕a2 a4 26 ♘b2 ♕d7 27 ♕c4 ♖c8 28 ♕e2 ♖ac7 29 ♘xa4 ♖c1+ 30 ♖xc1 ♖xc1+ 31 ♔f2 ♕c6 32 ♔g3 ♘f6 33 ♖a2 ♕e8 34 h3 ♘e4+ 35 ♔h2 ♖h1+ 36 ♔xh1 ♘g3+ 37 ♔h2 ♘xe2 38 ♖xe2 ♕xa4 **0-1**
L/N6047-1852

**1851-LON3-7**
**Szabó, G.– Anderssen, A.**
[Anderssen & Nathan]
1 e4 e5 2 ♘f3 ♘c6 3 d4 exd4 4 ♗c4 ♗c5 5 ♘g5 ♘h6 6 ♘f3 ♕f6 7 0-0 d6 8 h3 0-0 9 ♗g5 ♕g6 10 ♗d3 f5 11 ♗xh6 ♕xh6 12 exf5 ♗xf5 13 ♔h2 ♘e5 14 ♘g1 ♘g4+ 15 ♔h1 ♗xd3 16 cxd3 ♘xf2+ 17 ♖xf2 ♖xf2 18 b4 ♗xb4 19 ♕b3+ ♔h8 20 ♕xb4 ♖af8 21 ♕xd4 ♖8f4 22 ♕xa7 ♕g5 23 ♕a8+ ♖f8 24 ♕xb7 d5 25 g4 ♕f4 **0-1**
L/N6047-1852

### 1851-LON3-8
**Ehrmann, A.–Anderssen, A.**

[Anderssen & Nathan]

1 e4 e5 2 ♗c4 ♘f6 3 d3 ♗c5 4 ♘f3 d6 5 h3 ♗e6 6 ♗b3 0-0 7 ♗e3 ♘bd7 8 ♗xc5 ♘xc5 9 ♘fd2 ♗xb3 10 axb3 ♘e6 11 0-0 ♘d7 12 ♕g4 ♘f4 13 ♘c3 f5 14 exf5 h5 15 ♕f3 ♖xf5 16 ♕xb7? ♘c5∓ 17 ♕f3 ♘ce6 18 ♕e4 ♖f8 19 ♔h2 ♕d7 20 ♘f3 ♘xg2 21 ♔xg2 ♘f4+ 22 ♔h1 d5 23 ♘xd5 ♘xd5 24 ♘h2 ♘f4 25 ♖g1 ♘xh3 26 ♖g2 ♖ae8 27 f3 c6 28 ♖a6 ♖f6 29 ♕h4 ♖f7 30 ♖a1 ♘f4 31 ♖g5 ♕d4 32 ♖ag1 ♕xb2 33 ♕g3 ♖ee7 34 ♕e1 ♕xc2 35 ♖xe5 ♘xd3 **0-1** L/N6047-1852

### 1851-LON3-9
**Löwenthal, J.J.=Ehrmann, A.**

[Walker]

1 e4 c5 2 f4 [◻ 2 ♗c4] 2 ... e6 3 ♘f3 a6 4 c3 b6 5 d4 ♗b7 6 d5 ♘f6 7 dxe6 fxe6 8 e5 ♘d5 9 ♗d3 ♗e7 10 ♘g5? ♗xg5 11 ♕h5+ ♔f8 12 fxg5 ♔g8 13 0-0 ♕e7 14 g6 hxg6 15 ♕xg6 ♘c6 16 ♗g5

16 ... ♘xe5 17 ♗xe7 ♘xg6 18 ♗d6 ♖h6 19 ♘d2 ♘e3 20 ♖f2 ♘g4 21 ♖e2 ♘f6 [21 ... ♘xh2?] 22 ♗xg6 ♖xg6 23 ♘c4 ♘d5 24 ♘e5 ♖g5 25 g4! [△ h4] 25 ... ♘f4 26 ♖e3 ♘g6 27 h3 ♘xe5 28 ♗xe5 ♖f8 29 ♖f1 ♖xf1+ 30 ♔xf1 ♔f7 31 ♔f2 ♔e7 32 c4 d6 33 ♗g3 ♖g6 34 g5! e5 [34 ... ♖xg5 35 ♗h4+–] 35 h4 ♖e6 36 h5 b5 37 b3 ♗c6 38 ♖e1 ♔f7 39 ♔e3 ♖e8 40 ♖e2 ♖h8 41 ♖h2 ♔e6 42 h6 gxh6 43 ♖xh6+ ♖xh6 44 gxh6 ♔f6 45 ♗h4+ ♔g6 46 ♗e7= d5 47 cxd5 ♗xd5 48 ♗xc5 ♔xh6 49 ♗d6 e4 50 ♔d4 ♗b7 51 a4 ♔g5 52 axb5 axb5 53 b4 ♔g4 54 ♔e3 ♔f5 55 ♗c5 ♔e5 56 ♗f8 **½-½** M749

### 1851-LON3-10
**Meyerhofer, K.+Harrwitz, D.**

[Walker]

1 e4 e5 2 ♘f3 ♘c6 3 ♗c4 ♗c5 4 ♘c3 d6 5 h3 ♘f6 6 d3 ♘e7 7 ♘e2 ♘g6 8 ♘g3 ♗b6 9 0-0 ♗e6? 10 ♗b3 ♕d7 11 ♔h2 h5 12 ♘g5 h4 13 ♘f5! ♘h5 14 ♕g4 0-0-0 15 ♘xe6 fxe6 16 ♗xe6! ♕xe6 17 ♘e7+ ♔d7 18 ♕xe6+ ♔xe6 19 ♘xg6 ♖h7 20 ♗g5 ♘f6 21 f4 exf4 22 ♖xf4 ♖g8 23 ♖xh4 ♖xh4 24 ♗xh4± ♔f7 25 ♗xf6 ♔xg6 26 ♗h4 ♖f8 27 ♖d1 ♔h5 28 ♗g3 g5 29 d4 g4 30 c3 gxh3 31 ♔xh3 ♖h8 32 ♗h4 ♖e8 33 g4+ ♔g6 34 ♖e1 c5 35 ♗f2 cxd4 36 cxd4 ♖c8 37 ♖e2 ♖c4 38 e5! dxe5 39 dxe5 ♗xf2 40 ♖xf2 ♖e4 41 ♖f5 ♖e2 42 ♔g3 ♖xb2 43 ♖f2 ♖b4 44 ♖f4 ♖b2 45 ♖a4 a6 46 ♔f4 ♖g2 47 ♔f3 ♖c2 48 ♔e4 ♖c5 49 ♖b4 b5 50 ♔d4 ♖c2 51 a4 ♖d2+ 52 ♔e3 ♖d5 53 ♔e4 ♖c5 54 ♔d4 ♖c1 55 axb5 axb5 56 ♔d5 ♖d1+ 57 ♔e6 ♖g1 58 ♔e7 ♔g7 59 e6 ♖g2 60 ♔e8 ♔g8 61 ♖d4 ♖a2 62 ♔e7 ♔g7 63 ♔d6 ♖a6+ 64 ♔e5 ♖a1 65 ♖d7+ ♔f8 66 g5 ♖e1+ 67 ♔d6 ♖d1+ 68 ♔c5 ♖e1 69 ♔d6 ♖d1+ 70 ♔e5 ♖e1+ 71 ♔f6 ♖f1+ 72 ♔g6 ♖e1 73 ♖f7+ ♔g8 74 ♔f6 ♖f1+ 75 ♔e7 ♖d1 76 ♔e8 ♖d6 77 ♖f6 ♔g7 78 ♔e7 ♖d5 79 ♖f8 ♖xg5 80 ♖f7+ ♔g8 81 ♔e8 ♖e5 82 e7 ♖e1 83 ♖f8+ ♔g7 84 ♔d7 ♖d1+ 85 ♔c6 **1-0** M749

### 1851-LON3-12
**Ehrmann, A.–Harrwitz, D.**

[Horwitz & Kling]

1 e4 e5 2 ♗c4 ♘f6 3 ♘c3 ♗c5 4 ♕e2 ♘c6 5 ♗xf7+!? ♔xf7 6 ♕c4+ d5 7 ♕xc5 dxe4 8 ♘xe4 ♘xe4 9 ♕c4+ ♗e6 10 ♕xe4 ♘d4 11 ♘f3 ♗f5 12 ♕xb7 ♘xc2+ 13 ♔d1 ♘xa1 14 ♘xe5+ ♔f6 15 ♕c6+ ♕d6 16 d4 ♕xc6 17 ♘xc6 ♗c2+ 18 ♔e1 ♖he8+ 19 ♗e3 ♗a4 20 ♘b4 ♘c2+ 21 ♘xc2 ♗xc2 22 ♔d2 ♗e4 23 ♖c1 c6 24 g3 ♖ab8 25 b3 a5 26 ♗f4 ♖b5 27 ♖c3 g5 28 ♗d6 ♖d5 29 ♗c5 ♖f5 30 ♔e1 ♗g2+ 31 ♖e3 ♖xe3+ 32 fxe3 ♖f1+ 33 ♔e2 ♖a1 34 a3 ♗e4 35 h3 ♖a2+ 36 ♔e1 ♔e6 37 h4 gxh4 38 gxh4 ♔f5 39 a4 ♔g4 40 ♗e7 ♔f3 41 ♗c5 ♗d5 **0-1** L/N6127

## BIRD✕HORWITZ London
**[1851-✕BH-1]**

| | | | | | | | | | | | | | | | |
|---|---|---|---|---|---|---|---|---|---|---|---|---|---|---|---|
| H.E. Bird | 1 | 0 | 1 | ½ | ½ | ½ | 0 | 0 | 0 | 0 | ½ | 1 | 0 | 0 | 5 |
| B. Horwitz | 0 | 1 | 0 | ½ | ½ | ½ | 1 | 1 | 1 | 1 | ½ | 0 | 1 | 1 | 9 |

### 1851-✕BH-1
**Bird, H.E.+Horwitz, B.**

[Staunton]

1 e4 e5 2 ♘f3 ♘c6 3 ♗b5 ♘f6 4 d4 [4 0-0; 4 ♘c3] 4 ... exd4 5 e5 ♘e4 6 0-0 f5 7 ♘xd4 ♘xd4 8 ♕xd4 ♗c5 9 ♕d3 0-0 10 ♘c3 ♘xc3 11 bxc3 ♕e7 12 ♗f4 ♔h8 13 ♕g3 h6 14 h4 a6 15 ♗d3 ♕e6 16 ♖fe1 b6 17 a4 ♗b7 18 ♖e2 ♖f7 19 ♖d1 ♖g8 20 ♖ed2 ♗c6 21 ♗xa6 g5? 22 hxg5 hxg5 23 ♗xg5 ♕g6 [23 ... ♖fg7? 24 ♕h4+ ♖h7 25 ♗f6++–] 24 ♗c4 ♖fg7 25 ♕h4+ ♖h7 26 ♗f6+ ♖g7 27 ♗xg7+ ♔xg7 28 ♖xd7+! ♗xd7 29 ♖xd7 **1-0** Staunton(1)

### 1851-✕BH-2
**Horwitz, B.+Bird, H.E.**

[Staunton]

1 e4 e6 2 d4 d5 3 exd5 exd5 4 ♗d3 ♘f6 5 ♘f3 ♗d6 6 0-0 0-0 7 ♗g5 ♗e6 8 c3 c6 9 ♘e5 ♘bd7 10 f4 ♕b6? 11 ♘xd7 ♗xd7 [11 ... ♘xd7?? 12 f5+–] 12 ♗xf6 gxf6 13 ♕h5 f5 14 ♕g5+ ♔h8 15 ♕f6+ ♔g8 16 ♕xd6 ♗e6 17 b3 ♖fe8 18 ♘d2 **1-0** Staunton(1)

### 1851-✕BH-3
**Bird, H.E.+Horwitz, B.**

[Staunton]

1 e4 e5 2 ♘f3 ♘c6 3 ♗b5 ♘f6 4 0-0 ♘xe4 5 d4 exd4 6 ♖e1 f5 7 ♘xd4 ♗c5? 8 ♖xe4+ fxe4 9 ♕h5+ g6 10 ♕xc5 ♕e7 11 ♕c3 ♘e5 12 ♗f4 0-0 13 ♗c4+ ♘xc4 14 ♕xc4+ ♖f7 15 ♗e3 c6 16 ♕b3 d5 17 ♘d2 c5 18 ♘e2 d4 19 ♗f4 d3! 20 cxd3 ♗e6 21 ♕c3 ♗g4 22 ♘xe4 ♗xe2 23 ♗g5 ♕d7 24 ♘f6+ ♖xf6 25 ♕xf6 ♗xd3 26 ♗h6 ± ♖e8 27 ♖d1 ♗f5 28 ♖c1 b6? [◻ 28 ... ♕d4] 29 h3 ♕f7 [◻ 29 ... ♕d4] 30 ♕c3 ♖d8 31 ♖e1 ♖d4? 32 ♕g3 ♖d8 33 ♕g5 ♖d7 34 ♖e3 ♖d1+? 35 ♔h2 ♖d7 36 ♕f4 ♖d8 37 ♕e5 ♕d7 38 f4 ♕f7 39 b3 ♗b1 40 ♖e2 ♗d3 41 ♖e3 ♗b1 42 g4 c4 43 ♕b2 ♗d3 44 ♕e5 ♖c8 45 ♕d6 g5 46 f5 [46 ♗xg5] 46 ... cxb3 47 ♖xd3 [47 ♖e7! ♖c2+ 48 ♔g3+–; 47 ... ♕c4 48 ♖g7+ ♔h8 49 ♖xh7+ ♔xh7 50 ♕g6+ ♔h8 51 ♕g7#] 47 ... ♕c7 48 ♕xc7 ♖xc7 49 axb3 a5 50 ♗xg5 b5 51 ♗f4 ♖c2+ 52 ♔g3 b4 53 ♔f3 ♖a2 54 ♔e4 ♖a3 55 ♔d4 a4 56 ♔c4 axb3 57 ♖xb3 ♖a7 58 ♖xb4 ♖a3 59 h4 ♖h3 60 ♗g5 h6 61 ♖b8+ **1-0** Staunton(1)

### 1851-✕BH-4
**Bird, H.E.=Horwitz, B.**

[Staunton]

1 e4 e5 2 ♘f3 d6 3 d4 exd4 4 ♗c4 ♗e7 5 ♘xd4 ♘f6 6 ♘c3 0-0 7 0-0 ♘xe4 8 ♘xe4 d5 9 ♗xd5 ♕xd5 10 ♘c3 ♕d8 11 ♗f4 ♘a6 12 ♖e1 ♗f6 13 ♘db5 ♗d7 14 ♕f3 ♗c6 15 ♕g3 ♗xc3 16 ♘xc3 ♕f6! 17 ♗xc7 ♘xc7 18 ♕xc7 ♕g6 19 ♕g3 ♕xc2 20 ♖e2 ♕f5 21 ♖ae1 ♖ad8 22 ♖e5 ♕f6 23 h3 h6 24 b4! [△ 25 b5] 24 ... a6 25 a4 ♖d4 26 b5 axb5 27 axb5 ♗d7 28 ♘d5 ♕d6 29 ♘e7+ ♔h8

30 ♕f3 b6 31 g4 ♖d3 32 ♖1e3 ♖xe3 33 ♕xe3 ♖e8 34 ♘g6+!? fxg6 35 ♖xe8+ ♗xe8 36 ♕xe8+ ♔h7 37 ♕c6 ♕d4 38 ♔g2 h5 39 gxh5 gxh5 40 ♕e6 g6 41 ♕f7+ ♔h6 42 ♕f8+ ♔h7 43 ♕e7+ ♔g8 44 ♕e6+ ♔g7 45 ♕c6 ½-½

Staunton(1)

**1851-✕BH-5**
**Horwitz, B.= Bird, H.E.**

[Staunton]

1 e4 c5 2 f4 ♘c6 3 ♘f3 e6 4 ♗b5 ♕b6 5 ♘c3 ♗e7 [□ 5 + g6 △ 6 ... ♗g7] 6 d3 ♘f6 7 ♗xc6 bxc6 8 0-0 0-0 9 ♘a4 [△ 10 c4; 10 ♘e2 d5!] 9 ... ♕c7 10 c4 d5 11 ♘c3 ♗a6? [□ 11 ... ♗b7] 12 b3 ♖ad8 13 ♕e2 ♖fe8 14 e5 ♘d7 15 ♗b2 f6 16 ♖ae1 fxe5 17 fxe5 ♖f8 18 ♘d1 ♕a5? [□ 18 ... ♖f7 △ 19 ... ♖df8] 19 ♗c3 ♕c7 20 ♗d2 ♘b6 21 ♗g5 ♗c8 22 ♗xe7 ♕xe7 23 ♖f2 ♗d7 24 g3 ♗e8 25 ♘h4 ♖xf2 26 ♘xf2 g5 27 ♘f3 ♗h5 28 ♕e3 h6 29 g4 ♗g6 30 h4 ♖f8 31 hxg5 d4 32 ♕e2 ♕f7 [32 ... hxg5 33 ♘h3] 33 ♔g2 h5 34 ♖h1 ♘d7 35 ♘h4 ♘xe5 36 ♘xg6 ♘xg6 37 ♔g1 ♘f4 38 ♕e4 e5 39 gxh5 ♘xh5 40 ♖h2 ♘g3 41 ♕h4 [□ 41 ♕xe5! ♘h5 42 g6+-; 41 ... ♕f4 42 ♖h8+ ♔f7 43 ♖h7+ ♔g6 44 ♕g7++-] 41 ... ♘e2+ 42 ♔f1 ♕f5 43 ♔xe2? [□ 43 g6!+-] 43 ... ♕f3+ 44 ♔f1 ♕xd3+ 45 ♔g1 ♕b1+ 46 ♔g2 ♕f5 47 ♖h3 e4

48 ♕xe4? [□ 48 g6! ♕xg6 49 ♖g3+-; 48 ... ♔g7 49 ♕h6++-; 48 ... ♕xf2+ 49 ♕xf2 ♖xf2+ 50 ♔xf2 ♔g7 51 ♖g3+-] 48 ... ♕xf2+ ½-½

Staunton(1)

**1851-✕BH-6**
**Horwitz, B.= Bird, H.E.**

[Staunton]

1 e4 c5 2 f4 e6 3 ♘f3 d5 4 e5 ♗e7 5 ♗b5+ ♗d7 6 ♗xd7+ ♘xd7 [6 ... ♕xd7] 7 c3 ♘h6 8 0-0 0-0 9 d4 ♕b6 10 b3 f6 11 ♗a3? ♖ad8 12 ♔h1 ♘f5 13 ♕e1 fxe5 14 fxe5 ♖f7 15 ♗c1 ♖df8 16 a4 a5 [□ 16 ... ♘h4] 17 ♘a3 cxd4 18 cxd4 ♗b4 19 ♗d2 ♗xa3 20 ♖xa3 ♘xd4 21 ♕e3 ♕b4 [21 ... ♘xf3!? ∞] 22 ♘xd4 ♕xa3 23 ♘xe6 ♖e8 24 ♘g5 ± ♖xe5 25 ♘xf7 ♔xf7 26 ♖f1+ ♘f6 27 ♗d4 ♖e6 28 ♗xf6 gxf6 29 ♕xd5 [□ 29 ♕h5+ △ 30 ♕xd5±] 29 ... b6 30 ♕f5 ♕xb3 31 ♕xh7+ ♔f8 ½-½

Staunton(1)

**1851-✕BH-7**
**Bird, H.E.– Horwitz, B.**

[Staunton]

1 e4 e5 2 ♘f3 d6 3 ♗c4 ♗e6 4 ♗xe6 fxe6 5 d4 exd4 6 ♘xd4 ♕d7 7 0-0 c5 8 ♘f3 ♘c6 9 ♘c3 0-0-0 10 a4 a6 11 a5 ♗e7 12 ♘a4 ♔b8 13 ♘b6 ♕c7 14 ♗d2 ♘f6? 15 ♘g5 ♘d4 16 c3 h6 17 ♘f7 ♘c6 18 ♘xh8 ♖xh8 19 ♕a4 ♗d8 20 ♖fe1 ♘xa5 21 ♕xa5 ♕c6! 22 ♕a4 ♕xb6 23 b4 ♘g4 24 h3 ♘e5 ...? **0-1**

Staunton(1)

**1851-✕BH-8**
**Horwitz, B.+ Bird, H.E.**

[Staunton]

1 e4 c5 2 d4 cxd4 3 ♘f3 e6 4 ♘xd4 ♘c6 5 ♗e3 g6 6 c3 ♗g7 7 ♘b5 ♗e5 8 f4 ♗b8 9 e5 ♘ge7 10 ♗e2 ♘d5 11 ♗d2 0-0 12 c4 ♘de7 13 ♗c3 ♗c7 14 ♘d6 ♗xd6 15 exd6 ♘f5 16 ♕d3 ♕b6 17 ♘a3 ♕e3 18 ♕xe3 ♘xe3 19 g4? ♘g2+ 20 ♔f2 ♘xf4 21 h4 f5 22 g5 ♘xe2 23 ♔xe2 e5 24 h5 b6 25 hxg6 hxg6 26 ♖h6 ♔f7 27 ♖h7+ ♔e6 28 ♘b5 ♖b8 29 ♖d1 [29 ♗b4! △ 30 ♘c7#±] 29 ... f4 30 ♘c7+ ♔f5 31 ♖g1 ♗b7 32 ♖xd7 ♖bd8 33 ♖h7 ♗a8 [33 ... ♖xd6 34 ♘b5+-] 34 d7 ♗b7 35 ♘b5 ♗a6 36 a4 ♗xb5 37 axb5 ♘b8 38 ♖e7 ♘xd7 39 ♖d1 ♘c5 40 ♖xe5+ ♔g4 41 ♖g1+ ♔h3 42 ♖e7 f3+ 43 ♔e3 ♖d7 44 ♖xd7 ♘xd7 45 ♔f2 ♘c5 46 ♗f6 ♘e4+ 47 ♔xf3 ♘xg5+ 48 ♔f4 ♔h2 49 ♖xg5 ♖xf6+ 50 ♔e5! ♖f2 51 ♖xg6 ♖xb2 52 ♔d5 ♖d2+ 53 ♔c6 ♖d4 54 ♔b7 ♖d7+ 55 ♔a6 ♔h3 56 ♖g8 ♖c7 57 ♖a8 ♔g4 58 ♖xa7 ♖xc4 59 ♖f7 +- ♔g5 60 ♔xb6 ♖c2 61 ♔b7 ♖c5 62 b6 ♖c3 63 ♔b8 **1-0**

Staunton(1)

**1851-✕BH-9**
**Bird, H.E.– Horwitz, B.**

[Staunton]

1 e4 e5 2 ♘f3 ♘c6 3 ♗b5 d6 4 c3 ♗d7 = 5 d4 exd4 6 cxd4 ♗e7 7 ♘c3 ♘f6 8 0-0 0-0 9 h3 a6 10 ♗d3 b5! 11 a3 ♘e8 12 b4 f5 13 ♕c2 fxe4 14 ♗xe4 ♘f6 15 ♘g5 ♘xe4 16 ♘cxe4 ♖f5!? 17 ♘f3 [□ 17 f4 △ 18 g4] 17 ... ♖xf3 18 gxf3 ♘xd4 19 ♕d3 c5 20 ♔h2 ♕f8 21 f4 ♕f5 [△ 22 ... d5-+] 22 ♖e1 d5 23 bxc5 [23 ♘xc5 ♗xc5 24 ♕xf5 ♗xf5 25 bxc5 ♘f3+-+] 23 ... dxe4 24 ♕xd4 ♗f6 25 ♕xe4 ♕xe4 26 ♖xe4 ♗xa1 27 ♖e7 ♖d8 28 ♗e3 ♗b2 29 ♔g3 ♔f8 30 ♖e4 ♗xa3 31 ♗d4 ♗f5 32 ♖e5 g6 33 ♗e3 ♗b2! 34 c6 ♗xe5 35 fxe5 ♖c8 **0-1**

Staunton(1)

**1851-✕BH-10**
**Horwitz, B.+ Bird, H.E.**

[Staunton]

1 e4 e6 2 d4 d5 3 exd5 exd5 4 ♗d3 ♘f6 5 ♘f3 ♗g4 6 0-0 ♗e7 7 h3 ♗xf3 8 ♕xf3 0-0 9 c3 c5 10 dxc5 ♗xc5 11 ♗g5 ♗e7 12 ♘d2 ♘c6 13 ♖fe1 ♕d6 14 ♕f5? [□ 14 ♗f4] 14 ... g6 15 ♕f3 ♘e5 16 ♕g3 ♘xd3 17 ♕xd3 ♖ae8? 18 ♗h6 ♗d8 19 ♗xf8 ♖xf8 20 ♖e2 ♗c7 21 ♘f3 ♘h5 22 ♖e5 ♘f4 23 ♕d4? ♕xe5! 24 ♕xe5 [24 ♘xe5 ♘e2+=] 24 ... ♗xe5 25 ♘xe5 ♖e8 26 ♖e1 ♖e6 27 ♔f1 ♔g7 28 h4 ♔f6 29 ♘g4+ ♔e7 30 ♘e3 ♔d6 31 g3 ♘d3 32 ♖e2 f5 33 ♖d2 ♘c5 34 ♖xd5+ ♔c6 35 ♖d4 ♘e4 36 ♔g2 b6 37 ♘d5 b5 38 ♘b4+ ♔b6 39 f3 ♘c5 40 ♔f2 ♘b7 41 ♘d5+ ♔c6 42 ♘f4 ♖d6 43 ♖xd6+ ♔xd6 44 ♔e3 ♘c5 45 b3 a5 46 ♔d4 a4 47 b4 ♘b3+?! 48 ♔d3! [△ 49 ♔c2 ... 50 axb3; 48 axb3?? a3-+] 48 ... ♘c1+ 49 ♔c2 ♘xa2 50 ♔b2 ♘xc3 51 ♔xc3 ♔e5 52 ♘d3+ ♔d5 53 ♘e1 h6 54 ♘c2 ♔e5 55 ♔d3 ♔d5 56 ♘a3 g5 57 hxg5 hxg5 58 ♘xb5 ♔e5 59 ♘a3 f4 60 g4 ♔d5 61 ♔c3 ♔d6 62 ♔c4 **1-0**

Staunton(1)

**1851-✕BH-11**
**Bird, H.E.= Horwitz, B.**

[Staunton]

1 e4 e5 2 ♘f3 ♘c6 3 ♗b5 d6 4 c3 ♗d7 5 d4 ♘f6 6 0-0 ♗e7 7 d5 ♘b8 8 ♗d3 0-0 9 ♘e1 b6 10 f4 ♗g4 11 ♕c2 exf4 12 ♗xf4 ♘bd7 13 ♘d2 ♗h5 14 ♘ef3 h6 15 ♖ae1 ♗g6 16 ♘d4 ♘c5 17 ♗c4 a6 18 b4 ♘b7 19 ♗d3 ♕d7 20 ♘2f3 ♖fe8 21 c4 a5 22 ♘h4 axb4 23 ♘xg6 fxg6 24 ♘c6 ♘c5 25 e5 ♘xd3 26 ♕xd3 [26 e6?! ♘xe1 27 ♕xg6∞] 26 ... dxe5 27 ♗xe5 ♗c5+ 28 ♔h1 ♔h7 29 ♗xf6 ♖xe1 30 ♖xe1 gxf6 31 d6 ♕xd6 [31 ... ♕xc6 32 ♖e7+-] 32 ♕f3 ♖a3 33 ♕e4 f5 34 ♕e8 ♖e3! 35 ♖xe3 ♗xe3 36 ♕xe3 ♕xc6 37 ♕e7+ ♔g8 38 ♕xb4 ♕d6 39 ♕b3 ♔f7 40 a4 ♕c5 41 h3 f4 42 ♕d3 ♕e3 43 ♕d7+ ♕e7 44 ♕d5+ ♕e6 45 ♕d4 g5 46 c5 ♔e7 47 ♕g7+ ♔d8 48 cxb6 ♕xb6 49 ♕f8+ ♔d7 50 ♕g7+ ♔c8 51 h4 ♕a5 52 ♕xh6 ♕e1+ 53 ♔h2 ♕g3+ 54 ♔g1 ½-½

Staunton(1)

**1851-✕BH-12**
**Horwitz, B.– Bird, H.E.**

[Staunton]

1 e4 c5 2 d4 cxd4 3 ♘f3 ♘c6 4 ♘xd4 e5 5 ♘xc6 bxc6 6 ♗c4 ♗a6 7 ♗xa6 ♕a5+ 8 ♗d2 ♕xa6 9 ♗c3 f6 10 b3 ♘h6 11 a4 ♖d8 12 ♘d2

♗c5 13 ♕f3 0-0 14 0-0-0?! [□ 14 ♕e2] 14 … d5 15 ♗b2 ♘f7 16 h4 ♗d4 17 ♗a3 ♖fe8 18 g4 ♕b6 19 ♖h2 ♗c5 20 ♗b2 ♘d6 21 ♖de1 ♗d4 22 c3? dxe4 23 ♘xe4 ♕xb3 24 ♘d2 ♕xa4 25 cxd4 exd4 26 ♖xe8+ ♖xe8 27 ♕b3+ ♕xb3 28 ♘xb3 c5 29 f3 d3 30 ♗a3? ♘c4 31 ♔d1 ♘xa3 32 ♘xc5 ♖e3 33 ♖d2 ♘c4 34 ♖f2 d2 35 ♘e4 ♖e1+ **0-1**

Staunton(1)

### 1851-✕BH-13
**Bird, H.E. – Horwitz, B.**

[Staunton]

1 e4 e5 2 ♘f3 d6 3 d4 exd4 4 ♕xd4 ♘c6 5 ♗b5 ♗d7 6 ♗xc6 ♗xc6 7 0-0 ♘f6 8 ♘c3 ♗e7 9 ♘d5 ♗xd5 10 exd5 0-0 11 ♗g5 ♕d7 12 ♖fe1 h6 13 ♗h4 ♖fe8 14 ♕d2 ♕b5 15 ♕d4 ♕d7 [15 … ♘xd5?? 16 c4!+-; 15 … ♕xd5?? 16 ♗xf6!+-] 16 c4 a5 17 ♖e2 g5 18 ♗g3 ♘h5 19 ♖ae1 ♗f6 20 ♕d1 ♖xe2 21 ♕xe2 ♘g7 22 ♕c2 b6 23 ♘d2 ♘f5 24 ♘e4 ♗g7 25 ♖d1? ♘d4 26 ♕d2 f5 27 ♘xg5 hxg5 28 ♕xg5 ♘e2+ 29 ♔f1 ♘xg3+ 30 ♕xg3 ♖e8 31 h4 ♖e4 32 h5 ♖xc4 33 f4 ♕a4 34 b3 ♖xf4+ 35 ♔g1 ♖g4! 36 ♕h3 ♕f4 37 ♖e1 ♗d4+ 38 ♔h1 ♖h4 **0-1**

Staunton(1)

### 1851-✕BH-14
**Horwitz, B. + Bird, H.E.**

[Staunton]

1 e4 e5 2 f4 exf4 3 ♘f3 g5 4 h4 g4 5 ♘e5 h5 6 ♗c4 ♘h6 7 d4 d6 8 ♘d3 f3 9 gxf3 ♗e7 10 ♗f4 [10 ♗e3] 10 … ♗xh4+ 11 ♔d2 gxf3 12 ♕xf3 ♗g4 13 ♕e3 ♗e7 14 ♘c3 [14 ♗xh6 ♖xh6 15 ♕xh6?? ♗g5+-+] 14 … ♘c6 15 ♖ag1 [△ 16 ♗xh6 ♖xh6 17 ♖xg4] 15 … ♗f8 16 ♘d5 ♗g7 17 c3 ♘e7 18 ♗g5 ♘hg8 19 ♖f1 ♗e6 20 ♘3f4 ♗xd5 21 ♘xd5 f6 22 ♘xf6+ ♘xf6 23 ♗xf6 ♗xf6 24 ♖xf6 ♕d7 25 ♕g5 d5 26 exd5 0-0-0 27 d6! [△ 28 ♗e6+-; 27 ♖f7 ♖de8 28 ♖e1] 27 … ♖dg8 28 ♗xg8 ♖xg8

29 ♕xg8+! [29 dxe7!+-] 29 … ♘xg8 30 ♖f8+ ♕d8 31 ♖xd8+ ♔xd8 32 dxc7+ ♔xc7 33 ♖xh5 ♘f6 34 ♖f5 ♘e4+ 35 ♔e3 ♘d6 36 ♔f4 **1-0**

Staunton(1)

## BUCKLE✕LÖWENTHAL

London

[1851-✕BL]

| | | | | | | | | |
|---|---|---|---|---|---|---|---|---|
| H.T. Buckle | 0 | 1 | 0 | 1 | 1 | 0 | 1 | 4 |
| J.J.Löwenthal | 1 | 0 | 1 | 0 | 0 | 1 | 0 | 3 |

### 1851-✕BL-1
**Buckle,H.T.–Löwenthal, J.J.**

[Staunton]

1 e4 e5 2 ♘f3 ♘c6 3 ♗c4 ♗c5 4 ♘c3 ♘f6 5 d3 d6 6 ♘e2 ♘e7 7 ♘g3 h6 8 c3 c6 9 0-0 ♗b6 10 d4 exd4 11 cxd4 0-0 12 ♗d3 ♗g4 13 ♗e3 ♘g6 14 h3 ♗xf3 15 ♕xf3 ♘h4 16 ♕e2 [16 ♕f4?? g5] 16 … ♖e8 17 f4 ♘g6 18 f5 ♘f8 19 ♖f4 c5! 20 dxc5 ♗xc5 21 ♗xc5 dxc5 22 ♗b5 ♕c7! 23 ♖f3 ♖e5 24 ♖d1 a6 25 ♗d3 ♖ae8 26 ♗c2 c4 27 ♔h1 b5 28 ♕d2 ♘8d7 29 ♘h5 ♘xh5! [29 … ♘xe4 30 ♗xe4 ♖xe4 31 ♖g3+-] 30 ♕xd7 ♕xd7 31 ♖xd7 ♘f6 32 ♖a7 ♘xe4 33 ♖xa6 ♘f6 34 ♖f2 ♖e1+ 35 ♔h2 ♖8e2 36 ♔g3 ♖xf2 37 ♔xf2 ♖c1 -+ 38 ♗a4 bxa4 **0-1**

Staunton(1)

### 1851-✕BL-2
**Löwenthal,J.J.–Buckle, H.T.**

[Staunton]

1 e4 e6 2 d4 d5 3 exd5 exd5 4 ♘f3 ♘f6 5 ♗d3 ♗d6 6 0-0 0-0 7 ♗e3 ♘c6 8 c3 ♖e8 9 c4?! ♘b4 10 ♘c3 [□ 10 c5] 10 … ♘xd3 11 ♕xd3 dxc4 12 ♕xc4 h6 13 ♕d3 ♗g4 14 ♘d2 ♕d7 15 f3 ♗f5 16 ♕e2 [16 ♘de4] 16 … ♖e6 17 ♕f2 ♖ae8 18 ♖fe1 ♕e7 19 ♘f1 ♗f4 20 ♗d2 ♗xd2 21 ♖xe6 ♕xe6 22 ♕xd2 c6 23 ♔f2 ♕d6 24 ♘g3 ♗e6 25 ♘ce4 ♘xe4+ 26 fxe4 ♖d8 27 ♔e3!? [27 ♖d1 ♗g4-+] 27 … h5 28 e5 [28 ♖f1] 28 … ♕e7 29 ♘e4 c5! 30 ♘d6 [30 ♘xc5? ♕g5+ 31 ♔e2 ♕xg2+-+] 30 … ♕g5+ 31 ♔d3 ♗f5+ 32 ♔c3 cxd4+ 33 ♕xd4 ♕xg2 34 ♖g1 ♕c2+ 35 ♔b4 ♗e6 36 ♕c5 a5+ 37 ♕xa5 ♖xd6 38 exd6 ♕c4+ 39 ♔a3 ♕xa2+ 40 ♔b4

40 … ♕xb2+ [□ 40 … ♕c4+ 41 ♔a3 ♕b3#] 41 ♔c5 ♕f2+ 42 ♔b5 ♕xg1 **0-1**

Staunton(1)

### 1851-✕BL-3
**Buckle,H.T.–Löwenthal, J.J.**

[Staunton]

1 e4 e5 2 ♘f3 ♘f6 3 ♘c3 ♘c6 4 ♗c4 ♗c5 5 d3 d6 6 ♘e2 ♘e7 7 ♘g3 h6 8 c3 ♗b6 9 0-0 0-0 10 ♗b3 ♘g6 11 d4 ♗g4 12 ♗e3 ♘h4 13 dxe5 ♗xf3 14 gxf3 dxe5 15 ♕xd8 ♖axd8 16 ♗d1 ♗xe3 17 fxe3 ♖d2 18 ♖b1 ♖fd8 19 ♗e2 ♖c2 20 ♖fd1 ♖xd1+ 21 ♗xd1 ♖g2+ 22 ♔h1 g6 23 ♗e2 ♘h5! 24 ♖e1 ♘xg3+ 25 hxg3 ♖xg3 26 ♔h2 ♖xf3 27 ♗c4 g5 28 ♖e2 g4 29 ♔g1 ♖h3 30 ♖f2 ♘f3+ 31 ♔g2 h5 32 ♖f1 h4 33 ♖h1 ♖xh1 34 ♔xh1 h3 35 ♗e2 ♔g7 **0-1**

Staunton(1)

### 1851-✕BL-4
**Löwenthal,J.J.–Buckle, H.T.**

[Staunton]

1 d4 e6 2 c4 ♗b4+ 3 ♘c3?! [□ 3 ♗d2] 3 … ♗xc3+ 4 bxc3 f5 5 e3 ♘c6 6 ♘f3 ♘f6 7 ♗d3 b6 8 0-0 ♗b7 9 h3 0-0 10 ♗a3?! ♘e7 11 ♖b1 ♖e8 12 c5 ♘g6 13 ♕e2 ♘e4 14 ♗xe4 ♗xe4 15 ♖b3 ♕f6 16 ♘d2 ♗d5!? 17 c4 ♗b7 18 ♗b2 ♕g5? 19 f4 ♕e7 [□ 19 … ♕g3 20 e4? ♘xf4!∓] 20 ♕f2 ♗c6 21 ♗a3 d6 22 cxd6 cxd6 23 ♘f3 ♕c7 24 ♖c1 ♕d7 25 ♖bc3 [25 d5] 25 … ♖ac8 26 ♘d2 ♗b7 27 ♘f3 ♖c7 28 ♘d2 ♖ec8 29 ♗b2 ♘e7 30 ♔h2 b5 31 cxb5 ♖xc3 32 ♗xc3 ♘d5 33 ♗b2 ♖xc1 34 ♗xc1 ♕xb5 35 ♘f3 ♘c3 36 ♘g5 ♕d5 37 a3 h6 38 ♘f3 a5 39 ♕c2 ♘e4 40 h4 ♗c6 41 ♗d2 a4 [□ 41 … g5 42 hxg5 hxg5 43 fxg5 ♘xg5∓] 42 ♗b4 ♘f6 43 ♗d2 ♕b5 44 ♗c1 ♗xf3 45 gxf3 ♕f1 46 d5!? ♕xf3 [46 … ♘xd5; 46 … exd5? 47 ♕c8+∞] 47 dxe6 ♘e4! [△ 48 … ♕g3+ 49 ♔h1 ♘f2+-+] 48 ♕g2 ♕h5 49 ♔h3? g5 50 fxg5 hxg5 51 ♔h2 g4 52 ♕c2 ♕xh4+ 53 ♔g2 ♕g3+ 54 ♔f1 ♕f3+ 55 ♔e1 ♕h1+ 56 ♔e2 ♕g2+ 57 ♔d3 ♕xc2+ 58 ♔xc2 g3 **0-1**

Staunton(1)

### 1851-✕BL-5
**Buckle,H.T.+Löwenthal, J.J.**

[Staunton]

1 e4 e5 2 ♗c4 ♘f6 3 ♘c3 ♗c5 4 ♘f3 ♘c6 5 d3 d6 6 h3 h6 7 ♘e2 ♘e7 8 ♘g3 0-0 9 0-0 c6 10 d4 exd4 11 ♘xd4 d5 12 exd5 cxd5 13 ♗b3 a5 14 a4 ♘e4 15 ♘xe4 dxe4 16 ♘b5 ♖a6 17 ♕xd8 [17 ♗xf7+? ♔xf7 18 ♕h5+ ♖g6 19 ♕xc5 ♗xh3∓] 17 … ♖xd8 18 ♗f4 ♖g6 19 ♗e3! ♗xe3 20 fxe3

♖f8 [20 ... ♗e6] 21 ♔h2 ♗e6 [□ 21 ... ♘f5] 22 ♗xe6 ♖xe6 23 ♖ad1 b6 24 ♖d7 f5 25 g3 ♖ff6 26 ♖fd1 ♘c6 27 ♘c7 ♖e7? 28 ♘d5 ♔f7 29 ♘xf6 gxf6 30 ♖xe7+ ♔xe7 31 ♔g2 ♘b4 32 ♖d2 h5 33 ♔f2 ♔e6 34 ♖d8 ♘xc2 35 ♖h8 ♘b4 36 b3 ♘d3+ 37 ♔f1 ♘c5 38 ♖xh5 ♘xb3 39 ♖h8 [□ 39 ♖h7] 39 ... ♘c5 40 ♖b8 ♘xa4 41 h4 ♘c3 [□ 41 ... ♔f7] 42 ♖xb6+ ♔f7 43 ♖a6 ♘d5 44 ♔f2 ♘b4 45 ♖xa5 ♘d3+ 46 ♔e2 ♘e5 47 ♖a6 ♔g7 48 ♖a8 ♘g4 49 ♔d2 ♔g6 50 ♖g8+ ♔h5 51 ♖g7 ♘e5 [51 ... ♔h6 52 ♖xg4!+-] 52 ♔c3 ♔h6 53 ♖e7 ♘f3 54 ♔c4 ♘d2+ 55 ♔d5 ♘f1 56 ♔e6 ♘xe3 57 ♖f7 ♘f1 58 ♖xf6+ ♔g7 59 ♖xf5 ♘d2 60 ♖e5 ♔h6 61 ♔f6 ♘f1 62 g4 **1-0**

Staunton(1)

**1851-✕BL-6**
**Löwenthal,J.J.+Buckle, H.T.**

[Staunton]

1 f4 e6 2 ♘f3 g6 3 e3 b6 4 ♗e2 ♗g7 5 0-0 ♗b7 6 c3 f5 7 ♘a3 ♘c6 8 d3 ♘h6 9 h3 0-0 10 e4 ♘e7 11 ♕c2 ♘f7 12 ♗e3 fxe4 13 dxe4 ♘d6 14 ♗d3 ♗h6 15 ♘e5 ♘c6 16 ♘g4 ♗g7 17 ♖ad1 ♕e7 18 b4 ♘f7 ± 19 ♘c4 d5 20 ♘b2 d4 21 cxd4 ♘xb4 [□ 21 ... ♘xd4] 22 ♕b3 ♘xd3 23 ♕xd3 ♖ad8 24 ♕c2 ♘d6 25 ♘f2 ♗h6 26 ♘g4 ♗g7 27 ♘f2 ♖f7 28 ♖fe1 ♖df8 29 ♘c4 h5? 30 ♘e5 ♗xe5 31 fxe5 ♘e8 32 ♖d2 ♕h4 33 ♔h2! ♔h7 34 g3 ♕e7 35 h4 a5 36 ♘h3 ♖f1 37 ♖xf1 ♖xf1 38 ♘g5+ ♔g8 39 ♖f2 ♖xf2+ 40 ♕xf2 ♗c8 41 d5 ♕f8 [41 ... exd5 42 exd5 ♕xe5?? 43 ♕f7++-] 42 ♕c2 exd5 43 exd5 ♗f5 44 ♕c6 ♕e7 45 ♗d4 ♕d7 46 ♕c4 ♔f8 47 a4 ♕e7 48 d6! cxd6 49 ♗xb6 ♕b7 [49 ... dxe5? 50 ♗c5 ♘d6 51 ♗xd6 ♕xd6 52 ♕f7#] 50 exd6 ♘f6 [50 ... ♘xd6 51 ♕d4 ♘f7 52 ♘h7+ ♔e8 53 ♕e3+ ♔d7 54 ♘f6++-] 51 ♕d4 ♘g4+ 52 ♔g1 ♘e5

53 d7! ♘xd7 [53 ... ♗xd7 54 ♗c5+ △ 55 ♕xe5] 54 ♕h8+ ♔e7 55 ♕g7+ ♔d6 56 ♘f7+ **1-0**

Staunton(1)

**1851-✕BL-7**
**Buckle,H.T.+Löwenthal, J.J.**

[Staunton]

1 f4 f5 2 b3 ♘f6 3 g3 e6 4 ♗b2 ♗e7 5 ♗g2 c6 6 ♘c3 ♘a6 7 ♘h3 d6 ∓ 8 0-0 0-0 9 e3 ♗d7 10 ♕e2 h6 11 ♖fe1 ♕c7 12 ♘f2 e5 13 fxe5 dxe5 14 ♘d3 ♗d6 15 e4! f4? [□ 15 ... fxe4] 16 gxf4 ♗g4 17 ♕f2 ♕d7 18 ♕h4 ♘h5? 19 f5 ♘f6 20 ♘e2 ♗xe2 21 ♖xe2 ♖ae8 22 ♔h1 b5 23 ♗f3 ♕f7 24 ♖g1 ♔h7 25 ♖g6 ♖g8 26 ♖eg2 ♘b8 27 ♘f2 [27 ♘f4!] 27 ... ♘bd7 28 d3 [△ 29 ♗c1; 28 ♘h3 ♔h8 29 ♘g5!] 28 ... ♔h8 29 ♗c1 ♗e7 30 ♗h5 ♕f8 31 ♕h3 ♘xh5 32 ♕xh5 ♘f6 33 ♕h3 ♗a3? 34 ♗xh6 [34 ♗xa3! ♕xa3 35 ♖xg7! ♕c1+ (35 ... ♖xg7 36 ♕xh6++-) 36 ♖g1 ♕xg1+ 37 ♖xg1+-; 34 ♖xf6! gxf6 35 ♗xa3 ♕f7 36 ♕xh6+ ♔h7 37 ♕xf6+ ♖g7 38 ♗f8+-] 34 ... ♘h7 35 ♗xg7+ ♖xg7 36 ♖xg7 ♕xg7 37 ♖xg7 ♔xg7 38 ♘g4 ♗c1 39 ♕h5 ♖e7 40 ♕g6+ ♔f8 41 f6 **1-0**

Staunton(1)

**DEACON✕LOWE** London
**[1851-✕DL]**

| | | | | | | | | | | | |
|---|---|---|---|---|---|---|---|---|---|---|---|
| F.H. Deacon | 1 | 1 | 0 | 1 | ½ | 1 | 0 | 1 | 1 | 1 | 7½ |
| E. Lowe | 0 | 0 | 1 | 0 | ½ | 0 | 1 | 0 | 0 | 0 | 2½ |

**1851-✕DL-1**
**Lowe, E.−Deacon, F.H.**

[Staunton]

1 e4 c5 2 ♘f3 e6 3 c4 ♘c6 4 ♘c3 g6 5 d3 b6 6 ♗e2 [6 ♗f4 ♗b7 7 ♘b5 ♖c8 8 ♘d6+ ♗xd6 9 ♗xd6 ♘ge7] 6 ... ♗g7 7 ♗g5 ♘ge7 8 h4 h6 9 ♗f4 a6 10 e5?! ♕c7 11 ♕d2 ♗b7 12 0-0-0 ♘xe5 13 d4 [13 ♘xe5 ♗xe5 14 ♗xe5 (14 ♗xh6? ♖xh6 15 ♕xh6? ♗f4+-+) 14 ... ♕xe5 15 f4 ♕c7] 13 ... cxd4 14 ♕xd4 ♘7c6 [□ 14 ... ♘xf3!-+] 15 ♕d2 0-0-0 16 ♘e4 d5 17 cxd5 ♖xd5 18 ♕c2 ♘d3+! 19 ♗xd3 ♕xf4+ 20 ♔b1 ♔b8 21 ♗c4 ♘b4 22 ♕e2 ♖xd1+ 23 ♖xd1 ♗xe4+ 24 ♗d3 ♘xd3 25 ♖xd3 ♖d8 26 ♘e1 ♕e5 27 ♔a1 ♖xd3 28 ♘xd3 ♗xd3 **0-1**

Staunton(1)

**1851-✕DL-2**
**Deacon, F.H.+Lowe, E.**

[Staunton]

1 f4 d5 2 ♘f3 ♘c6 3 e3 a6 4 b3 ♘f6 5 ♗b2 ♗f5 6 ♘c3 e6 7 ♘e2 ♗c5 8 ♘g3 ♗g6 9 ♖c1 d4 10 exd4 ♘xd4 11 c3 ♘f5 12 d4 ♗d6 13 ♘e5 ♘d5 14 ♘xf5 [14 ♕f3 ♕h4!-+] 14 ... ♗xf5 15 g3? f6? [□ 15 ... ♘xf4! 16 gxf4 ♕h4+ 17 ♔e2 ♗xe5 18 fxe5 ♗g4+-+; 17 ♔d2 ♕xf4+ 18 ♔e1 ♗xe5-+] 16 ♘d3 c6 17 ♕d2 h5 18 c4 ♘e7 19 h4 ♔f7 20 ♗g2! ♗xd3 21 ♕xd3 ♕a5+ 22 ♗c3 ♕xa2? 23 0-0 b5 [23 ... ♕xb3 24 ♖b1 ♕a4 25 ♖a1 ♗a3 26 ♗b2+-] 24 c5 ♗c7 25 ♕d1 ♘f5 26 ♖f2 ♕a3 27 ♖a1 ♕xa1 28 ♕xa1 ♘xg3 29 ♗xc6 ♖a7 30 ♕e1 ♖hd8 31 f5 exf5 32 d5 g6 33 ♕e6+ ♔g7 34 ♕xf6+ ♔~ 35 ♕g7# **1-0**

Staunton(1)

**1851-✕DL-3**
**Lowe, E.+Deacon, F.H.**

[Staunton]

1 e4 c5 2 ♘f3 e6 3 c4 ♘c6 4 ♘c3 a6 5 ♗e2 g6 6 d4 cxd4 7 ♘xd4 ♗g7 8 ♘xc6 bxc6 9 ♕d3 ♖b8 10 0-0 ♘e7 11 f4 0-0 12 c5! ♔h8 13 ♕d6 ♖b4 14 e5 f6 15 a3 ♘f5 16 ♕xf8+! ♕xf8 17 axb4 ♘d4 18 ♗d3 ♕d8 [□ 18 ... f5] 19 ♘e4 fxe5 20 ♘d6! ♔g8 21 fxe5 ♗xe5? 22 ♘f7 ♕c7 23 ♘h6+ ♔g7 24 ♖f7+ ♔h8 25 ♖f8+ ♔g7 26 ♖g8+ ♔f6 27 h4! [△ 28 ♗g5#] 27 ... ♗g3 28 ♗g5+ ♔e5 29 ♘g4+ ♔d5 30 ♘f6+ ♔e5 31 ♘e8 ♕b8 32 ♗d2 ♘f5 33 ♗c3+ ♔f4 34 ♖f1+ ♔g4 35 ♗e2+ ♔xh4 36 ♗f6+ g5 37 ♗xg5# **1-0**

Staunton(1)

**1851-✕DL-4**
**Deacon, F.H.+Lowe, E.**

[Staunton]

1 c4 c5 2 e3 e5 3 ♘c3 ♘f6 4 g3 ♘c6 5 ♗g2 ♗e7 6 ♘ge2 d6 7 f4 ♗d7 8 0-0 0-0 9 a3 ♖b8 10 ♕c2 g6 11 ♖b1 ♗e6 12 ♘d5 ♗f5 13 d3 ♕d7 14 b4 [14 e4!? ♗g4 15 fxe5 ♘xd5 (15 ... ♗xe2 16 exf6±) 16 exd6 ♗xe2 17 ♕xe2 ♘d4 18 ♕d1 ♗xd6 19 cxd5±] 14 ... ♘xd5 15 cxd5 ♘d8 16 e4 ♗g4 17 bxc5 [17 fxe5 △ 18 ♗h6] 17 ... exf4 18 gxf4! dxc5 19 ♘g3 h5 20 f5 ♗d6 21 f6 h4 22 ♕d2

22 ... ♖e8 23 ♕h6 ♗f8 24 ♕xh4 ♖c8 25 ♗h6 ♗h5 26 ♗h3 ♘e6 27 ♗xf8 ♖xf8 28 ♘xh5 gxh5 29 ♖b2 ♖fe8 30 ♖g2+ ♔f8 31 ♕xh5 **1-0**

Staunton(1)

**1851-✕DL-5**
**Lowe, E.=Deacon, F.H.**

[Staunton]

1 e4 c5 2 f4 e6 3 ♘f3 d5 4 ♘c3 ♘c6 5 ♗b5 a6 6 ♗xc6+ bxc6 7 d3 g6 8 ♕e2 ♗g7 9 e5 ♘h6 10 ♕f2 ♗f8 [10

… d4 11 ♘e2 △ 12 c3±] 11 h3 f6 12 g4 ♘f7 13 ♗d2 f×e5 14 f×e5 ♕c7 15 0-0 ♗g7 16 ♕×c5 ♘×e5 17 ♘×e5 ♗×e5 18 ♖ae1 ♗×c3 19 ♗f4 ♕a7 20 ♕×a7 ♖×a7 21 b×c3± ♖f8 22 ♗d6 ♖×f1+ 23 ♖×f1 ♖f7 24 ♖b1 ♔d7 25 ♗e5 ♖f3 26 h4 ♖h3 27 ♔g2 ♖e3 [27 … ♖×h4? 28 ♔g3±] 28 d4 ♖e2+ [□ 28 … ♖×c3] 29 ♔f3 ♖×c2 30 ♔f4 h5 31 g×h5 g×h5 32 ♔g5 ♖×a2 33 ♔×h5 ♖g2 34 ♖b8 ♖g1 35 ♔h6 a5 36 ♖a8 ♖a1 37 ♖a7++− ♔e8 38 h5 c5 39 ♔h7 ♗d7 40 h6 ♗a4 41 ♔g8 ♗c2 42 d×c5 ♖h1 43 ♗g7 [43 c6! ♖×h6 44 ♖a8+ ♔e7 45 c7 ♖g6+ 46 ♗g7+−; 43 … ♖g1+ 44 ♗g7 e5 45 ♖a8+ ♔e7 46 c7 ♗f5 47 h7+−] 43 … e5 44 c6 ♗f5 45 ♖×a5? [□ 45 ♗×e5! ♖g1+ 46 ♗g7 ♖g6 47 ♖a8+ ♔e7 48 c7 ♖c6 49 c8♕ ♖×c8 50 ♖×c8 ♗×c8 51 ♗f6+! (51 h7? ♗e6+ 52 ♔h8 ♔f7=) 51 … ♔∼ 52 h7+−; 49 … ♗×c8 50 ♗f8+ ♔f6 51 ♖×c8+−; □ 45 ♗f6 ♗e6+ (45 … ♖g1+ 46 ♖g7 ♖×g7+ 47 ♔×g7 a4! 48 ♗×e5 a3 49 ♔f6 ♗e4 50 ♔e6 ♔d8=) 46 ♔g7 ♖g1+ 47 ♗g5 ♖×g5+ 48 ♔f6 ♔d8 49 ♔×g5+−] 45 … ♗e6+ 46 ♔h8 e4 47 ♖a8+ ♔f7 48 ♖f8+ ♔e7 49 ♖f2 ♔d6 50 ♗f8+ ♔×c6 51 ♖f6 ♔d7 52 ♗c5 ♖h3 53 h7 ♖g3 54 ♗f2 ♖g2 55 ♖f8 ♔c7 56 ♗d4 ♖g5 57 ♖f1 ♖g6 58 ♖g1 ♖×g1 59 ♗×g1 ♗f5 60 ♔g7 ♗×h7 61 ♔×h7 ♔c6 62 ♔g6 ♔b5 **½-½** Staunton(1)

**1851-⚔DL-6**
**Deacon, F.H.+Lowe, E.**

[Staunton]

1 c4 e5 2 e3 f5 3 d4 ♘c6 4 a3 ♘f6 5 ♘c3 d6 6 g3 ♗e7 7 ♗g2 0-0 8 ♘ge2 ♕e8 9 b3 ♗d7 10 ♗b2 e4 11 ♕c2 ♕f7 12 f3 e×f3 13 ♗×f3 ♖ae8 14 0-0 ♗d8 15 ♕d3 ♕g6 16 ♖ae1 ♕h6 17 ♘f4 ♔h8 18 ♖e2 ♖f7 19 ♖fe1 ♖fe7 [△ 20 … ♘e4] 20 e4 [□ 20 ♘cd5] 20 … f×e4 21 ♘×e4 ♗f5 22 ♗c1! g5 23 ♘d5 ♘×d5 24 c×d5 ♘b8 25 ♗×g5?? [□ 25 ♕b5! ♗×e4 26 ♖×e4 b6 (26 … ♖×e4 27 ♗×e4 ♖f8 28 ♕×b7) 27 ♕×e8+ ♖×e8 28 ♖×e8+ ♔g7 29 ♖1e6 ♗f6 30 ♖×b8∓] 25 … ♕×g5 26 ♘×g5 ♗×d3 27 ♖×e7 ♖×e7 28 ♘e6 c6? 29 ♖d1 ♗c2? [□ 29 … ♖×e6∞] 30 ♖d2 ♗×b3 31 ♘×d8 ♗×d5 32 ♗×d5 c×d5 33 ♖b2 ♘c6 34 ♘×b7 ♘×d4 35 ♘×d6 ♖d7 36 ♘e8 ♘c6 37 ♖f2! ♖g7 [37 … h5 38 ♖f8+ ♔h7 39 ♘f6++−; 37 … ♘e7 38 ♖f8+ ♘g8 39 ♖×g8+ ♔×g8 40 ♘f6++−] 38 ♘×g7 ♔×g7 39 ♔f1 ♘e5 40 ♔e2 ♘g4 41 ♖f4 ♘f6 42 ♖a4 ♔g6 43 ♖×a7 ♔f5 44 ♔f3 ♔e5 45 ♖f7 ♘e4 46 ♔e3 d4+ 47 ♔d3 ♘c5+ 48 ♔c4 ♘e4 49 ♖e7+ **1-0**

Staunton(1)

**1851-⚔DL-7**
**Lowe, E.+Deacon, F.H.**

[Staunton]

1 e4 e6 2 c4 c5 3 ♘c3 ♘c6 4 ♘f3 g6 5 d4 c×d4 6 ♘×d4 ♗g7 7 ♗e3 ♘ge7 8 f4 0-0 9 ♘×c6 b×c6 10 ♗e2 [□ 10 ♗c5] 10 … d6 11 0-0 f5 12 ♕d2 ♗×c3 13 ♕×c3 f×e4 14 ♕d4 d5 15 ♗g4 ♘f5 16 ♗×f5 e×f5 17 ♖fd1 ♗e6 [□ 17 … ♗b7] 18 ♕e5 ♕f6 19 ♕d6 ♖ad8 20 ♕c5 [20 ♕×c6?] 20 … ♕f7 21 ♗d4∓ 21 … ♕c7 22 b3 ♖f7 23 g3 d×c4 24 b×c4 ♖fd7 25 ♔f2 ♔f7 26 ♖ab1! h6 [26 … ♕d6 27 ♕a5 ♕e7 28 ♕e5±] 27 ♗e5 ♕c8 28 ♖b8?! ♕×b8? [□ 28 … ♖×d1 29 ♖×c8 ♖8d2+ 30 ♔e3 ♖d3+=] 29 ♖×d7+ ♗×d7 30 ♗×b8 ♖×b8 31 ♕×a7 ♖b2+ 32 ♔e3 ♔e6 33 ♔d4 ♖×h2 34 a4 ♖g2 35 ♕b8 ♖×g3 36 ♔c5 ♔f7 37 a5 **1-0** Staunton(1)

**1851-⚔DL-8**
**Deacon, F.H.+Lowe, E.**

[Staunton]

1 e4 e5 2 ♘f3 ♘c6 3 d4 e×d4 4 ♗c4 d6 5 c3 d3 6 ♕b3 ♕f6 7 0-0 h6 8 ♗e3 ♗e7 9 ♘bd2 ♕g6 10 ♔h1 ♘f6 11 ♖ae1 0-0 12 ♗×d3 ♘g4 13 ♗f4 ♘ge5 14 ♘×e5 d×e5 15 ♗g3 ♕d6 16 ♕d5 [□ 16 ♕c2] 16 … ♗e6 17 ♕×d6 ♗×d6 18 ♗c4 ♖ae8 19 ♖d1 g5 20 ♗b5 f5 21 e×f5 ♗×f5 22 ♘c4 ♖f6 23 ♖fe1 ♖fe6 24 ♖d5 [24 ♘e3 ♖f6 25 ♘×f5 ♖×f5 26 ♗d3 ♖f6 27 ♖e4±] 24 … h5 25 h3 h4 26 ♗h2 ♔h7 27 ♗×c6 b×c6 28 ♖a5 ♗d3 29 ♘d2 ♔g6 30 ♘e4 ♗×e4 31 ♖×e4 ♔f5 32 f3 ♖b8 33 b3 ♖b5 34 ♖×a7 ♖d5 35 ♖e1 e4 36 ♗×d6 [36 f×e4+?! ♖×e4 37 ♖×e4?! ♖d1+ 38 ♗g1 ♔×e4 39 ♖a5 ♗f4 △ 40 … ♗e3] 36 … c×d6 37 f×e4+ ♔g6 38 e×d5 ♖×e1+ 39 ♔h2 c×d5 40 ♖d7 ♖e6 41 a4 ♔f5 42 a5 ♔e4 43 a6 ♔d3 44 a7 ♖e8 45 ♖c7 d4 46 c×d4 ♔×d4 47 b4 ♖a8 48 b5 ♔e3 49 b6 d5 50 ♖b7 d4 51 ♖b8 **1-0** Staunton(1)

**1851-⚔DL-9**
**Lowe, E.−Deacon, F.H.**

[Staunton]

1 e4 e6 2 c4 c5 3 f4 ♘c6 4 ♘f3 g6 5 ♘c3 ♗g7 6 ♗e2 d6 7 0-0 ♘h6 8 d3 f5 9 ♘g5? ♘d4 10 ♗e3 0-0 11 h3 ♘f7 12 ♘f3 ♗d7 13 ♗×d4 c×d4 14 ♘b1 f×e4 15 d×e4 d3!→ 16 ♕×d3 ♗×b2 17 ♘c3 ♗×a1 18 ♖×a1 ♗c6 19 ♖f1 ♘h6 20 ♘d4 ♖f6 21 g4 g5 22 f×g5 [□ 22 h4] 22 … ♖×f1+ 23 ♗×f1 ♘f7 24 ♘×e6 ♕e7 25 ♘d4 ♕×g5 26 ♘f5 h5 27 ♗g2 h×g4 28 h×g4 ♖e8 29 ♘d5 ♖e6 30 ♕g3 ♕c1+ 31 ♔h2 ♕×c4 32 ♘de7+ ♔f8 33 ♘c8 ♗×e4 34 ♘c×d6 ♘×d6 35 ♘×d6 ♖h6+ **0-1** Staunton(1)

**1851-⚔DL-10**
**Deacon, F.H.+Lowe, E.**

[Staunton]

1 d4 d5 2 c4 c6 [□ 2 … e6] 3 e3 ♘f6 4 ♘c3 e6 5 a3 ♗d6 6 f4 h5 7 ♗d3 g5?! 8 f×g5 ♘g4 9 ♘f3 ♕c7 10 ♘e2 ♘×h2 11 ♘f4 ♗×f4 12 e×f4 ♘g4 13 ♘e5 d×c4 14 ♗×c4 f5 15 ♘×g4 f×g4 16 ♕e2 [□ 16 ♕×g4 h×g4 (16 … ♕a5+ 17 b4) 17 ♖×h8+ ♔d7 18 ♖h7+ ♔d6 19 ♖×c7 ♔×c7 20 ♗e2+−] 16 … ♕d6 17 f5 ♕×d4 18 ♗×e6 ♗×e6 19 ♕×e6+ ♔d8 20 ♗e3 ♕×b2 21 ♖d1+ ♔c7 22 ♕e7+ ♔c8 23 ♗f4 ♕c3+ 24 ♔f2 g3+ 25 ♔g1 **1-0**

Staunton(1)

## JAENISCH⚔STAUNTON

London

[1851-⚔JS]

| | | | | | | | | | | | |
|---|---|---|---|---|---|---|---|---|---|---|---|
| C.F. Jaenisch | 0 | 0 | 1 | ½ | 1 | 1 | 0 | 0 | 0 | 0 | 3½ |
| H. Staunton | 1 | 1 | 0 | ½ | 0 | 0 | 1 | 1 | 1 | 1 | 6½ |

**1851-⚔JS-1**
**Staunton, H.+Jaenisch, C.F.**

[Staunton]

1 e4 e5 2 ♘f3 ♘c6 3 d4 e×d4 4 ♗c4 ♗c5 5 0-0 d6 6 c3 d×c3 7 ♘×c3 ♗e6 8 ♗×e6 f×e6 9 ♕b3 ♕c8 10 ♘g5 ♘d4 11 ♕a4+ c6 12 ♗e3 b5? [□ 12 … e5] 13 ♕d1 e5 14 b4 ♗×b4 [14 … ♗b6 15 ♖c1; 15 a4] 15 ♗×d4 e×d4 16 ♕×d4 ♗×c3 17 ♕×c3 ♘f6 18 e5 ♘d5 19 ♕f3 ♕d7 20 e6 ♕e7 21 ♘f7 ♖f8 22 ♖fe1 ♕f6 23 ♘×d6+ [23 ♕g3? ♖×f7!=] 23 … ♔e7 24 ♕g3 ♕×f2+ [24 … ♕f4 25 ♕×g7+ ♔×d6 26 ♕d7+ ♔c5 27 ♖ac1++−] 25 ♕×f2 ♖×f2 26 ♔×f2 ♔×d6 27 ♖ac1 ♖e8 28 ♖c2 c5 29 ♖e4 c4 30 ♖b2 a6 31 a3 [31 a4 c3!∓] 31 … ♖×e6 32 ♖×e6+ ♔×e6 33 ♔e2 ♔e5 34 ♔d1 ♘e3+ 35 ♔c1 g6? [□ 35 … g5] 36 g3 g5 37 a4 b×a4 38 ♖a2 ♘f1 39 g4 ♔f4?! 40 ♖f2+ ♔×g4 41 ♖×f1 ♔h3 42 ♖f5 h6 43 ♖f6 ♔×h2 44 ♖×h6+ ♔g3 45 ♔d2 g4 46 ♔e3 ♔g2 47 ♔f4 ♔f2! 48 ♖h2+ ♔e1 49 ♔e3 ♔d1 [49 … ♔f1 50 ♔f4] 50 ♔d4 **1-0** Staunton(1)

**1851-⚔JS-2**
**Jaenisch, C.F.−Staunton, H.**

[Staunton]

1 e4 e5 2 f4 d5 3 e×d5 e4! 4 ♘c3 [4 ♗b5+ c6 5 d×c6 b×c6 6 ♗c4 ♘f6 7 d4 ♘bd7! (7 … ♗d6?!±; 7 … ♕b6!?∞) 8 ♘e2 ♘b6 9 ♗b3 ♗a6 10 ♘bc3 ♗b4 11 0-0 ♗×c3 12 b×c3 ♘fd5∓; 11 ♗d2 0-0 12 0-0! ♗×c3 13 ♗×c3 ♘bd5∓] 4 … ♘f6 5 d3 ♗b4 6 d×e4 ♘×e4 7 ♕d4 ♗×c3+ 8 b×c3 0-0 9 ♘f3 ♖e8 10 ♗e2 ♘d6! [10 … ♘f6] 11 ♗b2 ♖e4 12 ♕f2 ♘c4 13 0-0-0± ♘×b2 14 ♔×b2 ♕d6 15 ♖d4 ♖×f4

16 ♖xf4 ♕xf4 17 ♕d4 ♕d6 18 ♖e1 ♗d7 19 ♗d3 h6 20 g4 ♘a6 21 g5 ♘c5 22 gxh6 ♘a4+ 23 ♔a1 ♕xh6 24 ♖g1 ♖e8 25 ♘e5 ♘b6 26 c4 ♕f6 27 ♘f3 ♕xd4+ 28 ♘xd4 ♘a4 29 ♘b3 b6 30 ♔b1 ♖e5 31 ♔c1 ♘c3 32 ♔d2 ♘e4+ 33 ♔e3 ♘g5+ 34 ♔f4 f6 35 ♖g2 ♘h3+ 36 ♔f3 g5 37 ♖d2 g4+ 38 ♔g2 ♖e1 [△ 39 ... ♖g1#] 39 ♔g3 ♖e3+ 40 ♔g2 f5 41 ♘d4 f4 42 ♔f1 f3 43 ♗f5 ♗xf5 44 ♘xf5 ♖a3! 45 ♘h6+ ♔f8 46 ♘xg4 ♖xa2 [△ 47 ... ♖a1+−+] 47 ♘f2 ♖a1+ 48 ♖d1 ♖xd1+ 49 ♘xd1 ♔e7 50 ♘e3 ♔d6 51 ♔e1 ♔e5 52 ♔d2 ♔e4 53 c3 a5 54 ♘g4 ♔f5 55 ♘e3+ ♔f4 56 d6! cxd6 57 ♘d5+ ♔e4 58 ♘xb6 ♘f4 [△ 59 ... f2−+] 59 ♔e1 ♘d3+ 60 ♔d2 ♘e5 61 h4 ♔f5 62 ♔e3 ♔g4 63 h5 ♔xh5 64 ♘c8 ♘xc4+ 65 ♔xf3 a4 66 ♔e4 a3 67 ♔d5 ♘e3+ 68 ♔e4 ♘d1 69 c4 ♘b2 70 ♘xd6 ♘xc4 **0-1**

Staunton(1)

**1851-⚔JS-3**
**Staunton, H.−Jaenisch, C.F.**

[Staunton]

1 e4 e5 2 ♗c4 ♗c5 3 ♘f3 d6 4 c3 ♘f6 5 d3 h6 6 0-0 0-0 7 d4 exd4 8 cxd4 ♗b6 9 ♘c3 ♘xe4 10 ♘xe4 d5 11 ♗d3 dxe4 12 ♗xe4 ♘d7 13 ♗e3 ♘f6 14 ♗c2 ♗g4 15 ♕d3 ♗xf3 16 gxf3 ♕d5 17 ♕f5 c6 18 ♖ad1 ♗c7 19 ♔h1 ♕d6 20 ♕h3 ♘d5 21 ♖g1 ♔h8 22 ♖g2 ♘f4 23 ♕f5± g6 24 ♗xf4 ♕xf4 25 ♕h3 ♔g7 26 ♖dg1 ♖h8 27 ♖g4 [△ 28 ♗xg6] 27 ... ♕d6 28 ♗xg6! ♖ag8 [28 ... fxg6 29 ♖xg6+ ♕xg6 30 ♕d7+ ♔f6 31 ♖xg6++−] 29 ♗e4+ [□ 29 ♕h5; □ 29 ♗c2+! ♔f8 30 ♖xg8+ ♖xg8 31 ♕c8+ ♕d8 32 ♖xg8+ △ 33 ♕xb7 ±] 29 ... ♔f8 30 ♖xg8+ ♖xg8 31 ♕c8+? [□ 31 ♖xg8+ △ 32 ♕g3+±] 31 ... ♔e7 32 ♕h3 ♖xg1+ 33 ♔xg1 ♕xd4 34 ♕xh6!? ♕xb2 35 ♕g5+ ♕f6 36 h4 ♕xg5+ 37 hxg5 ♗f4 38 g6 fxg6 39 ♗xg6 c5 40 ♗d3 ♔d6 41 ♔f1 a6 42 a4 ♔e5 43 ♔e2 ♔d4 44 ♗f5 [44 a5! ♗c7 45 ♗e4 b6 46 axb6 ♗xb6 47 ♗b7 a5 48 ♗c6∞] 44 ... b5 45 axb5 axb5 46 ♔d1 ♔c3 47 ♗e4 b4 48 ♗h7 c4 49 ♗g8 b3 50 ♗e6 ♔b4 51 ♗d5 c3 52 ♗e4 ♔a3 **0-1**

Staunton(1)

**1851-⚔JS-4**
**Jaenisch, C.F.=Staunton, H.**

[Staunton]

1 e4 e5 2 ♘f3 ♘c6 3 ♗c4 ♗c5 4 c3 ♘f6 5 d4 exd4 6 e5 d5 7 ♗b5 ♘e4 8 ♗xc6+ bxc6 9 cxd4 ♗b6 10 ♘c3 ♗g4 11 ♗e3 0-0 12 ♕a4!? ♕d7 [12 ... ♘xc3 13 bxc3 ♗xf3 14 gxf3 ♕d7 △ 15 ... f6∓] 13 ♘xe4 dxe4 14 ♘d2 ♕d5 15 ♖c1 ♗d7 16 ♕c4 ♖ae8 17 0-0 ♔h8 [17 ... f6? 18 ♘xe4] 18 ♘b3 f6 19 ♘c5 [△ 20 ♕xd5 cxd5 21 ♘xd7+−] 19 ... ♗c8 20 ♕xd5 cxd5 21 exf6 ♖xf6 22 b4 c6 23 a4 ♗g4 [△ 24 ... ♗e2 25 ♖f∼ ♗c4] 24 ♖fe1 h6 25 h3 ♗c8 26 ♖e2 [±; △ 27 ♖ec2] 26 ... ♗xc5 [26 ... a6 27 ♖ec2 g5 28 b5 axb5 29 axb5 cxb5 30 ♘xe4 dxe4 31 ♖xc8±] 27 bxc5!? [□ 27 ♖xc5! △ 28 ♖ec2±] 27 ... g5 28 ♖b2 ♗a6 29 ♖cb1 ♖ff8 30 ♖b4 ♔g7 31 ♔h2 ♔g6 32 g3 h5 33 h4 ♗d3 34 ♖1b2 gxh4 35 gxh4 ♖f3 36 ♖b8 ♖xb8 37 ♖xb8 ♗c2 38 a5 ♖f7 39 ♖c8 ♗a4 40 ♖h8 ♖h7 41 ♖g8+ ♖g7 42 ♖h8 ♖h7 43 ♖xh7 ♔xh7 44 ♔g3 ♔g6 45 ♗f4 ♔f5 **½-½**

Staunton

**1851-⚔JS-5**
**Staunton, H.+Jaenisch, C.F.**

[Staunton]

1 e4 e5 2 ♘f3 ♘c6 3 d4 exd4 4 ♗c4 ♗c5 5 0-0 d6 6 c3 dxc3 7 ♘xc3 ♗e6 8 ♗xe6 fxe6 9 ♕b3 ♕c8 10 ♘g5 ♘d4 11 ♕a4+ c6 12 ♗e3 e5 13 ♗xd4 ♗xd4 14 ♕b3 ♕d7 15 ♘e2 ♗b6 16 ♖ad1 ♘h6 17 ♘f3 ♕e7 18 a4 0-0-0 19 ♕a3 ♖he8 20 a5 ♗c7 21 a6 ♗b6 22 axb7+ ♔xb7 23 ♖a1 d5 24 ♕a6+ ♔b8 25 ♘c3 ♘f7 26 ♖fc1 ♖d6 27 b4 d4 28 ♘a4 ♕b7 29 ♕c4 ♖c8 30 ♘c5 ♕e7 31 ♘e1 ♖g6 [△ 32 ... ♘d6] 32 ♘ed3! ♘d6 33 ♕b3 ♘b5? 34 ♘xe5 ♖d6 35 ♘c4 ♗xc5 36 bxc5 ♖e6 37 e5 ♕xc5 [□ 37 ... ♖xe5] 38 ♘b6! [38 ♘d6] 38 ... ♕xb6! 39 ♕xe6 ♘c3 40 ♖e1 c5 41 ♕c4 ♖e8 42 e6 a5 43 e7 ♕b4 44 ♕f7 **1-0**

Staunton(1)

**1851-⚔JS-6**
**Jaenisch, C.F.+Staunton, H.**

[Staunton]

1 e4 e5 2 ♘c3 ♗c5 [2 ... ♘f6] 3 f4 ♗xg1 4 ♖xg1 d6 5 d4 ♘c6 6 dxe5 dxe5 7 ♕xd8+ ♔xd8 8 fxe5 ♘xe5 9 ♗f4 ♘g6 10 0-0-0+± ♗d7 11 ♗g3 a6 12 ♗c4 ♘h6 13 ♘d5 ♖c8 14 ♖gf1 ♖e8 15 ♖d4 ♘e5?? 16 ♗h4+ f6 17 ♖xf6! [17 ♘xf6!] 17 ... gxf6 18 ♗xf6+ ♖e7 19 ♘xe7 ♘hg4 20 ♗h4 c5 21 ♘xc8+ ♔xc8 22 ♖d5 ♘xc4 23 ♖xc5+ ♗c6 24 ♖xc4 ♘e3 25 ♖d4 ♘xg2 26 ♗g3 h5 27 h4 ♘e3 28 e5 ♘f5 29 ♖d3 ♗e4 30 ♖c3+ ♔d7 31 ♔d2 ♔e6 32 ♔e2 ♘xg3+ 33 ♖xg3 ♗xc2 34 ♖g5 ♗f5 35 ♔f3 ♔xe5 36 ♖xh5 ♔f6 37 ♔f4 ♗d7 38 ♖g5 ♗b5 39 ♖xb5 axb5 40 b4 ♔g6 41 ♔g4 b6 42 a3 **1-0**

Staunton(1)

**1851-⚔JS-7**
**Staunton, H.+Jaenisch, C.F.**

[Staunton]

1 e4 e5 2 ♘f3 d6 3 ♗c4 ♗g4 [3 ... ♗e7] 4 c3 ♗xf3 5 ♕xf3 ♘f6 6 0-0 ♗e7 7 ♕e2 [△ 8 f4] 7 ... 0-0 8 d4 ♘bd7 9 f4 c6 10 ♗d3 ♕c7 11 ♘a3 ♖fe8 12 ♘c2 h6 13 ♘e1 exd4 14 cxd4 ♕b6 15 ♗e3 d5 16 e5 ♘h7 17 ♕g4 ♘df6!? 18 exf6 ♗xf6 19 ♗f2 [19 ♕f3? ♖xe3!−+; 19 ♕f5 g6 20 ♕h3 ♖xe3!−+] 19 ... ♗xd4 20 ♗xh7+ ♔xh7 21 ♘f3 ♗xf2+ 22 ♖xf2 ♖e2? 23 ♘g5+ hxg5 24 ♕xe2 d4 25 fxg5 **1-0**

Staunton(1)

**1851-⚔JS-8**
**Jaenisch, C.F.−Staunton, H.**

[Staunton]

1 e4 e5 2 ♘c3 ♘f6 [2 ... ♗c5] 3 f4 d5 4 exd5 e4 5 d4 ♗b4 6 ♗c4 ♘xd5 7 ♗xd5 ♕xd5 8 ♘ge2 ♗g4 9 0-0 ♗xc3 10 ♘xc3 [10 bxc3?!] 10 ... ♕d7 11 ♕e1 f5 [11 ... ♕xd4+ 12 ♗e3 ♕c4 13 h3 ♗d7 14 ♖ad1 ♘c6 15 ♗d4±] 12 ♗e3 0-0 13 ♕h4 ♖f6 14 h3 ♖h6 15 ♕f2 ♗h5 16 g4 ♗f7 [□ 16 ... ♖g6 17 ♘xe4 ♗xg4 18 ♘c5 (18 hxg4 fxe4 19 g5 ♕f5∓) 18 ... ♗xh3+ 19 ♔h2 ♕f7 20 ♔xh3 ♖g4−+] 17 h4 ♗c4 18 ♖fe1 fxg4 19 ♘xe4 ♗d5 20 f5 ♖b6 21 ♗g5 ♘a6 22 c4 ♗xc4 23 ♘c5 g3! 24 ♕xg3 ♕xf5 [24 ... ♘xc5 25 dxc5 ♖xb2 26 ♕c3+−; 24 ... ♕xd4+? 25 ♗e3+−] 25 ♖e5 ♕g6 26 b3 ♗f7 27 ♘d7 ♖d6 28 h5 [□ 28 ♖e7 (△ 29 ♘e5) 28 ... ♗d5 29 ♘e5 ♕e4 30 ♕xg7+ ♔xg7 31 ♗h6++−] 28 ... ♕xh5 29 ♘f6+ [29 ♗f6 ♕h6=] 29 ... gxf6 30 ♗xf6+ ♕g6 31 ♖g5 ♖xf6 32 ♔h2 ♖ae8 33 ♖g1 ♕xg5 34 ♕xg5+ ♖g6 35 ♕d2 c6 36 ♖xg6+ ♗xg6 37 ♕g5 ♘c7 38 ♕a5 ♘b5 39 d5 b6 40 ♕d2? [□ 40 ♕a6] 40 ... ♖d8 41 a4 ♖xd5 42 ♕f4 ♘d6 43 ♕f6 ♖d2+ 44 ♔g1 ♖d1+ 45 ♔h2 ♖d2+ 46 ♔g1 ♖d1+ 47 ♔h2 ♖d5 48 ♕d8+ ♘e8 49 ♕e7 ♖d2+ 50 ♔g1 ♖d3 51 b4 ♖d4 52 b5 cxb5 53 axb5 ♖d5 54 ♕e6+ ♗f7 55 ♕g4+ ♔f8 56 ♕b4+ ♘d6 57 ♕a3 ♔e8 58 ♕xa7 ♖xb5 59 ♕c7! ♖b1+ 60 ♔h2 ♖b2+ 61 ♔g1 ♘c4 62 ♕c6+ ♔e7 63 ♕e4+ ♗e6 64 ♕xh7+ ♔d6 65 ♕g7 b5 66 ♕f8+ ♔d5 67 ♕d8+ ♔c6 68 ♕e8+ ♗d7 69 ♕e4+ ♔c7 70 ♕d4 ♗c6 71 ♕c5 ♔b7 72 ♔f1 ♖d2 73 ♔e1 ♖d7 74 ♔e2 ♖d2+ 75 ♔e1 ♖d5 76 ♕f8 ♘e5 77 ♕g7+ ♔a6 78 ♕c7 b4 79 ♕c8+ ♔b5 80 ♕b8+ ♔c4 81 ♕b6 b3 82 ♔e2 ♗b5 83 ♕c7+ ♔b4+ 84 ♔e3 ♖c5 85 ♕d8 ♘d3 86 ♕d4+ ♗c4 87 ♔d2 b2 88 ♕c3+ ♔a4 89 ♔c2 [89 ♕c2+ ♗b3 90 ♕xd3 ♖d5 91 ♕xd5 ♗xd5−+] 89 ... ♗b3+ 90 ♔b1 ♗a2+ [90 ... ♖xc3??] 91 ♔xa2 ♖xc3 **0-1**

Staunton(1)

**1851-✕JS-9**
**Staunton, H.+Jaenisch, C.F.**

[Staunton]

1 e4 e5 2 ♘f3 ♘c6 3 d4 exd4 4 ♗c4 ♗c5 5 0-0 d6 6 c3 dxc3 7 ♘xc3 ♗e6 8 ♗xe6 fxe6 9 ♕b3 ♕c8 10 ♗e3 [10 ♘g5 ♘d4!] 10 ... ♗xe3 11 fxe3 ♘f6 12 ♘g5 ♘d8 13 ♖ac1 [△ 14 ♘b5!] 13 ... a6 14 ♘a4 ♕d7! 15 e5 h6 16 ♘f3 b5 17 exf6 [17 ♘c5±] 17 ... bxa4 18 ♕c2 gxf6 19 ♕g6+

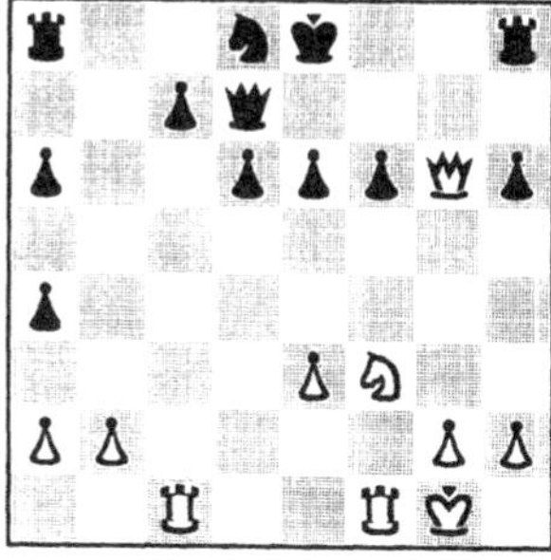

19 ... ♔e7? 20 ♘e5!+- dxe5 21 ♕xf6+ **1-0**

Staunton(1)

**1851-✕JS-10**
**Jaenisch, C.F.-Staunton, H.**

[Staunton]

1 e4 e5 2 ♘f3 ♘c6 3 ♗b5 ♘f6 4 ♕e2 d6 5 d4 ♗d7 6 d5 ♘e7 7 ♗g5 ♗xb5 8 ♕xb5+ c6 9 ♕xb7 ♖b8 10 ♕xa7 cxd5 11 ♗xf6 gxf6 12 ♕a4+ ♕d7 13 ♕xd7+ ♔xd7 14 ♘c3 d4 [14 ... ♖xb2!?] 15 ♘a4 ♗h6 16 ♔e2 [16 0-0 ♖hc8 17 c3 dxc3 18 ♘xc3 ♖xb2∓; 17 ♘e1 ♗d2] 16 ... ♖b4 17 b3 ♖c8 18 a3 ♖bb8? [◻ 18 ... ♖xa4! 19 bxa4 ♖xc2+ 20 ♔d3 ♖xf2 21 ♖hg1 ♘g6∓] 19 ♔d3 f5 20 exf5 ♘xf5 21 g4 ♘e7 22 g5 ♗g7 23 ♖he1 ♘d5 24 ♖a2 f5 25 gxf6 ♗xf6 26 ♖eg1 ♖c3+! 27 ♘xc3 [27 ♔e4 ♔e6-+] 27 ... ♘xc3 28 ♘xe5+ dxe5 29 ♖aa1 e4+ 30 ♔d2 h6! 31 ♖af1 ♗g5+ 32 f4 ♗e7 [32 ... exf3+ 33 ♖xg5!?] 33 ♖g7 ♘d5 34 ♖h7? [◻ 34 f5∓] 34 ... ♖g8 35 ♖xh6 ♖g2+ 36 ♔e1 ♗xa3 37 ♖h7+ [37 ♖f2? ♗b4+!-+] 37 ... ♔c6 38 ♖h6+ ♔c5 39 ♖h5 e3 40 ♖e5 ♗b4+ 41 ♔d1 e2+ 42 ♖xe2 ♘c3+ **0-1**

Staunton(1)

## LÖWENTHAL✕WILLIAMS

London

[1851-✕LW]

J.J. Löwenthal
½ 0 1 ½ 1 1 0 0 1 1 ½ 0 1 0 1 8½
E. Williams
½ 1 0 ½ 0 0 1 1 0 0 ½ 1 0 1 0 6½

**1851-✕LW-1**
**Williams, E.=Löwenthal, J.J.**

[Staunton]

1 f4 e6 2 e3 b6 3 ♘f3 ♗b7 4 b3 ♘c6 5 ♗b2 f6 6 ♗e2 ♘h6 7 0-0 ♗e7 8 ♗b5 0-0 9 ♗xc6 ♗xc6 10 c4 d6 11 d3 e5 12 d4 e4 13 ♘e1 f5 14 ♘c3 [◻ 14 d5] 14 ... ♗d7 15 ♕h5 ♗f6 [15 ... ♘g4 16 h3?? g6-+] 16 g3 ♘g4 17 ♘g2 [△ 18 ♘d5] 17 ... c6 18 ♘d1 ♕e7 [◻ 18 ... d5 △ 19 ... ♕e7 20 ... ♖f6 21 ... ♖h6] 19 ♘f2 g6 20 ♕h3 ♕g7 21 ♖ad1 [21 ♘xg4?? fxg4-+] 21 ... h6 [◻ 21 ... c5!] 22 ♗c1 g5 [△ 23 ... ♘xf2 24 ♖xf2 g4 25 ♕h5 ♗e8-+] 23 ♘xg4 fxg4 24 ♕h5 gxf4 25 ♖xf4 ♗g5 26 ♖ff1 ♖f3 [26 ... ♗e8 27 ♕xg4! ♗xe3+? 28 ♘xe3+-] 27 ♘f4 ♔h7 28 d5 ♗xf4 29 exf4 c5 30 ♖fe1 ♖ae8 31 ♖e2 ♕g6 32 ♕xg6+ ♔xg6 33 ♖de1 ♗f5 34 ♖e3 h5 35 h4 ♖xe3 36 ♖xe3 ♗d7 37 ♔f2 ♔f5 38 ♗d2 b5 39 ♗a5 ♖c8 40 ♖e2 ♗e8 41 ♖d2 a6 42 ♗c3 ♖c7 43 ♗a5 ♖b7 44 ♔e3 b4 45 ♗d8 ♗g6 46 ♖b2 ♖d7 47 ♗g5 a5 48 ♗h6 ♔f6 49 ♗g5+ ♔f7 50 ♖b1 ♗f5 51 ♖a1 ♖b7 52 a4 ½-½

Staunton(1)

**1851-✕LW-2**
**Löwenthal, J.J.-Williams, E.**

[Staunton]

1 e4 e6 2 d4 d5 3 exd5 exd5 4 ♘f3 ♘f6 5 ♗d3 ♗d6 6 0-0 0-0 7 ♘c3 ♗g4 8 ♗e2 h6 9 ♗e3 ♘c6 10 ♘e1 ♗xe2 11 ♘xe2 ♘g4 12 ♗f4 f5 13 ♗xd6 ♕xd6 14 ♘g3 ♕f4 15 c3 ♖ae8 16 ♕f3 [◻ 16 ♕b3; ◻ 16 ♘f3; 16 ♘d3?! ♕d6 △ 17 ... f4] 16 ... ♕xf3 17 gxf3!? f4 18 fxg4 fxg3 19 hxg3 ♖e2 20 ♖ab1 ♘a5 21 f4 ♖fe8 22 ♘f3 ♘c4 23 ♖f2 ♖8e3 24 ♔f1∓ ♖xf2+ 25 ♔xf2 ♖xf3+ 26 ♔xf3 ♘d2+ 27 ♔e2 ♘xb1 28 ♔d1 [◻ 28 ♔d3] 28 ... ♘xc3+ 29 bxc3 ♔f7 30 ♔e2 ♔e6 31 ♔e3 b6 32 ♔d3 c5 33 ♔e3 [◻ 33 c4] 33 ... ♔d6 34 f5? ♔e7 35 ♔f3 cxd4 36 cxd4 b5 37 g5 hxg5 38 g4 ♔d6 39 ♔e3 ♔c6 40 ♔d3 ♔b6 41 ♔c3 ♔a5 42 ♔b3 b4 **0-1**

Staunton(1)

**1851-✕LW-3**
**Williams, E.-Löwenthal, J.J.**

[Staunton]

1 f4 e6 2 e3 b6 3 ♘f3 ♗b7 4 b3 ♘h6 5 ♗b2 f6 6 ♗e2 ♗e7 7 0-0 0-0 8 c4 c5 9 ♘c3 d5 10 ♕c2 ♘a6 11 a3 ♘c7 12 ♖ae1 f5 13 ♘d1 ♗f6 14 ♗e5 ♗xe5 15 ♘xe5 ♘e8 16 ♘f2 ♘f7 17 d4 ♖c8 18 ♕d1 ♘ed6 19 ♗f3 dxc4 20 ♗xb7 ♘xb7 21 ♘xc4 ♘fd6 22 ♘e5 cxd4 23 ♕xd4 ♕e7 24 b4 ♖fd8 25 ♕b2 ♘c4 26 ♘xc4 ♖xc4 27 ♖c1 ♘d6 28 ♖fd1 ♖dc8 29 ♖xc4 ♘xc4 30 ♕b3 b5 31 e4 ♖d8 32 exf5 exf5 33 ♖xd8+ ♕xd8 34 a4 ♕d2 35 g3 ♔f8! 36 ♕f3? [◻ 37 ♕d1] 36 ... ♘e3 37 ♕a8+ ♔f7 38 ♕xa7+ ♔g6 39 ♕b6+ ♔h5 **0-1**

Staunton(1)

**1851-✕LW-4**
**Löwenthal, J.J.=Williams, E.**

[Staunton]

1 e4 e5 2 ♘f3 ♘c6 3 ♗c4 ♗c5 4 0-0 ♘f6 5 d3 d6 6 h3 ♘e7 7 c3 0-0 8 d4 ♗b6 9 dxe5 ♘xe4 10 ♘g5 ♘xg5 11 ♗xg5 ♗e6 12 exd6 cxd6 13 ♗d3 ♕d7 14 ♘d2 f6 15 ♗h4 ♘f5 16 ♗xf5 ♗xf5 17 ♘c4 ♗c7 18 ♗g3 ♖ad8 19 ♘e3 [19 ♕d5+ ♗e6 20 ♕xb7?? ♗xc4-+] 19 ... ♗e6 20 ♘d5 ♕f7 21 ♘xc7 ♕xc7 22 ♖e1 ♗f7 23 ♕d4 ♕c5 24 ♕xc5 [24 ♖ad1] 24 ... dxc5 25 ♖e7 ♗d5 26 ♗c7 ♖de8 27 ♖ae1 ♖xe7 28 ♖xe7 ♖f7 29 ♖e8+ ♖f8 30 ♖xf8+ ♔xf8 31 ♗d6+ ♔f7 32 ♗xc5 b6 33 ♗d4 ♗xa2 34 ♔f1 ♔e6 35 ♔e2 ♗c4+ 36 ♔e3 ♗f1 37 ♔f3 g6 38 h4 h5 39 g3= ♗c4 40 ♔f4 ♗b3 41 ♔e4 ♗c4 42 ♗e3 ♗f1 43 ♔f4 ♗e2 44 b4 ♗d3 45 ♗d4 ♗c4 46 ♔e3 ♔f5 47 ♔d2 g5 48 ♔c2 gxh4 49 gxh4 ½-½

Staunton(1)

**1851-✕LW-5**
**Williams, E.-Löwenthal, J.J.**

[Staunton]

1 e4 d6 2 f4 e5 3 ♘f3 ♗g4 4 ♗c4 ♘f6 5 fxe5 ♗xf3 6 ♕xf3 dxe5 7 ♕b3 ♗c5 8 ♗xf7+ ♔e7 9 ♕e6+ ♔f8 10 ♖f1 ♘c6 11 c3 ♕e7 12 d3?? ♕xf7 ...? **0-1**

Staunton(1)

**1851-✕LW-6**
**Löwenthal, J.J.+Williams, E.**

[Staunton]

1 e4 e6 2 f4 d5 3 e5 c5 4 ♗b5+ ♗d7 5 ♗xd7+ ♕xd7 6 ♘f3 ♘c6 7 d3 ♗e7 8 0-0 ♘h6 9 ♘c3 0-0 10 ♘e2 f5 11 c3 ♖ab8? [11 ... ♖ac8; 11 ... ♖fd8] 12 h3 ♕e8 13 d4 ♕g6 14 ♔h1 cxd4 15 cxd4 ♖bc8 16 ♗d2 ♔h8 17 ♖c1 ♘f7 18 ♖c3 ♕h6 19 ♖b3? ♖c7 20 a3 ♖g8 21 ♖c3 g5 22 fxg5 ♘xg5? 23 h4 ♕h5 24 ♘f4 ♕g4 25 hxg5 ♗xg5 26 ♘h2 [◻ 26 ♘xe6] 26 ... ♕xd1 27 ♖xd1 ♗xf4 28 ♗xf4 ♖cg7 29 ♖c2 [◻ 29 g3] 29 ... h5 30 ♘f3 ♖g6 31 g3 ♔g7 32 ♖h2 ♖h8 33 ♔g2 ♖g4 34 ♔f2 [34 ♘g5] 34 ... ♔g6 35 b4 a6 36 ♖h3 [△ 37 ♘h2] 36 ... ♘a7 37 ♘h2 ♘b5 38 ♖d3 ♖c8 39 ♘xg4 fxg4 40 ♖h1 ♖c2+ 41 ♖d2 ♖c4 42 ♖d3 ♖c2+ 43 ♔e1 ♖a2 44 ♗c1 ♖c2 45 ♔d1 ♖c4 46 ♗b2 ♖c6 47 ♔d2 ♖c8 48

♖f1 ♘c7 49 ♖c3 ♔g5 50 ♖f7 h4 51 gxh4+ ♔xh4 52 ♖cxc7 ♖g8 53 ♖g7 ♖f8 54 ♖cf7 **1-0** Staunton(1)

**1851-⚔LW-7**
**Williams,E.+Löwenthal, J.J.**

[Staunton]

1 e4 c5 2 f4 a6 3 ♘f3 e6 4 ♗e2 ♘c6 5 0-0 f6 6 d3 ♗d6 7 f5 ♘ge7 8 ♘h4 ♕c7 9 g3 ♘d8 10 ♗h5+ ♔f8 11 fxe6 dxe6?

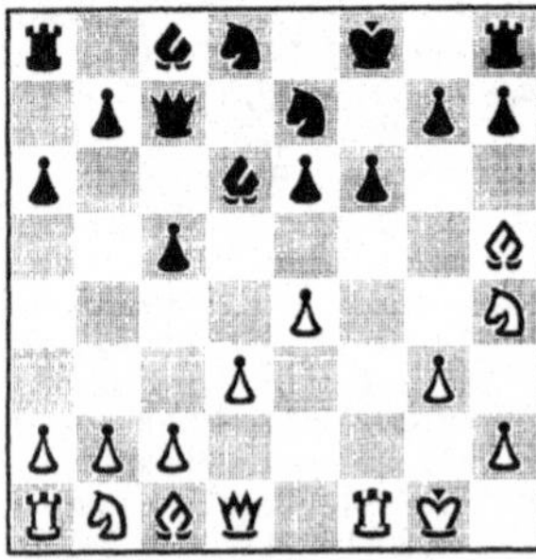

12 ♖xf6+! ♔g8 [12 ... gxf6 13 ♗h6+ ♔g8 14 ♕g4++-] 13 ♖f2 g6 14 ♕f3 ♘ec6 15 ♗g4 ♕g7 16 ♗g5 ♕xb2 17 ♗h6 ♕d4 18 ♔g2 ♕xf2+ 19 ♕xf2 **1-0** Staunton(1)

**1851-⚔LW-8**
**Löwenthal,J.J.–Williams, E.**

[Staunton]

1 e4 e5 2 ♘f3 ♘c6 3 ♗c4 ♗c5 4 d3 d6 5 h3 ♘f6 6 0-0 h6 7 ♘c3 0-0 8 ♘e2 d5 9 exd5 ♘xd5 10 c3 ♗b6 11 b4 a6 12 ♗xd5 ♕xd5 13 c4 ♕e6 14 c5 ♗a7 15 a3 ♕f6 16 ♘e1 ♗f5 17 ♗b2 ♕g6 18 ♘g3 ♖ad8 19 ♘xf5 ♕xf5 20 ♕e2 ♘d4 21 ♗xd4 ♖xd4 22 g4 ♕f6 23 ♘f3 ♖d5 24 ♖ae1 ♖fe8 25 ♕e4 c6 26 d4 ♗b8 27 ♖e3 ♖e6 28 dxe5 ♗xe5 29 ♕f5?? ♗h2+ **0-1** Staunton(1)

**1851-⚔LW-9**
**Williams, E– Löwenthal, J.J.**

[Staunton]

1 f4 d5 2 e3 e6 3 ♘f3 ♗d6 4 b3 ♘f6 5 ♗b2 0-0 6 ♗d3 ♘c6 7 a3 ♕e7 8 g4!? e5 [8 ... ♘xg4!?∞] 9 g5 ♘e8 10 fxe5 ♘xe5 [10 ... ♗xe5] 11 ♘xe5 ♗xe5 12 ♗xh7+ ♔xh7 13 ♕h5+ ♔g8 14 g6 fxg6 15 ♕xe5 ♕h4+ 16 ♕g3 ♕e4 17 ♖g1 ♖f3 18 ♕xg6 ♕h4+ 19 ♔d1 ♗f5 20 ♕g5?? ♖f1+ 21 ♖xf1 ♕xg5 22 ♘c3 ♘f6 23 d3 ♗g4+ 24 ♔d2 d4 25 ♘d1 ♗xd1 26 ♖axd1? ♕xe3# **0-1** Staunton(1)

**1851-⚔LW-10**
**Löwenthal,J.J.+Williams, E.**

[Staunton]

1 e4 e6 2 d4 d5 3 exd5 exd5 4 ♘f3 ♘f6 5 ♗d3 ♗d6 6 0-0 0-0 7 ♘c3 h6 8 ♗e3 ♗g4 9 h3 ♗h5 10 g4 ♗g6 11 ♗xg6 fxg6 12 ♘h4 ♔h7 13 g5 ♕d7 14 ♔g2 [14 gxf6? ♕xh3 15 ♘f3 ♖xf6 16 ♘e5 ♗xe5 17 dxe5 ♖f5-+] 14 ... hxg5 15 ♗xg5± ♕f7 16 ♕f3 ♘c6 17 ♖ad1 ♘e7 18 ♖fe1 c6 19 ♖e3 ♘h5 20 ♕xf7 ♖xf7 21 ♖e6 ♘f4+ 22 ♗xf4 ♗xf4 23 ♘f3 ♖af8 24 ♖f1 ♘f5 25 ♘e2 ♘d6 26 c3 [26 ♘xf4 ♖xf4 27 ♘g5+ ♔h6 28 ♖xd6 ♔xg5=] 26 ... ♘e4 27 ♘xf4 ♖xf4 28 ♖xe4! [28 ♘∼ ♖xf2+∓] 28 ... ♖xf3! [28 ... ♖xe4 29 ♘g5+ ♔h6 30 ♘xe4 dxe4 31 ♖e1 ♖f4]; 28 ... dxe4 29 ♘g5+ ♔h6 30 ♘e6±] 29 ♖e7 ♖3f7 30 ♖xf7 ♖xf7 31 ♖e1 g5 32 ♔g3 ♔h6 33 ♖e6+ ♔h5 34 f3 a6 35 a4 ♖d7 36 a5 ♖f7 37 b3 ♖c7 38 ♖e5 ♖f7 39 h4 ♔g6 40 hxg5 ♔h7 41 f4 g6 42 ♔g4 ♔g7 43 f5 gxf5+ 44 ♖xf5 ♖e7 45 ♖e5 ♖f7 46 ♖e6 ♖c7 47 ♔f5 c5 48 ♔e5 cxd4 49 cxd4 ♖c3 50 ♖b6 ♖g3 51 ♖xb7+ ♔g6 52 ♖b6+ ♔xg5 53 ♔xd5 ...? **1-0** Staunton(1)

**1851-⚔LW-11**
**Williams,E.=Löwenthal, J.J.**

[Staunton]

1 e4 e5 2 ♘f3 ♘c6 3 ♗b5 ♗c5 4 c3 ♕e7 5 0-0 a6 6 ♗xc6 dxc6 7 d4 ♗d6 8 dxe5 ♗xe5 9 ♘xe5 ♕xe5 10 f4 ♕c5+ 11 ♔h1 ♘f6 12 e5 ♗g4 13 ♕e1 ♘d5 14 ♕g3 h5 15 h3 0-0-0! 16 b4 ♕c4 17 ♘d2 ♕xc3! 18 ♕xc3 ♘xc3 19 hxg4 hxg4+ 20 ♔g1 ♘e2+ [20 ... g3!] 21 ♔f2 ♘xc1 22 ♖fxc1 ♖xd2+ 23 ♔g3 ♖hd8 24 ♖g1 ♖b2 25 a3 ♖dd2 [□ 25 ... f6] 26 ♔xg4 ♖xg2+ 27 ♖xg2 ♖xg2+ 28 ♔f3 ♖d2 29 f5 ♖d8 [29 ... ♔d7 30 ♖g1] 30 ♖g1 ♖g8 31 ♖d1 g6 32 f6 ♖d8 33 ♖h1 ♔d7? [□ 33 ... b6; 33 ... ♖d3+ 34 ♔e4 ♖xa3 35 ♖h8+ ♔d7 36 ♖f8 ♔e6 37 ♖e8+ ♔d7 38 ♖e7+ ♔d8 39 ♖xf7+-] 34 ♖d1+ ♔e8 35 ♖h1 ♖d5 [□ 35 ... ♖d4 36 ♖h8+ ♔d7 37 ♔e3 ♖c4 38 ♔d3 ♖g4 39 ♖f8 ♔e6 40 ♖e8+ (40 ♖c8 ♔xe5 41 ♖xc7 ♖g3+ 42 ♔c2 ♔xf6 43 ♖xb7 ♔e6-+) 40 ... ♔d5 41 ♖e7 ♖g3+ 42 ♔∼ ♖xa3-+] 36 ♔e4 ♖d8 37 ♖h7 b6 38 e6 fxe6 39 ♖e7+ ♔f8 40 ♖xc7 ♖d5 41 ♖xc6 ♖b5 42 ♖xe6 ♔f7 43 ♖c6 a5 44 bxa5 bxa5 45 ♖a6 ♖c5 46 ♔f4 g5+ 47 ♔g4 ♔g6 48 f7+ ♔xf7 49 ♔h5 ♔e7 50 ♔g4 ♔d7 51 ♔f3 ♔c7 52 ♔e4 ♔b7 53 ♖g6 a4 54 ♔d4 ♖b5 55 ♔c4 ♖f5 56 ♔b4 ♖f4+ 57 ♔b5 g4 58 ♖g7+ ♔c8 59 ♔c6 ♔d8 60 ♔d6 ♔e8 61 ♔e5 ♖c4 62 ♔d5 ♔f8 63 ♖g5 ♖f4 64 ♔e5 ♖f3 65 ♖xg4 ♖xa3 66 ♔d5 ♔e7 67 ♖g7+ ♔d8 68 ♔c4 ♖f3 **½-½** Staunton(1)

**1851-⚔LW-12**
**Löwenthal,J.J.–Williams, E.**

[Staunton]

1 e4 e6 2 f4 d5 3 exd5 exd5 4 ♘f3 ♘f6 5 d4 ♗d6 6 ♗d3 0-0 7 0-0 c5 8 c3 ♘c6 9 ♔h1 ♗g4 10 dxc5 ♗xc5 11 b4 ♗b6 12 a4 a6 13 a5 ♗a7 14 h3 ♗xf3 15 ♕xf3 ♖e8 16 ♗d2 ♘e4 17 ♗e1 ♖c8 18 ♘a3 ♕f6 [△ 19 ... ♘xb4] 19 ♖ad1 ♕e7 [19 ... ♘xc3 20 ♗xc3 ♕xc3?? 21 ♗xh7+!+-] 20 ♘c2 f5 21 c4 dxc4 22 ♗xc4+ ♔h8 23 b5? ♘xa5 24 ♗d3 ♘c4 25 bxa6 bxa6 26 ♗xc4 ♖xc4 27 ♘e3 ♗xe3 28 ♕xe3 ♖c2 29 ♕d3 ♖c6 30 ♕b3 ♕f6 31 ♕a4 ♖ec8 32 ♔h2 ♖c2 33 ♖f3? ♕b2 34 ♗f2 ♘xf2 35 ♖g1 ♕b5 36 ♕d4 ♘e4 37 ♖d3 h6 38 ♖a3 ♕c5 39 ♕a1 ♕f2 **0-1** Staunton(1)

**1851-⚔LW-13**
**Williams,E.–Löwenthal, J.J.**

[Staunton]

1 e4 e5 2 ♘f3 ♘f6 3 ♘xe5 d6 4 ♘f3 ♘xe4 5 d3 ♘f6 6 d4 ♗e7 7 ♗d3 0-0 8 c4 d5 9 h3 ♗b4+ 10 ♘c3 ♖e8+ 11 ♗e3 ♗e6 12 cxd5 ♘xd5 13 ♕c2 h6 14 0-0 ♗xc3 15 bxc3 ♘c6 16 ♗b5 ♗d7 17 ♗xc6 ♗xc6 18 ♘e5 ♕d6 19 c4 ♘f6 20 f4 ♗e4 21 ♕b3 ♘d7 22 ♖ae1 ♖e7 23 ♗c1 ♘xe5? [23 ... ♕xd4+!] 24 fxe5 ♕g6? [24 ... ♕xd4+!] 25 ♖f2 ♖e6 26 ♗b2 ♖b6 27 ♕e3 ♗c6 28 d5± ♗e8 29 ♕e4 ♕g5 30 ♖ef1 ♖g6 31 h4 ♕h5 32 ♖f5 ♖g4 33 ♖1f4 ♖xf4 34 ♕xf4 ♕g6 35 h5 ♕b6+ 36 ♗d4 c5 37 ♗c3 ♕b1+ 38 ♔h2 ♕d3 39 ♗d2 ♕e2 40 ♗e3 ♗d7 41 ♕f3 [41 ♖xf7?? ♕xh5+-+] 41 ... ♕xc4∓ 42 ♖f4 ♕c3 43 ♖e4 ♖e8 44 ♗f2 ♕c2 45 ♖e2 ♕c4 [△ 46 ... ♗g4] 46 ♔g3 ♗b5 47 ♖e3 b6 48 a3 ♗a6 49 d6 ♕e6 50 ♕g4 ♗c8 51 ♕xe6 ♖xe6 52 ♔f4 f6 53 exf6 ♖xf6+ 54 ♔g3 ♗d7 55 ♖d3 ♖f5 56 ♗e3 ♖xh5 57 ♗f4 ♖f5 58 ♖d2 g5 59 ♗e3 ♔f7 60 ♔h2 h5 61 g4 hxg4 62 ♔g3?? ♖e5? [□ 62 ... ♖f3+] 63 ♖d3 c4 64 ♖c3 ♗e6 65 a4 ♖a5 66 ♖a3 b5 67 ♗d2 ♖xa4 68 ♖xa4 bxa4 69 ♗b4 ♔e8 70 ♔f2 ♔d7 71 ♔e3 **0-1** Staunton(1)

**1851-⚔LW-14**
**Löwenthal,J.J.–Williams, E.**

[Staunton]

1 e4 e5 2 d4 exd4 3 ♗c4 ♘f6 4 ♕e2 ♗c5 5 ♘f3 d6 6 0-0 0-0 7 ♗f4

♗g4 8 h3 ♗h5 9 ♘bd2 ♘c6 10 g4 ♗g6 11 ♗g5 ♖e8 12 ♖fe1 ♘e5 13 ♗d3 h5 14 ♘h2 hxg4 15 hxg4 d5 16 ♕f1∓ dxe4 17 ♗xe4 ♕d6 18 ♗xf6 ♕xf6 19 f4 ♘c6 20 f5 [20 g5] 20 ... ♗h7 21 ♘hf3 ♕d6 22 ♕h3 ♕f4 23 ♔g2? ♘e5 24 g5 [24 ♘xe5? ♕xd2+→] 24 ... ♘xf3 25 ♘xf3 ♖xe4 26 ♖xe4 ♕xe4 27 g6 ♕e2+ 28 ♔h1 fxg6 29 ♖e1 ♕f2 30 ♖e5 ♕xc2 31 f6 gxf6 32 ♕e6+ ♔g7 **0-1** Staunton(1)

### 1851-✕LW-15̂
### Löwenthal, J.J.+Williams, E.

[Staunton]

1 e4 e5 2 ♘f3 ♘c6 3 ♗b5 ♘f6 4 0-0 ♗e7 5 ♘c3 d6 6 d4 exd4 7 ♘xd4 ♗d7 8 ♗xc6 bxc6 9 f4 0-0 10 h3 c5 11 ♘f3 ♗c6 12 e5 ♘e4 [12 ... dxe5?!] 13 ♕e1 f5 14 exf6 ♘xf6 15 ♕e6+ ♔h8 16 ♘g5 ♕e8 17 ♖e1 ♗d8 18 ♗d2 h6 19 ♕xe8 ♘xe8 20 ♘e6! ♖f7 21 ♖e2 ♗f6 22 ♖ae1 ♖b8 23 b3 ♗d7 24 ♔h2 ♔h7 25 ♘d5 c6 26 ♘xf6+ ♘xf6 27 c4 ♗xe6 28 ♖xe6 ♖d8 29 g4 [△ 30 g5 ♘~ 31 g6+-] 29 ... ♔g8 30 ♗a5 ♖dd7 31 f5 ♔f8 32 ♗c3 ♖d8 33 ♗xf6 ♖xf6 34 ♖xf6+ gxf6 35 ♖e6 ♔f7 36 ♔g3 ♖d7 37 ♔f4 a5 38 h4 ♖d8 39 g5 hxg5+ 40 hxg5 fxg5+ 41 ♔xg5 d5 42 ♖xc6 d4 43 ♖h6 d3 44 ♖h7+ ♔e8 45 ♖h1 d2 46 ♖d1 ♖d4 47 ♔f6 ♔f8 48 ♔e6 ♔e8 49 f6 ♖d3 50 ♔f5 ♔f7 51 ♔e4 ♖d4+ 52 ♔e3 a4 53 ♖xd2 axb3 54 axb3 ♖h4 55 ♖f2 ♖g4 [55 ... ♖h3+ 56 ♖f3! ♖xf3+ 57 ♔xf3 ♔xf6 58 ♔f4!+-] 56 ♔d3 ♖g3+ 57 ♔c2 ♖g5 58 b4! cxb4 59 ♔b3 ♖g1 60 ♔xb4 ...? **1-0** Staunton(1)

## STAUNTON✕WILLIAMS

London

[1851-✕SW]

| | | |
|---|---|---|
| H. Staunton | 1 0 1 0 1 ½ ½ 1 1 1 0 ½ 0 | 7½ |
| E. Williams | 0 1 0 1 0 ½ ½ 0 0 0 1 ½ 1 | 5½ |

### 1851-✕SW-1
### Williams, E.– Staunton, H.

[Staunton]

1 f4 c5 2 e3 e6 3 ♘f3 g6 4 ♗e2 ♗g7 5 0-0 ♘e7 6 ♘c3 d5 7 ♗b5+ ♘bd7 8 ♘e2 0-0 9 c4 ♘f6 10 ♘e5? a6 11 ♗a4 dxc4 12 ♘g3 b5 13 ♗c2 ♗b7 14 ♕e2 ♘fd5 15 ♘f3 f5 16 a3 ♘c6 17 ♖b1 ♕d6 18 h4 ♖ae8 19 h5 e5 20 hxg6 hxg6 [20 ... ♕xg6? 21 ♘xf5!] 21 fxe5 ♘xe5 22 b3 ♘f4 [22 ... ♘g4 23 ♕e1 c3∓] 23 ♕d1 ♘xf3+ 24 gxf3 ♘d3 [24 ... ♘h3+ △ 25 ... ♘g5∓] 25 f4 ♕d5 26 ♕e2 ♘xc1 27 ♖fxc1 c3! 28 ♖d1 cxd2 29 ♖xd2 ♗d4 30 ♔f1! ♕c6 31 ♖d3 ♖f7 32 ♕f2 ♗g7 [32 ... ♗xe3 33 ♖xe3 ♖xe3 34 ♕xe3 ♕g2+ 35 ♔e1 ♕xc2 36 ♕e8+ ♔g7 37 ♕e5+ ♔h7 38 ♖b2 ♕c1+ 39 ♔f2 ♖d7 40 ♖e2 (△ 41 ♘xf5) 40 ... ♕b1 41 ♕e8±] 33 ♖bd1 ♗f8 34 ♔e2 c4 35 bxc4 bxc4 36 ♖c3? [◻ 36 ♖d4] 36 ... ♗g7 37 ♔d2 ♖d7+ **0-1** Staunton(1)

### 1851-✕SW-2
### Staunton, H.– Williams, E.

[Staunton]

1 c4 e6 2 e3 f5 3 g3 ♘f6 4 ♗g2 ♘c6 5 d4 [◻ 5 f4] 5 ... ♗b4+ 6 ♘d2 0-0 7 ♘e2 d6 8 0-0 ♗xd2 9 ♗xd2 ♕e8 10 b4 e5 11 b5 ♘e7 12 dxe5 dxe5 13 ♗b4 ♖f7 14 ♕c2 ♘g6 15 ♖ad1 e4 16 ♗c3 ♘g4 17 ♘d4 ♘4e5! 18 ♗a1 ♗e6 19 ♘xe6 ♕xe6 20 ♗xe5 ♘xe5∓ 21 ♖d4 g5! 22 ♕d1! g4 23 ♖d8+ ♖f8 24 ♕d5 ♕xd5 25 ♖xd5 ♘xc4 26 ♖c1 [26 ♖c5 ♘d2 △ 27 ... ♘f3+∓] 26 ... ♘b6 27 ♖dc5 ♖f7 28 ♖xc7 ♖d8 29 ♗f1 ♖xc7 30 ♖xc7 ♖b8 31 ♗e2 [△ 32 ♗d1 ~ 33 ♗b3+] 31 ... a6 32 bxa6 bxa6 33 ♖a7? [◻ 33 ♗xa6 ♖a8 34 ♗f1 ♖xa2 35 ♖c5+-; 33 ♖c5 ♖f8 34 ♗xa6 ♖a8 35 ♗f1±] 33 ... ♖c8 34 ♗xa6 [◻ 34 ♖xa6 ♖c1+ 35 ♔g2 ♘d5 36 ♖a5 ♖c2 37 ♖xd5 ♖xe2 38 a4+-] 34 ... ♖c1+ 35 ♔g2 ♘d5 36 a4? [36 ♖b7!+-] 36 ... ♘b4! 37 ♖a8+ ♔g7 38 ♖c8? ♘c2 39 a5? [39 ♗e2=] 39 ... ♘e1+ 40 ♔f1 ♖a1! 41 f4 [41 ♔e2? ♘f3! △ 42 ... ♖e1#] 41 ... gxf3 42 ♔f2 ♘g2 43 ♗c4 ♖xa5 44 g4 fxg4 45 ♖g8+? [◻ 45 ♖e8±] 45 ... ♔f6 46 ♖xg4 ♔f5 47 ♖g8 ♖c5 48 ♖f8+ ♔g6 49 ♖g8+ ♔h6 50 ♗a6 ♖c2+ 51 ♔g3 ♘xe3 52 ♔f4 ♘d5+ 53 ♔e5 [53 ♔xe4 ♘f6+ 54 ♔d3 ♖a2-+] 53 ... ♘b4 54 ♔xe4 ♘xa6 55 ♔xf3 ♖xh2 56 ♖c8 ♘b4 57 ♖c4 ♘d5 58 ♖c6+ ♔g7 59 ♖c5 ♘f6 60 ♖g5+ ♔f7 61 ♖a5 ♖h4 62 ♔g3 ♖d4 63 ♔h3 ♔g6 64 ♖a6 ♔g5 65 ♖a7 ♖d3+ 66 ♔g2 h5 67 ♖a5+ ♘d5 68 ♖a8 ♘f4+ 69 ♔f2 ♘h3+ 70 ♔g2 ♔g4 71 ♖g8+ ♔h4 72 ♔h2 ♖d2+ 73 ♔h1 ♘f2+ 74 ♔g2 ♘g4+ 75 ♔f1 ♔g3 76 ♖a8 ♘h2+ 77 ♔e1 ♘f3+ 78 ♔f1 ♖f2# **0-1**

Staunton(1)

### 1851-✕SW-3
### Williams, E.– Staunton, H.

[Staunton]

1 e4 e5 2 ♘f3 ♘f6 3 ♘xe5 d6 4 ♘f3 ♘xe4 5 d4 d5 6 ♗d3 ♗d6 [6 ... ♘f6] 7 0-0 0-0 8 c4 c6 9 ♕c2 f5 10 ♕b3 ♔h8 11 ♘c3 dxc4 12 ♗xc4 ♘xc3 13 ♕xc3?! [13 bxc3] 13 ... b5 14 ♗b3 f4! 15 ♘e5 ♕f6 16 ♘xc6? f3 17 ♗d5 ♗b7! 18 g3 ♖c8 [18 ... ♗xc6 19 ♗xc6 ♘xc6 20 ♕xc6 ♕f5! (△ 21 ... ♕h3) -+] 19 ♕xf3 ♕xf3 20 ♗xf3 ♗xc6 21 d5 ♗b7 22 ♖e1 ♖f8 23 ♔g2 ♘a6 24 ♖e6 ♖ad8 25 ♗g5 ♖d7 26 ♖c1! ♗b8! 27 ♗e7 ♖xf3! [27 ... ♖e8 28 ♗h4 ♖xe6? 29 dxe6+-] 28 ♔xf3 ♗xd5+ 29 ♖e4 ♗xe4+ 30 ♔e3 ♗b7 **0-1** Staunton(1)

### 1851-✕SW-4
### Staunton, H.– Williams, E.

[Staunton]

1 e4 e6 2 d4 d5 3 exd5 exd5 4 ♘f3 ♘f6 5 ♗d3 ♗d6 6 0-0 0-0 7 ♗g5 ♗g4 8 c3 c5 9 dxc5 ♗xc5 10 ♘bd2 ♘bd7 11 ♕c2 ♕c7 12 ♗h4 ♗d6 13 ♗g3 ♘c5 14 ♘d4 ♗xg3 15 fxg3 ♘xd3 16 ♕xd3 ♖fe8 17 ♖ae1 ♗h5 18 ♕b5 a6 19 ♕a4 b5 20 ♖xe8+ ♘xe8 21 ♘xb5? ♕c6 [◻ 21 ... ♕d7!] 22 ♕h4 axb5 23 ♕xh5 ♘f6 24 ♕e5 ♕b6+ 25 ♔h1 ♖xa2 26 ♕f5 ♕e6 27 ♕b1 ♖a8 28 ♕d3 ♕c6 29 ♕f5∞ ♕e6 30 ♕d3 ♕c6 31 ♘f3 ♕c4 32 ♕d1 ♖e8 33 ♘d4 b4 [33 ... ♘g4 34 b3!+-] 34 ♘f5 ♖e6 35 ♕f3 bxc3 36 bxc3 ♕e4 37 h3 ♕xf3 38 gxf3 ♖e2 39 ♘d4 ♖d2 40 g4 g6 41 ♖a1 [41 ♔g1 △ 42 ♖f2] 41 ... ♘d7 42 ♖a8+ ♔g7 43 ♖d8 ♘e5 44 ♖xd5?? [◻ 44 f4±] 44 ... ♘xf3! 45 ♘xf3 ♖xd5 46 ♔g2 ♖c5 47 ♔g3 ♖xc3 48 h4 h5 49 g5 f6 50 ♔f4 ♖xf3+?? 51 ♔xf3= fxg5 52 hxg5 ♔f7 53 ♔e3 ♔e6 54 ♔e4 ♔d6 55 ♔d4 ♔c6 56 ♔e5?? [56 ♔e4=] 56 ... ♔c5 57 ♔f6 h4 58 ♔xg6 h3 59 ♔f7 h2 60 g6 h1♕ 61 g7 ♕d5+ 62 ♔f8 ♕f5+ 63 ♔e8 ♕g6+ 64 ♔f8 ♕f6+ 65 ♔g8 ♔d6 66 ♔h7 ♕f7 67 ♔h8 ♕h5+ 68 ♔g8 ♔e6 **0-1**

Staunton(1)

### 1851-✕SW-5
### Williams, E.– Staunton, H.

[Staunton]

1 e4 c5 2 f4 e6 3 ♘f3 g6 4 ♗e2 ♗g7 5 0-0 ♘e7 6 ♘c3 0-0 7 ♖b1 b6 8 d3 ♗b7 9 ♕e1 ♘bc6 10 a3 ♖c8 11 ♗d2 f5 12 ♕g3 ♘d4 13 ♗d1 ♘ec6 14 ♗e3 ♗a6! 15 ♗xd4 cxd4 16 ♘e2 fxe4 17 dxe4 d3! 18 cxd3 ♗xd3 19 ♖a1 ♗xe4 20 ♖a2 ♗b1 21 ♖a1 ♗d3 22 ♖a2 ♘e7 23 b4 ♘f5 24 ♕h3 ♗xe2 25 ♗xe2 ♖c3 26 ♖d1 ♘d4 27 g3 ♘xf3+ 28 ♗xf3 ♖xf3 29 ♖ad2 ♖xa3 30 ♖xd7 ♕f6 31 ♕g2 ♖a1 **0-1** Staunton(1)

### 1851-✕SW-6
### Staunton, H.= Williams, E.

[Staunton]

1 c4 e5 2 e3 ♘f6 3 g3 d5 4 cxd5 ♕xd5 5 f3 ♗c5 6 ♘c3 ♕d6 7 ♕c2 a6 8 a3 ♘c6 9 ♘h3 0-0 10 ♘f2 ♗b6 11 ♗e2 ♘e7 12 0-0 ♕c6 13 ♗d3 ♖b8 14 b4 ♖d8 15 ♗b2 h5 [15 ... ♕xf3 16 ♘fe4 ♗xe3+ 17 dxe3 ♕xe3+ 18 ♘f2±] 16 ♖ad1 h4 [△ 17 ... hxg3, 18 ...

♕xf3] 17 ♘ce4 ♘xe4 18 ♕xc6 ♘xc6 19 ♗xe4 hxg3 20 hxg3 ♗d7 21 ♔g2 f6 22 ♗d5+ ♔f8 23 ♗b3 ♔e7 24 ♖fe1? [□ 24 d4±] 24 ... ♗e6 25 ♗a4 ♔f7 26 ♗xc6 bxc6 27 d4 exd4 28 exd4 a5 29 ♘e4 axb4 30 axb4 ½-½ Staunton(1)

**1851-⚔SW-7**
**Williams, E.= Staunton, H.**
[Staunton]

1 e4 e5 2 ♘f3 d6 3 d4 exd4 4 ♘xd4 d5 5 ♘f3 ♗e6 6 exd5 ♕xd5 7 ♗d3 ♘c6 8 0-0 0-0-0 9 ♘c3 ♕h5 10 ♘g5 ♕xd1 [10 ... ♗g4?? 11 ♗f5+!+-] 11 ♖xd1 ♘f6 12 ♘xe6 fxe6 13 ♗e3 ♗d6 14 h3 h6 [□ 14 ... a6] 15 ♗c4 ♖he8 16 ♗b5 a6 17 ♗xc6 bxc6 18 ♘a4 ♘d5 19 ♗c5 ♖f8 20 g3 ♖f5 21 b4 ♘f6 22 ♔g2 ♘e4 23 g4 ♖d5 24 c4! ♖xd1 25 ♖xd1 e5 26 f3 ♘g5 [26 ... ♘xc5=] 27 a3 ♘e6 28 ♗e3 ♖f8 29 c5 ♗e7 30 ♘b2 ♗g5 31 ♗xg5 ♘xg5 32 ♖d3 ♖f4 33 ♖e3 ♖d4∞ 34 ♘d3 e4 35 fxe4 ♘xe4 36 ♘e5 ♔b7 37 h4 ♘f6 38 ♔f3 g5 39 hxg5 [39 h5] 39 ... hxg5 40 ♖d3 ♖f4+ 41 ♔g3 ♖e4 42 ♖f3 ♖xe5 43 ♖xf6 ♖d5 44 ♖f5 ♖d3+ 45 ♔f2 ♖xa3 46 ♖xg5 ♖b3 47 ♖g8 ♖xb4 48 ♔f3 ♖c4 49 g5 ♖xc5 50 g6 ♖c1 51 ♔f4 ♖g1 52 ♔f5 a5 53 ♖h8 [△ 54 ♖h4 ~ 55 ♖g4]

53 ... ♖f1+ [□ 53 ... a4 54 ♖h4 a3 55 ♖a4 (55 ♖g4 ♖xg4 56 ♔xg4 a2-+) 55 ... ♖g3 56 ♔f6 ♔b6 57 ♖a8 ♔b5 58 g7 ♔b4 59 g8♕ ♖xg8 60 ♖xg8 ♔b3 61 ♔e5=] 54 ♔e5 ♖e1+ 55 ♔f6 ♖f1+ 56 ♔e5 ♖g1 57 ♔f6 ½-½ Staunton(1)

**1851-⚔SW-8**
**Staunton, H.+Williams, E.**
[Staunton]

1 f4 e6 2 e3 f5 3 g3 ♘f6 4 ♗g2 d5 5 ♘f3 c5 6 b3 ♘c6 7 0-0 ♗d6 8 ♗b2 0-0 9 ♕e2 ♗c7 10 ♘a3 a6 11 ♖ad1 b5 12 c4! bxc4 13 bxc4 ♖b8 14 ♗xf6 ♕xf6 15 cxd5 exd5 16 d4 c4 17 ♘e5 ♘b4 18 ♘axc4 dxc4 19 a3! [19 ♕xc4+ ♖f7 20 ♘xf7 ♕xf7±] 19 ... ♗xe5 20 dxe5 [20 fxe5?!] 20 ... ♕f7 21 axb4 ♖xb4 22 ♖d6 ♗b7 23 e6! ♕c7 24 ♖d7 ♕c8 25 ♕d1 [25 ♕d2 c3 26 ♕d6+-] 25 ... ♗c6 26 ♗xc6 ♕xc6 27 ♕d4 ♖f6 28 ♖d6! [+-; 28 ♖d8+!?; 28 ♕a7] 28 ... ♕b5 [28 ... ♕a4?!] 29 ♖d8+ ♖f8 30 ♖xf8+ ♔xf8 31 ♕d6+ ♔e8 32 ♖d1 **1-0** Staunton(1)

**1851-⚔SW-9**
**Williams, E.– Staunton, H.**
[Staunton]

1 e4 c5 2 ♘f3 e6 3 d4 cxd4 4 ♘xd4 ♘c6 5 ♗e3 ♘f6 6 ♗d3 ♗e7 7 0-0 0-0 8 ♘c3 d5 9 ♘xc6 bxc6 10 e5 ♘e8 11 ♘e2 f5 12 c3 a5 13 f4 c5 14 b3 ♗b7 15 h3 ♕d7 16 ♔h2 ♕c6 17 ♖g1 ♖d8?! [□ 17 ... g6 △ 18 ... ♘g7] 18 g4 g6 19 gxf5 exf5 20 ♕c2 ♘g7 21 ♘g3 ♔h8 22 ♕e2 [△ 23 ♗b5] 22 ... ♘e6 23 ♖ac1 d4!? 24 cxd4 ♘xd4! [24 ... ♖xd4? 25 ♗c4 ♘xf4 26 ♕f1±] 25 ♗xd4 ♖xd4 26 ♖c4! ♖fd8 [26 ... ♕d5 27 ♖xd4 ♕xd4 28 ♖f1 ♖d8 29 ♗c4 ♕c5 30 ♖d1=] 27 ♖xd4 ♖xd4 28 ♗b5 ♕f3 29 ♖f1 ♕d5 [29 ... ♕xe2+?; 29 ... ♕c3 30 ♖d1 ♗h4 31 ♖d3=] 30 ♗c4 ♕d8 31 ♕e3 ♕d7 32 ♘e2 ♖d2! 33 a4 [33 e6 ♕d4-+] 33 ... ♕c6 [33 ... ♕d4!] 34 ♖g1 ♕f3 35 ♕xf3 ♗xf3 36 ♖g2 [36 ♔g3 ♗xe2 37 ♖g2 ♗xc4 38 ♖xd2 ♗xb3 39 ♖d7 ♗f8-+] 36 ... ♗h4 37 ♔g1 ♗xg2 38 ♔xg2 ♔g7 39 ♔f3 ♖d8 40 ♘c3 ♖d2 41 ♘e2 ♖d1 42 ♔g2 h6 43 ♘g3 ♗xg3 44 ♔xg3 g5 45 ♔f3 ♖c1 46 fxg5 hxg5 47 e6 ♖c3+ 48 ♔g2 ♔f6 49 ♗d5 ♔e7 50 ♗c4 f4 51 ♗d5 ♔d6 52 ♗c4 ♖e3 53 ♔h2 ♖g3 **0-1** Staunton(1)

**1851-⚔SW-10**
**Staunton, H.+Williams, E.**
[Staunton]

1 f4 f5 2 e3 ♘f6 3 ♘f3 e6 4 b3 b6 5 ♗b2 ♗b7 6 ♗e2 ♗e7 7 0-0 0-0 8 c4 ♘e4 9 d3 ♗f6 10 ♗e5 ♗xe5 11 ♘xe5 ♘f6 12 ♘c3 d6 13 ♘f3 ♕e7 14 ♕d2 e5 15 ♖ae1 ♘bd7 16 ♗d1 ♖ae8 17 b4 c5 18 b5 h6? 19 ♘h4 ♕e6 20 fxe5 ♘xe5 21 ♘xf5 ♘fg4 22 e4 ♕g6 23 h3 ♘f6 24 ♖e3 [24 ♘xd6 ♖d8 25 ♘f5] 24 ... ♘h5 25 ♕f2 ♘f7 26 ♕h4 ♕f6 27 ♗xh5 ♕xc3 28 ♘e7+ ♔h7 29 ♗g6+ ♔h8 30 ♗xf7 ♕d4 31 ♘f5 ♕b2 32 ♗xe8 ♖xe8 33 ♘xh6 **1-0** Staunton(1)

**1851-⚔SW-11**
**Williams, E.+ Staunton, H.**
[Staunton]

1 d4 d5 2 c4 e6 3 ♘c3 ♘f6 4 e3 ♗e7 5 ♘f3 b6 6 ♗d3 0-0 7 0-0 h6 8 ♘e5 ♗b7 9 cxd5 exd5 10 f4 c5 11 ♘e2 ♘e4 12 ♘g3 f5 [□ 12 ... ♘xg3] 13 ♕h5 ♗c8 14 b3 cxd4 15 exd4 ♕d6 16 ♗e3 ♘c6 17 ♖ac1 ♘d8 18 ♖c2 ♕e6 19 ♖fc1 ♗d6 20 ♕h4 a6 [20 ... ♗b7 21 ♗b5! △ 22 ♗d7] 21 ♗d2 ♗b7 22 ♕h3 ♗a3 23 ♖d1 ♗d6 24 ♖dc1 ♖ac8? [24 ... ♗a3=] 25 ♖xc8 ♗xc8 26 ♘xe4 fxe4 27 ♖xc8 ♕xh3 28 gxh3 ♗xe5 29 dxe5 exd3 30 h4 ♘e6 [□ 30 ... ♔f7] 31 ♖xf8+ ♔xf8 32 ♔f2 d4 33 ♔f3 ♔f7 34 ♔e4 g6 35 ♔xd3 h5 36 ♔e4 ♘g7 37 ♔xd4 ♔e6 38 ♗e1 ♘f5+ 39 ♔e4 ♘e7 40 ♗f2 b5 41 ♔d4 ♘d5 42 ♗g3 ♘b4 43 a4 bxa4 44 bxa4 ♘d5 45 ♔c5 ♘c3 46 a5 ♘d5 47 ♔c6 ...? **1-0** Staunton(1)

**1851-⚔SW-12**
**Staunton, H.=Williams, E.**
[Staunton]

1 f4 d5 2 ♘f3 e6 3 e3 c5 4 ♗b5+ ♗d7 5 ♗xd7+ ♘xd7 6 b3 ♘gf6 7 c4 ♗e7 8 cxd5 exd5 9 0-0 0-0 10 ♘c3 ♕b6 11 ♘e2 ♘e4 12 ♗b2 ♗f6 13 ♗xf6 ♘dxf6 14 ♘e5 ♕a5 15 d3 ♘c3 16 ♘xc3 ♕xc3 17 ♖f3 ♖ad8 18 ♖c1 ♕a5 19 ♖g3 ♕b6 20 ♘g4 ♘xg4 21 ♕xg4 ♕f6 22 h4 [22 ♖xc5 ♕a1+∓] 22 ... b6 23 ♖f1 ♖fe8 24 f5 ♖e7 25 ♖f4 ♖de8 26 ♕xg7+ ♕xg7 27 ♖xg7+ ♔xg7 28 f6+ ♔g6 29 fxe7 ♖xe7 30 ♔f2 h5 31 ♔f3 ♖e5 32 b4! ♖f5 33 bxc5 bxc5 34 e4! ♖e5! [34 ... ♖xf4+ 35 ♔xf4 c4 36 exd5+-] 35 exd5 ♖xd5 36 ♔e3 f5? 37 ♖a4 ♖d7 38 ♖a6+ ♔g7 39 ♖a5 ♖c7 40 g3 c4 41 dxc4 ♖xc4 42 ♖xa7+ [42 ♖xf4+-] 42 ... ♔g6 43 a4 ♖b4 44 a5 ♖a4 45 ♖a6+ ♔g7 46 ♖a8 ♔h7 47 a6 ♔g7 48 a7 ♖a3+ 49 ♔d4 ♖a5 50 ♔c4 ♔h7 51 ♔b4 ♖a1 52 ♔c5 ♔g7 53 ♔d6 ♔h7 54 ♔e5 ♖a5+ 55 ♔f6 ♖a6+ 56 ♔g5 ♔g7 57 ♔xh5 ♖a3 58 ♔g5? [58 ♖b8!+-] 58 ... ♖xg3+ 59 ♔xf5 ♖a3 60 h5 ♔h7 61 h6 ½-½ Staunton(1)

**1851-⚔SW-13**
**Williams, E.+ Staunton, H.**
[Staunton]

1 d4 f5 2 c4 ♘f6 3 ♘c3 e6 4 e3 ♗b4 5 ♗d2 ♗xc3 6 ♗xc3 b6 7 ♘f3 0-0 8 ♗d3 d6 9 0-0 g6 10 ♘g5 ♕e7 11 ♕f3 c6 12 ♕h3 ♘a6 13 f4 ♘c7 14 ♖ad1 ♖b8 15 a3 ♘ce8 16 ♖fe1 a5 17 ♕h4 ♘e4 18 ♗xe4 fxe4 19 d5! exd5 20 cxd5 c5 21 ♖d2 ♘c7 22 ♕h6 ♘e8 [22 ... ♘b5? 23 ♘xe4!] 23 h3! ♘f6 24 g4 ♖b7 25 ♖ed1 b5 26 ♗xa5 b4 27 axb4 ♖b5! [△ 28 ... cxb4-+; 27 ... cxb4 28 ♖d4!] 28 ♘e6!

28 … ♗xe6 [28 … ♖f7 29 ♗d8; 28 … ♖e8 29 ♘c7; 28 … cxb4 29 ♕xf8+ ♕xf8 30 ♘xf8 ♔xf8 (30 … ♖xa5 31 ♘e6) 31 ♗d8] 29 dxe6 d5 30 g5 d4? 31 gxf6 ♖xf6 [△ 32 … cxb4 33 ~ ♖h5−+] 32 ♕g5 d3 33 ♕d5 ♕xe6 34 ♕xe6+ ♖xe6 35 ♗c7 ♖c6 36 ♗e5 cxb4 37 ♔f1 ♖bc5 38 ♗d4 ♖c2= 39 b3 ♖xd2 40 ♖xd2 ♖c1+ 41 ♔f2 ♔f7 [41 … ♖h1 42 ♔g2 ♖b1 43 ♗b2 ♔f7=] 42 ♖a2 ♖h1 43 ♖a1 ♖h2+ [43 … ♖xh3=] 44 ♔g3 ♖c2 45 h4 h6 [45 … h5=] 46 h5 gxh5 47 f5 h4+ 48 ♔xh4 ♖f2 49 ♔g4 h5+ 50 ♔xh5 ♖xf5+ 51 ♔g4 ♖f3 52 ♗c5 ♔e6 53 ♖e1 ♖f5 54 ♗xb4 ♖b5 55 ♗d2 ♖xb3 56 ♔g3 ♖b2 57 ♖d1 ♔d5 58 ♔f2 ♖b8 59 ♗c3 ♖f8+ 60 ♔e1 ♖g8 61 ♖c1 ♖g1+ 62 ♔d2 ♖g2+ 63 ♔d1 ♖g3 64 ♗d4 ♖g1+ 65 ♔d2 ♖g2+ 66 ♔c3 ♖g8 67 ♖a1 ♖c8+ 68 ♔d2 ♖c2+ 69 ♔d1 ♖g2 70 ♖a4 ♖g1+ 71 ♔d2 ♖g2+ 72 ♔c3 ♖c2+ 73 ♔b3 ♖c8 74 ♗c3 ♖b8+ 75 ♖b4 ♖e8 76 ♖b5+ ♔d6 77 ♔c4 ♖a8 78 ♔d4 ♖a2 79 ♔xe4 **1-0** Staunton(1)

**59** Bird, H.E. M58.BL

### 1851-★AB-1
**Bird, H.E.+ Anderssen, A.**
London

1 e4 e5 2 ♘f3 ♘c6 3 ♗b5 ♘f6 4 d4 ♘xd4 5 ♘xd4 exd4 6 e5 ♘e4 7 0-0 ♕h4 8 g3 ♕h3 9 ♗e2 d5 10 exd6 ♗xd6 11 ♕xd4 ♗f5 12 ♘c3 0-0-0 13 ♕xa7 ♘xc3 14 bxc3 c6 15 ♗e3 ♗e4 16 ♕a8+ ♔d7 17 ♕xb7+ ♔e8 18 f3 ♗xg3 19 ♖f2 ♗xf2+ 20 ♗xf2 ♗d5 21 c4 ♗e6 22 ♕xc6+ ♔e7 23 ♗c5+ ♔f6 24 ♕c7 ♔g6 25 ♔h1 h6 26 ♖g1+ ♔h7 27 ♖g3 ♕h5 28 ♗d3+ ♗f5 29 ♕e5 g6 30 ♕f6 ♖hg8 31 ♕xf7+ ♖g7 32 ♕f6 ♖dd7 33 ♗d4 ♖de7 34 c5 ♗xd3 35 cxd3 g5 36 c6 ♖e1+ 37 ♗g1 ♖f7 38 ♕d8 ♖xf3 39 c7 ♖xg3 40 ♕d7+ ♔g6 41 ♕d6+ ♔f7 42 ♕xg3 ♖e8 43 ♕f2+ ♔g8 44 ♕f5 **1-0** L/N3034

### 1851-★AB-2
**Buckle, H.T.+ Anderssen, A.**
London

1 e4 e5 2 ♘f3 ♘c6 3 ♗c4 ♗c5 4 c3 ♘f6 5 d4 exd4 6 cxd4 ♗b4+ 7 ♗d2 ♗xd2+ 8 ♘bxd2 d5 9 exd5 ♘xd5 10 ♕b3 ♘ce7 11 0-0 0-0 12 ♖fe1 ♘f4 13 ♖e4 ♘eg6 14 ♖ae1 ♕f6 15 ♘e5 ♕g5? 16 ♗xf7+ ♔h8 17 ♘xg6+ hxg6 18 ♕g3! ♕xg3 19 hxg3 ♖xf7 20 ♖xf4 ♖xf4 21 ♖e8+ ♔h7 22 gxf4 …? **1-0** L/N3034

### 1851-★AC-1
**Anderssen, A.– Craske**
London [Staunton]

⟨♘b1⟩1 e4 e5 2 ♘f3 ♘c6 3 ♗c4 ♗c5 4 b4 ♗xb4 5 c3 ♗a5 6 0-0 ♘f6 7 ♕c2 0-0 8 d4 exd4 9 e5 d5 10 cxd4 ♘e4 11 ♗a3 ♗b4 12 ♗b2 ♗g4 13 a3 ♗xf3 14 gxf3 ♘d2! 15 ♗e2 ♗a5 16 ♖fd1 ♕g5+ 17 ♔h1 ♕f4 18 ♕d3 ♘c4 19 ♗c1 ♕h4 20 ♖g1 ♕xd4 21 ♗h6 g6 22 f4 ♕xd3 23 ♗xd3 ♖fe8 24 h4 ♗d2 25 ♖ad1

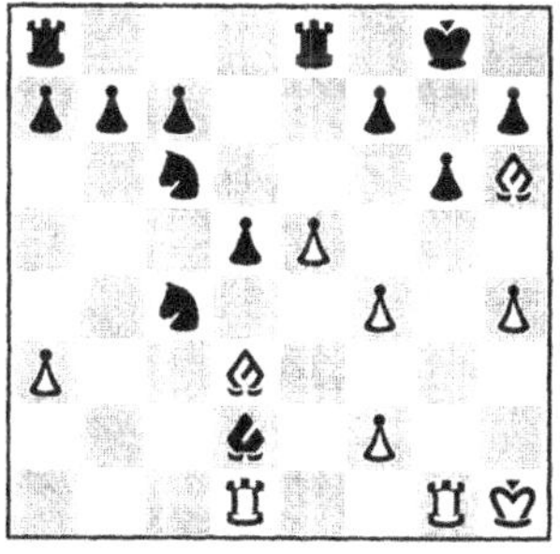

25 … ♘6xe5 26 ♖xd2 ♘f3 27 ♖dd1 ♘xg1 28 ♖xg1 ♘xa3 29 h5 c5 30 f5 c4 31 ♗f1 ♖e5 32 ♗h3 ♖ae8 33 ♔h2 c3 34 ♖g2 c2 35 ♗c1 ♘c4 36 hxg6 ♖e1 37 gxh7+ ♔xh7 38 f6 ♖xc1 39 ♖g7+ ♔h6 40 ♗f5 ♖h1+ 41 ♔xh1 c1♕+ 42 ♔g2 ♕g5+ **0-1** M954-1852

### 1851-★AD-1
**Anderssen, A.– Deacon, F.H.**
London [Staunton]

⟨♘b1⟩1 e4 e5 2 f4 exf4 3 ♘f3 g5 4 h4 g4 5 ♘e5 h5 6 ♗c4 ♘h6 7 d4 d6 8 ♘d3 f3 9 gxf3 ♗e7 10 ♗g5 ♗xg5 11 hxg5 ♕xg5 12 f4 ♕g6 13 f5 ♕g5 14 ♕e2 ♘c6 15 c3 ♗d7 16 b4 0-0-0 [△ 17 … ♗xf5] 17 d5 ♘e7 18 ♔d1 h4?! [18 … ♘exf5! (19 exf5 ♗xf5 20 ♗b3 ♖de8 21 ♕f2 ♘e3+∓)] 19 ♕f2 ♗a4+ 20 ♗b3 ♗xb3+ 21 axb3 ♘hxf5 22 exf5 ♕xf5 23 ♕d2 ♕xd5 24 ♔c2 ♘f5 25 ♖he1 [25 ♖xa7?! (25 … ♕xh1 26 ♖a8+ ♔d7 27 ♘e5+ ♔e6∓)] 25 … h3 [□ 25 … a6 25 … ♔b8] 26 ♖xa7 ♘d4+! 27 cxd4 h2 28 ♕e2 ♔b8! 29 ♖ea1 b6 30 ♕e7 ♕c6+ 31 ♘c5 h1♕ [31 … ♖de8?? (32 ♕xc7+ ♕xc7 33 ♖a8#)] 32 b5 **0-1** M954

### 1851-★AD-2
**Dufresne, J.– Anderssen, A.**
Berlin

1 e4 e5 2 ♘f3 ♘c6 3 ♗c4 ♗c5 4 b4 ♗xb4 5 c3 ♗a5 6 0-0 ♘f6 7 d4 0-0 8 ♕c2 ♕e7 9 dxe5 ♘xe5 10 ♘xe5 ♕xe5 11 ♗d3 ♘g4 12 g3 ♗b6 13 ♘a3 d5 14 ♗f4 ♕h5 15 h4 h6 16 ♔g2 g5 17 f3 gxf4 18 fxg4 ♕xg4 19 ♖xf4 ♕h3+ 20 ♔f3 h5 21 ♖f6 ♗g4+ 22 ♔f4 c6 23 e5 ♗c7 24 ♖ae1 ♖ae8 25 ♕f2 ♖xe5 26 ♖xe5 ♖e8 27 ♔g5 ♖xe5+ 28 ♔h6 ♖e6 29 ♖xe6 ♗xe6 30 ♕c5 ♗f4+ 31 gxf4 ♕xd3 32 ♕g1+ ♗g4 33 ♕b1 ♕xb1 34 ♘xb1 f5 **0-1** L/N6047

### 1851-★AD-3
**Anderssen, A.+ Dufresne, J.**
Berlin [Anderssen & Nathan]

1 e4 e5 2 ♘f3 ♘c6 3 ♗c4 ♗c5 4 b4 ♗xb4 5 c3 ♗a5 6 d4 exd4 7 0-0 d3 8 ♘g5 ♘h6 9 e5 d5 10 ♗xd3 ♗f5 11 ♗xf5 ♘xf5 12 e6 fxe6 13 ♘xe6 ♕d6 14 ♖e1 ♘ce7 15 ♗a3 ♕d7 16 ♘d2 g6 [16 … ♗xc3 17 ♖c1 d4 18 ♘xg7+±] 17 ♖c1 c6 18 g4 ♘d6 19 ♗xd6 ♕xd6 20 ♘c4 ♕d7 21 ♕d4 ♖g8 22 ♘xa5 b6 23 ♘b3 c5 24 ♕f6 ♖c8 25 ♖e3 ♖c6 26 ♖ce1 h5 27 ♖f3 ♕c8 28 ♕f7+ ♔d7 29 ♘6xc5+ ♖xc5 30 ♕xe7+ ♔c6 31 ♘d4# **1-0** L/N6047

### 1851-★AD-4
**Anderssen, A.– Dufresne, J.**
Berlin [Anderssen & Nathan]

1 e4 e5 2 f4 exf4 3 ♘f3 g5 4 h4 g4 5 ♘e5 h5 6 ♗c4 ♖h7 7 d4 f3 8 gxf3 d6 9 ♘d3 ♗e7 10 ♗e3 ♗xh4+ 11 ♔d2 gxf3 12 ♕xf3 ♗g4 13 ♕f4 ♖g7 14 ♖xh4 ♕xh4 15 ♘c3 ♘c6 16 d5 ♘ce7 17 ♗b5+ ♔d8 18 e5 ♘g6 19 ♗f2 ♕e7 20 exd6 cxd6 21 ♕h2 ♘e5 22 ♘xe5 ♕xe5 23 ♕h4+ [□ 23 ♗g3] 23 … ♔c7 24 ♖e1 ♕g5+

25 ♖e3 ♕xh4 26 ♗xh4 f5 27 ♗e8 a6 28 ♘a4 ♖c8 29 ♗f2 ♘e7 30 ♘b6 ♖xe8 31 ♖c3+ ♔d8 32 ♗h4 f4 **0-1** L/N6047

**1851-★AD-5**
**Dufresne, J.– Anderssen, A.**
Berlin
1 e4 e5 2 f4 exf4 3 ♘f3 g5 4 ♗c4 g4 5 ♘c3 gxf3 6 ♕xf3 d6 7 d4 ♗e6 8 d5 ♗c8 9 ♗xf4 ♗g7 10 0-0 ♕e7 11 e5 dxe5 12 d6 cxd6 13 ♘d5 ♕f8 14 ♘c7+ ♔d8 15 ♘xa8 exf4 16 ♕xf4 ♗e5 17 ♕g5+ ♕e7 18 ♕d2 ♘f6 19 ♖fe1 ♘c6 20 b4 ♖g8 21 b5 ♘d4 22 ♔h1 b6 23 c3 ♗b7 24 ♖g1 ♘f3 **0-1** L/N6047

**1851-★AD-6**
**Dufresne, J.– Anderssen, A.**
Berlin [Anderssen & Nathan]
1 e4 e5 2 ♘f3 ♘c6 3 ♗c4 ♗c5 4 0-0 d6 5 c3 ♕e7 6 d4 ♗b6 7 ♘g5 ♘h6 8 ♗e3 0-0 9 h3 ♘a5 10 ♗d3 f5 11 ♘f3 f4 12 ♗d2 ♘c6 13 d5 ♘d8 [□ 13 ... ♘b8] 14 a4 a6 15 ♘a3 g5 16 ♘h2 ♕g7 17 ♗e2 ♘df7 18 ♘c2 ♔h8 19 a5 ♗a7 20 ♔h1 ♘g8 21 c4 ♘f6 22 ♗f3 ♕g6 23 ♕e2 h5 24 g4 fxg3 25 fxg3 ♗xh3 26 ♖fe1 g4 27 ♗g2 ♗xg2+ 28 ♔xg2 ♘g5 29 ♗xg5 ♕xg5 30 ♕d3 ♖f7 31 ♘e3 ♖af8 32 ♘f5 ♘xe4 33 ♖xe4 ♖xf5 **0-1** L/N6047

**1851-★AD-7**
**Dufresne, J.– Anderssen, A.**
Berlin
1 e4 e5 2 ♘f3 ♘c6 3 ♗c4 ♘f6 4 d4 exd4 5 e5 d5 6 ♗b5 ♘e4 7 0-0 ♗c5 8 b4 ♗b6 9 ♘xd4 ♗d7 10 ♗xc6 bxc6 11 f4 ♗g4 12 ♕d3 ♗e2 13 ♕e3 ♗xf1 14 ♔xf1 ♕h4 15 ♗b2 ♕xh2 16 ♘d2 ♕h1+ 17 ♔e2 ♕xg2+ 18 ♔d3 ♘xd2 19 ♕xd2 ♕e4+ 20 ♔c3 c5 21 bxc5 ♗a5+ **0-1** L/N6047

**1851-★AD-8**
**Dufresne, J.= Anderssen, A.**
Berlin
1 e4 e6 2 d4 d5 3 exd5 exd5 4 c4 c6 5 ♘c3 ♗e6 6 cxd5 cxd5 7 ♘f3 ♘c6 8 ♗d3 ♘f6 9 0-0 ♗e7 10 h3 0-0 11 ♗e3 a6 12 a3 ♕d6 13 ♖fe1 ♗d8 14 ♘e5 ♘d7 15 f4 f5 16 ♖ac1 ♘f6 17 ♘a4 ♘e4 18 ♗xe4 fxe4 19 ♘c5 ♗c8 20 b4 ♗h4 21 ♖f1 ♘e7 22 g4 b6 23 ♘b3 ♗d7 24 ♘xd7 ♕xd7 25 ♕e2 ♕d6 26 ♕g2 ♖ac8 27 f5 ♕g3 28 ♕xg3 ♗xg3 29 ♔g2 ♗d6 30 ♖xc8 ♖xc8 31 ♖c1 ♖xc1 32 ♘xc1 ♔f7 33 ♘e2 g6 34 ♗g5 gxf5 35 ♗xe7 ♗xe7 36 gxf5 ♔f6 37 ♘c3 ♔xf5 38 ♘xd5 ♗d8 39 ♔g3 e3 40 ♔f3 e2 41 ♘e3+ ♔g5 42 ♔xe2 ♔h4 43 ♔f3 ♔xh3 44 d5 ♔h4 45 d6 ♔g5 46 ♔e4 h5 47 d7 h4 48 a4 a5 49 bxa5 bxa5 **½-½** L/N6047

**1851-★AD-9**
**Anderssen, A.– Dufresne, J.**
Berlin
1 e4 e5 2 ♘f3 ♘c6 3 ♗c4 ♗c5 4 b4 ♗xb4 5 c3 ♗a5 6 0-0 ♘f6 7 d4 ♘xe4 8 dxe5 0-0 9 ♕c2 d5 10 ♗a3 ♖e8 11 ♖d1 ♗e6 12 ♗xd5 ♗xd5 13 c4 ♘g5 14 ♘e1 ♘h3+ 15 gxh3 ♕g5+ 16 ♔f1 ♕xe5 17 cxd5 ♕xh2 18 ♘f3 ♕xh3+ 19 ♔g1 ♕g4+ **0-1** L/N6047

**1851-★AD-10**
**Anderssen, A.+ Dufresne, J.**
Berlin [Anderssen & Nathan]
1 e4 e5 2 ♘f3 ♘c6 3 d4 exd4 4 ♗c4 ♘f6 5 0-0 ♘xe4 6 ♖e1 d5 7 ♗xd5 ♕xd5 8 ♘c3 ♕d8 9 ♘xe4 ♗e7 10 ♗g5 ♗e6 11 ♗xe7 ♕xe7 12 ♘xd4 ♘xd4 [□ 12 ... ♖d8] 13 ♕xd4 0-0 14 ♖e3 ♖fd8 15 ♕c3 ♔h8 16 ♖ae1 c6 17 ♘c5 ♖d6 18 f4 b6 19 ♘e4 ♖d5 20 ♘g5 ♕d7 21 ♘xe6 fxe6 22 ♖xe6 ♖d1 23 ♖xd1 ♕xe6 24 ♖e1 ♕d7 25 ♕e5 h6 26 f5 ♖f8 27 ♖f1 ♖f6 28 g4 c5 29 h4 ♕a4 30 ♖f4 ♕xc2 31 g5 ♕d1+ 32 ♔g2 hxg5 33 hxg5 ♕d2+ 34 ♔g3 ♕d3+ 35 ♖f3 ♕d6 36 ♖e3 ♕xe5+ 37 ♖xe5 ♖f8 38 g6 ♔g8 39 ♔f4 ♖d8 40 ♖e7 a5 [40 ... ♖a8 +-] 41 ♖b7 a4 42 ♖xb6 c4 43 ♖b4 a3 44 ♖xc4 **1-0** L/N6047

**1851-★AD-11**
**Anderssen, A.– Dufresne, J.**
Berlin
1 e4 e5 2 ♘f3 ♘c6 3 ♗c4 ♗c5 4 b4 ♗xb4 5 c3 ♗a5 6 d4 exd4 7 0-0 dxc3 8 ♕b3 ♕f6 9 e5 ♕g6 10 ♘xc3 ♘ge7 11 ♘e2 ♗b6 12 ♗a3 0-0 13 ♖ad1 ♖e8 14 ♘h4 ♕h5 15 ♘g3 ♕xh4 16 ♗xf7+ ♔f8 17 ♗xe8 ♔xe8 18 ♖fe1 ♕f4 19 ♖e4 ♕f7 20 ♕c2 ♘d8 21 ♖d3 ♘e6 22 ♖f3 ♕g6 23 ♕b3 c5 24 h4 h5 25 ♔h2 ♗c7 26 ♖d3 b6 27 ♗c1 ♗b7 28 ♖e1 ♘f5 29 f4 ♕g4 30 ♔g1 ♘xh4 31 ♖ed1 ♗c6 32 ♖f1 ♔e7 33 ♖f2 ♖f8 34 ♘f1 ♘d4 **0-1** L/N3034

**1851-★AD-12**
**Anderssen, A.= Dufresne, J.**
Berlin
1 e4 c5 2 d4 cxd4 3 ♘f3 ♘c6 4 ♘xd4 e6 5 ♘f3 ♘ge7 6 ♗d3 ♘g6 7 0-0 ♗c5 8 ♘c3 a6 9 ♘e2 0-0 10 ♘g3 d6 11 ♔h1 ♔h8 12 ♘g5 h6 13 ♕h5 ♔g8 14 ♘f3 ♕f6 15 ♖b1 ♘ce5 16 ♘xe5 ♕xe5 17 ♕g4 ♕f6 18 f4 ♕h4 19 ♕e2 ♗d7 20 f5 exf5 21 exf5 ♖ae8 22 ♕d1 ♘e5 23 ♖f4 ♘xd3 24 cxd3 ♕d8 25 d4 ♗b4 26 ♗d2 ♕a5 27 ♗xb4 ♕xb4 28 ♘h5 f6 29 a3 ♕c4 30 h3 ♕e2 31 ♕b3+ ♖f7 32 ♖g4 ♔f8 33 ♕g3 ♖e3 34 ♕xd6+ ♔g8 35 ♘xf6+ ♖xf6 36 ♕xf6 ♖xh3+ 37 gxh3 ♗c6+ 38 ♕xc6 bxc6 39 ♖bg1 ♕f3+ 40 ♔h2 ♕xf5 41 ♖xg7+ ♔f8 42 ♖g8+ ♔e7 43 ♖1g7+ ♔e6 44 ♖e8+ ♔d6 45 ♖d8+ ♔e6 **½-½** L/N6047

**1851-★AD-13**
**Anderssen, A.– Dufresne, J.**
Berlin [Anderssen & Nathan]
1 e4 e5 2 f4 ♗c5 3 ♘f3 d6 4 c3 ♗g4 5 ♗c4 ♘c6 6 d3 ♘f6 7 h3 ♗xf3 8 ♕xf3 0-0 9 f5 d5 10 ♗b3 ♕d6 11 ♗g5 dxe4 12 dxe4 ♖ad8 13 ♘d2 [□ 13 ♗c2] 13 ... ♕d3 14 0-0-0 ♕xf3 15 gxf3 h6 16 ♗xf6 gxf6 17 ♖de1 b5 18 ♗c2 a5 19 ♘f1 a4 20 h4 ♔h7 21 ♘g3 ♗f2 22 ♘h5 ♗xe1 23 ♘xf6+ ♔h8 [□ 23 ... ♔g7] 24 ♖xe1 ♖d6 25 ♘d5 ♖d7 26 ♖g1 ♘e7 27 ♘f6 ♖d6 28 ♘g4 ♖g8 29 h5 f6 30 b3 a3 31 ♖g3 c5 [□ 31 ... ♖g5] 32 ♘xh6 ♖xg3 33 ♘f7+ ♔g7 34 ♘xd6 b4 35 c4 ♘c6 36 ♘b7 ♘d4 37 ♘xc5 ♔h6 38 ♘d3 ♖g1+ 39 ♗d1 ♘xb3+ 40 ♔c2 ♘d4+ 41 ♔d2 ♖xd1+ 42 ♔xd1 b3 **0-1** L/N6047

**1851-★AE-1** 16 x 51
**Eichborn, L.+ Anderssen, A.**
Breslau
1 e4 e5 2 ♘f3 ♘c6 3 ♗c4 ♗c5 4 c3 ♘f6 5 d4 exd4 6 e5 d5 7 ♗b5 ♘e4 8 cxd4 ♗b4+ 9 ♗d2 ♘xd2 10 ♘bxd2 0-0 11 ♗xc6 bxc6 12 0-0 c5 13 a3 ♗xd2 14 ♕xd2 cxd4 15 ♕xd4 f6 16 ♖ad1 c6 17 ♖fe1 fxe5 18 ♖xe5 ♗b7 19 ♖de1 ♕f6 20 ♖e7 ♖ab8 21 ♕xf6 gxf6 22 ♘d4 ♖f7 23 ♖e8+ ♖xe8 24 ♖xe8+ ♔g7 25 ♘f5+ ♔g6 26 ♘d6 ♖d7 27 ♖g8+ ♔h5 28 g4+ ♔h4 29 ♘f5+ ♔h3 30 f3 d4 31 ♖f8 c5 32 ♔f2 ♗d5 33 ♖xf6 h5 34 gxh5 d3 35 ♖g6 ♗e6 36 ♖xe6 d2 37 ♖e4 d1♘+ 38 ♔g1 ♖d4 39 ♘xd4 **1-0** L/N3034

**1851-★AE-2** 13 xi 51
**Eichborn, L.+ Anderssen, A.**
Breslau
1 e4 e5 2 ♘f3 ♘c6 3 ♗c4 ♗c5 4 c3 ♘f6 5 d4 exd4 6 e5 d5 7 ♗b5 ♘e4 8 cxd4 ♗b4+ 9 ♗d2 ♘xd2 10 ♘bxd2 0-0 11 ♗xc6 bxc6 12 0-0 c5 13 a3 ♗xd2 14 ♕xd2 cxd4 15 ♕xd4 ♖b8 16 b4 ♖b6 17 ♖ad1 ♗b7 18 ♖c1 ♖e8 19 ♖c3 ♖e7 20 ♘h4 a6 21 ♖g3 f6 22 f4 ♖d7 23 ♖e1 ♖e6 24 ♖ge3 ♔f7 25 ♘f3 g6 26 exf6 ♖xe3 27 ♘g5+ ♔g8 28 ♖xe3 **1-0** L/N3034

**1851-★AF-1** iv 51
**Falkbeer,E.K.+Anderssen, A.**
Berlin
1 e4 e5 2 ♘c3 f5 3 exf5 ♘f6 4 g4 ♗c5 5 g5 0-0 6 gxf6 ♕xf6 7 ♕f3 ♗b6 8 d3 c6 9 ♘e4 ♕e7 10 ♗d2 d5 11 f6 ♕c7 12 0-0-0 dxe4 13 dxe4 ♖xf6 14 ♗c4+ ♔h8 15 ♕h5 ♘d7 16 f4 ♖f8 17 ♘f3 ♘f6 18 ♕h4 ♗g4 19 ♘xe5 ♗h5 20 ♗c3 ♗e3+ 21 ♔b1 ♗xf4 22 ♕xf4 ♘d5 23 ♖xd5 ♖xf4 24 ♖d7 ♕c8 25 ♘g6+ hxg6 26 ♖xg7 ♖f3 27 ♗e5 ♕f8 28 ♖f7+ ♔g8 29 ♖xf3+ ♔h7 30 ♖xf8 **1-0** L/N6047

**1851-★AF-2**
**Anderssen,A.+Falkbeer, E.K.**
Berlin [Anderssen & Nathan]
1 e4 e5 2 f4 d5 3 exd5 e4 4 ♗b5+ ♗d7 5 ♕e2 ♘f6 6 ♘c3 ♗c5 7 ♘xe4 0-0 8 ♗xd7 ♘bxd7 9 d3 ♘xd5 10 ♘f3 ♖e8 11 f5 ♗b4+ 12 ♔f2 [□ 12 ♗d2] 12 ... ♘7f6 13 g3 ♕d7 14 c4 ♘xe4+ 15 dxe4 ♘f6 16 e5 ♕xf5 17 ♔g2 ♖ad8 18 a3 ♗d6 19 ♖d1 ♕h5 20 c5 ♖xe5? 21 ♕xe5 ♕g4 22 cxd6 ♖e8 23 ♕xe8+ ♘xe8 24 d7 ♕e4 25 d8♕ ♕c2+ 26 ♗d2 **1-0** L/N6047

**1851-★AF-3**
**Anderssen,A.+Falkbeer, E.K.**
Berlin [Anderssen & Nathan]
1 e4 e5 2 ♘f3 ♘c6 3 ♗c4 ♘f6 4 ♘g5 d5 5 exd5 ♘a5 6 ♗b5+ ♗d7 7 ♕e2 ♗d6 8 ♗xd7+ ♕xd7 9 ♘c3 0-0 10 d3 ♗b4 11 0-0 ♗xc3 12 bxc3 ♕xd5 13 c4 ♕d6 14 f4 ♖fe8 15 f5 ♘c6 16 ♗e3 e4 17 ♖f4 exd3 18 ♕f2 dxc2 19 ♖e1 ♘b4 20 c5 ♕xc5!? 21 ♗xc5 ♖xe1+ 22 ♕xe1 ♘d3 23 ♖f1 ♘xe1 24 ♖xe1 ♖d8 25 ♗a3 b5 26 ♗c1 ♖d1 27 ♔f1 h6 28 ♘f3 ♘d5 29 ♔f2 b4 30 g4 a5 31 g5 a4 32 ♖e8+ ♔h7 33 ♘e5 hxg5 34 ♘xf7 g6 35 ♘xg5+ ♔h6 36 ♘e6+ ♔h5 37 ♘g7+ ♔g4 38 ♖e4+ ♔h3 39 ♗g5 ♘f4 [△ 40 ... ♖f1+] 40 ♖e3+ ♔g4 41 ♖g3# **1-0** L/N6047

**1851-★AF-4**
**Anderssen, A.–Finch, J.G.**
London
1 e4 e5 2 ♘f3 ♘c6 3 ♗c4 ♗c5 4 b4 ♗xb4 5 c3 ♗c5 6 0-0 d6 7 d4 exd4 8 cxd4 ♗b6 9 h3 ♘a5 10 ♘c3 ♘xc4 11 ♕a4+ ♗d7 12 ♕xc4 ♘e7 13 e5 dxe5 14 dxe5 ♗e6 15 ♕f4 0-0 16 a4 a5 17 ♘e4 h6 18 ♗b2 ♘g6 19 ♕g3 ♕d3 20 ♖fe1 ♖ad8 21 h4 ♔h8 22 ♗a3 ♖fe8 23 h5 ♘e7 24 ♗xe7 ♖xe7 25 ♘f6 gxf6 26 exf6 ♖g8 27 fxe7 ♖xg3 28 e8♕+ ♔h7 29 ♘h4 ♕d4 30 ♕e7 ♕xf2+ 31 ♔h1 ♕xg2+ 32 ♘xg2 ♖h3# **0-1** +1

**1851-★AH-1** 30/31 xii 51
**Hirschbach,H.ΦAnderssen, A.**
Leipzig
1 d4 d5 2 c4 dxc4 3 e3 e5 4 ♗xc4 exd4 5 exd4 ♗d6 6 ♘f3 ♘f6 7 ♘c3 0-0 8 0-0 h6 9 ♕d3 ♘c6 10 a3 ♘e7 11 ♘h4 ♔h8 12 f4 c6 13 ♗d2 b5 14 ♗a2 ♗c5 15 ♗e3 ♗b6 16 ♖ad1 ♗g4 17 ♖d2 ♘ed5 18 ♘xd5 cxd5 19 g3 ♖c8 20 ♖c2 ♖xc2 21 ♕xc2 ♗h3 22 ♖e1 ♘g4 23 ♕d2 ♖e8 24 ♘f3 ♕f6 25 ♗b1 ♖xe3 26 ♖xe3 ♘xe3 27 ♕xe3 ♗f5 28 ♗xf5 ♕xf5 29 ♔g2 ♕e4 30 ♕xe4 dxe4 31 ♘e5 f5 32 d5 ♔g8 33 g4 ♔f8 34 d6 fxg4 35 ♘xg4 ♔f7 L/N3034

**1851-★AJ-1** 24 vi 51
**Jeney, E.–Anderssen, A.**
1 e4 e5 2 ♗c4 ♘f6 3 ♕f3 [3 d3; 3 d4; 3 ♘c3; 3 ♘f3] 3 ... ♗c5 4 h3 0-0 5 d3 c6 6 ♘c3 d5? 7 ♗b3 [7 exd5!] 7 ... ♗b4 8 ♗d2 ♗e6 9 ♘ge2 a5 10 a3 ♗xc3 11 ♗xc3? [□ 11 bxc3] 11 ... ♘bd7 12 ♘g3 d4 13 ♗d2 ♗xb3 14 cxb3∓ ♕b6 15 b4 axb4 16 ♗xb4 c5 17 ♗d2 ♕xb2 18 ♔e2 ♖xa3 19 ♖ab1 [19 ♖hb1 ♕xa1!] 19 ... ♕a2 20 ♖xb7 c4!−+ 21 ♖d1 ♖xd3 22 ♕f5 ♘c5 23 ♖c7 c3 24 ♘f1 ♕a6 25 ♔e1 cxd2+ 26 ♘xd2 ♖xd2 27 ♖xd2 ♘d3+ 28 ♔d1 ♕a1+ 29 ♔e2 ♘f4+ 30 ♕xf4 exf4 31 f3 ♕g1 32 ♔d3 ♕e3+ 33 ♔c2 ♖b8 34 ♖d3 ♕e2+ 35 ♖d2 ♕e1 36 ♖d1 d3+ **0-1** L/N6014

**1851-★AK-1** 13 vi 51
**Anderssen,A.–Kieseritsky, L.**
London [Staunton]
1 e4 e5 2 f4 exf4 3 ♘f3 g5 4 h4 g4 5 ♘e5 h5 6 ♗c4 ♖h7 7 d4 d6 8 ♘xf7 ♖xf7 9 ♗xf7+ ♔xf7 10 ♗xf4 ♗h6 11 0-0 ♗xf4 12 ♖xf4+ ♔g7 13 ♘c3 ♕xh4 14 ♘d5 ♘a6 15 ♕d3 c6 16 ♖af1 ♗e6 [16 ... cxd5 17 ♖f7+ +−] 17 ♘e3 ♘b4?! [□ 17 ... ♘h6] 18 ♕a3 c5 19 dxc5 [19 d5!] 19 ... ♘xa2 20 ♖f7+? [□ 20 ♕xa2! (20 ... ♗xa2 21 ♘f5+ +−)] 20 ... ♔h8 21 b4 ♕g5 22 cxd6 [□ 22 ♖1f5 (22 ... ♗xf5 23 ♕b2+ ♘f6 24 ♘xf5 +−)] 22 ... ♗xf7 23 ♖xf7 ♘f6 24 d7 ♘xe4 25 ♕d3 ♘ac3 26 ♖f5 ♕d8 27 ♕d4+ ♔g8 28 ♕c4+ ♔h8 29 ♖xh5+ ♔g7 30 ♘f5+ ♔f6 [30 ... ♔g6? (31 ♕e6+ ♘f6 32 ♘h4+ ♔xh5 33 ♕f5+ ♔xh4 34 g3+ ♔h3 34 ♕f1+ ♔xg3 35 ♕f2+ ♔h3 36 ♕h2#)] 31 ♘g3 ♕b6+ 32 ♔h2 ♔g6 33 ♖e5 ♖h8+ 34 ♘h5 ♖xh5+ 35 ♖xh5 ♕d6+ **0-1**

M954-1852

**1851-★AK-2** 3 vi 51
**Kieseritsky,L.+Anderssen, A.**
London
1 e4 e5 2 ♗c4 ♘f6 3 ♘f3 ♘c6 4 ♘g5 d5 5 exd5 ♘a5 6 d3 ♘xd5? 7 ♕f3 ♗e6 8 ♘xe6 fxe6 9 ♕h5+ g6 10 ♕xe5 ♘xc4 11 ♕xe6+! [11 ♕xh8] 11 ... ♕e7 12 ♕xe7+ ♗xe7 13 dxc4 ♘b6 14 b3± ♗f6 15 c3 0-0-0 16 ♔e2! ♘d7 17 ♗e3 ♖he8 18 ♖d1 [△ 19 b4] 18 ... c5 19 a4 ♖e6 20 ♖a2 ♖de8 21 ♖ad2 ♖6e7 22 b4 b6 23 a5 ♘e5 24 axb6 axb6 25 ♖d6 ♘g4 26 ♖xb6 ♘xe3 27 fxe3 ♖xe3+ 28 ♔f1 ♗h4 29 g3 ♖f8+ 30 ♔g2 ♖e2+ 31 ♔h3 ♗e7 32 ♖d2 ♖e1 33 ♘a3 ♔c7 34 ♖a6 cxb4 35 ♘b5+ ♔b7 36 ♖a7+ ♔b6 37 ♖dd7 bxc3 38 ♘xc3 **1-0** L/N6014

**1851-★AK-3** 3 vi 51
**Anderssen,A.=Kieseritsky, L.**
London
1 e4 e5 2 f4 exf4 3 ♘f3 g5 4 h4 g4 5 ♘e5 h5 6 ♗c4 ♖h7 7 d4 d6 8 ♘xf7 [8 ♘d3] 8 ... ♖xf7 9 ♗xf7+ ♔xf7 10 ♗xf4 ♘d7 11 0-0 ♔g7 12 g3 ♕e8 13 ♘c3 ♘e7 14 ♕d2 ♘g6 15 ♗h6+ ♔h7 16 ♗xf8 ♘gxf8 17 ♖f5 ♘b6 18 ♖f6 ♘g6 19 ♖af1 ♗e6 20 ♕g5 ♘d7 21 ♕xh5+ ♔g7 22 ♖6f2 ♗c4? 23 ♖e1 ♗e6 24 d5 ♗f7 25 ♕xg4 ♘e5 26 ♕f5 ♕e7 27 h5 ♘f8 28 ♘b5 ♘h7 29 ♘d4 ♖g8 30 ♕h3 [△ 31 ♘f5+] 30 ... ♔h8 31 ♖ef1 ♘g5 32 ♕g2 ♘g4 33 ♖e2 ♗xh5?! 34 ♕h1 ♕h7 35 ♖f4 ♖e8 36 ♘e6 ♘xe6 37 ♖xg4 ♘d4 [37 ... ♗xg4 38 ♖h2 ♘g5 39 ♖xh7+ ♘xh7] 38 ♖h2 ♖e5 39 ♖gh4 ♔g7 40 ♖xh5 ♖xh5 41 ♖xh5 ♕g6 42 ♔f2 ♕f6+ 43 ♔e3 ♘xc2+ 44 ♔d2 ♘b4 45 ♖h7+ ♔g8 46 ♖h4 ♕f2+ 47 ♔c3 ♕c2+ 48 ♔xb4 ♕xb2+ 49 ♔c4 ♕c2+ 50 ♔d4 ♕d2+ **½-½** L/N6014

**1851-★AK-4** 21 vi 51
**Anderssen,A.+Kieseritsky, L.**
London
1 e4 e5 2 f4 exf4 3 ♗c4 ♕h4+ 4 ♔f1 b5 5 ♗xb5 ♘f6 6 ♘f3 ♕h6 7 ♘c3 c6 8 ♗c4 d6 9 d4 ♘h5 10 ♘e2 ♗e7 11 e5 d5 12 ♗d3 0-0 [□ 12 ... ♗g4] 13 ♖g1! g5 14 ♔e1 f6? [14 ... g4] 15 g3 fxg3 16 ♘xg3 ♗g4

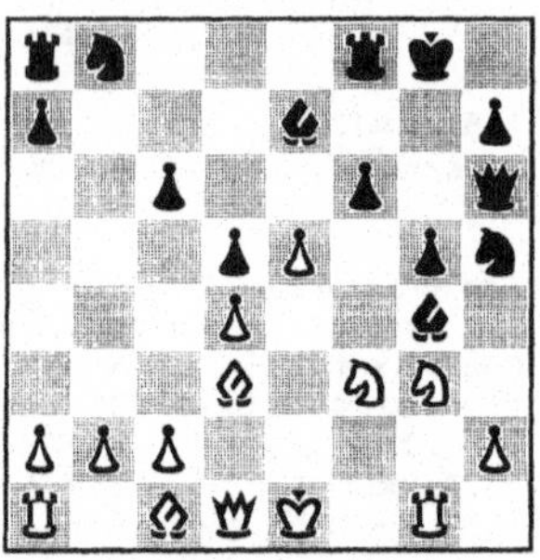

17 ♘xg5!! ♗xd1 18 ♘f5 fxg5 [⌓ 18 ... ♗b4+ △ 19 ... ♕g6] 19 ♘xh6+ ♔g7 20 ♗xg5 ♗xg5 21 ♘f5+ ♖xf5 22 ♗xf5 ♔h6 23 ♖xd1 ♘a6 24 ♖d3 ♖f8 25 ♗g4 ♖f4? [25 ... ♘f4] 26 ♖h3 ♖e4+ 27 ♔f1 ♖f4+ 28 ♔e2 ♖e4+ 29 ♔d3 ♘b4+ 30 ♔c3 ♘xa2+ 31 ♔b3 ♘c1+ 32 ♔a4 ♖xd4+ 33 ♔a5 ♗d8+? [33 ... ♖xg4 34 ♖xg4 ♘e2] 34 ♔a6 ♖xg4 35 ♖xg4 ♗b6 36 ♖g8 ♘e2 37 e6 ♘f4 38 e7 ♘e6 39 ♖xh5+ ♔xh5 40 e8♕+ **1-0**

L/N6014

**1851-★AK-5** 2 vii 51

**Kieseritsky,L.+Anderssen,A.**

London

1 d4 d5 2 c4 dxc4 3 e3 e5 [⌓ 3 ... ♗e6] 4 ♗xc4 exd4 5 exd4 ♗d6 6 ♘f3 ♘f6 7 ♘c3 0-0 8 0-0 h6 9 ♘e5 ♘c6 10 f4 [10 ♘xc6=] 10 ... ♘e7 11 ♕b3 ♗xe5 12 dxe5 ♕d4+ 13 ♔h1 ♘g4 14 ♘d1? [14 ♘b5! ♘f2+ (14 ... ♕c5 15 ♕c2) 15 ♖xf2 ♕xf2 16 ♗e3 ♕h4 17 ♘xc7±] 14 ... b5?! 15 ♗e2? [15 ♗xb5] 15 ... ♗e6 16 ♕g3 h5 17 h3 ♘h6 18 ♗xh5 f6 19 ♗f3 ♖ad8 20 ♕f2 fxe5 21 ♗e3 ♕d3 22 fxe5 ♘hf5 23 ♔h2 ♘g6 24 ♗g5 ♖d7 25 ♖c1 ♘xe5 26 ♖c3 ♕d6 27 ♗f4 g5 28 ♖c6?! ♘g4+ 29 hxg4 ♖h7+ 30 ♔g1 ♕xf4 31 g3 ♘xg3 32 ♖xe6 ♘xf1 33 ♔xf1

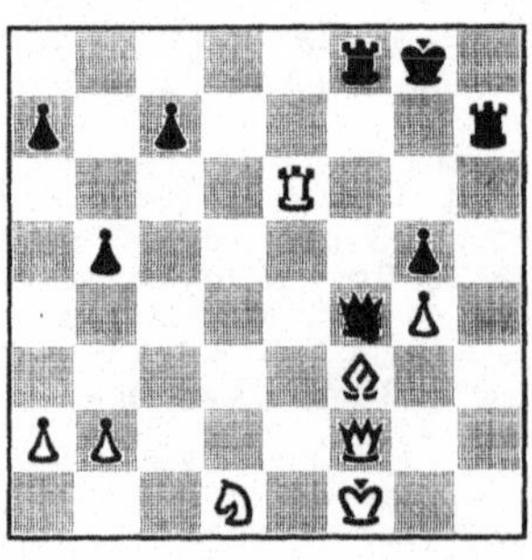

33 ... ♖h1+?? [33 ... ♕xf3] 34 ♗xh1 ♕c4+ 35 ♖e2 ♕xg4 36 ♗d5+ **1-0**

L/N6014

**1851-★AK-6** 2 vii 51

**Anderssen,A.–Kieseritsky,L.**

London

1 e4 e5 2 f4 exf4 3 ♗c4 ♕h4+ 4 ♔f1 b5! 5 ♗xb5 ♘f6 6 ♘f3 ♕h6 7 ♘c3 c6 8 ♗c4 d6 9 d4 ♗e6 10 d5 cxd5 11 exd5 ♗g4 12 g3 g5 13 h4 ♕h5 14 ♕e1+ ♗e7 15 ♘xg5 fxg3 16 ♗f4 [△ 17 ♗xd6] 16 ... ♔f8 17 ♕xg3 ♘bd7 18 ♖e1 [⌓ 18 ♗xd6] 18 ... h6 19 ♖xe7!? hxg5 20 ♗xd6 ♔g7 21 ♗e5 gxh4 22 ♕f4 ♖ae8 23 ♘e4 ♖xe7 24 ♗xf6+ [24 ♘xf6 ♕xe5] 24 ... ♘xf6 25 ♕xf6+ ♔f8 26 ♘g3 ♕h6 27 ♕xh6+ ♖xh6 28 ♔g2 ♖e3 29 ♘f1 h3+ 30 ♔h2 ♖f3 31 ♗d3 f5 32 ♔g1 f4 33 ♖h2 ♖h5 34 ♗e4 ♖g3+!→ 35 ♘xg3 [35 ♔f2 ♖e5 36 ♘xg3 fxg3+ 37 ♔xg3 ♖xe4; 35 ♔f2 ♖e5 36 ♗d3 ♖f3+ 37 ♔g1 ♖e1] 35 ... fxg3 36 ♖d2 ♖e5 37 ♗d3 ♖e1+ 38 ♗f1 ♗f3 **0-1**

L/N6014

**1851-★AK-7** 4 viii 51

**Kieseritsky,L.–Anderssen,A.**

London

1 e4 c5 2 ♗c4 e6 3 ♘c3 ♘e7 4 ♕e2 ♘bc6 5 ♘f3 a6 6 d3 ♘g6 7 0-0 ♗e7 8 ♗e3 0-0= 9 d4? [9 a4] 9 ... b5 10 dxc5 [⌓ 10 ♘xb5] 10 ... bxc4 11 ♕xc4 f5 12 ♖fd1 f4 13 ♗d4 ♘xd4 14 ♕xd4 ♕c7 15 b4 ♗f6 16 ♕c4 ♘e5 17 ♘xe5 ♗xe5 18 ♖ab1 ♗xc3 19 ♕xc3 ♗b7 20 f3 ♗c6 21 ♖d6 ♕d8 22 ♕d2 ♕g5 23 c4 ♕e5 24 ♔f1 ♖ab8 25 a4 ♗xa4 26 ♖xa6 ♖a8 27 ♖d6 ♖a7 28 ♖d3 ♖fa8 29 ♖a3? ♗b5! 30 ♖c3 ♖a2 31 ♕d3 ♕g5 32 ♖c2 ♖a1 33 ♖bc1 ♖8a2 **0-1**

L/N6014

**1851-★AK-8**

**Kieseritsky,L.+Anderssen,A.**

London [Staunton]

1 e4 e5 2 f4 exf4 3 ♘f3 g5 4 h4 g4 5 ♘e5 h5 6 ♗c4 ♘h6 7 d4 d6 8 ♘d3 f3 9 g3 [9 gxf3!? △ 10 ♗e3] 9 ... d5 10 exd5 ♘f5 11 ♗f4 ♗d6 12 ♔f2 ♘xd4 13 ♘c3 c6 14 ♗xd6 [⌓ 14 ♖e1+] 14 ... ♕xd6 15 ♘e4 ♕h6 16 ♘f4 ♘f5 17 ♕d3 0-0?! 18 ♘xh5 ♘d7 19 ♘f4 ♘e5 20 ♕c3 ♘xc4 21 ♕xc4 cxd5 22 ♘xd5 ♗e6 23 ♘ef6+ ♔h8 24 ♕f4 ♕xf4 25 ♘xf4 ♘h6 26 ♖he1 ♗f5 27 c3 ♖ad8 28 ♖ad1 ♘g8 29 ♘xg8 [⌓ 29 ♖xd8 △ 30 ♖e8] 29 ... ♔xg8 30 ♖d5 ♖xd5 31 ♘xd5 ♗e6 32 ♖e5 ♗xd5 33 ♖xd5 f5 34 c4 ♖f7? 35 c5 ♔g7 36 b4 ♔f6 37 b5 ♖c7 38 c6 bxc6 39 ♖c5 ♖e7 40 bxc6 f4? [⌓ 40 ... ♖e2+ (41 ♔g1 f4 42 c7 fxg3 43 ♖c1 ♖g2+ 44 ♔f1 ♖h2 45 ♔e1 f2+ 46 ♔e2 f1♕+ 47 ♔xf1 ♖h1+ △ 48 ... ♖xc1 →)] 41 ♖c2 **1-0**

M954-1852

**1851-★AK-9**

**Anderssen,A.+Kieseritsky,L.**

London [Steinitz]

1 e4 e5 2 f4 exf4 3 ♗c4 ♕h4+ 4 ♔f1 b5?! 5 ♗xb5 ♘f6 6 ♘f3 ♕h6 [△ ... ♘h5] 7 d3 ♘h5 8 ♘h4! ♕g5 9 ♘f5 c6? [9 ... g6?! (10 h4 ♘g3+ 11 ♔e1 ♕f6 (11 ... ♕h5? 12 ♘xg3 △ 13 ♕xh5 +−) 12 ♘xg3 fxg3 13 ♕e2±)]

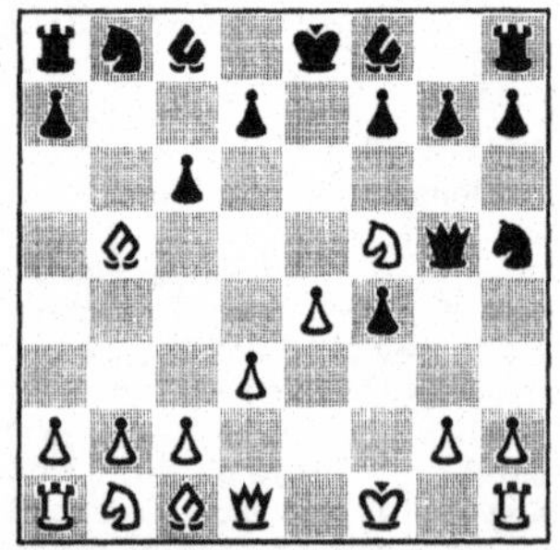

10 ♖g1!! cxb5 [10 ... g6±] 11 g4 ♘f6 12 h4 ♕g6 13 h5 ♕g5 14 ♕f3 ♘g8 15 ♗xf4 ♕f6 16 ♘c3 ♗c5 [16 ... ♗b7 17 ♕g3!] 17 ♘d5! ♕xb2 18 ♗d6! ♕xa1+ [18 ... ♗xd6? (19 ♘xd6+ ♔d8 20 ♘xf7+ ♔e8 21 ♘d6+ ♔d8 22 ♕f8#)] 19 ♔e2 ♗xg1 [19 ... ♕xg1? 20 ♘xg7+ +− 19 ... ♕b2! ∞] 20 e5! ♘a6? [20 ... f6? (21 ♘xg7+ ♔f7 22 ♘xf6 ♔xg7 23 ♘e8+ ♔h6 24 ♕f4#) 20 ... ♗a6! (21 ♘c7+ (21 ♘xg7+?! ♔d8 △ ... ♔c8 ... ♔b7 ∞) 21 ... ♔d8 22 ♘xa8 ♕c3 23 ♕xb8+ ♗c8 24 ♘d5 ♕xc2+ 25 ♔e1 ♕c1+=)] 21 ♘xg7+ ♔d8 22 ♕f6+! ♘xf6 23 ♗e7# **1-0**

L/N6125-1879

**1851-★AK-10**

**Anderssen,A.–Kieseritsky,L.**

London [Staunton]

1 e4 e5 2 ♘f3 ♘c6 3 ♗c4 ♗c5 4 b4 ♗xb4 5 c3 ♗d6? 6 0-0 ♕e7 7 d4 ♘f6 8 ♘g5 0-0 9 f4 exf4 10 e5 ♗xe5 11 dxe5 ♕c5+ 12 ♔h1 ♘xe5 13 ♗b3 ♘eg4 14 ♘h3 d6 15 ♗xf4 ♘e4 16 ♕d4 ♖e8 17 ♘d2 [⌓ 17 ♗xf7+ (17 ... ♔xf7 18 ♗xd6+ +−)] 17 ... ♕xd4 18 cxd4 ♘xd2 19 ♗xd2 ♗e6 20 ♘g5 ♗xb3 21 axb3 ♖e2 22 ♘f3 a6 23 ♖ae1 ♖ae8 24 ♖xe2 ♖xe2 25 ♖e1 ♖xe1+ 26 ♗xe1 f6 27 ♔g1 ♘e3 28 ♔f2 ♘d5 29 ♗d2 ♔f7 30 ♔e2 ♔e6 31 ♔d3 c5 32 g3 g5 33 ♔e4 f5+ 34 ♔d3 h6 35 ♘e1 b5 36 ♗e3 ♘b4+ 37 ♔c3 ♔d5 38 ♘f3 g4 39 ♘e1 h5 40 ♘d3 ♘xd3 41 ♔xd3 c4+ 42 bxc4+ bxc4+ 43 ♔c3 ♔e4 44 ♗d2 d5 **0-1**

L/N6123

**1851-★AK-11** 28 xii 51

**Anderssen, A.+Klaus, K.**

Leipzig

1 e4 e5 2 f4 ♗c5 3 ♘f3 d6 4 c3 ♘c6 5 d4 exd4 6 cxd4 ♗b4+ 7 ♘c3 ♗g4 8 ♗e3 ♘f6 9 ♗d3 ♕e7 10 0-0 ♗xc3 11 bxc3 ♘xe4 12 ♕c2 d5 13 ♘e5 ♗f5 14 g4 ♘xe5 15 fxe5 ♗xg4 16 ♗xe4 dxe4 17 ♕xe4 ♗c8 18 ♔h1 ♖b8 19 ♖g1 b6 20 ♖xg7 ♗b7 21 d5 ♖d8 22 c4 ♕b4 23 ♕f5 ♖d7 24 ♖ag1 ♖f8 25 ♖g8 b5 26 ♗h6 bxc4 27 ♗xf8 ♕xf8 28 e6 **1-0** L/N6047-1860

**1851-★AL-1** 18 viii 51

**Lange, M.+Anderssen, A.**

Berlin

1 e4 e5 2 f4 exf4 3 ♗c4 ♕h4+ 4 ♔f1 g5 5 ♘c3 ♗g7 6 d4 ♘e7 7 g3 fxg3 8 ♔g2 ♕h6 9 hxg3 ♕g6 10 ♘f3 h6 11 ♖f1 ♖f8 12 b3 d6 13 e5 ♗g4 14 ♘b5 ♘a6 15 exd6 cxd6 16 ♗a3 0-0-0 17 ♘xa7+ ♔b8 18 ♘b5 ♘f5 19 ♕d3 ♖fe8 20 ♖ae1 ♖xe1 21 ♖xe1 ♕h5 22 ♘g1 ♘c7 23 ♘xc7 ♗xd4 24 ♘a6+ ♔a7 25 ♗c1 d5 26 ♘c7 dxc4 27 bxc4 ♗xg1 28 ♘b5+ ♔b6 29 ♕xd8+ ♔a6 30 ♘c7+ ♔a7 31 ♔xg1 ♗f3 32 ♗e3+ ♘xe3 33 ♕a8+ ♔b6 34 ♘d5+ ♗xd5 35 ♖b1+ ♔c5 36 ♕f8+ ♔d4 37 cxd5 ♕e2 38 ♖b4+ ♔c3 39 ♕c5+ ♔d2 40 ♕d4+ ♔c1 41 ♕b2+ **1-0** L/N3034

**186** Lange, M. M1647.BL

**1851-★AL-2** 18 viii 51

**Lange, M.+Anderssen, A.**

Berlin

1 e4 e5 2 f4 exf4 3 ♗c4 ♕h4+ 4 ♔f1 g5 5 ♘c3 ♗g7 6 d4 ♘e7 7 g3 fxg3 8 ♔g2 ♕h6 9 hxg3 ♕g6 10 ♘f3 h6 11 ♖f1 0-0 12 ♘e5 ♗xe5 13 dxe5 ♘bc6 14 ♖f6 ♕g7 15 ♕h5 ♘xe5 16 ♖xh6 ♘xc4 17 ♗xg5 ♘g6 18 ♘d5 ♘e3+ 19 ♗xe3 d6 20 ♖h1 ♖e8 21 ♗d4 **1-0** L/N3034

**1851-★AL-3**

**Löwenthal, J.J.+Anderssen, A.**

London

1 e4 e5 2 ♘f3 ♘c6 3 ♗c4 ♗c5 4 b4 ♗xb4 5 c3 ♗a5 6 d4 exd4 7 0-0 d6 8 cxd4 ♗b6 9 h3 ♘f6 10 ♘c3 0-0 11 ♗g5 h6 12 ♗h4 g5 13 ♘xg5 hxg5 14 ♗xg5 ♗xd4 15 ♘d5 ♗e6 16 ♖b1 ♖b8 17 ♖b3 ♔h7 18 ♗xf6 ♗xf6 19 ♕h5+ ♔g8 20 ♖g3+ **1-0** L/N3034

**1851-★AL-4**

**Anderssen, A.−Löwenthal, J.J.**

London [Staunton]

1 e4 e5 2 ♘f3 ♘f6 3 ♘xe5 d6 4 ♘f3 ♘xe4 5 ♘c3 d5 6 ♗b5+?! c6 7 ♗a4 ♗c5 8 0-0 0-0 9 ♗b3 ♗g4 10 d4 ♗d6 11 ♕d3 ♘xc3 12 bxc3 ♕f6 13 ♘e1 ♗f5 14 ♕f3 ♕g6 15 ♗f4 ♗e4 [□ 15 ... ♗g4 △ ... ♗e2] 16 ♕g3 ♗xf4 17 ♕xf4 ♘d7 18 f3 ♗f5 19 c4?! dxc4 20 ♗xc4 ♗xc2 21 ♖f2 ♗f5 22 g4 ♗e6 23 ♗d3 ♕f6 24 ♕e4 g6 25 ♘g2 ♗d5 26 ♕f4 g5! 27 ♕d2 ♔h8 [△ ... ♖g8] 28 ♗c2 ♘c5 29 h4 ♘e6 30 ♖d1 gxh4 31 ♕d3 ♕g7 32 ♘xh4 ♘f4 33 ♕f1 ♗e6 [△ 34 ... ♗xg4] 34 ♖h2 f5 35 ♘g2 ♘g6 36 ♕d3! ♖ad8 37 ♕e3 ♖fe8 38 gxf5 ♗xf5 39 ♗e4 ♗xe4 40 fxe4 ♘e5 41 ♖h3 ♖g8 42 ♕e2 ♖d6 43 ♖d2 ♕d7 44 ♕h5 ♘g4 45 ♕c5 ♖dg6 46 ♕c3 ♘f6 47 ♖e3 ♕g7 48 ♕b2! ♘h5! 49 ♖h3 ♘f4 50 ♖h2 ♘xg2 51 ♖dxg2 c5! 52 e5 ♖xg2+ **0-1** L/N6123

**1851-★AL-5**

**Löwenthal, J.J.+Anderssen, A.**

London [Staunton]

1 e4 e5 2 f4 exf4 3 ♗c4 ♕h4+ 4 ♔f1 g5 5 ♘c3 ♗g7 6 d4 ♘e7 7 g3 fxg3 8 ♔g2 ♕h6 9 h4 ♕f6 10 ♗e3 gxh4 11 ♘f3 h3+ 12 ♖xh3 d5 13 ♖xg3 dxc4 14 ♗g5± ♕e6 15 ♗xe7 ♔xe7 16 ♖xg7 ♕h3+ 17 ♔f2 ♗g4 18 ♘d5+ ♔f8

19 ♖xf7+ ♔xf7 20 ♘e5+ ♔f8 21 ♕xg4 ♕xg4 22 ♘xg4 ♘a6 23 e5 c6 24 ♘f4 ♘c7 25 ♔f3 ♔g7 26 ♖g1 ♖hf8 27 ♘f6+ ♔h8 28 ♘g6+! hxg6 [29 ♖h1+ ♔g7 30 ♖h7#] **1-0** L/N6123

**1851-★AL-6**

**Löwenthal, J.J.−Anderssen, A.**

London [Staunton]

1 e4 e5 2 ♘f3 ♘c6 3 ♗c4 ♗c5 4 c3 ♘f6 5 d4 exd4 6 cxd4 ♗b4+ 7 ♗d2 ♗xd2+ 8 ♘bxd2 d5 9 exd5 ♘xd5 10 0-0 0-0 11 h3 ♘f4 12 ♘e4 ♗e6 13 ♗xe6 fxe6 14 ♖e1 ♕d5 15 a3 ♖ad8 16 ♖c1 h6 17 ♔h2 ♕h5 18 ♖e3 ♖d5 19 ♘g3 ♕f7 20 ♖b3 ♘xd4 21 ♘xd4 c5 22 ♖xc5 ♖xc5 23 ♕f3 ♖c7 24 ♘e4 e5 25 ♘b5 ♖d7 26 ♘bd6 ♕g6 27 ♘xb7 ♘d3 28 ♕e3 ♘f4 29 g3 ♖d1 30 ♘bc5 ♘xh3! 31 ♕e2 ♘xf2 32 ♔g2 ♖c1 33 ♖c3 ♖xc3 34 bxc3 ♘xe4 35 ♘xe4 ♖f4 36 ♘f2 ♕c6+ 37 ♔g1 ♕f3 **0-1** L/N6123

**1851-★AL-7**

**Anderssen, A.+Löwenthal, J.J.**

London

1 e4 e5 2 ♘f3 ♘c6 3 ♗c4 ♗c5 4 b4 ♗xb4 5 c3 ♗a5 6 d4 exd4 7 0-0 d6 8 cxd4 ♗b6 9 h3 ♘f6 10 ♘c3 0-0 11 ♗g5 h6 12 ♗h4 g5 13 ♘xg5 hxg5 14 ♗xg5 ♗xd4 15 ♘d5 ♗e6 16 ♖b1 ♖b8 17 ♖b3 ♔h7 18 ♗xf6 ♗xf6 19 ♕h5+ ♔g8 20 ♘xf6+ **1-0** L/N6123

**1851-★AL-8**

**Anderssen, A.+Löwenthal, J.J.**

London

1 e4 e5 2 f4 exf4 3 ♗c4 b5 4 ♗xb5 ♕h4+ 5 ♔f1 g5 6 ♘c3 ♗g7 7 d4 ♘e7 8 ♘f3 ♕h5 9 h4 h6 10 e5 ♘f5 11 ♔g1 ♘g3 12 ♖h2 ♕g6 13 ♘d5 ♔d8 14 hxg5 hxg5 15 ♖xh8+ ♗xh8 16 ♘xg5 ♕xg5 17 ♗xf4 ♕h4 18 ♗xg3 ♕xg3 19 ♕h5 ♕g8 20 ♕h4+ **1-0** L/N6047

**1851-★AL-9**

**Löwenthal, J.J.−Anderssen, A.**

London

1 e4 e5 2 d4 exd4 3 ♗c4 ♘c6 4 ♘f3 ♗c5 5 c3 ♘f6 6 e5 d5 7 ♗b5 ♘e4 8 cxd4 ♗b4+ 9 ♗d2 ♘xd2 10 ♘bxd2 0-0 11 ♗xc6 bxc6 12 0-0 ♗e7 13 ♕c2 ♖b8 14 ♘b3 ♖b6 15 ♘fd2 ♗a6 16 ♖fe1 f6 17 ♘f3 fxe5 18 ♘xe5 ♗c8 19 ♘xc6 ♖xc6 20 ♕xc6 ♖f6 21 ♕c3 ♕f8 22 ♖e3 ♗b4 23 ♕c2 **0-1** L/N6123

### 1851-★AL-10
**Anderssen, A.–Löwenthal, J.J.**
London [Staunton]

1 e4 e5 2 ♘f3 ♘c6 3 d4 exd4 4 ♗c4 ♗c5 5 0-0 d6 6 c3 d3?! 7 b4 ♗b6 8 a4 [◻ 8 b5] 8 ... a5 9 b5 ♘e5 10 ♘xe5 dxe5 11 ♕h5 ♕f6 12 ♗a3 ♘e7 13 ♘d2 ♗e6 14 ♗xd3 0-0-0 15 ♕e2 ♘g6 16 g3 ♗h3 17 c4 ♘f4 **0-1** L/N6123

### 1851-★AM-1
**Anderssen, A.+Mayet, K.**
Berlin

1 e4 e5 2 ♘f3 ♘c6 3 ♗c4 ♗c5 4 b4 ♗xb4 5 c3 ♗a5 6 0-0 ♘f6 7 d4 exd4 8 e5 d5 9 ♗b5 ♘e4 10 ♗a3 ♗xc3 11 ♘xd4 ♗xa1 12 ♘xc6 bxc6 13 ♗xc6+ ♗d7 14 ♕xd5 ♖b8 15 e6 ♘d6 16 ♗xd7+ ♔f8 17 ♗xd6+ cxd6 18 ♕xd6+ ♔g8 19 e7 ♕b6 20 ♕xb8+ ♕xb8 21 e8♕+ ♕xe8 22 ♗xe8 g6 23 ♘a3 ♗f6 24 ♘b5 ♔g7 25 ♖e1 **1-0** L/N6047

### 1851-★AM-2
**Mayet, K.+Anderssen, A.**
Berlin

1 e4 e5 2 ♘f3 ♘c6 3 ♗b5 ♘f6 4 d3 ♗d6 5 c3 h6 6 ♘bd2 0-0 7 0-0 ♕e7 8 a4 a6 9 ♗c4 ♗c5 10 b4 ♗a7 11 ♘h4 d5 12 exd5 ♘xd5 13 ♘g6 fxg6 14 ♗xd5+ ♔h7 15 ♗a3 ♖d8 16 ♗e4 ♕f7 17 b5 ♘b8 18 ♘f3 ♕f6 19 ♕e2 ♖e8 20 ♔h1 c6 21 ♖ab1 ♘d7 22 g3 ♘b6 23 a5 ♘d5 24 bxc6 bxc6 25 ♗b2 ♗g4 26 ♔g2 ♖ad8 27 h3 ♗xf3+ 28 ♗xf3 ♘e7 29 ♗e4 ♘f5 30 ♗c1 ♖b8 31 ♗e3 ♗xe3 32 ♖xb8 ♖xb8 33 fxe3 ♖b2 34 ♕xb2 ♘xe3+ 35 ♔h2 ♘xf1+ 36 ♔g2 ♘e3+ 37 ♔h2 h5 38 ♕e2 ♘f5 39 h4 c5 40 ♕f2 ♘h6 41 ♕xf6 gxf6 42 ♗b7 ♘f7 43 ♗xa6 ♘d6 44 ♗c4 ♘c8 45 ♔g2 ♔g7 46 ♔f3 f5 47 ♔e3 g5 48 hxg5 ♔g6 49 d4 exd4+ 50 cxd4 cxd4+ 51 ♔xd4 ♔xg5 52 ♔c5 f4 53 gxf4+ ♔xf4 **1-0** L/N6047

### 1851-★AM-3 vii 51
**Mongredien, A.+Anderssen, A.**
London [Löwenthal]

1 e4 e5 2 ♗c4 b5 3 ♗xb5 f5 4 d4 exd4 5 ♕xd4 ♘f6 6 exf5 ♗b7 7 f3 ♗d6?! 8 ♘e2 ♘a6 9 ♕e3+ ♔f7 10 ♕b3+ ♗d5 11 ♗c4 c6 12 ♗xd5+ ♘xd5 13 0-0 ♖he8 14 ♕c4 ♕b6+ 15 ♔h1 ♖e5 16 ♗f4 ♖xe2 17 ♗xd6 ♖ae8 18 ♘c3! ♖xc2 19 ♕h4 ♔g8 20 ♘e4 ♘e3 21 ♕h5! ♕d8 22 ♘g5 h6 23 ♕f7+ ♔h8 24 f6! ♘f5 25 fxg7+ ♘xg7 26 ♕b3 ♕xg5 27 ♕xc2 ♘f5 28 f4 ♕h5 29 ♗e5+ ♔h7 30 a3 **1-0** M324-1856

### 1851-★AP-1
**Perigal, G.–Anderssen, A.**
London

1 d4 d5 2 c4 dxc4 3 ♘c3 e5 4 d5 ♗c5 5 e3 ♘f6 6 ♗xc4 a6 7 a3 0-0 8 ♘ge2 ♘bd7 9 b4 ♗a7 10 ♗b2 ♘g4 11 ♘g3 f5 12 h3

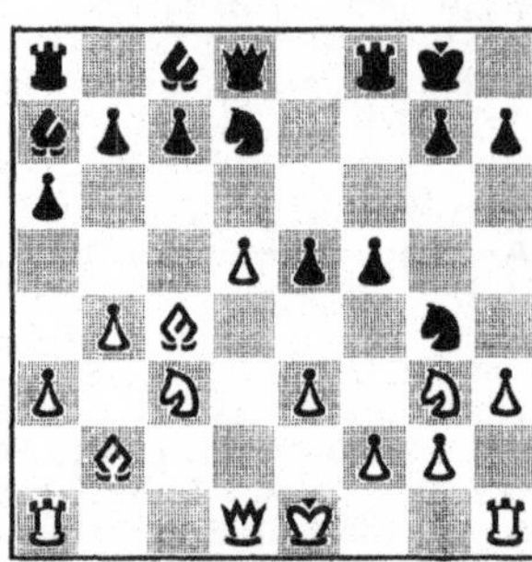

12 ... ♘xf2 13 d6+ ♔h8 14 ♔xf2 ♕h4 15 ♕h5 ♕xc4 16 ♔e1 f4 17 ♘ge4 ♗xe3 18 ♖d1 cxd6 19 ♘xd6 ♕b3 20 ♗a1 ♗d4 21 ♖d3 ♘f6 22 ♕e2 ♕e6 23 ♘xc8 ♕xc8 24 ♔d2 ♕f5 25 ♖d1 ♗xc3+ 26 ♗xc3 e4 27 ♖d4 ♖ac8 28 ♗a1 f3 29 ♕e3 fxg2 30 ♔e1 ♖c2 31 ♕g1 ♘g4 32 ♖d8 ♕f1+ 33 ♕xf1 gxf1♕# **0-1** L/N6047

### 1851-★AP-2
**Anderssen, A.+Perigal, G.**
London [Anderssen & Nathan]

1 e4 e5 2 ♘f3 ♘c6 3 ♗c4 ♗c5 4 b4 ♗xb4 5 c3 ♗c5 6 0-0 d6 7 d4 exd4 8 cxd4 ♗b6 9 h3 h6 10 ♘c3 ♘ge7 11 d5 ♘e5 12 ♘xe5 dxe5 13 ♘e2 ♗c5 14 ♔h1 g5 15 ♗b2 ♘g6 16 ♕b3 ♗d6 17 ♖ae1 0-0 18 ♕f3 ♔h7 19 ♕h5 f5 20 ♘g3 ♘f4 21 ♕d1 g4 22 ♘xf5 ♘xg2 [22 ... gxh3 23 g3±] 23 ♔xg2 ♗xf5 24 exf5 ♕h4 25 hxg4 ♖xf5 26 ♖e4 ♖g8 27 ♗d3 ♔h8 28 f3 **1-0** L/N6047

### 1851-★AP-3
**Anderssen, A.+Perigal, G.**
London [Anderssen & Nathan]

1 e4 e5 2 f4 exf4 3 ♘f3 g5 4 h4 g4 5 ♘e5 h5 6 ♗c4 ♘h6 7 d4 d6 8 ♘d3 f3 9 gxf3 ♗e7 10 ♗e3 ♗xh4+ 11 ♔d2 ♗e6 12 ♗xe6 fxe6 13 ♘f4 ♕f6 14 ♘xe6 ♕xe6 15 ♖xh4 gxf3 16 ♖xh5 f2 [16 ... ♕xe4 17 ♘c3 △ 18 ♕h1] 17 ♘c3 ♘f7 18 ♖xh8+ ♘xh8 19 ♕h5+ ♘f7 20 ♖f1 ♘d7 21 ♖xf2 ♘f6 22 ♕g6 ♔e7 23 ♖xf6 **1-0** L/N6047

### 1851-★AP-4
**Pitschel, K.–Anderssen, A.**
Leipzig [Minckwitz]

1 e4 e5 2 f4 exf4 3 ♘f3 g5 4 h4 g4 5 ♘e5 h5 6 ♗c4 ♖h7 7 d4 f3 8 g3 d6 9 ♘d3 ♗h6 10 ♘c3 ♗xc1 11 ♕xc1 ♗e6 12 ♗xe6 fxe6 13 ♘f4 ♕e7 14 ♘g6 ♕g7 15 ♕g5 ♘c6 16 0-0-0 ♔d7 17 ♘f4 ♕h6 18 ♘xh5 ♕xg5+ 19 hxg5 ♖f8 20 ♘f4 ♖xh1 21 ♖xh1

21 ... ♖xf4!→ 22 gxf4 g3 23 ♘e2 g2 24 ♘g3 f2 **0-1** L/N6047-1871

### 1851-★AP-5 ii 51
**Pitschel, K.=Anderssen, A.**
Leipzig

1 e4 e5 2 f4 exf4 3 ♗c4 ♕h4+ 4 ♔f1 g5 5 ♘c3 ♗g7 6 d4 ♘e7 7 g3 fxg3 8 ♔g2 ♕h6 9 hxg3 ♕g6 10 ♘f3 h6 11 ♖f1 ♖f8 12 e5 g4 13 ♘d2 b5 14 ♗d3 ♗b7+ 15 ♔g1 ♕b6 16 ♘e2 ♗xe5 17 c3 ♘bc6 18 ♘e4 0-0-0 19 ♕c2 ♗a8 20 a4 f5 21 ♘c5 ♗d6 22 axb5 ♗xc5 23 bxc6 ♕xc6 24 ♔f2 ♗b6 25 c4 f4 26 ♗xf4 ♗xd4+ 27 ♘xd4 ♕c5 28 ♕c3 ♘c6 29 ♗e4 ♘xd4 30 ♗xa8 ♖de8 31 ♔g2 ♖e2+ 32 ♖f2 ♖fe8 33 ♖xe2 ♖xe2+ 34 ♔f1 ♖c2 35 ♖e1 ♕h5 36 ♕xd4 ♕h3+ **½-½** L/N3034

### 1851-★AS-1
**Anderssen, A.+Simons, A.**
London

1 e4 e5 2 f4 exf4 3 ♘f3 g5 4 h4 g4 5 ♘e5 h5 6 ♗c4 ♘h6 7 d4 d6 8 ♘d3 f3 9 gxf3 ♗e7 10 ♗e3 ♗xh4+ 11 ♔d2 gxf3 12 ♕xf3 ♗g4 13 ♕f4 ♘c6 14 ♘c3 ♘xd4 15 ♖af1 ♘e6 16 ♗xe6 fxe6 17 ♖xh4 ♕xh4 18 ♗d4 0-0-0 19 ♗f6 ♕h3 20 ♗xd8 ♖xd8 21 ♔e1 ♘g8 22 ♕f2 e5 23 ♕xa7 b6 24 ♘d5 ♕h4+ 25 ♖f2 ♔d7 26 ♕xc7+ ♔e6 27 ♕f7# **1-0** +1

### 1851-★AS-2 24 vii 51
**Anderssen, A.+Slous, F.L.**
London [Staunton]

1 e4 e5 2 f4 exf4 3 ♗c4 ♕h4+ 4 ♔f1 g5 5 ♘c3 ♗g7 6 ♘f3 ♕h5 7 h4 h6 8 d4 d6 9 e5 ♗g4 10 exd6

c×d6 11 ♘b5 ♔d7 12 ♕d3 ♘e7 [12 ... a6? (13 ♕b3 ♗xf3 14 gxf3 g4 15 ♘xd6 ♔xd6 16 ♗xf4++-)] 13 ♗d2 [13 ♘e5+!?] 13 ... a6 14 ♘xd6 ♔xd6 15 ♘e5 ♗e2+ 16 ♕xe2 ♕xe2+ 17 ♔xe2 ♗xe5 18 dxe5+ ♔c5 [18 ... ♔xe5? 19 ♗c3++-] 19 ♗xf7 ♘bc6 20 e6 ♘f5 21 ♗c3 ♘g3+ 22 ♔f3 ♘xh1 23 ♗xh8 ♖xh8 24 ♖xh1 ♘e5+ 25 ♔e4 ♘xf7 26 exf7 ♖f8 27 hxg5 hxg5 28 ♖h7 **1-0** L/N6123

### 1851-★AZ-1
### Anderssen,A.–Zytogorski,A.

London [Staunton]

1 e4 e5 2 f4 exf4 3 ♗c4 ♕h4+ 4 ♔f1 d6 5 ♘f3 ♕h5 6 d4 b5 7 ♗e2 c6 8 ♗xf4 f6!? 9 ♘g5 ♕h4 10 g3 ♕h6 11 ♗h5+ g6 12 ♗g4 fxg5 13 ♗xc8 gxf4 14 ♗b7 fxg3 15 ♔g2 gxh2 16 ♖xh2 ♕f4! 17 ♘d2 ♗g7 18 ♘f3 ♘f6 [18 ... ♕xe4?! 19 ♕e1 ∞] 19 ♗xa8 ♘g4 20 ♕d3 ♘xh2 21 ♘xh2 0-0 22 ♔h1 ♕e8 23 ♖e1 g5 24 a4 a6 25 d5 c5 26 axb5 axb5 27 ♕xb5 ♖f8 28 ♗c6 ♗e5 29 ♕e2 ♕h4 30 ♖g1 ♖f2 31 ♖xg5+ ♔h8 32 ♖h5 ♕f4 **0-1** L/N6123-1859

### 1851-★JM-1
### Jaenisch,C.F.+Mongredien,A.

London

1 e4 e5 2 f4 exf4 3 ♘f3 g5 4 h4 g4 5 ♘e5 h5 6 ♗c4 ♖h7 7 d4 d6 8 ♘d3 f3 9 gxf3 ♗e7 10 ♗e3 ♗xh4+ 11 ♔d2 gxf3 12 ♕xf3 ♗g4 13 ♕f4 ♘c6 14 ♘c3 ♘xd4 15 ♖af1 ♗e7 16 ♗xf7+ ♔d7 17 ♗xh5 ♗xh5 18 ♖xh5 ♖xh5 19 ♕g4+ ♘e6 20 ♕xh5 ♘f6 21 ♕b5+ c6 22 ♕xb7+ ♘c7 23 e5 ♘g4 24 e6+ ♔xe6 25 ♕xc6 ♘xe3 26 ♔xe3 ♗g5+ 27 ♘f4+ ♔f7 28 ♔d3 ♗f6 29 ♘e4 ♘e8 30 ♕d5+ ♔g7 31 ♘e6+ **1-0** L/N6047-1851

### 1851-★KS-1 31x51
### Schulten, J.W.– Kieseritsky, L.

[Kieseritsky]

1 e4 c5 2 ♗c4 e6 3 ♘c3 ♘c6 4 f4 ♘ge7 5 ♘f3 d5 6 exd5 exd5 7 ♗b5 a6 8 ♗xc6+ ♘xc6 9 0-0 ♗e7 10 d4 0-0 11 ♘g5? ♘xd4 12 ♗e3 b6 [□ 12 ... f6 13 ♘f3 ♘f5 14 ♗f2 d4] 13 ♔h1 ♗b7 14 ♗xd4 cxd4 15 ♕xd4 ♗c5 16 ♕d3 f5 17 ♖ad1 d4∓ 18 ♕c4+ ♔h8 19 ♘f7+ ♖xf7 20 ♕xf7 ♕c8 21 ♘e2 ♕c6

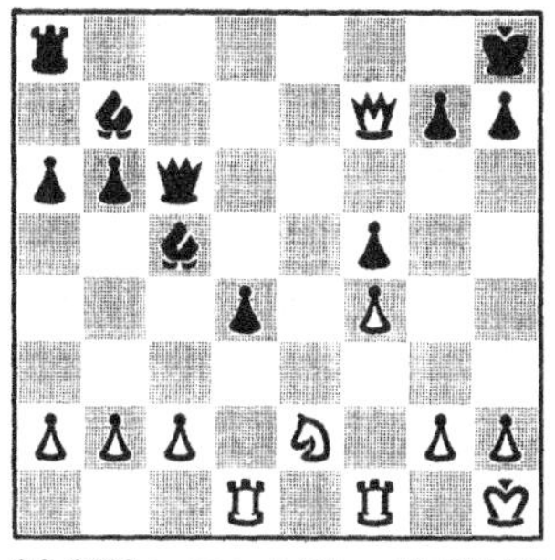

22 ♖f3? [□ 22 ♖g1] 22 ... ♕xf3! 23 gxf3 ♗xf3+ 24 ♔g1 d3+ 25 ♔f1 dxe2+ 26 ♔e1 exd1♕# **0-1** L/N6014

### 1851-★MS-1 v51
### Mayet, K.= Staunton, H.

London

1 e4 e5 2 ♘f3 ♘c6 3 ♗c4 ♗c5 4 0-0 d6 5 c3 ♘f6 6 d4 exd4 7 cxd4 ♗b6 8 h3 h6 9 e5 dxe5 10 dxe5 ♕xd1 11 ♖xd1 ♘e4 12 ♗e3 ♗xe3 13 fxe3 ♗e6 14 ♗xe6 fxe6 15 ♘a3 a6 16 ♘c2 0-0 17 ♖d7 ♖ac8 18 ♖ac1 ♖xf3 19 gxf3 ♘xe5 20 ♖xg7+ ♔xg7 21 fxe4 c5 22 ♘d4 ♔f6 23 ♔f1 ♔e7 24 ♔e2 b6 25 b4 c4 26 ♖g1 ♖f8 27 a4 b5 28 axb5 axb5 29 ♖g7+ ♘f7 30 e5 ♖a8 31 ♘xb5 ♔f8 32 ♖g6 ♖b8 33 ♘d6 ♘xd6 34 exd6 ♔f7 35 ♖xh6 ♖xb4 36 ♖h7+ ♔e8 37 e4 ♖b5 38 ♖e7+ ♔d8 39 ♖xe6 ♔d7 40 ♖g6 ♖e5 41 ♔e3 c3 42 ♖g2 ♔xd6 43 ♖c2 ♖h5 44 ♖xc3 ♖xh3+ ½-½ L/N6047

### 1851-★MS-2
### Mayet, K.– Staunton, H.

London [Staunton]

1 e4 e5 2 ♘f3 ♘c6 3 ♗c4 ♗c5 4 b4 ♗xb4 5 c3 ♗c5 6 0-0 d6 7 d4 exd4 8 cxd4 ♗b6 9 h3 ♘f6 10 ♘c3 h6 11 a4 a6 12 ♗a3 0-0 13 e5 ♘h7 14 ♘d5! ♗a7 15 ♖c1 ♖e8 16 ♗d3 dxe5 17 ♗xh7+ ♔xh7 18 dxe5 ♗f5 19 ♕b3 ♗e6 20 ♖fd1 ♔h8 21 ♖d3 ♕c8 22 ♕d1 ♗xd5 23 ♖xd5 ♕e6 24 ♖c4 ♖ab8 [24 ... ♖ad8 25 ♖xc6?? ♖xd5-+] 25 ♖h4 ♖bd8 26 ♖xd8 ♖xd8 27 ♕b1 ♘xe5 28 ♕xb7 ♕f6! 29 ♖h5 ♖d1+ 30 ♔h2 ♕f4+ 31 g3 ♘xf3+ **0-1** L/N6123

### 1851̂-★AZ-1
### Anderssen,A.+Zytogorski,A.

London

1 e4 e5 2 ♘f3 ♘c6 3 ♗c4 ♘f6 4 ♘g5 d5 5 exd5 ♘a5 6 ♗b5+ c6 7 dxc6 bxc6 8 ♗e2 ♗d6 9 ♘c3 ♗f5 10 d3 0-0 11 0-0 ♖c8 12 a3 ♗b8 13 b4 ♘b7 14 ♘ge4 ♗xe4 15 dxe4 ♕c7 16 f4 ♖cd8 17 ♕e1 ♖fe8 18 f5 ♕b6+ 19 ♔h1 ♘d6 20 ♗g5 ♔f8 21 ♗xf6 gxf6 22 ♕h4 ♔e7 23 ♖ad1 a6 24 ♖d3 ♖g8 25 ♘a4 ♕c7 26 ♘c5 a5 27 ♖fd1 axb4 28 axb4 ♗a7

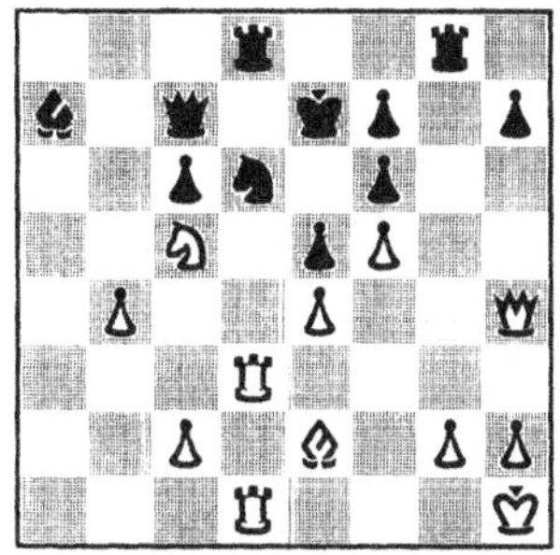

29 ♘e6! ♕b6 [29 ... fxe6 30 ♖xd6 ♖xd6 31 ♕xh7+ ♔d8 32 ♕xg8+ ♔e7 33 ♕g7+ ♔d8 34 ♕f8+ ♔d7 35 fxe6+ ♔xe6 36 ♗g4++-] 30 ♘xd8 ♖xd8 31 ♕e1 ♘xe4 32 ♖xd8 ♘f2+ 33 ♕xf2 ♕xf2 34 ♖1d7# **1-0** L/N6126-1884

### 1851̂-★AZ-2
### Zytogorski,A.+Anderssen,A.

London

1 e4 e5 2 ♘f3 ♘c6 3 ♗c4 ♗c5 4 b4 ♗xb4 5 c3 ♗a5 6 d4 exd4 7 0-0 dxc3 8 ♕b3 ♕f6 9 ♗g5? [□ 9 e5] 9 ... ♕g6 10 ♘xc3 ♗xc3 11 ♕xc3 ♘ge7 12 ♗xe7 ♘xe7 [□ 12 ... ♔xe7] 13 ♘e5 ♕f6 14 ♗xf7+ ♔d8 [14 ... ♔f8? (15 ♕xc7 ♘c6 16 ♘xc6 ♕xc6 17 ♕f4 ♔e7 18 ♗d5±)] 15 ♖ac1 ♘c6 16 f4 ♖f8 17 ♗d5 a5 18 ♘xc6+ bxc6 19 e5 ♕e7 20 ♗xc6 ♖a7 21 ♖cd1 ♕b4 22 ♕d4 ♔e7? [□ 22 ... ♕xd4] 23 ♕xa7 **1-0** L/N6126-1884

### 1851̂-★LS-1
### Löwenthal,J.J.+Staunton,H.

London [Staunton]

1 d4 e6 2 e4 c5 3 ♘f3 cxd4 4 ♕xd4 ♘c6 5 ♕d1 ♗c5 6 ♗d3 ♘ge7 7 0-0 ♘g6 8 ♕e2 0-0 9 ♗e3 ♗xe3 10 ♕xe3 e5 11 ♗c4 d6 12 ♘c3 ♗e6 13 ♗xe6 fxe6 14 ♖ad1 ♕e7 15 ♖d2 ♘f4? 16 g3 ♘g6 17 ♖fd1 ♖ad8 18 ♘b5 a6 19 ♘xd6

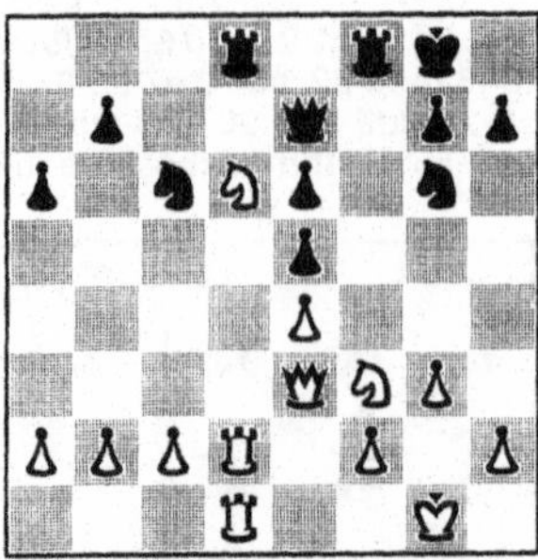

19 ... ♖xf3 20 ♕xf3 ♘d4 21 ♖xd4 exd4 22 ♘c4 b5 23 ♘d2 ♘e5 24 ♕b3 d3 25 ♘f1 ♘f3+ 26 ♔g2 dxc2 27 ♕xc2 ♘d4 28 ♕c3 e5 29 ♘e3 ♕b7 30 ♘d5 ♕f7 [30 ... ♖c8?? 31 ♕xc8+ ♕xc8 32 ♘e7+] 31 f4 ♕h5 32 ♖d2 ♖f8 33 fxe5 ♘f3 34 ♘f4 ♖xf4 35 ♖d8+ ♔f7 36 ♖d7+ ♔g6 37 ♕c6+ ♖f6 38 ♖xg7+ ♔xg7 39 ♕xf6+ **1-0** L/N6123-1851

### 1851-★LS-2
**Löwenthal,J.J.−Staunton, H.**
London [Staunton]

1 e4 e5 2 ♘f3 ♘c6 3 ♗c4 ♗c5 4 d3 d6 5 h3 h6 6 0-0 ♘f6 7 ♘c3 0-0 8 ♘e2 ♘e7 9 g4 ♘h7 10 ♘h4 c6 11 ♘g3 d5 12 ♗b3 ♗e6 13 ♕f3 ♘g6 14 ♘hf5 ♘g5 15 ♗xg5 hxg5 16 ♘h5 ♘h4 17 ♕g3?! g6 18 ♘xh4 [18 ♕xe5?? ♘f3+-+] 18 ... gxh4 19 ♕xe5 gxh5 20 ♕xh5 ♔g7 **0-1** L/N6123-1851

### 1851-★LS-3
**Löwenthal,J.J.=Staunton, H.**

1 e4 c5 2 ♘f3 ♘c6 3 d4 cxd4 4 ♘xd4 e5 5 ♘f3 ♘f6 6 ♗c4 ♗c5 7 a3 a5 8 h3 h6 9 ♕d3 0-0 10 0-0 d6 11 ♘c3 ♗e6 12 ♘e2 d5 13 ♗xd5 ♗xd5 14 exd5 e4 15 ♕c4 exf3 16 ♘c3 fxg2 17 ♔xg2 ♘d4 18 ♗e3 ♘xc2 19 ♗xc5 ♘xa1 20 ♗xf8 ♕xf8 21 ♖xa1 ♖c8 22 ♕d4 ♕d6 23 ♖d1 ♖d8 24 ♖d3 ♔f8 25 ♖g3 ♘h5 26 ♖f3 ♖d7 27 b4 axb4 28 axb4 b6 29 ♕g4 ♘f6 30 ♕d4 ♘xd5 31 ♘xd5 ♕xd5 32 ♕xb6 ♖b7 33 ♕c5+ ♕xc5 34 bxc5 ♖c7 35 ♖c3 ♔e7 36 ♔f3 ♔d7 37 ♔e4 ♔c6 38 ♔d4 ♖a7 39 ♖b3 ♖a4+ 40 ♔e3 ♖h4 41 ♖b6+ ♔xc5 42 ♖b7 ♖xh3+ 43 f3 g5 44 ♖xf7 **½-½** L/N6123

### 1851-★LS-4
**Löwenthal,J.J.+Staunton, H.**
[Staunton]

1 e4 e5 2 f4 d5 3 ♘f3 dxe4 4 ♘xe5 ♘f6 5 ♗c4 ♗e6 6 ♗xe6 fxe6 7 d4 exd3 8 ♘xd3 ♗d6 9 0-0 0-0 10 ♕e2 ♕d7 11 c4 ♘c6 12 ♗e3 ♖ad8 13 ♘c3 b6 14 ♖ad1 ♕e7 15 ♕f3 ♘b4 16 a3 ♘xd3 17 ♖xd3 ♘d7 18 ♖fd1 ♘e5?+- 19 fxe5 ♖xf3 20 exd6 cxd6 21 gxf3 ♕c7 22 ♘b5 ♕xc4 23 ♘xd6 ♕c2 24 ♖3d2 ♕g6+ 25 ♖g2 ♕h5 26 ♖d3 ♕e5 27 ♘c4 **1-0** L/N6123-1853

### 1851-★AP-1
**Anderssen, A.= Pitschel, K.**
Leipzig

1 e4 e5 2 ♘f3 ♘c6 3 d4 exd4 4 ♗c4 ♗b4+ 5 c3 dxc3 6 0-0 cxb2 7 ♗xb2 ♗f8 8 ♕d5 ♘h6 9 e5 ♗e7 10 ♘bd2 0-0 11 ♘e4 d6 12 exd6 cxd6 13 ♘eg5 ♘e5 14 ♗xe5 dxe5 15 h4 ♕xd5 16 ♗xd5 ♗f6 17 ♖ae1 ♖e8 18 ♘d2 ♗e6 19 ♘xe6 fxe6 20 ♗xb7 ♖ab8 21 ♗c6 ♖ed8 22 ♘e4 ♖d4 23 ♖b1 ♖c8 24 ♖fc1 ♘f7 25 ♔h2 h6 26 ♔h3 ♘d6 27 ♗d7 ♖xe4 28 ♗xe6+ ♔h7 29 ♗xc8 ♖xh4+ 30 ♔g3 ♘e4+ 31 ♔f3 ♘d2+ 32 ♔e2 ♘xb1 33 ♗f5+ ♔g8 34 ♖xb1 ♖a4 35 ♗g6 ♖xa2+ 36 ♔f3 ♔f8 37 ♖b7 ♖a4 38 ♔e3 ♗g5+ 39 ♔d3 ♖d4+ 40 ♔e2 ♖d6 41 ♗e4 a6 42 ♖a7 ♗d2 43 ♗d3 a5 44 ♔xd2 e4 **½-½** M954-1872

### 1851-★HS-1
**Horwitz, B.− Staunton, H.**
London [Staunton]

1 e4 e5 2 ♘f3 ♘c6 3 d4 exd4 4 ♗c4 ♗c5 5 c3 ♘f6 6 e5 d5 7 ♗b3 ♘e4 8 cxd4 ♗b6 9 h3 0-0 10 0-0 f6? 11 ♘c3 ♘xc3 12 bxc3 fxe5 13 dxe5 ♘e7 14 ♗g5 c6 15 ♗h4 ♕e8 16 ♗g3 ♕g6 17 ♔h2 ♘f5 18 ♗c2 ♕h5 19 ♗xf5 ♗xf5 20 ♘h4 ♕xd1 21 ♖fxd1 ♗e4 22 f3 ♗c2 23 ♖dc1 ♗d3 24 ♖d1 ♗c4 25 f4 g6 26 ♖e1 ♗a5 27 ♖e3 ♗b6 28 ♖ee1 ♖ae8 29 ♘f3 h5 30 h4 c5 31 a4 ♗d3 32 ♔h1 ♗a5 33 ♖ac1 d4

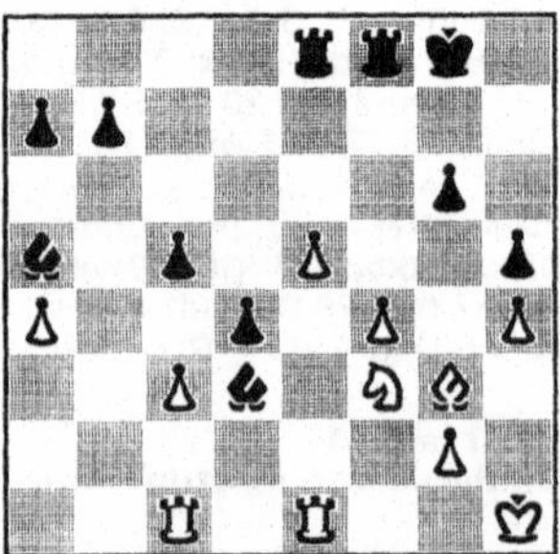

34 cxd4! ♗xe1 35 ♘xe1 ♗e4 36 dxc5 ♖c8 37 a5 b6 38 axb6 axb6 39 ♖c4 ♗d5 40 ♖d4 ♖xc5 41 ♘d3 ♖b5 42 ♘b4 ♗e6 43 ♗f2 ♖c8 44 g3 ♔f7 45 ♔g2 ♖c4 46 ♖xc4 ♗xc4 47 ♗e1 ♔e6 48 ♔f3 ♖a5 49 ♘c2 ♖a4 50 ♔e3 b5 51 ♘b4 ♖a3+ 52 ♔d4 ♖a1 53 ♘c2 ♖d1+ 54 ♔c5 ♖c1 55 ♘d4+ ♔d7 56 ♗d2 ♖g1 57 f5 gxf5 58 ♗f4 ♗d3 59 ♘xb5 [59 e6+?] 59 ... ♗xb5 60 ♔xb5 ♔e6 61 ♔c5 ♖d1 62 ♔c4 ♖d5 63 ♔c3 ♖c5+ 64 ♔d4 [64 ♔b4? ♖xe5] 64 ... ♖c6 65 ♔d3 ♔d5 66 ♔e3 ♖c8 67 ♔d3 ♖c4 68 ♔e3 ♖d4 69 ♔e2 ♔c4 [69 ... ♔e4? 70 e6 ♖d8 71 e7 ♖e8! 72 ♗d6=] 70 ♔e3 ♔c3 71 ♔e2 ♖e4+ 72 ♔f2 [72 ♔d1 ♔d3 73 ♔c1 ♖b4 74 ♗g5! ♖b3 75 ♗d2 ♖a3 76 ♗f4 ♖a1+ 77 ♔b2 ♖e1 78 ♔b3 ♖e2 79 ♔b4 ♔d4. Δ 80 ... ♖xe5-+] 72 ... ♔d3 73 ♔f1 [73 ♔f3 ♖e2] 73 ... ♖e2 74 ♔g1 ♔e4 75 ♔f1 ♔f3 76 ♔g1 ♖e1+ 77 ♔h2 ♔f2 78 e6 ♖xe6 79 ♗b8 ♖e2 80 ♗f4 ♔f1+ 81 ♔h1 [81 ♔h3 ♔g1-+] 81 ... ♖g2 82 ♗b8 ♔f2 83 ♗f4 ♖xg3 **0-1** L/N6123-1851

### 1851-★HS-2
**Horwitz, B.− Staunton, H.**
London [Staunton]

1 e4 c5 2 f4 e6 3 ♘f3 ♘c6 4 c3 g6 5 ♗e2 ♗g7 6 0-0 ♘h6 7 d3 0-0 8 ♘a3 d5 9 ♗e3 b6 10 h3 ♕e7 11 ♕c1 ♔h8 12 f5 ♘g8 13 fxe6 ♗xe6 14 exd5 ♗xd5 15 ♘g5 ♖ae8 16 ♗f3 ♗xf3 17 ♖xf3 ♘e5 18 ♗f4 ♘xf3+ 19 ♘xf3 ♖d8 20 ♕c2 ♕d7 21 ♖d1 b5 22 ♕b3 a6 23 c4 ♕f5 24 ♗e3 ♖fe8 25 ♘c2 b4 26 d4 ♘f6 27 ♖f1 cxd4 28 ♗xd4 ♘e4 29 ♗xg7+ [29 ♘g5?? ♕xf1+ 30 ♔xf1 ♘d2+] 29 ... ♔xg7 30 ♕xb4 ♘g3 31 ♖f2 ♖d1+ 32 ♘fe1 ♕e5 33 ♖f3 ♖b8 34 ♕a3 ♖xe1+ 35 ♘xe1 ♕xe1+ **0-1** L/N6123-1851

### 1851-★HS-3
**Horwitz, B.− Staunton, H.**
London

1 e4 e5 2 d4 exd4 3 ♕xd4 ♘c6 4 ♕d1 ♗c5 5 ♗d3 ♘f6 6 ♘f3 d6 7 h3 h6 8 0-0 0-0 9 ♘bd2 ♗e6 10 c3 ♕d7 11 b4 ♗b6 12 a4 a5 13 b5 ♘e5 14 ♘xe5 dxe5 15 ♕e2 ♖ad8 16 ♗c4 ♖fe8 17 ♗xe6 ♖xe6 18 ♘c4 ♕d3 19 ♖e1 ♕xe2 20 ♖xe2 ♖d1+ 21 ♔h2 ♘h5 22 g3 ♘f6 23 ♘b2 ♖d8 24 ♘c4 ♖d3 25 ♗b2 ♘d7 26 ♔g2 ♖f6 27 ♖a2 ♖df3? 28 ♗a1 ♖d3 29 ♖ac2 [□ 29 ♖ad2] 29 ... ♖d1 30 ♖a2 ♘c5 31 ♘xe5? ♖e6 32 ♘c4 ♖xe4 33 ♘e3 ♖d3 34 c4 ♘b3 35 ♖a3 ♗c5 36 ♖aa2 ♗xe3 37 ♖xe3 ♖dxe3 38 fxe3 ♖xe3 39 c5 ♖e1 [39 ... ♘xc5?? 40 ♗d4+-] 40 ♗c3 ♖c1 41 c6! bxc6 42 ♗e5 cxb5 43 axb5 ♖c5 **0-1** L/N6123-1851

### 1851-★HS-4
**Horwitz, B.+ Staunton, H.**
London [Staunton]

1 e4 e5 2 ♘f3 ♘c6 3 d4 exd4 4 ♗c4 ♗c5 5 c3 ♘f6 6 e5 d5 7 ♗b5

♘e4 8 c×d4 ♗b6 9 0-0 0-0 10 ♘c3 ♗g4 11 ♗×c6 b×c6 12 ♗e3 f6 13 ♘×e4 d×e4 14 ♕b3+ ♕d5 15 ♘d2 [△ 16 ♘×e4] 15 ... ♔h8 16 e×f6 ♖×f6 17 ♖fe1 ♖g6 18 ♕×d5 c×d5 19 ♔h1 ♖f8 20 h3 ♗c8 21 ♖ec1 ♖f5 22 a4 c6 23 g4 ♖f8 24 a5 ♗c7 25 b4 ♗a6 26 ♖a3 ♗e2 27 ♖ac3 ♗b5 28 ♘b3 ♖f3 29 ♔g2 h5 30 g5 h4 **1-0** L/N6123-1851

**1851-★HS-5**
**Horwitz, B.– Staunton, H.**
London [Staunton]

1 e4 e5 2 ♘f3 ♘c6 3 ♗c4 ♗c5 4 c3 ♘f6 5 d3 d5 6 e×d5 ♘×d5 7 b4 ♗b6 8 b5 ♘ce7 9 ♘×e5 0-0 10 ♗b2 ♗e6 11 0-0 ♔h8 12 a4 f6 13 ♘f3 ♘g6 14 ♗a3 ♖e8 15 ♕b3 ♘gf4 16 ♖a2 a6 17 b×a6 b×a6 18 ♗c1 ♖b8 19 ♕c2 ♗g4 20 ♗×d5 ♘e2+ 21 ♔h1 ♕×d5 22 c4? ♕×f3 23 h3 [23 g×f3??] 23 ... ♗×f2 24 ♘d2 [24 g×f3−+] 24 ... ♘g3+ 25 ♔h2 **0-1** L/N6123-1851

**1851-★JL-1**
**Jaenisch, C.F.= Lasa, T. von H. u. von d.**
Berlin?

1 e4 e5 2 f4 e×f4 3 ♘f3 g5 4 h4 g4 5 ♘e5 ♘f6 6 ♗c4 ♕e7 7 ♗×f7+ ♔d8 8 d4 d6 9 ♗b3 d×e5 10 d×e5+ ♗d7 11 e×f6 ♕×f6 12 ♘c3 ♗b4 13 ♗d2 ♖e8 14 ♕e2 f3 15 g×f3 g×f3 16 ♕c4 f2+ 17 ♔e2 ♗g4+ 18 ♔f1 ♕f3 19 ♕d3+ ♗d6 20 ♗g5+ ♔c8 21 ♕×f3 ♗×f3 22 ♖h3 ♗×e4 23 ♖e3 ♗g6 24 ♗e6+ ♘d7 25 ♖d1 a5 26 ♘b5 ♖a6 27 ♖×d6 c×d6 28 ♖c3+ ♖c6 29 ♘×d6+ ♔c7 30 ♘×e8+ ♗×e8 31 ♗f4+ ♔d8 32 ♖×c6 b×c6 33 ♔×f2 ♗g6 34 c3 ♘c5 35 ♗f5 ♘d3+ 36 ♗×d3 ♗×d3 37 ♔e3 ♗b1 38 a3 a4 39 ♔d4 ♔c8 40 ♔c5 ♔b7 **½-½** L/N6047-1851

**193** Löwenthal, J.J. M58.BL

**1851-★JL-2**
**Löwenthal, J.J.+ Jaenisch, C.F.**

1 e4 e5 2 f4 e×f4 3 ♗c4 ♕h4+ 4 ♔f1 g5 5 ♘c3 ♗g7 6 d4 d6 7 ♘f3 ♕h5 8 h4 h6 9 ♘d5 ♔d8 10 e5 ♕g6 11 h×g5 h×g5 12 ♖×h8 ♗×h8 13 ♘×g5 ♕×g5 14 ♗×f4 ♕h4 15 e×d6 ♕h1+ 16 ♔f2 ♕×d1 17 d×c7+ ♔e8 18 ♖×d1 ♘c6 19 c3 ♘f6 20 ♘×f6+ ♗×f6 21 d5 ♘e7 22 ♖e1 ♔f8 23 d6 ♘g6 24 ♗h6+ ♗g7 25 ♗×g7+ ♔×g7 26 ♖e8 ♗e6 27 ♖×e6 f×e6 28 d7 **1-0** L/N6047-1851

**1851-★JS-1**
**Shumov, I.S.– Jaenisch, C.F.**
St. Petersburg

1 e4 e5 2 f4 e×f4 3 ♘f3 g5 4 h4 g4 5 ♘e5 h5 6 ♗c4 ♖h7 7 d4 f3 8 g×f3 d6 9 ♘d3 ♗e7 10 ♗e3 ♗×h4+ 11 ♔d2 g×f3 12 ♕×f3 ♗g4 13 ♕g2 ♖g7 14 ♘c3 ♗g5 15 ♖af1 ♗×e3+ 16 ♔×e3 ♕g5+ 17 ♖f4 ♘d7 18 e5 d×e5 19 d×e5 0-0-0 20 ♗d5 c6 21 ♘e4 ♕e7 22 ♘d6+ ♔c7 23 ♘×f7 ♘gf6 24 ♗×c6 b×c6 25 ♘×d8 ♘d5+ 26 ♔f2 ♘×f4 27 ♕×c6+ ♔×d8 28 ♕a8+ ♔c7 29 ♕×a7+ ♔c8 30 ♕a6+ ♔b8 31 ♕b5+ ♔c7 32 ♕a5+ ♘b6 33 ♘×f4 ♔b7 34 ♘d3 ♕f7+ 35 ♔e1 ♕f3 36 ♖h2 ♕e3+ 37 ♔f1 ♗h3+ 38 ♖×h3 ♖g1# **0-1** L/N6123-1851

**1851-★JS-2**
**Shumov, I.S.+Jaenisch, C.F.**
St. Petersburg

1 e4 c5 2 d4 c×d4 3 ♘f3 e5 4 ♘×e5 ♕a5+ 5 b4 ♗×b4+ 6 ♗d2 ♗×d2+ 7 ♘×d2 ♕×e5 8 ♗d3 ♘f6 9 0-0 0-0 10 f4 ♕c5 11 e5 ♘d5 12 ♗×h7+ ♔×h7 13 ♕h5+ ♔g8 14 ♘e4 ♕×c2 15 ♖ae1 ♘e3 16 ♖×e3 d×e3 17 ♕f5 ♕e2 18 ♘f6+ g×f6 19 e×f6 ♕c2 20 ♕×c2 d5 21 ♕d3 d4 22 ♕b5 ♖d8 23 ♖f3 ♗f5 24 ♕×f5 ♘c6 25 ♕c5 **1-0** L/N6123-1851

**1851-★JS-3**
**Shumov, I.S.+Jaenisch, C.F.**
St. Petersburg

1 e4 e5 2 ♘f3 ♘c6 3 ♗c4 ♗c5 4 c3 ♘f6 5 0-0 ♘×e4 6 d4 e×d4 7 c×d4 ♗b6 8 ♗d5 ♘f6 9 ♖e1+ ♘e7 10 ♘c3 ♗a5 11 b4 ♗×b4 12 ♗×f7+ ♔f8 13 ♕b3 ♗×c3 14 ♘g5 ♗×e1 15 ♗h5 ♗×f2+ 16 ♔×f2 d5 17 ♗a3 ♘×h5 18 ♖e1 ♕d7 19 ♖×e7 ♕×e7 20 ♕×d5 ♔e8 21 ♗×e7 ♔×e7 22 ♕e5+ ♔f8 23 ♕×c7 ♗e6 24 ♕d6+ ♔e8 25 ♕×e6+ ♔d8 26 ♘f7+ ♔c7 27 ♕d6+ ♔c8 28 ♘×h8 ♘f6 29 ♕f8+ **1-0** L/N6123-1851

**1851-★P?-1**
**Petrov, A.D.+?**

1 e4 c5 2 d4 c×d4 3 ♘f3 e5 4 ♗c4 ♕c7 5 ♕e2 ♘c6 6 ♘g5 ♘h6 7 f4 ♗e7 8 0-0 d6 9 ♕h5 ♗g4 10 ♗×f7+ ♔d8 11 ♕h4 ♗f6 12 ♗e6 ♗e2 13 ♖f2 d3 14 ♘c3 ♘d4 15 ♘d5 ♕×c2 16 ♗e3 ♘×e6 17 ♖c1 d2 18 ♗×d2 ♕×d2 19 ♘×e6+ ♔e8 20 ♘×g7+ ♔f7 21 ♕×f6+ ♔g8 22 ♘e7# **1-0** L/N6123-1851

**1851-★S?-1**
**?– Staunton, H.**

1 e4 e5 2 ♘f3 ♘c6 3 d4 e×d4 4 ♗c4 ♗c5 5 ♘g5 d5 6 ♗×d5 ♘e5 7 f4 ♗g4 8 ♗×f7+ ♔e7 9 ♘e6 ♕c8 10 ♕d2 ♘c4 11 ♕d3 ♗×e6 12 ♗×e6 ♕×e6 **0-1** L/N6123-1851

**1851-★S?-2**
**Staunton, H.– ?**
Reading

⟨♘b1⟩1 e4 e5 2 ♗c4 ♗c5 3 ♕e2 ♕e7 4 c3 c6 5 f4 d6 6 ♘f3 ♗g4 7 d3 ♘d7 8 ♗d2 ♘gf6 9 f5 ♘b6 10 ♗b3 ♗×f3 11 ♕×f3 ♖d8 12 0-0-0 0-0 13 g4 d5 14 g5 ♘e8 15 f6 ♕d6 16 h4 g×f6 17 g×f6 ♕×f6 18 ♕g4+ ♕g7 19 ♕f3 ♔h8 20 d4 e×d4 21 ♖hg1 ♕e5 22 ♗h6 d×c3 23 ♗×f8 c×b2+ 24 ♔b1 ♗×f8 25 ♖g5 ♕e6 26 ♕g3 f6 27 e×d5 c×d5 28 ♖g4 ♘g7 29 ♖dg1 ♖d7 30 ♕b8 ♕d6 31 ♕e8 ♖c7 32 ♗c2 ♘c4 33 ♖×g7 **0-1** L/N6123-1851

**1851-★S?-3**
**Staunton, H.+?**
Cambridge

⟨♘b1⟩1 e4 e5 2 ♘f3 ♘c6 3 ♗c4 ♗c5 4 b4 ♗×b4 5 c3 ♗c5 6 d4 e×d4 7 0-0 d6 8 c×d4 ♗b6 9 a4 ♘f6 10 a5 ♗×a5 11 d5 ♗c3 12 ♖a3 ♗b4 13 ♖b3 ♗c5 14 d×c6 b×c6 15 e5 ♘e4 16 e×d6 c×d6 17 ♕c2 d5 18 ♗d3 ♕e7 19 ♗×e4 d×e4 20 ♗a3 ♗×a3 21 ♕×c6+ ♕d7 22 ♕×e4+ ♗e7 23 ♕×a8 0-0 24 ♕e4 ♗f6 25 ♖e1 ♕d6 26 ♖d3 ♕c5 27 ♖d5 ♕c6 28 ♘d4 ♕b6 29 ♖b1 ♕a6 30 ♕c2 g6 31 ♘b5 ♗f5 32 ♖×f5 g×f5 33 ♕×f5 ♗g7 34 ♘c7 ♕g6 35 ♕b5 ♗d4 36 ♖b3 ♔h8 37 ♕b4 ♗×f2+ 38 ♔×f2 ♕c2+ 39 ♔e3 ♕c1+ 40 ♔e4 ♕c2+ 41 ♔e3 **1-0** M954-1851

**1851-★S?-4**
**Staunton, H.+?**
Reading

⟨♘b1⟩1 e4 c5 2 ♘e2 e5 3 ♘g3 d5 4 c3 ♘f6 5 ♗b5+ ♗d7 6 ♗×d7+ ♕×d7 7 e×d5 ♘×d5 8 0-0 ♗d6 9 d4 cxd4 10 ♕f3 ♘e7 11 cxd4 exd4 12 ♘e4 ♘bc6 13 ♖e1 0-0 14 ♗g5 ♘e5 15 ♕g3 ♘7g6 16 ♗f4 ♘f3+ 17 ♕xf3 ♘xf4 18 ♔h1 ♔h8 19 g3 ♘e6 20 ♕f5 ♖ad8 21 ♖ac1 b6 22 ♕f3 ♘c5 23 ♘g5 ♕b7 24 ♕xb7 ♘xb7 25 a3 ♘c5 26 ♖ed1 ♘b3 27 ♖c2 h6 28 ♘f3 ♗c5 29 ♖d3 ♗xa3 30 bxa3 ♘c5 31 ♖xd4 ♖xd4 32 ♘xd4 ♖d8 33 ♘c6 ♖d1+ 34 ♔g2 a6 35 ♘e5 ♖d5 36 ♘c4 ♘d3 37 ♖e2 b5 38 ♖e8+ ♔h7 39 ♘e3 ♖c5 40 ♖a8 ♖c6 41 ♖a7 ♔g6 42 f4 f6 43 h4 ♘e1+ 44 ♔h3 ♖d6 45 h5+ ♔h7 46 ♘f5 ♖d5 47 ♔g4 ♘c2 48 ♖xg7+ ♔h8 49 ♖g6 ♖d3 50 ♖xh6+ ♔g8 51 ♖xf6 ♖xa3 52 ♔g5 b4 53 ♔g6 **1-0** M954-1851

## HARRWITZ✕WILLIAMS

[1852-✕HW1]

| | | | | | | | | | | | |
|---|---|---|---|---|---|---|---|---|---|---|---|
| D. Harrwitz | 1 | ½ | 1 | 1 | ½ | ½ | 1 | 1 | 1 | 1 | 8½ |
| E. Williams | 0 | ½ | 0 | 0 | ½ | ½ | 0 | 0 | 0 | 0 | 1½ |

### 1852-✕HW1-1 29 x 52

**Harrwitz, D.+Williams, E.**

[Harrwitz]

1 e4 e6 2 d4 d5 3 exd5 exd5 4 c4 ♘f6 5 ♘c3 ♘c6 6 ♘f3 h6 7 cxd5 ♘xd5 8 ♗c4 ♘xc3 9 bxc3 ♗d6 10 0-0 0-0 11 h3 ♕f6 12 ♗d3 ♘e7 13 ♗e3 ♘d5 14 c4 ♘e7 15 c5 ♗f4 16 ♕d2 ♘g6 17 ♗xg6 fxg6 18 ♗xf4 ♕xf4 19 ♕xf4? ♖xf4 20 ♔h2 ♗e6 21 ♖ad1 ♗d5 [◻ 21 ... ♗xa2] 22 ♘e5 ♔h7 23 a3 ♖af8 24 f3 ♖8f6 25 ♖d3 ♖a6 26 g3 ♖ff6 27 ♖e1 ♖a4 28 ♖ee3 ♖a5 29 ♔g2 ♖b5 30 ♔f2 c6 31 ♖d2 [31 h4] 31 ... g5 32 h4 gxh4 33 gxh4 ♖b1! 34 ♘g4 ♖f7 35 ♔g2 ♖f4 36 ♔g3 ♖f5 37 ♔g2 ♖h5 38 ♔g3 ♖g1+ 39 ♔h2 ♖b1 40 ♔g3 ♖f5 [△ 41 ... ♖h1] 41 ♔g2 b5 42 cxb6 ♖xb6 43 ♖dd3 ♖b7 44 ♖e5 ♖f4 45 ♔g3 ♖bf7 46 ♖ee3 ♖4f5 47 ♘e5 ♖7f6 48 ♖d2 ♖e6 [△ 49 ... c5] 49 ♖c3 ♖ef6 50 ♖b2 ♖f4 51 ♖b4 a6 52 ♖a4 a5 53 ♖xc6 ♗xf3 54 ♖xa5!+- ♖f8 55 ♖c7 ♗e4 56 ♖aa7 ♖f1 57 ♖xg7+ ♔h8 58 ♖af7! ♖1xf7 59 ♖xf7 ♖a8 60 ♔f4 ♗g2 61 ♘g4 ♗d5 [61 ... ♖xa3? 62 ♘f6+-] 62 ♖f6 ♔g7 63 ♖xh6 ♖xa3 64 ♖d6 ♗f7 65 ♖d7 ♔f8 66 ♘e5 ♗e6 67 ♘g6+ ♔g8 68 ♖e7 ♗d5 69 h5 ♗f7 70 ♔g5 ♖d3 71 ♖xf7! ♖g3+ 72 ♔f4 ♖g1 73 ♖f5 ♔g7 74 d5 ♖d1 75 ♔e5 ♖e1+ 76 ♔d6 **1-0** L/N6128-1853

### 1852-✕HW1-2

**Williams, E.=Harrwitz, D.**

[Harrwitz]

1 f4 d5 2 e3 c5 3 ♘f3 ♘c6 4 b3 ♘f6 5 ♗b5 ♗d7 6 0-0 e6 7 ♕e2 ♗e7 8 d3 0-0 9 c4 a6 10 ♗xc6 ♗xc6 11 ♘bd2 ♘d7 12 e4 d4 13 e5 f5 14 exf6 ♖xf6 15 ♘e4 ♖g6 16 ♗d2 ♕c7 17 ♖ae1 ♖e8 18 ♖f2 [18 ♘eg5? ♗xg5 19 ♘xg5 h6 20 ♕h5 ♘f8 21 ♘f3 ♗xf3 22 ♖xf3 ♕c6∓] 18 ... h6 19 h4 ♗xe4 20 ♕xe4 ♖f6 21 g4!? ♗d6 22 g5 ♖f5 23 gxh6 ♘f6 24 ♕e2 gxh6 [24 ... ♗xf4 25 ♖g2] 25 ♘e5 ♗xe5 26 ♖g2+! ♔h7 27 fxe5 ♘h5 28 ♕e4 ♕f7? [28 ... ♖g8] 29 ♔h2 ♖f8 30 ♖eg1 ♕c7 31 ♖g6 ♖8f6! 32 ♖xf6 ♘xf6 33 ♕g2 ♕xe5+ 34 ♔h1 ♕c7 35 ♕g6+ ♔h8 36 ♗xh6 ♕h7! 37 ♗g7+ ♔g8 38 ♕g3! ♘d7! 39 ♗xd4+ ♔f7 40 ♗e3 [◻ 40 ♗c3 △ 41 ♕g7+] 40 ... ♘e5 41 ♗g5 [41 ♗xc5 ♖f3 42 ♕g5 ♖h3+ 43 ♔g2 ♖h2+ 44 ♔g3 ♕xd3+ 45 ♕e3 ♕xe3+ 46 ♗xe3 ♖xa2=] 41 ... b5 42 ♖e1 ♕h8 43 ♕e3 ♕a8+ 44 ♕e4 ♕xe4+ 45 dxe4 ♖f2 [△ 46 ... ♘f3] 46 ♔g1 ♖xa2 47 ♖f1+ ♔g6 48 cxb5 [48 ♖f6+ ♔h5 49 ♖xe6 bxc4 50 ♖xe5 cxb3] 48 ... axb5 49 ♖f6+ ♔h5 50 ♖xe6 ♘f3+ 51 ♔f1 c4 52 bxc4 bxc4 53 ♖c6 ♖c2 54 ♖c5 ♔g4 55 e5 ♔g3 56 ♗e3 ♖h2 57 ♖xc4 ♖h1+ 58 ♔e2 ♖e1+ 59 ♔d3 ♘xe5+ 60 ♔d2 ♘xc4+ 61 ♔xe1 **½-½** L/N6128-1853

### 1852-✕HW1-3

**Harrwitz, D.+Williams, E.**

[Harrwitz]

1 e4 e5 2 ♘f3 d6 3 d4 exd4 4 ♗c4 ♗e7 [4 ... c5?] 5 ♘xd4 ♘f6 6 ♘c3 0-0 [△ 7 ... ♘xe4 8 ♘xe4 d5] 7 ♗b3 ♘c6 8 f4 ♘g4 9 ♘xc6 bxc6 10 0-0 ♗f6? 11 h3 ♗xc3 12 hxg4 ♗a5 13 g3? [13 g5!±] 13 ... ♗a6 14 c4 ♕e7 [14 ... d5!] 15 ♕d3 ♖ae8 16 ♗c2 ♕e6 17 b3 ♕xg4 18 ♔g2 f5 19 ♗d1 [19 exf5? ♖e2+] 19 ... fxe4 20 ♕e3 ♕c8 [◻ 20 ... ♕g6; 20 ... ♕d7] 21 ♗b2 ♖e7 22 f5!± ♗b6 [22 ... ♖xf5 23 ♗g4] 23 ♕g5 ♕d7 24 ♗g4 ♕e8 25 f6!+- ♖ef7 26 ♗h5 ♗c8 [26 ... g6? 27 ♗xg6!] 27 ♗xf7+ [27 ♕xg7+] 27 ... ♖xf7 28 fxg7 ♕d7 29 ♕h4 ♖f3 30 ♖ae1 d5 31 ♖xf3 exf3+ 32 ♔xf3 ♕f5+ 33 ♕f4 d4 34 ♕xf5 ♗xf5 35 c5 [35 b4!+-] 35 ... ♗a5 36 ♖e7 ♗c3 37 ♗xc3 dxc3 38 ♔e2 ♗b1 39 ♔d1 a5 [39 ... ♗xa2? 40 ♔c2+-] 40 ♖xc7 ♗e4 41 a3 h6 42 ♖e7 ♗f5 43 ♔c1 ♔h7 44 ♖b7 ♗e4 45 b4 axb4 46 ♖xb4 ♗d5 47 ♖b7 ♗e4 48 a4 ♗d3 49 a5 h5 50 ♖d7 ♗a6 51 ♔c2 ♗c8 52 ♖c7 ♗f5+ 53 ♔xc3 h4 54 gxh4 ♗e6 55 a6 ...? **1-0** L/N6128-1853

### 1852-✕HW1-4

**Williams, E.−Harrwitz, D.**

[Harrwitz]

1 d4 d5 2 c4 e6 3 ♘c3 ♘f6 4 e3 c5 5 ♘f3 ♘c6 6 ♗d3 a6 7 a3 cxd4 8 exd4 dxc4 9 ♗xc4 b5 10 ♗b3 ♘a5 11 ♗c2 ♗b7 12 0-0 ♖c8 13 ♗e3 ♘c4 14 ♘e5 [14 ♕c1 ♘xa3] 14 ... ♘xb2 15 ♕e1 ♘d5 16 ♗d2 [16 ♘xd5?? ♕xd5-+] 16 ... ♘c4 17 ♘xc4 ♖xc4 18 ♗b3 ♖xd4

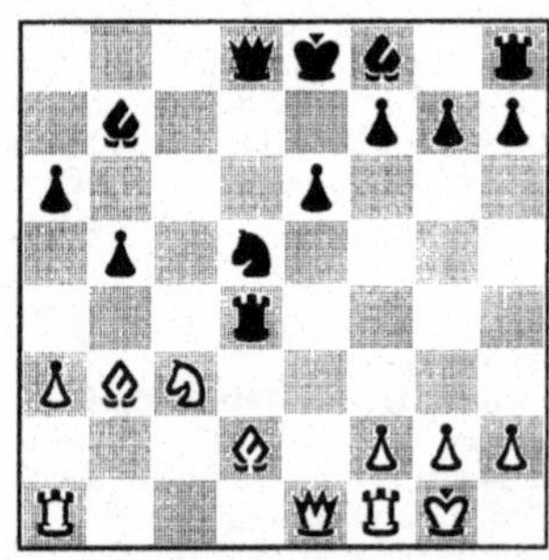

19 ♘e4 [19 ♘e2 ♖d3 20 ♗xd5 ♕xd5 21 ♘f4 ♕g5 22 g3 ♗c5 23 ♘xe6 (23 ♘xd3 ♕d5-+) 23 ... ♖xg3+ 24 hxg3 ♕xg3#] 19 ... ♘c7 20 ♗a5 ♖xe4 21 ♕c3 ♖c4 [21 ... ♗b6; 21 ... ♘d5!] 22 ♗xc4 bxc4 23 ♖fd1 [23 ♕xc4? ♕g5-+] 23 ... ♕g5 24 g3 ♕c5 25 ♖ab1 ♕c6 26 ♖xb7 ♕xb7 27 ♕xc4 ♘d5 28 ♖c1 f6 29 ♕c2 ♔f7 30 ♖b1 ♕a8 31 ♕a4 ♗e7 32 ♕d7 ♕c8 33 ♕a7 ♕c2 34 ♖b7 ♖c8 35 ♗b4 ♕b1+ 36 ♔g2 ♕e4+ 37 ♔h3 ♘f4+ **0-1** L/N6128-1853

### 1852-✕HW1-5

**Harrwitz, D.=Williams, E.**

[Harrwitz]

1 e4 e5 2 f4 ♗c5 3 ♘f3 d6 4 ♗c4 ♘c6 5 c3 ♘f6 6 b4 ♗b6 7 d3 a6 8 ♕e2 0-0 9 f5 d5 10 ♗b3 dxe4 11 dxe4 ♕d6 12 ♘bd2 ♗a7 13 ♘c4 ♕e7 14 ♗g5 b5 15 ♘e3 ♗xe3 16 ♕xe3 ♗b7 17 0-0 ♖ad8 18 h3 ♖d6 19 ♘h2 ♖fd8 20 ♘g4 ♔h8 [20 ... ♘xg4?? 21 hxg4+-] 21 ♘xf6 [◻ 21 ♗xf6] 21 ... gxf6 22 ♗h4 ♕f8 23 ♖f3 ♘e7 24 ♖e1 ♕g7 25 ♖g3 ♖d3 26 ♖xg7 ♖xe3 27 ♖xh7+ [27 ♗xf6? ♖xe1+ △ 28 ... ♖d6] 27 ... ♔xh7 28 ♖xe3 ♖d6 29 ♗xf7 ♔g7 30 ♗e6 ♗c8 31 ♖g3+ ♔f8 32 ♗xf6 ♗xe6 33 ♗xe7+ ♔xe7 34 fxe6 ♖xe6 35 ♖g7+ ♔d6 36 ♔f2 ♖f6+ 37 ♔e3 c6 38 ♖a7 ♖f1 39 ♖xa6 ♖e1+ 40 ♔f3 ♖c1 41 ♖a3 ♖f1+ 42 ♔e2 ♖h1 43 c4 bxc4 44 ♖c3 ♖b1 45 ♖xc4 ♖b2+ 46 ♔f3 ♖xa2 47 h4 ♖a8 48 g4? [48 ♔g3+-; 48 h5+-] 48 ... ♖a3+ 49 ♔f2 ♖a2+ 50 ♔f1 ♖h2 51 ♖c3 ♖xh4 52 ♖g3 ♖h2 53 g5 ♖h7 54 ♖f3? [54 g6; 54 ♔f2] 54 ... ♖h4 55 ♖g3 ♖xe4 56 g6 ♖f4+ 57 ♔e2 ♖f8 58 g7 ♖g8 59 ♔d3 ♔d5 60 ♖g5 c5 61 bxc5 [61 b5=] 61 ... ♔xc5 62 ♔e4 ♔d6 63 ♔f5 ♔d5! 64 ♔f6 ♔d4! 65 ♔f7 ♖xg7+ 66 ♖xg7 e4 67 ♔f6 e3 68 ♔f5 e2 69 ♖e7 ♔d3 70 ♔f4 ♔d2 71 ♖d7+ ♔c1 72 ♖c7+ ♔d2 73 ♖d7+ ♔c1 **½-½** L/N6128-1853

**1852-✕HW1-6** 25 xi 52
**Williams, E.= Harrwitz, D.**
[Harrwitz]
1 e3 d5 2 f4 a6 3 ♘f3 c5 4 d4 e6 5 ♗d3 ♘f6 6 0-0 ♘c6 7 c3 ♗e7 8 ♘e5 0-0 9 ♘d2 ♕c7 10 ♘df3 ♘e4 11 ♕c2 f5 12 ♘xc6 bxc6 13 ♘e5 ♗d6 14 b3 [△ 15 ♗a3] 14 ... cxd4 15 cxd4 ♗d7 16 ♗d2 ♗xe5 17 fxe5 ♕b6 18 ♖ac1 h6 19 ♗xe4 fxe4 20 ♖xf8+ ♖xf8 21 ♕c5 ♕b5 22 ♕xb5 [22 ♕d6?? ♕e2−+; 22 ♕e7?? ♕e2−+] 22 ... axb5 23 a4 bxa4 24 bxa4 c5 25 ♖xc5 ♗xa4 ½-½
L/N6128-1853

**1852-✕HW1-7**
**Harrwitz, D.+ Williams, E.**
[Harrwitz]
1 e4 e5 2 f4 ♗c5 3 ♘f3 d6 4 c3 ♘c6 [□ 4 ... ♗g4] 5 b4 ♗b6 6 b5 ♘a5 [□ 6 ... ♘b8] 7 d4 exd4 8 cxd4 ♘f6 9 ♗d3 ♗g4 10 ♗b2 0-0 11 ♘bd2 [11 h3] 11 ... ♘h5 12 h3?! [12 g3] 12 ... ♗xf3 [12 ... ♘xf4] 13 ♕xf3 ♕h4+ 14 ♔d1 ♕g3 [14 ... ♕xf4?? 15 ♕xh5; 14 ... ♘xf4?? 15 g3] 15 ♖f1 ♖fe8 16 ♕xg3 ♘xg3 17 ♖f3 ♘h5 18 e5 g6 19 g4 ♘g7 20 f5 dxe5 21 dxe5 ♖ed8 22 ♔c2 ♗d4 23 ♗xd4 ♖xd4 24 e6± fxe6 25 f6 ♘f5 26 gxf5 exf5 27 ♔c3 ♖d6 28 ♘c4 ♘xc4 29 ♗xc4+ ♔f8 30 f7 ♖ad8 31 ♖e1 ♖c8 32 ♖fe3 ♖dd8 33 ♗e6 ♖b8 34 h4 c6 35 bxc6 bxc6 36 ♖d3 ♖xd3+ 37 ♔xd3 ♖b4 38 ♗c4 ♖b8 39 ♔d4 ♖d8+ 40 ♔c5 ♖c8 41 ♔d6 ♖d8+ 42 ♔c7 ♖a8 43 ♔b7 [43 ♔d7!] 43 ... ♖d8 44 ♔xa7 h6 45 ♔b7 ♖d7+ 46 ♔xc6 ♖xf7 47 ♗xf7 ♔xf7 48 ♔d5 g5 49 hxg5 hxg5 50 ♔e5 ♔g6 51 a4 ...? 1-0
L/N6128-1853

**1852-✕HW1-8**
**Williams, E.− Harrwitz, D.**
[Harrwitz]
1 e4 e5 2 ♘f3 ♘c6 3 ♗b5 ♗c5 4 c3 ♕f6 [□ 4 ... ♕e7] 5 0-0 [5 d4! exd4 6 e5 ♘xe5?? 7 ♕e2+−] 5 ... ♘ge7 6 d4 exd4 7 ♗g5 ♕g6 8 ♗xe7 ♘xe7 9 cxd4 ♗b6 10 ♘c3 c6 11 ♗d3 ♕h6 12 e5 d5 13 exd6 ♕xd6 14 ♘e4 ♕c7 15 h3 h6 16 ♘g3 ♗e6 17 ♕d2 0-0-0 18 ♘e2 g5 19 a4 a5 20 b4 axb4 21 ♕xb4 ♘d5 22 ♕d2 ♗a5 23 ♕c2 ♘b4 24 ♕b1 g4 25 hxg4 ♘xd3 [25 ... ♗xg4 26 ♗f5+] 26 ♕xd3 ♗xg4 27 ♖fd1 ♖he8 28 ♕c2 ♗xf3 29 ♕f5+ ♖e6 30 ♕xf3 ♖g8 31 d5! ♖eg6 32 ♘f4 ♖g4 33 d6 ♕d7 34 ♖ac1! h5 35 ♖c5 ♗b6 36 ♖xh5 f5! 37 ♖h6 ♗d8 [△ 38 ... ♗g5] 38 ♖h2 ♗f6 39 ♕e3 ♖e8

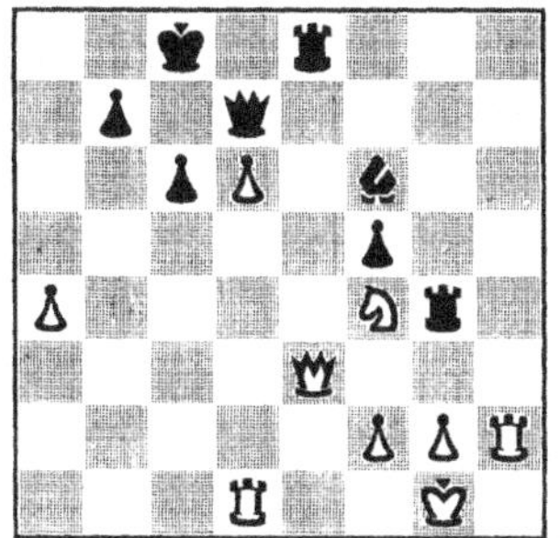

40 ♕a7? [40 ♖h8!!+− ♗xh8 41 ♕a7 ♕d8 (41 ... ♖e1+ 42 ♖xe1 ♕xd6 43 ♕a8+ ♔c7 44 ♘e6++−; 41 ... ♕g7 42 ♕a8++−) 42 ♕a8+ ♕c8 43 ♕a5+ ♔d7 44 ♕xf5+ ♔d8 45 d7+−] 40 ... ♕xd6!!−+ 41 ♘d3 ♗e5 42 ♖h7 ♖xg2+ 43 ♔xg2 ♕g6+ 44 ♔f3 ♕g4+ 45 ♔e3 ♗d4+ 46 ♔d2 ♗xa7 ...? 0-1
L/N6128-1853

**1852-✕HW1-9**
**Harrwitz, D.+ Williams, E.**
[Harrwitz]
1 e4 e5 2 f4 exf4 3 ♘f3 g5 4 h4 g4 5 ♘e5 h5 6 ♗c4 ♘h6 7 d4 d6 8 ♘d3 f3 9 gxf3 ♗e7 10 ♗e3 ♗xh4+ 11 ♔d2 gxf3 12 ♕xf3 ♗g4 13 ♕f4 ♕f6 14 ♘c3 ♘d7 15 ♘d5 ♕xf4 16 ♘3xf4 ♗d8 17 ♘xh5± ♔f8 18 ♖af1 ♗e6 19 ♘hf4 ♔e8 20 ♘xe6 fxe6 21 ♖xh6 ♖xh6 22 ♘xc7+ ♗xc7 23 ♗xh6 ♗a5+ 24 ♔d3 e5 25 ♗b5 ♖b8 26 ♖f5 ♗c7 27 ♖g5+− ♖d8 28 ♖g8+ ♔e7 29 ♖g7+ ♔f6 30 ♖xd7 ♖c8 31 c3 a6 32 ♗a4 ♔e6 33 ♗g5 1-0
L/N6128-1853

**1852-✕HW1-10** 30 xi 52
**Williams, E.− Harrwitz, D.**
[Harrwitz]
1 f4 d5 2 e3 e6 3 ♘f3 ♘f6 4 b3 ♗d6 5 ♗b2 0-0 6 ♗d3 c5 7 0-0 ♘c6 8 a3 d4 9 ♕e2 ♘d5 10 ♗e4 dxe3 11 dxe3 f5 12 ♗xd5 exd5 13 ♕d3 ♗e7 [13 ... ♗e6 14 ♘g5] 14 ♘c3 ♗e6 15 ♖ad1 ♗f6 16 ♗a1 h6 17 ♖d2 [17 ♘xd5?? ♗xa1−+] 17 ... ♗xc3 18 ♕xc3 ♕e7 19 ♘e5 ♘xe5 20 ♕xe5 ♖f7 21 ♖f3 ♖e8 22 ♖g3 ♔h7 23 c4?! dxc4 24 ♖d6 ♕f6 25 ♕xf6 gxf6 26 bxc4 ♗xc4 27 ♗xf6 ♖e6 28 ♗e5?? [28 ♖xe6] 28 ... ♖xd6 29 ♗xd6 ♖d7 30 e4 [30 ♗ ♖d1+ 31 ♔f2 ♖f1#] 30 ... ♖xd6 31 exf5 ♗d3 32 f6 c4 33 ♖g7+ ♔h8 34 ♖xb7 ♖xf6 35 ♖xa7 ♖xf4 36 g3 ♖f6 37 ♖c7 ♖a6 38 ♔f2 ♖xa3 39 ♔e3 ♖a2 40 h4 ♖e2+ 41 ♔f4 ♖e4+ 42 ♔f3 ♖e6 43 ♔g4 ♖g6+ 44 ♔h5 ♖xg3 45 ♔xh6 ♖g6+ 46 ♔h5 ♖g7 47 ♖c6 ♔g8 48 ♖d6 ♖c7 49 ♔h6 c3 50 ♖xd3 ♖c6+ 51 ♔h5 c2−+ 52 ♖g3+ ♔f7 53 ♖f3+ ♔e6 54 ♖e3+ ♔d5 55 ♖e1 c1=♕ 56 ♖xc1 ♖xc1 57 ♔g6 ♔e6 58 h5 ♖g1+ 59 ♔h7 ♔f7 60 ♔h6 0-1
L/N6128-1853

## HARRWITZ✕WILLIAMS
[1852-✕HW2]

| | | | | | | | | | | | | | |
|---|---|---|---|---|---|---|---|---|---|---|---|---|---|
| D. Harrwitz | 0 | 0 | 1 | ½ | ½ | 1 | 1 | 1 | ½ | 1 | 1 | 1 | 8½ |
| E. Williams | 1 | 1 | 0 | ½ | ½ | 0 | 0 | 0 | ½ | 0 | 0 | 0 | 3½ |

**1852-✕HW2-1** 4 xii 52
**Williams, E.+ Harrwitz, D.**
[Harrwitz]
1 e4 e5 2 ♘f3 ♘c6 3 ♗c4 ♗c5 4 d3 d6 5 ♘c3 ♘f6 6 h3 ♗e6 7 ♗b3 ♘e7 8 d4 exd4 9 ♘xd4 ♗xb3 10 axb3 c6 11 0-0 b5?± 12 ♗g5 ♕d7 13 ♗xf6 gxf6 14 ♕d3 0-0 15 ♘ce2 ♔h8 [□ 15 ... ♔g7; 15 ... ♘g6] 16 ♕f3 ♔g7 17 ♖ad1!± ♗xd4 18 ♖xd4 c5? [18 ... ♘g6] 19 ♕g3+ ♘g6 20 ♖xd6 ♕e7 21 ♘f4 ♕xe4? [21 ... ♕e5] 22 ♘h5+ ♔h8 23 ♖xf6 ♕xc2 24 ♕g5+− ♕xb2 25 ♕h6 ♖g8 26 ♖xf7 ♘f8 27 ♘f6 ♕c2 28 ♘xg8 ♕g6 29 ♕xg6 hxg6 30 ♘f6 a5 31 ♖e1 ♖a6 32 ♖ee7 ...? 1-0
L/N6128-1853

**1852-✕HW2-2** xii 52
**Harrwitz, D.− Williams, E.**
[Harrwitz]
1 e4 e5 2 f4 ♗c5 3 ♘f3 d6 4 c3 ♗g4! 5 ♗c4 ♗xf3 [5 ... ♕e7] 6 ♕xf3 ♘f6 7 d3 c6 8 ♗b3 ♘bd7 9 ♘d2 ♕e7 10 f5 g6 11 g4 h5 12 g5 ♘h7 13 f6 ♕d8 14 h4 ♗b6 15 ♘f1 ♘c5 16 ♗c4 ♕d7 17 ♕h3 ♕xh3 18 ♖xh3 ♘f8 19 b4 ♘ce6 20 a4 0-0-0 21 a5 ♗c7 22 a6 b6 23 ♗e3 d5 24 exd5 cxd5 25 ♗b5 d4 26 cxd4 exd4 27 ♗d2± ♖d5 28 ♗c6 ♖e5+ 29 ♗e4 ♘d8 30 ♖c1 ♔d7 31 ♖xc7+ ♔xc7 32 ♗f4 ♘d7 33 ♖h2 ♘e6 34 ♖c2+ ♔d8 35 ♗xe5 ♘xe5 36 ♘g3 ♔d7∓ 37 ♘e2 ♖c8 38 ♖xc8 ♔xc8 39 ♔d2 ♔d7 40 ♗d5 ♔d6 41 ♗xe6 ♘f3+ 42 ♔c2 ♔xe6 43 ♔b3 b5 44 ♘f4+ ♔d6 [44 ... ♔e5?? 45 ♘xg6+] 45 ♔c2 ♘xh4 46 ♔d1 ♔e5 47 ♘h3 ♘g2 48 ♘f2 ♘e3+ 49 ♔d2 ♘d5 50 ♘e4 ♘xb4 51 ♘c5 ♔d5 52 ♘b7 ♘c6!−+ 53 ♔e2 b4 ...? 0-1
L/N6128-1853

**1852-✕HW2-3** 10 xii 52
**Williams, E.− Harrwitz, D.**
London [Harrwitz]
1 e4 e5 2 ♘f3 ♘c6 3 ♗c4 ♗c5 4 ♘c3 d6 5 d3 ♘f6 6 h3 ♘e7 7 d4 exd4 8 ♘xd4 c6 9 ♘f3 ♘g6 10 0-0 0-0 11 ♕d3 ♘h5 12 ♘e2 ♔h8 [△ 13 ... f5] 13 g4 ♘f6 14 ♘g3 ♘d7 [△ 15 ... ♘ge5] 15 ♗b3 ♘ge5 16 ♘xe5 ♘xe5

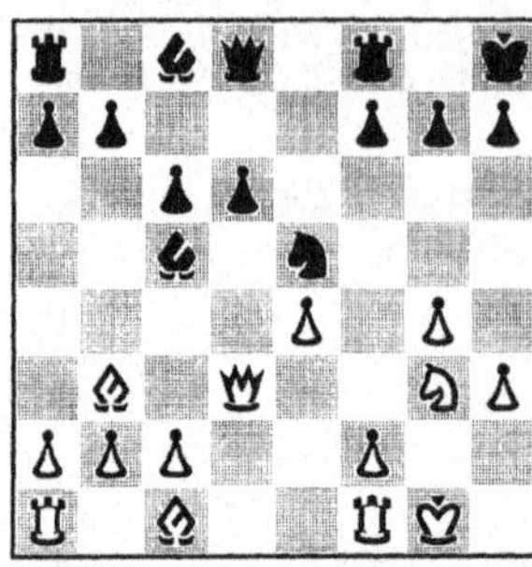

17 ♕c3?? [17 ♕e2 ♕h4] 17 ... ♗d4 18 ♕b4 a5 ...? **0-1** L/N6128-1853

### 1852-⚔HW2-4 xii 52
**Harrwitz, D.= Williams, E.**
[Harrwitz]

1 e4 e5 2 ♘f3 d6 3 c3 ♘f6 4 ♗c4 ♗e7 [4 ... ♘xe4 5 ♕a4+ △ 6 ♗xf7+ 7 ♕xe4] 5 d3 0-0 6 ♘bd2 ♘c6 7 b4 a6 8 a4 d5 9 exd5 ♘xd5 10 ♘e4 f5? [10 ... ♔h8] 11 ♕b3 fxe4 12 ♗xd5+ ♔h8 13 ♗xe4 ♕d6 14 ♗e3 ♗e6 15 ♕c2 ♗d5 16 ♘d2 ♗xe4 17 ♘xe4 ♕g6 18 0-0 ♘d8 19 f4 exf4 20 ♗xf4 ♘e6 21 ♗e3 ♖ad8 22 ♕e2 h6 23 ♖xf8+ ♗xf8 24 ♖f1 ♗e7 25 ♖f3?! ♗g5 26 ♗xg5 ♘xg5 27 ♖g3 ♕b6+ 28 ♕e3? [28 d4?? ♕e6; 28 ♕f2; 28 ♘f2] 28 ... ♖xd3 29 ♕xb6 ♖d1+ 30 ♔f2 ♘xe4+ 31 ♔f3 cxb6 32 ♔xe4 ♔h7 33 ♔e5 ♖a1 34 ♔d6 ♖xa4 35 ♔c7 a5 36 b5 ♖c4+ 37 ♔xb6 a4∞ 38 ♖f3 a3 39 ♖f2 ♖xc3 40 ♔xb7 ♖b3 41 b6 ♖b2 42 ♖f3 a2 43 ♖a3 ♖xg2 44 ♔a7 ♖xh2= 45 b7 ♖b2 46 b8=♕ ♖xb8 47 ♔xb8 g5 48 ♔c7 ♔g6 49 ♔d6 ♔f5 50 ♔d5 g4 51 ♖xa2 g3 52 ♖a8 ♔f4 53 ♖f8+ ♔e3 **½-½** L/N6128-1853

### 1852-⚔HW2-5 xii 52
**Williams, E.= Harrwitz, D.**
[Harrwitz]

1 e4 e5 2 ♗c4 ♗c5 3 ♘f3 ♘c6 [3 ... d6?! 4 d4] 4 d3 d6 5 c3 ♘f6 6 h3 0-0 7 0-0 ♗b6 8 ♗g5 ♗e6 9 ♘bd2 h6 10 ♗h4 ♔h7 11 ♔h2 ♖g8 12 ♗g3 g5 13 ♗xe6! fxe6 14 ♘c4 g4 15 ♘xb6 axb6 16 ♘h4 ♘h5 17 hxg4 ♘f4 18 ♖h1! ♕g5 19 f3 ♖g7 20 ♗xf4! exf4 21 ♔g1 ♘e5 22 b3 ♔g8 23 d4 ♘f7 24 d5 exd5 25 ♘f5 ♖g6 26 ♕xd5 c6 27 ♕d2 ♘e5± 28 ♖h5? ♕xh5! 29 gxh5 ♘xf3+ 30 ♔f2 ♖xg2+ 31 ♔xg2 ♘xd2 32 ♘xd6 ♘xb3!∓ 33 ♖d1 ♖xa2+ 34 ♔f3 ♘c5 35 ♔xf4 ♖h2 36 ♔g4 b5 37 e5 ♔f8 38 ♘f5 ♖g2+ 39 ♔h4 ♖e2 40 ♖d8+ ♔f7 41 ♘xh6+ ♔e7 42 ♖g8 ♖xe5 43 ♘g4 ♖e1 44 h6 ♘e4 45 ♔h3 ♖h1+ 46 ♘h2 ♘f6 47 ♖g7+ ♔e6 48 ♖xb7 ♖c1 49 h7 ♖xc3+ 50 ♔g2 ♘xh7 51 ♖xh7 b4 52 ♘f3 c5 53 ♔f2 b3 54 ♘d2= c4 55 ♔e2 b2 56 ♖b7 ♖c2 57 ♔e3 ♔d5 58 ♘b1 ♔c5 59 ♖b8 **½-½** L/N6128-1853

### 1852-⚔HW2-6 xii 52
**Harrwitz, D.+ Williams, E.**
London [Harrwitz]

1 e4 e5 2 f4 d5 3 exd5 e4!? 4 c4 f5 5 d4 ♘f6 6 ♘c3 ♗e7 7 ♗e2 0-0 8 ♘h3 c6 9 dxc6 ♘xc6 10 d5 ♘b8 11 a3 a5 12 ♗e3 ♘a6 13 ♘a4 ♘d7 14 d6 ♗h4+ 15 g3 ♗f6 16 c5± ♘ab8 17 ♖c1 ♘c6 18 0-0 ♔h8 19 ♕d2 ♕e8 20 ♗b5 ♕f7 [20 ... ♕h5] 21 ♗c4 ♕h5 22 ♘f2 ♕e8 23 ♔g2 ♗d8 24 ♘c3 ♘f6 25 ♖fd1 ♗d7 26 ♕c2 ♕h5 27 ♗e2 ♕f7 28 h3 ♕g6 29 b3 ♗e6 30 ♖b1 ♘d7 31 ♔h2 ♗f6 32 ♘d5 ♘d4 33 ♗xd4 ♗xd5 34 ♗e3 ♗c6 35 ♗c4 h5 36 ♖g1 ♕h6 37 h4 ♗d8 38 ♘h3 ♘f6 39 ♘f2 ♘g4+ 40 ♘xg4 hxg4 41 ♔g2 ♕g6 42 ♔f2 b5 43 ♗e2 ♗f6 44 a4 b4 45 ♗b5 ♕e8 46 ♕c4 ♗c3 47 ♖gd1 ♕d7 48 ♗xc6 ♕xc6 49 d7+– ♕c7 50 ♖d6 ♗f6 51 ♗d4 ♗xd4+ 52 ♕xd4 ♔g8 53 ♖d1 ♖fd8 54 ♖g6 ♖xd7 55 ♕xd7 ♕xc5+ 56 ♕d4 ♕xd4+ 57 ♖xd4 ♖c8 58 ♖d7 ♖c2+ 59 ♔e1 ♖c3 60 ♖gxg7+ ♔f8 61 ♖df7+ ♔e8 62 ♖a7 ♔f8 63 ♖gb7 ♖c8 64 ♖xa5 ...? **1-0** L/N6128-1853

### 1852-⚔HW2-7 xii 52
**Williams, E.– Harrwitz, D.**
[Harrwitz]

1 e4 e5 2 ♘f3 ♘c6 3 ♗b5 ♗c5 4 c3 ♕f6 5 0-0 [◻ 5 d4] 5 ... ♘ge7 6 d4 exd4 7 ♗g5 ♕g6 8 ♗xe7 ♗xe7 9 ♗xc6 bxc6 10 ♕xd4 [10 cxd4 ♕xe4? 11 ♖e1±] 10 ... d6 11 ♕a4 ♗d7 12 e5 0-0 13 ♘bd2 ♗h3 14 ♘e1 dxe5 15 ♘df3 ♗d6∓ 16 ♕xc6 e4 17 ♘d4 ♕h6 [△ 18 ... ♗d7–+] 18 gxh3!? [18 f4] 18 ... ♕f4 19 ♘ef3 exf3 20 ♘xf3 ♖ab8 21 b3 ♕f5 22 ♔g2 ♖b6 23 ♕c4 ♗e7 24 ♘d4 ♖g6+ 25 ♔h1 ♕xh3 26 ♕d5 ♕xc3 27 ♖ac1 ♕h3 28 ♕f3 [28 ♖xc7?? ♗d6] 28 ... ♕xf3+ 29 ♘xf3 ♗d6 30 ♖c4 ♖e8 31 ♖c2 ♖ge6 32 ♘d4 ♖h6 33 f4 ♖h5 34 f5 a6 35 ♘c6 ♖e4 36 ♖d1 h6 37 ♖f1 f6 38 ♘b8 a5 39 ♘c6 a4 40 bxa4 ♖xa4 41 ♖e2 ♖c4 42 ♘d8 ♗e5 43 ♘e6 ♖hh4 44 ♖d2 ♗d6 45 ♖b1 ♖b4 46 ♖g1 ♖hg4 47 ♖c1 h5 48 ♖dc2 ♖b5 49 ♖f1 ♖e5! 50 ♘xc7 ♗xc7 51 ♖xc7 ♖e2 52 ♖g1 ♖xg1+ 53 ♔xg1 ♖xa2 54 ♖c4 ♔h7 55 ♖f4 ♔h6 56 h4 g5 57 fxg6 ♔xg6 58 ♔h1 f5 59 ♔g1 ♔f6 60 ♔f1 ♔e5 61 ♖b4 ♖d2 62 ♖b3 ♖d4 63 ♖h3 ♔f4 64 ♔e2 ♔g4 65 ♖h1 ♔g3 66 ♖g1+ ♔xh4 67 ♔f3 ♖g4 68 ♖h1+ ♔g5 69 ♖a1 h4 70 ♖a8 ♖g3+ 71 ♔f2 ♔g4 72 ♖g8+ ♔f4 73 ♖h8 ♖f3+ 74 ♔g2 h3+ 75 ♔h2 [75 ♖xh3 ♖xh3 76 ♔xh3 ♔e3–+] 75 ... ♔e3 76 ♖e8+ ♔f2 77 ♖e5 ♔f1 78 ♖e8 f4 79 ♖e4 ♔f2 80 ♖a4 ♔e3 81 ♖a3+ ♔e4 82 ♖a4+ ♔f5 83 ♖a8 ♖e3!–+ 84 ♖f8+ ♔g4 85 ♖g8+ ♔f3 86 ♖f8 ♖e4 87 ♔xh3 ♔f2 88 ♔h2 f3 89 ♖h8 ♔e2 90 ♖a8 f2 91 ♖a2+ ♔f3 92 ♖a3+ ♖e3 93 ♖a1 ♖e1 94 ♖a3+ ♔e4 ...? **0-1** L/N6128-1853

### 1852-⚔HW2-8
**Harrwitz, D.+ Williams, E.**
[Harrwitz]

1 e4 e5 2 f4 ♗c5 3 ♘f3 d6 4 ♗c4 ♘f6 5 ♕e2 ♗g4 6 fxe5 ♗xf3 7 gxf3 dxe5 8 ♗xf7+± ♔xf7 9 ♕c4+ ♔e7 10 ♕xc5+ ♕d6 11 ♕f2 ♘c6 12 d3 ♖ad8 13 ♘c3 h6 14 ♗e3 ♔f7 15 0-0-0 a6 16 ♖hg1 ♕e6 17 f4 exf4 18 ♗xf4 ♖d7 19 d4+– ♘xe4?! 20 ♕g2 ♕f6 21 ♕xe4 ♖e8 22 ♗e5 ♘xe5 23 dxe5 ♖xd1+ 24 ♖xd1 ♖xe5 25 ♕c4+ ♔g6 26 ♖g1+ ♔h7 27 ♘d5 ♕f2 28 ♖d1 c6 29 ♕f4 ♕e2 30 ♘c3 ♕h5 31 ♘e4 ♖f5 32 ♕g3 ♖f3 33 ♕g2 ♕f5 34 ♖g1 ♕f7 35 b3 a5 36 ♔b1 a4 37 ♘d6 ♕f8 38 ♕g6+ ♔h8 39 ♘e8 ♖f7 40 ♘xg7??= ♕xg7 41 ♕xg7+ ♖xg7 42 ♖xg7 ♔xg7 43 ♔b2 axb3 44 cxb3 ♔f6 45 ♔c3 ♔g5 46 ♔d4 ♔g4 47 ♔c5 ♔h3 48 ♔b6 ♔xh2 49 ♔xb7 h5 50 a4 h4 51 a5 h3 52 a6 ♔g3 53 a7 h2 54 a8=♕ h1=♕ 55 ♕g8+ ♔f4 56 ♕c4+ ♔e5 57 ♕c5+ ♔f4 58 ♕xc6 ♕e1 59 ♕c4+ ♔e5 60 b4 ♔d6 61 ♕c6+ ♔e7 62 b5 ♔d8 63 ♕c7+ ♔e8 64 b6 ♕a5 65 ♕d6 ♕a2 66 ♔b8 ♕c4 67 ♕e5+ ♔f8 68 ♕c7 ♕b5 69 b7 ♔e8 70 ♕d6 ♕a5 71 ♕c6+ **1-0** L/N6128-1853

### 1852-⚔HW2-9 4 i 53
**Williams, E.= Harrwitz, D.**
[Harrwitz]

1 e4 e5 2 ♗c4 ♗c5 3 ♘f3 ♘c6 4 d3 d6 5 ♘c3 ♘f6 6 h3 ♗e6 7 ♗b3 h6 8 0-0 ♕d7 9 ♗e3 ♗b6 [△ 10 ... ♗xh3!?] 10 ♗xe6 fxe6 11 ♘a4 0-0 12 ♘xb6 axb6 13 c3 d5 14 ♕c2 ♘h5 15 b4 b5 16 a4 bxa4 17 ♖xa4 ♘d4!∓ 18 ♘xd4 ♖xa4? [18 ♕xa4–+] 19 ♘xe6 ♖fa8 [◻ 19 ... ♕xe6] 20 ♘c5 ♕b5 21 ♘xa4 ♕xa4 22 ♕xa4 ♖xa4 23 exd5 ♘f6 24 ♗d2 ♖a2! [24 ... ♘xd5 25 ♖e1] 25 ♖d1 ♘xd5 26 c4 ♘e7 27 f4 [27 ♗c3 ♘g6] 27 ... exf4 28 ♗xf4 c6 29 d4 g5 30 ♗c7 ♖c2 31 c5 [31 d5?] 31 ... ♘d5 32 ♗e5 ♖b2! [32 ... ♖xg2+? 33 ♔xg2 ♘e3+ 34 ♔f3 ♘xd1 35 d5 cxd5 36 ♔e2+–] 33 ♖a1 ♖xb4 34 ♖a8+ ♔f7 35 ♖h8 ♔g6 36 g4 ♘f4 37 h4 ♖b1+ 38 ♔h2 ♖b2+ 39 ♔h1 ♘d3 [◻ 39 ... ♖b1+=] 40 h5+

♔f7 41 ♖h7+ ♔f8 42 ♗d6+ ♔g8 43 ♖xh6 ♘f2+ 44 ♔g1 ♘xg4 45 ♖g6+ ♔h7 46 ♖xg5 ♘f6 47 ♗e5 ♘e4 48 ♖f5 b5 49 ♖f8 ♔h6 50 ♖h8+ ♔g5 51 h6 ♔g6 52 ♖c8 ♔xh6 53 ♖xc6+ ♔g5 54 ♖b6 ♘d2 55 c6 ♘f3+ 56 ♔f1 ♘xe5 57 c7 ♖c2 58 ♖xb5 ♖xc7 59 ♖xe5+ ♔f4 60 ♔e2 ♖c3 61 ♔d2= ♖h3 62 ♖e8 ♔f5 63 ♔e2 ♔f6 64 ♔d2 ♔f7 65 ♖e4 ♔f6 66 d5 ♖h5 **½-½** L/N6128

**1852-✕HW2-10** 8 iii 53
**Harrwitz, D.+Williams, E.**
[Harrwitz]

1 e4 e5 2 f4 exf4 3 ♘f3 d5 4 exd5 ♕xd5 5 ♘c3 ♕d8 6 ♗c4 ♘f6 7 d4 ♗d6 8 ♕e2+ ♕e7 9 0-0 ♕xe2 10 ♘xe2 0-0 11 ♘xf4 ♘c6 12 c3 ♗f5 13 b4 ♘e4 14 ♘e2 ♘e7 15 ♘g5 ♖ae8 16 ♘xf7! ♖xf7 17 ♗xf7+ ♔xf7 18 g4 ♘f6 19 gxf5 ♘ed5 20 ♘f4 ♘xc3 21 a3 ♖e4 [△ 22 ... ♗xf4 23 ♗xf4 ♖xf4 24 ♖xf4 ♘e2+] 22 ♘e6 h6 23 ♗b2 ♗xh2+ 24 ♔xh2 ♖e2+ 25 ♔h3 ♖xb2 26 ♘xc7 ♘ce4 27 ♘e6 g5 [△ 28 ... g4+ 29 ♔h4 ♖h2#] 28 fxg6+! ♔xe6 29 ♖ae1 ♔d5 30 ♖f5+ ♔d4 31 ♖f4 ♖c2 32 g7 ♖c8 33 ♖exe4+ ♘xe4 34 ♖f8 ♖c3+ 35 ♔h2 [35 ♔h4+ ♖c1 36 g8=♕ ♖h1+ 37 ♔g4 ♘f6+ 38 ♖xf6 ♖g1+ 39 ♔~ ♖xg8∓] 35 ... ♖g3 36 g8=♕ ♖xg8 37 ♖xg8 ♘d6 38 ♖d8 ♔d5 39 ♔g3 ♔c6 40 ♔f4 ♔c7 41 ♖h8 ♘c4 42 a4 ♘b6 43 ♖h7+ ♔c8 44 ♔e5!+− ♘xa4 45 ♔d6 b5 46 ♔c6 ♔d8 47 ♔xb5 ♘c3+ 48 ♔c6 a6 49 ♖xh6 ♔e7 50 ♖h7+ ♔e6 51 ♖a7 ♘d5 52 ♔c5 ♘e7 53 ♖xa6+ ♔d7 54 ♖a7+ ♔d8 55 ♖xe7 **1-0** L/N6128

**1852-✕HW2-11** 15 iii 53
**Williams, E.− Harrwitz, D.**
[Harrwitz]

1 e4 e5 2 ♗c4 ♘f6 3 ♘f3 ♘xe4 4 d3 ♘f6 5 ♘xe5 d5 6 ♗b3 ♗d6 7 f4 0-0 8 0-0 c5 9 c3 ♘c6 10 d4 ♕b6 11 ♔h1 cxd4 12 ♘xc6 bxc6 13 cxd4 ♗a6 14 ♖f3 ♖ae8 15 ♘c3 ♖e7 16 f5 ♖fe8 17 ♗f4 [17 ♗g5?!; □ 17 ♗d2] 17 ... ♗xf4 18 ♖xf4 ♖e1+ 19 ♕xe1 ♖xe1+ 20 ♖xe1 h5 21 h3 ♗d3 22 ♔h2 ♕b8! [22 ... ♕c7 23 ♖e5 ♘d7 24 ♖e8+] 23 g3 [23 ♖e5 ♘d7∓] 23 ... ♗c4! [23 ... ♕c8] 24 ♗xc4 ♕xb2+ 25 ♖e2 ♕xc3 26 ♗b3 ♘e4 27 ♖g2 ♕xd4 28 ♖f1 ♕e5 [28 ... c5? 29 ♖d1] 29 ♗c2 ♘xg3 30 ♖xg3 h4 31 ♖g1 hxg3+ 32 ♖xg3 c5 ...⊕ **0-1** L/N6128

**1852-✕HW2-12** 18 iii 53
**Harrwitz, D.+Williams, E.**
[Harrwitz]

1 e4 e5 2 f4 exf4 3 ♗c4 d5 4 ♗xd5 ♘f6 5 ♕e2 ♗d6 6 ♘c3 0-0 7 ♗b3 ♘c6 8 ♘f3 ♗g4 9 d3? [9 ♕f2] 9 ... ♘d4 10 ♕f2 ♗xf3 11 gxf3 ♗c5 12 ♕g2 ♘h5 13 ♕g4 ♕h4+ 14 ♔d1 ♕xg4 15 fxg4 ♘f6 16 h3 g5 17 ♘e2 ♘xb3 18 axb3 ♖ad8 19 ♘c3 ♖fe8 20 ♔e2 [△ 21 ♖a5] 20 ... ♗b6 21 ♘a4 ♘d5 22 ♘xb6 axb6 23 ♗d2 c6 24 h4!± h6 25 hxg5 hxg5 26 ♖h5 f6 27 ♖ah1 [△ 28 ♖h8+ ♔f7 29 ♖1h7+ ♔e6 30 ♖xe8+ ♖xe8 31 exd5+] 27 ... ♘e7 28 ♗c3 ♔f7 29 ♖h6 ♖d6 30 ♖h7+ ♔e6 31 ♖1h6 ♘g8 32 ♖g6 ♖d7 33 ♖xd7 ♔xd7 34 ♗xf6 ♘xf6 35 ♖xf6 ♖h8 36 ♖f5! [36 ♖g6 ♖h2+ 37 ♔d1 f3 38 ♖xg5? ♖h1+ 39 ♔d2 f2−+; 36 ♖g6 ♖h2+ 37 ♔d1 f3 38 ♖f6 f2 39 ♔e2 ♖g2±] 36 ... ♖h2+ 37 ♔d1 ♖h1+ 38 ♔d2 ♖h2+ 39 ♔c3 ♖g2 40 ♖xg5 f3 41 ♖f5 f2 42 g5 ♔e6 43 g6 b5 44 b4 b6 45 g7 c5 46 ♖xf2 ♖xg7 47 bxc5 bxc5 48 ♖f5 ♔d6 49 b4 **1-0** L/N6128

**9** Dufresne, J. M1647.BL

**1852-★AD-1** vii 52
**Anderssen, A.+Dufresne, J.**
Berlin [Steinitz]

1 e4 e5 2 ♘f3 ♘c6 3 ♗c4 ♗c5 4 b4 ♗xb4 5 c3 ♗a5 6 d4 exd4 7 0-0 d3?! 8 ♕b3 ♕f6 9 e5 ♕g6 10 ♖e1 ♘ge7 11 ♗a3 b5 12 ♕xb5 ♖b8 13 ♕a4 ♗b6 14 ♘bd2 ♗b7? [□ 14 ... 0-0 (15 ♘e4 ♔h8 16 ♗xd3 f6 17 ♖ad1 ♕e8±)] 15 ♘e4 ♕f5? [15 ... 0-0 (16 ♗xd3 ♔h8 (16 ... ♕h5? 17 ♘g3! 16 ... ♕h6? 17 ♗c1! 16 ♕e6? 17 ♘eg5!+−) 17 ♘c5 f5 18 ♘xd7 ♘d4 19 cxd4 ♗xf3 20 g3±)] 16 ♗xd3 ♕h5 17 ♘f6+! gxf6 18 exf6 ♖g8 19 ♖ad1!! ♕xf3? [19 ... ♖xg2+ (20 ♔xg2 ♘e5 21 ♕xd7+ ♔f8 (21 ... ♔xd7 22 ♗g6+ 21 ... ♘xd7 22 ♖xe7+ ♔d8 23 ♖xd7+ ♔c8 24 ♖d8+ ♔xd8 25 ♗f5++−) 22 ♕xe7+ ♔g8 23 ♗e4+−)] 20 ♖xe7+ ♘xe7 [20 ... ♔d8 (21 ♖xd7+ ♔c8 22 ♖d8+ ♘xd8 23 ♕d7+ ♔xd7 24 ♗f5++−)]

21 ♕xd7+ ♔xd7 22 ♗f5+ ♔e8 23 ♗d7+ ♔f8 24 ♗xe7# **1-0** L/N6125

**1852-★AE-1** 23 i 52
**Eichborn, L.+Anderssen, A.**
Breslau

1 e4 e5 2 ♘f3 ♘c6 3 c3 d5 4 ♗b5 dxe4 5 ♗xc6+ bxc6 6 ♘xe5 ♕d5 7 f4 f6 8 c4 ♕d4 9 ♕h5+ g6 10 ♘xg6 hxg6 11 ♕xh8 ♗e6 12 ♕h7 0-0-0 13 ♕xg6 ♘e7 14 ♕g3 ♘f5 15 ♕c3 ♗xc4 16 b3 ♗d3 17 ♗b2 ♗c5 18 ♕xd4 ♗xd4 19 ♗xd4 ♘xd4 20 ♘a3 ♘e2 21 g3 ♖h8 22 ♔f2 ♘d4 23 ♖ac1 f5 24 ♔e3 ♘f3 25 h4 ♖g8 26 ♖h3 c5 27 ♔f2 ♘xd2 28 ♖xc5 ♘f1 29 ♘c4 ♖d8 30 ♖h1 ♗xc4 31 ♖xc4 ♘d2 32 ♖c2 **1-0** L/N3034

**1852-★AE-2** 30 iv 52
**Anderssen, A.− Eichborn, L.**
Breslau

1 e4 e5 2 ♘f3 ♘c6 3 d4 exd4 4 ♗c4 ♗c5 5 0-0 d6 6 c3 dxc3 7 ♕b3 ♕d7 8 ♕xc3 ♘f6 9 ♗g5 ♗b4 10 ♕b3 ♘g4 11 ♗b5 ♗c5 12 ♘c3 0-0 13 ♘d5 a6 14 ♗xc6 bxc6 15 ♘e7+ ♔h8 16 h3 ♘e5 17 ♘xe5 dxe5 18 ♖ad1 ♗d6 19 f4 ♕e8 20 ♘f5 ♗xf5 21 exf5 f6 22 fxe5 ♗xe5 23 ♗e3 ♖b8 24 ♕c4 ♗xb2 25 ♗c5 ♖g8 26 g4 ♕e5 27 ♔g2 ♗c3 28 ♖d7 ♖b2+ 29 ♔f3 ♖e8 30 ♖f2 ♗e1 31 ♖xb2 ♕g3# **0-1** L/N3034

**1852-★AE-3** 30 v 52
**Eichborn, L.+Anderssen, A.**
Breslau

1 e4 e5 2 ♘f3 ♘c6 3 ♗c4 ♗c5 4 c3 ♘f6 5 d4 exd4 6 e5 d5 7 ♗b5 ♘e4 8 cxd4 ♗b6 9 ♗xc6+ bxc6 10 0-0 0-0 11 ♘c3 f5 12 ♔h1 ♗a6 13 ♘e2 g5 14 a4 g4 15 ♘fg1 ♕h4 16 a5 ♘xf2+ 17 ♖xf2 ♕xf2 18 axb6 axb6 19 ♗h6 ♗xe2 20 ♖xa8 ♖xa8 21 ♕c1 ♕h4 22 ♕xc6 ♕d8 23 ♕e6+ ♔h8 24 ♕f7 **1-0** L/N3034

**1852-★AE-4** 17 vi 52
**Anderssen, A.– Eichborn, L.**
Breslau
1 e4 e5 2 ♘f3 ♘c6 3 ♗c4 ♗c5 4 b4 ♗xb4 5 c3 ♗a5 6 d4 exd4 7 0-0 d6 8 h3 h6 9 cxd4 ♗b6 10 d5 ♘e5 11 ♘xe5 dxe5 12 ♗b2 ♕g5 13 ♗b5+ ♔f8 14 ♔h1 ♘f6 15 ♘d2 ♗g4 16 ♕c2 ♔g8 17 hxg4

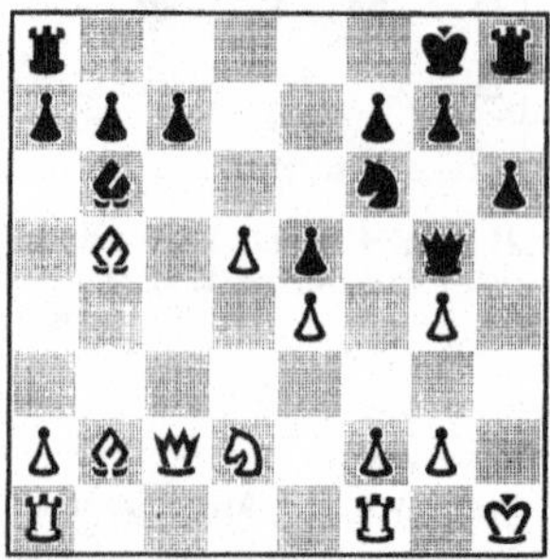

17 ... h5 18 g3 h4 19 ♔g2 hxg3 20 ♖h1 ♖h2+ 21 ♖xh2 gxh2 22 ♘f1 h1♕+ 23 ♔xh1 ♕h4+ 24 ♔g2 ♘xg4 25 ♗d7 ♘xf2 26 ♔f3 ♕h5+ 27 ♔g2 ♕h1+ 28 ♔g3 ♘xe4+ ...? **0-1** L/N3034

**1852-★AE-5** 4 xii 52
**Anderssen, A.– Eichborn, L.**
Breslau
1 e4 e5 2 f4 exf4 3 ♗c4 ♕h4+ 4 ♔f1 g5 5 ♘c3 ♗g7 6 d4 ♘e7 7 g3 fxg3 8 ♔g2 ♕h6 9 hxg3 ♕g6 10 ♘f3 h6 11 ♖f1 ♖f8 12 ♕e2 d6 13 ♗d2 c6 14 ♖ae1 ♗g4 15 e5 d5 16 ♗d3 ♕h5 17 ♖f2 ♕h3+ 18 ♔g1 ♕xg3+ 19 ♔h1 ♕h3+ 20 ♔g1 ♕g3+ 21 ♔h1 ♘d7 22 ♖ef1 0-0-0 23 ♖g2 ♗xf3 24 ♖xf3 ♕h4+ 25 ♖h2 ♕xd4 26 ♘b5 cxb5 27 ♗c3 ♕g4 28 e6 fxe6 29 ♖xf8 ♕xe2 30 ♖xd8+ ♔xd8 31 ♗xe2 d4 32 ♗d2 a6 33 ♗g4 e5 34 ♗e6 b6 35 ♗b4 a5 36 ♗d6 e4 37 ♖f2 ♘f6 38 ♗e5 e3 39 ♖e2 ♘c6 40 ♗h2 ♔e7 41 ♗f5 ♘h5 42 c3 ♘f4 43 ♖e1 ♔d6 **0-1** L/N3034

**1852-★AE-6** 4 xii 52
**Anderssen, A.– Eichborn, L.**
Breslau
1 e4 e5 2 f4 exf4 3 ♘f3 g5 4 h4 g4 5 ♘e5 h5 6 ♗c4 ♖h7 7 d4 f3 8 g3 ♘c6 9 ♘xc6 dxc6 10 ♘c3 ♗h6 11 ♗xh6 ♖xh6 12 ♕d2 ♕e7 13 0-0-0 b5 14 ♗b3 a5 15 a4 ♗a6 16 axb5 ♗xb5 17 d5 a4 18 ♗a2 ♕e5 19 dxc6 ♖d6 20 ♗d5 a3 21 ♕g5 axb2+ 22 ♔xb2 ♕xg5 23 hxg5 ♗xc6 24 ♖xh5 ♗xd5 25 ♘xd5 ♔f8 26 ♖h8 ♖g6 27 ♘f6 ♔g7 28 ♖h7+ ♔f8 29 ♖d7 ♘xf6 30 ♖hxf7+ ♔g8 31 ♖xf6 ♖xg5 32 ♖xc7 ♖f8 33 ♖cc6 ♖g7 34 ♖xf8+ ♔xf8 35 ♖d6 ♖e7 36 ♖d4 f2 37 ♖d1 ♖xe4 38 ♖f1 ♖e2 39 ♔c3 ♖e3+ 40 ♔d4 ♖f3 41 ♔e4 ♔e7 42 c4 ♔d6 43 ♔d4 ♔c6 44 c5 ♖f5 45 ♔e3 ♖f3+ 46 ♔e2 ♔xc5 47 ♖xf2 ♖xf2+ 48 ♔xf2 ♔d4 ...? **0-1** L/N3034

**1852-★AL-1** vii 52
**Lange, M.+ Anderssen, A.**
Berlin
⟨♙f7⟩ 1 e4 ... 2 d4 g6 3 ♗d3 ♗g7 4 ♘f3 c5 5 d5 b5 6 c4 bxc4 7 ♗xc4 ♗a6 8 ♘bd2 ♘h6 9 0-0 0-0 10 ♕e2 ♗b7 11 ♖b1 a5 12 b3 ♕e8 13 ♗b2 e5 14 dxe6 dxe6 15 ♕e3 ♗xb2 16 ♖xb2 ♘f7 17 ♕xc5 ♘d7 18 ♕c7 ♘d8 19 ♗b5 ♖f7 20 ♘e5 ♘xe5 21 ♕xe5 ♕e7 22 ♘c4 ♖f8 23 ♘d6 ♗c6 24 ♗c4 ♕c7 25 ♕g3 ♗b7 26 ♖c2 ♕b6 27 ♕e5 ♗c8 28 ♖d1 ♕b8 29 f4 ♗d7 30 f5 ♖e8 31 fxg6 ♖e7 32 ♕f6 ♕a7+ 33 ♔h1 ♗c6 34 ♘f5 ♖d7 35 ♘h6# **1-0** L/N6047

**1852-★AL-2** vii 52
**Lange, M.– Anderssen, A.**
Berlin
⟨♙f7⟩ 1 e4 ... 2 d4 g6 3 h4 d5 4 h5 g5 5 h6 ♗e6 6 exd5 ♕xd5 7 ♘c3 ♕a5 8 ♕h5+ ♗f7 9 ♕xg5 ♕b6 10 ♕e5 ♘f6 11 ♕b5+ ♘bd7 12 ♗e3 0-0-0 13 ♕xb6 ♘xb6 14 0-0-0 ♖g8 15 ♘ge2 ♘bd5 16 ♘xd5 ♗xd5 17 ♘c3 ♗xg2 18 ♖g1 ♗xf1 19 ♖dxf1 ♘g4 20 ♖h1 ♘xe3 21 fxe3 ♖g6 22 ♖f7 ♗xh6 23 ♖xe7 ♖xd4 24 ♘b5 ♖d7 25 ♖e8+ ♖d8 26 ♘xa7+ ♔d7 27 ♖e4 c6 28 ♖f1 ♔c7 29 b4 ♔b6 30 ♘xc6 ♖xc6 31 a4 ♖dc8 32 ♖f2 ♖c4 33 a5+ ♔b5 34 ♖f5+ ♔a4 35 ♖xc4 ♗xe3+ 36 ♔b2 ♖xc4 37 c3 ♖f4 **0-1** L/N6047

**1852-★AL-3** vii 52
**Lange, M.+ Anderssen, A.**
Berlin
1 e4 e5 2 f4 exf4 3 ♗c4 ♕h4+ 4 ♔f1 g5 5 ♘c3 ♗g7 6 g3 fxg3 7 ♔g2 ♕h6 8 hxg3 ♕g6 9 d4 d6 10 ♘f3 h6 11 ♖f1 ♗e6 12 ♕d3 ♘d7 13 ♘b5 ♔d8 14 ♗xe6 ♕xe6 15 ♗xg5+ ♗f6 16 ♗f4 a6 17 ♕a3 ♘e7 18 d5 ♕xe4 19 ♕c3 axb5 20 ♕xh8 ♘df8 21 ♗xh6 ♔d7 22 ♖ae1 ♕xd5 23 ♖xe7+ ♔xe7 24 ♗g5+ **1-0** L/N6047

**1852-★AL-4** vii 52
**Lange, M.– Anderssen, A.**
Berlin
⟨♙f7⟩ 1 e4 ... 2 d4 g6 3 ♗d3 ♗g7 4 ♘f3 b6 5 0-0 e6 6 c4 ♗b7 7 ♘c3 ♘e7 8 ♗g5 0-0 9 d5 ♕e8 10 ♕c2 ♘a6 11 a3 ♘c5 12 ♖ae1 a5 13 ♘b5 ♘a6 14 ♘fd4 ♘c8 15 f4 c6 16 f5 cxb5 17 f6 ♗h8 18 e5 ♘c5 19 ♗h6 ♘xd3 20 ♕xd3 ♖f7 21 ♘xb5 d6 22 dxe6 ♕xe6 23 exd6 ♕d7 24 ♘c7 ♘xd6 25 ♘xa8 ♗xa8 26 ♕xd6 ♕xd6 27 ♖e8+ ♕f8 28 ♗xf8 ♖xf8 29 f7+ ♔g7 30 ♖fe1 ♔xf7 31 ♖1e7+ ♔g8 32 b4 ♗d4+ 33 ♔h1 axb4 34 axb4 ♗c6 35 ♖xf8+ ♔xf8 36 ♖xh7 ♗g7 37 ♖h3 ♔e7 38 ♖a3 ♗d4 39 ♖a6 ♔d7 40 ♖a3 ♔e6 41 ♖a6 ♗b7 42 ♖a7 ♗e4 43 ♖a2 ♗c3 44 ♖e2 ♔f5 45 ♖f2+ ♔e5 46 c5 b5 47 ♖a2 ♔d5 48 ♖a5 ♔c4 49 ♖a6 ♗xb4 50 c6 ♗d6 51 ♔g1 b4 52 h4 ♔b5 53 c7 ♗xc7 54 ♖e6 ♗d3 55 g4 b3 **0-1** L/N6047

**1852-★AM-1**
**Mayet, K.– Anderssen, A.**
Berlin
1 e4 e5 2 f4 exf4 3 ♘f3 g5 4 ♗c4 g4 5 ♘c3 gxf3 6 ♕xf3 d5 7 ♘xd5 ♗e6 8 ♕xf4 ♕d6 9 ♘xc7+ ♔d8 10 ♘xe6+ fxe6 11 ♕xd6+ ♗xd6 12 ♗xe6 ♘f6 13 d3 ♖e8 14 ♗f5 ♘bd7 15 ♗g5 ♔c7 16 0-0 ♖g8 17 ♗xf6 ♘xf6 18 c3 ♖g7 19 d4 ♗e7 20 c4 ♖ag8 21 ♖f2 ♘g4 22 ♖e2 ♖d8 23 h3 ♘h6 24 d5 ♗c5+ 25 ♔h1 ♘xf5 26 exf5 h5 27 ♖f1 ♖f8 28 ♖e6 ♖gf7 29 ♖fd1 ♖xf5 30 d6+ ♔d8 31 g4 ♖f3 32 ♖d5 ♗e3 33 ♖xh5 ♖g3 34 ♔h2 ♗f4 35 ♔h1 ♔d7 36 ♖e7+ ♔xd6 37 ♖xb7 ♖e8 38 ♖d5+ ♔c6 39 ♖f7 ♖e1+ 40 ♔h2 ♖xg4+ 41 ♖xf4 ♖xf4 42 b3 ♖e3 43 ♖a5 ♖f2+ **0-1** L/N6047

**1852-★JS-1** iii 52
**Shumov, I.S.– Jaenisch, C.F.**
St. Petersburg
1 e4 e5 2 f4 exf4 3 ♗c4 ♕h4+ 4 ♔f1 g5 5 ♘c3 ♗g7 6 d4 d6 7 ♘b5 ♔d8 8 e5 ♘c6 9 ♘f3 ♕h5 10 h4 h6 11 b4 ♘ge7 12 ♘xc7 ♔xc7 13 exd6+ ♔xd6 14 b5 ♘a5 15 ♗a3+ ♔d7 16 ♘e5+ ♗xe5 17 ♕xh5 ♘xc4 18 ♗xe7 ♘e3+ 19 ♔f2 ♔xe7 20 hxg5 ♗g4 21 ♕h4 ♗xd4 22 gxh6+ ♔f8 23 ♕g5 ♘f5+ 24 ♔e1 ♖e8+ 25 ♔d2 ♖g8 26 ♕xf5 ♗e3+ **0-1** M954-1852

**1852-★SS-1** 7 xi 52
**Stanley, C.H.+ Saint-Amant, P.C.F.de**
New York [Staunton]
1 e4 c5 2 c4 ♘c6 3 ♘c3 e5 4 ♗d3 d6 5 ♘d5 ♘f6 6 ♘e2 ♘xd5 7 cxd5 ♘b4 8 ♗b1 f5? 9 a3 ♘a6 10 exf5 ♘c7 11 ♘c3 ♕g5 12 0-0!?± [12 ♕f3±] 12 ... ♗xf5 13 d4 ♕g6 14 dxe5 ♗xb1 15 ♕a4+! ♔d8 16 ♖xb1 dxe5 17 f4 b5

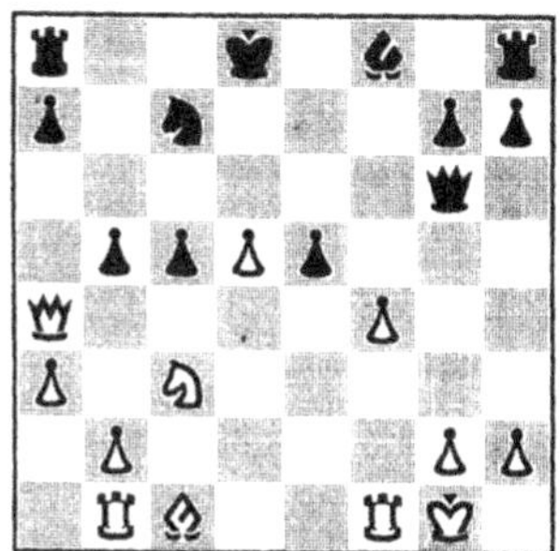

18 ♘xb5! ♘xb5 19 ♕xb5 ♕xb1 20 ♕b7 ♖c8 21 f5 [△ 22 ♗g5+] 21 ... ♗e7 22 d6 ♗f6 23 ♗d2 **1-0** M954

**1852-★SS-2** 8 xi 52
**Saint-Amant, P.C.F. de+ Stanley, C.H.**
New York [Staunton]
1 e4 e5 2 d4 exd4 3 ♘f3 d5 4 e5 ♘c6 5 ♗b5 ♗b4+ 6 c3 dxc3 7 0-0 c2 8 ♕xc2 ♘e7 9 a3 ♗f5 10 ♕a4 ♗c5 11 ♗g5 ♗d7 12 ♕h4!? h6? 13 b4 ♗b6 14 ♗xc6 ♗xc6 15 ♘c3 d4 16 ♖ad1 ♗xf3 17 gxf3 ♕d7 18 ♗xe7 g5?? 19 ♗xg5 ♕f5 20 ♘e4 ♔d7 21 ♗f4 ♖hg8+ 22 ♗g3 ♖g6 23 ♘f6+ ♔e6 24 ♕e4 ♕h3 25 ♕d5+ ♔e7 26 f4 h5 27 ♕f3 h4 28 ♕h5 d3 29 ♘d5+ ♔f8 30 ♕h8+ ♖g8 31 ♕h6+ ♖g7 32 ♘xb6 axb6 33 ♖xd3 ♕f5 34 ♖fd1 hxg3 35 ♖xg3 ♕h7 36 ♕xh7 ♖xh7 ...? **1-0** M954

**127** Donaldson, J. L/N6135. BL

**1852̂-★DS-1**
**Donaldson, J.– Staunton, H.**
[Staunton]
⟨△f7⟩ 1 e4 ... 2 d4 e6 3 ♗d3 ♕e7 4 h4 d6 5 e5 dxe5 6 dxe5 ♘c6 7 ♘c3? ♘xe5 8 ♕h5+ ♘f7 9 ♗e3 ♘f6 10 ♕e2 ♗d7 11 0-0-0 ♕b4 12 ♘b5 ♗d6 13 a3 ♕a5 14 ♗d2 ♕b6 15 ♘xd6+ cxd6 16 ♗g5 ♖c8 17 ♘f3 0-0 18 ♗e3 [□ 18 g4; 18 h5] 18 ... ♕a5 19 ♘g5 ♘e5 20 f4 ♘xd3+ 21 ♕xd3 d5 22 ♗d2 ♕a4 23 c3 b5 24 ♗e3 b4 25 axb4 ♕a1+ 26 ♔b1

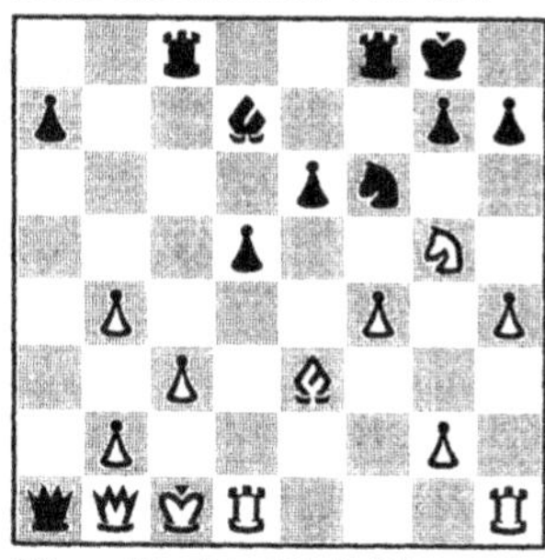

26 ... ♖xc3+ 27 ♔d2! [27 bxc3 ♕xc3+ 28 ♔c2 ♕xe3+∓] 27 ... ♕xb1 28 ♖xb1 ♖c4 29 ♗c5 ♖c8 30 g3 h6 31 ♘f3 ♘e4+ 32 ♔e3 ♘xg3 33 ♖hg1 ♘f5+ 34 ♔d2 ♖xf4 35 ♘e5 ♗e8 36 ♘g6 ♗xg6 37 ♖xg6 ♔f7 38 h5 ♘h4 39 ♖g3 e5 40 ♔d3 ♘f5 41 ♖g6 e4+ 42 ♔e2 d4 **0-1** M954-1852

**1852̂-★DS-2**
**Donaldson, J.– Staunton, H.**
[Staunton]
⟨△f7⟩ 1 e4 ... 2 d4 e6 3 ♗d3 c5 4 e5 g6 5 h4 cxd4 6 f4! ♘e7 7 h5 g5 8 h6 ♕a5+ 9 ♗d2 ♕b6 10 ♘a3 ♘f5 11 ♘c4 ♕c6 12 ♕h5+ ♔d8 13 ♗xf5? exf5 14 ♕e2? [□ 14 ♕xg5!?] 14 ... g4 15 0-0-0 b6 16 c3 ♗a6 17 b3 ♗a3+ 18 ♔c2 ♖e8 19 cxd4 d5 20 ♕e1 dxc4 21 b4 ♘d7 22 d5 ♕a4+ 23 ♔b1 ♘c5!-+ 24 ♗c3 ♘d3 25 ♕d2 ♗xb4 26 ♗xb4 ♘xb4 27 ♘e2 ♘d3 28 ♘c3 ♕a3 29 ♔a1 b5 30 ♖h5 b4 31 ♘b1 ♕a5 32 ♖xf5 ♕xd5 **0-1** M954-1852

**1852̂-★DS-3**
**Donaldson, J. & Gordon, T. & Meikle– Staunton, H.**
Edinburgh [Staunton]
⟨△f7⟩ 1 e4 ... 2 d4 ♘c6 3 d5 ♘e5 4 f4 ♘f7 5 ♘f3 d6 6 ♗d3 c6 7 c4 ♗g4 8 0-0 g6 9 ♘c3 ♗g7 10 ♗e3 ♘f6 11 ♕c2? [11 h3!] 11 ... ♗xf3 12 ♖xf3 ♘g4 [△ 13 ... ♘xe3 14 ♖xe3 ♗d4] 13 ♘e2 ♘xe3 14 ♖xe3 ♕b6 15 ♕d2

15 ... ♘e5! 16 h3 [16 fxe5? ♗h6 17 ♔f2 0-0+ 18 ♔~ ♗xe3-+] 16 ... 0-0 17 ♔h2 ♗h6 18 ♖f1 ♖f7 19 g4 ♖af8 20 ♖g3 ♗g5! 21 b3 ♗h4 22 ♖e3 [□ 22 ♖g2∓] 22 ... g5 23 f5 h5! 24 gxh5 ♖h7 25 ♖g1 ♗f2! 26 ♖gg3 [26 ♖xg5+ ♔f7∓] 26 ... ♖xh5 27 ♔g2! [27 ♘f4 ♗xe3 28 ♖xe3 (28 ♕xe3 ♘g4+-+) 28 ... gxf4-+] 27 ... ♗xe3 28 ♖xe3 ♔f7 29 ♖g3 ♖fh8 30 ♘g1 g4 31 ♗f1 ♖g8! 32 ♔h2 ♖hh8! 33 ♕f4 gxh3 34 ♖xg8 ♖xg8 35 ♘xh3 ♖g4 36 ♕f2 ♕xf2+ 37 ♘xf2 ♖g8 38 ♗e2 cxd5 39 exd5 ♔f6 **0-1** M954-1852

**1852̂-★DS-4**
**Donaldson, J. & McCoombe= Staunton, H.**
Glasgow [Staunton]
⟨△f7⟩ 1 e4 ... 2 d4 e6 3 ♗d3 ♕e7 4 f4 d5 5 e5 ♘h6 6 ♘f3 c5 7 c3 ♘c6 8 0-0 g6 9 ♗b5? ♗g7 10 ♗e3 cxd4 11 ♘xd4 ♗d7 12 ♗xc6 bxc6 13 ♘a3? [13 ♘b3] 13 ... ♖c8 14 ♖c1 0-0 15 ♘ac2 c5 16 ♘e2 a5! 17 ♔h1 ♗b5 18 ♕d2 ♘f5 19 ♗g1 ♕h4 [△ 20 ... ♗xe2] 20 ♖f3 ♗c6 21 ♘e3 [21 ♖h3?? ♕xh3] 21 ... d4 22 ♘xf5 ♖xf5 23 ♖g3 ♗b5 24 c4 [24 cxd4] 24 ... ♗c6 25 ♕d3 [25 ♕xa5] 25 ... ♖cf8 26 ♖h3 ♕g4 27 ♖g3 ♕h4 28 ♖h3 ♕e7 29 ♖g3 ♗h6 30 ♖f1 ♔g7? [30 ... ♗xf4] 31 ♖g4 ♔h8 32 h3 ♕b7 33 b3 ♗e4 34 ♕d1 ♗g7 35 ♖e1 g5!∓. 36 ♗h2 [36 ♖xg5 ♖xg5 37 fxg5 ♗xg2+ 38 ♔h2 ♗h1!-+ 39 ♘f4 ♖xf4; 36 fxg5 ♗f3! 37 gxf3 (37 ♖g3 ♗xe5) 37 ... ♖xf3! 38 ♖g2 ♖xh3+ 39 ♗h2 ♖f2 40 ♖g1 ♗xe5-+] 36 ... h5 37 ♖g3 [37 ♖xg5 ♖xg5 38 fxg5 ♗xg2+ 39 ♔g1 ♗h1 40 ♘f4 ♖xf4 41 ♕xh5+ ♔g8 42 ♕e8+ ♖f8 43 ♕xe6+ ♔h8 44 ♕g4 d3-+] 37 ... gxf4 38 ♘xf4 [38 ♖g6 f3-+] 38 ... ♖xf4 39 ♕xh5+ ♔g8 40 ♔g1 d3 41 ♕d1 ♖f2 42 ♕g4 d2 43 ♖a1 ♕f7 44 ♔h1 ♗c2?? [44 ... ♖f1+ 45 ♖xf1 ♕xf1+ 46 ♗g1 ♖f7-+] 45 ♗g1 d1♕ 46 ♖xd1 ♗xd1 47 ♕xd1 ♖xa2 48 ♕g4 ♖a1 49 ♔h2 ♖c8 50 ♗e3 ♖c7 51 ♗h6 ♕f5 52 ♕h4! ♖d1 53 ♕f6! ♖dd7 54 ♖g5! ♖f7= 55 ♕d8+ ♖f8 56 ♕xc7 ♕f4+ 57 ♔h1 ♕f1+ ½-½ M954-1852

**1852̂-★GJ-1**
**Goltz, von d.= Jaenisch, C.F.**
Frankfurt
1 e4 e5 2 ♘f3 ♘c6 3 d4 exd4 4 ♗c4 ♗c5 5 c3 ♘f6 6 cxd4 ♗b4+ 7 ♗d2 ♗xd2+ 8 ♘bxd2 d5 9 exd5 ♘xd5 10 ♕b3 ♘ce7 11 0-0 0-0 12 ♘e5 c6 13 ♖ac1 ♕b6 14 ♕g3 ♕xd4 15 ♘df3 ♕f4 16 ♕xf4 ♘xf4 17 ♘g5 ♘fd5 18 ♖fe1 h6 19 ♘e4 ♗e6 20 ♘c5 b5

21 ♘xe6 fxe6 22 ♗b3 ♖ac8 23 ♘g4 c5 24 ♖xe6 c4 25 ♗c2 ♘f5 26 ♗xf5 ♖xf5 27 ♖xh6 ♖g5 28 ♖h4 ♖e8 29 ♔f1 ♘b4 30 ♘e3 ♘xa2 31 ♖a1 ♘b4 32 ♖xa7 ♘d3 33 g4 ♘xb2 34 ♘f5 ♘d3 35 ♘e7+ ♔f7 36 ♘d5+ ♔g6 37 ♖a6+ ♔f7 38 ♖a7+ ½-½ M954-1852

**1852̂-★GS-1**
**Gordon, T.– Staunton, H.**
Edinburgh [Staunton]
⟨♙f7⟩ 1 e4 ... 2 d4 ♘c6 3 d5 ♘e5 4 f4 ♘f7 5 c4 e6 6 ♘c3 ♗c5 7 ♘f3 ♘f6 8 h3 0-0 9 ♗d3 c6 10 g4 ♔h8 11 g5 ♘g8 12 e5 d6 13 dxe6 ♗xe6 14 f5 ♗c8 [14 ... ♗xf5?] 15 e6 ♘e5 16 ♘xe5 dxe5 17 ♕e2 ♕d4 18 ♗d2 [△ 19 0-0-0] 18 ... ♗xe6 [18 ... ♖d8? 19 ♗e4] 19 fxe6 ♖ad8 20 ♘e4 [20 ♗c2? ♖f2–+] 20 ... ♗e7 21 ♗c2 ♕xb2 22 ♗c3 [22 ♖c1? ♖xd2! (22 ... ♗a3? 23 ♗d3; 22 ... ♗b4? 23 ♖b1 ♗xd2+ 24 ♕xd2 ♕xa2 25 ♘d6+–) 23 ♔xd2 (23 ♕xd2?? ♗b4–+; 23 ♘xd2?? ♕xc1+–+) 23 ... ♖d8+ 24 ... ♗xg5+! 25 ♘xg5 (25 ♔~ ♗xc1) 25 ... ♕d4+ 26 ♔f3 ♕f4+ 27 ♔g2 ♕xg5+ 28 ♕g4! ♕d2+ (28 ... ♖d2+?±) 29 ♔g3! ♖d4 30 ♗e4 (30 ♕f5 e4) 30 ... ♘f6 31 e7 ♕e3+ 32 ♕f3 (32 ♔h4–+; 32 ♔h2–+) 32 ... ♘xe4+–+; 22 ♕d1 ♖xd2 23 ♘xd2! ♗xg5 24 ♖b1 (24 ♖h2 ♕c3–+) 24 ... ♕d4 25 ♖f1 ♗xd2+ 26 ♕xd2 ♖xf1+–+] 22 ... ♗b4 23 ♗xb4 ♕xb4+ 24 ♘d2 ♕b2 25 ♕e4 ♕xa1+! [25 ... g6? 26 ♕e2 ♖f4 27 ♕e3 ♕xc2±] 26 ♔e2 ♖xd2+ 27 ♔xd2 ♕d4+ 0-1 M954-1852

**1852̂-★GS-2**
**Gordon, T.= Staunton, H.**
Edinburgh [Staunton]
⟨♙f7⟩ 1 e4 ... 2 d4 e6 3 ♗d3 c5 4 e5 ♘e7 5 f4 cxd4 6 ♘f3 ♘bc6 7 0-0 g6 8 ♘a3 [◻ 8 c3] 8 ... ♗g7 9 ♘c4 0-0 10 ♘d6 ♘d5 11 ♘g5± ♘ce7 [11 ... ♘e3 12 ♗xe3 dxe3 13 c3] 12 ♖f3 ♘e3 13 ♕e2 ♘7d5 14 g3 ♘f5 [14 ... ♗xe5? 15 ♘gf7 ♖xf7! 16 ♘xf7 ♔xf7 17 fxe5+–] 15 ♘ge4 ♘fe7 16 ♗d2 b6 17 ♖af1 [17 c4±] 17 ... ♖b8 18 g4 ♗b7 19 ♘xb7 ♖xb7 20 g5 ♘f5 21 ♘f6+ ♗xf6 22 exf6 ♖c7 23 ♗xf5 exf5 24 ♕d3 [◻ 24 ♕e5!±] 24 ... ♕a8 25 ♕xd4 b5 [△ 26 ... ♘b6] 26 ♖d3 ♘b6 27 f7+ ♔xf7 [27 ♖xf7 28 ♗c3 ♖xc3] 28 ♗c3 ♖c4 29 ♕g7+ ♔e8 30 ♗f6? [◻ 30 ♖e3+ ♕e4 31 ♖xe4+ fxe4 (31 ... ♕xe4? 32 ♖e1+–) 32 ♗b4+–] 30 ... ♕e4 31 ♕xh7 ♖xc2 32 ♕xg6+ ½-½ M954-1852

**1852̂-★GS-3**
**Gordon, T.+ Staunton, H.**
Edinburgh [Staunton]
⟨♙f7⟩ 1 e4 ... 2 d4 e6 3 ♗d3 ♕e7 4 c4 c5 5 d5 d6 6 ♘c3 g6 7 f4 ♗g7 8 ♘f3 ♘h6 9 ♗d2 0-0 10 ♕c2 ♘a6 11 a3 ♘c7 12 0-0-0 a6 [△ ... b5] 13 h3 ♗d7 14 g4 b5 15 dxe6 ♘xe6 [◻ 15 ... ♗xe6] 16 ♘d5 ♕d8 17 f5± ♘d4 18 ♘xd4 cxd4 19 g5? [◻ 19 f6] 19 ... ♘xf5 20 exf5 ♗xf5 21 ♗xf5 ♖xf5 22 ♔b1 ♖c8 23 ♘f4 ♕d7 24 h4 bxc4 25 ♗c1 d3? [◻ 25 ... c3∓] 26 ♘xd3 cxd3 27 ♕xd3 ♕b7 28 ♖h2 [28 ... ♖xc1+ △ 29 ... ♕xb2#] 28 ... d5 29 h5 ♖c3 30 ♕e2 ♖e5 31 ♕f2 ♖xa3 32 hxg6 hxg6 33 ♕c5! ♖f3 34 ♖c2 ♖f8 35 ♕d6 ♕f7 36 ♕xa6 ♖e6 37 ♕d3 d4 38 ♕c4 ♗e5 39 ♖f1! ♕e7 40 ♖xf8+ ♔xf8 41 ♕f1+! [△ ♕h3; 41 ♖f2+?] 41 ... ♕f7?? [◻ 41 ♔g7=] 42 ♖f2 ♗f6 43 ♖xf6 ♖xf6 44 ♕xf6 ♕xf6 45 gxf6 ♔f7 46 ♗g5 1-0 M954-1852

**1852̂-★GS-4**
**Gordon, T.– Staunton, H.**
Edinburgh [Staunton]
⟨♙f7⟩ 1 e4 ... 2 d4 e6 3 ♗d3 ♕e7 4 c4 d6 5 ♘c3 c6 6 f4 g6 7 ♘f3 ♗g7 8 0-0 ♘h6 9 e5 d5 10 cxd5 cxd5 11 ♘b5 ♘f7 12 b3! [△ 12 ... 0-0? 13 ♗a3] 12 ... ♘c6 13 ♗a3 ♕d8 14 ♘g5 ♗f8 15 ♘xf7 [◻ 15 ♗xf8 ♖xf8 16 ♘xf7 ♔xf7 17 ♘d6+ ♔g7 18 ♕g4 △ 19 h4] 15 ... ♔xf7 16 ♘d6+ ♔g7 17 ♗c2 ♗e7 18 ♕d3 ♖f8 19 ♖ac1 ♕a5! 20 b4! ♘xb4 21 ♗xb4 ♕xb4 22 ♖b1 ♕a5 23 ♘xc8 ♖axc8 24 ♖xb7 ♖f7 25 ♖b3 ♗c5! 26 ♗b1 [26 dxc5? ♕xc5+ 27 ♖f2 (27 ♔h1 ♕xc2 28 ♕xc2 ♖xc2 29 a3 ♖xf4) 27 ... ♖xf4 28 ♕e2 ♕xf2+ 29 ♕xf2 ♖xf2 30 ♔xf2 ♖xc2+ 31 ♔~ ♖xa2–+] 26 ... ♗b6 27 g3 ♖c4 28 ♔h1 ♖xd4 29 ♕e2 ♖d2 30 ♕f3 ♖c7 31 g4 ♗d4 32 g5 ♖c3 33 ♖b7+ ♔f8 34 ♕g4 ♕a6 35 ♖b8+ ♔f7 [35 ... ♔e7 36 ♖d1 ♖xd1 (36 ... ♖f2!–+) 37 ♕xd1 ♕c4 38 ♔g2 ♖e3 39 ♖b7+ ♔d8 40 ♖xh7 ♖e2+ 41 ♔f3 ♕c3+ 42 ♗d3 (42 ♔xe2?? ♕e3+, 43 ... ♕f2#) 42 ... ♖e3+ 43 ♔g4 ♕xd3 44 ♕xd3 ♖xd3 45 ♖g7 ♖d2 46 ♖xg6 ♔d7 47 h4 ♖g2+ 48 ♔f3 ♖xa2 49 h5 ♖a3+ 50 ♔g4 ♗f2 51 h6 ♖g3+ 52 ♔h5 ♖h3+=] 36 ♖e1 ♖f2 37 f5 [37 ♕h4–+] 37 ... ♖f1+ 38 ♔g2 ♖xe1 0-1 M954-1852

**1852̂-★GS-5**
**Gordon, T.– Staunton, H.**
Edinburgh [Staunton]
⟨♙f7⟩ 1 e4 ... 2 d4 e6 3 ♗d3 ♕e7 4 c4 c5 5 d5 e5 6 f4 d6 7 ♘f3 ♗g4 8 0-0 ♘d7 9 ♘c3 a6 10 ♕c2 g6 11 f5 ♗xf3 [12 ♘g5 △ 13 ♘e6] 12 ♖xf3 ♘h6 13 ♗xh6 ♗xh6 14 ♖af1 0-0-0 15 a3 ♖df8 16 b4 ♖hg8 17 ♔h1? ♘f6 18 h3 ♘h5 19 ♘e2? [◻ 19 ♕f2] 19 ... ♕g5 20 g4! ♘f6 21 ♖g1 [◻ 21 ♕c1] 21 ... ♕h4 22 ♔g2! gxf5 23 exf5 e4 [23 ... ♘xg4! 24 hxg4 ♖xg4+ 25 ♔f1! (25 ♖g3?–+; 25 ♘g3?–+) 25 ... ♖fg8! 26 ♖xg4! ♖xg4! (△ 27 ... e4; 26 ... ♕xg4+?; 26 ... ♕h1+?) 27 ♘c3 ♗e3 28 ♖f2 (28 ♖xe3?? ♕h1+ △ 29 ... ♖g2+–+) 28 ... ♕h1+ 29 ♔e2 ♗xf2–+] 24 ♗xe4 ♖e8 25 ♘g3 ♖e5 26 ♗d3 ♖ge8 27 ♖gf1 ♗e3 28 ♖e1? h5 29 ♗e2 hxg4 30 hxg4 ♘xg4 31 ♖h1 ♕e7 32 ♖h3 ♗d4 33 f6 ♘xf6 34 ♗d3 ♖e1 35 ♗f5+ ♔b8 36 ♖f1 ♖e3 37 ♗e6 ♕g7 38 bxc5 dxc5 39 ♕f5 ♔a7 40 ♔h2 ♖xa3 41 ♕f4 ♗e5 42 ♕f2 ♘e4 0-1 M954-1852

64 Journoud, P. L/N6018. BL

**1852̂-★JK-1**
**Journoud, P.–Kieseritsky, L.**
Paris [Staunton]
1 e4 e5 2 d4 exd4 3 ♘f3 c5 4 ♗c4 b5 5 ♗d5 [5 ♗xb5 ♕a5+→] 5 ... ♘c6 6 0-0 ♖b8 7 ♗f4 ♖b6 8 ♘bd2 d6 9 c4 ♘b4 10 cxb5 ♘xd5 11 exd5 ♘f6 12 ♘c4 ♘xd5 [12 ... ♖xb5 13 ♕e2+ ♔d7 14 ♘ce5+ ♔c7 15 ♕xb5+-] 13 ♘xb6 ♕xb6 14 ♕e2+ ♗e6 15 ♗g3 ♗e7 16 a4 0-0 17 ♘d2 ♘b4 18 ♖ac1 d5 19 ♔h1 c4 20 f4 d3 21 ♕f3 ♗f5 22 ♖fe1 ♗f6 23 ♗f2 ♗d4 24 ♔g1 ♘c2 25 ♖e5 ♗g4! 26 ♕xg4 [◻ 26 ♕g3] 26 ... ♗xf2+ 27 ♔h1 ♗e3 28 ♖d1 ♗d4 29 ♖xd5 ♘e3 30 ♕f3 ♗xb2 31 ♘xc4 ♘xc4 32 ♕xd3 [◻ 33 ♖5xd3=] 32 ... ♘e3 33 a5 ♘xd1 34 axb6 ♘f2+ 35 ♔g1 ♘xd3 36 bxa7 ♘xf4 37 ♖d7 ♗d4+ 38 ♔f1 ♗b6 39 ♖b7 ♘d5 40 ♔e2 ♗xa7 41 ♖xa7 ♘c3+ 42 ♔d3 ♘xb5 **0-1**
M954-1852

**1852̂-★KS-1**
**Kieseritsky, L.+Szén, J.**
[Staunton]
1 e4 e5 2 f4 exf4 3 ♘f3 g5 4 h4 g4 5 ♘e5 h5 6 ♗c4 ♖h7 7 d4 d6 8 ♘d3 f3 9 g3 ♗e6 10 ♗g5 ♗e7 11 ♗xe6 fxe6 12 ♘f4 ♔d7 13 d5 e5 14 ♘e6 ♕e8 15 ♕d3 a6 16 ♘c3 ♔c8 17 ♕c4 ♗xg5 18 hxg5 b5 19 ♕b4 c5?! 20 ♕a5! ♖aa7 21 ♕b6 [21 g6!] 21 ... ♖hd7 22 ♘d1 ♖ab7 23 ♕a5 ♖e7 24 ♘e3 ♖xe6 25 dxe6 ♕xe6 26 ♘d5 ♘e7 27 ♖xh5 ♘xd5 28 ♖h8+ ♔d7 29 exd5 ♕xd5 30 ♕d8+ ♔c6 31 ♕c8+ ♔b6 32 ♕xg4 ♖f7?! 33 ♖xb8+ ♔a7 34 ♖h8 e4 35 g6 e3! 36 ♖h2 ♖e7 37 ♖d1 f2+ 38 ♔f1 ♕e5 39 ♔e2 ♕xb2 40 ♕f5 ♕b4 41 ♖h4 ♕c3 42 ♕d3 ♕b2 43 ♖h7 ♖xh7 44 gxh7 **1-0**
M954-1852

**1852̂-★GS-1**
**Gordon, T.+Staunton, H.**
⟨♙f7⟩ 1 e4 ... 2 d4 e6 3 ♗d3 c5 4 e5 ♕a5+ 5 ♗d2 ♕b6 6 ♕h5+ ♔d8 7 ♕f7 ♘e7 8 ♘c3 cxd4 9 ♘b5 ♘bc6 10 ♘f3 a6 11 ♘d6

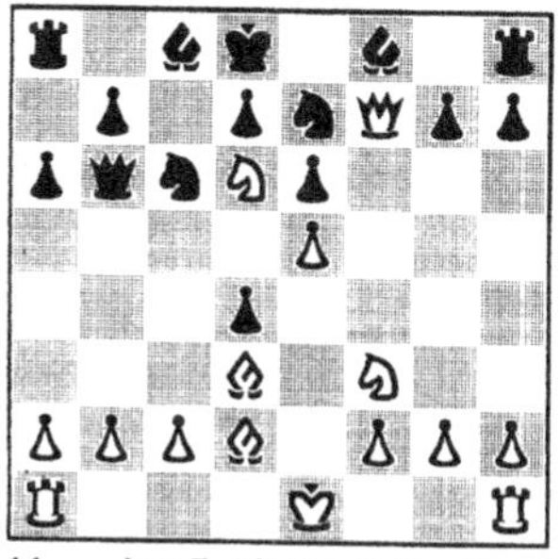

11 ... ♘xe5 12 ♘xe5 ♕xd6 13 ♘c4 **1-0**
M954

**1852̂-★JP-1**
**Jaenisch, C.F.=Petrov, A.D.**
1 e4 e5 2 f4 exf4 3 ♗c4 ♕h4+ 4 ♔f1 g5 5 ♘c3 ♗g7 6 d4 d6 7 ♘b5 ♘a6 8 ♗e2 ♕h6 9 h4 c6 10 ♘c3 ♘c7 11 ♘f3 g4 12 ♘e1 ♕f6 13 ♗xg4 ♕xd4 14 ♕xd4 ♗xd4 15 ♗xc8 ♖xc8 16 ♗xf4 ♗xc3 17 bxc3 d5 18 e5 ♘e6 19 ♘d3 ♘e7 20 ♖b1 b6 21 ♔f2 ♘xf4 22 ♘xf4 ♘g6 23 g3 ♔d7 24 ♖be1 ♖ce8 25 ♘d3 h5 26 ♔g2 ♖e7 27 ♖hf1 c5

28 ♘f4 ♘xf4+ 29 gxf4 ♖g8+ 30 ♔f3 ♖g4 31 ♖h1 ♔e6 32 ♖eg1 ♔f5 33 ♖xg4 hxg4+ 34 ♔g3 f6 35 ♖e1 fxe5 36 ♖xe5+ ♖xe5 37 fxe5 ♔xe5 38 ♔xg4 ♔f6 39 h5 b5 40 h6 ♔g6 41 ♔f4 ♔xh6 42 ♔e5 b4 43 ♔xd5 bxc3 44 ♔xc5 ♔g5 45 ♔d4 ♔f4 46 ♔xc3 ♔e5 47 ♔c4 ♔d6 48 ♔b5 ♔c7 49 ♔c5 ♔d7 50 ♔d5 ♔c7 51 ♔c5 ♔d7 52 ♔b5 ♔c7 53 a4 ♔b7 54 c4 ♔c7 55 ♔c5 ♔d7 56 ♔b5 ♔c7 57 ♔a5 ♔b8 58 c5 ♔a8 59 ♔b5 ♔b7 60 a5 ♔c7 61 ♔a6 ♔b8 62 ♔b5 ♔b7 63 c6+ ♔c7 64 ♔c5 ♔c8 65 ♔d6 ♔d8 66 c7+ ♔c8 **½-½**
M954-1852

**1852̂-★JS-1**
**Shumov, I.S.=Jaenisch, C.F.**
St. Petersburg
1 e4 e5 2 ♘f3 ♘c6 3 ♗c4 ♗c5 4 0-0 ♘f6 5 c3 ♘xe4 6 ♗d5 ♘xf2 7 ♖xf2 ♗xf2+ 8 ♔xf2 d6 9 d4 exd4 10 ♕e2+ ♕e7 11 ♗xc6+ bxc6 12 ♕xe7+ ♔xe7 13 cxd4 ♖b8 14 b3 ♖e8 15 ♘c3 ♗a6 16 ♗e3 f6 17 h4 ♔f7 18 g4 h6 19 g5 hxg5 20 hxg5 ♖h8 21 ♘e4 ♗d3 22 ♘g3 a5 23 ♖c1 ♖b6 24 ♖d1 ♗g6 25 gxf6 gxf6 26 ♖c1 ♔e7 27 ♘d2 d5 28 ♘f3 ♔d7 29 ♘e2 a4 30 ♖g1 axb3 31 axb3 ♗e4 32 ♖g7+ ♔c8 33 ♗f4 ♗xf3 34 ♖xc7+ ♔d8 35 ♔xf3 ♖xb3+ 36 ♔g4 ♖e8 37 ♘g3 ♖g8+ 38 ♔f5 ♖f3 39 ♖xc6 ♖gxg3 40 ♖xf6 ♖g7 41 ♔e6 ♖e7+ 42 ♔xd5 ♖a3 43 ♗d6 ♖a5+ 44 ♔c6 ♖a6+ 45 ♔c5 ♖ea7 46 ♔d5 ♖a2 **½-½**
M954-1852

**1852̂-★JS-2**
**Shumov, I.S.=Jaenisch, C.F.**
St. Petersburg
1 e4 e5 2 ♘f3 ♘c6 3 ♗c4 ♗c5 4 c3 ♘f6 5 d4 exd4 6 e5 d5 7 exf6 dxc4 8 fxg7 ♖g8 9 cxd4 ♘xd4 10 ♘xd4 ♕xd4 11 0-0 ♖xg7 12 ♕h5 ♕g4 13 ♕e5+ ♗e6 14 g3 ♗d6 15 ♕b5+ ♔e7 16 ♕xb7 ♖ag8 17 ♘c3 ♕h5 18 ♘e4 ♗d5 19 ♕b5 c6 20 ♕b7+ ♔e6 21 ♘xd6 f5 22 ♖e1+ ♔f6 23 ♕b4 ♕h3 24 ♕c3+ ♔g6 25 f3 ♔h5 26 ♗f4 ♖xg3+ 27 ♗xg3 ♖xg3+ 28 hxg3 ♕xg3+ 29 ♔f1 ♗xf3 30 ♕d2 ♕h3+ 31 ♔g1 ♕h1+ 32 ♔f2 ♕g2+ 33 ♔e3 f4+ 34 ♔xf4 ♕xd2+ 35 ♔xf3 ♕xd6 36 ♖h1+ ♔g6 37 ♖ag1+ ♔f7 38 ♖xh7+ ♔f8 39 ♖h8+ ♔f7 40 ♖h7+ **½-½**
L/N6047-1852

**1852̂-★S?-1**
**Staunton, H.+?**
1 e4 c5 2 d4 cxd4 3 ♘f3 e6 4 ♘xd4 a6 5 g3 ♗c5 6 ♘b3 ♗a7 7 ♗g2 ♘e7 8 ♗f4 ♘bc6 9 ♗d6 0-0 10 ♘c3 b5 11 e5 ♗b7 12 ♘e4 ♖e8 13 ♘ec5 ♗c8 14 0-0 ♘f5 15 c3 ♘xd6 16 exd6 ♗xc5 17 ♘xc5 ♕b6 18 b4 a5 19 ♖e1 axb4 20 cxb4 ♖a7 21 a3 ♘b8 22 ♕d4 ♘a6 23 ♘xe6 ♕xd4 24 ♘xd4 ♖xe1+ 25 ♖xe1 **1-0**
M954-1852

## Harrwitz✕Löwenthal

**1853-✕HL-1** 53
**Löwenthal, J.J.–Harrwitz, D.**
London [Staunton]
1 e4 e5 2 f4 ♗c5 3 ♘f3 d6 4 b4 ♗xb4 5 c3 ♗c5 6 ♗c4 ♘c6 7 d4 exd4 8 cxd4 ♗b6 9 0-0 ♗g4 10 ♗b2 ♗xf3 11 ♖xf3 ♘f6 12 ♔h1! 0-0 [12 ... ♘xe4 13 ♖e3 (13 d5? ♘a5 14 ♗xg7 ♖g8 15 ♗d4 ♘xc4 16 ♕a4+ ♔f8 17 ♕xc4 ♕h4 18 ♗xb6 axb6 19 ♕xe4 ♖e8→) 13 ... ♕e7 (13 ... d5 14 ♗xd5 ♕xd5 15 ♘c3±) 14 ♕e1 f5 15 ♗d5 ♔d8 16 ♘d2 ♘b4 (16 ... ♖e8 17 ♘xe4 ♘xd4 18 ♘xd6 ♕xe3 19 ♘xe8 ♕xe8 20 ♗xb7±) 17 ♖xe4±] 13 d5 ♘a5 14 ♗d3 ♘g4 15 ♕e1 f6! 16 ♘d2 c6 17 ♕g3± ♕d7 18 dxc6?! ♘xc6 19 ♘b3 ♖ae8 20 ♖af1 ♔h8 21 h3 ♘h6 22 ♕h4! d5 23 e5 d4?! 24 exf6 [24 ♗a3 ♘e7 25 f5 fxe5 26 f6 ♘g6 27 ♗xg6+-] 24 ... ♖xf6 25 g4 ♕d5 26 ♕f2? [◻ 26 ♕g3!±; 26 ♗xh7?] 26 ... ♖xf4 27 ♕g2 ♖xf3 28 ♖xf3 ♖e1+ 29 ♗f1 ♘f7! 30 ♖f5 ♕e6 31 ♕g3 ♔g8 32 ♘d2 g6 33 ♖f3 ♘g5 34 ♔g2 ♘xf3→ [34 ♗c4+-] 35 ♕xf3 ♔g7 36 ♗c4 ♕f6 37 ♕d5 ♘e7 38 ♕xb7 ♕c6+ 39 ♕xc6 ♘xc6 40 ♘f3 ♖b1 41 ♗a3

## HARRWITZ ✕ LÖWENTHAL
**London** [1853 – ✕ HL]

| | D. Harrwitz | J. J. Löwenthal |
|---|---|---|
| *1* | 1 | 0 |
| *2* | 1 | 0 |
| *3* | 0 | 1 |
| *4* | 0 | 1 |
| *5* | 0 | 1 |
| *6* | 0 | 1 |
| *7* | 0 | 1 |
| *8* | ½ | ½ |
| *9* | 0 | 1 |
| *10* | 0 | 1 |
| *11* | ½ | ½ |
| *12* | ½ | ½ |
| *13* | 1 | 0 |
| *14* | 1 | 0 |
| *15* | ½ | ½ |
| *16* | 1 | 0 |
| *17* | ½ | ½ |
| *18* | ½ | ½ |
| *19* | 1 | 0 |
| *20* | 1 | 0 |
| *21* | ½ | ½ |
| *22* | ½ | ½ |
| *23* | ½ | ½ |
| *24* | 1 | 0 |
| *25* | ½ | ½ |
| *26* | 0 | 1 |
| *27* | ½ | ½ |
| *28* | 1 | 0 |
| *29* | 1 | 0 |
| *30* | ½ | ½ |
| *31* | 1 | 0 |
| *Total* | 17 | 14 |

♗a5 42 ♗d5 ♘b4 43 ♗e4 ♖a1 44 ♗xb4 ♖xa2+ 45 ♔f1 ♗xb4 46 ♘xd4 ♔f6 47 ♘c2 ♗c5 48 ♔e2 ♔e5 49 ♔f3 a5 50 h4 a4 51 h5 gxh5 52 gxh5 a3 **0-1** L/N6123

### 1853-✕HL-2 x53
**Harrwitz,D.+Löwenthal, J.J.**

London [Staunton]

1 e4 e5 2 ♘f3 ♘c6 3 ♗b5 ♘f6 4 0-0 ♗e7 5 d4 ♘xe4 6 d5 ♘d4 7 ♘xd4 exd4 8 ♕xd4 ♘f6 9 ♘c3 0-0 10 ♗d3! d6 11 f4 c5 12 ♕e3 ♘g4 13 ♕f3 f5 14 h3 ♘h6? 15 ♘e2 ♗d7 16 c4 ♗f6 17 ♖b1 a6 18 b4 axb4 19 ♖xb4 b5 20 a3 ♖b8 21 cxb5 ♗xb5 22 ♗xb5 ♖xb5 23 ♖xb5 axb5 24 ♕b3 ♕d7 25 ♗b2 ♖e8 26 ♖f2 ♕a7 27 ♕c2 ♗xb2 28 ♕xb2 ♕c5 29 ♘d4 ♕xd5 30 ♘xb5 ♖b8 31 ♘c3 ♕b3 32 ♕a1 ♖c8 33 ♖f3 ♕c4 34 a4 ♖a8? [34 ... d5 35 a5 ♘f7 36 a6 ♘d6±] 35 ♕e1 ♔f7 36 ♕b1! ♕c5+ 37 ♔h2 ♖c8 38 ♘b5 ♖b8 39 ♕b3+ ♔f8 40 ♕e6 ♘f7 41 ♖c3 ♖e8 42 ♖xc5 ♖xe6 43 ♖xf5 g6 44 ♖d5 ♖e4 45 ♘d4 ♔e7 46 ♔g3 ♖e3+ 47 ♔f2 ♖a3 48 ♖a5 ♘d8 49 ♖a7+ ♔f6 50 g4 h6 51 h4 g5 52 fxg5+ hxg5 53 h5 ♘f7 54 ♘f3 ♘h6 55 ♔g3 ♘f7 56 ♖a8 ♘e5 57 ♖f8+ ♔g7 58 ♖f5 ♔h7 59 a5 ♘xf3 60 ♖xf3 ♖xa5 61 ♖f6 ♖a3+ 62 ♔f2 ♖d3 63 ♖g6 ♖d5 64 ♔e3 ♖e5+ 65 ♔d4 ♖a5 66 ♔e4 ♖e5+ 67 ♔f3 ♖d5 68 ♖f6 ♖d4 69 ♖e6 ♖d5 70 ♖e7+ ♔h6 71 ♔e4 ♖d1 72 ♖e6+ ♔h7 73 ♖g6 ♖e1+ 74 ♔f5 ♖e2 75 ♖xd6 ♖e7 76 ♔xg5 ♖f7 77 ♖f6 ♖a7 78 ♖f4 ♖a5+ 79 ♔h4 ♔g7 80 g5 ♖a6 81 ♖c4 ♖a7 82 h6+ ♔h7 83 ♔h5 ♖a8 84 g6+ ♔h8 85 ♖c5 ♖d8 86 ♔g5 ♖a8 87 ♖f5 ♔g8 88 h7+ **1-0** L/N6123

### 1853-✕HL-3 x53
**Löwenthal,J.J.+Harrwitz, D.**

London [Staunton]

1 e4 e5 2 ♘f3 ♘c6 3 ♗b5 ♗c5 4 c3 ♕e7 5 0-0 ♘f6 6 d4 ♗b6 7 ♗g5 h6 8 ♗xf6 gxf6 9 d5 ♘d8 [⌓ 9 ... ♘b8] 10 ♘h4! ♕c5 11 ♕f3!± ♕xb5? 12 ♕xf6 ♖g8! [12 ... ♖h7?; 12 ... ♖f8?] 13 ♘f5 ♗c5 14 ♕xe5+ ♔f8 15 ♕f6 ♔e8 16 b4 ♗f8 17 a4 ♕d3 18 ♕e5+ ♘e6 19 dxe6 dxe6 20 ♕d4! ♕xd4 21 ♘xd4 ♗d7 22 ♘d2 c5 23 bxc5 ♗xc5 24 ♘2b3 ♗d6 25 ♘a5! b6 26 ♘c4 ♗c7 27 f4 ♖c8 28 e5 ♗b8 29 ♘d2 ♖g4 [29 ... ♖xc3?? 30 ♘e4! △ ♘f6+] 30 h3 [♘e4? ♗xe5] 30 ... ♖g6 [⌓ 30 ... ♖g3] 31 ♘e4 ♔e7 32 ♖f3 ♖c4 33 ♘f6 ♖xa4 34 ♖ad1! ♖a2 35 ♖fd3 ♖gxg2+ 36 ♔f1 ♗a4? [36 ... ♗e8 37 ♘xe8 ♔xe8 38 ♘e2 ♗c7 39 ♔xg2 ♖xe2+ 40 ♔f3+–; 36 ... ♗b5 37 ♘e2 ♖axe2 38 ♖d7+! ♗xd7 39 ♖xd7++–]

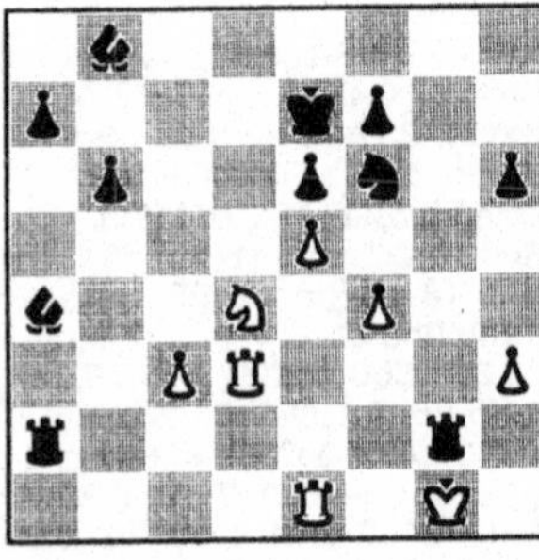

37 ♘c6+ ♗xc6 38 ♖d7+ ♔f8 39 ♖d8+ ♔e7 40 ♖1d7+ **1-0** L/N6123

### 1853-✕HL-4 x53
**Harrwitz,D.–Löwenthal, J.J.**

London [Staunton]

1 e4 e5 2 f4 exf4 3 ♘f3 g5 4 h4 g4 5 ♘e5 ♘f6 6 ♗c4 d5 7 exd5 ♗d6 8 d4 ♕e7! [⌓ 8 ... ♘h5] 9 ♗xf4??→ ♘h5 10 0-0 ♘xf4 11 ♖xf4 f6 12 g3 fxe5 13 dxe5 ♗xe5 14 ♖e4 ♗f5 15 ♖e2 ♘d7 16 ♘d2 0-0-0 17 ♔g2 ♕g7 18 c3 ♘b6? [⌓ 18 ... ♖he8] 19 a4 ♘xd5 20 ♕e1! ♗f6 21 ♕f2 ♗g6 22 ♕xa7 c6 23 a5 ♕c7! 24 ♖f1 ♖hf8 25 ♗xd5 cxd5! [25 ... ♖xd5? 26 ♘c4 △ ♘b6+] 26 ♖e6 ♗e7! 27 a6 ♔d7! 28 ♕b6 ♗c5 29 ♕xc7+ ♔xc7 30 b4 ♖xf1 31 ♔xf1 ♖f8+ 32 ♔e2 ♗d6 33 axb7 ♗xg3 34 ♘b3 ♖e8→ [34 ... ♖f2+→] 35 ♖xe8 ♗xe8 36 ♘c5 ♗xh4 37 ♔e3 ♗f6 **0-1** L/N6123

### 1853-✕HL-5 x53
**Löwenthal,J.J.+Harrwitz, D.**

London [Staunton]

1 e4 e5 2 ♘f3 ♘c6 3 ♗b5 ♘f6 4 0-0 ♗d6? 5 ♖e1! a6 6 ♗a4 b5 7 ♗b3 ♘a5? 8 d4 ♘xb3 9 axb3 ♕e7 10 ♗g5 h6 11 ♗h4 ♗b7 12 ♘bd2 c5 13 ♗g3!± cxd4 14 ♘xd4 g6! 15 ♘4f3 ♘h5 16 ♘f1 [△ ♘e3] 16 ... ♘xg3 17 hxg3 0-0? 18 ♕d2 ♖ac8 19 ♖ad1 ♖c6 20 ♕xh6 ♗c7 21 ♘e3 ♗d8! 22 ♘d5 ♕e8 23 ♘g5 ♗xg5 24 ♕xg5 ♔g7 25 ♘e3 ♖e6 26 ♘f5+ ♔g8 27 ♘d6 ♕b8 28 ♘xb7 ♕xb7 29 ♖d5 d6 30 ♖ed1 ♕c7 31 c3 ♔g7?? 32 ♖xd6! f6 33 ♖d7+ ♖f7 34 ♖xc7 fxg5 35 ♖1d7 ♖xd7 36 ♖xd7+ ♔f6 37 ♔f1 ♖c6 38 ♔e2 ♔e6 39 ♖d5 ♖c8 40 g4 ♖h8 41 c4 bxc4 42 bxc4 ♖b8 43 ♖d2 a5 44 ♔d1 [⌓ 44 ♔d3] 44 ... ♖b4 45 ♖c2 ♔d6 46 c5+ ♔c6 47 f3 ♖b5 48 ♔d2 ♖xc5 49 ♖c3 ♔b5 50 ♖d3 a4 51 ♖d6 ♖c6 52 ♖d5+ ♖c5 53 ♔d3 ♔b4 54 ♖xc5 ♔xc5 55 ♔c3 ♔b5 56 b4! ♔c6 57 ♔b2! ♔b6 58 ♔a3 ♔b5 59 g3 **1-0** L/N6123

### 1853-✕HL-6 x53
**Harrwitz,D.–Löwenthal, J.J.**

London [Staunton]

1 e4 e5 2 ♗c4 ♘f6 3 ♕e2?! ♗c5 4 f4 exf4?! 5 ♘f3 0-0 6 ♘c3 ♘c6 7 d3 ♗b4 8 0-0 ♖e8?! 9 ♘d5 ♘xd5 10 ♗xd5 ♘e7? 11 ♗b3? [11 ♗xf7+ ♔xf7 12 ♘g5+ ♔g8 (12 ... ♔g6 13 ♕g5!+–) 13 ♕h5 h6 14 ♘f7 g6 15 ♘xh6++–] 11 ... ♘g6 12 c3 ♗a5 13 ♘d4 c5 14 ♘b5 d5 15 ♗xf4 a6 16 ♘a3 c4! [17 ♗c2 ♕b6+ △ ♕xb2→; 17 ♗d1 cxd3 18 ♕xd3 ♕b6+ 19 ~ ♕xb2∓] 17 dxc4 ♖xe4→ 18 ♕d2 ♗b6+ 19 ♔h1 ♘xf4 20 ♖xf4 ♗e3 21 ♖xe4 ♗xd2 22 cxd5

♗f5 23 ♖e2 ♗f4 24 ♖ae1 g6 25 g3 ♗d6 26 ♘c4 [Δ 26 ♖e8+] 26 ... ♕c7 27 ♘xd6 ♕xd6 28 ♔g2 ♔f8 29 h3 b5 30 ♖e3 ♖d8 31 g4 ♗c8 32 ♖f3 ♗b7 33 ♖e6 ♕xe6 34 dxe6 ♖d3 **0-1** L/N6123

**1853-⚔HL-7** ×53
**Löwenthal,J.J.+Harrwitz,D.**
London [Staunton]
1 e4 c5 2 ♗c4 e6 3 ♘c3 a6 4 a4 ♘e7 5 d3 d5 6 exd5 exd5 7 ♗b3 ♗e6 8 ♘f3 ♘bc6 9 ♘g5 ♘g6± 10 0-0 ♗e7 11 ♘xe6 fxe6 12 f4 d4? 13 ♘e4 ♕d7 14 ♕g4 ♘d8 15 ♗d2 [Δ ♗a5] 15 ... ♕c6 16 a5 0-0 17 f5 ♘e5 18 ♕g3+- ♘d7 [18 ... ♗d6 19 f6, 20 ♗f4] 19 ♗a4 ♕c8 20 ♗xd7 ♕xd7 21 f6 ♖f7 22 fxe7 ♕xe7 23 ♗g5 ♕d7 24 ♗xd8 **1-0** L/N6123

**1853-⚔HL-8**
**Harrwitz,D.=Löwenthal,J.J.**
London [Staunton]
1 d4 d5 2 c4 e6 3 ♘c3 ♘f6 4 ♘f3 c5 5 ♗f4!? ♘c6? 6 e3 [□ 6 ♘b5+-] 6 ... a6! 7 a3 ♗e7 8 dxc5?! ♗xc5 9 b4 ♗e7 [□ 9 ... ♗a7] 10 h3 0-0 11 ♕c2 dxc4 12 ♗xc4 b5 13 ♗d3 ♗xb4!∓ 14 0-0 ♗xc3 15 ♕xc3 ♗b7 16 ♗g5 h6 17 ♗xf6 ♕xf6 18 ♕xf6 gxf6 19 ♗e4 f5 20 ♗xc6 ♗xc6 21 ♘e5 ♖fc8! 22 ♖fc1 ♗e8 23 f4 f6 24 ♘f3 ♗c6 25 ♘d4 ♗d5 26 ♖d1 [Δ ♘xf5] 26 ... ♖c3 27 ♔f2 ♔f7 28 ♖d2! [Δ ♘xf5] 28 ... ♗e4 29 ♘e2 ♖d3 30 ♖xd3 ♗xd3 31 ♖c1 ♗c4 32 ♘d4 h5 33 a4 ♖a7 34 g3 ♖d7 35 ♖c3 ♔e8? 36 axb5 axb5 37 ♖a3 ♖b7 38 ♖a8+ ♔f7 [□ 38 ... ♔d7] 39 ♘c6 ♖d7 40 ♘d4 ♖b7 41 ♘c6 ♔g7 42 ♘a5 ♖d7 43 ♘xc4 bxc4 44 ♔e2 c3 45 ♖a2 ♔f8 46 ♖c2 ♖g7 47 ♔f3 ♖c7 48 g4 fxg4+ 49 hxg4 hxg4+ 50 ♔xg4 f5+? [□ 50 ... ♔e7∓] 51 ♔f3 ♔e7 52 ♔e2 ♔d6 53 ♔d3 ♔d5 54 ♖xc3 ♖xc3+ 55 ♔xc3 ♔e4 56 ♔d2 ♔f3 57 ♔d3 ♔f2 58 ♔d2 ♔g3 59 ♔e2 ♔g2 60 ♔e1 ♔f3 61 ♔d2 ♔f2 62 ♔d3 ♔e1 63 ♔d4 ♔f2 64 ♔d3 **½-½** L/N6123

**1853-⚔HL-9**
**Löwenthal,J.J.+Harrwitz,D.**
London [Staunton]
1 e4 e5 2 ♘f3 d6 3 d4 cxd4 4 ♕xd4 ♘f6 5 ♘c3 ♗e7 6 ♗f4 0-0 7 ♗c4 a6 [Δ b5, c5] 8 a4 ♘c6 9 ♕d2 ♗e6 10 ♗d3 ♘d7 11 0-0 f6 12 ♗g3 ♘de5 13 ♗e2! f5 14 exf5 ♘xf3+ 15 ♗xf3 ♗xf5 16 ♘d5 ♗g5? 17 ♕c3 ♕d7 18 h4! ♗h6 19 ♖ad1 ♔h8 20 ♖fe1? [□ 20 ♘xc7! ♕xc7 21 ♖xd6 ♖ac8 22 ♖xh6 ♕f7 23 ♗h5 ♕g8 24 ♗d6 ♘e7 25 ♕e5+-] 20 ... ♖ad8 21 b4 ♖f7 22 ♘xc7! ♕xc7 23 ♖xd6 ♕c8 24 ♖xh6 ♘d4 25 ♖d6! ♘xf3+ 26 gxf3 ♖df8 27 ♕xc8 ♖xc8 28 c3 ♗c2 29 a5 ♗a4 [29 ... ♖xf3 30 ♖e7±] 30 ♖e3 ♗c6 31 ♖dd3 ♗b5 32 ♖d4 ♗c6 33 ♗f4!+- ♖cf8 34 ♗d6 ♖d8 35 f4 ♖f6 36 ♗e5 ♖g6+ 37 ♔f1 ♖xd4 38 ♗xd4 ♔g8 39 ♖e7 ♔f8 40 ♖c7 ♗f3 41 ♔e1 ♖g4 42 f5! ♖xh4 43 ♗xg7+ ♔g8 44 ♗d4 h5 45 ♖g7+ ♔f8 46 f6 ♖h1+ 47 ♔d2 ♗d5 48 ♗c5+ ♔e8 49 ♖e7+ ♔d8 50 ♗b6+ ♔c8 51 f7 [□ 51 ♖c7+ ♔b8 52 ♖d7 ♗e6 53 ♖d8+ ♗c8 54 f7+-] 51 ... ♗xf7 52 ♖xf7 ♖g1 53 ♖c7+ ♔b8 54 ♖d7 ♖g8 55 ♖d8+ ♖xd8+ 56 ♗xd8 **1-0** L/N6123

**1853-⚔HL-10**
**Harrwitz,D.−Löwenthal,J.J.**
London [Staunton]
1 e4 e5 2 ♗c4 ♘f6 3 ♕e2 ♗c5 4 f4?! d6 5 ♘f3 0-0 6 d3 ♗g4 7 c3 d5!∓ 8 fxe5 [□ 8 ♗b3] 8 ... dxc4 9 d4 ♘fd7 10 dxc5 ♘xe5 11 0-0 ♕e7 12 ♗e3 ♘bd7 13 ♘bd2 ♘xc5 14 ♗d4 ♘xf3+ 15 gxf3 ♗h3 16 ♖fb1 [16 ♗xc5 ♕g5+ 17 ♔h1 ♗xf1-+] 16 ... ♘d3 17 ♘f1 f5 18 ♘g3 c5 19 ♗f2 f4-+ 20 b3 ♘e5 21 ♕d2 ♘xf3+ **0-1** L/N6123

**1853-⚔HL-11**
**Löwenthal,J.J.=Harrwitz,D.**
London [Staunton]
1 e4 c5 2 ♗c4 e6 3 ♘c3 ♘c6 4 d3 a6 5 a4 g6 6 f4 ♗g7 7 ♗d2 ♘ge7 8 e5 0-0 9 ♘e4 f6 10 exf6 ♗xf6 11 ♘xf6+ ♖xf6 12 ♘f3 d5 13 ♗b3 ♕b6? 14 a5 ♕a7 15 c4! b5 16 axb6 ♕xb6 17 0-0 ♖b8 18 ♖a3 ♗b7 19 ♔h1! ♖bf8 20 cxd5 ♘xd5 21 ♗xd5 exd5 22 ♖e1 ♕c7 23 ♕c1 ♕d6 24 ♖b3 ♘b4 25 d4 a5 26 dxc5 ♕c7 27 ♗c3? [□ 27 ♘d4] 27 ... ♘d3 28 ♕e3 ♘xe1 29 ♕xe1 ♖xf4 [□ 29 ... ♖e7] 30 ♗e5 ♖e4 [30 ... ♖e8 31 ♖e3!±] 31 ♕xe4 dxe4 32 ♗xc7 exf3 33 gxf3 ♗xf3+ 34 ♔g1 a4 35 ♖b4 ♗c6 36 ♗d6 ♖c8 37 ♖f4 ♖e8 38 ♔f2 ♔g7 39 ♖b4 ♔f6 40 ♖b6 ♖c8 41 ♔e3 ♔e6 42 ♔d4 ♔d7 43 ♔c4 ♖a8 44 ♔b4 g5 45 ♔a3 h5 46 ♖b4 ♖e8 47 ♖b8 ♖xb8 48 ♗xb8 ♔e6 49 ♔b4 ♔d5 50 ♗d6 g4 **½-½** L/N6123

**1853-⚔HL-12**
**Harrwitz,D.=Löwenthal,J.J.**
London [Staunton]
1 d4 d5 2 c4 e6 3 ♘c3 ♘f6 4 ♗f4 c5 5 e3 ♕a5 6 ♗d3 dxc4 7 ♗xc4 ♘e4 8 ♘e2 cxd4 9 exd4 ♗d6 10 ♗xd6 ♘xd6 11 ♗d3 ♘d7 12 0-0 ♘f6 13 ♘g3 0-0 14 ♕d2 e5?! [□ 14 ... ♗d7] 15 ♕g5 ♖e8 16 ♘ge4 ♘dxe4 17 ♘xe4 ♘xe4 18 ♗xe4 ♕b4!∓ 19 ♖ad1 exd4 20 ♕h4 g6 21 ♗d5 ♗e6 22 ♗xe6 ♖xe6 23 ♕xd4 ♕xd4 24 ♖xd4 ♖e2 25 ♖b4 b6 26 a4 ♖d8 27 ♖b5 ♖dd2 28 b4 ♖b2 29 a5 bxa5 30 ♖xa5 ♖e7 31 ♖b5 ♖e4 32 ♖a5 ♖e7 33 ♖b5 ♖e6! 34 g3 ♖a6 35 ♔g2 ♔g7 36 h4 ♖a4 37 h5 a6 38 ♖b7 gxh5 39 ♖b6 ♖bxb4 40 ♖xb4 ♖xb4 41 ♖a1 ♖b6 42 ♖a5 h6 43 ♖xh5 ♔g6? [□ 43 ... ♖b5; 43 ... ♖b7; 43 ... ♖b8 Δ 44 ... ♖a7; 44 ... ♖a8∓] 44 ♖a5 ♔f6 45 ♔f3 ♔e6 46 ♔g4 ♔e7 47 f4 ♖g6+ 48 ♔h4 ♖f6 49 f5 ♔d7 50 g4 ♔c7 51 ♖e5 ♔d6 52 ♖a5 ♔e7 53 ♖e5+ ♔f8 54 g5 hxg5+ 55 ♔xg5 ♖b6 56 ♖d5 ♔g7 57 ♖d7 ♖b5 58 ♖a7 a5 59 ♖a6 ♖b1 50 ♖xa5 **½-½** L/N6123

**1853-⚔HL-13**
**Löwenthal, J.J.− Harrwitz, D.**
London [Staunton]
1 e4 e5 2 f4 ♗c5 3 ♘f3 d6 4 ♗c4 ♘f6 5 d4 exd4 6 e5!? dxe5 7 fxe5 ♘d5 [□ 7 ... ♘g4 Δ 8 h3 ♘xe5!∓] 8 0-0 ♗e6 9 ♘g5 ♕d7 10 ♕f3 ♘c6 11 ♕g3 [11 ♘xe6 fxe6 12 ♗xd5 exd5 13 ♕h5+ g6 14 ♕h4 ♗e7∓] 11 ... 0-0-0 12 ♘d2 h6 13 ♘ge4 ♗b6 14 ♘b3 g5 15 ♔h1 ♘cb4 16 ♗d2 ♕c6 17 ♗d3 ♔b8 18 a4 a5 19 ♖fc1 [□ 19 ♗xb4∓] 19 ... ♘e3 20 ♘f6 ♘xd3 21 cxd3 ♕xg2+! 22 ♕xg2 ♘xg2 23 ♘xa5 ♘e3 24 ♘c4 ♘xc4 25 dxc4 c5 26 ♘e4 ♗d7! 27 ♘d6 ♖hf8 28 ♖f1 f6 29 ♘f5 ♗xf5 30 ♖xf5 fxe5 31 ♖xe5 ♖f2 32 ♗e1 ♖xb2 33 ♖e6 ♗c7 34 ♖xh6 d3 35 ♖d1 ♖c2 36 ♗d2 ♗f4 **0-1** L/N6123

**1853-⚔HL-14**
**Harrwitz,D.+Löwenthal,J.J.**
London
1 e4 e5 2 ♘f3 ♘c6 3 ♗b5 f5 4 d3 ♘f6 5 0-0 fxe4 6 dxe4 d6 7 ♘c3 ♗e7 8 ♗c4 ♗g4 9 h3 ♗xf3 10 ♕xf3 ♕d7 11 a3 ♘d4 12 ♕d3 ♘e6 13 f4 exf4 14 ♗xf4 0-0-0 15 ♗e3 ♔b8 16 e5 ♘e8 17 ♕f5 d5 18 ♗xd5 ♗c5 19 ♗xe6 ♗xe3+ 20 ♔h1 ♕e7 21 ♘d5 ♖xd5 22 ♗xd5 c6 23 ♗f3 ♗d4 24 ♖fe1 ♗xb2 25 ♖ab1 ♕xa3 26 ♖ed1 ♖f8

27 ♖d8+ ♔c7 28 ♕d7+ ♔b6 29 ♕d4+ **1-0** L/N6123

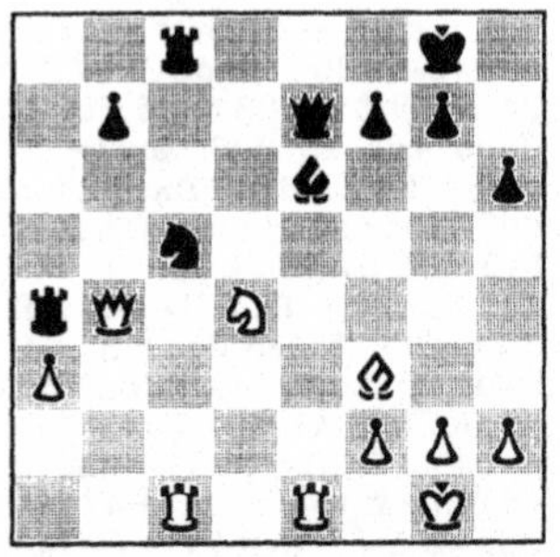

27 ♕xa4! ♘xa4 28 ♖xc8+ ♔h7 29 ♘xe6 fxe6 30 ♗e4+ g6 31 ♖ec1 **1-0** L/N6123

### 1853-⚔HL-15
**Löwenthal,J.J.=Harrwitz, D.**

London [Staunton]

1 e4 c5 2 ♘f3 ♘c6 3 ♗b5 ♘d4? 4 ♘xd4 cxd4 5 0-0 e6 6 d3 ♘e7 7 ♘d2 a6 8 ♗a4 b5 9 ♗b3 ♘c6 10 ♘f3 [□ 10 f4 △ 11 ♘f3] 10 ... ♗e7 11 ♗d2 0-0 12 c3 ♗c5 13 ♖c1 d6 14 cxd4 ♘xd4 15 ♘xd4 ♗xd4 16 ♗c3 ♕b6 17 ♕d2 a5 18 a3 h6 19 ♗xd4 ♕xd4 20 ♕c3 [□ 20 ♖c7] 20 ... ♕xc3 21 ♖xc3 a4 22 ♗a2 ♗d7 23 ♖c7 ♖fd8 24 f4 ♖ac8 25 ♖fc1 ♔f8 26 ♔f2 ♔e7 27 d4? [□ 27 ♔e3] 27 ... ♖xc7 28 ♖xc7 ♖b8 29 ♔e3 b4 30 axb4 ♖xb4 31 ♖c2 f6 32 ♗c4 g6 33 g3 ♖b6 34 ♔d2 ♗c6 35 ♗d3 ♔d7 36 g4 ♖b4 37 ♔c3 ♖b3+ 38 ♔d2 ♗b5 39 ♗xb5+ ♖xb5 40 ♔c1 ♖b4 41 ♖d2 ♔c6 42 ♖d3 ♔b5 43 f5 gxf5 44 gxf5 exf5 45 exf5 ♔c6 [□ 45 ... ♔c4] 46 ♖h3 ♖xd4 47 ♖xh6 ♔d5 48 ♖xf6 ♖h4 49 ♖g6 ♖xh2 50 ♖g4 ♔e5 51 ♖xa4 ♔xf5 52 ♖d4 ♔e5 53 ♖d2 **½-½** L/N6123

### 1853-⚔HL-16
**Harrwitz,D.+Löwenthal, J.J.**

London [Staunton]

1 d4 d5 2 c4 e6 3 ♘c3 ♘f6 4 ♗f4 a6 5 e3 c5 6 ♘f3 ♘c6 7 a3 ♗e7 8 dxc5 ♗xc5 9 b4 ♗d6 10 ♗xd6 ♕xd6 11 c5 ♕e7 12 ♗e2 0-0 13 0-0 ♖d8 14 ♖c1 e5 15 ♖e1! h6? 16 ♕c2 ♗e6 17 b5! axb5 18 ♘xb5 ♘e4 19 ♘d2 ♘xd2 20 ♕xd2 d4 [□ 20 ... ♘a5] 21 ♗f3 ♘a5 22 ♕b4 ♘b3 23 ♖b1 ♘xc5 24 exd4 exd4 25 ♖bc1 ♖dc8 26 ♘xd4 ♖a4??

### 1853-⚔HL-17
**Löwenthal,J.J.=Harrwitz, D.**

London [Staunton]

1 e4 e5 2 ♘f3 d6 3 ♗c4 ♗e7 [3 ... c6 4 d4 d5=] 4 ♘c3 ♘f6 5 d3 0-0 6 h3 ♘c6 7 ♗g5 ♗e6± 8 ♗xf6 ♗xf6 9 ♗b3 ♘e7 10 ♘e2 c6 11 ♗xe6 fxe6 12 c3 d5 13 ♕b3 ♕b6 14 0-0 ♘g6 15 ♕xb6 axb6 16 g3 dxe4 17 dxe4 ♖a4∞ 18 ♘d2 ♗g5 19 b3 ♖a6 20 ♖fd1 b5 [20 ... ♖d8? 21 ♘f3] 21 h4 ♗xd2 22 ♖xd2 ♖fa8 23 ♘c1 ♘f8 24 ♖b1 c5 25 ♖bb2 ♔f7 26 c4? [26 ♘d3+- ♘d7 27 ♘b4 cxb4 28 ♖xd7+ ♔e8 29 ♖xb7 bxc3 (29 ... ♖xa2 30 ♖xa2 ♖xa2 31 cxb4 ♖b2 32 ♖xb5+-; 31 ... ♖e2 32 f3) 30 ♖c2 ♖c6 31 ♖xb5 ♖d8 32 ♔f1 ♖d2 (32 ... ♖d4 33 ♖xe5) 33 ♖xd2 cxd2 34 ♔e2+-] 26 ... ♖a5 27 b4 cxb4 28 ♖xb4 ♖c8 29 ♘d3? [□ 29 ♘b3 ♖a4 30 ♖xb5 ♖axc4 31 ♖xb7+-] 29 ... bxc4 30 ♖xb7+ ♔f6 31 ♖c2 ♖a3 32 ♘b2? [□ 32 ♘e1+- △ 33 ♘g2, 34 ♘e3, 35 ♘g4+] 32 ... ♖xa2 33 ♖xc4 ♖xb2 34 ♖xc8 ♖xb7 35 ♖xf8+ ♔e7 36 ♖a8? [□ 36 ♖f3] 36 ... ♖b4 37 f3 ♖b2! 38 ♖a5 ♔f6 39 g4 h6 40 ♖a7 g5 41 h5 ♖g2+!= [42 ♔xg2◇] **½-½** L/N6123

### 1853-⚔HL-18
**Harrwitz,D.=Löwenthal, J.J.**

London [Staunton]

1 e4 e5 2 ♘f3 d6 3 d4 exd4 4 ♕xd4 ♘f6 5 e5 ♕e7 6 ♗e3 dxe5 7 ♘xe5 ♕b4+ 8 ♘d2 ♕xd4 9 ♗xd4 ♗e6 10 ♗d3 ♗e7 11 c4 0-0 12 f4 ♖d8∓ 13 ♗c3 ♘bd7 14 ♘xd7 ♖xd7 15 ♗c2 g6 16 ♗xf6 ♗xf6 17 0-0-0?→ ♗d4? [□ 17 ... ♖ad8 18 ♘e4 (18 b3 ♗d4→) 18 ... ♗d4→] 18 ♖he1 ♗g7? 19 b3 ♗h6? 20 g3 ♖ad8 21 ♖f1 ♗g7 [21 ... ♗g4? 22 ♘e4 △ 23 ♘f6+] 22 ♘e4!= ♖xd1+ 23 ♖xd1 ♖xd1+ 24 ♔xd1 **½-½** L/N6123-1854

### 1853-⚔HL-19
**Löwenthal, J.J.– Harrwitz, D.**

London [Staunton]

1 c4 f5 2 e3 c5 3 ♘c3 ♘f6 4 g3 ♘c6 5 ♗g2 e6 6 ♘h3 ♗e7 7 0-0± ♕b6? 8 d3 0-0 9 a3 d6 10 ♗d2 ♗d7 11 ♖b1 a5 12 ♘e2 h6 13 ♗c3 g5 14 d4 cxd4 15 exd4 ♕a6 16 c5 dxc5 17 dxc5 ♖ad8 18 ♕c2 ♘g4? 19 ♗xc6? [□ 19 b4±] 19 ... ♗xc6 20 b4?? ♗e4 21 ♕b2 ♗xb1 22 ♖xb1 axb4 23 axb4 ♕d3 24 ♖e1 ♗f6 25 ♗xf6 ♖xf6 26 ♘c1 ♕d5 27 ♕c3 ♕d2 28 ♕xd2 ♖xd2 29 ♘b3 ♖b2 30 ♘a5 e5 31 ♘xb7 e4 32 ♖c1 ♘e5 33 ♘d6 ♘f7 34 ♘xf7 ♖xf7 35 c6 ♖c7 36 f4 exf3 37 ♖c5 f4 38 gxf4 g4 39 ♘g5 hxg5 40 ♖xg5+ ♔f7 41 b5 ♖a2 **0-1** L/N6123-1854

### 1853-⚔HL-20
**Harrwitz,D.+Löwenthal, J.J.**

London [Staunton]

1 d4 d5 2 c4 e6 3 ♘c3 ♘f6 4 ♗f4 ♗b4 5 e3 dxc4 6 ♗xc4 ♗xc3+ 7 bxc3 ♘d5 8 ♘e2 ♘c6 9 0-0 ♘xf4 10 ♘xf4 e5 11 ♘h5 0-0 12 f4 exd4 13 cxd4± ♕e7 14 ♕f3 g6 15 ♘g3 ♕h4 [△ 16 f5 ♘xd4→] 16 ♘e4! ♔g7 17 g3 ♕e7 18 d5 ♘a5 19 ♗e2?? ♗f5?? [□ 19 ... ♖e8] 20 ♘f2 ♖fe8 21 e4 f6 [21 ... ♗xe4 22 ♕c3+-; 21 ... ♗d7; 21 ... ♗c8 22 ♕c3+-] 22 ♕c3 b6 23 ♗f3 ♗d7 24 ♖fe1 ♖ac8 25 e5 ♘b7 26 d6 ♘xd6 27 exd6 ♕xd6 28 ♖ad1 ♖xe1+ 29 ♕xe1 ♕e6 30 ♕c3 [△ 31 ♘g4+-] 30 ... ♕e7 31 ♗b7 ♖e8 32 ♕xc7 ♗a4 33 ♖c1 ♔f8 34 ♕xe7+ ♖xe7 35 ♖c8+ ♔g7 36 ♗d5 h5 37 ♘e4 ♗e8 38 ♘d6 ♗a4 39 f5 ♖e1+ 40 ♔f2 ♖d1 **1-0**

L/N6123-1854

### 1853-⚔HL-21
**Löwenthal,J.J.=Harrwitz, D.**

London [Staunton]

1 e4 e5 2 ♘f3 d6 3 ♗c4 ♗e7 4 d4 exd4 5 ♘xd4 ♘f6 6 ♗d3 0-0 7 ♘c3 c5 8 ♘de2 ♗e6 9 ♘g3 ♘c6 10 0-0 [□ 10 f4] 10 ... d5! 11 exd5 ♘xd5 12 ♘xd5 ♕xd5 13 ♗e3 f5 14 f4 c4 15 ♗e2 ♗c5∓ 16 ♕c1 ♘b4? [□ 16 ... ♘d4→] 17 ♗f3 ♕d6 18 ♗xc5 ♕xc5+ 19 ♔h1 ♗d5 20 a3 ♘a6 [20 ... ♘c6 21 b4 cxb3 22 cxb3 ♕d6 23 ♖fd1 ♘e7 24 ♖xd5 ♘xd5 25 ♕c4 ♖ad8 26 ♖d1+-] 21 b4 cxb3 22 cxb3 ♗xf3 23 ♖xf3 ♖ac8 24 ♕b2 g6 25 ♘h5! ♕e7 [25 ... gxh5? 26 ♖g3+-] 26 ♖e3 ♕f7 27 ♖ae1 ♖c7 28 b4 h6 29 ♘g3? [□ 29 ♖e6!!+-

29 ... gxh5 30 Rxh6 Qg7 31 Qb3+ Rcf7 32 Rxh5 Qf6 (32 ... Qd4 33 Rxf5 Nc7 34 h3+-; 33 ... Qd2 34 Rg5+ Kh8 35 Rd1 Qxf4 (35 ... Re8 36 Rh5+ Kg8 37 Qg3++-) 36 Qh3+ Rh7 37 Qc3++-) 33 Re5 Qc6 34 Rg5+ Kh8 35 Qb2 Rf6 (35 ... Qf6 (35 ... Kh7 36 Rexf5+-) 36 Rgxf5+-) 36 Rexf5+-] 29 ... Rd7 30 Nf1 Nc7 31 Re5 Nd5 32 Qf2 b6 33 h3 Nf6 34 Qh4? Ne4 35 Rc1 [35 Qxh6? Qf6-+] 35 ... g5! 36 Qe1 [36 Qxh6?? Rd6-+] 36 ... Qg7 37 Qe3? Rd3! 38 Qe2? gxf4 39 Re6 Rd2 40 Qxd2 [40 Qf3 Rf2; 40 Nxd2 Ng3+] 40 ... Nxd2 41 Nxd2 Qd7 42 Rg6+ Kh7 43 Nf3 Rc8 [43 ... Kxg6? 44 Ne5++-] 44 Re1 Re8 45 Rxe8 Qxe8 46 Rd6 Kg7 47 Kh2 Qa4? [⊡ 47 ... Qb5! △ ... Qa6-+] 48 Rd3= Kf7 49 Ng1! Qa6 50 Rf3 Qc8 51 h4 Kf6 52 Nh3 Ke5 53 Nf2 Qc7 54 Nd3+ Ke4 55 Nf2+ Ke5 56 Nd3+= ½-½

L/N6123-1854

## 1853-⚔HL-22
## Harrwitz,D.=Löwenthal, J.J.

London [Staunton]

1 e4 e5 2 Nf3 Nf6 3 Nc3 Nc6 4 Bc4 Bc5 5 d3 d6 6 Bg5 h6 7 Bh4 g5 8 Bg3 a6 9 Ne2 Bg4 10 c3 Qe7 11 b4 Bb6 12 Nd2 Nh5 13 f3 Bd7 14 Bf2 Bxf2+ 15 Kxf2 Qf6∓ 16 Nf1 Ne7 17 Ne3 g4 18 Ng3 Nf4 19 Rf1 h5 20 Kg1 h4 21 Ne2 g3 22 h3 Nxe2+ 23 Qxe2 Ng6 24 Nd5 Qd8 25 Qe3 Be6? [⊡ 25 ... c6 26 Nb6 Bxh3 27 Nxa8 Bxg2 28 Kxg2 (28 Qb6 Qxb6-+; 28 ... Qxa8-+; 28 Nc7+ Kd7-+) 28 ... Nf4+ 29 Kg1 h3-+] 26 f4 Bxd5 27 exd5 Kf8 28 fxe5 dxe5? [⊡ 28 ... Nxe5] 29 d6 Rh7 30 Bxf7!+- Rxf7 31 Qh6+ Kg8 32 Qxg6+ Rg7 33 Qe6+ Kh8 34 Rf5 Qxd6 35 Rh5+ Rh7 36 Rxh7+ Kxh7 37 Qf7+ Kh8 38 Qh5+ Kg7 39 Qg5+ Qg6 40 Qxe5+ Kh6 41 Qf4+? [⊡ 41 Rf1] 41 ... Qg5 42 Qxc7 Qe3+ 43 Kh1 Re8 44 Qd6+ Kh7 45 Qd7+ Kh6 46 Qd6+ Kh7 47 Qd7+ Kh6 48 Qd6+ ½-½ L/N6123-1854

## 1853-⚔HL-23
## Löwenthal,J.J.=Harrwitz, D.

London [Staunton]

1 e4 c5 2 Nf3 e6 3 d4 cxd4 4 Nxd4 Nc6 5 Be3 Nf6 6 Nxc6 bxc6 7 Bd3 d5 8 e5 Nd7 9 Bf4 g6 10 0-0 Bg7 11 Re1 0-0 12 Nd2 f6 13 exf6 Qxf6 14 Bg3 e5 15 f3 Qg5∓ 16 Nf1 Nc5? 17 c3 Bf5 18 Bxf5 Rxf5 19 h4? [19 b4! Nd7; 19 ... Ne6 20 b5±] 19 ... Qe7 20 b4 Ne6 21 Qb3 h5 22 Rad1 Rb8 23 Ne3 Rf7 24 Qc2 Kh7 25 Kh2 Nf4 26 a4 a6 27 Nf1? Qf6 28 Qd2 Bf8 29 Bf2 Bh6 30 Qc2 Rbf8 31 Bg3 Kh8 32 Kh1 g5 33 Qf2 Rg8 34 hxg5 Qxg5 35 Bh2 h4 36 Ne3 Nh5 37 Ng4 Qxg4 38 fxg4 Rxf2 39 gxh5 Bf4 [⊡ 39 ... e4] 40 Bxf4 exf4 41 Rd4 Rgxg2 42 Rxf4 Rh2+ 43 Kg1 Rfg2+ 44 Kf1 h3 [⊡ 44 ... Rg6] 45 Re8+ Kg7 46 h6+! Kxh6 47 Rh4+ Kg5 48 Rxh3 Rxh3 49 Kxg2 Rxc3 50 b5! axb5 51 axb5 cxb5 52 Re5+ Kf4 53 Rxd5 Rb3 54 Kf2 Rb2+ 55 Ke1 Ke4 56 Rd8 Rb4 57 Kd1 Rc4 58 Rh8 Kd4 59 Rh5 Rc5 60 Rxc5 Kxc5 61 Kc1 ½-½ L/N6123-1854

## 1853-⚔HL-24
## Harrwitz,D.+Löwenthal, J.J.

London [Staunton]

1 d4 d5 2 c4 dxc4 3 e4 e5 4 d5 f5 5 Nc3 Nf6 6 Bg5 Bd6 7 Bxc4 0-0 8 Nf3 h6 9 Bxf6 Qxf6 10 Qe2 Nd7 11 exf5 Qxf5 12 Bd3 Qh5 13 Ne4 [13 Qe4? Nf6] 13 ... Nc5 14 Nxc5 Bxc5 15 0-0 Bg4 16 Be4 Rf4∓ 17 Rac1 Bd6? [⊡ 17 ... Bb6] 18 h3 Raf8??+- 19 hxg4 Qxg4 20 Rfe1 Bb4 21 Nh2 Qg5 22 Rf1 Rxf2 23 Rxf2 Qxc1+ 24 Rf1 Rxf1+ 25 Nxf1 Bc5+ 26 Kh2 Bd4 27 b3 Qg5 28 g3 Kf8 29 Qf3+ Ke7 30 Qf5 Qxf5 31 Bxf5 c6 32 dxc6 bxc6 33 Nd2 g5 34 Kh3 h5 35 Bg6 h4 36 gxh4 gxh4 37 Kxh4 Kd6 38 Kg4 Kc5 39 Kf5 Kb4 40 Nc4 c5 41 Bf7 a5 42 Nb6 Ka3 43 Bc4 Bc3 44 Nd5 Bb4 45 Nxb4 cxb4 46 Bb5 **1-0** L/N6123-1854

## 1853-⚔HL-25
## Löwenthal,J.J.=Harrwitz, D.

London [Staunton]

1 e4 e5 2 Nf3 d6 3 d4 exd4 4 Qxd4 Nc6 5 Bb5 Bd7 6 Bxc6 [6 Qd1] 6 ... Bxc6 7 Bg5 f6 8 Bh4 Nh6 9 Nc3 Be7 10 0-0 0-0 11 Qc4+?! Kh8 12 Nd4 Bd7 13 Rad1± c6 14 Ne6? [⊡ 14 Bg3] 14 ... Bxe6 15 Qxe6 Nf7 16 Ne2 Qe8 17 Qb3 [⊡ 17 Bg3; 17 Nd4] 17 ... f5! 18 Bg3 fxe4 19 Qxb7 Rb8 20 Qxa7 Rxb2 21 Rfe1 d5 [21 ... Rxc2?] 22 Nd4 Bf6 23 c3 [⊡ 23 Rb1 Bxd4 (23 ... Rxb1 24 Rxb1 Be5 25 Bxe5 Nxe5 26 Rb7±) 24 Qxd4 Rxa2 (24 ... Rxc2 25 Rb8 Qe7 26 Qa7+-) 25 Rb8 Qe7 26 Reb1±] 23 ... Bxd4 24 Rxd4 Nh6 25 Qa3± Rb7 26 Bd6 Rf6 27 Ra4 Ng8 28 Ra8 Qe6 29 Bc5 h5 30 Bd4 Rg6 31 Qf8 Kh7 32 Re8 Qf7 33 Qxf7 Rxf7 34 Rb1 Rd6 35 Rbb8 Nh6 36 Bc5 Rdd7 37 a4 Nf5 38 a5 d4 39 cxd4 Nxd4 40 h3! Nb5 41 Rxe4 Rd1+ 42 Kh2 Ra1 43 Bb6 Rf5 44 g4 hxg4 45 hxg4 Rf3 46 Kg2 Rc3 47 Re5? [⊡ 47 Rb7 Nd6 48 Rxg7+ Kxg7 49 Bd4+ Kg8 50 Bxc3 Rxa5 51 Re6 Rd5 52 Bb4+-] 47 ... Ra4 48 f3 Ra2+ 49 Kg3 Nd6 50 Re7 Ra4 51 Rd8 [⊡ 51 Rf8] 51 ... Ne4+ 52 Kh4 Nf6 53 Rd4 Raa3 54 g5 Nd5 55 Rxd5?! cxd5 56 Bd4 Rc4 57 Kh5 [△ 58 g6+, 59 Re8#] 57 ... Kg8 58 Bxg7 Rxf3 59 Kg6 Rc8 60 Bf6 Kf8 61 a6 Ra3 62 a7 d4 63 Rb7 Ke8 64 Bxd4 Ra5 65 Bf6 Ra6

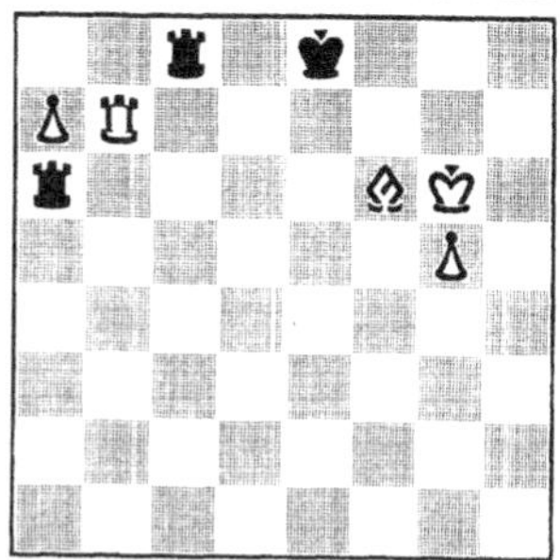

66 Kg7?? [66 Kh7+-] 66 ... Rxa7= [△ 67 Rxa7 Rc7+! 68 Rxc7◊; 68 K~ Rxa7=] ½-½ L/N6123-1854

## 1853-⚔HL-26
## Harrwitz,D.−Löwenthal, J.J.

London [Staunton]

1 e4 e5 2 Nf3 Nf6 3 Nc3 [⊡ 3 Nxe5] 3 ... Bb4! 4 Bc4 d6 5 0-0 0-0 6 d3 Bxc3 7 bxc3 h6 8 h3 Nc6 9 Nh2 d5 10 exd5 Nxd5 11 Qe1 Re8 12 Bd2 Bf5 13 f3 Qd6 14 g4 Be6 15 Qf2 Nf4 16 Bxf4 exf4∓ 17 Bb3 a5 18 Rfe1 a4 19 Bxe6 Rxe6 20 a3 Rxe1+ 21 Qxe1 Kf8! 22 Nf1 Re8 23 Qf2 Qe5 24 d4 Qe2 25 Rb1 Qc4 26 Qd2 Re2 27 Qd1 b6 28 Nd2 Qa6 29 Ne4 Re3 30 Kf2 Qc4 31 Qd2 Qd5 32 Re1 Na5! 33 Qc1 Nc4 34 Qb1??

34 ... ♖xf3+ 35 ♔g2 ♖e3 **0-1**
L/N6123-1854

**1853-✕HL-27**
**Löwenthal,J.J.=Harrwitz, D.**
London [Staunton]

1 d4 d5 2 c4 e6 3 ♘c3 ♘f6 4 a3 c5 5 e3 ♘c6 6 ♘f3 a6 7 b3 b6 8 ♗b2 cxd4 9 exd4 ♗d6 10 ♖c1 0-0 11 ♗d3 [11 cxd5 exd5 12 ♘xd5?? ♘xd5 13 ♖xc6 ♕e8+–+] 11 ... ♖a7 12 0-0 dxc4 13 bxc4 ♖d7 14 ♕e2 ♖e8 15 ♘e4± ♘e7 [15 ... ♘xe4?? 16 ♕xe4+–] 16 ♘xf6+ gxf6 17 ♘h4?! [□ 17 g3] 17 ... ♘g6 18 ♘xg6? [□ 18 ♕h5] 18 ... fxg6 19 ♗e4? f5 20 ♗c2 [20 ♗c6? ♗xh2+ 21 ♔xh2 ♕c7+ 22 ♕e5 ♕xc6 23 d5 ♕d6–+] 20 ... ♖c7 21 ♗a4 ♗d7 22 ♗xd7 ♕xd7 23 g3 ♕c6 24 ♖fe1 [△ 25 d5] 24 ... ♕b7 25 c5 bxc5 26 dxc5 ♗f8 27 c6 ♕b5 28 ♕xb5?± [28 ♕e5! ♕xe5 29 ♗xe5 ♖cc8 30 ♖ed1 ♗xa3 (30 ... ♗g7 31 ♗xg7 ♔xg7 32 ♖d7+ ♔g8 33 c7+–; 30 ... ♖ed8 31 ♖xd8 ♖xd8 32 c7 △ 33 ♖b1+–) 31 ♖a1 ♗f8 32 ♖xa6+–] 28 ... axb5 29 ♗e5 ♖cc8 30 ♖e3 ♖ed8 31 ♗b8? ♖d5 32 ♗a7 e5 33 ♖b3 ♔f7= 34 c7 ♗d6 35 ♗b6 ♔e7 36 ♖bc3 ♔d7 37 ♔f1 g5 38 h3 h5 39 ♔e2 e4 40 h4 g4 41 ♖1c2 **½-½**
L/N6123-1854

**1853-✕HL-28**
**Harrwitz,D.+Löwenthal, J.J.**
London [Staunton]

1 d4 d5 2 c4 dxc4 3 ♘c3 ♘f6 4 e4 e5 5 d5 ♗d6 6 ♗xc4 h6 7 ♘f3 0-0 8 h3 a6 9 0-0 b5 10 ♗d3 c6 11 dxc6 ♘xc6 12 ♘e2 ♘e7 13 ♘g3 ♗e6 14 ♘h4 g5?! 15 ♘hf5 ♘xf5 16 exf5 ♗d5 17 ♘h5 e4 18 ♗c2 ♘xh5 19 ♕xh5 ♕f6 20 ♖d1+– ♗c6 21 ♗xg5 [□ 21 ♖xd6! ♕xd6 22 ♗xg5+–] 21 ... ♕xg5 22 ♕xg5+ hxg5 23 ♖xd6 ♖ac8 24 ♖ae1 ♖fe8 25 ♖e3 ♔g7 26 ♗b3 ♖ed8 27 ♖xd8 ♖xd8 28 ♖c3 ♗d5 29 g4 b4 30 ♖e3 ♗c6= 31 ♗c4 ♖d1+ 32 ♔h2 a5 33 a3 ♖c1! 34 ♗a6 ♖c2 35 ♖e2 b3∓ 36 ♔g3 ♗b7 37 ♗b5 ♗c6 38 ♗a6 a4 39 h4 gxh4+ 40 ♔xh4 e3?? [40 ... ♔f6! 41 ♔h3 (41 ♔g3 ♔g5) 41 ... ♔e5 42 ♔g3 (42 f3 ♖xe2 43 ♗xe2 exf3–+) 42 ... ♔d4 43 g5 ♗b7 44 ♗b5 ♔c5–+] 41 ♔g3! ♗b7 42 ♗d3 ♖d2 43 ♖xe3 ♖xb2 44 g5 ♗c6 45 f6+ ♔f8 46 ♗e4 ♗b5 47 ♖c3 ♗d7 48 ♖d3 ♖e2 49 ♔f3 ♗g4+ 50 ♔f4 ♖xe4+ 51 ♔xe4 ♔e8 52 ♖d4 ♗d7 53 f4 ♗e6 54 ♖xa4 **1-0**
L/N6123-1854

**1853-✕HL-29**
**Löwenthal,J.J.–Harrwitz, D.**
London [Staunton]

1 e4 e5 2 ♘f3 d6 3 d4 exd4 4 ♕xd4 ♘c6 5 ♗b5 ♗d7 6 ♗xc6 ♗xc6 7 ♗g5 f6 8 ♗h4 ♘e7 9 0-0 ♘g6 10 ♗g3 ♕d7 11 ♘c3 h5 12 h3 h4 13 ♗h2 ♘e5 14 ♘d2 [△ 15 f4] 14 ... g5 15 f3 b6 16 ♗xe5 fxe5 17 ♕d3 0-0-0 18 ♘c4? [□ 18 ♘d5±] 18 ... ♗b7 19 ♖fd1 c6 20 a4 ♕e6 21 ♘e3 ♖h7 22 ♘e2? [□ 22 ♖d2 △ 23 ♖ad1] 22 ... ♖hd7 23 c4 d5∓ 24 cxd5 cxd5 25 ♖dc1+ ♔b8 26 exd5 ♗xd5 27 ♘xd5 [□ 27 ♕b5] 27 ... ♖xd5 28 ♕e4 ♗c5+ 29 ♔h2 a5 30 f4? g4 31 hxg4 ♕xg4 32 ♖c2 exf4 33 ♖f1 ♗d6 34 ♖f3 [34 ♕xd5 f3+–+] 34 ... ♗c7 35 ♖xc7! ♔xc7 36 ♘xf4? [□ 36 ♖xf4=] 36 ... ♔b8 37 ♖b3 ♔a7 38 ♕e3 ♖5d6 39 ♖c3 ♖c8 40 ♖b3 ♖c4 41 ♘h3 ♖g6 42 ♕d2 ♖xa4 43 ♖d3 ♖g7 44 ♖f3

44 ... ♕g3+ 45 ♔h1 [45 ♖xg3 hxg3+ 46 ♔h1 ♖a1+ 47 ♕~1 ♖x~1+ 48 ♘g1 ♖h7#] 45 ... ♖a1+ 46 ♘g1 ♖xg1+ 47 ♔xg1 ♕xf3 **0-1** L/N6123-1854

**1853-✕HL-30**
**Harrwitz,D.=Löwenthal, J.J.**
London [Staunton]

1 e4 e5 2 ♘f3 ♘f6 3 ♘xe5 d6 4 ♘f3 ♘xe4 5 d4 d5 6 ♗d3 ♗d6 7 0-0 0-0 8 c4 ♘f6 9 ♘c3 dxc4 10 ♗xc4 ♘c6 11 h3 h6 12 ♗e3 ♗f5 13 ♘h4 ♗h7 14 f4 ♘e4 15 ♘f3 ♘g3 16 ♖f2 ♘e7 17 ♕d2 ♗b4 18 ♗d3 ♗xd3 19 ♕xd3 ♘ef5? 20 ♖e1 c6 21 ♘e5 ♘d6 22 ♗d2 ♘gf5 23 g4 ♘e7 24 f5 f6 25 ♘f3 ♕d7 26 ♖fe2 ♖ae8 [□ 26 ... ♖fe8] 27 ♘h4 ♗xc3 28 bxc3 ♘b5 29 ♘g2? ♘c8 30 ♘f4 ♖xe2 31 ♖xe2 ♘cd6 32 ♘e6 ♖c8 33 ♗f4 ♘e8 34 ♘c5 ♕f7 35 c4 ♘bd6 36 ♖e6 ♖d8 37 d5 cxd5 38 ♕xd5 b6 39 ♗xd6 bxc5 40 ♕xc5 ♘xd6 41 ♖xd6 ♖xd6 42 ♕xd6 ♕xc4 43 ♕b8+ ♔h7 44 ♕xa7 ♕c1+ 45 ♔g2 ♕c6+= [45 ... ♕c2+; 45 ... ♕d2+ 46 ♕f2+–] **½-½**
L/N6123-1854

**1853-✕HL-31**
**Löwenthal,J.J.–Harrwitz, D.**
London [Staunton]

1 e4 c5 2 ♗c4 e6 3 ♘c3 a6 4 a4 ♘c6 5 d3 g6 6 f4 ♘ge7 7 ♘f3 d5 8 ♗a2 ♗g7 9 ♗d2 ♘d4 10 0-0 0-0 11 a5 dxe4 12 dxe4 ♗d7 13 e5 ♗c6 14 ♘g5 ♕c7 15 ♗c4 ♖ad8 16 ♖c1 ♘d5 17 ♗xd5 exd5 18 ♖e1 ♖fe8 19 ♕g4? h6 20 ♘f3 ♘xf3+ 21 ♕xf3 ♔h7? 22 ♕f2 d4 23 ♘e4 ♗xe4 24 ♖xe4 ♕c8 25 ♖ce1 ♖d5 26 h3 h5 27 c4 dxc3 28 ♗xc3 ♔g8 29 ♕f3 c4 30 ♖d4 [□ 30 e6!±] 30 ... ♖xd4 31 ♗xd4 ♖d8 32 ♕e4 ♕e6 33 ♗b6 ♖d7 34 ♖c1 g5 35 ♖xc4 ♖d1+ 36 ♔f2? [□ 36 ♔h2+–] 36 ... gxf4 37 ♖d4 ♖xd4 38 ♗xd4= f6 39 ♕g6 ♕d7 40 ♗c3 fxe5 41 ♗xe5?? ♕d2+ 42 ♔f1 ♕c1+ 43 ♔e2 ♕e3+ **0-1** L/N6123-1854

## LASA✕STAUNTON Bruxelles
**[1853-✕LS]**

| | | |
|---|---|---|
| T. von H.u. von d. Lasa | 1 0 1 ½ 0 1 ½ 1 1 0 ½ 0 Φ | 6½ |
| H. Staunton | 0 1 0 ½ 1 0 ½ 0 0 1 ½ 1 Φ | 5½ |

**16** Lasa, T. von H.u.von d. M1647 . BL

**1853-✕LS-1**
**Staunton,H.–Lasa,T. von H.u. von d.**
[Staunton]

1 e4 e5 2 ♘f3 ♘c6 3 ♗c4 ♘f6 4 ♘c3 [4 ♘g5?! d5 5 exd5 ♘a5 6 ♗b5+ c6 7 dxc6 bxc6] 4 ... ♗b4 5 0-0 0-0 6 d3 d6 7

♗g5 ♗xc3 8 bxc3 ♗e6 9 ♗b3 a5 10 a4 h6 11 ♗h4 ♗xb3 12 cxb3 ♕e7 13 ♘e1 g5 14 ♗g3 ♖ad8 15 h4 d5 16 hxg5 hxg5 17 ♕f3 d4! 18 c4 ♔g7 19 ♕f5 ♘h5 20 ♘f3 f6 21 ♕g4 ♖h8 22 ♘h4 ♔f7! 23 ♘f5 ♕e6 24 ♗h2 ♖dg8 25 ♕d1 ♘f4 26 g3 ♘h3+ 27 ♔g2 ♘e7 28 g4 ♖h7 29 ♖h1 ♖gh8 30 ♕d2 ♕b6 31 ♕c2 ♘g6−+ 32 ♔f3 ♘hf4 33 c5 ♕a6 34 ♗xf4 ♖xh1 35 ♖xh1 ♖xh1 36 ♗d2 ♘f4 37 ♗xf4 gxf4 38 ♔g2 ♖h7 39 b4 axb4 40 ♕b3+ ♕e6 41 ♕xb4 ♔g6 42 ♕xb7 ♔g5 43 a5 [□ 43 ♕f3 ♖h3+ 44 ♔g2 ♔xg4 45 f3+ ♖xf3 46 ♘h6+ ♔g5 47 ♔xf3 ♔xh6∓] 43 ... ♔xg4 44 a6 f3+ 45 ♔g1 ♕a2 46 ♘e3+ dxe3 47 ♕c8+ ♔h4 **0-1** L/N6123

**1853-⚔LS-2**
**Lasa,T.von H.u.von d.− Staunton, H.**

[Staunton]

1 e4 e5 2 d4 exd4 3 ♗c4 ♘f6 4 e5 d5 5 ♗b3 ♘e4 6 ♘e2 c5 7 0-0 ♘c6 8 f3 ♘g5 9 ♘f4 c4 10 ♗a4 ♗c5 11 ♔h1 ♘e6 12 b4 ♗b6 [12 ... ♗xb4 13 ♘xe6 Δ 14 ♕xd4] 13 ♘xe6 ♗xe6 14 f4 ♗f5 15 ♗a3 0-0 16 ♘d2 d3 17 b5 ♘e7 [□ 17 ... ♘d4 18 ♗xf8 ♘e2 (Δ 19 ... ♕h4) 19 ♕e1! ♕xf8 20 cxd3 cxd3 21 ♗d1 ♗d4 22 ♖b1 ♕a3] 18 cxd3 ♗xd3 19 ♖f3 ♖e8 20 ♗c2 ♗xc2 21 ♕xc2 ♘g6 22 ♖d1 [Δ 23 ♘xc4] 22 ... ♕c8 23 ♗b2 ♕c5 24 ♘b1 ♖ad8 25 ♘a3 ♕e7 26 ♖h3 h6 27 ♖f1 ♕c5 28 e6!! ♖d6! [28 ... ♘xf4 (28 ... fxe6?? 29 ♕xg6; 28 ... ♖xe6?? 29 f5) 29 exf7+ ♔xf7 30 ♖xf4+±] 29 ♕c3 f6 30 ♖g3 ♖dxe6 31 ♘c2 [31 ♖xg6 ♕f2−+] 31 ... ♘xf4 32 ♕f3 ♕c7 33 ♖g4 g5 34 g3 h5 35 ♖xf4 gxf4 36 ♕xh5 ♕h7 37 ♕g4+ ♔f7 38 ♕xf4 ♕xc2 39 ♗xf6 ♕e4+ **0-1** L/N6123

**1853-⚔LS-3**
**Staunton,H.−Lasa,T.von H. u. von d.**

[Staunton]

1 e4 e5 2 ♘f3 ♘c6 3 d4 exd4 4 ♗c4 ♗c5 5 0-0? [□ 5 c3] 5 ... d6 6 c3 dxc3 7 ♘xc3 ♘ge7 8 ♘d5 0-0 9 h3 h6 10 ♘f4 ♔h8 11 ♘d3 ♗b6 12 b4 ♘g6 13 ♗b2 ♗e6 14 ♗b5 [Δ 15 ♗xc6 bxc6 16 ♕c1] 14 ... ♘ce7 15 ♕d2?! ♔h7 16 ♕c3 f6 17 ♘d4?! ♗xd4 18 ♕xd4 d5 19 ♘c5 ♕c8 20 exd5 ♗xd5 21 ♖ae1 [□ 21 ♖fe1] 21 ... c6 22 ♗d3 ♖f7 23 ♗b1 f5 24 ♖e3 ♕c7 25 ♖fe1 ♖d8 26 ♕c3 ♘f4 27 ♕e5! ♕xe5 28 ♖xe5 ♘fg6! 29 ♖5e3

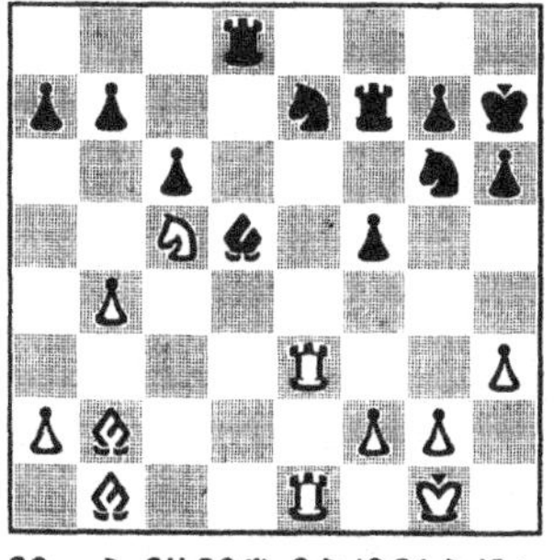

29 ... ♘c8!! 30 ♖g3 ♘d6 31 ♘d3 [Δ 32 ♖xg6 ♔xg6 33 ♘e5+] 31 ... ♘c4 32 ♘e5 ♘gxe5 33 ♗xe5 ♘xe5 34 ♖xe5 g6 35 ♖d3 ♔g7 36 g4?? fxg4 37 hxg4 ♖df8 38 ♖d2 ♖f4 39 ♖e7+ ♖8f7 40 ♖xf7+ ♔xf7 41 ♔h2 ♖xb4 42 ♗c2 ♖xg4 **0-1** L/N6123

**1853-⚔LS-4**
**Lasa,T.von H.u.von d.= Staunton, H.**

[?]

1 e4 e5 2 f4 exf4 3 ♘f3 g5 4 h4 g4 5 ♘e5 d6 6 ♘xg4 ♗e7 7 d4 ♗xh4+ 8 ♘f2 ♕g5 9 ♕f3 ♗g3 10 ♘c3 ♘f6 11 ♘e2 [11 ♗d2 Bilguer] 11 ... ♗g4 12 ♗xf4 ♗xf3 13 ♗xg5 ♗xf2+ 14 ♔xf2 ♘xe4+ 15 ♔e3! [15 ♔xf3] 15 ... ♘xg5 16 gxf3 ♘d7 17 f4 ♘e6 18 d5 ♘g7 19 ♘d4 0-0-0 20 ♖h3 ♔b8 21 ♗d3 ♘e8 22 c4 ♘ef6 23 ♔f3 ♖dg8 24 ♖ah1 [□ 24 ♗f5 ♖g7 25 ♖e1 ♖hg8 26 ♖e7] 24 ... ♖g7 25 ♗e4 ♖hg8 26 ♘e2 ♖h8 27 ♘d4 ♖hg8 28 ♘e2 ♖h8 29 ♘d4 [□ 29 ♘g3 ♖hg8 30 ♖1h2] **½-½** L/N6047

**1853-⚔LS-5**
**Staunton,H.+Lasa,T. von H u. von d.**

[Staunton]

1 e4 e5 2 ♘f3 ♘c6 3 ♗b5 ♘f6 4 ♕e2 [□ 4 0-0] 4 ... a6 5 ♗a4 b5 6 ♗b3 ♗c5 7 c3 0-0 8 d3 d6 9 ♗g5 ♗e6 10 ♘bd2 ♕e7?! 11 ♗d5 ♗d7 [11 ... ♗xd5?!] 12 ♘h4 ♖ab8 13 ♘f5 ♕d8 [13 ... ♗xf5?!] 14 b4 ♗b6 15 ♕f3?! ♗xf5 16 exf5 ♘e7 17 ♗b3 d5 18 ♗xf6 gxf6 19 0-0 ♕d7 20 g4 ♔h8 21 ♔h1 c6 22 ♖g1 ♖g8 23 ♘f1 a5 24 a3 ♕d6 25 ♘g3 ♗c7 26 ♖g2 ♖a8 27 ♘h5 axb4 28 cxb4 h6? [□ 28 ... e4 29 dxe4 (29 ♕e3 ♘xf5−+) 29 ... ♕e5 30 ♖a2 dxe4 31 ♕g3 ♘d5∓] 29 ♕e3 ♔h7 30 ♕c5 ♖gd8 [30 ... ♕xc5 31 ♘xf6+] 31 ♕c1 ♗b6 32 ♖a2 ♖a6 33 ♖g3 ♗d4 34 ♖h3 ♘g8 35 ♘g3 ♔g7 36 ♘h5+ ♔f8 37 f4 ♖e8 38 g5 exf4 39 gxh6 ♘xh6 [39 ... ♗e3? 40 ♖xe3 Δ 41 h7] 40 ♘xf4 ♘xf5 41 ♖h8+ ♔e7 42 ♖e2+ ♗e5 43 ♘xd5+ ♕xd5+ [□ 43 ... ♔d7 (43 ... cxd5?)] 44 ♗xd5 ♖xh8 45 ♕f4! cxd5 46 ♖xe5+ fxe5 47 ♕xe5+ ♔d7 48 ♕xh8 ♖xa3 49 ♕e5 ♘d6 50 ♕xd5 ♖a4 51 ♕d4 ♔e6 52 h4 ♖a6 53 ♔h2 ♘f5 54 ♕c5 ♘d6 55 ♔h3 ♖a3 56 ♕e3+ ♔f5 57 ♕f2+ ♔e6 58 ♕e2+ ♔f5 59 ♕f1+ ♔e6 60 ♕e2+ ♔f5 61 h5 ♘c4 62 ♕f3+ ♔g5 63 ♕g4+ ♔f6 64 ♕f3+ ♔g5 65 ♕xf7 ♖xd3+ 66 ♔g2 ♖d2+ 67 ♔f1 ♖d6 68 ♕e8 ♖f6+ 69 ♔e2 ♖b6 70 ♔d3 ♖d6+ 71 ♔c3 ♖b6 72 ♔d4 ♖d6+ 73 ♔c5 ♖f6 74 ♕xb5 ♘d6 [74 ... ♖f5+ 75 ♔xc4 ♖xb5 76 ♔xb5+−] 75 ♕b8 ♘e4+ 76 ♔d4 ♘d6 77 ♔d5 ♘f7 78 b5 ♔xh5 79 b6 **1-0** L/N6123

**1853-⚔LS-6**
**Lasa,T.von H u.von d.+ Staunton, H.**

[Staunton]

1 e4 e5 2 f4 exf4 3 ♘f3 g5 4 h4 g4 5 ♘e5 d6 6 ♘xg4 ♗e7 7 ♘f2 ♗xh4 8 d4 ♕g5 9 ♕f3 ♗g3 10 ♘c3 ♘f6 11 ♗d2 ♗d7 12 0-0-0 ♘c6 13 ♘e2 ♗xf2 14 ♗xf4 ♕a5∓ 15 ♕xf2 ♕xa2 16 ♘c3 ♕a1+ 17 ♘b1 0-0-0 18 ♗d3 ♘g4 19 ♕g1 ♖de8 20 d5 ♘b4 21 ♕d4 ♕a4 22 ♕g1 ♗b5? [□ 22 ... f5] 23 ♘c3 ♘xd3+? [□ 23 ... ♘a2+ 24 ♔d2 ♘xc3 25 bxc3 ♗xd3∓] 24 cxd3 ♕a1+ [□ 24 ... ♕a6] 25 ♔c2 ♕a6 26 ♖a1 ♗xd3+ 27 ♔d2 ♕c4 28 ♖a4 ♕c5 29 ♔xd3 ♘f2+ 30 ♔d2 ♕b6 [30 ... ♘xh1 31 ♗e3] 31 ♔c2 ♘xh1 32 ♗e3 c5 33 dxc6 ♕xc6 34 ♕xh1 a6 35 ♔d3 b5 [□ 35 ... ♔b8] 36 ♖d4 ♖e6 37 ♕h5+− ♖g6 38 ♘d5 ♕e8 39 ♘f4 ♖f6 40 ♕d5 ♔c7 41 ♕g5 ♖e6 42 ♘xe6+ fxe6 43 ♕g7+ ♔c6 44 ♕a7 ♕c8 45 ♔d2 [Δ 36 ♖d3] 45 ... ♕a8 46 ♕e7 ♕d8 47 ♕xe6 ♕a5+ 48 b4 ♕c7 49 ♗f4 ♖d8 50 ♕d5+ **1-0** L/N6123-1854

**1853-⚔LS-7**
**Staunton,H.=Lasa,T.von H. u. von d.**

[Staunton]

1 e4 e5 2 ♘f3 ♘c6 3 ♗b5 ♘f6 4 ♕e2 a6 5 ♗a4 b5 6 ♗b3 ♗c5 7 c3 0-0 8 d3 d6 9 ♗g5 ♗e6 10 ♘bd2 h6 11 ♗h4 ♖e8 12 0-0 ♖a7? 13 ♗d5 ♘b8 14 b4 ♗b6 15 a4 c6 16 ♗xe6 ♖xe6 17 a5 ♗c7 18 d4 g5 19 ♗g3 [19 ♘xg5?!] 19 ... ♘bd7 20 ♖ad1? [□ 20 h4±] 20 ... ♘h5 21 h4 ♘f4 22 ♕e3 ♗b8! 23 hxg5 hxg5 24 dxe5 dxe5 25 ♘b3 ♕e7 26 ♖d2 ♖c7 27 ♖fd1 ♗a7 28 ♕e1 ♖h6? 29 ♘h2 f6? 30 ♘g4 ♖g6 31 ♘e3 ♗xe3 32 ♕xe3 [32 fxe3 ♖h6 (□ 32 ... ♘e6) 33 exf4 ♕h7 34 ♕e2 ♖h1+ 35 ♔f2 ♖xd1 36 ♕xd1 exf4 37 ♗xf4 gxf4 38 ♕g4+−] 32 ... ♖g7 33 ♖d6 ♘d5 34 ♖6xd5 cxd5 35 exd5 ♖c8 [□ 35 ...

♕d6] 36 ♘c5! ♘xc5 37 d6 ♕a7 38 bxc5 ♖xc5 39 d7 ♖xd7 40 ♖xd7 ♕xd7 41 ♕xc5 ♕d1+ 42 ♔h2 ♕h5+ 43 ♔g1 ♕d1+ ½-½
L/N6123

**1853-⚔LS-8**
**Lasa,T.von H.u.von d.+Staunton, H.**
[Anderssen & Kossak]

1 e4 e5 2 f4 d5 3 exd5 e4 4 c4 [4 ♗b5+] 4 ... ♘f6 [□ 4 ... c6 5 d4] 5 d4 c6 6 dxc6 bxc6 7 ♘c3 ♗b4 8 ♗e3 0-0 9 ♘e2 ♘g4 10 ♕d2 f5 11 a3 ♗a5 12 0-0-0 ♘a6 13 ♗g1 [□ 13 h3] 13 ... ♕e7 14 d5 e3 15 ♕c2 cxd5 16 ♘xd5 ♗d2+ 17 ♔b1 ♕e8 18 ♘d4 ♗d7 [18 ... ♗e6 19 h3∓] 19 c5! ♘xc5 [19 ... ♗c8 20 ♗b5±] 20 ♕xc5 ♗a4 [20 ... ♕e4+ 21 ♕c2 (□ 21 ♔a1 ♖ac8 22 ♘e7+ ♔h8 23 ♘xc8 ♖xc8 24 ♕xa7) 21 ... ♕xd4 22 ♗xe3 ♘xe3 23 ♘xe3 ♕xe3 24 ♕xd2 ♕xd2 25 ♗c4+ ♔h8 26 ♖xd2] 21 b3 ♕e4+ 22 ♔b2 ♔h8 23 ♘c3 ♗xc3+ 24 ♕xc3 ♖fc8 25 ♕d3 **1-0** L/N6047-1854

**1853-⚔LS-9**
**Staunton,H.−Lasa,T.von H u. von d.**
[Staunton]

1 e4 e5 2 ♘f3 ♘c6 3 ♗b5 ♘f6 4 ♕e2 ♗d6? 5 c3 0-0 6 d3 h6 7 0-0 ♖e8 [6 0-0 ♖e8 7 d3 h6 L/N6047] 8 ♘h4 ♘e7 9 ♗c4 c6 10 ♕f3?! [□ 10 f4] 10 ... ♗c7 11 ♗xh6 d5 12 ♗b3 ♗g4 13 ♕g3 gxh6 14 h3?! [□ 14 f3] 14 ... ♔h7 15 hxg4 ♖g8 16 ♕f3 [□ 16 f3] 16 ... ♘xg4 17 ♕xf7+ ♖g7 18 ♕f3 [□ 18 ♕e6] 18 ... ♕d7 19 ♕e2 ♖f8 20 ♘d2 ♘g6 21 ♘xg6 ♖xg6 22 ♘f3 ♖gf6! 23 ♗d1 ♖xf3 24 gxf3 ♘h2−+ 25 ♔xh2 [25 f4 ♕h3 26 f3 ♖g8+−+] 25 ... ♖f4 26 ♖g1 ♖h4+ 27 ♔g2 ♕h3# **0-1** L/N6123

**1853-⚔LS-10**
**Lasa,T.von H.u.von d.−Staunton, H.**
[Staunton]

1 e4 e5 2 f4 exf4 3 ♘f3 g5 4 h4 g4 5 ♘e5 ♘f6 6 ♗c4 d5!? [6 ... ♕e7] 7 exd5 ♗d6 8 d4 ♘h5!∓

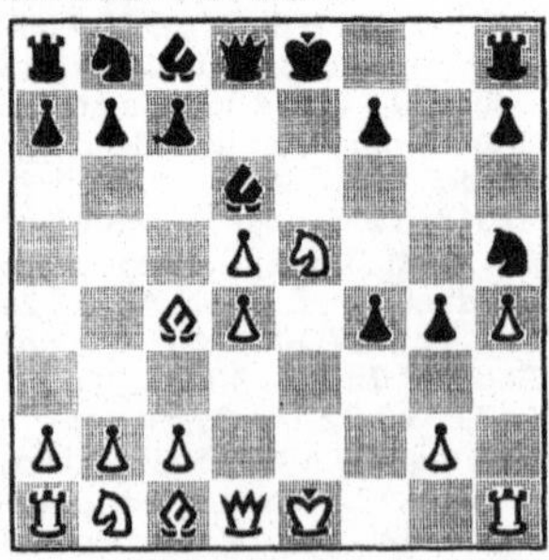

9 ♘xg4 ♘g3 10 ♖g1 ♕xh4 11 ♘f2 ♕e7+ [11 ... ♕h2 12 ♕d2] 12 ♗e2 0-0 13 ♘c3 ♖e8 14 ♘h1 ♘xe2 **0-1**
L/N6123

**1853-⚔LS-11**
**Staunton,H.=Lasa,T. von H.u. von d.**
[Staunton]

1 e4 e5 2 ♘f3 ♘c6 3 ♗b5 ♘f6 4 ♕e2 ♗d6? 5 c3 0-0 6 d3 ♖e8 7 ♗g5 h6 8 ♗h4 ♕e7 9 0-0 ♗c5 10 ♘bd2 a6 11 ♗a4 [□ 11 ♗xc6 △ 12 d4] 11 ... b5 12 ♗b3 ♗b7 13 ♗g3 g5 14 h4 ♘h5! 15 ♔h2 ♘f4 16 ♗xf4 exf4 17 d4 ♗b6 18 hxg5 hxg5 19 g3 [□ 19 ♘h4=] 19 ... g4 20 ♘h4 [□ 20 ♖h1 ♘d8! (20 ... gxf3?)] 20 ... ♕g5 21 ♕d3 ♘e7 22 ♖h1 ♔g7 23 ♔g1 f3 24 ♘hxf3? gxf3−+ 25 ♕xf3 f5 26 ♕d3 ♖h8 27 ♔g2 ♘g6 28 ♕e3 ♕xe3 29 fxe3 fxe4 30 ♖af1 d5 31 ♖xh8 ♖xh8 32 a4 ♗c8 33 ♖f2 c6 34 axb5 axb5 35 ♔g1 ♗c7 [□ 35 ... ♖f8] 36 ♘xe4 ♖e8 37 ♘g5 ♗xg3 38 ♖f7+ ♔h6 39 ♘f3 ♖xe3 40 ♔g2 ♗d6 41 ♔f2 ♖e7 42 ♖f6 ♖e6 43 ♖f7 ♗e7 44 ♗c2 ♗g5 45 ♖c7 [45 ♗f5 ♖e7] 45 ... ♘e7 46 ♔g3 ♖e2 47 ♗d3 ♖e3 48 ♗b1 ♗f5 [□ 48 ... ♔h5] 49 ♗xf5 ♘xf5+ 50 ♔g4 ♖e4+ 51 ♔xf5 ♖f4+ 52 ♔e5 ♖xf3 53 ♖xc6+ ♔g7 54 ♖b6 ♗c1 55 ♖xb5 ♖f2 56 b4 ♗b2 57 ♖c5 ♖f3 58 ♖c7+ ♔f8 59 b5 ♖xc3 60 b6 ♖d3 61 ♔xd5 ♖xd4+ 62 ♔e6 ♖e4+ 63 ♔d5 ♖e8 64 b7 ♗e5 65 ♖c8 ♗g3 66 ♖c3 ♗b8 67 ♖f3+ ♔e7 68 ♖e3+ ♔d7 69 ♖xe8 ½-½
L/N6123-1854

**1853-⚔LS-12**
**Lasa,T.von H.u.von d.−Staunton, H.**
[Staunton]

1 e4 c5 2 d4 cxd4 3 ♘f3 ♘c6 4 ♗c4 e6 5 ♘xd4 ♗c5 6 ♘b3?! ♗b6 7 0-0 ♘ge7 8 ♘c3 a6 [□ 8 ... 0-0] 9 ♗f4 e5 10 ♗e3 ♗xe3?! 11 fxe3 0-0 12 ♕h5 ♕e8! [12 ... ♘g6 13 ♖xf7 ♖xf7 14 ♖f1±] 13 a4 ♘g6 14 ♖ad1 ♕e7 15 ♘d5 ♕d8 16 a5 d6 [16 ... ♘xa5?? 17 ♘xa5 ♕xa5 18 ♘e7+ ♘xe7 19 ♖xf7+−] 17 h3 [17 ♘b6!? ♘xa5 18 ♖xf7 ♖xf7 19 ♗xf7+ ♔xf7 20 ♘xa8 (20 ♖f1+?) 20 ... ♘c4 (20 ... ♘xb3 21 ♕xh7! ♘c5 22 ♖f1++; 20 ... ♔g8 21 ♘xa5 ♕xa5 22 ♕g5 △ 23 b4+−) 21 ♕xh7 ♘xe3 22 ♖d2 ♘g4−+] 17 ... ♗e6 18 ♖a1 ♖c8 19 ♕e2 ♔h8 20 c3 ♘ce7 21 ♖ad1 f5 22 ♘b6 ♗xc4 23 ♘xc4 ♖c6 24 exf5 ♘xf5 25 g4 ♘g3 26 ♖xf8+ ♕xf8 27 ♕g2 ♖xc4 28 ♕xg3 ♕e7 29 ♕f3 ♖c8 30 ♘d2 ♖f8 31 ♕g3 h6 32 ♘c4 d5 33 ♘b6 [33 ♖xd5 ♕f7−+] 33 ... d4 34 exd4 exd4 35 ♖f1 [35 cxd4 ♘f4; 35 ♖xd4 ♕e2] 35 ... ♖d8 36 cxd4 ♖xd4 37 ♕c3 ♕d6 38 ♕a3 ♕d8 [38 ... ♕xa3 39 bxa3 ♖d3−+] 39 ♕e3 ♖d3 40 ♕e4 ♕d6 41 ♖f3 [□ 41 ♘c4 ♕g3+ 42 ♕g2 ♕h4 43 ♖f3 (43 ♔h2 ♕d8 △ 44 ... ♕c7+; 44 ... ♘h4) 43 ... ♘f4 44 ♖xf4 ♖g3−+] 41 ... ♕c5+ 42 ♔f1 ♕c1+ **0-1** L/N6123-1854

**1853-⚔LS-13**
**Staunton,H.⊕Lasa,T.von H. u. von d.**
[Anderssen & Kossak]

1 e4 e5 2 ♘f3 ♘c6 3 ♗b5 ♘f6 [3 ... a6 4 ♗xc6 (4 ♗a4 ♘f6) 4 ... dxc6=] 4 ♕e2 [4 0-0 ♘xe4 (4 ... ♗d6) 5 ♖e1 ♘f6 (□ 5 ... ♘d6) 6 ♘xe5 ♘xe5 (□ 6 ... ♗e7) 7 ♖xe5+ (□ 7 d4 △ 8 dxe5)] 4 ... a6 5 ♗a4 b5 6 ♗b3 ♗c5 7 c3 0-0 8 d3 ♗b7 9 0-0 h6 10 ♘h4 ♔h8 11 ♔h1 d5 12 ♘f5 dxe4 13 dxe4 ♘e7 14 ♘g3 ♗d6 15 ♗c2 c5 16 b3 ♕c7 17 ♘d2 ♗c8=
L/N6047-1854

**SHUMOV⚔URUSOV**
**[1853-⚔SU]**

| | | | | | | | | |
|---|---|---|---|---|---|---|---|---|
| I.S. Shumov | 1 | 0 | 0 | 0 | 0 | 0 | 1 | 2 |
| D.S. Urusov | 0 | 1 | 1 | 1 | 1 | 1 | 0 | 5 |

**1853-⚔SU-1**
**Urusov, D.S.−Shumov, I.S.**
[Staunton]

1 e4 e6 2 d4 d5 3 exd5 exd5 4 ♘f3 ♗e6 5 ♗e3 ♘f6 6 ♗d3 ♗d6 7 ♘bd2 c6 8 0-0 ♕c7 9 c3 h6 10 h3 ♘bd7 11 ♘h4 g5 12 ♘f5 0-0-0 13 ♘xd6+ ♕xd6 14 f4 gxf4 15 ♗xf4± ♕e7 16 ♕a4 ♘h5 17 ♗h2 ♕g5 18 ♕xa7+− ♕e3+ 19 ♖f2 ♘g3

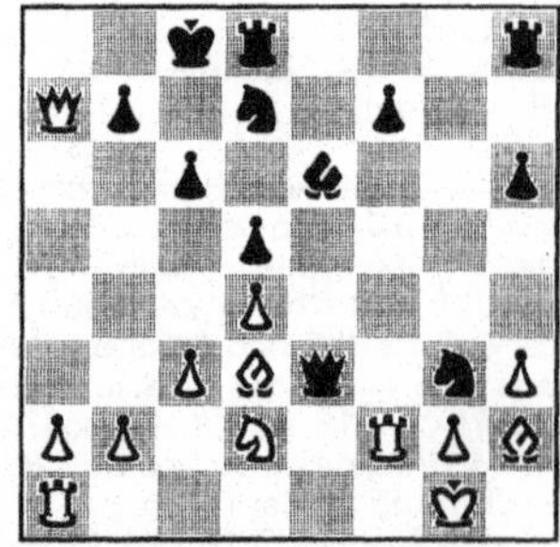

20 ♘f1 ♕xd3 21 ♕a8+ ♔c7 22 ♗xg3+ [22 ♕a5+!+−] 22 ... ♔b6 23 ♕a3 ♖dg8 24 ♕b4+ [24 ♕d6] 24 ...

♔a6 25 ♕a4+ ♔b6 26 b4 ♕a6 27 ♕b3 ♖g6 28 a4 ♖hg8 29 ♔h2 ♘f6 30 ♗d6?? [30 b5 cxb5 31 ♖xf6 ♖xf6 32 ♕b4 ♖c8 (32 ... ♔a7 33 ♖a3+-) 33 ♗b8!+- ♗f5 35 ♘e3 ♗e4 36 ♘g4 ♖e6 37 a5+ ♔c6 38 ♘e5+ ♖xe5 39 ♕d6#] 30 ... ♘e4 31 ♗c5+ ♔c7 32 ♖fa2?→ ♖xg2+!! 33 ♖xg2 ♖xg2+ 34 ♔xg2 ♕e2+ 35 ♔g1 ♕f2+ 36 ♔h1 ♕f3+ 37 ♔h2 ♕xh3+ 38 ♔g1 ♕g4+ 39 ♔h1 ♕f3+ 40 ♔h2 ♕f2+41 ♔h1 ♗g4 ...⚲ **0-1** M954-1854

**1853-✕SU-2̂**
**Shumov, I.S.– Urusov, D.S.**

1 e4 e5 2 ♘f3 ♘c6 3 ♗c4 ♗c5 4 c3 ♘f6 5 d3 d6 6 b4 ♗b6 7 a4 a5 8 b5 ♘b8?! [8 ... ♘e7] 9 0-0 ♗g4 10 ♕b3 0-0 11 ♘bd2 ♘bd7 12 ♗a3 ♕e7 13 ♖ae1 h6 14 d4 ♗xf3 15 ♘xf3 ♔h8 16 ♘h4! ♘h5 17 ♘f5 ♕f6 18 ♔h1 exd4 19 cxd4 ♗xd4 20 f4 ♗c5 21 g4 ♗xa3 22 ♕xa3 g6 23 ♘xh6 ♘xf4 24 ♕g3 g5 25 ♘f5 ♘e5 26 ♖xf4! gxf4! 27 ♕h3+ ♔g8

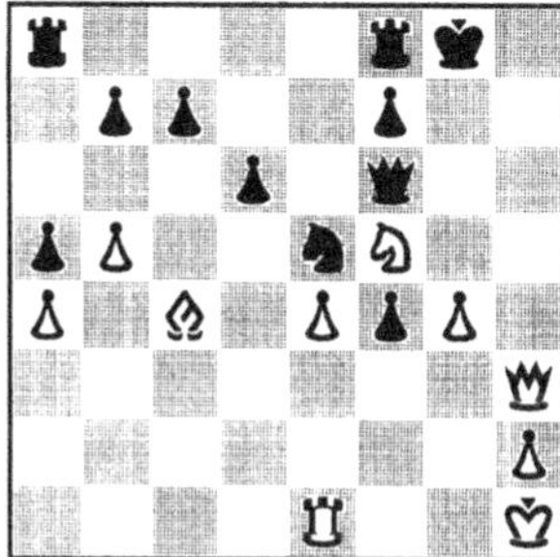

28 g5 [28 ♘h6+! ♔g7? 29 g5 ♕d8 (29 ... ♕xg5?? 30 ♖g1; 29 ... ♕g6?? 30 ♘f5+ ♔g8 31 ♘e7+) 30 ♘f5+ ♔g8 31 ♕h6+-; 28 ♘h6+! ♔h7? 29 g5 ♕d8 30 ♘f5+ ♔g8 31 ♕h6+-; 28 ♘h6+! ♔h8!! 29 ♘f5+= (29 ♘xf7+?!; 29 g5?!)] 28 ... ♕h8! 29 ♘h6+ [29 ♘e7+ ♔g7 30 ♕f5 ♕h5] 29 ... ♔g7 30 ♗b3 ♕h7 31 ♕h4 ♘d3 32 ♖e2 ♖ae8 33 ♗c2 f3!∓ 34 ♖e3 ♘e5 35 ♕f4 ♖e6 36 ♖e1 [Δ 37 g6] 36 ... ♖h8 37 ♖g1 ♔f8 38 ♗b3 ♖xh6!→ 39 gxh6 ♕xh6 40 ♕xh6+ ♖xh6 41 ♗d5 f2 42 ♖f1 ♘g4 43 h3 ♖xh3+ 44 ♔g2 ♖e3 45 ♗xb7 ♖e1 46 ♖xf2 ♘xf2 47 ♔xf2 ♖a1 ...⚲ **0-1** L/N6123-1854

**1853-✕SU-3̂**
**Urusov, D.S.+Shumov, I.S.**
[Staunton]

1 e4 e6 2 d4 d5 3 exd5 exd5 4 c4 ♗e6 5 ♘c3 c6 6 ♘f3 ♘f6 7 ♗g5 ♗b4 8 ♕b3 ♗xc3+ 9 bxc3 ♘bd7 10 ♕xb7 0-0 11 c5 ♖b8 12 ♕a6 ♕c7 13 ♗d3 ♗g4 14 0-0 ♗xf3 15 gxf3 ♘h5 16 ♗e7± ♕f4 17 ♗xf8 ♘xf8 18 ♖ab1 ♖d8 19 ♗e2 ♘g6 20 ♔h1 ♘h4 21 ♕d3 ♖e8 22 ♖g1 f5 23 ♖be1 ♕h6 24 ♗d1 ♖f8 25 ♕e3 ♘f4 26 ♖g3 ♘hg6 27 ♗c2 ♕h5 28 ♖eg1 ♘h3 29 ♕e6+ ♔h8 30 ♖f1 ♘g5 31 ♕e2 ♘h4 32 ♕e7 ♘e6 33 ♕xe6 ♘xf3 34 ♖g2 h6 35 ♕g6+- ♕xg6 36 ♖xg6 **1-0** M954-1854

**1853-✕SU-4̂**
**Shumov, I.S.– Urusov, D.S.**
[Brien]

1 e4 e5 2 ♘f3 ♘c6 3 ♗c4 ♗c5 4 c3 ♘f6 5 0-0!? ♘xe4∓ 6 ♗d5 ♘f6 7 ♗xc6 dxc6 8 ♘xe5 0-0 9 d4 ♗b6 10 ♗g5 c5 11 ♘bd2 cxd4 12 ♘e4 ♗f5 13 ♘g3± [13 ♘xf6+ gxf6 14 ♗h4+-] 13 ... ♗g6 14 ♘g4 ♕d6 15 ♗xf6 gxf6 16 ♘h6+ [◻ 16 cxd4] 16 ... ♔h8 17 ♘gf5 ♗xf5 18 ♘xf5 ♕f4 19 ♕h5 ♖ad8 20 ♖ae1 ♕g5 21 ♕f3 dxc3 22 bxc3 ♖g8 23 ♖e4? [23 ♘e7 ♖d3 24 ♕xb7±] 23 ... ♖d3 24 ♘e3 ♖xc3 25 h3 ♗xe3 26 fxe3 ♖g6 27 ♖d1 ♔g7 28 ♖d7 ♖c2 29 ♖g4 ♖c1+ 30 ♔f2 ♕b5 31 ♖xg6+ hxg6 32 ♕g4 ♖f1+ 33 ♔g3 ♕e5+ 34 ♔h4 g5+ 35 ♔h5 ♕e8 **0-1** L/N6123-1854

**1853-✕SU-5̂**
**Urusov, D.S.+Shumov, I.S.**
[Brien]

1 e4 e6 2 d4 c5 3 ♘f3 cxd4 4 ♘xd4 ♗c5 5 ♗e3 ♕b6 6 ♘c3 ♘c6 [6 ... ♕xb2?] 7 ♘db5!± ♗xe3 8 fxe3 ♕xe3+ 9 ♗e2 ♔d8 10 ♕d6 ♘f6 11 ♕c7+ ♔e8 12 ♖d1 ♘b4? 13 ♘d6+ ♔e7 14 ♘xc8+ ♖hxc8 15 ♕d6+ ♔e8 16 ♕xb4 ♘g4 17 ♕d4! ♕xd4 18 ♖xd4 ♘e3 19 ♔f2 ♘xc2 20 ♖d6 ♘b4 21 ♖hd1 ♘c6 22 ♖xd7 ♘e5 23 ♖xb7 ♖cb8 24 ♖xb8+ ♖xb8 25 b3 ...⚲ **1-0** L/N6123-1854

**1853-✕SU-6̂**
**Shumov, I.S.– Urusov, D.S.**
[Brien]

1 e4 e5 2 ♗c4 ♘f6 3 d3 ♗c5 4 ♘f3 d6 5 c3 0-0 6 ♗g5 c6 7 ♘bd2 ♗g4 8 h3 ♗e6 9 ♗xe6 fxe6 10 ♕b3 ♕d7 11 d4 exd4 12 cxd4 ♗b6 13 ♗xf6 gxf6 14 e5? fxe5 15 dxe5 d5 16 0-0-0 ♘a6 [16 ... ♗xf2? 17 ♘e4!±] 17 ♕c3 ♕g7 18 ♖df1 ♘c5 19 ♘h2 ♕g6!∓ 20 ♕g3 ♘d3+ 21 ♔b1 ♘xf2+ 22 ♕xg6+ hxg6 23 ♖hg1 ♘d3 24 ♘g4 ♗xg1 25 ♖xg1 ♔g7 26 ♘f3 ♖ae8 27 ♘f6 ♖xf6 [27 ... ♖e7 Δ 28 ... ♘xe5] 28 exf6+ ♔xf6 29 ♖f1 ♔e7 30 ♔c2 ♘c5 31 ♘e5 g5 32 ♖f7+ ♔d6 33 ♘f3 ♖g8 34 b4 ♘d7 35 g4 b6 36 ♖h7 [Δ 37 ♖h5] 36 ... ♘e5 37 ♘xe5 ♔xe5 38 ♖xa7 ♖h8 39 ♖c7 ♔d6 40 ♖g7 ♖xh3 41 ♖xg5 c5 42 bxc5+ bxc5 43 ♖g8 c4 44 g5 ♖h2+→ 45 ♔c3 ♖xa2 46 g6 ♖g2 47 g7 ♔e7 48 ♔d4 ♔f7 ...⚲ **0-1** L/N6123-1854

**1853-✕SU-7̂**
**Urusov, D.S.– Shumov, I.S.**
[Brien]

1 e4 c5 2 f4 ♘c6 3 ♘f3 e6 4 c4 d5? 5 cxd5 exd5 6 exd5 ♕xd5 7 ♘c3 ♕d8 8 ♗c4 ♗g4 9 0-0 ♗xf3 10 ♕xf3 ♕d4+ 11 ♕e3+ ♕xe3+ 12 dxe3 ♘f6 13 e4 ♗e7 14 e5 ♘d7 15 ♘d5 0-0-0 16 ♘xe7+ ♘xe7 17 ♗xf7+- ♘f5 18 g4 ♘d4 19 ♗e3? [19 ♖f2] 19 ... ♘c2 20 ♗xc5!? ♘xa1? [◻ 20 ... ♘xc5 21 ♖ac1 ♖d2] 21 ♗d6 b6 22 ♖c1+? [22 ♗d5 Δ 23 ♖xa1±] 22 ... ♔b7 23 ♖c7+?→ [23 ♖xa1] 23 ... ♔a6 24 a4 ♘c5 25 ♗c4+ ♔a5 26 ♖xa7+ ♔b4 27 ♗f7 ♘c2 28 a5 ♘d4 29 axb6 ♘b5 30 ♗xc5+ ♔xc5 31 ♖a5 ♔xb6 32 ♖a4 ♖d2 33 b3 ♖c8 34 ♗c4 ♘d4 35 ♖a6+ ♔b7 36 ♖a1 ♘f3+ 37 ♔f1 ♘xh2+ **0-1** L/N6123-1854

**1853-★AE-1** 22 iii 53
**Anderssen, A.– Eichborn, L.**
Breslau

1 e4 e5 2 ♗c4 ♘f6 3 ♕e2 ♗c5 4 b4 ♗xb4 5 c3 ♗c5 6 f4 d6 7 ♘f3 ♗g4 8 fxe5 ♗xf3 9 ♕xf3 dxe5 10 d4 ♗d6 11 dxe5 ♗xe5 12 ♗a3 ♘c6 13 ♗b5 ♕d7 14 ♘d2 0-0-0 15 ♘c4 ♖he8 16 0-0 ♕g4 17 ♗xc6 ♕xf3 18 gxf3 bxc6 19 ♗b4 ♖d3 20 ♖ad1 ♖xd1 21 ♖xd1 ♗f4 22 ♗c5 ♖d8 23 ♖xd8+ ♔xd8 24 ♗xa7 ♘d7 25 ♗f2 c5 26 h3 ♔c8 27 ♔f1 ♔b7 28 ♔e2 ♔c6 29 ♗e3 ♔b5 30 ♘a3+ ♔a4 31 ♘c2 ♗xe3 32 ♔xe3 ♘e5 33 f4 ♘c4+ 34 ♔e2 ♘a3 35 ♔d1 ♘b1 36 ♔e2 ♘xc3+ 37 ♔d2 ♘xe4+ 38 ♔d3 ♘f2+ 39 ♔e3 ♘d1+ 40 ♔e4 ♘c3+ 41 ♔e5 ♘xa2 42 ♔d5 ♘b4+ **0-1** L/N3034

**1853-★AE-2** 29 vi 53
**Anderssen, A.– Eichborn, L.**
Breslau

1 e4 e5 2 f4 exf4 3 ♘f3 g5 4 h4 g4 5 ♘e5 h5 6 ♗c4 ♖h7 7 d4 f3 8 gxf3 d6 9 ♗g5 ♗e7 10 ♘xf7 ♖xf7 11 ♗xf7+ ♔xf7 12 f4 d5 13 ♕d3 ♘f6 14 ♗xf6 ♗xf6 15 e5! ♗xh4+ 16 ♔d2 ♔g7 17 ♘c3 ♘c6 18 ♘xd5 ♕xd5 19 ♖xh4 ♘xd4 20 ♖xh5 ♘f3+ 21 ♔e3 ♕c5+ 22 ♔e2 ♘d4+ 23 ♔f1 ♗f5 24 ♖xf5 ♘xf5 25 ♕xf5 ♕c4+ 26 ♔f2 ♕d4+ 27 ♔g3 ♕e3+ 28 ♔xg4 ♕e2+ 29 ♔g5 ♖g8 30 ♕d7+ ♔h8+ 31 ♔f6 ♕h5 32 ♕f7 ♕h6+ 33 ♔e7 ♖g7 34 e6 ...⚲ **0-1** L/N3034

**1853-★AE-3** 19 vi 53
**Eichborn, L.+Anderssen, A.**
Breslau

1 e4 e5 2 ♘f3 ♘c6 3 ♗c4 ♗c5 4 c3 ♘f6 5 d4 exd4 6 e5 d5 7 ♗b5 ♘e4 8 cxd4 ♗b4+ 9 ♗d2 ♗xd2+ 10

♘fxd2 0-0 11 ♘xe4 dxe4 12 ♗xc6 bxc6 13 0-0 ♗a6 14 ♖e1 ♗d3 15 ♕a4 f6 16 ♕xc6 fxe5 17 ♕e6+ ♔h8 18 ♕xe5 ♖b8 19 ♘c3 ♖e8 20 ♕d5 ♕h4 21 b3 ♖f8 22 ♘xe4 ♖bd8 23 ♕g5 ♕xg5 24 ♘xg5 ♗f5 25 ♖ad1 h6 26 ♘e6 ♗xe6 27 ♖xe6 ♖f4 28 d5 ♖f5 29 d6 ♖a5 30 d7 **1-0** L/N3034

**1853-★AE-4** 20 viii 53
**Anderssen, A.– Eichborn, L.**
Breslau
1 e4 e5 2 ♘f3 ♘c6 3 d4 exd4 4 ♗c4 ♗c5 5 0-0 d6 6 c3 dxc3 7 ♕b3 ♕f6 8 ♘xc3 ♘ge7 9 ♘d5 ♘xd5 10 exd5 ♘e5 11 ♘xe5 ♕xe5 12 ♕a4+ ♗d7 13 ♗b5 0-0-0 14 ♗xd7+ ♖xd7 15 ♖d1 ♖he8 16 ♗d2 ♕xb2 **0-1** L/N3034

**1853-★AE-5** 22 viii 53
**Eichborn, L.+ Anderssen, A.**
Breslau
1 e4 e5 2 ♘f3 ♘c6 3 ♗c4 ♗c5 4 0-0 d6 5 c3 ♗b6 6 d4 ♕e7 7 ♗b5 ♗d7 8 ♗xc6 ♗xc6 9 d5 ♗d7 10 ♗g5 ♘f6 11 ♘bd2 a6 12 ♘c4 ♗a7 13 ♘e3 h6 14 ♗xf6 ♕xf6 15 ♘d2 ♕g6 16 ♕e2 0-0 17 ♔h1 f5 18 ♘xf5 ♗xf5 19 exf5 ♖xf5 20 g4 ♖f4 21 f3 h5 22 gxh5 ♕xh5 23 ♕g2 ♖af8 24 ♖ae1 ♖h4 25 ♖e4 ♖h3 26 ♖g4 ♗e3 27 ♘e4 ♗f4 28 ♖xg7+ ♔h8 29 ♘g3 ♕h6 30 ♖g4 ♕h7 31 ♖e1 ♖f5 32 ♖e2 ♖f6 33 ♕g1 ♗xg3 34 ♖xg3 ♖xf3 35 ♖xf3 ♖xf3 36 ♖g2 ♕f7 37 c4 c6 38 ♖g4 ♖h3 39 ♕g2 ♕f3 40 ♖h4+ **1-0** L/N3034

**1853-★AE-6** 7 ix 53
**Anderssen, A.– Eichborn, L.**
Breslau
1 e4 e5 2 f4 exf4 3 ♘f3 g5 4 h4 g4 5 ♘e5 h5 6 ♗c4 ♖h7 7 d4 f3 8 g3 d6 9 ♘d3 ♗e6 10 d5 ♗c8 11 e5 dxe5 12 ♘xe5 ♗d6 13 ♗f4 ♘e7 14 ♘c3 a6 15 ♘e4 ♗xe5 16 ♗xe5 ♘g8 17 ♕d4 ♖h6 18 d6 ♘c6 19 ♕c3 cxd6 20 0-0-0 ♘xe5 21 ♖xd6

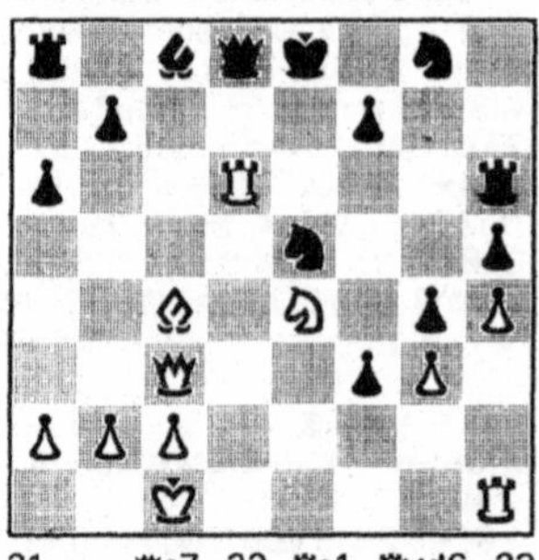

21 ... ♕e7 22 ♖e1 ♖xd6 23 ♘xd6+ ♕xd6 24 ♖xe5+ ♔f8 25 ♖xh5 ♗e6 26 ♗xe6 ♕xe6 27 ♖g5 f6 28 ♕b4+ ♘e7 **0-1** L/N3034

**1853-★AE-7** 30 viii 53
**Eichborn, L.+ Anderssen, A.**
Breslau
1 e4 e5 2 ♘f3 ♘c6 3 ♗c4 ♗c5 4 0-0 d6 5 c3 ♗b6 6 d4 ♕e7 7 h3 h6 8 ♗e3 g5 9 ♘h2 ♕f6 10 ♕e2 ♕g6 11 ♘d2 ♘d8 12 ♖ad1 ♘e7 13 ♕f3 f6 14 ♘g4 ♗xg4 15 ♕xg4 h5 16 ♕g3 ♕h7 17 dxe5 dxe5 18 ♗xb6 axb6 19 ♕d3 ♘g6 20 ♕d5 g4 21 ♔h2 gxh3 22 gxh3 ♘f4 23 ♕b5+ c6 24 ♕xb6 ♕d7 25 ♕e3 ♘de6 26 ♘f3 ♕c8 27 ♘h4 ♕c7 28 ♗xe6 ♘xe6 29 a3 ♘f4 30 ♘f5 ♖d8 31 ♖g1 ♖d7 32 ♖xd7 ♕xd7 33 ♖g7 ♕d8 34 ♖xb7 ♖g8 35 ♘g7+ ♖xg7 36 ♖xg7 ♕a5 37 ♕d2 **1-0** L/N3034

**1853-★AE-8** 18 x 53
**Anderssen, A.– Eichborn, L.**
Breslau
1 e4 e5 2 ♘f3 ♘f6 3 d4 ♘xe4 4 dxe5 ♗b4+ 5 c3 ♗c5 6 ♕d5 ♗xf2+ 7 ♔e2 f5 8 exf6 ♘xf6 9 ♕e5+ ♔f8 10 ♗g5 ♗b6 11 ♔d1 d6 12 ♕f4 ♗e6 13 ♗d3 ♘c6 14 ♘bd2 ♘e5 15 ♗e4 ♘g6 16 ♗xg6 hxg6 17 ♘h4 ♗f7 18 ♘e4 ♕d7 19 ♘xf6 gxf6 20 ♗xf6 ♖h7 21 ♖f1 ♔g8! 22 ♕g3? ♕b5 23 ♖f5 ♕xb2 24 ♘xg6 ♕xa1+ 25 ♔d2 ♕xa2+ 26 ♔d3 ♗c4+ 27 ♔e4 ♕e2+ 28 ♔f4 ♕f2+ **0-1** L/N3034

**1953-★AE-9** 18 x 53
**Eichborn, L.+ Anderssen, A.**
Breslau
1 e4 e5 2 ♘f3 ♘c6 3 d4 exd4 4 ♗c4 ♗c5 5 0-0 d6 6 c3 ♗g4 7 ♕b3 ♗xf3 8 ♗xf7+ ♔f8 9 ♗xg8 ♖xg8 10 gxf3 ♘e5 11 cxd4 ♗xd4 12 f4 ♘g4 13 ♕h3 ♘f6 14 ♕f3 ♕e7 15 ♘d2 g5 16 fxg5 ♖xg5+ 17 ♔h1 ♔g7 18 ♘b3 ♘xe4 19 ♘xd4 ♖f8 20 ♗xg5 **1-0** L/N3034

**1853-★AE-10** 19 x 53
**Anderssen, A.Φ Eichborn, L.**
Breslau
1 e4 e5 2 ♘f3 ♘f6 3 d4 ♘xe4 4 dxe5 d5 5 ♗e3 c5 6 h3 d4 7 ♗f4 ♗e6 8 ♘bd2 ♘xd2 9 ♕xd2 ♗e7 10 0-0-0 0-0 11 ♗d3 c4 12 ♗e4 c3 13 ♕xd4 cxb2+ 14 ♕xb2 ♕a5 15 ♖d3 ♘c6 16 ♗g5 ♘xe5 17 ♗xe7 ♘xd3+ 18 ♗xd3 ♖fe8 19 ♗b4 ♕c7 20 ♘g5 ♕f4+ 21 ♗d2 ♕xf2 22 ♗xh7+ ♔h8 23 h4 ♖ad8 24 ♗c3 f6 25 ♗g6 ♖e7 26 ♕b5 ♖d6 27 ♘e4 ♕e3+ 28 ♗d2 ♕a3+ 29 ♕b2 ♕xb2+ 30 ♔xb2 ♖b6+ 31 ♔c1 ♗d5 32 ♘c3 ♗xg2 33 ♖h2 ♗c6 34 h5 ♖e5 35 ♗f4 ♖e1+ 36 ♔d2 ♖f1 37 ♗c7 ♖b4 38 ♘e2 ♖g4 39 ♗d6 ♖g2 40 ♖h3 ♗f3 41 ♗d3 ♖ff2 42 ♖xf3 ♖xf3 43 ♗e4 ♖ff2 44 ♗xg2 ♖xg2 45 ♔e3 ♖g5 46 ♘f4 a5 47 ♔e4 ♖b5 48 c4 L/N3034

**1853-★BS-1** 8 v 53
**Blunden, J.& Burnell, J.& Grey & King+ Staunton, H.**
Manchester [Williams]
⟨♙f7⟩1 e4 ... 2 d4 ♘c6 3 d5 ♘e5 4 f4 ♘f7 5 ♗d3 e6 6 dxe6 dxe6 7 ♘f3 ♗c5 8 ♕e2 ♘e7 9 ♗e3 ♗xe3 10 ♕xe3 0-0 11 ♘c3 c6 12 ♖ad1 ♕c7 13 0-0 ♘h6 14 ♘e5 ♘f7 15 ♘xf7 ♖xf7 16 ♖f2 b5 17 ♘e2 ♗d7 18 ♘g3 ♖af8 19 ♖df1 a5 20 b3 c5 21 c4 b4 22 e5 ♘f5 [◻ 22 ... g6] 23 ♘xf5± exf5 24 ♖e1 ♗e6 25 h3 ♖d8 26 g4! g6 27 g5 ♖d4 28 ♗c2 ♖fd7 29 ♖ee2 ♕d8 30 h4 a4 31 ♕f3 axb3 32 axb3 ♕c7 33 h5 ♖d8 34 ♖h2 ♗c8 35 hxg6 hxg6 36 ♖h6 ♗b7 37 ♖xg6+ ♔f8 38 ♕h5 **1-0** M392-1853

**1853-★GS-♀** ii 53
**Gordon, T.– Staunton, H.**
London [Staunton]
⟨♙f7⟩1 e4 ... 2 d4 ♘c6 3 d5 ♘e5 4 f4 ♘f7 5 c4 e6 6 ♘c3 ♗c5 7 ♘f3 ♘gh6 8 h3 d6 9 dxe6 ♗xe6 10 f5 ♗d7 11 g4 ♘e5! 12 g5 [12 ♘xe5 (12 ♗xh6 ♘xf3+ 13 ♕xf3 ♕h4+ 14 ♔~ ♕xh6) 12 ... ♕h4+ 13 ♔~ dxe5] 12 ... ♘hf7 13 h4 c6 [Δ ... ♕e7] 14 ♘xe5 ♘xe5 15 ♗f4 ♕e7 16 ♕e2 ♗b4 17 ♗d2 0-0-0 18 0-0-0 ♖he8 19 ♔b1 [Δ 20 ♘d5] 19 ... ♕f7 20 ♖c1 ♔b8 21 ♔a1 [21 ♗f4? ♗xf5] 21 ... ♗c8 22 ♗f4 ♔a8 23 ♘d1

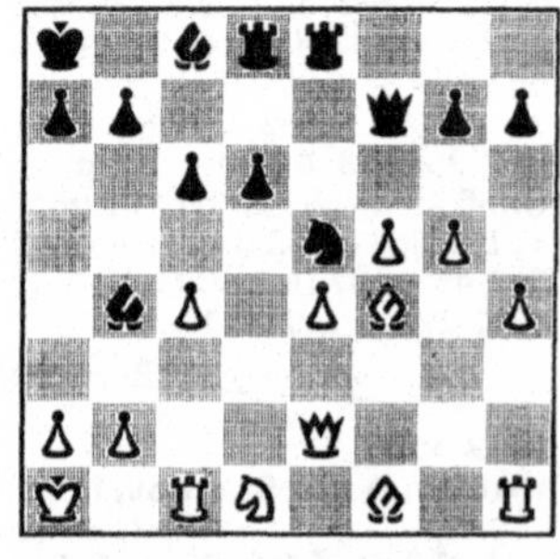

23 ... ♘g6∓ 24 ♕f3 [24 ♕h5 ♖xe4 25 fxg6 ♕xf4∓] 24 ... ♗xf5 25 ♗xd6! ♖xd6 26 ♕xf5 ♕e7 27 ♗g2 ♖f8 28 ♕g4 ♘e5 29 ♕h3 ♖d3 30 ♕h2 ♖d2 [30 ... ♗c5? (Δ 31 ... ♘g4) 31 ♖f1] 31 ♕h3 [◻ 31 ♕g3] 31 ... ♘d3 32 ♘e3 ♖xb2 **0-1** M954

**1853-★PU-1** vi 53

**Urusov, D.S.– Petrov, A.D.**

St. Petersburg

1 e4 e5 2 d4 exd4 3 ♗c4 ♘c6 4 ♘f3 ♗c5 5 c3 ♘f6 6 ♗g5 h6 7 ♗xf6 ♕xf6 8 e5 ♕g6 9 0-0 dxc3 10 ♘xc3 0-0 11 ♖e1 d6 12 ♘d5 ♗g4 13 ♗b5 ♗xf3 14 ♕xf3 dxe5 15 ♗xc6 bxc6 16 ♘xc7 ♖ac8 17 ♘a6 ♗d6 18 ♖ac1 ♖fe8 19 ♖xc6 e4 20 ♖xc8 ♖xc8 21 ♕h3 ♖c6 22 g3 f5 23 ♕f1 ♗xg3 24 fxg3 ♖xa6 25 ♕c4+ ♔h7 26 b4 ♕e6 27 ♕xe6 ♖xe6 28 ♖e3 g5 29 ♖c3 ♔g6 30 ♔f2 f4 31 a4 e3+ 32 ♔e1 ♔f5 33 b5 f3 34 a5 g4 35 ♖c5+ ♔f6 36 ♖c2 e2 37 ♖c1 ♔e5 38 ♖b1 ♖e7 39 b6 axb6 40 axb6 ♖b7 41 ♖b5+ ♔d4 42 ♔f2 ♔c4 43 ♖b1 ♔c5 44 ♖c1+ ♔xb6 45 ♖c4 ♖e7 46 ♖c1 e1♕+ 47 ♖xe1 ♖xe1 48 ♔xe1 ♔c5 49 ♔d1 ♔d4 50 ♔d2 ♔e4 51 ♔d1 ♔e3 52 ♔e1 f2+ 53 ♔f1 ♔f3 **0-1** L/N6123-1853

**1853-★RS-1** viii 53

**Staunton, H.+ Rives, de**

Bruxelles

1 e4 e5 2 ♘f3 ♘c6 3 c3 ♗c5 4 d4 exd4 5 cxd4 ♗b6 6 ♗c4 d6 7 h3 ♕f6 8 ♗e3 ♘ge7 9 ♘c3 0-0 10 a3 a6 11 ♘e2 h6 12 ♖c1 ♗d7 13 ♘g3 ♖ad8 14 0-0 ♘g6 15 ♘h5 ♕e7 16 ♕d3 ♘a5 17 b3 ♘xc4 18 bxc4 ♖fe8 19 ♘g3 ♕f6 20 ♘h2 ♘f4 21 ♕d2 ♘e6 22 ♘g4 ♕g6 23 f4 ♘xf4 24 ♗xf4 ♗xg4 25 hxg4 ♕xg4 26 ♖f3 ♖e6 27 ♖cf1 ♖g6 28 ♖1f2 ♖e8 29 ♕d3 ♖e6 30 ♖e2 c6 31 ♖b2 d5 32 exd5 cxd5 33 c5 ♗a5 34 ♖e3 ♕d7 35 ♖xe8+ ♕xe8 36 ♖e2 ♕d7 37 ♘f5 ♗d8 38 ♘d6 ♕g4 39 ♖e8+ ♔h7 40 g3 ♕xf4 41 ♕xg6+ ♔xg6 42 gxf4 **1-0** M954

**1853-★RS-2** viii 53

**Staunton, H.+ Rives, de**

Bruxelles [Staunton]

1 e4 e5 2 ♘f3 ♘c6 3 c3 ♘f6 4 d4 ♘xe4 5 dxe5 d5 6 ♗d3 ♗f5 7 0-0 ♗c5 8 b4 ♗b6 9 b5 ♘e7 10 ♘d4 ♗g6 11 ♗xe4 dxe4 12 ♗a3 0-0 13 ♘d2 ♖e8 14 ♘c4 ♘d5 15 ♕d2

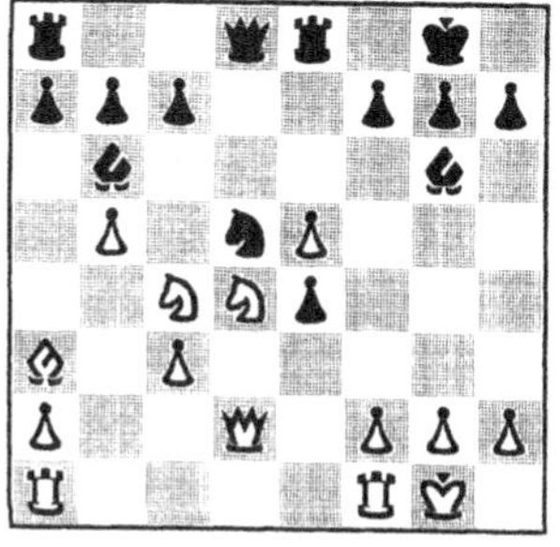

15 ... ♘xc3!? 16 ♘xb6 ♘xb5 17 ♘xa8 ♘xd4 18 ♖ad1 ♘f3+ 19 gxf3 ♕xa8 20 fxe4 ♗xe4 21 f4 ♕c8 22 ♕d7 ♕b8 23 e6 fxe6 24 ♗b2 **1-0** M954-1854

**1853-★RS-3** viii 53

**Rives, de= Staunton, H.**

Bruxelles [Staunton]

⟨♙f7⟩ 1 e4 ... 2 d4 ♘c6 3 d5 ♘e5 4 f4 ♘f7 5 c4 e6 6 ♗e3 b6 7 ♗d3 ♘gh6 8 ♘c3 ♗e7 9 ♘f3 ♘g4 10 ♗d4 0-0 11 0-0 c5 12 ♗f2 e5 13 fxe5 ♘fxe5 14 ♘xe5 ♘xe5 15 ♗g3 ♖xf1+ 16 ♕xf1 ♗f6 17 ♖c1 [17 d6!? △ 18 ♘d5] 17 ... d6 18 b3 ♕e7 19 ♗e2 ♗d7 20 ♘d1 ♖f8 21 ♕e1 ♔h8 [21 ... ♗g4 22 ♗xg4 ♘d3 23 ♗e6+] 22 ♘f2 ♘g6 23 ♗f3 ♗d4 24 ♔h1 ♘h4 25 ♕e2 ♕f6 26 ♘g4 ♕g5 27 ♖f1 ♘xf3 28 ♖xf3 ♖xf3 29 gxf3 h5 30 ♘f2 h4 31 ♗xd6 ♕c1+ [□ 31 ... ♗xf2 32 ♕xf2 ♗h3 33 e5 (33 f4 ♕g4→) 33 ... ♕c1+ 34 ♕g1 ♕c3 35 ♕f2 (35 ♕d1 ♕b2 36 ♕g1 ♕e2→) 35 ... ♔g8 36 ♕d3→] 32 ♔g2 h3+ 33 ♘xh3 ♗xh3+ 34 ♔xh3 ♕h6+ 35 ♔g3 ♕xd6+ **½-½** M954

**1853-★RS-5**

**Rives, de+ Staunton, H.**

Bruxelles [Anderssen & Kossak]

⟨♙f7⟩1 e4 ... 2 d4 d6 3 f4 ♘d7 4 ♘f3 ♘h6 5 ♗c4 c6 6 ♘c3 ♘b6 7 ♗b3 ♗g4 8 f5 g6 9 h3 ♗xf3 10 ♕xf3 ♔d7 11 ♗e6+ ♔c7 12 ♗e3 ♗g7 13 a4 ♖f8 14 a5 ♘d7 15 b4 a6 16 0-0 ♕e8 17 ♘a4 ♖d8 18 c4 gxf5 19 exf5 ♘xf5 20 ♗xf5 e6 21 ♕g4 [□ 21 ♕g3] 21 ... exf5 22 ♕f4 ♖f6 23 d5 ♗h6 24 ♗b6+ ♔b8 25 ♕f3 ♘xb6 26 ♘xb6 [□ 26 ♖fe1] 26 ... ♗e3+ 27 ♔h1 ♗xb6 28 axb6 cxd5 29 ♕xd5 ♕e5 30 ♖ad1 ♕b2 31 b5 ♖c8 32 ♖b1 ♕a2 33 bxa6 ♕xa6 34 ♖fc1 f4 35 ♕d4 ♖f5 36 ♕xd6+ ♔a8 37 ♕b4 [□ 37 ♕d7 ♖cf8 38 ♖d1] 37 ... f3 38 ♖a1 fxg2+ 39 ♔xg2 ♖g8+ 40 ♔h1 ♖f3 41 ♖xa6+ bxa6 42 b7+ ♔b8 43 ♕d6+ ♔a7 44 ♕d7 **1-0** L/N6047

**1853-★RS-6** viii 53

**Rives, de+ Staunton, H.**

Bruxelles [Anderssen & Kossak]

⟨♙f7⟩1 e4 ... 2 d4 ♘c6 3 d5 ♘e5 4 f4 ♘f7 5 c4 e6 6 ♗e3 c6 7 ♘c3 ♗b4 8 ♘f3 ♘f6 9 ♗d3 cxd5 10 cxd5 exd5 11 e5 ♘g4 [11 ... ♘e4 12 ♗xe4 dxe4 13 ♘d2 ♗xc3 14 bxc3 d5 15 exd6 ♘xd6 16 ♕h5+] 12 ♗d4 0-0 13 0-0 ♗xc3 14 bxc3 d6 15 ♕c2 dxe5 [15 ... h6?? 16 h3] 16 ♗xh7+ ♔h8 17 fxe5 ♗e6 18 h3 ♘gh6 19 ♗g6 ♘g5 20 ♕e2 ♗xh3 21 gxh3 ♘xh3+ 22 ♔h1 ♘f4 23 ♕c2 ♕d7 24 ♕h2 [△ 25 e6 ♕xe6 26 ♕xh6+] 24 ... ♔g8 25 ♗c2 ♕g4 26 ♘h4 ♘e2 27 ♖g1 ♘xg1 28 ♖xg1 ♕e6 29 ♕g2 [□ 29 ♖g6] 29 ... ♖f7 30 ♗g6 ♖c7 31 ♖f1 ♕e7 32 ♕xd5+ ♔h8 33 ♕e4 ♖f8 34 ♗f5 ♖c6 35 e6 ♖xe6 36 ♘g6+ **1-0** L/N6047

**1853-★RS-7** viii 53

**Rives, de+ Staunton, H.**

Bruxelles [Staunton]

⟨♙f7⟩1 e4 ... 2 d4 ♘c6 3 d5 ♘e5 4 f4 ♘f7 5 c4 e5 6 ♘f3 d6 7 fxe5 dxe5 8 ♗e3 ♘f6 9 ♗d3 ♘g4 10 ♕e2 ♗b4+ 11 ♘c3 b6 12 h3 ♘xe3 13 ♕xe3 0-0 14 0-0-0 a5 15 a3 ♗c5 16 ♕e2 a4 17 g4 ♕e7 18 ♘b1 ♗d7 19 ♘fd2 ♘d6 20 ♖df1 ♖fb8 21 ♘c3 ♗d4 22 ♘db1 ♘b7 23 ♖f3 ♘c5 24 ♖hf1 ♖a5 25 ♗c2 b5?! 26 ♖f7 ♕g5+ 27 ♔d1 h6 28 ♖xd7!? ♘xd7 29 ♘xb5 ♗xb2 30 ♕d2! ♕xd2+ 31 ♔xd2 ♖b7 32 ♘1c3 ♗xc3+ [□ 32 ... ♘c5] 33 ♔xc3 ♖a8 34 ♔b4 ♘f6 35 ♖f5 ♘d7 36 ♗xa4 g6 37 ♖f3 ♖a6 38 ♗b3 ♘f6 39 d6! [□ 39 c5!] 39 ... ♔g7 40 dxc7 ♖c6 41 c5 ♖cxc7 42 ♗d5! ♖b8 43 a4 ♖a7 44 c6 ♘e8 45 ♔c5 ♖e7 46 a5 ♖a8 47 ♖a3 ♖a6 48 ♗c4 ♖a8 49 a6 ♔f6 50 a7 **1-0** L/N6123

**1853-★RS-8** viii 53

**Rives, de= Staunton, H**

Bruxelles [Anderssen & Kossak]

1 e4 e5 2 ♘f3 ♘c6 3 d4 exd4 4 ♗c4 ♗c5 5 c3 ♘f6 6 ♗g5 d6 [6 ... h6 7 ♗h4 g5; 7 ♗xf6 ♕xf6 8 e5 ♕g6 9 cxd4 ♕e4+] 7 cxd4 ♗b6 8 h3 0-0 9 ♘c3 ♘e7 10 ♗xf6 gxf6 11 ♕d2 ♗e6 12 d5 ♗d7 13 ♘h4 ♘g6 14 ♘xg6 fxg6 15 0-0-0 ♕e7 16 f4 ♖ae8 17 ♖de1 ♔h8 18 ♖e2 ♕g7 19 g4 ♖e7 20 ♖he1 a6 21 ♔b1 ♗a7 22 a4 ♖b8 23 ♕d3 b5 24 axb5 axb5 25 ♘xb5 ♗xb5 26 ♗xb5 ♗c5 27 ♗c6 ♖b6 28 h4 ♕f8 29 e5 fxe5 30 fxe5 ♕g7 31 exd6 ♗xd6 32 b3 ♗e5 33 ♖e4 ♗d6 34 ♖xe7 ♗xe7 35 ♔a2 ♖b8 36 g5 ♗f8 37 ♕e3 ♕f7 38 ♕e6 ♕f2+ 39 ♖e2 ♕a7+ 40 ♗a4 ♗g7 41 ♕f7 ♕c5 42 ♖e8+ ♖xe8 43 ♕xe8+ ♗f8 **½-½** L/N6047

**1853-★RS-9** viii 53

**Staunton, H.+ Rives, de**

Bruxelles [Staunton]

1 e4 e5 2 ♘f3 ♘c6 3 d4 exd4 4 ♗c4 ♗b4+ 5 c3 dxc3 6 0-0 c2 7 ♕xc2 d6 8 a3 ♗a5 9 b4 ♗b6 10 ♕b3 [10 ♗b2 ♘f6 11 e5 dxe5 12 ♘xe5 ♘xe5 13 ♗xe5 0-0 14 ♘c3 ♘g4 15 ♗g3] 10 ... ♕e7 11 ♘c3 ♗e6 12 ♘d5 ♕d7 13 ♗b2 ♘ge7 14 ♗xg7 ♗xd5 15 exd5 ♘e5 16 ♘xe5 dxe5 17 ♗xh8 ♘g6 18 ♗f6 ♕f5 19 ♗b5+ ♔f8 20 ♕f3 ♘f4 21 ♗h4 e4 22 ♕c3 ♔g8 23 ♕f6 **1-0** M954-1853

### 1853-★RS-10 viii 53
**Rives, de– Staunton, H.**
Bruxelles [Staunton]
1 e4 e5 2 ♘f3 ♘c6 3 ♗c4 ♗c5 4 c3 ♘f6 5 d4 exd4 6 cxd4 ♗b6 [□ 6 ... ♗b4+] 7 e5 d5 8 exf6 dxc4 9 fxg7 ♖g8 10 d5 ♘e7 11 ♘c3 ♖xg7 12 0-0 ♗g4 [12 ... ♗h3!?] 13 ♕a4+ ♕d7 14 ♕xd7+ ♗xd7 15 ♖e1 f5 16 d6 cxd6 17 ♘d5 ♗c6 18 ♗h6 ♖f7 19 ♘xb6 axb6 20 ♘g5 ♖f6 21 ♖e3 ♔d7 22 ♖ae1 ♘d5 23 ♖e6 ♖xe6 24 ♘xe6 ♖xa2 25 ♗g7 b5 26 ♘f8+ ♔c7 27 ♘xh7 ♘f4 28 f3 ♘d3 29 ♖b1 b4 30 h4 ♘f4 31 ♘f6 c3 32 h5 c2 33 ♖c1 ♘e2+ 34 ♔h2 ♘xc1 35 h6 ♘e2 36 h7 c1♕ 37 h8♕ ♕f4+ **0-1** M954-1854

### 1853-★RS-11 viii 53
**Rives, de– Staunton, H.**
Bruxelles [Staunton]
⟨♙f7⟩ 1 e4 ... 2 d4 ♘c6 3 d5 ♘e5 4 f4 ♘f7 5 ♗d3 e5 6 ♘f3 d6 7 f5 ♘f6 8 0-0 c6 9 ♘g5 [□ 9 c4] 9 ... ♘xg5 10 ♗xg5 ♗d7 11 ♘d2 ♕b6+ 12 ♔h1 0-0-0 13 ♘c4 ♕c7 14 b4 cxd5 15 exd5 ♗e7 16 ♗xf6 ♗xf6 17 ♖b1 ♖df8 18 b5 b6 19 a4 g6!? 20 ♖b4 [△ 21 ♘xe5 ♗xe5 22 ♖c4] 20 ... ♔b8 21 ♘d2 ♗e7 22 fxg6 hxg6 23 ♖c4 ♕b7 24 ♗e4 [24 ♖xf8+ ♖xf8 25 ♗e4] 24 ... ♗f5 25 ♖c6 ♖h4 26 ♗xf5 gxf5 27 g3 ♖xa4 28 c4 ♖a2 29 ♘f3 f4 30 ♕b1 [30 ♘xe5 dxe5 31 d6 ♖h8 32 h4 ♕d7−+] 30 ... ♖e2 31 ♕h7 fxg3 32 hxg3 e4 33 ♘h2 ♖xh2+ 34 ♔xh2 ♖xf1 **0-1** L/N6123

### 1853-★RS-12 viii 53
**Rives, de– Staunton, H.**
Bruxelles [Staunton]
⟨♙f7⟩ 1 e4 ... 2 d4 ♘c6 3 f4 e6 4 ♘f3 d5 5 e5 ♘h6 6 ♗d3 ♘b4 7 0-0 ♘xd3 8 ♕xd3 c5 9 b3 ♗d7 10 c4 cxd4 11 ♘xd4 ♗c5 12 cxd5 ♘f5 13 ♗e3 ♘xe3 14 ♕xe3 ♗b5 15 ♖d1 0-0 16 ♘c3 ♗d7 17 d6 ♕h4 18 ♘ce2 ♗c6 19 ♔h1 ♖ac8 20 ♖ac1 ♗xd4 21 ♖xd4 ♖f5 22 ♕g3 ♕h5 23 ♕e3 ♖f7 24 ♘g3 ♕g6 25 b4 ♖cf8 26 ♖cf1 h5 27 h3 h4 28 ♘e4 ♕f5 29 ♘g5 ♕g6 30 ♕d2

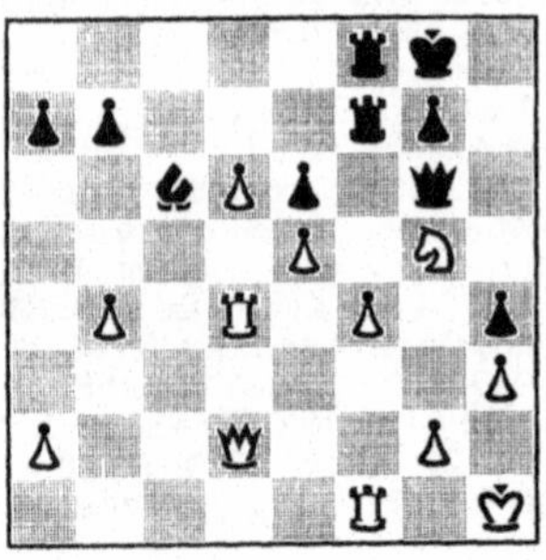

30 ... ♕xg5! 31 fxg5 ♖xf1+ 32 ♔h2 ♖1f2 [33 ♕xf2 (33 d7 ♖xd2 34 ♖xd2 ♖d8−+) 33 ... ♖xf2 34 d7 ♖xg2+ 35 ♔h1 ♖d2+−+] **0-1** M954

### 1853-★RS-13 viii 53
**Rives, de– Staunton, H.**
Bruxelles [Staunton]
⟨♙f7⟩ 1 e4 ... 2 d4 ♘c6 3 d5 ♘e5 4 f4 ♘f7 5 c4 e5 6 ♘f3 ♗b4+ 7 ♘c3 ♗xc3+ 8 bxc3 d6 9 ♗d3 ♘f6 10 0-0 0-0 11 fxe5 dxe5 12 c5! ♗g4 13 ♕b3! ♖b8 14 ♗e3 [□ 14 d6] 14 ... ♔h8 15 a4? ♗xf3 16 ♖xf3 ♘g4 17 ♖af1 ♘xe3 18 ♖xe3 ♕e7 19 ♕b4 ♘g5 20 d6 cxd6 21 cxd6 ♖xf1+ 22 ♗xf1 ♕f6 [△ 23 ... ♖f8] 23 ♕b1 [□ 23 ♗e2] 23 ... ♖f8 24 ♕e1 ♕xd6 25 ♗c4 ♕c5 26 ♗d5 ♖f3! **0-1** L/N6123

### 1853-★RS-14
**Rives, de= Staunton, H.**
Bruxelles
1 e4 e5 2 ♘f3 ♘c6 3 d4 exd4 4 ♗c4 ♗c5 5 c3 d6 6 0-0 d3 7 ♕xd3 ♘f6 8 ♗g5 h6 9 ♗h4 g5 10 ♗g3 ♘h5 11 b4 ♗b6 12 a4 a6 13 e5 ♘xg3 14 hxg3 dxe5 15 ♕xd8+ ♘xd8 16 ♘xe5 ♗e6 17 ♖e1 a5 18 ♘d2 axb4 19 cxb4 ♗d4 20 ♖ac1 0-0 21 a5 ♗xc4 22 ♖xc4 ♘e6 23 ♘d7 ♖fd8 24 ♖xe6 ♖xd7 25 ♖e2 b6 26 ♘f3 ♗g7 27 axb6 cxb6 28 ♖c6 ♖a1+ 29 ♖e1 ♖xe1+ 30 ♘xe1 ♖d1 31 ♔f1 ♖b1 32 ♖xb6 ♗c3 33 ♖b8+ ♔g7 34 ♖e8 ♗xb4 35 g4 ♔g6 36 f3 h5 37 gxh5+ ♔xh5 38 ♔f2 ♗c5+ 39 ♔g3 f5 40 ♘d3 ♗b6 41 ♖h8+ ♔g6 42 ♖g8+ ♔f6 43 ♖f8+ ♔e6 ...? **½-½** L/N6123-1854

### 1853-★RS-15
**Rives, de– Staunton, H.**
Bruxelles
1 e4 e5 2 c3 d5 3 exd5 ♕xd5 4 ♘f3 ♘c6 5 d3 ♗g4 6 ♗e2 ♘f6 7 0-0 ♖d8 8 ♕c2 ♗e7 9 ♘bd2 0-0 10 c4 ♕d7 11 a3 ♘h5 12 b4 ♘f4 13 ♘e4 ♘xe2+ 14 ♕xe2 ♘d4 15 ♕d1 ♗xf3 16 gxf3 f5 17 ♘g3 f4 18 ♘e4 ♕h3 19 ♘d2 ♖f5

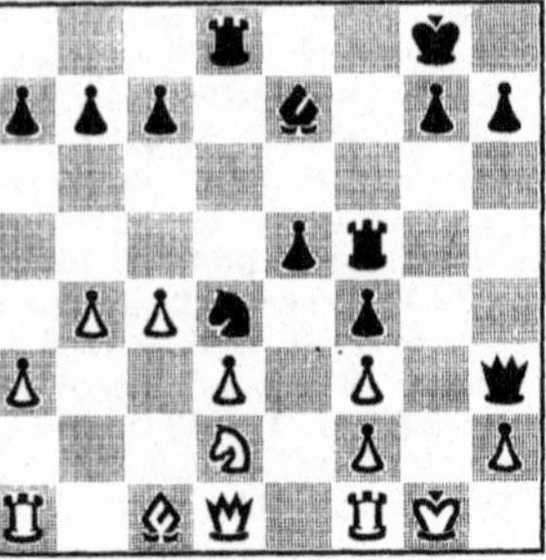

**0-1** L/N6123-1854

### 1853-★RS-16
**Rives, de+ Staunton, H.**
Bruxelles
⟨♙f7⟩ 1 e4 ... 2 d4 ♘c6 3 d5 ♘e5 4 f4 ♘f7 5 c4 e5 6 ♘f3 ♗b4+ 7 ♘c3 ♗xc3+ 8 bxc3 d6 9 fxe5 dxe5 10 c5 ♘f6 11 ♗d3 0-0 12 a4 ♗g4 13 0-0 a6 14 ♕b3 ♖b8 15 a5 h6 16 ♖a4 ♘d7 17 ♗e3 ♕e7 18 ♕c4 ♔h7 19 h3 ♗h5 20 ♖b4 b5 21 axb6 cxb6 22 cxb6 ♖fc8 23 ♕xa6 ♘c5 24 ♗xc5 ♕xc5+ 25 ♔h2 ♗xf3 26 ♖xf3 ♘g5 27 ♖f1 ♕xc3 28 b7 ♖d8 29 ♖b6 ♕d2 30 h4 ♖f8 31 hxg5 ♖xf1 32 g6+ ♔h8 33 ♗xf1 ♕f4+ 34 ♔g1 ♕e3+ 35 ♔h1 ♕xe4 36 ♕c4 **1-0** L/N6047

### 1853-★RS-17
**Rives, de+ Staunton, H.**
Bruxelles
⟨♙f7⟩ 1 e4 ... 2 d4 e6 3 ♗d3 ♕e7 4 f4 d6 5 ♘f3 g6 6 0-0 ♗g7 7 c4 b6 8 ♘c3 ♗b7 9 f5 e5 10 ♗g5 ♘f6 11 ♘d5 ♗xd5 12 exd5 ♘bd7 13 fxg6 hxg6 14 ♗h4 0-0-0 15 dxe5 ♘xe5 16 ♗f5+ ♔b8 17 ♘d4 ♖de8 18 ♖e1 ♕f8 19 ♕a4 ♔b7 20 ♘e6 ♕e7 21 b4 a6 22 c5 ♖hg8 23 cxb6 cxb6 24 ♖ac1 ♖c8 25 ♖c6 ♖xc6 26 dxc6+ ♔a7 27 ♘d4 **1-0** L/N6047

### 1853-★RS-18
**Staunton, H.– Rives, de**
Bruxelles
1 e4 e5 2 ♘f3 ♘c6 3 ♗c4 ♗c5 4 b4 ♗xb4 5 c3 ♗c5 6 0-0 d6 7 d4 exd4 8 cxd4 ♗b6 9 ♕b3 ♕f6 10 e5 dxe5 11 dxe5 ♕g6 12 ♗a3 ♗e6 13 ♘c3 ♘ge7 14 ♖ad1 0-0 15 ♘d5 ♗xd5 16 ♗xd5 ♘xd5 17 ♖xd5 ♖fd8 18 ♖fd1 ♖xd5 19 ♖xd5 ♖d8 20 h3 h6 21 ♖xd8+ ♘xd8 22 ♕d5 ♘c6 23 ♕d1 ♕e6 24 ♕a1 a5 25 ♕b2 ♕d5 26 ♕e2 ♘d4 27 ♕d3 ♘xf3+ 28 ♕xf3 ♕xe5 29 ♕xb7 ♕e1+ 30 ♔h2 ♕xf2 31 ♕a8+ ♔h7 32 ♕d5 ♕g1+ 33 ♔g3 ♕e3+ 34 ♕f3 ♕e1+ 35 ♔g4 h5+ 36 ♔xh5 g6+ 37 ♔g4 f5+ 38 ♔g5 ♗e3+ 39 ♔f6 ♕c3+ 40 ♔f7 ♕xa3 41 ♕d5 ♗h6 **0-1** L/N6047

### 1853̂-★CS-1
**Con & Saul & Schwab– Staunton, H.**
Liverpool [Staunton]
⟨♙f7⟩ 1 e4 ... 2 d4 ♘c6 3 ♗d3 e5 4 d5 ♘ce7 5 f4 exf4 6 ♗xf4 ♘g6 7 ♗g3 ♗c5 8 ♘f3 d6 9 ♘bd2 c6 [9 ... ♗g4 10 ♗b5+] 10 c4 ♗g4 11 ♕c2 ♘f6 12 h3 ♗xf3 13 ♘xf3 0-0 14 0-0-0 a6?! [14 ... ♘h5] 15 e5! ♘xe5 16 ♘xe5 dxe5 17 ♗xe5 [△ 18 dxc6] 17

... cxd5 18 ♗xf6 ♕xf6 19 ♗xh7+ ♔h8 20 ♖xd5 ♕h6+ 21 ♔b1 ♖f2 22 ♕d3? [22 ♕g6 ♕xh7?? 23 ♖h5] 22 ... ♕b6! 23 b3 ♕f6 24 ♔c1 ♖af8 25 ♖e1 ♕a1+ 26 ♕b1 ♕c3+ 27 ♔d1 ♗b4 **0-1** M954-1853

**1853̂-★DS-1**
**Duval & Kipping,J.S.– Staunton,H.**
[Staunton]

1 e4 e5 2 ♘f3 ♘c6 3 ♗c4 ♗c5 4 b4 ♗xb4 5 c3 ♗c5 6 d4 exd4 7 cxd4 ♗b6 8 0-0 d6 9 ♗a3? [9 ♕b3] 9 ... ♗g4 10 ♕b3 ♘h6 11 e5 0-0 12 exd6 ♘a5 13 ♕c3 ♗xf3 14 gxf3 cxd6 15 d5 ♖c8 16 ♘d2 ♘f5 17 ♕d3 ♕f6 [△ 18 ... ♗xf2+; 18 ... ♖xc4] 18 ♖ac1 ♘xc4? [18 ... ♕g6+!→] 19 ♖xc4 ♖xc4 20 ♕xc4 ♘d4 21 ♕d3 ♖e8 22 ♘e4 ♘xf3+ 23 ♔h1 ♕f4 24 ♘g3 ♘d4 25 ♖g1 ♕xf2 26 ♘h5 g6 27 ♕g3 ♕xg3 28 ♘f6+ ♔h8 29 ♖xg3 ♖e1+ 30 ♔g2 ♘f5 31 ♖c3 ♔g7 32 ♘d7 ♘e3+?! 33 ♔f2 ♗d4 [33 ... ♘d1+?? 34 ♔xe1 ♘xc3 35 ♘xb6 axb6 36 ♗b2+–] 34 ♖d3 ♘c2+ 35 ♖xd4 ♘xd4 36 ♗xd6 ♖e2+ 37 ♔f1 f6 38 ♗c5 ♖d2 39 ♗e7 ♘f3 40 ♘xf6 ♘xh2+ 41 ♔g1 ♘f3+ 42 ♔f1 ♔f7 43 d6 ♖xd6 44 ♗xd6 ♔xf6 **0-1**
L/N6123-1853

**1853̂-★S?-1**
**Staunton,H.+?**
Reading [Staunton]

1 e4 c5 2 ♘f3 ♘c6 3 ♘c3 e5 4 ♗c4 ♗e7 5 a3 h6 6 d3 ♘f6 7 0-0 d6 8 h3 0-0 9 ♗e3 a6 10 ♕d2 ♔h7 11 ♖ad1 ♘d4 12 ♘h2 b5 13 ♗a2 ♗b7 14 f4 c4 15 ♗xd4 exd4 16 ♘e2 ♕b6 [△ 17 ... c3] 17 ♔h1 ♘d7 18 ♘f3 ♗f6 19 g4 g6 20 h4 ♖h8 21 ♔g2 ♗g7 22 ♘g3 d5 23 e5 ♖ae8 24 ♕f2 ♘f8 25 ♘xd4 ♕d8 26 ♖h1 ♕d7 27 ♕f3 ♘e6 28 ♘xe6 d4?! [28 ... fxe6] 29 ♘g5+ hxg5 30 hxg5+ ♔g8 31 ♘e4 ♕d5 32 ♖xh8+ ♗xh8 33 ♖h1 ♗g7 34 ♔f2 ♕d7 35 ♕h3 ♗xe4 36 dxe4 d3 37 c3± [37 cxd3?? ♕d4+ 38 ♔~ ♕xb2] 37 ... ♖d8 38 ♗b1 a5 39 f5 ♕a7+ 40 ♔f3 gxf5 41 gxf5 ♕e7 42 f6 ♕xe5 43 ♕h7+ **1-0**
M954-1853

**185̂3̂-★BS-1**
**Brien,R.B.– Staunton,H.**
London [Staunton]

⟨△f7⟩ 1 e4 ... 2 d4 ♘c6 3 ♘c3 d6 4 ♗c4 e6 5 f4 g6 6 h4 ♗g7 7 ♗e3 ♘ge7 8 h5 d5 9 ♗b5 ♗d7 10 hxg6 hxg6 11 ♖xh8+ ♗xh8 12 ♘f3 dxe4 13 ♘xe4 ♘f5 14 ♗f2 ♘cxd4 [14 ... ♘fxd4 15 ♗xd4 ♘xd4 16 ♘xd4 ♕h4+ (16 ... ♗xd4 17 ♕xd4 ♕h4+ 18 g3+–) 17 ♘f2+–] 15 ♘xd4 ♘xd4 16 ♗xd4 ♗xb5 17 ♗xh8 ♕h4+ 18 ♘f2 ♕xh8 19 ♕g4 0-0-0 20 c3 ♕h2 ...? **0-1** L/N6123-1853

**1853̂-★BS-2**
**Brien,R.B.= Staunton,H.**
London [Staunton]

⟨△f7⟩ 1 e4 ... 2 d4 ♘c6 3 d5 ♘e5 4 f4 ♘f7 5 c4 d6 6 ♗d3 c6 7 ♘c3 g6 8 ♘f3 ♗g7 9 0-0 ♘gh6 10 h3 0-0 11 ♕c2 ♗d7 12 ♗d2 cxd5 13 exd5 ♖c8 14 ♖ae1 b5 15 b3 bxc4 16 bxc4 ♗f5 17 ♘e4 e6 18 dxe6 ♗xe6 19 ♘eg5 ♗f5 20 ♔h1 ♘xg5 21 fxg5 [□ 21 ♘xg5] 21 ... ♗xd3 22 ♕xd3 ♘f5 23 ♘h2 ♕c7 24 ♖e4 ♕c6 25 ♗f4 ♗e5 26 ♗xe5 dxe5 27 ♖fe1 ♖cd8 28 ♕c3 ♖d4 29 ♖xe5 ♖xc4 30 ♕b3 ♔h8 31 ♖e6 ♕c7 32 ♕b2+ ♔g8 33 ♘g4 ♘g3+ 34 ♔g1 ♕c5+ 35 ♔h2 ♖xg4 36 hxg4 ♕xg5 37 ♔xg3 **½-½** M954-1853

**185̂3̂-★BS-3**
**Brien,R.B.– Staunton,H.**
London [Staunton]

⟨△f7⟩ 1 e4 ... 2 d4 e6 3 c4 ♗b4+ 4 ♘c3 ♘e7 5 ♗g5 0-0 6 ♘f3 b6 7 ♗d3 d6 8 0-0 ♗xc3 9 bxc3 ♘d7 10 e5 ♗b7 11 ♘h4 h6 12 ♕h5 dxe5 [12 ... ♕e8 13 ♘g6 ♘xg6 (13 ... hxg5?) 14 ♗xg6 ♕b8 15 ♗e7 ♖c8 16 ♗f7+ ♔h8 17 ♗xe6 ♖e8 18 ♗xd7 ♖xe7 19 e6±] 13 ♘g6 ♘f6 14 ♗xf6 ♖xf6 15 ♘xe7+ ♕xe7 16 dxe5 ♕c5 17 ♖ae1 ♖af8 [□ 17 ... ♖d8] 18 ♖e2 ♖f4 19 ♕g6 ♕c6 20 ♕h7+ ♔f7 21 ♗g6+ ♔e7 22 ♕xg7+ ♔d8 23 ♗e4 [□ 23 ♗d3] 23 ... ♕xc4 24 ♖d2+ ♔c8 25 ♗xb7+ ♔xb7 26 ♖d6?? ♖4f7 **0-1** L/N6123-1853

**185̂3̂-★JU-1**
**Jaenisch,C.F.– Urusov,D.S.**

1 e4 e5 2 f4 exf4 3 ♘f3 g5 4 h4 g4 5 ♘e5 h5 6 ♗c4 ♖h7 7 d4 ♕f6 8 ♘c3 ♘e7 9 ♘e2 d6 10 ♗xf7+ ♖xf7 11 ♘xf7 ♕xf7 12 ♗xf4 ♘bc6 13 0-0 ♕h7 14 ♗g5 ♗d7 15 ♕d2 0-0-0 16 ♖f4 ♖e8 17 ♖af1 ♗g7 18 c3 ♘g6 19 ♖f7 ♗e6 20 ♖7f2 ♗c4 21 b3 ♗a6 22 ♕e3 ♕h8 23 ♖e1 ♗xe2 24 ♕xe2 ♘xd4 25 cxd4 ♗xd4 26 ♗e3 ♖xe4 27 ♕d3 ♕e5 28 ♖fe2 ♘f4 29 ♗xd4 ♘xe2+ 30 ♖xe2 ♕xd4+ 31 ♕xd4 ♖xd4 32 ♖e8+ ♔d7 33 ♖h8 g3 34 ♔f1 ♖xh4 35 ♔e2 ♖f4 36 ♖xh5 ♖f2+ 37 ♔e3 ♖xg2 38 ♔f3 ♖xa2 39 ♔xg3 ♖a3 40 ♖b5 ♔c6 41 ♖b4 a5 42 ♖c4+ ♔d7 **0-1** L/N6123-1853

**185̂3̂-★LS-1**
**Löwenthal,J.J.=Staunton, H.**
London [Staunton]

1 e4 e5 2 f4 d5 3 exd5 e4 4 ♗c4 ♘f6 5 ♘c3 ♗b4 6 ♘ge2 ♗g4 7 0-0 0-0 8 d4 c6 9 dxc6 ♘xc6 10 ♗e3 ♘a5 11 ♗b3 ♖c8?! [□ 11 ... ♘xb3 12 axb3 ♗xc3 13 bxc3 ♘d5] 12 ♕c1 ♘c4 13 h3 ♗xe2 14 ♘xe2 ♘d5 15 ♗xc4 ♖xc4 16 c3 ♗a5 17 ♕d2 b5 18 a3 f5 19 ♖ac1 ♖f7 20 ♘g3 ♗b6 21 b3 ♘xe3 22 bxc4 [22 ♕xe3?? ♖xd4–+] 22 ... ♘xf1 [22 ... ♘xc4!?] 23 ♘xf1 bxc4 24 ♘e3 ♕c8 [24 ... ♕c7 25 ♕e2 ♕xf4? 26 ♖f1 ♕g5 27 ♘xf5 ♖xf5 28 ♕xc4+–] 25 ♕e2 ♖c7 26 ♘d5 ♖d7 27 ♘e3 ♖c7 28 ♖b1 g6 29 ♖b4? [□ 29 ♘d5 ♖b7 30 ♖b4] 29 ... ♗a5 30 ♖xc4 ♖xc4 [30 ... ♗xc3?? 31 ♘d5+–] 31 ♕xc4+ ♕xc4 32 ♘xc4 ♗xc3 33 d5 ♔f7 34 ♔f1 ♗d4 35 ♔e2 ♔e7 36 a4 h6 37 ♘e5 ♔f6 [□ 37 ... ♗xe5=] 38 d6 ♔e6 39 ♘xg6 ♔xd6 40 g4 ♔e6 41 ♘h4 fxg4 42 hxg4 ♗c5 43 ♘f5 ♗f8 44 ♔e3 h5 45 ♔xe4 hxg4 46 ♘e3 **½-½** L/N6123-1853

**185̂3̂-★LS-2**
**Löwenthal,J.J.=Staunton, H.**
London [Staunton]

1 e4 e5 2 ♘f3 ♘c6 3 ♗c4 ♗c5 4 c3 ♘f6 5 d4 exd4 6 e5 d5 7 ♗b5 ♘e4 8 cxd4 ♗b6 9 0-0 0-0 10 ♗e3 ♗g4 11 h3 ♗h5 12 ♘c3 ♘e7 13 ♗d3 f5 14 exf6 ♘xf6 15 ♗e2 ♗xf3 16 ♗xf3 ♕d7 17 ♗g5 c6 18 ♖e1 ♘g6 19 ♕d3 ♗c7 20 ♗xf6 ♖xf6 21 ♗g4 ♕d6 22 g3 ♖af8 23 ♖e2 ♘h4 24 f4 [24 gxh4?? ♕h2+] 24 ... ♘f5 25 ♔g2 ♘h6 [25 ... ♘xg3+? 26 ♕xg3 ♖xf4 27 ♖h1+–] 26 ♖ae1 ♘f5 27 ♗xf5 ♖xf5 28 ♖e8 ♖f6 29 ♖xf8+ ♖xf8 30 ♕e3 ♗b6 31 a3 ♕f6 32 ♖d1 ♕g6 33 ♖e1 ♕f6 34 ♖d1 ♔f7 35 ♕e5 ♖e8 36 ♕xf6+ ♔xf6 37 ♔f3 a6 38 g4 h6 39 b4 ♗c7 40 ♘e2 ♖e4 41 ♖d3 a5 42 b5! cxb5 43 ♖b3 b4 44 axb4 a4! 45 ♖c3 ♗d6 46 b5 a3 47 ♖c8 ♗b4 48 ♖a8! [48 ♖c7?? ♖xe2 49 ♔xe2 a2–+] 48 ... b6 [□ 48 ... ♔e7] 49 ♖a4 [49 h4?? ♗a5–+] 49 ... ♗c5 50 h4 ♔e6 51 g5 hxg5 52 hxg5 a2 53 ♖xa2 [□ 53 f5+] 53 ... ♗xd4 54 ♘xd4+ ♖xd4 55 ♖a6 ♔f5 56 ♖xb6 ♖xf4+ 57 ♔e3 ♖b4 58 g6 ♔e5 59 ♔d3 ♖g4 60 ♖c6 ♖b4 61 b6 ♖b3+ 62 ♔c2 ♖b5 63 ♔c3 **½-½** L/N6123-1853

**185̂3̂-★LS-3**
**Löwenthal,J.J.–Staunton, H.**
London [Staunton]

1 e4 e5 2 d4 exd4 3 ♗c4 ♘c6 4 ♘f3 g6 5 0-0 ♗g7 6 ♗f4 ♘ge7 7 c3 d3 8 ♕xd3 d6 9 ♘bd2 0-0 10 ♗b3 a5 11 a4 b6 12 ♕e3 ♗a6 13 ♖fd1 ♕e8 14 ♗h6 ♖d8 15 ♕g5 ♔h8 16 ♕h4 [△ 17 ♘g5+–] 16 ... ♗xh6 17 ♕xh6 ♘g8 18 ♕h4 ♕e7 19 ♕h3 ♘e5 20 ♘d4 c5 21 ♘c2 ♘f6 22 f4

♘d3 23 c4 ♘xf4 24 ♕f3 ♕e6 25 ♖f1 ♘4h5 26 g4 ♕g5 27 ♘e3

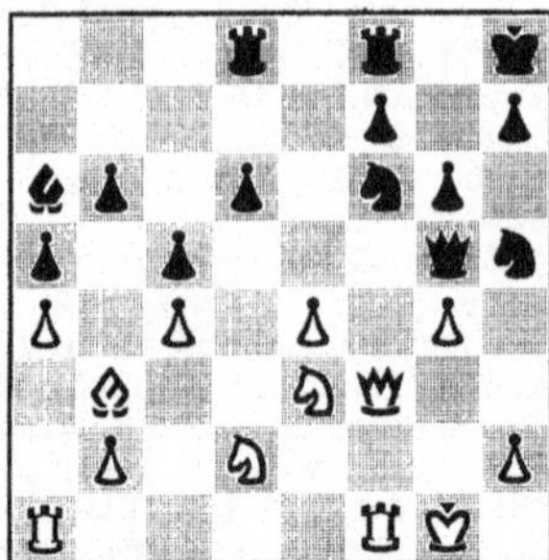

27 ... ♘xg4 28 ♘xg4 ♕xd2 29 ♖f2 ♕g5 30 ♖g2 ♗b7 [◻ 30 ... ♗c8] 31 ♖af1 f6 [31 ... ♗c8? 32 ♕c3+] 32 ♗c2 ♗c8 33 h3 ♗xg4 34 hxg4 ♘g7 35 ♖d1 ♘e6 36 ♖d5 ♕c1+ 37 ♔h2 ♘d4 [37 ... ♘f4?? 38 ♖d1] 38 ♕g3 ♘xc2 39 ♖xd6 ♘e3 40 ♖xd8 ♘f1+ 41 ♔h3 ♖xd8 **0-1** L/N6123-1853

**1853-★PS-1**
**Petrov, A.D.+Szymanski**
Warszawa
1 e4 e6 2 d4 d5 3 exd5 exd5 4 c4 ♗b4+ 5 ♘c3 ♘e7 6 ♘f3 ♗g4 7 ♗e2 dxc4 8 0-0 ♗xf3 9 ♗xf3 c6 10 ♕e2 ♕xd4 11 ♖d1 ♕f6 12 ♘e4 ♕e6 13 a3 ♗a5 14 ♗g4 ♕g6 15 ♗f5 ♘xf5 16 ♘f6+ ♔f8 17 ♕e8# **1-0** L/N6047-1853

**1853-★PU-1**
**Petrov, A.D.=Urusov, D.S.**
St. Petersburg
1 e4 e5 2 ♘f3 ♘c6 3 ♗c4 ♗c5 4 0-0 d6 5 h3 ♘f6 6 d3 ♘a5 7 ♗b3 ♘xb3 8 axb3 ♗e6 9 ♗g5 h6 10 ♗h4 g5 11 ♗g3 g4 12 hxg4 ♗xg4 13 ♗h4 ♕e7 14 ♘c3 ♕e6 15 b4 ♗b6 16 ♗xf6 ♕xf6 17 ♘d5 ♕g7 18 c3 ♖g8 19 g3 ♗xf3 20 ♕xf3 ♕xg3+ 21 ♕xg3 ♖xg3+ 22 ♔h2 ♖xd3 23 ♖g1 0-0-0 24 ♖g7 ♖f3 25 ♖f1 ♖xf2+ 26 ♖xf2 ♗xf2 27 ♘xc7 ♔xc7 28 ♖xf7+ ♖d7 29 ♖xf2 ♔c6 30 ♖f6 ♖h7 31 c4 b6 32 ♔g3 ♖g7+ 33 ♔f3 ♖g1 34 ♖xh6 ♖c1 35 c5 bxc5 36 bxc5 ♖xc5 37 ♖h8 a5 38 ♔e3 ♔b5 39 ♖b8+ ♔c4 40 ♖b6 ♖b5 41 ♖xd6 ♖b3+ 42 ♔d2 ♖xb2+ 43 ♔c1 ♖b5 44 ♔c2 a4 45 ♖a6 ♔b4 46 ♔b2 ♖a5 47 ♖c6 a3+ 48 ♔a2 ♖c5 49 ♖b6+ ♔c3 50 ♖d6 ♖b5 51 ♖d1 ♔b4 52 ♖d3 ♖c5 53 ♖d8 ♖c2+ 54 ♔b1 a2+ 55 ♔a1 ♖c4 56 ♔xa2 ♖xe4 57 ♔b2 ♖e2+ 58 ♔c1 ♔c3 59 ♔d1 ♖e4 60 ♖a8 ♖e3 61 ♖a3+ ♔d4 62 ♖a4+ ♔d3 63 ♖b4 e4 64 ♖a4 ♖f3 65 ♔e1 ♔e3 66 ♖a8 ♖f7 67 ♖a3+ ♔f4 68 ♔f2 ♖c7 69 ♖a2 ♖h7 70 ♔g2 **½-½** M954-18??

**1853-★PU-2**
**Petrov, A.D.+Urusov, D.S.**
St. Petersburg
1 e4 e5 2 ♘f3 ♘c6 3 ♗c4 ♗c5 4 c3 ♘f6 5 0-0 ♘xe4 6 ♗d5 ♘f6 7 ♗xc6 dxc6 8 ♘xe5 0-0 9 d4 ♗b6 10 ♗g5 ♗e6 11 ♘d2 c5 12 ♘df3 cxd4 13 cxd4 c5 14 dxc5 ♗xc5 15 ♕xd8 ♖axd8 16 ♖ac1 ♗b6 17 ♘c4 ♗xc4 18 ♖xc4 ♖d6 19 ♗xf6 ♖xf6 20 ♖e1 ♖d6 21 g3 ♖d7 22 b4 f6 23 a4 a6 24 a5 ♗a7 25 ♔g2 ♔f7 26 ♖ec1 ♖fd8 27 ♖c7 ♗b8 28 ♖xd7+ ♖xd7 29 ♖c4 ♗d6 30 ♘d4 ♖c7 31 ♘f5 ♗e5 32 ♖xc7+ ♗xc7 33 ♔f3 g6 34 ♘e3 ♗d6 35 ♘d5 f5 36 ♔e3 ♔e6 37 ♔d4 g5 38 ♔c4 h6 39 ♘b6 ♗c7 40 ♘a4 ♔d6 41 ♘c5 ♔c6 42 ♘e6 b5+ 43 axb6 ♗xb6 44 f4 ♔d7 45 ♘c5+ ♗xc5 46 ♔xc5 ♔c7 47 h4 gxh4 48 gxh4 h5 49 ♔d5 ♔b6 50 ♔e5 ♔b5 51 ♔xf5 ♔xb4 52 ♔g6 a5 53 f5 a4 54 f6 a3 55 f7 a2 56 f8♕+ ♔b3 57 ♕f6 **1-0** L/N6123-1854

**1853-★PU-3**
**Urusov, D.S.−Petrov, A.D.**
St. Petersburg
1 e4 e5 2 ♘f3 ♘c6 3 ♗c4 ♗c5 4 c3 ♘f6 5 d4 exd4 6 cxd4 ♗b4+ 7 ♔f1 d5 8 exd5 ♘xd5 9 ♘c3 ♗xc3 10 bxc3 0-0 11 ♕c2 h6 12 h4 ♗e6 13 ♗d3 ♘f6 14 ♘g5 ♕d5 15 c4 ♕xd4 16 ♗b2 ♕d8 17 a3 ♘d4 18 ♗xd4 ♕xd4 19 ♖d1 ♕c5 20 ♘xe6 fxe6 21 ♕e2 e5 22 ♗f5 ♖ad8 23 ♖b1 ♖fe8 24 ♖h3 ♖d4 25 ♖xb7 ♖xc4 26 ♔g1 e4 27 ♖b1 ♖c2 28 ♖b5 ♕c6 **0-1** L/N6123-1853

**1853-★SS-1**
**Stanley, C.H.+Saint-Amant, P.C.F.de**
1 e4 c5 2 c4 ♘c6 3 ♘c3 e5 4 ♗d3 d6 5 ♘d5 ♘f6 6 ♘ge2 ♘xd5 7 cxd5 ♘b4 8 ♗b1 f5 9 a3 ♘a6 10 exf5 ♘c7 11 ♘c3 ♕g5 12 0-0 ♗xf5 13 d4 ♕g6 14 dxe5 ♗xb1 15 ♕a4+ ♔d8 16 ♖xb1 dxe5 17 f4 b5 18 ♘xb5 ♘xb5 19 ♕xb5 ♕xb1 20 ♕b7 ♖c8 21 f5 ♗e7 22 d6 ♗f6 23 ♗d2 **1-0** L/N6047-1853

**1853-★SS-3**
**Stanley, C.H.+Saint-Amant, P.C.F.de**
1 e4 c5 2 c4 ♘c6 3 ♘f3 e5 4 ♘c3 d6 5 ♗d3 ♗g4 6 h3 ♗h5 7 ♘d5 ♘f6 8 g4 ♗g6 9 ♕c2 ♘xd5 10 cxd5 ♕f6 11 dxc6 ♕xf3 12 cxb7 ♕xh1+ 13 ♔e2 ♖ad8 14 ♕a4+ ♔e7 15 ♕c6 ♔f6 16 ♗c2 ♕xh3 17 ♕c8 ♔g5 18 d4+ ♔h4 19 ♕xd8+ **1-0** L/N6047-1853

**1853-★SS-4**
**Saint-Amant, P.C.F.de+Stanley, C.H.**
1 d4 d5 2 c4 dxc4 3 ♘c3 ♘f6 4 e3 e6 5 ♘f3 ♗d6 6 ♗xc4 ♘c6 7 0-0 0-0 8 e4 e5 9 ♗e3 ♗g4 10 d5 ♘e7 11 ♗e2 ♘g6 12 h3 ♗d7 13 ♖c1 h6 14 ♕b3 ♖b8 15 ♗xa7 ♖a8 16 ♗e3 ♘h7 17 ♗d3 f5 18 exf5 ♗xf5 19 ♗xf5 ♖xf5 20 ♘e4 ♘h4 21 ♘h2 ♘f6 22 ♘g3 ♖f4 23 ♗xf4 exf4 24 ♘e2 ♕e7 25 ♖fe1 ♕d7 26 ♘d4 ♖a5 27 ♘df3 ♖b5 28 ♕c4 ♖b4 29 ♕d3 ♘f5 30 ♖e6 ♘e7 31 ♘e5 ♗xe5 32 ♖xe5 ♘exd5 33 ♘g4 ♖xb2 34 ♘xf6+ ♘xf6 35 ♕xd7 ♘xd7 36 ♖e7 **1-0** L/N6047-1853

**1853-★S?-1**
**Staunton, H.+?**
Richmond
⟨♘b1⟩ 1 e4 e5 2 ♘f3 ♘c6 3 ♗c4 ♗c5 4 b4 ♗xb4 5 c3 ♗a5 6 0-0 ♗b6 7 d4 exd4 8 e5 d5 9 exd6 ♕xd6 10 ♖e1+ ♘ge7 11 a4 dxc3 12 ♕b3 ♘a5 13 ♗xf7+ ♔f8 14 ♕a2 ♕f6 15 ♗h5 h6 16 ♗a3 ♘ac6 17 a5 g6 18 ♖xe7 ♗xf2+ 19 ♔xf2 ♘xe7 20 ♖e1 gxh5 21 ♖xe7 ♕xe7 22 ♘e5 c5 23 ♘g6+ ♔e8 24 ♘xe7 ♔xe7 25 ♗xc5+ ♔d8 26 a6 ♖b8 27 ♕d5+ ♗d7 28 ♕e5 **1-0** M954-1853

## JAENISCH✕SHUMOV
**[1854-✕JS]**

| | | | | | | | | | |
|---|---|---|---|---|---|---|---|---|---|
| C.F. Jaenisch | 0 | 0 | 1 | 1 | ? | ½ | ? | ½ | ? |
| I.S. Shumov | 1 | 1 | 0 | 0 | ? | ½ | ? | ½ | ? |

**1854-✕JS-1**
**Shumov, I.S.+Jaenisch, C.F.**
[Anderssen & Kossak]
1 e4 e5 2 ♘f3 ♘c6 3 ♗c4 ♗c5 4 c3 ♘f6 5 0-0 d6 [5 ... ♘xe4 Bilguer] 6 b4 ♗b6 7 a4 a5 8 b5 ♘e7 9 d4 exd4 10 e5 dxe5 11 ♘xe5 0-0 [11 ... ♗e6] 12 ♕b3 ♕e8 [12 ... ♘ed5! Δ 13 ♗g5 ♗e6] 13 ♗a3 ♘e4 14 ♖e1 ♗f5

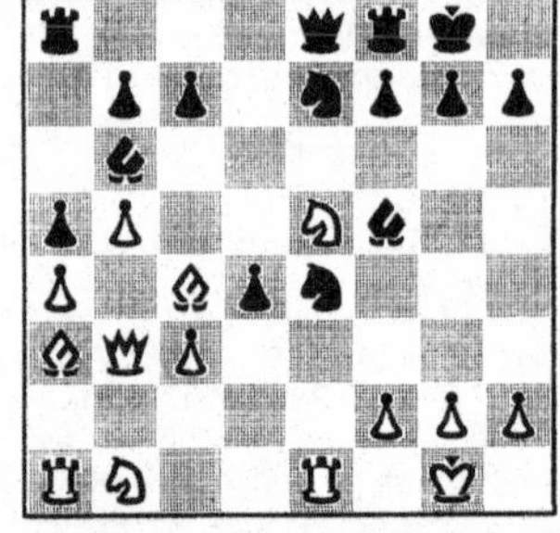

15 ♖xe4! ♗xe4 16 ♘d2 ♗g6 17 ♖e1 ♕d8 18 ♘df3 ♘f5 19 ♗xf8 ♕xf8 20 ♘xg6 hxg6 21 ♘e5 ♘d6

22 ♘xg6 ♖e8 23 ♖d1 ♘xc4 24 ♘xf8 ♘d2 25 ♕c2 dxc3 26 ♕h7+ ♔xf8 27 ♕h8+ ♔e7 28 ♖e1+ ♔f6 29 ♕xe8 **1-0** L/N6047

### 1854-⚔JS-2̂
**Jaenisch, C.F.– Shumov, I.S.**
[Anderssen & Kossak]

1 e4 e5 2 f4 exf4 3 ♗c4 ♕h4+ 4 ♔f1 g5 5 ♘f3 ♕h5 6 h4 h6 7 d4 d6 8 ♘c3 ♘e7 9 ♔g1 g4 10 ♘e1 f3 11 gxf3 gxf3 12 ♕xf3 ♖g8+ 13 ♔f1 ♗g4 14 ♕f2 ♘bc6 15 ♘b5 [□ 15 ♗e3] 15 ... 0-0-0 16 d5 ♘e5 17 ♕xa7 ♘xc4 18 ♕a8+ ♔d7 19 ♕xb7 ♖c8 20 ♘a7 ♗e2+ 21 ♔f2 ♗g7 22 ♕b5+ ♔d8 23 ♗e3 ♗e5 24 ♖h3 ♕g4 25 ♖f3 ♗xf3 26 ♘xf3 ♕g2+ 27 ♔e1 ♗g3+ 28 ♗f2 ♕xf2+ **0-1** L/N6047

### 1854-⚔JS-3̂
**Shumov, I.S.– Jaenisch, C.F.**
[Anderssen & Kossak]

1 e4 e5 2 ♘f3 ♘c6 3 ♗c4 ♗c5 4 c3 d6 [4 ... ♘f6; 4 ... ♗b6] 5 b4 ♗b6 6 a4 a5 7 b5 ♘ce7 [□ 7 ... ♘b8; 6 ... a6, 7 ... ♘a5] 8 ♕b3 f6 9 d4 ♗g4 10 ♗f7+ ♔f8 11 ♗xg8 ♘xg8 12 ♘bd2 ♕e8 13 dxe5 ♗e6 14 c4 fxe5 15 ♘g5 ♘f6 16 f4 h6 17 fxe5 hxg5 18 exf6 gxf6 19 ♗b2 ♔e7 20 ♖f1 ♖h6 21 0-0-0 ♕h5 22 e5 fxe5 23 ♗xe5 ♕g4 24 ♕d3 ♖g8 25 ♗b2 [□ 25 ♗g3] 25 ... ♕xg2 26 ♘e4 ♖h3 27 ♘g3 ♖xh2 28 ♘f5+ ♗xf5 29 ♖de1+ ♔d8 30 ♗f6+ ♔c8 31 ♕xf5+ ♔b8 32 ♗c3 ♗c5 33 ♖e7 ♕a2 34 ♕e4 ♕b3 **0-1** L/N6047

### 1854-⚔JS-4̂
**Jaenisch, C.F.+Shumov, I.S.**
[Anderssen & Kossak]

1 e4 c5 2 d4 cxd4 3 ♗c4 e6 [3 ... ♕c7, 4 ... ♘c6 Lasa] 4 ♕xd4 ♘c6 5 ♕d1 ♗c5 6 ♘f3 a6 7 0-0 ♘ge7 8 ♘c3 b5 9 ♗b3 0-0 10 ♗f4 f5 11 ♕d2 ♘g6 12 ♗d6 ♗xd6 13 ♕xd6 ♗b7 14 ♖ad1 fxe4 15 ♘xe4 ♖xf3 16 gxf3 ♘ce5 17 ♗xe6+ ♔h8 18 ♗d5 ♘xf3+ 19 ♔h1 ♘ge5 20 ♘d2 ♘xd2 21 ♖xd2 [□ 21 ♗xb7] 21 ... ♘c4 22 ♕f4 ♘xd2 23 ♕xd2 ♗xd5+ 24 ♕xd5 ♖c8 25 c3 ♕c7 26 ♖d1 ♕c6 27 f3 h6 28 ♔g2 ♖f8 29 ♖d3 ♕g6+ 30 ♔f2 ♖f5 31 ♕e4 ♕h5 32 ♖xd7 ♕xh2+ 33 ♔e3 ♕g1+ 34 ♔e2 ♕g2+ 35 ♔e3 ♕g5+ 36 ♔e2 h5 37 ♖d8+ ♔h7?? 38 ♖f8 ♕g2+ 39 ♔d1 ♕f1+ 40 ♔c2 ♕f2+ 41 ♔b3 ♕xf3 42 ♕xf3 **1-0** L/N6047-1855

### 1854-⚔JS-6̂
**Jaenisch, C.F.= Shumov, I.S.**
[Anderssen & Kossak]

1 e4 e5 2 f4 exf4 3 ♗c4 ♕h4+ 4 ♔f1 g5 5 ♕f3 d6 [□ 5 ... ♘c6] 6 g3 ♕h6 7 gxf4 gxf4 8 d4 ♕f6 9 ♕xf4 ♘c6 10 c3 ♗d7 11 ♘f3 ♕xf4 12 ♗xf4 f6 13 ♘bd2 ♗h6 14 ♗xh6 ♘xh6 15 ♔e2 0-0-0 16 ♖ae1 f5 17 exf5 ♗xf5 18 ♔d1 ♗g4 19 ♗e6+ ♗xe6 20 ♖xe6 ♘g4 21 ♖he1 ♔d7 22 ♘g5 ♖de8 23 ♖xe8 ♖xe8 24 ♖xe8 ♔xe8 25 ♘xh7 ♘xh2 26 ♘f6+ ♔e7 27 ♘d5+ ♔d7 28 ♘e3 ♘e7 29 ♔e2 ♘g6 30 ♔f2 ♘f4 31 ♔g3 ♘d3 32 b3 [32 ♘d1!] 32 ... ♘c1 33 ♔xh2 ♘xa2 34 ♘d1 ♔e6 35 ♔g3 c5 36 dxc5 dxc5 37 ♔f4 b5 38 ♘e4 ♔d5 39 ♘e3+ [39 ♘df2 b4 40 c4+ ♔d4] 39 ... ♔c6 40 ♘g4 a5 41 c4 ♘c1 42 ♘e5+ ♔b6 43 ♘d7+ ♔c6 44 ♘dxc5 ♘xb3 45 cxb5+ [45 ♘xb3=] 45 ... ♔xb5 46 ♘xb3 ♔b4 47 ♘c1 a4 48 ♘a2+ ♔c4 49 ♔e3 a3 ½-½ L/N6047-1855

### 1854-⚔JS-8̂
**Jaenisch, C.F.= Shumov, I.S.**
[Anderssen & Kossak]

1 e4 d5 2 exd5 ♘f6 3 ♗c4 c6!? [3 ... ♘xd5] 4 dxc6 e5 5 cxb7 ♗xb7 6 ♘f3 e4 7 ♘g5 ♗c5 8 ♗xf7+ ♔e7 9 0-0 ♕b6 10 ♗b3 ♕c6 11 d4 [11 ♕e2] 11 ... exd3 12 ♖e1+ ♔d8 13 ♕xd3+ ♘bd7 14 ♘f3 ♘g4 15 ♗g5+ ♔c8 16 ♗h4 ♘ge5 17 ♗d5 ♘xd3 18 ♗xc6 ♘xe1 19 ♗xb7+ ♔xb7 20 ♘xe1 ♘e5 21 ♘d2 ♖hf8 22 ♘ef3 ♘xf3+ 23 ♘xf3 ♖ae8 24 ♔f1 h6 25 h3 g5 26 ♗g3 ♖e7?? 27 b4 ♗b6 28 ♗d6 ♖xf3 29 gxf3 ♖d7 30 ♗g3 h5 31 h4 gxh4 32 ♗xh4 ♖d4 33 ♗g3 ♖xb4 34 ♔e2 h4 35 ♗e5 ♔c6 36 f4 ♔d5 37 ♖h1 ♖c4 38 ♖d1+ ♔e6 39 ♖d6+ ♔f7 40 c3 ♖a4 41 ♖d2 ♔g6 42 ♔f3 ♔h5 43 ♔g2 ♖e4 44 f3 ♖e1 45 ♗d4 ♖c1 46 ♖e2 ♗xd4 47 cxd4 ♖d1 48 ♖e5+ ♔g6 49 d5 ♖d4 50 ♖e4 ♖xd5 51 ♔h3 ♖h5 52 a4? [52 ♖e6+ ♔f7 53 ♖a6+–; 52 ... ♔f5 53 ♖e5+ ♔g6 54 ♖xh5 ♔xh5 55 f5 ♔g5 56 f6 ♔xf6 57 ♔xh4+–] 52 ... ♔f6 53 ♖c4 ♖h7 54 ♖c5 ♔g6 55 a5? [□ 55 ♔g4] 55 ... ♖f7 ½-½ L/N6047-1855

### 1854-★AE-1
18 ii 54
**Eichborn, L.+ Anderssen, A.**
Breslau

1 e4 e5 2 ♘f3 ♘c6 3 ♗c4 ♗c5 4 c3 ♘f6 5 d4 exd4 6 e5 ♘e4 7 cxd4 ♗b4+ 8 ♗d2 0-0 9 ♗xb4 ♘xb4 10 ♘c3 d5 11 ♗b3 ♗f5 12 0-0 c6 13 a3 ♘a6 14 ♗c2 ♗g6 15 ♘d2 ♕h4 16 g3 ♘xc3 17 bxc3 ♗xc2 18 ♕xc2 ♕h3 19 f4 ♘c7 20 f5 g6 21 ♖f4 f6 22 fxg6 fxe5 23 ♖h4 ♕e6? 24 g7 ♖f5 25 g4 e4 26 gxf5 ♕xf5 27 ♘xe4 dxe4 28 ♕xe4 ♕g5+ 29 ♖g4 ♕d2 30 ♖f1 **1-0** L/N3034

### 1854-★AE-2
2 iii 54
**Anderssen, A.– Eichborn, L.**
Breslau

1 e4 e5 2 f4 exf4 3 ♗c4 f5 4 ♕e2 fxe4 5 ♘c3 ♘f6 6 ♘xe4 ♘xe4 7 ♗d5 c6 8 ♗xe4 ♕e7 9 c4 g6 10 d4 ♗h6 11 c5 ♔d8 12 ♗d2 b6 13 ♘f3

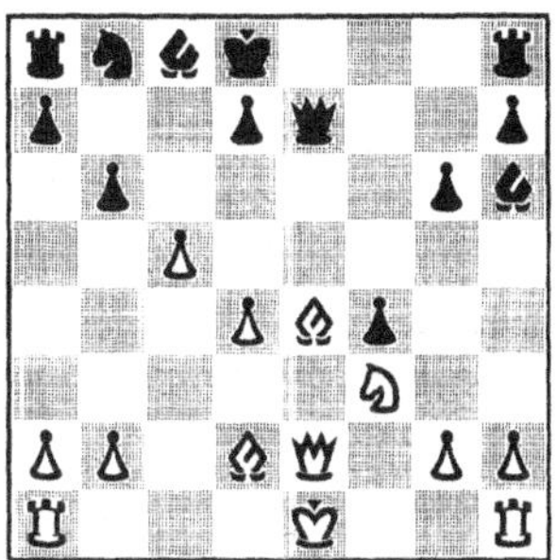

13 ... ♗a6 14 cxb6 **0-1** L/N3034

### 1854-★AE-3
25 iii 54
**Anderssen, A.– Eichborn, L.**
Breslau

1 e4 e5 2 f4 exf4 3 ♗c4 f5 4 ♘c3 d5 5 ♗xd5 ♘f6 6 d3 ♗b4 7 ♗b3 fxe4 8 ♗xf4 ♗g4 9 ♘ge2 ♘d5 10 ♕d2 ♗xe2 11 ♔xe2 ♗xc3 12 bxc3 exd3+ 13 cxd3 0-0 14 ♗xc7 ♕e7+ 15 ♔d1 ♕xc7 16 ♗xd5+ ♔h8 17 ♖b1 ♘c6 18 ♖b5 ♖f6 19 ♗e4 ♖d8 20 ♖h5 g6 21 ♖h4 ♖df8 22 ♕g5 ♕f7 23 ♗d5 ♖f1+ 24 ♖xf1 ♕xf1+ 25 ♔c2 ♖f2+ 26 ♔b3 ♕b1+ 27 ♔c4 ♕xa2+ 28 ♔c5 ♖f5 **0-1** L/N3034

### 1854-★AE-4
16 ix 54
**Eichborn, L.+ Anderssen, A.**
Breslau

1 e4 e5 2 ♘f3 ♘c6 3 c3 d5 4 exd5 ♕xd5 5 ♗e2 e4 6 ♘d4 ♘xd4 7 cxd4 ♕xd4 8 ♕c2 ♗d7 9 ♘c3 ♗c6 10 ♗b5 f5 11 ♗xc6+ bxc6 12 0-0 ♗d6 13 ♖e1 ♘f6 14 d3 0-0 15 dxe4 fxe4 16 ♘xe4 ♘g4 17 ♘xd6 cxd6 18 ♗e3 ♕d5 19 b3 ♕h5 20 h3 ♘e5 21 ♕e2 ♕g6 22 f4 ♘d3 23 ♖f1 ♖ae8 24 ♕d2 ♕e4 25 ♖f3 ♖f5 26 ♖af1 ♖d5 27 ♕c3 c5 28 ♕c4 ♘b4 29 ♖e1 ♘c2 30 ♖e2 ♕xc4 31 bxc4 ♖d1+ 32 ♔f2 ♘a3 33 ♗xc5 ♖xe2+ 34 ♔xe2 ♖a1 35 ♗xa3 ♖xa2+ 36 ♔f1 ♖c2 37 ♗xd6 ♖xc4 38 ♖a3 ♖c6 39 ♗e5 a6 40 ♖c3 ♖g6 41 g4 h6 42 ♖c8+ ♔f7 43 ♖c7+ ♔g8 44 ♖xg7+ ...? **1-0** L/N3034

**129** Kipping, J.S. L/N6135. BL

### 1854-★BK-1 21 vii 54

**Rivière,J.A.de & Kylman & Staunton,H.+ Blunden,J. & Kipping,J.S. & Löwenthal,J.J.**

Liverpool [Brien]

1 e4 e5 2 ♘f3 ♘c6 3 ♗c4 ♗c5 4 b4 ♗xb4 5 c3 ♗a5 6 d4 exd4 7 ♕b3 ♕e7 8 0-0 ♗b6 9 ♗a3 ♕f6 10 e5 ♕g6 11 cxd4 ♘xd4 12 ♘xd4 ♗xd4 13 ♘c3 ♗xc3 [13 ... ♗xe5?? 14 ♖ae1 △ 15 f4] 14 ♕xc3 ♘e7 15 ♖ad1 b6 16 ♖fe1? [16 e6!? fxe6 17 ♗xe6 dxe6 18 ♗xe7 (18 ♕xc7 0-0!) 18 ... ♕xe7 19 ♕xc7+ ♔f6 20 ♖d4 h5 21 ♖f4+ ♔g5 22 ♕c1+−] 16 ... ♗b7 17 f3 ♘c6? [17 ... c5!] 18 ♗d3 [18 ♖xd7! ♔xd7 19 ♗xf7 ♕xf7 20 e6+ ♕xe6 21 ♕xg7++−] 18 ... ♕h6 19 ♗c1 ♕h4 20 ♖e4 ♕h5 21 g4 ♕h4 22 e6! [22 g5!] 22 ... fxe6 [22 ... dxe6 23 ♗b5±] 23 ♕xg7 0-0-0 24 ♗g5 ♕h3 25 ♗xd8 ♖xd8 [25 ... ♕xf3 26 ♗h4 ♕xd1+ 27 ♖e1+−] 26 ♕f6 [△ 27 ♗f1] 26 ... ♖g8 27 ♗f1 ♕h5 28 ♖xd7! ♕c5+ [28 ... ♔xd7 29 ♕xe6+ ♔d8 30 ♕xg8++−] 29 ♔h1! ♘d8 30 ♖c4 ♔xd7 [30 ... ♕f2 31 ♖cxc7+ ♔b8 32 ♖xd8+ ♔xc7 33 ♕e7+ ♔c6 34 ♕d6#] 31 ♖xc5 bxc5 32 ♔g1 ♗d5 33 a3 ♘c6 34 ♗b5 ♖b8 35 ♗a4 ♔d6 36 f4 c4 37 h4 ♔c5 38 ♕g7 **1-0**

L/N6123

### 1854-★CM-1

**Cochrane, J.+ Mohischunder**

[Staunton]

1 e4 e5 2 ♘f3 d6 3 d4 exd4 4 ♕xd4 ♘c6 [4 ... ♗d7] 5 ♗b5 ♗d7 6 ♗xc6 ♗xc6 7 ♗g5 f6 8 ♗f4 [8 ♗h4] 8 ... ♕e7 9 ♘c3 ♕e6 10 0-0 ♘e7 11 ♖fe1 h6 12 ♘d5 ♕d7 13 ♘h4 ♔f7 14 c4 ♗xd5 15 exd5 g5 16 ♖e6 ♗g7 17 ♖ae1 ♖he8 18 ♕e4 gxf4 19 ♕h7 c6 20 ♖1e4 cxd5 21 ♖xf6+ ♔xf6 22 ♖xf4+ ♔e6 23 ♕xg7 ♕c6 24 ♕g4+ ♘f5 25 ♘xf5 **0-1** M954-1859

### 1854-★MM-1

**Morphy, E.= Morphy, P.C.**

New Orleans [Maróczy]

1 e4 e5 2 ♘f3 ♘c6 3 ♗c4 ♗c5 4 0-0 ♘f6 5 b4 ♗xb4 6 c3 ♗d6 [□ 6 ... ♗a5, 7 ... d6] 7 d4 ♕e7 8 ♗g5 [□ 8 ♖e1] 8 ... 0-0 9 ♖e1 a6 10 ♕c2 [□ 10 ♘bd2] 10 ... h6 11 ♗xf6 ♕xf6 12 ♘bd2 g5 [□ 12 ... exd4!] 13 dxe5 ♗xe5 14 ♖ac1 g4 [□ 14 ... d6] 15 ♘xe5 ♘xe5 16 ♗b3 h5 17 ♖e3 h4 18 ♖f1 ♔g7 19 f4 ♕b6 20 ♖fe1 ♘g6 21 g3 hxg3 22 hxg3 ♖h8 23 ♘c4 ♕c5 24 e5 b5 25 ♘d2 ♖h3 26 ♘e4 ♕b6 27 ♗xf7 ♗b7 28 ♘f2 ♘xf4 29 ♕f5 ♖f8 [30 e6!+−] **½-½** L/N3203

### 1854-★MM-2

**Morphy, P.C.− Maurian, C.A.**

New Orleans

⟨♕d1⟩ 1 e4 e5 2 ♘f3 ♘c6 3 ♗c4 ♗c5 4 0-0 d6 5 c3 ♘f6 6 b4 ♗b6 7 a4 a6 8 a5 ♗a7 9 b5 axb5 10 ♗xb5 0-0 11 d4 ♘xe4 12 ♖e1 f5 13 ♗b2 ♕f6 14 a6 ♘e7 15 axb7 ♗xb7 16 ♘a3 ♘g5 17 ♘d2 e4 18 ♘ac4 f4 19 ♘a5 e3 20 ♘f1 exf2+ 21 ♔xf2 ♘e4+ 22 ♔g1 f3 23 ♘xb7 f2+ 24 ♔h1 fxe1♕ 25 ♖xe1 ♘f2+ 26 ♔g1 ♘d3 **0-1** L/N3203

### 1854-★MM-3

**Morphy, P.C.Φ Maurian, C.A.**

New Orleans

⟨♖h1,♘g1⟩ 1 e4 e5 2 ♗c4 ♗c5 3 b4 ♗xb4 4 c3 ♗a5 5 ♗a3 d6 6 ♕b3 ♕e7 7 ♕a4+ ♘c6 8 ♗b5 ♗d7 9 ♗xc6 ♗xc6 10 ♕xa5 ♘f6 11 d3 0-0 12 0-0 b6 13 ♕b4 a5 14 ♕b2

L/N3203

### 1854-★MM-4

**Morphy, P.C.− Maurian, C.A.**

⟨♖a1,♘b1⟩ 1 e4 c5 2 f4 ♘c6 3 ♘f3 e6 4 c3 d5 5 e5 ♘h6 6 ♗d3 f5 7 ♘g5 ♘f7 8 h4 c4 9 ♗c2 ♗c5 10 b4 ♗b6 11 b5 ♘e7 12 ♗a3 0-0 13 g4 h6 14 gxf5 ♘xg5 15 hxg5 exf5 16 ♕h5 ♕e8 17 ♕h2 ♗e6 18 gxh6 g6 19 h7+ ♔h8 20 ♕h4 ♖f7 21 ♕g5 ♖xh7 22 ♖xh7+ ♔xh7 23 ♕h4+ ♔g7 24 ♗xe7 ♗d8 25 ♕f6+ ♔h7 26 ♗xd8 ♖xd8 27 b6 axb6 28 ♗a4 ♗d7 29 ♗d1 b5 30 ♔f2 ♗c6 31 ♗e2 d4 32 a4 d3 33 axb5 dxe2 34 bxc6 bxc6 35 ♔xe2 ♕d7 36 d4 cxd3+ 37 ♔d2 ♕d5 38 c4 ♕d4 39 ♕h4+ ♔g8 **0-1**

L/N3203

### 1854-★MM-5

**Morphy, P.C.+ Maurian, C.A.**

New Orleans

⟨♖a1,♘b1⟩ 1 e4 e5 2 ♗c4 ♗c5 3 d4 ♗xd4 4 ♘f3 ♘c6 5 c3 ♗b6 6 ♘g5 ♘h6 7 ♕h5 ♕f6 8 ♖f1 0-0 9 f4 ♕g6 10 ♕f3 d6 11 f5 ♕f6 12 ♕g3 ♗d7 13 ♘xh7 ♔xh7 14 ♗g5 ♕xg5 15 ♕xg5 f6 16 ♕h5 **1-0** L/N3202

### 1854-★MM-6

**Maurian, C.A.− Morphy, P.C.**

New Orleans

⟨♖a8,♙f7⟩ 1 e4 g6 2 d4 c5 3 d5 ♗g7 4 ♗d3 b5 5 c4 b4 6 a3 ♕a5 7 ♕d2 d6 8 ♘e2 ♘h6 9 0-0 0-0 10 ♕c2 ♘g4 11 ♗g5 ♗e5 12 h3 ♘h2 13 ♗h6 ♖f7 14 ♖d1

14 ... ♗xh3 15 gxh3 ♘f3+ 16 ♔h1 ♕d8 17 ♘d2 ♕d7 18 ♘g1 ♘xg1 19 ♔xg1 ♕xh3 **0-1**

L/N3203

### 1854-★MM-7

**Maurian, C.A.+ Morphy, P.C.**

New Orleans

⟨♖a8,♙f7⟩ 1 e4 e6 2 d4 d5 3 ♗d3 dxe4 4 ♗xe4 ♕h4 5 ♘c3 ♗b4 6 ♕e2 ♘e7 7 ♘f3 ♕h5 8 0-0 0-0 9 ♘e5 ♕h4 10 ♕g4 ♕xg4 11 ♘xg4 ♘d7 12 ♘e5 ♘f6 13 ♗d3 b6 14 ♗c4 ♘f5 15 d5 ♗d6 16 dxe6 ♘e7 17 ♘d7 ♗xd7 18 exd7+ ♔h8 19 ♗f7 ♘xd7 20 ♗b3 ♘f5 21 ♘b5 ♗c5 22 c3 ♘e5 23 ♗e3 c6 24 ♗xc5 bxc5 25 ♘a3 ♘h4 26 ♘c4 ♘d3 27 ♖ad1 **1-0** L/N3202

### 1854-★MM-8

**Maurian, C.A.− Morphy, P.C.**

New Orleans

⟨♖a8,♙f7⟩ 1 e4 ♘h6 2 d4 ♘f7 3 ♗c4 e6 4 ♘c3 c6 5 ♗d3 ♗b4 6 ♘f3 d5 7 0-0 ♘d7 8 a3 ♗a5 9 b4 ♗c7 10 e5 g5 11 ♘e1 ♕e7 12 f4 ♗b6 13 ♗e2 gxf4 14 ♗xf4 ♘dxe5 15 ♗xe5 ♘xe5 16 ♔h1 ♘g6 17 ♗h5 ♕h4 18 ♕g4 ♕xg4 19 ♗xg4 ♗xd4 20 ♖f3 h5 21 ♗xe6 ♗xe6 22 ♖d3 ♗b6 23 ♘f3 ♘f4 24 ♖d2 ♗e3 25 ♖dd1 ♖g8 26 ♖e1 d4 27 ♖ad1 ♘xg2 28 ♖xe3 dxe3 29 ♖g1 ♗g4 **0-1** L/N3203

### 1854-★MM-9

**Maurian, C.A.+ Morphy, P.C.**

New Orleans

⟨♖a8,♙f7⟩ 1 e4 ... 2 d4 e6 3 ♗d3 d5 4 e5 c5 5 ♘f3 c4 6 ♗e2 b5 7

0-0 ♘h6 8 ♗e3 ♘f5 9 a4 b4 10 ♘bd2 ♗e7 11 h3 h5 12 ♘h2 g6 13 ♘xc4 dxc4 14 ♗xc4 ♘a6 15 d5 ♘xe3 16 fxe3 ♕b6 17 ♗b5+ ♔d8 18 dxe6+ ♔c7 19 ♖f7 ♕xe6 20 ♕d6+ ♕xd6 21 exd6+ ♔xd6 22 ♖d1+ ♔e6 23 ♗c4+ ♔e5 24 ♖xe7+ ♔f5 25 ♖f7+ ♔e5 26 ♘f3+ ♔e4 27 ♖d4+ ♔xe3 28 ♖e7+ ♗e6 29 ♖xe6# **1-0** L/N3203

### 1854-★MM-10
### Maurian, C.A.– Morphy, P.C.

New Orleans

⟨♖a8,♙f7⟩ 1 e4 ... 2 d4 e6 3 c4 ♘c6 4 d5 ♘e5 5 f4 ♘g6 6 ♗e3 ♗b4+ 7 ♘c3 e5 8 ♕h5 ♘f6 9 ♕g5 ♗e7 10 f5 ♘xd5 11 ♕h5 ♘xe3 12 ♔f2 0-0 13 ♔xe3 ♗g5+ 14 ♔f3 ♘f4 15 ♕g4 h5 16 ♕g3 ♗h4 **0-1** L/N3203

### 1854-★MM-11
### Maurian, C.A.+ Morphy, P.C.

New Orleans

⟨♖a8,♙f7⟩ 1 e4 ... 2 d4 e6 3 ♗d3 g6 4 ♘f3 c5 5 c3 d5 6 e5 ♘c6 7 ♕a4 c4 8 ♗g5 ♕b6 9 ♗xc4 dxc4 10 b3 cxb3 11 axb3 ♗d7 12 ♘bd2 ♘xe5 13 ♕xa7 ♘d3+ 14 ♔e2 ♕b5 15 c4 ♕f5 16 ♕xb7 ♘e7 17 ♖a8+ ♘c8 18 ♖xc8+ ♗xc8 19 ♕xc8+ ♔f7 20 ♕c7+ ♔g8 21 g4 ♕xg4 22 ♔xd3 ♕f5+ 23 ♔e2 h6 24 ♗f4 g5 25 ♗d6 ♖h7 26 ♕d8 ♖f7 27 ♖f1 ♕c2 28 ♘e5 ♖f4 29 f3 g4 30 ♘xg4 ♖xd4 31 ♕xf8+ ♔h7 32 ♕f7+ **1-0** L/N3203

### 1854-★MM-12
### Morphy, P.C.+ Maurian, C.A.

New Orleans

⟨♖a1,♘b1⟩ 1 e4 e6 2 f4 d5 3 e5 ♘e7 4 ♘f3 ♘ec6 5 g4 ♗e7 6 d4 0-0 7 c3 f5 8 exf6 ♗xf6 9 h4 ♘a5 10 g5 ♗e7 11 h5 ♘d7 12 ♗d3 ♘b6 13 ♕c2 h6 14 gxh6 gxh6 15 ♖g1+ ♔h8 16 ♖g6 ♖f6 17 ♕g2 ♕f8 18 ♘h4 ♕f7 19 f5 ♗d7 20 ♗xh6 ♖g8 21 ♗g5 ♖fxg6 22 ♘xg6+ ♖xg6 23 hxg6 ♕g7 24 ♕h1+ ♔g8 25 f6 **1-0** L/N3203

### 1854-★MM-13
### Morphy, P.C.= Maurian, C.A.

New Orleans

⟨♖a1,♘b1⟩ 1 e4 e5 2 ♘f3 ♘c6 3 d4 exd4 4 ♗c4 ♗c5 5 0-0 ♘ge7 6 ♘g5 d5 7 exd5 ♘xd5 8 ♘xf7 ♔xf7 9 ♕h5+ ♔f8 10 ♗xd5 ♕f6 11 ♖e1 ♗f5 12 h4 ♗g6 13 ♕g4 ♕f5 14 ♕xf5+ ♗xf5 15 ♗xc6 bxc6 16 ♖e5 ♗xc2 17 ♖xc5 d3 18 ♖xc6 ♔g8 19 ♖xc7 h6 20 ♗d2 ♖e8 21 ♔f1 ♖e2 22 ♖xc2 dxc2 23 ♔xe2 ♔h7 24 ♔d3 ♖c8 25 ♗c1 ♔g6 26 b4 ♔f5 27 a4 a6 28 b5 axb5 29 axb5 ♖c5 30 b6 ♖b5 31 ♔xc2 ♖xb6 32 f3 ♖c6+ 33 ♔d1 ♖xc1+ 34 ♔xc1 ♔f4 35 ♔d2 ♔g3 36 ♔e3 ♔xh4 37 ♔f4 g6 38 g4 h5 39 g5 ♔h3 40 ♔e5 ♔g3 41 ♔f6 ♔xf3 42 ♔xg6 h4 43 ♔f6 h3 44 g6 h2 45 g7 h1♕ 46 g8♕ **½-½** L/N3203

### 1854-★MM-14
### Morphy, P.C.+ Maurian, C.A.

New Orleans

⟨♖a1,♘b1⟩ 1 e4 e6 2 f4 d5 3 e5 c5 4 ♘f3 ♘e7 5 c3 ♘ec6 6 ♗e2 ♗e7 7 0-0 f5 8 exf6 ♗xf6 9 g4 e5 10 g5 e4 11 ♘h4 ♗e7 12 f5 0-0 13 f6 ♗d6 14 ♗h5 gxf6 15 g6 f5 16 gxh7+ ♔h8 17 ♘g6+ ♔xh7 18 ♘xf8+ ♕xf8 19 ♔h1 f4 20 ♖g1 f3 21 ♗g6+ ♔h8 22 ♖g3 ♗g4 23 ♖xg4 ♕h6 24 ♕g1 ♕xh2+ 25 ♕xh2+ ♗xh2 26 ♔xh2 ♘d7 27 d4 **1-0** L/N3203

### 1854-★OS-1 25̂ x 54
### Oldham, T.C. & Skipworth, A.B. & ♀+ Staunton, H.

Caistor [Staunton]

⟨♙f7⟩ 1 e4 ... 2 d4 ♘c6 3 d5 ♘e5 4 f4 ♘f7 5 ♗d3 e5 6 fxe5 ♘xe5 7 ♕h5+ ♘f7 8 e5 g6 9 ♕e2 ♕e7 10 ♘f3 ♗g7 11 e6! dxe6 12 ♗b5+ ♔f8 13 dxe6 ♗xe6 14 0-0 ♘f6 15 ♖e1 c6 16 ♗d3 [16 ♕xe6?!] 16 ... ♖e8 17 ♘c3 ♘g4 18 ♘e4 ♕d8 19 h3 ♘ge5 20 ♗g5! ♕b6+ [20 ... ♘xf3+ 21 ♕xf3±] 21 ♗e3 ♘xf3+ 22 ♕xf3 ♗d4 23 ♘f6 ♖e7 24 b3 ♔g7 25 ♔h1! ♗xe3 26 ♖xe3 ♕d4? 27 ♖f1 ♘d6 [27 ... ♖f8 28 ♖e4 ♕~ 29 ♘h5++−; 27 ... ♘g5 28 ♕g3 △ 29 h4+−; 27 ... ♘e5 28 ♘h5+ △ 29 ♕f6+−] 28 ♕g3 ♖f8 29 c3!+− ♕b6 [29 ... ♕c5 30 b4] 30 ♕xd6 ...♀ **1-0** M954

### 1854-★OS-2 26̂ x 54
### Oldham, T.C. & Skipworth, A.B. & ♀– Staunton, H.

Caistor [Staunton]

⟨♙f7⟩ 1 e4 ... 2 d4 ♘c6 3 ♗d3 e5 4 d5 ♘ce7 5 c4 ♘g6 6 ♗e3 ♗b4+ 7 ♘d2 ♘f6 8 ♘e2 0-0 9 0-0 ♘g4 10 h3 ♘xe3 11 fxe3 ♗c5 12 ♖xf8+ ♘xf8 13 ♘f1 d6 14 ♕d2 ♘g6 15 ♔h2 ♕g5 16 ♘g1 ♘h4 17 ♕f2 ♗d7 18 ♕g3 ♕h6 19 ♗e2 ♖f8 20 ♗g4 ♗xg4 21 ♕xg4 ♕f6! [△ 22 ... ♕f2] 22 ♘f3 ♘xf3+ 23 gxf3 ♕xf3 24 ♕xf3 ♖xf3 25 ♔g2 ♖f6 26 ♖e1 c6 27 ♖e2 h5 28 ♖f2 ♖g6+ 29 ♔h2 h4 30 ♖f3 cxd5 31 exd5 a6 32 ♘d2 ♔h7! 33 ♘e4 b6 34 ♘xc5 bxc5 35 e4 a5 36 a3 [36 ♖a3 ♔h6 37 ♖xa5 ♔g5 38 a3 (38 ♖a3 ♔f4−+) 38 ... ♔f4 39 b4 ♔f3 40 bxc5 ♖g2+ 41 ♔h1 ♖g3−+] 36 ... a4! 37 b4 [37 b3−+] 37 ... ♖g3!!−+ 38 bxc5 [38 ♖xg3 hxg3+ 39 ♔xg3 cxb4 40 c5! bxa3 41 cxd6 a2 42 d7 a1♕ 43 d8♕ ♕g1+ 44 ♔f3 ♕f1+ 45 ♔g3 (45 ♔e3 ♕xh3+−+) 45 ... ♕f4+ 46 ♔g2 ♕xe4−+] 38 ... ♖xf3 39 cxd6 ♔g8 40 d7 ♖f8 41 c5 ♔f7 42 d6 ♔e6 **0-1** M954

### 1854-★RS-1
### Rogers & Smith+ Staunton, H.

Liverpool

⟨♙f7⟩ 1 e4 ... 2 d4 ♘c6 3 ♗d3 e5 4 dxe5 ♘xe5 5 ♕h5+ ♘f7 6 f4 ♘f6 7 ♕e2 d6 8 ♘f3 ♗g4 9 0-0 ♗e7 10 h3 ♗xf3 11 ♖xf3 0-0 12 ♘c3 c6 13 ♗d2 ♕d7 14 ♖af1 ♖ae8 15 g4 g6 16 ♕g2 ♗d8 17 ♗e1 b5 18 b4 a5 19 a3 axb4 20 axb4 ♕a7+ 21 ♔h1 ♕a3 22 ♖g3 g5 23 fxg5 ♘xg5 24 ♘xb5 ♕a8 25 ♘xd6 ♗c7 26 ♘xe8 ♕xe8 27 ♖e3 ♕e6 28 ♖f5 ♘f7 29 ♗c3 ♘e5 30 ♗xe5 ♗xe5 31 ♕f1 ♔g7 32 ♗c4 ♕e7 33 g5 ♘h5 34 ♖xf8 ♕xf8 35 ♕xf8+ ♔xf8 36 ♖f3+ ♘f4 37 ♗b3 ♔g7 38 ♗a4 ♔g6 39 ♗xc6 ♔xg5 40 ♗d7 ♔h4 41 c4 h5 42 c5 ♘e2 43 ♔g2 ♘f4+ 44 ♖xf4+ ♗xf4 45 b5 ♗e3 46 c6 ♗b6 47 ♔f3 ♔g5 48 e5 ♔g6 49 ♗e6 ♔g7 50 ♔e4 ♔f8 51 ♔f5 ♔e7 52 ♗d7 ♗c7 53 e6 ♗d8 54 ♔g5 h4 55 ♔xh4 ♔f6 56 ♔g4 ♗b6 57 h4 ♗d8 58 h5 **1-0** M392

### 1854-★SS-1 25̂ x 54
### Staunton, H.= Skipworth, A.B.

Caistor [Staunton]

⟨♘b1⟩ 1 e4 c5 2 f4 ♘c6 3 ♘f3 d6 4 ♗c4 e6 [4 ... ♗g4 5 ♗xf7+!] 5 0-0 ♗e7 6 ♗b3 h6 7 c3 ♘f6 8 e5 dxe5 9 fxe5 ♘h7 10 d4 cxd4 11 cxd4 ♘g5 12 ♗e3 ♘xf3+ 13 ♖xf3 ♗g5 14 ♗f2 0-0 15 ♗c2 f5 16 exf6 ♗xf6 [□ 16 ... ♖xf6] 17 ♕d3 ♖f7 18 ♕h7+ ♔f8 19 d5 ♘d4! 20 dxe6 [□ 20 ♕h8+ ♔e7 21 ♕xd8 ♔xd8 22 ♗xd4] 20 ... ♗xe6 21 ♖ad1 ♘xf3+ 22 gxf3 ♖d7 23 ♖xd7 ♗xd7 24 ♗c5+ ♗e7 25 ♗d4 ♗f6 26 ♗c5+ **½-½** M954

### 1854̂-★DK-1
### Devinck, F.J.= Kieseritsky, L.

[Staunton]

1 e4 e5 2 f4 exf4 3 ♘f3 g5 4 ♗c4 g4 5 ♘c3 gxf3 6 ♕xf3 ♘c6 [6 ... d5!] 7 0-0 ♗h6 8 d4 ♘xd4 9 ♕h5 ♘e6 10 ♗xe6?! dxe6 11 ♗xf4 ♗xf4 12 ♖xf4 ♕d4+ 13 ♔h1 ♘f6 14 ♕h6 [14 ♕g5 ♖g8 15 ♕xf6 ♕xf6 16 ♖xf6 ♔e7 17 ♖af1 ♖g7∓; 18 ♘b5 ♗d7] 14 ... ♘d7 [14 ... ♔e7 15 ♖af1] 15 ♖af1 ♖f8 [15 ... ♘e5? 16 ♖d1 (16 ♕g7 ♖f8 17 ♖xf7±) △ 17 ♕f6±] 16 ♖xf7! ♖xf7 [16 ... ♕c5 (16 ... ♕d6 17 ♕h5 ♖xf7 18 ♕xf7+ ♔d8 19 ♕g8++−; 17 ... ♔d8 18 ♖xf8+ ♘xf8 19 ♖d1±) 17 b4 ♖xf7 (17 ... ♕xb4 18 ♕xe6+ ♔d8 19 ♘d5 ♖xf7 20 ♕xf7 ♕xe4 21 ♕g8+ ♕e8 22 ♕g5+ ♘f6 23

# 1854̂-★DS-1/1854̂-★KS-1



♕xf6+ ♔d7 24 ♘b6+ cxb6 25 ♖d1+ ♔c7 26 ♕d6#; 18 ♕h5 ♔d8 19 ♕g5+ ♔e8 20 ♘b5 ♖xf7 21 ♘xc7+ ♔f8 22 ♘xe6+ ♔e8 23 ♕d8#; 18 ♕h5 ♖xf7 19 ♕xf7+ ♔d8 20 ♕g8+ ♔e7 21 e5+−) 18 ♖xf7 ♕c4 (18 ... ♕e5 19 ♕xh7 ♕g5 20 h4 ♕g3 21 ♖g7+−; 18 ... ♕xb4 19 ♕xe6+, 20 ♖g7±; 18 ... ♕d6 19 ♕h5 ♔d8 20 ♘b5; 18 ... ♕c6 19 ♕xh7+−) 19 ♕xh7+−] 17 ♕xe6+ ♔d8 [17 ... ♖e7 18 ♕g8++−] 18 ♖xf7 c6 19 e5 ♔c7 20 h3 a5 21 ♕e7 ♔b6 22 e6 ♘e5 23 ♕c7+ ♔a6 24 ♖f8 ♕e3 25 ♖xc8 ♕e1+ 26 ♔h2 ♘g4+ 27 hxg4 ♕h4+ ½-½ L/N6123-1854

## 1854̂-★DS-1
**Donaldson, J.− Staunton, H.**

[Staunton]

⟨♙f7⟩ 1 e4 e6 2 f4 d5 3 e5 c5 4 d4 ♘c6 5 ♗b5 ♕a5+ 6 ♘c3 cxd4 7 ♗xc6+ bxc6 8 ♕xd4 ♗c5∓ 9 ♕a4 ♕b6 10 ♘h3 ♘e7 11 ♗d2 ♖b8 12 ♘d1 0-0 13 ♘hf2 ♗a6 14 ♕b3 ♕c7 15 ♕h3 ♘f5 16 c3 ♕b6 17 g4 ♗xf2+ 18 ♘xf2 ♕xb2 19 ♖c1 ♘h6 20 ♘d3 ♕b5 21 c4 dxc4 **0-1**

L/N6123-1854

## 1854̂-★GS-1
**Gordon, T.+ Staunton, H.**

Edinburgh [Staunton]

⟨♙f7⟩ 1 e4 ... 2 d4 ♘c6 3 d5 ♘e5 4 f4 ♘f7 5 ♘f3 d6 6 f5 ♘f6 7 ♗d3 c6 8 c4 g6 9 ♘c3 gxf5 10 exf5 ♖g8 11 ♕e2 ♘g4 12 ♗f4 ♗g7 13 dxc6 bxc6 14 ♖d1 ♕a5 [△ 14 ... ♗xf5] 15 0-0!? ♗xf5 16 ♗xf5 ♕xf5 17 ♗g3 ♕c5+ 18 ♔h1 ♗xc3 19 bxc3 ♕e3? [⌓ 19 ... e5 △ 20 0-0-0] 20 ♕c2!± ♕h6 21 ♕e4 ♖c8 22 ♖de1 e5 23 ♘d4 ♕g6 24 ♘f5 h5 25 ♕b1!! ♘d8 26 ♕d1 ♘b7 27 c5 h4 28 cxd6! ♖d8 29 ♗xh4 ♘xd6 30 ♗xd8 ♘xf5 31 ♗c7 ♘g3+ [⌓ 31 ... ♕f6±] 32 ♔g1 ♘xf1 33 ♕d8+ **1-0**

M954-1854

## 1854̂-★GS-2
**Gordon, T.− Staunton, H.**

[Brien]

⟨♙f7⟩ 1 e4 ... 2 d4 ♘c6 3 d5 ♘e5 4 f4 ♘f7 5 c4 e6 6 ♘c3 ♗c5 7 ♘f3 d6 8 ♗d3 e5 9 f5 a6 10 h4 h6 11 ♕e2 ♘f6 12 ♘h2? [⌓ 12 ♗d2; 12 ♗e3] 12 ... ♖g8 13 a3 ♕e7 14 ♗e3 ♗d4 15 g4 g5 16 h5 ♗d7 17 ♔d2 c6 18 ♖ab1 ♖c8 19 ♖hg1 ♘d8 20 ♘f3 c5 21 b4 ♗xc3+ 22 ♔xc3 cxb4+ 23 ♖xb4 b5 24 ♘d2 ♘b7 25 ♔b2 ♘c5 26 ♗xc5 dxc5 27 ♖b3 b4 28 axb4 cxb4 29 ♖a1 ♕d6 30 ♔c1 ♔f7 31 ♔d1 ♕c5 32 ♖xa6?+ ♖a8 33 ♖xa8 ♖xa8 34 ♖b1 ♖a2 35 ♕f3 ♕g1+ 36 ♔e2 ♕h2+ **0-1**

L/N6123-1854

## 1854̂-★GS-3
**Gordon, T.+ Staunton, H.**

[Brien]

⟨♙f7⟩ 1 e4 ... 2 d4 e6 3 ♗d3 ♕e7 4 c4 d6 5 ♘c3 c6 6 f4 a6 7 ♘f3 g6 8 0-0 ♗g7 9 ♕c2 ♘h6 10 e5 d5? 11 cxd5 0-0 [11 ... cxd5? (11 ... exd5? 12 ♘xd5 cxd5? 13 ♕xc8+) 12 ♘xd5 exd5? 13 ♕xc8+] 12 d6+− ♕d8 13 ♘g5 ♘f5 14 ♗xf5 [14 g4 ♘xd4 15 ♕f2 ♕b6 16 ♗e3 c5 17 ♗xg6 hxg6 18 ♕h4] 14 ... ♖xf5 15 ♗e3 b6 16 ♖f3 ♕e8 17 g4 ♖f8 18 ♖af1 ♖a7 19 ♘ge4 h6 20 g5 h5 21 ♘f6+ ♗xf6 22 gxf6 ♔h8 23 ♖g3 ♖g8 24 ♘e4 c5 25 dxc5 [⌓ 25 ♘g5!] 25 ... ♕c6 26 ♘f2 ♖h7 27 h4 ♗b7 28 ♔h2 ♘d7 29 ♖fg1 ♘f8 30 ♘h3 bxc5 31 ♘g5 ♖d7 32 ♕xc5 [32 ♘xe6 ♘xe6 33 ♖xg6 ♖xg6 34 ♕xg6 ♕c8 35 f7] 32 ... ♕d5 33 a3 ♕b3 34 ♕c3 ♕d5 35 ♖c1 ♕b5 36 ♕c2 ♖d8 37 a4 ♕a5 38 ♗c5 ♖d7 39 b4 ♕d8 40 a5 ♗a8 41 ♗b6 ♕b8 42 ♕c4! [42 ♖c3!] 42 ... ♕b7 43 ♘xe6 ♘xe6 44 ♕xe6 ♕e4 45 ♕xd7 ♕e2+ 46 ♔h3 ♗e4 47 ♖cg1 ♕c2 [47 ... ♗f5+??] 48 ♖g5 ♕d3+ 49 ♔h2 ♕d2+ 50 ♖1g2 ♕xf4+ 51 ♖5g3 ♕xh4+ 52 ♕h3 ♕f4 53 d7 **1-0** L/N6123-1854

## 1854̂-★GS-4
**Gordon, T.− Staunton, H.**

Edinburgh [Staunton]

⟨♙f7⟩ 1 e4 ... 2 d4 ♘c6 3 ♗d3 e5 4 ♘f3 d6 5 d5 ♘ce7 6 c4 ♘g6 7 ♘c3 ♗e7 8 ♗e3 ♘f6 9 h3 c6 10 0-0 0-0 11 ♘h2 ♗d7 12 f4 exf4 13 ♗xf4 ♕b6+ 14 ♔h1 ♕xb2 15 ♘e2 ♘h5 16 ♖b1 ♕a3 17 ♖xb7?! ♘gxf4 18 ♖xd7 ♘xe2 19 ♖xf8+ ♖xf8 **0-1**

M954-1854

## 1854̂-★GS-5
**Gordon, T.+ Staunton, H.**

Edinburgh [Staunton]

⟨♙f7⟩ 1 e4 ... 2 d4 ♘c6 3 d5 ♘e5 4 f4 ♘f7 5 ♘f3 e5 6 ♗d3 [6 fxe5 ♘xe5 7 ♘xe5? ♕h4+] 6 ... d6 7 f5 ♗e7 8 c4 ♘f6 9 ♘c3 c6 10 ♗d2 ♗d7 11 ♕e2 0-0 12 0-0-0?!∓ cxd5 13 cxd5 a6 14 h3 b5 15 ♖dg1 b4 16 ♘d1 ♕a5? 17 ♔b1 ♖fc8? 18 a3 ♕a4? [⌓ 18 ... ♕b6] 19 ♗xb4 ♘h5 20 g3 ♗b5! [21 ♘c3 △ 22 ♘d2+−] 21 ♗xb5 axb5 22 ♘c3 ♕a6 23 h4 ♗d8 24 ♕xb5 ♗b6 25 ♕xa6 ♖xa6 26 ♖g2 ♖c4 27 ♖c1 ♗e3 28 ♖cc2 ♘f6 29 g4 ♖a8 [29 ... ♘xe4??+−] 30 g5? [⌓ 30 ♖ce2 △ 31 g5] 30 ... ♘xe4 31 ♘xe4 ♖xe4 32 g6 hxg6 33 fxg6 ♘h6 34 ♗xd6 ♘f5 35 ♗xe5 ♘xh4 36 ♘xh4 ♖xe5 37 d6 ♖d5 38 ♖g4 ♖xd6 39 ♘f5 ♖d1+ 40 ♔a2 ♗c1 41 ♖gc4 ♗g5 42 ♖c8+ ♖xc8 43 ♖xc8+ ♗d8 44 ♘e7+ **1-0** M954-1854

## 1854̂-★GS-6
**Gordon, T.− Staunton, H.**

Edinburgh [Staunton]

⟨♙f7⟩ 1 e4 ... 2 d4 e6 3 ♗d3 ♕e7 4 f4 d5 5 e5 ♘h6 6 ♘f3 g6 7 0-0 c5 8 c3 ♘c6 9 ♘g5?∓ cxd4 10 cxd4 ♘xd4 11 ♗xg6+ hxg6 12 ♕xd4 ♘f5 13 ♕d1?? ♕c5+ 14 ♔h1 ♘g3# **0-1** M954-1854

## 1854̂-★KL-1
**Kieseritsky, L.+ Laroche**

[Staunton]

1 e4 c5 2 b3 e6 3 ♗b2 d5 4 exd5 exd5 5 ♘f3 ♘f6 6 ♗b5+ ♘c6 [6 ... ♗d7 7 ♕e2+ ♕e7 (7 ... ♗e7 8 ♗xf6±) 8 ♗xf6 ♗xb5 9 ♗xe7 ♗xe2 10 ♗xf8 ♗xf3 11 ♗xc5 (11 ♗xg7±) 11 ... ♗xg2 12 ♖g1 ♗e4 13 d3 ♗g6 14 ♘c3 ♘d7 15 ♗d4 ♖c8 16 ♗xg7 ♖g8 17 ♗d4±] 7 ♕e2+ ♕e7 [7 ... ♗e6 8 ♘g5±] 8 ♗xf6 ♕xe2+ 9 ♔xe2 gxf6 10 ♖e1 ♗e6 11 d4 a6 12 ♗xc6+ bxc6 13 ♘bd2 ♔d7 14 c4 ♖g8 15 g3 ♖e8 16 ♔d3 ♗f5+ 17 ♔c3 ♖b8 [△ 18 ... cxd4 19 ♔xd4 (19 ♘xd4 ♗b4+, dxc4) 19 ... ♖g4+ 20 ♔c3 (20 ♔e3 ♖e8+) 20 ... ♗a3∓] 18 a3 [⌓ 18 cxd5 cxd4+ 19 ♘xd4 ♗b4+ 20 ♔b2 ♗xd2 21 dxc6+ ♔c7 22 ♖e7+ (22 ♘xf5 ♗xe1 23 ♖xe1 ♖ge8 24 ♖xe8 ♖xe8 25 ♘d4∓) △ 23 ♘xf5±] 18 ... ♗g6 19 ♖e2 cxd4+ 20 ♘xd4 [20 ♔xd4 c5+ 21 ♔c3] 20 ... c5 21 ♘4f3 d4+ 22 ♔b2 a5 [⌓ 22 ... ♗d3] 23 ♘e4 ♗e7 24 ♖d1 ♔c6 25 g4 ♖b7 26 h4 ♖gb8 27 ♖d3 h5 28 g5 a4 [⌓ 28 ... f5 29 ♘e5+ ♔b6 30 ♘xg6 fxe4∓] 29 b4 cxb4 30 ♘xd4+ ♔b6 [30 ... ♔c7 31 ♘b5+] 31 gxf6 bxa3+ [⌓ 31 ... ♗xf6] 32 ♔a2 ♗xf6 33 f3 ♗xd4 34 ♖xd4 ♔a7 35 ♔xa3 ♖b3+ 36 ♔xa4 ♖xf3 37 ♘d6 ♗d3 38 ♖e7+ ♔a8? [⌓ 38 ... ♔b6=] 39 ♘b5 ♗c2+ 40 ♔a5 ♖xb5+ 41 cxb5 **1-0**

L/N6123-1854

## 1854̂-★KS-1
**Kieseritsky, L.+Schulten, J.W.**

[Staunton]

1 e4 e5 2 f4 exf4 3 ♘f3 g5 4 h4 g4 5 ♘e5 h5 6 ♗c4 ♘h6 7 d4 d6 8 ♘d3 f3 9 g3 ♗e6 10 ♗xe6 fxe6 11 ♘f4 e5 [⌓ 11 ... ♕f6 12 ♘xh5 ♕g6∓] 12 dxe5 dxe5 13 ♕xd8+ ♔xd8 14 ♘xh5 ♗c5 15 ♗g5+ ♔c8 16 ♘f6 ♘c6 17 ♘c3 [17 ♗xh6 ♖xh6 18 ♘xg4 ♖g6] 17 ... b5 18 0-0-0 [18 ♘xb5 ♖b8 19 a4 a6 20 ♘c3 ♖xb2∓] 18 ... b4 19 ♘cd5 ♘d4 20 ♗xh6 ♖xh6 21 ♘xg4 ♖g6 22 ♘xe5 ♖xg3 23 h5 ♘e2+ 24 ♔b1 f2? [⌓ 24 ... ♔b7] 25 ♘d3 ♖g1 26 ♘xc5 ♖xh1 27 ♖xh1 ♘g3 28 ♖d1 f1♕ 29 ♘e7+ ♔b8 30 ♘c6+ ♔c8 31 ♖xf1 ♘xf1 32 h6 ♘d2+ 33 ♔c1 ♘xe4 34 h7 ♘xc5 35 h8♕+ **1-0**

L/N6123-1854

### 1854-★KS-2
**Kieseritsky, L.–Schulten, J.W.**

[Staunton]

1 e4 e5 2 ♗c4 f5 3 ♘f3 ♘c6 4 d3 ♘f6 5 ♘c3 fxe4 6 dxe4 ♗c5 7 0-0 d6 8 ♘g5 ♖f8 9 ♘xh7 ♖h8 [9 ... ♘xh7 10 ♕h5+±] 10 ♘g5 ♗g4 11 ♗f7+ ♔f8 12 ♘e6+ ♗xe6 13 ♗xe6 ♘d4 14 ♗h3 ♘h5 15 ♘e2 [□ 15 ♗e3] 15 ... ♘f3+ 16 gxf3 ♕h4 17 ♗g4 [17 ♗g2 ♘f4 (17 ... ♘g3 18 h3 ♘xf1 19 ♕xf1) 18 ♗xf4 exf4 19 h3±] 17 ... ♘f6 **0-1**

L/N6123-1854

### 1854-★LS-1
**Liddell, H.T.–Staunton, H.**

London [Staunton]

⟨♙f7⟩ 1 e4 ... 2 d4 ♘c6 3 ♗e3 e5 4 dxe5 ♘xe5 5 f4 ♘f7 6 ♗d3 ♘f6 7 ♘f3 c6 8 0-0 ♗e7 9 h3 b6 10 ♘g5 ♘h6 [10 ... 0-0? 11 e5] 11 f5 [11 e5 ♘d5] 11 ... ♘fg4! 12 hxg4 ♗xg5 13 ♗f2 ♘f7 14 ♘d2 ♘e5 15 ♘c4 ♘f7 16 e5 b5 17 ♘d6+ ♘xd6 18 exd6 0-0 19 ♗d4 ♗b7 20 c3 a5 21 ♕c2 ♖f6? [□ 21 ... ♗f6] 22 ♖ae1 [□ 22 ♗xf6 ♗e3+ 23 ♔h1 ♕xf6 24 ♖f3 ♖e8 (24 ... c5 25 ♘e4) 25 ♖af1 c5] 22 ... ♖h6 23 f6 gxf6 24 ♖e7 ♕f8 25 ♗xh7+ ♔h8 26 ♕f5 [△ 27 ♕xg5] 26 ... c5 27 ♗e5?? ♗e3+ 28 ♖f2 ♗xf2+ 29 ♕xf2 fxe5 **0-1**

M954-1854

### 1854-★HS-1
**Staunton, H.+H♀**

⟨♖a1⟩ 1 e4 e5 2 ♘f3 ♘c6 3 ♗c4 ♗c5 4 c3 d6 5 d4 exd4 6 cxd4 ♗b4+ 7 ♔f1 ♗g4 8 ♕a4 ♗xf3 9 gxf3 ♕d7 10 ♗b5 0-0-0 11 ♔g2 d5 12 e5 ♘e7 13 ♗f4 a6 14 ♗xa6 bxa6 15 ♕xa6+ ♔b8 16 e6 fxe6 17 ♖c1 ♘a7 18 ♖xc7 ♕xc7 19 ♕b6+ **1-0**

M954-1854

### 1854-★JS-1
**Shumov, I.S.–Jaenisch, C.F.**

1 ♘f3 d5 2 c4 d4 3 e4 c5 4 d3 ♘c6 5 ♗f4 e6 6 ♗e2 ♗d6 7 ♕d2 ♕c7 8 ♗xd6 ♕xd6 9 ♕g5 g6 10 ♘a3 a6 11 0-0 f6 12 ♕h4 e5 13 ♘d2 h5 14 f4 exf4 15 ♕xf4 ♕xf4 16 ♖xf4 ♘e5 17 h3 ♗e6 18 ♘c2 b5 19 b4 bxc4 20 bxc5 cxd3 21 ♘xd4 ♗xa2 22 ♖xa2 dxe2 23 ♘xe2 ♘d3 24 ♖f3 ♘xc5 25 ♖c3 ♘d7 26 ♘f4 ♘e7 27 ♘e6 ♔f7 28 ♘c7 ♖hc8 29 ♘xa8 ♖xc3 30 ♖xa6 ♘c5 31 ♖d6 ♘c8 32 ♖d8 ♘e6 33 ♖d7+ ♔e8 34 ♖b7 ♖c2 35 ♘b3 ♘d6 36 ♖b8+ ♖c8 37 ♖xc8+ ♘xc8 38 ♔f2 ♔d7 39 ♘a5 ♔d6 40 ♔e3 ♔c5 41 ♘b3+ ♔c6 42 ♘d4+ ♘xd4 43 ♔xd4 ♘e7 **0-1**

L/N6123-1854

### 1854-★JU-1
**Urusov, S.S.+Jaenisch, C.F.**

St. Petersburg♀

1 e4 e5 2 ♘f3 ♘c6 3 ♗c4 ♗c5 4 b4 d5 5 ♗xd5 ♘xb4 6 ♗b3 ♕e7 7 a3 ♗d7 8 ♗b2 ♘c6 9 d3 0-0-0 10 ♗d5 f5 11 ♗xc6 ♗xc6 12 ♘xe5 ♗xe4 13 0-0 ♕g5 14 ♘f3 ♗xf3 15 ♕xf3 ♘f6 16 ♘c3 h5 17 ♘a4 ♗d6 18 ♖ab1 c6 19 ♗c1 f4 20 ♗d2 ♘g4 21 d4 ♘h6 22 ♘c3 ♕f5 23 ♘e4 g5 24 ♖b3 ♗b8 25 ♕d3 g4 26 ♖fb1 ♖h7 27 ♖xb7 ♖xb7 28 ♕a6 ♕f7 29 ♘c5 ♖dd7 30 ♘xb7 ♖xb7 31 ♕xc6+ ♖c7 32 ♕xh6 ♖b7 33 ♕h8+ ♔c7 34 ♗xf4+ ♕xf4 35 ♕h7+ **1-0**

L/N6047-1858

### 1854-★JU-2
**Jaenisch, C.F.+Urusov, S.S.**

St. Petersburg♀

1 e4 e5 2 ♘f3 ♘c6 3 ♗b5 a6 4 ♗a4 ♗c5 5 c3 ♕e7 6 0-0 b5 7 ♗b3 ♘f6 8 d4 ♗a7 9 ♗g5 h6 10 ♗h4 g5 11 ♗g3 d6 12 dxe5 ♘xe5 13 ♘xe5 dxe5 14 a4 ♗b7 15 axb5 axb5 16 ♘a3 ♗xe4 17 ♘xb5 ♖d8

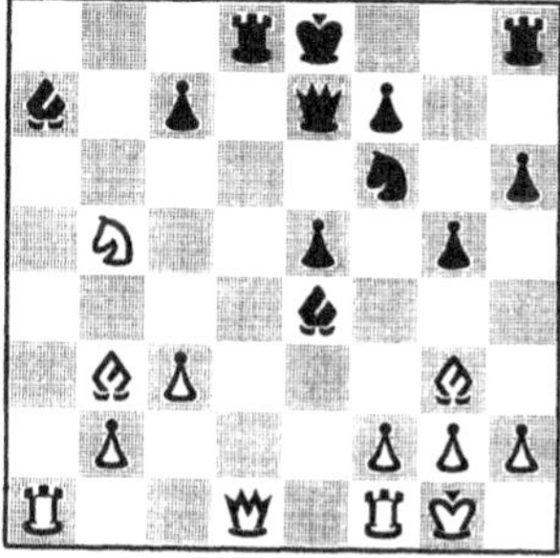

18 ♗xf7+ ♔f8 19 ♕b3 ♗c5 20 ♗c4 ♖b8 21 ♕a4 c6 22 ♘a3 ♖xb2 23 ♖fe1 ♖b7 24 ♗a6 ♖a7 25 ♘c4 ♗d3 26 ♖xe5 ♗xc4 27 ♕xc4 ♗xf2+ 28 ♔xf2 ♕d7 29 ♕c5+ ♔g7 30 ♖xg5+ hxg5 31 ♕xg5+ ♔f7 32 ♗c4+ ♘d5 33 ♕f4+ ♔g7 34 ♕d4+ **-0**

L/N6047-1858

### 1854-★JU-3
**Jaenisch, C.F.+Urusov, S.S.**

St. Petersburg♀

1 e4 e5 2 f4 exf4 3 ♗c4 ♕h4+ 4 ♔f1 g5 5 ♘c3 ♗g7 6 d4 d6 7 ♘f3 ♕h5 8 e5 dxe5 9 ♘d5 e4 10 ♕e1 ♔d8 11 ♕xe4 ♘c6 12 c3 ♘ge7 13 ♘xe7 ♘xe7 14 h4 h6 15 ♔g1 f5 16 ♕e1 ♕g6 17 hxg5 hxg5 18 ♖xh8+ ♗xh8 19 ♘e5 ♗xe5 20 ♕xe5 ♗d7 21 ♗d2 ♘c6 22 ♕h8+ ♗e8 23 ♖e1 ♘e7 24 ♖e6 ♕h5 25 ♕f6 ♕h7 26 ♕xg5 ♕f7 27 ♖d6+ cxd6 28 ♗xf7 **1-0**

L/N6047-1854

### 1854-★JU-4
**Urusov, S.S.+Jaenisch, C.F.**

St. Petersburg♀

1 e4 e5 2 d4 exd4 3 ♗c4 ♘c6 4 ♘f3 ♗c5 5 0-0 d6 6 c3 dxc3 7 ♘xc3 ♘ge7 8 ♗g5 0-0 9 ♘d5 ♔h8 10 b4 ♗b6 11 b5 f6 12 bxc6 fxg5 13 cxb7 ♗xb7 14 ♘xb6 axb6 15 ♘xg5 d5 16 ♘e6 ♕c8 17 exd5 ♖f6 18 ♖e1 ♕d7 19 ♖c1 ♕d6 20 ♕c2 ♖g6 21 ♗d3 ♕xd5 22 ♗e4 ♕xe6 23 ♗xb7 ♖xa2 24 ♕xc7 ♕f5 25 ♕c8+ **1-0**

L/N6047-1858

### 1854-★SW-1
**Wyvill, M.=Staunton, H.**

London

⟨♙f7⟩ 1 e4 ♘c6 2 d4 e5 3 ♗b5 ♘f6 4 ♘f3 ♘xd4 5 ♘xd4 exd4 6 e5 ♘d5 7 ♕xd4 c6 8 ♗c4 ♕b6 9 ♕e4 ♗c5 10 0-0 ♘e7 11 ♘c3 ♕c7 12 ♕f4 ♖f8 13 ♕g5 ♖f5 14 ♕xg7 ♕xe5 15 ♗f7+ ♔d8 16 ♕xe5 ♖xe5 17 ♘a4 ♗b4 18 a3 ♗a5 19 h4 d5 20 ♗g5 ♖f5 21 ♗h5 h6 22 g4 ♖e5 23 ♗xh6 ♗xg4 24 ♗xg4 ♖e4 25 f3 ♖xa4 26 ♗g5 ♔c7 27 ♗xe7 ♖e8 28 ♗g5 ♖e2 29 b4 ♗b6+ 30 ♔h1 ♗d4 31 ♖a2 a5 32 f4 ♖e3 33 ♖d1 axb4 34 ♖xd4 b3 35 cxb3 ♖xd4 36 f5 ♖e1+ 37 ♔g2 ♖xg4+ 38 ♔f2 ♖eg1 39 ♖e2 ♖1g2+ 40 ♔e1 ♔d6 41 ♖e6+ ♔c5 42 f6 ♖g1+ 43 ♔e2 ♖1g2+ 44 ♔d3 ♖xg5 45 hxg5 ♖xg5 46 b4+ ♔b5 47 ♖e7 b6 48 f7 ♖f5 49 ♔d4 c5+ 50 ♔e3 cxb4 51 axb4 ♔xb4 52 ♔d4 b5 **½-½**

M954-1854

### 1854-★SW-2
**Staunton, H.–Wyvill, M.**

London [Staunton]

⟨♙f2⟩ 1 ... e5 2 ♘c3 d5 3 e4 ♗b4 4 exd5?! ♗xc3 5 dxc3 ♕h4+ 6 ♔d2 ♘f6 7 ♕e1 ♘e4+ 8 ♔e2 ♕h5+ 9 ♘f3 ♗g4 10 ♗e3 0-0 11 h3 f5 12 ♖g1 ♗xf3+ 13 gxf3 f4 14 ♗f2 ♘g5 15 ♖g4 ♘xf3 16 ♔xf3 ♘d7 17 ♗h4 e4+! 18 ♔g2 e3 19 ♖g5 ♕f7 20 ♗d3 ♖ae8 21 ♖d1 ♘e5 22 ♗f5 h6 23 ♗e6 f3+ 24 ♔h1 ♖xe6 25 dxe6 ♕xe6 26 ♖g3 f2 [□ 26 ... e2] 27 ♕xe3 [□ 27 ♕e2] 27 ... ♕c6+ 28 ♔h2 f1♕ 29 ♖xf1 ♖xf1 30 ♖xg7+ ♔xg7 31 ♕xe5+ ♔g8 32 ♕g3+ ♔f8 **0-1**

L/N6123-1854

### 1854-★SW-3
**Staunton, H.+Wyvill, M.**

London [Brien]

⟨♙f2⟩ 1 ... e5 2 ♘c3 d5 3 d4 ♗b4 4 e3 e4 5 ♗b5+ c6 6 ♗a4 ♘h6 [6 ... ♕a5 7 ♗b3 ♗xc3+ 8 bxc3 ♕xc3+ 9 ♗d2 ♕b2 10 ♗b4 △ 11 ♖b1+−] 7 ♘e2 ♕h4+ 8 g3 ♕f6 9 ♗d2 b5 10 ♗b3 ♗g4 11 a4 ♗xc3 12 bxc3 bxa4 13 ♖f1 ♗f3 14 ♖xa4 ♕d6 15 c4 ♘g4 16 h3

♘h2 17 ♖f2 ♗xe2 18 ♔xe2 ♕xg3 19 ♕h1 dxc4 [◻ 19 ... ♘f3] 20 ♕xe4+ ♔d8 21 ♗a5+ ♔c8 22 ♖xf7 **1-0** L/N6123-1854

**1854-★S?-1**
**?– Staunton, H.**
Halifax
⟨♙f7⟩ 1 e4 ... 2 d4 e6 3 ♗d3 ♕e7 4 e5 d6 5 f4 ♘c6 6 h4 ♘xd4 7 ♗xh7 ♖xh7 8 ♕xd4 ♖xh4 9 exd6 cxd6 10 ♖xh4 ♕xh4+ 11 ♕f2 ♕h1 12 ♗e3 ♘f6 13 ♘d2 ♘g4 14 ♕e2 ♘xe3 15 ♕xe3 ♕xg2 16 0-0-0 ♗d7 17 f5 e5 18 ♖f1 ♗e7 19 ♘h3 ♕c6 20 ♘g5 0-0-0 21 ♘e6 ♗xe6 22 fxe6 ♔b8 23 ♕g3 ♗f6 24 ♕g6 ♖c8 25 c3 d5 26 ♖xf6 gxf6 27 ♕xf6 ♕d6 28 ♘f3 d4 29 ♘xe5 dxc3 30 ♘d7+ ♔a8 31 bxc3 ♕a3+ 32 ♔b1 ♕xc3 33 ♕xc3 ♖xc3 34 ♔b2 ♖e3 35 ♘c5 ♖e5 **0-1** M954-1854

**1854-★S?-2**
**Staunton, H.+?**
⟨♘b1⟩ 1 e4 e5 2 ♘f3 ♘c6 3 ♗c4 ♗c5 4 b4 ♗xb4 5 c3 ♗c5 6 d4 exd4 7 0-0 d6 8 cxd4 ♗b6 9 ♗b2 ♘f6 10 d5 ♘e7 11 ♗xf6 gxf6 12 ♘d4 ♗xd4 13 ♕xd4 ♘g6 14 f4 0-0 15 ♖ab1 a6 16 ♖b3 ♕e7 17 ♖g3 ♔h8 18 f5 ♘e5 19 ♕d2 ♖g8 20 ♖xg8+ ♔xg8 21 ♕h6 ♕f8 22 ♕xf6 ♕g7 23 ♕d8+ ♕f8 24 ♕xc7 ♘xc4 25 ♕xc4 ♗d7 26 ♕b3 ♗b5 27 ♖f3 ♖c8 28 ♖g3+ ♔h8 29 ♕b2+ f6 30 a4 ♗xa4 31 ♕xb7 ♖c1+ 32 ♔f2 ♗b5 33 ♖h3 ♖f1+ 34 ♔e3 ♕g8 35 ♖g3 ♕f8 36 ♔d4 ♖d1+ 37 ♔c3 ♖c1+ 38 ♔b2 ♖c8 39 ♖h3 ♕g8 40 g4 ♗f1 41 ♖h6 ♖b8 42 ♖xh7+ ♕xh7 43 ♕xb8+ ♕g8 44 ♕xd6 ♕xg4 45 ♕xf6+ ♕g7 46 ♕xg7+ ♔xg7 47 e5 **1-0** M954-1854

## BRIEN✕FALKBEER

**[1855-✕BF]**

| | | | | | | | | | | | | | | | | |
|---|---|---|---|---|---|---|---|---|---|---|---|---|---|---|---|---|
| R.B. Brien | ½ | 0 | 1 | 1 | 0 | 1 | 0 | 1 | 0 | 0 | ½ | 1 | ½ | 1 | 1 | 8½ |
| E.K. Falkbeer | ½ | 1 | 0 | 0 | 1 | 0 | 1 | 0 | 1 | 1 | ½ | 0 | ½ | 0 | 0 | 6½ |

**1855-✕BF-1**
**Falkbeer, E.K.= Brien, R.B.**
[Brien]
1 e4 e5 2 ♘f3 ♘c6 3 d4 exd4 4 ♗c4 ♗c5 5 0-0 d6 6 c3 dxc3 7 ♘xc3 ♘f6 [◻ ... ♘ge7] 8 ♗g5 ♘e7 9 e5 ♘d7 10 ♗xe7 ♕xe7 11 ♘d5 ♕d8 12 exd6 ♗xd6 13 ♖e1+ ♔f8 14 ♘d4 ♘b6 [14 ... ♗xh2+ 15 ♔xh2 ♕h4+ 16 ♔g1 c5 17 ♘f3 ♕xc4 18 ♗c7+–] 15 ♘xb6 axb6 16 ♕b3 ♕f6 17 ♘b5 ♗d7 18 ♘xd6 cxd6 19 ♗d5 ♖a5 20 ♖ac1 [20 ♕xb6 ♖xd5 21 ♕xb7 ♕f5 22 ♕b8+ ♗c8 23 ♖ac1+–] 20 ... g6 21 ♖c7 ♖b5 22 ♖xd7 ♖xb3 23 ♗xb3 ♔g7 24 ♖xf7+ ♕xf7 25 ♗xf7 ♔xf7 26 ♖c1 ♖e8 27 ♖c7+ ♖e7 28 ♖xe7+ ♔xe7 29 f4 [◻ 29 ♔f1] 29 ... ♔f6 30 ♔f2 ♔f5 31 ♔e3 h5 32 b4 [◻ 32 a4] 32 ... b5 33 h3 h4 34 ♔f3 d5 35 ♔e3 d4+ 36 ♔f3 d3 37 ♔e3 d2 38 ♔xd2 ♔xf4 39 ♔e2 ♔e4 40 a3 ♔d4 41 ♔f3 ♔c3 42 ♔g4 ♔b3 43 ♔xh4 ♔xa3 44 ♔g5 ♔xb4 45 g4 ♔a3 46 h4 b4 47 h5 gxh5 48 gxh5 b3 49 h6 b2 50 h7 b1♕ 51 h8♕ **½-½** L/N6123

**1855-✕BF-2**
**Brien, R.B.– Falkbeer, E.K.**
[Brien]
1 e4 e5 2 ♘f3 ♘c6 3 ♗c4 ♗c5 4 c3 ♘f6 5 d3 d6 6 h3 ♗e6 7 ♗b3 ♗xb3 8 axb3 h6 9 ♘a3 0-0 10 ♘c2 ♘h7 11 ♗e3 f5 12 exf5 ♖xf5 13 ♗xc5 dxc5 14 ♘e3 ♖f7 15 ♕c2 ♘g5 16 ♘xg5 ♕xg5 17 0-0 ♘e7 18 ♖a4 ♖f4 19 ♕e2 ♘g6 20 ♔h1 ♖xa4 21 bxa4 ♘f4 22 ♕c2 [◻ 22 ♕d1] 22 ... ♔h8 23 ♔h2 ♖d8 24 ♖d1 ♕g6 25 g3 ♘xd3 26 f3 e4 27 fxe4 ♕xe4 28 ♘g2 c4 29 ♖e1 ♕f3 30 ♖e3 ♕f1 31 ♘h4 ♖d6 [31 ... ♘f2 32 ♘g6+ ♔g8 33 ♘e7+ ♔h8 34 ♘g6+=] 32 ♖f3 ♕e1 33 ♖f8+ ♔h7 34 ♖f4 ♖e6 35 ♘g2 ♖e2 36 ♖e4 ♖xc2 **0-1** L/N6123

**1855-✕BF-3**
**Falkbeer, E.K.– Brien, R.B.**
[Brien]
1 e4 e5 2 ♘f3 ♘c6 3 ♗c4 ♗c5 4 c3 ♘f6 5 d4 exd4 6 0-0 0-0 [6 ... d3] 7 cxd4 ♗b6 8 d5 ♘b8 9 e5 ♘e8 10 d6 cxd6 11 ♗g5 ♕c7 12 ♘a3 dxe5 13 ♗e7 d5 [13 ... d6 14 ♗xf8 ♔xf8 15 ♘g5 f6 16 ♘xh7+ ♔e7 17 ♕d5±] 14 ♗xf8 dxc4 15 ♗b4 ♘c6 16 ♗c3 ♗g4 17 ♕d5 ♗e6 18 ♕e4 ♘d6 19 ♕h4 f6 20 ♖ad1 ♗c5 21 ♘c2 b5 22 a3 a5 23 ♖fe1 ♗f5 24 ♘e3 ♗d3 25 b4 axb4 26 axb4 ♗xe3 27 fxe3 ♖a3 28 ♗d2 e4 29 ♘d4 ♘xd4 30 exd4 c3 31 ♗c1 ♖b3 32 ♕h5! ♕c4? [◻ 32 ... c2] 33 ♖xd3 g6 [33 ... ♕xd3 34 ♕d5+–; 33 ... exd3 34 ♖e8++–] 34 ♕c5 ♕xc5 35 dxc5 exd3 36 cxd6 d2 37 ♖d1 ♖xb4 38 ♗xd2 ♖d4 39 ♔f2 ♖xd6 40 ♔e2 ♖xd2+ 41 ♖xd2 cxd2 42 ♔xd2 ♔f7 **0-1** L/N6123

**1855-✕BF-4**
**Brien, R.B.+ Falkbeer, E.K.**
[Brien]
1 e4 e5 2 ♘f3 ♘c6 3 c3 ♘f6 4 d4 ♘xe4 5 d5 ♗c5 6 dxc6 ♘xf2 7 ♕d5 d6 8 cxb7 ♗xb7 9 ♕xb7 ♘xh1 10 ♕c6+ ♔f8 11 ♗e2 f6 12 b4 ♗b6 13 ♗c4 ♘f2 14 ♕d5 ♕e8 15 ♘h4 ♖d8 16 b5 ♘g4 17 ♘f5 e4 18 ♘d4 ♗xd4 19 cxd4 ♘xh2 20 ♗f4 ♘g4 21 ♘c3 g5 22 ♗xg5 ♕h5? 23 ♗h6+ **1-0** L/N6123

**1855-✕BF-5**
**Falkbeer, E.K.+ Brien, R.B.**
[Brien]
1 e4 e5 2 ♘c3 ♗b4 3 f4 exf4 4 ♘f3 g5 5 ♗c4 g4 6 0-0 ♗xc3 7 bxc3 gxf3 8 ♕xf3 ♕e7 [◻ 8 ... d5] 9 d4 d6 10 ♗xf4 ♗e6 11 d5 ♗d7 [◻ 11 ... ♗c8] 12 ♖ae1 f6 13 e5 dxe5 14 ♗xe5 ♗g4 15 ♕xg4 ♔d8 16 d6 cxd6 17 ♗xd6 ♕d7 18 ♕g3 ♘c6 19 ♗e6 **1-0** L/N6123

**1855-✕BF-6**
**Brien, R.B.+ Falkbeer, E.K.**
[Brien]
1 e4 e5 2 ♘f3 ♘c6 3 ♗b5 ♘ge7 4 0-0 d6 5 d4 exd4 6 ♕xd4 ♗d7 7 ♕c4 ♘g6 8 ♗xc6 ♗xc6 9 ♘d4 ♕d7 10 ♘xc6 ♕xc6 11 ♕xc6+ bxc6 12 ♘c3 ♗e7 13 ♗e3 0-0 14 ♖ad1 ♗f6 15 ♗d4 ♗xd4 16 ♖xd4 ♖fb8 17 b3 a5 18 f4 ♖b4 19 ♖d2 f6 20 a3 ♖bb8 21 g4 ♘f8 22 ♔g2 ♖e8 23 h4 ♘d7 24 g5 ♖e7 25 ♔f3 ♖ae8 26 ♖e2 fxg5 27 hxg5 g6 28 b4 axb4 29 axb4 ♖b8 30 ♖b1 ♖f7 31 ♔g3 ♖bf8 32 ♖f2 ♖a8 33 ♖f3 ♖a3 34 ♖bf1 h6 35 gxh6 ♘f6 36 ♔h4 ♔h7 [36 ... ♖h7 37 ♔g5 ♖xc3 38 ♖xc3 ♘xe4+ 39 ♔xg6 ♘xc3 40 ♖a1+–] 37 e5 ♘d5 38 ♘e4 ♖xf3 39 ♘g5+ ♔g8 40 ♖xf3 ♖xf4+ 41 ♖xf4 ♘xf4 42 e6 ♘d5 43 ♘e4 ♔h7 44 ♔g5 ♘e7 45 ♘f6+ ♔h8 46 ♘e8 ♔h7 47 ♘xc7 ♘f5 48 ♘e8 ♘xh6 49 ♘f6+ ♔g7 50 e7 ♘f7+ 51 ♔f4 g5+ 52 ♔g3 **1-0** L/N6123

**1855-✕BF-7**
**Falkbeer, E.K.+ Brien, R.B.**
[Brien]
1 e4 e6 2 d4 d5 3 exd5 cxd5 4 ♗e3 ♗d6 5 c4 dxc4 6 ♗xc4 ♘f6 7 ♘c3 0-0 8 h3 c6 9 ♘f3 ♘bd7 10 0-0 ♘b6 11 ♗b3 ♘fd5 12 ♘e4 f5 13 ♘xd6 ♕xd6 14 ♖e1 ♗d7 15 ♘e5 f4 16 ♗d2 ♔h8 17 ♕h5 ♗e8 18 ♕f3 ♕d8 19 ♖e4 ♕h4 20 g4 g5 21 ♔g2 ♔g7 22 ♖ae1 ♘f6? 23 ♗b4 ♖h8 24 ♘d3 ♘xe4 25 ♕xe4 ♗g6 26 ♕e7+ ♔h6 27 ♘xf4 ♖ae8 28 ♘xg6 hxg6 29 ♕xe8 ♖xe8 30 ♖xe8 ♔h7 31 ♖e7+ ♔h8 32 ♖e8+ ♔h7 33 ♗d6 **1-0** L/N6123

**1855-✕BF-8**
**Brien, R.B.+ Falkbeer, E.K.**
[Brien]
1 d4 d5 2 c4 dxc4 3 e3 e5 4 ♗xc4 exd4 5 exd4 ♗d6 6 ♕b3 ♕e7+ 7 ♗e3 ♘c6 8 ♗b5 ♗d7 9 ♘c3 [9 ♗xc6

♗xc6 10 d5 ♕e4 11 dxc6 ♕xg2 12 cxb7 ♖b8 13 ♕b5+ ♔f8 14 ♕f5 ♕xb7∓; 9 d5 ♘a5 10 ♗xd7+ ♕xd7 11 ♕c3 ♕g4∓] 9 ... ♘f6 [9 ... ♘xd4 10 ♗xd7+ ♔xd7 11 ♕xb7 ♘f6 12 0-0-0±] 10 ♗xc6 bxc6 11 ♘ge2 0-0 12 ♗g5 ♗f5 13 ♕c4 ♖ab8 14 ♕xc6 ♖xb2 15 ♕f3 ♖e8 16 0-0 ♗g4 17 ♗xf6 [17 ♕xg4 ♘xg4 18 ♗xe7 ♗xh2+ 19 ♔h1 ♖xe7 20 f3 ♘e3 21 ♖fb1±] 17 ... ♗xf3 18 ♗xe7 ♗xe2 19 ♘xe2 ♖xe7 20 ♘c3 f5 21 ♖ab1 ♖c2 22 ♖fc1 ♖xc1+ 23 ♖xc1 ♗a3 24 ♖d1 [□ 24 ♖b1] 24 ... ♗b2 25 ♘d5 ♖d7 26 ♘f4 ♖xd4 27 ♖xd4 ♗xd4 28 ♘e6 c5 29 ♔f1 ♔f7 30 ♘d8+ ♔f6 31 ♘c6 a6 32 ♔e2 ♔e6 33 f3 ♗g1 34 h3 f4 35 ♘a5 ♔d6 36 ♘c4+ ♔e6 37 ♔d3 ♔f5 38 ♘d6+ ♔g5 39 ♔c4 ♔h4 40 ♘e4 g5 41 ♔d3 ♔h5 [□ 41 ... h5] 42 ♘d6 h6 43 a4 ♔g6 44 ♘e4 h5 45 ♔c4 ♔f5? 46 ♘xc5 g4 [□ 46 ... a5] 47 ♘xa6 gxh3 48 gxh3 ♗a7 [48 ... ♗b6 49 ♔b5 ♗d8 50 ♘c5 ♗c7 51 ♘e4+-] 49 a5 ♔g5 50 ♘b4 ♔h4 51 ♘c6 ♔xh3 52 ♘xa7 ♔g2 53 ♘c6 h4 54 ♘e5 h3 55 ♘g4 ♔xf3 56 a6 ♔xg4 57 a7 h2 58 a8♕ f3 59 ♕a1 ♔g3 60 ♕f1 f2 61 ♔d3 ♔f3 62 ♕h1+ ♔g3 63 ♔e2 **1-0** L/N6123

**1855-⚔BF-9**
**Falkbeer, E.K.+ Brien, R.B.**
[Brien]

1 e4 e6 2 d4 d5 3 exd5 cxd5 4 ♗e3 ♗d6 5 c4 dxc4 6 ♗xc4 ♘f6 7 ♘c3 0-0 8 ♘f3 h6 9 0-0 ♘c6 10 h3 ♗f5 11 g4 ♗c8 12 ♘e2 ♕e7 13 ♔g2 ♖e8 14 ♘g3 ♗xg3 15 fxg3 ♕b4 [15 ... ♕xe3 16 ♖e1 ♘xg4 17 hxg4 ♗xg4 18 ♖xe3 ♖xe3] 16 ♕d3 ♖xe3 17 ♗xf7+ ♔xf7 18 ♕xe3 ♗d7 19 g5 [19 ♘e5+ ♘xe5 20 dxe5 ♖e8] 19 ... hxg5 20 ♘xg5+ ♔g8 21 ♖ad1 ♕d6 22 ♔h2 ♕d5 23 ♕f4 ♖e8 24 ♖f2 ♘e7 25 ♖e5 ♕c6 26 ♕c5 ♘ed5 27 ♕xc6 ♗xc6 28 ♖c1 ♘b4 29 ♖a1 ♘e4 30 ♘xe4 ♖xe4 31 ♖d1 ♖e3 32 ♖dd2 ♗f3 33 a3 ♘d3 34 ♖f1 c6 [34 ... ♔f7 △ ♖e6 d5xd4→] 35 g4 ♔h7 36 ♖g1 ♔g6 37 h4 ♔f6 38 ♖g3 ♖e6 39 h5 ♔d5 40 g5 ♔xd4 41 h6 gxh6 42 gxh6 ♗e4 43 ♖xe3 ♔xe3 44 ♖g2 ♘e1 [44 ... b5=] 45 ♖g7 ♔f2 46 ♖f7+ [46 ... h7 47 ♘f3+ ♔h3 48 ♗xh7] 46 ... ♘f3+ 47 ♔h3 ♔e3 48 ♖xb7 ♔f4 49 ♖xa7 ♘g5+ 50 ♔h4 ♗g6 51 ♖a4+ ♘e4 52 ♖c4 [□ 52 ♖a6] 52 ... c5 53 a4 ♔e5 54 a5 ♔d6 55 a6 ♔c6 56 ♖a4 **1-0** L/N6123

**104** Falkbeer, E.K. M1647.BL

**1855-⚔BF-10**
**Brien, R.B.– Falkbeer, E.K.**
[Brien]

1 d4 d5 2 c4 dxc4 3 e3 e5 4 ♗xc4 exd4 5 exd4 ♗d6 6 ♕b3 ♕e7+ 7 ♗e3 ♘f6 8 ♘f3 0-0 9 0-0 ♘c6 10 ♘c3 ♘a5 11 ♕a4 ♘xc4 12 ♕xc4 c6 13 ♗g5 ♗e6 14 ♕d3 [□ 14 ♕e2] 14 ... h6 15 ♗xf6 ♕xf6 16 ♘e4 ♕g6 17 ♕e3 ♗c7 18 ♘e5 ♗xe5 19 dxe5 ♗d5 20 ♘g3 f6 21 f4 [□ 21 exf6] 21 ... fxe5 22 fxe5 h5 23 ♖f4 ♖xf4 24 ♕xf4 ♖f8 25 ♕d2 h4 26 ♘f1 ♖f5 27 ♘e3 ♖xe5 28 ♘xd5 ♖xd5 29 ♕e3 a5 30 ♖e1 ♖d3 31 ♕e8+ ♕xe8 32 ♖xe8+ ♔f7 33 ♖e2 c5 34 b3 ♔f6 35 h3 ♖d5 [△ 36 ... ♖e5] 36 ♖e8 ♖d1+ 37 ♔h2 ♔f7 38 ♖a8 b6 39 ♖b8 ♖d6 40 ♖b7+ ♔f6 41 ♖b8 ♔e5 42 ♖g8 ♔d5 43 ♖xg7 ♔c6 44 ♖f7 ♔b5 45 ♖f4 ♖d4 46 ♖f2 a4 47 bxa4+ ♔xa4 48 g3 c4 49 ♖c2 b5 50 gxh4 b4 51 ♔g3 c3 52 h5 ♖d2 53 ♖c1 ♖xa2 **0-1** L/N6123

**1855-⚔BF-11**
**Falkbeer, E.K.= Brien, R.B.**
[Brien]

1 e4 e5 2 ♘c3 ♗c5 3 ♗c4 d6 4 d3 ♘f6 [□ 4 ... h6] 5 ♗g5 ♗e6 6 ♘d5 ♗xd5 7 exd5 0-0 8 ♕f3 ♘bd7 9 ♘e2 a6 10 ♘g3 h6 11 ♗d2 b5 12 ♗b3 ♘h7 13 ♘f5 ♔h8 14 h4 ♕f6 15 0-0-0 a5 16 c3 g6 17 ♘xh6 ♕xf3 18 gxf3 ♗xf2 19 h5 g5 20 ♘f5 a4 21 ♗c2 ♘b6? 22 ♖df1 ♗h4 [22 ... ♗c5 23 d4+-] 23 ♘xh4 gxh4 24 ♖xh4 ♘xd5 25 c4 bxc4 26 dxc4 ♘e7 27 f4 f6 28 c5 a3 29 cxd6 [□ 29 b4] 29 ... axb2+ 30 ♔xb2 ♖fb8+ 31 ♗b3 cxd6 32 fxe5 dxe5 33 ♖g4 ♘g8 34 ♖fg1 ♖d8 35 ♖1g2 ♘e7 36 h6 ♘f5 37 ♗c1 ♘d4 38 ♖g7 ♘xb3 39 axb3 ♖g8 40 b4 ♖xg7 41 ♖xg7 ♖g8 42 ♖f7 ♖f8 43 ♖e7 ♘g5 44 ♗xg5 fxg5 45 ♖xe5 g4 46 ♖e1 g3 47 ♖g1 ♖f3 48 b5 ♔h7 49 ♖h1 ♖f5 50 ♔c3 ♖xb5 51 ♔d3 **½-½** L/N6123

**1855-⚔BF-12**
**Brien, R.B.+ Falkbeer, E.K.**
[Brien]

1 e4 e5 2 ♘f3 ♘c6 3 c3 ♘f6 4 d4 d5 5 ♗b5 ♘xe4 6 ♘xe5 ♗d7 7 ♘xd7 ♕xd7 8 ♕a4 ♗e7 9 0-0 0-0 10 ♘d2 ♘d6 11 ♗xc6 bxc6 12 ♘f3 f6 13 ♕c2 ♘e4 14 ♗e3 g5 [□ 14 ... c5] 15 ♖ad1 g4 16 ♘d2 f5 17 f3 ♘xd2 18 ♕xd2 h5 19 ♗g5 ♕d8 20 ♗xe7 ♕xe7 21 ♖de1 ♕g7 22 fxg4 fxg4 23 ♖xf8+ ♔xf8 24 ♕f4+ ♔g8 25 ♖e5 ♖f8 26 ♕g5 ♕xg5 27 ♖xg5+ ♔f7 28 ♖xh5 ♖b8 29 ♖h7+ ♔e6 30 ♖xc7 ♔d6 31 ♖xa7 ♖xb2 32 ♖g7 ♖c2 33 ♖xg4 ♖xc3 34 h4 ♖a3 35 h5 ♖xa2 36 h6 ♖a8 37 ♖g6+ ♔d7 38 g4 ♔e7 39 g5 ♖f8 40 h7 ♖h8 41 ♖xc6 ♔f7 42 g6+ ♔g7 43 ♔f2 ♖e8 44 ♔f3 ♖f8+ 45 ♔g4 ♔h6 46 ♖f6! ♖e8 47 ♔f5 ♔g7 48 ♖e6 ♖d8 49 ♔e5 ♔h8 50 ♖d6 **1-0** L/N6123

**1855-⚔BF-13**
**Falkbeer, E.K.= Brien, R.B.**
[Brien]

1 e4 e6 2 d4 d5 3 exd5 exd5 4 ♗d3 ♗d6 5 ♘f3 ♘f6 6 ♗e3 0-0 7 c4 dxc4 8 ♗xc4 ♘c6 9 0-0 ♗f5 10 ♘c3 h6 11 ♘e2 ♗g4 12 ♘g3 ♕e7 13 ♖e1 ♖ae8 14 h3 ♗xg3 15 fxg3 [15 hxg4 ♕b4 16 fxg3 ♕xc4∓] 15 ... ♕b4 16 ♖c1 ♗xf3 17 ♕xf3 ♘xd4 18 ♕f4 c5 19 ♕f1 ♕xb2 20 ♕d3 ♕b6 [20 ... b5] 21 ♖b1 ♕c6 22 ♗xd4 ♖xe1+ 23 ♖xe1 cxd4 [23 ... ♖d8 24 ♗b5 ♕c8 25 ♖c1] 24 ♕xd4 ♖c8 25 ♗b3 ♕c7 26 ♕xa7 ♕xg3 27 ♖f1 ♕c7 28 ♕a4 **½-½** L/N6123

**1855-⚔BF-14**
**Brien, R.B.+ Falkbeer, E.K.**
[Brien]

1 d4 d5 2 e3 c5 3 c4 e6 4 a3 ♘c6 5 ♘f3 ♕b6 6 ♘c3 cxd4 7 exd4 dxc4 8 ♗xc4 ♘f6 9 0-0 ♗e7 10 b4 0-0 11 ♗b2 ♖d8 12 ♕c2 ♗d7 [12 ... ♘xd4 13 ♘xd4 ♕xd4 14 ♘d5+-] 13 d5 exd5 14 ♘xd5 ♘xd5 15 ♗xd5 ♗g4 16 ♖e4 ♗xf3 17 ♕xf3 ♖f8 18 ♖ae1 ♗g5 19 h4 ♗h6 20 ♖e4 ♖ad8 21 ♕h5 [△ 22 ♕xh6] 21 ... ♘b8 22 ♖fe1 ♘d7 23 ♖e8 [23 ♖g4 ♘f6 24 ♕xh6 ♕xf2+ 25 ♔xf2 ♘xg4+→] 23 ... ♕g6 24 ♕xg6 hxg6 25 ♖xd8 ♖xd8 26 ♗xb7 ♘f6 27 ♗f3 ♖d2 28 ♗xf6 gxf6 29 ♖e7 a5 30 bxa5 ♗f8 31 ♖b7 ♗xa3 [31 ... ♗c5] 32 a6 ♗c5 33 a7 ♗xf2+ 34 ♔h2 ♗xa7 35 ♖xa7 ♔g7 36 ♖a5 f5 37 ♖d5 ♖a2 38 ♔g3 ♖a4 39 ♖d7 g5 40 hxg5 ♔g6 41 ♗d5 ♖a3+ 42 ♔h2 ♔xg5 43 ♖xf7 ♔f4 44 ♗f3 ♖b3 45 ♔h3 ♖b8 46 ♔h2 ♖b3 47 ♖d7 ♖b8 48 ♖d4+

♔e3 49 ♖d5 f4 50 ♔h3 ♖g8 51 ♔h4 ♖h8+ 52 ♔g4 ♖g8+ 53 ♖g5 ♖e8 54 ♗d5 ♖e7 55 ♖g6 ♔d4 56 ♗f3 ♔e3 57 ♔f5 ♖f7+ 58 ♖f6 ♖g7 59 ♖e6+ ♔d2 60 ♔xf4 **1-0**

L/N6123

**1855-✕BF-15**
**Falkbeer, E.K.– Brien, R.B.**

[Brien]

1 e4 e6 2 d4 d5 3 exd5 cxd5 4 ♘f3 ♘f6 5 c4 dxc4 6 ♗xc4 ♗d6 7 0-0 0-0 8 ♗g5 ♘c6 9 h3 h6 10 ♗h4 g5 11 ♗g3 g4?! 12 hxg4 ♗xg4 13 ♕d3 ♗xf3 14 ♕g6+ ♔h8 15 ♕xh6+? ♘h7 16 gxf3 ♗xg3 17 ♔g2

17 ... ♕h4 18 ♖h1 ♕xh6 19 ♖xh6 ♗d6? 20 ♘c3 ♖g8+ 21 ♔h1 ♘xd4 22 ♗xf7 ♖g7 23 ♗d5 ♖f8 24 ♖h3 c6 25 ♗e4 ♘e6 26 ♖h6 ♖f6 27 ♖h5 ♘g5 28 ♖d1 ♗c7 29 ♖g1! ♘xe4 30 ♘xe4 ♖xg1+ [30 ... ♖xf3 31 ♖xg7 ♔xg7 32 ♖xh7+ ♔xh7 33 ♘g5+] 31 ♔xg1 ♖g6+ 32 ♔f1 ♔g7 33 ♖f5 b6 34 b4 ♘f6 35 ♘g5 ♘d5 36 b5 ♖f6 37 ♖xf6 ♔xf6 38 ♘e4+ ♔e5 39 bxc6 ♘b4 40 a4 ♘xc6 41 ♔e2 ♔d4 [⌓ 41 ... ♔f4] 42 ♘g5 ♔c4 43 ♔e3 ♔b4 44 ♘e6 ♗b8 45 f4 ♔xa4 46 ♔e4 ♔b4 47 f5 ♘e5 48 ♘d8 ♔c5 49 f6 ♔d6 50 f4 ♔d7 51 fxe5 ♔xd8 52 e6 ♗d6 53 ♔f5 ♔e8 54 ♔g6 ♗e7 55 f7+ ♔f8 56 ♔f5 a5 **0-1**

L/N6123

**FALKBEER & LÖWENTHAL & RIVIÈRE✕KENNEDY & STAUNTON & WYVILL**

Leamington

**[1855-✕FK]**

| | | | | |
|---|---|---|---|---|
| E.K. Falkbeer & J.J. Löwenthal & J.A. de Rivière | ½ | 1 | ½ | 2 |
| H.A. Kennedy & H. Staunton & M. Wyvill | ½ | 0 | ½ | 1 |

**1855-✕FK-1** vi 55
**Kennedy, H.A. & Staunton, H. & Wyvill, M.=Rivière, J.A. de & Falkbeer, E.K. & Löwenthal, J.J.**
Leamington [Brien]

1 c4 e5 2 e3 ♘f6 3 ♘c3 ♗b4 4 ♘ce2 d5 5 cxd5 ♕xd5 6 ♘g3 ♘c6 7 ♕c2 ♗e6 8 ♘1e2 0-0 9 ♘c3 ♕d7 [⌓ 9 ... ♗xc3] 10 ♗e2 ♗d6 [△ 11 ... ♘b4?!] 11 0-0 a6 12 b3 [12 a3? ♘a5] 12 ... ♘g4? 13 ♘ce4± ♕e7 [13 ... f5 14 ♘g5] 14 ♘xd6 cxd6 15 ♗a3 ♖fd8 16 ♖ac1 ♕h4 17 ♗xg4 ♕xg4 18 f3! ♕h4 19 f4 f6 20 ♘f5! [20 ♖f3?! ♗g4 (20 ... ♕h6) 21 ♘f5 ♕h5 22 ♘xd6 ♖xd6 23 ♗xd6 ♗xf3 24 gxf3 ♕xf3=] 20 ... ♗xf5 21 ♕xf5 [△ 22 ♕e6+] 21 ... ♔f7 22 ♖f3 [22 fxe5! dxe5 23 ♖c4 ♕h6 24 ♖g4 (24 ♖xc6!? bxc6 25 ♕xe5±) 24 ... ♖xd2 25 ♗c1 ♕xe3+ (25 ... ♘e7 26 ♕e4) 26 ♔h1 ♕d3 27 ♗xd2 ♕xd2 28 ♕xh7+–; 22 fxe5! dxe5 23 d4 exd4 24 ♖f4 ♕h6 25 ♖e4! ♔g8 26 exd4 ♕d2 27 ♖ce1 h6 28 ♕g6+–] 22 ... g6 23 ♕d3 ♕g4 24 f5 d5 25 ♕f1 ♖g8 26 ♕f2 d4 27 ♖cf1 [27 h3! ♕g5 (27 ... ♕e4 28 fxg6+ ♖xg6 29 ♖cf1+–) 28 exd4 exd4 29 ♖c5 ♕h6 30 ♖d5 ♖ad8 31 fxg6+ ♖xg6 (31 ... ♕xg6 32 ♖df5+–) 32 ♖xd8 ♘xd8 33 ♕xd4±] 27 ... g5 28 ♖g3 dxe3 29 ♖xe3 h5 30 ♗c5! h4 31 d3 ♖ad8 32 ♖e4 ♕h5 33 a4?? [33 d4+–; 33 ♕c2+–] 33 ... ♖xd3 34 b4 ♖gd8 35 ♕a2+ ♔g7 36 b5 axb5 37 axb5 ♘d4 38 ♗e7 ♖d5! 39 ♕a8 ♕f7 40 ♕xb7 ♖xb5?? [40 ... ♖d7→] 41 ♗xf6+!!± ♔xf6 42 ♕a6+ ♔g7 43 ♖xd4 ♖xd4 44 ♕xb5 ♖d5 45 f6+ ♔h6 46 ♕b8 ♖d2! 47 ♕h8+ ♔g6 48 ♕a8 ♖d4 [△ 49 ... ♖f4] 49 g3 h3 50 ♕c8 ♖d2 51 ♕f5+ ♔h6 52 ♕xh3+ ♔g6 53 ♕f5+ ♔h6 54 h4 gxh4 55 gxh4?? [55 ♕f3+–] 55 ... ♕a7+ 56 ♔h1 ♕a8+ 57 ♕f3 ♕xf3+ 58 ♖xf3 ♖d8 59 ♖f5 ♔g6 ...? **½-½**

L/N6123

**166** Löwenthal, J.J., Rivière, J.A. de, Wyvill, M., Falkbeer, E.K., Staunton, H., Lyttleton, G.W., Kennedy, H.A. Leamington 1855

M954.BL

**1855-✕FK-2** 4/5 vii 55

**Rivière, J.A. de & Falkbeer, E.K. & Löwenthal, J.J.+ Kennedy, H.A. & Staunton, H. & Wyvill, M.**

Leamington [Löwenthal]

1 e4 e6 2 d4 b6 [2 ... d5] 3 d5! exd5 4 exd5 ♘f6 5 ♘f3 ♗b7 6 ♗c4 ♗e7? [6 ... ♗c5 △ 7 ... d6, 8 ... c6] 7 0-0 0-0 8 ♘c3 h6 [△ 9 ... ♘h7] 9 ♕d3 d6 10 ♘d4! [△ 11 ♘f5] 10 ... ♘bd7! [△ 11 ... ♘c5; 11 ... ♘e5] 11 f4 ♘h7 12 ♗d2 ♗f6 13 ♘f5 ♔h8 14 ♕h3! ♗c8 15 g4! ♘c5 16 ♘g3! [△ 17 b4] 16 ... a5 17 ♖ae1 ♗h4 [△ 18 ... ♗xg3] 18 ♖e2 f5? 19 ♘xf5 ♗xf5 20 gxf5 ♗f6 21 ♗b5! ♗d4+ 22 ♔h1! [22 ♔g2?!] 22 ... ♖b8 23 ♘d1! [△ 24 c3] 23 ... ♕c8 24 c3 ♗f6 25 b4 ♘b7 26 ♖fe1 ♘d8 27 ♖e8 ♕b7 28 ♕g2 ♔g8 [28 ... ♘f7 29 ♖xb8 ♖xb8 (29 ... ♕xb8 30 ♗d7 ♕d8 31 ♗e6+-) 30 ♗c6 ♕a7 (30 ... ♕a6 31 b5) 31 b5 ♘f8 (31 ... a4 32 c4) 32 c4 ♘d8 33 ♗e8 △ 34 ♘c3+-] 29 ♖xf8+ ♘xf8 [29 ... ♔xf8? 30 ♖e8+ ♔f7 31 ♕g6#] 30 ♘e3! [△ 31 ♘g4] 30 ... ♘f7 31 ♘g4 ♗h4 32 ♖g1+- c5 33 dxc6 ♕e7 34 ♘e3 [△ 35 ♘d5] **1-0** M324

**1855-✕FK-3** 5/6 vii 55

**Kennedy, H.A. & Staunton, H. & Wyvill, M.=Rivière, J.A.de & Falkbeer, E.K. & Löwenthal, J.J.**

Leamington [Löwenthal]

1 c4 e5 [1 ... e6; 1 ... f5] 2 e3 [2 ♘c3] 2 ... d5 3 cxd5 ♘f6 4 ♗b5+ ♗d7 5 ♗c4 ♗c5 [5 ... b5! 6 ♗b3 (6 ♕b3 bxc4 7 ♕b7 ♘c6 8 dxc6 ♗f5∓) 6 ... ♗f5 7 ♕f3 (7 ♘c3 b4=; 7 ♘f3 ♗g4 8 h3 ♗xf3 9 ♕xf3 e4∓) 7 ... ♗d3 8 ♘e2 ♘bd7 9 ♘bc3 b4 10 e4 ♘c5∓] 6 b4! ♗d6 7 ♗b2 c6 8 ♘c3! [8 dxc6?!] 8 ... 0-0 9 a3 ♗c7 10 ♘ge2 ♗f5 11 ♘g3 ♗g6 12 ♕f3± e4? 13 ♘gxe4 ♘xe4 14 ♘xe4 ♘d7 15 dxc6 bxc6 16 0-0??

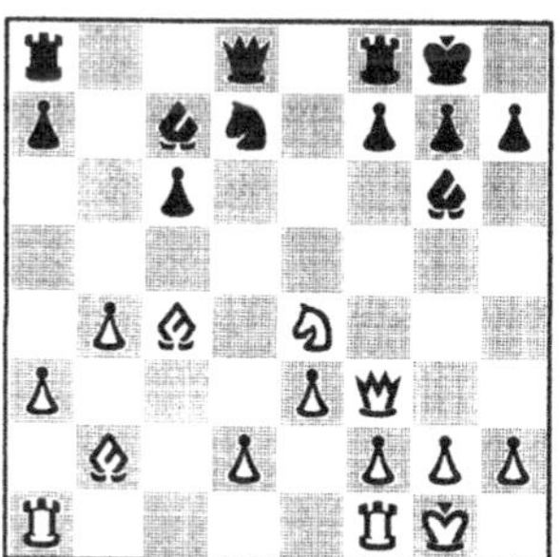

16 ... ♕h4!∓ 17 ♘g3 ♗xg3 18 ♕xg3 ♕xc4 19 f4 [△ 20 f5] 19 ... f5! [△ 20 ... ♘f6∓] 20 d3 ♕c2 21 ♗d4 ♘f6 22 ♖fd1 [□ 22 ♖fc1] 22 ... ♗h5 [22 ... ♕b3!] 23 ♖dc1! ♕xd3 24 ♖xc6 ♗g6 25 ♖ac1 ♘e4 26 ♕h4 ♖ad8 27 ♗xa7 ♕xa3? [27 ... ♖a8] 28 ♗b6 ♖d6 29 ♕e1 ♖xc6 30 ♖xc6 ♗f7 31 ♗d4 ♗d5? [31 ... ♘e8 △ 32 ... ♖f7, 33 ... ♖e7-+] 32 ♖c7 ♖f7 33 ♖c8+ ♖f8 34 ♖c7 ♗f7 35 b5 ♕b3 36 b6 ♖b8 37 h3 h6 38 ♕a5 ♕d1+ [38 ... ♕b1+ 39 ♔h2 ♘f2 40 ♔g3 (40 ♕e5?? ♕h1+ 41 ♔g3 ♘e4+-+) 40 ... ♕g1 41 ♖xf7 ♘e4+ 42 ♔h4 ♕f2+ 43 ♔h5 g6+ 44 ♔xh6 ♕h4+ 45 ♔xg6 ♕g3+=] 39 ♔h2 ♘d2= 40 ♕e5 **½-½** M324

**1855-★AD-1**

**Dufresne, J.– Anderssen, A.**

Berlin

1 e4 e5 2 ♘f3 ♘c6 3 ♗c4 ♗c5 4 b4 ♗xb4 5 c3 ♗a5 6 d4 exd4 7 0-0 dxc3 8 ♕b3 ♕f6 9 e5 ♕g6 10 ♘xc3 ♘ge7 11 ♗a3 ♗xc3 12 ♕xc3 0-0 13 ♗d3 ♕h6 14 ♖fe1 d5 15 exd6 cxd6 16 ♖ad1 ♗g4 17 ♗b1 ♗xf3 18 ♕xf3 ♖ad8 19 ♗c1 ♕f6 20 ♕h3 ♘g6 21 ♖e4 d5 22 ♖f4 ♕e6 23 ♕h5 ♖fe8 24 ♗e3 d4 25 ♖e4 ♕d7 26 ♖h4 ♘xh4 27 ♕xh7+ ♔f8 28 ♕h8+ ♔e7 29 ♕xh4+ f6 30 ♗c1 ♕e6 31 ♗a3+ ♔d7 32 ♗d3 ♔c8 33 ♗c1 ♔b8 34 ♗f4+ ♔a8 35 ♗g3 ♕e1+ 36 ♖xe1 ♖xe1+ 37 ♗f1 d3 **0-1** L/N6047

**1855-★AD-2**

**Dufresne, J.– Anderssen, A.**

Berlin

1 e4 e5 2 ♘f3 ♘c6 3 ♗c4 ♗c5 4 b4 ♗bxb4 5 c3 ♗a5 6 d4 exd4 7 0-0 dxc3 8 ♕b3 ♕f6 9 e5 ♕g6 10 ♗a3 ♘ge7 11 ♖fe1 0-0 12 ♘xc3 ♗xc3 13 ♕xc3 d5 14 exd6 cxd6 15 ♗d3 ♕h6 16 ♖e4 ♗f5 17 ♖h4 ♕g6 18 ♖d1 ♗xd3 19 ♖xd3 ♘f5 20 ♖h3 ♖fe8 21 ♘h4 ♘xh4 22 ♖hg3 ♕f6 **0-1** L/N6047

**1855-★AD-3**

**Anderssen, A.+ Dufresne, J.**

Berlin

1 e4 e5 2 ♘f3 ♘c6 3 ♗c4 ♗c5 4 b4 ♗xb4 5 c3 ♗a5 6 d4 exd4 7 0-0 d3 8 ♕b3 ♕f6 9 ♖e1 ♗b6 10 e5 ♕g6 11 ♕d1 ♘h6 12 ♗xd3 ♕h5 13 h3 ♘e7 14 ♘bd2 d5 15 exd6 cxd6 16 ♘c4 ♗c5 17 ♗g5 f6 18 ♘xd6+ ♗xd6 19 ♗b5+ ♔f8 20 ♕xd6 ♘hf5 21 ♕d8+ ♔f7 22 ♖xe7+ ♘xe7 23 ♘e5+ **1-0** L/N6047

**1855-★AD-4**

**Anderssen, A.+ Dufresne, J.**

Berlin [Anderssen & Kossak]

1 e4 e5 2 ♘f3 ♘c6 3 ♗c4 ♗c5 4 b4 ♗xb4 5 c3 ♗a5 6 d4 exd4 7 0-0 d3 8 ♕b3 ♕f6 9 ♖e1 b5?! 10 ♗xb5 ♖b8 11 e5 ♕g6 12 ♕a4 ♘ge7 13 ♗a3 ♗b6 14 ♘bd2 a6 15 ♗c4 0-0 16 ♘e4 d5 17 exd6 ♗h3 18 ♘h4 ♕g4 19 dxe7 ♘xe7 20 ♗xe7 d2 21 ♘xd2 g5 22 ♘e4 ♕xh4 23 ♗xg5 ♗xf2+ 24 ♘xf2 ♕xg5 25 ♘xh3 **1-0** L/N6047

**1855-★AD-5**

**Dufresne, J.– Anderssen, A.**

Berlin

1 e4 e5 2 f4 exf4 3 ♘f3 g5 4 ♗c4 g4 5 ♘e5 ♕h4+ 6 ♔f1 f3 7 ♗xf7+ ♔e7 8 ♗b3 ♗g7 9 d4 ♘f6 10 ♘c3 ♘c6 11 ♘xc6+ bxc6 12 ♗c4 ♘h5 13 ♔g1 f2+ 14 ♔f1 d5 15 exd5 ♖f8 16 ♘e4 h6 17 ♕e2 ♔d8 18 d6 cxd6 19 ♗d2 ♗f5 20 ♗a5+ ♔d7 21 d5 ♖ac8 22 dxc6+ ♖xc6 23 ♕e3 ♗xe4 24 ♕xa7+ ♔e8 25 ♕b8+ ♔e7 26 ♕b7+ ♔f6 27 ♗d8+ ♖xd8 28 ♕f7+ ♔g5 29 ♕e7+ ♗f6 30 ♕xe4 ♖xc4 31 ♕xc4 ♖e8 32 ♕b5+ ♖e5 33 ♕b4 ♘g3+ 34 hxg3 ♕xh1+ 35 ♔xf2 ♕xa1 36 ♕f4+ ♔g6 37 ♕xg4+ ♗g5 **0-1** L/N6047

**1855-★AE-1** 1 i 55

**Eichborn, L.+ Anderssen, A.**

Breslau

1 e4 e5 2 ♘f3 ♘c6 3 ♗c4 ♗c5 4 c3 ♘f6 5 d4 exd4 6 e5 ♘e4 7 cxd4 ♗b4+ 8 ♗d2 ♗xd2+ 9 ♘bxd2 d5 10 ♗b5 0-0 11 ♗xc6 bxc6 12 0-0 c5 13 dxc5 ♘xc5 14 ♘b3 ♘e4 15 ♕d4 ♗b7 16 ♖ac1 ♕e7 17 ♖fe1 f6 18 exf6 ♖xf6 19 ♘c5 ♗c6 20 ♘e5 ♖d8 21 ♘xc6 ♖xc6 22 ♘xe4 ♖xc1 23 ♖xc1 dxe4 24 ♕xa7 ♖d2 25 ♕b8+ ♔f7 26 ♔f1 ♔g6 27 ♖c6+ ♔h5 28 ♕xc7 ♕g5 29 ♖c5 ♖d1+ 30 ♔e2 ♖d2+ 31 ♔e1 ♖d5 32 ♕f7+ **1-0** L/N3034

**1855-★AE-2** 7 xi 55

**Eichborn, L.+ Anderssen, A.**

Breslau

1 e4 e5 2 ♘c3 ♗c5 3 ♗c4 b5 4 ♗xb5 c6 5 ♗c4 ♘f6 6 ♘f3 d5 7 exd5 cxd5 8 ♗b5+ ♗d7 9 ♗xd7+ ♘bxd7 10 d4 exd4 11 ♘xd4 0-0 12 0-0 h6 13 ♗e3 ♘e5 14 ♘c6 ♘xc6 15 ♗xc5 ♖e8 16 ♗d4 ♘e4 17 ♖e1 ♕g5 18 ♗e3 ♘xc3 19 bxc3 ♕f5 20 ♕d3 ♕h5 21 ♗d4 ♖e6 22 ♖e3 ♖ae8 23 ♖ae1 ♕g5 24 h3 ♖e8e7 25 ♖xe6 fxe6 26 ♗c5 ♖b7 27 ♖xe6 ♘e5 28 ♖e8+ ♔f7 29 ♖f8+ ♔e6 30 ♕a6+ ♖b6 31 ♕c8+ ♘d7 32 ♕e8+ ♕e7 33 ♕xe7# **1-0** L/N3034

**1855-★AE-3** 10 xi 55

**Eichborn, L.Φ Anderssen, A.**

Breslau

1 e4 e5 2 ♘c3 ♗c5 3 ♗c4 c6 4 ♘f3 ♕e7 5 d3 ♘f6 6 0-0 d6 7 h3 ♗b6 8 d4 0-0 9 ♗e3 ♗c7 10 dxe5 dxe5 11 a3 ♖d8 12 ♕e2 b5 13 ♗d3 ♘bd7 14 ♘h2 ♘f8 15 f4 ♘g6 16 f5

♘f4 17 ♗xf4 exf4 18 ♕f3 ♘d7 19 ♘g4 h5 20 ♘f2 ♕h4 21 ♔h1 ♘e5 22 ♕e2 ♕g3 23 ♕xh5 f3 24 gxf3 ♘xf3 25 ♘g4 ♘h4 26 ♖f2 ♕xh3+ 27 ♘h2 g6 28 ♖g1 ♗xh2 29 ♖xh2 ♕f3+ 30 ♕xf3 ♘xf3 31 fxg6 ♘xh2 32 gxf7+ ♔xf7 33 ♔xh2 ♖h8+ 34 ♔g3 ♔f6 35 ♔f4 ♖h4+ 36 ♔e3 ♗g4 L/N3034

**1855-★AM-1** 1 iii 55
**Morphy, P.C.+Ayers, D.**
Mobile [Maróczy]

1 e4 e5 2 ♘f3 ♘c6 3 ♗c4 ♗c5 4 b4 ♗xb4 5 c3 ♗a5 6 d4 d6! 7 ♕b3 [7 dxe5 dxe5 8 ♕xd8+ ♘xd8 9 ♘xe5 ♗e6; 7 ♘g5 ♘h6 8 0-0 ♗b6 9 ♗e3 exd4 10 cxd4 ♘xd4 11 ♘xf7 ♘xf7 12 ♗xf7+ ♔xf7 13 ♗xd4 ♖e8 14 ♘c3 ♗d7; 7 ♕a4 exd4 8 ♘xd4 ♘e7 9 ♗g5 ♕d7! 10 ♗xe7 (10 ♗b5 a6! 11 ♗xc6 ♘xc6 12 ♘xc6 ♗b6!) 10 ... ♘xd4 11 ♕xa5 ♘c6 12 ♕g5 ♕xe7 13 ♕xg7 ♕xe4+ 14 ♗e2 ♕e5∓] 7 ... ♕e7 [7 ... ♕d7 8 dxe5 ♘xe5 (8 ... ♗b6 9 e6! fxe6 10 ♘g5 ♘a5 11 ♗xe6 ♘xb3 12 ♗xd7+±) 9 ♘xe5 dxe5 10 ♗xf7+ ♕xf7 11 ♕b5+ ♗d7 12 ♕xa5 ♘e7 13 ♕xe5 0-0] 8 d5 ♘d4 9 ♗b5+ [9 ♕a4+ ♗d7 10 ♕xa5 b6 11 ♕a6 ♘c2+ 12 ♔d1 ♘xa1 13 ♗b2 ♘f6, 13 ... f5] 9 ... c6 10 ♘xd4 exd4 11 dxc6 ♕xe4+ 12 ♔d1 ♗g4+ 13 f3 ♗xf3+ 14 gxf3 ♕xf3+ 15 ♔c2 ♕e4+ 16 ♔b2 ♗xc3+ [□16 ... bxc6 17 ♖e1! (17 ♖d1 ♘e7 18 ♗d3 ♕h4) 17 ... ♕xe1 18 ♗xc6+ ♔e7 19 ♗xa8 ♘f6∓] 17 ♘xc3 dxc3+ 18 ♕xc3 0-0-0 19 ♖e1 ♕d5 20 cxb7+ ♔xb7 21 ♖b1 ♘f6

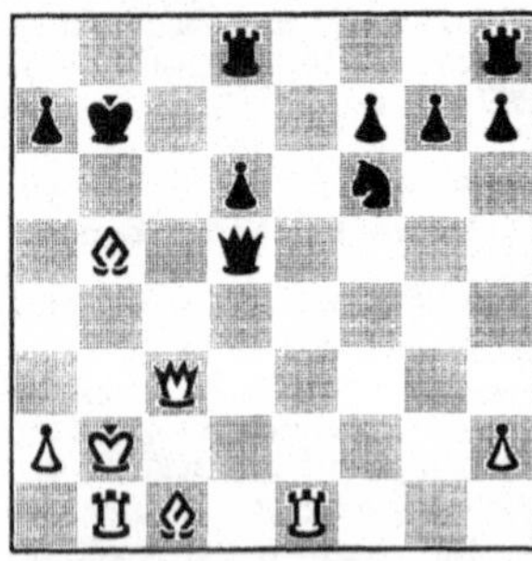

22 ♗c6+ ♕xc6 23 ♔a1+ ♔c7 24 ♕a5+ ♔c8 25 ♕xa7 ♘d7 26 ♗d2 **1-0** L/N3203

**1855-★AM-2**
**Anderssen, A.– Mayet, K.**
Berlin

1 e4 e5 2 ♘f3 ♘c6 3 ♗c4 ♗c5 4 b4 ♗xb4 5 c3 ♗a5 6 d4 exd4 7 0-0 dxc3 8 ♕b3 ♕f6 9 e5 ♕g6 10 ♘xc3 ♘ge7 11 ♘e2 0-0 12 ♗a3 ♗b6 13 ♖ad1 ♘a5 14 ♕c3 ♖e8 15 ♘g3 ♕c6 16 ♗xe7 ♖xe7 17 ♕a3 ♕c5 18 ♕xc5 ♗xc5 19 ♗d3 d5 20 ♖fe1 h6 21 ♗b1 ♗e6 22 ♘h4 g6 23 ♔f1 c6 24 f4 ♗g4 25 ♖d3 ♘c4 26 h3 ♗d7 27 ♘f3 ♖ae8 28 ♖b3 b5 29 ♘h1 a5 30 g4 a4 31 ♖d3 h5 32 gxh5 ♗xh3+ 33 ♔e2 gxh5 34 ♘f2 ♗g4 35 ♘xg4 hxg4 36 ♘h4 ♘xe5 **0-1** L/N6047

**1855-★AM-3**
**Mayet, K.– Anderssen, A.**
Berlin

1 e4 e5 2 ♘f3 ♘c6 3 ♗c4 ♗c5 4 0-0 ♘f6 5 ♘g5 0-0 6 ♔h1 d5 7 exd5 ♘a5 8 ♗d3 h6 9 ♘e4 ♘xe4 10 ♗xe4 f5 11 f3 fxe4 12 fxe4 ♗g4 13 ♕e1 ♕h4 14 d4 ♖xf1+ 15 ♕xf1 ♖f8 16 ♕g1 ♗xd4 **0-1** L/N6047

**1855-★AM-4**
**Mayet, K.– Anderssen, A.**
Berlin

1 d4 d5 2 c4 e6 3 a3 c5 4 dxc5 ♗xc5 5 ♘f3 a5 6 e3 ♘c6 7 cxd5 exd5 8 ♗b5 ♘f6 9 ♘e5 0-0 10 ♘xc6 bxc6 11 ♗xc6 ♗a6 12 ♗xa8 ♕xa8 13 ♕f3 ♘d7 14 ♘c3 ♘e5 15 ♕xd5 ♘d3+ 16 ♔d2 ♕c8 17 ♔c2 ♖d8 18 ♕h5

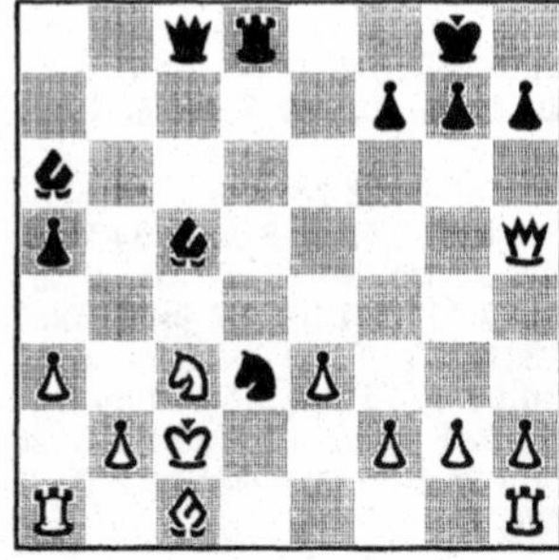

18 ... ♘f4 19 exf4 ♗d3+ 20 ♔b3 ♕e6+ 21 ♔a4 ♕c4+ 22 b4 ♗c2+ 23 ♔xa5 ♖a8‡ **0-1** L/N6047

**1855-★AM-5**
**Anderssen, A.+Mayet, K.**
Berlin

1 e4 e5 2 ♘f3 ♘c6 3 ♗c4 ♗c5 4 b4 ♗xb4 5 c3 ♗a5 6 d4 exd4 7 0-0 dxc3 8 ♕b3 ♕f6 9 e5 ♕g6 10 ♘xc3 ♘ge7 11 ♘e2 0-0 12 ♗a3 d5 13 ♗xd5 ♘xd5 14 ♗xf8 ♗e6 15 ♕xb7 ♖xf8 16 ♕xc6 ♗b6 17 ♖ad1 ♘e7 18 ♕a4 ♗g4 19 ♕f4 f6 20 exf6 gxf6 21 ♘h4 ♕h5 22 ♕g3 ♔h8 23 ♘f4 ♕g5 24 ♘f3 ♘f5 25 ♘xg5 ♘xg3 26 ♘ge6 ♘xf1 27 ♖xf1 ♖g8 28 ♖e1 a5 29 ♔f1 ♖e8 30 f3 ♗f5 31 g4 ♗xe6 32 ♘xe6 a4 33 f4 ♔g8 34 f5 h6 35 ♖d1 h5 36 ♖d7 hxg4 37 ♖g7+ ♔h8 38 ♖xg4 ♖a8 39 ♖g6 a3 40 ♖xf6 ♖a4 41 ♖f7 ♖c4 42 f6 ♖c1+ 43 ♔g2 ♖c2+ 44 ♔g3 ♖xa2 45 ♘f4 **1-0** L/N6047

**1855-★AM-6**
**Anderssen, A.– Mayet, K.**
Berlin

1 e4 e5 2 f4 exf4 3 ♘f3 g5 4 h4 g4 5 ♘g5 d5 6 exd5 h6 7 ♗b5+ c6 8 dxc6 bxc6 9 ♘xf7 ♔xf7 10 ♗c4+ ♔g7 11 ♕e2 ♘f6 12 d3 ♗b4+ 13 ♔d1 ♗d6 14 ♘c3 g3 15 ♕f1 ♗g4+ 16 ♔d2 ♕b6 17 ♘d1 ♖e8 **0-1** L/N6047

**1855-★AM-7**
**Mayet, K.+Anderssen, A.**
Berlin

1 e4 e5 2 ♘f3 ♘c6 3 ♗b5 ♗c5 4 0-0 ♘ge7 5 c3 ♘g6 6 d4 exd4 7 cxd4 ♗b6 8 ♘c3 0-0 9 ♗e3 d6 10 h3 h6 11 ♕b3 ♕f6 12 ♘d5 ♕e6 13 ♘xb6 axb6 14 d5 ♕f6 15 dxc6 bxc6 16 ♗xc6 ♖a5 17 ♗d4 ♕e7 18 ♕c3 ♘f4 19 ♔h2 ♖h5 20 ♘g1 ♖g5 21 e5 ♖d8 22 g3 ♘xh3 23 ♗d5 ♘xg1 24 ♔xg1 c5 25 ♗e3 ♖xe5 26 ♗g2 g5 27 ♖fe1 **1-0** L/N6047

**1855-★AM-8**
**Anderssen, A.+Mayet, K.**
Berlin

1 e4 e5 2 f4 exf4 3 ♘f3 c6 4 e5 f6 5 d4 fxe5 6 dxe5 g5 7 ♗c4 h6 8 0-0 ♗c5+ 9 ♔h1 ♘e7 10 ♘c3 d5 11 exd6 ♕xd6 12 ♕e2 ♗f5 13 ♘e5 b5 14 ♕h5+ ♗g6 15 ♗f7+ ♗xf7 16 ♕xf7+ ♔d8 17 ♗xf4 gxf4 18 ♖ad1 ♗d4 19 ♕xf4 ♕e6 20 ♕xd4+ ♔c8 21 ♖f7 ♘f5 22 ♕c5 ♘a6 23 ♕xc6+ ♕xc6 24 ♘xc6 ♘e3 25 ♘xb5 ♘c4 26 ♖dd7 **1-0** L/N6047

**1855-★AM-9**
**Anderssen, A.+Mayet, K.**
Berlin [Staunton]

1 e4 e5 2 f4 exf4 3 ♘f3 g5 4 ♗c4 ♗g7 5 d4 h6 6 c3 ♘e7 7 ♕b3 0-0 8 h4 g4 9 ♘g1 d5 10 exd5 ♕d6 11 ♘d2 f5 12 ♘e2 ♗f6 13 ♘f1 ♘g6 14 h5 ♗h4+ 15 ♔d1 f3 16 gxf3 gxf3 17 hxg6 fxe2+ 18 ♗xe2 ♗g5 19 ♗xg5 hxg5 20 ♖h7 [Δ 21 ♖xc7!] 20 ... ♘d7 21 ♖e7 [Δ 22 ♖e6] 21 ... ♘f6 [21 ... ♕xe7?? 22 d6+] 22 ♗c4 a6 23 ♕c2 b5 24 ♗b3 ♘xd5 25 ♗xd5+ ♕xd5 26 ♕h2 **1-0** L/N6123

**1855-★AP-1** 9 iv 55
**Anderssen, A.+Pitschel, K.**
Leipzig

1 e4 e5 2 f4 exf4 3 ♘f3 g5 4 h4 g4 5 ♘e5 h5 6 ♗c4 ♘h6 7 d4 d6 8 ♘d3 f3 9 gxf3 d5 10 ♗xd5 c6 11 ♗xh6 ♗xh6 12 ♗xf7+ ♔xf7 13 c3 ♕f6 14 f4 ♖e8 15 ♘d2 ♔g7 16 ♕e2 ♗xf4 17 0-0 ♕xh4 18 ♘xf4 ♕g5 19 e5 ♗f5 20 ♘e4 ♗xe4 21 ♕xe4 ♘d7 22 ♖f2 g3 23 ♖f3 h4 24 ♖af1 ♔h6 25 ♕d3 ♕g4 26 ♘h3 ♕xh3

27 ♖f6+ **1-0** L/N6047

**1855-★AP-2** 9 iv 55
**Pollmächer,H.–Anderssen, A.**
Leipzig
1 e4 e5 2 f4 d5 3 exd5 e4 4 ♗b5+ ♗d7 5 ♗c4 ♘f6 6 d4 ♗g4 7 ♘e2 ♘xd5 8 0-0 f5 9 c3 ♘c6 10 ♖e1 ♕d7 11 b4 ♘f6 12 ♕b3 ♗xe2 13 ♗e6 ♕e7 14 ♖xe2 g6 15 ♘d2 ♘d8 16 ♗c4 a6 17 a4 ♘f7 18 ♘f3 ♘d6 19 ♗e6 exf3 20 ♗f7+ ♘xf7 21 ♖xe7+ ♗xe7 22 gxf3 0-0 23 c4 ♘h5 24 c5 ♗f6 25 ♗e3 ♘xf4 26 ♖ad1 ♘h5 27 d5 ♖ad8 28 f4 ♖fe8 29 ♔g2 ♖e4 30 ♔f3 ♖de8 31 ♗c1 g5 32 d6 g4+ 33 ♔f2 cxd6 34 cxd6 ♗d4+ 35 ♔f1 ♖e2 36 d7 ♖f2+ 37 ♔g1 ♖f3+ 38 ♔h1 ♖e1+ 39 ♖xe1 ♖xb3 40 ♖e8+ ♔g7 41 ♖e7 ♖b1 42 ♖xf7+ ♔xf7 43 d8♕ ♖xc1+ 44 ♔g2 ♖g1# **0-1** L/N6047

**1855-★AP-3** iv 55
**Pollmächer,H.+Anderssen, A.**
Leipzig
1 e4 e5 2 ♘f3 ♘c6 3 c3 d5 4 ♗b5 dxe4 5 ♘xe5 ♕d5 6 ♕a4 ♘ge7 7 f4 exf3 8 ♘xf3 ♕h5 9 0-0 ♗g4 10 d4 0-0-0 11 ♗f4 ♔b8 12 ♘bd2 a6 13 ♗d3 ♘d5 14 ♗g3 ♗d6 15 ♘e4 ♗xg3 16 hxg3 ♘e3 17 ♘c5 ♖d6 18 ♘xb7 ♖h6 19 ♘h4 ♕d5 20 ♘c5 ♖e8 21 ♘xa6+ ♔c8 22 ♘c5 ♔d8 23 ♖ae1 ♗c8 24 ♕a8 g6 25 ♗a6 ♘a7 26 ♕xd5+ ♘xd5 27 ♗xc8 ♘xc8 28 ♘b7+ ♔d7 29 ♖xf7+ **1-0** L/N6047

**1855-★AP-4** iv 55
**Pollmächer,H.–Anderssen, A.**
Leipzig
1 e4 e5 2 ♘f3 ♘c6 3 d4 exd4 4 ♗c4 ♗c5 5 c3 ♘f6 6 cxd4 ♗b4+ 7 ♗d2 ♗xd2+ 8 ♘bxd2 d5 9 exd5 ♘xd5 10 ♕b3 ♘ce7 11 0-0 0-0 12 ♖ae1 c6 13 ♘e5 ♘f5 14 ♘df3 a5 15 a3 a4 16 ♕c2 ♘d6 17 ♗d3 h6 18 ♖e3 ♘f4 19 ♗h7+ ♔h8 20 ♖fe1 f5 21 ♘g6+ ♘xg6 22 ♗xg6 ♕f6 23 ♘e5 f4 24 ♖3e2 ♘f5 25 ♕c4 ♗e6 26 ♕c5 ♘h4 27 ♗h5 ♗d5 28 f3 ♕g5 29 ♗g4 h5 30 ♗e6 b6 31 ♕d6 ♖ad8 32 ♗d7 ♘xf3+ 33 ♘xf3 ♗xf3 34 ♖f2 ♗g4 35 ♖e7 f3 36 h4 ♕c1+ 37 ♔h2 fxg2 38 ♖xf8+ ♖xf8 39 ♖e1

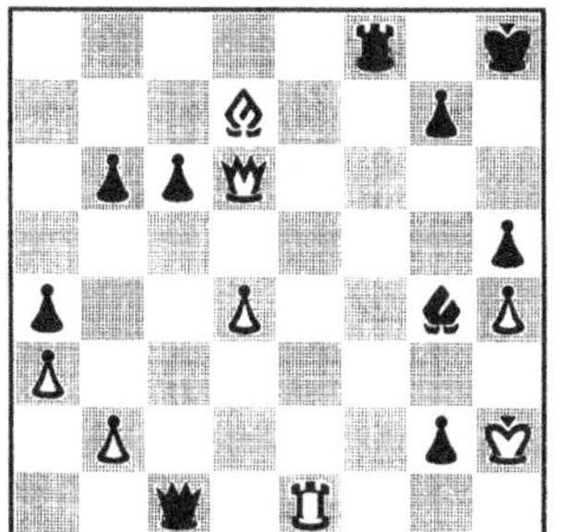

39 ... ♖f1 **0-1** L/N6047

**1855-★AP-5** iv 55
**Anderssen, A.+ Pollmächer, H.**
Leipzig
1 e4 e5 2 d4 exd4 3 ♘f3 ♗b4+ 4 ♗d2 ♕e7 5 ♗d3 ♘c6 6 0-0 ♗xd2 7 ♘bxd2 d6 8 ♗b5 ♗d7 9 ♗xc6 ♗xc6 10 ♘xd4 ♘h6 11 ♕h5 0-0 12 ♖ae1 ♖ae8 13 f4 ♕f6 14 ♘xc6 bxc6 15 c3 ♖b8 16 f5 ♖xb2 17 e5 dxe5 18 ♘e4 **1-0** L/N6047

**1855-★AS-1** iv 55
**Anderssen, A.+Saalbach, A.**
Leipzig
1 e4 e5 2 ♘f3 ♘c6 3 ♗c4 ♗c5 4 b4 ♗xb4 5 c3 ♗a5 6 d4 exd4 7 0-0 d6 8 cxd4 ♘f6 9 ♕a4 ♗d7 10 ♗b5 ♗b6 11 e5 a6 12 exf6 axb5 13 ♖e1+ ♗e6 14 fxg7 ♖g8 15 ♕d1 d5 16 ♗g5 ♕d7 17 ♗f6 ♗a5 18 ♘bd2 ♗b4 19 ♘g5 ♗e7 20 ♘xe6 fxe6 21 ♕h5+ ♔d8

22 ♕f7 **1-0** L/N6047

**1855-★AS-2** iv 55
**Schurig, R.–Anderssen, A.**
Leipzig
1 e4 e5 2 f4 exf4 3 ♗c4 ♕h4+ 4 ♔f1 b5 5 ♗xb5 g5 6 ♘f3 ♕h5 7 ♗e2 g4 8 ♘g1 f5 9 d3 ♗d6 10 ♘f3 ♘c6 11 e5 ♘xe5 12 ♗xf4 ♘c4 13 dxc4 ♗xf4 14 ♕d5 ♖b8 15 ♕d4 ♗c1 16 b3 ♗b7 17 ♘e1 ♕g5 18 ♕xh8 ♕f4+ 19 ♘f3 gxf3 20 ♕xg8+ ♔e7 21 ♕xh7+ ♔f6 22 ♔e1 ♖e8 **0-1** L/N6047

**1855-★AS-3**
**Smigielski– Anderssen, A.**
Berlin [Anderssen & Kossak]
1 e4 e5 2 ♘f3 ♘c6 3 ♗c4 ♗c5 4 c3 ♘f6 5 d4 exd4 6 cxd4 ♗b4+ 7 ♗d2 ♗xd2+ 8 ♘bxd2 d5 9 e5 dxc4 10 exf6 ♕d5 11 0-0 gxf6 12 ♖e1+ [◻ 12 ♘e4!] 12 ... ♗e6 13 ♘e4 0-0-0 14 ♘xf6 ♕f5 15 ♘e4 ♖hg8 16 ♘c3 ♕h3 17 g3 ♗g4 18 d5 ♘d4 19 ♖e3 ♘xf3+ 20 ♖xf3 ♖g6 **0-1** L/N6047

**1855-★AS-4**
**Anderssen, A.+Smigielski**
Berlin [Anderssen & Kossak]
1 e4 e6 2 d4 d5 3 exd5 exd5 4 ♗d3 ♘f6 5 ♘f3 ♗e6 6 0-0 c5 7 c3 ♗d6 8 h3 h6 9 ♗e3 b6 [◻ 9 ... ♕c7] 10 ♘e5 ♘e4 11 f4 ♗f5 12 ♗b5+ ♗d7 13 ♘xd7 ♘xd7 14 dxc5 ♗xc5 15 ♗xc5 ♘xc5 16 b4 ♕c7 17 ♕xd5 ♘b7 18 ♖e1+ ♔d8 19 ♕xf7 ♘d6 20 ♕e7+ ♔c8 21 ♘a3 g6 22 ♖ad1 ♘xb5 23 ♘xb5 ♕c6 24 ♘d4 ♕c7 25 ♘e6 ♕c6 26 ♖d6 ♕b7 27 ♖ed1 **1-0** L/N6047

**1855-★LM-1**
**Morphy,P.C.=Le Carp & Maurian,C.A.**
New Orleans [Maróczy]
⟨♘b1⟩ 1 e4 e5 2 ♘f3 ♘c6 3 ♗c4 ♗c5 4 b4 ♗xb4 5 c3 ♗a5 6 0-0 ♘f6 7 ♘g5 0-0 8 f4 d5 9 exd5 ♘xd5 10 ♗a3 ♘xf4 11 ♘xf7 ♖xf7 12 ♕b3 ♕xd2 13 ♗xf7+ ♔h8 14 ♖f2 ♗b6 15 ♕xb6 ♘h3+ 16 gxh3 ♕g5+ 17 ♖g2 ♕xg2+ 18 ♔xg2 axb6 19 ♗b2 ♗f5 20 ♖f1 ♗e4+ 21 ♔g3 ♖d8 22 ♗e6 h6 23 ♖f7 ♖d3+ [◻ 23 ... ♖d2] 24 ♔g4 ♖d8 25 ♖xc7 ♖e8 26 ♗d7 ♖f8 27 ♗xc6 ♖f4+ 28 ♔g3 bxc6 29 c4 ♖f3+ 30 ♔g4 ♖f4+ **½-½** L/N3203

**1855-★MM-1**
**Morphy, P.C.– Maurian, C.A.**
Springhill [Maróczy]
⟨♖a1⟩ 1 e4 e5 2 f4 exf4 3 ♘f3 g5 4 ♗c4 ♗g7 5 0-0 h6 6 c3 d6 7 ♕b3 ♕e7 8 d4 c6 9 a4 ♗e6 10 ♗xe6 fxe6 [10 ... ♕xe6 11 ♕xb7] 11 e5 d5 12 g3 ♘a6 13 gxf4 gxf4 14 ♗xf4 0-0-0 15 ♕c2 ♕e8 16 b4 ♘e7 17 ♕e2 ♘b8 18 b5 ♖g8 19 ♔h1 ♕g6 20 ♘bd2 ♖df8 21 ♗g3 ♘f5 22 bxc6 ♘xg3+ 23 hxg3 ♘xc6 24 ♖g1 b6 25 ♕b5 ♔b7 26 c4 ♖xf3 27 ♘xf3 ♕e4 28 ♖f1 ♘xd4 29 ♕d7+ ♔b8 30 cxd5 ♗xe5 31 ♕f7 ♖g7 32 ♕e8+ ♔b7 33 a5 ♕xd5 34 a6+ ♔xa6 35 ♕c8+ ♔a5 36 ♕c3+ ♔a6 37 ♕c8+ ♖b7 38 ♕c3 ♖c7 39 ♕a3+ ♔b7 40 ♔h2 ♘xf3+ 41 ♖xf3 ♖c2+ 42 ♔h3 ♗d6 **0-1** L/N3203

**1855-★MM-2**
**Morphy, P.C.– Maurian, C.A.**
[Maróczy]
⟨♖a1⟩ 1 e4 e5 2 f4 exf4 3 ♗c4 ♕h4+ 4 ♔f1 b5 5 ♗d5 ♘c6 6 ♘f3 ♕h5 7 d4 ♘f6 8 ♗b3 ♗a6 9 ♕e2 ♘xd4! 10 ♘xd4 b4 11 ♕xa6 ♕d1+ 12 ♔f2 ♘g4# **0-1** L/N3203

**1855-★MM-3** 1 iii 55
**Morphy, P.C.+ Meek, A.B.**
Mobile [Löwenthal]
1 e4 e5 2 f4 exf4 3 ♘f3 g5 4 ♗c4 ♗g7 5 h4 g4 6 ♘g5 ♘h6 7 d4 f6 8 ♗xf4 fxg5 9 ♗xg5 ♗f6 10 ♕d2 ♗xg5 11 hxg5 ♘f7 12 ♗xf7+ [12 ♕f4 ♖f8 13 ♖xh7 d5 14 ♗xd5 ♕d6 15 ♗xf7+ ♔d8 16 ♕xd6+ cxd6 17 g6+–] 12 ... ♔xf7 13 ♕f4+ ♔g8 14 0-0 ♕e7 15 ♘c3 c6 16 ♖ae1 d6 17 ♘d5! cxd5 18 exd5 **1-0** L/N3161

**1855-★MM-4** 1 iii 55
**Meek, A.B.– Morphy, P.C.**
Mobile [Löwenthal]
1 e4 e5 2 ♘f3 ♘c6 3 d4 exd4 4 ♗c4 ♗c5 5 ♘g5 ♘h6 [5 ... ♘e5 6 ♘xf7 ♘xf7 7 ♗xf7+ ♔xf7 8 ♕h5+ g6 9 ♕xc5± Heydebrandt] 6 ♘xf7 ♘xf7 7 ♗xf7+ ♔xf7 8 ♕h5+ g6 9 ♕xc5 d6 [◻ 9 ... d5] 10 ♕b5 ♖e8 11 ♕b3+ [◻ 11 0-0] 11 ... d5 12 f3? ♘a5 13 ♕d3 dxe4 14 fxe4 ♕h4+ 15 g3 ♖xe4+ 16 ♔f2 ♕e7 17 ♘d2 [17 ♗d2 ♗f5; 17 ♖f1 ♗h3] 17 ... ♖e3 18 ♕b5 c6! 19 ♕f1 ♗h3! 20 ♕d1 ♖f8 21 ♘f3 ♕e8 **0-1** L/N3161

**1855-★M?-1**
**Morphy, P.C.+?**
New Orleans [Maróczy]
⟨♖a1⟩ 1 e4 e5 2 ♘f3 ♘c6 3 ♗c4 ♗c5 4 b4 ♗xb4 5 c3 ♗c5 6 d4 exd4 7 cxd4 ♗b6 8 0-0 d6 9 ♘c3!? ♘a5 [◻ 9 ... ♗g4 Morphy M730-1860] 10 ♗d3 ♗g4 11 ♗e3 ♕f6 12 ♘d5 ♕d8 13 h3 ♗xf3 14 ♕xf3 ♘f6 [△ 15 ♗g5 ♗xd4∓ Morphy M730-1860] 15 ♗g5 ♗xd4 16 e5! ♗xe5 17 ♖fe1 0-0 18 ♖xe5 dxe5 19 ♘xf6+ gxf6 [19 ... ♔h8 20 ♕h5+–] 20 ♗xf6 [◻ 20 ♗h6! ♕xd3! 21 ♕xd3 ♔h8 22 ♕f5+–] **1-0** L/N3203

**1855̂-★AH-1**
**Anderssen, A.= Horwitz, B.**
[Brien]
1 e4 e5 2 f4 exf4 3 ♗c4 ♕h4+ 4 ♔f1 g5 5 ♘c3 d6 6 ♘d5 ♔d8 7 d4 ♗e6 8 ♕d3 ♕h5 9 ♘f3 ♘e7 10 ♘xe7 ♗xc4 11 ♕xc4 ♗xe7 12 ♕b5 b6 13 ♗xf4 f5 14 ♘xg5 ♗xg5 15 ♕xf5 h6 16 h4 ♘d7 17 ♔g1 ♖f8 18 ♕d5 c6 19 ♗xg5+ hxg5 [◻ 19 ... ♕xg5∓] 20 ♕xd6 gxh4 21 e5 ♕e2 22 ♖h3 ♖g8 23 ♕xc6 ♖c8 24 ♕d5 ♕c4 25 ♕xc4 ♖xc4 26 c3 ♖g4 27 ♖af1 ♖c6 28 ♖f2 ♖cg6 29 ♖hf3 ♔e7 30 ♔h2 a5 31 ♖f7+ ♔e8 32 ♖7f4 ♔e7 **½-½** L/N6123

**1855̂-★GK-1**
**Guttceit, von+ Kieseritsky, L.**
1 e4 e5 2 f4 exf4 3 ♘f3 ♗e7 4 ♗c4 ♗h4+ 5 g3 fxg3 6 0-0 gxh2+ 7 ♔h1 ♗f6 8 e5 d5 9 exf6 ♘xf6 10 ♗b3 ♗e6 11 d4 ♘e4 12 ♗f4 f5 13 ♘bd2 0-0 14 c4 c6 15 ♖c1 ♘d7 16 cxd5 cxd5 17 ♘xe4 fxe4 18 ♘g5 ♕e7 19 ♕h5 ♘f6 20 ♕xh2 ♖ad8 21 ♗c7 ♖d7 22 ♗a4 h6 23 ♘xe6 ♕xe6 24 ♗xd7 ♕xd7 25 ♗e5 **1-0** L/N6047-1855

**1855̂-★GL-1**
**Green– Löwenthal, J.J.**
London? [Löwenthal]
⟨♙f7⟩1 e4 d6 2 d4 ♘f6 3 ♘c3 e5 4 ♘f3 exd4 5 ♘xd4 a6! 6 f4 [6 ♗c4! b5 7 ♗d3? c5 8 ♘f3 c4 9 ♗e2 ♗b7 10 ♗g5 ♗e7∓; 6 ♗c4! b5 7 ♗e6? c5 8 ♗xc8 cxd4 9 ♗b7 ♖a7–+; 6 ♗c4! b5 7 ♗d5 ♘xd5; 6 ♗c4! b5 7 ♘e6! ♕e7 (7 ... ♕d7 8 ♘d5 △ 9 ♘exc7+) 8 ♘d5 ♘xd5 (8 ... ♕xe6?? 9 ♘xc7+) 9 ♗xd5 c6 10 ♗g5 ♕a7 (10 ... ♕f7 11 ♘d8+–) 11 ♗b3±; 6 ♗c4! b5 7 ♗b3! c5 8 ♘e6 ♕e7 9 ♘d5 ♘xd5 10 ♗xd5 ♖a7 11 ♗g5±] 6 ... ♗e7 7 e5 dxe5 8 fxe5 ♘g4 9 e6? ♘f6! [9 ... ♘e5? 10 ♕h5+ ♘g6 11 ♗d3±] 10 ♗c4 b5 11 ♗b3 c5 12 ♕f3 ♖a7 13 ♘c6 ♘xc6 14 ♕xc6+ ♔f8 15 0-0 c4 16 ♘d5 [16 ♖xf6+!? ♗xf6 (16 ... gxf6?? 17 ♗h6++–) 17 ♘d5 ♖e7! (17 ... ♗b7?? 18 ♕c5+) 18 ♘xe7 (18 ♘xf6 gxf6 19 ♗h6+ ♔g8 20 ♕f3 ♕d4+ 21 ♔h1 ♕h4–+) 18 ... ♕d1+ 19 ♔f2 ♗d4+ 20 ♗e3 ♕d2+ 21 ♔f1 ♕xe3 22 ♘g6+ hxg6 23 ♕xc8+ ♔e7 24 ♕c7+ ♔f6 25 ♕f7+ ♔g5–+] 16 ... ♗b7 17 ♕d7 ♕xd7 18 exd7 ♗xd5 **0-1** M324-1855

**1855̂-★JL-1**
**Journoud, P.+ Laroche**
Paris [de Rivière]
1 e4 c5 2 ♘f3 ♘c6 3 c3 e6 4 ♗d3 d5 5 exd5 exd5 6 ♗c2 ♗d6 7 h3 h6 8 0-0 ♘f6 9 d4 0-0 10 ♗e3 ♕b6 11 dxc5 ♗xc5 [11 ... ♕xb2? 12 cxd6 ♕xa1 13 ♕d2+–] 12 ♗xc5 ♕xc5 13 ♘bd2 ♗e6 14 ♘b3 ♕b6 15 ♘fd4 a5 16 a4 ♖ac8 17 f4 ♖fe8 18 ♖fe1 ♗d7 19 ♕d2 ♘e4 20 ♗xe4 dxe4 21 ♔h1 f5 22 ♘b5 ♗e6 23 ♘3d4 ♘xd4 24 ♘xd4 ♖cd8 25 ♕e3 ♖d5 26 ♖ab1 ♕c5 27 b4 axb4 28 ♖xb4 ♗c8 29 ♖eb1 ♖ed8 30 ♔h2 ♖8d6 31 ♕f2∓ ♕xc3? 32 ♘b5 ♖d2 33 ♕f1 ♕d3 34 ♘xd6 ♕xd6 35 ♖b6 ♕c7 36 a5 g5 37 ♖c1 ♖c2 38 ♖xc2 ♕xc2 39 ♖xh6 ♔g7 40 ♖h5 ♔f7 41 ♖xg5 ♕c7 42 ♕f2 ♕xa5 43 ♕d4 ♗e6 44 ♖g7+ ♔e8 45 ♕f6 **1-0** M954-1856

**1855̂-★KS-1**
**Schulten, J.W.– Kieseritsky, L.**
[Staunton]
1 e4 e5 2 f4 exf4 3 ♗c4 ♕h4+ 4 ♔f1 b5 5 ♗xb5 ♗b7 6 ♘c3 ♘c6 7 ♘f3 ♕h6 8 ♘d5 0-0-0 9 ♕e2 ♘b8 [◻ 9 ... ♘f6] 10 d4 g5 [10 ... c6 11 ♕c4±; 11 ♗xf4±] 11 ♘e5! ♕g7 12 ♕c4 ♗d6 13 ♘xf7! ♕xf7 14 ♘b6+ axb6 15 ♕xf7 ♗xe4 16 c4 ♗g6 17 ♕g7 ♘e7 18 c5 ♖hg8 19 ♕h6 bxc5 20 ♗c4 ♘f5 21 ♕h3 [21 ♕xg5 ♘e3+ 22 ♗xe3 ♗d3+ 23 ♗xd3 ♖xg5] 21 ... ♖gf8 22 d5 ♘e3+ 23 ♗xe3 fxe3+ 24 ♔g1 ♗e5 25 ♖e1 [◻ 25 ♗e2] 25 ... e2 26 ♖xe2 ♗d4+ 27 ♕e3 [27 ♖e3 ♖de8] 27 ... ♖f4! 28 b3 ♖df8 29 h3 ♗xe3+ 30 ♖xe3 ♖e4 31 ♖g3 h6 32 ♔h2 ♖d4 33 a4 d6 34 a5 ♘d7 35 ♖a1 ♔b8 36 ♗b5 ♘e5 37 a6 ♔a7 38 ♖c3 ♗e4 39 ♖a4 ♖xa4 40 bxa4 ♖f2 41 ♖g3 ♗xd5 42 h4 c6 43 hxg5 hxg5 44 ♖xg5 ♘f3+ 45 ♔g3 ♖xg2+ 46 ♔xg2 ♘xg5+ **0-1** L/N6123-1855

**1855̂-★KS-2**
**Kieseritsky, L.+Schulten, J.W.**
[Staunton]
1 e4 e5 2 d4 exd4 3 ♘f3 ♘c6 4 ♗c4 ♗c5 5 c3 d6 [◻ 5 ... ♘f6] 6 cxd4 ♗b4+ [◻ 6 ... ♗b6] 7 ♘c3 [7 ♔f1] 7 ... ♗g4 8 ♗e3 ♘f6 9 ♕c2 ♗xf3 10 gxf3 0-0 11 ♖g1 ♖e8 12 0-0-0 ♗xc3 13 bxc3 d5 14 ♗h6! g6 15 ♗b3 ♘a5 [15 ... dxe4 16 fxe4 ♘xe4 17 f3 ♘f6 18 ♖xg6+] 16 e5 ♘xb3+ 17 axb3 ♘h5 18 ♖g4 c5 19 f4 ♖e6 20 f5 ♖a6? 21 fxg6 fxg6 22 dxc5 ♖c8 23 b4 ♖cc6 24 ♔b2 [24 b5 ♖a1+ 25 ♔b2 ♖xd1 26 bxc6 ♖e1 27 ♕f5±] 24 ... b5 25 ♕b3 ♖a4 26 ♖xd5 **1-0** L/N6123-1855

**1855̂-★NS-1**
**Staunton, H.– Newman**
Hull [Staunton]
⟨♖a1⟩1 e4 e5 2 ♗c4 ♘f6 3 d3 ♗c5 4 ♘f3 d6 5 h3 ♗e6 6 ♗b3 ♗xb3 7 axb3 ♘bd7 8 c3 c6 9 0-0 0-0 10 ♔h2 h6 11 g4 ♘h7 12 ♕e2 d5 13 ♖g1 ♗e7 14 ♘a3 ♕c7 15 ♘c2 d4 16 ♘ce1 ♖ae8 17 ♘g2 ♘c5 18 ♘gh4?! [◻ 18 ♕d1; ◻ 18 b4] 18 ... ♘xb3 19 ♗xh6?! gxh6 20 ♘f5 ♗g5 21 ♘xg5 hxg5 22 h4 ♖e6! 23 hxg5 ♘xg5 24 ♔g3 ♖g6 25 ♖h1 f6 26 ♕d1 ♘c5 27 cxd4 exd4+ 28 f4 ♔f7 29 e5 fxe5 30 fxg5 e4+ 31 ♔g2 ♕e5 32 ♖h7+ ♔e8 33 ♕h1 [33 ♖e7+–+] 33 ... ♖xf5 34 gxf5 ♖xg5+ **0-1** M954-1856

**1855̂-★SS-1**
**Stella– Staunton, H.**
London [Staunton]
1 f4 d5 2 e3 c5 3 c4 d4 4 ♗d3 ♘c6 5 a3 e5 6 ♘f3 exf4 7 exf4 ♗d6 8 ♘g5 ♗xf4 9 ♕e2+ ♘e5 10 ♘f3 ♗g4 11 0-0 ♘e7 12 ♗e4 f5 13 ♕e1 ♗xf3 [13 ... fxe4 ♘xe5 ♗xe5 15 ♕xe4] 14 ♗xf3 ♕d6 15 ♗h5+ g6 16 ♕h4 ♘d3 17 ♗d1 0-0 18 a4 g5 19 ♕h5 ♖f6 20 ♖xf4 ♘xf4 **0-1** M954-1856

**1855̂-★BS-1**
**Deviner & Delondre & Whillermet & Benoit-Saint-Amant, P.C.F.de**
1 e4 e5 2 d4 exd4 3 ♗c4 ♘c6 4 ♘f3 ♘f6 5 0-0 ♗e7 6 ♘xd4 0-0 7 ♘c3 ♗c5 8 ♗e3 ♘e5 9 ♗b3 ♘fg4 10 ♗f4 d6 11 h3 ♘f6 12 ♗e3 c6 13 f4 ♘g6 14 ♕d3 a5 15 a4 ♘h5 16 ♘ce2 ♕e8 17 g4 ♘f6 18 ♘g3 b6 19 g5 ♘d7 20 ♘xc6 ♗a6 21 c4 d5 22 ♘d4 dxc4 23 ♗xc4 ♘de5 24 fxe5 ♘xe5 25 ♗b5 ♘xd3 26 ♗xe8 ♖fxe8 27 ♖f3 ♘e5 28 ♖f4 ♖ad8 29 ♘df5 ♘d3 30 ♗xc5 ♘xf4 31 ♗xb6 ♖d2 32 ♗xa5 ♘xh3+ 33 ♔h1 ♖xb2 34 ♘xg7 ♖c8 35 ♘7f5 ♖8c2 36 ♘h6+ ♔f8 37 ♘g4 ♘xg5 38 ♖d1 ♗d3 **0-1** M954-1855

**1855̂-★BS-2**
**Brien, R.B.+Staunton, H.**
London♀ [Staunton]
⟨♙f7⟩1 e4 ... 2 d4 e6 3 c4 ♗b4+ 4 ♘c3 ♘e7 5 ♕h5+ g6 6 ♕h6 ♘g8 7 ♕h3 d6 8 ♕g3 ♘c6 9 ♗g5 ♗xc3+ 10 bxc3 ♕d7 11 ♗e2 ♕g7 12 h4 h6 13 ♗e3 ♘ge7 14 ♘h3 ♗d7 15 a4 0-0-0 16 a5 a6 17 ♔d2 d5 18 cxd5 exd5 19 f3 ♖he8 20 ♖hb1 dxe4 21 fxe4 ♘g8?! 22 ♖xb7 ♔xb7 23 ♖b1+ ♔a8 24 ♕xc7 ♖b8 25 ♖b6 ♖xb6 26 axb6 ♖b8 27 ♗xa6 ♖xb6 28 ♕xb6 ♗e8 29 d5+- [29 ... ♘b8 30 ♕a5 ♘d7 (30 ... ♘xa6 31 ♕xa6+ ♔b8 32 ♗f4+) 31 ♕c7△#] ... **1-0**
L/N6123-1855

**1855̂-★BS-3**
**Brien, R.B.=Staunton, H.**
London♀ [Staunton]
⟨♙f7⟩1 e4 ... 2 d4 e6 3 ♗d3 ♕f6 4 ♗e3 d6 5 ♘d2 ♗e7 6 e5 ♕f7 7 ♘gf3 d5 8 0-0 g6 9 c4 c6 10 c5 ♕g7 11 b4 ♘h6 12 ♗xh6 ♕xh6 13 b5 0-0 14 a4 b6 15 ♘b3 ♗d7 16 ♕c2 ♗d8 17 ♖fe1 ♖f7 18 ♖e3 a6 19 cxb6 axb5 20 a5 ♘a6 21 ♕c3 ♗e7 22 ♘c5 ♗xc5 23 dxc5 ♕f8

24 ♘g5 ♖f4 [24 ... ♖xf2 25 ♘xh7 ♔xh6 26 ♗xg6+ ♔xg7 27 ♖g3+ ♔f7 28 ♔xf2 ♕xc5+ 29 ♕xc5 ♘xc5 30 ♔g1 ♔e7 31 h4] 25 ♘xh7 ♔xh7 26 ♖h3+ ♔g7 [26 ... ♔g8 27 ♗xg6 (△ 28 ♖h8) 27 ... ♕g7 (27 ... ♕xc5 28 ♕g3) 28 ♕g3 ♕xe5 29 ♖h7 ♕f6 (29 ... ♕xa1+ 30 ♗b1++-) 30 ♖xd7] 27 ♗xg6 ♖g4 [27 ... ♔xg6 28 ♕g3+ ♔f7 29 ♕xf4+ ♔e7 30 ♖h7+ ♔e8 31 ♕xf8+ ♔xf8 32 ♖h8++-; 27 ... ♕xc5 28 ♕g3 ♕xf2+ 29 ♕xf2 ♖xf2 30 ♖g3± ♖f7 31 ♗xf7+ ♔xf7 32 ♖f1+ ♔e7 33 ♖g7+ ♔d8 34 ♖f8+ ♗e8 35 ♖xe8+ ♔xe8 36 ♖g8++-] 28 ♖h7+ ♔xg6 29 ♕h3 ♖g5 30 ♖xd7 ♕g8 [30 ... ♖xe5 31 f4 ♖f5 32 g4 ♖xf4 (32 ... ♖f7 33 ♕h5+ △ 34 ♖xf7+ 35 ♖a3) 33 ♕h5+ ♔f6 34 ♖e1+-] 31 ♖h7 [◻31 f4; 31 ♖d6] 31 ... ♕xh7 32 ♕xe6+ **½-½**
L/N6123-1855

**1855̂-★BS-4**
**Brien, R.B.+Staunton, H.**
London♀ [Staunton]
⟨♙f7⟩1 e4 ... 2 d4 e6 3 ♗d3 d5 4 e5 b6 5 ♕h5+ ♔d7 6 ♘e2 ♗a6 7 ♕h3 ♗xd3 8 ♕xd3 ♘c6 9 a3 ♕e8 10 ♗e3 ♖d8 11 ♘d2 ♔c8 12 0-0 ♘ge7 13 ♗g5 h6 14 ♗xe7 ♗xe7 15 c4 ♖f8 16 b4 dxc4 17 ♕xc4 ♕d7 18 ♖ac1 ♔b7 19 ♘b3 ♕d5 20 b5 ♕xc4 21 ♖xc4 ♘b8 22 ♖fc1 ♖d7 23 a4 a5 24 g3 [◻24 ♖c6△ 25 ♖xe6] 24 ... g5 25 ♔g2 ♗d8 26 ♘d2 ♖df7 27 ♘e4 ♖f3?? 28 ♘f4

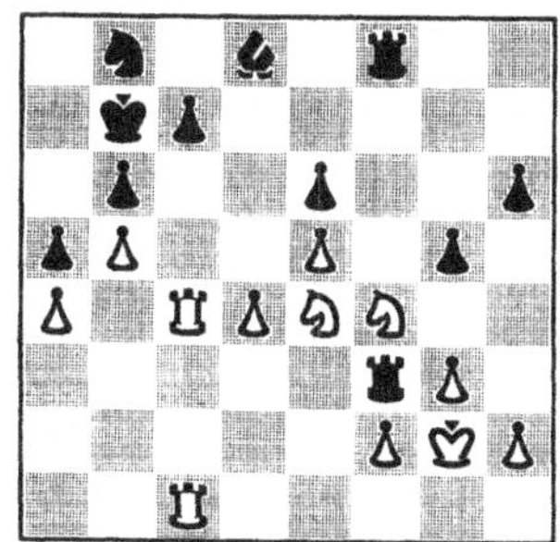

28 ... ♖3xf4 29 gxf4 ♖xf4 30 ♘g3 ♘d7 31 f3 ♘f8 32 ♘h5 ♖f7 33 ♖c6 ♘g6 34 ♖xe6 ♘h4+ 35 ♔h1 ♖xf3 36 ♖xh6 ♖d3 37 ♖h7 ♖xd4 38 ♘f6 ♔c8 39 ♘e8 ♖xa4 40 ♘d6+ ♔b8 41 ♖d7 cxd6 42 ♖xd8+ ♔b7 43 exd6 ...♀ **1-0** L/N6123-1855

**1855̂-★BS-5**
**Brien, R.B.+Staunton, H.**
London [Staunton]
⟨♙f7⟩1 e4 ... 2 d4 e6 3 ♗d3 ♕f6 4 ♘f3 g6 5 0-0 ♗e7 6 c4 ♕g7 7 ♘c3 ♘h6 8 ♘b5?! ♘a6 9 ♗f4 d6 10 ♕d2 ♘f7 11 e5 g5 12 exd6 cxd6 [12 ... gxf4 13 dxe7 ♖g8 14 ♘e1 f3 15 g3 ♘g5 16 ♕e3] 13 ♗e3 ♗d7 14 ♕a5 ♗d8 15 ♕a3 ♗xb5 16 cxb5 ♘c7 17 b6 axb6 18 ♗b5+ ♔e7 19 ♕b3 h5 20 ♗c4 d5 21 ♕b4+ ♔e8 22 ♗d3 ♖h6 23 ♕xb6 e5 24 ♗b5+ ♔f8 25 ♕c5+ ♔g8 26 dxe5 b6 27 ♕b4 ♘xe5 28 ♘xe5 ♕xe5 29 ♖fe1 ♖e6 30 ♗xb6 ♕f5 [30 ... ♖xa2 31 ♖xe5 ♖xa1+ 32 ♗f1 ♖xe5 33 ♕d6 ♖ee1 34 ♕xd8+ ♔f7 35 ♕xc7+ ♔g8 36 ♕c8+ ♔f7 37 ♕d7+ ♔g1 38 ♕b5] 31 ♗xc7 ♗xc7 32 ♖xe6 ♕xe6 33 ♖e1 ♕f5 34 ♗c6 ♖d8 35 ♕b7 ♕f4 36 g3 ♕d2 37 ♖e7 g4 [37 ... ♖f8 38 ♗xd5+ ♔h8 39 ♖h7+ ♔xh7 40 ♕xc7+-] 38 ♕xc7 ♕d1+ 39 ♔g2 ♕f3+ 40 ♔f1 ♕d3+ 41 ♖e2 ♖f8 42 ♕e5 ♖f5 43 ♕e3+- ...♀ **1-0**
L/N6123-1855

**1855̂-★S♀-1**
**Staunton, H.+♀**
London
1 e4 e5 2 ♘f3 ♘c6 3 d4 exd4 4 ♗c4 ♘f6 5 ♗g5 h6 6 ♗xf6 ♕xf6 7 0-0 ♗c5 8 e5 ♕g6 9 c3 dxc3 10 ♘xc3 0-0 11 ♘d5 ♗b6 12 b4 ♔h8 13 b5 ♘a5 14 ♗d3 ♕e6 15 ♗c2 c6 16 ♘f4 ♕c4 17 g3 ♕xb5 18 ♘g6+ ♔g8 19 ♕d6 ♕c5 20 ♘e7+ ♔h8 21 ♕d3 g6 22 ♘xg6+ fxg6 23 ♕xg6 ♕e7 24 ♕xh6+ ♔g8 25 ♘g5 ♕g7 26 ♗h7+ ♔h8 27 ♕h5 ♗d8 28 ♗g6+ ♔g8 29 ♘h7 ♗e7 30 ♘xf8 ♗xf8 31 ♖ad1 ♘c4 32 ♖fe1 d5 33 e6 ♗d6 34 ♖d4 ♘e5 35 ♖xe5 ♗xe5 36 ♗f7+ ♔f8 37 ♖g4 ♕f6 38 ♗g6 **1-0** M954-1855

## BIRD✕FALKBEER London
**[1856-✕BF]**

| | | | | | | | | | |
|---|---|---|---|---|---|---|---|---|---|
| H.E. Bird | ½ | 1 | 0 | 0 | 0 | 1 | 0 | 1 | ? |
| E.K. Falkbeer | ½ | 0 | 1 | 1 | 1 | 0 | 1 | 0 | ? |

**1856-✕BF-1̂**
**Bird, H.E.=Falkbeer, E.K.**
[Falkbeer]
1 f4 d5 2 ♘f3 ♘c6 3 d4 ♗f5 4 e3 a6 5 ♗d3 ♘h6 6 ♘c3 e6 7 a3 ♗e7 8 0-0 ♗xd3 9 ♕xd3 ♘f5 10 ♘xd5! ♕xd5 11 e4 ♕d7 12 exf5 exf5 13 c4 f6 14 ♗e3 0-0-0?! 15 b4 ♖he8 16 ♖fe1 ♗f8 17 ♖ad1 h6 18 d5 g5 19 ♕c2 ♘xb4! 20 axb4 ♗xb4 21 ♖e2 ♖e4 22 ♗f2 ♖de8! [22 ... ♖xf4] 23 ♖xe4 fxe4 24 ♘d4 e3 25 ♗g3

♗c5 26 ♕e2! ♖e4 27 ♘b3 ♗a7 28 ♔h1 gxf4 29 ♗h4 ♕a4? 30 ♗xf6! ♗b6 [30 ... ♕xb3?? 31 ♕g4++-] 31 c5 ♕xb3 32 cxb6 ♕xb6 33 d6? cxd6 34 ♖c1+ ♔b8 35 ♕d3 ♖e8 36 ♕g6 ♕b5 37 ♗d4 ♕d7 38 ♕xh6 e2 39 ♖e1 ♕e7?! 40 ♕xf4 ♖f8 41 ♖xe2 [41 ♕g3!] 41 ... ♖xf4 42 ♖xe7 ♖xd4 43 h3 b5 44 g4 b4 45 g5 b3 46 g6 ♖d1+ 47 ♔g2 b2 48 g7 ♖g1+ 49 ♔xg1 b1♕+ 50 ♔g2 [50 ... ♕g6+=] ...? ½-½

M1431-1857

## 1856-✕BF-2

**Falkbeer, E.K.– Bird, H.E.**

[Falkbeer]

1 d4 d5 2 c4 e6 3 e3 ♘f6 4 ♘f3 c6 [4 ... c5] 5 ♘c3 ♗d6 6 ♗d3 ♘bd7 7 cxd5 exd5 8 ♗d2 b5 9 ♕c2 ♗b7 10 ♘e2 ♖c8 11 ♘g3 ♗xg3 12 hxg3 ♕e7 13 ♖c1 [Δ 14 ♗xb5] 13 ... a6 14 ♘h4 g6 15 a3 [Δ 15 ♗b4] 15 ... c5 16 ♗b4? 0-0! [16 ... cxb4? 17 ♕xc8+ ♗xc8 18 ♖xc8+ ♕d8 19 ♖xd8+ ♔xd8 20 axb4] 17 ♗xc5 [17 dxc5 a5!] 17 ... ♘xc5 18 dxc5 d4!∓ 19 b4 dxe3 20 0-0 ♘g4 21 f4 ♖cd8 22 ♖ce1 ♘f2 23 ♗e2 ♘e4 24 ♔h2 ♘d2 25 ♖h1 ♕f6 26 ♔g1 ♗e4 27 ♕c1 ♖fe8 28 ♕a1 ♕c6 29 ♕c3 f6 [Δ 30 ... g5] 30 ♗g4 [□ 30 g4] 30 ... ♖d3 31 ♕c1 ♕d5 32 ♗e2 ♖d4 33 ♕c3 g5 34 fxg5 fxg5 35 ♕xe3 [35 ♘f3 ♗xf3 36 gxf3 ♘xf3+ 37 ♗xf3 ♕xf3-+] 35 ... ♗g6 36 ♕f2 gxh4 37 ♖xh4 ♖xh4 38 gxh4 ♕f7 39 ♕d4 [39 ♗d1∓] 39 ... ♖xe2!-+ 40 ♕d8+ ♔g7 41 ♕d4+ ♔h6 42 ♖xe2 ♕f1+ 43 ♔h2 ♕xe2 44 ♕f4+ ♔g7 45 ♕d4+ ♔f7 46 ♕d5+ ♔f6 47 ♕d6+ ♔f5 48 ♕d7+ ♔f4 49 ♕d6+ ♔e3 50 ♕g3+ ♘f3+ ...?
**0-1**

M1431-1857

## 1856-✕BF-3

**Bird, H.E.– Falkbeer, E.K.**

[Falkbeer]

1 f4 c5 [1 ... f5] 2 ♘f3 e6 3 e3 a6 4 b3 d5 5 ♗b2 ♘f6 6 ♗d3? ♘c6 7 0-0 ♗d6 8 ♕e2 ♘b4 9 ♘c3 ♘xd3 10 ♕xd3 ♕c7 11 ♖ae1 ♗d7 12 ♕e2 ♗c6 13 d4 b5 14 ♘d1 [Δ 15 ♘e5] 14 ... ♗b7 15 ♘f2 c4 16 ♘e5 c3 17 ♗c1 b4 18 ♘fd3 [Δ 19 f5] 18 ... g6 19 ♘g4 ♕e7 20 ♘de5 h5 21 ♘f2 ♔f8 [Δ 22 ... a5; 21 ... a5?! 22 ♕b5+] 22 ♘h3 a5 23 ♘g5 ♗a6 24 ♘d3 [24 ♕f3?! ♗xf1 25 ♘gxf7 (25 ♘exf7 ♖g8 26 ♖xf1 ♔g7) 25 ... ♖g8 26 ♖xf1 ♖a7 27 ♕g3 ♘e4] 24 ... ♘e4∓ 25 ♕f3 f5! [25 ... ♘xg5? 26 fxg5 Δ 27 e4] 26 ♖d1 h4 27 ♖fe1 ♘xg5 28 fxg5 ♗xd3 29 cxd3 [Δ 30 e4] 29 ... ♕c7 30 h3 ♗g3 31 ♖e2 ♔g7 32 e4 dxe4 33 dxe4 ♖ad8 34 e5 [34 d5 ♖he8] 34 ... ♕b6 35 ♗e3 ♖d5 36 ♗f2 ♖hd8 37 ♖d3 ♗xf2+ 38 ♕xf2 ♖xd4 39 ♔h2 ♖8d5 [39 ... ♖8d7 Δ 40 ... ♕d8] 40 ♖e4!? fxe4 [40 ... c2?? 41 ♖exd4 c1=♕ 42 ♖xd5 ♕xf2 43 ♖d7++-] 41 ♕f6+ ♔g8 42 ♕xg6+ ♔f8 43 ♕f6+ ♔e8 44 ♖xd4 ♕xd4 45 ♕xe6+ ♔d8 46 ♕f6+ ♔c7 47 ♕g7+ ♖d7 48 ♕f6 c2 49 ♕f4 e3
**0-1**

M1431-1857

## 1856-✕BF-4

**Falkbeer, E.K.+ Bird, H.E.**

[Falkbeer]

1 d4 g6?! 2 e4 ♗g7 3 e5 d6 4 f4 ♘h6 5 ♘c3 0-0 6 ♘f3 c6 7 ♗d3 ♗g4 8 h3 ♗e6 9 g4 dxe5 10 dxe5 f5 11 g5 ♘f7 12 ♗e3 b6 13 ♕e2 b5? 14 ♕g2! ♘a6 15 h4 ♘b4 16 ♖d1 ♘d5 17 ♘xd5 ♗xd5 18 h5 ♕a5+ 19 ♔f2 ♗xf3 20 ♕xf3 ♕xa2?! 21 hxg6 hxg6 22 ♕h3 ♘h8 23 ♕h7+ ♔f7 24 b3 [Δ 25 e6++-] 24 ... e6 25 ♗xf5!+- [? Δ 26 ♖d7+] 25 ... ♖fd8 26 ♗d3 ♖d5 27 ♗e4 ♖ad8 28 ♖a1± ♕b2 29 ♗xd5 ♕xc2+ 30 ♔g3 [Δ 31 ♖xa7+] 30 ... ♖d7 31 ♗f3 ♔f8

32 ♕xh8+! ♗xh8 33 ♖xh8+ ♔g7 34 ♖ah1 **1-0**

M1431-1857

## 1856-✕BF-5

**Bird, H.E.– Falkbeer, E.K.**

[Anderssen & Dufresne]

1 f4 d5 2 ♘f3 c5 3 b3 ♘c6 4 e3 e6 5 ♗b5 ♗d7 6 ♗b2 ♘f6 7 0-0 ♗e7 8 d3 ♕b6 9 ♗xc6 ♗xc6 10 ♘bd2 ♖c8 11 ♘e5 0-0 12 ♕e2 ♘e8 13 ♖f3 a5 [13 ... f5] 14 ♖h3 g6 15 ♕g4 ♘g7 16 ♖f1!? d4 17 e4 ♕c7! 18 ♖h6?! f5 19 ♕h3 ♘h5?? 20 g4?? [20 ♘xg6 hxg6 21 ♖xg6+ ♘g7 22 ♕h6 ♖f7 (22 ... ♗~ 23 ♖xg7+ ♕xg7 24 ♕xe6++-) 23 ♖f3+-] 20 ... ♘xf4! 21 ♖xf4 ♕xe5 22 ♖f3-+ ♗g5! 23 ♖xh7 fxg4 24 ♕xg4 ♔xh7 25 ♘c4 ♕c7 26 ♖h3+ ♔g7 27 ♕xg5 ♕f4 28 ♕g2 ♖f6 29 ♖g3 ♖cf8 30 ♖g5 b5 31 ♖g4 ♕f1+
**0-1**

L/N6047-1857

## 1856-✕BF-6

**Falkbeer, E.K.– Bird, H.E.**

London [Staunton]

1 e4 e6 2 d4 d5 3 exd5 exd5 4 ♗e3 ♘f6 5 c4 ♗b4+ 6 ♘c3 0-0 7 ♕b3 ♘c6 8 ♘f3 ♗e6 9 c5 ♖b8 10 ♗b5 ♗xc5! 11 ♕c2 [11 dxc5? d4] 11 ... ♗d6 12 ♗xc6 bxc6 13 0-0 ♗g4 14 ♘e5 ♗xe5 15 dxe5 ♘d7 16 f4 ♘b6 17 ♗c5 ♖e8 18 ♖ae1 ♕d7 19 h3 ♗f5 20 ♕f2 ♗d3 21 ♘e2 ♘a4 22 b3 ♗xe2 23 ♖xe2 ♘c3 24 ♖c2 ♘e4 25 ♕e3 a6 26 ♗d4 ♖b5 27 ♖fc1 ♖e6 28 f5 ♖h6 29 ♕f4 [□ 26 g4] 29 ... ♖b4 30 ♗c5 ♖b8 31 ♗e3 g5!? 32 ♕f3 ♖e8 33 e6 fxe6 34 ♖xc6 ♕f7 35 ♖xa6 [□ 35 g4 Δ 36 ♖xc7; Δ 36 ♖xe6] 35 ... ♖f6 36 ♖xe6 ♖exe6 37 fxe6 ♖xf3 38 exf7+ ♖xf7 39 ♖c6 h5

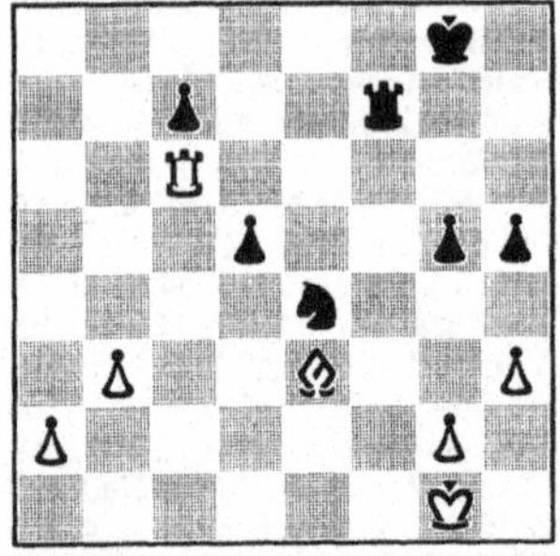

40 ♖g6+ [40 a4+-] 40 ... ♔h7 41 ♖c6 h4 42 ♗d4 ♔g8! [42 ... ♘g3 43 ♖f6] 43 a4 ♘g3 44 ♗f6 ♘e4 [□ 44 ... d4-+] 45 ♗e5 ♖f5 46 ♗xc7 d4 47 ♖c4 ♖d5-+ 48 ♔f1 ♘d2+ [□ 48 ... d3] 49 ♔e2 ♘xc4 50 bxc4 ♖c5 51 ♗d8 ♖xc4 52 ♗xg5 ♖xa4 53 ♔d3 ♔f7 54 ♗xh4 ♔e6 55 ♗g5 ♔d5 56 h4 ♖a3+ 57 ♔e2 ♔e4 58 h5 ♖a5
**0-1**

M954-1857

## 1856-✕BF-7

**Bird, H.E.– Falkbeer, E.K.**

London [Staunton]

1 f4 c5 2 e3 e6 3 b3 ♗e7 4 ♘c3 ♗h4+ 5 g3 ♗f6 6 ♘f3 d5 7 d4 cxd4 8 exd4 a6 9 ♗d3 ♘c6 10 ♗e3 b5 11 a4 b4 12 ♘e2 ♗b7 13 ♖c1 h5 14 ♕d2 ♘h6 15 h3 ♕d6 16 ♘e5 ♗xe5 17 fxe5 ♕e7 18 ♗g5 ♕d7 19 0-0± ♖c8 20 ♖f4 ♘f5 21 ♖cf1 g6 22 g4 hxg4 23 hxg4 ♖g8?! 24 gxf5 gxf5 25 ♖4f2 [□ 25 ♖h4 Δ 25 ... ♕e7 26 ♖h8+-] 25 ... ♘xe5!? 26 dxe5 d4 27 ♘xd4? f6 28 exf6 ♕xd4 29 f7+ [29 ♗b5+ ♔f7-+] 29 ... ♔xf7 30 ♗xf5 ♕xd2 31 ♗g6+ ♔xg6 32 ♗xd2 ♔h7+ 33 ♔h2 ♖c5 34 ♖f7+ ♔h8 **0-1**

M954-1857

## 1856-✕BF-8

**Bird, H.E.+ Falkbeer, E.K.**

London [Staunton]

1 e4 e5 2 ♗c4 ♗c5 3 ♘f3 d6 4 0-0 ♗g4 5 c3 ♘c6 6 b4 ♗b6 7 b5 ♘a5 8 ♗e2 f5 9 exf5 ♗xf5 10 d4 e4 11 ♗g5 ♘f6 12 ♘h4 ♗d7 13 c4 0-0 14 ♗e3 ♘d5 15 cxd5 ♕xh4 16 ♘c3

♖ae8 17 ♖c1 c6 18 dxc6 bxc6 19 ♕d2 [△ 20 ♗g5] 19 ... h6 20 bxc6 ♘xc6 21 ♘d5 ♗a5 22 ♕c2 [◻ 22 ♕d1] 22 ... ♖f5 23 g3 ♕d8 24 ♘f4 ♔h7 25 ♗g4 ♘b4 26 ♗xf5+ ♗xf5 27 ♕e2 g5 28 ♘g2 ♘d3 29 ♖b1 ♕d7 30 f4 ♗g4 31 ♕c2 ♗b6 32 fxg5 hxg5 33 ♘e1 ♗f5 34 a4 ♔g6 35 ♖b5 d5 36 ♕b3 ♖d8 37 a5! ♗c7 38 ♖b7 ♕h7 39 ♘xd3 exd3 40 ♖xf5 ♖e8 41 ♕xd3 ♖e4 42 ♖xd5 **1-0** M954-1857

**1856-★AD-1**
**Dufresne,J.♀–Anderssen, A.**
Breslau
1 e4 e5 2 ♗c4 b5 3 ♗xb5 c6 4 ♗c4 ♘f6 5 ♘c3 ♗b4 6 d3 d5 7 exd5 cxd5 8 ♗b5+ ♔f8 9 ♗d2 ♕a5 10 a4 a6 11 ♘f3 axb5 12 ♘xe5 ♗xc3 13 bxc3 ♕c7 14 f4 bxa4 15 0-0 a3 16 c4 a2 17 cxd5 ♘xd5 18 c4 ♘f6 19 ♗c3 ♘c6 20 d4 ♗f5 21 d5 ♘e4 22 ♕b3 ♕a7+ 23 ♔h1 ♘d4 24 ♕b2 ♘c2 25 ♘c6 ♕c5 26 ♖xa2 ♖e8 27 ♖a5 ♕d6 28 ♗xg7+ ♔g8 29 ♗xh8 f6 30 ♘e5 fxe5 31 ♗xe5 ♕h6 32 ♖f3 ♘e1 33 ♖a7 ♘xf3 34 gxf3 ♘g3+ 35 ♔g1 ♘h5 36 ♕g2+ ♗g6 37 d6 ♘xf4 ...♀ **0-1** L/N3034

**1856-★AE-1** 7 xi 56
**Eichborn, L.+Anderssen, A.**
Breslau
1 e4 e5 2 f4 exf4 3 ♘f3 g5 4 h4 g4 5 ♘e5 h5 6 ♗c4 ♖h7 7 d4 f3 8 gxf3 d6 9 ♘d3 ♗e7 10 ♗f4 ♗xh4+ 11 ♔d2 ♗g5 12 ♗xg5 ♕xg5+ 13 f4 ♕g7 14 ♕g1 h4 15 ♘c3 g3 16 e5 dxe5 17 ♘xe5 ♗e6 18 ♗xe6 fxe6 19 ♕g2 c5 20 ♘e4 ♘f6 21 ♘xc5 ♕e7 22 ♖ae1 ♕d6 23 ♘xe6 ♖e7 24 ♘d3 ♘c6 25 ♘g7+ ♔f7 26 ♘f5 ♕c7 27 ♘xe7 ♘xe7 28 ♖xh4 ♘f5 29 ♖hh1 ♖d8 30 ♘e5+ ♔g7 31 c3 ♕b6 32 ♔c1 ♖c8 33 ♖h3 ♕xd4 34 ♕xb7+ **1-0** L/N3034

**1856-★AE-2** 10 xii 56
**Eichborn, L.+Anderssen, A.**
Breslau
1 e4 e5 2 f4 exf4 3 ♘f3 g5 4 h4 g4 5 ♘e5 h5 6 ♗c4 ♖h7 7 d4 f3 8 gxf3 d6 9 ♘d3 ♗e7 10 ♗e3 ♗xh4+ 11 ♔d2 ♗g5 12 f4 ♗h6 13 ♘c3 ♗g7 14 e5 ♗f5 15 ♗d5 c6 16 ♗e4 ♘e7 17 ♗xf5 ♘xf5 18 ♘e4 ♘bd7 19 ♘xd6+ ♘xd6 20 exd6 ♕a5+ 21 c3 0-0-0 22 ♕c2 f5 23 ♘c5 ♖f8 24 b4 ♕d8 25 ♘e6 ♕f6 26 ♘xf8 ♗xf8 27 ♕a4 a6 28 b5 cxb5 29 ♕b3 ♗xd6 30 ♕g8+ ♘f8 31 a4 b4 32 cxb4 ♗xb4+ 33 ♔d3 a5 34 ♖ac1+ ♔b8 35 ♖c4 h4 36 ♖hc1 ♕a6 37 ♕d5 h3 38 ♕d8+ ♔a7 39 d5+ b6 40 ♗xb6+ ♔b7 41 ♗c7 ♘d7 42 ♔e3 h2 43 ♗xa5 ♖e7+ 44 ♔f2 ♗c5+ 45 ♔g2 ♖e2+ 46 ♔h1 ♕d6 47 ♖xc5 **1-0** L/N3034

**1856-★AH-1**
**Hillel, D–Anderssen, A.**
Breslau [Anderssen & Kossak]
1 e4 e5 2 f4 exf4 3 ♗c4 ♕h4+ 4 ♔f1 g5 5 ♘c3 ♗g7 6 d4 ♘e7 7 ♘b5 ♘a6 8 ♘f3 ♕h5 9 ♕e2 d6 10 h4 h6 11 e5 dxe5 12 dxe5 ♗e6 13 ♗xe6 fxe6 14 ♘bd4 0-0 15 ♘xe6 g4 16 ♘xg7 ♔xg7 17 ♘d4 ♘c5 18 b4 ♖ad8 19 c3 ♖xd4 20 cxd4 f3 21 gxf3 ♖xf3+ 22 ♔g2 ♘d3 23 ♗e3 ♘d5 24 ♕xd3 ♘xe3+ 25 ♔g1 ♖g3+ 26 ♔f2 ♕f7+ 27 ♔e1 ♕f3 28 ♔d2 ♕g2+ 29 ♔c3 ♘d5+ 30 ♔c4

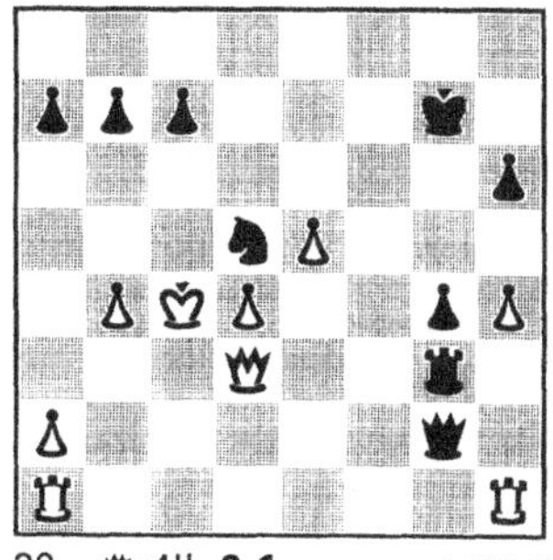

30 ... ♕e4!! **0-1** L/N6047

**1856-★A♀-1**
**♀– St. Amant, P.C.F. de**
[Staunton]
1 e4 c5 2 d4 cxd4 3 ♕xd4 ♘c6 4 ♕d1 e5 5 ♘f3 ♗c5 6 ♗c4 ♘f6 7 0-0 0-0 8 ♗g5 h6 9 ♗h4 d6 10 ♘c3 ♗e6 11 ♘d5 ♗xd5 12 ♗xd5 [◻ 12 exd5] 12 ... ♕e7 13 c3 ♘d8 14 ♕b3? g5 15 ♗g3 ♘e6 16 ♖ad1 ♘xd5 17 exd5 ♘f4 18 ♗xf4 gxf4 19 ♕c2 f5 20 ♖fe1 ♕f6 21 ♕d2 ♔h7 22 ♔h1 ♖g8 23 g3 e4 24 ♘d4 ♗xd4 25 ♕xd4 ♕g5 26 ♕b4 [◻ 26 ♕d2] 26 ... ♖ad8 27 ♕xb7+ ♖g7 28 ♕b5 e3 29 fxe3 fxg3 30 ♕e2 ♖e8 31 ♕f3 gxh2 32 ♕f2 ♕h5 33 ♖d2 ♖g1+ **0-1** M954-1856

**1856-★BC-1** 19 vii 56
**Barnes,T.W. & Staunton,H.– Cunningham & Löwenthal,J.J.**
London [Anderssen & Kossak]
1 e4 e6 2 d4 d5 3 exd5 exd5 4 c4 c5? [4 ... ♗b4+! 5 ♘c3 c5] 5 ♘f3 cxd4 6 ♕xd4 ♘c6 7 ♕e3+ ♗e6 8 cxd5 ♕xd5 9 ♘c3 ♕c5 10 ♗b5 ♕xe3+ 11 ♗xe3 ♗b4 12 ♗xc6+ bxc6 13 ♗d4 f6 14 a3 ♗xc3+ 15 ♗xc3 ♗d5 16 ♘d4 ♘h6 17 0-0 ♔f7 18 h3 ♖he8 19 ♖ac1 ♔g6 20 ♗d2 ♘f5! 21 ♘xc6 ♖e2 22 ♗b4 a5 [◻ 22 ... ♖xb2] 23 ♘xa5 ♖xb2 24 ♘c4 ♗xc4 25 ♖xc4 ♖e8

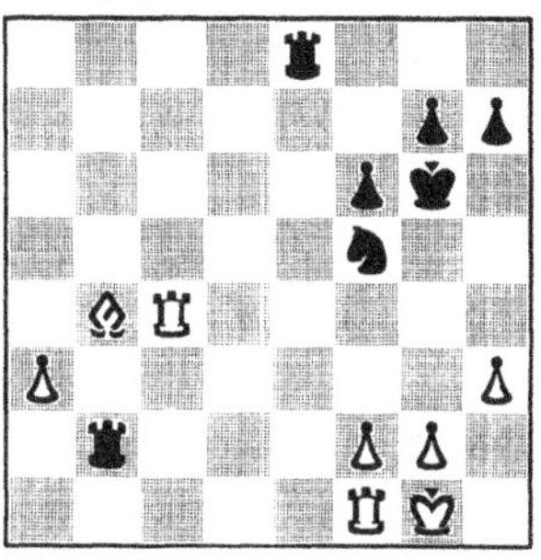

26 ♖e1?? ♖xb4! 27 ♖xb4 ♖xe1+ 28 ♔h2 ♖a1 29 g4 ♘e7 [29 ... ♘h4 30 ♔g3 ♖g1+ 31 ♔xh4 ♔h6–+] 30 a4 ♘d5 31 ♖d4 ♘c3 ... 50 **0-1** L/N6047

**1856-★BC-2**
**Cunningham & Löwenthal,J.J.+ Barnes,T.W. & Staunton,H.**
London [♀]
1 e4 e6 2 d4 d5 3 exd5 exd5 4 ♘f3 ♘f6 5 ♗e3 ♗d6 6 ♗d3 0-0 7 0-0 ♗e6 8 ♘g5 ♗g4 9 f3 ♗h5 10 ♕d2 b6 11 ♕f2 ♘bd7 12 ♘d2 c5 13 c3 ♕c7 14 g4 ♗g6 15 ♗xg6 hxg6 16 ♖ac1 [16 ♔g2] 16 ... ♖ae8 17 ♖fe1 ♖xe3 18 ♖xe3 cxd4! [18 ... ♗f4] 19 ♖d3 [19 ♖ee1? dxc3 △ 20 ... ♗c5] 19 ... ♘e5 20 ♖xd4 ♗c5 21 ♕f1 [21 ♔g2 ♘d3] 21 ... ♘c6 22 ♘b3 ♘xd4 23 cxd4 ♗xd4+ 24 ♘xd4 ♕f4 25 ♘c6 [25 ♘de6?? fxe6 26 ♘xe6 ♕e3+] 25 ... ♕xg5 26 ♘e7+ ♔h8 27 ♖e1 ♕h4 28 ♖e5 ♖d8 29 ♕d3 [△ 30 ♕xg6] 29 ... ♕h3 30 g5 ♘g4 31 ♖e2 d4 32 ♖g2 ♘e3 [32 ... ♘e5!] 33 ♖g3 ♕e6 34 ♕e4! ♘f5 35 ♖h3+ ♘h6 36 ♕xe6 fxe6 37 ♔f2 ♔h7 38 ♔e1 ♖d7 39 ♘c6 ♖c7 40 ♘e5 ♖c2 41 ♘d3 a5 42 f4 b5 43 ♔d1 ♖g2 44 ♔c1 b4 45 gxh6 gxh6 46 ♘c5 ♖e2 47 ♖d3 e5 48 fxe5 ♖xh2 49 ♖xd4 ♖e2 50 ♘d3 g5 51 ♔d1 ♖g2 52 e6 ♔g7 53 ♖e4 ♔f8 54 ♘e5 b3 55 axb3 ♖xb2 56 ♘g6+ ♔e8 57 ♖c4 ♔d8 58 e7+ **1-0** L/N6123-1859

**1856-★BL-1**
**Barnes,T.W. & Staunton,H.– Löwenthal,J.J. & Owen,J.**
London [Staunton]
1 e4 e5 2 ♘f3 ♘c6 3 ♗c4 ♗c5 4 ♘c3 d6 5 d3 ♘f6 6 ♘e2 ♗e6 7 ♗b3? [7 ♗xe6] 7 ... h6 8 ♘g3 0-0 9 0-0 d5 10 exd5 ♘xd5 11 ♗a4 ♘de7 12 ♘e4? ♗b6 13 c3 f5 14 ♘g3 ♕d6 15 ♗e3 ♖ad8 16 ♗c2 ♘d5 17 ♕e1?? [17 ♗xb6] 17 ... ♘xe3 18 fxe3 f4∓ 19 ♘e4 ♕e7 20 ♔h1 ♗xe3 21 ♘h4

♕e8 22 d4 exd4 23 ♘c5 d3 24 ♘xe6 dxc2 25 ♘xf8 ♕xf8 [25 ... ♔xf8?? 26 ♘g6+ ♕xg6 27 ♕xe3±] 26 ♕e2 c1♕ 27 ♖axc1 ♗xc1 28 ♖xc1 ♖e8 29 ♕b5 ♕d6 30 ♖f1 b6 31 ♕c4+ ♔h7 32 ♘f5 ♕e5! 33 ♕f7 [33 ♘xg7 ♘a5 34 ♕f7 ♖e7–+] 33 ... ♖e6 34 h3 ♕f6 35 ♕h5 ♕g5 36 ♕g4 ♕xg4 37 hxg4 ♖e4 38 ♖d1 ♘e5 ...♀ **0-1** M954

### 1856-★BL-2 1 xi 56

**Barnes, T.W. & Staunton, H.+ Löwenthal, J.J. & ♀**

London [Löwenthal]

1 e4 e5 2 ♘f3 ♘c6 3 d4 exd4 4 ♗c4 ♗c5 5 0-0 d6 6 c3 dxc3? 7 ♘xc3 ♘ge7 8 ♗g5! [8 ♘d5] 8 ... h6? [8 ... 0-0] 9 ♗h4 g5 10 ♗g3 ♘g6 11 e5± g4 12 exd6 cxd6 13 ♖e1+ ♔f8 14 ♘d2 ♘ge5 15 ♗b5 ♗f5 16 ♗xc6 ♘xc6 17 ♘de4 ♕d7 18 ♘f6 ♕c7 19 ♖c1 ♘b4 20 ♘cd5 ♘xd5 21 ♕xd5 ♗e6 22 ♖xc5 dxc5 23 ♗d6+ ♔g7 24 ♕e5 ♕xd6 25 ♘e8+ **1-0** M324

### 1856-★BL-3

**Barnes, T.W. & Staunton, H.= Löwenthal, J.J. & Owen, J.**

London [Staunton]

1 e4 e5 2 ♘f3 ♘c6 3 ♗c4 ♗c5 4 b4 d5 5 ♗b5 dxe4 6 bxc5 exf3 7 ♕xf3 [7 ♗xc6+!] 7 ... ♘e7 8 ♗b2 0-0 [△ 9 ... ♘d4] 9 c3 ♗e6 10 0-0 f5 11 ♕e2 ♕d5? 12 d4! exd4 13 cxd4 ♖f6 [13 ... ♘xd4?? 14 ♗xd4 ♕xb4 15 ♕xe6+] 14 ♖d1? [14 ♘c3! ♘xd4 (14 ... ♕d8 15 d5 ♘xd5 16 ♘xd5 ♗xd5 17 ♗xf6) 15 ♘xd5 ♘xe2+ 16 ♗xe2 ♗xd5 17 ♗xf6] 14 ... ♖g6 15 f3 ♖d8 16 ♘a3 f4 17 ♖d2 ♕h5! [17 ... ♘e5 18 ♔h1] 18 ♗d3 ♖h6 19 h3 ♘f5∓ 20 ♗c4 ♘e3 21 ♗xe6+ ♖xe6 22 ♘c2 ♕d5 23 ♘xe3 ♖xe3 24 ♕f2 ♘e5 25 ♖ad1 ♘c4 [25 ... ♘xf3+?!] 26 ♖c2 ♘xb2 27 ♖xb2 b6 28 ♖bd2 ♖de8 29 cxb6 axb6 30 ♕h4? g5 31 ♕g4 ♔g7 [◻ 31 ... c5 32 dxc5 ♕xc5] 32 h4 h6 33 ♔h2 [33 ♔f2?? ♕b5!] 33 ... ♔g6 34 ♔h3 ♕f5 35 d5 ♖e2 36 d6 ♖xd2 37 h5+ ♔f6 38 ♕xf5+ ♔xf5 39 ♖xd2 cxd6 40 ♖xd6± ♖e6 41 ♖d5+ ♖e5 42 ♖d8 ♖e6 43 a4 ♔f6 44 ♔g4 ♖e2 45 ♖f8+ ♔g7 46 ♖b8 ♖xg2+ 47 ♔f5 g4 48 ♖b7+ ♔g8 49 ♔xf4 gxf3 50 ♔xf3 ♖g5 51 ♖xb6 ♖xh5 ...♀ **½-½** M954

### 1856-★BO-1

**Barnes, T.W. & Löwenthal, J.J.– Staunton, H. & Owen, J.**

London [♀]

1 e4 e5 2 ♘f3 d6 3 d4 exd4 4 ♕xd4 ♘c6 5 ♗b5 ♗d7 6 ♗xc6 ♗xc6 7 ♘c3 ♘f6 8 0-0 ♗e7 9 ♗e3 0-0 10 h3 ♕d7 11 ♖ad1?! ♖ae8 [△ 12 ... ♗d8] 12 ♘d2 ♗d8 13 f4 ♘h5! [△ 14 ... ♗f6] 14 ♕d3 [◻ 14 ♔h2] 14 ... f5 15 ♔h2 [15 exf5 ♘g3] 15 ... fxe4 16 ♕e2 [16 ♘dxe4?? ♕e6 17 g4 ♗xe4 18 ♘xe4 ♕xe4–+] 16 ... ♘f6 17 ♘b3 ♕f7? [17 ... b6!] 18 ♘a5 ♕d7 19 ♗xa7 ♔h8 [19 ... b6? 20 ♕c4+] 20 ♗e3 b6 21 ♘xc6 ♕xc6 22 g4 ♕d7 23 g5 ♘g8 24 ♖d4 ♕f5 [△ 25 ... ♗xg5] 25 ♖g1? [25 ♖d5; 25 ♖fd1] 25 ... c6! 26 ♖xd6 ♗c7 27 ♖xc6 ♗xf4+ 28 ♗xf4 ♕xf4+ 29 ♔h1 ♘e7 30 ♖e6 ♘f5 31 ♖xe4 ♘g3+ 32 ♖xg3 ♕xg3 33 ♖xe8 [33 ♕g2 ♕d6–+] 33 ... ♕xh3+ 34 ♔g1 ♕g3+ 35 ♔h1 ♕h4+ 36 ♕h2 ♕xh2+ 37 ♔xh2 ♖xe8 38 ♔g3 ♖e5 39 ♔f4 ♖c5 40 a4 ♔g8 41 ♔g4 ♔f7 42 ♔f4 ♔g6 43 ♔e3 ♖xg5 ...♀ **0-1** L/N6123-1859

### 1856-★BO-2

**Owen, J. & Staunton, H.+ Barnes, T.W. & Löwenthal, J.J.**

London [Anderssen & Kossak]

1 e4 e5 2 ♘f3 ♘c6 3 ♗c4 ♗c5 4 b4 ♗xb4 5 c3 ♗a5 6 d4 exd4 7 0-0 d6 [7 ... dxc3; 7 ... d3] 8 ♕b3 ♕f6 9 cxd4 ♗b6 10 ♗b5 ♗d7 11 e5 dxe5 12 ♖e1 ♘ge7 13 dxe5 ♕g6 14 ♗d3 ♕h5 15 ♖e4 ♘g6? [15 ... ♗f5] 16 ♕a4 ♗e6 17 ♘bd2 ♗d5 18 ♖g4 h6 19 ♖xg6 ♗xf3 [19 ... fxg6? 20 g4 ♕h3 21 ♗f1!+–] 20 ♘xf3 fxg6 21 g4 ♕h3 22 ♗xg6+ ♔d8 23 ♕f4 ♘e7 24 ♗f7 ♔c8 [24 ... ♖f8 25 ♗a3 ♖xf7 26 ♕xf7 ♕xg4+ 27 ♔h1+–] 25 ♗a3 ♘c6

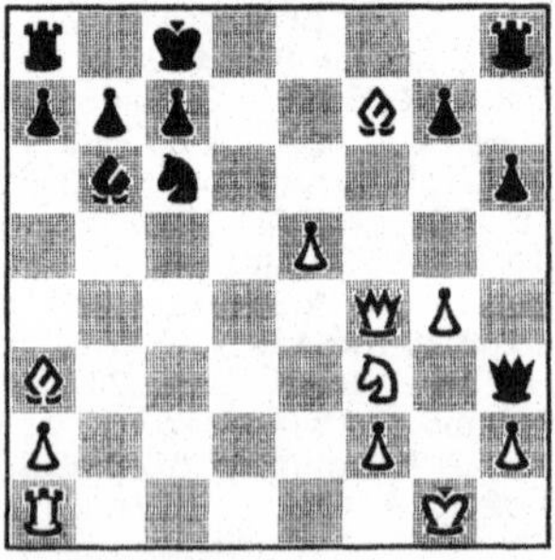

26 ♗f8!!+– [26 ♖d1? ♘d4 27 ♘xd4 ♕xa3] 26 ... ♘d8 27 ♗xg7 ♘xf7 28 ♗xh8 ♘xh8 29 ♕f5+ ♔d8 30 ♕f6+ ♔e8 31 ♕xh8+ ...♀ **1-0** L/N6047

### 1856-★BR-1

**Rivière, J.A.de & Staunton, H. & Wayte, W.= Barnes, T.W. & Löwenthal, J.J. & Owen, J.**

London [Staunton]

1 e4 e5 2 ♘f3 ♘c6 3 d4 exd4 4 ♗c4 ♗c5 5 c3 ♘f6 6 0-0 d6 7 cxd4 ♗b6 8 ♘c3 h6? [8 ... 0-0] 9 h3 0-0 10 ♕d3 ♘e7 11 a4 c6 12 ♗b3! d5 13 e5 ♗f5 14 ♕e2 ♘e4 15 ♗e3 ♘g6 16 g4 ♘xc3 17 bxc3 ♗e6 18 ♘h2 f5 19 f4± ♕h4? 20 ♕g2 ♕e7 21 ♗c2 ♖f7 22 g5 hxg5 23 a5 [23 fxg5? ♘xe5!] 23 ... ♗c7 24 fxg5 ♔h7?? 25 ♕e2 ♖h8 26 ♕h5+ ♔g8 27 ♕xg6+– ♖f8 28 ♘g4? [28 ♔g2 ♗d7 29 ♖xf5 ♖xf5 30 ♗xf5+–] 28 ... fxg4 29 ♖xf8+ ♔xf8 30 ♖f1+ ♔g8 31 ♖f6! ♗f7 32 ♕f5 ♖xh3 33 ♕xg4?? [33 ♗f4!+–; 33 ♗c1; 33 g6?!] 33 ... ♖xe3 34 ♖xf7?? [34 ♕h4 ♖e4!; 34 a6! bxa6 35 ♖xf7 ♕xf7 (35 ... ♔xf7 36 ♕f4+±) 36 ♕c8+ ♕f8 37 ♗h7+ ♔f7 38 ♗g6+ ♔g8 39 ♗h7+=] 34 ... ♕xf7 35 ♕c8+ ♕f8 36 ♗h7+ ♔f7 **0-1** M954-1856

### 1856-★CH-1 18 x 56

**Horwitz, B. & Löwenthal, J.J.+ Cunningham & Staunton, H.**

London [Löwenthal]

1 e4 e5 2 ♘f3 ♘c6 3 d4 exd4 4 ♗c4 ♗c5 5 c3 [5 0-0] 5 ... ♘f6 6 e5 d5 7 ♗b5 ♘e4 8 ♘xd4?! [8 cxd4] 8 ... 0-0 9 ♗xc6 bxc6 10 0-0 ♗a6 11 ♖e1 ♕h4!∓ [11 ... f6 12 f3 fxe5 13 fxe4 exd4 14 cxd4 ♕f6 15 ♗e3 (15 dxc5?? ♕f2+ 16 ♔h1 ♗f1–+) 15 ... ♗b4 16 e5±] 12 ♗e3 [△ 13 ♘f5] 12 ... ♗xd4 13 cxd4 ♖ab8 14 ♕c1 f6 15 f3 ♖xb2!? 16 ♘a3! [16 fxe4 ♖xg2+ 17 ♔xg2 ♕g4+=] 16 ... ♖fb8 17 ♕xc6 ♘g5 [17 ... ♗d3?! 18 ♖ac1 ♘g5 19 ♕xd5+ ♔h8 20 exf6 ♘xf3+ (20 ... gxf6 21 ♕c6±) 21 ♕xf3 ♗e4 22 fxg7+ ♔g8 23 ♗f2+–] 18 ♘c2! ♗b7 19 ♕c3 ♗a6 20 ♗f2 ♕h5 21 ♗g3 [21 ♘e3?? ♖xf2 22 ♔xf2 ♕xh2–+] 21 ... fxe5 22 ♖xe5 ♕g6 23 ♘e3 [23 ♘e1] 23 ... ♖b1+ 24 ♖xb1 ♕xb1+ 25 ♗e1 ♕g6 26 ♘xd5 ♔h8 27 ♕e3 h6 28 h4 ♘h3+!? [28 ... ♘f7 29 ♖e8+ ♖xe8 30 ♕xe8+ ♔h7 31 ♘e7+–; 28 ... ♘h7 29 ♘f4 ♕b6 30 ♖e6 ♕b5 31 ♘g6+ ♔g8 32 ♖e5 ♕b6 (32 ... ♕a4 33 ♖a5; 32 ... ♕d7 33 ♗b4) 33 ♖b5+–] 29 ♔h2 ♖b2 30 ♗d2 ♗f1 31 ♖e8+ ♔h7 32 ♘f6+!+– ♕xf6 [32 ... gxf6 33 ♕e7+ ♔g7 34 ♕e4+ ♕g6 35 ♖e7++–] 33 ♕e4+ ♕g6 [33 ... g6 34 ♖e7++–] 34 ♖h8+ ♔xh8 35 ♕xg6 ♖xd2 36 ♕e8+ ♔h7 37 ♕e4+ ♔h8 38 ♔xh3 ♖xg2 39 ♕e1 ♖f2+ 40 ♔g3 ♖g2+ 41 ♔f4 ♗d3 42 ♕c3 ♗h7 43 ♕xc7 ♗g8 44 a4 a6 45 ♕c6 ♖h2 46 ♕xa6 ♖xh4+ 47 ♔e3 ♖h1 48 a5 ♖e1+ 49 ♔f2 ♖a1 50 ♕b6 ♗c4 51 ♕d8+ ♔h7 52 d5 **1-0** M324

### 1856-★CL-1 8 xi 56

**Cunningham & Staunton, H.– Löwenthal, J.J. & ♀**

London [Löwenthal]

1 e4 e5 2 ♘f3 ♘c6 3 d4 exd4 4 ♗c4 ♗c5 5 0-0 [5 c3 ♘f6!; 5 ♘g5?!] 5 ... d6! 6 c3 d3! [6 ... ♘f6 7 cxd4 ♗b6 8 ♘c3

0-0 9 ♗b3 ♗g4 10 ♗e3±; 6 ... dxc3] 7 b4 ♗b6 8 a4 a5! [8 ... a6] 9 b5 ♘e5 10 ♘xe5 dxe5 11 ♕b3 ♕f6 12 ♘d2 ♘e7 13 h3 ♘g6 14 ♘f3 h6 15 ♗xd3 ♗e6∓ 16 ♕c2 ♖d8 [16 ... ♗xh3!] 17 ♗e3?! ♗xe3 18 fxe3 ♕e7 19 ♖ae1 ♕c5 20 ♔h1 0-0 21 c4 ♖d7 22 ♕c3 f6 23 ♖f2 b6 24 ♖d2 ♘e7 25 ♗e2 ♖fd8 26 ♖ed1 [□ 26 ♖xd7 △ 27 ♘d2, 28 ♘b3] 26 ... ♘c8 27 ♖xd7 ♖xd7 28 ♖xd7 ♗xd7 29 ♕d3 ♘d6 30 ♘d2 [30 ♕d5+ ♕xd5 31 exd5 ♘f5∓] 30 ... ♗e6 31 ♔h2 ♔f8 32 g4 ♔e7 33 ♕c3 ♕b4 34 ♕c2 [34 ♕xb4? axb4 △ 35 ... ♘b7∓] 34 ... ♘b7 35 ♘b1 ♘c5 36 ♘c3 ♕b3 37 ♕xb3 ♘xb3 38 ♔g3 ♔d6 39 ♔f2 ♘d2 40 ♔e1 ♘xc4 41 ♗xc4 ♗xc4 42 ♔d2 ♗f1 43 h4 ♗h3 44 g5 fxg5 45 hxg5 hxg5 46 ♘e2 ♗g4 47 ♘g3 g6 48 ♔c3 ♗d1 ...♀ **0-1** M324

**1856-★CL-2**
**Cunningham & Staunton, H.+ Löwenthal, J.J. & ♀**
London [Staunton]

1 e4 e5 2 ♘f3 ♘c6 3 d4 exd4 4 ♗c4 ♗e7 [□ 4 ... ♗c5] 5 0-0 d6 6 ♘xd4 ♘xd4 7 ♕xd4 ♗f6 8 ♕d3 [□ 8 ♕e3] 8 ... ♘e7 9 f4 ♘g6 10 ♘c3 c6 11 ♗e3? [11 ♘d1] 11 ... b5! 12 ♗b3 a5 13 a3 ♗a6 14 ♘d1 0-0 15 c3 ♖e8 16 ♖f3 ♕e7 17 ♘f2 a4 18 ♗a2 b4 19 ♗c4 ♗xc4 20 ♕xc4 bxc3 21 bxc3 d5 22 exd5 cxd5 23 ♕d3 ♖ac8 24 ♗d2 ♖c6 25 ♘g4 ♕c5+ 26 ♔f1 ♗d8 27 ♗e1! ♖e4 28 g3 f5 29 ♘e3 ♘e7 30 ♘c2! ♖h6? 31 h4 ♘c6 32 ♖d1 ♖d6 33 ♗f2 ♕c4 34 ♘e3 ♕xd3+ 35 ♖xd3 ♘e7 36 ♘c2 ♗b6 37 ♗xb6 ♖xb6 38 ♘b4 ♖b5 39 ♖d1 ♔f7 40 ♖fd3 ♔e6 41 ♔f2 h5 [41 ... g6? 42 h5 △ 43 ♖h1] 42 ♔f3 ♔d6 43 ♘c2 g6 44 ♘d4!? [44 ♘b4] 44 ... ♖b2 45 c4 dxc4 46 ♘xf5+ ♔c5 [46 ... ♔e6?! 47 ♘g7+ ♔f7 48 ♘e8] 47 ♘e3 [47 ♔xe4?; 47 ♘xe7?] 47 ... ♖xf4+ 48 ♔xf4 cxd3 49 ♖xd3 ♖b3 50 ♖d7 ♘f5 51 ♘xf5 [51 ♖d5+?] 51 ... gxf5 52 ♖f7 ♖xa3 53 ♖xf5+ ♔b4 54 ♖xh5 ♖c3 55 ♖h8 ♖c5 ⊠ 56 g4! a3 57 ♖e8 a2 58 ♖e1 ♖a5 59 ♖a1 ♔c4 60 ♔e5 ♔c6 61 ♔e6 ♖a4 62 g5! ♖e4+ 63 ♔f5 ♖xh4 64 ♖xa2 ♔d7 65 ♖e2 ♖h1 66 ♔f6 ♖f1+ 67 ♔g7 ♖g1 68 g6 ♖g3 69 ♔h7 ♖h3+ 70 ♔g8 ♖g3 71 g7 ♖g1 72 ♖e4 ♖g2 73 ♔h7 ♖h2+ 74 ♔g6 ♖g2+ 75 ♔h6 ♖h2+ 76 ♔g5 **1-0** M954-1856

**1856-★CL-3**
**Cunningham & Staunton, H.− Löwenthal, J.J. & ♀**
London [Staunton]

1 e4 e5 2 ♘f3 ♘c6 3 d4 exd4 4 ♗c4 ♗c5 5 0-0 d6 6 c3 d3 7 b4 ♗b6 8 a4 a5 9 b5 ♘e5 10 ♘xe5 dxe5 11 ♕b3 ♕f6 12 ♗xd3 ♗e6 13 ♕c2 [□ 13 c4] 13 ... ♘e7 14 ♘d2 ♘g6 15 ♘f3 h6 16 ♗e3 ♗xe3 17 fxe3 ♕e7 18 ♖ae1 ♕c5 [△ 19 ... ♘f4] 19 ♔h1 ♖ad8 20 c4 b6 [20 ... ♖xd3? 21 ♕xd3 ♗xc4 22 ♕c3] 21 ♖f2 0-0 22 ♖d2 ♖d7 23 ♕c3 ♖fd8 24 ♗e2 f6 25 h3 ♘e7 26 ♖ed1 ♘c8 27 ♖xd7 ♖xd7 28 ♖xd7 ♗xd7 29 ♕d3 ♘d6 30 ♘d2 ♗e6 31 ♔h2 ♔f8 32 g4 ♔e7 33 ♕c3 ♕b4 34 ♕c2 ♘b7 35 ♘b1 ♘c5 36 ♘c3 ♕b3 37 ♕xb3 ♘xb3 38 ♔g2 ♔d6 39 ♔f2 ♘d2 40 ♔e1 ♘xc4 **0-1** M954-1856

**1856-★DR-1**
**Dubois, S.+ Rivière, J.A. de**
Paris [Staunton]

1 e4 e5 2 ♘f3 ♘c6 3 c3 ♘f6 4 d4 ♘xe4 5 dxe5 d5 6 ♗e3 ♗c5 7 ♗b5 ♗xe3 8 fxe3 0-0 9 0-0 ♗g4 10 ♗xc6 bxc6 11 ♕a4 ♕d7 12 ♘bd2 ♘xd2 13 ♘xd2 ♗e2 14 ♖f2 ♗b5 15 ♕h4 ♕e6 16 ♘f3 h6 17 ♖d1 ♖ae8 18 ♕g3 [□ 18 ♘d4 △ ♘f5] 18 ... f6 19 exf6 ♖xf6 20 ♘d4 ♕xe3 21 ♕xe3 ♖xe3 22 ♖xf6 gxf6 23 ♘xb5 cxb5 24 ♖xd5 ♖e5 25 ♖xe5 fxe5 26 ♔f2 ♔f7 27 ♔f3 c5 28 ♔e4 ♔e6 29 g4 b4 30 c4 a6 31 h4 **1-0** M954-1856

**1856-★DR-2**
**Dubois, S.+ Rivière, J.A. de**
Paris [Staunton]

1 e4 e5 2 f4 exf4 3 ♘f3 g5 4 ♗c4 ♗g7 5 d4 d6 6 ♘c3 [6 c3] 6 ... c6? 7 0-0 ♗g4 8 g3 ♗h5 9 ♖f2 g4 10 ♘h4 f3 11 ♘f5 ♔f8 12 ♗f4 ♗f6 13 ♗xd6+ ♗e7 14 ♗f4 **1-0** M954-1856

**1856-★FR-1**
**Falkbeer, E.K. & Löwenthal, J.J.− Ranken, C.E. & Staunton, H.**
London [Anderssen & Kossak]

1 e4 e5 2 d4 exd4 3 ♘f3 ♘c6 4 ♗c4 ♗c5 5 0-0 [5 c3] 5 ... d6 6 c3 ♕f6 7 ♗b5 ♗g4 8 ♕a4 [8 ♗xc6+] 8 ... ♘e7 9 ♘xd4 0-0 10 ♗e3 [10 ♘xc6?! ♘xc6 11 ♗xc6 bxc6 12 ♕xc6∓] 10 ... ♕g6 11 ♔h1 [□ 11 ♕c2 ♗h3 12 f3] 11 ... ♗xd4 12 ♗xd4 ♗d7 13 ♘d2 f5 14 ♖ae1 fxe4 15 ♘xe4 a6 16 ♗xc6 ♗xc6 17 ♕c4+ ♗d5 18 ♕e2 ♖ae8 19 f3 ♗xa2! 20 c4 ♘f5 21 ♗f2 d5 22 cxd5 ♘d6∓ 23 ♕d2 ♗c4 24 ♖g1 ♖xe4! 25 ♖xe4 ♕xe4!!−+ 26 fxe4 ♘xe4 27 ♗e3 ♘xd2 28 ♗xd2 ♖f2 29 ♗c3 ♗xd5 30 h3 h5 31 h4 ♔f7 32 ♖d1 c6 33 ♖d2 ♗xg2+ 34 ♔g1 ♖xd2 35 ♗xd2 ♗e4 36 ♔f2 ♔e6 37 ♗c3 g6 38 ♗d4 b5 39 b4 ♔d5 40 ♔e3 ♗f5 41 ♗b6 ♔c4 42 ♗a5 c5 43 bxc5 ♔xc5 44 ♔d2 b4 45 ♗d8 ♔b5 46 ♔c1 a5 47 ♔b2 a4 48 ♗f6 a3+ 49 ♔a1 b3 **0-1** L/N6047

**1856-★F♀-1**
**Fraser, G.B.+♀**
[Staunton]

1 e4 e5 2 ♘f3 ♘c6 3 ♗c4 ♗c5 4 b4 ♗xb4 5 c3 ♗c5 6 d4 exd4 7 0-0 d6 8 cxd4 ♗b6 9 ♘c3 ♗g4 10 ♕a4 ♔f8 [□ 10 ... ♗d7 11 ♕b3 △ 11 ... ♘a5 12 ♗xf7+ Fraser] 11 ♘g5 ♘h6 12 d5 ♘e5 13 ♔h1 ♗d7 14 ♕b3 ♘hg4 15 f4 ♘xc4 16 ♕xc4 ♘f2+ 17 ♖xf2 ♗xf2 18 e5 ♕e7 19 ♘ce4 ♗c5 20 ♗b2 h6 21 ♘f3 b5 22 ♕c3 b4 23 ♕c4 a6 24 ♘xc5 dxc5 25 a3 [□ 25 e5 △ ♘e5+−] 25 ... ♗b5 26 ♕e4 ♖d8 27 axb4 cxb4 28 ♗d4 c5?! 29 d6 ♕a7 30 ♖c1 cxd4 31 ♖c7 ♕a8 32 ♕f5 ♗d7 [□ 32 ... ♕d5] 33 ♖xd7 ♖xd7 34 ♕xd7 a5 35 ♕e7+ ♔g8 36 d7 ♔h7 37 ♕xf7 ♖f8 38 ♕c4 ♕b8 39 ♕xd4 b3 40 ♘d2 b2 41 ♕e4+ ♔h8 42 h3 ♕d8 43 e6 ♕e7 44 f5 a4 45 ♘c4 a3 46 ♘xa3 ♕xa3 47 e7 ♕a1+ 48 ♔h2 b1♕ 49 exf8♕+ ♔h7 50 f6+ ♕xe4 51 ♕xg7# **1-0** M954-1856

**1856-★HO-1**
**Owen, J. & Staunton, H.+ Horwitz, B. & Löwenthal, J.J.**
London [Staunton]

1 e4 e5 2 ♘f3 ♘c6 3 d4 exd4 4 ♗c4 ♗e7?! 5 0-0 d6 6 ♘xd4 ♘xd4 7 ♕xd4 ♗f6 8 ♕d5 ♕d7 9 f4 c6 10 ♕d1 ♘h6 11 c3 0-0 12 ♘a3 [12 f5? d5] 12 ... ♕e7 13 ♗d3 g6 14 f5 ♗g5 15 f6 ♕e5 16 ♘c4 ♕c5+ 17 ♔h1 ♗xc1 18 ♕xc1 ♕h5 19 ♘xd6 ♖d8 20 ♕f4 ♗g4 21 ♗c4 b5 22 ♗b3 ♖d7 23 ♖f2 ♖ad8 24 ♖d2 c5 25 ♖d5 ♕h4 26 ♘xf7! ♘xf7 27 ♖xd7 c4 28 ♖xd8+ ♘xd8 29 ♖f1 ♘e6 [29 ... cxd3+−] 30 ♕b8+ ♔f7 31 ♕xa7+ ♔g8 32 ♕b8+ ♔f7 33 ♕b7+ ♔g8 34 ♕c8+ **1-0** M954-1856

**1856-★HS-1** 4 xi 56
**Horwitz, B. & Löwenthal, J.J.+ Staunton, H.**
London [Löwenthal]

1 e4 e5 2 ♘f3 ♘c6 3 d4 exd4 4 ♗c4 ♕f6?! [4 ... ♗c5] 5 0-0 ♗c5? 6 e5 ♕g6 7 ♖e1± ♘h6 8 h3 ♘e7 9 c3 dxc3 10 ♘xc3 0-0 11 ♘e4 ♗b6 12 ♗g5 ♘hf5 13 g4 h6 14 gxf5 ♘xf5 15 ♗d3 hxg5 16 ♘g3 ♗xf2+ 17 ♔xf2 ♕b6+ 18 ♔g2 ♘e3+ 19 ♖xe3 ♕xe3 20 ♕b3 ♕c5 21 ♘e4 ♕e7 22 ♘exg5 d6 23 ♕c4 g6 24 ♕h4 **1-0** M324

**1856-★HS-2** 11 xi 56
**Staunton, H. & ♀+ Horwitz, B. & Löwenthal, J.J.**
London
1 e4 e5 2 ♘f3 ♘c6 3 d4 exd4 4 ♗c4 ♗e7 5 0-0 d6 6 ♘xd4 ♘xd4 7 ♕xd4 ♗f6??+– 8 ♕d5 ♕d7 9 f4 c6 10 ♕d1 ♘h6 11 c3 0-0 12 ♘a3 ♕e7 13 ♗d3 g6 14 f5 ♗g5 15 f6 ♕e5 16 ♘c4 ♕c5+ 17 ♔h1 ♗xc1 18 ♕xc1 ♕h5 19 ♘xd6 ♖d8 20 ♕f4 ♗g4 21 ♗c4 b5 22 ♗b3 ♖d7 23 ♖f2 ♖ad8 24 ♖d2 c5 25 ♖d5 ♕h4 26 ♘xf7 ♘xf7 27 ♖xd7 c4 28 ♖xd8+ ♘xd8 29 ♖f1 ♘e6 30 ♕b8+ ♔f7 31 ♕xa7+ ♔g8 32 ♕b8+ ♔f7 33 ♕b7+ ♔g8 34 ♕c8+ ...♀ **1-0** M324

**1856-★KM-1**
**Morphy, P.C+ Knight, T.**
New Orleans [Maróczy]
⟨♖a1,♘b1⟩ 1 e4 e5 2 f4 exf4 3 ♘f3 g5 4 ♗c4 ♕e7 5 d4 d5 6 ♗xd5 c6 7 ♗xf7+ ♕xf7 8 ♘e5 ♕f6 9 ♕h5+ ♔e7 10 h4 gxh4 11 0-0 ♗h6 12 b3 ♘d7 13 ♗a3+ c5 14 ♖d1! ♘xe5 15 ♗xc5+ ♔e6 16 ♕e8+ ♘e7 17 d5# **1-0** L/N3203

**1856-★MM-1** x 56
**Maurian, C.A.+ Morphy, P.C.**
New Orleans
⟨♘b8⟩ 1 e4 e5 2 ♘f3 d5 3 ♘xe5 ♘f6 4 exd5 ♗d6 5 ♗b5+ c6 6 dxc6 0-0 7 ♘f3 ♖e8+ 8 ♗e2 ♕e7 9 ♘c3 ♗b4 10 d4 ♘d5 11 ♗d2 ♗xc3 12 bxc3 bxc6 13 ♘e5 f6 14 ♘d3 ♗a6 15 f3 ♖ad8 16 ♖f1 ♖d6 17 ♖f2 ♖e6 18 ♔f1 g5 19 ♘c1 ♕a3 20 c4 ♘c3 21 ♗xc3 ♕xc3 22 d5 ♖e3 23 ♘b3 ♗xc4 24 ♗xc4 ♕xc4+ 25 ♔g1 cxd5 26 ♕d2 ♖e2 27 ♕d3 ♖2e3 28 ♕xc4 dxc4 29 ♘d2 ♖e1+ 30 ♖xe1 ♖xe1+ 31 ♖f1 ♖e2 32 ♖d1 c3 33 ♔f1 ♖xd2 34 ♖xd2 cxd2 35 ♔e2 ♔f7 36 ♔xd2 ♔e6 37 ♔d3 ♔d5 38 c4+ ♔c5 39 ♔e4 ♔xc4 40 ♔f5 ♔c3 41 ♔xf6 h6 42 ♔g6 ♔b4 43 ♔xh6 ♔a3 44 ♔xg5 ♔xa2 45 h4 a5 46 h5 ♔b1 47 h6 a4 48 h7 a3 49 h8♕ a2 50 f4 a1♕ 51 ♕xa1+ ♔xa1 52 f5 **1-0**
M1481-1899

**1856-★MM-2** xi 56
**Morphy, P.C.+ Morphy, E.**
New Orleans [Löwenthal]
1 e4 e5 2 ♘f3 ♘c6 3 ♗b5 ♗c5 4 c3 ♕e7 5 0-0 ♘f6 6 d4 ♗b6 [6 ... exd4 7 e5] 7 ♗g5 h6 8 ♗xf6 gxf6 9 d5 ♘d8 10 ♘h4 c6 11 ♘f5 ♕c5 12 b4 ♕f8 13 dxc6 dxc6 14 ♘d6+ ♔e7 15 ♕d3! cxb5 [◻ 15 ... ♗e6] 16 ♘xc8+ ♖xc8 17 ♖d1 ♕g7 [◻ 17 ... ♗d4] 18 ♕d7+ ♔f8 19 ♕xc8 **1-0** L/N3161

**1856-★MR-1**
**Raphael+ Montgomery, W.**
[Staunton]
1 e4 c5 2 f4 e5 3 ♘f3 ♘c6 4 ♗c4 d6 5 d3 ♗g4 6 0-0 ♘d4 7 ♗xf7+! ♔e7 [7 ... ♔xf7 8 ♘g5+] 8 fxe5 ♗xf3 9 ♗g5+ ♔d7 10 e6+ ♔c6 11 ♗xd8 ♗xd1 12 ♗e8# **1-0** M954-1856

**1856-★MS-1** 12 v 56
**Medley, G.W.+ Saint-Amant, P.C.F.**
London♀ [Staunton]
⟨♙f7⟩ 1 e4 ♘c6 2 d4 d5 3 e5 [3 ♗b5] 3 ... ♗f5 4 ♗e3 e6 5 ♘f3 ♘ge7 6 ♘c3 [6 ♗d3] 6 ... ♗g4 7 h3 ♗xf3 8 ♕xf3 ♘f5 9 ♗b5 ♗b4 10 ♕g4 0-0 11 ♗d3 ♘ce7 12 0-0 c5 13 ♘e2 c4 14 ♗xf5 ♘xf5 15 c3 ♗e7 16 ♘f4 ♕d7 17 ♘h5 ♖f7 18 ♗g5 ♔h8 19 ♗xe7 ♕xe7 20 ♘g3 ♘h6 21 ♕h5 ♖f4 22 ♖ae1 ♖af8 23 ♖e3 g6 24 ♕e2 [24 ♕xh6? ♖h4–+] 24 ... ♕h4 25 ♕c2? g5 [25 ... ♘f5] 26 ♕e2 g4 27 ♘h1∓ ♖g8! [27 ... ♘f5 28 g3; 27 ... gxh3 28 ♖xh3] 28 hxg4

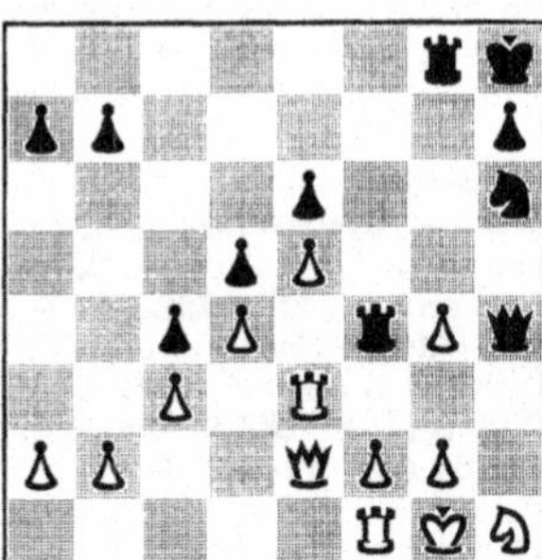

28 ... ♘xg4? [28 ... ♖fxg4! 29 g3 ♘f5 30 ♖f3 ♖8g5–+; 28 ... ♖fxg4! 29 f3 ♖4g5 30 ♕f2 ♕h3±; 28 ... ♖fxg4! 29 f4 ♘f5 30 ♖f3 ♖8g6 31 ♕f2 ♕h5 32 g3 (32 ♕e2 ♖h6 33 ♔f2 ♖xg2+ 34 ♔xg2 ♕h2#) 32 ... ♖h6 33 ♕g2 ♘h4∓; 28 ... ♖fxg4! 29 ♘g3 ♘f5 30 ♖f3 ♖8g6–+; 28 ... ♖fxg4! 29 ♕f3 ♘f5 30 ♖ee1 ♖f4 31 ♕e2 ♖g6 32 g3 ♕h3–+; 28 ... ♖fxg4! 29 ♖g3! ♖8g5 30 f4? (30 ♖xg4 ♘xg4) ♖h5–+; 28 ... ♖fxg4! 29 ♖g3! ♖8g5 30 ♕f3! ♖h5?! 31 ♕f6+ ♕xf6 32 exf6 ♖gh4 33 ♖h3 ♖xh3 34 gxh3 ♖f5 (34 ... ♖xh3 35 ♖e1!) 35 ♘g3 ♖xf6 36 ♖e1±; 28 ... ♖fxg4! 29 ♖g3! ♖8g5 30 ♕f3! ♖f4! 31 ♖h3 ♖xf3 32 ♖xh4 ♘f5 33 ♖h2 ♖d3∓] 29 ♖h3 ♕g5 [29 ... ♕xh3 30 gxh3 ♘e3+ 31 ♘g3 ♘xf1 32 ♕xf1 ♖xg3+ 33 fxg3 ♖xf1+ 34 ♔xf1+–] 30 ♘g3 ♕g6 31 ♕d2 ♖gf8 32 f3 ♕g5?+– 33 ♘h5 ♘h6 34 ♘xf4 ♖xf4 35 g3 ♕f5 36 ♖xh6 ♖xf3 37 ♖xf3 ♕xf3 38 ♕f2 ...♀ **1-0**
L/N6123

**1856-★MS-2** 14 v 56
**Medley, G.W.+ Saint-Amant, P.C.F.de**
London♀
⟨♙f7⟩ 1 e4 ♘c6 2 d4 d5 3 e5 ♗f5 4 ♗e3 e6 5 ♘f3 ♘b4 6 ♘a3 c5? 7 dxc5 ♕a5 8 c3 ♘c6 9 ♘b5 ♗g4 10 b4 ♕d8 11 ♗d4 [11 ♘d6+] 11 ... ♘h6 12 h3 ♗h5 13 ♗e2 ♗e7 14 0-0 0-0 15 ♘h2 ♗xe2 16 ♕xe2 a5 17 a3 ♖f4 18 g3 ♖e4?! 19 ♕h5 [19 ♕d3] 19 ... ♘f7 20 f4 ♕d7 21 ♕f3 ♘xb4 22 axb4 ♕xb5 23 ♘g4 a4 24 ♖a2 [△ 25 ♘f2] 24 ... ♕c4 25 ♖1a1 ♖e1+ 26 ♔g2 ♖f8 27 ♖xe1 ♕xa2+ 28 ♕e2 ♕b3 29 ♖a1+– h5 30 ♘e3 h4 31 ♕a2 ♘d8 32 ♕xb3 axb3 33 ♖b1 ♘c6 34 ♖xb3 ♖a8 35 ♖b2 ♖a1 36 g4 ♘xd4 37 cxd4 ♖a3 38 ♘c2 ♖g3+ 39 ♔h2 ♖d3 40 b5 ♗d8 41 b6 ♔f7 42 f5 ♔e7 43 c6 bxc6 44 b7 ♗c7 45 ♘b4 ♖c3 46 ♘a6 ...♀ **1-0** L/N6123

**1856-★MS-3**
**Stanley, C.H.+ Montgomery, W.**
[Staunton]
1 e4 e5 2 f4 exf4 3 ♗c4 ♕h4+ 4 ♔f1 g5 5 ♘c3 ♗g7 6 ♘f3 ♕h5 7 h4 h6 8 d4 d6 9 e5 dxe5 10 ♘d5 e4? [10 ... ♔d8] 11 ♘xc7+? [11 ♕e1+–] 11 ... ♔d8 12 ♘xa8 ♘e7 [◻ 12 ... exf3] 13 ♗xf4 gxf4 14 ♘e5 ♕xd1+ 15 ♖xd1 ♗xe5 16 dxe5+ ♗d7 17 ♗xf7 ♔c8 [△ 18 ... ♗b5+] 18 b3 ♘f5 19 e6 ♗c6 20 ♖h3 ♘e3+ 21 ♖xe3 fxe3 22 ♔e2 ♘a6 23 e7 **1-0**
M954-1856

**1856-★MS-4**
**Stanley, C.H.– Montgomery, W.**
1 e4 e5 2 f4 exf4 3 ♗c4 ♕h4+ 4 ♔f1 g5 5 ♘c3 ♗g7 6 ♘f3 ♕h5 7 h4 h6 8 d4 d6 9 e5 dxe5 10 ♘d5 e4 11 ♘xc7+ ♔d8 12 ♘xa8 exf3 13 ♕xf3 ♕xf3+ 14 gxf3 ♗xd4 15 ♗xf4 gxf4 16 ♖d1 ♘c6 17 c3 ♗e6 18 ♗b5 ♘ge7 19 cxd4 ♗d5 20 ♔f2 ♘f5 21 h5 ♔c8 22 ♖he1 ♘e3 23 ♖c1 ♔b8 24 ♗xc6 bxc6 25 b4 ♖g8 26 ♖g1 ♖xg1 27 ♖xg1 ♔xa8 28 a4 ♘c2 29 ♖g8+ ♔b7 30 ♖h8 ♘xd4 31 ♖xh6 ♘xf3 32 ♖f6 ♘e5 33 ♖f5 ♘g4+ 34 ♔g1 f3 35 b5 f2+ **0-1** M954-1856

**1856-★M♀-1**
**Morphy, P.C.+ ♀**
New Orleans
⟨♘b1⟩ 1 e4 e5 2 ♗c4 ♘f6 3 ♘f3 d6 4 d4 d5 5 exd5 ♗g4 6 dxe5 ♗xf3 7 gxf3 ♘fd7 8 0-0 ♗c5 9 e6 ♘e5 10 exf7+ ♘xf7 11 ♗b5+ c6 12 dxc6 bxc6 13 ♖e1+ ♗e7 14 ♗d3 0-0 15 f4 ♗d6 16 ♕h5 h6 17 ♕g6

♖e8 18 ♗d2 ♘d7 19 ♗c3 ♘f6 20 ♖xe8+ ♘xe8 21 ♖e1 ♗e7 22 ♗c4 ♗f6 23 ♕xf7+ ♔h7 24 ♕g8+ ♔g6 25 ♗d3+ ♔h5 26 ♕f7+ ♔g4 27 ♕g6+ ♔h4 28 ♕g3+ ♔h5 29 ♗g6# **1-0** M268-1860

**1856-★M♀-2**
**Morphy, P.C.+♀**
New Orleans
⟨♖a1⟩ 1 e4 e5 2 f4 exf4 3 ♗c4 ♕h4+ 4 ♔f1 g5 5 ♘c3 ♗g7 6 d4 ♘c6 7 ♘f3 ♕h5 8 ♘d5 ♔d8 9 c3 ♘f6 10 ♘xf6 ♗xf6 11 e5 ♗g7 12 h4 f6 13 ♔g1 g4 14 ♘h2 fxe5 15 ♘xg4 exd4 16 ♗xf4 ♖f8 17 ♗g5+ ♘e7 18 ♕e2 ♖e8 19 ♘e5 ♕xe2 20 ♘f7# **1-0** M268-1858

**1856-★M♀-3**
**Morphy, P.C.+♀**
New Orleans
⟨♖a1⟩ 1 e4 e5 2 ♘f3 ♘c6 3 ♗c4 d6 4 c3 ♗e6 5 ♗b5 a6 6 ♗a4 ♘e7 7 0-0 h6 8 a3 ♗a2 9 ♗c2 ♘g6 10 d4 d5 11 ♘bd2 dxe4 12 ♘xe4 exd4 13 b3 b6 14 cxd4 ♘h4 15 ♗b2 ♘xf3+ 16 ♕xf3 ♘xd4 17 ♗xd4 ♕xd4 18 ♖d1 ♕b2 19 ♘f6+ gxf6 20 ♕xa8+ ♔e7 21 ♖e1+ ♔d6 22 ♕d8+ ♔c6 23 ♗e4+ ♔b5 24 ♕d5+ ♗c5 25 ♕c4+ ♔a5 26 ♕a4# **1-0** M268-1860

**1856-★M♀-4**
**Morphy, P.C.+♀**
New Orleans
⟨♖a1⟩ 1 e4 e5 2 ♘c3 ♘c6 3 ♗c4 ♗c5 4 ♘ge2 ♘f6 5 f4 ♘g4 6 ♘g3 ♘f2 7 ♕h5 0-0 8 f5 ♘xh1 9 d4 ♘xd4 10 ♗g5 ♗e7 11 ♗xe7 ♕xe7 12 ♘d5 ♕d6 13 f6 ♘e6 14 ♘e7+ ♔h8 15 ♗xe6 ♕xe6 16 fxg7+ ♔xg7 17 ♘gf5+ ♔h8 18 ♕g5 ♕g6 19 ♘xg6+ fxg6 20 ♕e7 ♖xf5 21 exf5 ♔g8 22 f6 **1-0** M268-1858

**1856-★S♀-1**
**♀Φ Staunton, H.**
London [Staunton]
⟨♙f7⟩1 e4 ♘c6 2 d4 e5 3 ♗c4 d6 4 ♘f3 ♕e7 5 0-0 ♘f6 6 ♘c3 ♗g4 7 ♗b5 a6 8 ♗a4 b5 9 dxe5 ♘xe5 10 ♗b3 c6 11 ♘xe5! dxe5 [11 ... ♗xd1 12 ♗f7+] 12 ♕d3 ♗e6 13 ♗e3 ♗xb3 14 axb3 ♕c7 15 f4 ♗e7 16 fxe5 ♕xe5 17 ♖f5 ♕e6 18 e5! ♘g4 19 ♗b6 ♘h6 20 ♖ff1 ♘f7 21 ♘e4 0-0 22 ♘c5 ♗xc5+ 23 ♗xc5 ♖fd8

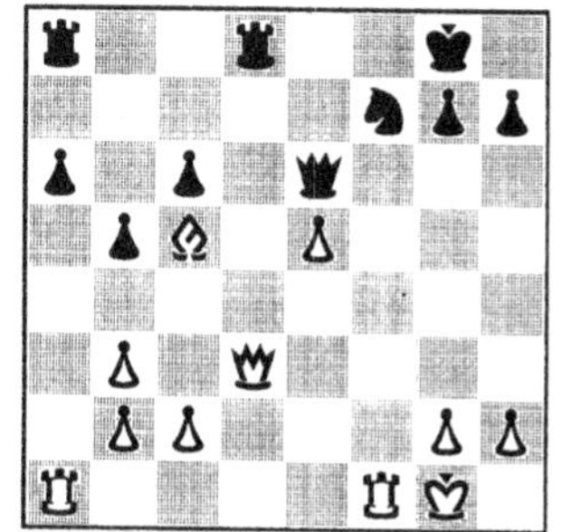

24 ♖xa6!! ♕xe5 [24 ... ♖xa6?+-; 24 ... ♖xd3?+-] 25 ♗b4 [25 ♗d4? ♖xa6-+] 25 ... ♖ac8 [□ 25 ... ♖ab8] 26 ♖xc6! ♖a8 27 ♕c3 ♕e2 28 ♖c7 ♘e5-+ M954-1856

**1856-★S♀-2**
**♀- Staunton, H.**
London [Staunton]
⟨♙f7⟩1 e4 e6 2 d4 d5 3 e5 c5 4 ♗d3 g6 5 c3 ♘c6 6 ♗e3 cxd4 7 cxd4 ♘b4 8 ♘e2 ♘xd3+ 9 ♕xd3 ♗d7 10 ♘bc3 ♘e7? [10 ... ♘h6] 11 ♗g5 ♕b6 12 0-0 ♘f5 13 g4 ♘e7 14 ♘f4 [□ 14 ♗f6] 14 ... 0-0-0 15 ♗xe7 ♗xe7 16 ♘fxd5? exd5 17 ♘xd5 ♕e6 18 ♘xe7+ [18 ♖c1+ ♔b8; 18 ... ♗c6?; 18 ♕c4+ ♔b8; 18 ... ♗c6?] 18 ... ♕xe7 19 d5 ♕xe5 20 ♖fe1 ♕d6 21 ♖e7 ♕xe7 22 ♕g3 ♕g5 23 ♖d1 ♗c6 **0-1** M954-1856

**1856-★S♀-3**
**♀+ Staunton, H.**
London [Staunton]
⟨♙f7⟩1 e4 d6 2 d4 ♘f6 3 ♗c4 e6 4 ♘c3 c6 5 ♘f3 ♗e7 6 0-0 0-0 7 ♗d3 b5? 8 e5 dxe5 9 ♘xe5 ♕e8 10 ♗g5 a5 11 ♘e4 ♖a7 12 ♗xf6 gxf6! 13 ♕g4+ ♔h8 14 f4! fxe5! [14 ... f5] 15 fxe5 ♘a6 16 ♖xf8+ ♕xf8 17 ♕h5 ♘b4 18 ♖f1 ♕g8 19 ♖f7 ♘xd3 20 ♘f6 ♗xf6 21 ♖xa7 ♘f4 22 ♕f3 ♗g5 23 ♕xc6 ♘e2+? [23 ... ♘d5 △ 24 ... ♘e7-+] 24 ♔h1 ♕f8 25 ♕f3 ♕xf3 26 gxf3 ♘xd4 27 ♖a8 ♘xf3 28 ♖xc8+ ♔g7 29 ♖c5± ...♀ **1-0** M954-1856

**1856-★S♀-4**
**♀- Staunton, H.**
London [Staunton]
⟨♙f7⟩1 e4 d6 2 d4 ♘f6 3 ♗d3 e5 4 f4 ♗g4 5 ♘f3 ♘bd7 6 c3 ♗e7 7 fxe5 dxe5 8 0-0 ♗xf3 9 ♕xf3 0-0 10 ♕g3 ♕e8 11 ♗e3 [11 dxe5?] 11 ... ♖d8 12 ♘d2 [12 dxe5?] 12 ... ♔h8 13 ♗e2 c5? 14 d5 a6 15 ♖f5 b5 16 a4 c4 17 axb5 axb5 18 ♖a6 ♖a8 19 ♖e6 ♖a1+ 20 ♔f2 [□ 20 ♗f1 ♘xe4∓] 20 ... ♘xe4+ 21 ♘xe4 ♖xf5+ 22 ♗f3 ♘f8? 23 ♘d6 ♖xf3+ 24 ♕xf3 ♕d7 25 ♘f7+ ♔g8 26 ♘xe5 ♕e8 27 ♖b6 [□ 27 ♕g4] 27 ... ♗h4+ 28 g3 ♕xe5 29 gxh4 ♕xh2+ 30 ♕g2 ♕xh4+ 31 ♔e2 ♕h5+ **0-1** M954-1856

**1856-★S♀-5**
**♀- Staunton, H.**
London [Staunton]
⟨♙f7⟩1 e4 d6 2 d4 ♘f6 3 ♘c3 ♘c6 4 ♗b5 ♗d7 5 f4 e5 6 ♘f3 [6 dxe5?!; 6 fxe5?!] 6 ... exd4 7 ♘xd4 ♘xd4 8 ♗xd7+ ♕xd7 9 ♕xd4 ♗e7 10 0-0 0-0 11 f5 b5 12 ♗g5 c5 13 ♕d3 c4 14 ♕f3 ♕c6 15 ♘e2 ♖ae8 16 ♘d4 ♕b7 17 ♖ad1 ♘d7! [17 ... ♕xe4] 18 ♗xe7 ♖xe7 19 ♘e6? ♖xe6 20 fxe6 ♖xf3 21 ♖xf3 ♘e5 22 ♖f5 ♕e7 23 ♖df1 h6 24 c3 ♕xe6 **0-1** M954-1856

**1856-★S♀-6**
**♀- Staunton, H.**
London [Staunton]
⟨♙f7⟩1 e4 d6 2 d4 ♘f6 3 ♘c3 ♘c6 4 ♗b5 ♗d7 5 f4 e5 6 ♘f3 exd4 7 ♘xd4 ♘xd4 8 ♗xd7+ ♕xd7 9 ♕xd4 ♗e7 10 0-0 0-0 11 f5 b5 12 ♗g5 c5 13 ♕d3 c4 14 ♕f3 ♕b7 15 ♖ad1 ♖ad8 16 ♘e2 ♘xe4?! 17 ♗xe7 ♕xe7 18 ♘d4 [△ 19 ♘c6; △ 19 ♘e6] 18 ... d5 19 ♘e6 [19 ♘c6 ♕c5+] 19 ... ♘g5 20 ♘xg5 ♕xg5 21 ♖xd5 a6 22 ♖xd8 ♕xd8 23 ♖d1 ♕b6+ 24 ♔h1 ♕f6 25 ♕d5+ ♔h8 26 ♕c5? [26 c3 g6; 26 ♕d4 g6] 26 ... h6 27 g4 ♖e8 28 c3 ♕h4! 29 ♕d4 ♖e2 30 ♕d8+ ♕xd8 31 ♖xd8+ ♔h7 32 ♖a8 [□ 32 ♖d7-+] 32 ... ♖xb2 33 ♖xa6 b4 34 cxb4 c3 **0-1** M954-1856

**HARRWITZ✕RIVIÈRE** Paris
**[1856̂-✕HR]**

| | | | | |
|---|---|---|---|---|
| D. Harrwitz | 1̂ | 0̂ | 1̂ | ? |
| J.A. de Rivière | 0̂ | 1̂ | 0̂ | ? |

**1856̂-✕HR-1̂**
**Harrwitz, D.+**
**Rivière, J.A. de**
Paris [de Rivière]
1 d4 f5 2 c4 ♘f6 3 ♘c3 d6 4 ♘f3 c6 5 ♗g5 [□ 5 ♗f4] 5 ... ♘e4 6 e3 ♕a5 7 ♕c2 ♘a6 8 a3 e5 [8 ... ♘b4?! 9 ♕c1] 9 ♖c1 ♘xc3 10 bxc3 h6 11 ♗h4 g5 12 ♗g3 f4? 13 ♕g6+ ♔d7 [13 ... ♔d8 14 ♕f6+; 13 ... ♕e7 14 c5 fxg3 (14 ... ♕c7 15 cxd6+ ♕xd6 16 ♕xd6+ ♔xd6 17 dxe5+; 14 ... ♗e6 15 cxd6+ ♔xd6 16 ♘xe5) 15 cxd6+ △ 16 ♘xe5+] 14 ♕f6 ♕xa3 15 ♖c2 ♔e8 [□ 15 ... ♔c7] 16 exf4 ♕a1+ [16 ... exf4 17 ♕e2+] 17 ♔d2 ♖g8 18 ♗d3! ♕xh1 19 ♗g6+ ♖xg6 20 ♕xg6+ ♔d8 21 ♕f7? [21 fxe5] 21 ... exf4 22 ♕xf8+ ♔c7 23 c5 dxc5 24 dxc5 ♔b8? [24 ... b5] 25 ♘e5 ♕xg2 **1-0** M954-1857

### 1856-✕HR-2
**Harrwitz, D.– Rivière, J.A. de**
Paris [de Rivière]
1 d4 f5 2 c4 ♘f6 3 ♘c3 d6 4 d5 ♘bd7 5 ♘f3 ♘b6 6 ♘g5 h6 7 ♘e6 ♗xe6 8 dxe6 ♕c8 [8 ... c6?! 9 e4] 9 ♘d5 c6 10 ♘xb6 [10 e4?!] 10 ... axb6 11 ♕b3 ♕xe6 12 ♕xb6 ♕xc4 13 e3 ♕c5 [□ 13 ... ♕c2] 14 ♕xb7 ♖xa2 15 ♕b8+ ♔d7 16 ♗a6? ♕a5+ 17 b4 ♕xa6 18 ♖xa2 ♕xa2 19 ♕b7+ ♔e6 20 ♕xc6 g6 21 0-0 ♗g7 22 f3 ♕d5 23 ♕c2 ♔f7 24 ♔h1 ♖a8 25 e4 ♕b5 26 ♕b3+ d5 27 ♖e1 fxe4 28 fxe4 ♘xe4 29 ♗e3 ♖a1 30 ♖xa1 ♗xa1 31 ♗g1 ♕c4 32 ♕f3+ ♗f6 33 ♕a3 ♕f1 34 ♕a7 ♗h4! 35 h3 ♗f2 **0-1**
M954-1857

### 1856-✕HR-3
**Rivière, J.A. de– Harrwitz, D.**
Paris [de Rivière]
1 f4 d5 2 ♘f3 c5 3 d3 [□ 3 e3] 3 ... ♘f6 4 c3 ♘c6 5 ♕c2 ♗f5 6 h3?! [6 ♘h4] 6 ... e6 7 g4 ♗g6 8 g5 ♘h5 9 ♖g1 ♗d6 10 e3 ♖c8 11 ♕h2 ♕c7 12 ♘a3 a6 13 ♘c2 0-0∓ 14 ♖g4 b5 15 ♗d2? c4 16 0-0-0?! cxd3 17 ♘cd4?! [17 ♘ce1] 17 ... ♘xd4 18 exd4 ♕a5 19 ♘e1 ♕xa2 20 ♗xd3 ♗a3 21 ♗e3 ♖xc3+ **0-1**
M954-1857

## LAROCHE✕RIVIÈRE
Paris
[1856-✕LR]

| | | | | | | |
|---|---|---|---|---|---|---|
| Laroche | 1 | 0 | 0 | 0 | 1 | 2 |
| J.A. de Rivière | 0 | 1 | 1 | 1 | 0 | 3 |

### 1856-✕LR-1
**Laroche+ Rivière, J.A. de**
Paris
1 f4 d5 2 c4 e6 3 e3 ♘f6 4 d4 c5 5 ♘f3 ♘c6 6 a3 a6 7 ♘c3 ♗e7 8 dxc5 ♗xc5 9 b4 ♗b6 10 c5 ♗c7 11 ♗d3 b6 12 0-0 bxc5 13 bxc5 ♕e7 14 ♘a4 ♘e4 15 ♕c2 f5 16 ♗b2 0-0 17 ♖ab1 ♗d7 18 ♖fc1 ♖fb8 19 ♗xe4 fxe4 20 ♘d4 ♘xd4 21 ♗xd4 ♖xb1 22 ♖xb1 ♗b5 23 ♘b2 a5 24 ♕d2 ♕d7 25 ♘d1 ♕c6 26 ♕c3 ♖a7 ♘f2 a4 28 ♘g4 ♗d3 29 ♖b2 ♗c4 30 ♗xg7 ♗xf4 31 ♖b8+ **1-0**
M954-1856

### 1856-✕LR-2
**Rivière, J.A. de+ Laroche**
Paris
1 d4 f5 2 e4 fxe4 3 ♘c3 ♘f6 4 ♗g5 c6 5 ♗xf6 exf6 6 ♘xe4 d5 7 ♘g3 ♗d6 8 ♕h5+ g6 9 ♕h6 ♔f7 10 0-0-0 ♕c7 11 ♘1e2 ♘a6 12 f4 ♗g4 13 ♕h4 ♗xe2 14 ♘xe2 ♔g7 15 g4 ♗xf4+ 16 ♔b1 ♖ae8 17 ♕f2 ♗e3 18 ♕f3 g5 19 h4 gxh4 20 ♖xh4 ♗g5 21 ♖h5 ♖e3 22 ♖xg5+ **1-0** M954-1856

### 1856-✕LR-3
**Rivière, J.A. de+ Laroche**
Paris [Staunton]
1 d4 f5 2 e4 d6 3 exf5 ♗xf5 4 ♗d3 ♗xd3 5 ♕xd3 ♘f6 6 ♕b5+ ♕d7 7 ♕xb7 ♕c6 8 ♕xc6+ ♘xc6 9 ♘e2 g6 10 a3 ♗g7 11 0-0 ♖b8 12 ♖a2! ♘a5 13 b3 ♘d7 14 ♗d2 [□ 14 ♗e3] 14 ... ♘c6 15 d5 ♘ce5 16 f4 ♘g4 17 b4 ♘b6 18 ♘bc3 ♘f6 19 ♗e3 ♘fxd5 20 ♘xd5 ♘xd5 21 ♗xa7 ♖a8 22 c4 ♘xf4 23 ♘xf4 ♖xa7 24 ♘e6 ♗f6 25 ♖d1 ♔f7 26 ♘d4 ♖ha8 27 ♘b5 ♖b7 28 ♖f2 c6 29 ♘d4 [□ 29 ♘xd6+ exd6 30 ♖xd6] 29 ... ♖b6 30 ♘c2 ♔g7 31 ♖f3 ♖a4 32 ♔f1 c5 33 ♔e2 ♖ba6 34 ♖b3 ♖a8 35 ♖dd3 h5 36 ♘e3 ♗d4 37 ♘d5 ♖f8 38 ♖f3 [38 ♘xe7? ♖e8] 38 ... ♖xf3 39 ♔xf3 cxb4 40 axb4 e6 41 ♘c7 ♔f6

42 ♔e4 ♗b6 43 ♘b5 ♔e7 [△ 44 ... ♖a2] 44 ♖b2 ♖a1 45 ♔d3 h4 46 h3 ♖d1+ 47 ♔c2 ♖a1 48 ♔b3 ♖c1 49 ♖c2 ♖b1+ 50 ♖b2 ♖c1 51 ♖c2 ♖b1+ 52 ♔c3 e5 53 ♖d2 ♖c1+ 54 ♔b3 ♖b1+ 55 ♔a3 ♖a1+ 56 ♔b2 ♖g1 57 ♔c2 ♗e3 58 ♖e2 ♗b6 59 ♘c3 ♗d4 60 ♘b5 ♗b6 61 ♔b3 ♖b1+ 62 ♔a4 ♖a1+ 63 ♘a3 ♗d4 64 ♔b3 ♖g1 65 ♘c2 ♗b6 66 ♔a4 ♖f1 67 ♔b5 ♗g1 68 ♔c6 ♖f2 69 ♖xf2 ♗xf2 70 ♔d5 ♔d7 71 ♘a3 ♗e1 72 b5 ♗b4 73 ♘c2 ♗c5 74 ♘e1 ♔c7 75 ♘d3 ♗d4 76 ♘e1 ♗c5 77 ♘f3 ♗f2 78 ♘g5 ♗e1 79 ♘e6+ ♔d7 80 ♘f8+ ♔e7 81 b6 ♗f2 82 b7 ♗a7 83 ♘xg6+ **1-0** M954-1856

### 1856-✕LR-4
**Rivière, J.A. de+ Laroche**
Paris
1 e4 e5 2 ♘f3 ♘c6 3 ♗c4 ♗c5 4 b4 ♗xb4 5 c3 ♗a5 6 d4 exd4 7 ♕b3 ♕f6 8 0-0 ♗b6 9 e5 ♕g6 10 ♗b2 d3 11 ♘bd2 ♘a5 12 ♕a4 ♘xc4 13 ♕xc4 ♘e7 14 ♗a3 ♕c6 15 ♕xd3 ♗c5 16 ♘d4 ♕d5 17 ♗xc5 ♕xc5 18 ♘2b3 ♕b6 19 c4 ♕g6 20 ♕c3 a6 21 f4 f5 22 ♖f3 0-0 23 ♖g3 ♕h5 24 ♖f1 b5 25 ♖h3 ♕g6 26 ♖ff3 ♗b7 27 ♖fg3 ♕f7 28 ♘c5 ♗c8 29 e6 dxe6 30 ♘dxe6 ♗xe6 31 ♘xe6 ♕f6 **1-0** M954-1856

### 1856-✕LR-5
**Laroche+ Rivière, J.A. de**
Paris [Staunton]
1 e4 e5 2 ♘f3 ♘c6 3 d4 ♘xd4 4 ♘xe5 ♘e6 5 f4 ♗c5 6 ♗c4 [□ 6 c3 △ 7 ♘f3] 6 ... d6 7 ♘d3 [7 ♗b5+] 7 ... ♘f6 8 e5 ♘e4 9 ♕f3 d5 10 ♘xc5 ♘6xc5 11 ♗d3 ♘xd3+ 12 cxd3 ♘c5 13 b4 ♘e6 14 ♗b2 c6 15 0-0 ♕b6+ 16 ♔h1 0-0 17 f5± ♘d4 18 ♕h5 [□ 18 ♗xd4 ♕xd4 19 ♕g3 ♕xa1 20 f6 g6 21 ♕e3 ♔h8 22 ♘d2 ♕xa2 23 ♕h6 ♖g8 24 ♘f3+–] 18 ... ♘xf5 19 ♖xf5 g6 20 ♖g5 ♕f2 21 ♘d2 ♕xd2 22 ♗d4 ♕xb4 23 ♗g1 ♕e7 24 ♕h4 [△ 25 ♖xg6+] 24 ... ♔h8 25 e6! c5 26 exf7 ♖xf7 27 ♖e1 ♗e6 28 ♕h6 ♖f6 29 ♖xd5 b6 30 ♖de5 ♕d7 31 d4! cxd4 32 ♖xe6 ♖xe6 33 ♖xe6 d3 [33 ... ♕xe6+–] 34 ♗e3 ♕a4 35 ♖e7
**1-0** M954-1856

## STAUNTON✕WORRALL
London
[1856-✕SW]

| | | | | | | | | | | | | | | | | | | |
|---|---|---|---|---|---|---|---|---|---|---|---|---|---|---|---|---|---|---|
| H. Staunton | 1 | 1 | 0 | 1 | 1 | ? | 0 | ? | ? | ? | ? | 1 | 0 | 1 | 0 | 1 | 1 | ? |
| T.H. Worrall | 0 | 0 | 1 | 0 | 0 | ? | 1 | ? | ? | ? | ? | 0 | 1 | 0 | 1 | 0 | 0 | ? |

### 1856-✕SW-1
**Staunton, H.+ Worrall, T.H.**
London [Staunton]
⟨♖a1⟩1 e4 e5 2 f4 d5 3 exd5 ♗c5 4 d4 ♗xd4 5 ♘f3 ♗g4 6 c3 ♗xf3 7 ♕xf3 ♗b6 8 fxe5 ♘e7 9 ♗c4 0-0 10 ♗g5 ♘d7 11 ♕e4 ♔h8 [□ 11 ... ♘c5±] 12 ♗d3 f5 13 exf6 ♘xf6 14 ♗xf6 **1-0** M954-1856

### 1856-✕SW-2
**Staunton, H.+ Worrall, T.H.**
London [Staunton]
⟨♖a1⟩1 e4 e5 2 ♘f3 ♘c6 3 ♗c4 f5 4 d4 f4 5 c3 ♘f6 6 ♘g5 d5 7 exd5 ♘xd5 8 h4 ♗f5 9 ♘d2 ♗e7 10 ♕f3 ♗xg5 11 ♗xd5 ♗f6 [11 ... ♗xh4? 12 ♗xc6+ △ 13 ♕h5+] 12 g4 ♗d7 13 g5 ♗e7 14 0-0 g6 15 ♖e1 ♗f5 16 dxe5 ♖f8 17 e6 ♗d6 18 ♗xc6+ bxc6 19 ♕xc6+ ♔e7 20 ♘b3 ♖b8 21 ♘d4 ♕e8 22 ♕c4 ♖b6 23 a4 ♕c8 24 a5 ♕a6 25 ♕a4 ♖d8 26 ♘xf5+ gxf5 27 ♕d4 **1-0**
M954-1856

### 1856-✕SW-3
**Staunton, H.– Worrall, T.H.**
London
⟨♖a1⟩1 e4 e5 2 d4 exd4 3 ♘f3 c5 4 ♗c4 ♘c6 5 0-0 h6 6 e5 d6 7 exd6 ♗xd6 8 ♖e1+ ♘ge7 9 ♘bd2 0-0 10 ♘e4 ♗g4 11 ♗xh6 gxh6 12 ♘f6+ ♔g7 13 ♘xg4 ♘g6 14 h3 ♖e8 15 ♖f1 ♖e7 16 g3 ♘ce5 17 ♘fxe5 ♘xe5 18 ♕c1 ♘xg4 19

hxg4 ♕d7 20 f3 ♗xg3 21 ♔g2 ♕d6 22 f4 ♖e3 **0-1** M954-1856

### 1856-✕SW-4
**Staunton, H.+Worrall, T.H.**
London [Staunton]

⟨♖a1⟩1 e4 e5 2 ♘f3 ♘c6 3 ♗c4 d6 4 c3 ♗g4 5 ♕b3 ♕d7 6 ♗xf7+ ♕xf7 7 ♕xb7 ♖d8 8 ♕xc6+ ♕d7 9 ♕c4 ♗xf3 10 gxf3 ♘f6 11 d4 d5 12 ♕e2 dxe4 13 dxe5 exf3 14 ♕xf3 ♘g4 15 0-0 ♗c5 16 h3 ♘h6 17 ♗g5 ♗e7 18 ♗xh6 gxh6 19 ♕h5+ ♔f8 20 ♕xh6+ ♔g8 21 ♔h2 ♗f8 22 ♖g1+ ♗g7 23 ♘d2 ♕e7 24 ♘e4 ♕xe5+ 25 f4 [25 ♖g3? ♕xg3+] 25 ... ♔f8! 26 ♕h4 ♕d5 27 ♘f6 ♕f7 28 ♘xh7+ ♔e8 29 ♖e1+ ♔d7 30 ♕g4+ ♔c6 31 ♖e6+ ♔b7 32 ♘g5 ♖d2+ 33 ♔g1 ♕d7 34 ♘e4 ♖d1+ 35 ♔g2 ♔b8 36 ♘f2 ♖d6 37 ♖xd6 ♕xg4+ 38 hxg4 cxd6 39 ♔g3 ♔c7 40 g5 ♖b8 41 f5 ♖xb2 42 f6 ♗f8 43 g6 **1-0** M954-1857

### 1856-✕SW-6
**Staunton, H.+Worrall, T.H.**
London [Staunton]

⟨♖a1⟩1 e4 e5 2 d4 exd4 3 ♘f3 ♘c6 4 ♗c4 d6 5 h3 ♗e6 6 ♗b5 ♗d7 7 ♗d3 ♘e5 8 ♘xd4 ♘xd3+ 9 cxd3 ♘e7 10 f4 c6 11 0-0 ♘g6 12 ♘f3 ♗e7 13 d4 ♘h4 14 ♘h2 0-0 15 f5 ♗g5 16 g3 ♗xc1 17 ♕xc1 ♕b6 18 ♕d2 ♖ae8 19 ♘c3 c5 20 gxh4 cxd4 21 ♘d5 ♕d8 22 f6! ♖e5 23 ♘g4 ♗xg4 [◻ 23 ... ♖h5+-] 24 hxg4 ♕d7 25 ♖f5 ♖xf5 26 gxf5 **1-0** M954-1857

### 1856-✕SW-7
**Staunton, H.−Worrall, T.H.**
London [Staunton]

⟨♖a1⟩1 e4 e5 2 ♘f3 ♘c6 3 ♗c4 ♗c5 4 b4 ♗xb4 5 c3 ♗c5 6 0-0 d6 7 d4 exd4 8 cxd4 ♗b6 9 ♕b3 ♗e6 10 ♗xe6 fxe6 11 ♕xe6+ ♕e7 12 ♕h3 ♘xd4 13 ♘xd4 ♗xd4 14 ♕h5+ ♕f7 15 ♕b5+ c6 16 ♕d3 ♗c5 17 ♔h1 ♘h6 18 f4 ♘g4 19 ♕e2 h5 20 ♘c3 ♕f6 21 e5 ♕h4 22 g3? [22 exd6+ ∆ 23 g3] 22 ... ♕e7 23 h3 0-0-0 24 hxg4 hxg4+ 25 ♔g2 ♕e6 26 ♘e4? **0-1** M954-1857

### 1856-✕SW-12
**Staunton, H.+Worrall, T.H.**
London [Staunton]

⟨♘b1⟩1 e4 e5 2 ♘f3 ♘c6 3 d4 d6 4 ♗b5 ♗d7 5 c3 ♗e7 6 h3 a6 7 ♗a4 b5 8 ♗c2 ♘f6 9 d5 ♘b8 10 0-0 0-0 11 ♘h2 h6 12 f4 exf4 13 ♗xf4 ♘h7 14 ♕h5 f5?! 15 exf5 ♘f6 16 ♕f3 c6 17 ♖ad1 cxd5 18 g4 ♗c6 19 ♖fe1 d4 20 ♗b3+ d5 21 g5 hxg5 22 ♗xg5 dxc3 23 bxc3 ♕b6+ 24 ♔g2 ♕c5 25 ♘g4 ♘bd7 26 ♖d4 ♖ae8 27 ♖e6 ♔h8 28 ♘xf6! ♘xf6 [28 ... ♗xf6 29 ♖xc6 (29 ♖xe8 ♖xe8 30 ♕h5+ ♔g8 31 ♕xe8+-) 29 ♕xc6 30 ♕h5+ ♔g8 31 ♗xd5+ ♕xd5 32 ♖xd5+-] 29 ♗xf6 ♖xf6 [29 ... ♗xf6 30 ♖xc6 ♕xc6 31 ♕h5+ ♔g8 32 ♗xd5++-] 30 ♕h5+ ♔g8 31 ♖xc6 **1-0** M954-1856

### 1856-✕SW-13
**Staunton, H.−Worrall, T.H.**
London [Staunton]

⟨♘b1⟩1 e4 e5 2 d4 ♘c6 3 d5 ♘ce7 4 ♘f3 d6 5 h3 ♘f6 6 ♗d3 ♘g6 7 0-0 h6 8 ♗e3 ♗e7 9 a4 0-0 10 ♖a3 ♘h7 11 c4 ♘g5 12 ♘h2 f5 13 exf5 ♗xf5 14 ♗xf5 ♖xf5 15 ♕g4 ♕f8 16 h4 ♘xh4! 17 f4 [17 ♕xh4? ♘f3+] 17 ... h5! 18 ♕g3 ♘e4 19 ♕e1 exf4 20 ♗d4 ♘g3 21 ♖f2 ♗f6 22 ♗xf6 ♕xf6 23 a5 ♖e5 24 ♕d2 ♖ae8 25 ♖xg3 ♖e1+ 26 ♘f1 ♖8e4 27 ♖h3 ♕g5 28 b4 ♘f5 29 c5 ♘g3 30 cxd6 cxd6 31 b5 ♖4e2 32 ♕xf4 [32 ♖xg3 ♖xf2 33 ♔xf2 (◻ 33 ♕xf2 ♖xf1+ 34 ♔xf1 fxg3-+) 33 ... ♖xf1+ 34 ♔xf1 ♕xg3-+] 32 ... ♕xf4 33 ♖xf4 ♖xf1+ 34 ♖xf1 ♘xf1 35 ♔xf1 ♖e5 **0-1** M954-1856

### 1856-✕SW-14
**Staunton, H.+Worrall, T.H.**
London [Staunton]

⟨♘b1⟩1 e4 e5 2 ♘f3 ♘c6 3 ♗c4 ♘f6 4 d4 ♘xd4 5 ♘xe5 ♘e6 6 0-0 ♗c5 7 ♘d3 ♗b6 8 e5 ♘e4 9 ♘f4 ♕h4 10 ♕f3 ♘6g5 11 ♕e2 0-0 12 ♗d3 d5 13 ♘xd5 ♗g4 14 ♗xg5 ♘xg5 [14 ... ♗xf3? 15 ♗xh4] 15 ♕d2 ♗f3! 16 ♕f4! [16 ♘f4 ♕g4; 16 ♘e3 ♗xg2] 16 ... ♕h5 17 ♘e7+ ♔h8 18 h4 ♗xg2 19 ♔xg2 ♘e6 20 ♕g3 ♗d4 21 f4 f6 22 ♗c4 ♘xf4+ 23 ♖xf4 ♗xe5 24 ♕g4 ♕e8 25 ♘d5 ♗xf4 26 ♘xf4 ♕e4+ 27 ♔g3 f5 [27 ... ♕xc4? 28 ♘g6+] 28 ♕e2 ♕d4 29 c3 ♕b6 30 ♘e6 f4+ 31 ♔h3 ♖f6 32 ♘g5 h6 33 ♘f7+ [33 ♕e1 hxg5? (33 ... ♕e3+) 34 ♕h5+ ♖h6 35 ♕e8+] 33 ... ♔h7 34 ♕e4+ g6 35 ♖f1 ♕xb2 [35 ... ♖f8 36 ♕e7+-; ◻ 35 ... ♖f5] 36 ♘g5+ hxg5 37 ♕e7+ ♔h6 38 hxg5+ ♔xg5 39 ♖g1+ ♔h6 40 ♕xf6 **1-0** M954-1856

### 1856-✕SW-15
**Staunton, H.−Worrall, T.H.**
London [Staunton]

⟨♘b1⟩1 e4 e5 2 ♘f3 ♘c6 3 ♗b5 ♗c5 4 c3 ♘ge7 5 0-0 0-0 6 d4 exd4 7 cxd4 ♗b6 8 d5 ♘b8 9 ♗d3 d6 10 h3 f5 11 ♗g5 h6 12 ♗h4 ♕e8 13 ♕c2 ♘d7 14 exf5 ♘f6 15 ♖ae1 ♕f7 16 ♖e2 ♗d7 17 g4? ♖ae8 18 g5 [18 ♖e6 ♘xd5] 18 ... hxg5 19 ♗xg5 ♕h5 20 ♔g2 ♔h8 21 ♗xf6 ♖xf6 22 ♖e4 ♘xf5 23 ♖g4 ♔g8 24 ♖g1 ♖e7 [◻ 24 ... ♘e3+ ∆ 25 ... ♗xg4-+] 25 ♔h2 ♖h6 26 ♘g5 ♗d4 27 ♗xf5 ♗e5+ 28 f4? [28 ♔h1∓] 28 ... ♗xf4+! 29 ♖xf4 ♖e2+ 30 ♔h1 ♖xc2 31 ♗xd7 ♕e2 32 ♘f3 ♖xb2 33 ♗e6+ ♖xe6 34 fxe6 ♕xe6 35 ♖fg4 ♕f7 **0-1** M954-1857

### 1856-✕SW-16
**Staunton, H.+Worrall, T.H.**
London [Staunton]

⟨♘b1⟩1 e4 c5 2 ♘f3 ♘c6 3 ♗c4 e6 4 c3 ♘f6 5 e5 ♘g4 6 ♕e2 ♕c7 7 d4 cxd4 8 cxd4 d5 9 ♗b3 ♗b4+ 10 ♔f1 a5 11 g3 b5 12 a3 ♗e7 13 ♗f4 a4 14 ♗c2 b4 15 axb4 ♘xb4 16 ♗xa4+ ♔f8 17 ♔g2 ♗a6 18 ♕d2 ♘d3 19 ♗b5 ♘xf4+ 20 ♕xf4 ♘xf2 21 ♖hc1! ♕b6 22 ♖xa6 ♖xa6 23 ♖c8+ ♗d8 24 ♗xa6 ♔e7 25 ♗e2 ♘e4 26 ♗d3 f5 [26 ... ♕xb2+?] 27 exf6+ ♘xf6 28 ♘e5 h6 29 ♖c2 [29 ♘g6+ ♔d7] 29 ... ♖g8 30 ♗h7 g5 31 ♕xf6+ ♔xf6 32 ♘d7+ ♔g7 33 ♘xb6 ♔xh7 34 ♘d7 **1-0** M954-1857

### 1856-✕SW-17
**Staunton, H.+Worrall, T.H.**
London [Staunton]

⟨♘b1⟩1 e4 e5 2 d4 exd4 3 ♘f3 c5 4 ♗c4 ♘c6 5 0-0 ♗d6 6 ♘g5 ♘h6 7 ♖e1 ♗e5 [◻ 7 ... ♘e5] 8 f4 ♗c7 9 ♕h5 ♕e7 10 ♗d2 0-0 11 a3 d6 12 h3 ♗e6 13 ♗d3 c4 14 ♗e2 f6 15 ♘xe6 ♕xe6 16 b3 b5 17 ♕xb5 ♕e8 18 ♗xc4+ ♔h8 19 ♕b7 ♗b6 20 ♔h1 ♖c8 21 ♗b5 ♖f7 22 ♕a6 ♖cc7 23 a4 ♖fe7 24 a5 ♗c5 25 b4!? ♗xb4 26 ♗xc6 ♖xc6 27 ♕d3 ♗xd2 28 ♕xd2 ♖c4 29 ♕d3 ♕c6 30 ♖ab1 ♖e8 31 ♖b2 ♘f7 32 ♖eb1 h6 33 e5 dxe5 34 ♕g6 ♘d6 35 ♖b8 ♖xc2 36 ♖xe8+ ♕xe8 [36 ... ♘xe8? 37 ♖b8+-] 37 ♕xc2 e4 38 ♕c7 ♕e6 39 ♕xa7! d3 40 ♕b8+ ♔h7 [40 ... ♘e8 41 a6+-; 40 ... ♘c8 41 ♖c1+-] 41 ♖b6 ♕c8 42 ♕xd6 ♕c1+ 43 ♔h2 d2 44 ♕d5 **1-0** M954-1857

### 1856-★AH-1
**Anderssen, A.+Hillel, D.**
Breslau

1 e4 e5 2 ♘f3 ♘c6 3 ♗c4 ♗c5 4 b4 ♗xb4 5 c3 ♗a5 6 d4 exd4 7 0-0 ♗b6 8 cxd4 d6 9 h3 ♕f6 10 ♗b2 ♘h6 11 ♘bd2 0-0 12 e5 dxe5 13 dxe5 ♕e7 14 ♘e4 ♗e6 15 ♗d3 ♗f5 16 ♘f6+ gxf6 17 exf6 ♕e8 18 ♕d2 ♗e3 19 fxe3 ♗xd3 20 ♕xd3 ♖d8 21 ♕a3 ♘f5 22 ♖ae1 ♕e4 23 ♘g5 ♕h4 24 e4 ♘fd4 25 ♘f3 ♘xf3+ 26 ♕xf3 ♖d2 27 ♗c3 ♖xa2 28 e5 ♘d4 29 ♗xd4 ♕xd4+ 30 ♔h1 ♔h8 31 ♖e4 ♕b2 32 ♖h4

♕xe5 33 ♕d3 h5 34 ♕f5 ♕xf5 35 ♖xf5 ♔h7 36 ♖g5 ♔h6 37 ♖hxh5# **1-0** L/N6047-1857

### 1856̂-★AH-2
**Hillel, D.+Anderssen, A.**

Breslau

1 e4 e5 2 f4 exf4 3 ♘f3 g5 4 ♗c4 g4 5 0-0 ♕e7 6 ♘c3 gxf3 7 d4 ♘c6 8 ♘d5 ♕d8 9 ♗xf4 d6 10 ♕xf3 ♗e6 11 c3 ♕d7 12 ♗g5 ♗g7 13 ♖ae1 h5 14 h3 ♘xd4 15 cxd4 ♗xd4+ 16 ♔h1 c6

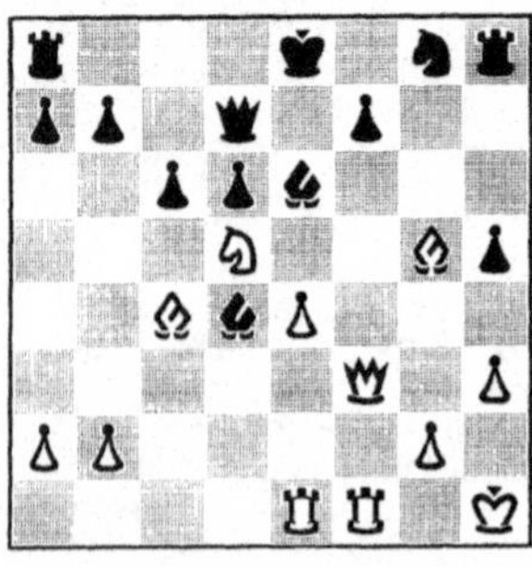

17 ♘c7+ ♕xc7 18 ♗xe6 ♖h7 19 ♗b3 ♕d7 20 e5 dxe5 21 ♗c2 ♖h8 22 ♗g6 ♘h6 23 ♕f6 **1-0** L/N6047

### 1856̂-★BC-1
**Cunningham & Löwenthal, J.J.+Barnes, T.W. & Staunton, H.**

London [Löwenthal]

1 e4 c5 2 ♗c4 e6 3 ♘c3 a6 4 a4 g6! 5 d4 [5 ♘ge2?!] 5 ... ♗g7 6 ♗e3 [6 dxc5!? ♗xc3+ 7 bxc3 ♕a5 (7 ... ♘c6 8 ♕d6) 8 ♕d4 f6 9 ♘e2 ♘c6 10 ♕d6] 6 ... ♕b6 7 ♘ge2 ♘c6 8 dxc5 ♕xb2 9 ♖b1! ♗xc3+ 10 ♔f1 ♕a3 11 ♖b3 ♕xa4 12 ♖xc3± ♘f6 13 f3 ♕a5 14 ♔f2 0-0 15 ♕d2 ♘e8 [△ 16 ... ♘g7] 16 ♘d4 e5 17 ♘b3 ♕c7 18 ♗h6 ♘g7 19 h4! d6 20 h5 ♗e6 21 cxd6 ♕b6+ 22 ♗e3 ♕d8 23 hxg6 ♗xc4 24 gxh7+ ♔h8 25 ♖xc4 ♘e6 26 ♘c5 ♘xc5 27 ♖xc5 f6 28 ♕d5 ♕d7 29 ♖h5 ♖ad8 30 ♖c4! ♕f7 [30 ... ♕xd6? 31 ♗h6 ♕xd5 (31 ... ♖fe8 32 ♕f7+-) 32 exd5+-] 31 g4 ♖d7 32 ♗b6 ♕e8 33 ♖a4 ♖ff7 34 ♖a1 ♘d8 35 c4 ♘e6 36 ♗e3 ♖xh7 37 ♖ah1 ♘f8 38 c5 ♖xh5 39 ♖xh5+ ♘h7 40 f4 exf4 41 ♗d4 ♕f7 [41 ... ♕g6 42 ♕e6+-] 42 ♕xf7 ♖xf7 43 g5 ♔g7 44 gxf6+ ♔g6 45 ♖e5+- ♘g5 [45 ... ♘xf6 45 ♖e6 ♔g5 46 ♗xf6+ ♖xf6 47 ♖e5+ △ 48 d7+-; 45 ... ♖xf6 46 d7+-; 45 ... ♔xf6 46 ♖e7++-] 46 ♖e8 ♖d7 47 ♖g8+ ♔h6 48 ♖g7 ♘xe4+ 49 ♔f3 ♘g5+ 50 ♔g4 ♘f7 51 ♔xf4 b6 52 ♔f5 **1-0** M324-1856

### 1856̂-★BC-2
**Cunningham & Staunton, H.–Barnes, T.W. & Owen, J.**

London

1 d4 d5 2 c4 e6 3 ♘c3 ♘f6 4 e3 c5 5 a3 a5 6 ♘f3 ♘c6 7 b3 ♗e7 8 ♗b2 cxd4 9 ♘xd4 0-0 10 ♘cb5 ♗d7 11 ♗d3 ♘e5 12 cxd5 ♘xd3+ 13 ♕xd3 ♘xd5 14 0-0 ♕b6 15 a4 ♗f6 16 ♘a3 ♗c6 17 ♘c4 ♕a6 18 ♖fc1 ♘b4 19 ♕d1 ♖fd8 20 ♕e2 ♗e8 21 ♖d1 ♖ac8 22 ♖ac1 h6 23 f4 ♘d5 24 g3 b5 25 ♘a3 ♖xc1 26 ♖xc1 ♕b6 27 axb5 ♘xe3 28 ♕xe3 ♗xd4 29 ♗xd4 ♖xd4 30 ♘c4 ♕c5 31 ♘b2 ♕d5 32 ♕e5 ♗xb5 33 ♕xd5 ♖xd5 34 ♘c4 ♖c5 35 ♖a1 ♗xc4 36 bxc4 ♔h7 37 ♔g2 ♔g6 38 ♔f3 h5 39 ♖a4 e5 40 h3 ♔f5 41 g4+ ♔g6 42 ♔e4 f6 43 ♔e3 hxg4 44 hxg4 exf4+ 45 ♔xf4 ♔f7 46 ♔e4 ♔e6 47 ♔d3 ♔e5 48 ♖a1 ♔d6 49 ♖f1 ♖g5 50 ♖f4 ♔c5 51 ♔c3 a4 52 ♖d4 a3 53 ♖f4 ♖e5 54 ♔b3 ♖e3+ 55 ♔a2 ♖g3 56 ♖e4 ♔b4 57 ♖f4 ♖g2+ 58 ♔a1 ♖c2 59 c5+ ♔xc5 60 g5 fxg5 61 ♖f5+ ♔b4 62 ♖xg5 ♖c7 ...♀ **0-1** M954-1856

### 1856̂-★BC-3
**Cunningham, & Löwenthal, J.J.+ Barnes, T.W. & Staunton, H.**

London [Staunton]

1 e4 e6 2 d4 d5 3 exd5 exd5 4 ♘f3 ♘f6 5 ♗e3 ♗d6 6 ♗d3 ♗e6 7 0-0 0-0 8 ♘g5? ♗g4 9 f3 ♗h5 10 ♕d2 b6 [△ 11 ... c5] 11 ♕f2 ♘bd7 12 ♘d2 c5 13 c3 ♕c7 14 g4 ♗g6 15 ♗xg6 hxg6 16 ♖ac1 ♖ae8 17 ♖fe1 ♖xe3 18 ♖xe3 cxd4 19 ♖d3 ♘e5 20 ♖xd4 ♗c5 21 ♕f1 ♘c6 22 ♘b3 ♘xd4 23 cxd4 ♗xd4+ 24 ♘xd4 ♕f4 25 ♘c6 ♕xg5 [◻ 25 ... ♕e3+ △ 26 ... ♕xg5] 26 ♘e7+ ♔h8 [◻ 26 ... ♔h7] 27 ♖e1 ♕h4 28 ♖e5 ♖d8 29 ♕d3 [△ 30 ♕xg6] 29 ... ♕h3 30 g5 ♘g4 31 ♖e2 d4 32 ♖g2 ♘e3? [32 ... ♘e5-+] 33 ♖g3 ♕e6? [33 ... ♕d7 34 ♕e4 ♘f5 35 ♖h3+ ♘h6 36 ♖h4 (36 ♔g2 ♕b5 37 ♘xg6+ fxg6 38 ♕xg6 ♕e8 39 ♕xe8 ♖xe8 40 gxh6 d3 41 hxg7+ ♔xg7 42 f4 ♖d8-+; 38 ... ♕e2+∓) 36 ... ♖e8 37 gxh6 (37 ♘xg6+?∓) 37 ... ♖xe7 38 hxg7+ ♔xg7 39 ♕xd4+ ♕xd4 40 ♖xd4 ♖e2∓] 34 ♕e4! [△ 35 ♕h4#] 34 ... ♘f5 [34 ... ♕xe4 35 ♖h3#] 35 ♖h3+ ♘h6 **1-0** M954-1856

### 1856̂-★BF-1
**Falkbeer, E.K. & Löwenthal, J.J.– Barnes, T.W. & Staunton, H.**

London [Staunton]

1 e4 e5 2 ♘f3 d6 3 d4 exd4 4 ♗c4 ♗g4 5 c3 ♗xf3 6 ♕xf3 ♕f6 7 cxd4 ♘c6 8 ♗e3 ♗e7 9 ♘c3 ♕xf3 10 gxf3 ♘f6 11 0-0-0 a6 12 ♖hg1 g6 13 f4 ♘a5 14 ♗e2 b5 15 e5 ♘d7 16 b3 c6 17 d5 c5 18 ♗f3 b4 19 ♘e4 ♘b7 20 ♖ge1 0-0 21 e6 ♘b6 22 ♘g3 f5! 23 ♔b1 a5 24 ♘e2 a4 25 ♘c1 axb3 26 axb3 ♗f6 27 ♖e2 ♖a1+ 28 ♔c2 ♖fa8 29 ♗d2 ♔f8 30 ♗e1 ♔e7 31 ♖e3 ♗d4 32 ♖ed3 ♗g7 33 ♖e3 ♗h6 34 ♖e2 [◻ 34 ♗e2 △ 35 ♖h3] 34 ... ♖8a3 35 ♗d2 c4 36 ♖e3 [36 ♗xb4 cxb3+ 37 ♔d2 (37 ♔d3 b2+; 37 ♘xb3 ♖3a2+) 37 ... b2-+] 36 ... c3 37 ♗e1 ♗xf4 38 ♖d4 ♗xe3 39 fxe3 ♘c5 40 ♖h4 ♖xc1+ [40 ... h5 41 ♖xh5!? gxh5 42 ♗h4+ ♔f8 43 e7+ ♔g7 44 e8♕ ♖xc1+ 45 ♔xc1 ♖a1+ 46 ♔c2 ♖a2+ 47 ♔c1 ♘xb3+ 48 ♔d1 c2+-+] 41 ♔xc1 ♖a1+ 42 ♔c2 ♖xe1 43 ♖xb4 ♖xe3 44 ♖xb6 ♖xf3 45 ♖c6 ♘e4 46 ♖c7+ ♔d8 47 ♖d7+ ♔e8 48 b4 ♖f2+ 49 ♔b3 c2 [49 ... ♖b2+ 50 ♔a3 ♖xb4 51 ♔xb4 c2 52 ♖c7 ♘c5-+] 50 ♖c7 ♘f6 [50 ... ♘c5+?? 51 bxc5 c1♕ 52 ♖c8+ ♔e7 53 cxd6+ ♔xd6 54 ♖xc1] 51 b5 ♘xd5 **0-1** M954-1856

### 1856̂-★BF-2
**Barnes, T.W. & Staunton, H.+Falkbeer, E.K. & Löwenthal, J.J.**

London

1 e4 e5 2 ♘f3 ♘c6 3 ♗b5 ♘ge7 4 c3 ♘g6 5 0-0 d6 6 d4 exd4 7 cxd4 ♗d7 8 ♘e1 ♗e7 9 f4 ♗f6 10 ♗e3 0-0 11 ♘c3 ♖e8 12 ♗c4 ♕c8 13 a3 ♘d8 14 ♖c1 c6 15 ♗d3 ♕b8 16 e5 dxe5 17 dxe5 ♘f8 18 ♗c5 ♗e7 19 ♗xe7 ♖xe7 20 ♘e4 ♕c7 21 ♔h1 ♘de6 22 ♕h5 ♘d4 23 ♘f6+ gxf6 24 exf6 ♖e6 25 ♕h6 ♖xf6 26 ♕xf6 ♘fe6 27 f5 **1-0** M954-1856

### 1856̂-★BL-1
**Löwenthal, J.J. & Owen, J.– Barnes, T.W. & Staunton, H.**

London [Staunton]

1 e4 e5 2 ♘c3 ♘f6 3 f4 d5 4 fxe5 ♘xe4 5 ♘f3 ♗g4 6 ♗e2 ♘c6 7 ♗b5 ♗b4 [7 ... ♗c5] 8 ♕e2 ♘g5 9 ♕f2 ♗xf3 10 gxf3 0-0 11 ♗xc6 bxc6 12 ♘e2 f6 13 h4 ♘e6 14 c3 ♗a5 15 d4 fxe5 16 dxe5 d4 17 ♗d2 ♕d5 18 ♖f1 ♗b6 19 ♕g3 d3 20 ♘c1 ♖ad8 21 ♘b3 a5 22 c4 ♕xc4 23 ♗c3 ♗d4? [23 ... d2+!] 24 ♘xd4 ♘xd4 25 ♔d2 ♘e6 26 f4 ♘c5 27 ♖ae1 ♘e4+ 28 ♖xe4 ♕xe4 29 ♖f2 ♖f7 30 ♕e3 ♕f5 ...♀ **0-1** L/N6123-1859

**1856̂-★BO-1**
**Owen, J. & Staunton, H.+ Barnes, T.W. & Löwenthal, J.J.**
London [Staunton]

1 e4 e5 2 ♘f3 ♘c6 3 ♗c4 ♗c5 4 b4 ♗xb4 5 c3 ♗a5 6 d4 exd4 7 0-0 d6 8 ♕b3 ♕f6 9 cxd4 ♗b6 10 ♗b5 ♗d7 11 e5 dxe5 12 ♖e1! ♘ge7 13 dxe5 ♕g6 14 ♗d3 ♕h5 15 ♖e4 ♘g6 [◻ 15 ... ♗f5] 16 ♕a4 [△ 17 g4] 16 ... ♗e6 17 ♘bd2 ♗d5 18 ♖g4 [18 g4 ♕h6 19 ♘c4 ♕h3] 18 ... h6

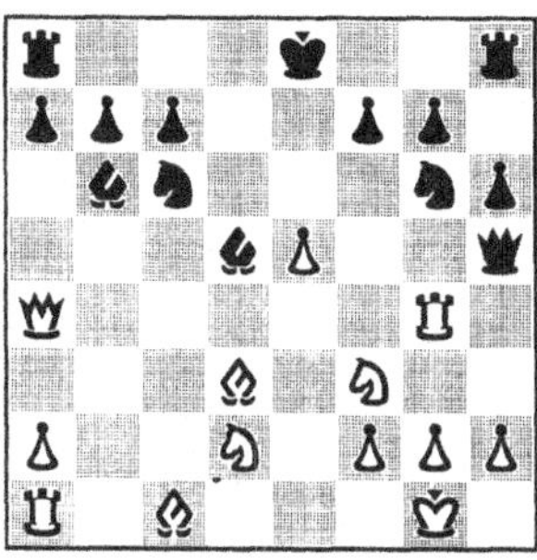

19 ♖xg6! ♗xf3 [19 ... fxg6 20 g4 ♕h3 21 ♗f1+−] 20 ♘xf3 fxg6 21 g4 ♕h3 22 ♗xg6+ [22 ♕e4? 0-0-0] 22 ... ♔d8 23 ♕f4 ♘e7 [△ 24 ... ♘d5] 24 ♗f7! ♔c8 [24 ... ♖f8 25 ♗a3 ♖xf7 26 ♕xf7 ♕xg4+ 27 ♔h1+−] 25 ♗a3 ♘c6 26 ♗f8! [26 ♖d1 ♘d4] 26 ... ♘d8 27 ♗xg7 ♘xf7 28 ♗xh8 ♘xh8 29 ♕f5+ ♔d8 30 ♕f6+ ♔e8 31 ♕xh8+ **1-0** M954-1856

**1856̂-★BO-2**
**Barnes, T.W. & Löwenthal, J.J.– Owen, J. & Staunton, H.**
London [Staunton]

1 e4 e5 2 ♘f3 d6 3 d4 exd4 4 ♕xd4 ♘c6 5 ♗b5 ♗d7 6 ♗xc6 ♗xc6 7 ♘c3 ♘f6 8 0-0 ♗e7 9 ♗e3 0-0 10 h3 ♕d7 11 ♖ad1?! ♖ae8 12 ♘d2 ♗d8 13 f4 ♘h5! 14 ♕d3 [◻ 14 ♔h2] 14 ... f5 15 ♔h2 [15 exf5 ♘g3] 15 ... fxe4 16 ♕e2 [16 ♘dxe4? ♕e7 17 g4 ♗xe4 18 ♘xe4 ♕xe4] 16 ... ♘f6 17 ♘b3 ♕f7 [◻ 17 ... b6] 18 ♘a5 ♕d7 19 ♗xa7 ♔h8 [19 ... b6? 20 ♕c4+] 20 ♗e3 b6 21 ♘xc6 ♕xc6 22 g4 ♕d7 23 g5 ♘g8 24 ♖d4 ♕f5 [△ 25 ... ♗xg5] 25 ♖g1 [◻ 25 ♖fd1; ◻ 25 ♖d5] 25 ... c6! 26 ♖xd6 ♗c7 27 ♖xc6 ♗xf4+ 28 ♗xf4 ♕xf4+ 29 ♔h1 ♘e7 30 ♖e6 ♘f5 31 ♖xe4 ♘g3+ 32 ♖xg3 ♕xg3 33 ♖xe8 [33 ♕g2 ♕d6−+] 33 ... ♕xh3+ 34 ♔g1 ♕g3+ 35 ♔h1 ♕h4+ 36 ♕h2 ♕xh2+ 37 ♔xh2 ♖xe8 38 ♔g3 ♖e5 39 ♔f4 ♖c5 40 a4 ♔g8 41 ♔g4 ♔f7 42 ♔f4 ♔g6 43 ♔e3 ♖xg5 **0-1** M954-1856

**1856̂-★BO-3**
**Boden, S.S.– Owen, J.**
London [Staunton]

1 d3? d5 2 f4 ♗g4? 3 h3 ♗d7 4 ♘f3 e6 5 b3 ♘h6 6 e4 ♗e7 7 ♗e2 ♗h4+ 8 ♔f1 dxe4 9 dxe4 f5 10 e5 0-0 11 ♗e3 ♗e7 12 ♘bd2 c5 13 a4 b6 14 ♘c4 ♘f7 15 g4 fxg4 16 hxg4 ♘c6 17 ♕d3 ♘h6 18 ♖d1 ♘d4 19 c3 ♘xe2 20 ♔xe2 ♗c6 21 ♘d6 ♗d5 22 c4 [◻ 22 ♘g5 ♗xg5 23 fxg5 ♗f3+ 24 ♔d2 ♗xh1 (24 ... ♗xd1 25 ♔xd1) 25 ♖xh1] 22 ... ♗xf3+ 23 ♔xf3 ♕c7 24 g5 ♘f5 25 ♕e4 ♗xd6 26 exd6 ♕d7 27 ♗c1 ♖ac8 28 ♗b2 ♖c6 29 ♗e5 g6 30 ♖h2 ♘xd6 31 ♕d3 ♕b7 32 ♔g4 ♘f7 33 ♕d7 [◻ 33 ♗b2 △ ♕c3] 33 ... ♘xe5+ 34 fxe5 ♖c7 35 ♕xe6+ ♖cf7 36 ♖d5 ♔g7 37 ♖hd2 ♖f3! 38 ♖d7+ ♔h8 **0-1** M954-1856

**1856̂-★BS-1**
**Barnes, T.W. & Owen, J.– Staunton, H.**
London [Staunton]

1 e4 e6 2 d4 d5 3 exd5 exd5 4 ♗d3 c5 5 dxc5 ♗xc5 6 ♘f3 ♘f6 7 0-0 0-0 8 ♗g5 ♗e6 9 ♘c3 ♘bd7 10 ♕d2 a6 11 ♘e2 ♕b6 12 c3 ♘e4 13 ♗xe4 dxe4 14 ♘fd4 ♗c4 15 ♗e3 ♖ad8 16 b4 ♗xd4 17 ♗xd4 ♕g6 18 ♘f4 ♕g5 19 ♖fe1 ♘e5 20 ♔h1 ♘d3 21 ♖xe4 f5 22 ♗f6! ♕xf6! 23 ♖xc4 ♘xb4 24 ♕e2 ♖fe8 25 ♕f3 ♘c6−+ 26 ♖d1 [26 ♖c5 ♕e7−+; 26 ♖a4 ♕e5−+] 26 ... ♘e5 27 ♖xd8 ♕xd8 28 ♕e2 ♘xc4 29 ♕xc4+ ♔h8 30 h3 ♖e4 31 ♕d5 ♕xd5 32 ♘xd5 ♖e2 **0-1** M954-1856

**1856̂-★BS-2**
**Staunton, H.+ Barnes, T.W. & Owen, J.**
London [Staunton]

1 e4 e5 2 ♘f3 ♘c6 3 ♗c4 ♘f6 4 0-0 ♗c5 5 b4 ♗xb4 6 c3 ♗e7 7 d4 d6 8 a4∓ 0-0 [8 ... ♘xe4] 9 ♕d3 d5! 10 ♗xd5 ♘xd5 11 exd5 ♕xd5 12 c4 ♕d8 13 d5 ♗g4 14 ♘bd2 ♘b4 15 ♕b1 ♗d6 16 ♗a3 a5 17 ♗xb4 axb4 18 ♖e1 f6 19 ♕c2 b6 20 a5?! ♗xf3 21 gxf3? bxa5 22 ♘e4 [22 c5 ♗e7 23 ♕c4] 22 ... f5 23 ♘g3 ♕g5 24 ♔h1 ♕f4 25 c5 ♕xf3+ 26 ♔g1 f4 27 ♘e4 ♗e7 28 ♕c4 ♔h8 29 ♕b5 ♕g4+ 30 ♔h1 f3 31 ♘g3 ♕d4 32 ♕d7

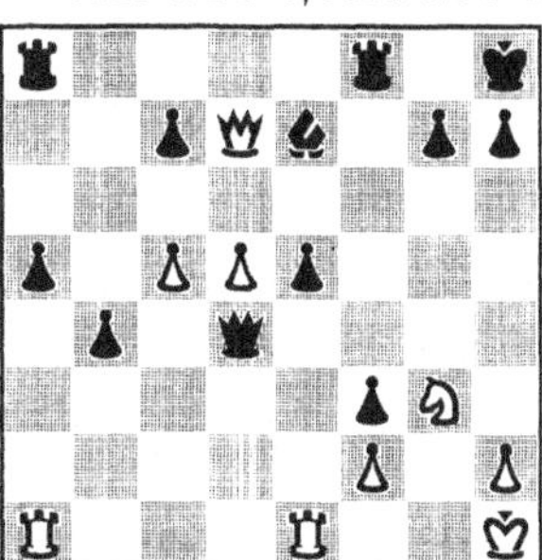

32 ... ♕xf2?? 33 ♖g1 ♕xc5??+− 34 ♘e4 ♕d4 35 ♕xe7 g6 36 ♘g5 [36 ... ♕h4 37 ♘f7++−; 36 ... ♖f7 37 ♘xf7++−] 36 ...? **1-0** M954-1856

**1856̂-★CS-1**
**Staunton, H. & ?+ Cunningham & Löwenthal, J.J.**
London

1 e4 e6 2 d4 d5 3 exd5 exd5 4 ♗e3 ♘f6 5 ♗d3 ♗d6 6 h3 ♗e6 7 ♘d2 0-0 8 ♘e2 ♘c6 9 c3 ♕d7 10 ♕c2 h6 11 f4 ♕e7 12 0-0-0 ♘e4 13 ♘f3 f5 14 ♘e5 ♕e8 15 g4 ♘e7 16 ♕b3 ♖b8 17 ♗xe4 fxe4 18 ♘g3 ♘c6 19 ♕c2 ♖d8 20 ♕e2 ♘a5 21 b3 ♗c8 22 h4 ♗xe5 23 dxe5 c5 24 ♖hf1 ♕e7 25 g5 hxg5 26 hxg5 g6 27 ♖h1 ♖f7

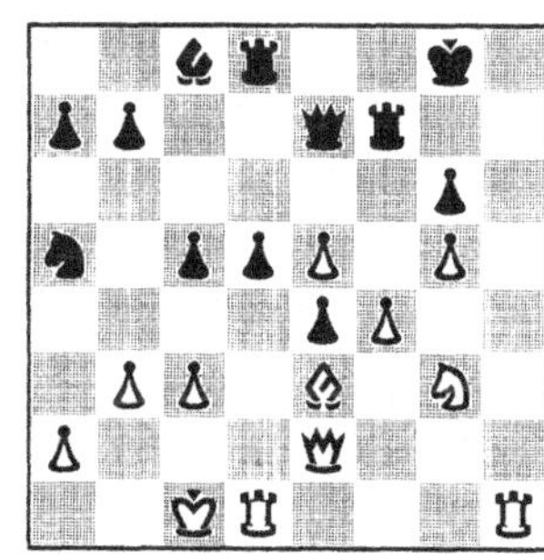

28 ♘xe4 **1-0** M954-1856

**1856̂-★FV-1**
**Vitzthum, C.+ Falkbeer, E.K.**
[Staunton]

1 e4 e5 2 ♘f3 ♘c6 3 d4 exd4 4 ♗c4 ♗c5 5 ♘g5 ♘h6 6 ♕h5 ♕e7 7 ♘f3 ♗b4+ 8 c3 dxc3 9 0-0 d6 10 bxc3 ♗c5 11 ♗g5 ♗g4 12 ♕h4 ♕d7 13 ♗xh6 gxh6 14 ♘bd2 ♗xf3 15 ♘xf3 ♕e7 16 ♕xh6 0-0-0 17 ♗d5 ♘e5 18 ♘xe5 ♕xe5 19 ♖ab1 ♗b6 20 ♕h3+ ♔b8 21 a4 a5 22 ♖b5 ♕f6 23 ♔h1 ♖dg8?? 24 ♖xb6 [24 ... cxb6 25 ♕d7] **1-0** M954-1856

**1856̂-★KS-1**
**Kennedy, H.A. & Löwenthal, J.J.–Staunton H. & ?**

[Staunton]

1 e4 e5 2 ♘f3 ♘c6 3 ♗b5 ♘d4?! 4 ♘xd4 exd4 5 0-0 ♗c5 6 d3 ♘e7 7 ♗g5 0-0 8 ♕h5 d6 9 f4 f6 10 ♗h4 ♗e6 11 f5 ♗f7 12 ♕g4 [△ 13 ♗xf6] 12 ... ♔h8 13 ♖f3± c6 14 ♗a4 ♕c7 15 ♗b3 ♘g8 16 ♘d2 ♘h6 17 ♕f4 [△ 18 ♗xf6] 17 ... ♕e7 18 ♖h3 ♗xb3 19 axb3 ♕e5 20 ♕f3 d5?! 21 ♖f1? [21 ♗g3! dxe4 (21 ... ♕e7 22 ♖e1±) 22 ♘xe4 ♕e7 (22 ... ♕xf5?? 23 ♕xf5 ♘xf5 24 ♘xc5+–) 23 ♖e1±] 21 ... ♗b4 22 ♗g3 ♕e7 23 ♗f4 ♗xd2 24 ♗xd2 dxe4 25 dxe4 ♘f7± 26 ♗f4 ♖ae8 27 ♖e1 ♕c5 28 ♕f2! ♕a5 29 ♗d2 ♕b6 30 b4 h6 31 ♔h1 ♘g5 32 ♗xg5 fxg5 33 ♕d2 ♕b5!? 34 ♖d3? [34 ♕xg5? ♖xf5!; 34 ♕xd4!? ♖xf5 35 ♖f3 ♖ff8=] 34 ... ♕e5 35 g4 g6 36 ♖f3 b6 37 h4 ♔g7 38 h5 gxh5 39 gxh5 ♖d8 [△ 40 ... ♕e8] 40 ♕g2 c5 41 bxc5 bxc5 42 ♕e2 ♖d7 43 ♔g2 ♖f6 44 ♔h3 ♖df7 45 b3 g4+ 46 ♔xg4 ♔h7 47 ♔h3 ♖g7 48 ♕h2 ♕e8 49 ♖g3 ♖e7! 50 ♕g1 ♕xh5+ 51 ♔g2 ♕e8 52 ♔f2 ♖xe4 53 ♖xe4 [53 ♖g7+ ♔h8 54 ♖g8+ ♕xg8 55 ♕xg8+ ♔xg8 56 ♖xe4 ♖xf5–+; 53 ♖f3 ♖xe1 54 ♕xe1 ♕xe1+ 55 ♔xe1 ♔g7–+] 53 ... ♖xf5+ 54 ♔e2 ♕xe4+ **0-1** M954-1856

**1856̂-★LP-1**
**Loyd, T.–Perrin, F.**

[Staunton]

1 d4 d5 2 c4 e6 3 ♘f3 c5 4 e3 ♘c6 5 ♘c3 cxd4 6 exd4 ♘f6 7 a3 ♗e7 8 b3 0-0 9 ♗d3 b6 10 0-0 ♗b7 11 cxd5? ♘xd5 12 ♘xd5 ♕xd5 13 ♗b2 ♖ad8 [△ ... e5] 14 ♕c2 ♕h5 15 ♗e4 ♖c8 16 ♕d2 f5 17 ♗d3 ♘a5 18 ♕e3 ♗d5 19 ♗a6 ♖c2 20 ♖ab1 ♘xb3 21 ♗b7 ♗xb7 22 ♕xb3 ♗xf3 23 gxf3 [23 ♕xc2??] 23 ... ♖f6! 24 ♗c1 ♖g6+ 25 ♔h1 ♕h3 26 ♖g1 ♖xf2 27 ♗f4 ♖h6 28 ♖b2 ♕xh2+ 29 ♗xh2 ♖hxh2# **0-1** M954-1856

**1856̂-★LP-2**
**Perrin, F.–Loyd, T.**

New York [Staunton]

1 e4 e5 2 ♘f3 ♘c6 3 ♗c4 ♗c5 4 b4 ♗xb4 5 c3 ♗a5 6 d4 exd4 7 0-0 ♗b6 8 e5 d5 9 exd6 cxd6 10 ♖e1+ ♘ge7 11 ♘g5 d5 12 ♕h5 g6 13 ♕h6 ♗e6

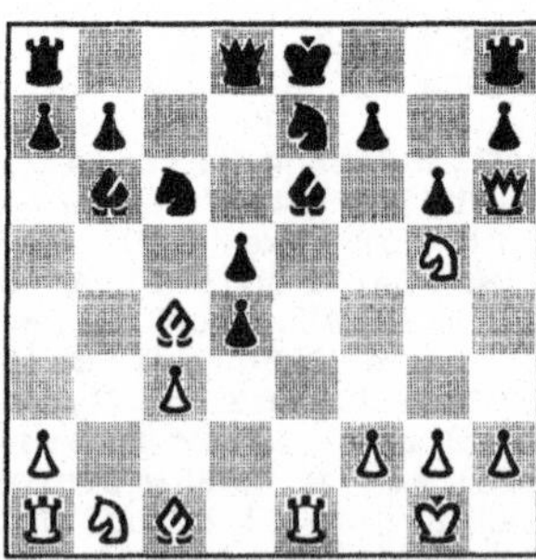

14 ♕g7? [14 ♖xe6 fxe6 (14 ... dxc4 15 ♕g7 fxe6 16 ♕f7+ ♔d7 17 ♕xe6+ ♔e8 18 ♘e4+–) 15 ♕g7 ♖g8 16 ♕f7+ ♔d7 17 ♕xe6+ ♔e8 18 ♘xh7+–] 14 ... ♖g8 15 ♕xh7 dxc4 16 ♘e4? [16 ♖xe6 fxe6 17 ♕f7+ ♔d7 18 ♕xe6+ ♔e8 19 ♘e4+–] 16 ... ♔d7 17 ♘f6+ ♔c8 18 ♘xg8 ♕xg8 19 ♕xg8+ ♘xg8 20 ♘d2 dxc3 21 ♘xc4 ♗xc4 22 ♖e8+ ♗d8 23 ♖xg8 b5 24 ♗g5 ♔b7 25 ♗xd8 ♖xd8 26 ♖xd8 ♘xd8 27 ♖c1 b4 28 a3 a5 **0-1** M954-1856

**1856̂-★LP-3**
**Loyd, T.+Perrin, F.**

New York

1 d4 d5 2 c4 e6 3 ♘f3 ♘c6 4 e3 ♗e7 5 ♗d3 ♘f6 6 0-0 0-0 7 a3 b6 8 b4 a6 9 ♘c3 ♗b7 10 ♕c2 h6 11 ♗b2 dxc4 12 ♗xc4 ♗d6 13 ♖ad1 ♕e7 14 e4 e5 15 ♘d5 ♘xd5 16 ♗xd5 ♘xd4 17 ♘xd4 ♗xd5 18 ♘f5 ♕e6 19 ♖xd5 ♖ad8 20 ♘xd6 cxd6 21 ♕c6 f5 22 ♖xe5 ♕b3 23 ♕d5+ **1-0** M954-1856

**1856̂-★LS-1**
**Staunton,H. & ?+ Löwenthal,J.J. & ?**

London [Staunton]

1 e4 e5 2 ♘f3 ♘c6 3 ♗b5 ♘ge7 4 c3 d6 5 d4 ♗d7 6 0-0 ♘g6 7 d5 ♘b8 8 ♗d3 ♗e7 9 ♘e1 ♗g5 10 g3 ♗h3 11 ♘g2 h5 12 f4 ♗xg2 13 ♔xg2 exf4 14 gxf4 ♗f6 [14 ... ♗xf4? 15 ♖xf4 ♕g5+ 16 ♔h1 ♗xf4 17 ♕f3±] 15 ♔h1 ♘d7 16 ♗e3 ♕e7 17 ♘d2 a6 18 ♕e2± ♗h4? 19 ♘f3 ♘c5 20 ♘d4 ♘xd3 21 ♕xd3 ♗f6 22 ♘f5 ♕d7 23 b4 ♘e7 24 ♘d4 ♗xd4 25 ♗xd4 f6 26 ♖g1 ♔f7 27 c4 ♖ag8 28 a4 h4 29 b5 a5 30 c5 dxc5 31 ♗xc5 ♖h6 32 ♗xe7 ♕xe7 33 e5 g6 34 ♖ac1 ♖d8 35 b6 c6 36 d6 ♕e6 37 ♖c5 f5 38 ♖e1 ♔g8 39 ♖xa5 ♖h7 40 ♖c5 ♖hd7 41 ♕e2 ♖e8

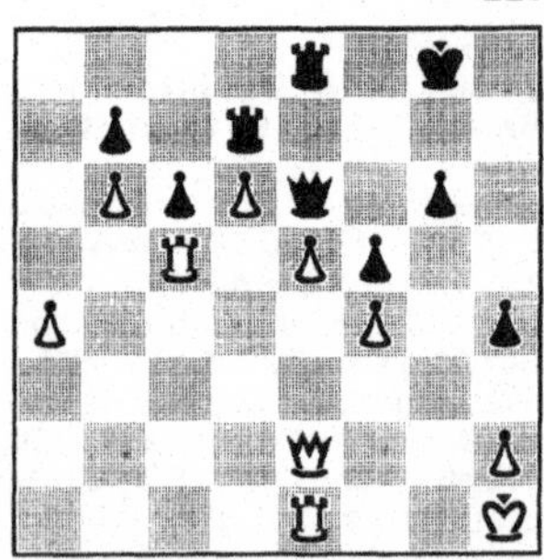

42 ♕f2? [42 a5!] 42 ... ♖xd6?? 43 ♕xh4?? [43 exd6 ♕xe1+ 44 ♕xe1 ♖xe1+ 45 ♔g2 ♖d1 (45 ... ♔f7 46 ♖e5 ♖a1 47 ♖e7++–) 46 a5 ♖xd6 47 a6 bxa6 48 b7 ♖d8 49 ♖xc6+–] 43 ... ♔g7 44 ♖g1 ♖dd8 45 a5 ♖d2 46 ♕g3 ♖h8 47 h3 ♖b2 48 ♖g2 ♖b1+ 49 ♔h2 ♖d8 50 ♖gc2 ♖dd1 51 ♕f3 ♕d7! 52 ♕c3 ♖h1+ 53 ♔g3 ♕d1 54 e6+ ♔h7 55 e7 ♖xh3+ 56 ♔xh3 ♕h5+ 57 ♔g2 ♕h1+ 58 ♔g3 ♖g1+ 59 ♔f2 ♖g2+ 60 ♔e3 ♕g1+ 61 ♔d3 ♕f1+ 62 ♔e3 ♖g3+ 63 ♔d2 ♕xf4+ 64 ♔d1? [64 ♔e2=] 64 ... ♖g1+ 65 ♕e1 ♕d4+ 66 ♖d2 ♕a1+ 67 ♖c1 ♕xc1+ 68 ♔xc1 ♖xe1+ 69 ♔c2 ♖xe7 70 ♖d8 ♔h6 71 ♖c8 ♖e5??+– 72 a6 bxa6 73 b7 ♖b5 74 b8=♕ ♖xb8 75 ♖xb8 f4 76 ♔d2 ♔g5 77 ♔e2 ♔g4 78 ♔f2 g5 79 ♖c8 **1-0** M954-1856

**1856̂-★RS-1**
**Recsi+ Szén, J.**

[Staunton]

1 e4 e5 2 ♘f3 ♘c6 3 ♗c4 ♗c5 4 b4 ♗xb4 5 c3 ♗c5 6 0-0 d6 7 d4 exd4 8 cxd4 ♗b6 9 ♗b2 ♘f6 10 ♘bd2 d5 11 exd5 ♘xd5 12 ♖e1+ ♗e6 13 ♘e4 0-0 [□ 13 ... h6] 14 ♘fg5 h6 15 ♘xe6 fxe6 16 ♕g4 ♕d7

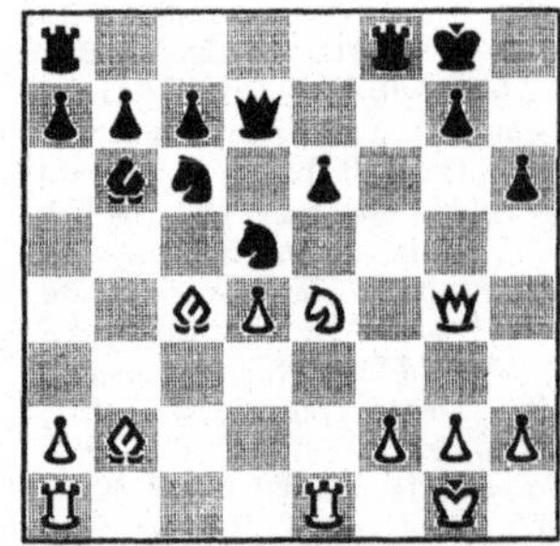

17 ♘c5 ♗xc5 18 dxc5 ♖ae8 19 ♖xe6 ♖xe6 20 ♗xd5 ♖e8 21 ♖ad1 ♕f7 22 f4! ♔h7 23 f5 ♖e1+ 24 ♖xe1 ♖xe1+ 25 ♔f2 **1-0**

M954-1856

**1856̂-★RS-2**
**Recsi–Szén, J.**
[Staunton]

1 e4 e5 2 ♘f3 ♘c6 3 ♗c4 ♗c5 4 b4 ♗xb4 5 c3 ♗c5 6 0-0 d6 7 d4 exd4 8 cxd4 ♗b6 9 ♗b2 ♘f6 10 ♘bd2 d5 11 exd5 ♘xd5 12 ♖e1+ ♗e6 13 ♘e4 h6 14 ♗a3 a6 15 ♕a4 ♗a5 16 ♘e5 ♗xe1 17 ♖xe1? [17 ♘xc6 b5 (17 ... ♘b6 18 ♘xd8+ ♘xa4 19 ♘xe6+−) 18 ♕c2 ♕h4 (18 ... ♕d7) 19 ♗xd5 ♗xd5 20 ♖xe1+−] 17 ... ♘b6 18 ♗xe6 fxe6 [18 ... ♘xa4?? 19 ♗xf7#] 19 ♕b3? [19 ♕c2 ♕d5 (19 ... ♘xd4 20 ♘d6+ cxd6 21 ♕g6++−; 19 ... ♘xe5 20 dxe5+−) 20 ♘c3 ♕xd4 21 ♕g6+ ♔d8 22 ♘xc6+ Δ 23 ♖d1+−; 22 ♕xg7 Δ 23 ♕xh8++−] 19 ... ♕d5 20 ♕xd5 ♘xd5 21 ♘g6 ♖g8 22 ♘c5 ♘xd4 23 ♖e4 ♘c3 24 ♖e3 0-0-0! 25 ♘e7+ ♔b8 26 ♔f1 ♘d5 27 ♘xg8 ♘xe3+ 28 fxe3 ♘b5 29 ♘xe6 ♖xg8 30 ♗b2 g6 **0-1**
M954-1856

**1856̂-★RS-3**
**Schulten, J.W.–Rivière, J.A. de**
Paris [Staunton]

1 e4 c5 2 ♗c4 e6 3 ♘c3 ♘c6 4 f4 ♘ge7 5 e5 ♘f5 6 ♘f3 d5 7 exd6 ♗xd6 8 d3 a6 9 a4 ♕c7 10 ♘e4 b6 11 ♘xd6+ ♘xd6 12 0-0 0-0 13 ♗b3 ♘d4 14 ♘xd4 cxd4 15 ♗d2 ♗b7 16 c3 ♘f5 17 ♖c1 ♕c5 18 ♖f2 ♖fd8 19 cxd4 ♕xd4 20 ♖c7 ♖ab8 21 ♗c3 ♕xd3 22 ♕g4 ♕d6 23 ♗e5 [□ 23 ♖xf7+−] 23 ... ♕f8 24 ♖e2 ♖bc8 25 ♖ec2 ♕b4 26 ♖2c3 ♖xc7 27 ♗xc7 ♖d2 28 ♗e5 h5 29 ♕xh5 ♖xg2+ 30 ♔f1 ♕e4 31 ♗c2 ♖g1+ **0-1**
M954-1856

**1856̂-★S♀-1**
**♀–Staunton, H.**
London [Staunton]

⟨Δf7⟩ 1 e4 d6 2 d4 ♘f6 3 ♗d3 ♘c6 4 ♘e2 e6 5 0-0 ♗e7 6 f4 0-0 7 e5 dxe5 8 fxe5 ♘xe5!? 9 dxe5 ♗c5+ 10 ♔h1 ♘g4 11 ♗f4 [11 ♖xf8+? ♕xf8−+] 11 ... ♘f2+ 12 ♖xf2 ♗xf2 13 ♘d2 ♗d7 14 ♘e4 ♗b6 15 ♘g5 h6 [15 ... ♖xf4? 16 ♘xe6! ♗xe6 17 ♘xf4 ♕e8 18 ♕e2 (Δ 19 ♘xe6) 18 ... ♗f7 19 ♖f1 ♗g6 (19 ... ♖d8 20 e6) 20 ♘xg6 hxg6 21 ♗c4+ ♔h8 22 ♖f3+−] 16 ♘h7 ♖f7 17 ♗g6 ♗b5 18 ♗d2? [18 ♗xf7+ Δ 19 ♘c3] 18 ... ♖f2 19 ♘f4 ♖f1+ 20 ♕xf1 ♗xf1 21 ♖xf1 ♕xd2 22 ♘xe6 [Δ 23 ♘hf8, 24 ♗f7+=] 22 ... ♕e2 23 ♗d3 ♕xf1+! 24 ♗xf1 ♔xh7 25 ♗d3+ ♔g8 26 ♗c4 ♔h8 27 ♘f4 g5 28 ♘d3 ♔g7 29 g4 ♖e8 30 c3 c6 31 ♔g2 ♗c7 32 e6 ♔f6 33 a4 ♔e7 34 ♘c5 ♖f8 35 h3 [35 ♘xb7 ♖b8] 35 ... b6 36 ♘b3 c5 37 ♘d2 ♖f4 38 ♗b3 a6 39 ♗c4 b5 40 axb5 axb5 41 ♗d5 ♔d6 42 b4 cxb4 [42 ... ♔xd5?? 43 e7] 43 cxb4 ♖d4 **0-1** M954-1857

**1856̂-★S♀-1**
**Staunton, H.+♀**

1 e4 e6 2 ♘f3 ♘c6 3 d4 d5 4 e5 a6 5 ♗d3 ♘b4 6 0-0 c5 7 ♗g5 f6 8 exf6 ♘xf6 9 c4 ♘xd3 10 ♕xd3 ♗e7 11 dxc5 0-0 12 ♘c3 dxc4 13 ♕xc4 b5 14 ♕e2 ♗xc5 15 ♗xf6 gxf6 16 ♘e4 ♗e7 17 ♖fd1 ♕b6 18 ♖ac1 ♗b7 19 ♘d6 e5 20 ♘f5 **1-0**
M954-1856

## MANCHESTER 1857

**1857-MNC-1** viii 57
**Horwitz, B.–Löwenthal, J.J.**
[Löwenthal]

1 e4 e5 2 ♘f3 d6 3 ♗c4 ♗e7 4 d4 exd4 5 ♘xd4 ♘f6 6 ♘c3 c6 7 0-0 0-0 8 ♗d3 d5 9 exd5 [□ 9 e5] 9 ... cxd5 10 ♗g5 ♘c6 11 ♘f5 ♗xf5 12 ♗xf5 d4= 13 ♘e2 ♕d5 14 ♘g3 g6 15 ♗xf6 ♗xf6 16 ♗e4 ♕c5 17 ♗xc6 ♕xc6 18 ♕d3 ♖ac8 19 ♖ac1 ♖fe8 20 ♘e2 ♕c4 21 ♘f4 ♕xd3 22 ♘xd3 ♖e2−+ 23 ♘b4! a5 24 ♘d5 ♗g7 25 c3 ♖c5 26 ♘f4 ♖d2! [26 ... ♖e4 27 ♘d3] 27 ♖b1! dxc3 28 bxc3 ♗xc3 29 ♖xb7 ♗e5 30 ♘h3 ♖xa2 31 ♘g5 ♗xh2+ 32 ♔xh2 ♖xg5 33 g3 ♖f5 34 ♔g2 h5

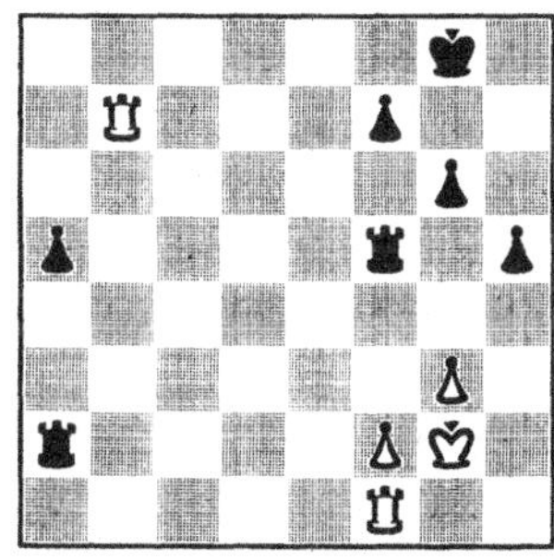

35 ♖a7 ♖b5 36 ♔h3 ♖bb2 37 ♔g2 ♔g7 38 ♔g1 g5 39 ♖a6 f6 40 ♖a7+ ♔g6 41 ♔g2 a4 42 ♔g1 a3 43 ♔g2 g4 44 ♖a5 ♖b3 45 ♖a4 ♖c3 46 ♔g1 ♖b2 47 ♔g2 a2 48 ♖a1 ♖cc2 49 ♖f1 ♖d2 50 ♖a6 ♖e2 51 ♖a7 ♖ec2 52 ♖a8 ♖d2 53 ♖a5! [53 ♔g1 ♖b1−+] 53 ... f5 [53 ... ♖b1 54 ♖xa2=] 54 ♖a6+ ♔g5 55 ♖a5 ♖d3 56 ♔g1 h4! 57 gxh4+ ♔xh4 58 ♖a8 [58 ♖xf5 ♖b1−+] 58 ... ♖dd2 59 ♔g2 g3 60 ♖a4+ ♔g5 61 ♔xg3 ♖b1 62 f4+ ♔h5 63 ♖xa2 ♖b3+ **0-1** +3

**1857-MNC-2** viii 57
**Anderssen, A.+Harrwitz, D.**
[Löwenthal]

1 e4 e5 2 ♘f3 d6! 3 ♗c4 ♗e7 4 d3 ♘c6 5 c3 ♘f6 6 h3 0-0 7 ♗b3 ♗e6 8 ♗g5 ♘h5 9 ♗xe7 ♕xe7 [Δ ... ♘f4; ... ♘g6] 10 g3 h6 11 ♘bd2 g6! [Δ ... ♘g7; ... ♘e6] 12 ♘h4 ♔h7 13 ♘g2 ♘g7 14 ♗xe6 ♘xe6 15 ♘e3 f5 16 ♕e2 ♕f7 17 h4 f4 18 ♘c2 h5 19 ♖f1 b5 20 ♘f3 ♔g8 [□ 20 ... ♔h8] 21 0-0-0 ♘c5 22 ♔b1 a5 23 ♘g5 ♕d7 24 d4 ♘a4 25 ♖g1 exd4? 26 cxd4 ♘e7 27 f3 b4 28 d5! [Δ 29 ♘d4] 28 ... ♖ab8 29 ♘d4 fxg3 30 ♘ge6 ♖fe8 31 ♖xg3 ♘c3+?! 32 bxc3 bxc3+ 33 ♔a1 ♖b2 [33 ... ♕a4 34 ♕c2] 34 ♕c4 ♖eb8 35 ♘b3 c2 36 ♖c1 ♖b1+ 37 ♖xb1 cxb1♕+ 38 ♔xb1 ♔f7 [38 ... a4 39 ♕c3 ♘f5 (39 ... ♘c8 40 ♖xg6++−) 40 exf5 axb3 41 ♖xg6++−] 39 ♕c3 ♖g8 40 ♕xa5 c6 41 ♘g5+ ♔g7 42 ♕c3+!!

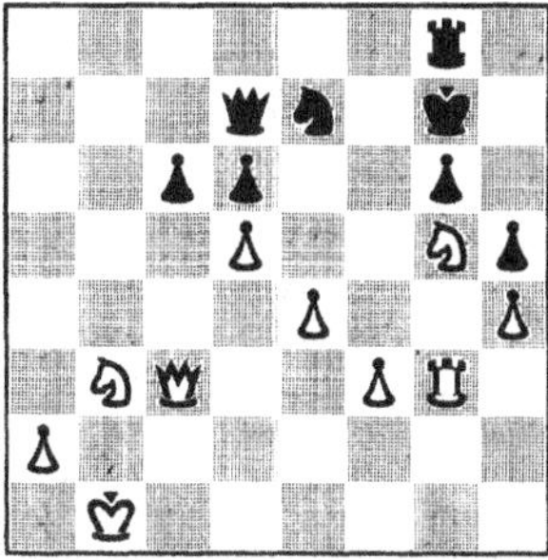

42 ... ♔h6 43 ♕f6 cxd5 44 ♕f7 ♖g7 45 ♕f8 ♘g8 46 ♘d4 ♕b7+ 47 ♔c2 ♕a6 48 ♘f5+ gxf5 49 ♘f7+ [49 ... ♔h7 50 ♕xg7#] **1-0** +3

**1857-MNC-4** viii 57
**Brien, R.B.–Pindar, E.**
[Löwenthal]

1 d4 d5 2 c4 e6 3 e3 c5 4 ♘f3 ♘f6 5 a3 a6 6 ♘c3 ♘c6 7 ♗d3 ♗e7 8 b3 b6 9 ♗b2 ♗b7 10 cxd5 exd5 11 0-0 cxd4 12 exd4 0-0 13 ♖c1 ♖c8 14 ♗b1 ♗d6 15 ♖e1 ♖e8 16 ♕d3 ♘e7= 17 ♘e5 ♘g6! 18 ♘xg6 hxg6 19 ♕f3 ♖xe1+ 20 ♖xe1 ♕c7!−+ 21 ♕h3 ♗xa3 22 ♘xd5 ♘xd5 23 ♗xa3 ♘f4 **0-1** +3

**1857-MNC-5** viii 57
**Löwenthal, J.J.+Anderssen, A.**
[Löwenthal]

1 e4 c5 2 ♘f3 e6 3 d4 cxd4 4 ♘xd4 [4 ♘xd4 ♘c6 5 ♘b5 d6 (5 ... d5 6 exd5 exd5 7 ♕xd5; 5 ... ♗c5 6 ♘d6+ ♗xd6 7 ♕xd6±) 6 ♗f4 e5 7 ♗g3±; 4 ... ♗c5 5 ♘b5 ♕b6 (5 ... d6 6 ♗e3) 6 ♗e3 ♗xe3 7 fxe3 ♕xe3+ 8 ♗e2±; 4 ... d5 5 exd5 exd5 6 ♗b5+ ♗d7 7 0-0] 4 ... ♘c6 5 ♘b5 a6 6 ♘d6+ ♗xd6 7 ♕xd6 ♘ge7 [7 ... ♕e7 8 e5] 8

♗e3 f5 9 ♗d3 0-0 10 ♘c3 fxe4 11 ♗xe4 ♘f5 12 ♗xf5 ♖xf5 13 0-0-0 ♕a5 14 g4 ♖f7 15 f4 b5 16 ♔b1 ♗b7 17 ♖hf1 ♖e8 18 ♗c5 ♕d8 19 ♘e4 [△ ♘g5] 19 ... h6 20 g5? [□ 20 ♕d3+-] 20 ... ♘e7 21 ♗b6 ♕a8 22 ♘g3 ♘c8 23 ♕d4 ♘xb6 24 ♕xb6 ♗g2 25 ♖g1 hxg5 26 fxg5 g6 27 ♕d6 ♕c6 28 ♕d3 ♔g7 29 ♕e2 ♗d5 30 ♕e5+ ♔g8 [30 ... ♔h7 31 ♖d4 △ 32 ♖h4+ 33 ♕h8#] 31 ♖d4 [△ 32 ♖h4] 31 ... ♕c5 [△ ... ♗xa2+] 32 ♖e1 ♖c8 [32 ... d6 33 ♖xd5+-] 33 ♖d2 ♕c7 34 b3 ♕xe5 35 ♖xe5 ♖f4 36 ♘e2 ♖f1+ 37 ♔b2 ♖e1 38 ♖e3 [38 ♘f4 ♖xe5 39 ♘xg6 ♖xg5 40 ♘e7+ ♔f7 41 ♘xc8 ♔e8] 38 ... ♖f8 39 ♖ed3 ♖f7 40 ♘c3 ♗c6 41 a3 ♖f5 42 h4 ♖h1 43 ♖d4 d5 44 ♖g4 ♔f7 45 ♘d1 ♖f3 46 ♖f2 d4?? 47 ♖f4+ ♔e7 48 ♖2xf3 ♗xf3 49 ♘f2 ♗d5 50 ♘xh1 **1-0** +3

**1857-MNC-6** viii 57
**Pindar, E.– Boden, S.S.**
[Löwenthal]

1 e4 e5 2 ♘f3 d6 3 d4 exd4 4 ♘xd4 ♘f6 [4 ... d5] 5 ♘c3 ♗e7 6 ♗d3 0-0 7 0-0 c5 8 ♘de2 ♘c6 9 f4 a6 10 a4 ♗g4 11 h3 ♗xe2 12 ♘xe2 ♘b4 13 c3 ♘xd3 14 ♕xd3 d5! 15 e5 [□ 15 exd5] 15 ... c4 16 ♕f3 ♘e4 17 ♘d4 ♗c5 18 ♔h2 ♗xd4 19 cxd4 f5 20 ♗e3 ♕b6 21 ♕e2 ♖ae8 22 ♖g1 ♔h8 23 g4 ♕e6 24 gxf5 ♕xf5 25 ♕g4 g6 26 ♖g2 ♖e6 27 ♖ag1 ♔g7 28 h4 ♕xg4 29 ♖xg4 ♖f5 30 ♖1g2?? ♖b6 [30 ... h5] 31 ♗c1 h5 32 ♖g5 ♘xg5 33 hxg5 ♔f7 34 ♖g3 ♔e6 35 a5 ♖b3 36 ♖xb3 cxb3 37 ♗d2 ♖f8 38 ♔g3 ♖c8 **0-1** +3

**1857-MNC-7** viii 57
**Boden, S.S.= Löwenthal, J.J.**
[Löwenthal]

1 e4 e5 2 ♘f3 d6 3 d4 exd4 4 ♕xd4 ♗d7 5 ♗e3 ♘c6 6 ♕d2 ♘f6 7 ♗d3 ♗e7 8 ♘c3 h6 9 h3 ♘e5 10 ♘h2!! [△ f4] 10 ... ♘h7 11 ♘e2 ♗f6 12 f4 ♘xd3+ 13 cxd3 ♗h4+ 14 g3 ♗e7 15 ♘f3 f5 [□ 15 ... 0-0] 16 ♖c1 ♗c6 17 ♘ed4 fxe4 18 dxe4 ♗d7 [18 ... ♗xe4?? 19 ♘e4 △ 20 ♘xc7+] 19 e5 dxe5 20 ♘xe5 0-0? [□ 20 ... ♗d6] 21 ♕c3! ♘f6 22 ♕xc7 ♗b4+ 23 ♔f2 ♕e7 24 ♕c4+! ♔h7 25 ♕d3+ ♔g8 26 ♘g6 ♕e4 27 ♕xe4 ♘xe4+ 28 ♔f3 ♖fe8 29 ♘e5 ♘f6 30 ♖c7 ♗d6 [□ 30 ... ♕e7] 31 ♖xd7 ♗xe5 32 ♖xb7 ♗d6 33 ♘f5 ♗f8 34 ♗d4 ♖e6 35 ♖c1 g6 36 ♗xf6 ♖xf6 37 ♘e7+ ♔h8 38 ♖cc7 a5 39 ♔g4 ♖aa6 40 h4 h5+ 41 ♔h3 a4 42 ♘d5 ♖f5 43 ♖f7 ♖xf7 44 ♖xf7 ♗g7!

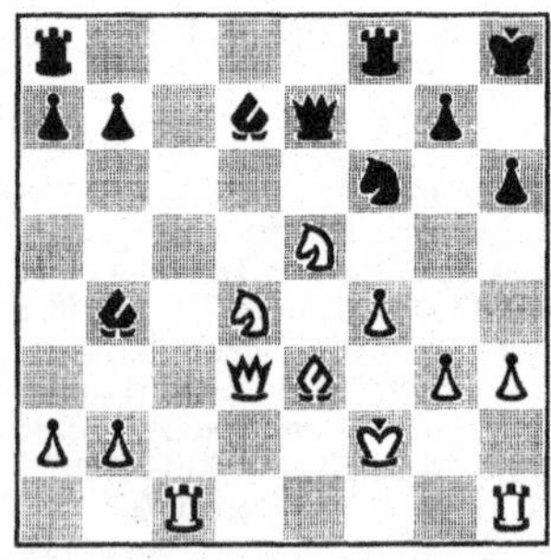

45 ♖b7 ♖d6 46 ♘b6 ♖d4 47 a3 ♖e4 48 ♖a7 ♗xb2 49 ♖xa4 ♖xa4 50 ♘xa4 ♗xa3 **½-½** +3

## NEW YORK CITY 1857

**1857-NYC1-1** 5x57
**Thompson, J.–Morphy, P.C**
[Fiske]

1 e4 e5 2 ♘f3 ♘c6 3 ♗c4 ♗c5 4 d3 ♘f6! [4 ... d6] 5 ♘c3 h6 6 ♘e2 d6 7 c3 0-0 8 h3 ♔h8 9 ♘g3 ♘h7 [△ 10 ... f5] 10 ♕c2? f5 11 exf5 d5! 12 ♗b3 e4 13 dxe4 dxe4 14 ♘g1 ♘e5 15 ♗e3 ♘d3+ 16 ♔e2 ♗xe3 17 fxe3 ♕h4 18 ♘xe4 ♕xe4 19 ♕xd3 ♕xg2+ 20 ♔d1 ♗xf5 21 ♕e2 ♕xh1 **0-1** L/N 5184

**1857-NYC1-2** 6x57
**Morphy, P.C.+Thompson, J.**
[Fiske]

1 e4 c5 2 ♘f3 ♘c6 3 d4 cxd4 4 ♘xd4 e6 5 ♗e3 ♗e7 6 ♘c3 h6 7 ♗d3 d5 8 ♗b5 ♗d7? [8 ... ♕d6 9 e5±] 9 exd5 exd5 10 ♘xd5 ♘f6 11 ♘xf6+ ♗xf6 12 c3 0-0 13 0-0 ♕c7 14 ♕a4 ♖fe8 15 ♖ad1 ♖e4 16 ♗xc6 ♗xc6 17 ♕c2 ♗e5 18 g3 ♗xd4 19 cxd4 ♕e7 20 d5 ♗d7 21 ♗c5 ♖ac8 22 ♗xe7 ♖xc2 23 ♗a3 b5 24 ♖fe1 f5 25 f3 ♖xe1+ 26 ♖xe1 ♖d2 27 d6 a5 28 ♗c5 b4 29 ♖e7 ♖d5 30 ♗xb4 axb4 31 ♖xd7 ♔f8 32 ♖b7 ♖d4 33 ♔f2 ♖xd6 34 ♖xb4 ♖d2+ 35 ♔e3 ♖xh2 36 a4 ♖c2 37 a5 ♖c5 38 ♖a4 ♔e7 39 b4 ♖c8 40 b5 ♖b8 41 a6 ♔d7 42 b6 ♔c6 43 b7 ♔b6 44 a7 ♖e8+ 45 ♔f4 ♔xb7 46 a8♕+ ♖xa8 47 ♖xa8 ♔xa8 48 ♔xf5 **1-0** L/N 5184

**1857-NYC1-3** 7x57
**Thompson, J.–Morphy, P.C.**
[Fiske]

1 e4 e5 2 ♘f3 ♘c6 3 ♗c4 ♗c5 4 c3 ♘f6 5 d3 [5 d4] 5 ... d6 6 h3 ♗e6 7 ♗b3 [□ 7 ♗xe6] 7 ... d5 8 exd5 ♗xd5 [8 ... ♘xd5] 9 0-0 0-0 10 ♗g5 ♗xb3 11 axb3 h6 12 ♗h4 g5 13 ♗g3 e4 14 ♘e5 ♘xe5 15 ♗xe5 exd3 16 ♗xf6 ♕xf6 17 ♕xd3 ♖ad8 18 ♕c2 ♖fe8 19 b4 ♗b6 20 ♘a3 ♕f4 21 ♖ad1 c6∓ 22 ♖d3? ♗xf2+ 23 ♔h1 ♖xd3 24 ♕xd3 ♖e3 25 ♕d8+ ♔g7 26 ♕d4+ ♕xd4 27 cxd4 ♖e2 28 ♘c4 ♖e1 29 ♖xe1 ♗xe1 30 ♘a5 ♗xb4 31 ♘xb7 ♔f6 32 ♘d8 c5 33 ♘c6 ♔e6 34 dxc5 ♗xc5 35 g4 ♔d5 36 ♘d8 f6 37 ♔g2 a5 38 ♔f3 a4 39 ♔e2 ♗d4 40 ♔d3 ♗xb2 41 ♘f7 ♗e5 42 ♔c2 ♔c4 43 ♘d8 a3 44 ♘b7 a2 45 ♘a5+ ♔b4 46 ♘b3 ♔a3 **0-1** L/N 5184

**1857-NYC1-4** 6x57
**Raphael, B.I.– Kennicott, H.**
[Fiske]

1 e4 e5 2 ♘f3 ♘c6 3 d4 cxd4 4 ♗c4 ♗c5 5 0-0 [□ 5 c3] 5 ... d6 6 c3 d3 [□ 6 ... dxc3 7 ♘xc3 ♘ge7 8 ♘g5 ♘e5 9 b4 ♗b6 10 ♕b3 0-0∓] 7 b4 ♗b6 8 ♕xd3 ♗e6 9 ♗xe6 fxe6 10 a4 a6 11 ♘a3 e5 12 ♘c4 ♗a7 13 ♗e3 ♘f6 14 ♗xa7 ♖xa7 15 ♖ad1 ♘d7 [15 ... 0-0 16 b5 axb5 17 axb5 ♘e7 18 ♘cxe5] 16 ♕e3 b6 17 b5 axb5 18 axb5 ♘cb8 19 ♘g5 h6 20 ♘h3 0-0 21 f4 ♕e7 22 ♖f3 ♖a4 23 ♘d2 ♘f6 24 fxe5 ♕xe5 25 c4 ♘bd7 26 ♘f2 ♖e8 27 h3 ♘c5 28 ♖f1 d5 29 ♖f5?? ♕xf5 30 ♘d3 ♕e6 31 ♘f4 ♕d7 32 ♘g6 ♘cxe4 33 ♘xe4 ♖xe4 34 ♕g3 ♖axc4 35 ♖xf6 gxf6 36 ♘e7+ ♔f7 **0-1** L/N5184

**1857-NYC1-5** 7x57
**Kennicott, H.– Raphael, B.I.**
[Fiske]

1 e4 e5 2 ♘f3 ♘f6 3 ♘xe5 d6 4 ♘f3 ♘xe4 5 d4 ♗e7 6 ♗d3 f5 7 c4 0-0 8 0-0 b6 9 ♕c2 ♘g5 10 ♘xg5 ♗xg5 11 f4 ♗f6 12 ♗e3 ♘c6 13 d5?? [□ 13 ♕c3] 13 ... ♘b4 14 ♕d2 ♘xd3 15 ♕xd3 ♗xb2 16 ♗d4 ♗xa1 17 ♗xa1 ♗b7 18 ♖f3 ♕d7 19 ♘d2 ♖ae8 20 ♔f2 ♕e7 21 ♖e3 ♕xe3+ 22 ♕xe3 ♖xe3 23 ♔xe3 ♖e8+ 24 ♔f2 ♗a6 25 a4 c6 26 dxc6 ♖c8 27 ♔e3 ♖xc6 28 ♔d4 ♖c8 29 ♗c3 ♔f7 30 ♔d5 ♗b7+ 31 ♔xd6 ♗xg2 32 ♔d7 ♖e8 33 ♗xg7 ♖e3 34 ♗d4 ♖d3 **0-1** L/N5184

**1857-NYC1-6** 8x57
**Raphael, B.I.= Kennicott, H.**
[Fiske]

1 d4 d5 2 c4 e6 3 e3 ♘f6 4 ♘c3 ♗e7 5 ♘f3 b6 6 b3 ♗b7 7 ♗b2 0-0 8 ♗e2 ♗b4 9 0-0 ♗xc3 10 ♗xc3 ♘e4 11 ♗b2 f5 12 ♕c2 ♘d7 13 ♖ac1 ♖c8 14 cxd5 exd5 15 ♗d3 c5 16 ♕b1 cxd4 17 ♖xc8 ♗xc8 18 ♗xd4 ♗b7 19 ♖c1 h6 20 ♕b2 ♖f7 21 ♗b5 ♘g5 22 ♘xg5 ♕xg5 23 ♖c7 ♘f6 24 ♗xf6 gxf6 25 ♖xf7 ♔xf7 26 ♕d4? [□ 26 ♕c3 ♕xg2+?? 27

♕xg2 d4+ 28 ♕c6 ♗xc6 29 ♗xc6+−] 26 ... ♕g4 27 ♗d7 ♕e2 28 ♕a1 f4 29 exf4 d4 30 ♕f1 ♕xa2 31 ♕c4+ ♔g7 32 h3 ♕a1+ 33 ♔h2 ♕c3 34 ♕e6 ♕c5 35 ♕g4+ ♔h8 36 ♕g6 ♕f8 37 ♗f5 ♕g7 38 ♔g1 ♕xg6 39 ♗xg6 ♗d5 40 ♗c2 d3 41 ♗xd3 ♗xb3 42 ♗a6 ♔g7 43 f3 ♔f7 44 ♔f2 ♔e6 45 ♔e3 ♔d6 46 g4 ♗e6 47 h4 ♗f7 48 g5 fxg5 49 fxg5 hxg5 50 hxg5 ♔c5 51 f4 b5 52 f5 b4 53 g6 ♗e8 54 ♗d3 ♔d6 55 ♗c4 ♔e7 56 g7 ♗f7 57 ♗xf7 ♔xf7 58 f6 a5 59 ♔d3 a4 60 ♔c4 a3 61 ♔b3 ½-½ L/N5184

**1857-NYC1-7** 9 x 57
**Raphael, B.I.– Kennicott, H.**
[Fiske]

1 e4 e5 2 f4 exf4 3 ♗c4 ♕h4+ 4 ♔f1 g5 5 ♘c3 ♗g7 6 g3 fxg3 7 ♔g2 ♕h6 8 hxg3 ♕g6 9 d4 d6 10 ♘f3 h6 11 ♘d5 ♔d8 12 ♖e1 c6 13 ♘c3 ♗g4 14 e5 ♗xf3+ 15 ♕xf3 d5 16 ♗d3 ♕e6 17 ♗f5 ♕e7 18 ♘a4 ♘a6 19 ♗d2 b5 20 ♘c5? [□ 20 ♘c3] 20 ... ♘xc5 21 ♗b4 ♗f8 22 ♗xc5 ♕e8 23 ♗d6 ♘e7 24 ♗h3 ♗g7 25 ♕a3 a5 26 ♕c5 ♘c8 27 e6 fxe6 28 ♖xe6 ♕d7 29 ♖ae1 ♖a6 30 ♖e8+ ♕xe8 31 ♖xe8+ ♖xe8 32 ♗xc8 ♔xc8 33 ♗e5 ♗xe5 34 dxe5 ♔b7 35 ♕d6 ♔b6 36 ♕xh6 ♖xe5 37 ♔f3 ♖a7 38 ♕d6 ♖ae7 39 c3 a4 40 ♕d8+ ♔c5 41 b3 axb3 42 axb3 ♖e4 43 ♕h8 **0-1** L/N5184

**1857-NYC1-8** 12 x 57
**Kennicott, H.– Raphael, B.I.**
[Fiske]

1 e4 c5 2 ♘f3 ♘c6 3 d4 cxd4 4 ♘xd4 e6 5 ♘b5 a6 6 ♘d6+ ♗xd6 7 ♕xd6 ♕e7 8 e5 f6 9 f4 fxe5 10 ♕c7 [10 fxe5 ♕h4+] 10 ... d5 11 ♕xe7+ ♘gxe7 12 fxe5 ♘xe5 13 b3 b5 14 ♗b2 ♘7c6 15 ♘d2 0-0 16 ♗e2 ♗b7 17 c3 ♖ac8 18 ♖c1 ♘g6 19 ♗f3 ♘ce5 20 ♔e2 ♘f4+ 21 ♔e3 ♘xf3 22 gxf3 e5 23 ♖hg1 b4

24 cxb4 d4+ **0-1** L/N5184

**1857-NYC1-9** 12 x 57
**Raphael, B.I.+ Kennicott, H.**
[Fiske]

1 e4 c5 2 ♘f3 e6 3 d4 d5 4 exd5 exd5 5 c4 ♘f6 6 ♗g5 ♗e7 7 ♗xf6 ♗xf6 8 cxd5 ♕xd5 9 ♘c3 ♕e6+ 10 ♗e2 ♗xd4 11 ♘xd4 cxd4 12 ♕xd4 0-0 13 0-0 ♘c6 14 ♕f4 ♕e5 15 ♕xe5 ♘xe5 16 f4 ♘g4 17 ♘d5 f5 18 h3 ♘h6 19 ♗c4 ♗e6 20 ♘e7+ ♔f7 21 ♗xe6+ ♔xe6 22 ♖fe1+ ♔f7 23 ♖e5 g6 24 ♘d5 ♘g8 25 g4 fxg4 26 hxg4 ♖ac8 27 ♖ae1 ♖fe8 28 ♖xe8 ♖xe8 29 ♖xe8 ♔xe8 30 ♔f2 ♔d7 31 ♔f3 ♔d6 32 ♘e3 ♘f6 33 g5 ♘d5 34 ♘c4+ ♔c5 35 ♘e5 ♔d6 36 ♔e4 ♔e6 37 a3 ♘e7 38 ♘d3 b6 39 b4 ♘f5 40 a4 ♘d6+ 41 ♔f3 ♔d5 42 ♘e5 ♘f5 43 b5 ♔c5?? 44 ♘d7+ ♔b4 45 ♘f8 ♔xa4 46 ♘xh7 ♔xb5 47 ♘f8 ♘e7 48 ♘xg6! ♘xg6 49 f5 ♘h4+ 50 ♔g4 ♘xf5 51 ♔xf5 a5 52 g6 a4 53 g7 a3 54 g8♕ **1-0** L/N5184

**30** Allison, W.S. M658.CPL

**1857-NYC1-10** 6 x 57
**Allison, W.S.– Montgomery, H.P.**
[Fiske]

1 e4 e5 2 ♘f3 ♘c6 3 ♗c4 ♗c5 4 c3 ♘f6 5 d3 0-0 6 a3? [□ 6 0-0] 6 ... d5 7 exd5 ♘xd5 8 0-0 ♔h8 9 b4 ♗b6 10 b5 ♘ce7 11 ♘xe5 ♘g6 12 ♕h5 ♕e6 13 ♘xg6+ fxg6 14 ♕e5 ♕d7 15 ♗h6 ♖f6 16 ♗e3 ♘xe3 17 fxe3 ♖xf1+ 18 ♔xf1 ♗xc4 19 dxc4 ♕d3+ 20 ♔e1 ♖f8 **0-1** L/N5184

**1857-NYC1-11** 6 x 57
**Montgomery, H.P.– Allison, W.S.**
[Fiske]

1 e4 e5 2 ♘f3 ♘c6 3 d4 exd4 4 ♗c4 ♗c5 5 ♘g5?! [□ 5 c3] 5 ... ♘h6 6 ♘xf7 ♘xf7 7 ♗xf7+ ♔xf7 8 ♕h5+ g6 9 ♕xc5 d6 10 ♕a3 a6? [□ 10 ... ♖e8] 11 0-0 ♖e8 12 ♘d2 b5 13 ♘f3 ♔g7 14 ♕d3 ♗e6 15 b3 d5 16 ♘xd4 dxe4 17 ♘xc6? [□ 17 ♘xe6+ ♖xe6 18 ♕h3] 17 ... exd3 18 ♘xd8 ♖axd8 19 cxd3 ♖xd3 20 ♗b2+ ♔g8 21 h3 ♖ed8 22 ♖fe1 ♔f7 23 ♖ac1 ♖8d7 24 ♖c6 ♖3d6 25 ♖ec1 ♖d2 26 ♖1c2 ♖xc2 27 ♖xc2 ♗d5 28 f4 c6 29 ♔f2 ♔e6 30 g4 ♖f7 31 ♖e2+ ♔d7 32 ♗e5 c5 33 ♔e3 c4 34 ♔d4 ♔c6 35 b4 a5 36 a3 a4 37 ♖f2 ♗h1 38 ♔c3 ♖d7 [Δ 39 ... ♖d3+] 39 ♗d4 [39 ♖d2 ♖d5] 39 ... ♖e7 40 f5 gxf5 41 ♖xf5 [□ 41 gxf5] 41 ... ♗d5 42 ♗e5 ♗e4 43 ♖f6+ ♔d5 44 ♗f4 ♗g6 45 ♖b6 ♔e4 46 ♗h2 ♗e8 47 h4 ♔f3 48 g5 ♖e3+ 49 ♔d4 [49 ♔b2 c3+→] 49 ... ♖xa3 50 h5 ♖d3+ 51 ♔c5 c3 52 ♗e5 ♔e4 53 ♖d6 ♖xd6 54 ♔xd6 c2 55 ♗b2 ♗xh5 56 ♔c5 ♗e2 57 ♗c1 ♗c4 58 ♔d6 ♔d3 59 ♔e5 ♔e2 **0-1** L/N5184

**1857-NYC1-12** 7 x 57
**Allison, W.S.– Montgomery, H.P.**

1 e4 e5 2 ♘f3 ♘c6 3 ♗c4 ♗c5 4 0-0 ♘f6 5 d3 h6 6 c3 d6 7 a4 a6 8 b4 ♗a7 9 a5 0-0 10 ♕b3 ♘e7 11 h3 c6 12 ♔h1?? [□ 12 d4] 12 ... d5 13 exd5 cxd5 14 ♘xe5 dxc4 15 ♕xc4 ♗e6 16 ♕f4 ♘g6 17 ♕h2 ♘xe5 18 ♕xe5 ♗b8 19 ♕e2 ♖e8 20 ♕c2 ♕d7 21 f3 ♘h5 22 ♖f2?? [□ 22 ♖e1→] 22 ... ♗b3 23 ♕d2 ♗f4 **0-1** L/N5184

**1857-NYC1-13** 7 x 57
**Montgomery, H.P.+ Allison, W.S.**
[Fiske]

1 e4 e5 2 ♘f3 ♘c6 3 ♗c4 ♗c5 4 b4 ♗xb4 5 c3 ♗a5 6 0-0 d6 7 d4 exd4 8 cxd4 ♗b6 9 d5 ♘a5? [□ 9 ... ♘ce7] 10 e5 ♘xc4 11 ♕a4+ ♗d7 12 ♕xc4 ♘e7 13 e6 fxe6 14 dxe6 ♗c6 15 ♗g5?! [□ 15 ♘g5] 15 ... 0-0? [□ 15 ... ♗xf3 16 gxf3 h6 17 ♕h4 ♖g8 18 ♗xe7 ♕xe7 19 ♕h5+ g6 20 ♕xh6 0-0-0; 18 ♗d2 ♘f5] 16 ♕h4 ♖e8 17 ♘bd2 h6 18 ♖fe1

18 ... hxg5 19 ♘xg5 ♕c8 20

♕h7+ ♔f8 21 ♕h8+ ♘g8 22 e7+ ♖xe7 23 ♖xe7 ♔xe7 24 ♕xg7+ ♔d8 25 ♕xg8+ ♗e8 26 ♖e1 ♔d7 27 ♘de4 ♔c6 28 ♕c4+ ♗c5 29 ♘xc5 dxc5 30 ♖e6+ **1-0** L/N5184

**1857-NYC1-14** 6x57
**Meek, A.B.+Fuller, W.J.A.**
[Fiske]

1 e4 e5 2 c3 ♘f6 [□ 2 ... d5] 3 d4 ♘xe4 4 dxe5 ♗c5? [□ 4 ... d5=] 5 ♕g4 ♘xf2 6 ♕xg7 ♖f8 7 ♗g5 f6 8 exf6 ♖f7 9 ♕g8+ ♗f8 10 ♔xf2 d5 11 ♘a3 ♕d6 12 ♖e1+ ♗e6 13 b4 [□ 13 ♘f3 ♕b6+ 14 ♘d4+-] 13 ... ♘d7 14 ♘f3 0-0-0 15 ♘b5 ♕b6+ 16 ♗e3 c5 17 ♕g3 ♘xf6 18 ♔g1 ♘e4 19 ♕e5 ♗g7 20 ♘xa7+ ♕xa7 21 ♕xe6+ ♖fd7 22 ♗b5 ♗xc3 23 ♗xd7+ ♖xd7 24 ♘e5 ♗xe5 25 ♕xe5 ♕xa2 26 ♖a1 **1-0** L/N5184

**1857-NYC1-16** 9x57
**Meek, A.B.–Fuller, W.J.A.**
[Fiske]

1 e4 e5 2 f4 exf4 3 ♘f3 g5 4 ♗c4 ♗g7 5 d4 d6 6 0-0 ♗e6? [□ 6 ... h6] 7 ♗b3? [□ 7 ♗xe6 △ c3, ♕b3] 7 ... h6 8 c3 ♘d7 9 ♗xe6 fxe6 10 ♕b3 ♘gf6 11 ♕xe6+ ♕e7 12 ♕xe7+ ♔xe7 13 ♘bd2 ♘g4 14 ♘c4 b6 15 h3 ♘gf6 16 e5 dxe5 17 ♘fxe5 ♖he8 18 b3 ♔d8 19 ♘c6+ ♔c8 20 ♗a3 ♘d5 21 ♗b2 ♔b7 22 ♘b4 ♗xd4+ 23 cxd4 ♘xb4 24 ♘e5?? ♘xe5 25 dxe5 ♘d3 26 ♗c3 ♘xe5 27 ♗xe5 ♖xe5 28 ♖ad1 ♖ae8 29 ♖d2 ♖e2 30 ♖fd1 ♖e1+ 31 ♖xe1 ♖xe1+ 32 ♔f2 ♖e6 33 ♔f3 h5 34 ♖e2 g4+ 35 hxg4 hxg4+ 36 ♔f2 ♖xe2+ 37 ♔xe2 ♔c6 38 ♔d3 ♔d5 39 a4 ♔e5 40 b4 f3 41 gxf3 gxf3 **0-1** L/N5184

**1857-NYC1-17** 9x57
**Meek, A.B.–Fuller, W.J.A.**
[Fiske]

1 e4 e6 2 d4 d5 3 e5 c5 4 f4 ♘c6 5 ♘f3 ♕b6 6 c3 ♘h6 7 ♕b3 ♘f5? [□ 7 ... ♕xb3] 8 ♕xb6 axb6 9 ♗b5 cxd4 10 ♘xd4 ♘xd4 11 cxd4 ♗d7 12 ♗xc6 [12 ♗e3 ♘xe5] 12 ... bxc6 13 ♗d2 c5 14 ♗c3 c4 15 0-0 b5 16 b4 cxb3?! 17 axb3 ♖xa1 18 ♗xa1 ♗b4 19 ♗c3 ♗xc3 20 ♘xc3 0-0 21 ♖a1 ♖c8 22 ♖a7 ♖xc3 23 ♖xd7 g6 24 ♖b7 ♖xb3 ...♀ **0-1** L/N5184

**1857-NYC1-18**
**Meek, A.B.+Fuller, W.J.A.**
[Fiske]

1 e4 e5 2 ♘f3 ♘c6 3 d4 exd4 4 c3 ♘f6 [□ 4 ... dxc3] 5 e5 ♕e7 6 cxd4 d6 7 ♗b5 ♗d7 8 0-0 dxe5 9 ♗xc6 ♗xc6 10 ♘xe5 ♗d7 11 ♖e1 ♗e6 12 ♘c3 0-0-0 13 ♗e3 ♘d5 14 ♘b5 a6 15 ♘a7+ **1-0** L/N5184

**1857-NYC1-19** 7x57
**Marache, N.–Fiske, D.W.**
[Fiske]

1 e4 c5 2 ♘f3 e6 3 d4 cxd4 4 ♘xd4 ♘c6 5 ♘f3 ♗c5 6 ♗d3 ♘ge7 7 0-0 0-0 8 ♘c3 h6 9 ♔h1 f5 10 exf5 ♘xf5 11 ♘e4 b6 12 c3 d5 13 ♘xc5? bxc5 14 ♕a4 ♘ce7 15 ♗b5 ♕c7 16 ♗f4 ♕b6 17 ♘e5 ♘d4 18 cxd4 ♖xf4 19 ♗d3 ♕d8 20 ♘c6 ♕c7 21 ♘xe7+ ♕xe7 22 ♕c6 ♖b8 23 dxc5 ♖fb4 24 ♖ae1 ♗d7 25 ♕xd5 ♖xb2 26 ♕e4 ♕xc5 27 ♕h7+ ♔f8 28 ♖e3 ♕d4 29 ♖f3+ ♔e7 30 ♖g3 ♖f8 31 ♖xg7+ ♔d8 32 ♖g8 ♕f6 33 f4 ♖d2 34 ♖g3 ♗c6 35 ♗e4 ♗b5 36 ♗d3 ♖f7 37 ♕e4 ♗xd3 38 ♖xd3+ ♖xd3 39 ♕xd3+ ♖d7 40 ♕e4 ♔e7 41 h3 ♕f5 42 ♕b4+ ♔f7 43 a4 ♔g6 44 ♖f3 ♖d3 45 g4?? ♕d5 46 f5+ ♔f7 47 fxe6+ ♔xe6 48 ♕e1+ ♔d7 **0-1** L/N5184

**1857-NYC1-20** 8x57
**Fiske, D.W.+Marache, N.**
[Fiske]

1 d4 d5 2 c4 e6 3 ♘c3 ♘f6 4 ♘f3 c5 5 e3 ♘c6 6 a3 b6 7 cxd5 exd5 8 ♗b5 ♗b7? [□ 8 ... ♗d7] 9 ♘e5 ♕c7 10 ♕a4 ♖c8 11 ♕xa7 ♖a8? [□ 11 ... ♗e7] 12 ♗xc6+ ♕xc6 13 ♕xa8+ ♗xa8 14 ♘xc6 ♗xc6 15 0-0 ♗d6 16 ♖d1 c4 17 f3 0-0 18 e4 dxe4 19 d5 ♗d7 20 fxe4 ♗g4 21 ♖e1 ♘d7 22 h3 ♗h5 23 ♗d2 ♗g3 24 ♖f1 ♗d6 25 ♖ae1? [□ 25 ♗f4] 25 ... f6 26 g4 ♗g6 27 ♔g2 ♖e8 28 ♖e2 ♘c5 29 ♗f4 ♗xf4 30 ♖xf4 ♘d3 31 ♖f1 ♖e5 32 ♔f3 ♗e8 33 ♖b1 ♔f7 34 ♖e3 ♘c5 35 a4 ♘xa4 36 b3 cxb3 37 ♖xb3 ♘xc3 38 ♖exc3 b5 39 ♖c7+ ♔g6 40 d6 ♗f7 41 d7 ♗xb3 42 d8♕ **1-0** L/N5184

**1857-NYC1-21** 16x57
**Marache, N.+Fiske, D.W.**
[Fiske]

1 e4 e6 2 d4 d5 3 exd5 exd5 4 ♘f3 ♘f6 5 c4 ♗b4+ 6 ♘c3 0-0 7 ♗e2 c5? [□ 7 ... ♗e6] 8 0-0 dxc4 9 ♗xc4 ♗xc3 10 bxc3 cxd4 11 ♗a3 ♖e8

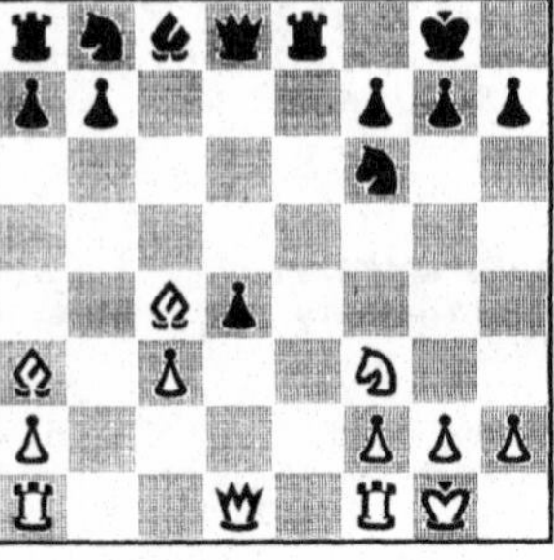

12 ♘g5 ♗e6 13 ♘xe6 fxe6 14 ♕b3 ♘d5 15 ♕xb7 ♘b6 16 ♗b5 ♘8d7 17 cxd4 ♖b8 18 ♕f3 ♘d5 19 ♗d3 ♕h4 20 ♖ac1 ♘7f6 21 ♗d6 ♖b7 22 ♗c2 ♖f7 23 ♕d3 ♘f4 24 ♗xf4 ♕xf4 25 f3 ♖d7 26 ♗a4 ♖ed8?? [□ 26 ... ♖xd4] 27 ♗xd7 ♖xd7 ...♀ **1-0** L/N5184

**1857-NYC1-22** 19x57
**Fiske, D.W.–Marache, N.**
[Fiske]

1 d4 e6 2 c4 f5 3 ♘c3 ♘f6 4 e3 b6 5 ♘f3 ♗b4 6 a3 ♗xc3+ 7 bxc3 0-0 8 ♗d3 ♗b7 9 0-0 ♘c6 10 ♗b2 ♘e7 11 ♘h4 d6 12 f4 ♕d7 13 ♕c2 ♘g4 14 ♖ae1 ♖f6 15 e4 ♖h6 16 ♘f3 ♖f8 17 h3 ♘f6 18 exf5 exf5 19 d5 c6 20 ♕e2? [□ 20 ♖e6] 20 ... ♘g6 21 dxc6 ♕xc6 22 ♘d4 ♕c5 23 ♕e6+ ♔h8 24 ♗xf5? [□ 24 ♕xf5±] 24 ... ♘h5 25 ♕e8 ♘f6 26 ♕e2 ♘h4 27 ♕e7 ♖b8 28 ♗d3? [□ 28 ♗g4] 28 ... ♗xg2 29 ♖f2 ♗xh3 30 f5 ♖h5 31 ♗c1 ♗xf5 32 ♗xf5 ♘xf5 33 ♘xf5 ♖xf5 34 ♗e3 ♕e5 35 ♕xa7 ♕g3+ **0-1** L/N5184

**1857-NYC1-23** 20x57
**Marache, N.+Fiske, D.W.**
[Fiske]

1 e4 c5 2 d4 cxd4 3 ♘f3 ♘c6 4 ♘xd4 e6 5 ♗e3 ♘ge7 6 ♗d3 ♘g6 7 0-0 ♗e7 8 c3 0-0 9 ♘d2 ♕c7 10 ♔h1 ♗d6?? 11 ♘b5 ♕b8 12 ♘xd6 ♕xd6 13 ♘c4 ♕c7 14 ♗c5 ♘ce7 15 ♗d6 ♕c6 16 e5 b5 17 ♘a5 ♕b6 18 ♗e4 ♖b8 19 ♗xb8 ♕xb8 20 f4 f5 21 ♗c2 ♘d5 22 ♕d4 ♕c7 23 ♘b3 ♗b7 24 ♖f2 ♗c6 25 ♕d2 ♕d8 26 ♘d4 ♗b7 27 ♘xb5 ♘h4 28 ♘d6 ♗c6 29 c4 ♘e7 30 b4 ♔h8 31 b5 ♗a8 32 ♖e1 ♘g8 33 ♖e3 ♘h6 34 h3 g5 35 ♔h2 gxf4 36 ♖ee2 f3 37 ♕xh6 fxe2 38 ♖xe2 ♕e7 39 c5 ♘g6 40 a4 ♗d5 41 a5 ♕d8 42 b6 axb6 43 axb6 ♕a8 44 ♕d2 ♕a3 45 ♕e3 ♕b4 46 ♕f2 ♘f4 47 ♕h4 ♕d4 48 ♖f2 ♘e2 49 ♕xd4 ♘xd4 50 ♗a4 ♗c6 51 ♗xc6 ♘xc6 52 b7 ♖b8 53 ♖e2 ♔g7 54 ♔g3 ♔f8 55 ♔f4 ♔g7 56 ♖e3 ♘a5 57 ♖g3+ ♔f8 58 ♔g5 ♔e7 59 ♔h6 ♔d8 60 ♖g8+ **1-0** L/N5184

**1857-NYC1-24** 9x57
**Stanley, C.H.–Lichtenhein, T.**
[Fiske]

1 e4 e5 2 ♘f3 ♘c6 3 ♗c4 ♗c5 4 d3 d6 5 h3 h6 6 ♘c3 ♘f6 7 ♗e3 ♗b6 8 0-0 ♗e6 9 ♗b3 0-0 10 ♕e2 ♘h7 11 ♘h2? ♘d4 12 ♕d2 ♗xb3 13 axb3 f5 14 exf5 ♖xf5 15 ♘g4 ♕h4 16 ♘d5 ♖af8 17 ♘xb6 axb6 18 ♗xd4 exd4 19 ♖ae1 ♘g5 [△ 20 ... ♕xh3 21 hxg3 ♘f3+ 22 ♔g2 ♘xd2 23 ♘f3]

20 f4 h5 21 fxg5 hxg4 22 hxg4 ♕xg4 23 ♖xf5 ♕xf5 24 ♕e2 ♕xg5 25 ♕e6+ ♖f7 26 ♕e8+ ♖f8 27 ♕e6+ ♔h7 28 ♕h3+ ♔g6 29 ♖e4 ♕c1+ 30 ♔h2 ♖f5 31 ♖xd4? [□ ♖e6+] 31 ... ♕xc2 32 ♕g4+ ♔f6 33 ♖c4 ♕xd3 34 ♖xc7 g6 35 ♕h4+ ♔e5 36 ♕h8+ ♖f6 37 ♖f7 ♕f1 38 ♕e8+ ♔d5 39 ♖xf6 ♕xf6 40 ♕b5+ ♔e6 41 ♕xb6 ♕e5+ 42 ♔g1?? [□ 42 ♔h3] 42 ... ♕c5+ 43 ♕xc5 dxc5 44 ♔f2 ♔f5 45 ♔f3 ♔g5 46 ♔g3 b6 47 ♔f3 ♔h4 48 ♔g2 ♔g4 **0-1** L/N5184

**1857-NYC1-25** 12x57
**Lichtenhein,T.– Stanley,C.H.**

[Morphy]

1 e4 e5 2 ♘f3 ♘c6 3 d4 exd4 4 ♗c4 ♗c5 5 c3 d3?! [□ 5 ... ♘f6] 6 ♘g5 [□ 6 b4 Δ 7 b5] 6 ... ♘h6 7 ♕h5 [7 ♘xf7 ♗xf2+ 8 ♔xf2 ♘xf7 9 ♗xf7+ ♔xf7 10 ♖f1= (10 ♕xd3=; 10 ♕b3+ ♔g6∓)] 7 ... ♘e5 8 ♗xf7+ ♘hxf7 9 ♘xf7 ♗xf2+ 10 ♔xf2 ♘xf7 11 ♖f1 0-0 12 ♔g1 c6 13 ♗e3 d6 14 ♘d2 ♗e6 15 ♖ae1 ♕d7 16 h3 a5 17 a4 c5 18 b3 c4 19 ♘xc4 ♗xc4 20 bxc4 ♘e5 21 ♗d4 ♕xa4 22 c5 d2 23 ♖xf8+ [□ 23 ♖d1] 23 ... ♖xf8 24 ♖d1 ♘f3+ **0-1** L/N5184

**1857-NYC1-26** 12x57
**Stanley,C.H.+Lichtenhein, T.**

[Fiske]

1 e4 c5 2 d4 cxd4 3 ♕xd4 ♘c6 4 ♕d1 e6 5 ♘f3 ♗c5 6 ♗c4 ♘ge7 [□ 6 ... ♘f6] 7 0-0 0-0 8 a3 a5 9 ♗d3 [□ 9 ♘c3] 9 ... f5 10 exf5 ♘xf5 11 ♗xf5 ♖xf5 12 ♘c3 d5 13 ♘e2 e5 14 ♘g3 ♖f7 15 ♘g5 ♖f6 16 ♕d3 ♖g6 17 ♗d2 ♘d4 [17 ... ♖xg5?? 18 ♗xg5 ♕xg5 19 ♕xd5+] 18 h4 b6

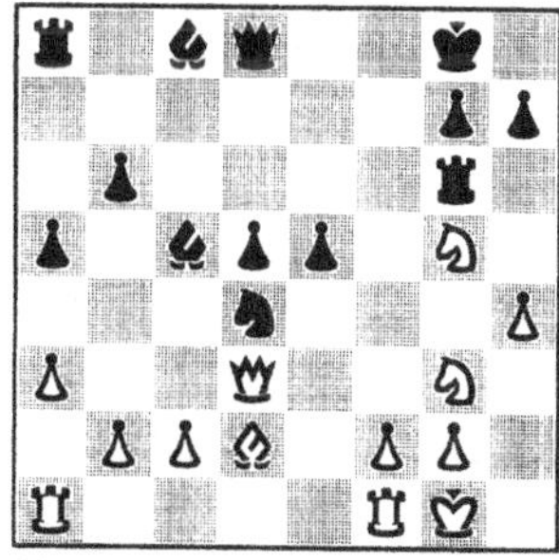

19 b4 [19 c4?? ♗a6 20 b3 e4 21 ♕b1 h6 22 ♘h3 (22 ♘f3 ♖xg3 23 fxg3 ♘xf3+) 22 ... ♖xg3 23 fxg3 ♘xb3+ 24 ♔~ ♘xd2-+; 21 ♕c3 h6 22 ♘h3 ♖xg3 23 ♕xg3 ♘e2+; 23 fxg3 ♘e2+] 19 ... ♗a6 20 ♕c3 axb4 21 axb4 ♗xf1 22 ♖xf1 h6? [□ 22 ... ♗e7∓] 23 bxc5 hxg5 24 ♗xg5 ♕e8 25 ♕d3 bxc5 26 c3 ♖a3 27 ♕d2 ♘b5 28 ♕xd5+ ♖e6 29 ♘f5 ♖xc3 30 ♘e7+ ♔f7 31 f4 **1-0** L/N5184

**1857-NYC1-27** 13x57
**Lichtenhein,T.+ Stanley,C.H.**

[Fiske]

1 d4 d5 2 c4 e6 3 ♘c3 dxc4 4 e3 ♗e7 5 ♗xc4 ♘f6 6 ♘f3 0-0 7 0-0 ♘d5 8 ♕b3 ♘xc3 9 bxc3 ♘c6 10 ♗d3 a5 11 a4 b6 12 ♗e4 ♗b7 13 ♕c2 f5 14 ♗xc6 ♗xc6 15 ♘e5 ♕d5 16 f4 ♕e4 17 ♕xe4 ♗xe4 18 ♗a3 ♗xa3 19 ♖xa3 ♖fd8 20 ♖f2 c5 21 ♖b3 cxd4 22 cxd4 ♖dc8 23 ♖fb2 ♖c1+ 24 ♔f2 ♖c2+ 25 ♔g3 ♖ac8 26 ♖xb6 ♖xb2 27 ♖xb2 ♗c2 28 ♖b5 ♗xa4 29 ♖xa5 ♗b3 30 ♖c5 ♖a8 31 ♘c4 h6 32 ♘b6 ♖a6 33 ♖b5 ♖a3 34 ♔h4 ♗a2 35 ♖e5 ♖a6 36 ♖b5 ♖a3 37 ♖b2 ♗b3 38 h3 ♔f7 39 g4 fxg4 40 hxg4 ♔e7 41 e4 ♔d6 42 f5 e5 43 dxe5+ ♔xe5 44 ♘d7+ ♔f4 45 e5 ♖a2?? 46 ♖xb3 **1-0** L/N5184

**1857-NYC1-28** 16x57
**Stanley,C.H.– Lichtenhein,T.**

[Fiske]

1 e4 e6 2 d4 d5 3 exd5 exd5 4 ♘f3 ♘f6 5 ♗e2 [□ 5 ♗d3] 5 ... ♗d6 6 0-0 h6 7 ♘e5 0-0 8 f4 c5 9 c3 ♘c6 10 ♗e3 ♕b6 11 ♘xc6 bxc6 12 dxc5 ♗xc5 13 ♗xc5 ♕xc5+ 14 ♕d4 ♕xd4+ 15 cxd4 ♖b8 16 b3 ♘e4 17 ♘a3 f5 18 ♖ac1 ♗d7 19 ♖fd1 ♖fe8 20 ♖e1 ♖e6 21 ♗d3 ♖be8 22 b4 ♖b8 23 ♘c2 g6 24 a3 ♖b6 25 ♘e3 a6 26 ♘c2 ♖e8 27 ♘a1 ♖a8 28 ♘b3 ♔f7 29 ♖c2 ♖e8 30 ♖ce2 ♖e6 31 ♘c5 ♘xc5 32 dxc5 ♖xe2 33 ♖xe2 ♖b7 34 ♖b2 a5 35 ♖b1 axb4 36 axb4 ♔e7 37 ♔f2 ♖b8 38 ♔e3 ♔f6 39 ♔d4 ♗e8 40 ♔c3 ♖a8 41 ♔b3 ♗f7 42 ♔c3 ♖b8 43 ♖a1 d4+ 44 ♔xd4 ♖xb4+ 45 ♔e3 ♗d5 46 ♖c1 ♖b2 47 ♗e2 g5 48 fxg5+ hxg5 49 g3 ♔e5 50 h4 f4+ **0-1** L/N5184

**1857-NYC1-29** 6x57
**Calthrop,S.R.– Paulsen,L.**

[Fiske]

1 e4 c5 2 f4 e6 3 ♘f3 d5 4 ♗b5+ ♘c6 5 ♗xc6+ bxc6 6 e5 ♗a6 7 d3 ♘h6 8 c3 ♘f5 9 0-0 ♕b6 10 g4 ♘h6 11 ♘h4 ♗e7 12 g5 ♘f5 13 ♘xf5 exf5 14 ♕b3? ♗xd3 15 ♖f2 ♕xb3 16 axb3 c4 17 b4 0-0 18 ♗e3 a5 19 ♗c5 ♗xc5 20 bxc5 ♖fb8 21 ♘a3 a4 22 ♖e1 ♗e4 23 h4 ♖a5 24 h5 ♖xc5 25 ♔h2 ♖a5 26 ♖g1 ♖a7 27 g6 fxg6 28 hxg6 h6 29 ♘b1 ♖ab7 30 ♘d2 ♖xb2 **0-1** L/N5184

**1857-NYC1-30** 7x57
**Paulsen,L.+Calthrop,S.R.**

[Fiske]

1 e4 e5 2 ♘f3 ♘c6 3 d4 exd4 4 ♗c4 ♗c5 5 c3 ♘f6 6 0-0 [□ 6 e5] 6 ... ♘a5?! [□ 6 ... d6] 7 cxd4 ♘xc4 8 dxc5 d5 9 cxd6 ♕xd6 10 e5 ♕xd1 11 ♖xd1 ♘d7 12 b3 ♘cb6 13 ♗a3 ♘f8 14 ♗xf8 ♖xf8 15 ♘c3 c6 16 ♘e4 ♘d5 17 ♘d6+ ♔e7 18 ♘d4 g6 19 ♖e1 ♖b8 20 ♖ab1 ♗d7 21 b4 f6 22 ♘c4 b5 23 ♘a5 ♖b6 24 e6 ♗e8 25 a3 ♔d6 26 ♖bc1 ♘e7 27 ♖ed1 ♔c7 28 ♘db3 f5 29 ♘c5 ♖f6 30 ♘d7 ♖xe6 31 ♘xb6 axb6 32 ♘b3 ♖e5 33 ♖e1 ♖xe1+ 34 ♖xe1 ♔d6 35 ♘d4 c5 36 ♘c2 ♗f7 37 ♖d1+ ♘d5 38 ♘e3 c4 39 ♘xd5 ♗xd5 40 f4

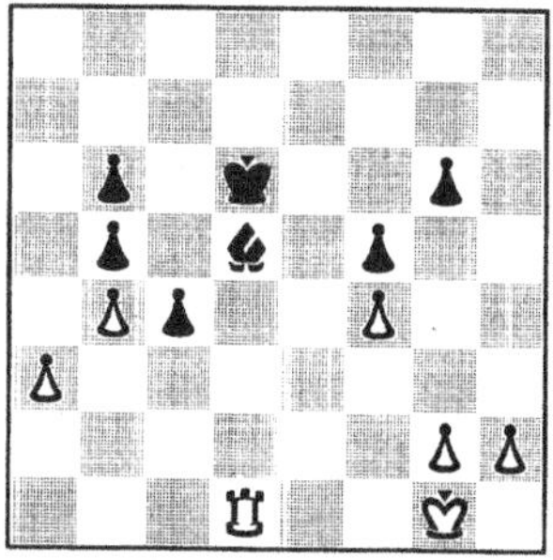

40 ... c3?? [□ 40 ... ♔c6 Δ 41 ... ♗e4] 41 ♖c1 ♗c4 42 ♖xc3 **1-0** L/N5184

**1857-NYC1-31** 7x57
**Calthrop,S.R.– Paulsen,L.**

[Fiske]

1 e4 e5 2 ♘f3 d5? 3 exd5 e4 4 ♗b5+?? [4 ♕e2 ♕e7 5 ♘d4 ♘f6 (5 ... ♕e5 6 ♘b5 Δ 7 d4) 6 ♘c3 ♕e5 7 ♘f3 ♕e7 8 ♘g5 ♗f5 9 ♕b5+±] 4 ... c6 5 dxc6 bxc6 6 ♕e2 cxb5 7 ♕xe4+ ♕e7 8 ♕xe7+ ♗xe7 9 ♘c3 a6 10 0-0 ♘f6 11 d4 0-0 12 ♗g5 ♖a7 13 ♖fe1 ♗e6 14 ♖ad1 h6 15 ♗xf6 ♗xf6 16 ♘e4 ♗d8 17 h3 ♗d5 18 b3 ♖e7 19 ♘fd2 ♖fe8 20 f3 f5 21 c4 ♗a8 22 d5 fxe4 **0-1** L/N5184

**1857-NYC1-32** 6x57
**Perrin,F.– Knott,H.**

[Fiske]

1 e4 e6 2 d4 d5 3 exd5 exd5 4 ♗e3 ♘f6 5 ♗d3 ♗d6 6 ♘c3 c6 7 ♘f3 ♗g4 8 h3 ♗xf3 9 ♕xf3 ♘bd7 10 0-0 h6 11 ♖fe1 0-0 12 ♕f5 g6 13 ♕f3 ♔g7 14 ♕e2 ♘h7 15 ♕d2 ♕h4 16 ♘e2 ♖ae8 17 ♘f4 ♘g5 [17 ... ♘df6??; 17 ... g5??] 18 ♔h1 [Δ 19 g3; 18 g3 ♘xh3+] 18 ... ♘e4 19 ♗xe4 ♖xe4 20 g3 ♕f6 21 f3 ♖e7 22 ♔g2 ♖fe8 23 ♘xd5?? [□ 23 ♖e2;; □ 23 h4] 23 ... cxd5 24 ♗xh6+ ♔h7 25 ♗g5 ♖xe1 26 ♖xe1 [26 ♗xf6 ♖1e2+ -+] 26 ... ♕h8 27 ♗e3 ♖e6 28 b3 ♕e8

29 c4 ♘f6 30 c5 ♗c7 31 ♗f2 ♖xe1 32 ♗xe1 ♕e6 33 ♗f2 ♘h5 34 ♕b4 b6 35 cxb6 axb6 36 ♕d2 ♕d6 37 ♕e1 ♘g7 38 a4 ♘f5 39 ♕d2 **0-1** L/N5184

**1857-NYC1-33** 7 x 57
**Knott, H.– Perrin, F.**
[Fiske]
1 d4 d5 2 c4 e6 3 ♘c3 ♘f6 4 e3 c5 5 ♘f3 ♘c6 6 a3 a6 7 dxc5 [7 b3 △ 8 ♗b2] 7 ... ♗xc5 8 b4 ♗e7 9 ♗e2 0-0 10 0-0 b6 11 ♗b2 ♗b7 12 cxd5 exd5 13 ♘d4 ♗d6 14 ♘xc6 ♗xc6 15 ♗f3 ♖c8 16 ♘e2 ♗b8 17 ♗xf6 ♕xf6 18 ♘d4 [18 ♗xd5?? ♕e5 19 ♘f4 g5 20 ♗xc6 ♖xc6 21 ♕g4 ♔h8–+] 18 ... ♕e5 19 g3 ♗b7 20 ♕d3 f5 21 ♖ac1 g6 22 ♘e2 ♖cd8 23 ♖fd1 ♖d6 24 ♕d4 ♕e7 25 ♘f4 ♖fd8 26 ♖c2 g5 27 ♘e2 ♕e6 28 ♖cd2 ♖6d7 29 ♕d3 ♗e5 30 ♘d4 ♕f6 31 ♘xf5 ♖f7 32 g4 h5 33 h3 hxg4 34 ♗xg4 ♖df8 35 ♘d4 ♗c7 36 ♗e6 ♔h8 37 ♗xf7 ♖xf7 38 f3 ♗c8 39 ♕f5?? ♗xf5 **0-1** L/N5184

**1857-NYC1-34** 11 x 57
**Perrin, F.= Knott, H.**
[Fiske]
1 e4 e6 2 d4 d5 3 exd5 exd5 4 c4 ♗b4+ 5 ♘c3 ♕e7+ 6 ♗e3 ♘f6 7 ♗d3 ♗e6 8 c5 0-0 9 h3 b6 10 ♖c1 bxc5 11 dxc5 ♘c6 12 ♘e2 ♖fd8 13 ♘d4 ♘xd4 14 ♗xd4 ♗g4+ 15 ♗e2 ♗xe2 16 ♕xe2 ♖e8 17 ♕xe7 ♖xe7+ 18 ♔d1 ♗xc3 19 bxc3 ♖e6 20 ♔d2 ♘e4+ 21 ♔d3 ♖c6 22 ♖he1 ♘xc5+ 23 ♗xc5 ♖xc5 24 ♔d4 ♖a5 25 ♖e2 ♖d8 26 ♖b1 c5+ 27 ♔d3 d4 28 ♖b7 dxc3+ 29 ♔xc3 ♖a3+ ...? **½-½** L/N5184

**1857-NYC1-35** 11 x 57
**Perrin, F.– Knott, H.**
[Fiske]
1 e4 e6 2 d4 d5 3 exd5 exd5 4 ♘f3 ♗d6 5 ♗d3 ♗e6 6 0-0 h6 7 ♕e2 ♘e7 8 ♗e3 0-0 9 c4 c6 10 ♘c3 ♘d7 11 ♖ac1 ♘f6 12 h3 ♘g6 13 ♗xg6 fxg6 14 c5 ♗c7 15 ♗xh6 ♕d7 16 ♗d2 ♖ae8 17 ♘e5 ♗xe5 18 dxe5 ♘e4 19 ♘xe4 dxe4 20 ♕e3 ♗d5 21 ♗c3 ♖f5 22 ♖cd1 ♕e6 23 f3??

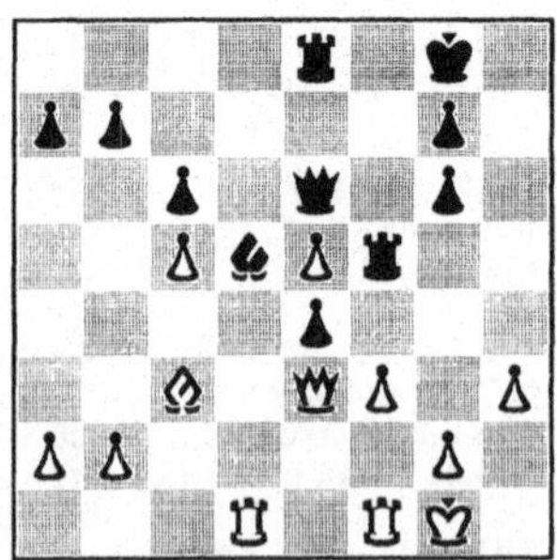

23 ... exf3 24 gxf3 ♖h5 25 ♖d2 ♕xh3 26 ♖g2 ♖f8 **0-1** L/N5184

**1857-NYC1-37** 14 x 57
**Knott, H.– Perrin, F.**
[Fiske]
1 d4 b6 2 e4 ♗b7 3 ♗d3 e6 4 c4 ♘c6 5 ♘f3 d6 6 0-0 ♕d7 7 a4 ♘b4 8 ♘c3 ♘xd3 9 ♕xd3 g6 10 ♗e3 ♗g7 11 ♖fd1 ♘e7 12 d5 0-0 13 ♗f4? e5 14 ♗g3 f5 15 exf5 ♘xf5 16 ♘e4 c6 17 ♘fg5 cxd5 18 cxd5 ♘e7 19 ♘e6 ♗xd5? 20 ♘xf8 ♖xf8 21 ♗h4 ♗xe4 22 ♕xe4 ♖f4 23 ♕a8+ ♖f8 24 ♕e4 d5?? 25 ♗xe7 ♕xe7 26 ♕xd5+ ♔h8 27 ♖a3 ♕b4 28 ♖f3 ♕xb2 29 ♖xf8+ ♗xf8 30 ♕f7 ♕b4 31 h3 ♕e7 32 ♕xe7 ♗xe7 33 ♖d7 ♗c5 34 ♖xa7 ♗d4 35 ♔f1 g5 36 f3 h6 37 ♔e2 ♔g8 38 ♔d3 h5 39 ♔c4?? b5+ 40 ♔xb5 ♗xa7 **0-1** L/N5184

**1857-NYC1-38** 16 x 57
**Perrin, F.+ Knott, H.**
[Fiske]
1 c4 f5 2 d4 e6 3 ♘c3 ♘f6 4 e3 ♗e7 5 ♗d3 0-0 6 a3 b6 7 ♘ge2 d5 8 0-0 c6 9 cxd5 cxd5 10 f3 ♗b7 11 ♘f4 ♗c8 12 ♗d2 ♔h8 13 ♔h1 g5 14 ♘h3 g4 15 ♘f4 ♗d6 16 fxg4 ♘xg4 17 ♕f3 ♕h4 18 h3 ♗xf4 19 ♕xf4 ♕h6 20 ♕xh6 ♘xh6 21 e4! dxe4 22 ♗xe4 ♗a6 23 ♗xa8 ♗xf1 24 ♗xh6 ♖f6 25 ♗f4 **1-0** L/N5184

**1857-NYC1-39**
**Meek, A.B.– Morphy, P.C.**
[Fiske]
1 e4 e5 2 ♘f3 ♘c6 3 ♗b5 ♘f6 4 d3 ♗c5 5 c3 d6 [□ 5 ... ♕e7 6 0-0 0-0 7 d4 ♗b6=] 6 b4? [6 d4 exd4 7 cxd4 ♗b4+ 8 ♔f1±] 6 ... ♗b6 7 a4 a6 8 ♗c4 ♗e6 9 ♗xe6 fxe6 10 0-0 0-0 11 ♘g5 ♕e7 12 ♔h1 h6 13 ♘h3 d5 14 ♗a3 ♘d8 15 b5 ♗c5 16 ♗b2 dxe4 17 d4 exd4 18 cxd4 ♗d6 19 ♘c3 axb5 20 axb5 ♘f7 21 ♕e2 ♕d7 22 ♘xe4 ♘xe4 23 ♕xe4 ♕xb5 24 ♖ab1 ♕d5 25 ♕g4 ♖a4 26 ♘f4 ♕e4 27 ♗c1 ♗xf4 [27 ... ♕xb1] 28 ♗xf4 ♖xd4 29 ♕h3 ♕xf4 **0-1** L/N 5184

**1857-NYC1-40**
**Morphy, P.C.+ Meek, A.B.**
[Fiske]
1 e4 e6 2 d4 g6 [□ 2 ... d5] 3 ♗d3 ♗g7 4 ♗e3 ♘e7 5 ♘e2 b6 6 ♘d2 ♗b7 7 0-0 d5 8 e5 0-0 9 f4 f5 10 h3 ♘d7 11 ♔h2 c5 12 c3 c4 13 ♗c2 a6? 14 ♘f3 h6 15 g4! ♔h7 16 ♖g1 ♖g8 17 ♕e1 ♘c6 18 ♘h4 ♕f8? [18 ... ♘f8+–]

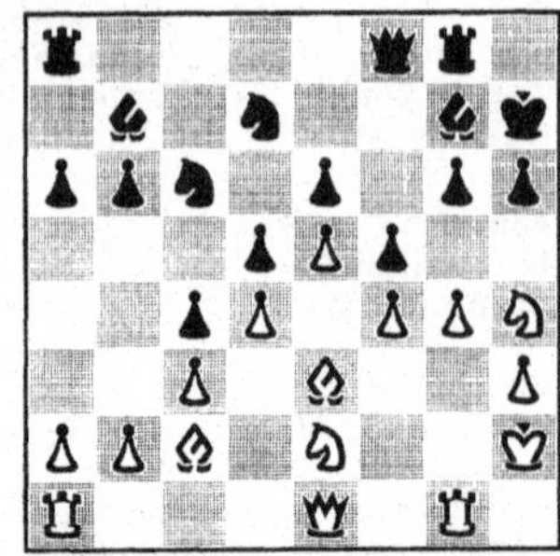

19 ♘xg6 ♔xg6 [19 ... ♕f7 20 gxf5 exf5 21 ♘h4 ♘e7 22 ♘xf5 ♘xf5 23 ♘g3+–] 20 gxf5+ ♔f7 21 fxe6+ ♔xe6 22 f5+ ♔e7 23 ♕h4+ ♔e8 24 f6 ♗xf6 25 exf6 ♖xg1 26 ♖xg1 ♘xf6 27 ♗g6+ ♔d7 28 ♗f5+ ♔e8 29 ♗xh6 ♕h8 30 ♖g7 ♘g8 **1-0** L/N 5184

**1857-NYC1-41**
**Meek, A.B.– Morphy, P.C.**
[Fiske]
1 e4 e5 2 ♘f3 ♘c6 3 d4 exd4 4 c3 dxc3 5 ♘xc3 ♗c5?! [5 ... ♗b4] 6 ♗c4 d6 7 h3? [7 ♕b3] 7 ... ♗e6 8 ♗b5 ♘e7 9 ♘g5 0-0 10 ♕h5 h6 11 ♘f3 ♘g6 12 g4 ♘ce5 13 ♘xe5 dxe5 14 g5 ♕d4 15 ♗e3 ♕b4 16 ♗xc5 ♕xb2 17 0-0 ♕xc3 18 ♗xf8 ♖xf8 19 ♖ac1 ♕b2 20 ♗c4 ♘f4 21 ♕d1 ♘xh3+ 22 ♔g2 ♘f4+ 23 ♔h1 ♕b6 24 gxh6 ♗xc4 25 h7+ ♔xh7 26 ♕g4 [26 ♖xc4 ♕h6+ 27 ♕h5 ♕xh5+ 28 ♔g1 ♕h3 △ 29 ... ♕g2#] 26 ... ♕h6+ 27 ♔g1 ♗xf1 28 ♖xf1 ♖d8 29 a4 ♖d6 30 f3 ♖g6 31 ♔f2 **0-1** L/N 5184

**1857-NYC1-42** 13 x 57
**Montgomery, H.P.– Paulsen, L.**
[Morphy]
1 e4 c5 2 d4 cxd4 3 ♘f3 ♘c6 4 ♗c4 e6 5 0-0 ♗c5 6 c3 dxc3 7 ♘xc3 ♘ge7 [□ 7 ... d5] 8 e5 ♘g6 [□ 8 ... d5] 9 ♘e4 ♘cxe5 [□ 9 ... ♗e7] 10 ♘xe5 ♘xe5 11 ♘xc5 ♕c7 [11 ... ♘xc4 12 ♕d4 d5 13 ♕xg7 ♖f8 14 ♗h6+–] 12 ♕d4 ♘xc4 13 ♕xc4 b6 14 ♘e4 [□ 14 ♕e4±] 14 ... ♕xc4 15 ♘d6+ ♔e7 16 ♘xc4 ♗a6 17 b3 d5 18 ♗a3+ ♔f6 19 ♘d6 [□ 19 ♗b2+ ♔e7! 20 ♗a3+ ♔f6!=] 19 ... ♗xf1 20 ♖xf1 ♖hd8 21 ♖c1 ♖d7 22 ♖c3 g5 23 ♖f3+ ♔g6

24 g4 ♖ad8 25 ♘b5 d4 26 ♗b2 e5 27 ♘a3 ♖d5 28 ♖d3 e4 29 ♖d1 e3 30 ♔f1 f5 31 ♘c2 e2+ 32 ♔xe2 d3+ 33 ♔f3 fxg4+? [□ 33 ... dxc2] 34 ♔e4 ♖f5 35 ♘e3 ♖xf2 36 ♗e5 ♖xa2 37 ♖f1 ♖e2 38 ♖f6+ ♔h5 39 ♖e6 d2 40 ♗g7 ♖e8! 41 ♖xe8 d1♕ 42 ♗d4 ♕h1+ 43 ♔e5 ♕f3 44 ♔d6 ♕f4+ 45 ♔d5 ♕f7+ 46 ♖e6 ♖d2 47 ♔e5 ♖xd4 **0-1** L/N5184

**1857-NYC1-43** 16x57
**Paulsen, L.+ Montgomery, H.P.**
[Fiske]

1 e4 d5 2 exd5 ♘f6 3 d4 [□ 3 ♗b5+ ♗d7 4 ♗c4] 3 ... ♕xd5 4 ♘f3 e6 5 c4 ♕d8 6 ♘c3 c6 7 ♗d3 ♘a6 8 a3 ♗e7 9 0-0 ♕c7 10 b4 b6 11 ♗b2 ♘b8 12 ♖c1 a5 13 b5 0-0 14 ♖e1 ♗b7 15 bxc6 ♗xc6 16 d5 ♗d7 17 ♘e4 ♘xe4 18 ♗xe4 ♖a7 19 ♘e5 ♗f6 20 ♕h5 g6 21 ♕h6 ♗c8 22 ♗b1 ♕d8 23 ♖cd1 ♗g5 24 ♘g4 f6 [□ 24 ... f5] 25 ♕xg5 e5 26 ♘xf6+ ♖xf6 27 ♗xe5 ♘d7 28 ♗xf6 ♘xf6 29 h4 ♕f8 30 d6 h6 31 ♕b5 **1-0** L/N5184

**1857-NYC1-44** 20x57
**Raphael, B.I.+ Marache, N.**
[Fiske]

1 e4 c5 2 d4 cxd4 3 ♘f3 ♘c6 4 ♘xd4 e5 5 ♘f3 ♘f6 6 ♗g5? [□ 6 ♗c4△ 7 0-0] 6 ... ♗e7 7 ♗xf6 ♗xf6 8 ♗c4 0-0 9 0-0 ♕b6 10 b3 ♘e7 11 ♘c3 d6 12 h3 ♗e6 13 ♗xe6 fxe6 14 ♘e2 d5 15 ♘g3 ♖ad8 16 ♕e2 d4 17 ♘h5 ♘g6 18 ♖ad1 ♗e7 19 ♖d3 ♕c7 20 ♖c1 ♗a3 21 ♖cd1 ♗b4 22 ♘g5 ♕e7 23 ♕g4 ♖d6 24 ♖g3 ♖f4??

25 ♘xf4 exf4 26 ♖gd3 ♘e5 27 ♕xf4 ♘xd3 28 cxd3 h6 29 ♘f3 ♕f6? 30 ♕xf6 gxf6 31 e5 fxe5 32 ♘xe5 ♔g7 33 f4 b5 34 ♖c1 ♗c3 35 ♖c2 h5 36 ♔f2 ♖d8 37 ♔f3 ♔f6 38 ♔e4 a5 39 g4 hxg4 40 hxg4 ♖h8 41 g5+ ♔g7 42 ♘c6 ♖h4 43 ♖f2 [△ 44 ♘xd4] 43 ... a4 44 ♘xd4 ♗e1 45 ♘xe6+ ♔f7 46 ♖f1 **1-0** L/N5184

**1857-NYC1-45** 22x57
**Marache, N.= Raphael, B.I.**
[Fiske]

1 e4 e5 2 c3 c5? [□ 2 ... d5] 3 ♘f3 ♘c6 4 ♗c4 ♘f6 5 ♘g5 d5 6 exd5 ♘xd5 7 ♕f3 ♕xg5 8 ♗xd5 ♕f6 9 ♗xc6+? [□ 9 ♕xf6 gxf6 10 ♗xc6+ bxc6] 9 ... ♕xc6 10 ♕xc6+ bxc6 11 d3 ♗a6 12 c4 0-0-0 13 ♔e2 e4 14 dxe4 ♗xc4+ 15 ♔f3 ♗d6 16 ♘c3 ♖hf8 17 ♖e1 ♖de8 18 ♗f4 ♗xf4 19 ♔xf4 f6 20 ♘a4 g5+ 21 ♔f3 ♖e5 22 ♖ac1 ♗xa2 23 ♖xc5 ♖xc5 24 ♘xc5 f5 25 e5 ♗d5+ 26 ♔g3 h5 27 f3 f4+ 28 ♔f2 ♔c7 29 ♖a1 ♖a8 30 ♖a6 ♗c4 31 ♖a4 ♗b5 32 ♖d4 ♖e8 33 e6 ♔b6 34 b4 a5 35 ♘d7+ ♔c7 36 ♖e4 axb4 37 ♘f6 ♖e7 38 ♘g8 ♖e8 39 ♘f6 ♖e7 **½-½** L/N5184

**1857-NYC1-46** 22x57
**Marache, N.– Raphael, B.I.**
[Fiske]

1 e4 e5 2 ♘f3 ♘f6 3 ♘c3 ♗b4 4 ♗c4 ♗xc3 5 dxc3 0-0 6 ♗g5 d6 7 ♕d3 h6 8 ♗h4 ♗e6 9 0-0-0 ♘bd7 10 ♗xe6 fxe6 11 ♕c4 ♕e8 12 ♕xc7 ♘xe4 13 ♕xb7?? ♘dc5 14 ♕b4 ♖b8 15 ♕c4 d5 16 ♕e2 ♘a4 17 ♘d2 ♘xd2 18 ♔xd2 ♖xb2 19 ♖b1 ♖f4 20 ♗g3 ♖e4 21 ♕f3 ♕b5 22 ♖be1 ♖xc2+! 23 ♔xc2 ♕b2+ 24 ♔d1 [24 ♔d3 ♕xc3#] 24 ... ♘xc3+ **0-1** L/N5184

**1857-NYC1-47** 22x57
**Raphael, B.I.– Marache, N.**
[Fiske]

1 e4 e6 2 d4 d5 3 exd5 exd5 4 ♘f3 ♘f6 5 ♗d3 ♗d6 6 0-0 0-0 7 h3 h6 8 ♗e3 ♗e6 9 c3 [□ 9 ♘e5] 9 ... ♘c6 10 ♘bd2 ♕d7 11 ♘h2 ♗xh3?! 12 gxh3 ♕xh3 13 ♘df3 g5 14 ♔h1 g4 15 ♖g1 ♔h8 16 ♘e5 ♘xe5 17 ♖g3 ♕h4 18 dxe5 ♗xe5 19 ♖g2 ♖ae8 20 ♖xg4?? [□ 20 ♕d2] **0-1** L/N5184

**1857-NYC1-48** 23x57
**Marache, N.+ Raphael, B.I.**
[Fiske]

1 e4 c5 2 d4 cxd4 3 ♘f3 ♘c6 4 ♘xd4 e6 5 ♗e3 ♘f6 6 ♗d3 d5 7 exd5 ♘xd5 8 ♘xc6 bxc6 9 ♘d2 ♗b4 10 0-0 0-0 11 a3 ♗d6 12 ♕h5 f5 13 ♘f3 ♘xe3 14 fxe3 ♖f6 15 ♕h4 ♕b6 16 ♕f2 ♗c5 17 ♘d4 e5 [17 ... f4!] 18 b4 ♗xd4 19 ♗c4+ ♔f8 20 cxd4 ♕xd4 21 ♕xd4 exd4 22 ♖ad1 c5 23 bxc5 ♗b7 24 ♖xd4 ♖c8 25 ♖fd1 ♗e4 26 ♗b3 ♖fc6 27 ♖d7 ♖6c7 28 ♖1d2 a5 29 ♔f2 ♖xd7 30 ♖xd7 ♖xc5 31 ♖f7+ ♔e8 32 ♖xg7 ♗xc2 33 ♗xc2 ♖xc2+ 34 ♔e1 ♖c3 35 ♖xh7 ♖xa3 36 ♖a7 ♖a2 37 ♔f1 a4 38 h4 ♔f8 39 h5 ♔g8 40 h6 ♔h8 [□ 40 ... a3] 41 ♖f7 f4 42 ♖xf4 ♔h7 43 ♖f6 a3 44 ♖a6 ♖a1+ 45 ♔f2 a2 46 ♔g3?! ♔h8 47 ♔g4 ♖h1 48 ♖xa2 ♖xh6 49 ♔g5 ♖b6 50 ♖a7 ♔g8 51 g4 ♔f8 52 ♔h5 ♔g8 53 g5 ♖b1 54 ♔h6 ♖h1+ 55 ♔g6 ♔f8 56 ♖a8+ ♔e7 57 ♔g7 ♖g1 58 g6 ♔e6 59 ♖a6+ ♔e7 60 ♖f6 ♖g2 61 ♖f3 ♖h2 62 ♔g8 ♖g2 63 ♔h7 ♖e2 64 ♖f7+ ♔e8 65 ♔g8 ♖g2 66 g7 ♖g3 67 ♖f2 ♖e3 68 ♖g2 ♖e4 [□ 68 ... ♖h3] 69 ♔h7 ♖h4+ 70 ♔g6 **1-0** L/N5184

**1857-NYC1-49** 24x57
**Raphael, B.I.+ Marache, N.**
[Fiske]

1 d4 f5 2 ♘c3 ♘f6 3 ♘f3 e6 4 ♗g5 ♗e7 5 ♗xf6 ♗xf6 6 e4 fxe4 7 ♘xe4 0-0 8 ♗d3 ♘c6 9 c3 d6 10 ♕c2 h6 11 0-0-0 ♔h8 12 h4! e5 13 d5 ♘e7 14 ♘fg5!! ♘xd5?? 15 ♗c4 c6 16 ♗xd5 cxd5 17 ♘xf6 e4 18 ♘xd5 hxg5 19 hxg5+ ♔g8 20 f4 ♗f5 21 ♘e3 ♗g6 22 g3 ♕a5 23 ♖xd6 ♗f7 24 g6 ♗xg6 [24 ... ♗~ 25 ♖h8+ ♔xh8 26 ♕h2+ ♔g8 27 ♕h7#] 25 ♖xg6 ♕xa2 26 ♕xe4 ♕a1+ 27 ♔c2 ♕a5 28 ♖xg7+

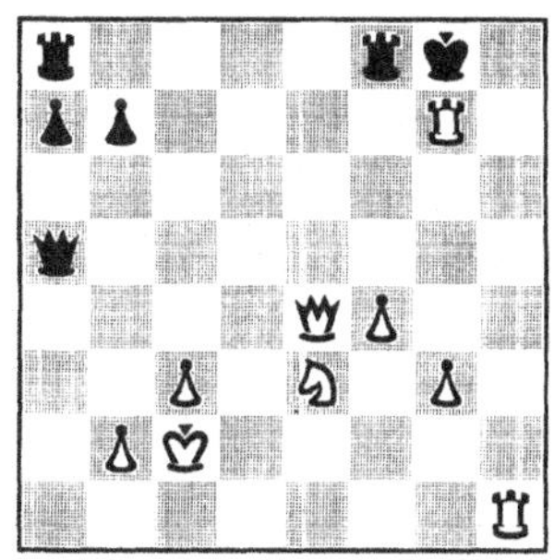

28 ... ♔xg7 29 ♕h7+ ♔f6 30 ♖h6# **1-0** L/N5184

**1857-NYC1-50** 19x57
**Lichtenhein, T.+ Perrin, F.**
[Fiske]

1 e4 e5 2 ♘f3 ♘c6 3 ♗b5 ♘f6 4 ♘c3 ♗c5 5 0-0 [5 ♗xc6] 5 ... d6 6 d4 exd4 7 ♘xd4 ♗d7 8 ♗xc6 ♗xc6 9 ♘xc6 bxc6 10 ♗g5 h6 11 ♗h4 ♕e7 12 ♕f3 ♕e5 13 ♗g3 ♕h5 14 ♕d3 0-0 15 ♔h1 ♘g4 16 f4 f5 17 e5 ♖ad8 18 ♖ae1 ♖fe8 [18 ... dxe5?? 19 ♕c4+] 19 b4 ♗b6 20 ♕c4+ ♔h8 21 ♕xc6 dxe5 22 fxe5 ♖d2 23 ♘d5! ♗f2 24 ♘f4 ♕f7 25 e6 ♕g8 26 ♗xf2 ♘xf2+ 27 ♔g1 ♘e4 28 ♘g6+ ♔h7 29 e7 ♖d6 30 ♘f8+ ♖xf8 31 exf8♕ ♖xc6 [31 ... ♕xf8 32 ♕xe4] 32 ♕xf5+ **1-0** L/N5184

**1857-NYC1-51** 19x57
**Perrin, F.– Lichtenhein, T.**
[Fiske]

1 e4 c5 2 d4 cxd4 3 ♘f3 ♘c6 4 ♘xd4 e6 5 ♗e3 ♘ge7 6 ♗d3 ♘g6 7 0-0 ♗e7 8 c3 0-0 9 ♘d2 ♘xd4 10 cxd4 f5 11 exf5 exf5 12 f4 d5 13 ♘f3 ♗e6 14 ♘e5 ♘xe5 15 fxe5 ♗g5 16 ♕d2 ♗xe3+ 17 ♕xe3 ♖f7 18 ♖ac1 ♕e7 19 ♖c3 ♖af8 20 g3 g5 21 ♗c2 f4 22 gxf4 gxf4 23 ♕f3 ♕b4 24 ♕f2 f3 25 ♔h1 ♖f4 26 ♖xf3?? ♖xf3 27 ♕g2+ ♔h8 28 ♖g1 [28 ♖xf3 ♕e1+] 28 ... ♕e7 29 a3 ♖f2 **0-1** L/N5184

**1857-NYC1-52** 19x57
**Lichtenhein, T.+ Perrin, F.**
[Fiske]

1 e4 b6 2 d4 ♗b7 3 ♗d3 e6 4 ♘e2 g6 5 0-0 ♗g7 6 c3 ♘e7 7 f4 f5 8 e5 d6 9 ♘d2 dxe5 10 fxe5 ♗xe5? 11 ♗c4 ♗d6 12 ♗xe6 ♗d5 [12 ... ♗xh2+ 13 ♔xh2 ♕d6+ 14 ♘f4 g5 15 ♕h5+ ♘g6 16 ♗xf5+-] 13 ♗xd5 ♘xd5 14 ♘f3 ♘c6 15 ♗g5 ♕d7 16 ♕b3 h6 17 ♗h4 ♘a5 18 ♕c2 ♘e3 19 ♕d3 ♘xf1 20 ♖xf1 g5 21 ♗g3 f4?? [□21 ... ♖f8 △ 22 ... 0-0-0] 22 ♕e4+ ♔f7 23 ♗xf4

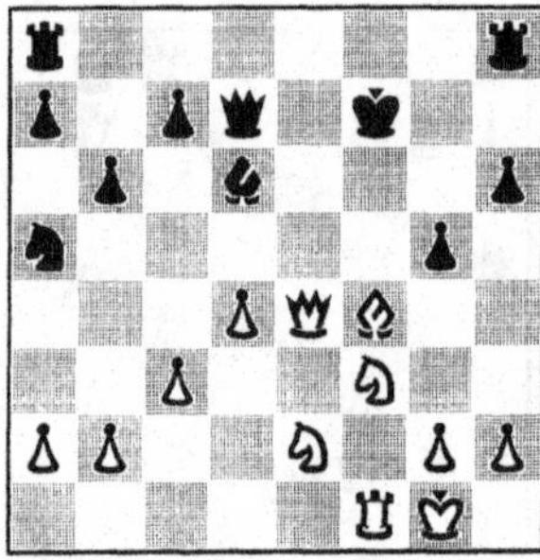

23 ... ♔g7 [23 ... gxf4 24 ♘xf4+-; 23 ... ♗xf4 24 ♘e5+] 24 ♗e5+ ♗xe5 [24 ... ♔g8 25 ♕g6+; 24 ... ♔f~ 25 ♘xg5+] 25 ♘xe5 ♕e6 26 ♖f7+ ♕xf7 [26 ... ♔g8 27 ♕xa8+ ♕e8 28 ♕xe8#] 27 ♘xf7 ♔xf7 28 b4 ♖ae8 29 ♕f3+ ♔g8 30 bxa5 **1-0** L/N5184

**1857-NYC1-53** 22x57
**Lichtenhein,T.– Morphy,P.C.**
[Löwenthal]

1 e4 e5 2 ♘f3 ♘c6 3 d4 exd4 4 ♗c4 ♘f6 5 e5 d5 6 ♗b5 ♘e4 7 ♘xd4 ♗d7 8 ♘xc6 bxc6 9 ♗d3 ♗c5 10 ♗xe4 ♕h4 11 ♕e2 dxe4 12 ♗e3 [□12 0-0] 12 ... ♗g4 13 ♕c4 [13 ♕d2? ♖d8-+] 13 ... ♗xe3 14 g3 ♕d8! 15 fxe3 ♕d1+ 16 ♔f2 ♕f3+ 17 ♔g1 ♗h3 18 ♕xc6+ ♔f8 **0-1** L/N3161

**1857-NYC1-54** 23x57
**Morphy,P.C.+ Lichtenhein,T.**
[Löwenthal]

1 e4 e5 2 ♘f3 ♘f6 3 ♗c4 ♘xe4 4 ♘c3 d5 5 ♗xd5 ♘f6 6 ♗b3 ♗d6 7 d3 0-0 8 h3 h6 9 ♗e3 ♘c6 10 ♕d2 ♘a5 11 g4 ♘xb3 12 axb3 ♗d7 13 ♖g1 ♘h7 14 ♘e4 ♔h8 15 g5 h5 16 ♘h4 g6 17 ♕e2 ♗c6? 18 f4 exf4 19 ♗d4+ ♔g8 20 ♘f5! ♖e8 [20 ... gxf5 21 g6+-; 21 ♘f6++-] 21 ♘h6+ ♔f8 22 0-0-0 ♗xe4 23 dxe4 ♕e7 24 e5! ♗xe5 [□ 24 ... ♗c5] 25 ♗xe5 ♕xe5 26 ♖d7! ♕g7? [□ 26 ... ♘xg5 27 ♖xg5 ♕f6 28 ♕xh5 f3 29 ♖xg6 fxg6 30 ♕d5 ♖e6 31 ♖f7+ ♕xf7 32 ♘xf7 f2 33 ♕c5+ ♔xf7 34 ♕xf2+=] 27 ♕c4 ♖e7 28 ♖xe7 ♔xe7 29 ♖e1+ **1-0** L/N3161

**1857-NYC1-55** 26x57
**Lichtenhein,T.= Morphy,P.C.**
[Fiske]

1 d4 d5 2 c4 e6 3 ♘c3 ♘f6 4 ♘f3 c5 5 e3 ♘c6 6 a3 ♗d6 7 dxc5 ♗xc5 8 b4 ♗d6 9 ♗b2 0-0 10 ♘b5 ♗e7 11 ♘bd4 ♘e4 12 ♘xc6 bxc6 13 ♗d3 c5 14 ♘d2 ♘xd2 15 ♕xd2 dxc4 16 ♗e4 ♕xd2+ 17 ♔xd2 ♖b8 18 ♗e5?! ♖b5 19 ♗c6 ♖b6 20 b5 ♗b7 21 ♗c7 c3+ 22 ♔xc3 ♗xc6 23 ♗xb6 ♗f6+ 24 ♔d2 axb6 25 bxc6 ♗xa1 26 ♖xa1 ♖c8 27 a4 ♖xc6 28 a5 bxa5 29 ♖xa5 g6 30 f3→ ♖b6? 31 ♖xc5 ...♀ **½-½** L/N5184

**1857-NYC1-56** 27x57
**Lichtenhein,T.– Morphy,P.C.**
[Fiske]

1 d4 f5 2 ♘c3 ♘f6 3 ♗g5 e6 4 e4 fxe4 5 ♘xe4 ♗e7 6 ♗xf6 ♗xf6 7 ♕h5+ g6 8 ♘xf6+ ♕xf6 9 ♕e5 ♕xe5+ 10 dxe5 b6 11 0-0-0 ♗b7 12 ♘h3 ♖f8 13 ♖g1 ♘c6 14 f4 ♔e7 15 g3 d6 16 ♗g2 dxe5 17 fxe5 ♖f5 18 ♖ge1 ♖d8 19 g4 ♖xd1+ 20 ♔xd1 ♖f8 21 ♗xc6 ♗xc6 22 ♔d2 h6 23 ♖e3 g5 24 b3 ♖f1 25 ♖e1 ♖xe1 26 ♔xe1 ♗e4 27 ♔d2 [27 c4 ♗b1] 27 ... ♔d7 28 c4 ♔c6 29 ♘f2 ♗b1 30 ♘d1?

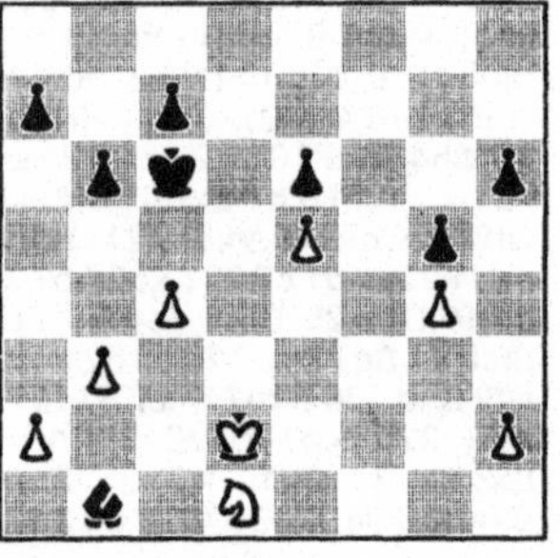

30 ... ♗xa2∓ 31 ♔c2 ♔c5 32 ♘c3 ♗xb3+ 33 ♔xb3 c6 34 ♘e2 ...♀ **0-1** L/N 5184

**1857-NYC1-57** 23x57
**Raphael, B.I.– Paulsen, L.**
[Fiske]

1 e4 c5 2 d4 cxd4 3 ♘f3 e6 4 ♘xd4 ♗c5 5 ♘c3 ♕b6 6 ♘a4 [6 ♗e3] 6 ... ♕a5+ 7 c3 ♗xd4 8 ♕xd4 ♘f6 9 f3 [9 ♗d3?? ♘c6] 9 ... ♘c6 10 ♕d1 0-0 11 b4 ♕e5 12 ♗d3?? [□12 ♗e3] 12 ... ♘xb4 13 cxb4? [□13 0-0] 13 ... ♕xa1 14 ♕c2 ♕d4 15 ♗b2 ♕e3+ 16 ♔d1 ♕h6 17 ♗c1 ♕h4 18 ♘c3 d5 19 g3 ♕h5 20 ♕f2 ♘xe4 21 ♗xe4 dxe4 22 ♘xe4 ♕d5+ 23 ♗d2 ♕xa2 24 ♖e1 ♗d7 25 ♕e3 ♗b5 **0-1** L/N5184

**1857-NYC1-58** 23x57
**Paulsen, L.= Raphael, B.I.**
[Fiske]

1 e4 e5 2 ♘c3 ♘f6 3 ♘f3 ♘c6 4 d4 ♗b4 5 d5 ♘e7 [5 ... ♘xe4!? 6 dxc6 ♘xc3 7 cxd7+ ♗xd7 8 bxc3 ♗xc3+ 9 ♗d2 ♗xa1 10 ♕xa1 0-0∞] 6 ♘xe5 d6 7 ♘f3 ♘xe4 8 ♕d4 ♗xc3+ 9 bxc3 ♘f6 10 ♗c4 0-0 11 0-0 h6 12 ♗b3 a5 13 a4 ♘g6 14 ♗a3 ♖e8 15 ♖fe1 ♗g4 16 ♘d2 ♘e5 17 c4 ♖e7 [□ 17 ... b6] 18 c5 ♕d7 19 cxd6 cxd6 20 c4 ♖ae8 21 c5

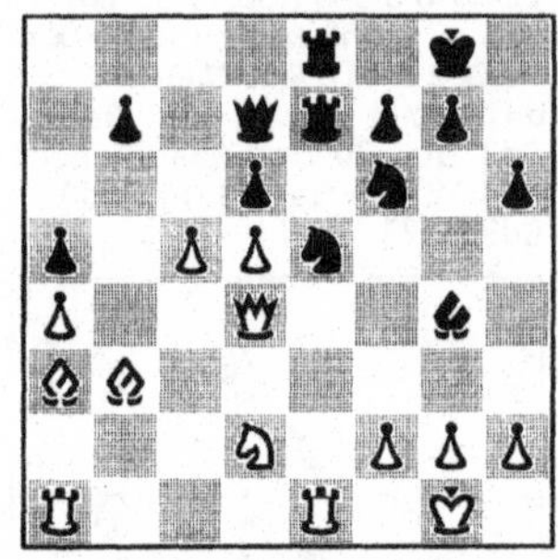

21 ... ♘c6! 22 ♖xe7 ♘xd4 23 ♖xd7 ♘xd7 24 f3 ♖e2 25 ♖d1 ♗h3! [26 gxh3 ♖xd2 27 ♖xd2 ♘xf3+ 28 ~ ♘xd2] 26 c6 ♖xg2+ 27 ♔h1 bxc6 28 dxc6 ♘e5 29 ♗xd6 ♘exc6 [△ 30 ... ♘e2; 29 ... ♘dxf3 30 ♘xf3 ♘xf3 31 ♗d5; 29 ♘exf3 30 ♗xf7+?? ♔xf7 31 ♘xf3 ♘xf3 32 ♖f1 ♖xh2+-+; □ 30 ♘xf3 ♘xb3 31 ♘g1+-] 30 ♗c4 ♖g6 31 ♗g3 ♘f5 [□ 31 ... h5] 32 ♘e4 ♘e3 33 ♖c1 ♗g2+ 34 ♔g1 ♗xf3 35 ♗d3 f5 [□ 35 ... ♘d4] 36 ♘d6 ♘d4 37 ♖c5 ♖f6 38 ♖xa5 f4 39 ♘c4 fxg3 40 ♘xe3 fxh2+ 41 ♔xh2 g5 42 ♖a7 ♔f8 43 a5 ♖f7 44 ♖a6 ♖e7 45 ♖f6+ ♔e8 46 ♘f5 ♘xf5 47 ♗xf5 **½-½** L/N5184

**1857-NYC1-59** 24 x 57
**Raphael, B.I.– Paulsen, L.**
[Fiske]

1 e4 e5 2 f4 d5 3 exd5 exf4 4 ♘f3 ♗e7 [□ 4 ... ♗d6!=; 4 ... ♕xd5 5 ♘c3 ♕e6+ 6 ♔f2 ♗d7 7 d4 ♗d6 8 ♗d3 ♘e7 9 ♘e4 f6 10 ♖e1 ♕f7 11 ♘xd6+ cxd6 12 ♗xf4±] 5 ♗c4 ♗h4+ 6 ♔f1 ♗g4 7 d3 ♘e7 8 ♗xf4 0-0 9 ♘c3 ♘g6 10 ♕d2 ♗xf3 11 gxf3 ♘d7 12 ♘e4 ♘de5 13 ♗xe5 ♘xe5 14 ♕g2 f5 15 ♖g1 ♘g4! [16 fxg4 fxe4+ 17 ♔e2 ♖f2+–+] 16 ♔e2 fxe4 17 ♖xg4 [17 dxe4 ♗f2 18 ♕xg4 ♗xg1 19 ♖xg1 ♕f6] 17 ... exf3+ 18 ♔d2 ♕f6 19 ♕e6+ ♔h8 20 ♕xf6 ♗xf6 21 ♖af1 ♖ae8 22 ♖xf3 ♗g5+ 23 ♖xg5 ♖xf3 24 ♖g2 h6 25 d6 cxd6 26 ♗d5 ♖f6 27 ♗xb7 ♖b8 28 ♗d5 ♖xb2 29 ♗b3 [Δ 30 ♖g1 31 ♔c3] 29 ... ♖b1 30 ♔c3 ♖e1 31 ♔d4 g5 32 a4 a5 33 ♗d5 ♖e5 34 c4 ♔g7 35 ♖b2 ♖e7 36 ♗e4 ♖a7 37 ♔d5 ♖a6 38 d4 ♖f7 39 c5 dxc5 40 dxc5 ♖a8 41 c6 ♖d8+ 42 ♔c5 ♖f4 43 ♖b7+ ♔f6 44 c7 ♖c8 45 ♗c6 ♔e7 46 ♖a7 [46 ♔b6 ♔d6 47 ♖b8 ♖ff8 (47 ... ♖xc7?? 48 ♖d8+) 48 ♖b7 ♖f7–+] 46 ... ♖f5+ 47 ♔b6 ♔d6 48 ♖a8 ♖xa8 49 ♗xa8 ♖c5 50 ♗f3 ♖xc7 51 ♔xa5 ♔c5 52 ♔a6 ♖f7 53 ♗g4 ♔b4 **0-1** L/N5184

**1857-NYC1-60** 29 x 57
**Lichtenhein, T.+ Raphael, B.I.**
[Fiske]

1 e4 e5 2 ♘f3 ♘c6 3 ♗b5 ♘f6 4 ♘c3 d6?? [□ 4 ... ♗c5] 5 d4 exd4 6 ♘xd4 ♗d7 7 ♗xc6 bxc6 8 0-0 ♗e7 9 f4 0-0 10 e5 ♘e8 11 ♕f3 c5 12 ♘de2 f6?? [□ 12 ... g6] 13 ♕d5+ ♔h8 14 e6 c6 15 ♕f5 ♗c8 16 ♘g3 g6 17 ♕e4 d5 18 ♕a4 ♕d6 [18 ... ♗xe6 19 ♕xc6] 19 f5 gxf5 20 ♗h6 ♖g8 21 ♘xf5 ♕c7 22 ♖ae1 d4 23 ♗f4 ♗d6 24 ♘xd6 ♘xd6 25 ♘e4 ♕g7 26 ♗g3 ♘xe4 27 ♖xe4 h6 28 ♖xf6! ♔h7 29 ♖f7 **1-0** L/N5184

**1857-NYC1-61** 30 x 57
**Raphael, B.I.+Lichtenhein, T.**
[Fiske]

1 e4 e5 2 f4 exf4 3 ♗c4 ♘f6 4 ♘c3 ♗b4 5 ♕f3 ♗xc3 6 dxc3 0-0 7 ♗xf4 ♘xe4 8 ♗xc7! ♕xc7 9 ♕xe4 d6 10 0-0-0 ♘d7 11 ♖f1 ♘e5 12 ♗b3 ♗e6 13 ♘f3 ♗xb3 14 cxb3 ♖ae8 15 h4 ♘xf3 16 ♕xf3 ♖e6 17 g4 ♖fe8 18 h5 ♖e3 19 ♕f2 ♕e7 20 h6 ♖e2 21 ♕f4 ♖e4 22 ♕d2 ♖e3 23 ♕f2 ♕e6 24 g5 ♖e2 25 ♕f4 ♕g6 26 ♕f5 ♕xf5 27 ♖xf5 gxh6 28 ♖xh6 ♖e1+ 29 ♔d2 ♖1e2+ 30 ♔d3 ♖xb2 31 ♖hf6 ♖e7 32 ♖xd6 ♖xa2 **0-1** L/N5184

**1857-NYC1-62** 31 x 57
**Lichtenhein, T.+Raphael, B.I.**
[Fiske]

1 d4 c5 2 d5 f5 [2 ... e5 3 e4 d6 4 f4 f5 5 ♗d3 fxe4 6 ♗xe4 ♘f6 7 ♘c3 ♗e7 8 ♘f3 0-0 9 fxe5 dxe5 10 0-0±] 3 e4 d6 4 ♗d3 fxe4 5 ♗xe4 ♘f6 6 ♘c3 g6 7 ♘f3 ♗g7 8 ♘g5 0-0 9 f4 h6 10 ♘f3 ♘xe4 11 ♘xe4 ♗f5 12 ♘g3 ♕d7 [□ 12 ... ♕a5+ 13 ♔f2 ♕b4 (13 ♗d2 ♕b5)] 13 0-0 ♘a6 14 ♘h4 ♖f6 15 ♘gxf5 gxf5 16 ♗d2 ♖f7 [16 ... e5 17 fxe5] 17 ♗c3 ♔h7 [□ 17 ... ♗xc3] 18 ♕h5 ♖af8 19 ♕g6+ ♔g8 [19 ... ♔h8 20 ♕xh6+] 20 ♖f3 ♘c7 [20 ... e5 21 dxe6; 20 ... ♖f6 21 ♗xf6] 21 ♖g3 e5 22 dxe6 ♕xe6

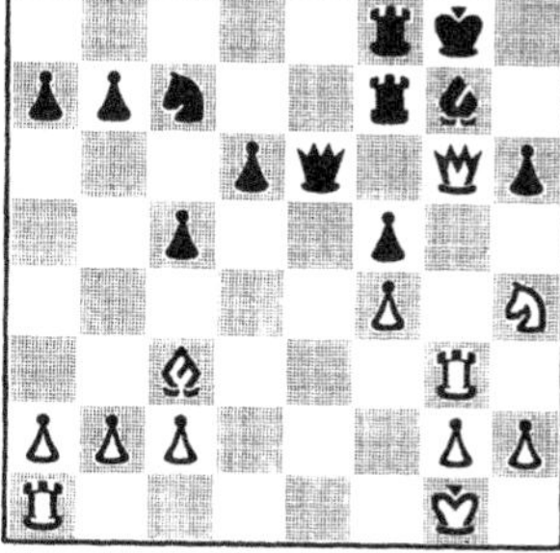

23 ♕xg7+! ♖xg7 24 ♖xg7+ ♔h8 25 ♘g6+ **1-0** L/N5184

**1857-NYC1-63** 29 x 57
**Morphy, P.C.+ Paulsen, L.**
[Fiske]

1 e4 c5 2 d4 cxd4 3 ♘f3 e6 4 ♘xd4 ♗c5 5 ♘b3 ♗b6 6 ♘c3 ♘e7 7 ♗f4 0-0 [□ 7 ... d5] 8 ♗d6 f5 9 e5 a6 10 ♗e2 ♘bc6 11 0-0 ♖f7 12 ♔h1 f4? 13 ♘e4 ♘f5 14 ♗h5 g6 15 ♗g4 ♘g7 16 ♕f3 h5 17 ♗h3 ♕h4 18 ♘f6+ ♔h8 19 ♕e4 ♕g5 20 g3 f3 21 ♘d2 ♗d8 22 ♘xf3 ♕h6 23 ♖g1 ♗xf6 24 exf6 ♘e8 25 ♗f4 ♘xf6 [25 ... ♕h7 26 ♘g5+–; 25 ... ♕f8 26 ♕xg6+–] 26 ♕xc6 ♕xf4 27 ♕xc8+ ♖xc8 28 gxf4 ♖xc2 29 ♖ac1 ♖xf2 30 ♖c8+ ♘g8 31 ♘e5 ♖g7 32 ♘xg6+ ♔h7 33 ♘f8+ ♔h6 [33 ... ♔h8 34 ♘xd7+–] 34 ♘xd7 ♖xd7 35 ♖cxg8 ♖xf4 36 ♗xe6 ♖e7 **1-0** L/N 5184

**1857-NYC1-64** 30 x 57
**Paulsen, L.= Morphy, P.C.**
[Fiske]

1 e4 e5 2 ♘f3 ♘c6 3 ♗b5 ♘f6 4 0-0 ♘xe4 5 d4 [5 ♖e1] 5 ... a6 [5 ... ♘xd4; 5 ... exd4; □ 5 ... ♗e7 Lange] 6 ♗d3 d5 7 ♘xe5 ♘xd4 [7 ... ♘xe5 8 dxe5±] 8 ♖e1 ♗e6 9 c3 [9 ♗xe4 dxe4 10 ♖xe4 ♘b3 11 ♕f3 ♘xa1 12 ♘xf7 ♕d7 13 ♘xh8 0-0-0] 9 ... ♘c6 10 ♘xc6 bxc6 11 ♕a4 ♕d7 12 ♗xe4 dxe4 13 ♕xe4 ♗d6 14 ♘d2 0-0 15 ♘f3 ♗d5∓ 16 ♕d3 ♖ae8 17 ♗g5 [□ 17 ♗d2] 17 ... ♕g4 18 h3 ♕h5 19 ♗d2 [19 ♗h4? ♗xf3; 19 ♗e3 ♗xf3 20 gxf3 ♕xh3] 19 ... ♖e6 20 ♘g5 ♖g6 21 ♘e4 ♖xg2+ 22 ♔xg2 f5 23 f3 ♕g6+? [23 ... fxe4 24 ♖xe4 (24 fxe4 ♕g6+ 25 ♔h1 ♖f2 26 ♖g1 ♗xe4+–+; 24 ... ♕e5–+; 24 ♕f1 ♖xf3–+) 24 ... ♕g6+ 25 ♔h1 (25 ♔f1 ♗xe4–+; 25 ♔f2 ♗xe4–+; 25 ♖g4 ♕xd3–+) 25 ... ♖xf3 26 ♖e8+ (26 ♕xf3 ♗xe4–+) 26 ... ♖f8+–+] 24 ♘g5 h6 25 c4 ♗f7 26 h4 ♖d8 27 ♕c2 hxg5 28 hxg5 ♗e6 29 ♖h1 ♗e7 30 f4 c5 31 ♖ae1 ♔f7 32 ♖h3 ♗c8 33 ♔g1 ♗b7 34 ♗c1 ♖d4 35 b3 ♗d6 36 ♕e2 ♖e4 37 ♕f2 ♕e6 38 ♖he3 ♕d7 39 ♕h4 ♔g6 40 ♕h3 ♗e7 41 ♖xe4 ♗xe4 42 ♕e3 [42 ♖xe4 ♕d1+ Δ 43 ... fxe4] 42 ... ♕d8 [Δ 43 ... ♕h8] 43 ♕h3 ♕d4+ 44 ♗e3 ♕c3 45 ♕f1 ♕a5 46 ♕f2 ♕b6 47 ♖e2 ♕c6 48 ♗c1 ♕d7 49 ♖d2 ♕e6 50 ♕e3 ♕c6 51 ♗b2 ♔f7 52 ♕h3 ♕g6 43 ♖h2 ♕d6 ... 56 **½-½** L/N 5184

**1857-NYC1-65** 2 xi 57
**Paulsen, L.+ Morphy, P.C.**
[Maroczy]

1 e4 e5 2 ♘f3 ♘c6 3 ♘c3 ♗c5 [□ 3 ... ♘f6] 4 ♗b5 [4 ♘xe5!] 4 ... d6 5 d4 exd4 6 ♘xd4 ♗d7 7 ♘xc6 bxc6 8 ♗a4 ♕h4? 9 0-0 ♘f6 10 ♕f3 ♘g4 11 ♗f4 ♘e5 12 ♕g3 ♕f6 13 ♖ad1 h6 14 ♔h1 g5? 15 ♗xe5 dxe5 16 b4! ♗d6 [16 ... ♗xb4? 17 ♖xd7 ♔xd7 (17 ... ♗xc3 18 ♖xc7) 18 ♘d5 ♕d6 19 ♕h3+ ♔d8 20 ♘xb4 ♕xb4 21 ♗xc6] 17 ♖d3 h5 18 ♖fd1 a6 19 ♘e2 ♖d8 20 a3 g4 21 c4 ♕h6 22 c5 h4 23 ♕e3 ♗e7 [23 ... ♕xe3 24 fxe3 Δ 24 ... ♗∼ 25 ♖xd7, 26 ♗xc6] 24 f4 exf4 25 ♕xf4 [Δ 26 ♕xc7] 25 ... ♕xf4 26 ♘xf4 ♖h6 27 ♘e2 f5 [27 ... ♗c8!] 28 e5 ♖e6 29 ♘f4 ♖xe5 30 ♖xd7 ♖xd7 31 ♗xc6 ♗d6 32 cxd6 cxd6 33 ♔g1 ♔d8 34 ♗xd7 ...⚲ **1-0**

**1857-NYC1-66** 4 xi 57
**Morphy, P.C.= Paulsen, L.**
[Maroczy]

1 e4 c5 2 ♘f3 e6 3 d4 cxd4 4 ♘xd4 ♗c5 5 ♘b3 [5 ♗e3] 5 ... ♗b6 6 ♘c3 ♘c7 7 8 ♗g3 ♘ge7 9 ♗c4 0-0 10 ♘b5 6 ♘c3 ♘c6 7 ♗f4 e5 8 ♗g3 ♘ge7 9 ♗c4 0-0 10 ♘b5 a6 11 ♘d6 ♗c7 12 a4 ♘g6 13 ♕d2 ♕f6 14 ♖d1 ♘f4 15 0-0 h5 16 ♘xc8 ♖axc8 17 ♕xd7 ♘d4 18 ♘xd4 exd4 19 ♕f5 [19 ♕xd4 ♗e5; 19 ♖xd4 ♗e5] 19 ... ♕xf5 20 exf5 ♗e5 21 ♗xf4 ♗xf4 22 ♖xd4 ♗e5 23 ♖e4 ♗xb2 24 ♖b1 ♖fd8 25 g3 ♖d4 26 ♗d3 ♖xe4 27 ♗xe4 ♖c4 28 ♗xb7 [28 ♖xb2 ♖xe4 29 ♖xb7±] 28 ... ♖xc2 29 ♗xa6 ♗d4 30 ♖f1 ♖a2 31 ♗b5 ♔h7 32 ♗c4 ♖xa4 33 ♗xf7 h4 34 ♔g2 ♖a1 35 ♗g6+ ♔g8 [35 ... ♔h6? 36 ♖xa1 ♗xa1 37 f4! hxg3 38 hxg3 ♗f6 39 ♔f3 Δ ♔e4, ♔d5, ♔e6, ♔f7, g5+–] 36 ♖xa1 ♗xa1 ...⚲ **½-½**

**1857-NYC1-67** 6 xi 57
**Morphy, P.C.+ Paulsen, L.**
[Fiske]

1 e4 c5 2 ♘f3 e6 3 d4 cxd4 4 ♘xd4 ♗c5 5 ♗e3 ♕b6 6 ♘b5 ♘f6 [6 ... ♗xe3 7 ♘d6+] 7 ♗xc5 ♕xc5 8 ♘d6+ ♔e7 9 ♘xc8+ ♖xc8 10 ♗d3 ♘c6 11 0-0 h5 12 ♘d2 h4 13 h3 g5 14 a3 ♖g8 15 b4 ♕b6 16 ♘c4 ♕c7 [Δ 17 ... g4] 17 f3 ♘e5 18 ♘xe5 ♕xe5 19 ♕d2 ♖g7 [□ 19 ... ♘h5] 20 ♖ad1 ♖d8 21 ♕f2 b6 22 f4 gxf4 23 ♕xf4 ♕g5 24 ♖f2 ♕xf4 25 ♖xf4 ♖dg8 26 ♖d2 [26 ♖f2?!] 26 ... ♖h8 27 e5 ♘d5 28 ♖d4 f6 29 exf6+ ♘xf6 30 ♖c4 [30 ♗b5 d5] 30 ... ♔d8 31 a4 ♘d5 32 ♗e4 ♘c7 33 ♗f3 d5 34 ♖c6 ♖d7 35 ♗g4 ♖h6 36 ♖e2 ♔e7 37 ♔h2 ♔f7 38 g3 hxg3+ 39 ♔xg3 ♖e7 40 h4 ♘e8 41 h5 ♘f6 42 ♖cxe6 ♖xe6 43 ♗xe6+ ♔g7? [43 ... ♔f8] 44 ♗g4 ♘xh5+ 45 ♗xh5 ♖xh5 46 ♖e7+ ♔f6 47 ♖xa7 ♔e5 48 ♖a6 ♖g5+ 49 ♔f3 ♖f5+ 50 ♔e2 b5 [50 ... ♖f6 51 a5 bxa5 52 ♖xf6 ♔xf6 53 bxa5+-] 51 axb5 ♖f4 52 c3 d4 53 c4! [53 cxd4] 53 ... ♖h4 54 c5 ♖h2+ 44 ♔d3 ♖h3+ 56 ♔c2 ♖h2+ 57 ♔b3 ♖h3+ 58 ♔d5 59 ♖d6+ ♔c4 60 c6 ♖h1 61 ♖xd4+ ♔xd4 62 c7 ♖h8 63 b6 ♔c4 64 b7 **1-0** L/N 5184

**1857-NYC1-68** 7 xi 57
**Paulsen, L.– Morphy, P.C.**
[Fiske]

1 e4 e5 2 ♘f3 ♘c6 3 ♘c3 ♘f6 4 ♗b5 ♗c5 5 0-0 0-0 6 ♘xe5 ♖e8 [6 ... ♘xe5 7 d4] 7 ♘xc6 [7 ♘d3=] 7 ... dxc6 8 ♗c4 b5 [8 ... ♘g4; 8 ... ♘xe4 9 ♘xe4 ♖xe4 10 ♗xf7+ Δ 10 ... ♔xf7 11 ♕f3+] 9 ♗e2 [9 ♗b3 ♗g4 10 ♕e1 b4∓] 9 ... ♘xe4 10 ♘xe4 [10 ♗f3 ♘xf2 11 ♖xf2 ♕d4 12 ♕f1 (12 ♘e4 ♖xe4 13 ♗xe4 ♕xf2+ 14 ♔h1 ♗g4 15 ♗f3 ♖e8-+) 12 ... ♕xf2+ 13 ♕xf2 ♖e1#] 10 ... ♖xe4 11 ♗f3 ♖e6 12 c3? [Δ 13 d4; 12 d3] 12 ... ♕d3 13 b4 ♗b6 14 a4 bxa4 15 ♕xa4 ♗d7 [15 ... ♖g6?!] 16 ♖a2? [Δ 17 ♕c2; 16 ♕a6] 16 ... ♖ae8 [Δ 17 ... ♕xf1+; 18 ... ♖e1#; Δ 17 ... ♕xf3] 17 ♕a6? [17 ♕d1]

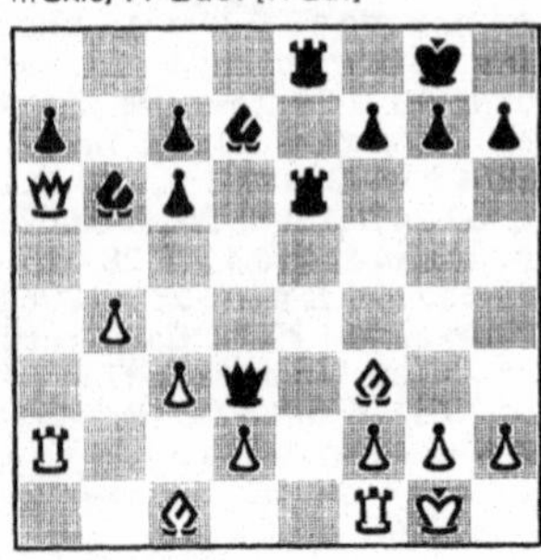

17 ... ♕xf3 18 gxf3 ♖g6+ 19 ♔h1 ♗h3 [Δ 20 ... ♗g2+, 21 ... ♗xf3#] 20 ♖d1 [20 ♖g1 ♖xg1+ 21 ♔xg1 ♖e1+ 22 ♕f1 ♖xf1#; 20 ♕d3 f5 (Δ 21 ... ♗g2+, 22 ... ♗xf3#) 21 ♕c4+ ♔f8 (21 ... ♔h8? 22 ♕f7+-) 22 ♕f4 (22 ♕h4 ♗xf1 23 h3 ♗g2+ 24 ♔h2 ♗xf3-+) 22 ... ♗xf2 23 ♕g3 ♗xg3-+] 20 ... ♗g2+ 21 ♔g1 ♗xf3+ 22 ♔f1 ♗g2+ 23 ♔g1 ♗h3+ 24 ♔h1 ♗xf2 25 ♕f1 ♗xf1 26 ♖xf1 ♖e2 27 ♖a1 [Δ 28 d4] 27 ... ♖h6 28 d4 ♗e3 **0-1** L/N 5184

**1857-NYC1-69** 9 xi 57
**Morphy, P.C.+ Paulsen, L.**
[Fiske]

1 e4 c5 2 ♘f3 e6 3 d4 cxd4 4 ♘xd4 ♗c5 5 ♗e3 ♕b6 6 ♘c3 ♕xb2? 7 ♘db5 ♗xe3 [7 ... ♕b4 8 ♖b1 ♕a5 9 ♗xc5; 7 ... ♗b4 8 ♗d2 ♗xc3 9 ♗xc3] 8 ♖b1 ♕xb1 9 ♘xb1 ♗f4 10 g3 a6 11 gxf4 axb5 12 ♘c3 ♘e7 13 ♘xb5 0-0 14 ♘d6 ♘bc6 15 ♖g1 ♖xa2 16 f5 f6 17 ♗c4 ♖a4 18 f4 b6 19 fxe6 dxe6 20 ♘xc8 ♘xc8 21 ♗xe6+ ♔h8 22 ♗xc8 ♖xc8 23 ♕d7 ♘e7 [23 ... ♖a1+ 24 ♔f2+-; 23 ... ♖g8+-] 24 ♕xe7 ♖a1+ 25 ♔f2 ♖xc2+ 26 ♔e3 **1-0** L/N 5184

**1857-NYC1-70** 10 xi 57
**Paulsen, L.– Morphy, P.C.**
[Fiske]

1 e4 e5 2 ♘f3 ♘c6 3 ♘c3 ♘f6 4 d4 [□ 4 ♗c4] 4 ... ♗b4 5 ♗b5 ♘xe4 6 ♕d3 d5 7 ♘xe5 0-0 8 0-0 ♘xe5 9 dxe5 ♗xc3 10 bxc3 c6 11 ♗a4 ♕a5 12 ♗b3 ♕xc3 13 ♗f4 ♗f5 14 ♖ac1 g5 15 ♕xc3 ♘xc3 16 ♗xg5 ♘e2+ 17 ♔h1 ♘xc1 18 ♖xc1 ♖fe8 19 ♗f6 b5 20 f3 a5 21 a3 ♗e6 [Δ 22 ... c5] 22 ♖d1 b4 23 axb4 axb4 24 h3 c5 25 c3 [25 ♗xd5 ♖ad8 26 ♗xd8 ♖xd8 27 c4 bxc3 28 ♗b3 ♖xd1+ 29 ♗xd1 ♗f5-+] 25 ... bxc3 26 ♗c2 ♖a2 27 ♖c1 ♖ea8 28 ♗g5 ♖a1 29 ♗b1 c2 30 ♗xc2 ♖xc1+ 31 ♗xc1 ♖a1 **0-1** L/N 5184

**1857-★AB-1** 7 viii 57
**Anderssen, A. & Horwitz, B. & Kling, J.– Boden, S.S. & Kipping, J.S. & Staunton, H.**
Manchester [Staunton]

1 e4 e6 2 d4 g6 3 ♗e3 ♗g7 4 ♘d2 ♘e7 5 ♗d3 b6 6 ♘e2 ♗b7 7 0-0 d6 8 c3 ♘d7 9 ♕b3?! 0-0 10 f4 d5 11 e5 [11 f5?] 11 ... ♖b8 [□ 11 ... ♕c8] 12 ♖ac1 c5 13 ♕a3 c4 14 ♗c2 [Δ 15 ♗a4] 14 ... a6 15 g4 b5 16 ♘g3 ♖e8 [Δ ... ♗f8] 17 b4 cxb3?! 18 axb3 ♖c8 19 ♗d3 ♕b6 20 ♕b2 f6 21 ♖ce1 ♕c6 22 ♘b1 fxe5 23 fxe5

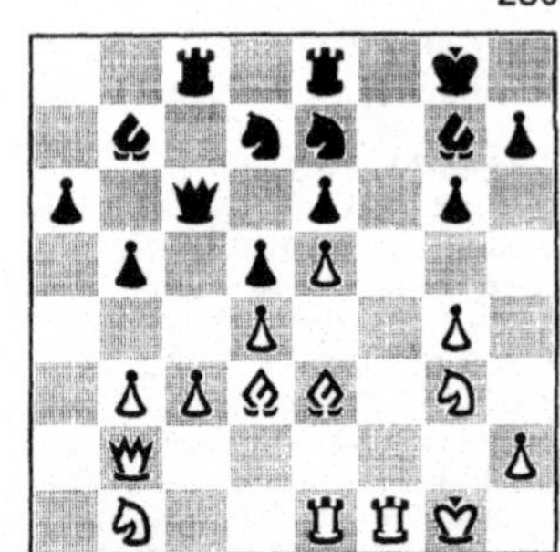

23 ... ♗xe5 24 dxe5 ♘xe5 25 ♗c2 [25 ♖d1? ♘xd3 26 ♖xd3 d4-+] 25 ... ♖f8 26 ♗g5 [□ 26 ♔g2 ♖xf1 Δ 27 ... ♘xg4∓] 26 ... ♘f3+ 27 ♖xf3 ♖xf3 28 ♗d1 [28 ♗xe7 ♕b6+ 29 ♔h1 ♕f2 30 ♖e2 ♖xg3 31 ♖xf2 d4+ 32 ♗e4 (32 ♖g2 ♖xg2 33 ♘d2 dxc3 34 ♕b1 cxd2-+) 32 ... ♗xe4+ 33 ♖g2 ♖xg2 34 ♕xg2 ♗xg2+ 35 ♔xg2 dxc3-+] 28 ... ♕c5+ 29 ♔g2 ♖f7 30 ♔h3 ♕d6 31 ♕e2 ♖c6 32 ♕e3 ♗c8 33 ♔g2 ♖c7 34 b4 ♘c6 35 ♕d2 [Δ 36 ♘e4] 35 ... ♖cd7 36 ♗b3 ♘e5 37 ♗f4 ♖xf4 38 ♕xf4 ♘d3 39 ♕e3 ♘xe1+ 40 ♕xe1 ♖c7 41 ♕e3 [41 ♘d2? ♕c6] 41 ... ♔g7 42 ♘d2 e5 43 ♕g5 [43 ♘f3 ♗xg4 44 ♕xe5+ ♕xe5 45 ♘xe5 ♖xc3 46 ♗xd5 ♖c2+ 47 ♔g1 ♗h3-+] 43 ... ♕e7 44 ♘h5+ ♔h8 45 ♘f6 ♗b7 46 ♔g1 ♖xc3 [46 ... ♔g7 Δ 47 ... ♕xf6] 47 h4 ♔g7 48 ♘h5+ ♔f7 49 ♕h6 ♔e8 [□ 49 ... gxh5] 50 ♘g7+ ♔d7 51 ♕xh7 ♖g3+ 52 ♔f2 ♖xg4 53 ♔e2 ♖g2+ [54 ♔e1 ♕f7-+; 54 ♔d1 e4-+; 54 ... ♔c6=; 54 ... ♕xb4??+-] **0-1** M954-1857

**1857-★AB-2**
**Anderssen, A.– Boden, S.S.**
Manchester [Wisker?]

1 e4 e5 2 f4 ♗c5 3 ♘f3 d6 4 ♗c4 ♘f6 5 d3 ♕e7 6 c3 a5 7 ♕e2 h6 8 f5 ♘c6 9 ♘bd2 ♗d7 10 ♘f1 a4 11 b4 axb3 12 ♗xb3 g6 13 fxg6 fxg6 14 h3± ♗e6 15 ♗xe6 ♕xe6 16 ♘e3 ♘h5 17 ♘d5 ♔d7 18 ♕b2 ♘g3 19 ♖h2 g5 20 ♗e3 ♗xe3 21 ♘xe3 ♘h5 22 g4 ♘f4 23 0-0-0 ♖a6 24 ♕b1!? ♖ha8 25 d4 exd4 26 cxd4 ♖b6 27 ♖b2 ♖xb2 28 ♔xb2 ♘b4 29 a3 ♖a4 30 d5 ♕f6+ 31 ♔b3 ♘e2 32 ♘d4 ♘xd4+ 33 ♔xa4 ♘a6 34 ♕a1 [34 ♖f1 ♕e5-+] 34 ... b5+ **0-1** L/N6131-1868

**1857-★AB-3**
**Pindar, E. & Beaver+ Anderssen, A.**
Manchester [Staunton]

1 e4 e5 2 ♘f3 ♘c6 3 d4 exd4 4 ♗c4 ♗c5 5 ♘g5 ♘h6 6 ♕h5 [6 ♘xf7; 6 ♗xf7+] 6 ... ♕e7 7 0-0 d6 8 h3 ♘e5 9 ♗b3 ♗d7 10 f4 ♗b5 11 fxe5 ♗xf1 12 ♘e6! ♗e2 13 ♘xg7+ ♔d7 14 e6+ ♔c6 15 ♕xh6 ♖af8 16

♗d5+ ♔b6 17 b4 **1-0** M954-1857

### 1857-★AB-4
**Burnell, J. & Owen, J. & Pindar, E.+Avery, T. & Brien, R.B. & Kylman**
Manchester [Staunton]
1 e4 e5 2 ♘f3 d6 3 ♗c4 ♗e7 4 d3?! ♘f6 5 ♘c3 ♘c6 6 h3 ♘a5 7 0-0 ♘xc4 8 dxc4 ♗e6 9 ♕e2 ♘d7 [◻ 9 ... c6] 10 ♘d5 f5 11 ♘xe7 ♕xe7 12 exf5 ♗xf5 13 ♗g5 ♕f7 14 ♘d4 0-0 15 ♘xf5 ♕xf5 16 ♗e3 ♖ae8 17 ♕d3 ♕xd3 18 cxd3= c6 19 ♖ac1 b6 20 ♖c2 ♖f7 21 d4 e4 [◻ 21 ... exd4] 22 b4 d5 23 a4 ♘f6 24 ♖fc1 ♖ef8?! 25 c5 ♘d7 26 b5! bxc5 27 bxc6 bxc6 28 ♗xc5 ♘b6 29 ♖c5! ♘xa4 [29 ... ♘c4?!] 30 ♖xd5 ♘b6 31 ♖b5 [◻ 31 ♖e5] 31 ... ♖c8 32 ♗xb6 axb6 33 ♖xb6 ♖f6 34 ♔f1 e3 35 f3 ♖e6 36 ♔e2 ♔f8 37 ♖c4 ♔g8?! 38 h4 g6 39 g4 ♔h8 40 f4 ♔g8 41 f5 gxf5 42 gxf5 ♖f6 43 ♔xe3 ♖xf5 44 c7 ♖f7 [◻ 44 ... ♖ff8] 45 ♖b8 ♖ff8 46 ♖xc8 ♖xc8 47 ♔d4 **1-0**
M954-1857

### 1857-★AE-1 15i57
**Eichborn, L.+Anderssen, A.**
Breslau
1 e4 e5 2 f4 exf4 3 ♘f3 g5 4 h4 g4 5 ♘e5 h5 6 ♗c4 ♖h7 7 d4 f3 8 gxf3 d6 9 ♘d3 ♗e7 10 ♗e3 ♗xh4+ 11 ♔d2 ♗g5 12 f4 ♗h6 13 ♘c3 ♗g7 14 ♕f1 c6 15 e5 d5 16 ♗b3 ♘e7 17 ♖e1 ♘f5 18 ♕g2 ♗e6 19 ♘c5 ♕e7 20 ♔c1 b6 21 ♘xe6 fxe6 22 ♗f2 ♘d7 23 ♘e2 b5 24 c3 ♘b6 25 ♗c2 b4 26 ♗xf5 exf5 27 ♗h4 ♕f8 28 ♕g3 bxc3 29 ♕xc3 ♘c4 30 ♘g3 ♖b8 31 ♖e2 a5 32 ♕d3 ♔d7 33 ♘xf5 ♗h6 34 e6+ ♔c7 35 ♗g3 ♕b4 36 ♘xh6 ♘xb2 37 ♕xh7+ **1-0** L/N3034

### 1857-★AE-2 18i57
**Eichborn, L.+Anderssen, A.**
Breslau
1 e4 e5 2 ♘f3 ♘c6 3 ♗b5 ♘f6 4 0-0 ♘xe4 5 ♗xc6 dxc6 6 ♘xe5 ♘f6 7 d4 h6 8 ♖e1 ♗e7 9 ♕e2 ♗e6 10 ♘g6 ♖g8 11 ♘c3 ♕d7 12 ♘xe7 ♕xe7 13 ♗f4 0-0-0 14 ♕e5 g5 15 ♗g3 h5 16 h3 h4 17 ♗h2 g4 18 ♗f4 gxh3 19 ♗g5 ♖xg5 20 ♕xg5 ♖g8 21 ♕xh4 ♖xg2+ 22 ♔h1 ♘g4 23 ♕h8+ ♔d7 24 ♘e4 ♗d5

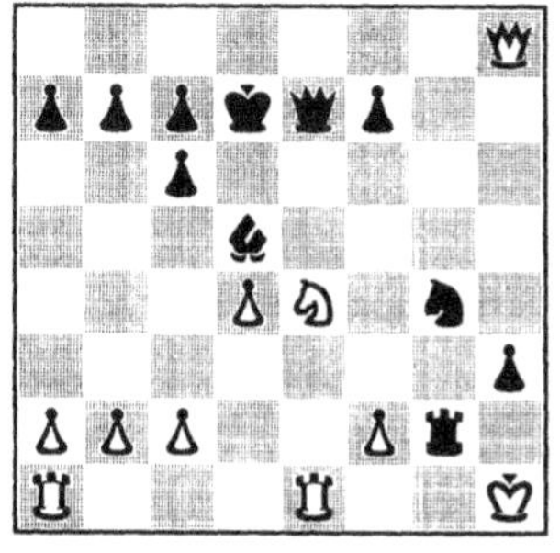

25 ♘c5+ ♔d6 26 ♘xb7+ ♔d7 27 ♖xe7+ ♔xe7 28 ♖e1+ ♗e6 29 ♕d8# **1-0** L/N3034

### 1857-★AE-3 10vi57
**Anderssen, A.– Eichborn, L.**
Breslau
1 e4 e5 2 f4 ♗c5 3 ♘f3 d6 4 ♗c4 ♘f6 5 d3 ♗g4 6 h3 ♗xf3 7 ♕xf3 a6 8 ♗b3 ♘c6 9 f5 ♕e7 10 ♗g5 ♖f8 11 c3 h6 12 ♗h4 g5 13 ♗g3 0-0-0 14 ♗c2 ♔b8 15 ♘d2 d5 16 b4 dxe4 17 dxe4 ♗a7 18 ♖b1 b5 19 a4 ♗b6 20 axb5 axb5 21 ♕e2 ♘a7 22 c4 c6 23 c5 ♗c7 24 0-0 ♔b7 25 ♖a1 ♖d4 26 ♖fb1 ♖a8 27 ♘f3 ♖xb4 28 ♖xb4 ♕xc5+ 29 ♕f2 ♕xb4 30 ♗xe5 ♗xe5 31 ♘xe5 ♕c3 32 ♖xa7+ ♖xa7 33 ♘d3 ♖a2 34 ♘c5+ ♔c8 35 e5 ♖xc2 **0-1** L/N3034

### 1857-★AE-4 16vi57
**Eichborn, L.+Anderssen, A.**
Breslau
1 e4 e5 2 ♘f3 ♘c6 3 ♗c4 ♗c5 4 c3 ♘f6 5 d4 exd4 6 e5 d5 7 ♗b5 ♘e4 8 cxd4 ♗b4+ 9 ♗d2 ♗xd2+ 10 ♘bxd2 0-0 11 ♗xc6 bxc6 12 0-0 ♖b8 13 ♘b3 f5 14 ♖c1 ♖b6 15 ♖c2 f4 16 ♕c1 c5 17 ♘xc5 ♖h6 18 ♘d3 g5 19 ♖xc7 g4 20 ♘xf4 gxf3 21 g3 ♗h3 22 ♖e1 ♔h8 23 ♘xd5 ♕h4 24 ♘f6 ♘xg3 25 hxg3 ♖fxf6 26 exf6 **1-0** L/N3034

### 1857-★AH-1 18viii57
**Harrwitz, D.+Anderssen, A.**
Manchester
1 e4 e5 2 f4 exf4 3 ♘f3 g5 4 h4 g4 5 ♘e5 h5 6 ♗c4 ♖h7 7 d4 f3 8 gxf3 d6 9 ♘d3 ♗e7 10 ♗e3 ♗xh4+ 11 ♔d2 ♗g5 12 ♕g1 ♘c6 13 ♗b5 ♗d7 14 ♗xc6 bxc6 15 ♘c3 ♕e7 16 e5 ♗xe3+ 17 ♕xe3 d5 18 ♖ag1 f5 19 ♘f4 ♕g5 20 ♘fxd5 ♕xe3+ 21 ♘dxe3 0-0-0 22 fxg4 fxg4 23 ♘e2 c5 24 d5 ♘e7 25 ♘f4 ♘xd5 26 ♘exd5 ♖f7 27 ♔e3 ♖e8 28 ♖xh5 ♗f5 29 e6 ♗xe6 30 ♖e5 **1-0**
L/N6126-1860

### 1857-★AK-1
**Kipping, J.S.+Anderssen, A.**
Manchester [Löwenthal]
1 e4 e5 2 ♘f3 ♘c6 3 ♗c4 ♗c5 4 b4 ♗xb4 5 c3 ♗a5 6 ♕b3 ♕e7 [◻ 6 ... ♕f6] 7 ♗a3 d6 8 d4 exd4 9 0-0 ♗b6 [◻ 9 ... ♘h6] 10 e5 ♘xe5 11 ♘xe5 ♕xe5 12 ♗xf7+ ♔f8 13 ♘d2+– ♘e7 14 ♖ae1 ♕f6 15 ♗c4 ♗f5 16 ♘e4 ♗xe4 17 ♖xe4 dxc3 18 g3 [△ 19 ♖f4] 18 ... g5 19 ♗b4! ♘c6 20 ♗xc3 ♘e5 21 a4 ♖e8 22 ♗e2 a5 23 ♔g2! [△ 24 f4] 23 ... ♕g6 24 f3 h5 25 ♗d3 ♘xd3 26 ♗xh8 ♘f4+ 27 gxf4 gxf4+ 28 ♔h1 ♖xe4 29 fxe4 ♕xe4+ 30 ♕f3 **1-0** M324

### 1857-★AK-2
**Anderssen, A.+Kipping, J.S.**
Manchester
1 e4 e5 2 f4 exf4 3 ♘f3 g5 4 h4 g4 5 ♘e5 h5 6 ♗c4 ♖h7 7 ♗xf7+ ♖xf7 8 ♘xf7 ♔xf7 9 d4 d6 10 ♗xf4 ♗e7 11 0-0 ♔g7 12 g3 ♗e6 13 ♕d3 ♘d7 14 ♘c3 c5 15 ♘e2 ♗f7 16 ♖f2 ♗g6 17 ♖af1 ♘df6 18 dxc5 ♗xe4 19 ♕e3 dxc5 20 ♗e5 ♕d5 21 ♕g5+ ♔h7 22 ♘c3 ♕c6 23 ♗xf6 ♗xf6 24 ♖xf6 ♘xf6 25 ♖xf6 **1-0**
+1

### 1857-★AK-3
**Anderssen, A.– Kipping, J.S.**
Manchester
1 e4 e5 2 ♘f3 ♘c6 3 ♗c4 ♗c5 4 b4 ♗xb4 5 c3 ♗c5 6 d4 exd4 7 cxd4 ♗b6 8 0-0 d6 9 h3? ♕f6 10 ♗b2 ♘ge7 11 e5 dxe5 12 dxe5 ♕g6 13 ♗d3 ♕g3 14 ♘d4 ♗xd4 15 ♗xd4 ♕f4 16 ♗c3 ♗e6 17 ♘d2 ♘d5 18 ♗b2 0-0 19 ♕c2 ♘db4 20 ♗xh7+ ♔h8 21 ♕e4 ♕h6 22 f4? ♕xh7 23 f5 ♗d5 24 ♕e2 ♖ae8 25 ♖f4 ♕h6 26 g3 ♕g5 27 ♔h2 ♘a6 28 ♖h4+ ♔g8 29 ♖af1 ♘xe5 30 ♗xe5 ♖xe5 31 ♕d1 ♖fe8 **0-1** +1

### 1857-★AK-4
**Kipping, J.S.– Anderssen, A.**
Manchester
1 e4 e5 2 ♘f3 ♘c6 3 ♗c4 ♗c5 4 b4 ♗xb4 5 c3 ♗a5 6 ♕b3 ♕e7 7 d4 ♘xd4 8 ♘xd4 exd4 9 0-0 ♘f6 10 ♗a3 c5 11 e5 ♕xe5 12 ♗xf7+ ♔d8 13 ♘d2 ♗xc3 14 ♖ae1 ♕f5 15 ♘f3 ♗xe1 16 ♖xe1 d6 17 ♘h4 ♕d7 18 ♗e6 ♕c6 19 ♕g3 g6 20 ♕g5 ♖f8 21 ♗b3 ♔c7 22 ♗d1 ♗d7 23 ♗f3 ♖ae8 24 ♖b1 ♘e4 25 ♕c1 g5 26 ♗xe4 ♕xe4 27 ♘f3 ♗c6 28 ♘e1 ♕e2 29 f3 g4 30 ♕g5 gxf3 **0-1** +1

**1857-★AK-5**
**Anderssen, A.– Kipping, J.S.**
Manchester
1 e4 e5 2 f4 e×f4 3 ♘f3 g5 4 h4 g4 5 ♘e5 d6 6 ♘×g4 ♗e7 7 ♘f2 ♗×h4 8 ♕f3 ♕f6 9 d3 ♗g3 10 ♘c3 ♘e7 11 ♘e2 ♘bc6 12 ♘×g3 ♘d4 13 ♕×f4 ♘×c2+ 14 ♔d1 ♕×f4 15 ♗×f4 ♘×a1 16 ♘h5? f5 17 ♘f6+ ♔f7 18 e5 ♘g6 19 ♘d5 ♗e6 20 ♘×c7 ♘×f4 21 ♘×a8 ♖×a8 22 g3 ♘g6 23 ♖×h7+ ♔g8 24 ♖×b7 ♗×a2 25 e×d6 ♗e6 26 ♘h3 ♖d8 27 ♖×a7 ♘b3 28 ♖a6 ♘e5 29 ♘f4 ♔f7 30 ♗g2 ♘c5 31 ♖a7+ ♔f6 32 d4 ♖×d6 33 ♘d5+ ♗×d5 34 d×e5+ ♔×e5 35 ♗×d5 ♔×d5 **0-1** +1

**1857-★AK-6**
**Anderssen, A.+ Kipping, J.S.**
Manchester
1 e4 e5 2 ♘f3 ♘c6 3 ♗c4 ♗c5 4 b4 ♗×b4 5 c3 ♗c5 6 d4 e×d4 7 c×d4 ♗b6 8 0-0 d6 9 d5 ♘ce7 10 e5 d×e5 11 ♘×e5 ♕d6 12 ♕e2 ♗d4 13 ♗f4 ♗f5 14 ♗b5+ c6 15 d×c6 0-0-0 16 c×b7+ ♔×b7 17 ♘d2 ♗×e5 18 ♗×e5 ♕×d2 19 ♗a6+ ♔a8 20 ♕f3+ ♘d5 21 ♖ab1 **1-0** L/N6047

**1857-★AK-7**
**Anderssen, A.– Kipping, J.S.**
Manchester [Staunton]
1 e4 e5 2 ♘f3 ♘c6 3 d4 e×d4 4 ♗c4 ♗c5 5 c3 d×c3 6 ♕b3 ♕f6 7 0-0 d6 8 ♘×c3 ♘ge7 9 ♘d5 ♘×d5 10 e×d5 ♘e5 11 ♘×e5 ♕×e5 12 ♕b5+ [□ 12 ♗b5+] 12 ... ♗d7 13 ♕×b7 0-0 14 ♕×c7 [□ 14 ♕b3] 14 ... ♗g4 15 ♕c6 ♖ac8 16 ♕a4 f5 17 ♗a6 ♖c7 18 h3?! ♗×h3 19 ♗f4 ♕f6 20 g×h3 ♕h4 21 ♔h2 g5 22 ♖g1 ♖g7 23 ♖g2 ♗×f2 24 ♖f1 ♗e3 25 ♗b5 g×f4 26 ♕c2 ♖g3 27 ♔h1? **0-1** M954-1857

**1857-★AK-8**
**Kipping, J.S.– Anderssen, A.**
Manchester [Staunton]
1 e4 e5 2 ♘f3 ♘c6 3 ♗c4 ♗c5 4 b4 ♗×b4 5 c3 ♗a5 6 ♕b3 ♕f6 7 d4 e×d4 8 0-0 ♘ge7 9 e5 ♕g6 10 c×d4 0-0 11 d5 ♘b4 12 ♗d2 [□ 12 ♗g5] 12 ... c5 13 a3 ♘c2 14 ♖a2 ♗×d2 15 ♖×c2 ♗f4 16 ♗d3 ♕h5 17 ♖×c5 d6 18 ♖c4 d×e5 19 g3 ♗h3 20 ♖e1 ♘×d5 21 ♖×e5 ♗×e5 22 ♘h4 ♖ac8 23 ♕d1 ♕×h4 24 ♘×h4 ♖fd8 25 ♘d2 ♘f6 26 ♘hf3 ♖×d3 27 ♘×e5 ♖d5 28 f4 ♘e4 **0-1** M954-1857

**1857-★AK-9**
**Kipping, J.S.+ Anderssen, A.**
Manchester [Staunton]
1 e4 e5 2 ♘f3 ♘c6 3 ♗c4 ♗c5 4 b4 ♗×b4 5 c3 ♗a5 6 ♕b3 ♕e7 [□ 6 ... ♕f6] 7 ♗a3 ♕f6 8 d4 ♘h6 9 0-0 ♗b6 10 ♕b5 a6 11 ♕d5 d6 12 d×e5 ♘×e5 13 ♘bd2 ♘hg4 [□ 13 ... ♘×f3+ △ 14 ... 0-0] 14 h3 ♘×f2 15 ♘×e5 d×e5 16 ♖ab1 ♗e3 17 ♖×f2 ♕×f2+ 18 ♔h1 ♗×h3 19 g×h3 ♖d8 20 ♕×e5+ ♔d7 21 ♖f1 **1-0** M954-1857

**1857-★AP-1**
**Pindar, E.+ Anderssen, A.**
Manchester [Löwenthal]
⟨♙f7⟩ 1 e4 e6 2 d4 d6 3 ♗d3 c5 4 c3 c×d4 5 c×d4 ♘c6 6 ♘f3 ♕b6 7 0-0 ♗d7 8 ♗c2 0-0-0 9 ♘c3 ♘ce7 10 ♘g5 ♘h6 11 ♗b3 e5 12 d5 ♘g6 13 ♗e3 ♕a5 14 ♖c1 ♔b8 15 ♗d2 ♖c8 16 ♕e2 ♗e7 17 ♘e6 ♖hg8 [17 ... ♗×e6? 18 d×e6 △ ♘d5] 18 ♘b1 ♕b5 19 ♕×b5 ♗×b5 20 ♖×c8+ ♖×c8 21 ♖c1 ♖g8 22 ♘a3 ♗e8 23 ♘×g7 ♖×g7 24 ♗×h6 ♖g8 25 ♖c3 b5 26 ♘c2 a5 27 a3 ♗d8 28 ♖f3 ♗b6 29 ♘e3 ♗d4 30 ♖f6!? ♘f4 31 ♖×f4! [31 g3 (31 ... ♖g6 32 ♖f8 ♘h3+ 33 ♔g2 ♖×h6 34 ♖×e8+ ♔c7 35 ♘f5±)] 31 ... e×f4 32 ♗×f4 ♗g6 [32 ... ♗c5? 33 e5!] 33 ♗×d6+ ♔b7 34 e5 ♖c8 35 h3 ♖c1+! 36 ♔h2 a4 37 ♗a2 ♖a1 38 e6! ♖×a2 39 ♗f4 ♗×b2? [□ 39 ... ♗c5∞] 40 d6 ♗×a3 41 d7 ♖d2 42 ♘c4 ♖d1 43 ♘×a3 ♔c6 44 ♗g5 b4 45 d8♕ ♖×d8 46 ♗×d8 b×a3 47 ♗f6 ♔d6 48 e7 ♔c6 49 ♗g7 ♔c5 50 g4 ♔c4 51 f4 ♔b3 52 f5 ♗f7 53 h4 ♔c2 54 h5 ♔b1 55 ♔g3 h6 56 g5 h×g5 [56 ... ♗×h5? 57 g6+-] 57 h6 a2 58 h7 a1♕ 59 ♗×a1 ♔×a1 60 h8♕+ ♔b1 61 e8♕ ♗×e8 62 ♕×e8 **1-0** M324

**1857-★AP-2**
**Anderssen, A.+ Pindar, E.**
Manchester [Staunton]
⟨♖a1, ♘g8⟩ 1 e4 e6 2 d4 d5 3 e×d5 e×d5 4 ♗d3 ♗e6 5 ♘f3 ♗d6 6 0-0 c6 7 ♘c3 h6 8 ♕e2 ♕c7 9 ♘e5 ♗×e5 10 d×e5 ♘d7 11 f4 g6 [□ 11 ... ♗g4] 12 ♘d4 ♘c5 13 ♗e3 ♘×d3 14 ♕×d3 ♖g8 15 ♕a3 a6 16 b4 b6 17 ♕c3 ♖c8 18 ♘b3 h5 19 a4 h4 20 a5 b×a5 21 ♘×a5 h3 22 g3 ♕b8 23 ♗c5 ♕b5 24 ♕d2 ♗f5 25 ♖e1 ♖d8 26 ♕d4 [△ 27 e6, 28 ♕f6] 26 ... ♔d7 27 c4 ♕a4 28 ♗d6 [△ 29 ♕a7+] 28 ... ♔e8 29 ♕a7 ♗d7 **1-0** M954-1857

**1857-★BC-1** 4 iv 57
**Barnes, T.W. & Staunton, H.= Cattley, H.G. & Löwenthal, J.J.**
London [Löwenthal]
1 e4 e5 2 ♘f3 ♘c6 3 d4 e×d4 4 ♗c4 ♗c5 5 0-0 d6 6 c3 d3 7 b4 ♗b6 8 ♕×d3 ♘f6 9 a4 a6 10 ♗f4 0-0 11 ♘bd2 ♗g4 12 ♖ae1 ♗×f3 13 ♘×f3 ♘g4 14 ♗b3 ♕f6 15 ♗g3 ♘ge5 16 ♘×e5 ♘×e5? [16 ... d×e5] 17 ♕d2 ♔h8 18 ♔h1 ♖ae8 [□ 18 ... ♖ad8] 19 f4 ♕h6? [19 ... ♘g6!=] 20 ♕d1 ♘d7 [20 ... ♘g6!] 21 e5!± ♖d8! [21 ... ♖e7? 22 e×d6 ♖×e1 23 ♖×e1 ♕×d6 24 ♕×d6 c×d6 25 ♖e7+-] 22 a5 ♗a7 23 ♕f3 c6 24 ♗×f7 ♖×f7 25 e6 ♖e7 26 e×d7 ♖e×d7 27 ♕g4! [△ 28 ♕×d7; 28 ♗h4] 27 ... ♖f7 28 ♖e6 ♖f6 29 f5 ♕g6 30 ♕f4 [30 ♕×g6?=] 30 ... ♕f7 31 ♗h4 ♖×e6 32 f×e6 ♕×f4 33 ♖×f4 ♖e8 34 ♖f7 g5 35 ♗×g5 ♖×e6 36 h3 ♗e3 37 ♗×e3?= ♖×e3 38 ♖×b7 ♖×c3 39 ♖b6 c5 40 b×c5 d×c5 41 ♖×a6 c4 42 ♔h2 ♖a3 43 ♖c6 ♖×a5 44 ♖×c4 ... ⚲ **½-½** M324

**1857-★BH-1 ●○⌂**
**Harrwitz, D.+Bonaparte, Prince A.**
Paris [Staunton]
1 e4 c5 2 d4 e6 [□ 2 ... c×d4] 3 d5 e5 4 f4 d6 5 ♘f3 ♗g4 6 ♗d3 g6?! 7 f×e5 ♗×f3 8 ♕×f3 d×e5 9 0-0 f6 10 ♘c3 a6 11 a4 ♕d6 [△ 12 ... c4 13 ♗×c4? ♕c5+] 12 ♔h1 h5 13 ♕g3 ♘e7 14 ♗e3 ♗h6 15 ♗×h6 [♗×c5?!] 15 ... ♖×h6 16 a5! ♘d7 17 ♘a4 g5 18 ♖a3 ♔f7? 19 ♕×g5 ♖g6 20 ♕h4 [20 ♕×h5?!] 20 ... ♔g7 21 ♖b3 ♖e8 22 ♖×b7 ♔h6 23 ♗e2 ♖g5 24 ♘b6 ♘g6 25 ♖×d7 ♘×h4 26 ♖×d6 ♘g6 27 ♖d×f6 ♖g8 28 h4 ♖g3 29 ♖1f5 ♔g7 **1-0** M954-1857

**1857-★BH-2 ●○⌂**
**Harrwitz, D.=Brunswick, Duke of**
Paris [Staunton]
1 e4 e5 2 ♘f3 ♘c6 3 ♗c4 ♗c5 4 b4 ♗×b4 5 c3 ♗a5 6 d4 e×d4 7 ♕b3 ♕e7 8 0-0 h6 9 ♗a3 d6 10 e5 ♕d7 11 c×d4 ♘d8 12 e×d6 c6 [12 ... c×d6?] 13 ♘e5 ♕f5 14 ♕e3 ♘e6 15 ♗×e6 ♕×e6 16 f4 f5 17 ♘c3 ♗×c3 18 ♕×c3 ♘f6 19 d7+ ♗×d7 20 ♖fe1 ♘e4 21 ♕b4 b5 22 ♕a5 [□ 22 ♘g6 c5 23 d×c5 ♕×g6 24 c6±] 22 ... g5 23 ♖ac1 g×f4 24 ♕c7 ♖c8 25 ♕×a7 ♖g8 26 ♖c5 ♖×g2+! **½-½** M954-1857

**1857-★BL-1**
**Löwenthal,J.J.–**
**Barnes,T.W. & Staunton, H.**
London [Staunton]

1 e4 e5 2 ♘f3 ♘c6 3 c3 d5 4 ♕a4 ♕d6 5 exd5 ♕xd5 6 ♗c4 ♕d6 7 d4 ♗d7 8 ♕b3 ♕f6 [△ 9 ... ♘a5] 9 dxe5 ♘xe5 10 ♘xe5 ♕xe5+ 11 ♗e3 0-0-0 12 ♘d2 [12 ♗xf7 ♗c5] 12 ... ♗c5 13 ♘f3 ♕e7 14 0-0 ♗xe3 15 ♖ae1 ♘h6 16 ♖xe3 ♕f6 17 ♘d4 ♖hf8 18 ♖f3 ♕e7 19 ♖e3 ♕h4 20 ♖e4 ♕g5 [20 ... ♕xe4? 21 ♗d5] 21 f4 ♕g6 22 ♖e5 ♘g4 23 ♖g5 ♕e4! 24 ♘c2 [24 ♗d5? ♕e3+ 25 ♔h1 ♘f2+ 26 ♔g1 ♘h3+ 27 ♔h1 ♕g1+ 28 ♖xg1 ♘f2#] 24 ... ♗f5 25 ♖xg4 [25 ♖xf5? ♖d2 26 ♗e6+ ♔b8 27 ♗d5→] 25 ... ♗xg4 26 ♖e1 ♕xf4 27 ♘d4 ♖fe8 28 ♖f1 ♕e3+ 29 ♔h1 ♗e6 30 ♕a4 ♗xc4 31 ♕xc4 f6 32 h3 ♖d7 33 b4 ♕e4 34 b5 ♖xd4?! [34 ... ♖ed8] 35 cxd4 ♕e2 36 ♖c1 ♕xc4 37 ♖xc4 ♔d7 38 ♖a4 ♖e1+ 39 ♔h2 ♖b1 40 ♖xa7 ♖xb5 41 ♔g3 ♔c6 42 ♔f3 ♖b2 43 g3 b5 44 ♖a8 ♖d2 45 ♖d8 ♖xa2 46 d5+ ♔c5 47 ♖d7 ♖a7 48 d6 ♔c6 49 ♖xg7 ♔xd6 50 ♖xh7 ♖b7 51 ♔e4 b4 52 ♖h5 c5 53 ♖f5 ♔c6 54 ♖xf6+ ♔b5 **0-1** M954-1857

**1857-★BL-2**
**Barnes,T.W.&**
**Staunton,H.+**
**Löwenthal,J.J.& Owen, J.**
London [Staunton]

1 e4 e5 2 f4 exf4 3 ♘f3 g5 4 ♗c4 ♗g7 5 c3 d6 6 0-0 [6 ♕b3 ♕e7 7 ♕b5+ c6 8 ♕xg5 ♕xe4+ 9 ♔f2 ♗h6 10 d3=] 6 ... h6 7 g3 g4 8 ♘h4 f3 9 d4 c6 10 ♕b3 ♕e7 11 ♘a3 a5 12 ♗f4! b5

13 ♘xb5 cxb5 14 ♕xb5+ [14 ♗d5?! ♖a6 15 ♕xb5+ ♘d7 16 ♘f5 ♕f8] 14 ... ♔d8 [14 ... ♕f8+-; 14 ... ♗d7 15 ♕b7+-; 14 ... ♘d7 15 ♘f5+-; 14 ... ♕d7 15 ♘f5 ♕xb5 16 ♗xb5++-] 15 ♗d5 ♕a7 16 ♗xa8 ♕xa8 17 ♕b6+ ♔e8 18 ♕xd6 ♘c6 19 ♘f5 ♗f8 20 ♕d5 ♘f6 21 ♘d6+ ♗xd6 22 ♕xd6 ♘xe4 23 ♖ae1 f5 24 ♕g6+ ♔f8 25 ♗d6+ [□ 25 ♖xe4 △ 26 ♗d6+, 27 ♕f6+, 28 ♗xe7] 25 ... ♘xd6 26 ♕xd6+ ♔g7 27 d5 ♘d8 28 ♖e7+ ♘f7 29 ♕e5+ ♔g6 30 ♖xf7 ♔xf7 31 ♕xh8 **1-0** M954-1857

**1857-★BL-3**
**Löwenthal,J.J.–**
**Barnes,T.W. & Staunton,H.**
London [Staunton]

1 e4 e5 2 ♘f3 ♘f6 3 ♘c3 [3 ♘xe5 ♘c6⇄] 3 ... ♗b4 4 ♗c4 d6 5 0-0 ♗g4 6 d3 ♘c6 7 ♘e2 ♗xf3 8 gxf3 ♕d7 9 c3 ♗a5 10 d4 ♗b6 11 ♗b5 a6 12 ♗a4 exd4 13 cxd4 d5 14 ♘f4 [14 ♗g5 ♘xe4 15 fxe4 ♕g4+] 14 ... 0-0-0 15 e5 g5 16 ♘g2 [□ 16 ♘d3] 16 ... ♘h5 17 ♗e3 ♖hg8 18 ♔h1 ♕h3 19 ♗xc6 bxc6 20 ♖g1 ♖g6 21 ♕e2 ♖h6 [△ 22 ... ♘f4] 22 ♘e1 [22 ♘h4 ♘f4 23 ♕xa6+ ♔d7 24 ♗xf4 gxf4→] 22 ... ♕xh2+ 23 ♔xh2 ♘f4+ 24 ♔g3 ♘xe2+ 25 ♔g2 ♘xg1 26 ♔xg1 f5 27 exf6 ♖xf6 28 ♔g2 ♖df8 29 ♘d3 ♖xf3 30 ♖h1 ♗xd4 31 ♘e1 ♖xf2+ 32 ♗xf2 ♖xf2+ 33 ♔g3 ♖xb2 34 ♘f3 ♗e3 **0-1** M954-1857

**1857-★BO-1**
**Owen, J.+Barnes, T.W.**
London [Staunton]

1 e4 e5 2 ♘f3 ♘f6 3 ♗c4 ♘xe4 4 ♘c3 ♘xc3 5 dxc3 f6 6 0-0 ♘c6 7 ♘h4 g6 8 f4 ♗c5+ 9 ♔h1 d6 10 f5 ♕e7 11 b4 [11 fxg6? hxg6 12 ♘xg6 ♖xh2+ 13 ♔xh2 ♕h7+→] 11 ... ♗b6 12 a4 a6 13 ♗h6 g5 14 ♕h5+ ♔d8 15 ♗xg5! fxg5 16 ♘g6 [16 f6 △ 17 ♕xg5+-] 16 ... hxg6 17 ♕xh8+ ♕e8 18 ♕f6+ ♘e7 19 ♗f7 ♕f8 20 fxg6 ♕h6 21 g7 ♕xf6 22 ♖xf6 ♗d7 23 ♖af1 ♗e3 24 ♖h6 ♗e8 25 ♗xe8 c5 26 ♖xd6+ ♔c7 27 ♖d7+ **1-0** M 954-1858

**1857-★BO-2**
**Barnes, T.W.+Owen, J.**
London [Staunton]

1 e4 e5 2 ♘f3 ♘c6 3 ♗c4 ♗c5 4 b4 ♗xb4 5 c3 ♗a5 6 d4 exd4 7 ♕b3 ♕f6 8 0-0 ♘h6?! 9 e5 ♕g6 10 ♗a3 [10 ♗xh6?] 10 ... dxc3 11 ♘xc3 ♗xc3 12 ♕xc3 b6 13 e6!? fxe6 [13 ... dxe6?] 14 ♗xe6 ♗b7 15 ♘h4 ♕f6 [□ 15 ... ♕g5 16 ♗xd7+ ♔xd7 17 f4∞] 16 ♗xd7+ ♔xd7 17 ♕h3+ ♔d8 18 ♖fe1 ♖e8 19 ♖ad1+ ♘d4 ...? **1-0** M954-1857

**1857-★CC-1**
**Cattley,H.G.&**
**Löwenthal,J.J.–**
**Cunningham & Staunton,H.**
London [Staunton]

1 e4 e5 2 ♘f3 ♘c6 3 c3 ♗c5 4 ♗b5! ♕e7 5 0-0 ♘d8 6 d4 ♗d6 7 ♗g5 f6 8 ♗h4 ♘f7 9 ♗c4 ♘gh6 10 ♘bd2 b6 11 ♖e1 ♗b7 12 ♗b3! g5 13 ♗g3 0-0-0 14 ♘c4 ♘g8?! [△ h5] 15 ♘xd6+ cxd6 16 h4? [16 ♗xf7 ♕xf7 17 dxe5 dxe5 18 ♘xe5 fxe5 (18 ... ♕e6 19 ♗c4+-) 19 ♗xe5 ♘f6 20 ♕d6+-] 16 ... gxh4 17 ♗xh4 ♘gh6 18 ♕d3 ♖de8 19 ♘d2 ♔b8 20 a4 ♖hg8 21 f3 ♖g6 22 a5 ♖eg8 23 ♖e2 bxa5 24 ♖xa5 ♕f8 25 ♘f1 ♕g7 26 g3 ♖c8 27 ♖b5 ♖c7 28 ♘e3 ♘d8 29 ♘c4 ♘e6 30 ♘xd6?

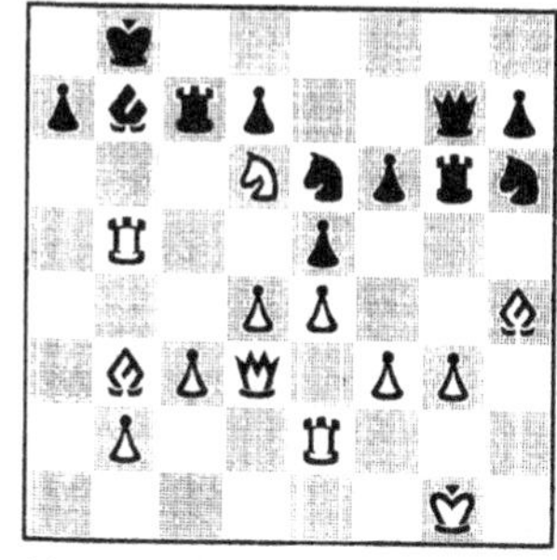

30 ... ♖xg3+ [30 ... ♘f4 31 ♕d2 (31 ♖xb7+?! △ 32 ♕a6) 31 ... ♖xg3+ 32 ♗xg3 ♕xg3+ 33 ♖g2 ♘xg2 34 ♕xg2 ♕e1+=] 31 ♔h1? [31 ♗xg3 ♘f4 32 ♕d2 ♕xg3+ 33 ♖g2 ♘xg2 34 ♕xg2 ♕e1+] 31 ... ♘f4 32 ♕d2 ♘xe2 33 ♗xg3 ♘xg3+ 34 ♔g1 ♘xe4+ **0-1** M954-1857

**1857-★CL-1**
**Löwenthal,J.J.&**
**?Φ Cunningham,&**
**Staunton,H.**
London [Staunton]

1 e4 e5 2 ♘f3 ♘c6 3 c3 d5 4 ♕a4 ♕d6 5 exd5 ♕xd5 6 ♗c4 ♕d6 7 0-0 ♗d7 8 ♕b3 ♘h6 9 ♘a3 ♕f6! [△ 10 ... ♘a5] 10 ♗d5! [10 ♕xb7?] 10 ... ♘a5 11 ♕c2 ♗xa3 12 bxa3 ♕d6 13 ♖e1 f6 14 ♗b3 ♗c6 15 ♘d4 ♘xb3 16 ♕xb3 ♗d5 17 ♘b5 [△ 18 ♕xd5, 19 ♘xc7+] 17 ... ♗xb3 18 ♘xd6+ cxd6 19 axb3 ♘f5 20 d4 ♖c8 21 dxe5 dxe5 22 f4 0-0 23 fxe5 ♖xc3 24 exf6 ♖c2!? 25 fxg7 ♖f7 26 ♖e4 ♖xg7 27 g3 h5 28 ♖f4∓ M954-1857

**1857-★DP-1**
**Dodge, R.J.=Paulsen, L.**
New York [Fiske]

1 e4 e5 2 ♘f3 d5 3 d3 dxe4 4 ♘g5 exd3 5 ♗xd3 h6 6 ♘e4 ♘f6 7 ♘bc3 ♗d6 8 0-0 0-0 9 h3 ♗e6 10 ♗e3 ♘c6 11 ♘g3 ♘e7 12 ♕d2 e4 13 ♘cxe4 ♘xe4 14 ♘xe4 f5 15 ♘xd6 ♕xd6 16 ♖ae1 ♘d5 17 ♗c5 ♕xc5 18 ♖xe6 ♘b4 19 ♕e3 ♕xe3 20 fxe3 ♘xd3 21 cxd3 ♖f7 22 ♖d1 ♖d8 23 ♖d2 f4 24 ♔f2 fxe3+ 25 ♔xe3 ♖fd7 26 ♖e4 b6 27 b4 ♖d6 28 ♖c4 ♖8d7 29 b5 ♖e6+ 30 ♖e4 ♖xe4+ 31 dxe4 ♖e7 32 ♖d8+ ♔f7 33 ♔d4 ♔f6 34 h4 g5 35 h5 ♖g7 36 g4 ♖h7 37 a4 ♔e6 **½-½** L/N5184

**1857-★EM-1**
**Elkin, L.– Morphy, P.C.**
New York [Maróczy]

1 e4 e5 2 f4 exf4 3 ♘f3 g5 4 h4 g4 5 ♘e5 ♘f6 6 ♗c4 d5 7 exd5 ♗d6 [◻ 7 ... ♗g7!] 8 d4 [8 0-0 ♗xe5 9 ♖e1 ♕e7! 10 c3 ♘h5! (10 ... g3 11 d4 ♘g4 12 ♘d2 ♕xh4 13 ♘f3 ♕h6 14 ♖xe5+ ♘xe5 15 ♕e2 ♘bd7 16 dxe5 ♘b8 17 ♕e4; 10 ... f3 11 d4 ♘e4 12 ♖xe4 ♗h2+ 13 ♔xh2 ♕xe4 14 g3; 10 ... ♕c5+ 11 d4 ♕xc4 12 ♖xe5+ ♔f8 13 ♗xf4 h6 14 ♕d2 ♘g8 15 ♘a3) 11 d4 ♘d7 12 ♗b5 ♔d8 13 ♗xd7 ♗xd7 14 ♖xe5 ♕xh4 15 ♖xh5 ♕xh5 16 ♗xf4∞] 8 ... ♘h5 9 ♕d2 [9 0-0 ♕xh4 10 ♕e1] 9 ... ♕e7 10 ♔d1 0-0 11 ♕e1 ♖e8 12 ♘d3 ♕d8 13 ♕c3 g3 14 ♘d2 ♗g4+ 15 ♘f3 ♘d7 16 ♗b5 ♖e7 17 ♗xd7 ♕xd7 18 ♗d2 ♖ae8 19 ♖e1 ♗xf3+ 20 gxf3 ♕h3 21 ♘e5 g2 22 ♗xf4 ♘xf4 23 ♕e3 ♗xe5 24 dxe5 ♖xe5 25 ♕xf4 ♖xd5+ **0-1** L/N3203

**1857-★FM-1** x57
**Fiske, D.W. & Fuller, W.J.A. & Perrin, F.+ Morphy, P.C.**
New York [Löwenthal]

1 e4 e5 2 ♘f3 ♘c6 3 ♗c4 ♘f6 4 ♘g5 d5 5 exd5 ♘a5 6 d3 h6 [◻ 6 ... ♗c5 Heydebrandt] 7 ♘f3 e4 8 ♕e2 ♘xc4 9 dxc4 ♗c5 10 h3 0-0 11 ♘h2 ♘h7 [11 ... e3 12 ♗xe3 ♗xe3 13 fxe3 ♘e4 14 0-0 ♘g3 15 ♕f3 ♘xf1 16 ♘xf1±] 12 ♗e3 ♗d6 13 0-0 ♕h4 14 f4! exf3 15 ♘xf3 ♕h5 16 ♘c3 ♖e8 17 ♕f2 ♘f6 18 ♗d4 ♘e4 19 ♘xe4 ♖xe4 20 ♖ae1 ♗f5 21 ♖xe4 [21 g4? ♕xh3 (21 ... ♗xg4 22 ♖xe4; 21 ... ♖xg4+ 22 hxg4 ♗xg4 23 ♕g2) 22 ♖xe4 ♗xe4 23 ♕g2 ♕xg2+ 24 ♔xg2 ♗xc2] 21 ... ♗xe4 22 ♘h4 ♖f8 [◻ 22 ... f5 Chess Monthly] 23 c5 ♗e5 24 ♗xe5 ♕xe5 25 c4 g5! [25 ... ♗d3 26 ♖e1] 26 ♘f3 ♗xf3 27 gxf3 ♖e8 28 f4 ♕e3 29 fxg5 hxg5 30 ♕xe3 ♖xe3 31 ♔g2 ♔g7 32 d6 cxd6 33 cxd6 ♖d3 34 c5 ♔g6 35 ♖f3 ♖d2+ 36 ♔g3 f5 37 ♖b3 f4+ 38 ♔f3 ♖h2 39 d7 ♖xh3+ 40 ♔e4 ♖h8 41 ♖xb7 ♔f6 42 ♖c7 ♔e7 43 ♖c8 ♖d8 44 ♖xd8 [◻ 44 c6] 44 ... ♔xd8 45 c6 a5 46 ♔d5 ♔e7 47 ♔e4 ♔d8 48 b3 ♔e7 49 a3 ♔d8 50 b4 **1-0** L/N3161

**1857-★FP-1** ○●⬠
**Frère, T.– Paulsen, L.**
New York [Fiske]

1 c4 f5 2 e3 ♘f6 3 ♘c3 e6 4 d4 ♗b4 5 ♘f3 ♘e4 6 ♗d2 ♘xd2 7 ♕xd2 d6 8 a3 ♗xc3 9 ♕xc3 0-0 10 g3 b6 11 ♗g2 ♗b7 12 0-0 ♘d7 13 ♖ad1 ♘f6 14 ♘d2 ♗xg2 15 ♔xg2 ♕e7 16 f4 c5 17 ♕d3 ♖ad8 18 ♖de1 d5 19 ♘f3 ♕b7 20 ♔g1 ♘e4 21 b3 ♖fe8 22 ♖e2 h6 23 a4 ♖db8 24 ♖g2 ♘f6 25 h3 dxc4 26 bxc4 ♕c6 27 ♕c2 ♖bc8 28 ♘e5 ♕c7 29 g4 cxd4 30 exd4 ♘e4 31 gxf5 exf5 32 ♕b3 ♔h7 33 ♖g6 ♖xe5 34 ♖xh6+ gxh6 35 fxe5 ♘d2 36 ♕d3 ♖g8+ 37 ♔h1 ♘xf1 38 ♕xf5+ ♔h8 39 ♕xf1 ♕g7 40 ♕f6 ♕xf6 41 exf6 ♖g6 **0-1** L/N5184

**1857-★HM-1**
**Hammond, G.– Morphy, P.C.**
New York [Maróczy]

1 e4 e5 2 ♘f3 ♘c6 3 ♗c4 ♗c5 4 c3 ♘f6 5 d4 exd4 6 e5 d5 7 ♗b3 ♘e4 8 cxd4 ♗b6 9 0-0 ♗g4 10 ♗e3 0-0 11 ♕d3 [◻ 11 ♘c3] 11 ... ♗xf3 12 gxf3 ♘g5 13 ♕f5 [13 ♘bd2 ♘e6 14 ♗c2 g6 15 ♘b3 f5∓] 13 ... ♘xd4 14 ♗xd4 [14 ♗xg5 ♘xf5 15 ♗xd8 ♖axd8∓] 14 ... ♗xd4 15 ♘c3 g6 [◻ 15 ... c6 △ ♘e6] 16 ♕g4 h5 17 ♕g2 [17 ♕g3 (17 ♕xd4? ♘xf3+) 17 ... ♗xe5∓] 17 ... ♗xe5 18 ♘xd5 c6

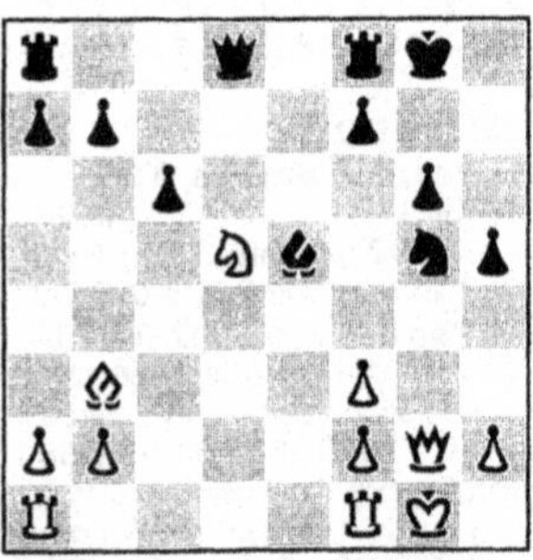

19 ♖fe1 [◻ 19 ♖ae1] 19 ... ♖e8 20 f4 cxd5 21 fxe5 ♘e6 22 ♕xd5 ♕xd5 23 ♗xd5 ♘f4 24 ♗xb7 ♖ab8 25 ♗c6 [◻ 25 ♗a6 ♖xb2 26 ♗f1=] 25 ... ♖e6 26 ♗d7 ♖e7 27 ♖ad1 ♖xb2 28 ♖e4? [◻ 28 a4] 28 ... ♖xd7 **0-1** L/N3203

**1857-★HM-2**
**Morphy, P.C.+ Hammond, G.**
New York [Maróczy]

1 e4 e5 2 ♘f3 ♘c6 3 ♗c4 ♗c5 4 b4 ♗xb4 5 c3 ♗a5 6 d4 exd4 7 0-0 ♗b6 8 cxd4 ♘ge7? 9 ♘g5 d5 10 exd5 ♘a5 [10 ... ♘xd5 11 ♘xf7 ♔xf7 12 ♕f3+±] 11 d6 ♘xc4 12 ♕a4+ c6 13 ♕xc4 ♕xd6 [13 ... ♘d5 14 ♖e1+±] 14 ♕xf7+ ♔d8 15 ♗a3 ♕f6 16 ♕xf6 gxf6 17 ♘f7+ ♔c7 18 ♘xh8 ♗xd4 19 ♗xe7 ♗xa1 20 ♘d2 ♗e5 21 ♘f7 ♗e6 22 ♘xe5 fxe5 23 a3+− h5 24 ♖fe1 ♖g8 [24 ... ♖e8 25 ♗f6+−] 25 ♖xe5 ♗d5 26 ♘e4 ♖e8 27 ♘f6 ♖h8 28 ♗c5 [◻ 28 ♘xh5] 28 ... ♖d8 29 h3 b6 30 ♖e7+ ♔b8 31 ♗e3 c5 32 ♗f4+ ♔a8 33 ♘e8 ♗c6 34 ♘c7+ ♔b7 35 ♘e6+ ♖d7 36 ♘d8+ ♔a6 37 ♘xc6 ♖d1+ 38 ♔h2 b5 39 ♘b4+ cxb4 40 ♗e3 **1-0** L/N3203

**1857-★HP-1**
**Harrwitz, D.+ Pindar, E.**
Manchester [Staunton]

1 d4 d5 2 c4 e6 3 ♘c3 ♘f6 4 ♗f4 a6 5 e3 c5 6 ♘f3 dxc4 7 ♗xc4 b5 8 ♗b3 ♗b7 9 0-0 ♘bd7 10 a4 c4 11 ♗c2 b4 12 ♘e2 a5 13 ♖c1 ♗e7 14 ♘g3 0-0 15 e4 b3 16 ♗b1 ♘b6 17 ♗e3 ♘xa4 18 d5 exd5 19 e5 ♘e4?! [19 ... ♘d7] 20 ♗xe4 dxe4 21 ♘d4 ♗c5 [21 ... ♘xb2 22 ♕g4] 22 ♘gf5 ♗xd4 23 ♗xd4 ♕g5 24 ♘d6 ♗d5 25 ♘xc4! ♖fd8 26 ♘e3 ♗e6 27 f4 exf3 28 ♕xf3 ♖ab8 29 ♗a7 ♖b4 30 ♖c7 ♕g6 31 ♘d5! ♖xd5 32 ♕xd5 h6 33 ♕xa5 ♖g4 34 ♕d2 h5 35 ♗e3 h4 36 h3 ♖g3 37 ♖a7 ♗xh3 38 ♕d8+ **1-0** M954-1857

**1857-★HP-2** ●○⬠
**Paulsen, L.+ Heilbuth, G.**
New York [Fiske]

1 e4 e5 2 ♘f3 ♘c6 3 d4 d5 4 ♘xe5 ♘xe5 5 dxe5 d4 6 ♗c4 ♗e6 7 ♗xe6 fxe6 8 0-0 ♕d7 9 f4 g6 10 f5 0-0-0 11 ♗g5 exf5 12 ♗xd8 ♔xd8 13 exf5 gxf5 14 e6 ♕d6 15 ♘a3 ♗g7 16 ♕f3 c6 17 c3 ♘e7 18 ♘c2 ♔c7 19 ♘xd4 ♗xd4+ 20 cxd4 ♕xe6 21 ♕f4+ ♕d6 22 ♖ae1 ♕xf4 23 ♖xf4 ♔d6 24 ♖f3 ♖f8 25 ♖g3 ♖f7 26 a4 b6 27 b4 ♔d5 28 ♖ge3 ♘g6 29 ♖c3 f4 30 ♖d1 ♘h4 31 ♖f1 ♘g6 32 g3 ♖g7 33 ♔h1 fxg3 34 hxg3 ♘e7 35 ♖f4 h5 36 ♖h4 ♘f5 37 ♖xh5 ♔xd4 38 ♖xf5 ♔xc3 39 b5 cxb5 40 axb5 ♖xg3 41 ♖f7 ♔b4 42 ♖xa7 43 ♔h2 ♖g7 **1-0** L/N 5184

**85** Julien, D. L/N6396. BL

**1857-★HP-3** ●○⬠
**Paulsen, L.+ Hawes, A.C.**
New York [Fiske]

1 e4 c5 2 ♘f3 e6 3 d4 cxd4 4 ♘xd4 ♗c5 5 ♗e3 ♕b6 6 b3 ♘e7 7 c3 ♘bc6 8 ♗e2 0-0 9 0-0 d5 10 exd5 ♘xd5 11 ♕d2 ♘xe3 12 fxe3

e5 13 ♘c2 a5 14 ♘ba3 ♗e6 15 ♘c4 ♕a7 16 ♖ae1 ♖ad8 17 ♕c1 f6 18 ♔h1 ♘e7 19 b4 axb4 20 cxb4 ♗d6 21 ♘xd6 ♖xd6 22 a3 ♘f5 23 ♗f3 ♖c8 24 ♕b2 ♖d2 25 ♖e2 ♖dxc2 26 ♖xc2 ♘xe3 27 ♖xc8+ ♗xc8 28 ♕b3+ ♔h8 29 ♖c1 ♕b8 30 ♕xe3 ♗e6 31 ♕b6 **1-0**

L/N 5184

**1857-★JM-1**
**Morphy, P.C.+ Julien, D.**
New York [Löwenthal]

⟨♘b1⟩ 1 e4 e5 2 f4 exf4 3 ♘f3 g5 4 ♗c4 ♗g7 5 0-0 h6 6 c3 d6 7 ♕b3 ♕e7 8 d4 c6 9 ♗d2 ♘d7 10 ♖ae1 ♘b6 11 ♗d3 ♗g4 12 a4 ♗xf3 13 ♖xf3 ♘d7 14 ♕xb7 ♖b8 15 ♕xc6 ♖xb2 16 e5! ♖xd2 17 ♕c8+ ♕d8 18 exd6+ ♗e5 19 ♖xe5+! ♘xe5 20 ♗b5+ **1-0**

L/N3161

**1857-★JM-2**
**Morphy, P.C.+ Julien, D.**
New York [Löwenthal]

⟨♘b1⟩ 1 e4 e5 2 ♘f3 d6 3 d4 exd4 4 ♗c4 c5 5 c3 dxc3 6 0-0 ♗e6 7 ♗xe6 fxe6 8 ♕b3 ♕d7 9 ♘g5 e5 10 f4 ♘c6 11 fxe5 ♘xe5 12 ♗f4 ♘f6 13 ♗xe5! dxe5 14 ♖ad1 ♗d6 15 ♖xd6! ♕xd6 16 ♕f7+ ♔d8 17 ♕xb7 ♕d7 18 ♕xa8+ ♕c8 19 ♘f7+ ♔e7 20 ♕xa7+ ♘d7 21 ♘xh8 ♕xh8 22 ♖d1 ♕c8 23 bxc3 **1-0**

L/N3161

**1857-★JM-3**
**Morphy, P.C.+ Julien, D.**
New York

⟨♘b1⟩ 1 e4 c5 2 d4 cxd4 3 ♘f3 ♘c6 4 ♗c4 e5 5 c3 ♗c5 6 b4 ♗b6 7 b5 ♘a5 8 ♗xf7+ ♔xf7 9 ♘xe5+ ♔f8 10 ♕h5 ♕f6 11 ♗a3+ ♘e7 12 f4 d3 13 0-0-0 ♗e3+ 14 ♔b1 ♗xf4 15 ♖hf1 g6 16 ♖xf4 ♕xf4 17 ♘xg6+ hxg6 18 ♕xh8+ ♔f7 19 ♕h7+ ♔f8 20 ♕xe7+ ♔g8 21 ♕d8+ ♔g7 22 ♕xa5 **1-0** +13

**1857-★KM-1** xi 57
**Morphy, P.C.+ Kennicott, H.**
New York

1 e4 e5 2 ♘f3 ♘c6 3 ♗c4 ♗c5 4 b4 ♗xb4 5 c3 ♗c5 6 0-0 d6 7 d4 exd4 8 cxd4 ♗b6 9 ♗b2 f6 10 ♖e1 ♘ce7 11 e5 d5 12 exf6 ♘xf6 13 ♗a3 ♘e4 14 ♖xe4 dxe4 15 ♘e5 ♕xd4 16 ♕h5+ g6 17 ♗f7+ ♔d8 18 ♗xe7+ ♔xe7 ...? **1-0**

M985-1859

**1857-★KM-2**
**Kennicott, H.– Morphy, P.C.**
New York [Löwenthal]

1 e4 e5 2 ♘f3 ♘c6 3 d4 exd4 4 ♗c4 ♗c5 5 ♘g5 [◻ 5 0-0] 5 ... ♘h6 6 ♘xf7 ♘xf7 7 ♗xf7+ ♔xf7 8 ♕h5+ g6 9 ♕xc5 d6 [◻ 9 ... d5 Shumov & Cochrane] 10 ♕b5 ♖e8 11 0-0 ♖xe4 12 ♕d5+ ♖e6 13 ♗g5 ♕e8 14 f4 ♔g7 15 f5 gxf5 16 ♕xf5 ♖g6 17 ♗f6+ ♔g8 18 ♕f4 ♗h3 19 ♗g5 ♕e3+! 20 ♕xe3 dxe3 21 gxh3 ♖xg5+ 22 ♔h1 e2 23 ♖e1 ♘d4 24 ♘a3 ♖e8 **0-1**

L/N3161

**68** Lichtenhein, T. L/N6396 . BL

**1857-★LM-1**
**Morphy, P.C.+ Lichtenhein, T.**
New York [Löwenthal]

1 e4 e5 2 ♘f3 ♘c6 3 ♗c4 ♗c5 4 b4 ♗xb4 5 c3 ♗c5 6 0-0 [◻ 6 d4 exd4 7 cxd4 ♗b6 8 ♗b2 Boden] 6 ... ♘f6 7 d4 exd4 8 cxd4 ♗b6 9 e5 d5 10 exf6 dxc4 11 fxg7 [11 ♖e1+ ♗e6 (11 ... ♔f8 12 ♗a3+ ♔g8 13 d5±) 12 fxg7 ♖g8 13 ♗g5 ♕d5 14 ♘c3 ♕a5 15 d5 ♕xc3 16 dxe6±] 11 ... ♖g8 12 ♖e1+ ♘e7 13 ♗g5 ♗e6 14 ♘c3 ♗a5 15 ♘e4 ♖xg7 16 ♘f6+ ♔f8 17 ♖e5 c6 18 ♗h6 ♘f5 19 ♖xe6!

19 ... fxe6 20 ♘e5 ♔e7 [20 ... ♕e7 21 ♕h5 ♘xh6 22 ♕xh6±] 21 ♗xg7 ♘xg7 22 ♕f3 ♕xd4 [◻ 22 ... ♘f5] 23 ♖d1 ♗d2 24 ♘g8+ ♖xg8 25 ♕f7+ ♔d8 26 ♘f3 **1-0**

L/N3161

**1857-★LM-2** ●0 x 57
**Morphy, P.C.+ Lichtenhein, T.**
New York [Löwenthal]

1 e4 e5 2 f4 exf4 3 ♘f3 d5 4 exd5 ♗e7 [4 ... ♗d6 5 d4 g5 6 c4 c6 7 ♗d3= Staunton] 5 ♗b5+ c6 6 dxc6 bxc6 7 ♗c4 ♗h4+ 8 g3 fxg3 9 0-0 gxh2+ 10 ♔h1 ♗f6 11 ♘e5 ♘h6 12 d4 ♗xe5 13 ♕h5!

13 ... ♕xd4 14 ♗xf7+ ♘xf7 [14 ... ♔d8? 15 ♖d1+-; 14 ... ♔f8 15 ♗e6++-; 14 ... ♔e7 15 ♗g5++-] 15 ♕xf7+ ♔d8 16 ♗g5+ ♗f6 17 ♘c3! ♗d7 18 ♖xf6! ♔c7 19 ♗f4+ ♔b7 20 ♖d6! ♕c5 21 ♘e4 ♕xc2 22 ♖xd7+ ♘xd7 23 ♕xd7+ ♔a6 24 ♘d6 ♖hd8 25 ♕b7+ ♔a5 26 ♗d2+ ♕xd2 27 ♘c4+ ♔a4 28 b3# **1-0** L/N3161

**1857-★LS-1** 21 ii 57
**Staunton, H. &?= Löwenthal, J.J. & Cattley, H.G.**
London [Boden]

1 e4 e5 2 ♘f3 ♘c6 3 ♗c4 ♗c5 4 b4 ♗xb4 5 c3 ♗a5 6 d4 exd4 7 ♕b3 [7 0-0! d6!; 7 0-0! dxc3 8 ♕b3 ♕f6 (8 ... ♕e7 9 ♗a3 d6 10 e5±) 9 e5 ♕g6 (9 ... ♘xe5 10 ♖e1 d6 11 ♕a4+ ♔f8 12 ♘xe5 c2 13 ♘g6++-; 9 ... ♘xe5 10 ♖e1 d6 11 ♘xe5 c2 12 ♗xf7+ ♔e7 13 ♘c6++-; 9 ... ♘xe5 10 ♖e1 d6 11 ♘xe5 dxe5 12 ♕b5+ ♗d7 13 ♖xe5++-) 10 ♘xc3 ♘ge7 (10 ... ♗xc3 11 ♕xc3 ♘ge7 12 ♘g5 0-0 13 ♗d3) 11 ♘e2 0-0 12 ♗a3 ♖e8 13 ♘h4 ♕h5 14 ♘g3 ♕xh4 15 ♗xf7+ ♔f8 16 ♗g8 ♘xe5 17 f4±] 7 ... ♕f6 [7 ... ♕e7? 8 ♗a3±] 8 0-0 d6 9 cxd4 ♗b6 10 ♗b5 ♗d7 11 e5 dxe5 12 ♘c3 ♘ge7 13 ♗g5 ♕f5! [13 ... ♕g6 14 ♗xe7± ♘xe7?? 15 ♗xd7+ ♔xd7 16 ♘xe5++-] 14 d5 [14 ♗xc6] 14 ... ♘a5! 15 ♕a3 f6 16 ♗e3 ♗xb5 17 ♘xb5 ♕d7 18 ♗xb6 axb6 19 ♖ab1 0-0→ 20 d6 ♘c4?? 21 ♕b3 cxd6 22 ♕xc4+ d5 23 ♕b3 ♔h8 24 ♖fd1 d4 25 ♘d2 ♘d5 26 ♘c4 ♖ac8 27 ♘cd6 ♖c5 28 ♘e4 ♖c6 29 ♘xd4!! exd4 30 ♖xd4 ♖d8 31 ♖bd1 f5 [31 ... ♕e6? 32 f3!±] 32 ♘c3 ♖xc3 33 ♕xc3 ♘xc3 34 ♖xd7 ♖e8 35 ♖d8 [◻ 35 ♖e7] 35 ... ♖g8 36 ♖xg8+ ♔xg8 37 ♖d7? [37 ♖d2] 37 ... ♘xa2 38 ♖xb7 ♘c3 39 ♖xb6

♔f7 40 ♔f1 h6 41 h4 ♘e4 42 f3 ♘f6 43 ♔e2 g5± 44 hxg5 hxg5 45 ♖a6 ♘d5 46 g3 ♘f6 47 ♔d3 ♔g7 48 f4 g4 49 ♔d4 ♘e4 50 ♔e5? [50 ♖a3] 50 ... ♘xg3 51 ♖a3 ♘f1 52 ♖a1 ♘e3 53 ♖e1 ♘g2 54 ♖h1 ♔g6 55 ♖h8 ♘e1!= 56 ♖g8+ ♔h7 57 ♖a8 g3 58 ♖a3 g2 59 ♖g3 ♘f3+ ½-½ M392

### 1857-★LS-2
**Staunton, H.= Löwenthal, J.J. & ?**

London [Staunton]

1 e4 e5 2 ♘f3 ♘c6 3 ♗c4 ♗c5 4 b4 ♗xb4 5 c3 ♗a5 6 d4 exd4 7 ♕b3 ♕f6 8 0-0 d6 9 cxd4 ♗b6 10 ♗b5 ♗d7 11 e5 dxe5 12 ♘c3 ♘ge7 13 ♗g5 ♕f5! 14 d5 ♘a5 15 ♕a3 f6 16 ♗e3 [16 ♖fe1!?] 16 ... ♗xb5 17 ♘xb5 ♕d7 18 ♗xb6 axb6 19 ♖ab1 0-0∓ 20 d6 ♘c4?? 21 ♕b3 cxd6 22 ♕xc4+ d5 23 ♕b3 ♔h8 24 ♖fd1 d4 25 ♘d2 ♘d5 26 ♘c4 ♖ac8 27 ♘cd6 ♖c5 28 ♘e4 ♖c6 29 ♘xd4! exd4 30 ♖xd4 ♖d8 31 ♖bd1 f5 32 ♘c3 ♖xc3 33 ♕xc3 ♘xc3 34 ♖xd7 ♖e8 35 ♖d8 ♖g8 36 ♖xg8+ ♔xg8+− 37 ♖d7 ♘xa2 38 ♖xb7 ♘c3 39 ♖xb6 ♔f7 40 ♔f1 h6 41 h4 ♘e4 42 f3 ♘f6 43 ♔e2 g5 44 hxg5 hxg5 45 ♖a6 ♘d5 46 g3 ♘f6 47 ♔d3 ♔g7 48 f4 g4 49 ♔d4 [□ 49 ♖xf6+−] 49 ... ♘e4 50 ♔e5 ♘xg3 51 ♖a3 ♘f1 52 ♖a1 ♘e3 53 ♖e1 ♘g2 54 ♖h1 ♔g6 55 ♖h8 ♘e1 56 ♖g8+ ♔h7 57 ♖a8 g3 58 ♖a3 g2 59 ♖h3+ ♔g6 60 ♖g3+ ♔f7 61 ♔xf5 ♘f3 ½-½ M954-1857

### 1857-★MM-1 30 i 57
**Morphy, P.C.+ Meek, A.B.**

New Orleans [Maróczy]

1 e4 e5 2 ♘f3 ♘c6 3 ♗c4 ♗c5 4 b4 ♗xb4 5 c3 ♗a5 6 0-0 ♘f6 [□ 6 ... d6; 6 ... ♕f6 7 d4 h6! (7 ... ♘ge7 8 d5 ♘d8 9 ♗g5 ♕d6 10 ♕a4 ♗b6 11 ♘a3 c6 12 ♖ad1 ♕b8 13 ♗xe7 ♔xe7 14 d6+ ♔f8 15 ♕b4!±; 7 ... d6 8 d5 ♘d8 9 ♕a4+±) 8 ♗e3! ♗b6 9 dxe5 ♘xe5 10 ♘xe5 ♕xe5 11 ♗d4 ♗xd4 12 cxd4 ♕e7 13 ♘c3±] 7 d4 ♘xe4 [□ 7 ... 0-0] 8 ♗a3 [8 ♘xe5 ♘xe5 9 dxe5 d5 10 ♗xd5 ♗xc3 11 ♘xc3 ♘xc3 12 ♗xf7+ ♔xf7 13 ♕f3±] 8 ... d6 9 d5 [□ 9 ♕c2] 9 ... ♘xc3 [□ 9 ... ♘e7! 10 ♕a4+ c6 11 dxc6 0-0 12 ♗xf7+ ♖xf7 13 ♕xe4 ♘xc6 14 ♖d1 ♗c7 15 ♕d5 ♕f6!∓; 16 ♗xd6? ♗xd6 17 ♕xd6 ♖d7!] 10 ♘xc3 ♗xc3 11 ♖c1 ♗b4 12 ♗xb4 ♘xb4 13 ♕a4+ ♘c6 14 dxc6 b6 [14 ... bxc6 15 ♗d5!] 15 ♖cd1 ♕f6 16 ♖fe1 a6 17 ♕a3 [□ 17 ♗d5] 17 ... 0-0 18 ♕b3 b5 19 ♗d5 ♗g4 20 h3 ♗e6 21 ♖e3 ♖ae8 22 ♘d2 ♕h6 23 ♘e4 ♔h8 24 ♕a3 f5

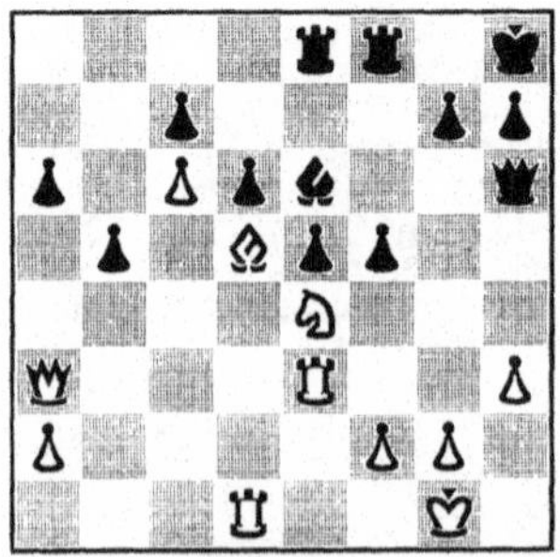

25 ♗xe6 ♖xe6 [□ 25 ... ♕xe6 26 ♘xd6 cxd6 27 ♖xd6 ♕e7 28 ♖ed3 e4 29 ♖d1] 26 ♘xd6 ♖xd6 27 ♖ed3! ♖fd8 28 ♖xd6 ♖xd6 29 ♖xd6 cxd6 30 c7 ♕e6 31 ♕xd6 ♕c8 32 ♕d8+ ♕xd8 33 cxd8♕# 1-0 L/N3203

### 1857-★MM-2
**Morphy, P.C.+ Meek, A.B.**

New York [Maróczy]

1 e4 e6 2 d4 c5 3 d5! e5? 4 f4 d6 5 ♘f3 ♗g4 6 fxe5 ♗xf3 7 ♕xf3 dxe5 8 ♗b5+ ♘d7 9 ♘c3 ♘f6 10 ♗g5 ♗e7 11 d6! ♗xd6 12 0-0-0 1-0 L/N3202

### 1857-★MM-3
**Mead, C.D.− Morphy, P.C.**

New York [Maróczy]

1 h3 e5 2 e4 ♘f6 3 ♘c3 ♗c5 4 ♗c4 b5 5 ♗xb5 c6 6 ♗a4 0-0 7 ♘ge2 [□ 7 ♘f3] 7 ... d5 8 exd5 cxd5 9 d4 [□ 9 d3 ♕a5 10 a3] 9 ... exd4 10 ♘xd4 ♕b6 11 ♘ce2 ♗a6 12 c3 ♗xe2 13 ♔xe2 [13 ♕xe2 (13 ♘xe2 ♗xf2+ 13 ♔f1 ♘a6∓) 13 ... ♗xd4 14 cxd4 ♕b4+−+] 13 ... ♗xd4 14 ♕xd4 ♕a6+ 15 ♔f3 ♖c8 16 b3 ♘e4 17 ♗b2 [□ 17 ♕xd5∓] 17 ... ♘c6 18 ♗xc6 ♖xc6 19 ♔e3 ♖e8−+ 20 ♖he1 ♘xc3+ 21 ♔f3 ♖f6+ 22 ♔g3 ♕d6+ 23 f4 ♘e2+ 24 ♖xe2 ♖xe2 25 ♖f1 ♖g6+ 26 ♔f3

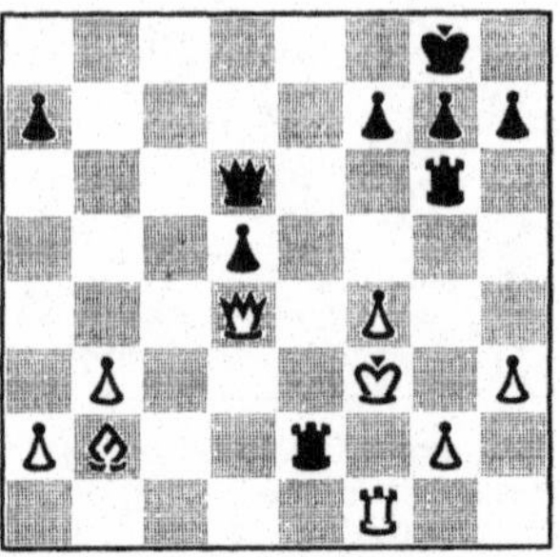

26 ... ♖gxg2 0-1 L/N3203

### 1857-★MM-4
**Montgomery, H.P.− Morphy, P.C.**

New York [Maróczy]

1 e4 e5 2 ♘f3 ♘c6 3 ♗c4 ♗c5 4 b4 ♗xb4 5 c3 ♗a5 6 0-0 ♘f6 7 d4 0-0 8 d5 ♘e7 9 ♕c2 [9 ♗d3 △ ♗g5] 9 ... d6 10 h3 ♘g6 11 ♗d3 ♘h5 12 ♔h2 ♘hf4 13 ♖g1 ♗b6 [□ 13 ... ♘h4] 14 ♗e3 ♘h4 15 ♘bd2 [15 ♗xf4 ♘xf3 16 gxf3 ♕h4 17 ♗f1 exf4∓] 15 ... ♕f6 [△ 16 ... ♘xh3] 16 ♘xh4 ♕xh4 17 ♘f3 ♕h6 18 ♗f1 [18 ♗xf4 ♕xf4+ 19 ♔h1 ♗xh3∓] 18 ... f5 19 g3 fxe4 20 ♗xf4 [20 gxf4 exf3∓] 20 ... exf4 21 ♘d4 e3 22 f3 ♗xd4 23 cxd4 ♗f5 24 ♕g2 [24 ♕xc7 ♖ac8 △ 25 ... ♖c2+∓] 24 ... fxg3+ 25 ♕xg3 ♖f6 26 f4 ♖e8 27 ♖ae1 ♖e4 28 ♖xe3 ♕xf4 29 ♗d3 ♖xd4 30 ♗xf5 ♖xf5 31 ♖e7 ♖d2+ 32 ♔h1 ♕xg3 33 ♖xg3 ♖f1+−+ 34 ♖g1 ♖xg1+ 35 ♔xg1 ♖xd5 36 ♖xc7 ♖d1+ 37 ♔g2 ♖d2+ 38 ♔f3 ♖xa2 39 ♖xb7 ♖a3+ 40 ♔g4 a5 41 ♖d7 a4 42 ♖xd6 ♖a1 0-1 L/N3203

### 1857-★MM-5
**Marache, N.− Morphy, P.C.**

New York [Maróczy]

⟨♙f7⟩ 1 e4 e6 2 d4 d5 3 exd5 exd5 4 ♗d3 ♘f6 5 ♘f3 ♗d6 6 0-0 0-0 7 c4 c6 8 c5 ♗c7 9 ♘e5 ♗xe5 10 dxe5 ♘g4 11 h3 [□ 11 f4] 11 ... ♘xe5 12 ♗xh7+ ♔xh7 13 ♕h5+ ♔g8 14 ♕xe5 ♘d7 15 ♕g3 ♘xc5 16 ♗g5 ♕e8 17 ♘d2 ♗d7 18 ♖ae1 ♕g6 19 ♗e7 ♕xg3 20 fxg3 ♖xf1+ 21 ♔xf1 ♘d3 22 ♖e3 c5 23 b3 ♖e8 24 a4 d4 25 ♖xd3 ♖xe7 26 ♘f3 a5 27 ♔f2 b5 28 axb5 ♗xb5 29 ♖d2 ♖e3 30 ♖b2 ♖c3 31 g4 a4 32 bxa4 ♗xa4 33 g5 [□ 33 ♖b8+ △ ♘g5+] 33 ... ♖c2+ 34 ♖xc2 ♗xc2 35 ♔e1 ♗e4−+ 36 ♔d2 ♗xf3 37 gxf3 ♔f7 38 ♔d3 ♔g6 39 h4 ♔h5 40 ♔e4 ♔xh4 41 f4 g6 42 ♔d3 ♔g4 43 ♔e4 d3 44 ♔xd3 ♔xf4 45 ♔c4 ♔xg5 46 ♔xc5 ♔f4 47 ♔d4 g5 0-1 L/N3203

### 1857-★MM-6
**Morphy, P.C.+ Maurian, C.A.**

New Orleans [Morphy]

⟨♘b1⟩ 1 e4 e5 2 f4 exf4 3 ♘f3 g5 4 ♗c4 g4 5 d4 gxf3 6 ♕xf3 d5 7 ♗xd5 c6 8 ♗xf7+ ♔xf7 9 ♕h5+ ♔g7 10 ♗xf4 ♗e7? [□ 10 ... ♘f6] 11 0-0 ♕xd4+ 12 ♔h1 ♕xe4 13 ♖ae1 ♕g6

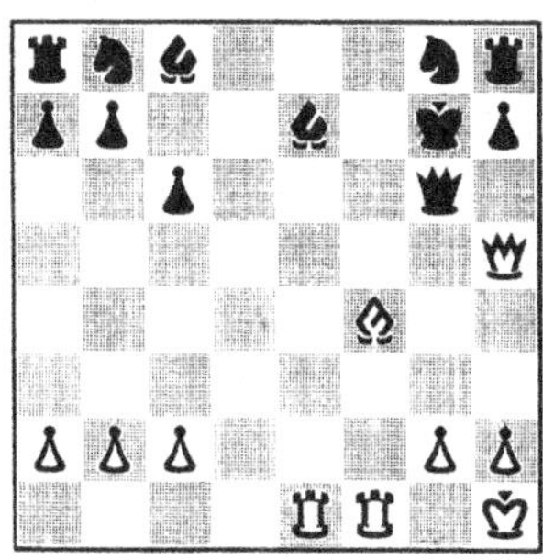

14 ♖xe7++- ♔f8 [14 ... ♘xe7 15 ♗h6+ ♔xh6 16 ♖f7#] 15 ♗d6+ **1-0** M730

### 1857-★MM-7
**Marache, N.– Morphy, P.C.**
New York [Löwenthal]

1 e4 e5 2 ♘f3 ♘c6 3 ♗c4 ♗c5 4 b4 ♗xb4 5 c3 ♗a5 6 d4 exd4 7 e5 d5 8 exd6 [□ 8 ♗b5] 8 ... ♕xd6 9 0-0 ♘ge7 10 ♘g5? [□ 10 ♗a3, 11 ♖e1] 10 ... 0-0 11 ♗d3 ♗f5! 12 ♗xf5 ♘xf5 13 ♗a3 ♕g6 14 ♗xf8 ♕xg5 15 ♗a3 dxc3 16 ♗c1 ♕g6 17 ♗f4 ♖d8 18 ♕c2 ♘cd4 19 ♕e4

[19 ♕d3 ♘g3-+; 19 ♖d1 ♘g3 20 ♕xg6 ♘de2#; 19 ♕a4 b5 20 ♕xa5 ♘e2+ 21 ♔h1 ♘xf4 22 ♖g1 (22 g3 ♕c6+ 23 f3 ♕xf3+ 24 ♖xf3 ♖d1+ 25 ♖f1 ♖xf1#) 22 ... ♖d1 23 g3 ♕c6+ 24 f3 ♕xf3#] 19 ... ♘g3!! **0-1** L/N3161

### 1857-★MP-1 10x57
**Paulsen, L.– Morphy, P.C.**
New York [Maróczy]

1 e4 e5 2 ♘f3 ♘c6 3 ♘c3 ♗c5 4 ♗b5 d6 5 d4 exd4 6 ♘xd4 ♗d7 7 ♘xc6 bxc6 8 ♗a4 ♕f6 9 0-0 ♘ge7 10 ♗e3 [□ 10 ♕e2; 10 ♔h1] 10 ... ♗xe3 11 fxe3 ♕h6 12 ♕d3 [□ 12 ♕e2] 12 ... ♘g6 13 ♖ae1 ♘e5 14 ♕e2 0-0 15 h3 ♔h8 16 ♘d1 g5 17 ♘f2 ♖g8 18 ♘d3 g4 19 ♘xe5 dxe5 20 hxg4 ♗xg4 21 ♕f2 ♖g6 22 ♕xf7 ♗e6 23 ♕xc7 ♖xg2+ [24 ♔xg2 ♕h3+-+] **0-1** L/N3203

### 1857-★MP-2 20x57
**Morphy, P.C.+ Paulsen, L.**
New York [Maróczy]

1 e4 e5 2 ♘f3 d5 3 exd5 [3 ♘xe5 dxe4 4 d4! (4 ♗c4 ♕g5!) 4 ... ♗e6 5 ♗c4 ♗xc4 6 ♘xc4 f5 7 0-0 ♘f6] 3 ... e4 [3 ... ♕xd5 4 ♘c3 ♕a5 5 d4 exd4] 4 ♕e2 f5 5 d3 ♗b4+ [5 ... ♕xd5 6 ♘c3 (6 ♘bd2 ♘f6 7 ♘g5±) 6 ... ♗b4 7 ♗d2 ♗xc3 8 ♗xc3 ♘e7 9 dxe4 fxe4 (9 ... ♕xe4 10 ♗xg7±) 10 ♘d2 ♗f5 11 ♕e3+-] 6 c3 ♗e7 7 dxe4 fxe4 8 ♕xe4± ♘f6 9 ♗b5+ ♗d7 [9 ... c6 10 dxc6!] 10 ♕e2 ♘xd5 11 ♗c4 c6 12 ♗g5 ♗g4 13 ♘bd2 ♘d7 14 0-0 ♘7b6 15 ♖fe1 ♗xf3 16 ♘xf3 ♘xc4 17 ♕xc4 ♕c7 18 ♗xe7 ♘xe7 19 ♖xe7+! ♕xe7 [19 ... ♔xe7 20 ♕e1+ ♔d8 (20 ... ♔f8 21 ♘g5 ♖e8 22 ♘e6+ ♖xe6 23 ♕xe6 ♕d8 24 g4!) 21 ♘e5 ♔c8 (21 ... ♖f8 22 ♖d1+) 22 ♕g4+ ♔d8 23 ♕g5+ ♔c8 24 ♕f5+ ♔b8 25 ♘d7+ ♔c8 26 ♘f8++-] 20 ♖e1 ♕xe1+ 21 ♘xe1 0-0-0 22 ♕g4+ ♖d7 23 ♘d3 h5 24 ♕e6 [□ 24 ♕f5 ♖h6 25 ♘e5 ♖d6 26 g3 ♖d5 27 ♕e6 ♖d6 28 ♕h3±] 24 ... ♖h6 25 ♕e4 ♖hd6 26 ♘e1 ♖d1 27 g3 ♔d8 28 ♕e5 ♖e7 29 ♕b8+ ♔d7 30 ♕xb7+ ♔d6 31 ♕b8+ ♔d7 32 ♕xa7+ ♔d6 33 ♕b8+ ♔d7 34 ♔g2 ♖dxe1 35 a4 ♖a1 36 ♕b7+ ♔d6 37 ♕b4+ ♔d7 38 a5 g6 39 a6 g5 40 ♕b7+ ♔d6 41 ♕b8+ ♔e6 42 b4 g4 43 c4 ♔f7 44 ♕b7 ♔f8 45 h3 ♖ee1 46 hxg4 hxg4 47 ♕c8+ ♔e7 48 ♕xg4 ♖g1+ 49 ♔f3 ♖xa6 50 ♕g7+ ♔e6 51 ♕c7 ♖ga1 52 ♔g4 ♖1a4 53 ♔g5 ♖a2 54 f4 **1-0** L/N3203

### 1857-★MP-3
**Morphy, P.C.= Paulsen, L.**
New York [Maróczy]

1 e4 e5 2 ♘f3 d5 3 exd5 e4 4 ♕e2 ♗e7 5 ♕xe4 ♘f6 6 ♗b5+ ♗d7 7 ♕e2 ♘xd5 8 ♗xd7+ ♕xd7 9 d4 0-0 10 0-0 ♘c6 11 c4 ♘f6 12 d5 ♘b4 13 ♘e5 [□ 13 a3 ♘a6 14 b4 ♖e8 15 ♕c2] 13 ... ♕f5 14 ♘c3 ♘c2 15 g4 ♘xg4 16 ♕xg4 ♕xg4+ 17 ♘xg4 ♘xa1 18 ♗f4 ♘c2 19 ♗xc7 ♖ac8 20 d6 ♗d8 21 ♘d5 ♔h8 22 ♖fd1 ♗xc7 23 ♘xc7 ♖fd8 24 a3 ♔g8 [24 ... ♖xc7 25 dxc7 ♖xd1+ 26 ♔g2+-] 25 c5 f6 26 ♖d2 ♘e1 27 ♔f1 [□ 27 ♖e2 ♘f3 28 ♔g2 ♘d4 29 ♖e7 ♘c6 30 ♘e3!] 27 ... ♘f3 28 ♖d3 ♘g5 29 b4 ♖d7 30 f4 ♘f7 31 ♘e3 ♘h6 32 b5 ♔f7 33 ♔e2 g6 34 a4 ♘g8 35 ♘c4 ♘e7 36 b6 axb6 37 ♘xb6 ♖cxc7 38 ♘xd7 ♖xd7 39 dxe7 ♔xe7 40 ♖e3+ ♔f7 41 ♖b3 ♔e6 42 ♖b6+ ♔d5 43 ♖xf6 ♔xc5 44 f5 gxf5 45 ♖xf5+ ♔b4 46 a5 ♖c7 47 ♖h5 ♔c4 48 ♔e3 ♔b4 49 h4 ♖c3+ 50 ♔d4 **½-½** L/N3203

### 1857-★MP-4
**Perrin, F.= Morphy, P.C.**
New York [Maróczy]

1 e4 e5 2 ♘f3 ♘c6 3 ♗c4 ♗c5 4 c3 ♘f6 [4 ... ♕e7 5 0-0 d6 6 d4 ♗b6] 5 d4 exd4 6 e5 [□ 6 cxd4 ♗b4+ 7 ♘c3! ♘xe4 (7 ... d5?) 8 0-0 ♗xc3 (8 ... ♘xc3 9 bxc3 ♗xc3 10 ♕b3 ♗xa1 11 ♗xf7+ ♔f8 12 ♗g5 ♘e7 13 ♘e5 ♗xd4 14 ♗g6 d5 15 ♕f3+ ♗f5 16 ♗xf5 ♗xe5 17 ♗e6+ ♗f6 18 ♗xf6) 9 d5! ♘e5 (□ 9 ... ♗f6 10 ♖e1 ♘e7 11 ♖xe4 d6 12 ♗g5 ♗xg5 13 ♘xg5 0-0 14 ♘xh7 ♔xh7 15 ♕h5+ ♔g8 16 ♖h4 f5 17 ♗e2 ♘g6! 18 ♕h7+ ♔f7 19 ♗h5 ♕g5! 20 ♖e1 ♕h6 21 ♗xg6+ ♕xg6 22 ♖e7+ ♔f6) 10 bxc3 (□ 10 ♕e2!) 10 ... ♘xc4 11 ♕d4 f5! (11 ... ♘cd6 12 ♕xg7 ♕f6 13 ♕xf6 ♘xf6 14 ♖e1+ ♔f8 15 ♗h6+ ♔g8 16 ♖e5 ♘fe4 17 ♘g5) 12 ♕xc4±] 6 ... d5 7 ♗b3 ♘e4 8 cxd4 ♗b6 9 0-0 ♗g4 10 ♗e3 0-0 11 ♘c3 ♘e7 12 h3 ♗xf3 13 ♕xf3 ♘xc3 14 bxc3 f6 15 e6 c6 16 ♗c1 ♗c7 17 ♗a3 ♗d6 18 ♗xd6 ♕xd6 19 ♖fe1 ♖fe8 20 ♗c2 ♘g6 21 ♗xg6 hxg6 22 ♕g4 g5 23 ♕f5 ♖e7 24 ♖e3 ♖ae8 25 ♖ae1 ♕f4 26 ♕g6 [26 ♕xf4 gxf4 27 ♖3e2 ♔f8 △ ♔e7, ♔d6∓] 26 ... ♕h4 27 ♕f5! ♕h7 28 ♕g4 g6 29 f4 ♕h4 30 f5 ♔g7 31 ♕xh4 gxh4 32 g4! ♔h6 33 ♖f3 ♔g5 34 ♔f2 ♖c7 35 ♖e2 **½-½** L/N3203

### 1857-★MP-5
**Perrin, F.– Morphy, P.C.**
New York [Maróczy]

⟨♙f7⟩ 1 e4 ... 2 d4 d6 3 ♗d3 ♗e6 4 ♕h5+ ♗f7 5 ♕b5+ ♘d7 6 ♕xb7 e5 7 d5 ♘gf6 8 ♘c3 ♗e7 9 ♘b5 [△ 10 ♕xa8, 11 ♘xc7+±] 9 ... 0-0 10 ♕xc7 ♕e8 11 ♘xd6 ♗xd6 12 ♕xd6 ♔h8 13 ♘f3 [□ 13 ♘e2] 13 ... ♗xd5 14 exd5 e4 15 ♕e6 ♕h5 16 ♗xe4 ♖ae8 17 ♕c6 ♘xe4 18 ♗e3 ♘xf2 19 ♔xf2 ♘e5 20 ♕xe8 [20 ♕c3 ♖xf3+ 21 gxf3 ♕xf3+ 22 ♔g1 ♕e2 23 ♗xa7 ♘f3+-+] 20 ... ♕xe8 21 h3 ♕h5 22 ♖he1 ♘xf3 23 gxf3 ♕xf3+ 24 ♔g1 ♕g3+ 25 ♔h1 ♕xh3+ 26 ♔g1 ♕g3+ 27 ♔h1 ♖f5 **0-1** L/N3203

### 1857-★MP-6
**Morphy, P.C.+ Perrin, F.**
New York [Maróczy]

⟨♘b1⟩ 1 e4 e5 2 f4 d5 3 exd5 ♕xd5 4 ♘f3 e4 5 ♘e5 ♗e6 6 ♗c4 ♕d6 7 ♕e2 ♘f6 8 d4 ♗xc4 [8 ... ♕xd4 9 ♗e3±] 9 ♘xc4 ♕e6 10 0-0 ♘c6 11 c3 ♗d6 12 f5 ♕e7 13 ♗g5 0-0-0 14 b4 ♘b8 15 a4 c6 [□ 15 ... ♘d7] 16 b5 ♕c7 17 h3 ♖de8 18 ♗xf6 gxf6 19 ♖fb1 b6 [□ 19 ... ♕e7 20 a5 c5!] 20 a5± cxb5 21 axb6 ♗h2+ 22 ♔h1 axb6 23 ♖xb5 ♘c6 [23 ... ♘d7 24 ♘xb6+ ♘xb6 25 ♖c5±] 24 ♖ab1 ♗f4 25 ♘xb6+ ♔d8 26 ♘d5 ♕d6 27 ♕a2 **1-0** L/N3203

## 1857-★MP-7
**Morphy, P.C.+ Perrin, A.**
New York [Maróczy]

⟨♖a1⟩ 1 e4 e5 2 f4 exf4 3 ♘f3 d5 4 exd5 ♕xd5 5 ♘c3 ♕e6+ 6 ♔f2 ♕f6 7 ♗c4 c6 8 ♘e4 ♕f5 9 ♖e1 ♗e6 10 d4 ♗e7 11 ♘fg5 ♘d7 12 ♘xf7! ♘gf6 [□ 12 ... ♕xf7 13 ♘d6+ (13 ♘g5 ♗xc4 14 ♘xf7 ♗xf7) 13 ... ♗xd6 14 ♗xe6 (14 ♖xe6+ ♘e7; 14 ... ♕xe6) 14 ... ♕f6; □ 12 ... ♔xf7 13 ♗xe6+ ♕xe6 14 ♘g5+ ♗xg5 15 ♖xe6 ♔xe6 16 ♕g4+ ♔f7] 13 ♘fd6+ ♔f8 14 ♘xf5 ♘xe4+ 15 ♖xe4 ♗xf5 16 ♕h5 g6 17 ♕h6+ ♔e8 18 ♖xe7+ ♔xe7 19 ♕g7+ ♔d6 20 ♗xf4+ ♘e5 21 ♗xe5# **1-0**

L/N3203

## 1857-★MP-8
xii 57

**Perrin, F.– Morphy, P.C.**
New York

⟨♙f7⟩ 1 e4 ... 2 d4 e6 3 ♗d3 c5 4 e5 g6 5 c3 ♘c6 6 ♗e3 ♕b6 7 ♕d2 d5 8 exd6 ♗xd6 9 ♘a3 cxd4 10 ♗xd4 ♘xd4 11 ♘c4 ♕c7 12 ♘xd6+ ♕xd6 13 cxd4 ♘e7 14 ♘f3 0-0 15 0-0 ♗d7 16 ♗e4 ♖f4 17 ♖ae1 ♖af8 18 ♘e5 ♗b5 19 g3 ♖xe4 20 ♖xe4 ♗xf1 21 ♔xf1 ♕d5 22 ♕c2 ♘f5 23 ♕c4 ♕xe4 24 ♕xe6+ ♔g7 25 ♕d7+ ♔h6 26 ♘f7+ ♔h5 27 ♘e5 ♘e3+ 28 ♔e2 ♘c4+ 29 ♔d1 ♕b1+ 30 ♔e2 ♕c2+ 31 ♔e1 ♕d2+ 32 ♔f1 ♕xf2# **0-1** L/N6141-1913

## 1857-★MP-9
xi 57

**Morphy, P.C.+ Perrin, A.**
New York

⟨♖a1⟩ 1 e4 e6 2 f4 d5 3 e5 ♘c6 4 d4 ♘h6 5 ♘f3 f6 6 c3 ♗e7 7 ♗d3 0-0 8 0-0 ♘a5 9 a3 a6 10 ♔h1 b5 11 ♖g1 ♕e8 12 g4 fxe5 13 dxe5 ♕f7 14 ♕f1 ♗d7 15 ♕h3 ♗g5 16 ♘xg5 ♕e7 17 ♘xh7 ♗e8 18 g5 ♘f5 19 ♘f6+ ♖xf6 20 gxf6 ♕f7

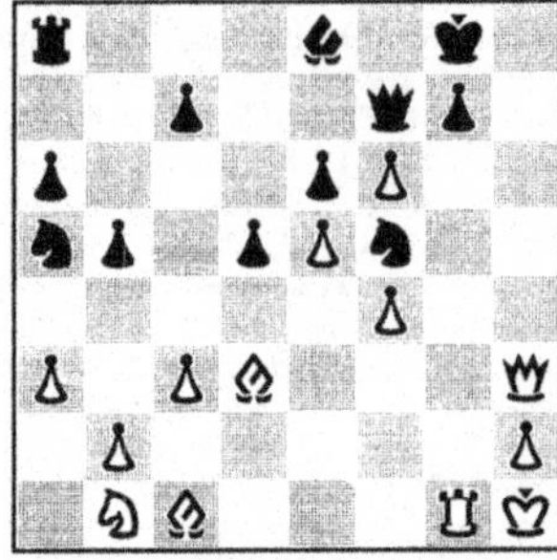

21 ♖xg7+ ♘xg7 22 ♕h7+ ♔f8 23 ♕h8+ ♕g8 24 fxg7+ ♔f7 25 ♗g6+ **1-0** +13

## 1857-★MP-10
**Morphy, P.C.+ Perrin, F.**
New York

1 e4 c5 2 ♘f3 e6 3 d4 cxd4 4 ♘xd4 ♘c6 5 ♗e3 [□ 5 ♘b5] 5 ... ♘f6 6 ♗d3 ♗b4+ 7 c3 ♗a5 8 0-0 ♗b6 9 ♘d2 ♘e5? 10 ♗e2 d5 11 f4 ♘c6 12 e5 ♗xd4 13 cxd4 ♘d7 14 ♗d3 f5 15 g4 g6 16 gxf5 exf5 17 ♔h1 ♘f8 18 ♖c1 ♘e6 19 ♗xf5 ♘exd4 20 ♗xc8 ♖xc8 21 f5 ♘xf5 22 ♖xf5 gxf5 23 ♕h5+ ♔d7 24 ♕f7+ ♕e7 25 e6+ ♔d8 26 ♗g5 **1-0** L/N3161

## 1857-★MP-11
**Morphy, P.C.+ Perrin, F.**
New York [Löwenthal]

⟨♘b1⟩ 1 e4 e5 2 ♘f3 ♘c6 3 ♗c4 ♗c5 4 b4 ♗xb4 5 c3 ♗c5 6 0-0 ♘f6 7 d4 exd4 8 cxd4 ♗b6 9 ♗a3 d6 10 e5 dxe5 11 ♕b3 ♕d7 12 dxe5 ♘e4 13 ♖ad1 ♘d4 14 ♘xd4 ♗xd4

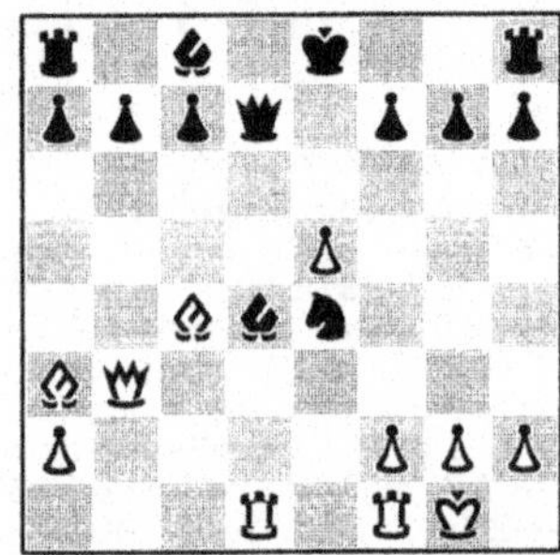

15 ♖xd4! ♕xd4 16 ♗xf7+ ♔d8 17 ♖d1 ♘d2 18 ♕c2 ♗d7 19 e6 ♗a4 20 ♖xd2! ♗xc2 21 ♖xd4+ ♔c8 22 e7 b6 23 e8♕+ ♖xe8 24 ♗xe8 ♔b7 25 ♗c6+ ♔xc6 26 ♖c4+ ♔b5 27 ♖xc2 **1-0** L/N3161

**44** Morphy, P.C. ○●● Paulsen, L.O M658. CPL

### 1857-★MR-1
**Raphael, J.B.– Morphy, P.C.**
New York [Maróczy]
1 e4 e5 2 f4 exf4 3 ♗c4 ♕h4+ 4 ♔f1 b5 5 ♗xb5 ♘f6 6 ♘f3 ♕h6 7 ♘c3 g5 8 d4 ♗g7 9 e5? ♘h5 10 ♔g1 ♗b7 11 ♗e2 ♖g8 [□ 11 ... g4 12 ♘e1 f5 13 h3 ♘g3 14 ♖h2 ♗xe5 15 hxg4 ♕b6!] 12 ♘e1 f3 13 ♗xf3 ♗xf3 14 ♕xf3 ♘c6 15 ♘d5 0-0-0 16 ♘e7+ [16 c3 ♔b8∓] 16 ... ♔b8 17 ♘xg8 ♖xg8 18 ♕xf7 [□ 18 c3] 18 ... ♖f8 19 ♕b3+ ♔c8 20 ♘f3 ♕g6 21 c3 g4 22 ♘h4 ♕d3 23 ♗g5 ♘f4 24 ♗xf4 ♖xf4 25 ♖e1 ♕d2 26 ♘f3 gxf3 **0-1** L/N3203

### 1857-★MR-2 xi 57
**Morphy, P.C.+ Reif, A.**
New York
⟨♘b1⟩ 1 e4 e5 2 ♘f3 ♘c6 3 d4 exd4 4 ♗c4 ♗c5 5 c3 dxc3 6 0-0 d6 7 ♕b3 ♕e7 8 ♗g5 ♘f6 9 ♖ae1 0-0 10 ♔h1 ♘e5 11 ♘xe5 dxe5 12 f4 ♗b6 13 ♕xc3 ♗d4 14 ♕g3 ♗e6 15 fxe5 ♗xc4 16 ♗xf6 ♕xf6 17 exf6 g6 18 ♕g5 ♗xf1 19 e5 ♗xg2+ 20 ♔xg2 ♔h8 21 ♖e4 ♖ad8 22 ♕h6 ♖g8 23 ♕xh7+ ♔xh7 24 ♖h4# **1-0** +13

### 1857-★MR-3
**Richardson, H.– Morphy, P.C.**
New York [Maróczy]
⟨♙f7⟩ 1 e4 ... 2 d4 e6 3 ♗d3 c5 4 e5 g6 5 c3 [□ 5 h4 Morphy L/N6389-1859] 5 ... ♘c6 6 ♘f3 d5 7 ♗e3 ♕b6 8 ♕c2 ♗d7 9 ♗g5? ♘ge7 10 ♗e3 c4 11 ♗e2 ♘f5 12 ♘bd2 ♘xe3 13 fxe3 ♗h6 14 ♘f1 [□ 14 e4] 14 ... 0-0∓ 15 ♕d2 ♖f7 16 ♘g3 ♖af8 17 0-0 ♕d8 18 ♖ae1 b5 19 ♗d1 a5 20 a3 ♕b6 21 b4 axb4 22 cxb4? [□ 22 axb4∓] 22 ... ♖a8 23 ♕b2 ♕a7 24 a4 bxa4 25 ♗xa4

25 ... ♘xb4! 26 ♕xb4 ♕xa4 27 ♕xa4 ♖xa4 28 ♖f2 ♖a3 29 ♘f1 ♗a4 30 g4 ♖b7 31 g5 ♗f8 32 ♖c1 c3 33 ♘e1 c2 34 ♘d2 [34 ♘xc2 ♖c3–+] 34 ... ♖c3 35 ♘ef3 ♖bc7 **0-1** L/N6389

### 1857-★MR-4 xi 57
**Richardson, H.– Morphy, P.C.**
New York
⟨♙f7⟩ 1 e4 ... 2 d4 d6 3 ♗d3 ♗e6 4 ♘f3 ♗g4 5 h3 ♗h5 6 g4 ♗f7 7 ♘g5 ♘h6 8 d5 c6 9 ♘c3 ♕d7 10 ♕f3 g6 11 ♗c4 ♕c8 12 ♘xf7 ♘xf7 13 dxc6 ♘e5 14 ♕e2 ♘bxc6 15 ♗e3 ♗g7 16 0-0-0 ♕d7 17 ♗b3 ♘a5 18 ♗a4 ♘ac6 19 f4 ♘f7 20 e5 0-0 21 ♗d4 e6 22 ♗xc6 ♕xc6 23 ♖he1 dxe5 24 ♗xe5 ♘xe5 25 fxe5 ♕c5 26 ♕b5 ♖ac8 27 ♖d7 a6 28 ♕xb7 ♗h6+ 29 ♔b1 ♖b8 30 ♕c7 ♕b4 31 b3 ♖bc8 32 ♕d6 ♕xc3 33 ♕xe6+ ♔h8 34 ♖ed1 ♕xc2+ 35 ♔a1 ♗c1 ...? **0-1** +13

### 1857-★MS-1
**Stanley, C.H.– Morphy, P.C.**
New York [Maróczy]
1 e4 e5 2 ♘f3 ♘c6 3 ♗c4 ♗c5 4 c3 ♘f6 5 d3 d6 6 h3 0-0 7 ♗g5 ♗b6 8 ♘bd2 ♗e6 9 0-0 [□ 9 ♕e2] 9 ... h6 10 ♗h4 ♔h8 11 ♘h2 g5 12 ♗g3 h5 13 ♘hf3 [□ 13 h4] 13 ... h4 14 ♘xh4 gxh4 15 ♗xh4 ♔g7 16 ♕f3 ♖h8 17 ♕g3+ ♔f8 18 ♕g5 ♘d7 19 ♗xe6 fxe6 20 ♕xd8+ ♘xd8 21 ♘f3 ♔g7 22 g4 ♘f8 23 ♔g2 ♘g6 24 ♗g5 [□ 24 ♗g3] 24 ... ♘f7 25 h4 ♘xg5 26 hxg5 ♘f4+ 27 ♔g3 [27 ♔g1 ♖h3 △ ♖ah8–+] 27 ... ♖h3# **0-1** L/N3203

### 1857-★MS-2 22 x 57
**Morphy, P.C.+ Stanley, C.H.**
New York [Maróczy]
1 e4 e5 2 ♘f3 ♘c6 3 ♗c4 ♗c5 4 b4 ♗xb4 5 c3 ♗a5 6 d4 exd4 7 0-0 d6 8 cxd4 ♗b6 9 ♘c3! [9 d5; 9 ♗b2] 9 ... ♘f6? [□ 9 ... ♘a5; 9 ... ♗g4; 9 ... a6!] 10 e5! dxe5 11 ♗a3! ♗xd4 12 ♕b3 ♗e6 13 ♗xe6 fxe6 14 ♕xe6+ ♘e7 15 ♘xd4 exd4 16 ♖fe1 ♘fg8 [16 ... dxc3 17 ♖ad1 ♘d7 18 ♗xe7 ♘f8 19 ♗xf8+ ♔xf8 20 ♖xd8+ ♖xd8 21 ♕e7++–] 17 ♘d5 [□ 17 ♗xe7 ♕d7 (17 ... ♘xe7 18 ♘d5+–) 18 ♕b3 ♘xe7 19 ♘d5+–] 17 ... ♕d7 18 ♗xe7 [□ 18 ♕xd7+ ♔xd7 19 ♘xe7+–] 18 ... ♕xe6 19 ♖xe6 ♔d7 20 ♖ae1 ♖e8 21 ♖6e4 c6 22 ♖xd4 cxd5 23 ♖xd5+ ♔c6 24 ♖d6+ ♔c7 25 ♖c1+ ♔b8 26 ♗h4+– ♘h6 27 ♗g3 ♔a8 28 h3 ♘f5 29 ♖d7 g6 [29 ... ♖e7 30 ♖xe7 ♘xe7 31 ♖c7 ♘f5 32 ♗e5 ♖g8 33 ♖f7 g6 34 ♖xh7+–] 30 ♖cc7 ♘xg3 31 fxg3 ♖b8 32 ♖xh7 ♖xh7 33 ♖xh7 a5 34 h4 ♖g8 35 g4 b5 36 h5 a4 37 h6 b4 38 ♖g7 ♖h8 39 h7 b3 40 ♖g8+ ♔b7 41 ♖xh8 b2 42 ♖b8+ ♔xb8 43 h8♕+ **1-0** L/N3203

### 1857-★MS-3
**Stanley, C.H.– Morphy, P.C.**
New York [Maróczy]
1 e4 e5 2 f4 exf4 3 ♗c4 ♕h4+ 4 ♔f1 b5 5 ♗b3 [□ 5 ♗xb5] 5 ... ♘f6 [5 ... a5 6 a4 b4 7 d3 ♗a6 8 ♘f3 ♕f6∓] 6 ♘f3 ♕h6 7 ♘c3 b4 8 ♘b5 ♗a6 9 ♗c4 ♗xb5 10 ♗xb5 ♘h5 11 ♔e2 [□ 11 d4] 11 ... g5 12 ♘e5 ♗g7 13 ♘g4 f3+ 14 ♔xf3 ♕b6 15 ♕e2 0-0 16 ♗c4 ♘c6 17 c3 ♔h8 18 ♕e3 f5 19 ♕xb6 fxg4+ 20 ♔xg4 ♘f6+ **0-1** L/N3203

### 1857-★MS-4 x 57
**Stanley, C.H.+ Morphy, P.C.**
New York [Maróczy]
1 e4 e5 2 f4 exf4 3 ♗c4 ♕h4+ 4 ♔f1 b5 5 ♗b3 ♘f6 6 ♘f3 ♕h6 7 ♘c3 b4 8 ♘b5 ♗a6 9 ♗c4 ♗xb5 10 ♗xb5 ♘h5 11 d4! ♘g3+ 12 ♔g1 ♘xh1 13 ♔xh1 c6 14 ♗c4 d6 [14 ... a5 △ 15 ... ♘a6; 15 ♘e5] 15 a3! g5 16 axb4 g4 17 ♘g1 g3 18 h3 ♗e7 19 ♖a5! ♗g5 20 ♕g4 [20 ... ♗d8 21 ♖f5 ♖f8 22 ♘f3 ♘d7 23 ♗xf4 ♕g6 24 ♘g5+–] **1-0** L/N3203

### 1857-★MS-5 28 xi 57
**Stanley, C.H.= Morphy, P.C.**
New York
⟨♙f7⟩ 1 e4 d6 2 d4 ♘f6 3 ♘c3 e6 4 ♗d3 ♘c6 5 ♗e3 e5 6 d5 ♘e7 7 h3 ♘g6 8 ♘ce2 ♘h4 9 ♖h2 ♗e7 10 g3 ♘g6 11 f4 exf4 12 ♘xf4 ♘e5 13 ♘f3 0-0 14 ♘xe5 dxe5 15 ♘g2 c6 16 c4 ♗b4+ 17 ♗d2 ♕b6 18 ♗xb4 ♘xe4 19 ♘f4 ♕g1+ 20 ♔e2 ♕xh2+ 21 ♔e3 ♕f2+ 22 ♔xe4 ♕d4+ 23 ♔f3 c5 24 ♗c3 ♖xf4+ 25 gxf4 ♕xf4+ 26 ♔g2 ♗xh3+ 27 ♔xh3 ♕h6+ 28 ♔g2 ♕g5+ 29 ♔h2 ♕h4+ **½-½** +13

### 1857-★MS-6 29 xi 57
**Stanley, C.H.– Morphy, P.C.**
New York
⟨♙f7⟩ 1 e4 d6 2 d4 ♘f6 3 ♗d3 e5 4 dxe5 dxe5 5 h3 ♗c5 6 ♘f3 ♘c6 7 ♘c3 ♗e6 8 0-0 ♕e7 9 ♗b5 0-0 10 ♗xc6 bxc6 11 ♗g5 ♗c4 12 ♖e1 ♖ad8 13 ♕c1 h6 14 ♗e3 ♗d6 15 ♘h4 ♘xe4 16 ♘g6 ♕f6 17 ♘xf8 ♘xc3 18 ♘d7 ♖xd7 19 bxc3 ♕g6 20 ♕d1 ♗e6 21 ♔h1 ♖f7 22 ♖b1 e4 23 ♖b8+ ♔h7 24 ♖g1 h5 25 f4 exf3 26 gxf3 ♕f5 27 ♕d3 ♕xd3 28 cxd3 ♖xf3 29 ♗d4 ♖xh3+ 30 ♔g2 c5 **0-1** +13

### 1857-★MS-7
**Morphy, P.C.+ Schulten, J.W.**
New York [Maróczy]
1 e4 e5 2 ♘f3 ♘c6 3 ♗c4 ♗c5 4 b4 ♗xb4 5 c3 ♗c5 6 0-0 d6 7 d4 exd4 8 cxd4 ♗b6 9 d5 ♘ce7 [□ 9 ...

♘a5] 10 e5 ♗g4 [□ 10 … ♘g6; 10 … ♘h6! 11 ♘c3 0-0 12 ♗xh6 gxh6 13 ♘e4 dxe5] 11 h3 [□ 12 ♗b2] 11 … ♗xf3 12 ♕xf3 ♗d4 13 ♘c3 ♗xe5 14 ♗b5+ ♔f8 15 ♗b2 c6 [□ 15 … ♘g6 Δ ♕f6] 16 ♗d3 ♘f6 17 ♖ae1 ♗xc3? [□ 17 … ♘exd5 18 ♘xd5 ♗xb2→+] 18 ♗xc3 ♘fxd5 19 ♗a1 f6? [□ 19 … ♘g6] 20 ♖e6 ♕d7 21 ♖fe1+– b5 22 ♖xe7 [□ 22 ♗xb5 cxb5 23 ♖xe7 ♘xe7 24 ♕xa8++–] 22 … ♘xe7 23 ♗xf6 ♘d5 24 ♗e7+ ♔g8 25 ♗f5 **1-0** L/N3203

## 1857-★MS-8
**Morphy,P.C.+**
**Schulten,J.W.**

New York [Maróczy]

1 e4 e5 2 ♘f3 ♘c6 3 ♗b5 ♗c5 [□ 3 … ♘f6 Morphy L/N6389-1858] 4 c3 ♘ge7 5 0-0 0-0 6 d4 exd4 7 cxd4 ♗b6 8 d5 ♘b8 9 d6! cxd6 10 ♗f4! ♗c7 11 ♘c3 a6 12 ♗c4 b5 13 ♗b3 ♗b7 14 ♗xd6 ♗xd6 15 ♕xd6 h6? 16 ♖ad1 ♘c8 17 ♕f4 ♘b6 18 ♘e5 ♕f6

19 ♕xf6 gxf6 20 ♘g4 ♔g7 21 ♘xf6! ♗c6 22 e5 a5 23 ♖d3 ♖h8 [23 … a4 24 ♖g3+ ♔h8 25 ♗xf7+–] 24 ♘cd5 ♘c4 25 ♗xc4 bxc4 26 ♖g3+ ♔f8 27 ♘b6 ♖a7 28 ♖d1 ♗b5 29 ♖d4 ♖c7 30 ♖dg4! **1-0** L/N3203

## 1857-★MS-9
**Schulten,J.W.+**
**Morphy,P.C.**

New York [Maróczy]

1 e4 e5 2 f4 d5 3 exd5 e4 4 ♘c3 ♘f6 5 ♗c4 c6 6 d3 ♗b4 7 dxe4 ♘xe4 8 ♗d2 ♗xc3 [8 … ♕h4+? 9 g3 ♘xg3 10 hxg3 ♕xh1 11 ♕e2+, 12 0-0-0±] 9 ♗xc3 0-0 10 ♕h5 ♖e8 11 0-0-0 ♘xc3 [11 … ♘f2 12 ♘h3! ♗g4? 13 ♕xf7+ ♔xf7 14 dxc6+ ♔g6 15 ♖xd8 ♖xd8 16 cxb7 ♘c6 (16 … ♘xh1 17 ♗d3+) 17 bxa8♕ ♖xa8 18 ♘xf2±] 12 bxc3 ♕a5 13 ♔b2 g6 14 ♕h6 ♗g4 15 ♘f3 ♗xf3 16 gxf3 b5 17 f5 bxc4 18 f6 **1-0** L/N3203

## 1857-★MS-10
29 xi 57

**Schulten,J.W.–**
**Morphy,P.C.**

New York

1 e4 e5 2 f4 exf4 3 ♗c4 d5 4 exd5 ♘f6 5 ♘c3 ♗d6 6 ♘f3 0-0 7 0-0 ♗g4 8 d4 ♘bd7 9 ♘ce2 ♘b6 10 ♗b3 ♘bxd5 11 c4 ♘e3 12 ♗xe3 fxe3 13 ♕d3 ♖e8 14 ♗c2 ♗h5 15 ♘h4 ♗g6 16 ♘xg6 hxg6 17 c5 ♗xh2+ 18 ♔xh2 ♘g4+ 19 ♔g3 ♕g5 20 ♖f5 gxf5 21 ♕xf5 ♕xf5 22 ♗xf5 ♘f6 23 ♔f3 g6 24 ♗c2 ♖ad8 25 ♖d1 ♔g7 26 ♘f4 ♘d5 27 ♘xd5 e2 28 ♖e1 ♖xd5 **0-1** +13

## 1857-★MS-11
29 xi 57

**Schulten,J.W.–**
**Morphy,P.C.**

New York

1 e4 e5 2 f4 exf4 3 ♗c4 d5 4 ♗xd5 ♘f6 5 ♘c3 ♗b4 6 ♘ge2 ♗xc3 7 bxc3 ♘xd5 8 exd5 ♕h4+ 9 ♔f1 f3 10 ♘g3 fxg2+ 11 ♔xg2 ♗h3+ 12 ♔f2 0-0 13 ♕h5 ♕f4+ 14 ♕f3 ♕h4 15 d4 f5 16 ♗a3 ♖f7 17 ♖he1 ♘d7 18 ♕h5 ♕f4+ 19 ♕f3 ♕d2+ 20 ♖e2 ♕g5 21 ♖ae1 ♘f6 22 ♖e7 f4 23 ♘f1 ♘g4+ 24 ♔e2 ♖xe7+ 25 ♗xe7 ♕xe7+ 26 ♔d2 ♕h4 27 ♕xf4 ♖f8 28 ♕g3 ♕h6+ 29 ♘e3 ♘xe3 30 ♖xe3 ♖e8 31 c4 ♗f1 32 c5 ♗c4 33 d6 cxd6 34 cxd6 ♖xe3 35 ♕xe3 ♕xe3+ 36 ♔xe3 ♔f7 **0-1** +13

## 1857-★MS-12
29 xi 57

**Morphy,P.C.+**
**Schulten,J.W.**

New York

1 e4 e5 2 ♘f3 ♘c6 3 ♗c4 ♗c5 4 b4 ♗xb4 5 c3 ♗c5 6 0-0 d6 7 d4 exd4 8 cxd4 ♗b6 9 d5 ♘ce7 10 e5 ♗g4 11 h3 ♗h5 12 g4 ♗g6 13 ♖e1 h5 14 ♘c3 hxg4 15 hxg4 ♕d7 16 e6 fxe6 17 dxe6 ♕d8 18 ♘g5 ♖h4 19 ♘f7 ♕b8 20 ♗g5 ♖h3 21 ♖c1 ♘f6 22 ♔g2 ♖h7 23 ♕f3 d5 24 ♗xf6 gxf6 25 ♘xd5 ♘xd5 26 ♕xd5 ♖h2+ 27 ♔xh2 c6+ 28 ♘d6+ ♔e7 29 ♕d2 ♗c7 30 ♖cd1 ♗xd6+ 31 ♔g2 b5 32 ♗b3 ♕c7 33 ♕h6 ♖g8 34 ♖e2 ♕b8 35 ♖ed2 ♗e4+ 36 f3 ♖xg4+ 37 ♔f1 ♕g8 38 fxg4 ♕xg4 39 ♖xd6 **1-0** +13

## 1857-★MS-13
29 xi 57

**Morphy,P.C.+Schulten, J.W.**

New York

1 e4 e5 2 ♘f3 ♘c6 3 ♗c4 ♗c5 4 b4 ♗xb4 5 c3 ♗c5 6 0-0 d6 7 d4 exd4 8 cxd4 ♗b6 9 ♘c3 ♗g4 10 ♗b5 ♔f8 11 ♗e3 ♗xf3 12 gxf3 ♘ge7 13 ♔h1 h5 14 ♖g1 ♘g6 15 f4 ♕h4 16 f5 ♘f4 17 ♕f3 ♗xd4 18 ♗xf4 ♘e5 19 ♗xe5 ♗xe5 20 ♖g2 ♗xc3 21 ♕xc3 ♕xe4 22 ♖e1 **1-0** +13

## 1857-★MS-14
29 xi 57

**Schulten,J.W.–**
**Morphy,P.C.**

New York

1 e4 e5 2 f4 exf4 3 ♗c4 ♘f6 4 ♘c3 ♗b4 5 e5 d5 6 exf6 dxc4 7 fxg7 ♖g8 8 ♘e4 ♘c6 9 b3 ♕d4 10 ♕e2

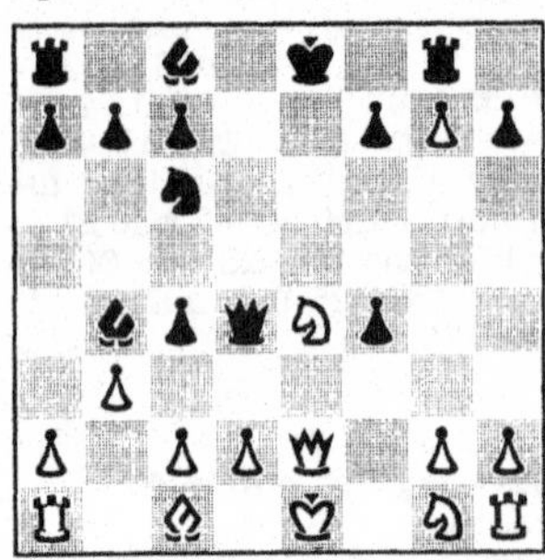

10 … ♕xa1 11 ♘f6+ ♔d8 12 c3 ♕xc1+ 13 ♔f2 ♗c5+ 14 ♔f3 ♘e5+ 15 ♕xe5 ♕f1+ 16 ♔e4 ♕d3+ 17 ♔xf4 ♗d6 **0-1** +13

## 1857-★MS-15
30 xi 57

**Morphy,P.C.+**
**Schulten,J.W.**

New York

1 e4 e5 2 f4 exf4 3 ♘f3 g5 4 ♗c4 ♗g7 5 0-0 d6 6 c3 ♗g4 7 ♕b3 ♘h6 8 ♕b5+ ♘d7 9 ♕xg5 ♕xg5 10 ♘xg5 ♘e5 11 ♗b3 ♗f6 12 h4 ♘d3 13 ♗c2 ♘xc1 14 ♖xc1 0-0-0 15 ♖f1 ♖dg8 16 ♖xf4 ♗xg5 17 hxg5 ♖xg5 18 ♔f2 ♖hg8 19 ♘a3 ♗e6 20 ♖g1 ♘g4+ 21 ♔e2 h5 22 d4 ♗xa2 23 b3 ♘h6 24 ♔f2 ♖g3 25 ♖f6 ♗xb3 26 ♗xb3 ♖xc3 27 ♖xh6 ♖xb3 28 ♘c4 ♖g4 29 ♘d2 ♖d3 30 ♔e2 ♖xd4 31 ♖xh5 ♖g3 32 ♖f5 ♖g7 33 ♔e3 c5 34 ♘f3 ♖a4 35 ♖d1 ♔c7 36 ♘g5 b5 37 ♖xf7+ ♖xf7 38 ♘xf7 b4 39 ♘xd6 b3 40 ♘b5+ ♔b6 41 ♘c3 ♖a3 42 e5 b2 43 ♔d2 ♖a1 44 ♔c2 ♖xd1 45 ♘xd1 b1♕+ 46 ♔xb1 ♔c6 47 ♘b2 ♔d5 48 ♘c4 a5 49 ♔a2 **1-0** +13

## 1857-★MS-16
30 xi 57

**Schulten,J.W.–**
**Morphy,P.C.**

New York

1 e4 e5 2 f4 exf4 3 ♗c4 d5 4 exd5 ♘f6 5 ♘c3 ♗d6 6 ♘f3 0-0 7 0-0 ♗g4 8 d4 ♘bd7 9 ♘e2 ♘b6 10 ♗b3 ♘bxd5 11 ♘e5 ♘e3 12 ♗xe3 ♗xe5 13 dxe5 ♕xd1 14 ♖axd1 ♗xe2 15 ♖xf4 ♗xd1 16 exf6 b6 17 fxg7 ♔xg7 18 h4 f5 19 ♗d4+ ♔g6 20 ♗e5 c5 21 ♗d6 ♖fe8 22 ♗a4 ♖e6 23 ♗c7 ♖c8 24 ♗d7 ♖e1+ 25 ♔f2 ♖e2+ 26 ♔f1 ♖xc7 27 ♗xf5+ ♔g7 28 ♖g4+ ♔f6 29 ♗d3 ♖e1+ 30 ♔xe1 ♗xg4 **0-1** +13

**1857-★MS-17**
**Morphy,P.C.+ Schulten,J.W.**
New York [Löwenthal]
1 e4 e5 2 ♘f3 ♘c6 3 ♗c4 ♗c5 4 b4 ♗xb4 5 c3 ♗c5 6 0-0 d6 7 d4 exd4 8 cxd4 ♗b6 9 ♘c3 ♗g4 10 ♗b5 [□ 10 ♕a4 Fraser] 10 ... ♗xf3 [□ 10 ... ♗d7 Morphy] 11 gxf3 ♔f8 12 ♗e3 ♘ce7 13 ♔h1 c6 14 ♗a4 d5 15 ♖b1 ♖b8 16 ♕d3 ♗c7 17 ♖g1 ♘g6 18 e5 ♕h4 19 ♗g5 ♕h3 20 ♘e2 f6 21 ♘f4 ♘xf4 22 ♗xf4 g5 23 ♕a3+ ♔e8 [23 ... ♔g7 24 exf6++-] 24 ♖xb7!

24 ... ♖xb7 25 ♗xc6+ ♔f7 26 ♗xd5+ ♔g6 27 ♕f8! ♕d7 28 ♗xb7 ♗d8 29 exf6 ♗xf6 30 ♗e4+ ♔h5 31 ♗e3 h6 32 ♖g3 ♗g7 33 ♕f7+! **1-0** L/N3161

**1857-★MS-18**
**Schulten,J.W.- Morphy,P.C.**
New York [Löwenthal]
1 e4 e5 2 f4 d5 3 exd5 e4 4 ♘c3 [4 d3 ♕xd5 5 ♘c3 ♗b4 6 ♕d2 (6 ♗d2 ♗xc3 7 ♗xc3 f6 8 dxe4 ♕xe4+ 9 ♕e2=) 6 ... ♕e6 7 dxe4 ♗xc3 8 ♕xc3 ♕xe4+ 9 ♔f2 ♘f6 10 ♗d3 ♕c6 11 ♕xc6 ♘xc6 12 ♘f3= Heydebrand] 4 ... ♘f6 5 d3 ♗b4 6 ♗d2 e3 7 ♗xe3 0-0 8 ♗d2 ♗xc3 9 bxc3 ♖e8+ 10 ♗e2 ♗g4 11 c4 c6 12 dxc6 ♘xc6 13 ♔f1 ♖xe2! 14 ♘xe2 ♘d4 15 ♕b1 ♗xe2+ 16 ♔f2 ♘g4+ 17 ♔g1 ♘f3+! 18 gxf3 ♕d4+ 19 ♔g2 ♕f2+ 20 ♔h3 ♕xf3+ **0-1** L/N3161

**1857-★MS-19**
**Schulten,J.W.- Morphy,P.C.**
New York [Löwenthal]
1 e4 e5 2 f4 exf4 3 ♗c4 ♘f6 4 ♘c3 ♗b4 5 e5 d5 6 exf6 dxc4 7 fxg7 ♖g8 8 ♕e2+ ♗e6 9 a3 ♗c5 10 ♘f3 ♘c6 11 ♘e4 ♘d4 12 ♘xd4 ♗xd4 13 c3 ♕h4+ 14 ♔f1 [14 ♔d1 △ 14 ... ♗g4 15 ♘f6+] 14 ... ♗b6 15 d4? cxd3 16 ♕xd3 ♖d8! 17 ♕e2 ♖d1+ [18 ♕xd1 ♗c4+] **0-1** L/N3161

**1857-★MS-20**
**Schulten,J.W.- Morphy,P.C.**
New York [Löwenthal]
1 e4 e5 2 f4 exf4 3 ♗c4 d5 4 exd5 ♘f6 5 ♘c3 ♗d6 6 d4 0-0 7 ♘ge2? [□ 7 ♘f3] 7 ... f3 8 gxf3 ♘h5 9 h4 ♖e8 10 ♘e4 ♗g3+ 11 ♔d2 ♗d6 12 ♔c3 b5 13 ♗xb5 c6 14 ♘xd6 ♕xd6 15 ♗a4 ♗a6 16 ♖e1 ♘d7 17 b3 ♘b6 18 ♗xc6 ♖ac8 19 ♔d2 ♖xc6! 20 dxc6 ♗xe2 21 ♖xe2 ♕xd4+ 22 ♔e1 ♕g1+ 23 ♔d2 ♖d8+ 24 ♔c3 ♕c5+ 25 ♔b2 ♘a4+ **0-1** L/N3161

**1857-★MS-21**
**Morphy,P.C.+Schulten, J.W.**
New York
1 e4 e5 2 ♘f3 ♘c6 3 ♗c4 ♗c5 4 0-0 f5 5 d4 exd4 6 e5 d6 7 exd6 ♕xd6 8 ♖e1+ ♘ge7 9 ♘g5 ♘e5 10 ♗f4 ♘7g6 11 ♗xe5 ♘xe5 12 ♘f7 **1-0** M212-1858

**1857-★MS-22**
**Stanley, C.H.- Morphy, P.C.**
New York [Löwenthal]
⟨♙f7⟩ 1 e4 e6 2 d4 d5 3 e5 [□ 3 ♕h5+] 3 ... c5 4 ♗e3 ♕b6 5 b3 ♘c6 6 ♘f3 cxd4 7 ♗xd4 ♘xd4 8 ♘xd4 ♗c5 9 c3 ♘e7 10 ♗b5+ ♘c6 11 ♗xc6+ bxc6 12 ♕h5+ [□ 12 b4] 12 ... g6 13 ♕g4 0-0 14 0-0 ♗a6 15 ♕xe6+ ♔h8 16 ♖d1 ♖ae8 17 ♕g4 ♖xe5 18 ♘d2 ♗c8 19 ♕g3 ♗d6 20 ♕d3 ♗a6 21 ♕c2 ♖h5 22 ♘2f3 c5 23 ♘e2 ♖xf3! 24 gxf3 ♕d8 25 c4 ♖xh2 26 ♖xd5 ♕h4 27 ♕c3+ ♔g8 28 ♘g3 ♕h3 **0-1** L/N3161

**1857-★MT-1**
**Thompson, J.- Morphy, P.C.**
New York [Maróczy]
1 e4 e5 2 ♘f3 ♘c6 3 ♗c4 ♗c5 4 b4 ♗xb4 5 c3 ♗a5 6 0-0 d6 7 d4 exd4 8 cxd4 [□ 8 ♕b3 Morphy L/N6389-1860] 8 ... ♗b6 9 d5 ♘ce7 10 e5 ♘g6 11 ♘g5 [□ 11 e6; 11 ♗b2] 11 ... ♘8e7 [11 ... ♘xe5 12 ♗f4 ♘g6 13 ♖e1+ ♔f8 14 ♗b5 ♗d7∓] 12 ♖e1 0-0 [12 ... ♘xe5? 13 ♗b2!±] 13 ♕h5? h6 14 ♘e4 [□ 14 ♘f3] 14 ... ♘xe5 15 ♗xh6 gxh6 16 ♘f6+ ♔g7 17 ♖xe5 [17 ♖e4; 17 ♗d3 ♔xf6] 17 ... dxe5 18 ♕xe5 ♔h8 [□ 18 ... ♘f5!] 19 ♗d3 [19 ♘h5+ f6 20 ♘xf6? ♘g6!∓] 19 ... ♕d6 20 ♕b2 ♕f4 [20 ... ♕c5∓] 21 ♘e4+ f6 22 g3 ♕e5 23 ♕d2 ♘g8 24 ♘bc3 f5 25 ♖e1 fxe4 26 ♖xe4 ♖xf2 **0-1** L/N3203

**1857-★MT-2**
**Thompson, J.- Morphy, P.C.**
New York [Löwenthal]
1 e4 e5 2 ♘f3 ♘c6 3 ♗c4 ♗c5 4 b4 ♗xb4 5 c3 ♗a5 6 d4 exd4 7 ♕b3 ♕f6 8 0-0 d6 9 e5 dxe5 10 cxd4 exd4 11 ♘bd2 ♘ge7 12 ♗b2 0-0 13 ♘e4 ♕g6 14 ♗d3 ♗f5 15 ♘h4 ♕h5 16 ♘xf5 ♘xf5 17 f4 ♖fe8 18 ♖f3 ♘b4 19 ♘g5 ♘xd3 20 ♕xd3 ♕g6 21 ♖h3 ♖e3 22 ♕b5 ♖xh3 23 ♕xb7 ♖e8 24 ♘xh3 ♗b6 25 ♖f1 ♘e3 26 f5 ♕g4 27 ♘f2 ♕e2 28 ♖b1 ♘d1! **0-1** L/N3161

**1857-★MT-3**
**Thompson, J.- Morphy P.C.**
New York [Löwenthal]
1 e4 e5 2 ♘f3 ♘c6 3 ♗c4 ♗c5 4 b4 ♗xb4 5 c3 ♗a5 6 d4 exd4 7 ♕b3 ♕f6 8 0-0 d6 9 cxd4 ♗b6 10 e5 dxe5 11 dxe5 ♕g6 12 ♗a3 ♗e6 13 ♘bd2 ♘ge7 14 ♗xe6 fxe6 15 ♖ae1 0-0 16 ♘e4 ♖ad8 17 ♘eg5 ♖xf3! 18 ♘xf3 ♖d3 19 ♕b2 ♖xf3 20 ♔h1 ♗d4 21 ♕c1 ♖c3 22 ♕b2 ♖g3 23 ♕c1 ♖xg2 24 ♕f4 ♘f5 25 ♕f3 ♖xh2+! 26 ♔xh2 ♗xe5+ 27 ♖xe5 ♘xe5 28 ♕h3 ♘h4 29 f3 ♕c2+ 30 ♔h1 ♘f5 31 ♗c1 ♕e2 32 ♗f4 ♘d3 33 ♗xc7 e5 34 ♔g1 ♘f4 35 ♕h2 ♕c4 36 ♗b8 ♘e2+ 37 ♔f2 ♕d4+ 38 ♔e1 ♘fg3 39 ♕h3 ♕c3+ 40 ♔f2 ♘e4+ 41 fxe4 ♕xh3 42 ♔xe2 ♕g2+ **0-1** L/N3161

**1857-★M♀-1**
**Morphy, P.C.**
New York [Maróczy]
⟨♘b1⟩ 1 e4 e5 2 ♘f3 ♘f6 3 d4 exd4 4 e5 ♕e7 [□ 4 ... ♘e4] 5 ♗e2 ♘e4 6 0-0 d5 7 exd6 ♘xd6 8 ♖e1 ♗e6 9 ♗g5 ♕d7 10 ♘e5 ♕c8 11 ♗h5 ♗e7 12 ♗xe7 ♔xe7 13 ♘xf7 ♘xf7 14 ♗g4 ♘d8 15 ♕xd4 ♖g8 16 ♖xe6+ ♘xe6 17 ♖e1 ♘c6 18 ♕c5+ ♔f6 19 ♕f5+ ♔e7 20 ♖xe6+ [20 ... ♕xe6 (20 ... ♔d8 21 ♕g5++-) 21 ♕xe6+ ♔f8 22 ♕f5+ ♔e7 23 ♕d7+ ♔f8 24 ♗e6 ♘e5 25 ♕xc7+-] **1-0** L/N3203

**1857-★M♀-2**
**Morphy, P.C.**
New York [Maróczy]
⟨♖a1⟩ 1 e4 e5 2 ♘f3 ♘c6 3 ♗c4 ♗c5 4 b4 ♗xb4 5 c3 ♗a5 6 d4 exd4 7 0-0 ♘f6 8 ♗a3 ♗b6? [□ 8 ... d6] 9 ♕b3 d5 10 exd5 ♘a5 11 ♖e1+ ♗e6 12 dxe6 ♘xb3 13 exf7+ ♔d7 14 ♗e6+ ♔c6 15 ♘e5+ ♔b5 16 ♗c4+ ♔a5 17 ♗b4+ ♔a4 18 axb3# **1-0** L/N3203

**1857-★M?-3**
**Morphy, P.C.+?**
New Orleans
⟨♖a1⟩ 1 e4 e5 2 ♘f3 ♘c6 3 ♗c4 ♗c5 4 b4 ♗xb4 5 c3 ♗c5 6 0-0 d6 7 d4 exd4 8 cxd4 ♗b6 9 ♘c3 ♘a5 10 ♗d3 ♗g4 11 ♗e3 ♕f6 12 ♘d5 ♕d8 13 h3 ♗xf3 14 ♕xf3 ♘f6 15 ♗g5 ♗xd4 16 e5 ♗xe5 17 ♖e1 0-0 18 ♖xe5 dxe5 19 ♘xf6+ gxf6 20 ♗xf6 **1-0** M730-1860

**1857-★M?-4**
**Morphy, P.C.+?**
New York [Löwenthal]
⟨♘b1⟩ 1 e4 e5 2 f4 exf4 3 ♘f3 g5 4 ♗c4 g4 5 0-0 gxf3 6 ♕xf3 ♕f6 7 e5 ♕xe5 8 ♗xf7+!? ♔xf7 [□ 8 ... ♔d8] 9 d4 ♕xd4+ 10 ♗e3 ♕f6 [10 ... ♕xb2 11 ♕d5+, 12 ♗d4] 11 ♕h5+ ♕g6 12 ♖xf4+ ♘f6 13 ♖xf6+ ♔xf6 14 ♗d4+ ♔e7 15 ♖e1+ ♔f7 16 ♕d5+ ♕e6 17 ♕f3+ ♔e8 18 ♕h5+ ♔d8 19 ♖xe6 dxe6 20 ♗xh8 **1-0** L/N3161

**1857-★M?-5**
**Morphy, P.C.+?**
New York [Löwenthal]
⟨♘b1⟩ 1 e4 e5 2 f4 exf4 3 ♘f3 g5 4 ♗c4 g4 5 d4 gxf3 [□ 5 ... d5 Lewis] 6 0-0 ♗h6 7 ♕xf3 ♘c6 8 ♗xf7+ ♔xf7 9 ♕h5+ ♔g7 10 ♗xf4 ♗xf4 11 ♖xf4 ♘h6 12 ♖af1 ♕e8 13 ♕h4 d6 14 ♕f6+ ♔g8 15 ♕xh6 ♗d7 16 ♖4f3 ♘e7 17 h4 ♘g6 18 h5 ♗g4 19 hxg6 hxg6 20 ♖f8+ **1-0** L/N3161

**1857-★M?-6**
**Morphy, P.C.+?**
New York [Löwenthal]
⟨♘b1⟩ 1 e4 e5 2 ♘f3 ♘c6 3 d4 ♘xd4 4 ♘xe5 ♘e6 5 ♗c4 ♘f6 6 ♘xf7 ♔xf7 7 ♗xe6+ ♔xe6 8 e5 ♗c5 9 0-0 ♘d5 10 ♕g4+ ♔xe5 11 ♗g5 ♕f8 12 ♖ad1 ♔d6 13 ♕e4 ♕f7 14 c4 ♔c6 15 ♖xd5 ♔b6 16 ♖xc5 c6 [16 ... ♔xc5 17 ♗e3++–] 17 ♕e5 ♖e8 18 ♖b5+ **1-0** L/N3161

**1857-★M?-7**
**Morphy, P.C.+?**
New York
⟨♘b1⟩ 1 e4 e5 2 ♘f3 ♘c6 3 ♗c4 ♗c5 4 b4 ♗xb4 5 c3 ♗c5 6 0-0 ♘f6 7 d4 exd4 8 cxd4 ♗b6 9 ♗a3 d6 10 e5 ♘e4 11 ♖e1 d5 12 ♗b5 ♗g4 13 ♖c1 ♕d7 14 ♕a4 ♗xf3 15 ♖xc6 0-0-0 16 e6 fxe6 17 ♖xb6 **1-0** L/N3161

**1857-★M?-8**
**Morphy, P.C.+?**
New York [Löwenthal]
⟨♘b1⟩ 1 e4 e5 2 ♘f3 ♘c6 3 ♗c4 ♗c5 4 b4 ♗xb4 5 c3 ♗c5 6 0-0 d6 7 d4 exd4 8 cxd4 ♗b6 9 ♗b2 ♗g4 10 ♗b5 ♗d7 11 d5 ♘e5 12 ♗xd7+ ♕xd7 13 ♗xe5 dxe5 14 ♘xe5 ♕b5? 15 ♖b1 ♕a5 16 ♕g4! ♘e7 17 ♕d7+ ♔f8 18 ♖b3 ♗d4 19 ♘f3 ♗c5 20 ♖c1 c6 21 d6 ♗xd6 [21 ... ♘g6 22 ♖xb7+–] 22 ♕xd6 ♖d8 23 ♕g3 b6 24 ♕c7 ♖c8 25 ♖d3 ♖e8 26 ♖d8 ♕a6 27 ♖cd1 **1-0** L/N3161

**1857-★M?-9**
**Morphy, P.C.+?**
New York
⟨♘b1⟩ 1 e4 e5 2 ♘f3 ♘c6 3 ♗c4 ♗c5 4 b4 ♗xb4 5 c3 ♗a5 6 0-0 d6 7 d4 exd4 8 ♕b3 ♗e6 9 ♗xe6 fxe6 10 cxd4 ♗b6 11 d5 ♘a5 12 ♕c3 e5 13 ♘g5 h6 14 ♘e6 ♕e7 15 ♗e3 ♘f6 16 ♗xb6 axb6 17 ♖ae1 ♖c8 18 f4 ♔d7 19 fxe5 dxe5 20 ♕xe5 ♘c4 21 ♕c3 b5 22 ♕h3 ♔e8 23 e5 ♘xe5 24 ♖xe5 ♔f7 25 ♘g5+ hxg5 26 ♖xe7+ ♔xe7 27 ♕e6+ **1-0** +13

**1857-★OP-1 ●○⬠**
**Paulsen, L.+Oscanyan, C.**
New York [Fiske]
1 e4 e5 2 ♘f3 ♘c6 3 d4 d6 4 dxe5 dxe5 5 ♕xd8+ ♔xd8 6 ♗c4 f6 7 ♗e3 ♗d6 8 ♘c3 ♗d7 9 0-0-0 ♘ge7 10 ♖d2 ♘c8 11 ♖hd1 ♘6e7 12 ♘e1 a6 13 f4 b6 14 fxe5 fxe5 15 ♘f3 ♘g6 16 h4 ♗g4 17 ♗d5 ♖a7 18 ♗c6 ♗xf3 19 gxf3 h6 20 ♘d5 ♘ge7 21 ♘xe7 ♔xe7 22 ♖g2 ♔f6 23 ♖dg1 ♗f8 24 ♖g6+ ♔e7 25 ♖d1 ♔f7 26 h5 ♗d6 27 ♗d5+ ♔f8 28 ♖dg1 c6 29 ♗e6 ♘e7 30 ♖xg7 c5 31 ♖f7+ ♔e8 32 ♖f6 ♔d8 33 ♖xh6 ♖e8 34 ♗f7 ♘f5 35 exf5 ♖xf7 36 ♖xd6+ ♔c7 37 ♖e6 ♖xe6 38 fxe6 **1-0** L/N5184

**1857-★S?-1**
**? & ?+Staunton, H.**
London [Staunton]
1 e4 e5 2 ♘f3 ♘f6 3 ♘xe5 ♘c6 4 ♘xc6 dxc6 5 d3 ♗c5 6 ♗e2 h5 7 h3 ♕d4 8 ♖f1 [8 0-0 ♘g4∓] 8 ... ♗e6 9 c3 ♕d7 10 e5 ♘d5 11 d4 ♗b6 12 ♗xh5 0-0-0 13 ♗g4 c5! 14 ♗xe6 ♕xe6 15 ♗e3 f5 16 ♗g5 ♖d7 17 ♕b3 cxd4 18 cxd4 ♗xd4 19 f4 ♕c6 20 ♘a3 ♘c3 [20 ... ♘e3 21 ♖f3 ♕e4–+] 21 ♕c2 ♘e3 [21 ... ♕d5 22 bxc3 ♗xc3+ 23 ♕xc3 ♕e4+ 24 ♔f2 ♖d3–+] 22 bxc3 ♗d2+?? [22 ... ♖d2 23 ♕xf5+ (23 ♕xd2 ♗xd2+ 24 ♔xd2 ♕xg2+ 25 ♔e1 ♖xh3–+) 23 ... ♔b8 24 ♖c1 (24 ♘b1 ♕xg2–+; 24 ♖f3 ♕xc3–+; 24 ♖d1 ♕xc3–+; 24 ♕g4 ♕xc3–+) 24 ... ♕a6–+] 23 ♔f2 ♕c5+ 24 ♔g3 ♕xa3 25 ♖f3 **1-0** M954-1857

**1857-★S?-2**
**? & ?– Staunton, H.**
London [Staunton]
1 e4 e5 2 f4 exf4 3 ♘f3 g5 4 h4 g4 5 ♘e5 h5 6 ♗c4 ♘h6 7 d4 d6 8 ♘d3 f5 9 ♘xf4 c6 10 ♘xh5 fxe4 11 ♗g5 ♗e7 12 0-0 ♗xg5 13 hxg5 ♕xg5 14 ♘f6+ ♔d8 15 ♕e1 d5 16 ♘c3 [16 ♗b3 g3–+] 16 ... ♘f5 17 ♘cxd5 g3 18 ♖xf5 ♗xf5 19 ♕b4 cxd5 20 ♘xd5 ♘d7 21 ♕xb7 ♖c8 22 ♕xa7 ♕d2 **0-1** M954-1857

**1857-★S?-3**
**? & ?= Staunton, H.**
London [Staunton]
1 e4 e5 2 ♘f3 d6 3 d4 exd4 4 ♘xd4 ♘f6 5 ♗d3 ♗e7 6 0-0 c5 [□ 6 ... 0-0] 7 ♗b5+ ♗d7 [□ 7 ... ♔f8] 8 ♗xd7+ ♕xd7 9 ♘f5 0-0 10 ♕f3 ♘c6 11 ♕g3 ♘e8 12 ♘c3 ♘d4 13 ♘xd4 cxd4 14 ♘d5 ♖c8 15 ♕d3 ♗d8! 16 ♗f4 f5 17 ♕xd4 fxe4 [17 ... ♖xc2 18 ♘e3] 18 ♕xe4 ♕f5! 19 ♕xf5 ♖xf5 20 ♖ad1 ♖c5 21 ♖fe1 ♖cxd5? [21 ... ♔f7 Δ 22 ... ♖cxd5] 22 ♖xd5 ♖xd5 23 ♖xe8+ ♔f7 24 ♖e1 ♗f6 25 g3 g5 [25 ... ♗xb2 26 ♖b1] 26 ♗e3 a6 27 c4 ♖a5 28 ♖d1 ♔e6 29 a3 ♗xb2 30 ♖b1 ♗xa3 31 ♖xb7 h5 32 ♖g7 g4 33 ♔f1 ♗c5 [□ 33 ... ♖a4] 34 ♖g5 ♖a1+ 35 ♔e2 ♖a2+ 36 ♔d3 ♖a3+ 37 ♔e4 ♗xe3 38 fxe3 ♖a2 39 ♖xh5 a5 40 ♔f4 a4± 41 ♔xg4 a3 42 ♖a5 ♖a1 43 h4 a2 44 h5 ♔f7 45 ♔g5 ♖g1 46 ♖xa2 ♖xg3+ 47 ♔f4 ♖h3 48 ♖a5 ♖h4+ 49 ♔g5 ♖xc4 50 h6 ♔g8 **½-½** M954-1857

**1857-★S?-4**
**Staunton, H.+? & ?**
London [Staunton]
1 e4 e5 2 ♘f3 ♘f6 3 ♘xe5 d6 4 ♘f3 ♘xe4 5 d4 d5 6 ♗d3 ♗d6 7 0-0 0-0 8 c4 ♘f6 9 ♗g5 dxc4 10 ♗xc4 h6 11 ♗h4 g5 12 ♗g3 ♗g4 13 ♕d3 [Δ 14 ♕g6+] 13 ... ♔g7 14 ♘bd2 ♘c6 15 a3 ♗xg3 16 fxg3 ♕d6 17 d5 ♖ad8 18 ♕c3 ♘e7 19 ♘e4 ♕b6+ 20 ♔h1 ♗f5 [20 ... ♘xd5 21 ♗xd5 ♖xd5 22 ♘h4+–] 21 d6 ♘g8 [□ 21 ... ♖xd6] 22 ♘xf6 ♘xf6 23 ♘xg5 ♔g6 24 ♕e5 ♕xd6 25 ♕xf5+ ♔g7 26 ♖ad1 ♕c6 [26 ... ♕xd1 27 ♕xf6++–] 27 ♖xd8 ♖xd8 28 ♘e6+ **1-0** M954-1857

**1857-★S?-5**
**?– Staunton, H.**
Manchester [Staunton]
⟨♙f7⟩ 1 e4 d6 2 f4 ♘c6 3 d4 e6 4 c3 g6 5 ♘f3 d5 6 e5 ♘ce7 7 ♗d3 ♘h6 8 ♗e3 ♘g4 9 ♗g1 c6 10 h3 ♘h6 11 g4 ♗d7 12 ♗e3 ♗g7 13 ♘bd2 ♕c7 14 ♘b3 b6 15 ♕d2 [Δ 16

f5] 15 ... Nf7 16 h4 0-0-0 17 Rc1 Kb8 18 c4 dxc4 19 Rxc4 Nd5 20 Be4 Rc8 21 Ke2 [□ 21 Kf2] 21 ... Rhd8 22 Rhc1 Qb7 23 a4 Bf8 24 a5 c5 25 Kf2 Bb5 26 R4c2 c4 27 Na1 Qa6 28 Bxd5 exd5 [28 ... Rxd5?!] 29 axb6 Qxb6 [29 ... axb6?!] 30 b3 Ba3 31 Rb1 c3 [31 ... Ba4? 32 Ra2+-] 32 Rxc3 Rxc3 33 Qxc3 Rc8 34 Qd2 Be7 35 Kg3 h5 36 Rc1 Rxc1 37 Qxc1 hxg4 38 Ng5 Nh6 39 Qc3 Bd7 40 Nc2 Nf5+ 41 Kf2 g3+ 42 Kg2 Qb5 43 Qd2 Qxb3 44 Kf3 g2 45 Kxg2 [45 Kf2 Ba4-+] 45 ... Qxc2 46 Qxc2 Nxe3+ 47 Kf3 Nxc2 ...♀ **0-1** M954-1857

**1857-★♀-6**
**♀+ Staunton, H.**
Manchester [Staunton]

⟨Δf7⟩ 1 e4 d6 2 Bc4 Nf6 3 Nc3 Nc6 4 Qe2 e6 5 Bb5 Bd7 6 Bxc6 Bxc6 7 d4 Be7 8 f4 0-0 9 Nf3 Qd7 10 0-0 d5 11 e5 Ne4 12 Rd1 Nxc3 13 bxc3 Bb5 14 Qf2 Rac8 15 Be3 b6 16 Ne1 c5 17 Nd3 Qc6 18 h3 cxd4 19 Bxd4 Rf7 20 g4 Rcf8 21 Rf1 Ba3 [□ 21 ... Bxd3 △ 22 ... Bg5∓] 22 Rab1 Bc4 23 Kh2 g6 24 Rbe1! Be7 25 Qg3 Bg5 26 f5 Bxd3 27 cxd3 gxf5 28 gxf5 Rg7 29 Re2 Bh6 30 Qh4 Bg5 31 Qg3 Bh6 32 Qh4 Bg5 33 Qg3 Qe8? [33 ... Bh6=] 34 Ref2 Be7 35 Qe3 **1-0** M954-1857

**1857-★S♀-7**
**♀– Staunton, H.**
Manchester [Staunton]

⟨Δf7⟩ 1 e4 d6 2 Bc4 Nf6 3 d3?! c6 4 Nc3 e6 5 Nge2 Be7 6 0-0 a5 7 a4 Na6 8 Ng3 Nc7 9 f4 d5 10 Bb3 0-0 11 e5 Nd7 12 d4 c5 13 Be3 b6 14 dxc5 Nxc5 15 Ba2 g6 16 Nce2 Ba6 17 Rf3 Qe8 18 b3 Rad8 19 Nd4 Ne4 20 Nxe4 dxe4 21 Rf2 Bc5 [21 ... Nd5] 22 c4 Rd7 [□ 22 ... Bxd4 △ 23 ... e3, 24 ... Qd7; 24 ... e2] 23 Qd2 Bb7 24 Rd1 Na6 25 Bb1 Nb4 26 Qe1 Qe7 27 Rfd2 Rfd8 28 Kh1 Nd3 29 Bxd3 exd3 30 Nb5 [30 Rxd3 Be4 △ 31 ... Bb4] 30 ... Bb4 31 Bxb6 Rf8 32 Qg1 Bxd2 33 Bc5 Qh4 34 Bxf8 Bxf4 35 Bd6 d2 36 Nd4 Qg4 [△ 37 ... Bxg2+; △ 37 ... Bxh2] 37 Rf1 d1Q 38 Rxd1 Bxg2+ **0-1** M954-1857

**1857-⊠AN-1**
**Athenaeum Chess Club Philadelphia+ New York Chess Club**
[Athenaeum Committee]

1 e4 e5 2 Nf3 Nc6 3 d4 Nxd4 4 Nxd4 exd4 5 Bc4 Qf6? 6 0-0 Bc5 7 e5 Qf5 [□ 7 ... Qd8] 8 c3 dxc3 9 Nxc3 Ne7 10 Bd3 Qe6 [10 ... Qxe5?!] 11 Ne4 Bd4 [11 ... Qxe5?!] 12 Ng5 Qb6 13 Qh5 g6 14 Qh6 [△ 15 Qg7] 14 ... Bxe5 15 Re1 Qf6 [15 ... d6 16 Rxe5 dxe5 17 Qg7 Rf8 18 Nxh7+-] 16 Nf3 [16 Nxh7 Rxh7; 16 ... Qg7?] 16 ... d6 17 Bg5 Qe6 18 Nxe5 dxe5 19 Rac1

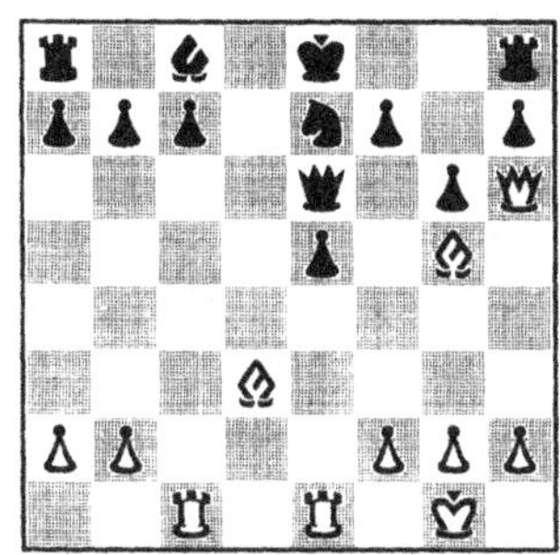

19 ... Rf8 [19 ... f6 20 Bc4 Qf5 21 Bxe6 Nxh6 22 Bxc8 fxg5 23 Rxe5+ Kf8 (23 ... Kd8 24 Bxb7 △ 25 Rd1#) 24 Rxc7+-; 19 ... Bd7 20 Bc4 Qf5 21 Qg7 Rg8 22 Qxe5+-; 19 ... Nf5 20 Bxf5 Qxf5 21 Qg7+-; 19 ... Rg8 20 Qxh7 Bd7 (20 ... Kf8 21 Bc4 △ 22 Rxe5; 20 ... Rf8 21 Rc5 f6 22 Bxf6 Qxf6 23 Rcxe5+-) 21 Bc4 Qf5 22 Rxe5+-; 19 ... c6 20 Bc4 Qf5 (20 ... Nd5 21 Qg7) 21 Qg7 Rg8 22 Qxe5+-; 19 ... Qd6 20 Red1 c6 (20 ... Qb6 21 Qg7 Rg8 22 Bb5+ c6 23 Rxc6 bxc6 24 Bxc6+ Bd7 25 Bxd7++-; 20 ... Qe6 21 Bc4 Qf5 22 Qg7 Rf8 23 Rd8+ Kxd8 24 Qxf8++-; 20 ... Nd5 21 Qg7 Rf8 22 Rxc7 Nxc7 23 Bb5+ Nxb5 24 Rxd6 Nxd6 25 Qxe5+ Kd7 26 Qe7++-; 22 ... Qxc7 23 Bb5+ Bd7 24 Rxd5 Bxb5 25 Rxe5++-; 22 ... Bd7 23 Bb5 Bxb5 24 Rxd5 Qxd5 25 Qe7++-) 21 Bb5 Nd5 22 Qg7 Rf8 23 Rxd5 Qxd5 24 Qf6 Qd7 25 Re1+-] 20 Bc4 [20 Qg7 f6 21 Bc4 Rf7] 20 ... Qf5 21 Bxe7 Kxe7 22 f4 [22 Qg7+-] 22 ... e4 [22 ... Be6+-; 22 ... Qg4+-; 22 ... f6+-] 23 Bd3 Be6 [23 ... Qh5 24 Rxe4+ Be6 25 Qxh5 gxh5 26 f5+-; 23 ... Qf6 24 Bxe4 Qd4+ (24 ... Be6 25 f5+-) 25 Kh1 Be6 26 f5 gxf5 27 Bxf5 Qd6 28 Rcd1 Qc6 29 Qh4+ Ke8 30 Qf6 Rg8 31 Rd2 △ 32 Bxe6+-; 23 ... Qa5 24 Qh4+ Ke8 (24 ... Kd7 25 Rxe4 Qb6+ 26 Kh1 Qd6 27 Be2+-; 25 ... Re8+-; 25 ... f6+-; 24 ... Kd6 25 Rxe4 Be6 26 Rd4+ Bd5 27 Qf6+ Kd7 28 Bf5+ gxf5 29 Qxf5+ Kd6 30 Qe5++-; 24 ... Ke6+-; 24 ... f6+-; 24 ... g5+-) 25 Rxc7 Qxc7 (25 ... Qb6+ 26 Kh1 Qd6+-) 26 Bb5+ Qd7 (26 ... Bd7 27 Rxe4#) 27 Rxe4++-] 24 Bxe4 Qa5 25 Qh4+ [25 f5?!] 25 ... Kd7 [25 ... Ke8+-] 26 Red1+ Ke8 [26 ... Kc8 27 Qe7 Rg8 28 Rd6 Kb8 29 b4+-] 27 Kh1 [△ 28 Bxb7] 27 ... c6 [27 ... Qb6+-] 28 Rxc6 Rd8 29 Rcc1 Rxd1+ 30 Rxd1 h5 31 Qf6 Bc8 32 Bxb7 [32 ... Bxb7 33 b4 Qb6 34 Re1+ Kd7 35 Qe7+ Kc6 36 a4+-; 32 ... Bd7 33 Bc6 Bxc6 34 Qxc6+ Ke7 35 Qd6+ Ke8 36 Qd7#] **1-0** M954-1857

**1857-⊠AN-2**
**New York Chess Club– Athenaeum Chess Club Philadelphia**
[Athenaeum Committee]

1 e4 c5 2 d4 cxd4 3 Nf3 e6 [3 ... e5] 4 Qxd4 Nc6 5 Qd1 Bc5 6 Bd3 Nge7 7 Nc3 d5 8 exd5 Nxd5 9 Ne4 Bb6 10 Bb5 0-0 11 Bxc6 bxc6 12 0-0 f5?! 13 Ng3 Qc7 14 c4 Nf6 15 Qc2 c5!? 16 b3 Bb7 17 Ng5 Qc6 18 f3 Bc7 19 Rfe1 Rae8 20 Bb2 g6 [20 ... Bd7 21 Nxf5] 21 Re2 e5 22 Rae1 e4 23 fxe4 Bf4 24 Nh3 Bxg3 25 hxg3 Nxe4 26 Ng5? [26 Nf4 h6 27 Nd5 (27 Rxe4 Rxe4 28 Rxe4 Qxe4 29 Qxe4 Bxe4 30 Nxg6 Rd8=; 29 Qc3 Qd4+) 27 ... Kh7 28 g4 (28 Rxe4=) 28 ... Re6 29 gxf5 gxf5 30 Rxe4 fxe4 31 Rxe4 Rxe4 32 Qxe4+ Qg6 33 Nf6+ Rxf6 34 Qxb7+ Rf7=] 26 ... Nxg5 27 Qc3 Qxg2+ 28 Rxg2 Rxe1+ 29 Qxe1 [29 Kh2?; 29 Kf2?!] 29 ... Nf3+ 30 Kf1 Nxe1 31 Rd2! f4! [31 ... Re8; 31 N~? 32 Rd7] 32 gxf4 [32 Kxe1 fxg3 33 Be5 (33 Ba3 Rf5 34 Rd8+ Kf7 35 Bc1 Re5+ 36 Kf1 g2+ 37 Kf2 Re1-+) 33 ... g2 34 Bh2 Rf1+ 35 Ke2 Be4 36 Ke3 Rh1 37 Kxe4 Rxh2 38 Rxg2 Rxg2-+; 32 Rd7 fxg3+ 33 Kxe1 (33 Kg1 Rf2-+) 33 ... Re8+ 34 Kf1 g2+ 35 Kf2 Re1-+; 32 g4 Re8 33 Rd7 Bg2+ 34 Kf2 Bf3-+] 32 ... Ng2 33 Rd7 Rxf4+ 34 Kg1 [34 Ke2-+] 34 ... Be4 35 Rg7+ Kf8 36 Rxh7 Ne3 37 Rh8+ Kf7 38 Be5 Rf1+ 39 Kh2 Nf5 40 Kh3 g5 41 Rc8 [41 ... Rh1+ 42 Kg4 (42 Bh2 Bf3 43 Rc7+ Kg6 44 Rc6+ Kh5 45 Rh6+ Kxh6 46 ~ g4#) 42 ... Rg1+ 43 Kh3 (43 Kh5 Bf3#; 43 Bg3 Rxg3+ △ 44 ... Bf3#) 43 ... g4+ 44 Kh2 Rh1#] **0-1** M954-1857

**1857̃-★AB-1**
**Bird, H.E.+ Anderssen, A.**
London [Löwenthal]

1 e4 e5 2 Nf3 Nc6 3 Bb5 Nf6 4 c3 Nxe4 5 d4 exd4 6 0-0 Be7 7 Re1 Nf6 8 cxd4 0-0 [□ 8 ... d5] 9 d5 Nb8 10 Nc3 a6 11 Ba4 b5 12 Bc2 d6 [□ 12 ... h6] 13 Bg5 h6 14 Bh4 Nbd7 15 Nd4 Bb7 16 Qd3 Re8 17 Nf5 Bf8 18 Ne4! Rxe4! 19 Rxe4 Nc5? [□ 19 ... g5!∞] 20 Nxh6+! gxh6 21 Rg4+ Bg7 22 Qg3! Nxg4 23 Bxd8 Rxd8 24 Qxg4 Bxd5 25 Re1 Be6 26 Qg3 a5 27 Re3 Kf8 28 Qf4 Bxa2 29 b3 a4 30 bxa4 bxa4 31 Qh4 f6 32 Bxa4 Bf7 33 Bc6 Rb8 34 h3 Rb6 35 Bf3 Nd7 36 Qa4 Ne5 37 Qa8+ Be8 38 Bh5 **1-0** M324

**1857̃-★AG-1**
**Anderssen, A.– Greenaway, F.E.**
London [Löwenthal]

1 e4 e5 2 f4 exf4 3 Bc4 Qh4+ 4 Kf1 d6 5 Nf3 Bg4 6 d4 Nf6 7 Nc3

♗xf3 8 ♕xf3 ♕g4 9 ♗xf4 ♕xf3+ 10 gxf3 ♗e7 11 ♖g1 ♘h5 12 ♗e3 a6 13 f4 g6 14 ♗e2! ♘f6 [14 ... ♘g7? 15 f5±] 15 e5 ♘fd7 16 ♘d5 ♔d8 17 c4 dxe5 18 fxe5 ♘c6 19 ♗g4 f5 20 ♗f3 ♖b8 21 e6 ♘f6 22 ♘xe7 ♔xe7 23 ♔g2 ♖hd8 24 ♖ad1 ♘a5 25 b3 ♔xe6 26 ♗f4 ♖d7 27 d5+ ♔f7 28 c5 ♖e8 29 c6 bxc6 30 dxc6 [30 ♗d2 ♘xd5−+] 30 ... ♖xd1 31 ♖xd1 ♖e6 32 ♗xc7 [32 ♖c1 ♘e4!] 32 ... ♘xc6 33 ♗d6 ♘e4 34 ♗a3 ♘e5 35 ♗xe4 fxe4 36 ♔f2 ♘d3+! 37 ♔e3 ♔f6 38 ♖g1 g5 39 ♗f8 ♔f5 40 h3 ♖c6 41 ♗g7 ♖c1 42 ♖g2 ♘f4 **0-1** M324

## BIRMINGHAM 1858

### 1858-BIR-1
**Löwenthal,J.J.+ Kipping,J.C.**

1 e4 b6 2 d4 e6 3 ♘f3 ♗b7 4 ♗d3 ♗e7 5 ♗e3 ♘f6 6 ♘bd2 d6 7 0-0 0-0 8 c3 ♘bd7 9 ♘e1 d5 10 e5 ♘e8 11 ♕h5 f5 12 exf6 ♘dxf6 13 ♕h3 ♗c8 14 ♕g3 ♘d6 [□ 14 ... ♘h5] 15 f4 ♘f5 16 ♕f3 ♗d7 17 ♗f2 ♗e8 18 g4 ♘d6 19 ♘g2 ♗b5 20 ♗xb5 ♘xb5 21 ♕e2 ♕d7 22 g5 ♘e8 23 ♖ae1± ♔f7? 24 ♘f3+− ♔g8 25 ♘e5 ♕d6 26 ♕xb5 **1-0** L/N6124

### 1858-BIR-2
**Kipping,J.C.−Löwenthal, J.J.**

1 e4 e5 2 ♘f3 ♘c6 3 ♗c4 ♗c5 4 b4 d5 5 ♗b5! [5 exd5?!] 5 ... dxe4 6 ♘xe5 ♗xf2+ 7 ♔xf2 ♕d4+ 8 ♔e1 ♕xe5 9 ♗xc6+ bxc6 10 ♘c3 ♘f6∓ 11 ♕e2 ♗g4! 12 ♕c4 0-0 13 ♗b2 e3 14 d3 ♕f5 15 ♖f1 ♕h5 16 ♖xf6 ♕h4+ 17 g3 ♕xf6 18 ♕f4 ♕xf4 19 gxf4 f5−+ 20 ♘e2 ♖ae8 21 ♗d4 ♖e6 22 a4 ♖fe8 23 ♘g3 ♖h6 24 ♘f1 ♖h3 25 ♗xa7 ♖f3 26 a5 ♖f2 27 ♘xe3 ♖xh2 28 ♖a2 g5 29 ♔f1 gxf4 30 ♔g1 ♖e2 31 ♘g2 ♖d2 32 ♗f2 ♖ee2 33 a6 ♖xc2 34 ♖xc2 ♖xc2 35 a7 ♖a2 36 ♘xf4 ♔f7 37 ♔f1 h5 38 ♘g2 ♗f3 39 ♘e1 ♗d5 40 ♗c5 h4 41 ♘c2 h3 42 ♔g1 ♖xc2 **0-1** L/N6124

### 1858-BIR-6
24 viii 58

**Hampton, T.I.−Owen, J.**

[Löwenthal]

1 e4 b6 2 d4 ♗b7 3 ♗d3 e6 4 ♘h3? [□ 4 ♘e2] 4 ... c5 5 c3 ♘c6 6 ♗e3 ♘f6 7 0-0 cxd4 8 cxd4 ♘b4 9 f3 ♘xd3 10 ♕xd3 ♗e7 11 ♘c3 0-0 12 ♖ad1 ♘e8= 13 ♕d2? ♘d6 14 b3 f5 15 e5 ♘f7 16 ♗f4? [□ 16 f4] 16 ... g5 17 ♗g3 ♗b4 18 ♖c1 ♗a6 19 ♖fd1 ♖c8 20 ♕b2 ♕e7 21 ♘b1 ♗a5 22 a3 b5 23 b4 ♗b6 24 ♔h1 ♗b7 25 ♘c3 a6 26 ♕d2 ♔h8 27 ♗f2 ♖c4 28 ♘g1 ♖fc8 29 h3 ♖8c6 30 ♘ge2 ♘h6 31 ♘g3 ♕f7∓ 32 ♘ce2 ♕g6 33 ♘f1 f4 34 ♖xc4 ♖xc4 35 ♕d3 ♘f5 36 ♘d2?? ♘g3+ **0-1** M324-1865

### 1858-BIR-7
24 vii 58

**Salmon, G.+Szabó, G.**

[Löwenthal]

1 e4 e5 2 ♘f3 d6 3 d4 f5 4 dxe5 fxe4 5 ♘g5 d5 6 e6 ♗c5? 7 ♘xe4 dxe4 8 ♕h5+ g6 9 ♕xc5 ♗xe6 10 ♕e5 ♕f6 11 ♕xe4 ♘c6 12 ♗c4 ♔f7 13 0-0 ♖e8 14 ♘c3 ♘ge7 15 ♘b5 ♖c8 16 ♗f4 ♗xc4 17 ♕xc4+ ♔g7 18 ♘xc7 h6 19 ♗d2 [Δ 20 ♗c3+− Staunton M954 1865] 19 ... ♘d4?? [□ 19 ... ♘e5] 20 ♕xd4 ♕xd4 21 ♘e6+ **1-0** M324-1865

### 1858-BIR-8
24 viii 58

**Szabó, G.−Salmon, G.**

[Löwenthal]

1 e4 e5 2 ♘f3 ♘c6 3 ♗c4 ♗c5 4 ♘c3 ♘f6 5 0-0 0-0 6 d3 d6 7 ♘e2 [□ 7 ♗g5] 7 ... ♗g4 8 c3 ♗xf3 9 gxf3 ♘h5 10 ♘g3 ♘f4 11 d4 ♗b6 12 ♗xf4 exf4 13 ♘e2 ♕h4 14 ♕d2 g5! 15 ♔h1 ♔h8 16 ♖g1 ♕xf2 17 ♖af1 ♕h4 18 ♖g4 ♕h5 19 ♖fg1 ♘e5!

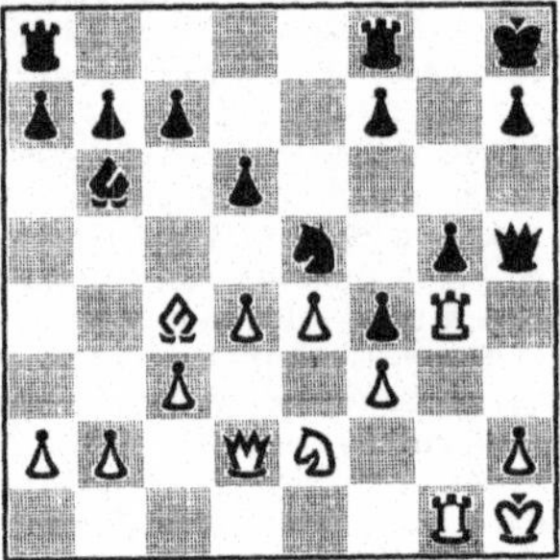

20 ♘xf4 [20 dxe5 ♗xg1 ∞ Staunton M954 1865] 20 ... gxf4 21 dxe5 ♗xg1 22 ♕xf4 ♕xh2+ 23 ♕xh2 ♗xh2 24 ♔xh2 dxe5 25 ♖g5 f6 26 ♖g4 ♖ad8 27 ♖g2 f5 28 ♔h3 fxe4 29 fxe4 ♖f4 **0-1** M324-1865

### 1858-BIR-9
24 vii 58

**Falkbeer,E.K.+ Ingelby,C.M.**

1 e4 e5 2 d4 exd4 3 ♗c4 c5 4 c3 ♘c6 5 ♘f3 d6 6 cxd4 b6? 7 dxc5 bxc5 8 ♗xf7+! ♔xf7 9 ♕d5+ ♔e8 10 ♕xc6+ ♗d7 11 ♕d5 ♘f6 12 ♕d3 ♕b6 13 ♘c3 ♗c6 14 0-0 ♖d8 15 ♘d5 ♕b7 16 ♖e1 ♗b5? 17 ♕xb5+ ♕xb5 18 ♘c7+ ♔d7 19 ♘xb5 a6 20 ♘c3 ♔c8 21 ♗f4 h6 22 e5 ♘h5 23 ♘d5 dxe5 24 ♖xe5 ♗d6 25 ♖xh5 g6 26 ♖e5 ♗xe5 27 ♗xe5 ♖he8 28 ♖d1 ♔b7 29 h4 ♔c6 30 ♘e7+ ♔b7 31 ♖xd8 ♖xd8 32 ♘xg6 ♖d1+ 33 ♔h2 a5 34 h5 ♔b6 35 g4 ♔b5 36 ♗g7 a4 37 ♗xh6 ♖d8 38 ♗g7 **1-0** M324-1865

### 1858-BIR-12
24 viii 58

**Beetlestone−Saint−Amant, P.C.F.de**

[Löwenthal]

1 e4 e6 2 ♘c3 c5 3 ♘f3 d5 4 exd5 exd5 5 d3 ♘c6 6 a3? ♗e7 7 ♗e2 h6 8 d4 ♘f6 9 h3 0-0 10 0-0 ♖e8 11 ♗e3 b6 12 ♕d2 ♘e4 13 ♘xe4? dxe4 14 ♘h2 cxd4 15 ♗f4 ♗f6 16 ♖ab1 ♗f5 17 ♘g4 ♘e5 18 ♘xf6+ ♕xf6 19 b4 ♖ac8 20 ♖b3 ♘c4 21 ♕c1 d3! 22 cxd3 ♘a5 23 bxa5 ♖xc1 24 ♗xc1 ♗e6 25 ♖b4 exd3 26 ♗xd3 ♕c3 27 ♗e4 bxa5 28 ♖b2 ♗b3 29 f3 a4!−+ 30 ♖d2 ♕c5+ 31 ♔h1 f5 32 ♗d3 ♔h8 33 ♗b2 ♖d8 34 ♖c1 ♕e3 35 ♗xg7+ ♔xg7 36 ♖c7+ ♔h8 37 ♖h7+ ♔xh7 38 ♗xf5+ ♔g7 39 ♖xd8 ♕c1+ 40 ♔h2 ♕c7+ 41 ♔h1 ♕xd8 **0-1** M324-1865

### 1858-BIR-13
**Brien, R.B.+Bird, H.E.**

1 c4 e5 2 e3 ♘f6 3 a3 c5 4 ♘c3 ♘c6 5 b3 d6 6 ♗d3 g6 7 ♗b2 ♗g7 8 ♘ge2 ♗e6 9 0-0 ♘h5 10 ♖e1 f5 11 ♘g3 ♘xg3 12 fxg3 h5 13 ♗e2 ♕g5 14 ♖f1 h4 15 g4 ♖h7 16 ♖b1 ♖d8 17 ♘d5 ♖d7 18 h3 ♖f7 19 b4 cxb4 20 axb4 e4 21 ♗xg7 ♖fxg7 22 ♘f4 ♗d7 23 d4 ♘e7 24 d5 fxg4 25 ♗xg4 ♘f5 26 ♗xf5 gxf5 27 ♕d4 b6 28 c5 ♕d8 29 cxd6 ♔f7 30 ♖a1 a5 31 bxa5 bxa5 32 ♕a7 ♖g3 33 ♖xa5 ♖hg7 34 ♖b1 ♖xe3 35 ♖b8 ♖e1+ 36 ♔f2 ♕xb8 37 ♕xb8 ♖c1 38 ♕a7 ♔e8 39 ♘h5 ♖c2+ 40 ♔e3 f4+ 41 ♘xf4 ♗f5 42 ♕b6 **1-0** L/N875

### 1858-BIR-14
25 viii 58

**Bird, H.E.+Brien, R.B.**

[Löwenthal]

1 e4 e6 2 d4 d5 3 exd5 exd5 4 ♗d3 ♘f6 5 ♘f3 ♗d6 6 0-0 0-0 7 ♗e3 h6 8 ♘e5 ♖e8 9 f4 a6 10 ♘d2 ♘c6 11 c3 ♘e7 12 ♘df3± ♘f5 13 ♗f2 ♘e4 14 ♕c2 f6 15 g4!± fxe5 16 fxe5 ♗f8 17 gxf5 ♗xf5 18 ♗g3 ♗h3 19 ♖fe1 ♘xg3 20 hxg3 g5 21 ♖e2 ♗g4 22 ♖f2 ♗xf3 23 ♖xf3 ♖e7 24 ♖af1+− ♕d7 25 ♕f2 ♗g7 26 ♗b1 ♕e6 27 ♕c2 ♗f8 28 ♖f6 ♕h3 29 ♕f2 ♗g7 30 ♗f5 ♕h5 31 ♗g6 ♕h3 32 ♖f7 ♖xf7 33 ♗xf7+ ♔h8 34 e6 ♗f8 35 ♕e3 ♗e7 36 ♕e5+ ♔h7 37 ♗h5 ♖f8 38 ♖xf8 ♗xf8 39 e7 ♗g7 40 ♗g6+ **1-0** M324-1865

**1858-BIR-15** 25/26 viii 58
**Staunton,H.–Löwenthal,J.J.**

[Löwenthal]

1 c4 e5 2 ♘c3 ♘f6 3 e3? ♗b4! 4 ♕b3 [4 ♘d5 ♘xd5∓; 4 ♘ge2 c5∓; 4 a3 ♗xc3 5 bxc3 c5 6 d4 e4∓] 4 ... c5! 5 ♘d5 ♘c6 6 ♘e2 d6 7 ♘g3 ♗e6 8 a3 ♗a5 9 ♕xb7? ♗d7 [9 ... ♖c8? 10 b4!] 10 ♕b3 [10 ♘xf6+ gxf6 11 ♕b3 f5∓] 10 ... 0-0 11 ♘xf6+ ♕xf6 12 ♗e2 ♕h4! [△ 13 ... f5∓] 13 ♗f3 ♖ab8 14 ♕d3 ♗c7 15 ♗xc6 ♗xc6 16 e4? f5 17 0-0 fxe4 18 ♕c2 ♖f4 19 b3 ♖bf8 20 ♗b2 ♖8f6 21 ♖ae1 ♖h6 22 h3 ♖hf6 23 ♖e3 ♗a5 24 ♕d1 ♕h6 25 ♕e2 ♕g6 26 ♗c1 ♖h4 27 ♖e1 ♖ff4 28 ♘f1 ♖f3 29 ♘g3 ♖xe3 30 ♕xe3 ♕f7 31 ♖e2 ♖f4 32 ♗b2 ♕g6 33 b4 ♗b6 34 b5 ♗b7 35 ♕c3 h5 36 ♖e3 h4 37 ♘h1 ♕f7 38 a4 ♕c7 39 d3 ♗a5 40 ♕c2 exd3 41 ♕xd3 e4 42 ♕d1 ♕e7 43 g3 hxg3 44 ♖xg3 ♖f7 45 ♖e3 d5 46 cxd5 ♕g5+ 47 ♘g3 ♗xd5 48 ♗c1 ♕e5 49 ♕c2 c4 50 ♗b2 ♕g5 51 ♗d4 ♗b6 52 ♕d2 ♕f4 53 ♘h5 c3!∓ 54 ♗xc3 ♕g5+ 55 ♘g3 ♗xe3 56 ♕xe3 ♕xe3 57 fxe3 ♖f3 58 ♗e5 ♖xe3 59 ♘f5 ♖d3 60 a5 e3 61 ♘d4 ♖d1+ 62 ♔h2 e2 63 ♘xe2 ♖d2 64 ♗b8 ♖xe2+ 65 ♔g3 ♖b2 [66 ♗xa7 ♗b7 Staunton L/N875]
**0-1** M980-1860

**1858-BIR-16** 28 viii 58
**Löwenthal,J.J.+Staunton,H.**

[Löwenthal]

1 e4 d5 2 exd5 ♘f6 3 ♗c4 ♘xd5 4 d4 e6? 5 ♘f3 ♗d6 6 0-0 0-0 7 ♗d3 ♗f4 8 ♘bd2 ♘c6 9 a3 ♘f6 10 ♘e4 ♗xc1 11 ♖xc1 ♕e7 [11 ... ♘xd4?] 12 ♖e1 b6? 13 ♘xf6+! gxf6 [13 ... ♕xf6 14 ♗e4 △ 15 ♘e5+−] 14 d5 ♘e5 15 ♘xe5 fxe5

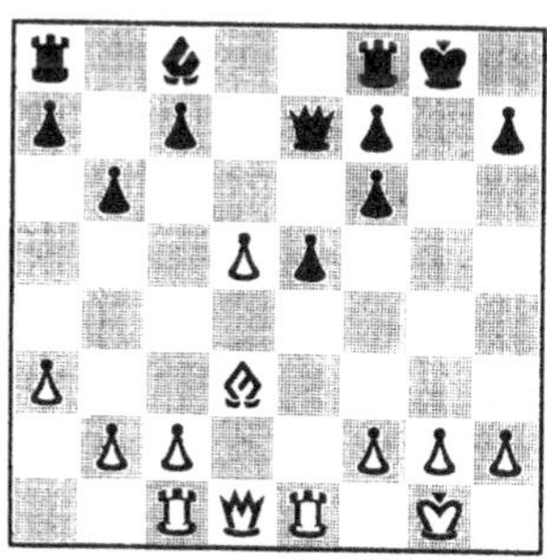

16 ♗xh7+! ♔xh7 [16 ... ♔h8 17 ♕h5+−] 17 ♕h5+ ♔g7 18 ♖e3 ♖g8 19 ♖g3+ ♔f8 20 ♕h6+− ♔e8 21 ♖xg8+ ♔d7 22 dxe6+ ♕xe6 23 ♖d1+ ♔c6 24 ♕xe6+ fxe6 25 ♖dd8 **1-0** M980-1860

**1858-BIR-19** 25 viii 58
**Saint-Amant,P.C.F.de–Falkbeer,E.K.**

1 e4 e6 2 d4 d5 3 exd5 exd5 4 ♗e3 ♘f6 5 c4 ♗e7 6 ♘c3 0-0 7 ♕b3 c6 8 ♗d3 b6 9 ♘ge2 ♗e6 10 h3 c5 11 g4 ♘c6 12 cxd5 ♘xd5 13 ♕c2 cxd4 14 ♗xd4 ♘db4 15 ♕d2 ♘xd4 16 ♘xd4 ♕xd4 17 ♗xh7+ ♔xh7 18 ♕xd4 ♘c2+ 19 ♔d2 ♘xd4 20 f4 ♖ad8 21 ♖af1 ♗c4 22 ♖f2 ♗c5 **0-1** L/N875

**1858-BIR-21** 25 viii 85
**Falkbeer,E.K.+Saint-Amant,P.C.F.de**

1 e4 e6 2 ♘f3 d5 3 exd5 exd5 4 d4 ♘f6 5 ♗d3 ♗g4 6 ♗e3 ♗e7 7 ♘bd2 0-0 8 h3 ♗h5 9 c3 b6 10 g4 ♗g6 11 ♗xg6 fxg6 12 ♘e5 ♗d6 13 ♘df3 c5 14 ♕c2 ♘fd7 15 0-0-0 ♕e8 16 ♖he1 c4 17 ♗g5 ♕c8 18 ♗h4 ♘f6 19 ♘g5 ♘bd7 20 ♗g3 ♖e8 21 f4 b5 22 f5 h6 23 ♘gf7 ♗f8 24 fxg6 ♘e4 25 ♗h4 b4 26 ♖xe4 dxe4 27 ♕xe4 ♖e6 28 g5 ♘xe5 29 ♘xe5 ♖b8 30 gxh6 gxh6 31 ♕f5 ♕e8 32 ♕f7+ ♕xf7 33 gxf7+ ♔h7 34 ♘d7 ♖c8 35 d5 ♖e2 36 ♖g1 ♗g7 37 ♗f6 ♗f8 38 ♖g8 b3 39 axb3 cxb3 40 ♘xf8+ ♖xf8 41 ♖xf8 ♔g6 42 ♖e8 ♖c2+ 43 ♔d1 ♔xf7 44 ♖e2 ♖xe2 45 ♔xe2 ♔xf6
**1-0** L/N875

**1858-BIR-24** 6 ix 58
**Owen, J.–Löwenthal, J.J.**
London [The Chess Player's Magazine]

1 e4 e5 2 d4 exd4 3 ♘f3 ♗c5 4 ♗c4 d6 5 c3 d3 6 ♕xd3 [⌓ 6 b4 △ 7 ♕b3] 6 ... ♘c6 7 0-0 ♗g4 8 ♗b5 ♘ge7 9 ♘d4 0-0 10 f4 f5 11 ♗xc6 ♘xc6 12 h3 ♗xd4+ 13 cxd4 ♗h5 14 exf5 ♕f6 15 ♗e3 [15 g4 ♕xd4+ 16 ♕xd4 ♘xd4 17 gxh5 ♘c2∓] 15 ... ♖ae8 16 ♗f2 [⌓ 16 g4 ♖xe3 17 ♕xe3 ♕xd4 18 ♕xd4 ♘xd4 19 ♘c3 ♗~=] 16 ... ♗e2 17 ♕b3+ ♔h8 18 ♖e1 ♘xd4 19 ♕c3 ♘c6 20 ♕xf6 gxf6 21 ♘c3 ♗c4 22 b3 ♗f7 23 ♘b5± ♖xe1+ 24 ♖xe1 ♖c8 25 g4 a6 26 ♘d4 ♘b4 27 ♖e7 ♔g8 28 ♗h4 ♘d5 29 ♖e4 c5 30 ♘e6 ♖e8 31 ♗e1 ♘c7 32 ♗c3? [⌓ 32 ♗a5] 32 ... ♗xe6 33 fxe6 d5 34 ♖e1 d4 35 ♗a5 ♖xe6 36 ♔f2 ♖xe1 37 ♔xe1 ♘d5 38 ♗d2 b5 39 ♔d1 c4 40 ♔c2 c3 41 ♗e1 ♘xf4 42 ♗g3 ♘e6 43 b4 ♔f7 44 ♔d3 ♔g6 45 h4 f5 46 g5 f4 47 ♗e1 ♔f5 48 a3 f3 49 ♗f2 ♘f4+ 50 ♔c2 ♔e4 51 ♗g1 ♘h3 52 h5 ♘xg5 **0-1** L/N6124-

**1858-BIR-26** 27 viii 58
**Falkbeer, E.K.+Brien, R.B.**

1 e4 e6 2 ♘f3 d5 3 exd5 exd5 4 d4 ♘f6 5 ♗g5 ♗d6 6 ♘c3 c6 7 ♗d3 0-0 8 0-0 ♗e6 9 ♘e2 ♘bd7 10 ♘f4 h6 11 ♘xe6 fxe6 12 ♕e2 ♕e7 13 ♗h4 ♖fd8 14 ♖ae1 ♘f8 15 ♘e5 ♖e8 16 f4 c5 17 c3 cxd4 18 cxd4 ♗b4 19 ♖c1 ♖ac8 20 ♘g4 ♘8d7 21 ♗b5 ♖f8 22 ♖xc8 ♖xc8 23 ♗xd7 ♕xd7 24 ♗xf6 ♕f7 25 ♗e5 ♕f5 26 ♘e3 ♕e4 27 ♕f3 ♕xf3 28 ♖xf3 ♖c1+ 29 ♖f1 ♗d2 30 ♘d1 b5 31 a3 a5 32 g4 b4 33 axb4 axb4 34 ♔g2 b3 35 h4 ♖c2 36 ♔f3 ♔f7 37 ♗d6 ♔e8 38 ♖f2 ♗c1 39 ♗b4 ♔d7 40 ♗c3 ♔c6 41 g5 ♔b5 42 gxh6 gxh6 43 ♖e2 ♗xf4 44 ♖xe6 ♗d2 45 ♖d6 ♗c1 46 ♖xd5+ ♔a6 47 ♖a5+ ♔b7 48 ♖a3 **1-0** L/N875

**1858-BIR-29**
**Brien, R.B.=Falkbeer, E.K.**

[Löwenthal]

1 d4 f5 2 c4 ♘f6 3 ♘c3 e6 4 a3 ♗e7 5 e3 b6 6 ♗d3 ♗b7 7 ♘f3 c5 8 0-0 0-0 9 b3 [⌓ 9 d5] 9 ... ♕e8 10 d5 ♕h5 11 ♘e5 exd5 12 cxd5 d6 13 ♗e2 ♕e8 14 ♘f3 ♘fd7! 15 ♗b2 ♘a6 16 ♕d2 ♘c7 17 ♘b5 ♘xb5 [17 ... ♘xd5?] 18 ♗xb5 a6 19 ♗xd7 ♕xd7 20 ♖fe1 ♖ae8 21 ♖ad1 g5 22 e4 h6 23 exf5 [⌓ 23 e5±] 23 ... ♕xf5 24 ♖e6 ♕f7! 25 ♖de1 ♗c8∞
½-½ M324-1865

**1858-BIR-31** 11 ix 58
**Falkbeer,E.K.=Löwenthal,J.J.**

1 e4 e5 2 ♗c4 ♗c5 3 ♕e2 ♘f6 4 d3 [4 f4 d5! 5 ♗xd5 ♘xd5 6 exd5 0-0 7 fxe5 ♕xd5 8 ♘c3 (8 c3 ♗xg1 9 ♖xg1 c5∓) 8 ... ♕d8 9 ♘f3 ♗g4 10 d3 ♗xf3 11 ♕xf3 ♕c8∓] 4 ... ♘c6 5 c3 h6 6 b4 ♗b6 7 a4 a6 8 ♘f3 d6 9 ♗e3 ♗xe3 10 fxe3 ♘e7 11 0-0 ♘g6 12 ♘bd2 0-0 13 h3 c6 14 ♕f2 d5

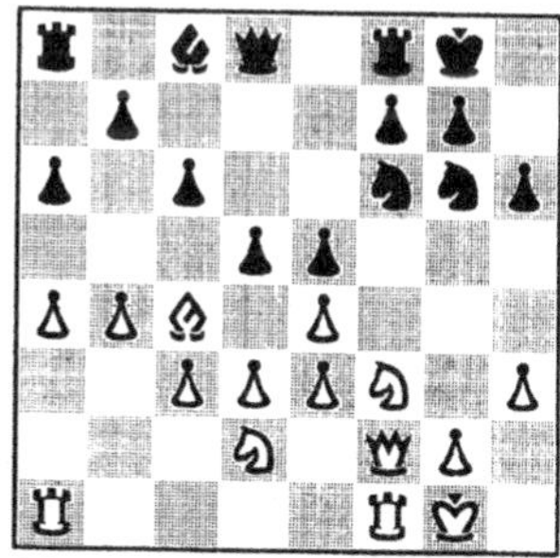

15 ♗b3 [⌓ 15 exd5 cxd5 16 ♗b3 e4 (16 ... ♗e6 17 d4 e4 18 ♘h4±) 17 dxe4 dxe4 18 ♘d4±] 15 ... dxe4 16 dxe4 ♕d3 17 ♖ac1 ♗e6 18 ♗xe6 fxe6 19 ♘e1 ♕d7 20 ♘ef3 ♖ad8 21 ♕g3 ♔h7 22 ♕xg6+ ♔xg6 23 ♘xe5+ ♔h7 24 ♘xd7 ♖xd7 25 ♘b3 e5 26 ♘c5 ♖e7 27 ♖cd1 b6 28 ♘d3 [28 ♘xa6 ♖a8 29 b5 cxb5 30 axb5 ♘xe4=] 28 ... ♖d8 29 ♘f2 ♖ed7 30 ♖xd7 ♖xd7

31 ♖b1 ♖d2 32 c4 ♖c2 33 b5 c×b5 34 c×b5 a5 35 ♖d1 ♖a2 36 ♖d8 [36 ♖d6?? ♖×f2! 37 ♔×f2 ♘×e4–+] 36 ... ♖×a4 37 ♖d6 ♖a1+ 38 ♔h2 ♖f1 39 ♘g4 ♘×g4+ 40 h×g4 ♖e1 41 ♖×b6 ♖×e3 42 ♖a6 ♖×e4 43 ♖×a5 ♖×g4 44 b6 ♖b4 45 ♖×e5 ♖×b6 ½-½ L/N6124-1863

**1858-BIR-32**
**Falkbeer,E.K.+**
**Löwenthal,J.J.**

1 e4 e5 2 ♘c3 ♘f6 3 ♗c4 ♗c5 4 d3 h6 5 f4 d6 6 ♘f3 0-0 7 ♘a4 c6 8 f×e5 d×e5 9 ♘×c5 ♕a5+ 10 ♗d2 ♕×c5 11 a3 b5 12 ♗b3 a5 13 ♕e2 ♘a6 14 ♗e3 ♕e7 15 0-0 ♘g4 16 ♗d2 ♘c5 17 ♗a2 ♘e6 18 c3 ♕d6 19 h3 ♘f6 20 d4 ♘d7 21 ♗e3 ♔h7 22 ♖ad1 ♕c7 23 ♘h4 ♘f6 24 ♗×h6! ♔×h6 25 ♖×f6+ g×f6 26 ♘f5+ ♔g6 27 ♗×e6 [27 ♕g4+ ♘g5 28 h4 ♖h8 29 h×g5 f×g5∞] 27 ... f×e6 28 ♕g4+ ♔h7 29 ♕h5+ ♔g8 30 ♕g6+ ♔h8 31 ♕h6+ ♔g8 32 ♖d3 e×d4 33 e5! [33 ♖g3+ ♕×g3∞] 33 ... e×f5 34 ♖g3+ ♔f7 35 ♕g7+ ♔e8 36 ♕×c7 ♗e6 37 ♖g7 ♖f7 38 ♖×f7 ♗×f7 39 ♕×c6+ **1-0** L/N6124-1863

**1858-BIR-33**
**Falkbeer,E.K.+**
**Löwenthal,J.J.**

1 e4 e5 2 ♘f3 d6 3 d4 e×d4 4 ♕×d4 ♗d7 5 ♗e3 ♘c6 6 ♕d2 ♘f6 7 ♘c3 ♘g4 8 0-0-0 ♘×e3 9 ♕×e3 ♗e7 10 ♗b5 a6 11 ♗a4 b5 12 ♗b3 0-0 13 ♗d5 ♖b8 14 ♗×c6 ♗×c6 15 ♘d4 ♗d7 16 ♘d5 c6 17 ♘×e7+ ♕×e7 18 ♖he1 a5 19 ♕g3 ♖fd8 20 e5 d5 21 e6! f×e6 22 ♖e5 c5 23 ♘f5 ♕f6 24 ♘×g7!+– ♔h8 25 ♘h5 ♕f7 26 ♖g5 **1-0** L/N6124-1863

**1858-BIR-34**
**Falkbeer,E.K.=**
**Löwenthal,J.J.**

[Staunton]

1 e4 e6 2 ♘f3 d5 3 e×d5 e×d5 4 d4 ♘f6 5 ♗g5 ♗e7 6 ♘c3 0-0 7 ♗d3 h6 8 ♗e3 ♘c6 9 a3 ♘g4 10 ♕d2 ♘×e3 11 f×e3 f5 12 0-0-0 a6 13 ♘e2 b5 14 ♘f4 b4 15 b3 ♖f7 [15 ... b×a3 16 ♘×d5± Chess Player's Magazine L/N6124 1863] 16 a4 ♕d6 17 ♕e2? ♗f6 18 ♖hf1 ♘a5 19 ♔b1 ♗d7 20 ♘h5 g6 21 ♘×f6+ ♖×f6 22 ♘e5!± ♘c6 23 ♘×d7 ♕×d7 24 g4 ♘e7 25 g×f5 ♘×f5 26 ♕g4 ♕e6 27 ♗×f5 ♖×f5 28 ♖×f5? [□ 28 ♕h3+–] 28 ... ♕×f5 29 ♕×f5 g×f5 30 ♖f1 ♖f8 31 a5? [□ 31 h4±] 31 ... ♔g7 32 c3 b×c3 33 ♔c2 ♔f6 34 ♔×c3 ♔e6 35 ♖g1 ♔f6 36 h4 ♖e8 37 ♔d3 ♖e6 38 ♖g8? [38 h5+–] 38 ... ♖c6 39 ♖d8 ♔e6 40 ♖e8+? [□ 40 h5±] 40 ... ♔f6 41 ♖e5? ♖d6 42 ♔c3? ♖e6 43 b4 c6 44 ♖×e6+ ♔×e6 45 ♔d3 ♔f6 46 ♔e2 f4 47 e×f4 ♔f5 48 ♔f3 h5 49 ♔g3 ♔e4 50 f5! ♔×f5 51 ♔f3 ½-½ L/N6123-1859

**1858-BIR-35**
**Falkbeer,E.K.=**
**Löwenthal,J.J.**

1 e4 e6 2 ♘f3 d5 3 e×d5 e×d5 4 d4 ♘f6 5 ♗d3 ♗d6 6 ♗e3 0-0 7 h3 ♘c6 8 c3 h6 9 ♘bd2 ♗e6 10 g4 ♕d7 11 ♕c2 ♘e8 12 ♘h4 ♘e7 13 ♘f5 ♗×f5 14 g×f5 ♘f6 15 0-0-0 b6 16 ♖dg1 ♔h8 17 ♘f3 c5 18 ♘e5 ♕c7 19 ♘g4 ♘eg8 20 ♘×f6 [□ 20 ♕d2±] 20 ... ♘×f6 21 ♕d2 ♖g8 22 ♔b1 [△ 23 ♗×h6±] 22 ... ♔h7 23 ♖g4 ♖ae8 24 ♖h4 ♗f8 25 ♗f4 ♕e7 26 f3 [□ 26 ♗e5±] 26 ... c4 [26 ... ♘e4 27 f6+–] 27 ♗c2 ♕e2 28 ♕×e2 [28 ♕c1] 28 ... ♖×e2 29 ♖g1 ♖e8 30 ♗e5 ♗e7 31 a4 ♗d8 32 b3 a6 [32 ... ♘e4 33 f6 g×f6 34 ♖×g8 ♖×g8 (34 ... ♔×g8 35 f×e4 f×e5 36 ♖g4+ ♔~ 37 e×d5±) 35 ♗f4+–] 33 b×c4 d×c4 34 ♗×f6 ♗×f6 35 ♖e4 b5 36 a×b5 a×b5 37 ♖×e8 ♖×e8 38 ♗e4 ♔g8 39 ♔c2 ♖b8 40 ♖a1 b4 41 ♖a8 ♖×a8 42 ♗×a8 b×c3 43 ♔×c3 ♔f8 44 ♔×c4 ♗e7 45 ♔b5 ♗a3 46 ♔c6 ♔e7 ½-½ L/N6124

**1858-BIR-37**
**Löwenthal,J.J.=**
**Falkbeer,E.K.**

1 e4 e5 2 ♘f3 ♘c6 3 ♗b5 f5 4 ♕e2 f×e4 5 ♗×c6 d×c6 6 ♕×e4 ♗d6 7 ♘×e5 ♘f6 8 ♕e2 0-0 9 d4 ♔h8 10 0-0 c5 11 c3 c×d4 12 c×d4 ♗f5∞ 13 ♘c4? [□ 13 ♘c3] 13 ... ♘g4 [13 ... ♗×h2+!?] 14 f4 ♖e8 15 ♘e5 ♗×e5 16 d×e5 ♕d4+ 17 ♔h1 ♗d3 18 ♕d2 ♖ad8 19 h3 ♗×f1–+ 20 ♕×d4 ♖×d4 21 h×g4 ♗e2 [□ 21 ... ♖d1–+] 22 ♘c3 ♗×g4 23 ♗e3 ♖d3 24 ♖e1 ♗f5 25 ♔g1 ♔g8 26 ♔f2 h5 27 g3 b6? [□ 27 ... a6–+] 28 ♘b5 c5 29 ♘d6 ♖f8 30 ♔f3 [△ 31 ♘×f5, 32 ♔e4] 30 ... g6 31 ♖c1 ♗g4+ 32 ♔e4 ♖d1 33 ♖×d1 ♗×d1

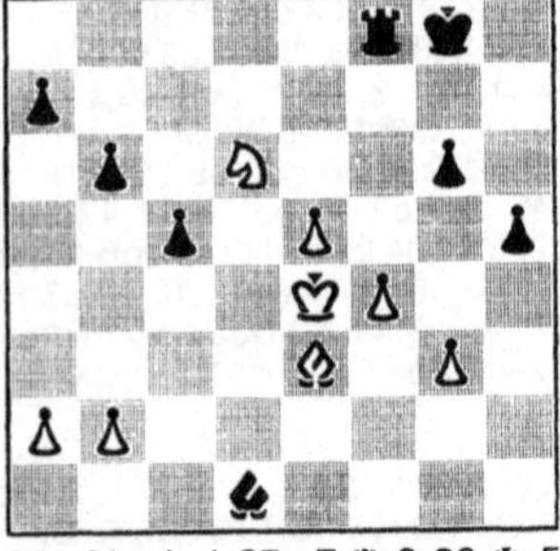

34 e6!= ♗a4 35 e7 ♖a8 36 ♔e5 ♔g7 37 ♔e6= ♗e8 38 ♗d2 b5 39 ♗c3+ ♔g8 40 ♘e4 ♗f7+ 41 ♔d7 [41 ♔d6?!] 41 ... ♗e8+ 42 ♔e6 ♗f7+ ½-½ L/N6124-1863

## ANDERSSEN✕MORPHY

Paris

**[1858-✕AM]**

| | | | | | | | | | | | | |
|---|---|---|---|---|---|---|---|---|---|---|---|---|
| A. Anderssen | 1 | ½ | 0 | 0 | 0 | 0 | 0 | ½ | 0 | 1 | 0 | 3 |
| P.C. Morphy | 0 | ½ | 1 | 1 | 1 | 1 | 1 | ½ | 1 | 0 | 1 | 8 |

**1858-✕AM-1** 20 xii 58
**Morphy, P.C.– Anderssen, A.**

[Hoffer & Zukertort]

1 e4 e5 2 ♘f3 ♘c6 3 ♗c4 ♗c5 4 b4 ♗×b4 5 c3 ♗a5 6 d4 e×d4 7 0-0 ♘f6? 8 e5 [□ 8 ♗a3 d6 9 e5 d5 10 ♗b5 ♘e4± Suhle] 8 ... d5 9 ♗b5 ♘e4 10 c×d4 [10 ♘×d4 ♗d7 11 ♗×c6 b×c6 12 ♗a3 ♗b6 13 f3 ♘c5 14 f4 ♘e4∓] 10 ... 0-0 11 ♗×c6 b×c6 12 ♕a4 ♗b6 13 ♕×c6∓ ♗g4 14 ♗b2 [□ 14 ♗e3] 14 ... ♗×f3 15 g×f3 ♘g5 16 ♘d2 ♖e8! 17 ♔h1 ♘h3! 18 f4 ♕h4 19 ♕×d5 ♘×f2+ 20 ♔g1 ♘d3 21 ♗c3 ♘×f4 22 ♕f3 ♘h3+ 23 ♔h1 ♘g5 24 ♕g2 ♖ad8 25 ♖g1 [□ 25 ♘f3 ♘×f3 26 ♕×f3 ♖d7 27 ♖ad1] 25 ... h6 26 ♖af1 ♕h3 [26 ... ♗×d4? 27 ♘f3] 27 ♕c6 ♕d7 28 ♕g2 ♗×d4 29 ♗×d4 ♕×d4 30 ♘f3 ♕d5 31 h4 ♘e6 32 ♕g4 ♕c6 [32 ... ♕×a2∓] 33 ♖g2 ♖d3 34 ♕f5 ♖ed8 35 ♕f6 [△ 36 ♖×g7+] 35 ... ♕d5 36 ♕f5 ♖d1 37 ♖×d1 ♕×d1+ 38 ♔h2 ♖d3 [□ 38 ... ♕d3! 39 ♕g4 (39 ♕f6? ♕f8) 39 ... h5 40 ♕g3 ♕e3 41 ♕f2 ♕×f2 42 ♖×f2 ♖d3–+] 39 ♖f2 ♖e3 40 ♘d2 ♖e2 41 ♕×f7+ ♔h8 42 ♘e4 ♖×f2+ [□ 42 ... ♖×e4 43 ♕×e6 ♕d8] 43 ♘×f2 ♕d5 44 ♘g4! ♕×a2+ 45 ♔g3 ♕b3+ 46 ♔h2 ♕c2+ 47 ♔g3 ♕c3+ 48 ♔h2 ♕c6 [48 ... ♕c4 49 ♕e8+ ♔h7 50 ♘f6+ g×f6 51 ♕f7+=] 49 h5 a5 [□ 49 ... ♕c2+ 50 ♔g3 (50 ♔h1 ♕d1+ 51 ♔~ ♕×g4–+) 50 ... ♕d3+ 51 ♔h2 ♕h3+ 52 ♔×h3 ♘g5+–+] 50 ♘f6 g×f6 [50 ... ♕c2+ 51 ♔g3 ♕d3+ 52 ♔h2 ♕d2+ 53 ♔g1! ♕g5+ 54 ♔f2 (54 ♔h1 g×f6 55 ♕×e6 ♕×h5+; 56 ... ♕×e5–+) 54 ... ♕f5+ 55 ♔g1 g×f6 56 e×f6 (56 ♕e8+ ♔g7 57 ♕e7+ ♔g8 58 ♕e8+ ♘f8–+) 56 ... ♕g5+ 57 ♔f2 ♕g8 58 ♕e7 ♘g5–+] 51 ♕×f6+ [51 e×f6 a4 52 ♕g6 ♕d6+ 53 ♔g1 (53 ♔h1 ♕d5+ 54 ♔h2 ♕e5+ 55 ♔h1 ♕e1+ 56 ♔h2 ♕h4+ 57 ♔g1 ♕g5+–+) 53 ... ♕d1+ 54 ♔f2 ♕e2+ 55 ♔g1 ♕e1+ 56 ♔h2 ♕h4+–+] 51 ... ♔g8 52 ♕g6+ ♔f8 53 ♕×h6+ ♔e8 54 ♕g6+ ♔d7 55 h6 ♕d5 56 h7 ♕×e5+ 57 ♔g1 ♘g5 58 h8♕ ♕×h8 59 ♕×g5 ♕d4+ 60 ♔f1 a4 61 ♕f5+ ♔c6 62 ♕c8 ♔b5 63 ♔e1 [63 ♕×c7 ♕c4+ 64 ♕×c4 ♔×c4 65 ♔e2 ♔c3 66 ♔d1 ♔b2–+] 63 ... c5 64 ♕b7+ ♔c4 65 ♕f7+ ♔c3 66 ♕f3+ ♕d3 67 ♕f6+ ♔b3 68 ♕b6+ ♔c2 69 ♕a7 ♕c3+ 70 ♔e2 a3 71

♕a4+ ♔b2 72 ♕b5+ ♕b3 **0-1**
L/N6138-1879

**1858-✕AM-2** 21 xii 58
**Anderssen, A.= Morphy, P.C.**
[Hoffer & Zukertort]

1 e4 e5 2 ♘f3 ♘c6 3 ♗b5 a6 4 ♗a4 ♘f6 5 d3 ♗c5 6 c3 [□ 6 0-0] 6 ... b5 7 ♗c2 [□ 7 ♗b3] 7 ... d5 8 exd5 ♘xd5 9 h3 0-0 10 0-0 h6 11 d4 exd4 12 cxd4 ♗b6 13 ♘c3 ♘db4 14 ♗b1 [□ 14 ♗e3; 14 d5 ♘e7∓] 14 ... ♗e6 [14 ... ♗xd4 15 ♘e2 ♗b6 16 a3 ♘d5 17 ♕c2+-; □ 14 ... ♘xd4 15 ♘xd4 ♗xd4 (15 ... ♕xd4 16 ♕f3 ♖b8 17 a3 ♗b7 18 ♕g3 ♘d5 19 ♗xh6±) 16 ♕f3 ♗e6 17 ♕e4 (17 ♖d1 c5∓; 17 a3 ♘d5 18 ♕e4 ♘f6∓) 17 ... ♖e8! 18 ♖d1 (18 a3 f5 19 ♕f3 ♗xc3 20 bxc3 ♘d5 21 ♗xf5 ♗xf5 22 ♕xf5 ♘xc3 23 ♗xh6 ♕f6 24 ♕xf6 gxf6∓) 18 ... c5 19 ♕h7+ ♔f8 20 ♗e3 ♕f6 21 ♘e4 ♕e5 22 ♗xd4 cxd4 23 f4 ♕xf4 24 ♕h8+ ♔e7 25 ♕xg7 ♖ad8 26 ♖f1 ♖g8∓] 15 a3 ♘d5 16 ♘e2 [16 ♘xb5 ♘f6 (16 ... axb5 17 ♕c2 ♘f6 18 ♕xc6±) 17 ♘c3 ♘xd4 18 ♘xd4 ♗xd4 19 ♘e4; 19 ♘e2±] 16 ... ♘f6 [16 ... ♖c8? 17 ♕c2+-] 17 ♗e3 ♖e8 18 ♘g3 ♗c4 19 ♘f5?! [□ 19 ♗d3=; 19 ♖e1 ♘xd4 20 ♘xd4 (20 ♗xd4? ♖xe1+-+) 20 ... ♗xd4 21 ♗xd4 ♖xe1+ 22 ♕xe1 ♕xd4-+] 19 ... ♗xf1 20 ♕xf1 ♘e7 21 ♘3h4 ♘xf5 22 ♘xf5 ♕d7 [□ 22 ... ♘e4 Δ 23 ... ♕f6] 23 ♗xh6 gxh6 24 ♕c1 ♗xd4 [□ 24 ... ♘h7 (24 ... ♘e4 25 ♕f4±) 25 ♕xh6 f6 26 ♗a2+ ♔h8 27 ♘h4 ♖g8 28 ♗xg8 ♔xg8∓] 25 ♕xh6 ♖e1+ 26 ♔h2 ♘e4 27 ♗xe4 ♖xe4 [27 ... ♖xa1? 28 ♘xd4 (28 ♘e7+=) 28 ... ♕d6+ (28 ... ♕xd4?? 29 ♗h7++-; 28 ... ♖? 29 ♗h7+, Δ 30 ♗f5++-; 28 ... f5 29 ♘xf5+-) 29 ♕xd6 cxd6 30 ♗xa8 ♖a2 31 ♗b7+-] 28 ♕g5+ ♔f8 29 ♕h6+ ♔e8 30 ♘xd4 ♕d6+ [30 ... ♖xd4 31 ♖e1+ Δ 32 ♕f8++-; 30 ... ♕xd4 31 ♕c6++-] 31 ♕xd6 cxd6 32 ♖d1! ♔f8 [32 ... ♖c8 33 ♘f5±] 33 ♖d2 ♖ae8 34 g4 ♖8e5 35 f3 ♖e1 36 h4 ♖d5 37 ♔g3 a5 38 h5 ♔g8 39 ♔f2 ♖e8 40 ♔g3 ♔h7 41 ♔f4 ♖e7 42 ♔g3 f6 43 ♔f4 ♖e8 44 ♔g3 ♖e7 **½-½** L/N6138-1879

**1858-✕AM-3**
**Morphy, P.C.+ Anderssen, A.**
[Staunton]

1 e4 e5 2 ♘f3 ♘c6 3 ♗b5 ♘f6 4 d4 ♘xd4 5 ♘xd4 exd4 6 e5 c6 7 0-0 cxb5 8 ♗g5 ♗e7 [□ 8 ... ♕b6] 9 exf6 ♗xf6 10 ♖e1+ ♔f8 11 ♗xf6 ♕xf6 12 c3 d5 13 cxd4 ♗e6 14 ♘c3 a6 15 ♖e5 ♖d8 16 ♕b3 ♕e7 17 ♖ae1 g5 18 ♕d1 ♕f6 19 ♖1e3 ♖g8?? 20 ♖xe6 fxe6 21 ♖f3 **1-0** M954-1859

**1858-✕AM-4** 22 xii 58
**Anderssen, A.– Morphy, P.C.**
[Hoffer & Zukertort]

1 e4 e5 2 ♘f3 ♘c6 3 ♗b5 a6 4 ♗a4 ♘f6 5 d3 ♗c5 6 c3 [□ 6 0-0] 6 ... b5 7 ♗c2 d5 8 exd5 ♘xd5 9 h3 0-0 10 0-0 h6 11 d4 exd4 12 cxd4 ♗b6 13 ♘c3 ♘db4 14 ♗b1 ♗e6 15 a3 ♘d5 16 ♗e3 ♘f6 [16 ... ♘xe3 17 fxe3±] 17 ♕d2 ♖e8 18 ♖d1 [18 ♗xh6 gxh6 19 ♕xh6 ♘xd4 20 ♘g5 ♘f5-+] 18 ... ♗d5 [18 ... ♘a5? 19 ♗xh6 gxh6 (19 ... ♘b3 20 ♕g5 ♘h5 21 ♕xh5 gxh6 22 ♕xh6 f6 23 ♘e4; 23 d5+-) 20 ♕xh6 ♘b3 21 d5 ♘xa1 22 dxe6 ♕e7 23 ♘d5+-] 19 ♘e5 ♕d6! 20 ♕c2 [20 ♗xh6 gxh6 21 ♕xh6 ♘xe5 22 dxe5 (22 ♘xd5 ♕xd5 23 ♕xf6 ♗xd4∓) 22 ... ♗xf2+! 23 ♔h1 ♖xe5∓; 20 ♘xd5 ♘xd5 (20 ... ♕xd5? 21 ♗a2±) 21 ♕c2 ♘xe3 22 fxe3 ♘xe5 23 exd5 ♗xe3+ 24 ♔h1 ♕xe5∓; □ 20 ♕d3 ♖ad8 (20 ... ♘xd4 21 ♗xd4 ♗xd4 22 ♕xd4 ♖xe5 23 f4 ♖h5 24 g4 c5 25 ♕d2 ♖g5 26 ♗e4 ♘xe4 27 ♘xe4+-) 21 f4=]

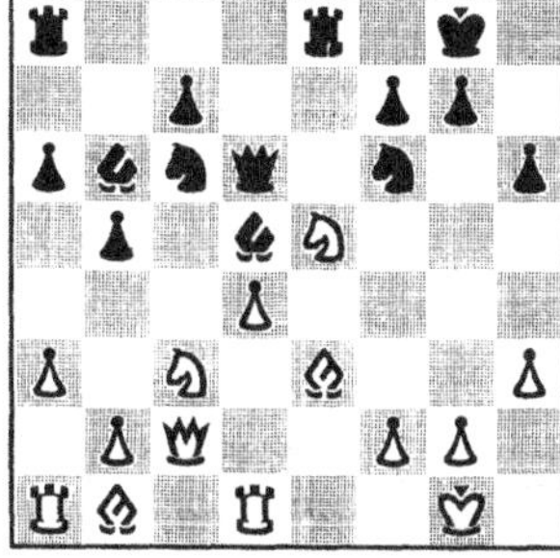

20 ... ♘xd4! 21 ♗xd4 ♗xd4 22 ♘xd5 [22 ♘g4 c6 23 ♘xf6+ ♕xf6 24 ♕h7+? ♔f8 25 ♕h8+ ♔e7 26 ♘xd5+ cxd5 27 ♖e1+ ♔d6 28 ♖xe8 ♖xe8 29 ♕xe8 ♕xf2+-+] 22 ... ♕xe5 [22 ... ♘xd5; 22 ... ♕xd5 23 ♘c6+-] 23 ♘xf6+ ♕xf6 24 ♕h7+ ♔f8 25 ♗e4 ♖ad8 26 ♔h1 [26 ♖f1 ♗xb2 27 ♖ae1 g5 28 f4 gxf4 29 g3 ♕g5 30 ♔h1 ♕xg3 31 ♕xh6+ ♗g7 32 ♕xf4 (32 ♕h5 ♖d2-+) 32 ... ♕xh3+ 33 ♕h2 ♕xh2+-+] 26 ... ♗xb2 27 ♖ab1 [27 ♖e1? ♗xa1 28 ♕h8+ ♔e7 29 ♗c6+ ♗e5-+] 27 ... ♖xd1+ 28 ♖xd1 ♕xf2 29 ♕h8+ ♔e7 30 ♕h7 ♗e5 [□ 30 ... ♖d8! 31 ♖b1 (31 ♖xd8?; 31 ♗~-+) 31 ... ♕g3 32 ♕f5 ♗e5 33 ♔g1 ♖d2-+; 31 ♗d3 ♗e5 32 ♕e4 ♕g3 33 ♔g1 (33 ♕b4+ ♔e8-+) 33 ... ♖d4 34 ♕e2 ♕h2+ 35 ♔f2 ♖f4+ 36 ♔e3 ♕g3+ 37 ♔d2 ♖f2-+; 31 ♗d5 ♖xd5 32 ♖xd5 ♕e1+ 33 ♔h2 ♗e5+ 34 ♖xe5 ♕xe5+ 35 ♔h1 ♕a1+ (35 ... c5-+) 36 ♔h2 ♕xa3 37 ♕xg7 (37 ♕e4+ ♔d8 38 ♕a8+ ♔d7-+) 37 ... ♕d6+ 38 ♔h1 b4-+] 31 ♗f3 ♕g3 32 ♔g1 ♕g6 33 ♕xg6 fxg6 34 ♗b7 ♖b8 [34 ... a5 35 ♖b1] 35 ♗xa6 c6 36 ♔f2 [□ 36 ♖b1] 36 ... ♗d6 37 ♖d3 [□ 37 ♖a1 Δ 38 a4] 37 ... ♔d7 38 ♔e2 ♖a8 [38 ... ♔c7 39 a4] 39 ♗b7 ♖xa3 40 ♗c8+ [40 ♖xa3 ♗xa3 41 ♔d3 ♔c7 42 ♗a6 ♔b6 43 ♗c8 c5 44 ♗e6 c4+ 45 ♔c2 ♔c5 46 ♗f7 g5 47 ♗g6 b4-+] 40 ... ♔c7 41 ♖d1 ♖a2+ 42 ♔f3 ♗c5 43 ♗e6 ♖f2+ 44 ♔g3 ♖f6 45 ♖d7+ ♔b6 46 ♗g4 ♗d6+ 47 ♔h4 c5 48 ♗f3 c4 49 ♖xg7 ♖f4+ 50 ♗g4 c3 51 g3 ♖xg4+ **0-1**
L/N6138-1879

**1858-✕AM-5** 23 xii 58
**Morphy, P.C.+ Anderssen, A.**
[Hoffer & Zukertort]

1 e4 d5 2 exd5 ♘f6? 3 d4 [3 ♗b5+ ♗d7 4 ♗c4 b5 5 ♗b3 ♗g4 (5 ... a5 6 a3 ♗g4 7 f3 ♗c8 8 ♘c3 ♗a6 9 d3 b4 10 axb4 axb4 11 ♘a2 ♗b7 12 ♗d2±) 6 f3 ♗f5 7 ♕e2 a6 8 c4 c6 9 ♘c3 b4 10 ♘a4±] 3 ... ♘xd5 4 c4 ♘f6 5 ♘c3 ♗f5 6 ♘f3 e6 7 ♗e3 [7 a3 c5 8 dxc5 ♕xd1+ 9 ♘xd1 ♗xc5 10 b4 ♗e7 11 ♗b2 ♘bd7 12 ♘e3±] 7 ... ♗b4? 8 ♕b3 [8 ♕a4+ ♘c6 9 ♘e5 0-0 10 ♘xc6 ♗xc3+ 11 bxc3 bxc6 12 ♕xc6= Morphy] 8 ... ♗xc3+ 9 bxc3 ♗e4 10 ♘d2 ♗c6 11 ♗d3 ♘bd7 [11 ... ♗xg2 12 ♖g1±] 12 ♕c2 h6? 13 0-0 0-0 14 ♖ae1 [□ 14 ♖fe1, 15 ♖ad1] 14 ... b6 15 h3 ♕c8 [□ 15 ... ♔h8] 16 ♔h2 ♔h8 17 ♖g1 ♖g8 18 g4 g5 19 f4 ♕f8! 20 ♖g3 ♖d8 21 ♘f3 ♗xf3 22 ♖xf3 ♕d6 23 ♔g2 ♘h5? 24 fxg5 [24 gxh5 gxf4+-+] 24 ... hxg5 25 gxh5 g4 26 hxg4 ♖xg4+ 27 ♔f1 f5 28 ♕f2 ♘e5 29 dxe5 [□ 29 ♗f4 ♘xd3 (29 ... ♖xf4 30 ♖xe5 ♖xf3 31 ♕xf3, 32 ♕e3+-) 30 ♗xd6 ♘xf2 31 ♗e5+ ♔h7 32 ♔xf2+-] 29 ... ♕xd3+ 30 ♕e2 ♕e4 31 ♗f2 ♕c6 32 ♖d1 ♖xd1+ 33 ♕xd1 ♕xc4+ 34 ♕d3 [□ 34 ♕e2 ♕xe2+ 35 ♔xe2 ♖a4 36 ♖d3 ♖xa2+ 37 ♔f3 c5 38 ♖d7 ♖c2 39 ♗h4 ♖xc3+ (39 ... ♖h2 40 ♔g3) 40 ♔f4 ♖c4+ 41 ♔g5 ♖g4+ 42 ♔h6 ♔g8 43 ♗g5, 44 ♔g6+-] 34 ... ♕xa2 35 ♖g3 ♕c4 36 ♕xc4 ♖xc4 37 ♖g6 ♖c6 [37 ... ♖xc3 38 ♖xe6 ♖h3 39 ♖f6 ♖xh5 40 e6 ♔g7 41 e7 ♖h8 42 ♗d4+-] 38 c4? a5 39 ♔e2 ♖xc4 40 ♖xe6 ♖c2+ 41 ♔f3 a4 42 ♖g6 [□ 42 ♖e8+ ♔g7 43 e6 ♖c4 44 h6+ ♔h7 45 ♗e3 ♖e4 46 ♖e7+ ♔g6 47 ♖g7+ ♔f6 48 ♗g5+ ♔xe6 49 h7+-] 42 ... ♖c4 43 ♖g1 a3 44 e6 a2 45 ♖a1 ♖e4 46 ♖xa2 ♖xe6 47 ♔f4 ♖d6 48 ♔xf5 ♖d5+ 49 ♔g4 b5 50 ♖a8+ ♔h7 51 ♖a7 ♖d7 52 ♗g3 ♖g7+ 53 ♔h4 ♖f7 54 ♖xc7 **1-0**
L/N6138-1879

**1858-✕AM-6** 24 xii 58
**Anderssen, A.– Morphy, P.C.**
[Hoffer & Zukertort]

1 a3 e5 [□ 1 ... d5] 2 c4 ♘f6 3 ♘c3 d5 4 cxd5 ♘xd5 5 e3 ♗e6 6 ♘f3 ♗d6 7 ♗e2 0-0 8 d4 ♘xc3 9 bxc3 e4 10 ♘d2 f5 11 f4 [□ 11 0-0] 11 ... g5?! 12 ♗c4 [□ 12 ♘c4] 12 ... ♗xc4 13 ♘xc4 gxf4 14 exf4 ♕e8 15 0-0 ♕c6 16 ♕b3 ♕d5 17 ♖b1 b6 18 ♕a2 c6 [18 ... b5? 19 ♖xb5+-] 19 ♕e2 ♘d7 20 ♘e3 ♕e6 21 c4! ♘f6 22 ♖b3! ♔f7 23 ♗b2! ♖ac8 24 ♔h1 ♖g8 25 d5 cxd5 26 cxd5 ♕d7 [26 ... ♘xd5 27 ♕h5+] 27 ♘c4! ♔e7 [27 ... ♘xd5 28 ♖d1 (28 ♕h5+ ♔e6!) 28 ... ♕c6 (28 ... ♘xf4 29 ♖xd6 ♘xe2 30 ♖xd7+ ♔e8 31 ♖e2; 28 ... ♗xf4 29 ♗e5; 28 ...

♗b8 29 ♘e3 ♖c5 30 ♕h5+ ♔f8 31 ♘xf5; 28 ... ♕e6 29 ♕h5++–) 29 ♕h5+ ♔e6 30 ♕h6+ ♖g6 (30 ... ♔d7 31 ♗e5 ♕xc4 32 ♕xd6+ ♔e8 33 ♖c3!; 30 ♔e7 31 ♕xh7+ ♔f8 32 ♕xf5+ ♔e7 33 ♘xd6 ♕xd6 34 ♖xd5+–) 31 ♕xh7 ♖ag8 32 ♘xd6 ♕xd6 (32 ... ♕xd6 33 ♖b5) 33 ♖c3!+–] **28 ♗xf6+** [□ 28 ♖h3 ♖g7 (28 ... ♕b5 29 ♗xf6+ ♔xf6 30 ♕f2! ♕xc4 31 ♕h4+ ♔f7 32 ♕xh7+ ♔f8 33 ♕xf5+ ♔e8 34 ♕e6+ ♔f8 35 ♕xd6+ ♔e8 36 ♕e6+ ♔f8 37 ♕f5+ ♔e8 38 ♕e1) 29 ♖h6 ♖f7 (29 ... ♖f8 30 ♘e5 ♕~ 31 ♘c6++–) 30 ♘e5 (30 ♗xf6+ ♖xf6 31 ♖xh7+ ♖f7 32 ♖xf7+ ♔xf7 33 ♕h5+ ♔f6? 34 ♕g5+ ♔f7 35 ♘xd6++– Lange) 30 ... ♗xe5 31 fxe5 ♘xd5 (31 ... ♘g4 32 ♕xg4 fxg4 33 ♖xf7+ ♔xf7 34 e6++–; 31 ... ♘g8 32 ♖d6 ♕b7 33 ♕h5 h6 34 e6 ♔xd6 35 exf7 ♘e7 36 ♕xh6+) 32 e6 ♕c6 33 ♕h5 ♖ff8 34 ♖xh7+ ♔d8 35 e7+ ♘xe7 36 ♖d1+ ♘d5 37 ♖xd5++–] **28 ... ♔xf6 29 ♕b2+ ♔f7 30 ♖h3** [□ 30 ♕d4 ♖c5 (30 ... ♗c5 31 ♕d1 ♔e8 32 ♘e5 ♕g7 33 ♕h5+ ♔e7 34 ♖g3; 30 ... ♖cd8 31 ♖h3 ♖g7 32 ♖h5+–) 31 ♖h3 ♖g7 32 ♖h6 ♗c7 33 d6 ♔g8 35 ♖d1 ♗d8 35 ♘e5 ♕b5 (35 ... ♕e8 36 d7 ♕e7 37 ♘c6 ♕xd7 38 ♖d6+–) 36 ♕e6 h6 37 d7 ♕e2 38 ♕g1 ♖c2 39 ♕e8+ ♔h7 40 ♖xd8 ♖xg2 41 ♖h8+ ♔xh8 42 d8♕++–] **30 ... ♖g7 31 ♕d4 ♔g8! 32 ♖h6 ♗f8 33 d6 ♖f7 34 ♖h3** [34 ♘e5 ♕b5] **34 ... ♕a4 35 ♖c1 ♖c5** [35 ... b5 36 d7 ♖d8 37 ♖g3+ ♗g7 38 ♖xg7+ ♖xg7 39 ♕d5+ ♔h8 40 ♘e5 ♕xa3 41 ♖d1 ♕e7 42 ♘c6 ♕f6 43 ♘xd8 ♕xd8 44 ♕xf5 b4 45 ♕xe4 a5 46 ♕e8+ ♖g8 47 ♕e1] **36 ♖g3+ ♗g7 37 h3 ♔h8 38 ♖xg7** [□ 38 ♕d2 ♕e8 (38 ... ♖xc4 39 ♖xc4 ♕xc4 40 d7; 38 ... ♗h6 39 ♘e5 ♖xe5 40 fxe5!; 38 ... h6 39 ♘e5 ♗xe5 40 fxe5 f4 41 e6 ♖c6 42 d7; 38 ... e3 39 ♖xe3 ♖xc4 40 ♖xc4 ♕xc4 41 d7 ♕f1+ 42 ♔h2 ♕xf4+ 43 g3) 39 ♘e5 ♗xe5 (39 ... ♖xe5 40 ♖xg7 ♔xg7 41 fxe5 f4 42 ♕d4 ♕e6 43 ♕xe4+–) 40 ♖xc5 bxc5 41 fxe5 ♕xe5 42 ♕g5 ♖f8 43 d7 ♕d4 44 ♕e7] **38 ... ♖xg7 39 ♖c3 e3** [39 ... ♖c8 (39 ... ♔g8 40 ♖g3 ♕d7 41 ♘e5 ♕d8 42 ♖xg7+ ♔xg7 43 d7 ♔g8 44 ♕d6 ♖xe5 45 fxe5 e3 46 ♕e6+ ♔~ 47 ♕f6+) 40 ♖g3 ♖g8 41 ♕f6! ♕e8 (41 ... ♕xc4 42 d7 ♕f1+ 43 ♔h2 ♕xf4 44 ♕xg7++–) 42 ♖xg7 (42 ♘e5 ♕f8) 42 ... ♖xg7 43 ♘e5 ♔g8! 44 ♕xf5 e3 45 d7 ♕d8 (45 ... ♕e7 46 ♕d3; 45 ... ♖xd7 46 ♘xd7 e2 47 ♘f6++–) 46 ♕e6+ ♔f8 47 ♕d6+ ♔g8 (47 ... ♕e7 48 ♕f6+ ♔g8 49 ♘c6+–) 48 ♔g1 e2 49 ♕d5+ ♔f8 50 ♔f2+–] **40 ♖xe3??** [40 ♕f6=; 40 ♕xe3 ♖xc4 (40 ... ♖c8 41 ♕d4 ♖g8 42 ♖g3 ♕e8 43 ♘e5) 41 ♖xc4 ♕xc4 42 ♕e8+ ♕g8 43 d7 ♖xd7 44 ♕xd7=] **40 ... ♖xc4 41 ♕f6??** [□ 41 ♕e5] **41 ... ♖c1+ 42 ♔h2 ♕xf4+ 0-1** L/N6138-1879

### 1858-XAM-7 — 25 xii 58

**Morphy,P.C.+Anderssen,A.**

[Hoffer & Zukertort]

**1 e4 d5 2 exd5 ♕xd5 3 ♘c3 ♕a5** [□ 3 ... ♕d8] **4 d4** [□ 4 ♘f3 e5 5 ♗b5+! ♗d7 (5 ... c6 6 ♗c4 ♗f5 7 0-0 ♘d7 8 ♖e1 f6 9 ♘h4±) 6 ♕e2! f6 (6 ... ♗xb5 7 ♕xe5+; 6 ... ♗d6 7 ♘xe5) 7 0-0 (7 d4 ♗b4 8 ♗d2 ♗xb5) 7 ... ♗d6 8 d4±] **4 ... e5! 5 dxe5 ♕xe5+ 6 ♗e2 ♗b4! 7 ♘f3** [7 ♗d2 ♗g4∓] **7 ... ♗xc3+ 8 bxc3 ♕xc3+ 9 ♗d2 ♕c5 10 ♖b1 ♘c6 11 0-0 ♘f6 12 ♗f4** [□ 12 ♖b5 ♕d6 13 ♖e1 0-0 14 ♕c1] **12 ... 0-0** [12 ... ♘b4 (12 ... ♕e7 13 ♖e1; 12 ... ♘d5 13 ♖b5) 13 ♕e1 ♘xc2 14 ♗b5+ ♔f8 15 ♕d2 ♗f5 16 ♖fc1 ♘d5 17 ♗a4±] **13 ♗xc7 ♘d4! 14 ♕xd4 ♕xc7 15 ♗d3 ♗g4?** [□ 15 ... b6 Δ 16 ... ♗b7] **16 ♘g5! ♖fd8** [16 ... h6 17 ♘e4!] **17 ♕b4 ♗c8** [□ 17 ... a5 18 ♕xb7 ♕xb7 19 ♖xb7 ♖d7] **18 ♖fe1! a5** [18 ... h6 19 ♕e7 ♖d7?? 20 ♕e8+ ♘xe8 21 ♗h7+ ♔h8 22 ♕f8#] **19 ♕e7! ♕xe7 20 ♖xe7 ♘d5** [20 ... ♗e6 21 ♘xe6 fxe6 22 ♖bxb7; 20 ... ♖f8 21 ♗c4 ♗e6 22 ♗xe6 fxe6 22 ♖bxb7] **21 ♗xh7+ ♔h8** [21 ... ♔f8 22 ♖xf7++–] **22 ♖xf7** [22 ♖d1? ♗g4] **22 ... ♘c3 23 ♖e1 ♘xa2 24 ♖f4 ♖a6 25 ♗d3 1-0** L/N6138-1879

### 1858-XAM-8 — 26 xii 58

**Anderssen, A.=Morphy, P.C.**

[Hoffer & Zukertort]

**1 a3 e5 2 c4 ♘f6 3 ♘c3 d5 4 cxd5 ♘xd5 5 e3 ♗e6 6 ♘f3 ♗d6 7 ♗e2 0-0 8 d4 ♘xc3? 9 bxc3 e4? 10 ♘d2 f5 11 f4? ♕h4+ 12 g3 ♕h3 13 ♗f1 ♕h6 14 c4** [□ 14 ♘c4] **14 ... c6 15 c5 ♗c7 16 ♗c4 ♘d7 17 0-0 b5 18 cxb6 axb6 19 ♕b3 ♖fe8 20 ♗b2 b5** [□ 20 ... ♕g6] **21 ♗xe6+ ♕xe6 22 ♕c2** [□ 22 ♖fc1 ♕xb3 (22 ... ♔h8 23 d5) 23 ♘xb3 ♖a6 (23 ... ♘b8 24 d5 ♗b6 25 ♗d4 ♗xd4 26 ♘xd4 cxd5 27 ♘xb5±) 24 ♘c5 ♘xc5 25 ♖xc5 g6 26 ♖ac1±] **22 ... ♕d5 23 ♖fc1** [□ 23 a4] **23 ... ♖a6 24 a4 ♖ea8 25 axb5 ♕xb5** [□ 25 ... ♖xa1] **26 ♕c4+** [□ 26 ♖xa6 ♖xa6 27 ♕c4+ ♕xc4 28 ♖xc4] **26 ... ♕xc4 27 ♘xc4 ♖xa1 28 ♗xa1 ♘f6 29 ♗c3 ♖a2 30 ♗d2 ♘d5 31 ♔f1 ♗d8 32 ♔e1 ♗e7 33 ♖b1 h6 34 ♘e5** [34 ♖b8+ ♔h7 35 ♖c8 ♗b4] **34 ... c5 35 dxc5** [35 ♖b5 ♖a1+ 36 ♔e2 ♖a2=] **35 ... ♗xc5 36 ♖b5 ♘xe3 37 ♖xc5 ♘g2+ 38 ♔e2** [38 ♔d1 e3 39 ♖c2 ♖xc2 40 ♔xc2 dxc2 41 ♔xd2 g5 42 fxg5 hxg5 43 ♘f3 f4 44 ♘xg5 fxg3 45 hxg3 ♔g7 46 ♔e2 ♔g6 47 ♘f3 ♔f5 48 ♔f2 ♘f4] **38 ... e3 39 ♘f3** [□ 39 ♘c4 exd2 40 ♖xf5 d1♕+ 41 ♔xd1 ♖a4 42 ♘b2] **39 ... g6 40 ♖d5 ♔f7 41 ♖d6 ♔g7 42 h4** [42 ♘e5 g5] **42 ... exd2 43 ♖xd2 ♖a4 44 ♔f2** [44 ♘d4 ♖a3] **44 ... ♘xf4 45 gxf4 ♖xf4 46 ♖d4 ♖xd4 47 ♘xd4 ♔f6 48 ♔e3 g5 49 h5 ♔e5 50 ♘f3+ ♔f6 51 ♘d4 ½-½** L/N6138-1879

### 1858-XAM-9 — 27 xii 58

**Morphy,P.C.+Anderssen, A.**

[Hoffer & Zukertort]

**1 e4 c5 2 d4 cxd4 3 ♘f3 ♘c6** [3 ... e5 4 ♗c4 ♘c6 5 0-0 ♗e7; 3 ... e6 4 ♘xd4 ♘f6] **4 ♘xd4 e6** [□ 4 ... ♘f6] **5 ♘b5! d6** [□ 5 ... ♘f6] **6 ♗f4 e5 7 ♗e3 f5** [□ 7 ... a6] **8 ♘1c3! f4** [8 ... a6 9 ♘d5 axb5 10 ♗b6+–; 8 ... ♘f6 9 ♗g5 a6 10 ♗xf6 gxf6 11 ♕h5+ ♔d7 12 ♕xf5+ ♔e8 13 ♕h5+ ♔d7 14 ♘a3+–] **9 ♘d5! fxe3 10 ♘bc7+ ♔f7 11 ♕f3+** [□ 11 ♘xa8] **11 ... ♘f6 12 ♗c4 ♘d4** [12 ... exf2+ 13 ♕xf2 ♗e6 14 ♘xe6 ♔xe6 15 ♘xf6+ ♔e7 16 ♘d5+ ♔e8 17 0-0+–] **13 ♘xf6+ d5! 14 ♗xd5+ ♔g6??**

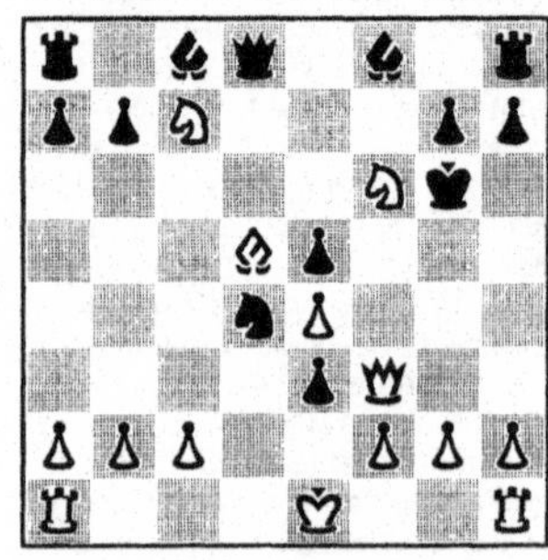

[□ 14 ... ♕xd5 15 ♘xd5+ ♘xf3+ 16 gxf3 exf2+ 17 ♔xf2 ♗c5+ 18 ♔e2 ♖b8=; 14 ... ♔e7 15 ♕h5 gxf6 16 ♕f7+ ♔d6 17 ♘xa8 (17 ♘e8+ ♕xe8! 18 ♕xe8 ♘xc2+ 19 ♔f1 e2+ 20 ♔g1 ♘xa1 21 ♕d8+ ♗d7 22 ♕xf6+ ♔c5 23 h3 e1♕+ 24 ♔h2 ♕d2) 17 ... ♘xc2+ (17 ... ♔e7 18 ♕xe7+ ♗xe7 19 0-0-0 e2 20 ♖d2) 18 ♔e2 ♕e7 (18 ... ♘xa1 19 ♖d1 ♘c2 20 ♗b3+ ♘d4+ 21 ♖xd4+ exd4 22 ♕d5+=) 19 ♕xe7+ ♗xe7 20 ♖ac1 ♘d4+ 21 ♔xe3 ♗d7 22 ♗xb7 ♖b8 23 ♗d5 ♖xb2 24 ♘c7 ♗d8 25 ♘a6 f5 26 ♔d3 ♗a5! 27 ♖c5 (27 ♖hd1 fxe4+ 28 ♗xe4 ♗b5+) 27 ... ♖d2+ 28 ♔c4 ♖c2+ 29 ♔d3 ♖xc5 30 ♘xc5 ♔xc5] **15 ♕h5+ ♔xf6 16 fxe3** [16 ♘e8+ ♕xe8!; 16 ♕f7+ ♔g5] **16 ... ♘xc2+ 17 ♔e2 1-0** L/N6138-1879

### 1858-XAM-10 — 27 xii 58

**Anderssen,A.+Morphy, P.C.**

[Hoffer & Zukertort]

**1 a3 e5 2 c4 ♘f6 3 ♘c3 d5 4 cxd5 ♘xd5 5 e3 ♗e6 6 ♘f3 ♗d6 7 ♗e2 0-0 8 0-0 ♘xc3? 9 bxc3 f5 10 d4 e4? 11 ♘d2 ♖f6? 12 f4 ♖h6 13 g3** [□ 13 ♖f2] **13 ... ♘d7 14 ♘c4** [14 c4] **14 ... ♗xc4 15 ♗xc4+ ♔h8 16 ♖a2 ♕e7 17 a4 ♘f6 18 ♕b3 b6 19 ♗e6 ♖e8! 20 ♗c4** [20 ♗xf5?? g6–+] **20 ... ♘g4 21 ♖g2 ♖b8 22 ♗e2 ♘f6 23 c4 c6 24 ♗b2 ♕f7** [Δ 25 ... b5] **25 ♕c2 ♗e7 26 ♗c3 ♖g8? 27 a5! ♗d6 28 axb6 axb6 29 ♖a1 g5? 30 fxg5 ♖xg5 31 ♖a8+** [□ 31 c5 bxc5 (31 ... ♗c7 32 ♖a7) 32 dxc5 ♗xc5 (32 ... ♗f8 33 ♖a8 ♔g7 34 ♗c4 ♕e7 35 ♖d2 ♕xc5 36 ♖d7+ ♔h8 37 ♗xf6+ ♖xf6 38 ♕c3 ♖g6 39 ♖f7) 33 ♖a8+ ♗f8 34 ♗c4 ♕g7 35 ♕b2 c5 36 ♕b8] **31 ... ♖g8 32 ♕a4 ♖xa8 33 ♕xa8+ ♕e8 34 ♕xe8+** [□ 34 ♕b7] **34 ... ♘xe8 35 c5! ♗c7 36 ♗c4** [36 ♖f2 Löwenthal] **36 ... ♔g7! 37 cxb6**

[◻ 37 d5+ ♘f6 (37 ... ♔f8 38 d6 ♗d8 39 ♖f2 bxc5 40 ♖xf5+ ♘f6 41 g4; 37 ... ♔g6! 38 d6 ♗d8 39 ♖a2 bxc5 40 d7 ♘c7 41 ♖a7 ♘b5 42 ♖a8 ♗g5 43 h4) 38 d6 ♗d8 39 ♖a2 ♔f8 40 ♖a8 ♔e8 41 ♗xf6 ♖xf6 42 cxb6+-] 37 ... ♗xb6 38 ♖b2 ♗c7 39 ♖b7 ♔f6 40 ♗b4 ♖g6 41 ♗f8! h5 42 ♔f2 h4 [42 ... ♖g4 43 ♔e2 ♖g8 44 ♗c5 ♖h8 45 d5] 43 gxh4 ♖g4 44 h5 ♖h4 45 h6 ♖xh2+ 46 ♔g1 ♖h3 47 ♗f1 [△ 47 ... ♖xe3 48 h7] 47 ... ♖g3+ 48 ♔f2 ♖g4 49 ♗c4 ♖h4 50 ♗g8 ♗d6 51 ♗xd6 ♘xd6 52 ♖d7 ♘e8 [52 ... ♘c8 53 ♖f7+ ♔g5 54 h7] 53 h7 ♔g5 54 ♖e7 ♘d6 [54 ... ♘f6?? 55 ♖g7++-] 55 ♖e6 [55 ♖c7 f4] 55 ... ♘c4 56 ♖xc6 ♘d2 57 ♔e2 ♖h2+ 58 ♔d1 ♘f3 [58 ... ♘f1 59 ♖c3 f4 60 exf4+ ♔xf4 61 d5 ♔e5 (61 ... e3 62 d6 ♘g3 63 ♖xe3 ♔xe3 64 d7 ♖d2+ 65 ♔c1 ♘e2+ 66 ♔b1 ♘c3+ 67 ♔a1+-; 61 ... ♘e3+ 62 ♖xe3 ♔xe3 63 d6 ♔d3 64 ♗c4+) 62 ♔e1! (62 ♖c6? ♘e3+ 63 ♔e1 ♘xd5 64 ♖c5 ♔f6 65 ♖xd5 ♔g7= Löwenthal) 62 ... ♘d2 63 ♖c6 ♘f3+ 64 ♔d1 ♘g5 65 d6 e3 66 ♖c5+ ♔xd6 67 ♖xg5 ♔e7 68 ♖g7+ ♔f8 69 ♖a7 ♖h3 70 ♗c4 ♖h2 71 ♖f7+ ♔e8 72 ♖g7] 59 ♖c7! ♔g6 [59 ... f4 60 ♖g7+ ♔f6 61 ♖f7+ △ 62 ♖xf4] 60 d5 f4 61 exf4 e3 62 ♖e7 e2+ 63 ♖xe2 ♖h1+ 64 ♔c2 ♘d4+ 65 ♔d2 ♘xe2 66 ♔xe2 ♔g7 [66 ... ♔f5 67 d6 ♔f6 68 ♔e3 ♖h3+ 69 ♔e4 ♖h5 70 f5 ♖h1 71 ♔d5 ♔xf5 72 d7] 67 ♔e3 ♖e1+ 68 ♔d4 ♖f1 69 ♔e5 ♖e1+ 70 ♔f5 ♖d1 71 ♗e6 ♖d4 [71 ... ♔xh7 72 ♔f6, 73 f5+-] 72 ♔e5 ♖d1 73 f5 ♖h1 74 f6+ ♔xh7 [74 ... ♔f8 75 d6 ♖e1+ 76 ♔f5 ♖f1+ 77 ♔g5 ♖g1+ 78 ♗g4] 75 ♔d6 ♖a1 76 ♔e7 ♖a7+ 77 ♗d7 **1-0** L/N6138-1879

## 1858-✕AM-11 — 28 xii 58

**Morphy,P.C.+ Anderssen,A.**

[Hoffer & Zukertort]

1 e4 e6 2 d4 g6 3 ♗d3 ♗g7 4 ♗e3 c5 5 c3 cxd4 6 cxd4 ♘c6 7 ♘e2 ♘ge7 8 0-0 0-0 9 ♘bc3 d5 [◻ 9 ... d6] 10 e5 f6 11 f4 fxe5? [◻ 11 ... a6 △ 12 ... ♗d7] 12 fxe5 a6 [◻ 12 ... ♖xf1+] 13 ♕d2 ♘b4? 14 ♗g5! ♘xd3 15 ♕xd3 ♗d7 16 ♕h3 ♕e8 17 ♘g3 ♖c8 [◻ 17 ... ♘f5 18 ♘xf5 ♖xf5 19 ♖xf5 gxf5 20 ♖f1 ♕g6] 18 ♖xf8+ ♕xf8 19 ♖f1 ♕e8 20 ♕h4 ♘f5 21 ♘xf5 gxf5 22 ♖f3 ♗b5 23 ♖g3 ♖c7 24 ♗f6 [△ 25 ♕h6 ♕f8 26 ♗xg7 ♖xg7 27 ♖xg7+ ♕xg7 28 ♕xe6+ ♔h8 29 ♘xd5+-] 24 ... f4 [24 ... ♔h8 25 ♖xg7 ♖xg7 26 ♘xb5 Löwenthal; ◻ 24 ... ♔h8 25 ♕h6 ♕f8 26 ♘xb5 axb5 27 ♖xg7 (27 ♔f2 ♕xf6) 27 ... ♖xg7 28 ♔f2 ♕f7 (28 ... ♔g8 29 ♗xg7 ♕xg7 30 ♕xe6+) 29 ♔e3 ♕g6 30 ♕xg6 hxg6 31 ♔d3 ♔g8 32 ♗xg7 ♔xg7 33 ♔c3] 25 ♕xf4 ♕f8 26 ♘xb5 [26 ♕h6 ♗d3] 26 ... axb5 27 ♕h6 ♔h8 28 ♖xg7 ♖xg7 29 ♔f2 ♔g8 30 ♕xg7+ ♕xg7 31 ♗xg7 ♔xg7 32 g4 b4 33 h4 b5 34 ♔e3 b3! 35 a3 [35 axb3 b4] **1-0** L/N6138-1879

## BODEN✕OWEN — London

**[1858-✕BO]**

| | | | | | | |
|---|---|---|---|---|---|---|
| S.S. Boden | ? | 1 | 1 | 1 | 1 | ? |
| J. Owen | ? | 0 | 0 | 0 | 0 | ? |

## 1858-✕BO-2

**Boden, S.S.+ Owen, J.**

London [Staunton]

1 e4 b6 2 d4 ♗b7 3 ♗d3 e6 4 c4 ♗b4+ 5 ♗d2 ♘c6?! 6 d5 ♗xd2+ 7 ♕xd2 ♘e5 8 ♘c3 ♘h6 9 f4 ♘xd3+ 10 ♕xd3 f5 11 e5 g5?! 12 ♘ge2 ♕e7 13 0-0-0 0-0-0 14 ♘b5 exd5 15 cxd5 ♕c5+ 16 ♔b1 ♗a6 17 ♘d6+ cxd6 18 ♕xa6+ ♔b8 19 ♘c3 [19 ♖c1!? ♕xd5 20 ♖c7 △ 21 ♕xa7+, 22 ♖c1+] 19 ... ♕c8 20 ♕a3 [△ 21 b4] 20 ... ♕c5 21 ♕a6 ♕c8 22 ♕a4 a6 23 ♕a3 ♘f7 24 e6! dxe6 25 dxe6 ♕xe6 26 ♕xa6 d5 27 ♖he1 ♕c6 28 ♖e7 ♘d6 29 ♕a7+ ♔c8 30 ♘xd5 **1-0** M954-1858

## 1858-✕BO-3̂

**Boden, S.S.+ Owen, J.**

London [Staunton]

1 e4 b6 2 g3 ♗b7 3 ♗g2 f5 4 ♘c3 ♘f6 5 d3 e5 6 ♘ge2 ♗b4 7 0-0 ♗xc3 8 ♘xc3 fxe4 9 ♘xe4 ♗xe4 10 dxe4 h6 11 f4 ♘c6 12 fxe5 ♘xe5 13 ♖f5 d6 14 ♗f4! ♕e7 [14 ... g6? 15 ♗xe5 gxf5 16 ♗xf6 ♕xf6 17 e5] 15 ♕d4 ♘fd7 16 ♗xe5 ♘xe5 17 a4 g6 18 ♖f2 ♖f8 19 a5 [◻ 19 ♖xf8+ △ 20 ♖f1] 19 ... ♖xf2 20 ♕xf2 b5 21 ♕e3! g5? 22 ♕b3 a6 23 ♕g8+ ♕f8 24 ♕e6+ ♕e7 25 ♕xh6 0-0-0 [△ ... ♘c5] 26 b3 ♔b8 27 ♖f1 ♘g4 28 ♕g6 ♕e5 29 ♕f5 ♕d4+ 30 ♔h1 ♘e3 31 ♕f2 ♖h8 32 h3 ♕c3 33 ♕f6 ♕xf6 34 ♖xf6 ♘xc2 35 e5 ♘e3 36 exd6 c5 37 d7 ♔c7 38 ♖c6+ ♔xd7 39 ♖xc5 g4 40 h4 ♔d6 41 ♖c6+ ♔e5

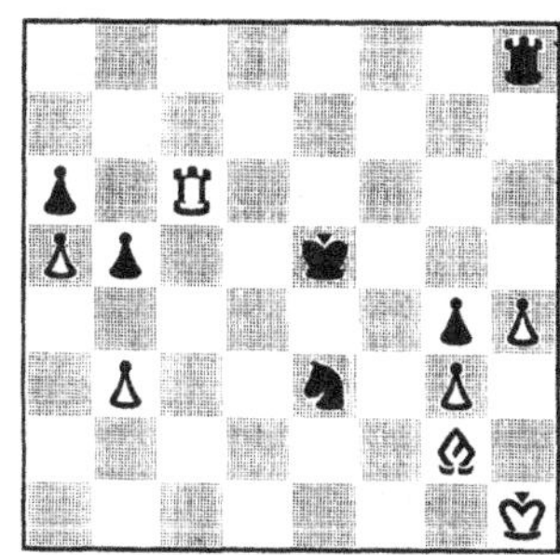

42 ♖xa6! ♖d8 43 ♖a7! ♖d1+ 44 ♔h2 ♖e1 [44 ... ♖d2 45 ♖e7+ △ 46 ♖d7+, 47 ♖xd2] 45 a6 ♔d6 46 ♖d7+! ♔xd7 47 a7 ♖a1 48 a8♕ ♖xa8 49 ♗xa8 ♘f5 50 ♗e4 ♘h6 51 b4 ♔d6 52 ♗d3 ♔c6 53 ♔g2 ♘f7 54 ♔f2 ♘e5 55 ♔e3 **1-0** M954-1858

## 1858-✕BO-4̂

**Boden, S.S.+ Owen, J.**

London [Staunton]

1 e4 b6 2 d4 ♗b7 3 ♗d3 e6 4 ♕e2 ♗e7 5 f4 c5 6 c3 ♘f6 7 ♘f3 0-0 8 ♘bd2 ♘g4 9 0-0 f5 10 e5 ♘c6 11 h3 ♘h6 12 ♘b3 cxd4 13 ♘bxd4 ♘xd4 14 cxd4 ♔h8 15 ♗d2 ♕e8 16 ♖ac1 ♖g8 17 b4 ♘f7 18 ♘g5 ♘xg5 19 fxg5 h6? 20 h4 hxg5 21 ♖c7 ♗c6 22 b5 ♗d8 23 bxc6 ♗xc7 24 cxd7 ♕f7 25 d5 g6 [25 ... exd5 26 e6 △ 27 ♗xg5] 26 ♗xg5 ♕xd7 [◻ 26 ... ♗d8] 27 ♗f6+ ♔h7 28 dxe6 ♕d4+ 29 ♔h1 ♖af8 [29 ... ♕g4 30 ♕xg4 △ 31 h5]

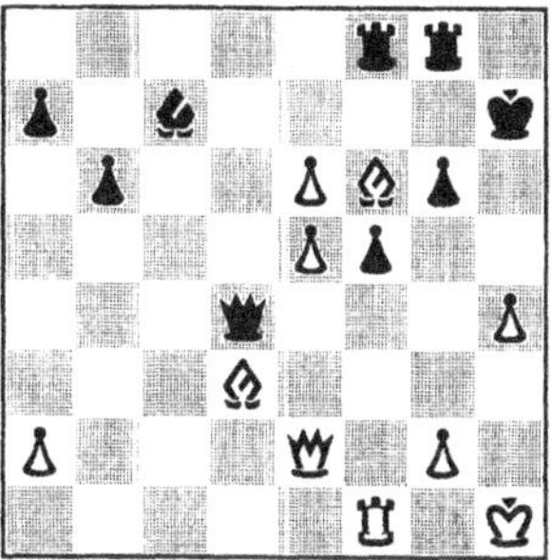

30 ♖xf5! ♖xf6 31 ♕h5+!! gxh5 32 ♖xh5+ ♔g7 33 ♖h7+ ♔f8 34 e7+ ♔e8 35 ♗b5+ ♕d7 36 ♗xd7+ ♔xd7 37 exf6 ♖g4 [37 ... ♖c8 38 f7 ♔xe7 39 f8♕+ ♔xf8 40 ♖h8+ ♔~ 41 ♖xc8+-; 37 ... ♖b8 38 e8♕+ △ 39 ♖xc7+-] 38 ♖h8 ♖e4 39 g4 **1-0** M954-1858

## 1858-✕BO-5̂

**Owen, J.– Boden, S.S.**

London [Staunton]

1 e4 b6 2 d4 ♗b7 3 ♗d3 e6 4 ♕e2 g6 5 f4 ♗g7 6 ♘f3 ♘e7 7 0-0 0-0 8 ♗e3 d6 9 ♘bd2 ♘d7 10 e5 d5 11 g4 c5 12 c3 ♕e8 13 f5 exf5 14 gxf5 ♘xf5 15 ♗xf5 gxf5 16 ♘h4 f6 17 ♘xf5 ♔h8 18 ♔h1? [18 ♘d6 ♕b8 (18 ... ♕g6+ 19 ♔h1 △ 20 ♖g1) 19 ♕h5+-] 18 ... ♘xe5! 19 ♖g1 ♖g8 20 ♖g2 ♗f8 21 ♖xg8+ ♔xg8 22 ♖g1+ ♔h8 23 ♕f2 ♕e6 24 ♖g3 ♖e8 25 ♗h6 ♗xh6 26 ♘xh6 ♘c4 27 ♕f5! ♗c8 28 ♘f3 ♘d6 29 ♘e5 fxe5 30 ♕g5? [30 ♕xe5+ ♕xe5 31 dxe5 ♗e6 32 exd6 ♖d8] 30 ... ♕g6 31 ♕e3 exd4 32 ♕g1 ♕xh6 33 cxd4 ♗f5 **0-1** M954-1858

## HARRWITZ✕MORPHY — Paris

**[1858-✕HM]**

| | | | | | | | | | |
|---|---|---|---|---|---|---|---|---|---|
| D. Harrwitz | 1 | 1 | 0 | 0 | 0 | 0 | ½ | 0 | 2½ |
| P.C. Morphy | 0 | 0 | 1 | 1 | 1 | 1 | ½ | 1 | 5½ |

**1858-✕HM-1** 5 ix 58
**Harrwitz, D.+Morphy, P.C.**
Paris [Löwenthal]
1 d4 e6 2 c4 d5 3 ♘c3 ♘f6 4 ♗f4 a6 5 e3 c5 6 ♘f3 ♘c6 7 a3 c×d4 8 e×d4 d×c4 9 ♗×c4 b5 10 ♗d3 ♗b7 11 0-0 ♗e7 12 ♗e5 0-0 13 ♕e2 ♘d5 14 ♗g3! ♔h8 [□14 ... ♗f6=] 15 ♖fe1 ♗f6 [15 ... f5 16 ♕×e6 ♘×c3 17 b×c3 f4 18 ♕e4 g6 19 ♗×f4+-] 16 ♕e4 g6 17 ♘×d5 ♕×d5 18 ♕×d5 e×d5 19 ♘e5 ♖ad8 20 ♘×c6 ♗×c6 21 ♖ac1 ♖c8 22 ♗d6 ♖g8 23 ♗e5 ♔g7? [23 ... ♗×e5=] 24 f4 ♗d7 25 ♔f2 h6 26 ♔e3 ♖×c1 27 ♖×c1 ♖c8 28 ♖c5 ♗×e5 29 f×e5 ♗e6 [29 ... ♖×c5? 30 d×c5+-] 30 a4 b×a4 31 ♗×a6 ♖b8 32 ♖b5 ♖d8 33 ♖b6 ♖a8 34 ♔d2 ♗c8 35 ♗×c8 ♖×c8 36 ♖b5 ♖a8 37 ♖×d5 a3 38 b×a3 ♖×a3 39 ♖c5 ♔f8 40 ♔e2 ♔e7 41 d5 ♔d7 42 ♖c6 h5 43 ♖f6 ♔e7 44 d6+ ♔e8 45 e6 f×e6 46 ♖×e6+ ♔f7 47 d7 ♖a8 48 ♖d6 ♔e7 49 ♖×g6 ♔×d7 50 ♖g5 ♖h8 51 ♔f3 ♔e6 52 ♔g3 h4+ 53 ♔g4 h3 54 g3 ♔f6 55 ♖h5 **1-0** L/N3161

**1858-✕HM-2** ix 58
**Morphy, P.C.–Harrwitz, D.**
Paris [Löwenthal]
1 e4 e5 2 ♘f3 d6 3 d4 e×d4 4 ♕×d4 ♘c6 [□4 ... ♗d7] 5 ♗b5 ♗d7 6 ♗×c6 ♗×c6 7 ♗g5 ♘f6 [□7 ... f6] 8 ♘c3 ♗e7 9 0-0-0 0-0 10 ♖he1 h6 11 ♗h4 ♘e8 12 ♗×e7 ♕×e7 13 e5 ♗×f3 14 g×f3 ♕g5+ 15 ♔b1 d×e5 16 ♖×e5 ♕g2 17 ♘d5 ♕×h2 18 ♖ee1 ♕d6 19 ♖g1 ♔h7 20 ♕e3 f5 21 ♘f4 ♕b6 22 ♕e2 ♖f7 23 ♕c4 ♕f6 24 ♘h5 [24 ♖g6 ♕e7] 24 ... ♕e7 25 ♖de1 ♕d7 26 a3 ♘d6 27 ♕d4 ♖g8 [27 ... ♖d8? 28 ♖×g7+ ♖×g7 29 ♘f6++-] 28 ♖g2 ♘e8 29 ♕c3 f4 30 ♖h1 g6 31 ♖hg1 ♕d5 32 ♕e1 ♕×h5 33 ♖g5 ♕×f3 34 ♕e6 ♖f6 35 ♕e7+ ♖g7 36 ♕×e8 h×g5 37 ♕e1 ♕c6 **0-1** L/N3161

**1858-✕HM-3** ix 58
**Harrwitz, D.–Morphy, P.C.**
Paris [Löwenthal]
1 d4 f5 2 c4 e6 3 ♘c3 ♘f6 4 ♗g5 ♗b4 5 ♕b3 c5 6 d5 e5 7 e3 0-0 8 ♗d3 d6 9 ♘ge2 h6 10 ♗×f6 ♕×f6 11 a3 ♗×c3+ 12 ♕×c3 ♕g6 13 0-0 ♘d7 14 b4 b6 15 f3 h5 16 ♗c2 ♗b7 17 ♗a4 ♕f7 18 ♗×d7 ♕×d7 19 b×c5 b×c5 20 f4 e4 21 ♖ab1 ♗a6 22 ♖fc1 ♕a4 23 ♘g3 h4 24 ♘f1 ♖ab8 25 ♘d2 ♖b6 26 ♖×b6 a×b6 27 ♕b3 ♕×b3 28 ♘×b3 b5!± 29 c×b5 ♗×b5 30 ♘a5 ♖a8 31 ♘b7 ♖a6 32 ♖c3 ♔f8 33 ♘d8 ♗d7 34 ♖b3 ♔e7 35 ♖b8 c4 36 ♔f2 c3 37 ♔e2 ♖×a3 38 ♘c6+ ♗×c6 39 d×c6 c2 40 ♔d2 ♖c3 41 ♔c1 ♖×c6 42 ♖b3 ♔f6 43 ♖a3 g5 44 g3 h×g3 45 h×g3 g×f4 46 g×f4 ♔g6 47 ♖a5 ♖c5 48 ♖a6 ♖c3 49 ♖×d6+ ♔h5 50 ♖d2 ♔g4 51 ♖g2+ ♔f3 52 ♖g5 ♖c5 53 ♖h5 ♔×e3 54 ♖h4 ♔f3 **0-1** L/N3161

**1858-✕HM-4** ix 58
**Morphy, P.C.+Harrwitz, D.**
Paris [Löwenthal]
1 e4 e5 2 ♘f3 d6 3 d4 e×d4 4 ♕×d4 ♘c6 [□4 ... ♗d7] 5 ♗b5 ♗d7 6 ♗×c6 ♗×c6 7 ♗g5 f6 8 ♗h4 ♘h6 9 ♘c3 ♕d7 10 0-0 ♗e7 11 ♖ad1± 0-0 12 ♕c4+ ♖f7 [□12 ... ♔h8] 13 ♘d4 [13 e5 △ 13 ... ♕f5 14 e6 ♖ff8 15 ♖fe1 ♖ad8 16 ♘d5 ♗×d5 17 ♖×d5+-; 13 ... ♗×f3 14 e6 d5 15 e×f7+ ♘×f7 16 g×f3±; 13 ... ♕g4 14 ♕×g4 ♘×g4 15 e6 ♖ff8 16 ♘d4±; 13 ... f×e5 14 ♘×e5+-] 13 ... ♘g4 14 h3 ♘e5 15 ♕e2 g5 16 ♗g3 ♖g7 17 ♘f5 ♖g6 18 f4 g×f4 19 ♖×f4 ♔h8 20 ♖h4 ♗f8 21 ♗×e5 f×e5 22 ♖f1 ♕e6 23 ♘b5 ♕g8 24 ♖f2 a6 25 ♘×c7 ♖c8 26 ♘d5 ♗×d5 27 e×d5 ♖c7 [27 ... ♕×d5 28 ♖×h7+ ♔×h7 29 ♕h5+ ♗h6 30 ♘×h6 ♖×h6 31 ♕f5++-] 28 c4 ♗e7 29 ♖h5 ♕e8 30 c5!+-

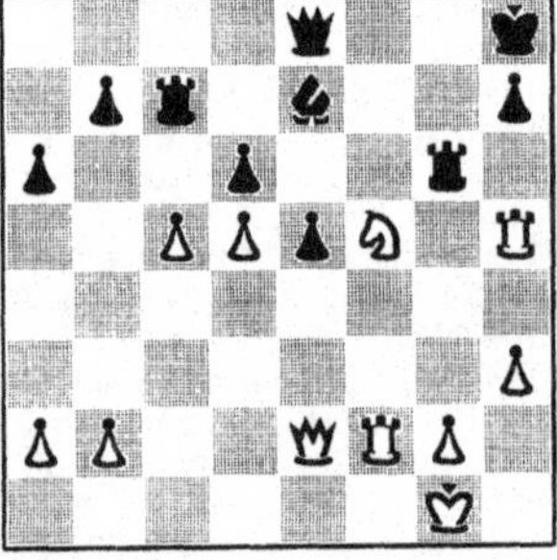

30 ... ♖×c5 31 ♖×h7+ ♔×h7 32 ♕h5+ ♔g8 33 ♘×e7+ ♔g7 34 ♘f5+ ♔g8 35 ♘×d6 **1-0** L/N3161

**1858-✕HM-5** ix 58
**Harrwitz, D.–Morphy, P.C.**
Paris [Löwenthal]
1 d4 f5 2 c4 e6 3 ♘c3 ♘f6 4 ♗g5 ♗e7 5 e3 0-0 6 ♗d3 b6 7 ♘ge2 ♗b7 8 0-0 ♘h5 9 ♗×e7 ♕×e7 10 ♘g3 ♘×g3 11 h×g3 d6 12 f4 [□12 e4] 12 ... ♘c6 13 g4 ♘b4 14 g×f5 e×f5 15 ♕d2 ♖ae8 16 ♖ae1 ♕h4∓ 17 ♗b1 ♖e6 18 ♕f2 ♕h5 19 d5 ♖h6 20 ♕f3 ♕h4 21 a3 ♘a6 22 b4 ♘b8 23 ♘e2 ♘d7 24 ♘g3 g6 25 ♔f2 ♘f6 26 ♖h1 ♘g4+ 27 ♔g1 ♕f6 28 ♖×h6 ♘×h6 29 ♕d1 ♘g4 30 ♕d2 ♕h4 31 ♘f1 ♖e8 32 g3 ♕h3 33 b5 ♘f6 34 ♕g2 ♕×g2+ 35 ♔×g2 a6 36 a4 a×b5 37 a×b5 ♖a8 38 ♘d2 ♖a3 39 e4 f×e4 40 ♘×e4 ♘×e4 41 ♗×e4 ♖c3 42 ♗f3 ♔f7 43 ♖e4 ♗c8 44 ♗e2 ♗f5 45 ♖d4 h5 46 ♔f2 ♔f6 47 ♖d2 ♗c2 48 ♔e1 ♗e4 49 ♔f2 ♔f5 50 ♖a2 h4! 51 g×h4 ♔×f4 52 ♖a7 ♖h3 53 ♖×c7 ♖h2+ 54 ♔e1 ♔e3 **0-1** L/N3161

**1858-✕HM-6** ix 58
**Morphy, P.C.+Harrwitz, D.**
Paris [Löwenthal]
1 e4 e5 2 ♘f3 d6 3 d4 e×d4 4 ♕×d4 ♘f6?! 5 e5 d×e5 [□5 ... ♕e7] 6 ♕×d8+ ♔×d8 7 ♘×e5 ♗e6 8 ♘c3 ♗d6 9 ♘c4 ♗×c4 10 ♗×c4 ♖e8+ 11 ♗e3 ♔e7 12 0-0-0 a6 13 ♗g5 ♘bd7 14 ♘e4 h6 [14 ... ♔f8 15 ♘×d6+-; 14 ... ♗e5 15 f4±] 15 ♗×f6+ [15 ♘×f6+ ♘×f6 16 ♖he1+ ♔f8 17 ♗×f6 g×f6=] 15 ... ♘×f6 16 ♘×d6 c×d6 17 ♖he1+ ♔f8 18 ♖×e8+ ♘×e8 19 ♗d5 ♖b8 20 ♗f3 g6 21 c3 ♔e7 22 ♖e1+ ♔f8 [22 ... ♔d7 23 ♗d5±] 23 ♔c2 ♘c7 24 ♔b3 ♘e6 25 ♔a4 b6 26 b4 h5 27 h4 ♔e7 28 ♖e3 ♔d7 29 ♗d5 ♖e8 30 ♔b3 ♖g8 31 ♖f3 ♔e7 32 a4 a5 33 ♗×e6 ♔×e6 34 ♔c4 g5 35 ♔b5! a×b4 36 c×b4 g×h4 37 ♔×b6 ♖b8+ 38 ♔a5 ♔d5 39 ♖d3+ ♔c4 40 ♖×d6 ♖×b4 41 ♖d4+ ♔×d4 42 ♔×b4 f5 43 f4 ♔e3 44 a5 ♔f2 45 a6 ♔×g2 46 a7 h3 47 a8♕+ ♔g1 48 ♕f3 [48 ... h2 49 ♕g3+ ♔h1 50 ♕f2 h4 51 ♕f1#] **1-0** L/N3161

**1858-✕HM-7** ix 58
**Harrwitz, D.=Morphy, P.C.**
Paris [Löwenthal]
1 d4 f5 2 c4 e6 3 ♘c3 ♘f6 4 ♗g5 ♗e7 5 e3 0-0 6 ♗d3 b6 7 ♘ge2 ♗b7 8 ♗×f6 ♗×f6 9 0-0 ♕e7 10 ♕d2 d6 11 f4? c5 12 d5 ♘a6 13 d×e6 ♕×e6 14 ♖ae1? ♗h4 15 ♘g3 ♕g6 16 ♘d5 ♗×d5 17 c×d5 ♗×g3 18 h×g3 ♘c7 19 ♔f2 ♖ae8 20 ♖h1 ♖e7 21 ♖h4 ♕f7 22 ♗e2 [22 g4 ♕×d5 (22 ... ♘×d5? 23 ♗c4+-) 23 ♕c2±] 22 ... ♘e8 23 ♕d3 ♘f6 24 ♗f3 g6 25 ♖e2 ♖fe8 [25 ... g5 26 f×g5 ♘e4+ 27 ♔g1 ♘×g3 28 ♖e1 ♕g7∓] 26 b3 ♕g7 27 ♖h1 h6 28 ♔g1 g5 29 f×g5 h×g5 30 ♗h5 ♘e4!

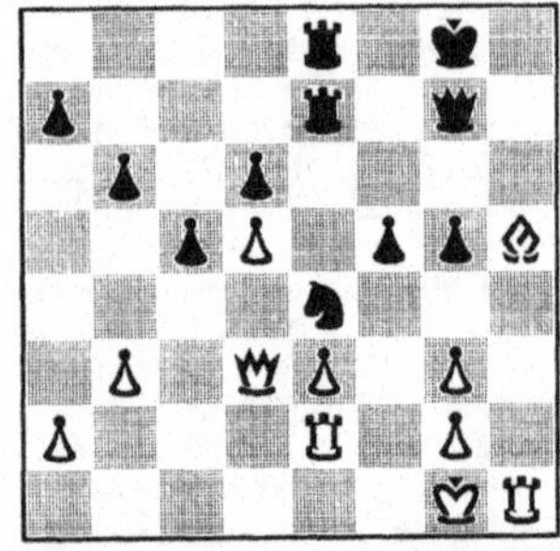

31 ♖e1 [31 ♗×e8? ♕a1+-+] 31 ... ♖f8 32 ♗f3 [32 g4 ♘b3 33 ♖h3 f4 34 e4 ♕e5 35 ♗g6 ♖f6 36 ♗f5 ♘×f5 37 g×f5 ♖×f5-+] 32 ... ♘×g3 33 ♖h3 ♕e5+- 34 ♖h6 g4 35

♗d1 ♔g7 36 ♖h4 ♖h8 37 ♖xh8 ♔xh8 38 ♗c2 ♖h7 39 ♕d2 ♕b2 40 ♖d1 ♖h1+ 41 ♔f2 ♖f1+? 42 ♔xg3 ♕e5+ 43 ♔h4 ♕f6+ 44 ♔g3 ♕e5+ ½-½ L/N3161

### 1858-✕HM-8 ix 58
**Morphy, P.C.+Harrwitz, D.**
Paris [Löwenthal]

1 e4 e5 2 ♘f3 d6 3 d4 ♗g4 [□ 3 ... exd4] 4 dxe5 ♗xf3 5 ♕xf3 dxe5 6 ♗c4 ♘f6 [□ 6 ... ♕d7] 7 ♕b3 ♗d6 8 ♗xf7+ ♔f8 9 ♗g5 ♘bd7 10 ♗h5 g6 11 ♗h6+ ♔e7 12 ♗f3 ♘c5 13 ♕c4 b5 14 ♕e2 ♘e6 15 ♗e3 a6 16 ♘d2 ♔f7 17 0-0-0 ♕e7 18 g3 ♖hb8 [□ 18 ... ♖hd8; 18 ... ♖he8] 19 ♗g2 a5 20 ♖hf1 a4 21 f4 a3 22 b3 ♔g7 23 f5 ♘f8 24 g4 ♕e8 25 ♗f3 ♕c6 26 ♘b1 b4 27 ♕f2 ♘8d7 28 g5 ♘g8 [28 ... ♘xe4? 29 ♕g2+-] 29 f6+ ♔h8 30 f7 ♘c5

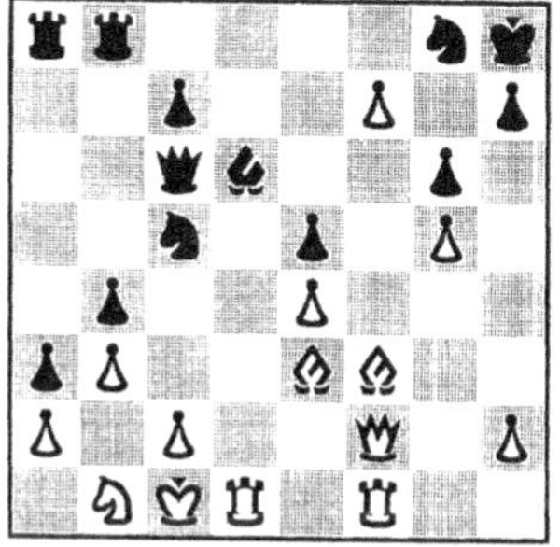

[30 ... ♘e7 31 ♗g4+-] 31 fxg8♕+ ♔xg8 32 ♗xc5 ♗xc5 33 ♕e2 ♕e6 34 ♘d2 ♔h8 35 ♗g4 ♕e7 36 ♘f3 ♖d8 37 h4 ♖d6 38 ♖xd6 cxd6 39 ♕c4 ♖f8 40 ♕e6 ♗e3+ 41 ♔d1 ♕c7 42 ♘d2 ♗f4 43 ♘c4 ♕c5 44 ♕d5 ♕xd5+ 45 exd5 ♖d8 46 ♖f3 ♔g7 47 c3! ♖b8 48 cxb4 ♖xb4 49 ♔c2 ♔f8 50 ♔c3 ♖b5 51 ♗e6 ♖c5 52 b4 ♖c7 53 b5 ♔e7 54 b6 ♖b7 55 ♗c8 ♖b8 56 b7 ♔d8 57 ♘xd6 ♔e7 58 ♘b5 h6 59 d6+ **1-0** L/N3161

## LÖWENTHAL✕MORPHY
London

[1858-✕LM]

| | | | | | | | | | | | | | | | |
|---|---|---|---|---|---|---|---|---|---|---|---|---|---|---|---|
| J.J. Löwenthal | ½ | 0 | 0 | 0 | 1 | 0 | 0 | 1 | 0 | 0 | 1 | 0 | ½ | 0 | 4 |
| P.C. Morphy | ½ | 1 | 1 | 1 | 0 | 1 | 1 | 0 | 1 | 1 | 0 | 1 | ½ | 1 | 10 |

### 1858-✕LM-1 19 vii 58
**Löwenthal,J.J.=Morphy,P.C.**
London [Löwenthal]

1 e4 e5 2 ♘f3 d6 3 d4 exd4 4 ♘xd4 ♘f6 5 ♘c3 ♗e7 6 ♗e2 0-0 7 0-0 c5 8 ♘f3 ♘c6 9 ♗f4 ♗e6 10 ♕d2 d5 11 exd5 [11 e5 ♘h5∓] 11 ... ♘xd5 12 ♖ad1 ♘xf4 13 ♕xf4 ♕a5 14 ♗d3 ♖ad8 15 ♘g5 ♗xg5 16 ♕xg5 h6 17 ♕h4 ♘d4 18 a3 [18 h3 ♕b4-+] 18 ... ♖fe8 19 ♖fe1 ♕b6 20 ♘a4 ♕a5 21 ♘c3 f5 22 ♖e5 ♗f7 23 ♖de1 ♕b6 24 ♖xe8+ ♖xe8 25 ♖xe8+ ♗xe8 26 ♕e7 ♗f7 27 ♘a4 ♕a5 28 ♘xc5 ♕d2 29 f3 [29 h3 ♕c1+=; 29 g3? ♕c1+-+] 29 ... ♘c6! 30 ♕e2 [30 ♕xb7?? ♕e3+-+] 30 ... ♕c1+ 31 ♔f2 ♕xb2 32 ♗xf5 [32 a4 ♕b4-+] 32 ... ♕xa3 33 ♕b5 [33 ♘xb7 ♕b4∓] 33 ... ♕c3 [33 ... ♘d4 34 ♕xb7 ♘xf5 35 ♕c8+±] 34 ♘b3 ♕f6 35 ♕xb7 g6 36 ♕c8+ ♔h7 37 ♗d3 ♘e5 38 ♘d2 ♕h4+ 39 ♔f1 ♕xh2 40 ♘e4 ♕h1+ 41 ♔f2 ♕c1 42 ♕c3 ♕f4 43 ♔e2 h5 44 ♘f2 h4 45 ♕d2 ♕g3 46 ♕e3 a5 47 ♕e4 ♗e6 48 f4 ♘xd3 49 cxd3 ♗g4+ 50 ♔f1 ♗f5 51 ♕e7+ ♔h6 ½-½ L/N3161

### 1858-✕LM-2 20 vii 58
**Morphy,P.C.+Löwenthal,J.J.**
London [Löwenthal]

1 e4 e5 2 f4 ♗c5 3 ♘f3 d6 4 c3 ♗g4 5 ♗c4 [5 ♗e2 ♗xf3 6 ♗xf3 ♘c6 7 b4 ♗b6 8 b5 ♘ce7 9 d4 exd4 10 cxd4 a6 11 bxa6 ♖xa6 12 ♗e2 ♖a7 13 0-0 ♘f6 14 ♗f3 ♘c6 15 ♗b2 0-0 16 ♔h1±] 5 ... ♗xf3 6 ♕xf3 ♘f6 7 b4 ♗b6 8 d3 ♘bd7 9 f5 ♕e7 10 g4 [□ ♗g5] 10 ... h6 11 ♔e2 c6 12 g5 hxg5∓ 13 ♗xg5 d5 14 ♗b3 [14 exd5 e4 15 ♕g2 (15 dxe4 ♘e5-+; 15 ♕g3 exd3+-+) 15 ... ♘e5-+] 14 ... ♕d6 15 ♘d2 a5 16 bxa5 ♖xa5 17 h4 ♘h5 18 ♘f1 ♘c5 19 ♗c2 ♖b5 [□ 19 ... ♖a3 20 ♗d2 ♗a5 21 ♖c1 ♗xc3 22 ♗xc3 (22 exd5 ♗xd2 23 ♔xd2 cxd5 24 ♗b3 e4-+) 22 ... ♖xc3 23 exd5 e4 24 ♕e3 ♘f4+-+] 20 ♗c1 dxe4 [□ 20 ... ♘f4+ 21 ♗xf4 ♖b2-+] 21 dxe4 ♖b2? 22 ♗xb2 ♘f4+ 23 ♔e1 ♘cd3+ 24 ♗xd3 ♘xd3+ 25 ♔d2 ♘xb2+ 26 ♔c2 ♕a3 [□ 26 ... ♘c4] 27 ♘d2 ♗c7? 28 ♘b1 **1-0** L/N3161

### 1858-✕LM-3 22 vii 58
**Löwenthal,J.J.–Morphy,P.C.**
London [Löwenthal]

1 e4 e5 2 ♘f3 ♘f6 3 ♘xe5 d6 4 ♘f3 ♘xe4 5 d4 d5 6 ♗d3 ♗e7 7 0-0 ♘c6 8 ♖e1 f5 [□ 8 ... ♘d6; 8 ... ♘f6 Morphy] 9 c4 ♗e6 10 cxd5 ♗xd5 11 ♘c3 ♘xc3 12 bxc3 0-0 13 ♗f4 ♗d6 14 ♗xd6 ♕xd6 15 ♘e5 ♖ae8 16 c4 [□ 16 f4] 16 ... ♗e6 17 ♘xc6 bxc6 18 ♗f1 ♗f7 19 ♕d2 ♖xe1 20 ♖xe1 ♖d8 [□ 20 ... c5 Morphy] 21 ♕a5 ♕xd4 22 ♕xc7 ♕b6 23 ♕f4 [23 ♖e7 ♖d1 (23 ... ♖f8 24 ♕xa7+-; 23 ... ♕xc7 24 ♖xc7+-) 24 ♖xf7 ♖xf1+ 25 ♔xf1 ♕b1+ 26 ♔e2 ♕c2+ 27 ♔e3 ♕c3+ 28 ♔f4 ♕xc4+ 29 ♔xf5 ♕xf7+ 30 ♕xf7+ ♔xf7 31 ♔e5 ♔e7=] 23 ... g6 24 h3 ♕b2 25 ♕c7 ♕b6 26 ♖e7 ♖d1 27 ♕c8+ ♖d8 28 ♕c7 ♖d1 29 ♕e5? [□ 29 ♕c8+=] 29 ... ♕b1 30 ♕e2 ♔f8 31 ♖e5 f4 32 f3 ♕c1 33 h4 h6 34 c5 ♔g7 35 ♖e4 ♕xc5+ 36 ♔h2 ♕c1 37 ♔g1 ♖d2 38 ♕a6 ♖xa2 39 ♕d3 ♖d2 40 ♕a6 ♖d1 41 g3 fxg3 42 ♔g2 ♕c5 43 ♔xg3 ♕g1+ 44 ♗g2 ♖d2 45 ♕f1 ♕xf1 46 ♗xf1 ♔f6 47 ♗c4 ♗xc4 48 ♖xc4 ♖d6 49 ♔f4 ♖e6 50 ♖d4 ♔e7 51 ♖a4 ♔d6 52 ♖xa7 c5 53 ♖a1 c4 54 h5 gxh5 [54 ... ♖f6+, 55 ... g5-+] 55 ♔f5 ♖e3 56 ♔f4 ♖e8 57 ♖a6+ ♔d5 58 ♖xh6 c3 59 ♖xh5+ ♔d4 60 ♖h7 ♖c8 61 ♖d7+ ♔c4 62 ♔e3 ♖e8+ 63 ♔f2? [□ ♔f4=] 63 ... c2 64 ♖c7+ ♔d3 65 ♖d7+ ♔c3 66 ♖c7+ ♔d2 67 ♖d7+ ♔c1 68 ♖b7 ♖e5 69 f4 ♖e4 70 ♔f3 ♖c4 71 ♖h7 ♔d2 72 ♖h1 c1♕ 73 ♖xc1 ♖xc1 74 ♔e4 ♖e1+ 75 ♔d4 ♔e2 76 f5 ♔f3 77 ♔d5 ♔f4 78 f6 ♔g5 79 f7 ♖f1 **0-1** L/N3161

### 1858-✕LM-4 23 vii 58
**Morphy,P.C.+Löwenthal,J.J.**
London [Löwenthal]

1 e4 e5 2 f4 ♗c5 3 ♘f3 d6 4 c3 ♗g4 5 ♗e2 ♗xf3 6 ♗xf3 ♘c6 7 b4 ♗b6 8 b5 ♘ce7 9 d4 exf4 10 ♗xf4 ♘g6 11 ♗e3 ♘f6 12 ♘d2 0-0 13 0-0 h6 14 a4 c6 15 ♕e2 ♖e8 16 ♕d3 d5 17 e5 ♘d7 18 ♗h5! ♖e6 19 a5 ♗c7 20 ♖xf7!

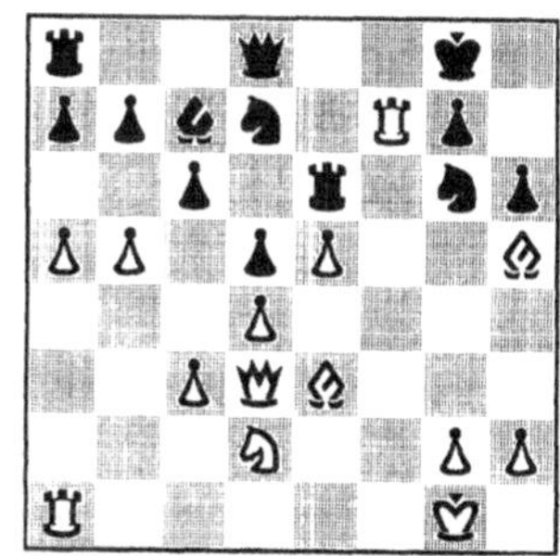

20 ... ♔xf7 [□ 20 ... ♔h8] 21 ♕f5+ ♔e7 22 ♗xg6 ♕g8 23 ♗f2 ♘xe5 [□ 23 ... ♘f8] 24 dxe5 ♖f8? 25 ♗c5+ ♔d8 26 ♗xf8 ♖xe5 27 ♕f2 ♕e6 28 b6 axb6 29 axb6 ♕xg6 30 bxc7+ ♔xc7 31 ♖b1 **1-0** L/N3161

### 1858-✕LM-5 26 vii 58
**Löwenthal,J.J.+Morphy,P.C.**
London [Löwenthal]

1 e4 e5 2 ♘f3 ♘f6 3 ♘xe5 d6 4 ♘f3 ♘xe4 5 d4 d5 6 ♗d3 ♗e7 7 0-0 ♘c6 8 c4 ♗e6 9 cxd5 ♗xd5 10 ♗e3 0-0 11 ♘c3 f5 12 ♘xd5 ♕xd5 13 ♗c2 ♔h8 14 ♗b3 ♕d6 15 d5 ♘a5 16 ♗d4 ♗f6 17 ♖e1 ♖ad8 18 ♗xf6 ♘xf6 19 ♘g5 ♘g4 20 g3 ♕c5 21 ♕e2 ♘xb3 22 axb3 ♖de8 23

♕f3 ♘e5 24 ♕h5 h6 25 ♖ad1 [25 ♘e6 ♕xd5 26 ♘xf8 ♘f3+] 25 ... ♕c2! 26 ♘e6 ♘g4 27 ♖f1 ♕xb2 28 ♘xf8 ♖xf8 29 h3 ♘f6 30 ♕xf5 ♕xb3 31 d6 cxd6 [31 ... ♘h7] 32 ♖xd6 ♕f7 33 ♖d2 a6 34 ♖e1 b5 35 ♕c5 ♖e8 36 ♖de2 ♖xe2 37 ♖xe2 ♕b3 38 ♕f8+ ♘g8 [□ 38 ... ♔h7 39 ♖e7 ♕b1+ 40 ♔h2 ♕g6=] 39 ♖e7 ♕d1+ 40 ♔h2 ♕d4 41 ♖e8 ♕c4 42 ♖a8 b4 43 ♖a7 ♕d4 44 ♖xa6 b3 45 ♖a8 ♕d5 46 ♖a7 ♕d4 47 ♖b7 ♕c3 48 ♕f7 ♔h7 49 ♖xb3 ♕e5 50 ♖b7 h5 51 ♖d7 ♘h6 52 ♕d5 ♕f6 53 ♕d3+ ♔h8 54 ♖d8+ ♘g8 55 ♕d4 ♕f3 56 ♔g1 ♔h7 57 ♕d5 ♕xd5 58 ♖xd5 ♘f6 59 ♖e5 ♔g6 60 f4 ♔f7 61 ♔g2 ♔g6 62 ♔f3 ♔f7 63 ♖a5 ♔g6 64 ♖a6 ♔f7 65 f5 ♘d5 66 g4 hxg4+ 67 hxg4 ♘e7 68 ♔f4 ♘d5+ 69 ♔e5 ♘f6 70 ♖a7+ **1-0** L/N3161

**1858-⚔LM-6** 28 vii 58
**Morphy,P.C.+ Löwenthal,J.J.**
London [Löwenthal]

1 e4 c5 2 d4 cxd4 3 ♘f3 ♘c6 4 ♘xd4 e5 5 ♘xc6 bxc6 6 ♗c4 ♘f6 [□ 6 ... ♗a6 7 ♗xa6 ♕a5+] 7 0-0 d5 [7 ... ♘xe4 8 ♖e1 d5? 9 ♖xe4 dxe4 10 ♗xf7++-] 8 exd5 cxd5 9 ♗b5+ ♗d7 10 ♗xd7+ ♕xd7 11 ♖e1 ♗d6 12 ♘c3 e4 [□ 12 ... d4] 13 ♗g5 ♘g4 14 ♕xd5 ♗xh2+ 15 ♔h1 ♕xd5 16 ♘xd5 0-0? 17 f3 exf3 18 gxf3 ♘e5 19 ♖e3 f6 20 ♔xh2 ♖ad8 21 ♖xe5! fxg5 22 ♔g3 h6 23 c4 ♖f7 24 ♖ae1 ♔f8 25 c5 g6 26 c6 ♖c8 27 c7 ♖cxc7 28 ♖e8+ ♔g7 29 ♘xc7 **1-0** L/N3161

**1858-⚔LM-7** 29 vii 58
**Löwenthal,J.J.–Morphy,P.C.**
London [Löwenthal]

1 e4 e5 2 ♘f3 d6 3 d4 exd4 4 ♕xd4 ♗e6 5 ♘c3 a6 6 ♗e3 ♘c6 7 ♕d2 ♘f6 8 ♖d1 ♗e7 9 ♗e2 0-0 10 0-0 b5 11 a3 ♘e5 12 ♘d4 c5 13 ♘xe6 fxe6 14 f4± ♘g6 15 ♗f3 ♖b8 16 ♕e2 ♕c7 17 h4? ♘xh4 18 ♗g4 ♘xg4 19 ♕xg4 ♕c8 20 g3 ♘g6 21 ♖f2 ♖f6 22 ♖df1 b4 23 axb4 cxb4 24 ♘a4? ♕c6 25 b3 ♕xe4 26 ♗a7 ♖bf8 27 ♕e2 ♕b7 28 ♗f2 ♘xf4 **0-1** L/N3161

**1858-⚔LM-8** 30 vii 58
**Morphy,P.C.–Löwenthal,J.J.**
London [Löwenthal]

1 e4 e5 2 ♘f3 d6 3 d4 exd4 4 ♕xd4 ♗d7 5 ♗e3 ♘f6 6 ♘c3 ♗e7 7 ♗c4 ♘c6 8 ♕d2 ♘e5 9 ♘xe5 dxe5 10 0-0-0 0-0 11 f4 ♗d6 [□ 11 ... exf4] 12 f5± ♗c6 13 ♕e2 h6 14 ♖ad1 ♕e7 15 ♗d5 ♗xd5 16 ♘xd5 ♘xd5 17 ♖xd5 f6 18 ♕g4 [□ 18 ♔h1 Morphy] 18 ... c6 19 ♖d3 ♗c5 20 ♕g3 ♖ad8 21 ♖fd1 ♖xd3 22 ♖xd3 ♖d8 23 ♗xc5 [23 ♖xd8+ ♕xd8 24 ♗xc5 ♕d1+ 25 ♔f2 ♕xc2+∓] 23 ... ♕xc5+ 24 ♕f2 ♕xf2+ 25 ♔xf2 ♖xd3 26 cxd3 c5! 27 g4 ♔f8 28 a4 b6 29 ♔g3 ♔f7 30 ♔h4 ♔f8 31 ♔h5 ♔f7 32 b3 ♔f8 33 ♔g6 ♔g8 34 h3 ♔f8 35 h4 ♔g8 36 g5 hxg5 37 hxg5 fxg5 38 ♔xg5 ♔f7 39 ♔h4 ♔e7 40 ♔g4 ♔f6 41 ♔h5 a6 42 ♔h4 g6 43 a5 bxa5 44 fxg6 ♔xg6 45 ♔g4 a4! 46 bxa4 a5 47 ♔f3 ♔f6 48 ♔f2 ♔f7 49 ♔g3 ♔g7 50 ♔f2 ♔f6 51 ♔g1? ♔g5 52 ♔g2 ♔f4 53 ♔f2 c4 54 dxc4 ♔xe4 55 ♔e2 ♔d4 56 ♔f3 ♔xc4 57 ♔e4 ♔b4 58 ♔xe5 ♔xa4 59 ♔d4 ♔b4 **0-1** L/N3161

**1858-⚔LM-9** viii 58
**Löwenthal,J.J.–Morphy,P.C.**
London [Löwenthal]

1 e4 e5 2 ♘f3 ♘c6 3 ♗b5 ♗c5 4 c3 ♕e7 5 0-0 f6 6 d4 ♗b6 7 ♘a3 ♘d8 8 ♘c4 ♘f7 9 ♘e3 c6 10 ♘f5 ♕f8 11 ♗d3 g6 12 ♘g3 d6 13 a4 ♗g4 14 a5 ♗c7 15 h3 ♗d7 16 ♕b3 ♘d8 17 ♖e1 ♗e6 18 ♕c2 ♘e7 19 b4 ♕g7 20 c4 ♘f7 21 ♗e3 0-0 22 d5 ♗d7 23 ♖ad1 ♔h8 24 ♔h1 cxd5 25 exd5 [25 cxd5 ♖ac8∓] 25 ... f5 26 ♗c1! ♖ae8 27 ♗b2 ♘g8 28 ♕c3 ♘f6 29 ♗b1 ♖g8 30 ♖d2 ♕h6 31 ♘h2 f4 32 ♘e4 ♘xe4 33 ♗xe4 g5 34 f3 ♕h4 35 ♖f1 ♘h6 36 ♖e2 ♘f5 37 ♗xf5 ♗xf5 38 c5 ♕h6 39 ♖fe1 ♖gf8 40 b5 ♖c8

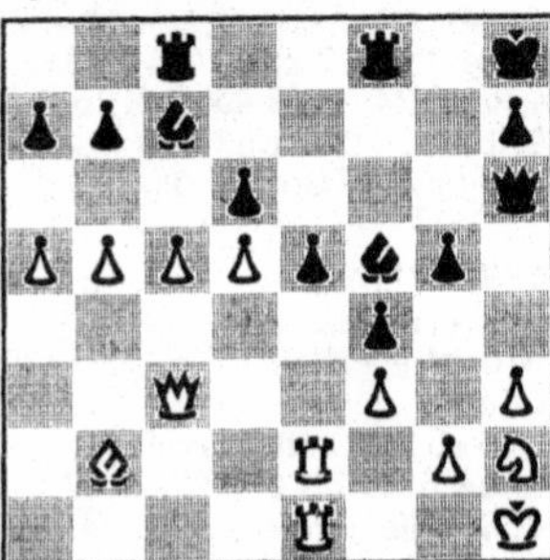

41 ♕a3 [□ 41 c6 bxc6 42 dxc6 ♖b8 (42 ... ♕g6 43 b6 axb6 44 axb6 ♗xb6 45 ♖xe5 dxe5 46 ♖xe5 ♕f6 47 ♕b3 ♖xc6 48 ♖xf5 ♖c1+ 49 ♗xc1 ♕xf5 50 ♗b2+ ♖f6 51 ♕xb6 ♕b1+ 52 ♘f1 ♕xf1+ 53 ♔h2+-) 43 ♕b4 ♕e6 44 ♖d2 ♖fd8 45 ♗d4+-] 41 ... ♔g8 42 b6 axb6 43 cxb6 ♗d8 44 ♖c1? [□ 44 a6 ♗xb6 (44 ... bxa6 45 b7 ♖b8 46 ♕xa6±) 45 axb7 ♖b8 46 ♕a6 ♗d4 (46 ... ♗c5? 47 ♖xe5!+-) 47 ♗a3±] 44 ... ♖xc1+ 45 ♗xc1 ♕g6 46 ♕b4 ♗d3 47 ♖e1 ♗e7 48 ♗b2 ♖e8 49 ♘g4 h5 50 ♘f2 g4 51 ♕c3 ♗f5 52 fxg4 hxg4 53 hxg4 ♗xg4 54 ♘xg4 ♕xg4 55 ♖c1 ♔f7 56 ♕h3? [□ 56 ♕f3±] 56 ... ♕xh3+ 57 gxh3 f3 58 ♖f1 e4 59 ♗d4 ♗f6 60 ♗e3 ♖a8 61 ♗d2 ♗d4 62 h4 ♔g6 63 ♔h2 ♖f8 64 ♔g3 f2 65 ♔g2 e3 66 ♗e1 ♔h5 67 ♔g3 fxe1♕+ **0-1** L/N3161

**1858-⚔LM-10** viii 58
**Morphy,P.C.+ Löwenthal,J.J.**
London [Löwenthal]

1 e4 e6 2 d4 d5 3 exd5 exd5 4 ♘f3 ♘f6 5 ♗d3 ♗d6 6 0-0 0-0 7 ♘c3 c6 8 ♗g5 h6 9 ♗h4 ♗g4 10 h3 ♗xf3 11 ♕xf3 ♘bd7 12 ♗f5 ♕c7 13 ♖ae1 ♖ae8 14 ♖e3 ♗f4 15 ♖e2 ♖xe2 16 ♘xe2 ♗d6 17 ♗xd7 ♘xd7 18 ♘g3! ♖e8 [18 ... g5 19 ♘f5!] 19 ♘f5 ♘f8 20 ♗g3! ♗xg3 21 fxg3 ♖e4 22 c3 ♘h7 23 h4 h5? 24 c4!± ♘f6? 25 ♘xg7 ♘g4 26 ♘xh5 ♖xd4 27 ♘f6+ ♘xf6 28 ♕xf6 ♖xc4 [□ 28 ... ♖g4] 29 ♖f5 ♖g4 30 ♖e5 ♕c8 31 ♖e7 ♕f8 32 ♕e5 ♕g7 33 ♖e8+ ♔h7 34 ♕h5+ **1-0** L/N3161

**1858-⚔LM-11** viii 58
**Löwenthal,J.J.+ Morphy,P.C.**
London [Löwenthal]

1 e4 c5 2 ♘f3 e6 3 d4 cxd4 4 ♘xd4 ♘c6 5 ♘b5 a6 6 ♘d6+ ♗xd6 7 ♕xd6 ♕e7 8 ♕g3 ♘f6 9 ♘c3 d5 [□ 9 ... d6 Morphy] 10 e5 ♘h5 11 ♕f3 g6 12 g4 ♘xe5?! 13 ♕e2 ♘xg4 14 ♕xg4 e5 15 ♕a4+ ♗d7 16 ♕b3 d4 17 ♕xb7 0-0 18 ♘d5 ♕d6 19 ♗g2 e4 20 c4 f5 21 ♕b4 ♕e5 22 ♕e7 ♗e6 23 ♕c7 ♕g7 24 ♕xg7+ ♘xg7 25 ♘b6 ♖ab8 26 c5 ♘h5 27 b4 ♔f7 28 0-0 g5 29 ♖d1 ♖fd8 [29 ... d3 30 f3] 30 ♗xg5 ♖g8 31 h4 ♖g6 32 ♖xd4 ♖bg8 33 ♘d7 ♖xg5 [33 ... ♗xd7 34 ♖xd7+±] 34 hxg5 ♖xg5 35 ♔h2 ♘f4 36 ♗f1 ♖h5+ 37 ♔g3 ♘d5 38 f4 exf3 39 ♘e5+ ♔f6 40 ♘xf3 ♖h6 41 ♖e1 ♖g6+ 42 ♔f2 ♘c3 43 ♗d3 ♗d5 44 ♗xa6 ♖g7 45 ♖f4 ♗xf3 46 ♖xf3 **1-0** L/N3161

**1858-⚔LM-12** viii 58
**Morphy,P.C.+Löwenthal,J.J.**
London [Löwenthal]

1 e4 e6 2 d4 d5 3 exd5 exd5 4 ♘f3 ♘f6 5 ♗d3 ♗e6 [□ 5 ... ♗d6] 6 0-0 ♗d6 7 ♘c3 c6 8 ♘e5± ♕b6 9 ♗e3 ♘bd7 10 f4 ♗xe5 11 fxe5 ♘g4 [11 ... ♘xe5 12 ♘a4+-] 12 ♕d2 ♘xe3 13 ♕xe3 ♕xb2 14 ♘e2 ♕a3 15 ♘f4 ♕e7 16 ♖ab1 0-0-0 17 ♗e2 ♘b6 18 ♕b3 ♖d7 19 ♘d3 ♘c4 20 ♘c5! ♖c7 [20 ... ♘d2 21 ♕a4!] 21 ♕a4 [□ 21 ♗xc4 dxc4 22 ♕a4 Morphy] 21 ... b6 22 ♗xc4 bxc5 [22 ... dxc4 23 ♖xb6!+-] 23 ♗a6+ ♔d7 24 ♗b7 ♖d8?? 25

♗xc6+! **1-0** L/N316

## 1858-✕LM-13 viii 58
**Löwenthal,J.J.= Morphy,P.C.**
London [Löwenthal]

1 e4 e5 2 ♘f3 ♘f6 3 ♘xe5 d6 4 ♘f3 ♘xe4 5 d4 d5 6 ♗d3 ♗e7 7 0-0 ♘c6 8 c4 ♗e6 9 cxd5 ♗xd5 10 ♘c3 ♘xc3 11 bxc3 0-0 12 ♗f4 ♗d6 13 ♗xd6 ♕xd6 14 ♘g5 f5 15 c4 ♗xg2 [15 ... ♗f7 16 d5 ♘e7 17 ♖e1±] 16 ♔xg2 ♕g6 17 f4 h6 18 d5 ♘d8 19 h4 hxg5 20 hxg5 ♘f7 21 ♕f3 ♘h6? 22 ♕g3 ♘f7 [22 ... ♘g4 23 ♕xg4+-] 23 c5 ♖ad8 24 ♗c4 b5 [◻ 24 ... b6] 25 ♗b3 a5 26 ♖ae1 ♖fe8 27 ♖e6! ♖xe6 [27 ... ♕h5 28 ♗d1+-] 28 dxe6 a4 29 exf7+ ♔f8 30 ♖d1 ♖xd1 31 ♗xd1 ♕c6+ [◻ 31 ... ♕xf7] 32 ♗f3 ♕xc5 33 g6 ♕d6 34 ♕g5 ♕d2+ 35 ♔h3 ♕d3 36 ♕h5 [◻ 36 ♔g3] 36 ... ♔e7 37 ♕h4+ ♔d7 38 ♔g3 ♕d6 39 ♕h8? ♕xg6+ 40 ♔f2 ♕xf7 41 a3 ♕e7 42 ♔g3 ♕e1+ 43 ♔g2 ♕d2+ 44 ♔g3 ♕e1+ **½-½**

L/N3161

## 1858-✕LM-14 viii 58
**Morphy,P.C.+Löwenthal, J.J.**
London [Löwenthal]

1 e4 e5 2 ♘f3 ♘c6 3 ♗b5 a6 4 ♗a4 ♘f6 5 d4 exd4 6 e5 ♘e4 7 0-0 [7 ♕e2 ♘c5] 7 ... ♘c5 8 ♗xc6 dxc6 9 ♘xd4 ♘e6 10 ♘xe6 ♗xe6 11 ♕e2 ♗c5 12 ♘c3 ♕e7 13 ♘e4 h6 14 ♗e3 ♗xe3 15 ♕xe3 ♗f5 16 ♘g3 ♗xc2!? 17 f4 g6

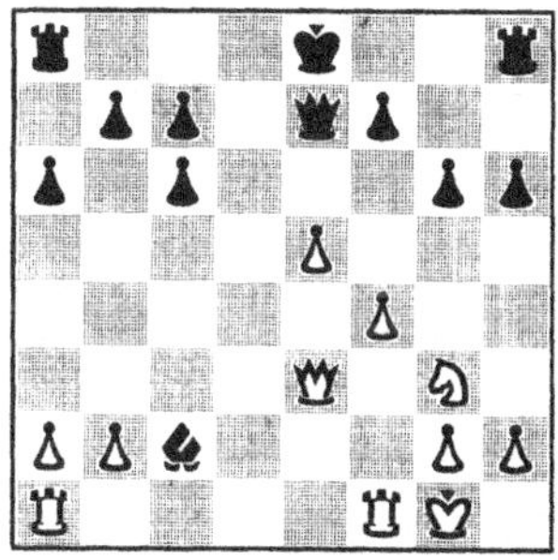

18 e6! ♗f5 [18 ... ♕xe6? 19 ♕c3+-] 19 ♘xf5 gxf5 20 exf7+ ♔xf7 21 ♕h3 ♕f6 22 ♖ae1 ♖he8 23 ♖e5! ♔g6 [23 ... ♖xe5? 24 fxe5 ♕xe5 25 ♖xf5++-] 24 ♖fe1 ♖xe5 25 ♖xe5 ♖d8 26 ♕g3+ ♔h7 27 h3 ♖d7 28 ♕e3 b6 29 ♔h2 c5 30 ♕e2 ♕g6 31 ♖e6 ♕g7 32 ♕h5 ♖d5 33 b3 b5 [33 ... ♕f8 34 g4±] 34 ♖xa6 ♖d6 35 ♕xf5+ ♕g6 36 ♕xg6+ ♔xg6 37 ♖a5 ♖b6 [◻ 37 ... c6] 38 g4 c6 39 ♔g3 h5 40 ♖a7 hxg4 41 hxg4 ♔f6 42 f5 ♔e5 43 ♖e7+ ♔d6 44 f6 ♖b8 45 g5 ♖f8 46 ♔f4 c4 47 bxc4 bxc4 48 ♔f5 c3 49 ♖e3 **1-0**

L/N3161

## MORPHY✕OWEN London
[1858-✕MO]

| | | | | | | | | |
|---|---|---|---|---|---|---|---|---|
| P.C. Morphy | 1 | ½ | 1 | 1 | 1 | ½ | 1 | 6 |
| J. Owen | 0 | ½ | 0 | 0 | 0 | ½ | 0 | 1 |

## 1858-✕MO-1 viii 58
**Owen, J.– Morphy, P.C.**
London [Löwenthal]

⟨♙f7⟩ 1 e4 d6 2 d4 ♘f6 3 ♗c4 ♘c6 4 ♘c3 e6 5 ♘f3 d5 6 ♗d3 ♗b4 7 ♗g5 h6 8 e5 [◻ 8 ♗xf6] 8 ... hxg5 9 ♗g6+ ♔f8 10 ♘xg5 ♖h6 11 ♗d3 ♔g8 12 exf6 ♕xf6 13 ♘f3 e5∓ 14 dxe5 ♘xe5 15 0-0? [15 ♘xe5 ♕xe5+, ♗xc3+∓] 15 ... ♕f4! 16 h4 ♘xf3+ 17 ♕xf3 ♕xh4 18 ♕xd5+ ♗e6 **0-1** L/N3161

## 1858-✕MO-2 viii 58
**Owen, J.= Morphy, P.C.**
London [Löwenthal]

⟨♙f7⟩ 1 e4 d6 2 d4 ♘f6 3 ♗c4 ♘c6 4 ♘c3 e6 5 ♘f3 d5 6 ♗d3 ♗b4 7 ♗g5 dxe4 8 ♗xe4 ♗d7 9 0-0 0-0 10 ♘e5 ♕e8 11 ♗xf6 ♖xf6 12 ♘g4 ♖f8 13 f4 ♕e7 14 ♖f3? ♘xd4 15 ♖h3 ♘f5 16 ♘e5 ♗e8 17 g4 ♘h4 [17 ... ♘h6 18 g5] 18 ♕e1 ♘g6 19 ♘xg6 hxg6 20 ♕g3 ♖d8 21 ♖f1 ♖d2 22 ♔h1 ♕d8 23 ♕e1 ♗b5 24 ♘xb5 ♖xf4 [24 ... ♖xh2+ 25 ♖xh2 ♗xe1 26 ♖xe1 ♖xf4 27 ♘c3 ♖xg4 28 ♖d1 ♕f6 29 ♗g2∞] 25 ♖xf4 ♖d1 26 ♕f1 ♖xf1+ 27 ♖xf1 ♕g5 28 ♗d3 ♕d5+ 29 ♖hf3 ♔h7 30 a3 ♗d2 31 ♔g2 e5 32 ♖d1 e4 33 ♖h3+ ♔g8 34 c4 ♕g5 35 ♗e2 e3 36 ♘xc7 ♕f4 37 ♗f3 [◻ 37 ♖f1] 37 ... ♕xc7 38 ♗d5+ ♔f8 39 ♖f1+ ♔e7 40 ♖f7+ ♔d6 41 ♖xe3 [41 ♖xc7 e2-+] 41 ... ♗xe3 42 ♖xc7 ♔xc7 43 ♔f3 ♗c1 44 b3 ♗xa3 45 h4 **½-½** L/N3161

## 1858-✕MO-3 vii 58
**Owen, J.– Morphy, P.C.**
London [Löwenthal]

⟨♙f7⟩ 1 e4 e6 2 d4 d5 3 e5 c5 4 c3 ♘c6 5 ♘h3? cxd4 6 ♗b5 dxc3 7 bxc3 ♗c5 8 0-0 ♘e7 9 ♘g5?! 0-0 10 ♕h5 h6 11 ♘f3 ♗d7 12 ♗d3 ♕e8! 13 ♕g4 ♖xf3!



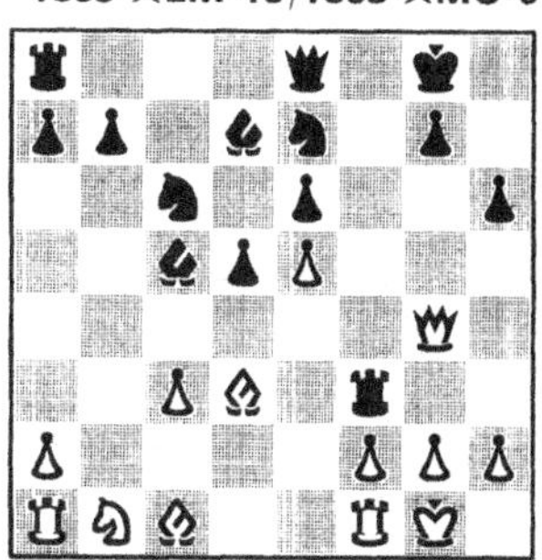

14 ♕xf3 [14 gxf3 ♘xe5-+] 14 ... ♘xe5 15 ♕g3 ♘xd3 16 ♕xd3 ♗b5 17 ♕h3 ♗xf1 18 ♕xe6+ ♔h7 19 ♔xf1 ♕h5 20 ♗f4 ♖f8 21 ♗g3 ♘f5! **0-1** L/N3161

## 1858-✕MO-4 viii 58
**Owen, J.– Morphy, P.C.**
London [Löwenthal]

⟨♙f7⟩ 1 e4 e6 2 d4 d5 3 e5 c5 4 c3 ♘c6 5 ♘f3 ♕b6 6 ♗d3 g6 7 0-0 ♗d7 8 a4 a5 9 ♘a3 c4 10 ♗c2 ♘h6 11 ♘b5 ♘f7 12 b3 cxb3 13 ♗xb3 ♗e7 14 ♖e1 [◻ 14 c4] 14 ... 0-0 15 ♗xd5 exd5 16 e6 ♗e8 17 exf7+ ♖xf7 18 ♗g5 ♗d7 19 ♖b1 ♕d8 20 ♗xe7 ♖xe7 21 ♕b3 ♗f5 22 ♖bc1 ♗d3 23 ♘a3 ♗e2 24 c4 ♗xf3 25 ♖xe7 ♕xe7 26 ♕xf3 dxc4 27 ♕c3 ♖e8 28 ♕xc4+ ♔g7 29 ♘c2 ♕g5 30 ♖d1 ♖e4 31 ♕c3 ♕f6 32 ♕d2 ♕d6 33 g3 h5 34 f3 ♖e7 35 ♕g5 ♘e5! 36 ♔f2 ♘xf3! 37 ♔xf3 ♕c6+ 38 d5 ♖f7+ 39 ♔g2 ♕xc2+ 40 ♖d2 ♕e4+ 41 ♔h3 ♕e1 42 d6 ♕f1+ 43 ♖g2 ♖d7 44 ♕e5+ ♕f6 45 ♕b2 ♖xd6 46 ♕xb7+ ♔h6 47 ♕b5 g5! **0-1** L/N3161

## 1858-✕MO-5 viii 58
**Owen, J.– Morphy, P.C.**
London [Löwenthal]

⟨♙f7⟩ 1 e4 e6 2 d4 d5 3 ♗d3 [◻ 3 ♕h5+ g6 4 ♕e5 ♘f6 5 ♗g5 ♗e7 6 ♗b5+ ♘c6 (6 ... c6 7 exd5 cxb5 8 d6±; 6 ... ♕f7 7 ♘c3 ♘xe4 8 ♘xe4 dxe4 9 ♗xe7 ♕xe7 10 ♕g7+ ♔d6 11 c4±) 7 exd5 a6 8 dxc6 axb5 9 cxb7+-] 3 ... g6 4 ♘f3 c5 5 c3 ♘c6 6 0-0 ♕b6 7 exd5 exd5 8 ♖e1+ ♗e7 9 ♘g5 ♘f6 10 ♘xh7?! ♖xh7 11 ♗xg6+ ♖f7 12 ♗g5 ♗g4! 13 ♕c2 [13 f3 ♗h5] 13 ... ♔f8 14 ♗xf7 ♔xf7 15 h3 ♗h5 16 ♗xf6 ♗g6! 17 ♕e2 ♗xf6 18 ♕e6+ ♔g7 19 ♕d7+ ♔h8 20 ♕d6 ♔g7 21 ♘d2 cxd4 22 ♘f3 ♘e5!

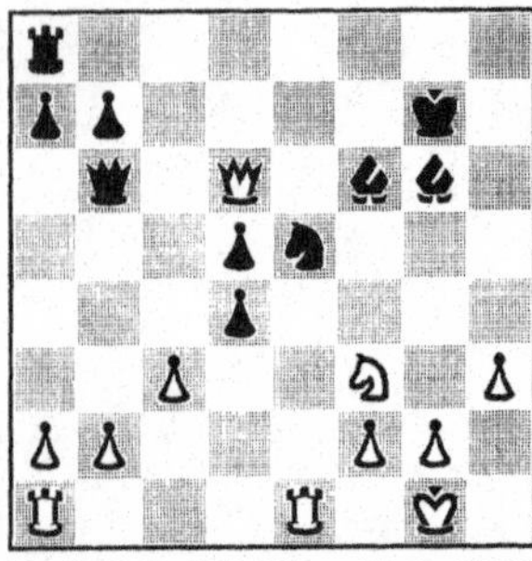

23 ♕a3 ♘xf3+ 24 gxf3 dxc3 25 bxc3 ♖g8 26 ♖e3 ♔h8 27 ♔h1 d4 28 cxd4 ♗xd4 29 ♖ae1 ♗xe3 30 ♖xe3 ♕b1+ 31 ♔h2 ♗e4! 32 ♕c3+ ♖g7 33 ♖e1 ♕b6 34 ♖e3 ♕d6+ 35 ♔h1 ♗xf3+ 36 ♖xf3 ♕d1+ 37 ♔h2 ♕g1# **0-1** L/N3161

**1858-✕MO-6** viii 58
**Owen, J.= Morphy, P.C.**
London [Löwenthal]

⟨♙f7⟩ 1 e4 e6 2 d4 d5 3 ♗d3 g6 4 ♘f3 c5 5 c3 ♘c6 6 e5 ♕b6 7 0-0 ♗d7 8 ♗e3? c4 [8 ... ♕xb2 9 ♕c2!] 9 ♗c2 ♕xb2 10 ♘bd2 ♕xc3 11 ♖b1 ♘b4 12 ♘e1 ♗h6 13 ♗xh6 ♘xh6 14 ♖c1 ♕xd4 15 ♘ef3 ♕c5 16 ♗e4 0-0 [16 ... dxe4 17 ♘xe4, 18 ♘d6+] 17 ♘xc4? dxe4 18 ♕xd7 exf3 19 ♕xe6+ ♔h8 20 ♘d6 ♕b6 21 g3 ♖ae8? 22 ♕h3 ♘f5 23 ♘xe8 ♖xe8 24 ♖fd1 ♖d8 25 g4 ♘d4 26 ♔h1 ♘e2? [◻ 26 ... ♕e6] 27 ♕xf3 ♘xc1 28 ♖d6 ♘c6 29 ♕f6+ ♔g8 30 ♕e6+ ½-½ L/N3161

**1858-✕MO-7** viii 58
**Owen, J.– Morphy, P.C.**
London [Löwenthal]

⟨♙f7⟩ 1 e4 ♘c6 2 d4 e5 3 ♘f3 [◻ 3 dxe5] 3 ... exd4 4 ♗c4 ♕f6 5 0-0 d6 6 ♘g5 ♘h6 7 c3 [7 f4!] 7 ... ♗g4 8 f3 ♗d7 9 ♗d5 dxc3 10 ♘xc3 ♗e7 11 ♘b5 ♗d8 12 f4 ♘e7 13 ♘c3 [13 e5 dxe5 14 fxe5 ♕b6+ 15 ♔h1 ♘xd5 16 ♕xd5 ♕xb5−+] 13 ... ♗g4 14 ♕b3 c6 15 e5 [15 ♕xb7 ♖c8 16 ♗~ ♗b6+ 17 ♔h1 ♖c7] 15 ... dxe5 16 ♘ce4 ♗b6+ 17 ♔h1 ♕g6 18 ♗f7+ ♘xf7 19 ♘xf7 ♘d5 [19 ... ♖f8? 20 ♘ed6+ ♔d7 21 ♘xe5+−] 20 ♘ed6+ ♔e7 21 f5 ♕h5 22 ♗g5+ ♔d7 23 ♕g3 ♗c7 24 ♕xe5 ♖ae8 25 ♕xg7 [25 ♕g3 ♖hf8]

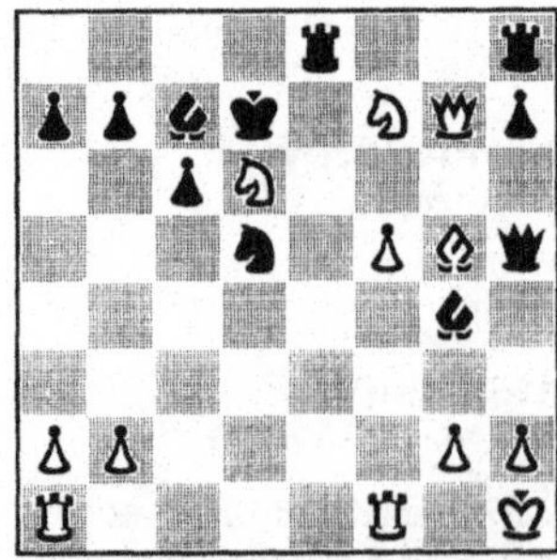

25 ... ♗xd6 [◻ 25 ... ♖hg8] 26 ♘e5+ ♔c8 27 ♕d7+ ♔b8 28 ♕xd6+ ♔a8 29 ♗f4 ♕xf5 30 ♘xc6 ♗h3 31 gxh3 ♕e4+ 32 ♔g1 ♘xf4 33 ♖xf4 ♖hg8+ **0-1** L/N3161

**1858-★AD-1** xii 58
**Anderssen, A.+ de Rivière, J.A. de**
Paris

1 e4 e5 2 ♘f3 ♘c6 3 d4 exd4 4 ♗c4 ♘f6 5 ♘g5 ♘e5 6 ♗b3 h6 7 f4 hxg5 8 fxe5 ♘xe4 9 0-0 d5 10 exd6 f5 11 ♘d2 ♕xd6 12 ♘xe4 ♕xh2+ 13 ♔f2 fxe4 14 ♕xd4 ♗e7 15 ♕xe4 ♗f5 16 ♗f7+ ♔xf7 17 ♕xf5+ ♔g8 18 ♕d5+ ♔h7 19 ♕e4+ ♔h6 20 ♗e3 ♖hf8+ 21 ♔e2 ♕h5+ 22 g4 ♕h2+ 23 ♖f2 ♖xf2+ 24 ♗xf2 ♖f8 25 ♖h1 ♖xf2+ 26 ♔d3 ♖d2+ 27 ♔c4 ♖xc2+ 28 ♔d5 ♗f6 29 ♔e6 ♗xb2 30 ♔f7 ♖f2+ 31 ♔g8

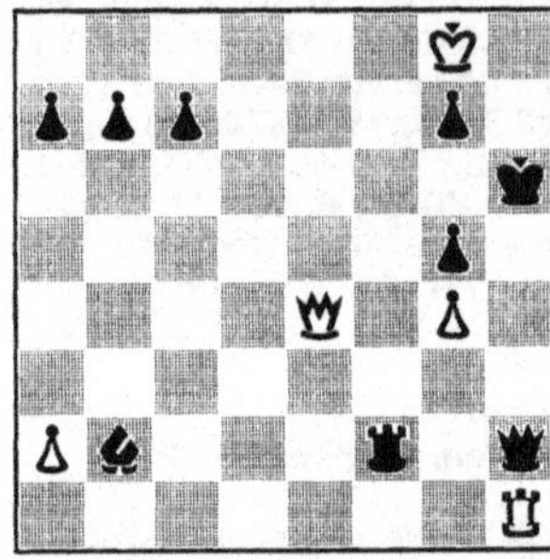

**1-0** +9

**1858-★AE-1** 23 iv 58
**Eichborn, L.+ Anderssen, A.**
Breslau

1 e4 e5 2 ♘f3 d5 3 exd5 e4 4 ♕e2 f5 5 ♘e5 ♘f6 6 ♕b5+ ♘bd7 7 d4 a6 8 ♕a4 ♗d6 9 ♗g5 0-0 10 ♘xd7 ♗xd7 11 ♕b3 h6 12 ♗xf6 ♕xf6 13 c3 ♕g5 14 ♘a3 ♖ae8 15 ♘c2 e3 16 fxe3 ♖xe3+ 17 ♘xe3 ♕xe3+ 18 ♗e2 ♖e8 19 ♕c2 ♗b5 20 c4 ♗b4+ 21 ♔f1 ♗d7 22 ♖d1 f4 23 ♕d3 ♕e7 24 ♗h5 f3 25 ♗xe8 fxg2+ 26 ♔xg2 ♕g5+ 27 ♕g3 **1-0** L/N3034

**1858-★AM-1** xii 58
**Anderssen, A.– Morphy, P.C.**
Paris [Löwenthal]

1 e4 e5 2 f4 exf4 3 ♗c4 ♘f6!? 4 e5 d5 5 ♗b3 ♘e4 6 ♘f3 ♗g4 7 0-0 ♘c6 8 ♗a4 [8 d4? ♘xd4] 8 ... g5 9 ♗xc6+ bxc6 10 d4 c5 11 c3 ♗e7 12 b4 cxb4 13 cxb4 0-0 14 ♕b3 [14 a3 a5∓] 14 ... ♖b8! 15 a3 c5 16 ♘c3 ♘xc3 17 ♕xc3 cxb4 18 axb4 ♗xb4 19 ♕d3 a5 20 h4 h6 21 hxg5 hxg5 22 g3 ♖b6 23 ♖a2 ♖g6 24 ♖g2 ♗h3 25 e6 ♗xg2 26 exf7+ ♔g7 27 ♔xg2 ♕c8!

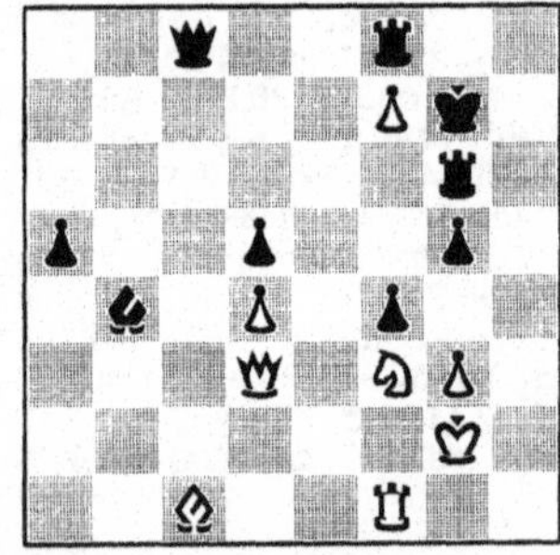

28 ♘e5 ♖h6 29 gxf4 ♖fh8 30 fxg5 ♖h2+ 31 ♔g1 ♖h1+ 32 ♔f2 ♖8h2+ 33 ♔e3 ♖h3+ 34 ♘f3 ♖xf3+ 35 ♖xf3 ♕xc1+ **0-1** L/N3161

**1858-★AM-2** xii 58
**Morphy, P.C.+ Anderssen, A.**
Paris [Löwenthal]

1 e4 e5 2 f4 exf4 3 ♘f3 g5 4 h4 g4 5 ♘e5 ♘f6 6 ♘xg4 ♘xe4 7 d3 ♘g3 8 ♗xf4 ♘xh1 [8 ... ♕e7+ 9 ♗e2 ♕b4+ 10 ♕d2 (10 ♗d2 ♕b6) 10 ... ♕xd2 11 ♘xd2 ♘xh1 12 ♗e5 f6 13 ♘xf6+±] 9 ♕e2+ ♕e7 10 ♘f6+ ♔d8 11 ♗xc7+ ♔xc7 12 ♘d5+ ♔d8 13 ♘xe7 ♗xe7 14 ♕g4 d6 [◻ 14 ... ♖e8] 15 ♕f4 ♖g8 16 ♕xf7 ♗xh4+ 17 ♔d2 ♖e8 18 ♘a3 ♘a6 [◻ 18 ... ♘g3 19 ♘b5 ♗e7] 19 ♕h5 ♗f6 20 ♕xh1 ♗xb2 21 ♕h4+ ♔d7 22 ♖b1 **1-0** L/N3161

**1858-★AM-3** xii 58
**Anderssen, A.– Morphy, P.C.**
Paris [Löwenthal]

1 e4 e5 2 f4 exf4 3 ♘f3 g5 4 h4 g4 5 ♘e5 ♘f6 6 ♘xg4 d5 7 ♘xf6+ ♕xf6 8 ♘c3 ♕g6 9 ♕f3 ♗d6 10 ♗d3 [10 ♘xd5 ♗g4? 11 ♕xg4+−] 10 ... ♗g4 11 ♕f2 ♘d7 12 exd5 f5 13 ♗b5 a6 14 ♗xd7+? [◻ 14 ♗e2] 14 ... ♔xd7 15 d3 ♖ae8+! 16 ♔f1 ♖hg8 17 ♖h2 [17 ♗xf4? ♗xf4 18 ♕xf4 ♗e2+ −+] 17 ... f3 18 g3 ♗h5 19 ♗g5 [19 ♗f4 ♗xf4 20 gxf4 ♖e2 21 ♘xe2 fxe2+ 22 ♔e1 ♕g1+ −+ Morphy] 19 ... h6 20 ♕a7 hxg5 21 ♘a4 gxh4 22 ♕xb7 hxg3 **0-1** L/N3161

**1858-★AM-4** xii 58
**Morphy,P.C.+ Anderssen,A.**
Paris [Löwenthal]
1 e4 e5 2 f4 exf4 3 ♘f3 g5 4 ♗c4 ♗g7 5 0-0 d6 6 c3 ♘c6 [□ 6 ... h6] 7 ♕b3 ♕e7 8 d4 ♘f6 [□ 8 ... h6] 9 ♘xg5 ♘xe4 10 ♗xf7+ ♔d8 11 ♘xe4 ♕xe4 12 ♗xf4 ♗h3! 13 gxh3 ♘xd4 14 ♘d2! ♘e2+ 15 ♔f2 ♕xf4+ 16 ♔xe2 ♕g5 17 ♖ae1 ♗h6 18 ♕d5 ♖e8+ 19 ♔d1 **1-0** L/N3161

**1858-★AM-5** xii 58
**Morphy,P.C.+ Anderssen,A.**
Paris [Löwenthal]
1 e4 e5 2 f4 exf4 3 ♘f3 g5 4 ♗c4 ♗g7 5 0-0 d6 6 c3 ♘c6 7 ♕b3 ♕e7 [7 ... ♘a5 8 ♗xf7+ ♔f8 9 ♕d5 c6 10 ♕xg5 ♕b6+ 11 d4 ♔xf7 12 ♕xf4+ ♘f6 (12 ... ♔e7 13 ♘g5 ♘f6 14 e5 dxe5 15 ♕xe5++-) 13 e5 dxe5 14 ♘xe5+ ♔e7 15 b4±] 8 d4 a6 [□ 8 ... h6] 9 ♘xg5 ♕xg5 10 ♗xf7+ ♔d8 [10 ... ♔f8 11 ♗xf4, 12 ♗xg8+-] 11 ♗xf4 ♕e7 12 ♗xg8 ♗g4 13 ♘d2 ♔d7 14 ♗d5 ♘d8 15 ♗xb7 ♘xb7 16 ♕xb7 a5 17 ♗xd6! ♗xd4+ 18 cxd4 ♕xd6 19 ♖f7+ **1-0** L/N3161

**1858-★AM-6** xii 58
**Anderssen,A.+ Morphy,P.C.**
Paris [Löwenthal]
1 e4 e5 2 f4 exf4 3 ♘f3 g5 4 h4 g4 5 ♘e5 ♘f6 6 ♘xg4 d5 7 ♘xf6+ ♕xf6 8 ♕e2 ♗d6 9 ♘c3 c6 10 d4! [10 exd5+ ♔d8 △ 11 ... ♖e8] 10 ... ♕xd4 11 ♗d2 ♖g8 12 exd5+ ♔d8 13 0-0-0! ♗g4 14 ♕e4 ♕xe4 15 ♘xe4 ♗xd1 16 ♘xd6 ♗h5 17 ♗xf4 cxd5 18 ♘xb7+ ♔e7 19 ♗b5 ♖xg2 20 ♖e1+ ♔f6 21 ♖e8 ♗g6 22 ♘d6! ♘c6 [22 ... ♗e4 23 ♗e5+, 24 ♘xe4+-] 23 ♖xa8 ♖xc2+ 24 ♔d1 ♘d4 25 ♖e8 ♗h5+ 26 ♔e1 ♘f3+ 27 ♔f1 ♖xb2 28 ♗e2 ♖xa2 29 ♗g5+ ♘xg5 30 hxg5+ ♔xg5 31 ♖e5+ ♔f6 32 ♖xh5 **1-0** L/N3161

**1858-★AM-7 ●○** 27 viii 58
**Morphy,P.C.= Avery,T.**
Birmingham [Löwenthal]
1 e4 c5 2 d4 cxd4 3 ♘f3 ♘c6 4 ♘xd4 e6 5 ♗e3 ♘f6 6 ♗d3 d5 7 ♘xc6 bxc6 8 e5 ♘d7 9 f4 ♗a6 10 0-0 [10 ♗xa6 ♕a5+] 10 ... ♗xd3 11 ♕xd3 ♗c5 12 ♘d2 ♗xe3+ 13 ♕xe3 ♕b6 14 ♖ae1 0-0 15 b3 f6 16 exf6 ♖xf6 17 g3 ♖af8 18 ♔g2 ♕xe3 19 ♖xe3 g6 20 ♖fe1 e5! 21 ♖1e2 exf4 22 ♖e7 ♖8f7 23 gxf4 ♖xf4 24 ♖e8+ ♔g7 25 ♖c8 ♖4f6 26 ♖c7 ♘f8 27 ♖ee7 ♖xe7 28 ♖xe7+ ♖f7 29 ♖e8 ♘d7 30 ♘f3 ♖f8 31 ♖e7+ ♖f7 32 ♖e8 ♖f8 33 ♖e7+ ♖f7 **½-½** L/N3161

**1858-★AP-1** iv 58
**Pitschel, K.= Anderssen, A.**
Leipzig
1 e4 e5 2 ♘f3 ♘c6 3 d4 exd4 4 ♗c4 ♗c5 5 c3 ♘f6 6 e5 ♘e4 7 cxd4 ♗b4+ 8 ♗d2 d5 9 ♗xb4 ♘xb4 10 ♕a4+ ♘c6 11 ♗e2 0-0 12 ♘c3 ♗e6 13 0-0 f5 14 ♖fd1 ♔h8 15 ♕c2 g5 16 a3 g4 17 ♘e1 ♕h4 18 ♗f1 f4 19 ♘xe4 ♗f5 20 f3 dxe4 21 fxe4 ♗g6 22 ♖d2 f3 23 ♖ad1 ♘xd4 24 g3 ♘xc2 25 gxh4 ♘e3 26 ♖c1 ♗xe4 27 ♔f2 ♘xf1 28 ♔xf1 c6 29 ♖c4 ♗f5 30 ♘c2 ♗xc2 31 ♖cxc2 ♖ae8 32 ♖c4 h5 33 ♖e4 ♖f5 34 e6 ♖f6 35 e7 ♔g7 36 ♖d7 ♔f7 37 ♖e5 ♖e6 38 ♖f5+ ♔g6 39 ♖g5+ ♔f6 40 ♖xb7 ♖e8xe7 41 ♖xe7 ♖xe7 42 ♖xh5 ♖e2 43 ♖g5 ♖xb2 44 ♖xg4 ♔f5 45 h3 ♔e5 46 h5 ♖b7 47 ♔f2 ♖f7 48 h6 ♖h7 49 ♖g6 c5 50 ♔xf3 ♔d4 51 ♖d6+ ♔c3 52 ♔g4 ♔b3 53 ♔g5 ♖c7 54 ♔g6 c4 55 h7 ♖c8 56 ♔g7 ♖c7+ 57 ♔g6 ♖c8 **½-½** +9

**1858-★AS-1** iv 58
**Saalbach, A.– Anderssen, A.**
Leipzig
1 e4 e5 2 ♘f3 ♘c6 3 ♗c4 ♗c5 4 c3 ♘f6 5 d4 exd4 6 cxd4 ♗b4+ 7 ♗d2 ♗xd2+ 8 ♘bxd2 d5 9 exd5 ♘xd5 10 0-0 0-0 11 ♖e1 ♘f4 12 ♕c2 ♕f6 13 ♘f1 ♘xg2 14 ♔xg2 ♕xf3+ 15 ♔g1 ♘xd4 16 ♕e4 b5 17 ♗d3 f5 18 ♕xd4 ♗b7 **0-1** +9

**1858-★BB-1** iv 58
**Staunton,H. & Barnes,T.W.– Bird,H.E. & Owen,J.**
London [Boden]
1 e4 e5 2 ♘f3 ♘c6 3 ♗c4 ♗c5 4 b4 ♗xb4 5 c3 ♗c5 6 0-0 d6 7 d4 exd4 8 cxd4 ♗b6 9 d5 ♘a5 10 ♗e2 [□ 10 ♗d3] 10 ... ♘e7 11 ♗b2 f6 12 ♕d2 0-0 13 ♘d4 ♘g6 14 ♔h1 ♗d7 15 f4 c5 16 ♘c2 ♖c8 17 ♘ba3 ♗c7 18 ♖ae1 ♖e8 19 ♗f3 b5 20 f5 ♘e5 21 ♘e3 b4 22 ♗xe5 ♖xe5 23 ♘ac4 ♘xc4 24 ♘xc4 ♖e7 25 ♕f4 ♗b5 26 ♗e2 ♗xc4 27 ♗xc4 ♖e5 28 ♖f3 ♕d7! 29 ♖g3 [29 ♖h3 ♖ce8 30 ♕h4 ♕xf5!] 29 ... ♖ce8 30 ♕g4 ♖8e7 [□ 30 ... ♕f7] 31 h4 ♕e8 32 h5 ♔h8 33 ♖ee3 ♗d8∓ [Staunton, H. & Barnes, T.W. v Bird, H.E. & Hampton, J.W.] 34 h6 g5 [34 ... gxh6? 35 ♕h4 ♕f8 36 ♖g4 △ 37 ♖eg3=] 35 fxg6 ♖xe4!? [35 hxg6!] 36 ♕f3? [36 g7+] 36 ... ♖h4+ 37 ♔g1 ♖xe3 38 ♕xe3 [□ 38 g7+] 38 ... ♕xe3+ 39 ♖xe3 hxg6-+ 40 ♖e8+ [40 ♗d3 c4-+; 40 ♗d3 ♗b6-+] 40 ... ♔h7 41 ♖xd8 ♖xc4 42 ♖xd6 ♖d4 [42 ... f5-+] 43 ♖xf6 ♖xd5 44 ♖f7+ ♔xh6 45 ♖xa7 c4 46 ♔f2 [46 ♖b7 c3] 46 ... ♖d2+ 47 ♔f3 c3 48 ♖b7 c2 49 ♖c7 ♖d3+ 50 ♔e2 ♖c3 **0-1** M392

**1858-★BM-1**
**Barnes, T.W.– Morphy, P.C.**
London [Löwenthal]
1 e4 e5 2 ♘f3 d6 3 d4 exd4 4 ♘xd4 ♘f6 [□ 4 ... d5 5 e5 c5 6 ♗b5+ ♗d7 7 e6 ♗xb5 (7 ... fxe6 8 ♘xe6 ♕e7 9 ♗xd7+ ♘xd7 10 0-0±) 8 exf7+ ♔xf7 9 ♘xb5 ♕e8+ 10 ♕e2 ♕xe2+ 11 ♔xe2=] 5 ♗d3 ♗e7 6 ♘c3 0-0 7 0-0 c5 8 ♘de2 ♘c6 9 f4 a6 10 a4 ♗g4 11 h3 ♗xe2 12 ♕xe2 ♖e8 13 ♕f2 ♖c8 14 g4 ♘b4 15 b3 d5! 16 ♔h1 [16 e5 c4 17 bxc4 ♗c5 18 e3 d4 19 exf6 ♖xe3∓] 16 ... dxe4 17 ♘xe4 ♘xe4 18 ♗xe4 ♗f6 19 ♗xb7 ♗xa1 20 ♗xc8 ♕xc8 21 ♗e3 ♕c6+ 22 ♔h2 ♗d4 **0-1** L/N3161

**1858-★BM-2** vii 58
**Morphy, P.C.– Barnes, T.W.**
London [Löwenthal]
1 e4 f6 2 d4 e6 3 ♗d3 ♘e7 4 ♗e3 d5 5 ♘c3 dxe4 6 ♘xe4 ♘d5 7 ♘h3 ♗e7 8 ♕h5+ g6 9 ♕h6 ♗f8 10 ♕h4 ♗g7 11 0-0 0-0 12 c4 ♘xe3 13 fxe3 f5 14 ♘eg5 h6 15 ♘f3 e5! [15 ... g5∞] 16 ♕xd8 ♖xd8 17 ♗c2 exd4 18 exd4 ♗xd4+ 19 ♘xd4 ♖xd4 20 ♖fe1 ♔f7 21 c5 ♗e6 22 ♖ad1 ♘c6 23 ♖xd4 ♘xd4 24 ♗a4 g5 25 ♖d1 ♖d8 26 a3 f4 27 ♘f2 ♘e2+ 28 ♔f1 ♖xd1+ 29 ♗xd1 ♘d4 30 ♔e1 ♔f6 31 ♔d2 ♘b3+ 32 ♗xb3 ♗xb3 33 ♘e4+ ♔g6 34 g3 h5 35 ♘f2 ♔f5 36 ♔c3 ♗d5 37 ♔d4 c6 38 b4 ♗g2 39 gxf4 ♔xf4 40 a4 ♗f1 41 ♘e4 h4 42 ♘d2 ♗e2 43 ♘e4 g4 44 ♘f2 ♔f3 45 ♘e4 ♗f1 [45 ... g3-+] 46 ♔e5 ♗d3 47 ♘g5+ ♔g2 48 ♔d6 ♔xh2 49 ♔c7 ♔g3 50 ♔xb7 h3 **0-1** L/N3161

**1858-★BM-3** vii 58
**Barnes, T.W.– Morphy, P.C.**
London [Löwenthal]
1 e4 e5 2 ♘f3 ♘c6 3 ♗b5 ♘f6 4 d4 exd4 5 e5 ♘e4 6 0-0 a6 7 ♗a4 ♘c5 8 ♗xc6 dxc6 9 ♘xd4 ♗e7 10 ♘c3 [□ 10 f4] 10 ... 0-0 11 ♗e3 f6 12 exf6 ♖xf6 13 ♕e2 ♖g6 14 ♔h1 ♗d6 15 ♖ad1 ♕h4 16 f4 ♗g4 17 ♘f3 ♕h5 18 ♗xc5 ♗xc5 19 ♘e4 ♗b6 20 ♘eg5 h6 21 ♕c4+ ♔h8 22 ♘f7+ ♔h7 23 ♘7e5 ♖f6 24 ♘xg4 ♕xg4 25 ♘e5 ♕e6 26 ♕e4+ ♕f5 27 ♕xf5+ ♖xf5 28 g4 ♖f6 29 f5 ♖e8

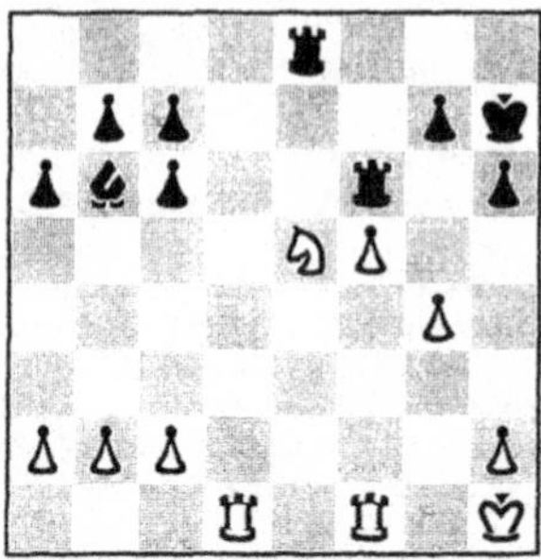

30 ♘g6 ♖e2 31 ♖d8 ♖xg6 32 fxg6+ ♔xg6 33 ♖d7 ♖xc2 34 ♖ff7 ♗d4 35 ♖xc7 ♖xb2 36 ♖xb7 ♖xa2 37 h4 a5 38 h5+ ♔g5 39 ♖xg7+ ♔h4 40 ♖ge7 a4 **0-1**

L/N3161

**1858-★BM-4**

**Morphy, P.C.+ Barnes, T.W.**

London [Löwenthal]

1 e4 e5 2 ♘f3 d6 3 d4 exd4 4 ♗c4 ♗e7 [□ 4 ... ♘f6] 5 c3 d3 6 ♕b3 ♗e6 7 ♗xe6 fxe6 8 ♕xb7 ♘d7 9 ♕b5 ♘f6 10 ♘g5 ♖b8 11 ♕a4 0-0 12 ♘xe6 ♘c5 13 ♘xc5 dxc5 14 ♕c4+ ♔h8 15 0-0 ♘g4 16 f4 d2 17 ♗xd2 ♖xb2 18 h3 ♖xd2 19 ♘xd2 ♘e3 20 ♕e2 ♘xf1 21 ♖xf1 ♕d7 22 ♘c4 ♕b5 23 e5 ♗h4 24 f5 ♗e7 25 ♕g4 ♕d7 26 ♖d1! ♕xf5 27 ♕xf5 ♖xf5 28 ♖d7 ♗f8 29 e6 **1-0** L/N3161

**1858-★BM-5**

**Morphy, P.C.– Barnes, T.W.**

London [Löwenthal]

1 e4 e5 2 f4 ♗c5 3 ♘f3 d6 4 b4 ♗b6 5 ♗c4 ♘f6 6 ♕e2 ♘c6 7 c3 0-0 8 d3 exf4 9 ♗xf4 d5∓ 10 ♗b3 dxe4 11 dxe4 ♗g4 [□ 11 ... ♘xe4 12 ♕xe4 ♖e8 13 ♗e5 (13 ♘e5 ♘xe5 14 ♗xe5 ♕e7–+) 13 ... ♕e7–+] 12 ♘bd2 ♘h5 13 ♗e3 ♘e5 14 0-0-0 ♘d3+ [□ 14 ... ♕d3∓] 15 ♔c2 ♘hf4 16 ♗xf4 ♘xf4 17 ♕f1 ♕e7 18 h3 ♗h5 19 g4 ♗g6 20 ♔b2 ♖ad8 21 ♘d4 ♗xd4 22 ♕xf4 ♗e5 23 ♕e3 ♕xb4 24 h4 h5 25 ♘c4 ♕e7 26 ♖xd8 ♖xd8 27 gxh5 ♗xh5 28 ♕g5 ♕xg5 29 hxg5 ♗f3 30 ♖f1 [30 ♖h3 ♗g2] 30 ... ♗e2 31 ♘xe5 ♗xf1 32 g6 ♔f8 33 gxf7 ♖d6 34 ♘f3 ♖f6 35 ♘g5 ♖f2+ 36 ♔a3 c5 37 ♗d5 b5 38 ♘h7+ ♔e7 39 f8♕+ ♖xf8 40 ♘xf8 ♔xf8 41 e5 g5 42 ♗f3 ♗h3 43 c4 bxc4! 44 ♔b2 g4 45 ♗d5 g3 46 ♔c3 ♗e6! [46 ... g2 47 ♗xg2=] 47 ♗c6 ♔e7 48 a3 ♗d7 49 ♗d5 ♗e6 50 ♗f3 ♔d7 51 ♔d2 ♗h3 52 ♔e3 ♔e6 53 ♗e2 c3 **0-1** L/N3161

**1858-★BM-6**

**Barnes, T.W.– Morphy, P.C.**

London [Löwenthal]

1 e4 e5 2 ♘f3 d6 3 d4 f5 4 dxe5 fxe4 5 ♘g5 d5 6 e6 ♗c5 7 ♘f7 [□ 7 ♘xe4] 7 ... ♕f6 8 ♗e3 d4! 9 ♗g5 ♕f5 10 ♘xh8 ♕xg5 11 ♗c4 ♘c6 12 ♘f7 ♕xg2 13 ♖f1 ♘f6 14 f3?! ♘b4 15 ♘a3 ♗xe6! 16 ♗xe6 ♘d3+ 17 ♕xd3 [17 cxd3 ♗b4+–+] 17 ... exd3 18 0-0-0 ♗xa3 19 ♗b3 d2+ 20 ♔b1 ♗c5 21 ♘e5 ♔f8 22 ♘d3 ♖e8 23 ♘xc5 ♕xf1 **0-1** L/N3161

**1858-★BM-7**

**Morphy, P.C.+ Barnes, T.W.**

London [Löwenthal]

1 e4 e5 2 ♗c4 ♘f6 3 ♘f3 ♘xe4 4 ♘c3!? ♘xc3 5 dxc3 f6 6 0-0 ♘c6? [□ 6 ... ♕e7∓; 6 ... d6 7 ♘h4 ♕e7 8 f4 ♗e6∓] 7 ♘h4 ♕e7 8 ♘f5 ♕c5 9 ♗b3 d5 10 ♗e3 ♕a5 11 ♘h4 ♗e6 12 ♕h5+ g6 [□ 12 ... ♗f7] 13 ♘xg6 ♗f7 14 ♕h4 ♗xg6 15 ♕xf6 ♖g8 16 ♖ad1 ♗e7 17 ♕e6! ♗f7 18 ♕h3 ♘d8 19 f4 e4 20 ♖xd5! ♗xd5 21 ♕h5+ ♔f8 22 ♗xd5 ♖g7 23 b4 ♕a6 24 f5 ♘f7 25 f6! ♗xf6 26 b5 ♕d6 27 ♗xf7 b6 [27 ... ♖xf7? 28 ♗c5+–] 28 ♗h6 ♔e7 29 ♗xg7 ♗xg7 30 ♗b3 ♖f8 31 ♖f7+ ♖xf7 32 ♕xf7+ ♔d8 33 ♕xg7 ♕d1+ 34 ♔f2 ♕d2+ 35 ♔g3 e3 36 ♕f6+ ♔c8 37 ♗e6+ **1-0**

L/N3161

**1858-★BM-8**

**Barnes, T.W.– Morphy, P.C.**

London [Maróczy]

1 e4 e5 2 ♘f3 ♘c6 3 ♗b5 a6 4 ♗a4 ♘f6 5 ♘c3 ♗b4 6 ♘d5 b5 7 ♗b3 d6 8 0-0 ♗g4 9 c3 ♗a5 10 d4 exd4 11 ♘xf6+ ♕xf6 12 ♗d5 ♘e5 13 ♗xa8 [13 ♗g5!] 13 ... ♘xf3+ 14 gxf3 ♗xf3 15 ♕d2 dxc3 16 ♕g5 cxb2 17 ♗c6+ ♔e7 18 ♕xf6+ gxf6 19 ♗f4 ♖g8+ 20 ♗g3 bxa1♕ 21 ♖xa1 f5 22 a4 ♗b6 23 axb5 f4 24 bxa6 fxg3 25 hxg3 ♖xg3+ 26 ♔h2 ♖g6 27 ♖f1 ♗d4 28 ♔h3 ♗e5 29 ♔h4 ♗f4 30 a7 ♖h6# **0-1**

L/N3202

**168** Morphy, P.C. ●○ Paris, 27 ix 1858 M979.BL

**1858-★BM-9 ∞○** 27 ix 58
**Morphy, P.C.+ Baucher, H.**
Paris [Löwenthal]

1 e4 e5 2 ♘f3 d6 3 d4 exd4 4 ♕xd4 ♘c6 5 ♗b5 ♗d7 6 ♗xc6 ♗xc6 7 ♗g5 f6 8 ♗h4 ♘h6 9 ♘c3 ♗e7 10 0-0 0-0 11 ♕c4+ ♔h8 12 ♘d4 ♕d7 13 ♖ad1 ♖f7 14 f4 a5 15 f5 ♖ff8 16 ♘e6 ♖g8 17 a4 ♘g4 18 ♕e2 ♘e5 19 ♗g3 ♕c8 20 ♗xe5 dxe5 21 ♖f3!

21 ... ♗d7 22 ♖h3 h6 [22 ... ♖e8 23 ♕h5 h6 24 ♘xg7 ♗f8 (24 ... ♔xg7 25 ♖g3++-) 25 ♕xh6+ ♔g8 26 ♕h7+ ♔f7 27 ♘h5+ ♗g7 28 ♕xg7#] 23 ♕d2! ♔h7 24 ♕xd7 ♗d6 25 ♖xh6+! ♔xh6 26 ♖d3 ♔h5 27 ♕f7+ **1-0** L/N3161

**1858-★BM-10** x 58
**Baucher, H.– Morphy, P.C.**
Paris [Löwenthal]

1 e4 e5 2 f4 exf4 3 ♘f3 g5 4 h4 g4 5 ♘e5 ♘f6 6 ♘xg4 ♘xe4 7 d3 ♘g3 8 ♗xf4 ♘xh1 [8 ... ♕e7+ 9 ♗e2 ♕b4+ 10 ♘d2 (10 ♕d2±) 10 ... ♕b6∓] 9 ♕e2+ ♕e7 10 ♘f6+ ♔d8 11 ♗xc7+ ♔xc7 12 ♘d5+ ♔d8 13 ♘xe7 ♗xe7∓ 14 ♕g4 d6 [◻ 14 ♖e8] 15 ♕f4 ♖g8 16 ♘c3 ♗e6 17 ♗e2 ♘c6 18 0-0-0 ♘g3 19 ♗f3 ♘f5 20 d4 ♘xh4 21 ♔b1 ♘xf3 22 gxf3 d5 23 ♘b5 ♖c8 24 c4 ♔d7 25 cxd5 ♗xd5 26 ♘c3 ♗d6 27 ♕f5+ ♗e6 28 ♕b5 ♔c7 29 ♔a1 ♗d7 30 ♘d5+ ♔b8 31 ♘f6 ♖gd8 32 d5 ♘e5 33 ♕e2 ♗f5 34 ♘e4 ♗xe4 35 fxe4 ♘c4 36 ♖c1 b5 37 e5 ♘xe5 38 ♕xb5+ ♔a8 39 ♖d1 ♖c2 40 ♕a6 f5 41 ♔b1 ♖c7 42 ♖f1 ♘c4 43 ♖f2 ♖b8 44 b3 ♗a3 **0-1** L/N3161

**1858-★BM-11 ∞○** 27 ix 58
**Morphy, P.C.+ Bierwith**
Paris [Löwenthal]

1 e4 e6 2 d4 c6 3 ♗d3 d5 4 exd5 exd5 5 ♘f3 ♗g4 6 0-0 ♗d6 7 h3 ♗h5 8 ♗e3 ♘d7 9 ♖e1 ♘e7 10 ♘bd2± ♗xf3 11 ♘xf3 h6 12 ♕d2 ♕c7 13 c4 dxc4 14 ♗xc4 f5 15 ♘e5 0-0-0 [15 ... ♗xe5 16 dxe5 ♘xe5 17 ♗e6 ♖d8 18 ♕c3 ♕d6 19 ♗c5±; 15 ... ♘xe5 16 dxe5 ♗xe5 17 ♗c5 ♖d8 18 ♕e2 ♗f6 19 ♕e6 ♖d7 (19 ... ♖f8 20 ♗xe7 ♗xe7 21 ♕g6+ ♔d7 22 ♗e6+-) 20 ♖ad1 ♖d5 (20 ... ♔d8 21 ♗xe7+; 20 ... ♖f8 21 ♗d6; 20 ... ♖xd1 21 ♖xd1 ♖f8 22 ♗xe7+-) 21 ♗xd5 cxd5 22 ♗xe7 ♗xe7 23 ♖c1+-] 16 ♗e6! ♗xe5 17 dxe5 ♔b8 18 ♕c3! ♘b6 19 ♕a3 ♘bc8 20 ♖ac1 g5 21 f4 gxf4 22 ♗xf4 ♖d4 23 ♕e3 ♖e4 24 ♕f3 ♕b6+ 25 ♔h2 ♖xe1 26 ♖xe1 ♕b4 27 ♖e2 ♘g6 28 ♗d2 ♕b5 29 ♗xc8 ♖xc8 30 ♗xh6 ♖h8 31 ♗g7 ♖h7 32 ♗f6 ♖f7 33 ♕h5 ♘f4 34 ♕xf7 **1-0** L/N3161

**1858-★BM-12**
**Morphy, P.C.+ Bird, H.E.**
London [Löwenthal]

1 e4 e5 2 f4 ♗c5 3 ♘f3 d6 4 c3 ♗g4 5 ♗c4 ♘c6 6 b4 ♗b6 7 a4 a6 8 h3 ♗xf3 9 ♕xf3 ♘f6 10 d3 ♕e7 11 f5 ♖d8 12 ♗g5 ♘b8 13 ♘d2 c6 14 ♘f1 d5 15 ♗b3 ♕d6 16 ♘g3 0-0 17 ♘h5 dxe4 18 dxe4 ♘xh5 [◻ 18 ... ♔h8] 19 ♖d1 ♕c7 20 ♗xd8 ♖xd8 21 ♖xd8+ ♕xd8 22 ♕xh5 ♗e3 23 ♕d1 ♕h4+ 24 ♔e2 ♗b6 25 ♔d3 ♘d7 26 ♕g4! ♕f2 27 f6 **1-0** L/N3161

**1858-★BM-13**
**Morphy, P.C.+ Bird, H.E.**
London [Löwenthal]

1 e4 e5 2 f4 exf4 3 ♘f3 g5 4 h4 g4 5 ♘e5 ♘f6 6 ♗c4 d5 7 exd5 ♗d6 8 d4 ♘h5 9 ♘c3 ♗f5 10 ♘e2 ♗xe5 11 dxe5 f3 12 gxf3 gxf3 13 ♗g5+- f6 [13 ... fxe2 14 ♕xe2] 14 exf6 ♕d6 15 ♕d4 fxe2 16 ♗xe2 ♕g3+ 17 ♔d2 0-0 18 ♖ag1 **1-0** L/N3161

**1858-★BM-14**
**Morphy, P.C.+ Bird, H.E.**
London [Löwenthal]

1 e4 e5 2 ♘f3 ♘c6 3 ♗c4 ♗c5 4 b4 ♗xb4 5 c3 ♗c5 6 d4 exd4 7 cxd4 ♗b6 8 0-0 [8 ♗b2 Boden] 8 ... d6 9 d5 ♘a5 10 e5 ♘xc4 11 ♕a4+ ♗d7 12 ♕xc4 dxe5 13 ♘xe5 ♕f6 14 ♘xd7! ♔xd7 15 ♕g4+ ♔e8 16 ♗g5 [◻ 16 ♗a3] 16 ... ♕g6 [16 ... ♕xa1 17 ♖e1++-] 17 ♘c3 ♘f6 18 ♖ae1+ ♔f8 19 ♕b4+ ♔g8 20 ♗xf6 ♕xf6 21 ♘e4 ♕g6 22 ♔h1 h5 23 f4 h4 24 f5 ♕h5 [24 ... ♕g4?? 25 ♘f6++-] 25 ♖f4!

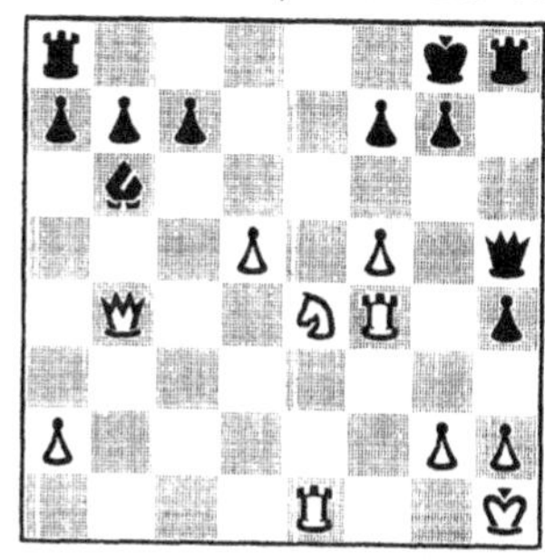

25 ... f6? [◻ 25 ... ♖h6∓] 26 ♘xf6+ gxf6 27 ♖g4+ ♕xg4 28 ♕xg4+ ♔f8 29 ♖e6 ♖h6 30 ♕f4 ♔g7 31 ♖e7+ **1-0** L/N3161

**1858-★BM-15**
**Bird, H.E.– Morphy, P.C.**
London [Löwenthal]

1 e4 e5 2 ♘f3 d6 3 d4 f5 4 ♘c3 [◻ 4 dxe5 fxe4 5 ♘g5 d5 6 e6 ♘h6 7 f3 ♗e7 8 fxe4 ♗xg5 9 ♕h5+ g6 10 ♕xg5 ♕xg5 11 ♗xg5±] 4 ... fxe4 5 ♘xe4 d5 6 ♘g3 e4∓ 7 ♘e5 ♘f6 8 ♗g5 ♗d6 9 ♘h5 0-0 10 ♕d2 [10 ♘xf6+? gxf6-+; 10 ♗xf6 gxf6 11 ♘g4 f5 12 ♘e5 f4∓] 10 ... ♕e8! 11 g4? ♘xg4 12 ♘xg4 [◻ 12 ♘xg7] 12 ... ♕xh5 13 ♘e5 ♘c6 14 ♗e2 ♕h3 15 ♘xc6 bxc6 16 ♗e3 ♖b8 17 0-0-0 ♖xf2! 18 ♗xf2 ♕a3!! 19 c3 [19 bxa3?? ♗xa3#] 19 ... ♕xa2 20 b4 [20 ♕c2 ♖xb2, 21 ... ♗a3-+] 20 ... ♕a1+ 21 ♔c2 ♕a4+ 22 ♔b2 ♗xb4 23 cxb4 ♖xb4+ 24 ♕xb4 ♕xb4+ 25 ♔c2 [◻ 25 ♔c1; 25 ♔a2=] 25 ... e3 26 ♗xe3 ♗f5+ 27 ♖d3 [27 ♔d3? ♕c4+-+] 27 ... ♕c4+ 28 ♔d2 ♕a2+ 29 ♔d1 ♕b1+ **0-1** L/N3161

**1858-★BM-16**
**Morphy, P.C.+ Boden, S.S.**
London [Löwenthal]

1 e4 e5 2 ♘f3 ♘c6 3 ♗c4 ♗c5 4 b4 ♗b6 5 a4 a6 [5 ... a5 6 b5 ♘d4 7 ♘xe5 ♕f6 8 ♘f3 ♗e6 9 e5±] 6 c3 d6 7 d3 ♘f6 8 ♕b3 ♕e7 9 ♗g5 h6 10 ♗h4 ♘d8 11 ♘bd2 g5 12 ♗g3 ♘h5 13 h3 ♕f6 14 ♘h2 ♘e6 [14 ... ♘xg3 15 fxg3 ♕f2+∞ Boden] 15 0-0-0 ♘hf4 16 ♘g4 ♕g7 17 ♔b1 h5 18 ♘e3 ♗xe3 19 fxe3 ♘xg2 20 ♗f2 ♘h4 21 ♗xh4 gxh4 22 ♖hg1 ♕h6 23 ♘f3 ♕xe3 24 ♘xh4 ♕xh3 25 ♘f5 ♗d7 26 ♕a2 ♘f4 27 ♖g3 ♗xf5 28 ♖xh3 ♗xh3 29 ♗xf7+ ♔d7 [◻ 29 ... ♔e7] 30 d4 ♗g4 31 ♖d2 ♔e7 32 ♕c4 c6 33 dxe5 dxe5 34 ♖f2 ♖ad8 35 ♕c5+ ♔f6 [35 ... ♔xf7 36 ♕xe5] 36 ♗b3 ♖he8 [◻ 36 ... h4] 37 a5 ♖d3 38 ♕c4 ♖d7 39 ♔a2 ♖ed8 40 ♔a3 ♔g5 41 ♕c5 ♔f6 [◻ 41 ... ♖e8=] 42 ♖xf4+ exf4 43 e5+ ♔g6 44 ♗c2+ ♖d3 [44 ... ♗f5 45 ♕g1++-; 44 ... ♔h6 45 e6 ♗xe6 46 ♕e5+-] 45 ♕e7 ♖d7 46 ♕f6+ ♔h7 47 e6

♖d6 48 ♕f7+ ♔h6 49 ♕xf4+ ♔g7 50 ♕g5+ ♔h8 51 ♕h6+ ♔g8 52 ♕g6+ ♔h8 53 ♗xd3 **1-0** L/N3161

### 1858-★BM-17
**Boden, S.S.= Morphy, P.C.**

London [Maróczy]

1 e4 e5 2 ♘f3 d6 3 d4 f5 4 ♗c4 ♘c6 5 dxe5 dxe5 6 ♕xd8+ ♘xd8 7 0-0 [7 exf5 e4 8 ♘d4!] 7 ... fxe4 8 ♘xe5 ♘f6 9 ♖e1 ♗d6 10 f4 ♗e6 11 ♘c3 0-0 12 ♘xe4 ♗xe5 13 fxe5 [13 ♗xe6+?] 13 ... ♘d7 [13 ... ♗xc4 14 exf6 gxf6 15 ♗h6 ♖f7 16 ♘d6!] 14 ♘d2 ♖f5 15 ♗xe6+ ♘xe6 16 ♘f3 ♖xf3 17 gxf3 ♘d4 18 ♗f4 [18 ♖f1 ♘xe5 19 ♔g2] 18 ... ♘xf3+ 19 ♔g2 ♘xe1+ 20 ♖xe1 ♖e8 21 ♖d1 ♘f8 [21 ... ♘xe5 22 ♖e1] 22 ♔f3 ♘g6 23 ♔e4 ♘xf4 24 ♔xf4 ♔f7 25 h4 ♔e6 26 ♔e4 ♖f8 27 ♖g1 g6 28 h5! gxh5 29 ♖g7 ♖f7 30 ♖g5 ♖f2 31 ♖xh5 ♖xc2 32 ♖h6+ ♔e7 33 ♖xh7+ ♔e6 34 ♖h6+ ♔e7 35 ♖h7+ ♔e6 ½-½ L/N3203

### 1858-★BM-18
**Morphy, P.C.+ Boden, S.S.** 9 vii 58

London [Steinitz]

1 e4 e5 2 f4 ♗c5 3 ♘f3 d6 4 c3 [4 ♗c4 ♘f6 5 d3 ♘g4 6 ♕e2! ♗f2+ 7 ♔f1 ♗b6 8 h3 ♘f6± (8 ... ♘f2 9 ♖h2 Δ g4±)] 4 ... ♗g4 5 ♗c4 [5 ♗e2 ♘c6∓] 5 ... ♕e7 [□5 ... ♘c6 6 b4 ♗b6 7 b5 (7 a4 a6) ♘a5] 6 d4?! exd4 7 0-0 ♘c6 [7 ... dxc3+?] 8 b4 ♗b6 9 a4 dxc3+ [9 ... a6 (9 ... a5 10 b5 dxc3+ 11 ♔h1 c2 12 ♕xc2 ♗xf3 13 gxf3 ♘d4 14 ♕d3±) 10 a5 ♗a7 11 b5 axb5 12 ♗xb5 Δ a6±] 10 ♔h1 c2 11 ♕xc2 ♗xf3 12 gxf3 ♘xb4 13 ♕b3 a5 [13 ... ♘c6 14 ♗b5 a5 15 ♘c3 ♘f6 16 e5 dxe5 17 ♗a3±] 14 ♘c3 ♘f6 15 e5 dxe5 [□ 15 ... ♘d7 Δ ♘c5] 16 fxe5 ♘h5 17 ♘e4 0-0 18 ♗b2 ♘f4 [□18 ... ♖ad8] 19 ♖g1 ♖ad8 [19 ... ♗xg1 20 ♖xg1 ♘g6 (□ 20 ... ♔h8) 21 ♘g5 ♕xe5 22 ♘xh7 ♔xh7 23 f4 ♘g6 24 ♖xg6 ♕e4+= (24 ... ♔xg6 25 ♕g3+ ♔f5 26 ♕h3+ ♔xf4 27 ♗c1+ ♔e5 28 ♕e3+ ♔d6 29 ♕d4++-)] 20 e6! ♗d4 [20 ... f6 21 ♘xf6+ ♖xf6 22 ♗xf6 ♕xf6 23 e7++-] 21 exf7+ ♔h8 22 ♖g4 ♗xb2 23 ♕xb2 ♖xf7 [23 ... ♘g6 24 ♕g2 (Δ 25 ♖xg6+-) 24 ... ♘e5 25 ♖xg7 ♘xc4 26 ♖xh7+ ♔xh7 27 ♖g1+-] 24 ♗xf7 ♕xf7 25 ♘g5 ♕d5 26 ♖xf4 ♕xg5 27 ♖g1 ♕h6 28 ♖f7 ♖g8 29 ♖xc7 ♘d3 30 ♕d4 **1-0** L/N6137

### 1858-★BM-19
**Morphy, P.C.= Boden, S.S.**

London [Löwenthal]

1 e4 e5 2 ♘f3 ♘c6 3 ♗b5 ♗c5 4 c3 ♕e7 5 0-0 f6 6 d4 ♗b6 7 ♘a3 ♘d8 8 ♘c4 ♘f7 9 ♘e3 c6 10 ♘f5 ♕f8 11 ♗a4 [□ 11 ♗d3] 11 ... g6 12 ♘e3 d6 13 d5 ♗d7 14 dxc6 bxc6 15 ♘c4 ♖c8 16 b3 ♗e6! 17 ♕d3 ♕e7 18 ♗a3 ♗xc4 19 ♕xc4 ♔f8 20 ♖ad1 c5 [□ 20 ... ♔g7] 21 ♖d3 ♘gh6 22 ♔h1 ♔g7 23 ♗c1 ♖hf8 24 g4?! ♘xg4 25 h3 ♘gh6 26 ♖g1 ♔h8 27 ♘h4 ♖g8 28 ♖dg3 g5 29 ♘f5 ♘xf5 30 exf5 ♕b7+ 31 ♖1g2 d5 32 ♕g4 ♘h6 33 ♕h5 ♘xf5 34 ♖f3 ♘g7 [34 ... ♘h4 35 ♖xf6 ♘xg2 36 ♖f7+-] 35 ♕h6 ♗d8 36 ♖xf6 ♗xf6 37 ♕xf6 ♖cf8 38 ♕xe5 ♖f5 39 ♕e3 d4 40 cxd4 ♖f3 41 ♕e2 cxd4 42 ♗xg5 d3 43 ♕d2 ♕d5 44 b4 ♖gf8 [44 ... ♖xh3+, 45 ... ♕e5∓] 45 ♗h6 ♖xh3+ [45 ... ♖xf2 46 ♗xg7+ ♔g8 47 ♗b3 ♖xd2 48 ♗xd5+-] 46 ♔g1 ♖g8 47 ♗g5 [47 ♕f4? ♖xh6 48 ♕xh6 ♕xg2+-+; 47 ♗b3 ♕h5-+] 47 ... ♕d4 [□ 47 ... ♕e5] 48 ♕f4 ♕a1+ 49 ♕c1 ♕e5 50 ♗h6 ♘e8 51 ♖xg8+ ♔xg8 52 ♗b3+ ♔h8 53 ♗f4 ♕g7+ 54 ♗g3 ♖h5 55 ♕d1 ♖e5 56 ♕xd3 ♖e1+ 57 ♔g2 ½-½ L/N3161

### 1858-★BM-20
**Morphy, P.C.+ Boden, S.S.**

London [Löwenthal]

1 e4 e5 2 f4 ♗c5 3 ♘f3 d6 4 c3 ♗g4 5 ♗e2 ♘c6 6 b4 ♗b6 7 b5 ♘a5 8 d4 ♗xf3 9 ♗xf3 exd4 10 cxd4 ♕f6 11 ♗e3 ♘c4 12 ♗f2 ♕xf4 13 0-0 ♘f6 14 ♕d3 ♘a5 15 ♘c3 0-0 16 g3 ♕h6 17 ♔g2 ♖ae8 18 ♖ae1 ♔h8 19 ♗e3 ♕g6 20 ♘e2 h6 [20 ... ♘xe4 21 ♘f4+-] 21 ♗d2 d5 22 ♘f4 ♕h7 23 e5 ♕xd3 24 ♘xd3 ♘c4 [24 ... ♘e4 25 ♗xe4 dxe4 26 ♗xa5 ♗xa5 27 ♖xe4±] 25 ♗b4 ♘e4 26 ♗xf8 ♖xf8 27 ♘f4 ♘ed2 28 ♗xd5 ♘xf1 29 ♗xc4 ♘d2 30 ♗d5 ♗xd4 31 e6! g5 32 e7 ♖e8 33 ♗xf7 gxf4 34 gxf4 ♖xe7 35 ♖xe7 **1-0** L/N3161

### 1858-★BM-21
**Boden, S.S.– Morphy, P.C.**

London [Löwenthal]

1 e4 e5 2 ♘f3 ♘c6 3 ♗b5 ♘f6 4 d4 exd4 5 e5 ♘d5 6 0-0 ♗c5 7 c3 0-0 8 cxd4 ♗b6 9 ♗c4 ♘ce7 10 ♗g5 ♕e8 11 ♖e1 h6 12 ♗h4 [□ 12 ♗xe7, 13 ♘h4] 12 ... ♘f4! 13 ♘c3 ♘f5 14 ♕d2 ♘g6 15 ♘e4 d5 [15 ... ♘gxh4 16 ♘xh4 ♘xh4 17 ♘f6+!+-] 16 exd6 ♕d7 17 ♘e5? [□ 17 ♗e7] 17 ... ♘xe5 18 dxe5 ♘xh4 19 ♘f6+ gxf6 20 e6 ♕xd6 21 ♕xh6 ♗xe6 22 ♗xe6? [□ 22 ♖e4] 22 ... fxe6 23 ♖e4 ♘f5 24 ♖g4+ ♔f7 **0-1** L/N3161

### 1858-★BM-22
**Boden, S.S.= Morphy, P.C.**

London [Löwenthal]

1 e4 e5 2 ♗c4 ♘f6 3 ♘f3 ♘xe4 4 ♘c3 ♘xc3 5 dxc3 c6 6 ♘xe5 d5 7 0-0 ♗d6 8 ♖e1 ♗e6 9 ♗d3 ♘d7 10 f4 ♘xe5 11 fxe5 ♗c5+ 12 ♔h1 ♕h4 13 ♗e3 ♗xe3 14 ♖xe3 0-0 15 ♕e1 ♕h6 16 ♕g3 ♖ae8 17 ♖ae1 c5 18 ♗e2 ♗d7 19 ♗f3 ♕e6 20 ♖d3 ♗c6 21 b4 b6 22 a4 f6 23 b5 ♗b7 24 c4 dxc4 25 ♖d6 ♕e7 26 ♗xb7 [26 ♗h5 g6 27 e6 ♗c8 (27 ... ♖d8 28 ♖xd8 ♖xd8 29 ♗xg6 hxg6 30 ♕xg6+=) 28 ♗e2 ♖d8 29 ♖xd8 ♖xd8 30 ♗xc4] 26 ... ♕xb7 27 e6 ♕c7 28 ♖ed1 ♖d8 29 ♔g1 ♖xd6 30 ♕xd6 ♕xd6 31 ♖xd6 ♖e8 32 ♔f2 ♔f8 33 ♔f3 ♔e7 34 ♖d7+ ♔xe6 35 ♖xa7 ♖e7 36 ♖a6 ♖b7 37 a5 ♔d6 38 axb6 ♔e6 39 ♔e3 g5 40 g4! ♔d6 41 ♔e4 ♔e6 ...? ½-½ L/N3161

### 1858-★BM-23
**Morphy, P.C.+ Boden, S.S.**

London [Löwenthal]

1 e4 e5 2 ♘f3 ♘c6 3 d4 exd4 4 ♗c4 ♗c5 5 0-0 d6 6 c3 ♘f6 7 cxd4 ♗b6 8 ♘c3 0-0 9 d5 ♘a5 [□ 9 ... ♘e5] 10 ♗d3 c5 11 ♗g5 h6 12 ♗h4 ♗g4 [12 ... g5 13 ♘xg5±] 13 h3 ♗h5 14 g4 ♗g6 15 ♕d2 ♖e8 16 ♖ae1 ♗c7 17 ♘b5 ♔h7 18 ♗xf6 gxf6 19 ♘xc7 ♕xc7 20 ♕c3 ♕d8 21 ♘h4! b6 22 f4 ♔g7 23 ♘xg6 fxg6 24 e5 ♖c8 25 ♗b1 ♔f7 26 e6+ ♔g7 27 ♕d3 f5 28 gxf5 ♕f6 29 fxg6 ♕xb2 30 f5 ♕f6 [30 ... ♕d4+ 31 ♕xd4 cxd4 32 f6++-] 31 e7 c4 32 ♕g3 c3 33 ♖e6 ♕d4+ 34 ♕f2 ♕xd5 35 f6+ **1-0** L/N3161

### 1858-★BM-24
**Morphy, P.C.+ Boden, S.S.**

London [Löwenthal]

1 e4 e5 2 ♘f3 ♘c6 3 ♗c4 ♘f6 4 ♘g5 d5 5 exd5 ♘a5 6 d3 h6 7 ♘f3 ♘xc4 8 dxc4 ♗d6 9 ♘c3 a6 10 ♗e3 b6 11 h3 0-0 12 a3 ♕e7 13 ♕d2 [13 0-0 e4, 14 ... ♕e5∓] 13 ... ♗f5 14 ♕e2 ♗h7 15 g4 ♘e4 16 ♘xe4 ♗xe4 17 ♖g1 ♕f6 18 ♖g3 ♗xf3 19 ♖xf3 [19 ♕xf3? ♕xf3 20 ♖xf3 e4] 19 ... ♕h4 20 ♖g3 e4 21 ♖g1 ♕xh3 22 0-0-0 ♕f3 23 ♕d2 a5 24 ♔b1 [Δ 25 ♗xh6] 24 ... f6 25 ♖h1 ♔f7 26 ♖dg1 ♔e7? [□ 26 ... ♖h8=] 27 ♕e1 ♗f4 28 ♖h4 ♖g8 [28 ... ♗xe3 29 fxe3+-] 29 ♖gh1 g5 30 ♖xh6 ♗xe3 31 fxe3 ♖af8 32 ♖f1 ♕xg4 33 ♕c3 ♔d7 34 ♖fxf6 ♖xf6 35 ♕xf6 ♔c8 36 ♖h7 ♔b8 37 ♕c6 ♖c8 38 ♖d7 ♕g1+ 39 ♔a2 ♕xe3 40 d6 ♕c5 41 ♕xe4 ♔a7 42 c3 a4 43 ♕d5 ♕xd5 44 cxd5 b5 45 dxc7 ♔b6 46 d6 g4 47 ♖d8 ♔b7 48 d7 ♖xc7 49 ♖b8+ ♔xb8 50 d8♕+ **1-0** L/N3161

### 1858-★BM-25
**Boden, S.S.+ Morphy, P.C.**

London [Löwenthal]

1 e4 e5 2 ♘f3 d6 3 d4 exd4 4 ♕xd4 ♗d7 5 ♗e3 ♘c6 6 ♕d2 ♘f6 7 ♗d3 ♗e7 8 ♘c3 0-0 9 0-0 h6 10 h3 ♘h7 11 g4 h5 12 ♘h2 hxg4 13 hxg4 ♘e5 14 f3 g5 15 ♔g2 c5 16

♖h1 ♔g7 17 ♘f1 ♖h8 18 ♘g3 f6 19 ♘d5 ♗f8 [◻ 19 ... ♖c8] 20 ♘h5+ ♔f7 21 ♖ad1 ♘fg6 22 ♗e2 ♘h4+ 23 ♔f2 ♗c6 24 ♘xe7 ♕xe7 25 ♕xd6 b6 26 ♕xe7+ ♔xe7 27 ♘g3 ♔f7 28 ♖d6 ♔e7 29 ♖d2 ♔f7 30 f4 gxf4 31 ♗xf4 ♘hg6 32 ♗h6 ♖h7 33 ♔e3 ♖ah8 34 ♘f5 ♘ge7 35 ♘xe7 ♔xe7 36 g5 ♔e6 37 ♖hd1!

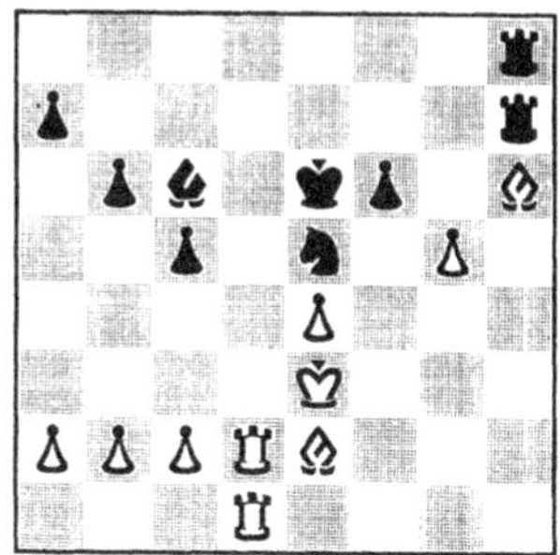

37 ... fxg5 38 ♖d6+ ♔f7 39 ♗h5+ ♔e7 40 ♗xg5+ ♔f8 41 ♖f1+ **1-0** L/N3161

**1858-★BM-26 ●o⬠** 27 ix 58

**Morphy, P.C.+ Bornemann**

Paris [Löwenthal]

1 e4 e5 2 f4 ♗c5 3 ♘f3 d6 4 c3 ♗g4 5 ♗c4 ♘f6 6 fxe5 ♗xf3 [6 ... dxe5? 7 ♗xf7++-] 7 ♕xf3 dxe5 8 d3 ♘c6 9 ♗g5 a6 10 ♘d2 ♕e7 11 0-0-0 ♕d7 12 ♘f1! 0-0-0 13 ♘e3 h6 14 ♗h4 g5 15 ♗g3 ♖df8 16 ♘d5 ♘e8 17 d4! exd4 18 cxd4 [18 ♗xc7!] 18 ... ♗d8 19 ♖hf1 ♘d6 20 ♗b3 ♘b5 21 ♕e3 f5?! 22 exf5 ♖xf5 23 ♘b6+! cxb6 24 ♕e6 ♖d5 25 ♖f7 ♘e7 26 ♔b1! ♕e8 27 ♖c1+ ♘c7 28 ♗xd7+ ♖xd7 29 d5 ♘c6 30 dxc6 ♖xe3 31 cxd7+ **1-0** L/N3161

**1858-★BM-27**

**Morphy, P.C.+ Bottin, A.**

Paris [Maróczy]

1 e4 e5 2 c3 ♘f6 [◻ 2 ... d5] 3 d4 ♘xe4 4 dxe5 ♗c5 5 ♕g4! [5 ♕d5 ♗xf2+ 6 ♔e2 f5 7 exf6 ♘xf6 8 ♕e5+ ♔f7!] 5 ... ♘xf2 [5 ... ♗xf2+ 6 ♔e2, ♕g7±] 6 ♕xg7 ♖f8 7 ♗g5 f6 8 exf6 ♖xf6? [8 ... d5 9 ♗e2 ♗g4! 10 ♗xg4 ♘xg4 11 f7+ ♖xf7+ 12 ♕xf7+ ♔xf7 13 ♗xd8 ♘f2 14 ♗h4 ♘xh1 15 ♘f3 ♘c6 16 ♘bd2 ♖g8 17 ♔f1 d4 18 cxd4 (18 ♘b3) 18 ... ♘xd4 19 ♘xd4 ♗xd4 20 ♘f3 ♗b6 21 ♖e1 h6 22 ♖e7+ ♔f8 23 ♘e5 ♖g7 24 ♘d7+ ♔g8 25 ♖xg7+ ♔xg7 26 ♘xb6 axb6 27 g4 ♔g6 28 ♔g2 h5 29 h3+- Morphy] 9 ♗xf6 ♕e7 10 ♕g8+ **1-0** L/N3203

**1858-★BM-28** 2 xi 58

**Morphy, P.C.+Braunschweig, C. & de Vauvenargue, J.**

Paris [Löwenthal]

1 e4 e5 2 ♘f3 d6 3 d4 ♗g4 4 dxe5 ♗xf3 5 ♕xf3 dxe5 6 ♗c4 ♘f6 7 ♕b3 ♕e7 8 ♘c3 [8 ♗xf7+ △ 9 ♕xb7±] 8 ... c6 9 ♗g5 b5 10 ♘xb5 cxb5 11 ♗xb5+! [11 ♗d5+-] 11 ... ♘bd7 12 0-0-0 ♖d8 13 ♖xd7 ♖xd7 14 ♖d1 ♕e6 15 ♗xd7+ ♘xd7 16 ♕b8+!! ♘xb8 17 ♖d8# **1-0** L/N3161

**1858-★BO-1** 23 vi 58

**Owen, J. & Staunton, H.–Barnes, T.W. & Morphy, P.C.**

London [Löwenthal]

1 e4 e5 2 ♘f3 d6 3 d4 f5!? 4 dxe5 [◻ 4 ♗c4 fxe4 5 ♘xe5±] 4 ... fxe4 5 ♘g5 d5 6 e6 ♘h6 7 ♘c3 [◻ 7 f3 ♗e7 8 fxe4 ♗xg5 9 ♕h5+ g6 10 ♕xg5 ♕xg5 11 ♗xg5 ♘g4 12 exd5±] 7 ... c6 8 ♘gxe4 dxe4 9 ♕h5+ g6 10 ♕e5 ♖g8 11 ♗xh6 [◻ 11 ♗g5 ♕b6 (11 ... ♕d6 12 ♕xd6 ♗xd6 13 ♘xe4 ♗f8 14 ♘f6+ ♔e7 15 ♘xg8+ ♔xe6 16 ♘xh6+-; 11 ... ♗g7 12 e7 ♕d7 13 ♕f4±) 12 0-0-0 ♘g4 13 ♕f4±] 11 ... ♗xh6 12 ♖d1 ♕g5 13 ♕c7 ♗xe6 14 ♕xb7 [◻ 14 ♘xe4 ♕e7 15 ♖d8+ ♕xd8 (15 ... ♔f7) 16 ♘d6+ ♕xd6 17 ♕xd6 ♔f7∞] 14 ... e3 15 f3 ♕e7 16 ♕xa8 ♔f7 17 ♘e4 ♗f4 18 ♗e2 [◻ 18 g3] 18 ... ♔g7! [18 ... ♕c7 19 g3 ♘a6 20 ♖d7+ ♕xd7 21 ♕xg8+ ♔xg8 22 ♘f6+ ♔f7 23 ♘xd7 ♗xd7 24 ♗xa6+-] 19 0-0 ♕c7 20 ♘c5 ♗xh2+ 21 ♔h1 ♗c8 22 ♖d4 ♗g3 23 ♕e4 ♔h8 24 ♖d1 ♕g7 25 ♖h4 ♗xh4 26 ♕xb8 ♗a6 27 ♕h2 ♗xe2 28 ♖d7 ♕h6 29 ♘e4 ♗c4 30 ♘f6 e2 31 ♕e7 ♕c1+ 32 ♕g1 ♕xg1+ 33 ♔xg1 e1♕+ 34 ♖xe1 ♗xe1 **0-1** L/N3161

**1858-★BO-2** 24 vi - 3 vii 58

**Barnes, T.W. & Morphy, P.C.+Owen, J. & Staunton, H.**

London [Löwenthal]

1 e4 d5 2 exd5 ♕xd5 3 ♘c3 ♕d8 4 d4 ♘f6 5 ♗d3 ♘c6 6 ♗e3 e6?! 7 ♘f3 ♗d6 8 0-0 0-0 9 ♕e2 b6 10 ♗g5 ♗b7 11 ♘e4 ♗e7 12 ♘xf6+ ♗xf6 13 ♕e4 g6 14 ♕h4 ♗xg5 15 ♘xg5 h5 16 c3 ♕f6 17 ♖ae1 ♘e7 18 f4 ♘f5 19 ♕h3 ♖fe8 20 ♖e5 ♖ad8 21 ♖fe1 ♘g7 22 g4 c5 [22 ... ♖d5 23 ♘e4 ♕e7 (23 ... ♕xf4 24 ♖f1 ♕xg4+ 25 ♕xg4 hxg4 26 ♘f6+ ♔f8 27 ♘xd5, 28 ♘xg6±) 24 g5 ♖xe5 25 ♘f6+ ♔f8 (25 ... ♕xf6 26 gxf6 ♖xe1+ 27 ♔f2±) 26 fxe5±] 23 ♘e4! ♗a6 [23 ... ♗xe4 24 ♘xe4!] 24 gxh5 ♘xh5 25 ♗f3! cxd4 26 ♗xh5 gxh5 27 ♕xh5 ♕g7 28 ♔f2 ♕f6 29 ♕h4 ♗d3 30 ♕g3 ♗g6 31 f5 ♗xf5 32 ♘e4+ ♕g6 33 ♘f6+ ♔f8 34 ♕xg6 ♗xg6 35 ♘xe8 ♔xe8 36 h4 d3 37 ♔e3 ♔e7 38 ♔d2 ♖d6 [◻ 38 ... ♖h8] 39 ♖g5! ♔f6 40 ♖f1+ ♗f5 41 ♖g8 ♖d5 42 h5 ♖e5 43 ♖f2 ♖e4 44 ♖h2 ♗h7 45 ♖h8 ♔g7 46 ♖a8 ♔h6 47 ♖xa7 ♖f4 48 ♖b7 e5 49 ♖xb6+ f6 50 a4 e4 51 ♖e6 ♖f3 52 a5 **1-0** L/N3161

**1858-★BR-1 ●o⬠**

**Rivière, J.A. de–de Basterot**

[Staunton]

1 e4 e5 2 f4 d5 3 exd5 exf4 4 ♘f3 ♘f6 5 ♗c4 ♗d6 6 d3 ♕e7+ 7 ♕e2 ♕xe2+ 8 ♔xe2 ♗g4 9 ♘c3 a6 10 ♖e1 0-0 11 ♔f1 ♗xf3 12 gxf3 ♘bd7 13 ♘e4 ♗e5 14 ♘xf6+ gxf6 15 ♖e4 f5 16 ♖e2 ♔h8 17 ♗d2 ♖g8 18 ♖ae1 ♗d4 19 ♖g2 ♖xg2 20 ♔xg2 ♖g8+ 21 ♔h1 ♘e5 22 ♖f1 ♘xf3 23 ♗xf4 ♖g4 24 ♗g3 f4 25 ♖xf3 fxg3 26 hxg3 f6 27 c3 ♗e5 28 ♔g2 ♔g7 29 d4 ♗d6 30 ♗d3 h5 31 ♔h3 ♖g5 32 c4 ♗b4 33 ♖e3 ♔f7 34 a3 ♗d2 35 ♖e2 ♗c1 36 ♖c2? [36 c5] 36 ... ♗e3 37 ♗e2 ♗xd4 38 b4 ♗e5 39 g4 hxg4+ 40 ♗xg4 ♔g6 41 a4 [◻ 41 ♗c8] 41 ... f5 42 ♗d1 ♖g3+ 43 ♔h4 f4 44 ♗h5+ ♔h6 **0-1** M954-1858

**1858-★BR-2 ●o⬠**

**Rivière, J.A. de+de Blemer**

[Staunton]

1 d4 d5 2 c4 ♘f6 3 ♘c3 a6 4 e3 e6 5 ♗d2 ♗d6 6 ♘f3 0-0 7 ♗e2 dxc4 8 ♗xc4 b5 9 ♗d3 ♗b7 10 0-0 ♘g4 11 h3 ♘h6 12 e4 ♕f6 13 e5 ♗xf3 14 gxf3 ♕h4 15 ♔h2 [15 exd6] 15 ... ♗e7 16 ♖g1 ♕xf2+ 17 ♖g2 ♕h4 18 ♕e1 ♘f5 19 ♗xf5 exf5 20 ♕xh4 ♗xh4 21 ♗h6 ♘c6 [◻ 21 ... g6] 22 ♗xg7 ♖fe8 23 ♗f6+ ♔f8 24 ♖ag1! ♘e7 25 ♗xh4 ♘g6 26 ♗f6 ♖e6 27 ♘d5 ♖a7 28 ♘f4 ♖c6 29 ♘xg6+ fxg6 30 d5 ♖c5 31 ♖d1 ♔f7 32 ♗g5 ♖a8 33 e6+ ♔g7 34 ♖e2 h6 35 ♗f4 g5 36 ♗xc7! ♖xc7 37 d6 ♖cc8 38 d7 ♖d8 39 e7 ♖xd7 40 ♖xd7 ♖e8 41 ♖d8 ♔f7 42 ♖xe8 ♔xe8 **1-0** M954-1858

**1858-★BS-1**

**Staunton, H.+ Barnes, T.W. & Owen, J.**

London [Staunton]

1 e4 e5 2 ♘f3 d6 3 ♗c4 ♗e7 4 d4 exd4 5 ♘xd4 ♘f6 6 ♘c3 0-0 7 ♗d3 d5 8 e5 ♘g4 9 e6 ♘e5 10 ♗f5 [10 ♗xh7+?! ♔xh7 11 ♕h5+ ♔g8 12 ♕xe5 ♗f6 13 ♕e2 ♖e8] 10 ... c5 11 exf7+ ♖xf7 12 ♗xc8 ♕xc8 13 ♘de2 d4 14 ♘d5 ♕d7?! [14 ... ♗d6] 15 ♘xe7+ ♖xe7 [◻ 15 ... ♕xe7] 16 0-0 ♘bc6 17 ♘g3 c4?! 18 b3 c3 19 a4 ♖c8 20 ♗a3 ♖e6 21 f4 ♘f7 22 ♕g4 ♘h6 23 ♕h3 ♕d5 24 f5± ♖f6 25 ♖ae1 [△ 26 ♖e6] 25 ... d3 26 cxd3 ♘d4 27 ♘e4

[27 ♗e7 ♖fc6] 27 ... ♖xf5 28 ♘d6! [28 ♘xc3 ♖xc3 29 ♖e8+ ♔f7; 28 ♘f6+?! gxf6 29 ♕xh6 ♖xf1+ 30 ♖xf1 c2∓] 28 ... ♖xf1+ 29 ♖xf1 ♖d8 30 ♕h4 ♖xd6? [30 ... ♘e6; 30 ... ♘c6] 31 ♕e7 ♘e2+ 32 ♔h1 ♔h8 33 ♗xd6 ♘g8 34 ♕xe2 ♕xd6 35 ♖c1 **1-0** M954-1858

### 1858-★BS-2
**Barnes,T.W. & Owen,J.– Staunton,H.**

London [Staunton]

1 e4 e5 2 ♘f3 ♘c6 3 ♗b5 ♘d4 4 ♘xd4 exd4 5 d3 ♗c5 6 0-0 a5 7 ♗c4 d6 8 f4 ♗d7 [Δ 9 ... b5] 9 a3 ♕e7 10 ♘d2 ♘h6 11 f5 f6 12 ♕h5+ ♔d8 13 ♘b3 b5 14 ♘xc5 bxc4 15 ♘xd7 ♔xd7 16 ♗xh6 gxh6 17 dxc4 ♖hg8 18 ♖fe1 ♖g5 19 ♕xh6 ♖ag8 20 ♖e2 ♖8g7 21 b4 ♕f7 22 c5 ♕c4 23 ♖ae1 axb4 24 ♕xf6 ♕c3! [Δ 25 ... ♖xg2+–+; 24 ... ♕xc5] 25 ♕e6+ ♔d8 26 ♖f1 [26 ♕f6+ ♔c8 27 ♕e6+ ♔b7 28 c6+ ♔a7 29 ♕c8 ♖xg2+ 30 ♔h1 ♖xh2+ 31 ♔xh2 ♕g3+ 32 ♔h1 ♕h4+ 33 ♖h2 ♕xe1#] 26 ... ♕h3 27 ♖ff2 ♖h5 28 ♔f1 ♕xh2 29 ♔e1 [29 ♖d2 ♕h1+ Δ 30 ... ♖xg2; ◻ 29 ♖e1 ♕g3 30 ♕b3 ♕e5 31 ♕e6 (31 ♔g1 ♕h2+ 32 ♔f1 ♖g3) 31 ... ♕xc5 32 ♔g1 ♕c3–+] 29 ... ♕g3 30 ♕f6+ ♔c8 31 ♕xd4 ♖h1+ 32 ♔d2 dxc5 **0-1** M954-1858

### 1858-★BS-3
**Staunton,H.–Barnes,T.W. & Owen,J.**

London [Staunton]

1 e4 e5 2 ♘f3 ♘c6 3 d4 exd4 4 ♗c4 ♗c5 5 0-0 d6 6 c3 ♕f6 7 ♗g5 ♕g6 8 ♗h4 ♗g4 9 ♘bd2 dxc3 10 bxc3∓ ♘ge7 11 ♗g3 0-0 12 ♕c2 ♕h5 [12 ... d5 13 ♘h4 Δ 14 exd5] 13 ♖ab1 ♘g6 14 ♗d5 ♘d8 15 ♘d4 c6 16 ♗c4 d5 17 exd5 ♗xd4 18 cxd4 cxd5 19 ♗d3 ♘c6 20 ♕a4 ♕g5 21 f4 ♕f6 22 f5 ♘ge7 23 ♖xb7 ♖ac8 24 ♖f4? [24 ♗e5] 24 ... ♗xf5 25 ♗b5 ♕e6 26 ♘f1 ♗e4 27 ♘e3 ♗d3! 28 ♘d1 ♗xb5 29 ♖xb5 ♖b8 30 ♖xb8 ♖xb8 31 ♖f1 ♖b4 32 ♕a3 ♖xd4 [32 ... ♘f5 33 ♖e1 ♕d7 34 ♕f3 ♘xg3 (34 ... ♘~xd4 35 ♕xd5) 35 ♕xg3 ♖xd4 (35 ... ♘xd4 36 ♕c7) 36 ♕c7] 33 ♗f2 ♖d2 **0-1** M954-1858

### 1858-★BS-4
**Staunton, H.+ Barnes, T.W. & Owen, J.**

London [Staunton]

1 e4 e5 2 ♘f3 ♘c6 3 ♗c4 ♗c5 4 b4 ♗xb4 5 c3 ♗c5 6 d4 exd4 7 cxd4 ♗b6 8 0-0 d6 9 d5 ♘ce7 10 ♗b2 f6 11 ♘d4 ♗xd4 12 ♗xd4 ♘h6 13 f4 ♗g4 14 ♕b3 b6 15 f5 0-0 16 ♘d2 ♔h8 17 ♖f4 ♗h5 18 ♕h3 ♗e8 19 ♖h4 ♘eg8 20 g4 ♕e7 21 g5 fxg5 22 ♖xh6 ♘xh6 23 ♕xh6 ♔g8 24 ♕e6+ ♕f7 25 ♖f1 ♗d7 26 ♕xf7+ ♖xf7 27 h4 gxh4 28 ♘f3 h6 29 ♘xh4 b5 30 ♗b3 a5 31 ♗c2 a4 32 ♗c3 c5 33 dxc6 ♗xc6 34 ♘g6 ♖c7 35 ♗b4 ♗d5 36 ♗b1 [36 ♗xd6] 36 ... ♗c4 37 ♖c1 ♖d7 38 a3 ♖e8 39 ♔f2 d5 40 e5 d4 41 e6 ♖dd8 42 ♖d1 d3 43 ♘f4 ♔h7 44 ♔e3 g5 45 ♘xd3 h5 46 e7 ♔h6 47 f6 g4 48 ♖f1 g3 49 ♗d2 ♖d6 50 ♘e5 **1-0** M954-1858

### 1858-★CM-1 ●○ 27 viii 58
**Morphy, P.C.+ Carr, G.S.**

Birmingham [Löwenthal]

1 e4 h6 2 d4 a5 3 ♗d3 b6 4 ♘e2 e6 5 0-0 ♗a6 6 c4 ♘f6 7 e5 ♘h7 8 f4 ♗e7 9 ♘g3 d5 10 ♕g4 0-0 11 ♘h5 g5 12 fxg5 hxg5 13 ♗xh7+ ♔h8 14 ♘f6 dxc4 15 ♗c2 ♕xd4+ 16 ♕xd4 ♗c5 17 ♕xc5 bxc5 18 ♗xg5 ♘c6 19 ♖f3 ♔g7 20 ♗h6+ ♔xh6 21 ♖h3+ ♔g5 22 ♖h5+ ♔f4 23 ♔f2 **1-0** L/N3161

### 1858-★CM-2 xi 58
**Morphy, P.C.+ Chamouillet, M. & Versailles**

Versailles [Löwenthal]

1 e4 e6 2 d4 d5 3 exd5 exd5 4 ♘f3 ♘f6 5 ♗d3 ♗d6 6 0-0 0-0 7 ♘c3 c5 8 dxc5 ♗xc5 9 ♗g5 ♗e6 10 ♕d2 ♘c6 11 ♖ad1 ♗e7 12 ♖fe1 a6 13 ♕f4 ♘h5 14 ♕h4 g6 15 g4 ♘f6 [◻ 15 ... ♘g7] 16 h3 ♖c8 17 a3 ♖e8 18 ♘e2 h5 19 ♘f4 ♘h7? 20 ♘xe6 fxe6 21 ♖xe6 ♗xg5 22 ♖xg6+! ♔f8 23 ♕xh5

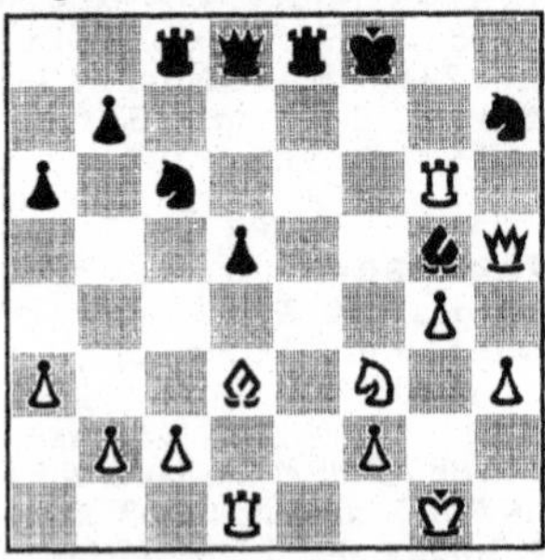

23 ... ♖c7 24 ♘xg5 ♖8e7 [24 ... ♘xg5 25 ♕h6++–] 25 ♕h6+ ♔e8 26 ♖g8+ **1-0** L/N3161

### 1858-★DM-1
**Devinck, A.–Morphy, P.C.**

Paris [Löwenthal]

⟨Δf7⟩ 1 e4 e6 2 d4 c5 3 d5 d6 4 c4 g6 5 ♘c3 ♗g7 6 ♗d3 ♘a6 7 a3 [◻ 7 ♘f3] 7 ... ♘h6 8 ♘ge2 [◻ 8 ♗xh6] 8 ... 0-0 9 0-0 exd5 10 exd5 [◻ 10 cxd5] 10 ... ♘g4 11 h3 ♘e5 12 f4 ♘xd3 13 ♕xd3 ♗f5 14 ♕f3 ♕b6 15 g4 [◻ 15 ♘b5] 15 ... ♗c2 16 ♘b5 ♖ae8 17 ♗e3? ♗d3 18 b3 ♗xe2 19 ♕xe2 ♗d4 20 ♖f3 ♗xa1 21 ♕d3 ♘c7 22 f5 ♘xb5 23 cxb5 ♖xe3 **0-1** L/N3161

### 1858-★DM-2
**Devinck, A.–Morphy, P.C.**

Paris [Maróczy]

⟨Δf7⟩ 1 e4 d6 2 d4 ♘f6 3 ♗d3 [◻ 3 ♘c3] 3 ... e5 4 dxe5 dxe5 5 ♗g5 ♗c5 6 ♘f3 h6 7 ♗h4 ♗g4 8 0-0 ♘bd7 9 ♘bd2 g5 10 ♗g3 h5 11 ♕e1 ♕e7 12 h4 ♘h7 13 c3 0-0-0 14 b4 ♗b6 15 a4 a6 16 ♕b1 ♖hf8 17 a5 [◻ 17 c4] 17 ... ♗a7 18 b5 ♗xf3 19 ♘xf3 ♖xf3 20 gxf3 gxh4 21 b6 [◻ 21 ♗h2; 21 bxa6] 21 ... cxb6 22 axb6 ♗xb6 23 ♖xa6? [23 ♗h2 ♘g5 24 ♔h1 ♘xf3 25 ♕a2 ♘c5∓] 23 ... bxa6 24 ♗xa6+ ♔c7 25 ♕b5 hxg3 **0-1** L/N3203

### 1858-★FM-1 ●○ 27 viii 58
**Morphy, P.C.+ Freeman, J.**

Birmingham [Löwenthal]

1 e4 e5 2 ♗c4 ♗c5 3 b4 ♗b6 4 ♘f3 d6 5 d4 exd4 6 ♘xd4 ♘f6 7 ♘c3 0-0 8 0-0 ♘xe4 9 ♘xe4 d5 10 ♗g5 ♕e8 11 ♗xd5 c6 12 ♖e1 ♕d7 13 ♘f6+ gxf6 14 ♗xf6 ♕d6

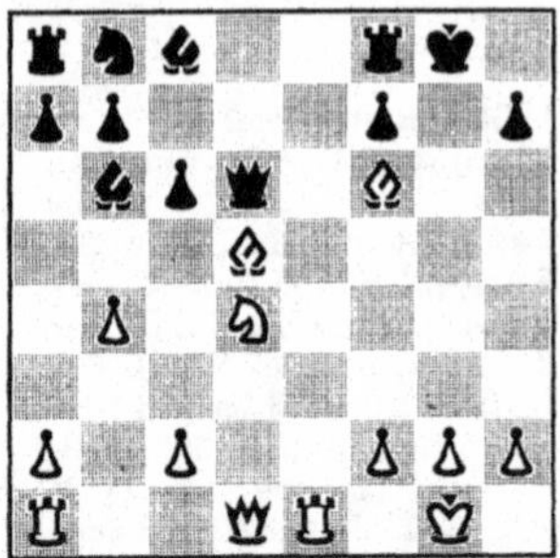

[14 ... ♕xd5? 15 ♖e5+–; 14 cxd5? 15 ♖e5 h6 16 ♕h5 (16 ♖g5+!+–) 16 ... ♔h7 17 ♘f5+–] 15 ♘e6 ♗xe6 16 ♕h5 ♗xf2+ 17 ♔h1 ♕f4 ♖xe6!! ♘d7 19 ♗b2! [Δ 20 ♖g6++–] 19 ... ♗d4 20 g3 ♘f6 [20 ... ♕g4++–] 21 gxf4 ♘xh5 22 ♗xd4 ♘xf4 23 ♖g1+ ♘g6 24 ♖exg6+ hxg4 25 ♖xg6+ ♔h7 26 ♖g7+ ♔h6 27 ♗e4 f5 28 ♗d3 b6 29 ♖g3 ♖f7 30 ♗e5 ♖e8 31 ♖f4+ ♔h7 32 ♖g5 ♖e1+ 33 ♔g2 ♖g7 34 ♗xf5+ ♔h8 35 h4 ♖xg5+ 36 ♗xg5 ♖e8 37 ♔f3 **1-0** L/N3161

### 1858-★GL-1 vii 58
**Morphy,P.C. & Walker,G. & Greenaway,F.E.=Löwenthal, J.J. & Medley,G.W. & Mongredien,A.**

London [Löwenthal]

1 e4 e5 2 f4 exf4 3 ♗c4 d5 4 ♗xd5 ♘f6 5 ♘f3 [5 ♘c3 ♗b4 6 ♕f3 ♕e7 7 ♘ge2 c6 8 ♗b3 g5∓] 5 ... ♘xd5 6 exd5 ♕xd5 7 ♘c3 ♕h5 8 d4 ♗d6 9 ♕e2+ ♔d8

10 0-0 g5 11 ♕b5 f5 12 ♕d5 ♘c6 13 ♘e5 ♖f8 14 ♗d2 ♘e7 15 ♕c4 ♖f6 16 ♖ae1 c6 17 ♘a4 ♗d7 18 ♘c5 ♗c8 19 ♖f3 g4 20 ♖b3 b6 **½-½** L/N3161

**1858-★GM-1 ●○** 27 ix 58
**Morphy, P.C.= Guibert**
Paris [Löwenthal]

1 e4 d5 2 exd5 ♕xd5 3 ♘c3 ♕d8 4 d4 e6⩲ 5 ♘f3 ♗d6 6 ♗d3 ♘e7 7 0-0 h6 8 ♗e3 c6 9 ♘e5! ♘d7 10 f4 ♘f6 11 ♘e4 ♘f5 12 ♗f2 ♗c7 13 c3 ♘d5 14 ♕f3 ♕e7 15 ♖ae1 ♗xe5 16 dxe5 h5 17 ♗c5 ♕d8 18 ♘d6+ ♘xd6 19 ♗xd6 g6 20 ♕g3 ♘e7 21 ♖d1 ♗d7 22 ♖d2 h4 23 ♕g4 ♘f5 24 ♗xf5 exf5 [24 ... gxf5 25 ♕g7] 25 ♕f3 ♕b6+ 26 ♔h1 0-0-0 27 c4 [⌓ 27 h3] 27 ... h3 28 g3 ♗e6 29 ♕c3 ♖d7 30 ♖fd1 c5 31 ♔g1 ♖hd8 32 ♕a3 a6 33 ♗xc5 ♕c6 34 ♗d6 f6 35 ♖d5! ♗xd5 36 ♖xd5 ♖xd6 37 exd6 ♔b8 38 ♕d3 ♖xd6 39 ♕d2 ♖xd5 40 cxd5 ♕c5+ 41 ♔f1 ♕c4+ 42 ♔f2 ♕c5+ **½-½** L/N3161

**1858-★HM-1** 4 ix 58
**Harrwitz, D.+ Morphy, P.C.**
Paris [Maróczy]

1 e4 e5 2 f4 exf4 3 ♘f3 g5 4 h4 g4 5 ♘e5 ♘f6 6 ♗c4 d5 7 exd5 ♗d6 8 d4 ♘h5 9 ♗b5+ [⌓ 9 ♘c3] 9 ... c6 10 dxc6 0-0 [⌓ 10 ... bxc6 11 ♘xc6 (11 ♗e2 ♘g3 12 ♖h2 ♗xe5 13 dxe5 ♕b6) 11 ... ♘xc6 12 ♗xc6+ ♔f8 13 ♗xa8 ♘g3 14 ♖h2 (14 ♔f2 ♘xh1+ 15 ♕xh1 ♗a6) 14 ... ♕e7+ 15 ♔f2 ♘e4+ 16 ♔g1 (⌓ 16 ♗xe4) 16 ... g3 17 ♖h1 ♘f2 18 ♕f1 ♘xh1 19 ♗xf4 ♗xf4 20 ♕xf4 ♕e1+ 21 ♕f1 ♕f2+ 22 ♕xf2+ gxf2+ 23 ♔f1 ♗a6+ 24 c4 ♗xc4#] 11 cxb7 ♗xb7 12 ♕xg4+ ♘g7 13 ♗xf4 ♕b6 14 ♘c3 ♗xe5 [14 ... ♕xd4? 15 ♖d1 ∆ 16 ♘d7; ∆ 16 ♘d3] 15 ♗xe5 f6 16 ♗g3 ♘a6 17 0-0 ♖ad8 18 ♖ad1± ♔h8 19 ♗xa6 [⌓ 19 ♖fe1] 19 ... ♗xa6 20 ♖fe1 ♗c8 21 ♕f3 ♗b7 [21 ... ♖xd4 22 ♗f2 ♖xd1 23 ♘xd1 (23 ♗xb6?) 23 ... ♕a6 24 ♘c3±] 22 ♕d3 ♖d7 23 ♕b5 ♕d8 24 d5 ♘f5 25 ♗f2 ♖g8 26 ♕d3 ♖dg7 [26 ... ♘e7 27 ♕f3 ♘xd5 28 ♗d4 ♖g6! 29 ♘e4 ♘f4 30 ♗xf6+ ♖xf6 (30 ... ♕xf6 31 ♖xd7) 31 ♖xd7 ♕xd7 32 ♘xf6 ♕d4+ 33 ♕e3 ♕xf6 34 ♕e8+ ♔g7 35 ♖e7+ ♔h6 36 ♖xb7] 27 ♕xf5 ♖xg2+ 28 ♔f1 ♗a6+ 29 ♘e2 [⌓ 29 ♖d3] 29 ... ♕d6 30 ♖d3 ♗xd3 31 cxd3 ♖h2 32 ♘f4 ♖h1+ 33 ♔e2 ♖h2 34 ♘e6 ♖g6 35 ♖c1 ♕b8 36 b3 ♖gg2 37 ♕xf6+ ♔g8 38 ♕e3 ♖h3+ 39 ♔e2 ♖xf2+ 40 ♕xf2 ♖h2 41 ♖g1+ ♔h8 42 ♖g2 ♕e5+ 43 ♔f3 ♕xd5+ 44 ♔g3 ♖xg2+ 45 ♕xg2 ♕xe6 46 ♕a8+ ♔g7 47 ♕xa7+ **1-0** L/N3203

**1858-★HM-2**
**Morphy, P.C.+ Hampton, H.**
London [Löwenthal]

1 e4 e5 2 ♘f3 ♘c6 3 ♗c4 ♗c5 4 b4 ♗xb4 5 c3 ♗c5 6 0-0 d6 7 d4 exd4 8 cxd4 ♗b6 9 ♘c3 ♘f6 10 e5 dxe5 11 ♗a3 ♗g4 12 ♕b3 ♗h5 [12 ... ♕d7 13 ♘xe5±] 13 dxe5 ♘g4 14 ♖ad1 ♕c8 15 e6! f6 16 ♕b5 ♗g6 17 ♗d5! **1-0** L/N3161

**1858-★JM-1** 5 xi 58
**Journoud, P. & Rivière, J.A. de+ Morphy, P.C.**
Paris [Maróczy]

1 e4 e5 2 ♘f3 ♘c6 3 ♗c4 ♗c5 4 b4 ♗xb4 5 c3 ♗c5 6 0-0 d6 7 d4 exd4 8 cxd4 ♗b6 9 ♗b2 [9 d5] 9 ... ♘f6 [⌓ 9 ... ♘a5 10 ♗d3 ♘e7] 10 ♘bd2 [⌓ 10 d5 ♘a5 11 ♗d3 0-0 12 ♘c3 c6 13 ♘e2 ♗g4 14 ♕d2⩲] 10 ... 0-0 11 e5 dxe5 12 dxe5 ♘d5 [12 ... ♘g4 13 h3 ♘h6, ♗f5] 13 ♘e4 ♗e6 [13 ... ♘f4 14 ♕c1 ♘e6 (14 ... ♘g6 15 ♖d1 ♕e8 16 ♘f6+±) 15 ♖d1 ♘ed4 16 ♘xd4 ♘xd4 17 ♗xd4 ♗xd4 18 ♕d2±] 14 ♘fg5 h6 15 ♘xe6 fxe6 16 ♕g4 ♔h8 [16 ... ♕e7 17 ♘f6+±] 17 ♖ad1 ♖f4 18 ♕xe6 ♖xe4 19 ♗xd5 ♘d4 20 ♖xd4 [20 ♕f7? ♖f4!] 20 ... ♖xd4 21 ♗xd4 ♗xd4 22 ♖e1 ♕g5 23 ♗f3 ♖f8 24 ♕c4 c5 [⌓ 24 ... ♗xe5!=] 25 e6! ♕e7 [25 ... ♖xf3 26 e7 ♗xf2+ 27 ♔h1 ♖e3 28 e8♕+] 26 ♕a4 ♕h4 27 ♕c2 ♕e7 28 ♕g6 [∆ 29 ♗e4] 28 ... ♖f6 29 ♕e4 ♖f8 30 g3 b5 31 ♖e2 b4 32 ♗h5 a5 33 ♗f7 a4 34 ♕c2 ♖a8 35 ♕e4 ♖b8 36 ♕d5 b3 37 axb3 axb3 38 ♗g6 b2 39 ♗b1 ♖d8 40 ♕f5 g5 41 ♕g6 ♗f6 42 ♕xh6+ ♔g8 43 ♕g6+ ♗g7 44 ♕h7+ ♔f8 45 h4 ♖d1+ 46 ♔g2 ♗f6 47 hxg5 ♗d4 48 ♕f5+ ♔g8 49 ♕g6+ ♔h8 50 ♖e4 ♕b7 51 e7 **1-0** L/N3203

**1858-★JM-2**
**Journoud, P.− Morphy, P.C.**
Paris [Staunton]

1 e4 e5 2 ♘f3 ♘c6 3 ♗c4 ♗c5 4 ♘c3 d6 5 h3 ♗e6 6 ♗b3 ♘f6 7 d3 ♕d7 8 0-0 0-0 9 ♔h1 h6 10 ♘h2 d5 11 f4 dxe4 12 fxe5 ♘xe5 13 ♘a4 [13 ♖xf6?] 13 ... ♗b6 14 ♘xb6 axb6 15 d4 ♘c6 16 ♖xf6 gxf6 17 ♗xh6 ♖fd8 18 ♕e1 ♘e7 19 ♕h4 ♘g6 20 ♕xf6 ♕xd4 21 ♕f1 ♗xb3 22 cxb3 ♖a5 23 ♘g4 f5 24 ♗e3 ♕d3 25 ♘h6+ ♔h7 26 ♕c1 ♖d7 27 ♗g5 ♕g3 28 ♕e3 ♕xe3 29 ♗xe3 f4 30 ♘g4 fxe3 31 ♘f6+ ♔g7 32 ♘xd7 ♖d5 33 ♖e1 ♖xd7 34 ♖xe3 ♖d4 35 ♔h2 ♘h4 36 g4 ♔f6 37 a4 ♔g5 38 ♔g3 ♖d2 **0-1** M954-1858

**1858-★JM-3**
**Morphy, P.C.+ Journoud, P.**
Paris [Löwenthal]

1 e4 c5 2 d4 cxd4 3 ♘f3 e5 4 ♗c4 ♗e7? [⌓ 4 ... ♕c7] 5 c3 d6 6 ♕b3 dxc3 7 ♗xf7+ ♔f8 8 ♘xc3 ♘c6 9 ♗xg8 ♖xg8 10 0-0 ♕e8 11 ♘g5 ♗xg5 12 ♗xg5 ♗e6 13 ♘d5 h6 14 f4! ♕d7 [14 ... hxg5? 15 fxg5+−] 15 fxe5+ ♔e8 16 ♘c7+ ♕xc7 17 ♕xe6+ **1-0** L/N3161

**1858-★KM-1**
**Kipping, J.S.− Morphy, P.C.**
Birmingham [Löwenthal]

1 e4 e5 2 ♘f3 ♘c6 3 ♗c4 ♗c5 4 b4 ♗xb4 5 c3 ♗c5 6 d4 exd4 7 cxd4 ♗b6 8 d5 ♘a5 9 ♗d3 d6 10 h3 ♘f6 11 ♗b2 0-0 12 0-0 ♘h5! 13 ♕d2 f5 14 ♘a3 ♘g3 15 ♖fe1 fxe4 16 ♗xe4 ♗f5 17 ♗xf5 ♘xf5 18 ♖e4 ♕d7 19 ♗c3 ♗c5 20 ♘c2 b6 21 ♕g5 [⌓ 21 ♗xa5] 21 ... ♖ae8 22 ♖ae1 ♖xe4 23 ♖xe4 h6 24 ♕g4 ♖f7 25 ♖e6 c6 26 ♘cd4 cxd5 27 ♕g6! ♘e7 28 ♕g3 [28 ♖xe7 ♕xe7 (28 ... ♖xe7 29 ♘f5 ♖e6 30 ♘xh6+ ♔f8 31 ♗xg7+ ♕xg7 32 ♕xe6) 29 ♘e6 ♖xf3 30 gxf3∞] 28 ... ♘ac6 29 ♘xc6 ♕xe6 30 ♘d8 ♕g6 **0-1** L/N3161

**1858-★KM-2**
**Morphy, P.C.+ Kipping, J.S.**
Birmingham [Löwenthal]

1 e4 e5 2 ♘f3 ♘c6 3 ♗c4 ♗c5 4 b4 ♗xb4 5 c3 ♗a5 6 d4 exd4 7 0-0 d6 8 ♕b3 ♕f6 [8 ... ♕e7? 9 e5±] 9 e5 dxe5 10 ♗g5 ♕f5 11 ♘xe5 ♘xe5 12 ♖e1 ♗b6 13 f4 dxc3+ 14 ♔h1 ♗d4 15 ♘xc3 ♔f8 16 ♖ad1 ♘xc4 [16 ... c5 17 ♖xd4±] 17 ♕xc4 ♗e6 18 ♕xd4 f6 19 ♘e4! b6 [19 ... fxg5? 20 ♘xg5+−] 20 ♘g3 ♕c5 21 ♕xc5+ bxc5 22 ♖xe6 fxg5 23 fxg5 g6 24 h4 ♔f7 25 ♖e5 h6 26 ♘e4 hxg5 27 ♘xg5+ ♔f6 28 ♖e6+ ♔f5 29 ♖d5+ ♔f4 30 ♖e4+ **1-0** L/N3161

**1858-★KM-3 ●○** 27 viii 58
**Morphy, P.C.− Kipping, J.S.**
Birmingham [Löwenthal]

1 e4 e5 2 ♘f3 ♘c6 3 d4 exd4 4 ♗c4 ♗c5 5 0-0 d6 6 c3 ♕f6 7 ♗g5 [7 b4 ♗b6 8 ♗b2 ♘e5 9 ♘xe5 dxe5 10 ♔h1 ∼ 11 f4±] 7 ... ♕g6 8 cxd4 ♘xd4 9 ♘xd4 ♕xg5 10 f4 ♕g6 11 ♔h1 ♘h6 12 h3? ♗xh3 13 gxh3 ♕xe4+ 14 ♕f3 ♕xd4 15 ♖e1+ ♔d7 16 ♘a3 ♗xa3 17 ♗b5+ c6 18 bxa3 ♖he8 [18 ... cxb5? 19 ♕xb7+, 20 ♕e7+, 21 ♖ac1+−] 19 ♖ac1 d5 20 ♕b3 ♔c7 21 ♗d3 ♖e3 22 ♖xe3 ♕xe3 23 ♖b1 ♕xh3+ 24 ♔g1 b6 25 ♖e1 ♕g3+ 26 ♔f1 ♕xf4+ 27 ♔g2 ♕g5+ 28 ♔f1 ♘g4 29 ♖e2 ♘e3+ **0-1** L/N3161

**1858-★LM-1 ●○⬠** 27 ix 58
**Morphy, P.C.= Lequesne, E.**
Paris
1 e4 b6 2 d4 ♗b7 3 ♗d3 e6 4 ♘h3 ♘e7 5 0-0 d5 6 e5 ♘ec6 7 c3 ♗e7 8 f4 g6 9 g4 h5 10 gxh5 ♖xh5 11 ♕g4 ♖h4 12 ♕g3 ♔d7 13 ♘d2 ♕h8 14 ♘g5 ♘d8 15 ♘df3 ♗xg5 16 fxg5 ♖h3 17 ♕g2 ♘bc6 18 ♗d2 ♘e7 19 ♖ac1 ♖c8 20 b4 a6 21 a4 ♕h5 22 ♘e1 ♘f5 23 ♖f3 ♖h4 24 ♖f4 ♖xf4 25 ♗xf4 c5 26 bxc5 bxc5 27 ♖b1 c4 28 ♗xf5 gxf5 29 ♘c2 ♗c6 30 a5 ♕h4 31 ♕g3 ♕h5 32 ♕g2 ♕h4 **½-½** L/N3161

**1858-★LM-2**
**Morphy, P.C.–Löwenthal, J.J.**
1 e4 e5 2 ♘f3 d6 3 d4 exd4 4 ♕xd4 ♗e7 5 ♗c4 ♘c6 6 ♕d1 ♗d7 7 0-0 ♘f6 8 ♘c3 0-0 9 h3 a6 10 ♗f4 b5 11 ♗d3 ♕c8 12 ♕d2 ♘d8 13 ♘d5 ♘xd5 14 exd5 f5 15 ♖ae1 ♗f6 16 c3 ♘f7 17 b3 h6 18 h4 ♕b7 19 ♗c2 ♖ae8 20 g3 ♘e5 21 ♗xe5 dxe5 22 c4 c5 23 ♖e2 e4 24 ♘e1 ♕b6 25 ♘g2 ♗e5 26 a3 ♕f6 27 ♘f4 g5 28 ♘g2 ♖e7 29 f4 exf3 30 ♖xf3 ♖fe8 31 hxg5 hxg5 32 ♘e3 ♗d4 33 ♔f1 f4 34 gxf4 g4 35 ♘xg4 ♗xg4 36 ♖g3 ♕h4 37 ♖eg2 ♖e1+ 38 ♕xe1 ♕h1+ 39 ♖g1 ♖xe1+ 40 ♔xe1 ♗xg1 41 ♖xg4+ ♔f8 ...? **0-1** L/N3161

**1858-★LM-3**
**Morphy, P.C.+ Löwenthal, J.J.**
London
1 e4 e5 2 ♘f3 ♘f6 3 d4 exd4 4 e5 ♘e4 5 ♗d3 d5 6 ♘xd4 c5 7 ♘e2 ♘c6 8 f3 ♘g5 9 f4 ♘e6 10 0-0 ♕b6 11 ♔h1 ♗e7 12 ♘bc3 ♘c7 13 b3 ♘b4 14 ♘g3 ♘xd3 15 ♕xd3 ♕c6 16 f5 g6 17 ♗f4 ♗xf5 18 ♘xf5 gxf5 19 ♕xf5 ♕g6 20 ♗g3 h5 21 ♕xg6 fxg6 22 e6 ♘xe6 23 ♖ae1 ♖f8 24 ♖xf8+ ♘xf8 25 ♘xd5 **1-0** L/N3161

**1858-★LM-4** vii 58
**Löwenthal, J.J. & Medley, G.W.=Mongredien, A. & Morphy, P.C.**
London [Löwenthal]
1 e4 e5 2 ♘f3 d6 3 ♗c4 f5 4 d4 ♘c6 5 dxe5 [◻ 5 ♘g5] 5 ... dxe5 6 ♕xd8+ ♘xd8 7 ♘xe5 fxe4 8 ♗d2 ♗d6 9 ♗c3 ♘f6 10 h3 ♗e6 11 ♘d2 0-0 12 0-0 ♘d5 13 ♗xd5 ♗xd5 14 ♘dc4 b5 15 ♘xd6 cxd6 16 ♖fd1 e3 17 fxe3 [◻ 17 ♖xd5 exf2+ 18 ♔f1 dxe5 19 ♖xe5 ♖c8 20 ♖xb5 ♖c7 21 ♖ad1 ±] 17 ... ♗xg2 18 ♔xg2 dxe5 19 ♗xe5 ♘c6 20 ♗d4 [◻ 20 ♗f4] 20 ... ♖ae8! 21 ♖d2 ♖e6 [21 ... ♘xd4 22 exd4 ♖e3; 23 ... ♖ff3] 22 ♖e1 ♖g6+ 23 ♔h2 ♖f3 24 ♖g2 ♘xd4 25 exd4 ♖h6 26 ♖e7 ♖fxh3+ 27 ♔g1 ♖h1+ 28 ♔f2 ♖f6+ 29 ♔e2 ♖f7 30 ♖e8+ ♖f8 **½-½** L/N3161

**1858-★LM-5 ●○⬠** 27 viii 58
**Morphy, P.C.+Lyttelton, G.W.**
Birmingham [Löwenthal]
1 e4 e5 2 f4 exf4 3 ♘f3 g5 4 h4 g4 5 ♘e5 d6 6 ♘xg4 ♗e7 7 d4 ♗xh4+ 8 ♘f2 ♗xf2+ [8 ... ♕g5 9 ♕f3 ♗g3 10 ♘c3 ♘f6 11 ♗d2 ♘c6 (11 ... ♗d7 12 d5 ♘g4 13 ♕xg3 fxg3 14 ♗xg5 gxf2+ 15 ♔d2 f6 16 ♗e3 0-0 17 ♗e2 ♘xe3 18 ♔xe3 f5∞) 12 ♗b5 ♗d7 13 ♗xc6 bxc6 14 0-0-0=] 9 ♔xf2 ♘f6 10 ♘c3 ♕e7 11 ♗xf4 ♘xe4+ 12 ♘xe4 ♕xe4 13 ♗b5+ ♔f8 14 ♗h6+ ♔g8 15 ♖h5 ♗f5 16 ♕d2 ♗g6 17 ♖e1 **1-0** L/N3161

**1858-★MM-1**
**Morphy, P.C.–Maurian, C.A.**
New Orleans [Maróczy]
⟨♘b1⟩ 1 e4 e5 2 ♘f3 ♘f6 3 ♘xe5 d6 4 ♘xf7 ♔xf7 5 ♗c4+ ♗e6 [◻ 5 ... d5 6 exd5 ♗d6] 6 ♗xe6+ ♔xe6 7 d4 ♗e7 8 0-0 ♖f8 9 ♕d3 ♔f7 10 ♕b3+ d5 11 e5 ♘bd7! 12 ♕xb7 [12 exf6 ♘xf6 13 ♕xb7 ♔g8∓] 12 ... ♖b8 13 ♕xa7 ♘e4 14 f3 ♘g5 15 ♗xg5 ♗xg5 16 f4 ♗e7 17 ♕a6 ♖b6 18 ♕e2 g6 19 c4 ♘b8 20 c5 ♖b4 21 f5 gxf5 22 ♖xf5+ ♔g8 23 ♕g4+ ♔h8 24 ♖xf8+ ♕xf8 25 ♕e6 ♖xd4 26 ♖f1 ♕e8 27 ♔h1 [27 ♖f7 ♖d1+, 28 ... ♗xc5−+] 27 ... ♖d2 28 ♕h6 ♕f7 29 ♖g1 ♕f2 [◻ 29 ... ♖xb2] 30 b4 ♖d4 31 ♕e6 ♕f8 32 a3 c6 33 h3 ♖f4 34 ♔h2 ♖f2 35 ♔h1 ♖f1 36 ♕g4 ♘a6 37 ♖xf1 ♕xf1+ 38 ♔h2 ♕f8 39 ♕e6 ♗h4 40 ♕xc6 ♕f4+ 41 ♔h1 ♕xe5 42 ♕c8+ ♔g7 43 ♕d7+ ♕e7 44 ♕g4+ ♔h6 45 g3 ♗f6 46 ♔h2 ♕e4 47 ♕d1 d4 48 ♕f1 ♔g7 49 ♕xa6 d3 50 ♕a7+ ♔g6 51 h4 ♕e2+ 52 ♔h3 d2 53 g4 d1♕ **0-1** L/N3203

**1858-★MM-2**
**Morphy, P.C.– Maurian, C.A.**
New Orleans [Maróczy]
⟨♘b1⟩ 1 e4 e5 2 f4 exf4 3 ♘f3 d5! 4 exd5 ♕xd5 5 ♗e2 ♘f6 6 0-0 ♗e7 7 d4 0-0 8 ♗xf4 c6 [◻ 8 ... c5 9 c4 ♕f5 10 ♗xb8 ♖xb8 11 d5 ♗d6] 9 c4 ♕d8 10 ♕c2 ♗g4 11 ♖ad1 ♗h5 12 ♘e5 ♗g6 13 ♕b3 ♕b6 14 ♕h3 ♘a6 15 c5 ♕d8 16 ♗xa6 bxa6 17 ♘xc6 ♕e8 18 ♘xe7+ ♕xe7 19 ♗d6 ♕e6 20 ♗xf8 [20 ♕xe6 fxe6 21 ♗xf8 ♔xf8] 20 ... ♕xh3 21 gxh3 ♔xf8 22 d5 ♖d8 23 c6 [23 d6] 23 ... ♖xd5 24 c7 ♖g5+ 25 ♔f2 ♖f5+ 26 ♔e3 [26 ♔g2 ♖g5+ 27 ♔f2 ♖f5+=] 26 ... ♖e5+ 27 ♔d4 ♖e8 28 ♔c4? [◻ 28 ♔c5! ♔e7 (28 ... ♗e4 29 ♖d8 ♗b7 30 ♖e1!) 29 ♖fe1+ ♗e4 30 ♖xe4+ ♘xe4+ 31 ♔c6] 28 ... ♔e7 29 ♖fe1+ ♗e4 30 ♔c5 ♖c8 31 ♖xe4+ ♘xe4+ 32 ♔c6 ♘c5! 33 b4 ♘e6 34 ♖d7+ ♔f6 [◻ 34 ... ♔e8, ♖c7!] 35 a4 ♖xc7+! 36 ♖xc7 ♘xc7 37 ♔xc7 ♔e6! 38 b5 axb5 39 axb5 f5 40 ♔b7 f4 41 ♔xa7 f3 42 b6 f2 43 b7 f1♕ 44 b8♕ ♕a1+ [45 ♔b7 ♕b2+ 46 ♔a7 ♕xb8+ 47 ♔xb8 ♔f6 48 ♔c7 ♔g5 49 ♔d6 ♔h4 50 ♔e7 ♔xh3 51 ♔f7 g5 52 ♔f6! h6! 53 ♔f5 ♔xh2 54 ♔g4 ♔g2 55 ♔h5 ♔h3 56 ♔xh6 g4−+] **0-1** L/N3203

**1858-★MM-3**
**Maurian, C.A.– Morphy, P.C.**
New Orleans [Maróczy]
⟨♘b8⟩ 1 e4 e5 2 f4 exf4 3 ♘f3 g5 4 h4 g4 5 ♘e5 ♘f6 6 ♗c4 d5 7 ♗xd5 [◻ 7 exd5] 7 ... ♘xd5 8 exd5 f3 9 0-0 ♕xh4 10 d4 f2+ 11 ♖xf2 g3 12 ♖f4 ♕h2+ 13 ♔f1 ♕h1+ 14 ♔e2 ♕xg2+ 15 ♔d3 ♕h3 16 ♕e1 ♗f5+ 17 ♔c4 0-0-0 18 ♕a5 [18 ♘xf7 g2 19 ♗e3 ♖e8 20 ♘e5 ♗h6 21 ♖xf5 ♕xf5 22 ♗xh6 ♕f1+−+; ◻ 18 ♖f3] 18 ... a6 19 ♘c3 ♗xc2 20 ♖xf7 ♗d6 21 ♘b5 axb5+ 22 ♔xb5 ♔b8 23 ♗g5 [23 ♘c6+ bxc6 24 ♔xc6 ♕c8!−+] 23 ... ♗xe5 24 ♗xd8 ♖xd8 25 ♕c3 ♖xd5+ 26 ♔c4 ♖xd4+ 27 ♕xd4 ♕e6+ 28 ♕d5 ♗d3+ **0-1** L/N3203

**1858-★MM-4**
**Morphy, P.C.+ Maurian, C.A.**
New Orleans [Maróczy]
1 e4 e5 2 f4 exf4 3 ♗c4 ♕h4+ 4 ♔f1 b5 5 ♗b3 ♘f6 6 ♘f3 ♕h6 7 ♘e5 d5 8 ♘c3 ♗d6 9 d4 ♘xe4 [◻ 9 ... 0-0] 10 ♘xe4 ♗xe5 11 ♗xd5 c6 12 dxe5 cxd5 13 ♘d6+ ♔d7 14 ♕xd5 ♔c7 [◻ 14 ... ♕e6! 15 ♕xa8 ♘c6! 16 ♗xf4 ♖d8 17 ♘xc8 ♔c7!] 15 c4! ♕e6 16 ♕xa8 ♘c6 17 cxb5 ♕d5 18 ♕xc6+ ♕xc6 19 bxc6 ♔xc6 20 ♗xf4 ♖d8 21 ♔f2 ♗e6 22 ♖ac1+ ♔b6 23 ♗e3+ ♔a6 24 ♖c6+ ♔a5 25 ♗d2+ ♔a4 26 ♖a6# **1-0** L/N3203

**1858-★MM-5**
**Morphy, P.C.+ Maurian, C.A.**
New Orleans [Maróczy]
⟨♖a1⟩ 1 e4 e5 2 f4 exf4 3 ♗c4 ♕h4+ 4 ♔f1 b5 5 ♗b3 ♘f6 6 ♘f3 ♕h6 7 d4 ♗e7 8 e5 ♘h5 9 ♔f2 g5 10 g4 ♘g7 [◻ 10 ... fxg3+ 11 hxg3 ♕g6] 11 h4 ♕g6 [◻ 11 ... gxh4!] 12 hxg5 ♗xg5 13 ♘xg5 ♕xg5 14 ♕f3 ♘c6 15 ♗xf4 ♘xd4

16 ♗xf7+ ♔f8 [16 ... ♔xf7 17 ♕d5+, 18 ♗xg5+−] 17 ♕e4 ♕xg4 18 ♗d5 ♕e2+ 19 ♕xe2 ♘xe2 20 ♗h6! c6 21 ♖f1 ♗a6 22 ♔e3+ ♔e7 23 ♗g5+ ♔e8 24 ♗f7+ ♔f8 25 ♔xe2 b4+ 26 ♗c4+ **1-0** L/N3203

**1858-★MM-6** i58
**Morphy, P.C.− Maurian, C.A.**
New Orleans [Maróczy]

⟨♖a1⟩ 1 e4 e5 2 ♘f3 ♘c6 3 ♗c4 ♗c5 4 b4 ♗xb4 5 c3 ♗a5 6 d4 exd4 7 0-0 d3 8 ♕b3 ♕f6 9 e5 ♕g6 10 ♖e1 b6 11 ♗a3 ♗b7 12 ♗xf7+ ♕xf7 13 e6 ♕f5 14 ♘h4 ♕h5 15 exd7+ ♔xd7 16 ♕e6+ ♔d8 17 ♘f5 ♘f6 18 ♗e7+ ♘xe7 19 ♕xe7+ ♔c8 20 ♕xg7 ♖e8 21 ♘e7+ ♖xe7 22 ♕xe7 ♕e8! 23 ♕xe8+ ♘xe8 24 ♖xe8+ ♔d7 25 ♖e3 ♗a6 26 f4 ♖e8 27 ♔f2 ♖xe3 28 ♔xe3 ♔e6 29 g4 c5 30 ♔e4 d2−+ 31 ♘xd2 ♗xc3 32 ♘b3 ♗f1 33 h4 a5 34 a4 ♗c4 35 ♘c1 ♗d2 **0-1** L/N3203

**1858-★MM-7**
**Medley, G.W.− Morphy, P.C.**
London [Löwenthal]

1 e4 e5 2 ♘f3 ♘c6 3 ♗b5 ♘ge7 4 c3 a6 5 ♗a4 b5 6 ♗b3 d5 7 exd5 ♘xd5 8 d4 exd4 9 ♘xd4 ♘xd4 10 ♕xd4 ♗e6 11 0-0 c5 12 ♕e5 c4 13 ♗c2 ♗d6 14 ♕d4 [14 ♕xg7 ♔d7∓] 14 ... 0-0 15 ♕e4 g6 16 ♕f3 ♕h4 17 g3 ♕h3 18 ♗e4 ♘c7 19 ♗f4 ♖ad8 20 ♗xd6 ♖xd6 21 ♕f4 ♖fd8 22 ♗g2 ♕h5 23 ♗f3 ♕c5 24 ♘a3 ♘d5 25 ♕e5 f6 26 ♕e2 ♘xc3 27 bxc3 ♕xa3 28 ♕e3 ♗h3 29 ♖fd1 ♕xa2! 30 ♕e7 ♕b2 31 ♕xd8+? ♖xd8 32 ♖xd8+ ♔g7 33 ♖e1 ♕xc3 34 ♖e7+ ♔h6 35 ♖e3 ♕b2 36 ♖d1 c3 37 ♖3e1 c2 38 ♖c1 b4 39 ♗e4 b3 **0-1** L/N3161

**1858-★MM-8**
**Morphy, P.C.+ Medley, G.W.**
London [Löwenthal]

1 e4 e5 2 f4 exf4 3 ♘f3 g5 4 h4 g4 5 ♘e5 ♘f6 6 ♗c4 d5 7 exd5 ♗d6 8 d4 ♘h5 [□ 8 ... ♕e7] 9 ♘c3 ♗f5 [□ 9 ... ♘g3] 10 ♘e2 ♕f6 11 ♘xf4 ♘g3 [□ 11 ... ♘xf4] 12 ♘h5 ♘xh5 13 ♗g5 ♗b4+ [□ 13 ... ♕g7] 14 c3 ♕d6 15 0-0 ♘g7 16 ♖xf5! ♘xf5 17 ♕xg4 ♘e7 18 ♖e1 h5 19 ♕f3 ♖h7 20 ♗b5+ c6 21 dxc6 bxc6 22 ♘xc6 ♘xc6 23 ♗xc6+ **1-0** L/N3161

**1858-★MM-9**
**Medley, G.W.− Morphy, P.C.**
London [Löwenthal]

1 e4 e5 2 ♘f3 ♘c6 3 ♗b5 ♘f6 4 d4 exd4 5 e5 ♘e4 6 0-0 a6 7 ♗xc6 dxc6 8 ♕xd4 ♗f5 9 ♗f4 ♗c5 10 ♕xd8+ ♖xd8 11 ♘bd2 0-0 12 ♘xe4 ♗xe4 13 ♘g5 ♗d5 [13 ... ♗xc2 14 e6; 14 ♖fc1] 14 ♖fe1 h6 15 ♘e4 ♗xe4 16 ♖xe4 g5 17 ♗g3 ♖d2 18 ♖c1 f5! 19 exf6 ♖xf6 20 h4 ♗xf2+ 21 ♗xf2 ♖fxf2 22 hxg5 [□ 22 ♖g4] 22 ... ♖xg2+ 23 ♔f1 hxg5 24 ♖e7 g4 25 ♖xc7 g3 **0-1** L/N3161

**1858-★MM-10**
**Medley, G.W.+ Morphy, P.C.**
London [Löwenthal]

⟨♙f7⟩ 1 e4 d6 2 d4 ♘f6 3 ♗c4 ♘c6 4 ♘c3 e5 5 d5 ♘e7 6 ♘f3 ♘g6 7 ♗g5 h6 8 ♗xf6 ♕xf6 9 ♗b5+ ♔f7 10 ♘d2 ♘h4 11 g3 ♘g2+!? 12 ♔e2 [12 ♔f1? ♘e3+−+] 12 ... ♗h3 13 f3 ♕g5 14 ♕g1 a6 15 ♗d3 h5 16 ♕f2 g6 17 ♖ag1 [□ 17 ♖hg1] 17 ... ♗h6 18 ♘f1 ♕c1 19 ♘d1 b5 20 ♖xg2 ♖hc8 21 ♘fe3 [21 ♖2g1 ♗xf1+−+] 21 ... c5 22 dxc6 ♖xc6 23 ♖e1 ♗xe3 24 ♘xe3 ♕xb2 25 ♖2g1 ♖ac8 26 ♖c1 [26 ♕b1 ♖xc2+=] 26 ... ♗e6 [26 ... ♕xa2 27 g4] 27 ♖gd1 ♖c3 28 ♔f1 ♗h3+ 29 ♔e1 [29 ♔g1 ♖xd3 30 cxd3 ♕xc1 31 ♖xc1 ♖xc1+ 32 ♘f1 ♔e6=] 29 ... ♗e6 30 ♘d5 ♖3c5 31 c3 ♕a3 32 ♕d2 ♗xd5 33 exd5 ♖xc3 [33 ... ♖xd5 34 ♗xg6+−] 34 ♖xc3 ♖xc3 35 ♗e4 ♕c5 36 ♔e2 b4 37 ♕h6 [□ 37 ♕g5] 37 ... ♔e7 38 ♕g5+ ♔d7 39 ♕d2 g5 40 ♕xg5 ♔c7 41 ♕d2 a5 42 h3 a4 43 g4 hxg4 44 hxg4 ♔b6 45 g5 ♕c4+ 46 ♔e1 **1-0** L/N3161

**1858-★MM-11**
**Morphy, P.C.+ Morphy, A.**
New Orleans [Löwenthal]

⟨♖a1⟩ 1 e4 e5 2 ♘f3 ♘c6 3 ♗c4 ♘f6 4 ♘g5 d5 5 exd5 ♘xd5 6 ♘xf7 ♔xf7 7 ♕f3+ ♔e6 8 ♘c3 ♘d4 [□ 8 ... ♘e7] 9 ♗xd5+ ♔d6 10 ♕f7 ♗e6 11 ♗xe6 ♘xe6 12 ♘e4+ ♔d5 13 c4+ ♔xe4 14 ♕xe6 ♕d4 15 ♕g4+

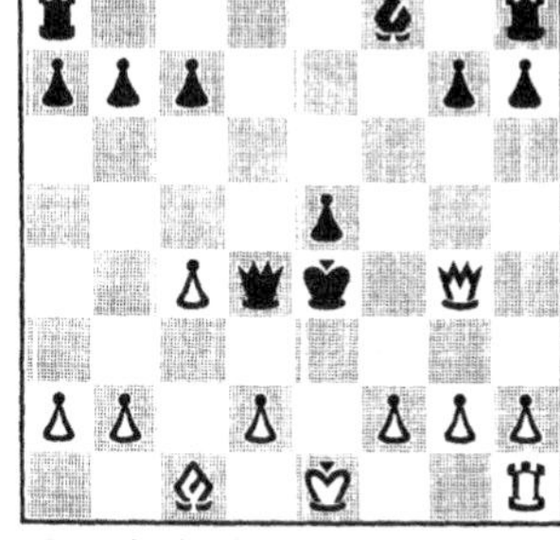

15 ... ♔d3 16 ♕e2+ ♔c2 17 d3+ ♔xc1 18 0-0# **1-0** L/N3161

**1858-★MO-1**
**Owen, J.− Morphy, P.C.**
London [Maróczy]

1 d4 e6 2 c4 d5 3 e3 [3 ♘c3 ♘f6 4 ♗g5 ♗e7 5 ♘f3 0-0 6 ♕c2∞] 3 ... ♘f6 4 ♘f3 c5 5 ♘c3 ♘c6 6 a3 ♗d6 7 dxc5 ♗xc5 8 b4 ♗d6 9 cxd5! exd5 10 ♗e2 0-0 11 0-0 a5 12 b5 ♘e7 13 ♗b2 ♗e6 14 ♘a4 ♘e4! 15 ♘d4 ♘c5 16 ♘xe6? fxe6 17 ♗g4 ♘f5 18 ♗xf5 ♖xf5 19 ♘xc5 ♗xc5 20 ♕g4 ♕e7 21 ♗d4 ♗xd4 [22 ... ♗xa3? 23 ♖xa3 △ ♕g7#] 22 ♕xd4 ♖c8 23 ♕b6 ♖c2 24 ♖ac1? [□ 24 ♕xa5 ♕f6 (24 ... h6 25 ♖d1 △ ♖d2) 25 ♕a8+ ♔f7 26 ♕xb7+ ♔g6 27 f4 ♕b2 28 ♔h1!] 24 ... ♖fxf2! 25 ♖xc2 ♖xc2 26 ♕xa5 h6 27 ♖f2 ♖c1+ 28 ♖f1 ♕c5 29 ♕d2 ♖c3! 30 ♕d4 ♕xd4 31 exd4 ♖xa3 32 ♖c1 ♔f7! [32 ... ♖b3 33 ♖c8+ ♔h7 34 ♖e8] 33 ♖c7+ ♔f6 34 ♖xb7 ♖d3 35 ♔f2 ♖xd4 36 ♔e3 e5 37 b6 ♖b4 38 ♖b8 ♔e7! 39 b7 ♔d7! 40 ♖g8 ♖xb7 41 ♖xg7+ ♔c6 42 ♖g6+ ♔c5 43 ♖xh6 ♖b3+ 44 ♔e2 e4 45 ♖h8 ♔d4 46 ♖g8 ♖b2+ 47 ♔d1 ♔d3 **0-1** L/N3203

**1858-★MO-2**
**Morphy, P.C.− Owen, J.**
London [Maróczy]

1 e4 b6 2 d4 ♗b7 3 ♗d3 e6 4 ♘h3 [□ 4 c3; 4 ♘e2] 4 ... c5 5 c3 cxd4 6 cxd4 ♘c6 7 ♗e3 ♘b4 8 ♘c3 ♘xd3+ 9 ♕xd3 ♗b4 10 0-0 ♗xc3 11 bxc3 ♘f6 12 e5 ♘d5 13 c4 ♗a6 14 ♗d2! ♖c8 [□ 14 ... 0-0] 15 ♖ac1 [□ 15 ♕g3] 15 ... 0-0 16 ♕b3 ♘e7 17 ♗b4 ♖e8 18 ♖fd1 ♘f5 19 g4 ♘h4 20 f4 f6 21 ♗e1 fxe5 22 dxe5 ♕e7 23 ♘g5 h6 24 ♘e4 [24 ♗xh4 hxg5 25 ♗xg5 ♕c5+] 24 ... ♗b7 25 ♕d3 [25 ♘d6 ♘f3+, ♕h4+, ♘xh2+] 25 ... ♖f8

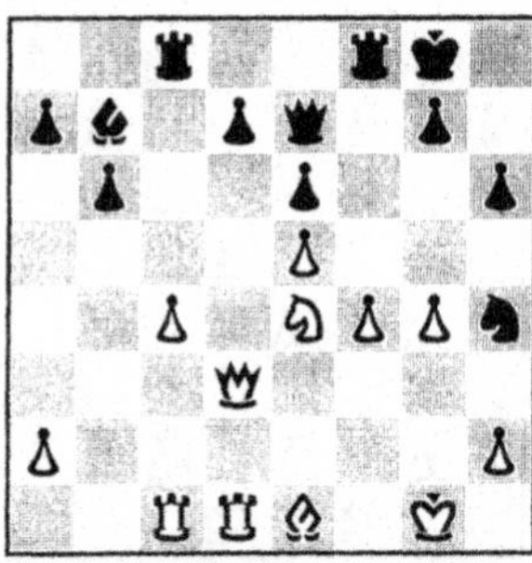

26 ♗xh4 ♕xh4 27 ♘f6+ ♖xf6! [27 ... gxf6 28 ♕g6+ ♔h8 29 ♖xd7+–] 28 exf6 ♕xg4+ 29 ♕g3 ♕xg3+ 30 hxg3 ♗c6 31 fxg7 ♔xg7 32 ♔f2 ♔f6 33 g4 [□ 33 ♖e1, 34 ♖e5] 33 ... h5! 34 g5+ [34 gxf5 ♖h8 35 ♖e1 ♖xh5 36 ♔g3 ♖h8 37 ♖e2 ♖g8+ 38 ♔h2 ♔f5 39 ♖f1=] 34 ... ♔f5 35 ♔e3 [35 ♔g3 ♖h8∓] 35 ... h4 36 ♖d2 h3 37 ♖h2 ♗g2 38 ♖c2 d5 39 g6 dxc4 40 g7 ♖g8 41 ♖cxg2 hxg2 42 ♖xg2 ♔f6 43 ♖c2 ♖xg7 44 ♖xc4 ♖g3+ 45 ♔e4 ♖a3 46 ♖c2 ♖a4+ **0-1** L/N3203

**1858-★MO-3**
**Morphy, P.C.+ Owen, J.**
London [Maróczy]

1 e4 b6 2 d4 ♗b7 3 ♗d3 [3 d5] 3 ... e6 4 ♘h3 c5! 5 c3 ♘c6 6 ♗e3 ♘f6 [□ 6 ... cxd4] 7 ♘d2 cxd4 8 cxd4 ♗b4 9 0-0 ♗xd2 10 ♕xd2 ♘e7 11 f3 ♘g6 12 ♖ac1 0-0 13 ♗g5 h6 14 ♗xf6 ♕xf6 15 e5 ♕h4 16 ♗b5 ♖fd8 17 ♖c7 ♗c6 18 ♗e2 [18 ♗xc6 dxc6 19 ♖xc6 ♖xd4∓] 18 ... ♘e7 19 ♘f4 ♕g5 [19 ... g5 20 g3] 20 ♖d1 ♖f8 21 ♕c1 ♘f5 22 g4 ♘h4 [□ 22 ... ♘xd4! 23 ♖xd4 ♕xe5 24 ♖dxd7 ♗xd7 25 ♖xd7 g5! 26 ♘g6 fxg6 27 ♕b1 ♕e3+ 28 ♔h1 ♖f6∓] 23 ♔f2 ♕d8 24 ♖xc6 dxc6 25 ♕xc6 ♖c8 26 ♕e4 ♕g5 27 ♗d3 g6 28 ♖g1 ♖c7 29 ♘e2 f5? [□ 29 ... ♔h8∓] 30 gxf5 ♕xf5 31 ♕xf5 exf5 32 ♘f4 ♖c6 33 d5 ♖c5 34 ♘xg6 ♘xg6 35 ♖xg6+ **1-0** L/N3203

**1858-★MP-1 ●○⬠** 27 ix 58
**Morphy, P.C.+ Potier**
Paris [Löwenthal]

1 e4 e5 2 ♘f3 ♘f6 3 ♗c4 [3 ♘c3 ♗b4 4 ♘xe5 ♗xc3 5 dxc3 d6 6 ♘f3 ♘xe4 7 ♗d3 ♘f6 8 0-0 0-0=] 3 ... ♘xe4 4 ♘c3 ♘f6 [4 ... ♘xc3 5 dxc3 f6 6 ♘h4 (6 0-0 ♕e7 7 ♘h4 g6, 7 ... c6∓) 6 ... ♕e7 7 ♕h5+ ♔d8 8 ♘g6 ♕e8 9 ♗d3 ♗e7→] 5 ♘xe5 d5 6 ♗b3 ♗e7 7 d4 c6 8 0-0 ♘bd7 9 f4 ♘b6 10 ♕f3 h5 11 f5 ♕c7 12 ♗f4 ♗d6 13 ♖ae1 ♔f8 14 ♕g3 h4 [14 ... ♗xf5 15 ♘g6+±] 15 ♘g6+! ♔g8 16 ♗xd6 hxg3 17 ♗xc7 fxg6 18 fxg6 gxh2+ 19 ♔h1 ♗g4 20 ♖e7 ♘bd7 21 ♗e5 ♔f8 22 ♖f7+ ♔g8 23 ♘xd5! cxd5 24 ♗xd5 ♘b6 25 ♗b3 **1-0**
L/N3161

Préti, J.L. L/N639.BL

**1858-★MP-2 ●○⬠** 27 ix 58
**Morphy, P.C.+ Préti, J.L.**
Paris [Löwenthal]

1 e4 c5 2 d4 cxd4 3 ♘f3 e5 4 ♗c4 ♗b4+ 5 c3 dxc3 6 bxc3 ♗c5 7 ♘xe5 ♕f6 8 ♗xf7+ ♔f8 9 ♘d3 ♗b6 [9 ... ♗xf2+? 10 ♘xf2 Δ 11 0-0±] 10 ♗b3 d6 11 ♗a3 ♘c6 12 0-0 ♘h6 13 e5! ♕g6 14 ♘f4 ♕g4 15 ♘e6+ ♗xe6 16 ♕xd6+ ♔f7 17 ♕d7+ ♔g6 18 ♗xe6 ♕g5 19 ♗d5! ♘xe5 20 ♗e4+ ♘f5 21 ♕e6+ ♕f6 22 ♗xf5+ ♔h5 23 g4+ ♘xg4 24 ♗xg4+ **1-0**
L/N3161

**1858-★MR-1 ●○⬠** 27 viii 58
**Morphy, P.C.+ Rhodes, J.**
Birmingham [Lowenthal]

1 e4 e5 2 f4 ♗c5 3 ♘f3 ♘c6 4 fxe5 d5 [4 ... ♘xe5 5 ♘xe5 ♕h4+ 6 g3 ♕xe4+ 7 ♕e2 ♕xh1 8 d4 (8 ♘g6+, 9 ♘xh8∓) 8 ... ♗e7 9 ♘f3 d6 10 ♗e3 ♗g4 11 ♘bd2±] 5 exd5 ♕xd5 6 ♘c3 ♕d8 7 ♘e4 ♗b6 8 c3 ♗g4 9 d4 ♕d5 10 ♘f2 ♘xe5 11 ♕e2 [11 dxe5 ♗xf2+∞] 11 ... ♗xf3 12 gxf3 ♕xf3 13 ♕xe5+ ♔f8 14 ♗e2 ♕c6 15 ♖g1 f6 16 ♕g3 g6 17 ♗e3 ♖e8 18 ♔d2 ♘e7 19 ♗d3 ♕d7 20 ♘g4 ♘d5 21 ♖ae1 ♘xe3 22 ♖xe3 ♕f7 23 ♘xf6 ♖xe3 24 ♕xe3 ♕xa2 25 ♕e8+ ♔g7 26 ♘h5+ ♔h6 27 ♕e3+ ♔xh5 28 ♕g5# **1-0**
L/N3616

**1858-★MR-2**
**Rivière, J.A.de– Morphy, P.C.**
Paris [Löwenthal]

1 e4 e5 2 ♘f3 ♘c6 3 ♗c4 ♗c5 4 b4 ♗xb4 5 c3 ♗c5 6 0-0 d6 7 d4 exd4 8 cxd4 ♗b6 9 ♗b2 ♘f6 10 ♘bd2 0-0 11 h3 d5 12 exd5 ♘xd5 13 ♘e4 ♗f5 14 ♘g3 ♗g6 15 ♘e5 ♘f6 16 ♘xg6 hxg6 17 ♗a3 ♖e8 18 ♕b3 ♕d7 19 ♖ad1 ♘a5 20 ♕d3 ♖ad8 21 ♗b2 ♘xc4 22 ♕xc4 ♕d5 23 ♕a4 c6 24 ♖d3 c5 25 ♖fd1 c4 26 ♖e3 ♗c7 27 ♘f1 a5 28 ♖xe8+ ♖xe8 29 ♘e3 ♕d6 30 ♕xc4 [30 g3 ♖xe3∓] 30 ... ♕h2+ 31 ♔f1 ♘e4 [31 ... ♖xe3 32 fxe3 ♘e4 33 ♔e2 (33 ♕c2 ♕h1+ 34 ♔e2 ♕xg2+ 35 ♔d3 ♘f2+ 36 ♔c3 ♕c6+ 37 ♔d2 ♕xc2+ 38 ♔xc2 ♘xd1 39 ♔xd1 ♗d6→) 33 ... ♕xg2+ 34 ♔d3 ♘f2+ 35 ♔c2 ♘xd1+ 36 ♔xd1 ♕xb2 37 ♕xc7 ♕b1+→] 32 ♗c1 ♗f4 33 ♕c2 ♗xe3 34 ♗xe3 ♕h1+ 35 ♔e2 ♕xg2 36 ♔d3 ♕f3 37 ♖e1 ♕f5 38 ♔e2 ♕h5+ 39 ♔d3 ♕b5+ 40 ♕c4 ♘xf2+! 41 ♗xf2 [41 ♔c3 ♖xe3+ 42 ♖xe3 ♘d1+ 43 ♔d3 ♘b2+→] 41 ... ♕f5+ 42 ♔d2 ♕xf2+ 43 ♖e2 ♖xe2+ 44 ♕xe2 ♕xe2+ **0-1** L/N3161

**1858-★MR-3**
**Morphy, P.C.+ Rivière, J.A.de**
Paris [Löwenthal]

1 e4 e5 2 ♘f3 ♘c6 3 ♗c4 ♗c5 4 b4 ♗xb4 5 c3 ♗c5 6 0-0 d6 7 d4 exd4 8 cxd4 ♗b6 9 ♘c3 ♘f6 10 e5 d5 11 exf6 dxc4 12 fxg7 [12 d5 ♘a5 13 ♕e2+ ♔f8 14 ♗a3+ ♔g8 15 ♗e7 ♕d7 (15 ... ♕e8 16 fxg7 ♔xg7 17 ♕e5+ f6 18 ♗xf6++–) 16 fxg7 ♔xg7 17 ♕e5++–] 12 ... ♖g8 13 ♖e1+ ♗e6 14 d5 ♕f6 15 ♗g5 ♕xc3 16 dxe6 ♕d3 17 exf7+ ♔xf7 18 ♖e7+ ♔g6 19 ♕e1 ♕d5 20 ♖d1 ♘d4 21 ♖xd4! ♗xd4 22 ♕b1+ **1-0** L/N3161

**1858-★MR-4**
**Rivière, J.A.de– Morphy, P.C.**
Paris [Maróczy]

1 e4 e5 2 ♘f3 ♘c6 3 ♗c4 ♗c5 4 b4 ♗xb4 5 c3 ♗c5 6 0-0 d6 7 d4 exd4 8 cxd4 ♗b6 9 d5 ♘a5 10 ♗d3 [10 ♗b2 ♘e7! (10 ... ♘xc4 11 ♗xg7 ♗d7 12 ♗xh8 f6 13 ♘fd2 ♘xd2 14 ♕h5+ ♔f8 15 ♘xd2 ♕e7∓) 11 ♗xg7? (11 ♗d3!) 11 ... ♖g8 12 ♗d4 ♘xc4 13 ♕a4+ ♕d7 14 ♕xc4 ♖xg2+ 15 ♔h1! (15 ♔g2 ♕g4+ 16 ♔h1 ♕xf3+ 17 ♔g1 ♗h3→) 15 ... ♕h3 16 ♘bd2 ♘g6! 17 ♖g1 ♘h4 18 ♗xb6 ♗g4→] 10 ... ♘e7 11 ♗b2 0-0 12 ♘bd2 [12 ♘c3 ♘g6 13 ♘e2 c5 14 ♕d2 ♗c7 15 ♘g3 f6! 16 ♖e1 ♖b8 17 ♔h1 b5 18 ♘f5 c4 19 ♗b1 b4 20 ♗d4 c3∓] 12 ... ♘g6 13 ♘d4 ♕f6 [□ 13 ... ♘f4 (13 ... ♗d7) 14 ♗c2? (14 ♘f3 ♘xd3 15 ♕xd3 c5) 14 ... ♗h3 15 ♕f3 ♕g5 16 ♕g3 ♕xg3 17 hxg3 ♗xd4 18 ♗xd4 ♘e2+ 19 ♔h2 ♘xd4∓] 14 ♘2f3 ♗g4 15 ♕c2 ♗xf3 16 ♘xf3 ♘e5 17 ♔h1 ♕e7 18 ♘xe5 dxe5 19 f4 f6 20 ♕c3 [□ 20 ♗e2; ♕d2, ♗c3] 20 ... ♗d4 21 ♕xa5 ♗xb2 22 ♖ab1 b6 23 ♕d2 ♗d4 24 f5 a6 [□ 24 ... g5] 25 ♗c4 ♕d6 26 a4 ♖fb8 27 ♖b3 ♔f8 28 ♕e2 b5 29 axb5 a5 30 ♖g3 a4 31 ♕h5 h6 32 ♕g6 ♕e7 33 d6 cxd6

34 ♕×h6 [⌓ 34 ♕h7!+−] 34 … ♕f7 35 ♕h8+ [⌓ 35 ♕h7 ♕×c4 36 ♕×g7+ ♔e8 37 ♕h8+, ♖g7++−] 35 … ♔e7 36 ♖×g7 [⌓ 36 ♕h7 (36 ♕×b8±) 36 … ♖h8 37 ♕×h8 ♖×h8 38 ♗×f7 ♔×f7 39 ♖a3 ♖a8 40 b6 ♗×b6 41 ♖fa1±] 36 … ♖×h8 37 ♖×f7+ ♔e8 38 ♖×f6 a3 39 ♗a2 ♖c8 40 b6 ♔d7 41 b7? [⌓ 41 ♗e6+ ♔c6 42 ♗×c8 ♖×c8 (42 … a2 43 b7 ♔c7 44 ♖×d6 a1♕ 45 ♖×a1 ♗×a1 46 ♖c6+ ♔b8 47 ♖a6) 43 ♖c1+ ♔b7 44 ♖f7+ ♔b8 45 ♖×c8+ ♔×c8 46 ♖a7±] 41 … ♖c2 42 ♗e6+ ♔c7 43 ♖b1 ♔b8 [43 … a2 44 b8♕+ ♖×b8 45 ♖f7+ ♔c6 46 ♗d5+ ♔c5 47 ♖c7#] 44 ♗b3 ♖b2 45 ♖×b2 a×b2 46 ♗a2 ♔×b7 47 ♖×d6 ♖a8 **0-1** L/N3203

## 1858-★MR-5
## Rivière,J.A.de=Morphy,P.C.

Paris

1 e4 e5 2 ♘f3 ♘c6 3 ♗b5 a6 4 ♗a4 ♘f6 5 ♘c3 ♗c5 6 d3 h6 7 ♗e3 ♗×e3 8 f×e3 d6 9 0-0 0-0 10 ♗×c6 b×c6 11 ♕e1 ♗e6 12 ♘h4 g6 13 ♖d1 ♕e7 14 d4 ♖ae8 15 h3 ♗c4 16 ♖f3 e×d4 17 ♖×d4 ♗b5 18 a4 c5 19 ♖d2 ♗c6 20 ♘d5 ♗×d5 21 e×d5 ♘e4 22 ♖e2 ♕e5 23 c4 ♖b8 24 ♖f4 ♖fe8 25 ♘f3 ♕g7 26 ♘d2 ♘×d2 27 ♕×d2 ♖b3 28 ♕a5 f5 29 ♕×a6 ♖×b2 30 ♖×b2 ♕×b2 31 ♕c6 ♖×e3 32 ♕×c7 ♖e1+ 33 ♔h2 ♕e5 34 ♕d8+ ♔f7 35 ♕d7+ ♔f6 36 ♕d8+ ♕e7 37 ♕h8+ ♕g7 38 ♕d8+ ½-½ M954-1858

## 1858-★MR-6
## Morphy,P.C.–Rivière,J.A.de

Paris [Staunton]

1 e4 e5 2 ♘f3 ♘c6 3 ♗c4 ♗c5 4 b4 ♗×b4 5 c3 ♗c5 6 0-0 d6 7 d4 e×d4 8 c×d4 ♗b6 9 d5 ♘ce7 10 e5 ♘g6 11 e6 f×e6 12 d×e6 ♘8e7 13 ♘g5 0-0 14 ♕h5 h6 15 ♘f7 ♖×f7 16 e×f7+ ♔h7 17 ♗d3 ♗e6 18 ♗g5 ♗×f7 19 ♖e1 ♔g8 20 ♗×e7 ♘×e7 21 ♕g4 ♕f8 22 ♘c3? ♗×f2+ 23 ♔h1 ♗×e1 24 ♖×e1 d5 25 ♖f1 ♖d8 26 ♘b5 c5 27 ♕g3 c4 28 ♗c2 ♘c6 29 ♗g6 ♖d7 30 ♗f5 ♖e7 31 ♘d6 ♕b8 32 ♗c8 ♘d8 33 ♗f5 b5

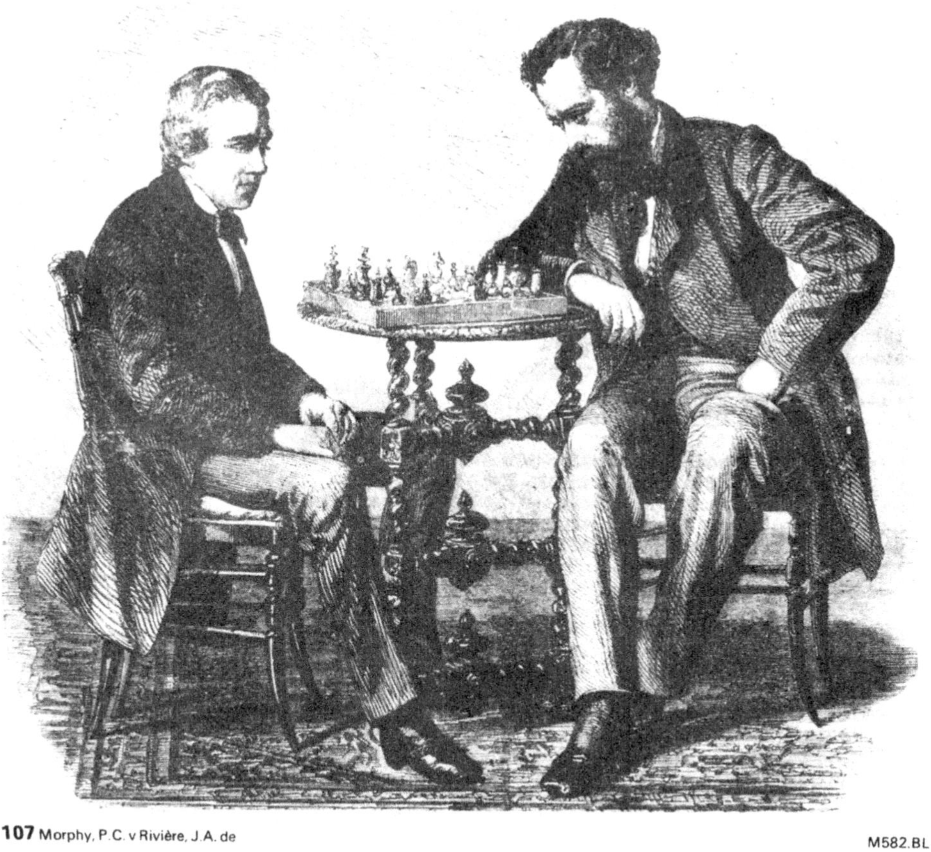

**107** Morphy, P.C. v Rivière, J.A. de M582.BL

34 ♗g6 ♗xg6 35 ♘f5 ♕xg3 36 ♘xe7+ ♔h7 37 hxg3 d4 38 ♘xg6 ♔xg6 39 a3 a5 40 ♔g1 ♘c6 41 ♖f8 c3 42 ♖c8 ♘e5 43 ♔f2 ♘c4 44 ♔e2 c2 **0-1** M954-1858

**1858-★MS-1** xi 58
**Saint-Amant, P.C.F. & ?– Morphy, P.C.**
Paris [Maróczy]

1 e4 e5 2 ♘f3 ♘c6 3 ♗c4 ♗c5 4 c3 ♘f6 5 d4 exd4 6 cxd4 [□ 6 e5 Morphy L/N6389-1859] 6 ... ♗b4+ 7 ♗d2 [7 ♘c3∞] 7 ... ♗xd2+ [7 ... ♘xe4 8 ♗xb4 ♘xb4 9 ♗xf7+ ♔xf7 10 ♕b3+ d5 11 ♘e5+ ♔e6 12 ♕xb4 c5 13 ♕a4±] 8 ♘bxd2 d5 9 exd5 ♘xd5 10 0-0 [□ 10 ♕b3 ♘ce7 11 0-0 0-0 12 ♖fe1 c6 13 a4!±] 10 ... 0-0 11 h3? [□ 11 ♖fe1] 11 ... ♘f4 12 ♔h2 [□ 12 ♘e4 Morphy L/N6389-1859] 12 ... ♘xd4 13 ♘xd4 ♕xd4 14 ♕c2 ♕d6 15 ♔h1 [□ 15 ♘e4] 15 ... ♕h6 16 ♕c3 ♗f5 17 ♔h2 ♖ad8 18 ♖ad1 [18 ♕e3 ♖fe8∓]

18 ... ♗xh3 19 gxh3 ♖d3! 20 ♕xd3 ♘xd3 21 ♗xd3 ♕d6+ 22 f4 ♕xd3 **0-1** L/N3203

**1858-★MS-2 ●o⬠** 27 viii 58
**Morphy, P.C.+ Salmon, G.**
Birmingham [Löwenthal]

1 e4 e5 2 ♘f3 ♘c6 3 ♗c4 ♗c5 4 b4 d5 5 exd5 [□ 5 ♗b5 dxe4 6 bxc5 exf3 7 ♗xc6+ bxc6 8 ♕xf3 ♘e7∓] 5 ... ♘xb4 6 0-0 ♘e7 [□ 6 ... ♗f5] 7 ♘xe5 0-0 [□ 7 ... ♗d4] 8 d4 ♗d6 9 ♘c3 ♗f5 10 ♗b3 a5 11 a3 a4 12 ♘xa4 ♘bxd5 13 c4 ♖xa4 14 cxd5 [14 ♗xa4 ♘c3; 15 ... ♘e2+] 14 ... ♖a5 15 ♕f3 ♗g6 16 ♖e1 ♗b4 17 ♖e2 ♘f5 18 ♗b2 ♕a8 19 g3 ♕a7 20 ♘xg6 hxg6 21 ♖e5 ♗xa3 22 d6! ♗b4 [22 ... ♘xd4? 23 ♗xf7+ ♔h8 24 ♕f4 ♖xe5 25 ♗xd4+-; 22 ... ♘xd4? 23 ♗xf7+ ♖xf7? 24 ♖e8+ ♔h7 25 ♕xf7 ♗xb2 26 ♕g8++-] 23 ♖exa5 ♗xa5 24 ♕d5 b6 25 d7 ♕a8 26 ♖c1 ♕xd5 27 ♗xd5 b5 28 ♗c6 ♘d6 29 d5 ♗d2 30 ♖d1 ♗g5 31 f4 ♗d8 32 ♗a3 f5 33 ♖e1 ♔f7 34 ♗xb5 ♖h8 35 ♗xd6 cxd6 36 ♖e8 ♖f8 37 ♔f2 g5 38 ♔e3 g4 39 ♔d3 g5 40 ♗c6 gxf4 41 gxf4 ♖g8 42 ♔c4 ♖f8 43 ♔b5 ♖g8 44 ♔a6 ♖f8 45 ♔b7 ♖g8 46 ♔c8 ♗b6 47 ♖xg8 ♔xg8 48 d8♕+ **1-0** L/N3161

**167** Morphy, P.C. M979.BL

**1858-★MS-3 ●o⬠** 27 ix 58
**Morphy, P.C.+ Séguin, C.A.**
Paris [Löwenthal]

1 e4 e5 2 ♘f3 d6 3 d4 exd4 4 ♘xd4 ♘f6 5 ♘c3 ♗e7 6 ♗d3 0-0 7 f4 c5 8 ♘f3 ♘c6 9 0-0 ♗g4 10 ♗e3 a6 11 a4 h6 12 h3 ♗xf3 13 ♕xf3 ♘b4 14 ♖ad1 ♕c7 15 b3 ♘xd3 16 cxd3 ♖fe8 17 d4 ♕c6 18 dxc5 dxc5 19 e5 ♕xf3 20 ♖xf3 ♘h7 21 ♖d7 ♖ab8 22 ♘d5 ♗f8 23 ♗f2 ♖ed8 24 ♘b6 ♖xd7 25 ♘xd7 ♖c8 26 ♖c3 ♖c7 27 ♘xf8 ♘xf8 28 ♖xc5 ♖xc5 29 ♗xc5 ♘e6 30 ♗e3 g6 31 g4 ♘d8 32 ♔f2 ♘c6 33 ♔e2 b5 34 axb5 axb5 35 ♔d3 ♔f8 36 ♗c5+ ♔e8 37 ♔e4 ♔d7 38 ♔d5 ♘d8 39 f5 gxf5 40 gxf5 h5 41 ♗b6 ♘b7 42 e6+ fxe6+ 43 fxe6+ ♔e7 44 ♔c6 ♘d8+ 45 ♗xd8+ ♔xd8 46 ♔d6 ♔e8 47 e7 **1-0** L/N3161

**1858-★MS-4** 25 x 58
**Smith, J.R.– Morphy, E.**
Cincinatti [Schmidt & French]

1 e4 e5 2 f4 exf4 3 ♘f3 g5 4 h4 g4 5 ♘e5 h5 6 ♗c4 ♘h6 7 d4 d6 8 ♘d3 d5 [□ 8 ... f3] 9 exd5 ♘f5 10 ♕e2+ ♗e7 11 ♗xf4 ♘xd4 12 ♕f2 ♘f5 13 g3 b6 14 ♘c3 ♘d6 15 ♗xd6 ♗xd6 16 0-0-0 0-0 17 ♘f4 ♗xf4+ 18 ♕xf4 ♕d6? 19 ♕xd6 cxd6 20 ♘e4 ♘d7 21 ♘xd6 ♘e5 22 ♗b3 a5 23 a4 ♖d8 24 ♘e4 ♔g7 25 ♘g5 ♗f5 26 ♖he1 ♘f3 27 ♖e7 ♘xg5 28 hxg5 ♖d6 29 ♗a2 ♔g6 30 c4 ♖f8 31 b3 ♔xg5 32 ♖de1 ♗g6 33 ♗b1 ♖f6 34 ♖1e5+ ♔h6 35 ♗xg6 ♔xg6 36 ♖e3 h4 37 gxh4 ♖h8 38 ♖g3 ♖xh4 39 ♖e4 ♔g5 40 ♖e5+ ♔g6 41 ♖e4 ♖f1+ 42 ♔d2 f5 43 ♖e6+ ♔f7 44 ♖ge3 [□ 44 ♖xb6] 44 ... ♖h2+ 45 ♔d3 ♖h3 46 ♔e2 ♖xe3+ 47 ♖xe3 ♖h1 48 ♔f2 f4 49 ♖e4 g3+ 50 ♔g2 ♖h2+ 51 ♔g1 ♖f2 52 d6 f3 53 d7 ♖g2+ 54 ♔f1 ♖d2 55 ♖f4+ ♔e7 56 ♖xf3 g2+ 57 ♔g1 ♔xd7 58 ♖f7+ ♔c6 59 ♖f6+ ♔c5 60 ♖f5+ ♔c6 61 ♖f6+ ♖d6 62 ♖f5 ♖g6 63 ♖b5? ♖g3 64 ♖f5 ♖xb3 65 ♔xg2 ♖b4 66 ♖f4 ♖xa4 **0-1** M291

**1858-★MW-1 ●o⬠** 27 viii 58
**Morphy, P.C.+ Wills, W.R.**
Birmingham [Löwenthal]

1 e4 c5 2 ♘f3 ♘c6 3 d4 cxd4 4 ♘xd4 e6 5 ♗e3 [□ 5 ♘b5 a6 (5 ... ♘f6 6 ♘1c3 ♗b4 7 ♘d6+±) 6 ♘d6+ ♗xd6 7 ♕xd6±; 5 ♘b5 d6 6 ♗f4 e5 7 ♗e3±] 5 ... ♘f6 6 ♗d3 e5 7 ♘xc6 bxc6 8 0-0 d6 9 f4 exf4 10 ♗xf4 ♗e7 11 ♘c3 ♖b8 12 e5 dxe5 13 ♗xe5 ♖b4 14 ♕f3 ♕b6+ 15 ♔h1 ♗g4 16 ♕f2 ♕xf2 17 ♖xf2 ♗c5 18 ♖ff1 ♗e7 19 a3 ♖b7 20 ♘e4 ♗d7 21 ♘xf6+ gxf6 22 ♗xf6 ♗xf6 23 ♖xf6 ♖xb2 24 ♖e1+ ♗e6 25 ♗f5 ♔e7 26 ♖h6 ♖hb8 27 ♗xe6 ♖b1 28 ♖g1 fxe6 29 ♖xh7+ ♔d6 30 ♖xa7 ♖xg1+ 31 ♔xg1 ♖b1+ 32 ♔f2 ♖b2 33 h4 ♖xc2+ 34 ♔f3 ♔e5 35 h5 ♔f5 36 h6 ♖d2 37 h7 **1-0** L/N3161

**1858-★MW-2**
**Morphy, P.C.+ Worrall, T.H.**
New Orleans [Löwenthal]

⟨♘b1⟩ 1 e4 e5 2 ♘f3 ♘c6 3 ♗c4 ♗c5 4 b4 ♗xb4 5 c3 ♗e7? 6 d4 [6 ♕b3±] 6 ... ♘f6 7 dxe5 ♘g4 8 0-0 ♘gxe5 9 ♘xe5 ♘xe5 10 ♗b3 0-0 11 f4 ♗c5+ 12 ♔h1 ♘g6 13 f5 ♘e5 14 f6 gxf6 15 ♗h6 d6 16 ♕e1 ♗e6 [□ 16 ... ♔h8] 17 ♕g3+ ♘g6 18 h4 ♔h8 19 h5 ♖g8 20 hxg6 ♖xg6 21 ♕h4 ♗xb3 22 axb3 ♕e7 23 ♖f5 ♖e8 24 ♖e1 ♖eg8 25 ♖h5! ♖xg2 26 ♗g5 ♖g7 27 ♗xf6 **1-0** L/N3161

**1858-★MW-3**
**Morphy, P.C.+ Worrall, T.H.**
New Orleans

⟨♘b1⟩ 1 e4 d6 2 f4 ♘c6 3 ♘f3 ♗g4 4 c3 ♗xf3 5 ♕xf3 e5 6 ♗c4 ♘f6 7 b4 a6 8 d3 ♗e7 9 f5 0-0 10 g4 b5 11 ♗b3 ♘e8 12 h4 ♔h8 13 g5 f6 14 ♕h5 d5 15 g6 h6 16 ♗xh6 **1-0** L/N3161

**1858-★MW-4**
**Morphy, P.C.+ Worrall, T.H.**
New Orleans [Löwenthal]

⟨♘b1⟩ 1 e4 e6 2 f4 d5 3 e5 ♘c6? [□ 3 ... c5] 4 d4 ♘h6 5 ♘f3 ♗e7 6 c3 f6 7 ♗d3 0-0 8 0-0 ♕e8 9 h3 ♕h5 10 ♕e1 ♗d7 11 ♗d2 ♖ae8 12 ♕g3 f5 13 ♖ae1 ♔h8 14 ♗e2 ♕g6 15 ♕h2 ♘d8 16 ♔h1 a6 17 b3 b6 18

♖g1 ♕f7 19 g4 c5 20 g5 ♘g8 21 h4 g6 22 h5 ♕g7 23 ♘h4 cxd4 24 ♘xg6+! hxg6 25 hxg6+ ♘h6 26 gxh6 ♕g8 27 g7+ ♔h7 28 ♗h5 **1-0** L/N3161

**1858-★MW-5**
**Morphy, P.C.+Worrall, T.H.**
New Orleans [Löwenthal]
⟨♘b1⟩ 1 e4 e5 2 f4 d5 3 exd5 e4 4 ♗c4 ♗d6 5 ♘e2 ♗g4 6 0-0 f5 7 d4 ♘f6 8 h3 ♗xe2 9 ♕xe2 0-0 10 ♗b3 ♔h8 11 c4 c5 12 dxc6 ♘xc6 13 ♗e3 ♗c7 14 ♖ad1 ♗b6 15 c5 ♗c7 16 d5 ♘a5 17 d6 ♗b8 18 ♗e6 ♘c6 19 ♗xf5 a5 20 g4 ♘b4 21 a3 ♘bd5 22 g5 ♘xe3 23 ♕xe3 ♘h5 24 ♗g4 g6 25 f5 b6 26 ♕c3+ ♔g8 27 ♕c4+ ♔h8 28 ♕d4+ ♘g7 [28 ... ♔g8? 29 ♕d5++-] 29 f6 ♖f7 30 fxg7+ ♖xg7 31 ♖f7 **1-0** L/N3161

**1858-★MW-6**
**Morphy, P.C.+Worrall, T.H.**
New Orleans [Schmidt & French]
⟨♘b1⟩ 1 e4 e5 2 f4 exf4 3 ♘f3 g5 4 ♗c4 g4 5 d4 gxf3 6 0-0 ♗h6 7 ♕xf3 ♘c6 8 ♗xf7+ ♔xf7 9 ♕h5+ ♔g7 10 ♗xf4 ♗xf4 11 ♖xf4 ♘h6 12 ♖af1 ♕e8 13 ♕h4 [△ 14 ♕f6++-] 13 ... d6 14 ♕f6+ ♔g8 15 ♕xh6+- ♗d7 16 ♖4f3 ♘e7 17 h4 ♘g6 18 h5 ♗g4 19 hxg6 hxg6 20 ♖f8+ ♕xf8 21 ♖xf8+ ♖xf8 22 ♕xg6# **1-0** M291

**1858-★M?-1**
**Morphy, P.C.+?**
New Orleans [Maróczy]
1 e4 e5 2 f4 exf4 3 ♘f3 g5 4 ♗c4 g4 5 0-0 gxf3 6 ♕xf3 ♕f6 7 e5 ♕xe5 8 d3 ♗h6 9 ♘c3 ♘c6 [□ 9 ... ♘e7 10 ♗d2 ♘bc6 11 ♖ae1 ♕f5 12 ♘d5 ♔d8 13 ♕e2! ♕e6 (13 ... ♘xd5 14 ♗c3!) 14 ♘xe7 ♕xe2 15 ♘xc6+ bxc6 16 ♖xe2 d5 17 ♗b3 ♗e6] 10 ♗xf4 [△ 11 ♖ae1] 10 ... ♕xf4 11 ♕h5 ♕g5 12 ♖ae1+ ♘ge7 13 ♕xf7+ ♔d8 14 ♘e4 ♕g7 15 ♕h5 d5 16 ♗xd5 ♕d4+ 17 ♔h1 ♕xd5 18 ♕xh6 ♘g6 [18 ... ♗f5] 19 ♘g5 ♗f5 20 ♕g7 ♖f8 21 ♘e6+ ♗xe6 22 ♖xf8+ ♘xf8 23 ♕xf8+ ♔d7 24 ♕xa8 ♘e5 [□ 24 ... ♘d8] 25 ♕h8 ♘g4 26 ♕xh7+ ♔d6 27 ♕g6 ♘e5 28 ♕g3 **1-0** L/N3203

**1858-★M?-2 ●o⬠**
**Morphy, P.C.+?**
New Orleans [Maróczy]
1 e4 e5 2 ♘f3 ♘c6 3 ♗c4 ♘f6 4 d4 [4 ♘g5] 4 ... exd4 [4 ... ♘xe4 5 ♗d5] 5 ♘g5 d5 [5 ... ♘e5 6 ♕xd4 (6 ♗b3 h6 7 ♕xd4 hxg5 8 ♕xe5+ ♕e7) 6 ... ♘xc4 7 ♕xc4 d5 8 exd5 ♕xd5 9 ♕e2+±] 6 exd5 ♘xd5 [□ 6 ... ♘e5; 6 ... ♕e7+] 7 0-0 ♗e7 [7 ... ♗e6 8 ♖e1 ♕d7 9 ♘xe6 fxe6 10 ♕h5+ ♔d8 11 ♗g5+±] 8 ♘xf7± ♔xf7 9 ♕f3+ ♔e6 10 ♘c3! [10 ♖e1+] 10 ... dxc3 11 ♖e1+ ♘e5 12 ♗f4 ♗f6 13 ♗xe5 ♗xe5 14 ♖xe5+ ♔xe5 15 ♖e1+ ♔d4 16 ♗xd5 ♖e8 [16 ... cxb2 (16 ... ♕xd5 17 ♕xc3#) 17 ♖e4+ ♔c5! 18 ♕a3+ ♔xd5 19 ♕d3+ ♔c5 20 ♖c4++-] 17 ♕d3+ ♔c5 18 b4+ ♔xb4! 19 ♕d4+ [19 ... ♔a5 20 ♕xc3+ ♔a4 21 ♕b3+ ♔a5 22 ♕a3+ ♔b5 23 ♖b1#] **1-0** L/N3203

**1858-★M?-3**
**Morphy, P.C.+?**
London [Maróczy]
1 e4 e5 2 ♘f3 ♘c6 3 ♗c4 ♗c5 4 b4 ♗xb4 5 c3 ♗c5 6 d4 exd4 7 cxd4 ♗b6 8 ♗g5 [□ 8 0-0] 8 ... ♘ge7 9 ♘c3 0-0 [□ 9 ... f5] 10 d5 ♘a5 11 d6 cxd6 12 ♘d5 ♘ac6 13 ♘xe7+ ♘xe7 14 ♕xd6 ♖e8 [△ 15 ... ♗c7] 15 ♖c1 ♗a5+ 16 ♔f1 ♔f8 17 ♕f4 d5 18 ♗b5 [□ 18 exd5] 18 ... ♗d7 19 ♘e5 ♗xb5+ 20 ♔g1 f5 21 exf5 ♕b6 22 f6 ♘g8 23 f7 ♖ec8 24 fxg8♕+ ♔xg8 25 ♕f7+ ♔h8 26 ♖xc8+ ♖xc8 27 ♕xd5 h6? [□ 27 ... ♗c4 (27 ... ♗e8) 28 ♘f7+ ♔g8 29 ♘h6+ ♔h8 30 ♘f7+=] 28 ♘f7+ ♔h7 29 ♕f5+ ♕g6 30 ♕xc8 ♕b1+ [□ 30 ... ♕xf7] 31 ♕c1 ♕f5 32 ♗e3 ♕xf7 33 ♕b1+ **1-0** L/N3203

**1858-★M?-4 ●o⬠** 17 iii 58
**Morphy, P.C.+?**
New Orleans
1 e4 e5 2 f4 exf4 3 ♘f3 g5 4 ♗c4 g4 5 d4 gxf3 6 0-0 d5 7 ♗xd5 c6 8 ♗xf7+ ♔xf7 9 ♕xf3 ♘f6 10 c3 ♗h6 11 ♗xf4 ♗xf4 12 ♕xf4 h5 13 e5 ♗e6 14 ♘d2 ♘d7 15 ♘e4 ♕e7 16 exf6 ♘xf6 17 ♘xf6 ♔f8 18 ♘d5+ ♕f7 19 ♕d6+ **1-0** +13

**1858-★P?-1 ●o⬠** 10 v 58
**Paulsen, L.+?**
Chicago
1 e4 e5 2 ♘f3 ♘c6 3 d4 exd4 4 ♘xd4 ♘xd4 5 ♕xd4 ♘e7 6 ♗c4 d6 7 ♘c3 ♗d7 8 ♘d5 ♘c6 9 ♕c3 ♖c8 10 0-0 h6 11 f4 ♘e7 12 ♗e3 b5 13 ♗b3 c5 14 ♘xe7 ♕xe7 15 a3 c4 16 ♗a2 ♗c6 17 e5 dxe5 18 fxe5 ♗d5 19 b4 ♕b7 20 ♖f2 ♖c6 21 ♖d1 ♗e6 22 ♗c1 ♗e7 23 ♕g3 g5 24 c3 ♖g8 25 ♗b1 ♖c7 26 ♕e1 h5 27 h4 ♗g4 28 ♗f5 gxh4 29 ♕h2 ♗f3 30 e6 fxe6 31 ♗xe6 ♖g6 32 ♗f5 ♖g8 33 ♗f4 ♖d7 34 ♗xd7+ ♔xd7 35 ♖d2+ ♔c8 36 ♖f2 ♗g4 37 ♗d6 ♗d8 38 ♕e5 ♗b6 39 ♗c5 ♗c7 40 ♕e7 ♕d5 41 ♖f7 ♗d8 42 ♕xa7 ♖g6 43 ♗d4 ♗h3 44 ♕c5+ ♕xc5 45 bxc5 ♖xg2+ 46 ♔h1 ♖g8 47 ♖g1 ♗g4 48 ♗e5 ♗g5 49 a4 ♗e3 50 ♖b1 ♗e6 51 ♖c7+ ♔d8 52 ♖d1+ ♔e8 53 ♗f6 ♖g1+ 54 ♖xg1 ♗xg1 55 ♔xg1 **1-0** M954-1858

**1858-★P?-2** 10 v 58
**Paulsen, L.+?**
Chicago [Staunton]
1 e4 e5 2 ♘f3 ♘c6 3 ♗c4 ♘f6 4 d4 d5 5 exd5 ♘xd5 6 dxe5 ♗e6 7 0-0 ♗c5 8 ♘bd2 0-0 9 ♘e4 ♗b6 10 ♗g5 ♕d7 11 ♕e2 ♕e8 12 ♖ad1 ♘de7 13 ♗d3 ♘g6 14 ♕d2 ♘cxe5 15 ♘xe5 f5 [15 ... ♘xe5??] 16 ♘xg6 ♕xg6 17 ♘g3 ♕f7 18 b3 f4 19 ♘e4 h6 20 ♗h4 ♖ae8 21 ♔h1 ♕h5 22 ♘f6+ gxf6 23 ♕xf4 f5 24 ♖de1 ♗d7 25 ♖xe8 ♖xe8 26 ♗f6 ♔f7 27 ♗b2 ♗e6 28 ♖e1 ♗d5 29 ♖f1 ♖g8 30 f3 ♗e6 31 g4 ♕h3 32 ♕e5 ♖g6 33 c4 c5 34 ♕h8 ♔e7 35 ♕h7+ ♗f7 36 ♖e1+ ♔f8 37 ♕h8+ ♗g8 38 ♖f1 ♗c7 39 ♗e5 ♗d8 40 ♖f2 ♗h4 41 ♗f1 **1-0** M954-1858

**1858̊-★BO-1**
**Owen, J.+Barnes, T.W.**
London [Staunton]
1 e4 c5 2 f4 e6 3 ♘f3 ♘h6 4 ♗c4 ♘c6 5 c3 f5 6 e5 ♗e7 7 0-0 a6 8 d4 b5 9 ♗b3 ♕b6 10 ♗e3 [□ 10 ♔h1] 10 ... ♘g4 11 ♗f2 ♗b7 12 d5! ♘xf2 13 ♖xf2 ♘a5 14 d6 ♗d8 15 ♘bd2 c4 16 ♗c2 ♕a7 17 ♘d4 ♗b6 18 ♕h5+ g6 19 ♕g5 0-0 20 h4 ♔h8 21 ♖d1 ♗xd4 22 cxd4 ♕xd4? 23 ♘e4 ♕e3 24 ♘f6 ♖f7 25 ♔f1 ♘c6 26 h5 gxh5 [26 ... ♘xe5 27 ♖e1+-] 27 ♖f3 ♕b6 28 ♖h3 ♘xe5 29 ♕xh5 ♗xg2+ 30 ♔xg2 ♖g7+ 31 ♔h1 **1-0** M954-1858

**1858̊-★CP-1 ●o⬠**
**Paulsen, L.+Chisslet**
1 e4 e5 2 ♘f3 ♘c6 3 d4 exd4 4 ♘xd4 ♗c5 5 ♘f5 ♕f6 6 ♘c3 ♘ge7 7 ♗d3 0-0 8 0-0 d6 9 ♕h5 ♗xf5 10 exf5 h6 11 g4 ♘b4 12 ♘e4 ♕e5 13 ♗xh6 ♘xd3 14 ♗xg7 ♕xg7 15 f6 ♕g6 16 fxe7 ♖fe8 17 ♕xg6+ fxg6 18 ♘f6+ ♔f7 19 ♘xe8 ♖xe8 20 cxd3 ♖xe7 21 ♖ae1 ♗d4 22 ♖xe7+ ♔xe7 23 b3 c5 24 ♔g2 g5 25 f4 ♔f6 26 fxg5+ ♔xg5 27 h3 ♗f6 28 h4+ ♔g6 29 h5+ ♔g7 30 h6+ **1-0** L/N6047-1858

**1858̊-★OS-1**
**Owen, J.=Staunton, H.**
London [Staunton]
⟨△f7⟩ 1 e4 ♘c6 2 d4 e5 3 d5 ♘ce7 4 f4 exf4 5 e5 ♘g6 6 ♘f3 ♗c5 7 ♗d3 ♘8e7 8 h4 [□ 8 d6] 8 ... 0-0?! 9 h5 ♘h8 10 ♘g5 ♘f5

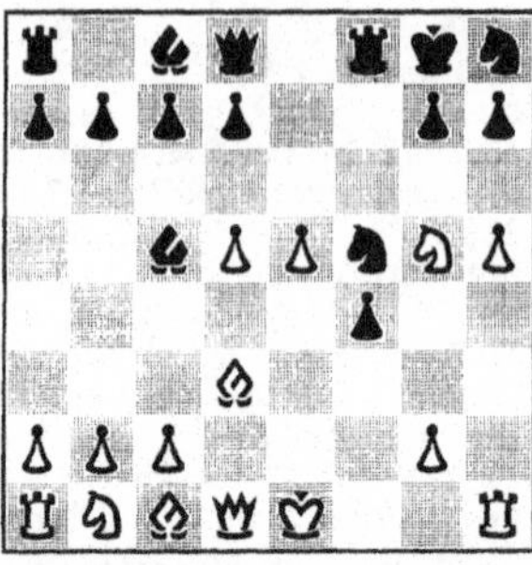

11 ♘xh7?! ♔xh7 12 ♕g4 d6 13 e6 ♕f6 14 ♘c3 ♕e5+ 15 ♔f1 ♔g8 16 ♗xf5 ♕xf5 17 h6! g6 18 h7+ ♔g7 19 ♕h4 ♕h5 20 ♕e7+ ♖f7 21 ♕xf7+ ♘xf7 22 ♖xh5 gxh5 23 exf7 ♗f5 24 ♘e2 ♗xh7 25 ♘xf4 ♔xf7 26 c3 ♖e8 27 ♗d2 ♖e5 28 ♖e1 ♗e4 29 ♗e3 ♗xd5 30 ♗xc5 ♗c4+ 31 ♔f2 ♖xc5 32 b3 ♖f5 33 ♔g3 ♗b5 34 ♖h1 ½-½

M954-1859

## 1858-★SW-1

**Staunton, H.= Worrall, T.H.**

London [Staunton]

⟨♘b1⟩ 1 b3 e5 2 ♗b2 ♘c6 3 e3 ♗c5 4 ♘e2 d6 5 ♘g3 ♘f6 6 ♗e2 0-0 7 0-0 ♗e6 8 a3 a5 9 c3 d5 10 d4 ♗d6 11 dxe5 ♗xe5 12 f4 ♗d6 13 ♗d3 ♗g4 14 ♕c2 ♕e7 15 ♖ae1 ♖ae8 16 b4 g6 17 c4 axb4 18 ♗xf6 ♕xf6 19 cxd5 ♘e7 20 ♘e4 ♕g7 21 ♕c4 bxa3 22 ♘c3 ♗d7 23 e4 b5 24 ♘xb5 ♗xb5 25 ♕xb5 ♕d4+ 26 ♔h1 ♖b8 27 ♕c4 ♗c5 28 f5 ♘c8 29 fxg6 hxg6 30 e5 ♕xc4 31 ♗xc4 ♖b4 32 ♖c1 ♗d4 33 d6 cxd6 34 e6 ♘e7 35 exf7+ ♔g7 36 ♗e6 ♗c5 37 ♖ce1 ♖h4 38 g4 ♗d4 [∆ 39 ... ♗e5] 39 ♖f3 ♗c5 40 h3 d5 41 ♖c1 ♗d4 42 ♖c2 ♖hh8 43 ♖xa3 ♖b8 44 ♔g2 ♔f6 45 ♗d7 ♔xf7 46 ♖f3+ ♔g7 47 ♗e6 ♗f6 48 g5 ♗xg5 49 ♖f7+ ♔h6 50 ♖c7 ♖b2+ 51 ♔f3 ♖b3+ 52 ♔g4 ♘g8 53 ♗xd5 ♘f6+ 54 ♖xf6 ♗xf6 55 ♗xb3 ♖b8 56 ♗c4 ♖b4 57 ♖c6 ...⚲ ½-½

M954-1858

## 1858-★SW-2

**Staunton, H.+ Worrall, T.H.**

London [Staunton]

⟨♘b1⟩ 1 b3 g6 2 ♗b2 ♘f6 3 e3 d6 4 ♘f3 e5 5 ♗c4 ♗g4 6 h3 ♗xf3 7 ♕xf3 ♗g7 8 ♕xb7 ♘bd7 9 ♕c6 0-0 10 0-0 ♘b6 11 ♗e2 ♘bd5 12 ♗f3 e4 13 ♗e2 [13 ♗xe4 ♘xe4 14 ♗xg7 ♔xg7 15 ♕xd5] 13 ... ♘e7 14 ♕a4 d5 15 ♖ad1 ♘f5 16 d3 ♕c8 17 ♗xf6 ♗xf6 18 dxe4 dxe4 19 ♕xe4 ♖e8 20 ♕a4 ♕e6 21 ♗g4 ♕e5 22 c4 ♖ad8 23 ♖xd8 ♖xd8 24 ♕xa7 ♖d2 [∆ 25 ... ♗g5] 25 ♗xf5 gxf5 26 a4 ♗e7 27 a5 ♗d6 28 g3 ♕e4 [∆ 29 ... ♕f3] 29 ♕b8+ ♔g7 30 ♕d8! f6 31 ♕d7+ ♔h6 32 c5 ♕e7 33 ♕xf5! [33 ♕xe7] 33 ... ♗xc5 34 ♖c1 ♗xe3

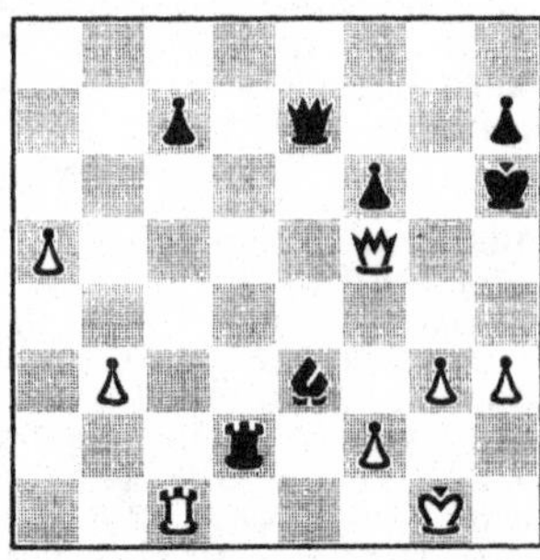

35 ♖e1 [35 fxe3?? ♕xe3+ 36 ♔h1 ♖f2-+; 35 ♖xc7!! ♗xf2+ (35 ... ♕xc7? 36 ♕xf6+ ♔h5 37 g4#) 36 ♕xf2 ♖d1+ 37 ♔h2+-] 35 ... ♖xf2 36 ♖xe3 ♖xf5 37 ♖xe7 ♖xa5 38 ♖xc7 ♖b5 39 ♖c3 ♔g5 40 ♔f2 f5 41 ♔f3 h5 42 h4+ ♔f6 43 ♖e3 ♖b4 44 ♔e2 f4 45 ♖f3 ♔e5 46 gxf4+ ♔e4 47 f5 ♔e5 48 f6 1-0

M954-1858

## 1858-★SW-3

**Staunton, H.= Worrall, T.H.**

London [Staunton]

⟨♘b1⟩ 1 e4 b6 2 d4 ♗b7 3 ♗d3 ♘f6 4 ♕e2 e6 5 ♘h3 h6 6 0-0 ♗e7 7 e5 ♘h7 8 f4 d6 9 ♗e3 ♘c6 10 c3 ♕d7 11 b4 a6 12 a4 0-0 13 b5?! axb5 14 ♗xb5 f5 15 ♖ad1 ♖ad8 16 g4 fxg4 17 ♕xg4 ♖f5 18 c4 d5 19 ♘f2 ♖df8 20 ♕g6 ♔h8 21 ♘h1 ♗h4 22 ♘g3 ♗xg3 23 hxg3 ♖8f7 24 ♕g4 [24 g4? ♘f8] 24 ... ♕d8 25 ♕h3 ♖f8 26 cxd5 ♕xd5 27 g4 [27 ♗d3? ♘xd4 28 ♗xd4 (28 ♗xf5 ♘f3+ 29 ♔f2 ♕a2+ 30 ♗d2 ♖xf5) 28 ... ♕xd4+ 29 ♖f2 (29 ♔h2 ♕b2+ ∆ 30 ... ♖h5) 29 ... ♘g5-+] 27 ... ♖5f7 28 g5 hxg5 29 fxg5 ♘e7 30 ♗d3 g6 31 ♖f6 ♘f5 32 ♗xf5 exf5 33 ♖xg6 f4 34 ♗f2 ♖f5 [∆ 35 ... ♖xe5] 35 ♖c1 ♕e4 36 ♖xc7 ♕b1+ 37 ♕f1 ♕xf1+ 38 ♔xf1 ♗a6+ 39 ♔e1 ♘xg5 40 ♖xb6 [40 ♖h6+=] 40 ... ♗d3 41 ♔d2 ♘e4+ 42 ♔xd3 ♘xf2+ 43 ♔e2 ♘g4 44 ♔f3 ♘xe5+ 45 dxe5 ♖xe5 ...⚲ ½-½

M954-1858

## 1858-★SW-4

**Staunton, H.+ Worrall, T.H.**

London [Staunton]

⟨♘b1⟩ 1 b3 c5 2 ♗b2 e6 3 e3 ♘c6 4 ♘h3 ♘f6 5 ♗e2 h6 6 0-0 ♗d6 7 f4 0-0 8 ♔h1 ♗c7 9 g4 d5 10 g5 ♘h7 11 ♗d3 e5 12 ♗xh7+ ♔xh7 13 f5 d4 14 e4 g6 15 ♕f3 h5 16 d3 ♗d7 17 ♖f2 ♘e7 [∆ 18 ... ♘xf5 19 exf5 ♗c6] 18 ♖e1 ♗c6 19 ♕e2

19 ... ♕d7 [19 ... ♘xf5? 20 ♖xf5! gxf5 21 ♕xh5+ ♔g8 22 g6 fxg6 23 ♕xg6+ ♔h8 24 ♕h6+ ♔g8 25 ♖g1++-] 20 ♔g1 ♖h8 21 ♖ef1 ♖af8 22 c3 gxf5 23 cxd4 cxd4 24 ♗a3 ♔g7 25 exf5 ♔g8 26 g6 ♕d5 27 ♕e4 ♖e8 28 ♗xe7 ♖xe7 29 f6 ♖e6 30 ♘g5 ♖h6 31 ♘xf7 ♖xg6+ 32 ♕xg6+ ♔f8 33 ♕g7+ ♔e8 34 ♘d6+ ♗xd6 35 f7+ ♔d8 36 f8♕+ ♗xf8 37 ♖xf8+ ...⚲ 1-0

M954-1858

## 1858-★SW-5

**Staunton, H.+ Worrall, T.H.**

London [Staunton]

⟨♘b1⟩ 1 b3 b6 2 e4 ♗b7 3 f3 e6 4 ♗b2 ♘f6 5 ♘h3 ♘h5 6 d4 ♕h4+ 7 ♘f2 e5 8 ♗c4 ♘c6 9 g3 ♕f6 [⌓ 9 ... ♕e7] 10 f4 exf4 11 ♕xh5 fxg3 12 hxg3 0-0-0 13 ♖f1 ♗b4+ 14 ♔d1 [14 c3 ♕xd4] 14 ... g6 15 ♕g4 h5 16 ♕e2 ♖he8 17 c3 ♗f8 18 ♘d3 ♕g5 19 ♗xf7 ♖e7 20 ♗d5 ♔b8 21 ♕f3 d6 22 ♗c1 ♕g4 23 ♕xg4 hxg4 24 ♗g5 ♖ee8 25 ♗xd8 ♘xd8 26 ♗xb7 ♔xb7 27 ♖f4 ♘e6 28 ♖xg4 g5 29 ♔d2 ♗g7 30 ♖f1 ♘d8 31 e5 dxe5 32 dxe5 ♗xe5 33 ♖e1 ♘c6 34 ♖ge4 ...⚲ 1-0

M954-1858

## 1858-★SW-6

**Staunton, H.- Worrall, T.H.**

London [Staunton]

⟨♘b1⟩ 1 e4 e5 2 ♘f3 ♘c6 3 ♗c4 ♗c5 4 b4 ♗xb4 5 c3 ♗c5 6 d4 exd4 7 0-0 d6 8 ♕b3 ♕e7 9 ♗g5 ♘f6 10 cxd4 ♘xd4 11 ♘xd4 ♗xd4 12 ♖ad1 ♗b6 13 e5 dxe5 14 ♗xf7+ ♔f8 [14 ... ♕xf7? 15 ♖d8+] 15 ♗c4 ♗g4 16 ♖d2 h6 17 ♗h4 g5 18 ♗g3 ♘e4 19 ♖d5 ♘xg3 20 ♕xg3 ♗h5 21 ♖xe5 ♕f6 22 ♕c3 [⌓ 22 ♖e6] 22 ... ♗f7 23 ♗xf7 ♔xf7 24 ♖d1 ♖hd8 25 ♖c1 ♖d6 26 ♕c4+ ♔g7 27 ♕e4 ♖ad8 28 ♖f1 ♕xf2+ 29 ♖xf2 ♖d1+ 30 ♕e1 ♖xe1+ 31 ♖xe1 ♖d2 32 ♖e7+ ♔g6 33 ♖e6+ ♔h5 34 g4+ ♔xg4 35 ♖xb6 ♖d1+ 36 ♔g2 axb6 37 ♖b2 ♖d7 ...⚲ 0-1

M954-1858

**1858̂-★SW-7**
**Staunton, H.–Worrall, T.H.**
London [Staunton]
⟨♘b1⟩ 1 b3 e5 2 ♗b2 ♘c6 3 e3 d5 4 ♗b5 ♗d6 5 ♘e2 ♘e7 6 0-0 ♗d7 7 ♘g3 0-0 8 a3 d4 9 ♗d3 f5 10 ♗c4+ ♔h8 11 f4 ♘g6 12 ♘h5 ♕h4 13 g3 ♕e7 14 b4 ♗e6 15 ♗e2 ♖ad8 16 b5 ♘b8 17 ♕e1 ♘d7 18 e×d4 e×d4 19 ♕f2 [19 ♗×d4 ♗c5] 19 ... ♗c5 20 d3 ♘f6 21 ♘×f6 ♕×f6 22 ♖ae1 ♘e7 23 ♗f3 ♘d5 24 ♖e5 b6 25 ♕g2 ♘c3 [25 ... ♘e3 26 ♖×e3 d×e3 27 ♗×f6 e2+ 28 d4 e×f1=♕+ 29 ♕×f1 ♖×f6 30 d×c5] 26 ♔h1 ♘×b5 27 ♖fe1 ♖de8 28 ♗c6 ♘d6 29 ♗×e8 ♖×e8 30 c3 ♘f7 31 ♖×e6 ♖×e6 32 ♖×e6 ♕×e6 33 ♕a8+ ♘d8 34 ♕×d8+ ♕g8 35 ♕×g8+ [35 ♕×c7?? ♕d5+ 36 ♔g1 d×c3+] 35 ... ♔×g8 36 c×d4 ♗d6 37 ♔g2 ♔f7 38 ♔f3 g6 39 h3 ♔e6–+ 40 g4 ♔d5 41 h4 ♗e7 42 g5 ♗f8 43 ♔g3 ♗g7 44 h5 ♗×d4 45 ♗c1 ♗c3 46 h×g6 h×g6 47 ♔f3 c5 48 ♔e2 b5 49 ♔d1 a5 50 ♔c2 ♗e1 51 ♗e3 c4 52 ♔d1 ♗c3 53 ♔c2 ♗g7 54 ♗d2 a4 55 ♗b4 ♗d4 56 ♗d2 ♗c5 57 ♗c1 b4 58 a×b4 ♗×b4 59 ♗b2 a3 60 d×c4+ ♔×c4 61 ♗e5 ♔d5 62 ♔b3 ♗c5 ...⚲ **0-1**
M954-1858

**1858̂-★SW-8**
**Staunton, H.+Worrall, T.H.**
London [Staunton]
⟨♘b1⟩ 1 e4 e5 2 ♘f3 ♘c6 3 ♗c4 ♗c5 4 b4 ♗×b4 5 c3 ♗c5 6 0-0 ♘f6 7 d4 e×d4 8 e5 d5 9 e×f6 d×c4 10 ♖e1+ ♗e6 11 ♘g5 ♕×f6?? 12 ♘×e6 f×e6 13 ♕h5+ ♔f8 14 ♕×c5+ ♔f7 15 ♖e4 e5 16 c×d4 ♖hd8 17 d5 ♖d7 18 ♗b2 ♘d4 19 ♕×c4 ♕d6 20 ♗×d4 e×d4 21 ♖×d4 ♔g8 22 ♖ad1 ♔h8 23 ♕b5 ♖e8 24 g3 [24 ♕×b7! c5 25 d×c6 ♕×d4 26 ♕×d7+–] 24 ... b6 25 ♕a6 ♖de7 26 ♕a4 h6 27 ♖1d3 a5 28 ♕c4 ♕d7 [△ 29 ... ♕h3–+] 29 ♔g2 ♖e2 30 ♖f3 ♖2e7 31 a4 ♖b8 32 ♖df4 ♖g8 33 ♖f8 ♕d6 34 ♖8f7 ♖×f7 35 ♖×f7 ♖d8 36 ♕e4 ♔g8 [36 ... ♕×d5?? 37 ♖f8++] 37 ♖f5 ♕d7 38 ♖e5 ♔h8 39 h4 ♖g8 40 g4 ♖f8 41 g5 ♕f7 42 f3 h×g5 43 h×g5 g6 44 ♔g3 ♔g8 45 ♖e6 ♕f5 46 ♖×g6+ ♔h7 47 ♖h6+ ♔g8 48 ♕e6+ ♕×e6 49 d×e6 ♖e8 50 f4 b5 51 a×b5 a4 52 f5 a3 53 ♖h2 ♖a8 54 ♖a2 **1-0** M954-1858

**1858̂-★SW-9**
**Staunton, H.+Worrall, T.H.**
London [Staunton]
⟨♘b1⟩ 1 b3 e5 2 ♗b2 ♘c6 3 e3 d5 4 ♗e2 ♘f6 5 f4 ♗d6 6 f×e5 ♗×e5 7 d4 ♗d6 8 ♘f3 ♗g4 9 0-0 ♘e4 10 a3 ♗×f3 11 ♗×f3 ♕h4 12 g3 ♘×g3 13 h×g3 ♕×g3+ 14 ♗g2 ♕h2+ 15 ♔f2 ♗g3+ 16 ♔f3 ♗d6 17 ♕e1 g5 18 ♖g1 0-0-0 19 ♕e2 ♖de8 20 ♔d3 ♘e7 21 ♕f1 f5 22 ♖e1 ♕h6 23 ♗c1 c5 24 ♔c3 ♔b8 25 ♔b2 ♖hf8 26 ♕b5 ♕e6 27 d×c5 ♗e5+ 28 ♔b1 ♘c6 29 ♖h1 h6 30 ♗d2 ♗g7 31 c3 a6 32 ♕d3 ♖d8 33 ♔a2 ♘a5 34 ♖ef1 ♖d7 35 ♖f2 ♗e5 36 ♖hf1 f4 37 e×f4 g×f4 38 ♗h3 ♕c6 39 ♗×d7 ♕×d7 40 c4 ♘c6 41 c×d5 ♖d8 42 ♗×f4 ♗×f4 43 ♖×f4 ♕×d5 44 ♕×d5 ♖×d5 45 b4 h5 46 ♖1f2 ♘d4 47 ♖d2 ♘e6 48 ♖×d5 ♘×f4 49 ♖f5 **1-0** M954-1858

**1858̂-★SW-10**
**Staunton, H.+Worrall, T.H.**
London
⟨♘b1⟩ 1 b3 e5 2 ♗b2 ♘c6 3 e3 ♗c5 4 ♘e2 d6 5 ♘g3 ♗e6 6 a3 ♘ge7 7 ♗e2 0-0 8 0-0 f5 9 d4 ♗b6 10 c4 e×d4 11 e×d4 ♗d7 12 b4 a5 13 b5 ♘b8 14 ♖c1 c6 15 c5 d×c5 16 d×c5 ♗c7 17 ♕d4 ♖f6 18 ♗c4+ ♘d5 19 ♖c3 ♗×g3 20 ♖×g3 ♔h8 21 ♕h4 ♗e6 22 ♖e1 ♗f7 23 ♗×d5 c×d5 24 ♗×f6 g×f6 25 ♕h6 ...⚲ **1-0** M954-1858

**1858̂-★SW-11**
**Staunton, H.+Worrall, T.H.**
London [Staunton]
⟨♘b1⟩ 1 b3 e5 2 ♗b2 ♘c6 3 e3 d5 4 ♘e2 ♗g4 5 f3 ♗e6 6 ♘g3 ♗d6 7 ♗b5 ♘f6 8 0-0 0-0 9 f4 ♗g4 10 ♕e1 e×f4 11 e×f4 ♖e8 12 ♕f2 ♘e4 13 ♘×e4 ♖×e4 14 ♕g3± ♗c5+ 15 ♔h1 ♗d4 16 c3 ♗d7 17 c×d4 g6 18 ♗d3 ♖e8 19 f5 ♖e7 20 ♗a3 ♖e8 21 f×g6 f×g6 22 ♗×g6 h×g6 23 ♕×g6+ **1-0** M954-1858

**1858̂-★SW-12**
**Staunton, H.–Worrall, T.H.**
London [Staunton]
⟨♘b1⟩ 1 b3 g6 2 ♗b2 ♘f6 3 e3 ♗g7 4 ♘e2 0-0 5 ♘g3 d5 6 ♗d3 c5 7 0-0 ♘c6 8 f4 d4 9 e4 a6 10 a4 ♘b4 11 ♗c4 b5 12 a×b5 ♗b7 13 d3 a5 14 f5 ♕d6 15 ♗c1 e5 16 f×g6 h×g6 17 h3 ♕d7 18 ♖f2 ♕d6 19 ♕f3 ♗c8 20 ♗g5 ♘h7 21 ♗c1 ♗e6 22 ♘f1 ♗×c4 23 b×c4 ♘f6 24 g4 ♘h7 25 h4 ♕e7 26 ♕h3 ♗f6 27 ♗h6 ♗g7 28 ♗×g7 ♔×g7 29 ♘g3 ♕e6 30 ♖af1 f6 31 h5 ♘g5 32 ♕h4 a4 33 ♖h2? [33 h×g6±] 33 ... ♖h8 34 ♖hf2 ♖af8 35 ♖a1 ♖a8 36 ♖af1 ♖af8 37 ♖a1 ♘×c2! 38 ♖×a4 [38 ♖×c2? ♘f3+–+] 38 ... ♘e1 ...⚲
M954-1858

**1858̂-★SW-13**
**Staunton, H.–Worrall, T.H.**
London [Staunton]
⟨♘b1⟩ 1 e4 e5 2 ♘f3 ♘c6 3 ♗c4 d6 4 c3 ♗e6 5 ♗×e6 f×e6 6 ♕b3 ♔d7?! 7 d4 e×d4 8 c×d4 ♘f6 9 d5 e×d5 10 e×d5 ♕e8+ 11 ♗e3 ♘e5 12 ♘d4 ♕g6 13 0-0 b6 14 ♖ac1 ♖c8 15 ♕b5+ ♔e7 16 ♖fe1 ♔f7 17 ♘e6 ♘f3+ 18 ♔h1 ♘×e1 19 ♖×e1 ♗e7 20 ♘g5+ ♔g8 21 ♗c1 h6 22 ♘f3 ♔f7 23 ♕e2 ♖he8 24 ♕e6+ ♔f8 25 ♘d4?? ♗d8 **0-1** M954-1858

**1858̂-★SW-14**
**Staunton, H.=Worrall, T.H.**
London
⟨♘b1⟩ 1 b3 e5 2 ♗b2 ♘c6 3 e3 ♗c5 4 ♘e2 ♗b6 5 ♘g3 d5 6 ♗b5 ♕d6 7 0-0 ♘e7 8 a4 a6 9 ♗e2 0-0 10 ♔h1 ♘f5 11 c4 ♘×g3+ 12 f×g3 d4 13 ♗d3 ♕e6 14 ♗a3 ♖d8 15 c5 ♗a7 16 ♗c4 ♕h6 17 ♗×f7+ ♔h8 18 e4 ♗e6 19 d3 ♖f8 20 ♗c1 g5 21 ♗×e6 ♕×e6 22 ♗×g5 ♗×c5 23 ♕h5 ♗e7 24 ♗h6 ♖×f1+ 25 ♖×f1 ♕g6 26 ♕h3 ♗g5 27 ♗f8 ♗f6 28 ♗a3 ♖g8 29 ♕d7 ♕g7 30 ♕e6 ♗d8 31 ♖f3 a5 32 h3 ♗g5 33 g4 ♗f4 34 g3 ♘d8 35 ♕d5 ♗e3 36 ♖f5 ♘c6 37 ♔g2 h6 38 ♖f7 ♕g6 39 ♖×c7 ♗g5 40 ♖×b7 ♖c8 41 ♗d6 ♗f6 42 ♕e6 ♖e8 43 ♕d7 ♘d8 44 ♖b8 ♖g8 45 ♗c7 ♕g5 46 h4 ♕d2+ 47 ♔h3 ♕d1 **½-½** M954-1858

## CAMPBELL✕WORMALD

London

[1859-✕CW]

Campbell

1 0 0 ½ ? 1 ? 0 ? ? ? ? ? ? ? ? ? ? ? ?
? 1 *Total* 12

R.B.Wormald

0 1 1 ½ ? 0 ? 1 ? ? ? ? ? ? ? ? ? ? ? ?
? 0 *Total* 9

**1859-✕CW-1̂**
**Campbell+Wormald, R.B.**
London [Staunton]
1 e4 e5 2 ♘f3 ♘c6 3 ♗b5 a6 4 ♗a4 ♘f6 5 0-0 ♗e7 6 c3 0-0 7 ♖e1 b5 8 ♗c2 d5 9 e×d5 ♕×d5 10 d4 e4 11 c4! ♕h5 12 ♗×e4 ♘×e4 13 ♖×e4 ♗f5 14 ♖e1 ♗b4? [14 ... ♗g4] 15 ♗d2 b×c4 16 ♕a4! ♗×b1 17 ♕×c6 ♗×d2 18 ♘×d2 ♕a5 19 ♖a×b1 ♕×d2 20 ♕×c4 ♖ad8 21 ♖ed1 ♕f4 22 g3 ♕e4 23 ♖bc1 ♖fe8 24 ♖c3 ♕e2 25 ♕×e2 ♖×e2 26 ♖×c7 ♖×b2 27 ♖e1 ♖b5 28 ♖d7 ♖bb8 29 ♖ee7 ♖×d7 30 ♖×d7 ♔f8 31 d5 ♔e8 32 ♖a7 ♖d8 33 ♖×a6 ♖×d5 34 ♖a7 g6 35 ♔g2 ♖d3 36 g4 ♔f8 37 f3 h6 38 h4 ♔g7 39 g5 h×g5 40 h×g5 ♖d5 41 f4 ♖d3 42 a4 ♖c3 43 a5 ♖d3 44 a6 ♖a3 45 ♔f2 ♔f8 46 ♖a8+ ♔e7 47 a7 ♖a4 48 ♔f3 ♖a1 49 f5! g×f5 50 g6 ♖a3+ 51 ♔f4 ♖a4+ 52 ♔×f5 ♖a5+ 53 ♔g4 ♖a4+ 54 ♔g5 ♖a5+ 55 ♔h6 ♖a6

56 ♔h7 ♖a1 57 g7 **1-0**

### 1859-⚔CW-2̂
**Campbell–Wormald, R.B.**
London

1 e4 e5 2 ♘f3 d6 3 d4 exd4 4 ♕xd4 ♘c6 5 ♗b5 ♗d7 6 ♗xc6 ♗xc6 7 ♗g5 f6 8 ♗e3 ♘e7 9 ♘c3 ♘g6 10 0-0-0 ♗e7 11 h4 ♘e5 12 ♘h2 ♕c8 13 g4 ♕e6 14 ♘d5 ♗xd5 15 exd5 ♕d7 16 f4 ♘f7 17 ♖hg1 c5 18 ♕c3 0-0-0 19 ♕a5 ♔b8 20 ♖d3 ♖c8 21 ♖a3 b6 22 ♕a6 g5 23 ♘f3 gxf4 24 ♗xf4 ♘e5 25 ♖e1 ♖c7 26 ♘xe5 fxe5 27 ♖xe5 ♕xg4 28 ♖e4 ♕xh4 29 ♖ae3 ♗g5 30 ♔b1 ♕h5 31 ♕d3 ♗xf4 32 ♖xf4 c4 33 ♕d2 ♖g8 34 a4 ♖g1+ 35 ♔a2 ♕h1 36 ♖e8+ ♔b7 37 ♔a3 ♖a1+ 38 ♔b4 ♖xa4+ 39 ♔xa4 ♕a1+ **0-1**

### 1859-⚔CW-3̂
**Campbell–Wormald, R.B.**
London

1 e4 e5 2 ♘f3 ♘c6 3 d4 exd4 4 ♗c4 ♗c5 5 0-0 d6 6 c3 dxc3 7 ♘xc3 ♘ge7 8 ♘g5 ♘e5 9 ♗f4 ♘xc4 10 ♕a4+ ♗d7 11 ♕xc4 0-0 12 ♖ad1 h6 13 ♘f3 ♘g6 14 ♗c1 ♗g4 15 ♕d3 ♘e5 16 ♘xe5 ♗xd1 17 ♖xd1 dxe5 18 ♕g3 ♕f6 19 ♘d5 ♕g6 20 ♕xe5 ♖fe8 21 ♕xc7 ♕xe4 22 ♗e3 ♖ac8 23 ♕g3 ♔h8 24 h3 ♖ed8 25 ♗xc5 ♖xc5 26 ♘e3 ♖xd1+ 27 ♘xd1 ♕e1+ **0-1** M954

### 1859-⚔CW-4̂
**Campbell=Wormald, R.B.**
London [Staunton]

1 e4 e6 2 d4 d5 3 exd5 exd5 4 ♘f3 ♗d6 5 c4 c6 [◻5 ... dxc4] 6 ♘c3 ♗e6 7 ♕b3 ♕e7 8 ♗e3 dxc4 9 ♗xc4 ♗xc4 10 ♕xc4 ♘f6 11 0-0 0-0 12 ♖fe1 ♕c7 13 ♖ac1 a6 14 d5 cxd5 15 ♘xd5 ♘xd5 16 ♕xd5 ♘c6 17 ♕h5 ♗f4 18 ♖c4 ♗xe3 19 ♖xe3 ♖ad8 20 ♘g5 h6 21 ♘e4 [△ 22 ♘f6++–] 21 ... ♕e5 22 g4 [22 ♕e2 ♕xb2] 22 ... ♕xh5 23 gxh5 f5 24 ♘c5 f4 25 ♖d3 ♖de8 26 ♖e4 ♖xe4 27 ♘xe4 ♖e8 28 ♘c3 ♘e5 29 ♖d5 ♔f7 30 ♔g2 ♔e6 31 ♖d4 ♔f5 32 f3 **½-½** M954

### 1859-⚔CW-6̂
**Campbell+Wormald, R.B.**
London

1 e4 e5 2 ♘f3 d6 3 d4 exd4 4 ♕xd4 ♗d7 5 ♗e3 ♘c6 6 ♕d2 ♘f6 7 ♘c3 ♗e7 8 h3 0-0 9 0-0-0 a6 10 g4 b5 11 ♗d3 b4 12 ♘e2 ♘e5 13 ♘xe5 dxe5 14 ♘g3 ♗e6 15 g5 ♘d7 16 ♘f5 c5 17 h4 ♖e8 18 ♕e2 ♕a5 19 ♗c4 ♘b6 20 ♗xe6 fxe6 21 ♘xe7+ ♖xe7 22 ♔b1 ♖c8 23 ♖d6 ♖a8 24 h5 ♘a4 25 ♕c4 ♕b5 26 ♕xb5 axb5 27 g6 h6 28 ♖hd1 ♔f8 29 ♖c6 ♖ea7 30 ♖xe6 ♘c3+ 31 bxc3 ♖xa2 32 ♗xc5+ ♔g8 33 ♖e8+ ♖xe8 34 ♔xe8 **1-0** M954

### 1859-⚔CW-8̂
**Wormald, R.B.+Campbell**
London

1 e4 e5 2 ♘f3 ♘f6 3 ♘xe5 d6 4 ♘f3 ♘xe4 5 d4 d5 6 ♗d3 ♗e7 7 0-0 ♗g4 8 c4 0-0 9 ♘c3 ♘xc3 10 bxc3 ♘c6 11 ♗f4 dxc4 12 ♗xc4 ♘a5 13 ♗d3 ♗d6 14 ♗xd6 cxd6 15 ♖e1 f5 16 h3 ♗h5 17 ♖c1 ♕f6 18 d5 ♖ac8 19 c4 ♖ce8 20 ♖xe8 ♖xe8 21 ♕a4 b6 22 ♕d7 ♖e7 23 ♕c8+ ♔f7 24 ♘d4 ♕xd4 25 ♕xf5+ ♔e8 26 ♕xh5+ g6 27 ♕f3 ♕b2 28 ♕f4 ♕xa2 29 c5 ♕xd5 30 ♗b5+ ♘c6 31 ♗xc6+ ♕xc6 32 cxd6 ♖e4 33 d7+ ♔xd7 34 ♕f7+ ♖e7 35 ♕xe7+ ♔xe7 36 ♖xc6 **1-0** M954

### 1859-⚔CW-21
**Campbell+Wormald, R.B.**
London [Staunton]

1 e4 e5 2 ♘f3 ♘c6 3 ♗c4 ♗c5 4 ♘c3 d6 5 h3 ♘f6 6 d3 h6 7 ♗e3 0-0 8 ♕d2 [8 ♗xc5] 8 ... ♗xe3 9 ♕xe3 ♘e7 10 d4! ♘g6 11 0-0-0 ♕e7 12 g3 ♗e6 13 d5 ♗d7 14 ♘d2 a6 15 f4 b5 16 ♗d3? b4 17 ♘e2 exf4 18 gxf4 ♘xd5 19 ♕g3 ♘b6 20 ♘f3 ♖fc8 21 ♖hg1 [△ 22 f5] 21 ... ♕f8 22 f5 ♘e5 23 ♘xe5 dxe5 24 ♕xe5 f6 25 ♕g3 ♗e8 26 ♘f4 ♗f7 27 ♘g6 ♗xg6 28 ♕xg6 ♔h8 29 e5!+– ♘d7 30 ♖de1 fxe5 31 f6 ♘xf6 32 ♖ef1! ♕g8 33 ♖xf6 ♖f8 34 ♕xh6+ **1-0** M954

## JOURNOUD⚔RIVIÈRE Paris
[1859-⚔JR]

| | | | | | | | | | | | | | | | |
|---|---|---|---|---|---|---|---|---|---|---|---|---|---|---|---|
| P.Journoud | 1 | 1 | ½ | 0 | 0 | ? | 0 | ½ | 0 | 1 | 0 | 0 | 0 | 1 | 0 | ? |
| J.A. de Rivière | 0 | 0 | ½ | 1 | 1 | ? | 1 | ½ | 1 | 0 | 1 | 1 | 1 | 0 | 1 | ? |

### 1859-⚔JR-1 x59
**Rivière,J.A.de–Journoud,P.**
Paris [Staunton]

1 e4 e5 2 f4 d5 3 exd5 exf4 4 ♘f3 ♕xd5 5 ♘c3 ♕d8 6 d4 ♗d6 7 ♗c4 ♘f6 8 0-0 0-0 9 ♘e5 ♗xe5 10 dxe5 ♕xd1 11 ♖xd1 ♘g4 12 ♗xf4 ♘c6 13 ♘d5 ♗e6 14 ♖e1 ♖fe8 15 h3 ♘gxe5 16 ♗xe5 ♗xd5 17 ♗xd5 ♘xe5 18 ♗xb7 ♖ab8 19 ♗d5 ♖xb2 20 ♗b3 c5 21 ♖ad1± ♔f8! 22 ♗a4 ♖e6 23 ♖d8+ ♔e7 24 ♖e8+ ♔f6 25 ♖f1+ ♔g6 26 ♖c8 c4 27 ♖c7 a6 28 ♖a1 ♖b4 29 ♗d7 ♖d6 30 ♗c8 ♖b2 31 g4 ♔g5 32 ♖c5 f6 33 ♖c7 ♖xc2 34 ♖xg7+ ♔f4 35 ♗b7 ♘f3+ 36 ♗xf3 ♔xf3 37 ♖f7 [△ 38 ♖xf6+ ♖xf6 39 ♖f1+] 37 ... ♔g3 38 a4 c3 39 ♖c7 ♖dd2 **0-1** M954-1859

### 1859-⚔JR-2 x59
**Journoud,P.+Rivière,J.A.de**
Paris [Staunton]

1 e4 e5 2 ♘f3 ♘c6 3 ♗b5 a6 4 ♗a4 ♘f6 5 0-0 b5 6 ♗b3 ♗e7 7 ♘c3 b4 8 ♘e2 d5 9 ♗a4! ♗d7 10 ♗xc6 ♗xc6 11 ♘xe5 ♗b5 12 exd5 ♕xd5 13 ♘f3 ♗d6 14 d3 g5 15 c4 bxc3 16 ♘xc3 ♕b7 17 ♖e1+ ♔d7 18 ♕b3 ♖af8 19 a4 ♗c6 20 ♕xb7 ♗xb7 21 ♘xg5 ♖hg8 22 g3 ♘g4 23 ♘ge4 ♗e7 24 ♗f4 f5 25 ♘d2 ♗g5 26 ♗xg5 ♖xg5 27 h4 ♖g6 28 ♘e2 f4 29 ♘e4 [29 ♘xf4? ♖xf4 30 gxf4 ♘e3+∓] 29 ... ♘e5 30 ♘c5+ ♔c8 31 ♘xf4 ♘f3+ 32 ♔f1 ♖b6 33 ♖e7 ♘d2+ 34 ♔g1 ♘f3+ 35 ♔g2 ♘xh4+ 36 ♔h3 ♘g6 37 ♘xg6 hxg6 38 ♖ae1 ♗c6 39 ♖xc7+! ♔xc7 40 ♘e6+ ♔d6 41 ♘xf8 ♖xb2 42 f4 g5 43 fxg5 ♗xa4 44 ♖e6+ ♔d5 45 g6 ♗d7 46 g7! ♗xe6+ 47 ♘xe6 ♖b8 48 ♘f8 **1-0** M954-1859

### 1859-⚔JR-3
**Rivière,J.A.de=Journoud,P.**
Paris [Staunton]

1 e4 d5 2 exd5 ♕xd5 3 ♘c3 ♕a5 4 ♗c4 ♘f6 5 d3 e6 6 ♘f3 h6 7 0-0 ♗d6 8 ♘e2 ♘c6 9 ♗d2 ♕h5 10 ♗c3 b6 11 ♘g3 ♗xg3 12 fxg3 ♗b7 13 ♕e1 0-0 14 ♗xf6 gxf6 15 ♕c3 ♔g7 16 b4 ♖ad8 17 ♖f2 ♘e7 18 ♖e1 ♘g8 19 ♘d2 ♔h7 20 d4 ♖d7 21 ♗d3+ ♔h8 22 ♕b2 ♕g5 23 c3 f5 24 ♘c4 ♖e7 25 b5! a5 26 a4 ♘f6? 27 ♗xf5 h5 28 ♗b1 h4 29 gxh4 [◻ 29 ♕c2 △ 30 ♖xf6+–] 29 ... ♕xh4 30 ♖e3 ♖g8 31 ♔f1 ♘h5 [◻ 31 ... ♘g4 △ 32 ♖h3? ♗xg2+–+] 32 g3 ♕g5 33 ♗e4 ♗d5 34 ♗xd5 exd5 35 ♖xe7 ♕xe7 36 ♕d2 ♔g7 37 ♘e3 ♕e6 38 ♘f5+ ♔h7 39 ♕d1 ♖g5 40 ♕f3 ♔h8 41 g4 ♘f6 42 ♘e3 ♖g6 43 h3 ♘e4 44 ♕xf7 ♘xf2 45 ♕xe6 ♖xe6 46 ♔xf2+– c6 47 bxc6 ♖xc6 48 ♘xd5 ♖c4 49 ♔e3 ♖xa4 50 ♘xb6 ♖a1 51 c4 a4 52 ♘xa4 ♖xa4 53 c5 ♔g7 54 h4 ♔f6 55 g5+ ♔e6 56 ♔e4 ♖a1 57 d5+ ♔d7 58 ♔e5 ♖h1 59 c6+ ♔c7 60 ♔f6 ♖xh4 61 g6 ♖f4+ 62 ♔e5 ♖g4 63 ♔f5 ♖d4 [△ 64 g7 ♖xd5+, 65 ... ♖d8=] 64 ♔e5 ♖g4 **½-½** M954-1859

### 1859-⚔JR-4
**Journoud,P.–Rivière, J.A.de**

Paris [Staunton]

1 e4 e5 2 ♘f3 ♘c6 3 ♗b5 a6 4 ♗a4 ♘f6 5 0-0 ♗e7 6 ♘c3 b5 7 ♗b3 d6 8 d4 ♗g4 9 ♗e3 exd4 10 ♗xd4 0-0 11 ♗d5 ♕d7 12 ♗xc6 ♕xc6 13 ♗xf6 ♗xf6 14 ♘d5 ♗d8 15 ♕d3 ♕d7± 16 h3 ♗e6 [16 ... ♗h5 17 ♘e5] 17 ♘d4 c5 18 ♘f5 g6? 19 ♘xd6! c4 20 ♕d4 ♗xh3 21 e5 ♕g4 22 ♕e4 ♕xe4 23 ♘xe4 ♗f5 24 ♘ef6+ ♗xf6 25 ♘xf6+ ♔g7 26 ♖ac1 h5 27 f3 h4 28 ♔f2 ♖ad8 29 ♔e3 g5 30 ♖g1 ♖h8 31 g4 ♗g6 32 ♖g2 b4 33 f4 gxf4+ 34 ♔xf4 a5 35 ♖h2 c3 36 bxc3 bxc3 37 ♖h3 ♖d4+ 38 ♔g5 ♖a4 39 ♖xc3 ♖xa2 40 ♖c7 ♖b2 41 ♘h5+ ♗xh5 42 gxh5 ♖b5 43 ♔xh4 ♖xe5 44 ♖g1+ ♔f6 45 ♖f1+? [45 ♖c6+ △ 46 h6+–] 45 ... ♔e6 46 ♖fxf7 ♖hxh5+ 47 ♔g4 ♔d5 48 ♖fd7+ ♔e4 ♖e7 ♖hg5+ 50 ♔h4 ♔f4 51 ♖c4+ ♔e3 52 ♖xe5+ ♖xe5 53 ♔g3 ♖g5+ 54 ♔h4 ♖b5 55 ♔g3 ♖g5+ 56 ♔h4 ♖d5 57 ♖c8 a4 58 c4 ♖a5 59 c5 a3 60 c6 a2 61 c7 a1♕ 62 ♖e8+ ♔f3 63 ♖f8+ ♔g2 64 ♖g8+ ♔h2 65 c8♕ ♕e1+ 66 ♔g4 ♕g3# **0-1**

M954-1859

### 1859-⚔JR-5
**Rivière,J.A.de+Journoud,P.**

Paris [Staunton]

1 e4 d5 2 exd5 ♘f6 3 ♗b5+ ♗d7 4 ♗c4 ♗g4 5 f3 ♗h5 6 ♘c3 a6 7 a4 ♘bd7 8 a5 b5 9 ♗b3 ♘c5 10 ♗a2 b4 11 d4 ♘b7 12 ♘ce2 ♘xd5 13 ♘g3 ♗g6 14 ♗c4 c6 15 ♕e2 ♘xa5 16 f4! f6 17 f5 ♗f7 18 ♘f3 ♘xc4 19 ♕xc4 ♕b6 20 ♕e2 g5 21 ♘e4 ♔d8 22 ♘c5 ♘c7 23 0-0+– e5? 24 ♘xe5 ♗e8 [24 ... fxe5+–] 25 ♘c4 ♕a7 26 ♗e3 ♗xc5 27 dxc5 ♘d5 28 ♖fd1 ♗d7 29 ♘b6 ♘xb6 30 cxb6 ♕b7 31 ♗c5 ♖he8 32 ♕c4 a5 33 ♕f7 ♔c8 34 ♖xd7 **1-0** M954-1859

### 1859-⚔JR-7
**Rivière,J.A.de+Journoud,P.**

Paris [Staunton]

1 e4 d5 2 exd5 ♕xd5 3 ♘c3 ♕d8 4 d4 e6 5 ♗c4 ♗d6 6 ♘f3 h6 7 ♗e3 ♘f6 8 h3 a6 9 a4 ♘c6 10 0-0 ♘e7 11 ♗d3 b6 12 ♘e4 ♘xe4 13 ♗xe4 ♖b8 14 ♕e2 0-0 15 ♗d3 a5 16 ♘h4 f5 17 f4 ♘d5 18 ♘g6 ♘xe3 19 ♕xe3 ♖f6 20 ♘h4 ♗b7 21 ♖ae1 c5!∓ 22 c3 ♔h8 23 ♗c4 cxd4 24 cxd4 ♗b4 25 ♖e2 ♗e4 26 ♘f3 ♗d5 27 ♗b5 ♗xf3 28 ♖xf3 ♕c7 29 ♕b3 ♕e7 30 ♗c4 ♕d6 31 ♖xe6 ♕xd4+ 32 ♔h1 ♗c5 33 ♖f1 ♖bf8 34 ♕c2 g5? 35 fxg5 hxg5 36 ♕e2 ♔g7 37 b3 g4 38 ♖xf6 ♕xf6? [38 ... ♖xf6] 39 ♗d3 ♕g5 40 ♕b2+ ♔g6 41 ♕e5 gxh3 42 gxh3 ♖f6 43 ♕d5 [◻ 43 b4 △ 44 a5+–] 43 ... ♕h5 44 ♗xf5+ ♔h6 45 ♕g8 ♖f7 [45 ... ♖f8 46 ♕h7+ ♔g5 47 ♕g7+ ♔h4 48 ♖f4+] 46 ♕h8+ ♔g5 47 ♕xh5+ ♔xh5 48 ♗g4+ ♔g6 49 ♗h5+ **1-0** M954-1859

### 1859-⚔JR-8
**Journoud,P.=Rivière,J.A.de**

Paris

1 e4 e5 2 ♘f3 ♘c6 3 ♗c4 ♘f6 4 d3 ♗e7 5 ♘c3 0-0 6 a3 d6 7 h3 ♗e6 8 ♘d5 ♕d7 9 c3 ♖ae8 10 ♘xf6+ ♗xf6 11 ♗b3 h6 12 0-0 g5 13 ♘h2 ♗g7 14 ♗xe6 ♕xe6 15 g4 d5 16 ♕b3 dxe4 17 ♕xe6 ♖xe6 18 dxe4 ♘a5 19 ♖d1 ♘b3 20 ♖b1 ♖c8 21 ♘f1 ♔f8 22 ♗e3 b6 23 ♘g3 ♔e8 24 ♘f5 ♗f8 25 ♖d3 a5 26 a4 ♖ec6 27 c4 ♘c5 28 ♗xc5 ♖xc5 29 b3 ♖d8 30 ♖bd1 ♖xd3 31 ♖xd3 ♖c6 32 ♖d5 ♖e6 33 ♔g2 c6 34 ♖d1 ♖g6 35 ♔g3 ♗c5 36 h4 ♖f6 37 hxg5 hxg5 38 ♖h1 ♖g6 39 ♖h8+ ♔d7 40 ♖h7 ♔e6 **½-½**

M954-1859

### 1859-⚔JR-9
**Rivière,J.A.de+Journoud,P.**

Paris [Staunton]

1 e4 d5 2 exd5 ♕xd5 3 ♘c3 ♕d8 4 d4 e6 5 ♗e3 ♗d6 6 ♘f3 h6 7 ♗d3 ♘f6 8 0-0 b6 9 ♘e4 ♗b7 10 ♘xd6+ cxd6 11 ♕e2 0-0 12 c4 ♘c6 [12 ... ♘bd7 △ 13 ... e5] 13 a3 ♘e7 14 ♘d2 ♘h7 15 f4 f5 16 ♗f2 ♖f6 17 ♖ae1 g5 18 d5 ♘g6 [◻ 18 ... ♘f8] 19 ♗d4 exd5 20 ♗xf6 ♕xf6 21 fxg5 ♘xg5 22 ♖xf5 ♕d4+ 23 ♕e3 ♕g7 24 cxd5 ♘e5 25 ♘e4 ♘g4 26 ♕g3 ♘xe4 27 ♖xe4 ♘e5 28 ♕h4! ♖e8 [28 ... ♗xd5 29 ♖fxe5] 29 ♗b5 ♖e7 30 ♖e3 ♘g6 31 ♖xe7 ♘xe7 32 ♖f4 ♗xd5 33 ♖g4 ♘g6 34 ♕d8+ ♔h7 35 ♗d3 ♗f7 36 ♕xd6 h5 37 ♖xg6 ♗xg6 38 ♗xg6+ ♕xg6 39 ♕xg6+ **1-0**

### 1859-⚔JR-10
**Journoud,P.+Rivière,J.A.de**

Paris [Staunton]

1 e4 e5 2 d4 exd4 3 ♘f3 ♘c6 4 ♘xd4 ♕f6 5 ♘xc6 dxc6 6 ♗d3 ♗c5 7 0-0 ♘h6 8 ♕h5 ♗e7 9 h3 ♕g6 10 ♕xg6 hxg6 11 ♗f4 g5 12 ♗xc7 g4 13 hxg4 ♗xg4 14 ♗f4 0-0-0 15 ♗e3 a6 16 ♘c3 ♗e6 17 f3 g5 18 ♔f2 c5? 19 ♘a4 f5 20 ♗xc5 ♗f6 21 exf5 ♘xf5 22 ♖ae1 ♘g7 23 ♗b6 ♖d6 24 b3 ♖xb6 25 ♘xb6+ ♔c7 26 ♘c4 g4 27 ♖h1 ♗d4+ 28 ♔e2 gxf3+ 29 gxf3 ♖e8 30 ♔d2 b5 31 ♘e3 b4 32 ♘d1 ♖d8 33 ♔c1 a5 34 ♖h7 ♔d6 35 ♖h6 ♗e5 36 ♔b1 ♖f8 37 ♘e3 ♗f4 38 ♖g6 ♗xe3 39 ♖xe3 ♖f7 40 ♗c4 ♖e7 41 ♖xg7 ♖xg7 42 ♖xe6+ ♔c5 43 ♖e5+ ♔d4 44 ♖d5+ ♔e3 45 ♖xa5 ♔xf3 46 ♖b5 ♔e3 47 ♖xb4 ♔d4 48 ♔b2 **1-0**

M954-1859

### 1859-⚔JR-11
**Rivière,J.A.de+Journoud,P.**

Paris [Staunton]

1 e4 c5 2 d4 cxd4 3 ♘f3 ♘c6 4 ♘xd4 e5 5 ♘b5 a6 6 ♘d6+ ♗xd6 7 ♕xd6 ♕e7 8 ♕c7 ♘f6 9 ♘c3 h6 [◻ 9 ... d5] 10 ♗d3 d6 [◻ 10 ... d5] 11 ♕b6 0-0 12 0-0 ♕d8 13 ♕e3 d5 14 exd5 ♘xd5 15 ♕e4 ♘f6 16 ♕h4 ♘h7 17 ♕g3 ♔h8 18 f4 exf4 19 ♗xf4 ♗e6 20 ♗e3 ♕a5 21 ♖ae1 ♖ae8 22 ♘e4 ♕xa2?

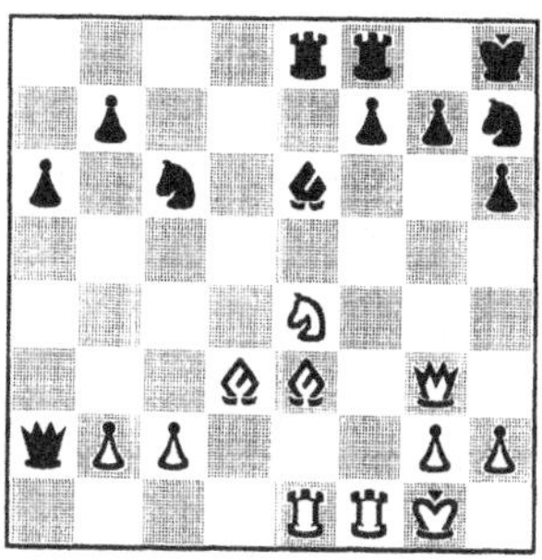

23 ♗xh6 g6 [23 ... gxh6 24 ♘f6 ♖d8 (24 ... ♘xf6 25 ♖xf6 △ 26 ♖xh6#) 25 ♕h4 ♘xf6 26 ♕xh6+ ♔g8 27 ♕g5+ ♔h8 28 ♖xf6+–] 24 ♗xf8 ♖xf8 25 ♕h4 ♕xb2 26 c3 ♕b6+ 27 ♔h1 ♔g7 28 ♘f6 ♖h8 29 ♘xh7 ♖xh7 30 ♕f6+ ♔g8 31 ♖xe6 **1-0** M954-1860

### 1859-⚔JR-12
**Journoud,P.–Rivière,J.A.de**

Paris [Staunton]

1 e4 e5 2 d4 exd4 3 ♘f3 ♘c6 4 ♘xd4 ♕h4 5 ♕d3 ♘f6 6 ♘xc6 dxc6 7 ♘d2 ♗c5 8 g3 ♕h5 9 ♘b3 ♗g4 10 ♘xc5? ♖d8 11 ♕xd8+ ♔xd8 12 ♘xb7+ ♔c8 13 ♗a6 ♔b8 14 b4 ♖e8 15 ♘c5 ♘xe4 16 ♗e3 ♗f3 17 ♖b1 ♘c3 [17 ... ♗xh1? 18 b5 ♘c3 19 bxc6+ ♘xb1 20 ♘d7+ ♔a8 21 ♗b7#] 18 ♔d2 ♘xb1+ 19 ♖xb1 ♖d8+ 20 ♗d3 ♗e2 21 b5 ♗xd3 22 cxd3 cxb5 23 ♖xb5+ ♔c8 24 a4 ♕d5 25 d4 ♕a2+ 26 ♔d1 ♖d5 27 ♖a5 ♕b1+ 28 ♔e2 ♕c2+ 29 ♔f1 ♕b1+ 30 ♔g2 ♕b8 31 h4 ♕a8 32 ♔h2 ♔d8 **0-1** M954-1860

**1859-✕JR-13**
**Rivière,J.A.de+Journoud, P.**
Paris [Staunton]

1 e4 e6 2 f4 c5 [□2 ... d5] 3 ♘c3 d5 4 ♗b5+ ♘c6 5 ♘f3 d4 6 ♘e2 ♗d7 7 0-0 ♗d6 8 d3 ♗c7 9 c4 ♘ge7 10 ♕e1 a6 11 ♗xc6 ♘xc6 12 ♕g3 g6 13 ♕h3 ♕e7 14 ♗d2 0-0-0 15 g3 f5 16 a3 fxe4 17 dxe4 e5 18 ♕h4 ♕xh4 19 ♘xh4 ♖de8 20 f5 gxf5 21 ♘xf5 ♘b8 22 ♖ae1 ♗c6 23 ♘c1 b5 24 b3 bxc4 25 bxc4 ♘d7 26 ♘d3 ♔b7 27 h3 ♔a7 28 g4 ♖b8 29 ♘e7 ♗a8 30 ♘d5 ♗xd5 31 exd5 ♖hf8 32 ♗h6 ♖xf1+ 33 ♖xf1 ♖b7 34 ♖f7 e4 35 ♖xd7 exd3 36 ♔f1 ♗a5 37 ♖xb7+ ♔xb7 38 ♗f8 ♔b6 39 g5 ♗d2 40 h4 ♗c1 41 ♗e7 ♗xa3 42 h5 ♗c1 43 ♗d8+ ♔b7 44 g6 hxg6 45 hxg6 ♗h6 46 ♗f6 a5 47 g7 ♗xg7 48 ♗xg7 d2 49 ♔e2 a4 50 ♔xd2 **1-0** M954-1860

**1859-✕JR-14**
**Journoud,P.+Rivière, J.A.de**
Paris [Staunton]

1 e4 e5 2 ♘f3 ♘f6 3 ♗c4 ♘c6 4 d3 ♗c5 5 h3 0-0 6 ♘c3 d6 7 ♗g5?! ♘d4 8 ♘d5?! c6? [8 ... ♘e6] 9 ♘xf6+ gxf6 10 ♗h4? [10 ♗h6 ♖e8 11 ♘xd4 exd4 12 ♕f3 ♔h8 13 ♗xf7] 10 ... ♘e6 11 ♘h2 d5 12 ♘g4 ♘g5 13 exd5 cxd5 14 ♗b3 ♗e6 15 ♗xg5 fxg5 16 ♘xe5 ♗d4 17 ♘f3 ♗xb2 18 ♖b1 ♗c3+ 19 ♔f1 f6 [□19 ... h6 △ 20 ... f5] 20 ♘g1 b5 21 a4 bxa4 [21 ... b4?!] 22 ♗xa4 ♕a5 23 ♗b3 ♗f7 24 ♕f3 ♕b6? [24 ... ♖ab8 25 ♘e2 ♖fe8 26 d4 ♗d2 27 ♕xf6 ♖e6 28 ♕f3 ♖be8 29 ♗xd5 ♕xd5 30 ♕xd5 ♖xe2 31 ♕e5 ♖8xe5 32 dxe5 ♖xe5 △ 33 ... a5∓] 25 ♘e2 ♗e5 26 ♕xd5 ♗xd5 27 ♗xd5+ ♔g7 28 ♖xb6 axb6 29 ♗xa8 ♖xa8 30 g3 ♖a2 31 f4 ♗d6 32 c3 gxf4 33 gxf4 ♔g6 34 ♖g1+ ♔f5 35 ♖g4 ♖d2 36 ♘d4# **1-0** M954-1860

**1859-✕JR-15**
**Rivière,J.A.de+ Journoud,P.**
Paris [Staunton]

1 e4 e6 2 d4 d5 3 exd5 exd5 4 ♘f3 ♘f6 5 ♗d3 ♗d6 6 0-0 ♗e6 7 ♘c3 c6 8 ♘e5 ♗xe5 9 dxe5 ♘g4 10 ♕e2 ♕h4 11 h3 ♘h6 12 ♗xh6 ♕xh6 13 f4± g6 14 ♖ae1 ♘d7 15 ♔h2 ♕h4 16 ♕e3 h5 17 b4 a5 18 ♘a4 axb4 19 ♘b6 ♘xb6 20 ♕xb6 ♕e7 21 ♖b1 c5 22 f5 gxf5 23 ♗xf5 ♖xa2 24 ♗xe6 fxe6 25 ♖f6 ♖a6 26 ♕b5+ ♔d8 27 ♖bf1 ♖h7 28 ♖f8+ ♔c7 29 ♖e8 ♕g7 30 ♕xc5+ ♖c6 31 ♕a5+ ♖b6 32 ♖xe6 **1-0**

**MONGREDIEN✕MORPHY**
Paris
[1859-✕MM]

| | | | | | | | | | |
|---|---|---|---|---|---|---|---|---|---|
| A.Mongredien | ½ | 0 | 0 | 0 | 0 | 0 | 0 | 0 | ½ |
| P.C. Morphy | ½ | 1 | 1 | 1 | 1 | 1 | 1 | 1 | 7½ |

**1859-✕MM-1** 26 ii 59
**Mongredien,A.= Morphy,P.C.**
Paris [Löwenthal]

1 e4 e5 2 ♗c4 ♗c5 3 b4 ♗xb4 4 f4 d5 5 exd5 e4 6 ♘e2 ♘f6 7 c3 ♗c5 8 d4 exd3 9 ♕xd3 0-0 10 ♗a3! ♗xa3 11 ♘xa3 ♗g4 12 0-0 ♗xe2 13 ♕xe2 ♘xd5 14 ♕f3! c6 15 ♖ab1 ♕e7 [15 ... ♕a5 16 ♗xd5 cxd5 17 ♖b3] 16 ♗xd5 cxd5 17 c4 dxc4 18 ♖xb7 ♘d7 19 ♔h1 ♖fe8 20 ♘xc4 ♕e6 21 ♘e5 ♘xe5 22 fxe5 ♖f8 23 ♕b3 ♕xb3 24 axb3 ♖ab8 25 ♖xa7 [25 ♖xb8? ♖xb8 26 ♖b1 ♖b5∓] 25 ... ♖xb3 **½-½** L/N3161

**1859-✕MM-2** ii 59
**Morphy,P.C.+ Mongredien,A.**
Paris [Löwenthal]

1 e4 e5 2 ♘f3 ♘c6 3 ♗c4 ♗c5 4 b4 ♗xb4 5 c3 ♗c5 6 0-0 d6 7 d4 exd4 8 cxd4 ♗b6 9 ♗b2 ♘f6 10 ♘bd2 0-0 11 d5 ♘e5? [□11 ... ♘a5] 12 ♘xe5 dxe5 13 ♗xe5 ♖e8 14 ♗xf6 ♕xf6 15 ♔h1 ♗a5?? 16 ♕a4 b5 17 ♕xb5 ♗a6 18 ♕xa5 ♗xc4 19 ♘xc4 ♖xe4 20 ♕xc7 ♖ae8 21 ♘d6 ♕xa1 22 ♕xf7+ **1-0** L/N3161

**1859-✕MM-3** ii 59
**Mongredien,A.-Morphy, P.C.**
Paris [Löwenthal]

1 d4 e6 2 c4 f5 3 f4 ♘f6 4 ♘f3 b6 5 a3 a5 6 ♘c3 ♗b7 7 e3 ♗e7 8 ♗e2 0-0 9 0-0 h6 10 b3 d6 11 ♗b2 ♘bd7 12 ♖c1 ♔h7 13 ♗d3 g6 14 h3 ♕e8 15 ♕e1 ♘e4 16 ♗xe4 [□16 d5±] 16 ... fxe4 17 ♘d2 ♘f6 18 ♔h2 ♕d7 19 ♖g1 d5 20 ♖c2 g5 21 ♘f1 gxf4 22 exf4 ♗d6 23 g3 c6 24 ♘e3 ♖g8 25 ♖cg2 ♖af8 26 ♘e2 ♗c8 27 g4 ♕c7 28 ♖f2 ♘e8 29 ♕f1 ♖f7 30 ♔h1 ♖gf8 31 ♘g2 ♗a6 32 ♕c1! ♕e7 33 ♘g3 ♘g7 34 ♖e1 c5 35 ♘e2 ♗b7 36 cxd5 exd5 37 f5 ♘e6 38 ♘gf4 ♘xf4 39 ♘xf4 ♖c8 40 ♕e3 cxd4 41 ♗xd4 ♗xa3 42 ♗xb6 [□42 ♘e6] 42 ... ♗b4 43 ♖d1 ♖c3! 44 ♕d4 ♕h4 45 ♖g1 ♖g7 46 ♕e5 ♖e7 47 ♕d4 ♗d6! 48 ♕xc3 d4 49 ♕xd4 ♗xf4 50 ♔g2 e3+ **0-1** L/N3161

**1859-✕MM-4** ii 59
**Morphy,P.C.+ Mongredien,A.**
Paris [Löwenthal]

1 e4 e5 2 ♘f3 ♘c6 3 ♗c4 ♘f6 4 ♘g5 d5 5 exd5 ♘a5 6 d3 h6 7 ♘f3 ♗g4 [□7 ... e4] 8 h3 ♗xf3 9 ♕xf3 ♗d6? [□9 ... e4] 10 ♗b5+ c6 11 dxc6 bxc6 12 ♗xc6+ ♘xc6 13 ♕xc6+ ♔e7 14 ♘c3 ♖c8 15 ♕f3 ♖e8 16 0-0 ♔f8 17 ♗d2 g5? 18 h4 ♘h7 19 ♕f5 ♔g7 20 hxg5 hxg5 21 g3 f6 22 ♔g2 ♖h8 23 ♖h1 ♖c7 24 ♖h2 ♕c8 25 ♕xc8 ♖hxc8 26 ♖ah1 ♘f8 27 ♘b5 ♖d7 28 ♘xd6 ♖xd6 29 ♗b4 **1-0** L/N3161

**1859-✕MM-5** iii 59
**Mongredien,A.- Morphy,P.C.**
Paris [Löwenthal]

1 e4 e5 2 f4 exf4 3 ♗c4 d5 4 ♗xd5 ♘f6 5 d3 [□5 ♘f3] 5 ... ♘xd5 6 exd5 ♕xd5 7 ♕e2+ ♗e6 8 ♗xf4 ♘c6 9 ♘f3 0-0-0 10 ♘c3 ♗b4 11 0-0 ♕h5 12 a3 [□12 ♘e5] 12 ... ♗c5+ 13 ♔h1 ♗g4 14 ♕d2 ♖he8 15 ♖ae1 ♗xf3 16 ♖xf3 ♖xe1+ 17 ♕xe1 ♘d4 18 ♖f1 [18 ♖h3 ♕f5∓] 18 ... ♘xc2 19 ♕c1 ♘d4 20 b4 [□20 ♗xc7] 20 ... ♗d6 21 ♗xd6 ♖xd6 22 ♕e3 ♘f5! 23 ♕f3 ♕xf3 24 ♖xf3 ♖c6 25 ♘e2?? ♘d4 **0-1** L/N3161

**1859-✕MM-6** iii 59
**Morphy,P.C.+ Mongredien,A.**
Paris [Löwenthal]

1 e4 e5 2 ♘f3 d5?! 3 exd5! e4 4 ♕e2 ♕e7 5 ♘d4 ♕e5 [□5 ... ♘f6] 6 ♘b5 ♗d6 7 d4 ♕e7 [7 ... exd3 8 ♕xe5±] 8 c4± ♗b4+ 9 ♗d2 ♗xd2+ 10 ♘xd2 a6 11 ♘c3 f5 12 0-0-0 ♘f6 13 ♖e1 0-0 14 f3 b5 15 fxe4 fxe4 16 ♘cxe4 bxc4 17 ♕xc4 ♔h8 18 ♗d3 ♗b7 19 ♘xf6 ♕xf6 20 ♖hf1 ♕d8 21 ♖xf8+ ♕xf8 22 ♕b4! **1-0** L/N3161

**1859-✕MM-7** iii 59
**Mongredien,A.-Morphy, P.C.**
Paris [Löwenthal]

1 e4 e5 2 ♘f3 ♘c6 3 ♗c4 ♗c5 4 b4 ♗xb4 5 c3 ♗a5 6 0-0 ♘f6 7 d4 0-0 8 d5 ♘e7 9 ♕d3 d6 10 h3 ♘g6 11 ♘h2 ♘h5∓ 12 ♗b3 ♘hf4 13 ♗xf4 ♘xf4 14 ♕f3 f5 15 exf5 ♗xf5 16 g4 ♗d3! 17 ♕e3 [17 ♖~ ♘e2−+] 17 ... ♗b6 18 ♕d2 ♕h4 **0-1** L/N3161

**1859-✕MM-8** 3 iii 59
**Morphy,P.C.+ Mongredien,A.**
Paris [Löwenthal]

1 e4 e5 2 ♘f3 d6 3 d4 exd4 4 ♕xd4 a6 5 ♗g5 f6 6 ♗e3 ♗e6 7

♘c3 ♘e7 8 ♗e2 ♘ec6 [□ 8 ... ♘bc6] 9 ♕d2 ♗e7 10 0-0 0-0 11 ♖ad1 ♘d7 12 ♘d4 ♘xd4 13 ♗xd4 f5 [□ 13 ... c5 14 ♗e3 f5] 14 exf5 ♗xf5 15 ♗c4+ ♔h8 16 ♘d5 ♘f6 17 ♘xe7 ♕xe7 18 ♖fe1 ♕d7 19 ♕g5 h6 20 ♕h4 ♖ae8 21 c3 ♖e4? 22 ♖xe4 ♘xe4 23 ♕xh6+ ♗h7 24 ♖e1 c5 25 ♖xe4 cxd4 26 ♕h5 g6 27 ♕h6 ♖e8 28 ♕f4! ♔g7 29 ♖xe8 ♕xe8 30 ♕xd4+ **1-0** L/N3161

**1859-★AC-1** i 59
**Carstanjen, A.+ Anderssen, A.**
Köln
1 e4 e5 2 ♘f3 ♘c6 3 ♗b5 ♘f6 4 d4 ♘xd4 5 ♘xd4 exd4 6 e5 c6 7 0-0 cxb5 8 ♗g5 ♗e7 9 exf6 ♗xf6 10 ♖e1+ ♔f8 11 ♗xf6 ♕xf6 12 ♕e2 ♕e6 13 ♕d2 ♕b6 14 c3 d5 15 cxd4 ♗e6 16 ♘c3 h5 17 a4 b4 18 ♘a2 a5 19 ♘c1 ♖h6 20 ♘b3 ♖g6 21 ♘c5 ♔g8 22 ♖e5 ♗h3 23 g3 f5 24 ♖ae1 ♖f8? 25 ♘e6 ♖xe6 26 ♖xe6 ♕d8 27 ♕f4 ♕d7 28 ♖e7 ♕xa4 29 ♕g5 ♖f7 30 ♖xf7 **1-0** L/N6051-1869

**1859-★AC-2** i 59
**Carstanjen, A.–Anderssen, A.**
Köln
1 e4 e5 2 ♘f3 ♘c6 3 ♗b5 ♘f6 4 d4 ♘xd4 5 ♘xd4 exd4 6 e5 c6 7 0-0 cxb5 8 ♗g5 ♗e7 9 exf6 ♗xf6 10 ♖e1+ ♔f8 11 ♗xf6 ♕xf6 12 ♕e2 ♕e6 13 ♕d2 ♕b6 14 c3 d5 15 cxd4 ♗e6 16 ♘c3 h6 17 a3 g6 18 b4 ♔g7 19 f4 ♖ac8 20 ♖e3 ♖hd8 21 ♘e2 ♗f5! 22 ♖c1 ♗e4 23 ♘c3 f5 24 g4 ♔h7 25 h4 ♖c4 26 ♘e2 fxg4 27 ♖xc4 bxc4 28 ♘g3 ♗f5 29 ♖e7+ ♔g8 30 ♕e3 ♕f6! 31 ♖xb7 ♖c8 32 h5 c3 33 hxg6 c2 34 ♘e2 ♗e4! 35 f5 g3! 36 ♘c1 ♕h4 **0-1** L/N6051-1869

**1859-★AC-3** iv 59
**Carstanjen, A.–Anderssen, A.**
Köln [Anderssen & Lange]
1 e4 e5 2 ♘f3 ♘c6 3 ♗c4 ♗c5 4 b4 ♗xb4 5 c3 ♗a5 6 d4 exd4 7 0-0 ♗b6 8 cxd4 d6 9 d5 ♘ce7 10 e5 ♗g4 11 ♕b3 [□ 11 ♗b2] 11 ... ♗xf3 12 ♕xf3 ♗d4 13 e6 ♘f6 [□ 13 ... fxe6 △ 14 ... ♘f6] 14 exf7+ ♔xf7 15 ♘c3 ♖f8 16 ♖d1 ♗e5 17 ♖b1 ♔g8 18 h3 ♕d7 19 ♖b3 ♘f5 20 ♗e3 ♘h4 21 ♕e2 ♖f7 22 f4 ♗xc3 23 ♖xc3 ♖af8 24 ♔h2 ♖e7 25 ♗b5 ♕c8 26 ♕c2 a6 27 ♗e2 ♕e8 28 ♖dd3 ♕g6 29 g4 ♕e4 30 ♗d1 ♘xd5 31 ♖c4 ♘f3+ 32 ♔g3 ♕e6 33 ♖e4 ♕xe4 34 ♗xf3 ♕xe3! 35 ♖xe3 ♖xe3 36 ♕d2 c6 37 f5 ♖fe8 38 ♕f2 g5 39 h4 ♘c3 **0-1** L/N6047

**1859-★AE-1** 28 iii 59
**Anderssen, A.– Eichborn, L.**
Breslau
1 e4 e5 2 ♘f3 ♘c6 3 ♗b5 ♘ge7 4 d4 ♘xd4 5 ♘xd4 exd4 6 0-0 c6 7 ♗a4 ♕b6 8 c3 dxc3 9 ♘xc3 ♘g6 10 ♗e3 ♗c5 11 ♗b3 ♗xe3 12 fxe3 ♕xe3+ 13 ♔h1 0-0 14 ♕d6 ♕g5 15 ♖f5 ♕e7 16 e5 ♕xd6 17 exd6 b6 18 ♖e1 ♗a6 19 ♖e7 ♘h8 20 ♖f3 ♖fe8 21 ♘e4 ♖xe7 22 dxe7 ♖e8 23 ♖e3 ♖xe7 24 ♘f6+ ♔f8 25 ♘xh7+ ♔e8 26 ♖xe7+ ♔xe7 **0-1** L/N3043

**1859-★AH-1** ii 59
**Anderssen, A.+ Hillel, D.**
Breslau [Boden]
⟨♘b1⟩ 1 e4 e5 2 ♘f3 ♘c6 3 c3 d5 4 ♗b5 dxe4 5 ♘xe5 ♗d7 6 ♘xd7 ♕xd7 7 0-0 0-0-0 8 f3 ♗c5+ 9 ♔h1 e3?! 10 d4 ♕e6 11 ♖e1 ♘xd4 12 cxd4 ♖xd4 13 ♕c2 ♗b6 14 ♗xe3 [□ 14 ♖xe3] 14 ... ♖d8 15 ♖ad1 ♕e5 16 ♗g5 ♕xg5 17 ♕f5+! ♕xf5 18 ♖xd8+ ♔xd8 19 ♖e8# **1-0** M392-1860

**1859-★AL-1** i 59
**Lange, M.+ Anderssen, A.**
Breslau
1 e4 e5 2 ♘f3 ♘c6 3 ♗c4 ♗c5 4 0-0 ♘f6 5 d4 ♗xd4 6 ♘xd4 ♘xd4 7 f4 d6 8 fxe5 dxe5 9 ♗g5 ♗e6 10 ♗xf6 gxf6 11 ♗xe6 ♘xe6 12 ♘c3 c6 13 ♕xd8+ ♖xd8 14 ♖xf6 ♔e7 15 ♖af1 ♖df8 16 g3 ♖hg8 17 ♖6f5 f6 18 ♘d1 ♖g4 19 ♘f2 ♖g6 20 ♘d3 a5 21 ♔g2 c5 22 b3 b5 23 ♘b2 ♖d8 24 ♘d1 b4 25 ♖5f2 ♖d4 26 ♘e3 ♖xe4 27 ♘d5+ ♔d6 28 ♘xf6 ♖e3 29 ♘xh7 ♖g7 30 ♘f6 **1-0** L/N6047

**1859-★AL-2** i 59
**Lange, M.–Anderssen, A.**
Breslau
1 e4 e5 2 ♘f3 ♘c6 3 ♗c4 ♗c5 4 b4 ♗xb4 5 c3 ♗a5 6 d4 exd4 7 0-0 ♘f6 8 e5 d5 9 ♗b5 ♘e4 10 ♘xd4 ♗d7 11 ♗xc6 bxc6 12 ♗a3 c5 13 ♘b3 ♗a4 14 e6 0-0 15 e7 ♕xe7 16 ♕xd5 ♗xb3 17 ♕xb3 ♕e5 18 ♖e1 ♕f4 19 ♕c2 ♖fe8 20 f3 ♘xc3 21 ♘xc3 ♕d4+ 22 ♔h1 ♗xc3 23 ♖xe8+ ♖xe8 24 ♖d1 ♕e3 25 h3 ♗d4 26 ♕a4 h5 27 ♗c1 ♕e2 28 ♗g5 ♗f2 29 ♕xe8+ ♕xe8 30 ♖d8 ♔f8 31 g4 hxg4 32 hxg4 f6 33 ♖xe8+ ♔xe8 34 ♗f4 ♔d7 35 ♔g2 ♗d4 **0-1** L/N6047

**1859-★AL-3** i 59
**Anderssen, A.+ Lange, M.**
Breslau [Löwenthal]
1 e4 e5 2 f4 exf4 3 ♘f3 g5 4 h4 g4 5 ♘e5 ♘f6 6 ♘xg4 ♘xe4 7 d3 ♘g3 8 ♗xf4 ♕e7+ [□ 8 ... ♘xh1] 9 ♗e2 ♕b4+ 10 ♕d2! ♕xd2+ 11 ♘xd2 ♘xh1 12 ♘f6+ ♔d8 13 ♘d5 ♗e7 14 0-0-0 ♘f2? [□ 14 ... d6] 15 ♖f1 ♗xh4 16 ♗xc7+ ♔e8 17 ♗d6! ♘a6 18 d4 b5! 19 g3 ♗b7 20 ♗f3 ♘d3+ 21 cxd3 ♗xd5 22 ♗xd5 ♖c8+ 23 ♔b1 ♗g5 24 ♘e4 f6 25 ♗b7 ♖c6 26 ♗xc6 dxc6 27 ♘xf6+ ♗xf6 28 ♖xf6 ♔d7 29 ♗e5 ♖e8 30 ♖d6+ **1-0** M324

**1859-★AL-4** i 59
**Anderssen, A.= Lange, M.**
Breslau
1 e4 e5 2 ♘f3 ♘c6 3 ♗b5 ♘f6 4 d3 ♗c5 5 c3 0-0 6 ♗xc6 bxc6 7 ♘xe5 ♖e8 8 ♘f3 d5 9 e5 d4 10 0-0 ♘g4 11 b4 ♗b6 12 c4 c5 13 bxc5 ♗xc5 14 ♖e1 ♗b7 15 ♘bd2 ♗b4 16 ♖b1 ♗xf3 17 ♕xf3 ♗xd2 18 ♗xd2 ♘xe5 19 ♕g3 ♖b8 20 ♖xb8 ♕xb8 21 f4 ♘d7 22 f5 ♖xe1+ 23 ♕xe1 c5 24 h3 ♕e5 25 ♕f2 h6 26 ♕f3 ♕b8 27 ♗f4 ♕b1+ 28 ♔h2 ♕xa2 29 ♗d6 ♕a6 30 ♕d5 ♕c8 31 f6 g6 32 h4 a5 33 h5 ♘xf6 34 ♕xc5 ♕xc5 35 ♗xc5 ♘g4+ 36 ♔g3 ♘e5 37 ♗xd4 ♘xd3 38 ♔f3 gxh5 39 ♔e4 ♘b4 40 ♗c3 ♔f8 41 ♗d2 ♔e7 42 ♗xh6 ♔e6 43 ♔f4 f6 44 ♗f8 ♘c6 45 ♗a3 ♘e5 46 c5 ♘c4 47 ♗c1 a4 48 c6 ♘d6 **½-½** L/N6047

**1859-★AL-5** i 59
**Anderssen, A.– Lange, M.**
Breslau
1 e4 e5 2 f4 exf4 3 ♘f3 g5 4 h4 g4 5 ♘e5 d6 6 ♘xg4 ♗e7 7 ♕f3 ♗xh4+ 8 ♘f2 ♕g5 9 d3 ♗g3 10 ♘c3 ♘c6 11 ♘e2 ♘b4 12 ♘xf4 ♘xc2+ 13 ♔d1 ♘d4 14 ♕e3 ♗xf2 15 ♕xf2 ♗g4+ 16 ♗e2 ♘xe2 17 ♘xe2 ♕b5 18 ♕d4 0-0-0 19 ♔e1 ♗xe2 20 ♔xe2 ♘e7 21 a4 ♕d7 22 ♕f2 f5 23 ♕xa7 ♘c6 24 ♕a8+ ♘b8 25 ♗e3 fxe4 26 ♗a7 ♕g4+ 27 ♔d2 ♕g5+ 28 ♔d1 ♕xg2 29 ♖g1 ♕f3+ 30 ♔c1 exd3 31 ♖a3 ♔d7 32 ♖b3 ♖hg8 33 ♕xb7 ♖xg1+ 34 ♗xg1 ♕f1+ 35 ♔d2 ♕e2+ 36 ♔c3 ♘c6 **0-1** L/N6047

**1859-★AL-6**
**Lange, M.+ Anderssen, A.**
Breslau
1 e4 e5 2 ♘f3 ♘c6 3 ♗c4 ♗c5 4 b4 ♗xb4 5 c3 ♗a5 6 d4 exd4 7 0-0 ♘f6 8 e5 d5 9 ♗b5 ♘e4 10 ♘xd4 ♘xc3 11 ♘xc3 ♗xc3 12 ♘xc6 ♕dd7 13 e6 fxe6 14 ♘e5 ♕xb5 15 ♕h5+ g6 16 ♘xg6 hxg6 17

♕xg6+ ♔d7 18 ♗f4 ♔c6 19 ♖ac1 d4 20 ♕g7 b6 21 ♖xc3+ dxc3 22 ♕xc7+ ♔d5 23 ♖d1+ ♔e4 24 f3+ ♔f5 25 ♕f7# **1-0** L/N6047

**1859-★AL-7**
**Lange, M.– Anderssen, A.**
Breslau♀
1 e4 e5 2 ♘f3 ♘c6 3 ♗b5 ♘f6 4 d4 exd4 5 e5 ♘e4 6 0-0 ♗e7 7 ♖e1 ♘c5 8 ♘xd4 ♘xd4 9 ♕xd4 0-0 10 ♘c3 d6 11 ♗e3 ♗f5 12 ♖ad1 a6 13 ♗c4 ♘d7 14 ♗f4 ♗xc2 15 exd6 cxd6 16 ♖d2 ♗g6 17 ♗xd6 ♗f6 18 ♕g4 ♘e5 19 ♕e2 ♘xc4 20 ♕xc4 ♖c8 21 ♕b3 ♗xc3 22 bxc3 ♖e8 23 ♖ed1 ♗e4 24 f3 ♗c6 25 c4 ♕g5 26 f4 ♕g6 27 ♖f2 ♖e4 28 f5 ♕g5 29 ♖df1 ♖g4 30 ♗g3 ♖e8 31 f6 ♕c5 32 fxg7 ♖xg7 33 ♕d3 h5 34 ♔h1 h4 35 ♗xh4 ♕xf2 36 ♗xf2 ♖xg2 37 ♕d5 ♖g6 38 ♗g3 ♖e2 39 ♖d1 ♔f8 40 ♔g1 ♗xd5 41 cxd5 ♔e8 42 d6 ♔d8 43 a4 ♖g4 44 a5 ♖e5 45 ♔f2 **0-1** L/N6047

**1859-★AM-1** 18 xi 59
**Morphy, P.C.+ Arnold, W.E.**
Baltimore [Maróczy]
⟨♘b1⟩ 1 e4 e6 2 f4 ♗c5 3 d4 ♗b6 4 ♘f3 d5 5 e5 f6 6 ♗d3 ♘c6 7 c3 ♗d7 8 0-0 ♕e7 9 ♗e3 ♘h6 10 h3 0-0 11 g4 fxe5 12 fxe5 ♘f7 13 ♕e2 ♕e8 14 ♖f2 ♘e7 15 ♖af1 ♘g6 16 ♗xg6 hxg6 17 ♘g5! ♕e7 18 ♖xf7 ♖xf7 19 ♖xf7 ♕e8 20 ♕f2 c6 21 ♕h4 **1-0** L/N3203

**1859-★AM-2** iv 59
**Mayet, K.– Anderssen, A.**
Berlin [Hoffer & Zukertort]
1 e4 e5 2 ♘f3 ♘c6 3 ♗b5 ♗c5 4 c3 ♘f6 5 ♗xc6 dxc6 6 0-0 ♗g4 7 h3 h5 8 hxg4 hxg4 9 ♘xe5 g3 10 d4

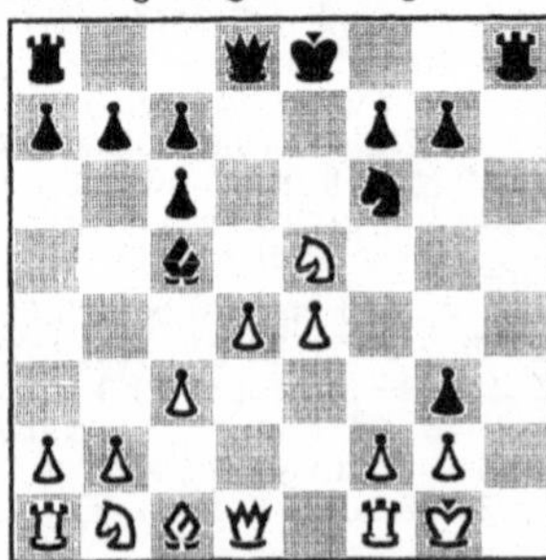

10 ... ♘xe4! [△ 11 ... ♖h1+ 12 ... ♕h4+−+] 11 ♕g4 [11 ♘f3? (11 ... gxf2+ 12 ♖xf2 ♖h1+ 13 ♔xh1 ♘xf2+−+); □ 11 fxg3 (11 ... ♘xg3 12 ♖e1 ♖h1+ 13 ♔f2 ♕h4 14 ♖xh1 ♘xh1+ 15 ♔g1 ♗d6 16 ♗e3∞)] 11 ... ♗xd4 [11 ... gxf2+−+] 12 ♕xe4 [12 ♗e3 (12 ... gxf2+ 13 ♗xf2 ♗xf2+ 14 ♖xf2 ♖h1+−+); 12 ♘d3 (12 ... ♖h4 13 ♗g5 ♖xg4 14 ♗xd8 ♗xf2+ 15 ♘xf2 gxf2+ 16 ♖xf2 ♘xf2−+)] 12 ... ♗xf2+ 13 ♖xf2 ♕d1+ **0-1** L/N6138-1882

**1859-★AM-3** v 59
**Anderssen, A.+ Mayet, K.**
Berlin
1 e4 c5 2 ♘f3 ♘c6 3 d4 cxd4 4 ♘xd4 e5 5 ♘xc6 bxc6 6 ♗c4 ♕h4 7 ♕d3 ♘f6 8 ♘d2 ♗c5 9 0-0 ♘g4 10 ♘f3 ♗xf2+ 11 ♔h1 ♕h5 12 ♕d6 ♗a6 13 ♗g5 f6 14 ♖ad1 ♗xc4 15 ♕xd7+ ♔f8 16 ♕xc6 ♘xh2 17 ♕xa8+ ♔f7 18 ♘xe5+ fxe5 19 ♕b7+ ♔g6 20 ♖d6+ ♔xg5 21 ♕xg7+ ♔f4 22 g3+ ♔xe4 23 ♕b7+ ♔f5 24 ♖xf2+ ♘f3+ 25 ♔g2 e4 26 ♕d7+ **1-0** L/N6047

**1859-★AR-1**
**Anderssen,A.+Rivière, J.A.de**
Paris
1 e4 e5 2 ♘f3 ♘c6 3 d4 exd4 4 ♗c4 ♘f6 5 ♘g5 ♘e5 6 ♗b3 h6 7 f4 hxg5 8 fxe5 ♘xe4 9 0-0 d5 10 exd6 f5 11 ♘d2 ♕xd6 12 ♘xe4 ♕xh2+ 13 ♔f2 fxe4 14 ♕xd4 ♗e7 15 ♕xe4 ♗f5 16 ♗f7+ ♔xf7 17 ♕xf5+ ♔g8 18 ♕e6+ ♔h7 19 ♕e4+ ♔h6 20 ♗e3 ♖hf8+ 21 ♔e2 ♕h5+ 22 g4 ♕h2+ 23 ♖f2 ♖xf2+ 24 ♗xf2 ♖f8 25 ♖h1 ♖xf2+ 26 ♔d3 ♖d2+ 27 ♔c4 ♖xc2+ 28 ♔d5 ♗f6 29 ♔e6 ♗xb2 30 ♔f7 ♖f2+ 31 ♔g8 g6 32 ♕e7

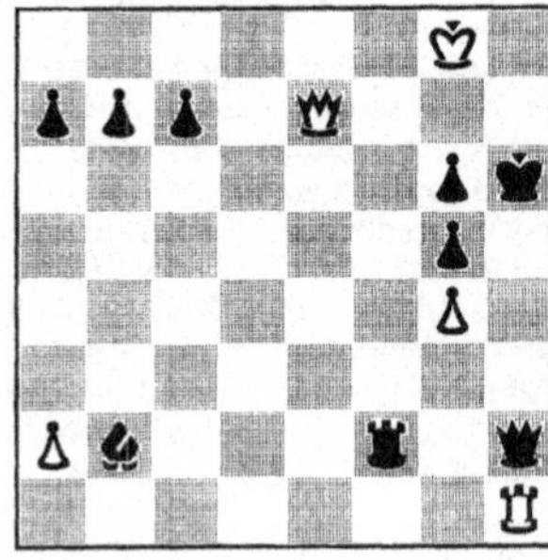

**1-0** M954-1859

**1859-★AR-2**
**Anderssen,A.– Rivière,J.A.de**
Paris [Staunton]
1 e4 e5 2 ♘f3 ♘c6 3 ♗c4 ♗c5 4 b4 ♗xb4 5 c3 ♗a5 6 d4 exd4 7 0-0 ♘f6 8 e5 d5 9 exf6 dxc4 10 ♖e1+ ♗e6 11 fxg7 ♖g8 12 ♗g5 ♕d5 13 ♘bd2 ♖xg7 [13 ... dxc3? 14 ♘e4 △ 15 ♘f6+] 14 ♘e4 ♔f8 15 ♗h6 d3 16 ♘fg5 ♕f5 17 ♘f6 ♗xc3 18 ♘gxh7+ ♔e7 19 ♗xg7 ♗xf6 20 ♘xf6 ♕g6 21 ♕g4 ♕xg4 22 ♘xg4 ♖g8 23 ♗f6+ ♔d6 24 ♘e5 b5 25 ♘xc6 ♔xc6 26 ♗c3 ♔c5 27 ♖ab1 a6 28 h4 ♔d5 29 f3 c5 30 a3 ♔c6 31 ♔f2 a5 32 h5 b4

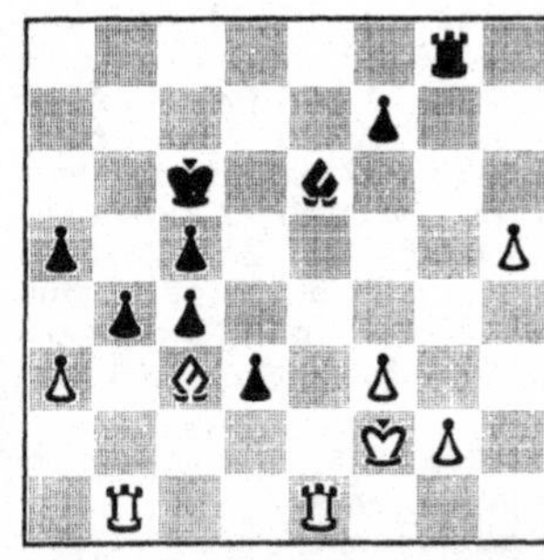

33 ♗f6 c3 34 g4 d2 35 ♖h1 ♗c4 36 ♖bd1 ♖e8 37 f4 ♖e2+ 38 ♔f3 c2 39 h6 cxd1♕ 40 ♖xd1 ♖h2 41 ♖xd2 ♖xh6 42 ♗a1 ♗d5+ 43 ♔g3 c4 44 axb4 axb4 45 f5 ♖h1 46 g5 ♖f1 47 ♔g4 ♗e4 48 ♗e5 ♗xf5+ 49 ♔g3 c3 50 ♖f2 ♖xf2 51 ♔xf2 ♔d5 52 ♗f6 ♔e4 53 ♔e2 ♗g4+ 54 ♔e1 ♔d3 55 ♗e5 b3 **0-1** M954-1859

**1859-★AR-3**
**Rivière,J.A.de– Anderssen,A.**
Paris [Staunton]
1 e4 e5 2 ♘f3 ♘c6 3 ♗c4 f5?! 4 d4! d6 5 dxe5 fxe4 6 ♕d5 ♕e7 7 ♗g5 ♗e6 8 ♕xe4 d5 9 ♗xd5 ♗xd5 10 ♕xd5 ♘f6 11 ♗xf6 gxf6 12 0-0 [□ 12 e6] 12 ... fxe5 13 ♘c3 ♕d6 14 ♘b5 ♕xd5 15 ♘xc7+ ♔d7 16 ♘xd5 ♗d6 17 ♖ad1 ♖af8 18 ♘d2 ♔c8 19 c3 ♗b8 20 b4 ♖f7 21 b5 ♘d8 22 ♖fe1 ♖hf8 23 f3 ♖g7 24 ♖e4 [□ 24 ♘c4] 24 ... b6 25 a4 ♘e6 26 a5 ♔b7 27 axb6 [□ 27 a6+; □ 27 ♘c4] 27 ... axb6 28 ♖c4 ♖d8 29 ♘e4 ♘f4 30 ♘ef6 ♖xg2+ 31 ♔h1 ♖b2 32 ♖g1 ♘xd5 [32 ... ♖xb5?] 33 ♘xd5 ♖d7 [33 ... ♖xb5?; 33 ... ♖xd5??] 34 ♘f6 e4! 35 ♖e1 ♖xh2+ 36 ♔g1 ♖g7+ 37 ♔f1 ♖h1+ 38 ♔e2 exf3+ 39 ♔d2 ♖gg2+ **0-1**
M954-1859

**1859-★AS-1** iv 59
**Suhle, B.– Anderssen, A.**
Köln
1 e4 e5 2 ♘f3 ♘c6 3 d4 exd4 4 ♗c4 ♗c5 5 0-0 d6 6 c3 ♗g4 7 ♕b3 ♗xf3 8 ♗xf7+ ♔f8 9 ♗xg8 ♖xg8 10 gxf3 g5 11 ♔h1 ♕f6 12 f4 gxf4 13 ♕xb7 ♖d8 14 ♕xc6 ♕g5 15 e5 dxe5 16 ♗xf4 exf4 17 cxd4 ♖d5 18 ♕a8+ ♔e7 19 ♕xg8 ♕xg8 20 dxc5 f3 **0-1** L/N6047

**1859-★AS-2** iv 59
**Suhle, B.= Anderssen, A.**
Köln
1 e4 e5 2 f4 exf4 3 ♗c4 ♕h4+ 4 ♔f1 g5 5 ♘c3 ♗g7 6 d4 ♘e7 7 g3 fxg3 8 ♔g2 ♕h6 9 ♘f3 ♕g6 10

♘xg5 ♖f8 11 hxg3 h6 12 ♘h3 d6 13 ♘f4 ♕h7 14 ♘h5 ♗h8 15 ♖f1 ♘bc6 16 ♗e3 ♗d7 17 ♘f6+ ♗xf6 18 ♖xf6 ♘g8 19 ♖f4 0-0-0 20 d5 ♘e5 21 ♕d4 c5 22 dxc6 ♘xc6 23 ♕d2 ♘e5 24 ♗d5 ♘e7 25 ♗xa7 ♖g8 26 ♘e2 ♘xd5 27 exd5 ♗g4 28 ♗b6 ♗xe2 29 ♕c3+ ♗c4 30 ♖xc4+ ♔d7 31 ♖c7+ ♔e8 32 ♖e1 ♕f5 33 ♖xb7 ♖c8 34 ♗c7 ♖g6 35 ♕c6+ ♔f8 36 ♗xd6+ ♖xd6 37 ♕xd6+ ♔g8 [38 ♕xe5 ♖xc2+ 39 ♖e2 ♕xe5] ½-½ L/N6047

**1859-★AS-3** iv 59

**Suhle, B.– Anderssen, A.**

Köln [Staunton]

1 e4 c5 2 ♘f3 e6 3 d4 cxd4 4 ♘xd4 a6 5 ♗d3 ♘c6 6 ♗e3 ♘f6 7 0-0 ♗e7 8 f4 d5 9 e5 ♘d7 10 ♘d2 ♗c5 11 c3 ♕b6 12 ♘2f3 f5 13 b4 ♗xd4 14 ♘xd4 ♘xd4 15 ♗xd4 ♕c7 16 g4 [□16 ♕h5+ g6 17 ♕h6 ♘f8 18 a4±] 16 ... ♘f8 17 ♗c5 g6 18 gxf5 gxf5 19 ♔h1 ♕f7 20 ♕e1 ♘g6 21 c4 dxc4 22 ♗xc4 ♗d7 [□22 ... b6 △ 23 ... ♗b7+] 23 ♗e2 ♗c6+ 24 ♗f3 ♕d7 25 ♕g3 0-0-0 26 ♖ac1 ♖hg8 27 ♕f2 ♘h4! 28 ♗d6 [28 ♕xh4? ♗xf3+ 29 ♖xf3 ♕d1+ 30 ♗g1+ ♕xc1 31 ♕f2 ♖d1 32 ♕c5+ ♕xc5–+] 28 ... ♘xf3 29 ♕xf3 ♖de8 30 b5 axb5 31 ♖fd1

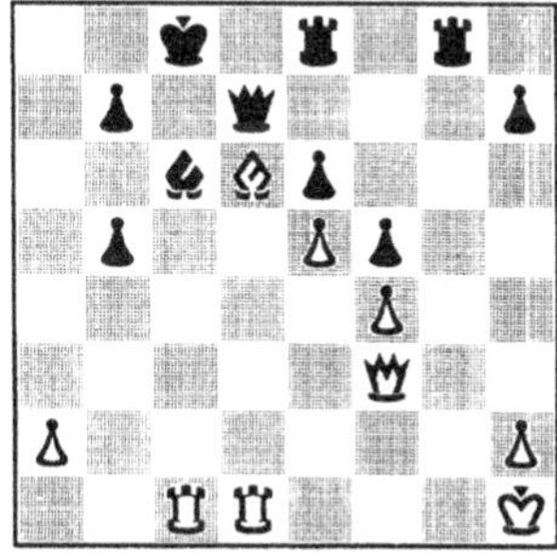

31 ... ♕c7! 32 ♖d5 ♕b6 33 ♖d3 ♖g1+ 34 ♖xg1 ♗xf3+ 35 ♖xf3 ♕c6 36 ♖gg3 b4 37 ♔g2 h5 38 ♗xb4 h4 39 ♖g7 ♔b8 40 ♗d6+ ♔a7 41 ♖c7 ♕e4 42 ♖c3 b5 43 ♖a3+ ♔b6 44 ♔h3 ♖c8 45 ♖ae3 ♕d5 46 a4 ♖c2 47 axb5 ♕a2 48 ♔xh4 ♖xh2+ 49 ♔g5 ♕a8 **0-1** M954-1859

**1859-★AS-4** ix 59

**Suhle, B.– Anderssen, A.**

Breslau

1 e4 e5 2 ♘f3 ♘c6 3 ♗b5 ♘f6 4 d4 exd4 5 e5 ♘e4 6 0-0 ♗e7 7 ♖e1 ♘c5 8 ♘xd4 ♘xd4 9 ♕xd4 0-0 10 ♗e3 d5 11 ♘c3 c6 12 ♗f1 ♘e6 13 ♕a4 b5 14 ♘xb5 cxb5 15 ♗xb5 ♗b7 16 c3 f5 17 ♗c6 f4 18 ♗xb7 fxe3 19 ♖xe3 ♘c5 20 ♕c6 ♘xb7 21 ♕xb7 ♖b8 22 ♕xa7 ♖xb2 23 ♖f1 ♗g5 24 ♖ee1 ♗d2 25 ♕a3 ♕b6 26 ♖d1 ♗xc3 27 ♕xc3 ♖2xf2 **0-1** L/N6047

**1859-★AS-5** ix 59

**Suhle, B.– Anderssen, A.**

Breslau [Anderssen & Lange]

1 b3 e5 2 ♗b2 ♘c6 3 e3 ♘f6 4 ♗b5 ♗d6 5 d3 ♘e7 6 d4 exd4 7 ♗xd4 ♘f5 8 ♗b2 ♘h4 9 ♗f1 b6 10 ♘f3 ♘g6 11 ♗d3 ♗b7 12 ♘bd2 0-0 13 ♕e2 ♘d5 14 0-0 ♕e7 15 ♗xg6 fxg6 16 ♕c4 ♖ab8 [△ 17 ... b5] 17 ♕g4 ♖f5 18 ♖fe1 ♖bf8 19 e4 ♖f4 20 ♕h3 ♘b4 21 ♖ac1 g5 22 ♕h5 ♗c5 23 a3 ♘c6 24 b4

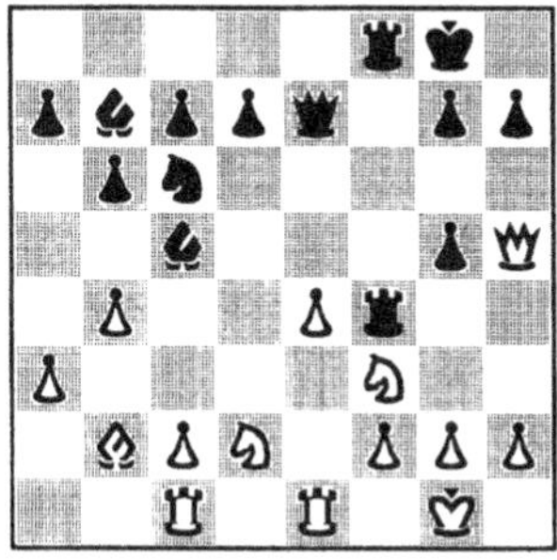

24 ... ♗xf2+ 25 ♔xf2 ♖h4 **0-1** L/N6047

**1859-★AS-6** ix 59

**Anderssen, A.– Suhle, B.**

Breslau

1 e4 e5 2 f4 exf4 3 ♘f3 g5 4 h4 g4 5 ♘e5 ♘f6 6 ♘xg4 ♘xe4 7 d3 ♘g3 8 ♗xf4 ♘xh1 9 ♕e2+ ♕e7 10 ♘f6+ ♔d8 11 ♗xc7+ ♔xc7 12 ♘d5+ ♔d8 13 ♘xe7 ♗xe7 14 ♕h5 ♘g3 15 ♕a5+ b6 16 ♕d5 ♘c6 17 ♘d2 ♘xf1 18 ♔xf1 ♗b7 19 ♖e1 ♖g8 20 ♘f3 ♔c7 21 ♕f5 ♖ae8 22 d4 ♔c8 23 ♕f4 ♘d8 24 ♖e3 ♗b4 25 ♖xe8 ♖xe8 26 d5 ♗a6+ 27 c4 ♘b7 28 b3 ♘d6 29 ♕h6 ♗c5 30 ♘d2 ♘f5 31 ♕g5 ♘e3+ 32 ♔e2 ♘xc4+ 33 ♔d1 ♗e3 34 ♕f6 ♘xd2 35 ♕xf7 ♖d8 36 ♕xh7 ♘f1 37 g4 ♔b8 38 ♔c2 ♖c8+ 39 ♔b1 ♗d4 **0-1** L/N6047

**1859-★AS-7** ix 59

**Anderssen, A.+ Suhle, B.**

Breslau

1 e4 e5 2 ♘f3 ♘c6 3 ♗b5 ♘ge7 4 d4 exd4 5 0-0 ♘g6 6 ♘xd4 ♗e7 7 ♘f5 0-0 8 ♘c3 ♗c5 9 ♕h5 d6 10 ♗g5 ♕e8 11 ♘xg7 ♔xg7 12 ♕h6+ **1-0** L/N6047

**1859-★AS-8**

**Anderssen, A.+ Suhle, B.**

Breslau

1 e4 e5 2 ♘f3 ♘c6 3 c3 ♘f6 4 d4 ♘xe4 5 dxe5 d5 6 ♗e3 ♗e7 7 ♗b5 0-0 8 ♗xc6 bxc6 9 ♘bd2 f5 10 ♘d4 ♕e8 11 f4 ♕g6 12 0-0 c5 13 ♘4f3 h5 14 ♖e1 h4 15 h3 ♖d8 16 ♕c2 c4 17 ♖ad1 ♗b7 18 b3 c5 19 ♘xe4 fxe4 20 bxc4 ♕g3 21 ♘h2 d4 22 ♘f1 ♕g6 23 cxd4 cxd4 24 ♖xd4 ♖xd4 25 ♗xd4 ♖d8 26 ♗e3 ♕c6 27 c5 ♖d3 28 ♕c4+ ♔h8 29 ♖c1 ♕g6 30 c6 ♗c8 31 c7 ♖xe3 32 ♘xe3 ♕b6 33 ♕xe4 ♗c5 34 ♔f2 ♕xc7 35 ♕d4 **1-0** L/N6047

**1859-★AS-9**

**Anderssen, A.= Suhle, B.**

Breslau

1 e4 e5 2 f4 exf4 3 ♗c4 ♕h4+ 4 ♔f1 g5 5 ♘c3 ♗g7 6 ♘d5 ♔d8 7 d4 d6 8 e5 c6 9 ♘c3 d5 10 ♘e2 f6 11 b3 ♘e7 12 ♘f3 ♕h6 13 exf6 ♗xf6 14 ♘e5 ♗xe5 15 dxe5 ♘d7 16 ♗b2 ♘f5 17 ♔g1 ♖e8 18 ♕d2 ♘xe5 19 ♘e4 ♔c7 20 ♘f2 ♘e3 21 c4 g4 22 h3 gxh3 23 ♘xh3 ♘xg2 24 ♘f2 ♕g7 25 ♖h2 ♘e3+ 26 ♔h1 ♘f5 27 ♖g2 ♘g3+ 28 ♔h2 ♕h6+ 29 ♔g1 ♕g5 30 ♘h1 ♖g8 31 ♘xg3 fxg3 32 ♕xg5 ♖xg5 33 ♔h1 ♗e6 34 ♖xg3 ♘f7 35 ♖ag1 ♖ag8 36 ♖xg5 ♖xg5 37 ♖xg5 ♘xg5 38 c5 ♘e4 39 ♗e5+ ♔d7 40 b4 a5 41 a3 axb4 42 axb4 ♗f5 43 ♔g2 ♔e6 44 ♗d4 ♗g6 45 b5 cxb5 46 ♗xb5 ♘d2 47 ♗a4 ♘c4 48 c6 bxc6 49 ♗xc6 ♘d6 50 ♔f2 ♘f5 51 ♗h8 ♔d6 52 ♗a4 ♔c5 53 ♔f3 ♔c4 54 ♔f4 d4 55 ♗d7 d3 56 ♗a4 ♘e7 57 ♔e3 ♘d5+ 58 ♔d2 h5 59 ♗d7 ♔c5 60 ♗e6 ♔d6 61 ♗c8 h4 62 ♗d4 ♘e7 63 ♗h3 ♗f5 64 ♗f1 h3 65 ♗xh3 **½-½** L/N6047

**1859-★AS-10**

**Anderssen, A.– Suhle, B.**

Breslau

1 e4 e5 2 ♘f3 ♘c6 3 ♗c4 ♘f6 4 ♘g5 d5 5 exd5 ♘a5 6 ♗b5+ c6 7 dxc6 bxc6 8 ♗e2 h6 9 ♘f3 e4 10 ♘e5 ♕d4 11 f4 ♗c5 12 ♖f1 ♗b6 13 c3 ♕d8 14 d4 exd3 15 ♗xd3 0-0 16 ♕e2 ♖e8 17 h3 ♘d7 18 ♘d2 ♗c7 19 b4 ♘b7 20 ♘df3 ♘d6 21 ♗e3 ♘b6 22 ♖d1 ♘d5

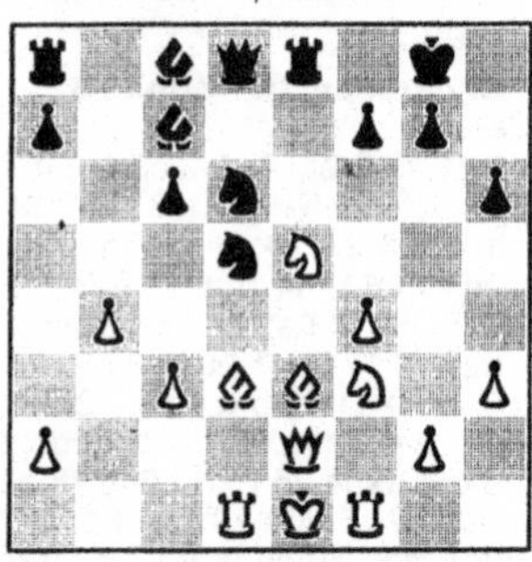

23 ♗c4 ♘f5 24 ♔f2 ♘fxe3 25 ♕xe3 ♗b6 **0-1** L/N6047

**1859-★AS-11**
**Anderssen, A.+Suhle, B.**

1 e4 e5 2 ♘f3 ♘c6 3 ♗b5 d6 4 ♗xc6+ bxc6 5 d4 f5 6 dxe5 fxe4 7 ♘g5 d5 8 e6 ♘h6 9 0-0 ♕f6 10 c4 ♗xe6 11 ♘c3 ♖d8 12 ♕a4 ♗d7 13 cxd5 cxd5 14 ♕a5 c6 15 ♘gxe4 dxe4 16 ♗g5 ♗b4 17 ♕xb4 ♕xg5 18 ♘xe4 c5 19 ♕c4 ♕e5 20 ♖fe1 ♔f8 21 ♘xc5 ♕f6 22 ♖ad1 ♗c8 23 ♕b4 ♔g8 24 ♘e4 ♕f8 25 ♕c4+ ♘f7 26 ♖xd8 ♕xd8 27 ♘d6 **1-0** L/N6047

**1859-★AS-12**
**Suhle, B.+Anderssen, A.**
Breslau

1 e4 c5 2 c4 ♘c6 3 ♘c3 a6 4 ♘f3 e6 5 ♗e2 ♘ge7 6 d4 exd4 7 ♘xd4 ♘g6 8 0-0 ♗c5 9 ♗e3 ♗a7 10 ♘xc6 dxc6 11 ♕xd8+ ♔xd8 12 ♗xa7 ♖xa7 13 c5 e5 14 ♘a4 ♘f4 15 ♗c4 ♗e6 16 ♘b6 ♔c7 17 ♖ad1 ♗xc4 18 ♘xc4 ♖e8 19 ♘b6 ♖e7 20 ♖d2 ♘e6 21 b4 a5 22 a3 axb4 23 axb4 f6 24 ♖fd1 ♘d4 25 f4 ♖a3 26 fxe5 fxe5 27 ♖f2 ♘e6 28 ♖f5 ♖e8 29 ♖xe5 ♖d8 30 ♖xd8 ♘xd8 31 ♖e7+ ♔b8 32 ♖xg7 **1-0** L/N6047

**1859-★BD-1**
**Deacon, F.H.+Baumann**
London [Staunton]

1 e4 e5 2 f4 exf4 3 ♘f3 d5 4 exd5 ♗d6 5 ♗c4 ♘f6 6 0-0 0-0 7 d4 c6 8 ♘c3 h6 9 ♘e5 a5 10 dxc6 ♘xc6 11 ♗xf4 ♘xe5 12 dxe5 ♗c5+ 13 ♔h1 ♘h7 14 ♕h5 ♗e6 15 ♖ad1 ♕c7 16 ♘d5 ♕c6

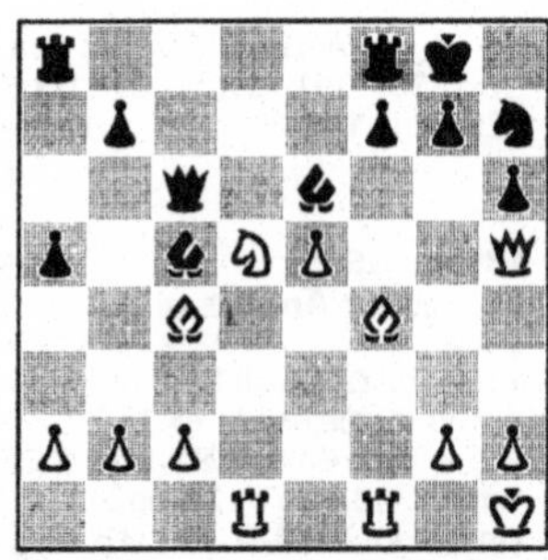

17 ♕h4 f5 [17 ... g5 18 ♗xg5 hxg5 (18 ... ♘xg5 19 ♕xh6) 19 ♘f6+ ♘xf6 20 ♕xg5+ ♔h7 21 ♖xf6] 18 a4 ♖ad8 [18 ... g5 19 ♕xh6] 19 ♗b5 ♕c8 20 ♘e7+ ♗xe7 21 ♕xe7 ♖xd1 22 ♖xd1 ♔h8 23 c3 ♖g8 24 h4 [24 ♗d7!? ♗xd7 25 ♖xd7 ♕c4 26 ♗e3 ♘g5 27 h3 f4] 24 ... g5 25 hxg5 hxg5 26 ♗e3 f4 27 ♗b6 g4 28 ♖d7 [28 ♗d7?! ♕c4 29 ♗xe6 ♕e2 30 ♖g1 g3 31 ♕f7 ♖f8] 28 ... ♗xd7 29 e6 **1-0** M954-1859

**1859-★BK-1**
**Brunswick, Duke of & Casabianca, Count−Kolisch, I.F. von**
[Staunton]

1 d4 d5 2 c4 e6 3 ♗f4 ♗d6 4 ♗g3 ♘f6 5 e3 0-0 6 ♘f3 ♘e4 7 ♗d3 f5 8 ♗xd6 ♕xd6 9 0-0 c5 10 cxd5 exd5 11 dxc5 ♕xc5 12 ♘bd2 ♘c6 13 ♘b3 ♕e7 14 ♘fd4 f4 15 exf4 ♖xf4 16 ♗xe4 dxe4 17 ♘xc6 bxc6 18 ♕c2 ♗a6 19 ♕xc6 ♗b7 20 ♕c5 ♕f7 21 ♕e3 ♖f8 22 ♘c5 ♗a8 23 b3 ♕g6 24 ♔h1

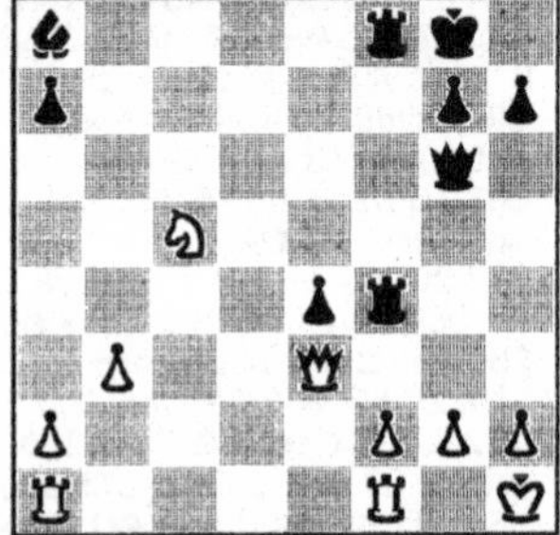

24 ... ♖f3! 25 gxf3 ♖xf3 26 ♖g1 ♕f7 27 ♕d4 e3 28 ♕d8+ ♕f8 29 ♕xf8+ ♔xf8 30 ♖g2 exf2 31 ♖f1 ♔g8 32 ♘e6 g6 33 ♘g5 ♖e3 34 h4 ♖e1 35 ♔h2 ♖xf1 36 ♔g3 ♖g1 **0-1** M954-1859

**1859-★BM-1** iii 59
**Morphy, P.C.+Budzinski, J.**
Paris [Maróczy]

1 e4 e5 2 ♘f3 ♘f6 3 ♘xe5 d6 4 ♘f3 ♘xe4 5 d4 d5 6 ♗d3 ♗e7 7 0-0 ♘c6 8 c4 ♗e6? [◻ 8 ... ♘b4 9 ♘c3 ♘xd3 10 ♕xd3 ♘xc3 11 bxc3 ♗e6; ◻ 8 ... ♗g4 9 ♗e3 0-0 10 ♘c3 ♘f6] 9 ♕b3! ♘a5 [◻ 9 ... dxc4 10 ♕b7 (10 ♗xc4 ♗xc4 11 ♕xc4 ♘d6) 10 ... ♗d5 11 ♗xe4 ♗xe4 12 ♘c3 ♖b8 13 ♕a6 ♗xf3 14 gxf3 ♖b6] 10 ♕a4+ c6 11 ♖e1 f5 12 cxd5 ♗xd5 13 ♗d2 ♘xd2 14 ♘bxd2 b5 15 ♕c2 g6 16 ♖xe7+!? [◻ 16 ♗xf5!±]

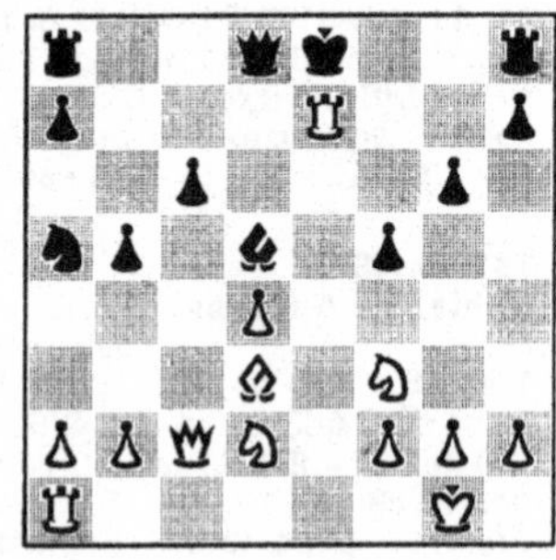

16 ... ♔xe7 [16 ... ♕xe7 17 ♖e1 ♗e6 18 d5 cxd5 19 ♘d4±] 17 ♖e1+ ♔f7 [◻ 17 ... ♔f6] 18 ♗xf5 gxf5 [18 ... ♕f6 19 ♗e4!±] 19 ♕xf5+ ♕f6 [19 ... ♔g7 20 ♕g4+, 21 ♖e5±] 20 ♘e5+ ♔g7 21 ♕g4+ ♔h6 22 ♖e3 ♗xg2 23 ♔xg2 ♖hg8 24 ♖h3+ **1-0** L/N3203

**1859-★BM-2**
**Morphy, P.C.+Broughton, W.R.**
Boston [Maróczy]

⟨♘b1⟩ 1 e4 e5 2 ♘f3 ♘c6 3 ♗c4 ♘f6 4 ♕e2 ♗c5 5 c3 d6 6 b4 ♗b6 7 d3 h6 8 a4 a5 9 b5 ♘e7 10 d4 ♗g4 11 dxe5 ♗xf3 [11 ... dxe5 12 ♗xf7+±] 12 ♕xf3 dxe5 13 ♗a3 ♘g6 14 ♖d1 ♕c8 [◻ 14 ... ♕b8, ♕a7, ♗c5] 15 h3 c5 16 bxc6 bxc6 17 ♖d6 ♗d8? [◻ 17 ... 0-0 18 ♖xf6 gxf6 19 ♕xf6 ♔h7 20 ♗xf7 ♖g8!] 18 ♖xc6 ♕xc6 19 ♗b5 ♕xb5 20 axb5 ♖c8 [◻ 20 ... ♗e7 21 ♗xe7 ♔xe7] 21 0-0 ♖c4 22 ♕d3 ♖c7 23 b6 ♖b7 24 ♖d1 ♖d7 25 ♕b5 ♗xb6 26 ♖xd7 ♘xd7 27 c4+ ♗c7 28 c5 ♔d8 29 c6 ♘b8 30 ♕b7 ♖e8 31 ♗c5 ♖e6 32 ♗b6 ♗xb6 33 ♕xb8+ ♔e7 34 ♕xb6 ♔d6 35 c7+ ♔d7 36 ♕b8 ♘e7 37 ♕d8+ **1-0** L/N3203

**1859-★BM-3** 28 v 59
**Morphy, P.C.+Broughton, W.R.**
Boston [Maróczy]

⟨♘b1⟩ 1 e4 e5 2 f4 d5 3 exd5 e4 4 ♗c4 ♗d6 5 d4 ♘f6 6 ♘e2 ♗g4 7 h3 ♗xe2 8 ♕xe2 c6 9 dxc6 ♘xc6 10 c3 0-0 11 ♗e3 ♘a5 12 ♗b5 a6 13 ♗a4 ♕c7 14 g3 ♕c4 15 ♕d1 ♘d5 16 ♔f2 ♘xe3 17 ♔xe3 b5 18 ♗c2 ♖ad8 19 ♗b3 ♕c7 20 ♖c1 ♘c6 21 ♕f1 ♘e7 22 ♕g2 ♘f5+ 23 ♔e2

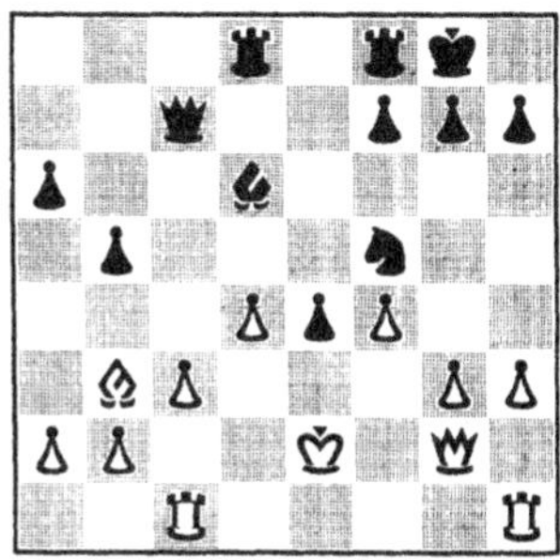

23 ... ♘xg3+! 24 ♕xg3 ♗xf4 25 ♕g2 ♗xc1 26 ♖xc1 ♔h8 [26 ... ♖xd4 27 ♖g1!] 27 h4 f5 28 ♖h1 f4 29 ♕h2 f3+ [⌂ 29 ... ♕d6] 30 ♔e3 ♕xh2 31 ♖xh2 ♖f6 32 c4 bxc4 33 ♗xc4 ♖h6 34 ♖c2 ♖xh4 35 ♗f7 f2? [⌂ 35 ... g5→] 36 ♖xf2 ♖h3+ [36 ... ♖f8 37 ♖c2 g5] 37 ♔e2 ♖c8 38 ♗c4 ♖f3 39 b3 ♖xf2+ 40 ♔xf2 g5 41 ♔e3 ♖e8 42 ♗e2 ♔g7 [⌂ 42 ... a5] 43 b4 ♔f6 44 a4 ♔f5 45 ♗xa6 g4 46 a5 g3 47 ♗f1 ♔g4 48 a6 ♖f8 49 ♗g2 ♖f2 50 ♗xe4 ♖a2 51 b5 h5 52 ♗b7 h4 53 ♗c8+ ♔g5 54 ♗h3 g2 55 ♗xg2 ♖xg2 56 a7 ♖a2 57 b6 **1-0**

L/N3203

### 1859-★BM-4
### Morphy, P.C.+ Bryan, T.J.

New York [Maróczy]

⟨♘b1⟩ 1 e4 e5 2 ♘f3 ♘c6 3 ♗c4 ♗c5 4 b4 ♗xb4 5 c3 ♗c5 6 0-0 d6 7 d4 ♗b6! 8 dxe5 dxe5 9 ♕b3 [9 ♕xd8+ ♘xd8 10 ♘xe5 ♗e6∓] 9 ... ♕f6? [9 ... ♕e7] 10 ♗b5 ♗e6 [10 ... ♗d7 11 ♗g5 ♕g6 12 ♗xc6 (12 ♖ad1 f6) 12 ... bxc6 13 ♘xe5 ♕e6 14 ♕xe6 ♗xe6 15 ♘xc6 f6∓] 11 ♕a4 ♘e7 12 ♗g5 ♕g6 13 ♗xe7 ♔xe7 14 ♗xc6 bxc6 15 ♘xe5 ♕f6 16 ♘xc6+ ♔f8 17 e5 ♕g5 18 h4 ♕g4 19 ♕a3+ ♔g8 20 ♘e7+ ♔f8 21 ♘g6+ ♔g8 22 ♕f8+ ♖xf8 23 ♘e7# **1-0** L/N3203

### 1859-★BM-5⌂ 20 iv 59
### Morphy, P.C.− Barnes, T.W.

London [Löwenthal]

1 e4 e5 2 ♘f3 ♘f6 3 ♗c4 ♘xe4 4 ♘c3 ♘xc3 5 dxc3 f6 6 0-0 ♕e7 7 ♘h4 d6 8 ♕h5+ ♔d8 9 f4 ♗e6 10 ♗xe6 ♕xe6 11 fxe5 dxe5 12 ♘g6 ♗c5+ [12 ... ♕f7 13 ♕d1++−] 13 ♔h1 ♖e8 14 ♕xh7 ♕g8 15 ♕h4 ♘d7 16 b4 ♗d6 17 ♗d2 [⌂ 17 ♗e3] 17 ... ♕f7 18 ♕g4 ♕e6 19 ♕e4 ♘b6! 20 ♕xb7? ♕g4 21 a4 ♖c8 22 ♖ad1 ♕xg6 23 ♗e3 ♘c4 24 ♕c6 ♕f7 [24 ... ♘xe3 25 ♖xd6+] 25 ♗xa7 e4 26 ♖d4 ♕h5! 27 ♖f4 e3 28 g4 e2! 29 gxh5 e1♕+ 30 ♔g2 ♖e2+ 31 ♔h3 f5 32 ♕xc4 ♕f1+!! 33 ♔h4 ♖xh2+ 34 ♔g5 ♕g2+ 35 ♖g4 fxg4 36 ♕f7 ♕c6 37 b5 ♕d7 38 ♖xd6 ♕xd6 **0-1** L/N3161

### 1859-★BM-6 ●○⌂ 20 iv 59
### Morphy, P.C.= Barnes, T.W.

London [Löwenthal]

1 e4 e5 2 ♘f3 ♘f6 3 ♘xe5 d6 4 ♘f3 ♘xe4 5 d4 d5 6 ♗d3 ♗d6 7 0-0 0-0 8 c4 ♘f6 [⌂ 8 ... c5 Jaenisch] 9 ♗g5 ♗e6 10 ♕b3 dxc4 11 ♗xc4 [11 ♕xb7? ♗d5 12 ♗xf6 (12 ♕xd5? ♗xh2+→) 12 ... gxf6 13 ♕b5 cxd3→] 11 ... ♗xc4 12 ♕xc4 ♘c6 13 ♘c3 h6 14 ♗h4 g5 15 ♗g3 ♕d7 16 ♘e5 ♕e6 17 ♕xe6 fxe6 18 ♘xc6 bxc6 19 ♖fe1± ♖fe8 20 ♖ac1 ♖ab8 21 b3 ♖e7 22 ♘a4 ♖b4 23 ♗e5 ♗xe5 24 dxe5 ♘d5 25 ♖xc6 ♖d4 26 ♖c2 ♘b4 27 ♖ce2 ♘d3= 28 ♖d2 ♖xa4 29 ♖xd3 ♖xa2 30 ♖c1 ♖f7 31 f3 **½-½** L/N3161

### 1859-★BM-7⌂ 20 iv 59
### Morphy, P.C.+ Bird, H.E.

London [Löwenthal]

1 e4 e5 2 f4 exf4 3 ♘f3 ♗e7 4 ♗c4 ♗h4+ 5 g3 fxg3 6 0-0 gxh2+ 7 ♔h1 d5 8 ♗xd5 ♘f6 9 ♗xf7+ [9 ♘xh4 ♘xd5] 9 ... ♔xf7 10 ♘xh4 ♖e8 [⌂ 10 ... ♔f8] 11 d3 ♗h3 12 ♕h5+! ♔g8 13 ♖xf6 gxf6 14 ♘c3 ♖e5 15 ♕f3 ♕d7 16 ♗f4 ♘c6 17 ♔xh2 ♗g4 18 ♖g1 h5 19 ♗xe5 fxe5 20 ♘d5 ♘d4 21 ♘f6+ ♔h8 22 ♕e3 ♕g7 23 ♘xh5 ♕h7 24 ♖xg4 ♕xh5 25 ♕h3! ♔h7 26 c3 ♘e6 27 ♖g6 [27 ♘g6+−] 27 ... ♖e8 28 ♖xe6 ♖xe6 29 ♕xe6 ♕xh4+ 30 ♕h3 ♕xh3+ 31 ♔xh3 c5 32 ♔g4 ♔g6 33 ♔f3 ♔f6 34 ♔e3 ♔e6 35 d4 exd4+ 36 cxd4 cxd4+ 37 ♔xd4 ♔d6 38 e5+ ♔e6 39 ♔e4 ♔e7 40 ♔d5 ♔d7 41 e6+ ♔e7 42 ♔e5 a6 43 a3 ♔e8 44 ♔d6 **1-0** L/N3161

### 1859-★BM-8⌂ 26 iv 59
### Morphy, P.C.= Boden, S.S.

London [Löwenthal & Boden]

1 e4 e5 2 ♘f3 ♘c6 3 d4 exd4 4 ♗c4 ♗c5 5 0-0 d6 6 c3 ♘f6 7 cxd4 ♗b6 8 ♘c3 ♗g4 9 ♗e3 0-0 10 ♕d3 ♕d7 11 ♘d2 ♘e7 12 ♗b3 d5 13 e5 ♘e8 14 h3 ♗h5 15 f4 f5 [15 ... ♕f5 16 ♕xf5 ♘xf5 17 ♘xd5 ♘xe3 18 ♘xe3 ♗xd4 19 ♖ae1 ♖ad8 20 ♖f2±] 16 ♔h2 c6 17 ♖g1 ♔h8 18 ♗c2 ♗g6 19 ♘f3 ♘c7 20 b4 ♘e6 21 ♘d2 ♘g8 22 ♘b3 ♘h6 23 ♘a4 ♕e7 24 ♘ac5 ♘xc5 25 bxc5 ♘g4+ 26 ♔h1 [26 ♔g3 ♗d8] 26 ... ♕h4 27 ♖gf1 ♘xe3 28 ♕xe3 ♗c7 29 ♘d2 ♕e7 30 ♘f3 ♖ae8 31 ♖ab1 b6 32 ♗a4 b5 33 ♗c2 a5 34 ♖g1 ♗d8 35 g4 ♕e6 36 g5 ♔g8 37 h4 h5? [⌂ 37 ... ♗h5] 38 gxh6 ♖f7 39 ♖g2 ♗h5 40 ♖bg1? ♕xh6 41 ♘g5 ♗xg5 42 hxg5 ♕h8 43 ♖h2 g6 44 ♖g3 ♖h7 45 ♖gh3 ♖ee7 46 ♔g1 ♗g4 47 ♖h6 ♖xh6 48 ♖xh6 ♖h7? [⌂ 48 ... ♕g7] 49 ♖xg6+? [⌂ 49 e6 ♔f8 (49 ... ♖xh6 50 gxh6 ♔f8 51 ♕e5+−) 50 ♖xh7 ♕xh7 51 ♕e5 ♕h3 52 ♕f6+ ♔g8 53 ♕xg6+ ♔h8 54 ♕h6++−] 49 ... ♔f7 50 ♖h6 [50 ♖f6+, 51 ♕g3 ♖h1+, 51 ... ♖c1→] 50 ... ♖xh6 51 gxh6 ♕xh6 **½-½**

L/N3161

### 1859-★BM-9
### Budzinski, J.− Morphy, P.

Paris

1 e4 e5 2 f4 exf4 3 ♗c4 d5 4 ♗xd5 ♘f6 5 ♘c3 ♗b4 6 d3 ♘xd5 7 exd5 0-0 8 ♕f3 ♖e8+ 9 ♘ge2 ♗xc3+ 10 bxc3 ♕h4+ 11 g3 ♗g4 **0-1**

L/N3161

### 1859-★BM-10 ●○⌂ ii 1859
### Morphy, P.C.+ Bousserolles, A.

Paris

1 e4 e5 2 ♘f3 ♘c6 3 ♗c4 h6 4 d4 exd4 5 c3 ♘ge7 6 ♕b3 d5 7 exd5 ♘b8 8 d6 ♕xd6 9 ♗xf7+ ♔d8 10 cxd4 ♘bc6 11 ♘c3 ♘a5 12 ♕a4 ♘ac6 13 0-0 ♗d7 14 ♗e3 ♕f6 15 ♗c4 ♔c8 16 ♖fe1 ♘d8 17 ♕b3 a6 18 ♘e5 b5 19 ♗d5 c6 20 ♘e4 ♕h4 21 g3 ♕h5 22 ♘d6+ ♔c7 23 ♗f3 ♕h3 24 ♖ac1 ♔xd6 25 ♗f4 ♗e6 26 ♘d3+ ♔d7 27 ♖xe6 ♘xe6 28 ♗g4 ♕xg4 29 ♘e5+ ♔e8 30 ♘xg4 ♘xd4 31 ♕e3 **1-0** M268

### 1859-★BR-1
### Rivière, J.A. de+ Baucher, H.

Paris [Staunton]

1 e4 e5 2 f4 exf4 3 ♘f3 g5 4 h4 g4 5 ♘e5 ♘f6 6 ♗c4 d5 7 exd5 ♗d6 8 d4 ♕e7 [⌂ 8 ... ♘h5] 9 0-0 [9 ♗xf4? ♘h5 10 0-0 ♘xf4 11 ♖xf4 f6] 9 ... ♘h5 10 ♖e1 [10 ♗b5+!] 10 ... 0-0 11 ♘xg4 [11 ♘g6+!?] 11 ... ♕xh4 12 ♘h2 f3 13 ♘xf3 ♕g3 14 ♘c3 ♗g4 15 ♗e3 ♗xf3 16 ♕xf3 ♕h2+ 17 ♔f1 ♘g3+ 18 ♔f2 ♕h4 19 ♘e2 ♘e4+ 20 ♔f1 ♕h1+ 21 ♘g1 f5 22 ♗f4 ♗xf4 23 ♕xf4 ♘d6 24 ♖e3 ♕h5 25 ♗e2 [⌂ 25 ♖g3+ ♔f7 26 ♗e2 ♕h2 (26 ... ♕h1 27 ♖h3+−) 27 ♖g7++−] 25 ... ♕f7 26 c4 ♘d7 27 ♘f3 ♘e4 28 ♘e5 ♕g7 29 ♖d1 ♖ae8 30 ♘xd7 ♕xd7 31 ♖h3 ♖e7 32 b3 ♖g7 33 ♖h4 ♘g3+ 34 ♔f2 ♘xe2 35 ♔xe2 ♖xg2+ 36 ♔d3 ♕e7 37 ♖dh1 ♕e2+ 38 ♔c3 ♕c2+ 39 ♔b4 a5+ 40 ♔b5 ♕xa2 41 ♖4h3 ♖g7 42 ♕e5 ♕a3 43 ♕e6+ ♔h8?? [43 ... ♖ff7] 44 ♖xh7+ ♖xh7 45 ♕e5+ ♔g8 46 ♖g1+ **1-0** M954-1859

### 1859-★BR-2
### Rivière, J.A. de− Baucher, H.

Paris [Staunton]

1 e4 e5 2 ♘f3 ♘f6 3 d4 ♘xe4 4 dxe5 d5 5 ♗d3 ♗g4 6 c3 [⌂ 6 ♗xe4] 6 ... ♘c6 7 ♗f4 ♗c5 8 0-0 0-0 9

♕e2 ♗xf3 10 gxf3 ♘g5 11 ♔h1 ♘e6 12 ♗g3 ♕g5 13 b4 ♗b6 14 ♘a3 ♘e7 15 ♖g1 ♕h6 16 ♘c2 ♘g6 17 ♘e3 ♘gf4 18 ♗xf4 ♘xf4 19 ♘f5 ♕h3 20 ♖xg7+? [20 ♕d1 ♗xf2 21 ♖g4 ♘g6 22 ♕e2 ♗b6 23 e6 fxe6 24 ♕xe6+ ♔h8 25 ♖g3 ♕h5 26 ♕d7 ♖g8 27 ♘d6+-] 20 ... ♔h8 21 ♕d1 ♗xf2 22 ♖g4 ♖g8 23 ♗f1 ♕h5 24 ♕d2 ♖xg4 25 fxg4 ♕xg4 26 ♕xf2 ♕xf5 27 ♖e1 ♖g8 28 e6 fxe6 29 ♕d4+ ♖g7 30 ♖e5 ♕g4 **0-1** M954-1859

### 1859-★BS-1
**Barnes,T.W.& Owen,J.– Staunton, H.**
London [Staunton]

1 e4 e5 2 ♘f3 ♘f6 3 ♘xe5 d6 4 ♘f3 ♘xe4 5 d4 d5 6 ♗d3 ♗e7 7 0-0 ♘c6 [7 ... ♘f6=] 8 c4 ♘f6 9 ♕e2 ♗g4 10 ♗e3 0-0 11 ♘c3 ♕d7 12 c5 ♖ad8 13 a3 a6 14 b4 ♖de8 15 ♕c2 ♗xf3 16 ♗f5??+ ♗e4 17 ♗xd7 ♗xc2 18 ♗xe8 ♖xe8 19 ♖ac1 ♗b3 20 h3 ♗d8 21 ♖fe1 ♔f8 22 f3 ♖e6 23 b5 axb5 24 ♘xb5 ♗c4 25 ♘c3 ♘a5 26 ♗f4 ♘d7 27 ♖xe6 fxe6 28 ♖b1 ♗a6 29 ♘b5 e5 30 dxe5 ♘xc5 31 ♔h2 ♔f7 32 ♗e3 ♘d3 33 f4 ♘c4 34 ♗c1 c6 35 ♘d4 g6 36 g4 ♗b6 37 ♘f3 h6 38 f5 ♘xc1 39 ♖xc1 gxf5 40 ♖e1 ♘e3 41 ♔g3 f4+ 42 ♔h2 d4 43 g5 hxg5 44 ♘xg5+ ♔e7 45 h4 d3 46 ♘f3 ♘f5 47 ♔h3 ♗e3 48 ♔g4 ♘h6+ 49 ♔g5 ♘f7+ 50 ♔f5 d2 51 ♖h1 ♗d3+ 52 ♔g4 ♗e2 **0-1** M954-1859

### 1859-★CK-1
**Kolisch,I.F.von+ Centurini & St.Bon**
Genoa

1 e4 e5 2 ♘f3 ♘c6 3 ♗c4 ♗c5 4 b4 ♗xb4 5 c3 ♗a5 6 d4 exd4 7 0-0 ♘f6 8 e5 d5 9 ♗b5 ♘e4 10 ♘xd4 ♗d7 11 ♘b3 ♘xc3 12 ♘xc3 ♗xc3 13 ♗a3 a6 14 ♗xc6 ♗xc6 15 ♖ac1 d4 16 ♕g4 ♕d7 17 ♕h4 f6 18 ♖fd1 ♗d5 19 e6 ♕xe6 20 ♘xd4 ♗xd4 21 ♕xd4 0-0-0 22 ♕a7 c6 23 ♖b1 b5 24 ♕xa6+ ♔b8 25 ♕b6+ ♔a8 26 ♗c5 ♖d7 27 ♖d3 ♖b7 28 ♕a6+ ♔b8 29 ♖e3 ♗e4 30 ♖be1 ♕d5 31 ♗b6 ♗f5 32 ♖a3 ♔c8 33 ♖c1 ♗d7 34 ♖d3 ♕e6 35 ♖xd7 ♕xd7 36 ♕a8+ ♖b8 37 ♖xc6+ **1-0** M954-1859

### 1859-★CM-1
**Morphy, P.C.– Cheney, G.N.**
New York [Maróczy]

⟨♘b1⟩ 1 e4 e5 2 ♘f3 ♘c6 3 ♗c4 ♗c5 4 b4 d5 5 exd5 ♘xb4 6 0-0 ♘f6 7 d4 exd4 8 ♖e1+ ♗e7 9 d6 cxd6 10 ♗a3 ♘c6 11 ♘xd4 0-0 12 ♘xc6 bxc6 13 ♕e2 ♕a5 14 ♗b2 ♖b8 15 ♖ab1 ♗d8 [15 ... ♗d7] 16 ♗c3 ♕xc3 17 ♖xb8 ♗a5 18 ♖eb1 ♗b6 19 a4 ♖e8 20 ♕d3 ♕xd3 21 ♗xd3 ♗d7 22 ♖xe8+ ♗xe8 23 ♖a1 g6 24 a5 ♗c5 25 h3 ♘d5 26 ♖b1 ♘b4 27 ♗e4 f5 28 c3 fxe4 29 cxb4 ♗d4 30 ♖d1 ♗e5 31 ♖e1 d5 32 f3 ♗d4+ 33 ♔f1 e3 34 ♖c1 a6 35 ♔e2 ♔f7 36 f4 ♔e6 37 ♔d3 ♗a7 38 g4 d4 39 ♔e4 ♔d6 40 f5 gxf5+ 41 gxf5 c5 42 bxc5+ ♗xc5 43 f6 ♗g6+ 44 ♔f4 d3 45 ♖xc5 ♔xc5 46 ♔xe3 ♔c4 **0-1** L/N3203

### 1859-★CM-2
**Morphy,P.C.+ Conway,M.D.**
New York [Maróczy]

⟨♖a1⟩ 1 e4 e5 2 f4 exf4 3 ♘f3 g5 4 ♗c4 g4 5 d4 gxf3 6 ♕xf3 ♗h6 [□ 6 d5; 6 ... d6 △ 7 ... ♗e6] 7 0-0 ♘e7 8 ♗xf4 [8 ♕h5± Morphy L/N6389] 8 ... ♗xf4 9 ♗xf7+ ♔xf7 10 ♕xf4+ ♔g7 [10 ... ♔g6 11 ♕f6+ ♔h5 12 g4+ ♔xg4 13 ♖f4+ ♔h3 14 ♕h4#] 11 ♕f6+ ♔g8 12 ♕f7# **1-0** L/N3203

### 1859-★CM-3 ●○⌂ 20 iv 59
**Morphy, P.C.+ Cattley, H.G.**
London [Löwenthal]

1 e4 e5 2 ♘f3 ♘c6 3 ♗b5 a6 4 ♗a4 ♘f6 5 0-0 ♗e7 [5 ... b5 6 ♗b3 d5 7 exd5 ♘xd5 8 ♖e1 ♗g4 9 h3 ♗xf3 10 ♕xf3±] 6 ♘c3 d6 7 d4 b5 8 ♗b3 ♗g4 9 d5 ♘d4 10 ♗e3 ♘xb3 [□ 10 ... ♘xf3+] 11 axb3 0-0 12 h3 ♗h5 13 b4 ♕d7 14 ♔h2 c6 15 dxc6 ♕xc6 16 ♗g5 ♖fe8 17 ♗xf6 ♗xf6 18 g4 ♗g6 19 ♕d3 ♗e7 20 ♖fd1 ♖ec8 21 ♖a3 ♕c4 22 ♖da1 d5 23 ♘xd5 ♗xb4 24 ♕xc4 ♖xc4 25 ♖xa6 ♖xa6 26 ♖xa6 h6 27 c3 ♗c5 28 ♘xe5 ♖xe4 29 ♘d7 ♖a4?? 30 ♘xc5 ♖xa6 31 ♘xa6 **1-0** L/N3161

### 1859-★CM-4 ●○⌂ 20 iv 59
**Morphy, P.C.+ Cremorne, R.**
London [Löwenthal]

1 e4 e5 2 f4 ♗c5 3 ♘f3 ♘c6 4 b4 ♗xb4 5 c3 ♗a5 6 ♗c4 ♗b6 7 d4 exd4 8 cxd4 d6 9 ♗b2 f6 10 f5! ♕e7 [10 ... g6 11 g4] 11 0-0 ♗d7 12 ♘c3 0-0-0 13 ♖e1 ♕e8 14 ♘d5 g6 15 ♘xb6+ axb6 16 ♕a4 ♘a5 [□ 16 ... ♘b8] 17 ♕a3 c6 18 ♗d3 ♕f8 [18 ... ♔c7? 19 e5] 19 ♗c3 ♔c7 20 ♗xa5 ♖a8 21 ♗xb6+ ♔xb6 22 ♖ab1+ ♔c7 23 ♕b3 ♖b8 24 ♕b6+ ♔c8 25 ♗a6! ♘e7 26 e5 [26 ♕a7 ♔c7 (26 ... d5 27 ♗xb7+ ♔c7 28 ♗c8++-) 27 ♗xb7+-] 26 ... dxe5 27 ♗xb7+ ♖xb7 28 ♕xb7+ ♔d8 29 dxe5 **1-0** L/N3161

### 1859-★CM-5 ●○⌂ 20 iv 59
**Morphy, P.C.+ Cunningham**
London [Löwenthal]

1 e4 e5 2 ♗c4 ♗c5 3 c3 ♘c6 4 ♘f3 ♘f6 5 d4 exd4 6 e5 ♕e7? [□ 6 ... d5] 7 0-0 ♘g8 8 cxd4 ♗b6 9 d5 ♕c5 10 ♘a3 ♘d4 11 ♗e3 ♘xf3+ 12 ♕xf3 ♕f8 13 ♗xb6 axb6 14 ♘b5 ♔d8 15 ♖ac1 d6 16 exd6 cxd6 17 ♕e3 ♖a6 18 ♘c7 ♕e7 19 ♘e6+! fxe6 20 ♗xa6 ♗d7 21 ♗b5 ♕e8 22 dxe6 ♘f6 23 ♖c8+ **1-0** L/N3161

### 1859-★DD-1
**Deacon, F.H.+ Discart**
Sienna [Staunton]

1 e4 e5 2 ♘f3 ♘c6 3 ♗c4 ♗c5 4 b4 ♗xb4 5 c3 ♗a5 6 0-0 ♘f6 7 ♘g5 0-0 8 ♕b3 ♕e7 9 f4 h6 10 ♘xf7 ♖xf7 11 ♗xf7+ ♕xf7 12 ♕xf7+ ♔xf7 13 fxe5 ♘xe5 14 d4 ♗b6 15 a4 [15 ♔h1 ♘d3 16 ♗a3 ♔g6 17 ♘d2 ♗a5] 15 ... a5 16 ♔h1 ♘d3 17 ♗a3 ♔g6 18 ♘d2 c5 19 ♖f3 ♘g4 20 ♖af1 ♘b4 21 ♘c4 ♗c7 22 e5 cxd4 23 cxd4 h5 24 h3 ♘h6 25 ♗c1 [△ 26 ♖f8, 27 ♗xh6, 28 ♖h8+, 29 ♖ff8] 25 ... b6 26 ♖g3+ ♔h7 27 ♗xh6 ♗a6 [27 ... ♔xh6 28 ♘e3; 28 ♖f8] 28 ♗xg7 ♗xc4 29 ♖f6 ♖b8 30 ♖g5 [△ e6] 30 ... ♗a6 31 e6 ♗xe6 32 ♖h6+ ♔g8 33 ♗e5+ ♔f8 34 ♖h8+ ♗g8 35 ♖g7 [△ 36 ♖hxg8#] **1-0** M954-1859

### 1859-★DM-1
**Morphy,P.C.– Rivière,J.A.de**
[Maróczy]

1 e4 e5 2 ♘f3 ♘c6 3 ♗c4 ♗c5 4 b4 ♗xb4 5 c3 ♗c5 6 0-0 d6 d4 exd4 8 cxd4 ♗b6 9 d5 ♘ce7 10 e5 ♘g6 11 e6 fxe6 12 dxe6 ♘8e7 13 ♘g5 0-0 14 ♕h5 h6 15 ♘f7 ♖xf7? [□ 15 ... ♕e8] 16 exf7+ ♔h7 17 ♗d3? [□ 17 ♗g5 ♕f8 18 ♘d2 ♗f5 19 ♖ae1 ♗c2 20 ♘f3 d5 21 ♗xe7 ♘xe7 22 ♗xd5 ♘xd5 (22 ... ♗g6 23 ♗e4±) 23 ♕xd5 ♖d8? 24 ♕xd8+-] 17 ... ♗e6 18 ♗g5 ♗xf7 19 ♖e1 ♔g8 20 ♗xe7 ♘xe7 21 ♕g4 ♕f8 22 ♘c3? ♗xf2+ 23 ♔h1 [23 ♕xf2 ♗h5+-+] 23 ... ♗xe1 24 ♖xe1 d5 25 ♖f1 ♖d8 26 ♘b5 c5 27 ♕g3 c4 28 ♗c2 ♘c6 29 ♗g6 ♖d7 30 ♗f5 ♖e7 31 ♘d6 ♕b8 32 ♗c8 [△ 33 ♗xf7 ♖xf7 34 ♗e6] 32 ... ♘d8 33 ♗f5 b5 34 ♗g6 ♗xg6 35 ♘f5 ♕xg3 36 ♘xe7+ ♔h7 37 hxg3 d4 38 ♘xg6 ♔xg6 39 a3 a5 40 ♔g1 ♘c6 41 ♖f8 c3 42 ♖c8 ♘e5 43 ♔f2 ♘c4 44 ♔e2 c2 **0-1** L/N3203

### 1859-★DM-2
**Devinck, A.= Morphy, P.C.**
Paris [Maróczy]

⟨♙f7⟩ 1 e4 e6 2 d4 d5 3 exd5 [3 ♕h5+ g6 4 ♕e5 ♘f6 5 ♗g5 ♗g7 6 exd5 0-0∓] 3 ... exd5 4 c4 ♘f6 5 ♘c3 ♗b4 6

♗d3 ♘c6 7 a3 ♗xc3+ 8 bxc3 0-0 9 ♘e2 ♗e6 10 cxd5 ♗xd5 11 0-0 ♘a5 12 h3 a6 13 ♘g3 g6 14 ♗g5 ♕d7 15 ♕c2 b5 16 ♖ab1 ♘c4 17 ♗xc4 ♗xc4 18 ♖fe1 ♖ae8 19 ♖e5 ♖xe5 20 dxe5 ♘d5 21 ♖e1 ♕e6 22 ♕d2 ♖e8 23 ♕d4 ♔h8 24 ♘e4 ♔g8 [24 ... ♕xe5 25 ♘c5!] 25 ♘f6+ [◻ 25 ♘c5] 25 ... ♘xf6 26 ♗xf6 ♗d5 27 ♕h4 a5 28 ♕h6 ♕f7 29 ♖e3 c5 30 ♖g3 ♗e4 31 h4 ♖b8 32 h5 b4 33 cxb4 cxb4 34 axb4 axb4 35 hxg6 ♗xg6 36 ♕d2 b3 37 ♕b2 ♕c4 38 ♖c3 ♕xc3 39 ♕xc3 b2 40 ♕c4+ ♗f7 41 ♕g4+ ♗g6 42 ♕e6+ ♗f7 ½-½ L/N3203

**71** Delannoy, A. L/N6396.BL

**1859-★DM-3**
**Morphy, P.C.+ Delannoy, A.**
Paris [Morphy]

⟨♘b1⟩ 1 e4 e6 2 f4 d5 3 e5 c5 4 ♘f3 ♘c6 5 c3 ♕b6 [◻ 5 ... f6] 6 ♗d3 d4 7 ♕e2 ♘h6 8 b3 ♗e7 9 ♗b2 ♗d7 10 g4 0-0 [10 ... ♘xg4 11 ♖g1±] 11 h3 ♕d8 12 0-0-0 ♔h8 13 ♗c2 ♘b8 14 cxd4 ♗c6 15 f5 exf5 16 gxf5 cxd4 17 f6 d3 18 fxg7+ ♔xg7 19 ♖hg1+ ♔h8 20 ♗xd3 ♗xf3 21 ♕xf3 ♕c8+ 22 ♔b1 ♕e6 23 ♕e4 ♘f5 [23 ... ♕g6 24 ♖xg6+−] 24 ♗c4! [24 ♕xf5±] 24 ... ♕c8 25 ♗xf7 ♖xf7 [25 ... ♕d8 26 e6+ ♗f6 27 e7 ♕xe7 28 ♕xe7+−] 26 e6+ ♖f6 27 ♕xf5 ♕f8 28 ♖df1 ♘c6 29 ♕xf6+ ♗xf6 30 ♖xf6 ♕g7 **1-0** L/N6389

**1859-★EM-1** 31 iii 59
**Ehrmann, A.= Morphy, P.C.**
Paris [Maróczy]

⟨♙f7⟩ 1 e4 ... 2 d4 e6 3 ♗d3 c5 [3 ... d5 4 e5 g6 5 h4] 4 dxc5 ♕a5+ 5 c3 ♕xc5 6 ♘e2 ♘c6 7 ♗e3 ♕h5 8 f4 ♘f6 9 ♘g3 ♕h4 10 ♕e2 ♘g4 11 ♗f2 ♘xf2 12 ♕xf2 ♗d6 13 e5 ♗c7 14 ♘e4 ♕e7 15 ♘bd2 0-0 16 ♕g3 d5 17 ♘g5 h6 18 ♘gf3 [18 ♘h3] 18 ... ♕f7 19 0-0 ♗d7 [19 ... ♕xf4 20 ♕g6±] 20 ♘h4 ♘e7 21 ♗c2 ♘f5 22 ♘xf5 exf5 23 ♖ae1 b5 24 ♔h1 ♗b6 25 ♕d3 a6 26 ♗b3 ♗e6 27 ♘f3 ♖fb8 28 ♘h4 ♗d8 29 ♘f3 ♗b6 30 ♗c2 [◻ 30 ♖d1] 30 ... g6 31 ♖e2 [31 g4 fxg4 32 ♘h4] 31 ... d4 32 b3 dxc3 33 ♘h4 b4 34 g4 ♖d8 35 ♕g3 ♔h7 36 gxf5 gxf5 37 ♕h3 ♖f8 38 ♖g2 ♖ad8 39 ♘f3 ♖g8 40 ♘g5+ ♖xg5 41 fxg5 ♕f8 42 gxh6 ♖d2 43 ♖xd2 cxd2 44 ♕g2 ♕xh6 45 ♕b7+ ♕g7 46 ♕xg7+ ♔xg7 47 ♔g2 ♗d4 48 ♖d1 ♗d5+ 49 ♔h3 ♗e3 50 ♗xf5 ♗f3 51 ♗g4 ♗xd1 52 ♗xd1 ♗f4 53 e6 ♔f6 54 ♗g4 d1♕ 55 ♗xd1 ♔xe6 56 ♔g2 ♔e5 ½-½ L/N3202

**1859-★GK-1**
**Kolisch, I.F. von+ Gastein**
Wien

1 e4 e5 2 ♘f3 ♘c6 3 ♗c4 ♗c5 4 b4 ♗xb4 5 c3 ♗a5 6 d4 exd4 7 0-0 ♘f6 8 e5 d5 9 ♗b5 ♘e4 10 ♗a3 ♗xc3 11 ♘xd4 ♗xa1 12 ♘xc6 bxc6 13 ♗xc6+ ♗d7 14 ♕xd5 ♘g5 15 f4 ♘e6 16 f5 ♘g5 17 e6 fxe6 18 fxe6 ♘xe6 19 ♕xe6+ **1-0** M954-1859

**1859-★GM-1 ●0⬠** 13 iv 59
**Morphy, P.C.=Greenaway, F.E.**
London [Löwenthal]

1 e4 e5 2 ♘f3 ♘c6 3 ♗c4 ♗c5 4 b4 ♗xb4 5 c3 ♗a5 6 d4 exd4 7 0-0 ♘f6 8 ♗a3 [8 ♗a3! Morphy] 8 ... d6 9 e5 d5 [0 ... dxe5 10 ♕b3 ♕d7 11 ♖e1±; 9 ... ♘e4 10 exd6 ♘xd6 (10 ... cxd6 11 ♖e1 d5 12 ♘xd4±) 11 ♖e1+ ♔f8 (11 ... ♘e7 12 ♕a4+ c6 13 ♗xd6 ♕xd6 14 ♕xa5+−) 12 ♘xd4± Chess Monthly] 10 ♗b5 ♘e4 11 cxd4 ♗d7 12 ♕b3 a6 [12 ... ♘e7 13 ♗xd7+ ♕xd7 14 ♗xe7+−] 13 ♗d3 [13 ♕xd5 axb5 14 ♕xe4 b4 15 ♗b2 ♗e6∞] 13 ... ♗c8 14 ♖c1 ♗b6 15 ♖xc6

15 ... bxc6 16 ♕c2 ♗b7 17 ♘bd2 ♘xd2 18 ♕xd2 h6 19 ♖e1 ♗c8 20 ♕c3 ♖b8 21 ♕xc6+ [◻ 21 e6 ♗xe6 22 ♖xe6+ fxe6 23 ♘e5 △ 24 ♗g6+ ( 23 ... c5 24 ♗g6+ ♔f8 25 ♕f3++−; 23 ... c5 24 ♗g6+ ♔e7 25 ♘xc6++−)] 21 ... ♕d7 22 ♕c2 ♕e6 23 ♘h4 g6 24 ♕c3 ♔d8 25 ♖c1 ♖e8 26 ♘f3 ♗b7 27 h3 ♖c8 28 ♕d2 ♖h8 ½-½ L/N3161

**1859-★HK-1**
**Kolisch, I.F. von+ Hamppe, C.**
Wien

1 e4 e5 2 ♘f3 ♘c6 3 d4 exd4 4 ♗c4 d6 5 0-0 ♗e7 6 ♘xd4 ♗f6 7 c3 ♘ge7 8 f4 0-0 9 ♗e3 d5 10 e5 dxc4 11 exf6 gxf6 12 f5 ♘xf5 13 ♕g4+ ♘g7 14 ♕g3 ♕d6 15 ♗f4 ♘xd4 16 cxd4 ♕xd4+ 17 ♔h1 ♗f5 18 ♘c3 ♗d3 19 ♗h6 f5 20 ♖f4 ♕f6 21 ♗g5 ♕g6 22 ♘d5 ♖ae8 23 ♘f6+ ♔h8 24 ♖h4 h5 25 ♘xh5 ♘xh5 26 ♗f6+ ♔g8 27 ♖xh5

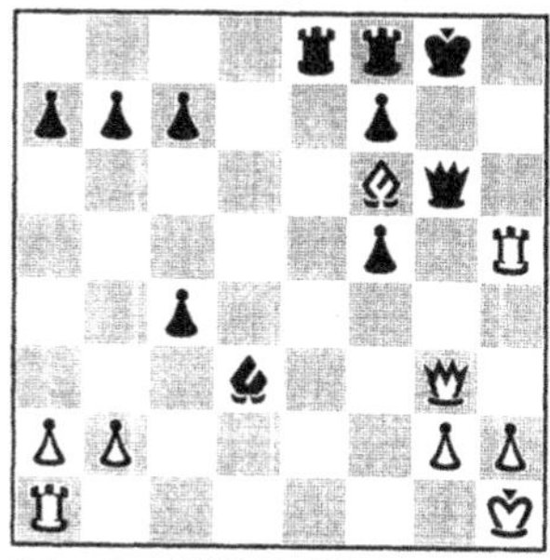

27 ... ♕xg3 28 ♖h8# **1-0** M954-1859

**1859-★HK-2**
**Harrwitz, D.– Kolisch, I.F. von**

1 d4 f5 2 c4 ♘f6 3 ♘c3 e6 4 ♘f3 ♗e7 5 e3 d5 6 ♘e5 0-0 7 ♗e2 c6 8 0-0 ♘e4 9 f3 ♘f6 10 ♗d2 ♘bd7 11 cxd5 cxd5 12 ♖c1 ♗d6 13 ♘d3 ♘h5 14 ♕e1 f4 15 e4 ♘g3 16 ♗xf4 ♘xe2+ 17 ♘xe2 ♗xf4 18 ♘exf4 ♕b6 19 ♔h1 ♕xd4 20 ♕g3 ♘b6 21 ♖c7 ♖f7 22 ♖fc1 ♗d7 23 ♘c5 ♕xb2 24 ♘fd3 ♕d2 25 f4 ♖af8 26 h3 ♗c6 27 ♘b3 ♕xa2 28 ♖xf7 ♖xf7 29 ♘e5 ♖f8 30 ♘xc6 bxc6 31 ♖a1 ♕b2 32 ♖xa7 ♘c4 33 ♘c5 ♘d2 34 ♘d3 ♘xe4 35 ♕g4 ♕f6 36 ♔h2 c5 37 ♖a6 ♖e8 38 ♘e5 ♕f5 39 ♔g1 ♕xg4 40 hxg4 g5 41 fxg5 ♘xg5 42 ♔f2 ♖b8 43 ♔e3 ♖b4 44 ♖a8+ ♔g7 45 ♖a7+ ♔h6 46 ♘d7 ♖e4+ 47 ♔f2 c4 48 ♔g3 c3 49 ♘f6 c2 50 ♖a1 d4 51 ♘xe4 ♘xe4+ 52 ♔f3 d3 **0-1** L/N6126-1859

**1859-★HK-3**
**Healey, F. & ♀+ Kling, J.**
London [Staunton]

1 e4 e5 2 ♘f3 ♘c6 3 ♗b5 f5 4 d4 ♘xd4 5 ♘xd4 exd4 6 ♕xd4 ♕e7 7 e5 c6 8 ♗d3 d6 9 ♗f4? dxe5? [9 ... g5 △ 10 ... dxe5] 10 ♗xe5 ♗e6 11 0-0 ♘h6 12 ♘d2 ♔f7 13 ♖fe1 ♕d7 14

♕f4 ♗e7 15 ♗xg7 ♔xg7 16 ♕e5+ ♔f7 17 ♗c4 ♗xc4 18 ♘xc4 ♖ad8 19 ♖ad1 ♕xd1 20 ♕xe7+ ♔g8

21 ♕g5+ ♔f8 [21 ... ♔f7 22 ♘e5+ +−] 22 ♕xh6+ ♔g8 23 ♕g5+ ♔f8 24 ♕xf5+ ♔g7 25 ♕g5+ ♔f8 26 ♕f4+ ♔g7 27 ♕g3+ ♔f6 28 ♕c3+ ♕d4 29 ♕f3+ ♔g5 30 h4+ ♔h6 31 ♖e6+ ♔g7 32 ♖e7+ ♔h6 33 ♘e3 ♖df8 34 ♘g4+ ♔g6 35 ♘e5+ ♕xe5 36 ♕g4+ **1-0** M954-1859

**1859-★HM-1** 1 vi 59
**Morphy, P.C.+ Hammond, G. & 4 Allies**
Boston [Morphy]
1 e4 e5 2 ♘f3 ♘c6 3 ♗b5 a6 4 ♗a4 b5 [◻ 4 ... ♘f6] 5 ♗b3 ♗c5 6 c3 d6 7 d4 ♗b6 [7 ... exd4±] 8 dxe5 ♕e7 9 ♗d5 ♗b7 10 ♗g5 f6 11 exf6 ♘xf6 12 0-0 ♕d7 13 ♗xf6 gxf6 14 ♘d4 ♗xd4 15 ♕h5+ ♔d8 16 cxd4 ♔c8 17 ♖c1! ♘xd4 18 ♗xb7+ ♔xb7 19 ♕d5+ ♘c6 20 a4 ♔b6 [20 ... b4 (20 ... bxa4 21 ♖xa4 △ 22 ♖b4+; 21 ... a5 22 ♕b5+ +−; 21 ... ♔b6 22 ♖xc6+ ♕xc6 24 ♖b4+ +−) 21 ♘d2 ♖hg8 (21 ... ♔b6 22 ♖xc6+ ♕xc6 23 ♘c4+ ♔b7 24 ♘a5+ +−) 22 ♘b3 (△ 23 ♘a5+, 23 ♘c5+) 22 ... ♔b6 (22 ... ♖xg2+ 23 ♔xg2 ♕g4+ 24 ♔f1 ♕h3+ 25 ♔e1 +−) 23 ♖xc6+ ♕xc6 24 ♕d4+ +−] 21 a5+ ♔b7 [21 ... ♘xa5 22 ♖xa5 ♔xa5 23 ♖c6 △ 24 ♕a2+, 25 ♕a3#] 22 ♖a3 **1-0** L/N6389

**1859-★HM-2** 20 iv 59
**Morphy, P.C.= Hay, Lord A.**
London [Löwenthal]
1 e4 e5 2 f4 d5 3 exd5 e4 4 ♘c3 f5 5 ♗c4 ♘f6 6 ♘ge2 ♗d6 7 d4 0-0 8 ♗e3 ♔h8 9 0-0 c6 10 dxc6 ♘xc6 11 a3 a6 12 ♕d2 ♘e7 13 ♗a2 b5 14 ♘d1 ♘g6 15 b3 a5 16 c4 bxc4 17 bxc4 ♗xa3 18 d5 ♕d6 19 ♘d4 ♗c5 20 ♘b5 ♕b6 21 ♗xc5 ♕xc5+ 22 ♕d4 ♕xd4+ 23 ♘xd4 ♖d8 24 ♘e3 ♘e7 25 ♖fd1 ♖a6 26 ♖ab1! g6 27 c5 ♘fxd5 28 ♘xd5 ♘xd5 29 ♘b5! ♖c6 [◻ 29 ... ♘e6 30 ♘c7 ♘xc7] 30 ♖xd5 ♖xd5 31 ♗xd5 ♖xc5 32 ♗a2 **½-½** L/N3161

**1859-★JK-1**
**Kolisch, I.F. von+ Jeney, E.**
Wien
1 ... e5 2 e4 ♗c5 3 ♘f3 ♘c6 4 c3 ♘f6 5 d4 exd4 6 e5 ♘d5 7 ♗c4 ♘ce7 8 ♕b3 c6 9 cxd4 ♗b4+ 10 ♘c3 0-0 11 0-0 ♗xc3 12 bxc3 h6 13 ♗a3 ♘f4 14 ♖ae1 b5 15 ♗e2 ♖e8 16 ♘h4 ♗a6 17 ♗b4 ♘ed5 18 g3 ♗b7 19 ♘f5 ♕g5 20 ♘d6 ♖eb8 21 h4 ♕g6 22 ♔h2 ♘xe2 23 ♖xe2 a5 24 ♗c5 ♗a6 25 f4 ♕d3 26 ♖ff2 a4 27 ♕c2 ♕xc2 28 ♖xc2 ♘e3 29 a3 ♘xc2 30 ♖xc2 g6 31 ♖f2 ♔g7 32 f5 g5 33 f6+ ♔g6 34 h5+ ♔xh5 35 ♘xf7 b4 36 cxb4 ♗d3 37 e6 dxe6 38 g4+ ♔h4 39 ♘e5 ♗e4 40 d5 h5 41 ♖e2 hxg4 42 ♖xe4 exd5 43 ♖xg4+ ♔h5 44 ♖g3 g4 45 ♖xg4 ♖e8 46 ♗e7 ♖xe7 47 fxe7 ♖e8 48 ♖g7 ♔h6 49 ♖f7 **1-0** M954-1859

**1859-★JM-1** iii 59
**Morphy, P.C.+ Journoud, P.**
Paris [Maróczy]
1 e4 e5 2 ♘f3 ♘c6 3 ♗c4 ♗c5 4 b4 d5 5 exd5 ♘xb4 6 c3 ♘xd5 7 ♕b3 c6 8 0-0 e4 9 ♖e1 f5 [◻ 9 ... ♘gf6, 10 ... 0-0] 10 d3 ♘gf6 11 ♗g5 ♕d6 12 ♗xf6 ♘xf6 13 ♘bd2 b5 14 ♗f7+ ♔f8 15 dxe4 fxe4 16 ♘xe4 ♘xe4 17 ♖xe4 ♗f5 18 ♖d1 ♕f6 [18 ... ♕xd1 19 ♕xd1 ♗xe4 20 ♘g5 ♗f5 21 ♕f3±] 19 ♘e5 ♗xf2+ [19 ... ♗d6 20 ♖de1, 21 ♗e6] 20 ♔h1 ♖d8 21 ♘d7+ ♗xd7 22 ♖xd7 ♖c8 23 ♗h5 g6 24 ♖ee7 ♕xe7 25 ♖xe7 ♔xe7 26 ♗g4 ♖cd8 27 ♕b4+ [◻ 27 ♕e6+, 28 ♕f6+] 27 ... c5 28 ♕e4+ ♔d6 29 ♕f4+ ♔c6 30 ♕xf2 ♖hf8 31 ♗f3+ ♔b6 32 h3 ♖d1+ 33 ♔h2 **1-0** L/N3203

**1859-★JM-2** v 59
**Morphy, P.C.+ Julien, D.**
New York [Maróczy]
⟨♘b1⟩ 1 e4 e5 2 ♘f3 d6 3 d4 exd4 [◻ 3 ... ♘c6, ♗e7, ♘f6, 0-0] 4 ♗c4 ♘c6 5 c3 ♘e5 6 ♘xe5 dxe5 7 ♕b3 ♕e7 8 f4 dxc3 9 0-0 c6 10 fxe5 ♗e6 11 ♗xe6 fxe6 [◻ 11 ... ♕xe6 12 ♕xb7 ♗c5+ 13 ♔h1 ♖d8! 14 ♗g5 ♘e7 −+]

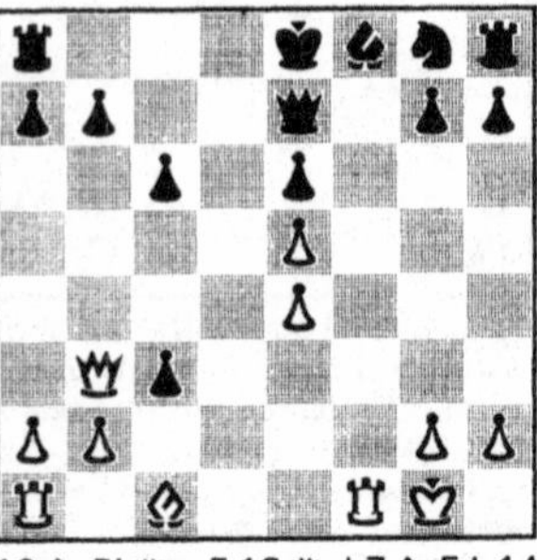

12 ♗g5! ♕xg5 13 ♕xb7 ♗c5+ 14 ♔h1 ♕xe5 15 ♕xa8+ ♔d7 16 ♕b7+ ♕c7 17 ♖ad1+ ♗d6 18 ♖xd6+ ♔xd6 19 ♖d1+ **1-0** L/N3203

**1859-★JM-3** 13 iv 59
**Morphy, P.C.= Janssens, F.G.**
London
1 e4 e5 2 f4 c6? 3 ♘c3 d6 4 ♘f3 ♗e7 5 ♗c4 exf4 6 d4 ♘f6 7 ♗xf4 0-0 8 0-0 ♗g4 9 ♗d3 ♘bd7 10 ♕d2 ♗h5 11 ♖ae1 ♗g6 12 e5 dxe5 13 dxe5 ♘e8 14 ♘e4 ♘c5 15 ♘xc5 ♗xc5+ 16 ♔h1 ♘c7 17 ♘g5 ♕e8 18 e6 ♘xe6 19 ♗xg6 hxg6 20 ♕c3 ♗e7 21 ♘xe6 fxe6 22 ♕b3 ♖f6 23 ♖xe6 ♖xe6 24 ♕xe6+ ♕f7 25 ♕xf7+ ♔xf7 26 g4 ♔g8 27 ♖e1 ♔f7 **½-½** L/N3161

**1859-★JM-4** 13 iv 59
**Morphy, P.C.+ Jones, J.P.**
London [Löwenthal]
1 e4 e5 2 f4 exf4 3 ♘f3 g5 4 ♗c4 g4 5 d4 ♕e7 6 0-0 gxf3 7 ♘c3 c6 8 ♕xf3 ♗g7 9 ♗xf4 ♗xd4+ 10 ♔h1 ♗g7 11 e5 ♗h6 12 ♘e4 d5 13 exd6 ♕f8 14 ♖ae1 ♗e6 15 ♗xe6 fxe6 16 ♕h5+ ♔d7 [16 ... ♕f7?? 17 d7+ +−] 17 ♘c5+ ♔c8 18 ♗xh6 ♘f6 19 ♕e5 ♘bd7 20 ♘xd7 ♕xh6 21 ♖xf6 ♕h4 22 ♘c5 **1-0** L/N3161

**1859-★JO-1**
**Journoud, P.+ O'Sullivan**
Paris [Staunton]
1 e4 e5 2 ♘f3 ♘c6 3 ♗c4 ♗c5 4 b4 ♗xb4 5 c3 ♗a5 6 0-0 [◻ 6 d4] 6 ... d6 7 d4 exd4 8 cxd4 ♗b6 9 ♕b3 ♕f6 10 e5 ♕g6 11 ♖e1 ♘ge7 12 exd6 cxd6 13 d5 ♘a5 14 ♗b5+ ♔f8 15 ♕a3 [△ 16 ♗d2] 15 ... ♗c7 16 ♖e3 ♗d8 17 ♗a3 a6 18 ♗d3 f5 19 ♕f4 ♗c7 20 ♘c3 ♕f6 21 ♖ac1 ♗b8 22 ♖c2 b5 23 ♗b4 ♘c4 24 ♗xc4 bxc4 25 ♖ce2 ♖a7 26 ♕xc4 ♖c7 27 ♕f4 ♖d7 28 ♖e6 ♕f7 29 ♘g5 ♕h5 30 h3 h6 31 ♘f3 g5 32 ♕d4 ♖h7 33 ♖f6+ ♖f7 34 ♖ee6 ♘g8 35 ♖xf7+ ♕xf7 [35 ... ♔xf7 36 ♕h8+ −] 36 ♘e5 ♗a7 37 ♘xd7+ ♗xd7 38 ♗xd6+ ♘e7 39 ♕h8+ ♕g8 40 ♗xe7+ **1-0** M954-1859

**1859-★JO-2**
**O'Sullivan= Journoud, P.**
Paris [Staunton]
1 e4 e5 2 ♘f3 ♘c6 3 ♗b5 ♗c5 4 ♗xc6 dxc6 5 d3 ♘f6 6 h3 h6 7 0-0 ♕e7 8 b3 0-0 9 ♗b2 ♗d6 10 ♘bd2 b5 11 d4 ♘d7 12 dxe5 ♘xe5 13 ♘xe5 ♗xe5 14 ♗xe5 ♕xe5 15 c4 ♗b7 16 ♕e2 ♖fe8 17 f4 ♕d4+ 18 ♕f2 ♖ad8 19 ♖ad1 ♕xf2+ 20 ♔xf2 a6 21 e5 c5 22 ♘f3 ♗e4 [◻ 22 ... ♗xf3 △ 23 ... ♖d4] 23 ♖fe1 ♗d3 24

cxb5 axb5 25 ♖d2 c4 26 ♖ed1 ♖a8 27 ♘d4 ♖eb8 28 ♘c6 ♖b7 29 ♘b4 c5 30 ♘xd3 cxd3 31 ♖c1 ♖c7 32 ♔e3 c4 33 bxc4 bxc4 34 ♖xd3 ♖xa2 35 ♖d2 ♖a3+ 36 ♔e4 c3 37 ♖dc2 ♖c4+ 38 ♔e3 g5 39 fxg5 hxg5 40 ♔d3 ♖c5 41 ♖e1 ♔f8 [△ 42 e6 f6, 43 ... ♔e7] 42 ♔e4 ♔g7 43 ♖e3 ♖aa5 44 ♔d4 ♖d5+ 45 ♔xc3 ♖xe5 46 ♖xe5 ♖xe5 47 ♔d4 f6 48 g4 ♔g6 ½-½ M954-1859

**1859-★KM-1**
**Morphy, P.C.+Knott, H.**
New York [Maróczy]

⟨♖a1⟩ 1 e4 e5 2 f4 exf4 3 ♘f3 g5 4 ♗c4 g4 5 d4 gxf3 6 0-0 d5 7 ♗xd5 ♗g4 8 ♕d3 fxg2 [□ 8 ... c6 9 ♗xf7+ ♔xf7 10 ♗xf4 ♗h6 11 ♕e3 ♕h4] 9 ♖f2 [9 ♖xf4 ♗e6, ♗h6] 9 ... c6 [9 ... f3 10 ♘d2] 10 ♗xf7+ ♔xf7 11 ♗xf4 ♘f6 12 e5 ♘bd7 13 ♘c3 ♗g7 14 ♘e4 h6 [□ 14 ... ♘xe4 15 ♕xe4 (15 ♗g5+ ♘xf2 16 ♕b3+ ♗e6 17 ♕f3+ ♘f6) 15 ... ♔g8 ... ♕h4 18 ♗xg7 ♔xg7 19 e6 (19 ♖xg2 h5) 19 ... ♕xf2+ 29 ♔xf2 ♖f8+ 21 ♔g1 ♖f1+ 22 ♔xg2 ♗f3+] 15 exf6 ♘xf6 16 ♗e5 ♖f8 17 ♘xf6 ♗xf6 18 ♗xf6 [18 ♖xf6+ ♕xf6 19 ♕h7+ ♔e6! (19 ... ♔e8? 20 ♗xf6 ♖xf6 21 ♕g8+, 22 ♕xg4) 20 ♗xf6 ♔xf6 21 ♕xh6+ ♔f5] 18 ... ♕d7 [18 ... ♕xf6 19 ♕h7+ ♔e6 20 ♕e4+] 19 ♕h7+ ♔e8 [19 ... ♔e6 20 ♕e4+ ♔f7 21 ♗e5+ ♔e8 (21 ... ♔e6 22 ♗g3#; 21 ... ♔e7 22 ♗d6+ ♔xd6 23 ♕e5#; 23 ♔d8 ♖xf8++-) 22 ♗g7+ ♔e6! (22 ... ♗e6 23 ♖xf8+ ♔e7 24 ♕h4+ ♔d6 25 ♗e5+ ♔d5 26 ♕g3!+-) 23 ♖xf8+ ♔d7 24 ♕xe6+ ♔xe6 25 ♖xa8+-] 20 ♕g6+ ♖f7

21 ♗g5! ♗f3 [21 ... ♔f8 22 ♗xh6++-; 21 ... hxg5 22 ♕g8+ ♔e7 23 ♖xf7+ ♔e6 24 ♕g6+ ♔d5 25 ♕xg5+ ♔xd4 26 ♖f4+ ♔e3 27 ♖f5+, 28 ♕xg4++-; 21 ... ♗f5 22 ♕g8+ ♖f8 23 ♖e2+ ♕e6 24 ♖xe6+ ♔d7 25 ♖e7+ ♔d6 26 ♕g7+-; 21 ... ♕e6 22 ♕g8+ ♔d7! 23 ♕xf7+ ♕xf7 24 ♖xf7+ ♔e6 25 ♖e7+ ♔d5 26 ♖e5+ ♔xd4 27 ♗f6 ♖f8 28 ♗g7 ♖g8 29 ♖g5++-] 22 ♖xf3 ♕xd4+ 23 ♖e3+ ♔f8 24 ♗xh6+ ♖g7 25 ♗xg7+ ♕xg7 26 ♕d6+ ♔g8 [26 ... ♔f7 28 ♖e7++-] 27 ♖g3 1-0 L/N3203

**1859-★KM-2** ●○ 20 iv 59
**Morphy, P.C.& Kennedy, H.A.**
London [Löwenthal]

1 e4 e5 2 ♘f3 ♘c6 3 ♗c4 ♗c5 4 b4 ♗xb4 5 c3 ♗c5 6 0-0 d6 7 d4 exd4 8 cxd4 ♗b6 9 d5 ♘ce7 [□ 9 ... ♘a5] 10 e5 ♘g6 11 e6 fxe6 12 dxe6 ♘8e7 13 ♘c3 c6 [□ 13 ... 0-0] 14 ♘g5 ♘e5 15 ♗f4! g6 16 ♘f7 0-0

17 ♗xe5! ♖xf7 18 exf7+ ♔f8 19 ♗xd6 ♗g4 20 ♕d2 g5 21 ♖ae1 1-0 L/N3161

**1859-★KM-3**
**Kolisch, I.F. von+Mandolfo**
Trieste?

1 ... e5 2 e4 ♗c5 3 ♘f3 ♘c6 4 c3 d6 5 b4 ♗b6 6 a4 a5 7 b5 ♘a7 8 d4 exd4 9 cxd4 ♘f6 10 ♘c3 ♕e7 11 ♗g5 0-0 12 ♗c4 ♗g4 13 h3 h6 14 h4 hxg5 15 hxg5 ♘xe4 16 ♘d5 ♕e8 17 ♘e5

17 ... ♗xd1 18 ♘g6 ♘g3+ 19 ♘de7+ ♕xe7+ 20 ♘xe7# 1-0 M954-1859

**1859-★KR-1**
**Kolisch, I.F. von–Rivière, J.A. de**
Paris

1 e4 e5 2 f4 d5 3 exd5 exf4 4 ♘f3 ♘f6 5 ♗c4 ♗d6 6 0-0 0-0 7 d4 ♗g4 8 ♕d3 ♘h5 9 c3 c6 10 dxc6 ♘xc6 11 h3 ♗xf3 12 ♕xf3 g6 13 ♘d2 ♕c7 14 ♗d3 ♘g3 15 ♘e4 ♘xf1 16 ♘xd6 ♕xd6 17 ♗xf4 ♘d2 18 ♗xd2 ♖ad8 19 ♖d1 ♘e5 20 ♕g3

**56** Kolisch, I.F. von M58.BL

♘xd3 21 ♕xd3 ♖fe8 22 ♗g5 f6 23 ♗h4 ♕f4 24 ♗g3 ♕e3+ 25 ♕xe3 ♖xe3 26 ♔f2 ♖e4 27 ♔f3 f5 28 ♗f2 ♔f7 29 c4 b5 30 cxb5 ♖c8 31 d5 ♖b4 32 d6 ♔e6 33 ♗xa7 ♖xb5 34 ♖d2 ♖d5 35 ♖xd5 ♔xd5 36 b4 ♔xd6 37 ♗c5+ ♔c6 38 a4 ♖d8 39 ♔e3 ♖d1 40 ♔e2 ♖a1 41 a5 ♔d5 42 ♗e7 ♔e4 43 ♗d8 ♖a2+ 44 ♔f1 ♔e3 45 ♗b6+ ♔d3 46 ♗c5 g5 47 ♗e7 g4 48 hxg4 fxg4 49 g3 h5 50 ♗c5 ♔c4 51 ♗d6 ♔d4 52 ♗c7 ♔e4 53 b5 ♔f3 54 ♔e1 h4 55 gxh4 g3 56 a6 ♖e2+ 57 ♔d1 g2 58 ♗h2 ♖a2 59 ♗g1 ♖a1+ 60 ♔c2 ♖xg1 61 a7 ♖a1 0-1 M954-1859

**1859-★KS-1**
**Kolisch, I.F. von+Schlemm, H.P.**
Wien

1 e4 e5 2 ♘f3 ♘c6 3 ♗c4 ♗c5 4 b4 ♗xb4 5 c3 ♗a5 6 d4 exd4 7 0-0 ♘f6 8 e5 d5 9 exf6 dxc4 10 fxg7 ♖g8 11 ♖e1+ ♗e6 12 ♘g5 ♕d5 13 ♖xe6+ fxe6 14 ♕h5+ ♔d7 15 ♕f7+ ♘e7 16 ♘xh7 ♕f5 17 ♘f6+ ♔d6 18 ♗a3+ c5 19 ♗xc5+ ♔xc5 20 ♕xe7+ ♔b6 21 ♕d6+ ♔b5 22 a4# 1-0 M954-1859

**97** Laroche L/N6396.BL

### 1859-★LM-1
**Morphy, P.C.+ Laroche**

Paris [Maróczy]

1 e4 e5 2 ♘f3 ♘c6 3 ♗c4 ♗c5 4 b4 ♗xb4 5 c3 ♗a5 6 d4 ♘f6? [□ 6 ... exd4] 7 dxe5 ♘g4 [7 ... ♘xe4 8 ♕d5+−] 8 ♗g5 f6 9 exf6 ♘xf6 [□ 9 ... gxf6] 10 e5 h6 11 exf6 hxg5 12 fxg7 ♕e7+ 13 ♕e2 **1-0** L/N3203

### 1859-★LM-2 vii 59
**Morphy,P.C.− Lichtenhein,T.**

New York [Maróczy]

⟨♘b1⟩ 1 e4 e5 2 ♘f3 ♘c6 3 ♗c4 ♗c5 4 b4 ♗xb4 5 c3 ♗a5 6 0-0 ♘f6 7 d4 0-0 8 ♕c2 exd4 9 cxd4 h6 10 d5 ♘e7 11 ♗b2 d6 12 h3 ♘g6 13 ♘d4 ♕e7 14 ♘b3 ♗b6 15 ♖ae1 ♔h8 16 ♘d2 ♘h5 17 ♘f3 ♘h4 [17 ... ♘g3 18 ♕c3 ♕f6 19 ♕b3 ♕f4 20 ♗c1 ♕f6 21 ♗b2 ♕e7 22 ♕c3 f6 23 ♘h4 ♘xh4 24 ♕xg3∞] 18 ♘xh4 ♕xh4 19 ♔h2 ♘f4 20 ♕c3 ♖g8 [□ 20 ... f6] 21 ♕g3 ♕g5 22 ♕xg5 [22 ♗c1 ♕xg3 △ 23 ... ♘g6, 24 ... ♘e5−+] 22 ... hxg5 23 g3 ♘g6 24 f4 gxf4 25 gxf4 f6 26 ♔g3 ♗d7 27 h4 ♖ae8 28 h5 ♘f8 29 ♖h1 ♘h7 30 ♔f3 ♖e7 31 ♖e2 ♖ge8 32 ♗d3 c6 33 h6 g5−+ 34 fxg5 ♘xg5+ 35 ♔f4 ♘h7 36 ♖g2 ♖g8 37 ♖g7 ♖gxg7 38 hxg7+ ♔xg7 39 ♖xh7+ ♔xh7 40 e5+ f5 41 e6 ♗xe6! 42 dxe6 ♖xe6 43 ♗xf5+ ♖g6 **0-1** L/N3203

### 1859-★LM-3 vii 59
**Morphy,P.C.−Lichtenhein, T.**

New York [Maróczy]

⟨♘b1⟩ 1 e4 e5 2 f4 exf4 3 ♘f3 d5 4 exd5 ♗d6 5 ♗c4 h6 6 d4 c6 7 dxc6 ♘xc6 8 ♗d3 ♘ge7 9 c4? [□ 9 0-0] 9 ... ♗b4+ 10 ♔f1 ♗d6 11 d5 ♘b8 12 b4 b6 13 ♕b3 a5 14 c5 bxc5 15 bxc5 ♗xc5 16 ♗xf4 ♕xd5 17 ♗b5+ ♘d7 18 ♕c2 ♗a6 19 ♗xa6 ♖xa6 20 ♖d1 ♕f5 21 ♕c4 ♖a7 22 h3 0-0 23 g4 ♘b6 24 ♕c1 ♕e4 **0-1** L/N3203

### 1859-★LM-4 vii 59
**Morphy,P.C.= Lichtenhein,T.**

New York [Maróczy]

⟨♘b1⟩ 1 e4 e5 2 ♘f3 ♘c6 3 ♗c4 ♗c5 4 c3 ♘f6 5 d4 exd4 6 0-0 ♘xe4 7 ♗xf7+ ♔xf7 8 cxd4 d5 9 dxc5 ♗g4 [□ 9 ... ♖f8, ♔g8] 10 ♘g5+ ♕xg5 11 f3 ♕g6 12 fxg4+ ♔e6 13 ♗f4 ♕f6 14 ♗e3 ♕d8 15 ♕f3 ♖f8 16 ♕h3 ♘g5 17 ♕h5 h6 18 h4 ♘e4 19 ♕g6+ ♖f6 20 ♕xg7 ♕e7 21 ♖xf6+ ♕xf6 22 ♕xc7 ♕f7 23 ♕xf7+ ♔xf7 24 ♗xh6 ♔g6 [□ 24 ... ♖h8] 25 ♗f4 d4 26 h5+ ♔h7 27 g5 d3 28 ♖f1 d2 29 ♗xd2 ♘xd2 30 ♖f7+ ♔g8 31 ♖xb7 ♘e4 32 h6 ♖c8 33 b4 ♘xb4 34 ♖xb4 ♘xg5 35 ♖b7 ♖xc5 36 ♖xa7 ♔h8 37 a4 ♖c6 38 a5 ♖xh6 39 a6 ♘e4 40 ♖a8+ ♔g7 41 a7 ♖a6 42 ♖e8 ♖xa7 43 ♖xe4 **½-½** L/N3203

### 1859-★LM-5 ●○⬠ 11 xi 59
**Morphy, P.C.+ Lewis, S.**

Philadelphia [Maróczy]

1 e4 b6 2 d4 ♗b7 3 ♗d3 e6 4 ♘h3 d5 [□ 4 ... c5; 4 ... ♘f6] 5 e5 ♘e7 6 0-0 ♘g6 7 f4 ♗e7 8 f5 exf5 9 ♗xf5 ♗c8 10 ♗xc8 ♕xc8 11 ♘c3 c6 12 ♗g5 0-0 13 ♗xe7 ♘xe7 14 ♕h5± h6 [14 ... g6 15 ♕h6 ♘f5 16 ♖xf5, 17 ♘g5±] 15 ♖f3 ♘g6 16 ♖af1 ♕e6 17 ♘e2 ♘d7 18 ♘ef4 ♘xf4 19 ♘xf4 ♕e7 20 ♖g3 ♔h7 21 ♖ff3 [△ 22 ♖xg7+ ♔xg7 23 ♖g3+ ♔h7 24 ♖h3+−] 21 ... ♖g8 22 ♘h3 g6 23 ♘g5+ ♕xg5 24 ♖xf7+ ♔h8 [24 ... ♖g7 25 ♖xg7+ ♔xg7 (25 ... ♔h8 26 ♖xg5 gxh5 27 ♖5g6 ♖d8 28 e6) 26 ♖xg5 hxg5 27 ♕g4+−] 25 ♕xg5 **1-0** L/N3202

### 1859-★LM-6
**Laroche− Morphy, P.C.**

Paris [Löwenthal]

1 f4 e6 2 e4 d5 3 e5 c5 4 ♘f3 ♘c6 5 c4 d4 6 d3 ♘h6 7 ♗e2 ♗e7 8 ♘bd2 0-0 9 ♘e4 f5 10 ♘eg5 [10 exf6 ♗xf6 11 ♘xc5 ♕a5+] 10 ... ♘f7 11 ♘xf7 ♖xf7 12 0-0 b6 13 ♗d2 ♗b7 14 h3 h6 15 ♘h2 g5! 16 ♗f3 ♖g7 17 a3 ♕c7 18 ♕e2 gxf4 19 ♗xf4 ♗g5 20 ♗xg5 ♖xg5 21 ♖ae1 ♔h7 22 ♔h1 ♖ag8 23 ♖f2 ♘e7 24 ♗xb7 ♕xb7 25 ♕f3 ♕c7 26 g4?! ♘g6 27 ♕e2 ♘h4 28 ♘f3 ♕b7 29 ♔h2 ♘xf3+ 30 ♕xf3 ♕xf3 31 ♖xf3 fxg4 32 ♖f6 ♖h5 33 ♖xe6 ♖xh3+ 34 ♔g2 ♖xd3 35 ♖f1 g3 36 ♖ff6 ♖d2+ 37 ♔g1 ♖h2 38 ♖f7+ ♖g7 39 ♖xg7+ ♔xg7 40 ♖f6 ♖e2 41 ♖f3 ♖e3 42 ♖f1 d3 43 ♔g2 d2 44 ♖d1 ♖d3 45 ♔f1 ♔f7 46 ♔e2 ♖d4 47 ♔f3 ♔e6 48 ♔xg3 ♔xe5 49 ♔f3 ♖d3+ **0-1** L/N3161

### 1859-★LM-7 21 vii 59
**Morphy,P.C.+ Lichtenhein,T.**

New York [Löwenthal]

⟨♘b1⟩ 1 e4 e5 2 ♘f3 ♘c6 3 ♗c4 ♗c5 4 b4 ♗xb4 5 c3 ♗c5 6 0-0 ♗b6 7 d4 d6 [□ 7 ... exd4] 8 dxe5 dxe5 9 ♕b3 ♕f6 10 ♗g5 ♕g6 11 ♗b5 ♗e6 [□ 11 ... f6] 12 ♕a4 ♗d7 13 ♖ad1 f6 14 ♖xd7! ♔xd7 [14 ... fxg5 15 ♘xe5 ♕e6 (15 ... ♘xe5 16 ♖xg7++−) 16 ♘xc6 bxc6 17 ♗xc6+−] 15 ♗xc6+ bxc6 16 ♖d1+ ♔e7 17 ♘xe5 ♕xg5 18 ♖d7+ ♔e8 [18 ... ♔f8 19 ♖f7+ ♔e8 20 ♕xc6+ ♔d8 21 ♕d7#; 18 ... ♔e6 19 ♕xc6+ ♔xe5 20 ♖d5+ ♔f4 21 ♖xg5+−] 19 ♕xc6 ♕xe5 [19 ... ♕c1+ 20 ♖d1+ ♔e7 (20 ... ♔f8 21 ♕xa8+ ♔e7 22 ♕d8+ ♔e6 23 ♕d7+ ♔xe5 24 ♕f5#) 21 ♕d7+ ♔f8 22 ♕f7#] 20 ♖xc7+ ♔f8 21 ♕xa8+ ♕e8 22 ♖c8 ♕xc8 23 ♕xc8+ ♔f7 24 c4 g5 25 c5 ♗a5 26 c6 **1-0** L/N3161

### 1859-★LM-8 vii 59
**Morphy,P.C.+Lichtenhein, T.**

New York [Löwenthal]

⟨♘b1⟩ 1 e4 e5 2 ♘f3 ♘c6 3 ♗c4 ♗c5 4 b4 ♗xb4 5 c3 ♗c5 6 0-0 ♘f6 [□ 6 ... d6] 7 d4 exd4 8 cxd4 ♗b6 9 ♗a3 d6 10 e5 dxe5 11 ♕b3 ♗e6 [11 ... ♕d7 12 ♘xe5 ♘xe5 13 dxe5 ♘e4 14 ♖ad1 ♕f5 15 ♗xf7+ ♕xf7 16 ♖d8+ ♔xd8 17 ♕xf7+−] 12 ♗xe6 fxe6 13 ♕xe6+ ♘e7 14 ♘xe5 ♖f8 15 ♖fe1 ♘d5 16 ♕g4 g6 17 ♕h4 a5 18 ♕xh7 ♗xd4 19 ♘xg6 c5 [19 ... ♗xf2+ 20 ♔h1 ♗xe1 21 ♖xe1+−] 20 ♘xf8 ♔xf8 21 ♖ad1 ♔e8 22 ♗xc5 ♗xc5 23 ♕g8+ ♔d7 24 ♖xd5+ ♘xd5 25 ♕xd5+ ♗d6 26 ♕xb7+ ♕c7 27 ♕xa8 **1-0** L/N3161

### 1859-★LM-9 16 iv 59
**Morphy,P.C.=Löwenthal, J.J.**

London [Löwenthal]

1 e4 e5 2 ♘f3 ♘c6 3 ♗c4 ♗c5 4 b4 ♗xb4 5 c3 ♗c5 6 0-0 d6 7 d4 exd4 8 cxd4 ♗b6 9 d5 ♘ce7 10 e5 ♘g6 11 e6 fxe6 12 dxe6 ♘8e7 13 ♘g5 0-0 14 ♕h5 h6 15 ♘f7 ♕e8 16 ♗b2 d5 17 ♗xg7 [17 ♗xd5 ♕b5] 17 ... ♖xf7 [□ 17 ... ♗xe6 18 ♗xf8 ♕xf8 19 ♘xh6+ ♔g7 20 ♗d3 ♕f6] 18 exf7+ ♕xf7 19 ♗b2 dxc4 20 ♘d2 ♗f5 21 ♖ae1 ♖d8 22 ♘f3 ♗d3 23 ♕xh6 ♕h7 24 ♕g5 ♖d5 25 ♖xe7 ♖xg5 26 ♖xh7 ♖xg2+ 27 ♔xg2 ♗xf1+ 28 ♔xf1 ♔xh7 29 ♘d2= ♗c5 30 ♘xc4 b5 31 ♘e5 ♘xe5 32 ♗xe5 ♗d6 33 ♗d4 c5 34 ♗e3 a5 35 ♔e2 a4 36 ♔d3 a3 37 ♗c1 ♔g6 38 ♔e4 c4 39 f4 b4 40 ♗xa3 bxa3 41 ♔d4 ♗xf4 42 ♔xc4 ♗xh2 43 ♔b3 ♗d6 44 ♔c2 **½-½** L/N3161

### 1859-★LM-10 ⬠ 20 iv 59
**Löwenthal,J.J.= Morphy,P.C.**

London [Löwenthal]

1 e4 e5 2 ♘f3 ♘c6 3 ♗b5 a6 4 ♗a4 ♘f6 5 0-0 ♗e7 6 d4 exd4 7 e5 ♘e4 8 ♗xc6 dxc6 9 ♕xd4 ♗f5 10 ♘c3 ♗c5 11 ♕xd8+ ♖xd8 12 ♘h4 ♘xc3 13 ♘xf5 ♘e2+ 14 ♔h1 g6 15 ♘g3 [15 ♗e3 gxf5 16 ♗xc5 ♖d2] 15 ... ♘xg3+ 16 hxg3 h6 17 ♖b1 ♔e7 18 b4 ♗d4 19 f4 ♔e6 20 ♖b3 h5 21 ♖d3 ♗b6 22 ♖fd1 ♖xd3 23 ♖xd3 ♔f5 24 ♗b2 ♖h7 25 ♗d4 h4 26 ♗xb6 hxg3+ 27 ♔g1 cxb6 28 ♖d7 ♔e6 [28 ... ♔xf4 29 e6] 29 ♖xb7 ♖h4 30 ♖xb6 ♖xf4 31 ♖xc6+

♔xe5 32 ♖c5+ ♔d6 33 ♖g5 ♖xb4 34 ♖xg3 ♖a4 35 a3 ♖c4 36 ♖d3+ ♔e6 37 ♖b3 ♖xc2 38 ♖b6+ ♔f5 39 ♖xa6 g5 40 ♖b6 ♖a2 41 ♖b3 g4 42 ♖b5+ ♔f4 43 ♖b3 f5 [43 ... g3 44 ♖f3+, 45 ♖xf7] 44 g3+ ♔e4 45 ♔f1 ♔e5 46 ♔g1 f4 47 ♖b4 ½-½

L/N3161

**1859-★LM-11** iv 59

**Löwenthal,J.J.+Morphy, P.C.**

London [Löwenthal]

1 e4 e5 2 ♘f3 ♘c6 3 ♗b5 a6 4 ♗a4 ♘f6 5 0-0 b5 6 ♗b3 ♗c5 7 c3 d6 8 d4 exd4 9 cxd4 ♗b6 10 ♗g5 ♗b7 11 ♘c3 ♘e7 12 ♖e1 h6 13 ♗h4 g5 14 ♗g3 ♔f8 15 ♕d3 c5 16 e5 dxe5 17 ♗xe5 ♔g7 [17 ... c4 18 ♕e2±] 18 ♘e4 ♗xe4 19 ♕xe4 ♘g6 20 ♕b7 ♖a7 21 ♕c6 c4 22 ♗c2 ♗c7 [□ 22 ... ♘xe5 23 dxe5 ♘g4] 23 ♖ad1 ♕e7 24 ♗xg6 ♔xg6 25 d5 ♗xe5 26 ♘xe5+ ♔g7 27 ♘g6 ♕d8 28 ♘xh8 ♔xh8 29 d6 ♔g7 30 a4 ♖d7 31 axb5 axb5 32 ♕xb5 ♖xd6 33 ♖xd6 ♕xd6 34 ♕xc4 h5 35 h3 ♘d7 36 ♖e3 ♘e5 37 ♖xe5! ♕xe5 38 ♕c3 **1-0**

L/N3161

**1859-★LM-12** iv 59

**Morphy,P.C.+ Löwenthal,J.J.**

London [Löwenthal]

1 e4 e5 2 ♘f3 ♘c6 3 ♗c4 ♗c5 4 b4 ♗xb4 5 c3 ♗c5 6 0-0 d6 7 d4 exd4 8 cxd4 ♗b6 9 d5 ♘e5 10 ♘xe5 dxe5 11 ♗b2 ♕e7 12 ♗b5+ ♗d7 13 ♗xd7+ ♔xd7 14 ♕g4+ f5 15 ♕xf5+ ♔e8 [□ 15 ... ♔d8] 16 ♗xe5 ♘h6 17 ♕f4 ♔d7 18 ♘d2 ♖ae8 19 ♘c4 ♗c5 20 ♖ad1 ♗d6 21 ♗xd6 cxd6 22 ♖b1 b6 23 ♖fc1 [△ 24 ♖xb6 axb6 25 ♘xb6+ ♔d8 26 ♖c8#] 23 ... ♕f6 24 ♕e3 ♘g4 25 ♘xb6+! axb6 [25 ... ♔e7 26 ♖c7+ ♔f8 27 ♘d7++-] 26 ♖c7+!! ♔d8 [26 ... ♔xc7 27 ♕xb6++-] 27 ♕xb6 ♕xf2+ 28 ♕xf2 ♘xf2 29 ♖a7 ♘h3+ 30 gxh3 ♔c8 31 ♔f2 **1-0**

L/N3161

**1859-★LM-13** 21 vii 59

**Morphy,P.C.+ Lichtenhein,T.**

⟨♘b1⟩ 1 e4 e5 2 ♘f3 ♘c6 3 ♗c4 ♗c5 4 b4 ♗xb4 5 c3 ♗c5 6 0-0 ♗b6 7 d4 d6 8 dxe5 ♘xe5 9 ♘xe5 dxe5 10 ♗xf7+ ♔e7 11 ♕b3 ♘f6 12 ♗a3+ c5 13 ♖ad1 ♕c7 14 f4 ♗g4 15 ♖de1 ♖hf8 16 ♗c4 ♗h5 17 h3 ♗f7 18 ♗xf7 ♖xf7 19 fxe5 ♕xe5 20 ♖f5 ♕e6 21 c4 ♖c8 22 ♗b2 ♘d7 23 ♕g3 ♗c7 24 ♕h4+ ♔e8 25 ♖ef1 ♖xf5 26 ♖xf5 ♕h6 27 ♕f2 ♗d8 28 ♖f7 ♗f6 29 ♕f5 ♗e7 30 ♖xg7 ♕d6 31 e5 ...? **1-0**

+13

**1859-★LR-1**

**Rivière,J.A.de+Lasseur,H.**

[Staunton]

1 e4 e5 2 ♘f3 ♘c6 3 ♗c4 ♗c5 4 b4 ♗xb4 5 c3 ♗c5 6 0-0 d6 7 d4 exd4 8 cxd4 ♗b6 9 d5 ♘a5 10 e5 ♘e7 [□ 10 ... ♘xc4 △ 11 ... ♘e7] 11 exd6 cxd6 12 ♘c3 ♗d7 13 ♗d3 f5 14 ♘g5 0-0 15 ♖e1 ♖c8 16 ♕e2 ♖e8 17 ♘e6 ♗xe6 18 ♕xe6+ ♔h8 19 ♗g5 ♖xc3 20 ♗xe7 ♕c8 21 ♗xf5 ♕xe6 22 ♖xe6 ♘c4 23 ♖ae1 ♗d4 24 g4 ♗e5 25 ♗h4 ♖f8 26 ♗g3 ♔g8 [□ 26 ... ♗xg3] 27 f4 ♗d4+ 28 ♔h1 h6 29 ♗b1 ♖e3 30 ♖1xe3 ♗xe3 31 f5 ♗c5 32 ♖e7 ♖f7 33 ♖e6 g5 34 h4+- h5 35 hxg5 hxg4 36 g6 ♖c7 37 f6 ♖c8 38 ♖e7 ♘e5 39 ♗xe5 dxe5 40 ♖g7+ ♔f8 41 ♖h7 **1-0**

M954-1859

**1859-★LS-1** 20 viii 59

**Steinitz,W.+Lenhof**

Wien [Bachmann]

1 e4 e5 2 ♘f3 ♘c6 3 ♗c4 ♗c5 4 b4 ♗xb4 5 c3 ♗a5 6 d4 exd4 7 0-0 d6 8 ♕b3 ♕d7? [□ 8 ... ♕f6; 8 ... ♘f6] 9 cxd4 ♗b6? 10 ♗b5 a6 11 ♗a4 ♗a7 12 d5 b5 13 dxc6 ♕xc6 14 ♕b2 ♘f6 15 ♗c2 0-0 16 ♘c3 ♖e8 [□ 16 ... h6] 17 ♗g5 ♘g4 18 ♘d5 ♕d7 19 h3 ♘e5 20 ♘xe5 dxe5 21 ♔h2 c6 22 ♘c3 ♗b8 23 ♗b3 ♗b7 24 ♖ad1 ♕c7 25 f4 c5 26 ♘d5 ♗xd5 27 ♗xd5 ♖a7 28 f5 h6 29 ♕d2! ♔h7 [29 ... hxg5 30 ♕xg5 △ 31 f6+-] 30 f6 ♕d6 31 ♕e2 ♕b6 32 ♕h5 **1-0**

L/N3131

**1859-★LS-2** 20 viii 59

**Lenhof−Steinitz,W.**

Wien [Bachmann]

1 e4 e5 2 ♗c4 f5 3 d3 ♘f6 4 ♘f3 d5 5 exd5 ♗d6 6 0-0 0-0 7 ♘c3 a6 8 a4 h6 9 d4 e4 10 ♘e5 ♘bd7 11 ♘xd7 ♗xd7 12 f3 ♕e8 13 fxe4 fxe4 14 ♗f4 ♕g6 15 ♗xd6 cxd6 16 ♕e2 ♖ae8 17 ♖f4 ♖e7 18 ♖e1 ♖fe8 19 ♕f2 ♘h5 20 ♖h4 ♖f7 21 ♕d2 ♘f6 22 h3 ♕g5 23 ♕f4 [23 ♕xg5?] 23 ... ♘h7 24 ♕xg5 ♘xg5 25 ♖f1 ♖fe7 26 ♖hf4 e3 27 ♖e1 [□ 27 ♔h2] 27 ... ♗xh3 28 ♗d3 ♗d7 29 b3 ♘h7 30 ♘d1 [30 ♘e4 g5] 30 ... ♘f6 31 c4 ♘g4 32 ♖f3 ♘f2! 33 ♗g6 ♘xd1 34 ♗xe8 ♖xe8 35 ♖xd1 ♗g4 36 ♖e1 ♗xf3 37 gxf3 ♔f7 38 c5 dxc5 39 dxc5 ♖e5 40 c6 bxc6 41 dxc6 ♔e6 42 ♔f1 [42 ♖c1 e2 43 ♔f2 e1♕+ 44 ♖xe1 ♖xe1 45 ♔xe1 ♔d6-+] 42 ... e2+ 43 ♖xe2 ♖xe2 44 ♔xe2 a5 45 f4 g6 **0-1**

L/N3131

**61** Marache, N. M58.BL

**1859-★MM-1**

**Morphy,P.C.+Marache,N.**

New York [Maróczy]

⟨♘b1⟩ 1 e4 e5 2 ♘f3 ♘c6 3 d4 exd4 4 ♗c4 ♘f6 5 0-0 ♗c5 6 e5 d5 7 exf6 dxc4 8 ♖e1+ ♗e6 9 ♘g5 ♕xf6 [□ 9 ... ♕d5] 10 ♘xe6 fxe6 11 ♕h5+ g6 12 ♕xc5 ♖f8 13 ♗g5 [13 ♗h6 ♕xf2+ 14 ♔h1 ♖f5 15 ♕xc4 0-0-0!] 13 ... ♕xf2+ 14 ♔h1 ♖f5? [□ 14 ... ♕f5] 15 ♕xc4 ♖xg5 16 ♕xe6+ ♔f8 17 ♖f1 ♖xg2 18 ♕h3! ♖g1+ 19 ♖xg1 ♔g7 20 ♖ae1 ♖f8 21 ♖gf1 ♕xc2 22 ♕d7+ ♔g8 23 ♖xf8+ ♔xf8 24 ♖e8# **1-0**

L/N3203

**1859-★MM-2**

**Morphy,P.C.−Michaelis, O.E.**

New York [Maróczy]

⟨♖a1⟩ 1 e4 e5 2 ♘f3 d6 3 d4 exd4 4 ♘xd4 ♘c6 5 ♘c3 ♘xd4 6 ♕xd4 c6 7 ♗e3 ♘f6 8 ♗e2 ♗e6 9 0-0 ♗e7 10 f4 0-0 11 f5 ♗d7 12 g4 c5 13 ♕d2 ♗c6 14 ♗f3 ♘d7! 15 g5 ♘e5 16 ♗e2 f6 17 h4 a6 18 ♖f2 b5 19 ♖g2 fxg5 20 hxg5 ♘c4 21 ♗xc4+ bxc4 22 ♕e2 d5 23 ♕h5

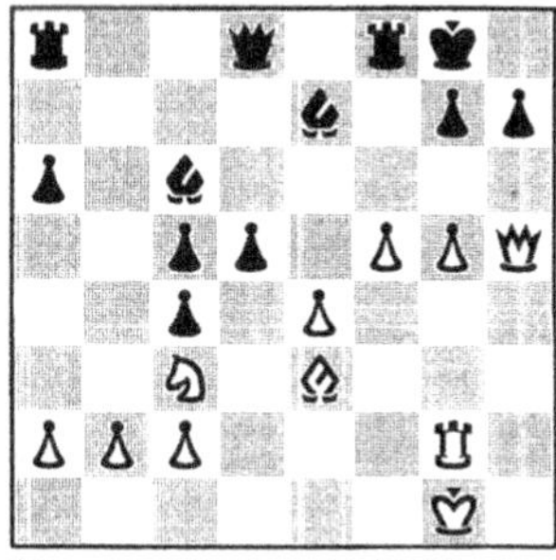

23 ... ♖xf5! 24 exf5 d4 25 g6 [25 ♖h2 dxe3! 26 ♕xh7+ ♔f8 27 ♕h8+ ♔f7 28 g6+ ♔f6 29 ♕h4+ ♔xf5 30 ♕h3+ ♔f6 31 ♕xe3 (31 ♕f1+ ♔xg6; 31 ♕h4+ ♔e6) 31 ... ♕d4 32 ♖f2+ ♔xg6 33 ♕xe7 (33 ♕g3+ ♗g5) 33 ... ♕g4+ 34 ♔f1 ♕h3+ 35 ♔e1 ♖e8] 25 ... h6 26 ♗xh6 dxc3 27 ♗xg7

♔xg7 28 ♕h7+ ♔f6 29 ♕f7+ ♔e5 30 ♕e6+ ♔f4 31 ♖f2+ ♗f3 32 ♕e2 ♕d5 33 ♕xe7 ♖h8 34 ♕c7+ ♔g4 35 ♕h7 ♕d1+ 36 ♖f1 ♕xf1+ [□ 36 ... ♕d4+ 37 ♖f2 ♕e3!-+] 37 ♔xf1 ♖xh7 38 gxh7 cxb2 39 h8♕ b1♕+ **0-1** L/N3203

### 1859-★MM-3
**Morphy,P.C.+ Michaelis,O.E.**

New York [Maróczy]

⟨♖a1⟩ 1 e4 e5 2 ♘f3 ♘c6 3 ♗c4 ♗c5 4 b4 ♗xb4 5 c3 ♗a5 6 d4 exd4 7 0-0 ♗b6 8 cxd4 d6 9 ♘c3 ♘f6 [□ 9 ... ♘a5; 9 ... ♗g4!] 10 e5 ♘g4 [10 ... dxe5 11 ♗a3] 11 h3 ♘h6 12 ♗g5 ♕d7 13 ♖e1 ♔f8 [13 ... 0-0 (13 ... dxe5 14 d5) 14 e6] 14 e6 ♕e8 [□ 14 ... fxe6] 15 e7+ [□ 15 exf7] 15 ... ♔g8 16 ♗xh6 gxh6 17 ♘g5 hxg5 18 ♕h5 ♘xe7 19 ♘d5 ♗xd4 20 ♘xe7+ ♔f8 21 ♕h6+ ♗g7 22 ♘g6+ hxg6 23 ♖xe8+ ♔xe8 24 ♕xg7 ♖f8 25 g4 ♗d7 26 ♕f6 ♗c6 27 ♔h2 ♔d7 [□ 27 ... ♖d8, ♖d7, ♔e7] 28 ♔g3 ♖ae8 29 ♗xf7 ♖e7 30 ♗e6+ ♔e8 31 ♕xg6+ ♔d8 32 ♗f5 ♗d7 33 ♗xd7 ♔xd7 34 ♕xg5 ♖ef7 35 ♕b5+ ♔c8 36 ♕e2 ♖xf2 37 ♕e6+ ♔d8 38 g5 ♖8f3+ 39 ♔g4 ♖f4+ 40 ♔h5 ♖f7 41 h4 ♖h7+ 42 ♔g4 ♖hf7 43 g6 ♖7f4+ 44 ♔g5 ♖f5+ 45 ♕xf5 ♖xf5+ 46 ♔xf5 ♔e7 47 h5 c5 48 h6 ♔f8 49 ♔f6 ♔g8 50 g7 ♔h7 51 ♔f7 **1-0** L/N3203

### 1859-★MM-4
**Morphy, P.C.+ Mead, C.D.**

New York [Maróczy]

⟨♘b1⟩ 1 e4 e5 2 f4 exf4 3 ♘f3 g5 4 ♗c4 ♗g7 5 c3 d6 6 d4 ♗g4 7 ♕b3 ♗xf3 8 ♗xf7+ ♔f8 9 gxf3 b6 [□ 9 ... ♘d7] 10 h4 ♕e7 11 ♗xg8 ♖xg8 12 ♕d5 c6 13 ♕f5+ ♕f7 14 ♕xg5 ♘d7 15 ♗xf4 ♗xd4 16 ♕h6+ ♗g7 17 ♕xd6+ ♔e8 18 0-0-0 ♗f8? 19 ♕xc6! ♕xf4+ 20 ♔b1 ♖d8 21 ♕e6+ ♗e7 22 ♕xg8+ ♘f8 23 ♖xd8+ ♔xd8 24 ♖d1+ ♔e8 25 ♕d5 ♕xf3 26 ♕b5+ ♘d7 [26 ... ♔f7 27 ♖f1+-] 27 ♕xd7+ **1-0** L/N3203

### 1859-★MM-5
**Morphy, P.C.+ Mead, C.D.**

New York [Maróczy]

⟨♘b1⟩ 1 e4 e5 2 f4 exf4 3 ♘f3 g5 4 ♗c4 ♗g7 5 0-0 d6 6 c3 ♘c6 7 d4 a6 [□ 7 ... h6] 8 ♕b3 ♘a5 9 ♗xf7+ ♔f8 10 ♕d5 c6 11 ♕xg5 ♕xg5 12 ♘xg5 h6 13 ♗xf4 ♔e7 14 ♗xg8 ♖xg8 15 ♘f3 ♘c4 16 b3 ♘b6 17 a4 ♗g4 18 ♘d2 ♖ad8 19 a5 ♘d7 20 ♘c4 ♘f8 21 ♗g3! d5 22 ♗h4+ ♔d7 23 ♘b6+ ♔e8 24 ♖ae1 ♘e6 25 exd5 ♖xd5 26 ♘xd5 cxd5 27 h3 ♗xh3 28 gxh3 ♗f6+ 29 ♔h1 ♗xh4 30 ♖xe6+ ♔d7 31 ♖xh6 **1-0** L/N3203

### 1859-★MM-6
**Morphy, P.C.+ Montgomery, H.P.**

New York [Maróczy]

⟨♘b1⟩ 1 e4 e5 2 ♘f3 d6 3 d4 exd4 4 ♗c4 ♗e7 5 c3 d3 6 ♕b3 ♗e6 7 ♗xe6 fxe6 8 ♘d4 [8 ♕xb7?] 8 ... ♗f6 9 ♘xe6 [9 ♕xb7 ♗xd4, 10 ... ♗b6] 9 ... ♕c8 10 f4 ♘c6 11 e5 dxe5 12 fxe5 ♗xe5 13 0-0 ♘f6 [13 ... ♘ge7 14 ♗g5±] 14 ♘xg7+ ♔d8 15 ♗g5 ♕d7 16 ♘e6+ ♔e7 [16 ... ♔c8 17 ♘c5] 17 ♘c5 ♘d4 18 cxd4! [18 ♘xd7] 18 ... ♕xd4+ 19 ♔h1 ♕xc5 20 ♖xf6 ♗xf6 21 ♖e1+ ♔f8 [22 ♗h6+ ♗g7 23 ♕e6 ♗h6! (23 ... ♕f2 24 ♕e7+, 25 ♕xg7#) 24 ♖f1+ ♕f2 25 ♖xf2+ ♗f4 26 ♖xf4+ ♔g7 27 ♕f6+ ♔g8 28 ♕f7#] **1-0** L/N3203

### 1859-★MM-7 ●○ 13 iv 59
**Morphy, P.C.+ Maude, P.**

London [Löwenthal]

1 e4 e5 2 ♗c4 ♘f6 3 ♘f3 ♘c6 4 ♘g5 d5 5 exd5 ♘a5 6 d3 e4 7 ♕e2 ♕e7 8 ♘xe4 ♘xe4 9 dxe4 ♕b4+ 10 ♘d2 ♘xc4 11 ♕xc4 ♕b6 12 0-0 ♗d7 13 a4 c6 14 ♘f3 ♗d6 15 ♗e3 ♕c7 16 ♕d4 f6 17 c4 c5 18 ♕d3 ♗g4 19 ♘d2 ♗xh2+ 20 ♔h1 ♗f4 21 g3 ♗xe3 22 ♕xe3 ♔d7 23 f4 b6 [□ 23 ... ♖ae8] 24 e5 f5 25 ♘f3 ♗xf3+ 26 ♕xf3 h5 27 ♖ad1 ♕d8 28 d6 ♖b8 29 ♖fe1 ♖h6 30 e6+! ♖xe6 31 ♖xe6 ♔xe6 32 ♕d5+ ♔f6 33 ♖e1 g6 34 ♖e7 **1-0** L/N3161

### 1859-★MM-8 ●○ 13 iv 59
**Morphy, P.C.= Medley, G.W.**

London [Löwenthal]

1 e4 e5 2 ♘f3 ♘c6 3 d4 exd4 4 ♗c4 ♗c5 5 0-0 d6 6 c3 d3 7 b4 ♗b6 8 a4 a5 9 b5 ♘e5 10 ♘xe5 dxe5 11 ♘d2 ♘f6 12 ♕b3 ♗e6 [12 ... 0-0? 13 ♗a3] 13 ♗xe6 fxe6 14 ♗a3! ♕d7! 15 ♘f3 0-0-0 [15 ... ♘xe4 16 ♘xe5±] 16 ♘xe5 ♕e8 17 ♕c4! d2 18 ♖ad1 ♕h5 19 ♘f3 [19 ♘c6? ♘g4!∓] 19 ... ♕g4 20 ♘xd2 ♘h5 21 e5 ♘f4 22 g3 ♖xd2 [□ 22 ... ♗xf2+ 23 ♔h1 ♗xg3 24 ♖g1 ♖xd2 25 ♖xd2 ♕f3+ 26 ♖1g2 ♕e1∓ (22 ... ♘e2+ 23 ♔g2 ♕xc4 24 ♘xc4 ♘xc3 25 ♘xb6+ cxb6 26 ♖c1+-)] 23 ♕xf4 [23 ♖xd2? ♘h3+-+] 23 ... ♕xf4 24 gxf4 ♗xf2+ 25 ♔g2 ♖xd1 26 ♖xd1 ♗h4 27 ♔h3 ♗d8 **½-½** L/N3161

### 1859-★MM-9 ●○ 13 iv 59
**Morphy,P.C.= Mongredien,A.**

London [Löwenthal]

1 e4 c5 2 d4 ♘c6? 3 d5 ♘b8 [3 ... ♘e5 4 f4 ♘g6 5 f5 ♘e5 6 ♗f4 d6 7 ♗xe5 dxe5 8 ♘f3±] 4 f4 d6 5 ♘f3 e6 6 c4 ♗e7 7 ♘c3 ♗d7 8 ♗d3 f5?! 9 dxe6 ♗xe6 10 exf5 ♗d7 11 ♘g5! ♘f6 12 0-0 ♘c6 13 ♘e6 ♗xe6 14 fxe6 ♘d4 15 f5 h5 16 ♗e3 ♘c6 17 ♘d5 ♘e5 18 ♗f4 ♘c6 19 ♗e2 h4 20 ♘xf6+ ♗xf6 21 ♕xd6 ♕xd6 22 ♗xd6 ♗xb2 23 ♖ab1 ♗d4+ 24 ♔h1 b6 25 ♗f3 ♖c8 26 ♖fd1 ♖h6 27 ♗f4 ♖h8 28 ♖d3 ♘a5 29 ♖c1 **½-½** L/N3161

### 1859-★MM-10
**Morphy,P.C.+ McConnell,J.**

New Orleans [Morphy]

⟨♘b1⟩ 1 e4 e5 2 ♘f3 ♘c6 3 ♗c4 ♗c5 4 b4 ♗xb4 5 c3 ♗c5 6 0-0 ♘f6 7 d4 exd4 8 cxd4 ♗b6 9 ♗a3 [9 e5; 9 d5] 9 ... d6 10 e5 ♘e4 11 ♖e1 d5 12 ♗b5 ♗g4 13 ♖c1 ♕d7 14 ♕a4 ♗xf3 15 ♖xc6 0-0-0 16 e6! [16 ♖xb6? ♕g4!∞] 16 ... fxe6 16 ♖xb6 **1-0** M730

### 1859-★MN-1 27 x 59
**Morphy,P.C.+ Bonaparte, Prince A.**

New York [Maróczy]

⟨♖a1⟩ 1 e4 e5 2 f4 ♗c5 3 ♘f3 ♘c6 4 b4 ♗b6 5 b5 ♘d4 6 ♘xd4 ♗xd4 7 c3 ♗b6 8 ♗c4 ♕e7 9 d4 d6 10 0-0 ♗e6 11 ♗xe6 ♕xe6 12 f5 ♕d7 13 ♕d3 c6 14 ♔h1 ♘f6 15 ♗g5 ♗d8 16 ♘d2 h6 17 ♗h4 ♘h7 18 ♗g3 ♗f6 19 bxc6 bxc6 20 ♘c4 ♕c7 21 h3 ♘f8? [21 ... 0-0] 22 dxe5 ♗xe5 23 ♗xe5 dxe5 24 f6 [24 ♘d6+ ♔e7! 25 f6+ gxf6 26 ♘f5+, 27 ♘g7+=] 24 ... ♖d8 [□ 24 ... ♘e6 25 fxg7 ♘xg7 26 ♘d6+ ♔f8 27 ♖xf7+ ♕xf7 28 ♘xf7 ♔xf7∓] 25 fxg7 ♖g8 26 gxf8♕+ ♖xf8 27 ♕e3 ♖h8 28 ♕c5 ♖f8 29 ♖f6 ♕e7 30 ♕xc6+ ♕d7 31 ♘d6+ ♔e7 32 ♘f5+ ♔e8 33 ♕c5 ♕d1+ 34 ♔h2 ♖d7 **1-0** L/N3203

### 1859-★MN-2 18 xi 59
**Morphy, P.C.+ Nicholson, C.**

Baltimore [Maróczy]

⟨♘b1⟩ 1 e4 e5 2 f4 exf4 3 ♘f3 g5 [□ 3 ... d5] 4 ♗c4 ♗g7 5 0-0 h6 6 c3 d6 7 ♕b3 ♕f6 [□ 7 ... ♕e7] 8 d4 ♘e7 9 ♗d2 0-0 10 ♗d3 ♘bc6 11 ♖ae1 ♗g4 12 h4 ♗xf3 13 ♖xf3 b6 14 hxg5 hxg5 15 ♖h3 ♘a5? 16 ♕d1 ♘g6 17 g3 [17 ♕h5 ♘h4] 17 ... fxg3 18 ♖xg3 ♗h6 19 e5 dxe5 20 ♗xg5 ♗xg5 21 ♕h5 ♘e7? [□ 21 ... exd4 22 ♖xg5 ♔g7 23 ♖f1 ♕e6 24 ♖xf7+ ♖xf7! 25 ♖xg6+ ♕xg6 26 ♕xg6+ (26 ♗xg6

♖h8 27 ♕g5 ♖g8!) 26 ... ♔f8 27 ♕h6+ ♖g7+]
22 ♕h7# **1-0** L/N3203

## 1859-★MP-1 iv 59
**Morphy, P.C.– Pindar, E.**
London [Maróczy]
⟨♘b1⟩ 1 e4 d5 2 exd5 ♕xd5 3 c4 ♕d8 4 d4 e5 5 ♗d3 [5 dxe5 ♗b4+ 6 ♗d2 ♕xd2+ 7 ♕xd2 ♗xd2+–+] 5 ... ♗b4+ 6 ♗d2 ♗xd2+ 7 ♕xd2 ♘c6 8 ♘e2 ♘f6 9 d5 ♘d4 10 ♘g3 0-0 11 0-0 ♖e8 12 ♖ae1 ♕d6 13 f4 c5 14 fxe5 ♖xe5 15 ♖xe5 ♕xe5 16 ♖e1 ♕d6 17 ♕g5 ♗d7 18 ♖f1 ♖e8 19 b4 b6 20 ♕h4 h6! 21 bxc5 bxc5 22 h3 ♖e3–+ 23 ♘e4 ♘xe4 24 ♕d8+ ♕f8 25 ♕xd7 ♖xd3 26 ♖e1 ♘f6 27 ♕c7 ♘f5 **0-1** L/N3203

## 1859-★MP-2 11 v 59
**Morphy, P.C.+ Perrin, F.**
New York [Maróczy]
⟨♘b1⟩ 1 e4 e5 2 ♘f3 ♘c6 3 d4 exd4 4 ♗c4 ♗c5 5 0-0 d6 6 b4 [6 c3 Morphy L/N6389] 6 ... ♗b6 7 b5 ♘e5 [◻ 7 ... ♘a5 Morphy L/N6389] 8 ♘xe5 dxe5 9 f4 d3+ 10 ♔h1 ♕d4

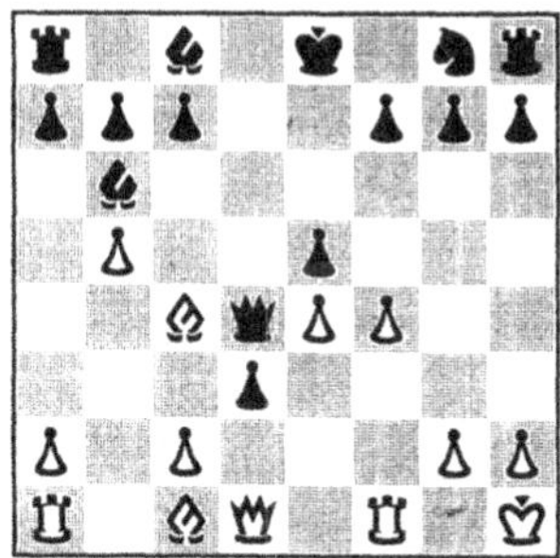

11 ♗xf7+ ♔xf7 12 fxe5+ ♔e8 13 ♕f3 ♘e7 14 ♕f7+ ♔d8 15 ♗g5 ♕xe5 16 ♖ad1 ♕xg5 17 ♖xd3+ ♗d7 18 ♕f8+ ♖xf8 19 ♖xf8# **1-0** L/N3203

**84** Perrin, F. L/N6396.BL

## 1859-★MP-3 11 v 59
**Morphy, P.C.+ Perrin, F.**
New York [Maróczy]
⟨♘b1⟩ 1 e4 e5 2 ♘f3 ♘c6 3 d4 exd4 [◻ 3 ... d6, 4 ... ♗e7] 4 ♗c4 d6 5 c3 d3 6 ♕b3 ♕f6 7 0-0 h6 8 ♗e3 g5 9 ♘d4 ♖h7 10 f4 g4 11 e5 ♕e7 12 e6 fxe6 13 ♘xe6 ♘f6 14 ♖ae1 ♗xe6 15 ♗xe6 ♖b8 16 ♗f5 ♔d8 17 ♗xa7 ♘xa7 18 ♖xe7 ♖xe7 19 ♗xd3 ♘c6 20 ♗f5 d5 21 ♗xg4 ♘xg4 22 ♕xd5+ ♔e8 [22 ... ♔c8; 22 ... ♖d7 23 ♕f5] 23 ♕h5+ ♖f7 24 ♖e1+ ♗e7 25 ♕xg4 ♖d8 26 ♕g8+ ♖f8 27 ♕g6+ ♔d7 28 ♕e6+ ♔e8 29 ♕xh6 ♖d6 30 ♕h5+ ♔d8 31 g3 ♔c8 32 b4 ♗f6 33 ♖e8+ ♖xe8 34 ♕xe8+ ♘d8 35 ♕e3 ♖c6 36 ♔g2 ♖xc3 37 ♕e4 ♖c6 38 g4 ♖e6 39 ♕f5 ♔b8 40 g5 ♗d4 41 ♕f8 ♖d6 42 f5 **1-0** L/N3203

## 1859-★MP-4 11 v 59
**Morphy, P.C.+ Perrin, F.**
New York [Maróczy]
⟨♘b1⟩ 1 e4 e5 2 ♘f3 ♘c6 3 d4 ♘xd4 4 ♘xe5 ♘c6 [4 ... ♘e6] 5 ♘xf7 ♔xf7 6 ♗c4+ d5 7 ♗xd5+ ♗e6 8 ♕h5+ g6 9 ♕f3+ ♘f6 10 ♗xe6+ ♔xe6 11 ♕b3+ ♔d7 12 ♗g5 ♗e7 [◻ 12 ... ♗d6] 13 0-0-0+ ♗d6 14 ♕xb7 ♕e7 [14 ... ♖b8 15 ♖xd6+ ♔xd6 16 ♖d1+, 17 ♖xd8±] 15 f4 h6? [◻ 15 ... ♖hb8 16 ♕a6 ♖b6 17 ♕f1! ♔c8 18 e5 ♘xe5] 16 e5 hxg5 17 ♖he1 [◻ 17 ♖xd6+] 17 ... ♖hb8 18 ♕a6 [18 exd6 ♖xb7 19 dxe7+ ♔e8 20 fxg5 ♘g8] 18 ... ♖b6 19 ♕c4 ♖b4 20 ♕a6 ♖d4 21 exd6 ♕xd6 22 ♕b5 ♕xf4+ 23 ♔b1 ♖e8 [◻ 23 ... ♖b8!–+] 24 ♖f1 ♘d5 25 a3 ♘c3+ [◻ 25 ... ♘e3!] 26 bxc3 ♖b8 27 ♖xd4+ ♕xd4 28 ♕xb8 ♕xc3 29 ♖d1+ ♘d4 30 ♕b2 **1-0** L/N3203

## 1859-★MP-5 21 x 59
**Morphy, P.C.+ Perrin, A.**
New York
⟨♖a1⟩ 1 e4 e5 2 f4 ♗c5 3 ♘f3 d6 4 ♗c4 ♘h6 5 f5 ♘c6 6 b4 ♘xb4 7 c3 b5 8 ♗xb5+ c6 9 cxb4 ♗f2+ 10 ♔xf2 ♕b6+ 11 d4 cxb5 12 ♗xh6 gxh6 13 ♘c3 ♗b7 14 ♕d3 a6 15 ♖d1 0-0 16 ♔f1 f6 17 ♕d2 ♔g7 18 d5 ♖ac8 19 ♘e2 ♖c4 20 ♘g3 ♖fc8 21 ♘h5+ ♔h8 22 ♕xh6 ♕c7 23 ♕xf6+ ♔g8 24 ♘g5 ♗xd5 25 exd5 ♖f4+ 26 ♘xf4 exf4 27 ♕e6+ ♔f8 28 ♘xh7+ ♔g7 29 ♕g6+ ♔h8 30 ♘f6 ♕c4+ 31 ♔g1 ♕c7 **1-0** L/N3203

## 1859-★MR-1 17 v 59
**Morphy, P.C.+ Richardson, H.**
New York [Morphy]
⟨♘b1⟩ 1 e4 e5 2 ♘f3 ♘c6 3 ♗c4 ♗c5 4 b4 ♗xb4 5 c3 ♗a5 6 0-0 d6 7 d4 exd4 [7 ... ♗xc3 8 ♕b3±] 8 cxd4 ♘f6? [◻ 8 ... ♗b6] 9 ♕b3 0-0 10 e5 dxe5 11 dxe5 ♘h5 12 ♗a3 ♘e7 13 ♖ad1 ♕e8 14 ♘g5 ♗f5 [14 ... h6 15 ♗xf7+ ♖xf7 16 ♖d8 ♕xd8 17 ♕xf7+ ♔h8 18 ♗xe7 ♕g8 19 ♕xh5+–] 15 e6 fxe6 16 ♗xe6+ ♗xe6 17 ♕xe6+ ♔h8 18 ♗xe7 ♖f6 [18 ... ♖f4 19 g3±] 19 ♗xf6 ♕xe6 20 ♘xe6 ♘xf6 21 ♖d8+ ♖xd8 22 ♘xd8 b5 23 ♖b1 a6 24 a4 ♗b6 [24 ... bxa4 25 ♖b8+–] 25 axb5 axb5 26 ♖xb5 h6 27 g3 ♘e4 28 ♔g2 ♔g8 [28 ... ♗xf2 (28 ... ♘xf2 29 ♖xb6+–) 29 ♖e5+–] 29 f3 ♘f6 30 ♘c6 ♔f7 31 ♖e5 ♘g8 32 f4 g6 33 ♔f3 ♔f6 34 g4 ♗g1 35 h4 ♗b6 36 g5+ hxg5 37 hxg5+ ♔f7 38 f5 gxf5 39 ♖xf5+ ♔g6 40 ♔g4 ♗e3 41 ♘e5+ ♔g7 42 ♖f7+ ♔h8 43 ♘g6# **1-0** L/N6389

## 1859-★MR-2
**Morphy, P.C.+ Richardson, H.**
New York [Löwenthal]
⟨♘b1⟩ 1 e4 c5 2 f4 d6 3 ♘f3 ♘c6 4 c3 e6 5 d4 cxd4 6 cxd4 ♗e7 7 ♗d3 ♘f6 8 0-0 0-0 9 e5 dxe5 10 fxe5 ♘d5 11 ♗d2 f6 12 ♕e2 fxe5 13 ♘xe5 ♘xe5 [13 ... ♘xd4 14 ♗xh7+] 14 dxe5 ♕b6+ 15 ♔h1 ♖xf1+ 16 ♖xf1 g6 [16 ... ♕d4 17 ♕h5+–] 17 ♗xg6

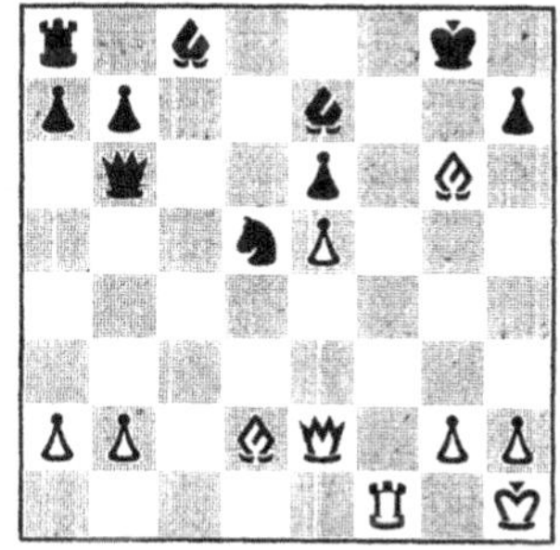

17 ... hxg6 18 ♕g4 ♔g7 19 ♕h3 g5 20 ♕h5 ♘f4 21 ♗xf4 gxf4 22 ♖xf4 ♕d8 23 ♖f7+ ♔g8 24 ♕h7# **1-0** L/N3161

## 1859-★MR-3 ⬠ 26 iv 59
**Rivière, J.A.de– Morphy, P.C.**
London [Löwenthal]
1 e4 e5 2 ♘f3 ♘c6 3 ♗c4 ♘f6 4 ♘g5 d5 5 exd5 ♘a5 6 d3 h6 7 ♘f3 e4 8 ♕e2 ♘xc4 9 dxc4 ♗c5 10 h3 0-0 11 ♘h2 ♘h7 12 ♘c3 f5 13 ♗e3 ♗b4 14 ♕d2 [14 ♗d4 c5, 14 ... ♖e8∓] 14 ... ♗d7 15 g3 ♕e7 16 a3 ♗d6 17 ♘e2 b5 18 cxb5 ♗xb5 19 ♘d4 ♗c4 20 ♘e6 ♖fe8 21 ♕d4 ♗a6 [21 ... ♗xd5 22 ♘xg7±] 22 c4 c5 23 ♕c3 ♗c8 24 ♘f4 ♖b8 25 ♖b1 g5 26 ♘e2 ♘f8 27 h4 ♘g6 28 hxg5 hxg5 29 ♕c1 ♘e5 30 ♗xg5! ♘d3+ 31 ♔f1 ♕g7

[31 ... ♘xc1 32 ♗xe7 ♘xe2 33 ♗xd6] 32 ♕d2 ♘xb2 33 ♕c2 ♗a6 34 ♗c1 ♘xc4 35 ♕a4 ♘d2+! 36 ♔g2 [36 ♗xd2 ♖xb1+ 37 ♔g2 ♗b5] 36 ... ♘xb1 37 ♕xa6 ♖b6 38 ♕a4 ♖eb8 39 ♘f1 ♗e5 40 ♘e3 f4 41 ♘xf4 ♗xf4 42 ♘f5 ♕f6 43 ♗xf4 ♕xf5 44 ♗xb8 ♖xb8 45 ♕xa7 ♖f8 46 ♕xc5 ♕f3+ 47 ♔g1 ♘c3 48 ♖h4 ♘e2+ 49 ♔h2 ♕xf2+ 50 ♕xf2 ♖xf2+ 51 ♔h3 ♘g1+ 52 ♔g4 e3 53 ♔h5 e2 54 ♖e4 ♖f1 **0-1**
L/N3161

**1859-★MR-4**
**Morphy,P.C.+ Rivière,J.A.de**
Paris [Löwenthal]

1 e4 e5 2 ♘f3 ♘c6 3 ♗c4 ♗c5 4 b4 ♗xb4 5 c3 ♗c5 6 0-0 d6 7 d4 exd4 8 cxd4 ♗b6 9 d5 ♘ce7 10 e5 dxe5 11 ♘xe5 ♘f6 12 ♗b5+ c6 13 dxc6 0-0 14 ♗a3 ♗xf2+! 15 ♔h1 ♕b6 16 ♗xe7 ♕xb5 17 ♘f3 ♘e4 18 ♘bd2 ♗c5 19 ♗xf8 ♘xd2 20 ♕xd2 ♗xf8 21 ♕d8 bxc6 22 ♘g5 [◻ 22 ♖ab1] 22 ... ♗h3 23 ♕d2 ♗f5 24 a4 ♕d3 25 ♕a2 ♗g6 26 ♘xf7 ♕d5 27 ♘e5 ♗e4 28 ♖fe1 ♕xa2 29 ♖xa2 **1-0**
L/N3161

**1859-★MS-1** 14 v 59
**Morphy, P.C.+ Stone, J.W.**
New York [Maróczy]

⟨♘b1⟩ 1 e4 e5 2 ♘f3 ♘c6 3 ♗c4 ♗c5 4 b4 ♗xb4 5 c3 ♗a5 6 0-0 ♕f6 [◻ 6 ... d6; 6 ... ♘f6] 7 ♕b3 ♘ge7 8 d4 exd4 9 cxd4 0-0 10 e5 ♕g6 11 d5 ♘b4 12 ♗d2 ♕c2 13 ♕xc2 ♘xc2 14 ♗xa5 ♘xa1 15 ♖xa1 b6 16 ♗b4 ♖e8 17 ♗xe7 ♖xe7 18 d6 cxd6 [◻ 18 ... ♖e8 19 ♘g5 ♖f8 20 dxc7 ♗b7 21 ♖d1 ♗c6 22 ♗a6 h6∓] 19 exd6 ♖e8 20 ♘g5 ♖f8 21 ♖e1 ♗b7 22 ♘xf7 ♖xf7 23 ♖e7 ♖af8 24 ♖xd7 ♗c8 25 ♖c7 ♗f5 [25 ... ♗a6 26 ♗xa6 ♖xf2 27 d7 ♖d2 28 ♗c4+, 29 h3+-] 26 d7 **1-0**
L/N3203

**1859-★MS-2** 14 v 59
**Morphy, P.C.+ Stone, J.W.**
New York [Maróczy]

⟨♘b1⟩ 1 e4 e5 2 ♘f3 ♘c6 3 ♗c4 ♗c5 4 b4 ♗xb4 5 c3 ♗c5 6 0-0 ♗b6 7 d4 exd4 8 cxd4 ♕f6? [◻ 8 ... d6 Morphy L/N6389] 9 e5 ♕g6 10 d5 ♘a5 11 ♗d3 ♕h5 12 ♗a3 ♘e7 13 d6 ♘g6 14 dxc7 ♘c6 15 ♗d6 ♘ge7 16 ♖e1 0-0 17 ♖e4

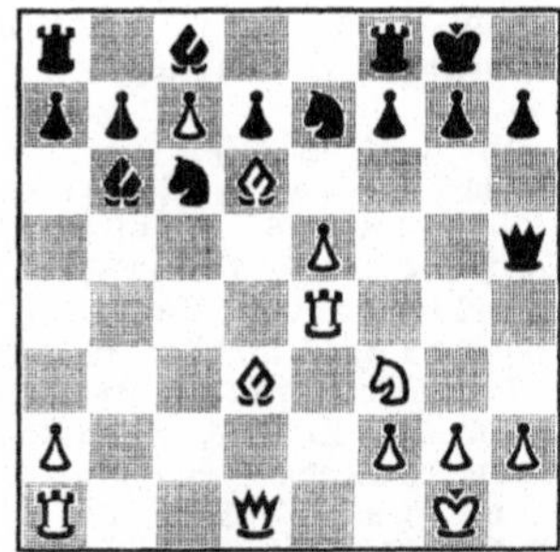

17 ... ♘g6 18 h4 ♖e8 19 g4 ♕h6 20 g5 ♕h5 21 ♗e2 ♘ge7 22 ♖f4 [△ 23 ♘d4 ♕g6 24 ♗h5+-] 22 ... ♕g6 23 ♗c4 [23 ♗d3 ♕h5] 23 ... ♘f5 [23 ... ♖f8 24 h5 ♕xh5 25 ♖h4 ♕g6 26 ♗d3 ♘f5 27 ♖f4+-] 24 ♗d3 ♘xe5 25 ♗xf5 ♘xf3+ 26 ♖xf3 ♕h5 27 ♕d5 ♕xh4 28 ♗xh7+ ♔xh7 29 ♕f5+ ♔h8 30 ♖h3 **1-0**
L/N3203

**1859-★MS-3 ●○** 11 xi 59
**Morphy, P.C.+ Smyth, S.**
Philadelphia [Maróczy]

1 e4 e6 2 d4 d5 3 exd5 exd5 4 ♘f3 ♗e6 5 ♗d3 ♘f6 6 0-0 h6 7 ♘e5 ♗d6 8 f4 ♘c6 [◻ 8 ... c5!] 9 c3 ♕e7 10 ♖e1 ♗xe5 11 fxe5 ♘d7 12 b4 0-0 13 b5 ♘a5 14 ♗a3 ♕g5 15 ♗xf8 ♖xf8 16 ♘d2 ♗g4 17 ♘df3 ♕e7 18 h3 ♗e6 19 ♕a4 b6 20 ♖ad1 g5 21 ♗b1 ♔g7 22 ♕c2 ♖h8 23 ♘d2 h5 24 ♘f1 h4 25 ♘e3 ♖h6 26 ♘f5+ ♗xf5 27 ♕xf5 ♘f8 28 ♖f1 ♘c4 29 ♖f3 ♘e6 30 ♕g4 ♕e8 31 ♖df1 ♕xb5 32 ♖xf7+ ♔h8 33 ♕xe6 ♖xe6 **1-0**
L/N3203

**1859-★MS-4 ●○** 13 iv 59
**Morphy, P.C.= Slous, F.L.**
London [Löwenthal]

1 e4 e5 2 ♘f3 d6 3 d4 exd4 4 ♘xd4 ♗e7 5 ♘c3 ♘f6 6 ♗d3 a6 7 a4 c5 8 ♘de2 ♘c6 9 f4 h5 10 0-0 ♗e6 11 b3 g6 12 f5 gxf5 13 exf5 ♗d7 14 ♘f4 ♘e5! 15 ♘cd5 ♘xd5 16 ♘xd5 ♗c6 17 ♗e4 ♗f6! 18 ♗b2 ♗xd5 19 ♗xd5 ♕c7 20 ♗xe5 ♗xe5 21 ♖b1 0-0-0 22 b4 cxb4 23 ♖b3 ♕c5+ 24 ♔h1 ♗c3 25 ♖f3 ♖d7 26 ♖f1 ♖e8 27 ♖b1 ♖de7 28 ♕d3 ♖e5 29 ♗f3 ♖e3 30 ♕d5 ♖8e7 **½-½**
L/N3161

**1859-★MT-1**
**Morphy, P.C.+ Thompson, J.**
New York [Maróczy]

⟨♘b1⟩ 1 e4 e5 2 ♘f3 ♘c6 3 ♗c4 d6 [◻ 3 ... ♗e7] 4 c3 ♘f6 5 ♕b3 ♕e7 6 0-0 a6 7 d4 b6 [△ 8 ... ♘a5 Morphy L/N6389] 8 ♗d3 h6 9 d5 ♘d8 10 ♗d2 ♘b7 11 ♕a3 ♘c5 12 ♗c2 ♘fxe4?? 13 ♗xe4 ♘xe4 14 ♕a4+ b5 15 ♕xe4 f5 16 ♕c2 g5 17 ♖fe1 ♕f7 18 c4 ♗e7 19 cxb5 ♕xd5 20 ♖ad1 ♕xb5 21 a4 ♕b7 22 ♘xe5 dxe5 23 ♖xe5 ♖h7 24 ♕c4 ♔f8 25 ♖xe7 ♖xe7 26 ♗b4 ♗e6 27 ♕c3 c5 [◻ 28 ... ♔f7 28 ♗xe7+ ♔xe7 29 ♕g7+ ♔e8 30 ♕g6+ (30 ♖e1? ♕d5) 30 ... ♔e7 31 ♕g7+=] 28 ♕f6+ ♗f7 29 ♕xh6+ ♔g8 30 ♕xg5+ ♔h7 31 ♖d3 ♗g6 32 ♖h3+ ♔g7 33 ♗c3+ ♔f7 34 ♕f6+ ♔e8 35 ♕xg6+ ♖f7 36 ♕e6+ ♕e7 37 ♖h8+ ♖f8 38 ♕c6+ **1-0**
L/N3203

**1859-★MT-2**
**Morphy, P.C.− Thompson, J.**
New York [Morphy]

⟨♘b1⟩ 1 e4 e5 2 ♘f3 ♘c6 3 ♗c4 ♗c5 4 b4 ♗xb4 5 c3 ♗a5 6 0-0 ♘f6 7 ♘g5 0-0 8 f4 exf4 9 d4 [9 ♕b3 ♘e5∓] 9 ... ♗xc3 10 ♘xf7 ♖xf7 11 ♗xf7+ ♔f8? [◻ 11 ... ♔h8] 12 ♗b3 ♗xd4+ 13 ♔h1 ♗xa1 14 ♗xf4! [14 ♗a3+∞] 14 ... ♗e5 15 ♗xe5 ♘xe5 16 ♕d5

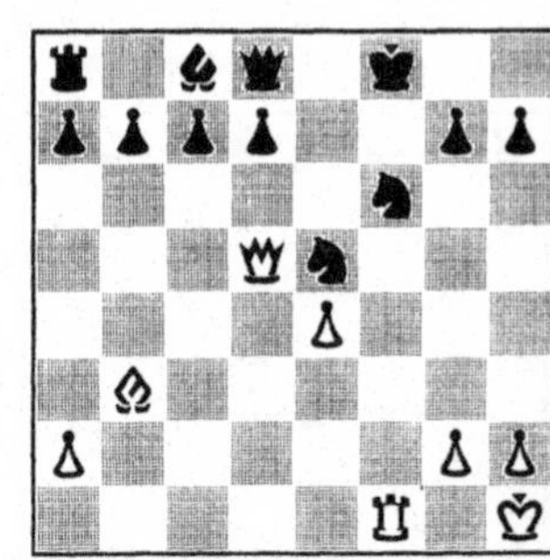

16 ... c6? [◻ 16 ... ♕e8! 17 ♕xe5+ ♕e7 18 ♕xc7 (18 ♕xe7+ ♔xe7 19 e5 d6 20 exf6+ gxf6-+) 18 ... d6-+] 17 ♕g8+ ♔e7 18 ♕xg7+ ♔d6 19 ♖xf6+ ♔c5 [19 ... ♔c7 20 ♖f8+-] 20 ♖f8 ♕c7 21 ♖f5 ♔d4 22 ♕g3 ♕d6 23 ♕f2+ ♔c3 24 ♕e1+ ♕d2 25 ♕xd2+? [26 ♕a1+=] 25 ... ♔xd2 26 ♖xe5 b5 27 g4 d6 28 ♖e8 ♗b7 29 ♖e7 ♖b8 30 ♖d7 c5 31 ♖xd6+ ♔e3 32 ♗d5 c4 **0-1**
L/N6389

**1859-★MT-3**
**Morphy, P.C.+ Thompson, J.**
New York [Morphy]

⟨♘b1⟩ 1 e4 e5 2 ♘f3 d6 3 d4 ♘c6 4 c3 ♘f6 5 ♗d3 ♗g4 6 0-0 exd4 7 cxd4 ♗xf3 8 gxf3 ♘xd4 9 ♕a4+ ♘c6 10 ♗g5 ♕d7 11 ♖fd1 a6 12 e5 ♘h5 13 ♗b5 [△ 14 ♖ac1] 13 ... h6 [13 ... ♗e7 14 ♗xe7 ♕xe7 (14 ... ♔xe7 15 ♕h4++-) 15 ♗xc6++-] 14 ♖ac1 [△ 15 ♖xc6+-] 14 ... ♖c8 15 ♕e4

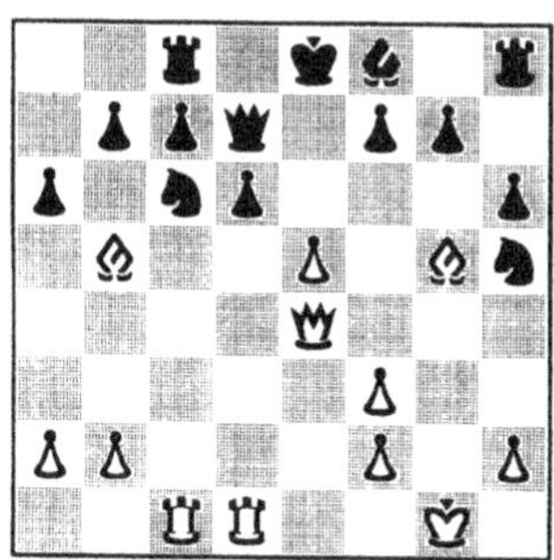

15 ... f5? [15 ... axb5 (15 ... d5 16 ♖xd5 ♕e6 17 ♖xc6 bxc6 18 ♗xc6+ ♕xc6 19 ♖d8+ ♖xd8 20 ♕xc6+ ♖d7 21 ♕a8+ ♖d8 22 ♕xd8#; 15 ... ♗e7 16 ♗xc6 bxc6 17 ♗xe7 ♕xe7 18 ♕xc6+ ♕d7 19 exd6 ♕xc6 20 ♖xc6 ♔d7 21 ♖xa6±; 15 ... hxg5 16 exd6+ ♗e7 17 dxe7 ♕e6 18 ♗xc6+ bxc6 19 ♕d3±; 17 ... ♕xe7 18 ♕g4 0-0 19 ♕xh5±) 16 exd6+ ♗e7 (16 ... ♕e6 17 d7#) 17 dxe7 ♕e6 (17 ... f5 18 ♕e3 f4 19 ♕e4+−) 18 ♕xc6+ ♕xc6 19 ♖d8+ ♖xd8 20 exd8♕#] 16 exf6+ ♔f7 17 ♗c4+ d5 18 ♖xd5 ♕e6 19 ♖d7+ **1-0** L/N6389

## 1859-★MT-4
**Morphy, P.C.+Thompson, J.**
New York [Maróczy]

⟨♘b1⟩ 1 e4 e5 2 ♘f3 ♘c6 3 ♗c4 ♗c5 4 b4 ♗b6 5 a4 a6 6 d4 exd4 7 c3 d6 8 ♕b3 ♕e7 9 0-0 ♗e6 10 a5 ♗a7 11 b5 ♗xc4 12 ♕xc4 ♘e5? [□ 12 ... axb5 13 ♕xb5 ♕d7→] 13 ♘xe5 dxe5 14 bxa6 c6 15 ♖b1 ♖b8 16 axb7 ♖xb7 17 ♕xc6+ ♖d7 18 ♖b7 ♔d8 19 ♗a3 ♕e6 20 ♖xd7+ ♕xd7 21 ♕a8+ ♕c8 22 ♕xa7 ♕c7 23 ♕a8+ ♔d7 24 ♖b1 **1-0** L/N3203

## 1859-★MT-5 
14 xi 59
**Morphy, P.C.=Thomas, W.G.**
Philadelphia [Maróczy]

⟨♘b1⟩ 1 e4 e5 2 ♘f3 d6 3 d4 f5 4 ♗c4 fxe4 [□ 4 ... ♘c6] 5 ♘xe5 dxe5 6 ♕h5+ g6 7 ♕xe5+ ♕e7 8 ♗b5+ ♗d7 9 ♕xh8 [9 ♗xd7+ ♘xd7 10 ♕xh8 ♘f6∓] 9 ... ♗xb5 10 ♕xg8 ♕b4+ 11 ♗d2 ♕c4 12 ♕xc4 ♗xc4 13 b3 ♗a6 14 c4 ♘c6 15 d5 ♘d4 16 0-0-0 ♗a3+ 17 ♔b1 c6? 18 ♗c1! ♗xc1 [18 ... ♗c5 19 b4] 19 ♖xd4 ♗g5 20 ♖xe4+ ♔d7 21 dxc6+ bxc6 22 ♖d1+ ♔c7 23 f4 ♗f6 24 ♖e6 ♖d8 25 ♔c2 ♖xd1 26 ♔xd1 ♗d8 27 ♖e8 ♗c8 28 ♖h8 h5 29 ♖h7+ ♔b6 30 ♔d2 ♗f5 31 b4 a5 32 a3 axb4 33 axb4 ♗f6 34 h3 ♗b2 35 ♔e3 ♗c3 36 c5+ ♔b5 37 ♖b7+ ♔c4 38 ♖b6 ♗xb4 39 ♖xc6 ♗xc5+ 40 ♔f3 ♔d4 41 ♖a6 ♗e4+ 42 ♔g3 ♔e3 43 ♖e6 ♗b4 44 ♔h4 ♔xf4 45 g3+ ♔f5 46 ♖xe4 ♔xe4 47 ♔g5 ♔f3 48 ♔xg6 [48 g4? h4 49 ♔xh4 (49 ♔xg6 ♔f4, ♔g3−+) 49 ... ♔f4 50 g5 ♗e1#] 48 ... ♔xg3 49 ♔xh5 ♔xh3 **½-½** L/N3203

## 1859-★MT-6
14 xi 59
**Morphy,P.C.+ Thomas,W.G.**
Philadelphia [Maróczy]

⟨♘b1⟩ 1 e4 e5 2 f4 d5 3 exd5 ♕xd5 4 ♘f3 e4 5 ♘e5 ♗e6 6 ♗c4 ♕d6 7 ♕e2 ♘c6 8 ♗b5 ♘f6 9 b3 ♗d7 10 ♗b2 ♗e7 11 0-0-0 a6 12 ♗c4 ♗e6 13 d4 exd3 14 ♖xd3 ♗xc4 15 bxc4 ♕e6 16 f5 ♕xf5 17 ♘xc6 bxc6 18 ♖e3 ♕g5 19 h4 ♕h6 20 ♔b1 0-0 21 ♖xe7 ♖ab8 22 ♔a1 ♕f4 23 ♕f1 ♕d6 24 ♕e3 ♖fd8 25 ♗e5 ♕d7 26 ♗xf6 gxf6 27 ♖g3+ ♔h8 28 ♖d3 ♕e8 29 ♖xd8 ♕xd8 30 ♕f3 ♔g7 31 ♕g4+ ♔h8 32 ♕f4 ♔g7 33 h5 f5 [33 ... h6, c5, ♖b6] 34 h6+ ♔h8 35 c3 ♕f6 36 ♕d4 ♕xd4 37 cxd4 ♖b4 38 ♖xf5 ♖xc4 39 ♖xf7 ♔g8 40 ♖g7+ ♔f8 41 ♖xh7 ♖xd4 42 ♖xc7 ♖d1+ 43 ♔b2 ♖d2+ 44 ♔b3 ♖xg2 45 a4 a5 [□ 45 ... ♔g8!=] 46 h7 ♖h2 47 ♔c4 ♖h5 48 ♖a7 ♖h4+ 49 ♔c5 ♖h5+ 50 ♔xc6 ♖h6+ 51 ♔b5 ♖h5+ 52 ♔b6 ♖h6+ 53 ♔xa5 **1-0** L/N3203

## 1859-★MT-7 ●○⬠
11 xi 59
**Morphy,P.C.+ Thomas,W.G.**
Philadelphia [Maróczy]

1 e4 e5 2 ♘f3 ♘c6 3 ♗c4 d6 4 c3 ♗e7 5 ♕b3 ♘h6 6 d4 ♘a5 7 ♕a4+ c6 8 ♗xh6 [□ 8 ♗e2] 8 ... b5 9 ♕c2 ♘xc4 10 ♗c1 [10 ♗xg7 ♖g8] 10 ... exd4? [□ 10 ... ♕c7] 11 cxd4 ♕c7 12 b3 ♘b6 13 0-0 h6 14 ♘c3 a6 15 ♗f4 g5 16 ♗e3 g4 17 ♘d2 h5 18 ♘d5 ♘xd5 19 exd5 c5 20 dxc5 h4 21 ♖fe1 ♔f8 22 ♗d4 ♖h5 23 ♕e4 g3 [23 ... ♗f5] 24 fxg3 hxg3 25 h3 f5 26 ♕f3 ♖h4 27 ♘e4 dxc5 28 d6! ♗xd6 29 ♘xd6 ♕xd6 30 ♗e5 ♕d7 31 ♕xg3 ♖e4 32 ♖xe4 fxe4 33 ♖f1+ **1-0** L/N3203

## 1859-★MT-8 ●○⬠
11 xi 59
**Morphy,P.C.+Tilghman, B.C.**
[Maróczy]

1 e4 e5 2 f4 exf4 3 ♘f3 g5 4 ♗c4 d6 [□ 4 ... g4; 4 ... ♗g7] 5 h4 g4 6 ♘g5 ♘h6 7 d4 f6 8 ♗xf4 ♘c6 [8 ... fxg5 9 ♗xg5 ♗e7 10 ♕d2] 9 0-0 ♕e7 10 ♘c3 ♕g7 11 ♘e6 ♗xe6 12 ♗xe6 ♔e7

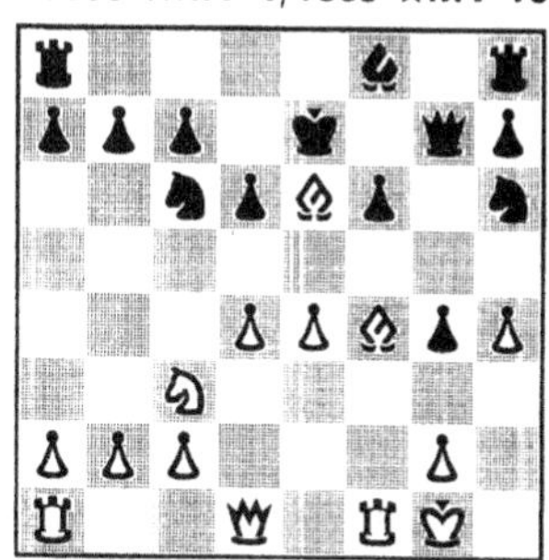

13 ♘d5+ ♔xe6 14 ♗xh6 ♕xh6 15 ♕xg4+ ♔f7 16 ♖xf6+ ♕xf6 17 ♘xf6 ♔xf6 18 ♖f1+ ♔e7 19 ♕g5+ ♔d7 20 ♕f5+ ♔e8 21 ♕f7+ ♔d8 22 ♕f6+ ♘e7 23 ♕xh8 ♘g6 24 ♖xf8+ **1-0** L/N3203

## 1859-★MT-9
**Morphy, P.C.− Thompson, J.**
New York [Löwenthal]

⟨♘b1⟩ 1 e4 c5 2 f4 e6 3 ♘f3 ♘c6 4 c3 d5 5 e5 d4! 6 ♗b5 ♗d7 7 ♕e2 ♕b6 8 ♗d3 f6 9 b3 ♗e7 10 f5 ♘xe5 11 ♘xe5 fxe5 12 ♕h5+ ♔d8 13 cxd4 ♘f6 14 ♕e2 exd4 15 0-0 e5! 16 ♕xe5 ♗d6 17 ♕e1 ♖e8 18 ♕h4 ♗b5 19 ♕h3 ♗xd3 20 ♕xd3 ♔d7 21 b4 c4 22 ♕xc4 d3+ 23 ♔h1 ♘e4 24 g3 ♖ac8 25 ♕d5 ♕c6 26 ♕xc6+ ♖xc6 27 ♗b2 ♗e5 28 ♗xe5 ♖xe5 29 ♖ae1 ♘f2+ 30 ♔g2 ♖xe1 31 ♖xe1 ♘g4 32 h3 ♘f6 33 ♖e3 ♖d6 34 ♔f3 ♘d5! 35 ♖e4 ♘c3 36 ♖h4 ♘b1 37 ♔e3 ♘a3 38 ♖xh7 ♘c4+ 39 ♔f2 ♘xd2 40 ♖xg7+ ♔c6 41 ♖g6 ♘e4+ 42 ♔e3 ♘f6 43 ♔d2 ♔b5 44 g4 ♔c4 45 g5 ♘e4+ 46 ♔e3 ♖d7 **0-1** L/N3161

## 1859-★MT-10
**Morphy, P.C.+ Thompson, J.**
New York [Löwenthal]

⟨♘b1⟩ 1 f4 d5 2 e3 ♘f6 3 ♘f3 ♗g4 4 h3 ♗xf3 5 ♕xf3 c5 6 b3 e6 7 ♗b2 ♘e4 8 0-0-0 ♘c6 9 d3 ♘d6 10 g4 d4! 11 ♗g2 ♕c7 12 ♖he1 ♖c8 13 c4 b5 14 ♔b1 a5 15 exd4 cxd4 16 cxb5 ♘xb5 17 ♖c1 ♘ba7 18 ♖c4 ♕d6 19 ♖ec1 ♔d7 20 ♗xd4

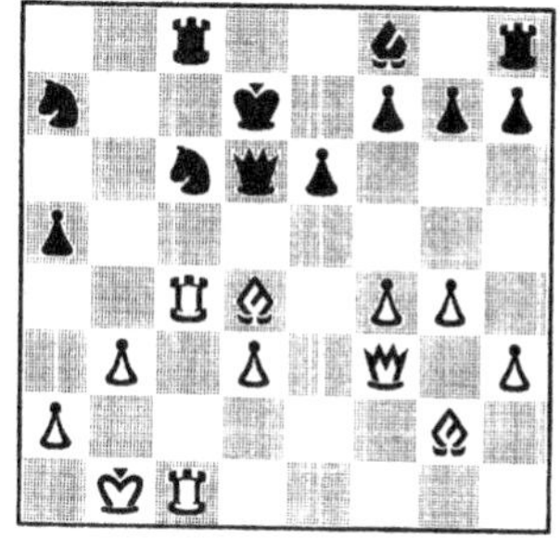

20 ... ♕b8 [20 ... ♘xd4? 21 ♕b7++-] 21 ♖xc6 ♘xc6 22 ♖xc6 ♗a3 23 f5 ♖he8 24 fxe6+ fxe6 25 ♗xg7 ♕h2 26 ♕f2! ♕b8 [26 ... ♖xc6 27 ♗xc6+-] 27 ♕d4+ ♗d6 [27 ... ♔e7 28 ♗e5+-] 28 ♖b6 ♕a7 29 ♖b7+ [29 ♕xd6#] 29 ... ♕xb7 30 ♗xb7 ♖c7 31 ♗e5 **1-0** L/N3161

**1859-★MT-11**
**Morphy, P.C.+Thompson, J.**
New York [Löwenthal]
⟨♘b1⟩ 1 f4 d5 2 e3 ♘f6 3 ♘f3 ♗g4 4 ♗e2 c5 5 0-0 ♘c6 6 b3 e6 7 ♗b2 ♗e7 8 h3 ♗xf3 9 ♗xf3 d4 10 ♕e1 ♕b6 11 ♖b1 ♘b4 12 ♕e2 ♖d8 13 a3 ♘bd5 [13 ... ♘xc2 14 ♕d3+-; 13 ... d3 14 cxd3 ♘xd3 15 ♗c3±] 14 ♔h1 dxe3 15 dxe3 h5 16 c4 ♘c7 17 b4 cxb4 18 axb4 ♗xb4 19 ♗d4 ♖xd4 20 exd4 a5 21 c5 ♕a7 22 ♕e5 ♘cd5 23 ♗xd5 ♘xd5 24 ♕xg7 ♖f8 25 f5 ♕a6 26 ♕e5 f6 27 ♕g3 ♕c6 28 fxe6 ♘e7 29 ♕b8+ ♕c8 30 ♕d6 ♕c6? ...? **1-0** L/N3161

**1859-★MT-12**
**Morphy, P.C.+Thompson ,J.**
New York [Löwenthal]
⟨♘b1⟩ 1 e4 e5 2 ♘f3 ♘c6 3 ♗c4 ♗c5 4 b4 ♗xb4 5 c3 ♗a5 6 0-0 ♗b6 [□ 6 ... ♘f6] 7 d4 d6 8 dxe5 ♘xe5 [□ 8 ... ♗e6] 9 ♘xe5 dxe5 10 ♗xf7+ ♔e7 11 ♕b3 ♘f6 12 ♗a3+ c5 13 ♖ad1 ♕c7 14 f4 ♖f8 15 ♗c4 ♖d8 16 ♖de1 ♗d7 17 ♗c1 ♖f8 18 fxe5 ♕xe5 19 ♗f4 ♕h5 20 ♖d1 ♔d8 [20 ... ♘e8 21 ♖d5 ♕ 22 ♗g5+ ♘f6 23 e5+-] 21 e5 ♘e8 22 ♕a4 ♕g4 23 e6 ♘f6 **1-0** L/N3161

**1859-★MT-13**
**Morphy, P.C.+Thompson, J.**
New York [Löwenthal]
⟨♘b1⟩ 1 e4 e5 2 ♘f3 ♘c6 [□ 2 ... d5] 3 ♗c4 ♗c5 4 b4 ♗xb4 5 c3 ♗a5 6 0-0 ♘f6 7 ♘g5 0-0 8 f4 h6 [□ 8 ... d6; 8 ... d5] 9 ♘xf7 ♖xf7 10 ♗xf7+ ♔xf7 11 fxe5 ♗b6+ 12 d4 ♘xe5 13 ♕h5+ ♘g6? [□ 13 ... ♔g8 14 ♕xe5 d6] 14 e5 c5 15 exf6 gxf6 16 ♗xh6 d5 17 ♗g5 **1-0** L/N3161

**1859-★MT-14**
**Morphy, P.C.-Thompson, J.**
New York [Löwenthal]
⟨♘b1⟩ 1 e4 e5 2 ♘f3 ♘c6 3 ♗c4 ♗c5 4 b4 ♗xb4 5 c3 ♗a5 6 ♕c2 ♘f6 7 0-0 d6 8 d4 ♗b6 [□ 8 ... 0-0; 8 ... exd4] 9 dxe5 ♘xe5 10 ♘xe5 dxe5 11 ♗a3 c5 12 f4 0-0 13 f5 ♕c7 14 h3 ♗d7 15 ♖ae1 ♗c6 16 g4 ♖ad8 17 g5 ♘h5 18 g6 ♘f4 19 gxf7+ ♔h8 20 ♗c1 ♘d3 21 ♗g5 [21 ♗xd3 c4+] 21 ... ♘xe1 22 ♖xe1 ♖d6 23 ♕e2 ♖xf7 24 ♕h5 ♖ff6 25 ♖f1 ♕d7 26 ♖e1 ♗d8 27 ♗xf6 ♗xf6 28 ♗f7 ♖d3 29 ♗c4 ♖g3+ 30 ♔h2 ♕d2+ **0-1** L/N3161

**1859-★MT-15**
**Morphy, P.C.-Thompson, J.**
New York [Maróczy]
⟨♘b1⟩ 1 e4 e5 2 ♘f3 ♘c6 3 ♗c4 ♗c5 4 b4 ♗xb4 5 c3 ♗a5 6 ♕b3 ♕f6 7 d4 ♗b6 [□ 7 ♘xd4] 8 dxe5 ♘xe5 9 ♘xe5 ♕xe5 10 ♗xf7+ ♔f8 11 0-0 [□ 11 ♗xg8, 12 0-0, ♗e3∞] 11 ... ♘f6 12 ♗a3+ d6 13 ♖ae1 ♘g4 14 g3 ♕f6 15 ♗c4 ♘e5 16 ♗e2 ♘f3+

17 ♔h1 [□ 18 ♗xf3 ♕xf3 18 ♖e3! ♕f7 (18 ... ♕h5 19 e5) 19 c4 ♔g8 20 ♖f3] 17 ... ♗h3 18 ♖d1 ♗xf1 19 ♗xf1 ♕h6 20 h3 ♘d2 21 ♕b5 ♘xf1 22 ♕xf1 ♔e7 23 e5 ♔d7 24 ♗xd6 ♖ae8 25 ♔g2 ♔c8 26 c4 cxd6 27 exd6 ♖ef8 28 c5 ♗xc5 29 ♕c4 ♕g5 **0-1** L/N3203

**1859-★MT-16**
**Morphy, P.C.+Thompson, J.**
New York [Maróczy]
⟨♘b1⟩ 1 f4 f5 2 ♘f3 ♘f6 3 e3 e6 4 ♗e2 ♗e7 5 0-0 b6 6 b3 d5 7 ♗b2 ♗a6 [□ 6 ... ♗b7] 8 c4 0-0 9 ♖c1 c5 10 ♕e1 ♘c6 11 ♘g5 ♕d7? [11 ... ♗c8] 12 cxd5 ♗xe2 13 dxc6 ♕xc6 14 ♕xe2 ♖ad8 15 ♖fd1 h6 16 ♘f3 ♖d5 17 ♘e5 ♕e8 18 d3 ♗d6 19 e4 fxe4 20 dxe4 ♖xd1+ 21 ♖xd1 ♗c7 22 g3 b5 23 ♔g2 ♕a8 24 ♘d7! ♘xe4 25 ♘xf8 ♘c3+ 26 ♕f3 ♕xf3+ 27 ♔xf3 ♘xd1 28 ♘xe6 ♗b6 29 ♗xg7 c4 30 bxc4 bxc4 31 ♗d4 ♔f7 32 ♗xb6 axb6 33 ♘d4 ♘c3 34 a3 ♘b1 35 ♘c2 b5 36 ♔e3 ♔f6 37 g4 ♘c3 38 h4 ♘d5+ 39 ♔e4 ♘c3+ 40 ♔f3 ♘b1 41 g5+ hxg5 42 fxg5+ ♔g6 43 ♔g4 c3 44 h5+ ♔g7 45 ♔f5 ♘xa3 46 h6+ ♔h8 47 ♘xa3 b4 48 g6 bxa3 49 ♔f6 ♔g8 50 h7+ ♔h8 51 ♔f7 **1-0**

**1859-★MT-17**
**Morphy, P.C.+Thompson, J.**
[Maróczy]
⟨♘b1⟩

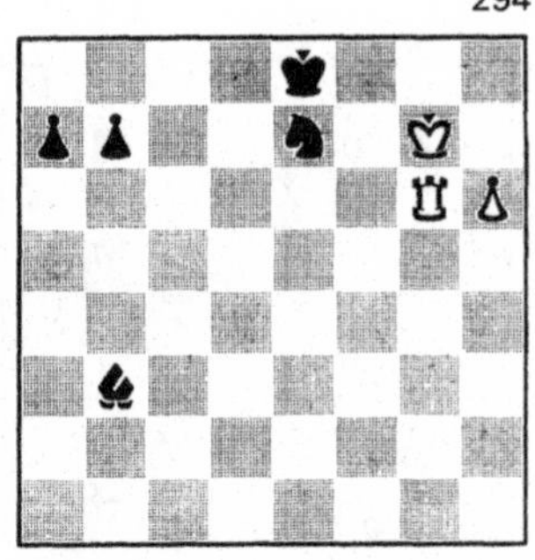

1 ♖e6 [1 h7? ♗xg6 2 ♔xg6 ♗c2+, 3 ... ♗xh7-+] 1 ... ♗xe6? [□ 1 ... ♗c2 2 ♔f6 ♔f8 3 ♖xe7 ♔g8 4 ♖xb7 a5 5 ♖c7 ♗d3 6 h7+ ♔h8=] 2 h7 ♘f5+ [2 ... ♘g6 3 ♔xg6 ♗f7+ 4 ♔f6+-] 3 ♔f6 [△ 4 h8♕] **1-0** L/N3203

**1859-★MT-18 ●○⬠** 20 iv 59
**Morphy, P.C.=Thrupp**
London [Löwenthal]
1 e4 e5 2 f4 c5 3 ♘f3 d6 4 ♗c4 ♕f6?! 5 ♘c3 ♗e6 6 ♗b5+ ♘c6 7 f5 ♗d7 8 0-0 ♕d8 9 d3 ♗e7 10 g4 h6 11 ♗e3 ♘d4 12 ♗xd7+ ♕xd7 13 ♘d5 ♘f6 14 ♘xf6+ ♗xf6 15 c3 ♘c6 16 c4 g5 17 ♘d2 b6 18 ♘b1 ♘e7 19 ♘c3 a6 20 ♖b1 ♕c6 21 b4 ♔d7 22 ♘d5 ♘xd5 [22 ... ♗g7? 23 f6+-] 23 cxd5 ♕c7 24 bxc5 bxc5 25 ♕a4+ ♔e7 26 ♖b3 ♖hb8 27 ♖fb1 ♖xb3 28 ♕xb3 ♔f8 29 ♕b7 ♕xb7 30 ♖xb7 ♗e7 31 ♔f1 **½-½** L/N3161

**1859-★MW-1**
**Morphy, P.C.+Ware, G.P.**
New York [Maróczy]
⟨♘b1⟩ 1 e4 e5 2 f4 exf4 3 ♘f3 g5 4 ♗c4 ♗g7 5 h4 h6 6 d4 ♘c6 7 c3 ♘a5 8 ♗d3 d5 9 ♕a4+ c6 10 exd5 ♕xd5 11 c4 ♕d8 [11 ... ♕e6+ 12 ♔f2 Morphy L/N6389-1860] 12 ♗d2 ♗xd4? [□ 12 ... b6 Morphy L/N6389-1860] 13 ♗xa5 ♕e7+ 14 ♔d2 ♕e3+ 15 ♔c2 ♕f2+ 16 ♗d2 ♗e6 17 ♖hf1+- ♕xg2 18 ♘xd4 ♘f6 19 ♖ae1 0-0 20 hxg5 b5

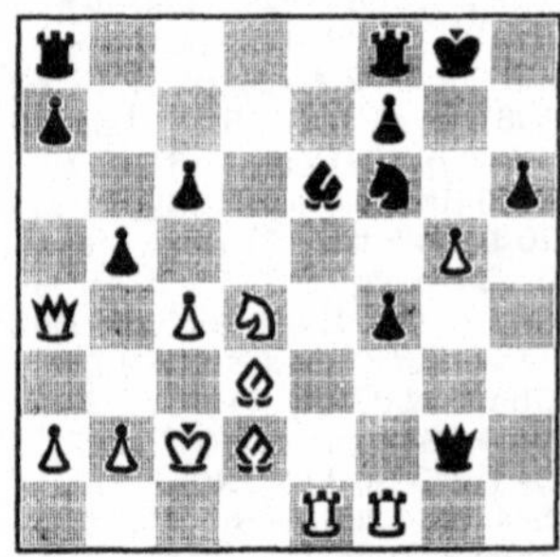

21 gxf6 bxa4 22 ♖g1 ♕xg1 23 ♖xg1+ ♔h8 24 ♘xe6 fxe6 25 f7 **1-0** L/N3203

**1859-★MW-2** 13 iv 59
**Morphy, P.C.= Walker, G.**
London [Löwenthal]
1 e4 e6 2 d4 d5 3 e×d5 e×d5 4 ♘f3 ♗d6 5 ♗d3 ♘f6 6 0-0 0-0 7 ♘c3 ♗g4 8 h3 ♗e6 9 ♗e3 ♘c6 10 ♕d2 ♕d7 11 ♗f4! ♖fe8 12 ♖ae1 ♖ad8 13 ♘e5! ♕c8 14 ♗b5 ♗×e5 15 ♗×e5 ♘×e5 [15 ... ♖d6 16 f4±] 16 d×e5 ♘e4 17 ♘×e4 d×e4 18 ♕f4 c6 19 ♗e2 ♗f5 20 ♗c4 ♖e7 21 g4 ♗g6 22 h4 h6 23 h5 ♗h7 24 g5 h×g5 25 ♕×g5 ♕f5 26 ♕×e7 **½-½** L/N3161

**142F** Ware, P. JGW.CPL

**1859-★MW-3**
**Morphy, P.C.+ Ware, G.P.**
New York [Löwenthal]
⟨♘b1⟩ 1 e4 e5 2 f4 e×f4 3 ♘f3 g5 4 ♗c4 ♗g7 5 h4 h6 6 d4 d6 7 c3 ♕e7 8 0-0 ♗g4 9 ♕b3 c6 10 ♗d2 ♗×f3 11 ♖×f3 ♘f6 12 ♖e1 ♘g4 13 ♖ef1 0-0 14 h×g5 h×g5 15 ♗d3 ♘h6 16 ♖h3 ♘a6 17 ♕d1 f5 18 ♕b3+ ♖f7 19 ♖e1 ♕d7 20 e×f5 ♖e8 [□ 20 ... ♘×f5] 21 ♖×e8+ ♕×e8 22 f6 d5 [□ 22 ... ♗f8] 23 f×g7 ♔×g7 24 ♕d1 g4 25 ♖×h6! ♔×h6 26 ♕×g4 ♖f6 27 ♗×f4+ ♖×f4 28 ♕×f4+ **1-0** L/N3161

**1859-★MW-4** 20 iv 59
**Morphy, P.C.+ Worrall, T.H.**
London [Löwenthal]
1 e4 e5 2 ♘f3 ♘c6 3 ♗c4 f5 4 d4 d6 5 d×e5 d×e5 [5 ... f×e4 6 ♕d5] 6 ♕×d8+ ♔×d8 7 ♗g5+ ♘f6 8 ♘c3 ♗b4 9 0-0-0+ ♗d6 10 ♖he1 h6 11 ♗×f6+ g×f6 12 ♘b5 ♔e7 13 ♘h4 ♖d8 14 e×f5 ♔e8 15 ♖e3 ♖d7 16 ♖g3 ♘e7 17 ♗e6 e4 18 ♗×d7+ ♗×d7 19 ♖×d6 ♗×b5 20 ♖×f6 **1-0** L/N3161

**1859-★M?-1** ii 59
**Morphy, P.C.+?**
Paris [Maróczy]
1 e4 e5 2 ♘f3 ♘c6 3 ♗c4 ♘f6 4 d4 e×d4 5 0-0 ♘×e4 6 ♖e1 d5 [6 ... ♗e7 7 ♖×e4 d5 8 ♖×e7+ ♘×e7 9 ♗b3 c5 10 c3 d×c3 11 ♘×c3 d4 12 ♘e4 ♕c7 13 ♗a4+ ♔f8 14 ♗g5 ♗g4! 15 ♖c1 b6 16 ♕×d4±] 7 ♗×d5 ♕×d5 8 ♘c3 ♕h5 [8 ... ♕d8 (8 ... ♕c4; 8 ... ♕f5±) 9 ♖×e4+ ♗e7 10 ♘×d4 f5 11 ♖f4 0-0 12 ♘×c6 ♕×d1+ 13 ♘×d1 b×c6 14 ♖c4±] 9 ♘×e4 ♗e6 [□ 9 ... ♗e7 10 ♗g5! ♗g4! 11 ♗×e7 ♗×f3!] 10 ♘eg5 [□ 10 ♗g5!] 10 ... ♗b4? [□ 10 ... 0-0-0] 11 ♖×e6+ f×e6 12 ♘×e6 ♕f7 [□ 12 ... ♔d7!] 13 ♘fg5 ♕e7 14 ♕e2 ♗d6 [14 ... ♔d7 15 ♕g4 ♘e5 16 ♕h3] 15 ♘×g7+ ♔d7 16 ♕g4+ ♔d8 17 ♘f7+ [□ 17 ♘5e6+] 17 ... ♕×f7 18 ♗g5+ ♗e7? [18 ... ♘e7! 19 ♘e6+ ♔e8-+] 19 ♘e6+ ♔c8 [□ 19 ... ♔d7] 20 ♘c5+ ♔b8 21 ♘d7+ ♔c8 22 ♘b6+ ♔b8 23 ♕c8+ ♖×c8 24 ♘d7# **1-0** L/N3203

**1859-★M?-2** 2 i 59
**Morphy, P.C.+?**
1 e4 e5 2 ♘f3 ♘c6 3 ♗c4 ♗c5 4 b4 ♗×b4 5 c3 ♗c5 6 0-0 d6 7 d4 e×d4 8 c×d4 ♗b6 9 ♘c3 ♗g4 10 ♗b5 ♗d7 11 ♖e1 ♘ge7 12 e5 d×e5 13 d5 ♘d4 14 ♗×d7+ ♕×d7 15 ♘×e5 ♕d6 16 ♕a4+ c6 17 ♗a3 ♗c5 18 ♘e4 ♕×e5 19 ♘×c5 ♘e2+ 20 ♔h1 ♕d4 21 ♕×d4 ♘×d4 22 ♘×b7 0-0 23 ♗×e7 ...? **1-0** +13

**1859-★NP-1** xi 58
**Lichtenhein, T.& Thompson, J.& Mead, C.D.& Perrin, A. &?= Montgomery, H.P.& Thomas, W.G.& Randolph, Lewis & S.& Elkin, L.**
[American Chess Monthly]
1 d4 e6 2 c4 d5 3 ♘c3 ♘f6 4 ♘f3 c5 5 e3 ♘c6 6 a3 b6?! [Staunton] 7 c×d5 ♘×d5 8 ♗b5 ♗d7 9 ♘×d5? [9 0-0] 9 ... e×d5 10 0-0 [10 d×c5 b×c5 11 ♕×d5 ♕a5+] 10 ... a6 11 ♗×c6 ♗×c6 12 ♘e5 ♕c7! [12 ... ♖c8 13 ♕g4; 12 ... ♗b7 13 ♕g4] 13 ♕g4 ♗d7 14 ♕f3? [14 ♕g3] 14 ... ♗e6 15 ♕e2 ♗d6 16 f4 ♗f5 17 b3 ♗e4 18 ♗b2 h5 19 ♘f3 [19 g4!?] 19 ... ♔f8 20 ♘g5 ♕e7! 21 ♖ad1 ♖h6 22 d×c5 b×c5 [22 ... ♗×c5?!] 23 ♘×e4?! ♕×e4 24 ♕d3 ♖b8! 25 ♕×e4 d×e4 26 ♖×d6! [26 ♖b1 ♗e7 27 ♖fc1 ♖hb6 28 ♖c3 ♔g8] 26 ... ♖×d6 27 ♗e5 ♔e7 28 ♖b1 f6 29 ♗×d6+ ♔×d6 30 ♔f2 ♔c6 31 ♔e2 a5! 32 ♔d2 ♖d8+ 33 ♔e2 ♖d3∓ 34 a4 h4?! 35 g4 h×g3 36 h×g3 f5 37 ♖b2 ♔d5 38 ♖b1 c4 39 b×c4+ ♔×c4 40 ♖b7 ♖b3 [□ 40 ... ♖a3] 41 ♖c7+ ♔b4 42 ♖×g7 ♔×a4 43 g4 ♖b2+ 44 ♔f1 f×g4 45 ♖e7! ♖b8? [45 ... ♖b4 46 f5 (46 ♔e2 ♔b3 47 ♔d2 ♔b2 48 f5 a4 49 f6 ♖b6 50 f7 ♖f6 51 ♖b7+ ♔a2-+) 46 ... ♔b3 47 f6 ♖b6 48 f7 ♖f6+ 49 ♔g2 a4 50 ♖b7+ ♔c3 51 ♖a7 ♔d3 52 ♖×a4 ♔×e3-+] 46 f5 ♖f8 47 ♖×e4+ ♔b3 48 ♖f4 a4 49 ♔g2 a3 50 e4 a2 51 ♖f1 ♖a8 52 f6 ♔c4 53 ♖a1 ♔d4 54 ♔g3 ♔×e4 55 f7 ♖f8 56 ♖×a2 ♖×f7 57 ♖a4+ ♔e3 **½-½** M954-1859

**1859̂-★PS-1**
**Paulsen, L.+ Shields, P.L.**
Pittsburgh
1 e4 e6 2 c4 ♗c5 3 ♘f3 ♘c6 4 d4 ♗b4+ 5 ♗d2 ♘f6 6 ♗×b4 ♘×b4 7 ♘c3 0-0 8 ♗d3 d5 9 c×d5 e×d5 10 0-0 ♘×d3 11 ♕×d3 d×e4 12 ♘×e4 ♗f5 13 ♘×f6+ ♕×f6 14 ♕c3 c6 15 ♖ad1 ♖fe8 16 ♘e5 ♖ad8 17 f4 ♗e4 18 ♕e3 ♗d5 19 a3 ♖d6 20 f5 c5 21 ♕g3 c×d4 22 ♘g4 ♕d8 23 f6 g6 24 ♘h6+ ♔f8 25 ♘f5 ♖×f6 26 ♘h6 ♖e2 27 ♖×f6 ♖×g2+

28 ♕×g2 ♗×g2 29 ♖×f7+ ♔e8 30 ♖e1+ **1-0** M954-1859

**1859̂-★P?-1**
**? & ?– Paulsen, L.**
1 e4 e5 2 ♘f3 ♘c6 3 ♗c4 ♘f6 4 ♘g5 d5 5 e×d5 ♘a5 6 ♗b5+ c6 7 d×c6 b×c6 8 ♕f3 ♕b6 9 ♗a4 ♗g4 10 ♕e3 ♗c5 11 ♕×e5+ ♔d7 12 0-0 ♗×f2+ 13 ♔h1 ♖ae8 14 ♕f4 ♗c5 15 ♘×f7 ♖hf8 16 ♘e5+ ♔d8 17 ♘×g4 ♘×g4 18 ♕g5+ ♗e7 19 ♖×f8 **0-1** L/N6047-1859

**1859̂-★P?-2**
**Paulsen, L.+?**
1 e4 e5 2 ♘f3 ♘c6 3 d4 e×d4 4 ♗c4 ♗b4+ 5 c3 d×c3 6 0-0 c×b2 7 ♗×b2 ♗f8 8 ♘c3 ♗e7 9 ♘d5 ♘f6 10 ♘g5 0-0 [10 ... ♘×d5 11 ♘×f7 ♕×f7 12 ♕×d5+ ♔g6 13 ♕f7+ ♔g5 14 ♗c1+ ♔h4 15 g3++-] 11 ♘f4 d6 12 ♗×f6 ♗×f6 13 ♘×h7 ♗×a1 [13 ... ♔×h7 14 ♕h5+ ♔g8 15 ♗×f7+ ♖×f7 16 ♘g6+-] 14 ♕h5 ♘e5 15 ♘g5 ♖e8 16 ♘×f7 ♘×f7 17 ♕×f7+ ♔h8 18 ♕h5# **1-0** L/N6047

**1859̂-★P?-3 ●○⌂**
**Paulsen, L.+?**
[Staunton]

1 e4 e5 2 ♘f3 ♘c6 3 d4 exd4 4 ♘xd4 ♗c5 5 ♘f5 ♕f6 6 ♘c3 ♘ge7 7 ♗d3 d6 8 0-0 0-0 9 ♕h5 ♗xf5 10 exf5 h6 11 g4 ♘b4 12 ♘e4 ♕e5 13 ♗xh6 ♘xd3 [13 ... gxh6 14 ♕xh6 f6 15 ♖ae1 ♘xd3 16 cxd3 ♕d4 17 ♖e3 ♖f7 18 ♖fe1 ♖e8 19 ♖h3 ♖g7 20 ♘xf6+−] 14 ♗xg7 ♕xg7 15 f6 ♕g6 16 fxe7 ♖fe8 17 ♕xg6+ fxg6 18 ♘f6+ ♔f7 19 ♘xe8 ♖xe8 20 cxd3 ♖xe7 21 ♖ae1 ♗d4 22 ♖xe7+ ♔xe7 23 b3 c5 24 ♔g2 g5 25 f4 ♔f6 26 fxg5+ ♔xg5 27 h3 ♗f6 28 h4+ ♔g6 29 h5+ ♔g7 30 h6+ **1-0** M954

**1859̂-★P?-4 ●○⌂**
**Paulsen, L.+?**

1 e4 e5 2 ♘f3 ♘c6 3 ♗c4 ♗c5 4 b4 ♗xb4 5 c3 ♗a5 6 0-0 ♗b6 7 d4 exd4 8 cxd4 ♘ge7 9 ♘g5 d5 10 exd5 ♘xd5 11 ♘xf7 ♔xf7 12 ♕f3+ ♕f6 13 ♗xd5+ ♔e8 14 ♖e1+ ♘e7 15 ♕h5+ ♔d8 16 ♗g5 g6 17 ♕h4 **1-0** M954

**1859̂-★P?-5**
**Paulsen, L.+?**
Rock Island

1 e4 e5 2 ♘c3 ♘c6 3 f4 exf4 4 ♘f3 a6 5 ♗c4 d6 6 0-0 ♗e6 7 d3 g5 8 ♘d5 h6 9 ♕e1 ♗e7 10 b4 ♗f6 11 ♖b1 ♗xd5 12 exd5+ ♘ce7 13 h3 ♕d7 14 b5 a5 15 b6 c6 16 dxc6 bxc6 17 b7 ♖b8 18 ♕xa5 d5 19 ♗a6 ♘g6 20 ♗a3 ♘8e7 21 ♗c5 0-0 22 ♗a7 g4 23 hxg4 ♕xg4 24 ♗xb8 ♖xb8 25 ♕c7 ♖xb7 26 ♖xb7 ♘f8 27 ♖b8 ♕g7 28 ♕xf4 ♔h7 29 ♖xf8 ♘g6 30 ♕f5 c5 31 c3 c4 32 d4 ♕xf8 33 ♕xf6 ♕e7 34 ♘e5 ♕xf6 35 ♖xf6 **1-0** M954-1859

**1859̂-★P?-6 ●○⌂**
**Paulsen, L.+?**
Rock Island [Staunton]

1 e4 e5 2 ♘f3 ♘f6 3 ♗c4 b6 4 0-0 ♗b7 5 ♘xe5 d5 6 exd5 ♘xd5 7 ♘c3 c6 8 ♖e1 ♗e7 9 d4 0-0 10 ♕h5 ♘d7 11 ♘xd5 cxd5 12 ♗d3 g6 13 ♕h6 ♗f6 14 f4 ♕e7 15 ♗d2 ♖fe8? 16 ♘xg6! ♗xd4+ 17 ♔h1 ♕f6 18 ♘e7+ ♖xe7 19 ♗xh7+ ♔h8 20 ♗g6+ ♔g8 21 ♖xe7 ♕xe7 22 ♕h7+ ♔f8 23 ♖e1 ♕f6 24 f5! ♘e5 25 ♗h6+ ♔e7 26 ♗g7 ♕d6 27 ♗xe5 ♗xe5 28 ♕xf7+ ♔d8 29 ♕xb7 ♖c8 30 ♕f7 ♖xc2 31 ♕e8+ ♔c7 32 ♖xe5 ♖c1+ 33 ♖e1 ♖xe1+ 34 ♕xe1 ♕c5 35 f6 ♕f8 36 ♕e7+ **1-0** M954

**1859̂-★SS-1**
**Salmon, G.−Staunton, H.**
London [Staunton]

⟨♙f7⟩ 1 e4 ... 2 d4 e6 3 ♗d3 ♕e7 4 ♘c3 ♘c6 5 ♘f3 g6 6 ♘b5 d6 7 ♗g5 ♕g7 8 0-0 a6 9 ♘c3 ♗e7 10 ♗e3 ♘h6 11 d5 ♘e5 12 ♘xe5 dxe5 13 f4 exf4 14 ♖xf4?! ♗g5 15 ♖f3 ♗xe3+ 16 ♖xe3 0-0 17 ♗c4! exd5 18 ♕xd5+ ♔h8 19 ♖f3 ♗g4 20 ♖xf8+ ♖xf8 21 ♖f1 ♖e8 22 h3 ♗d7 23 e5?? ♗e6 24 ♕d4 ♗xc4 25 ♕xc4 ♕xe5 26 ♘d5 ♘f5 27 ♕c3 ♘d4 28 ♘f4 g5 29 ♖d1 c5 30 ♘d3 ♘e2+ **0-1** M954-1859

**1859̂-★SS-2**
**Salmon, G.+Staunton, H.**
London [Staunton]

⟨♙f7⟩ 1 e4 ... 2 d4 e6 3 ♗d3 c5 4 e5 g6 5 h4 cxd4 6 f4 ♗g7 7 h5 ♘e7 8 ♕g4 ♕a5+ 9 ♔f2 ♘bc6 10 hxg6 h6 11 ♘f3 0-0 12 ♘a3 ♘f5 13 ♕h5! [△ 14 g4] 13 ... ♘e3 14 ♘c4 ♘xc4 15 ♗xc4 b5 16 ♗d2 ♕b6 17 ♗d3 ♘e7 18 g4 ♗b7 19 ♖ae1 ♘d5 20 f5 exf5 21 gxf5 ♘e3 22 ♗xe3 ♗xf3 23 ♔xf3 dxe3 24 ♖xe3 ♖ae8 25 ♔e2 [25 f6?? ♗xf6−+] 25 ... ♕c5 26 e6 a6 [□ 26 ... dxe6] 27 f6 ♕xh5+ 28 ♖xh5 ♖xf6 29 exd7 ♖d8 30 ♖d5 **1-0** M954-1859

**1859̂-★SW-1**
**Staunton, H.−Worrall, T.H.**
London

⟨♘b1⟩ 1 b3 e5 2 ♗b2 ♘c6 3 e3 d5 4 ♘e2 ♗d6 5 ♘g3 ♘f6 6 ♗e2 h6 7 f3 0-0 8 a3 a6 9 0-0 ♘h7 10 c4 d4 11 ♗d3 ♕g5 12 c5 ♗e7 13 ♘e4 ♕h4 14 ♕c2 ♘g5 15 ♘g3 ♗d7 16 f4 e4 17 ♗c4 d3 18 ♕c1 ♘h7 19 ♘xe4 ♗f5 20 ♘g3 ♗e6 21 ♗xd3 ♗f6 22 ♕c2 ♗xb2 23 ♕xb2 ♘f6 24 ♗e2 ♗g4 25 ♗d3 ♖ad8 26 ♕c2 ♘e7 27 ♗c4 ♖d7 28 d4 c6 29 ♖ae1 ♗e6 30 ♗d3 ♘g4 31 h3 ♕xg3 32 hxg4 ♗xg4 33 f5 ♘d5 34 ♕d2 ♘f6 35 b4 ♖e8 36 ♗b1 h5 37 e4 h4 38 ♖e3 ♕b8 39 ♕f2 ♖xd4 40 ♕xh4 ♕e5 41 ♖g3 ♗e2 42 ♖h3 ♔f8 43 ♖e1 ♗g4 44 ♖he3 ♖d2 45 ♕g5 ♔e7 46 ♕h4 ♔d7 47 ♖g3

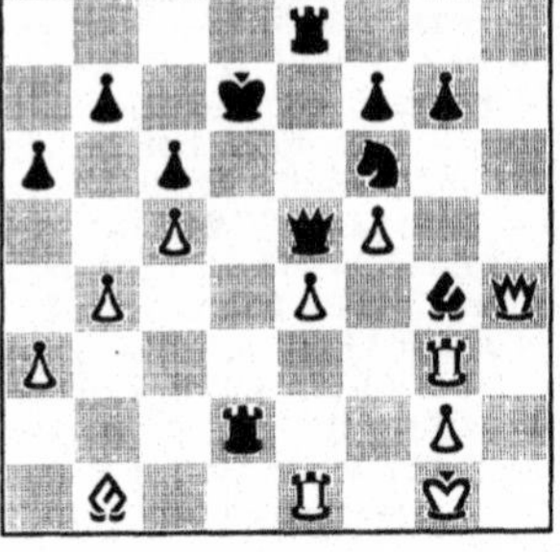

47 ... ♖h8 **0-1** M954

**1859̂-★S?-1 ●○⌂**
**Suhle, B.+?**

1 e4 e5 2 f4 exf4 3 ♘f3 g5 4 h4 g4 5 ♘e5 h5 6 ♗c4 ♖h7 7 d4 ♗h6 8 ♘c3 c6 9 ♘d3 ♕f6 10 e5 ♕f5 11 ♘c5 ♕g6 12 ♗d3 ♕g7 13 ♗xh7 ♕xh7 14 ♘3e4 b6 15 ♘d6+ ♔d8 16 ♘d3 f6 17 ♗xf4 ♗a6 18 ♕d2 ♗f8 19 ♖f1 ♗xd6 20 exd6 ♕e4+ 21 ♕e3 f5 22 ♕xe4 fxe4 23 ♗g5+ ♔e8 [24 0-0-0 c5 25 ♖de1 ♗b7 26 ♘e5 ♗d5 27 ♘g6 ♗f7 28 ♖xe4+ ♘e7 29 ♗xe7 ♘c6 30 ♗g5+ ♘e7 31 ♗xe7 ∼ 32 ♗g5+ ♗e6 33 ♖f8# Suhle] **1-0** M954-1859

**185?-★P?-1 ○●**
**?−Paulsen, L.**
Dubuque

1 e4 e5 2 d4 exd4 3 ♗c4 ♘f6 4 e5 d5 5 ♗b3 ♘e4 6 ♘e2 ♘c6 7 f4 ♗c5 8 c3 ♗g4 9 ♕d3 ♗xe2 10 ♕xe2 dxc3 11 g3 ♘d4 12 ♕g2 cxb2 13 ♗xb2 c6 14 ♘a3 ♕a5+ 15 ♔d1 ♘f2+ 16 ♕xf2 ♘xb3 17 ♕e2 ♘xa1 18 ♗xa1 ♗xa3 19 e6 0-0 20 e7 ♗xe7 21 ♕xe7 ♕xa2 22 ♕e5 f6 23 ♕e6+ ♔h8 24 ♗xf6 ♖xf6 25 ♕e3 ♕b1+ **0-1** M324-1861

**185̂?-★GS-1**
**Gordon, T.−Staunton, H.**
[Löwenthal]

⟨♙f7⟩ 1 e4 ... 2 d4 e6 3 ♗d3 c5 4 e5 ♘e7 5 f4 cxd4 6 ♘f3 ♘bc6 7 0-0 g6 8 ♘bd2 ♗g7 9 ♘e4 0-0 10 ♘d6 ♘d5 11 ♘g5 [△ 12 ♘xh7 ♔xh7 13 ♕h5+] 11 ... ♘ce7 12 ♖f3 ♘e3 13 ♕e2 ♘7d5 14 g3 ♘f5 15 ♘ge4 ♘fe7 16 ♗d2 b6 17 ♖af1 ♖b8 18 g4 ♗b7 19 ♘xb7 ♖xb7 20 g5 [20 c4!] 20 ... ♘f5 21 ♘f6+ ♗xf6 22 exf6 ♖c7 23 ♗xf5 exf5 24 ♕d3 ♕a8 25 ♔g2?? [□ 25 ♕xd4 ♖xc2 26 ♖d3+−] 25 ... ♖fc8 26 ♖c1 ♖e8 27 ♔f2 ♖e4 28 a3 ♕c6 29 ♕b3 ♔f8 30 c4 ♘e3 31 ♗xe3 dxe3+ 32 ♔g3 ♕d6 33 ♖d1 e2 34 ♖xd6 e1♕+ [35 ♔h3! ♕g1 36 ♖g3 ♕f1+ 37 ♖g2 ♖xf4 38 ♖d3! ♖cxc4−+] **0-1** L/N6124-1866

**185̂?-★HM-1**
**Morphy, P.C.+Hart**

1 e4 e5 2 ♘f3 ♘c6 3 d4 exd4 4 ♗c4 d6 5 c3 dxc3 6 ♕b3 ♕e7 7 0-0 b6 8 ♘xc3 ♘a5 9 ♕b4 ♘xc4 10 ♕xc4 ♗b7 11 ♖e1 0-0-0 12 ♗f4 f6 13 ♖ac1 ♔b8 14 ♘d5 ♗xd5 15 exd5 ♕d7 16 ♘d4 ♘e7 17 ♕a6 c5 18 dxc6 ♕c8 19 c7+ ♔a8 20 cxd8♕ ♕xd8 21 ♘b5 ♕b8 22 ♖c7 **1-0** +13

### 185?-★KV-1
**Kolisch,I.F.von+ Vitzthum,C.**
Genoa
1 e4 c5 2 ♘f3 e6 3 d4 cxd4 4 ♘xd4 ♘c6 5 ♘b5 a6 6 ♘d6+ ♗xd6 7 ♕xd6 ♘f6 8 ♘c3 ♕e7 9 e5 ♕xd6 10 exd6 0-0 11 ♗g5 h6 12 ♗xf6 gxf6 13 0-0-0 ♘e5 14 ♗e2 b5 15 f4 ♘g6 16 ♗f3 ♖b8 17 g3 ♗b7 18 ♗xb7 ♖xb7 19 ♘e4 ♔g7 20 ♘c5 ♖a7 21 h4 ♖c8 22 b4 a5 23 a3 axb4 24 axb4 ♖a1+ 25 ♔b2 ♖xd1 26 ♖xd1 ♘f8 27 ♖a1 f5 28 ♖a7 ♖c6 29 ♖a6 ♖c8 30 ♔b3 ♔f6 31 c4 bxc4+ 32 ♔xc4 e5 33 ♔d5 e4 34 b5 e3 35 b6 ♖e8 36 b7 e2 37 ♖a1 **1-0** L/N6124-1864

### 185?-★KV-2
**Kolisch,I.F.von+ Vitzthum,C.**
Genoa
1 e4 e6 2 d4 d5 3 ♗d3 dxe4 4 ♗xe4 ♘f6 5 ♗d3 h6 6 ♘f3 ♗d6 7 c3 0-0 8 0-0 b6 9 ♗e3 ♗b7 10 ♘bd2 ♘bd7 11 ♕e2 ♘d5 12 ♘c4 ♘f4 13 ♗xf4 ♗xf4 14 ♖ad1 ♕e7 15 ♖fe1 ♖ad8 16 ♗b1 ♘f6 17 ♘ce5 ♘d7 18 ♕c2 g6 19 ♘xd7 ♖xd7 20 ♖d3 f5 21 ♕b3 ♖e8 22 g3 ♗d6 23 ♖de3 ♗d5 24 ♕c2 ♕f6 25 ♘e5 ♗xe5 26 ♖xe5 b5 27 ♕e2 a6 28 b3 ♖de7 29 c4 bxc4 30 bxc4 ♗b7 31 ♗c2 ♔f7 32 ♗a4 ♖d8 33 d5 ♖d6 34 ♗d7 ♖exd7 35 dxe6+ ♖xe6 36 ♖xe6 ♕d8 37 ♖e8 ♕f6 38 ♖b8 ♗e4 39 f3 ♕d4+ 40 ♔h1 ♗c6 41 ♕e6+ ♔g7 42 ♖g8+ ♔h7 43 ♕xg6# **1-0** L/N6124-1864

### 185?-★M?-1
**Morphy, P.C.+?**
1 e4 e5 2 ♘f3 ♘c6 3 ♗c4 ♗c5 4 b4 ♗xb4 5 c3 ♗c5 6 0-0 d6 7 d4 exd4 8 cxd4 ♗b6 9 ♘c3 ♗g4 10 ♗b5 ♗d7 11 ♖e1 ♘ge7 12 e5 dxe5 13 d5 ♘d4 14 ♗xd7+ ♕xd7 15 ♘xe5 ♕d6 16 ♕a4+ c6 17 ♗a3 ♗c5 18 ♘e4 ♕xe5 19 ♘xc5 ♘e2+ 20 ♔h1 ♕d4 21 ♕xd4 ♘xd4 22 ♘xb7 0-0 23 ♗xe7 ...? **1-0** M268-1859

### 185?-★M?-2
**?–Morphy, P.C.**
New Orleans
1 e4 e5 2 ♘f3 ♘c6 3 ♗b5 ♘f6 4 d3 ♗c5 5 0-0 0-0 6 ♗xc6 dxc6 7 ♘xe5 ♕d6 8 ♗f4 ♘g4 9 ♘xg4 ♕xf4 10 h3 f5 11 d4 fxg4 12 g3 ♕xe4 13 dxc5 gxh3 14 f3 ♕e3+ 15 ♔h2 ♗e6 16 ♘c3 ♖ad8 17 ♕e1 ♖d2+ 18 ♔h1 ♖xf3 19 ♖d1 ♖xd1 20 ♕xd1 ♖f1+ 21 ♕xf1 ♕xg3 22 ♕g1 ♗d5+ 23 ♘xd5 ♕xg1+ 24 ♔xg1 cxd5 **0-1** M268-1859

### 185?-★S?-1
**?+Staunton, H.**
⟨♙f7⟩ 1 e4 ... 2 d4 e6 3 ♗d3 c5 4 e5 g6 5 c3 ♘c6 6 h4 cxd4 7 cxd4 ♗g7 8 h5 ♘xd4 9 hxg6 ♕a5+ 10 ♔f1 h6 11 ♕h5 ♕xe5 12 ♘c3 d5 13 ♕d1 ♗d7 14 ♖h5 ♕f6 15 ♘h3 ♖c8 16 ♗f4 ♘e7 17 ♗e5 ♕f8 18 ♗xd4 ♗xd4 19 ♘b5 ♗c5 20 ♖c1 ♕g7 21 ♖xc5 ♖xc5 22 ♘d6+ ♔f8 23 ♕f3+ ♘f5 24 g4 ♖c1+ 25 ♔g2 ♕xb2 26 gxf5 ♕g7 27 ♔h2 ♕e5+ 28 ♕f4 **1-0** L/N6047-1863

### 185?-★S?-2
**?–Staunton, H.**
⟨♙f7⟩ 1 e4 ... 2 d4 e6 3 ♗d3 c5 4 d5 d6 5 c4 ♘f6 6 f4 exd5 7 cxd5 ♗g4 8 ♕c2 ♘bd7 9 h3 ♗h5 10 g4 ♗f7 11 ♘c3 a6 12 a4 ♖c8 13 b3 ♗e7 14 ♘f3 0-0 15 ♗e3 ♕a5 16 ♔e2 ♕c7 17 ♘g5 ♘b6 18 e5 dxe5 19 ♗xh7+ ♔h8 20 ♘xf7+ ♖xf7 21 ♗g6 ♖ff8 22 ♕f5 ♗d6 23 a5 ♘bd7 24 ♕g5 exf4 25 ♕h4+ ♔g8 26 g5 fxe3 27 ♘e4 ♘e5 28 gxf6 ♘xg6 29 ♕g4 ♘f4+ 30 ♔f3 ♗e5 31 ♖hg1 ♗xf6 32 d6 ♕c6 33 d7 ♖cd8 34 ♖af1 ♗d4 **0-1** L/N6047-1863

### 185?-★S?-3
**?–Staunton, H.**
London
⟨♙f7⟩ 1 e4 ... 2 d4 e6 3 ♗d3 c5 4 dxc5 ♕a5+ 5 ♘c3 ♕xc5 6 ♗e3 ♕a5 7 ♘e2 ♗d6 8 0-0 ♘f6 9 a3 0-0 10 b4

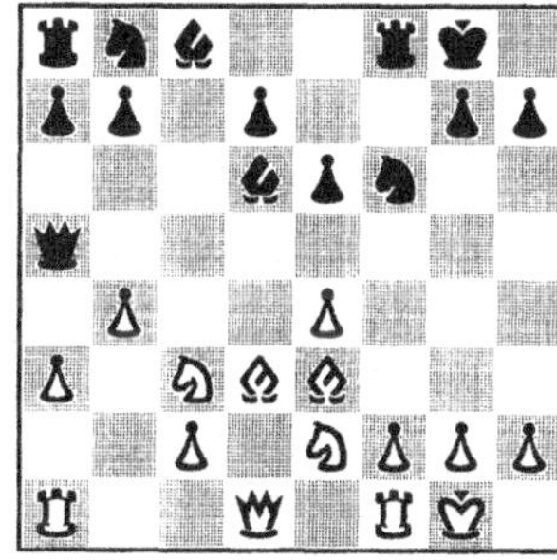

10 ... ♗xh2+ 11 ♔xh2 ♕h5+ 12 ♔g1 ♘g4 **0-1** M954-1863

### 185?-★S?-4
**Staunton, H.+?**
⟨♖a1⟩ 1 e4 e5 2 ♘f3 ♘c6 3 ♗c4 ♗c5 4 b4 ♗xb4 5 c3 ♗a5 6 0-0 ♗b6 7 d4 exd4 8 e5 d5 9 exd6 ♕xd6 10 ♗a3 ♗c5 11 ♗xf7+ ♔xf7 12 ♘g5+ ♔e8 13 ♖e1+ ♘ge7 14 ♘e4 ♕d5 15 ♗xc5 ♗f5 16 c4 ♕xc4 17 ♘a3 ♕d5 18 ♘b5 ♖c8 19 ♘bc3 ♕d7 20 ♗xe7 ♗xe4 21 ♘xe4 ♘xe7 22 ♕h5+ ♔d8 23 ♘c5 ♕f5 24 ♘xb7+ ♔d7 25 ♖xe7+ ♔xe7 26 ♕xf5 **1-0** M954-1863

### 185?-★S?-5
**Staunton, H.+?**
London
1 e4 e5 2 ♘f3 ♘c6 3 ♗c4 ♗c5 4 b4 ♗xb4 5 c3 ♗a5 6 0-0 ♗b6 7 d4 exd4 8 ♘xd4 ♗xd4 9 cxd4 d6 10 f4 ♘f6 11 e5 dxe5 12 fxe5 ♘d5 13 ♗a3 ♗e6 14 ♕d3 ♘ce7 15 ♘d2 0-0 16 ♘e4 h6 17 ♗xd5 ♗xd5 18 ♘f6+ gxf6 19 ♗xe7 ♕xe7 20 ♕g3+ ♔h7 21 exf6 ♖g8 22 fxe7 ♖xg3 23 hxg3 ♖e8 24 ♖ae1 ♗e6 25 ♖e5 **1-0** M954-1863

### 185?-★S?-6
**Staunton, H.+?**
1 e4 e5 2 ♘f3 ♘c6 3 d4 exd4 4 c3 d3 5 ♘d4 ♗c5 6 ♗e3 ♗b6 7 ♗xd3 ♘f6 8 f4 d6 9 h3 0-0 10 0-0 ♕e7 11 ♕f3 ♖e8 12 ♘d2 ♘d5 13 ♗f2 ♘f6 14 ♖ae1 ♘xd4 15 ♗xd4 ♗xd4+ 16 cxd4 c5 17 e5 dxe5 18 fxe5 ♘d7 19 e6 f6 20 d5 ♘e5 21 ♖xe5 **1-0** L/N6047-1863

### 185?-★S?-7
**Staunton, H.+?**
London
1 e4 e5 2 ♘f3 ♘c6 3 ♗c4 ♗c5 4 b4 ♗xb4 5 c3 ♗c5 6 d4 exd4 7 0-0 d6 8 cxd4 ♗b6 9 ♘c3 ♗g4 10 ♕a4 ♗d7 11 ♕b3 ♘a5 12 ♗xf7+ ♔f8 13 ♕c2 ♔xf7 14 e5 ♔f8 15 ♖e1 ♕c8 16 d5 ♗f5 17 ♕d2 ♘h6 18 ♕f4 ♘g4 19 e6 ♗xf2+ 20 ♔h1 ♗xe1 21 ♕xf5+ ♘f6 22 ♘e4 ♗c3 23 ♗h6 ♕d8 24 ♖c1 ♗b2 25 ♗xg7+ ♔xg7 26 ♕g5+ ♔f8 27 ♕h6+ ♔e8 28 ♕g7 ♖f8 29 ♖xc7 ♘xd5 30 ♖d7 ♘c4 31 ♕xh7 ♘f4 32 e7 ♖f7 33 ♕xf7+ ♔xf7 34 exd8♕+ **1-0** M954-1868

### 185?-★S?-8
**Staunton, H.+?**
1 e4 e5 2 ♘f3 ♘c6 3 d4 exd4 4 ♗c4 ♗c5 5 0-0 ♘ge7 6 ♘g5 d5 7 exd5 ♘e5 8 ♗b3 h6 9 ♘e4 ♗b6 10 h3 ♘xd5 11 ♕h5

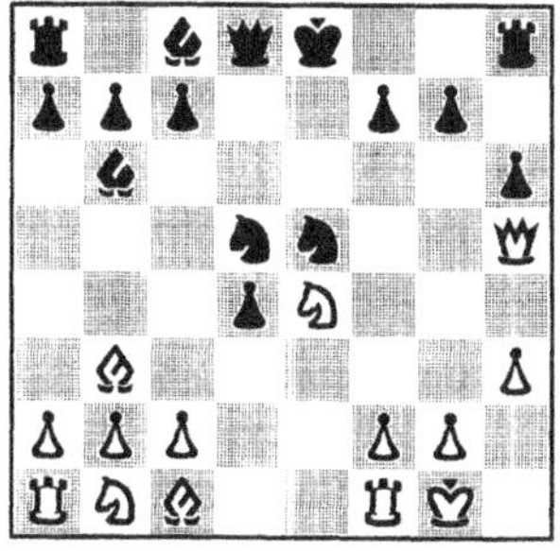

11 ... 0-0 12 ♕xe5 ♗e6 13 ♗xh6 **1-0** M954-1863

**185?-★S?-9**
**Staunton, H.+?**
1 e4 e5 2 ♘f3 ♘c6 3 d4 exd4 4 ♗c4 ♗c5 5 0-0 ♘ge7 6 ♘g5 d5 7 exd5 ♘e5 8 ♗b3 h6 9 ♘e4 ♗b6 10 h3 ♘xd5 11 ♕h5 0-0 12 ♕xe5 ♗e6 13 ♗xh6 **1-0** L/N6047-1865

**185?-★S?-10**
**Staunton, H.+?**
1 e4 e5 2 ♘f3 ♘c6 3 d4 exd4 4 ♗c4 ♘f6 5 ♗g5 h6 6 ♗xf6 ♕xf6 7 0-0 ♗c5 8 c3 d3 9 e5 ♕f4 10 ♕xd3 0-0 11 b4 ♗b6 12 a4 a5 13 g3 ♕g4 14 b5 ♘e7 15 ♘bd2 ♘g6 16 ♔h1 d5 17 ♗xd5 ♗e6 18 ♗xb7 ♖ad8 19 ♕e4 ♕h5 20 ♕e2 ♗g4 21 ♖ad1 ♖fe8 22 ♘c4 ♖xd1 23 ♖xd1 ♘xe5 24 ♘cxe5 ♖xe5 25 ♕d3 ♖f5 26 ♘h4 ♖xf2 27 ♕d8+ ♔h7 28 ♗e4+ f5 29 ♗d5 ♗f3+ 30 ♘xf3

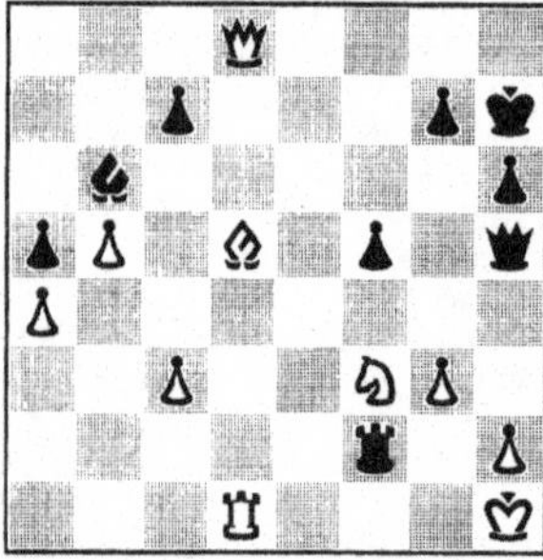

30 ... ♖xh2+ 31 ♘xh2 ♕xd1+ 32 ♔g2 ♕e2+ 33 ♔h3 ♕h5+ 34 ♕h4 **1-0** M954-1864

**185?-★S?-11**
**Staunton, H.+?**
1 e4 e5 2 ♘f3 ♘c6 3 d4 exd4 4 ♘xd4 ♕h4 5 ♘b5 ♗c5 6 ♕f3 ♘d4 7 ♘xc7+ ♔d8 8 ♕f4 ♘xc2+ 9 ♔d1 ♕xf4 10 ♗xf4 ♘xa1 11 ♘xa8 d6 12 ♘c3 ♘e7 13 ♗c4 ♗g4+ 14 f3 ♗h5 15 ♔d2 ♔d7 16 b4 ♗xb4 17 ♖b1 ♗xc3+ 18 ♔xc3 ♖xa8 19 ♖xb7+ ♔d8 20 ♗xd6 ♘c6 21 ♗xf7 ♗xf7 22 ♖xf7 ♖c8 23 ♔b2 ♘c2 24 ♖f8+ ♔d7 25 ♖xc8 ♔xc8 26 ♔xc2 **1-0** M954-1864

**185?-★S?-12**
**Staunton, H.+?**
1 e4 e5 2 f4 exf4 3 ♘f3 g5 4 ♗c4 ♗g7 5 h4 h6 6 hxg5 hxg5 7 ♖xh8 ♗xh8 8 d4 d6 9 ♘c3 c6 10 ♘e5 dxe5 11 ♕h5 ♕f6 12 dxe5 ♕g7 13 e6 ♘f6 14 exf7+ ♔f8 15 ♗xf4 ♔e7 16 ♗xg5 ♘bd7 17 ♖d1 ♘e5 18 ♕h2 ♕xg5 19 f8♕+ ♔xf8 20 ♕xh8+ ♘g8 21 ♖d8+ ♕xd8 22 ♕xg8+ ♔e7 23 ♕g7+ ♔d6 24 ♕h6+ ♔c7 25 ♕g7+ ♘d7 26 ♕g3+ ♔b6 27 ♘a4+ ♔a5 28 ♕c3+ ♔xa4 29 ♕a3# **1-0** M954-1864

## CAMBRIDGE 1860

**1860-CMB-1** 28 viii 60
**Kolisch, I.F. von+Geake**
1 e4 e5 2 ♘f3 d6 3 d4 ♗g4 4 dxe5 ♗xf3 5 ♕xf3 dxe5 6 ♗c4 ♘f6 7 ♕b3 ♕d7 8 ♕xb7 ♕c6 9 ♗b5 **1-0** +4

**1860-CMB-2** 28 viii 60
**Geake−Kolisch, I.F. von**
1 e4 e5 2 ♘f3 ♘c6 3 ♗c4 ♘f6 4 ♘c3 ♗c5 5 0-0 d6 6 d3 ♗g4 7 ♗xf7+ ♔xf7 8 ♘g5+ ♔e8 9 ♘f3 ♘d4 10 ♗g5 ♕d7 11 ♘d5 ♘xd5 12 exd5 ♗xf3 13 gxf3 ♕h3 **0-1** +4

**1860-CMB-3** 28 viii 60
**Zytogorski, A.+Bateman**
1 e4 e5 2 ♘f3 ♘c6 3 c3 ♗c5 4 ♗c4 ♘f6 5 d4 exd4 6 e5 ♘e4 7 0-0 d6 8 cxd4 ♗b6 9 ♗d5 f5 10 exf6 ♘xf6 11 ♗xc6+ bxc6 12 ♖e1+ ♔d7 13 ♗g5 ♖e8 14 ♘c3 ♖xe1+ 15 ♕xe1 h6 16 ♗xf6 ♕xf6 17 ♖d1 ♗b7 18 ♘e4 ♕f7 19 ♘c5+ ♗xc5 20 dxc5 ♕f6 21 cxd6 cxd6 22 ♘e5+ ♔c7 23 ♕a5+ ♔c8 24 ♘c4 d5 25 ♘e3 ♕xb2 26 ♕c5 ♕b6 27 ♕f8+ ♕d8 28 ♕xg7 ♕g5 29 ♕f7 a5 30 ♘f5 ♔b8 31 ♖b1 ♖a7 32 ♕f8+ ♔c7 33 ♕d6+ **1-0** +4

**1860-CMB-4** 28 viii 60
**Bateman,−Zytogorski, A.**
1 e4 e5 2 ♘f3 ♘c6 3 ♗b5 a6 4 ♗a4 ♗c5 5 c3 b5 6 ♗b3 ♘f6 7 d4 exd4 8 cxd4 ♗b4+ 9 ♗d2 ♗xd2+ 10 ♘bxd2 0-0 11 0-0 ♗b7 12 d5 ♘e7 13 e5 ♘fxd5 14 ♗xd5 ♘xd5 15 a4 h6 16 ♘d4 c5 17 ♘f5 ♕g5 18 g4 h5 19 h3 hxg4 20 ♕xg4 ♕xg4+ 21 hxg4 g6 22 ♘d6 ♗c6 23 axb5 axb5 24 ♖xa8 ♖xa8 25 ♘2e4 ♔g7 26 ♘xc5 ♘f4 27 f3 ♖a2 28 ♘e8+ ♔f8 29 ♘f6 ♖xb2 30 ♘cxd7+ ♔e7 31 ♘c5 b4 32 g5 ♘h3+ 33 ♔h1 ♘xg5 34 ♘ce4 ♘xe4 35 ♘xe4 ♗xe4 36 fxe4 ♖e2 37 ♖f4 b3 **0-1** +4

**1860-CMB-5** 28 viii 60
**Stanley, C.H.+Rainger, F.G.**
1 e4 e6 2 d4 d5 3 exd5 exd5 4 ♘f3 h6 5 h3 ♗e6 6 ♗d3 ♘e7 7 0-0 ♘f5 8 ♖e1 ♗e7 9 c3 ♘d7 10 ♕c2 ♘d6 11 ♘e5 c6 12 ♘g6 ♖g8 13 f4 ♘e4 14 ♗xe4 fxg6 15 ♗xg6+ ♗f7 16 b3 ♕c7 17 ♗a3 c5 18 dxc5 ♘xc5 19 ♗xf7+ ♔xf7 20 ♕f5+ ♔e8 21 ♕xd5 **1-0** +4

**1860-CMB-6** 28 viii 60
**Rainger, F.G.−Stanley, C.H.**
1 e4 e5 2 ♘f3 ♘c6 3 ♗c4 ♗c5 4 b4 ♗xb4 5 c3 ♗a5 6 0-0 ♘f6 7 d4 0-0 8 d5 ♘e7 9 ♘xe5 d6 10 ♘d3 ♘xe4 11 ♗b2 f5 12 f3 ♘g5 13 ♘d2 ♔h8 14 ♘f4 c6 15 ♔h1 b5 16 ♗b3 cxd5 17 ♘xd5 ♗b7 18 ♘xe7 ♕xe7 19 ♖e1 ♕f6 20 ♕c2 ♕h6 21 ♖e7 ♗c6 22 c4 ♘f7 23 cxb5 ♗xd2 24 bxc6 ♘e5 25 ♗d5 ♗f4 26 g3 ♗xg3 27 ♖g1 f4 28 ♖g2 ♕g5 29 c7 ♕xe7 30 ♗xa8 ♖c8 31 hxg3 fxg3 32 ♗d5 ♖xc7 33 ♕e4 ♕g5 34 ♗c4 ♕h5+ 35 ♔g1 ♘xf3+ 36 ♔f1 ♕h1+ 37 ♔e2 ♕xg2+ **0-1** +4

**1860-CMB-7** 28 viii 60
**Horne+Puller, A.G.**
1 e4 e5 2 ♘f3 ♘c6 3 c3 ♗c5 4 ♗c4 d6 5 0-0 ♗g4 6 d3 h6 7 ♗e3 ♕f6 8 ♘bd2 ♘ge7 9 b4 ♗b6 10 a4 a6 11 b5 ♘a5 12 ♗xb6 cxb6 13 ♖c1 ♘xc4 14 ♘xc4 ♗xf3 15 ♕xf3 ♕xf3 16 gxf3 ♘c8 17 ♔h1 0-0 18 ♖g1 f6 19 ♖g6 ♘e7 20 ♖g2 ♘c8 21 ♖cg1 ♖f7 22 ♘e3 ♘e7 23 d4 axb5 24 dxe5 fxe5 25 axb5 g5 26 h4 ♖xf3 27 hxg5 ♖h3+ 28 ♖h2 ♖xh2+ 29 ♔xh2 hxg5 30 ♖xg5+ ♔f7 31 ♖h5 ♔g6 32 ♖h4 ♖f8 33 ♔g2 ♔g5 34 ♖g4+ ♔f6 35 ♖g3 ♘g6 36 ♖f3+ ♘f4+ 37 ♔f1 ♖a8 38 ♘d5+ ♔g5 39 ♘xf4 exf4 40 ♖d3 ♖a1+ 41 ♔e2 ♔g4 42 f3+ ♔g3 43 ♖xd6 ♖a2+ 44 ♖d2 ♖xd2+ 45 ♔xd2 ♔xf3 46 e5 ♔g2 47 e6 f3 48 e7 f2 49 e8♕ f1♕ 50 ♕g6+ ♔f3 51 ♕f7+ ♔g2 52 ♕xb7+ ♔g3 53 ♕g7+ ♔h2 54 ♕h6+ ♔g2 55 ♕g5+ ♔h1 56 ♕h5+ ♔g2 57 ♕e2+ ♕f2 58 ♕xf2+ ♔xf2 59 c4 **1-0** +4

**1860-CMB-8** 28 viii 60
**Puller, A.G.+Horne**
1 e4 e5 2 d4 exd4 3 ♘f3 ♗c5 4 ♗c4 ♘f6 5 e5 ♘e4 6 ♗d5 ♘xf2 7 ♔xf2 0-0 8 g3 c6 9 ♗b3 d6 10 ♔g2 dxe5 11 ♘xe5 ♗e6 12 c3 ♗d5+ 13 ♗xd5 ♕xd5+ 14 ♘f3 d3 15 ♖f1 ♘d7 16 h4 ♘e5 17 ♗f4 ♘xf3 18 ♖xf3 ♖fe8 19 ♕xd3 ♕xd3 20 ♖xd3 ♖e2+ 21 ♔h3 ♖xb2 22 ♘d2 b5 23 ♖d1 ♖xa2 24 ♘b3 ♗b6 25 ♘c5 h6 26 ♘d7 ♖e2 27 ♘xb6 axb6 28 ♖d8+ ♖ee8 29 ♖xe8+ ♖xe8 30 ♗c7 c5 31 ♗xb6 b4 32 ♗xc5 bxc3 33 ♖c1 ♖c8 34 ♖xc3 f6 35 g4 ♔f7 36 ♔g3 ♔g6 37 h5+ ♔f7 38 ♔f4 g6 39 ♔e4 ♖e8+ 40 ♔f4 ♖c8 41 hxg6+ ♔xg6 42 ♔e4 h5 43 gxh5+ ♔xh5

44 ♔f5 **1-0** +4

**1860-CMB-9** 28 viii 60
**Horne+Puller, A.G.**
1 e4 e5 2 ♘f3 ♘c6 3 ♗c4 ♗c5 4 d3 h6 5 ♗e3 d6 6 h3 ♕f6 7 a3 ♗e6 8 ♗a2 ♘ge7 9 ♘c3 ♗xe3 10 fxe3 ♕g6 11 ♕e2 0-0-0 12 ♘d5 f5

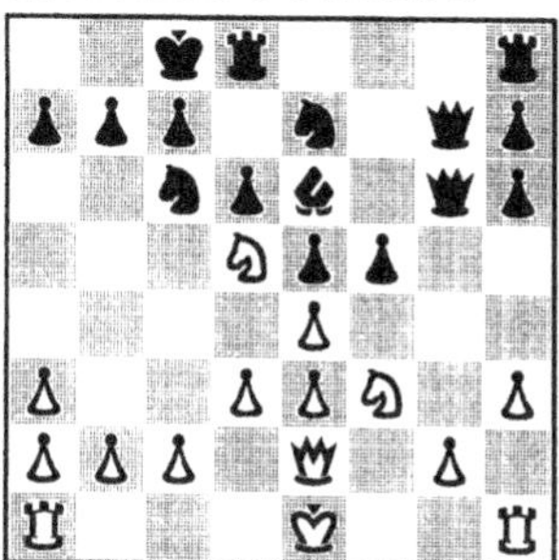

13 ♘xe7+ ♘xe7 14 ♗xe6+ ♕xe6 15 exf5 ♕xf5 16 e4 ♕g6 17 0-0-0 ♘c6 18 c3 ♕e6 19 ♔b1 d5 20 exd5 ♖xd5 21 d4 e4 22 c4 ♕g6 23 ♘h4 ♕g3 24 cxd5 ♕xh4 25 dxc6 **1-0** +4

**1860-CMB-10** 29 viii 60
**Horne−Stanley, C.H.**
1 e4 e5 2 ♘f3 ♘c6 3 ♗c4 ♗c5 4 d3 d6 5 ♗e3 ♗b6 6 h3 h6 7 ♘c3 ♘f6 8 ♘d5 ♘xd5 9 ♗xd5 ♘e7 10 ♗b3 ♘g6 11 ♕d2 0-0 12 0-0-0 ♗e6 13 h4 ♗xb3 14 cxb3 f5 15 h5 ♘h8 16 ♗xh6 gxh6 17 ♕xh6 ♕f6 18 ♕xf6 ♖xf6 19 exf5 ♗xf2 20 g4 ♗e3+ 21 ♔b1 ♘f7 22 ♖h3 ♘g5 23 ♘xg5 ♗xg5 24 ♖dh1 ♔h7 25 ♔c2 d5 26 h6 ♖e8 27 ♖h5 ♖c6+ 28 ♔d1 ♖c1+ 29 ♔e2 ♖c2+ 30 ♔d1 ♖xb2 31 ♖1h3 ♖g8 32 ♖f3 e4 33 dxe4 dxe4 **0-1** +4

**1860-CMB-11** 29 viii 60
**Stanley, C.H.−Horne**
1 e4 d5 2 exd5 ♘f6 3 ♘c3 ♘xd5 4 ♗c4 e6 5 ♘f3 ♘xc3 6 bxc3 b6 7 0-0 ♗b7 8 ♘e5 ♗d6 9 f4 g5 10 ♗xe6 ♗xe5 11 ♗xf7+ ♔xf7 12 fxe5+ ♔g7 13 ♕h5 ♖f8 14 ♗a3 c5 15 ♖xf8 ♕xf8 16 ♖f1 ♕e7 17 ♖f6 ♘d7 18 ♕h6+ ♔g8 19 ♖e6 ♕f8 20 ♕xg5+ ♔h8 21 ♖e7 ♗c6 22 ♕h4 ♕g8 23 g3 ♖e8 24 c4 ♖xe7 25 ♕xe7 ♕f8 26 ♕xf8+ ♘xf8 27 d4 ♘g6 28 dxc5 bxc5 29 ♗xc5 a6 30 ♔f2 ♔g8 31 ♔e3 ♘xe5 32 h4 ♘xc4+ 33 ♔d4 ♘d2 34 ♗d6 ♔f7 35 ♔c5 ♗f3 36 ♗f4 ♘f1 37 ♔d4 ♔f6 38 g4 ♗xg4 39 ♔e4 ♔g6 40 ♗g5 ♗f5+ 41 ♔f3 ♗xc2 42 ♔f2 ♗d3 43 a3 ♔h5 44 ♗d8 a5 45 ♗xa5 ♔xh4 46 ♗d8+ ♔g4 47 ♔g1 h5 48 ♗c7 ♘d2 49 a4 h4 50 a5 ♘f3+ 51 ♔h1 h3 52 a6 ♗f1

**0-1** +4

**1860-CMB-12** 29 viii 60
**Horne−Stanley, C.H.**
1 d4 e6 2 e4 d5 3 exd5 exd5 4 ♘c3 ♘f6 5 ♗g5 ♗e7 6 ♗e3 0-0 7 ♗d3 ♗e6 8 ♕d2 b6 9 0-0-0 c5 10 dxc5 bxc5 11 ♗g5 d4 12 ♘e4 ♘bd7 13 ♘f3 ♗xa2 14 b3 c4 15 ♘xf6+ ♘xf6

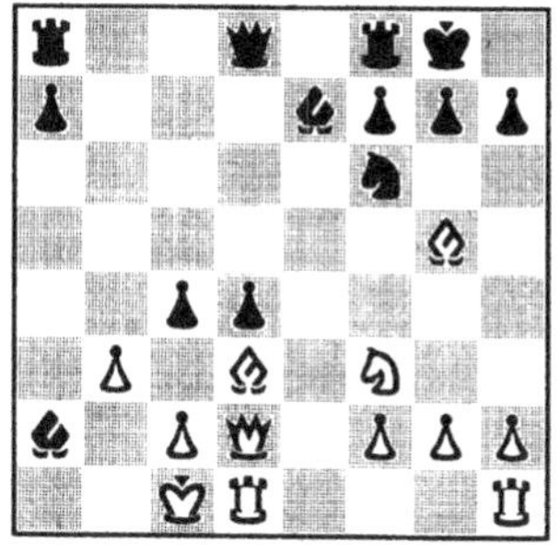

16 ♖de1 ♗a3+ 17 ♔d1 cxd3 18 ♕xd3 ♖c8 19 ♕a6 d3 20 ♕xa3 ♖xc2 21 ♕b4 ♘d5 22 ♗xd8 ♘xb4 23 ♗a5 ♗xb3 24 ♗xb4 ♖c4+ 25 ♔d2 ♖xb4 26 ♖b1 a5 27 ♘d4 ♖xd4 28 ♖xb3 ♖fd8 29 ♖a1 a4 30 ♖c3 h5 31 ♖aa3 h4 32 ♖xd3 ♖xd3+ 33 ♖xd3 ♖xd3+ 34 ♔xd3 g5 35 g3 hxg3 36 hxg3 g4 **0-1** +4

**1860-CMB-13** 30 viii 60
**Kolisch, I.F.von+Stanley, C.H.**
[Löwenthal]
1 e4 e6 2 d4 d5 3 exd5 exd5 4 ♘f3 ♘f6 5 ♗d3 ♘c6 6 0-0 ♗d6 7 ♖e1+ ♗e6 8 ♗f5 0-0! 9 ♗xe6 fxe6 10 ♘g5! [10 ♖xe6 ♘e4 11 c4 ♖xf3 12 gxf3 ♕h4−+] 10 ... ♕d7 11 f4 ♖ae8 12 ♘c3 h6 13 ♘f3 ♘h5 14 g3 ♕f7 15 ♗e3 g5? 16 ♘e5 ♗xe5 17 fxe5 a6 18 ♕e2 ♕g6 19 a3 [△ 20 g4] 19 ... g4! [△ ... ♘g7; ... ♘f5] 20 ♖f1 ♘e7 21 ♕d2 ♘f5 22 ♗f4 ♘hg7 23 ♘e2 h5 [△ ... h4; ... ♘h5] 24 ♗g5 ♕h7 25 ♗f6 h4 26 ♕g5 hxg3 27 hxg3 ♖f7 28 ♖f2 [△ 29 ♔h2] 28 ... ♕h5 [28 ... ♕h6 29 ♖xf5] 29 ♕d2 ♕h6 30 ♕xh6!+− ♘xh6 31 ♖h2 ♘gf5 32 ♔f2!! ♖h7 33 ♖ah1 ♔f7 34 ♘f4 ♖g8 35 ♖h5 b6 36 ♗g5+− [36 ♘xd5 exd5 37 ♖xf5 ♘xf5 38 ♖xh7+ ♔g6 39 ♖xc7 ♘xd4 40 c3 ♘f5 41 ♖c6+−] 36 ... ♖gh8 37 b4 c5! 38 bxc5 bxc5 39 dxc5 ♖c8 40 ♘d3! [40 ♗xh6 ♖xc5 41 ♗g5 ♖xc2+ 42 ♘e2 ♖xe2+ 43 ♔xe2 ♖xh5−+] 40 ... ♖ch8 41 c3! a5 42 c6 ♔g6 43 ♘f4+ ♔f7 44 c7 ♖c8 45 ♗xh6 ♖xc7 46 ♘e2 d4 [46 ... ♔g6 47 ♗d2 ♖xh5 48 ♘f4+ +−] 47 ♗d2 ♖xh5 48 ♖xh5 dxc3 49 ♖h7+ ♘g7 50 ♗h6 **1-0** M979

**1860-CMB-14** 31 viii 60
**Stanley, C.H.−Kolisch, I.F.von**
[Löwenthal]
1 e4 e5 2 ♘c3 ♘f6 3 ♗c4 c6 4 ♕e2 b5 5 ♗b3 a5 6 a4 b4 7 ♘d1 ♗c5 8 ♘f3 d6 9 0-0 0-0 10 d3 ♗a6 11 ♗g5 ♘bd7 12 ♘e3 ♕c7 13 ♘f5! d5 14 ♕d2! [14 exd5 e4∓] 14 ... dxe4 15 ♗xf6 ♘xf6 [15 ... e3? 16 ♗xe5] 16 ♕g5 ♘e8 17 ♘xe5 ♔h8! 18 ♘h4? ♗e7! 19 ♕h5 ♗xh4 20 ♗xf7 [◻ 20 ♘xf7+] 20 ... ♖xf7 21 ♘xf7+ ♔g8 22 ♘h6+ gxh6 23 ♕xh4 exd3 24 cxd3 ♗xd3 25 ♖fe1 ♗g6 26 ♖e7∞ ♕d6 27 ♖ae1 ♘g7 28 ♕g4 ♖d8 29 h3 ♘f5 30 ♖7e6 ♕d4! 31 ♕f3 ♕xb2 32 ♕xc6 ♕d4 33 ♕a6 ♘g7 34 ♖6e5 b3 35 ♕xa5 b2 36 ♖b5 ♖c8 37 ♖d5 ♕f6 38 ♖dd1 ♖b8 39 ♕d5+ ♕f7 40 ♕e5 ♕b3 41 ♖d7 ♘e8 42 ♔h2 b1♕ 43 ♖xb1 ♗xb1 44 a5 ♖a8 [△ 45 ... ♕b8] 45 g3 ♕a2 46 ♕e3 ♘f6 47 ♖d2 ♕xa5 48 ♕b3+ ♔h8 49 ♕b2 ♖f8 50 ♖d6 ♕f5!! 51 ♔g1 ♗e4 **0-1** M979

**1860-CMB-15** 1 ix 60
**Kolisch, I.F.von+Stanley, C.H.**
[Löwenthal]
1 e4 e6 2 d4 d5 3 ♗d3 dxe4 4 ♗xe4 ♘f6 5 ♗d3 ♗e7 6 ♘f3 0-0 7 0-0 ♘c6 8 ♗e3 ♗d6 9 ♘c3 ♘e7 10 ♕e2 c6 11 ♗g5 ♘g6 12 ♖ad1 h6 13 ♗xf6 ♕xf6 14 ♘e4 ♕e7 15 ♘xd6 ♕xd6 16 ♘e5 ♘e7 17 ♖fe1 f5 18 ♗c4 b5 19 ♗b3 a5 20 a3 f4? 21 ♕e4 ♘d5 22 ♖d3 ♗b7 23 ♘g4 ♖f7 [23 ... ♖ae8 24 ♘xh6+ gxh6 25 ♕g6+ ♔h8 26 ♕xh6+ ♔g8 27 ♕g6+ ♔h8 28 ♖h3#] 24 ♕g6 ♔f8 25 ♖xe6 ♕e7!+− 26 ♕f5+ ♔e8 27 ♗xd5 cxd5 28 ♘f6+ **1-0** M979

## HAMPPE✕HARRWITZ
[1860-✕HH]

| | | | | | |
|---|---|---|---|---|---|
| C. Hamppe | 0 | 0 | ½ | 0 | ½ |
| D. Harrwitz | 1 | 1 | ½ | 1 | 3½ |

**1860-✕HH-1** 13 xi 60
**Hamppe, C.−Harrwitz, D.**
[Steinitz]
1 e4 c5 2 d4 cxd4 3 ♕xd4? ♘c6 4 ♕d1 ♘f6 5 ♗d3 e6 6 f4 ♗c5 7 e5? ♘d5 8 ♘f3 f5? 9 ♕e2 ♕b6 10 c3 a5 11 g3 0-0 12 ♘bd2 a4 13 ♘c4 ♕c7? [13 ... ♕a7] 14 ♗e3 ♘xe3 15 ♘xe3 ♕b6 16 ♘c4 ♕a7 17 h4 ♖b8? 18 a3 ♘e7 19 ♘d6 ♗xd6 20 exd6 ♘d5 21 ♗c4 ♘f6 22 ♗d3 ♕b6 23 0-0-0 ♘e8 24 ♗b5 ♖a8 25 ♖d4 ♘xd6 26 ♗xa4∓ ♘e4 27 ♖g1 d5 28 ♖g2 ♕c5 29 ♕b5 b6 30 ♕d3 [30 ♕xc5? bxc5−+] 30 ... ♗a6 31 ♕d1 ♗c4 32 ♗c2

32 ... ♖xa3!! 33 ♗xe4 [33 bxa3? ♕xa3+ 34 ♔b1 ♘xc3#] 33 ... ♗b3 [33 ... fxe4 34 bxa3 ♕xa3+ 35 ♔b1 exf3 36 ♕xf3 e5 37 ♖dd2 (37 ♖xc4 ♕b3+) 37 ... e4 38 ♕e3 ♖a8−+] 34 ♕g1 [◻ 34 ♗c2 ♖a1+ 35 ♔d2 ♖xd1+ 36 ♔xd1∓] 34 ... fxe4 35 bxa3 [35 ♘d2 ♖a1+ 36 ♘b1 ♖xb1+ 37 ♔xb1 ♕a5−+] 35 ... ♕xc3+ 36 ♔b1 exf3 37 ♖gd2 ♖c8 38 ♖b2 f2!! **0-1** M392-1877

### 1860-⚔HH-2̂
**Harrwitz, D.+Hampe, C.**

[Steinitz]

1 e4 e6 2 d4 d5 3 exd5 exd5 4 ♗d3 ♘f6 5 ♘f3 ♗d6 6 0-0 0-0 7 c4? c6 8 ♘c3 ♗c7?! [8 ... ♗e6 9 ♘g5 ♗g4 10 ♗xh7+ ♔h8 11 f3 ♘xh7 12 ♘xh7 ♕h4 13 g3 (13 h3? ♗xh3 △ 14 ... ♗xg2−+) 13 ... ♗xg3 14 ♕e2 ♔xh7 15 fxg4 ♗d6 16 cxd5?! cxd5 17 ♘xd5 ♘c6 △ 18 ... ♖ae8∓] 9 ♗g5 ♗e6 10 cxd5 ♗xd5 11 ♘e5 ♕d6 12 ♗xf6 ♕xf6 13 f4 ♕d8 14 ♕h5 h6?? [14 ... g6 15 ♘xg6?? fxg6 16 ♗xg6 ♕d7 (16 ... ♖f7); 14 ... g6 15 ♕h6! ♗e6 16 f5 ♕xd4+ 17 ♔h1 ♗xe5 18 fxe6 ♕xd3 19 exf7+ ♖xf7 20 ♖xf7 ♔xf7 21 ♕xh7+ ♗g7 22 ♖d1! (22 ♘e4?! ♘d7 23 ♘g5+ ♔f6) 22 ... ♕c4 23 ♘e4 △ 24 ♘d6+−] 15 ♕f5 g6 16 ♘xg6+− ♗e6 17 ♘e7+ ♔g7 18 ♕h7+ ♔f6 19 ♘f5! [△ 20 ♕g7#, 20 ♕xh6#] 19 ... ♗xf5 [19 ... ♖g8 20 ♕xh6+ ♖g6 21 ♕h4+] 20 ♕xf5+ ♔e7 21 ♖ae1+ ♔d6 22 ♕e5+ ♔d7 23 ♗f5# **1-0** M392-1877

### 1860-⚔HH-3̂
**Hampe, C.=Harrwitz, D.**

[Steinitz]

1 e4 c5 2 d4 cxd4 3 ♕xd4 ♘c6 4 ♕d1?∓ e6 5 ♗d3 ♗c5 6 ♘e2 ♘f6 7 0-0 d5 [7 ... ♘g4 8 h3 h5 9 hxg4 hxg4 10 g3 (10 ♘g3 ♕h4 △ 11 ... ♕h2#, 11 ... ♕xg3) 10 ... ♕f6 (△ 11 ... ♕f3) 11 ♗f4 g5∓] 8 exd5 ♘xd5 9 ♘bc3 0-0 10 ♘xd5 ♕xd5 11 ♘f4 ♕d6 12 ♗e3! f5? [12 ... ♗xe3?? 13 ♗xh7+; 12 ... g6! △ 13 ... e5] 13 ♗c4 ♕xd1 14 ♖axd1 ♗xe3 15 fxe3 ♖e8 16 ♖d6 ♔f7 17 ♖fd1 g5? [17 ... ♘e5 18 ♗b3 b5] 18 ♘h3 h6 19 ♗b5 ♖e7 20 ♗xc6 bxc6 21 ♖xc6 ♗b7 22 ♖c5 ♖c8 [22 ... ♖b8 △ 23 ... ♗a8, 23 ... ♗a6] 23 ♖xc8 ♗xc8 24 c4 ♖d7 25 ♘f2 ♔e7 26 ♔f1 ♗b7 27 g3 ♖xd1+ 28 ♘xd1 ♗e4 29 ♔e2 ♔d6 30 b4 e5 31 ♘c3 ♗c6? [31 ... ♗g2 32 c5+? ♔c6; 31 ... ♗g2 32 a4? a5!] 32 c5+ ♔c7 33 b5 [33 e4! fxe4 34 ♔e3] 33 ... ♗g2 34 e4 f4 35 a4 fxg3 36 hxg3 h5 37 a5 h4 38 gxh4 gxh4 39 ♔f2 ♗h3 40 ♘d5+ ♔b8 41 c6 ♗e6 42 ♘e7? [42 b6+−] 42 ... ♔c7 43 ♘d5+ ♔d6 44 ♘e7?! ♔c7 45 ♘d5+ ♗xd5! [45 ... ♔d6 46 c7 ♗c8 (46 ... ♔d7 47 b6 axb6 48 a6 ♔c8 49 ♘xb6+ ♔xc7 50 a7+−) 47 a6 △ 48 b6+−] 46 exd5 e4 47 b6+ axb6 48 a6 h3 49 a7 e3+!! 50 ♔xe3 [50 ♔g3 e2 51 ♔f2 e1♕+ 52 ♔xe1 h2=] 50 ... h2 51 a8♕ h1♕ 52 ♕b7+ ♔d6 53 ♕d7+ ♔c5 54 c7 ♕g1+ 55 ♔e4 ♕g2+ 56 ♔e5 ♕g5+ 57 ♔e6 ♕g4+ 58 ♔e7 ♕g7+ 59 ♔d8 ♕g8+ 60 ♕e8 ♕xd5+ **½-½** M392-1880

### 1860-⚔HH-4̂
**Harrwitz, D.+Hampe, C.**

[Steinitz]

1 e4 e5 2 f4 exf4 3 ♘f3 g5 4 h4 g4 5 ♘e5 h5 6 ♗c4 d5?! 7 ♗xd5 ♖h7 8 d4 c6 9 ♗b3? [9 ♗xf7+! ♖xf7 10 ♘xf7 ♔xf7±] 9 ... ♗h6 10 ♘c3 ♘e7 11 ♘e2 f6 12 ♘d3 f3 13 gxf3 gxf3 14 ♘ef4 ♕xd4 15 ♕xf3 ♗g4 16 ♕e3 ♕d7 17 ♗d2 ♕c7 18 ♕f2 ♘d7 19 ♘e6 ♗xd2+ 20 ♔xd2 ♕d6 [20 ... ♗xe6? 21 ♗xe6 ♕d6 22 ♗xd7+ ♔xd7 23 ♖ad1 ♔c7 24 ♔c1 b6 25 ♖he1 △ 26 e5±] 21 ♕f4 ♕xf4+ 22 ♘dxf4 ♖c8 23 ♔e3 ♘e5 24 ♖af1 c5 25 ♗d5 b5 26 b3 c4 27 b4 ♗xe6 28 ♗xe6 ♖c6 29 a4!? bxa4 [29 ... ♘g4+ 30 ♔e2; 29 ... a6 30 axb5 axb5 31 ♖a1] 30 ♖a1 ♖a6 31 ♖a3 ♖g7 32 ♔d4! ♘7c6+? [32 ... ♖d6+! 33 ♔c5 ♖c6+ 34 ♔b5 ♖b6+=; 32 ... ♖d6+! 33 ♔c3 ♖g3+ 34 ♔b2 ♖xa3 35 ♔xa3=; 32 ... ♖d6+! 33 ♗d5 ♖g4 34 ♔c5 ♖b6 35 ♘xh5?? ♘d7+ 36 ♔xc4 ♘xd5 37 ♔xd5 ♖b5+−+] 33 ♔c5 ♘d8 34 ♗d5 ♖c7+ 35 ♔d4 ♖b6 36 ♖xa4 ♘dc6+ 37 ♔c3 ♔e7 38 ♘xh5 ♖cb7 39 ♖g1 ♖xb4 40 ♖xb4 ♖xb4 41 ♖g7+ ♔d6 42 ♘xf6 a5 43 ♘e8+ ♔c5 44 ♖g5! [△ 45 ♗xc6] 44 ... ♔b6 45 ♗xc6 ♘xc6 46 ♘d6 ♖b1 47 ♘xc4+ ♔b7 48 ♘xa5+ ♘xa5 49 ♖xa5+− ♖h1 50 ♖h5 ♔c6 51 ♔d4 ♖d1+ 52 ♔c4 ♖e1 53 ♖h6+ ♔d7 54 ♔d5 ♖d1+ 55 ♔e5 ♖c1 56 ♖h7+ ♔d8 57 ♔d6 ♔e8 58 ♖c7 ♖h1 59 e5 ♖xh4 60 ♖c8+ ♔f7 61 e6+ ♔f6 62 ♖f8+ ♔g7 63 e7 **1-0** M392-1878

## HORWITZ⚔KOLISCH

Manchester

[1860-⚔HK]

| | | | | | |
|---|---|---|---|---|---|
| B. Horwitz | 0 | 1 | 0 | 0 | 1 |
| I.F. von Kolisch | 1 | 0 | 1 | 1 | 3 |

### 1860-⚔HK-1
**Horwitz,B.−Kolisch, I.F.von**

Manchester [Staunton]

1 e4 e5 2 f4 d5 3 exd5 e4 4 ♗b5+ c6 5 dxc6 bxc6 6 ♗c4 ♘f6 7 d4 ♗d6 8 ♘e2 0-0 9 0-0 ♗g4 10 ♘bc3 ♘bd7 11 h3 ♗xe2 12 ♘xe2 ♘b6 13 ♗b3 c5! 14 dxc5 ♗xc5+ 15 ♔h2? [15 ♔h1] 15 ... ♘g4+ 16 ♔g3 [16 ♔h1] 16 ... ♗f2+ 17 ♖xf2 [17 ♔xg4? f5+ 18 ♔h5 ♕h4#] 17 ... ♕xd1 18 hxg4 e3 19 ♖f3 ♕e1+ 20 ♔h3 ♕xe2 21 ♗xe3 ♖fe8 22 ♗d4 ♖ad8 23 ♗c3 ♘d5 24 ♖e1 ♘xc3 25 ♖xe2 ♘xe2 26 ♖f2 ♖d1 27 g5 ♖e3+ 28 ♔h2 ♘g3 29 ♖f3 ♖xf3 30 gxf3 ♘e2 31 f5 ♘d4 32 ♗c4 ♘xf3+ 33 ♔g3 ♘xg5 34 b4 ♘e4+ **0-1** M954-1860

### 1860-⚔HK-2
**Kolisch,I.F.von−Horwitz,B.**

Manchester [Staunton]

1 e4 e5 2 ♘f3 ♘c6 3 ♗b5 ♘f6 4 0-0 ♗e7 5 ♘c3 d6 6 d4 exd4 7 ♘xd4 ♗d7 8 f4 ♘xd4 9 ♗xd7+ ♕xd7 10 ♕xd4± 0-0 11 f5 b6 12 ♕d3 ♘g4 13 ♗f4 f6 14 ♖ad1 ♘e5 15 ♗xe5 fxe5 16 ♕d5+ ♔h8 17 ♕xe5? ♗f6 18 ♕g3 ♖ae8 19 ♖fe1 ♕c6 20 ♕d3 ♗xc3 21 bxc3 ♖e5 22 ♖e3 ♖fe8 23 ♖de1 ♕a4 24 g4 ♕xa2 25 g5 ♕f7 26 ♖h3 g6 27 ♖h6? ♖xf5 28 ♕g3 ♖fe5 29 ♕h4 ♖f8 30 h3 ♖xg5+ **0-1** M954-1869

### 1860-⚔HK-3
**Horwitz,B.−Kolisch,I.F. von**

Manchester [Staunton]

1 e4 e5 2 ♘f3 ♘f6 3 ♘xe5 d6 4 ♘f3 ♘xe4 5 c3 [5 d4] 5 ... d5 6 ♗e2 ♗d6 7 d3 ♘f6 8 ♗g5 ♗e6 9 ♘a3 c6 [9 ... ♗xa3 10 ♕a4+] 10 ♘c2 ♘bd7 11 0-0 ♕c7 12 ♗h4 0-0-0 13 ♘cd4 ♖de8 14 b4 ♘g4 15 h3 ♘ge5 16 ♘xe6 fxe6 [△ 17 ... ♘xf3+, 18 ... ♗f4] 17 ♗g5 h5 18 ♘xe5 ♗xe5 19 ♗xh5 g6! 20 ♗xg6? [20 ♗g4=] 20 ... ♖eg8 21 ♗f7 ♖xg5 22 ♗xe6 ♗xc3 23 ♖c1 ♗d4 24 ♕f3 ♕d6 25 ♕f7 ♖f8 26 ♕xd7+ ♕xd7 27 ♗xd7+ ♔xd7 28 ♖c2 ♖f3 29 ♔h2 ♗e5+ 30 g3 ♗xg3+ 31 ♔g2 ♖gf5 32 fxg3 ♖xf1 **0-1** M954-1860

### 1860-⚔HK-4
**Kolisch,I.F.von+Horwitz,B.**

Manchester [Staunton]

1 e4 e5 2 ♘f3 ♘c6 3 ♗b5 ♘f6 4 0-0 d6 5 d4 exd4 6 e5 dxe5 7 ♘xe5 ♗d7 8 ♗xc6 ♗xc6 9 ♘xc6 bxc6 10 ♖e1+ ♗e7 11 ♕e2 ♘d5 12 c4 ♘b4 13 a3 ♘a6+− 14 b4 ♕d7 15

♘d2 0-0?? 16 ♕xe7 ♖ae8?? 17 ♕xd7 ♖xe1+ 18 ♘f1 **1-0**

M954-1860

## HARRWITZ✕MONGREDIEN

[1860-✕HM]

| | | |
|---|---|---|
| D. Harrwitz | 1 1 1 1 1 ½ 1 1 | 7½ |
| A. Mongredien | 0 0 0 0 0 ½ 0 0 | ½ |

### 1860-✕HM-1
**Mongredien,A.–**
**Harrwitz,D.**

1 e4 e5 2 ♗c4 ♘f6 3 d3 ♗c5 4 ♘f3 ♘c6 5 c3 d6 6 b4 ♗b6 7 ♗g5 h6 8 ♗h4 g5 9 ♗g3 ♗e6 10 ♘bd2 ♘e7 11 h3 ♘g6 12 ♗xe6 fxe6 13 ♘c4 0-0 14 ♘xb6 axb6 15 ♕c2 ♕e8 16 d4 ♕c6 17 d5 exd5 18 exd5 ♕e8 19 c4 ♘h5 20 0-0 ♖xf3?! [20 ... ♖a3] 21 gxf3 ♘gf4 22 ♗xf4 [◻ 22 ♕f5] 22 ... ♘xf4 23 ♕f5 ♖a3 24 ♕g4 ♘e2+ 25 ♔g2 ♘d4 26 ♖ae1 [◻ 26 ♖fe1] 26 ... ♘xf3 27 ♖e3 ♘h4+ 28 ♔g3 ♖xa2 29 c5?! [29 ♕e6+=] 29 ... bxc5 30 bxc5 ♕f7 31 ♖d3 ♔g7 32 c6?→ [32 cxd6=] 32 ... bxc6 33 dxc6 ♖c2 34 ♕d7 ♖xc6 35 ♕xf7+ ♔xf7 36 ♖b1 ♖c2 37 ♖db3 h5 38 ♖1b2 ♖c4 39 ♖a2 ♔e6 40 ♖a8 ♖c1 41 ♖h8 ♖g1+ 42 ♔h2 ♖g2+ 43 ♔h1 ♖xf2 44 ♔g1 ♖c2 45 ♖xh5 ♔f5 46 ♖g3 ♔f4 47 ♖a3 e4 48 ♖h7 ♘f3+ 49 ♔f1 ♔g3 **0-1**

L/N6123

### 1860-✕HM-2
**Harrwitz,D.+Mongredien,**
**A.**

1 d4 d5 2 c4 dxc4 3 e4 b5 4 a4 c6 5 axb5 cxb5 6 b3 ♗b7 7 f3 [◻ 7 d5] 7 ... e6 8 bxc4 bxc4 9 ♗xc4 ♘f6 10 ♗e3 ♗b4+ 11 ♘d2 ♘fd7 12 ♘e2 a5 13 0-0 0-0 14 ♘g3 ♘c6 15 ♗a2 ♘b6 16 ♘b1 ♗a6 17 ♖f2 ♘c4 18 ♗xc4 ♗xc4 19 ♕c1 ♗b5 20 ♘c3 ♗xc3 21 ♕xc3 ♘b4 22 ♕c5 ♕d7 23 ♕g5 f6 24 ♕h5 f5 25 f4 ♗d3 26 e5 a4 27 ♕d1 ♖fc8 28 ♖b2 ♘c2 29 ♖ab1 ♘xe3 30 ♕xd3 ♘d5 31 ♘e2 a3 32 ♖a2 ♕a4 33 ♖b7 ♘b4? 34 ♕g3 **1-0** L/N6123

### 1860-✕HM-3
**Mongredien,A.–**
**Harrwitz,D.**

1 e4 e5 2 ♗c4 ♘f6 3 d3 ♗c5 4 ♗g5 h6 5 ♗h4 d6 6 h3 ♘bd7 7 ♘f3 ♘f8 8 c3 g5 9 ♗g3 ♘g6 10 b4 ♗b6 11 ♘bd2 ♕e7 12 a4 a6 13 ♕c2 ♘h5 14 d4 ♘gf4 15 ♗xf4 ♘xf4 16 ♗f1 exd4 17 ♘xd4 f5 18 g3 ♘d5 19 a5 ♗xd4 20 cxd4 c6 21 ♖b1 ♘f6 22 f3 fxe4 23 fxe4 0-0 24 ♔d1 ♘h5 25 ♖b3 ♕f6 26 ♗e2 ♘g7 27 ♘f3 ♗e6 28 ♖e3 ♖ad8 29 g4 ♗f7 30 h4 [◻ 30 ♔c1] 30 ... gxh4 31 ♖xh4 [◻ 31 ♘xh4] 31 ... ♘e6 32 g5? ♘xg5 33 ♖g4 ♗h5 34 e5 dxe5 35 ♘xg5 hxg5 36 ♖h3 ♖xd4+ 37 ♖xd4 ♕f1+ 38 ♔d2 ♕xe2+ 39 ♔c1 exd4 **0-1** L/N6123

### 1860-✕HM-4
**Harrwitz,D.+**
**Mongredien,A.**

1 e4 e5 2 f4 exf4 3 ♗c4 ♘f6 4 ♘c3 ♗b4 5 ♘f3 ♗xc3 6 dxc3 d6 7 ♗xf4 0-0 8 ♗g5 ♘bd7 9 0-0 h6 10 ♗xf6 ♘xf6 11 ♕d3 ♗e6 12 ♗b3 a5 13 ♘d4 ♖e8 14 ♖ae1 a4 15 ♗xe6 fxe6 16 ♕h3 ♕e7 [◻ 16 ... ♕d7] 17 e5 dxe5 18 ♖xe5 ♖a6 19 ♖fe1 ♕d7 20 ♖xe6 ♖axe6 21 ♖xe6 ♖xe6 22 ♕xe6+ ♕xe6 23 ♘xe6 ♘d5 24 ♔f2

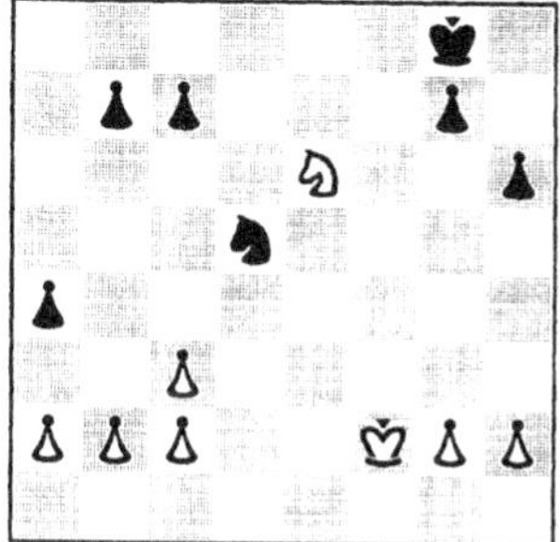

24 ... a3 [◻ 24 ... b6, ... ♔f7] 25 bxa3 ♘xc3 26 ♘xc7 ♘xa2 27 ♘b5 ♔f8 [◻ 27 ... g5] 28 ♔e3 ♔e7 29 ♔d2 ♔d7 30 ♘c3 ♘xc3 31 ♔xc3 ♔c6 32 ♔c4 g5 33 g4 b6 34 a4 **1-0**

L/N6123

### 1860-✕HM-5
**Mongredien,A.–**
**Harrwitz,D.**

1 e4 c5 2 f4 e6 3 ♘f3 ♘c6 4 ♗b5 ♘ge7 5 0-0 d5 6 exd5 ♕xd5 7 c4? ♕d3 8 ♘e5? ♕d4+ 9 ♔h1 f6 10 ♗xc6+ [◻ 10 ♘xc6] 10 ... bxc6 11 ♘f3 ♕xc4 12 d3 ♕a6 13 ♘c3 ♘d5 14 ♘a4?! ♗e7 15 ♖e1 0-0 16 ♗e3 ♕b5 17 ♖c1 ♘xe3 18 ♖xe3 ♗d6 19 ♖e4 ♖e8 20 ♖ec4 ♕b8 21 g3 ♗a6 22 ♖4c3 ♖d8 23 ♖b3 ♕c7 24 ♘xc5 ♗xc5 25 ♖xc5 ♕d6 26 ♖cc3 c5 27 ♕e2 ♖ac8 28 ♘d2 ♖d7 29 ♘e4 ♕d5 30 ♔g1 ♗b7 [◻ 30 ... c4] 31 ♖b5 f5 32 ♘xc5 ♖xc5 33 ♖bxc5 ♕h1+ 34 ♔f2 ♕xh2+ 35 ♔f1 ♕h1+ 36 ♔f2 ♕g2+ 37 ♔e1 ♕xg3+ 38 ♕f2 ♕h3 39 ♔d2 h5 40 ♕e2 ♖d6 41 ♖c7 ♖b6 42 b3 ♗f3 43 ♕e5 ♕g2+ 44 ♔c1 ♔h7 45 ♖e7 h4 46 ♖c2 ♕g4 47 ♖h2? ♕g1+ **0-1** L/N6123

### 1860-✕HM-6
**Harrwitz,D.=**
**Mongredien,A.**

1 e4 e5 2 f4 exf4 3 ♘f3 g5 4 h4 g4 5 ♘e5 ♘f6 6 ♗c4 d5 7 exd5 ♗d6 8 d4 ♗xe5 [◻ 8 ... ♘h5] 9 dxe5 ♘h5 10 ♘c3 ♕e7 11 e6? [11 ♕d4±] 11 ... fxe6 12 ♗b5+ ♗d7 13 ♕xg4 ♘g3 14 ♖h3 exd5+ 15 ♔d1 c6 16 ♕xf4 ♗xh3 17 ♕xg3 ♗e6 18 ♗d3 ♖g8 19 ♕f2 ♘d7 20 ♗g5 ♕g7 21 ♕e3 ♕e5 22 ♕f3 ♘c5 23 ♕h5+ ♔d7 24 ♔d2 ♖af8 25 ♖e1 ♖f2+ 26 ♔d1 ♕d4 27 ♕h6 ♗g4+ 28 ♘e2 ♗xe2+ 29 ♖xe2 ♖xe2 30 ♔xe2 ♖e8+ 31 ♔f3 ♘xd3 32 ♕xh7+ ♔d6 33 cxd3 ♖f8+ 34 ♔g3 ♕e5+ 35 ♔g4 ♕e2+ 36 ♔g3 ♕e6 37 d4 ♖f7 38 ♕h8 c5 39 dxc5+ ♔xc5 40 ♕c3+ ♔d6 41 ♗f4+ ♔e7 42 ♕c7+ ♔f8 43 ♕b8+ ♔g7 **½-½**

L/N6123

### 1860-✕HM-7
**Mongredien,A.–**
**Harrwitz,D.**

1 d4 f5 2 c4 e6 3 f4 ♘f6 4 ♘c3 ♘e4 5 ♘f3? [5 ♘xe4; 5 ♘h3] 5 ... ♗b4 6 ♗d2 ♗xc3 7 ♗xc3 d5 8 e3 0-0 9 ♗e2 ♘c6 10 0-0 ♘e7 11 ♘e5 ♖f6 12 ♗h5? [12 c5] 12 ... dxc4 13 g4 ♘d5 14 g5 ♖f8 15 ♗d2 b5 16 ♗f3 ♗b7 17 ♗xe4 fxe4 18 ♕g4 ♖f5 19 ♖f2 ♕e7 20 h4 c5 21 dxc5 ♕xc5 22 ♖e1 b4 23 ♕e2 ♖c8 24 ♖c1 c3 25 bxc3 bxc3 26 ♘g4 ♕a3 27 ♖b1 ♗a6 28 ♗c1 ♗xe2 29 ♗xa3 ♗xg4 **0-1** L/N6123

### 1860-✕HM-8
**Harrwitz,D.+**
**Mongredien,A.**

1 e4 e5 2 f4 exf4 3 ♘f3 g5 4 h4 g4 5 ♘e5 ♘f6 6 ♗c4 d5 7 exd5 ♗d6 8 d4 ♕e7? 9 ♗xf4 ♘h5 10 0-0 ♕xh4 [◻ 10 ... ♗xf4] 11 ♕e2 0-0 12 ♗h6 ♘g3 [◻ 12 ... ♗xe5, 13 ... g3] 13 ♕e3 ♘f5 14 ♖xf5 ♗xf5 15 ♗xf8 ♔xf8 16 g3 ♕h5 17 ♘d2 f6? 18 ♖f1+– ♔g7 19 ♘d3 ♘d7 20 ♘f4 ♗xf4 21 ♕xf4 ♔g6 22 ♕xc7 ♖e8 23 ♖xf5 ♔xf5 24 ♗d3+ ♔g5 25 ♕f4# **1-0** L/N6123

## KOLISCH✕MAUDE

[1860-✕KM1]

| | | |
|---|---|---|
| I.F. von Kolisch | 1 0 1 0 1 0 1 | 4 |
| P. Maude | 0 1 0 1 0 1 0 | 3 |

## 1860-✕KM1-1
**Kolisch, I.F. von+ Maude, P.**

⟨♘b1⟩ 1 e4 e5 2 ♘f3 ♘c6 3 ♗c4 ♗c5 4 b4 ♗xb4 5 c3 ♗a5 6 0-0 ♘f6 7 ♕c2 0-0 8 d4 d6 9 dxe5 ♘xe5 10 ♘xe5 dxe5 11 ♗a3 c5 12 f4 ♕c7 13 f5 ♗d7 14 ♖f3 b5 15 ♗f1 b4 16 ♗c1 ♗c6 17 ♖e3 ♗b6 18 c4 ♖ad8 19 ♗b2 ♖d4 20 ♗d3 ♖d7 21 ♕e2 ♖fd8 22 ♖d1 ♗a4 23 ♖e1 b3 24 axb3 ♗xb3 25 g4 ♘xe4 26 ♗xe4 ♕xe5 27 ♖xe5 ♕d6 28 ♖e8+ ♖xe8 29 ♕xe8+ ♕f8 30 ♕xd7 **1-0** L/N6126

## 1860-✕KM1-2
**Kolisch, I.F. von– Maude, P.**
[Löwenthal]

⟨♘b1⟩ 1 e4 e5 2 ♗c4 ♘f6 3 f4 ♗c5 4 fxe5? ♘xe4 5 d4?→ [5 ♕f3] 5 ... ♕h4+ 6 g3 ♘xg3 7 ♘f3 ♕e4+ 8 ♔f2 ♘xh1+ 9 ♔g1 ♗b6 10 ♗xf7+ ♔f8 11 c3 d5 12 ♘g5 ♕g4+! 13 ♕xg4 ♗xg4 14 ♗xd5 ♘c6 15 b3 ♘xd4 16 ♗a3+ ♔e8 17 ♔xh1 ♘c2 **0-1** M324

## 1860-✕KM1-3
**Kolisch, I.F. von+ Maude, P.**
[Staunton]

⟨♘b1⟩ 1 e4 e5 2 f4 exf4 3 ♘f3 g5 4 ♗c4 ♗g7 5 0-0 d6 6 c3 c6 7 ♕b3 ♕e7 8 d4 h6 9 ♗d2 b5 10 ♗d3 ♗g4 11 a4 ♗xf3 12 ♖xf3 bxa4 13 ♕xa4 ♕c7 14 ♖e1 ♘d7 15 ♗b1 ♘e7 16 ♕a3 0-0 17 e5 ♗xe5 18 dxe5 ♘xe5 19 ♖f2 ♘g4 20 c4 [20 ♖fe2] 20 ... ♘xf2 21 ♔xf2 ♕b6+ 22 c5 ♕b7 23 ♕d3 ♘g6 24 ♗c3 ♕b5?? 25 ♕xd6 ♖fd8 26 ♕f6 ♕xc5+ 27 ♔f1 ♕f8 28 ♗xg6 ...⚲ **1-0** M954-1860

## 1860-✕KM1-4
**Kolisch, I.F. von– Maude, P.**
[Staunton]

⟨♘b1⟩ 1 e4 e5 2 f4 ♗c5 3 ♘f3 d6 4 c3 ♘c6 [◻ 4 ... ♗g4] 5 d4 exd4 6 cxd4 ♗b6 7 ♗b5 ♗d7 8 0-0 ♘f6 9 ♔h1 0-0 10 d5 ♘e7 11 ♗d3 c6 12 e5 dxe5 13 fxe5 ♘exd5?! [13 ... ♘g4!; 13 ... ♘fxd5? 14 ♗xh7+ ♔xh7 15 ♘g5+ ♔g6 16 ♕d3+ ♗f5 17 ♕g3+–] 14 exf6 ♘xf6 15 ♗g5 ♗g4 16 ♕d2 h6 17 ♗xh6? gxh6 18 ♕xh6 ♕xd3 19 ♘e5 ♕h7 20 ♕xf6 ♗h5 21 ♘d7 ♕g6! 22 ♕e7 ♗d4 [22 ... ♖fd8 23 ♘f6+ △ 24 ♕e5] 23 ♘xf8 ♖xf8 24 ♕xb7 ♖e8! 25 ♖ac1 c5 26 ♕xa7 ♖e2 27 ♕a8+ ♔g7 28 b3 ♗g4 29 a4 ♗f5 30 ♕f3 ♖b2 31 ♖fe1 ♗d7 32 ♖e7 ♖f2 33 ♕xf2 [33 ♕g3 ♕xg3 34 hxg3 ♖f6–+] 33 ... ♗xf2 34 ♖xd7 ♕e6 35 ♖b7 ♕e3 36 ♖d1 ♕e2 37 ♖bd7 ♗d4 38 ♖c1 ♕b2 39 ♖f1 ♕xb3 40 a5 ♕c4 41 ♖b1 ♕a4 42 ♖a7 c4 43 ♖c7 c3 44 ♖f1 c2? [44 ... ♗f6; 44 ... ♗e5] 45 ♖cxf7+ ♔g6 46 ♖7f4 ♕c6 [◻ 46 ... ♕c4] 47 ♖xd4 c1♕ 48 ♖d6+ ♕xd6 49 ♖xc1 ♕a3 50 ♖f1 ♕xa5 51 ♔g1? [51 h3=] 51 ... ♕c5+ 52 ♔h1 ♔g5 53 ♖a1 ♔f4 54 ♖a4+? [54 ♖f1+ △ 55 h3 56 ♖f3=] 54 ... ♔e3 55 ♖a1 ♕c2 56 ♖f1 ♔e2 57 ♖g1 ♔f2 58 ♖a1 ♕d2 59 ♖b1 ♕d4 60 ♖c1 ♕e4 ...⚲ **0-1** M954-1860

## 1860-✕KM1-5
**Kolisch, I.F. von+ Maude, P.**
[Staunton]

⟨♘b1⟩ 1 e4 e5 2 f4 ♗c5 3 ♘f3 d6 4 c3 ♗g4 5 ♗c4 ♘f6 6 fxe5 dxe5 7 ♗xf7+ ♔f8 8 ♗c4 ♘xe4 9 d4 [9 ♖f1!] 9 ... exd4 10 b4 ♘xc3 11 ♕d3 ♕e7+ 12 ♔f1 ♗xb4 13 ♗d2 ♗xf3 14 gxf3 ♘c6 15 ♖e1 ♕c5 [15 ... ♕f6? 16 ♖e6; 15 ... ♕d7? 16 ♗e6; 15 ... ♕d6?? 16 ♕f5+ ♕f6 17 ♕xf6+ gxf6 18 ♗h6#] 16 ♖g1 ♘a5 17 ♗e6 h6 18 ♕g6 ♕e7

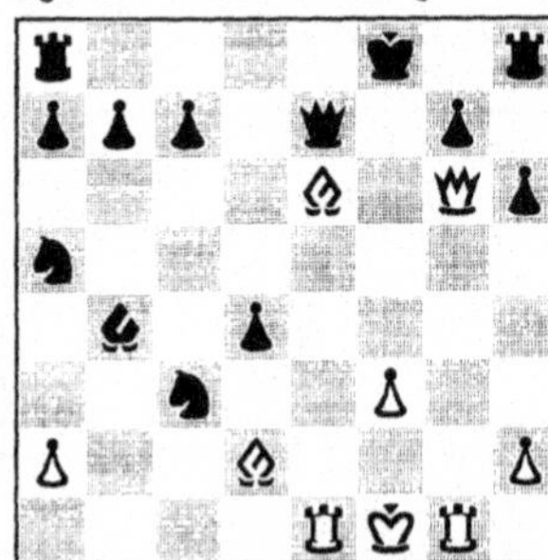

19 ♗xh6 ♖xh6 20 ♕xh6 ♕f6 21 ♕h8+ ♔e7 22 ♖xg7+ ♔d6 23 ♖d7+ ...⚲ **1-0** M954-1860

## 1860-✕KM1-6
**Kolisch, I.F. von– Maude, P.**
[Staunton]

⟨♘b1⟩ 1 e4 e5 2 f4 exf4 3 ♘f3 d5 4 exd5 ♕xd5 5 d4 ♘f6 6 ♗e2 c5 7 c4 ♕d8 8 d5 ♗d6 9 0-0 0-0 10 ♗d3 ♗g4 11 ♕e1 ♘bd7 12 ♗c2 ♖e8 13 ♕h4 ♗xf3 14 ♖xf3 ♘e4 15 ♕xd8 ♖axd8 16 ♗xf4 ♗xf4 17 ♖xf4 ♘d6 18 b3 ♖e2 19 ♗d3 ♖d2 20 ♗f1 ♖e8 21 a3 ♖b2 22 b4 cxb4 23 axb4 ♖xb4 24 ♖xa7 ♘e5 25 ♖d4 ♘exc4 26 ♗xc4 ♘xc4 27 d6 ♖b2 28 h3 ♘e5 29 d7? ♖d8? [29 ... ♘f3+!] 30 ♖a8 ♘c6 31 ♖xd8+ ♘xd8 32 ♖e4 f6 33 ♖e8+ ♔f7 34 ♖xd8 ♖d2 35 ♖h8 ♖xd7 36 ♖xh7 b5 37 ♖h5 ♖b7 38 ♖c5 b4 39 ♖c2 ♔e6 40 ♔f2 ♔d5 41 ♔e3 b3 42 ♖b2 ♔c4 43 ♔d2 ♖a7 44 ♔c1 ♖a1+ 45 ♖b1 ♖xb1+ ...⚲ **0-1** M954-1860

## 1860-✕KM1-7
**Kolisch, I.F. von+ Maude, P.**
[Staunton]

⟨♘b1⟩ 1 e4 e5 2 ♘f3 ♘c6 3 ♗c4 ♗c5 4 0-0 d6 5 b4 ♗xb4 6 c3 ♗c5 7 d4 exd4 8 cxd4 ♗b6 9 ♗b2 ♘f6 10 e5 dxe5 11 ♗a3 ♗e6 12 ♗xe6 fxe6 13 ♕a4 ♗xd4 14 ♖ab1 ♗b6 15 ♖fd1 ♘d7 16 ♖bc1 ♘d4 17 ♘xe5 c6 [17 ... c5 18 ♖xd4 cxd4 19 ♖c6 ♘xe5 20 ♖xe6+ ♔f7 21 ♕b3!+–] 18 ♖xd4 ♗xd4 19 ♖xc6 ♕f6 20 ♖c8+ **1-0** M954-1860

## KOLISCH✕MAUDE
|1860-✕KM2|

| | | | | |
|---|---|---|---|---|
| I.F. von Kolisch | 1̂ | 1̂ | 1̂ | 3̂ |
| P. Maude | 0̂ | 0̂ | 0̂ | 0̂ |

## 1860-✕KM2-1̂
**Maude, P.– Kolisch, I.F. von**
[Staunton]

1 e4 e5 2 ♘f3 ♘c6 3 ♗b5 a6 4 ♗a4 ♘f6 5 0-0 b5 [5 ... ♘xe4?!] 6 ♗b3 ♗c5 7 c3 d6 8 d4 exd4 9 cxd4 ♗b6 10 ♗g5 [10 ♕c2 △ 11 e5] 10 ... h6 11 ♗xf6 ♕xf6 12 e5 dxe5 13 dxe5 ♕g6 14 ♗d5 ♗b7 15 e6 0-0-0! 16 ♕b3 fxe6 17 ♗xe6+ ♔b8 18 ♗f7 ♕f6 19 ♘c3 ♖hf8 20 ♗h5?? ♕f5 21 a4 ♕xh5 22 axb5 axb5 23 ♘xb5 ♖xf3 24 gxf3 ♘e5 **0-1** M954-1861

## 1860-✕KM2-2̂
**Kolisch, I.F. von+ Maude, P.**
[Staunton]

1 e4 e5 2 ♘f3 ♘c6 3 ♗c4 ♗c5 4 b4 ♗xb4 5 c3 ♗c5 6 0-0 d6 7 d4 exd4 8 cxd4 ♗b6 9 ♘c3 ♗g4 10 ♕a4 ♗xf3 11 d5 ♗g4 12 dxc6 bxc6 13 ♕xc6+ ♗d7 14 ♕d5 ♗e6 15 ♗b5+ ♔f8 16 ♕d3 ♘e7 17 ♘d5 ♗xd5 18 exd5 ♘g6 19 ♗b2 ♕g5 20 ♖ae1 ♘f4 21 ♕e4 f5 22 ♕f3 ♘g6 23 ♖e6 ♔f7 24 ♖fe1 ♖hf8 25 ♕c3 ♘e5

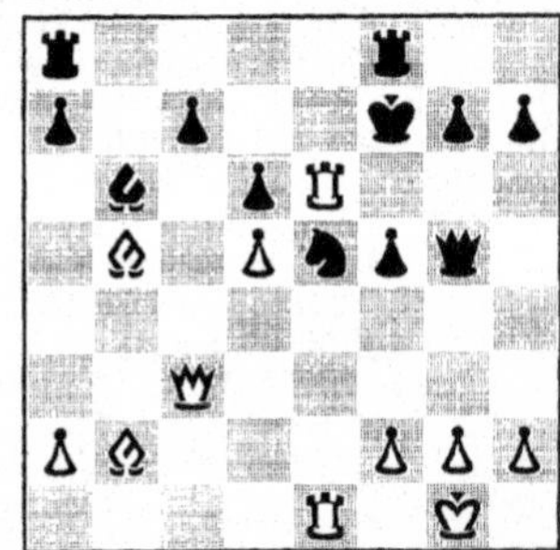

26 ♖1xe5! dxe5 27 ♕xe5 ♔g8 28 ♖e7 ♖f7 29 ♖xf7 ♔xf7 30 ♕e6+ ♔f8 31 ♗a3+ **1-0** M954-1861

## 1860-✕KM2-3̂
**Maude, P.– Kolisch, I.F. von**
[Löwenthal]

1 e4 e5 2 ♘f3 ♘c6 3 ♗b5 a6 4 ♗a4 ♘f6 5 0-0 b5? 6 ♗b3 ♗c5 7 ♗d5 [7 c3!±] 7 ... 0-0 8 c3 ♗b6 9 d4 exd4 10 cxd4 ♘xd5 11 exd5 ♘e7 12

♕b3 d6 13 ♗e3 ♗g4 14 ♘bd2 h6 15 h3 ♗c8 16 a4 ♗b7 17 a×b5 ♗×d5 18 ♕d3 a5 19 ♘h4 ♕d7 20 f4 f5 21 ♘df3 ♖ae8? [21 ... ♕e6 △ 22 ... ♗e4] 22 ♗d2 ♖a8 23 ♔h2 ♔h7 24 g4 ♗e4 25 ♕e2 ♗×f3 [25 ... d5? 26 ♘e5] 26 ♘×f3 f×g4 27 h×g4 ♖ae8 [27 ... ♕×g4?? 28 ♘g5+] 28 ♕d3+ ♔h8 29 ♔g3 ♖f7 30 ♖h1 ♘d5 31 ♘g5!→ ♘f6 32 ♘×f7+ ♕×f7 33 ♖ae1 ♖f8 34 ♖h4 d5! 35 ♖e5 ♘e4+ 36 ♔g2 ♘d6 37 ♕e3 ♘c4 38 ♕e2 ♗×d4! [38 ... ♘×e5] 39 ♖f5∞ ♗f6 40 ♗c3 ♖e8 41 ♗e5 d4 42 ♔g1 ♔g8 43 ♖h3 ♘e3 44 ♖×e3 d×e3 45 ♕×e3 g6 46 ♖×f6 ♕×f6 47 ♕b3+ ♕e6 48 ♕×e6+ ♖×e6 49 ♗×c7 ♖e1+ 50 ♔f2 ♖c1 51 ♗e5 ♖c5 52 b6 ♖b5 53 ♗d4 ♔f7 54 ♔e3 ♔e6 55 ♔e4 h5 56 g×h5 g×h5 57 ♔f3 ♔f5 58 ♔g3 a4 59 ♔h4 ♔×f4 60 b7 ♖×b7 61 ♔×h5 ♔f5 62 ♔h6 ♔e4 ...? **0-1** M324

**KOLISCH✕MEDLEY**
[1860-✕KM3]

| | | | | | |
|---|---|---|---|---|---|
| I.F. von Kolisch | 1 | ½ | 1 | ½ | 3 |
| G.W. Medley | 0 | ½ | 0 | ½ | 1 |

**1860-✕KM3-1** 2 x 60
**Kolisch,I.F.von+ Medley,G.W.**
[Löwenthal]

1 e4 e5 2 ♘f3 ♘c6 3 ♗c4 ♗c5 4 b4 ♗b6 5 0-0 d6 6 a4 a6 [□ 6 ... a5] 7 c3 ♘f6 [□ 7 ... ♗g4 △ 8 ... ♘ge7] 8 d4 0-0 9 ♗g5 ♗g4 10 a5 ♗a7 11 b5 a×b5 12 ♗×b5 e×d4 13 a6 ♗b6 14 ♗×c6 b×c6 15 c×d4 h6 16 ♗×f6 ♕×f6 17 ♖a4 ♗×f3 18 g×f3 ♕f4! 19 ♕d3 f5 20 ♘c3 f×e4 21 f×e4 ♕f3? 22 ♕×f3! ♖×f3 23 ♘e2 ♖d3 24 ♖c1 c5 [24 ... ♖d2 25 ♔f1] 25 d×c5 ♗×c5 26 ♖c2 ♖a3 27 ♖×a3 ♗×a3 28 ♖×c7 ♖×a6 29 ♘g3 ♗c5 30 e5 ♖a1+ 31 ♔g2 ♖e1 32 f4 g5 33 ♘f5 ♖e2+ 34 ♔h3 g×f4 35 e×d6 ♗b6 36 ♖b7 ♗d8 37 ♘×h6+ [37 ... ♔f8 38 ♖f7+ ♔e8 39 d7#] **1-0** M324

**1860-✕KM3-2**
**Medley,G.W.= Kolisch,I.F.von**
[Löwenthal]

1 e4 e5 2 ♘f3 ♘f6 3 ♘×e5 d6 4 ♘f3 ♘×e4 5 d4 d5 6 ♗d3 ♗e7 7 h3 0-0 8 0-0 ♘c6 9 c4 ♗e6 10 c×d5 ♗×d5 11 ♘c3 f5 12 ♗f4 ♖c8 13 ♘×d5 ♕×d5 14 ♖c1 ♔h8 15 ♗c4 ♕d7 16 ♗b5± ♖cd8 17 ♗×c6 [□ 17 ♕a4] 17 ... b×c6 18 ♕a4 c5 19 ♕a5 [□ 19 ♕×d7 ♖×d7 20 ♘e5 ♖×d4 21 ♘c6 ♖d7 22 f3 ♘f6 23 ♘×e7] 19 ... ♗d6 20 ♗×d6 c×d6 21 d×c5 d×c5 22 b4 c×b4 23 ♖c7 ♕d6 24 ♖×a7 ♕c5 25 ♕×c5 ♘×c5 26 ♖c1 ♖d7 27 ♖×d7 ♘×d7 28 ♖c7 ♘f6 29 ♖b7 ♖a8 30 ♖×b4 ♖×a2 31 ♖b8+ ♘g8 **½-½** M324

**1860-✕KM3-3**
**Kolisch,I.F.von+ Medley,G.W.**
[Löwenthal]

1 e4 e5 2 ♘f3 ♘c6 3 c3 d5? [3 ... ♘f6!] 4 ♕a4! ♗d7? 5 e×d5 ♘d4 6 ♕d1 ♘×f3+ 7 ♕×f3 ♘f6 8 ♗c4 ♗c5 9 d3 ♕e7 10 ♗g5 c6 11 ♘d2 h6 12 ♗×f6 ♕×f6 13 ♕×f6 g×f6 14 ♘e4 ♗e7 15 d×c6 ♗×c6 16 f3+− ♖d8 17 0-0-0 ♗×e4 18 d×e4 ♗d6 19 ♖d3 ♔e7 20 ♖hd1 ♖hg8 21 g3 ♖g5 22 ♗×f7 ♗c7 23 ♖×d8 ♗×d8 24 ♗d5 b6 25 ♗c6 ...? **1-0** M324

**1860-✕KM3-4**
**Medley,G.W.= Kolisch,I.F.von**
[Löwenthal]

1 e4 e5 2 ♘f3 ♘f6 3 ♘×e5 d6 4 ♘f3 ♘×e4 5 d4 d5 6 ♗d3 ♗e7 7 0-0 0-0 8 ♖e1 ♘f6 [8 ... f5!? 9 c4 ♗e6] 9 ♗f4 ♗g4 10 ♘bd2 ♘c6 11 c3 ♘h5 12 ♗e3 ♗d6! [12 ... f5?! 13 h3±] 13 h3 ♗d7 14 ♘e5 g6! [14 ... ♘f6 15 ♗g5!] 15 g4 ♘g7 16 f4 ♗×e5 17 f×e5 f6 18 e×f6 ♕×f6 19 ♖f1 ♕d6 20 ♔g2 ♘e6 21 ♕e2 ♖ae8 22 ♖×f8+ ♕×f8 23 ♖f1 ♕d6 24 ♕f2 ♖f8 25 ♕g3 ♕×g3+ 26 ♔×g3 ♖×f1 27 ♗×f1 **½-½** M324-1861

**1860-★AB-1**
**Budzinski, J.− Anderssen, A.**
Paris [Journoud]

1 e4 e5 2 ♘f3 ♘c6 3 ♗c4 ♗c5 4 c3 ♘f6 5 0-0 ♕e7 6 d4 ♗b6 7 ♗g5 d6 8 a4 a6 9 ♖e1 h6 10 ♗×f6 ♕×f6 11 ♘a3 g5 12 ♖e2 ♘e7 13 ♗d3 ♘g6 14 ♘c4 ♗a7 15 ♗c2 ♗g4 16 ♖e3 0-0-0 17 h3 h5!? 18 h×g4 h×g4 19 ♘h2 ♖h4 20 ♘×g4! [20 g3 ♖×h2 21 ♔×h2 ♕×f2−+] 20 ... ♕e6 21 ♖g3 [□ 21 d5 ♕×g4 22 ♕×g4 ♖×g4 23 ♖h3 ♘f4 24 ♖h2=] 21 ... ♖dh8 22 ♖h3 ♕×c4 23 ♖×h4 ♖×h4 24 ♗b3 ♕c6 25 g3 ♖h8 26 ♕f3 e×d4 27 ♗×f7 ♘e5 28 ♘×e5 d×e5 29 ♕f5+ ♔b8 30 ♕×e5 ♕h6! 31 ♔f1 d3 32 ♔g2? [□ 32 ♔e1] 32 ... g4!−+ 33 ♗h5 ♕×h5 34 ♕×h5 ♖×h5 35 ♖d1 ♖h8 36 ♖×d3 ♖f8 37 f4 g×f3+ 38 ♖×f3 ♖g8 39 ♖f5 ♔c8 40 ♔f3 ♔d7 41 ♖f7+ ♔c6 42 b4 ♗b8 43 c4 ♔d6 44 g4 ♔e6 45 ♖f5 c6 46 b5 ♗e5 47 g5 ♖d8 48 g6 ♖g8 49 ♖f7 c×b5 50 c×b5 a×b5 51 a×b5 b6 52 ♖b7 ♗d4 53 ♔e2 ♖×g6 54 ♔d3 ♗c5 55 ♖h7 ♖g3+ 56 ♔c4 ♔e5 57 ♖h5+ ♔×e4 58 ♖×c5 b×c5 59 ♔×c5 ♔e5 60 ♔c6 ♔e6 61 b6 ♖c3+ 62 ♔b7 ♔d7 **0-1** L/N6016

**1860-★AC-1**
**Chapelle− Anderssen, A.**
Paris [Journoud]

1 e4 e5 2 ♘f3 ♘c6 3 d4 e×d4 4 ♗c4 ♗c5 5 0-0 d6 6 c3 ♗g4 7 h3 ♗h5 8 g4 ♗g6 9 ♗g5 f6 10 ♗h4 h5 11 g5 d×c3 12 ♘×c3 ♘ge7 13 ♗d5 ♘×d5 14 e×d5 ♘e5 15 ♖e1 ♕d7 16 ♘×e5 d×e5 17 ♘a4 ♗b4 18 ♖e3 0-0-0 19 ♕b3 ♗d6 20 ♖c1 [□ 20 g×f6] 20 ... f5! 21 ♖ec3 e4 22 ♘c5 ♗×c5 23 ♖×c5 f4 24 ♖×c7+ ♕×c7 25 ♖×c7+ ♔×c7 26 ♕c3+ ♔b8 27 ♕×g7 ♖hg8 28 ♕e5+ ♔a8 29 d6 e3 30 f×e3 f3 31 b4 [□ 31 ♗g3 (31 ♗f2) △ 32 h4±] 31 ... ♗e8 32 b5 ♗d7∓ 33 ♔h2 ♖df8 34 ♗f2 ♖f5 35 ♕d4 ♖f×g5 36 e4 b6 37 e5 ♔b8 38 a4 ♖c8 39 ♕e3 ♖g2+ 40 ♔h1 ♖c2 41 ♗g1 ♖g3 42 ♗f2 ♖×h3+ 43 ♔g1 ♖c8−+ 44 e6 ♖g8+ 45 ♔f1 ♖h1+ 46 ♗g1 ♖g×g1+ 47 ♕×g1 ♖×g1+ 48 ♔×g1 ♗×e6 **0-1** L/N6016

**1860-★AG-1** iv 60
**Anderssen, A.+ Guibert**
Paris

1 e4 c5 2 ♘f3 e6 3 d4 d5 4 e×d5 e×d5 5 ♗b5+ ♘c6 6 0-0 ♗d6 7 ♘c3 ♘e7 8 ♗g5 f6 9 d×c5 ♗×c5 10 ♗f4 0-0 11 ♕d2 ♗e6 12 ♖fe1 ♗f7 13 a3 ♘g6 14 ♗g3 ♘ce7 15 ♗d3 a6 16 h4 ♕d7? [16 ... h5] 17 h5 ♘h8 18 h6 g5 19 ♘e2 ♗h5 20 ♘ed4 ♗×f3 21 ♘×f3 ♘f5 22 ♗×f5 ♕×f5 23 b4 ♗b6 24 ♖e7 ♖f7 25 ♖ae1 ♖af8 26 ♖7e6 ♗a7 [□ 26 ... ♗c7] 27 ♗d6! ♘g6 28 ♗×f8 ♖×f8 29 c4 g4 30 ♘d4 ♕h5 31 c5 ♗b8 32 g3 ♗e5 33 c6 ♕h3 [△ 34 ... ♘h4] 34 ♘f5! b×c6

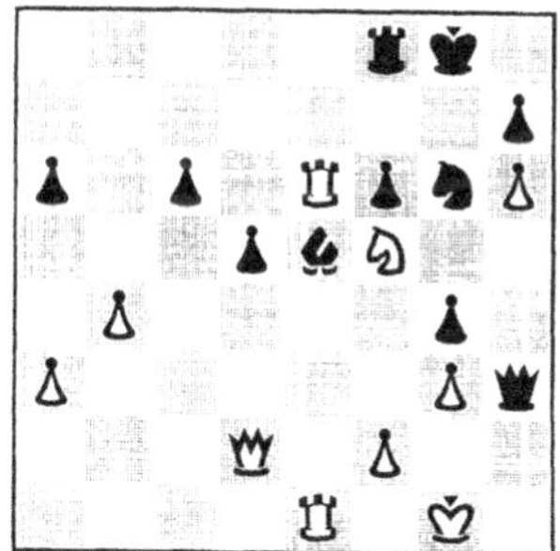

35 ♖1×e5 f×e5 36 ♕g5 ♔h8 37 ♖×g6 h×g6 38 ♕×g6 ♖g8 39 ♕f6+ ♔h7 40 ♕f7+ ♔h8 41 ♘h4 **1-0** L/N6016

**1860-★AH-1** viii 60
**Anderssen,A.− Hirschfeld,P.**
Berlin

1 e4 e5 2 f4 e×f4 3 ♘f3 g5 4 h4 g4 5 ♘e5 ♘f6 6 ♗c4 d5 7 e×d5 ♗d6 8 d4 ♘h5 9 0-0 ♕×h4 10 ♕e1 ♕×e1

11 ♖xe1 0-0 12 ♘c3 ♗f5 13 ♗b3 ♘d7 14 ♔f2 ♖ae8 15 ♖h1 ♘df6 16 g3 fxg3+ 17 ♔g2 ♗xe5 18 dxe5 ♖xe5 19 ♗h6 ♖fe8 20 ♗a4 ♖8e7 21 ♗g5 ♗e4+ 22 ♘xe4 ♖xe4 23 ♗b5 ♘f4+ 24 ♔xg3 ♖e3+ **0-1** L/N6047-1861

### 1860-★AH-2 viii 60

**Hirschfeld,P.+ Anderssen,A.**

Berlin

1 e4 e5 2 ♘f3 ♘c6 3 ♗c4 ♗c5 4 b4 ♗xb4 5 c3 ♗a5 6 d4 exd4 7 0-0 ♗b6 8 cxd4 d6 9 ♘c3 ♗g4 10 ♗b5 ♗d7 11 e5 dxe5 12 dxe5 ♘ge7 13 ♗g5 h6 14 ♗h4 g5 15 ♘e4 ♗e6 16 ♘f6+ ♔f8 17 ♕a4 gxh4 18 ♖ad1 ♘d4 19 ♘xd4 ♗xd4 20 ♖xd4 ♕c8 21 ♖fd1 ♔g7 22 ♗d7 ♗xd7 23 ♖xd7 **1-0** L/N6047-1861

### 1860-★AH-3 vii 60

**Hirschfeld,P.+ Anderssen,A.**

Berlin

1 e4 e5 2 ♘f3 ♘c6 3 ♗c4 ♗c5 4 b4 ♗xb4 5 c3 ♗a5 6 d4 exd4 7 0-0 dxc3 8 ♕b3 ♕f6 9 e5 ♕g6 10 ♘xc3 ♗xc3 11 ♕xc3 ♘ge7 12 ♘g5 ♘d8 13 ♗e3 h6 14 ♘h3 b6 15 ♘f4 ♕c6 16 ♕b3 ♘e6 17 ♘xe6 fxe6 18 ♖fd1 ♕e4 19 ♖d4 ♕xe5 20 ♖ad1 ♘f5 21 ♗xe6 ♘xd4 22 ♗f7+ ♔f8 23 ♗xd4 ♕f5 24 ♗d5 c6 25 ♕a3+ ♔e8 26 ♖e1+ ♔d8 27 ♕e7+ ♔c7 28 ♗e5+ ♔b7 29 ♗xc6+ ♔xc6 30 ♕d6+ ♔b7 31 ♕d5+ ♔a6 32 ♖e4 b5 33 a4 ♖b8 34 axb5+ ♖xb5 35 ♖a4+ ♔b6 36 ♕d6+ **1-0** L/N3034

### 1860-★AH-4

**Anderssen,A.− Hirschfeld,P.**

[Lange & Suhle & Hirschfeld]

1 e4 e5 2 f4 exf4 3 ♘f3 g5 4 h4 g4 5 ♘e5 ♘f6 6 ♗c4 d5 7 exd5 ♗d6 8 d4 ♘h5 9 ♗b5+ ♔f8 10 ♘c3 ♘g3 11 ♖h2 ♕f6 12 ♘e2 ♘xe2 13 ♕xe2 a6 14 ♗d3 ♘d7 15 ♘xg4 ♕xd4 16 ♖h1 ♘f6 [◻ 16 ... ♘c5] 17 ♘xf6 ♕xf6 18 ♗d2 ♕xb2 19 ♖d1 ♕g7 20 ♗c1 ♗g4 21 ♗b2 ♕g8 22 ♕f2 ♖e8+ 23 ♔d2 ♗xd1 24 ♖xd1 h5 25 ♗f6 ♖h6 26 ♗g5 ♕g7 27 c3 ♖g6 28 ♗xg6 ♕xg6 29 ♕d4 ♗e5 30 ♕b4+ ♔g8 31 ♕xb7 ♕e4 32 ♕c6 ♖b8 **0-1** L/N6047-1861

### 1860-★AH-5 9 viii 60

**Anderssen,A.− Hirschfeld,P.**

Berlin [Bachmann]

1 e4 e5 2 f4 exf4 3 ♘f3 g5 4 h4 g4 5 ♘e5 ♘f6 6 ♗c4 d5 7 exd5 ♗d6 8 d4 [8 ♗b5+ c6 9 dxc6 0-0!] 8 ... ♘h5 9 0-0 ♕xh4 [9 ... f3] 10 ♕e1 ♕xe1 11 ♖xe1 0-0 12 ♘c3 [◻ 12 ♗d3 ♖e8] 12 ... ♗f5 13 g3 f3 [13 ... fxg3 14 ♔g2!] 14 ♗h6 ♖fe8 15 ♘xf3 ♘d7 16 ♘h4 ♘xg3 17 ♗b5 ♖xe1+ 18 ♖xe1 ♘f8 19 ♔f2 ♗xc2 20 ♖g1 ♘e4+ 21 ♔e3 ♘xc3 22 ♖xg4+ ♘g6 23 bxc3 a6 24 ♗d3 ♖e8+ 25 ♔d2 ♗xd3 26 ♔xd3 b5 27 ♘f5 f6 28 ♖g1 ♔f7 29 ♖f1 [△ 30 ♘xd6+ cxd6 31 ♗g5] 29 ... ♘e7 30 ♘xe7 ♗xe7 [30 ... ♖xe7 31 ♗g5] 31 ♖b1 ♗d6 32 a4 ♔g6 33 ♗d2 ♖b8 34 axb5 axb5 35 ♔e4 f5+ 36 ♔f3 [△ 37 c4] 36 ... ♖b6 37 ♗f4 ♗xf4 38 ♔xf4 ♔f6 39 ♖h1 b4 40 c4? [◻ 40 cxb4 ♖xb4 41 ♖xh7 ♖xd4+ 42 ♔e3] 40 ... b3 41 ♖h6+ ♔g7 42 ♖xb6 cxb6 43 d6 ♔f7 44 c5 b2 **0-1** L/N3033

### 1860-★AH-6

**Hirschfeld,P.+ Anderssen,A.**

Berlin? [Lange & Suhle & Hirschfeld]

1 e4 e5 2 f4 exf4 3 ♘f3 g5 4 ♗c4 ♗g7 5 0-0 h6 6 d4 d6 7 g3 ♗h3 8 ♖f2 ♕e7 9 gxf4 g4 10 ♘e1 ♘f6 11 e5 g3 12 hxg3 ♘e4 13 ♕f3 ♘xf2 14 ♕xb7 0-0 15 ♕xa8 c6 16 ♔xf2 dxe5 17 dxe5 ♕c5+ 18 ♗e3 ♕xc4 19 ♘d2 ♕d5 20 ♕xa7 ♕h1 21 ♔e2 ♘d7 [◻ 21 ... ♖d8] 22 ♖d1 ♘xe5 23 fxe5 ♗xe5 24 ♘ef3 ♕g2+ 25 ♗f2 ♗g4 26 ♖g1 ♕h3 27 ♕e7 ♕h5 28 ♗c5 ♖a8 29 ♔f2 f6 30 ♖g2 ♖e8 31 ♖h2 ♗xg3+ 32 ♔xg3 ♗h3 33 ♖xh3 **1-0** L/N6047-1861

### 1860-★AJ-1 iv 60

**Anderssen, A.+ Journoud, P.**

Paris [Journoud]

1 e4 e5 2 f4 exf4 3 ♗c4 d5 4 ♗xd5 ♘f6 5 ♘c3 ♗b4 6 ♘f3 c6? [◻ 6 ... 0-0 △ 7 ... c6] 7 ♗b3 ♗xc3 8 bxc3 ♘xe4± 9 ♗a3 ♘g5 10 0-0 ♘xf3+ 11 ♕xf3 ♗e6 12 ♗xe6 fxe6 13 ♕h5+ ♔d7 14 ♖xf4 ♔c8 15 ♖d4 ♘d7 16 ♖f1 ♕e8 17 ♖f7 ♘f6 18 ♗d6!! ♘d5 19 ♖xd5 cxd5 20 ♖c7+ [20 ... ♔d8 21 ♕g5+] **1-0** L/N6016

### 1860-★AJ-2

**Anderssen, A.− Journoud, P.**

Paris

1 e4 e5 2 ♘f3 d6 3 d4 exd4 4 ♕xd4 ♗d7 5 ♗c4 ♘c6 6 ♕d3 ♗e7 7 0-0 ♘f6 8 ♘c3 0-0 9 a3 ♗g4 10 ♗a2 ♗xf3 11 ♕xf3 ♘e5 12 ♕e2 c6 13 f4 ♘g6 14 ♗e3 ♕c7 15 ♖f3 ♘g4 16 ♗d4 ♗f6 17 ♗xf6 ♘xf6 18 ♖h3 ♘xf4 19 ♕f3 ♘xh3+ 20 ♕xh3 ♖ae8 21 ♖e1 ♖e5 **0-1** L/N6016

### 1860-★AK-1 iv 60

**Anderssen, A.+ Kolisch, I.F. von**

Paris

1 e4 e5 2 ♘f3 ♘f6 3 ♘xe5 ♕e7 4 ♘f3 ♕xe4+ 5 ♗e2 ♗c5 6 0-0 0-0 7 d4 ♗b6 8 c4 c6 9 ♘c3 ♕e7 10 ♗g5 h6 11 ♗h4 g5 12 ♗g3 d5 13 ♘e5 ♘bd7 14 cxd5 ♘xd5 15 ♘xd5 cxd5 16 f4 gxf4 17 ♘xd7 fxg3 18 ♘f6+ ♔g7 19 ♕d3 ♖h8 20 ♗h5 ♗e6 21 ♕xg3+ ♔f8 22 ♕e5 ♕c7 23 ♕e3 ♕d6 24 ♖f4 ♖c8 25 ♖af1 ♖c7 26 ♕g3 ♖c4 27 ♘h7+ ♔e8 28 ♕g7 ♖xh7 29 ♕xh7 ♖xd4 30 ♗xf7+ ♗xf7 31 ♕xf7+ ♔d8 32 ♕g8+ ♔c7 33 ♖f7+ ♔c6 34 ♕e8+ ♔c5 35 ♔h1 ♖h4 36 ♖c1+ ♖c4 37 b4+ ♔xb4 38 ♖b1+ ♔a3 39 ♖f3+ **1-0** L/N6047

### 1860-★AK-2 iv 60

**Kolisch,I.F.von+ Anderssen,A.**

Paris [Boden]

1 e4 e5 2 f4 exf4 3 ♘f3 g5 4 h4 g4 5 ♘e5 h5 6 ♗c4 ♖h7 7 d4 f3 8 gxf3 d6 9 ♘d3 ♗e7 10 ♗e3 ♗xh4+ 11 ♔d2 ♗g5 12 ♘c3 [◻ 12 f4] 12 ... ♗xe3+ 13 ♔xe3 ♕g5+ 14 f4 ♕g7 15 e5 ♗f5 16 ♘b5! ♘a6 17 exd6 0-0-0 18 ♘e5 cxd6 19 ♘xf7 ♖e8+ 20 ♔d2 ♔b8 21 ♘fxd6 ♖f8 22 ♕e2 [△ 23 ♘xf5, 24 ♕e8‡] 22 ... ♗g6 23 ♖ae1 ♘b4? [◻ 23 ... ♕f6±] 24 f5 ♕h6+ 25 ♔c3 **1-0** M392

### 1860-★AK-3 iv 60

**Kolisch,I.F.von+ Anderssen,A.**

Paris [Boden]

1 e4 e5 2 f4 exf4 3 ♘f3 g5 4 h4 g4 5 ♘e5 h5 6 ♗c4 ♖h7 7 d4 f3 8 gxf3 d6 9 ♘d3 ♗e7 10 ♗e3 ♗xh4+ 11 ♔d2 ♗g5 12 f4 ♗h6 13 ♘c3 ♗g7 14 f5 ♘c6 15 ♕g1 ♗d7 16 ♕e1 [◻ 16 a3] 16 ... ♘a5 17 ♗b3 ♘xb3+ 18 axb3 ♗c6 19 ♘f4 ♘f6 20 ♔c1 ♗h6 21 e5! ♗xh1 22 exf6 ♗f3 23 ♘fd5 ♔f8 24 ♗xh6+ ♖xh6 25 ♕e3 ♖xf6 26 ♕g5! ♖g6 27 ♕xd8+ ♖xd8 28 fxg6 fxg6 [◻ 28 ... h4] 29 ♘xc7 ♔g8 30 ♘e6 ♖e8 31 ♔d2 h4 32 ♘g5 ♖f8 33 ♘ce4 d5 34 ♘f2 g3 35 ♘fh3 ♗g4 36 c4 ♖f5 37 cxd5 ♖xd5 38 ♖e4 ♗xh3 39 ♘xh3 ♖h5 40 ♖f4 ♔g7 41 ♔d3 a6 42 ♔e4 ♖b5 43 ♖xh4 ♖xb3 44 ♖g4 ♔h6 [◻ 44 ... ♔f6] 45 ♘f4 g5 46 ♘d3 ♔h5 47 ♖xg3 ♔h4 48 ♖g1 g4 49 d5 ♖b6 50 ♔e5 ♖h6 51 d6 ♔g5 52 d7 **1-0** M392

**1860-★AK-4**
**Anderssen,A.–Kolisch, I.F.von**
Paris
1 e4 e5 2 ♘f3 ♘c6 3 ♗b5 a6 4 ♗a4 ♘f6 5 d4 e×d4 6 0-0 ♗e7 7 ♖e1 0-0 8 e5 ♘e8 9 c3 d×c3 10 ♘×c3 d6 11 ♘d5 ♘×e5 12 ♘×e5 d×e5 13 ♘×e7+ ♕×e7 14 ♗c2 ♘d6 15 ♗f4 f6 16 ♕h5 g6 17 ♕h4 g5 18 ♖×e5 f×e5 19 ♗×g5 ♕f7 20 ♗h6 ♖e8 21 g4 ♔h8 22 ♗g5 e4 23 f3 ♗d7 24 ♖f1 ♖f8 25 ♗e3 ♖ae8 26 ♗d4+ ♔g8 27 f4 ♘b5 28 ♗c5 ♕f6 29 ♕f2 b6 30 ♗e3 c5 31 f5 ♘d4 32 g5 ♕×f5 33 ♗×d4 c×d4 34 ♗b3+ ♗e6 35 ♕×f5 ♖×f5 36 ♗×e6+ ♖×e6 37 ♖×f5 e3 38 ♔f1 d3 39 ♖d5 d2 40 ♔e2 ♔g7 41 h4 a5 42 a4 ♔g6 43 ♖d7 h6 44 g×h6 ♔×h6 45 ♖d5 ♖e8 46 ♖d6+ ♔h5 47 b4 a×b4 48 ♖×b6 ♖d8 49 ♖b5+ ♔h6 **0-1** +14

**1860-★AK-5** iv60
**Kolisch, I.F.von–Anderssen, A.**
Paris [Staunton]
1 e4 e5 2 ♘f3 ♘c6 3 d4 e×d4 4 ♗c4 ♗c5 5 0-0 d6 6 c3 ♗g4 7 ♕b3? [7 ♗e2] 7 ... ♗×f3 8 ♗×f7+ ♔f8 9 ♗×g8 ♖×g8 10 g×f3 g5 11 ♕d1 ♕d7 12 b4 ♗b6 13 ♗b2 d3 14 ♕×d3 ♘e5 15 ♕e2 ♕h3 16 ♘d2 g4 **0-1** M954-1860

**1860-★AK-6** iv60
**Kolisch,I.F.von+Anderssen,A.**
Paris [Staunton]
1 e4 e5 2 f4 e×f4 3 ♘f3 g5 4 ♗c4 ♗g7 5 d4 d6 6 h4 h6 7 h×g5 h×g5 8 ♖×h8 ♗×h8 9 ♕d3 [9 ♘c3; 9 ♘e5?] 9 ... ♘h6 [Δ 10 e5 ♗f5] 10 g3 ♕e7 11 ♘c3 c6 12 g×f4 g4 13 ♘g5 ♘d7 [13 ... f6!?] 14 e5 ♘f6 [14 ... d5 15 ♗×d5 c×d5 16 ♘×d5 ♕d8 17 ♕h7] 15 ♗e3 d5 16 ♗b3 ♘f5 17 0-0-0 ♘×e3? 18 e×f6 ♗×f6 19 ♖e1 ♗×g5 20 f×g5 ♗e6 21 ♕×e3 0-0-0 22 g6 ♕h4 23 ♖f1 ♖e8 24 g×f7 ♗×f7 25 ♕f2 ♕g5+ 26 ♕f4 ♕×f4+ 27 ♖×f4 ♗h5 28 ♖f5 ♖h8 29 ♖g5 ♔d7 30 ♘e2 ♔e7 31 ♘f4 ♗f7 32 ♖×g4 ♔f6 33 ♘d3 ♗g6 34 ♘e5 ♗f5 35 ♖f4 a5 36 ♖f2 ♖h1+ 37 ♔d2 ♖b1 38 ♘g4+ ♔e6 39 ♘e3 ♗g6 40 ♖f1 ♖×f1 41 ♘×f1 b5 42 a4 ♔d6 43 a×b5 c×b5 44 ♘e3 ♗f7 45 ♔e2 a4 46 ♗×d5 ♗×d5 47 ♘×d5 ♔×d5 48 ♔d3 b4 49 c3 **1-0** M954-1860

**1860-★AL-1**
**Laroche+Anderssen, A.**
Paris [Journoud]
1 f4 f5 2 ♘f3 ♘f6 3 c4 e6 4 ♘c3 ♗b4 5 d3 ♗×c3+ 6 b×c3 c5 7 e3 0-0 8 ♗e2 ♘c6 9 0-0 b6 10 ♘e5 ♘e7 11 ♗f3 ♖b8 12 ♕a4 a6 13 d4 ♕c7 14 ♗a3 b5 15 ♕c2 d6 16 ♘d3 b×c4 17 ♘b2 c×d4 18 c×d4 d5 19 ♘a4 ♗d7 20 ♘c5 ♗c8 21 ♖ab1 ♖×b1 22 ♖×b1 ♘e4 23 ♗×e4 f×e4 24 ♕a4 ♕c6 25 ♕×c6 ♘×c6 26 ♖b6 ♘d8 27 ♗b4 ♖e8 28 a4 g5 29 g3 g×f4 30 g×f4 ♔f7 31 ♔f2 ♖g8 32 ♘×a6 h5 33 ♘c5 h4 34 ♗c3 h3 35 ♔f1 ♖g2 36 ♖b2 [36 ♖b8!+-] 36 ... ♖×b2 37 ♗×b2 ♘c6 38 ♗c3 ♔e7 39 ♔f2 ♔d6 40 a5 ♘e7 41 a6 ♘c6 42 ♔g3 ♔c7 43 ♔×h3 e5+ 44 ♔g3 e×d4 45 ♗×d4 ♘×d4 46 e×d4 ♔b6 47 h4 ♗f5 48 ♔f2 ♔a7 49 ♘a4 ♔×a6 50 ♘c3 ♔a5 51 ♘×d5 ♔a4 52 ♔e3 ♔b3 53 ♔d2 ♗h7 54 ♘e3 ♔b4 55 h5 c3+ 56 ♔c2 ♗g8 57 f5 **1-0** L/N6016

**1860-★AL-2**
**Laroche–Anderssen, A.**
Paris [Journoud]
1 e4 e5 2 ♘f3 ♘c6 3 d4 e×d4 4 ♗c4 ♗c5 5 c3 ♘f6 6 e5 d5 7 ♗b5 ♘e4 8 c×d4 ♗b4+ 9 ♗d2 ♗×d2+ 10 ♘b×d2 0-0 11 0-0 f5 12 ♗×c6 b×c6 13 ♘b3 f4 14 ♖ac1 ♕e8 15 ♕c2 ♗d7 16 ♘c5 ♗f5 17 ♘×e4 d×e4 18 ♘h4 ♕e6 19 ♕×c6!? [19 ♕×e4 ♗d5] 19 ... g5 20 ♕×e4 g×h4 21 ♖×c7 ♕h5 22 d5 ♗f5 23 ♕×f4? ♗d3 24 ♕d4 ♗×f1 25 e6 ♕g6 26 ♔×f1 ♖ac8 27 ♖×c8 ♖×c8 28 e7 ♔f7 29 g3 h3 30 ♕e5 ♕d3+ **0-1** L/N6016

**1860-★AL-3**
**Allix–Lasa, T. von H.u.von d.**
Brussels [Staunton]
⟨Δf7⟩ 1 e4 ... 2 d4 ♘c6 3 ♘c3 d6 4 ♗d3 e5 5 d5 ♘ce7 6 h3 c6 7 f4 ♘g6 8 ♘f3 e×f4 9 0-0 ♘8e7 10 ♔h1 ♗d7 11 ♘d4 ♕c8 12 ♕h5 [12 ♗×f4 ♗×h3 13 g×h3 ♘×f4 14 ♖×f4 ♕×h3+ 15 ♔g1 ♕g3+ 16 ♔~ ♕×f4-+] 12 ... ♔d8 13 ♗×f4 ♘×f4 14 ♖×f4 ♘g6 15 ♖f2 [15 ♖f7 ♘e5 16 ♕g5+ ♔c7 (16 ... ♔e8 17 ♖×g7 ♗×g7 18 ♕×g7 ♖f8 19 ♗e2) 17 ♘e6+ ♔b8 (17 ... ♔b6+-) 18 ♖×f8 ♖×f8 19 ♕e7 ♗×e6 20 ♕×d6+] 15 ... ♗e7 16 ♘f5 ♗×f5 17 ♖×f5 ♗f6 18 ♖af1 ♕d7 19 ♖×f6 [◻ 19 ♗e2 ♔c7 20 ♗g4 ♕e7 21 d×c6 b×c6 22 ♖×f6 g×f6 23 ♕a5+ ♔b8 24 ♖f3 Δ 25 ♘d5] 19 ... g×f6 20 ♖×f6 ♘e5 21 ♕h6 ♔c7 22 ♗e2 b5 23 a3 ♖ag8 24 ♗h5 ♖g3 25 ♘e2 ♖×h3+ 26 g×h3 ♕×h3+ 27 ♔g1 ♖g8+ 28 ♔f2 ♖g2+ **0-1** M954-1860

**1860-★AP-1**
**Pollmächer,H.=Anderssen,A.**
Leipzig
1 e4 e5 2 f4 ♗c5 3 ♘f3 d6 4 ♗c4 ♘f6 5 d3 ♗g4 6 f×e5 ♗×f3 7 ♕×f3 d×e5 8 ♗e3 ♗×e3 9 ♕×e3 ♘bd7 10 ♘d2 ♕e7 11 0-0 ♘f8 12 ♘f3 ♘g6 13 ♘g5 0-0 14 g3 h6 15 ♘f3 b5 16 ♗b3 c5 17 ♔h1 ♖ac8 18 ♕e2 ♕c7 19 ♘d2 ♔h7 20 ♖f2 ♘e8 21 ♖af1 ♘d6 22 ♗d5 c4 23 ♕h5 f6 24 ♘f3 ♕d7 25 d4 ♖fe8 26 d×e5 ♘×e5 27 ♘h4 ♕g4 28 ♕×g4 ♘×g4 29 ♖e2 ♖c5 30 ♖d1 ♘×e4 31 ♗f7 ♘gf2+ 32 ♔g2 ♘×d1 33 ♗×e8 ♘d6 34 ♗g6+ ♔g8 35 ♖e6 ♖d5 36 ♘f5 ♖×f5 37 ♖×d6 ♖d5 38 ♖e6 ♖d8 39 b3 c×b3 40 a×b3 a5 41 ♔f3 ♘c3 42 ♖a6 a4 43 b×a4 b×a4 44 ♖c6 ♘d5 45 ♖a6 ♘c3 46 ♖c6 ♘d5 **½-½** L/N6047

**1860-★AR-1** iv60
**Anderssen,A.+Rivière,J.A.de**
Paris
1 e4 e5 2 ♘f3 ♘c6 3 ♗c4 ♘f6 4 ♘g5 d5 5 e×d5 ♘a5 6 ♗b5+ [6 d3] 6 ... c6 7 d×c6 b×c6 8 ♗e2 [8 ♗a4? h6 9 ♘f3 e4 10 ♘e5 ♕d4 11 ♗×c6+ ♘×c6 12 ♘×c6 ♕c5-+] 8 ... h6 9 ♘f3 e4 10 ♘e5 ♕d4 11 f4 ♗c5 12 ♖f1 [Δ 13 c3, 14 b4] 12 ... ♕d6 13 c3 ♘b7 14 b4 ♗b6 15 ♘a3 0-0 16 ♘ac4 ♕c7 17 a4 a6 18 ♘×b6 ♕×b6 19 a5 ♕c7 20 ♔f2 ♘d5 21 ♔g1 ♘×f4 22 ♖×f4 ♕×e5 23 ♕f1 ♘d6 24 ♗a3 f5 25 ♖d1 g5 26 ♖f2 ♖a7 27 ♗c4+ ♘×c4 28 ♕×c4+ ♕e6 29 ♕×e6+ ♗×e6 30 b5 a×b5 31 ♗×f8 ♔×f8 32 ♖a1 ♔e7 33 ♖e2 [Δ 33 g4] 33 ... h5 34 h4 g×h4 35 ♔h2 ♔f6 36 ♖a3 ♗c4 37 ♖e1 ♗d3 38 ♔g1 ♔g5 39 ♔f2 ♔g4 40 ♖h1 ♗c2 41 ♔e3 ♗a4 42 ♖aa1! ♖×a5

43 ♖×h4+! ♔g5 [43 ... ♔×h4 44 ♔f4+-] 44 ♖ah1 ♗b3 45 ♖×h5+ ♔f6 46 ♔f4 ♗e6 47 ♖h7 ♗f7 48 ♖1h6+ ♗g6 49 ♖d7 e3 50 ♔×e3 [50 ♖d6+ Δ 51 ♖h×g6] 50 ... ♔g5 51 ♖h8 ♖a4 52 ♖g8 ♖e4+ 53 ♔f2 ♖e6 54 ♖dg7 ♔h6 55 ♖c7 ♔g5 56 d4 ♔f4 57

♖gc8 ♗e8 58 ♖xe8 ♖xe8 59 ♖xc6 ♔e4 60 ♖c5 ♔d3 61 ♖xb5 ♔xc3 62 ♖xf5 ♔xd4 ...? **1-0** L/N6016

### 1860-★AR-2
**Rivière,J.A.de+**
**Anderssen,A.**

Paris [Journoud]

1 e4 e5 2 ♘f3 ♘c6 3 ♗c4 ♗c5 4 b4 ♗xb4 5 c3 ♗c5 6 0-0 d6 7 d4 exd4 8 cxd4 ♗b6 9 d5 ♘ce7 10 e5 ♗g4 11 ♗b2 dxe5 12 ♕b3 ♗xf3 13 ♕xf3 ♕d6 14 ♘d2 ♗d4? [14 ... ♘f6 △ 15 ... 0-0] 15 ♘e4 ♕g6 16 ♗xd4 exd4 17 d6 f5 [17 ... cxd6? 18 ♗xf7+!+-] 18 d7+! ♔d8 19 ♘g5 ♕c6 [□ 19 ... ♘h6; 19 ... ♕xg5 20 ♕xb7+-] 20 ♘f7+ ♔xd7 21 ♘e5+ **1-0**

L/N6016

### 1860-★AR-3
**Rivière,J.A.de+**
**Anderssen,A.**

Paris [Journoud]

1 e4 e5 2 ♘f3 ♘c6 3 ♗c4 ♘f6 4 ♘g5 d5 5 exd5 ♘a5 6 d3 h6 7 ♘f3 ♗d6 8 b4 ♘xc4 9 dxc4 ♗xb4+ 10 ♗d2 ♗xd2+ 11 ♘bxd2 e4 12 ♘e5 ♕e7 13 f4 e3 [13 ... exf3 14 ♘dxf3 ♘g4 15 ♕e2 ♕b4+ 16 ♘d2 ♕e7] 14 ♘df3 ♕b4+ 15 ♔e2 ♗f5 16 ♖ab1 ♕a5 17 ♖b3 ♘e4 18 ♕a1 0-0 19 g4 ♗c8 20 ♖xe3 f5?! 21 gxf5 ♗xf5 22 ♖hg1 ♖ae8 [□ 22 ... ♘f6] 23 ♖xe4 ♗xe4 24 ♖xg7+ ♔xg7 25 ♘c6+ ♔h7 26 ♘xa5 ♖xf4 27 ♘e5 ♖f5 28 ♘d3 ♗xd5+ 29 ♔d2 ♗f3 30 ♕d4?! ♖e2+ 31 ♔c3 ♖xa5 32 ♕d7+ ♔g6 33 ♘f4+ ♔f6 34 ♘xe2 ♗xe2 35 ♕d8+ ♔f5 36 ♕f8+ ♔e4 37 ♕e7+ ♔f3 38 ♕xc7 b6 39 ♔d2! **1-0**

L/N6016

### 1860-★AR-4
**Rivière,J.A.de−**
**Anderssen,A.**

Paris [Journoud]

1 e4 e5 2 ♘f3 ♘c6 3 d4 f5?! 4 ♗c4 d6 5 dxe5 fxe4 6 ♕d5 ♕e7 7 ♗g5 ♗e6 8 ♕xe4 d5 9 ♗xd5 ♗xd5 10 ♕xd5± ♘f6 11 ♗xf6 gxf6 12 0-0 [12 e6!] 12 ... fxe5 13 ♘c3 ♕d6 14 ♘b5 ♕xd5 15 ♘xc7+ ♔d7 16 ♘xd5 ♗d6 17 ♖ad1 ♖af8 18 ♘d2 ♗b8 19 c3 ♔c8 20 b4 ♖hg8 21 b5 ♘d8 22 a4? [22 ♘e7+] 22 ... ♖g7 23 ♖fe1 b6 24 ♖e4 [24 ♘c4] 24 ... ♔b7 25 a5 ♘e6 26 axb6 [26 a6+] 26 ... axb6 27 f3 ♖c8 28 ♖c4 ♖d8 29 ♘e4? [29 ♘d3] 29 ... ♘f4 30 ♘ef6 ♖xg2+ 31 ♔h1 ♖b2 32 ♖g1 ♘xd5 [32 ... ♖xb5? 33 ♖g7+-] 33 ♘xd5 ♖d7 [33 ... ♖xd5 34 ♖g7+-] 34 ♘f6 e4!-+ 35 ♖e1 ♖xh2+ 36 ♔g1 ♖g7+ 37 ♔f1 ♖h1+ 38 ♔e2 exf3+ 39 ♔d1 ♖gg1 **0-1** L/N6016-1861

### 1860-★AR-5
**Rivière,J.A.de=**
**Anderssen,A.**

Paris [Journoud]

1 e4 e5 2 f4 exf4 3 ♘f3 g5 4 h4 g4 5 ♘e5 ♘f6 6 ♘xg4 ♘xe4 7 d4 [□ 7 d3] 7 ... h5 8 ♕e2 d5 [□ 8 ... hxg4 9 ♕xe4+ ♕e7 10 ♕xe7+ ♗xe7 11 ♗xf4 ♖xh4 12 ♖xh4 ♗xh4+ 13 g3 ♗f6∓ (13 ... ♗d8∓)] 9 ♘f2 ♕e7 10 ♗xf4 ♘c6 11 ♘xe4 dxe4 12 ♕b5 ♗g7 13 ♘c3 a6 14 ♕a4 ♗e6 15 0-0-0 ♖d8 [15 ... 0-0-0? 16 ♗xa6] 16 ♘xe4 ♖xd4 17 ♖xd4 ♗xd4 18 ♗d3 ♕b4 19 ♕xb4 ♘xb4 20 a3 ♘xd3+ 21 cxd3 ♔d7 22 ♔c2 c5 23 ♖e1 ♖c8 24 ♗e3 ♗g7 25 ♖f1 ♗d4 26 ♘f6+ ♔e7 27 ♗g5 c4 28 ♖f4 cxd3+ 29 ♔xd3 ♗xb2 30 ♘xh5+ ♔d6 31 ♖b4 ♗f5+ 32 ♔e3 ♗c1+ 33 ♔f3 ♖c3+ 34 ♔f2 ♗xg5 35 hxg5 b5 36 a4 ♖c4 37 ♖xc4 bxc4 38 ♔e3 c3? [38 ... ♔c5-+] 39 ♘g3 ♗g6 40 ♔d4 c2 41 ♘e2 ♗h5 42 ♘c1 ♗g4 43 ♔c3 ♗d1 44 ♔d4 a5 45 g3 ♗g4 46 ♔c3 ♗d7 47 ♔xc2 ♗xa4+ 48 ♔c3 ♔e5 49 ♘d3+ ♔f5 50 ♘c5 [50 g6 fxg6 51 ♘f4 g5 52 ♘h3 g4 53 ♘f2 △ 54 ♘xg4=] **½-½**

L/N6016

### 1860-★AR-6
**Rivière,J.A.de+**
**Anderssen,A.**

Paris [Journoud]

1 e4 e5 2 ♘f3 ♘c6 3 ♗c4 ♗c5 4 c3 ♘f6 5 d4 exd4 6 e5 d5 7 ♗b5 ♘e4 8 cxd4 ♗b4+ 9 ♔f1! [△ 10 ♕a4] 9 ... 0-0 10 ♕a4 ♗e7 11 ♘c3 ♘b8 12 ♗d3 ♗f5 [12 ... f5? 13 ♘xd5] 13 ♕c2 ♘c6 14 a3 ♗g6 15 h4 ♘xc3 16 ♗xg6 fxg6 17 ♕xc3 a5 18 ♗e3 a4 19 ♖c1 ♕d7 20 ♖h3 ♕f5 21 ♕c2 ♕xc2 22 ♖xc2 ♖ac8 23 ♘d2 h6 24 g4 g5 25 h5 ♘d8 26 ♘b1 c6 27 ♘c3 ♖a8 28 ♘e2 ♘e6 29 ♘g3 ♖fc8 30 ♘f5 ♗f8 31 ♗c1 b6 [△ 32 ... c5] 32 ♖d3 ♖a7 33 ♗e3 ♔h7 34 ♗d2 ♖d7 35 b4 g6 36 ♘g3 ♖dd8 37 ♘e2 gxh5 38 gxh5 ♗e7 39 ♖f3 ♔g7? [39 ... ♔g8] 40 ♗e3 c5 41 bxc5 bxc5 42 ♘g3 ♔g8 43 ♘f5 ♗f8 44 ♘xh6+ ♗xh6 45 ♖f6 ♘xd4 46 ♗xd4 ♗g7 47 ♖g6 cxd4 48 ♖xc8 ♖xc8 49 h6 d3 50 ♖xg7+ ♔h8 51 ♔e1 ♖c2 52 ♔d1 ♖xf2?+- [52 ... ♖e2 53 ♖xg5 ♖xf2 54 e6 ♖e2=] 53 e6 ♖f6 54 e7 ♖xh6 55 ♖f7 **1-0** L/N6016

### 1860-★AR-7
**Anderssen,A.+**
**Rivière,J.A.de**

Paris [Staunton]

1 e4 e5 2 ♘f3 ♘c6 3 ♗c4 ♗c5 4 c3 ♘f6 5 d4 exd4 6 e5 d5 7 ♗b5 ♘e4 8 cxd4 ♗b4+ 9 ♔f1 0-0 10 ♕a4 ♗e7 11 ♘c3 ♘b8 12 ♗d3 ♗f5 13 ♕c2 ♘c6 14 a3 ♗g6

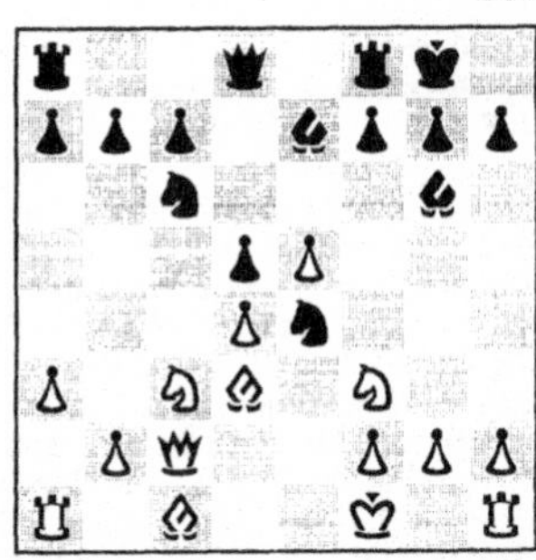

15 h4! ♘xc3 16 ♗xg6 fxg6 17 ♕xc3 a5 18 ♗e3 a4 19 ♖c1 ♕d7 20 ♖h3 ♕f5 21 ♕c2 ♕xc2 22 ♖xc2 ♖ac8 23 ♘d2 h6 24 g4 g5 25 h5 ♘d8 26 ♘b1 c6 27 ♘c3 ♖a8 28 ♘e2 ♘e6 29 ♘g3! ♖fc8 30 ♘f5 ♗f8 31 ♗c1 b6 32 ♖d3 ♖a7 33 ♗e3 ♔h7 34 ♗d2 ♖d7 35 b4 g6 36 ♘g3 ♖dd8 37 ♘e2 gxh5 38 gxh5 ♗e7 39 ♖f3 ♔g7 [□ 39 ... ♔g8] 40 ♗e3 c5 41 bxc5 bxc5 42 ♘g3 ♔g8 43 ♘f5 ♗f8 44 ♘xh6+ ♗xh6 45 ♖f6 ♘xd4 46 ♗xd4 ♗g7 47 ♖g6 cxd4 48 ♖xc8 ♖xc8 49 h6 d3 50 ♖xg7+ ♔h8 51 ♔e1 ♖c2 52 ♔d1 ♖xf2 [□ 52 ... ♖e2] 53 e6 ♖f6 54 e7 ♖xh6 55 ♖f7 **1-0** M954

### 1860-★AR-8
**Rivière,J.A.de=**
**Anderssen,A.**

Paris

1 e4 e5 2 f4 exf4 3 ♘f3 g5 4 h4 g4 5 ♘e5 ♘f6 6 ♘xg4 ♘xe4 7 d4 h5 8 ♕e2 d5 9 ♘f2 ♕e7 10 ♗xf4 ♘c6 11 ♘xe4 dxe4 12 ♕b5 ♗g7 13 ♘c3 a6 14 ♕a4 ♗e6 15 0-0-0 ♖d8 16 ♘xe4 ♖xd4 17 ♖xd4 ♗xd4 18 ♗d3 ♕b4 19 ♕xb4 ♘xb4 20 a3 ♘xd3+ 21 cxd3 ♔d7 22 ♔c2 c5 23 ♖e1 ♖c8 24 ♗e3 ♗g7 25 ♖f1 ♗d4? 26 ♘f6+ ♔e7 27 ♗g5 c4 28 ♖f4 cxd3+ 29 ♔xd3 ♗xb2 30 ♘xh5+ ♔d6 31 ♖b4 ♗f5+ 32 ♔e3 ♗c1+ 33 ♔f3 ♖c3+ 34 ♔f2 ♗xg5 35 hxg5 b5 36 a4 ♖c4 37 ♖xc4 bxc4 38 ♔e3 c3? 39 ♘g3 ♗g6 40 ♔d4 c2 41 ♘e2 ♗h5 42 ♘c1 ♗g4 43 ♔c3 ♗d1 44 ♔d4 a5 45 g3 ♗g4 46 ♔c3 ♗d7 47 ♔xc2 ♗xa4+ 48 ♔c3 ♔e5 49 ♘d3+ ♔f5 50 ♘f4 **½-½** +14

### 1860-★AR-9
**Allix+ de Rives**

Bruxelles [Staunton]

⟨♙f7⟩ 1 e4 ♘c6 2 ♘c3 ♘e5 3 d4 ♘f7 4 ♗d3 e6 5 a3 c5 6 d5 e5 7 ♘f3 [□ 7 f4 d6 8 ♘f3 ♗e7 9 0-0] 7 ... d6 8 h3 a6 9 ♗e3 b5 10 ♕d2 ♘f6 11 ♘g5 ♘xg5 12 ♗xg5 ♗e7 13 0-0 ♘xd5 14 ♗xe7 ♘xe7 15 f4 0-0 16 f5 ♗b7 17 ♖f3 c4 18 ♗e2 d5 19 ♖g3 d4 20 ♕g5 ♖f7 21 ♗h5 ♕f8 22 ♗xf7+ ♕xf7 23 ♘d5 ♘xd5 24 exd5 ♗xd5 25 ♖f1 ♖e8 26 f6 g6 27 h4 [□ 27 ♖f5 ♕c7 28 ♕h5 e4 (28 ... ♗f7 29 ♕h6+−) 29 ♖xg6+ hxg6 30 ♕xg6+ ♔f8 31 ♕h6++−] 27 ... ♔h8 28 h5 gxh5 29 ♕h6 ♖g8 30 ♖xg8+ ♕xg8 31 ♖f2 ♕f7 32 ♖f5 ♗e4 33 ♖xe5 **1-0** M954-1860

**1860-★BD-1**
**Deacon, F.H.+ Blachière, L.**
Bruges [Staunton]
⟨♘b1⟩ 1 e4 e5 2 f4 exf4 3 ♘f3 g5 4 ♗c4 ♗c5 5 d4 ♗b6 6 c3 d6 7 0-0 c6 8 ♕b3 ♕e7 9 ♘xg5 ♕xg5 10 ♗xf7+ ♔d8 11 ♗xf4 ♕g7 12 ♗xd6 ♗h3 [12 ... ♗xd4+? 13 cxd4 ♕xd4+ 14 ♔h1 ♕xd6 15 ♖ad1] 13 ♗g3 h5 14 ♗xg8 ♖xg8 15 ♖f7 ♕g5 16 ♖af1 ♘d7 17 ♖1f4 [△ 18 ♗h4] 17 ... ♔e8 18 gxh3 ♘c5 19 ♕c4 [19 dxc5? ♕xc5+ 20 ♖f2 ♕e5 21 ♔h1 ♗xf2∓] 19 ... h4 20 ♖g4 ♕e3+ 21 ♗f2 ♖xg4+ 22 hxg4 ♕xe4 23 ♖g7 ♕b1+ 24 ♔g2 ♕e4+ 25 ♔h3 ♕f3+ 26 ♗g3 hxg3 27 ♕g8+ ♕f8 28 dxc5 ♗xc5 29 ♕e6+ ♗e7 30 ♖g8 **1-0** M954-1860

**1860-★BD-2**
**Burden, F.− Deacon, F.H.**
London [Staunton]
1 e4 g6 2 d4 ♗g7 3 c4 e6 4 f4 ♘e7 5 ♘f3 c5 6 d5 d6 7 ♘c3 ♗xc3+ 8 bxc3 f5 9 e5 dxe5 10 d6 e4 11 ♘e5 ♘ec6 12 ♗e3 b6 13 h4 ♕f6 14 ♕a4 ♗d7 15 ♘xd7 ♕xc3+ 16 ♔f2 ♔xd7 17 ♗e2 h5 18 ♖hd1 ♔d8 19 ♖ab1 ♖h7 20 g3 ♕a5 21 ♕c2 ♘d7 22 ♕b2 ♕a4 23 a3 ♘a5 24 ♕c3 ♖c8 25 ♖d2 ♖c6 26 ♖c1 [△ 27 ♗d1] 26 ... ♘b7 [26 ... ♘b3 27 ♗d1; 26 ... ♕b3 27 ♕a1] 27 ♖cd1 ♔e8 28 ♔g2 ♔f7 29 ♔h3 ♖g7 [△ ... ♖g8, ... ♖d8, ... ♘f6] 30 ♕b2 a6 31 ♖c1 ♖xd6 32 ♖xd6 ♘xd6 33 ♖d1 ♕c6 34 ♕d2 ♔e7 35 ♕c3 ♖g8 36 ♗c1 ♘e8 37 ♗b2 ♘ef6 38 ♕d2 ♔f7 39 ♕d6 ♖c8 40 ♗xf6 ♘xf6 41 ♕e5 ♘d7 42 ♕a1 ♕c7 [△ ... ♘b8, ... ♘c6, ... ♘d4] 43 ♖d2 ♘b8 44 ♕d1 ♖e8 45 ♗xh5 ♖e7 [45 ... gxh5??+−] 46 ♗e2 [46 ♕a1 ♕c8 △ 47 ... ♖d7] 46 ... ♖d7 47 h5 ♖xd2 48 ♕xd2 ♘c6 49 g4 ♘d4 50 ♗d1 fxg4+ 51 ♗xg4 gxh5 52 ♗xh5+ ♔f6 53 ♕f2 ♘f5 54 ♕b2+ ♔e7 55 ♕h8 ♕d8 56 ♕h7+ ♔d6 57 ♗g4 ♕f6 58 ♕h5 ♕c3+→ 59 ♔g2 ♕g3+ 60 ♔h1 ♕e1+ 61 ♔g2 ♘e3+ 62 ♔h3 [62 ♔h2 ♕f2+ 63 ♔h3 ♕g2+ 64 ♔h4 ♕xg4+ 65 ♕xg4 ♘xg4 66 ♔xg4 b5−+] 62 ... ♕h1+ 63 ♔g3 ♘f5+ 64 ♔f2 e3+ 65 ♔e2 ♘g3+ **0-1** M954-1860

**1860-★BD-3**
**Deacon, F.H.+ Baucher, H.**
Paris [Staunton]
1 e4 e5 2 f4 exf4 3 ♗c4 ♘f6 4 ♘c3 ♗c5 5 d4 ♗b6 6 ♗xf4 d6 7 ♘f3 ♗e6 8 ♕d3 0-0 9 0-0 ♘c6 10 a3 ♘g4 11 ♘e2 ♗xc4 12 ♕xc4 ♘ce5 13 ♕b3 ♔h8 14 ♔h1 ♘g6 15 ♗g3 ♘f6 16 ♘g5 ♕e7 17 e5 dxe5 18 dxe5 ♘xe5 19 ♗xe5 ♕xe5 20 ♘xf7+ ♖xf7 21 ♕xf7 ♕xe2 22 ♖ae1 ♕b5 [22 ... ♕h5 23 ♖xf6; 22 ... ♕xc2 23 ♖e8+] 23 ♖xf6 ♗c5 24 ♖f5 [△ 25 ♖xc5; △ 25 b4] 24 ... g6 25 ♖e7 **1-0** M954-1860

**1860-★BD-4**
**Burden, F.− Deacon, F.H.**
London [Staunton]
1 e4 e5 2 f4 exf4 3 ♗c4 d5 4 ♗xd5 ♘f6 5 ♘f3 ♘xd5 6 exd5 ♕xd5 7 d4 ♗e6 8 0-0 [8 ♗xf4? ♕e4+ 9 ♕e2 ♕xf4 10 d5 ♕c1+] 8 ... ♘c6 9 ♗xf4 0-0-0 10 ♘c3 ♕h5 11 ♖e1 ♗c5 12 ♘e5 ♕xd1 13 ♖axd1 ♘xd4 14 ♔h1 [14 ♗e3 ♗f5 △ 15 ... ♖he8−+] 14 ... ♘xc2 15 ♖xd8+ ♖xd8 16 ♖c1 ♗e3 17 ♖xc2 ♗xf4 18 ♘xf7 ♗xf7 19 ♖f2 ♗e5 **0-1** M954-1860

**1860-★BK-1**
**Kolisch, I.F. von+ Barnes, T.W.**
London?
1 e4 e5 2 ♘f3 ♘c6 3 ♗c4 ♗c5 4 b4 ♗xb4 5 c3 ♗a5 6 d4 exd4 7 0-0 d6 8 ♕b3 ♕f6 9 e5 dxe5 10 ♖e1 ♘ge7 11 ♗g5 ♕g6 12 ♗xe7 ♘xe7 13 ♘xe5 ♕b6 14 ♗b5+ c6 15 ♕xf7+ ♔d8 16 ♘xc6+ ♘xc6 17 ♗xc6 ♕c5 18 cxd4 ♕d6 19 ♕xg7 ♖f8 20 ♕g5+ ♔c7 21 ♕xa5+ ♔xc6 22 d5+ ♔d7 23 ♘c3 b6 24 ♕a4+ ♔d8 25 ♘b5 ♕f6 26 ♕c2 ♖f7 27 ♖ad1 ♗b7 28 d6 ♗xg2 29 ♕c7+ ♖xc7

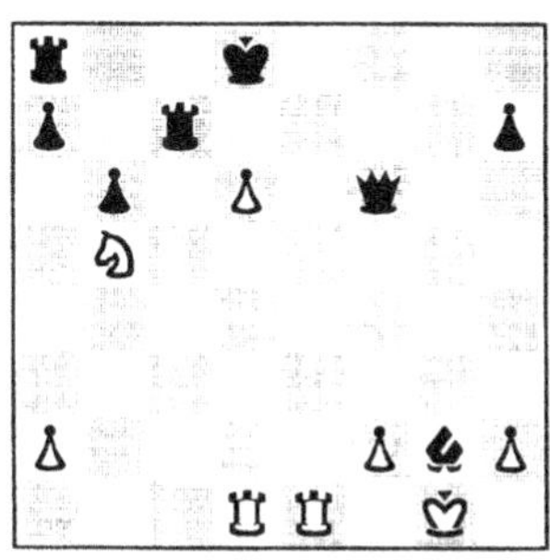

30 dxc7+ ♔c8 31 ♖e8+ ♔b7 32 ♖xa8 ♗h3 33 ♖xa7+ ♔c6 34 ♖d6+ **1-0** L/N6131-1872

**1860-★BK-2** vii 60
**Kolisch, I.F. von+ Burden, F.**
London
1 e4 e5 2 f4 ♗c5 3 ♘f3 d6 4 b4 ♗b6 5 a4 a5 6 b5 c6 7 ♗b2 ♕e7 8 ♘a3 ♗g4 9 ♘c4 ♘d7 10 h3 ♗xf3 11 ♕xf3 ♗c5 12 c3 ♘gf6 13 ♗d3 exf4 14 0-0-0 ♘e5 15 ♘xe5 dxe5 16 ♗c4 0-0 17 d4 cxb5 18 ♗xb5 ♗d6 19 ♖he1 exd4 20 cxd4 ♗b4 21 ♖e2 ♖fd8 22 ♔b1 ♖ac8 23 d5 ♖c5 24 ♗d4 ♖cc8 25 ♗b6 ♖c3 26 ♗xd8 ♕e5 27 ♗xf6 gxf6 28 ♖c2 ♖xf3 29 gxf3 f5 30 ♖g1+ ♔f8 31 ♖c8+ ♔e7 32 ♖e8+ **1-0** M392

**1860-★BN-1** ⌛
**Lichtenhein,T.& Loyd,S.& Marache,N.& Perrin,A.& Thompson,J.− Hammond,G.& Howard,A.G.& Richardson,H.& Stone,J.W.& Ware,G.P.**
[Staunton]
1 e4 e5 2 ♘f3 d6 3 d4 exd4 4 ♕xd4 ♗d7 5 ♗c4 [5 ♗f4 △ ♕d2] 5 ... ♘c6 6 ♕d3 ♘f6 7 0-0 ♗e7 8 ♘g5?! [8 ♗d2] 8 ... ♘e5 9 ♕b3 ♘xc4 10 ♕xc4 0-0 11 f4 h6 12 ♘f3 [12 ♘xf7? ♖xf7 13 e5 d5 14 ♕b3 ♗c5+ 15 ♔h1 ♘e4−+] 12 ... ♗c6 13 ♘c3 [13 e5 d5 △ 14 ... ♘e4] 13 ... ♘xe4 14 ♘d4 [14 ♘xe4?! d5] 14 ... ♘xc3 [□ 14 ... d5] 15 ♘xc6 bxc6 16 ♕xc3 ♕d7 17 f5 ♗f6 18 ♕g3 ♔h7 19 ♕d3 ♖fe8 20 ♗d2 ♖e5 21 ♗c3 ♖d5 22 ♕f3 ♗xc3 23 ♕xc3 f6 24 ♖ae1 ♖e8 25 ♖xe8 ♕xe8 26 ♕g3 ♕h5 27 ♕f2 c5 28 h3 ♖e5 29 ♕f3 ♕xf3 30 ♖xf3 ♖e2 31 ♖c3 a5 32 b3 ♖e4 33 g3 g6 34 fxg6+ ♔xg6 35 ♔f2 f5 36 ♔f3 h5 37 ♖e3 ♖xe3+ 38 ♔xe3 ♔f6 39 ♔f4 d5 40 a3 d4 41 a4 c6 42 ♔f3 ♔e5 43 ♔e2 ♔e4 44 h4 c4 45 b4 ♔d5 46 bxa5 c5 47 ♔d2 c3+ 48 ♔e2 c4 49 a6 ♔c6 **0-1** M954-1860

**1860-★BN-2** ⌛
**Hammond,G.& Howard,A.G.& Richardson,H.& Stone,J.W.& Ware,G.P.− Lichtenhein,T.& Loyd,S.& Marache,N.& Perrin,& Thompson,J.**
[Staunton]
1 e4 e5 2 ♘f3 ♘c6 3 ♗b5 a6 4 ♗a4 ♘f6 5 d4 ♘xe4 6 ♕e2 f5 7 d5 ♘e7 8 ♘xe5 ♘c5 9 ♗b3 [9 d6 ♘xa4 (9 ... cxd6 10 ♘c4 ♔f7 11 ♘xd6+ ♔g8 12 ♗b3+ ♘e6 13 0-0+−) 10 ♕c4 ♘d5 11 ♕xd5 ♕f6 12 0-0± Philadelphia Daily Evening Bulletin] 9 ... d6 10 ♘f3 h6 11 0-0 ♔f7 12 c4 ♘xb3 13 axb3 g6 14 ♘d4 ♗g7 15 ♘e6 ♗xe6 16 ♕xe6++− ♔f8 17 ♖e1 ♕e8 18 ♕e2?! [18 ♘a3 △ 19 ♘b5; 18 b4 △ 19 ♖a3] 18 ... ♕d7 19 ♘c3 ♔f7 20 ♗e3 ♖he8 21 ♕d2 g5 22

♗d4 ♗xd4 23 ♕xd4 ♘g6± 24 ♖e3 ♖e7 25 ♖ae1 ♖ae8 26 b4 ♘e5 27 f3 ♘g6 28 c5 ♖xe3 29 ♖xe3 ♖xe3 30 ♕xe3 ♕e7 31 ♔f2 ♕xe3+ 32 ♔xe3 ♔f6 33 g3 ♔e5 34 b3 b5 35 cxd6 cxd6 36 ♔d3 ♘e7 37 ♔e3 ♘g6 38 ♔d3 f4 39 ♘e2 fxg3 40 hxg3 ♔xd5 41 ♔e3 ♘e7 42 ♘d4 h5 43 f4 gxf4+ 44 gxf4 ♘c6 45 ♘xc6 ♔xc6 46 f5 d5 47 ♔f4 d4 48 ♔g5 d3 49 f6 ♔d7 50 ♔g6 d2 **0-1** M954-1860

**1860-★BP-1**
**Pindar, E.+ Birch**
Manchester [Staunton]
1 e4 e5 2 d4 exd4 3 ♗d3 ♘c6 4 f4 d5 5 e5 ♘h6 6 ♘f3 ♘g4 7 0-0 ♘e3 8 ♗xe3 fxe3 9 ♘c3 ♗c5 10 ♔h1 ♗g4 11 h3 ♗xf3 12 ♕xf3 d4 13 ♘e4 ♗b6 14 ♕g3 ♕e7 15 ♕xg7 0-0-0 16 ♘f6 h6? [16 ... ♔b8] 17 g4 ♔b8 18 ♗f5 ♔a8 19 a3 ♘xe5!? 20 dxe5 ♕xe5 21 ♖f3 d3 [21 ... ♖dg8?; 21 ... ♖hg8?] 22 ♗xd3 ♕xb2 23 ♖ff1 ♕e5 24 ♕xf7 ♕g3?? [24 ... e2 △ 25 ... ♖hf8−+] 25 ♕h5 ♖xd3 26 ♘e4 **1-0** M954-1861

**1860-★CH-1**
**Casabianca, Count– Harrwitz, D.**
Paris [Staunton]
⟨♙f7⟩ 1 e4 ... 2 d4 e6 3 ♗d3 c5 4 e5 g6 5 h4 cxd4 6 f4 ♘e7 7 h5 ♖g8 8 ♕g4 d5 9 ♘f3 ♘bc6 10 hxg6 hxg6 11 ♘g5 ♕a5+ 12 ♗d2 ♕b6 13 b3 ♗d7 14 ♖h7 0-0-0 15 ♘f7 a6 16 ♘xd8 ♕xd8 17 ♕f3 ♘f5 18 ♖h1? [18 g4] 18 ... ♗e7 19 ♗xf5 gxf5 20 g3 ♖g4 21 ♖h3 ♕g8 22 ♔f2 ♗c5 23 ♕d3 ♕g7 24 ♔f3

24 ... ♘xe5+! 25 fxe5 ♗b5 26 c4 dxc4 [◻ 26 ... dxc3 27 ♕xc3 ♖c4 28 bxc4 ♕g4+ 29 ♔g2 ♕e2+ 30 ♔h1 ♕f1+ 31 ♔h2 ♕g1#] 27 bxc4 ♗c6+ 28 ♔f2 ♗e4 29 ♕b3 ♗c2 30 ♕f3 [30 ♕xc2? d3+] 30 ... ♕xe5 [△ 31 ... d3+] 31 ♔f1 ♗e4 32 ♗f4 ♕g7 33 ♕f2 b6 34 ♗h6 ♕h8 35 ♕d2 f4! 36 ♕e2 f3 37 ♕d2 ♕h7 38 ♕e1 ♗d3+ 39 ♔g1 ♗e2 40 ♔h2 d3 41 ♘d2 ♕f5 42 a4 ♖g6−+ 43 a5? ♕xh3+ 44 ♔xh3 ♖xh6+ 45 ♔g4 f2+ **0-1** M954-1860

**1860-★CK-1** v60
**Carstanjen, A.+ Kolisch, I.F. von**
1 e4 e5 2 ♘f3 ♘c6 3 ♗c4 ♘f6 4 d4 exd4 5 0-0 d5 6 exd5 ♘xd5 7 ♖e1+ ♗e6 8 ♘xd4 ♘xd4 9 ♕xd4 c6 10 ♗xd5 ♕xd5 11 ♕xd5 cxd5 12 ♗f4 ♗e7 13 ♘d2 0-0 14 ♘f3 ♗f6 15 ♗e5 ♗xe5 16 ♖xe5 ♖ad8 17 ♖d1 ♖d6 18 ♘d4 a6 19 ♖de1 ♖e8 20 f4 ♔f8 21 ♖1e3 ♗d7 22 ♖xe8+ ♗xe8 23 ♔f2 ♗d7 24 f5 g6 25 g4 ♔g7 26 ♔g3 ♔f6 27 ♔f4 gxf5 28 gxf5 ♖b6 ... ? **1-0** M954

**1860-★CK-2**
**Kolisch, I.F. von+ Coke**
London
⟨♘b1⟩ 1 e4 e5 2 ♘f3 ♘c6 3 d4 exd4 4 ♗c4 h6 5 0-0 ♗c5 6 c3 dxc3 7 ♗xf7+ ♔xf7 8 ♕d5+ ♔f8 9 ♕xc5+ d6 10 ♕xc3 ♘f6 11 e5 dxe5 12 ♗e3 ♘d7 13 ♖ad1 ♕f6 14 ♖d5 ♔f7 15 ♖fd1 ♖d8 16 ♕c4 ♔f8 17 ♘xe5 ♘dxe5 18 ♗c5+ ♔e8 19 ♖xe5+ ♘xe5 20 ♕g8+ **1-0** M954-1860

**1860-★CK-3**
**Kolisch, I.F. von+ Cremorne, R.**
1 e4 e5 2 ♘f3 ♘c6 3 ♗c4 ♗c5 4 b4 ♗xb4 5 c3 ♗a5 6 d4 exd4 7 0-0 d6 8 ♕b3 ♕f6 9 e5 dxe5 10 ♖e1 ♗b6 11 ♗g5 ♕f5 12 ♘xe5 ♘xe5 13 ♕b5+ c6 14 ♖xe5+ ♗e6 15 ♗xe6 fxe6 16 ♕e2 ♕f7 17 ♘d2 ♔d7 18 ♘c4 ♖e8 19 ♖a5 ♕f8 20 ♖b1 ♗xa5

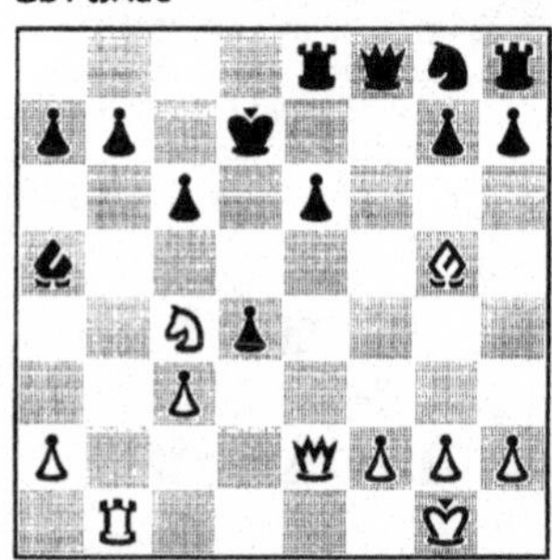

21 ♖xb7+ ♗c7 22 ♕e5 ♖c8 23 ♕xd4+ ♔e8 24 ♖xc7 ♖xc7 **1-0** L/N6131-1870

**1860-★DD-1**
**Deacon, F.H.+ Detmold**
London
⟨♘b1⟩ 1 e4 e5 2 f4 exf4 3 ♘f3 d5 4 e5 a6 5 d4 g5 6 ♗d3 h6 7 0-0 ♗e6 8 b3 g4 9 ♗xf4 gxf3 10 ♕xf3 ♗e7 11 ♗g3 h5 12 ♗f5 ♕d7 13 ♕d3 ♗xf5 14 ♖xf5 h4 15 ♖af1 ♖h7 16 ♖5f4 ♖g7 17 ♖xf7 ♖xf7 18 ♕g6 hxg3 19 ♕xf7+ ♔d8 20 ♕xg8+ ♕e8 21 ♕xd5+ ♔c8 22 hxg3 c6 23 ♕e6+ ♕d7 24 ♕g8+ ♔c7 25 c3 ♕d5 26 ♕g7 ♔d7 27 ♖f7 ♕e6 28 c4 a5 29 ♖f6 **1-0** M954-1860

**1860-★DF-1**
**Forbes– Deacon, F.H.**
London [Staunton]
⟨♙f7⟩ 1 e4 ... 2 d4 g6 3 e5 e6 4 ♗d3 b6 5 h4 ♗b7 6 ♕g4 ♕e7 7 ♘c3 [7 h5?!] 7 ... ♘h6 8 ♕h3 [8 ♗xh6?!] 8 ... ♘f7 9 ♘e4? [9 ♘f3] 9 ... ♘xe5 10 dxe5 ♗xe4 11 ♘e2 ♗xd3 12 ♕xd3 ♘c6 13 f4 0-0-0 14 ♗d2 ♔b7 15 0-0-0 d6 16 exd6 ♖xd6 17 ♕f3 ♗g7 18 g3 ♖hd8 19 ♗c3 ♗xc3 20 ♘xc3 [20 bxc3? ♖xd1+ △ 21 ... ♕a3+−+; 20 ♕xc3 ♘b4] 20 ... ♕f8 21 ♘e4 ♖d5 22 ♘g5 ♕g8 23 ♕e4 ♖e8 24 ♖he1 ♖xd1+ 25 ♔xd1 e5 26 b3 ♖d8+ 27 ♔c1 ♖d4 28 ♕f3 h6 29 ♖xe5 [29 ♘e4 ♕d5∓] 29 ... hxg5 30 ♖xg5 ♕e6 31 ♖e5 ♕d6 32 h5 gxh5 33 ♖xh5 a5 34 ♖h1 [34 ♔b2 ♖d1; 34 f5 ♖d5 35 g4 ♕a3+ 36 ♔b1 ♘b4−+] 34 ... ♔a7 35 ♔b2 ♖d2 36 ♖h8 [36 ♕e4 ♘b4 37 ♖c1 ♘d3+−+] 36 ... ♖xc2+ **0-1** M954-1860

**1860-★DK-1**
**Deacon, F.H.– Kolisch, I.F. von**
London
1 e4 e5 2 ♘f3 ♘c6 3 ♗c4 ♘f6 4 ♘g5 d5 5 exd5 ♘a5 6 d3 h6 7 ♘f3 e4 8 ♕e2 ♘xc4 9 dxc4 ♗e7 10 ♘d4 0-0 11 0-0 c6 12 ♘c3 ♗c5 13 ♘b3 ♗g4 14 ♕e1 ♗b4 15 ♗d2 ♗xc3 16 ♗xc3 ♖e8 17 h3 ♗h5 18 ♗xf6 ♕xf6 19 c3 ♖e5 20 ♘c5 ♗f3 21 g3 ♖h5 22 ♔h2 ♖xh3+ 23 ♔xh3 ♕f5+ 24 ♔h2 ♕h5+ **0-1** M954-1860

**1860-★DM-1**
**Deacon, F.H.+ Maude, P.**
London [Staunton]
1 e4 e5 2 ♗c4 ♗c5 3 ♘f3 d6 4 c3 ♘f6 5 d4 exd4 6 cxd4 ♗b6 7 ♘c3 h6 8 h3 0-0 9 0-0 ♘c6 10 ♗e3 ♘e7 11 ♗d3 ♘g6 12 ♘h2 ♘h7 13 ♕c2 ♕h4 [△ 14 f4 ♗xh3 15 gxh3 ♕g3+] 14 ♘e2 ♗d7 15 f4 ♕e7 [△ 16 ... f5; △ 15 f5 ♘e5] 16 ♖f3 ♘f6 [△ 17 ... ♘h4 18 ♖g3 ♘h5] 17 ♗f2 ♖fe8 18 ♘c3 ♗c6 19 ♖e1 ♖ad8 20 g4 ♘h7 21 b4 ♘hf8 22 b5 ♘e6 [25 ... ♗d7? 26 ♘d5] 23 bxc6 ♘xd4 24 ♗xd4 ♗xd4+ 25 ♔h1 bxc6 26 ♘e2 ♗c5 27 ♘g3 ♘h4 28 ♖ff1 ♖b8 29 ♖e2 ♖b6 30 e5 d5 31 ♘f3 ♘xf3 32 ♘f5 ♕f8 33 ♖xf3 ♗a3 34 g5 hxg5 35 fxg5 [△

36 e6; Δ 36 ♖g2; Δ 36 ♘h4; Δ 36 ♕a4, 37 ♕h4] 35 ... c5 [35 ... ♕b4 36 ♘h6+ Δ 37 ♗h7+, 38 ♖xf7] 36 ♘h4 ♕e7 37 ♗h7+ ♔h8 38 ♖xa3 ♕xg5 39 ♘f3 ♕h5 40 ♗f5 ♖eb8 41 ♗g4 ♖b1+ 42 ♔g2 ♕h6 43 ♕xc5 **1-0**

M954-1860

**1860-★DM-2**
**Michaels–Deacon, F.H.**
Bruxelles [Staunton]

⟨Δf7⟩ 1 e4 ♘h6 2 d4 ♘f7 3 e5 d6 4 f4 e6 5 g3 c5 6 c3 dxe5 7 fxe5 cxd4 8 ♕xd4 ♘c6 9 ♕xd8+ ♔xd8 10 ♘f3 ♘cxe5 11 ♘xe5 ♘xe5 12 ♗e2 b6 13 ♗f4 ♗b7 14 ♖f1 ♘f7 15 ♘a3 ♗xa3 16 0-0-0+ ♔e7 17 bxa3 ♖ac8 18 ♔b2 ♖c5 19 ♗g4 ♖hc8 20 ♖fe1 ♗d5 21 ♖d4 g5 22 ♗e5 ♘h6 [22 ... ♖xc3? 23 ♖xd5] 23 ♗e2 ♘f5 [23 ... ♖xc3? 24 ♗a6 Δ ♖xd5] 24 ♖a4 a5 25 ♗a6 ♖d8 26 ♗d4 ♖c7 27 ♗d3 ♖f8 28 ♗e5 ♖d7 29 ♖g4 ♗f3 30 ♗xf5 ♖xf5 31 ♖d4 g4 32 ♖e3 ♖h5 33 h4 gxh3 34 g4 h2 **0-1** M954-1860

**1860-★DM-3**
**Deacon, F.H.+Mayet, K.**
[Staunton]

1 e4 e5 2 ♘f3 ♘c6 3 ♗c4 ♗c5 4 b4 ♗xb4 5 c3 ♗c5 6 d4 exd4 7 cxd4 ♗b6 8 ♗b2 ♘f6 9 e5 d5 [9 ... ♘e4 10 ♗d5 ♘g5 11 h4 ♘e6 12 ♗e4] 10 exf6 dxc4 11 d5 ♗a5+ 12 ♘fd2 ♕xd5 13 fxg7 ♖g8 14 0-0 ♗e6 15 ♗f6 ♘e5 16 ♕e2 ♗xd2 17 ♘xd2 c3 18 ♘e4 ♕c4 19 ♕c2 ♘d7 20 ♖fe1 b5 21 ♖ad1 ♕c6 [21 ... b4 22 ♕a4] 22 f4 ♘c5 23 f5 ♘xe4 24 ♖xe4 ♕c5+ 25 ♖ed4 ♗d5 26 ♔h1 c6 27 ♕e4+ **1-0** M954-1860

**1860-★DR-1**
**Rivière, J.A.de=Deacon, F.H.**
[Staunton]

1 e4 e5 2 ♗c4 ♘f6 3 f4 d5 4 exd5 e4 5 d4 ♘xd5 6 ♕h5 c6 7 ♘c3?! [7 ♕e5+] 7 ... ♗b4 8 ♘e2 0-0 9 0-0 ♘xc3 10 bxc3 ♗xc3 11 ♗a3 g6 12 ♕g5 ♗xd4+ 13 ♔h1 ♗xa1 14 ♗e7 ♕d7 15 ♖xa1 ♖e8 16 ♗f6 ♕f5 17 ♕h4 ♘d7 18 ♗c3 b5 19 ♘g3 ♕c5 20 ♗xf7+ ♔xf7 21 ♕xh7+ ♔e6 22 ♘xe4 ♕h5 23 ♘g5+ ♔d6 24 ♕f7 ♖e7 25 ♗e5+ ♘xe5 26 ♘e4+ ♔c7 27 ♕xe7+ ♘d7 28 ♘f6 ♕c5 29 ♘e8+ ♔b8 30 ♘d6 a5 31 ♘xc8 ♔xc8 32 ♕e8+ ♔b7 33 ♕xd7+ **½-½** M954-1860

**1860-★DS-1** i60
**Schroeder–Deacon, F.H.**
London [Staunton]

⟨Δf7⟩ 1 e4 ... 2 d4 g6 3 e5 e6 4 ♗d3 b6 5 ♕g4 ♕e7 6 ♘h3 ♗b7 7 c3 ♘h6 8 ♗xh6 ♗xh6 9 0-0 ♘c6 10 b4 0-0-0 11 a4 ♔b8 12 ♗e4 d6 13 ♗xc6 ♗xc6 14 b5 ♗b7 15 f4 ♖hf8 16 ♘a3 [16 ♘d2 dxe5] 16 ... dxe5 17 ♘c2 [17 fxe5 ♗e3+ 18 ♘f2 (18 ♔h1 ♖xf1+ Δ 19 ... ♕xa3) 18 ... ♖xf2 19 ♖xf2 ♖f8; 17 dxe5 ♖d2 18 ♖f2 ♖xf2 19 ♔xf2 ♕c5+] 17 ... exf4 18 ♘xf4 ♖f5 19 ♘h3 [19 ♘e3 ♖g5 20 ♕h4 e5 21 ♘fd5 ♗xd5 22 ♕xh6 ♗b7 Δ 23 ... ♖h5] 19 ... ♖dd5 20 ♖f2 ♖xf2 21 ♔xf2 e5 22 c4 [22 ♖e1 ♗d2; 22 ♖d1 exd4 23 cxd4 ♖f5+ 24 ♔g1 ♗c8 25 ♖e1 ♕xe1+ 26 ♘xe1 ♗e3+ 27 ♘f2 ♖xf2−+; 22 ♘b4 ♗e3+ 23 ♔xe3 exd4+ 24 ♔d2 ♕e3+ 25 ♔d1 dxc3−+] 22 ... ♖d8 23 ♕e2 [23 d5 ♕c5+ Δ 24 ... ♗xd5] 23 ... ♕f8+ 24 ♔g1 exd4 25 ♖f1 ♕d6 26 ♕d3 ♖e8 27 ♔h1 ♗e3 28 ♘f2 c5 29 ♖e1 ♕f4 30 ♕e2 [30 ♘h3 ♗xg2+−+; 30 ♘d1 ♗xg2+−+; 30 ♕f1 ♖f8−+; 30 ♖f1 ♖f8−+; 30 ♖e2 ♖f8 31 ♘xe3 dxe3 32 ♘h3 ♕f1+ 33 ♘g1 ♗xg2+−+] 30 ... ♖f8 31 ♘xe3 ♕xf2 32 ♕xf2 ♖xf2 33 ♘d5 ♗xd5 34 cxd5 d3 35 ♔g1 ♖f7 36 d6 ♔c8 37 ♖d1 c4 38 ♖c1 ♖f4 39 g3 ♖e4 40 ♔f2 d2 41 ♖d1 c3 **0-1**

M954-1860

**1860-★DT-1**
**Thorold, E.–Deacon, F.H.**
London [Staunton]

1 e4 e5 2 ♘f3 d5 3 ♘xe5 ♗d6 4 ♘xf7 ♔xf7 5 ♕h5+ g6 6 ♕xd5+ ♗e6 7 ♕xb7 ♘d7 8 d4 ♘b6 9 ♘c3 ♘e7 [Δ 10 ... ♗c8] 10 e5 ♗b4 11 ♕f3+ ♔e8 12 ♕f6 ♔d7 13 ♗e3 ♘bd5 14 ♕f3 ♘xc3 15 a3 ♖f8 16 ♕b7 ♖b8 17 ♕a6 ♖b6 18 ♕d3 ♗f5 19 ♕c4 ♗a5 20 bxc3 ♖c6 21 ♕a4 ♗xc3+ 22 ♔d1 ♗xa1 23 ♗b5 a6 24 ♗xc6+ ♘xc6 25 d5 ♗xe5 26 ♕xc6+ ♔e7 27 ♗g5+?? [27 ♖e1+−] 27 ... ♗f6 28 ♖e1+ ♔f7 29 ♗xf6 ♕xf6 30 ♕xc7+ ♔g8 31 ♕c4 ♖c8 32 ♕b4 ♖xc2 [32 ... ♕a1+? 33 ♔e2 ♖xc2+ 34 ♔f1 ♗d3+ 35 ♔g1 ♖c1=] 33 ♖e8+ ♔g7 34 ♖e7+ ♔h6 35 ♕f4+ g5 36 ♖e6 ♕xe6 **0-1** M954-1860

**1860-★D?-1** i60
**Deacon, F.H.+?**
London [Staunton]

1 e4 e5 2 ♘c3 c6 3 f4 ♗b4 4 d4 ♘f6 5 fxe5 ♘xe4 6 ♕f3 d5 7 exd6 ♘xd6 8 ♗d2 ♘f5 [8 ... ♕h4+ 9 g3 ♕xd4 10 0-0-0; 8 ... 0-0 9 ♗d3 ♕h4+ 10 g3 ♕xd4 11 ♘ge2 Δ 12 0-0] 9 0-0-0 0-0 [9 ... ♘xd4? 10 ♕e4+; 9 ... ♕xd4? 10 ♗g5] 10 ♗d3 ♘xd4 11 ♕h5 g6 12 ♕h6 ♕f6 [12 ... ♗e7 13 ♘e4 (13 ♗e3 c5 14 ♘f3 ♘xf3 15 ♗xg6±) 13 ... ♘d7 (13 ... ♘f5 14 ♕f4) 14 ♗g5 ♗xg5 15 ♘xg5 ♘f6 16 ♘1f3 ♘e6 (16 ... ♘xf3 17 ♗xg6+−) 17 ♗xg6+−] 13 ♗g5 ♕g7 14 ♕h4 ♘d7 15 ♘ge2! [15 ♗h6] 15 ... ♘xe2+ 16 ♘xe2 ♕e5 [Δ 17 ♗h6 ♗e7] 17 ♘f4 ♖e8 [17 ... f6 18 ♗c4+ Δ 19 ♘xg6] 18 ♗c4 b5 [18 ... ♗e7 19 ♘e6] 19 ♗b3 a5 20 ♖hf1 ♖f8 [20 ... ♖e7 21 ♘d3 Δ 22 ♗xe7]

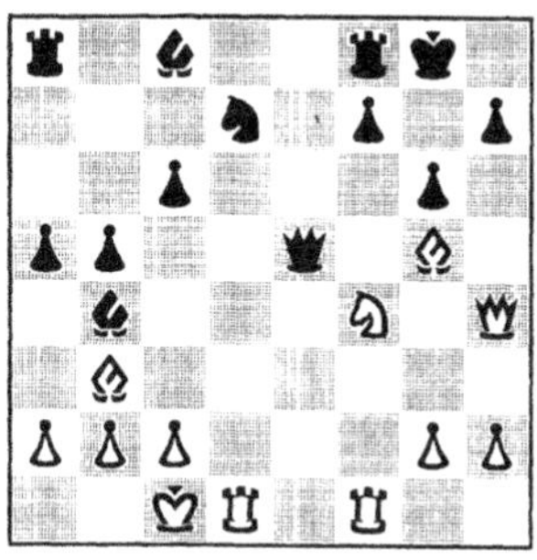

21 ♘xg6 hxg6 22 ♖xd7 ♕h8 23 ♗xf7+ ♖xf7 24 ♖d8+ ♗f8 **1-0**

M954-1860

**1860-★EK-1**
**Kolisch, I.F. von+Epstein, L.**
Paris?

1 e4 c5 2 d4 e6 3 ♗d2 cxd4 4 ♘f3 ♘c6 5 c3 dxc3 6 ♗xc3 h6 7 ♗c4 ♗b4 8 0-0 ♘f6 9 a3 ♗xc3 10 ♘xc3 a6 11 ♗a2 d6 12 ♖e1 0-0 13 ♖e3 ♕c7 14 ♖d3 ♖d8 15 ♕d2 b6 16 ♖d1 ♘e8 17 ♘h4 ♗b7 18 ♖g3 ♔h7 19 f4 ♘e7 20 f5 exf5 21 exf5 f6 22 ♘g6 ♘xg6 23 fxg6+ ♔h8 24 b4 a5 25 ♖h3 d5 26 ♖xh6+ gxh6 27 ♕xh6+ ♔g8 28 ♘xd5 ♕g7 29 ♘xf6+ **1-0** M954-1860

**1860-★FK-1**
**Kolisch, I.F.von–Fraser, G.B.**

1 e4 e5 2 ♘f3 ♘f6 3 ♗c4 ♘xe4 4 ♘c3 ♘xc3 5 dxc3 f6 6 0-0 ♘c6 7 ♘h4 ♘e7 8 f4 d5 9 ♗b5+ c6 10 fxe5 ♕b6+ 11 ♔h1 ♕xb5 12 exf6 gxf6 13 ♕h5+ ♔d8 14 ♖xf6 ♗d7 15 a4 ♕c4 16 ♗f4 ♕e4 17 ♗g3 ♗g7 18 ♖f7 ♗e8 19 ♘f3 ♗xf7 20 ♕xf7 ♕g6 21 ♕f4 ♖c8 22 ♖ae1 ♘f5 23 ♗f2 ♔d7 24 ♗xa7 ♖he8 25 ♖f1 ♖e4 26 ♕d2 ♖ce8 27 ♗f2 ♖e2 **0-1** M324-1860

**1860-★FK-2**
**Kolisch, I.F.von=Fraser, G.B.**

1 e4 e5 2 ♘f3 ♘f6 3 d4 ♘xe4 4 dxe5 d5 5 ♗d3 ♗e7 6 0-0 ♘c5 7 h3 ♘xd3 8 cxd3 ♘c6 9 d4 ♗e6 10 ♘h2 ♕d7 11 f4 0-0-0 12 ♗e3 h6 13 ♕d2 ♖dg8 14 ♘c3 g5 15 f5 ♗xf5 16 ♘xd5 g4 17 hxg4 ♗xg4 18 ♘xe7+ ♘xe7 19 ♖xf7 ♗e6 20 ♖f2 ♗d5 21 ♖ac1 ♕h3 22 ♖f8+ ♔d7 23 ♖xc7+ ♔xc7 24 ♕a5+ ♔d7 25 ♕d8+ ♔c6 26 ♕d6+ ♔b5 **½-½** M324-1861

### 1860-★F?-1
**Fraser, G.B.+?**
[Staunton]
1 e4 e5 2 ♘f3 ♘c6 3 d4 e×d4 4 ♗c4 ♗c5 5 0-0 d6 6 b4 ♗×b4 7 c3 d×c3 [7 ... ♗×c3 8 ♘×c3 d×c3 9 ♕b3] 8 ♕b3 ♕e7 9 ♗b5 ♗c5 10 ♘×c3 ♗e6 11 ♘d5 ♕d8 12 ♗b2 ♔f8 13 ♕c3 f6 14 ♘g5 ♗f7 15 ♘×f7 ♔×f7 16 ♗c4 ♔e8 17 ♕g3 ♕d7 18 ♘f4! ♘d8 19 ♘h5 d5 20 ♗×d5 ♗f8 21 ♖ad1 [21 ♗×g8 △ 22 ♘×f6+] 21 ... ♕e7 22 e5 [22 ♗×g8 △ 23 ♘×f6+] 22 ... f5 23 ♗a3 c5 [23 ... ♕×a3 24 ♘×g7+] 24 ♘f4 ♕c7 25 ♘g6 h×g6 26 ♕×g6+ ♘f7 27 ♕e6+ ♕e7 28 ♗c6+ **1-0**
M954-1860

### 1860-★F?-2
**Fraser, G.B.+?**
[Staunton]
1 e4 e5 2 ♘f3 ♘c6 3 d4 e×d4 4 ♗c4 ♗c5 5 0-0 ♘f6 6 b4 ♗×b4 7 c3 ♗×c3 [□ 7 ... d×c3] 8 ♘×c3 d×c3 9 e5 d5 10 ♗b5 ♘e4 11 ♗a3 ♗g4 12 ♕a4 ♗d7 [12 ... ♕d7 13 ♘d4; 13 e6] 13 ♕b3 a6 [13 ... ♘a5 14 ♕×d5] 14 ♗×c6 ♗×c6 15 ♖fe1 ♕d7 16 e6 f×e6 17 ♘e5 ♕c8 [17 ... ♕d8 18 ♖×e4] 18 ♖×e4 d×e4 19 ♕×c3 ♗d5 20 ♕g3 g6 21 ♕f4 c5 22 ♕f7+ ♔d8 23 ♗×c5 ♕c7 24 ♗b6 **1-0**
M954-1860

### 1860-★F?-3
**Fraser, G.B.+?**
[Staunton]
1 e4 e5 2 ♘f3 ♘c6 3 d4 e×d4 4 ♗c4 ♗c5 5 0-0 ♘f6 6 b4 ♗×b4 7 c3 ♗×c3 8 ♘×c3 d×c3 9 e5 d5 10 ♗b5 ♘e4 11 ♗a3 a6! 12 ♗×c6+ b×c6 13 ♘d4 c5 [13 ... ♗d7?!] 14 f3 c×d4 [14 ... ♘d2 15 ♗×c5] 15 f×e4 d×e4 16 ♖×f7?! ♔×f7 17 ♕b3+ ♔e8? [17 ... ♔g6] 18 e6 c6 19 e7 ♕d5 20 ♖f1! ♗f5 21 ♕b7 ♖c8 22 ♕×c8+ ♗×c8 23 ♖f8+ **1-0**
M954-1860

### 1860-★HK-1
**Kolisch, I.F.von+ Harrwitz, D.**
1 e4 e5 2 ♘f3 ♘c6 3 d4 e×d4 4 ♗c4 ♗c5 5 0-0 d6 6 c3 d×c3 7 ♕b3 ♘a5 8 ♗×f7+ ♔f8 9 ♕×c3 ♔×f7 10 ♕×a5 ♘f6 11 e5 ♘e4 12 b4 ♗×f2+ 13 ♖×f2 ♘×f2 14 ♔×f2 ♖f8 15 ♗g5 ♕d7 16 ♕d5+ ♔g6 17 ♔g1 ♖×f3 18 g×f3 c6 19 ♕d2 ♕f5 20 f4 d×e5 21 ♕d6+ ♗e6 22 ♘d2 h6 23 ♗h4 e×f4 24 ♘f3 ♔h7 25 ♖e1 ♖e8 26 ♔f2 ♕g4 27 ♖e4 ♗d5 28 ♖×f4 ♕h5 29 ♗g3 ♖e6 30 ♕d8 ♕g6 31 ♘d4 ♖e8 32 ♕d7 ♖e5 33 ♕g4 ♕b1 34 ♘e2 h5 35 ♕h3 ♕×a2 36 ♕f1 ♕d2 37 ♕b1+ ♔h6 38 ♖f6+ g×f6 39 ♗f4+ **1-0**
L/N6384-1860

### 1860-★HL-1
**Harrwitz, D.+ Laroche**
Paris [Staunton]
1 e4 c5 2 ♘f3 ♘c6 3 d4 c×d4 4 ♘×d4 e5 5 ♘f3 [5 ♘b5] 5 ... ♘f6 6 ♗c4 ♗c5 [6 ... ♘×e4 7 ♗×f7+ ♔×f7 8 ♕d5+] 7 0-0 0-0 8 ♘c3 d6 9 ♗g5 ♗g4 10 ♘d5 ♘d4 11 ♗e2 ♗×f3 12 ♗×f3 ♘e6 13 ♗×f6 g×f6 14 ♗g4 ♖e8 15 ♗f5 ♘c7 16 ♕h5 ♘×d5 17 ♕h6 [17 ... ♕c7 18 ♗×h7+ ♔h8 19 e×d5+-] **1-0**
M954-1860

### 1860-★HL-2
**Harrwitz, D.+ Laroche**
Paris
1 e4 c5 2 ♘f3 ♘c6 3 d4 c×d4 4 ♘×d4 e5 5 ♘f3 ♘f6 6 ♗c4 ♗c5 7 0-0 h6 8 ♘c3 d6 9 ♘e2 ♗g4 10 ♘g3 ♘d4 11 c3 ♘×f3+ 12 g×f3 ♗e6 13 ♗b5+ ♗d7 14 ♗×d7+ ♕×d7 15 b4 ♗b6 16 ♘f5 0-0-0 17 a4 g6 18 ♘g3 ♕h3 19 a5 ♗c7 20 a6 b6 21 ♕a4 h5 22 ♗g5 h4 23 ♖a2 h×g3 24 f×g3 ♘h5 25 ♗×d8 ♔×d8 26 ♕c6 ♕c8 27 c4 ♔e7 28 c5 b×c5 29 b×c5 d×c5 30 ♕×c5+ ♗d6 31 ♕×a7+ ♔e6 32 ♕b6 ♕c5+ 33 ♕×c5 ♗×c5+ 34 ♔g2 ♘f6 35 ♖b1 ♘d7 36 ♖b7 ♖a8 37 a7 ♔d6 38 ♖a6+ ♔e7 39 f4 ♗d4 40 ♔f3 ♔e8 41 ♖d6 ♖×a7 42 ♖d×d7 **1-0**
M954-1860

### 1860-★HL-3
**Laroche− Harrwitz, D.**
Paris [Staunton]
1 f4 d5 2 c4 d4 3 d3 c5 4 e4 e6 5 ♗e2 ♘c6 6 ♘f3 f6 7 a3 ♗d6 8 0-0 ♘h6 9 ♗d2 0-0 10 h3 ♘f7 11 ♕e1?! ♕b6 12 ♕c1 ♗d7 13 ♗d1 ♘h8 14 ♗a4 ♗e8 15 ♗×c6 ♗×c6 16 a4 a5 17 ♕c2 ♖f7 18 b3? [18 ♘a3 △ 19 ♘b5=] 18 ... ♘g6 19 ♘e1 ♕c7 20 g3 h5 21 ♘f3 [□ 21 ♕d1] 21 ... ♕d7 22 ♗e1 ♖af8 23 ♗×a5 h4! 24 ♘×h4 ♘×h4 25 g×h4 e5 26 f5 g6! 27 ♗e1 g×f5 28 ♖×f5 ♖g7+ 29 ♔h2 ♕×f5 **0-1**
M954-1860

### 1860-★HS-1
**Hammond, G.+ Stone, J.W.**
Boston [Staunton]
1 e4 e5 2 ♘f3 ♘c6 3 d4 e×d4 4 ♗c4 ♗c5 5 b4 ♗×b4+ 6 c3 d×c3 7 0-0 h6 8 ♕b3 ♕f6 9 e5 ♕g6 10 ♘×c3 ♘ge7 11 ♘b5 ♗a5 12 ♗d3 ♕h5 [□ 12 ... ♕e6] 13 ♗b2 a6 14 ♘c3 0-0 15 ♘e4 ♘f5 16 ♘g3 ♘×g3 17 f×g3 d6 18 e×d6 c×d6 19 ♘h4 ♘e5 20 ♗×e5 ♕×e5 21 ♖ad1 b5 22 ♗c2 ♗e6? [22 ... ♕c3] 23 ♕d3 g6 24 ♘×g6 f×g6 25 ♕×g6+ ♕g7 26 ♕×e6+ ♔h8 27 ♕×d6 ♖×f1+ 28 ♖×f1 ♗c3 29 ♔h1 a5 30 ♕c6 ♖b8 31 ♖f7! ♕×f7 32 ♕×h6+ ♔g8 33 ♗b3 **1-0**
M954-1860

### 1860-★JS-1 3 ix 60
**Steinitz, W.+ Jeney, E.**
Wien [Bachmann]
1 c4 e6 2 ♘c3 c5 3 e3 d5 4 c×d5 e×d5 5 d4 ♘f6 6 ♘f3 ♘c6 7 ♗e2 c4 8 0-0 ♗d6 9 b3 c×b3 10 ♕×b3 0-0 11 ♗b2 [11 ♘×d5?? ♘×d5 12 ♕×d5 ♗×h2+] 11 ... ♘a5 12 ♕c2 [□ 12 ♕d1] 12 ... ♗e6 13 ♖fc1 ♖c8 14 ♕d1 a6 15 ♘a4? b5 16 ♘c3 ♘c4 17 ♕b3 ♕a5 [△ 18 ... ♘×b2 19 ♕×b2 ♗a3] 18 a3 ♗f5 19 a4 b4 [□ 19 ... ♘×b2 20 ♕×b2 b4] 20 ♘×d5! ♘×d5 21 ♗×c4 ♘b6 22 ♗d3 ♗e6 23 ♕d1 b3 24 e4 ♘×a4 25 d5 ♗d7 26 ♕×b3 ♖×c1+ 27 ♖×c1 ♖b8 28 ♗c3 ♘×c3 29 ♕×c3 ♗b4 30 ♕c7 ♕×c7 31 ♖×c7 ♗e8 32 ♖a7 a5 33 ♔f1 **1-0**
L/N3131

### 1860-★JS-2 3 ix 60
**Jeney, E.− Steinitz, W.**
Wien [Bachmann]
1 e4 e5 2 ♘f3 ♘c6 3 d4 e×d4 4 ♗c4 ♘f6 5 ♗g5 h6 6 ♗h4 g5 7 ♗g3 ♘×e4 8 0-0 ♘×g3? 9 f×g3 d5 10 ♗b5 ♗c5 11 ♘e5 ♗e6 [□ 11 ... ♗d7 (11 ... a6 Steinitz 12 ♘×c6 ♕d7 13 ♘×d4 a×b5 14 ♖e1+±)] 12 ♘×c6 b×c6 13 ♗×c6+ ♔e7 14 ♗×a8 ♕×a8 15 ♔h1 g4! 16 ♘d2 ♗b6 17 ♕e2 h5 18 ♕e5 ♔d7 19 ♖ae1 [△ 20 ♖×f7+ ♗×f7 21 ♕e7+] 19 ... ♕g8 20 b4 [△ 21 ♘b3, 22 ♘c5] 20 ... h4 21 g×h4 ♖×h4 22 g3 ♖h3 23 ♖f6 [□ 23 ♖e2] 23 ... d3 [△ 24 ... ♖×h2+] 24 ♘f1 d×c2 25 ♖f4 [25 ♕c3 d4 26 ♕×c2 ♗d5+−+] 25 ... c6 26 ♕e2 d4 27 ♕d3 ♗d5+ 28 ♔g1 ♕g6 29 ♕d2 [□ 29 ♕×g6] 29 ... d3+ 30 ♘e3 [□ 30 ♖e3]

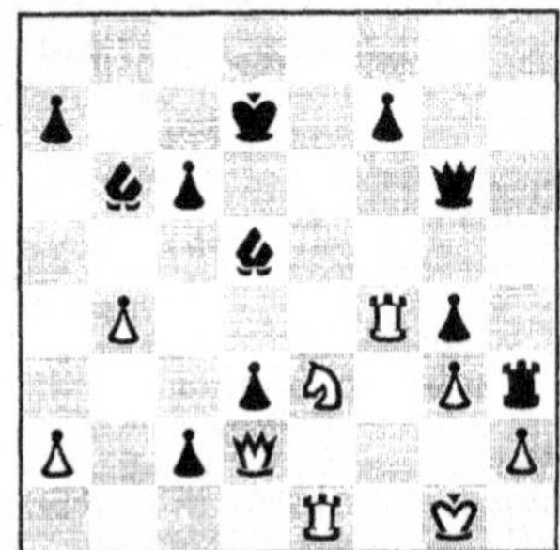

30 ... ♖×g3+! 31 h×g3 ♕h5 32 ♖c1 [32 ♕h2 ♗×e3+−+] 32 ... ♕h1+ 33 ♔f2 ♕g2+ 34 ♔e1 ♕×g3+ 35 ♖f2 ♗×e3 **0-1**
L/N3131

### 1860-★JS-3 3 ix 60
**Steinitz, W.− Jeney, E.**
Wien [Bachmann]
1 c4 e6 2 ♘c3 c5 3 e3 d5 4 c×d5 e×d5 5 d4 ♘f6 6 d×c5 ♗×c5 7 ♘f3 ♘c6 8 ♗e2 0-0 9 0-0 ♗f5 10 ♕b3 ♘b4 11 a3?? [□ 11 ♕d1 ♘c2] 11 ... ♗c2 12 a×b4 ♗×b3 13 b×c5 a6 14 ♘d4 ♕c7?? 15 ♘×b3 ♖fd8 16 ♖d1

h5 17 ♗f3 ♕e5 18 ♖a4 g5 19 ♖ad4 ♔g7 20 ♗xd5 ♘g4 21 f4 gxf4 22 exf4 ♕c7 23 ♘e4 a5 24 h3 ♘h6 25 ♗e3 ♘f5 26 ♖4d3?? [◻ 26 ♗f2] 26 ... ♖xd5 27 ♖xd5 ♘xe3 28 ♖g5+ ♔f8 29 ♖d6 ♖d8 30 ♔f2 ♘c4 31 ♖f6 ♕e7 32 ♖e5?? ♘xe5 **0-1** L/N3131

**1860-★JS-4** 4 ix 60
**Jeney, E.+Steinitz, W.**
Wien [Bachmann]

1 e4 e5 2 ♘f3 ♘c6 3 ♗c4 ♗c5 4 c3 ♘f6 5 d3 d6 6 h3 ♗b6 7 0-0 ♗e6 [◻ 7 ... 0-0] 8 ♗xe6 fxe6 9 ♕b3 ♕e7 10 ♘g5 h6 [◻ 10 ... ♔d7] 11 ♘xe6 ♔d7 12 d4 exd4 [12 ... ♕xe6? 13 d5] 13 ♘xd4 ♘xd4 14 cxd4 ♕xe4 [14 ... ♘xe4 15 ♖e1] 15 ♘c3 ♕xd4 [◻ 15 ... ♕e7] 16 ♕f7+ ♔c6 [◻ 16 ... ♔c8] 17 ♗e3 ♕e5 18 ♗xb6 ♔xb6 19 ♖ae1 [19 ♕xg7 ♖ag8 20 ♕xf6 ♕xf6 21 ♘d5+] 19 ... ♕a5 20 b4 ♕a3 [◻ 20 ... ♕a6] 21 ♖e3 ♖af8 22 ♕c4 **1-0** L/N3131

**1860-★JS-5** 4 ix 60
**Steinitz, W.Φ Jeney, E.**
Wien

1 c4 e6 2 ♘c3 d5 3 e3 ♘f6 4 ♘f3 ♘c6 5 d4 ♗b4 6 ♕b3 0-0 7 ♗d2 a5 8 a3 ♗xc3 9 bxc3 a4 10 ♕c2 ♗d7 11 cxd5 exd5 12 ♗e2 ♘a5 13 0-0 ♘b3 14 ♖a2 b5 15 ♗e1 ♖c8 16 ♘d2 ♘a5 17 ♖b2 c6 18 ♕c1 ♕e7 19 ♕a1 ♗f5 20 ♖b4 h6 21 ♕b2 ♘e8 22 ♕a1 ♘c7 23 ♖b2 ♘e6 24 ♕a2 g5 25 ♘b1 ♘b3 26 ♗d2 ♖b8 27 ♗d1 ♗xb1 28 ♕xb1 ♘xd2 29 ♖xd2 ♕xa3 30 ♕f5 ♘g7 31 ♕f6 ♖fd8 ...? L/N3151

**1860-★KK-1 ⬠**
**Kolisch, I.F. von−Kylman**
Manchester

1 e4 e5 2 f4 d5 3 exd5 e4 4 ♗b5+ c6 5 dxc6 bxc6 6 ♗c4 ♘f6 7 d4 ♘bd7 8 ♘e2 ♘b6 9 ♗b3 ♗g4 10 c3 ♗d6 11 0-0 ♕c7 12 h3 ♗xe2 13 ♕xe2 0-0 14 ♗e3 ♘bd5 15 ♗xd5 ♘xd5 16 ♘d2 f5 17 ♕f2 ♘xe3 18 ♕xe3 c5 19 ♖ac1 ♖ac8 20 ♘c4 ♗e7 21 d5 ♖cd8 22 ♖cd1 ♖f6 23 ♔h1 ♖h6 24 ♘e5 ♗d6 25 ♘c6 ♖d7 26 ♔h2 g5 27 g3 gxf4 28 gxf4 ♖g7 29 ♖f2 ♖h4 30 ♖df1 ♖gg4 31 ♖g1 ♕g7 32 ♖fg2 ♕h6 **0-1** M392

**1860-★KM-1**
**Kolisch, I.F.von+Maude, P.**
London

1 e4 e5 2 ♘f3 ♘c6 3 ♗c4 ♗c5 4 b4 ♗xb4 5 c3 ♗c5 6 0-0 d6 7 d4 exd4 8 cxd4 ♗b6 9 ♘c3 ♗g4 10 ♕a4 ♗xf3 11 d5 ♗g4 12 dxc6 bxc6 13 ♕xc6+ ♗d7 14 ♕d5 ♗e6 15 ♗b5+ ♔f8 16 ♕d3 ♘e7 17 ♘d5 ♗xd5 18 exd5 ♘g6 19 ♗b2 ♕g5 20 ♖ae1 ♘f4 21 ♕e4 f5 22 ♕f3 ♘g6 23 ♖e6 ♔f7 24 ♖fe1 ♖hf8 25 ♕c3 ♘e5

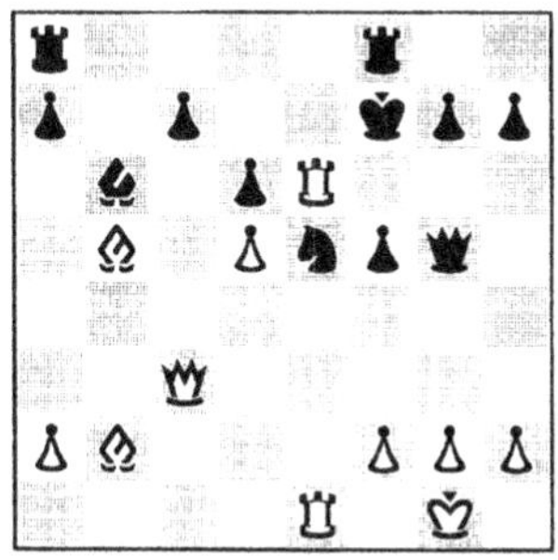

26 ♖1xe5 dxe5 27 ♕xe5 ♔g8 28 ♖e7 ♖f7 29 ♖xf7 ♔xf7 30 ♕e6+ ♔f8 31 ♗a3+ **1-0** M954-1860

**1860-★KM-2**
**Maude, P.−Kolisch, I.F.von**
London [Staunton]

1 e4 e5 2 ♘f3 ♘c6 3 ♗b5 a6 4 ♗a4 ♘f6 5 0-0 b5 [5 ... ♘xe4!?] 6 ♗b3 ♗c5 7 c3 d6 8 d4 exd4 9 cxd4 ♗b6 10 ♗g5 h6 11 ♗xf6 ♕xf6 12 e5 dxe5 13 dxe5 ♕g6 14 ♗d5 ♗b7 15 e6 0-0-0! 16 ♕b3 fxe6 17 ♗xe6+ ♔b8 18 ♗f7 ♕f6 19 ♘c3 ♖hf8 20 ♗h5? ♕f5 21 a4 ♕xh5 22 axb5 axb5 23 ♘xb5 ♖xf3 24 gxf3 ♘e5 **0-1** M954-1861

**1860-★KP-1**
**Pindar, E.+Kolisch, I.F. von**
Manchester

⟨♘b1,♖a8⟩ 1 ... e5 2 e3 d5 3 d4 e4 4 c4 ♘f6 5 ♕b3 c6 6 ♗d2 ♗d6 7 f4 0-0 8 c5 ♗c7 9 ♘e2 ♘h5 10 0-0-0 b5 11 h3 a5 12 g4 a4 13 ♕c2 ♘f6 14 ♘g3 ♘a6 15 ♗e2 ♗a5 16 g5 ♗xd2+ 17 ♕xd2 ♘e8 18 h4 ♘ec7 19 f5 b4 20 ♖dg1 ♘b5 21 ♗xb5 cxb5 22 f6 g6 23 h5 b3 24 a3 ♗e6 25 ♕h2 ♕d7 26 hxg6 fxg6 27 ♘h5 ♔h8 28 ♘f4 ♗f5 29 ♘xd5 ♖f7 30 ♘b6 ♕c6 31 ♕e5 **1-0** M392

**1860-★KR-1**
**Rivière, J.A. de−Kolisch, I.F. von**
Paris

1 e4 e5 2 ♘f3 ♘c6 3 ♗b5 ♗c5 4 0-0 ♘d4 5 ♘xd4 ♗xd4 6 c3 ♗b6 7 d4 c6 8 ♗a4 ♘f6 9 ♗c2 ♕e7 10 ♗g5 d6 11 ♘d2 h6 12 ♗h4 g5 13 ♗g3 h5 14 dxe5 dxe5 15 ♘c4 ♗c7 16 h4 b5 17 ♘e3 ♘g4 18 ♘xg4 hxg4 19 hxg5 ♕xg5 20 ♖fe1 ♗a6 21 ♗b3 ♖ad8 22 ♕c2 ♕h6 23 ♔f1 ♕d2 **0-1** M954-1860

**1860-★KS-1**
**Kolisch, I.F. von−Sabourov**
London

⟨♘b1⟩ 1 e4 e5 2 ♗c4 ♘f6 3 f4 d5 4 exd5 ♗g4 5 ♘e2 exf4 6 0-0 f3 7 gxf3 ♗h3 8 ♖e1 ♗e7 9 ♘f4 ♕d6 10 d4 ♗d7 11 ♕e2 c6 12 ♘g6 ♘xd5 13 ♘xh8 ♗e6 14 c3 ♘d7 15 ♗xd5 ♕xd5 16 ♗f4 17 c4 ♕xd4+ 18 ♗e3 ♕e5 19 f4 ♕f4 20 ♖ad1 ♗b4 21 ♖f1 0-0-0 22 a3 ♗c5 23 b4 ♗xe3+ 24 ♕xe3 ♗xc4 25 ♖f3 ♖xh8 26 ♖g3 ♖g8 27 ♖g5 ♕e6 28 ♕xa7 ♕e2 29 ♖c1 b6 30 ♕a8+ ♘b8 31 ♖e5 ♕g4+ 32 ♔h1 ♕xf4 33 ♖ce1 ♖d8 34 b5 ♕f2 35 bxc6 ♗d5+ 36 ♖xd5 ♕xe1+ 37 ♔g2 ♕e4+ 38 ♔g1 ♕b1+ 39 ♔g2 ♕c2+ 40 ♔g1 ♖xd5 41 ♕b7+ ♔d8 42 c7+ ♕xc7 43 ♕xd5+ ♔e8 44 ♕e4+ ♕e7 45 ♕xh7 ♕e1+ 46 ♔g2 ♕d2+ 47 ♔g1 ♕c1+ 48 ♔g2 ♕c6+ 49 ♔f1 ♘d7 50 ♕xg7 ♕f6+ 51 ♕xf6 ♘xf6 **0-1** M324-1860

**1860-★KS-2**
**Kolisch, I.F. von+Sabourov**
London

⟨♘b1⟩ 1 e4 d5 2 e5 d4 3 ♗c4 e6 4 ♘f3 a6 5 a4 ♗c5 6 0-0 f6 7 ♕e2 ♘h6 8 d3 ♘f7 9 c3 0-0 10 b4 ♗a7 11 cxd4 fxe5 12 dxe5 ♘c6 13 ♗b2 b5 14 axb5 axb5 15 ♗xb5 ♘xb4 16 ♕e4 ♘d5 17 ♗c6 ♖b8 18 ♗a3 ♘c3 19 ♕c4 ♘e2+ 20 ♔h1 ♗d4 21 ♖ae1 ♘xe5 22 ♘xe5 ♗xe5 23 ♗xf8 ♕xf8 24 ♖xe2 ♖b4 25 ♕c1 ♗f4 26 ♕c3 ♕d6 27 ♗e4 ♗d7 28 ♖a2 ♗e5 29 ♖a8+ ♔f7 30 ♕c2 ♗b2 31 ♕d1 ♗b5 32 ♕h5+ ♔e7 33 ♕xh7 ♕f4 ♕h8 ♖xe4 35 ♕d8+ **1-0** M324-1860

**1860-★KS-3**
**Kolisch, I.F. von+Schroeder**
London

⟨♘b1⟩ 1 e4 e5 2 ♘f3 ♘c6 3 ♗c4 ♗e7 4 d4 d6 5 c3 ♘f6 6 d5 ♘a5 7 ♗d3 b6 8 h3 c5 9 ♗e3 0-0 10 g4 h6 11 g5 hxg5 12 ♘xg5 ♘h7 13 ♘xh7 ♔xh7 14 ♕h5+ ♔g8 15 ♖g1 ♗f6 16 f4 c4 17 ♗c2 ♖e8 18 f5 ♔f8 19 0-0-0 ♔e7 20 ♖xg7 ♗xg7 21 ♗g5+ f6 22 ♕h7 ♖g8 23 ♗h6 ♕f8 24 ♖g1 ♕f7 25 ♗xg7 ♗xf5 26 ♗xf6+ ♔f8 27 ♖xg8+ ♕xg8 28 ♕e7++ **1-0** M392-1960

**1860-★KS-4**
**Kolisch, I.F. von+Schroeder**

⟨♘b1⟩ 1 e4 e5 2 ♘f3 ♘c6 3 ♗c4 ♗e7 4 d4 exd4 5 c3 d6 6 ♕b3 ♘a5 7 ♗xf7+ ♔f8 8 ♕a4 c5 9 ♗xg8 ♔xg8 10 cxd4 cxd4 11 ♕xd4 ♗e6 12 0-0 h6 13 ♗f4 ♘c6 14 ♕a4 a6 15 ♖ad1 ♕c7 16 ♖fe1 ♘e5 17

♘d4 ♗d7 18 ♕b3+ ♔h7 19 ♗g3 ♖hf8 20 f4 ♘g6 21 ♖c1 ♕b8 22 ♘f5 ♗c6 23 ♘xe7 ♘xe7 24 f5 ♕a7+ 25 ♗f2 ♕b8 26 ♕e6 ♖e8 27 ♗d4 ♕d8 28 ♖e3 ♕d7 29 ♖g3 ♖g8 ♕f7 ♘xf5 31 ♕g6+ ♔h8 32 exf5 **1-0** M954-1860

**1860-★KS-5**
**Schulten, J.W.– Kolisch, I.F. von**

1 e4 e5 2 f4 d5 3 exd5 e4 4 ♘c3 ♘f6 5 d3 ♗b4 6 ♗d2 e3 7 ♗xe3 0-0 8 ♘ge2 ♖e8 9 ♗d2 ♗xc3 10 ♗xc3 ♘xd5 11 ♕d2 ♘e3 12 ♗e5 ♘xf1 13 ♖xf1 f6 14 ♗c3 g5 15 ♖f2 ♕d5 16 ♔f1 ♘c6 17 h3 ♗xh3 18 gxh3 ♖xe2 19 ♔xe2 ♖e8+ 20 ♗e5 ♘xe5 21 ♕e3 ♔f7 22 ♕g3 ♘c4+ 23 ♔f1 ♕h1+ 24 ♕g1 ♕xh3+ 25 ♖g2 ♘d2+ 26 ♔f2 ♕e3# **0-1** M324-1860

**1860-★KS-6**
**Kolisch,I.F.von+ Stanley,C.H.**
London

1 e4 e6 2 d4 d5 3 ♗d3 dxe4 4 ♗xe4 ♘f6 5 ♗d3 ♗e7 6 ♘f3 0-0 7 0-0 ♘c6 8 ♗e3 ♗d6 9 ♘c3 ♘e7 10 ♕e2 c6 11 ♗g5 ♘g6 12 ♖ad1 h6 13 ♗xf6 ♕xf6 14 ♘e4 ♕e7 15 ♘xd6 ♕xd6 16 ♘e5 ♘e7 17 ♖fe1 f5 18 ♗c4 b5 19 ♗b3 a5 20 a3 f4 21 ♕e4 ♘d5 22 ♖d3 ♗b7 23 ♘g4 ♖f7 24 ♕g6 ♔f8 25 ♖xe6 ♖e7 26 ♕f5+ ♔e8 27 ♗xd5 cxd5 28 ♘f6+ **1-0** L/N6047-1860

**1860-★KW-1**
**Kolisch,I.F.von+ Worrall,T.H.**
London

⟨♘b1⟩ 1 e4 e6 2 f4 d5 3 e5 f5 4 d4 c5 5 c3 ♘c6 6 ♘f3 ♗d7 7 ♗d3 ♗e7 8 0-0 ♘h6 9 h3 0-0 10 ♗e3 b6 11 ♔h2 ♗e8 12 ♘g5 ♕d7 13 ♖c1 ♗g6 14 ♕a4 c4 15 ♗e2 ♘f7 16 b3 ♘xg5 17 fxg5 b5 18 ♕xb5 ♘xe5 19 ♕xd7 ♘xd7 20 bxc4 ♗d6+ 21 g3 ♗a3 22 ♖ce1 ♖ac8 23 c5 ♖b8 24 ♗a6 ♖b2+ 25 ♖f2 f4 26 gxf4 ♗e4 27 ♔g3 ♘b8 28 ♗e2 ♘c6 29 ♗g4 ♔f7 30 ♗f3 ♗f5 31 h4 ♖fb8 32 h5 ♖xf2 33 ♔xf2 ♖b2+ 34 ♗e2 ♖xe2+ 35 ♔xe2 ♗b1 36 ♔d1 ♗xa2 37 ♔c2 ♘a5 38 ♗f2 ♘c4 39 f5 a5 40 g6+ hxg6 41 fxg6+ ♔f6 42 ♗h4+ ♔f5 43 ♗g4+ ♔xg4 44 h6 ♘e3+ 45 ♔d2 ♘c4+ 46 ♔e2 gxh6 47 g7 ♔xh4 48 g8♕ ♗c1 49 c6 ♗f4 50 ♕f3 ♗g5 51 c7 **1-0** L/N6047-1862

**1860-★KW-2**
**Kolisch,I.F.von+ Worrall,T.H.**
London♀

⟨♘b1⟩ 1 e4 c5 2 ♗c4 e6 3 ♕e2 ♗d6 4 ♘f3 ♘c6 5 0-0 ♘d4 6 ♘xd4 cxd4 7 f4 ♗c7 8 d3 ♘e7 9 f5 d5 10 ♗b3 0-0 11 f6 ♘g6 12 ♗g5 ♕d6 13 g3 ♕e5 14 fxg7 ♕xg5 15 gxf8♕+ ♔xf8 16 ♔h1 dxe4 17 ♕xe4 ♗e5 18 ♖f3 f5 19 ♖af1 ♔e7 20 ♕e1 ♗d7 21 ♕b4+ ♗d6 22 ♕xb7 ♖b8 23 ♕xa7 ♖f8 24 ♗a4 ♖d8 25 ♗xd7 ♖xd7 26 ♕xd4 ♘e5 27 ♖3f2 h5 28 ♕e2 ♘g4 29 ♖fe1 e5 30 h3 ♔f6 31 ♕a4 ♖e7 32 ♕c6 ♖e6 33 hxg4 ♕xg4 34 ♕g2 ♖e8 35 ♖f1 ♖g8 36 ♖ef2 ♖g5 37 ♕f3 ♕d4 38 ♕e4 **1-0** L/N6047-1860

**1860-★KW-3**
**Kolisch,I.F.von+ Worrall,T.H.**
Cambridge

⟨♘b1⟩ 1 e4 e5 2 f4 ♘c6 3 ♘f3 d6 4 c3 ♗g4 5 ♗c4 ♗xf3 6 ♕xf3 ♘f6 7 f5 ♗e7 8 d3 0-0 9 g4 ♘e8 10 h4 ♗xh4+ 11 ♔e2 ♗g5 12 ♖h5 ♗xc1 13 ♖xc1 ♘a5 14 ♖xh7 ♘xc4 15 ♕h3 f6 16 ♕h5 **1-0** M954-1860

**1860-★K♀-1**
**Kolisch, I.F.von+♀**
Paris [Staunton]

1 e4 e5 2 ♘f3 ♘c6 3 ♗c4 ♗c5 4 b4 ♗xb4 5 c3 ♗a5 6 d4 exd4 7 0-0 d6 8 ♕b3 ♕f6 9 e5 dxe5 10 ♖e1 ♗b6 11 ♗g5 ♕f5 12 ♘xe5 ♘xe5 13 ♕b5+ c6 14 ♖xe5+ ♗e6 15 ♗xe6 fxe6 16 ♕e2 ♕f7 17 ♘d2! ♔d7 18 ♘c4 ♖e8 19 ♖a5 [△ 20 ♘e5+] 19 ... ♕f8

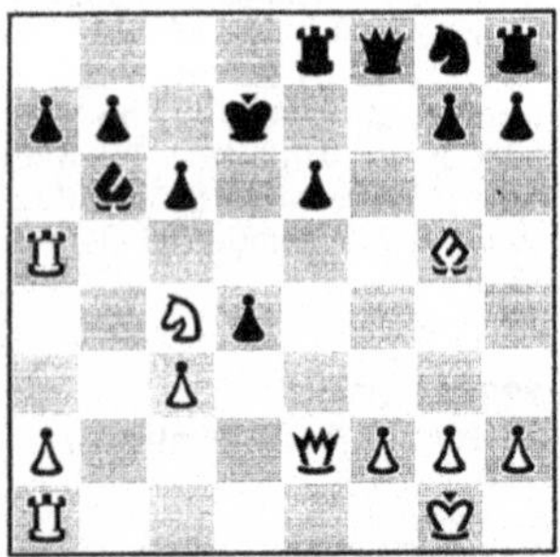

20 ♖b1! ♗xa5 21 ♖xb7+ ♗c7 22 ♕e5 ♖c8 23 ♕xd4+ ♔e8 24 ♖xc7 ♖xc7 25 ♕d8+ ♔f7 26 ♘e5# **1-0** M954-1860

**163** Paulsen, L. M1647.BL

**1860-★LP-1**
**Littleton, H.A.– Paulsen, L.**
[Fiske]

1 e4 e5 2 ♘f3 ♘c6 3 d4 exd4 4 ♗c4 ♗c5 5 0-0 d6 6 c3 dxc3 7 ♘xc3 ♘ge7 8 ♗g5 0-0 9 ♘d5 ♗e6 10 ♘f6+ ♔h8 [10 ... gxf6 11 ♗xf6 h6 12 ♘e5+–] 11 ♗d3 h6 12 ♘h4 ♘g8 13 e5 [13 ♕h5 ♘xf6] 13 ... ♘xe5 14 ♘h7 hxg5 15 ♘xf8 gxh4 16 ♘xe6 fxe6 17 ♕h5+ ♘h6 18 ♗c2 ♕f6 19 h3 ♖f8 20 ♔h1 ♕f4 21 ♖ae1 ♔g8 22 ♖e4 ♕g3

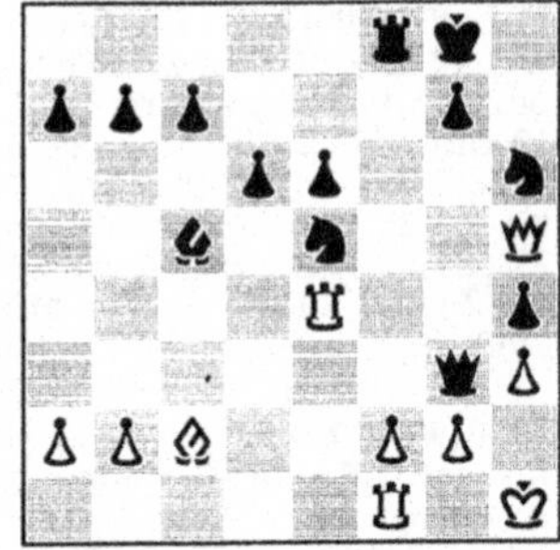

23 fxg3 ♖xf1+ 24 ♔h2 ♗g1+ 25 ♔h1 ♗f2+ 26 ♔h2 hxg3# **0-1** L/N6389-1860

**1860-★LR-1**
**deRives= Lasa,T.von H.u.von d.**
Bruxelles [Staunton]

1 e4 e5 2 ♗c4 f5 3 exf5 ♘f6 4 g4 d5 5 ♗b3 ♗c5 6 d3 h5 7 ♗e3 ♗xe3 8 fxe3 ♘xg4 9 ♕f3 ♕h4+ 10 ♔e2 ♖f8 11 e4 ♘c6 12 c3 dxe4 13 dxe4 ♗d7 [◻13 ... ♘f2] 14 ♘d2 g6 15 h3 ♘h6 16 ♕e3 ♘g8 [◻16 ... ♗xf5 17 ♕xh6 ♗xe4 18 ♖h2 ♕g3 19 ♘xe4 (19 ♕xf8+ ♔xf8 20 ♖f2+ ♗f5 21 ♘e4 ♕h4–+) 19 ... ♕xh2+ 20 ♔e3 ♘e7 21 ♗e6 ♕xb2–+] 17 ♘gf3 ♕f6 18 fxg6 ♕xg6 19 ♖ag1 ♕h7 20 ♖g5 0-0-0 21 ♘xe5 ♘f6 22 ♘xd7 ♕xd7 23 ♖hg1 ♖fe8 24 ♖g7 ♕d6 25 ♖1g2 ♘xe4 26 ♘xe4 ♕e5 27 ♗c2 ♕b5+ 28 ♗d3

♕xb2+ 29 ♔f3 ♘e5+ 30 ♔g3 ♖xd3 31 ♕xd3 ♕xg2+ **0-1**
M954-1860

**1860-★LS-1** 5 ii 60
**Steinitz, W.+Lang**
Wien [Bachmann]
1 e4 e5 2 f4 exf4 3 ♘f3 g5 4 ♗c4 ♘c6 5 d4 g4?! 6 c3 gxf3 7 0-0 fxg2 [□ 7 ... d6] 8 ♗xf7+ ♔xf7 9 ♕h5+ ♔e7 10 ♖xf4 ♘h6 [□ 10 ... ♘f6] 11 ♖xf8?! ♕xf8 12 ♗g5+ ♔e6 [12 ... ♔d6] 13 d5+ ♔d6 14 ♘d2 ♔c5 [□ 14 ... ♘e5] 15 ♗e3+ ♔b5 16 ♕e2+ ♔a5 17 ♘b3+ ♔a4 18 ♕c4+ ♘b4 19 ♘c5+ **1-0** L/N3131

**1860-★LS-2** 26 iii 60
**Steinitz, W.+Lang**
Wien [Bachmann]
1 e4 e5 2 ♘c3 ♘c6 3 f4 ♗c5 4 fxe5 ♗xg1 5 ♖xg1 ♕h4+ 6 g3 ♕xh2 7 ♖g2 ♕h6 8 d4 ♕g6 9 ♗f4 ♘h6? 10 ♗d3 b5 11 ♕f3 0-0 12 0-0-0 f6 13 exf6 ♕xf6 14 e5 ♕e6 15 ♖h1 ♘a5 16 ♕e4 ♘f5 17 g4 d5

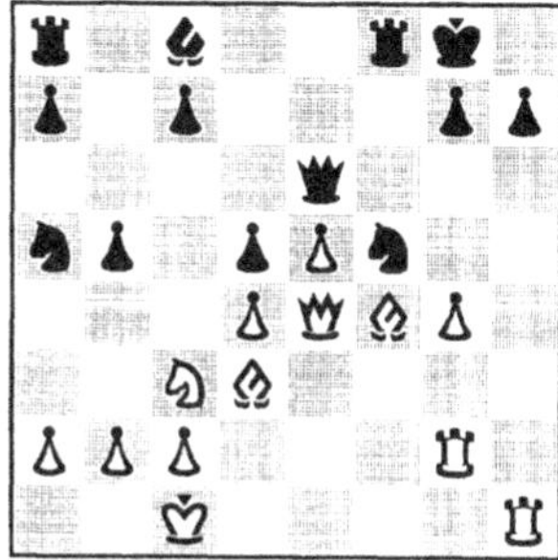

18 ♕xf5! ♖xf5 19 gxf5 ♕f7 20 e6! [△ 21 ♗e5] 20 ... ♗xe6 21 ♗e5 g6 [□ 21 ... ♗xf5 22 ♖xg7+ ♕xg7 23 ♗xg7 ♗xd3] 22 fxg6 ♕f3 [22 ... ♕d7 23 ♖xh7] 23 gxh7+ ♔f8 [23 ... ♕f7 24 ♖g7++−] 24 h8♕+ ♔e7 25 ♖g7+ ♗f7 26 ♖xf7+ ♔xf7 [26 ... ♕xf7 27 ♕xa8] 27 ♕g7+ ♔e6 [27 ... ♔e8 28 ♖h8+ ♕f8 29 ♖xf8#] 28 ♖h6+ ♕f6 29 ♖xf6# **1-0** L/N3131

**1860-★LS-3** 15 iv 60
**Steinitz, W.+Lang**
Wien [Bachmann]
1 e4 e5 2 ♘f3 ♘c6 3 d4 exd4 4 ♗c4 ♕e7 5 0-0 ♘e5 6 ♘xe5 ♕xe5 7 c3 c5 8 f4 ♕f6 9 e5 ♕b6 10 ♔h1 ♗e7 11 f5 d5 [11 ... d6 12 e6] 12 ♗xd5 ♘h6 13 f6 ♗f8 14 ♗xh6 gxh6 15 ♗xf7+! ♔xf7 16 ♕h5+ ♔e6 [16 ... ♔g8? 17 ♖f3] 17 ♕e8+ ♔d5 18 cxd4 ♗e6 [□ 18 ... cxd4] 19 ♘c3+ ♔c4 [19 ... ♔xd4 20 ♕xa8] 20 d5! ♖xe8 21 ♖f4+ ♔d3 22 ♖d1+ ♔c2 [22 ... ♔e3 23 ♖f3#] 23 ♖f2# **1-0** L/N3131

**1860-★MM-1** 7 v 60
**Morphy, P.C.+Meunier, J.**
⟨♖a1⟩ 1 e4 e5 2 f4 d5 3 exd5 exf4 4 ♘f3 ♗d6 5 ♗e2 ♗g4 6 0-0 ♗xf3 7 ♗xf3 ♘e7 8 d4 0-0 9 c4 c6 10 dxc6 ♘bxc6 11 c5 ♗b8 12 d5 ♘e5 13 d6 ♘xf3+ 14 ♕xf3 ♘c6 15 ♗xf4 a5 16 ♘c3 ♗a7 17 ♗e3 a4 18 ♘d5 ♕a5 19 ♖c1 ♔h8 20 ♘f6 g6 21 ♕h3 h5 22 ♘xh5 gxh5 23 ♕xh5+ ♔g7 24 ♕g5+ ♔h8 25 ♕h4+ ♔g8 26 ♕g3+ ♔h7 27 ♖c4 **1-0** +13

**1860-★MP-1** x 60
**Morphy, P.C.+Perrin F.**
New York [Maróczy]
⟨♘b1⟩ 1 e4 e5 2 f4 d5 3 exd5 exf4 4 ♘f3 ♕xd5 5 ♗e2 ♘f6 6 0-0 ♗d6 7 d4 c5 [□ 7 ... 0-0] 8 c4 ♕c6 9 ♘e5 ♗xe5 10 dxe5 ♘fd7 11 ♗f3 ♕b6 [11 ... ♕e6 12 ♗d5] 12 e6 fxe6 13 ♗h5+ g6 14 ♗xf4 ♘c6 [□ 14 ... 0-0 15 ♗g4 (15 ♗h6 ♖xf1+ 16 ♕xf1 gxh5 17 ♕f3 e5 18 ♕d5+ ♔h8 19 ♗e3 ♕c6 20 ♕f7 ♕g6) 15 ... ♘f6 16 ♗h6 ♖f7 17 ♗g5 (17 ♕c2 ♘c6!) 17 ... ♕xb2 18 ♖b1 ♕d4+ 19 ♕xd4 cxd4 20 ♗xf6 ♘c6 △ 21 ... e5] 15 ♕g4 ♘e7 [15 ... ♘e5 16 ♗xe5 ♘xe5 17 ♕f4 ♕c7 18 ♖ae1] 16 ♗g5 gxh5 17 ♕f3! [17 ♕xh5+] 17 ... ♘e5 [17 ... ♖f8 18 ♕xh5+ ♘g6 19 ♕xh7] 18 ♕f6 ♘7g6 19 ♖ad1 ♗d7 20 ♕g7 ♕c7 21 ♖de1 ♕d6 22 ♖d1 ♘f3+?? 23 gxf3! ♕c6 24 f4 ♖f8 25 ♕xh7 e5 26 ♖xd7 ♕xd7 27 ♕xg6+ ♕f7 28 ♕d6 ♖g8 29 ♖fe1 **1-0** L/N3203

**1860-★MP-2** x 60
**Morphy, P.C.+Perrin, F.**
New York [Maróczy]
⟨♘b1⟩ 1 e4 e5 2 ♘f3 ♘c6 3 ♗c4 ♘f6 4 d4 exd4 5 0-0 ♘xe4 6 ♗d5 [□ 6 ♖e1] 6 ... ♘f6 7 ♘g5 ♘xd5 8 ♖e1+ ♗e7 9 ♕h5 ♖f8 [9 ... g6 10 ♕h6] 10 ♘xh7 ♘f6 11 ♘xf6+ gxf6 12 ♕h7 ♘e5 [□ 12 ... d6, ♗e6, ♔d7] 13 ♗h6 ♘g6 14 h4 d5 15 h5 ♖h8 16 hxg6! ♖xh7 17 gxh7 ♔d7 18 ♗g7 ♔d6 19 h8♕ ♕xh8 20 ♗xh8 ♗f5 21 ♗g7 ♖g8 22 ♗h6 ♗xc2 23 ♗f4+ ♔d7 24 ♗xc7 ♗e4 [24 ... ♔xc7] 25 ♗g3 ♗d6 26 ♗xd6 ♔xd6 27 f3 ♗xf3 28 ♔f2 ♗e4 29 ♖g1 d3 [□ 29 ... f5 △ f4] 30 ♔e3 ♔e5 31 ♖ac1 f5 32 ♖c7 f4+ 33 ♔d2 f3 34 g4 f5 35 g5 ♔f4 36 g6 ♖xg6? [□ 36 ... f2] 37 ♖xg6 f2 38 ♖c1 ♔f3 39 ♖h1 ♔f4 40 ♖f1 ♔f3 41 ♖g7 d4 42 a4 a6 43 b4 b5 44 a5 ♗d5 45 ♖g6 ♔f4 46 ♖c1 ♗e4 47 ♖xa6 ♗g2 48 ♔xd3 f1♕+ 49 ♖xf1+ ♗xf1+ 50 ♔xd4 ♗c4 51 ♖f6 ♔g5 52 ♔e5 ♗d3 53 a6 ♗e4 54 a7 ♔g4 55 ♖xf5 **1-0** L/N3203

**1860-★MT-1**
**Morphy, P.C.+Thompson, J.**
New York [Maróczy]
⟨♘b1⟩ 1 e4 e5 2 ♘f3 ♘c6 3 ♗c4 ♗c5 4 b4 ♗xb4 5 c3 ♗a5 6 0-0 ♘f6 7 d4 exd4 [□ 7 ... 0-0] 8 ♗a3 ♗xc3 9 ♕b3 d5 10 exd5 ♘e7 11 ♖ae1 ♗xe1 12 ♖xe1 ♘g8 13 d6 [13 ♘g5] 13 ... cxd6 14 ♗xf7+ ♔f8 15 ♘g5 ♘h6 16 ♗e6 ♕b6 17 ♕f3+ ♘ef5 18 ♗xf5 ♗xf5 19 ♘e6+

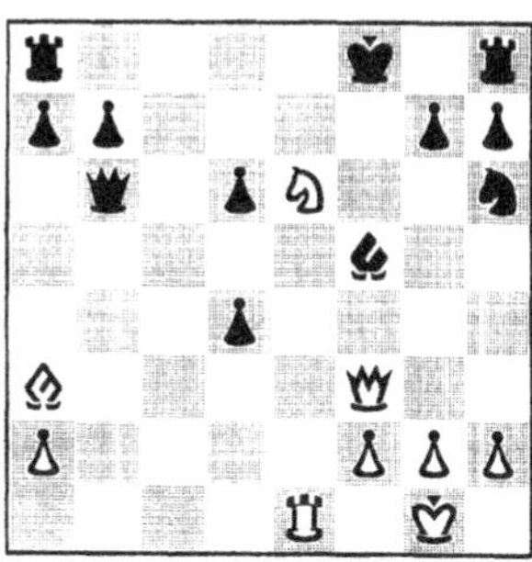

19 ... ♔g8? [□ 19 ... ♔e7 20 ♘xg7+ ♔d7 21 ♘xf5 ♖af8∓] 20 ♕d5 ♕c6 [□ 20 ... ♘f7] 21 ♘d8+ ♕xd5 22 ♖e8# **1-0** L/N3203

**1860-★MT-2** 18 ix 60
**Morphy, P.C.–Thompson, J.**
New York [Maróczy]
⟨♘b1⟩ 1 e4 e5 2 f4 d5 3 exd5 ♕xd5 4 ♘f3 ♗g4 5 ♗e2 ♗xf3 6 ♗xf3 e4 7 ♕e2 f5 8 d3 ♘f6 9 dxe4 ♘xe4 10 ♗e3 ♘c6 11 ♖d1 ♕e6 12 0-0 ♗e7 [□ 12 ... ♗d6] 13 g4 g6 14 ♕g2 h5! 15 gxf5 gxf5 16 ♕h3 ♗d6 17 ♖fe1 0-0-0 18 ♔h1 ♖de8 [□ 18 ... ♗xf4−+] 19 ♕f1 ♕f6 20 ♕b5 a6 21 ♕d5 ♕e6 22 ♕d3 ♗xf4 23 ♗g1 ♖d8 24 ♕f1 ♖xd1 25 ♖xd1 ♘d2 26 ♖e1 [26 ♕h3 ♘xf3 27 ♕xf3 ♕e4] 26 ... ♘xf1 27 ♖xe6 ♔d7 28 ♖f6 ♘e3 29 ♗xe3 ♗xe3 30 ♖xf5 ♘d4 31 ♖f7+ ♔c8 [31 ... ♔e6? 32 ♖xc7 ♘xf3 33 ♖c3] 32 ♗d1 ♖g8 33 ♖f1 h4 34 c3 ♘c6 35 ♖e1 ♗b6 36 h3 ♗f2 37 ♖f1 ♗g3 38 b4 ♘e5 39 ♗e2 ♖d8 40 ♗d1 ♖d2 41 ♗b3 ♖f2 42 ♗e6+ ♔b8 43 ♖xf2 [43 ♖d1 ♘f3−+] 43 ... ♗xf2 44 c4 c6 45 a4 ♔c7 46 ♔g2 ♗e1 47 b5 axb5 48 cxb5 cxb5 49 axb5 ♔d6 50 ♗c8 b6 51 ♔f1 ♗g3 52 ♔e2 ♔c5 53 ♗a6 ♘c4 54 ♔d3 ♘d6 55 ♔e3 ♘xb5 56 ♗c8 ♘d6 57 ♗e6 b5 58 ♔d3 ♘c4 59 ♔c3 ♗e5+ 60 ♔b3 ♘a5+ 61 ♔c2 ♔b4 62 ♗g8 ♔a3 63 ♗f7 b4 64 ♗d5 b3+ 65 ♔b1 ♔b4 66 ♗g8 ♘c4 67 ♗h7 ♔c3 68 ♔c1 ♗f4+ 69 ♔d1 [69 ♔b1 ♘a3+ 70 ... ♗e5−+] 69 ... ♘e3+ 70 ♔c1 ♘g4+ 71 ♔b1 ♘f2 72 ♗f5 ♘d3 73 ♗h7 ♘e5 74 ♗f5 ♘c4 75 ♔a1 ♗c1 76 ♔b1 ♗b2 77 ♗h7 ♘d2# **0-1** L/N3203

**95** Thompson, J. L/N6396.BL

### 1860-★MT-3 ix 60
**Morphy, P.C.+Thompson, J.**
New York [Maróczy]

⟨♘b1⟩ 1 e4 e5 2 ♘f3 ♘c6 3 ♗c4 ♗c5 4 b4 ♗b6 5 a4 a6 6 d4 exd4 [6 ... ♗xd4 7 ♘xd4 ♘xd4 8 f4 d6] 7 c3 d3 8 0-0 d6 9 ♕b3 ♕e7 10 a5 ♗a7 11 b5 axb5 12 ♕xb5 ♘f6 [□ 12 ... ♕d7, ♘ge7] 13 e5 dxe5 14 ♗a3 ♕d7 15 ♖ad1 [15 ♘xe5 ♘xe5 16 ♕xe5+ ♔d8! 17 ♖ad1 ♖e8 18 ♕g3 ♕g4 19 ♖xd3+ ♗d7] 15 ... e4 16 ♗xd3 ♕f5 [16 ... exd3 17 ♖fe1+ ♔d8 18 ♖xd3 ♕xd3 19 ♕xd3+ ♔c8] 17 a6 ♕xb5 18 ♗xb5 ♘d7 19 ♖fe1 f5 20 ♖d5 ♘e7? [20 ... ♘f6! 21 axb7 ♗xb7 22 ♖e5+ (22 ♖f5 0-0-0) 22 ... ♔f7] 21 axb7 ♗xb7 22 ♖xd7 ♗xf2+ [22 ... ♘c6 23 ♖xc7±] 23 ♔xf2 ♖xa3 24 ♖xc7+ ♔f7 25 ♖xb7 **1-0** L/N3203

### 1860-★MT-4 ix 60
**Morphy, P.C.+Thompson, J.**
New York [Maróczy]

⟨♘b1⟩ 1 e4 e5 2 ♘f3 d6 3 d4 exd4 4 ♗c4 ♘c6 5 c3 ♘e5 6 ♘xe5 [6 cxd4 ♘xc4 7 ♕a4+ c6 8 ♕xc4 d5∓] 6 ... dxe5 7 ♕b3 ♕e7 8 0-0 c6 9 f4 b5 10 ♗d3 ♗e6 11 ♕c2 dxc3 12 fxe5 ♕c5+ 13 ♔h1 cxb2 14 ♕xb2 ♖d8 15 ♖d1 ♗c4 16 ♕e2 ♕d4 [□ 16 ... ♖xd3 17 ♖xd3 ♗xd3 18 ♕xd3 ♕xe5 19 ♖b1 ♘f6 20 ♗b2 ♕xe4 21 ♕f1 ♗e7 22 ♖e1 ♕b4 23 ♕e2 0-0∓] 17 ♗g5 ♗xd3 18 ♗xd8 ♗xe2 19 ♖xd4 ♗c5 20 ♖d2 ♗g4 21 ♗a5 ♗b6 22 ♗xb6 axb6 23 h3 ♗e6 24 ♖ad1 ♔e7 25 ♖d8 f6 26 exf6+ ♔xf6 27 ♖a8 g5 [□ 27 ... ♔e5 28 ♖dd8 h5] 28 ♖d6 ♔f7 29 ♖dd8 [□ 19 ♖xc6! ♘e7 30 ♖xh8 ♘xc6 31 ♖xh7+, 32 ♖b7] 29 ... h5 30 ♖db8 ♔g7 31 ♖a7+ ♔f6 [31 ... ♗f7 32 e5 ♘h6!] 32 ♖xb6 ♘e7 33 e5++− ♔f7 34 ♖xc6 ♖c8 35 ♖b6 ♗c4 36 ♖f6+ ♔e8 37 ♖h6 g4 38 e6 ♘g8 39 ♖g6 **1-0** L/N3203

### 1860-★M♀-1
**Morphy, P.C.+♀**

1 e4 e5 2 f4 exf4 3 ♘f3 g5 4 ♗c4 g4 5 d4 gxf3 6 ♕xf3 ♗h6 7 0-0 c6 8 ♗xf7+ ♔xf7 9 ♗xf4 ♗xf4 10 ♕xf4+ ♔g6 11 ♕f7+ ♔h6 12 ♖f5 ♕h4 13 ♘d2 ♘e7 14 ♘f3 ♕g4 15 ♖g5 ♕xg5 16 ♘xg5 ♔xg5 17 ♕xe7+ ♔g6 18 ♖f1 **1-0** M1109

### 1860-★PS-1
**Stanley, C.H.+Pindar, E.**
Manchester [Staunton]

1 e4 e5 2 ♘f3 ♘c6 3 d4 exd4 4 ♗c4 ♗c5 5 0-0 d6 6 c3 ♗g4 7 cxd4 ♘xd4 8 ♘bd2 ♕f6? 9 e5 dxe5 10 ♘e4 ♕g6 11 ♕a4+ ♗d7 12 ♕xd7+ ♔xd7 13 ♘xe5+ ♔e7 14 ♘xg6+ hxg6 15 ♗g5+ f6 16 ♘xc5 fxg5 17 ♖fe1+ ♔f6 18 ♘d7+ **1-0** M954-1860

### 1860-★PS-2
**Pindar, E.−Stanley, C.H.**
Manchester [Staunton]

1 e4 e5 2 ♘f3 ♘c6 3 ♗c4 ♗c5 4 b4 ♗xb4 5 c3 ♗a5 6 d4 exd4 7 0-0 d6 8 ♕b3 ♕f6 9 cxd4 ♗b6 10 e5 dxe5 11 dxe5 ♕g6 12 ♘g5 ♘h6 13 e6 ♗xe6 14 ♗xe6 fxe6 15 ♘xe6 ♘f5 16 ♗b2 ♔d7!? 17 ♖d1+ [□ 17 ♘f4] 17 ... ♘d6 18 ♘f4 ♕f5 19 g3 ♖ae8 20 ♘a3 ♔c8 21 ♖ac1 ♘e4 22 ♖c2 g5?! 23 ♖d5 ♕g4 24 h3? ♕xg3+ 25 ♕xg3 ♘xg3 26 ♗xh8 gxf4 27 ♔h2 ♘e4 28 f3 ♖xh8 29 fxe4 ♘d4 30 ♖c1 ♖g8 31 ♘c4 ♘f3+ 32 ♔h1 ♗f2 33 ♖f1? [33 ♘d6+] 33 ... ♖g3 34 ♖d3 ♘h4 35 ♖xg3 fxg3 36 ♖xf2 gxf2 37 ♘e3 ♔d7 38 ♔h2 ♘f3+ 39 ♔g2 ♘d2 40 e5 f1♕+ **0-1** M954-1860

### 1860-★RS-1 25 ii 60
**Steinitz, W.+Reiner**
Wien [Bachmann]

1 e4 e5 2 ♘f3 ♘c6 3 ♗c4 ♗c5 4 0-0 d6 5 b4 ♗xb4 6 c3 ♗c5 7 d4 exd4 8 cxd4 ♗b6 9 d5 ♘e5 10 ♘xe5 dxe5 11 ♗b2 f6 12 ♔h1 ♘h6 13 ♕h5+ ♘f7 14 f4 g6 15 ♕e2 ♗c5 16 fxe5 ♘xe5 17 ♗xe5 fxe5 18 d6 ♕xd6 [18 ... ♗d4 19 ♕f3 ♕xd6 (19 ... ♕d7) 20 ♘c3] 19 ♗f7+ ♔d8 20 ♘c3 ♗d4 21 ♘b5 ♕d7 22 ♘xd4 exd4 23 e5 c5 24 ♖f6 ♔c7 25 ♖c1 b6 26 ♗c4 ♔b8 27 ♖f7 ♕c6 28 e6 ♕d6? 29 ♗a6 ♗xa6? [□ 29 ... h5 30 ♖cf1 (30 ♗xc8 ♔xc8 (30 ... ♖xc8 31 ♕e4 ♕c6 32 ♕e5+ ♖c7 33 e7!+−) 31 ♕e4 ♖b8 32 ♖d7+−) 30 ... ♖e8 31 ♖1f6 ♖xe6 32 ♖xe6 ♕xe6 33 ♖b7+ ♗xb7 34 ♕xe6+−] 30 ♕xa6 ♕c6 31 ♖xc5 ♕e4 32 ♖c1 [Δ 33 ♖fc7, 34 ♖c8+] **1-0** L/N3131

### 1860-★RS-2 29 iv 60
**Steinitz, W.+Reiner**
Wien [Bachmann]

1 e4 e5 2 ♘f3 ♘c6 3 ♗c4 ♗c5 4 0-0 d6 5 b4 ♗xb4 6 c3 ♗c5 7 d4 exd4 8 cxd4 ♗b6 9 d5 ♘e5 10 ♘xe5 dxe5 11 ♗b2 f6 12 ♔h1 ♘h6 13 f4 ♘f7 14 fxe5 fxe5?

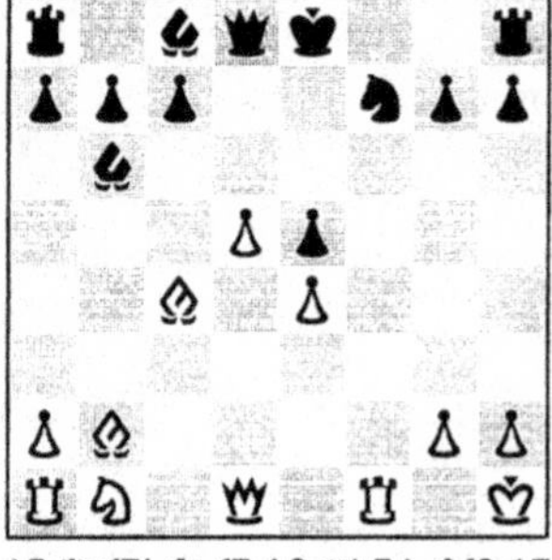

15 ♖xf7! ♔xf7 16 ♕h5+ ♔f8 17 d6 ♕d7 18 ♘c3 g6 19 ♕xe5 **1-0** L/N3131

### 1860-★RS-3 iv 60
**Reiner−Steinitz, W.**
Wien [Bachmann]

1 e4 e5 2 ♘f3 ♘c6 3 d4 exd4 4 ♗c4 ♗c5 5 0-0 d6 6 c3 ♗g4 7 ♕b3 ♗xf3 8 ♗xf7+ ♔f8 9 ♗xg8 ♖xg8 10 gxf3 g5 11 ♕e6 ♘e5 12 ♕f5+ ♔g7 13 ♔h1 [13 ♗xg5 (13 ♕xg5+? ♔h8 14 f4 ♘f3+ 15 ♔h1 ♘xg5) 13 ... ♔h8 14 h4 h6 15 f4 ♘f3+ 16 ♔h1 hxg5 17 hxg5 dxc3 18 bxc3 ♘xg5 19 fxg5 ♖xg5 20 ♕h3+ ♔g7] 13 ... ♔h8 14 ♖g1 g4! 15 f4 [15 fxg4 ♕h4 16 ♗f4! ♘xg4 17 ♗g3 ♕h6 18 ♘a3 dxc3 19 bxc3 ♖af8 20 ♕d5 ♖xf2 21 ♖g2 ♖xg2 22 ♔xg2 ♘e3+] 15 ... ♘f3 16 ♖xg4 ♕h4! 17 ♖g2 [17 ♔g2 dxc3 18 ♘xc3 ♕xf2+ 19 ♔h3 ♕h2#] 17 ... ♕xh2+ 18 ♖xh2 ♖g1# **0-1** L/N3131

### 1860-★SS-1
**Salmon, G.−Staunton, H.**
[Staunton]

⟨♙f7⟩ 1 e4 ... 2 d4 e6 3 ♗d3 c5 4 e5 g6 5 h4 cxd4 6 f4 ♘e7 7 h5 ♖g8 8 ♕g4 ♕a5+ 9 ♔f2 ♘bc6 10 hxg6 hxg6 11 ♘a3 ♘f5 12 ♘f3 ♗xa3 13 bxa3 ♘ce7 14 ♖h7 b6 15 ♕g5 ♗b7 16 g4 ♕d5 17 ♘h4 0-0-0 18 gxf5 ♘xf5 19 ♕g2 ♕a5 20 ♕f1?! ♘xh4 21 ♖xh4 g5 22 fxg5 ♖df8+ 23 ♖f4 ♕xe5 24 g6 ♖xf4+ 25 ♗xf4 ♕xf4+ 26 ♔e1 ♕e3+ 27 ♕e2 ♕g5 **0-1** M954-1860

### 1860-★SS-2
**Steele, J.−Stanley, C.H.**
Liverpool [Staunton]

1 e4 e5 2 ♘f3 ♘c6 3 d4 exd4 4 ♗c4 ♗c5 5 c3 d3 6 b4 ♗b6 7 b5

♘ce7 [7 ... ♕e7 8 0-0 ♘d8 9 e5 ♘e6 10 a4 ♗c5 11 ♘bd2 ♘h6 12 ♘e4 ♘f5 13 ♕xd3 d6 14 ♖e1 0-0 15 exd6 ♗xd6 16 ♘xd6 ♘xd6 17 ♘g5 Staunton - Harrwitz] 8 ♕b3 d5 9 exd5 ♘f6 10 d6 [10 ♗a3; 10 ♗g5]

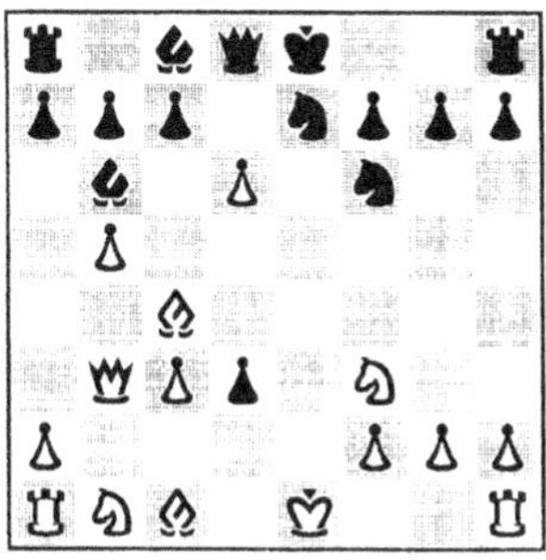

10 ... 0-0 11 ♘e5 ♕xd6 12 ♘xf7 ♗xf2+ 13 ♔xf2 [13 ♔f1 ♕c5 14 ♘g5+ ♔h8 15 ♘f7+ ♖xf7 16 ♗xf7 ♗h4 17 ♕b2 ♘e4→] 13 ... ♘fd5 14 ♗xd3 ♖xf7+ **0-1** M954-1860

**1860-★SW-1**
**Staunton, H.+Worrall, T.H.**
Cambridge [Staunton]

⟨♘b1⟩ 1 e4 b6 2 d4 ♗b7 3 ♗d3 d6 4 ♘f3 ♘d7 5 0-0 e5 6 d5 h6 7 c4 ♘c5 8 ♗c2 a5 9 ♕e2 ♘f6 10 ♗d2 ♗e7 11 a3 0-0 12 ♖ab1 ♘h7 13 ♘e1 ♗g5 14 ♗c3 ♗c8 15 b4 axb4 16 axb4 ♘d7 17 g3 ♗e7 18 f4 f6 19 f5 ♘g5 20 h4 ♘h7 21 ♘g2 ♕e8 22 ♘e3 ♔h8 23 ♔g2 g6 24 ♗d2 ♖g8 25 ♖f3 ♕f7 [25 ... g5 26 h5 ♕xh5 27 ♖h1 ♕~ 28 ♖xh6] 26 ♘g4 g5? 27 ♘xh6 ♕g7 28 ♘xg8 ♔xg8 29 ♖h1 ♘df8 30 ♖b3 ♗d7 31 g4 gxh4 32 ♖xh4 ♘g5 33 ♗xg5 fxg5 34 ♖h1 ♗f6 35 ♖bh3 c6 36 dxc6 ♗xc6 37 c5! bxc5 38 ♗b3+ d5 39 exd5 ♗e8 [□ 39 ... ♗b7] 40 bxc5 ♕b7 41 c6 ♕b6 42 d6+ ♗f7 43 ♗xf7+ ♔xf7 44 ♕c4+ ♔g7 45 ♖b3? [45 ♖c1+−] 45 ... ♖a2+ 46 ♔h3 ♕f2! 47 ♖g3 ♖c2 48 ♕e4! [48 ♕a6?! e4! △ 49 ... ♗e5] 48 ... ♕d2 49 c7 [△ 50 c8♕ ♖xc8 51 ♕b7+] 49 ... ♘d7 50 ♕a4 ♘b6 51 ♕a7 ♘c8 [△ 52 ... ♕d5] 52 ♕b7 ♕xd6 53 ♕xc8 ♖xc7 54 ♕e8 ♗e7 55 ♖a1 ♕h6+ 56 ♕h5 ♕xh5+ 57 gxh5 ♔h6 58 ♖e3± [58 f6!+−] 58 ... ♔xh5 59 ♔g3 g4 60 ♖h1+ ♔g5 61 ♖h7 e4! 62 ♖g7+ ♔xf5 63 ♖xg4 ♗d6+ 64 ♔h3 ♗f4 65 ♖b3 e3 66 ♖b5+ ♗e5 67 ♖g8 ♖c2 68 ♖f8+ ♔e4 69 ♖e8 ♖h2+ 70 ♔g4 ♖g2+ 71 ♔h5 ♖h2+ 72 ♔g6 ♖g2+ 73 ♔f7 ♖g5 74 ♖b1 ♔f3 75 ♔e6 e2 76 ♖f8+ ♔g2 77 ♖e1 ♗d4 78 ♖xe2+ ♔g3 79 ♖e4 ♗b6 80 ♖b4 ♗c5 81 ♖b3+ ♔g2 82 ♖c8 ♗g1 83 ♖c2+ ♗f2 84 ♖bb2 **1-0**
M954-1860

**1860-★SW-2**
**Staunton, H.−Worrall, T.H.**
Cambridge [Staunton]

⟨♘b1⟩ 1 e4 c5 2 ♘f3 d5 3 e5 ♘c6 4 h3 h6 5 c3 ♗f5 6 ♗b5 e6 7 0-0 a6 8 ♗a4 b5 9 ♗c2 ♗xc2 10 ♕xc2 ♕c7 11 d4 cxd4 12 cxd4 ♖c8 13 ♕d1 ♗b4 14 a3 ♗a5 15 b4 ♗b6 16 ♗e3 ♘ge7 17 g4 0-0 18 ♖c1 ♕d7 19 ♕d2 ♔h7 20 h4 a5? 21 ♔g2 axb4 22 axb4 f5 23 exf6 ♖xf6 24 g5 ♖f5 25 ♖c2 ♖cf8 26 ♘h2 h5 27 ♕e2 g6 28 ♕xb5 ♗c7 29 ♖fc1 ♗xh2 30 ♔xh2 ♕d6+ 31 ♔g2 ♖c8 32 ♕b7 [□ 32 ♕a6] 32 ... ♖f7 [32 ... ♖c7?? 33 ♖xc6!+−] 33 ♕a6 [△ 34 b5] 33 ... e5! 34 b5 exd4 35 ♗xd4 ♕f4 36 ♗f6 ♕e4+ [36 ... ♘d4 37 ♖xc8 ♕g4+; 36 ... ♘d4 37 ♗xd4?? ♖xc2 38 ♖xc2 ♕e4+→] 37 f3 ♕xh4 38 bxc6 ♘f5! 39 ♕e2!? [39 ♕xc8=] 39 ... ♕g3+ 40 ♔h1 ♕h3+ 41 ♔g1 ♘h4! 42 ♖c3?? [42 ♖f1=] 42 ... d4! 43 ♖d3 ♖e8! 44 ♕f2 [44 f4 ♖e3!→] 44 ... ♖e3 45 ♖xe3 dxe3 ...? **0-1** M954-1860

**1860-★SW-3**
**Staunton, H.+Worrall, T.H.**
Cambridge? [Staunton]

⟨♘b1⟩ 1 e4 e6 2 d4 b6 3 ♗d3 ♗b7 4 ♘f3 ♘f6 5 ♕e2 d5 6 e5 ♘e4?! 7 0-0 h6 8 c4 c5 9 cxd5 exd5 10 ♗e3 c4 11 ♗c2 ♗e7 12 ♘e1 0-0 13 f3 ♘g5 14 ♕d2 ♘d7 15 g4 a5 16 a3! ♗a6 17 ♕c3 b5 18 b4 axb4 [□ 18 ... cxb3] 19 axb4 ♗b7 20 ♖xa8 ♗xa8 21 ♘g2 ♘h3+ 22 ♔h1 ♗g5? 23 f4 ♗e7 24 ♖f3 ♘g5 25 fxg5 ♗xg5 26 ♗b1? ♘xe5! 27 ♗xg5 ♕xg5 28 ♖f5 [28 dxe5? d4 29 ♕c2 d3 30 ♕~ ♗xf3→] 28 ... ♕xg4 [□ 28 ... ♕g6±] 29 ♖xe5 f5 30 ♖e7 ♕g5 31 ♕e1 ♗c6 32 ♕e6+ ♔h7 33 ♘e3 ...? **1-0** M954-1860

**1860-★SW-4**
**Staunton, H.+Worrall, T.H.**
Cambridge [Staunton]

⟨♘b1⟩ 1 e4 e5 2 ♘f3 ♘c6 3 ♗c4 ♗c5 4 b4 ♗xb4 5 c3 ♗e7 6 0-0 d6 7 d4 exd4 8 cxd4 ♗g4 9 ♕b3 ♖b8 10 ♗xf7+ ♔f8 11 ♗xg8 ♖xg8 12 d5 ♘e5 13 ♘d4 c5 14 f4 ♘g6 15 f5 [△ 16 ♘e6+] 15 ... cxd4 16 fxg6+ ♗f6

17 e5!+− dxe5 18 ♗a3+ ♔e8 19 gxh7 ♖h8 20 d6 ♔d7 [20 ... ♕~ 21 ♕g8++−] 21 ♕f7+ ♔c6 22 ♖fc1+ **1-0** M954-1860

**1860-★SW-5**
**Staunton, H.−Worrall, T.H.**
Cambridge [Staunton]

⟨♘b1⟩ 1 e4 e6 2 ♘f3 c5 3 c3 ♘c6 4 ♗e2 ♘ge7 5 d4 cxd4 6 cxd4 h6 7 0-0 ♘g6 8 ♘e1 ♗b4 9 ♘d3 ♗a5 10 ♗e3 ♗c7 11 f4 0-0 12 f5? exf5 13 ♖xf5 [13 exf5 ♕h4] 13 ... ♕h4 14 e5 ♘xd4→ 15 ♖f2 ♘xe2+ 16 ♕xe2 d5 17 ♖c1 ♗b6! 18 ♗xb6 axb6 19 ♖c7 ♖xa2 20 h3 ♕g3 21 ♖f1 ♗xh3 22 ♘c1 ♗g4 23 ♕d2 ♖a1 24 ♕b4 ♕e3+ 25 ♔h1 ♘xe5 26 ♕e7 ♗e6 27 ♕h4 ♘c6 ...? **0-1** M954-1860

**186ô-★CS-1**
**Saumchurn Guttock−Cochrane,J.**
[Staunton]

1 d4 d5 2 g3 c5 3 c3 e6 4 ♗g2 f5 5 ♘f3 ♘f6 6 0-0 cxd4 7 cxd4 ♘c6 8 a3 ♗e7 9 b4 a6 10 ♘c3 ♗d7 11 ♔h1 0-0 12 ♘e5 ♘xe5 13 dxe5 ♘e4 14 ♘xe4 fxe4 15 f3 exf3 16 exf3 ♕c7 17 ♗b2 ♖ac8 18 ♖c1 ♕b6 19 ♕d2 ♗b5 20 ♖fe1 ♖c4 21 ♖xc4 ♗xc4 22 f4 ♕c6 23 h4 g6 24 ♔h2 ♕d7 25 ♖c1 b5 26 ♗h3 ♗d8 27 ♕d4 ♕f7 28 ♕c5 ♗xh4 29 gxh4 ♕xf4+ 30 ♔g1 ♕g3+ 31 ♗g2 ♕xh4 32 ♕d4 ♖f4 33 ♕e3 ♕g5 [△ 34 ... ♖f1+] 34 ♕h3 ♖g4 35 ♖c2 h5 36 ♖f2 ♕e7 37 ♕e3 d4 38 ♗xd4 ♗d5 39 ♗c5 ♕h4 40 ♖f8+ ♔g7 41 ♖f2 ♖g3 42 ♕d2 ♕g4 43 ♗f8+ ♔g8 44 ♗e7 h4 45 ♔h2 ♖h3+ 46 ♔g1 [46 ♔xh3 ♕g3#] 46 ... ♖g3 47 ♕c2 ♕d4 48 ♔h1?? [48 ♔h2] **0-1** M954-1860

## BRISTOL 1861

### 1861-BRI-1 10 ix 61
**Kolisch, I.F. von= Paulsen, L.** [Suhle]

1 e4 e5 2 ♘f3 ♘c6 3 ♗b5 a6 4 ♗a4 ♘f6 5 0-0 ♗e7 6 d3 d6 7 ♘c3 [□ 7 ♗xc6+] 7 ... 0-0 8 h3 h6 9 ♘h2 ♘h7 10 f4 exf4 11 ♗xf4 ♗g5 12 ♕d2 ♘d4 13 ♘f3 ♘xf3+ 14 ♖xf3 c6 15 ♗b3 ♗e6 16 ♘e2 ♗xb3 17 axb3 d5 18 ♘g3 dxe4 19 ♘xe4 ♕d4+ 20 ♔h1 ♕xb2 21 ♖af1 ♗xf4 22 ♕xf4 ♘g5 23 ♘xg5 hxg5 24 ♕xg5 ♖ae8 **½-½** L/N5186

### 1861-BRI-2 11 ix 61
**Paulsen, L.= Kolisch, I.F. von** [Suhle]

1 e4 c5 2 ♘f3 e6 3 ♘c3 d5 4 exd5 exd5 5 d4 ♗e6 6 ♗e3 c4 7 ♗e2 ♗d6 [7 ... ♗b4 Paulsen-Kolisch, Match] 8 0-0 ♘e7 9 b3 cxb3 10 axb3 ♘bc6 11 ♘b5 ♗b8 12 c4 a6 13 ♘c3 ♗a7 14 ♖e1 0-0 15 ♗d3 ♕d7 16 c5 ♖ad8 17 ♗f4 ♗b8 18 ♗xb8 ♖xb8 19 ♘a4 h6 20 ♕d2 ♕c7 21 ♘b6 ♖bd8 22 ♔h1 ♘c8 23 ♘xc8 ♗xc8 24 ♗c2 a5 25 ♘h4 b6 26 ♘f5 ♗xf5 27 ♗xf5 bxc5 28 dxc5 ♘e7 29 ♗b1 ♕xc5 30 ♖xa5 ♕d6 31 b4 ♘c6 32 ♖a4 ♖fe8 33 b5 ♖xe1+ 34 ♕xe1 ♘e5 35 f4 ♘c4 36 ♕f2 ♖e8 37 h3 ♕b6 38 ♕xb6 ♘xb6 39 ♖a6! ♖b8 **½-½** L/N5186

### 1861-BRI-3
**Kolisch, I.F. von− Paulsen, L.** [Suhle]

1 e4 e5 2 ♘f3 ♘c6 3 ♗c4 ♗c5 4 b4 ♗xb4 5 c3 ♗a5 6 d4 exd4 7 0-0 d6 8 cxd4 ♗b6 9 d5 ♘a5 10 ♗b2 ♘e7 11 ♗d3 [11 ♗xg7 ♖g8 12 ♗f6 ♘xc4 13 ♕a4+ ♕d7 14 ♕xc4 ♖xg2+∓] 11 ... 0-0 12 ♘c3 ♘g6 13 ♘e2 c5 14 ♕d2 f6 15 ♔h1 ♗d7 16 ♖ac1 [□ 16 ♗c3] 16 ... a6 17 ♘e1 ♗b5 18 f4 c4 19 ♗b1

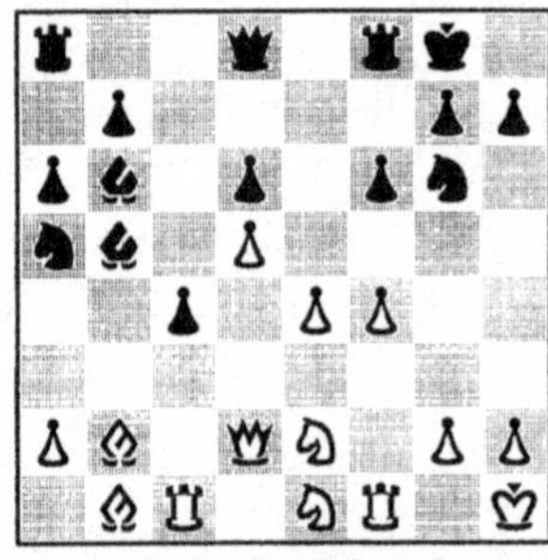

19 ... c3! 20 ♖xc3 ♘c4 21 ♕c1 ♖c8 22 ♗d3 ♗e3 23 ♕c2 ♘d2 24 ♖g1 ♖xc3 25 ♕xc3 ♕b6 26 ♗c1 [26 ♗xb5 ♘xe4∓] 26 ... ♗xg1 27 ♘xg1 ♗xd3 28 ♘xd3? [□ 28 ♕xd3] 28 ... ♘xe4 **0-1** L/N5186

### 1861-BRI-4 10 ix 61
**Wilson, H.+ Stanley, C.H.** [Suhle]

1 e4 e5 2 ♘f3 ♘c6 3 ♗c4 ♗c5 4 0-0 ♘f6! 5 d3 h6 6 ♗e3 ♗b6 7 h3 d6 8 ♘c3 0-0 9 ♕d2 ♗e6 10 ♗b3 ♘e7 11 ♘h4 c6 12 ♗xh6 gxh6 13 ♕xh6 ♘h7? 14 ♗xe6 fxe6 15 ♕xe6+ ♔h8?? 16 ♕xe7 ♕xe7 17 ♘g6+ ♔g7 18 ♘xe7 ♖f6 19 ♘f5+ ♔f7 20 ♔h2 ♖g8 21 f4 ♖fg6 22 g4 ♔e6 23 fxe5 dxe5 24 ♘a4 ♘f6 25 ♘xb6 ♘xg4+ 26 hxg4 ♖xg4 27 ♖f3 ♖g2+ 28 ♔h3 axb6 29 ♘e3 ♖2g5 30 ♔h2 **1-0** L/N5186

### 1861-BRI-5 10 ix 61
**Boden, S.S.+ Horwitz, B.** [Suhle]

1 e4 e5 2 ♘f3 ♘c6 3 d4 exd4 4 ♗c4 ♗c5 5 0-0 d6 6 c3 dxc3 [□ 6 ... ♗g4] 7 ♕b3 ♕e7? [□ 7 ... ♕d7] 8 ♘xc3 ♘f6 9 ♗g5 0-0 10 ♘d5 ♕d8 11 ♘xf6+ gxf6 12 ♗h6 ♘a5! 13 ♕c3 ♘xc4! 14 ♗xf8 ♕xf8 15 ♕xc4 ♕g7 16 ♕d3 ♗e6 17 ♘h4 ♔h8 18 ♘f5 ♕g5 19 ♕g3 ♖g8 20 ♕xg5 ♖xg5 21 ♘g3 h5 22 ♔h1! ♗c4 23 ♖fc1 ♗a6 24 f4 ♖g6 25 ♘xh5 ♗d3 26 ♘g3 ♗f2 27 f5 ♖h6 28 ♖c3! ♗xg3 29 ♖xd3 ♖xh2+ 30 ♔g1 ♗e5 31 ♖c1 c6 32 ♖c2 ♔g7 33 ♖h3 ♖xh3 34 gxh3 ♔h6 35 ♖g2 b5 36 b3 a5 37 ♔f2 ♔h5 38 ♖g7 c5 39 ♖xf7 c4 40 bxc4 bxc4 41 ♔f3! c3 42 ♖h7+ ♔g5 43 h4# **1-0** L/N5186

### 1861-BRI-6 10 ix 61
**Wayte, W.+ Hampton, T.I.** [Suhle]

1 e4 e5 2 ♘f3 ♘c6 3 d4 exd4 4 ♗c4 ♗c5 5 0-0 d6 6 c3 dxc3 7 ♕b3 ♕d7! 8 ♕xc3 f6 9 a3 ♘ge7 10 b4 ♗b6 11 ♕b3 ♖f8 12 ♘c3 ♘d4 13 ♘xd4 ♗xd4 14 ♖a2 ♗xc3 15 ♕xc3 b6 16 ♖c2 [□ 16 f4] 16 ... c6 17 a4 ♗b7 18 ♗f4 ♘g6 19 ♗g3 ♘e5 20 ♗b3 0-0-0 21 f4 ♘f7 22 ♖d1 ♕e7 23 ♗d5 c5 24 bxc5 dxc5 25 ♗xb7+ ♕xb7 26 ♖xd8+ ♖xd8 27 ♕c4 ♖d4?? 28 ♕xd4 **1-0** L/N5186

### 1861-BRI-7
**Wilson, H.− Paulsen, L.** [Suhle]

1 e4 e5 2 ♘f3 ♘c6 3 d4 exd4 4 ♘xd4 ♕h4 5 ♘b5? [□ 5 ♕d3] 5 ... ♗b4+ [□ 5 ... ♕xe4+, 6 ... ♔d8] 6 ♗d2! ♕xe4+ 7 ♗e2 ♔d8 8 0-0 ♘f6 9 ♘1c3 ♕h4 10 g3 ♕h3 11 ♗g5 ♕f5 12 ♕d5 ♕e6 13 ♖ad1 ♗e7 14 ♕g2 d6 15 ♗f3 ♗d7 16 ♔h1? ♕h3 17 ♕g1? ♕f5! 18 ♗f4 g5 19 ♘xc7 ♔xc7 20 ♘d5+ ♘xd5 21 ♖xd5 ♘e5 22 ♕g2 gxf4 **0-1** L/N5186

### 1861-BRI-8 11 ix 61
**Boden, S.S.+ Wayte, W.** [Suhle]

1 e4 e5 2 ♘f3 d6 3 d4 exd4 4 ♕xd4 ♗d7 5 ♗e3 ♘c6 6 ♕d2 ♘f6 7 ♘c3 ♗e7 8 ♗d3 0-0 9 h3 ♗e6 10 ♖d1 ♘e5 11 ♘xe5 dxe5 12 0-0 c6 13 ♘e2 ♕c7 14 ♘g3 ♖ad8 15 ♕e2 ♘d7 16 ♗c4 ♗xc4 17 ♕xc4 ♘b6 18 ♕e2 g6 19 b3 ♗h4 20 ♗h6 ♖xd1 21 ♕xd1 ♖d8 22 ♕f3 ♗xg3?? 23 ♕f6 **1-0** L/N5186

### 1861-BRI-9
**Boden, S.S.− Paulsen, L.** [Suhle]

1 e4 e5 2 ♘f3 ♘c6 3 ♗b5 ♘ge7 4 0-0 g6 5 c3 ♗g7 6 d4 exd4 7 cxd4 d5 8 exd5 ♘xd5 9 ♖e1+ ♗e6 10 ♗xc6+? bxc6 11 ♘c3 0-0 12 h3 c5 13 ♗e3 c4 14 ♘xd5 ♕xd5 15 ♖c1 ♖ab8 16 ♖c2 ♖b5 17 a4? ♖b3 18 ♘e5 ♖b4 19 ♖d2 ♖fb8 20 ♘c6? ♕xc6 21 d5 ♕xa4 22 dxe6 ♕xd1 23 exf7+ ♔xf7 24 ♖exd1 ♗xb2 25 ♖d7+ ♔g8 26 ♗xa7 ♖c8 27 ♖e1 c3 28 ♖ee7 c2 29 ♗e3 ♗c3!

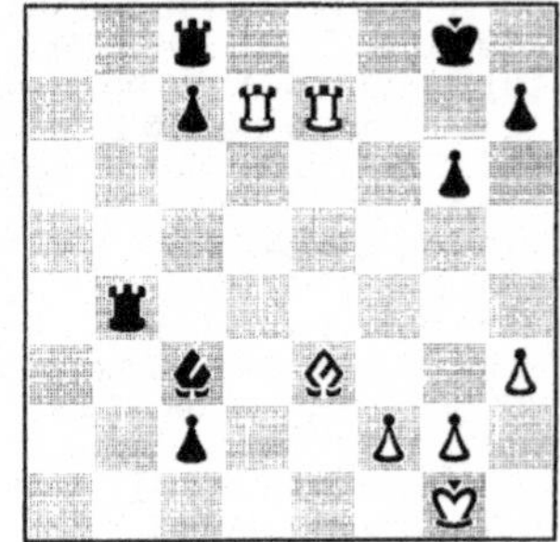

30 ♖xh7 ♖b1+ 31 ♔h2 ♖e1 32 ♗f4 c1♕ 33 ♗xc1 ♖xc1 34 ♖h6 ♗e5+ 35 g3 ♖c6 36 ♖h4 ♖d6 37 ♖hh7 ♖xd7 38 ♖xd7 c5 39 f4 ♗g7 40 ♖d2 c4 41 ♖c2 c3 42 ♔g2 ♖d8 43 ♔f3 ♖d3+ 44 ♔g4 ♖d2 45 ♖c1 c2 46 ♔g5 ♗b2 **0-1** L/N5186

## MANCHESTER 1861

### 1861-MNC-1
**Horwitz, B.− Stanley, C.H.** [Boden]

1 e4 e6 2 f4 d5 3 e5 c5 4 ♘f3 d4 5 c3 d3? 6 ♕a4+ ♗d7 7 ♕c4 a6 8 ♕xd3 [8 ♗xd3? ♗b5] 8 ... ♘e7 9 ♕c2 ♘bc6 10 ♗e2 ♘d5 11 d3 ♗e7 12 0-0 ♖c8 13 a3 0-0 14 c4 ♘b6 15 ♘c3 f6 16 exf6? ♗xf6 17 ♘e4

♗d4+ 18 ♘xd4? ♘xd4 19 ♕d1 ♗a4! 20 b3 ♘xb3 21 ♖b1 ♘d4 22 ♕d2 ♗c2 23 ♖b2 ♘xe2+ 24 ♕xe2 ♗xd3 25 ♕g4 ♗xf1 26 ♕xe6+ ♔h8 27 ♘g5? ♗xc4 28 ♕e4 ♕xg5 29 ♖xb6 [29 fxg5?? ♖f1 #] 29 ... ♕d5 30 ♕c2 ♖ce8 31 ♕d2 ♖xf4 32 ♕xf4 ♖e1+ 33 ♔f2 ♖f1+ 34 ♔g3 ♖xf4 35 ♗xf4 ♕d3+ 36 ♔g4 h5+ 37 ♔xh5 ♕f5+ 38 ♗g5 ♗e2+ **0-1** M392

**1861-MNC-2**
**Stanley, C.H.– Horwitz, B.**
[Boden]

1 e4 e5 2 ♘f3 ♘c6 3 ♗b5 ♘f6 4 ♕e2 ♗e7 5 ♗xc6 dxc6 6 ♘xe5 ♕d4 7 ♘d3? ♕xe4 8 ♕xe4 ♘xe4 9 0-0 ♘c5 10 ♘e1? 0-0 11 b4 ♘a4 12 c3 ♗f6 13 ♘a3 ♗f5 14 ♘ec2 ♗g6 15 f4 ♖ae8 16 ♘e3 ♖xe3 17 dxe3 ♗xc3 18 f5 ♗xa1 19 fxg6 hxg6 20 e4 ♖e8 **0-1** M392

**1861-MNC-3**
**Horwitz, B.+ Stanley, C.H.**
[Boden]

1 e4 e5 2 f4 exf4 3 ♗c4 d5 4 ♗xd5 ♘f6 5 ♘c3 ♗b4! 6 ♕e2 0-0 7 ♗b3 ♗xc3 8 dxc3 ♘xe4 9 ♗xf4 ♖e8 10 ♖d1 ♘d6 11 ♗e3 ♕e7 12 ♔d2 ♗g4 13 ♘f3 a5?! [⌓ 13 ... ♘c6 △ 14 ... ♘f5] 14 a4 ♘c6 15 ♖he1 ♘f5 16 ♗d4 ♕d7? [⌓ 16 ... ♘cxd4 17 ♕xe7 ♘xb3+−+; 16 ... ♘cxd4 17 cxd4 ♕b4+−+] 17 ♕d3 ♗xf3 18 gxf3 ♘fxd4 19 cxd4 ♕xd4 20 ♖xe8+ ♖xe8 21 ♔c1 ♕f4+? [⌓ 21 ... ♕xd3] 22 ♔b1 h6 23 ♕b5 ♕xf3??

24 ♖f1! **1-0** M392

**1861-MNC-4**
**Stanley, C.H.– Horwitz, B.**
[Boden]

1 e4 e5 2 ♘c3 ♘f6 3 f4 exf4 4 d4 [⌓ 4 e5] 4 ... ♗b4 5 ♗d3 d5 6 e5 ♗g4 7 ♘f3 ♘e4 8 ♗d2 ♘xd2 9 ♕xd2 ♗xf3 10 gxf3 ♕h4+ 11 ♔e2 c5 12 a3 ♗xc3 13 ♗b5+ ♘d7 14 ♗xd7+ ♔xd7 15 bxc3 c4? 16 ♖ag1 g5 17 ♖g4 ♕h5 18 h4 [⌓ 18 ♖hg1 ♕xh2+ 19 ♖1g2; 18 ♖hg1 h6] 18 ... h6 19 hxg5?? ♕xh1 20 ♕xf4 ♖af8 21 ♕f5+ ♔c7 22 ♕f4 hxg5 23 ♕xg5 ♖h2+ 24 ♔e3 ♖c1# **0-1** M392

**1861-MNC-8**
**Birch– Pindar, E.**
[Boden]

1 d4 f5? 2 c4 e6 3 e3 ♗b4+ 4 ♗d2 ♗xd2+ 5 ♕xd2 ♘f6 6 ♘c3 b6 7 f3 ♗b7 8 ♗d3 d6? 9 ♘ge2 ♘bd7 10 ♘f4 ♕e7 11 ♘b5 ♘f8 12 d5 a6 13 ♘d4 exd5 14 ♘xf5 ♕d7 15 cxd5 ♘xd5 16 ♘xd5 ♗xd5 17 e4 ♗e6 18 0-0 ♘g6 19 f4 0-0 20 ♘d4 ♗f7 21 ♘f5 ♘e7 22 ♘d4 c5 23 ♘f3? c4 24 ♗c2 b5 25 ♔h1 ♕c7 26 ♘g5 h6 27 ♘xf7 ♖xf7 28 f5 ♘c6 29 f6 ♖af8 30 ♕d5 ♘b4 **0-1** M392

**1861-MNC-10**
**Birch– Pindar, E.**
[Boden]

1 d4 e6 2 e4 c5 3 d5! d6 4 f4? [⌓ 4 c4] 4 ... g6 [4 ... exd5 5 exd5 ♗f5=] 5 ♘f3 ♗g7 6 ♗b5+ ♗d7 7 ♗xd7+ ♕xd7 8 c4 ♘a6 9 0-0 ♘e7 10 a3 0-0 11 ♕d3 exd5 12 cxd5 b5 13 ♘c3 c4 14 ♕e2 ♘c5 15 ♗e3 ♘b3 16 ♖ad1 ♖fc8 [⌓ 16 ... ♖ac8] 17 e5 ♘f5 18 ♗f2 ♖e8 19 ♖fe1 a5 20 ♘g5 dxe5 21 ♕g4 exf4 22 ♕h3 h6 23 ♘ge4 b4 24 axb4 axb4 25 ♘b1 ♗xb2 26 ♗d4 [△ 27 ♘f6+] 26 ... ♖xe4 27 ♖xe4 ♕xd5 **0-1** M392

**1861-MNC-14**
**Pindar, E.– Kipping, J.S.**
[Boden]

1 e4 e5 2 d4 exd4 3 f4 ♗b4+ 4 ♗d2 ♕e7 5 ♗d3 d5! 6 e5 ♘h6 7 ♘f3 ♗xd2+ 8 ♕xd2 c5 9 0-0 ♘c6 10 ♘a3 a6 11 ♖ad1 b5 12 ♘g5 ♘g4 13 f5? ♘cxe5 14 ♘f3 f6 [14 ... ♘e3 15 ♘xe5] 15 c3 dxc3 16 bxc3 0-0 17 h3 ♘h6 [⌓ 17 ... ♘xf3 18 ♖xf3 ♘e5] 18 g4 ♗b7 [18 ... c4 19 ♗c2 △ 20 ♕xd5+] 19 g5 [19 ♘xe5 ♕xe5−+] 19 ... ♘hf7 20 g6 ♘xf3+ 21 ♖xf3 ♘e5 22 gxh7+ ♔h8 23 ♖g3 c4 24 ♘c2 ♕c5+ 25 ♘d4 cxd3 26 ♔h1 ♕d6 27 ♖dg1 ♖f7 **0-1** M392

**1861-MNC-15**
**Kipping, J.S.– Pindar, E.**
[Boden]

1 e4 e5 2 ♘f3 ♘c6 3 ♗c4 d6 4 d3 [⌓ 4 d4] 4 ... ♗g4 5 c3 ♕d7 6 h3 ♗xf3 7 ♕xf3 ♘f6 8 b4 ♗e7 9 ♗e3 a5 10 b5 ♘d8 11 a4 c6 12 0-0 d5 13 exd5 cxd5 14 ♗b3 0-0 15 ♗g5 e4 16 ♕e3 ♖fe8 17 ♖d1 ♕f5 18 ♖a2 ♖c8 19 d4 ♘e6 20 ♗xf6 ♗xf6 21 g4 ♕g6 22 ♗xd5 ♘g5 23 ♗xb7? ♘f3+ 24 ♔g2 ♗g5 25 ♕e2 ♕d6 26 ♖h1 ♘h4+ 27 ♔f1 ♖c7 28 ♗c6 ♖e6 29 ♘a3 e3 30 ♘c4 ♕f4 31 ♘e5 ♖cxc6 32 ♘xc6 ♕e4 33 ♕b2 **0-1** M392

**1861-MNC-16**
**Pindar, E.+ Kipping, J.S.**

1 c4 e5 2 e3 ♘c6 3 d4 exd4 4 exd4 d5 5 ♘f3 ♗e6 6 c5 g6 7 ♗b5 ♗d7 8 ♘c3 ♘ce7 9 ♗xd7+ ♕xd7 10 ♘e5 ♕f5 11 ♕b3 0-0-0 12 ♘b5 ♘c6 13 ♘xc6 bxc6 14 ♘xa7+ ♔d7 15 0-0 ♗g7 16 ♘xc6 ♔xc6 17 ♕a4+ ♔b7 18 c6+ ♔b6 19 ♗d2 **1-0** M324

**1861-MNC-17**
**Kipping, J.S.= Pindar, E.**
[Löwenthal]

1 e4 e5 2 ♘f3 ♘c6 3 ♗c4 ♗c5 4 c3 ♘f6 5 d4 exd4 6 cxd4 [⌓ 6 e5] 6 ... ♗b4+ 7 ♗d2 ♘xe4 8 ♗xb4 ♘xb4 9 ♗xf7+ ♔xf7 10 ♕b3+ d5 11 ♘e5+ ♔f6 12 ♕xb4 c5 13 ♕a4 ♕e8 14 ♕d1 cxd4 15 f4 ♗e6 16 ♕xd4 ♔e7 17 0-0 g6 18 ♘a3 ♖c8 19 ♖ac1 a6 20 ♘f3 [⌓ 20 ♕b6] 20 ... h6 21 ♘h4 ♖g8 22 ♕e5 ♕d8 23 h3 [⌓ 23 f5] 23 ... ♕d6 24 ♘f3 g5 25 ♘d4 ♕xe5 26 fxe5 g4 27 hxg4 ♗xg4 28 ♘ac2 ♖c4? 29 b3 ♖cc8 30 ♘e3 ♗e6 31 ♖xc8 ♖xc8 32 g4 ♖g8 33 ♔h2 h5 34 ♘ef5+ ♔d7 35 gxh5 ♖g5 36 h6 ♖h5+ 37 ♔g2 ♖g5+ 38 ♔h3 ♖h5+ 39 ♔g4 ♖xh6 40 ♔f4 ♗xf5 41 ♘xf5 ♖h2 42 a3 ♘c5 43 ♖d1 ♖f2+ 44 ♔g5 ♔e6 45 ♘e3 ♘xb3 46 ♖xd5 ♖a2 47 ♖d6+ ♔xe5 48 ♘c4+ ♔e4 49 ♖b6 ♘c5 50 ♘d6+ ♔d5 51 ♘xb7 ♘xb7 ½-½ M324

**1861-MNC-18**
**Pindar, E.+ Kipping, J.S.**
[Boden]

1 e4 e5 2 f4 d5 [⌓ 2 ... ♗c5] 3 exd5 exf4 4 ♘f3 ♕xd5 5 d4 ♗d6 6 c4 ♕e4+ 7 ♗e2 c6? 8 ♘c3 ♕f5 9 0-0 ♘e7 10 ♗d3 ♕h5 11 ♘e4 ♗c7 12 ♕e1 0-0 13 ♘f6+!

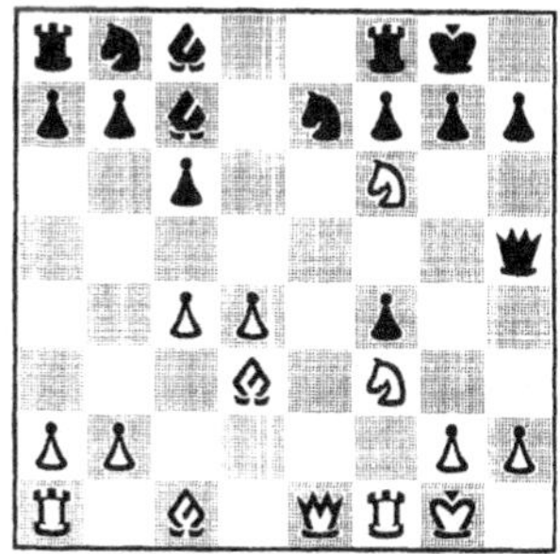

13 ... gxf6 14 ♕xe7 ♘d7 15 ♗d2 c5 16 d5 ♗e5 17 ♖ae1 a5 18 ♖e4 ♗c7 19 ♗c3 ♗d8 20 ♕d6 f5 21 ♖e2 ♕g4 22 h3 ♕g3 23 ♗e1 ♕g6 24 ♕xf4 ♖a6 25 ♗c3 ♘f6 26 ♘h4 ♕h5 27 ♘xf5 ♗xf5 28 ♕xf5 ♕xf5 29 ♖xf5 **1-0** M392

## 1861-MNC-19
23 iii 61
**Horwitz, B.+ Pindar, E.**
[Boden]

1 e4 e6 2 f4 d5 3 e5 c5 4 ♘f3 ♘c6 5 b3 ♘h6 6 c3 f6 7 ♘a3 ♕b6 8 ♗b5 ♗d7 9 ♕e2 ♗e7 10 ♗xc6 bxc6 11 ♘c2 ♘f7 12 d3 0-0 13 0-0 c4+ 14 ♗e3 cxd3 15 ♕xd3 ♕c7 16 ♖fe1 fxe5 17 fxe5 ♘xe5 18 ♘xe5 ♕xe5 19 ♗xa7 ♕c7 20 ♗f2 ♖xf2!

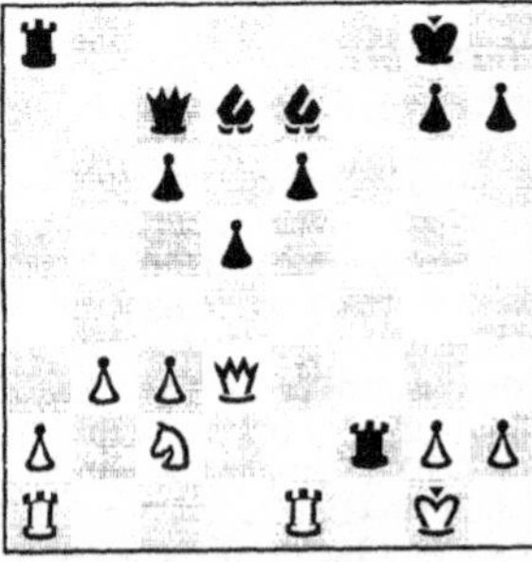

21 ♔xf2 ♕xh2 22 ♖g1 e5 23 ♘e3 e4 24 ♕d4 ♗g5 25 ♔e2 ♕h5+ 26 ♔d2 ♗e6 27 a4 ♖d8? [□ 27 ... c5 28 ♕xc5 d4 29 cxd4 ♗xe3+ 30 ♔xe3 ♕h6+ 31 ♔xe4 ♖e8 32 ♔d3 ♖c8∓] 28 ♕c5 ♕e8 29 b4 ♗f6 30 ♘c2 ♗g5+ 31 ♔e1 ♗g4 32 ♘e3 ♗xe3 33 ♕xe3 ♕e5 34 ♖f1 h5 35 ♖f4 g5 36 ♖f2 d4 37 cxd4 ♖xd4 38 ♖b1 ♕d5 39 ♖d2 ♖d3 40 ♖xd3 exd3 41 ♖b2 ♗e2 42 g3 ♕h1+ 43 ♔d2 ♕d5 44 a5 ♗f1 45 ♔c3 d2 46 ♕e8+ ♔g7 47 ♕e7+ ♔g6 48 ♖xd2 ♕c4+ 49 ♔b2 **1-0** M392

## 1861-MNC-20
**Pindar, E.= Horwitz, B.**
[Boden]

1 e4 e5 2 ♘c3 ♘f6 3 f4 d6 4 ♘f3 ♗g4 5 d4 exd4 6 ♕xd4 ♘c6 7 ♗b5 ♗d7 8 ♗xc6 ♗xc6 9 0-0 ♗e7 10 ♘d5 0-0 11 c4 b6 12 a4 a5 13 ♖a3 ♕d7 14 ♘xe7+? ♕xe7 15 e5 dxe5 16 ♘xe5 ♗b7 17 ♖h3 ♖ad8 18 ♕c3 ♘e4 19 ♕c2 f5 20 ♗e3 ♘g5! 21 ♖g3 ♗e4 22 ♕f2 ♘e6 23 h4 g6 24 h5 g5 25 ♕e2 g4 26 ♘xg4! fxg4 27 ♕xg4+ ♔h8 28 f5 ♘c5 29 ♗g5 [□ 29 f6 ♖xf6 30 ♗d4 ♘d7 31 ♖xf6 ♘xf6 32 ♕xe4+−] 29 ... ♕d7 30 ♗xd8 ♖xd8 31 ♕f4 ♕d4+ 32 ♔h2 ♕d6 33 f6 ♕xf4 34 ♖xf4 ♖f8 35 ♖g7 [□ 35 ♖e3] 35 ... ♖xf6 36 ♖fg4 ♖f8 37 ♖xc7 ♗c2 38 ♖g3 ♘xa4 39 b3 ♘c5 40 ♖c6 ♖b8 41 ♖c3 ♘xb3! 42 c5 [42 ♖xc2? ♘d4] 42 ... bxc5 43 ♖xc2 ♘d4 44 ♖2xc5 ♘xc6 45 ♖xc6 ♖a8 46 ♖c1 a4 47 ♖b1 ♔g7 48 ♔g3 ♔f6 49 ♔f4 ♖a5 50 g3 h6 51 g4 ♔e6 52 ♔e4 ♔d6 53 ♔f4 ♔c5 54 g5 hxg5+ 55 ♔g4 ♔c4 56 ♖a1 a3 57 h6 **½-½** M392

## 1861-MNC-21
**Horwitz, B.− Pindar, E.**
[Boden]

1 e4 e5 2 ♘f3 ♘c6 3 ♗c4 ♘f6 4 ♘g5 d5 5 exd5 ♘a5 6 ♗b5+ [□ 6 d3] 6 ... c6 7 dxc6 bxc6 8 ♗a4 [8 ♕f3∓] 8 ... h6 9 ♘f3 e4 10 ♕e2 ♗d6 11 ♘d4 [11 d3 ♗a6 12 ... 0-0] 11 ... ♕b6 12 c3 0-0 13 b4? ♗xb4 14 cxb4 ♕xd4 15 ♘c3 ♕xb4 16 ♖b1 ♕d6 17 0-0 ♗e6 18 ♘xe4 ♘xe4 19 ♕xe4 ♗c4 20 ♖e1 ♗d3 21 ♕b4 ♖ae8 22 ♗a3 ♗xb1 23 ♖xb1 ♖b8 **0-1** M392

## 1861-MNC-22
**Pindar, E.+ Horwitz, B.**
[Boden]

1 e4 e5 2 ♘c3 ♘f6 3 f4 d6 4 ♘f3 ♗g4 5 ♗e2 exf4 6 d4 ♘h5? 7 0-0 g5? 8 ♘h4! ♗xe2 9 ♕xe2 ♘g7 10 ♘f5 c6 11 g3 fxg3 12 e5! gxh2+ 13 ♔h1 ♘e6 [13 ... dxe5?+−] 14 ♕h5 ♗e7 [14 ... ♕d5 15 ♘ce4] 15 ♘xd6+ ♔d7 16 ♖xf7 ♖f8 17 ♗xg5!

17 ... ♖xf7 18 ♘xf7 ♕g8 19 ♗xe7 ♔xe7 20 ♖f1 ♘a6 21 d5 ♘f4 22 ♕h4+ ♔xf7 23 ♕xf4+ ♔e8 24 ♘e4 ♔d8 25 e6 **1-0** M392

## 1861-MNC-23
**Horwitz, B.− Pindar, E.**
[Boden]

1 e4 e6 2 b3 d5 3 e5 c5 4 f4 ♘c6 5 ♘f3 ♘h6 6 c3 ♕b6 7 ♘a3 f6 8 ♗b5 ♗e7 9 ♗b2 0-0 10 ♗xc6 ♕xc6 11 0-0 ♗d7 12 d4 ♗e8 13 ♘c2 ♗h5 14 ♗a3 ♗xf3 15 ♖xf3 fxe5 16 dxe5 ♘f5 17 g3 ♖ad8 18 ♕e2 b5 19 ♖af1 b4 20 cxb4 cxb4 21 ♗b2 ♖c8 22 ♖c1 ♕b6+ 23 ♔h1 ♖c7 24 ♕d3 ♖fc8 25 g4 ♘h4 26 ♖ff1 d4 27 ♖f2 [27 ♗xd4 ♕c6+−+; 27 ♘xd4 ♕b7+ 28 ♘f3 ♖xc1−+] 27 ... ♖c3! 28 ♗xc3 ♖xc3 29 ♕xd4? [29 ♕f1 ♕c6+ 30 ♔g1 d3; 29 ♕d1 ♕c6+ 30 ♔g1 d3] 29 ... ♖xc2 **0-1** M392

# ANDERSSEN⚔KOLISCH
London

[1861-⚔AK]

| | | | | | | | | | | |
|---|---|---|---|---|---|---|---|---|---|---|
| A. Anderssen | 1 | 0 | 0 | 1 | 0 | ½ | 1 | ½ | 1 | 5 |
| I.F. von Kolisch | 0 | 1 | 1 | 0 | 1 | ½ | 0 | ½ | 0 | 4 |

## 1861-⚔AK-1
vii 61
**Kolisch, I.F.von− Anderssen, A.**
London [Boden]

1 e4 c5 2 ♘f3 e6 3 d4 cxd4 4 ♘xd4 ♘f6 5 ♗d3 ♘c6 6 ♗e3 d5 7 exd5 exd5 8 h3 h6 9 0-0 ♗d6 10 ♕f3 [10 ♕e2] 10 ... 0-0 11 ♘c3 ♘e5 12 ♕e2 a6 13 ♖ad1 ♖e8 14 ♗f5 ♗d7 15 ♗xd7 ♕xd7 16 ♘f3 ♖ad8 17 ♔h1 ♗b8 18 ♘xe5 ♖xe5 19 f4 ♖ee8 20 ♕d3 ♕d6 21 ♗d4 ♘e4 22 ♘xe4 dxe4 23 ♕g3 ♕f8 24 ♕e3 f5 25 ♖g1 ♖d7 26 ♖df1 ♖f7 27 g4 fxg4 28 ♖xg4 g5 29 f5 ♔h7 30 f6 ♕d6 31 ♖f2 ♕d5 32 h4 ♗f4 33 ♕b3 ♕d7 34 hxg5 ♗xg5 35 ♖h2 ♖g8 36 ♖xe4 ♖xf6 37 ♕d3 [37 ♗xf6−+] 37 ... ♖fg6 38 ♖g2 ♕c6 39 ♖eg4 ♖e8 40 ♔g1 ♖e1+ 41 ♔f2 ♖h1 42 ♕e4 ♕xe4 43 ♖xe4 ♗h4+ 44 ♖xh4 [44 ♔f3 ♖h3+] 44 ... ♖xg2+ 45 ♔xg2 ♖xh4 **0-1** M392

## 1861-⚔AK-2
vii 61
**Anderssen, A.− Kolisch, I.F. von**
London [Lange & Suhle & Hirschfeld]

1 e4 e6 2 d4 d5 3 exd5 exd5 4 ♘f3 ♘f6 5 ♗d3 ♗d6 6 0-0 0-0 7 h3 h6 8 c4 c6 9 ♘c3 ♗e6 10 cxd5 cxd5 11 ♗e3 ♘c6 12 ♕d2 ♖e8 13 ♖ae1 ♘e7 14 ♘e5 ♗f5 15 f4 ♖c8 16 g4 ♘e4 17 ♕g2 ♘xc3 18 gxf5 ♘e4 19 ♗xe4 [19 f6!?] 19 ... dxe4 20 ♕xe4 [20 f6] 20 ... f6 21 ♘g4 ♗b4 22 ♖e2 ♘d5 23 ♕d3 ♔h8 24 ♗c1 ♕d7 [24 ... ♖xc1 25 ♖xc1 ♘xf4 26 ♖xe8+ ♕xe8∓ Boden M392] 25 ♖xe8+ ♖xe8 26 ♘e3 ♗a5 27 a3 ♘xe3 28 ♗xe3 ♗b6 29 ♗f2 ♕d5 30 ♔h2 ♖e4 31 ♗e3 ♕xf5 32 b4 ♗c7−+ 33 d5 ♖xf4 34 ♕xf5 ♖xf5+ 35 ♔g2 ♖xd5 36 ♗xa7 ♖g5+ 37 ♔f2 ♖g3 38 ♖d1 ♖xa3 39 ♗c5 [39 ♖d7 ♗e5 40 ♖xb7 ♖xa7 41 ♖xa7 ♗d4+] 39 ... b6 40 ♗e3 ♖b3 41 ♖d4 ♗e5 42 ♖d8+ ♔h7 43 ♗xb6 ♖xb4 44 ♗e3 ♖b2+ 45 ♖d2 ♖xd2+ 46 ♗xd2 ♔g6 47 ♔f3 f5 48 ♗b4 ♔h5 49 ♔g2 g5 50 ♗d2 ♔g6 51 ♗c1 h5 52 ♗a3 g4 53 ♗c1 f4 54 ♗d2 ♔f5 55 ♔f2 ♔e4 56 ♗e1 g3+ 57 ♔g1 f3 **0-1** L/N6047

## 1861-⚔AK-3
vii 61
**Kolisch, I.F.von+ Anderssen, A.**
London [Gottschall]

1 e4 c5 2 ♘f3 e6 3 d4 cxd4 4 ♘xd4 ♘f6 5 ♗d3 ♘c6 6 ♗e3 d5 7

exd5 exd5 8 0-0 ♗d6 9 h3 h6 10 ♘c3 0-0 11 ♕d2 ♖e8 12 ♖ad1 ♗c7 13 ♖fe1 ♕d6 14 ♘f3 a6? [14 ... d4! 15 ♘b5 dxe3 16 ♘xd6 exd2 17 ♘xe8 dxe1♕+ 18 ♖xe1; 15 ♗xh6 dxc3 16 ♕g5 ♕f8; 15 ♕c1 dxe3 16 ♗h7+ ♔xh7 17 ♖xd6 exf2+ 18 ♔xf2 ♗xd6]

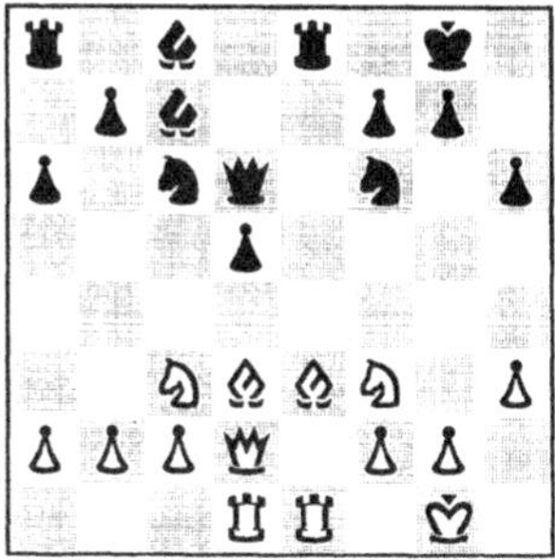

15 ♗xh6! ♖xe1+ [15 ... ♘d4±] 16 ♖xe1 gxh6 17 ♕xh6 ♘e4 18 ♕h5 f5 [18 ... ♗e6 Anderssen N392] 19 ♘xd5! ♕xd5 20 ♗xe4 ♕d7 [20 ... ♕xe4 21 ♖xe4 fxe4 22 ♘g5] 21 ♗d5+! ♔g7 [21 ... ♕xd5 22 ♖e8+ ♔g7 23 ♕h8+ ♔g6 24 ♘h4+ ♔g5 25 ♕g7+] 22 ♕g5+ [22 ... ♔h7 23 ♕g8+ ♔h6 24 ♗f7] **1-0** L/N3034

### 1861-✕AK-4 vii 61
**Anderssen, A.+ Kolisch, I.F. von**

London [Boden]

1 f4 e6 2 ♘f3 d5 3 e3 c5 4 ♗b5+ ♘c6 5 ♗xc6+ bxc6 6 c4 ♗a6 7 ♘a3 ♗d6 8 0-0 ♘f6 9 b3 0-0 10 ♗b2 ♘e8 11 ♕c2 f5 12 ♖ae1 ♘f6 13 ♘b1 ♕a5 14 ♗c3 ♕c7 15 d3 ♖ae8 16 ♗b2 ♘d7 17 ♘bd2 e5 18 g3 d4?! 19 fxe5 ♘xe5 20 ♘xe5 ♗xe5 21 ♘f3 ♗f6 22 exd4 cxd4 23 ♗xd4 ♗xd4+ 24 ♘xd4 c5 25 ♖xe8 [25 ♘e6 ♕c6 Δ 26 ... ♗b7] 25 ... ♖xe8 26 ♘xf5 ♗b7 27 ♕f2!+− h6 [27 ... ♕c6 28 ♘e7+] 28 d4 cxd4 29 ♕xd4 ♖e2 30 ♘xh6+ ♔h7 31 ♖f7 **1-0** M392

### 1861-✕AK-5 vii 61
**Kolisch, I.F. von+ Anderssen, A.**

London [Boden]

1 e4 e5 2 ♘f3 ♘c6 3 ♗b5 a6 4 ♗a4 ♘f6 5 0-0 ♗e7 6 ♘c3?! b5 7 ♗b3 d6 8 d3 0-0 9 ♗e3 h6 10 ♕d2 ♔h8 11 ♘e2 [11 ♘d5!? Lange/Suhle/Hirschfeld L/N6047] 11 ... ♕e8 [11 ... d5 Gottschall L/N3034] 12 ♘g3 ♘h7 13 ♗d5 ♖b8 14 ♘e1 ♗g5 15 f4 exf4 16 ♗xf4 ♘e7 17 ♗xg5 ♘xg5 18 ♗b3 f5 19 ♘f3 ♘h7 [19 ... f4 20 ♘e2 Gottschall L/N3034] 20 ♘h4 f4? 21 ♖xf4 ♖xf4 22 ♕xf4 g5 23 ♕d2!+− ♕c6 [23 ... gxh4 24 ♕c3+] 24 ♕f2 ♕b6 25 ♕xb6 ♖xb6 26 ♘hf5 ♗xf5 27 exf5 c5 28 ♖e1 ♖b7 29 ♖e6 d5 30 f6 ♘xf6 31 ♖xf6 c4 32 dxc4 dxc4 33 ♖xh6+ ♔g8 34 ♖xa6 cxb3 35 cxb3 ♖c7 36 ♖e6 ♔f7 37 ♖e5 ♖c1+ 38 ♔f2 ♖c2+ 39 ♖e2 ♖c5 40 ♘e4 ♖d5 41 ♔g3 ♘f5+ 42 ♔f2 ♔g6 43 ♘c3 ♖c5 44 b4 ♖c4 45 ♖e6+ ♔h5 46 ♖e4 ♘d4 47 a3 ♔g6 48 ♘e2 **1-0** M392

### 1861-✕AK-6 vii 61
**Anderssen, A.= Kolisch, I.F. von**

London [Gottschall]

1 f4 f5 2 ♘f3 ♘f6 3 e3 e6 4 ♗e2 ♗e7 5 0-0 0-0 6 b3 b6 7 ♘e5 ♗b7 8 ♗f3 c6 9 ♘c3 ♕c7 10 ♗b2 d6 11 ♘d3 ♘bd7 12 ♘f2 e5 13 g3 ♖ae8 14 ♕e2 d5 15 ♘h3?! e4 16 ♗g2 ♘c5 [Δ 17 ... ♗a6] 17 ♕d1 ♗a6 18 ♘e2 ♘e6 19 ♖c1 ♕d7 20 ♘f2 d4 [20 ... c5] 21 exd4 ♗xe2 22 ♕xe2 ♘xd4 23 ♕c4+ ♘e6 24 ♖cd1 ♘d5 25 ♖fe1 ♗f6 26 c3 ♔h8 27 ♕e2 ♕f7 28 d4!? ♖d8 29 ♘d3 ♘xc3! 30 ♗xc3 ♗xd4+ 31 ♗xd4 ♘xd4 32 ♕f1 exd3 33 ♖xd3 c5 34 ♖de3 ♖de8 35 ♖e5 ♖xe5 36 ♖xe5 h6 37 ♕e1 ♕h5 38 ♖e7 ♖d8 39 ♕e5 [39 ♖xa7? ♘f3+ 40 ♗xf3 ♕xf3] 39 ... ♕d1+ 40 ♔f2 ♕c2+ 41 ♔f1 ♕b1+ 42 ♕e1 ♘xb3!!−+ 43 ♕xb1 [43 axb3? ♖d1] 43 ... ♘d2+ 44 ♔e1 ♘xb1 45 ♖xa7 ♘c3 46 ♗f3 b5 47 ♖c7 c4 48 ♖c5 ♖b8 49 a3 ♔g8? [49 ... ♘b1] 50 ♖xf5 ♘b1 51 a4 b4?! [51 ... bxa4] 52 ♗d5+ ♔h8 53 ♗xc4 b3 54 ♖b5 [54 ♗xb3! ♖xb3 55 ♖b5 ♖xb5 56 axb5 ♘a3! 57 b6 ♘c2+ 58 ♔d2 ♘b4 59 b7 ♘c6 60 ♔c3+−] 54 ... ♖e8+ 55 ♔f2 ♘a3 56 ♖b4 ♘xc4 57 ♖xc4 ♖b8 58 ♖c1 ♖b4 59 ♖b1 ♖xa4 60 ♖xb3 ♖a2+ 61 ♔g1 ♔h7 **½-½** L/N3034

### 1861-✕AK-7 vii 61
**Kolisch, I.F. von– Anderssen, A.**

London [Boden]

1 e4 c5 2 ♘f3 e6 3 d4 cxd4 4 ♘xd4 ♘f6 5 ♗d3 ♘c6 6 ♗e3 d5 7 exd5 exd5 8 0-0 ♗d6 9 h3 h6 10 c4 0-0 [10 ... dxc4±] 11 ♘c3 ♗e5 12 ♘f3 [12 ♘ce2] 12 ... ♗xc3 13 bxc3 ♗e6 14 cxd5 ♘xd5 15 ♕d2 ♕f6 16 ♘d4 ♘e5 17 ♗c2 ♖fd8 [17 ... ♘c4 18 ♕d3+−] 18 ♘xe6?! fxe6 19 ♗d4

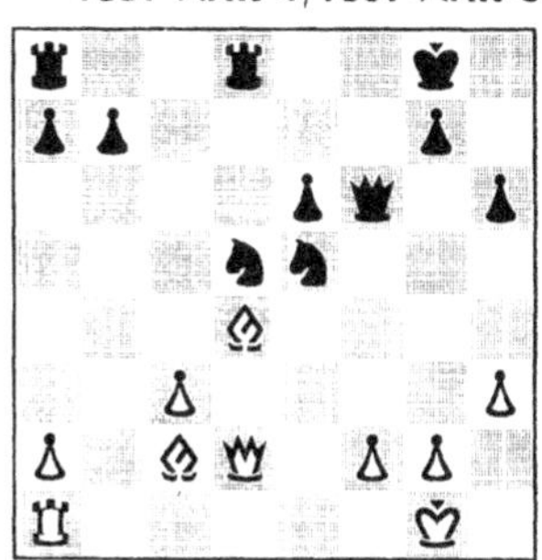

19 ... ♘xc3 20 ♕xc3 ♖xd4 21 ♖ae1 [21 ♕xd4 ♘f3+−+] 21 ... ♖c4 22 ♕xe5 ♕xe5 23 ♖xe5 ♖xc2 24 ♖xe6 ♖xa2 25 ♖e7 b5 26 ♖c1 ♖f8 27 ♖cc7 ♖fxf2 28 ♖xg7+ ♔f8 29 ♖xa7 ♖xg2+ 30 ♖xg2 ♖xa7∞= 31 ♖g6? ♖g7 **0-1** M392

### 1861-✕AK-8 vii 61
**Anderssen, A.= Kolisch, I.F. von**

London [Boden]

1 e4 c5 2 ♗c4 e6 3 ♘c3 a6 4 a4 ♘c6 5 d3 ♘ge7 6 ♗f4 d5 7 ♗a2 [□ 7 ♗b3] 7 ... ♘g6 8 ♗g3 ♘b4 9 ♗b3 ♗d6 10 ♘ge2 0-0 11 0-0 ♗b8 12 f3 ♔h8 13 a5 d4 14 ♘b1 f5 15 ♘d2 f4 16 ♗e1 ♗c7 17 ♘c4 ♘c6 18 ♗d2 ♕g5 19 ♔h1 ♕h5 20 ♖f2 ♖f6 21 ♕g1 ♗d7 22 g3 fxg3 23 ♘xg3 ♕h3 24 ♕f1 ♕h4 [Δ 25 ... ♗xg3] 25 ♕g1 ♖af8 26 ♖af1 ♕h3 [□ 26 ... ♘ge5 Lange/Suhle/Hirschfeld L/N 6047] 27 ♗a4! ♘ce5 28 ♗xd7 ♘xd7 29 b4 ♘de5 30 ♘xe5 ♘xe5 31 ♕g2 ♕xg2+ 32 ♔xg2 cxb4 33 ♗xb4 ♖c8 34 ♖b1 ♘c6 35 ♗d2 ♖b8 36 ♖a1 ♖ff8 [□ 36 ... ♖f7 Gottschall L/N3034] 37 f4 g6 38 c4 dxc3 39 ♗xc3+ ♔g8 40 ♘e2 ♖f7 41 d4 ♖bf8 42 e5 ♖d8 43 ♔f3 ♖d5 44 ♔e4 ♗xa5 45 ♗xa5 ♖xa5 46 ♖xa5 ♘xa5 47 ♘c3 ♖c7 [47 ... ♘c6 48 d5 Gottschall] 48 ♘a4 ♖c4 49 ♘c5 ♔f7 50 ♖b2 b5 51 ♘xa6 ♘c6 52 ♖d2 b4 53 ♘c5 ♘xd4 ...? **½-½** M392

### 1861-✕AK-9 vii 61
**Kolisch, I.F. von– Anderssen, A.**

London [Gottschall]

1 f4 f5 2 ♘f3 e6 3 e3 ♘f6 4 ♗e2 ♗e7 5 0-0 0-0 6 b3 d6 7 ♗b2 c5 8 h3? ♘c6 9 c4 ♘e4 10 ♔h2 ♗f6 11 d4 cxd4 12 exd4 ♗d7 13 ♘a3 [□ 13 ♘c3 Boden M392] 13 ... ♕e8 14 ♘b5 [□ 14 ♘c2] 14 ... ♕g6 15 ♕e1 ♕h6 16 ♗d3 ♔h8 [16 ... ♕xf4+ 17 g3 ♕h6 18 ♗xe4 fxe4 19 ♕xe4] 17 ♘a3 [17 ♗xe4 ♕xf4+; 17 g3] 17 ... ♗e8 18 ♘c2 d5 19 g3 ♗h5 20 ♘e5 ♗e7! 21 ♘e3? ♗b4 22 ♕c1 ♗d2 23 ♕c2 ♘xe5 [23 ... ♗xe3!?] 24 ♗xe4 fxe4 25 ♕xd2

♘f3+ 26 ♖xf3 ♗xf3 27 cxd5 exd5 28 ♘xd5 ♖ad8 29 ♘e3 ♖d6 [△ 30 ... ♕xh3+ 31 ♔xh3 ♖h6#] 30 h4? [30 ♘g2] 30 ... ♖xf4! 31 ♕e1 [31 gxf4? ♕xh4+ 32 ♔g1 ♖g6+] 31 ... ♖g6 32 ♗c1 [32 gxf4 ♕xf4+ 33 ♔h3 ♗g2+ 34 ♘xg2 ♕g4+; 32 ♘g2 ♖fg4 (32 ... ♗xg2 33 ♗c1) 33 ♗c1 ♖xg3! (33 ... ♕h5 34 ♘f4) 34 ♗xh6 (34 ♕xg3 ♖xg3–+) 34 ... ♖xg2+ 35 ♔h3 gxh6 36 ♖c1 e3! 37 ♖c3 (37 ♖c8+ ♔g7 38 ♖c7+ ♔f6) 37 ... ♗e4 38 ♖c5 e2 (38 ... ♖g1–+) 39 h5 ♖6g3+–+] 32 ... ♖xh4+ 33 gxh4 ♕f4+ 34 ♔h3 ♗g2+ 35 ♘xg2 ♕f3+ 36 ♔h2 ♕xg2# **0-1**

L/N3034

## KOLISCH ✕ PAULSEN
**London** [1861 – ✕ KP]

| | I. F. von Kolisch | L. Paulsen |
|---|---|---|
| *1* | ½ | ½ |
| *2* | 1 | 0 |
| *3* | 0 | 1 |
| *4* | ½ | ½ |
| *5* | 0 | 1 |
| *6* | 0 | 1 |
| *7* | ½ | ½ |
| *8* | ½ | ½ |
| *9* | ½ | ½ |
| *10* | ½ | ½ |
| *11* | 0 | 1 |
| *12* | ½ | ½ |
| *13* | ½ | ½ |
| *14* | 0 | 1 |
| *15* | ½ | ½ |
| *16* | 0 | 1 |
| *17* | ½ | ½ |
| *18* | 1 | 0 |
| *19* | 1 | 0 |
| *20* | 1 | 0 |
| *21* | ½ | ½ |
| *22* | 1 | 0 |
| *23* | ½ | ½ |
| *24* | 0 | 1 |
| *25* | ½ | ½ |
| *26* | 1 | 0 |
| *27* | ½ | ½ |
| *28* | ½ | ½ |
| *29* | ½ | ½ |
| *30* | ½ | ½ |
| *31* | ½ | ½ |
| *Total* | 15 | 16 |

### 1861-✕KP-1 x61
**Paulsen, L.= Kolisch, I.F. von**
London [Lange & Hirschfeld]

1 e4 c5 2 ♘f3 e6 3 ♘c3 d5 4 exd5 exd5 5 d4 ♗e6 6 ♗e3 c4 7 ♗e2 ♗b4 8 ♗d2 ♘f6 9 0-0 ♗xc3 10 ♗xc3 ♘e4 11 ♗e1 0-0 12 b3 ♘c6 13 ♘e5 ♘xe5 14 dxe5 f6 15 f3 ♕b6+ 16 ♔h1 ♘c5 17 exf6 ♖xf6 18 ♗f2 ♕c6 19 ♕d4 ♘d7 20 ♖fd1 ♖f7 [20 ... ♘b6] 21 bxc4 dxc4 22 ♕d6 ♘b6 23 ♕b4 ♘d5? 24 ♕xc4 ♘c3 25 ♕xc6 bxc6 26 ♖d6 ♗d5 27 ♗f1 ♖b8 28 ♗d4 ♘b5? 29 ♗xb5 ♖xb5 30 ♖d8+ ♖f8 31 ♖xf8+ ♔xf8 32 a4 ♖b7 33 a5 a6 34 ♗b6 ♔f7 35 ♔g1 ♖e7 36 ♔f2 ♗c4 37 ♗e3 ♖b7 38 ♖a4 ♗d5 [38 ... ♗b5 39 ♖b4 △ 40 c4+–] 39 ♖f4+ ♔g8 40 ♗c5 ♖f7 41 ♖b4 h6 42 ♖b6 ♖f5 43 ♗e3 ♗c4 44 ♖xc6 ♗b5 45 ♖c8+ ♖f8 46 ♖c5 ♖f6 47 c4 ♗a4 48 ♖d5 ♖c6 49 c5 ♗b5 50 ♗d4 ♖c7 51 ♖d6 ♖d7 52 f4 ♖xd6 53 cxd6

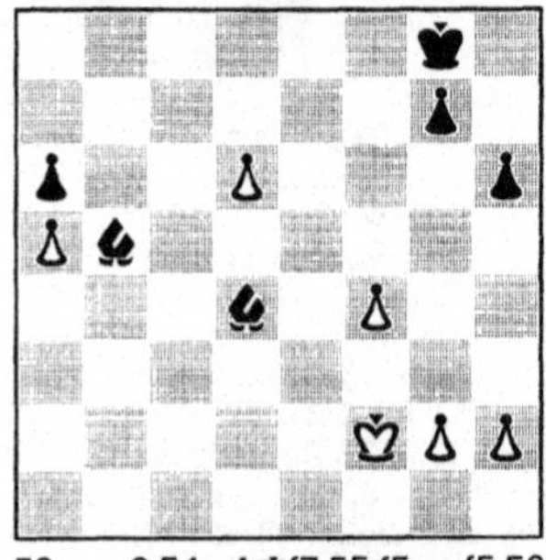

53 ... g6 54 g4 ♔f7 55 f5 gxf5 56 gxf5 ♗d7 57 f6 ♔e6 58 ♗e5 ♗c6 59 ♔g3 ♗b5 60 ♔g4 ♗e8 61 h4?? [61 ♔f4+–] 61 ... ♔xe5 62 f7 ♗xf7 63 d7 ♗e6+ 64 ♔h5 ♗xd7 65 ♔xh6 ♔f6 66 ♔h5 ♗f5 67 ♔h6 ♗g6 68 h5 ♗e8 69 ♔h7 ♗xh5 70 ♔h6 ♗f7 71 ♔h7 ♔g5 72 ♔g7 ♗a2 73 ♔h7 ♗b1+ 74 ♔g7 ♗c2 75 ♔f7 ♔f5 76 ♔e7 ♔e5 77 ♔f7 ♔d6 78 ♔f6 ♔c5 79 ♔e5 ♔b5? [□ 79 ... ♗d3–+] 80 ♔d4 ♔xa5?? 81 ♔c4 ♔a4 82 ♔c3 **½-½**

L/N6047-1862

### 1861-✕KP-2 x61
**Kolisch, I.F. von+ Paulsen, L.**
London [Lange & Hirschfeld]

1 e4 e5 2 ♘f3 ♘c6 3 ♗c4 ♗c5 4 0-0 ♘f6? [□ 4 ... d6] 5 b4 ♗xb4 6 c3 ♗e7 7 d4 exd4 8 cxd4 ♘xe4 9 d5 ♘a5 10 ♗d3 ♘c5 11 ♗a3 ♘xd3 12 ♕xd3 0-0 13 d6 cxd6? [□ 13 ... ♗xd6] 14 ♘c3 b6 15 ♘d5 ♘b7 16 ♗b2 ♘c5 17 ♕e3 ♘e6 18 ♘d4 ♗f6

19 ♘c6! dxc6 20 ♘xf6+ gxf6 21 ♕h6 d5 22 ♗xf6 ♕d6 23 f4 ♖e8 24 ♖f3 **1-0**

L/N6047-1862

### 1861-✕KP-3 x61
**Paulsen, L.+ Kolisch, I.F. von**
London [Lange & Hirschfeld]

1 e4 e5 2 f4 exf4 3 ♗c4 ♕h4+ 4 ♔f1 g5 5 ♘c3 ♗g7 6 d4 ♘e7 [□ 6 ... d6] 7 g3 fxg3 8 ♔g2 d6 [8 ... ♕h6 9 h4 ♕f6 10 ♗e3±] 9 hxg3 ♕g4 10 ♗e2 ♕d7 11 ♗xg5 ♘bc6 12 ♘f3 f6 13 ♗e3 d5 14 exd5 ♘b4 15 d6 ♘ed5 [□ 15 ... ♕xd6] 16 ♗d2 c6 17 ♘xd5 ♘xd5 18 c4 ♘b6 19 ♗d3 ♗f8 20 ♘g5 ♗xd6 21 ♕h5+ **1-0**

L/N6047-1862

### 1861-✕KP-4 x61
**Kolisch, I.F. von= Paulsen, L.**
London

1 e4 e5 2 ♘f3 ♘c6 3 ♗c4 ♗c5 4 0-0 ♘f6 5 c3 ♘xe4 6 ♗d5 ♘f6 7 ♗xc6 dxc6 8 ♘xe5 0-0 9 d4 ♗d6 10 ♗g5 c5 11 f4 cxd4 12 cxd4 c5 13 d5 h6 14 ♗h4 ♗e7 15 ♗xf6 ♗xf6 16 ♘c3 ♖e8 17 ♖e1 ♗f5 18 ♕b3 ♖b8 19 ♖ad1 ♕d6 20 ♘b5 ♕b6 21 ♘c4 ♗c2 22 ♕xc2 ♖xe1+ 23 ♖xe1 ♕xb5 24 ♘e5 ♖d8 25 ♖d1 c4 26 ♕xc4 ♕xb2 27 ♕c7 ♕e2 28 ♕xf7+ ♔h8 29 ♖f1 ♗xe5 30 fxe5 ♕xe5 31 ♕xb7 ♕d4+ **½-½**

L/N6047-1862

### 1861-✕KP-5 x61
**Paulsen, L.+ Kolisch, I.F. von**
London [Lange & Hirschfeld]

1 e4 e6 2 d4 d5 3 ♘c3 dxe4 4 ♘xe4 ♘f6 5 ♘xf6+ ♕xf6 6 ♗d3 ♗d6 7 ♘f3 h6 8 0-0 ♘c6 9 c3 ♗d7 10 ♖e1 0-0-0 11 b4 g5 12 b5 ♘e7 13 ♘e5 [△ 14 ♘xd7 ♖xd7 15 ♕a4±] 13 ... ♔b8 [□ 13 ... ♘d5] 14 c4 ♕g7 15 ♖b1 ♗xe5 16 dxe5 ♘g6 17 ♕a4 ♘xe5 18 ♗e4 b6 19 ♖b3 a5 20 c5 [□ 20 ♗d2 △ 21 ♗xa5+–] 20 ... ♗c8 21 ♗b2 f6 22 ♗c3 ♗b7 23 ♗xb7 ♔xb7 24 c6+ ♔a7 25 ♗xa5 ♖a8 26 ♗xb6+ ♔b8 [26 ... ♔xb6 27 ♕d4+ +–] 27 ♗a5 g4 [△ 28 ... ♘f3+] 28 ♖xe5 fxe5 29 b6 ♖a6 30 bxc7+ ♔a8 31 ♕b5 **1-0**

L/N6047-1862

**1861-⚔KP-6** x61
**Kolisch, I.F. von– Paulsen, L.**
London
1 e4 e5 2 f4 exf4 3 ♘f3 g5 4 ♗c4 g4 5 0-0 gxf3 6 ♕xf3 ♕f6 7 e5 ♕xe5 8 d3 ♗h6 9 ♗d2 ♘e7 10 ♘c3 ♘bc6 11 ♖ae1 ♕f5 12 ♘d5 ♔d8 13 ♗c3 ♖g8 14 ♗f6 ♗g5 15 ♖xe7 ♗xf6 16 ♖e4 ♗g5 17 g4 ♕g6 18 h4 ♗xh4 19 ♕xf4 d6 20 ♕xf7 ♕xf7 21 ♖xf7 ♘e5 22 ♖xh7 ♘xc4 23 ♖xc4 c6 24 ♘c7 ♖b8 25 ♖f4 ♗e7 26 ♖ff7 ♔xc7 27 ♖xe7+ ♔b6 28 ♖hg7 ♖xg7 29 ♖xg7 ♗e6 30 ♖g6 ♗xa2 31 ♖xd6 ♖g8 32 ♔f2 ♖xg4 33 ♔e2 ♖g2+ 34 ♔d1 ♗b1 35 c3 ♖xb2 **0-1** L/N6047-1862

**1861-⚔KP-7** x61
**Paulsen, L.= Kolisch, I.F. von**
London [Lange & Hirschfeld]
1 e4 e6 2 d4 d5 3 exd5 exd5 4 ♘f3 ♘f6 5 ♗d3 ♗e6 6 0-0 ♗d6 7 ♘c3 0-0 8 ♘e2 c6 9 ♘g3 ♘bd7 10 c3 ♕c7 11 ♘h4 ♘e4 12 h3 ♗xg3 [◻ 12 ... ♘xf2 13 ♖xf2 ♗xg3 14 ♖f1 ♗xh4 15 ♕h5 g6 16 ♕xh4 f5; 13 ♗xh7+ ♔xh7 14 ♕c2+ ♔g8 15 ♕xf2 ♗xg3!∓] 13 fxg3 ♕xg3 14 ♘f5 ♗xf5 15 ♖xf5 ♖ae8 16 ♕f1 ♕d6 17 ♗f4 ♕e6 18 ♗c7 g6 19 ♗xe4 dxe4 20 ♖a5 a6 21 ♖e1 f5 22 ♗f4 ♘b6 23 ♗h6 ♖f7 24 ♖e5 ♕d7 25 ♖xe8+ ♕xe8 26 ♕f2 ♘c4 27 b3 ♘d6 28 c4 ♖d7 29 ♗c1 ♘f7 30 ♗b2 h6 31 h4 h5 32 d5 ♔h7 33 ♕d4 ♕h8 34 ♕f2 ♕e8 35 ♕d4 ♕h8 36 ♕f2 **½-½** L/N6047-1862

**1861-⚔KP-8** x61
**Kolisch, I.F. von= Paulsen, L.**
London [Lange & Hirschfeld]
1 e4 e5 2 ♘f3 ♘c6 3 ♗c4 ♗c5 4 0-0 ♘f6 5 d4 ♗xd4! 6 ♘xd4 ♘xd4 7 f4 d6 8 fxe5 dxe5 9 ♗g5 ♗e6! 10 ♗xe6 ♘xe6 11 ♕xd8+ [◻ 11 ♗xf6 gxf6 12 ♘c3] 11 ... ♖xd8 12 ♗xf6 gxf6 13 ♘c3 c6 14 ♖xf6 ♖d2 15 ♖f2 ♖xf2 16 ♔xf2 ♘d4 17 ♖c1 ♖g8 18 ♘b1 ♔e7 19 ♘d2 f6 **½-½** L/N6047-1862

**1861-⚔KP-9** x61
**Paulsen, L.= Kolisch, I.F. von**
London [Lange & Hirschfeld]
1 e4 e5 2 f4 exf4 3 ♗c4 ♘f6 4 ♘c3 [◻ 4 ♕e2 △ 5 ♘f3, 6 c3] 4 ... ♗b4 5 ♘f3 0-0 6 0-0 ♗xc3 7 dxc3 ♘xe4 8 ♗xf4 d6 9 ♗d5 ♘f6 10 ♗g5 c6 11 ♗b3 ♗f5 [11 ... ♕b6+ 12 ♔h1 ♘e4 13 ♗e7 ♖e8 14 ♗xf7+ ♔xf7 15 ♘g5+±; 12 ♘d4 ♘e4 13 ♗e7±] 12 ♘d4 ♗g6 13 ♗xf6 gxf6 14 ♘f5 d5 15 ♕d2 [◻ 15 c4 ♗xf5 16 ♖xf5 d4 17 ♕g4+ △ 18 ♖d1±; 15 ... ♕d7 16 ♕g4 d4 17 ♖ad1 c5 18 c3±] 15 ... ♔h8 16 ♖ae1 ♘d7 17 ♘g3 ♖g8 18 ♖e3 ♘c5 19 ♕e2 ♘e4 20 c4 ♕b6 21 ♘xe4 ♗xe4 22 ♖f2 ♖g6 23 g3 ♖ag8 24 cxd5 cxd5 25 ♖xe4 dxe4 26 ♗xf7 e3 27 ♖f3 ♖d8 28 ♕xe3 ♕xe3+ 29 ♖xe3 ♖g7 30 ♗c4 ♖d1+ 31 ♔g2 ♖c7 32 ♖e8+ ♔g7 33 ♖g8+ ♔h6 34 ♗d3 ♖a1 35 ♖g4 ♖xa2 36 b4 ♖axc2+ 37 ♗xc2 ♖xc2+ 38 ♔h3 ♖a2 39 ♖h4+ ♔g6 40 ♖g4+ **½-½** L/N6047-1862

**1861-⚔KP-10** x61
**Kolisch, I.F. von= Paulsen, L.**
London
1 e4 e5 2 d4 exd4 3 ♗c4 ♘f6 4 ♘f3 ♘xe4 5 ♕xd4 ♘f6 6 0-0 d5 7 ♗d3 ♗e7 8 ♗g5 0-0 9 ♘c3 ♗e6 10 ♕h4 g6 11 ♖fe1 ♘c6 12 ♗b5 ♘h5 13 ♗xc6 ♗xg5 14 ♘xg5 bxc6 15 g4 h6 16 gxh5 hxg5 17 ♕g3 ♗f5 18 ♘e2 c5 19 c3 ♖e8 20 f4 g4 21 hxg6 fxg6 22 ♕f2 ♕d6 23 ♘g3 ♗d7 24 ♖e5 ♖xe5 25 fxe5 ♕xe5 26 ♕xc5 ♖f8 27 ♖f1 ♖xf1+ 28 ♘xf1 a6 29 ♘e3 ♗e6 30 ♕d4 ♕g5 31 ♔g2 **½-½** L/N6047-1862

**1861-⚔KP-11** x61
**Paulsen, L.+ Kolisch, I.F. von**
London [Boden]
1 e4 e5 2 f4 exf4 3 ♗c4 ♘f6 4 ♘c3 ♗b4 5 e5 d5 6 ♗b5+! c6 7 exf6 cxb5 8 ♕e2+ ♗e6 9 ♕xb5+ ♘c6 10 ♘f3 ♕xf6 [◻ 10 ... ♗xc3 11 dxc3 ♕xf6] 11 ♕xb7 ♖c8 12 ♘xd5! ♕f5 13 ♘c7+? [◻ 13 ♘xb4 ♕e4+ 14 ♔f2±] 13 ... ♖xc7? [◻ 13 ... ♔d8 14 ♕xc6 ♖xc7∓] 14 ♕xc7 ♕e4+ 15 ♔d1 0-0 16 d3 ♕g6

17 ♕xf4 [17 ♕xc6? ♖c8 △ 18 ... ♕xg2→ Lange & Hirschfeld] 17 ... f6 18 ♕e4 ♕xg2! 19 ♖g1 ♕h3 20 ♕xc6 ♖d8 [△ 21 ... ♗d5→] 21 ♔e2! ♗d5 22 ♕xf6 ♖e8+ 23 ♗e3 g6 24 ♖g3 ♕h6 25 ♕g5 ♗xf3+ 26 ♔xf3 **1-0** M392

**1861-⚔KP-12** x61
**Kolisch, I.F. von= Paulsen, L.**
London [Boden]
1 f4 d5 2 ♘f3 ♘c6 3 e3 ♗g4 4 ♗e2 ♗xf3 5 ♗xf3 e5 6 fxe5 ♘xe5 7 0-0 ♘f6 8 d4 ♘xf3+ 9 ♕xf3 ♗d6 10 c4 c6 11 cxd5 cxd5 12 ♘c3 0-0 13 ♗d2 ♕d7 14 ♕f5 ♕e6! 15 ♖f3 ♖ac8 16 ♖af1 ♗b4 17 ♕g5 [△ 18 ♖xf6+−] 17 ... h6 18 ♕g3 ♗d6 19 ♕h4 ♗e7 20 ♕e1 ♖c6 21 ♖f5 ♕d7 22 ♔h1 ♗b4 23 ♕g3 ♗xc3 24 ♗xc3 ♔h7 25 ♕f3 a6 26 g4 ♔g8 27 h4 ♕c7! [△ 28 ... ♘e4, 29 ... ♘g3∓] 28 ♕f4 ♘e4 29 ♕xc7 ♖xc7 30 ♔g2 ♘xc3 31 bxc3 ♖xc3 32 ♖xd5 ♖xe3 33 ♖d7 b5 34 d5 ♖e2+ 35 ♖f2 ♖xf2+ 36 ♔xf2 ♖a8 37 ♔e3 a5 38 ♔d4 b4 39 ♖b7 ♔f8 40 ♔c5 **½-½** M392

**1861-⚔KP-13** x61
**Paulsen, L.= Kolisch, I.F. von**
London
1 e4 e6 2 c4 e5 3 ♘f3 ♘c6 4 ♘c3 d6 5 ♗e2 f5 6 d3 ♘f6 7 exf5 ♗xf5 8 0-0 ♗e7 9 ♘h4 ♗e6 10 f4 0-0 11 ♘f3 ♕d7 12 d4 exd4 13 ♘xd4 ♘xd4 14 ♕xd4 ♔h8 15 ♗e3 d5 16 cxd5 ♘xd5 17 ♘xd5 ♕xd5 18 ♗f3 ♕xd4 19 ♗xd4 ♗f6 20 ♗xf6 ♖xf6 21 b3 c6 22 ♖ae1 ♔g8 **½-½** L/N6047-1862

**1861-⚔KP-14** xi 61
**Kolisch, I.F. von– Paulsen, L.**
London [Boden]
1 e4 e5 2 ♘f3 ♘c6 3 ♗c4 ♗c5 4 b4 ♗xb4 5 c3 ♗a5 6 d4 exd4 7 0-0 d6 8 ♕b3 ♕f6 9 cxd4 ♗b6 10 e5 dxe5 11 dxe5 ♕g6 12 ♘g5 ♘h6 13 e6 0-0 14 ♘xf7 ♘xf7 15 exf7+ ♔h8 16 ♗a3 [16 ♗b2] 16 ... ♘d4! 17 ♕c3 c5 18 ♘d2 ♗e6 19 ♔h1 ♗xc4 20 ♘xc4 ♕xf7 21 ♖ab1 ♕h5! 22 ♘xb6 axb6 23 ♖xb6 ♖xf2 24 ♖bb1 [24 ♖xf2?? ♕d1+−+] 24 ... ♖xf1+ [◻ 24 ... ♘f3! 25 h3 ♕xh3+! 26 gxh3 ♖h2#; 25 ♕xf3 ♖xf3−+] 25 ♖xf1 b6 26 ♗b2 ♕e2 27 ♕e1 ♖f8 28 h3 ♖f1+ 29 ♖xf1 ♕xf1+ 30 ♔h2 ♕f4+ 31 ♕g3 g5 32 ♕xf4 gxf4 33 g3 fxg3+ 34 ♔xg3 ♔g7 35 ♔f4 ♔g6 36 ♔e5 ♘c6+ 37 ♔d6 ♘b4 38 a4 ♔f5 39 ♔c7 ♘d5+ 40 ♔c6 ♔e4 41 a5 bxa5 42 ♔xc5 ♘f4 43 ♔b5 ♘xh3 44 ♔xa5 h5 45 ♗f6 ♔f4 46 ♔b5 ♘g5 47 ♔c4 h4 48 ♔d5 h3 49 ♗e5+ ♔f3 50 ♗h2 ♘e4 51 ♔e5 ♔g2 52 ♔xe4 ♔xh2 53 ♔f3 ♔g1 54 ♔g3 h2 **0-1** M392

**1861-⚔KP-15** xi 61
**Paulsen, L.= Kolisch, I.F. von**
London
1 e4 e6 2 c4 e5 3 ♘f3 ♘c6 4 d4 exd4 5 ♘xd4 d6 6 ♘c3 ♗e7 7 ♗e2 ♗f6 8 ♗e3 ♘ge7 9 0-0 0-0 10 ♘d5 ♗xd4 11 ♗xd4 ♘xd4 12 ♕xd4 f5 13 exf5 ♗xf5 14 ♖ae1 ♘c6 15 ♕d2 ♕d7 16 ♗d3 ♗xd3 17 ♕xd3 ♖ae8 18 ♖xe8 ♖xe8 19 f4 ♘e7 20 ♘e3 ♔h8 21 ♖f3 ♘g8 22 ♖h3 ♘f6 23 ♘d5 c6 24 ♘xf6 gxf6 **½-½** L/N6047-1862

**1861-⚔KP-16** xi 61
**Kolisch, I.F. von– Paulsen, L.**
London [Boden]
1 e4 e5 2 ♘f3 ♘c6 3 ♗c4 ♗c5 4 d3 ♘f6 5 0-0 d6 6 c3 0-0 7 ♗g5 ♗e6 8 ♘bd2 ♕e7 9 ♔h1 h6 10 ♗h4 ♔h7 11 d4 exd4 12 ♗d3 ♔g8 13 cxd4 ♘xd4 14 e5 dxe5 15 ♘e4 ♗g4 16 ♗xf6 gxf6 17 ♕c1! ♔g7 18 ♕xc5 ♕xc5 19 ♘xc5 ♘xf3 20 h3 ♘d2 21 hxg4 ♘xf1 22 ♖xf1 b6 23 ♘e4 ♖ad8 24 ♗c2 ♖d4 25 f3 ♖fd8 26 ♔g1 c5 27 ♔f2?? ♖d2+ 28 ♔e3 ♖xc2 29 ♘g3 c4 **0-1** M392

**1861-⚔KP-17** xi 61
**Paulsen, L.= Kolisch, I.F. von**
London
1 e4 e6 2 c4 d5 3 cxd5 exd5 4 exd5 ♕xd5 5 ♘c3 ♕a5 6 ♘f3 ♘f6 7 ♗c4 ♗d6 8 0-0 0-0 9 d4 ♗g4 10 ♘b5 a6 11 ♘xd6 cxd6 12 ♕b3 ♘c6 13 ♖d1 ♖ae8 14 ♗f4 b5 15 ♗f1 ♕b6 16 ♗xd6 ♗xf3 17 ♕xf3 ♘xd4 18 ♕c3 ♕xd6 19 ♖xd4 ♕b6 20 ♖ad1 ♖e6 21 ♕b4 ♕c7 22 a4 bxa4 23 ♕xa4 a5 24 ♗c4 ♖e5 25 h3 ♕b7 26 b3 ♖g5 27 ♗f1 ♖e5 28 ♖d6 ♖fe8 29 ♖6d4 ♖5e7 **½-½** L/N6047-1862

**1861-⚔KP-18** xi 61
**Kolisch, I.F. von+ Paulsen, L.**
London [Lange & Hirschfeld]
1 e4 e5 2 ♘f3 ♘c6 3 ♗c4 ♗c5 4 d3 ♘f6 5 ♗g5 d6 6 0-0 0-0 7 ♘c3 ♗e6 8 ♘e2 ♗xc4 9 dxc4 h6 10 ♗h4 g5 11 ♘xg5 hxg5 12 ♗xg5 ♔g7 13 ♘g3 ♔g6 [◻ 13 ... ♖h8] 14 b4 ♗b6 [14 ... ♔xg5] 15 ♗xf6 ♔xf6 16 ♕f3+ ♔e7 17 ♘f5+ ♔e8 [◻ 17 ... ♔d7] 18 c5 dxc5 19 ♘g7+ ♔e7 20 ♖ad1 ♘d4 21 ♕h5 ♖g8 22 bxc5 ♔f8 23 ♕xe5

23 ... ♘e2+ [◻ 23 ... ♘f3+ 24 gxf3 ♕h4 25 ♔h1 ♖xg7 26 ♖g1 ♖xg1+ 27 ♖xg1 ♗a5∓] 24 ♔h1 ♕h4 25 cxb6 ♖xg7 26 bxc7 ♖h7 27 ♖d3 ♘f4 28 ♖d8+ ♖xd8 29 cxd8♕+ ♕xd8 30 ♕xf4 **1-0** L/N6047-1862

**1861-⚔KP-19** xi 61
**Paulsen, L.– Kolisch, I.F. von**
London [Löwenthal]
1 e4 e6 2 c4 d5 3 exd5 exd5 4 cxd5 ♕xd5 5 ♘c3 ♕a5 6 ♘f3 ♘f6 7 ♗c4 ♗e7 8 0-0 0-0 9 d4 c6 10 ♘e5 ♘bd7 11 ♘xf7? [◻ 11 ♘xd7 △ 12 ♗f4±] 11 ... ♖xf7 12 ♕b3 ♕h5! 13 ♗f4 ♘b6 14 ♗xf7+ ♕xf7 15 ♕xf7+ ♔xf7 16 ♗e5 ♘bd5 17 h3 h5 18 f3 ♘xc3 19 bxc3 ♘d5 20 ♖fc1 ♗a3 21 ♖cb1 ♘xc3 22 ♖b3 ♘b5 23 g4 ♗e6 24 ♖e3 ♗d5 25 ♖d1? [◻ 25 ♖b1 △ 26 ♖xb5] 25 ... a5 26 ♖dd3 ♗f8 27 a4 ♘d6 28 ♗g3 ♘c4 29 ♖e2 ♘b6 30 ♖e5 ♘xa4 31 ♖xh5 b5 **0-1** M324

**1861-⚔KP-20** xi 61
**Kolisch, I.F. von+ Paulsen, L.**
London [Lange & Hirschfeld]
1 e4 e5 2 ♘f3 ♘c6 3 ♗c4 ♗c5 4 0-0 ♘f6 5 d3 d6 6 ♗g5 h6 7 ♗h4 ♗g4? 8 h3 ♗h5 9 c3 g5 10 ♗g3 ♕d7 11 b4 ♗b6 12 ♘bd2 g4 13 hxg4 ♗xg4 14 a4 a5 15 ♗b5 axb4 16 cxb4 ♘h7 17 ♕c2 ♘g5 18 ♘h4? [◻ 18 a5 △ 19 a6+–] 18 ... ♘e6 19 ♘b3 ♔e7 20 a5 ♗d4 21 ♖ac1 ♘xb4 22 ♕c4 c6 23 ♕xb4 cxb5 24 ♘f5+ ♗xf5 25 exf5 ♘c5 26 ♘xd4 ♘xd3 27 ♕d2 ♘xc1 28 ♖xc1 exd4 29 ♕xd4 ♖hg8 30 ♖e1+ ♔d8 31 ♕f6+ ♔c8 32 ♖c1+ ♔b8 33 ♗xd6+ ♔a7 34 ♕d4+ **1-0** L/N6047-1862

**1861-⚔KP-21** xi 61
**Paulsen, L.= Kolisch, I.F. von**
London
1 e4 e6 2 d4 d5 3 ♘c3 ♗b4 4 exd5 exd5 5 ♘f3 ♘f6 6 ♗d3 0-0 7 0-0 ♗g4 8 ♗g5 c6 9 ♗e2 ♘bd7 10 ♘e5 ♗xe2 11 ♘xe2 ♕c7 12 ♘xd7 ♘xd7 13 ♗f4 ♗d6 14 ♕d2 ♖ae8 15 ♗xd6 ♕xd6 16 ♖ae1 f5 17 ♘f4 ♖e4 18 g3 ♖fe8 19 f3 ♖4e7 20 ♔g2 ♕f7 21 ♘d3 ♖xe1 22 ♖xe1 ♖xe1 23 ♕xe1 ♕e7 24 ♕e5+ ♔g8 25 ♔f2 **½-½** L/N6047-1862

**1861-⚔KP-22** xi 61
**Kolisch, I.F. von+ Paulsen, L.**
London [Boden]
1 e4 e5 2 ♘f3 ♘c6 3 ♗c4 ♗c5 4 0-0 ♘f6 5 d3 d6 6 ♗g5 0-0 7 ♘c3 ♗e6 8 ♗b3! ♕e7 9 ♘h4 h6 10 ♘f5 ♗xf5 11 ♘d5 ♕d7 12 ♗xf6 ♗e6 13 ♕h5 ♔h7 14 ♔h1 ♗xd5 15 exd5 ♘d4 16 f4! ♕f5 [16 ... gxf6 17 fxe5+–] 17 ♕xf5+ ♘xf5 18 fxe5 ♘e3 19 ♗e7 ♘xf1 20 ♖xf1 ♖ae8 21 ♗xf8 ♖xf8 22 c3 ♖e8 23 d4 ♗b6 24 exd6 cxd6 25 g3 ♔g8 26 ♔g2 ♖e2+ 27 ♖f2 ♖xf2+ 28 ♔xf2 ♗d8 29 ♗a4 ♗g5 30 c4 ♔f8 31 c5 ♔e7 32 c6 bxc6 33 dxc6 ♔d8 34 b4 ♗d2 35 b5 ♗a5 36 ♔e3 [36 d5?=] 36 ... ♔e7 37 ♗b3 ♗c7 38 ♔e4 ♔e8 39 ♔d5 ♔d8 40 ♗d1 ♔e8 41 ♗h5 ♔e7 42 ♔c4 ♗b6 43 a4 ♗a5 44 ♔d5 ♗c7

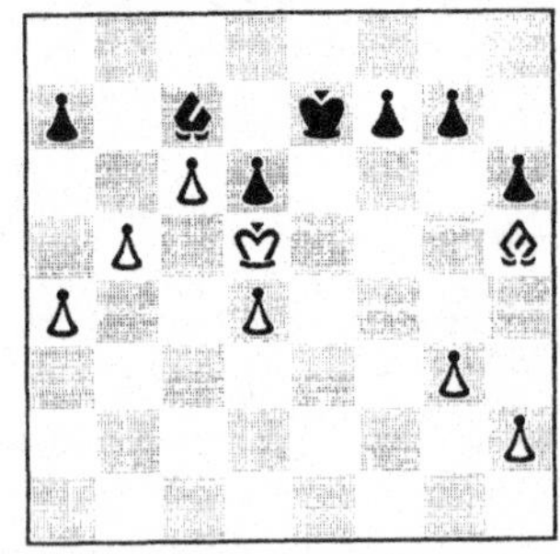

45 ♗xf7! ♔xf7 46 a5 ♔e7 47 b6 ♗xb6 [47 ... axb6 48 a6 ♗b8 49 c7+– Lange & Hirschfeld] 48 axb6 axb6 49 ♔c4 ♔d8 50 d5 ♔c7 51 ♔b5 **1-0** M392

**1861-⚔KP-23** xi 61
**Paulsen, L.= Kolisch, I.F. von**
London
1 d4 e6 2 ♘f3 d5 3 e3 ♗d6 4 ♗d3 ♘f6 5 0-0 0-0 6 c4 b6 7 b3 ♗b7 8 ♗b2 ♘bd7 9 ♘bd2 ♕e7 10 ♘e5 ♖ad8 11 ♕e2 ♘e4 12 f4 f5 13 ♘df3 ♘df6 14 ♖ac1 ♕e8 15 ♘e1 c5 16 ♖c2 ♖c8 **½-½** M392

**1861-⚔KP-24** xi 61
**Kolisch, I.F. von– Paulsen, L.**
London [Löwenthal]
1 e4 e5 2 ♘f3 ♘c6 3 ♗c4 ♗c5 4 0-0 ♘f6 5 d3 d6 6 ♗g5 ♕e7! 7 d4 exd4 8 ♗xf6 gxf6 9 ♘xd4 0-0 10 ♘c3 f5! 11 ♔h1 f4 12 ♘de2 ♘g6 13 ♕d2 ♗e6 14 ♗d3 ♕f6 15 ♘g1 ♔h8 16 ♖ae1 ♖g8 17 ♘f3 ♘e5 18 ♘xe5? dxe5 19 ♘d5 ♗xd5 20 exd5 ♖g5 21 ♕e2 ♖ag8 22 g3 ♕h6

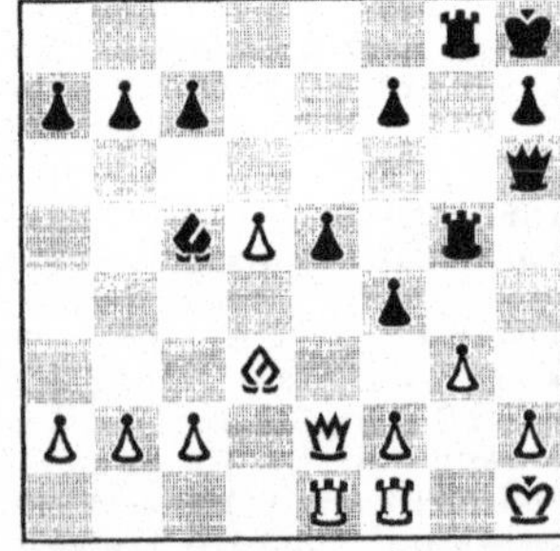

23 ♖g1 [23 gxf4 ♖g2!–+] 23 ... ♖h5 24 ♖g2 ♗d6 25 ♖eg1 fxg3 26 fxg3 f5 27 c4 e4 28 ♗b1 ♖g7 29 a3 a5 30 ♗c2 b6 31 ♗a4 ♖hg5 32 ♕e1 ♕h3 33 ♕c3 f4 34 gxf4 ♖xg2! [35 ♕xh3 ♖xg1#] **0-1** M324

**1861-⚔KP-25** xi 61
**Paulsen, L.= Kolisch, I.F. von**
London
1 d4 f5 2 ♘c3 e6 3 e4 ♗b4 4 exf5 exf5 5 ♗d3 d5 6 ♕f3 ♘e7 7 ♘ge2 0-0 8 0-0 c6 9 ♗f4 ♘g6 10 ♖ae1 ♘d7 11 a3 ♘xf4 12 ♘xf4 ♗xc3 13 bxc3 ♘f6 14 c4 ♘e4 15 ♕e2 ♕a5 16 f3 ♘f6 17 cxd5 cxd5 18 ♕e7 ♗d7 19 ♕b4 ♕xb4 20 axb4 g5 **½-½** M392

**1861-⚔KP-26** xi 61
**Kolisch, I.F. von+ Paulsen, L.**
London [Löwenthal]
1 e4 e5 2 ♘f3 ♘c6 3 ♗c4 ♗c5 4 0-0 ♘f6 5 d3 d6 6 c3 0-0 [◻ 6 ... ♘e7] 7 ♗g5 h6 8 ♗h4 ♗e6 9 ♘bd2 ♕e7 10 ♔h1 ♗xc4 11 ♘xc4 ♕e6 12 ♘e3 ♗xe3 13 fxe3 ♘d7 [◻ 13 ... ♘g4] 14 ♘d2

14 ... f5? 15 exf5 ♖xf5 16 ♖xf5 ♕xf5 17 ♕b3+ ♔h7 18 ♕xb7 ♖f8 19 ♕xc6 ♕xd3 20 ♕e4+ **1-0** M324

**1861-⚔KP-27** xi 61
**Paulsen, L.= Kolisch, I.F. von**
London
1 e4 e6 2 d4 d5 3 ♘c3 ♗b4 4 exd5 exd5 5 ♗d3 ♘f6 6 ♘ge2 0-0 7 0-0 c6 8 ♘g3 ♗d6 9 ♘f5 ♗xf5 10 ♗xf5 ♕c7 11 g3 ♘bd7 12 ♘e2 ♖fe8 13 c3 ♘f8 14 ♘f4 ♘g6 15 ♘g2 ♘e4 16 ♗xg6 hxg6 17 ♗f4 ♗xf4 18 ♘xf4 g5 19 ♘d3 ♖e6 20 ♔g2 ♖h6 21 ♖h1 f5 22 ♘e5 ♖f8 23 f3 ♘f6 **½-½** L/N6047-1862

**1861-⚔KP-28** xi 61
**Kolisch, I.F. von= Paulsen, L.**
London
1 f4 e6 2 ♘f3 f5 3 e3 ♘f6 4 ♗e2 ♗e7 5 0-0 0-0 6 b3 d6 7 ♗b2 c5 8 d3 ♘c6 9 ♕d2 ♗d7 10 c4 ♕c7 11 ♘c3 a6 12 ♗d1 d5 13 ♘e5 ♗d6 14 ♘xd7 ♕xd7 15 ♗f3 ♗e7 16 ♖ad1 ♖ad8 17 ♕f2 ♕c7 18 ♘e2 ♖f7 19 ♕g3 b6 20 ♗e5 ♕c8 21 a3 ♖ff8 22 h3 ♖f7 23 ♔h2 ♘e8 24 ♘c3 ♘xe5 25 fxe5 d4 26 exd4 cxd4 27 ♘a4 ♗xa3 28 ♘xb6 ♕b8 29 ♖a1 ♗f8 30 ♘a4 ♕xb3 31 ♗h5 ♖b7 32 ♖fb1 ♕xb1 33 ♖xb1 ♖xb1 34 ♕f4 ♖db8 35 ♕xd4 g6 36 ♗f3 ♖e1 37 ♘c5 ♗g7 38 ♘d7 ♖d8 39 ♕h4 ♖xd7 40 ♕xe1 ♖xd3 41 ♔g1 ♖a3 42 ♕c1 ♖a5 43 ♕d2 ♖a1+ 44 ♔f2 ♗xe5 45 ♕d8 ♖a2+ 46 ♔e3 ♖a3+ 47 ♔f2 ♖a2+ 48 ♗e2 ♔f8 49 c5 a5 50 ♔f1 ♖a1+ 51 ♔f2 ♖a2 **½-½** L/N6047-1862

**1861-⚔KP-29** xi 61
**Paulsen, L.= Kolisch, I.F. von**
London
1 e4 e6 2 d4 d5 3 exd5 exd5 4 ♘f3 ♘f6 5 ♗d3 ♗d6 6 0-0 0-0 7 b3 ♗g4 8 c4 c6 9 ♘bd2 ♕c7 10 ♕c2 ♖e8 11 ♗b2 ♘bd7 12 ♖ae1 ♖e6 13 h3 ♗xf3 14 ♘xf3 ♖ae8 15 ♖xe6 fxe6 16 ♖e1 ♘f8 17 ♘e5 ♘6d7 18 a3 ♕d8 19 c5 ♗xe5 20 dxe5 b6 21 cxb6 ♕xb6 22 b4 c5 23 bxc5 ♕xc5 24 ♕d2 ♘b6 **½-½** L/N6047-1862

**1861-⚔KP-30** xi 61
**Kolisch, I.F. von= Paulsen, L.**
London [Boden]
1 e4 e5 2 ♘f3 ♘c6 3 ♗c4 ♘f6 4 d4 exd4 5 0-0 ♗e7 6 e5 ♘e4 7 ♗d5 ♘c5 8 ♗xc6 dxc6 9 ♕xd4 ♗f5 10 b4 ♘e6 11 ♕c3 0-0 12 ♗e3 f6 [12 ... ♕d5!∓] 13 ♘bd2 fxe5 14 ♘xe5 ♗d6 15 f4 ♕e7 16 ♖ad1 ♗xb4 17 ♕c4 ♗xd2 18 ♗xd2 ♕c5+ 19 ♕xc5 ♘xc5 20 ♗b4 b6 21 ♗xc5 bxc5 22 ♘xc6 ♗xc2 23 ♖c1 ♗d3 24 ♖fd1 c4 25 g3 [25 ... ♖f6 △ 26 ... ♖a6∓] **½-½** M392

**1861-⚔KP-31** xi 61
**Paulsen, L.= Kolisch, I.F. von**
London
1 e4 e6 2 d4 d5 3 exd5 exd5 4 ♘f3 ♘f6 5 ♗d3 ♗d6 6 0-0 0-0 7 ♗g5 ♗g4 8 ♘bd2 ♘bd7 9 c3 c6 10 ♕c2 ♕c7 11 ♖ae1 ♖ae8 12 h3 ♗h5 13 ♘h4 ♗f4 14 ♗xf4 ♕xf4 15 g3 ♕c7 16 ♔g2 ♗g6 17 ♘f5 ♖xe1 18 ♖xe1 ♖e8 19 ♖xe8+ ♘xe8 20 ♘e7+ ♔f8 21 ♘xg6+ hxg6 22 ♘f3 ♘ef6 23 ♘g5 ♕d6 24 ♕a4 ♕b8 **½-½** M392

## THOROLD⚔WATKINSON
Sheffield/Huddersfield
[1861-⚔TW]

| | | | | | | | | | | | | | |
|---|---|---|---|---|---|---|---|---|---|---|---|---|---|
| E. Thorold | 1̂ | 0̂ | 0̂ | 0̂ | ? | ? | ? | ? | ? | ? | ? | 0 | 4 |
| J. Watkinson | 0̂ | 1̂ | 1̂ | 1̂ | ? | ? | ? | ? | ? | ? | ? | 1 | 7 |

**1861-⚔TW-1̂**
**Thorold, E.+ Watkinson, J.**
Sheffield
1 e4 e5 2 ♘f3 ♘c6 3 ♗c4 ♗c5 4 b4 ♗xb4 5 c3 ♗c5 6 0-0 d6 7 d4 exd4 8 cxd4 ♗b6 9 ♘c3 ♗g4 10 ♕a4 ♗xf3 11 d5 ♗g4 12 dxc6 bxc6 13 ♕xc6+ ♗d7 14 ♕d5 ♗e6 15 ♗b5+ ♔f8 16 ♕d3 f6 17 ♔h1 ♘e7 18 ♗a3 h6 19 f4 ♔g8 20 e5 ♘f5 21 ♗c4 ♗xc4 22 ♕xc4+ ♔h7 23 ♘d5 fxe5 24 fxe5 ♕g5 25 ♕e4 ♖hf8 26 g4 ♖ae8 27 ♖xf5 ♖xf5 28 e6 ♖xe6 29 ♕xf5+ ♕xf5 30 gxf5 ♖e5 31 ♘xb6 axb6 32 ♖c1 c5 33 ♖b1 ♖e3 34 ♗c1 ♖e1+ 35 ♔g2 b5 36 ♔f2 ♖d1 37 ♔e2 ♖h1 38 a3 ♖xh2+ 39 ♔d1 ♖f2 40 ♖xb5 ♖xf5 41 a4 h5 42 a5 h4 43 a6 ♖f8 44 a7 ♖a8 45 ♖b7 h3 46 ♗f4 ♔g6 47 ♗xd6 ♖d8 48 ♖b8 ♖xd6+ 49 ♔e2 ♖a6 50 a8♕ ♖xa8 51 ♖xa8 ♔f5 52 ♖a5 g5 53 ♖xc5+ **1-0** M954-1861

**1861-⚔TW-2̂**
**Watkinson, J.+ Thorold, E.**
Sheffield
1 e4 e5 2 ♘f3 ♘c6 3 ♗c4 ♗c5 4 b4 ♗b6 5 c3 ♘f6 6 d4 ♘xe4 7 ♗d5 f5 8 ♗xe4 fxe4 9 ♗g5 ♘e7 10 ♘xe5 0-0 11 ♕b3+ d5 12 ♗xe7 ♕xe7 13 ♕xd5+ ♗e6 14 ♕xe4 ♖ad8 15 0-0 ♗d5 16 ♕g4 c6 17 ♘d2 ♗e6 18 ♕g3 ♖f5 19 f4 ♖df8 20 ♖ae1 ♕d6 21 ♘e4 ♕c7 22 a3 ♗d5 23 h3 a6 24 ♔h2 ♕e7 25 ♘g4 ♔h8 26 ♘ef6 ♕f7 27 ♘xd5 cxd5 28 ♘e5 ♕c7 29 ♖e3 g5 30 ♖ef3 gxf4 31 ♖xf4 ♖g8 32 ♕xg8+ ♔xg8 33 ♖xf5 **1-0** M954-1861

**1861-⚔TW-3̂**
**Thorold, E.− Watkinson, J.**
Sheffield [Staunton]
1 e4 e5 2 ♘f3 ♘f6 3 ♘xe5 d6 4 ♘f3 ♘xe4 5 ♗c4? d5 6 ♕e2 ♕e7 7 ♗b3 0-0 8 0-0 ♗g4∓ 9 d3 ♘g5 10 ♗xg5 ♗xg5 11 h3 ♖e8 12 ♕d1 ♗h5 13 ♘c3 c6 14 g4!? ♗g6 15 ♘xg5 ♕xg5 16 f4 ♕h4 17 ♕f3 h6 18 f5 ♗h7 19 ♘e2 ♘d7 20 d4 ♖e7 21 ♕g3 ♕f6 22 ♖ae1 ♖ae8 23 ♕h2 ♖e3 24 h4 ♕e7 25 ♖f2 ♘f6 26 ♖g2 ♖f3! 27 ♕e5 ♕d8 28 ♕h2 ♖ee3 29 g5 ♘h5 [△ 30 ... ♖h3] 30 ♖f2 ♖h3 31 ♕g2 ♖hg3 32 ♘xg3 ♖xg3 33 g6 fxg6 34 ♕xg3 ♘xg3 35 fxg6 ♗xg6 36 ♖f4 ♔h7 37 c4 ♗d3 38 ♔f2 dxc4 39 ♗xc4 ♗xc4 40 ♔xg3 ♕d6 41 ♖e5 ♗d5 42 h5 c5 43 ♖ff5 cxd4 44 ♔f2 ♗xa2 **0-1** M954-1861

**1861-⚔TW-4̂**
**Watkinson, J.+ Thorold, E.**
Sheffield [Staunton]
1 e4 e6 2 d4 d5 3 exd5 exd5 4 ♘f3 ♗d6 5 ♘c3 ♗e6 6 ♗d3 ♘f6 7 ♗g5 c6 8 ♘e5 h6 9 ♗h4 ♕b6 10 ♕d2 ♕xd4?

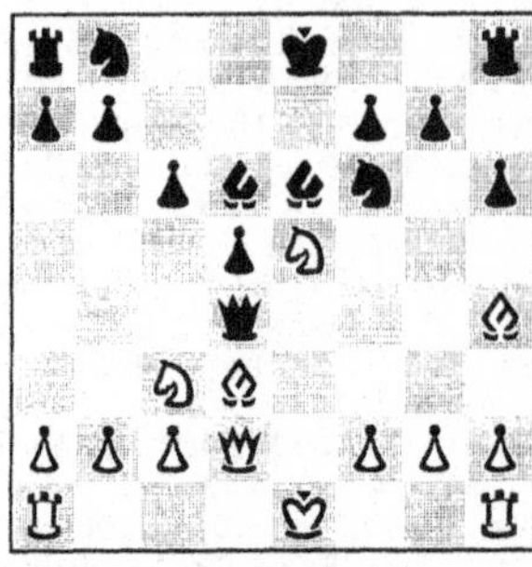

11 ♘g6 ♖g8 12 ♘b5 ♕xb2 13 ♘xd6+ ♔d7 14 0-0 fxg6 15 ♖ab1 ♕a3 16 ♖xb7+ ♔d8 [16 ... ♔xd6 17 ♗g3+-] 17 ♕f4 ♘bd7 18 ♖e1 g5 19 ♘f7+ ♔e7 20 ♕e3 ♖ge8 21 ♘d6 [21 ♕xe6+?] 21 ... ♔f8 [21 ... ♕xd6 22 ♗g3] 22 ♘xe8 ♖xe8 23 ♗g3 a5 24 ♗g6 **1-0** M954-1861

## 1861-⚔TW-11 4 viii 61

**Thorold, E.–Watkinson, J.**

Huddersfield

1 e4 e5 2 f4 ♗c5 3 ♘f3 d6 4 c3 ♗g4 5 ♗e2 ♘c6 6 b4 ♗b6 7 d4 ♗xf3 8 ♗xf3 ♘xd4 9 a4 ♘xf3+ 10 ♕xf3 a6 11 f5 h6 12 ♘a3 ♘f6 13 a5 ♗a7 14 c4 ♕e7 15 ♘c2 c6 16 ♘e3 d5 17 c5 ♘xe4 18 0-0 0-0-0 19 ♗b2 ♘d2 20 ♕e2 ♘xf1 21 ♖xf1 f6 22 ♔h1 ♗b8 23 ♕c2 h5 24 ♖a1 ♕d7 25 ♖d1 ♗c7 26 b5 axb5 27 ♖a1 d4 28 ♘f1 h4 29 h3 ♖h5 30 ♕d3 ♕xf5 31 ♕a3 ♖g5 32 a6 ♕f2 33 axb7+ ♔d7 34 ♕f3 ♕xf3 35 gxf3 ♗b8 36 f4 exf4 37 ♗xd4 ♔c7 38 ♗f2 ♔xb7 39 ♗xh4 ♖h5 40 ♗f2 ♖xh3+ 41 ♔g2 ♖dh8 **0-1** M954-1861

## 1861-★AC-1 vi 61

**Campbell, J.G.+ Anderssen, A.**

London♀ [Löwenthal]

1 e4 e5 2 ♘f3 ♘c6 3 ♗b5 a6 4 ♗a4 ♘f6 5 d3 ♗c5 6 ♘c3 h6 7 ♗e3 ♕e7 8 ♕d2 ♘d4 9 ♗xd4 exd4 [◻ 9 ... ♗xd4] 10 ♘e2 0-0 11 0-0 d5 12 exd5 ♘xd5 13 ♘fxd4 ♕f6 14 c3 ♗d6 15 ♗b3 ♘f4 16 ♘xf4 ♗xf4 17 ♕e2 c5 18 ♘c2 ♗d7 19 ♘e3 ♗c6 20 ♕h5! ♖ad8 21 ♖ad1 ♗b8?! 22 ♕xc5 ♖fe8 23 d4 ♖e4 24 ♕f5! ♕e7± 25 g3 ♕e8 26 ♗c2 g6 27 ♕h3 ♖xe3 28 fxe3 ♕xe3+ 29 ♖f2 ♖e8 30 ♗b3! ♔g7 [30 ... ♖e7 31 ♕c8++] 31 ♖d3! ♕g5 32 ♖xf7+ ♔h8 33 ♕f1 **1-0** M324

## 1861-★AD-1 vii 61

**Anderssen, A.–Dufresne, J.**

Rotterdam♀ [Boden]

1 e4 e5 2 ♘f3 ♘c6 3 ♗c4 ♘f6 4 ♘g5 d5 5 exd5 ♘a5 6 d3?! h6 7 ♘f3 ♘xc4 8 dxc4 e4 9 ♘e5 ♗d6 10 f4 exf3 11 ♘xf3 0-0 12 0-0 ♗c5+ 13 ♘d4 [13 ♔h1 ♘e4∓] 13 ... b5!? 14 b4 ♗xb4 15 ♘c6 ♗c5+ 16 ♔h1 ♕e8 17 ♘c3 [△ 18 ♖e1] 17 ... ♘g4 18 ♘xb5 ♘f2+ 19 ♖xf2 ♗xf2 20 ♗b2? [20 ♗a3!±] 20 ... ♕e4 21 ♕f1 ♕xc2 22 ♖b1 ♖e8! 23 ♘xc7 ♗f5 24 ♘xe8 ♖xe8 25 ♖c1 ♕xb2 26 d6 ♗d7 27 ♘e7+ ♔f8 28 ♖b1 ♕f6 29 ♘d5 ♕d4 30 ♖d1 ♕xd1 31 ♕xd1 ♖e1+ 32 ♕xe1 ♗xe1 **0-1** M392-1863

## 1861-★AD-2 vii 61

**Dufresne, J.–Anderssen, A.**

Rotterdam♀ [Boden]

1 e4 e5 2 ♘f3 ♘c6 3 ♗b5 a6 4 ♗a4 ♘f6 5 ♘c3 ♗c5 6 d3 0-0 7 ♗e3 ♕e7 8 0-0 ♗a7 9 ♖e1 d6 10 d4 ♗g4 11 d5 ♘b8 12 ♗xa7 ♖xa7 13 ♖e3 [◻ 13 ♕d3] 13 ... b5 14 ♗b3 ♘h5 15 ♕e1 ♘d7 16 ♘d2 ♘f4 17 f3 ♗h5 18 ♘e2 ♕g5 19 ♘g3 ♗g6 20 ♕f2 h5 21 ♔h1 h4 22 ♘gf1 ♘f6 23 g3 hxg3 24 ♕xg3 ♕h6 25 h4 ♘h7 26 c4 f5 27 c5 ♘h5 28 ♕g1 fxe4 29 fxe4 ♖f4 30 ♖h3 ♘7f6 31 cxd6

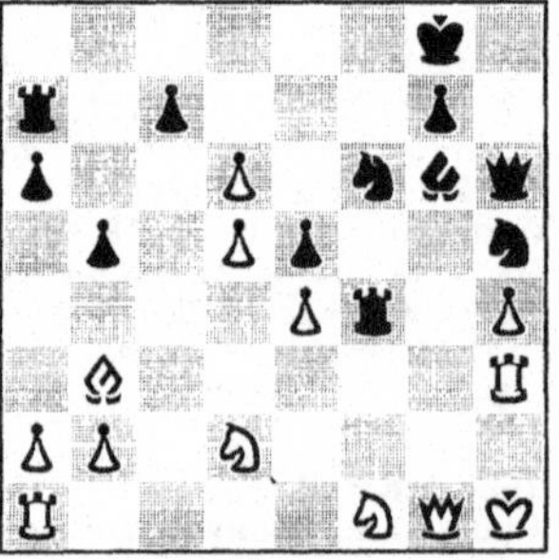

31 ... cxd6!! 32 ♕xa7 ♘g4 33 ♖f3 ♖xf3 34 ♘xf3 ♗xe4 35 ♔g1 ♗xf3 36 ♗d1 ♕f4 37 a4 ♗xd5 38 ♕b8+ ♔h7 39 ♗c2+ g6 40 ♕a7+ ♔h6 41 ♖a3 ♕c1 42 ♖c3 ♘f4 **0-1** M392-1863

## 1861-★AD-3 vii 61

**Dufresne, J.–Anderssen, A.**

Rotterdam [Journoud]

1 e4 e5 2 ♘f3 ♘c6 3 c3 d5 [3 ... ♘f6] 4 ♗b5 dxe4 5 ♘xe5 ♕d5 6 ♗xc6+ [6 ♕a4!] 6 ... bxc6 7 d4 ♗a6! 8 b3 ♘f6 9 c4?! ♗b4+! 10 ♗d2 ♕xd4 11 ♘xc6 [◻ 11 ♗xb4 ♕xa1 12 ♗c3 ♕xa2 13 ♘xc6 0-0 14 ♘b4 ♕a5 15 ♘d5 ♕c5 (15 ... ♕a2 16 ♘xf6+ gxf6 17 ♕g4++) 16 ♗b4 ♕c6 17 ♘e7++] 11 ... ♗xd2+ [11 ... ♕xa1? 12 ♘xb4 △ 13 ♗c3+-] 12 ♘xd2 ♕c5 13 b4 ♕xc6 14 b5 ♕d7! 15 bxa6 ♖d8 16 ♘b3 ♕e7 17 ♕c2 ♕b4+ 18 ♔e2 0-0 19 ♖hd1 ♖de8 20 a4 ♘g4 21 ♖d4 f5! 22 c5 ♕b8 23 h3 ♘f6 24 ♖b1 [◻ 24 c6!] 24 ... f4∓ 25 ♘d2 f3+ 26 ♔e3

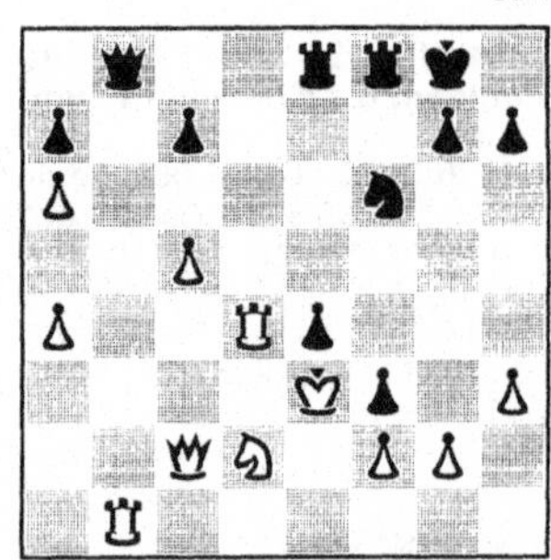

26 ... fxg2! 27 ♕c4+ ♔h8 28 ♖g1? [28 ♖xb8! g1=♕ 29 ♖xe8 ♕e1+ 30 ♕e2 ♕xe2+=] 28 ... c6 29 ♖xg2 ♘d5+ 30 ♖xd5 [30 ♔e2 ♘f4+-+] 30 ... cxd5 31 ♕xd5 ♕f4+ 32 ♔e2 e3!-+ 33 fxe3 ♕xe3+ 34 ♔d1 ♖d8 35 ♕a2 ♖f1+ 36 ♔c2 ♕d3+ 37 ♔b2 ♖b8+ **0-1** L/N6016

## 1861-★AD-4 17 vii 61

**Dufresne, J. & Dupré–Anderssen, A.**

Rotterdam

1 e4 e5 2 f4 exf4 3 ♗c4 ♕h4+ 4 ♔f1 g5 5 ♘c3 ♗g7 6 g3 fxg3 7 ♔g2 ♕h6 8 hxg3 ♕g6 9 d4 ♘e7 10 ♘f3 h6 11 b3 d6 12 e5 ♗f5 13 ♕e2 ♘bc6 14 exd6 cxd6 15 ♘b5 0-0-0 16 ♘xa7+ ♔b8 17 ♘b5 ♗e4 18 ♗xf7 g4 19 ♗xg6 ♗xf3+ 20 ♕xf3 gxf3+ 21 ♔xf3 ♘xg6 22 c3 ♖hf8+ 23 ♔g2 ♖de8 24 ♗a3 ♖e2+ 25 ♔h3 ♖f5 26 ♘xd6 ♖f3 27 ♘b5 h5 28 ♗d6+ ♔c8 29 ♖ae1 ♖ef2 30 ♖e6 ♗f6 31 ♖he1 ♘d8 32 ♖6e2 ♘f7 33 ♖xf2 ♖xf2 34 ♗f4 ♔d7 35 ♗e3 ♘g5+ 36 ♗xg5 ♗xg5 37 a4 ♘e7 38 ♖e5 ♘f5 39 ♖d5+ ♔e7 40 ♖e5+ ♔f6 41 ♘c7 ♘h6 42 ♘d5+ ♔g6 43 ♖e6+ ♔f7 44 ♖e4 ♘g4 45 ♖xg4 hxg4+ 46 ♔xg4 ♗d2 47 c4 ♔e6 48 b4 ♔d6 49 a5 ♗e1 50 ♔g5 ♖b2 **0-1** L/N3031

## 1861-★AD-5 17 vii 61

**Dufresne, J. & Dupré, C.E.A.–Anderssen, A.**

Rotterdam

1 e4 e5 2 ♘f3 ♘c6 3 d4 exd4 4 ♗c4 ♘f6 5 e5 d5 6 ♗b5 ♘e4 7 ♘xd4 ♗c5 8 0-0 0-0 9 ♘xc6 bxc6 10 ♗xc6 ♗a6 11 ♗xa8 ♗xf1 12 ♗e3 ♗xe3 13 fxe3 ♕g5 14 ♔xf1 [14 ♕f3? ♗xg2!-+] 14 ... ♕xe3 15 ♕e2 ♕f4+ 16 ♔g1 ♕c1+ 17 ♕f1 ♕e3+ 18 ♔h1 ♘f2+ 19 ♔g1 ♘g4+ 20 ♔h1 ♕xe5 21 ♕g1 ♕f4 22 g3 ♕f3+ 23 ♕g2 ♕d1+ 24 ♕g1 ♕xc2 25 ♘c3 ♖xa8 26 ♕g2 ♕xg2+ 27 ♔xg2 d4 28 ♘d5 c5 29 ♖c1 ♖d8 30 ♖xc5 h5 31 h3 ♖xd5 32 ♖c8+ ♔h7 33 hxg4 d3 34 ♖c1 d2 35 ♖d1 hxg4 36 ♔f2 f5 37 ♔e3

g5 38 ♖xd2 f4+ 39 gxf4 gxf4+ 40 ♔e2 ♖xd2+ 41 ♔xd2 ♔g6 42 ♔e2 ♔f5 43 b4 ♔e4 44 ♔f2 g3+ 45 ♔g2 ♔e3 46 a4 ♔e2 **0-1**
L/N3303

**1861-★AD-6** 17 vii 61
**Dufresne, J. & Dupré, C.E.A.– Anderssen, A.**
Rotterdam

1 e4 e5 2 ♘f3 ♘c6 3 d4 exd4 4 ♗c4 ♘f6 5 e5 d5 6 ♗b5 ♘e4 7 ♘xd4 ♗c5 8 0-0 0-0 9 ♘xc6 bxc6 10 ♗xc6 ♗a6 11 ♗xa8 ♗xf1 12 ♗e3 ♗xe3 13 fxe3 ♕g5 14 ♔xf1 ♕xe3 15 ♕e2 ♕f4+ 16 ♔g1 ♕c1+ 17 ♕f1 ♕e3+ 18 ♔h1 ♘f2+ 19 ♔g1 ♘g4+ 20 ♔h1 ♕xe5 21 ♕g1 ♕f4 22 g3 ♕f3+ 23 ♕g2 ♕d1+ 24 ♕g1 ♕xc2 25 ♘c3 ♖xa8 26 ♕g2 ♕xg2+ 27 ♔xg2 d4 28 ♘d5 c5 29 ♖c1 ♖d8 30 ♖xc5 h5 31 h3 ♖xd5 32 ♖c8+ ♔h7 33 hxg4 d3 34 ♖c1 d2 35 ♖d1 hxg4 36 ♔f2 f5 37 ♔e3 g5 38 ♖xd2 f4+ 39 gxf4 gxf4+ 40 ♔e2 ♖xd2+ 41 ♔xd2 ♔g6 42 ♔e2 ♔f5 43 b4 ♔e4 44 ♔f2 g3+ 45 ♔g2 ♔e3 46 a4 ♔e2 **0-1** L/N3031

**1861-★AD-7** vii 61
**Dupré, C.E.A.=Anderssen, A.**
Rotterdam [Boden]

1 e4 e5 2 ♘f3 ♘c6 3 ♗c4 ♗c5 4 c3 ♘f6 5 d4 exd4 6 cxd4 [□ 6 e5] 6 ... ♗b4+ 7 ♗d2 ♗xd2+ 8 ♘bxd2 d5 9 exd5 ♘xd5 10 0-0 0-0 11 h3 [□ 11 ♘b3] 11 ... ♘f4 [□ 11 ... ♘b6] 12 ♘e4 ♗e6 13 ♗b5 ♕d5 14 ♗xc6 bxc6 15 ♘eg5 ♖ab8 16 ♕c2 g6 17 ♕d2 ♕f5 18 ♖fe1 ♗d5 19 ♖e5 ♕f6 20 ♘e4 ♘xh3+ 21 ♔h2! ♕f4+ 22 ♔xh3 ♗e6+ 23 ♖xe6 ♕f5+ 24 ♔h2 fxe6 25 ♘g3 ♕d5 26 ♖e1 [□ 26 b3] 26 ... ♕xa2 27 ♕h6 [△ 28 ♘g5] 27 ... ♖xf3 28 gxf3 ♖xb2 29 ♘e4 ♖xf2+ 30 ♔g3 ♖g2+ 31 ♔f4 g5+ 32 ♘xg5 ♕d2+ 33 ♖e3 ♕xd4+ 34 ♘e4 ♖g6 35 ♕h5 ♖f6+ 36 ♔g3 ♖f5 37 ♕e8+ ♔g7 38 ♕e7+ ♖f7 39 ♕g5+ ♔h8 40 ♔f2 e5 41 ♕g4 ♖f8 42 ♕e6 ♖b8 43 ♕f6+ ♔g8 44 ♕e6+ ♔h8 **½-½** M392-1863

**1861-★AD-8** vii 61
**Dupré, C.E.A.–Anderssen, A.**
Rotterdam [Boden]

1 e4 e5 2 ♘f3 ♘c6 3 ♗c4 ♗c5 4 c3 ♘f6 5 d4 exd4 6 cxd4 ♗b4+ 7 ♗d2 ♗xd2+ 8 ♘bxd2 d5 9 exd5 ♘xd5 10 ♕b3 ♘ce7 [10 ... ♘a5!?] 11 0-0 0-0 12 ♖fe1 c6 13 ♘e4 ♖b8 14 ♖ad1 b5 15 ♗d3 ♗g4 16 ♗b1! ♘g6 17 h3 ♗xf3 18 ♕xf3 ♘gf4 19 ♘c5 ♕d6 20 ♖e4 f5 21 ♖e5 ♖f6 22 ♗xf5!? ♘g6 [□ 22 ... ♖bf8] 23 ♖e6! ♖xe6 24 ♗xe6+ ♔h8 25 ♗xd5 cxd5 26 ♖e1 ♖f8 27 ♕e3 h6 28 g3 ♔h7 29 ♔g2?! ♖f5 30 ♘e6 ♕e7 31 f4 ♕f7 32 ♖f1 ♖f6 33 ♘c5 h5 34 ♘d3 ♘e7 35 ♘e5 ♕e6 36 ♕d3+ g6 37 ♕xb5 ♘f5 38 ♕d7+? [□ 38 ♕d3+–] 38 ... ♕xd7 39 ♘xd7 ♖d6 40 ♘e5 ♘e3+ 41 ♔f2 ♘xf1 42 ♔xf1 ♖a6 43 a3 ♖a4 44 ♘c6 [□ 44 ♘f3] 44 ... ♖c4 45 ♘xa7 ♖c1+ 46 ♔e2 ♖c2+ 47 ♔e3 ♖xb2 48 a4 ♖b3+ 49 ♔f2 ♖a3 50 ♘b5 ♖xa4 51 ♔e3 ♔g7 52 ♘c3 ♖a5 53 g4 ♔f6 54 ♔d3 ♔e6 55 ♔e3 ♖a1 56 ♔f2 ♖a3 57 ♘e2 ♖xh3 58 f5+ [△ 59 ♘f4+–] 58 ... ♔f6 59 ♘f4 hxg4! 60 ♘xd5+ [60 ♘xh3? gxh3–+] 60 ... ♔xf5 61 ♘e7+ ♔g5 62 d5 ♖a3 63 d6 ♖d3 64 ♘c8 g3+ 65 ♔e2 ♖d4 66 ♔f3 ♔h4 **0-1** M392-1863

**1861-★AD-9** vii 61
**Anderssen, A.+ Dupré, C.E.A.**
Rotterdam [Boden]

1 e4 e6 2 d4 d5 3 exd5 exd5 4 ♘f3 ♗d6 5 ♗d3 ♘c6 6 0-0 ♗e6 7 ♘c3 h6 8 ♖e1 ♘f6 9 ♘xd5!? ♘xd5 10 c4 0-0! 11 cxd5 ♗xd5 12 ♗e3 f5∓ 13 ♗c2 ♕f6 14 ♘e5 ♘xe5 15 dxe5 ♕xe5 16 f4 ♕e6 17 g4 c6 18 h4 ♖ae8 19 g5 hxg5 20 hxg5 ♕g6 21 ♔f2 ♔f7 22 ♖h1 ♖h8 23 ♗b3 ♕e6 24 g6+!? ♕xg6 25 ♗xd5+ cxd5 26 ♕xd5+ ♕e6 27 ♕xb7+ ♖e7 28 ♕f3 ♖he8 29 ♖ae1 ♕f6 30 ♖h7 ♕xb2+ 31 ♖e2 ♕f6 32 ♕d5+ ♕e6 33 ♖xg7+?! ♔xg7 34 ♗d4+ ♗e5 35 ♗xe5+ ♔f7 36 ♕h1 ♕b6+? 37 ♖e3 ♖xe5 38 fxe5 ♖xe5 39 ♕h7+ ♔e6 40 ♕g6+ ♔d5 41 ♕f7+ ♔d4 42 ♕g7 [△ 43 ♔f3 44 ♕f4+–] **1-0** M392-1863

**1861-★AG-1** vii 61
**Gouda & Messemaker, C.– Anderssen, A.**
Rotterdam? [Bachmann]

1 e4 e5 2 ♘f3 ♘c6 3 ♗c4 ♗c5 4 c3 ♘f6 5 d4 exd4 6 cxd4 ♗b4+ 7 ♗d2 ♗xd2+ 8 ♘bxd2 d5 9 exd5 ♘xd5 10 ♕b3 ♘ce7 11 0-0 0-0 12 ♘e4 c6 13 ♘c3 h6 14 ♘e5 f6 15 ♘d3 ♕d6 16 ♖ae1 ♗e6 17 ♘e4 [17 ♖xe6!? △ 18 ♘f4] 17 ... ♕c7 18 ♘ec5 ♗f7 19 ♕xb7 ♕xb7 20 ♘xb7 ♘f5 21 ♖e4 ♖ab8 22 ♘bc5 ♖fd8 23 ♗xd5 ♖xd5 24 ♘b3 a5 25 ♘dc5 ♖b4 26 a3 ♖b6 27 ♘xa5 ♘xd4 28 b4 f5 29 ♖e7 f4 30 ♘c4 ♖b8 31 ♘e5 ♗h5 32 f3 ♖a8 33 ♘c4 ♖g5 34 ♔f2 ♗f7 35 ♘d6 [△ 36 ♘xf7] 35 ... ♖xa3 36 ♖fe1 ♗d5 37 ♘ce4 ♖a2+ 38 ♔f1 ♖gxg2 39 ♖e8+ ♔h7 40 ♖e7 ♘xf3 41 ♖e2 ♖gxe2 42 ♘f6+ ♔g6 43 ♖xe2 ♘xh2+ 44 ♔e1 ♖xe2+ 45 ♔xe2 ♔xf6 **0-1**
L/N3303

**1861-★AH-1** 14 vii 61
**Anderssen, A.+ Heer, K. de**
Amsterdam [Lange & Hirschfeld]

1 e4 c5 2 ♗c4 e6 3 ♘c3 ♘c6 4 d3 d6 [□ 4 ... a6] 5 ♘ge2 ♘f6 6 0-0 ♗e7 7 ♘g3 a6 8 a4 0-0 9 ♗d2 d5 10 ♗a2 dxe4 11 dxe4 ♕c7 12 ♘ce2 b6 13 c3 ♗b7 14 ♕c2 ♖ad8 15 ♖ae1 ♖d7 16 ♗b1 ♖fd8 17 ♗c1 b5 18 f4 e5 19 fxe5 ♘xe5 20 ♘f4 c4 21 ♗e3 ♘d3 22 ♘xd3 cxd3 23 ♕f2 ♕c4 24 ♗d4 ♘g4 25 ♕f4 ♖xd4 26 cxd4 ♕xd4+ 27 ♔h1 d2 28 ♕xf7+ ♔h8 29 ♖d1 ♗f6 30 ♕xb7 ♘f2+ 31 ♖xf2 ♕xf2 32 ♗c2 ♗d4 33 ♖f1 ♕e3 34 ♕f7 h6 35 e5 d1♕ 36 ♗xd1 ♗xe5 37 ♗c2 ♗d6 38 ♕g6 **1-0** L/N6047-1862

**1861-★AH-2** 14 vii 61
**Heer, K.de+ Anderssen, A.**
Amsterdam [Lange & Hirschfeld]

1 c4 f5 2 ♘c3 ♘f6 3 d4 e6 4 e3 ♗b4 5 f3 ♗xc3+ 6 bxc3 c5 7 ♗d3 ♘c6 8 ♘e2 b6 9 0-0 0-0 10 ♗a3 ♕e7 [□ 10 ... ♕c7] 11 ♕c2 ♗b7 12 ♖ae1 ♖ac8 13 ♘f4 ♘a5 14 e4 g6 15 exf5 gxf5 16 ♗xf5 ♘xc4 17 ♗c1 cxd4 18 ♘xe6 ♖fe8 19 ♘xd4 ♕xe1 20 ♖xe1 ♖xe1+ 21 ♔f2 ♖ce8 22 ♗g5 ♘e3 23 ♗xh7+ ♔f8 24 ♗h6+ **1-0** L/N6047-1862

**1861-★AK-1** 12 vii 61
**Anderssen, A.– Kloos, H.**
Amsterdam [Boden]

1 e4 e5 2 ♘f3 ♘c6 3 ♗c4 ♗c5 4 b4 ♗xb4 5 c3 ♗c5 6 0-0 d6 7 d4 ♗b6 8 ♕b3 ♕e7 9 dxe5?! dxe5 10 ♗a3 ♕f6 11 ♘bd2 ♘a5 12 ♕b4 c5 13 ♕a4+ ♗d7 14 ♕c2 ♘e7 15 ♗d5 0-0 16 ♘b3 ♘xb3 17 axb3 ♗c6 18 c4 ♘g6 19 ♗b2 ♖fe8 20 ♘xe5?! ♗xd5 21 exd5 [21 ♘d7? ♕g5∓] 21 ... ♖xe5 22 f4 ♘xf4 23 ♖f2 ♕g5 24 h4 ♕f5 25 ♕d2 ♖e4 26 ♖af1 ♖ae8! 27 ♖xf4 ♖xf4 28 ♖xf4 ♕b1+ 29 ♖f1 ♕e4 30 ♕c3 ♕e3+ 31 ♕xe3 ♖xe3 32 ♖f3 ♖xf3 33 gxf3 ♗c7 34 ♔f2 f5 35 ♔e3 ♔f7 36 f4 g6 37 ♗e5 ♗d8→ 38 ♗d6 b6 39 h5 gxh5 40 ♔f3 ♔e8 41 ♗e5 ♔d7 42 ♗c3 ♗e7 43 ♗e5 a6 44 ♗c3 b5 45 ♗e5 bxc4 46 bxc4 a5 47 ♗c3 a4 48 ♗b2 ♗d8 49 ♔g3 ♗a5 50 ♗c1 ♗b4 51 ♔h4 a3 52 ♔xh5 a2 53 ♗b2 ♗d2 54 ♔g5 ♗e3 **0-1** M392-1863

**1861-★AK-2** 12 vii 61
**Kloos, H.– Anderssen, A.**
Amsterdam

1 e4 e5 2 ♗c4 ♘f6 3 ♘c3 ♗c5 4 ♘f3 ♘c6 5 d3 d6 6 h3 h6 7 a3 ♗b6 8 0-0 g5 9 ♗e3 g4 10 hxg4 ♗xg4

11 ♘e2 ♗xf3 12 gxf3 ♖g8+ 13 ♔h1 ♘xe4 14 ♘g3 ♕h4+ 15 ♔g2 ♖xg3+ 16 fxg3 ♕xg3+ 17 ♔h1 ♕h3+ 18 ♔g1 ♗xe3+ 19 ♖f2 ♗xf2# **0-1** +9

**1861-★AK-3** vii 61
**Kloos, H.– Anderssen, A.**
Amsterdam [Boden]
1 e4 e5 2 ♗c4 ♗c5 3 ♘f3 ♘c6 4 d3 ♘f6 5 ♘c3 d6 6 h3 h6 7 ♗e3 ♗b6 8 ♘a4? ♗xe3 9 fxe3 0-0 10 0-0 ♘e7 11 ♕e1 c6 12 ♘c3 b5 13 ♗b3 b4 14 ♘a4? [□ 14 ♘e2] 14 ... ♘g6 15 ♕g3 ♔h7 16 ♖ad1 ♘h5 17 ♕h2 f5 18 exf5

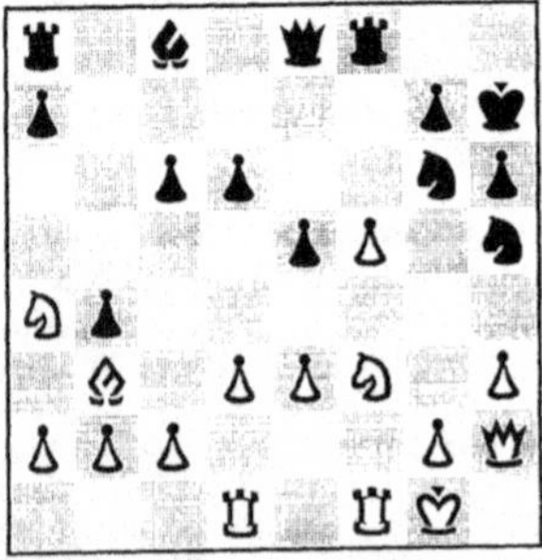

18 ... ♖xf5! 19 g4 ♖xf3 20 ♖xf3 ♘h4 21 ♖f2 ♕g5 22 ♖df1? [□ 22 ♖e1] 22 ... ♕xe3 [△ 23 ... ♘f3+→] 23 ♔h1 ♘g3+ 24 ♔g1 ♘f3+ **0-1** M392-1863

**1861-★AK-4** vii 61
**Anderssen, A.+ Kolisch, I.F. von**
London [Lange & Hirschfeld]
1 e4 e5 2 ♘f3 ♘c6 3 ♗c4 ♗c5 4 b4 ♗xb4 5 c3 ♗c5 6 0-0 d6 7 d4 exd4 8 cxd4 ♗b6 9 d5 ♘a5 10 ♗b2 ♘f6 11 ♗d3 c6 12 ♘c3 0-0 13 ♘a4 [□ 13 ♘e2 △ ♘g3] 13 ... ♗c7 14 h3 a6 15 ♘c3 b5 16 ♖c1 c5 17 ♘e2 c4 18 ♗b1 ♕e7 19 ♘g3 ♘b7 20 ♘d4 ♘c5 [□ 20 ... ♗b6] 21 ♘gf5 ♗xf5 22 ♘xf5 ♕d8 23 ♖e1 ♘cd7 24 f4 ♖e8 25 ♖c3 ♗a5 26 ♖g3 ♗xe1 27 ♖xg7+ ♔h8 28 ♕xe1 ♘e5 29 ♕h4 ♖g8 30 ♕h6 ♕f8 31 ♕xf6 ♖xg7 32 fxe5 ♖c8 33 exd6 c3 34 ♗xc3 ♖xc3 35 ♕xc3 ♔g8 36 ♕xg7+ **1-0** L/N6047-1862

**1861-★AL-1** 13 vii 61
**Anderssen, A.+ Lelie, A. de**
Amsterdam [Lange & Hirschfeld]
1 e4 e5 2 ♘f3 ♘c6 3 d4 exd4 4 ♗c4 ♗c5 5 0-0 ♘f6 [□ 5 ... d6 △ ... ♗g4] 6 e5 d5 7 exf6 dxc4 8 ♖e1+ ♔f8 9 ♗g5 ♕d5 10 ♘c3 ♕f5 11 ♘e4 ♗e6 12 fxg7+ ♔xg7 13 ♘h4 ♕d5 14 ♗f6+ ♔g8 15 ♕f3 ♘e7 16 ♘xc5 ♕xc5

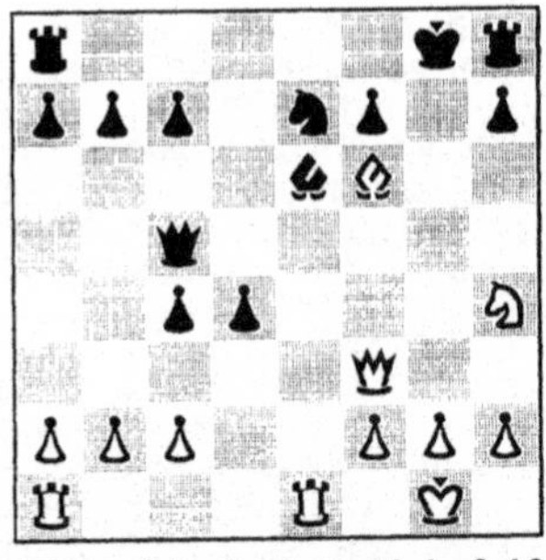

17 ♖xe6 fxe6 18 ♕g4+ ♘g6 19 ♕xe6+ ♔f8 20 ♘f5 **1-0** L/N6047-1862

**1861-★AL-2** 15 vii 61
**Lelie, A. de– Anderssen, A.**
Amsterdam [Lange & Hirschfeld]
1 e4 e5 2 ♘f3 ♘c6 3 ♗b5 a6 4 ♗a4 ♘f6 5 d4 exd4 6 0-0 ♗e7 7 e5 ♘e4 8 ♘xd4 ♘xd4 9 ♕xd4 ♘c5 10 f4 0-0 11 ♘c3 b5 12 ♗b3 ♘xb3 13 axb3 ♗b7 14 ♘e4 f6 15 ♗e3 ♕e8 16 b4 fxe5 17 fxe5 ♕g6 18 ♘g3 ♕c6 19 ♕d2 ♗xb4 20 c3 ♗e7 21 ♘f5 ♖fe8 22 ♖f3 ♕e6 23 ♘xg7? ♔xg7 24 ♖g3+ ♔h8 25 ♖f1 ♖g8 26 ♗h6

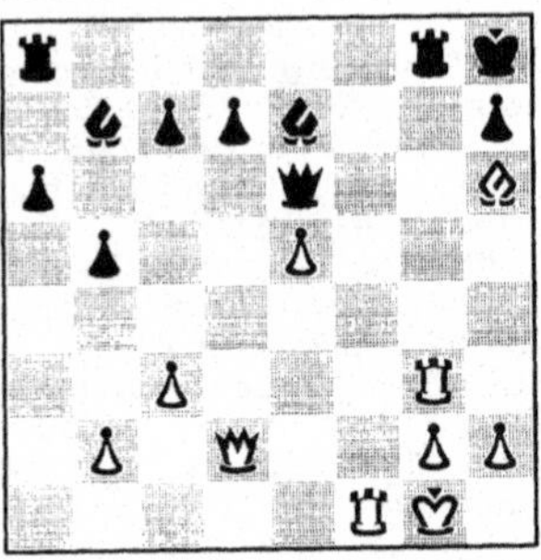

26 ... ♗c5+ 27 ♔h1 ♖xg3 28 hxg3 ♕h3# **0-1** L/N6047-1862

**1861-★AL-3** vii 61
**Lelie,A. de & Pinedo,J.– Anderssen,A.**
Amsterdam
1 e4 e5 2 ♘f3 ♘c6 3 ♗b5 a6 4 ♗a4 ♘f6 5 d4 exd4 6 0-0 ♗e7 7 e5 ♘e4 8 c3 dxc3 9 ♘xc3 ♘xc3 10 bxc3 0-0 11 ♕d3 d5 12 ♗c2 g6 13 ♕e3 ♖e8 14 ♘d4 ♗c5 15 ♘xc6 ♗xe3 16 ♘xd8 ♗xc1 17 ♖axc1 ♖xd8 18 f4 b5 19 h3 c5 20 g4 a5 21 a3 c4 22 ♖fd1 b4 23 cxb4 axb4 24 axb4 ♖a3 25 ♗e4 ♖xh3 26 ♔g2 ♗xg4 27 ♖xd5 ♖a8 28 ♖xc4 ♖aa3 29 ♖d2 h5 30 ♖f2 h4 31 b5 ♖a1 32 ♖f1 ♖g3+ 33 ♔f2 ♖a2+ 34 ♖c2 ♖a4 35 ♖e1 ♖b4 36 ♖c5 ♖b2+ 37 ♗c2 ♖d3 38 ♖c1 h3 39 b6 ♖f3+ 40 ♔g1 ♖xb6 41 ♗d1 ♖xf4 42 ♗xg4 ♖xg4+ 43 ♔h2 ♖h4 44 ♖1c3 ♖b2+ 45 ♖c2 ♖xc2+ 46 ♖xc2 ♖e4 47 ♖c5 ♖e3 48 ♖a5 ♔f8 **0-1** L/N3030

**1861-★AM-1** vii 61
**Anderssen,A.+ Messemaker,C.**
Rotterdam [Löwenthal]
1 e4 e5 2 ♘f3 ♘c6 3 ♗b5 a6 4 ♗a4 b5?! 5 ♗b3 ♗c5 6 c3 ♘f6 7 0-0 d6 8 d4 ♗b6 9 ♕d3 h6 10 a4 ♘a5 11 ♗a2 ♗b7 12 ♘bd2 exd4 13 cxd4 bxa4 14 e5 dxe5 15 ♘xe5 0-0 16 ♘df3 ♗xf3 17 ♕xf3 ♕xd4 18 ♗xf7+ ♖xf7 19 ♘xf7 [19 ♕xa8+ ♖f8!] 19 ... ♖f8 20 ♘xh6+ gxh6 21 ♗xh6 ♖f7 22 ♖ad1 ♕g4 23 ♕a8+ ♔h7 24 ♖d3! ♘e4 25 ♗e3 ♖g7 26 g3 ♘g5 27 ♖d8 ♕f3 28 ♖h8+ ♔g6 29 ♖h6+! ♔f7 [29 ... ♔xh6? 30 ♕xf3+−] 30 ♕d8 ♕f5 31 ♖d1 ♘f3+ 32 ♔g2 ♘e5 33 ♕d5+ ♔e7 34 ♗c5+ ♗xc5 35 ♕xc5+ ♔e8 36 ♖h8+ ♔f7 37 ♖f8+ **1-0** L/N6124-1863

**1861-★AM-2** vii 61
**Messemaker,C.– Anderssen,A.**
Rotterdam [Boden]
1 e4 e5 2 ♘f3 ♘c6 3 ♗b5 a6 4 ♗a4 ♘f6 5 d4 exd4 6 e5 ♘e4 7 ♘xd4 ♘xd4 8 ♕xd4 ♘c5 9 0-0 ♗e7 10 ♘c3 0-0 11 ♘d5 d6 12 ♗b3 dxe5 13 ♕xe5 ♗d6 14 ♕h5 ♘xb3 15 axb3 c6 16 ♘c3 f5 17 f4 ♗e6 18 ♗e3 ♖f6 19 ♖ad1 ♖h6 20 ♕f3 ♕e7 21 ♕f2 b5 22 ♖fe1 a5 23 g3 a4 24 ♕f3 ♖c8 25 bxa4 b4 26 ♘b1 c5 27 b3 c4 28 bxc4 ♖xc4 29 ♕f2 ♕c7 30 ♖e2 ♖e4 31 ♖ed2 ♗c8! 32 ♗b6?! ♕c6 33 a5 ♗b7 34 ♕g2 [□ 34 ♖d5] 34 ... ♖he6 35 h4? ♖e1+ 36 ♖xe1 ♖xe1+ 37 ♔h2 ♕xg2+ 38 ♖xg2 ♗xg2 39 ♔xg2 ♖xb1 40 a6 ♖b2 41 a7 ♖xc2+ 42 ♔f3 ♖a2 43 ♔e3 b3 44 ♔d3 ♖a3 **0-1** M392-1863

**1861-★AM-3** vii 61
**Messemaker,C.+ Anderssen,A.**
Rotterdam [Boden]
1 e4 e5 2 ♘f3 ♘c6 3 d4 exd4 4 ♗c4 ♗c5 5 c3 ♘f6 6 e5 d5 7 ♗b5 ♘e4 8 cxd4 ♗b4+ 9 ♗d2 ♗xd2+ 10 ♘bxd2 0-0 11 ♗xc6 bxc6 12 0-0 f5 13 ♖c1 ♕e8 14 ♘b3 f4 15 ♕c2 ♗d7 16 ♘c5 ♘xc5 17 ♕xc5 h6 18 ♖fe1 ♕e6 19 ♕c3 g5 20 h3 ♖f7 21 ♘h2 h5 22 f3 ♖g7 23 ♕d2 a5 24 b3 a4 25 ♖c5 axb3 26 axb3 ♖b8 27 b4 ♖b6 28 ♖a1 ♗e8 29 ♖ac1 ♕c8 30 ♕e1 ♕b7 31 ♖b1 ♗g6 32 ♖b2 ♖e7 33 h4 ♕c8 34 hxg5 ♕f5 35 ♕c3 ♗e8 36 ♘f1 ♕xg5 37 g3 fxg3 38 ♕e3 ♕h4?!

39 ♖g2 ♖g7 40 f4 ♖xb4 41 ♖xg3 ♖g4 42 ♖c2 ♖b1 43 ♖cg2 ♗g6 44 ♕f2 ♖xg3 45 ♖xg3 ♔f7 46 f5 ♖xf1+ 47 ♔xf1 ♕h1+ 48 ♔e2 ♕e4+ 49 ♖e3 ♕c2+ 50 ♔f1 ♕b1+ 51 ♔g2 ♗xf5 52 e6+ ♔e8 53 ♔h2! ♕c2 54 ♕xc2 ♗xc2 55 ♔g3 ♔e7 56 ♔f4 ♗e4? [□ 56 ... ♗d1=] 57 ♔e5 ♗c2 58 ♖g3 ♗a4 59 ♖g7+ ♔d8 60 ♔f6 c5 61 e7+ ♔d7 62 ♔f7 ♔c8 63 dxc5 d4 64 ♖g6 **1-0**
M392-1863

**1861-★AM-4** vii 61
**Anderssen, A.+ Mohr, C.E.**
Amsterdam

1 e4 e5 2 f4 exf4 3 ♗c4 ♕h4+ 4 ♔f1 g5 5 ♘c3 ♘f6 6 ♘f3 ♕h5 7 d4 d6 8 h4 ♗g4 9 ♔f2 ♗xf3 10 ♕xf3 h6

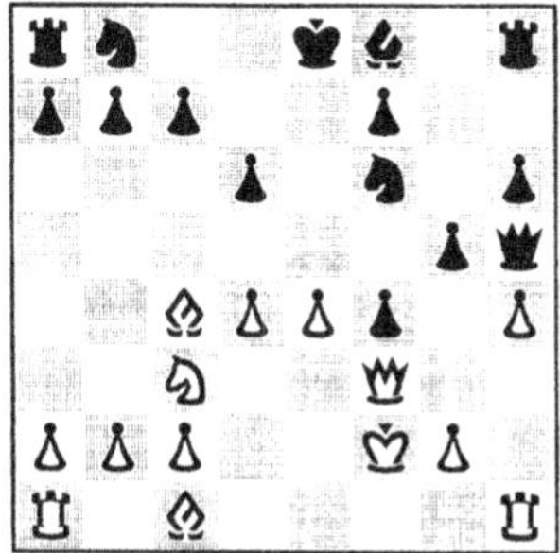

11 hxg5 ♕xh1 12 gxf6 ♕h4+ 13 ♔g1 ♕e1+ 14 ♗f1 ♕g3 15 ♕h5 f3 16 ♘d5 ♘a6 17 ♗c4 ♕g6 18 ♕xf3 0-0-0 19 ♗xa6 bxa6 20 ♕c3 ♖d7 21 ♕c6 **1-0** L/N3030

**1861-★AM-5** vii 61
**Mohr, C.E.- Anderssen, A.**
Amsterdam

1 e4 e5 2 f4 exf4 3 ♗c4 ♕h4+ 4 ♔f1 g5 5 ♘c3 ♗g7 6 d4 ♘e7 7 g3 fxg3 8 ♔g2 ♕h6 9 hxg3 ♕g6 10 ♘f3 h6 11 ♖f1 ♖f8 12 e5 g4 13 ♗d3 gxf3+ 14 ♕xf3 ♕b6 15 ♕g4 ♖g8 16 ♕f4 ♕e6 17 ♗d2 d5 18 ♖h1 ♗d7 19 ♘e2 ♘bc6 20 b3 0-0-0 21 b4 ♔b8 22 ♗c3 ♘g6 23 ♕e3 f5 24 b5 f4 25 ♘xf4 ♘xf4+ 26 ♕xf4 ♗xe5 27 dxe5 d4 28 ♗b2 ♘xe5 29 ♖xh6 ♘xd3 30 cxd3 ♕e2+ 31 ♕f2 ♖xg3+ **0-1**
L/N3030

**1861-★AM-6** vii 61
**Molebreok- Anderssen, A.**
Rotterdam

1 e4 e5 2 ♘f3 ♘c6 3 ♗c4 ♗c5 4 0-0 ♘f6 5 d3 d6 6 h3 h6 7 ♘c3 ♗b6 8 a3 g5 9 ♘d5 ♘xd5 10 ♗xd5 ♘e7 11 ♗e3 ♘g6 12 ♘h2 h5 13 ♗xb6 axb6 14 d4 ♘f4 15 dxe5 dxe5 16 f3 ♕e7 17 ♕d2 f5 18 exf5 ♕c5+ 19 ♖f2 ♗xf5 20 ♖e1 0-0-0 21 c4 ♘d3 22 ♖e3 ♘xf2 23 ♕xf2 ♕d6 24 ♘f1 c6 25 ♗e4 ♗e6 26 ♗d3 g4 27 fxg4 hxg4 28 h4 e4 29 ♗xe4 ♖df8 30 ♕g3 ♕d4 31 b3 ♕f6 32 ♕e1 g3 33 ♖f3 ♕xh4 34 ♖xf8+ ♖xf8 35 ♘xg3 ♗d7 36 ♕e3 ♖h8 37 ♕d4 ♕h2+ 38 ♔f2 ♖f8+ 39 ♗f3 ♗h3 40 ♘f5 ♗xf5 41 ♕g7 ♕h4+ 42 ♔g1 ♖e8 **0-1** L/N3031

**1861-★AP-1** 14 vii 61
**Anderssen, A.+ Paddenburg, M. van**
Amsterdam? [Boden]

1 e4 e5 2 ♘f3 ♘c6 3 ♗c4 ♗c5 4 b4 ♗b6 5 b5 ♘d4 6 ♘xe5 ♘e6 7 ♗b2 ♘f6 8 0-0 0-0 9 d3 d6 10 ♘g4 ♘xg4 11 ♕xg4 ♗d4 12 ♘c3 ♘g5 13 ♕g3 ♕f6? [□ 13 ... h5] 14 ♘d5 ♕e5 15 ♗xd4 ♕xg3 16 fxg3 ♘e6 17 ♗b2 c6 18 ♘e7+ ♔h8 19 ♖f5 cxb5 20 ♗b3 ♘c5 21 ♖g5 f6 22 ♖f1 ♘d7 23 ♖h5 h6 24 ♖f4 ♘e5 25 ♗xe5 **1-0** M392-1863

**1861-★AP-2** 14 vii 61
**Paddenburg, M. van+ Anderssen, A.**
Amsterdam? [Boden]

1 e4 e5 2 ♘f3 ♘c6 3 ♗c4 ♗c5 4 d3 d6 5 0-0 ♘f6 6 ♘g5 0-0 7 ♘c3 h6 8 ♘f3 ♗g4 9 ♘d5?! ♘xd5 10 ♗xd5 ♘d4 11 ♗e3 ♘xf3+ 12 gxf3 ♗h3 13 ♔h1 ♗xf1 14 ♕xf1 c6 15 ♗b3 ♗b4 16 ♕g2 ♕f6 17 ♖g1 ♖ad8 18 ♕h3 ♔h8?! 19 ♗g5 ♕g6 20 ♗xd8 ♕h7 21 ♗e7 ♖a8 22 ♗xf7 ♗d2 23 ♕h4 ♗f4 24 ♖xg7! **1-0** M392-1863

**1861-★AP-3** 15 vii 61
**Pinedo, J.- Anderssen, A.**
Amsterdam

1 e4 e5 2 ♘f3 ♘c6 3 d4 exd4 4 ♗c4 ♘f6 5 e5 d5 6 ♗b5 ♘e4 7 ♘xd4 ♗c5 8 ♘xc6 ♗xf2+ 9 ♔f1 bxc6 10 ♗xc6+ ♔f8 11 c4 ♗a6 12 b3 dxc4 13 ♗a3+ ♔g8 14 ♕xd8+ ♖xd8 15 ♗xe4 ♗d4 16 ♘c3 cxb3+ 17 ♘e2 ♗xa1 18 ♔f2 ♖d2 19 ♗f3 ♗d4+ 20 ♔g3 ♗xe2 21 ♗xe2 bxa2 22 e6 ♖xe2 **0-1**
L/N6047-1862

**1861-★AP-4** vii 61
**Anderssen, A.+ Pinedo, J.**
Amsterdam

1 e4 c5 2 ♘f3 ♘c6 3 d4 cxd4 4 ♘xd4 a6 5 f4 e6 6 ♗e3 d6 7 ♘f3 ♘ge7 8 ♘c3 b5 9 ♗d3 ♗b7 10 a3 ♘g6 11 0-0 ♗e7 12 ♕e2 0-0 13 ♖ad1 ♕d7 14 e5 d5 15 f5 ♘gxe5 16 ♘xe5 ♘xe5 17 f6 gxf6 18 ♕h5 f5 19 ♖xf5 ♘xd3 20 ♖g5+ ♗xg5 21 ♕xg5+ ♔h8 22 ♕f6+ ♔g8 23 ♗h6 **1-0** L/N3030

**1861-★AP-5** vii 61
**Pinedo, J.- Anderssen, A.**
Amsterdam [Journoud]

1 e4 e5 2 ♘f3 d6 3 ♗c4 [3 d4] 3 ... f5 4 d4 ♘c6 5 dxe5 ♘xe5 6 ♘xe5 dxe5 7 0-0 ♗d6 8 ♘c3 f4! 9 ♘b5 ♘f6 10 ♕d3 ♗g4 11 b3 ♗c5 12 ♗f7+ ♔f8 13 h3 h5! 14 ♗g6 ♕e7 15 ♘c3 c6∓ 16 ♖e1 b5 [△ 17 ... ♗e6] 17 ♗xf4!? exf4 18 e5 ♘d7 19 e6 ♘f6 20 hxg4 hxg4 21 ♘e4 ♘xe4 22 ♖xe4 ♖h1+!! 23 ♔xh1 ♕h4+ 24 ♕h3 gxh3 25 g3! ♕g5 26 ♖xf4+ ♔e7 27 ♖f7+ ♔e8 28 ♖f6+ ♔d8 29 ♖d1+ ♔c7 30 ♖f7+ ♔b6 31 ♗e4 ♕e5 32 ♗f3 ♗xf2 33 e7 ♕xg3 34 ♖f8 ♖e8 35 c4 ♖xe7 36 b4 ♖e2 37 a4 ♗d4 38 c5+ ♔a6 39 axb5+ cxb5 **0-1** L/N6016

**1861-★AR-1** vii 61
**Anderssen, A.+ Raland, F.**
Rotterdam [Journoud]

1 e4 e5 2 ♘f3 ♘c6 3 ♗c4 ♗c5 4 b4 ♗xb4 5 c3 ♗a5 6 d4 exd4 7 0-0 ♘f6 8 ♗a3! d6 9 e5 dxe5 10 ♕b3 ♕d7 11 ♖e1 e4 12 ♘bd2 ♔d8 13 ♘xe4 ♘xe4 14 ♖xe4 ♖e8 15 ♖ae1 ♖xe4 16 ♖xe4 ♕f5 17 ♗d5 ♗e6 18 ♗xc6!! bxc6 [18 ... ♗xb3 19 ♖e8#; 18 ... ♕xe4 19 ♕xb7+-] 19 ♖xd4+ ♔c8 20 ♕d1 ♗d5 21 c4 ♗xf3 22 gxf3 c5 23 ♖d5 ♕g6+ 24 ♔h1 ♗b6 25 ♖d8+ ♔b7 26 ♕d5+ **1-0**
L/N6016-1862

**1861-★AR-2** vii 61
**Anderssen, A.+ Raland, F.**
Rotterdam

1 e4 e5 2 ♘f3 ♘c6 3 ♗c4 ♗c5 4 b4 d5 5 ♗xd5 ♘xb4 6 ♗b3 ♘c6 7 d3 ♘ge7 8 ♘g5 ♖f8 9 ♕h5 ♘g6 10 ♕xh7 ♕f6 11 0-0 ♖h8 12 ♗xf7+ ♕xf7 13 ♕xh8+ ♘xh8 14 ♘xf7 ♘xf7 15 ♘c3 ♘d4 16 ♗e3 ♗b6 17 ♘d5 ♗e6 18 ♘xb6 axb6 19 c4 ♘c2 20 ♖ac1 ♖xa2 21 h3 ♘d4 22 ♗xd4 exd4 23 f4 ♔e7 24 ♖ce1 ♗d7 25 ♖f3 b5 26 e5 ♘h6 27 cxb5 ♗xb5 28 g4 ♖d2 29 f5 ♗c6 30 f6+ ♔e6 31 ♖g3 gxf6 32 exf6+ ♔xf6 33 g5+ ♔g6 34 ♖e6+ ♔f7 35 ♖f6+ ♔e7 36 gxh6 **1-0** L/N3031

**1861-★AR-3** vii 61
**Raland, F.- Anderssen, A.**
Rotterdam

1 e4 e5 2 ♘f3 ♘c6 3 ♗c4 ♗c5 4 b4 ♗xb4 5 c3 ♗a5 6 d4 exd4 7 0-0 dxc3 8 ♕b3 ♕f6 9 ♗g5 ♕g6 10 e5 b5 11 ♗d5 c2 12 ♘c3 ♗xc3 13 ♕xc3 ♗b7 14 ♖fe1 ♘h6 15 ♗e4 ♕h5 16 ♗d5 0-0 17 ♖e4 ♕g6 18 ♕d2 ♘f5 19 g4 ♘h6 20 ♘h4

20 ... ♕xe4 21 ♗xe4 ♘xg4 22 ♗xc2 ♘cxe5 23 ♗f4 ♖fe8 24 ♗xe5 ♘xe5 25 ♖e1 ♖e6 26 ♔f1 d5 27 ♕f4 ♖ae8 28 ♕g3 b4 29 ♘f5 g6 30 ♘d4 ♖6e7 31 f4 ♘c4 32 ♖xe7 ♖xe7 33 ♔f2 c5 34 ♘f5 ♖e6 35 ♘h6+ ♔g7 36 ♘f5+ ♔f8 37 ♘h4 ♘d6 38 ♘f3 d4 39 ♘e5 c4 40 ♕g5 ♔g7 41 h4 d3 **0-1** L/N3031

**1861-★AR-4** vii 61
**Raland, F.– Anderssen, A.**
Rotterdam
1 e4 e5 2 ♘f3 ♘c6 3 ♗c4 ♗c5 4 c3 ♘f6 5 0-0 ♘xe4 6 d4 exd4 7 cxd4 ♗b6 8 ♗d5 ♘f6 9 ♖e1+ ♘e7 10 ♗g5 0-0 11 ♘c3 ♘g6 12 ♘e5 c6 13 ♗e4 d5 14 ♗c2 ♕d6 15 ♗xf6 gxf6 16 ♘f3 ♗c7 17 ♕d3 ♗g4 18 g3 ♔g7 19 ♘h4 ♖h8 20 ♘f5+ ♗xf5 21 ♕xf5 h5 22 h4 ♖h6 23 ♕h3 ♖g8 24 ♖e3 ♔h8 25 ♗xg6 ♖hxg6 26 ♘e2 ♖g4 27 ♔g2 b6 28 ♖d1 c5 29 b3 cxd4 30 ♖xd4 ♕c5 31 ♖xg4 hxg4 32 ♕h1 d4 33 ♖d3 ♗e5 34 ♔h2 f5 35 ♕c1 ♕xc1 36 ♘xc1 f4 37 ♘e2 f3 38 ♘f4 f5 39 ♘e6 ♖e8 40 ♘g5 ♔g7 41 ♔g1 ♔f6 42 ♔f1 f4 43 gxf4 ♗xf4 44 ♖xd4 ♗xg5 45 hxg5+ ♔xg5 46 ♖d2 ♖c8 47 ♔g1 ♔h4 48 ♔h2 ♖e8 49 ♖d7 ♖e2 50 ♖h7+ ♔g5 **0-1** L/N3031

**1861-★AV-1** 18 vii 61
**Van't Kruijs, M.+ Anderssen, A.**
Amsterdam
1 a3 e5 2 c4 ♗c5 3 ♘c3 a5 4 e3 ♘c6 5 ♘ge2 d6 6 d4 ♗b6 7 ♘a4 ♗a7 8 d5 ♘ce7 9 b4 f5 10 ♘ec3 ♘f6 11 ♗e2 0-0 12 ♘b5 ♗b8 13 ♘bc3 c6 14 b5 cxd5 15 cxd5 b6 16 ♗c4 ♘g6 17 0-0 f4 18 ♗d3 ♘d7 19 ♕h5 ♕e8 20 ♘e4 ♗c7 21 exf4 exf4 22 ♗b2 ♘de5 23 ♘g5 h6 24 ♗xg6 ♘xg6 25 ♖fe1 ♘e5 26 ♕xe8 ♖xe8 27 ♗xe5 dxe5 28 ♘e4 ♗d7 29 ♘ac3 a4 30 ♖ab1 ♖ec8 31 d6 ♗d8 32 ♖b4 ♔f7 33 f3 ♔e6 34 ♖d1 g5 35 g4 fxg3 36 hxg3 h5 37 ♔f2 ♖a7 38 ♔e3 ♗e8 39 f4 exf4+ 40 gxf4 g4 41 ♖d5 ♗f6 42 f5+ ♔f7 43 ♘xa4 ♖b8 44 ♘xf6 ♔xf6 45 ♔f4 ♖g7 46 ♘c3 ♗d7 47 ♘e4+ ♔f7 48 f6 ♖gg8 49 ♖xh5 ♖h8 50 ♖e5 ♖bd8 51 ♖e7+ ♔f8 52 a4 ♖h1 53 ♖b2 ♗e8 54 ♖d2 ♗f7 55 ♔xg4 ♗b3 56 ♘g5 ♖a8 57 ♘h7+ ♔g8 58 ♘g5 ♖xa4+ 59 ♔f5 ♖f1+ 60 ♔g6 ♖a8 61 ♖g7+ ♔f8 62 d7 **1-0** L/N3030

**1861-★AV-2** 24 vii 61
**Van't Kruijs, M.= Anderssen, A.**
Amsterdam
1 c4 f5 2 d4 e6 3 ♘c3 ♘f6 4 e3 ♗b4 5 ♗d2 c5 6 a3 cxd4 7 exd4 ♗a5 8 b4 ♗b6 9 ♗f4 a6 10 ♘f3 ♗c7 11 ♗xc7 ♕xc7 12 ♗d3 b5 13 c5 ♗b7 14 0-0 0-0 15 h3 ♘c6 16 ♕b3 ♘e7 17 ♘e5 ♘e4 18 ♗xe4 fxe4 19 ♖fe1 ♘f5 20 ♖ad1 ♖ad8 21 ♘xe4 ♘xd4 22 ♖xd4 ♕xe5 23 ♕e3 ♖f4 24 g3 ♖f3 25 ♕xf3 ♕xd4 26 ♕c3 ♕d5 27 f4 ♖f8 28 ♕d2 ♕f5 29 ♘f2 ♗c6 30 ♖e5 ♕b1+ 31 ♕e1 ♕a2 32 ♕e3 ♖f6 33 g4 ♕b1+ 34 ♔h2 ♕f1 35 ♔g3 ♕g2+ 36 ♔h4 h6 37 ♘e4 ♗xe4 38 ♖xe4 ♔h7 39 ♖d4 e5 40 fxe5 ♖f3 41 ♕e4+ ♔h8 42 ♕a8+ ½-½ L/N3030

**1861-★AV-3** 17 vii 61
**Anderssen, A.+ Van't Kruijs, M.**
Amsterdam
1 e4 c5 2 d4 d5 3 exd5 ♕xd5 4 dxc5 ♕xc5 5 ♗e3 ♕e5 6 ♘c3 ♘c6 7 ♘f3 ♕a5 8 ♗b5 ♗g4 9 ♕d5 ♕c7 10 ♘e5 e6 11 ♕c4 ♕xe5 12 ♗xc6+ bxc6 13 ♕xc6+ ♔e7 14 ♕xa8 ♘h6 15 0-0 ♘f5 16 ♗g5+ f6 17 ♕xa7+ ♔e8 18 ♖fe1 ♕d4 19 ♖xe6+ **1-0** L/N3030

**1861-★AV-4** 17 vii 61
**Van't Kruijs, M.= Anderssen, A.**
Amsterdam
1 c4 f5 2 d4 e6 3 a3 ♘f6 4 ♘c3 c5 5 d5 ♕b6 6 f3 e5 7 e4 d6 8 ♗d3 f4 9 g4 ♗e7 10 h4 ♕d8 11 ♕e2 ♘a6 12 ♗d2 ♘c7 13 b4 cxb4 14 axb4 0-0 15 b5

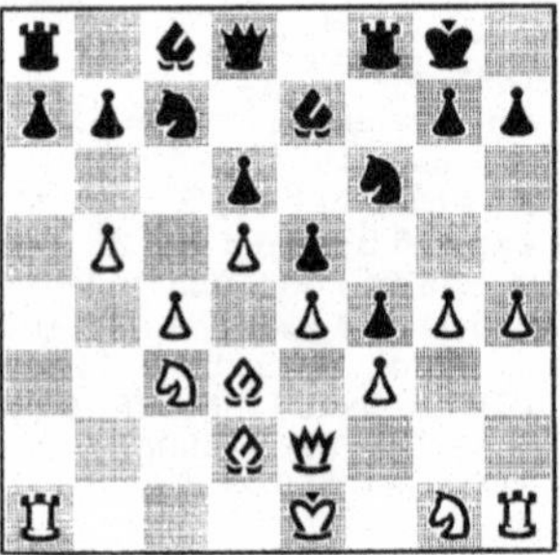

15 ... ♘xg4 16 fxg4 f3 17 ♕f2 ♗xg4 18 ♘d1 ♘e8 19 ♕g3 h5 20 ♘f2 ♕b6 21 ♘gh3 ♘f6 22 ♘g5 ♕d4 23 0-0 a6 24 bxa6 ♖xa6 25 ♖xa6 bxa6 26 ♖b1 ♗d8 27 ♖b7 ♗b6 28 ♔f1 ♘d7 29 ♗e1 ♕e3 30 ♘e6 ♖f7 31 c5 dxc5 32 ♗xa6 c4 33 ♗xc4 ♕c1 34 ♗d3 ♕a1 35 ♘g5 ♖e7 36 d6 ♖e8 37 ♗c4+ ♔h8 38 ♘f7+ ♔h7 39 ♘g5+ ♔h8 40 ♘f7+ ♔h7 ½-½ L/N3030

**1861-★AV-5** 16 vii 61
**Van't Kruijs, M.– Anderssen, A.**
Amsterdam
1 c4 f5 2 d4 e6 3 ♘c3 ♗b4 4 f3 ♗xc3+ 5 bxc3 ♘f6 6 ♗g5 c5 7 e4 fxe4 8 ♗xf6 ♕xf6 9 fxe4 ♕h4+ 10 ♔d2 0-0 11 ♔d3 cxd4 12 ♘f3 ♕f4 13 cxd4 d5 14 ♕e2 ♘a6 15 e5 ♗d7 16 ♖b1 ♕f5+ **0-1** L/N3030

**1861-★AV-6** vii 61
**Anderssen, A.+ Van't Kruijs, M.**
Amsterdam
1 e4 e6 2 d4 d5 3 exd5 exd5 4 ♘f3 ♘f6 5 ♗d3 c5 6 0-0 ♘c6 7 ♗g5 c4 8 ♖e1+ ♗e7 9 ♗xf6 gxf6 10 ♗e2 ♗f5 11 ♘c3 a6 12 ♘h4 ♗e6 13 ♗g4 ♕d7 14 ♗xe6 fxe6 15 ♕h5+ ♔d8 16 ♖ad1 ♔c7 17 ♕f7 ♔d6

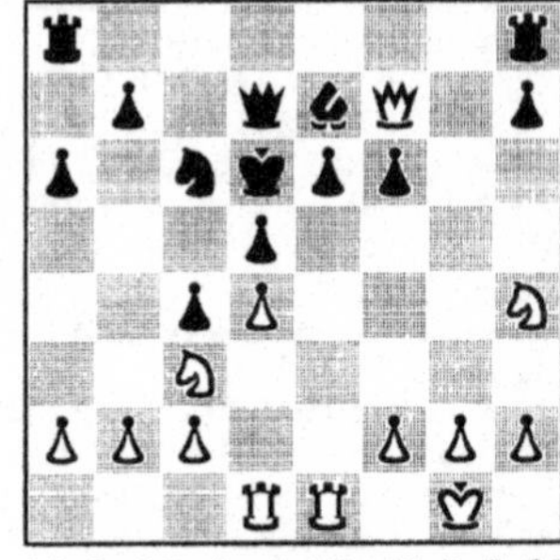

18 ♘e4+ dxe4 19 d5 ♘e5 20 dxe6+ ♔c6 21 ♖xd7 ♘xf7 22 ♖xe7 ♘d6 23 f3 f5 24 g4 fxg4 25 fxe4 ♖ae8 26 ♘f5 ♘xf5 27 ♖xe8 ♖xe8 28 exf5 ♔d6 29 f6 ♖xe6 30 ♖d1+ ♔e5 31 f7 **1-0** L/N3030

**1861-★AV-7** vii 61
**Anderssen, A.+ Van't Kruijs, M.**
Amsterdam [Journoud]
1 e4 e6 2 d4 d5 3 exd5 exd5 4 ♘f3 ♗d6 5 ♗d3 ♘f6 6 0-0 0-0 7 h3 h6 8 c4 c6 9 ♘c3 b6 10 cxd5 ♘xd5 11 ♘xd5 cxd5 12 ♘e5 ♗xe5 13 dxe5 f5 14 f4 ♘a6 15 b4 ♘xb4 16 ♗a3 ♘xd3 [□ 16 ... a5] 17 ♗xf8 ♗a6 [17 ... ♘xf4? 18 ♗d6 (△ 19 ♖xf4) 18 ... ♘~ 19 ♕xd5++–] 18 ♗d6 ♗c4 19 ♕h5 ♕d7 20 ♖f3 ♕f7 21

♕h4 ♘c5! [△ 22 ... ♘e4] 22 ♗xc5 bxc5 23 ♖g3 ♔h7 24 ♖g5 ♗d3 25 g4 ♖b8 26 gxf5 ♗xf5 27 ♖g2 ♕e6 [□ 27 ... ♖b1+ 28 ♖xb1 ♗xb1 △ 29 ... d4] 28 ♕g3 g6 29 ♔h2 ♖b4? [29 ... d4] 30 h4 h5 31 ♕g5 a5 32 ♖c1 c4 33 ♕d8 ♖b5 34 ♖d2 ♕c6 35 a4 ♖c5 36 ♖cd1 ♗e6 37 ♕e7+ ♔h6 38 ♖b2 ♗c8 39 f5!! [△ 40 ♕f8+ ♔h7 41 fxg6+ ♕xg6 42 ♖g2] 39 ... ♕c7 [39 ... ♗xf5 40 ♖b7+−] 40 ♕g5+ ♔h7 41 ♕xg6+ ♔h8 42 ♕xh5+ [42 ♕h6+!] **1-0** L/N6016

**1861-★AV-8** vii 61
**Anderssen,A.– Versteeven,J.F.**
Rotterdam
⟨♖a1⟩ 1 e4 e5 2 ♘f3 d6 3 d4 f5 4 ♗c4 c6 5 ♘c3 ♘f6 6 dxe5 ♘xe4 7 ♘xe4 fxe4 8 ♘g5 d5 9 ♗b3 ♗e7 10 ♕h5+ g6 11 ♕h6 ♗f8 12 ♕h4 h6 13 0-0 ♗g7 14 ♕g3 hxg5 15 ♗xg5 ♕c7 16 f4 ♗f5 17 c4 d4 18 c5 ♘a6 19 ♖c1 ♔d7 20 ♖c4 ♖ae8 21 ♖xd4+ ♔c8 22 ♕c3

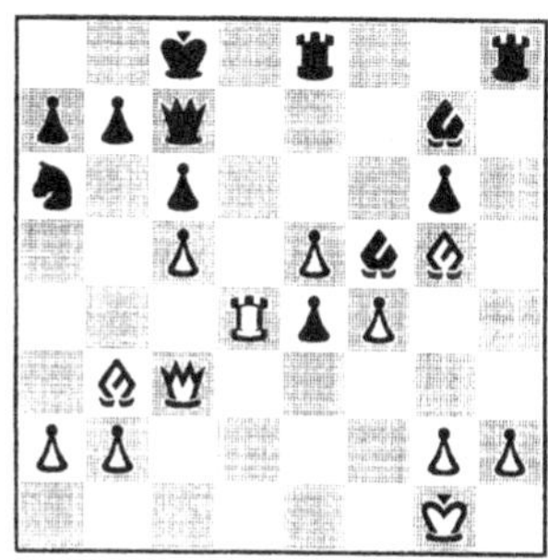

22 ... ♖xe5 23 fxe5 ♗xe5 24 g3 ♕g7 25 ♗e3 ♘c7 26 ♕d2 ♕e7 27 ♖a4 a6 28 ♗c4 ♕h7 29 ♕f2 ♖d8 30 ♗e2 ♘b5 31 g4 ♗e6 32 ♖xe4 ♕g7 33 ♗g5 ♖f8 34 ♕xf8+ ♕xf8 35 ♖xe5 ♘d4 36 ♗d1 ♗d5 37 ♗e7 ♕f4 **0-1** L/N3031

**1861-★A?-1** vii 61
**?– Anderssen, A.**
Rotterdam [Journoud]
1 e4 e5 2 ♗c4 f5 3 exf5 ♘f6 4 g4 d5 5 ♗b3 ♗c5 6 d3 h5 7 g5 ♘g4 8 ♘h3 ♗xf5 9 f3 0-0 10 ♘c3 [10 fxg4 ♗xg4 11 ♕d2 ♗xh3−+] 10 ... c6 11 ♕e2 ♘a6 12 a3 [12 ♗d2 △ 13 0-0] 12 ... ♘c7 13 ♘d1 ♕d6 14 ♘hf2 ♘xf2 15 ♘xf2 ♘e6 16 h4 ♘d4 17 ♕d1 e4 18 dxe4 ♕g3 19 ♕d3 ♗xe4 20 fxe4 ♕xf2+ 21 ♔d1 ♘xb3 22 ♕xb3 ♖f3 23 ♕a4 ♖af8 24 exd5 [24 ... ♖e3 25 ♗xe3 ♗xe3 26 ♕b4 ♕f3+ 27 ♔e1 ♖e8−+] **0-1** L/N6016

**1861-★A?-2** vii 61
**Anderssen, A.+?**
Rotterdam
1 e4 e5 2 ♘f3 ♘c6 3 ♗c4 ♗c5 4 b4 ♗xb4 5 c3 ♗c5 6 0-0 d6 7 d4 exd4 8 cxd4 ♗b6 9 d5 ♘a5 10 ♗b2 ♘f6 11 ♗d3 0-0 12 ♘c3 ♗g4 13 ♘a4 ♘d7 14 ♘xb6 axb6 15 ♕c2 ♗xf3? 16 gxf3 ♘e5 17 ♔h1 ♕f6 18 ♖g1! ♕xf3+ 19 ♖g2 ♕xd3? 20 ♕xd3 ♘xd3 21 ♖xg7+ ♔h8 22 ♖g8+ ♔xg8 23 ♖g1# **1-0** L/N6016

**1861-★A?-3** vii 61
**Anderssen, A.+?**
Rotterdam
1 e4 e5 2 ♘f3 ♘c6 3 ♗c4 ♗c5 4 b4 ♗xb4 5 c3 ♗c5 6 0-0 d6 7 d4 exd4 8 cxd4 ♗b6 9 d5 ♘a5 10 ♗b2 ♘f6 11 ♗d3 0-0 12 ♘c3 ♗g4 13 ♘a4 ♘d7 14 ♘xb6 axb6 15 ♕c2 ♗xf3 16 gxf3 ♘e5 17 ♔h1 ♕f6 18 ♖g1 ♕xf3+ 19 ♖g2 ♕xd3 20 ♕xd3 ♘xd3 21 ♖xg7+ **1-0** L/N3031

**1861-★A?-4** vii 61
**Anderssen, A.+?**
Rotterdam
1 e4 e5 2 f4 exf4 3 ♘f3 g5 4 h4 g4 5 ♘g5 h6 6 ♘xf7 ♔xf7 7 ♕xg4 ♘f6 8 ♕xf4 ♗d6 9 ♕f2 ♖g8 10 ♗c4+ ♔f8 11 ♗xg8 ♔xg8 12 d3 ♕f8 13 ♖h3 ♕g7 14 ♘c3 ♘h5 15 ♘d5 ♘a6 16 ♗e3 ♗g3 17 ♖xg3 ♕xg3 18 ♘f6+ ♔h8 19 ♘xh5 ♕xf2+ 20 ♔xf2 d6 21 ♗d4+ ♔h7 22 ♘f6+ ♔g6 23 h5+ ♔f7 24 ♔g3 c5 25 ♗c3 b5 26 ♖f1 b4 27 ♘d5+ ♔e8 28 ♗d2 ♔d7 29 c4 ♔c6 30 ♖f6 **1-0** L/N3031

**1861-★A?-5** vii 61
**?– Anderssen, A.**
Rotterdam
1 d4 d5 2 c4 dxc4 3 e4 e5 4 d5 f5 5 ♘c3 ♘f6 6 ♗xc4 ♗c5 7 ♗g5 ♕d6 8 ♘f3 a6 9 0-0 f4 10 a3 ♗g4 11 b4 ♗a7 12 b5 ♘bd7 13 ♗xf6 ♕xf6 14 ♖c1 g5 15 ♗e2 h5 16 ♘a4 ♗xf3 17 ♗xf3 g4 18 ♗e2 g3 19 ♗xh5+ ♔e7 20 bxa6 gxf2+ 21 ♔h1 ♕h4 22 ♖xc7 ♖xh5 23 d6+ ♔f6 24 h3 ♖g8 25 ♕f3 ♖g3 **0-1** L/N3031

**1861-★A?-6** vii 61
**?– Anderssen, A.**
Rotterdam
1 e4 e5 2 c3 d5 3 exd5 ♕xd5 4 b4 f5 5 ♕e2 ♘d7 6 ♗b2 ♘gf6 7 f3 c5 8 c4 ♕e6 9 b5 ♗d6 10 ♘h3 0-0 11 ♘g5 ♕e8 12 h4 b6 13 ♕e3 ♗b7 14 ♘c3 e4 15 f4 ♘g4 16 ♕g3 e3 17 d3 ♘f2 18 ♖g1 ♘f6 19 ♗e2 ♘6g4 20 ♘f3 ♖d8 21 ♘h2 ♗b8 22 ♘xg4 fxg4 23 ♗xg4 ♘xd3+ 24 ♔d1



♘xb2+ 25 ♔c2 ♖d2+ 26 ♔b3 ♘xc4 27 ♕h3 ...? 30 **0-1** L/N3031

**1861-★A?-7** vii 61
**Anderssen, A.+?**
Rotterdam
1 e4 e5 2 ♘f3 ♘c6 3 ♗c4 ♘f6 4 ♘g5 d5 5 exd5 ♘a5 6 d3 h6 7 ♘f3 ♗d6 8 0-0 c6 9 dxc6 ♘xc6 10 ♘c3 0-0 11 h3 ♗f5 12 ♗e3 ♖c8 13 ♕d2 ♔h7 14 a3 ♗b8 15 ♖ae1 ♘d4 16 ♗xd4 exd4 17 ♘e2 ♕c7 18 ♘exd4 ♗g6 19 ♘e5 ♕c5 20 ♘xg6 fxg6 21 ♘e6 ♕d6 22 ♘xf8+ ♖xf8 23 f4 ♘h5 24 ♖e6 ♕c5+ 25 ♕f2 ♕xf2+ 26 ♖xf2 ♘xf4 27 ♖e7 ♗d6 28 ♖d7 ♗c5 29 d4 ♗b6 30 c3 ♖f6 31 ♔h2 ♘h5 32 ♖fe2 ♖f8 33 ♖xb7 **1-0** L/N3031

**1861-★A?-8** vii 61
**?– Anderssen, A.**
Rotterdam
1 e4 e5 2 ♘f3 ♘c6 3 ♗c4 ♗c5 4 0-0 ♘f6 5 d3 h6 6 ♘c3 d6 7 h3 g5 8 ♘a4 g4 9 hxg4 ♗xg4 10 ♘xc5 dxc5 11 c3 ♕d6 12 ♗e3 0-0-0 13 ♕e2 ♖dg8 14 ♖ad1 ♖g7 15 ♔h1 ♖hg8 16 d4 ♘xe4 17 dxc5 ♕g6 18 ♗d3 ♕h5+ 19 ♔g1 ♗xf3 **0-1** L/N3031

**1861̂-★BK-1**
**Kolisch,I.F.von+ Barnes,T.W.**
London
1 e4 g6 2 d4 f6 3 ♗d3 e6 4 ♘f3 ♘h6 5 e5 fxe5 6 ♗g5 ♗e7 7 ♗xh6 exd4 8 ♗g7 ♖g8 9 ♗xd4 c5 10 ♗e5 ♘c6 11 0-0 a6 12 c4 ♘xe5 13 ♘xe5 ♗f6 14 f4 d6 15 ♘f3 ♗xb2 16 ♘bd2 ♗xa1 17 ♕xa1 b6 18 ♖e1 ♖a7 19 ♘g5 ♕e7 20 ♘de4 ♖f8 21 ♕b2 b5 22 cxb5 d5 23 bxa6 dxe4

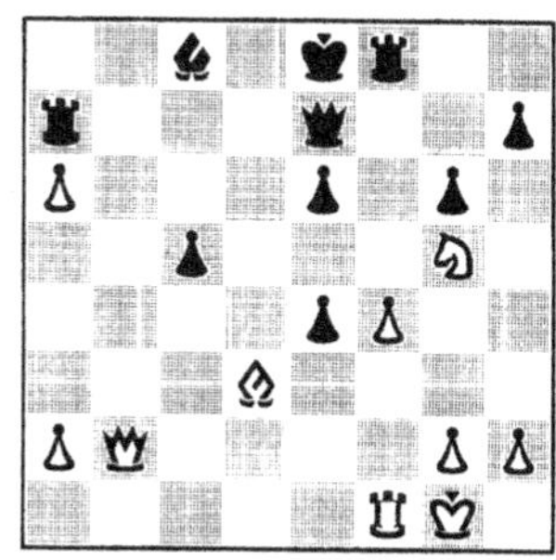

24 ♗b5+ ♗d7 25 ♖xe4 ♖f6 26 ♗xd7+ ♔xd7 27 ♕b6 ♔c8 28 ♖e5 ♕d7 29 ♖xc5+ ♖c7 30 ♕b7+ ♔d8 31 ♕b8+ ♖c8 32 ♖xc8+ ♕xc8 33 a7 **1-0** L/N6047-1864

**1861-★BK-2**
**Kolisch,I.F.von= Boden,S.S.**
London [Staunton]
1 e4 e5 2 ♘f3 d6 3 d4 e×d4 4 ♗c4 ♗e7 5 0-0 ♘f6 6 ♕×d4 0-0 7 ♘c3 ♘c6 8 ♕d3 h6 9 ♗f4 ♘h5 10 ♗e3 ♗g4 11 ♘d5 ♗×f3 12 g×f3 ♘e5 13 ♕e2 [△ 14 f4] 13 ... ♘×c4 14 ♕×c4 c6 15 ♘×e7+ ♕×e7 16 ♔h1 ♕f6 17 ♕e2 ♘f4 18 ♕d2 ♘g6 19 f4 d5! 20 f5 [20 e×d5?-+] 20 ... d×e4 21 f×g6 ♕f3+ 22 ♔g1 ♖ad8 23 g×f7+ [23 ♕c1? ♖d6 24 g×f7+ (24 ♗f4 ♖×g6+ 25 ♗g3 f5-+) 24 ... ♖×f7 25 ♖fd1 ♖g6+ 26 ♔f1 ♖g2 27 ♖d2 ♖×h2-+] 23 ... ♔h7 24 ♕c1 ♕g4+ [24 ... ♖d6 25 ♗f4] 25 ♔h1 ♕f3+ ½-½ M954-1861

**1861-★BP-1 ●○**
**Paulsen,L.+ Blackburne,J.H.**
Manchester [Blackburne]
1 e4 d6 2 d4 e6 3 ♗d3 b6 4 ♘e2 ♗b7 5 0-0 g6 6 ♗e3 ♗g7 7 ♘d2 ♘d7 8 f4 ♘h6 9 ♘f3 f5 10 e5 ♕e7 11 ♕d2 ♘f7 12 ♖ad1 0-0-0 13 a4 d×e5 14 f×e5 h6 15 a5 b5 16 a6 ♗a8 17 ♗×b5 ♘d×e5 18 ♘×e5 ♘×e5 19 ♕c3 ♘g4 20 ♗f4 e5 21 d×e5 ♘×e5 22 ♘d4 c5 23 ♖fe1 ♖×d4 24 ♖×d4 ♘f3+ 25 g×f3 ♗×d4+ 26 ♔g2 ♕h4 27 ♗g3 ♕g4? 28 ♕b3 f4 29 ♗c4 ♕g5 30 ♗g8! ♗e3 31 ♖×e3 f×e3 32 ♕b8+ ♔d7 33 ♕×a7+ 1-0 L/N3036

**1861-★BP-2** 25 xi 61
**Paulsen,L.+Blackburne, J.H.**
Manchester [Löwenthal]
1 e4 e6 2 d4 d5 3 ♘c3 ♗b4 4 ♗d3 c5 5 e×d5 e×d5 [5 ... c×d4 6 ♗b5+±] 6 ♗b5+ ♘c6 7 ♘e2 ♘f6 8 0-0 0-0 9 d×c5 ♗×c5 10 ♗g5 ♗e6 [10 ... d4 11 ♗×f6 ♕×f6 12 ♘e4 ♕e7 13 ♗×c6 b×c6 14 ♘×c5 ♕×c5 15 ♕×d4±] 11 ♘f4 d4 12 ♘e4 ♗e7 13 ♗×f6 ♗×f6 14 ♘×e6 f×e6 15 ♕g4 ♕d5 16 ♗a4 ♘e5 17 ♕e2 ♘g6 18 ♗b3 ♕c6 19 ♕g4 ♖ae8 20 ♖ae1 ♕b6 21 ♘×f6+ ♖×f6 22 ♖e4 ♖d8 23 ♖×e6 ♖×e6 24 ♕×e6+ ♕×e6 25 ♗×e6+ ♔f8 26 f4 d3 27 c×d3 ♖×d3 28 g3 ♖d2 29 ♖f2 ♖d6 30 ♗f5 h6 31 ♗×g6 ♖×g6 32 ♖c2 ♖b6 33 b3 ♔e7 34 ♔f2 ♔f6 35 ♔f3 ♖d6 36 h4 ♖d3+ 37 ♔g4 h5+ 38 ♔h3 ♖d7 39 ♖c3 a6 40 a4 ♖d6 41 g4 h×g4+ 42 ♔×g4 g6 43 ♖c4 b6 44 b4 ♖e6 45 b5 a×b5 46 a×b5 ♖d6 47 ♖c6 ♖×c6 48 b×c6 ♔e6 49 c7 ♔d7 50 f5 1-0 M324

**1861-★BP-3 ●○**
**Paulsen,L.+ Blackburne,J.H.**
Manchester [Löwenthal]
1 e4 d6 2 d4 e6 3 ♗d3 b6 4 ♘e2 ♗b7 5 0-0 g6 6 ♗e3 ♗g7 7 ♘d2 ♘d7 8 f4 ♘h6 9 ♘f3 f5 10 e5 ♕e7 11 ♕d2 ♘f7 12 ♖ad1 0-0-0 13 a4 d×e5 14 f×e5 h6 15 a5 b5 16 a6 [16 ♗×b5 ♘d×e5] 16 ... ♗a8 [16 ... ♗×a6 17 ♖a1±] 17 ♗×b5 ♘d×e5 18 ♘×e5 ♘×e5 19 ♕c3 ♘g4 20 ♗f4 e5 21 d×e5 ♘×e5 22 ♘d4 c5 23 ♖fe1

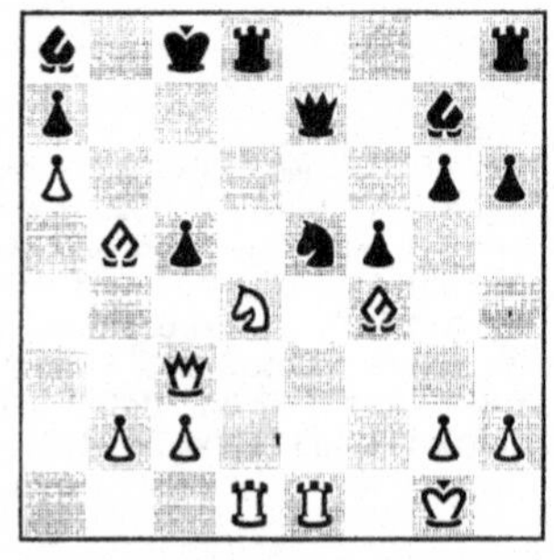

23 ... ♖×d4 24 ♖×d4 ♘f3+ 25 g×f3 ♗×d4+ 26 ♔g2 ♕h4 27 ♗g3 ♕g4 28 ♕b3 f4 29 ♗c4 ♕g5 30 ♗g8 ♗e3 31 ♖×e3 f×e3 32 ♕b8+ ♔d7 33 ♕×a7+ 1-0 M324

**1861-★BS-1**
**Steinkühler, A- Blackburne, J.H.**
Manchester [Blackburne]
1 e4 e5 2 ♘f3 ♘c6 3 d4 e×d4 4 ♗c4 ♗c5 5 ♘g5 ♘h6 6 ♘×f7 ♘×f7 7 ♗×f7+ ♔×f7 8 ♕h5+ g6 9 ♕d5+!? ♔g7 10 ♕×c5 d5!∓ 11 e×d5 ♖e8+ 12 ♔d1 ♕f6 13 f3 [13 d×c6 ♗g4+-+] 13 ... ♕e5 14 ♕c4 d3 15 ♕×d3 ♗f5 16 ♕c4 b5 17 ♕f1 ♘d4 18 ♘a3 b4 19 g4 ♗×g4 20 f×g4 ♕×d5! 21 ♗d2 b×a3 22 ♗c3 ♔g8 23 ♗×d4 a×b2 24 ♖b1 ♕×d4+ 0-1 L/N3036

**1861-★B?-1**
**Barnes,T.W.& Staunton,H.+? & ?**
London [Staunton]
1 e4 e5 2 ♘f3 ♘c6 3 ♗c4 ♗c5 4 0-0 d6 5 h3 [5 c3 ♗g4∓] 5 ... f5? 6 d4 e×d4 7 ♘g5 ♕f6 [7 ... ♘e5 8 ♗×g8 ♖×g8 9 ♕h5+] 8 ♘f7 ♘e5 9 ♗g5! [9 ♘×h8] 9 ... ♕g6 10 ♘×h8 ♕×g5 11 f4 d3+ 12 ♔h1 ♕h4 13 f×e5 f×e4 14 ♕e1 ♕×e1 15 ♖×e1 ♘e7 16 e×d6 c×d6 17 ♗f7+ ♔f8 18 c×d3 e×d3 19 ♘c3 d2 20 ♖f1 ♘f5 21 ♗b3 ♔e8 22 ♘e4 ♘e3 23 ♖f3 ♗d7 24 ♘×c5 1-0 M954-1861

**1861-★CM-1**
**Chapelle- Mosenge**
[Staunton]
1 e4 e5 2 ♘f3 ♘c6 3 c3 f5? 4 e×f5? [4 d4 d6 5 d×e5 f×e4 6 ♘g5 d5 7 e6 ♘e5 (7 ... ♘h6 8 f3) 8 ♕d4 ♕d6 9 ♘a3±] 4 ... d5 5 ♗b5 ♗d6 6 d4 e4 7 ♘e5 ♗×e5 8 ♕h5+ ♔f8 9 ♗×c6 ♘f6 10 ♕g5 h6 11 ♕g6 ♗d6 12 ♗a4 c6 13 0-0 ♗d7 [△ 14 ... ♗e8] 14 f4 ♕c8 15 ♕g3 h5 16 b4 b5 17 ♗c2 ♗×f5 18 a4 h4 19 ♕e1 a6 20 a×b5 c×b5 21 ♘a3 ♖h6 22 ♖f2 ♖g6 23 ♗b3 ♖g4 24 ♖fa2 ♗×f4 25 ♗×f4 ♖×f4 26 ♘×b5 ♔e7 27 ♕e3 g5 28 ♖a5 h3 29 g3 ♘g4 30 ♕c1

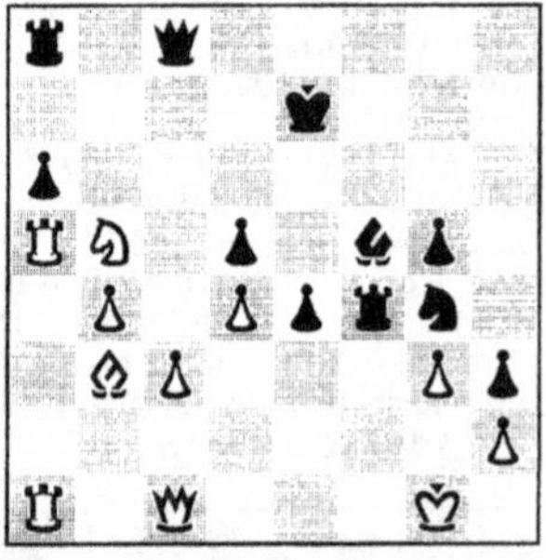

30 ... e3! 31 g×f4 g×f4 32 ♗×d5 ♘f2 33 ♕e1 ♗d3 34 ♖1a2 ♕g8+ 35 ♗×g8 ♖×g8# 0-1 M954-1861

**1861-★CP-1** ix 61
**Carstanjen, A.- Paulsen, L.**
Köln [Anderssen & Zukertort]
1 e4 e5 2 ♘f3 ♘c6 3 ♗c4 ♗c5 4 b4 ♗×b4 5 c3 ♗a5 6 d4 e×d4 7 0-0 d6 8 ♕b3 ♕f6 9 e5 d×e5 10 ♖e1 ♘h6 11 ♗a3 ♗d7 12 ♘bd2 0-0-0 13 ♘e4 ♕g6 14 ♘c5 ♗b6 15 ♘×d7 ♖×d7 16 ♖×e5 d×c3 17 ♗b5 ♘f5 18 ♖ae1 ♖hd8 19 ♖5e2 ♘fd4 20 ♘×d4 ♗×d4 21 ♗e7 ♖×e7 22 ♗×c6 ♕×c6 23 ♖×e7 c2 24 ♖c1 [24 ♕a3 ♗×f2+ 25 ♔×f2 ♖d2+ 26 ♖7e2 ♖×e2+ 27 ♔×e2 ♕×g2+ 28 ♔d3 ♕f3+ 29 ♖e3 ♕d1+ 30 ♔e4 c1♕-+] 24 ... ♗×f2+ 25 ♔f1 ♗c5 26 ♖×f7 ♕a6+ 27 ♔e1 ♖e8+ 28 ♔d2 ♕e2+ 29 ♔c3 ♖e3+ 30 ♔b2 ♗d4+ 31 ♔a3 ♕a6+ 32 ♔b4 c5# 0-1 L/N6051-1868

**1861-★CP-2** ix 61
**Paulsen, L.= Carstanjen, A.**
Köln [Anderssen & Zukertort]
1 e4 e5 2 ♘f3 ♘c6 3 ♗c4 ♗c5 4 b4 ♗b6 5 0-0 d6 6 a4 a6 7 c3 ♗g4 8 a5 ♗a7 9 b5 a×b5 10 ♗×b5 ♘e7 11 d4 e×d4 12 c×d4 ♗×f3 13 g×f3 0-0 14 d5 ♘d4 15 ♗a4 ♘g6! 16 ♖a3 ♕h4 17 ♔h1 ♘e5 18 ♗b2 ♘d×f3 19 ♖×f3 ♘g4 20 h3 ♘×f2+ 21 ♖1×f2 ♗×f2 22 ♗c2 ♖×a5 23 ♕d2 ♗b6 24 ♘a3 f6 25 ♘c4 ♖a6 26 ♘×b6 ♖×b6 27 ♗d4 ♖a6 28

♕c3 ♖f7 ½-½ L/N6051-1868

**1861-★DP-1 ●○** xii 61
**Paulsen, L.+De Vere, C.**
London
1 e4 e6 2 d4 d5 3 ♘c3 ♗b4 4 exd5 exd5 5 ♘f3 ♘f6 6 ♗d3 ♘c6 7 0-0 0-0 8 ♘e2 ♗g4 9 c3 ♗d6 10 ♘g3 h6 11 h3 ♗e6 12 ♕e2 ♕e7 13 ♘e5 ♘h7 14 f4 ♕h4 15 ♘g6 ♕xg3 16 ♖f3 ♗g4 17 hxg4 ♕xg4 18 ♘xf8 ♘xf8 19 ♕f2 ♘e7 20 f5 ♘h7 21 ♗f4 ♗xf4 22 ♖xf4 ♕g5 23 ♖e1 ♕f6 24 ♖f3 ♘g5 25 ♖fe3 ♘e4 26 ♗xe4 dxe4 27 ♖xe4 ♘xf5 28 ♖e8+ ♖xe8 29 ♖xe8+ ♔h7 30 g4 ♘d6 31 ♕xf6 gxf6 32 ♖e7 **1-0**
M324

**1861-★D?-1**
**Deacon, F.H.+?**
London [Staunton]
⟨♘b1⟩ 1 e4 e5 2 f4 ♗c5 3 ♘f3 d6 4 ♗c4 ♗g4 5 fxe5 dxe5 6 ♗xf7+ ♔f8 7 d4 exd4 [7 ... ♕xd4 8 ♘xd4 ♗xd1 9 ♗d5 c6 10 ♘e6+] 8 0-0 ♘f6 9 ♗b3 ♘c6 10 ♕d3 ♗xf3 11 ♕xf3 ♘e5 12 ♕h5 ♕e7 13 ♗g5 ♘ed7 14 e5 ♘xe5 15 ♖xf6+ ♕xf6 16 ♗xf6 gxf6 17 ♖e1 d3+ 18 ♔h1 d2 19 ♕h6+ ♔e8 20 ♕xd2 ♖d8 21 ♕f4 ♖f8 22 ♕c4 ♗e7 23 ♕xc7 ♖d7 24 ♗a4 ♘c6 25 ♕c8+ ♖d8 26 ♕xb7 **1-0** M954-1861

**1861-★HO-1**
**Hay, Lord A.+Owen, J.**
London [Staunton]
⟨♙f7⟩ 1 e4 d6 2 d4 ♘f6 3 ♘c3 ♗e6 4 f4 ♗f7 5 ♘f3 ♗h5?! 6 ♗c4 ♘xe4?! 7 ♘xe4 d5 8 ♘g3 ♗xf3 9 ♕xf3 dxc4 10 c3 [10 ♕xb7] 10 ... c6 11 f5! [△ 12 ♕h5+] 11 ... ♕d5! 12 ♘e4 ♘d7 13 ♗f4 0-0-0 14 ♗g5? [14 0-0-0] 14 ... ♘f6 15 ♗xf6 exf6 16 0-0-0 ♗e7 17 ♕g4 g5 18 ♖he1 [18 fxg6? f5] 18 ... ♖de8 19 ♕e2 h5 20 ♕c2 ♔b8 [20 ... ♕xf5? 21 ♘d6+] 21 ♕f2 ♕a5 22 ♔b1 h4 23 g4 ♕d8 24 h3 ♗d6 25 d5! ♕c7 26 dxc6 ♗g3 27 ♘xg3 ♖xe1 28 ♕xe1 hxg3 29 cxb7 ♖xh3 30 ♕e8+ ♔xb7 31 ♖d7 ♖h1+ 32 ♔c2 ♖h2+ 33 ♔d1 g2 34 ♖xc7+ ♔xc7 35 ♕e7+ ♔c6 36 ♕xf6+ **1-0** M954-1861

**1861-★KM-1**
**Kolisch, I.F.von+ Mortimer, J.**
Paris
⟨♘b1⟩ 1 e4 e5 2 ♘f3 ♘c6 3 ♗c4 ♗c5 4 b4 ♗xb4 5 c3 ♗a5 6 0-0 ♘f6 7 ♕c2 0-0 8 d4 exd4 9 cxd4 d6 10 ♗g5 h6 11 ♗h4 ♗g4 12 e5 ♗xf3 13 ♗xf6 ♘xd4 14 ♕g6 ♘e2+ 15 ♔h1 ♗xg2+ 16 ♕xg2 **1-0**
M324-1862

**1861-★KM-2**
**Kolisch, I.F.von+ Mortimer, J.**
Paris
⟨♘b1⟩ 1 e4 e5 2 ♘f3 ♘c6 3 ♗c4 ♗c5 4 b4 ♗xb4 5 c3 ♗a5 6 0-0 d6 7 d4 ♗xc3 8 ♗xf7+ ♔xf7 9 ♕b3+ ♗e6 10 d5 ♗xa1 11 dxe6+ ♔e7 12 ♗g5+ ♘f6 13 ♖xa1 ♖b8 14 ♖d1 h6 15 ♗xf6+ gxf6 16 ♘h4 ♘d4 17 ♖xd4 exd4 18 ♘f5+ ♔e8 19 ♕g3 ♕e7 20 ♕g6+ ♔d8 21 ♘xe7 ♔xe7 22 ♕f7+ **1-0**
M324-1862

**1861-★KO-1**
**Owen, J.+Kolisch, I.F. von**
London [Staunton]
1 e4 e5 2 d4 exd4 3 ♘f3 ♘c6 4 ♗c4 ♗c5 5 0-0 ♘f6 6 c3 ♘xe4?! 7 cxd4 ♗e7 8 d5! ♘a5 9 ♗d3 ♘f6 10 b4!? ♗xb4 11 ♕a4 ♘xd5 12 a3 c5 13 axb4 ♘xb4 14 ♖e1+ ♔f8 15 ♗b5 ♘ac6 16 ♗f4 b6 17 ♗d6+ ♔g8 18 ♗c7 ♕f8 19 ♘c3 ♗b7 20 ♖ad1 ♕c8 21 ♗d6 h6 [21 ... a6 22 ♗c4 b5 23 ♗xf7+ ♔xf7 24 ♕b3+ c4 25 ♕b1+-] 22 ♘e5 ♘xe5 23 ♖xe5 ♗c6 24 ♕b3! [△ 25 ♖e7] 24 ... ♔h7 25 ♕xf7 ♖e8 26 ♗e7! [△ 27 ♗f6; △ 27 ♖d6] 26 ... d5 [26 ... ♗xb5 27 ♗f6 (27 ♖d6+-) 27 ... ♖g8 28 ♖g5+-] 27 ♗xc6 [27 ♗f6] 27 ... ♘xc6 [□ 27 ... ♕xc6+-] 28 ♗f6 ♖g8 29 ♖g5 **1-0** M954-1861

**1861-★KP-1** 25 xi 61
**Kipping, J.S.−Paulsen, L.**
Manchester
1 e4 e5 2 ♘f3 ♘c6 3 ♗c4 ♗c5 4 b4 ♗xb4 5 c3 ♗a5 6 ♕b3 ♕f6 7 0-0 d6 8 d4 exd4 9 cxd4 ♗b6 10 e5 dxe5 11 dxe5 ♕g6 12 ♗d2 ♘ge7 13 a4 0-0 14 ♗c3 ♘f5 15 ♕b2 a5 16 ♘bd2 ♗e6 17 ♗d3 ♖ad8 18 ♗e4 ♕h5 19 ♕b5 ♘fd4 20 ♕b2 ♘e2+ 21 ♔h1 ♘xc3 22 ♕xc3 ♘xe5 23 ♘xe5 ♗d4 24 ♕f3 ♕xe5 25 ♖ae1 ♕g5 26 ♕e2 ♗c3 27 ♘f3 ♕f6 28 ♖c1 ♗g4 29 ♕c2 ♗xf3 30 ♗xf3 ♗d2 31 ♖b1 b6 32 ♕xc7 ♗b4 33 ♖bc1 ♗c5 34 ♖c4 ♖d2 35 ♔g1 ♖xf2 36 ♖fc1 ♖xf3+ 37 ♖xc5 bxc5 **0-1** M324

**1861-★KP-2 ●○**
**Paulsen, L.−Kylman**
Manchester [Löwenthal]
1 e4 e6 2 d4 b6 3 ♗d3 ♗b7 4 ♘h3 g6 5 0-0 ♗g7 6 c3 d6 7 ♗e3 ♘d7 8 ♘d2 ♘gf6 9 f4 ♕e7 10 c4 h5 11 ♘f2 0-0-0 12 h3 h4 13 a4 ♘h5 14 ♘h1 f5 15 a5 c5 16 axb6 [16 a6 ♗a8 17 d5 exd5 18 cxd5 ♗xd5] 16 ... cxd4 17 bxa7 ♔c7 18 ♗f2 ♘xf4 19 ♕f3 g5 20 ♗e1 ♘e5 21 ♕d1 ♘exd3 22 ♘b3 ♘xe1 23 ♕xe1 ♗xe4 24 ♕a5+ ♔d7 25 ♘f2 ♘e2+ 26 ♔h1 ♗c6 27 ♘d3 ♔e8 28 ♘b4 ♗a8 29 ♘a6 ♗xg2+ 30 ♔xg2 ♕b7+ 31 ♖f3 ♔d7 32 ♕b5+ ♕xb5 33 cxb5 g4 34 ♖f2 d3 35 ♘a5 [□ 35 hxg4 ♖a8 (35 ... ♖hg8 36 ♘b8+ ♖xb8 37 axb8♕ ♖xb8 38 ♖a7+, 39 ♖xg7) 36 gxf5] 35 ... ♖a8 36 ♘c6 ♗d4 37 ♘xd4 ♘xd4 38 b6 ♔c6 39 ♘c7 ♔xb6 40 ♘xa8+ ♖xa8 41 hxg4 fxg4 42 ♖f4 e5 43 ♖xg4 ♘c2 **0-1** M324

**1861-★KP-3** ix 61
**Kolisch, I.F. von=Paulsen, L.**
London [Staunton]
1 e4 e5 2 ♘f3 ♘c6 3 ♗b5 a6 4 ♗a4 ♘f6 5 0-0 ♗e7 6 d3 d6 7 ♘c3 0-0 8 h3 h6 9 ♘h2 ♘h7 10 f4 exf4 11 ♗xf4 ♗g5! 12 ♕d2 ♘d4 13 ♘f3 ♘xf3+ 14 ♖xf3 c6 15 ♗b3 ♗e6 16 ♘e2 ♗xb3 17 axb3 d5= 18 ♘g3 dxe4 19 ♘xe4 ♕d4+ 20 ♔h1 ♕xb2 21 ♖af1 ♗xf4 22 ♕xf4 ♘g5 23 ♘xg5 hxg5 24 ♕xg5 ♖ae8= **½-½** M954-1861

**1861-★KP-4** ix 61
**Kolisch, I.F. von−Paulsen, L.**
London [Staunton]
1 e4 e5 2 ♘f3 ♘c6 3 ♗c4 ♗c5 4 b4 ♗xb4 5 c3 ♗c5 6 d4 exd4 7 0-0 d6 8 cxd4 ♗b6 9 d5 ♘a5 10 ♗b2 ♘e7 11 ♗d3 [11 ♗xg7!?] 11 ... 0-0 12 ♘c3 ♘g6 13 ♘e2 f6 14 ♕d2 c5∓ 15 ♔h1 ♗d7 16 ♖ac1 a6 17 ♘e1 ♗b5 18 f4 c4 19 ♗b1 c3 20 ♖xc3 ♘c4 21 ♕c1 ♖c8−+ 22 ♗d3 ♗e3 23 ♕c2 ♘d2 24 ♖g1 ♖xc3 25 ♕xc3 ♕b6 26 ♗c1 ♗xg1 27 ♘xg1 ♗xd3 28 ♘xd3 [□ 28 ♕xd3−+] 28 ... ♘xe4 **0-1**
M954-1861

**1861-★KR-1 ○**
**Kolisch, I.F.von− Rainger, F.G.**
Norwich [Staunton]
⟨♘b1⟩ 1 e4 b6 2 d4 ♗b7 3 ♗d3 e6 4 ♘e2 d5 5 e5 c5 6 c3 ♘c6 7 0-0 ♕c7 8 ♗e3 ♗e7 9 ♖c1 c4 10 ♗b1 0-0-0!? 11 b3 ♔b8 12 b4 ♘h6 13 f3 ♘f5 14 ♗f2 g5 15 a4 h5 16 a5 b5 17 ♗c2 ♘xb4!? [17 ... a6] 18 cxb4 ♗xb4 19 ♖b1 ♕xa5 20 ♖a1 ♕b6 21 ♗xf5 exf5 22 ♕b1 ♗e7 23 ♕xf5 ♕g6 24 g4 hxg4 25 fxg4 ♗c8 26 ♕f3 ♕e6 27 ♗g3 ♖h7 [27 ... ♕xg4? 28 e6+] 28 ♖fb1 b4 29 ♖a5 a6 30 ♘c3 ♗b7 31 ♘a4 ♔a7 32 ♗f2 ♖h6 33 ♕e2 [△ 34 ♕xc4 dxc4 35 d5+] 33 ... ♔a8 34 ♕f3 b3! 35 ♘b2 ♗b4 36 ♖a4 ♕g6! 37 ♖ba1 ♕c2 38 ♘d1 b2 39 ♘xb2 ♕xb2 40 ♕xf7 ♖f8 **0-1** M954-1861

**1861-★KR-2 ⬠**
**Rainger, F.G. & Taylor– Kolisch, I.F. von**
Norwich [Staunton]
1 a3 e5 2 c4 ♘f6 3 ♘c3 d5 4 cxd5 ♘xd5 5 e3 ♘f6 6 ♗c4 ♗d6 7 ♘ge2 0-0 8 d4 exd4 9 ♘xd4 ♘c6 10 ♘xc6 bxc6 11 ♕c2 ♕e7 12 ♗d3 h6 13 ♘e4 c5 14 ♘xf6+ ♕xf6 15 ♗d2 ♗b7 16 ♗c3 ♗e5 17 ♗xe5 ♕xe5 18 0-0 ♖ad8 19 ♖ad1 ♖d6 20 ♕e2 f5 21 f4 ♕e7 22 ♗c4+? ♔h8 23 ♖xd6? cxd6 24 ♖d1 ♖f6 25 ♗d5 ♗xd5 26 ♖xd5 ♖e6 27 ♖d3 d5 28 ♕d2 d4 29 exd4 ♖e2 30 ♕c3 ♖e1+ 31 ♔f2 ♕e2+ 32 ♔g3 ♕g4+ 33 ♔f2 ♖e2+ **0-1**
M954-1861

**1861-★KS-1**
**Kolisch, I.F. von– Sabourov**
London
⟨♘b1⟩ 1 e4 e5 2 f4 d5 3 exd5 e4 4 ♗b5+ c6 5 dxc6 bxc6 6 ♗c4 ♘f6 7 d4 ♘bd7 8 ♘e2 ♘b6 9 ♗b3 ♗a6 10 ♘g3 h5 11 ♗e3 ♘g4 12 ♗g1 ♕h4 13 ♕d2 e3 14 ♗xe3 ♘xe3 15 ♕xe3+ ♕e7 16 ♕xe7+ ♗xe7 17 0-0-0 ♗c4 18 ♖he1 ♗xb3 19 axb3 g6 20 f5 ♔d7 21 ♘e4 ♖he8 22 fxg6 fxg6 23 c4 ♔c7 24 ♖f1 ♖f8 25 ♖fe1 ♖ae8 26 ♖e2 ♗g5+ 27 ♔c2 ♖f4 28 ♔d3 ♘d7 29 d5 ♖fxe4 **0-1** M324-1861

**1861-★KS-2**
**Kolisch, I.F. von+ Sabourov**
⟨♘b1⟩ 1 e4 e5 2 ♘f3 d6 3 ♗c4 ♗e7 4 d4 exd4 5 c3 ♘f6 6 ♘g5 0-0 7 0-0 d5 8 exd5 ♘xd5 9 ♘xh7 ♘b6 10 ♗d3 ♖e8 11 ♕h5 g6 12 ♗xg6 hxg6 13 ♕xg6+ ♔h8 14 ♘g5 ♗xg5 15 ♗xg5 ♕xg5 16 ♕xg5 ♗d7 17 f4 ♘c6 18 ♖f3 ♖e7 19 ♕h6+ ♖h7 20 ♕f6+ ♖g7 21 ♖g3 ♖ag8 22 ♖g5 ♗e8 23 ♖xg7 ♖xg7 24 ♕f8+ ♖g8 25 ♕h6# **1-0**
M324-1861

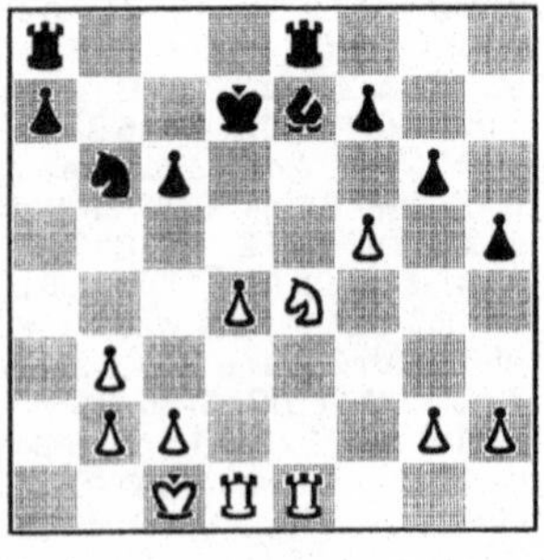

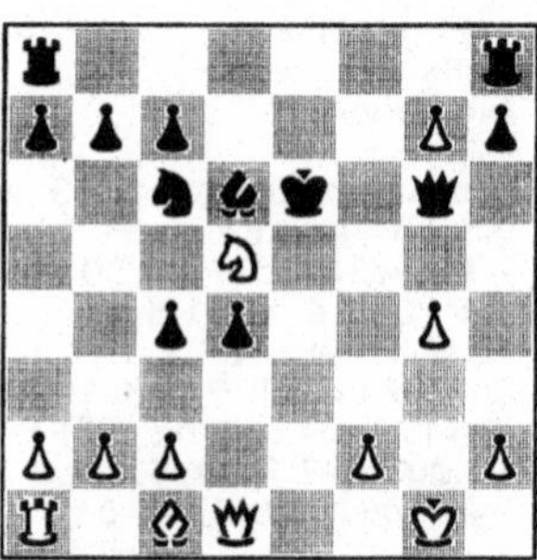

**1861-★KS-3 ⬠**
**Kolisch, I.F. von+ Steel**
Liverpool [Staunton]
1 e4 e5 2 ♘f3 ♘c6 3 ♗c4 ♘f6 4 d4 exd4 5 0-0 ♗c5 6 e5 d5 7 exf6 dxc4 8 ♖e1+ ♗e6 9 ♘g5 ♕d5 [9 ... ♕xf6? 10 ♘xe6 △ 11 ♕h5+] 10 ♘c3 ♕f5 11 g4 ♕g6 [11 ... ♕xf6?! 12 ♘d5 ♕d8 13 ♖xe6+] 12 ♘xe6 fxe6 13 ♖xe6+ ♔f7 14 ♘d5 ♗d6 15 fxg7 ♔xe6 16 gxh8♕ ♖xh8 17 ♘f4+ ♗xf4 18 ♗xf4 ♔d7 19 ♗g3 ♔c8 20 b3 cxb3 21 axb3 h5 22 gxh5 ♖xh5 23 ♕f3 ♖h8 24 ♕f4 ♕h7 25 b4 ♘xb4 26 ♖xa7 ♔b8 27 ♖a4 ♘c6 28 ♕c1 b6 29 ♕b1 ♔c8 30 ♕b5 ♘b8 31 ♖c4 ♖g8 32 ♕xb6 ♖g7 33 ♕e6+ ♔d8 34 ♕f6+ ♔c8 35 ♕f8+ **1-0** M954-1861

**1861-★KS-4 ⬠**
**Kolisch, I.F. von+ Steel**
Liverpool [Staunton]
1 e4 e5 2 ♗c4 ♗c5 3 b4 ♗xb4 4 c3 ♗c5 5 ♘f3 ♘c6 6 d4 exd4 7 0-0 d6 8 cxd4 ♗b6 9 d5 ♘a5 10 e5 ♘e7 [10 ... ♘xc4 11 ♕a4+] 11 exd6 cxd6 12 ♗b2 0-0 13 ♗d3 ♗f5 14 ♘c3 ♖c8 15 ♗xf5 ♘xf5 16 ♕d3 ♘e7 17 ♘e4 ♘g6 18 ♖ac1 ♘f4 19 ♕d2 ♖xc1 20 ♖xc1 ♘g6 21 ♘d4 ♕d7 22 ♘g3 ♘e5 23 ♕g5 ♕g4 24 ♕xg4 ♘xg4 25 ♘df5 ♘xf2 26 ♗xg7 ♘e4+ [26 ... ♘d3+ 27 ♔f1 ♘xc1 28 ♘h5 △ 29 ♘f6#; △ 29 ♘h6#] 27 ♔f1 ♘xg3+ 28 hxg3 ♖b8 [⌓ 28 ... ♖e8] 29 ♗f6 ♗c5 30 g4 b6 31 ♖c3 ♖e8 32 ♖h3 ♘c4 33 ♘e7+ ♔f8 34 ♖xh7 ♘d2+ 35 ♔e1 ♖xe7+ 36 ♔xd2 ♔e8 37 ♖h8+ ♔d7 38 ♗xe7 **1-0** M954-1861

**1861-★KT-1 ⬠**
**Kolisch, I.F. von– Taylor**
Norwich [Staunton]
⟨♘b1⟩ 1 e4 b6 2 d4 ♗b7 3 ♗d3 e6 4 ♗e3 ♘f6 5 f3 d5 6 e5 ♘fd7 7 ♘h3 c5 8 c3 cxd4 9 cxd4 ♗b4+ 10 ♔e2 ♘c6 11 ♖f1 0-0 12 a3 ♗e7 13 ♕e1 f5 14 ♘f4 ♕c8! 15 ♕g3 [15 ♘xe6 ♘dxe5] 15 ... ♘dxe5!? 16 dxe5 ♘xe5 17 ♘h5 ♘g6 18 ♖fc1 ♕d8 19 f4 ♗d6 [⌓ 19 ... d4 △ 20 ... ♗h4] 20 ♔f1 ♖f7 21 b4 ♕e7 22 ♗d4 e5 23 fxe5 f4! 24 ♕e1 ♘xe5 25 ♗xe5 ♗xe5 26 ♖a2 ♕g5 27 ♖e2 f3 **0-1**
M954-1861

**1861-★KW-1**
**Kolisch, I.F. von+ Wormald, R.B.**
London [Staunton]
1 e4 e5 2 ♘f3 ♘c6 3 d4 exd4 4 ♗c4 ♗c5 5 ♘g5 ♘h6 6 ♕h5 ♕e7! 7 0-0 d6 8 h3 ♗d7 9 f4 0-0-0!= 10 f5 ♘e5 [10 ... f6? 11 ♘e6±] 11 ♗b3 ♘g8 12 ♗f4 ♘f6 13 ♕h4 ♖df8 [⌓ 13 ... ♘xe4 14 f6 (14 ♗xe5 ♘xg5) 14 ... ♕xf6 15 ♗e3 (15 ♗xe5 d3+→) 15 ... dxe3 16 ♖xf6 e2+ 17 ♔h2 ♘xg5 18 ♖f4 ♗e3 19 ♘c3 ♘g6∓] 14 ♘d2 h6 15 ♗xe5 dxe5 [⌓ 15 ... hxg5] 16 ♘gf3 ♗b5 17 ♖fe1 ♖fg8 18 a4 ♗a6 19 ♗c4 ♗xc4 20 ♘xc4 ♗d6 21 ♔h1 ♕d7? 22 ♘fxe5 ♗xe5 23 ♘xe5 ♕e7 24 ♘f3 ♘d5 25 f6 ♘xf6 26 e5 ♘d5 27 ♕xd4 **1-0**
M954-1861

**1861-★K♀-1**
**♀– Kolisch, I.F. von**
London [Staunton]
1 e4 e5 2 ♘f3 ♘c6 3 d4 exd4 4 ♗c4 ♗c5 5 0-0 d6 6 c3 ♗g4 7 ♕b3 ♗xf3 8 ♗xf7+ ♔f8 9 ♗xg8 ♖xg8 10 gxf3 g5 11 ♕e6 ♖g6 12 ♕f5+ ♔g7 13 h4 gxh4+ 14 ♔h1 ♕e7 15 b4 ♗b6 16 ♗b2 ♖f8 17 ♕h3 ♘e5 18 f4 ♖xf4 19 ♘d2

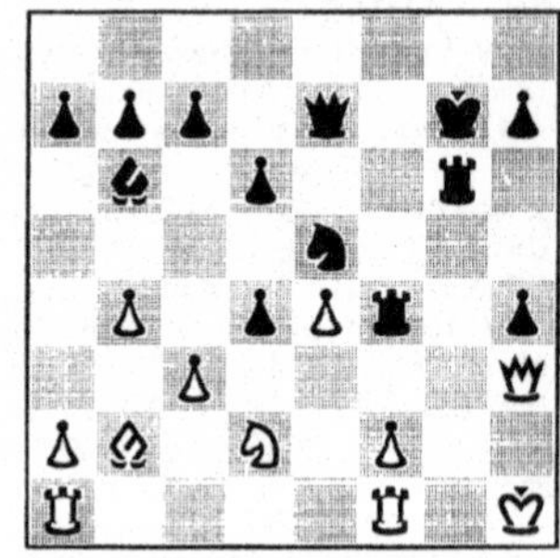

19 ... ♘f3! 20 ♘xf3 ♕xe4 21 ♖ae1 ♕xf3+ 22 ♔h2 ♕xh3+ 23 ♔xh3 dxc3 24 ♗xc3+ ♔f7 25 ♗d2 ♖f3+ 26 ♔h2 ♗d4 **0-1** M954-1861

**1861-★K♀-2**
**♀– Kolisch, I.F. von**
London [Staunton]
1 e4 e5 2 ♘f3 ♘c6 3 c3 ♘f6 4 d4 ♘xe4 5 d5 ♗c5 6 dxc6 ♗xf2+ 7 ♔e2 d5 8 cxb7 ♗xb7 9 ♕a4+ c6 10 ♘bd2 ♕b6 11 ♘xe4 dxe4 12 ♕xe4 0-0 13 b3 f5 14 ♕b4 ♗a6+ 15 ♔d1 ♗b5 16 ♗xb5 cxb5 17 a4 e4 18 ♘d4 a5 19 ♕xb5 ♗xd4 20 ♕xb6 [20 ♕c4+ ♔h1 21 cxd4 ♖ac8→] 20 ... ♗xb6 21 ♗f4 ♖ac8 22 c4 h6 23 h4 ♗d4 24 ♖c1 ♗f6 25 ♔e2 ♖fd8

26 Rhd1 Bxh4 27 Rxd8+ Bxd8 28 c5 Kf7 29 c6 g5 30 Be5 Ke6 31 Rc5 Bb6 32 Rb5 Rxc6 33 Bg7 Kf7 34 Bc3 f4 35 Bxa5 Bxa5 36 Rxa5 Rb6 37 Re5 e3 38 Rf5+ Ke6 39 Ra5 Rxb3 **0-1** M954-1861

**1861-★LP-1**
**Lichtenhein, T.– Paulsen, L.**
1 e4 e5 2 Nf3 Nc6 3 Bb5 Nf6 4 d4 exd4 5 e5 Ne4 6 0-0 Be7 7 Nxd4 0-0 8 Nxc6 dxc6 9 Bd3 f5 10 Qe2 Nc5 11 Be3 f4 12 Bxc5 Bxc5 13 Nc3 Qh4 14 Bc4+ Kh8 15 e6 f3 16 gxf3 Bd6 17 f4 Rxf4 18 f3 Rxc4 **0-1** M954-1862

**1861-★MM-1** 11 ix 61
**Morphy, P.C.– Maurian, C.A.**
New Orleans [Maróczy]
⟨Nb1⟩ 1 b3 e5 2 Bb2 Nc6 3 e3 d5 4 g3 f5 5 Bg2 Nf6 6 Ne2 Be7 7 0-0 0-0 8 Rc1 e4 9 Nf4 g5 10 Ne2 Ne8 11 d3 Qd6 12 c4 Ne5 13 c5 Qe6 14 Nd4 Qg6 15 dxe4 dxe4 16 Nb5 Nd3 17 Bd4 Nxc1 18 Qxc1 Bf6 19 f3 exf3 20 Bxf3 c6 21 Nc3 Bxd4 22 exd4 Be6 23 d5 cxd5 24 Nxd5 Qg7 25 c6 Qd4+ 26 Ne3 bxc6 27 Rd1 Qb6 28 Kh1 Rd8 29 Re1 Ng7 30 Nd1 Bd5 31 Bxd5+ Rxd5 32 Qxg5 f4 33 Qg4 f3 34 Rf1 f2 35 Qe2 Qd4 36 Nxf2 Qd2

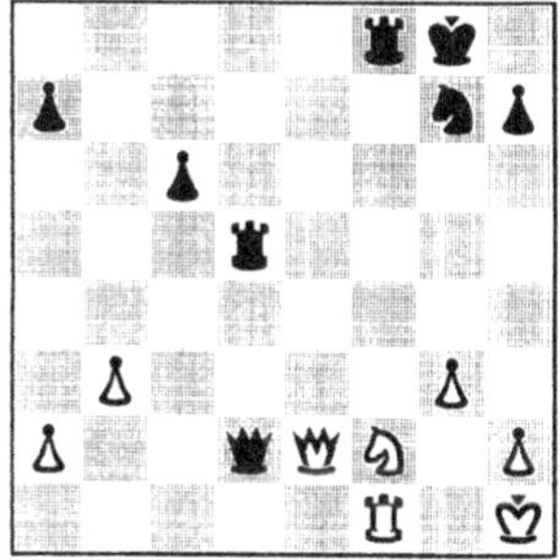

37 Ng4 Rxf1+ [37 ... Qxe2? 38 Nh6+ Kh8 39 Rxf8#] 38 Qxf1 Rf5 39 Qc4+ Qd5+ 40 Qxd5+ cxd5 [□ 40 ... Rxd5] 41 Nh6+ Kf8 42 Nxf5 Nxf5 43 Kg2 Kf7 44 Kf3 Kf6 [□ 44 ... Ke6] 45 Kf4 Ke6 [□ 45 ... Nd6] 46 g4 Nd6 47 h4 Ne4 48 a3 h6 49 b4 Nf2 50 Kf3 Nd3 51 Ke3 Ne5 52 Kf4 Ng6+ 53 Kg3 Kd6 54 h5 Ne5 55 Kf4 d4 56 g5 d3 57 Ke3 d2 58 Ke2 hxg5 59 h6 Nf7 60 h7 Ke6 61 b5 Kf6 62 a4 Kg7 63 a5 Ne5 64 b6 Nc6 65 Kxd2 axb6 66 axb6 Kxh7 67 Kd3 Kg6 68 Ke4 Kf6 69 Kd5 Na5 70 Kc5 Ke6 71 Kb5 Nb7 72 Kc6 Nd6 73 Kc5 g4 74 Kd4 g3 75 Ke3 Kd7 76 b7 Kc7 77 Kf3 Nf5 **0-1** L/N3203

**1861-★NP-1**
**Paulsen, L.+ Neumann, G.R.**
[Staunton]
1 e4 e5 2 Nf3 Nc6 3 Bc4 Bc5 4 b4 Bb6 [□ 4 ... d5] 5 b5 Na5 6 Nxe5 Qf6 7 Bxf7+ Kf8 8 d4 d6 9 Bxg8 dxe5 10 Bd5 Bxd4 11 0-0 Bxa1 12 f4 Bd4+ 13 Kh1 Ke8+– 14 fxe5 Bg4 15 Qd3 Qb6 16 Bf7+ Ke7 17 c3 Bxe5 18 Qd5 Nc4 19 Qxc4 Rad8 20 Ba3+ Bd6 21 e5 Bxa3 22 Qxg4 Bc5 23 Qxg7 Rdf8 28 Rf6 **1-0** M954-1861

**1861-★NR-1**
**Neumann, G.R.+ Robin, L.**
Berlin [Anderssen & Neumann]
⟨Nb1⟩ 1 e4 e5 2 f4 exf4 3 Nf3 g5 4 Bc4 d6 5 h4 g4 6 Ng5 Nh6 7 d4 f6 8 Bxf4 fxg5 9 Bxg5 Qd7 10 0-0 Bg7 11 Qd2 d5 12 exd5 Nf7 13 Rae1+ Kf8 14 Re7 Qxe7 15 Bxe7+ Kxe7 16 d6+ Nxd6 17 Qg5+ Ke8 18 Re1+ Kd7 19 Re7+ Kc6 20 Qc5# **1-0** L/N6051-1864

**1861-★NR-2** vi 61
**Neumann, G.R.+ R?**
Berlin [Anderssen & Neumann]
⟨Ng1⟩ 1 e4 e5 2 Bc4 Bc5 3 c3 Qg5 [□ 3 ... Nc6] 4 0-0 [△ 5 d4] 4 ... Qg6 5 d4 exd4 [5 ... Qxe4 6 Re1] 6 cxd4 Bb6 7 Nc3 d6 8 Kh1 Nf6 9 f4 0-0 10 f5 Qh5 11 Be2 Qh4 12 Rf4 Qh6 13 e5 [□ 13 Rf3 Qh4 14 Rh3 Qf2 15 Be3+–] 13 ... dxe5 14 dxe5 Ne8 15 Re4 Qc6 16 Bb5 Qc5 17 Be3 Qe7 18 f6 gxf6 [□ 18 ... Qe6] 19 Nd5 Qe6 20 Bxe8 Rxe8 21 Nxf6+ Kf8 [21 ... Kh8 22 Rh4] 22 Bh6+ Ke7 23 Nd5+ Kd8 24 Bg5+ Kd7 25 Nxb6+ Kc6 26 Rc1+ Kxb6 27 Rb4+ Ka6 28 Qa4# **1-0** L/N6051-1864

**1861-★NW-1** iii 61
**Neumann, G.R.+ Weise, von**
Berlin [Anderssen & Neumann]
⟨Ra1⟩ 1 e4 e5 2 Nf3 Nc6 3 Bc4 Bc5 4 c3 Nf6 5 d4 exd4 6 0-0 Nxe4 7 cxd4 Bb6? [□ 7 ... d5] 8 Bd5 f5? 9 Re1 Ba5? 10 Bg5 Ne7 11 Rxe4 fxe4 12 Ne5 **1-0** L/N6051-1864

**1861-★O?-1**
**?– Owen, J.**
London [Staunton]
1 e4 b6 2 d4 Bb7 3 Bd3 Nc6 4 c3 e5 5 Be3 exd4 6 cxd4 Nb4 7 Nc3 Nxd3+ 8 Qxd3 f5 9 Nf3 fxe4 10 Nxe4 Nf6= 11 Ned2 Be7 12 0-0 0-0 13 Rac1 Bd5 14 Bf4 d6 15 Qf5? [15 Bg3; 15 Bg5] 15 ... c6 16 Qh3 Ne4! 17 Be3 [17 Nxe4 Rxf4] 17 ... Nxd2 18 Nxd2 Qe8 19 f4 Qf7 20 b3 Rae8 21 g4 Bf6! 22 g5?

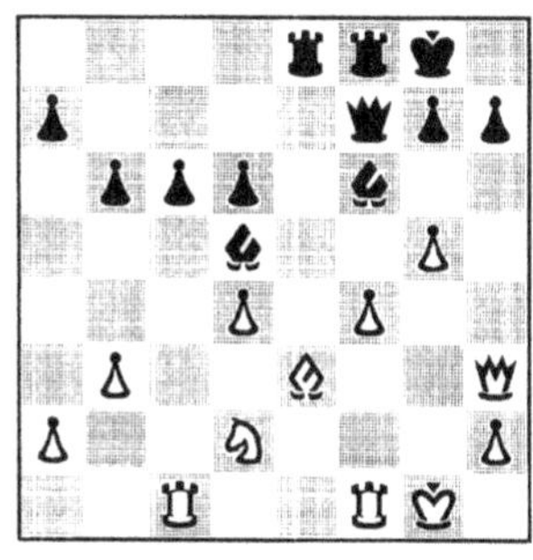

22 ... Qe6! 23 Qxe6+ Rxe6 24 Bf2 Re2 25 Rfe1 [25 Nc4 Bxd4] 25 ... Rxd2 26 gxf6 Rxf6 27 Kf1 Rxa2 28 Re2 Rxe2 29 Kxe2 Rxf4 30 b4 a6 31 Ra1 g5 32 Rg1 h6 33 h4 g4 **0-1** M954-1861

**1861-★PR-1 ●○** xii 61
**Paulsen, L.+ Roby**
London
1 e4 e5 2 Nf3 Nf6 3 Nxe5 d6 4 Nf3 Nxe4 5 d4 Be7 6 Bd3 Ng5 7 0-0 0-0 8 Nxg5 Bxg5 9 Nd2 f5 10 f4 Bf6 11 Nf3 Nc6 12 c3 Ne7 13 Ng5 Bxg5 14 fxg5 Bd7 15 Qb3+ Kh8 16 Qxb7 Bc6 17 Qb3 h6 18 gxh6 gxh6 19 Qe6 Ng8 20 Rxf5 Qh4 21 Bd2 Nf6 22 g3 Qh3 23 Bf1 Bd7 24 Rxf6 Qxe6 25 Rxe6 Bxe6 26 Bxh6 Rf6 27 Bg5 Rg6 28 h4 Kg7 29 Bd3 Rxg5 30 hxg5 Rf8 31 Re1 Rf3 32 Rxe6 Rxg3+ 33 Kf2 Rxd3 34 Re7+ Kg6 35 Rxc7 Rd2+ 36 Ke3 Rxb2 37 Rxa7 Kxg5 38 Ra6 **1-0** M324

**1861-★P?-1**
**Paulsen, L.+?**
1 e4 e5 2 Nf3 Nc6 3 Bc4 Bc5 4 b4 Bxb4 5 c3 Ba5 6 0-0 d6 7 d4 exd4 8 cxd4 Bb6 9 a4 Nf6 10 a5 Nxa5 11 e5 Nxc4 12 exf6 Be6 13 fxg7 Rg8 14 Bg5 Qd7 15 d5 Bg4 16 Re1+ Ne5 17 Nxe5 Bxd1 18 Ng4+ Qe6 19 Nf6+ Kd8 20 Nxg8+ Kd7 21 dxe6+ fxe6 22 Nf6+ Kc6 23 Rxd1 **1-0** M324-1861

**1861-★P?-2 ●○**
**Paulsen, L.+?**
1 e4 e5 2 f4 exf4 3 Nf3 g5 4 Bc4 g4 5 d4 gxf3 6 Qxf3 d5 7 Bxd5 Nf6 8 0-0 c6 9 Bxf7+!! Kxf7 10 Qxf4 Rg8 [10 ... Qxd4+ 11 Be3] 11 e5 Be7 12 Qh4 Kg7 13 Bg5!

13 ... ♘d5 14 ♕h6+ ♔h8 15 ♖f7 ♗f5 16 ♗xe7 ♖xg2+! [16 ... ♘xe7 17 ♕f6++-] 17 ♔f1 [17 ♔xg2 ♘e3+] 17 ... ♖g1+ 18 ♔f2 ♖g2+ 19 ♔f3 ♕g8 20 ♗f6+ ♘xf6 21 ♕xf6+ ♖g7 22 ♖f8 ♗g4+ 23 ♔e3 ♘d7 24 ♖xg8+ ♖axg8 25 ♕h4 ♘b6 26 ♘a3 ♘d5+ 27 ♔d2 ♗f3 28 ♖e1 ♖g4 29 ♕h6 ♖xd4+ 30 ♔c1 ♖e4! 31 ♖f1 [31 ♖xe4 ♖g1+-+] 31 ... ♗g4 32 c4 ♘b4 33 ♖f8! ♖e1+ 34 ♔d2 ♖e2+ 35 ♔c3 ♘xa2+ 36 ♔b3 ♘c1+ 37 ♔a4 b5+ 38 ♔a5 ♘b3+ 39 ♔b4 a5+ 40 ♔xb3 a4+ 41 ♔a2 **1-0**

L/N6016-1861

**1861-★S?-1**
**Steinitz, W.+?**
London? [Bachmann]

1 e4 e5 2 f4 ♕h4+ 3 g3 ♕e7 4 fxe5 ♕xe5 5 ♘c3 ♘f6 6 ♘f3 ♕h5 7 d4 ♗b4 8 ♗c4 0-0 9 e5 ♘e4 10 0-0 ♘xc3 11 bxc3 ♗xc3

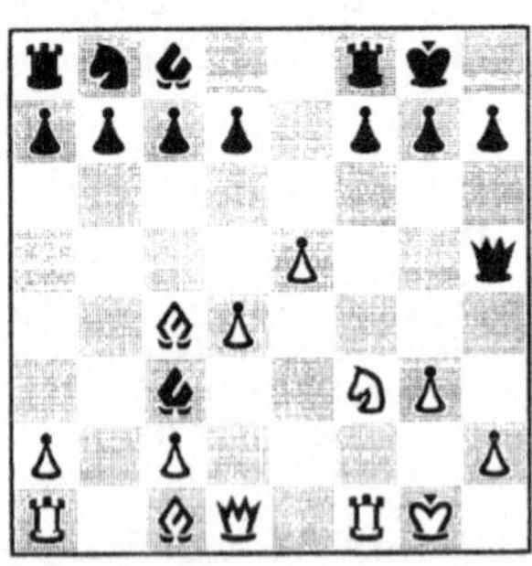

12 ♕d3 ♗xa1 13 ♘g5 d5 14 exd6 cxd6 15 ♘xf7 ♗xd4+ 16 ♕xd4 ♘d7 17 ♗b2 ♘f6 [17 ... ♕c5 18 ♘xd6+ ♔h8 19 ♖xf8+ ♔♘xf8 20 ♕xc5] 18 ♘h6+ ♔h8 19 ♖xf6 ♖xf6 20 ♕xf6 ♕c5+ 21 ♔g2 ♕c6+ 22 ♔f2 ♕c5+ 23 ♔f3 ♕c6+ 24 ♔e3 ♕c5+ 25 ♔d2 ♕b4+ 26 ♔d1 ♗g4+ 27 ♘xg4 ♖g8 28 ♕f7 d5 29 ♘h6 ♕f8 30 ♗xd5 ♕d8 31 ♕xb7 **1-0** L/N3131

**1861-☒EL-1**
**Elberfeldu Schaakclub–Schaakclub La Bourdonnais**
[Staunton]

1 e4 e5 2 ♘f3 ♘c6 3 ♗b5 a6 4 ♗a4 ♘f6 5 d4 exd4 6 0-0 ♗e7 7 e5 ♘e4 8 ♘xd4 0-0 9 c3 f6 10 ♗c2 d5 11 ♘xc6 bxc6 12 ♗xe4 dxe4 13 exf6

13 ... ♗d6! 14 fxg7 ♖f7 15 g3 ♗h3 16 ♖e1 ♗c5 17 ♗f4 ♖xf4! 18 gxf4 [18 ♕xd8+ ♖xd8 19 gxf4 ♖d7-+] 18 ... ♕h4 [18 ... ♗xf2+ 19 ♔xf2 ♕h4+ Δ 20 ... ♖d8-+] 19 ♔h1 ♕xf2 20 ♖g1 ♕xg1+ 21 ♕xg1 ♗xg1 22 ♔xg1 ♖d8 23 ♘a3 ♖d2 24 b4 e3 25 ♘c4 ♖g2+ 26 ♔h1 e2 27 ♘e3 ♖f2 28 ♔g1 ♖f3 29 ♘g2 ♖d3 30 ♖e1 ♖d1 31 ♔f2 ♗xg2 32 ♖xe2 ♗d5 33 ♖e8+ ♔xg7 34 ♖e7+ ♔h6 35 ♖xc7 ♖c1 36 ♖a7 ♖c2+ 37 ♔e1 ♖xa2 38 ♔d1 ♔g6 **0-1** M954-1861

## DÜSSELDORF 1862

**1862-DUS-1** ix 62
**Schultz, G.+ Hanneken, von**
[Lange]

1 e4 e5 2 ♘f3 ♘c6 3 ♗c4 d6 4 d4 exd4 5 ♘xd4 ♘f6 6 ♘c3 ♗e7 7 0-0 ♘e5 8 ♗b3 a6 9 f4 ♗g4 10 ♕e1 ♘c6 11 ♘xc6 bxc6 12 e5 dxe5 13 fxe5 ♕d4+ 14 ♔h1 ♘d5 15 ♘xd5 cxd5 16 ♖f4 ♕d1 17 ♕xd1 ♗xd1 18 ♗xd5 0-0-0 19 ♗xf7 ♗xc2 20 ♗e3 ♖d3 21 ♗f2 ♖hd8 22 ♗g3 ♖d1+ 23 ♖f1 ♖xa1 24 ♖xa1 ♗e4 25 ♗c4 ♖d2 [□ 25 ... ♔b7] 26 ♗xa6+ ♔d7 27 ♗f1 ♖xb2 28 a4 c5 29 a5 c4 30 a6 c3 31 a7 c2 32 ♖e1 ♖b1 33 e6+ ...? **1-0** L/N5187

**1862-DUS-2** ix 62
**Hipp, F.A.+ Lichtenscheidt, R.**
[Lange]

1 e4 e5 2 ♘f3 ♘c6 3 ♗c4 ♗c5 4 b4 ♗xb4 5 c3 ♗a5 6 d4 exd4 7 0-0 dxc3 8 ♕b3 ♕f6 9 ♗g5 ♕g6 [□ 9 ... e5] 10 ♘xc3 ♗xc3 11 ♕xc3 f6? [□ 11 ... ♘ge7] 12 ♗h4 d6 13 ♗d5 ♘ge7 14 ♖fe1 ♗d7 15 ♖ab1 b6 [15 ... 0-0-0] 16 ♘d4 ♘xd5 17 exd5+ ♘e7 18 ♕xc7 ♖c8 19 ♕xd6 ♕f7 20 f4 ♖d8 21 ♕b4? [□ 21 ♖xe7+ ♕xe7 22 ♖e1+-] 21 ... 0-0 22 ♖xe7 ...? **1-0**

L/N5187

**1862-DUS-3** ix 62
**Kohtz, J.– Lange, M.**
[Lange]

1 e4 e5 2 ♘f3 ♘c6 3 ♗c4 ♗c5 4 0-0 d6 5 c3 ♘f6 6 b4 ♗b6 7 d4 exd4 8 cxd4 ♗g4 9 ♗b2 0-0 10 b5 ♘e7 11 ♘c3 ♘g6 12 ♕d2 ♕d7 13 ♕e3? ♖fe8 14 ♖ad1 ♘xe4 15 ♘xe4 [15 ♘g5 ♘e5∞; 15 ... ♗e6∞] 15 ... d5 16 ♗e2? [□ 16 ♘c5 ♗xc5 17 ♕g5 dxc4 18 ♕xc5! ♘f4∓] 16 ... ♖xe4 17 ♕d2 ♘f4 18 ♘e5 [□ 18 ♖fe1∓] 18 ... ♘xe2+ 19 ♔h1 ♖xe5 [20 dxe5 ♕f5! 21 f3 ♘g3+-+] **0-1** L/N5187

**1862-DUS-4** ix 62
**Paulsen, W.+ Wülfing, O.**
[Lange]

1 e4 e6 2 d4 d5 3 exd5 exd5 4 ♗d3 ♗e6 5 ♘f3 ♘f6 6 0-0 ♗e7 7 ♘c3 0-0 8 ♗f4 c5 9 dxc5 ♗xc5 10 ♕d2 ♘c6 11 a3 a6 12 ♖ad1 ♕d7 13 ♘e5 ♘xe5 14 ♗xe5 ♘g4 15 ♗g3 ♖ad8 16 ♔h1 b5 17 ♘e2 ♗b6 18 ♘f4 h6 19 ♖fe1 ♗c7? [□ 19 ... ♖fe8!] 20 f3 ♘f6

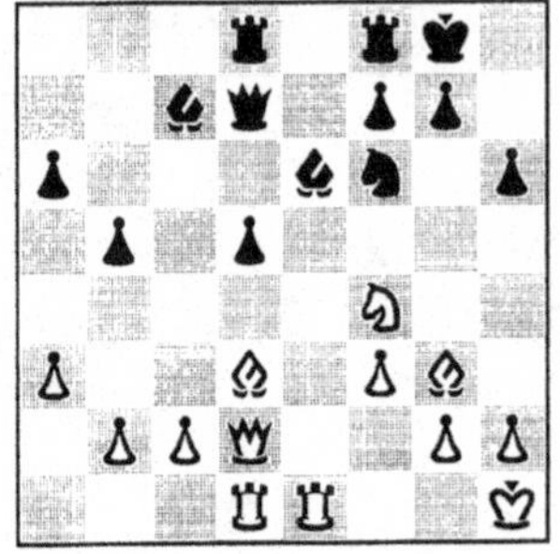

21 ♘xe6 ☒

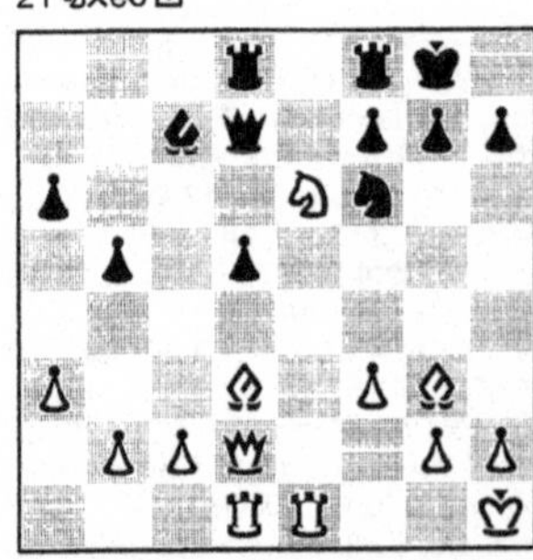

21 ... fxe6 22 ♗xc7 ♕xc7 23 ♖xe6 ♖f7 24 ♕g5 ♖d6 25 ♕e5 ♖xe6 26 ♕xe6 ♕b7 27 ♗e4 ♕e7 28 ♗xd5 ♘xd5 29 ♕xd5 h6 30 ♕d8+ ♕xd8 31 ♖xd8+ ♔h7 32

♔g1 ♖f6 33 ♔f2 g5 34 ♖d7+ ♔g6 35 g4 **1-0** L/N5187

**1862-DUS-5** ix 62
**Lichtenscheidt, R.– Lange, M.**
[Lange]
1 e4 e5 2 ♘f3 ♘c6 3 ♗c4 ♗c5 4 0-0 d6 5 h3 [□ 5 c3] 5 ... ♘f6 6 d3 ♗e6 7 ♗b5 0-0 8 ♗g5 ♘e7 9 ♗xf6 gxf6 10 ♘bd2 ♘g6 11 ♔h1 ♔h8 12 ♗c4 ♕d7 13 ♗xe6 fxe6 14 ♘b3 ♗b6 15 d4 f5! 16 dxe5 fxe4 17 ♘g5 ♘xe5 [□ 17 ... d5] 18 ♘xe4 ♖f4! 19 ♕e2 ♕g7 20 ♘bd2 ♖g8 21 g3 d5 22 ♖g1 ♕h6 23 ♖g2 ♖ff8 [23 ... ♖xe4?! 24 ♘xe4 dxe4 25 ♕xe4 ♘g4 26 ♖f1 ♕xh3+ 27 ♔g1] 24 ♖h2 [24 ♘c3 ♘g4!∓] 24 ... dxe4 25 ♕xe4 ♕f6! 26 f4 ♘c6 27 ♖g2 ♕h6 28 h4 ♖g4 29 ♖f1 e5 30 ♕f3 ♖fg8 31 fxe5 ♘xe5 32 ♕f6+ ♕xf6 33 ♖xf6 ♖xg3 **0-1** L/N5187

**1862-DUS-6** ix 62
**Wülfing, O.– Lange, M.**
[Lange]
1 e4 e5 2 ♘f3 ♘c6 3 ♗b5 ♘f6 4 d4 exd4 5 e5 ♘e4 6 0-0 ♗e7 7 ♖e1 ♘c5 8 ♘xd4 ♘xd4 9 ♕xd4 0-0 10 ♘c3 c6 11 ♗d3 ♘xd3 12 ♕xd3 f6 13 f4 fxe5 14 fxe5 d5 15 ♖f1? [□ 15 exd6; □ 15 ♗e3] 15 ... ♖xf1+ 16 ♕xf1 ♕b6+ 17 ♔h1 ♗e6 18 b3 ♖f8 19 ♕d3 d4! [19 ... ~ 20 ♗e3!] 20 ♘e2 c5 21 ♗f4 ♗d5 22 c4 ♗c6 23 ♔g1 g5 24 ♕g3 ♔h8 25 ♗d2 ♕d8 26 ♖f1 ♖xf1+ 27 ♔xf1 ♕f8+ 28 ♔g1 ♕f5 29 ♘c1 ♗e4 30 h4 gxh4 31 ♕f4 ♕g6 32 ♕h2 ♕g4 33 ♔f2 ♔g7 [33 ... h3] 34 ♘e2 h3 35 ♕xh3 ♗h4+ 36 ♔f1 ♕xh3 37 gxh3 ♗d3 38 ♗f4 ♔f7 39 ♗h2 ♔e6 40 a3 a5 41 a4 b6 42 ♗g1 [42 ♗f4 ♔f5 43 ♗h2 ♔e4–+] 42 ... ♔xe5 43 ♗f2 ♗xf2 44 ♔xf2 ♗xe2 45 ♔xe2 ♔e4 **0-1** L/N5187

**1862-DUS-7** ix 62
**Schultz, G.– Lange, M.**
[Lange]
1 e4 e5 2 ♘f3 ♘c6 3 d4 exd4 4 ♘xd4 ♗c5 5 ♘f5 ♕f6 6 ♘c3 ♘ge7 7 ♗d3 d6 8 0-0 0-0 9 ♕f3 ♘e5 10 ♘xe7+ ♕xe7 11 ♕g3 c6 12 ♔h1 f5 13 ♗g5 ♕f7 14 exf5 ♘xd3 15 ♕xd3 ♗xf5 16 ♕d2 d5 17 ♖ae1 h6 ...? **0-1** L/N5187

**1862-DUS-8** ix 62
**Hanneken, von– Lange, M.**
[Lange]
1 e4 e5 2 f4 exf4 3 ♘f3 g5 4 ♗c4 ♗g7 5 d4 d6 6 0-0 h6 7 c3 ♘c6 8 b3 ♕e7 9 ♘bd2 ♗d7 10 ♗d5 ♘f6 11 ♗a3 ♘g4 12 ♕c1 ♘e3 13 ♖e1 g4 14 e5 gxf3 15 exd6 f2+ 16 ♔xf2 ♕h4+ 17 ♔g1 0-0-0 18 ♘e4? ♘xd5–+ 19 dxc7 ♘xc7 20 ♘d6+ ♔b8 21 ♘xf7 ♘xd4 22 ♘xd8 ♘f3+ 23 gxf3 ♗d4+ 24 cxd4 ♖g8+ 25 ♔h1 ♕f2 26 ♕xc7+ [26 ♕b2 ♕f3+] 26 ... ♔xc7 27 ♖ac1+ ♗c6 28 ♘e6+ ♔c8 **0-1** L/N5187

**1862-DUS-9** ix 62
**Wülfing, O.+ Kohtz, J.**
[Lange]
1 e4 e5 2 ♘f3 ♘c6 3 ♗b5 a6 4 ♗a4 ♗e7 5 d4 exd4 6 0-0 ♘f6 7 e5 ♘e4 8 ♘xd4 ♘xd4 9 ♕xd4 ♘c5 10 ♕g4 ♘e6 [□ 10 ... 0-0 11 ♗h6 ♘e6 12 f4 f5!] 11 f4 b5 12 ♗b3 0-0 13 f5 ♗c5+ 14 ♔h1 ♘d4 15 ♗h6 g6 16 fxg6 ♘e6 17 ♗xe6 **1-0** L/N5187

**1862-DUS-10** ix 62
**Wülfing, O.+ Schultz, G.**
[Lange]
1 e4 e5 2 f4 exf4 3 ♗c4 ♕h4+ 4 ♔f1 g5 5 ♘c3 ♗g7 6 g3 fxg3 7 ♔g2 ♕h6 8 hxg3 ♕g6 9 d4 d6 10 ♘f3 h6 11 e5 ♗g4 12 exd6 cxd6 13 ♘d5 ♔d8 14 c3 ♘c6 15 ♘e3 ♗xf3+ 16 ♕xf3 ♘ge7 17 b4 f5 18 b5 g4 19 ♕f4 ♘a5 20 ♗d3 ♖f8 21 ♗a3 ♔c7 22 ♗b4 b6 23 ♗xa5 bxa5 24 a4 h5 25 c4 ♗h6 26 ♕f2 ♗xe3 27 ♕xe3 ♖ae8 28 ♕f4 ♖f6 29 ♖ac1 ♕h6 30 ♕xh6 ♖xh6 31 c5 d5 32 ♖ce1 ♔d8 33 ♖e5 ♖eh8 34 ♖he1 ♖6h7 35 b6 axb6 36 cxb6 ♔d7 37 ♗b5+ ♔d8 38 b7 ♔c7 39 ♖xe7+ ♖xe7 40 ♖xe7+ ♔b8 41 ♗c6 ♖d8 42 ♖e5 ♔c7 43 ♖xd5 ♖b8 44 ♖c5 ♖d8 45 d5 **1-0** L/N5187

**1862-DUS-11** ix 62
**Hipp, F.A.– Wülfing, O.**
[Lange]
1 e4 e6 2 d4 d5 3 exd5 exd5 4 ♘f3 ♘f6 5 ♗d3 ♗e6 6 0-0 c5 7 dxc5 ♗xc5 8 ♘c3 0-0 9 h3 a6 10 ♗g5 ♘bd7 11 a3 h6 12 ♗h4 ♕c7 13 ♗xf6 ♘xf6 14 b4 ♗a7 15 ♖e1? ♕xc3 16 ♘d2 ♕c7 17 ♖c1 ♗xh3 18 ♘f1 ♗e6 19 c3 ♘g4 20 ♖e2 ♘e5 21 ♕c2 ♘xd3 22 ♕xd3 ♕c4 23 ♕xc4 dxc4 24 ♘g3 b5 25 ♔f1 ♖fd8 **0-1** L/N5187

**1862-DUS-12** ix 62
**Wülfing, O.– Hanneken, von**
[Lange]
1 e4 e5 2 ♘f3 ♘c6 3 ♗b5 d6 4 d4 exd4 5 ♘xd4 ♗d7 6 ♗xc6 bxc6 7 0-0 c5 8 ♘f5 [□ 8 ♘e2] 8 ... ♗xf5 9 exf5 ♕d7 [□ ♘f6 △ 10 ... ♗e7] 10 ♕f3 ♖d8 11 ♖e1+ ♗e7 12 ♕g3 ♔f8 13 ♕f3 ♗f6 14 g4 h6 15 ♘c3 ♗e5 16 ♗f4 ♗xc3 17 ♕xc3 ♘f6 18 h3 h5 19 f3 hxg4 20 fxg4 ♘d5 21 ♕f3 ♘xf4 22 ♕xf4 ♖xh3 23 ♔g2 ♖h8 24 ♖h1 ♕c6+ 25 ♕f3 ♕xf3+ 26 ♔xf3 ♖xh1 27 ♖xh1 f6 28 ♖h8+ ♔e7 29 ♖xd8 ♔xd8 30 ♔e4 ♔d7 31 c3 a5 32 ♔d5 c6+ 33 ♔c4 ♔c7 34 a4 ♔b6 35 ♔d3 d5 36 ♔d2 ♔c7 37 ♔e2 ♔d7 38 ♔d3 ♔d6 39 ♔e3 c4 40 ♔d4 c5+ 41 ♔e3 ♔e5 **0-1** L/N5187

**1862-DUS-13** ix 62
**Paulsen, W.+ Schultz, G.**
[Lange]
1 e4 e5 2 ♘f3 ♘c6 3 ♗c4 d6 4 c3 ♘f6? [□ 4 ... ♗e7] 5 ♘g5 d5 6 exd5 ♘a5 [6 ... ♘xd5 7 ♕b3! (7 ♘xf7?! ♔xf7 8 ♕f3+ ♔e6∞)] 7 ♕a4+ c6 8 dxc6 ♘xc6 9 ♘xf7 ♕e7 10 ♘xh8 ♗e6 11 ♗b5 ♗d7 12 0-0 g6 13 d4 ♗g7 14 ♘xg6 hxg6 15 ♗g5 ♔f7 16 ♘d2 a6? 17 f4 exd4 18 ♖ae1 ♕c5 19 ♗c4+ ♔f8 20 ♘b3 ♕a7? [21 ♕a3+ ♘b4 22 ♕xb4 ♕c5 23 ♕xc5#] **1-0** L/N5187

**1862-DUS-14** ix 62
**Schultz, G.+ Lichtenscheidt, R.**
[Lange]
1 e4 e5 2 ♘f3 ♘c6 3 ♗c4 ♗c5 4 b4 ♗xb4 5 c3 ♗e7 6 d4 ♘a5 7 ♘xe5 ♘xc4 8 ♘xc4 d6 9 0-0 ♘f6 10 e5 dxe5 11 dxe5 ♕xd1 12 ♖xd1 ♘d7 13 ♘ba3 a6 14 f4 b5 15 ♘a5 ♗c5+ 16 ♔h1 0-0 17 ♘b3 ♗b6 18 ♘c2 ♘c5 19 ♗a3 ♘e4 20 ♖f1 ♖e8 21 h3? ♘g3+ 22 ♔h2 ♘xf1+ 23 ♖xf1 ♗b7 24 ♘c5 ♗d5 25 ♘b3 a5 26 ♘cd4 b4 27 ♗b2 a4 28 ♘c1 bxc3 29 ♗xc3 c5 30 ♘f5 c4 31 ♘d6 ♖ed8 32 ♘e2 ♗c5 33 ♘f5 ♗e4 34 ♘eg3 ♗d3 35 ♖f3 ♖ab8 36 e6 ♖b1 37 exf7+ ♔xf7 38 ♘e3 ♗e4? 39 ♘xe4 ♗xe3 40 ♘g5+ ♔g6 41 ♖xe3 h6 42 ♘e6 ♖d3 43 ♖g3+ ♔f7 44 f5 g5 45 ♗g7 ♖3d1 46 ♖a3 ♖h1+ 47 ♔g3 ♖hg1 48 ♖xa4 ♖gf1 49 ♖a7+ ♔e8?? [□ 49 ... ♔g8] 50 ♗f6 [△#] **1-0** L/N5187

**1862-DUS-15** ix 62
**Lichtenscheidt, R.+ Kohtz, J.**
1 a3 e5 2 e3 d5 3 c4 d4 4 h3 ♘f6 5 ♘f3 ♘c6 6 b4 e4 7 ♘g1 d3 8 ♗b2 ♗d6 9 ♘c3 ♕e7 10 ♘d5 ♘xd5 11 cxd5 ♘e5 12 ♕b3 ♗d7 13 0-0-0 c5 14 dxc6 ♖c8 15 ♔b1 ♖xc6 16 f3 b5 17 ♖c1 ♗e6 18 ♕d1 ♖xc1+ 19 ♕xc1 f5 20 fxe4 fxe4 21 g4 0-0 22 ♗g2 ♗d5 23 h4 ♖f2 24 ♘h3 ♖xg2 25 ♘f4 ♖g3 26 ♘xd5 ♕b7 27 ♗xe5 ♗xe5 28 ♕c5 ♔f7 29 g5 ♔e6 30 ♘f4+ ♗xf4 31 exf4 e3 32 ♖e1 e2 33 ♕e5+ ♔f7 34 ♖c1 ♕d7 35 h5 ♖g2 36 ♔b2 e1♕ 37 ♕xe1 ♕d4+ 38 ♖c3 ♕xf4 39 ♖xd3 ♕xg5 40 ♖f3+ ...? **1-0** L/N5187

**1862-DUS-16** ix 62
**Lichtenscheidt, R.= Hanneken, von**

1 a3 e5 2 h3 d5 3 e3 f5 4 c4 c6 5 b4 ♘f6 6 ♗b2 ♗d6 7 ♘f3 ♘bd7 8 ♘h4 f4 [▢ 8 ... 0-0 9 ♘xf5? ♘e4!→] 9 ♘f5 ♗f8 10 exf4 e4 11 cxd5 cxd5 12 ♗b5 ♔f7 13 ♕b3 ♘b6 14 ♘e3 ♗d6 15 f5 a6 16 ♗e2 ♗f4 17 0-0 ♖f8 18 ♗xf6 ♔xf6 19 ♘c3 d4 20 ♘xe4+ ♔e7 21 f6+ gxf6 22 ♘c5 dxe3 23 dxe3 ♗e5 24 ♖ad1 ♕c7 25 f4 ♗d6 26 ♖c1 ♗xc5 27 ♖xc5 ♕d7 28 ♖d1 ♕e6 29 ♖c7+ ♘d7 30 ♕xe6+ ♔xe6 31 f5+ ♔e7 32 ♗c4

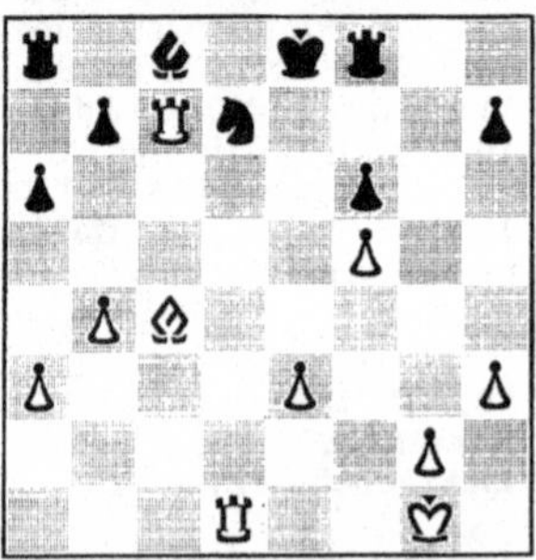

32 ... ♔d8 33 ♖c5 [▢ 33 ♖cxd7+ ♗xd7 34 ♗e6] 33 ... ♔e8 34 ♖cd5 b5 35 ♗a2 ♖a7 36 ♖d6 ♖c7 37 ♖e6+ ♔d8 38 ♖ed6 ♗b7 39 ♗e6 ♗c8 40 ♔h2 ♔e7 41 ♔g3 ♘e5 42 ♗xc8 ♖fxc8 43 ♖e6+ ♔f7 44 ♖dd6 ♖c6 45 ♖xf6+ ♔g7 46 ♔f4 ♖xd6 47 ♖xd6 ♘c6 48 g4 a5 49 ♖d7+ ♔g8 50 g5 axb4 51 axb4 ♘xb4 52 f6? ♖c4+ [▢ 52 ... ♖f8!] 53 e4 ♘c6 54 h4 ♘d4 55 h5 ♘e6+ 56 ♔f5 ♖xe4 57 ♔xe4 ♘c5+ 58 ♔e5 ♘xd7+ 59 ♔e6 ♘f8+ 60 ♔e7 b4 61 f7+ ♔g7 62 h6+ ♔g6 63 ♔xf8 b3 64 ♔g8 b2 65 f8♕ b1♕ ½-½ L/N5187

**1862-DUS-17** ix 62
**Hanneken, von= Kohtz, J.**

1 e4 e5 2 ♘f3 ♘c6 3 ♗c4 ♘f6 4 d4 exd4 5 0-0 ♗e7 6 ♗d5 d6 7 ♗xc6+ bxc6 8 ♘xd4 ♗d7 9 ♘c3 0-0 10 f4 ♘e8 11 f5 ♗f6 12 ♗e3 c5 13 ♘de2 ♗c6 14 ♕e1 ♖b8 15 b3 ♕e7 16 ♘g3 ♗xc3 17 ♕xc3 ♗xe4 18 ♖ae1 ♖b5 19 a4 ♖b4 20 ♖f4 ♘f6 21 ♕b2 d5 22 ♗d2 ♖bb8 23 ♘xe4 ♘xe4 24 ♖g4 ♕f6 25 ♕xf6 ♘xf6 26 ♖g3 ♖be8 27 ♖xe8 ♖xe8 28 ♗h6 g6 29 fxg6 fxg6 30 ♗g5 ♘e4 31 ♖e3 ♖f8 32 ♗e7 ♖f7 33 ♗d8 g5 34 c4 ♘d2 35 h3 d4 36 ♖e8+ ♔g7 37 ♗xg5 ♘xb3 38 ♖b8 ♘a5 39 ♖b5 ♘xc4 40 ♖xc5 ♘d6 41 ♖d5 ♖f5 42 ♖xf5 ♘xf5 43 ♔f2 ♔f7 44 ♔e2 ♔e6 45 ♗f4 c5 46 a5 a6 47 g4 ♘e7 48 h4 ♘c6 49 ♗c7 ♔d7 50 ♗b6 ♘e5 51 ♗xc5 d3+ 52 ♔e3 ♔c6 53 ♗d4 ♘xg4+ 54 ♔xd3 ♔b5 55 ♗c3 h5 56 ♔e4 ♔c4 57 ♗e1 ♘h2 58 ♔f4 ♔b3 59 ♗g3 ♘f1 60 ♗f2 ♘d2 61 ♗e3 ♘c4 62 ♗b6 ♔a4 63 ♔g5 ♘d6 64 ♗c7 ♘b5 65 ♗d8 ♘d6 66 ♔xh5 ♘f5 67 ♔g5 ♘xh4 68 ♔xh4 ♔b5 ½-½ L/N5187

## LONDON 1862

**1862-LON1-2**
**Anderssen, A.+ Blackburne, J.H.**
[Löwenthal]

1 e4 e6 2 d4 d5 3 exd5 exd5 4 ♘f3 ♘f6 5 ♗d3 ♗d6 6 0-0 0-0 7 h3 h6 8 c4 c6 [▢ 8 ... c5; 8 ... dxc4] 9 ♘c3 ♗e6 10 cxd5 ♘xd5 11 ♘e4 ♗c7 12 ♗e3 ♘d7 13 ♕e2 ♖e8 14 ♖fe1 ♗f5 15 ♘fd2 ♗a5? 16 ♘d6

16 ... ♗xd3 [▢ 16 ... ♘f4 17 ♕f3 ♘xd3 18 ♕xf5 ♘xe1 19 ♖xe1 (19 ♘xb7 ♕c7 20 ♘xa5 g6 21 ♕b1 ♕xa5 22 ♕xe1∓; 19 ♕xf7+ ♔h8 20 ♘xe8 ♕xe8 21 ♕f5 ♘xg2=; 19 ♘xe8 ♕xe8 20 ♖xe1 ♗b6 21 ♘f3) 19 ... ♗xd2 20 ♕xf7+ ♔h8 21 ♗xd2 ♖xe1+ 22 ♗xe1 ♘b6 23 ♘xb7 ♕d7] 17 ♕xd3 ♗xd2 18 ♗xd2 ♖xe1+ 19 ♖xe1 ♕f6 20 ♘xb7 ♖b8 21 ♘a5 g5 [21 ... ♖xb2?? 22 ♖e8+ ♘f8 23 ♖xf8 ♔xf8 24 ♕a3+] 22 ♘c4 ♘5b6 23 ♘e5 ♘xe5 24 dxe5 ♕e6 25 ♕g3 ♘c4 26 ♗c1 ♘d6! [26 ... ♘xb2 27 h4±] 27 f4 ♘f5 28 ♕f2 [28 ♕g4 ♖b4!] 28 ... gxf4 29 ♕xf4 ♔h7 30 ♖f1 ♘g7 31 ♕g3 ♕g6 32 ♕h4 ♘f5 [▢ 32 ... ♘e8 Blackburne] 33 ♕f4 ♘g3 34 ♕xf7+ ♕xf7 35 ♖xf7+ ♔g8 36 ♖f2 ♖d8 37 ♖d2 ♖e8 38 ♖c2 ♖e6 39 ♗f4 ♘h5 40 g3 ♔f7 41 ♔f2 ♔g6 42 ♔f3 ♘g7 43 ♖d2 ♘e8 44 ♖d7 a6 45 g4 c5 46 h4 h5 47 gxh5+ ♔xh5 48 ♖h7+ ♔g6 49 ♖h6+ ♔f7 50 ♖xe6 ♔xe6 51 ♔e4 ♘c7 52 h5 ♘d5 53 ♗g5 ...⚲ **1-0** L/N5188

**1862-LON1-4** 4 vii 62
**Anderssen, A.+ Dubois, S.**
[Löwenthal]

1 e4 e5 2 f4 exf4 3 ♗c4 d5 4 exd5 ♕h4+ 5 ♔f1 f3? 6 ♗b5+ c6 7 ♘xf3 ♕f6 8 dxc6 bxc6 9 ♗e2 ♗d6 10 d4 ♘e7 11 ♗g5 ♕g6 12 c4 f6 13 ♗d2 0-0 14 ♘c3 ♗f5?? 15 c5 ♗c7 [15 ... ♗c2 16 ♕c1 17 ♘h4] 16 ♕b3+ ♔h8 17 ♕b7 ♗d3 18 ♕xc7 ♘d5 19 ♕g3 ♘xc3 20 bxc3 ♕e4 21 ♗xd3 ♕xd3+ 22 ♔f2 ♘d7 23 ♖he1 ♘e5 24 dxe5 fxe5 25 ♔g1 e4 26 ♗h6!!

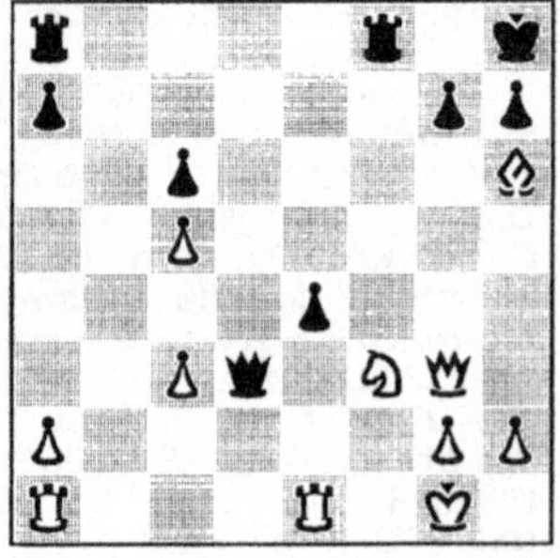

26 ... gxh6 27 ♕e5+ ♔g8 28 ♖xe4 ♖f6 29 ♕xf6 ♕xe4 30 ♖e1 ♕g6 31 ♕xg6+ hxg6 32 ♖e6 ...⚲ **1-0** L/N5188

**1862-LON1-5**
**Anderssen, A.+ Green, V.**
[Löwenthal]

1 e4 e5 2 f4 exf4 3 ♘f3 g5 4 h4 g4 5 ♘e5 ♘f6 6 ♗c4 d5 7 exd5 ♗d6 8 d4 ♕e7 9 ♗xf4 ♘h5 10 g3 ♘xf4? [▢ 10 ... f6∓] 11 gxf4 f6 12 ♕e2 fxe5 13 fxe5 ♗b4+ 14 c3 ♗a5 15 ♘d2 ♗f5 16 ♗b3 ♗b6 17 ♘c4! h5 18 d6 ♕h7 19 0-0-0 ♘c6 20 d5 ♗e4 21 exc6 ♗xh1 22 ♖xh1 bxc6 23 ♕g2 0-0-0 24 ♕xc6 ♔b8 25 ♘xb6 axb6 26 ♗d5 ...⚲ **1-0** L/N5188

**1862-LON1-6**
**Hannah, J.W.– Anderssen, A.**
[Löwenthal]

1 e4 c5 2 ♘f3 e6 3 d4 cxd4 4 ♘xd4 ♘f6 5 ♗d3 [▢ 5 ♘c3] 5 ... ♘c6 6 ♗e3 d5 7 ♘d2 [▢ 7 ♘xc6 bxc6 8 e5] 7 ... ♗d6 8 0-0 0-0 9 f4? ♗c5! 10 c3 [10 e5? ♘xd4∓; 10 ♘2b3 ♗xd4∓] 10 ... e5! 11 ♘c2 ♗xe3+ 12 ♘xe3 ♕b6! 13 ♕e1 ♘g4 14 ♖f3 exf4 15 exd5 ♘ce5 16 ♗xh7+ ♔xh7 17 ♖h3+ ♘h6 18 ♖h5 fxe3 19 ♘e4 ♗g4 20 ♖xe5 ♖ae8 21 ♕b1 e2+ 22 ♔h1 e1♕+ 23 ♕xe1 ♖xe5 24 ♕b1 ♕g6 25 ♘g3 ♘f5 ...⚲ **0-1** L/N5188

**1862-LON1-7**
**MacDonnell, G.A.– Anderssen, A.**
[Löwenthal]

1 e4 c5 2 ♘f3 e6 3 d4 cxd4 4 ♘xd4 ♘f6 5 ♗d3 ♘c6 6 ♗e3 d5 7 ♘xc6 bxc6 8 e5 ♘d7 9 f4 f5 10 0-0 ♗c5 11 ♕e2 0-0 12 ♖f3

♗xe3+ 13 ♖xe3 ♘c5 14 ♘d2 ♘e4 15 ♖f1 a5 16 ♖ff3 ♖a7 17 ♖h3 ♕b6 18 ♘f1 g6 19 g4?! [□ 19 c3] 19 ... ♖g7 20 ♔g2? [□ 20 g5] 20 ... c5 21 ♗xe4 fxe4 22 ♖b3 ♕c7 23 ♔g3 c4 24 ♖a3 g5 25 fxg5 ♕xe5+ 26 ♔g2 d4 27 ♖h5 e3 28 ♘g3 ♕d5+ 29 ♔g1 ♖f2 30 ♕xf2 exf2+ 31 ♔xf2 ♖f7+ ... **0-1**

L/N5188

## 1862-LON1-9
**Anderssen, A.+ Mongredien, A.**

[Löwenthal]

1 e4 g6 2 d4 ♗g7 3 f4 e6 4 ♘f3 b6 5 c4 ♗b7 6 ♘c3 ♘e7 7 ♗d3 d6 8 0-0 0-0 9 ♗e3 ♘d7 10 f5 ♕e8! 11 ♘g5?! exf5 12 ♕d2 [12 exf5? ♘xf5] 12 ... fxe4 13 ♘gxe4 ♘f5! 14 ♖xf5 [14 ♖f3 ♘xe3 15 ♕xe3 f5!] 14 ... gxf5 15 ♘g3 f4 16 ♗xf4 ♗xd4+ 17 ♔h1 ♗xc3 18 bxc3 f6 19 ♖e1 ♘e5 20 ♘f5 ♕h5 21 ♘h6+ ♔h8 22 ♗c2 ♖g8? [□ 22 ... ♖ae8] 23 ♘xg8 ♖xg8 24 ♖e2

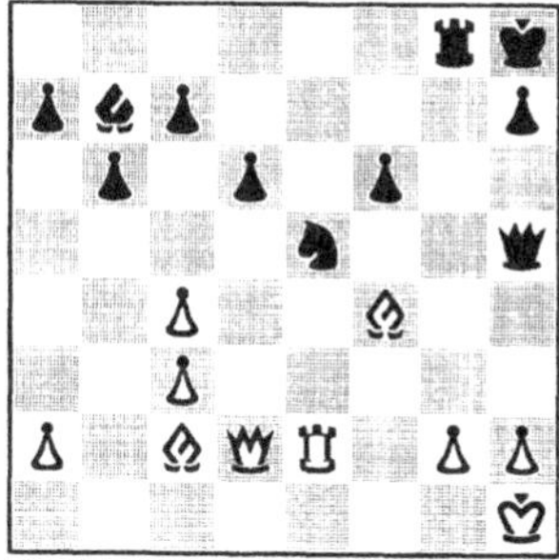

24 ... ♕g4? [24 ... ♕f3 25 gxf3 ♘xf3 26 ♕e3 ♘d2+ 27 ♗e4 ♗xe4+ 28 ♕xe4 ♘xe4 29 ♖xe4+−; 25 ♗e3 ♕f1+ 26 ♗g1 ♘f3 27 ♕d1 ♘e1−+; 25 ♔g1 ♘xc4 26 ♗g3 ♘xd2 27 gxf3 ♘xf3+∓; 25 ♖f2 ♖xg2!−+; 24 ... ♘f3 25 ♕e3! (25 ♕d3 ♘e1 26 ♖xe1 ♖xg2 27 ♕xh7+ ♕xh7 28 ♗xh7 ♔xh7−+; 25 ♕d1 ♘h4 26 ♕d4 ♖xg2 27 ♕xf6+ ♖g7+ 28 ♗e4 ♗xe4+ 29 ♖xe4 ♕f3#) 25 ... ♘h4 26 ♕e7 ♘xg2=] 25 ♗g3 ♕h5 26 ♔g1 ♖xg3!? 27 hxg3 ♘g4 28 ♖e7! ♕h2+ 29 ♔f1 ♕h1+ 30 ♔e2 ♕xg2+ 31 ♔d1 ♕f1+ 32 ♕e1 ♗f3+ 33 ♔d2 ♕xe1+ 34 ♔xe1 c6 35 ♖xh7+ ♔g8 36 ♖xa7 ♘e5 37 ♗f5 ♔f8 38 ♗e6 ♗e4 39 ♔d2 f5 40 ♔e3 ♔e8 41 ♔f4 ♗d3 42 ♗xf5 ♗xc4 43 ♔g5 ♘f7+ 44 ♔f6 ... **1-0**

L/N5188

## 1862-LON1-10
28 vi 62

**Owen, J.+ Anderssen, A.**

[Löwenthal]

1 d4 f5 2 e4 fxe4 3 ♘c3 e6 [□ 3 ... ♘f6 4 ♗g5 c6 5 ♗xf6 exf6 6 ♘xe4 d5 7 ♘g3 ♗d6 8 ♗d3 0-0=] 4 ♕h5+ g6 5 ♕e5 ♘f6 6 ♗g5 ♗e7 7 d5 0-0 8 ♗h6 d6 9 ♕d4 e5 10 ♕d2 ♖f7 11 h3 ♘bd7 12 0-0-0 ♘c5 13 ♗c4 a5 14 ♘ge2 ♗d7 15 g4 ♕e8 16 ♘g3 b5! 17 ♗e2 b4 18 ♘b1 c6 19 ♗e3! ♘xd5 20 ♗xc5 dxc5 21 ♘xe4 ♖f4 22 ♗c4! ♗e6 23 ♕e2 ♕f7 24 ♘bd2 a4 25 ♔b1! ♘b6 26 ♗xe6 ♕xe6 27 f3 c4 28 c3 a3 29 ♕f2 c5 [□ 29 ... ♘a4!; 30 b3 (30 bxa3 bxc3 31 ♘f1 ♖b8+ 32 ♔a1 ♖b2∓; ♗xa3∓; 30 cxb4 ♘xb2 31 ♘c5 ♕d5 32 ♖hf1 ♖d4∓) 30 ... cxb3 31 ♘xb3 (31 axb3 ♘xc3+ 32 ♘xc3 bxc3 33 ♘c4 ♖xc4 34 bxc4 ♕xc4−+) 31 ... ♕c4 32 ♕f1 (32 ♘ed2 ♕d3+−+) 32 ... ♖xe4 33 fxe4 ♕xe4+ 34 ♕d3 ♘xc3+ 35 ♔c2 ♕g2+ 36 ♕d2 ♘xd1 37 ♖xd1 ♕xh3∓; 29 ... ♕d5 30 ♕f1 axb2 31 ♔xb2 ♕a5 32 ♖a1 bxc3+ 33 ♘xc3 ♘a4+−+] 30 ♘xc5 ♗xc5 31 ♕xc5 bxc3 32 bxc3 ♘d7 33 ♕c7 ♘f8 34 ♖he1 ♖f7 35 ♕c5 ♕a6 36 ♔a1 ♖b7 37 ♕xe5 ♖b5 38 ♕d4 ♘e6 39 ♕d7 ♖b6 40 ♘e4 ♖f8 41 g5 ♖b7 42 ♕d5 ♖b5 43 ♕d6 ♖b6 44 ♕e5 ♘f4 45 ♖d7 ... **1-0**

L/N5188

## 1862-LON1-11
30 vi 62

**Anderssen, A.+ Paulsen, L.**

[Löwenthal]

1 e4 e5 2 ♘f3 ♘c6 3 ♗b5 ♘f6 4 d3 d6 5 ♗xc6+ bxc6 6 h3 ♗e7 7 ♘c3 0-0 8 0-0 ♘e8 9 d4! exd4 10 ♘xd4 ♗b7 11 ♗e3 d5 12 ♘f5 ♗f6 13 ♗c5 ♘d6 14 ♖e1! ♖e8 15 ♕g4 ♘xf5 16 exf5 ♕d7 17 ♕f3 a5 18 ♘e2 a4 [□ 18 ... ♖e5!] 19 c3 ♖a5? 20 ♗d4! ♕d6 21 ♘g3 ♗e5 22 f6 ♕xf6 23 ♕h5 g5 24 ♕e2 [□ 24 h4!] 24 ... ♕h8? [□ 24 ... ♕g6 25 ♗xe5 f6!] 25 ♗xe5 f6 26 ♕h5 ♖xe5 27 ♖xe5 fxe5 28 ♕e8+ ♔g7 29 ♘f5+ ... **1-0**

L/N5188

## 1862-LON1-12
**Robey, J.− Anderssen, A.**

[Löwenthal]

1 e4 e5 2 ♘f3 ♘c6 3 ♗b5 ♘f6 4 0-0! ♘xe4 5 d4! ♗e7 6 d5 ♘d6 7 ♗e2 e4 8 dxc6 exf3 9 cxd7+ ♗xd7 10 ♗xf3 0-0 11 ♗f4 ♗f5 12 ♘c3 ♕d7 13 ♘d5 ♗d8 [□ 13 ... ♗e6] 14 b3 ♗e6 15 ♕d2 f5 16 ♖ad1 ♘e8 17 ♕b4! ♕c8 18 ♖fe1 c6 19 ♘e7+ ♗xe7 20 ♕xe7 ♗f7 21 ♖d7 ♗g6 22 ♖ed1? [□ 22 ♗e2 b4 23 ♖xa7±] 22 ... ♖f7 23 ♕e6 ♘f6 24 ♖d8+ ♕xd8 25 ♖xd8+ ♖xd8 26 h4 ♖e8 27 ♕c4 h6 28 ♗e3 ♔h7 29 ♗d4 ♘g4 30 ♗c3 h5 31 g3 ♖fe7 32 ♕d4 ♘e5 33 ♗g2 ♖d7 34 ♕xa7 ♖d1+ 35 ♔h2 ♘g4+ 36 ♔h3 ♖e2 37 ♗d4 ♘xf2+ 38 ♔h2 ... **0-1**

L/N5188

## 1862-LON1-13
**Anderssen, A.+ Steinitz, W.**

[Löwenthal]

1 e4 e5 2 ♘f3 ♘c6 3 ♗b5 ♘f6 4 0-0 [4 ♕e2 a6 5 ♗a4 b5 6 ♗b3 ♗c5 7 a4 ♖b8 8 axb5 axb5 9 ♘c3 ♗b4 10 ♘d5 0-0 11 0-0=; 4 d4! ♘xe4 (4 ... ♘xd4 5 ♘xd4 exd4 6 e5 c6 7 0-0) 5 d5 ♘d6 6 ♗xc6 bxc6 7 dxc6 ♘c4 8 ♘d4 dxc6 9 ♘xc6 ♕d7=; 4 c3 ♘xe4 5 ♕e2 ♘d6 6 ♗xc6 dxc6 7 ♘xe5 ♗e7∓] 4 ... ♘xe4 [4 ... a6 5 ♗a4 ♗e7 6 d4 exd4 7 e5 ♘e4 8 ♖e1 ♘c5=] 5 d4 ♗e7 6 d5 ♘b8 7 ♘xe5 0-0 8 ♖e1 ♘f6 9 ♘c3 d6 10 ♘f3 c6? [□ 10 ... ♗d7] 11 ♗a4 ♗g4 12 ♕e2! ♗xf3 13 gxf3 ♖e8 14 ♗g5 b5 15 ♗xf6 bxa4 16 dxc6 gxf6 17 c7! ♕d7! [17 ... ♕xc7 18 ♘d5 ♕d8 19 ♘xe7+ 20 ♕e4±] 18 cxb8♕ ♖axb8 19 ♘d5 ♔f8 20 ♕e3 ♔g7 21 ♘xe7 [□ 21 ♔h1!] 21 ... ♖b5!! 22 ♘f5+ [□ 22 f4 ♔f8 23 f5 ♖xe7 24 ♕h6+ ♔g8 (24 ... ♔e8 25 ♕xf6!−+) 25 ♕xf6 ♖xe1+ 26 ♖xe1 ♖xf5 27 ♖e7±] 22 ... ♖xf5 23 ♕d3 [23 ♕xe8 ♖g5+ 24 ♔h1 (24 ♔f1 ♕h3+ 25 ♔e2 ♖e5+!) 24 ... ♕h3−+] 23 ... ♖ee5 24 ♔h1 ♖f4 25 ♖g1+ ♖g5 26 ♖g3 ♕f5? [□ 26 ... h6; 26 ... ♕b7] 27 ♕xf5 ♖fx5 28 ♖d1 ♖b5 29 b3 axb3 30 axb3 ♖bc5 31 c4 ♖c6 32 f4 ♖g6 33 f5 ♖g5 34 f4 ♖xg3 35 hxg3 ♖c5 [□ 35 ... ♖b6] 36 ♖xd6 ♖xf5 37 b4 h5 38 ♖a6 h4 39 ♔g2 hxg3 40 ♔xg3 ♖h5 41 ♖xa7 ♖h8 42 ♖c7 ... **1-0**

L/N5188

## 1862-LON1-14
5 vii 62

**Blackburne, J.H.− Barnes, T.W.**

[Löwenthal]

1 e4 c5 2 d4 cxd4 3 ♘f3 g6 4 ♘xd4 ♗g7 5 b3 ♘c6 6 ♗b2 ♕b6 7 c3 ♘f6 8 ♗d3 d5 9 ♘d2 ♘xd4 10 cxd4 dxe4 11 ♘xe4 ♘d5 12 0-0 0-0 13 ♗c4 ♗e6 [□ 13 e6 △ ♗c6] 14 ♘c5 ♖ad8 15 ♖e1 [□ 15 ♕f3] 15 ... ♘f4 16 ♗xe6 ♘xe6 17 ♘xe6 fxe6 18 ♕e2 ♗xd4 19 ♗xd4 ♖xd4 20 ♕xe6+ ♕xe6 21 ♖xe6 ♖d2 22 ♖f1 ♖xa2 23 ♖xe7 b5 24 ♖e3 a5 25 f3 ♖c8 26 f4 b4 27 f5 ♖cc2 28 ♖g3 ♔g7 29 fxg6 hxg6 30 h4 ♖c5 31 ♖d3 ♔h6 32 ♖f6 ♖c3 33 ♖ff3 ♖ac2 34 ♔f1 ♔h5 35 ♖d5+ ♔xh4 36 ♖d4+ ♔h5 37 ♖d5+ ♔h6 38 ♖xc3 ♖xc3 39 ♖xa5 ♖xb3 40 ♖b5 g5 41 g4 ♖f3+ 42 ♔g2 ♖f4 43 ♔g3 ♖c4! 44 ♖b6+ ♔g7 45 ♖b5 ♔f6 46 ♖b6+ ♔e5 47 ♖b5+ ♔d4 48 ♖xg5 b3 49 ♖b5 ♔c3 50 ♔h4 b2 51 ♖xb2 ♔xb2 52 ♔h5? [□ 52 ♔g5=] 52 ... ♔c3 53 g5 ♔d4 ... **0-1**

L/N5188

## 1862-LON1-15
**Barnes, T.W.= Deacon, F.H.**

[Löwenthal]

1 e4 e6 2 d4 d5 3 exd5 exd5 4 ♗d3 ♗e7 5 ♘f3 ♘f6 6 0-0 0-0 7 ♗e3 ♗g4 8 ♘bd2 ♘bd7 9 c3 ♗xf3 10 ♘xf3 [□ 10 ♕xf3] 10 ... ♘e4 11 ♕c2 ♘df6 12 ♘e5 c6 13 f3 ♘d6 14 ♗g5 h6! 15 ♗xf6 ♗xf6 16 f4 ♕c7 17 ♖ae1 ♖fe8 18 ♘g4 ♗e7 19 ♖e5 f6 20 ♖h5 ♗f8 21 ♗g6 ♖e7 22 ♕d3

♘e4 23 ♘e3 ♖d8 24 ♘f5 ♖ed7 25 ♘h4 ♖e7 26 ♗f5 c5 27 ♘g6 ♖ee8 28 ♗xe4 dxe4 29 ♕c4+ ♕f7 30 ♕xf7+ ♔xf7 31 ♘xf8 cxd4 32 cxd4 ♖xd4 33 ♖b5 ♖e7 34 ♖e1 ♔xf8 35 ♖b3 f5 36 ♔f2 ♖ed7 37 ♖e2 g5? 38 ♖b5 ♖4d5 39 ♖xd5 ♖xd5 40 fxg5 hxg5 41 g4! fxg4 42 ♔e3 ♔e7 43 ♔xe4 ♔e6 ... ½-½ L/N5188

**1862-LON1-16**
**Deacon, F.H.– Barnes, T.W.**
[Löwenthal]

1 e4 c5 2 ♘f3 g6 3 ♗e2 ♗g7 4 ♘c3 ♘f6 5 d4 cxd4 6 ♘xd4 ♘c6 7 ♘xc6 bxc6 8 0-0 0-0 9 ♕d3 d6 10 ♗e3 ♘g4 11 ♖ad1 [□ 11 ♗xg4] 11 ... ♘xe3 12 ♕xe3 ♕b6 13 ♘a4 ♕xe3 14 fxe3 ♗e6 15 c4 c5 16 b3 ♖ab8 17 g4 ♖b4 18 ♖c1 ♖fb8 19 ♘c3 ♗xc3 20 ♖xc3 a5 21 h3 a4 22 ♗d1 axb3 23 ♗xb3 [23 axb3? ♖a8] 23 ... h5 24 ♖f4 hxg4 25 hxg4 ♔g7! [25 ... g5 26 ♖f5!] 26 ♔g2 ♗d7 27 ♔g3 ♗a4! 28 ♗xa4 ♖xa4 29 ♖f2 ♖bb4 30 ♖fc2 ♔f6 31 a3 ♖b1 32 ♖f2+ ♔e6 33 ♖a2 ♔e5 34 ♔f3 ♖f1+ 35 ♔g2 ♖e1 36 ♔f2 ♖h1 37 ♔g2 ♖h4 38 ♔g3 g5 39 ♖b2 f6 40 ♖b7 ♖h7 41 ♔f3 ♖a8 42 ♖d3 ♖ah8 43 ♖d5+ ♔e6 44 ♖f5 ♖h2 45 e5 ♖8h3+ 46 ♔e4 ♖e2 [46 ... ♖g2!] 47 ♖f3 ♖xf3 48 ♔xf3 ♖c2 49 exf6 exf6 50 a4 ♖xc4 51 a5 ♖a4 52 ♖a7 ♔d5 53 ♖a8 ♔c4 54 a6 d5 55 a7 ♖a3 56 ♔f2 ♖a1 57 ♔f3 ♖a2 58 ♔g3 ♔d3 59 ♖c8 ♖xa7 60 ♖xc5 ♔e4 61 ♖c3 ♖a1 62 ♖b3 ♖g1+ 63 ♔f2 ♖xg4 64 ♖b6 ♔e5 65 ♔f3 ♖a4 ... 0-1 L/N5188

**1862-LON1-17** 2 vii 62
**Barnes, T.W.– Dubois, S.**
[Löwenthal]

1 e4 e5 2 ♘f3 ♘c6 3 ♗b5 ♘f6 4 d4 ♘xe4 5 dxe5 ♗e7 6 0-0 0-0 7 ♕d5 ♘c5 8 ♗e3 ♘e6 9 ♘c3 a6 10 ♗xc6 bxc6 11 ♕b3 d5 12 exd6 cxd6 13 ♘a4 d5 14 ♖ad1 ♕c7 15 c4! ♖b8 16 ♕c2 dxc4 17 ♕xc4 c5 18 b3 ♖b4! 19 ♕c2 ♗b7 20 ♘d2 ♗d6 21 g3 ♖g4 22 f4 ♘xf4!

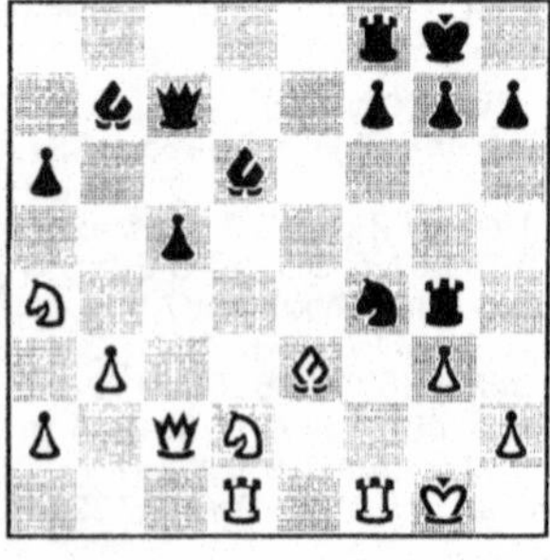

23 ♗xf4 ♗xf4 24 ♘f3 ♗xg3 25 ♔h1 ♖h4 26 ♖d2 ♕f4 27 ♕d3 ♗e4 28 ♕c3 ♗e1 29 ♖xe1 ♗xf3+ 30 ♔g1 ♖g4+ 31 ♔f1 ♗g2+ 32 ♔e2 ♖e8+ 33 ♔d3 [33 ♔d1 ♖xe1+ 34 ♔xe1 ♕f1#] 33 ... ♖xe1 34 ♕xc5 ♗e4+ 35 ♔c3 ♖c1+ ... 0-1 L/N5188

**1862-LON1-18** 30 vi 62
**Barnes, T.W.+ Green, V.**
[Löwenthal]

1 e4 e5 2 ♘f3 ♘c6 3 ♗b5 ♗c5? 4 0-0 ♕f6 5 c3 ♘ge7 6 ♗xc6! ♘xc6 7 d4 exd4 8 e5 ♕g6 9 cxd4 ♗b6 10 ♘c3 ♕h5! 11 d5 ♘d8 12 ♘e4 0-0 13 ♘g3 ♕g4 14 ♔h1 [△ h3] 14 ... d6 15 h3 ♕d7 16 ♗f4 dxe5 17 ♘xe5 ♕e7 18 ♕h5 f6 19 ♘g4 ♕f7 20 ♕h4! ♕xd5 21 ♘h5 ♗xg4 22 ♕xg4 ♕f7 23 ♖ae1! ♘c6 24 ♗h6 ♘e5 25 ♕xg7+ ♕xg7 26 ♗xg7 ♖f7 27 ♗xf6 ♘d3 28 ♖e2 ♖af8 29 ♖d2 ♘c5 30 ♗h4 ♘e4 31 ♖e2 ♘xf2+ 32 ♗xf2 ♗xf2 [□ 32 ... ♖xf2∓] 33 g4 ♗d4 34 ♖xf7 ♖xf7 35 ♔g2 ♔f8 36 ♘g3 c5 37 ♘f5 a6 38 ♖d2 ♖d7 39 ♔f3 ♔e8 40 ♘xd4 cxd4 41 ♔e4 ♖g7 42 ♖xd4 h5 43 ♔f5 hxg4 44 hxg4 ♖f7+ 45 ♔g6 ♖f2 46 ♖b4 b5 47 g5 ♔f8 48 ♖b3 ♖g2 49 ♖f3+ ♔e8 50 ♖b3 ♔f8 51 a3 ♖f2 52 ♖b4 ♖g2 53 ♖f4+ ♔e8 54 b3 ♖g3 55 ♖b4 ♔f8 56 a4 bxa4 57 bxa4 ♖a3 58 ♔f6 ♖f3+ 59 ♔e6 ♖e3+ 60 ♔f5 ♖f3+ 61 ♖f4! ♖g3 62 ♔e5+ ♔g8 63 ♖f5 ♖g4 64 a5 ♔g7 65 ♔d6 ♔g6 66 ♖c5 ♖xg5 67 ♖xg5+ ♔xg5 68 ♔c6 ... 1-0 L/N5188

**1862-LON1-19**
**Barnes, T.W.= Hannah, J.W.**
[Löwenthal]

1 c4 e5 2 e3 ♘f6 3 a3 c5 4 ♘c3 d5 5 cxd5 ♘xd5 6 ♘f3 ♘c6 7 ♗b5 ♕d6 8 0-0 ♗g4 9 h3 ♗h5 10 ♗xc6+ bxc6 11 ♘xd5 ♕xd5 12 d3 ♖d8 13 g4 ♗g6 14 e4 ♗xe4 15 ♘xe5 ♕xe5 [□ 15 ... ♗xd3] 16 ♖e1 ♗d6! 17 ♗f4! [17 ♖xe4? ♕xe4 18 dxe4 ♗h2+!] 17 ... ♕xf4 18 ♖xe4+ ♕xe4 19 dxe4 ♗h2+ 20 ♔xh2 ♖xd1 21 ♖xd1 ♔e7 22 f4 ♖b8 23 ♖d2 ♖b3 24 ♔g2 f6 25 ♖c2 ♔d6 26 h4 ♖e3 27 e5+ fxe5 28 fxe5+ ♖xe5 29 ♔f3 ♖e7 30 ♖d2+ ♔e5 31 ♖e2+ ♔d6 32 ♖d2+ ... ½-½ L/N5188

**1862-LON1-20**
**Hannah, J.W.– Barnes, T.W.**
[Löwenthal]

1 e4 c5 2 ♘f3 g6 3 d4 cxd4 4 ♘xd4 ♗g7 5 ♗c4 ♘c6 6 ♘xc6 bxc6 7 ♕f3 e6 8 0-0 ♘e7 9 ♘c3 0-0 10 ♗f4 d5 11 ♖ad1 ♗d7 12 ♗b3 h5 [□ 12 ... d4 △ e5] 13 ♗d6 ♖e8 14 ♖d3 ♗c8 15 ♗xe7 ♕xe7 16 exd5 cxd5 17 ♖e1 ♗xc3 18 ♖xc3 ♗b7 19 ♕e3 a5 20 ♗a4 ♖ed8 21 ♕g3 ♕b4! 22 ♖xe6!? ♖a6 23 ♖e8+ [23 ♖xa6 ♗xa6!] 23 ... ♖xe8 24 ♗xe8 ♖e6 25 ♗xf7+ ♔xf7 26 ♖f3+ ♔g7 27 h4 d4 28 c3 ♕c5 29 ♖d3 dxc3 30 ♖xc3 ♕b4 31 ♖c7+ ♔g8 32 ♖d7 ♗c6 33 ♖d8+ ♔g7 34 ♕c7+ ♕e7 35 ♕c8 ♖e1+ 36 ♔h2 ♕xh4+ [□ 36 ♕e5+!] 37 ♕h3 ♕xh3+ [□ 37 ♖h1+!] 38 ♔xh3 ♖e2 39 f3 ♖xb2 40 ♖d6 ♗b5 41 ♖d5 a4 42 a3 ♗f1 43 ♖g5 ♔f6 44 f4 ♖b3+ [□ 44 ... ♖xg2] 45 ♔h2 ♖xa3 46 ♖a5 ♖a2 47 ♖a8 a3 48 f5 ♗xg2 49 ♖a5 ♗e4+ 50 ♔g1 h4 51 ♖a4 ♔xf5 52 ♖a5+ ♔f4 53 ♖a6 h3 54 ♖f6+ ♗f5 ... 0-1 L/N5188

**1862-LON1-21**
**Löwenthal, J.J.+ Barnes, T.W.**
[Löwenthal]

1 e4 e5 2 ♘f3 ♘f6 3 ♘xe5 [3 ♗c4 ♘xe4 (3 ... ♘c6 4 d4!) 4 ♘c3 ♘xc3 5 dxc3 f6 6 ♘h4 (6 0-0 ♕e7 7 ♘h4 g6 8 ♔h1 c6∓) 6 ... g6 7 0-0 ♕e7∓; 4 ... ♘f6 5 ♘xe5 d5 6 ♗b3 ♗e7 7 d4 0-0 8 0-0=; 4 ... d5 5 ♗xd5 ♘f6 6 ♗b3 ♗d6 7 d3 0-0 8 h3=] 3 ... d6 4 ♘f3 ♘xe4 5 d4 ♗e7 6 ♗d3 ♘f6 7 0-0 0-0 8 h3 ♘c6 9 ♗e3 ♘b4 10 ♘c3 d5 11 a3 ♘xd3 12 ♕xd3 ♗e6 13 ♘g5 ♕d7 14 ♘xe6 ♕xe6 15 f4 ♕b6 16 f5 c5? 17 ♘a4 ♕c6 18 ♘xc5 ♗xc5 19 dxc5 ♘e4 20 b4 a6 21 ♖ad1 ♖ad8 22 c4 dxc4? 23 ♕xd8 ... 1-0 L/N5188

**1862-LON1-22** 14 vi 62
**Barnes, T.W.+ Mongredien, A.**
[Löwenthal]

1 e4 e5 2 ♘f3 ♘c6 3 ♗b5 ♗c5? 4 0-0 ♘ge7 5 c3 d6?? 6 d4 exd4 7 cxd4 ♗b6 8 d5 a6 9 ♗a4 0-0 10 dxc6 bxc6 11 ♗g5 f6 12 ♗h4 d5 13 ♘c3 d4 14 ♘e2 c5 15 ♕d3 a5 16 ♘d2 ♗a6 17 ♗b3+ ♔h8 18 ♗c4 ♗b7 19 ♘f4 ♕d7 20 ♘e6 ♖fe8 21 ♗g3 ♘c6 22 ♘f4 ♘e5 23 ♕e2 ♘xc4! [□ 23 ... f5!! 24 ♗d5 (24 ♘d5 ♘xc4 25 ♕xc4 fxe4!; 24 f3 g5 25 ♘d3 f4!) 24 ... c6 25 ♗b3 g5!] 24 ♘xc4 ♗xe4 25 ♕d2 ♕f7 26 b3 g5! 27 ♘d3 ♕g6 28 ♖ad1 h5 29 f3 ♗f5 30 h4 ♖g8! 31 hxg5 ♗xd3 32 ♕xd3 ♕xg5 33 ♖f2 ♕xg3 34 ♖e1 ♖ae8 35 ♖xe8 ♖xe8 36 ♖e2 ♖g8 37 ♕f5 ♕g5 38 ♕d7 h4 39 ♔h1 ♖g7 40 ♕e8+ ♔h7 41 ♘d2 f5 42 f4 ♕g6? [□ 42 ... ♕xf5] 43 ♘f3 ♕xe8 44 ♖xe8 ♖g4? [□ 44 ... ♖d7] 45 ♘g5+ ♔g7 46 ♖e7+ ♔g6 47 ♖e6+ ♔h5 48 ♘f7 ♖g6 49 ♖e8! ♖g7 50 ♘e5 ♔h6 51 ♖f8 c6 52 ♖xf5 ♗c7 53 ♖f6+ ♔h7 54 ♖xc6 ♗xe5 55 fxe5 ♖d7 56 ♖d6 ♖e7 57 ♖d5 ♔g7 58 ♖xc5 ♖d7 59

e6 ♖d6 60 ♖e5 ♔f8 61 ♖e2 d3 62 ♖d2 ♔e7 63 ♔g1 ♔xe6 64 ♔f2 ♔f5 65 ♔f3 ♖d5 66 a3 ♔e5?? [□ 66 ♖d6=] 67 ♔e3 ♔f5 68 ♖xd3 ♖xd3+ 69 ♔xd3 ♔g4 70 ♔e2 h3 71 gxh3+ ♔xh3 72 b4 ...⚲ **1-0**

L/N5188

### 1862-LON1-23
**Barnes, T.W.– Owen, J.**

[Löwenthal]

1 e4 b6 2 d4 ♗b7 3 ♗d3 e6 4 f4 c5 5 c3 ♘f6 6 ♕e2 cxd4 7 cxd4 ♘c6 8 ♘f3 ♘b4 9 ♘c3 ♘xd3+ 10 ♕xd3 ♗b4 11 ♘d2 0-0 12 0-0 ♖c8 13 e5 ♘d5 14 ♘de4 f5 15 exf6 ♘xf6 16 ♘g3 ♗xc3 17 bxc3 ♘d5 18 ♘e4 ♕c7 19 ♘g5 [□ 19 ♗d2] 19 ... ♘f6 20 ♗a3 ♖fe8 21 ♖ac1 h6 22 ♕h3 ♘d5 23 ♘e4 ♘xf4 24 ♘f6+

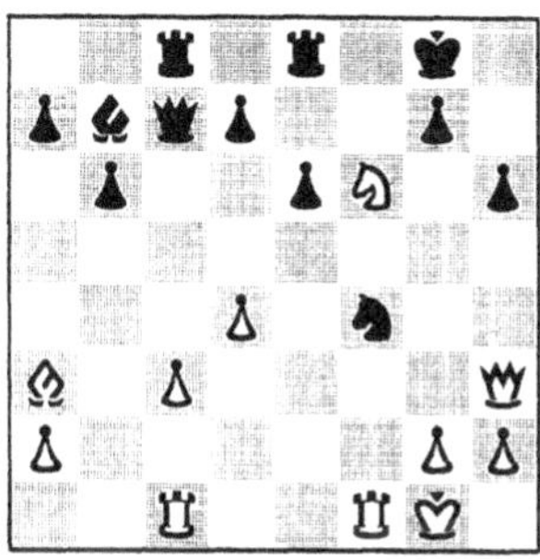

24 ... ♔h8? [□ 24 ... gxf6] 25 ♕g4? [□ 25 ♖xf4 ♕xf4 26 ♖f1 ♕d2 27 ♘xe8 ♖xe8 28 ♗d6 29 ♗e5=] 25 ... gxf6 26 ♖xf4?? [□ 26 ♕xf4=] 26 ... ♖g8 27 ♕h4 ♖xg2+ 28 ♔f1 ♕c4+ ...⚲ **0-1**

L/N5188

### 1862-LON1-24
**Paulsen, L.= Barnes, T.W.**

[Löwenthal]

1 e4 c5 2 ♘f3 e6 3 ♘c3 g6 4 d4 cxd4 5 ♕xd4 f6 6 ♗c4 ♘c6 7 ♕d3 ♘h6 8 ♘b5 a6 9 ♘d6+ ♗xd6 10 ♗xh6 ♗f8 11 ♗xf8 ♖xf8 12 h4 b5 13 ♗b3 h5 14 a4 ♕a5+ 15 c3 b4 16 0-0 bxc3 17 bxc3 ♘e5 18 ♘xe5 ♕xe5 19 f4 ♕c5+ 20 ♔h1 ♗b7 21 ♖ab1 ♗c6 22 ♗c2 f5 23 exf5! gxf5 24 ♖b2 ♖g8 25 ♗d1 ♔e7 26 ♔h2 ♖g7 27 ♕d4 ♕xd4 28 cxd4 ♖ag8 29 ♖ff2 ♖g3 30 ♗xh5 ♖d3 31 ♖bd2 ♖xd2 32 ♖xd2 ♖h8 33 ♗e2 ♖xh4+ 34 ♔g3 ♖h8 35 ♗xa6 ♖g8+ 36 ♔h2 ♗xa4 37 ♗c4 ♖c8 38 ♗a2 d5 39 ♗b1 ♖c4 40 ♔h3 ♖c1 41 ♗d3 ♗d1 42 ♔g3 ♔f6 43 ♔f2 ♔g6 44 ♗b5 ♗b3 45 ♗d3 ♗c4 46 ♖c2 ♖xc2 47 ♗xc2 ♔f6 48 ♔f3 ♔e7 49 g4 fxg4+ 50 ♔xg4 ♔f6 ...⚲ **½-½**

L/N5188

### 1862-LON1-25
4 vii 62

**Barnes, T.W.– Paulsen, L.**

[Löwenthal]

1 f4 d5 2 b3 e6 3 ♗b2 ♘f6 4 e3 c5 5 ♘f3 g6 6 ♘a3? ♗g7 7 ♗b5+ ♗d7 8 ♗e5 ♕a5! 9 ♗xd7+ ♘bxd7 10 ♗b2 0-0 11 0-0 ♖ad8 12 ♘b1 ♘b8 13 ♕e2 ♘c6 14 d3 b5 15 a4 b4 16 ♘bd2 ♕c7 17 ♗e5 [□ 17 ♘e5] 17 ... ♘xe5! 18 ♘xe5 ♘d7 19 ♘xd7 ♖xd7 20 ♖ac1 e5 21 fxe5 [□ 21 f5] 21 ... ♗xe5 22 ♘f3 ♗c3 23 d4 ♖e7 24 ♕d3 ♖fe8 [□ 24 ... c4!] 25 dxc5 ♕xc5 26 ♖cd1 ♖d8 27 ♘d4 ♖e4 28 ♔h1 ♖de8 29 ♘b5 ♖8e5 30 ♘xc3 bxc3 31 ♕a6 ♕xe3 32 ♕f6 ♖f5! 33 ♖xf5 gxf5 34 h3 ♖e5 35 ♖d3 ♕f4 36 ♖d1 ♕g3 37 b4 ♖e2 38 ♕d8+ ♔g7 39 ♖g1 ♖d2 40 b5 ♕e3! 41 a5 ♖xc2 42 ♕xd5 ♖c1 43 ♖xc1 ♕xc1+ 44 ♔h2 ♕f4+ 45 g3 ♕d2+ ...⚲ **0-1**

L/N5188

### 1862-LON1-26
**Robey, J.– Barnes, T.W.**

[Löwenthal]

1 e4 e5 2 ♘f3 ♘f6 3 ♘xe5 d6 4 ♘f3 ♘xe4 5 d4 d5 6 ♗d3 ♗d6 7 0-0 0-0 8 c4 ♘f6 9 c5? ♗e7 10 ♗f4 ♘c6 [10 ... b6!] 11 h3 b6 12 ♗b5 ♗d7 13 ♗xc6 ♗xc6 14 b4 ♘e4 15 ♘e5 ♗b5 16 ♖e1 ♗g5 17 ♗h2 f6 18 ♘f3 bxc5 19 bxc5 c6 20 a4 ♕a5 21 ♖a3 [□ 21 ♘bd2] 21 ... ♗a6 22 ♗g3? [□ 22 ... ♘xg5] 22 ... ♗h6 23 ♘h4 g6 24 ♔h2 ♖ae8 [△ 25 ... ♘xg3 26 ♖xe8 ♗f1+] 25 ♖g1 ♘xg3 26 fxg3 ♖e2 27 ♘f3 ♖fe8 28 ♘c3 ♖2e3 29 ♖e1 ♖xe1 30 ♘xe1 ♖e3 31 ♕c1 ♔g7 32 ♕a1 f5 33 ♘f3 ♕b4 34 ♘e5 f4 35 g4 [35 ♘xc6? fxg3+ △ ♕xa3!] 35 ... f3 36 ♘xf3 ♗f4+ 37 ♔h1 ♔g8 38 ♔g1 ♖xf3 39 gxf3 ♕xd4+ 40 ♔h1 ♕f2 41 ♕g1 ♕xf3+ 42 ♕g2 ♕e3 43 ♘b1 ♗d3 44 ♖xd3 ♕xd3 45 ♕b2 ♕xh3+ 46 ♔g1 ♗e3+ ...⚲ **0-1**

L/N5188

### 1862-LON1-27
1 vii 62

**Steinitz, W.+ Barnes, T.W.**

[Löwenthal]

1 e4 c5 2 ♘f3 e6 3 ♗e2 g6 4 0-0 ♗g7 5 ♘c3 a6 6 e5 f5 7 b3 ♘h6 8 ♘a4 ♕c7 9 ♗a3 ♗f8 10 d4 b6 11 dxc5! bxc5 12 ♕d2 ♘f7 13 ♕c3 ♘c6 14 ♖fe1 ♘fxe5 15 ♘xe5 ♘xe5 16 ♗c4 ♘xc4 17 ♕xh8 ♘xa3 18 ♕xh7 ♕c6 [18 ... ♘xc2 19 ♖xe6+ dxe6 20 ♕xc7 ♘xa1 21 ♕c6++-] 19 ♖ad1 d5 [□ 19 ... d6] 20 ♘b6?! ♕xb6 21 ♕xg6+ ♔d8 22 ♕f6+ ♔c7 [22 ... ♗e7 23 ♖xd5+ ♗d7 (23 ♔e8 24 ♕h8+ ♔f7 25 ♕h7+ ♔e8 26 ♕g8+ ♗f8 27 ♖xf5 ♕d6 28 ♕f7+=) 24 ♕h8+ ♔c7 25 ♖xd7+ ♔xd7 26 ♕xa8±] 23 ♕xf8 ♕d6 24 ♕g7+ ♗d7 25 c4 d4? [□ 25 ... ♘c2∓] 26 b4 ♘c2 27 bxc5 ♕xc5 28 ♖xe6 ♕f8 29 ♕e5+ ♔c8 30 ♖b1! ♘b4 [30 ... ♗xe6 31 ♕xe6+ ♔c7 (31 ... ♔d8 ♖b7) 32 ♕b6+ ♔d7 33 ♕b7+ ♔d6 34 ♖b6+ ♔e5 (34 ... ♔c5 ♕c7#) 35 ♕d5+ ♔f4 36 ♖g6+-]

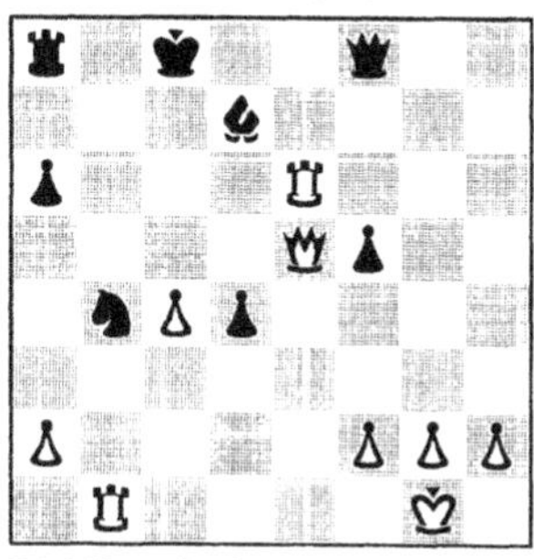

31 ♖f6 ♕e8 32 ♕c5+ ♘c6 33 ♖f8 ...⚲ **1-0**

L/N5188

### 1862-LON1-28
**Blackburne, J.H.– Deacon, F.H.**

[Löwenthal]

1 e4 e5 2 ♘f3 d6 3 d4 exd4 4 ♕xd4 ♗d7 5 ♗f4! ♘c6 6 ♕d2 ♗e7 7 ♗c4 ♘f6 8 ♘c3 0-0 9 0-0 [□ 9 0-0-0] 9 ... ♘g4 10 ♖ad1! ♗f6 11 ♖fe1 ♘ge5 12 ♗xe5 ♗xe5 13 h3 ♗e6 14 ♗d3 ♘e7 15 ♘xe5 dxe5 16 ♖e3 ♘g6 17 ♘e2 c6 18 ♖g3 ♕h4 19 ♔h2 ♖ad8 20 ♕e3 b6 21 ♖f1 ♘f4 22 ♘g1 h6 23 ♕e1 [△ ♕c3; ♖e3] 23 ... c5 24 ♖e3 [24 ♕c3 ♘h5 25 ♖e3 (25 ♖f3 ♖d4 26 ♘e2 ♗g4∓) 25 ... ♖d4 26 ♘f3 ♕f4+ △ ♘g3; g5∓] 24 ... ♕h5 25 g3? [□ 25 ♗e2 ♕g5 26 g3 ♘g6 27 h4] 25 ... ♗xh3! 26 gxf4 ♗xf1+ 27 ♘h3 exf4 28 ♗e2 ♗xe2 29 ♖xe2 f3 30 ♖e3 ♕g4 31 ♕h1 ♖d1 32 ♕xf3 ♕xf3 33 ♖xf3 ♖e8 34 ♖d3 ♖xd3 35 cxd3 c4 36 dxc4 ♖e4 37 b3 ♖e2 38 a3 ♖a2 39 ♘f4 ♖xa3 40 b4 ♖c3 41 ♘d5 ♖xc4 42 ♔g3 ♔f8 43 ♔f3 ♖d4 44 ♘f4 ♖xb4 ...⚲ **0-1**

L/N5188

### 1862-LON1-29
30 vi 62

**Dubois, S.= Blackburne, J.H.**

[Löwenthal]

1 e4 e6 2 d4 b6 3 ♘f3 ♗b7 4 ♗d3 c5 5 c3 cxd4 6 cxd4 d6 7 0-0 g6 8 ♘c3 ♗g7 9 ♖e1 ♘e7 10 ♗f4 a6 11 ♕b3 0-0 12 ♖ad1 ♘bc6 13 e5 d5 14 ♘a4 ♘c8 15 ♖c1 ♘a5 16 ♕c3 ♗c6! 17 ♕b4 ♗xa4 18 ♕xa4 b5 19 ♕b4 ♘e7 20 ♗g5 ♘ec6! 21 ♕c5 ♕d7 22 b3 ♖fc8 23 ♕a3 ♖a7 24 ♗d2 ♗f8 25 ♕b2 ♖ac7 26 ♗xa5 ♘xa5 27 ♖xc7 ♕xc7 28 ♕d2 ♕c3 29 ♕xc3 ♖xc3 30 ♖d1 ♗h6 31 ♔f1 ♘c6 32 ♔e2 ♖c1 33 ♖xc1 ♗xc1 34 ♗b1 ♗b2 35 ♔e3 h6 36 a4 bxa4 37 bxa4 ♔f8 38 ♗d3 ♘b4 39 ♘e1 ♔e7 40 ♘c2 ♘xd3 41 ♔xd3 ...⚲ **½-½**

L/N5188

## 1862-LON1-30
**Blackburne, J.H.+Green, V.**

[Löwenthal]

1 e4 e5 2 ♘f3 ♘c6 3 ♗b5 ♗c5? [◻ 3 ... a6 4 ♗a4 ♘f6 5 d4 (5 0-0 ♗e7 6 ♘c3 0-0=; 5 0-0 ♘xe4 6 ♖e1 ♘c5) 5 ... exd4 6 e5 ♘e4 7 0-0 ♘c5 8 ♗xc6 dxc6 9 ♘xd4±] 4 c3 ♕f6 5 0-0 [◻ 5 d4 exd4 6 e5 ♕g6 7 cxd4 ♗b4+ 8 ♗d2 ♗xd2+ 9 ♘bxd2 ♕xg2 10 ♖g1 ♕h3 11 ♖xg7±] 5 ... ♘ge7 6 d4 exd4 7 e5! ♘xe5 8 ♘xe5 ♕xe5 9 ♖e1 ♕f6 10 ♕h5! b6 [10 ... c6?; 10 ... a6?; 10 ... ♕b6?±] 11 ♗d3! dxc3 12 ♖e2 ♗b7 13 ♘xc3 0-0-0 [◻ 13 ... h6] 14 ♗g5 ♕c6 15 ♗e4 d5 16 ♗xe7 dxe4 17 ♗xd8 ♖xd8 18 ♕xh7 ♔b8 19 ♕xg7 f5 20 ♕g5 ♖f8 21 ♖d1 ♗a6 22 ♖ed2 ♗d3 23 a3 ♗xa3 24 ♘xe4 ♗xb2 25 ♖xb2 ♗xe4 26 ♖c1 ♕f6 27 ♕d2 ♖g8 28 g3 ♖d8 29 ♕f4 ♖d1+ [29 ... ♕c3!] 30 ♖xd1 ♕xb2 31 ♖c1 ♕g7 32 h4 ♔b7 33 h5 c5 34 h6 ♕g6 35 ♕h4 f4 36 ♕xf4 ♗c6 37 ♕h4 ♕f5 38 h7 ♕d5 39 ♕e7+! ♔a6 40 ♖a1+ ♔b5 41 ♕e2+ c4 42 ♕b2+ ♔c5 43 ♕a3+ ...? **1-0**

L/N5188

## 1862-LON1-31
**Hannah,J.W.+ Blackburne,J.H.**

[Löwenthal]

1 e4 e5 2 ♘f3 ♘f6 3 ♘xe5 d6 4 ♘f3 ♘xe4 5 d3 ♘f6 6 d4 d5 7 ♗d3 ♗d6 8 0-0 0-0 9 ♗g5 ♗g4 10 ♘c3 c6 11 h3 ♗h5 12 ♗f5 ♘bd7 [△ 13 ♗xd7? ♕xd7] 13 ♕d3 ♕c7 14 ♖ae1 ♖ae8 15 ♖e3 ♗g6 16 ♖fe1 ♖xe3 17 ♖xe3 ♗f4! 18 ♗xf4 ♕xf4 19 ♗xg6 fxg6 20 ♘e2 ♕d6 21 ♘e5 ♘e4? 22 ♖xe4 dxe4 23 ♕b3+ ♔h8 24 ♘f7+ ♖xf7 25 ♕xf7 h6 26 ♘f4 ♕f6 27 ♕e8+ ♔h7 28 ♘e6 c5 29 c3 g5 30 ♕xd7 cxd4 31 cxd4 h5 32 ♕e8 ♔h6 33 ♕g8 g4 34 h4 g3 35 f4 exf3 36 gxf3 b5 37 ♔g2 a5 38 ♘f8 ♕xh4 39 ♕h7+ ♔g5 40 ♕xg7+ ♔f5 41 ♕e5# **1-0**

L/N5188

## 1862-LON1-32
**MacDonnell,G.A.+ Blackburne,J.H.**

[Löwenthal]

1 e4 e5 2 d4 exd4 3 ♘f3 ♘c6 4 ♗c4 ♗c5 5 c3 ♘f6 [5 ... ♕f6 6 e5 ♘xe5? 7 ♕e2 ~ 8 cxd4] 6 cxd4 ♗b4+ 7 ♗d2 ♗xd2+ [7 ... ♘xe4 8 ♗xb4 ♘xb4 9 ♗xf7+ ♔xf7 10 ♕b3+ d5 11 ♘e5+ ♔~ 12 ♕xb4±] 8 ♘bxd2 d5 9 exd5 ♘xd5 10 0-0 0-0 11 h3 [◻ 11 ♗xd5 ♕xd5 12 ♕b3] 11 ... ♗f5 12 ♘b3 ♘f4 13 ♕d2 ♘g6 14 ♖fe1 ♕d6 15 ♖e3 ♘b4 16 ♘e1 ♖ad8 17 a3 ♘d5 18 ♗xd5 ♕xd5 19 ♘f3 ♗e4 20 ♖c1 ♗xf3 21 ♖xf3 ♘h4 22 ♖g3 c6 23 ♖c5 ♕d6 24 ♖cg5 ♘g6 25 h4 f6 26 ♖5g4 f5 27 ♖g5 ♖f7 28 h5 ♘f8 29 ♕c2 [◻ 29 ♘c5] 29 ... ♕f6 30 h6 g6 31 ♖h5 ♘e6 32 ♖hh3! ♘xd4 [◻ 32 ... ♘f4!] 33 ♘xd4 ♖xd4 34 ♖d3 ♖fd7 35 ♕c3 ♔f7? [◻ 35 ... f4] 36 ♕b3+ ♔f8 37 ♕c3 ♕d6 [◻ 37 ... f4]

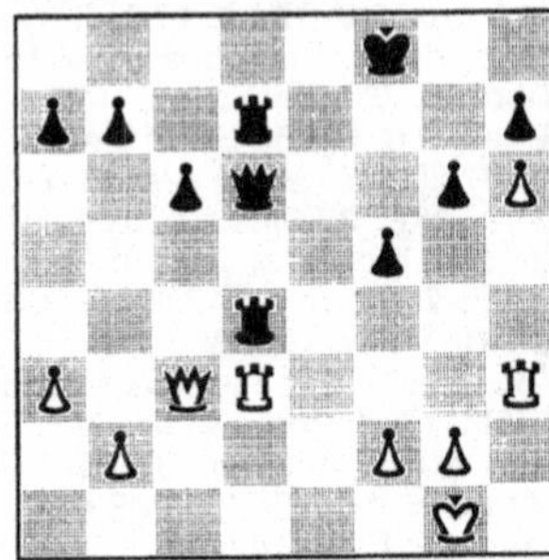

38 ♖he3! c5 [38 ... ♖xd3?? 39 ♕h8+ ♔f7 40 ♕g7#] 39 b4 c4 40 ♖d2 ♔f7 41 ♖e1 ♕f6 42 ♕e3! ♖e4 43 ♖xd7+ ♔e6 [43 ... ♔e8 44 ♖xh7 ♖xe3 45 ♖xe3+ ♔f8 46 ♖ee7+-] 44 ♖ed1 ♖xe3 45 ♖1d6+ ♔e5 46 f4+ ♔xf4 47 ♖xf6 ♖xa3 48 ♖xg6 hxg6 49 h7 ♖a1+ 50 ♔h2 ...? **1-0**

L/N5188

## 1862-LON1-33
**Mongredien,A.= Blackburne,J.H.**

[Löwenthal]

1 e4 e5 2 f4 exf4 3 ♗c4 ♘f6 4 ♘c3 d5 5 ♗xd5 c6 6 ♗b3 ♗d6 7 ♘f3 ♗g4 8 0-0 0-0 9 d4 ♘h5 10 e5 ♗c7 11 ♘e2 ♗xf3 12 ♖xf3 ♗xe5 13 c3! g5? 14 dxe5 ♕b6+ 15 ♔h1 c5 16 ♕d6 ♕xd6 17 exd6 ♘c6 18 ♗c2 [◻ 18 ♗d2] 18 ... ♖ae8 19 ♖f2 ♘e5 20 h3 ♖e6 21 b3 ♖xd6 22 ♘g1 ♘g3+ 23 ♔h2 ♖h6 24 ♗d1 ♖d8 25 ♗xf4! gxf4 26 ♖xf4 ♘g6 27 ♖f3! [27 ♔xg3 ♘xf4 28 ♔xf4 ♖f6+ 29 ♔~ ♖f1!; 27 ♖g4 ♘f1+ 28 ♔h1 ♘e3∓] 27 ... ♘e4 28 ♗c2 ♘g5 29 ♖g3 ♘e6 30 ♘f3 ♖h5 31 ♖e1 ♖hd5 32 ♗e4 ♖5d7 33 ♗f5 ♖d6 34 h4 ♘g7 35 ♗e4 b6 ...? **½-½**

L/N5188

## 1862-LON1-34
**Blackburne,J.H.= Mongredien,A.**

[Löwenthal]

1 e4 d5 2 exd5! [2 e5=] 2 ... ♕xd5 [2 ... ♘f6 3 ♗b5+ (3 d4!) 3 ... ♗d7 4 ♗c4 b5 5 ♗b3 ♗g4 6 f3 ♗c8 7 ♕e2 a6 8 c4 a5 9 cxb5 a4 10 ♗c4 ♘xd5 11 ♘c3±] 3 ♘c3 ♕d8 [3 ... ♕e5+?] 4 d4 e6 5 ♘f3 ♘f6 6 ♗d3 ♗e7 7 0-0 0-0 8 ♗e3 a6 9 ♘e5 b5 10 f4 ♗b7 11 f5 ♘bd7 12 ♘e2 [12 ♘xf7 ♕xf7 (12 ... ♖xf7 13 fxe6 ♖f8 14 exd7) 13 fxe6+ ♔xe6 14 d5+ ♔f7 ♗xh7 g6 16 ♕g4 ♘e5 17 ♕e6+ ♔g7 18 ♕xe5 ♔xh7 19 ♖f3!?] 12 ... ♘d5 13 ♗f4 c5! 14 ♘g3 ♘7f6 [◻ 14 ... ♘xf4] 15 ♘h5 c4 16 ♗e2 exf5 17 ♕e1 ♘xh5 18 ♗xh5 ♘f6 19 ♗f3 ♕xd4+ 20 ♗e3 ♕xe5 21 ♗xb7 ♖ad8 22 ♔h1 ♘g4 23 ♗f4 ♕xe1? [◻ 23 ♕c5] 24 ♖axe1 ♗c5 25 h3 ♘f2+ 26 ♔h2 a5 27 ♗a6 ♘e4 28 ♗xb5 g5 29 ♗c7 ♗d6+ 30 ♗xd6 ♘xd6 31 ♖e5! f6 32 ♖d5 ♘xb5 33 ♖xb5 ♖d2 34 ♖fxf5 ♖xc2 35 ♖b7 ♖f7 36 ♖b8+ ♔g7 37 ♖b6 ♔g6 38 ♖xa5 ♖d7 39 ♖a3 ♖dd2 40 ♖g3 h5 41 b4 ♖xa2 42 ♖c6 ♖dc2 43 b5 ♖ab2 44 b6 h4 45 ♖f3 ♖xg2+ 46 ♔h1 ♖gd2 47 ♖fxf6+ ♔g7 48 ♖g6+ ♔f7 49 ♖xg5 ♖d1+ 50 ♖g1 ♖xg1+ 51 ♔xg1 c3 52 ♖xc3 ...? **½-½**

L/N5188

## 1862-LON1-35
**Blackburne, J.H.+ Owen, J.**

[Löwenthal]

1 e4 b6 2 d4 ♗b7 3 ♗d3 e6 4 ♘f3 c5 5 c3 ♘f6 6 ♗g5 h6 7 ♗xf6 ♕xf6 8 0-0 cxd4 9 cxd4 ♘c6 10 ♗b5 a6 11 ♗xc6 ♗xc6 12 ♘c3 ♗b4 13 ♖e1 0-0 14 ♖c1 ♖ac8 15 ♖e3 b5 16 ♘e5! ♖fd8 17 ♖f3! ♕h4 18 ♘xf7 ♖f8 19 ♘e5 ♗xe4 20 ♖xf8+ ♖xf8 21 g3 ♕h3 22 ♘xe4 d5 23 ♘c5 ...? **1-0**

L/N5188

## 1862-LON1-36
**Paulsen,L.= Blackburne,J.H.**

[Löwenthal]

1 e4 e6 2 d3 b6 3 g3 g6 4 ♗g2 ♗b7 5 ♘c3 ♗g7 6 ♘ge2 ♘e7 7 0-0 0-0 8 ♗g5? f6 9 ♗d2 f5 10 ♕c1 ♘bc6 11 ♗h6 ♘e5 12 ♗xg7 ♔xg7 13 ♕f4? [◻ 13 d4] 13 ... d6 14 ♘d4 ♕d7 15 ♕c1 fxe4 16 dxe4 c5 17 ♘de2 ♘f3+ 18 ♔h1 e5? [◻ 18 ... d5] 19 ♘g1 ♘d4 20 ♕d2 ♖f6 21 ♘ce2 ♘xe2 22 ♘xe2 ♖af8 23 ♔g1 ♘c6 24 f4! ♗a6 25 fxe5 ♘xe5 26 ♖xf6 ♖xf6 27 ♘f4 ♕f7 28 b3 ♗b7 29 ♕c3 ♔g8 30 ♕e3 ♘g4 31 ♕e2 ♘e5 32 ♖d1 ♕e7 33 ♘d3 ♗a6 34 c4 ♗b7 35 ♘f4 ♘f7 36 ♘d3 ♘e5 ...? **½-½**

## 1862-LON1-37
**Blackburne,J.H.− Paulsen,L.**

[Löwenthal]

1 d4 d5 2 ♗f4 e6 3 c4 ♘f6 4 e3 b6 5 ♘c3 ♗b7 6 ♘f3 ♗d6 7 ♗g5 0-0 8 cxd5 exd5 9 ♗d3 ♘bd7 10 0-0 h6 11 ♗h4 c5 12 ♖c1 a6 13 ♗f5! ♗e7 14 ♗xd7 ♘xd7 15 ♗xe7 ♕xe7 16 dxc5 ♕xc5 17 ♘d4 [17 e4 dxe4 18 ♕xd7 (18 ♘xe4 ♕d5!) 18 ... ♗c6 19 ♕exf3!] 17 ... ♕b4 18 ♖c2 ♘f6 19 a3 ♕d6 20 ♘f5 ♕e5 21 ♕d3 g6 22 ♘g3 ♖fe8 23 ♖d1 ♖ac8 24 ♖cd2 ♖c4? 25 e4 b5 26 exd5 ♕d6 27 a4? [◻ 27 ♘f1 △ 28 ♘e3] 27 ... ♕c5 28 axb5 axb5 29 ♘f1 b4! 30 ♘a4 ♕xd5 31

♘e3 ♕xd3 32 ♖xd3 ♖c7 33 ♖b3 ♖e4 34 f3 ♖e5 35 ♔f2 ♘d5 36 ♘xd5 ♗xd5 37 ♖xb4 ♖c2+ 38 ♔g3 ♖g5+ 39 ♖g4 ♖xg4+ 40 fxg4 ♗c6 41 b3 ♖xg2+ 42 ♔h3 ♖f2 43 ♖d3 g5 44 ♘c5 ♖c2 45 b4 ♖c4 46 ♖b3 ♗d5 47 ♖d3 ♗c6 48 ♖b3 h5 49 gxh5 f5 50 ♔g3 ♖g4+ 51 ♔f2 ♖g2+ 52 ♔f1 ♖xh2 53 b5 ♗d5 54 b6? [□ 54 ♖b4 ♖c2 55 b6 ♖xc5 56 b7 ♗xb7 57 ♖xb7=] 54 ... ♗xb3 55 b7 ♗c4+ ...? **0-1** L/N5188

### 1862-LON1-38 — 2 vii 62
**Blackburne, J.H.– Robey, J.**

[Löwenthal]

1 e4 e5 2 ♘f3 ♘c6 3 c3 f5 4 exf5 [4 d4 d6 (4 ... fxe4? 5 ♘xe5 ♕f6 6 f4 d6 7 ♘xc6 bxc6 8 d5 ♗d7 9 ♗c4) 5 dxe5 fxe4 6 ♘g5 ♘xe5 7 ♘xe4=] 4 ... e4 5 ♘g1 ♘f6 6 d4 d5 7 g4 g6 8 g5 ♘h5 9 f6 ♗d6 10 h4 0-0 11 ♘h3 ♗e6 12 ♗e3 ♕d7 13 ♘d2 ♗g4 14 ♕b3 ♗e6 15 0-0-0 [15 ♕xb7?] 15 ... a6 16 ♘g1 ♘a5 17 ♕c2 b6 18 ♗h3 ♗xh3 19 ♘xh3 b5 20 ♘b3 ♘c4 21 ♘c5 ♕c6 22 ♕e2 ♕b6 23 b3 [23 ♘d7? ♕a5 24 ♘xf8 ♕xa2 25 ♕c2 ♖xf8∓] 23 ... ♘a3 24 ♕b2 b4 25 cxb4 ♘b5 [25 ... ♕xb4 26 ♗d2±] 26 a4 ♘a7 27 ♕c3 ♖f7 28 ♔b2 ♘c6 29 ♔a3 ♖b8 30 ♗d2 a5! 31 b5 [31 bxa5 ♘xa5 32 b4 (32 ♕xa5 ♕xb3#) 32 ... ♘c4+ 33 ♔a2 ♘xd2 34 ♕xd2 ♕xb4∓] 31 ... ♘xd4!

32 ♖c1 ♘e2 33 ♕e3 ♘xc1 34 ♖xc1 c6 35 bxc6 d4 36 ♗xa5 ♗xc5+ ...? **0-1** L/N5188

### 1862-LON1-39
**Steinitz,W.– Blackburne,J.H.**

[Blackburne]

1 e4 e6 2 d4 d5 3 exd5 exd5 4 ♘f3 ♘f6 5 ♗d3 ♗d6 6 0-0 h6 7 ♖e1+ ♗e6 8 ♘e5 [8 ♗f5] 8 ... ♘bd7 [8 ... 0-0] 9 ♘g6 [□ 9 f4] 9 ... fxg6 10 ♖xe6+ ♔f7 11 ♖e1 c6 12 ♗e3 ♕c7 13 ♕f3? ♗xh2+ 14 ♔h1 ♗d6 15 c4 ♖he8 16 cxd5 [□ 16 ♘c3 Δ 17 cxd5] 16 ... cxd5 17 ♘c3 ♘b6 18 ♖ac1 ♕d8 19 g4? a6 20 ♖g1 g5 21 ♗f5 g6 22 ♗b1 ♖c8 23 a3 ♗b8 24 ♗a2 ♔g7 25 ♔g2 ♕d7 26 ♔f1 ♖e7 [Δ 27 ... ♕f8] 27 ♔e2 ♗f4 28 ♔d2 ♘e4+ 29 ♔c2 [29 ♘xe4? dxe4 Δ 30 ... ♕xd4+] 29 ... ♘xc3 30 bxc3 ♘a4 31 ♔d2 ♗xe3+ 32 fxe3 ♘b6 33 ♖gf1 ♕d6 34 ♖f2 ♖ec7 [34 ... ♕xa3?] 35 e4 dxe4 36 ♕xe4 ♖e7 37 ♕f3 ♖ce8 38 ♖h1! [Δ 39 ♕f7+ ♖xf7 40 ♖xf7+ ♔h8 41 ♖xh6++–] 38 ... ♕f4+ 39 ♕xf4 gxf4 40 ♖b1 ♘c8 41 ♗d5 ♘d6 42 ♖b6 ♖d8 43 ♖e2 [43 ♖xf4?] 43 ... ♖xe2+ 44 ♔xe2 ♖d7 45 c4 g5 46 ♔d3 ♔f8 47 ♗h1 ♔e8 48 a4 ♔d8 49 c5 ♘f7 50 ♖xb7 ♘e5+ 51 ♔c3 ♘xg4 52 ♖xd7+ ♔xd7 53 d5 h5 54 d6 ♘f2 55 ♗b7 h4 56 ♔d4 h3 57 ♔e5? [□ 57 ♔d5 h2 58 c6+ ♔e8 59 ♔e6 h1♕ 60 d7+ ♔d8 61 c7+ ♔xc7 62 ♗xh1 ♔d8 63 ♗b7=] 57 ... ♘d3+ 58 ♔f5 ♘xc5 59 ♗f3 ♘e6 60 ♔g4 h2 61 ♔h3 ♘d4 62 ♗h1 ♔xd6 63 ♔xh2 g4 64 ♗b7 a5 65 ♗c8 ♘f3+ 66 ♔g2 ♘h4+ 67 ♔g1 g3 68 ♗b7 ♔e5 69 ♔f1 f3 70 ♔g1 ♔f4 **0-1** L/N3036

### 1862-LON1-40
**Deacon, F.H.+ Green, V.**

[Löwenthal]

1 g3 d5 2 ♗g2 ♘f6 3 e3 e6 4 ♘e2 c5 5 b3 ♘c6 6 ♗b2 ♗d6 7 d3 ♗d7 8 0-0 0-0 9 c4 dxc4 10 dxc4 ♗e7 11 ♘d2 ♕c7 12 a3 ♖ad8 13 ♕c2 b6 14 ♖ae1 ♘e8 15 f4 f5 16 e4 fxe4? [□ 16 ... e5] 17 ♗xe4 h6 18 ♘f3 ♗f6 19 ♘e5 ♘xe5 20 fxe5 ♗e7 21 ♘f4 ♗c6 22 ♗h7+

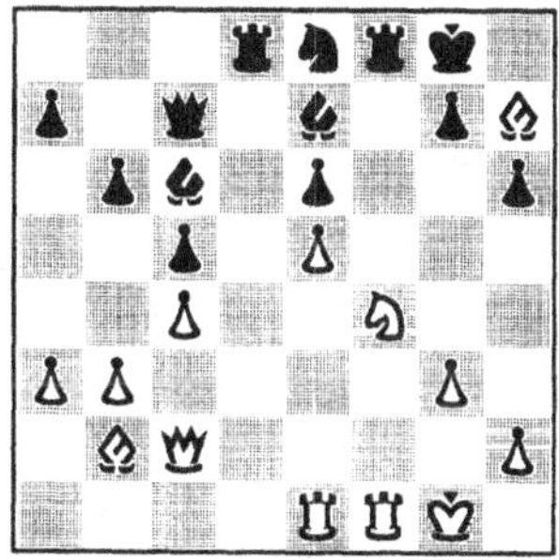

22 ... ♔h8 23 ♘g6+ ♔xh7 24 ♘xe7+ ♖f5 25 ♖xf5 exf5 26 ♕xf5+ ♔h8 27 ♕f8+ ♔h7 28 ♕g8# **1-0** L/N5188

### 1862-LON1-41
**MacDonnell,G.A.+ Deacon,F.H.**

[Löwenthal]

1 e4 c5 2 ♘f3 e6 3 ♘c3 a6 4 a4 ♘c6 5 d4 cxd4 6 ♘xd4 ♕b6 7 ♘xc6 bxc6 8 ♗d3 ♗c5 9 0-0 ♘e7 [□ 9 ... ♗b7 Δ 0-0-0] 10 ♔h1 0-0 [10 ... ♗xf2? 11 ♕f3] 11 f4 f5 12 ♗d2 fxe4 13 ♘xe4 ♘f5 14 ♕h5 ♗e7 [□ 14 ... g6] 15 ♗c3 g6 16 ♕h3 ♗b7 17 ♖ae1 ♖ae8 18 ♘f2 [Δ ♘g4; ♗xf5; ♘h6#] 18 ... ♗f6! 19 ♗xf6 ♖xf6 20 ♘g4 ♖ff8 21 ♗xf5 gxf5 [21 ... exf5 22 ♘f6+!] 22 ♘h6+ ♔g7 23 ♕g3+ ♔h8 24 ♕c3+ e5 25 ♖xe5 ...? **1-0** L/N5188

### 1862-LON1-42
**Mongredien,A.+ Deacon,F.H.**

[Löwenthal]

1 e4 e5 2 f4 exf4 3 ♗c4 d5 4 exd5 ♗d6 [4 ... ♕h4+ 5 ♔f1 f3 6 ♗b5+ c6 7 ♘xf3 ♕g4 8 ♕e2+] 5 ♘f3 ♘e7 [5 ... ♗g4 6 0-0 ♘e7 7 d4 ♘d7 8 ♗b3 g5 9 c4 b6 10 ♘c3 0-0 11 ♘e4 f6= Heydebrand] 6 ♘c3 0-0 7 0-0 ♘d7 8 d4 ♘b6 9 ♗b3 ♗g4 10 ♘e2! ♘bxd5? 11 c4 ♗xf3 12 ♖xf3 ♘e3 13 ♗xe3 fxe3 14 c5 ♗xh2+ 15 ♔xh2 ♘g6 16 ♖xe3 c6 17 ♕d3 ♕c7+ 18 ♔h1 ♖ae8 19 ♖f1 ♖xe3 20 ♕xe3 ♔h8 21 ♗c2 [21 ♗xf7!] 21 ... ♘e7 22 ♘f4 ♕d7 23 ♘e6 ♖g8 24 ♖xf7 ♘d5 25 ♕h3 ...? **1-0** L/N5188

### 1862-LON1-43 — 1 vii 62
**Deacon, F.H.– Robey, J.**

[Löwenthal]

1 e4 e5 2 f4 ♗c5 3 ♘f3 d6 4 c3 ♗g4 5 ♗c4 ♘f6 6 fxe5 ♗xf3 7 ♕xf3 dxe5 8 d3 0-0 9 ♗g5 ♘bd7 10 ♘d2 c6 11 0-0-0 b5 12 ♗b3 a5 13 ♖df1 a4 14 ♗d1 b4 15 ♘c4! bxc3 16 bxc3 ♕e7 17 ♕g3 ♗a3+ 18 ♔d2 ♔h8 19 ♖f5 ♖ad8 20 ♖hf1 ♖fe8 21 ♕h4 ♕c5 22 ♘xa3 [□ 22 ♗xa4] 22 ... ♕xa3 23 ♖xf6 ♕xa2+ 24 ♗c2? [□ 24 ♔e3±] 24 ... ♘xf6 25 ♖xf6 [□ 25 ♗xf6]

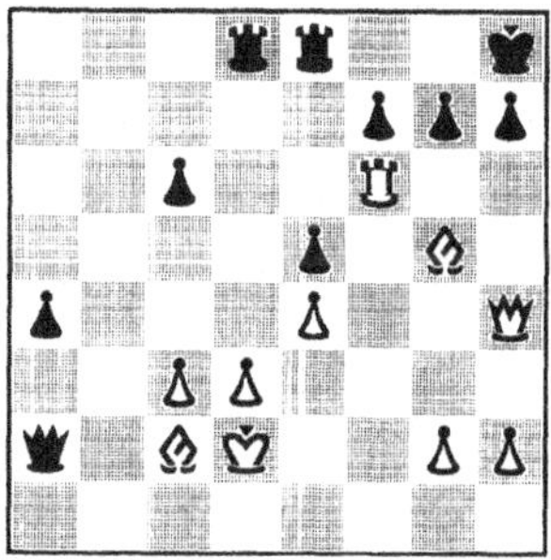

25 ... ♖xd3+ 26 ♔xd3 ♖d8+ 27 ♔e3 ♕xc2 28 ♕e1 ♖d3# **0-1** L/N5188

### 1862-LON1-44
**Dubois, S.+ Green, V.**

[Löwenthal]

1 e4 e5 2 ♘f3 ♘c6 3 d4 exd4 4 ♘xd4 ♗c5 5 ♗e3 ♗xd4 6 ♗xd4 ♘f6 7 ♘c3 0-0 8 ♗xf6 ♕xf6 9 ♗d3 ♘e7 10 ♕d2 c6 11 f4 d6 12 0-0-0 b5 13 ♗e2 b4 14 ♘b1 ♗e6 15 g3 [□ 15 ♕xd6] 15 ... ♗xa2 16 ♕xd6 ♕xd6 17 ♖xd6 ♗xb1 18 ♔xb1 a5

19 ♖d7 ♘g6 20 ♗c4! h6 21 ♖hd1 a4 22 ♖b7 c5 23 ♖dd7 ♘h8 24 e5 ♖ad8 25 f5 ♖xd7 26 ♖xd7 ♖e8 27 e6 fxe6 28 ♗xe6+ ♔f8 29 ♖c7 ♖d8 30 ♖xc5 ♘f7 31 ♔c1 ♘g5 32 ♖c4 ♖b8 33 h4 ♘xe6 34 fxe6 a3 35 bxa3 bxa3 36 ♖a4 ♖e8 37 ♖xa3 ♖xe6 38 ♔d2 ♖e7 39 ♖f3+ ...⚲ **1-0** L/N5188

### 1862-LON1-45
**Dubois, S.+Hannah, J.W.**

[Löwenthal]

1 e4 e6 2 d4 d5 3 exd5 exd5 4 ♗d3 ♘f6 5 ♘f3 ♗d6 6 0-0 0-0 7 ♗g5 ♗g4 8 ♘bd2 ♘c6 9 c3 h6 10 ♗h4 ♗f4 11 ♕c2 ♕d6 12 ♗g3 ♗xf3 13 ♘xf3 ♗xg3 14 fxg3 ♖ae8 15 ♘h4 ♘e4 16 ♖ae1 ♕e6 17 ♘f5 ♔h7 18 ♕c1! ♕f6 19 ♕f4 ♕d8 20 ♗xe4 dxe4 21 ♖xe4 ♖xe4 22 ♕xe4 g6 23 ♘e3 f5 24 ♕f3 ♖e8 25 h4 h5 26 ♘d5 ♖e4 27 ♘f4 ♕e8 28 ♔h2 ♕f7? 29 ♘xh5! ♘d8? [□ 29 ... ♖e7] 30 ♘f6+ ♕xf6 31 ♕xe4 ♘e6 32 ♕e5 ♕xe5 33 dxe5 ♔g7 34 h5 ♘f8 35 hxg6 ♔xg6 36 g4 ...⚲ **1-0** L/N5188

### 1862-LON1-46
**Mongredien, A.= Dubois, S.**

[Löwenthal]

1 d4 f5 2 c4 [2 e4 fxe4 3 ♘c3 ♘f6 (3 ... d5 4 ♕h5+) 4 ♗g5 c6 5 ♗xf6 exf6 6 ♘xe4 d5 7 ♘g3 ♗d6 8 ♗d3 0-0±] 2 ... e6 3 ♘c3 ♘f6 4 e3 b6 5 ♘f3 ♗b4 6 ♗d2 ♗b7 7 ♗e2 0-0 8 0-0 d6 9 ♖c1 c5 10 a3!? [10 ♘g5 △ ♗f3] 10 ... ♗xc3 11 ♗xc3 ♘e4 12 b4 ♘d7 13 ♘d2 ♘xd2 14 ♕xd2 ♕g5 15 f3 ♖ad8 16 ♖f2 ♘f6 17 d5 exd5 [□ 17 ... e5] 18 ♗xf6 ♕xf6 19 cxd5 ♖de8 20 ♗b5 ♖e7 21 ♗c6 ♕e5 22 ♗xb7 ♖xb7 23 ♖e2 ♖e7 24 ♖ce1 ♖fe8 25 ♕d3 ...⚲ **½-½** L/N5188

### 1862-LON1-48
**Owen, J.= Dubois, S.**

[Löwenthal]

1 c4 e5 2 e3 ♘f6 3 a3 c6? [□ 3 ... d5] 4 ♘c3 ♗e7 [□ 4 + d5] 5 d4 d6 6 d5! ♗f5 7 ♘f3 0-0 8 ♗e2 ♘bd7 9 0-0 ♘c5 10 ♘e1 ♘ce4 11 ♘xe4 ♗xe4 12 f3 ♗g6 13 e4 ♘d7 14 g4 cxd5 15 ♕xd5! ♘c5 16 ♗e3 ♘e6 17 b4 ♗g5 18 ♗xg5 ♕xg5 19 ♘g2 ♘d4 20 ♖a2 ♕e7 21 ♗d1 ♕e6 22 ♘e3 ♕xd5 23 ♘xd5 ♖fd8 24 ♔f2 f6 25 ♗e2 ♔f8 26 ♔e3 ♖ac8 27 ♗d3 ♘e6 28 ♖c2 ♗f7 29 ♖c3 h6 30 ♖fc1 b6 31 h4 h5 32 gxh5 ♗xh5 33 ♗f1 ♘d4 34 ♗h3 ♖c6 35 ♗g4 ♗xg4 36 fxg4 ♖d7 37 a4 ♘e6 38 b5 ♖c8 39 a5 bxa5 40 ♖a1 ♘c7 41 ♖xa5 ♘xd5+ 42 exd5 ♖dc7 43 ♔d3 g6 44 ♖a6 ♔e7 45 c5? [□ 45 ♖c6!] 45 ... ♖xc5 46 ♖xa7+ ♔d8 47 ♖b3 ♖xd5+ 48 ♔e3 ♖d4 49 b6 ♖xg4 50 ♔f3 ♖xh4 51 ♔g3 ♖hc4 52 ♔f2 ♖c1 53 ♔e2 d5 54 ♖g7 ♖8c2+ 55 ♔d3 e4+ 56 ♔d4 ♖d1+ 57 ♔e3 ♖d3+ 58 ♖xd3 exd3 59 ♖g8+ ♔d7 60 b7 ♖b2 61 b8♕ ♖xb8 62 ♖xb8 ♔e6 63 ♔xd3 ♔f5 64 ♔e3 g5 65 ♔d4 ♔f4 66 ♔xd5 g4 67 ♖f8 f5 68 ♔d4 g3 69 ♖g8 ♔f3 70 ♔e5 g2 71 ♖g5 f4 ...⚲ **½-½** L/N5188

### 1862-LON1-50
**Dubois, S.– Steinitz, W.**

[Löwenthal]

1 e4 e5 2 ♘f3 ♘c6 3 ♗c4 ♗c5 4 0-0 ♘f6 5 d3 d6 6 ♗g5? h6 7 ♗h4 g5 8 ♗g3 h5 9 h4 [9 ♘xg5? h4 10 ♘xf7 ♕e7 11 ♘xh8 hxg3 12 ♗f7+ ♔d8 13 ♘d2 (13 ♕d2 gxf2+ 14 ♔h1 ♘g4∓) 13 ... ♗xf2+ 14 ♔h1 ♘g4 15 ♘f3 ♕f6–+; 12 ♘f7 ♗xf2+ 13 ♖xf2 gxf2+ 14 ♔xf2 ♘g4+ 15 ♔g3 ♕f6 16 ♕f3 ♕g7–+; 12 ♔h1 ♗xf2 13 ♗f7+ ♔d8 14 ♘d2 ♘g4 15 ♘f3 ♕f6–+] 9 ... ♗g4 10 c3 ♕d7 11 d4 exd4 12 e5 dxe5 13 ♗xe5 ♘xe5 14 ♘xe5 ♕f5! 15 ♘xg4? [□ 15 ♗xf7+ ♔~ 16 ♕e1] 15 ... hxg4 16 ♗d3 ♕d5 17 b4 0-0-0 18 c4 [18 bxc5? ♖xh4 △ ♖dh8] 18 ... ♕c6 19 bxc5 ♖xh4 20 f3 ♖dh8 21 fxg4 ♕e8

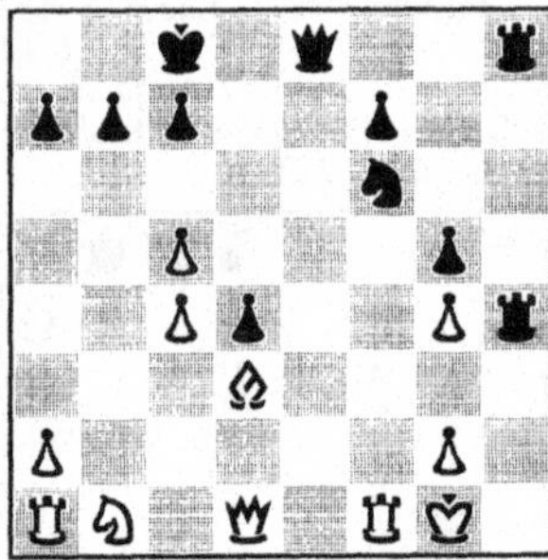

22 ♕e2 [22 ♖e1? ♕f8 23 ♗f5+ ♔b8 24 ♕xd4 ♘xg4 25 ♗xg4 f5–+] 22 ... ♕e3+ 23 ♕xe3 dxe3 24 g3 ♖h1+ 25 ♔g2 ♖8h2+ 26 ♔f3 ♖xf1+ 27 ♗xf1 ♖f2+ 28 ♔xe3 ♖xf1 29 a4 ♔d7 30 ♔d3 ♘xg4 31 ♔c3 ♘e3 32 ♖a2 ♖xb1 33 ♖d2+ ♔c6 34 ♖e2 ♖c1+ 35 ♔d2 ♖c2+ 36 ♔xe3 ♖xe2+ 37 ♔xe2 f5 ...⚲ **0-1** L/N5188

### 1862-LON1-51
**Green, V.– Löwenthal, J.J.**

[Löwenthal]

1 e4 e5 2 d3? ♗c5 3 ♘f3 ♘c6 4 ♘c3 d6 5 ♗e2 h6 6 ♗e3 ♗b6 7 0-0 ♘f6 8 d4 0-0 9 dxe5 dxe5 10 ♗xb6 axb6 11 ♕xd8 ♖xd8 12 a3 ♗g4 [△ ♘d4] 13 ♖ad1 ♗xf3 14 ♗xf3 ♘d4 15 ♖c1 ♘xf3+ 16 gxf3 ♖d2 17 ♖fd1 ♖ad8 18 ♖xd2 ♖xd2 19 ♖d1 [□ 19 ♔f1 △ ♔e1] 19 ... ♖xc2 20 ♖d8+ ♔h7 21 ♖b8 ♘h5 22 ♔g2 ♘f4+ 23 ♔g3 ♖c1 ...⚲ **0-1** L/N5188

### 1862-LON1-52
**Green, V.– MacDonnell, G.A.**

[Löwenthal]

1 e4 e5 2 ♘f3 d6 3 d4 exd4 4 ♘xd4 ♘f6 5 ♘c3 ♗e7 6 f4 0-0 7 ♗e2 ♘bd7 8 0-0 b6? 9 h3 [□ 9 ♘c6 ♕e8 10 ♗f3±] 9 ... ♗b7 10 ♗f3 ♖e8 11 ♘f5 ♗f8 12 ♖e1 g6 13 ♘g3 ♘c5 14 ♘d5 ♗g7 15 c3 ♘xd5 16 exd5 ♕h4 17 ♔h2 ♗h6 18 ♖xe8+ ♖xe8 19 b4 ♘d7 20 ♕a4? ♘f6 21 c4 ♖e1 22 ♕xa7 ♖xc1 23 ♘e2 ♗xf4+ 24 g3 ♗xg3+ 25 ♘xg3 ♖c2+ 26 ♗g2 ♗c8 27 ♘f5 ♘g4+ ...⚲ **0-1** L/N5188

### 1862-LON1-53
**Green, V.– Mongredien, A.**

[Löwenthal]

1 e4 e5 2 f4 exf4 3 ♗c4 ♕h4+ 4 ♔f1 d6 [□ 4 ... g5] 5 d4 [5 ♕f3!] 5 ... ♘c6 6 ♘c3 ♗g4 7 ♕d2? g5 8 ♗e2 [8 g3! fxg3 9 ♔g2; 8 ... ♕h6 9 ♗b5 ♗d7 10 ♗xc6 ♗xc6 11 h4] 8 ... ♘f6 9 ♘f3 ♗xf3 10 ♗xf3 ♗g7 11 e5 dxe5 12 ♗xc6+ bxc6 13 dxe5 ♘g4 14 ♕e2 0-0 15 ♗d2 ♗xe5 16 ♗e1 ♕h5 17 ♔g1 ♖fe8 18 ♕f3 ♗d4+ 19 ♔f1 ♘e3+ [□ 19 ... ♕xh2 20 g3 ♘e3+ 21 ♕xe3 ♕xh1+ 22 ♔f2 ♖xe3–+] 20 ♔e2 ♘xc2+ 21 ♔d2 ♕xf3 22 gxf3 ♘xa1 23 ♔c1 ♗xc3 24 ♗xc3 ♖e2 25 ♔b1 ♘c2 26 h4 ♖ae8 27 a3 ♖e1+ 28 ♗xe1 ♖xe1+ 29 ♖xe1 ♘xe1 ...⚲ **0-1** L/N5188

### 1862-LON1-54
**Owen, J.= Green, V.**

[Löwenthal]

1 c4 e6 2 e3 c5 3 ♘c3 ♘c6 4 ♗e2 ♗d6? 5 ♘e4 ♗e7 6 ♘g3 ♘f6 7 b3 d5 8 cxd5 exd5 9 ♗b2 ♗e6 10 ♘f3 0-0 11 0-0 ♘e4 12 ♘h5 d4 13 d3 ♘f6 14 ♘xf6+ ♗xf6 15 e4 ♕d6 16 ♘d2 ♗e5 17 g3 g5 18 ♗g4 ♔g7 19 ♗xe6 ♕xe6 20 f4 gxf4 21 gxf4 ♗c7 22 ♕f3 ♔h8 23 ♔h1 f5 24 e5 ♖g8 25 ♖g1 ♖ab8 26 ♖ac1 b6 27 a3 a5 28 ♘c4 ♖xg1+ 29 ♖xg1 ♘e7 30 ♖g5 ♖g8 31 ♖xg8+ ♕xg8 32 b4 axb4 33 axb4 ♕d5 34 ♕xd5 ♘xd5 35 bxc5 bxc5 36 ♗a3 ♘xf4 37 ♗xc5 ♔g8 38 ♗xd4 ♘xd3 39 ♔g2 ♔f7 40 ♔f3 ♔e6 41 ♗a7 ♘xe5+ 42 ♘xe5 ♗xe5 43 h3 h5 44 ♗f2 ♔f6 45 ♗e3 ♔g6 46 ♗d2 ♗f6 47 ♗e3 ♗g5 48 ♗b6 ...⚲ **½-½** L/N5188

**1862-LON1-55**
**Green, V.=Owen, J.**

[Löwenthal]

1 f4 f5 2 b3 ♘f6 3 ♘f3 e6 4 e3 b6 5 g3 ♗b7 6 ♗g2 ♗e7 7 ♘c3 c5 8 0-0 0-0 9 ♗b2 ♘a6 10 ♕e2 ♘c7 11 d3 ♕e8 12 ♖ae1 ♖c8 13 ♘d1 d6 14 c4 ♕d7 15 ♘e5? [◻ 15 ♘f2 Δ e4] 15 ... dxe5 16 ♗xb7 ♖b8 17 ♗g2 exf4 18 exf4 ♖bd8 19 ♗e5 ♘fe8 20 ♘b2 ♗f6 21 ♖d1 ♗xe5 22 ♕xe5 ♘f6 23 ♗f3 ♕d4+ 24 ♕xd4 ♖xd4 25 ♖fe1 ♖fd8 26 ♔f2 ♔f7 27 ♖e3 g6 28 ♖de1 h6 ...♀ **½-½** L/N5188

**1862-LON1-56**
**Green, V.–Owen, J.**

[Löwenthal]

1 e4 b6 2 ♘f3 e6 3 ♘c3 ♗b7 4 a3 c5 5 ♗e2 ♗e7 6 d3 ♘f6 7 e5 ♘d5 8 ♘xd5 ♗xd5 9 c4 ♗b7 10 0-0 0-0 11 ♗f4 ♘c6 12 d4 cxd4 13 ♘xd4 ♗c5 14 ♘b5 f6 15 exf6 ♕xf6 16 ♗g3 [◻ 16 ♗d6] 16 ... ♘d4 17 b4 ♘xb5 18 bxc5 ♘c3 19 ♕d2 ♘xe2+ 20 ♕xe2 bxc5 21 ♗d6 ♕g6 22 f3 ♖f5 23 ♕e3 ♖c8 24 ♖ad1 ♗c6 25 ♗xc5? ♗a4 26 ♗xa7 ♗xd1 27 ♖xd1 ♖f7 28 c5 ♕c2 29 ♖xd7! ♖xd7 30 ♕xe6+ ♔f8 31 ♕xd7 ♖e8 32 ♕d6+? [◻ 32 h3] 32 ... ♔g8 33 h3 ♕c1+ 34 ♔h2 ♕xa3 35 ♕d5+ ♔h8 36 ♕f7 ♖a8 37 ♗b6 ♕a6 38 ♕c7 ♖c8 39 ♕a7 ♕b5 40 ♕b7 ♕e8 41 ♕d5 h6 42 f4? ♖c6 43 ♕d4 ♔h7 44 ♔g3 ♖g6+ 45 ♔f3 ♕a8+ 46 ♕e4 ♕a3+ 47 ♔f2 h5 48 f5 ♖f6 49 ♔g1 ♕c1+ 50 ♔h2 ♕g5 51 ♗d8 ♕xf5 52 ♕xf5+ ♖xf5 53 c6 ♖c5 54 c7 ♖c3 55 h4 ♔g6 56 g3 ♔f5 57 ♔g2 ♔g4 58 ♔f1 ♖c2 59 ♗e7 ♔f3 ...♀ **0-1**

L/N5188

**1862-LON1-57**
**Green, V.–Paulsen, L.**

[Löwenthal]

1 e4 e5 2 d3 ♗c5 [◻ 2 ... f5] 3 ♘f3 d6 4 ♘c3 ♘e7 5 ♗e2 0-0 6 ♗g5 ♘bc6 7 ♕d2 f6 8 ♗h4 ♘g6 9 ♗g3 f5 10 exf5 ♗xf5 11 h4 h6 12 0-0-0 ♗b4! 13 h5 ♘ge7 14 ♗h4 ♕d7 15 ♗xe7 ♘xe7 16 ♖dg1 ♘d5 17 ♘h4 ♗xc3 18 bxc3 ♕a4 19 ♔b2 ♕b5+ 20 ♔a1 ♕a5 21 ♔b2 ♗e6 22 ♖a1 ♖xf2 23 ♖he1 ♕b5+ 24 ♔c1 ♕a4! 25 a3 ♕xh4 ...♀ **0-1** L/N5188

**1862-LON1-58**
**Green, V.+Robey, J.**

1 e4 e5 2 ♘c3 ♗c5? 3 f4 d6 4 ♘f3 ♗g4 5 h3 ♗xf3 6 ♕xf3 a6 7 ♗c4 ♘c6 8 ♘e2 ♘f6 9 c3 0-0 10 d3 ♘a5 11 f5! ♘xc4 12 dxc4 h6 13 g4 ♘h7 14 h4 f6 15 ♘g3 ♕e7 16 g5 fxg5 17 hxg5 ♘xg5 18 ♕h5 ♘f7 19 ♗d2 ♕f6 20 0-0-0 b5 21 ♖h4 bxc4 22 ♖g4 ♔h7 23 ♖g6 ♕e7 24 ♖h1 ♖h8

25 ♗xh6 ♗e3+ 26 ♗xe3+ ♔g8 27 ♖xg7+ ♔xg7 28 ♕g6+ ♔f8 29 ♖xh8+ ♘xh8 30 ♗h6+ ...♀ **1-0**

L/N5188

**1862-LON1-59**
**Green, V.=Steinitz, W.**

[Löwenthal]

1 e4 e5 2 ♘f3 ♘c6 3 ♗c4 ♗c5 4 c3 ♘f6 5 d4 exd4 6 cxd4 [◻ 6 e5] 6 ... ♗b4+ 7 ♗d2 ♗xd2+ 8 ♘bxd2 d5 9 exd5 ♘xd5 10 ♕b3 ♘ce7 11 0-0 0-0 12 ♖fe1 ♘f4 13 ♖e4 ♘eg6 14 ♖ae1 ♗f5 15 ♖4e3 ♕d6 16 ♘e5 [16 ♘g5 ♕f6] 16 ... ♘xe5 17 ♖xe5 ♗g6 18 ♘f3 ♔h8 19 ♕e3 ♘h5 20 ♖e8 ♖axe8 21 ♕xe8 ♘f6 22 ♕e7 h6 23 ♕xd6 cxd6 24 h3 [24 ♖e7 d5 25 ♗b3 ♖c8 26 h3 ♖c1+ 27 ♔h2 ♖f1 28 ♖xb7 ♖xf2=] 24 ... ♖e8 25 ♖xe8+ ♘xe8 26 ♔f1 ♔g8 27 ♘d2 ♔f8 28 ♔e2 ♔e7 29 ♔e3 ♘c7 30 f4 d5 31 ♗d3 ♗xd3 32 ♔xd3 ♔f6 33 ♔e3 ♘e6 34 ♘f3 g5 35 g3 h5 36 fxg5+ ♘xg5 37 ♘xg5 ♔xg5 38 ♔f3 ♔f5 39 ♔e3 ♔g5 40 ♔f3 h4 41 g4 ...♀ **½-½**

L/N5188

**1862-LON1-60**
**Steinitz, W.=Green, V.**

[Lowenthal]

1 e4 e5 2 f4 exf4 3 ♘f3 g5 4 h4 g4 5 ♘e5 ♘f6 [◻ 5 ... ♘c6? 6 d4! (6 ♘xg4 d5 7 exd5 ♕e7+ 8 ♔f2 ♕c5+ 9 ♔e1 ♘d4 10 ♘a3 ♕xd5 11 ♘f2 ♗xa3 12 bxa3 ♕e5+∓; 6 ♘xc6 dxc6 10 d4∓) 6 ... ♕e7 7 ♘c3 ♘xe5 8 ♘d5 ♕d6 9 dxe5 ♕xe5 10 ♗xf4 ♕xe4+ 11 ♕e2 ♕xe2+ 12 ♗xe2±] 6 ♗c4 d5 7 exd5 ♗d6 8 d4 ♕e7 9 0-0 ♘h5 10 ♖e1 0-0 11 ♘g6 ♕f6 12 ♘xf8 ♔xf8 13 c3? ♕xh4 14 ♘d2 f3 [◻ 14 ... ♘g3!] 15 ♘xf3! gxf3 16 ♗h6+ ♘g7 17 ♗xg7+ ♔xg7 18 ♕xf3 ♗g4 19 ♕e3 ♗g3 20 ♗e2 ♕h2+ 21 ♔f1 ♕h1+ 22 ♕g1 ♕xg1+ 23 ♔xg1 ♗xe1 24 ♗xg4 ♗g3 25 ♗c8 ♘a6?? [◻ 25 ... a5] 26 ♗xb7 ♖b8 27 ♗xa6 ♖xb2 28 ♗c4 ...♀ **½-½** L/N5188

**1862-LON1-61**
**Green, V.–Steinitz, W.**

[Löwenthal]

1 e4 c5 2 ♘f3 e6 3 ♘c3 d5 4 exd5 exd5 5 d4 ♗e6 6 ♗b5+ ♘c6 7 0-0 ♘f6 8 ♖e1 ♗e7 9 ♗e3 ♘g4 10 dxc5? [◻ 10 ♕d2=] 10 ... ♘xe3 11 fxe3 ♗xc5 12 ♘d4 ♕d6 13 ♘xe6? fxe6 14 ♕g4 0-0 15 ♗xc6 bxc6 16 ♔h1 ♖f2 17 ♖ad1 ♖af8 18 h3 [18 ♘e4? dxe4 19 ♖xd6 ♖f1+→] 18 ... ♕e5 19 e4 h5 20 ♕h4 ♗d6 21 g3 d4 22 ♘e2 g5 23 ♕xh5 ♕xe4+ ...♀ **0-1** L/N5188

**1862-LON1-62**
**MacDonnell, G.A.–Hannah, J.W.**

[Löwenthal]

1 e4 e6 2 d4 d5 3 exd5 exd5 4 ♘f3 ♘f6 5 ♗d3 ♗d6 6 0-0 0-0 7 ♘c3 ♗g4 8 h3 ♗h5 9 ♗g5 ♗e7 10 ♗xf6 ♗xf6 11 g4 ♗g6 12 ♘e5 ♗xe5 [◻ 12 ... ♗xd3 13 ♕xd3 c5] 13 dxe5 c6 14 f4 f5? 15 g5? [◻ 15 gxf5 ♗xf5 16 ♗xf5 ♖xf5 17 ♕g4 ♖f7 (17 ... ♕d7 18 ♘e2±) 18 f5 ♕b6+ 19 ♔h1 ♕xb2 20 f6+–] 15 ... ♕b6+ 16 ♖f2 ♘d7 17 ♕e1 ♘c5 18 ♔h2 ♘e4 19 ♘xe4 [◻ 19 ♖g2] 19 ... fxe4 20 ♗f1 e3 21 ♖f3 ♗e4 22 ♖xe3 ♖xf4 23 ♗g2 ♕xb2 24 ♗xe4 dxe4 25 ♕c3 ♕xc3 26 ♖xc3 ♖e8 27 ♖b1 ♖xe5 28 ♖xb7 e3 29 ♖xc6 e2 30 ♖c8+ ♖f8 31 ♖cc7 ♖xg5 32 ♖e7 ♖f2+ 33 ♔h1 h6 34 ♖b8+ ♔h7 35 ♖be8 ♖gg2 36 c4 ♖h2+ ...♀ **0-1** L/N5188

**1862-LON1-63**
**Hannah, J.W.–Mongredien, A.**

[Löwenthal]

1 e4 e6 2 b3 d5 3 e5 c5 4 d4 ♕b6 5 ♗e3 ♘c6 6 c3 cxd4 7 ♗xd4 ♘xd4 8 ♕xd4 ♗c5 9 ♕d2 [◻ 9 ♕h4] 9 ... a5 10 ♘f3 ♘h6 11 ♗d3 0-0 12 0-0 ♗d7 13 ♕c2 f5? 14 exf6 ♖xf6 15 ♘e5 ♗e8 16 ♗xh7+ ♔h8 17 ♗d3 ♖d8 18 a3 ♗h5 19 b4 ♗d6 20 ♗e2 ♗xe2 21 ♕xe2 ♖f5 22 ♘g6+ ♔g8 23 ♘d2 ♖e8 24 ♘b3 ♕d8 25 g3 ♕g5 26 ♘h4 ♖f4 27 ♘g2 ♖e4 28 ♕d2 ♕h5 29 ♖ae1 ♘g4 30 ♘h4 ♖xe1 31 ♖xe1 ♘xh2?! 32 ♕e2 [◻ 32 ♔xh2] 32 ... ♘g4 33 ♘xa5 g5 34 ♘f3 ♕h3 35 ♕f1 ♕h7 36 ♔g2 ♖e7 37 ♕e2 ♕g6 38 ♕d2 ♗f4? 39 gxf4 gxf4 40 ♔f1 ♖h7 41 ♔e2?? [◻ 41 ♕xf4+–] 41 ... ♕e4+ 42 ♔d1 [42 ♔f1 ♖h1+ 43 ♔g2 ♖h2+ 44 ♔~ ♕xf3→] 42 ... ♕xf3+ 43 ♔c1 ♘xf2 44 ♖xe6 ♖h2 45 ♔b1 ♖h1+ 46 ♔b2 b5 47 ♖e2 ♘d3+ 48 ♔a2 ♘c1+ ...♀ **0-1**

L/N5188

### 1862-LON1-64
**Owen, J.+Hannah, J.W.**

[Löwenthal]

1 e4 e6 2 f4 d5 3 e5 c5 4 ♘f3 ♕b6 5 c4 ♘c6 6 b3 d4 7 d3 ♘h6 8 ♗e2 ♗e7 9 0-0 0-0 10 ♘bd2 f6 11 ♘e4 ♘f7 [□ 11 ... f5 12 ♘eg5 ♘f7] 12 exf6 gxf6 13 ♗d2 ♕c7? [□ 13 ... f5 Δ ... e5] 14 ♕e1 ♔h8 15 ♕h4 ♘d6 16 ♘xd6 ♗xd6 17 ♖ae1 ♘e7 18 ♕h5 ♗d7 19 ♘h4 ♗e8 20 ♕g4 ♗f7 21 ♗f3 ♖g8 22 ♕h3 ♖ab8 [□ 22 ... ♖g7] 23 ♔h1 b5 24 cxb5 ♖xb5 25 f5 e5? [□ 25 ... exf5] 26 ♗e4! ♕d8 27 ♖f3 ♗h5 28 ♘g6+!

28 ... hxg6 [□ 28 ... ♗xg6 29 fxg6 ♘xg6 30 ♖ef1 ♗e7 31 ♖f5 ♕d7 (31 ... ♕c7 32 ♗d5 ♖d8 33 ♕xh7+ ♔xh7 34 ♖h5+ ♔g7 35 ♗h6+ ♔~ 36 ♗f8#) 32 ♖h5 ♕xh3 33 ♖xh3 Δ ♖f5; ♖fh5+-] 29 fxg6 ♔g7 30 ♕xh5 ♖h8 31 ♕g4 ♕c8 32 ♕g3 ♖h5 33 ♕f2 ♕h8 34 g4 ♖h3 35 ♖xh3 ♕xh3 36 ♖f1 ♘g8 37 ♕f5 ♗e7 38 ♖f3 ...⚲ **1-0** L/N5188

### 1862-LON1-65
**Hannah, J.W.–Paulsen, L.**

[Löwenthal]

1 e4 e5 2 ♘f3 ♘c6 3 ♗b5 ♘f6 4 c3 ♘xe4 5 ♕e2! ♘d6 6 ♗xc6 dxc6 7 ♕xe5+ [□ 7 ♘xe5] 7 ... ♕e7 8 d4 f6 9 ♕xe7+ ♗xe7 10 ♗f4 ♗g4 11 ♘bd2 0-0-0 12 0-0 g5 13 ♖fe1 ♖de8 14 ♗g3 ♗d8 15 ♗xd6? [□ 15 h3] 15 ... cxd6 16 ♘e4? [□ 16 ♖xe8 ♖xe8 17 ♖e1±] 16 ... ♔c7 17 ♘fd2 f5 18 ♘g3 f4 19 ♘gf1 h5 20 f3 ♗f5 21 ♔f2 d5 22 ♖xe8 ♖xe8 23 ♖e1 ♖xe1 24 ♔xe1 ♗f6 25 ♘b3 b6 26 ♔e2 a5 27 ♘c1 ♔d6 28 ♘d3 c5 29 dxc5+ bxc5 30 ♔d2 c4 31 ♘c1 g4 32 ♔e2 a4 33 a3 ♔c5 34 ♔d2 gxf3 35 gxf3 d4 36 ♘e2? ♗h3 37 ♔e1 ♗h4+ 38 ♘fg3 fxg3 39 cxd4+ ♔d5 40 hxg3 ♗g5 41 f4 ♗f6 42 ♘c3+ ♔xd4 43 ♘xa4 ♔d3 44 ♔d1 ♗d4 45 ♘c3 ♗xc3 46 bxc3 ♔xc3 47 a4 ♔b4 48 ♔d2 ♔xa4 49 ♔c3 ♔b5 50 ♔b2 ♔b4 ...⚲ **0-1** L/N5188

### 1862-LON1-66
**Steinitz, W.+Hannah, J.W.**

[Löwenthal]

1 e4 e6 2 d4 d5 3 exd5 exd5 4 ♗d3 ♘f6 5 ♘f3 ♗d6 6 0-0 0-0 7 ♘c3 ♗g4 8 h3 ♗h5 9 g4 ♗g6 10 ♗g5 ♗e7 11 ♕d2 ♘c6 12 ♖ae1 ♗b4 13 ♘e5 ♕d6 14 ♗xf6 gxf6 15 ♘xg6 fxg6 16 ♕h6 f5 17 ♘b5 ♕d7 18 c3 ♗e7 [□ 18 ... a6] 19 ♔h1 ♖f6 20 gxf5 ♗f8 21 ♕h4 ♗g7 22 ♖g1 a6 23 fxg6? h6 [□ 23 ... axb5 24 ♕xh7+ (24 gxh7+ ♔h8 25 ♖g4 ♖h6 26 ♕g3 ♖f8 27 ♖g1 ♖f7∓)] 24 ♘a3 ♔f8 25 ♖g3 [□ 25 ♖e3 Steinitz] 25 ... ♖xf2 26 ♘c2 ♖e8 27 ♖eg1 ♖e6 28 ♘e3 ♕e7! 29 ♕xe7+ ♘xe7 30 ♖1g2 ♖xg2 31 ♔xg2 ♗f6 32 ♘g4 ♗g5 33 h4 ♗xh4 34 ♘xh6 ♔g7 35 ♖h3 ♔xh6 [35 ... ♘xg6 36 ♘f5+ ♔f6 37 ♘xh4 ♘f4+ 38 ♔h2 ♘xh3 39 ♘f5 ♘g5=] 36 ♖xh4+ ♔g5 37 ♖h7 ♘xg6 38 ♗xg6 ♔xg6 39 ♖xc7 ♖e2+ 40 ♔f3 ♖xb2 41 a4 ♔f5 42 ♖c5 ♔e6 43 a5 ♔d6 44 ♔f4 ♖a2 45 ♔e3 ♖a3 46 ♔f4 ♖a4 47 ♔e3 ♖a3 48 ♔f4 ♖b3 49 ♔e3 ♖b5? 50 ♖xb5 axb5 51 ♔f4 ♔c6 52 ♔e5 b4 53 cxb4 ♔b5 54 ♔xd5 ♔xb4 55 ♔e6 ♔xa5 56 d5 b5 57 d6 ...⚲ **1-0** L/N5188

### 1862-LON1-68
**MacDonnell, G.A.+Mongredien, A.**

[Löwenthal]

1 e4 e5 2 d4 exd4 3 ♘f3 d6 4 c3 dxc3 [□ 4 ... d3] 5 ♘xc3 ♗g4 6 ♗c4 ♕d7 7 0-0 c6 8 ♗f4 ♗xf3 9 ♕xf3 ♘f6 10 e5 dxe5 11 ♖fe1 ♗e7 12 ♖xe5 ♔f8 13 ♖d1 ♕c8 14 ♖xe7 ♔xe7 15 ♗d6+ ♔d8 16 ♗xb8+ ♔e8 17 ♗d6 ♘d5 18 ♘xd5 cxd5 19 ♕xd5 ♕e6 20 ♕xb7 ...⚲ **1-0** L/N5188

### 1862-LON1-69
4 vii 62

**Owen, J.–MacDonnell, G.A.**

[Löwenthal]

1 c4 c5 2 ♘c3 ♘c6 3 e3 f5 4 f4 ♘f6 5 ♗e2 e6 6 ♘f3 b6 7 b3 ♗b7 8 ♗b2 ♗e7 9 a3? 0-0 10 0-0 ♖c8 11 ♕c2 ♗d6 12 ♖ae1 ♗b8! 13 ♘d1 ♘e7 14 ♘f2 ♘g6 15 ♘d3 ♘g4 16 ♘g5 h6 17 ♗xg4 hxg5 18 ♕c3 ♕e7 19 ♗f3 ♗xf3 20 ♖xf3 g4 21 ♖g3? ♖f7 22 ♔f2 ♕h4 23 ♕c1 d6 24 ♕d1 ♖e8 25 ♖h1 e5 26 h3 exf4 [□ 26 ... ♖fe7] 27 exf4 ♘xf4 28 ♘xf4 gxh3 29 ♕f3? [□ 29 ♘g6+-] 29 ... d5 30 ♖hxh3 ♕xf4 31 ♕xf4 ♗xf4 32 ♖d3 d4 33 ♖h1 ♖fe7 34 ♖d1 ♖e2+ 35 ♔f1 g5 36 ♗c1 g4 37 b4 ♗h2 38 bxc5 bxc5 39 ♖b3 f4 40 ♖b8 ♖xb8 41 ♔xe2 ♖e8+ 42 ♔f1 [42 ♔d3 f3-+] 42 ... d3! 43 ♖e1 ♖b8 44 a4 ♗g3 45 ♖d1 ♖b1 46 ♔g1 ♔f7 47 ♖f1 ♔e6 48 ♗a3 ♗h2+ 49 ♔xh2 ♖xf1 50 ♗xc5 ♔f5 51 g3 f3 52 ♗xa7 ♖e1 ...⚲ **0-1** L/N5188

### 1862-LON1-70
**MacDonnell, G.A.+Paulsen, L.**

[Löwenthal]

1 e4 e5 2 f4 ♗c5 3 ♘f3 d6 4 c3 ♗g4 5 ♗e2 ♗xf3 6 ♗xf3 ♘c6 7 d3 [□ 7 b4 ♗b6 8 b5 ♘ce7 9 d4 exd4 10 cxd4±] 7 ... ♘f6 8 ♕b3 ♗b6 9 ♘a3 a5? 10 ♘c4 0-0 [□ 10 ... ♖a6] 11 ♘xb6 cxb6 12 0-0 h6 13 f5 a4 14 ♕d1 ♕c7 15 ♗e3 ♖fe8 16 ♖c1 ♖a5 17 ♖c2 ♕d8 18 ♖d2 ♖e7 19 g4 ♘h7 20 ♖g2 f6 21 b4 ♖a8 22 b5 ♘b8 23 h4 ♖f7 24 g5 fxg5 25 ♗h5 ♖d7 26 hxg5 d5 27 f6 gxf6 28 gxf6+ ♔h8 29 ♗xh6 ♘xf6 30 ♖g6 ♖f7 31 ♖fxf6 ♕xf6 32 ♖xf6 ♖xf6 33 ♕g4 ♖xh6 34 ♕c8+ ♔g7 35 ♕xb7+ ♘d7 36 ♕xa8 ♖xh5 37 ♕b7 dxe4 38 ♕xd7+ ♔g6 39 ♕e6+ ...⚲ **1-0** L/N5188

### 1862-LON1-71
3 vii 62

**Robey, J.–MacDonnell, G.A.**

[Löwenthal]

1 e4 e5 2 ♘f3 d6 3 d4 exd4 4 ♕xd4 ♗d7 5 ♗e3 ♘f6 6 ♘c3 ♗e7 7 ♗e2 0-0 8 0-0 ♘c6 9 ♕d2 ♘e5 10 ♘e1! ♗c6 11 f4 ♘g6 12 ♗d3 ♘g4 13 ♘f3 ♘xe3 14 ♕xe3 ♗f6 15 ♖ad1 ♗xc3 16 bxc3 ♕e7 17 f5 ♘e5 18 ♘xe5 ♕xe5 19 ♕e2 [□ 19 f6] 19 ... f6 20 c4 [□ 20 ♗c4+] 20 ... ♖fe8 21 ♖de1 ♖e7 22 ♕g4 ♖ae8 23 ♖f3? d5! 24 cxd5 ♗xd5 25 ♖g3 ♗xa2 26 h4 ♗d5 27 ♖e2 ♗c6 28 h5 h6 29 ♔h2 b5 30 ♔h3 a5 31 ♖ee3 ♔h8 32 ♕e2 ♗d7 33 ♕f1! ♕c5 34 ♖ef3 ♖e5 35 ♖g6 ♖xe4! 36 ♗xe4 ♖xe4 37 c3 ♖e5 38 g4 ♖e3 39 ♕f2 ♖xf3+ 40 ♕xf3 ♗c6 41 ♕d3 ♕d5 42 ♕xd5 ♗xd5 43 g5 ♗f7 44 gxf6 ♗xg6 45 fxg7+ ♔xg7 46 hxg6 a4 ...⚲ **0-1** L/N5188

### 1862-LON1-72
**MacDonnell, G.A.+Steinitz, W.**

[Löwenthal]

1 e4 e5 2 d4 exd4 3 ♘f3 ♘c6 4 ♗c4 ♗c5 5 0-0 d6 6 c3 ♗g4 7 b4! [7 ♕b3 ♘a5∓] 7 ... ♗b6 8 a4 a5 9 b5 ♘e5 10 ♗e2 d3 11 ♗xd3 ♗xf3 [□ 11 ... ♘xf3] 12 gxf3 ♕h4 13 ♔h1 [Δ ♗e3] 13 ... ♗xf2? [□ 13 ... ♘f6] 14 ♖a2! ♗b6 [14 ... ♗g3 15 f4] 15 ♖g2 ♘f6 16 ♗e2 [16 ♖xg7 ♘g6∓] 16 ... h6 17 f4! ♘g6? 18 f5 ♘e5 19 ♖f4!

19 ... ♕h3 20 ♖g3 ♕xg3 21 hxg3 h5 22 ♘d2 ♘fg4 23 ♘c4 ♘f2+ 24 ♖xf2 ♗xf2 25 ♗f4 h4 26 g4 f6 27 ♕d5 0-0-0 28 ♗e3 ♗g3 29 ♘xa5 ...⚲ **1-0** L/N5188

### 1862-LON1-73 1 vii 62

**Owen, J.= Mongredien, A.**

[Löwenthal]

1 e4 g6 2 d4 ♗g7 3 ♘f3 b6 4 ♗d3 e6 5 c3 ♗b7 6 ♗e3 d6 7 ♘bd2 ♘e7 8 0-0 0-0 9 ♕e2 ♕d7 10 ♘g5 f6 11 ♘h3 f5 12 f3 e5 13 dxe5 ♗xe5 [13 ... dxe5? 14 ♗c4+ Δ ♘g5±] 14 ♗h6 ♗g7 15 ♗c4+ d5 16 ♗xg7 ♔xg7 17 exd5 ♗xd5 18 ♕e5+ ♔g8 19 ♘f4 ♗xc4 20 ♘xc4 ♘bc6 21 ♕b5 [□ 21 ♕e6+] 21 ... ♖f6 22 ♖ad1 ♕e8 23 ♘e5 [□ 23 ♖fe1] 23 ... a6 24 ♘d5?

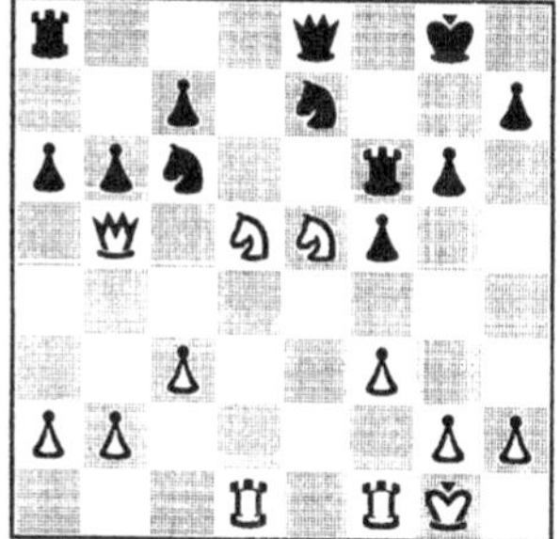

24 ... ♖e6 25 ♘xe7+ ♕xe7 26 ♕d5 ♕c5+ 27 ♕xc5 bxc5 28 ♘xc6 ♖xc6 29 ♖d7 ♖e8 30 ♖fd1 ♖ee6 31 ♔f2 ♖ed6 32 ♖1xd6 ♖xd6 33 ♖e7 ♖d2+ 34 ♖e2 ♖d6 35 ♔e1 ♔f7 36 ♖e5 ♖e6 37 ♖xe6 ♔xe6 38 ♔d2 c4 39 ♔e3 ♔e5 40 f4+ ♔d5 41 b4 c5 42 a4 ...⚲ **½-½** L/N5188

### 1862-LON1-74 2 vii 62

**Mongredien, A.= Owen, J.**

[Löwenthal]

1 e4 c5 2 ♗c4 e6 3 ♘c3 a6 4 a4 ♗e7 5 ♘f3 ♘c6 6 0-0 ♗f6 7 d3 ♘ge7 8 ♗f4 d6 9 ♖e1 ♘g6 10 ♗g3 0-0 11 ♖b1? [□ 11 h3] 11 ... ♗xc3 12 bxc3 e5 13 d4 [□ 13 h3] 13 ... cxd4 14 cxd4 ♗g4 15 c3 ♗xf3 16 gxf3 h5 17 h3 ♕f6 18 d5 ♘a5 19 ♗e2 ♖ac8 20 ♕d2 ♖c7 21 ♗h2 ♖fc8 22 ♖ec1 ♘h4 23 ♕e3 ♘c4 24 ♕d3 ♕g5+ 25 ♗g3 ♘d2? 26 f4 exf4 27 ♕xd2 ♘g6 28 ♔h1 ♕e5 29 ♗h2 ♕xe4+ 30 f3 ♕xa4 31 c4 ♕d7 32 ♗f1 ♕f5 33 ♕d3 ♕g5 34 ♕d4 ♕f5 35 ♖b6 ♖d8 36 ♖e1 ♕g5 37 ♖e4 f5 38 ♖xf4 [□ 38 ♖e6 ♘e5 (38 ... ♖e7 39 ♖xe7 ♕xe7 40 ♗xf4 ♕e8 41 ♔g1 ♘h4 42 ♕f2+−; 38 ... ♖cd7 39 ♖b2 ♘h4 40 ♗xf4 ♘xf3 41 ♕e3+−) 39 ♗xf4 ♕h4 40 ♗xe5 ♕e1 41 ♔g2 dxe5 42 ♖xe5+−] 38 ... ♘xf4 39 ♗xf4 ♕h4 40 ♕d2 ♖e8 41 ♔h2 ♖d7 42 ♗g3 ♕d8 43 ♕b4 [□ 43 ♗f2 Δ ♗d4±] 43 ... f4 44 ♗xf4 ♕f6 45 ♕d2 ♖f7 ...⚲ **½-½** L/N5188

### 1862-LON1-75 3 vii 62

**Owen, J.+ Mongredien, A.**

[Löwenthal]

1 c4 f5 2 e3 ♘f6 3 d4 e6 4 a3 c5 5 d5 e5 6 ♘c3 d6 7 ♗e2 ♗e7 8 ♘h3 ♗d7 9 0-0 ♘a6 10 ♗d2 ♘c7 11 f3 0-0 12 ♘f2 ♔h8 13 ♔h1 g5! 14 ♕e1 ♖g8 15 ♘cd1 ♕e8 16 ♗c3 g4 17 g3 ♕h5 18 ♘d3 ♖g6 19 ♖f2 ♖ag8 20 f4 e4 [20 ... ♘e4? 21 fxe5] 21 ♘c1 ♖6g7 22 b4 ♕f7 23 bxc5 dxc5 24 ♕d2 ♘ce8 25 a4 h5 26 ♗f1 ♖h7 27 ♕b2 h4 28 ♘e2 ♘g7 [□ 28 ... ♗c8] 29 ♕xb7 ♗c8 30 ♕xa7 hxg3 31 ♘xg3 ♘gh5 32 ♘xh5 ♕xh5 33 ♕b6 ♖f7 34 ♖g2 ♔h7 35 ♖g3 ♘d7 36 ♕c6 ♗h4 37 ♖g2 ♗f6 38 ♗e2 ♗xc3 39 ♘xc3 ♘f6 40 ♕xc5 ♕h4 41 ♕d4 ♖g6 42 ♕d2 ♘h5 43 ♕e1 ♕h3 44 ♖d1 ♕xe3 45 ♗f1 ♕xf4 46 ♖f2 ♕e5 47 ♘xe4 ♖e7 48 d6 ♕xe4+ 49 ♕xe4 ♖xe4 50 d7 ♗xd7 51 ♖xd7+ ♖g7 52 ♖xg7+ ♘xg7 53 a5

53 ... ♖e5? [53 ... ♖e1 54 a6 ♖a1 55 c5 ♔g6 56 ♔g2 (56 c6 ♘e6 57 ♔g2 ♘c7=) 56 ... ♔g5 57 ♗c4 ♘e8 58 ♖a2 ♖c1 59 a7 ♘c7 60 ♗d5 ♖xc5=] 54 ♖a2 ♘e8 55 a6 ♘c7 56 a7 ♖e8 57 ♖b2 ♔h6 58 ♖b7 ♖e1 59 ♔g2 ♘a8 60 ♖b8 ♘c7 61 ♖c8 f4 62 ♖xc7 f3+ 63 ♔g3 ...⚲ **1-0** L/N5188

### 1862-LON1-76

**Paulsen, L.+ Mongredien, A.**

[Löwenthal]

1 e4 g6 2 ♘c3 ♗g7 3 g3 e6 4 ♗g2 c6 5 ♘ge2 d5 6 d4 dxe4 7 ♘xe4 f5 8 ♘g5 ♗f6 [□ 8 ... e5] 9 ♘f3 ♘d7 10 b3 e5 11 ♗b2 e4 12 ♘d2 ♘e7 13 0-0 0-0 14 c4 c5 15 ♕c2 cxd4 16 ♘xd4 ♘c5 17 ♘e2 ♗xb2 [□ 17 ... ♘c6] 18 ♕xb2 ♘c6 19 ♘f4 ♘b4 20 ♖ad1 ♗d7 21 ♕e5 ♘cd3 22 ♘xd3 ♘xd3 23 ♕d5+ ♖f7 24 ♕xb7 ♗e8 25 ♕d5 ♕xd5 26 cxd5 ♖d8 27 ♘c4 ♖xd5 28 a4 ♖e7 29 ♖d2 ♗f7 30 ♖fd1 ♖d4 [□ 30 ... ♖c5] 31 a5 ♔g7 [31 ... ♗xc4? 32 bxc4 ♖xc4 33 ♖xd3 exd3 34 ♗d5+] 32 ♗f1 ♗xc4 33 bxc4 ♖xc4 34 ♗xd3 exd3 35 ♖xd3 ♖a4 36 ♖d7 ♔f7 37 ♖1d5 ♔e8 38 ♖7d6 ♖ae4 39 ♖b5 ♖4e6 40 ♖xe6 ♖xe6 41 ♖b8+ ♔f7 42 ♖b7+ ♖e7 43 a6 ♔e6 44 ♔g2 ♔d6 45 ♖b2 ♖c7 46 h4 h6 47 h5 gxh5 48 ♖b5 ♖f7? [□ 48 ... ♔e6] 49 ♔f3 ♔c6 50 ♖b8 ♔d6 51 ♔f4 ♔c6 52 f3 ♖d7 53 ♖b4 ♖f7 54 ♔e5 f4 55 ♖xf4 ♖g7 56 ♖f6+ ♔b5 57 ♔f4 ♖c7 58 ♖xh6 ♖c4+ 59 ♔g5 ♖c3 60 ♖f6 ♖a3 61 ♔xh5 ♖xa6 62 ♖xa6 ♔xa6 63 g4 ♔b5 64 g5 a5 65 g6 a4 66 g7 ...⚲ **1-0** L/N5188

### 1862-LON1-77

**Robey, J.– Mongredien, A.**

[Lowenthal]

1 e4 g6 2 d4 ♗g7 3 ♘f3 b6 4 ♗d3 e6 5 ♗e3 ♗b7 6 ♘c3 ♘e7 7 ♘e2 0-0 8 ♘g3? f5 9 ♕d2 fxe4 10 ♘xe4 ♗xe4 11 ♗xe4 d5 12 ♗d3 ♘f5 13 0-0 ♘d7 14 c3 c6 15 ♗f4 ♖e8 16 g4 ♘h4 17 ♘xh4 ♕xh4 18 g5 e5? 19 ♗g3? ♕h3 20 dxe5 ♘xe5 21 f4 ♘xd3 22 ♕xd3 ♖e4 23 ♖fe1 ♖ae8 24 ♕a6 ♖xe1+ 25 ♗xe1 ♗f8 26 ♗g3 ♗c5+ 27 ♔h1 b5 28 ♖g1 [□ 28 ♕xc6] 28 ... ♕g4 29 ♖f1 ♕e2 30 ♖g1 ♕f3+ ...⚲ **0-1** L/N5188

### 1862-LON1-78

**Steinitz, W.+ Mongredien, A.**

[Löwenthal]

1 e4 d5 2 exd5 ♕xd5 3 ♘c3 ♕d8 4 d4 e6 5 ♘f3 ♘f6 6 ♗d3 ♗e7 7 0-0 0-0 8 ♗e3 b6 9 ♘e5 ♗b7 10 f4 ♘bd7 11 ♕e2 ♘d5 12 ♘xd5 exd5 13 ♖f3! f5 14 ♖h3 g6 15 g4! fxg4? [□ 15 ... ♘xe5 Δ ... ♗c8] 16 ♖xh7!!

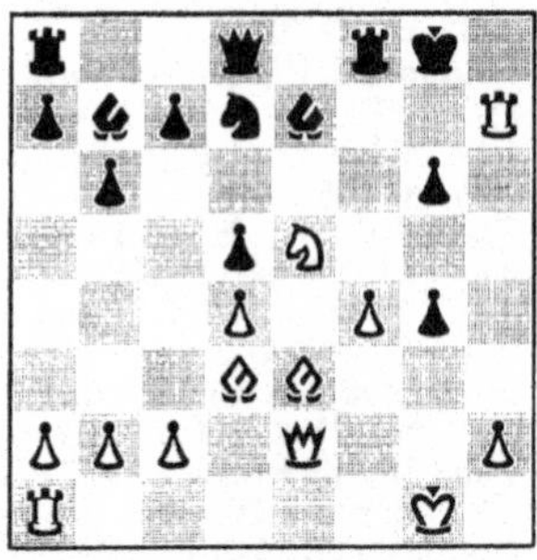

16 ... ♘xe5 [16 ... ♔xh7 17 ♕xg4 ♘xe5 18 fxe5] 17 fxe5 ♔xh7 18 ♕xg4 ♖g8 [18 ... ♕e8 19 ♕h5+ ♔g8 20 ♗xg6 ♖f7 21 ♔h1 ♗f8 22 ♖g1 ♗g7 23 ♗h6+-] 19 ♕h5+ ♔g7 20 ♕h6+ ♔f7 21 ♕h7+ ♔e6 22 ♕h3+ ♔f7 23 ♖f1+ ♔e8 24 ♕e6 ♖g7 25 ♗g5 ♕d7 26 ♗xg6+ ♖xg6 27 ♕xg6+ ♔d8 28 ♖f8+ ♕e8 29 ♕xe8# **1-0** L/N5188

**1862-LON1-79**
**Paulsen, L.+Owen, J.**
[Löwenthal]

1 e4 b6 2 g3 e6 3 ♗g2 ♗b7 4 ♘c3 f5 5 ♘ge2 ♘f6 6 d3 ♗b4 7 0-0 ♗xc3 8 ♘xc3 fxe4 9 ♘xe4 ♘xe4 10 ♕h5+! g6 11 ♕e5 0-0 12 dxe4 ♘c6 13 ♕c3 e5 14 ♗h6 ♖f7 15 f4! ♗a6 [□ 15 ... ♕e7] 16 fxe5 ♗xf1 17 ♖xf1 ♕e7 18 ♖xf7 ♕xf7 19 e6! ♕e7 20 exd7 ♘e5 [20 ... ♕xd7 21 e5!] 21 ♗h3 g5 22 ♕xc7 g4 23 d8♕+ ♕xd8 24 ♕g7# **1-0** L/N5188

**1862-LON1-80**
**Robey, J.–Owen, J.**
[Löwenthal]

1 e4 b6 2 d4 ♗b7 3 ♗d3 e6 4 ♘f3 c5 5 c3 ♘f6 6 ♗g5? h6 7 ♗xf6 ♕xf6 8 ♕d2 [□ 8 ♕e2] 8 ... ♕g6 9 0-0 [□ 9 ♕e2] 9 ... ♗xe4 10 ♗xe4 ♕xe4 11 ♖e1 ♕b7 12 d5 ♗e7 13 c4 ♗f6 14 ♘c3 ♗xc3 15 ♕xc3 0-0 16 ♖ad1 ♕c7 17 ♖e4 ♕d6 18 ♖g4 [□ 18 ♖d3] 18 ... f6 19 ♖g6 ♘c6 20 ♕c1 ♘e7 21 ♖g3 ♘f5 22 ♖h3 ♖ae8 23 g4 ♘e7 24 dxe6 ♕xe6 25 ♖g3 ♘g6 26 ♖d5 ♕e4! 27 ♖f5 ♖f7 28 b3 ♖fe7 29 h4 h5! 30 ♖xf6 hxg4 31 ♖d6 gxf3 32 ♖dxg6 ♕xh4 33 ♔f1 ♕h1+ 34 ♖g1 ♕h3+ 35 ♖6g2 fxg2+ ...⚑ **0-1** L/N5188

**1862-LON1-81**
**Steinitz, W.=Owen, J.**
[Löwenthal]

1 e4 c5 2 ♘f3 e6 3 d4 cxd4 4 ♘xd4 ♘f6 5 ♘c3 ♗b4 6 ♗d3 ♘c6 7 ♘xc6 dxc6 8 0-0 ♗xc3 9 bxc3 ♕a5 10 c4 h6 11 f4 e5 12 fxe5 [□ 12 f5] 12 ... ♕xe5 13 ♗f4 ♕d4+ 14 ♔h1 ♗e6 15 ♕e2 ♘g4 16 h3 [16 e5 g5 (16 ... f5 17 exf5 ♕xf6 18 ♗d6!) 17 ♗g3 h5 18 h4 ♕e3∓] 16 ... ♘e5 17 ♖ab1 b6 18 ♗e3 ♕d7 19 c5 b5 20 ♖fd1 ♘xd3 21 ♖xd3 ♕c8 22 ♕h5 ♔f8 23 ♖bd1 ♔g8 24 ♖d8+ ♕xd8 25 ♖xd8+ ♖xd8 26 c3 ♗xa2 27 ♗d4 ♔h7 28 ♕f5+ g6 29 ♕f2 ♗e6 30 ♗xh8 ♖xh8 31 ♕f4 ♖c8 32 ♔g1 a5 33 ♔f2 a4 34 ♕c1 ♖d8 35 ♔e3 ♗b3 36 h4 h5 37 ♔f4 ♖d1 38 ♕b2 ♖d3 39 ♔e5 ♔g7 40 ♕c1 ...⚑ **½-½** L/N5188

**1862-LON1-82** 30 vi 62
**Owen, J.+Steinitz, W.**
[Löwenthal]

1 c4 f5 2 e3 e6 3 a3 ♘f6 4 ♘c3 ♗e7 5 ♘f3 0-0 6 d4 b6 7 d5 ♗d6 8 ♗d3 ♗b7 9 0-0 ♔h8 10 ♗c2 ♘a6 11 b4 ♕e8 12 ♗b2 ♕h5 13 ♘b5 exd5 14 ♘xd6 cxd6 15 ♗xf6 ♖xf6 16 cxd5 ♘c7 17 ♗b3 ♖h6 18 ♖c1 ♘e8 19 ♖c4 g5 20 h4 g4 21 ♘g5 ♗a6 22 ♖f4 ♗xf1 [□ 22 ... ♘g7 23 e4 (23 ♗c4? ♗xc4 24 ♖xc4 ♖f6∓) 23 ... ♖f6 24 exf5 ♗xf1 25 ♔xf1] 23 ♖xf5 ♖f6 24 ♕d4 ♕g6 25 ♗c2 ♕g7 26 ♖xf6 ♘xf6 27 ♔xf1 ♖e8 28 ♕f4 h6 29 ♘e4 ♖f8 30 ♔g1 g3 31 ♘xg3 ♘g4 32 ♕d4 ♕xd4 33 exd4 ♖c8 34 ♗f5 ♖c1+ 35 ♘f1 ♘f6 [□ 35 ... ♘h2] 36 f3 ♘xd5 37 ♗xd7 ♘e3 38 ♗b5 ♖a1 39 ♔f2 ♘xf1 40 ♗xf1 ♖xa3? [□ 40 ... a5] 41 b5 ♔g7 42 g4 ♔f6 43 f4 ♖b3 44 ♗e2 h5? 45 g5+ ♔f5 46 ♗xh5 ♔xf4 47 ♗f7 ♖a3 [□ 47 ... ♖b2+] 48 g6 ♖f3+ 49 ♔e2 ♖g3 50 h5 ♔f5 51 ♔f2 ♖g5 52 ♔f3 ♔f6 53 h6 ♖xb5 54 ♗e8 ♖g5 55 g7 b5 56 ♔f4 b4 57 h7 ♔xg7 58 ♔xg5 ♔xh7 59 ♗a4 ♔g7 60 ♗b3 ♔f8 61 ♔f6 ...⚑ **1-0** L/N5188

**1862-LON1-83**
**Robey, J.–Paulsen, L.**
[Löwenthal]

1 e4 e5 2 ♘f3 ♘c6 3 ♗b5 ♘f6 4 0-0 ♗e7 5 c3 ♘xe4 6 ♖e1 ♘f6 7 ♗xc6 dxc6 8 ♘xe5 0-0 9 d4 c5 10 ♗e3 cxd4 11 ♕xd4 [□ 11 ♗xd4] 11 ... ♗e6 12 ♘d2 ♘d5 13 ♘b3 ♗f6 14 ♖ad1 ♕d6 11 ♗xd4] 15 ♗c1 ♖ad8 16 f4 ♕b6 17 ♕f2 ♗e7 18 ♘d4 ♗c5 19 f5 ♗c8 20 ♗e3 ♘xe3 21 ♕xe3 ♗xf5 22 ♕f4 ♗e6 23 ♔h1 ♗xd4 24 cxd4 ♕xb2 25 ♖e3 [□ 25 ♖d3] 25 ... c5 26 ♖g3 ♖xd4 27 ♖xg7+? ♔h8 28 ♘g6+ ♔xg7 29 ♕e5+ f6 ...⚑ **0-1** L/N5188

**1862-LON1-84**
**Steinitz, W.–Paulsen, L.**
[Löwenthal]

1 e4 c5 2 ♘f3 g6 3 ♘c3 ♗g7 4 ♗c4 ♘f6 5 e5 ♘g8 [□ 5 ... ♘g4] 6 0-0 ♘c6 7 ♕e2 ♘h6 8 ♘e4 0-0 [8 ... ♗xe5? (8 ... ♘xe5 9 ♘xe5 ♗xe5 10 d4!±) 9 d4 ♗g7 10 ♗xh6 ♗xh6 11 ♘d6+ ♔f8 12 ♘xf7±] 9 ♘xc5 d5 [□ 9 ... d6 10 exd6 exd6 11 ♘b3 d5] 10 ♗b5 ♕b6 11 ♘a4 ♕a5 12 d4 ♘f5 13 c3 ♗d7 14 ♗xc6 [□ 14 b4 Δ ♘c5] 14 ... ♗xc6 15 ♘c5 ♗b5 16 ♘d3 ♕a6 17 ♖d1 e6 18 g4! ♘e7 19 g5 ♘f5 20 ♕c2 ♖ac8 21 a4 ♗e8 22 b3 ♗d7 23 ♗a3 ♖fd8 24 h4 ♕c6 25 ♗b2 ♕b6 26 ♘c5 ♗e8 27 ♔g2 ♕c7 28 b4? ♕e7 29 h5 gxh5 30 ♖h1 h4 31 ♕d2 h6 32 ♖ag1 hxg5 33 ♔f1 b6 34 ♘d3 f6 35 exf6 ♕xf6 36 ♘de5 ♗h5 37 ♘xg5 ♖c7 38 ♔e1 ♖f8 39 ♖h2 a5 40 b5 ♕h6 41 ♗c1 ♕f6 42 ♘h3 ♖fc8 43 ♘f4 ♗e8 44 ♗b2 ♘d6 45 ♖hg2 ♕f5 46 ♕e3 ♕b1+ 47 ♗c1? [□ 47 ♕c1] 47 ... ♘f5 48 ♕d2 ♖xc3 49 ♖xg7+ ♘xg7 50 ♖xg7+ ♔xg7 51 ♘xe6+ ♔g8 ...⚑ **0-1** L/N5188

**1862-LON1-85**
**Steinitz, W.+Robey, J.**
[Löwenthal]

1 e4 e5 2 f4 ♗c5 3 ♘f3 d6 4 c3 ♗g4 5 ♗e2 ♘c6 6 b4 ♗b6 7 a4 a6 8 d3 ♕e7 9 ♘a3! ♘f6 10 ♘c4 ♗xf3 11 ♗xf3 ♗a7 12 b5 ♘d8 [12 ... axb5 13 axb5±] 13 bxa6 bxa6 14 ♘e3 0-0 15 f5 ♖b8 16 0-0 ♘c6 17 ♔h1 ♘a5 18 ♘g4 ♘xg4 19 ♗xg4 f6 20 ♗a3 ♖b7 21 ♕c2 ♖fb8 22 ♖ab1 ♕e8 23 h3 ♖xb1 24 ♖xb1 ♖xb1+ 25 ♕xb1 ♕xa4 26 ♗b4 ♘c6 27 ♗d1 ♕b5 28 ♕a2+ ♔f8 29 ♕e6! ♘xb4 [29 ... ♕xd3 30 ♕c8+ ♔e7 31 ♕xc7++-] 30 ♗h5! g6 31 fxg6 hxg6 32 ♗xg6 ...⚑ **1-0** L/N5188

## LONDON 1862

**1862-LON2-1**
**Mackenzie,G.H.+ Medley,G.W.**
[Löwenthal]

1 e4 e5 2 ♘f3 ♘f6 3 ♘xe5 d6 4 ♘f3 ♘xe4 5 d4 d5 6 ♗d3 ♗e7 7 0-0 0-0 8 h3 ♗e6 9 c4 ♘c6 10 cxd5 ♗xd5 11 ♘c3 ♘xc3 12 bxc3 f5 13 ♖e1 ♗d6 14 ♗d2 ♕f6 15 ♖b1 ♖ae8? 16 ♖xb7 ♖xe1+ [16 ... ♘xd4 17 cxd4 ♗xb7 18 ♕b3+±] 17 ♗xe1 ♕f7 18 ♖b2 ♕h5 19 ♗e2 f4 20 ♖b5 a6 21 ♘e5 f3 22 ♖xd5 ♘xe5 23 ♗c4 ♔h8 24 dxe5 ♕g5 25 g3 ♗xe5 26 ♕d2 ♕f6 27 ♕e3 ♗d6 28 ♗d3 ♖b8 29 ♕e4 g6 30 ♗d2 ♖b2 31 ♗e3 **1-0** L/N5188

**1862-LON2-2**
**Mackenzie,G.H.– Medley,G.W.**
[Löwenthal]

1 e4 e6 2 d4 d5 3 exd5 exd5 4 ♘f3 ♘f6 5 ♗d3 ♗d6 6 0-0 0-0 7 h3

h6 8 ♗e3 ♗e6 9 ♕d2 [□ 9 ♘c3] 9 ... ♘e4 [Δ f5] 10 ♗xe4 dxe4 11 ♘h2 [□ 11 ♘e5] 11 ... f5 12 f4 c6 13 ♘c3 ♗b4 14 ♕f2 ♗xc3 15 bxc3 ♘d7 16 ♕g3 ♗c4 17 ♖fe1 ♘b6 18 ♘f1 ♗xf1 [□ 18 ... ♕d5] 19 ♖xf1 ♘c4! 20 ♖fb1 b5 21 a4 a6 22 ♗f2 ♔h7 23 h4 ♕d6 24 h5 ♖g8 25 ♕h3 ♕xf4 26 ♖e1 g6 27 axb5 cxb5 28 d5 gxh5 29 ♗d4 ♕g4 30 ♕h2 ♕g3 31 ♕xg3 ♖xg3 32 ♔h2 ♖gg8 33 ♖f1 ♔g6 34 ♖f4 ♖gd8 35 ♖af1 ♖xd5 36 ♔h3 ♔g5 37 ♖h4 ♖f8 [□ 37 ... a5∓] 38 g3 ♘d2 39 ♗e3+ [□ 39 ♖d1∓] 39 ... ♔g6 40 ♖d1 ♖fd8 41 ♖a1 ♘f3 42 ♖xa6+ ♖8d6→ **0-1** L/N5188

### 1862-LON2-3
### Mackenzie,G.H.+ Medley,G.W.

[Löwenthal]

1 e4 g6 2 d4 ♗g7 3 ♘f3 [□ 3 f4] 3 ... e6 4 ♗d3 ♘e7 5 0-0 0-0 6 ♗g5 b6 [□ 6 ... f6 7 ♗h4 d5] 7 c3 ♗b7 8 ♘bd2 d6 9 ♕e2 f6 10 ♗h4 e5 [□ 10 ... ♘d7] 11 ♖ae1 ♕e8 [□ 11 ... ♔h8; 11 ... c5] 12 ♖d1 ♘d7 13 ♘e1 ♘c6? 14 ♗b5! ♘d8 15 ♕c4+ ♘e6 16 d5 ♘d8 17 ♕xc7 ♖f7 18 ♘c4 ♘c5 19 ♕xc5! ♕f8 20 ♕xd6 a6 21 ♕xf8+ ♔xf8 22 ♗c6 ♘xc6 23 dxc6 ♗xc6 24 f3 ♗b5 25 ♘xb6 ♖b8 26 c4 ♗e8 27 c5 ♗b5 28 ♖f2 ♗h6 29 ♖c2 ♖c7 30 ♗f2 ♔e7 31 ♘d5+ **1-0** L/N5188

### 1862-LON2-4
### Salter, D.– Cole, A.J.

[Löwenthal]

1 e4 e6 2 ♘f3 d5 3 e5 c5 4 d4 ♘c6 5 ♗b5 ♕b6 6 ♗xc6+ bxc6 7 0-0 ♗a6 8 ♖e1 cxd4 9 ♘xd4 c5 10 ♘f3 c4? 11 b3 ♘e7 12 ♗e3 ♕c7 13 ♕d4 ♘g6 14 c3 ♗e7 15 b4 0-0 16 ♗g5 ♗b7 17 ♘bd2 h6 18 ♗h4 ♖ae8 19 ♗g3 ♗d8! 20 ♕xa7 ♕c6 21 ♘d4 ♕d7 22 ♘2f3 ♗e7! 23 ♕a3 f5 24 h3 ♘h8 25 ♕c1 g5 26 ♔h1 f4 27 ♗h2 ♘g6 28 ♕c2 ♔g7 29 ♖g1 ♗d8 30 g3? fxg3 31 ♖xg3 ♖f7 32 h4 ♖ef8 33 hxg5 h5 34 ♖h3 ♖xf3! 35 ♘xf3 ♖xf3 36 ♖xf3 d4 37 cxd4 ♗xf3+ 38 ♔g1 ♕xd4 39 ♖e1 ♕g4+ 40 ♗g3 ♕h3→ ...? **0-1** L/N5188

### 1862-LON2-5
### Cole, A.J.+ Salter, D.

[Löwenthal]

1 e4 e5 2 ♘f3 ♘c6 3 d4 exd4 4 ♘xd4 ♗c5 5 ♗e3 ♘xd4? 6 ♗xd4 ♗xd4 7 ♕xd4 ♕f6 8 e5 ♕g6 9 ♘a3 ♘h6 10 0-0-0 0-0 11 ♗d3 ♕b6 12 ♕e4 g6 13 ♕f4 ♔g7 14 h4 f5 15 h5 d5 16 hxg6 ♕xg6 17 ♖h3 ♘g4 18 ♖g3 ♕h6 19 ♕xh6+ ♔xh6 20 ♖h1+ ♔g5 21 f3 f4 22 ♖xg4+ ♗xg4 23 fxg4 h6 24 ♗f5 c6 25 ♖h5# **1-0** L/N5188

### 1862-LON2-6
### Solomons,S.+ Blackburne,J.H.

[Löwenthal]

⟨♙f7⟩ 1 e4 d5? 2 ♕h5+ g6 3 ♕xd5 ♕xd5 4 exd5 ♘f6 5 ♘c3 ♗g7 6 ♗c4 ♗f5 7 d3 ♘bd7 8 ♗g5 0-0-0 9 ♗xf6 ♗xf6 10 ♘ge2 ♘b6 11 ♗b3 g5 12 0-0-0 ♗g6 13 f4? ♗h5 14 ♖de1 ♗xe2 15 ♖xe2 gxf4 16 a4 a5 17 ♘e4 ♘xd5 18 ♗xd5 ♖xd5 19 ♘xf6 exf6 20 ♖f1 ♖e5 21 ♖e4 ♖g8 22 ♖fxf4 ♖xg2 [□ 22 ... ♖xe4] 23 ♖xe5 fxe5 24 ♖f8+ ♔d7 25 ♖f7+ ♔d6 26 ♖xh7 b6 27 b3 c5 28 h4 ♖h2 29 h5 ♔c6 30 ♔b2 ♔d6 31 ♔c3 ♔c6 32 h6 ♔d6 33 ♖h8 ♔c7 34 h7 ♔b7 35 ♔b2 ♔a7 36 ♔c1 ♔b7 37 ♔d1 ♔a7 38 ♔e1 ♔b7 39 ♔f1 ♔a7 40 ♔g1 ♖h6 41 ♔g2 ...? **1-0** L/N5188

### 1862-LON2-7
### Solomons,S.– Blackburne,J.H.

[Löwenthal]

⟨♙f7⟩ 1 e4 d6 2 d4 ♘f6 3 ♗d3 e5 4 d5 ♗e7 5 f4 ♗g4 6 ♗e2 ♗xe2 7 ♕xe2 0-0 8 f5 c6 9 c4 cxd5 10 cxd5 ♘bd7 11 ♘f3 ♘c5 12 ♘c3 h6 13 0-0 a6 14 b4 ♘cd7 15 a3 ♖c8 16 ♗d2 ♘b6 17 ♖a2 ♘c4 18 ♖c1 b5 19 a4 ♕b6+ 20 ♔h1 ♘xd2 21 a5 ♕a7 22 ♖xd2 ♖c4 23 ♖dc2! ♖xb4 24 ♘a2 ♖xe4 25 ♕d3 ♖e3 26 ♕d2 ♘e4 27 ♖c7 ♕xc7! 28 ♕xe3 ♘c5 29 ♕a3 ♖xf5 30 ♘b4 ♕b7 31 ♕e3 e4 32 ♘d4 ♗g5 33 ♕g3 ♖f6 34 ♖d1 ♕f7 35 ♔g1 ♗d2 36 ♘bc6 ♗f4 37 ♕h3 ♘d3 38 ♘f5 ♖xf5 39 ♕xf5 ♗e3+ 40 ♔h1 ♘f2+ 41 ♔g1 ♘xd1+ 42 ♔h1 ♕xf5 43 ♘e7+ ♔f7 44 ♘xf5 ♗c5 45 ♘g3 ♘c3 46 ♘f1 e3 47 ♘g3 e2 48 ♘xe2 ♘xe2 49 g4 b4 ...? **0-1** L/N5188

### 1862-LON2-8
### Solomons,S.+ Blackburne,J.H.

[Löwenthal]

⟨♙f7⟩ 1 e4 d6 2 d4 ♘f6 3 ♗d3 e5 4 d5 ♗e7 5 f4 exf4 6 ♗xf4 0-0 7 ♘f3 c6 [□ 7 ... ♘xe4] 8 dxc6 ♘xc6 9 ♕d2 ♗g4 10 0-0 ♘h5 11 ♗e3 ♗xf3 12 ♖xf3 ♖xf3 13 gxf3 ♘e5 14 ♕g2 ♕f8 15 ♘d2 ♘f4 16 ♗xf4 ♕xf4 17 ♖f1 ♖c8 [□ 17 ... ♘xd3 Δ ... ♕e3+∓] 18 ♕e2 ♗g5 19 ♘c4 ♘g6 20 a4 d5? 21 exd5 ♕d4+ 22 ♔h1 ♕xd5 23 ♕e4 ♕d7 24 ♕g4 ♕d8 [□ 24 ... ♕xg4] 25 ♕e6+ ♔f8 26 ♘d6 ♖c7 27 ♗c4 ♗f6 28 ♕g8+ ...? **1-0** L/N5188

### 1862-LON2-9
### Heathcote,J.H.– Wilson,G.W.R.

[Löwenthal]

1 d4 d5 2 c4 e6 3 e3 ♘f6 4 a3 ♗e7 5 ♘f3 0-0 6 ♘bd2 [□ 6 ♘c3] 6 ... c5 7 dxc5 ♗xc5 8 b4 ♗d6 9 ♗b2 b6 10 ♗d3 ♗b7 11 0-0 h6 12 h3 ♘bd7 13 ♕c2? ♖ac8 14 ♘d4 e5 15 ♘f5 ♗b8 16 ♕b3 e4 17 ♗e2 ♘e5 18 ♖ac1 ♕d7 19 ♘d4 ♕d6 20 f4? exf3 21 ♘2xf3 ♘xf3+ 22 ♘xf3 dxc4 23 ♗xc4 ♗xf3 24 ♖xf3 ♕h2+ 25 ♔f1 ♕h1+ 26 ♔e2 ♕xg2+ 27 ♖f2 ♕g5 28 ♗xf7+ ♔h8 29 ♖xc8 ♖xc8 30 ♗xf6 gxf6 31 ♗d5 ♖d8 32 e4 ♗e5 33 ♕f3 ♖c8 34 ♕g4 ♖c2+ 35 ♔f1 ♕c1+ 36 ♔g2 ♖xf2+ 37 ♔xf2 ♗d4+ 38 ♔g3 ♕e1+ 39 ♔f4 ♕f2+ 40 ♕f3 ♗e5+ 41 ♔g4 h5+ 42 ♔xh5 ♕xf3+ **0-1** L/N5188

### 1862-LON2-10
### Heathcote,J.H.– Wilson,G.W.R.

[Löwenthal]

1 e4 c5 2 ♘f3 e6 3 d4 cxd4 4 ♘xd4 ♘c6 5 ♘b5 d6 6 ♗c4 [□ 6 ♗f4] 6 ... a6 7 ♘5c3 ♘f6 8 0-0 h6 9 f4 b5 10 ♗b3 [□ 10 ♗d3] 10 ... b4 11 e5 ♕b6+ 12 ♔h1 dxe5 13 fxe5 ♘xe5 14 ♘e2 ♗e7 15 ♗f4 ♘g6 16 ♘d2 0-0 17 ♘c4 ♕c5 18 ♗e3 ♕c7 19 ♘f4 ♘xf4 20 ♗xf4 ♕c5 21 ♕f3 ♘d5 22 a3 ♗b7 23 axb4 ♕xb4 24 ♖a4 ♕b5 25 ♖a5 ♘xf4 26 ♕xf4 ♕c6 27 ♖f2 ♕e4 28 ♖e5 ♕xf4 29 ♖xf4 ♖ad8 30 ♖e1 ♗d5 31 ♖f2? ♗h4 32 ♔g1 ♗xf2+ 33 ♔xf2 ♗xc4 34 ♗xc4 ♖d2+ 35 ♖e2 ♖xe2+ 36 ♔xe2 a5 37 ♔d3 ♖b8 38 b3 ♔f8 39 ♔d4 ♔e7 40 c3 ♔d6 41 g3 f5 42 ♔d3 e5 43 ♔c2 e4 44 ♔b2 g5 45 ♔a3 f4 46 ♔a4 f3 **0-1** L/N5188

### 1862-LON2-11
### Cremorne, R.– Deacon, F.H.

[Löwenthal]

1 e4 g6 2 d4 ♗g7 3 f4 e6 4 ♘f3 ♘e7 5 c3 [Δ ♗e3] 5 ... b6 6 ♗d3 ♗b7 7 ♘bd2! c5 8 0-0 cxd4 9 cxd4 ♘bc6 10 e5 f6 11 ♘e4! 0-0 12 ♘d6 ♕c7 13 ♘xb7 ♕xb7 14 ♗e4 fxe5 15 fxe5 ♘f5 [□ 15 ... ♖ad8] 16 g4 ♘fe7 17 ♗g5 ♖ae8 18 ♕b3 [□ 18 ♗xe7 ♖xe7 19 d5 exd5 20 ♕xd5+ ♔h8 21 ♘g5 ♕b8±] 18 ... ♕b8 [Δ 19 ... ♘xd4 20 ♘xd4 ♕xe5∓] 19 ♗xe7 ♖xe7 [□ 19 ... ♘xe7] 20 ♗xc6 dxc6 21 ♘g5 ♖fe8 22 ♕h3 ♗xe5 23 dxe5! ♕xe5 24 ♘f3 ♕xb2 25 ♕g2 ♕a3 26 ♕e2 ♕a4 27 h3 e5 28 ♖ad1 c5 29 ♕d2 ♕c6 30 ♕d5+! [30 ♕h6 ♕f6 31 ♘g5 ♕g7 32 ♕xg7+ ♔xg7 33 ♘e4 ♖f8 34 ♖d5 ♖ff7=] 30 ... ♕xd5 31 ♖xd5 e4 32

♘e1 ♖f8 33 ♖xf8+ ♔xf8 34 ♔f2 ♔f7 35 ♔e3 ♔e6 36 ♖d1 ♔e5 37 ♖d8 b5 38 a3 ♖e6 39 ♖d7 ♖a6 40 ♘c2 ♖e6 41 ♖xa7 ♔d5 42 ♖xh7 ♔c4 43 ♖f7 ♔b3 44 ♖f2 g5 45 ♖f5 ♖c6 46 ♘e1 ♔xa3 47 ♖xg5 b4 48 ♖g8 b3 49 ♔d2 ♔b2 50 ♖d8 c4 51 h4 c3+ 52 ♔e3 c2 53 ♖d2 ♔c1 54 ♘xc2 ♖c3+ 55 ♔e2 ♖xc2 ...⚲ **0-1** L/N5188

### 1862-LON2-12
**Cremorne, R.+ Deacon, F.H.**
[Löwenthal]

1 e4 c5 2 f4 e6 3 ♘f3 ♘c6 4 c3 d5 5 e5 ♗d7 6 d4 ♕b6 7 b3 cxd4! [7 ... ♖c8 8 ♗b2] 8 cxd4 ♗b4+ 9 ♔f2 ♘h6 10 h3 0-0 [10 ... ♘f5 11 ♗b2 h5 12 a3 ♗e7 △ ... h4∓] 11 g4! f6 12 exf6 gxf6 13 ♗e3 ♘f7 14 ♕d3! [14 g5? fxg5 15 fxg5 e5 16 dxe5 d4 17 ♗f4 (17 ♗xd4 ♘xd4∓) 17 ... ♘fxe5∓] 14 ... ♘d6 15 a3 ♘e4+ 16 ♔g2 ♗d6 17 ♖g1 ♕c7 18 ♘bd2 ♘xd2 [□ 18 ... ♗xf4] 19 ♕xd2 ♘e7 20 ♗d3 e5 21 ♖ac1 ♗c6 22 fxe5 fxe5 23 ♘g5 ♕d7 [□ 23 ... e4 24 ♘e6 ♕c8±] 24 ♗xh7+ ♔h8 25 ♖cf1 ♗xa3 26 ♖xf8+ ♖xf8 27 ♖f1 ♘g8 28 ♖xf8 ♗xf8 29 ♕f2 ♗h6 30 ♗f5 ♕g7 31 ♕h4 ♗d7 32 ♘e6! ♕f7 33 ♗xh6 **1-0** L/N5188

### 1862-LON2-13
**Cremorne, R.− Deacon, F.H.**
[Löwenthal]

1 e4 c5 2 f4 e6 3 ♘f3 d5 4 e5 ♘c6 5 c3 ♕b6 6 d4 ♗d7 7 ♗e2 ♘h6 8 0-0 cxd4 9 cxd4 ♘f5 10 ♔h1! ♘5xd4 11 ♘c3 ♘xe2 12 ♘xe2 ♗e7 13 ♘fd4 [13 f5 f6=] 13 ... 0-0 14 ♖f3 f6 15 ♗e3! ♗c5 16 ♕g1 [△ 17 ♘xc6 ♗xe3 18 ♘e7+±] 16 ... ♘xd4 17 ♘xd4 fxe5 18 fxe5 ♖ac8 19 ♖af1 ♖xf3 20 gxf3 ♕c7 21 f4 ♗xd4! 22 ♗xd4 ♗e8 23 f5 [23 ♗xa7 ♗g6 24 ♕e3 ♖c7 27 ♖f2 ♕c7∓] 23 ... exf5 24 ♕g2 ♕c4 25 ♗xa7 f4 [□ 25 ... ♗c6 26 ♔g1 d4 27 ♕ ♕d5∓] 26 b3 ♕d3 27 ♕f3 [27 ♖xf4 ♖c1+ 28 ♗g1 ♗c6−+] 27 ... ♕xf3+ 28 ♖xf3 g5 29 h4 ♗g6 30 ♔g1 ♗e4 31 ♖f2 ♖c1+ 32 ♔h2?? ♖h1# **0-1** L/N5188

### 1862-LON2-14
**Green, S.J.= Lyttelton, G.W.**
[Löwenthal]

1 e4 e5 2 ♗c4 ♘f6 3 ♘c3 ♗c5 4 ♘f3 d6 5 d3 h6 6 h3 0-0 7 0-0 ♔h8 8 ♗e3 ♗b6 9 ♗xb6 axb6 10 a3 ♘h7 11 ♘h2 f5 12 f4 ♘c6 13 fxe5 ♘xe5 14 ♗b3 ♕g5 15 d4 ♘g6 16 ♘f3 ♕e3+ 17 ♔h1 fxe4 18 ♖e1 ♕f4 19 ♖xe4 ♕f5 20 ♖e1 c6 21 d5 ♗d7 22 ♘e4 ♕f4 23 dxc6 ♗xc6 24 ♖xd6 [24 ♘xd6 ♗xf3 (24 ... ♖ad8 25 ♘f7+ ♖xf7 26 ♗xf7 ♖xd1 27 ♗xg6) 25 gxf3 ♘g5∓] 24 ... ♗xe4 25 ♕xf4 ♖xf4 26 ♘d2 ♘f6 27 ♘xe4 ♘xe4 28 ♗d5 ♖e8 29 ♔h2 ♘d6 30 ♖xe8+ ♘xe8 31 ♗xb7 ♖f2 32 ♖d1 ♘f6 33 ♖d6 ♖xc2 34 ♖xb6 ♘e5 35 ♗a6 ♘c4 36 ♖c6 ♘e3 37 ♖xc2 ♘xc2 38 a4 ♘b4 39 ♗c4 ♘d7 40 b3 ♘b6 41 ♗e6 ♔h7 42 a5 ♘a8 43 ♔g3 ♔g6 44 ♗c4 ♘c7 45 ♔f4 ♔f6 46 ♔e4 h5 47 ♔d4 ♘c6+ 48 ♔c5 ♘xa5 49 ♗g8 ♘e6+ 50 ♗xe6 ♔xe6 51 b4 ♘b7+ 52 ♔c6 ♘d6 53 g3 ♘e4 [□ 53 ... ♔e5∓] 54 b5 g5 55 b6 ♘d6 56 ♔c5 ♔d7 57 ♔d5 ♘f5 58 g4 hxg4 59 hxg4 ♘e3+ 60 ♔e4 ♘xg4 61 ♔f5 **½-½** L/N5188

### 1862-LON2-15
**Green, S.J.= Lyttelton, G.W.**
[Löwenthal]

1 e4 e5 2 ♘f3 ♘c6 3 ♘c3 ♗c5 4 ♗b5 d6 [□ 4 ... ♘ge7 5 ♗xc6 dxc6∓] 5 ♗xc6+ bxc6 6 d4 exd4 7 ♘xd4 ♘e7 8 0-0 0-0 9 a3 ♗a6 10 ♖e1 h6 11 b4 ♗xd4 12 ♕xd4 d5 13 ♗b2 dxe4 14 ♕xe4 ♖e8 15 ♕g4 ♗c8 16 ♕g3 ♘f5 17 ♖xe8+ ♕xe8 18 ♕xc7 ♘d4 19 ♖d1 ♘e2+ 20 ♔h1 ♗a6 21 ♕d7 ♘xc3 22 ♗xc3 ♕e2 23 ♕d4 f6 24 ♕d2 ♖e8 25 ♖e1 ♕h5 26 ♖xe8+ ♕xe8 27 ♕e3 ♕d7 28 ♗d4 ♗b7 29 h3 a6 30 c3 ♕d5 31 ♕g3 ♕e6 32 a4 ♔h7 33 f4 ♕c4 34 f5 ♕f1+ 35 ♔h2 ♕xf5 36 ♕c7 ♕c8 37 ♕f7 ♔h8 **½-½** L/N5188

### 1862-LON2-16
**Green, S.J.= Lyttelton, G.W.**
[Löwenthal]

1 e4 e5 2 f4 exf4 3 ♘f3 d5 4 e5 ♗c5 5 d4 ♗b6 6 ♗xf4 ♗g4 7 ♗e2 ♘c6 8 c3 h6 9 h3 ♗h5 10 0-0 ♘ge7 11 ♕c1 [□ 11 ♘bd2; □ 11 ♔h2] 11 ... ♕d7 12 a4 g5! 13 ♗h2 0-0-0! [□ 13 ... g4∓] 14 ♗b5 a6! [□ 14 ... g4∓] 15 a5 ♗a7 16 ♗d3 ♖dg8 17 g4 ♗g6 18 ♗e2 ♗e4 19 b4 ♗xf3 20 ♖xf3 ♘xd4! 21 cxd4 ♗xd4+ 22 ♔g2 ♗xa1 23 ♖xf7 ♕e6! [23 ... ♕c6!] 24 ♖f6 ♕d7 25 e6 ♕c6 26 ♕xc6 ♘xc6 27 ♖f7 ♖g7 28 ♖xg7 ♗xg7 29 b5 ♘d4 30 bxa6 bxa6 31 ♗xa6+ ♔b8 32 ♗d3 ♘xe6 33 ♗f5 ♘d4 [□ 33 ... ♘f4+! 34 ♗xf4 gxf4 △ ... c5∓] 34 ♘a3 ♘xf5 35 gxf5 ♖f8 36 ♘b5 ♖f7 37 a6 ♔a8 38 ♘xc7+ ♔a7 39 ♗g1+ d4 40 ♘b5+ ♔xa6 41 ♘xd4 ♗xd4 42 ♗xd4 ♖xf5 43 ♗g7 h5 44 ♔g3 ♔b6 45 ♗h6 ♔c6 46 ♗g7 ♔d5 47 ♗h6 ♔e4 48 ♗g7 ♖f3+ 49 ♔g2 h4? [□ 49 ... ♖d3 50 ♗h6 ♖d2+ 51 ♔g3 (51 ♔g1 ♔f4 52 h4 ♔g3 53 ♔f1 ♖f2+ 54 ♔∼ g4−+) 51 ... h4+ 52 ♔g4 ♖g2+ 53 ♔h5 ♔f5 54 ♗g7 ♖g3 55 ♗h6 g4−+] 50 ♗b2 ♖g3+ 51 ♔h2 ♔f3 52 ♗e5 ♖g2+ 53 ♔h1 g4 54 hxg4 ♖xg4 ...⚲ **½-½** L/N5188

### 1862-LON2-17
**Lyttelton, G.W.− Green, S.J.**
[Löwenthal]

1 d4 e6 2 ♘f3 ♘f6 3 ♗g5 ♘c6 4 e3 h6 5 ♗h4 ♗e7 6 ♗c4 [□ 6 ♗d3] 6 ... d5 7 ♗b3 ♗d7 8 0-0 g5 9 ♗g3 ♘e4 10 ♘bd2 ♘xg3 11 fxg3 f6 12 c4 [□ 12 ♘e5±] 12 ... ♘a5 13 cxd5 ♘xb3 14 ♕xb3 exd5 15 ♕xd5 c6 16 ♕e4 ♖g8 17 ♘c4 [□ 17 d5±] 17 ... ♕c7 18 ♕h7? ♗e6 19 ♖ac1 0-0-0 20 ♘cd2 ♖h8 21 ♕e4 ♗d5 22 ♕f5+ ♔b8 23 a3 h5 24 e4 ♗f7 25 d5 ♕b6+ 26 ♔h1 cxd5 27 b3?? [□ 27 ♘xg5±] 27 ... ♗e6 28 ♕g6 ♖dg8 ...⚲ **0-1** L/N5188

### 1862-LON2-18
**Lyttelton, G.W.− Green, S.J.**
[Löwenthal]

1 e4 e5 2 f4 exf4 3 ♗c4 ♕h4+ 4 ♔f1 ♗c5 5 d4 ♗b6 6 c3 [□ 6 ♘c3] 6 ... d6 7 ♘f3 ♕f6 8 h3 [□ 8 a4] 8 ... ♗e6 9 ♗xe6 fxe6 10 ♘a3 a6 11 ♔f2 ♘e7 12 ♕a4+ ♘bc6 13 ♖e1 0-0 14 ♔f1 e5 15 dxe5 dxe5 16 ♘c4 ♗a7 17 ♕b3! ♔h8 18 ♕xb7 ♕f7 [□ 18 ... ♖fb8 19 ♕xc7 ♕e6 20 b3 ♗c5∓] 19 ♘cxe5 [□ 19 b3] 19 ... ♘xe5 20 ♘xe5 ♕e6 21 ♘f3 ♕c4+ 22 ♖e2 ♖fb8 23 ♘e5 ♕xe2+ **0-1** L/N5188

### 1862-LON2-19
**Young, H.T.− Hannah, J.W.**
[Löwenthal]

1 e4 e5 2 ♘f3 ♘f6 3 ♘xe5 d6 4 ♘f3 ♘xe4 5 d3 ♘f6 6 ♗e2 ♗e7 7 h3 0-0 8 ♘c3 ♗e6 9 ♘e4 ♘xe4 10 dxe4 f5 11 exf5 ♗xf5 12 ♕d5+ ♔h8 13 ♕xb7? ♘d7 14 ♕c6 ♘c5 15 ♘d4 ♗e4 16 ♕b5 ♖b8 17 ♕c4 d5 18 ♕c3 ♘d3+

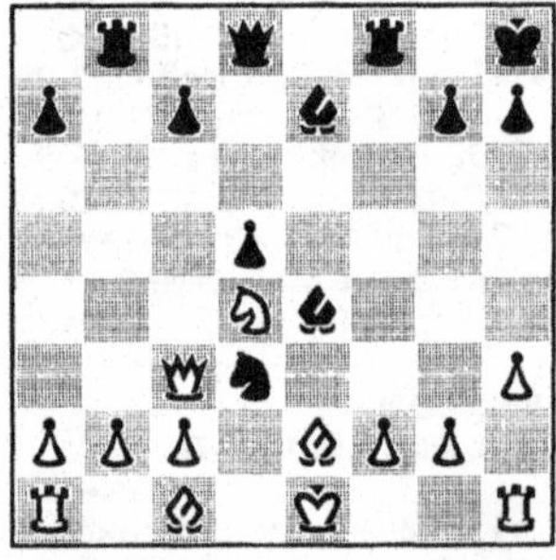

19 cxd3 ♗b4 20 dxe4 ♗xc3+ 21 bxc3 dxe4 22 0-0 ♕h4 23 ♗e3 ♖b6 24 ♔h2 ♖g6 25 g3 ♕e7 26 ♖ab1 ♕a3 27 ♖fc1 c5 28 ♘f5 ♖gf6 29 g4 g6 30 ♘g3 ♕xa2 31 ♗xc5 ♖xf2+ 32 ♗xf2 ♖xf2+ 33 ♔g1 e3 34 ♖e1 ♕d5 35 ♗f1 ♕e5 36 ♖xe3 ♕xe3 **0-1** L/N5188

**1862-LON2-20**
**Young, H.T.– Hannah, J.W.**

[Löwenthal]

1 e4 e5 2 ♘f3 ♘f6 3 ♘xe5 d6 4 ♘f3 ♘xe4 5 d3 [◻ 5 d4] 5 ... ♘f6 6 ♗e2 ♗e7 7 0-0 0-0 8 ♘c3 ♔h8 9 ♘e4 ♘xe4 10 dxe4 f5 11 exf5 ♗xf5 12 ♗e3 ♘c6 13 c3 ♕e8 14 ♘e1 ♗f6 15 ♕d2 ♕g6 16 f4 ♗e4 17 ♗f3 ♗f5 18 ♖d1 ♖ae8 19 ♕f2 ♖e7 20 ♔h1 ♖fe8 21 ♗xc6 bxc6 22 ♗c1 ♖e2 23 ♕g1 ♗h4 24 ♘f3 ♕h5 25 ♘xh4 ♕xh4 26 ♖f3 ♗e4 27 ♖g3 ♗xg2+ 28 ♖xg2 ♖e1 29 ♖xg7 ♖xg1+ 30 ♖dxg1 ♕h3 31 ♖7g3 ♕e6 32 a3 ♕d5+ 33 ♖3g2 ♖e2 34 f5 h5! 35 ♗g5 ♕e4 36 ♗h4? [◻ 36 f6] 36 ... ♖xg2 37 ♗f6+ ♖g7+ 38 ♖g2 ♕xg2# **0-1** L/N5188

**1862-LON2-21**
**Stockil, W.– Falkbeer, E.K.**

[Löwenthal]

⟨♙f7⟩ 1 e4 ... 2 d4 ♘c6 3 f4 e6 4 c3 d5 5 e5 ♘h6 6 ♗d3 ♘e7 7 ♘f3 ♘ef5 8 0-0 ♗d7 9 ♘g5 g6 10 g4 ♘e7 11 f5 exf5 12 e6 ♗c6 13 gxf5 gxf5 14 ♗xf5 ♘exf5 15 ♖xf5! ♕e7 16 ♕h5+ ♔d8 17 ♖xf8+ ♕xf8 18 ♕xh6 ♕xh6 19 ♘f7+ ♔e7 20 ♗xh6 ♖hg8+ 21 ♔h1 ♖g6 22 ♘d2 ♔xe6 23 ♖f1 ♖ag8 24 ♗e3 ♗e8 25 ♘e5 ♖g2 26 ♘d3 ♔d7 27 ♘f4 ♖2g5 28 ♘f3 ♖f5 29 ♘e5+ ♔c8 30 ♖g1 ♖xg1+ 31 ♔xg1 c6 32 ♘e6 ♖f6 33 ♘g7 ♗g6 34 h4 ♗e4 35 ♗g5 ♖f8 36 h5 a5 37 h6 a4 38 ♘e6 ♖g8 39 ♔f2 a3 40 bxa3 ♗b1 41 ♘g4? ♖g6 42 ♘f6 ♗f5 43 ♔e3 ♗xe6 44 ♔f4 ♗g8 45 ♔f5 ♔c7 46 a4 ♔b6 47 ♘d7+ ♔a5 48 ♘f8 ♖d6 49 ♗e7 ♖xh6 50 ♗b4+ ♔xa4 **0-1** L/N5188

**1862-LON2-22**
**Stockil, W.– Falkbeer, E.K.**

[Löwenthal]

⟨♙f7⟩ 1 e4 ... 2 d4 e6 3 f4 d5 4 e5 c5 5 c4? cxd4 6 ♕xd4 ♘c6 7 ♕f2 d4 8 b3 ♗c5 9 ♘f3 ♕b6 10 ♗d3 ♘b4 11 ♕e2 ♘xd3+ 12 ♕xd3 ♘e7 13 0-0 ♘f5 14 ♔h1 0-0 15 a3 a5 16 ♗b2 ♘e3 17 ♘g5 g6 18 ♖f3 ♘f5 19 ♘d2 ♗d7 20 ♘de4 ♗c6! 21 ♖h3 h6 22 ♘f3 ♔g7 23 g4? ♘e3 24 ♘xc5? ♕xc5 25 ♗xd4 ♖fd8 26 ♕xe3 ♕xd4 27 ♖e1 ♕xe3 28 ♖xe3 ♖d4 29 ♔g2 ♖xf4 30 ♔g3 g5 31 ♔f2 ♖xg4 32 ♖g3 ♖xg3 33 ♔xg3 ♖d8 34 ♘e1 ♖d4 35 ♘d3 b6 36 c5 b5 37 b4 a4 38 ♘f2 h5 39 h3 ♖f4 40 ♘d3 h4+ 41 ♔h2 ♖f1 42 ♖e1 ♖f3 43 ♖d1 ♔g6 44 ♖d2 ♔f5 45 ♖f2 ♖xf2+ 46 ♘xf2 ♔xe5 47 ♘g4+ ♔f4 48 ♔g1 ♔g3 49 ♘e5 ♗d5 50 c6 ♔xh3 51 c7 ♗b7 52 ♘c6 g4 53 ♘a7 ♔g3 54 c8♕ ♗xc8 55 ♘xc8 h3 56 ♘d6 h2+ **0-1** L/N5188

**1862-LON2-23**
**Anderssen,A.+ Pearson,A.C.**

⟨♘b1⟩ 1 e4 ♘f6 2 e5 ♘d5 3 ♗c4 c6 4 ♘f3 e6 5 0-0 ♗c5 6 d4 ♗b6 7 ♗b3 h6 8 c4 ♘c7 9 ♗c2 c5 10 d5 d6 11 ♗f4 exd5 12 exd6 ♘e6 13 ♖e1 ♘c6 14 cxd5 ♘d4 15 ♘xd4 cxd4 16 dxe6 ♗xe6

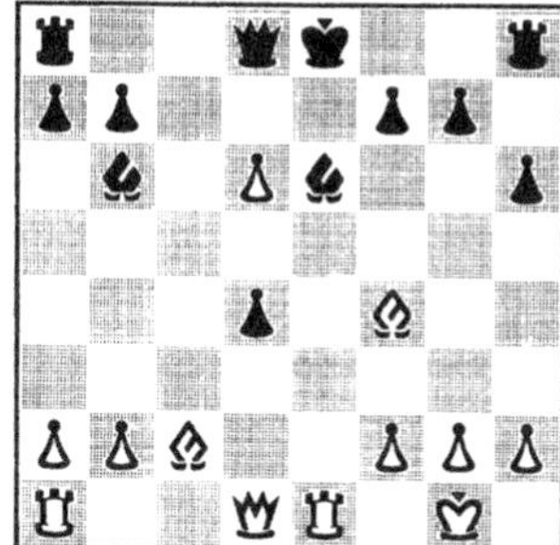

17 d7+ ♔e7 18 ♕g4 ♕xd7 19 ♗f5 ♖hf8 20 ♕xg7 ♖ae8 21 ♖xe6+ ♕xe6 22 ♗xe6 ♔xe6 23 ♕e5+ ♔d7 24 ♕d6+ ♔c8 25 ♖c1+ **1-0** L/N5188

**1862-LON2-24**
**Anderssen,A.+ Pearson,A.C.**

[Löwenthal]

⟨♘b1⟩ 1 e4 ♘f6 2 e5 ♘d5 3 ♗c4 ♘b6 4 ♗b3 e6 5 ♘f3 g6 6 d4 ♗g7 7 c4 d6 8 ♗g5 f6 9 exf6 ♗xf6 10 ♗h6 ♕e7 11 ♕d2 ♘6d7 12 0-0 b6 13 ♖fe1 ♗b7 14 c5 d5 15 c6!

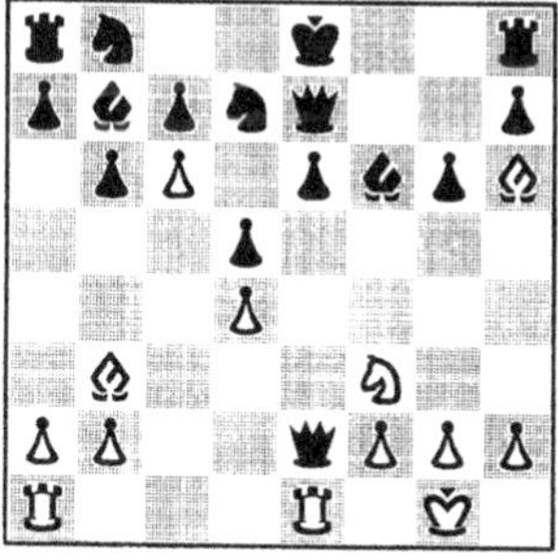

15 ... ♘xc6 [15 ... ♗xc6 16 ♖ac1±] 16 ♗xd5 0-0-0 17 ♖xe6 ♕b4 18 ♗xc6 ♕xd2 19 ♗xd2 ♗xc6 20 ♖xc6 ♗xd4 21 ♗f4 ♗xb2 22 ♖xc7+ ♔b8 23 ♖c2+ ♗e5 24 ♘xe5 ♘c5 25 ♘xg6+ ♔b7 26 ♘xh8 ♖xh8 27 ♗e3 ♖c8 28 ♗xc5 bxc5 29 ♖b1+ ♔c6 30 ♖xc5+ ♔xc5 31 ♖c1+ **1-0** L/N5188

**1862-LON2-25**
**Lamb, F.E.– Schröder, A.**

[Löwenthal]

1 e4 e5 2 ♘f3 ♘c6 3 ♗b5 d6 4 ♗xc6+ bxc6 5 ♘c3 ♗e7 6 d3 ♗g4 7 ♘e2 f5 [◻ 7 ... ♗xf3] 8 exf5 ♗xf5 9 ♘g3 ♗g6 10 0-0 ♘f6 11 ♘h4 d5 12 ♘xg6 hxg6 13 ♗g5 ♘h5 14 ♗xe7 ♕xe7 15 ♕g4 ♘f4 16 ♖fe1 ♖h4 17 ♕f3 ♔d7 18 ♘f1 ♖ah8 19 ♕e2! ♕g5 20 ♕f3 [◻ 20 g3] 20 ... ♖h3! 21 ♖xe5! ♕xe5 22 gxh3 ♖xh3 23 ♕g4+ ♔d6 24 ♘g3 ♖h8 25 c3 ♕f6 26 ♕f3 ♖f8 27 ♕e3 ♘h3+ 28 ♔g2 ♘f4+ 29 ♔h1 c5 30 ♖d1 ♘h5 31 ♖e1 ♘xg3+ 32 hxg3 g5 33 d4 cxd4 34 cxd4 ♔d7 35 ♔g2 g4 36 ♖e2 c6 37 ♕e5 ♖h8 38 ♕f4! ♕xf4 39 gxf4 ♖h3 40 ♖e3 [◻ 40 ♖e5] 40 ... ♖xe3 41 fxe3 ♔e6 42 a4 ♔f5 43 ♔g3 a5 44 ♔f2 ♔e4 45 b3 g3+ 46 ♔xg3 ♔xe3 47 b4 axb4 48 a5 b3 49 a6 b2 50 a7 b1♕ 51 a8♕ ♕g1+ ...? **0-1** L/N5188

**1862-LON2-26**
**Lamb, F.E.+ Schröder, A.**

[Löwenthal]

1 e4 e5 2 ♘f3 ♘c6 3 ♗b5 ♘f6 4 0-0 ♗e7 5 d3 d6 6 ♗xc6+ bxc6 7 h3 0-0 8 ♘c3 ♗b7 9 ♘e2 ♘h5 10 ♗e3 f5 11 exf5 ♖xf5 12 ♘h2 ♘f4 13 d4 ♘xe2+ 14 ♕xe2 exd4 15 ♗xd4 c5 16 ♗c3 ♖g5 17 f3 ♗f6 18 ♕e6+ ♔h8 19 ♗xf6 gxf6 20 ♖fe1 ♗d5 21 ♕e7 ♖g7 22 ♕xd8+ ♖xd8 23 ♖ad1 ♗c6 24 ♖d3 ♖dg8 25 g4 f5 26 ♔f2 f4 27 ♖a3 ♖a8 28 h4 a6 29 ♖e6 ♖f7 30 h5 ♗b5 31 g5 ♖f5 32 g6 ♖xh5 33 ♘g4 ♖h1 34 gxh7 ♖f8 35 b3 ♖xh7 36 c4 ♗d7 37 ♖f6 ♖ff7 38 ♖xf7 ♖xf7 39 ♖xa6 ♗xg4 40 fxg4 ♔g7 41 ♔f3 ♔g6 42 ♖a8 ♔g5 43 ♖g8+ ♔h6 44 ♖e8 ♔g5 45 ♖e4 c6! 46 ♖e6 ♖a7 [◻ 46 ... ♖h7±] 47 ♖xd6 ♖xa2 48 ♖xc6 ♖a5 49 ♖d6 ♖a3 50 ♖d5+ ♔g6 51 ♖xc5 ♖xb3+ 52 ♔xf4 **1-0** L/N5188

**1862-LON2-27**
**Lamb, F.E.+ Schröder, A.**

[Löwenthal]

1 e4 e5 2 ♘f3 ♘c6 3 d4 exd4 4 ♘xd4 ♘xd4 5 ♕xd4 ♘f6 [◻ 5 ... ♘e7] 6 ♗c4 ♗e7 7 e5 c5? [◻ 7 ... d5] 8 ♕f4 d5 9 exf6 0-0? 10 fxe7 ♕xe7+ 11 ♗e2 d4 12 f3 ♖fe8 13 ♕e4 ♕xe4 14 fxe4 ♖xe4 15 ♔f2 ♖e6 16 ♖e1 ♗d7 17 ♔g1 ♖ae8 18 ♔f2 ♗b5 19 ♗xb5 ♖f6+ 20 ♗f4 ♖xf4+ 21 ♔g3 ♖xe1 22 ♔xf4 h6 23 a4 ♖e3 24 ♖a3 g5+ 25 ♔f5 ♖e1 26 ♘d2 ♔g7 27 ♘f3 ♖e6 28 ♗c4 ♖f6+ 29 ♔e5 g4 30 ♘h4 ♖f2 31 ♘f5+ ♔g6 32 ♗d3 ♔g5 33 ♗e4 f6+ 34 ♔e6 **1-0** L/N5188

**1862-LON2-28**
**Chinnery, W.M.–Green, V.**
[Löwenthal]

⟨♙f7⟩ 1 e4 ♘c6 2 d4 d6 3 d5 ♘e5 4 f4 ♘f7 5 ♘f3 ♘gh6 6 ♗d3 c6 7 c4 g6 8 ♗d2 ♗g7 9 ♗c3 0-0 10 h4? [□ 10 ♗xg7 △ ♘c3] 10 ... ♗g4 11 ♗xg7 ♔xg7 12 ♘bd2 ♕b6 13 ♕e2 ♖ae8! 14 0-0-0 cxd5 15 exd5 e5 16 dxe6 ♖xe6 17 ♘e4 ♘f5 18 b3 ♗xf3 19 ♕xf3 ♘d4 20 ♕f2? ♖xe4 21 ♔b2 ♖xf4 22 g3 ♖f2 23 ♕c3 ♘e5 24 ♔b1 ♖8f3 25 ♖he1 ♖c2!

**0-1** L/N5188

**1862-LON2-29**
**Chinnery, W.M.= Green, V.**
[Löwenthal]

⟨♙f7⟩ 1 e4 d6 2 d4 ♘f6 3 ♘c3 e5 4 dxe5 dxe5 5 ♕xd8+ ♔xd8 6 a3 c6 7 ♘f3 ♗d6 8 ♗e3 ♗e6 9 0-0-0 ♔e7 10 ♘g5 ♗g8 11 ♘h3 h6 12 f4 ♘g4 13 fxe5 ♗xe5 14 ♗c5+ ♔e8 15 g3 g5 [□ 15 ... ♘d7] 16 ♗e2 ♗e6 17 ♖d2 ♘d7 [□ 17 ... ♗xc3] 18 ♗d6 ♘gf6 19 ♘f2 ♖d8 20 ♘cd1? [□ 20 ♗xe5 ♘xe5 21 ♖hd1] 20 ... ♗xd6 21 ♖xd6 ♔e7 22 ♖d2 ♘c5 23 e5? ♘fe4 24 ♘xe4 ♘xe4 25 ♖xd8 ♖xd8 26 ♗d3 ♘c5 27 ♘f2 ♖d5 28 ♖e1 ♘d7 29 b4 ♖xe5 30 ♖f1 ♘f6 31 ♔d2 ♗d5? 32 c4 ♗g2 33 ♖g1 ♗f3 34 g4 c5 35 b5 b6 36 ♖g3 ♗b7 37 ♖h3 h5 38 gxh5 g4 39 ♖g3 [□ 39 ♖e3] 39 ... ♖xh5 40 ♘xg4 ♘xg4 41 ♖xg4 ♖xh2+ 42 ♔c3 ♖g2 43 ♖h4 ♖g7 **½-½** L/N5188

**1862-LON2-30**
**Chinnery, W.M.+Green, V.**
[Löwenthal]

⟨♙f7⟩ 1 e4 ♘c6 2 d4 e5 3 dxe5 ♘xe5 4 f4 ♘f7 5 ♗c4 ♘gh6 6 ♘f3 ♗c5 7 h3 c6 8 ♕e2 0-0 9 ♗d3 d5 10 e5 ♗f5? 11 g4 ♗d7 12 ♘c3 g6 13 ♗d2 ♘xe5? 14 fxe5 ♖xf3 15 ♕xf3 ♕h4+ 16 ♔e2 ♖f8 17 ♗f4 g5 18 ♘xd5! cxd5 19 ♕xd5+ ♖f7 20 ♕xc5 ♖xf4 21 ♕d5+ ♖f7 22 ♖af1 ♗xg4+ 23 hxg4 ♕xg4+ 24 ♔e1 ♕g3+ 25 ♔d1 **1-0** L/N5188

**1862-LON2-31**
**Chinnery, W.M.–Green, V.**
[Löwenthal]

⟨♙f7⟩ 1 e4 e6 2 d4 ♘c6 3 f4 d5 4 e5 g6 5 ♘f3 ♘h6 6 c3 ♗g7 7 ♗d3 ♘e7 8 0-0 ♗d7 9 ♕c2 ♘ef5 10 h3 ♕e7 11 ♘a3 0-0 12 g4 ♘h4 13 ♘g5 ♘f7 14 ♘f3 ♘xf3+ 15 ♖xf3 ♗h6 [△ ... ♘g5, ... ♘e4] 16 g5? ♘xg5 17 ♖g3 ♘e4 18 ♖g4 ♗c6 19 ♗e3 ♖f5 20 ♕g2 ♖af8 21 ♖af1 ♖5f7? 22 c4 ♔h8 23 cxd5 exd5 24 ♗xe4 dxe4 25 ♕g3 g5 26 ♘c2 ♗d7 27 f5 ♖xf5 [□ 27 ... ♗xf5 28 ♗xg5 ♗xg4 20 ♗xe7 ♖xf1+-+] 28 ♖xf5 ♗xf5 [28 ... ♖xf5 29 ♖xe4±] 29 ♗xg5! ♗xg5 30 ♖xg5 ♗g6 31 a3 ♖f3 32 ♕g4 ♕f8 33 ♘b4 ♖f1+ 34 ♔h2 e3 35 ♖xg6! hxg6 36 ♘d3 ♖f2+ 37 ♔g1 ♖d2 38 ♘f4 ♖d1+! 39 ♔g2 ♖d2+ 40 ♔g1 ♕g7 41 ♕h4+ ♔g8 42 ♕e1 ♕h6 43 ♕xe3 ♕g5+ [□ 43 ... ♖xb2] 44 ♔f1 ♖xb2 45 ♕e4 ♕f5 46 ♕xf5 gxf5 47 h4 ♖b3 48 e6? [48 ♔f2=] 48 ... ♖f3+ 49 ♔g2 ♖xf4 50 d5 ♖xh4 ...? **0-1** L/N5188

**1862-LON2-32**
**Harris, E.+Puller, A.G.**
[Löwenthal]

1 e4 e5 2 ♘f3 d6 3 d4 exd4 4 ♘xd4 ♗e7 5 ♗c4 ♘f6 6 ♘c3 0-0 7 0-0 a6 8 a4 c5 9 ♘de2 h6? [□ 9 ... ♘c6] 10 h3 ♘c6 11 f4 ♗e6 12 ♗a2? ♘b4 13 ♘g3 ♘xa2 14 ♘xa2 ♗xa2 15 ♖xa2 d5 16 e5 ♘e4? 17 ♘f5 [17 ♘xe4!±] 17 ... ♔h7! [17 ... ♖e8 18 ♕g4±] 18 ♘xe7 ♕xe7 19 ♕xd5 ♘g3? [□ 19 ... f5=] 20 ♕d3+ ♔h8 21 ♕xg3 ♕e6 22 b3 c4 23 ♗b2 ♖ad8 24 f5 ♕b6+ 25 ♔h2 ♖d7 26 e6 fxe6 27 f6! g5 28 ♕f3 ♖df7 29 ♖aa1 cxb3 30 cxb3 ♕c7+ 31 ♔h1 ♔g8 32 ♕e4 ♕c6 33 ♕g6+ ♔h8 34 ♕xh6+ ♔g8 35 ♕xg5+ ♔h8 36 ♖f4 **1-0** L/N5188

**1862-LON2-33**
**Harris, E.+Puller, A.G.**
[Löwenthal]

1 e4 e5 2 ♘f3 d6 3 d4 exd4 4 ♘xd4 ♗e7 5 ♗c4 ♘f6 6 ♘c3 0-0 7 0-0 a6 8 a4 c5 9 ♘de2 ♗e6 10 ♗d5 ♕c7 11 ♘f4 ♗xd5 12 ♘fxd5 ♘xd5 13 ♘xd5 ♕d8 14 ♗f4 ♘d7? [□ 14 ... ♖e8±] 15 ♘xe7+ ♕xe7 16 ♗xd6 ♕xe4 17 ♗xf8 ♘xf8 18 ♖e1 ♕c6 19 c4 ♘e6 20 ♕d5 ♕c7 21 ♖a3 ♖d8 22 ♕f3 ♘d4 23 ♕e4 h6 24 ♖ae3 b6 25 ♕b1 [△ ♖e8+] 25 ... ♕c6 26 b3 ♘e6 27 ♕e4 ♕c7 28 ♕e5 ♕c6 29 f4 ♖d4 30 ♖g3 ♖xf4 31 ♕b8+! ♔h7 32 ♖xe6 ♖f1+ 33 ♔xf1 ♕xe6 34 ♕f4 g5 35 ♕e3 ♕d7 36 ♕d3+ ♕xd3+ 37 ♖xd3 **1-0** L/N5188

**1862-LON2-34** 3 vii 62
**Cole, A.J.–Mackenzie, G.H.**
[Löwenthal]

1 e4 e5 2 ♘f3 ♘c6 3 ♗b5 a6 4 ♗a4 ♘f6 5 0-0 ♗e7 6 d4 exd4 7 e5 ♘e4 8 ♗xc6 dxc6 9 ♘xd4 0-0 10 f4 f5 11 ♗e3 ♕e8 12 ♘d2 c5 13 ♘4f3 ♕c6 14 ♕e2 ♘xd2 15 ♗xd2 b6 16 ♗c3 [□ 16 c4] 16 ... ♗e6 17 b3 b5 18 ♗b2 c4 19 ♗d4 ♖ad8 20 ♖ab1 ♖d7 21 c3 ♗d5 22 b4? ♗e4 23 ♖be1 [□ 23 ♖bd1] 23 ... ♗d3 24 ♕e3 ♗xf1 25 ♔xf1 ♕e6 26 ♖d1 ♖fd8 27 h3 c5 28 bxc5 ♗xc5 29 ♘g5 ♗xd4 30 cxd4 ♕d5 31 ♔f2 h6 32 ♘f3 ♕e6 33 ♘e1 b4 34 ♘c2 a5 35 ♖b1 ♕b6 36 g4 fxg4 37 hxg4 ♕g6 38 ♕e2 ♕c6 39 e6 ♖e7 40 f5 ♖f8 41 ♔g3 h5 42 ♕e5 hxg4 43 d5 ♕c5 44 ♕e4 b3 45 axb3 cxb3 46 ♖xb3 ♕g1+ 47 ♔h4 ♕d1 48 ♖g3 ♕d2 49 ♖xg4?? ♕h2+ **0-1** L/N5188

**1862-LON2-35**
**Cole, A.J.–Mackenzie, G.H.**
[Löwenthal]

1 e4 e5 2 ♘f3 ♘f6 3 ♗c4 ♘xe4 4 d3 ♘f6 5 ♘xe5 d5 6 ♕e2 ♗e7 [□ 6 ... ♗e6] 7 ♗b3 0-0 8 0-0 c5 9 ♘c3 ♘c6 10 f4 ♗f5 11 g4? ♗c8 [△ ... ♘xe5, ... ♘xg4∓] 12 g5 ♘d4 13 ♕d1 ♘d7 14 ♗xd5 ♘xe5 15 fxe5 ♗xg5 16 ♕h5 ♗xc1 17 ♗xf7+ ♔h8 18 ♖axc1 ♗e6 19 ♗g6 [□ 19 ♗xe6=] 19 ... ♗g8 20 ♘e4 ♕e7 21 ♘g5 ♘e2+ 22 ♔g2 h6 23 ♘e4 ♘f4+ 24 ♖xf4 ♖xf4 25 c3 ♖h4 26 ♕e2 ♕e6 27 ♘f2 ♕xg6+ ...? **0-1** L/N5188

**1862-LON2-36** 30 vi 62
**Solomons, S.–Wilson, G.W.R.**
[Löwenthal]

1 e4 c5 2 ♘f3 e6 3 ♗e2 ♘c6 4 c3 d5 5 d3 ♗e7 6 0-0 b6 7 h3 ♗b7 8 ♘h2 ♕c7 9 exd5 exd5 10 a3 0-0-0 11 b4 ♗d6 12 ♘g4 f5 13 ♘e3 ♘ce7 14 d4 c4 15 ♕c2 ♖f8 16 f4 g6 17 ♘d1 ♘f6 18 ♗e3 ♘e4 19 ♖f3 h6 20 ♘f2 g5 21 fxg5 f4 22 ♗d2 hxg5 23 a4 ♘f5 24 ♘g4 ♘fg3 25 ♗e1 ♕d7 26 a5 ♕xg4!

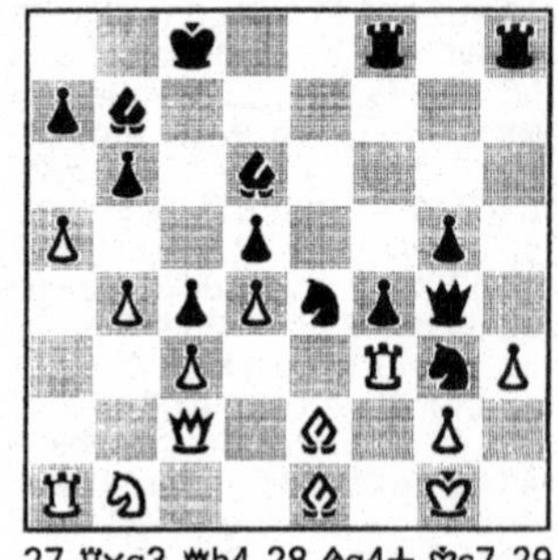

27 ♖xg3 ♕h4 28 ♗g4+ ♔c7 29

♖e3 ♕h7 30 ♖e2 b5 31 a6 ♗c8 32 ♗f3 ♗f5 33 ♕a2 g4 34 ♕a5+ ♔c6 35 ♗xe4 ♗xe4 36 ♘a3 ♖b8 37 ♘xb5 ♖xb5 38 ♕a2 gxh3 39 gxh3 ♕xh3 **0-1** L/N5188

**1862-LON2-37** 3 vii 62
**Wilson,G.W.R.– Solomons,S.**
[Löwenthal]

1 e4 e5 2 ♘f3 ♘c6 3 d4 d5? 4 exd5 [◻ 4 ♗b5±] 4 ... ♕xd5 5 ♘c3 ♗b4 6 ♗d2 ♗xc3 7 ♗xc3 exd4 8 ♘xd4 ♘f6 9 ♘xc6 [◻ 9 ♗b5±] 9 ... ♕xc6 10 ♕d3 ♗d7 11 0-0-0 0-0-0 12 ♕c4 ♘e4 13 ♗d4 ♕h6+ 14 ♗e3 ♕c6 15 f3 ♘d6 16 ♕xc6 ♗xc6 17 ♗d3 ♖he8 18 ♖he1 ♗b5 19 ♗xb5 ♘xb5 20 ♗f2 ♖xd1+ 21 ♔xd1 ♖xe1+ 22 ♔xe1 ♔d7 23 ♔d2 ♔e6 24 ♔d3 a6 25 ♗g3 c6 26 ♗f2 ♘c7 27 ♔d4 ♘d5 28 ♔c5 ♔d7 29 c4 ♘f4 30 ♗d4? ♘e6+ 31 ♔b6 ♘xd4 32 ♔xb7 a5 33 ♔b6 a4 34 ♔a5 a3 35 bxa3 ♔c7 36 ♔a6 ♘c2 37 a4 ♘b4+ 38 ♔a7 ♘xa2 39 ♔a6 h5 40 ♔a5 ♔b7 41 f4 h4 42 g4 h3 43 f5 f6 44 c5 ♔c7 45 ♔a6 ♘c3 46 ♔a5 ♘d5 47 ♔a6 ♘e3 48 a5 ♘xg4 49 ♔a7 ♘xh2 50 a6 ♘f3 51 ♔a8 h2 52 a7 ♔d7 53 ♔b8 h1♕ 54 a8♕ ♕b1+ 55 ♔a7 ♔c7 ...⚲ **0-1** L/N5188

**1862-LON2-38**
**Solomons,S.+ Wilson,G.W.R.**
[Löwenthal]

1 c4 c5 2 d4 cxd4 3 ♕xd4 ♘c6 4 ♕d1 e6 5 ♘c3 ♗b4 6 ♘f3 ♘f6 7 ♗d2 0-0 8 e3 b6 9 ♕c2 ♘e8? 10 ♗d3 f5 11 a3 ♗e7 12 h3 ♗b7 13 ♘b5 ♖c8 14 ♗c3 a6 15 ♘bd4 ♘xd4 16 exd4 ♘d6 17 b3 ♘e4 18 ♗b2 ♕e8 19 ♕e2 ♕g6 20 g4 d5 [◻ 20 ... fxg4∓; 20 ... ♗g5∓] 21 0-0-0 dxc4 22 bxc4 fxg4 23 hxg4 ♕xg4? 24 d5 ♗xd5 25 ♖dg1 ♗g5+ [◻ 25 ... ♕f4+ 26 ♔g1 ♗f6 27 cxd5 ♗xb2 28 ♕xe4±] 26 ♘xg5 ♕xe2 27 ♗xe2 ♘xf2 28 ♖xh7 ♖c7 29 ♗e5 ♖fc8 30 ♗xc7 ♖xc7 31 ♖h2 ♘e4 32 ♘xe4 ♗xe4 33 ♔b2 **1-0** L/N5188

**1862-LON2-39**
**Green, S.J.= Deacon, F.H.**
[Löwenthal]

⟨♙f7⟩ 1 e4 ... 2 d4 e6 3 ♘c3 g6 4 ♗c4 ♗g7 5 ♘f3 ♘e7 6 ♗g5 0-0 7 d5 [△ 8 dxe6 dxe6 9 ♕xd8 ♖xd8 10 ♗xe7±] 7 ... ♕e8 [7 ... ♗f6 8 dxe6; 7 ... ♖f7 8 dxe6] 8 ♘b5 ♘a6 9 d6 [9 ♘xc7 ♘xc7 10 d6 ♘c6 11 dxc7 d5 12 exd5 exd5+ 13 ♗e2 ♗e6=] 9 ... ♘c6 10 dxc7 d5 11 ♗d3 [11 ♘d6 ♕d7 12 ♘xc8 ♘xc7] 11 ... ♕d7 12 c3 ♘xc7 13 ♘xc7 ♕xc7 14 0-0 dxe4 [14 ... ♗d7 15 exd5 exd5 16 ♗c2 ♗e6 17 ♗b3 ♕d7 18 ♖fe1 ♗f7 19 ♕d2±] 15 ♗xe4 ♘e5 [◻ 15 ... ♗d7] 16 ♘xe5 ♗xe5 17 h3 ♗d7 18 ♕c2 ♗e8 19 h4 ♗b5 20 ♖fe1 ♖f7 21 ♗xb7

21 ... ♗xc3 22 ♕xc3 ♕xb7 23 ♖ac1 ♕d5 24 ♖e5 ♕d3 25 ♕xd3 ♗xd3 26 ♗h6 ♖d7 27 ♖ec5 ♖f7 28 ♗g5 ♖b8 29 b3 ♗e4 ...⚲ ½-½ L/N5188

**1862-LON2-40**
**Green, S.J.= Deacon, F.H.**
[Löwenthal]

⟨♙f7⟩ 1 e4 ... 2 d4 e6 3 ♘c3 g6 4 ♗d3 ♘h6 5 h3? ♘f7 6 e5 ♗b4 7 a3 ♗xc3+ 8 bxc3 d6 9 ♘f3 dxe5 10 dxe5 ♘c6 11 ♗f4 ♗d7 12 h4 ♕e7 13 c4! 0-0-0 14 ♕b1 ♕c5! 15 ♕b2 ♕b6 16 ♕c3 ♕a5 17 ♗d2 ♕xc3 18 ♗xc3 ♘e7 19 0-0 c5 [19 ... ♗c6 20 ♘d4±] 20 a4 ♗c6 21 ♘d2 ♘f5 22 g3 ♘d4 23 f4 ♘h6 24 ♗xd4 cxd4 25 a5 ♘f5 26 ♔h2 ♘e3 27 ♖fe1 ♖hg8 28 ♘b3 h6 29 ♘c5 [29 ♘xd4 ♘g4+ 30 ♔h3 ♘f2+ 31 ♔h2 ♖xd4∓] 29 ... g5! [30 ♘xe6 gxh4 31 ♘xd8 hxg3+ 32 ♔g1 ♔xd8∓] 30 ♖g1 ½-½ L/N5188

**1862-LON2-41**
**Green, S.J.= Deacon, F.H.**
[Löwenthal]

⟨♙f7⟩ 1 e4 ... 2 d4 ♘c6 3 c3 e5 4 d5 ♘ce7 5 ♗g5 d6 6 ♘f3 ♘f6 7 ♘bd2 ♘g6 8 ♕a4+ ♗d7 9 ♗b5 ♗e7 10 ♗xf6 gxf6 11 g3 ♘f8? 12 ♘h4 a6 13 ♗xd7+ ♘xd7? [◻ 13 ... ♕xd7] 14 ♕d1 ♘b6 15 ♕h5+ ♔d7 16 ♕g4+ ♔e8 17 ♘f5 ♕d7 18 ♕g7 ♖f8 19 ♕xh7 ♔d8 20 ♕xe7+? [◻ 20 ♘g7 △ ♘e6±] 20 ... ♕xe7 21 ♘xe7 ♔xe7 22 0-0-0 f5! 23 f3 c6 24 c4 ♖ac8 25 ♔b1 ♘a4 26 ♖c1 fxe4 27 fxe4 ♖f2 28 ♖c2 ♖e2!! 29 b4 ♖h8 30 h3 ♖e3 31 c5 ♘c3+ 32 ♔b2 ♘xe4 33 ♘xe4 [◻ 33 cxd6+ ♔~ 34 dxc6±] 33 ... ♖xe4 34 cxd6+ ♔xd6 35 dxc6 bxc6 36 ♖d1+ ♔c7 37 a3 ♖xh3 38 ♖dc1 ♖d4 ½-½ L/N5188

**1862-LON2-42**
**Green, S.J.– Deacon, F.H.**
[Löwenthal]

⟨♙f7⟩ 1 e4 ... 2 d4 ♘c6 3 c3 e5 4 d5 ♘ce7 5 ♗g5 d6 6 ♕a4+ ♗d7 7 ♗b5 c6 8 dxc6 bxc6 9 ♗d3 ♕c7 10 b4 ♘g6 11 g3 ♗e7 12 ♗e3 ♘f6 13 h4 h5 14 ♕d1 ♖d8! 15 ♘d2 ♘g4 16 ♗e2 d5 17 ♕c2 [17 exd5 cxd5 18 ♕c2 e4 19 ♗xg4 ♗xg4 △ ... ♘e5∓] 17 ... d4! 18 cxd4 [18 ♗xg4 dxe3 19 ♗xd7+ ♕xd7 20 fxe3 ♕g4 21 ♘e2 ♘xh4 22 gxh4 ♗xh4+ 23 ♔d1 ♕g2 24 ♖g1 ♖f8∓] 18 ... ♘xe3 19 fxe3 exd4 20 ♘f1 [20 e5 ♘xe5 21 exd4 ♘g4−+] 20 ... ♗xb4+ 21 ♔f2 ♕e5 [◻ 21 ... ♗c3 22 ♖c1 dxe3+ 23 ♘xe3 ♗e5−+] 22 ♘f3 ♕f6 23 exd4 ♗g4 24 e5 ♕e6 25 ♗c4 ♕f5 26 ♕xf5 ♗xf5 27 ♘e3 ♗e4 28 ♖ad1 [28 ♖hd1 ♗c3 △ ... ♗xf3; 28 ♗f7+ ♔xf7 29 ♘g5+ ♔e7 30 ♘xe4 ♖hf8+ 31 ♔~ ♖xd4∓] 28 ... ♖f8 29 ♗e2 c5 30 ♘c4 cxd4 31 ♘d6+ ♗xd6 32 exd6 ♖xd6 33 ♖hf1 ♘e5 34 ♔g2 d3 35 ♖d2 [35 ♗xd3 ♗xf3+∓; 35 ♖xd3 ♘xd3∓; 35 ♖f2 dxe2∓; 35 ♖fe1 ♔d7∓] 35 ... ♖df6 36 ♗xd3 ♘xf3 37 ♗b5+ ♔e7 38 ♖d7+ ♔e6 39 ♔h3 ♘g5+ 40 hxg5 ♖xf1 41 ♖d2 ♖h1+ 42 ♖h2 ♖xh2+ 43 ♔xh2 ♖f2+ **0-1** L/N5188

**1862-LON2-43**
**Green, S.J.– Deacon, F.H.**
[Löwenthal]

⟨♙f7⟩ 1 e4 ... 2 d4 ♘c6 3 c3 e5 4 d5 ♘ce7 5 ♗g5 d6 6 h4 h5 7 ♗e2 g6 8 f4 exf4 9 ♗xf4 ♗g7 10 ♘d2 ♘f6 11 ♗g5 c6 12 ♕b3 ♕c7 13 0-0-0 ♗d7 14 ♘h3 cxd5 15 ♗xf6 ♗xf6 16 exd5 ♕b6 17 ♕xb6 axb6 18 ♘e4 ♗e5 19 a3 ♖a5 20 c4 0-0 21 ♖hf1 ♗f5 22 ♘hg5 ♖c8 23 ♖d2 [◻ 23 ♔b1 b5 24 cxb5 ♖a4 25 ♗f3 ♖c5∓] 23 ... ♖xd5

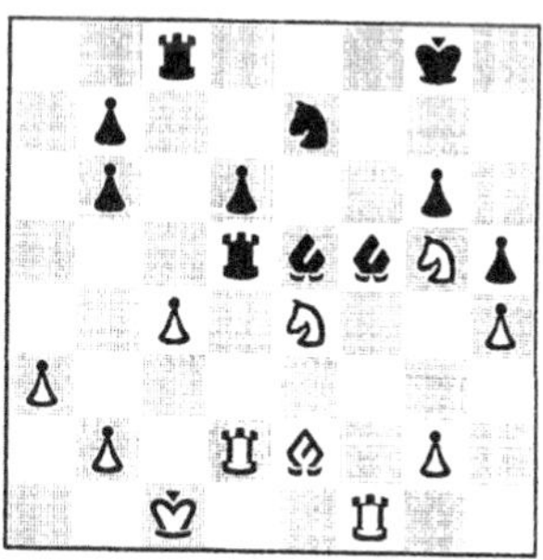

24 ♖xd5 [24 ♖fd1 ♗f4∓; 24 ♔~ ♖xd2∓] 24 ... ♘xd5 25 ♔b1 ♘e3 26 ♖c1 ♘xg2 27 ♔a1 ♘f4 [◻ 27 ... ♘xh4∓] 28 ♗f1 d5 29 ♘g3 [29 ♘f2 b5 30 ♖e1 ♗d4∓; 29 ♘d2 ♘d3 30 ♗xd3 (30 ♖c2 ♘b4 31 ♖c1 b5 32 ♘gf3 ♗f4 33 b3 ♗h6∓) 30 ... ♗xd3 31 ♖e1 ♗f4∓] 29 ... ♗d3 30 ♖e1! ♗xf1! 31 ♘xf1! [31 ♖xe5 ♗xc4 32 ♖e7 ♗b3 33 ♔b1

♘d3 34 ♘e2∓] 31 ... ♘d3! [□ 31 ... ♗xb2+ 32 ♔a2 (32 ♔xb2 ♘d3+∓) 32 ... dxc4 33 ♖e4 ♘d3∓] 32 ♖e2 dxc4 33 ♖c2 b5 34 ♘e3 ♖d8 [Δ 35 ... ♘xb2+ 36 ♖xb2 ♖d2∓] 35 ♖g2 ♘f4! 36 ♖c2 ♖d3 37 ♘g2 ♖d1+ 38 ♔a2 ♘d3 39 ♘f3 [39 ♘e3 ♖h1 40 ♖d2 ♗f4 41 ♖d1 ♖h2 42 ♘d5 ♖xb2+ 43 ♔a1 ♘e5∓] **0-1** L/N5188

**1862-LON2-44** 3 vii 62
**Hannah, J.W.+ Falkbeer, E.K.**
[Löwenthal]

1 e4 e5 2 ♘f3 ♘c6 3 ♗b5 f5? 4 d4 [□ 4 ♕e2±] 4 ... exd4 [□ 4 ... fxe4] 5 ♘xd4 ♘xd4 6 ♕xd4 c6 7 ♗d3 fxe4 8 ♗xe4 d5 9 ♗d3 ♘f6 10 ♗g5 ♗e7 11 ♕h4 ♕b6 [□ 11 ... ♘e4] 12 ♗g6+ ♔d8 13 0-0 ♕xb2 14 ♘d2 ♕b4 15 c4 ♕d6 16 ♖fe1 ♗e6 17 ♖ad1 ♘g4 18 ♗xe7+ ♕xe7 19 ♕xe7+ ♔xe7 20 ♗f5 ♔f6 21 ♗xe6 ♘e5 22 cxd5 cxd5 23 ♗xd5 ♖hd8 24 ♘e4+ ♔f5 25 ♘g3+ ♔f6 26 ♖d4 ♖e8 27 ♖f4+ ♔g6 28 ♗e4+ ♔g5 29 ♖f5+ **1-0** L/N5188

**1862-LON2-45**
**Hannah, J.W.+ Falkbeer, E.K.**
[Löwenthal]

1 e4 e5 2 ♘f3 ♘c6 3 ♗b5 a6 4 ♗a4 ♘f6 5 d4 exd4 6 e5 ♘e4 7 ♘xd4 ♘xd4 8 ♕xd4 ♘c5 9 ♘c3 ♘xa4 10 ♘xa4 ♗e7 11 0-0 0-0 12 ♗f4! f6? 13 exf6 ♖xf6 14 ♕c4+ d5 15 ♕xc7 ♕xc7 16 ♗xc7 ♗f5 [□ 16 ... ♗e6; 16 ... ♖c6] 17 ♘b6 ♖xb6 18 ♗xb6 ♗xc2 19 ♖fe1 ♗f6 20 ♖ac1 ♗a4 21 ♖c7 ♗c6 22 b3 h5 23 ♖e6 ♖f8 [23 ... ♗d8 24 ♖cxc6 Δ ♖e8++-] 24 ♗c5 ♖d8 25 ♗b6 ♖f8 26 ♔f1 ♗d8 27 ♖cxc6 bxc6 28 ♗c5 ♔f7 29 ♖xc6 ♖e8 30 ♖d6 a5 31 ♖xd5 ♔g6 32 ♖d6+ ♔f5 33 ♗d4 ♗e7 34 ♖a6 ♗b4 35 ♗e3 ♖c8 36 a3 ♗c3 37 ♔e2 ♖b8 38 ♖b6 ♖c8 39 ♖b5+ ♔e6 40 ♖c5 ♖xc5 41 ♗xc5 ♔d5 42 ♔d3 a4 43 bxa4 ♔e5 44 ♗b6 ♗xh2 45 g3 g5 46 ♗d8 h4 47 gxh4 gxh4 48 ♗xh4 ♗d6 49 ♗g5 ♗xa3 50 a5 ♗c5 51 ♗e3 ♗e7 52 ♔c3 ♗h4 53 ♔b4 ♔c6 54 a6 ♔c7 55 f4 ♗f6 56 ♗a7 ♗h4 57 ♔c4 ♔c6 58 f5 ♗d8 59 ♗d4 ♔c7 60 ♔d5 ♗h4 61 ♔e6 ♔c6 62 ♗c5 ♔c7 63 ♗e7 ♗f2 64 f6 ♗d4 65 f7 ♗g7 66 ♔f5 ...? **1-0** L/N5188

**1862-LON2-46** 30 vi 62
**Anderssen, A.+ Lamb, F.E.**
[Löwenthal]

⟨♘b1⟩ 1 e4 d5 2 e5 e6 3 f4 c5 4 ♘f3 ♕b6 5 d3 ♘h6 6 ♗e2 ♘c6 7 c3 ♗d7 8 0-0 ♗e7 9 ♔h1 d4 [□ 9 ... f6] 10 ♘d2 f5 [□ 10 ... f6; 10 ... ♕c7; 10 ... ♘f5] 11 h3 0-0 12 ♕e1 ♔h8 [□ 12 ... ♘f7 Δ ... ♘xe5] 13 ♘f3 ♖g8 14 ♖g1 ♗e8 15 g4 ♗g6 16 g5 ♘f7 17 ♘h4 ♖gf8 [□ 17 ... ♘xe5] 18 ♘xg6+ hxg6 19 h4 ♔h7 20 h5 ♖h8 21 ♔g2 ♕d8 22 ♖h1 b5? 23 ♗f3 ♖c8 24 ♗d2 c4 25 hxg6+ ♔xg6 26 ♕e2 ♘h6 27 ♗h5+ ♔h7 28 ♗f7 ♕d5+ 29 ♔f2 ♖hf8 30 ♕h5 **1-0** L/N5188

**1862-LON2-47** 4 vii 62
**Anderssen, A.– Lamb, F.E.**
[Löwenthal]

⟨♘b1⟩ 1 e3 e5 2 c4 ♘c6 3 b3 ♗c5 4 a3 ♗e7 5 ♘e2 d5 6 cxd5 ♕xd5 7 ♘c3 ♕d8 8 ♗e2 ♗f5 9 d3 ♘f6 10 0-0 ♕d7 11 b4 a6 12 f4 ♖d8 13 fxe5 ♘xe5 14 d4 ♘g6 15 ♗c4 ♗e6 16 ♗d3 ♕c6 17 ♗d2 [□ 17 ♗b2] 17 ... ♗c4 18 ♗c2? ♗xf1 19 ♕xf1 0-0 20 ♖e1 ♘d5 21 ♕d3 ♘xc3 22 ♗xc3 ♗f6 23 a4 ♕d5 24 ♖f1 b5 25 ♕d2 ♖fe8 26 ♖f5 ♕c6 27 axb5 axb5 28 ♗d3 ♖xe3! 29 ♖c5 [29 ♕xe3 ♕xc3 Δ ... ♗xd4∓] 29 ... ♖xd3 30 ♕xd3 [30 ♖xc6 ♗xd4+ 31 ♔f1 ♖xd2 32 ♗xd2 ♗b6 Δ 33 ... ♘e5; Δ 33 ... ♘e7∓] 30 ... ♕xg2+!

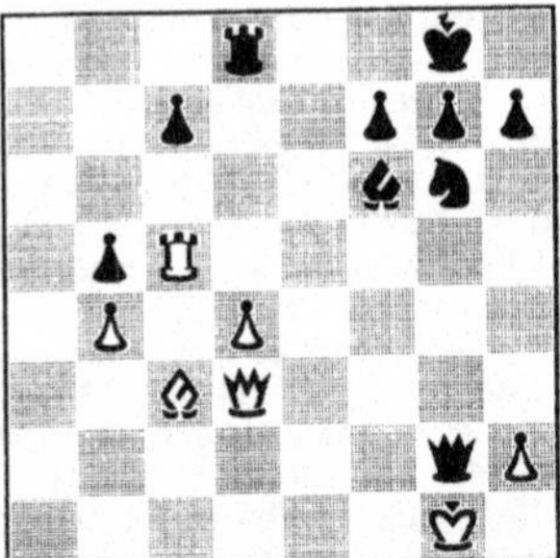

31 ♔xg2 ♘f4+ 32 ♔f3 ♘xd3 33 ♖xb5 h6 [Δ ... ♗xd4] 34 ♔e3 ♘c1 35 ♖b7 ♘b3 36 ♖xc7 ♘xd4 37 ♔e4 ♘b5 [□ 37 ... ♖e8+∓] 38 ♗xf6 gxf6! 39 ♖c2 ♖d4+ 40 ♔f5 ♖xb4 41 ♔xf6 ♖f4+ 42 ♔e5 ♖f5+ 43 ♔e4 ♔g7 44 ♖d2 ♔g6 ...? **0-1** L/N5188

**1862-LON2-48**
**Anderssen, A.+ Lamb, F.E.**
[Löwenthal]

⟨♘b1⟩ 1 e4 e5 2 f4 ♗c5 3 ♘f3 d6 4 b4 ♗xb4 5 c3 ♗c5 6 ♗c4 ♘c6 7 d3 a6 8 a4 h6 9 f5 ♘f6 10 ♕e2 ♘e7 11 h4 d5 12 ♗b3 ♗d6 13 ♘h2 ♗d7 14 g4 dxe4 15 dxe4 ♘xe4 16 ♗e3 ♗c6! 17 0-0 ♘g3 18 ♕a2 f6 [18 ... ♘xf1 19 ♗xf7+ ♔f8 20 ♖xf1 Δ f6] 19 ♗f7+ ♔f8 20 ♖fe1 e4 21 ♖ad1 ♕c8 22 ♔g2 [Δ ♖xd6] 22 ... ♘gxf5 23 gxf5 ♕xf5 24 ♖f1 ♕e5 25 ♖xd6 cxd6 26 ♘g4 ♕xc3 27 ♕e6 ♗d5 28 ♕xd6 ♔xf7 29 h5 ♘c6?? 30 ♕xd5+ ♔e8 31 ♕xe4+ ♔d7 32 ♕d5+ ♔c8 33 ♕e6+ ♔b8 34 ♕d6+ ♔c8 35 ♗f4 ♕a5 36 ♕e6+ **1-0** L/N5188

**1862-LON2-49**
**Harris, E.– Green, V.**
[Löwenthal]

⟨♙f7⟩ 1 e4 e6 2 d4 ♘c6 3 ♗e3 [□ 3 ♗d3] 3 ... d5 4 e5 g6 5 ♗d3 ♗d7 6 f4 [□ 6 h4] 6 ... ♘h6 7 c3 ♗g7 8 ♘h3 [□ 8 ♘f3] 8 ... ♕e7 9 ♘d2 0-0-0 10 ♘b3 b6 11 a4 ♘f5 12 ♗f2 ♖hf8 13 g3 h6 14 a5 ♗e8 15 ♘g1? g5 16 ♘f3 ♗h5 17 h3 gxf4 18 ♗xf5 fxg3!

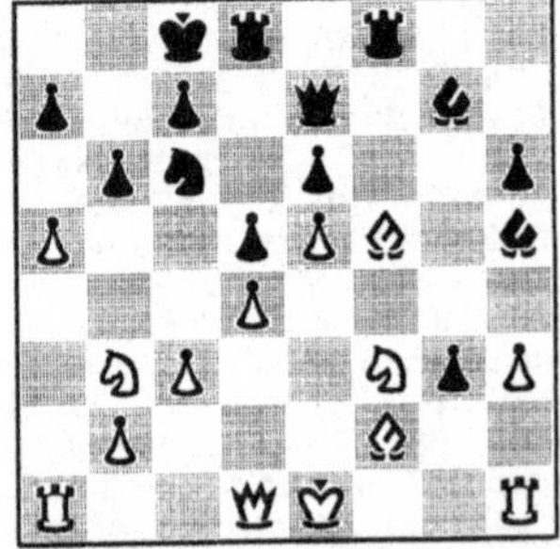

19 ♗xg3 ♖xf5 20 0-0 ♖df8 21 ♘bd2 ♕f7 22 ♔g2 ♘xa5 23 ♕e2 ♘c4 24 ♖f2 [□ 24 b3] 24 ... ♘xd2 25 ♕a6+ ♔d8 26 ♗h4+ ♗f6 27 ♗xf6+ ♖xf6 28 exf6 ♕xf6 29 ♕e2 ♖g8+ 30 ♔h1 ♗xf3+ 31 ♖xf3 ♕xf3+ 32 ♕xf3 ♘xf3 33 ♖f1 ♖g3 34 h4 ♔e7 **0-1** L/N5188

**1862-LON2-50**
**Harris, E.+ Green, V.**
[Löwenthal]

⟨♙f7⟩ 1 e4 ♘c6 2 d4 e5 3 dxe5 ♘xe5 4 f4 ♘f7 5 ♗c4 ♘gh6 6 ♘f3 ♗c5 7 ♕d3 d6 8 ♗e3 0-0? 9 ♗xc5 dxc5 10 ♕xd8 ♖xd8 11 0-0 c6 12 ♘e5 ♗e6?? 13 ♗xe6 **1-0** L/N5188

**1862-LON2-51**
**Harris, E.– Green, V.**
[Löwenthal]

⟨♙f7⟩ 1 e4 e6 2 d4 ♘c6 3 ♘f3 d5 4 e5 ♗d7 [□ 4 ... g6] 5 ♗e3 ♗b4+ 6 ♘c3 ♘ge7 7 ♗d3 ♘f5 8 ♗xf5 exf5 9 ♗g5 ♘e7 10 0-0 ♗xc3 11 bxc3 0-0 12 ♖e1 ♗e6 13 ♕d3 ♕d7 14 ♗xe7 ♕xe7 15 ♘d2 f4! 16 c4 dxc4 17 ♘xc4 f3 18 gxf3 ♖f4 19 ♖e4 ♖af8 20 ♖xf4 ♖xf4 21 ♔h1 ♕f7 [□ 21 ... ♕h4] 22 ♘d2 ♗d5 23 ♔g2 ♕h5 24 ♖h1 ♕g4+ 25 ♔f1 ♗xf3 26 ♘xf3 ♕xf3 27 ♕xf3 ♖xf3 28 ♔e2 ♖a3 29 f4 ♔f7 30 f5 ♖xa2 31 ♔d2 c6 32 ♖f1 b5? 33 f6 gxf6! 34 ♖xf6+ ♔e7 35 ♖xc6 h5 36 d5 ♖a4 37 ♔d3 ♖h4 38 ♖c7+ ♔d8 39 ♖xa7 ♖xh2 40 ♖b7 ♖h3+ 41 ♔d4 b4! 42 ♖xb4 ♖h4+ 43 ♔c3 ♖xb4

44 ♔xb4 h4 45 c4 h3 46 ♔c5 h2 47 e6 h1♕ 48 ♔c6 ♕e4 49 ♔b5 ♔c7 50 ♔b4 ♔d6 51 e7 ♕xe7 **0-1** L/N5188

**1862-LON2-52**
**Solomons,S.– Mackenzie,G.H.**
[Löwenthal]

1 c4 f5 2 e3 e6 3 a3 ♘f6 4 ♘c3 ♗e7 5 ♘f3 [◻ 5 f4] 5 ... d6 6 d4 0-0 7 ♗d3 b6 8 b3 ♗b7 9 ♗b2 ♘e4 10 ♕c2 d5 11 h3 ♘d7 12 ♘d2 a6 13 g4? ♘xc3 14 f3 [14 ♗xc3? dxc4] 14 ... ♗h4+ 15 ♔f1 ♘e4 16 cxd5 ♗xd5 17 ♔g2 ♘xd2 18 ♕xd2 fxg4 19 e4 ♕f6 20 f4 gxh3+ 21 ♖xh3 ♗b7 22 d5 e5 23 ♖f1 ♕g6+ 24 ♔h2 exf4 25 ♖xf4 ♖xf4 26 ♕xf4 ♗g5 27 ♕xc7 ♖f8 28 ♗d4 ♗f4+ 29 ♕xf4 ♖xf4 30 ♖g3 ♖g4 31 e5 ♕h6+ 32 ♔g2 ♕d2+ 33 ♔h3 ♖xg3+ 34 ♔xg3 ♕xd3+ ...? **0-1** L/N5188

**1862-LON2-53**
**Solomons,S.+ Mackenzie,G.H.**
[Löwenthal]

1 c4 e6 2 a3 c5 3 e3 ♘c6 4 ♘c3 ♘f6 5 ♘f3 ♗e7 6 ♗e2 0-0 7 0-0 b6 8 b3 ♗b7 9 ♗b2 d5 10 d4 ♖c8 11 ♖c1 ♗d6 12 ♘b5 ♗b8 13 dxc5 bxc5 14 cxd5 exd5 15 ♖xc5 a6 16 ♘bd4 ♕d6 17 ♖c1 ♘e7 18 ♕d2 ♘e4 19 ♕b4 ♘c5 [◻ 19 ... ♕xb4] 20 ♖xc5 ♖xc5 21 ♕xb7 f5 22 ♕xa6 ♘c6 23 b4! ♘xd4 24 ♕xd6 ♘xe2+ [24 ... ♘xf3+?] 25 ♔h1 ♗xd6 26 bxc5 ♗xc5 27 ♖e1 ♗xa3 28 ♗xa3 ♖a8 29 ♗b2 **1-0** L/N5188

**1862-LON2-54**
**Solomons,S.–Mackenzie, G.H.**
[Löwenthal]

1 c4 f5 2 f4 e6 3 a3 ♘f6 4 ♘c3 ♗e7 5 ♘f3 d6 6 e3 b6 7 b3 ♗b7 8 ♗b2 0-0 9 ♗e2 c5 10 ♕c2 a6 11 ♘g5? ♕d7 12 ♗f3 ♘c6 13 0-0 h6 14 ♘h3 ♖ae8 15 ♖ae1 ♗d8 16 d3 d5 17 ♘e2 ♘e7 18 ♘g3 ♘g6 19 ♗h5 ♘xh5 20 ♘xh5 ♖f7! 21 cxd5 ♕xd5 22 e4?? fxe4 23 dxe4 ♕xh5 24 ♕c4 b5 25 ♕c2 ♗b6 26 ♔h1 ♖ef8 27 ♕c3 ♕g4 28 ♖f3 ♘xf4 29 ♖g3 ♘xh3! 30 gxh3 ♗xe4+ 31 ♔g1 c4+ 32 ♕d4 ♗xd4+ 33 ♗xd4 ♕e2 **0-1**

**1862-LON2-55**
**Hannah, J.W.– Deacon, F.H.**
[Löwenthal]

1 e4 c5 2 ♘f3 g6 3 ♗c4 ♗g7 4 c3 ♘c6 5 d4 cxd4 6 ♘xd4 ♘f6 7 ♕c2 0-0 8 ♗e3 e6 9 0-0 d5 10 ♗b5? ♘xd4 11 cxd4 ♘xe4 12 ♘c3 ♘d6 13 ♗d3 ♗d7 14 f4 ♖c8 15 ♖f3 f5 16 ♕b3 ♖c6 17 ♖d1 ♕b6 18 ♗c2 ♘c4 19 ♕xb6 ♖xb6 20 b3 ♘xe3 21 ♖xe3 ♖c8 22 ♗b1 [22 ♖dd3 ♖bc6 △ ... ♗xd4∓] 22 ... ♔f7! 23 ♔f1 ♖b4 24 ♘e2 ♗b5 25 ♗d3 ♗xd4 26 ♖h3 ♗xd3 27 ♖dxd3 ♖c2 28 ♖xh7+ ♗g7 29 ♖hh3 ♖e4 30 ♖he3 ♖xa2 31 g3 [31 ♖xe4? fxe4∓] 31 ... ♗f8 32 ♘c3 ♖xe3 33 ♖xe3 ♖xh2 34 ♘b5 ♖c2 35 ♖xe6 [35 ♘d4 ♖c1+ 36 ♔~ ♗c5∓] 35 ... ♖c5 36 ♘d4 ♗g7 37 ♖d6 ♗xd4 ...? **0-1** L/N5188

**1862-LON2-56**
**Hannah, J.W.= Deacon, F.H.**
[Löwenthal]

1 e4 c5 2 ♘f3 g6 3 ♘c3 [3 d4 cxd4 4 ♕xd4 ♘f6 5 e5 ♘c6 6 ♕h4 (6 ♕c3 e6) 6 ... ♘xe5 7 ♘xe5 ♕a5+ 8 ♘c3 ♕xe5+ 9 ♗e2 △ ♗f4±] 3 ... ♗g7 4 ♗c4 ♘c6 5 ♘e2 e6 [5 ... ♘f6 6 ♘g3 (6 d3 b5 7 ♗xb5 ♕a5+ 8 ♘c3 ♘xe4 9 dxe4 ♗xc3+ 10 bxc3 ♕xb5 △ ♗a6∓) 6 ... 0-0 7 c3 (7 0-0 ♘xe4 8 ♘xe4 d5 9 ♘xc5 dxc4 10 d4 cxd3 11 ♘xd3 e5∓] 6 c3 ♘ge7 7 d4 cxd4 8 ♘fxd4 a6 9 ♕a4 0-0 10 ♗e3 b6 11 ♘xc6 ♘xc6 12 ♖d1 ♗b7 13 ♕c2 ♖c8 14 0-0 ♕c7 15 f4 ♘e7 16 ♗b3 [16 ♕d3 ♕xc4 17 ♕xc4 ♖xc4 18 ♖xd7 ♖xe4 19 ♔f2 ♘d5∓] 16 ... d5 17 e5 f6 18 ♘d4 ♕d7 19 exf6 ♗xf6 [◻ 19 ... ♖xf6] 20 ♕e2 b5 [20 ... e5 21 fxe5 ♗xe5 22 ♘f3 ♗c7 23 ♗g5±] 21 ♗f2 ♗xd4 22 ♗xd4 ♘f5 23 ♖fe1 ♘xd4 24 ♖xd4 ♖ce8 25 ♕g4 ♕f7 [△ ... e5] 26 ♖e5 ♔h8 27 ♗c2 ♗c8 28 h4 ♖g8 29 ♕g5 ♖ef8 30 h5 gxh5 31 ♕xh5 ♕xh5 32 ♖xh5 ♖g7 33 f5 exf5 34 ♖xd5 ♗b7 35 ♖d2 ♖fg8 36 ♖h2 f4 37 ♔f1! ♖e7 [37 ... ♖e8 38 ♗xh7 ♖xh7 39 ♖xh7+ ♔xh7 40 ♖d7+±] 38 ♔f2 ♖eg7 39 ♔f1 ♖e7 40 ♖h6 ♖eg7 41 ♖f2 ♖e7! 42 ♖f6 ♖xg2! 43 ♗b3 f3

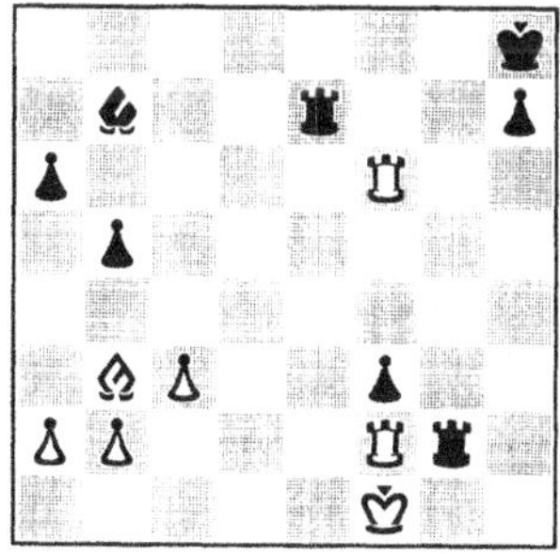

½-½ L/N5188

**1862-LON2-57**
**Hannah, J.W.= Deacon, F.H.**
[Löwenthal]

1 e4 c5 2 ♘f3 g6 3 ♘c3 ♗g7 4 ♗c4 ♘c6 5 0-0 ♘f6? 6 e5 ♘g8! [6 ... ♘g4 7 ♗xf7+ ♔xf7 8 ♘g5+ ♔e8 9 ♕xg4 ♘xe5 10 ♕e4 △ f4±] 7 ♖e1 e6 8 ♘b5 ♗f8 9 d4 cxd4? 10 ♘fxd4 a6 [10 ... d5 11 exd6 △ ♘xc6±] 11 ♘d6+ ♗xd6 12 exd6 ♕h4 [12 ... f5 13 ♘xe6±; 12 ... ♘f6 13 ♘xc6 bxc6 14 ♕d4 h6 15 ♗f4 ♖h7 16 ♗e5 ♘d5 17 ♗xd5 cxd5 18 ♕xd5 ♖b8 19 c4±] 13 ♗e3 ♘f6 14 f3 0-0 15 g3 ♕h5 16 ♕d2 ♕c5! 17 ♗b3 [17 ♕c3 ♘e5=; 17 ♘xe6 ♕xc4 18 ♘xf8 ♘e5 (18 ... ♔xf8 19 ♗h6+ ♔g8 20 ♕g5 ♕d4+ 21 ♔h1 ♕xd6 22 ♕xf6+-) 19 ♕a5 b5 20 ♕d8 ♗b7 21 ♕xf6 ♘xf3+=] 17 ... ♕xd6 18 ♕c3 ♘e7 19 ♘f5! [◻ 19 ♘xe6] 19 ... ♘xf5 20 ♕xf6 ♘xe3 21 ♖xe3 ♕c5 22 ♖ae1 b5 23 ♔g2 ♖e8 ½-½ L/N5188

**1862-LON2-58**
**Deacon, F.H.+Hannah, J.W.**
[Löwenthal]

1 c4 b6 2 e3 ♗b7 3 f4 g6 [3 ... e5!?] 4 ♘f3 ♗g7 5 d4 e6 6 ♘c3 ♘e7 7 e4 f6 8 ♗d3 0-0 9 ♗e3 d6 10 0-0 ♘d7 11 ♕d2 ♖e8 12 ♖ae1 c6 13 ♗c2 d5 14 cxd5 exd5 15 e5 f5 16 ♔h1 ♘f8 17 ♖g1 h5 18 h3 ♘e6 19 ♕f2 ♔f7 20 ♘e2! ♖h8 21 ♘g5+ ♘xg5 22 fxg5 c5 23 ♘f4 ♕c7 24 e6+ [24 ♖gf1? ♖af8=] 24 ... ♔g8 [24 ... ♕e8 25 ♘xg6 ♘xg6 26 ♕xf5 ♘f8 27 e7+-] 25 dxc5 [25 ♘xg6 ♘xg6 26 ♕xf5 cxd4 (26 ... ♘h4 27 ♕f2 cxd4 28 ♗f4 ♕c6 29 ♗d6+-) 27 ♕xg6 dxe3 28 ♖xe3 ♗c6 29 ♖c3±] 25 ... ♖c8 26 ♗a4! bxc5 27 ♗d7 d4 28 ♗d2 ♖d8 29 ♖c1

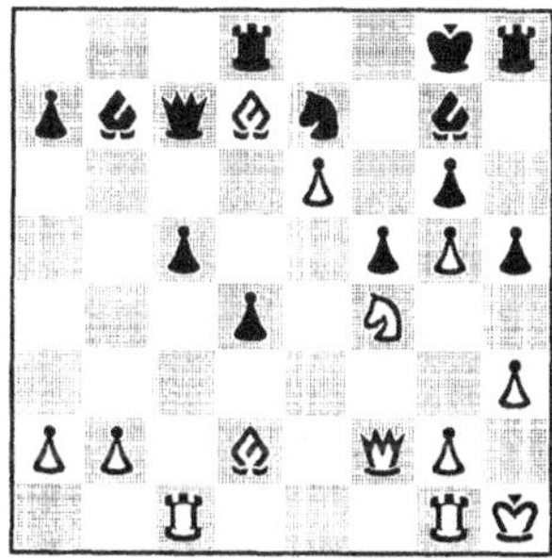

29 ... ♔h7 [◻ 29 ... a5 30 ♗b5 ♕b6 31 ♗c4 ♖d6 (31 ... ♔h7 32 ♕e2 ♖hf8 33 ♘xh5 gxh5 34 ♕xh5+ ♔g8 35 g6 ♖fe8 36 ♕h7+ ♔f8 37 ♗h6+-) 32 ♘xg6 ♘xg6 33 ♕xf5 ♔h7 34 ♕xg6+ ♔xg6 35 ♗d3++-; 29 ... a5 30 ♘d3 c4 31 ♗f4 ♕b6 32 ♖xc4 ♕a6 33 ♖gc1 ♗d5 34 ♘c5 ♕a7 (34 ... ♕b6 35 ♘a4 ♕a6 36 ♖c7 ♗xa2 37 ♘c5 ♕a8 38 b3+-) 35 ♖a4 ♘c6 36 b4 ♔h7 37 ♗xc6 ♗xc6 38 ♖xa5 ♕e7 39 b5+-] 30 ♗b4 ♗e5 31 ♖xc5 ♕b8 32 ♘d3! [32 ♖xe5 ♕xe5 33 ♗xe7 ♖xd7 34 exd7 ♕xe7 35 ♕xd4 ♖d8±] 32 ... ♗g3 [32 ... ♗d6 33 ♖b5 ♗xb4 (33 ... ♖xd7 34 exd7 ♗xg2+ 35 ♖xg2 ♕xb5 36 ♗xd6+-) 34 ♖xb4 ♘d5 35 ♖b3 ♘e3 36 ♗c6 ♘g4 37 ♕f4 ♕xf4 38 ♖xb7+ ♔g8 39 ♘xf4 d3 40 e7+-] 33 ♕xd4 ♗h2 34 ♕f6 ♖hg8 [34 ... ♖df8 35 ♕xe7+ ♔g8 36 ♖c8+-] 35 ♗c3 **1-0** L/N5188

**1862-LON2-59**
**Green, V.– Anderssen, A.**

[Löwenthal]

⟨♙f7⟩ 1 e4 e6 2 ♘c3 c5 3 ♘f3 ♘c6 4 d4 c×d4 5 ♘×d4 ♘f6 6 ♘db5 a6 7 ♘d6+ ♗×d6 8 ♕×d6 ♕a5 9 ♗d3 ♕h5 10 ♗e3 ♘g4 11 ♗e2 ♕g6 12 ♗c5 ♘ge5 13 0-0-0 b5 14 f4 ♘f7 15 ♕d3 ♕f6 16 ♖hf1 ♖b8 17 e5 ♕h6 18 ♔b1 d5! 19 e×d6 ♗d7 20 ♖f3 e5 21 f5 0-0 22 ♘e4! ♘g5? 23 ♘×g5? [◻ 23 ♗e3±] 23 ... ♕×g5 24 ♖df1 ♔h8 25 g3? e4! 26 ♕×e4 ♖be8 27 ♕d3 ♘e5 28 ♗e3 ♕d8 29 ♕c3 ♘×f3 30 ♗×f3 b4 31 ♕d4 ♖×f5 32 b3 ♕a5 33 ♗f4 ♖f6 34 a4? b×a3 35 ♔a2 ♕f5 36 ♕d3 ♕×d3 37 c×d3 ♗b5 38 h4 h6 39 ♖d1 [◻ 37 h5±] 39 ... g5 40 h×g5 h×g5 41 ♗h5 g×f4 42 ♗×e8 ♗×e8 43 g×f4 ♖×d6 44 d4 ♔g7 45 ♔×a3 ♗f7 46 b4 ♖b6 47 d5 ♖d6 48 ♔a4 ♔f6 49 ♔a5? ♗e8! 50 ♖d2 ♗b5 51 ♖d1 ♔f5 52 ♖c1 ♔×f4 53 ♖e1 ♖×d5 ...? **0-1** L/N5188

**1862-LON2-60**
**Green, V.– Anderssen, A.**

[Löwenthal]

⟨♙f7⟩ 1 e4 e6 2 ♘c3 c5 3 ♘f3 ♘c6 4 d4 c×d4 5 ♘×d4 d6 6 ♗c4 ♘×d4 7 ♕×d4 ♗d7 8 ♗e3 ♕a5 9 a3 [◻ 9 0-0] 9 ... ♘f6 10 b4 ♕c7 11 ♘b5? ♕c6! 12 ♖d1 [◻ 12 a4] 12 ... a6 13 ♘×d6+ ♗×d6 14 ♕×d6 ♕×c4 15 ♗c5 ♕×e4+ 16 ♔f1 0-0-0 17 ♔g1 ♗c6 **0-1** L/N5188

**1862-LON2-61**
**Mackenzie,G.H.+ Anderssen,A.**

[Löwenthal]

⟨♙f7⟩ 1 e4 e6 2 d4 d6 3 ♘f3 c5? 4 d×c5 ♕a5+ 5 ♘c3 ♕×c5 6 ♗e3 ♕a5 7 ♗c4 ♘c6 8 0-0 a6 9 ♘g5 ♘d8 10 f4 ♘f6 11 f5! e×f5 12 e×f5 ♗×f5 13 ♘d5 ♘×d5 14 ♗×d5 ♗g6 15 ♕f3 ♖c8 16 ♖ad1 [◻ 16 ♗d4] 16 ... ♔d7 [◻ 16 ... ♗e7] 17 b4 ♕×b4 18 ♖db1 ♕c3 19 ♕g4+ ♔e8 20 ♗d4 ♕a5 21 ♖be1+ ♗e7 22 ♕×c8 ♕×d5 23 ♗b6 **1-0** L/N5188

**1862-LON2-62**
**Mackenzie,G.H.+ Anderssen,A.**

[Löwenthal]

⟨♙f7⟩ 1 e4 ♘c6 2 ♘f3 e6 3 d4 d6 4 ♗d3 e5 5 c3 ♘f6 6 ♗e3 ♗e7 7 0-0 ♗g4 [◻ 7 ... 0-0] 8 ♘bd2 ♕c8 9 ♕b3 h6 10 ♖ae1 a6 11 ♗c4! g5 12 h3 ♗d7 13 ♗f7+ ♔f8 14 ♗g6 ♗e6 15 d5 ♗g8 16 ♕c2 ♘b8 17 c4 ♘bd7 18 ♗f5

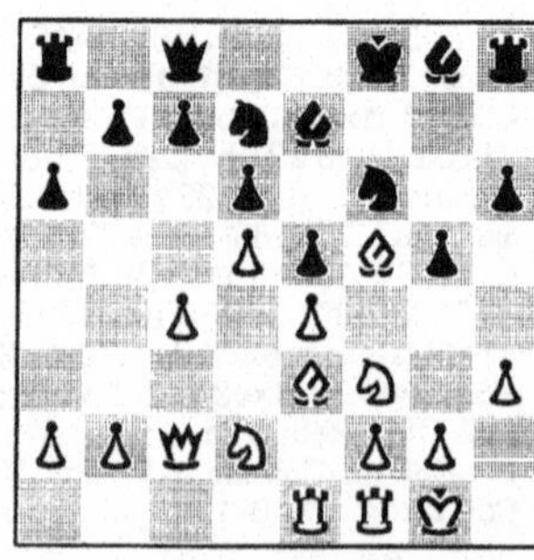

18 ... ♕d8 19 c5 d×c5 20 ♘c4 ♗d6 21 ♗d2 b5 22 ♘e3 ♕e7 23 ♗c1 ♖e8 24 ♘h2 ♕g7 25 ♗×d7 ♘×d7 26 ♘f5 ♕g6 27 ♖e3 ♗f7 28 ♖g3 ♘f6 29 ♖a3 ♖a8 30 ♖e1 ♔g8 [◻ 30 ... ♘h5] 31 ♖g3 ♘h5 32 ♖g4 ♔h7 33 h4 ♖hf8?? 34 h×g5 ♗×d5?? 35 ♘h4 ♗b3 36 ♕×b3 ♕e8 37 g6+ ♔g7 38 ♘f5+ ♖×f5 39 e×f5 ♘f6 40 ♖h4 h5 41 ♕e3 ♕h8 42 g4 e4 43 g5 ♗×h2+ 44 ♖×h2 ♘g4 45 ♕c3+ **1-0** L/N5188

**1862-LON2-63**
**Mackenzie,G.H.=Deacon, F.H.**

[Löwenthal]

1 e4 d5 2 e×d5 ♕×d5 3 ♘c3 ♕d8 4 d4 e6 5 ♘f3 ♗d6 6 ♗d3 f5?! 7 0-0 ♘f6 8 ♕e2 0-0 9 ♗g5 ♔h8 10 ♖ad1 ♕e8 11 ♗c4 ♕g6 12 ♖fe1! ♖e8 13 ♗c1 ♘c6 14 ♘e5 ♗×e5 15 d×e5 ♘d7 16 ♗f4 [16 ♘b5 ♖e7 17 ♘×c7 ♖b8 18 f4 a6∓] 16 ... ♘b6 17 ♗b3 ♗d7 18 ♖d3 ♘e7 19 ♖g3 ♕f7 20 ♖h3 ♗c6 21 ♕e3 ♖ad8 22 ♗g5 ♖d7 23 ♗×e7 ♕×e7 24 ♘e2 a5! 25 ♘f4 ♕f7 26 a3 ♗d5 27 ♘×d5 ♘×d5 28 ♗×d5 ♖×d5 29 ♕b3 b6 30 ♖d3 ♖ed8 31 ♖ed1 ♖×d3 32 ♖×d3 ♖×d3 33 ♕×d3 h6 **½-½** L/N5188

**1862-LON2-64**
**Mackenzie,G.H.= Deacon,F.H.**

[Löwenthal]

1 e4 c5 2 ♘f3 g6 3 c3 ♗g7 4 d4 b6 5 ♗e3 ♕c7? [◻ 5 ... d6] 6 ♘a3 a6 7 ♗d3 d6 8 0-0 ♘f6 9 e5 d×e5 10 ♘×e5 0-0 11 f4 e6 12 ♖c1 ♗b7 13 ♕e2 [13 b4 ♘d5 14 ♕d2 c×d4 15 c×d4 ♕d6∓] 13 ... ♘bd7 14 ♘ac4 b5 15 ♘d2 c4 16 ♗b1 ♘d5 17 ♘e4 ♘×e3 18 ♕×e3 ♗d5 19 ♖ce1 [△ 19 ... f6 20 ♘×d7 ♕×d7 21 ♘c5±] 19 ... ♖ae8 20 ♕h3 f5 [◻ 20 ... f6] 21 ♘g5 ♘f6 22 ♖e3 ♘h5 23 ♘×h7

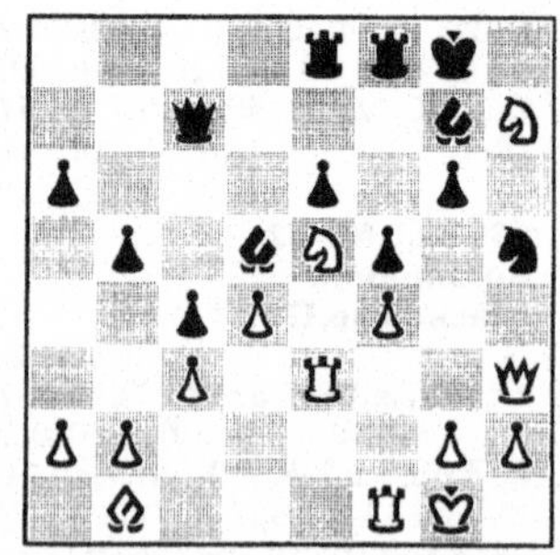

23 ... ♔×h7 [23 ... ♘×f4 24 ♖×f4 ♗×e5 25 ♖h4 ♗f4 26 ♘f6+ ♕f7 27 ♘×d5 ♗×e3+ 28 ♔f1+–; 23 ... ♗×e5 24 ♘×f8 ♗×f4 25 ♘×g6 ♗×e3+ 26 ♕×e3 ♕g7 27 ♗×f5+–] 24 g4 ♗×e5 25 f×e5 ♖g8 26 g×h5 g×h5+ 27 ♖g3 ♕f7 28 ♖f4 [28 ♗×f5!?] 28 ... ♔h6 29 ♗c2 ♖g7? [◻ 29 ... ♖×g3+=] 30 ♗d1 ♖eg8 31 ♗×h5 ♕×h5 32 ♖h4 ♗f3 33 ♖×h5+ ♗×h5 34 ♔f2 ♖g4 35 ♖×g4 ♖×g4 36 ♕e3+ ♔g6 37 h3 ♖e4 38 ♕g3+ ♔h6 39 ♕g8! ♖e2+ 40 ♔f1 ♗f3 41 ♕×e6+ [◻ 41 ♕g3 △ h4] 41 ... ♔g5 42 d5 ♔f4 43 d6 ♔e3 44 ♕g6 ♖f2+ 45 ♔g1 ♖d2 46 ♕×f5 [46 e6? ♖d1+ 47 ♔h2 ♖h1+ 48 ♔g3 ♖g1+ 49 ♔h2 (49 ♔h4 ♖×g6 50 d7 ♖g2+ 51 ♔h1 ♔f2–+) 49 ... ♖×g6–+] 46 ... ♖g2+ 47 ♔f1 [47 ♔h1 ♖c2+ (47 ... ♖×b2+?) 48 ♕×f3+ ♔×f3 49 d7 ♔g3–+] 47 ... ♖f2+ 48 ♔e1 ♖e2+= [49 ♔d1 ♖g2+ 50 ♕×f3+ (50 ♔c1 ♖g1+ 51 ♔c2 ♗d1+–+) 50 ... ♔×f3 51 d7=] **½-½** L/N5188

**1962-LON2-65**
**Mackenzie,G.H.+ Deacon,F.H.**

[Löwenthal]

1 e4 c5 2 ♘f3 g6 3 c3 ♗g7 4 d4 c×d4 5 c×d4 e6 6 ♘c3 ♘e7 7 ♗d3 0-0 8 0-0 ♘bc6 9 ♗e3 d5 10 e5 f6 11 e×f6 ♖×f6 12 ♖c1 [12 ♗g5?] 12 ... ♖f8 13 ♕d2 ♘f5 14 ♗×f5 ♖×f5 15 ♘e2 ♗d7 16 ♘g3 ♖f8 17 ♖fe1 ♖c8 [△ ... ♕a5] 18 h4 ♖×f3! 19 g×f3 ♕×h4 20 ♔g2 ♕f6 21 f4 [21 ♖cd1 ♖f8 22 f4 h5∓] 21 ... ♘×d4 22 ♖×c8+ ♗×c8 23 ♗×d4 ♕×d4 24 ♕a5 ♕×f4 25 ♖e2 ♕c4? [◻ 25 ... ♕d6 26 ♖c2 (26 ♕×a7 ♕c6 △ ... h5∓) 26 ... ♗d7 27 ♕d8+ ♗f8 28 ♖c7 ♗c6 29 ♕b8 d4+ 30 ♔∼ d3–+] 26 ♕d8+ ♔f7 27 ♖e3 e5 28 ♖c3 ♗f6 29 ♕×c8 ♕×c8 30 ♖×c8 ♔e6 31 ♖c7 h5 32 ♖×b7 h4 33 ♘f1 e4 34 ♖×a7 ♗×b2 35 ♖b7 ♗c3 36 a4 ♔d6 37 ♖b5 ♔c6 38 ♘e3 d4 39 ♘d5 ♗e1 40 ♘e7+ ♔c7 41 ♘×g6 h3+ 42 ♔f1 ♗c3 43 ♖h5 ♔d6 44 ♖×h3 **1-0** L/N5188

**1862-LON2-66**
**Mackenzie,G.H.+Deacon, F.H.**

[Löwenthal]

1 e4 e5 2 ♘f3 ♘c6 3 ♗c4 ♗c5 4 0-0 ♘f6 5 d4 ♗xd4 6 ♘xd4 ♘xd4 [◻6 ... exd4] 7 f4 d6 8 fxe5 dxe5 9 ♗g5 ♗e6 10 ♘d2 [10 ♗xe6 ♘xe6 11 ♕xd8+ ♖xd8 12 ♗xf6 gxf6 13 ♖xf6 ♔e7 14 ♖f5 ♖d1+ 15 ♖f1 ♖hd8 16 ♘c3 ♖xa1 17 ♖xa1 ♖d2∓] 10 ... ♕e7 11 c3 ♘c6 [11 ... ♕c5 12 b4 ♕b6 13 ♗e3 ♘g4∓]

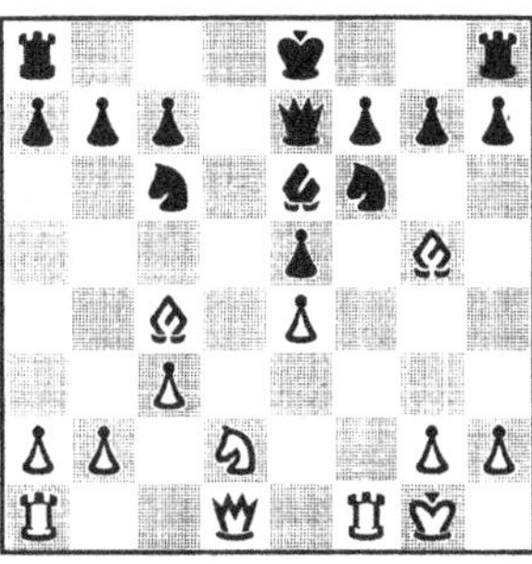

12 ♕e2 0-0-0 [◻12 ... h6] 13 b4 h6 14 ♗e3 ♘g4 15 ♗c5 ♕h4 16 h3 [16 ♗xe6+? fxe6 17 ♘f3 ♕h5 △ ... ♘xh2] 16 ... ♗xc4 17 ♘xc4 ♘f6 18 ♖ae1 b6 19 ♗f2 ♕h5 20 ♕c2 ♘e8 [◻20 ... ♔b7] 21 ♕a4 ♔b7 22 ♘a5+ ♘xa5 23 bxa5 ♕g6 24 c4 a6 [◻24 ... c5] 25 axb6 c6 26 ♖e3 ♕e6 27 ♖a3 ♖a8 28 ♖d1 ♘f6 29 c5 ♖hc8 30 ♖d6 ♕e8 31 ♗g3 ♘d7 32 ♕c4 ♖d8? [◻32 ... ♘b8] 33 ♖xc6! ♖dc8 34 ♖xc8 ♕xc8 35 ♗f2 ♕c6 36 ♖d3 ♖d8 37 ♖d6 ♘xb6 38 ♕xf7+ ♖d7 39 ♖xc6 ♖xf7 40 ♖xb6+ ♔a7 41 ♖e6 **1-0** L/N5188

**1862-LON2-67**
**Solomons, S.+Green, V.**

[Löwenthal]

1 c4 c5 2 f4 e6 3 ♘c3 ♘c6 4 ♘f3 g6 5 e3 ♗g7 6 a3 ♘ge7 7 ♗d3 0-0 8 b3 d5 9 ♗b2 d4! 10 ♘a4 b6 [◻10 ... ♕d6 △ ... e5] 11 0-0 f5? 12 ♕e2 ♕d6 13 ♖ae1 ♗b7 14 ♔h1 dxe3 15 dxe3 e5 16 ♖d1 ♕c7 17 ♘g5 ♗c8 18 ♘c3! a6 19 ♘d5 ♘xd5 20 cxd5 ♘a5 21 d6 ♕c6 22 ♗c4+ ♔h8 23 ♗d5 **1-0** L/N5188

**1862-LON2-68**
**Solomons, S.=Green, V.**

[Löwenthal]

1 c4 e6 2 e3 c5 3 ♘c3 ♘c6 4 f4 ♘f6 5 ♘f3 d5 6 ♗d3 d4 7 ♘e2 dxe3 8 dxe3 ♘b4 9 ♘e5 ♘xd3+ [◻9 ... ♗d6] 10 ♘xd3 ♗e7 11 0-0 0-0 12 ♘g3 b6 13 b3 g6 14 ♗b2 ♗b7 15 ♕e2 ♘e4? 16 ♘xe4 ♗xe4 17 ♘f2 ♗b7 18 ♖ad1 ♕c7 19 ♘g4 h5 20 ♘f6+ ♗xf6 21 ♗xf6 ♔h7 22 ♖d2 ♕c6 23 f5 exf5 24 ♖xf5 ♕xg2+! 25 ♕xg2 ♗xg2 26 ♖e5 ♗h3 27 ♖e7 ♔g8 28 ♔f2 ♖fe8 29 ♖xe8+ ♖xe8 30 ♔g3 ♗f5 31 ♔f4 ♔h7 32 h4 ♖e4+ 33 ♔f3 ♖e6 34 ♗g5 ♖e8 35 ♗f6 ♗e6 36 ♖d6 ♗g4+ 37 ♔f4 ♖e6 38 ♗e5 ♖xd6 39 ♗xd6 ♗d1 40 ♗b8 ♗c2 41 ♗xa7 ♗b1 42 a3 ♗a2 43 ♗xb6 ♗xb3 44 ♗xc5 ♗xc4 45 e4 ♗b3 **½-½** L/N5188

**1862-LON2-69**
**Solomons, S.–Green, V.**

1 c4 d5? 2 cxd5 ♕xd5 3 ♘c3 ♕d8 4 e3 ♘f6 5 ♗c4 e6 6 f4 ♗e7 7 ♘f3 ♘bd7 8 a3 0-0 9 0-0 b6 10 b3 ♗b7 11 ♗b2 ♘c5 12 ♕c2 a6 13 b4 ♘ce4 14 ♗d3 ♘xc3 15 ♗xc3 h6 16 f5 exf5 17 ♗xf5 ♕d5 18 ♖f2 a5 19 bxa5 bxa5 20 ♘h4 ♘e4 21 ♖f4 ♘xc3 22 dxc3 ♗xh4 23 ♗e4? ♕c5 24 ♖xh4 ♕xe3+ 25 ♔h1 ♗xe4 26 ♖xe4 ♕c5 27 a4 ♖ae8 28 ♖g4 ♖e3 29 ♖c1 ♖fe8 30 h3 ♖e1+ 31 ♖xe1 ♖xe1+ 32 ♔h2 ♕e5+ 33 ♖g3 ♖e3 34 ♕f2 ♕xg3+ 35 ♕xg3 ♖xg3 36 ♔xg3 ♔f8 37 ♔f4 ♔e7 ...? **0-1** L/N5188

**1862-LON2-70**
**Solomons, S.=Green, V.**

[Löwenthal]

1 c4 e6 2 e3 f5 3 f4 ♘f6 4 a3 ♗e7 5 ♘c3 b6 6 b3 ♗b7 7 ♗b2 0-0 8 ♘f3 c5 9 ♗d3 ♘c6 10 0-0 a6 11 ♖c1 d6 12 ♘e2 ♕d7 13 ♘g3 g6 14 ♕e2 ♖ad8 15 ♗b1 d5 16 d3 ♘e8 17 ♔h1 ♗f6 18 d4 cxd4 19 exd4 dxc4 20 bxc4 ♘c7 21 c5 bxc5 22 dxc5 ♗xb2 23 ♕xb2 ♘d5 24 ♘e5 ♕g7!

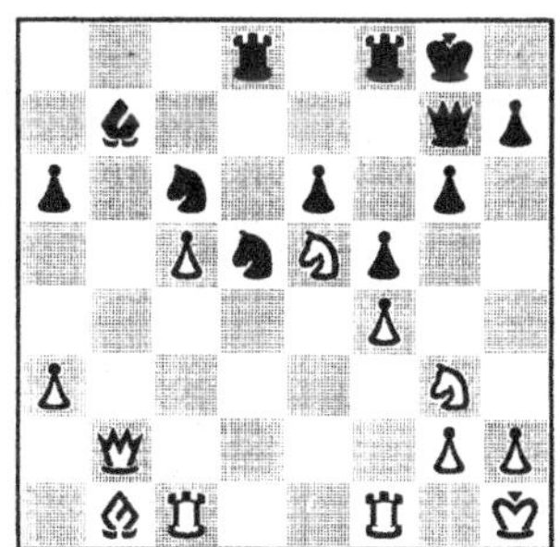

25 ♕e2 ♘xf4 26 ♖xf4 ♕xe5 27 ♕xe5 ♘xe5 28 ♖e1 ♘d3 [◻28 ... ♘g4] 29 ♗xd3 ♖xd3 30 ♖xe6 ♖xa3 31 ♔g1 ♖c3 32 c6 ♗a8 33 ♖a4 ♗xc6 34 ♖xa6 ♖c1+ 35 ♔f2 ♖c2+ 36 ♘e2 ♗b5 37 ♖a7 ♗xe2 38 ♖xe2 ♖xe2+ 39 ♔xe2 ♖f7 40 ♖xf7?? ♔xf7 41 ♔e3 g5 42 ♔d4 ♔e6 ...? **½-½** L/N5188

**1862-LON2-71**
**Solomons, S.–Green, V.**

[Löwenthal]

1 c4 f5 2 f4 ♘f6 3 ♘c3 e6 4 e3 b6 5 b3 ♗b7 6 ♘f3 ♗e7 7 ♗b2 0-0 8 ♗d3 ♘c6 9 a3 a6 10 0-0 g6? 11 ♖c1 d5? 12 ♘g5! ♕d7

13 ♘xe6 ♕xe6 14 cxd5 ♕d6 15 dxc6 ♗xc6 16 ♗c4+ ♔g7 17 b4 b5 18 ♗b3 ♗b7 [◻18 ... ♖ac8] 19 ♘e2 ♖ac8 20 ♘d4 ♗d5 21 ♖c5 c6 22 ♗xd5 cxd5 23 ♕c2 ♕d7 24 ♖c7! ♖xc7 25 ♕xc7 ♕xc7 26 ♘e6+ ♔f7 27 ♘xc7 ♖c8 28 ♖c1 ♗d8 29 ♘xa6 ♖xc1+ 30 ♗xc1 ♗b6 31 ♗b2 ♘e4 32 ♗c3? ♘xc3 33 dxc3 ♗xe3+ 34 ♔f1 ♗xf4 35 ♔f2! ♗xh2 36 g3 f4 37 ♔g2 ♗xg3 38 ♘c7 ♗e1 39 ♘xb5 [◻39 ♘xd5] 39 ... ♔e6 40 ♔f3 ♗d2 41 ♔e2 ♗e3 42 a4 ♔d7 43 ♘a3 ♔c6 44 ♘c2 ♗a7 45 ♘e1 g5 46 ♔f3 h5 47 ♘d3 ♗e3 48 ♘e5+ ♔b7 49 c4 g4+ 50 ♔e2 dxc4 51 ♘xc4 ♗d4 52 ♘d6+ ♔a6 53 ♘e4 h4 54 ♔f1 f3 55 ♘g5 h3 56 ♘e4 h2 57 ♘g3 ♗e5 58 ♘h1 g3 59 b5+ ♔a5 60 b6 g2+ **0-1** L/N5188

**1862-LON2-72** 2×62
**Solomons, S.–Hannah, J.W.**

[Löwenthal]

1 f4 d6 2 c4 e5 3 fxe5 dxe5 4 e3 ♗c5 5 ♘c3 ♘c6 6 ♘f3 ♘f6 7 ♗e2 e4 8 ♘g5 ♗f5 9 0-0 ♕d7 10 ♖f4 0-0-0! 11 ♘gxe4 ♗xe4 12 ♘xe4 ♗xe3+ 13 dxe3 ♕xd1+ 14 ♗xd1 ♖xd1+ 15 ♔f2 ♘xe4+ 16 ♖xe4 f5 17 ♖f4 ♘b4 18 ♔e2 ♖hd8 19 ♖f1 [19 ♖xf5 ♘c2 20 ♖b1 ♖e1+ 21 ♔~ ♖dd1–+] 19 ... ♖xf1 20 ♔xf1 ♖d1+ 21 ♔e2 ♖g1

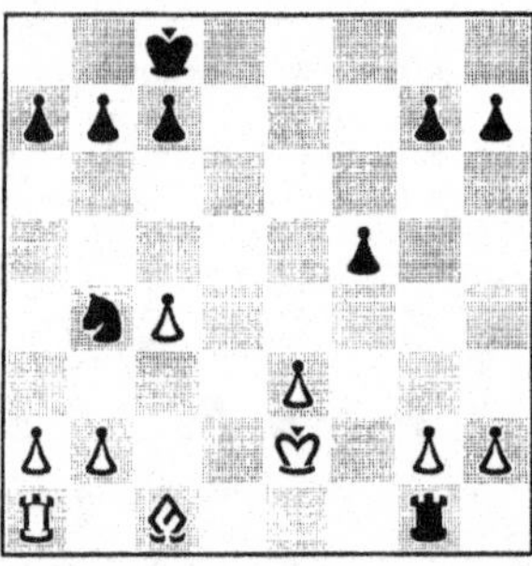

22 g3? [□ 22 a3 ♘c2 23 ♖b1 ♖xg2+ 24 ♔d1 ♖xh2 25 ♗d2 ♘xe3+ 26 ♗xe3] 22 ... ♖g2+ 23 ♔d1 ♖xh2 24 ♗d2 ♖h1+ 25 ♗e1 ♖xe1+ 26 ♔xe1 ♘c2+ 27 ♔d1 ♘xa1 28 ♔c1 h5 29 ♔b1 g5 ...⚲ **0-1** L/N5188

## ANDERSEN⚔PAULSEN

London

|1862-⚔AP|

| | | | | | | | | | |
|---|---|---|---|---|---|---|---|---|---|
| A. Anderssen | 1 | ½ | 0 | 0 | ½ | 0 | 1 | 1 | 4 |
| L. Paulsen | 0 | ½ | 1 | 1 | ½ | 1 | 0 | 0 | 4 |

### 1862-⚔AP-1
**Anderssen, A.+ Paulsen, L.**

[Löwenthal]

1 e4 e5 2 ♘f3 ♘c6 3 ♗b5 ♘f6 4 d3 d6? 5 ♗xc6+!± bxc6 6 ♘c3 g6 7 h3 ♗g7 8 ♗e3 0-0 9 ♘e2 ♕e7 10 0-0 d5 11 ♘g3 ♘e8 [Δ 12 ... f5] 12 ♖e1 d4 [□ 12 ... f5] 13 ♗d2 c5 14 b3 ♘d6 15 ♕c1 [Δ 16 ♕a3 ♘b5 17 ♕a5, 18 b4] 15 ... ♗b7 16 ♕a3 ♘b5 17 ♕a5 a6 18 a4 ♘a7 19 ♗c1 [19 b4? c4! 20 dxc4 ♘c6 21 ♕c5 ♕xc5 22 bxc5] 19 ... ♘c6 20 ♕d2 ♘d8? [□ 20 ... a5] 21 a5! ♘e6 22 ♗a3 f5 [Δ 23 ... fxe4 24 dxe4 ♖xf3 25 gxf3 ♕h4] 23 ♕d1 f4? 24 ♘f1 ♖f7 25 ♘1d2 ♘f8 26 ♖b1 g5 27 b4 cxb4 28 ♖xb4 c5 29 ♖b6 h5? 30 ♘h2 h4 31 ♘c4 ♖d8 32 ♕h5 ♗c8 33 ♖c6 ♘e6 34 ♘g4! f3 35 ♘cxe5 ♗xe5 36 ♘xe5 ♖g7 37 ♗xc5! ♘xc5 38 ♖h6 ♔f8 [38 ... ♖h7] 39 ♖h8+ **1-0** M324

### 1862-⚔AP-2
**Paulsen, L.= Anderssen, A.**

[Löwenthal]

1 e4 c5 2 ♘c3 e6 3 g3!? ♘e7 4 ♗g2 d6 5 d3 ♘bc6 6 ♘h3 a6 7 0-0 ♗d7 8 f4 f5 9 ♗e3 [□ 9 exf5 exf5 (9 ... ♘xf5) 10 ♘g5 Δ 11 ♖e1±] 9 ... b6 10 ♘g5 h6 11 ♘f3 g6 12 ♘h4 h5 13 d4 ♗g7 14 dxc5 dxc5 15 e5 ♕c7 16 ♕e2 g5 17 ♘f3 gxf4 18 gxf4 ♘b4 19 ♘g5 ♘bd5 20 ♘xd5 exd5 21 c4 0-0-0 22 cxd5 ♗b5 23 d6 [□ 23 ♕d2+-] 23 ... ♗xe2 24 dxc7 ♖d3! 25 ♖f2 ♖xe3 26 ♖ae1 ♘g6 27 ♖exe2 ♖xe2 28 ♖xe2 ♘xf4 29 ♖e3 ♖e8 [□ 29 ... ♘xg2] 30 ♗f1 b5 31 ♘f7 ♖e7 32 ♘d6+ ♔xc7 33 ♘xf5 ♖xe5 34 ♖xe5 ♗xe5 35 b3 ♔b6 36 ♔f2 ♔a5 37 ♘e7 ♗d6 38 ♘f5 ♗c7 39 a3 ♔b6 40 ♘e3 ♔c6 41 h3 ♔d6 42 ♔f3 ♔e5 43 ♘g2 ♘e6 44 ♔e3 ♗d8 45 ♘e1 ♗g5+ 46 ♔d3 ♔f4 47 a4 ♔g3 48 ♔e4 ♘d4 49 ♗d3 ♗d2 50 ♘c2 ♘xc2 51 ♗xc2 ♔xh3 52 ♔f3 c4 53 bxc4 bxc4 54 ♗f5+ ♔h2 55 ♗c2 h4 56 ♗e4 **½-½** M324

### 1862-⚔AP-3
**Anderssen, A.− Paulsen, L.**

[Löwenthal]

1 e4 e5 2 ♘f3 ♘c6 3 ♗c4 ♗c5 4 b4 ♗xb4 5 c3 ♗c5 6 0-0 d6 7 d4 exd4 8 cxd4 ♗b6 9 d5 ♘a5 10 ♗b2 ♘e7 11 ♗d3 0-0 12 ♘c3 ♘g6 13 ♘a4?! [□ 13 ♘e2] 13 ... c5 14 ♘xb6 axb6 15 ♕d2 f6 16 ♖ac1 ♗d7 17 ♗a1 b5 18 ♕b2 b4 19 ♖fe1 b5 20 ♗f1 ♕e7 21 g3 ♖a7 22 ♘d2 ♖fa8! 23 ♕b1 ♘b7 24 ♖c2 ♘d8 25 f4 ♘f7 26 ♘f3? b3! 27 ♖f2 [27 ♕xb3?? (27 axb3?? ♖xa1) 27 ... ♖a3 Δ 28 ... ♖xf3] 27 ... ♖xa2 28 ♗b2 ♕d8 29 h4 ♕c7 30 h5 ♘e7 31 ♕c1 ♘h6 32 ♗d3 ♘g4 33 ♖fe2 ♕b6 34 ♗b1 ♖2a4 35 ♔g2 b4 36 e5 ♘xd5 37 ♕c4 [□ 37 e6∞] 37 ... ♗e6 38 ♕d3 f5 39 exd6 c4 40 ♕d4 ♕xd4 41 ♗xd4 ♗d7 42 ♘g5 ♘gf6 43 ♖e5 c3 44 ♗d3 ♖a2+ 45 ♖5e2 ♖xe2+ 46 ♖xe2 b2 47 ♖e1 ♖a1 48 ♖b1 ♖xb1 [□ 48 ... b3] 49 ♗xb1 b3 50 ♗d3 ♗b5 51 ♗xf5 b1♕ 52 ♗xb1 c2 53 ♗xc2 bxc2 54 ♗b2 ♘b4 55 h6 ♘d3 56 ♗a3 gxh6 57 ♘f3 c1♕ 58 ♗xc1 ♘xc1 59 ♘e5 ♘d3 60 ♔f3 ♘c5 **0-1** M324

### 1862-⚔AP-4
**Paulsen, L.+ Anderssen, A.**

[Löwenthal]

1 e4 c5 2 ♘c3 e6 3 g3 d6 4 ♗g2 ♗d7 5 ♘ge2 ♘c6 6 0-0 ♗e7 7 d4 cxd4 8 ♘xd4 ♘xd4 9 ♕xd4 h5?! 10 h3 ♗c6 11 ♖d1 e5 [□ 11 ... ♕c7 Anderssen] 12 ♕d3 ♕d7 13 b4 b6 14 a4 ♖c8 15 a5 b5 16 a6! g6 17 ♗f1 ♘f6 18 f3 0-0 19 ♗e3! ♖b8

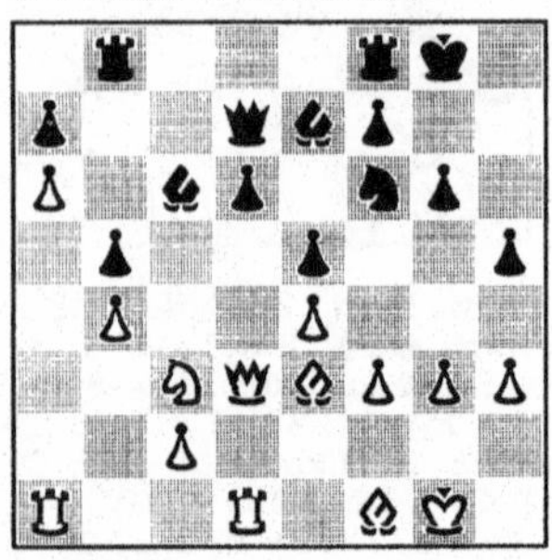

20 ♖a5 d5 [20 ... ♗d8? 21 ♕xd6 ♕xd6! 22 ♖xd6 ♗xa5 23 bxa5 (Δ 24 ♖xc6; 24 ♖xf6)] 21 ♘xd5 ♘xd5 22 exd5 ♗xb4 23 ♖a2 ♗a8 24 ♖b2 ♗d6 25 ♖xb5 ♖xb5 26 ♕xb5 ♕f5 27 ♕e2 e4 28 fxe4 ♕xe4 29 ♗xa7 ♕a4 30 ♗f2 ♖c8 31 ♕b5 ♕xc2 32 ♖e1 ♗f8 33 a7 ♕f5 34 ♗g2 [□ 34 ♖e8 ♖xe8! 35 ♕xe8 ♕xd5 36 ♕xa8 ♕xa8 37 ♗g2+-] 34 ... ♖c2 35 ♖f1 ♔h7 36 ♕b8 ♗c5 37 ♕f4 [37 ♗xc5 ♖xg2+ 38 ♔xg2 ♕xd5+∞] 37 ... ♕d7 38 ♗xc5 ♖xg2+ 39 ♔xg2 ♕xd5+ 40 ♕f3 ♕d2+ 41 ♔g1 ♗xf3 42 ♖xf3 **1-0** M324

### 1862-⚔AP-5
**Anderssen, A.= Paulsen, L.**

[Löwenthal]

1 e4 e5 2 ♘f3 ♘c6 3 ♗b5 ♘f6 4 d3 d6 5 ♗xc6+ bxc6 6 h3 g6 7 ♘c3 ♗g7 8 0-0 0-0 9 ♘e2 c5 10 ♘g3 ♗b7 11 b3 ♘e8 12 ♖b1 ♕e7 13 ♖e1 f5 14 b4! cxb4 15 ♖xb4 c5 16 ♖b1 f4?! [□ 16 ... fxe4] 17 ♘f1 ♗c8 18 c3 ♕f6 19 d4 cxd4 20 cxd4 exd4 21 ♕a4 ♗e6 22 ♖b2 d3 23 ♖b7 ♖f7 24 e5 dxe5 25 ♖xf7 ♕xf7 26 ♘xe5 ♗xe5 27 ♖xe5 ♖c8 28 ♗b2 ♖c4 29 ♕b3 ♕d7 [Δ 30 ... d2 31 ♘xd2 ♖c1+ 32 ♗xc1 ♗xb3] 30 ♔h2 ♘g7 31 ♖e1 f3 32 ♘d2 ♖c8 33 ♕b4 fxg2 34 ♘e4 ♘e8 35 ♗a3 ♕f7 36 ♕d4 ♕f4+ 37 ♔g1 [□ 37 ♔xg2] 37 ... d2 38 ♕xd2 ♕xd2 39 ♘xd2 ♗xh3 40 ♔h2 ♘g7 [□ 40 ... ♘f6] 41 ♘e4 ♗f5 42 ♔xg2 ♗xe4+ 43 ♖xe4 ♖c2 44 ♖e7 ♖xa2 45 ♖xa7 g5 46 ♖a8+ ♔f7 47 ♖a7+ ♔g6 48 ♖a6+ ♔h5 49 ♖a7 h6 50 ♖xg7 ♖xa3 **½-½** M324

### 1862-⚔AP-6
**Paulsen, L.+ Anderssen, A.**

[Löwenthal]

1 e4 c5 2 ♘c3 e6 3 g3?! ♘c6 4 ♗g2 g6 5 ♘ge2 ♗g7 6 0-0 ♘ge7 7 d3 d6 8 ♗e3 ♕b6 9 ♖b1 [Δ 10 b4] 9 ... a5 10 ♕d2 0-0 11 a3 [Δ 12 ♗h6] 11 ... ♗d7 12 ♗h6 ♘d4 13 ♗xg7 ♔xg7 14 ♘xd4 cxd4 15 ♘e2 ♗b5 16 b4 [□ 16 c3] 16 ... ♘c6 17 f4 axb4 18 axb4 e5 19 ♔h1 ♖a2 20 f5 f6 21 fxg6 hxg6 22 ♗h3 ♘d8 23 ♖a1 ♕a6 24 ♕c1 ♖h8? 25 ♗g2 ♘c6 26 c4 dxc3 27 ♖xa2 ♕xa2 28 ♘xc3 ♕a6 29 ♘d5 ♗xd3 30 ♖xf6 ♕a2 [Δ 31 ... ♗xe4] 31 h4 ♕e2 32 ♖xd6 ♖f8 [32 ... ♕c2 33 ♕g5+-] 33 ♘c3 ♕g4 34 ♖xd3 ♘xb4 35 ♖d6 ♕xg3 36 ♕g5 ♕xg5 37 hxg5 ♖h8+ 38 ♔g1 ♖h5 39 ♖d7+ ♔f8 40 ♖xb7 ♘d3 41 ♘b5 ♖xg5 42 ♘d6 ♖g3 43 ♔h2 ♖e3 44 ♖b3 **1-0** M324

**1862-✕AP-7**
**Anderssen, A.+Paulsen, L.**

[Löwenthal]

1 e4 e5 2 ♘f3 ♘c6 3 ♗b5 ♘f6 4 d3 d6? 5 ♗xc6+± bxc6 6 h3 g6 7 ♘c3 ♗g7 8 0-0 0-0 9 ♘e2 c5 10 ♘g3 ♗b7 11 ♖e1 ♘d7 12 ♖b1 [△ 13 b4] 12 ... f5 13 b4 [□ 13 c3 (△ 14 ♕b3+ ♔h8 15 ♕xb7), 14 ♘g5±] 13 ... fxe4 14 dxe4 cxb4 15 ♖xb4 ♘b6 16 ♖b3 ♕e7 17 a4 a5 18 ♗e3 ♖a6 19 ♕e2 ♗c8 20 ♖eb1 ♕d8 21 ♘g5 ♕e7 22 ♘f3 ♕d8 23 h4 ♔h8 [23 ... ♘d7 24 ♕c4+ △ 25 ♘g5] 24 ♖a3 ♖a8 [△ 25 ... ♗a6] 25 h5 ♗a6 [25 ... ♗g4 26 h6] 26 ♕e1 ♘c4 27 ♖ab3 ♕d7 28 hxg6 hxg6 29 ♗g5 ♕xa4 30 ♘h4 ♕e8 31 ♘f1 a4 32 ♖h3 ♔g8 33 ♖g3! a3 34 ♖a1 ♗f6 35 ♘xg6 ♗xg5 36 ♘xf8 ♔xf8 37 ♖xg5 ♔e7 38 ♘e3 ♔f6 39 ♖g3 c6 40 ♘xc4 ♗xc4 41 ♕c3 d5 42 ♖xa3 **1-0** M324

**1862-✕AP-8**
**Paulsen, L.–Anderssen, A.**

[Löwenthal]

1 e4 e5 2 f4 exf4 3 ♗c4 d5 4 ♗xd5 c6 5 ♗b3 ♕h4+ 6 ♔f1 g5 7 d4 ♗g7 8 ♘c3 ♘e7 9 ♘f3 ♕h5 10 h4 h6 11 ♖h2? g4 12 ♘g1 f3∓ 13 gxf3 gxf3 14 ♕xf3 ♗g4 15 ♕f2 ♖f8 16 ♘ge2 ♘d7 17 e5 0-0-0 18 ♘e4 ♘xe5!–+ 19 ♘2g3 [19 dxe5? ♖d1+ 20 ♔g2 ♘f5–+] 19 ... ♕g6 20 dxe5 ♖d1+ 21 ♔g2 ♗xe5 22 h5 ♕g7 23 ♖h1 ♗f5 24 ♗g5! ♗xe4+ 25 ♘xe4 ♖xa1 26 ♖xa1 f5 27 ♖f1 ♔b8 28 ♔h1 hxg5 29 ♘c5 ♖h8 30 ♕e2 ♗d6 31 ♘d7+ ♔c7 32 ♖d1 ♕h6 33 ♗e6 g4 34 ♗f7 ♔xd7 35 c4 ♕f6 36 ♕d2 ♘c8 37 ♕b4 ♕h4+ 38 ♔g2 ♕h3+ 39 ♔f2 ♕f3+ 40 ♔e1 ♕xd1+ 41 ♔xd1 ♗xb4 **0-1** M324

**BLACKBURNE✕STEINITZ** London

**[1862-✕BS]**

| | | | | | | | |
|---|---|---|---|---|---|---|---|
| J.H. Blackburne | 0 | ½ | ? | 0 | 0 | ½ | ? |
| W. Steinitz | 1 | ½ | ? | 1 | 1 | ½ | ? |

**1862-✕BS-1** xii 62
**Steinitz,W.+**
**Blackburne,J.H.**

[Löwenthal]

1 e4 b6 2 d4 ♗b7 3 ♗d3 e6 4 ♘c3 g6 5 ♗e3 ♗g7 6 ♕d2 d6 7 ♘ge2 ♘d7 8 0-0 ♘e7 9 f4 0-0 10 f5! exf5 11 exf5 ♘f6 12 ♗h6 ♕d7 13 ♘g3 ♖ae8 14 ♕g5 [15 ♗xg7 ♔xg7 16 fxg6+–] 14 ... ♗xh6! 15 ♕xh6 ♔h8 16 ♘ce2 ♘eg8 17 ♕h4 ♕d8 18 ♘f4 ♘d5 19 ♕xd8 ♖xd8 20 ♖ae1 ♘xf4 21 ♖xf4 g5 22 ♖f2 f6 23 ♖fe2 ♗d5 24 c4 ♗f7 25 d5 ♖fe8 26 ♔f2 ♖e5 27 b3 h5= 28 ♖xe5 dxe5 29 ♘e4 ♔g7 30 ♘c3 c6 31 ♗e4 cxd5 32 ♘xd5 ♗xd5 33 cxd5 ♘e7 34 ♖d1 ♘c8 35 ♖c1 ♘d6 36 ♖c7+ ♔f8 37 ♗d3 e4 38 ♗c4 ♘xf5 39 ♖xa7 e3+ 40 ♔e2 ♖e8 41 ♖h7 ♘d4+ 42 ♔d3 ♔g8 43 ♖e7?! ♖xe7 44 d6+ ♖f7 45 ♔xd4 ♔f8 46 ♔d5 ♔e8 47 ♔c6 ♔d8 48 ♔xb6 [48 ♗xf7?? e2–+] 48 ... f5 49 a4 ♖f6? [□ 49 ... ♔d7 △ 50 ... ♖f8] 50 ♔c6 f4 51 a5 ♔c8 52 a6 ♔b8 53 b4 ♖f8 54 d7 ♖f6+ 55 ♔d5 ♔c7 56 d8♕+ ♔xd8 57 a7 **1-0** M324

**1862-✕BS-2** xii 62
**Blackburne,J.H.=**
**Steinitz,W.**

[Lange]

1 d4 f5 2 e4 fxe4 3 ♘c3 e6 4 ♘xe4 ♘f6 [4 ... d5 5 ♕h5+ g6 6 ♕e5 dxe4 7 ♕xh8 ♘f6 8 ♗h6! ♘bd7 9 ♗xf8 ♘xf8 10 0-0-0±] 5 ♗d3 ♗e7 6 ♘f3 ♘xe4 7 ♗xe4 d5 8 ♗d3 [□ 8 ♘e5 dxe4 9 ♕h5+ g6 10 ♘xg6 hxg6 11 ♕xh8+ ♔d7 12 ♕h7 ♕e8 13 ♗g5±] 8 ... ♗f6 9 0-0 0-0 10 ♘e5 ♕e7 11 f4 c5 12 c3 ♘c6 13 ♗e3 cxd4 14 cxd4 ♗d7 15 ♖c1 g6 16 ♕g4 ♗xe5 17 fxe5 ♖xf1+ 18 ♖xf1 ♖f8 19 ♖xf8+ ♕xf8 20 ♗d2 **½-½** L/N6047

**1862-✕BS-4** xii 62
**Blackburne,J.H.–**
**Steinitz,W.**

1 d4 f5 2 e4 fxe4 3 ♘c3 e6 4 ♘xe4 ♘f6 5 ♗g5 ♗e7 6 ♗d3 ♘xe4 7 ♗xe7 ♕xe7 8 ♗xe4 0-0 9 c3 ♘c6 10 ♕e2 d5 11 ♗c2 ♕g5 12 g3 e5 13 dxe5 ♗g4 14 ♕e3 ♕h5 15 f4 ♘xe5 16 fxe5 ♖ae8 17 ♗xh7+ ♔xh7 18 ♕d4 ♕g5 19 h4 ♕xe5+ **0-1** M324

**1862-✕BS-5** xii 62
**Steinitz,W.+**
**Blackburne, J.H.**

[Löwenthal]

1 e4 e6 2 d4 d5 3 ♘c3 ♗b4 4 exd5 exd5 5 ♘f3 ♘f6 6 ♗d3 0-0 7 0-0 ♗g4 8 ♔h1 c6 [□ 8 ... ♘c6] 9 ♘e2 ♗d6 10 ♘e5 ♘bd7 11 f4 ♖e8 12 ♗d2 ♘f8 13 h3 ♗xe2 14 ♕xe2 ♘6d7 15 ♕f2 f6 16 ♖ae1 fxe5 17 fxe5 ♗c7 [17 ... ♘xe5 18 dxe5 ♖xe5 (18 ... ♗xe5 19 ♕f7+ ♔h8 20 ♕h5 ♗f6∓) 19 ♕f7+ ♔h8 20 ♗c3 ♖g5 21 ♖f5 ♖g3 (21 ... ♖g6 22 ♖h5 ♖g3 23 ♖e3±) 22 ♕h5+–] 18 ♕f7+ ♔h8 19 ♕h5 ♖e6 [19 ... g6 20 ♗xg6 ♘xg6 21 ♖f7+–] 20 ♖f7 ♕e8 21 ♖ef1 h6 [□ 21 ... ♘g6 22 ♗h6 gxh6 23 ♕xh6 ♕g8 24 ♖xd7 ♘f8 25 ♖xf8 ♖xh6 26 ♖xg8+ ♔xg8 27 ♖xc7±] 22 ♕g4! [22 ♗f5 ♘f6 23 exf6 ♖xf6 24 ♗g6 ♖xf1+ 25 ♖xf1 ♕xg6–+] 22 ... ♗xe5 23 dxe5 ♘g6 24 ♗xh6 [□ 24 ♗xg6] 24 ... gxh6 25 ♗xg6 ♘xe5 26 ♖f8+ ♔g7 27 ♖xe8 [□ 27 ♗xe8+ ♘xg4 28 ♖1f7+ ♔g6 29 ♖g8+ ♔h5 30 ♖f5+ ♔h4 31 ♖xg4#] 27 ... ♖axe8 28 ♕d4 ♔xg6 29 ♕xa7 ♖6e7 30 ♕f2 ♖e6 31 ♕f5+ ♔g7 32 g4 b5 33 c3 ♖8e7 34 b3 ♘d7 35 a4 bxa4 36 bxa4 ♘c5 37 ♕f8+ ♔g6 38 a5 h5 39 gxh5+ ♔xh5 40 ♖g1 ♘e4 41 ♕f5+ ♔h6 42 ♕f4+ **1-0** M324

**1862-✕BS-6** xii 62
**Blackburne,J.H.=**
**Steinitz,W.**

1 e4 e5 2 ♘f3 ♘c6 3 ♗b5 ♘f6 4 0-0 ♘xe4 5 ♖e1 ♘d6 6 ♘xe5 ♗e7 7 ♗a4 ♘xe5 8 ♖xe5 0-0 9 d4 ♗f6 10 ♖e1 ♖e8 11 c3 b5 12 ♗c2 ♗b7 13 ♗f4 ♖xe1+ 14 ♕xe1 ♕e8 15 ♘d2 ♕xe1+ 16 ♖xe1 ♖e8 **½-½** L/N6051

**DUBOIS✕STEINITZ** London

**[1862-✕DS]**

| | | | | | | | | | | |
|---|---|---|---|---|---|---|---|---|---|---|
| S. Dubois | 0 | ½ | 0 | 1 | 1 | 0 | 1 | 0 | 0 | 3½ |
| W. Steinitz | 1 | ½ | 1 | 0 | 0 | 1 | 0 | 1 | 1 | 5½ |

**1862-✕DS-1** 24 vii 62
**Dubois, S.–Steinitz, W.**

[Löwenthal]

1 e4 e5 2 f4 exf4 3 ♗c4 d5 4 ♗xd5 c6 5 ♗b3 ♕h4+ 6 ♔f1 g5 7 ♘f3 ♕h5 8 d4 ♗g7 9 ♘c3 ♘e7 10 e5 [△ 11 ♘e4] 10 ... ♗f5! 11 d5? g4 12 ♘d4 ♗xe5 13 ♘xf5 ♘xf5 14 ♕e1 0-0 15 ♘e4 ♘d7 16 ♕f2 ♖ae8 17 ♗xf4 ♗d4 18 ♘g3 ♘xg3+ 19 ♕xg3 ♕f5 20 ♖e1 ♗e5 21 ♖xe5 ♖xe5 22 ♕f2 ♖e4 23 ♗d6 ♕g5 24 g3 ♖fe8 25 dxc6 ♕b5+ 26 ♔g2 ♖e2 27 ♗xf7+ ♔g7 28 ♗xe8 ♕xc6+ 29 ♔g1 ♖xf2 30 ♔xf2 ♕xh1 31 ♗xd7 ♕f3+ **0-1** M324-1863

**1862-✕DS-2**
**Steinitz, W.=Dubois, S.**

[Löwenthal]

1 e4 e5 2 ♘f3 ♘c6 3 ♗c4 ♗c5 4 b4 ♗b6 5 b5 ♘a5 6 ♘xe5 ♘h6 7 d4 d6 8 ♗xh6 dxe5 9 ♗xg7 ♖g8 10 ♗xf7+ ♔xf7 11 ♗xe5 ♕g5 12 ♘c3 [12 ♗g3 ♕xb5; 12 g3 ♗g4] 12 ... ♘c4 13 ♕f3+ ♔e8 14 ♘d5 ♗a5+ [14 ... ♕d2+? 15 ♔f1±] 15 c3 ♘xe5 [15 ... ♕xg2 16 ♕xg2 ♖xg2 17 ♗g3!] 16 dxe5 ♕xg2 17 ♕h5+ ♕g6 18 ♕h4 ♖g7 19 ♔d2 ♕g5+ 20 ♕xg5 ♖xg5 21 ♖hg1 ♖xg1 22 ♖xg1 ♔f7 23 ♘f6 ♗e6 [23 ... h6 24 ♖g8!] 24 ♘xh7 ♖h8 25 ♘g5+ ♔e7 26 h3 [26 ♘xe6? ♔xe6] 26 ... ♗b6 27 ♖g2 ♖f8 28 f3 ♗xa2 29 ♖g4 ♖d8+! 30 ♔c2 ♗e3 [△ 31 ... ♖d2+] 31 ♖g2 ♗f4 32 h4 ♗c4 33 ♘h3 ♗xe5 34 f4 ♗f1? [□ 34 ... ♖d3 35 ♘f2 (35 fxe5 ♖xh3 36 ♖g7+ ♗f7 37 ♖h7 ♖e3∓) 35 ... ♖xc3+ 36 ♔d2 ♗d4 37 ♘g4 ♖a3–+] 35 ♖g5 ♗f6 36 ♖g3 ♗xh4 37 ♖g7+ ♔f6 38 ♖xc7 ♗d3+ 39 ♔b3 ♗xe4 40 ♔b4 ♔e6 41 ♘g5+ ♗xg5

42 fxg5 ♖d7 43 ♖c8 b6 44 c4 ♖d1 [◻ 44 ... ♗b7 45 ♖g8 ♖c7→] 45 ♖e8+ ♔f5 46 g6 ♖d7 47 c5 ♖d4+ 48 ♔c3 bxc5 49 g7 ♗d5 50 g8♕ ♗xg8 51 ♖xg8 ½-½ M324-1863

### 1862-⚔DS-3
**Dubois, S.– Steinitz, W.**

[Löwenthal]

1 e4 e5 2 ♘f3 ♘c6 3 ♗c4 ♗c5 4 0-0 ♘f6 5 b4 ♗xb4 6 c3 ♗e7 7 d4 ♘xe4 8 dxe5 0-0 9 ♗d5 ♘c5 10 ♗e3 ♘e6 11 ♕c2 ♔h8 12 ♘bd2 d6 13 ♗xc6 bxc6 14 ♖ad1 d5 15 ♘d4 ♕e8 16 f4 g6 17 f5?! [◻ 17 ♘2f3] 17 ... ♘xd4 18 cxd4 ♗xf5 19 ♖xf5 gxf5 20 ♕xf5 f6 21 ♗h6 ♕g6 22 ♕xg6 hxg6 23 ♗xf8 ♖xf8 24 ♘f3 [24 ♖c1 c5 25 exf6 ♗xf6 26 dxc5 ♗g5 27 ♖d1 ♗e3+→] 24 ... c5 25 exf6 ♖xf6 26 dxc5 ♗xc5+ 27 ♔f1 c6 28 a4 ♔g8 29 ♔e2 ♔f8 30 ♔d3 ♔e7 31 ♖e1+ ♔d6 32 ♖e8 ♗b6 33 ♖g8 c5 34 ♘h4 c4+ 35 ♔c2 d4 36 ♖xg6 d3+ 37 ♔d2 ♗a5+ 38 ♔e3 ♖xg6 39 ♘xg6 d2 40 ♔e2 c3 41 ♔d1 ♔c5 42 ♘e5 ♗c7 43 ♘f3 ♔b4 44 ♔c2 ♔xa4 45 g4 ♗f4 46 g5 d1♕+ 47 ♔xd1 ♔b3 48 ♘d4+ ♔b2 49 g6 ♗h6 50 h4 a5 51 h5 a4 52 ♘c2 a3 53 ♘d4 a2 54 ♘c2 ♗g7 55 ♘a1 ♔xa1 56 ♔c2 ♗h6 **0-1** M324-1863

### 1862-⚔DS-4
**Steinitz, W.– Dubois, S.**

[Löwenthal]

1 e4 e5 2 ♘f3 ♘c6 3 ♗c4 ♗c5 4 b4 ♗b6 5 b5 [5 a4 a5 6 b5 ♘d4 7 ♘xe5 ♕f6 8 ♘f3 ♘e6 9 e5± Boden; 5 a4 a6 6 c3 d6 7 d3 ♘f6 8 ♕b3 ♕e7 9 ♗g5 h6 10 ♗h4= Heydebrand] 5 ... ♘a5 6 ♘xe5 ♘h6 [6 ... ♕f6 7 ♗xf7+ ♔f8 8 d4 d6 9 ♗xg8 dxe5 10 ♗d5 ♗xd4 11 f4 ♗xa1 12 fxe5±; 6 ... ♗d4 7 ♗xf7+ ♔f8 8 ♗xg8 ♔xg8 9 ♕h5 (9 c3 ♗xe5 10 d4 ♗f6 11 e5 ♗e7 12 0-0 d6 13 f4 dxe5 14 fxe5 ♗e6∓) 9 ... ♕e7 10 ♘c4 ♕xe4+ (10 ... ♘xc4 11 ♕d5+ △ 12 ♕xd4) 11 ♔d1 g6 12 ♕g5 h6 13 ♕d8+ (13 ♕g3 ♘xc4) 13 ... ♔h7 14 ♕xc7 ♘xc4 15 ♕xc4 d5 16 ♕c7+ ♗g7 17 f3 ♗g4 18 ♕g3 (18 ♖e1 ♗xf3+ 19 gxf3 ♕xf3+ 20 ♖e2 ♖e8→) 18 ... ♖he8 19 ♖e1 (19 ♕f2 ♗d4 20 d3 ♕e5→) 19 ♗xf3+ 20 gxf3 ♕xe1+ 21 ♕xe1 ♖xe1+ 22 ♔xe1 ♗xa1→; 6 ... ♗d4 7 ♘xf7 ♕f6 8 0-0 ♘xc4 9 ♘xh8 ♗xa1 10 c3 g6 11 ♕b3 d5 12 exd5 ♘d6 13 ♖e1+ ♔f8 14 d4 ♗f5 15 ♗a3 ♖e8 16 ♖d1 (16 ♖xe8+ ♔xe8 17 ♘d2 ♕e7) 16 ... ♖e2∓; 6 ... ♗d4 7 ♕f3 ♕f6 8 ♗xf7+ ♔d8 9 ♕a3 ♕xf2+ 10 ♔d1 d6→] 7 d4 d6 8 ♗xh6 dxe5 9 ♗xg7 ♕g5 10 ♗xh8 ♘xc4 11 0-0 ♗g4 12 ♗f6 ♕g6 13 ♕d3 ♕xf6 14 ♕xc4 0-0-0 15 dxe5 ♕xe5 16 ♘a3 ♗e6 17 ♕e2 ♕c3 18 ♕f3 ♕xf3 19 gxf3 ♗c5 20 ♘b1? ♗h3 **0-1** M324-1863

### 1862-⚔DS-5
**Dubois, S.+ Steinitz, W.**

[Löwenthal]

1 e4 e5 2 ♘f3 ♘c6 3 d4 exd4 4 ♗c4 ♗c5 5 c3 ♘f6 6 cxd4 ♗b4+ 7 ♗d2 ♗xd2+ 8 ♘bxd2 d5 9 exd5 ♘xd5 10 0-0 0-0 11 ♖e1 ♘f4! 12 ♘e4 ♗g4 13 ♕d2 ♘h3+ 14 gxh3 ♗xf3 15 d5 ♘e5 16 ♕f4 f6 17 ♗b3 ♔h8 18 ♖e3 g5 [△ 19 ♘xg5 ♖g8∓] 19 ♕f5 ♗h5 20 ♘xf6 ♕xf6 21 ♕xe5 ♔g7 22 ♕xc7+ ♖f7 23 ♕e5 ♖af8 24 ♖f1 ♖d7 25 ♕xf6+ ♖xf6 26 ♖fe1 ♗g6 27 ♖e7+ ♖xe7 28 ♖xe7+ ♖f7 29 ♖xf7+ ♔xf7 30 ♔g2 ♔f6 31 ♔g3 ♔e5 32 h4 gxh4+ 33 ♔xh4 b5 34 ♔g3 a5 35 f4+ ♔d4 36 d6 ♗f5 37 ♗d1 **1-0** M324-1863

### 1862-⚔DS-6
**Steinitz, W.+ Dubois, S.**

[Löwenthal]

1 e4 e5 2 ♘f3 d6 3 d4 exd4 4 ♕xd4 ♗d7 5 ♗e3 [◻ 5 ♗f4] 5 ... ♘c6 6 ♕d2 ♘f6 7 ♘c3 ♗e7 8 h3 0-0 9 g4 ♘e5 10 ♘xe5 dxe5 11 g5 ♘h5 [◻ 11 ... ♘e8] 12 0-0-0 ♗d6 13 ♗e2 ♘f4 [◻ 13 ... g6] 14 ♗xf4 exf4 15 e5 ♗c6 16 exd6 ♗xh1 17 ♖xh1 ♕xg5 [◻ 17 ... ♕xd6] 18 dxc7 ♖ac8 19 ♘d5 ♖fe8 20 ♗f3 ♕e5 21 ♖d1 g5 22 ♕d4 ♕xd4 23 ♖xd4 ♔g7 24 ♗g4 ♖e6 25 ♖c4 ♔f8 26 ♗xe6 fxe6 27 ♘f6 h6 28 ♔d2 ♔f7 29 ♘e4 ♔e7 30 ♔e2 ♔d7 31 ♔f3 ♖xc7 32 ♖xc7+ ♔xc7 33 ♔g4 ♔c6 34 c4 **1-0** M324-1863

### 1862-⚔DS-7
**Dubois, S.+ Steinitz, W.**

[Löwenthal]

1 e4 e5 2 ♘f3 ♘c6 3 d4 exd4 4 ♘xd4 ♗c5 5 ♗e3 ♕f6 6 c3 ♘ge7 7 ♗c4 ♗b6 8 0-0 0-0 9 f4 d6 10 ♕d3 ♗e6! 11 ♗b5 [◻ 11 ♘d2] 11 ... d5 12 e5 ♕g6 13 ♕e2 [◻ 13 ♘d2] 13 ... ♘xd4 14 cxd4 ♘f5 15 ♕f2? [◻ 15 ♖d1] 15 ... ♘xe3 16 ♕xe3 ♕e4 17 ♕xe4 dxe4 18 ♘c3 ♖ad8?! 19 ♔h1 c6 20 f5 ♗c8 [◻ 20 ... ♗d5] 21 ♗c4 ♖xd4 22 ♗b3 ♖e8 23 e6 fxe6

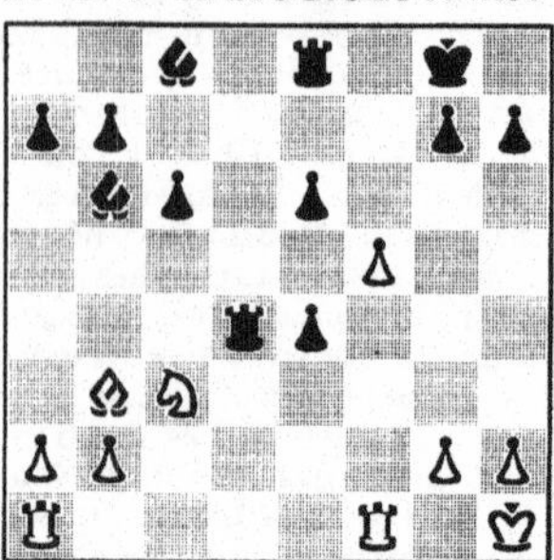

24 ♖ae1! ♗a5 25 ♖e3 ♗xc3 26 bxc3 ♖d3 27 ♖xe4 g6 [◻ 27 ... b5 △ 28 ... c5] 28 fxe6 ♗xe6 29 ♖f6 **1-0** M324-1863

### 1862-⚔DS-8
**Steinitz, W.+ Dubois, S.**

[Löwenthal]

1 e4 e5 2 ♘f3 ♘c6 3 ♗c4 ♗c5 4 b4 ♗b6 5 b5 ♘a5 6 ♘xe5 ♘h6 7 d4 d6 8 ♗xh6 dxe5 9 ♗xg7 ♕g5 10 ♗xh8 ♕xg2 11 ♖f1 ♘xc4 12 ♕e2 ♗g4! 13 f3 [13 ♕xc4? ♕xe4+ △ 14 ... 0-0-0] 13 ... ♕xe2+ 14 ♔xe2 ♗h3 15 ♖d1 0-0-0 16 ♗xe5 ♖g8 17 ♗g3 f5 18 ♘d2 ♘a3 19 c3 ♘xb5 20 ♖ac1 fxe4 21 ♘xe4 ♖e8 22 ♔f2 a6 23 a4 ♘a7 24 ♖e1 ♖f8 25 ♘g5 ♗f5 26 ♖e7 ♘c6 27 ♖f7 ♖xf7 28 ♘xf7 ♘e7 29 ♖e1 ♘d5 30 ♖e5! ♗g6 31 ♘d6+ cxd6 32 ♖xd5 ♗c2 33 ♖xd6 ♗d8 34 ♖h6 ♗g6 35 h4 ♗e7 36 h5 ♗c2 37 d5 ♗d3 38 d6 ♗d8 39 d7+ ♔xd7 40 ♖d6+ **1-0** M324-1863

### 1862-⚔DS-9
8 vii 62

**Dubois, S.– Steinitz, W.**

[Löwenthal]

1 e4 e5 2 ♘f3 ♘c6 3 d4 exd4 4 ♘xd4 ♗c5 5 ♗e3 ♕f6 6 c3 ♘ge7 7 ♗c4 ♗b6 8 0-0 d6 9 ♔h1 [◻ 9 ♘b5] 9 ... ♘e5 10 ♗e2 h5 11 f4 ♘g4 12 ♗g1 ♘c6 13 ♘a3 g5 14 fxg5 [◻ 14 e5] 14 ... ♕xg5 15 ♘c4 ♗d7 16 ♘xb6 axb6 17 ♘f5 0-0-0 18 b4 [◻ 18 ♕d5 △ 19 ♘xd6+] 18 ... ♖dg8 19 ♗f3 ♘ce5 20 a4 ♗c6 21 b5 ♘xf3 22 ♕xf3 ♘e5 23 ♕e2 ♗d7 24 ♖a2? [◻ 24 ♗e3] 24 ... ♗e6 25 ♗e3 ♕d8 26 ♖fa1 ♗c4 27 ♕e1 ♗xa2 28 ♖xa2 ♕f6 29 ♗d4 ♕e6 30 ♖a1 ♖g6 31 a5 bxa5 32 ♖xa5 ♖hg8 33 g3 ♘c4 [33 ... h4 (△ 34 ♘xh4 ♖xg3 35 hxg3 ♕h3+→) 34 ♖a8+! ♔d7 35 ♖xg8 ♖xg8 36 ♘xh4±] 34 ♖a8+ ♔d7 35 ♖xg8 ♖xg8 36 ♕e2 ♖e8 37 ♘g7 ♕xe4+ 38 ♕xe4 ♖xe4 39 ♘xh5 ♔e6 40 ♔g2 ♔f5 41 h3 ♘a3 42 b6 c5 43 ♗f6 ♘c4 44 g4+ ♔g6 45 ♗d8 ♖e2+ 46 ♔g3 ♖e3+ 47 ♔h4 ♖xc3 48 ♘f4+ ♔h7 49 g5 ♘e5 50 ♘d5 ♖d3 51 ♘f6+ ♔g6 52 ♘e8 c4 53 ♗f6 c3 54 ♘xd6 c2 **0-1**

M324-1864

## KOLISCH⚔SHUMOV
Saint Petersburg

[1862-⚔KS]

| | | | | | | | | | |
|---|---|---|---|---|---|---|---|---|---|
| I.F. von Kolisch | 0 | 0 | 1 | 1 | 1 | 1 | 1 | 1 | 6 |
| I.S. Shumov | 1 | 1 | 0 | 0 | 0 | 0 | 0 | 0 | 2 |

### 1862-⚔KS-1
8 v 62

**Shumov, I.S.+ Kolisch, I.F. von**

[Mikhailov]

1 e4 e5 2 ♘f3 ♘c6 3 ♗c4 ♗c5 4 0-0 ♘f6 5 d4 ♗xd4 [5 ... exd4 6 e5 d6 7 exf6

dxc4 8 ♖e1+; 5 ... ♘xd4?] 6 ♘xd4 ♘xd4 7 f4 d6! 8 fxe5 dxe5 9 ♗g5 ♕e7 10 ♗xf6 gxf6 11 b4 ♗e6 12 ♗xe6 fxe6 13 ♕h5+ ♕f7 14 ♕h4 0-0-0 15 ♘a3 [15 ♖xf6 ♕e7] 15 ... f5 16 ♕f2 ♕h5 17 ♖ae1 f4 18 c3 ♘c6 19 b5 ♘b8 20 ♕xa7? b6 21 ♕a4 ♖hg8 22 ♖d1 22 ... ♖xg2+ 23 ♔xg2 ♕e2+ 24 ♔h1 ♕xe4+?? [24 ... ♖d2→] 25 ♕xe4 **1-0** L/N6308

**1862-⚔KS-2** 10 v 62
**Kolisch,I.F.von–Shumov,I.S.**
[Mikhailov]
1 e4 e5 2 ♘f3 ♘c6 3 ♗c4 ♗c5 4 b4 ♗xb4 5 c3 ♗a5 6 d4 exd4 7 0-0 d6 8 ♕b3 ♕f6 9 e5 ♕g6 10 exd6 cxd6 11 ♘g5 ♘h6 12 ♖e1+ ♔f8 13 ♗a3 ♗c7± [13 ... ♕xg5?+-] 14 f4 b6 15 ♗d5 ♗d7 16 ♗xc6 ♗xc6 17 ♕c4 ♗xg2 18 ♕xc7 ♘f5 19 ♘d2 h6 20 ♕xf7+ ♕xf7 21 ♘xf7 ♔xf7 22 ♔xg2 ♘e3+ 23 ♔f3 ♘c2 24 ♗xd6 ♘xa1 25 ♖xa1 dxc3 26 ♘e4 ♖hd8 27 ♖c1 ♖ac8 28 ♗e5 ♔e6 29 ♘xc3 ♔f5 30 ♗xg7 ♖d3+ 31 ♔e2 ♖h3 32 ♗e5 ♖xh2+ 33 ♔d3 b5 34 ♖b1 ♖d8+ 35 ♔e3 ♖h3+ 36 ♔e2 a6 37 a4 ♖h2+ 38 ♔e3?? ♖hd2 **0-1** L/N6308

**1862-⚔KS-3** v 62
**Shumov,I.S.–Kolisch,I.F.von**
[Mikhailov]
1 e4 e5 2 ♘f3 ♘c6 3 d4 exd4 4 ♗c4 ♗c5 5 0-0 d6 6 c3 ♗g4 7 ♘bd2 dxc3 8 bxc3 ♘e5 9 ♕a4+ c6 10 ♘xe5 dxe5 11 ♗xf7+ ♔xf7 12 ♕c4+ ♔e8 13 ♕xc5 ♕e7 14 ♗a3 ♕xc5 15 ♗xc5 b6 16 ♗d6 ♖d8 17 ♗xe5 ♘f6 18 ♗xf6 gxf6 19 ♘c4? [19 ♘b3; 19 f3] 19 ... ♗e2 20 ♘e3 ♗xf1 21 ♔xf1 ♔f7 22 ♔e2 ♖d7 23 ♖c1 ♖e8 24 f3 ♖e5 25 ♖c2 ♖c5 26 ♘f5 b5 27 g4 b4 28 c4 a5 29 ♔e3 a4 30 h4 ♖d1 31 f4 ♖b1 32 ♖d2 ♖a5 33 g5 fxg5 34 fxg5 b3 35 axb3 ♖xb3+ 36 ♔f4 a3 37 ♖d7+ ♔e8 38 ♖xh7 a2 39 g6 a1♕ 40 g7 ♕e5+ 41 ♔g5 ♖g3+ 42 ♔h5 ♖xg7 43 ♖xg7 ♕xg7 **0-1** L/N6308

**1862-⚔KS-4** 18 v 62
**Kolisch,I.F.von+Shumov,I.S.**
1 e4 e5 2 ♘f3 ♘c6 3 ♗c4 ♗c5 4 b4 ♗xb4 5 c3 ♗c5 6 0-0 d6 7 d4 exd4 8 cxd4 ♗b6 9 d5 ♕f6 10 dxc6 ♕xa1 11 ♕b3 ♕f6 12 e5 dxe5 13 ♖e1 bxc6 14 ♗g5 ♕d6 15 ♘xe5 ♗e6 16 ♘xf7 ♔xf7 17 ♖xe6 ♗xf2+ 18 ♔xf2 ♕d4+ 19 ♔f1 ♔f8 20 ♕a3+ c5 21 ♕f3+ **1-0** L/N6308

**1862-⚔KS-5**
**Shumov,I.S.–Kolisch,I.F.von**
[Mikhailov]
1 e4 e5 2 ♘f3 ♘c6 3 ♗b5 a6 4 ♗a4 ♘f6 5 d4 exd4 6 e5 ♘e4 7 ♗xc6 dxc6 8 ♘xd4? c5 9 ♕f3 [9 ♘? ♕xd1+ 10 ♔xd1 ♘xf2+; 9 ♕e2? ♕xd4 10 f3 ♘g5 11 ♗xg5 ♕xb2] 9 ... ♕xd4 10 0-0 ♗e7 11 ♖e1 ♘g5 12 ♕g3 ♕g4 13 ♕b3 c4 14 ♕e3 ♗f5 15 ♘c3 ♖d8 16 h3 ♕h4 17 ♖e2 0-0 18 ♗d2 [◻ 18 b3] 18 ... ♗xc2 19 ♗e1 ♖d3 20 f4 ♖xe3 21 ♗xh4 ♖xe2 22 ♗xg5? [22 ♗xe2→] 22 ... ♗c5+ 23 ♔h2 ♖f2 **0-1** L/N6308

**1862-⚔KS-6** 4 vi 62
**Kolisch, I.F. von+ Shumov, I.S.**
[Mikhailov]
1 e4 e5 2 ♘f3 ♘c6 3 ♗c4 ♘f6 4 0-0 d6? [4 ... ♗c5] 5 ♘g5 d5 6 exd5 ♘a5 7 d3 ♗d6 8 f4 ♘xc4 9 dxc4 h6? [9 ... 0-0] 10 ♘xf7 ♔xf7 11 fxe5 ♗c5+ [◻ 11 ... ♗xe5 12 ♕h5+] 12 ♔h1 ♖e8 13 exf6 g6 14 ♗xh6 ♖e4 15 ♘d2 ♖h4 16 ♗g5 ♗g4 17 ♕e1 ♖h5 18 ♕e7+ ♗xe7 [18 ... ♕xe7+-] 19 fxe7+ **1-0** L/N6308

**1862-⚔KS-7** 6 vi 62
**Shumov,I.S.–Kolisch,I.F.von**
[Mikhailov]
1 e4 e5 2 ♘f3 ♘c6 3 ♗b5 a6 4 ♗a4 ♘f6 5 0-0 ♗e7 6 d4 exd4 7 e5 ♘e4 8 ♘xd4 0-0 9 ♘xc6 dxc6 10 ♕xd8 ♖xd8 11 ♗e3 ♗f5 12 ♘c3 ♘xc3 13 bxc3 a5 14 c4 ♗e6 15 c5 ♖d5 16 ♖ab1 ♗c8 17 ♖fe1 ♔f8 [17 ... ♖xe5?] 18 ♗b3 [18 f4?!] 18 ... ♖xe5 19 ♗d4 ♖xe1+ 20 ♖xe1 f6 21 a4 ♖b8 22 ♖b1 ♗f5 23 ♖b2 b6 24 cxb6 cxb6 25 h3 b5 26 axb5 cxb5 27 ♗a4? ♖d8 28 ♖xb5 ♖xd4 29 ♖xa5 ♖d1+ 30 ♔h2 ♗d6+ 31 g3 ♗e4 **0-1** L/N6308

**1862-⚔KS-8** 13 v 62
**Kolisch,I.F.von+Shumov,I.S.**
[Mikhailov]
1 e4 e5 2 ♘f3 ♘c6 3 ♗c4 ♘f6 4 0-0 ♗e7 5 d4 d6 6 ♗b5 ♗d7 7 ♘c3 0-0 8 d5 ♘b8 9 ♗xd7 ♘bxd7 10 ♘e1 c6 11 dxc6 bxc6 12 f4 ♕b6+ 13 ♔h1 ♖ad8 14 ♘d3 exf4 15 ♗xf4 ♘e5 16 ♗xe5 dxe5 17 ♖f5 ♘d7 18 ♕e2 f6 19 ♖af1 ♘c5 20 ♘xc5 ♕xc5 21 ♕g4 ♖d2 22 ♖h5 ♖f2 23 ♕e6+ ♔h8 24 ♖d1 h6 25 ♖f5 ♖xc2 26 ♕b3 ♖f2 27 ♖xf2 ♕xf2 28 ♕b7 ♗c5 29 ♕xc6 ♗d4 30 ♕b5 ♗xc3 31 bxc3 ♕xa2 32 ♕d5 ♕c2 33 ♕d3 ♕xd3 34 ♖xd3

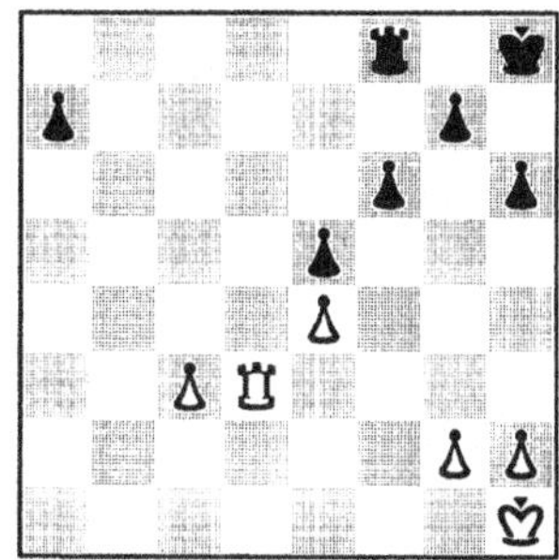

34 ... ♖c8 35 ♔g1 ♖c4 36 ♖e3 a5 37 ♔f2 a4 38 ♔e2 a3? 39 ♔d3 a2 40 ♖e1 ♖a4 41 ♖a1 ♔g8 42 c4 ♔f7 43 ♔c3 ♔e6 44 ♔b3 ♖a6 45 ♖xa2 ♖xa2? 46 ♔xa2 ♔d6 47 ♔b3 ♔c5 48 g4 ♔d4 [48 ... ♔c6 49 ♔b4 ♔b6 50 c5+ ♔c6 51 ♔c4 ♔c7 52 ♔b5 ♔b7 53 c6+ ♔c7 52 ♔c5 ♔c8 55 ♔b6 ♔b8 56 c7+ ♔c8 57 ♔c6+-] 49 ♔b4 ♔xe4 50 c5 ♔d5 51 ♔b5 e4 52 c6 ♔d6 [52 ... e3 53 c7 e2 54 c8♕ e1♕ 55 ♕d8++-] 53 ♔b6 e3 54 c7 e2 55 c8♕ e1♕ 56 ♕d8+ ♔e5 57 ♕e8+ **1-0** L/N6308

## KOLISCH⚔URUSOV
**[1862-⚔KU]**

| | | | | | | | |
|---|---|---|---|---|---|---|---|
| I.F. von Kolisch | 1̂ | 1̂ | ? | 1̂ | ? | 0̂ | ? |
| S.S. Urusov | 0̂ | 0̂ | ? | 0̂ | ? | 1̂ | ? |

**1862-⚔KU-1̂** 20 v 62
**Kolisch,I.F.von+Urusov,S.S.**
[Mikhailov]
1 e4 e5 2 ♘f3 ♘c6 3 ♗c4 ♘f6 4 d4 exd4 5 0-0 ♘xe4 6 ♖e1 d5 7 ♗xd5 ♕xd5 8 ♘c3 ♕h5 9 ♘xe4 ♗e6 10 ♘eg5 0-0-0 11 ♘xe6 fxe6 12 ♗f4 ♗d6 13 ♘e5 ♕xd1 14 ♖axd1 ♗xe5 15 ♗xe5 ♘xe5 16 ♖xe5 ♖he8 17 f4 g6 18 ♔f2 ♖d6 19 ♔f3 ♔d7 20 ♔e4 ♖f8 21 g3 ♖f5 22 ♖xd4 c5 23 ♖xd6+ ♔xd6 24 c4 ♖f7 25 ♔f3 a6 26 ♖e2 b5 27 cxb5 axb5 28 ♖d2+ ♔c6 29 ♔e4 ♖f5 30 g4 ♖d5?+- 31 ♖xd5 exd5+ 32 ♔e5 c4 33 a3 ♔c5 34 f5 b4 35 axb4+ ♔xb4 36 ♔xd5 **1-0** L/N6308

**1862-⚔KU-2̂** 22 v 62
**Urusov,S.S.–Kolisch,I.F.von**
[Mikhailov]
1 e4 e5 2 ♘f3 ♘c6 3 ♗b5 a6 4 ♗a4 ♘f6 5 0-0 ♗e7 6 d4 exd4 7 ♖e1

0-0 8 e5 ♘e8 9 ♘xd4 [9 ♗xc6 dxc6 10 ♕xd4] 9 … ♘xd4 10 ♕xd4 c5 [Δ … b5] 11 ♕e4 ♖b8 12 c4 b5 13 ♗c2 g6 14 ♘c3 [□ 14 ♗h6] 14 … ♗b7 15 ♘d5 bxc4 16 ♗h6 ♗xd5 17 ♕xd5 ♘c7 18 ♕xc4 ♖e8 19 ♖ad1 ♖b4 20 ♕c3 [Δ e6; □ 20 ♕e2] 20 … ♘b5 21 ♕h3? ♖h4 22 ♖xd7 ♕c8 23 ♕d3 ♖xh6 24 ♕d5 ♖h4 25 e6 f5 26 ♗xf5? gxf5 27 ♕xf5 ♖f8 28 ♕e5 ♕e8 29 ♖e3 ♖g4 30 ♕d5 ♖d4 31 ♕b3 c4 32 ♕c2 ♖xd7 33 exd7 ♕xd7 34 ♕xc4+ ♔h8 35 g3 ♘d4 36 f4 ♘f5 37 ♖d3 ♕a7+ 38 ♔h1 ♕b7+ 39 ♔g1 ♖c8 40 ♕d5 ♕b6+ 41 ♔h1 ♖c1+ 42 ♔g2 ♘e3+ **0-1**

L/N6308

**1862-✕KU-4̂** 23 v 62
**Urusov,S.S.– Kolisch,I.F.von**

[Mikhailov]

1 e4 e5 2 ♘f3 ♘c6 3 ♗c4 ♗c5 4 b4 ♗xb4 5 c3 ♗a5 6 d4 ♕e7 [6 … ♕f6 7 ♗g5] 7 ♗a3 ♕f6 8 0-0 ♗b6 9 dxe5 ♘xe5 10 ♘xe5 ♕xe5 11 ♔h1 [Δ f4] 11 … g5 12 ♕h5 ♕g7 13 f4 gxf4 14 ♖xf4 d6 15 e5 [□ 15 ♗xf7+] 15 … ♘h6 16 exd6 0-0 17 d7 ♗xd7 18 ♗xf8 ♖xf8 19 ♘a3 ♖e8 20 ♗e2 ♖e5 21 ♕f3 ♗c6 22 ♕f1 ♖f5 23 ♖ad1 [23 ♖xf5?] 23 … ♕g5 24 ♖xf5 ♘xf5 25 ♖d3 ♗e3 26 ♖xe3 ♘xe3 27 ♕f2 ♗xg2+ 28 ♔g1 ♗f3+ 29 ♕g3 ♕xg3+ 30 hxg3 ♗xe2 31 ♔f2 ♘c4 **0-1**

L/N6308

**1862-✕KU-6̂** 24 v 62
**Urusov,S.S.+Kolisch, I.F.von**

1 e4 e5 2 ♘f3 ♘c6 3 ♗b5 a6 4 ♗a4 ♘f6 5 0-0 ♗e7 6 d4 exd4 7 e5 ♘e4 8 ♘xd4 ♘xd4 9 ♕xd4 ♘c5 10 ♘c3 0-0 11 ♗e3 d6 12 ♖ad1 ♘xa4 13 ♕xa4 ♗d7 14 ♕e4 ♗c6 15 ♘d5 dxe5 16 ♕xe5 ♗d6 17 ♕h5 ♖fe8 18 c4 ♖e4 19 ♖d4 ♖e5 20 ♕f3 ♗c5 21 ♖g4 ♗xe3 22 fxe3 ♗xd5 23 ♕g3 ♕e7 24 ♖xg7+ ♔h8 25 cxd5 ♖xe3 26 ♖gxf7 ♖xg3 27 ♖xe7 ♖g7 28 ♖ff7 ♖ag8 29 ♖xg7 ♖xg7 30 ♖e8+ ♖g8 31 ♖xg8+ ♔xg8 32 ♔f2 **1-0**

L/N6308

**MACDONNELL✕MACKENZIE** [1862-✕MM]

| | | |
|---|---|---|
| G.A. MacDonnell | 1 0 0 1 1 0 0 0 ½ 0 | 3½ |
| G.H. Mackenzie | 0 1 1 0 0 1 1 1 ½ 1 | 6½ |

**1862-✕MM-1**
**MacDonnell,G.A.+ Mackenzie,G.H.**

1 e4 e5 2 ♘f3 ♘c6 3 ♗c4 ♗c5 4 0-0 ♘f6 5 d3 h6 6 c3 d6 7 h3 ♗b6 8 ♗e3 ♗e6 9 ♘bd2 ♕d7 10 ♗xe6 fxe6 11 ♘c4 ♕f7 12 ♘xb6 axb6 13 ♘h2 g5 14 ♘g4 ♘h5 15 g3 0-0-0 16 ♔h1 ♖df8 17 ♖g1 ♖h7 18 ♖g2 ♕g6 19 a4 ♖hf7 20 b4 ♘g7 21 a5 b5 22 ♕b1 h5 23 ♘h2 d5 24 a6 bxa6 25 ♗c5 ♖d8 26 ♖xa6 ♔d7 27 ♕a2 dxe4 28 c4 ♘b8 29 ♖a5 exd3 30 ♖xb5 ♔e8 31 ♗e3 ♕e4 32 ♘f1 ♕f5 33 ♔h2 ♘d7 34 ♕d2 ♘f6 35 ♕b2 ♘d7 36 ♘d2 ♕g6 37 g4 h4 38 c5 c6 39 ♖b7 ♘f6 40 ♖xf7 ♔xf7 41 ♕xe5 ♘d5 42 ♗xg5 ♖d7 43 ♗xh4 ♔g8 44 f4 ♔h7 45 ♘e4 ♖b7 46 ♗e1 ♘xb4 47 ♗xb4 ♖xb4 48 ♘f6+ ♔h8 49 ♖a2 **1-0**

M392

**1862-✕MM-2**
**Mackenzie,G.H.+ MacDonnell,G.A.**

[Boden]

1 e4 e5 2 ♘f3 d6 3 d4 exd4 4 ♘xd4 ♘f6 5 ♘c3 ♗e7 6 f4 0-0 7 ♗e2 [□ 7 ♗d3] 7 … c5 [□ 7 … ♘c6] 8 ♘f3 ♗g4? [□ 8 … ♘c6] 9 h3 ♗xf3 10 ♗xf3 ♕c7 11 0-0 ♘bd7 12 ♗e3 ♖ad8 13 ♕e2 a6 14 a4 ♖fe8 15 ♖ad1 h6 16 ♕f2 ♗f8 [□ 16 … ♘f8] 17 ♔h1 ♘b6 18 g4 ♕c8 19 ♗c1 ♘h7 20 h4 f6 21 ♕g3 ♗e7 22 ♗e2 g6 23 a5 ♘d7 24 ♗c4+ ♔g7 25 ♘d5 ♕c6 26 ♖de1 b5 27 axb6 ♘xb6 28 ♘xb6 ♕xb6 29 b3 ♖a8 30 ♗b2 ♕d8 [□ 30 … g5] 31 g5 hxg5 32 fxg5 ♖h8 33 ♖f4 ♕d7 34 ♖g1 ♕e8 35 ♖gf1 [□ 35 h5] 35 … ♖f8 36 h5 ♖a7 37 hxg6 ♕xg6 38 gxf6+ ♘xf6 39 ♖g4 ♖h8+ 40 ♔g2 ♖h6 41 ♔f2 ♔h7 42 ♖xg6 ♖xg6 43 ♖h1+ ♔g7 44 ♕h4 ♔f8 45 ♕h8+ ♘g8 46 ♖g1 ♗g5 47 ♔e2 **1-0**

M392

**1862-✕MM-3**
**MacDonnell,G.A.– Mackenzie G.H.**

[Boden]

1 e4 e5 2 ♘f3 ♘f6 3 ♘xe5 d6 4 ♘f3 ♘xe4 5 d4 d5 6 ♗d3 ♗e7 7 c4 ♗e6 8 cxd5 ♗xd5 9 0-0 0-0 10 ♘c3 ♘f6 11 ♗e3 ♘c6 12 ♘e5 ♗d6 13 f4 ♘b4 14 ♗b1 ♗c6 15 ♘xc6?! ♘xc6 16 ♖f3 ♕d7 17 ♖h3 ♘e7 18 ♕f3 h6 19 f5 ♖fe8 20 ♗d3 c6 21 ♔h1 [□ 21 ♖f1] 21 … ♖ad8 22 ♖g1 ♗b8 23 ♘e2 ♕d5 24 ♘c3 [□ 24 g4] 24 … ♕xf3 25 gxf3 ♔f8 26 ♖xh6? ♘eg8 27 ♘e4 [27 ♖xf6? ♖xe3–+] 27 … gxh6 28 ♘xf6 ♘xf6 **0-1**

M392

**1862-✕MM-4**
**Mackenzie,G.H.– MacDonnell, G.A.**

[Boden]

1 e4 e5 2 ♘f3 d6 3 d4 exd4 4 ♕xd4 ♗e6 5 ♘c3 a6 6 ♗e3 ♘c6 7 ♕d2 ♗e7 8 ♗d3 ♘f6 9 h3 ♘e5 10 ♘xe5 dxe5 11 0-0 0-0 12 f4 exf4 13 ♖xf4 ♘d7 14 ♕e2 ♗g5 15 ♖ff1 ♗xe3+ 16 ♕xe3 f6 17 ♖ad1 ♕e7 18 ♖f2 ♖ae8 19 a3 ♘e5 20 ♘e2 ♔h8 21 ♘d4 ♗c8 22 g4 ♗xg4 23 hxg4 ♘xg4 24 ♕g3 ♘xf2 25 ♕xf2 g6 26 ♖e1 c5 27 ♘f3 b5 28 c3 c4 29 ♗b1 ♕c7 30 ♘d4 ♖e5 31 ♖e3 ♕d6 32 ♗c2 ♖fe8 33 ♘f3 ♖5e7 34 ♕h4 ♕b6 35 ♔f2 ♖g7 36 ♔e2 ♕d6 37 ♘d4 ♖e5 38 ♕f4 ♖d5! 39 ♖f3 ♕xf4 40 ♖xf4 ♖d6 41 ♔f3 ♖b7 42 ♖g4 a5 43 b4 cxb3 44 ♗xb3 b4 45 ♗d5 ♖b8 46 axb4 axb4 47 cxb4 ♖xb4 48 ♘c2 ♖a4 49 ♘e3 ♖a3 50 ♔f4 g5+ 51 ♔f3 h6 [□ 51 … h5] 52 ♖g1 ♔h7 53 ♖h1? ♖d8 54 ♗e6 ♖d2 55 ♖c1 h5 56 e5 g4+ 57 ♔e4 ♖e2 58 ♗f5+ ♔h6 59 exf6 ♖exe3+ 60 ♔d4 ♖f3 61 ♖c5 ♖a4+ 62 ♔e5 ♖af4 63 ♔e6 g3 64 f7 ♔g7 **0-1**

M392

**1862-✕MM-5**
**MacDonnell,G.A.+ Mackenzie, G.H.**

[Boden]

1 e4 e5 2 ♘f3 ♘c6 3 ♗c4 ♗c5 4 ♘c3 ♘f6 5 d3 h6 6 0-0 d6 7 h3 ♗e6 8 ♗b3 ♕d7 9 ♗e3 ♗b6 10 ♘h2 ♘d4 11 ♗a4 c6 12 ♘e2 ♘xe2+ 13 ♕xe2 g5 14 g4 ♘h7 15 c3 ♗c7 16 d4 b5 17 ♗b3 f6 18 d5 cxd5 19 exd5 ♗f7 20 a4 b4 21 cxb4 ♔f8 22 ♖ac1 ♔g7 23 ♖fd1 ♘f8 24 ♘f1 h5 25 ♘g3 hxg4 26 hxg4 ♘g6 27 ♘f5+ ♔g8 28 ♗c2 [□ 28 ♖c6, 29 ♖dc1] 28 … ♖b8 29 b5 ♗b6 30 ♗e4 ♗e8 31 ♔g2 ♗xe3 32 fxe3 ♕h7 33 ♖h1 ♘h4+ 34 ♔g3 ♘xf5+ 35 ♗xf5 ♕xh1 36 ♖xh1 ♖xh1 37 ♕c4 ♗f7 38 ♕c7 ♖f8 39 ♕xd6 ♔g7 40 ♕c7 ♖d1 41 ♗e6 ♔g8 42 ♕xa7 ♖d2 43 b4 ♗xe6 44 dxe6 ♖d6 45 b6 ♖xe6 46 b7 ♖ee8 47 a5 **1-0**

M392-1863

**1862-✕MM-6**
**Mackenzie,G.H.+ MacDonnell G.A.**

[Boden]

1 e4 e5 2 ♘f3 d6 3 d4 exd4 4 ♗c4 ♗e7 5 ♘xd4 ♘f6 6 ♘c3 ♘c6 7 f4 0-0 8 0-0 ♗g4 9 ♘f3 ♕d7 10 ♗e3 ♖ad8 11 ♕e2 a6 12 a4 ♔h8 13 h3 ♗xf3 14 ♕xf3 ♘e8 15 g4 ♗f6 16 ♗f2 ♗d4 17 ♖ad1 ♗xf2+ 18 ♖xf2 f6 19 h4 g6 20 h5 g5 21 ♗b3 h6 22 ♕g3 ♕e7 23 ♖e2 ♕g7 24 ♘d5 ♘e7 25 ♘e3 c6 26 c3 ♖d7 27 ♖ed2 gxf4 28 ♕xf4 ♕g5 29 ♕xg5 hxg5 [□ 29 … fxg5] 30 ♗e6 ♖c7 [□ 30 … ♖d8] 31 a5 ♘c8 32 ♗xc8 ♖xc8 33 ♘f5 ♖c7 34 ♔f2 ♖ff7 35 ♘xd6 ♘xd6 36 ♖xd6 ♔g7 37 ♔e3 ♖ce7 38 ♖f1 ♖e5 39 ♖f5 ♖e8 40 ♔d3 ♖ee7 41

e5 fxe5 42 ♖g6+ ♔h7 43 ♖gxg5 e4+ 44 ♔e3 ♔h6 45 ♖g6+ ♔h7 46 ♖xf7+ ♖xf7 47 ♔xe4 **1-0** M392

**1862-✕MM-7**
**MacDonnell, G.A.– Mackenzie, G.H.**
[Boden]
1 e4 e6 2 d4 d5 3 exd5 exd5 4 ♘f3 ♘f6 5 ♗d3 ♗d6 6 0-0 0-0 7 ♗g5 ♗e6 8 c3 [□ 8 ♘c3] 8 ... ♘bd7 9 ♖e1 c6 10 ♘e5 ♕c7 11 f4 ♘e4!

12 ♗xe4 dxe4 13 ♖xe4 ♗d5 14 ♖e1 [□ 14 ♖e3] 14 ... f6 15 ♗h4 [□ 15 ♘xd7] 15 ... fxe5 16 fxe5 ♘xe5 17 dxe5 ♗xe5 18 ♔h1? ♗xh2 19 ♕g4 ♗d6 20 ♘d2 ♖f4 21 ♕h3 ♖af8 22 ♖e2 ♕f7 23 ♗g3 ♖f5 24 ♗xd6 ♖h5 25 ♗xf8 ♖xh3+ 26 ♔g1 ♕h5 27 ♔f2 ♕h4+ **0-1** M392

**1862-✕MM-8**
**Mackenzie, G.H.+ MacDonnell, G.A.**
[Boden]
1 e4 g6 2 d4 ♗g7 3 ♘f3 e6 4 ♘c3 b6 5 ♗d3 ♗b7 6 ♗e3 d6 7 ♕d2 ♘e7 8 ♘e2 ♘d7 9 0-0 ♘f6 10 ♘g3 ♕d7 11 c4 0-0 12 ♖ad1 ♘g4 13 h3 ♘xe3 14 fxe3 ♖ad8 15 ♖f2 f5 16 exf5 ♘xf5 17 ♘e2 ♗h6 18 ♗xf5 exf5 19 d5 c5 20 ♘f4 ♗c8 21 ♘e6 ♕e8 22 ♘fg5 ♗xg5 23 ♘xg5 h6 24 ♘f3 ♕e4 25 ♕c3 ♖de8 26 ♖e1 ♖f7 27 ♘d2 ♕h4 28 ♖ef1 ♕g3? 29 ♖f3 ♕g5 30 ♔h2 ♕e7 31 e4 ♖ef8 32 exf5 ♖xf5 33 ♖e3 ♕h4? 34 ♘f3 ♕d8 35 ♖fe1 ♖5f7 36 ♖1e2 ♗d7 37 ♕e1 ♕f6 38 ♕g3 ♔h7 39 b3 ♖g8 40 ♘d2 ♗f5 41 ♘e4 ♗xe4 42 ♖xe4 ♖d8 43 ♖e6 ♕g5 44 ♕xg5 hxg5 45 ♔g3 ♔h6 46 ♖f2 ♖df8 47 ♖xf7 ♖xf7 48 ♖xd6 **1-0** M392-1863

**1862-✕MM-9**
**MacDonnell, G.A.= Mackenzie, G.H.**
[Boden]
1 c4 f5 2 ♘c3 ♘f6 3 f4 e6 4 ♘f3 ♗e7 5 e3 0-0 6 ♗e2 d6 7 b3 b6 8 ♗b2 ♗b7 9 0-0 ♘c6 10 d4 ♕d7 11 ♕e1 ♘d8 12 ♖d1 ♘f7 13 ♕d2? [□ 13 d5] 13 ... ♘e4 14 ♕c2 ♗f6 15 ♗d3 d5 16 ♘e5 ♘xe5 17 dxe5 ♘xc3 18 ♕xc3 ♗e7 19 cxd5 ♗xd5 20 e4 fxe4 21 ♗xe4 c6 22 ♕d3 [□ 22 b4] 22 ... ♗c5+ 23 ♔h1 g6 24 a3 b5 25 b4 ♗b6 26 ♗xd5 cxd5 27 ♖c1 ♖ac8 28 ♖cd1 ♖c4 29 ♕g3 ♕f7 30 ♗c1 ♕f5 31 ♖d3? ♖fc8 [□ 31 ... ♕xe5!] 32 ♗d2 ♖d4 33 ♖ff3 ♖c2 34 ♖xd4 ♖xd2 35 ♖dd3 ♗f2 36 ♕h3 ♕e4 37 ♕xe6+ **½-½** M392-1863

**1862-✕MM-10**
**Mackenzie, G.H.+ MacDonnell, G.A.**
[Boden]
1 e4 g6 2 d4 ♗g7 3 ♗e3 e6 4 ♗d3 ♘e7 5 ♘c3 b6 6 ♘ge2 ♗b7 7 0-0 0-0 8 ♕d2 d6 9 ♘g3 ♘d7 10 ♖ae1 c5 11 ♘ce2 ♕c7 12 c3 ♖ae8 13 ♗h6 ♕c6 14 ♗xg7 ♔xg7 15 f3 ♖h8 16 h4 h6 17 ♘f4 ♕c7 18 ♖f2 ♕d8 19 h5 ♖eg8 [□ 19 ... e5; 19 ... g5] 20 hxg6 ♘xg6 21 e5 d5 22 ♗xg6 ♔f8 23 ♘xe6+ fxe6 24 ♕f4+ ♘f6 25 ♗c2 ♖xg3 26 ♕xg3 ♘e8 27 f4 ♖g8 28 ♕h3 ♘g7 29 ♕xh6 ♔e8 30 ♗a4+ ♔f7 31 f5! ♘xf5 32 ♖xf5+ exf5 33 e6+ ♔e7 34 ♕h4+ ♔d6 35 ♕xd8+ ♖xd8 36 e7 **1-0** M392-1863

**1862-★AA-1** 9 vi 62
**Amelung, F.– Anderssen, A.**
Berlin
1 e4 e5 2 ♘f3 ♘c6 3 ♗b5 ♘f6 4 d3 ♗c5 5 0-0 ♘d4 6 ♘xd4 ♗xd4 7 c3 ♗b6 8 ♗g5 0-0 9 d4 exd4 10 cxd4 d6 11 ♘a3 ♕e7 12 b3 ♕xe4 13 ♗xf6 gxf6 14 ♗d3 ♕xd4 15 ♔h1 ♔h8 16 f4 ♖g8 17 ♕c2 ♗d7 18 ♖ad1 ♗c6 19 ♖d2 ♕d5 20 ♕b2 ♖xg2 21 ♖xg2 ♗d4 22 ♕c2 ♖g8 23 ♖g1 ♗xg1 24 ♗f1 ♖xg2 25 ♗xg2 ♕xg2+ ...? **0-1** L/N3034

**1862-★AA-2** 9 vi 62
**Anderssen, A.– Amelung, F.**
Berlin
1 e4 e5 2 f4 exf4 3 ♘f3 d6 4 d4 g5 5 h4 g4 6 ♘g5 h6 7 ♘xf7 ♔xf7 8 ♗c4+ ♔g7 9 ♗xf4 ♖h7 10 ♘c3 ♔h8 11 ♕d2 c6 12 0-0-0 b5 13 ♗d3 ♖f7 14 ♗g5 hxg5 15 hxg5+ ♔g7 16 e5 ♗f5 17 ♘e4 ♗e7 18 ♘f6 ♘xf6 19 ♗xf5 ♘e4 20 ♗xe4 ♗xg5 21 e6 ♗xd2+ 22 ♔xd2 ♕a5+ 23 ♔c1 ♖f8 24 ♖h7+ ♔g8 25 e7 ♖e8 26 ♖dh1 ♘d7 27 ♗f5 ♘f8 28 exf8♕+ ♔xf8 29 c3 b4 30 ♖d7 ♖e1+ 31 ♖xe1 ♕xf5 **0-1** +9

**1862-★AB-1** vi 62
**Barnes, T.W.+ Anderssen, A.**
London [Boden]
1 e4 e5 2 ♘f3 d6 3 ♗c4 f5 4 d3 ♘f6 5 0-0 c6?! 6 ♘c3 ♗e7 7 ♘g5 d5 8 exd5 cxd5 9 ♗b3 h6 10 ♘f3 ♘c6 11 ♘h4 g5 12 ♘g6 ♖h7 13 ♖e1 e4 14 dxe4 dxe4 15 ♗e3 ♗d6 16 ♘d5 ♗d7 17 ♗d4 ♘xd5 18 ♗xd5 ♗e6?! 19 ♗xe6 ♘xd4 20 ♗xf5! ♘xf5 21 ♖xe4+ ♔d7? 22 ♕d5 ♔c7 23 ♕xf5 ♖c8 24 ♘f8 ♕xf8 25 ♕xh7+ ♔b8 26 ♖ae1 a6 27 ♕d7 ♗c5 28 ♕xc8+ **1-0** M392

**1862-★AB-2** vi 62
**Anderssen, A.+ Barnes, T.W.**
London [Boden]
1 e4 f6? 2 d4 e6 3 ♗d3 ♘e7 4 ♕h5+ g6 5 ♕h4 ♗g7 6 ♘c3 0-0 7 ♘f3 d5 8 g4 dxe4 9 ♘xe4 f5 10 ♗g5 fxe4 11 ♗xe7 ♗f6 12 ♗xf6 ♕xf6 13 ♘g5 ♖f7 14 ♗xe4 h6 15 ♕xh6 ♕xf2+ 16 ♔d1 ♕xd4+ 17 ♔c1 ♖g7 18 ♗xg6 ♘c6 19 ♖f1 ♗d7 20 ♗h7+ ♔h8 21 ♘f7+ ♖xf7 22 ♗g6+ **1-0** M392

**1862-★AB-3** vii 62
**Bird, H.E.– Anderssen, A.**
London [Bachmann]
1 e4 e5 2 ♘f3 ♘c6 3 ♗b5 ♘f6 4 d4 exd4 [□ 4 ... ♘xe4] 5 0-0 ♗e7 6 e5 ♘e4 7 ♖e1 [7 ♘xd4 ♘xd4 8 ♕xd4 ♘c5 9 f4 c6] 7 ... ♘c5 8 c3 dxc3 9 ♘xc3 0-0 10 ♘d5 f6 11 ♗f4 fxe5 12 ♗xe5 ♘xe5 13 ♘xe5 ♘e6 14 ♗c4 ♗c5 15 ♘d3 ♕h4 16 ♕c2 ♗d6 17 g3 ♕h6 18 ♖e4 b5 19 ♗b3 ♘g5 20 ♕e2 ♘xe4 21 ♕xe4 ♔h8 22 ♘e3 ♖ab8 23 ♖e1 ♗b7 24 ♘d5 c5 25 ♘e5 ♗xe5 26 ♕xe5 c4 27 ♗c2 ♕d2 28 ♕e4 ♕xf2+ 29 ♔h1 ♗xd5 **0-1** L/N3033

**1862-★AB-4** vii 62
**Anderssen, A.+ Blackburne, J.H.**
London [Boden]
1 e4 e5 2 f4 exf4 3 ♗c4 ♕h4+ 4 ♔f1 g5 5 ♘c3 ♗g7 6 d4 d6 7 e5 ♗e6 8 ♗e2 [8 d5? ♗g4∓] 8 ... d5 [□ 8 ... dxe5] 9 g3 ♕h6 10 h4 fxg3 11 ♔g2 ♕g6 12 hxg5 ♘e7 13 ♗h5 ♕f5 14 ♗e3 ♘g6 15 ♘ge2 ♗d7 16 ♕d2 ♗c6 17 ♖af1 ♕d7 18 ♘f4 ♘xe5 19 ♕e2 0-0 20 ♖h3 ♘a6 21 dxe5 d4+ 22 ♔xg3 dxc3 23 ♗g4! ♕e7 24 ♖xh7! ♗xe5 [24 ... ♔xh7? 25 ♗f5+ ♔g8 26 ♕h5+-] 25 g6 ♖ae8 26 ♕h2 ♕g5 27 ♖h8+ ♔g7 28 ♕h7+ ♔f6

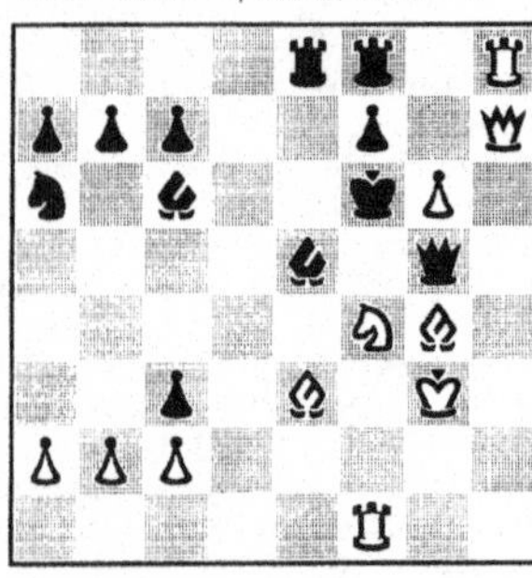

29 ♔h3!! [29 ... ♖xh8 30 ♘h5+ ♔e7 31 ♕xf7+ △ 32 ♗xg5+–] **1-0** M392

**1862-★AB-5**
**Blackburne,J.H.+ Anderssen,A.**
London [Boden]
1 e4 e5 2 f4 exf4 3 ♘f3 g5 4 ♗c4 g4 5 0-0 gxf3 6 ♕xf3 ♕e7 7 d3?! ♘c6 [□ 7 ... d6] 8 ♗xf4 ♘d4 9 ♕f2 ♘e6 10 ♗e3 ♗g7 11 d4 ♘f6 12 ♕f3 d6 13 ♘c3 0-0 14 d5 ♘c5 15 ♗g5 ♘cd7 16 ♖ae1 [△ e5] 16 ... ♘e5 17 ♕g3 ♔h8 18 ♕h4 ♘xc4 19 ♖xf6 ♕d7 20 ♖h6 ♕g4?! [□ 20 ... f6=] 21 ♖xh7+ ♔g8 22 ♖xg7+ ♔xg7 23 ♕h6+ [23 ♗f6+? ♔g6–+] 23 ... ♔g8 24 ♗f6 **1-0** M392

**1862-★AB-6**
**Boden, S.S. & Kennedy, H.A. & Löwenthal, J.J.– Anderssen, A. & Dubois, S. & Paulsen, L.**
London
1 e4 c5 2 ♘f3 e6 3 d4 cxd4 4 ♘xd4 ♘f6 5 ♘c3 ♗b4 6 ♗d3 0-0 7 0-0 d5 8 e5 ♘e8 9 ♕h5 f5 10 f4 ♘c6 11 ♘f3 ♘c7 12 ♘e2 b6 13 a3 ♗e7 14 b4 a5 15 b5 ♘b8 16 a4 ♘d7 17 ♘ed4 ♗b7 18 ♗e3 g6 19 ♕h3 ♘c5 20 ♘b3 ♘xb3 21 cxb3 d4 22 ♗f2 ♘d5 23 ♕g3 ♗c5 24 ♖fe1 ♘e3 25 ♖ac1 ♕e7 26 ♘xd4 ♘g4 27 ♘c6 ♗xf2+ 28 ♕xf2 ♗xc6 29 ♕xb6 ♗d5 30 h3 ♘h6 31 ♗c4 ♖fb8 32 ♕f2 ♗e4 33 ♖ed1 ♘f7 34 ♖d2 ♖d8 35 ♖cd1 ♖xd2 36 ♖xd2 g5 37 ♕b6 gxf4 38 ♗xe6 ♕a7 39 ♕xa7 ♖xa7 40 ♖f2 ♖e7 41 ♗c4 ♔g7 42 e6 ♘g5 43 b4 axb4 44 a5 ♘xe6 45 ♖b2 ♘c5 46 ♖xb4 ♔f6 47 a6 ♖g7 48 b6 ♗xg2 49 ♔f2 ♗e4 50 ♗f1 ♔e5 51 b7 ♘xb7 52 axb7 ♖xb7 53 ♖xb7 ♗xb7 54 ♗e2 f3 55 ♗c4 ♔f4 56 ♗d3 ♗e4 57 ♗c4 ♔e5 58 ♔g3 f4+ 59 ♔f2 ♗b7 60 ♗f1 ♗c8 61 ♔xf3 ♗b7+ 62 ♔f2 ♗c8 63 ♔f3 ♗b7+ 64 ♔f2 h6 65 ♗c4 ♗c8 66 ♗f1 ♗d7 67 ♔f3 ♗c6+ 68 ♔f2 ♔f5 69 ♗g2 ♗xg2 70 ♔xg2 ♔e4 **0-1** L/N3034

**1862-★AB-7**
**Burden, F.+Anderssen, A.**
London
⟨Δf7⟩1 e4 ... 2 d4 e6 3 ♗d3 d6 4 e5 g6 5 h4 ♘h6 6 ♗g5 ♕d7 7 h5 ♘f7 8 ♗f6 ♖g8 9 hxg6 hxg6 10 ♘c3 ♘c6 11 ♕g4 dxe5 12 ♗xg6 exd4 13 ♘b5 a6 14 ♖h7 ♖xg6 15 ♕xg6 axb5 16 ♖h8 ♕d6 17 ♘f3 e5 18 ♘g5 ♕b4+ 19 ♔f1 ♕c4+ 20 ♔g1 ♘cd8 21 ♘h7 ♘e6 22 ♗h4 ♗d7 23 ♘f6+ ♔e7 24 ♘xd7+ ♔xd7 25 ♕xf7+ ♔c6 26 b3 ♕d5 27 ♗e7 ♕d7 28 ♕f3+ ♕d5 29 ♕xd5+ ♔xd5 30 f3 c5 31 ♖e1 ♖e8 32 ♗xf8 ♘xf8 33 g4 c4 34 g5 ♔e6 35 f4 ♔f7 36 f5 e4 37 bxc4 bxc4 38 ♖b1 ♔g7 39 ♖h6 e3 40 f6+ ♔g8 41 ♖xb7 **1-0** L/N6047

**1862-★AB-8**
**Bird, H.E.– Anderssen, A.**
London [Staunton]
1 e4 e5 2 ♘f3 ♘c6 3 ♗b5 ♘f6 4 d4 exd4 5 0-0 [5 e5!?] 5 ... ♗e7 6 ♖e1 0-0 7 e5 ♘e8 8 ♘xd4?! ♘xd4 9 ♕xd4 d5 10 ♘c3 c6 11 ♗d3 ♗e6 12 ♕f4 f5 13 exf6 ♖xf6 14 ♕g3 ♗d6 15 ♕h4 [□ 15 f4] 15 ... h6 16 ♗e3 ♕c7 17 ♘e2 g5 18 ♕a4 [18 ♗xg5!?] 18 ... b5 19 ♕d4 c5 20 ♕c3 c4 21 ♗d4 b4 22 ♕d2 cxd3 23 ♗xf6 ♘xf6 24 ♘d4 ♗d7 25 ♕xd3 ♔h8 26 ♕g6 ♗xh2+ 27 ♔f1 [27 ♔h1? ♘g4] 27 ... ♕c4+ 28 ♕d3 ♖f8 29 ♕xc4 dxc4 30 ♖e7 ♗d6 31 ♖e2 ♘g4 32 ♖d1 ♗c5 33 c3 ♖f4 34 f3 ♗xd4 35 cxd4 ♗b5 36 ♔e1 ♘f6 37 ♖e5 ♗a4 38 b3 cxb3 39 axb3 ♗xb3 40 ♖b1 ♗d5 41 ♖xb4 ♔g7 42 ♖e7+ ♔g6 43 ♖xa7 h5 44 ♖a6 h4 45 ♖bb6 g4 46 ♔f2 h3 47 ♔g3 ♔g5 [47 ... hxg2 (48 ♔xf4 g1♕ 49 ♖xf6+ ♔g7 50 ♖g6+ ♔f7 51 ♖gf6+ ♔e7–+)] 48 ♖xf6 ♖xf6 49 ♖a5 ♖f5 50 f4+ [50 fxg4? (50 ... hxg2 51 ♔h2 ♔xg4–+); 50 gxh3? (50 ... ♖xf3+ 51 ♔h2 ♖xh3+ 52 ♔g1 ♖g3+ 53 ♔f1 ♖f3+ △ 54 ... ♖f5–+)] 50 ... ♔f6 51 gxh3 gxh3 52 ♖b5 ♗e6 53 ♖e5 ♗d7 54 ♖e3 ♖d5 55 ♖d3 ♔f5 56 ♔f3 ♗c6 57 ♔g3 ♔e4 58 ♖d1 ♗d7 59 ♖e1+ ♔xd4 60 ♖e7 ♔c3 61 ♖e2 ♖d2 62 ♖e5 ♖g2+ 63 ♔f3 ♗c6+ 64 ♔e3 h2 **0-1** M392-1866

**1862-★AB-9**
**Belareff– Anderssen, A.**
London [Löwenthal]
1 e4 e5 2 ♘f3 ♘c6 3 c3 f5 4 ♗b5 [□ 4 d4] 4 ... fxe4 5 ♗xc6 bxc6 6 ♘xe5 ♘f6 7 d4 ♗a6 8 ♗e3 ♗e7 9 ♘d2 ♖b8 10 b4 ♖b6 11 d5 ♖b5 12 c4 ♖xb4 13 a3 ♖b2 14 ♗d4 ♖b8 15 ♘xe4! cxd5 16 ♘xf6+ ♗xf6 17 ♕h5+ g6 18 ♘xg6 hxg6 19 ♕xg6+ ♔f8 20 ♗xf6 ♕e8+ 21 ♕xe8+ ♖xe8+ 22 ♔d2 ♖h6 23 ♗g5 ♖g6 24 f4 dxc4 25 ♖ae1 ♖d6+ 26 ♔c2 ♖de6 27 ♖d1 ♖e2+ 28 ♖d2 d5 29 ♖hd1 d4 30 ♔c1 d3 [31 ♖xe2 ♖xe2 32 ♖d2 ♖xd2 33 ♔xd2∞] **0-1** M713-1871

**1862-★AD-1** vi 62
**Anderssen, A.– Dubois, S.**
London [Lowenthal]
1 e4 e5 2 f4 exf4 3 ♘f3 g5 4 ♗c4 ♗g7 5 d4 d6 6 h4 h6 7 ♕d3 [□ 7 c3] 7 ... g4 8 ♘g1 ♕f6 9 c3 h5 10 ♘a3 ♗d7 11 ♗d2 ♘c6 12 0-0-0 ♘ge7 13 ♔b1 [□ 13 ♘c2] 13 ... d5 14 ♗b3 dxe4 15 ♕f1 e3 16 ♗c1 g3 17 ♘f3 0-0-0 18 ♘g5 ♗e6 19 ♘xe6 fxe6 20 ♘c2 ♘a5 21 ♗a4 ♕f5 22 b4 ♘d5! 23 ♗b2 ♘b6 24 ♗b5 ♘c6 25 a4 ♘d5 26 ♗d3 ♕f6 27 ♕e1 [△ 28 c4] 27 ... ♖hf8 28 c4 ♘b6 29 b5 ♘b8 30 ♕a5! c5 31 ♕xa7 ♖d6 32 ♗a3 ♘8d7 33 a5 ♘a4! 34 ♔a1 ♖xd4 35 ♔b1 ♘c3+ 36 ♔c1 e2 37 a6 exd1♕+ 38 ♖xd1 b6 39 ♕b7+ ♔d8 40 ♖d2 f3 41 a7 ♔e7 42 ♘b4 ♕f4 43 ♘c6+ ♔f6 44 ♘xd4 fxg2 45 ♘f3 ♗h6 46 ♗b2 ♕xd2+ 47 ♘xd2 g1♕+ 48 ♔c2 ♕d1+ 49 ♔xc3 ♗xd2# **0-1** M324-1864

**1862-★AD-2** vi 62
**Dubois, S.– Anderssen, A.**
London [Boden]
1 e4 e5 2 f4 exf4 3 ♘f3 g5 4 ♗c4 g4 5 0-0 gxf3 6 ♕xf3 ♕e7 7 d3?! d6 8 ♗xf4 ♗e6 9 ♗g5 f6 [9 ... ♕xg5? 10 ♗xe6±] 10 ♗xe6 ♕xe6 11 ♘c3 ♘d7 12 ♘d5 0-0-0 13 ♗e3 ♘h6 14 b4 ♘g4 15 ♗d4 h5 16 c4 ♗h6 17 h3 ♘ge5 18 ♕e2 ♖dg8 19 ♗e3 [□ 19 ♗xe5] 19 ... ♕xh3 20 ♗xh6 ♖g3! 21 ♗f4 ♘g4 22 ♗xg3 ♕xg3 **0-1** M392

**1862-★AD-3** vi 62
**Dubois, S.– Anderssen, A.**
London [Lange & Hirschfeld]
1 e4 e5 2 f4 exf4 3 ♘f3 g5 4 ♗c4 g4 5 0-0 gxf3 6 ♕xf3 ♕e7 7 d4 ♘c6 8 c3 ♘e5 9 dxe5 ♕c5+ 10 ♔h1 ♕xc4 11 ♗xf4 ♕e6 12 ♘d2 b6 13 ♕g3 ♕g6 14 ♕d3 ♗b7 15 e6 fxe6 16 ♗xc7 ♘f6 17 ♖ae1 ♖g8 18 ♖e2 ♖c8 19 ♗e5 ♘g4 20 ♗g3 ♖c5! 21 ♖f5 ♗xe4 22 ♖xf8+ ♖xf8 23 ♕xe4 ♕xe4 24 ♖xe4 ♘f2+ 25 ♗xf2 ♖xf2 26 ♖d4 e5 27 ♖d3 e4 28 ♖d4 e3 29 ♘f3 ♖f1+ 30 ♘g1 ♖e5 **0-1** L/N6047

**1862-★AD-4**
**Anderssen, A.+ Dubois, S.**
London [Staunton]
1 e4 e5 2 f4 exf4 3 ♘f3 g5 4 ♗c4 ♗g7 5 d4 d6 6 c3 c6 7 h4 h6 8 ♕b3 ♕e7 9 0-0 g4 10 ♘e1 f3 11 gxf3 b5 12 ♗d3 ♕xh4 13 ♘g2

♕h3 14 fxg4 ♘f6 15 ♗e2 ♗e6∓ 16 ♕c2 ♗xg4 17 ♗f4 ♖g8! 18 ♗xg4 ♘xg4 19 ♕e2 ♘d7 20 ♘d2 ♘de5 21 dxe5 ♗xe5 22 ♗xe5 dxe5 23 ♘f3 0-0-0 24 ♖f2 ♖g5?! 25 ♕e1 ♖h5 26 ♔f1 ♕h1+ 27 ♔e2 ♘xf2 28 ♔xf2 ♕h3 29 ♕e3 ♖g8 30 ♘ge1 ♕g3+?! 31 ♔e2 ♖d8 32 a4 ♖h2+ 33 ♘xh2 ♕xh2+ 34 ♔f1 ♖d6 35 ♕f3 ♖g6 36 ♕f2 ♕h1+ 37 ♔e2 ♕xe4+ 38 ♔d1 ♖d6+ 39 ♔c1 ♕d5 40 ♕e2 a6 41 axb5 cxb5 42 ♔c2 f5 43 ♘f3 e4 44 ♘d4 ♖f6 45 ♖g1 b4 46 ♖g7 bxc3 47 ♕h2! ♖d6 48 ♕h5 cxb2 49 ♔b1 e3 50 ♖e7 ♖d7 51 ♕e8+ ♖d8 52 ♕a4 a5 53 ♕c2+ **1-0** M954

**1862-★AH-1** v62
**Hamel, S.– Anderssen, A.**
Breslau [Harrwitz]
1 e4 e5 2 ♘f3 ♘c6 3 ♗c4 ♗c5 4 b4 ♗xb4 5 c3 ♗c5 6 0-0 [□ 6 d4] 6 ... d6 7 d4 exd4 8 cxd4 ♗b6 9 ♗a3 ♘h6 10 e5 0-0 11 d5 ♘e7 12 e6 fxe6 13 dxe6 ♗a5 14 ♘g5 ♖f6 15 ♕d3 ♖g6 16 f4 b5 17 ♗d5 ♗b6+ 18 ♔h1 ♖b8 19 ♗e4! ♗b7 20 ♗xg6 hxg6 21 ♘d2 ♕f8 22 ♖ae1 ♕f5 23 ♕c3 [□ 23 ♕xf5] 23 ... ♕g4 24 ♘df3 ♘hf5 25 ♗b2 ♖f8 26 ♘f7 [□ 26 ♕d2 △ 27 ♘e4, 28 h3±] 26 ... ♘d4 27 ♖f2? b4 28 ♕d3 ♘xe6 29 ♖fe2 ♘xf4 30 ♕b3 ♗d5 **0-1** M392-1863

**1862-★AH-2** v62
**Hamel, S.+ Anderssen, A.**
Breslau
1 e4 e5 2 f4 exf4 3 ♘f3 g5 4 h4 g4 5 ♘e5 ♘f6 6 ♗c4 d5 7 exd5 ♗d6 8 d4 ♘h5 [□ 8 ... ♕e7] 9 ♘c3 0-0 10 ♘e4 [10 ♘xg4? ♖e8+ △ ... ♘g3∓] 10 ... ♖e8 11 ♕d3 f6 12 ♗b5 ♖e7 [□ 12 ... fxe5] 13 ♘xf6+ ♘xf6 14 ♗xf4 ♘a6 15 ♗xa6 bxa6 16 0-0 ♗b7 17 c4 ♖g7 18 ♗g5 ♗e7 19 ♖ae1 ♘xd5 20 cxd5 ♕xd5 21 ♖e2 ♗xg5 22 hxg5 ♖d8 [□ 22 ... ♖xg5] 23 ♘xg4 ♕xg5 24 ♘f6+ ♔h8 25 d5 ♖f8 26 ♖f5 ♕g6 27 ♕f3 c6 28 ♖e8 ♖gf7 29 ♘d7! ♖xe8 30 ♖xf7 cxd5 31 ♕f6+ ♕xf6 32 ♘xf6 **1-0** M392-1863

**1862-★AK-1** vii 62
**Kennedy, H.A. & Löwenthal, J.J.– Anderssen, A. & Paulsen, L.**
London
1 e4 c5 2 ♘f3 e6 3 d4 cxd4 4 ♘xd4 ♘f6 5 ♘c3 ♗b4 6 ♘db5 0-0 7 e5 ♘e8 8 ♕g4 ♘c6 9 ♗d3 f5 10 ♕g3 ♕a5 11 0-0 a6 12 ♘d6 ♕xe5 13 ♗f4 ♕f6 14 ♘xe8 ♖xe8 15 ♖ae1 ♖f8 16 ♗d6 ♗xd6 17 ♕xd6 b5 18 ♖e3 ♕f7 19 f4 ♗b7 20 ♗e2 ♖ae8 21 ♗f3 g6 22 ♖d1 ♗c8 23 ♗xc6 dxc6 24 ♕xc6 ♕a7 25 ♖dd3 e5 26 ♔f1 e4 27 ♕d5+ ♗e6 28 ♕d4 ♕c7 29 ♖d1 ♕xf4+ 30 ♔g1 ♖d8 31 ♕b6 ♖xd1+ 32 ♘xd1 ♗c4 33 ♘f2 ♕e5 34 c3 ♖b8 35 ♕a7 ♖d8 36 ♖h3 ♕g7 37 ♕xa6 ♕d7 38 ♖g3 f4 **0-1** L/N3034

**1862-★AK-2** vii62
**Kolisch, I.F. von+ Anderssen, A.**
London
1 e4 e5 2 ♘f3 ♘c6 3 ♗c4 ♗c5 4 b4 ♗xb4 5 c3 ♗a5 6 d4 exd4 7 0-0 dxc3 8 ♕b3 ♕f6 9 e5 ♕g6 10 ♘xc3 b5 11 ♘xb5 ♖b8 12 ♗e3 ♘ge7 13 ♕e2 ♕h5 14 ♗a3 ♗b7 15 ♖ad1 ♘f5

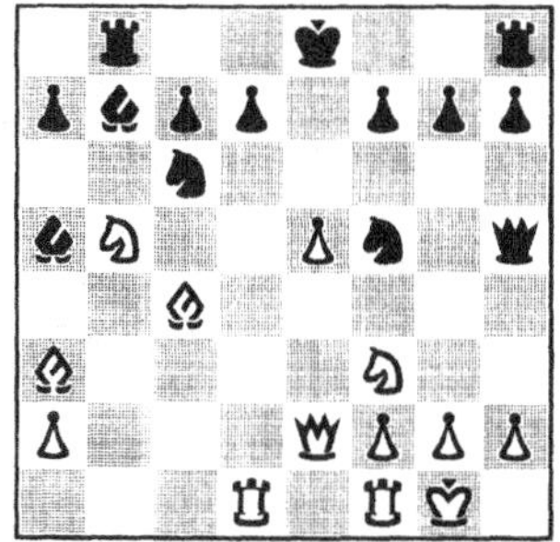

16 ♖xd7 ♔xd7 17 e6+ ♔c8 18 exf7 ♗a8 19 ♘xa7+ ♘xa7 20 ♕e6+ ♔d8 21 ♖d1+ ♘d6 22 ♖xd6+ cxd6 23 ♕xd6+ ♔c8 24 ♗e6+ ♔b7 25 ♗d5+ ♕xd5! 26 ♕xd5+ ♔a6 27 ♕c4+ ♔b7 28 ♕e4+ ♘c6 29 ♘e5 ♔a6 30 ♕c4+ ♔a7 31 ♗c5+ ♖b6 32 ♗xb6+ ♗xb6 33 ♘xc6+ ♗xc6 34 ♕xc6 **1-0** L/N6047

**1862-★AL-1** vii 62
**Lelie, A. de– Anderssen, A.**
Amsterdam
1 e4 e5 2 ♘f3 ♘c6 3 ♗b5 a6 4 ♗a4 ♘f6 5 d4 exd4 6 0-0 ♗e7 7 e5 ♘e4 8 c3 dxc3 9 ♖e1 cxb2 10 ♗xb2 ♘c5 11 ♗c2 ♘e6 12 ♘bd2 b5 13 ♘e4 ♗b7 14 h3 a5 15 ♘h2 a4 16 a3 ♘a5 17 ♘g4 ♘c4 18 ♗c3 ♗xe4 19 ♗xe4 c6 20 ♘e3 ♘xa3 21 ♘f5 ♘c4 22 ♘d6+ ♗xd6 23 exd6 ♗f6 24 ♖a3 ♗xc3 25 ♖xc3 0-0 26 ♕h5 g6 27 ♖g3 ♕f6 28 ♖ee3 a3 29 ♕d1 a2 30 ♖a3 b4 **0-1** L/N6047

**1862-★AM-1**
**MacDonnell, G.A.+ Anderssen, A.**
London♀
1 e4 e5 2 ♘f3 ♘c6 3 ♗c4 ♗c5 4 b4 ♗xb4 5 c3 ♗c5 6 0-0 d6 7 d4 exd4 8 cxd4 ♗b6 9 ♘c3 ♗g4 10 ♗b5 ♗xf3 11 gxf3 ♔f8 12 ♘e2 [□ 12 ♗e3] 12 ... ♘ce7 [□ 12 ... ♕f6] 13 f4 d5 14 e5 ♘h6 15 ♔h1 ♘hf5 16 ♖g1 g6 17 ♗a3 c6 18 ♗a4 ♔g7 19 ♗c2 ♕d7 20 ♕d3 h5 21 ♕h3 ♕e6 22 ♗xe7 ♘xe7 23 f5! ♕c8 24 f6+ ♔g8

25 e6! ♕xe6 26 ♕xe6 fxe6 27 fxe7 ♔f7 28 ♖xg6 ♔xe7 29 ♖g7+ ♔d6 30 ♖ag1 c5 31 dxc5+ ♗xc5 32 ♖xb7 ♗xf2 33 ♖gg7 ♗b6 34 ♖bd7+ ♔e5 35 ♖g5+ ♔f6 36 ♖g6+ ♔e5 37 ♖de7 **1-0** M392

**1862-★AM-2**
**Mayet, K.– Anderssen, A.**
Berlin [Anderssen & Neumann]
1 e4 e5 2 ♘f3 ♘c6 3 ♗b5 ♘f6 4 d3 ♗c5 5 c3 [□ 5 0-0] 5 ... 0-0 6 0-0 d5 7 ♗xc6 bxc6 8 ♘xe5 dxe4 9 d4 ♗b6 10 f4 c5 11 dxc5 ♗xc5+ 12 ♔h1 ♗b7 13 c4! ♖e8 14 a3 [□ 14 ♘c3] 14 ... e3 15 ♕e2 ♕d4 16 ♘c3 ♖ad8 17 ♘b5 ♕e4 18 b4 [□ 18 ♘c3 ♕f5 19 ♗xe3 ♗xe3 20 ♕xe3 ♘g4 21 ♕g3]

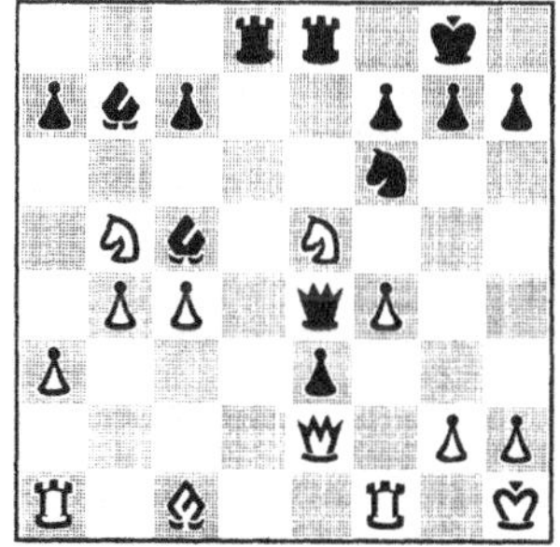

18 ... ♘h5 19 bxc5 ♘xf4 20 ♖xf4 ♕xg2+ 21 ♕xg2 ♖d1+ 22 ♖f1 ♖xf1# **0-1** L/N6051-1864

**1862-★AM-3**
**Anderssen, A.+ Mayet, K.**
Berlin [Anderssen & Neumann]
1 e4 e5 2 ♘f3 ♘c6 3 ♗c4 ♗c5 4 b4 ♗xb4 5 c3 ♗a5 6 d4 exd4 7 0-0 dxc3 8 ♕b3 ♕f6 9 e5 ♕g6 10 ♘xc3 ♗xc3 [□ 10 ... ♗b6] 11 ♕xc3 ♘ge7 12 ♗a3 0-0 13 ♖ad1 ♖e8 14 ♖fe1 a6 [□ 14 ... h6] 15 ♗d3 ♕h5 16 ♖e4 ♘g6 [16 ... ♘f5 17 g4 ♕g6 18 ♖f4 d6 19 exd6 cxd6 20 ♔h1] 17 g4 ♕h3 18 ♗f1 ♕h6 19 ♗c1 **1-0** L/N6051-1864

### 1862-★AM-4
3 vii 62

**Medley,G.W.–Anderssen,A.**

London [Bachmann]

1 e4 e5 2 ♘f3 ♘c6 3 d4 exd4 4 ♗c4 ♗c5 5 0-0 d6 6 c3 ♗g4 7 ♕b3 ♗xf3 8 gxf3 ♘e5 9 f4 ♘xc4 10 ♕xc4 ♕h4 11 cxd4 ♘f6 12 f3 ♗b6 13 ♘c3 h6 14 ♘a4? g5 15 f5 g4 16 ♘xb6 ♖g8 17 ♖f2 g3 18 hxg3 ♕xg3+ 19 ♔f1 axb6 20 ♔e2 d5 21 ♕d3 0-0-0 22 e5 ♘h5 23 ♗d2 ♕h3 24 f6 ♘g3+ 25 ♔d1 ♘e4 26 ♖f1 ♖g2 [26 ... ♖g1 27 ♔c2!] 27 ♗e3 ♖xb2 28 ♔c1 ♖h2 29 a4 ♖g8 30 fxe4 dxe4 **0-1**

L/N3033

### 1862-★AM-5

**Anderssen,A.–Medley,G.W.**

London

1 e4 e5 2 f4 exf4 3 ♘f3 g5 4 h4 g4 5 ♘e5 ♘f6 6 ♗c4 d5 7 exd5 ♗d6 8 d4 ♕e7 9 ♗xf4 ♘h5 10 g3 f6 11 ♕e2 fxe5 12 dxe5 ♗c5 13 ♘d2 ♗f5 14 0-0-0 ♘xf4 15 gxf4 ♘d7 16 e6 ♘f6 17 ♕e5 ♗g6 18 ♗b5+ ♔f8 19 f5 ♗d6 20 ♕d4 ♗c5 21 ♕d3 ♗e8 22 ♗c4 ♕d6 23 ♖hf1 b5 24 ♕c3 ♕e7 25 ♘e4 ♔g7 26 d6 cxd6 27 b4 bxc4 28 bxc5 dxc5 29 ♖d6 ♖f8 30 ♖fd1 ♔g8 31 ♕xc4 ♘xe4 32 ♕xe4 ♖b8 33 ♕xg4+ ♔h8 34 ♖g1 ♕f6 35 e7 ♕xe7 36 ♖e6 ♕b7 37 ♕g5 ♕b2+ 38 ♔d2 ♗a4 39 ♖e7 ♕xc2+ 40 ♔e3 ♕c3+ 41 ♔f4 ♖b4+ 42 ♖e4 ♖xe4+ 43 ♔xe4 ♗c6+ 44 ♔f4 ♕d4+ **0-1**

L/N6047

### 1862-★AM-6

**Mieses, S.–Anderssen, A.**

Breslau

1 e4 e5 2 ♘f3 ♘c6 3 ♗c4 ♗c5 4 b4 ♗xb4 5 c3 ♗a5 6 d4 exd4 7 0-0 ♗b6 8 cxd4 d6 9 d5 ♘a5 10 ♗b2 ♘e7 11 ♗d3 0-0 12 h3 ♘g6 13 ♕d2 c5 14 ♘a3 ♗d7 15 ♖ac1 ♕e7 16 ♖fe1 ♖ae8 17 ♔h2 ♕d8 18 g3 f6 19 ♘h4 ♘xh4 20 gxh4 ♖f7 21 ♖g1 ♔h8 22 ♖g3 c4 23 ♗b1 ♖e5 24 f4 ♖h5 25 f5 ♖xh4 26 ♖e1 ♗c5 27 ♖e2 b5 28 ♘c2 c3 29 ♗xc3 ♘c4 30 ♕e1 ♘e5 31 ♘e3 g5 32 ♗xe5 dxe5 33 ♘g2 ♖h5 34 ♖g4 ♗d6 35 ♕f2 ♖g7 36 ♗d3 ♖g6 37 ♕xa7 ♖gh6 38 ♖e3 ♕c8 39 ♖eg3 ♗xf5 40 ♗e2 ♗xe4 41 ♘e3 ♗g6 42 ♕b6 ♕f8 43 ♗f1 e4 **0-1**

L/N6047-1863

### 1862-★AM-7
vi 62

**Mongredien, A.– Anderssen, A.**

London [Bachmann]

1 e4 e5 2 f4 exf4 3 ♗c4 d5 4 exd5 ♕h4+ 5 ♔f1 g5 6 d4 ♘e7 7 ♘f3 ♕h5 8 ♘c3 ♗f5 9 ♘b5 ♘a6 10 d6 0-0-0 11 dxe7 ♗xe7 12 ♘xa7+ ♔b8 13 ♘c6+ bxc6 14 ♗xa6 ♗c5 15 c3 ♗b6 16 a4 ♔a8 17 ♗e2? [□ 17 a5 ♗a7 18 ♕a4 ♖d6 19 ♘e5] 17 ... f6 18 b4 ♕g6 19 b5 ♗a5 20 ♗d2 ♖he8 21 bxc6 ♗c2 22 ♕c1 ♖xe2! 23 ♔xe2 g4 24 ♘e1 ♖e8+ 25 ♔f2 g3+ 26 ♔g1 ♖e2 27 ♘f3? [□ 27 ♕b2 ♗b6 28 a5] 27 ... ♖xg2+ 28 ♔xg2 gxh2+ 29 ♔f1 ♗d3+ 30 ♔e1 ♕g3+ 31 ♔d1 ♕xf3+ 32 ♔e1 ♕e2# **0-1**

L/N3033

### 1862-★AM-8

**MacDonnell,G.A.–Anderssen,A.**

London [Boden]

1 e4 e5 2 ♘f3 ♘c6 3 ♗c4 ♗c5 4 b4 ♗xb4 5 c3 ♗a5 6 d4 exd4 7 0-0 d6 8 cxd4 ♗b6 9 ♘c3 ♗g4 10 ♗b5 ♗xf3 11 gxf3 ♔f8 12 ♘e2 ♕f6 13 ♗xc6 bxc6 14 f4 h5 15 ♔h1 ♕h4 16 e5 ♘h6 17 ♕d3∓ ♘g4 18 ♕g3 ♕xg3 19 hxg3 h4 20 ♔g2 hxg3 21 fxg3 ♖h2+ 22 ♔f3 f5 23 ♗a3 ♔f7 24 ♖ac1 c5 25 e6+?! ♔xe6 26 dxc5

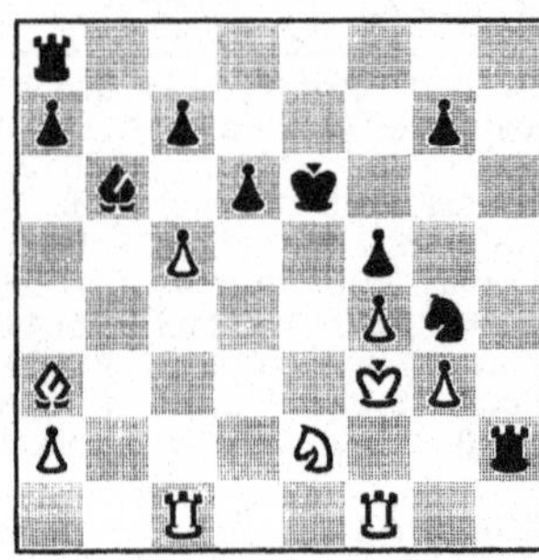

26 ... ♔f7! 27 cxb6 ♖e8 28 ♖xc7+ ♔g6 29 ♗c5 dxc5 **0-1**

M392

### 1862-★AM-9

**MacDonnell,G.A.=Anderssen,A.**

London [Boden]

1 e4 e5 2 f4 exf4 3 ♘f3 g5 4 h4 g4 5 ♘g5?! h6 6 ♘xf7 ♔xf7 7 ♗c4+ [7 ♕xg4] 7 ... d5 8 ♗xd5+ ♔e8 9 d4 c6?! 10 ♗b3 f3 11 gxf3 ♗e7 12 0-0 g3 13 f4 ♘f6 14 f5 h5 15 e5 ♘g4 16 f6 ♘f2 17 ♕d2 ♗h3 18 ♖e1 ♘a6 19 fxe7 ♕xe7 20 ♕g5 ♕xg5 21 ♗xg5 ♗g4 22 ♗f6 [□ 22 ♘d2] 22 ... ♗f3 [Δ 23 ... ♘h3+, 24 ... g2#] 23 ♗e6 ♘c7 24 ♘d2 ♘xe6 25 ♘xf3 ♘f4 26 ♗xh8 ♘2h3+ 27 ♔h1 ♘f2+ 28 ♔g1 **½-½**

M392

### 1862-★AM-10

**Mongredien, A.= Anderssen, A.**

London [Löwenthal]

1 f4 f5 2 ♘f3 ♘f6 3 c4 e6 4 d4 ♗b4+ 5 ♗d2 ♗xd2+ 6 ♘bxd2 c5 7 e3 b6 8 ♗d3 ♘c6 9 0-0 0-0 10 ♘b3 ♘e7 11 ♕d2 d6 12 ♖ad1 ♗b7 13 ♗e2 ♘e4 14 ♕c2 ♔h8 15 ♘bd2 ♖f6 16 ♘g5! [Δ ♗f3] 16 ... h6? [□ 16 ... ♘xd2 Δ 17 ... h6] 17 ♘gxe4 fxe4 18 ♘xe4 ♖f8 19 dxc5 ♘f5 20 ♕d3 dxc5 21 ♗f3 ♕c7 22 ♕e2 ♘h4! 23 ♘d2 ♘xf3+ 24 ♘xf3 ♗e4 25 ♘e5 ♖ad8 26 ♕h5 ♔g8 27 ♕g4 ♗f5 28 ♕f3 ♕c8 29 ♖xd8 ♖xd8 30 h3 ♖d2 31 ♖f2 ♕d8 32 ♔h2 ♖xf2 33 ♕xf2 ♗e4 34 ♕e2 ♕d6± **½-½**

M324-1863

### 1862-★AM-11

**Mongredien, A.– Anderssen, A.**

London [Staunton]

1 e4 e5 2 f4 exf4 3 ♗c4 d5 4 exd5 ♕h4+ 5 ♔f1 g5 6 d4 ♘e7 7 ♘f3 ♕h5 8 ♘c3 ♗f5 9 ♘b5 ♘a6 10 d6!? 0-0-0? 11 dxe7 ♗xe7 12 ♘xa7+ ♔b8 13 ♘c6+ bxc6 14 ♗xa6 ♗c5 15 c3 ♗b6 16 a4 ♔a8 17 ♗e2 [□ 17 a5] 17 ... f6 18 b4 ♕g6 19 b5 ♗a5 20 ♗d2 ♖he8 21 bxc6 ♗c2 22 ♕c1 ♖xe2!? 23 ♔xe2 g4 24 ♘e1 ♖e8+ 25 ♔f2 g3+ 26 ♔g1 ♖e2 27 ♘f3?? [□ 27 ♕b2+-]

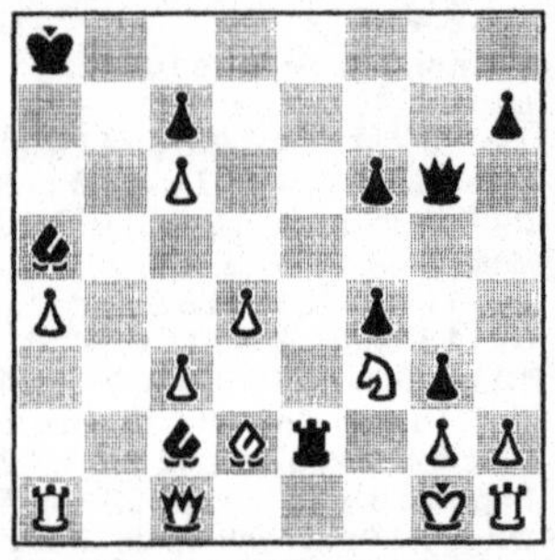

27 ... ♖xg2+ 28 ♔xg2 gxh2+ 29 ♔f1 ♗d3+ 30 ♔e1 ♕g3+ **0-1**

M954-1863

### 1862-★AP-1
vi 62

**Anderssen, A.– Paulsen, L.**

London

1 e4 e5 2 ♘f3 ♘c6 3 ♗c4 ♗c5 4 b4 ♗xb4 5 c3 ♗c5 6 0-0 d6 7 d4 exd4 8 cxd4 ♗b6 9 h3 ♘a5 10 ♗d3 ♘e7 11 d5 0-0 12 ♘c3 ♘g6 13 ♘a4 c5 14 ♘xb6 axb6 15 ♗b2 f6 16 ♘d2 ♘e5 17 ♗e2 ♗d7 18 f4 ♘g6 19 ♗d3 b5 20 ♕h5 ♕b6 21 ♔h1 c4 22 ♗c2 ♕e3 23 ♖ad1 c3 24 ♖f3 ♕e2 25 e5 cxb2 26 e6 b1♕ 27 ♖xb1 ♕xd2 28 ♗f5 ♗e8 29 ♖bf1 ♘c4 30 ♖d3 ♕b2 31 ♖g3

♖xa2 32 ♖ff3 ♘d2 33 e7 ♕c1+ 34 ♔h2 ♘xf3+ 35 ♖xf3 ♖xg2+ 36 ♔xg2 ♘xf4+ **0-1** L/N6047

**1862-★AP-2** vi 62
**Paulsen, L.= Anderssen, A.**
Köln [Löwenthal]

1 e4 e5 2 ♘f3 ♘c6 3 d4 exd4 4 ♘xd4 ♘xd4 5 ♕xd4 ♘e7 6 ♗c4 [□ 6 ♗g5] 6 ... ♘c6 7 ♕d5 ♕f6 8 0-0 ♗b4 9 c3 ♗a5 10 e5 ♕f5 11 ♘d2 0-0 12 ♘f3 ♗b6 13 ♗d3 ♕h5 14 ♗f4 d6 15 ♖ae1 ♗e6 16 ♕e4 dxe5 17 ♘xe5 ♘xe5 18 ♗xe5 f5 19 ♕a4 [□ 19 ♕f4 (19 ... g5 20 ♕g3±)] 19 ... ♖ae8 20 ♗c4 ♕f7 21 ♗xe6 ♖xe6 22 ♗d4 c5 23 ♖xe6 ♕xe6 24 ♗e3 h6 25 h4 ♔h7 26 ♖d1 ♖f6 27 ♕d7 ♕e4 28 g3 ♖g6 29 ♔h2 ♕f3 30 ♖d6 ♖xd6 [30 ... ♖g4? 31 ♖xh6+] 31 ♕xd6 c4 32 ♗xb6 axb6 33 ♕xb6 f4 34 ♕d4 fxg3+ 35 fxg3 ♕e2+ 36 ♔g1 ♕e1+ 37 ♔g2 ♕e2+ 38 ♕f2 ♕d3 39 a4 h5 **½-½** M324

**1862-★AP-3** viii 62
**Anderssen, A.– Paulsen, L.**
Breslau [Löwenthal]

1 e4 e5 2 f4 exf4 3 ♘f3 g5 4 h4 g4 5 ♘e5 ♗g7 6 ♘xg4 d5 7 ♘f2 ♘e7 8 ♘c3 0-0 9 d3 f5 10 exd5 ♘xd5 11 ♘xd5 ♕xd5 12 ♕f3 ♕c5 13 ♔d1 ♘c6 14 ♕xf4 ♔h8 15 c3 ♗e6 16 ♗e3 ♕b5 17 ♔c1 ♖ae8 18 d4 ♗c4 19 ♘d1 [19 ♗xc4? ♕xc4 △ ... ♘b4∓] 19 ... ♖e4 20 ♗xc4 ♕xc4 21 ♕f1 ♕e6 22 ♕d3 ♘e7 23 ♗d2 ♘d5 24 ♔c2 [□ 24 c4] 24 ... ♖e2 25 ♔b1 f4 26 c4 ♘b6 27 ♘c3 ♖xg2 28 b3 ♕g6 29 ♔c2 ♗xd4 30 ♖ad1 f3! 31 ♘e4 c5 32 h5 ♕f5 33 b4 ♘xc4 34 bxc5 ♘e3+ 35 ♔c1 ♕e5 36 ♖de1 f2 **0-1** M324-1863

**1862-★AP-4 ○●**
**Anderssen, A.– Paulsen, L.**
London

⟨♘b1⟩ 1 f4 d5 2 e3 g6 3 h3 e6 4 ♘f3 ♗g7 5 ♗e2 ♘h6 6 0-0 a5 7 c4 ♘c6 8 a3 0-0 9 g4 e5 10 cxd5 ♕xd5 11 f5 e4 12 ♘e1 ♕d8 13 fxg6 hxg6 14 ♘g2 ♘e5 15 ♖b1 f5 16 b4 fxg4 17 hxg4 ♗xg4 18 ♗xg4 ♘hxg4 19 ♖xf8+ ♕xf8 20 ♕e2 ♘f3+ 21 ♔h1 ♗f6 22 ♕c4+ ♔h8 23 ♘h4 ♕h6 24 ♔g2 ♕xh4 **0-1** M324-1863

**1862-★AP-5**
**Anderssen, A.– Paulsen, L.**
[Boden]

1 e4 e5 2 ♘f3 ♘c6 3 ♗c4 ♗c5 4 b4 ♗xb4 5 c3 ♗a5 6 d4 exd4 7 0-0 ♗b6 8 cxd4 d6 9 d5 ♘a5 [9 ... ♘e5!?] 10 ♗b2 ♘e7 11 ♗d3 0-0 12 ♘c3 ♘g6 13 ♘a4 c5 14 ♘xb6 axb6 15 ♕c1 f6 16 ♘e1 ♗d7 17 f4 c4 18 ♗c2 ♕c7 19 ♗d4 b5 [△ ... b4] 20 ♘f3 b4 21 ♕e3 b3 22 ♗b1 c3? 23 axb3 ♘xb3 24 ♖xa8 ♖xa8 25 ♗xc3 ♗b5 26 ♖e1 ♘a5 27 ♘d4 ♗d7 28 ♘e6 ♗xe6 29 bxe6 ♘c4 30 ♕f2 ♘a3 31 ♗d4 ♘xb1 32 ♖xb1 ♕c4 33 f5 ♖a2 34 ♕e3? ♕c2 **0-1** M392-1863

**1862-★AP-6**
**Anderssen, A.– Paulsen, W.**
[Löwenthal]

1 e4 e5 2 ♘f3 ♘c6 3 ♗c4 ♗c5 4 b4 ♗xb4 5 c3 ♗a5 6 d4 exd4 7 0-0 ♗b6 8 cxd4 d6 9 ♘c3 ♘a5 [□ 9 ... ♗g4] 10 ♗d3 ♘e7 11 ♘a4 0-0 12 ♘xb6 axb6 13 ♘h4 [△ ♕h5] 13 ... f6 14 f4 f5 15 ♕h5 g6 16 ♕h6 d5 17 e5 ♘b3 18 ♘f3 ♖f7 19 ♘g5 ♕f8 20 ♘xf7 ♘xa1 21 ♗b1? [□ 21 ♗b2] 21 ... ♕xf7 22 ♖f2 ♖a4 23 ♗b2 ♖b4 24 ♕h3 ♗d7 25 ♕a3 ♘c6 26 ♖f1 ♕f8 27 ♗xa1 ♘xd4 28 ♗d3 ♕c5 29 ♕a8+ ♔g7 30 ♔h1 ♘e6 31 ♕xb7 ♖xf4 32 ♖xf4 ♘xf4 33 e6+ ♔h6 34 ♗f1 [34 ... ♘e2–+] **0-1** M324-1863

**1862-★AR-1** vi 62
**Rivière, J.A. de+ Anderssen, A.**
London [Staunton]

1 e4 e5 2 ♘f3 ♘c6 3 ♗c4 ♗c5 4 ♘c3 ♘f6 5 d3 d6 6 h3 h6 7 ♕e2 0-0 8 g4 ♘h7 [8 ... ♘xg4 (9 hxg4 ♗xg4 10 ♖g1 ♘d4 11 ♖xg4 ♘xe2 12 ♔xe2 ♔h8 13 ♗d2 △ 14 ♖h1 +–)] 9 ♗d2 a6 10 0-0-0 ♘d4 11 ♘xd4 exd4 [□ 11 ... ♗xd4] 12 ♘d5 b5 13 ♗b3 c6 14 ♘f4 a5 15 c4 a4 16 ♗c2 b4 17 b3 axb3 18 ♗xb3 ♕b6 [△ 19 ... ♖xa2!] 19 ♔b1 ♗e6 20 ♗c1 ♖a7 21 ♖d2 g5 22 ♘h5 f6 23 f4 ♖e7 24 ♕f3 d5 25 exd5 cxd5 26 cxd5 ♗f7 27 ♖c2 ♖fe8 28 fxg5 fxg5 29 ♖f1 ♔h8 30 ♘f6 ♖d8 31 ♘e4 [31 ♘xh7 (31 ... ♔xh7 32 d6 ♗xb3 33 dxe7 ♗xc2+ 34 ♔xc2+–)] 31 ... ♗d6 [31 ... ♗xd5 (32 ♗xd5 ♖xd5 33 ♘xg5 ♖xg5 34 ♗xg5 hxg5 35 ♕a8+ ♔g7 36 ♕d5 ♖c7 37 ♖xc5 ♖xc5 38 ♕f7+ ♔h8 39 ♕e8+ ♔g7 40 ♖f7+ ♔h6 41 ♖e7+–)] 32 ♖c6 ♕b8 33 ♘xd6 ♖xd6 34 ♕g3 ♗g6 35 ♗b2 ♘f8 36 ♗xd4+ ♔h7 37 ♖xd6 **1-0** M954

**1862-★AR-2**
**Rosanes, J.+ Anderssen, A.**
Breslau

1 e4 e5 2 ♘f3 ♘c6 3 ♗b5 ♘f6 4 0-0 ♘xe4 5 ♖e1 ♘f6 6 d4 e4 7 d5 a6 8 ♗a4 b5 9 ♗b3 ♘a5 10 ♘c3 ♘xb3 11 ♘xe4 ♘xe4 12 ♖xe4+ ♗e7 13 d6 cxd6 14 ♗g5 f6 15 ♗xf6 gxf6 16 ♘h4 0-0 17 ♘f5 ♔h8 18 ♖xe7 ♕xe7 19 ♘xe7 ♘xa1 20 ♕h5 ♗b7 21 ♘g6+ ♔g7 22 ♘xf8 ♖xf8 23 ♕d1 ♖c8 24 c3 ♔f7 25 ♕xa1 ♖g8 26 g3 ♗c6 27 ♕d1 ♖e8 28 ♕h5+ ♔f8 29 f4 **1-0** L/N6047-1863

**1862-★AR-3**
**Rosanes, J.= Anderssen, A.**
Breslau

1 e4 e5 2 ♘f3 ♘c6 3 ♗b5 ♘f6 4 0-0 ♘xe4 5 ♖e1 ♘f6 6 d4 e4 7 d5 a6 8 ♗a4 b5 9 ♗b3 ♘a5 10 ♘c3 ♗e7 11 d6 cxd6 12 ♘xe4 ♘xe4 13 ♖xe4 ♘xb3 14 axb3 0-0 15 ♖g4 ♔h8 16 ♕d5 ♖b8 17 ♘g5 f5 18 ♖g3 ♕e8 19 ♘xh7 ♗b7 20 ♖h3 ♗h4 21 ♕d1 ♔xh7 22 ♖xh4+ ♔g8 23 ♗f4 ♖f6 24 ♗xd6 ♕g6 25 ♗g3 f4 26 ♖g4 ♕f7 27 ♗h4 ♖e6 28 f3 ♖be8 29 ♕d4 ♖e2 30 ♖xf4 ♕h5 31 ♕xd7 ♖xc2 32 ♗f2 ♗c6 33 ♕g4 ♕h6 34 ♕f5 ♖ee2 35 ♕f7+ ♔h8 36 ♖h4 ♕xh4 37 ♗xh4 ♖xg2+ 38 ♔f1 ♖xh2 **½-½** L/N3034

**1862-★AR-4**
**Rosanes, J.– Anderssen, A.**
Breslau

1 e4 e5 2 f4 d5 3 exd5 e4 4 ♗b5+ c6 5 dxc6 ♘xc6 6 ♘c3 ♘f6 7 ♕e2 ♗c5 8 ♘xe4 0-0 9 ♗xc6 bxc6 10 d3 ♖e8 11 ♗d2 ♘xe4 12 dxe4 ♗f5 13 e5 ♕b6 14 0-0-0 ♗d4 15 c3 ♖ab8 16 b3 ♖ed8 17 ♘f3 ♕xb3 18 axb3 ♖xb3 19 ♗e1 ♗e3+ **0-1** L/N3034

**1862-★AR-5**
**Rosanes, J.+ Anderssen, A.**
Breslau

1 e4 e5 2 ♘f3 ♘c6 3 ♗c4 ♗c5 4 b4 ♗xb4 5 c3 ♗c5 6 0-0 d6 7 d4 exd4 8 cxd4 ♗b6 9 d5 ♘a5 10 ♗b2 ♘f6 11 ♗d3 0-0 12 ♘c3 ♗d7 13 ♕d2 c5 14 ♘e2 ♗c7 15 ♕g5 h6 16 ♕f4 ♘h5 17 ♕e3 b5 18 ♘f4 ♘xf4 19 ♕xf4 c4 20 ♕g3 f6 21 ♗c2 ♕e7 22 ♖ae1 b4 23 ♘d4 c3 24 ♘f5 ♗xf5 25 exf5 ♕f7 26 ♗c1 ♔h7 27 ♖e4 ♖ae8 28 ♖g4 ♖e7 29 ♖g6 ♖fe8 30 ♗xh6 gxh6 31 ♕h4 ♕f8 32 ♖xf6 ♖f7 33 ♖xh6+ ♕xh6 34 f6+ ♔g8 35 ♕xh6 ♖e5 36 ♗g6 ♖xf6 37 ♕h7+ ♔f8 38 ♕h8+ ...? **1-0** L/N3034

**1862-★AS-1** vi 62
**St. Bon– Anderssen, A.**
London [Journoud]

1 e4 e5 2 f4 exf4 3 ♘f3 g5 4 ♗c4 g4 5 0-0 gxf3 6 ♕xf3 ♕e7 7 d3 d6 8 ♗xf4 ♗e6 9 ♗g5 f6 10 ♗xe6 ♕xe6 11 ♘c3 ♘d7 12 ♘d5 0-0-0 13 ♗e3 ♘h6 14 h3 ♘f7 15 ♗d4 ♘fe5 16 ♕e2 h5 17 c4 ♗h6 18 b4 ♖dg8 19 ♗e3? ♕xh3 20 ♗xh6 ♖g3! [20 ... ♖xh6? 21 ♕e7+] 21 ♗f4 ♘g4 **0-1** L/N6016-1863

**1862-★AS-2**
**St.Bon & Stewart+**
**Anderssen,A.**
London [Journoud]
1 e4 e5 2 f4 exf4 3 ♘f3 g5 4 ♗c4 g4 5 0-0 gxf3 6 ♕xf3 ♕e7 7 d4 ♘c6 8 ♕f2 [8 c3 ♘e5! 9 dxe5 ♕c5+] 8 ... ♗g7 9 e5 d6 10 ♗xf4 dxe5 11 d5!? exf4? [11 ... ♘a5] 12 dxc6 ♕e3?± 13 ♖e1 ♗d4 14 ♔h1! ♘f6 15 ♖xe3+ ♗xe3 16 ♕h4 ♘e4 17 ♘c3 ♘f2+ 18 ♔g1+− ♖g8 [18 ... ♘e4+ 19 ♔f1 ♘d2+ 20 ♔e2 ♘xc4 21 ♘d5] 19 ♘d5 ♘g4+ 20 ♔f1 ♔f8 21 ♕e7+ ♔g7 22 h3 bxc6 23 ♘xc7 ♘h6 24 ♕g5+ ♔h8 25 ♕xh6 ♖xg2!? 26 ♘xa8 [26 ♔xg2?? f3+] 26 ... ♖g1+ 27 ♔e2 ♖g2+ 28 ♔f3 ♖g3+ 29 ♔e4 ♗xh3 30 ♕f6+ ♖g7 31 ♖d1 **1-0**
L/N6016-1863

**1862-★AS-3** vii 62
**Anderssen, A.− Steinitz, W.**
London [Löwenthal]
1 e4 e5 2 ♘f3 ♘c6 3 ♗c4 ♗c5 4 b4 ♗xb4 5 c3 ♗c5 6 0-0 d6 7 d4 exd4 8 cxd4 ♗b6 9 d5!? ♘ce7 [□ 9 ... ♘a5] 10 e5 [□ 10 ♗d3] 10 ... ♘g6 11 ♗b2 ♘8e7 12 ♕a4+ [12 exd6?! ♕xd6 13 ♗xg7 ♖g8 14 ♗b2 ♘f4 15 g3 ♕d7 16 ♔h1 ♕h3 17 ♖g1 ♗xf2−+] 12 ... ♗d7 13 ♕a3 dxe5 14 ♘xe5 0-0 15 ♕c3 [□ 15 d6 cxd6 16 ♕xd6 ♗e6 17 ♕a3 ♗xc4 18 ♘xc4 ♖c8 19 ♘bd2±] 15 ... ♘f5 16 ♘xd7 ♕xd7 17 g4 ♗d4 18 ♕c2 ♗xb2 19 ♕xb2 ♘fh4 20 f3? ♘xf3+ 21 ♔h1 [21 ♖xf3? ♕xg4+−+] 21 ... ♘fe5 22 ♗b3 ♕xg4 23 ♘d2 ♘d3 24 ♕c3 ♘h4 **0-1**
L/N6124-1863

**1862-★AS-4**
**Steinitz, W.− Anderssen, A.**
[Löwenthal]
1 e4 e5 2 ♘c3 ♗c5 3 ♗c4 [3 f4!?] 3 ... ♘f6 4 d3 d6 5 ♘f3 ♘c6 6 0-0 ♗g4 7 ♗e3 a6 8 ♔h1 ♗a7 9 ♖g1 h6 10 h3 ♗h5 11 g4 ♗g6 12 ♘e2 d5 13 exd5 ♘xd5 14 ♗xa7 ♖xa7 15 d4 ♘b6 16 ♗b3 h5 17 g5? [□ 17 ♘xe5=] 17 ... ♕d7 18 ♔h2 exd4 19 ♘exd4 ♕d6+ 20 ♔g2 0-0 21 ♘e2 ♕c5 22 ♖e1 ♖aa8 [□ 22 ... ♗e4] 23 ♘f4 ♖ad8 24 ♕e2 ♘d4 25 ♕e7 ♕c6 26 ♖e3? [□ 26 ♘xg6∞] 26 ... ♘xf3 27 ♖xf3 ♗e4 28 g6 ♗xf3+ 29 ♔g3 ♘d5 30 gxf7+ ♔h8 31 ♗xd5 ♗xd5 **0-1**
M324-1863

**1862-★AS-5**
**Steinitz, W.− Anderssen, A.**
London [Bachmann]
1 e4 e5 2 f4 exf4 3 ♘f3 g5 4 ♗c4 g4 5 0-0 gxf3 6 ♕xf3 ♕e7? 7 d4 ♘c6 8 ♘c3 ♘xd4 9 ♕d3? ♘e6 10 ♘d5 ♕c5+ 11 ♔h1 b5 12 ♗b3 ♗h6 13 ♗d2 ♕f8 14 ♕c3 ♕g7 15 ♘xc7+ ♘xc7 16 ♕xc7 ♘e7 17 ♗c3 f6 18 e5 ♖f8 19 ♖ae1 [□ 19 ♗a5!] 19 ... ♗a6 20 exf6? ♖xf6 21 ♗b4 ♖c6

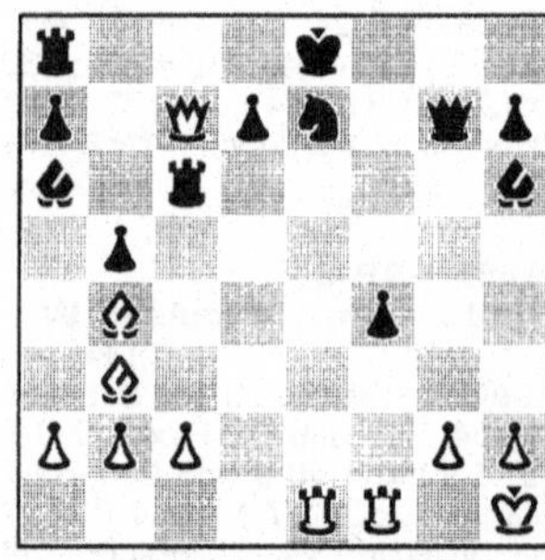

22 ♕a5? [□ 22 ♗xe7! ♖xc7 23 ♗g5+ ♔f8 24 ♖xf4+−] 22 ... ♗g5 23 ♗xe7 ♗xe7 24 ♖xf4 ♖f6 25 ♕c3 ♔d8 26 ♕a5+ ♔c8 27 ♗d5 [27 ♖xe7? ♖xf4!] 27 ... ♖b8 28 ♖fe4 ♖bb6 29 h3 ♖fe6 30 ♗xe6 dxe6 31 a4 b4 32 ♕h5 ♗d8 33 ♖d1 ♕e7 34 ♖ed4 ♗c7 35 ♖g4 ♔b7 36 ♖g8 ♖c6 37 ♕f3 ♗c4 38 ♖g4 ♗d5 39 ♕e2 ♕d6 40 ♔g1 ♕h2+ 41 ♔f1 ♗b6 **0-1**
L/N3033

**1862-★A?-1**
**Anderssen, A.=?**
Breslau
⟨♘b1⟩1 e4 e5 2 ♘f3 ♘c6 3 ♗b5 ♗c5 4 c3 ♘ge7 5 0-0 a6 6 ♗a4 b5 7 ♗c2 0-0 8 d4 exd4 9 cxd4 ♗b6 10 d5 ♘a7 11 b4 d6 12 ♗b2 ♘g6 13 ♔h1 f5 14 e5 ♘xe5 15 ♘xe5 dxe5 16 ♗xe5 ♗b7 17 ♗b3 ♔h8 18 f4 ♘c8 19 ♖f3 ♘d6 20 ♖h3 ♕e8 21 ♕c2 ♖d8 22 ♕b2 ♖f7 23 ♖d1 ♘c4 24 ♕e2 ♘xe5 25 fxe5 ♖f6 26 e6 c6 27 d6 ♗c8 28 e7 ♖dxd6 29 ♖xd6 ♖xd6 30 ♕h5 ♕xh5 31 ♖xh5 ♗d7 32 ♖xf5 ♖f6 33 ♖xf6 gxf6 34 ♗f7 ♔g7 35 e8♕ ♗xe8 36 ♗xe8 **½-½**
L/N3034

**1862-★A?-2**
**Anderssen, A.+?**
1 e4 e5 2 ♘f3 ♘c6 3 ♗c4 ♘f6 4 ♘g5 d5 5 exd5 ♘a5 6 ♗b5+ c6 7 dxc6 bxc6 8 ♗e2 h6 9 ♘f3 e4 10 ♘e5 ♕d4 11 f4 ♗c5 12 ♖f1 ♘b7 13 c3 ♕d6 14 ♕a4 ♗d7 15 b4 ♗b6 16 ♘a3 0-0 17 ♘ac4 ♕c7 18 ♗a3 ♘d5 19 ♘xd7 ♕xd7 20 ♘e5 ♕e7 21 b5 ♕h4+ 22 g3 ♕xh2 23 ♗xf8 ♕xg3+ 24 ♔d1 ♘xc3+ 25 dxc3 ♕xc3 26 ♗e7 ♗e3 27 ♘c4 cxb5 28 ♕a3 **1-0**
L/N3034

**1862-★A?-3**
**?− Anderssen, A.**
1 e4 e5 2 ♘f3 ♘c6 3 ♗c4 ♗c5 4 c3 ♘f6 5 d4 exd4 6 cxd4 ♗b4+ 7 ♗d2 ♗xd2+ 8 ♘bxd2 d5 9 exd5 ♘xd5 10 ♕b3 ♘ce7 11 0-0 0-0 12 ♖fe1 a5 13 a4 h6 14 ♘e4 ♘f4 15 ♘e5 ♗e6 16 ♖ad1 ♗xc4 17 ♕xc4 ♖a6 18 ♖e3 ♘f5 19 ♖f3 ♕h4 20 ♘c5 ♖d6 21 g3 ♘h3+ 22 ♔g2 ♕h5 23 g4 ♖g6 24 ♘xg6 ♕xg4+ 25 ♖g3 ♘xg3 26 ♘e7+ ♔h8 27 f3 ♘f4+ 28 ♔f2 ♘h1+ 29 ♖xh1 ♕g2+ 30 ♔e3 ♖e8 31 ♔xf4 ♕g5+ 32 ♔e4 ♖xe7+ 33 ♔d3 ♖e3+ 34 ♔c2 ♕g2+ 35 ♔b1 ♕xh1+ 36 ♔a2 ♕xf3 ... ? **0-1**
L/N3034

**1862-★BC-1 ●o⌂** 4 vii 62
**Blackburne, J.H.+ Chinnery, W.M.**
London [Blackburne]
1 e4 e5 2 ♘f3 ♘c6 3 ♗b5 ♘f6 4 0-0 ♗c5 5 d3 ♕e7 6 ♗g5 h6 7 ♗xf6 ♕xf6 8 ♘c3 a6 9 ♘d5 ♕d8 10 ♗a4 b5 11 ♗b3 d6 12 c3 ♗g4 13 ♘e3 ♗xf3 14 ♕xf3 0-0 15 ♗d5 ♕d7 16 ♘f5 ♔h7 17 d4 ♗b6 18 ♕g4 ♖g8+− 19 ♘xh6 ♕xg4 20 ♘xg4 ♘e7 21 ♗xa8 ♖xa8 22 dxe5 dxe5 23 ♘xe5 f6 24 ♘g4 ♖e8 25 ♔h1 ♘g6 26 ♖fe1 ♘f4 27 g3 ♘d3 28 ♖e2 f5 29 ♖d1 ♘c5 30 ♘e3 ♘xe4 31 ♔g2 ♘f6 32 ♖ee1 g5 33 ♘d5 ♖xe1 34 ♘xf6+ ♔g7 35 ♘h5+ ♔h6 36 ♖xe1 ♔xh5 37 f4 ♗c5 38 ♖e8 ♔h6 39 ♖a8 ♗d6 40 ♖xa6 **1-0**
L/N3036

**1862-★BE-1 ●o⌂** 4 vii 62
**Blackburne,J.H.+ Evelyn,W.J.**
London [Blackburne]
1 e4 e5 2 d4 exd4 3 ♗c4 ♗c5 [3 ... ♘c6] 4 ♗xf7+ ♔xf7 5 ♕h5+ g6 6 ♕d5+ ♔g7 7 ♕xc5 d5 8 ♕xd4+ ♘f6 9 ♗g5 dxe4 10 ♗xf6+ ♕xf6 11 ♕xf6+ ♔xf6 12 ♘c3 ♔f5 [12 ... ♗f5? 13 ♘d5+] 13 ♘ge2 ♗e6 14 ♘g3+ ♔f4 15 ♘gxe4± ♘c6 16 0-0 ♖ad8 17 g3+ ♔f5 18 f4 ♘d4 19 ♖f2 h5 20 h3 ♗c4 21 ♖e1 ♖hf8 22 ♘d2 ♗e6 23 ♖e5+ ♔f6 24 ♘de4+ ♔g7 25 ♘g5 ♗f7 26 ♖e7 ♖c8 27 ♖d7 c5 28 ♘ce4 ♖cd8 29 ♖xb7 ♔g8 30 ♘f6+ ♔g7 31 ♘d7! ♗d5 32 ♘xf8+ **1-0**
L/N3036

**1862-★BG-1 ●o⌂** 4 vii 62
**Blackburne,J.H.− Gillam,J.F.**
London [Blackburne]
1 e4 c5 2 ♘f3 e6 3 d4 d5 4 ♗b5+ ♗d7 5 ♗xd7+ ♘xd7 6 dxc5 ♘xc5 7 exd5 ♕xd5 8 ♕xd5 exd5 9 0-0 ♗d6 10 ♘c3 ♖d8 11 a3 ♘e7 12 ♗g5 f6 13 ♗h4 0-0 14 ♖ad1 ♘e4 15 ♘d4 ♘xc3 16 bxc3 ♖c8 17 ♖d3 ♖c4 18 f4 ♘g6 19 ♗g3 ♗c5 20 ♗e1 ♖e8 21 ♔h1 ♗xa3 22 f5 ♘e5 23 ♖g3 ♗d6 24 ♘e6 ♘g4 25 ♖d3 ♗xh2 26 g3 g6 27 ♘d4 ♖e3 28 ♘f3 ♖ce4 29 ♖d1 ♖e2 30 ♗f2?? [30

♘d4; 30 ♖xd5=] 30 ... ♖xf2 31 ♖xf2 ♘xf2+ 32 ♔xh2 ♘xd1 **0-1**
L/N3036

**1862-★BH-1 ●○**
**Blackburne, J.H.+Hamilton**
Manchester [Blackburne]
1 e4 e5 2 f4 exf4 3 ♘f3 g5 4 ♗c4 ♗g7 5 c3 d6 6 0-0 c6 7 d4 b5 8 ♗b3 ♗b7 9 ♘xg5 ♕xg5 10 ♗xf4 ♕e7 11 ♕f3 f6 12 ♕g3 ♘a6 13 ♗xd6 ♕d7 14 e5! 0-0-0 [14 ... fxe5 15 ♕xe5+!!+-] 15 ♘d2 f5 16 ♘f3 ♗h6 17 ♖ae1 ♘e7 18 ♕h4 ♗f8 19 ♘g5 ♘g6 20 ♕h3 ♖e8 21 ♘f7 ♖g8 22 ♗xf8 ♖exf8 23 ♘d6+ ♔b8 24 ♗xg8 ♖xg8 25 ♖xf5 ♘f4 26 ♖f8+ ♔c7 27 ♕xd7+ ♔xd7 28 ♖xg8 **1-0**
L/N3036

**1862-★BH-2**
**Blackburne, J.H.+Harley**
Manchester
⟨♕d1⟩ 1 b3 e5 2 ♗b2 ♗d6 3 ♘c3 ♘e7 4 e3 0-0 5 0-0-0 c5 6 ♘ge2 b6 7 f4 ♘bc6 8 g4 a6 9 f5 ♕c7 10 ♘g3 e4 11 ♘cxe4 ♗xg3 12 hxg3 ♗b7 13 ♗c4 d5

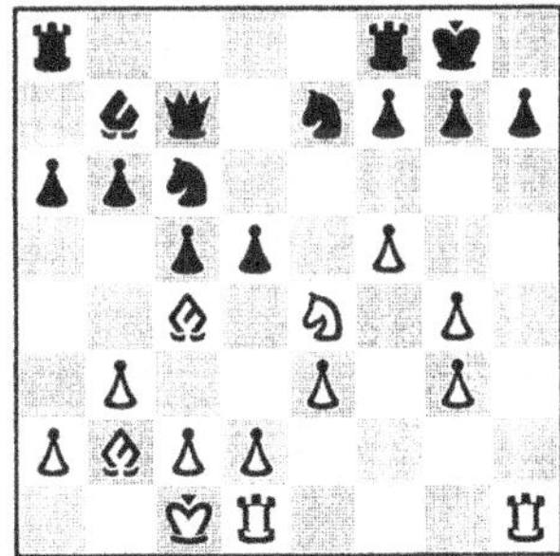

14 ♖xh7 ♔xh7 15 ♖h1+ ♔g8 16 ♘f6+ gxf6 17 ♗xf6 ♘g6 18 fxg6 fxg6 19 ♗xd5+ ♖f7 20 ♖h8# **1-0**
L/N3036

**1862-★BH-3 ●○** 4 vii 62
**Blackburne, J.H.+ Howard, A.G.**
London [Blackburne]
1 e4 e5 2 d4 exd4 3 ♘f3 ♘c6 4 ♗c4 ♗c5 5 c3 ♘f6 6 e5 ♘g4 7 0-0 0-0 8 cxd4 d5 9 ♗b3 ♗b6 10 ♘c3 ♘e7 11 h3 ♘h6 12 ♗xh6 gxh6 13 ♕d2 ♔g7 14 ♘e2 f6 15 ♘g3 ♕e8 16 ♖ae1 ♗e6 17 ♖e3 f5 18 ♘e2 f4 19 ♖c3 ♗a5 20 ♘xf4 ♕f7 21 ♘xe6+ ♕xe6 22 ♗c2 ♘g6 23 b4! ♗b6 24 ♘h2 h5 25 ♔h1 ♖f4 26 ♖d3 c6 27 g3 ♖f7 28 f4 ♔h8 29 ♖df3 ♕xh3 30 g4 ♕h4 31 g5 ♘xf4 32 ♖xf4 ♕xg5 33 ♕d3! ♖g8 34 ♖g4 hxg4 35 ♖xf7 ♕g6 36 ♖xh7+ **1-0**
L/N3036

**1862-★BJ-1 ●○**
**Blackburne, J.H.+ Jebson**
Manchester [Blackburne]
1 e4 c5 2 ♘f3 e6 3 d4 f5 4 e5 cxd4 5 ♕xd4 ♘c6 6 ♕a4 ♗c5 7 ♗d3 ♕b6 8 0-0 ♘ge7 9 ♘c3 0-0 10 ♕h4 ♘g6 11 ♕g3 f4 12 ♕h3 ♘ce7 13 ♘g5 h6 14 ♘ce4 d5 15 ♘f6+ ♔h8 16 ♕h5 ♘xe5 17 ♗xf4 ♘xd3 18 ♕f7

18 ... ♕d8 19 ♗c7 **1-0**
L/N3036

**1862-★BK-1**
**Kolisch, I.F. von+ Barbies**
Paris
⟨♘b1⟩ 1 e4 e5 2 ♘f3 ♘c6 3 ♗c4 ♗c5 4 b4 ♗xb4 5 c3 ♗c5 6 0-0 ♘f6 7 d4 exd4 8 cxd4 ♗b6 9 ♗a3 ♘a5 10 ♗d3 d6 11 e5 dxe5 12 ♖e1 e4 13 ♗xe4 ♘xe4 14 ♖xe4+ ♗e6 15 d5 ♕f6 16 dxe6 fxe6 17 ♘g5 e5 18 ♕d5 ♘c6 19 ♖f4 ♖d8 20 ♕b3 exf4 21 ♖e1+ ♔d7 22 ♕h3+ **1-0**
M324

**158** Blackburne, J.H. M1647.BL

**1862-★BL-1 ●○**
**Blackburne, J.H.+ Lomax**
Manchester [Blackburne]
1 e4 e6 2 d4 d5 3 exd5 [3 ♘c3] 3 ... exd5 4 ♘f3 ♘c6 5 ♗e3 a6 6 ♗d3 ♗g4 7 c3 h6 8 ♘bd2 ♗d6 9 ♕c2 ♗xf3 10 ♘xf3 ♘f6 11 0-0 ♘e7 12 ♘e5 ♗xe5 13 dxe5 ♘e4? 14 ♗xe4 dxe4 15 ♕xe4 ♕d5? 16 ♕xd5 ♘xd5 17 ♗d4 ♘f4 18 g3 ♘e2+ 19 ♔g2 ♘xd4 20 cxd4 0-0-0 21 ♖fd1 ♖d5 22 ♖d3 ♖hd8 23 ♖ad1 c5 24 ♔f3 c4 [24 ... ♖xd4 25 ♖xd4 ♖xd4 26 ♖xd4 cxd4 27 ♔e4+-] 25 ♖3d2 b5 26 ♔e4 g6 27 f4 ♖8d7 28 g4 ♔d8 29 f5 ♔e7 30 f6+ ♔e6 31 a3 a5 32 h4 b4 33 axb4 a4 [33 ... axb4 34 ♖a1] 34 b5 ♖b7 35 ♖c1 ♖dxb5 36 ♖xc4 ♖a7 37 ♖dc2 ♖b6 38 ♖c7 ♖xc7 39 ♖xc7 [△ 40 ♖e7#] **1-0**
L/N3036

**1862-★BP-1 ●○** 4 vii 62
**Blackburne, J.H.– Parminter, H.B.**
London [Blackburne]
1 e4 e5 2 ♗c4 ♘c6 [2 ... ♘f6] 3 ♘f3 ♗c5 4 b4 ♗xb4 5 c3 ♗c5 6 d4 exd4 7 0-0 d6 8 cxd4 ♗b6 9 ♘c3 ♗g4 10 ♗b5 ♗d7 11 e5 dxe5 12 d5 ♘d4 13 ♗xd7+ ♕xd7 14 ♘xe5 ♕f5 15 ♕a4+ ♔d8 16 ♗g5+! ♘e7 17 d6? [17 ♖fe1!+-] 17 ... cxd6 18 ♘d5 ♘f3+ 19 ♘xf3 ♕xd5 20 ♖ad1 ♕c6 21 ♕xc6 bxc6 22 ♖xd6+ ♔e8 23 ♖e1 f6 24 ♗c1 ♔f7 25 ♖d7 ♖he8 26 ♗a3 c5!∓ 27 ♘d2 ♖ad8 28 ♖xd8 ♖xd8 29 ♘b3 ♖d5 30 ♖c1 c4 31 ♖e1 cxb3 32 ♖xe7+ ♔g6 33 h3 bxa2 34 ♗b2 ♗d4 35 ♗xd4 ♖xd4 **0-1**
L/N3036

**1862-★BP-2 ●○**
**Blackburne, J.H.+ Payne**
Manchester [Blackburne]
1 e4 e5 2 ♘f3 ♘c6 3 d4 exd4 4 ♗c4 ♗c5 5 c3 dxc3 6 ♘xc3 ♗b4 7 0-0 ♗xc3 8 bxc3 ♘ge7 9 e5 h6 10 ♗a3 ♘a5 11 ♗d3 0-0 12 ♘h4 ♖e8 13 f4 ♘g6 14 ♘xg6 fxg6 15 ♗xg6 c6 16 ♗xe8 ♕xe8 17 ♗d6 b6 18 ♖f3 ♗b7 19 ♖g3 c5 20 ♕g4 ♕f7 21 f5 ♔h7 22 ♖e1 ♖g8 23 e6 dxe6 24 ♖xe6! ♘c6 25 ♗f4 [△ 26 ♗xh6 gxh6 27 ♖xh6++-] 25 ... ♘d8 26 ♖g6 ♗c8 27 ♕h5 ♕f8 28 f6 ♘f7 29 fxg7 ♖xg7 30 ♗xh6 **1-0** L/N3036

**1862-★BP-3 ●○** 4 vii 62
**Blackburne, J.H.+Pigott, A.S.**
London [Blackburne]
1 e4 e5 2 f4 exf4 3 ♘f3 d6 4 d4 ♕e7 5 ♘c3 c6 6 ♗xf4 h6 7 ♗d3 d5 8 0-0 ♘f6 9 exd5 ♘xd5 10 ♖e1 ♗e6 11 ♘xd5 cxd5 12 c4 ♕d8 13 cxd5 ♕xd5 14 ♖e5 ♕d8 15 d5 ♕b6+ 16 ♔h1 ♗d6 17 dxe6 ♗xe5 18 exf7+ ♔f8 19 ♘xe5 ♕f6

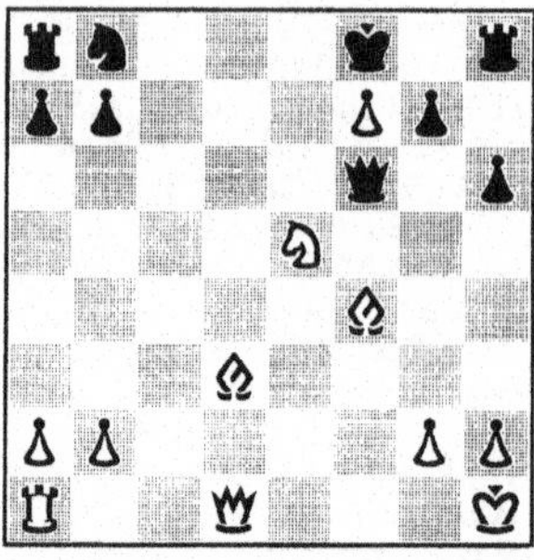

20 ♗c4! g5 21 ♘g6+ **1-0** L/N3036

**1862-★BP-4 ●○** 4 vii 62
**Blackburne,J.H.+ Puller,A.G.**
London [Blackburne]
1 e4 e5 2 f4 d5 3 exd5 e4 4 ♘c3 ♘f6 5 d3 ♗b4 6 ♗d2 exd3 7 ♗xd3 0-0 8 ♘ge2 ♗g4 9 0-0 ♗xc3 10 ♗xc3 ♘xd5 11 ♕d2 ♖e8 12 ♗d4 ♘c6 13 ♗f2 ♘db4 14 ♗c3 ♘xd3 15 ♕xd3 ♘b4 16 ♕g3 ♗e2 17 ♘xe2 ♖xe2 18 c3 ♘c2 19 ♖ad1 ♕e7 20 f5 f6 21 ♕d3 ♖e8 22 ♕d5+ ♔h8 23 ♕d3 ♕e4 24 ♕xe4 ♖2xe4 25 ♖d2 ♘e3? 26 ♖fe1 h5 27 ♖de2 ♖8e5 28 ♖xe3 ♖xe3 29 ♖xe3 ♖xf5 30 ♖e7 ♖b5 31 b4 a5 32 a3 axb4 33 axb4 ♖d5 34 ♗d4 c6 35 ♖xb7 ♖d8 36 ♖c7 ♖d6 37 ♔f2 ♖e6 38 ♖d7 ♔g8 39 ♗c5 g6 40 ♖d6 ♖xd6 41 ♗xd6 ♔f7 42 ♔e3 ♔e6 43 ♗c5 ♔d5 44 ♗d4 ♔e6 45 ♔d3 f5 46 ♗f2 ♔d5 47 c4+ ♔d6 48 ♔d4 ♔e6 49 b5 cxb5 50 cxb5 **1-0** L/N3036

**1862-★BR-1 ●○** 4 vii 62
**Blackburne,J.H.= Ravensworth**
London [Blackburne]
1 e4 c5 2 d4 cxd4 3 ♘f3 ♘c6 4 ♘xd4 e5 5 ♘b5 ♗c5 6 ♘d6+ ♗xd6 7 ♕xd6 ♘ge7 8 ♗c4 0-0 9 0-0 ♘a5 10 ♗g5 ♘xc4 [10 ... ♖e8 11 ♗d5±] 11 ♕xe7 ♕b6 12 ♘c3 f6! [12 ... ♕xb2 13 ♘d5 h6 14 ♘f6+ gxf6 15 ♗xh6 ♕a3 16 ♕xf6+-] 13 ♘d5 ♕c6 14 ♕b4 a5 15 ♕c3 ♖f7 16 ♗h4 ♘d6 17 ♕b3 ♔f8 18 ♕d3 ♘e8 19 ♗g3 d6 20 f4 b6 21 fxe5 dxe5 22 ♖f3 ♖aa7 **½-½** L/N3036

**1862-★BR-2 ●○** 4 vii 62
**Blackburne,J.H.= Rimington-Wilson**
London
1 e4 c5 2 f4 e6 3 ♘f3 ♘c6 4 d4 cxd4 5 ♘xd4 ♘xd4 6 ♕xd4 ♘e7 7 ♗e3 ♘c6 8 ♕d2 ♗e7 9 ♗d3 b6 10 0-0 ♗b7 11 ♘c3 0-0 12 ♖f3 ♘b4 13 ♖af1 f5 14 ♖h3 ♘xd3 15 cxd3 ♕e8 16 ♕e2 ♕f7 17 g4 fxg4 18 ♕xg4 ♕g6 19 ♕xg6 hxg6 20 ♖g3 ♔f7 21 ♘d1 d5 22 e5 ♖fc8 23 ♘c3 ♗a6 24 ♖d1 ♗b4 25 ♗d4 ♗c5 26 ♗f2 ♗b4 27 d4 ♖c6 28 a3 ♗e7 29 ♖g2 ♗c4 30 ♗g3 ♗b3 31 ♖d3 ♖ac8 32 h3 ♖h8 **½-½** L/N3036

**1862-★BS-1 ●○**
**Blackburne,J.H.+ Steinkühler,A.**
Manchester [Blackburne]
1 e4 e5 2 ♘f3 ♘c6 3 ♗c4 ♗c5 4 b4 ♗xb4 5 c3 ♗a5 6 0-0 d6 7 d4 exd4 8 cxd4 ♗b6 9 ♘c3 ♘a5 10 ♗d3 ♘e7 11 e5 [11 d5] 11 ... dxe5 12 dxe5 ♗g4 13 ♗g5 ♘ac6 14 ♖e1 0-0 15 ♖e4 ♗f5? [□ 15 ... ♕d7=] 16 ♕d2 ♗xe4 17 ♘xe4 ♘d4 18 ♘f6+ gxf6 19 ♗xf6 ♘xf3+ 20 gxf3 ♕d4 21 ♖f1 **1-0** L/N3036

**1862-★BW-1** ii 62
**Blackburne,J.H.+ Wellington, S.**
Manchester [Blackburne]
1 e4 e5 2 ♘f3 ♘c6 3 ♗b5 a6 4 ♗a4 ♘f6 5 0-0 ♗e7 6 d4 exd4 7 e5 ♘e4 8 ♘xd4 ♘c5 9 ♗xc6 dxc6 10 ♘c3 ♘e6 11 ♗e3 ♘xd4 12 ♗xd4 0-0 13 ♘e4 ♗e6 14 f4 ♗d5 15 ♘g3 f5 16 b3 c5 17 ♗b2 ♗h4 18 ♕h5 ♗f7 19 ♕f3 ♕d5 20 ♘xf5 ♗d8 21 ♕g4 ♗g6 22 ♘h6+ gxh6 23 f5 h5 24 ♕g3 ♕f7 25 e6 ♕e8 26 fxg6 ♕xg6 27 ♕e5 **1-0** L/N3036

**1862-★BY-1 ●○** 4 vii 62
**Blackburne,J.H.= Young,H.T.**
London
1 e4 e5 2 ♘f3 d6 3 d4 exd4 4 ♕xd4 ♗d7 5 ♗f4 ♕f6 6 ♕xf6 ♘xf6 7 ♘c3 ♘c6 8 ♗d3 a6 9 0-0 ♗e6 10 ♖fe1 0-0-0 11 a3 ♘g4 12 b4 ♘ce5 13 ♗xe5 ♘xe5 14 ♘xe5 dxe5 15 b5 a5 16 ♘a4 ♖d4 17 ♘b2 ♗c5 18 c3 ♖d6 19 ♗c4 ♖hd8 20 ♗xe6+ ♖xe6 21 ♔f1 g5 22 ♔e2 b6 23 ♘c4 h5 24 h3 f6 **½-½** L/N3036

**1862-★B?-1 ●○**
**Blackburne, J.H.+?**
Manchester [Blackburne]
1 e4 e5 2 f4 exf4 3 ♘f3 g5 4 ♗c4 ♗g7 5 c3 c6 6 d4 h6 7 0-0 ♘e7 8 g3 d5 9 exd5 fxg3 10 dxc6 0-0 11 ♗xg5 ♘bxc6 12 hxg3 hxg5 13 ♘xg5 ♘f5 14 ♕h5 ♗h6 15 ♕g6+ [Δ 16 ♕h7#] **1-0** L/N3036

**1862-★B?-2 ⊠** 62/63
**Bloch,P. & Rosanes,J. & Zukertort,J.H.+?**
Breslau-Berlin [Anderssen & Neumann]
1 e4 e5 2 ♘f3 ♘c6 3 ♗b5 ♘f6 4 0-0 ♘xe4 5 d4 ♗e7 6 d5 ♘d6 7 dxc6?! ♘xb5 8 c4 ♘d4 9 ♘xd4 exd4 10 ♕xd4 0-0 11 cxb7 ♗xb7 12 ♘c3 f5 13 ♘d5 d6? [□ 13 ... ♗f6 14 ♘xf6+ ♕xf6] 14 ♖e1! ♗xd5 15 ♕xd5+ ♔h8 16 b3 ♗f6 17 ♖b1 ♗c3 18 ♖e6 f4 19 ♗b2 ♗xb2 20 ♖xb2 ♕h4 21 ♖be2! [Δ 22 ♕xa8+-] 21 ... h6 22 f3 ♖ac8 23 ♖g6 ♔h7 24 ♖ee6 [Δ 25 ♖g4 ♕d8 26 ♕e4+ ♔h8 27 ♖xg7 ♔xg7 28 ♕g6+ ♔h8 29 ♕xh6+ ♔g8 30 ♖g6+ ♔f7 31 ♕g7++-] 24 ... ♖f7 [24 ... ♖g8 25 ♖g4 ♕d8 26 ♕f5+ ♔h8 27 ♖xg7 ♖xg7 (27 ... ♔xg7 28 ♖g6++-) 28 ♖xh6+ ♔g8 29 ♕d5+ ♖f7 30 ♕h5+-] 25 ♖g4 ♕d8 26 ♖xh6+ [26 ♕e4+ ♔h8 27 ♖xg7+-] 26 ... ♔xh6 27 ♕xf7 ♕f6 28 ♕xf6+ gxf6 29 ♖xf4 ♔g6 30 ♖e4 ♔f7 31 g4 **1-0** L/N6051

**1862-★CD-1**
**Steinitz, W. & Chevalier & St Bon & Kling, J.+ Deacon, F.H. & Medley, G.W. & Walker, G.**
London [Bachmann]
1 e4 g6 2 f4 e6 3 ♘f3 c5 4 d4 d5 5 ♘c3 ♗g7 6 exd5 exd5 7 dxc5 ♗xc3+ 8 bxc3 ♘e7 9 ♗e3 0-0 10 ♗e2 ♘bc6 11 0-0 ♘f5 12 ♗f2 [12 ♗d4? ♘cxd4 Δ 13 ... ♘e3] 12 ... ♖e8 13 ♕d2 ♗e6 [13 ... ♕e7 14 ♖ae1 Δ 15 ♗d3] 14 ♗b5 ♕c7 15 ♗xc6 bxc6 16 g4 ♘e7 17 f5 gxf5 18 ♕h6 f6 19 g5 f4 20 ♗d4 ♘f5 21 ♕xf6 ♘xd4 22 ♘xd4 ♗h3 23 ♕xf4 ♕d7 24 ♖fe1 ♖xe1+ 25 ♖xe1 ♖f8 26 ♕g3 ♕e7 27 ♔h1 [27 ♘xc6 ♕e2-+] 27 ... ♕d7 28 g6 h5 29 g7 ♖f6 30 ♕b8+ ♔xg7 31 ♖g1+ ♗g4 [31 ... ♖g6 32 ♕e5+ ♔h6 33 ♕h8+ ♕h7 34 ♖xg6+ ♔xg6 35 ♕xh7+ ♔xh7 36 ♘xc6+-] 32 h3 ♕e7 33 ♕g3 ♕e4+ 34 ♔h2 ♕h7 35 ♖e1 ♕h6 36 hxg4 h4 37 ♕e5 ♔g8 38 ♘f5 ♕f8 39 ♕e8 **1-0** L/N3131

**1862-★CK-1**
**Keon+ Connell**
Bermuda
1 e4 e5 2 f4 exf4 3 ♗c4 ♕h4+ 4 ♔f1 g5 5 ♘c3 ♗g7 6 d4 d6 7 e5 dxe5 8 ♘d5 ♔d8 9 dxe5 ♗d7 10 ♘f3 ♕h5 11 h4 h6 12 ♔g1 ♕g6 13 hxg5 hxg5 14 ♖xh8 ♗xh8 15 ♘xg5 ♕xg5 16 ♗xf4 ♕g6 17 e6 fxe6 18 ♘xc7 e5 19 ♘e6+ ♔e8 20 ♗g5 ♘a6 21 ♕d6 ♗xe6 22 ♖f1 ♗f5 23 ♗b5+ ♔f7 24 ♕d7+ **1-0**
M954-1862

**1862-★CP-1**
**Carstanjen, A.– Paulsen, L.**
Köln [Hirschfeld & Lange]
1 e4 e5 2 ♘f3 ♘c6 3 ♗c4 ♗c5 4 b4 ♗xb4 5 c3 ♗a5 6 d4 exd4 7 0-0 d6 8 ♕b3 ♕f6 9 e5 dxe5 10 ♖e1 ♘h6 11 ♗a3 [□ 11 ♘xe5 0-0 12 ♘xc6 bxc6 13 ♗a3] 11 ... ♗d7 12 ♘bd2

0-0-0 13 ♘e4 ♕g6 14 ♘c5 ♗b6 15 ♘xd7 ♖xd7 16 ♖xe5! dxc3 17 ♗b5 ♘f5 18 ♖ae1 ♖hd8 19 ♖5e2 ♘fd4 20 ♘xd4 ♗xd4 21 ♗e7 ♖xe7 22 ♗xc6 ♕xc6 23 ♖xe7 c2 24 ♖c1 ♗xf2+! 25 ♔f1 ♗c5 26 ♖xf7 ♕a6+ 27 ♔e1 ♖e8+ 28 ♔d2 ♕e2+ 29 ♔c3 ♖e3+ 30 ♔b2 ♗d4+ 31 ♔a3 ♕a6+ 32 ♔b4 c5# **0-1** L/N6047-1863

**1862-★HP-1**
**Paulsen, L.=Höing, C.**

1 e4 d6 2 d4 g6 3 ♗d3 e5 4 dxe5 dxe5 5 f4 exf4 6 ♗xf4 ♗g7 7 ♘c3 c6 8 ♘f3 ♘e7 9 0-0 ♕b6+ 10 ♔h1 ♕xb2 11 ♗e5 ♗xe5 12 ♘xe5 ♕xc3 13 ♘xf7 0-0 14 ♕f3 ♘d7 15 e5 ♘f5 16 e6 ♘f6 17 ♘g5 ♘d4 18 ♕h3 ♘xe6 19 ♘xe6 ♖e8 20 ♖ae1 ♘d5 21 ♖e4 ♗xe6 22 ♖xe6 ♖f8 23 ♖xg6+ hxg6 24 ♕e6+ ♔h8! 25 ♕h3+ ♔g7 26 ♕d7+ **½-½** L/N6047-1862

**175** Schallopp, E. M1647.BL

**1862-★KS-1** 20 xiii 62
**Kolisch, I.F. von+Schallopp, E.**
Berlin [Anderssen & Neumann]

1 e4 e5 2 ♘f3 ♘c6 3 ♗c4 ♗c5 4 b4 ♗xb4 5 c3 ♗a5 6 d4 exd4 7 0-0 ♗b6 8 cxd4 d6 9 ♘c3 ♗g4 10 ♕a4 [□10 ♗b5] 10 ... ♗d7 11 ♕b3 ♘a5 12 ♗xf7+ ♔f8 13 ♕d5 ♘f6 14 ♕g5 ♔xf7 15 e5 h6 [□15 ... ♘g4] 16 ♕f4 g5 17 ♕xf6+ ♕xf6 18 exf6

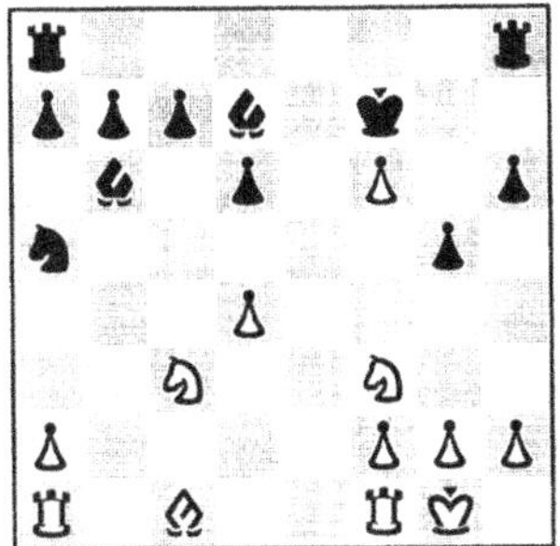

18 ... ♔xf6 [□18 ... g4 19 ♘h4 (19 ♘e1 ♗xd4, 20 ... ♘c4→; 19 ♗d2 ♗xd4 20 ♗b2 ♖he8∓) 19 ... ♗xd4 20 ♗d2 ♘c4 21 ♗e1 ♗xf6 22 g3 ♗xh4 23 gxh4 ♖hg8 24 ♘e2 ♘e5 25 ♘d4 c5∓] 19 ♘d5+ ♔g6 20 h4 g4 21 h5+ ♔f7 [21 ... ♔xh5?? 22 ♘f4#] 22 ♘xb6 axb6 23 ♘h4 ♘b3 24 ♖b1 ♘xd4 25 ♘g6 ♖hg8 26 ♖e1 [26 ♗xh6 ♗f5 27 ♖b2 ♗xg6 28 hxg6+ ♖xg6 29 ♗f4! ♖e8→] 26 ... ♘f5 27 ♗xh6 ♗c6 28 ♖b4 ♘xh6 [28 ... g3 29 ♖f4 ♖xg6 30 hxg6+ ♔xg6 31 ♖e6+ ♔f7 32 ♖e1 ♗d7=] 29 ♖f4+ ♔g7 30 ♖e7+ ♘f7 31 ♖exf7+ ♔h6 32 ♘e7 ♖ge8 33 ♖4f6+ ♔g5 34 ♖g6+ ♔h4 35 ♘f5+ ♔xh5 36 ♖fg7 **1-0** L/N6051-1864

**1862-★KS-2**
**Kolisch,I.F.von+Schulten,J.W.**
Paris

1 e4 e5 2 ♘f3 ♘c6 3 ♗c4 ♗c5 4 b4 ♗xb4 5 c3 ♗c5 6 d4 exd4 7 cxd4 ♗b6 8 0-0 d6 9 ♘c3 ♗g4 10 ♕a4 ♗xf3 11 d5 ♗g4 12 dxc6 bxc6 13 ♕xc6+ ♗d7 14 ♕d5 ♗e6 15 ♗b5+ ♔f8 16 ♕d3 ♘e7 17 ♘d5 ♗c5 18 ♔h1 c6 19 ♘xe7 cxb5 20 ♘d5 a6 21 f4 f6 22 ♗b2 h5 23 ♖ad1 ♖h6 24 f5 ♗f7 25 ♗c1 ♖h7 26 ♗f4 ♕d7 27 h4 b4 28 ♕g3 ♖d8 29 ♖d2 a5 30 ♖fd1 ♕c6 31 ♘e3 ♔e7 32 e5 fxe5 33 ♗g5+ ♔e8 34 ♕xe5+ **1-0** M954

**1862-★KS-3**
**Kolisch,I.F.von+Shumov,I.S.**
St. Petersburg

1 e4 e5 2 ♘f3 ♘c6 3 ♗c4 ♗c5 4 b4 ♗xb4 5 c3 ♗c5 6 0-0 d6 7 d4 exd4 8 cxd4 ♗b6 9 d5 ♕f6 10 dxc6 ♕xa1 11 ♕b3 ♕f6 12 e5 dxe5 13 ♖fe1 bxc6 14 ♗g5 ♕d6 15 ♘xe5 ♗e6 16 ♘xf7 ♔xf7 17 ♖xe6 ♗xf2+ 18 ♔xf2 ♕d4+ 19 ♔f1 ♔f8 20 ♕a3+ c5 21 ♕f3+ **1-0** L/N6047-1863

**1862-★KS-4**
**Kolisch,I.F.von+Shumov,I.S.**
St. Petersburg

1 e4 e5 2 ♘f3 ♘c6 3 ♗c4 ♗e7 4 d4 d6 5 0-0 ♘f6 6 ♗b5 ♗d7 7 ♘c3 0-0 8 d5 ♘b8 9 ♗xd7 ♘bxd7 10 ♘e1 c6 11 dxc6 bxc6 12 f4 ♕b6+ 13 ♔h1 exf4 14 ♘d3 ♖ad8 15 ♗xf4 ♘e5 16 ♗xe5 dxe5 17 ♖f5 ♘d7 18 ♕e2 f6 19 ♖af1 ♘c5 20 ♘xc5 ♕xc5 21 ♕g4 ♖d2 22 ♖h5 ♖f2 23 ♕e6+ ♔h8 24 ♖d1 h6 25 ♖f5 ♖xc2 26 ♕b3 ♖f2 27 ♖xf2 ♕xf2 28 ♕b7 ♗c5 29 ♕xc6 ♗d4 30 ♕b5 ♗xc3 31 bxc3 ♕xa2 32 ♕d5 ♕c2 33 ♕d3 ♕xd3 34 ♖xd3 ♖c8 35 ♔g1 ♖c4 36 ♖e3 a5 37 ♔f2 a4 38 ♔e2 a3 39 ♔d3 a2 40 ♖e1 ♖a4 41 ♖a1 ♔g8 42 c4 ♔f7 43 ♔c3 ♔e6 44 ♔b3 ♖a6 45 ♖xa2 ♖xa2 46 ♔xa2 ♔d6 47 ♔b3 ♔c5 48 g4 ♔d4 49 ♔b4 ♔xe4 50 c5 ♔d5 51 ♔b5 e4 52 c6 e3 53 c7 e2 54 c8♕ e1♕ 55 ♕d8+ **1-0** L/N6047-1863

**1862-★KS-5**
**Shumov,I.S.−Kolisch, I.F.von**
St. Petersburg

1 e4 e5 2 ♘f3 ♘c6 3 ♗c4 ♗c5 4 0-0 ♘f6 5 d4 ♗xd4 6 ♘xd4 ♘xd4 7 f4 d6 8 fxe5 dxe5 9 ♗g5 ♕e7 10 b4 ♗e6 11 ♗xf6 gxf6 12 ♗xe6 fxe6 13 ♕h5+ ♕f7 14 ♕h4 0-0-0 15 ♘a3 f5 16 ♕f2 ♕h5 17 ♖ae1 f4 18 c3 ♘c6 19 b5 ♘b8 20 ♕xa7 b6 21 ♕a4 ♖hg8 22 ♖d1 ♖xg2+ 23 ♔xg2 ♕e2+ 24 ♔h1 ♖d2 **0-1** L/N6126-1880

**1862-★KS-6**
**Kolisch,I.F.von+Schulten,J.W.**
Paris

1 e4 e5 2 f4 exf4 3 ♘f3 g5 4 h4 g4 5 ♘e5 ♗e7 6 ♗c4 ♗xh4+ 7 ♔f1 ♘h6 8 ♘xg4 ♘xg4 9 ♕xg4 ♗g5 10 ♕h5 ♕f6 11 ♘c3 c6 12 e5 ♕g6 13 ♕xg6 fxg6 14 ♘e4 ♗e7 15 d4 b5 16 ♗b3 a5 17 a3 g5 18 ♗d2 ♘a6 19 ♖e1 ♘c7 20 ♘d6+ ♗xd6 21 exd6+ ♘e6 22 d5 cxd5 23 ♗xd5 ♖a6 24 ♗c3 ♖g8 25 ♗e5 ♖b6 26 ♖xh7 g4 27 ♖d1 ♖f8 28 ♗xe6 f3 29 ♗xg4 fxg2+ 30 ♔g1 **1-0** M954-1862

**1862-★LP-1** ●○
**Paulsen, L.+Lafontaine**
London [Löwenthal]

1 e4 e5 2 ♘f3 d6 3 d4 exd4 4 ♗c4 ♗d7 5 ♘xd4 ♘f6 6 0-0 ♗e7 7 ♘c3 0-0 8 f4 ♗g4 9 ♕d3 c5 10 ♘f3 ♘c6 11 ♗e3 ♘b4 12 ♕d2 ♗xf3 13 gxf3 ♘d7 14 a3 ♘b6 15 ♗e2 ♘c6 16 ♔h1 ♕d7 17 ♖g1 ♖ad8 18 ♘d5!

♘xd5 19 exd5 ♘b8 20 ♗d3 f5 21 ♖g2 ♖f7 22 ♖ag1 b6 23 c4 g6 24 ♕c2 ♖e8 25 ♗d2 ♗f8 26 ♗c3 ♗g7 27 ♗xg7 ♖xg7 28 ♗xf5 ♕c7 29 ♗e6+ ♔h8 30 f5 ♘d7 31 fxg6 h6 32 ♕d2 **1-0** M324-1862

**1862-★LP-2**
**Paulsen, L.+ Lemke & Seifert**

1 e4 e5 2 ♘f3 ♘c6 3 ♗c4 ♗c5 4 b4 ♗xb4 5 c3 ♗a5 6 d4 exd4 7 0-0 d6 8 cxd4 ♗b6 9 ♘c3 ♘a5 10 ♗d3 ♘e7 11 ♘d5 ♘xd5 12 exd5 0-0 13 ♘g5 h6 14 ♕h5! ♗xd4 15 ♖b1 c6 16 ♘f3 ♕f6 17 ♗g5 ♗xf2+ 18 ♖xf2 ♕c3 19 ♗c2 ♘c4 20 ♖c1 ♕a3 21 ♗xh6 gxh6 22 ♕xh6 f5 23 ♖e1 ♘e5 24 ♘g5 ♖f7 25 ♖xe5 **1-0** M324-1862

**1862-★MP-1**
**Mackenzie, G.H.+Paulsen, L.**
London [Boden]

1 e4 e5 2 ♘f3 ♘c6 3 ♗c4 ♗c5 4 b4 ♗xb4 5 c3 ♗c5 6 0-0 d6 7 d4 exd4 8 cxd4 ♗b6 9 ♘c3 ♘a5 10 ♗d3 ♘e7 11 e5 dxe5 12 dxe5 0-0 13 ♕c2 h6 [□ 13 ... ♘g6] 14 ♗a3 c5 15 ♖ad1 ♗d7 16 e6! fxe6 17 ♗h7+ ♔h8 18 ♘e5 ♘d5 19 ♘xd5 exd5 20 ♖xd5 ♗f5 21 ♖xd8 ♗xc2 22 ♖xf8+ ♖xf8 23 ♗xc2 **1-0** M392-1862

**39** Mackenzie, G.H. JGW.CPL

**1862-★MP-2**
**Mackenzie, G.H.−Paulsen, L.**
[Löwenthal]

1 e4 e5 2 f4 exf4 3 ♘f3 g5 4 h4 g4 5 ♘e5 ♗g7 6 ♘xg4 d5 7 exd5 [□ 7 ♘f2] 7 ... ♕e7+ 8 ♔f2 ♗d4+ 9 ♔f3 h5 10 ♗b5+ ♔d8 11 ♘f2 ♗g4+ 12 ♘xg4 hxg4+ 13 ♔xg4 ♘f6+ 14 ♔h3 ♖xh4+! 15 ♔xh4 ♘e4+ 16 ♔g4 ♘f2+ 17 ♔h5 ♕e5+ 18 ♔h4 ♕f6+ 19 ♔h5 ♕g6+ 20 ♔h4 ♗f6# **0-1** M324-1863

**1862-★MP-3**
**Paulsen, L.=Mackenzie, G.H.**
London [Boden]

1 e4 e5 2 ♘f3 ♘c6 3 ♗b5 a6 4 ♗a4 ♘f6 5 d4 ♘xe4 6 d5 ♘d4 7 ♘xe5 ♗c5 8 0-0 0-0 9 c3 ♘f5 10 ♗c2 d6! 11 ♘g4 ♘g5 12 ♘e3 ♘h4 13 ♔h1 f5 14 f4 ♘e4 15 ♕e1 ♕e7 16 ♘d2 ♗d7 17 ♘xe4 fxe4 18 ♕g3 ♗xe3 19 ♗xe3 ♘f5 20 ♕f2 ♖f6 21 ♖ae1 ♖e8 22 c4 ♖h6 23 ♖e2 ♕f6 24 ♖fe1 ♕g6 25 ♖d2 ♕g4 26 ♔g1 [26 ♗d1 ♘g3+!−+] 26 ... ♕g6 27 ♖de2 ♘h4 28 ♔h1 ♗g4 29 f5! ♘xf5 30 ♗xh6 ♗xe2 31 ♕xe2 ♕xh6 32 ♕f2 ♕h4 33 ♕xh4 ♘xh4 34 ♖xe4 ♖xe4 35 ♗xe4 ♔f7 36 ♔g1 ♘g6 37 ♗xg6+ ♔xg6 38 ♔f2 ♔f5 39 ♔e3 **½-½** M392-1862

**1862-★MP-4**
**Paulsen, L.+ Mackenzie, G.H.**
London

1 e4 e5 2 ♘f3 ♘c6 3 ♗c4 ♗c5 4 b4 ♗xb4 5 c3 ♗c5 6 0-0 d6 7 d4 exd4 8 cxd4 ♗b6 9 ♗b2 ♘f6 10 d5 ♘a5 11 ♗d3 0-0 12 ♘c3 ♗g4 13 ♘e2 ♗xf3 14 gxf3 c5 15 ♕d2 c4 16 ♗c2 ♖c8 17 ♗c3 ♖c5 18 ♔h1 ♘e8 19 ♖g1 f6 20 ♘f4 ♘c7 21 ♘h5 ♖f7 22 ♕h6 ♕f8 23 ♗a4 ♔h8 24 ♗xf6 **1-0** M392-1862

**1862-★MS-1** 18x62
**Sicre, F.−Morphy, P.C.**
Habana [Maróczy]

1 e4 e5 2 ♘f3 ♘c6 3 ♗b5 a6 4 ♗a4 ♘f6 5 d3 [□ 5 0-0] 5 ... ♗c5 6 0-0 b5 7 ♗b3 d6 8 c3 h6 9 ♗e3 ♗xe3 10 fxe3 0-0 11 ♘bd2 d5 12 exd5 [□ 12 ♕c2; 12 ♕e2] 12 ... ♘xd5 13 ♕e2 ♗e6 14 ♗xd5 ♕xd5 15 ♘e4 [□ 15 d4] 15 ... f5 16 ♘f2 ♕d8 17 b3 g5 18 ♔h1 g4 19 ♘g1 ♕g5 20 ♖ad1 ♘e7 21 ♕d2 ♖ad8 22 d4 c5 23 e4 ♕xd2 24 ♖xd2 cxd4 25 ♖fd1 fxe4 26 ♘xe4 ♗d5! 27 cxd4 ♗xe4 28 dxe5 ♖xd2 29 ♖xd2 ♖f1 30 e6 ♔g7 31 ♖d4 ♖e1 32 ♖d2 ♘d5 33 e7 ♔f7 34 ♖f2+ ♔xe7 **0-1** L/N3203

**1862-★MS-2 ●○** 22x62
**Morphy, P.C.+Sicre, J.M.**
Habana [Maróczy]

1 e4 e6 2 d4 d5 3 exd5 exd5 4 ♘f3 ♗d6 5 ♗d3 ♘f6 6 0-0 0-0 7 ♘c3 c6 8 ♗g5 ♗g4 9 h3 ♗xf3 10 ♕xf3 ♘bd7 11 ♖fe1 ♕c7 12 g4 ♖fe8 13 ♗e3 ♔h8? [□ 13 ... ♘f8] 14 g5 ♘g8 15 ♕xf7 ♖e7 16 ♕h5 ♘f8 17 ♕g4 ♘e6? 18 ♗xh7+− ♘f6 19 gxf6 gxf6 20 ♗g6 ♖g7 21 ♕h5+ ♔g8 22 ♔h1 ♘f8 23 ♗f5 ♗f4 24 ♖g1 ♗xe3 25 fxe3 ♖g5 26 h4 ♘h7 27 hxg5 ♘xg5 28 ♖xg5+ fxg5 29 ♖g1 **1-0** L/N3203

**1862-★MS-2** x̂62
**MacDonnell, G.A.=Steinitz, W.**
London [Boden]

1 e4 e5 2 ♘f3 ♘c6 3 ♗c4 ♗c5 4 b4 ♗xb4 5 c3 ♗c5 6 d4 exd4 7 0-0 d6 8 cxd4 ♗b6 9 ♘c3 ♗g4 10 ♕a4 ♗d7 11 ♕b3? ♘a5 12 ♗xf7+ ♔f8 13 ♕d5 ♘f6 14 ♕g5 ♔xf7 15 e5 ♘e8? [□ 15 ... ♘g4] 16 ♕f4+ ♔g8 17 ♘g5 ♕e7 18 e6 ♗c8 [18 ... ♗xe6 19 ♖e1] 19 ♘d5 ♕f8 20 ♕f7+ ♕xf7 21 exf7+ ♔f8 22 ♖e1! ♗d7 23 fxe8♕+ ♖xe8 24 ♗b2 ♖xe1+ 25 ♖xe1 h6 26 ♖e7 hxg5 27 ♖xd7 ♖h4 28 ♘xc7 ♖e4 29 ♗c3 ♘c6 30 d5 ♘e5 31 ♘e6+ ♔e8 32 ♖xg7 ♖e2 33 h3 ♖xf2 34 ♗d4 ♗xd4 35 ♘xd4 ♖xa2 36 ♖xb7 g4 37 ♘f5 gxh3 38 ♘xd6+ ♔f8 39 ♖b8+ ♔e7 40 ♘f5+ ♔d7 41 gxh3 ♘f3+ **½-½** M392

**1862-★OZ-1 ●○** x62
**Zukertort, J.H.+Oppler, S.**
Posen [Anderssen & Neumann]

1 e4 e5 2 ♘f3 ♘c6 3 ♗c4 ♗c5 4 b4 ♗b6 5 b5 ♘a5 6 ♘xe5 ♘h6 7 d4 d6 8 ♗xh6 dxe5 9 ♗xg7 ♖g8 10 ♗xf7+ ♔xf7 11 ♗xe5 ♕h4 [□ 11 ... ♕g5] 12 ♕f3+ ♔e8 13 ♗g3? ♕g5 14 d5 ♗d4? [□ 14 ... ♕c1+ (14 ... ♗g4 15 ♕f4 ♗xf2+ 16 ♔f1∓)] 15 c3 ♗f6 [15 ... ♕c1+] 16 ♘d2 ♗g4 17 ♕d3 c6 18 bxc6 bxc6 19 f4 ♕g7 20 e5 ♕e7 21 d6 ♕e6 22 0-0 ♗g7 [□ 22 ... ♗f5] 23 f5 ♕f7 24 e6 ♕f6 25 ♘e4 ♕h6 [25 ... ♕d8 26 d7+ ♔f8 27 ♗d6+−] 26 d7+ ♔d8 27 ♗c7+! ♔xc7 28 ♕d6+ ♔b7 29 ♖ab1+ ♔a6 [29 ... ♘b3 30 ♖xb3+ ♔a6 31 ♕a3#] 30 ♘c5# **1-0** L/N6051-1867

**1862-★PS-1 ●○⬠**
**Paulsen, L.+St. Bon**
London

1 e4 e5 2 ♗c4 f5 3 d3 [□ 3 d4; 3 ♘f3] 3 ... ♗c5 [□ 3 ... ♘f6] 4 ♗xg8 ♖xg8 5 ♕h5+ ♔f8 6 ♘f3 ♕f6 7 ♘g5 ♖h8 8 ♘xh7+ ♖xh7 9 ♕xh7 fxe4 10 0-0 d5 11 ♘c3 ♗e6 12 ♕h8+ ♔e7 13 dxe4 c6 14 exd5 cxd5 15 ♗e3 ♗d6 [15 ... d4 16 ♘e4] 16 ♖ad1 ♕f7 17 b4 ♗xb4?

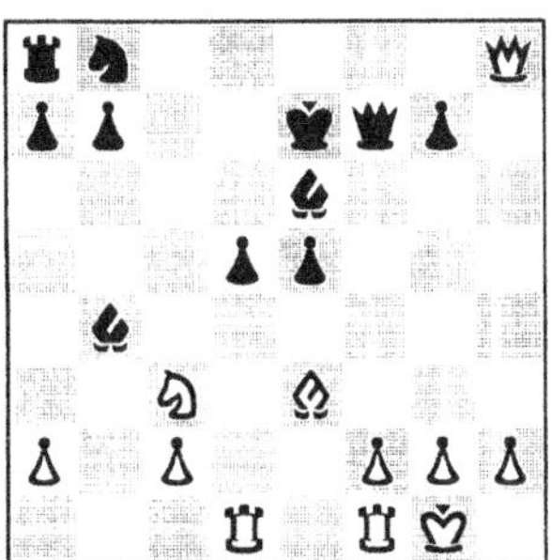

18 ♘e4 ♕f8 19 ♕h4+ ♔d7 20 f4 ♘c6 21 fxe5 ♕h8 22 ♕g3 **1-0** M954-1863

**1862-★PS-2**
**Paulsen, L.= Schultz, G.**
1 e4 e5 2 d4 exd4 3 c3 d6 4 cxd4 ♗e7 5 ♘f3 ♘f6 6 ♗d3 0-0 7 0-0 ♗g4 8 ♘c3 ♘c6 9 ♗e3 ♘b4 10 a3 ♘xd3 11 ♕xd3 ♗xf3 12 gxf3 ♕d7 13 ♔h1 ♕h3 14 ♗d2 ♘g4 15 ♗f4 ♗g5! 16 ♗g3 ♘xh2 17 ♔g1! ♘xf1 18 ♖xf1 ♖ae8 19 ♘d5 ♖e6 20 f4! ♖h6 21 ♕f3 ♗h4 22 ♕g2! ♕xg2+ 23 ♔xg2 c6 24 ♘e3 ♗xg3 25 fxg3 ♖e6 26 ♔f3 ♖fe8 27 e5 dxe5 28 dxe5 f6 29 ♘g4 h5 30 ♘e3 fxe5 31 f5 ♖d6 32 ♖f2 g6 33 g4 hxg4+ 34 ♔xg4 ♖d4+ 35 ♔g5 ♖f4 36 ♖d2 ♖d4 37 ♖g2 gxf5 38 ♔f6+ ♔f8 39 ♘xf5 ♖d7 40 ♖h2 ♖f7+ 41 ♔g5 ♖xf5+ 42 ♔xf5 e4 [□ 42 ... ♖e7] 43 ♔f6 ♔g8 44 ♖g2+ ♔h7 45 ♖h2+ ♔g8 46 ♖g2+ ♔f8 47 ♖h2 **½-½** L/N6047-1862

**1862-★SW-1** 25 x 62
**Steinitz, W.+ Wilson**
London [Bachmann]
1 e4 e5 2 ♘f3 ♘c6 3 ♗c4 ♘f6 4 ♘g5 ♘xe4 5 ♗xf7+ ♔e7 6 d3 [□ 6 d4] 6 ... ♘f6 7 ♗b3 d5 8 0-0 ♗g4 9 f3 ♗h5 10 ♘c3 ♘d4 11 ♕e1 ♔d7 12 ♕xe5 ♗c5 13 ♔h1 ♖e8 14 ♕g3 c6 15 f4 ♘f5 16 ♕h3 ♗g6 [16 ... ♗g4] 17 ♘f3 ♗d6 18 ♘e5+ [□ 18 ♘d4] 18 ... ♔c7 19 ♗d2 ♕c8 20 ♖ae1 ♗h5 21 g4 ♗xe5 22 fxe5 ♗xg4 23 ♕g2 ♘h5 24 e6 [24 ♕xg4 ♘fg3+ △ 25 ... ♕xg4] 24 ... ♖xe6 25 ♕xg4 ♖xe1 26 ♗xe1 **1-0** L/N3131

**1862-★SW-2** x̆ 62
**Steinitz, W.+ Wilson**
London
1 e4 e5 2 f4 exf4 3 ♘f3 g5 4 h4 g4 5 ♘e5 ♘f6 6 ♗c4 d5 7 exd5 ♗d6 8 d4 ♘h5 9 ♗b5+ ♔f8 10 0-0 ♕xh4 11 ♗xf4 g3 12 ♗h6+ ♔g8 13 ♖f3 ♕h2+ 14 ♔f1 ♕h1+ 15 ♔e2 ♕xg2+ 16 ♔e3 f6 17 ♗c4 fxe5 18 ♖f8+ ♗xf8 19 d6+ ♗e6 20 ♗xe6# **1-0** M324

**1862-★S?-1**
**?– Steinitz, W.**
London
1 e4 e5 2 ♘f3 ♘c6 3 ♗c4 ♗c5 4 b4 ♗xb4 5 c3 ♗c5 6 0-0 d6 7 d4 exd4 8 cxd4 ♗b6 9 ♘c3 ♗g4 10 d5 ♘e5 11 h3 h5 12 ♗e2 ♗xf3 13 gxf3 ♕h4 14 ♔h2 ♘f6 15 ♖g1 ♗xf2 16 ♖g2 ♘fg4+ **0-1** M324

**1862-★S?-2**
**?– Staunton, H.**
London
⟨♙f7⟩1 e4 ... 2 d4 e6 3 ♗d3 c5 4 d5 d6 5 c4 ♘f6 6 f4 exd5 7 cxd5 ♗g4 8 ♕c2 ♘bd7 9 h3 ♗h5 10 g4 ♗f7 11 ♘c3 a6 12 a4 ♖c8 13 b3 ♗e7 14 ♘f3 0-0 15 ♗e3 ♕a5 16 ♔e2 ♕c7 17 ♘g5 ♘b6 18 e5 dxe5 19 ♗xh7+ ♔h8 20 ♘xf7+ ♖xf7 21 ♗g6 ♖ff8 22 ♕f5 ♗d6 23 a5 ♘bd7 24 ♕g5 exf4 25 ♕h4+ ♔g8 26 g5 fxe3 27 ♘e4 ♘e5 28 gxf6 ♘xg6 29 ♕g4 ♘f4+ 30 ♔f3 ♗e5 31 ♖hg1 ♗xf6 32 d6 ♕c6 33 d7 ♖cd8 34 ♖af1 ♗d4 **0-1** M954-1863

**1862-★S?-3**
**?– Staunton, H.**
London
⟨♙f7⟩1 e4 ... 2 d4 e6 3 ♗d3 c5 4 dxc5 ♕a5+ 5 ♘c3 ♕xc5 6 ♗e3 ♕a5 7 a3 a6 8 ♘e2 ♘c6 9 0-0 ♘f6 10 f4 ♘g4 11 ♗f2 ♘xf2 12 ♔xf2 ♗c5+ 13 ♔g3 ♕d8 14 h3 b5 15 b4 ♗a7 16 e5 0-0 17 ♘e4 ♘e7 18 ♘d6 ♘d5 19 ♖f3 ♗e3 20 ♗e4 ♗xf4+ 21 ♘xf4 ♕g5+ 22 ♔h2 ♘xf4 23 ♖g3 ♕xe5 24 ♗xa8 ♘h5 25 ♘xc8 ♘xg3 26 ♕d6 ♘f1+ 27 ♔g1 ♕xa1 28 ♘e7+ ♔f7 29 ♕xd7 ♘d2+ 30 ♔h2 ♕e5+ 31 ♔h1 ♕e1+ 32 ♔h2 ♖xa8 **0-1** M954-1862

**1862-★S?-4**
**?+ Staunton, H.**
London
⟨♙f7⟩1 e4 ... 2 d4 e6 3 ♗d3 c5 4 e5 g6 5 c3 ♘c6 6 h4 cxd4 7 cxd4 ♗g7 8 h5 ♘xd4 9 hxg6 ♕a5+ 10 ♔f1 h6 11 ♕h5 ♕xe5 12 ♘c3 d5 13 ♕d1 ♗d7 14 ♖h5 ♕f6 15 ♘h3 ♖c8 16 ♗f4 ♘e7 17 ♗e5 ♕f8 18 ♗xd4 ♗xd4 19 ♘b5 ♗c5 [□ 20 ... ♘c6] 20 ♖c1 ♕g7 21 ♖xc5 ♖xc5 22 ♘d6+ ♔f8 23 ♕f3+ ♘f5 [□ 23 ... ♔g8] 24 g4 ♖c1+ [□ 24 ... ♕xg6 25 gxf5 ♖c1+, 26 ... ♕f6] 25 ♔g2 ♕xg6 26 ♔h2 ♕g7 27 gxf5 ♕e5+ 28 ♕f4 **1-0** M954-1863

**1862-★Z?-1** iv 62
**?– Zukertort, J.H.**
Posen [Anderssen & Neumann]
1 e4 e5 2 ♗c4 ♘f6 3 ♘f3 ♘xe4 4 ♘xe5 d5 5 ♗b3 ♕g5 6 0-0 ♕xe5 7 d3 [7 ♖e1 ♗d6 8 g3 (8 d3 ♕xh2+ 9 ♔f1 ♕h1+ 10 ♔e2 ♕xg2) 8 ... ♕f5 9 ♕e2 (9 d3 ♕xf2+ 10 ♔h1 ♗h3) 9 ... 0-0∓] 7 ... ♗d6! 8 g3 [8 f4 ♕d4+] 8 ... ♘g5! 9 ♖e1? ♘f3+ 10 ♔f1 ♗h3# **0-1** L/N6051-1867

**1862-★Z?-2** x 62
**Zukertort, J.H.+?**
Posen [Anderssen/Neumann]
1 e4 e5 2 f4 exf4 3 ♘f3 g5 4 ♗c4 g4 5 0-0 gxf3 6 ♕xf3 ♕e7 [□ 6 ... ♕f6] 7 d4 ♘c6 8 c3? ♘e5! 9 ♕e2 ♘xc4 10 ♕xc4 c6? [□ 10 ... d6] 11 ♗xf4 ♕xe4 12 ♗g3 [□ 12 ♘d2] 12 ... ♕d5 13 ♖e1+ ♘e7 14 ♕e2 ♔d8 [□ 14 ... d6, 15 ... ♗e6] 15 ♗h4 ♕d6 16 ♘a3 b5 17 ♖ad1 ♗b7 18 ♖d3 f6 19 ♖f3! ♗g7 20 ♗g3! ♕e6 21 ♖e3! ♕f7 22 ♖xe7 ♕g6 23 ♘xb5! ♗a6! 24 ♖xd7+! [24 ... ♔xd7 25 ♕e7+ ♔c8 26 ♕c7#; 24 ... ♔c8 25 ♖c7+ ♔b8 26 ♖xg7++–] **1-0** L/N6051-1867

## DÜSSELDORF 1863

**1863-DUS-1** 30 viii 63
**Lange, M.+ Schultz, G.**
[Lange]
1 e4 e5 2 ♘f3 ♘c6 3 ♗b5 a6 4 ♗a4 d6 5 0-0 [□ 5 d4!] 5 ... ♗d7 6 d4 ♘xd4 7 ♗xd7+ ♕xd7 8 ♘xd4 exd4 9 ♕xd4 ♘f6 10 ♘c3 ♗e7 11 b3 0-0 12 ♗b2 c6 13 ♖ad1 ♖ad8 14 f4 ♘e8 15 ♖d3 ♕e6 16 ♕b6 [□ 16 f5, ♕f2] 16 ... ♕d7! 17 ♔h1 f5 18 e5 ♕c7 19 ♕d4 [19 ♕xc7 ♘xc7 20 exd6=] 19 ... dxe5 20 ♕c4+ ♔h8 21 ♖xd8 ♗xd8 22 ♕c5 ♗e7 23 ♕xe5 ♗d6! 24 ♕d4 ♘f6 25 ♘e2 ♘e4!∓ 26 ♕e3 ♖e8 [26 ... ♗c5 27 ♗d4] 27 ♘g1! ♕d8 [△ ♗c5] 28 ♕d4 ♕e7 29 ♘h3! ♗c5 30 ♕d1 ♕h4 [□ 30 ... ♖d8] 31 ♕d7 ♕e7 32 ♕xf5 ♘f2+ [32 ... ♘d2 33 ♘g5±] 33 ♘xf2 ♗xf2 34 ♗e5 ♗b6 35 ♖d1 ♖d8 36 ♖e1 ♗d4 37 h3 ♕h4 38 ♖f1 ♗b6 39 ♕f7 ♕g3 40 ♕xb7 ♗e3 41 ♕e7 ♖g8 42 f5 ♕g5 43 f6 h5 44 fxg7+ ♔h7 45 ♗f6 ♕g3 46 ♕e4+ ♔h6 47 ♗e5 ♖e8 48 g8♘+ **1-0** L/N5192

**1863-DUS-2** 30 viii 63
**Hengstenberg, C.+ Möhringer, C.**
[Lange]
1 e4 e5 2 ♘f3 ♘c6 3 ♗c4 ♗c5 4 b4 ♗xb4 5 c3 ♗c5 6 d4 exd4 7 0-0 ♗e7? 8 ♕b3 ♘a5 9 ♗xf7+ ♔f8 10 ♕d5 ♘f6 11 ♕xa5 ♔xf7 12 e5 b6 13 ♕a4 ♘d5 14 ♕xd4 [14 cxd4] 14 ... c6 15 e6+ dxe6 [□ 15 ... ♔g8] 16 ♘e5+ ♔g8 17 ♘xc6 ♕c7 18 ♘xe7+ ♕xe7 19 ♖e1 ♔f7 20 c4 ♘f6 21 ♘d2 ♖e8 22 ♘f3 h6 23 ♗b2

♗b7 24 ♘e5+ ♔g8 25 ♖e3 ♖ad8 26 ♕f4 ♔h7 27 ♕g3 g5? 28 ♖ae1± ♕c7 29 ♕h3 ♗c8 30 ♘g4 ♘xg4 31 ♕xg4 ♕f7 32 ♕e4+ ♕g6 33 ♕e5 ♖e7 34 ♖g3 ♖f7 35 h4 ♕f5 36 hxg5 hxg5 37 ♖h3+ ♔g6 38 ♕e2 g4 39 ♖g3 ♔h5 40 ♗c1 ♗b7 41 ♖h3+! ♔g6 42 ♖h6+ ♔g7 43 ♖xe6 ♖df8? 44 ♗h6+ ♔g8 45 ♗xf8 ♖xf8 46 ♖e7 ♗a6 47 ♖xa7 ♗c8 48 ♖e7 ♖f6 49 ♖e8+ ♔g7 50 ♕e3 ♗d7 51 ♖e7+ ♖f7 52 ♖xf7+ ♔xf7 53 ♕e7+ ♔g6 54 ♕d6+ **1-0** L/N5192

**1863-DUS-3** 30 viii 63
**Schultz, G.– Paulsen, W.**
[Lange]

1 e4 e5 2 ♘f3 ♘c6 3 ♗c4 ♗c5 4 c3 ♘f6 5 d4 exd4 6 cxd4 ♗b4+ 7 ♗d2 ♗xd2+ 8 ♘bxd2 d5 9 exd5 ♘xd5 10 0-0 0-0 11 h3 ♗f5 12 ♖e1 ♘f4 13 ♘e4 ♘a5 14 ♗f1 ♘c6 15 ♘g3 ♗g6 16 ♕d2 ♕f6 17 ♘e5 ♘xe5 18 dxe5 ♕g5 19 ♕d7 [□ 19 ♕e3, ♘e2] 19 ... ♘e6 20 ♕b5? ♘d4 21 ♕c4 [21 ♕xb7] 21 ... ♘c2 22 ♕xc7 ♘xa1 23 ♖xa1 ♖fc8 24 ♕a5 [24 ♕xb7] 24 ... b6 25 ♕e1 ♖e8 26 ♕b4 ♕xe5 27 f4 ♕e3+ 28 ♔h2 ♕f2 29 ♗b5 ♖e3 30 ♘h1 ♕c2 31 ♗a4 ♖e4 32 ♗xc2 ♖xb4 33 f5 ♖xb2 34 ♗e4 ♖e8 35 ♗c6 ♖c8 36 ♗b7 ♖b8 37 ♖d1 ♗xf5 38 ♘g3 ♗e6 **0-1** L/N5192

**1863-DUS-4** 30 viii 63
**Knorre, V.– Schwengers, P.**
[Lange]

1 e4 e5 2 ♘f3 ♘c6 3 d4 exd4 4 ♗c4 ♗c5 5 c3 dxc3 [□ 5 ... ♘f6] 6 ♗xf7+ ♔xf7 7 ♕d5+ ♔e8 8 ♕h5+ ♔f8 9 ♕xc5+ d6 10 ♕xc3 ♘f6 11 ♕e3? [□ 11 ... ♘bd2] 11 ... ♕e7 12 ♘c3 ♗e6 13 0-0 ♘g4 14 ♕f4+ ♕f6

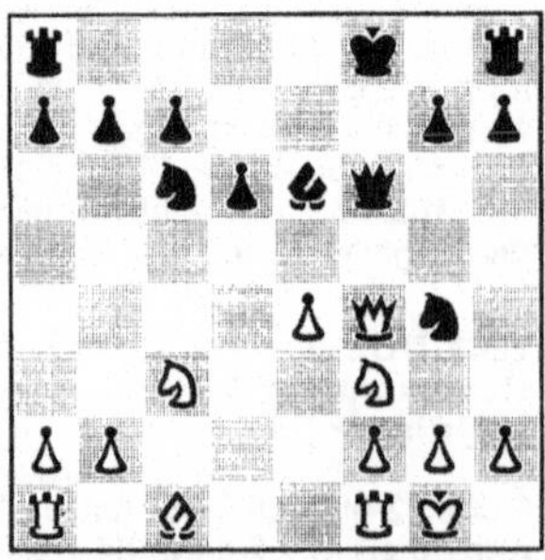

15 ♘g5 ♔e7 16 ♘d5+ ♗xd5 17 exd5 ♕xf4 18 ♗xf4 ♘ce5 19 ♘e6 [□ 19 h3, 20 ♗xe5] 19 ... ♘f6 20 ♗g5 ♔d7 21 ♗xf6 gxf6 22 ♖ac1 ♖ac8 23 ♘d4 [□ 23 ♘f4] 23 ... ♘d3 24 ♖c3 ♘f4 25 ♖b3 ♖b8 26 ♖g3 ♖hg8 27 ♖f3 ♘xd5 28 ♖f5 ♖g5 29 ♖e1 ♖xf5 30 ♘xf5 ♖e8 31 ♖xe8 ♔xe8 32 g3 ♔d7 33 ♔g2 c5 34 ♔f3 ♘b4 35 a3 ♘d3 36 ♔e4 c4 37 ♔d4 ♘xb2 38 ♔c3 ♘d1+ 39 ♔xc4 ♘xf2 40 ♔d5 ♘d1 41 ♘xd6 ♘c3+ 42 ♔c4 ♔xd6 43 ♔xc3 ♔c5 44 a4 a5 45 g4 b6 46 h3 h6 47 ♔b3 ♔d4 **0-1** L/N5192

**1863-DUS-5** 30 viii 63
**Busch, von d.– Höing, C.**
[Lange]

1 e4 e5 2 ♗c4 ♘f6 3 d3 ♗e7 4 ♘f3 d6 5 ♘g5 0-0 6 h3 c6 7 ♘c3 d5 8 ♗b3 dxe4 9 ♘gxe4 ♘a6 10 ♗e3 ♘d5 11 ♕d2 f5∓ 12 ♘xd5 cxd5 13 ♘g3 f4 14 ♘h5 fxe3 15 ♕xe3 ♗c5 16 ♕d2 ♗xf2+ 17 ♔e2 ♘c5 18 ♖af1 ♘xb3 19 cxb3 ♕h4 20 ♘xg7 ♕g4+ 21 hxg4 ♗xg4# **0-1** L/N5192

**1863-DUS-6** 30 viii 63
**Rossy, M.=Lichtenscheidt, R.**
[Lange]

1 e4 e5 2 ♘f3 ♘c6 3 ♗c4 ♗c5 4 ♘c3 ♘f6 5 d3 d6 6 ♗g5 0-0 7 ♘a4 [7 ♘d5] 7 ... ♗b6 8 ♘xb6 axb6 9 0-0 ♗e6 10 ♗b3 h6 11 ♗h4 ♘e7 12 ♗xf6 gxf6 13 ♘h4 ♔h7 14 f4 ♗xb3 15 axb3 ♖xa1 16 ♕xa1 exf4 17 ♖xf4 ♘g6 18 ♘xg6 fxg6 19 ♕f1 c5 20 ♕e1 ♕e7 21 ♕c3 ♕e5 22 ♖f3 ♔g7 23 g3 f5 24 exf5 ♖xf5 25 ♖e3 ♕xc3 26 bxc3 ♔f7 27 ♔g2 h5 28 ♖e4 d5 29 ♖a4 ♔e6 30 b4 d4 31 cxd4 cxd4 32 ♖a7 ♖f7 33 ♖a8 ♖c7 34 ♖a2 ♔f5 35 ♔f3 **½-½** L/N5192

**1863-DUS-7** 30 viii 63
**Lichtenscheidt, R.– Rossy, M.**
[Lange]

1 e4 e5 2 ♘f3 ♘c6 3 ♗b5 ♘d4 4 ♘xd4 exd4 5 c3 [□ 5 d3] 5 ... c6 6 ♗e2 ♗c5 7 cxd4 ♗xd4 8 ♘c3 ♘f6 9 d3 b5 10 ♗e3 ♕b6 11 ♗xd4 ♕xd4 12 ♕d2 0-0 13 0-0 ♗b7 14 ♕e3 ♕b4 15 ♖ab1 ♖ae8? 16 ♕xa7 ♖b8 17 a3 ♕d6 18 ♕e3 ♖fe8 19 f3 ♕c7 20 d4 ♗a6 21 b4 d6 22 ♗d3 ♕a7 23 ♖fe1 d5 24 e5 ♘d7 25 f4 ♘b6 26 ♕h3 g6 27 f5 ♘c4!

28 ♔h1 ♕xd4 29 f6 ♔h8 30 ♗xc4 bxc4 31 ♕h6 ♖g8 32 ♖f1 ♕xe5 33 ♖f3 ♕h5 34 ♕f4 g5 35 ♕f5 ♕g6 36 ♕xg6 ♖xg6 37 ♖e1 ♖d8 38 ♘a4 d4 39 ♘c5 ♗c8 [39 ... d3] 40 a4 d3 41 ♘xd3 cxd3 42 ♖d1 ♗a6 43 ♖f5 ♗c4 44 ♖d2 ♖d4 [44 ... ♖e8] 45 ♔g1 h6 46 g3 ♖g8 47 ♖c5 ♖b8 48 ♖xc6 ♖xb4 49 a5 ♖a4 50 ♔f2 ♖e4 51 ♖xc4 ♖axc4 52 ♖xd3 ♖a4 53 ♔f3 ♖e6 54 ♖d5 ♖xf6+ 55 ♔e3 ♔g7 **0-1** L/N5192

**1863-DUS-8** 30 viii 63
**Lange, M.+ Hengstenberg, C.**
[Lange]

1 e4 c5 2 ♘f3 e6 3 ♘c3 a6 4 d4 cxd4 5 ♘xd4 ♘c6 6 ♘xc6 bxc6 7 e5 h6 [□ 7 ... ♕c7 8 f4] 8 ♗d3 ♘e7 9 0-0 ♘d5

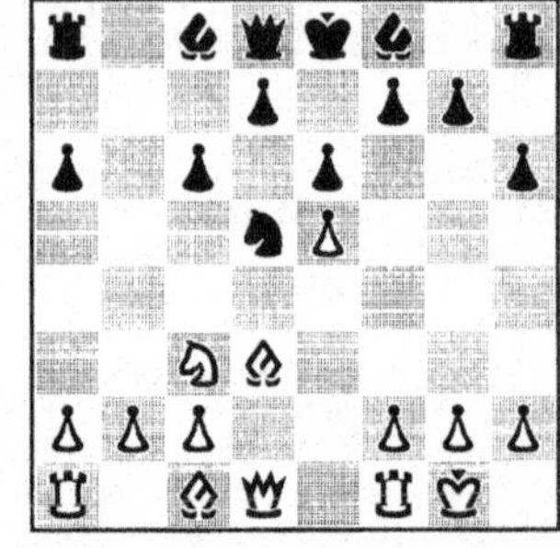

10 ♘e4 [10 ♘xd5 cxd5 11 c4 dxc4 12 ♗xc4 ♕c7 13 ♕e2 d5 14 exd6 ♗xd6, 15 ... 0-0=] 10 ... ♗b7 11 f4 c5 12 f5 exf5 13 ♖xf5 ♕b6 14 c4 [14 ♗c4 ♕e6] 14 ... ♘b4 15 ♖f2 ♘xd3 16 ♕xd3 ♕g6 [□ 16 ... ♕e6!] 17 ♘d6+ ♗xd6 18 ♕xg6 fxg6 19 exd6 a5 [19 ... ♖f8 20 ♖e2+ ♔d8! 21 ♗d2 a5! 22 ♖ae1, 23 ♖e7±] 20 ♗e3 ♗a6 21 b3 ♖c8 22 ♗d2 ♖c6 23 ♖e1+ ♔d8 24 ♗xa5+ ♔c8 25 ♗c7 ♖xc7 26 dxc7 ♔xc7 27 ♖e7 ♗b7 28 ♖ff7 ♗c6 29 ♖xg7 ♖a8 30 ♖e2 g5 31 ♖h7 ♖f8 32 ♖xh6 g4 33 ♖h4 ♖f4 34 h3 ♖d4 35 ♖xg4 ♖d1+ 36 ♔h2 ♖f1 37 h4 ♖f5 38 ♖g5 ♖f4 39 ♔g3 **1-0** L/N5192

**1863-DUS-9** 30 viii 63
**Paulsen, W.+ Schwengers, P.**
[Lange]

1 e4 e5 2 ♘f3 ♘c6 3 ♗c4 ♗c5 4 b4 ♗xb4 5 c3 ♗c5 6 d4 exd4 7 0-0 d6 8 cxd4 ♗b6 9 d5 ♘a5 10 ♗b2 ♘f6 11 ♗d3 ♗g4 12 ♘c3 0-0 13 ♘a4 ♕e7 [□13 ... c6] 14 ♖e1 ♖fe8 15 ♕d2 ♗xf3 [□15 ... c6] 16 gxf3 ♘h5 17 ♔h1 ♕h4 18 ♘xb6 axb6 19 ♖g1 ♕e7 [□19 ... ♔h8] 20 ♕h6 g6 21 ♕xh5 f6 22 e5 dxe5 23 ♗xg6 **1-0** L/N5192

**1863-DUS-10** 30 viii 63
**Rossy, M.– Höing, C.**
[Lange]

1 e4 e5 2 ♘c3 ♘f6 3 ♗c4 ♗c5 [3 ... ♘xe4 4 ♗xf7+ (4 ♘xe4 d5)] 4 d3 0-0 5 ♘f3 d6 6 0-0 c6 7 a3 b5 8 ♗a2 a5 9 ♕e2 ♗g4 10 ♘d1 ♘bd7 11 ♗g5 ♕b6 12 c3 [12 ♗e3; 12 ♘e3] 12 ... d5 13 h3 dxe4 14 dxe4 ♗xf3 15 ♕xf3 ♘e8 16 ♘e3 ♔h8 17 ♘f5 f6 18 ♗h4 [□18 ♗e3!] 18 ... ♕c7 19 ♖ad1 ♗b6 20 ♖d2 c5 21 ♗e6 ♘b8 22 ♕h5 ♖a7 23 ♘e3 ♘d6 24 ♘d5 ♕c6 25 ♗f5 ♘xf5 26 ♕xf5 ♖af7 27 ♖fd1 [27 f4?] 27 ... g6 28 ♕f3 f5 29 ♕g3 ♗c7 30 ♗e7 ♖e8 31 ♕g5 ♘d7 32 f3 ♔g7 33 exf5 ♖xf5 34 ♕e3 ♖f7 35 ♗h4 ♘b6 36 ♘xb6 ♗xb6 37 ♗f2 ♕f6 38 ♖d5 ♖e6 39 ♕e4 ♖c7 40 ♖e1 ♖cc6 41 ♖xe5 ♖xe5 42 ♕xe5 ♕xe5 43 ♖xe5 ♔f6 44 f4 [□44 ♖e2!] 44 ... h6 45 h4 ♗c7 46 ♖d5 ♗xf4 47 b3 ♖d6 48 ♖xd6+ ♗xd6 49 g3 [□49 ♗e3, 50 ♔f2] 49 ... ♔f5 50 ♔g2 ♔e4 51 g4 ♔d3 52 b4 axb4 53 axb4 cxb4 54 cxb4 ♗xb4 55 ♔f3 ♗d2 56 ♗c5 b4 57 h5 g5 58 ♗f8 b3 59 ♗xh6 b2 60 ♗g7 b1♕ 61 h6 ♕f1+ 62 ♔g3 ♗f4# **0-1** L/N5192

**1863-DUS-11** 30 viii 63
**Lange, M.= Paulsen, W.**
[Lange]

1 e4 e5 2 ♘f3 ♘c6 3 ♗c4 ♗c5 4 0-0 ♘f6 5 d3 h6 6 ♘c3 d6 7 ♘e2 ♘h5! 8 ♗e3 ♗b6 9 ♕d2 ♕f6 10 ♘c3 ♘e7 11 ♘d5 ♘xd5 12 ♗xd5 c6 13 ♗c4 ♗c7 14 d4 ♗g4 15 ♗e2 ♘f4 16 ♗xf4 ♕xf4 17 ♕b4 ♖b8 18 dxe5 ♗xf3 19 ♗xf3 ♕xe5 [19 ... d5 20 ♖ae1 ♗xe5 21 g3 ♕xf3 22 exd5 f6! 23 ♖e3 ♕xd5 24 f4±] 20 g3 0-0 21 ♗g2 **½-½** L/N5192

**1863-DUS-12** 31 viii 63
**Höing, C.– Paulsen, W.**
[Lange]

1 e3 e5 2 ♘c3 ♘f6 3 ♗e2 d5 4 d4 exd4 5 exd4 ♗e7 6 ♗f3 ♘c6 7 a3 0-0 8 ♘ge2 ♖e8 9 0-0 ♘a5 10 ♗e3 ♘c4 11 ♕c1 ♘xe3 12 fxe3 c6 13 ♘d1 [□13 e4 dxe4 14 ♗xe4] 13 ... ♘g4 14 ♘g3 ♘xh2 15 ♔xh2 ♗d6 16 ♔g1 ♗xg3 **0-1** L/N5192

**1863-DUS-13** 1 ix 63
**Lange, M.+ Höing, C.**
[Lange]

1 e4 e6 2 d4 g6 3 ♗d3 ♗g7 4 ♗e3 ♘e7 5 f4 d5 6 e5 ♘bc6 7 ♘c3 0-0 8 ♘f3 f6 9 ♕d2 ♘a5 10 b3 b6 11 0-0 ♘f5 12 ♗xf5 exf5 13 ♖ae1 fxe5 14 fxe5 ♗e6 15 ♗f2 ♘b7 16 ♔h1 c5? 17 ♘g5 ♕d7 18 dxc5 bxc5 19 ♘xe6 ♕xe6 20 ♕xd5 ♕xd5 21 ♘xd5 ♖ad8 22 c4 ♖fe8 23 ♗h4 ♖d7 24 e6 ♖d6 25 ♘c7 **1-0** L/N5192

**1863-DUS-14** 2 ix 63
**Paulsen, W.= Lange, M.**
[Lange]

1 e4 e5 2 ♘f3 ♘c6 3 ♗c4 ♗c5 4 b4 ♗b6 5 b5 ♘a5 6 ♘a3 ♘f6! 7 0-0 0-0 8 ♕e2 d5 9 ♗xd5! [9 exd5 e4 10 ♘g5 ♗g4 11 ♕e1 ♘xc4 12 ♘xc4 ♕xd5 13 ♘xb6 ♕xg5 14 d3 ♕g6 15 ♘xa8 ♗f3∓] 9 ... ♘xd5 10 exd5 ♕xd5 11 ♗b2 ♗d4! 12 c4 ♕d6 13 ♘xd4 exd4 14 ♕d3 ♗e6! 15 ♕xd4 [15 ♖fc1 ♖fd8 16 c5 ♕f4=] 15 ... ♕xd4 16 ♗xd4 ♘xc4 17 ♘xc4 ♗xc4 18 ♖fc1 ♗xb5 19 ♖xc7 ♗c6 **½-½** L/N5192

**1863-DUS-15** 2 ix 63
**Lange, M.+ Paulsen, W.**
[Lange]

1 e4 e5 2 f4 exf4 3 ♘f3 g5 4 h4 g4 5 ♘e5 ♗g7 6 d4 ♘f6 7 ♗c4! d5 8 exd5 0-0 [8 ... ♘xd5; 8 ... ♘h5] 9 ♗xf4 ♘h5 [9 ... ♘xd5 10 ♕d2] 10 ♕d2 c5! 11 dxc6 [□11 c3] 11 ... ♘xf4 12 ♕xf4 [12 cxb7 ♗xb7∓] 12 ... ♘xc6 13 ♘xc6 bxc6 14 c3

14 ... c5! 15 dxc5 ♖e8+! [15 ... ♕e7+ 16 ♔f1] 16 ♔f2 ♕e7 [16 ... ♖e5 17 ♕xf7+ ♔h8 18 ♖d1 ♖f5+ 19 ♔e2 ♖e5+ 20 ♔f2 ♕xh4+ 21 ♔g1 ♗a6!∓] 17 ♘d2! ♕xc5+ 18 ♔f1 ♗e6 19 ♗e2! f5! 20 ♗c4 ♖ad8 21 ♗xe6+ ♖xe6 22 ♖e1! ♖de8 23 ♖xe6 ♖xe6 24 g3! ♗h6 25 ♕b8+ ♔g7 26 ♖h2 ♕e3! 27 ♖f2 ♕e1+ [□27 ... ♕d3+ 28 ♔g2 ♗e3! 29 ♕c7+ ♔~ 30 ♕c4 ♕xc4 31 ♘xc4 ♗xf2–+] 28 ♔g2 ♗xd2 [28 ... ♗e3 29 ♘e4!=] 29 ♕xa7+ ♔g6 30 h5+ ♔h6 [30 ... ♔xh5 31 ♕xh7+=; 30 ... ♔f6? 31 ♕d4+±; 30 ... ♔g5 31 ♕g7+=] 31 ♕f7 ♖e2 32 ♕f6+ ♔xh5 33 ♕xf5+ ♔h6 [33 ... ♗g5 34 ♕xh7+ ♗h6 35 ♕f7+, 36 ♕f5#] 34 ♕f6+ ♔h5 35 ♕h4+ ♔g6 36 ♕xg4+ ♔h6 37 ♕xe2 **1-0** L/N5192

## DEACON✕STEINITZ London

**[1863-✕DS]**

| | | |
|---|---|---|
| F.H. Deacon | 0 0 0 1 ½ 0 0 | 1½ |
| W. Steinitz | 1 1 1 0 ½ 1 1 | 5½ |

**1863-✕DS-1** 29 iv 63
**Steinitz, W.+ Deacon, F.H.**
[Löwenthal]

1 e4 e5 2 f4 exf4 3 ♘f3 g5 4 h4 g4 5 ♘e5 ♘f6 6 ♗c4 d5 7 exd5 ♗d6 8 d4 ♘h5 [□8 ... ♕e7] 9 ♘c3 ♕e7 10 ♗b5+ c6 11 dxc6 bxc6 12 ♘d5 ♕e6 13 ♘c7+ ♗xc7 14 ♗c4 ♕e7 [□14 ... ♕f5] 15 ♗xf7+ ♔f8 16 ♗xh5 ♗xe5 17 dxe5 ♕xe5+ 18 ♕e2 ♕xh5 19 ♗xf4 ♗f5 [19 ... ♔f7 20 0-0 ♖e8 21 ♗h6+ ♔g8 (21 ... ♗f5 22 ♕c4+ ♔g6 23 ♗g5 ♘d7 24 ♕xc6+ ♗e6 25 ♖ae1 ♘f8 26 ♖xf8 ♖xf8 27 ♖xe6+ ♔g7 28 ♖e7+ ♔g8 29 ♕d5++–) 22 ♕c4+ ♕d5 23 ♕f4 ♕c5+ 24 ♔h1 ♗e6 25 ♖ae1+–; 19 ... ♗a6 20 ♗h6+ ♔g8 21 0-0 ♕c5+ 22 ♕f2 ♘d7 23 ♕xc5 ♘xc5 24 ♖f5 ♘e6 25 ♖d1+–] 20 0-0 ♘d7 21 ♗h6+ ♔f7 22 ♖xf5+ ♕xf5 23 ♖f1 ♕xf1+ 24 ♕xf1+ ♔g6 [□24 ... ♔e6] 25 ♗g5 h6 26 ♕d3+ ♔h5 27 ♗e7 **1-0** L/N6124

**1863-✕DS-2** v 63
**Deacon, F.H.– Steinitz, W.**
[Löwenthal]

1 f4 e5 2 fxe5 d6 3 ♘f3 dxe5 4 ♘xe5 ♗d6 5 ♘f3 ♘f6 6 g3 ♘g4 7 ♖g1 h5 8 c3 [8 h3? h4!±] 8 ... h4 9 ♕a4+ ♘c6 10 ♔d1 hxg3 11 hxg3 ♕f6 12 d4 ♘f2+ 13 ♔e1 ♘e4 14 ♘bd2 [14 d5? ♗c5] 14 ... ♘xd2 15 ♗xd2 ♗g4 16 ♘e5 ♗xe5 17 dxe5 ♕e6 18 ♗g2 f5 19 ♗g5 ♕xe5 **0-1** L/N6124

**1863-✕DS-3** v 63
**Steinitz, W.+ Deacon, F.H.**
[Löwenthal]

1 e4 e5 2 ♘f3 ♘c6 3 ♗c4 ♗c5 4 b4 ♗xb4 5 c3 ♗c5 6 0-0 d6 7 d4 exd4 8 cxd4 ♗b6 9 d5 ♘a5 10 e5 ♘xc4 11 ♕a4+ ♕d7 [□11 ... ♗d7] 12 ♕xc4 ♘e7 13 ♘c3 0-0 14 ♗a3 ♘f5 15 ♘e4 ♖d8 16 ♖ad1 ♕e7 17 ♖fe1 ♔h8 18 ♘fg5 **1-0** L/N6124

**1863-⚔DS-4** v63
**Deacon, F.H.+ Steinitz, W.**
[Löwenthal]

1 e4 e5 2 f4 exf4 3 ♘f3 g5 4 h4 g4 5 ♘e5 ♘f6 6 ♗c4 d5 7 exd5 ♗d6 8 d4 ♘h5 9 ♘c3 ♕e7 10 ♗b5+ c6 11 dxc6 bxc6 12 ♘d5 ♕b7 [□ 12 ... ♕e6] 13 ♘c4 ♗e7 [□ 13 ... ♗f8] 14 ♕e2 ♗e6 15 ♕e5 ♖f8 16 ♘a5 ♕d7 17 ♘c7+ ♔d8 18 ♘xa8 ♗d6 19 ♕xd6 ♕xd6 20 ♘b7+ ♔d7 21 ♘xd6 ♔xd6 22 ♗d2 ♖e8 23 ♗d3 ♗d5+ 24 ♔d1 ♗xg2 25 ♗b4+ c5 26 ♗xc5+ ♔c6 27 ♖g1 f3 28 ♗b5+ ♔xb5 29 ♘c7+ ♔c6 30 ♘xe8 f2 31 ♔d2 fxg1♕ 32 ♖xg1 ♗h3 33 ♘d6 f6 34 ♘f5 a6 35 ♗d6 ♘d7 36 c4 ♘b6 37 b3 a5 38 ♗a3 a4 39 ♖e1 axb3 40 axb3 ♘c8 41 ♖e8 ♘b6 42 ♖e6+ ♔b7 43 ♖e7+ ♔a6 44 ♖xh7 g3 45 ♘xg3 ♘f4 46 ♘e4 ♘e6 47 ♘c5+ **1-0** L/N6124

**1863-⚔DS-5** v63
**Steinitz, W.= Deacon, F.H.**

1 e4 e5 2 f4 exf4 3 ♗c4 d5 4 exd5 ♕h4+ 5 ♔f1 ♗d6 6 ♘c3 ♘e7 7 d4 ♗g4 8 ♘f3 ♕h5 9 ♘b5 g5 10 ♔f2 ♘d7 11 ♖e1 ♗xf3 12 ♕xf3 ♕xf3+ 13 ♔xf3 ♔f8 14 ♘xd6 cxd6 15 g3 ♘b6 16 ♗b3 ♘bxd5 17 ♗d2 a5 18 c4 a4 19 ♗d1 ♘e3 20 ♗xe3 fxe3 21 ♔xe3 ♔g7 22 ♔d3 ♘c6 23 a3 **½-½** L/N6124

**1863-⚔DS-6** v63
**Deacon, F.H.– Steinitz, W.**
[Löwenthal]

1 e4 e5 2 ♘c3 ♗c5 3 f4 d6 4 ♘f3 ♘f6 5 d4 exd4 6 ♘xd4 0-0 7 ♗e2 ♖e8 8 ♕d3 ♕e7 9 ♘db5 [□ 9 ♘b3] 9 ... ♘c6 10 ♗f3 a6 11 ♘a3 b5 12 ♘d5 ♘xd5 13 ♕xd5 ♗b7 14 ♗d2 b4 15 ♘c4? ♘a5 **0-1** L/N6124

**1863-⚔DS-7** v63
**Steinitz, W.+ Deacon, F.H.**

1 e4 e5 2 f4 exf4 3 ♘f3 g5 4 h4 g4 5 ♘e5 ♘f6 6 ♗c4 d5 7 exd5 ♗d6 8 d4 ♘h5 9 ♘c3 ♕e7 10 ♗b5+ ♔d8 11 0-0 ♗xe5 12 dxe5 ♕xe5 13 ♖e1 ♕f6 14 ♕e2 c6 [□ 14 ... ♘d7 15 ♘e4 ♕d4+ 16 ♔h2 ♖e8 17 ♕xg4 ♖xe4 18 ♖xe4 ♕xe4 19 ♕xh5 ♘f6 20 ♕g5 ♕f5 21 ♗xf4 h6 22 ♕g3] 15 dxc6 bxc6 16 ♘e4 ♕xh4?

17 ♗xf4! ♘xf4 18 ♕d2+ ♗d7 19 ♕xf4 cxb5 20 ♘d6 ♗e6 21 ♖ad1 ♘d7 22 ♘xf7+ ♔e7 23 ♕d6+ ♔xf7 24 ♕xe6+ **1-0** L/N6124

## GURETSKY-CORNITZ⚔NEUMANN [1863-⚔GN]

| | | | |
|---|---|---|---|
| B. v. Guretsky-Cornitz | 0̂ | 1̂ | ? |
| G.R. Neumann | 1̂ | 0̂ | ? |

**1863-⚔GN-1̂** x63
**Neumann, G.R.+ Guretsky-Cornitz, B.v.**
[Anderssen/Neumann]

1 e4 e5 2 ♘f3 ♘c6 3 ♗c4 ♗c5 4 c3 ♘f6 5 d4 exd4 6 0-0?! ♘xe4 7 cxd4 ♗e7? [7 ... d5!] 8 d5 ♘b8 [8 ... ♘a5?!] 9 ♖e1 ♘d6 [9 ... f5 10 ♘c3 d6; 9 ... f5 10 ♘c3 ♘xc3? 11 bxc3 h6 (11 ... ♔f8 12 d6 cxd6 13 ♕d5 ♕e8 14 ♗g5+-) 12 d6 cxd6 13 ♕xd6 ♔f8 14 ♕g6 ♕e8 15 ♕xf5++-] 10 ♗b3 0-0 11 ♘c3 ♘e8 [△ 12 ... d6] 12 d6! cxd6 [12 ... ♘xd6 13 ♖xe7 ♕xe7 14 ♗g5 ♕e8 15 ♕d3 △ 16 ♖e1+-; 12 ... ♗xd6 13 ♗g5 ♘f6 14 ♘d5 ♘c6 (14 ... c6 15 ♘xf6+ gxf6 16 ♕xd6 fxg5 17 ♖e7) 15 ♘d4 ♗e5 16 ♘f5 d6 17 ♖xe5 dxe5 18 ♘xg7+-] 13 ♖xe7 ♕xe7 14 ♗g5 ♘f6 15 ♘d5 ♕d8 16 ♕d4 ♘c6 17 ♕h4 **1-0** L/N6051-1864

**1863-⚔GN-2̂** xi63
**Neumann, G.R.– Guretsky-Cornitz, B.v.**
[Anderssen/Neumann]

1 e4 e5 2 f4 d5 3 exd5 e4 4 ♗b5+ c6 5 dxc6 bxc6 6 ♗a4? [6 ♗c4 ♘f6 (6 ... ♗c5? 7 ♗xf7+) 7 d4] 6 ... ♗c5 [△ 7 ... ♕d4] 7 ♘e2 [7 ♘c3 ♗xg1 8 ♖xg1 ♕h4+ 9 g3 ♕xh2 10 ♘e2 ♗g4∓] 7 ... ♕h4+ 8 g3 ♕h3 9 d4 exd3 10 cxd3 ♕g2 11 ♔d2 ♘f6 12 ♘c3 0-0 13 a3 ♘a6 14 ♕f1 ♗h3 15 ♕xg2 ♗xg2 16 ♖e1? ♗f2 17 ♖d1 ♘c5 18 ♔c2 ♖fe8 19 ♘g1 ♖ad8 20 ♗b3 ♘g4 21 h3 ♘h2! [△ 22 ... ♗xg3; 22 ... ♗xg1 23 ♖xg1 ♘f3] 22 ♖d2 [22 ♘ge2 ♘f3–+; 22 ♘ce2 ♘f3] 22 ... ♗xg1 23 ♖xg2 ♘f3 [24 ♗d2 ♘d4+–+; 24 ♖xg1 ♘xg1 25 ♗d2 ♘f3 26 ♗c4 ♘d4+ 27 ♔d1 ♘xd3 28 ♗xd3 ♘b3–+] 24 ...? **0-1** L/N6051-1864

## GREEN⚔STEINITZ London [1863-⚔GS]

| | | | | | | | | | | |
|---|---|---|---|---|---|---|---|---|---|---|
| V. Green | 0 | 0 | 0 | 0 | ½ | 0 | 0 | ? | 0 | ? |
| W. Steinitz | 1 | 1 | 1 | 1 | ½ | 1 | 1 | ? | 1 | ? |

**1863-⚔GS-1**
**Green, V.– Steinitz, W.**
[Löwenthal]

1 e4 e5 2 ♘f3 ♘c6 3 ♗c4 ♘f6 4 ♘c3 ♗c5 5 d3 d6 6 0-0 ♗g4 7 ♘e2 ♗xf3 8 gxf3 ♘h5 9 ♘g3 ♕h4 10 ♘xh5 ♕xh5 11 c3 g5∓ 12 ♔g2 ♖g8 13 h3 ♖g6 14 ♗e3 ♖h6 15 ♖h1 ♘e7 16 d4 ♗b6 17 ♗e2 ♕h4 18 ♕g1 f5 19 dxe5 dxe5 20 ♗xb6 cxb6 21 b4 0-0-0 22 ♖d1 ♖f8! 23 ♔f1 ♘g6 24 ♗d3 ♘f4 25 exf5 ♘xd3! 26 ♖xd3 ♕c4 27 ♔e2 ♖d6 28 ♕b1 ♖fd8 29 ♖d1 e4 30 fxe4 ♕xe4+ 31 ♖e3

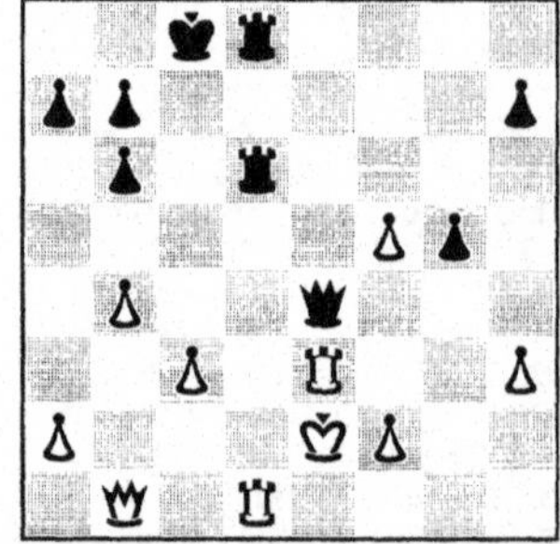

31 ... ♖d2+ **0-1** M324-1864

**1863-⚔GS-2**
**Steinitz, W.+ Green, V.**
[Löwenthal]

1 e4 e5 2 f4 ♗c5 3 ♘f3 d6 4 c3 ♗g4 5 ♗e2 ♘c6 6 b4 ♗b6 7 b5 ♗xf3 8 ♗xf3 ♘ce7 9 d4 exf4 [□ 9 ... exd4] 10 ♗xf4 ♘g6 11 ♗g3! [11 ♗e3] 11 ... ♘f6 12 ♘d2 0-0 13 0-0 ♕d7 14 a4 c6 15 ♘c4± ♗c7 16 e5 dxe5 17 ♘xe5 ♘xe5 18 dxe5 ♕xd1 19 ♖fxd1 ♘d5 20 ♗xd5 cxd5 21 ♖xd5 ♖ad8 22 ♖ad1 ♖xd5 23 ♖xd5 ♖d8 24 c4 ♔f8 25 ♔f2 ♔e7 26 ♗h4+ f6 27 exf6+ gxf6 28 ♖xd8 ♗xd8 29 ♔e3 ♔e6 30 ♔d4 b6 31 ♗g3 ♗e7 32 ♗b8 ♗c5+ 33 ♔d3 ♔d7 34 ♗xa7 ♔c7 35 a5 **1-0** M324-1864

**1863-⚔GS-3**
**Green, V.– Steinitz, W.**
[Löwenthal]

1 e4 e5 2 ♘f3 ♘c6 3 ♗c4 ♘f6 4 0-0 ♘xe4 5 d4 ♘d6 6 ♗d5 e4 7 ♖e1 ♗e7 8 ♘e5 0-0 9 ♘c3 ♗f6 10 ♗f4 ♘f5 11 ♕h5 [11 ♖xe4 ♘fxd4 12 ♖xd4 ♘xd4 13 ♕xd4 d6 14 ♘xf7 ♖xf7!] 11 ... g6 12 ♘xg6 ♘g7! [12 ... hxg6? 13 ♕xg6+ ♘g7 14 ♘xe4 ♗e7 15 ♘g5 ♗xg5 16 ♗xg5+-] 13 ♕h6 hxg6 14 ♘xe4 [14

♕xg6 ♗xd4 15 ♗g5 ♘e5 16 ♕h6 ♗xf2+ 17 ♔f1 ♘g4 18 ♗xd8 ♘xh6–+] 14 ... ♘e6 15 ♗xc6 ♗g7! [15 ... dxc6? 16 ♘xf6+ ♕xf6 17 ♗e5+–] 16 ♕h3 ♘xf4 17 ♕f3 dxc6 18 ♕xf4 ♗f5 19 ♘g5 ♗h6 **0-1** L/N6124-1864

**1863-✕GS-4**
**Steinitz, W.+Green, V.**
[Lange]

1 e4 e5 2 f4 exf4 3 ♘f3 g5 4 h4 g4 5 ♘e5 ♘f6 6 ♗c4 d5 7 exd5 ♗d6 [□ 7 ... ♗g7] 8 d4 ♕e7 [□ 8 ... 0-0; 8 ... ♘h5] 9 ♗xf4 ♘h5 10 g3 f6 11 ♕e2 fxe5 12 dxe5 ♗c5 13 ♘c3 ♗b4 [□ 13 ... ♗f5 Δ 14 ... ♘d7, 15 ... 0-0-0] 14 0-0 ♗xc3 15 bxc3 ♘xf4 16 ♖xf4 ♖f8?! [□ 16 ... ♘d7 17 ♗b5 (17 e6 ♘f6) 17 ... c6] 17 ♖xf8+ ♕xf8 18 ♖f1 ♕c5+ 19 ♔h2 b5 20 ♗xb5+ ♗d7

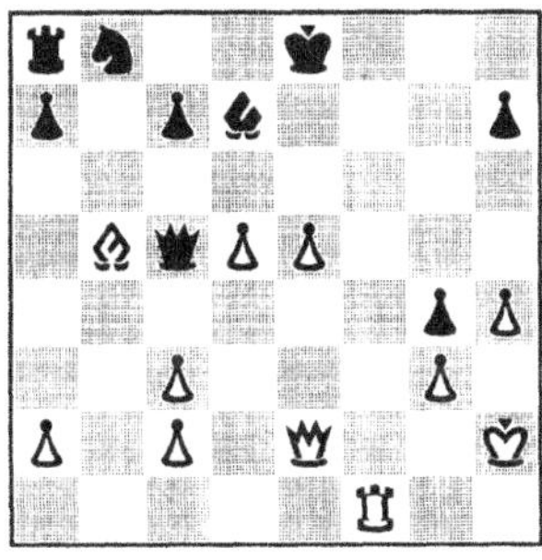

21 ♕xg4!! ♕xd5 22 ♕h5+ ♔e7 [22 ... ♔d8 23 ♖f8+ ♔e7 24 ♖e8++–] 23 ♕xh7+ ♔e6 **1-0** L/N6047-1864

**1863-✕GS-5**
**Green, V.=Steinitz, W.**
[Löwenthal]

1 e4 e5 2 ♘f3 ♘c6 3 ♗c4 ♗c5 4 0-0 ♘f6 5 d3 d6 6 c3 ♗b6 7 ♗e3 ♗e6 8 ♘bd2 ♕d7 9 ♕e2 0-0 10 ♖ad1 ♖ad8 11 ♔h1 ♖fe8 12 ♗xe6 ♕xe6 13 a3 ♕a2 14 ♘c4 d5 15 ♘xb6 axb6 16 ♗g5 ♖d6 17 ♘h4 h6 18 ♗xf6 ♖xf6 19 ♘f5 ♘e7 20 ♘xe7+ ♖xe7 21 exd5 ♕xd5 22 f3 ♖d6 23 ♖fe1 f6 24 ♕e4 ♖ed7 25 ♕xd5+ ♖xd5 26 ♖e3 b5 27 ♔g1 c5 28 ♔f2 c4 29 ♔e2 f5 30 d4! ♔f7 [30 ... exd4 31 ♖xd4 ♖xd4 32 cxd4 ♖xd4 33 ♖e5±] 31 ♖xe5 ♖xe5+ 32 dxe5 ♖xd1 33 ♔xd1 f4 34 ♔e2 ♔e6 35 ♔f2 ♔xe5 36 ♔e2 ♔f5 37 ♔f2 g5 38 ♔f1 h5 39 ♔e2 g4 40 ♔f2 ♔e5 41 ♔e2 gxf3+ 42 gxf3 [42 ♔xf3? ♔f5 43 g3 fxg3 44 hxg3 ♔g5 45 ♔f2 ♔g4 46 ♔g2 b6 47 ♔f2 ♔h3 48 ♔f3 ♔h2 49 ♔f2 b4 50 axb4 (50 cxb4) 50 ... b5 51 ♔f3 ♔g1 52 ♔f4 ♔f2–+] ½-½ L/N6124-1864

**1863-✕GS-6**
**Steinitz, W.+Green, V.**
[Löwenthal]

1 e4 e5 2 f4 exf4 3 ♘f3 g5 4 h4 g4 5 ♘e5 d6 6 ♘xg4 ♗e7 7 d4 ♗xh4+ 8 ♘f2 ♕g5 9 ♘c3 ♘f6 [9 ... ♗xf2+ 10 ♔xf2 ♕g3+ 11 ♔g1 Δ 12 ♘e2±; 12 ♘d5±] 10 ♕f3 ♗g3 11 ♗d2 ♘c6 12 ♗b5 ♗d7 13 ♗xc6 bxc6 14 0-0-0 0-0-0?! [□ 14 ... ♗xf2 15 ♕xf2 ♘g4 Δ 16 ... ♘e3=] 15 ♘d3 ♖hg8 16 e5 ♘g4 17 ♘e4 ♕e7 18 ♘dc5 dxc5 19 ♘xc5 ♘e3 20 ♕e2 ♖df8 21 ♗b4 [Δ 22 ♕a6+ ♔d8 23 ♘b7+ ♔ 24 ♗xe7] 21 ... ♕g5 22 ♕a6+ ♔d8 23 ♕xa7 ♗c8 [23 ... ♕f5 (Δ 24 ... ♕xc2#) 24 ♖d3 ♘d5 25 ♗a5 f3 26 gxf3 ♗f4+ 27 ♔b1 ♖g2 28 c4 ♘b6 29 ♕b8+ ♗c8 30 ♗xb6 cxb6 31 ♘b7+ ♔e7 (31 ... ♔e8 32 ♘d6+ ♔~ 33 ♘xf5) 32 ♕d6+ ♔e8 33 ♕d8#] 24 ♗a5 ♕e7! [24 ... ♘d5 25 c4 f3+ 26 ♔b1 ♗f5+ 27 ♔a1 fxg2 28 cxd5 gxh1♕ 29 ♕xc7+ ♔e8 30 ♕b8+ ♔e7 31 d6#] 25 ♕b8 ♘d5 26 c4 ♘b6 27 ♘a6!+– ♖g6 28 ♘xc7 ♕xc7 29 ♗xb6 **1-0** L/N6124-1864

**1863-✕GS-7**
**Green, V.–Steinitz, W.**
[Bachmann]

1 e3 f5 2 f4 ♘f6 3 ♘f3 e6 4 b3 ♗e7 5 ♗b2 0-0 6 c4 c5 7 ♘c3 ♘c6 8 ♗e2 d5= 9 cxd5 exd5 10 0-0 ♔h8 [Δ 11 ... d4 12 ♘c~ d3, 13 ... dxe2] 11 ♘g5 h6 12 ♘h3 d4 13 ♘b5 a6 14 ♘a3 ♘e4 15 ♘f2 ♗f6 16 ♘d3 ♗e6 17 ♘c4 ♗xc4 18 bxc4 ♕a5–+ 19 ♗f3 ♘xd2 20 ♖e1 ♘xc4 21 ♗xc6 bxc6 **0-1** L/N3131

**1863-✕GS-9**
**Green, V.–Steinitz, W.**
[Löwenthal]

1 e4 e5 2 ♘f3 ♘c6 3 ♗c4 ♗c5 4 d3 ♘f6 5 ♘c3 d6 6 h3 ♗e6 7 ♗g5?! h6 8 ♗h4 g5 9 ♗g3 ♗xc4 10 dxc4 ♗b4 11 ♕d3 ♗xc3+ 12 bxc3 ♕e7 13 h4 g4 14 ♘h2 ♕e6 15 ♘f1 ♘e7 16 ♘e3 ♘d7 17 f3 gxf3 [□ 17 ... h5] 18 gxf3 ♖g8 19 ♗f2 ♘c5 20 ♕e2 0-0-0 21 ♘d5 c6 22 ♘xe7+ ♕xe7 23 ♗xc5 dxc5 24 ♖d1 ♕c7 25 ♖xd8+ ♖xd8 26 0-0 ♕e7! [26 ... ♕a5] 27 ♕f2 ♕e6 28 f4! ♕h3 29 ♕g2 ♕e3+ 30 ♖f2?? [□ 30 ♔h1=] 30 ... ♖d2 31 fxe5 ♔d7 32 ♕f3 ♕xf2+ 33 ♕xf2 ♖xf2 34 ♔xf2 ♔e6 35 a4 ♔xe5 36 ♔e3 b6 37 ♔f3 h5 38 ♔e3 f6 39 ♔f3 f5 40 exf5 ♔xf5 **0-1** M324-1864

**1863-★AH-1**
**Anderssen, A.+Hamel, S.**
Breslau [Bachmann]

1 e4 e5 2 ♘f3 ♘c6 3 ♗c4 ♗c5 4 b4 ♗xb4 5 c3 ♗c5 6 0-0 ♗b6 7 d4 exd4 8 cxd4 d6 9 d5 ♘ce7 10 e5 ♗g4 11 ♕a4+ ♕d7 12 ♗b5 c6 13 e6 ♗xe6? [□ 13 ... fxe6] 14 dxe6 fxe6 15 ♗d3 ♘f6 16 ♘bd2 e5 17 ♗a3 ♘g6 18 ♘c4 ♗c7 19 ♖ab1 b5 20 ♖xb5 cxb5 21 ♘xd6+ ♔d8 22 ♗xb5 **1-0** L/N3033

**1863-★AL-1**
**Anderssen, A.– Lasa, T. von H. u. von d.**
[Journoud]

1 e4 e5 2 ♘f3 ♘c6 3 ♗c4 ♘f6 4 ♘g5 d5 5 exd5 ♘a5! 6 ♗b5+ [□ 6 d3] 6 ... c6 7 dxc6 bxc6 8 ♗a4 [8 ♕f3 ♕b6; 8 ♕f3 cxb5!?; 8 ♗e2 h6 9 ♘f3 e4 10 ♘e5 ♕d4 11 ♘g4 ♗xg4 12 ♗xg4 ♘c4 13 c3 ♕b6 14 b3 ♘e5∓] 8 ... ♗d6?! 9 d3 h6 10 ♘e4 [10 ♘f3 e4] 10 ... ♘xe4 11 dxe4 ♗a6! 12 ♘c3 [12 ♗d2 0-0; 12 ♗d2 ♖b8] 12 ... ♖b8 13 ♗b3 0-0 14 ♗d2 ♗c5 15 ♕g4! ♔h8 16 0-0-0 ♗d4 [16 ... ♗xf2? 17 ♗xh6 ♕f6 18 ♖d6 ♗e3+ 19 ♔b1 ♗c8 20 ♕d1] 17 f4 ♘xb3+ 18 axb3 f6 19 f5 ♕b6∓ 20 ♘a4 ♕b7 21 h4 c5 22 ♖h3 c4 23 ♖g3? ♗b5 24 ♘c3 ♗c6 25 ♘e2 ♗f2 [25 ... ♗xe4?!] 26 ♖f3 ♗c5 27 ♘g3 cxb3 28 ♖xb3 ♕a6! 29 ♔b1 ♖xb3 30 cxb3 ♕d3+ 31 ♔c1 ♖c8!–+ 32 ♕xg7+ ♔xg7 33 ♗xh6+ ♔xh6 34 ♖xd3 ♗f2 ...? **0-1** L/N6016-1863

**1863-★AM-1**
**Anderssen, A.=Mieses, S.**
Breslau

1 e4 c5 2 ♗c4 e6 3 ♘c3 ♘c6 4 d3 ♘f6 5 ♗f4 d5 6 ♘b5 dxc4 7 ♘c7+ ♔e7 8 ♘xa8 e5 9 ♗e3 b6 10 dxc4 ♗b7 11 ♕xd8+ ♔xd8 12 ♘xb6 axb6 13 0-0-0+ ♔c7 14 f3 ♗d6 15 ♘e2 ♖a8 16 ♘c3 ♗a6 17 b3 ♘d4 18 ♖hf1 b5 19 ♗xd4 exd4 20 cxb5 dxc3 21 bxa6 ♖xa6 22 ♔b1 c4 23 ♖d4 cxb3 24 axb3 ♗xh2 25 f4 ♘g4 26 ♖d3 ♖f6 27 ♖xc3+ ♔b7 28 g3 g5 29 ♖cf3 gxf4 30 gxf4 h5 31 ♖h3 ♖h6 32 ♖d1 ♗xf4 33 ♖d7+ ♔c6 34 ♖xf7 ♗e5 35 ♔c1 h4 36 ♖f5 ♗g3 37 ♔d2 ♖d6+ 38 ♔e2 ♖e6 39 ♖h1 ♖d6 40 ♖a1 ♘e5 41 ♖a6+ ♔d7 42 ♖xd6+ ♔xd6 43 ♖h5 ♔e6 44 ♖h6+ ♔f7 45 c4 ♘g4 46 ♖a6 h3 47 ♔f3 h2 48 ♖a1 ♗e5 49 ♖e1 ♘f6 50 b4 ♔e7 51 c5 ♔d7 52 b5 ♔c7 53 ♔g2 ♘d7 54 c6 ♘f6 55 ♖b1 ♔b6 56 ♖f1 ♘xe4 57 ♖e1 ♘g3 58 ♔xh2 ♗c7 59 ♔g2 ♔xb5 ½-½ L/N6047-1864

**1863-★AM-2**
**Mieses, S.+Anderssen, A.**
Breslau

1 e4 e5 2 ♘f3 ♘c6 3 ♗c4 ♗c5 4 b4 ♗xb4 5 c3 ♗a5 6 d4 exd4 7 0-0 ♗b6 8 cxd4 d6 9 ♕b3 ♕f6 10 e5 dxe5 11 ♖e1 ♘xd4 12 ♖xe5+ ♘e7 13 ♗xf7+ ♕xf7 14 ♘xd4 ♗xd4 15 ♕a4+ ♗d7 16 ♕xd4

0-0-0 17 ♕xa7 ♘c6 18 ♕a8+ ♘b8 19 ♗e3 ♗c6 20 ♘c3 b6 21 ♕a7 ♕g6 22 ♖g5 ♕c2 23 ♖xg7 ♖d7 24 ♖xd7 ♘xd7 25 ♗f4 ♗b7 26 ♖c1 ♖e8 27 h3 ♕g6 28 ♘d5 ♘c5 29 ♗g3 ♕c6 20 ♖d1 ♘a6 31 ♔h2 ♘b4 32 ♖c1 ♕xc1

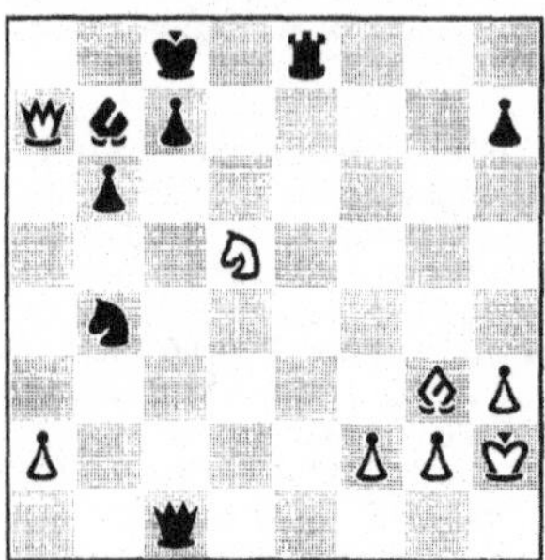

33 ♘xb6+ ♔d8 34 ♗h4+ ♖e7 35 ♕b8+ ♗c8 36 ♕xc8# **1-0**

L/N6047-1864

**1863-★AP-1 ●○⬠** 31 viii 63
**Paulsen, L.=Asbeck, J.**
Dusseldorf [Lange]

1 e4 e5 2 ♗c4 ♗c5 3 b4 ♗xb4 4 c3 ♗a5 5 ♘f3 ♘f6 6 d4 0-0 7 0-0 d6 8 ♗a3 ♘xe4 9 dxe5 ♘xc3 10 ♕d3 ♘xb1 11 ♖axb1 ♘c6 12 exd6 cxd6 13 ♗xd6 ♖e8 14 h4 h6 15 ♖fd1 ♕f6 16 ♗a3 [□ 16 ♕b3] 16 ... ♗f5 17 ♕b3 ♗xb1 18 ♖xb1 ♗b6 19 ♗b2 ♕f5 20 ♗d3 ♕f4 21 ♕c3 f6 22 ♕b3+ ♔h8 23 ♖f1 ♘e5 24 ♘xe5 fxe5 25 ♗b1 ♕xh4 26 ♕f7 ♖f8 27 ♕g6 ♗xf2+ 28 ♖xf2 ♕xf2+ 29 ♔h1 ♕h4+ **½-½**

L/N5192

**1863-★AR-1** i 63
**Rosanes, J.–Anderssen, A.**
Breslau

1 e4 e5 2 f4 exf4 3 ♘f3 g5 4 h4 g4 5 ♘e5 ♘f6 6 ♗c4 d5 7 exd5 ♗d6 8 d4 ♘h5 9 ♗b5+ c6 10 dxc6 bxc6 11 ♘xc6 ♘xc6 12 ♗xc6+ ♔f8 13 ♗xa8 ♘g3 14 ♖h2 ♗f5 15 ♗d5 ♔g7 16 ♘c3 ♖he8+ 17 ♔f2 ♕b6 18 ♘a4 ♕a6 19 ♘c3

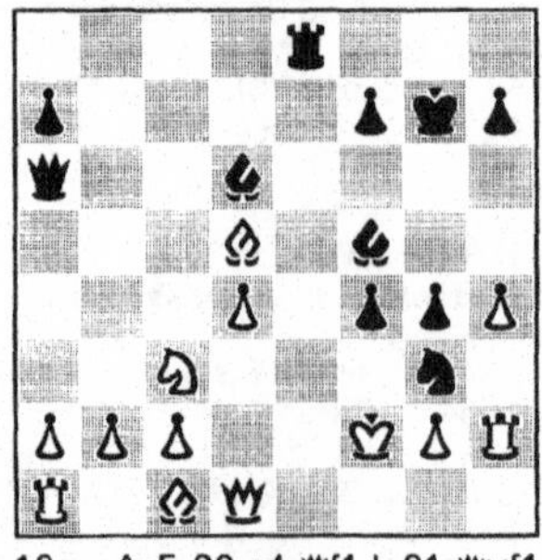

19 ... ♗e5 20 a4 ♕f1+ 21 ♕xf1 ♗xd4+ 22 ♗e3 ♖xe3 23 ♔g1 ♖e1# **0-1**

L/N3034

**1863-★BB-1 ●○⬠**
**Blackburne, J.H.+ Butterfield**
Manchester

1 e4 e5 2 f4 ♗c5 3 ♘f3 d6 4 c3 ♗g4 5 ♗c4 ♗xf3 6 ♕xf3 ♘c6 7 b4 ♗b6 8 a4 a6 9 ♘a3 ♕f6 10 d3 exf4 11 d4 ♘ge7 12 ♗xf4 ♘g6 13 ♗e3 ♕xf3 14 gxf3 ♘h4 15 ♔e2 ♖f8 16 ♖hg1 ♘g6 17 f4 f5 18 e5 ♘ce7 19 ♗e6 dxe5 20 dxe5 ♖d8 21 ♖ad1 ♖xd1 22 ♖xd1 ♘c6 23 ♘c4 ♔e7 24 ♘xb6 ♔xe6 25 ♘d7 ♖d8 26 ♘c5+ ♔f7 27 ♖xd8 ♘xd8 28 a5 ♘e7 29 b5 ♘d5 30 ♘xb7 ♘xc3+ 31 ♔e1 **1-0**

L/N3036

**1863-★BP-1 ●○⬠** 31 viii 63
**Paulsen, L.+Bollen, C.**
Düsseldorf [Lange]

1 e4 e5 2 ♘f3 ♘c6 3 d4 d6? 4 d5 ♘d4? 5 ♘xd4 exd4 6 ♕xd4 ♗e7 7 ♗b5+ ♗d7 8 ♗xd7+ ♕xd7 9 0-0 ♗f6 10 ♕b4 0-0-0 11 ♘c3 a6 12 a4 ♘e7 13 ♘b5 ♔b8 14 ♗e3 c5 15 ♕c4 ♗xb2 16 ♖a2 ♗f6 17 ♘c3 ♗xc3 18 ♕xc3 f6 19 ♖b1 ♖c8 20 ♖ab2 ♖c7 21 ♕a5 ♔a8 22 f4 ♘g6 23 ♕b6 ♖e8 24 ♖b4 ♘xf4

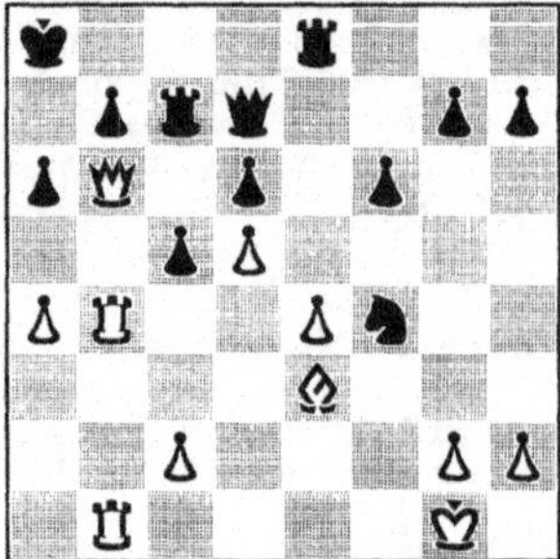

25 ♖c4 [25 ♗xf4 cxb4 26 ♗e3 ♖c5! 27 ♖xb4±] 25 ... ♘xd5 26 exd5 ♖xe3 27 ♖f4 ♕e7 28 ♖4f1 ♖d7 29 ♕a5 ♕e4 30 ♖b6 ♕xd5 31 ♖fb1 ♖ee7 32 ♖xa6+! bxa6 33 ♕xa6+ ♖a7 34 ♕c8# **1-0**

L/N5192

**1863-★BP-2** xi 63
**Paulsen, L.+Beuthner, R.**
Leipzig

1 e4 e5 2 ♘f3 ♘c6 3 d4 exd4 4 ♘xd4 ♘xd4 5 ♕xd4 d6 6 ♗c4 ♘f6 7 ♘c3 ♗e7 8 0-0 0-0 9 f4 c6 10 ♗e3 ♘g4 11 h3 b5 12 ♗e2 ♗f6 13 ♕d2 ♘xe3 14 ♕xe3 b4 15 ♘d1 ♕c7 16 a3 c5 17 ♔h1 ♖e8 18 ♗f3 ♗d4 19 ♕d3 bxa3 20 ♖xa3 ♗b7 21 c3 ♗f6 22 ♘e3 a5 23 ♘f5 ♗e7 24 ♖d1 ♖ad8! 25 ♖da1 ♖a8 26 ♕b5 ♗c6 27 ♕d3 ♗f8 28 c4 a4 29 ♖d1 ♕b7 30 ♘xd6 ♗xd6 31 ♕xd6 ♗xe4 32 ♗xe4 ♕xe4 33 ♕xc5 ♖ac8 34 ♕b5 ♕xc4 35 ♕xa4 ♕xa4 36 ♖xa4 ♖c2 37 b4 g6 38 ♖a7 ♖ee2 39 ♖d8+ ♔g7 40 ♖dd7 ♖xg2 41 ♖xf7+ ♔g8 42 ♖fd7 ♖h2+ 43 ♔g1 ♖hg2+ 44 ♔f1 ♖cf2+ 45 ♔e1 ♖xf4 46 ♖d8+ ♖f8 47 ♖xf8+ ♔xf8 48 ♖xh7 **1-0**

L/N6047-1865

**1863-★BP-3** xi 63
**Beuthner, R.+Paulsen, L.**
Leipzig [Minckwitz & von Schmidt]

1 e4 e5 2 ♘f3 ♘c6 3 ♗b5 ♘f6 4 d3 d6 5 0-0 ♗d7 6 ♘e1 ♗e7 7 f4 exf4 8 ♗xf4 0-0 9 ♘c3 ♘d4 10 ♗xd7 ♕xd7 11 ♗e3 ♘c6 12 h3 h6 13 d4 ♖fe8 14 ♕f3 ♗f8 15 ♘d3 b5 16 e5 dxe5 17 ♘xe5 ♘xe5 18 dxe5 ♘h7 19 ♖ae1 c6 20 ♕g3 ♔h8 21 ♕f4 f6 22 exf6 ♘xf6 23 ♗d4 ♗d6 24 ♕h4 ♗g3 25 ♕xg3 ♕xd4+ 26 ♔h1 b4 27 ♘d1 ♘e4 28 ♕e3 ♕d5 29 ♕f4 ♖e6 30 ♘f2! ♘xf2+ 31 ♕xf2 ♖f6 32 ♕e2 ♖xf1+ 33 ♖xf1 ♕xa2 34 b3 ♕b2 35 ♕c4 ♕c3 36 ♕xc3 bxc3 37 ♖f3 ♖e8 38 ♖xc3 ♖e6 39 ♖c4 ♔h7 40 ♔h2 a6 41 h4 h5 42 ♔h3 g6 43 g4+ hxg4 44 ♔xg4 ♔h6 45 ♖c5 ♔g7 46 h5 gxh5+ 47 ♔xh5 ♔f6 48 ♔g4 ♔e7 49 ♔f5 ♔d6? 50 ♖xc6+ ♔xc6 51 ♔xe6 ♔c5 52 c3 ♔c6 53 b4 ♔b5 54 ♔d5 ♔a4 55 ♔c4 ♔a3 56 ♔c5 [□ 56 b5] 56 ... ♔b3 57 c4 ♔c3 58 b5 a5 59 b6 **1-0**

L/N6047-1865

**1863-★BS-1**
**Blackburne, J.H.+ Steinitz, W.**
London [Blackburne]

1 e4 e5 2 ♘f3 ♘c6 3 ♗c4 ♗c5 4 b4 ♗xb4 5 c3 ♗c5 6 d4 exd4 7 cxd4 ♗b6 8 0-0 d6 9 ♘c3 ♗g4 10 ♕a4 ♗d7 11 ♕b3 ♘a5 12 ♗xf7+ ♔f8 13 ♕c2?! ♔xf7 14 e5 ♗g4? [14 ... h6!] 15 ♖e1 ♗xf3 16 ♕f5+ ♘f6 17 ♕xf3 ♖e8 18 ♗g5 ♘c6 19 exf6 ♖xe1+ 20 ♖xe1 gxf6 21 ♕h5+ ♔g8 22 ♗h6 ♕d7 23 ♖e4 ♔h8 24 ♕h4 ♕f7 25 ♘d5 ♕g6 26 ♘f4 ♕f5 27 ♕g3 ♕d7 28 ♘h5 **1-0** L/N3036

**1863-★BS-2**
**Blackburne, J.H.+ Steinkühler, A.**
Manchester [Blackburne]

1 e4 e5 2 ♘f3 ♘c6 3 ♗c4 ♗c5 4 b4 ♗xb4 5 c3 ♗c5 6 d4 exd4 7 0-0 d6 8 cxd4 ♗b6 9 ♘c3 ♗g4 10 ♗b5 ♗d7 [□ 10 ... ♔f8] 11 e5 dxe5 12 d5 ♘d4 [□ 12 ... ♘ce7] 13 ♗xd7+ ♕xd7 14 ♘xe5 ♕d6 15 ♕a4+ c6 16 ♗a3 ♕f6 17 dxc6 bxc6 18 ♘d5 ♕xe5 19 ♖fe1 ♘e2+ 20 ♖xe2 ♕xe2 21 ♕xc6+ ♔d8 22 ♘xb6 axb6 23 ♖c1 **1-0**

L/N3036

**1863-★BS-3**
**Steinkühler, A.– Blackburne, J.H.**
Manchester [Blackburne]
1 e4 e5 2 ♘f3 ♘c6 3 ♗c4 ♗c5 4 c3 ♘f6 5 d4 exd4 6 cxd4 ♗b4+ 7 ♗d2 ♗xd2+ 8 ♘fxd2? [◻ 8 ♘bxd2] 8 ... ♘xd4 9 0-0 d6 10 ♘b3 ♘xb3 11 ♕xb3 0-0 12 ♖e1 ♘h5 13 e5 ♕g5 14 exd6 ♘f4 15 ♗xf7+? ♔h8 16 g3 cxd6 17 ♘c3 ♘h3+ 18 ♔g2 ♕f6 19 ♗d5

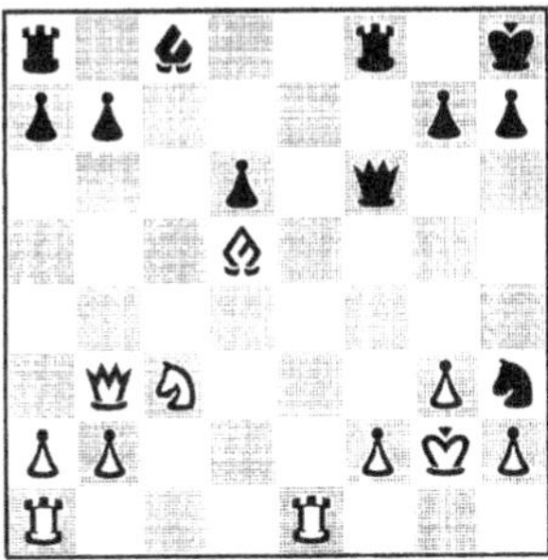

19 ... ♕xf2+ 20 ♔h1 ♕g1+ 21 ♖xg1 ♘f2+ 22 ♔g2 ♗h3# **0-1** L/N3036

**1863-★B?-1 ●○△**
**Blackburne, J.H.+?**
Kidderminster
1 e4 e5 2 d4 exd4 3 c3 dxc3 4 ♗c4 d6 5 ♘xc3 ♘c6 6 ♘f3 ♘e5 7 ♘xe5 dxe5 8 ♗xf7+ ♔e7 9 ♗g5+ ♘f6 10 ♕h5 c6 11 ♖d1 ♕a5 12 f4 ♕c5 13 fxe5 ♕xe5 14 0-0 h6 15 ♗e8 ♗e6 16 ♖xf6 gxf6 17 ♖d7+ ♗xd7 18 ♕f7+ ♔d6 19 ♕xd7+ ♔c5 20 ♗e3+ ♔b4 21 ♕xb7+ ♔a5 22 b4+ ♗xb4 23 ♗b6+ axb6 24 ♕xa8# **1-0** L/N3036

**1863-★B?-2 ●○△**
**Blackburne, J.H.+?**
Manchester [Blackburne]
1 e4 e5 2 f4 d5 3 ♘f3 dxe4 4 ♘xe5 ♘d7 5 d4 exd3 6 ♗xd3 ♘xe5 7 fxe5 ♗c5 8 ♘c3 c6 9 ♘e4 ♕e7 10 ♕e2 [△ 11 ♗g5] 10 ... h6 [10 ... ♕xe5? 11 ♘xc5+–] 11 ♗e3 ♗xe3 12 ♕xe3 ♗e6 13 0-0 ♕c7 14 ♖ad1 ♕xe5? 15 ♗c4 [△ 16 ♘d6+] 15 ... ♔f8 16 ♕a3+ ♘e7 17 ♕xa7

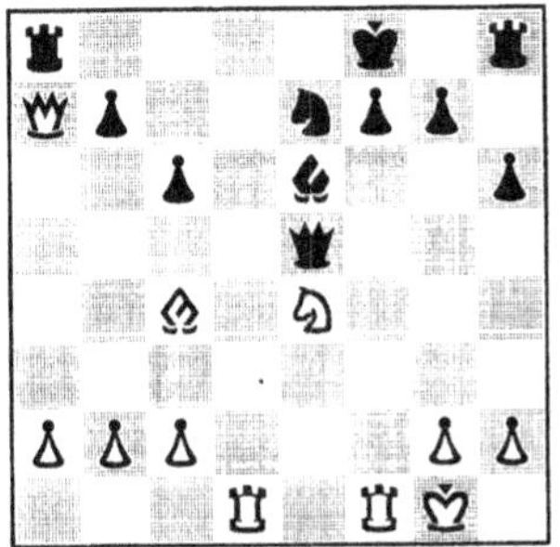

17 ... ♖e8 18 ♗xe6 ♕xe6 19 ♘d6 ♖d8 20 ♕a5 ♕e3+ 21 ♔h1 b6 22 ♕a7 ♔g8 23 ♖de1 ♕c5 24 ♘xf7 ♖e8 25 ♕d7 **1-0** L/N3036

**1863-★DN-1** x63
**Dufresne,J.– Neumann,G.R.**
Berlin
1 e4 e5 2 ♘f3 ♘c6 3 ♗c4 ♗c5 4 b4 ♗xb4 5 c3 ♗c5 6 0-0 d6 7 d4 exd4 8 cxd4 ♗b6 9 ♘c3 ♗g4 10 ♗b5 ♗d7 11 e5 dxe5 12 dxe5 ♘ge7 13 ♗g5 h6 14 ♗h4 g5 15 ♘e4 ♗f5 16 ♘f6+ ♔f8 17 ♗g3 ♕xd1 18 ♖axd1 ♔g7 19 h4 g4 20 ♘h2 h5 21 ♔h1 ♘d4 22 ♗c4 ♖ad8 23 f3 ♗c2 24 ♖c1 ♘ef5 **0-1** L/N6051-1864

**1863-★DN-2** x63
**Neumann,G.R.+Dufresne, J.**
Berlin
1 e4 e5 2 f4 ♗c5 3 ♘f3 d6 4 ♗c4 ♘c6 5 ♘c3 ♘f6 6 d3 ♘g4 7 ♕e2 ♗f2+ 8 ♔f1 ♗b6 9 h3 ♘f6 10 f5 h5 11 ♗g5 ♘e7 12 ♖d1 c5 13 ♔f2 a6 14 g4 ♗d7 15 ♗h4 hxg4 16 hxg4 ♘xg4+ 17 ♔g3 ♘h6 18 ♗g5 f6 19 ♗xh6 ♖xh6 20 ♖xh6 gxh6 21 ♘xe5 ♘xf5+ 22 exf5 dxe5 23 ♕h5+ ♔e7 24 ♕f7+ ♔d6 25 ♘e4+ ♔c7 26 ♘xf6 **1-0** L/N6051-1864

**1863-★DN-3** x63
**Neumann,G.R.+ Dufresne,J.**
Berlin
1 e4 e5 2 f4 ♗c5 3 ♘f3 d6 4 ♗c4 ♘f6 5 ♘c3 0-0 6 d3 ♘g4 7 ♖f1 ♘xh2 8 ♖h1 ♘g4 9 ♕e2 ♗f2+ 10 ♔f1 ♘c6 11 f5 ♗c5 12 ♘g5 ♘h6 13 ♕h5 ♕e8 14 ♘xh7 ♔xh7 15 ♗xh6 g6 16 ♕xg6+ fxg6 17 ♗xf8# **1-0** L/N6051-1864

**1863-★EN-1** xi63
**Neumann, G.R.+ Erner**
Berlin [Anderssen & Neumann]
⟨♗f1⟩ 1 e4 e5 2 d4 exd4 3 ♘f3 c5? [◻ 3 ... ♘c6] 4 0-0 ♘c6 5 c3 dxc3 6 ♘xc3 ♗e7 7 ♗f4 a6 8 e5 h6 9 ♘e4 g5 10 ♗g3 g4 11 ♘fd2 h5 12 ♘c4 b5 13 ♘cd6+ ♗xd6 14 ♘xd6+ ♔f8 15 ♖e1 ♘h6 16 ♗f4 ♘d4 17 ♕d2 ♘hf5 18 ♗g5 ♕c7 19 ♗f6 ♖h7 20 ♕g5 ♘xd6 21 exd6 ♕b6 [22 ♕e5+–] **1-0** L/N6051-1864

**1863-★GN-1** 9xi63
**Neumann, G.R.+ Göhle, A.**
Berlin [Anderssen & Neumann]
⟨♘b1⟩ 1 e4 e5 2 ♘f3 ♘c6 3 ♗c4 ♗c5 4 b4 ♗xb4 5 c3 ♗c5 6 0-0 d6 7 d4 exd4 8 cxd4 ♗b6 9 d5 ♘a5 10 ♗d3 ♘f6 11 ♗b2 0-0 12 ♔h1 ♗g4 13 ♕d2 ♗xf3? 14 gxf3 ♔h8 15 ♖g1 [△ ♖xg7] 15 ... ♘e8 16 ♖xg7+– ♘xg7 17 ♕h6 f6 18 e5 f5 19 e6 ♕e7 20 ♖g1 ♖g8 21 ♗xf5 **1-0** L/N6051-1864

**1863-★HS-1** ix63
**Steinitz, W.+ Holstein**
London [Löwenthal]
⟨♖a1⟩ 1 e4 e5 2 ♘f3 ♘c6 3 ♗c4 h6 4 d4 exd4 5 0-0 ♗c5 6 c3 d3 7 b4 ♗b6 8 b5 ♘a5 9 ♗xf7+!± ♔xf7 10 ♘e5+ ♔f6 [10 ... ♔e6 11 ♕g4+; 10 ... ♔e7] 11 ♕f3+ ♔xe5 12 ♕f5+ ♔d6 13 e5+!+– [13 ♗a3+? c5; 13 ♗f4+? ♔e7] 13 ... ♔e7 [13 ... ♔d5? 14 e6+ ♔d6! 15 ♗f4++–] 14 ♗a3+ d6 15 exd6+ ♔e8 16 d7+ ♕xd7 17 ♕f8# **1-0** M324

**1863-★JK-1**
**Jaenisch, C.F.+ Kolisch, I.F. von**
St. Petersburg
1 d4 f5 2 e4 d6 3 exf5 ♗xf5 4 ♗d3 ♗xd3 5 ♕xd3 ♘f6 6 ♕b5+ ♕d7 7 ♕xb7 ♕c6 8 ♕xc6+ ♘xc6 9 ♘e2 g6 10 a3 ♗g7 11 0-0 ♖b8 12 ♖a2 ♘a5 13 b3 ♘d7 14 ♗d2 ♘c6 15 d5 ♘ce5 16 f4 ♘g4 17 b4 ♘b6 18 ♘bc3 ♘f6 19 ♗e3 ♘fxd5 20 ♘xd5 ♘xd5 21 ♗xa7 ♖a8 22 c4 ♘xf4 23 ♘xf4 ♖xa7 24 ♘e6 ♗f6 25 ♖d1 ♔f7 26 ♘d4 ♖ha8 27 ♘b5 ♖b7 28 ♖f2 c6 29 ♘d4 ♖b6 30 ♘c2 ♔g7 31 ♖f3 ♖a4 32 ♔f1 c5 33 ♔e2 ♖ba6 34 ♖b3 ♖a8 35 ♖dd3 h5 36 ♘e3 ♗d4 37 ♘d5 ♖f8 38 ♖f3 ♖xf3 39 ♔xf3 cxb4 40 axb4 e6 41 ♘c7 ♔f6 42 ♔e4 ♗b6 43 ♘b5 ♔e7 44 ♖b2 ♖a1 45 ♔d3 h4 46 h3 ♖d1+ 47 ♔c2 ♖a1 48 ♔b3 ♖c1 49 ♖c2 ♖b1+ 50 ♖b2 ♖c1 51 ♖c2 ♖b1+ 52 ♔c3 e5 53 ♖d2 ♖c1+ 54 ♔b3 ♖b1+ 55 ♔a3 ♖a1+ 56 ♔b2 ♖g1 57 ♔c2 ♗e3 58 ♖e2 ♗b6 59 ♘c3 ♗d4 60 ♘b5 ♗b6 61 ♔b3 ♖b1+ 62 ♔a4 ♖a1+ 63 ♘a3 ♗d4 64 ♔b3 ♖g1 65 ♘c2 ♗b6 66 ♔a4 ♖f1 67 ♔b5 ♗g1 68 ♔c6 ♖f2 69 ♖xf2 ♗xf2 70 ♔d5 ♔d7 71 ♘a3 ♗e1 72 b5 ♗b4 73 ♘c2 ♗c5 74 ♘e1 ♔c7 75 ♘d3 ♗d4 76 ♘e1 ♗c5 77 ♘f3

♗f2 78 ♘g5 ♗e1 79 ♘e6+ ♔d7 80 ♘f8+ ♔e7 81 b6 ♗f2 82 b7 ♗a7 83 ♘xg6+ **1-0** L/N6047-1863

**1863-★JP-1**
**Petrov, A.D.= Journoud, P.**
Paris
1 e4 e5 2 f4 exf4 3 ♘f3 g5 4 h4 g4 5 ♘e5 ♘f6 6 ♗c4 d5 7 exd5 ♗d6 8 d4 ♘h5 9 ♗b5+ ♔f8 10 ♘c3 ♘g3 11 ♗xf4 ♘xh1 12 ♕d2 ♕xh4+ 13 g3 ♘xg3 14 ♕f2 ♘f5 15 ♕xh4 ♘xh4 16 ♗h6+ ♔g8 17 ♘e4 ♗e7 18 ♗e8 ♘f3+ 19 ♔f2 ♘xe5 20 dxe5 ♗f5 21 ♘f6+ ♗xf6 22 exf6 ♘d7 23 ♗xd7 ♗xd7 24 ♖e1 ♖e8 25 ♖xe8+ ♗xe8 26 ♔g3 ♗d7 27 c4 a5 28 a3? a4 29 c5 ♗c8 30 d6 cxd6 31 cxd6 ♗d7 32 ♔f4 ♗e6 33 ♔g3 **½-½** L/N6047-1863

**1863-★KP-1 ●○** 31 viii 63
**Paulsen, L.= Knorre, V.**
Düsseldorf [Lange]
1 e4 e5 2 ♘f3 ♘c6 3 ♗c4 ♘f6 4 d4 exd4 5 0-0 ♗e7 6 e5 ♘e4 7 ♗d5 [□ 7 ♖e1 d5 8 ♘xd4] 7 ... ♘c5 8 ♖e1 ♘e6 9 ♘bd2 d6 10 exd6 ♗xd6 11 ♔h1 [11 ♘e4 ♗xh2+] 11 ... ♗b4 12 ♗xc6+ bxc6 13 a3 ♗e7 14 b4 c5 15 bxc5 ♘xc5 16 ♗b2 ♘e6 17 ♕e2 0-0 18 ♘xd4 ♘xd4 19 ♗xd4 [19 ♕xe7 ♘xc2∓] 19 ... ♕xd4 20 ♕xe7 ♕xf2 [20 ... ♕xd2? 21 ♖ad1 △ 22 ♕xf8++-] 21 ♘e4 ♕b6 22 ♖ab1 ♕c6 23 ♖b3 ♗f5 24 ♖c3 ♕e6 [24 ... ♕d7 (24 ... ♖fe8 25 ♘f6+) 25 ♘f6+ △ 26 ♖g3++-]

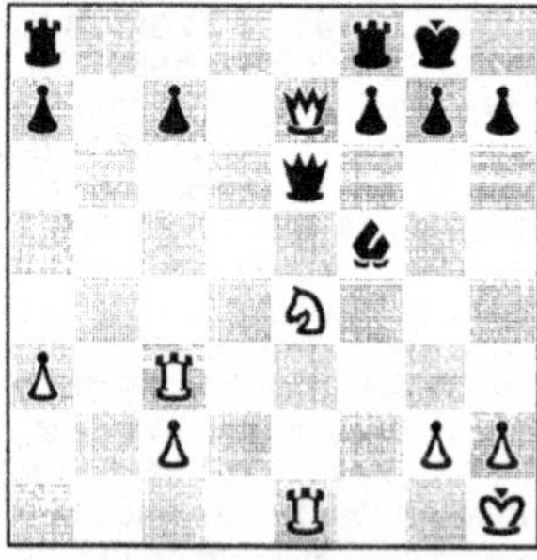

25 ♖xc7 ♖ac8 [25 ... ♖fe8 26 ♘f6++-] 26 ♘d6 ♖xc7 27 ♖xe6 ♖xe7 28 ♖xe7 ♗xc2 29 ♖xa7 ♖d8 30 ♔g1 h5 31 ♘xf7 ♖d1+ 32 ♔f2 ♖d2+ 33 ♔f3 ♗d1+ [33 ... ♖d3+ 34 ♔e2 ♖xa3 35 ♖xa3 ♔xf7=] 34 ♔g3 ♗e2 35 ♘g5 g6 36 ♘f3 ♖a2 37 ♔f4 ♗f1 38 ♘h4 ♖f2+ 39 ♔g5 [39 ♔e3 ♖a2; 39 ♔g3 ♖a2; 39 ♔e5 g5=] 39 ... ♗xg2 40 ♘xg6 ♗e4 41 ♘f4 ♖xh2 42 ♘xh5 ♗h1 43 ♘f6+ ♔f8 44 ♘g4 ♖g2 45 ♖h7 ♖g3 46 a4 ♗f3 47 ♖h4 ♖xg4+ 48 ♖xg4 ♗xg4 49 ♔xg4 ♔e7 50 a5 ♔d6 51 a6 ♔c7 52 a7 ♔b7 53 a8♕+ ♔xa8 **½-½** L/N5192

**1863-★LM-1**
**Löwenthal, J.J. & Steinitz, W.= Medley, G.W. & Mongredien, A.**
London [Löwenthal]
1 e4 e5 2 f4 exf4 3 ♘f3 g5 4 h4 g4 5 ♘e5 h5 [5 ... ♘f6] 6 ♗c4 ♖h7! [6 ... ♘h6] 7 d4 d6 [7 ... ♗e7 8 ♗xf4 d6! 9 ♘xf7 ♖xf7 10 ♗xf7+ ♔xf7 11 0-0 ♔g7 12 g3] 8 ♘d3 f3 9 gxf3 ♗e7 10 ♗e3 ♗xh4+ 11 ♔d2 gxf3 12 ♕xf3 ♗g4 13 ♕f4 ♘c6 14 c3 [□ 14 ♗b5] 14 ... ♖g7 15 ♘a3 ♗g5 16 ♕f2 ♗xe3+ 17 ♕xe3 a6 18 ♖af1 ♕e7 19 ♘f4! ♘f6! 20 ♘d5 ♘xd5 21 ♗xd5 ♘d8 22 ♘c4! ♕g5! [22 ... c6? 23 ♕h6 cxd5 (23 ... ♖g6 24 ♗xf7+±) 24 ♘b6±] 23 ♕xg5 [23 ♖f4] 23 ... ♖xg5 24 e5 dxe5 25 ♘xe5 ♖g7 26 ♘xg4? [□ 26 ♖e1 ♔f8 27 ♖xh5 ♗xh5 28 ♘d7+ ♔g8+-] 26 ... hxg4 27 ♖h8+ ♔e7 28 ♖e1+ ♔d6 29 ♗g2 [29 ♗xb7? ♖b8 30 ♗~ ♖xb2+∓] 29 ... c6 30 ♖ee8 [□ 30 c4] 30 ... ♔d7 31 c4 ♖c8 32 ♖ef8 ♖g6 33 ♗e4 ♖f6 34 a4 b5! 35 axb5 axb5 36 c5 ♔c7 37 ♖hg8 ♖f2+ 38 ♔c3 ♖f4 39 ♔d3 ♖f2 40 ♔c3 [□ 40 ♔e3 ♖xb2? 41 ♗f5 ♖a8 42 ♖e8+-] **½-½** M324

**1863-★LN-1** xii 63
**Neumann, G.R.+ Lichtenstein, A.**
Berlin [Anderssen & Neumann]
1 e4 e6 2 d4 d5 3 exd5 exd5 4 ♘f3 ♗e6 5 ♗d3 ♘f6 6 0-0 ♗d6 7 ♗e3 0-0 8 ♘bd2 h6 9 c4 c6 10 ♖e1 ♘bd7 11 ♖c1 ♗g4 12 ♕b3 b6 13 cxd5 cxd5 14 ♖c6 ♗e7 15 ♘e5 ♗e6? 16 ♖xe6 fxe6 17 ♘c6 ♕e8 18 ♗g6 ♖f7 19 ♗xh6 gxh6 [□ 19 ... ♕f8] 20 ♖xe6 ♕f8 21 ♗xf7+ ♕xf7 22 ♖xe7 **1-0** L/N6051-1864

**1863-★LP-1 ●○** 31 viii 63
**Paulsen, L.+ Lange, A.**
Düsseldorf [Lange]
1 e4 e5 2 ♘f3 ♘c6 3 ♗c4 ♗c5 4 b4 ♗xb4 5 c3 ♗c5 6 0-0 d6 7 d4 exd4 8 cxd4 ♗b6 9 d5 ♘e5 [□ 9 ... ♘a5!] 10 ♘xe5 dxe5 11 ♘c3 ♘e7 12 ♘e2 0-0 [□ 12 ... ♗g4] 13 ♔h1 ♗g4 14 f3 ♗h5 15 ♗b2 ♕d6 16 ♘g3 ♗g6 17 ♕e2 ♖fe8 [□ 17 ... ♔h8, △ ... f6] 18 ♖ad1 a6 [□ 18 ... ♖ad8] 19 f4 exf4 20 e5 ♕c5 21 ♖xf4 ♖ad8 22 e6 ♘xd5 23 ♖xf7 ♘f6 24 ♖fd7! ♘xd7 25 exd7+ ♔h8 26 dxe8♕+ ♖xe8 27 ♕g4 ♕f2 28 ♗c3 ♕c5 29 ♕f4 ♕e7 30 ♖f1 ♗c5 31 ♘f5 ♗xf5 32 ♕xf5 ♖f8 33 ♗f7! ♗d6 34 ♖f3 **1-0** L/N5192

**1863-★LP-2** 18 xi 63
**Paulsen, L.= Lepge, C.**
Leipzig
1 e4 e5 2 ♘f3 d6 3 d4 exd4 4 ♘xd4 d5 5 exd5 ♕xd5 6 ♕e2+ ♗e7 7 ♘b5 ♘a6 8 ♘1c3 ♕f5 9 ♗e3 ♘f6 10 ♘d4 ♕g6 11 ♕b5+ ♘d7 12 ♗d3 c6 13 ♗xg6 cxb5 14 ♗d3 b4 15 ♘d5 ♘dc5 16 ♗xa6 ♘xa6 17 ♘b5 ♗d8 18 ♘d6+ ♔f8 19 0-0-0 b6 20 ♗d2 ♗e6 21 ♘xb4 ♘xb4 22 ♗xb4 ♗e7 23 ♖d3 ♗xd6 24 ♖xd6 ♔g8 25 f4 h5 26 ♖f1 ♔h7 27 f5 ♗c4 28 ♖f4 ♗b5 29 g4 hxg4 30 ♖xg4 ♖hd8 31 f6 g6 32 c4 ♖xd6 33 ♗xd6 ♖c8 34 ♖h4+ ♔g8 35 b3 ♗c6 36 ♗e7 ♗d7 37 ♔b2 ♗f5 38 ♖d4 ♔h7 39 ♔c3 g5 40 ♖d8 ♔g6 41 a4 ♖xd8 42 ♗xd8 ♗e4 43 b4 ♔f5 44 ♔d4 ♗f3 45 c5 bxc5+ 46 ♔xc5 ♔e6 47 b5 ♔d7 48 ♗e7 ♔c8 49 a5 ♔c7 50 a6 ♔b8 51 ♗d6+ ♔a8 52 b6 axb6+ 53 ♔xb6 g4 **½-½** L/N6047-1863

**1863-★LP-3** xii 63
**Lepge, C.– Paulsen, L.**
Leipzig [Minckwitz & von Schmidt]
1 e4 e5 2 ♘f3 ♘c6 3 ♗b5 ♘f6 4 0-0 ♘xe4 5 d4 ♗e7 6 ♕e2 ♘d6 7 ♗xc6 dxc6 8 dxe5 ♘f5 9 ♖d1 ♗d7 10 e6 fxe6 11 ♘e5 ♗d6 12 ♕h5+ g6 13 ♘xg6 ♘g7 14 ♕h6 ♘f5 15 ♕h3 ♖g8 16 ♕xh7 ♖g7 17 ♕h5 ♕f6 18 ♘e5+ ♔d8 19 ♘f3 [□ ♗g5 ♖xg5 20 ♕xg5 ♕xg5 21 ♘f7+] 19 ... ♘e7 20 ♗g5 ♕f8 21 ♘c3 ♔c8 22 ♘e4 ♘f5 23 g4 ♘e7 24 ♗h6 ♖xg4+ 25 ♕xg4 ♕xh6 26 ♕g5 ♕f8 27 ♘e5 ♘d5

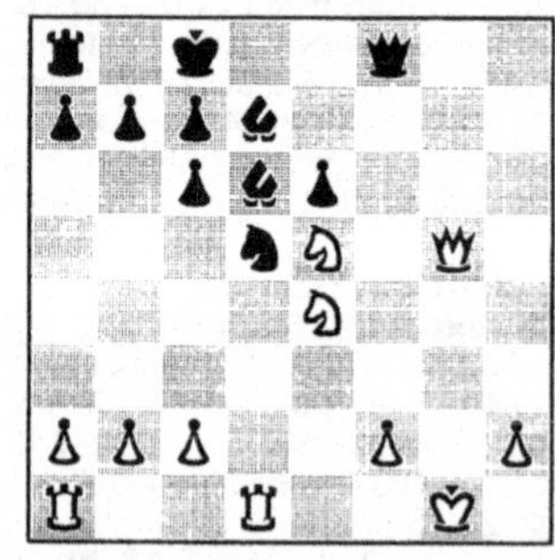

28 c4 ♘f4 29 ♘xd7 ♘h3+ 30 ♔g2 ♔xd7 31 ♕h4 ♕g7+ 32 ♔h1 ♕g6 33 ♘f6+ [□ 33 ♘xd6] 33 ... ♔e7 34 ♘h7+ ♔d7 35 ♕xh3 ♖h8 36 c5 ♖xh7 37 ♕g2 ♕xg2+ 38 ♔xg2 ♖xh2+ 39 ♔f1 e5 40 cxd6 cxd6 41 ♔e2 ♖h4 42 ♖h1 ♖e4+ 43 ♔d3 ♖d4+ 44 ♔e3 c5 45 ♖ad1 ♖b4 46 ♖d2 a5 47 ♖h6 ♖b6 48 ♔e4 ♔c7 49 ♔d5 ♖c6 50 ♖h7+ ♔c8 51 ♔e6 c4 52 ♖xd6 ♖c5 53 ♖dd7 ♖c6+ 54 ♔xe5 a4 55 ♖df7 ♔b8 56 ♖xb7+ ♔c8 57 ♖bc7+ ♖xc7 58 ♖xc7+ ♔xc7 59 ♔d5 a3 **0-1** L/N6047-1864

**1863-★LP-4** 31 viii 63
**Paulsen, L.= Lichtenscheidt, R.**
Düsseldorf [Lange]
1 e4 e5 2 f4 d5 3 exd5 exf4 4 ♘f3 ♕xd5 5 ♘c3 ♕e6+ 6 ♗e2 [6 ♔f2] 6 ... ♗d6 7 0-0 ♘e7 8 d4 0-0 9 ♘b5 ♘d5 10 ♘g5 ♕e7 11 ♘xd6 cxd6 12 ♘f3 ♘e3 13 ♗xe3 fxe3 14 c4 f5 15 ♕b3 f4 16 c5+ ♔h8 17 cxd6 ♕xd6 18 ♘g5 ♕e7 19 ♘f3 b6 20 ♘e5 ♗b7 21 ♗f3 ♘a6 22 ♗xb7 ♕xb7 23 ♖f3 ♖f6 24 ♕b5 ♘b8 25 ♖af1 ♕e4 26 ♕c4 h6 27 ♘g4 ♖c6 28 ♖xe3? ♕xe3+ 29 ♘xe3 ♖xc4 30 ♘xc4 ½-½ L/N5192

**1863-★LP-5**
**Lange, M.= Paulsen, L.**
1 e4 e5 2 ♘f3 ♘c6 3 ♗c4 ♗c5 4 0-0 ♘f6 5 d3 h6 6 ♘c3 d6 7 ♘e2 ♘h5 8 ♗e3 ♗b6 9 ♕d2 ♕f6 10 ♘c3 ♘e7 11 ♘d5 ♘xd5 12 ♗xd5 c6 13 ♗c4 ♗c7 14 d4 ♗g4 15 ♗e2 ♘f4 16 ♗xf4 ♕xf4 17 ♕b4 ♖b8 18 dxe5 ♗xf3 19 ♗xf3 ♕xe5 20 g3 0-0 21 ♗g2 ½-½ M392-1863

**1863-★LP-6**
**Paulsen, L.+ Lemke**
1 e4 e5 2 f4 exf4 3 ♗c4 ♕h4+ 4 ♔f1 d6 5 d4 ♘f6 6 ♘f3 ♕h6 7 ♘c3 ♗e7 8 ♔g1 ♘h5 9 ♘d5 ♗d8 10 g3 g5 11 h4 gxh4 12 ♘xf4 ♖g8 13 ♘e6 ♖xg3+ 14 ♔f2 ♕f6 15 ♘xd8 ♔xd8 16 e5 ♕e7 17 ♘xh4 ♗g4 18 ♗e2 ♕e6 19 d5 ♗xe2 20 dxe6 ♗xd1 21 exf7 ♔e7 22 ♘f5+ ♔xf7 23 ♘xg3 ♘xg3 24 ♔xg3 ♗xc2 25 exd6 cxd6 26 ♗f4 d5 27 ♖ac1 ♗f5 28 ♖c7+ ♔f6 29 ♖h6+ ♗g6 30 ♖c8 **1-0** M392-1863

**1863-★LP-7**
**Lindehn, H.A.W.– Petrov, A.D.**
1 e4 e5 2 f4 exf4 3 ♘f3 g5 4 h4 g4 5 ♘e5 ♘f6 6 ♗c4 d5 7 exd5 ♗d6 8 d4 ♘h5 9 ♗b5+ ♔f8 10 ♘c3 ♘g3 11 ♖g1 ♕xh4 12 ♗xf4 ♘e4+ 13 g3 ♕h2 14 ♖f1 ♗b4 15 ♕d3 ♗f5 16 0-0-0 ♘d6 17 ♕d2 ♕xd2+ 18 ♗xd2 ♗g6 19 ♗h6+ ♔e7 20 ♖de1 ♔d8 21 ♗e2 f5 22 ♗d3 ♖e8 23 ♖e2 ♘d7 24 ♘b5 ♘b6 25 c3 ♘xd5 26 cxb4 ♘xb4 27 ♗xf5 ♘xf5 28 ♘f7+ ♗xf7 29 ♖xe8+ ♗xe8 30 ♖xf5 ♘xa2+ 31 ♔d2 c6 32 ♘d6 ♔d7 33 ♘xb7 ♗g6 34 ♘c5+ ♔c7 35 ♗f4+ ♔b6 36 ♘a4+ ♔a6 37 ♖c5 ♘b4 38 ♖c4 ♔b5 39 b3 a5 40 ♗c7 ♘d3 41 ♘c3+ ♔a6 42 ♖xc6+ ♔b7 43 ♖c4 ♗f7 44 d5 ♘b4 45 ♗f4 ♘xd5 46 ♘xd5 ♗xd5 47 ♖c7+ ♔b6 48 ♔c3 ♗e4 49 ♖e7 ♖c8+ 50 ♔d4 ♗c2 51 ♖e6+ ♔b5 52 ♖e5+ ♔b6 53 ♖e6+ ♔b7 54 ♖e5 ♗xb3 55 ♖xa5 ♔b6 56 ♖h5 ♗c2 57 ♖h6+ ♗g6 58 ♔e5 ♖f8 59 ♖h1 ♖f5+ 60 ♔e6 ♔c5 61 ♖h2 ♔d4 62 ♖f2 ♔d3 63 ♖d2+ ♔e4 64 ♖f2 h5 65 ♖b2 ♗f7+ 66 ♔e7

66 ... h4 67 ♗b8 h3 68 ♗f4 ♗c4 69 ♖b4 ♖c5 70 ♗d6 h2 71 ♗xc5 h1♕ 72 ♖xc4+ ♔d5 73 ♖xg4 ♕e1+ 74 ♔f6 ♔xc5 75 ♖g5+ ♔d6 76 g4 ♕e4 77 ♖g6 ♕e7+ 78 ♔f5+ ♔d5 79 ♖h6 ♕e5+ 80 ♔g6 ♕e6 81 ♖h5 ♕f4 82 ♖g5 ♕e4+ 83 ♔g7 ♕e7 84 ♖g6 ♕f4 85 g5 ♕f8+ 86 ♔h7 ♕f5 87 ♔g7 ♕e8 88 ♔h8 ♕h3+ 89 ♔g7 ♕h5 90 ♔f6 ♕f8 91 ♖h6 ♕f3+ 92 ♔e5 ♕g7 93 ♖f6 ♕g4 94 ♖f5 ♔g6 **0-1** L/N6016-1863

**1863-★MM-1** 16 i 63
**Mongredien, A.– Morphy, P.C.**
Paris [Maróczy]
1 e4 e5 2 f4 exf4 3 ♗c4 d5 4 exd5 ♘f6 5 ♘f3 [◻ 5 ♘c3] 5 ... ♘xd5 6 0-0 ♗e6 7 ♗xd5 ♗xd5 8 d4 ♘c6 9 ♗xf4 ♗e7 [9 ... ♗xf3 10 ♕xf3 ♕xd4+ (10 ... ♘xd4 11 ♖e1+, 12 ♕xb7) 11 ♔h1 0-0-0 12 ♘c3±] 10 ♘bd2 0-0 11 c4 ♗xf3 12 ♘xf3 ♗f6 13 d5 ♘e7 14 ♗e5 ♘f5 15 ♕d3 g6 16 ♗xf6 [◻ 16 ♕c3] 16 ... ♕xf6 17 ♕b3 ♖fe8 18 ♖ae1 ♘d4 19 ♘xd4 ♕xd4+ 20 ♔h1 ♖xe1 21 ♖xe1 ♕d2 22 ♖f1 [◻ 22 ♖g1] 22 ... ♖e8 23 ♕f3 f5 24 ♕d1 ♖e2 [25 ♕xd2 ♖xd2 26 ♖b1 ♖c2 27 b3 ♖xa2−+] **0-1** L/N3203

**1863-★MN-1** 28 xii 63
**Mayet, K.– Neumann, G.R.**
Berlin [Anderssen & Neumann]
1 e4 e5 2 f4 d5 3 exd5 e4 4 ♗b5+ c6 5 dxc6 bxc6 6 ♗c4 ♘f6 7 d4 ♗d6 8 ♘e2 0-0 9 h3 ♘bd7 10 0-0 ♘b6 11 ♗b3 c5 12 dxc5 ♗xc5+ 13 ♔h1 ♕e7 14 ♘bc3 ♗b7 15 ♕e1 e3 16 ♘g3 ♖ad8 17 f5 [17 ♘a4 ♕d7∓] 17 ... ♖fe8 18 ♘a4 ♘xa4 19 ♗xa4 e2 **0-1** L/N6051-1864

**1863-★MN-2** xii 63
**Neumann, G.R.+ Mayet, K.**
Berlin [Anderssen & Neumann]
1 e4 e5 2 f4 exf4 3 ♗c4 f5 4 ♘c3 ♕g5?! 5 ♕e2! fxe4 6 ♘f3 ♕d8 7 0-0 ♗c5+ 8 d4 ♕e7? 9 ♘xe4 ♗b6 10 ♗xf4 ♘c6 11 c3 ♘f6 12 ♘xf6+ gxf6 13 ♕f2 ♔d8 14 ♖ae1 ♕g7 15 ♘g5 d5 [15 ... ♖f8 16 ♘f7+ ♖xf7 16 ♗xf7 ♕xf7 17 ♗g5 d5 19 ♗xf6+ ♔d7 20 ♕f5+ ♔d6 21 ♗e5+−] 16 ♗xd5 fxg5 17 ♗xc6 gxf4 [17 ... bxc6 18 ♗e5 ♕g8 19 ♗f6+−] 18 ♕h4+ **1-0** L/N6051-1864

**1863-★MN-3** vii 63
**Neuman, G.R.+ Mieses, S.**
[Anderssen/Neuman]
1 e4 c5 2 ♗c4 e6 3 ♘c3 a6 4 a4 ♘c6 5 d3 d5?? 6 exd5 exd5 7 ♗xd5 ♘b4 8 ♗b3 ♗d6 9 ♘f3 ♘f6 10 0-0 0-0 11 ♗g5 h6 12 ♗h4 ♗e7 13 ♖e1 ♗g4 14 h3 ♗h5 15 g4 ♗g6 16 ♕d2 [△ 17 ♘e5] 16 ... ♘c6 17 ♖xe7! ♘xe7 [17 ... ♕xe7 18 ♘d5+−] 18 ♗xf6 gxf6 19 ♕xh6 ♕d6 20 ♖e1 ♗h7 21 ♖xe7 c4 [21 ... ♕xe7 22 ♘d5 ♕d6 23 ♘xf6+−] 22 ♗xc4 b5 23 ♘d5 ♗g6

24 ♕xg6+!! **1-0** L/N6051-1864

**1863-★MP-1**
**Paulsen, L.+ Mackenzie, G.H.**
[Löwenthal]
1 e4 e5 2 ♘f3 ♘c6 3 ♗c4 ♘f6 4 d4 exd4 5 0-0 ♗c5 6 e5 d5 7 exf6 dxc4 8 fxg7 [8 ♖e1+ ♗e6 9 ♘g5 ♕d6 10 ♘xe6 fxe6 11 fxg7±] 8 ... ♖g8 9 ♗g5 ♕d6 10 ♘bd2 ♗f5 11 ♖e1+ ♔d7 12 ♘xc4 ♕d5 13 ♘ce5+ ♔c8 14 c4 ♕d6 15 ♘xc6 ♕xc6 16 ♘xd4 ♗xd4 17 ♕xd4 b6 18 b4 ♕g6 19 ♗f4 ♗e6 20 ♕e5!

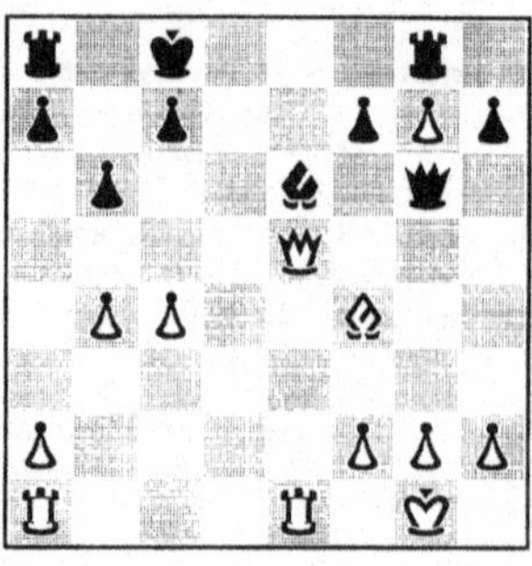

20 ... ♔b7 21 ♕xc7+ ♔a6 22 b5+ ♔a5 23 ♗d2+ ♔a4 24 ♕d6 a5 25 bxa6 **1-0** M324-1863

**1863-★MR-1**
**Rivière,J.A.de–**
**Morphy,P.C.**

Paris [Maróczy]

1 e4 e5 2 ♘f3 ♘c6 3 ♗c4 ♗c5 4 c3 ♘f6 5 d3 d6 6 h3 h6 7 b4 ♗b6 8 a4 a6 9 ♘a3 [◻ 9 a5 ♗a7 10 ♗e3!] 9 ... 0-0 10 ♘c2 ♗e6 11 ♕e2 d5 12 exd5 [◻ 12 ♗a2] 12 ... ♗xd5 13 0-0 e4 14 ♗xd5 ♕xd5 15 dxe4 ♘xe4 16 c4 ♘g3∓ 17 cxd5 ♘xe2+ 18 ♔h2 ♘e7 19 ♖e1 ♘xc1 20 ♖xe7 ♘d3 21 a5 ♗a7 22 g3 ♖fe8 23 ♖xc7 ♖e2 24 ♘cd4 ♖xf2+ **0-1** L/N3203

**1863-★MR-2** i63
**Morphy,P.C.+**
**Rivière,J.A.de**

Paris [Maróczy]

1 e4 e5 2 ♘f3 ♘c6 3 ♗c4 ♗c5 4 c3 ♕e7 [4 ... ♘f6 5 d4 exd4 6 cxd4 ♗b4+ 7 ♘c3 ♘xe4 8 0-0 d6 7 h3 [◻ 7 a4 a5 8 0-0 ♗xc3 9 d5!∞] 5 d4 ♗b6 6 0-0 d6 7 h3 [◻ 7 a4 a5 8 ♘a3 ♗g4 9 ♘c2 ♘f6 10 ♖e1 0-0 11 ♘e3!] 7 ... ♘f6 8 ♖e1 h6 9 a4 a5 10 ♘a3 ♘d8 [10 ... 0-0] 11 ♘c2 ♗e6 12 ♘e3 ♗xc4 13 ♘xc4 ♘d7 14 ♘e3 g6 [14 ... c6 15 ♘f5 ♕f6 16 dxe5 dxe5 17 ♘d6+] 15 ♘d5 ♕e6 [15 ... ♕f8 16 ♘xb6±] 16 ♗xh6 f6 [16 ... ♖xh6 17 ♘g5++-] 17 ♗g7 [◻ 17 ♗e3] 17 ... ♖h5 [17 ... ♖~ 18 ♗xf6 ♘xf6 19 ♘g5] 18 g4 ♖xh3 19 ♘xf6+ ♘xf6 20 ♘g5 ♕d7 [20 ... ♕xg4+ 21 ♕xg4 ♘xg4 22 ♘xh3 ♔f7 23 f3 ♔xg7 24 fxg4 exd4 25 ♔g2 ♘e6=] 21 ♗xf6 ♖h4 22 f3 exd4 23 cxd4 ♖h6 24 ♔g2 ♘f7 25 ♖h1 ♘xg5 [25 ... ♖xh1 26 ♕xh1±] 26 ♖xh6 ♘h7 27 ♕h1 ♘xf6 28 ♖h8+ ♔e7 29 ♖xa8 ♗xd4 30 ♕h6! ♕c6 31 ♖c1 ♕b6 32 ♖xc7+ ♔e6 33 ♖e8+ ♘xe8 34 ♕xg6+ ♔e5 35 ♕f5# **1-0** L/N3203

**1863-★MR-3**
**Rivière,J.A.de+**
**Morphy,P.C.**

Paris [Maróczy]

1 e4 e5 2 ♘f3 ♘c6 3 ♗c4 ♗c5 4 d3 ♘f6 5 0-0 h6 [◻ 5 ... d6] 6 c3 d6 7 b4 ♗b6 8 a4 a5 [8 ... a6 9 a5 ♗a7 10 b5 axb5 11 ♗xb5] 9 b5 ♘e7 10 ♗b3 0-0 11 ♘bd2 ♘g6 12 ♘c4 ♗g4 [◻ 12 ... ♗a7] 13 ♘xb6 cxb6 14 ♕e2 ♘h4 15 ♔h1 ♕c8 16 ♗d2 ♗xf3 17 gxf3 ♕h3 18 ♖g1 ♘xf3 [◻ 18 ... ♕xf3+ 19 ♕xf3 ♘xf3 20 ♖gd1 ♖ac8 21 ♖ac1 ♘d7] 19 ♖g2 ♘g4 20 ♖ag1 g5

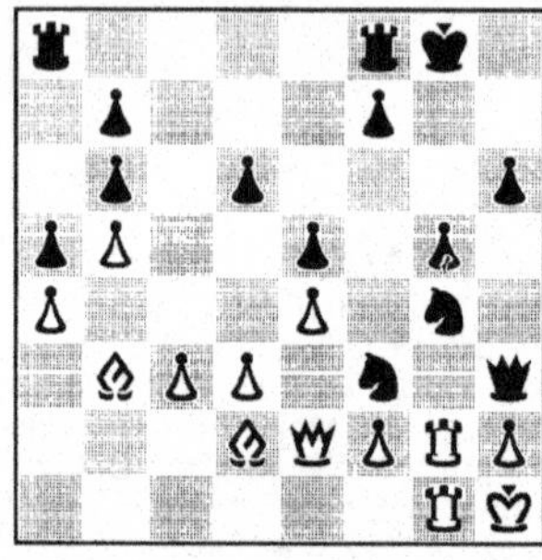

[◻ 20 ... ♘gxh2 (20 ... ♘xg1 21 ♔xg1 ♘f6 22 ♖g3 ♕h5 24 ♕f1 g5 25 f4±) 21 ♖xg7+ (21 ♖g3 ♕h5 22 ♗d1 ♘f1+ 23 ♔g2 ♘1xd2 24 ♖h1 ♘h4+∓) 21 ... ♔h8 22 ♖1g3 ♕h5 23 ♗d1! ♘f1+ 24 ♔g2 ♘1xd2 25 ♖h3! ♖g8! 26 ♖xh5 ♖xg7+ 27 ♔h3 ♘g1+ 28 ♔h4 ♘xe2∓] 21 ♗d1 ♘gxh2 22 ♖g3 ♕h4 [◻ 22 ... ♕h5 23 ♔g2 g4 24 ♖h1 f5 25 exf5 ♖xf5 26 ♗e3 ♖af8 27 ♗xb6 ♘d4∓] 23 ♔g2 g4 24 ♖h1 f5 25 exf5 ♖xf5 26 ♕e4! ♖af8 27 ♗xf3 ♖xf3 28 ♕g6+ ♔h8 29 ♕xh6+ ♕xh6 30 ♗xh6 ♖xf2+ 31 ♔g1 ♖f1+ 32 ♔xh2 ♖8f2+ 33 ♖g2 g3+ 34 ♔xg3 ♖f3+ [34 ... ♖xh1 35 ♖xf2 ♖xh6 36 ♖f7 ♖g6+ 37 ♔f3 d5 38 ♖xb7; 35 ♔xf2? ♖xh6 36 c4 ♔h7 37 ♔e3 ♖h4!∓] 35 ♔g4 [35 ♔h2 ♖xh1+ 36 ♔xh1 ♖xd3] 35 ... ♖xh1 36 ♔xf3 ♖xh6 37 c4 ♔h7 38 ♔e4 ♖h4+ 39 ♔f5± ♖f4+ 40 ♔e6 ♖d4 41 ♖g3 e4 42 ♖g4 ♖xd3 43 ♖xe4 ♔g6 44 ♖g4+ ♔h7 45 ♔d7 ♖a3 46 ♔xd6 ♖xa4 47 ♔c7 ♖b4 [47 ... ♖a1 48 ♔xb6 a4 49 c5 a3 50 ♖a4 a2 51 ♔xb7 ♖b1 52 b6] 48 ♔xb6 a4 49 ♔a5 ♖b1 50 c5 a3 51 ♖a4 ♖b3 52 ♔b6 ♔g6 53 ♖a5 ♖c3 54 ♖a7 ♔f5 55 ♖xb7 **1-0** L/N3203

**1863-★MR-4**
**Morphy,P.C.+**
**Rivière,J.A.de**

Paris [Maróczy]

1 e4 e5 2 ♘f3 ♘c6 3 ♗c4 ♗c5 4 b4 ♗xb4 5 c3 ♗c5 6 0-0 d6 7 d4 exd4 8 cxd4 ♗b6 9 ♘c3 ♕f6? 10 ♘d5± ♕g6 11 ♘f4 ♕f6 12 e5 dxe5 13 dxe5 ♕f5 14 e6 f6 [14 ... fxe6 15 ♘xe6±] 15 ♘h4 ♕c5 16 ♗e3 ♕g5 [16 ... ♕17 ♕h5++-] 17 ♘f3 ♕a5 18 ♗xb6 ♕xb6 19 ♘d5 ♕a5 20 ♘d2! [△ 21 ♘b3 ♕a3 22 ♘xc7++-] 20 ... ♘d4 21 ♘b3 ♘xb3 22 axb3 ♕c5 23 ♕h5+ ♔d8 24 ♖ad1 **1-0** L/N3203

**1863-★MR-5**
**Rivière,J.A.de–**
**Morphy,P.C.**

Paris [Maróczy]

1 e4 e5 2 ♘f3 ♘c6 3 ♗c4 ♗c5 4 b4 ♗xb4 5 c3 ♗c5 6 0-0 d6 7 d4 exd4 8 cxd4 ♗b6 9 ♘c3 ♗g4 10 ♗b5 ♗d7 11 ♗g5 [11 e5 dxe5 12 ♖e1 ♘ge7 13 d5 ♘b8 (13 ... ♘d4 14 ♗xd7+ ♕xd7 15 ♘xe5 ♕f5 16 ♘d3±) 14 ♗c4 0-0 15 ♘xe5 ♗f5 16 ♗g5 ♗c5 17 ♘xf7±] 11 ... ♘ce7 [◻ 11 ... ♘ge7 12 ♘d5 f6 13 ♗xf6 gxf6 14 ♘xf6+ ♔f8 15 ♘xd7+ ♕xd7 16 d5 ♕g4 17 dxc6 bxc6 18 ♗c4 ♘g6 19 ♘d4] 12 ♗c4 ♗e6 13 ♕a4+ [◻ 13 ♗xe6 fxe6 14 ♘h4] 13 ... ♕d7 14 ♗b5 c6 15 ♗d3 f6 16 ♗h4 [◻ 16 ♗e3] 16 ... ♘g6 17 ♗g3 [◻ 17 d5 ♗f7 18 dxc6 bxc6 19 ♘d5] 17 ... ♘8e7 18 d5 ♗f7 19 ♘b5 [◻ 19 ♖ad1] 19 ... ♗c5 20 ♖ac1 0-0 21 ♘bd4 ♔h8 22 ♗c4 ♘e5 23 ♘xe5 fxe5 24 dxc6 bxc6 25 ♘b3 ♗b6 26 ♖fd1 [◻ 26 ♗xf7 ♖xf7 27 ♖cd1 ♕e6 28 ♘d2] 26 ... ♗h5 27 ♖d2 a5! 28 ♕a3 [28 ♗xe5 ♖xf2] 28 ... ♖ad8 29 ♗xe5 ♖xf2 30 ♔h1 [30 ♗d4 ♗xd4 31 ♖xd4 (31 ♖xf2 ♗xf2+, ♕a7+) 31 ... ♖xg2+ 32 ♔xg2 ♕g4+ 33 ♔f1 ♕f3+ 34 ♔e1 ♕e3+ 35 ♔f1 ♖f8+] 30 ... ♖xd2 31 ♗xg7+ ♔xg7 32 ♘xd2 ♕a7 33 ♕g3+ ♗g6 34 ♖f1 ♗d4 35 ♘f3 ♕c5 36 ♗b3 ♖f8 37 h4 ♗e5 38 ♕g4 ♕e3 **0-1** L/N3203

**1863-★MR-6**
**Morphy,P.C.+**
**Rivière,J.A.de**

Paris [Maróczy]

1 e4 e5 2 ♘f3 ♘c6 3 ♗c4 ♗c5 4 b4 ♗xb4 5 c3 ♗c5 6 0-0 d6 7 d4 exd4 8 cxd4 ♗b6 9 ♘c3 ♗g4 10 ♗b5 ♔f8 [◻ 10 ... a6! 11 ♗a4 ♔f8! 12 ♗xc6 bxc6] 11 ♗e3 [◻ 11 ♗xc6 bxc6 12 a4] 11 ... ♘ce7 12 h3 ♗h5 13 ♗d3 f6 14 a4 c6 15 ♕b3 ♗f7 16 ♕a3 ♗a5 17 ♘e2 ♘c8? [◻ 17 ... ♗c7] 18 ♖ab1 b6 19 ♗a6! ♘ge7 20 e5 ♗d5 21 ♘f4! fxe5 22 dxe5 dxe5 23 ♘xd5 cxd5 24 ♘xe5 ♕d6 25 ♕b2 ♘f5 26 ♗f4 ♕e7 27 ♘c6 ♕e4 [27 ... ♕f7 28 ♘xa5 bxa5 29 ♗b7±] 28 ♗b7 ♕xf4 29 ♗xa8 ♕xa4 30 ♖bd1 ♕e4 31 ♕a3+ ♔f7 32 ♘xa5 bxa5 33 ♖fe1 [◻ 33 ♗xd5++-] 33 ... ♕b4 34 ♗xd5+ ♔g6 35 ♖e6+ ♔g5 36 ♕c1+ ♕f4 37 h4+ ♘xh4 38 ♖e5+ ♘f5 39 ♖xf5+ ♔xf5 40 ♗e6+ **1-0** L/N3203

### 1863-★MR-7
**Rivière,J.A.de–Morphy,P.C.**

Paris [Maróczy]

1 e4 e5 2 ♘f3 ♘c6 3 ♗c4 ♘f6 4 ♘g5 d5 5 exd5 ♘a5 6 d3 h6 [◻6 ... ♘xc4 7 dxc4 ♗d6, 0-0] 7 ♘f3 e4 8 ♕e2 ♘xc4 9 dxc4 ♗c5 [9 ... ♗e7; ♗d6] 10 h3 0-0 11 ♘h2 ♘h7 12 ♘d2 [◻12 ♗e3] 12 ... f5 13 ♘b3 ♗d6 14 0-0 ♗xh2+ 15 ♔xh2 f4!

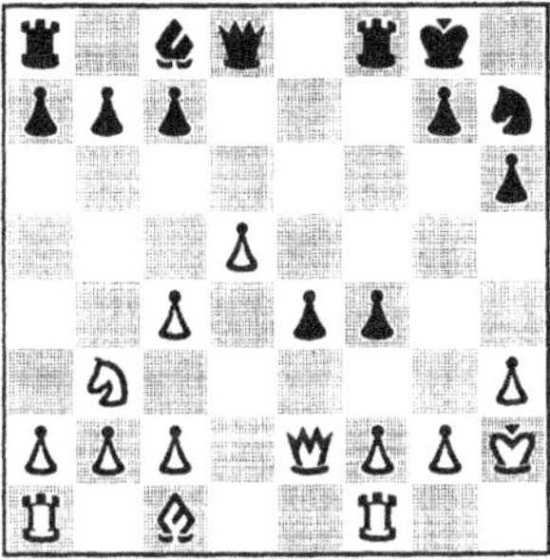

16 ♕xe4 ♘g5 17 ♕d4 [◻17 ♕d3 ♗f5 18 ♕d4] 17 ... ♘f3+ 18 gxf3 ♕h4 19 ♖h1 ♗xh3 20 ♗d2 ♖f6 **0-1** L/N3203

### 1863-★MR-8
**Morphy,P.C.+Rivière,J.A.de**

Paris [Maróczy]

1 e4 e5 2 ♘f3 ♘c6 3 ♗c4 ♘f6 4 d4 exd4 5 0-0 ♗e7 [◻5 ... ♗c5; 5 ... ♘xe4] 6 ♘xd4 0-0 [6 ... ♘xe4 7 ♘f5 0-0 (7 ... d5 8 ♘xg7+ ♔f8 9 ♗h6 ♔g8 10 ♗xd5±; 7 ... ♔f8 8 ♕d5±) 8 ♕g4 g6 (8 ... ♘g5 9 ♘xe7+ ♕xe7 10 ♕xg5) 9 ♘h6+ ♔g7 10 ♕xe4±] 7 ♘c3 ♘e5? [◻7 ... d6] 8 ♗e2 [◻8 ♗b3] 8 ... d5 [◻8 ... d6] 9 f4 ♘c6 10 ♘xc6 bxc6 11 e5 ♗c5+ 12 ♔h1 ♘d7 [12 ... ♘e8, 13 ... g6, 14 ... ♘g7] 13 ♗d3 ♖e8 14 ♗d2 ♘f8 15 ♕h5 g6 16 ♕h6 ♘e6? 17 f5 ♗f8 18 ♕h3 ♘c5 [18 ... ♘g7 19 e6 fxe6 20 f6 ♘f5 21 f7+ ♔xf7 22 g4 e5 23 gxf5 e4 24 ♕xh7+ ♗g7 25 fxg6++–] 19 e6 fxe6 [19 ... ♘xd3 20 exf7+ ♔xf7 21 fxg6+ ♔xg6 22 ♕g3+ ♔h5 23 ♕xd3] 20 f6 e5 21 f7+ ♔h8 22 fxe8♕ ♕xe8 23 ♗xg6 ♗xh3 24 ♗xe8 ♗xg2+ 25 ♔xg2 ♖xe8 26 ♖ae1 **1-0** L/N3203

### 1863-★MR-9
**Rivière,J.A.de–Morphy,P.C.**

Paris [Maróczy]

1 e4 e5 2 ♘f3 ♘c6 3 ♗c4 ♘f6 4 ♘c3 [◻4 d3] 4 ... ♗c5 [◻4 ... ♘xe4! 5 ♗xf7+ (5 ♘xe4 d5 6 ♗xd5 ♕xd5 7 d3 f5) 5 ... ♔xf7 6 ♘xe4 d5 7 ♘fg5+ (7 ♘g3 e4 8 ♘g1) 7 + ♔g8 8 ♕f3 ♕d7! 9 ♘c3 ♘b4] 5 d3 h6 [◻5 ... d6] 6 ♕e2 0-0 7 ♘a4 [7 h3; 7 ♗e3!] 7 ... ♗e7 8 a3 d5 9 exd5 ♘xd5 10 0-0 [10 ♘xe5 ♘d4 11 ♕d1 ♗f6] 10 ... ♗g4 11 ♗e3 ♔h8 12 ♘c3 ♘xc3 13 bxc3 f5 14 ♗c1 ♗d6 15 ♖ab1 e4 16 dxe4 ♘e5 17 ♘xe5 [17 ♗d3 (17 h3 ♗xf3 18 gxf3 fxe4 19 f4! ♘f3+ 20 ♔g2 ♕e8 21 ♗d5 ♕g6+ 22 ♔h1 ♕f5 23 ♔g2 ♕xd5) 17 ... ♕e8! 18 ♕d1 ♘xd3 19 exd3 fxe4 20 dxe4 ♗xf3 21 gxf3 ♕h5 22 f4 ♕g6+ 23 ♔h1 ♕xe4+] 17 ... ♗xe2 18 ♘g6+ ♔h7 19 ♘xf8+ ♕xf8 20 ♗xe2 fxe4 21 ♖xb7 ♗xa3 22 ♗e3 a5 23 ♖xc7 ♗d6 24 ♖d7 ♗e5 25 f3 [25 ♗d4 ♕f5! 26 ♖d5 ♗xh2+] 25 ... ♕c8 26 ♖e7 ♕xc3 27 ♗f2 a4 28 f4 ♗d4 29 ♖xe4 ♗xf2+ f30 ♖xf2 a3 31 ♗d3 g6 32 f5 a2 33 fxg6+ ♔h8 **0-1** L/N3203

### 1863-★MR-10
**Morphy,P.C.–Rivière,J.A.de**

Paris [Maróczy]

1 e4 e5 2 f4 exf4 3 ♘f3 g5 4 ♗c4 ♗g7 5 0-0 h6 6 c3 d6 7 d4 [7 ♕b3] 7 ... ♘e7 8 h4 ♘g6 9 h5 ♘e7 10 g3 ♗g4 [◻10 ... ♗h3, 11 ... fxg3] 11 gxf4 ♗xh5 12 fxg5 ♕d7 13 ♘e5 ♕h3 14 ♕d3 [14 ♕xh5 ♕g3+ 15 ♔h1 hxg5] 14 ... ♕xd3 15 ♘xd3 hxg5 16 ♘a3 c6 17 ♗xg5 ♗xd4+ 18 cxd4 ♖g8 19 ♖f6 ♖xg5+ 20 ♔f2 ♘d7! 21 ♖xd6 0-0-0 [◻21 ... ♗g6 22 ♖h1 0-0-0 [◻21 ... ♗g6 22 ♖h1 0-0-0 (22 ... ♘c8 23 ♖h8+ ♔e7 24 e5 ♖b8∓)] 22 ♖g1 ♖xg1 23 ♔xg1 ♔c7 24 ♖h6 ♗g6 25 ♘f4 ♗xe4 26 ♗xf7 ♗f5 27 ♗e6 ♘f8 28 d5 ♘xe6 29 ♘xe6+ ♗xe6 30 dxe6 ♖d5 [30 ... ♖d1+ 31 ♔f2 ♖d2+ 32 ♔f3 ♖xb2 33 ♖h7 ♖xa2! 34 ♘c4 ♔d8 35 ♖h8+ ♔c7 36 ♖h7] 31 ♔f2 b5 32 ♔f3 ♖d2 33 ♘b1 ♖xb2 34 ♘c3 ♔d6 35 ♔f4 ♘d5+ 36 ♘xd5 cxd5 37 e7+ ♔xe7 38 ♖a6 ♖e2! 39 a3 ♔d7 40 ♖xa7+ ♔c6 41 ♔f3 ♖e4 42 ♖a8 ♖a4 43 ♖c8+ ♔d6 44 ♖c3 d4

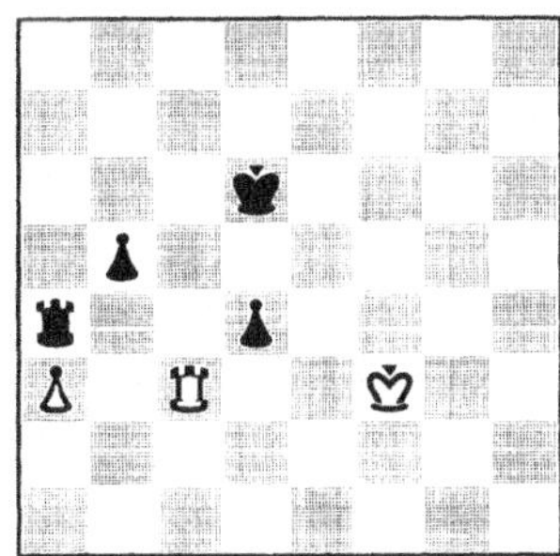

45 ♖b3 ♔c5 46 ♔e4 ♖a8 47 ♔d3 ♖h8 48 ♔d2 ♖h2+ 49 ♔c1 [49 ♔d1 ♔c4 50 ♖b4+ (50 ♖g3 ♖b2, 51 ... ♖b3) 50 ... ♔c3 51 ♖xb5 ♖h1+ 52 ♔e2 d3+ 53 ♔e3 ♖e1+ 54 ♔f2 d2] 49 ... ♔c4 50 ♖g3 [50 ♖b4+ ♔c3] 50 ... d3 51 ♖g8 ♖a2 52 ♖c8+ ♔b3 53 ♖b8 ♖c2+ 54 ♔d1 ♖c5 55 ♔d2? [◻55 ♖a8! ♔b2 56 ♔d2! ♖c2+ 57 ♔xd3 ♖c3+ 58 ♔d2? (58 ♔d4! ♖xa3 59 ♖b8 ♖b3 60 ♔c5 ♖c3+ 61 ♔b4=) 58 ... ♖xa3 59 ♖b8! ♖b3 60 ♖b7 b4 61 ♖b8 ♔a2 62 ♖a8+ (62 ♔c2 ♖c3+ 63 ♔d2 ♔b3 64 ♖b7 ♖c8 65 ♔d1 ♔a3–+; 62 ♖b7 ♖b2+ 63 ♔c1 ♖b1+ 64 ♔c2 b3+–+) 62 ... ♖a3 63 ♖b8 b3 64 ♔c1 (64 ♔c3) 64 ... ♖a7 65 ♖b6 ♖c7+ 66 ♔d2 b2 67 ♖a6+ ♔b1 68 ♖a8 ♖c5 69 ♖a7 ♖d5+ 70 ♔e2 (70 ♔c3 ♔c1) 70 ... ♔c2 71 ♖c7+ ♔b3 72 ♖b7+ ♔c3 73 ♖c7+ ♔b4 74 ♖b7+ ♖b5] 55 ... ♔xa3 56 ♔xd3 b4 **0-1** L/N3203

### 1863-★MR-11
**Rivière,J.A.de+Morphy,P.C.**

Paris [Maróczy]

1 e4 e5 2 f4 exf4 3 ♗c4 ♘f6 [◻3 ... d5! 4 exd5 ♕h4+ 5 ♔f1 g5 6 ♘c3 ♘e7 7 d4 ♗g7] 4 ♘c3 ♗b4 5 ♘f3 0-0 6 ♘d5 ♘xd5 [◻6 ... ♗a5] 7 exd5 ♖e8+ 8 ♔f2 d6 9 d4 ♕f6 10 c3 ♗a5 11 ♕a4 ♗d7 12 ♕xa5 b6 13 ♕a3 g5 14 h3 h5 15 ♗d2 g4 16 hxg4 hxg4 17 ♘g1 [◻17 b3] 17 ... b5 18 ♗d3 ♗f5 19 ♗xb5 [◻19 ♗e2] 19 ... ♘d7 20 ♕a4 ♖ab8 21 ♗xd7 g3+ 22 ♔f3 [22 ♔f1 ♗d3+ 23 ♘e2 ♗xe2+ 24 ♔e1 (24 ♔g1 f3) 24 ... ♗b5+ 25 ♗xe8 ♖xe8+, 26 ... ♗xa4∓] 22 ... ♗e4+ 23 ♔g4 [23 ♔e2 f3+ 24 ♔d1! fxg2] 23 ... ♗xd5 24 ♗xe8 ♕g6+ 25 ♔xf4 ♕e4+ 26 ♔g5 ♔g7? [◻26 ... ♕g6+ 27 ♔h4 (27 ♔f4! ♕e4+ 28 ♔g5 ♕g6+; 28 ♔xg3 ♕xg2+ 29 ♔f4 ♕e4+=) 27 ... ♕e4+ 28 ♔h3 ♕xg2+ 29 ♔g4 ♕e4+ 30 ♗f4 ♕g6+ 31 ♔h3 (31 ♗g5 f5+!) 31 ... ♕h7+ 32 ♔xg3 ♕g6+ 33 ♔h4 (33 ♔f2? ♖xb2+ 34 ♔e1 ♕g2 35 ♗b5 ♕f2+, ♕xf4–+; 35 ♗e3 ♕g3+, ♕xe3–+) 33 ... ♕h7+ 34 ♔g3 ♕g6+] 27 ♖h6 ♗e6 28 ♖xe6 ♕xe6 29 ♕d7 ♖xb2 30 ♘f3 **1-0** L/N3203

### 1863-★MR-12
**Morphy,P.C.+Rivière,J.A.de**

Paris [Sergeant]

1 e4 e5 2 ♘f3 ♘c6 3 ♗b5 ♘f6 4 0-0 d6 [◻4 ... ♘xe4] 5 d4 exd4 6 ♘xd4 ♗d7 7 ♗xc6 bxc6 8 ♘c3 ♗e7 9 h3 [◻9 b3] 9 ... c5 10 ♘de2 0-0 11 f4 ♗c6 12 ♘g3 ♘d7! 13 ♕d3 ♖b8 14 b3 ♗f6 15 ♗d2 ♗d4+ [◻15 ... g6; 15 ... a5 Hoffer] 16 ♔h1 g6 17 ♖ae1 ♕h4 18 ♘ce2 ♗g7 19 c4 ♘f6 [◻19 ... f5! Maroczy] 20 ♘c3 ♗d7? 21 ♘ge2 ♘h5 22 ♔h2 f5 23 e5 ♗c6 24 g3 ♕d8

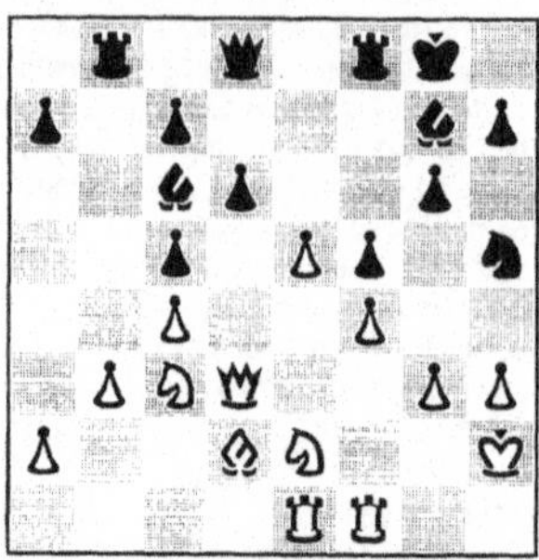

25 e6!? ♖e8 26 ♘g1 ♕c8 [◻ 26 ... ♗xc3 27 ♗xc3 ♘g7 Hoffer] 27 ♘d5! ♘f6 [27 ... ♖xe6? 27 ♘e7+±] 28 ♗c3 ♘xd5 29 ♗xg7 ♘xf4? [◻ 29 ... ♔xg7 (29 ... ♘b4 30 ♕c3 ♘xa2 31 ♕f6+-) 30 cxd5 ♘b5 31 ♕c3+ ♔g8 32 ♖f3 (32 ♕f6 ♖f8) c6∞] 30 ♖xf4 ♔xg7 31 ♕c3+ ♔g8 32 e7! ♕a6 [32 ... ♗e4 33 ♖exe4 fxe4 34 ♕f6 ♕d7 35 ♕f7+ ♔h8 36 ♖h4 h5 37 ♖xe4 △ 37 ♖e6; 37 ♘f3+- Hoffer] 33 ♖e2 ♔f7 34 g4 [◻ 34 ♕e3 ♗d7 35 ♘f3 h6 36 ♖h4+- Hoffer] 34 ... ♖xe7 35 ♖xe7+ ♔xe7 36 ♕g7+ ♔d8 37 ♕g8+ ♔d7 [◻ 37 ... ♗e8 38 ♖f2 ♕c8] 38 ♕xh7+ [38 ♕xb8 ♕xa2+ 39 ♔g3 g5! Mlotkowski] 38 ... ♔c8 39 ♖f2 fxg4 40 hxg4 ♗e4 41 ♕e7 ♕c6 42 ♖e2 d5 43 cxd5 ♗xd5 44 ♘h3 ♔b7 45 ♘f4 ♖h8+ 46 ♔g3 ♗h1 47 ♖e3 g5 [◻ 47 ... ♕d6] 48 ♕xg5 ♕a6 49 ♕xc5 ♕xa2 [49 ... ♕f1 50 ♕b4+ ♔a8 51 ♕e1] 50 ♕b5+ ♔a8 51 ♖e8+ ♖xe8 52 ♕xe8+ ♔b7 53 ♕b5+ ♔c8 54 g5 c6 55 ♕f5+ ♔b7 56 ♕f7+ ♔b6 57 g6 ♕d2 58 g7 ♕e1+ 59 ♔g4 ♕g1+ 60 ♔f5 ♕c5+ 61 ♔f6 ♕d4+ 62 ♔e7 ♕c5+ 63 ♔d7 ♕d4+ 64 ♔c8 **1-0** LIN3098

### 1863-★MS-1
**Morphy, P.C.+ St. Leon, C.**
Paris [Maróczy]

⟨♘b1⟩ 1 e4 e5 2 f4 exf4 3 ♘f3 g5 4 ♗c4 g4 5 d4 gxf3 6 ♕xf3 ♗h6 7 0-0 ♕f6 8 e5 ♕g7 9 ♗xf4 ♗xf4 10 ♕xf4 ♘h6 11 ♖f3 ♖g8 12 ♖g3 ♕f8 13 ♖xg8 ♘xg8 14 ♖f1 ♘h6 15 g4 d6 [15 ... d5 16 ♗xd5 c6 17 ♗b3 ♕g7!∓] 16 e6 f6 17 g5 ♕g7 18 ♕xf6 ♕xf6 19 ♖xf6 ♘g8 20 ♖f7 c6 21 ♖g7 ♘e7 22 ♖xh7 ♔d8 23 ♖h8+ ♔c7 24 ♖e8 d5 [24 ... ♘d5 (24 + ♘f5 25 g6) 25 ♗xd5 cxd5 26 h4 ♗xe6 27 ♖xe6 ♘d7 28 h5] 25 ♖xe7+ ♔d6 26 ♖e8 dxc4 27 ♖xc8 ♔xe6 28 h4 ♔f5 29 ♖g8 **1-0** L/N3203

### 1863-★MS-2 x 63
**Mongredien, A.− Steinitz, W.**
London [Löwenthal]

1 e4 e5 2 c3 d5 3 ♘f3 ♘c6 4 ♗b5 dxe4 5 ♘xe5 ♗d7 6 ♘xd7 ♕xd7 7 0-0 0-0-0 8 c4 ♘f6 9 ♘c3 ♗c5 10 b4 ♗xb4 11 ♕b3 ♗c5 12 ♖b1 ♕f5 [◻ 12 ... ♕d3] 13 ♗xc6 bxc6 14 ♘a4 ♗d6 15 ♗a3 ♗xa3 16 ♕xa3 ♕a5 17 ♕h3+ ♘d7 18 ♘c3 f5 19 ♖b2 g6 20 ♖fb1 ♘b6? [◻ 20 ... ♘c5 21 ♖b8+ ♔d7, 22 ... ♘d3] 21 ♘xe4! ♖d4 22 d3 ♖hd8 23 ♖b3 ♕xa2 24 ♘c5 ♕a5 25 ♘e6 ♖e8!∓ 26 ♕xh7 ♕e5 27 ♕xg6 ♖xe6 **0-1** L/N6124

### 1863-★MS-3
**Steinitz, W.+ Mongredien, A.**
London [Löwenthal]

1 e4 g6 2 d4 ♗g7 3 c3 b6 4 ♗e3 ♗b7 5 ♘d2 d6 6 ♘gf3 e5 7 dxe5 dxe5 8 ♗c4 ♘e7 9 ♕e2 0-0 10 h4 ♘d7 11 h5 ♘f6 12 hxg6 ♘xg6 13 0-0-0 c5 14 ♘g5 a6 15 ♘xh7 ♘xh7 16 ♖xh7 ♔xh7 17 ♕h5+ ♔g8 18 ♖h1 ♖e8 19 ♕xg6 ♕f6

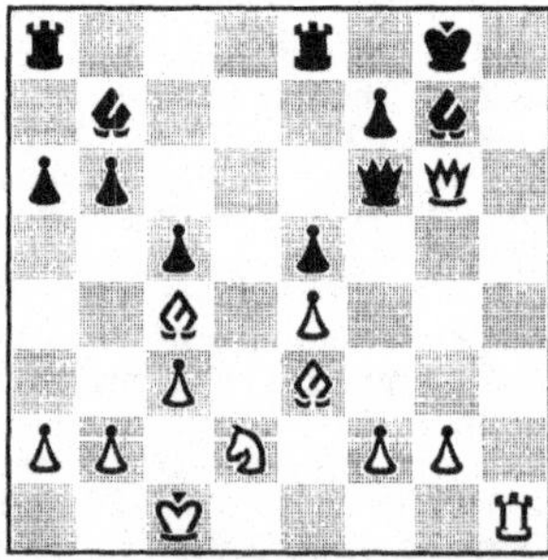

20 ♗xf7+ ♕xf7 [20 ... ♔f8 21 ♗xe8 ♖xe8! 22 ♖h8+ ♗xh8 23 ♗h6++-] 21 ♖h8+ ♔xh8 22 ♕xf7+- **1-0** L/N6124

### 1863-★NP-1 xi 63
**Neumann, G.R.+ Pomtow**
Berlin [Anderssen & Neumann]

⟨♘b1⟩ 1 e4 e5 2 f4 ♗c5 3 ♘f3 d6 4 ♗c4 ♗g4 5 fxe5 dxe5? [◻ 5 ... ♕e7] 6 ♗xf7+ ♔f8 [6 ... ♔xf7 7 ♘xe5+] 7 d3 [◻ 7 ♗b3] 7 ... ♗xf3 8 ♕xf3 ♕f6 9 ♖f1 ♕xf3 [9 ... ♔xf7 10 ♕h3] 10 ♖xf3 ♘f6 11 ♗b3 h6 12 ♗d2 ♘c6 [△ 13 ... ♘d4] 13 c3 ♔e7 14 0-0-0 ♖hf8 15 ♖df1 ♘g4? 16 ♖f7+ ♖xf7 17 ♖xf7+ ♔d6 18 ♖xg7 ♘xh2 19 d4 ♗b6 [19 ... exd4 20 ♗f4+] 20 ♖g6+ ♔d7 21 ♖xh6 ♘f1 22 ♗e6+ ♔e7 [22 ... ♔d6 23 ♗c4+] 23 ♗g5+ ♔f8 24 ♗f6 **1-0** L/N6051-1864

### 1863-★NP-2 xi 63
**Neumann, G.R.+ Pomtow**
Berlin [Anderssen & Neumann]

⟨♘b1⟩ 1 e4 e5 2 ♘f3 d6 3 d4 ♗g4 4 dxe5 ♗xf3 5 ♕xf3 dxe5 6 ♗c4 ♕f6 7 ♕b3 b6 8 0-0 ♗c5 9 ♔h1 [△ 10 f4] 9 ... g5 10 ♗e3 ♘d7 11 ♖ad1 c6 [11 ... h6] 12 ♗xg5 ♕xg5 13 ♗xf7+ ♔d8 14 ♕e6 ♕e7 [14 ... ♘f6 15 f4 exf4 16 e5+-] 15 ♗xg8 ♔c7 16 ♖xd7+ ♕xd7 17 ♕xe5+ ♗d6 18 ♕xh8 **1-0** L/N6047-64 L/N6051-1864

### 1863-★NR-1 xi 63
**Neumann, G.R.+ Ritter**
Berlin [Anderssen & Neumann]

⟨♘b1⟩ 1 e4 e5 2 ♘f3 ♘c6 3 ♗c4 f5 4 d4 fxe4 5 ♘xe5 ♘xe5 6 dxe5 ♕e7 7 ♕d4 d6 8 ♗f4 dxe5 9 ♗xe5 ♘f6 10 0-0-0 ♗f5 11 f4 [△ 11 ... ♖d8 12 ♗f7+] 11 ... ♕c5? 12 ♗xf6 gxf6 13 ♕xf6 ♕xc4 14 ♕xf5 ♗d6 15 ♖he1 ♕f7 16 ♖xe4+ ♔f8 17 ♕g5 ♖g8 18 ♕h6+ ♕g7 [◻ 18 ... ♖g7] 19 ♖xd6 cxd6 20 ♕xd6+ ♔f7 21 ♖e7+ ♔f8 22 ♖e5+ ♔f7 23 ♕e6+ ♔f8 24 ♖f5+ **1-0** L/N6051-1864

### 1863-★NS-1 viii 63
**Schallopp, E.−Neumann, G.R.**
Berlin [Anderssen & Neumann]

⟨♙f7⟩ 1 e4 c5 2 ♕h5+ g6 3 ♕xc5 ♘c6 4 f4 [◻ 4 e5] 4 ... e5 5 ♕f2 ♘f6 6 d3 d5 7 exd5 ♕xd5 8 ♘c3 ♗b4 9 fxe5 ♘g4 10 ♕e2 0-0 11 ♘f3 ♘gxe5 12 ♘xe5 ♘xe5 13 ♗d2 ♗xc3 14 ♗xc3 ♗g4 15 ♕d2 ♘xd3+ **0-1** L/N6051-1864

### 1863-★NS-2 5 xii 63
**Neumann, G.R.+Schallopp, E.**
[Andersson & Neumann]

1 e4 e5 2 ♘f3 ♘c6 3 ♗c4 ♗c5 4 b4 ♗xb4 5 c3 ♗a5 6 d4 exd4 7 0-0 ♗b6 8 cxd4 d6 9 ♘c3 ♗g4 10 ♗b5 ♗d7 11 e5 dxe5 12 ♖e1 ♘ge7 13 d5 ♘d4 [◻ 13 ... ♘b8] 14 ♗xd7+ ♕xd7 15 ♘xe5 ♕f5 16 ♘d3 ♖d8 17 ♗a3 ♖d7 18 ♖e5 ♕g6 19 ♘c5 ♗xc5 20 ♗xc5 ♘f5 21 ♕e2 b6 22 ♗a3 ♘d6 23 ♖ae1 ♕f6 24 ♘b5 a6 25 ♘d4 **1-0** L/N6051-1864

### 1863-★NW-1 x 63
**Neumann, G.R.+ Wernich**
Berlin [Anderssen & Neumann]

1 e4 e5 2 f4 exf4 3 ♗c4 g5 4 h4 c6 5 ♗xf7+± ♔xf7 6 ♕h5+ ♔e6 [◻ 6 ... ♕g7] 7 hxg5 d6 8 d4 ♔d7 9 ♗xf4 ♔c7 10 ♘c3 ♗g7 11 ♘f3 ♘e7 12 0-0-0 a6 13 e5 d5 14 e6+ ♔b6 15 ♖he1 ♘g6 16 ♗g3 ♕e7 17 ♕h2 ♔a7 18 ♗d6 ♕e8 [18 ... ♕d8 19 e7 ♕d7 20 e8♕ ♖xe8 21 ♖xe8+-] 19 ♗c5+ b6 20 ♕c7+ ♗b7 21 ♗xb6# **1-0** L/N6051-1864

### 1863-★PP-1 ●○ 31 viii 63
**Paulsen, L.= Pflaum, M.**
Düsseldorf [Lange]

1 e4 e5 2 ♘f3 ♘c6 3 d4 exd4 4 ♘xd4 ♗c5 5 ♗e3 ♗b6 [◻ 5 ... ♕f6] 6 ♗c4 ♘e5 7 ♗b3 ♘f6 8 ♘d2 0-0 9 0-0 ♘fg4 10 ♘2f3 ♘xe3 11 fxe3 d6 12 ♔h1 ♗g4 13 ♕e1 ♕e7 14

♕g3 ♗d7 15 ♘h4 ♗xd4 16 exd4 ♘c6 17 ♘f5 ♗xf5 18 exf5 ♕f6! 19 c3 ♔h8 20 ♖f4 ♘e7 21 ♕f2 ♘g8 22 ♖g1 ♖ae8 23 g4 ♕e7 24 g5 ♕e2 25 ♕h4 ♖e4 26 g6 ♘h6 27 ♖xe4 ♕f3+ 28 ♖g2 ♕f1+ ½-½

L/N5192

**1863-★PR-1 ●○⌂** 31 viii 63

**Paulsen, L.– Rossy, M.**

Düsseldorf [Lange]

1 e4 e5 2 f4 exf4 3 ♗c4 ♕h4+ 4 ♔f1 g5 5 ♘c3 ♘e7 [□ 5 ... ♗g7] 6 d4 d6 7 ♘f3 ♕h6 8 h4 f6 9 ♔g1 ♕g6 10 e5 h6 11 exf6 ♕xf6 12 ♘e4 [□ 12 hxg5 hxg5 13 ♖xh8 ♕xh8 14 ♘xg5±] 12 ... ♕g6 13 ♗d3 ♗f5 14 ♕e2 g4 15 ♘e1 f3 16 gxf3? gxf3+ **0-1**

L/N5197

**1863-★PS-1** 13 xi 63

**Paulsen, L.+ Schmorl, A.**

Leipzig

1 e4 e6 2 d3 d5 3 exd5 exd5 4 g3 ♘f6 5 ♗g2 ♗d6 6 ♘e2 ♗e6 7 0-0 c6 8 b3 ♕c7 9 c4 dxc4 10 bxc4 ♘a6 11 ♘bc3 0-0-0 12 ♖b1 h5 13 ♗g5 h4 14 ♘e4 hxg3 15 hxg3 ♖h7 16 ♕a4 ♖dh8 17 ♘xd6+ ♕xd6 18 ♖xb7 ♘c5 19 ♕xa7 ♘xb7 20 ♗f4 ♕b4 21 ♕b8+ ♔d7 22 ♕c7+ ♔e8 23 ♗xc6+ ♘d7 24 ♗xb7 ♕c5 25 ♗c6 ♖h1+ 26 ♗xh1 ♕h5 27 ♕c8+ ♔e7 28 ♕xh8 ♕xh8 29 ♘d4 ♘c5 30 ♘xe6 ♘xe6 31 ♗e3 g5 32 ♗d5 f5 33 ♖e1 ♘g7 34 ♗xg5+ ♔d6 35 ♗e7+ ♔d7 36 ♗f6 ♕f8 37 ♖e7+ ♔d6 38 ♖f7 **0-1** L/N6047

**1863-★PS-2 ●○⌂** 31 viii 63

**Paulsen, L.– Schultz, G.**

Düsseldorf [Lange]

1 e4 e5 2 d4 exd4 3 c3 d6 [3 ... dxc3] 4 cxd4 ♘f6 5 ♘c3 ♗e7 6 ♗d3 ♘c6 7 ♘ge2 0-0 8 0-0 b6 9 f4 ♘b4 10 d5 ♘xd3 11 ♕xd3 a5 12 ♖f3 ♗a6 13 ♕c2 ♘d7 14 ♘d4 ♗f6 15 ♘c6 ♕e8 16 ♗e3 [□ 16 ♗d2] 16 ... ♗xc3 17 bxc3 ♘f6 18 ♗d4 ♕xe4 19 ♕f2 ♘xd5∓ 20 ♖e1 ♕f5 21 ♖g3 f6 22 ♖ge3 ♗b5 23 ♘e7+ ♘xe7 24 ♖xe7 ♖f7 25 ♕g3 ♖xe7 26 ♖xe7 ♕b1+ 27 ♖e1 ♕xa2 28 ♗xf6 ♕f7 29 ♗d4 c5 30 ♗e3 a4 31 f5 ♕f6 32 ♗f4 ♕xf5 33 ♗xd6 ♕d3 34 ♕e5 [□ 34 ♕f4] 34 ... ♖e8 35 ♗e7 ♕d7 36 ♕e3 a3 37 c4 ♖xe7 38 ♕xe7 ♕xe7 39 ♖xe7 ♗xc4 40 ♖a7 a2 41 ♔f2 b5 42 ♔e3 ♗b3 43 ♔d2 [43 ♖a3−+] 43 ... ♗a4 **0-1** L/N5192

**1863-★PS-3 ●○⌂** 31 viii 63

**Paulsen, L.– Schwengers, P.**

Düsseldorf [Lange]

1 e4 e5 2 f4 ♗c5 3 ♘f3 d6 4 c3 ♘c6 5 d4 exd4 6 cxd4 ♗b6 7 ♗b5 ♗d7 8 0-0 ♕e7 9 ♘c3 0-0-0 10 ♔h1 f5 11 d5 ♘b8 12 ♗xd7+ ♘xd7 13 exf5 ♕f7 14 ♘d4 g6 15 ♘e6 ♖e8 16 ♘a4 gxf5 17 ♘xb6+ ♘xb6 18 b3 ♘xd5 19 ♘g5 ♕g7 20 ♗b2 ♕xb2 21 ♕xd5 ♕f6 22 ♕f7 ♖e7 23 ♕c4 h6 24 ♘f3 ♖e4 25 ♕d3 ♘e7 26 ♖ae1 ♕e6 27 ♘d4 ♕d5 28 ♘xf5? ♕xd3 29 ♘xe7+ ♖xe7 **0-1** L/N5192

**1863-★PS-4**

**Paulsen, L.= Saalbach, A.**

Leipzig

1 e4 e6 2 d4 d5 3 ♘c3 ♘c6 4 ♘f3 dxe4 5 ♘xe4 ♘f6 6 ♘xf6+ ♕xf6 7 ♗d3 h6 8 0-0 ♗d6 9 c3 0-0 10 ♕e2 e5 11 ♕e4 ♕g6 12 ♕xg6 fxg6 13 dxe5 ♘xe5 14 ♘xe5 ♗xe5 15 f4 ♗d6 16 ♗xg6 ♗f5 17 ♗xf5 ♗c5+ 18 ♔h1 ♖xf5 19 g4 ♖f6 20 f5 ♖e8 21 ♗f4 ♗d6 22 ♗xd6 ♖xd6 23 ♖f2 ♔f7 24 ♔g2 ♖ed8 25 ♖e1 ♖e8 26 ♖xe8 ♔xe8 27 a4 ♔f7 28 b4 ♔f6 29 ♔g3 h5 30 h3 hxg4 31 hxg4 ♔g5 32 ♖f3 ♖d1 33 ♔f2 ♖d2+ 34 ♔e3 ♔xg4 35 f6 gxf6 36 ♖xf6 ♖d7 ½-½

L/N6047-1863

**1863-★PS-5**

**Schurig, R.– Paulsen, L.**

Leipzig

1 e4 e5 2 f4 exf4 3 ♗c4 ♕h4+ 4 ♔f1 d6 5 d4 ♘f6 6 ♘c3 ♘g4 7 ♘h3 g5 8 ♕f3 ♗e6 9 ♘d5 ♔d8 10 ♗e2 ♗g7 11 c3 ♘d7 12 ♗d2 ♗xd5 13 exd5 f5 14 ♗d3 ♖f8 15 ♖e1 ♘df6 16 ♖e6 ♘e3+ 17 ♔e2 ♘fxd5 18 ♗xe3 ♘xe3 19 ♖xd6+ cxd6 20 ♕xb7 ♕g4+ 21 ♔f2 ♕xg2+ 22 ♕xg2 ♘xg2 23 ♘xg5 ♗h6 24 ♘e6+ ♔e7 25 ♘xf8 ♘e3 26 ♘xh7 ♖h8 27 ♖e1 ♔f7 28 c4 ♖xh7 29 c5 ♗g5 30 c6 ♗h4+ 31 ♔e2 ♗xe1 32 c7 ♖xh2+ 33 ♔xe1 f3 34 ♗f1 ♖c2 35 ♗c4+ ♔f6 **0-1** L/N6047-1863

**1863-★PV-1 ●○⌂** 31 viii 63

**Paulsen, L.= Busch, von d.**

Düsseldorf

1 e4 e5 2 ♘f3 ♕f6 3 ♗c4 ♘h6 4 0-0 ♗c5 5 ♘c3 c6 6 d4 ♗xd4 7 ♘xd4 exd4 8 e5 ♕g6 9 ♕xd4 ♘f5 10 ♕f4 0-0 11 ♗d3 d6 12 exd6 h5 13 ♘e4 h4 14 d7 ♘xd7 15 g4 ♘h6 16 f3 f5 17 ♘d6 ♘b6 18 g5 ♘f7 19 ♘xc8 ♘xc8 20 ♗xf5 ♕h5 21 ♗e6 ♔h8 22 ♕b4 ♘cd6 23 ♗f4 ♖ad8 24 ♖ad1 ♘xg5 25 ♗g4 ♖xf4 26 ♕xf4 ♕g6 27 ♖xd6 ♘h3+ 28 ♔h1 ♘xf4 29 ♖xg6 ♘xg6 ½-½

L/N5192

**1863-★P?-1**

**Paulsen, L.+ ? & ?**

1 e4 e5 2 f4 exf4 3 ♗c4 ♘f6 4 ♘c3 c6 5 ♕f3 ♗b4 6 ♘ge2 0-0 7 0-0 d5 8 exd5 ♗g4 9 ♕xf4 ♗xc3 10 ♘xc3 cxd5 11 ♘xd5 ♘bd7 12 d4 ♗e6 13 ♘xf6+ ♘xf6 14 ♗d3 ♖c8 15 b3 ♖e8 16 ♕h4! h6 17 ♗xh6 ♘g4 18 ♗g5 ♕xd4+ 19 ♔h1 f6 20 ♖ad1 ♕e5 21 ♗f4 ♕c3 22 ♕h7+ ♔f8 23 ♗d6+ ♖e7 24 ♗xe7+ ♔xe7 25 ♕xg7+ ♗f7 26 ♕xg4 ♖g8 27 ♖fe1+ ♔f8 28 ♕d7 ♕c6 29 ♕e7+ ♔g7 30 ♖e3 ♔h6 **1-0**

M324-1863

**1863-★P?-2**

**Paulsen, L.+ ?**

1 e4 e5 2 f4 exf4 3 ♗c4 b5 4 ♗b3 a5 5 ♘c3 a4 6 ♗xf7+! ♔xf7 7 ♕h5+ g6 [7 ... ♔e7 8 ♕e5+, 9 ♕d5+] 8 ♕d5+ ♔g7 9 ♕xa8 ♕h4+ 10 ♔d1 [□ 10 ♔f1] 10 ... ♕f2 11 ♘ge2 ♕xg2 12 ♖g1 ♕xh2 13 ♕xb8 f3 14 ♕xc8 ♗c5 15 ♕xd7+ ♘e7 16 d4 ♕xg1+?? 17 ♘xg1 f2 18 ♗h6+ **1-0** M324-1863

**1863-★P?-3**

**?– Paulsen, L.**

[Löwenthal]

1 e4 e5 2 f4 exf4 3 ♘f3 g5 4 ♗c4 g4 5 ♘e5 ♕h4+ 6 ♔f1 f3 7 g3 ♕h3+ 8 ♔f2 ♘f6 9 ♘xf7 d5 10 ♗f1 ♘xe4+ 11 ♔e1 f2+ 12 ♔e2 ♕h5 13 ♘xh8 ♕e5 14 d4 ♘c3+ 15 ♔d3 ♕e1! [△ 16 ... ♗f5#]

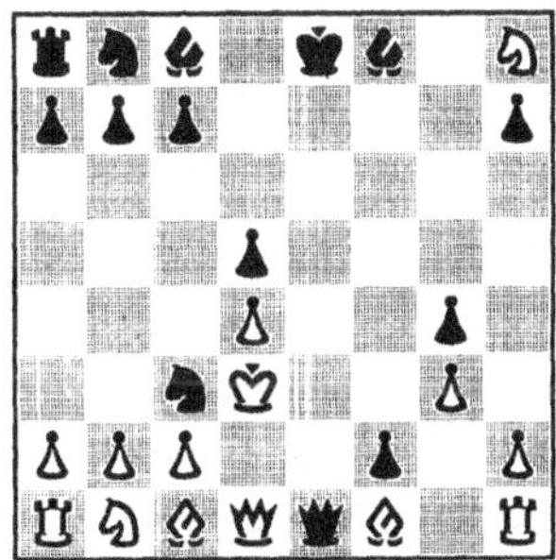

16 ♕d2 ♗h6 17 ♔xc3 ♗xd2+ 18 ♘xd2 ♘c6 19 b3 ♕e3+ 20 ♔b2 ♕xd4+ 21 c3 ♕xh8 22 ♗b5 ♗f5 23 ♖f1 d4 **0-1** M324-1863

**1863-★P?-4**

**?– Paulsen, L.**

1 e4 e5 2 f4 exf4 3 ♘f3 g5 4 ♗c4 g4 5 ♘e5 ♕h4+ 6 ♔f1 f3 7 g3 [□ 7 d4] 7 ... ♕h3+ 8 ♔f2 ♘f6 9 ♘xf7 d5 10 ♗f1 ♘xe4+ 11 ♔e1 f2+ 12 ♔e2 ♕h5 13 ♘xh8 ♕e5 14 d4 ♘c3+ 15 ♔d3 ♕e1! 16 ♕d2 ♗h6 17 ♔xc3 ♗xd2+ 18 ♘xd2 ♘c6 19 b3 ♕e3+ 20 ♔b2 ♕xd4+ 21 c3 ♕xh8 22 ♗b5 ♗f5 23 ♖f1 d4 **0-1**

L/N6016-1863

**1863-★P?-5**
**?– Paulsen, L.**
[Löwenthal]
1 e4 e5 2 f4 exf4 3 ♗c4 b5 4 ♗xf7+ ♔xf7 5 ♕h5+ g6 6 ♕d5+ ♔g7 7 ♕xa8 ♘c6 8 ♘f3 ♗c5 9 b4 ♗b6 10 ♗b2+ ♘f6 11 e5 ♘e4 12 e6+ [□ 12 d3, 13 e6+] 12 ... ♘f6 13 ♘e5 ♕e7 14 ♔d1 ♕xe6 15 ♖e1 ♕d6 16 ♘xc6 dxc6 17 ♗e5? ♕xe5 18 ♖xe5 ♗g4+ 19 ♔e1 ♖xa8 20 c3 f3 21 gxf3 ♗xf3 22 d4 a5 23 ♘d2 ♗d5 24 a4 axb4 **0-1**
M324-1863

**1863-★P?-6**
**?– Petrov, A.D.**
1 e4 e5 2 f4 exf4 3 ♘f3 g5 4 h4 g4 5 ♘e5 ♘f6 6 ♗c4 d5 7 exd5 ♗d6 8 d4 ♘h5 9 ♗b5+ ♔f8 10 ♘c3 ♘g3 11 ♖g1 ♕f6 12 ♘e2 ♗xe5 13 dxe5 ♕b6 14 ♘d4 c5 15 dxc6 ♘xc6 16 ♗xc6 bxc6 17 ♗xf4 ♘f5 18 ♘e2

18 ... ♗a6 19 ♖h1 ♖d8 20 ♕c1 ♕b4+ 21 ♔f2 g3+ 22 ♔f3 ♗xe2+ 23 ♔xe2 ♕e4+ 24 ♗e3 ♘d4+ 25 ♔e1 ♘xc2+ 26 ♔e2 ♕xg2+ **0-1**
L/N6016-1863

**1863-★SS-1**
**Steinitz, W.+Schlesser**
London? [Boden]
⟨♘b1⟩ 1 e4 e5 2 ♘f3 ♘c6 3 ♗c4 ♗c5 4 b4 ♗xb4 5 c3 ♗c5 6 0-0 d6 7 d4 exd4 8 cxd4 ♗b6 9 h3 h6 10 ♗b2 ♘a5 11 ♗d3 ♘f6 12 ♕e2 0-0 13 e5! dxe5 [□ 13 ... ♖e8] 14 dxe5 ♘d5 15 ♕e4 f5 16 exf6 ♘xf6 17 ♗xf6 ♕xf6 18 ♕h7+ ♔f7 19 ♖fe1 ♗e6 20 ♘e5+ ♔e8 21 ♘g4! ♗xf2+ 22 ♔f1 ♕e7 23 ♘xf2 ♔d8 24 ♖ad1 ♔c8 25 ♔g1 ♕c5 26 ♖xe6 ♕xf2+ 27 ♔h1 ♕g3 28 ♕f5 **1-0** M392

**1863-★S?-1** x63
**Steinitz, W.+?**
London
⟨♖a1⟩1 e4 e5 2 ♘f3 ♘c6 3 ♗c4 ♗c5 4 b4 ♗xb4 5 c3 ♗c5 6 0-0 d6 7 d4 ♗b6 [□ 7 ... exd4] 8 dxe5 dxe5 9 ♕b3 [9 ♗xf7+! ♔xf7 10 ♘xe5+] 9 ... ♕f6 10 ♗g5 ♕g6 11 ♗b5 ♕e6 12 ♕a4 ♘e7 13 ♗c4 ♕d7 14 ♖d1 ♕g4 15 ♘xe5 ♕xg5 16 ♗xf7+ ♔f8 17 ♖d8+ ♘xd8 18 ♕e8# **1-0**
L/N6124

**1863-★S?-2** x63
**Steinitz, W.+?**
London
⟨♖a1⟩1 e4 e5 2 ♘c3 ♘c6 3 f4 exf4 4 ♘f3 ♗b4 5 ♘d5 ♗a5 6 ♘xf4 d6 7 c3 ♗b6 8 d4 ♗g4 9 ♗b5 ♔f8 10 0-0 ♘e5

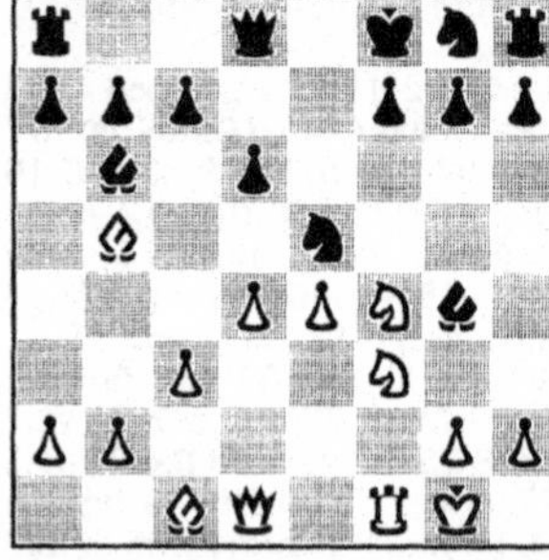

11 ♘xe5 ♗xd1 12 ♘eg6+ **1-0**
L/N6124

**1863-★S?-3** x63
**Steinitz, W.+?**
London [Löwenthal]
⟨♖a1⟩ 1 e4 e5 2 ♘f3 ♘f6 3 d4 exd4 4 e5 ♘d5 [□ 4 ... ♘e4] 5 ♕xd4 c6 6 ♗c4 ♕b6 7 ♕e4 ♗c5 8 0-0 ♘e7?? [□ 8 ... ♘c7 ∆ ... ♘e6] 9 ♘g5 g6 10 ♘xf7 ♖f8 11 ♘d6+ ♔d8 12 ♕h4 ♕c7 13 ♕xe7+!! ♔xe7 14 ♗g5+ ♖f6 15 exf6+ ♔f8 [15 ... ♔d8 16 f7#] 16 ♗h6# **1-0** L/N6124

## DÜSSELDORF 1864

**1864-DUS-1**
**Wülfing, O.= Lange, M.**
[Lange]
1 e4 e5 2 ♘f3 ♘c6 3 ♗b5 ♗c5 4 c3 ♘f6 5 d4 exd4 6 e5 ♘e4 7 0-0 [7 cxd4 ♗b4+ 8 ♗d2 ♘xd2 9 ♘bxd2 0-0 (9 ... d5) 10 0-0 d5] 7 ... d5! [7 ... dxc3 8 ♕e2 ♘xf2! 9 ♖xf2 ♗xf2+ 10 ♕xf2 cxb2 11 ♗xb2] 8 exd6 0-0! 9 ♗xc6 bxc6 10 dxc7 ♕xc7 11 ♘xd4 [11 cxd4 ♗g4] 11 ... ♗a6 12 ♖e1 ♖ae8 13 ♗e3 ♗d6 14 ♘f3 f5 15 ♘bd2 c5 16 ♖c1 ♖f6 17 b4 [17 ♕a4 ♖ef8∓ 18 ♕xa6? ♗xh2+–+] 17 ... c4 18 h3 ♗b7 19 ♗xa7 ♖d8! 20 ♗d4 ♘xd2 21 ♘xd2! ♖g6 22 f3 ♗h2+! 23 ♔h1

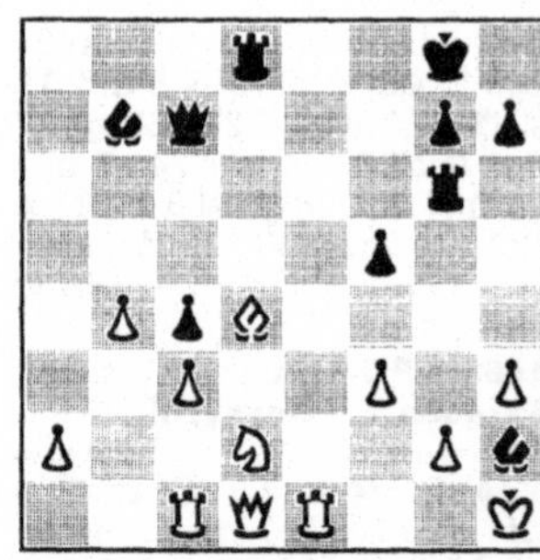

23 ... ♖xg2 24 ♔xg2 ♕g3+ 25 ♔h1 [25 ♔f1 ♖xd4 26 cxd4 ♕g1+ 27 ♔e2 ♕g2+ 28 ♔e3 f4#] 25 ... ♕xh3 [25 ... ♖xd4? 26 cxd4 ♕xh3 27 ♖e8+ ♔f7 28 ♕e2±] 26 ♕e2! ♗e5+ [26 ... ♗f4+ 27 ♔g1 ♕g3+ 28 ♕g2 ♕xg2+ 29 ♔xg2 ♗xd2 30 ♖e7±] 27 ♔g1 ♖xd4 28 ♕xe5! ♖g4+ 29 ♔f2! ♖g2+ 30 ♔e3 ♕h6+ 31 ♔d4 [31 ♔f4 (31 f4 ♕b6+, 32 ... ♕e6=) 31 ... ♕b6+ 32 ♕d4 f4+ 33 ♔xf4 ♕h6+ 34 ♔f5 ♕g6+–+] 31 ... ♖xd2+ 32 ♔xc4 ♕a6+! 33 b5! ♕a4+! 34 ♔c5 ♖d5+! 35 ♕xd5+ ♗xd5 36 ♔xd5 ♕xb5+ 37 ♔d6 ♕b6+ 38 ♔e5 ♕f6+ 39 ♔d5 ♕f7+ **½-½**
L/N6047

**1864-DUS-2**
**Lange, M.+Wülfing, O.**
[Lange]
1 e4 e5 2 f4 exf4 3 ♗c4 ♕h4+ 4 ♔f1 d6 5 d4 ♘c6 6 ♘c3 [□ 6 c3, 7 ♕f3] 6 ... ♗g4 7 ♘f3 ♗xf3 8 gxf3 g5 9 ♗b5 ♕h3+ 10 ♔f2 a6! 11 ♗xc6+ bxc6 12 ♖g1! h6 13 ♘e2 ♗g7 14 ♗d2 ♘e7 15 c3 ♘g6 16 ♖g2 ♕xg2+ [16 ... ♕h5 17 ♖g4] 17 ♔xg2 ♘h4+ 18 ♔f2 f5! 19 exf5 ♘xf5 20 h4 ♘xh4 21 ♘xf4 ♔d7 [21 ... 0-0 22 ♖h3±] 22 ♘h5! ♘f5 23 ♖h3 ♖af8 24 ♘xg7 ♘xg7 25 ♖ah1 g4 26 ♗xh6 ♖xf3+ 27 ♖xf3 gxf3 28 ♖h2! ♘f5 29 ♗f4 ♖xh2+ 30 ♗xh2 a5 31 ♔xf3 ♔e6 32 ♔e4 ♘e7 33 ♗f4 ♘d5 34 ♗d2 a4 35 c4 ♘b6 36 ♔d3 d5 37 c5 ♘c4 38 ♔c3 ♘xd2 [□ 38 ... ♔f5] 39 ♔xd2 ♔f5 40 ♔e3 ♔g4 41 a3 ♔f5 42 ♔d3 ♔f4 43 b3 axb3 44 a4 b2 45 ♔c2 b1♕+ 46 ♔xb1 ♔e4 47 a5 ♔xd4 48 a6 ♔xc5 49 a7 d4 50 a8♕ ♔d5 51 ♔c2 **1-0**
L/N6047

**1864-DUS-3**
**Neuhaus– Hipp, F.A.**
[Lange]
1 e3 e5 2 a3 [□ 2 c4] 2 ... d5 3 d4 exd4 4 ♕xd4 [□ 4 exd4] 4 ... ♘c6 5 ♕d1 [□ 5 ♗b5] 5 ... ♘f6 6 h3 ♗c5 7 ♘f3 0-0 8 ♘bd2 ♖e8 9 ♘b3 ♗b6 10 ♗d3 d4 11 ♕e2 dxe3 12 fxe3 ♘d5 13 e4 ♕d6 14 ♔f1 ♘f4 15 ♗xf4 ♕xf4 16 ♖e1 ♗e6 17 ♘bd2 ♖ad8

18 b3 ♘d4 19 ♕d1 ♕g3 20 ♘xd4 ♗xd4 21 ♕e2 f5! 22 ♘f3 ♗b6 23 e5 ♗xb3 24 ♗c4+ ♗xc4 25 ♕xc4+ ♔h8 26 ♖e2? [□ 26 ♕e2 △ 27 h4, 28 ♖h3] 26 ... ♖d1+ 27 ♘e1 ♖xe1+ 28 ♖xe1 ♕f2# **0-1**

L/N6047

### 1864-DUS-4
**Schnitzler, G.– Vitzthum, C.**

[Lange]

1 e4 e5 2 ♘f3 ♘c6 3 ♗b5 ♘d4 4 ♘xd4 exd4 5 d3! c6 6 ♗c4 b5 7 ♗b3 ♕f6 8 0-0 a5 9 a3 [□ 9 c3] 9 ... d6 10 f4 ♗e6 11 ♕f3 ♖c8 12 f5 ♗xb3 13 cxb3 g6 14 ♕g4 h5 15 ♕h3 g5 16 ♗d2 ♖a8 17 ♕g3 ♗e7 18 ♗e1 ♘h6 19 ♘c3 ♘g4 20 ♘d1 ♘e5 21 ♖c1 h4 22 ♕f2 ♘xd3 23 ♕c2 ♘e5 24 ♘f2 c5 25 b4? axb4 26 axb4 c4 27 ♗d2 ♔d7 28 ♖a1 ♖hc8 29 ♘h3 ♕g7 30 ♖a5 ♖xa5 31 bxa5 f6 32 ♖a1 ♖a8 33 ♘f2 ♕g8 34 ♖c1 ♗d8 35 b4? c3 36 ♘d3 ♕c4! 37 ♘xe5+ dxe5 38 ♕b1 ♗e7 39 ♕a1 ♕xb4 40 ♕a2 ♕c4 41 ♕a1 ♖a6 42 ♗xc3 dxc3 43 ♖xc3 ♕d4+ 44 ♔f1 ♖c6 **0-1**

L/N6047

### 1864-DUS-5
**Schwengers, P.+ Höing, C.**

[Lange]

1 e4 e6 2 d4 d5 3 ♘f3 f6 4 ♗d3 ♗d6 5 e5 fxe5 6 ♘xe5 [△ 7 ♕h5++-] 6 ... ♘f6 7 ♘c3 ♗b4 8 ♗g5 0-0 9 ♕f3 a5 10 ♕h3 g6 11 0-0 ♗e7 12 ♗h6 ♖e8 13 ♘xg6!? e5 14 ♕g3 ♘g4 15 ♘xe5 ♗h4 16 ♕f4 ♕f6 17 ♘xg4 ♕xf4 18 ♗xf4 ♗xg4 19 ♖ae1 ♘d7 20 h3 ♗h5 21 ♗f5 ♘f8 22 ♖xe8 ♖xe8 23 g3 ♗f6 24 ♗e3 ♗f3 25 ♘b1 ♗h5 26 c3 ♔g7 27 ♘d2 b6 28 g4 ♗g6 29 ♗xg6 hxg6 30 ♘f3 ♘h7 31 ♖e1 g5 32 h4 ♔g6 33 h5+ ♔g7 34 ♔g2 ♖e4 35 ♔g3 ♗e7 36 ♘e5 ♗d6 37 f3 ♗xe5+ 38 dxe5 ♖c4 39 ♗d4 ♖a4 40 a3 c5? 41 e6+ ♔f8 42 ♗e5 ♔e8 43 ♖d1? ♔e7! 44 ♖e1 ♔xe6 45 f4 gxf4+ 46 ♗xf4+ ♔f6 47 ♔f3 d4 48 ♖e4 ♘g5+ 49 ♗xg5+ ♔xg5 50 cxd4 cxd4 51 ♔e2 ♖c4 52 ♔d3 ♖c1 53 ♖xd4 ♖d1+ 54 ♔c4 ♖c1+ 55 ♔b5 ♖c2 56 b4 **1-0**

L/N6047

### 1864-DUS-6
**Lange, M.+ Hipp, F.A.**

[Lange]

1 e4 e5 2 ♘f3 ♘c6 3 ♗b5 d6 4 0-0 ♘f6 5 ♘c3 ♗d7 6 ♗c4 ♗e6 7 ♗xe6 fxe6 8 d4 exd4 9 ♘xd4 ♘xd4 10 ♕xd4 e5 11 ♕c4 c6 12 ♖e1 ♕d7 13 h3 0-0-0 14 ♕a4 ♔b8 15 ♗e3 a6 16 ♗b6 ♖c8 17 b4 d5 18 ♖ab1 d4 19 ♘d1 ♘e8 20 ♘b2 ♘d6 21 ♕a5 ♗e7 22 ♕xe5 ♔a8 23 ♕xd4 ♖he8 24 ♗c5 ♕e6 25 c4 ♗f6 26 ♕xd6 ♗xb2 27 ♖xb2 ♕xc4 28 e5 ♖cd8 29 ♕c7 ♕b5 30 a4 ♕xa4 31 ♕b6 ♔b8 32 ♕a7+ ♔c8 33 ♖bb1! ♕a2 34 ♗b6 ♖d5 [35 e6 ♖xe6 36 ♕a8+ ♔d7 37 ♕d8#] **1-0**

L/N6047

### 1864-DUS-7
**Vitzthum, C.+Schwengers, P.**

[Lange]

1 e4 e5 2 ♘f3 ♘c6 3 ♗c4 ♗c5 4 c3 d6 5 0-0 ♘f6 6 d3 ♗e6 7 ♗xe6 fxe6 8 b4 ♗b6 9 a4 a5 [□ 9 ... a6] 10 b5 ♘b8 11 ♕b3 ♕e7 12 ♗a3 ♘bd7 13 ♘g5 ♘f8 14 ♘d2 h6 15 ♘gf3 ♘g6 16 ♘c4 ♘d7 17 ♘xb6 cxb6 18 d4 0-0 19 dxe5 ♖xf3?! 20 ♗xd6 ♕f7 21 gxf3 ♘h4 22 ♖fd1 ♕g6+ [□ 22 ... ♕xf3] 23 ♔f1 ♕g2+ 24 ♔e2 ♕xf3+ 25 ♔d2 ♕f4+ 26 ♔c2 ♕xe4+ 27 ♔b2 ♔f7 28 ♖d4 ♕f3 29 ♖xh4 ♕xf2+ 30 ♔a3 ♕xh4 31 ♖f1+ ♘f6 32 exf6 gxf6 33 ♗e5 ♕h3 34 ♖xf6+ ♔e7 35 ♕c2 **1-0**

L/N6047

### 1864-DUS-8
**Vitzthum, C.– Lange, M.**

[Lange]

1 e4 e5 2 ♗c4 ♗c5 3 ♘f3 ♘c6 4 c3 ♘f6 5 d3 d6 6 ♗g5 h6 7 ♗h4 ♕e7 8 ♘bd2 ♗d7 9 h3 ♗b6 10 b4 a6 11 a4 ♘d8 12 0-0 g5 13 ♗g3 ♘h5 14 ♔h2 ♘g7 15 ♕e2 ♘de6 [△ ♘f8, ♘g6, h5] 16 ♗xe6 ♗xe6 17 b5 axb5 18 axb5 ♖xa1 19 ♖xa1

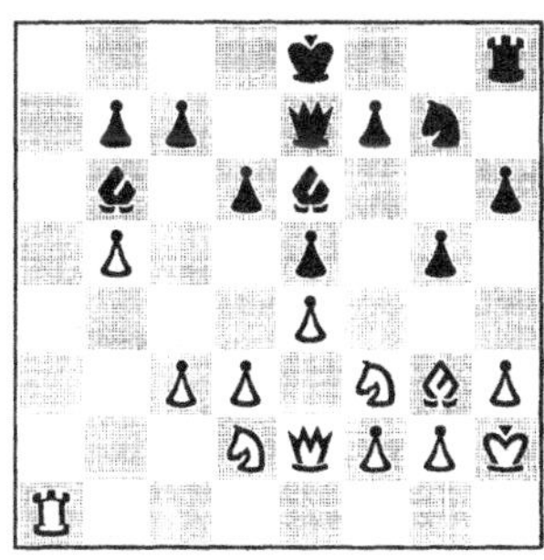

19 ... 0-0! 20 d4 f6 [20 ... f5?] 21 ♘c4 ♗xc4 22 ♕xc4+ ♕e6 23 ♕xe6+ ♘xe6 24 ♖d1 [24 ♖a4 exd4 25 ♘xd4 (25 cxd4 g4) 25 ... ♘c5] 24 ... exd4 25 ♘xd4 ♘xd4 26 cxd4 ♖a8 27 f3 ♖a4 28 d5 [28 ♗f2 ♖b4] 28 ... ♖b4 29 ♖a1 ♖xb5 30 ♖a8+ ♔g7 31 h4 ♗d4! 32 ♖d8 ♖c5 33 h5 f5! 34 ♖d7+ ♔f8 35 exf5 [35 ♖h7 (35 ♖xc7? ♖xc7 36 ♗xd6+ ♖e7-+) 35 ... ♗g7, ♔g8-+] 35 ... b5 36 ♖h7 b4 37 ♖xh6 b3 38 ♖e6 b2 **0-1**

L/N6047

## ANDERSSEN⚔SUHLE
Berlin

[1864-⚔AS]

| | | | | | | | | | |
|---|---|---|---|---|---|---|---|---|---|
| A. Anderssen | 0 | 0 | 1 | 1 | ½ | 1 | 0 | ½ | 4 |
| B. Suhle | 1 | 1 | 0 | 0 | ½ | 0 | 1 | ½ | 4 |

### 1864-⚔AS-1
vii 64

**Anderssen, A.– Suhle, B.**

[Anderssen & Neumann]

1 e4 e5 2 ♘f3 ♘c6 3 ♗c4 ♗c5 4 b4 ♗b6 5 a4 a6 6 0-0 d6 7 c3 ♘f6 8 d3 0-0 9 ♗b3 [□ 9 ♗e3] 9 ... ♗g4 10 ♘a3 d5 11 h3 dxe4 12 hxg4 exf3 13 gxf3 ♘d7 14 ♔g2 ♘e7 15 ♖h1 ♘g6 16 d4? exd4 17 cxd4 ♕f6 18 ♘c2 h6 19 ♖h3 ♖ad8 20 a5 ♗a7 21 ♖b1 ♘f4+ 22 ♗xf4 ♕xf4 23 ♕d3? ♘e5 24 ♕e3 ♘g6 25 ♖d1 ♖fe8 26 ♕c3 ♕f6 27 ♔f1 ♘f4 28 ♖h2 ♘e2 29 ♕c4 ♕xf3 30 ♖d3 ♕f4 31 ♘e3 ♕xh2 **0-1**

L/N6051

### 1864-⚔AS-2
vii 64

**Suhle, B.+ Anderssen, A.**

[Anderssen & Neumann]

1 e4 e5 2 f4 exf4 3 ♗c4 d5 4 ♗xd5 c6 5 ♗b3 ♕h4+ 6 ♔f1 g5 7 ♘c3 ♗g7 8 d4 ♘e7 9 ♘f3 ♕h5 10 h4 h6 11 ♘e5 ♕xd1+ 12 ♘xd1 ♗xe5 13 dxe5 ♖g8 14 hxg5 hxg5 15 ♘f2 ♗e6 16 ♗xe6 fxe6 17 ♖h5 ♘d7 18 ♘h3 ♘xe5 19 ♘xg5 0-0-0 20 ♘xe6 ♖de8 21 ♗xf4 ♘7g6 22 ♗xe5 ♖xe6 23 ♗h2 ♖xe4 24 ♖h7 ♘f4 25 ♗xf4 ♖xf4+ 26 ♔g1 ♖fg4 27 ♖h2 ♔c7 [□ 27 ... ♖d4=] 28 ♖d1 ♔b6 29 ♖d2 a5 30 ♖h3 ♔b5 31 ♔h2 a4 32 a3 c5 33 g3 b6 34 ♖g2 ♔a5 35 ♖h4 ♖4g5 36 g4 ♔b5 37 ♔h3 ♔c4 38 ♖h5 ♖5g6 39 g5 b5 40 ♖g4+ ♔d5 41 ♔h4 ♖e6 42 g6+ ♔d6 43 g7 ♖e1 44 ♖g6+ ♔e7 45 ♔g5 b4 46 ♔h6 bxa3 47 bxa3 ♖f1 48 ♔h7 ♔f7 49 ♖gg5 ♖f6 50 ♖h6 ♖f2 51 ♖gg6 **1-0**

L/N6051

### 1864-⚔AS-3
vii 64

**Anderssen, A.+ Suhle, B.**

[Anderssen & Neumann]

1 e4 c5 2 ♗c4 e6 3 ♘c3 a6 4 a4 ♘c6 5 d3 ♘f6 6 ♗d2 d5 7 ♗a2 dxe4 8 dxe4 b6 9 ♘f3 ♗b7 10 0-0 ♗e7 11 ♖e1 0-0 12 ♗c4 ♘d4 13 ♗f4 h6 14 ♗e5 ♖c8 15 ♕d3 ♘c6 16 ♕f1 ♘xe5 17 ♘xe5 ♕c7 18 f4 ♖a8 19 ♖ad1 ♖fd8 20 ♖d3 ♖d4 21 b3 ♖ad8 22 ♖de3 ♖d2? 23 ♗d3 c4 24 ♘xc4 ♗c5 25 ♘xd2 ♘g4?? 26 ♘d1 g5 27 ♔h1 ♘xe3 28 ♘xe3 gxf4 29 ♘g4 ♔g7 30 e5 h5 31 ♘f6 ♗e3 32 ♘xh5+ ♔f8 [32 ... ♔h6 33 ♖xe3+-] 33 ♘xf4 **1-0**

L/N6051

**1864-✕AS-4** vii 64

**Suhle, B.– Anderssen, A.**

1 e4 e5 2 f4 exf4 3 ♗c4 d5 4 ♗xd5 c6 5 ♗b3 ♕h4+ 6 ♔f1 g5 7 d4 ♗g7 8 ♘c3 h6 9 e5 ♗f5 10 ♗d2 ♘e7 11 h3 ♗g6 12 ♗e1 ♕h5 13 ♕xh5 ♗xh5 14 ♘e4 ♘f5 15 ♗f2 ♘a6 16 c3 ♘c7 17 h4 ♘d5 18 ♗xd5 cxd5 19 ♘c5 0-0-0 20 hxg5 hxg5 21 ♘h3 b6 22 ♘d3 f6 23 exf6 ♗xf6 24 ♖e1 ♗g6 25 ♔e2 ♘d6 26 ♘e5 ♗h5+ 27 ♔d3 ♘e4 28 ♔c2 ♗xe5 29 dxe5 ♗g6 30 ♔b3 ♖xh3 31 ♖xh3 ♘xf2 32 ♖h6 ♗e4 33 e6 ♖f8 34 c4 ♘d3 35 ♖d1 d4 36 ♔a3 ♘c5 37 ♖xd4 ♗xg2 38 b4 ♘xe6 39 ♖d2 f3 40 ♖g6 ♖d8 41 ♖xd8+ ♔xd8 42 ♖xe6 f2 **0-1** L/N6051

**1864-✕AS-5** vii 64

**Anderssen, A.= Suhle, B.**

[Anderssen & Neumann]

1 e4 e5 2 ♘f3 ♘c6 3 ♗c4 ♗c5 4 b4 ♗b6? 5 a4 a6 6 0-0 d6 7 a5 ♗a7 8 b5 axb5 9 ♗xb5 ♘ge7 10 d4 0-0 [◻ 10 ... exd4] 11 dxe5 ♘xe5 12 ♘xe5 dxe5 13 ♗a3 ♕xd1 14 ♖xd1 ♗g4 15 ♖d3 c5 16 ♘c3 ♖fd8 17 ♘a4 ♘g6 18 ♗xc5 ♖xd3 19 ♗xd3 ♗xc5 20 ♘xc5 b6 21 ♘b3 bxa5 22 f3 ♗d7 23 ♖xa5 ♖xa5 24 ♘xa5 ♘f4 25 ♗f1 ♔f8 26 ♔f2 ♔e7 27 ♔e3 f6 28 ♔d2 ♔d6 29 ♔c3 ♘e6 30 ♔b4 ♘d4 31 ♘c4+ ♔c7 32 c3 ♘e6 33 ♘e3 ♗c6 34 ♗c4 ♘f4 35 g3 ♘h3 36 ♔c5? [◻ 36 ♗e2±] 36 ... ♘g1 37 ♗d5 ♗d7 38 f4 exf4 39 gxf4 ♘e2 40 ♗g8 ♘xc3 41 ♗xh7 ♔d8 42 ♘d5 ♘xd5 43 exd5 g5 44 f5 ♔e7 45 d6+ ♔d8 46 ♔d5 ♗c8 47 ♗g6 ♗d7 48 h3 ♗c8 49 ♗h5 ♗xf5 50 ♗g4 ♗xg4 51 hxg4 ♔d7 52 ♔c5 f5 53 gxf5 g4 54 f6 g3 55 f7 g2 **½-½** L/N6051

**1864-✕AS-6** vii 64

**Suhle, B.– Anderssen, A.**

[Anderssen & Neumann]

1 e4 e5 2 f4 exf4 3 ♗c4 d5 4 ♗xd5 c6 [4 ... ♘f6] 5 ♗b3 ♕h4+ 6 ♔f1 g5 7 d4 ♗g7 8 ♘c3 ♘e7 9 ♘f3 ♕h5 10 h4 h6 11 ♘e5 ♕xd1+ 12 ♘xd1 ♗xe5 13 dxe5 ♖g8 14 hxg5 hxg5 15 ♘f2 ♘g6 16 ♘d3 b6! 17 ♔f2 ♗e6 18 ♗d2 ♘d7 19 ♗c3 0-0-0 20 ♖ag1 ♖de8 21 ♗xe6 fxe6 22 g3 fxg3+ 23 ♔xg3 ♘h4 24 ♖f1 c5! 25 b3 b5 26 ♖h2 c4 27 bxc4 bxc4 28 ♘b2 ♘c5 29 ♖e1 ♖ef8

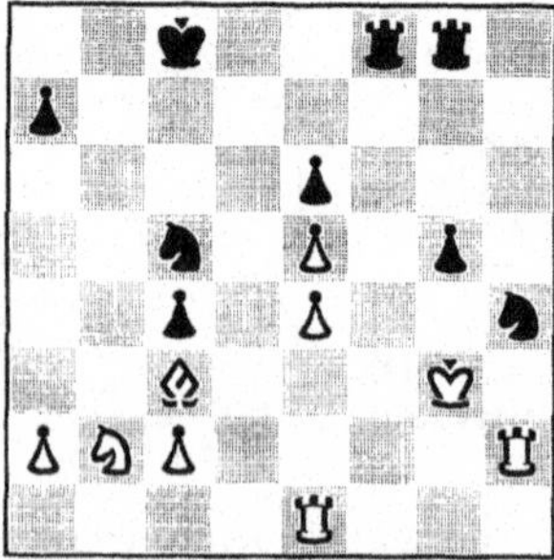

30 ♖e3 ♖f4 31 ♘xc4 ♘xe4+ 32 ♖xe4 ♘f5+ 33 ♔g2 ♖xe4 **0-1** L/N6051

**1864-✕AS-7** vii 64

**Anderssen, A.– Suhle, B.**

[Anderssen & Neumann]

1 e4 e5 2 ♘f3 ♘c6 3 ♗c4 ♗c5 4 b4 ♗b6? 5 a4 a6 6 0-0 d6 7 a5 ♗a7 8 b5 axb5 9 ♗xb5 ♘ge7 10 d4 exd4 11 ♘xd4 ♗d7 12 ♘b3? 0-0 13 ♗b2 ♘g6 14 ♘c3 ♕g5 15 ♔h1 f5 16 ♗c4+ ♔h8 17 ♗d5 f4 18 ♕d2 ♕h5 19 ♘b5? f3 20 e5 ♘cxe5 21 ♘xa7 fxg2+ 22 ♗xg2 ♘f3 23 ♗xg7+ ♔xg7 24 ♕c3+ ♘ge5 25 ♗xf3 ♕xf3+ 26 ♕xf3 ♘xf3 27 ♖fd1 ♖xa7 28 ♘c5 ♗f5 29 ♘d3 ♗e4 **0-1** L/N6051

**1864-✕AS-8** vii 64

**Suhle, B.= Anderssen, A.**

[Anderssen & Neumann]

1 e4 c5 2 ♘f3 e6 3 c3 ♘c6 4 d4 d5 5 exd5 exd5 6 ♗e2 ♘f6 7 0-0 cxd4 8 cxd4 ♗e7 9 ♘c3 0-0 10 ♗e3 ♗d6 11 ♕d2 ♗e6 12 ♘g5 ♖e8 13 f4? ♗f5 14 h3 ♖c8 15 ♘f3 ♘e4 16 ♘xe4 ♗xe4 17 a3 ♘a5∓ 18 ♖ac1 ♘b3 19 ♖xc8 ♕xc8 20 ♕e1 ♗xf3 21 ♖xf3 ♕c2 22 ♗b5 ♖e7? [◻ 22 ... ♖e6] 23 ♖f2 ♕e4 24 ♕c3! g6 25 ♖e2 ♕b1+ 26 ♖e1 ♕a2 27 ♗a4 ♘a1 28 b4 [◻ 28 f5 △ 29 ♗h6±] 28 ... b5 29 ♖xa1 ♕c4 30 ♕xc4 dxc4 31 ♗xb5 ♖xe3 32 ♗xc4 ♗xf4 33 d5 ♔f8 34 ♗b5 ♗g3 35 ♗c6 ♔e7 36 a4 ♔d6 37 b5 ♖e1+ 38 ♖xe1 ♗xe1 39 ♔f1 ♗a5 40 g4 f6 41 h4 ♔e5 42 ♔g2 ♔f4 43 ♔h3 ♗c7 44 ♗d7 f5 45 h5 fxg4+ 46 ♗xg4 gxh5 47 ♗xh5 ♔g5 48 ♗f3 ♔f4 49 ♗g2 ♔g5 50 ♗h1 ♔f4 51 ♔h4 ♔e5 52 ♔h5 ♔d6 53 ♔h6 ♔c5 54 ♗f3 ♔b4 55 ♗d1 ♔c5 56 ♔xh7 ♔xd5 **½-½** L/N6051

## HIRSCHFELD✕KOLISCH

Paris

**[1864-✕HK]**

| | | | | | | | | | |
|---|---|---|---|---|---|---|---|---|---|
| P. Hirschfeld | 1̂ | 0̂ | 1̂ | ? | 0̂ | 0̂ | ? | 1̂ | ? |
| I.F. von Kolisch | 0̂ | 1̂ | 0̂ | ? | 1̂ | 1̂ | ? | 0̂ | ? |

**1864-✕HK-1̂** vii 64

**Kolisch, I.F.von+Hirschfeld, P.**

[Löwenthal]

1 e4 e5 2 ♘f3 ♘c6 3 ♗c4 ♗c5 4 b4 ♗xb4 5 c3 ♗c5 6 0-0 d6 7 d4 exd4 8 cxd4 ♗b6 9 ♘c3 ♗g4 10 ♕a4 ♗d7 11 ♕b3 ♘a5 12 ♗xf7+ ♔f8 13 ♕c2 ♔xf7 14 e5 ♔f8? [14 ... h6] 15 ♖e1 ♕c8 16 d5 ♗f5 17 ♕d2 ♘h6 18 ♕f4 ♘g4 19 e6 ♗xf2+ 20 ♔h1 ♗xe1 21 ♕xf5+ ♘f6 22 ♘e4 ♔e7 23 ♗g5 ♕f8 24 ♖xe1 ♖e8 25 ♖c1 ♔d8

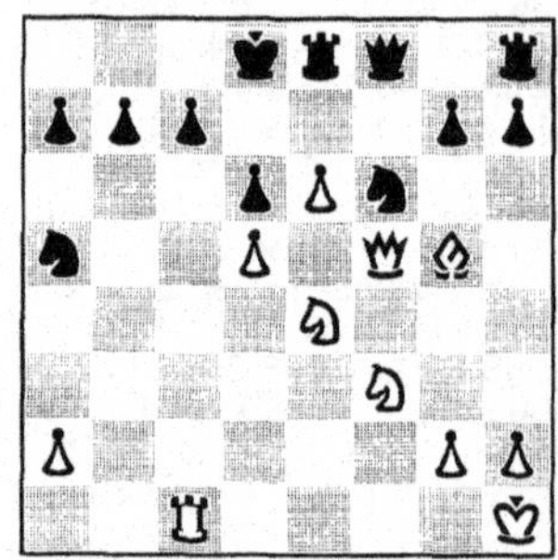

26 ♘e5 dxe5 27 d6 ♘c6 28 ♖xc6 bxc6 29 ♘xf6 gxf6 30 ♗xf6+ ♔c8 31 e7+ **1-0** L/N6124

**1864-✕HK-2̂**

**Hirschfeld,P.+Kolisch,I.F. von**

[Löwenthal]

1 e4 e5 2 ♘f3 ♘c6 3 ♗c4 ♗c5 4 b4 ♗xb4 5 c3 ♗c5 6 0-0 d6 7 d4 exd4 8 cxd4 ♗b6 9 ♘c3 ♗g4 10 ♗b5 ♗d7 [◻ 10 ... ♔f8] 11 e5 dxe5 [11 ... ♘ge7 12 ♗g5] 12 d5 ♘ce7 13 ♗xd7+ ♕xd7 14 ♘xe5 ♕f5 15 ♕a4+ ♔d8 16 ♗f4 ♘g6 17 g4 ♕c8 18 ♖fe1 ♘xe5 19 ♗xe5 f6 20 ♗xc7+ ♔xc7 21 ♘b5+ ♔d8 22 ♘d6 ♕d7 23 ♖e8+ ♕xe8 24 ♕xe8+ ♔c7 25 ♘b5# **1-0** L/N6124

**1864-✕HK-3̂** viii 64

**Kolisch,I.F.von+ Hirschfeld,P.**

[Löwenthal]

1 e4 e5 2 ♘f3 ♘c6 3 ♗c4 ♗c5 4 b4 ♗xb4 5 c3 ♗c5 6 0-0 d6 7 d4 exd4 8 cxd4 ♗b6 9 ♘c3 ♗g4 [◻ 9 ... ♘a5] 10 ♗b5 [10 ♕a4?!] 10 ... ♗d7 [◻ 10 ... ♔f8] 11 e5 [11 ♗g5 ♘ge7 12 e5 0-0 13 ♘d5 ♕e8 14 ♘f6++–] 11 ... dxe5 12 d5 ♘b8+– 13 ♘xe5 ♘e7 14 ♕g4 g6 15 ♘e4 ♘xd5 16 ♗g5 f6 17 ♕e6+ ♕e7 18 ♕xd5 c6 19 ♘xf6+ ♕xf6 20 ♕d2 ♕f5 21 g4 ♕f8 22 ♘xd7 ♘xd7 23 ♖ae1+ ♔f7 24 ♗c4+ ♔g7 25 ♕xd7+ **1-0** L/N6124

**1864-⚔HK-5** viii 64
**Kolisch,I.F.von–Hirschfeld,P.**
[Löwenthal]

1 e4 e5 2 f4 exf4 3 ♘f3 g5 4 h4 g4 5 ♘e5 ♘f6 6 ♗c4 d5 7 exd5 ♗d6 8 d4 ♘h5 9 ♗b5+ c6 10 dxc6 bxc6 11 ♘xc6 ♘xc6 12 ♗xc6+ ♗d7!? 13 ♗xa8 ♘g3 14 ♔f2? ♘xh1+ 15 ♕xh1 ♕e7 16 ♘c3 0-0 17 ♗d5 g3+ 18 ♔f1

18 ... ♗b5+ 19 ♘xb5 ♖e8 20 ♗xf7+ ♔xf7 21 ♘xd6+ ♕xd6 22 ♗d2 ♕xd4 23 ♗e1 ♕e3 24 ♕h3 ♕e2+ 25 ♔g1 ♕xe1+ 26 ♖xe1 ♖xe1# **0-1** L/N6124

**1864-⚔HK-6** viii 64
**Hirschfeld,P.+Kolisch,I.F. von**
[Löwenthal]

1 e4 e5 2 ♘f3 ♘c6 3 ♗c4 ♗c5 4 b4 ♗xb4 5 c3 ♗c5 6 0-0 d6 7 d4 exd4 8 cxd4 ♗b6 9 ♘c3 ♗g4 10 ♕a4 ♗d7 11 ♕b3 ♘a5 12 ♗xf7+ ♔f8 13 ♕c2 ♔xf7 14 e5 g6 15 e6+± ♗xe6 16 ♘g5+ ♔f6 17 d5 ♗f5 18 ♘ce4+ ♗xe4+– [18 ... ♕e7+–] 19 ♕c3+ ♔f5 [19 ... ♕e7 20 ♕g7+, #] 20 g4+ ♔xg4 21 ♕h3# **1-0** L/N6124

**1864-⚔HK-8** vii 64
**Hirschfeld,P.–Kolisch,I.F. von**

1 e4 e5 2 f4 exf4 3 ♘f3 g5 4 h4 g4 5 ♘e5 ♘f6 6 ♗c4 d5 7 exd5 ♗d6 8 d4 ♘h5 9 ♗b5+ c6 10 dxc6 bxc6 11 ♘xc6 ♘xc6 12 ♗xc6+ ♗d7 13 ♗xd7+ [13 ♗xa8?!] 13 ... ♕xd7 14 0-0 0-0 15 ♘c3 ♖ae8 16 ♘d5 ♕f5 17 c4 ♘g3 18 ♖e1? [18 ♕xg4+ ♕xg4 19 ♘f6+ ♔h8 20 ♘xg4 ♘xf1 21 ♔xf1 ♖e4 22 ♗d2, 23 ♗c3∞] 18 ... f3 19 gxf3 gxf3 20 ♗e3 ♖xe3 21

**LANGE⚔PAULSEN** [1864-⚔LP]

| | | | | | | | | |
|---|---|---|---|---|---|---|---|---|
| M. Lange | 1 | 0 | 0 | 0 | 0 | 1 | 0 | 2 |
| L. Paulsen | 0 | 1 | 1 | 1 | 1 | 0 | 1 | 5 |

**1864-⚔LP-1** 2 ii 64
**Paulsen, L.–Lange, M.**
[Lange]

1 e4 e5 2 ♘f3 ♘c6 3 ♗b5 ♘f6 4 d3 d6 [4 ... ♗c5 5 c3! 0-0 6 ♗xc6 bxc6 7 ♘xe5 ♖e8 (7 ... d5)] 5 ♘c3 ♗d7 6 0-0 ♗e7 7 ♘e1 0-0 8 f4 ♗g4 [□ 8 ... exf4 △ 9 ... ♘e5] 9 ♕d2 ♘d4 10 ♗c4 ♗e6 [10 ... exf4 △ 11 ... ♘e6] 11 ♗xe6 ♘xe6 12 f5 ♘d4! [12 ... ♘f4 13 ♕d1] 13 ♘f3 ♘xf3+ 14 ♖xf3 d5 15 ♕e2 ♕d6 16 ♔h1 [16 ♖h3 △ 17 g4] 16 ... ♖ad8 17 ♗g5 dxe4 18 dxe4 ♕c6 [□ 18 ... c6 △ 19 ... ♕c7] 19 ♖af1 ♖d4 20 ♘d5 ♘xd5 21 exd5 ♕d6! 22 ♗xe7 [22 f6 ♗xf6 23 ♖xf6 gxf6 24 ♗xf6 ♕xd5 25 ♕h5 ♕e4] 22 ... ♕xe7 23 f6 gxf6 24 ♖h3 [24 c3 ♖h4 (24 ... ♖xd5? 25 ♖g3+ △ 26 ♕g4)] 24 ... f5 25 ♖xf5 f6 26 ♖fh5 ♖f7 27 c4 ♕b4! 28 ♖g3+ ♔f8! [28 ... ♔h8 29 ♖xe5 ♖d1+! 30 ♕xd1 fxe5] 29 b3 ♖xc4→ 30 ♕e3 ♖f4 31 h3 ♕d4 32 ♕c1 ♕xd5 33 ♔h2 [33 ♕a3+?, 34 ♕xa7 ♕d1+ △ 35 ... ♕xh5] 33 ... ♕d6 34 ♕c2 e4! 35 ♕c3 b6 36 ♕c4 ♖f3! 37 ♕xf7+! [37 gxf3 ♖g7 38 f4 (38 ♖e5 ♕d2+) 38 ... ♕d2+! 39 ♔h1 ♕e1+] 37 ... ♔xf7 38 gxf3 exf3 39 ♖xh7+ ♔e6 40 ♖g7 ♕d2+ 41 ♔h1 ♕e1+ 42 ♔h2 [42 ♖g1 f2→] 42 ... ♕e2+ 43 ♔h1 f2 44 ♖g1 ♕f3+ 45 ♔h2 ♕f4+ 46 ♔g2 fxg1♕+ 47 ♔xg1 ♕c1+ 48 ♔h2 ♕d2+ 49 ♔g3 ♕xa2 50 h4 ♕xb3+ 51 ♔g4 ♕d1+ 52 ♔h3 ♕h1+ **0-1** L/N6047

**1864-⚔LP-2** 4 ii 64
**Lange, M.–Paulsen, L.**
[Lange]

1 e4 e5 2 d4 exd4 3 ♕xd4 ♘c6 4 ♕d1 ♘f6 5 ♗d3 d5 6 exd5 ♕xd5 7 ♘f3 ♗g4 8 ♗e2 ♕h5 9 ♗f4! ♘d5 10 ♗g3 0-0-0 11 ♘bd2 ♗b4 12 0-0 ♖he8 13 h3 ♗xf3 14 ♗xf3 ♕h6 15 c3 ♗c5 [15 ... ♘xc3?! 16 bxc3] 16 ♕b3! ♘f4 [16 ... ♕xd2 17 ♖ad1] 17 ♕xf7 ♖f8 18 ♗xf4 ♕xf4 19 ♕xf4 ♖xf4 20 ♘b3 ♗b6 21 ♗xc6 bxc6 22 ♖ae1! ♖df8 23 ♖e2! h5 24 ♘c1 g5 25 ♘d3 ♖4f5 26 ♖e5 g4 27 hxg4 hxg4 28 ♖xf5 ♖xf5 29 ♔h2! ♖d5 30 ♖d1 c5 31 c4 ♖d4 32 b3 c6 33 ♘b2 ♖e4 34 ♖d2 ♗c7+ 35 g3 ♗e5 36 ♘d1 ♗d4 37 ♔g2? [△ 38 f4, 39 ♘f2] 37 ... ♖e1 38 f3?? [□ 38 f4] 38 ... ♖g1+ 39 ♔h2 gxf3 40 ♖xd4?? [□ 40 ♔h3] 40 ... ♖g2+ 41 ♔h3 cxd4 42 g4 ♖d2 **0-1** L/N6047

**1864-⚔LP-3** ii 64
**Paulsen, L.+Lange, M.**
[Lange]

1 e4 e5 2 ♘f3 ♘c6 3 ♗b5 ♘f6 4 d3 d6 5 ♘c3 ♗e7 6 0-0 0-0 7 ♗xc6 bxc6 8 d4 ♘d7 9 dxe5 dxe5 10 ♗e3 ♕e8 11 ♕d3 ♘c5 12 ♗xc5 ♗xc5 13 ♘a4 ♗d6 14 c4 f5 [□ 14 ... ♕e7 △ 15 ... c5] 15 c5 fxe4 16 ♕xe4 ♖f4 17 ♕e3

17 ... ♗g4! 18 cxd6 ♗xf3 19 gxf3! cxd6! 20 ♘c3 ♕h5! 21 ♘e2 ♖xf3 22 ♘g3 ♕g4 23 ♕d2 [23 h3 ♕xg3+; 23 ♕e2 ♖xg3+] 23 ... d5 24 ♖ac1 ♖c8 25 b4 h5 26 b5 h4 27 bxc6 d4! 28 ♖fe1 hxg3= 29 hxg3! ♖f5? [□ 29 ... e4 30 ♕xd4! ♖xg3+ 31 fxg3 ♕xg3+ 32 ♔h1! (32 ♔f1 ♖f8+ 33 ♔e2 ♖f2+ 34 ♔d1 (34 ♕xf2 ♕d3#) 34 ... ♕f3+→) 32 ... ♕h3+=] 30 ♖c5 ♕h3 31 ♖exe5 ♖xe5 32 ♖xe5 ♖xc6 33 ♖e8+ ♔f7 34 ♖d8 ♕h6 [□ 34 ... ♖b6=] 35 ♕xh6 ♖xh6 36 ♖d7+ ♔e8 37 ♖xd4 [37 ♖xa7 d3 38 ♖b7 (38 ♖a3 ♖d6; 38 ♔f1 ♖h1+) 38 d2 39 ♖b1 ♖c6→; 37 ♖xg7 d3 38 ♖g4 ♖d6→] 37 ... ♖a6 38 a4 ♔e7 39 f4 ♔e6 [□ 39 ... g6] 40 g4 ♖b6 41 ♔f2 ♖b3 42 f5+ ♔e7 43 g5 ♖c3 44 ♖d5! ♖h3 45 ♖a5 **1-0** L/N6047

**1864-⚔LP-4** ii 64
**Lange, M.–Paulsen, L.**
[Lange]

1 e4 e5 2 ♘f3 ♘c6 3 ♗b5 ♘f6 4 d4 exd4 5 e5 ♘e4 6 0-0 ♗e7 7 ♘xd4 0-0 8 ♘xc6 [□ 8 ♘f5] 8 ... dxc6 9 ♗d3 f5 10 ♗xe4 [10 ♗f4; 10 ♕e2 (10 ♗e3 f4)] 10 ... ♕xd1 11 ♖xd1 fxe4 12 ♘c3 ♗f5 13 ♗e3 ♗b4 14 ♘a4 ♖fe8 15 a3! [15 c3 ♗f8 16 ♗d4 b5 17 ♘c5 ♗xc5 18 ♗xc5 ♖xe5] 15 ... ♗f8 16 ♗f4 e3! 17 ♖ac1! [17 fxe3 ♗xc2 18 ♖d4 c5] 17 ... exf2+ 18 ♔xf2 b5 19 ♘c3 ♗c5+ 20 ♔g3 h6! 21 h4 ♖e6 22 ♔h2 ♖f8 23 g3 ♗e7 24 ♖e1 g5 25 hxg5 hxg5 26 ♗e3 a5 27 ♗a7 [27 ♗f2? ♗g4 △ 28 ... ♖h6+, 29 ... ♗f3] 27 ... ♗g4 28 ♘e4 ♖xe5 [28 ... ♖h6+ 29 ♔g1 ♗f3 30 ♗f2] 29 ♘f2 ♗e2! [29 ... ♖xe1?] 30 c4 ♗d6 31 ♗d4 ♖e6 32 c5 ♗e7 33 ♖c2 ♗c4 34 ♖xe6 ♗xe6 35 ♖e2 ♗f6 [35 ... ♔f7 36 ♘d3] 36 ♗xf6 [36 ♖xe6? ♗xd4 37 ♘e4 ♗xb2 38 ♖xc6 ♖f7] 36 ... ♖xf6 37 b4 a4 38 ♘e4 ♖g6 39 ♘xg5 ♗d5 40 ♘h3 ♖h6 41 g4 ♗c4 [41 ... ♗f3 42 ♖e5 ♗xg4 (42 ... ♖g6 43 g5) 43 ♖g5+] 42 ♖e1 ♖h7 43 ♔g3 ♖d7 44 ♘f4 ♖d2 45 ♖a1 ♔g7! 46 g5 ♗f7 47 ♖e1 ♔f8 48 g6 ♗c4 49 ♔g4 ♖f2 50 ♔g5 ♖f3 51 ♖h1? [□ 51 ♖a1] 51

... ♖xa3 52 ♔f6 ♔e8! 53 ♖e1+ ♔d7 54 g7 ♖f3 55 ♖d1+ ♔c8 56 ♔g5 ♖g3+ 57 ♔h6 a3 58 ♔h7 a2 59 ♖a1 ♔b7 60 ♘h5 ♖h3 61 ♔g6? [□ 61 g8♕ ♗xg8+! 62 ♔xg8 ♖xh5 63 ♖xa2 ♔c8 64 ♔f7=] 61 ... ♖f3 62 ♔g5? ♖f1! 63 ♖xf1 ♗xf1 64 g8♕ a1♕ 65 ♕b3 [65 ♕g7 ♕c1+ △ 66 ... ♕c2−+] 65 ... ♕e5+ 66 ♔h4 ♗e2 67 ♕f7 [67 ♘g3 ♕h8+ 68 ♔g5 ♕g7+] 67 ... ♗xh5 68 ♕xh5 ♕e1+ 69 ♔g4 ♕xb4+ **0-1** L/N6047

**1864-⚔LP-5** ii 64

**Paulsen, L.+ Lange, M.**

[Lange]

1 e4 e5 2 ♘f3 ♘c6 3 d4 exd4 4 ♘xd4 ♗c5 5 ♗e3 ♕f6 6 c3 ♘ge7 7 ♗e2 0-0 [□ 7 ... d5] 8 0-0 ♗xd4 9 cxd4 d5 10 e5 ♕h4 11 ♘c3 ♗e6 12 g3 ♕h3 13 ♗f3 ♕f5 14 ♗g2 f6 15 f4 ♘b4 16 ♗f2! fxe5? [16 ... c5? 17 exf6 △ 18 dxc5] 17 fxe5 ♖ad8! 18 ♕b3 c5 19 ♘b5 ♘bc6 20 ♕c3!± a6! [20 ... cxd4 21 ♗xd4] 21 ♘d6 cxd4 22 ♗xd4 ♕g4 23 ♗b6 ♖a8! 24 a3 [24 ♘xb7 ♖fb8] 24 ... ♘g6 25 ♘xb7 ♘gxe5 [25 ... ♘cxe5 26 ♗d4] 26 ♗c7! ♘d4?! 27 ♔h1! ♘ef3 28 ♗f4 ♘xh2 [□ 28 ... g5 29 ♗xf3 ♘xf3 30 ♕xf3! ♕xf3 31 ♖xf3 gxf4 32 gxf4 ♖ab8 33 ♘c5±] 29 ♕xd4 ♘xf1 30 ♖xf1 ♔h8 31 ♔g1 ♖ac8 32 ♘c5 ♗g8 33 ♘xa6 h5 34 ♘b4 ♖c4 35 ♕d3 ♖d8 36 ♗f3 ♕h3 37 ♕g6 ♗h7 38 ♕xh5 ♕xh5 39 ♗xh5 d4 40 ♗g5 ♖b8 41 ♗f7 ♖cc8 42 ♗e6 ♖f8 43 ♖d1 d3 44 ♗c4 ♖b6 45 ♗xd3 ♗xd3 46 ♖xd3 ♖e6 47 b3 ♖e1+ 48 ♔g2 ♖f5 49 ♗f4 g5 50 ♗d2 ♖e2+ 51 ♔h3 ♖e4 52 ♘d5 ♔h7 53 g4 **1-0** L/N6047

**1864-⚔LP-6** ii 64

**Lange, M.+ Paulsen, L.**

[Lange]

1 e4 e5 2 f4 exf4 3 ♗c4 ♕h4+ 4 ♔f1 d6 5 d4 ♘f6 6 ♘f3 ♕h6 7 ♘c3 c6 8 e5 [□ 8 ♔g1 △ 9 g3; 8 ♕e1; 8 ♗d2] 8 ... ♘h5 9 ♕e1 d5! 10 ♗d3 ♗e7 11 ♔g1 g5 12 ♘e2 ♗g4 [□ 12 ... ♕g7 △ 13 ... h6∓] 13 ♕f2 ♘d7 14 h3 ♗e6 [□ 14 ... ♗xf3] 15 h4 g4 16 ♘g5 ♗xg5 17 hxg5 ♕xg5 18 g3! f5 [18 ... ♗f5 19 ♘xf4 ♘xf4 20 ♗xf4 ♕g6 21 ♖h6 △ 22 ♗xf5; 18 ... ♘xg3 19 ♕xg3 (19 ♘xg3?)] 19 ♗xf4! [19 ♘xf4 ♘xf4 20 ♗xf4 ♕g8; 19 exf6 ♘hxf6 20 ♘xf4 ♕g8] 19 ... ♕g6 [19 ... ♘xf4?! 20 ♘xf4 △ 21 ♘xe6, 22 ♗xf5] 20 ♕h2 ♗f7! [20 ... ♘g7 20 ♗h6 △ 21 ♗f4] 21 ♖f1!+− 0-0-0 [21 ... ♘g7 22 ♗h6] 22 ♗c1! [22 e6?] 22 ... c5 [22 ... ♗e8 23 ♖xf5] 23 ♗xf5 [23 ♖xf5 c4] 23 ... ♕a6 24 ♗xg4! ♖hf8 25 ♗xh5 ♗e6 26 c3 cxd4 27 cxd4 ♖xf1+ 28 ♔xf1 ♖f8+ 29 ♔g2 ♗f5 30 ♘c3 ♕b6 31 ♖d1 ♘xe5 32 dxe5 d4 33 ♕g1 ♕c6+ 34 ♗f3 ♗h3+ 35 ♔xh3 ♕xf3 36 ♕xd4 h5 37 ♕d7+ ♔b8 38 ♗f4 a6 39 ♕d6+ ♔a7 40 ♕c5+ **1-0** L/N6047

**1864-⚔LP-7** ii 64

**Paulsen, L.+ Lange, M.**

[Lange]

1 e4 e5 2 ♘f3 ♘c6 3 ♗b5 ♘f6 4 ♕e2 ♗d6? 5 0-0 0-0 6 c3 ♖e8 7 d3 ♘e7 8 ♗c4 [8 ♗g5?!] 8 ... ♘g6 [8 ... h6 9 ♘h4] 9 ♘g5 ♖e7 10 d4 ♕e8 [10 ... h6 11 ♘xf7 ♖xf7 12 ♗xf7+ ♔xf7 13 f4 exd4 14 e5 ♕e8 15 ♕c4+] 11 f4 exd4 [11 ... exf4? 12 e5 c6 13 ♘xf7] 12 cxd4 [12 e5 ♗c5] 12 ... ♗b4 [12 ... ♘xe4 13 ♘xf7 ♖xf7 (13 ... ♔f8 14 f5) 14 ♗xf7+ ♔xf7 15 f5 ♘f8 16 ♕h5+ ♔e7 17 ♕h4+ ♔f7 (17 ... ♘f6) 18 ♖e1±] 13 e5 d5 14 ♗d3 ♕c6 15 f5 ♘f8 16 ♕f3 ♘e8 17 a3! ♗a5 18 b4 ♗b6 19 ♗e3 h6 [19 ... a6 20 a4] 20 b5 ♕d7 21 e6+− ♕d8 [21 ... fxe6 22 fxe6 ♘xe6 23 ♗h7+ ♔h8 24 ♕f8+ ♘xf8 25 ♖xf8#] 22 exf7+ ♖xf7 23 ♘xf7 ♔xf7 24 ♘c3 ♘f6 25 ♘a4 c6 26 ♘xb6 axb6 27 a4 ♗d7 28 ♖fe1 ♖c8 29 ♗f4 ♗e8 30 ♕e2 c5 31 ♖ac1 ♔g8 32 ♕e7! ♕xe7 33 ♖xe7 ♘8d7 34 ♗d6 ♖a8 35 dxc5 bxc5 36 ♗xc5 ♖xa4 37 ♗d6 ♖a8 38 h3 ♖d8 39 ♖c7 b6 40 ♖b7 ♖a8 41 ♗e5 ♘xe5 42 ♖xe5 ♖a3 43 ♗e2 d4 44 ♖xb6 d3 45 ♖xf6 ♗xb5 46 ♖xb5 gxf6 47 ♗f3 ♔f7 48 ♖d5 **1-0** L/N6047

## NEUMANN⚔PAULSEN

**[1864-⚔NP]**

| | | |
|---|---|---|
| G.R. Neumann | 0 0 0 0 1 ½ 1 ½ ½ 0 1 | 4½ |
| L. Paulsen | 1 1 1 1 0 ½ 0 ½ ½ 1 0 | 6½ |

**1864-⚔NP-1** v 64

**Paulsen, L.+ Neumann, G.R.**

[Anderssen & Neumann]

1 e4 e5 2 ♘f3 ♘c6 3 ♗b5 ♘f6 4 0-0 d6 5 d3 [□ 5 ♗xc6+] 5 ... ♗d7 6 ♘c3 ♗e7 7 ♘e1 0-0 8 f4 exf4 9 ♗xf4 ♘e5 10 ♗xd7 ♕xd7 11 d4 ♘g6 12 ♗g3 c6 13 ♘d3 d5 14 e5 ♘e8 15 ♘e2 ♘c7 16 ♘ef4 ♘xf4 17 ♘xf4 ♘e6 18 ♕g4 ♖ad8 19 ♘xe6 ♕xe6 20 ♕h5 c5 21 dxc5 ♗xc5+ 22 ♔h1 ♖fe8 23 ♖ae1 d4 24 ♖f3 g6 25 ♕h4 ♗e7 26 ♕f4 ♕xa2 27 e6 f5 28 ♖b3 ♕a6 29 ♗f2 ♗f6? [29 ... ♕d6] 30 ♕c7 ♗e7 [30 ... ♖xe6 31 ♖xe6 ♕xe6 32 ♖xb7±] 31 ♖xb7 ♕d6 32 ♖xa7 ♕xc7 33 ♖xc7 ♖d6 34 ♖d7 ♖c6 35 ♗xd4 ♖xc2 36 ♗c3 ♗f8 37 h3 ♗h6 38 ♖a1 ♖c1+ 39 ♖xc1 ♗xc1 40 ♖d6 ♖b8 41 g3 ♔f8! 42 ♖d1 ♗g5 43 h4 ♗e7 44 ♔g2 ♖b6 45 ♖e1 ♗d6 46 ♖a1 ♗b8 47 ♖e1 ♔e7? 48 ♗f6+ ♔e8 49 b4 ♗d6 [□ 49 ... ♗c7] 50 ♖c1 ♖b8 51 b5 ♗e7 52 ♗e5 **1-0** L/N6051

**1864-⚔NP-2** v 64

**Neumann, G.R.− Paulsen, L.**

[Anderssen & Zukertort]

1 e4 e5 2 ♘f3 ♘c6 3 ♗b5 ♘f6 4 0-0 ♗e7 5 ♘c3 ♘d4 6 ♘xd4 exd4 7 e5 dxc3 8 exf6 ♗xf6 9 ♖e1+ ♗e7 10 ♕e2 c6 11 ♗d3 d5 12 dxc3 [□ 12 f4] 12 ... ♗e6 13 ♗f4 [13 f4] 13 ... 0-0 14 ♕h5 g6 15 ♕h6 ♗f6 16 ♗e5 ♗xe5 17 ♖xe5 [△ 18 ♖h5] 17 ... ♕f6 18 ♖ae1 ♖ae8 19 f4 ♗d7 20 ♖xe8 ♖xe8 21 ♖xe8+ ♗xe8 22 f5 b6 23 ♕f4 ♔f8 24 g4 g5 25 ♕f3 c5 26 ♗f1 [26 ♕xd5 ♗c6 27 ♕c4 ♕e5∓] 26 ... d4 27 c4 ♗c6 28 ♕f2 ♕e5 29 ♗g2 ♗xg2 30 ♔xg2 ♕e4+ 31 ♔g3 h5 32 gxh5?? [32 h3] 32 ... ♕h4+ 33 ♔g2 ♕g4+ 34 ♔f1 ♕xh5 35 ♔e1 ♔g7 36 ♔d2 ♕g4 37 f6+ ♔g6 38 ♕e1 ♕f4+ 39 ♔d1 ♕xh2 40 ♕e7 ♕g1+ 41 ♔d2 ♕e3+ 42 ♕xe3 dxe3+ 43 ♔xe3 ♔xf6 44 c3 ♔e5 45 b4 f5 **0-1** L/N6051

**1864-⚔NP-3** v 64

**Paulsen, L.+ Neumann, G.R.**

[Anderssen & Neumann]

1 e4 e5 2 ♘f3 ♘c6 3 d4 exd4 4 ♘xd4 ♗c5 5 ♗e3 ♘xd4 [□ 5 ... ♕f6] 6 ♗xd4 ♗xd4 7 ♕xd4 ♕f6 8 e5 ♕b6? 9 ♕xb6 axb6 10 ♘c3 ♖a5 11 f4 f6 12 0-0-0 fxe5 13 b4 ♖a8 14 fxe5 ♘h6 15 ♗c4 ♘f5 16 ♘d5 ♔d8 17 ♖hf1 g6 18 g4 ♘e7 19 ♘xe7 ♔xe7 20 ♖f7+ ♔e8 21 e6 dxe6 22 ♖xc7 **1-0** L/N6051

**1864-⚔NP-4** v 64

**Neumann, G.R.− Paulsen, L.**

[Anderssen & Neumann]

1 e4 e5 2 ♘f3 ♘c6 3 ♗b5 ♘f6 4 0-0 ♗e7 5 ♘c3 ♘d4 6 ♘xd4 exd4 7 e5 dxc3 8 exf6 ♗xf6 9 ♖e1+ ♗e7 10 ♕e2 c6 11 ♗d3 d5 12 dxc3 ♗e6 13 f4 ♗c5+ 14 ♔h1 0-0 15 f5 ♗d7 16 ♕h5 f6 17 ♗d2 ♗e8 18 ♕h4 ♗f7 19 ♖f1 ♕d7 20 ♖f3 ♔h8 21 ♖h3 ♗g8 22 ♗e2 [△ ♗h5, ♗g6] 22 ... ♕xf5 23 ♗d3 ♕f2 24 ♕h5 f5 [24 ... ♕xd2 25 ♗xh7±] 25 ♖d1 [△ 26 ♖f3] 25 ... ♗b6 26 b4 [26 ♗e3 ♗xe3 27 ♖f3 ♕xf3 28 ♕xf3 f4∞] 26 ... ♖ae8? 27 ♖f3 ♖e1+ 28 ♖xe1 ♕xd2 29 ♖ef1 g6 30 ♕h4 [□ 30 ♕h3] 30 ... ♕xc3 31 ♕e7 [31 ♗xf5 ♖xf5] 31 ... ♖f7 32 ♕e8? [□ 32 ♕e1] 32 ... ♕xb4 33 ♕e5+ ♖g7 34 ♕e8 ♕e7 35 ♖e1 ♕d6 36 h4 ♗c7 37 ♖h3 h5 38 c4 ♗a5 39 ♖f1 ♖e7 40 ♕f8 ♔h7 41 ♖hf3 ♗c7 42 g3 dxc4 43 ♖xf5 cxd3 **0-1** L/N6051

**1864-✕NP-5** v64
**Paulsen, L.– Neumann, G.R.**
[Anderssen & Neumann]
1 e4 c5 2 ♘c3 ♘c6 3 g3 d6 4 ♗g2 e5! 5 ♘ge2 ♘f6 6 0-0 h5 7 d3 h4 8 ♗g5 h3 9 ♗h1 ♗e7 10 f4 ♘g4 11 ♗xe7 ♘xe7 12 ♕d2 f6 13 ♗f3 ♘h6 14 f5 ♘f7 15 ♘d1 ♘g5 16 ♗h1

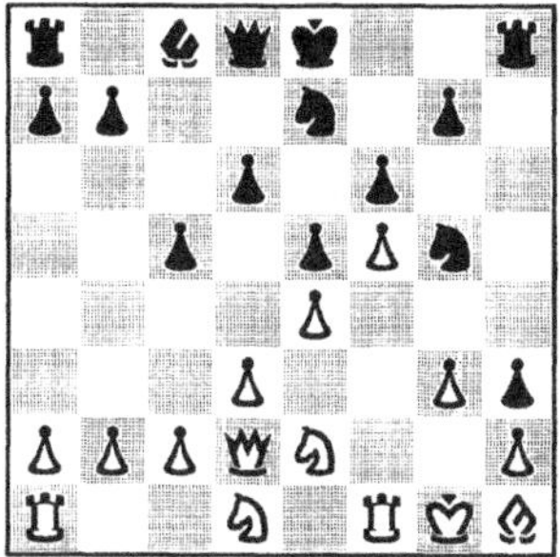

16 ... ♗d7 17 c3 ♖c8 18 d4 cxd4 19 cxd4 ♕b6 20 ♘f2 ♗b5 21 dxe5 dxe5 22 ♖fd1 ♗xe2 23 ♕xe2 ♘c6 24 ♖ac1 ♔e7 25 b3 ♘d4 26 ♕b2 ♖hd8 27 b4 ♕b5 [27 ... ♖xc1 28 ♖xc1 ♘df3+ 29 ♗xf3 ♘xf3+ 30 ♔h1 ♖d2 31 ♕a3 ♖xf2 32 b5+ ♔d7! 33 ♖d1+ ♕d4∓] 28 ♖xc8 ♘df3+ 29 ♗xf3 ♘xf3+ 30 ♔h1 ♖xd1+ 31 ♘xd1 ♕f1# **0-1**
L/N6051

**1864-✕NP-6** v64
**Neumann, G.R.= Paulsen, L.**
[Anderssen & Neumann]
1 e4 e5 2 ♘f3 ♘c6 3 ♗b5 a6 4 ♗a4 ♘f6 5 0-0 ♗e7 6 d4 exd4 7 e5 ♘e4 8 ♘xd4 0-0 9 ♘f5 d5 10 ♗xc6 bxc6 11 ♘xe7+ ♕xe7 12 ♖e1 f6 13 f3 ♘c5 14 exf6 ♕xf6 15 ♘c3 ♗f5 16 ♗e3 ♘e6 17 ♗f2 ♕g6 [17 ... ♖ab8] 18 ♗g3 ♖ab8 19 b3 h6 20 ♖c1 d4 21 ♘e2 ♖bd8 **½-½**
L/N6051

**1864-✕NP-7** v64
**Paulsen, L.– Neumann, G.R.**
1 e4 b6 2 ♘c3 ♗b7 3 g3 e6 4 ♗g2 ♘f6 5 ♘ge2 c5 6 d3 ♗e7 7 0-0 d6 8 e5 ♘d5 9 exd6 ♕xd6 10 ♘e4 ♕d7 11 b3 ♘c6 12 ♗b2 e5 13 ♕d2 f5 14 ♘4c3 ♘d4 15 f4 ♘xc3 16 ♘xc3 exf4 17 ♗xb7 ♕xb7 18 ♕xf4 0-0 19 ♖f2 ♗f6 20 h4 ♖ae8 21 ♖g2 ♗e5 22 ♕f1 f4 23 ♘e4 fxg3 24 ♕c1 ♘f3+ 25 ♔h1 ♕d7 26 ♘g5 ♘xg5 27 hxg5 ♕h3+ 28 ♔g1 ♗f4 **0-1**
L/N6051

**1864-✕NP-8** v64
**Neumann, G.R.= Paulsen, L.**
[Anderssen & Neumann]
1 e4 e5 2 ♘f3 ♘c6 3 ♗b5 a6 4 ♗a4 ♘f6 5 0-0 ♗e7 6 ♘c3 b5 7 ♗b3 d6 8 h3 ♗b7 9 d3 0-0 10 a3 ♘d7 11 ♘e2 ♘c5 12 ♗a2 ♔h8 13 ♘g3 ♗f6 14 ♗e3 ♘e6 15 ♕d2 ♘e7 16 d4 exd4 17 ♘xd4 d5 18 ♘xe6 fxe6 19 c3 dxe4 20 ♗xe6 ♘d5 21 ♗c5 [□ 21 ♖ad1] 21 ... ♖e8 22 ♗f7 ♖e5 23 ♗d4 ♖e7 24 ♗xd5 ♕xd5 25 ♖ad1 ♗xd4 26 ♕xd4 ♕xd4 27 ♖xd4 c5 28 ♖d2 e3 29 fxe3 ♖xe3 30 ♘f5 ♖e5 31 ♘d6 ♖e7 32 ♘xb7 ♖xb7 33 ♖fd1 h6 34 ♖d8+ ♖xd8 35 ♖xd8+ ♔h7 **½-½**
L/N6051

**1864-✕NP-9** v64
**Paulsen, L.= Neumann, G.R.**
[Anderssen & Neumann]
1 e4 b6 2 d4 ♗b7 3 ♗d3 e6 4 ♘h3 ♘f6 5 f3 c5 6 c3 ♘c6 7 ♗e3 d5 8 e5 ♘d7 9 0-0 ♗e7 10 ♘d2 cxd4 11 cxd4 ♘b4 12 ♗e2 ♖c8 13 ♗f2 ♗h4 14 g3 ♗e7 15 f4 g6 16 a3 ♘c6 17 ♖c1 h5 18 ♘b3 a6 19 ♗d3 b5 20 ♕f3 ♕b6 21 ♗e3 a5 22 ♕f2 [22 ♘c5 ♘xd4∓] 22 ... a4 23 ♘d2 [23 ♘c5 ♘xc5 24 dxc5 ♕a6 25 ♕e2 ♘a7 26 c6 ♗xc6 27 ♗xa7 ♕xa7+ 28 ♔h1 ♕b6 29 ♖xc6 ♖xc6 30 ♗xb5 0-0∓] 23 ... ♘a5 24 ♖xc8+ ♗xc8 25 ♘g5 ♘c4 26 ♘xc4 [26 ♘xf7 ♕xf7 27 ♗xg6+∓] 26 ... bxc4 27 ♗c2 ♕a6 28 h3 ♘b8 29 ♘f3 ♘c6 30 ♘d2 ♗d7 31 ♘b1 ♘a5 32 ♘c3 ♘b3 33 ♕e2 ♗d8 34 ♕d1 **½-½**
L/N6051

**1864-✕NP-10** v64
**Neumann, G.R.– Paulsen, L.**
[Anderssen & Neumann]
1 e4 e5 2 ♘f3 ♘c6 3 ♗b5 a6 4 ♗a4 ♘f6 5 0-0 ♗e7 6 ♘c3 b5 7 ♗b3 d6 8 h3 ♘a5 9 d3 c5 10 ♕e2 0-0 11 ♘h2 [□ 11 ♘d5] 11 ... ♗b7 12 f4 ♘xb3 13 axb3 ♘d7 14 f5 [□ 14 fxe5] 14 ... ♘b6 15 ♘g4 f6 16 ♘d1 d5! 17 ♘df2 c4! 18 bxc4 dxc4 19 ♗e3 ♖c8 20 ♘h2 ♗c5 21 ♗xc5 ♖xc5 22 ♖ad1 ♕e7 23 ♘f3 cxd3 24 ♖xd3 b4 25 ♖fd1 ♖c7 26 ♘e1 ♗c6 27 ♕d2 a5 28 b3 ♘c8 [△ ... ♘a7, ... ♘b5, ... ♘d4] 29 ♖d8 ♘a7 30 ♖xf8+ ♔xf8 31 ♘ed3 ♖c3 32 ♖c1 ♗b5 33 ♘d1 ♕b6+ 34 ♔h2 ♖c8 35 ♘e3? [□ 35 c4] 35 ... ♕d4 36 ♘g4 ♔g8 37 ♖d1 ♖c3 38 ♘e1 ♘c6 39 ♘f3 ♕xd2 40 ♖xd2 a4∓ 41 bxa4 ♗xa4 42 ♘e1 ♘d4 43 ♘f2 ♗xc2 44 ♘xc2 ♖xc2 45 ♖xc2 ♘xc2 46 ♘d3 b3 47 ♔g1 h5 48 ♔f2 ♔h7 49 ♔e2 ♘b4! 50 ♘b2 g6 51 ♔d2 gxf5 52 ♔c3 ♘c2 53 exf5 ♘d4 54 ♘c4 ♔h6 55 ♘d6 ♔g5 56 h4+ ♔g4 **0-1**
L/N6051

**1864-✕NP-11** v64
**Neumann, G.R.+ Paulsen, L.**
[Anderssen & Neumann]
1 e4 e5 2 ♘f3 ♘c6 3 ♗b5 a6 4 ♗a4 ♘f6 5 0-0 ♗e7 6 ♘c3 b5 7 ♗b3 d6 8 h3 ♘a5 9 d3 0-0 10 ♕e2 ♘xb3 11 axb3 ♘e8?? 12 ♘xb5 f5 13 ♘c3 fxe4 14 dxe4 ♘f6 15 ♗g5 [15 ♕c4+ ♔h8 16 ♘g5 ♕e8!∞] 15 ... ♔h8 16 ♗xf6 ♗xf6 17 ♘d5 c6 18 ♘xf6 ♕xf6 19 ♘h2! ♕g6 20 ♔h1 ♖a7 21 ♖ad1 ♖af7 22 ♖d3 ♖f4 23 f3 h6 [23 ... h5] 24 c4 ♖4f6 25 ♖fd1 ♖d8 26 ♕d2 h5 27 c5 d5 28 exd5 ♗f5 29 ♕a5 ♖ff8 30 ♖3d2 cxd5 31 ♖xd5 ♖xd5 32 ♖xd5 e4 33 ♖d8 ♖xd8 34 ♕xd8+ ♔h7 35 ♕d4 ♕e6 36 ♕e3 ♕d5 37 fxe4 ♗xe4 38 ♘f3 ♗xf3 39 gxf3 ♕d1+? 40 ♔g2 ♕c2+ 41 ♔g3 ♕xb2 42 c6 ♕f6 43 ♕e4+ g6 44 ♕d5 ♕c3 [□ 44 ... g5] 45 ♕f7+ ♔h6 46 ♕f8+ ♔h7 47 ♕e7+ ♔g8 48 c7 h4+ 49 ♔xh4 g5+ 50 ♔xg5 ♕d2+ 51 ♔h5 ♕c3 52 ♕d8+ ♔f7 53 c8♕ **1-0**
L/N6051

**1864-★AE-1** vii64
**Eliason– Anderssen, A.**
Berlin [Anderssen & Neumann]
1 e4 e5 2 ♘f3 ♘c6 3 ♗c4 ♗c5 4 0-0 ♘f6 5 d4 ♗xd4 6 ♘xd4 ♘xd4 7 f4 d6 8 fxe5 dxe5 9 c3? ♗e6 10 cxd4 ♗xc4 11 ♖fe1 ♕xd4+ 12 ♕xd4 exd4 13 e5 ♘d5 14 ♘a3 ♗a6 15 ♗g5 h6 16 ♗h4 g5 17 ♗g3 0-0-0 18 ♖ad1 ♘e3 19 ♖d2 h5 20 ♗f2 ♘f5 21 g3 g4 22 ♘c2 c5 23 b4 b6 24 bxc5 bxc5 25 e6 fxe6 26 ♖xe6 ♗b7 27 ♘a3 h4 28 gxh4 ♘xh4 29 ♗xh4 ♖xh4 30 ♘b5 ♔b8 31 ♘d6 g3 32 ♘xb7 gxh2+ 33 ♔h1 ♖g8 **0-1**
L/N6051

**1864-★AG-1**
**Anderssen,A.+ Guretsky-Cornitz,B.v.**
Berlin [Bachmann]
1 e4 e5 2 ♘f3 ♘f6 3 ♘xe5 d6 4 ♘f3 ♘xe4 5 d4 d5 6 ♗d3 ♘c6 7 0-0 ♗e7 8 c4 ♗e6 9 cxd5 ♗xd5 10 ♘c3 f5 11 ♕e2 ♘xc3 12 bxc3 0-0 13 ♖b1 ♕d7 14 ♗c4 ♔h8 15 ♗xd5 ♕xd5 16 ♖xb7 ♗d6 17 ♖b5 ♕f7 18 ♘g5 ♕g6 19 f4 ♖ae8 20 ♕c4 ♘d8 21 ♘f3 a6 22 ♖b1 ♖e4 23 ♕xa6 ♘e6 24 ♘e5 ♕h5 25 ♗a3 ♖xf4 26 ♗xd6 cxd6 27 ♕xd6 **1-0**
L/N3033

**1864-★AK-1** vii64
**Knorre, V.+ Anderssen, A.**
Berlin
1 e4 e5 2 ♘f3 ♘c6 3 ♗c4 ♗c5 4 0-0 ♘f6 5 c3 ♘xe4! 6 ♗d5 ♘xf2 7 ♗xf7+ ♔xf7 8 ♘xe5+ ♘xe5 9 d4 ♘g4 10 ♕xg4 ♗e7 11 ♖xf2+ ♗f6 12 ♗g5 h5 13 ♗xf6 gxf6 14 ♕g5 d5 15 ♘d2 a5 16 ♖af1 ♖a6 17 ♖f4 ♗g4 18 ♘f3 ♗xf3 19 ♖4xf3 ♖e6 20 ♖g3 ♕e7 21 ♕f5 ♕d6 22 ♖g7+ ♔d8 23 c4 dxc4 24 ♕xa5 **1-0**
L/N6051-1865

**1864-★AK-2** vii 64

**Anderssen, A.+Knorre, V.**

Berlin [Anderssen & Neumann]

1 e4 e5 2 ♘f3 ♘c6 3 d4 exd4 4 ♗c4 ♗c5 5 0-0 d6 6 c3 d3 [◻ 6 ... ♗g4] 7 b4 ♗b6 8 b5 ♘a5 9 ♗xd3 ♘e7 10 ♘d4 c5 11 ♘e2 ♗e6 12 ♔h1 f6 13 f4 0-0 14 ♘d2 c4 15 ♗c2 d5 16 f5 ♗f7 17 ♗a3 ♖e8 18 e5 ♗h5 19 exf6 gxf6 20 ♘f3 ♗e3 21 ♘ed4 ♕b6 22 ♘e6 d4 23 ♗c5 ♕xb5 24 ♗a4 ♕b2 25 ♗xe8 ♖xe8 26 ♗xd4 ♘xf5 27 ♖b1 ♕xa2 28 ♖a1 ♕b2 29 ♖xa5 **1-0**

L/N6051-1865

**1864-★AM-1** vii 64

**Anderssen, A.+Mayet, K.**

Berlin [Löwenthal]

1 e4 e5 2 ♘f3 ♘c6 3 ♗c4 ♗e7 4 d4 d6 5 d5 [5 c3!?] 5 ... ♘b8 6 ♗d3 ♘bd7 [6 ... ♗g4 (7 0-0 ♘f6 8 c4 c6 9 ♘c3 ♘a6=)] 7 c4 ♘c5 8 ♗c2 [△ 9 b4] 8 ... a5 9 ♘c3 h6 10 h3 ♘f6 11 0-0 0-0 12 ♔h2 c6 13 ♕e2 ♗d7 14 ♘g1 g5 15 g3 ♘h7 16 f4 f6 17 ♗e3 ♔g7 18 ♗xc5 dxc5 19 fxe5 fxe5 20 ♖xf8 ♕xf8 21 ♖f1 ♗f6 22 ♘a4 ♕d6 23 ♘f3 ♖f8 24 ♘d2 ♗e8 25 ♘b3! cxd5 26 exd5 ♗xa4 27 ♕e4! ♖h8 28 ♕g6+ ♔f8 29 ♕xh6+ ♔e7 30 ♗xh7 b6 [◻ 30 ... ♗xb3] 31 ♘d2 ♗c2? 32 ♖xf6 ♕xf6 33 ♕xf6+ ♔xf6 34 ♗xc2 g4 35 h4 e4 36 ♘xe4+ ♔e5 37 ♘g5 ♖f8 38 ♔g2 ♖f6 39 b3 ♔d4 40 ♗d1 ♔e3 41 ♗xg4 ♖f2+ 42 ♔h3 ♖xa2 43 d6 ♖d2 44 d7 **1-0** M324-1865

**1864-★AM-2**

**Mieses, S.−Anderssen, A.**

Breslau [Bachmann]

1 e4 e5 2 ♘f3 ♘c6 3 ♗c4 ♗c5 4 b4 ♗xb4 5 c3 ♗c5 6 0-0 d6 7 d4 exd4 8 cxd4 ♗b6 9 d5 ♘a5 10 ♗b2 ♘e7 11 ♗d3 0-0 12 h3 ♘g6 13 ♕d2 c5 14 ♘a3 ♗d7 15 ♖ac1 ♕e7 16 ♖fe1 ♖ae8 17 ♔h2 ♕d8 18 g3 f6 19 ♘h4 ♘xh4 20 gxh4 ♖f7 21 ♖g1 ♔h8 22 ♖g3 c4 23 ♗b1 ♖e5 24 f4 ♖h5 25 f5 ♖xh4 26 ♖e1 ♗c5 27 ♖e2 b5 28 ♘c2 c3 29 ♗xc3 ♘c4 30 ♕e1 ♘e5 31 ♘e3 g5 32 ♗xe5 dxe5 33 ♘g2 ♖h5 34 ♖g4 ♗d6 35 ♕f2 ♖g7 36 ♗d3 ♖g6 37 ♕xa7 ♖gh6 38 ♖e3 ♕c8 39 ♖eg3

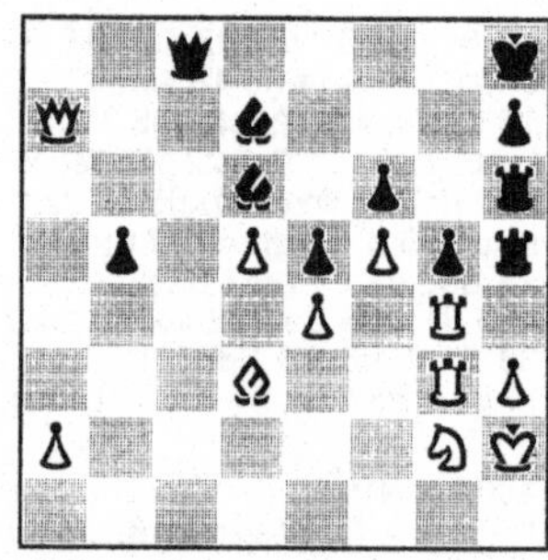

39 ... ♗xf5! 40 ♗e2 ♗xe4 41 ♘e3 ♗g6 42 ♕b6 ♕f8 43 ♗f1 e4 **0-1**

L/N3033

**1864-★AN-1**

**Anderssen,A.=Neumann, G.R.**

[Anderssen & Neumann]

1 e4 e5 2 ♗c4 ♗c5 3 d4 ♗xd4 4 ♘f3 ♘c6 5 ♘c3 ♗xc3+ 6 bxc3 h6 7 ♗d5 d6 8 0-0 ♘ge7 9 ♘d2 g5 10 ♕h5 ♘xd5 11 exd5 ♘e7 12 ♘e4 ♘g6 13 g3 ♗f5 14 f3 ♔f8 15 ♖b1 ♖b8 16 a4 ♔g7 17 ♖b4 ♕d7 18 a5 f6 19 ♖c4 ♘e7 20 f4 exf4 [20 ... ♗g4 21 ♘xf6] 21 gxf4 ♖bf8 22 fxg5 hxg5 23 ♕f3 ♖h3 24 ♕g2 ♗xe4 25 ♖xe4 ♖h6 26 h4 ♖fh8 27 ♖e6 ♖xh4 28 ♗xg5 ♖h1+ 29 ♔f2 ♖xf1+ [29 ... ♖1h2 30 ♗h6+] 30 ♔xf1 fxg5 31 ♕xg5+ ♔f8 32 ♕f6+ ♔g8 33 ♖xe7 ♕h3+ 34 ♔f2 ♕h2+ 35 ♔e1 ♕h1+ **½-½**

L/N6051-1864

**1864-★AN-2** iv 64

**Anderssen,A.−Neumann, G.R.**

Breslau [Anderssen & Neumann]

1 e4 e5 2 ♗c4 ♘f6 3 ♕e2 [◻ 3 ♘f3] 3 ... ♘c6 4 c3 ♗c5 5 f4 d6 6 ♗b3 0-0 7 ♘f3 exf4 8 d4 ♖e8 9 ♘bd2 ♗b6 10 0-0 ♗g4 11 ♔h1 ♘xe4 12 ♗xf7+ ♔xf7 13 ♘xe4 ♔g8 14 ♕c2 ♗xf3 15 gxf3 d5 16 ♘f2 ♖f8 17 ♖g1 ♘e7 18 ♘h3 ♘g6 19 ♘g5 [△ 20 ♘xh7] 19 ... ♕d6 20 a4 c6 21 b3 ♕f6 22 ♗a3 ♕f5 23 ♕d2 ♖f6 24 ♕g2 h6 25 ♘h3 ♔h7 26 ♖ae1 ♖g8 27 ♕e7 ♖f7 28 ♗d6 ♗c7 29 ♗xc7 ♖xc7 30 ♕e2 ♖f7 31 ♖ge1 ♘h4 32 ♕f1 ♕d3 33 ♘g1 ♕xc3 34 ♖e7 ♖xe7 35 ♖xe7 ♕xd4 36 ♕h3 ♕f6 37 ♖xb7 ♖e8 38 ♖xa7 ♖e1 39 ♕g4 ♕g5 **0-1** L/N6051

**1864-★AN-3** iv 64

**Anderssen,A.=Neumann, G.R.**

Breslau

1 e4 e5 2 ♗c4 ♗c5 3 d4 ♗xd4 4 ♘f3 ♘c6 5 ♘c3 ♗xc3+ 6 bxc3 h6 7 ♗d5 d6 8 0-0 ♘ge7 9 ♘d2 g5 10 ♕h5 ♘xd5 11 exd5 ♘e7 12 ♘e4 ♘g6 13 g3 ♗f5 14 f3 ♔f8 15 ♖b1 ♖b8 16 a4 ♔g7 17 ♖b4 ♕d7 18 a5 f6 19 ♖c4 ♘e7 20 f4 exf4 21 gxf4 ♖bf8 22 fxg5 hxg5 23 ♕f3 ♖h3 24 ♕g2 ♗xe4 25 ♖xe4 ♖h6 26 h4 ♖fh8 27 ♖e6 ♖xh4

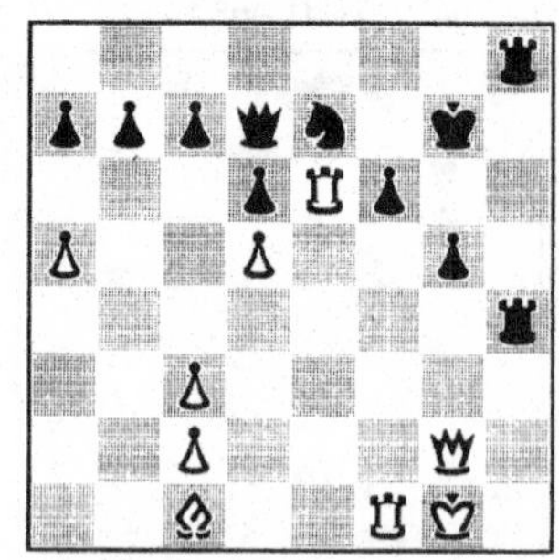

28 ♗xg5 ♖h1+ 29 ♔f2 ♖xf1+ 30 ♔xf1 fxg5 31 ♕xg5+ ♔f8 32 ♕f6+ ♔g8 33 ♖xe7 ♕h3+ 34 ♔f2 ♕h2+ 35 ♔e1 ♕h1+ 36 ♔e2 ♖h2+ 37 ♔e3 ♕e1+ 38 ♔d3 ♖h3+ 39 ♔c4 ♖h4+ 40 ♔b3 ♕b1+ **½-½** L/N3034

**1864-★AN-4** iv 64

**Anderssen,A.+Neumann, G.R.**

Breslau [Neumann]

1 e4 e5 2 ♘f3 ♘c6 3 ♗c4 ♗c5 4 b4 ♗xb4 5 c3 ♗c5 6 0-0 d6 7 d4 exd4 8 cxd4 ♗b6 9 d5 ♘a5 10 ♗b2 ♘e7 11 ♗d3 [11 ♗xg7 ♖g8 12 ♗f6 ♘xc4 13 ♕a4+ ♕d7 14 ♕xc4 ♖xg2+] 11 ... 0-0 12 ♘c3 ♘g6 13 ♕d2 c5 14 ♘e2 ♗d7 [◻ 14 ... a6] 15 ♘g3 [△ 16 ♗xg7 ♔xg7 17 ♘h5+ ♔h8 18 ♕h6 ♖g8 19 ♘g5+−] 15 ... f6 16 ♔h1 c4 [◻ 16 ... ♗c7 △ 17 ... b5] 17 ♗e2 ♗c7 18 ♘d4 b5 19 f4 ♘b7 20 ♘e6 ♗xe6 21 dxe6 ♘c5 22 ♕d5 ♕e7?+− [22 ... ♘e7] 23 ♗g4 ♔h8 24 ♕h5 ♘d3 25 ♗f5 ♕e8 26 ♗d4 ♗b6 [◻ 26 ... ♗d8] 27 e7! ♖g8 28 ♘e2 ♕f7 29 ♖f3 [29 ... ♖ge8 30 ♖af1 △ 31 ♖h3] **1-0**

L/N6020-1868

**1864-★AN-5** iv 64

**Anderssen,A.−Neumann, G.R.**

Breslau

1 e4 e5 2 ♘f3 ♘c6 3 ♗c4 ♗c5 4 b4 ♗xb4 5 c3 ♗c5 6 0-0 d6 7 d4 exd4 8 cxd4 ♗b6 9 d5 ♘a5 10 ♗b2 ♘e7 11 ♗d3 0-0 12 ♘c3 ♘g6 13 ♘a4 c5 14 ♘xb6 axb6 15 ♘e1 ♗d7 16 f4 f6 17 f5 ♘e5 18 ♗b1 b5 19 ♕e2 ♕e7 20 ♕f2 ♖fc8 21 ♕g3 b4 22 ♖f4 c4 23 ♗d4 c3 24 ♗c2 ♘ac4 25 ♖h4 ♘d2 26 ♖h3 b3 27 ♗xc3

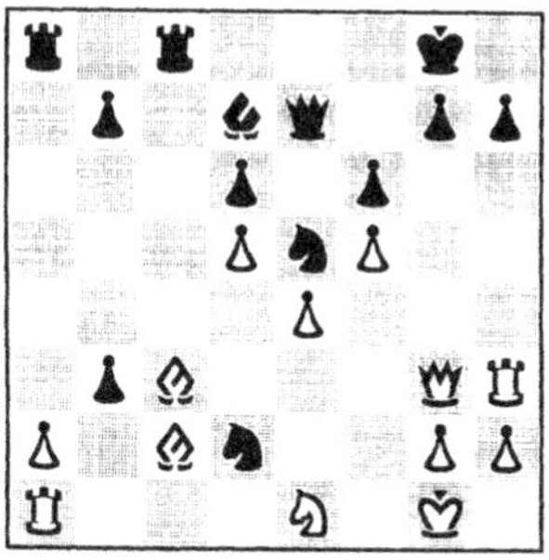

27 ... ♘ef3+ **0-1** L/N6051

**1864-★AN-6** iv 64
**Anderssen,A.–Neumann, G.R.**
Breslau [Anderssen & Neumann]

1 e4 e5 2 f4 d5 3 e×d5 e4 4 ♗b5+ c6 5 d×c6 b×c6 6 ♗c4 ♘f6! 7 d4 ♗d6 8 ♘e2 0-0 9 0-0 ♘bd7 10 c3 ♘b6 11 ♗b3 c5 12 a4 c4 13 ♗c2 a5 14 ♘a3 ♗×a3 15 ♖×a3 ♖e8 16 b3 ♕d5 17 b×c4 ♘×c4 18 ♖b3 e3 19 ♖f3 ♗d7 20 ♖b1 ♗c6 21 ♗d3 ♘g4 22 ♕c2 g6 23 ♖g3 ♘f2 24 ♗×c4 ♕×c4 25 ♗×e3 ♗×a4 26 ♕b2 ♘e4 27 ♖f3 ♗c6 28 f5? ♘d6 29 ♖h3 ♘×f5 30 ♔f2 a4 31 ♖e1 a3 32 ♕a1 a2 33 ♘f4 ♖eb8 34 ♗d2 ♗e4 **0-1** L/N6051

**1864-★AN-7** vii 64
**Anderssen,A.+Neumann, G.R.**
Berlin

1 e4 e5 2 ♘f3 ♘c6 3 ♗c4 ♗c5 4 b4 ♗×b4 5 c3 ♗a5 6 d4 e×d4 7 0-0 ♗b6! 8 c×d4 d6 9 d5 ♘a5 10 ♗b2 ♘e7 11 ♗d3 0-0 12 ♘c3 f6 13 ♘a4 c5 14 ♘×b6 a×b6 15 ♘e1 ♘g6 16 f4 ♗d7 17 g4 b5 18 ♘g2 c4 19 ♗e2 ♖e8 20 f5 ♘e5 21 ♘f4 b4 22 ♗×e5 f×e5 23 ♘e6 ♗×e6 24 d×e6 ♕b6+ 25 ♔h1 ♕d4 26 ♖b1 b3 27 a×b3 ♘×b3 28 ♕×d4 e×d4 29 ♗×c4 ♘d2 30 ♗b5 ♖e7 31 ♖a1 **1-0** L/N6051-1865

**1864-★AN-8** vii 64
**Anderssen,A.–Neumann, G.R.**

1 e4 e5 2 ♘f3 ♘c6 3 ♗c4 ♗c5 4 b4 ♗×b4 5 c3 ♗c5 6 0-0 d6 7 d4 e×d4 8 c×d4 ♗b6 9 d5 ♘a5 10 ♗b2 ♘e7 11 ♗d3 0-0 12 ♘c3 f6 13 ♘a4 c5 14 ♘×b6 a×b6 15 ♘e1 ♘g6 16 f4 ♗d7 17 ♗e2 b5 18 f5 ♘e5 19 ♗×e5 f×e5 20 g4 c4 21 ♔h1 ♕g5 22 ♘g2 c3 23 h4 ♕d2 24 ♕×d2 c×d2 25 ♖ad1 ♘c4 26 ♗×c4 b×c4 27 ♖×d2 b5 28 ♖c1 ♖a3 29 ♖b2 ♖fa8 30 ♖cc2 ♖d3 31 ♔g1 ♖d4 32 ♖e2 c3 33 ♖bc2 b4 34 ♔f2 ♗b5 35 ♖e3 ♗d3 **0-1** L/N6051

**1864-★AN-9** vii 64
**Anderssen,A.+Neumann, G.R.**
Berlin [Anderssen & Neumann]

1 e4 e5 2 f4 e×f4 3 ♘f3 g5 4 ♗c4 ♗g7 5 h4 h6 6 d4 d6 7 ♕d3 ♘c6 8 h×g5 h×g5 9 ♖×h8 ♗×h8 10 g3 ♘h6 11 g×f4 g4 12 ♘g5 ♘×d4 13 ♘c3 ♗e6 14 ♗×e6 f×e6 [⌓ 14 ... ♘×e6] 15 ♗e3 ♕f6 16 0-0-0 ♘c6 17 e5 ♕f5 18 ♖h1 ♗g7 19 ♕×f5 ♘×f5 20 ♘×e6 ♘×e3 21 ♘×c7+ ♔d7 22 ♘×a8 d×e5 23 ♖h7 ♘f5 24 ♘d5 e×f4 25 ♘×f4 ♔c8 26 ♘c7 **1-0** L/N6051

**1864-★AN-10** vii 64
**Anderssen,A.–Neumann, G.R.**
Berlin [Anderssen & Neumann]

1 e4 e5 2 ♘f3 ♘c6 3 ♗c4 ♗c5 4 b4 ♗×b4 5 c3 ♗c5 6 0-0 d6 7 d4 e×d4 8 c×d4 ♗b6 9 d5 ♘a5 10 ♗b2 ♘e7 11 ♗d3 0-0 12 ♘c3 f6 13 ♘e2 ♘g6 14 ♕d2 c5 15 ♔h1 a6 16 ♖ac1 ♗c7 17 ♘e1 b5 18 f4 ♗d7 19 ♘f3 ♘b7 20 f5 ♘e5 21 ♘f4 c4 22 ♗e2 ♘c5 23 ♕e3 ♘g4 24 ♕g1 ♘×e4 25 ♘d4 ♘e5 26 ♘fe6 ♗×e6 27 ♘×e6 ♕e7 28 ♕e3 ♘c5 29 ♘×f8 ♕×f8 30 ♗×e5 d×e5 31 ♕h3 e4 32 ♕e3?! ♕d6 33 ♕g3 ♕×g3 34 h×g3 ♖d8 35 ♔h2 ♘d3 36 ♖b1 ♖×d5 37 ♔h3 a5 38 ♔h4 b4 39 g4 ♗f4 40 ♖×f4 ♘×f4 41 ♗×c4 ♘×g2+ 42 ♔g3 ♘e3 43 ♗×d5+ ♘×d5 44 ♖d1 ♘c3 45 ♖d8+ ♔f7 46 ♖d7+ ♔f8 47 ♔f4 a4 48 ♖a7 g5+ 49 ♔e3 b3 50 a×b3 a×b3 51 ♖b7 b2 **0-1** L/N6051

**1864-★AN-11** vii 64
**Anderssen,A.–Neumann, G.R.**
Berlin [Staunton]

1 e4 e5 2 f4 e×f4 3 ♘f3 g5 4 ♗c4 g4 5 0-0 g×f3 6 ♕×f3 ♕e7 [6 ... ♕f6!?] 7 d4 ♘c6 8 ♕×f4 ♘×d4 9 ♗×f7+ ♔d8 10 ♘c3 c6 11 ♕f2 ♗g7 12 ♗e3 ♘e6 13 ♖ad1 ♘c7 14 ♕g3 ♘e8 15 ♗×g8 ♖×g8 16 e5!? ♕e6 [16 ... ♕×e5+-] 17 ♘e4 ♗×e5 18 ♕h4+ ♔c7 19 ♘g5 ♕g6 20 ♖f7 h6 21 ♗f4? ♗d6 22 ♕f2 h×g5 23 ♗×d6+ ♘×d6 24 ♖f6 ♘e4 **0-1** M954-1865

**1864-★AN-12**
**Anderssen,A.+Neumann, G.R.**
Berlin [Bachmann]

1 e4 e5 2 ♘f3 ♘c6 3 ♗c4 ♗c5 4 b4 ♗×b4 5 c3 ♗c5 6 0-0 d6 7 d4 e×d4 8 c×d4 ♗b6 9 d5 ♘a5 10 ♗b2 ♘e7 11 ♗d3 [11 ♗×g7? ♖g8 12 ♗f6 ♘×c4 13 ♕a4+ ♕d7 14 ♕×c4 ♖×g2+ 15 ♔h1 (15 ♔×g2? ♕g4+ 16 ♔h1 ♕×f3+ 17 ♔h1 ♗h3–+) 15 ... ♕h3 16 ♘bd2 ♗g4 17 ♕b3 0-0-0 △ 18 ... ♖dg8] 11 ... 0-0 12 ♘c3 ♘g6 13 ♕d2 c5 14 ♘e2 ♗d7 15 ♘g3 [△ 16 ♗×g7 ♔×g7 17 ♘h5+ ♔h8 18 ♕h6 ♖g8 19 ♘g5+–] 15 ... f6 16 ♔h1 c4? [⌓ 16 ... ♗c7] 17 ♗e2 ♗c7 18 ♘d4 b5 19 f4 ♘b7 20 ♘e6 ♗×e6 21 d×e6 ♘c5 22 ♕d5 ♕e7 23 ♗g4 ♔h8 24 ♕h5 ♘d3 25 ♗f5 ♕e8 26 ♗d4 ♗b6? 27 e7 ♖g8 28 ♘e2 ♕f7 29 ♖f3 **1-0** L/N3033

**1864-★AN-13** iv 64
**Neumann,G.R.–Anderssen, A.**
Breslau [Anderssen & Neumann]

1 e4 e5 2 ♘f3 ♘c6 3 ♗b5 a6 4 ♗a4 ♘ge7 5 0-0 ♘g6 6 d4 ♗d6 7 d×e5 ♘c×e5 8 ♘×e5 ♗×e5 9 f4 ♗f6 10 e5 ♗e7 11 ♘c3 b5 12 ♗b3 ♗c5+ 13 ♔h1 ♗b7 14 ♗d5! c6 15 ♗b3 ♕e7 16 ♘e4 0-0-0 17 ♘d6+ ♗×d6 18 e×d6 ♕f6 19 ♗e3 ♖de8 20 ♕d4 ♕×d4 21 ♗×d4 f6 22 f5 c5 23 ♗×c5 ♘h4 24 ♖f2 ♘×g2 25 ♖×g2? ♖e2 **0-1** L/N6051

**1864-★AN-14** iv 64
**Neumann,G.R.+Anderssen, A.**
Breslau

1 e4 e5 2 ♘f3 ♘c6 3 ♗c4 ♗c5 4 b4 ♗×b4 5 c3 ♗c5 6 0-0 d6 7 d4 e×d4 8 c×d4 ♗b6 9 ♘c3 ♘a5 10 ♗d3 ♘e7 11 e5 d5 12 ♗a3 ♗e6 13 ♘a4 0-0 14 ♘g5 h6 15 ♘×e6 f×e6 16 ♕g4 ♕d7 17 ♘×b6 a×b6 18 ♗×e7 ♕×e7 19 ♕g6 **1-0** L/N6051

**1864-★AN-15** iv 64
**Neumann,G.R.–Anderssen, A.**
Breslau

1 e4 e5 2 ♘f3 ♘c6 3 ♗c4 ♗c5 4 b4 ♗×b4 5 c3 ♗c5 6 0-0 d6 7 d4 e×d4 8 c×d4 ♗b6 9 ♗b2 ♘a5 10 ♗d3 ♘e7 11 ♘c3 0-0 12 d5 ♘g6 13 ♘e2 c5 14 ♖c1 ♗d7 15 ♘g3 f6 16 ♕d2 ♖c8 17 h4 c4 18 ♗b1 ♘e5 19 ♘d4 a6 20 f4 c3 21 ♗×c3 ♘ac4 22 ♕e1 ♘g4 23 f5 ♘ce5 24 ♔h1 ♗×d4 25 ♗×d4 ♗b5 26 ♖f4 ♕d7 27 ♖d1

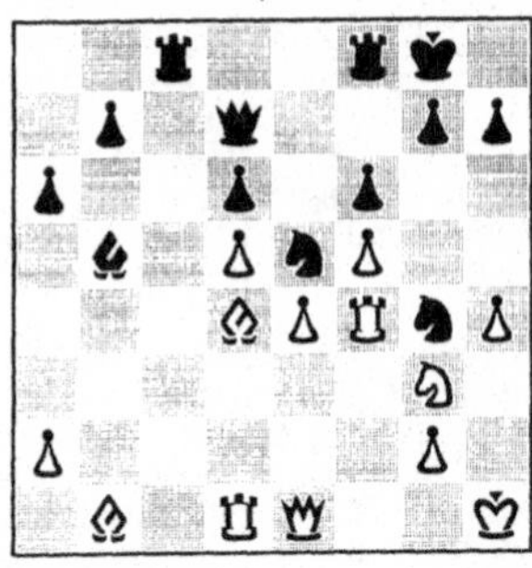

27 ... g5 **0-1** L/N6051

### 1864-★AN-16 iv 64
**Neumann,G.R.–Anderssen, A.**

Breslau [Anderssen & Neumann]

1 e4 e5 2 ♘f3 ♘c6 3 ♗b5 ♘ge7 4 0-0 ♘g6 5 d4 exd4 6 ♘xd4 ♗c5 7 ♘e2 [□ 7 ♘f5] 7 ... 0-0 8 ♔h1 ♘ce5 9 ♘g3 d6 10 ♗e2 ♕h4 11 ♘d2? [□ 11 f4] 11 ... f5 12 exf5 ♗xf5 13 ♘xf5 ♖xf5 14 ♘f3 ♘xf3 15 ♗xf3 ♗xf2 16 ♕e2 ♗g3 17 h3 ♖af8 18 ♗d2 c6 19 ♗g4 ♖f2 20 ♖xf2 ♖xf2 21 ♕e6+ ♔h8 22 ♖g1 h5 23 ♗f5 ♘f8 24 ♕f7 ♕xh3+ 25 ♗xh3 ♖xf7 **0-1** L/N6051

### 1864-★AN-17 iv 64
**Neumann,G.R.=Anderssen, A.**

Breslau

1 e4 e5 2 ♘f3 ♘c6 3 ♗c4 ♗c5 4 b4 ♗xb4 5 c3 ♗c5 6 0-0 d6 7 d4 exd4 8 cxd4 ♗b6 9 ♘c3 ♘a5 10 ♗d3 ♘e7 11 e5 dxe5 12 dxe5 ♗e6 13 ♕c2 ♕d7 14 ♗b5 c6 15 ♖d1 ♘d5 16 ♘xd5 ♗xd5 17 ♗d3 ♗xf3 18 gxf3 ♕e7 19 ♗f5 ♖d8 20 ♖xd8+ ♕xd8 21 ♗a3 ♕g5+ 22 ♔h1 ♕f4 23 ♔g2 ♘c4 24 ♕d3 ♕g5+ 25 ♔f1 ♘xa3 26 ♗d7+ ♔f8 27 ♕xa3+ ♕e7 28 ♕d6 g6 29 ♗c8 ♗c7 30 ♕xe7+ ♔xe7 31 ♗xb7 ♗xe5 32 ♖e1 ♔d6 33 ♗xc6 ♗xh2 34 ♗a4 h5 35 ♗b3 ♖h7 36 ♖e4 g5 37 ♖a4 f6 38 ♖a6+ ♔e5 39 ♖e6+ ♔f5 40 ♗c2+ ♔xe6 41 ♗xh7 ½-½ L/N6051

### 1864-★AN-18 vii 64
**Neumann,G.R.=Anderssen, A.**

Berlin [Anderssen & Neumann]

1 e4 e5 2 ♘f3 ♘c6 3 ♗b5 ♘f6 4 0-0 ♘xe4 5 d4 ♗e7 6 ♕e2 ♘d6 7 ♗xc6 bxc6 8 dxe5 ♘b7 9 ♗e3 0-0 10 ♖d1 ♕e8 11 ♘c3 ♘d8 12 ♘d4 d5 13 f4 ♘e6 14 ♘f5 ♗b4 15 ♘g3 d4 16 ♖xd4! ♘xd4 17 ♗xd4 a5 18 ♘ce4 c5 19 ♘xc5 ♕c6 20 ♕f2 ♖d8 21 c3 ♗xc5 22 ♗xc5 ♗b7 23 ♗d4 ♕d5 24 ♘f5 ♖d7

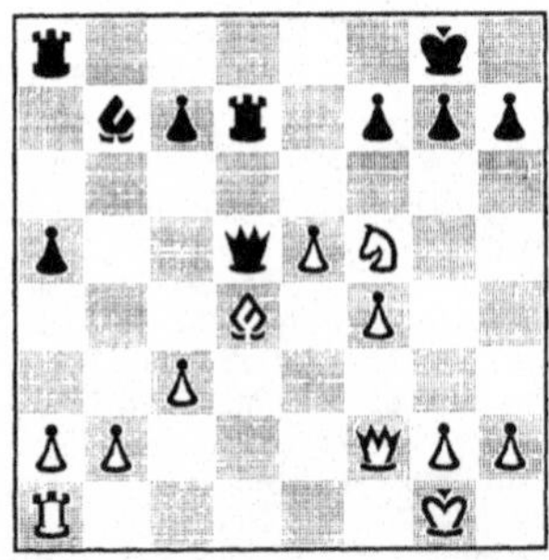

25 ♘xg7 ♕xg2+ [25 ... c5 26 ♘h5] 26 ♕xg2 ♗xg2 27 ♔xg2 [27 ♘h5 ♗c6! 28 ♘f6+ ♔f8! 29 ♘xd7+ ♗xd7] 27 ... ♔xg7 28 e6+ ♖xd4 29 cxd4 fxe6 30 ♔f3? ♔f6 31 ♔e4 ♖g8 32 ♖c1 ♖g2 33 ♖xc7 ♖xh2 34 ♖a7 ♖xb2 35 ♖xa5 h5 36 ♖xh5 ♖xa2 ½-½ L/N6051

### 1864-★AN-19 vii 64
**Neumann,G.R.=Anderssen, A.**

Berlin [Anderssen & Neumann]

1 e4 e5 2 ♘f3 ♘c6 3 ♗b5 ♘f6 4 d3 ♗c5 5 0-0 d6 6 ♗xc6+ bxc6 7 h3 ♗b6 8 ♘c3 h6 9 ♘e2 ♘h5 10 d4 f5 11 dxe5 fxe4 12 ♘fd4 0-0 13 ♗e3 ♕h4 14 ♔h2 dxe5 15 ♘xc6 ♗xh3 16 gxh3 ♖f3 17 ♘g1 ♗xe3 18 ♘xf3 ♕f4+ 19 ♔g2 ♖f8 20 ♕d5+ ♔h7 21 ♘cxe5 ♗b6 22 ♖ae1 exf3+ 23 ♘xf3 ♖f5 24 ♕e4 c6 25 ♕xf4? ♘xf4+ 26 ♔h2! ♗c7 27 ♘g1 ♘d3+ 28 ♔g2 ♖g5+ 29 ♔f3 ♘xe1+ 30 ♖xe1 ½-½ L/N6051

### 1864-★AN-20 vii 64
**Neumann,G.R.–Anderssen, A.**

Berlin [Anderssen & Neumann]

1 e4 e5 2 ♘f3 ♘c6 3 ♗b5 ♘f6 4 d3 ♗c5 5 c3 0-0 6 ♗xc6 bxc6 7 ♘xe5 d5! 8 0-0 dxe4 9 d4 ♗d6 10 ♘xc6? ♕e8 11 ♘a5 ♕b5! 12 ♘b3 ♗g4 13 ♕d2 ♗xh2+ 14 ♔xh2 ♕xf1 15 ♕f4 ♗f3 16 gxf3 ♕xf2+ 17 ♔h1 exf3 18 ♕h2 ♕e1+ **0-1** L/N6051-1865

### 1864-★AN-21 vii 64
**Neumann,G.R.=Anderssen, A.**

Berlin

1 e4 e5 2 ♘f3 ♘c6 3 ♗b5 ♘f6 4 0-0 ♘xe4 5 d4 ♗e7 6 ♕e2 ♘d6 7 ♗xc6 bxc6! 8 dxe5 ♘b7 9 ♗e3 0-0 10 ♖d1 ♕e8 11 ♘c3 ♘d8 12 ♘d4 f5 13 f4 c5 14 ♘db5 ♘e6 15 ♘d5 ♗d8 16 c4 a6 17 ♘a3 ♗b7 18 ♕f2 ♖b8 19 ♖d2 ♗a8 20 ♖ad1 ♕h5 21 ♔h1? ♖xb2 22 ♗xc5 ♖xa2 23 ♘b1 d6? 24 exd6 ♗xd5 25 cxd5 ♘xc5 26 ♕xc5 cxd6 27 ♕xd6 ♗a5 28 ♖d3 ♕g4 29 ♖g1 ♖b2 30 ♕e6+ ♔h8 31 ♖g3 ♕h4 32 ♕e5 ♖b7 33 d6 ♗b6 34 ♖f1 ♖bf7 35 ♖gf3 ♕d8 36 ♖e1 ♖f6 37 ♖d3 ♗c7 38 ♖ed1 ♗b8 39 ♕c5 ♕d7 40 ♕b6 ♕a4 41 ♘c3 ♕xf4 42 ♕xa6 ♕g4 43 ♘b5 f4 44 ♕b7 ♖g6 45 d7 ♖d8 46 ♖e1 ♖e6 47 ♖c1 ♕h4 48 h3 f3 49 ♕xb8 ♖xb8 50 ♖c8+ ♕d8 51 ♖xd8+ ♖xd8 52 ♖xf3 ♔g8 53 ♘d4 ♖e1+ 54 ♔h2 ♖xd7 55 ♘f5 ♖f7? 56 g4 h6 57 ♘h4 ♖xf3 58 ♘xf3 ♖e3 59 ♔g3 g5 60 ♔f2 ♖a3 61 h4 gxh4 62 ♘xh4 ♔f7 63 ♘f3 ♔f6 64 ♔g3 ♖a4 65 ♔h4 ♖a1 66 ♔g3 ♔e6 67 ♔f4 ♔d5 68 g5 h5 69 g6 ♔e6 70 ♔g5 ♖a5+ 71 ♔h6 ½-½ L/N6051

### 1864-★AN-22 vii 64
**Neumann,G.R.=Anderssen, A.**

Berlin

1 e4 e5 2 ♘f3 ♘c6 3 ♗b5 ♘f6 4 0-0 ♘xe4 5 d4 ♗e7 6 ♕e2 ♘d6 7 ♗xc6 bxc6 8 dxe5 ♘b7 9 ♗e3 0-0 10 ♖d1 ♕e8 11 ♘c3 ♘d8 12 ♘d4 f5 13 f4 c5 14 ♘db5 ♘e6 15 ♘d5 ♗d8 16 c4 a6 17 ♘a3 d6 18 exd6 cxd6 19 ♕e1 ♗a5 20 ♗d2 ♗xd2 21 ♕xd2 ♕d8 22 ♖ad1 ♖a7 23 ♘c2 ♖af7 24 a3 g5 25 fxg5 ♘xg5 26 ♘e7+ ♖xe7 27 ♕xg5+ ♖g7 28 ♕xd8 ♖xd8 29 ♖f1 ♗b7 30 ♘e3 ♖e8 31 ♘d5 ♗xd5 32 ♖xd5 ♖e2 33 ♖f2 ♖e1+ ½-½ L/N6051

### 1864-★AN-23 vii 64
**Neumann,G.R.+Anderssen, A.**

Berlin

1 e4 e5 2 ♘f3 ♘c6 3 ♗b5 ♘f6 4 0-0 ♘xe4 5 d4 ♗e7 6 ♕e2 ♘d6 7 ♗xc6 bxc6 8 dxe5 ♘b7 9 ♗e3 0-0 10 ♖d1 ♕e8 11 ♘c3 ♘d8 12 ♘d4 f5 13 f4 ♕g6 14 ♘a4 a5 15 c4 d6 16 ♘f3 ♘e6 17 b3 h6 18 c5 dxc5 19 ♖ac1 ♗a6 20 ♕f2 c4 21 bxc4 ♗a3 22 ♖c2 ♖ad8 23 ♖f1 ♖f7 24 ♔h1 ♖fd7 25 ♗c5 ♖d3 26 ♗xa3 ♖xa3 27 ♘c5 ♗c8 28 ♘xe6 ♗xe6 29 ♘d4 ♗c8 30 ♘b3 a4 31 ♘c5 ♗e6 32 ♕e1 ♖d4 33 ♕c1 ♗xc4 34 ♖xc4 ♖xa2 35 ♖c2 ♖c4 36 ♖xa2 ♖xc1 37 ♖xc1 ♕g4 38 ♖xa4 **1-0** L/N6051-1865

### 1864-★AN-24 vii 64
**Neumann,G.R.–Anderssen, A.**

Berlin [Anderssen & Neumann]

1 e4 e5 2 f4 exf4 3 ♘f3 g5 4 ♗c4 g4 5 0-0 gxf3 6 ♕xf3 ♕e7 7 ♕xf4 ♘c6 8 ♕xf7+ ♕xf7 9 ♗xf7+ ♔d8 10 ♘c3 ♘e5 11 d4 ♘xf7 12 ♖xf7 ♔e8! 13 ♖xf8+?! ♖xf8 14 ♘d5 c6 15 ♘c7 ♖b8 16 ♗f4

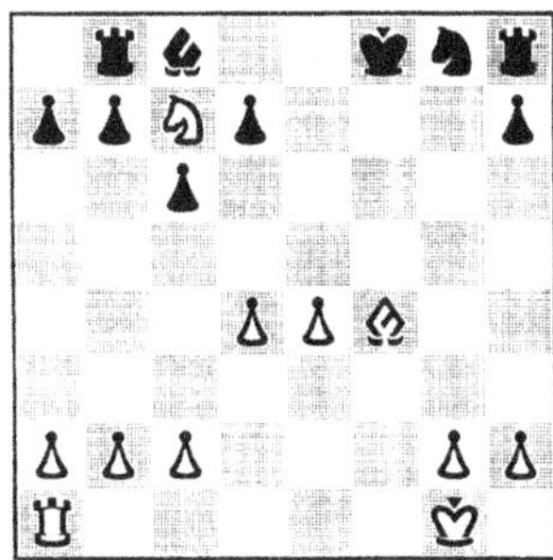

16 ... ♘f6! 17 ♖f1 ♔e7! 18 ♗g5 ♖f8 19 e5 ♔d8 20 exf6 ♔xc7 21 ♖e1 d6 22 ♖e7+ ♗d7 23 ♖xh7 ♖be8 24 f7 ♖e1+! 25 ♔f2 ♖e6 26 ♔g3 ♖g6 27 ♔h4 ♗f5 **0-1**

L/N6051

**1864-★AN-25** vii 64

**Neumann,G.R.–Anderssen, A.**

Berlin [Anderssen & Neumann]

1 e4 e5 2 f4 exf4 3 ♗c4 d5 4 exd5? ♕h4+ 5 ♔f1 ♗d6 6 ♘f3 ♕h5 7 ♘c3 ♘e7 8 d4 ♗f5 9 ♗b5+ ♘d7 10 ♘e5 ♕xd1+ 11 ♘xd1 f6 12 ♘xd7 ♗xd7 13 ♗xd7+ ♔xd7 14 c4 b6 15 ♘f2 g5 16 ♘e4 ♘g8 17 ♘xd6 cxd6 18 h4 ♘e7 19 hxg5 fxg5 20 ♔f2 ♘f5 21 ♖d1 ♖ae8 22 ♖d3 ♘g3 23 b3? ♖e2+ 24 ♔f3 h5 25 ♗d2 ♖f8 **0-1** L/N6051

**1864-★AN-26** vii 64

**Neumann,G.R.+Anderssen, A.**

Berlin [Anderssen & Neumann]

1 e4 e5 2 f4 exf4 3 ♘f3 g5 4 ♗c4 g4 5 0-0 gxf3 6 ♕xf3 ♕e7 7 ♕xf4 ♘h6 [◻ 7 ... ♘c6] 8 ♘c3 ♗g7 9 e5 b5 10 ♘xb5 ♘a6 11 d4 ♗b7 12 ♘d6+ cxd6 13 exd6 ♕e4 14 ♗xf7+ ♔d8 15 ♕g5+ ♔c8 16 ♕xg7 ♘xf7 17 ♖xf7 ♖d8 18 ♗d2 ♗c6 19 ♗a5 ♔b7 20 ♗xd8 ♖xd8 21 c4 ♘b4 22 d5 ♗a4 23 b3 ♖g8 24 ♕xg8 ♕d4+ 25 ♖f2 ♕xa1+ 26 ♖f1 ♕d4+ 27 ♔h1 ♘d3 28 ♕f7 **1-0** L/N6051

**1864-★AP-1 ●○** 8 v 64

**Paulsen, L.=Alexi**

Berlin [Anderssen & Neumann]

1 e4 e5 2 ♘f3 ♘c6 3 d4 d6 4 d5 [◻ 4 dxe5 dxe5 5 ♕xd8+] 4 ... ♘b8 5 ♗d3 ♗g4 6 h3 ♗h5 7 c4 c6 8 ♘c3 ♕c7 9 ♗e3 h6 10 ♕e2 ♘f6 11 g4 ♗g6 12 ♘h4 ♗e7 13 ♘f5 ♗xf5 14 gxf5 ♘a6 15 0-0-0 ♖c8 16 ♔b1 c5 17 f4 ♘d7! 18 ♖hg1 ♗f6 19 ♘b5 ♕b6 20 ♖g2 ♘b4 21 a3 ♘xd3 22 ♕xd3 a6 23 ♘c3 exf4 24 ♗xf4 ♘e5 25 ♗xe5 ♗xe5 26 ♕c2 ♕a5 ½-½

L/N6051

**1864-★AR-1**

**Rosanes, J.–Anderssen, A.**

Breslau [Bachmann]

1 e4 e5 2 f4 exf4 3 ♘f3 g5 4 h4 g4 5 ♘e5 ♘f6 6 ♗c4 d5 7 exd5 ♗d6 8 d4 ♘h5 9 ♗b5+ c6 10 dxc6 bxc6 11 ♘xc6 ♘xc6 12 ♗xc6+ ♔f8 13 ♗xa8 ♘g3 14 ♖h2 [14 ♔f2 ♘xh1+ 15 ♕xh1 g3+ (15 ... ♗f5 16 ♗d5 ♔g7 17 ♘c3 ♖e8) 16 ♔e1 ♕e7+ 17 ♔d1 ♗g4+ 18 ♗f3 ♗xf3+ 19 gxf3 ♖g8→] 14 ... ♗f5 15 ♗d5 ♔g7 16 ♘c3 ♖e8+ 17 ♔f2 ♕b6 [△ 18 ... ♗e5] 18 ♘a4 ♕a6 [△ 19 ... ♕e2+ 20 ♕xe2 ♖xe2+ 21 ♔g1 ♖e1+ 22 ♔f2 ♖f1#] 19 ♘c3 [19 c4 ♕xa4!→] 19 ... ♗e5 20 a4

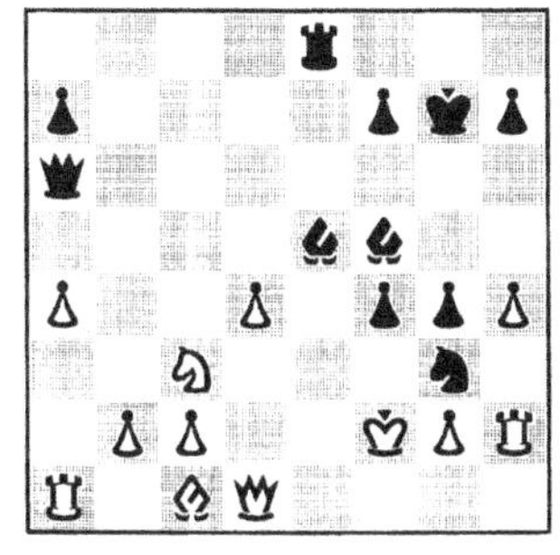

20 ... ♕f1+ 21 ♕xf1 ♗xd4+ 22 ♗e3 ♖xe3 **0-1** L/N3033

**1864-★AS-1** vii 64

**Anderssen, A.+Schallopp, E.**

Berlin

1 e4 e5 2 ♘f3 ♘c6 3 d4 exd4 4 ♗c4 ♗c5 5 0-0 d6 6 c3 ♗g4! 7 b4 ♗b6 8 ♗b2 ♘e5 9 ♗b3 ♘xf3+ 10 gxf3 ♗h3 11 ♔h1 ♗xf1 12 ♕xf1 ♕f6 13 ♕d3 ♘e7 14 cxd4 ♘g6 15 ♘d2 ♘f4 16 ♕e3 a5 17 ♘c4 a4 18 ♘xb6 cxb6 19 ♗c4 0-0 20 ♖g1 d5 21 ♖g4 g5 22 ♗xd5 ♘xd5 23 ♖xg5+ ♔h8 24 ♖xd5 ♖g8 25 f4 ♖g7 26 ♗c3 ♖ag8 27 ♖g5 h6 28 d5 **1-0** L/N6051

**1864-★AS-2** vii 64

**Anderssen, A.+Schallopp, E.**

Berlin [Anderssen & Neumann]

1 e4 e5 2 ♘f3 ♘c6 3 ♗b5 ♘f6 4 d3 ♗c5? 5 c3 0-0 6 0-0 ♗d6 7 ♗g5? h6 8 ♗xf6 ♕xf6 9 d4 ♘e7 10 ♗d3 ♘g6 11 ♕d2 ♘f4 12 dxe5 ♗xe5 13 ♘xe5 ♕xe5 14 g3 ♘h3+ 15 ♔g2 d5 16 f4 ♕d6 17 e5 ♕b6 18 f5 ♘g5 19 h4 ♘e4 20 ♗xe4 dxe4 21 ♘a3 e3 22 ♕e2 ♗d7 23 ♘c4 ♗c6+ 24 ♔h2 ♕b5 25 a4 ♕d5 26 ♖ad1

26 ... ♕g2+ 27 ♕xg2 ♗xg2 28 ♖fe1 e2 29 ♖d2? ♗f3 30 ♔g1 ♖fe8? 31 ♔f2 ♗h5 32 ♖d4 c5 33 ♖e4 g6 34 f6 g5 35 hxg5 hxg5 36 g4 ♗g6 37 ♖4xe2 ♗d3 38 ♖e3 ♗xc4 39 ♖h1 ♖ad8 40 ♖eh3 ♖d2+ 41 ♔e1 ♖e2+ 42 ♔d1 ♖d8+ 43 ♔c1 ♖e1+ 44 ♖xe1 ♖d3! 45 ♖h5 ♗d5 46 ♖xg5+ ♔f8 47 ♖d1 **1-0**

L/N6051

**1864-★AS-3** vii 64

**Anderssen, A.–Schallopp, E.**

Berlin [Anderssen & Neumann]

1 e4 c5 2 ♘f3 e6 3 ♘c3 ♘c6 [◻ 3 ... a6] 4 d4 cxd4 5 ♘xd4 d5 6 ♗b5 ♘e7 7 exd5 exd5 8 0-0 a6 9 ♗a4 b5 10 ♘xc6 ♘xc6 11 ♖e1+ ♗e7 12 ♘xd5?! bxa4 13 ♗g5 ♗e6 14 ♗xe7 ♘xe7 15 ♘f4 ♕xd1 16 ♖axd1 0-0 17 ♖d4 a3 18 b3 ♖ad8 19 ♖a4 ♖d2 20 ♖xa6 ♖xc2 21 ♖xa3 ♘g6 22 ♘h5 ♗g4 23 ♘g3 ♘f4 24 h3 ♘e2+ 25 ♔h2 ♘xg3 26 hxg4 ♘e2 27 ♖a7 f5 28 g5 f4 29 f3 ♖f5 30 ♖e7 ♘d4 31 ♔h3 ♖xg5 32 ♖d7 **0-1** L/N6051-1865

**1864-★AS-4** vii 64

**Anderssen, A.+Schallopp, E.**

Berlin

1 e4 e5 2 f4 d5 3 ♘f3 dxe4 4 ♘xe5 ♗d6 5 ♗c4 ♗xe5 6 fxe5 ♕d4 7 ♕e2 ♕xe5 8 d4 ♕xd4 9 ♘c3 ♘f6 10 ♗e3 ♕d8 11 0-0 h6 12 ♗c5 ♘bd7 13 ♕xe4+ **1-0**

L/N6051-1865

**1864-★AS-5** vii 64

**Schallopp, E.–Anderssen, A.**

Berlin [Anderssen & Neumann]

1 e4 e5 2 ♘f3 ♘c6 3 ♗b5 ♘ge7 4 0-0 ♘g6 5 d4 exd4 6 ♘xd4 ♗c5 7 ♘f5 ♕f6 8 ♘c3 ♘ce7 9 ♘d5 ♘xd5 10 ♕xd5 ♗e7 11 ♕d3 0-0 12 ♗d2 c6 13 ♗a4 ♖e8 14 ♗c3 ♘e5 15 ♕g3 ♗c5 16 ♔h1! b5! 17 f4 ♕g6 18 ♗b3 ♕xg3 19 hxg3 ♘g4 20 ♘xg7 ♖xe4 21 ♖ae1 d5 22 ♖xe4 dxe4 23 ♘h5 a5 24 a3 ♘f2+ 25 ♔h2 ♗f5 26 ♘f6+ ♔f8 27 g4 ♘xg4+ 28 ♘xg4 ♗xg4 29 ♔g3 ♗f5 30 ♔h4 ♗e7+ 31 ♔h5 b4 32

axb4 axb4 33 ♗e5 f6 34 g4 ♗g6+ 35 ♔h6 fxe5 36 f5 ♗f7 37 f6 ♗c5 38 ♗xf7 ♔xf7 39 ♔xh7 ♖g8 **0-1** L/N6051

**1864-★AS-6** vii 64
**Schallopp, E.= Anderssen, A.**
Berlin
1 e4 e5 2 ♘f3 ♘c6 3 ♗b5 a6 4 ♗a4 b5 5 ♗b3 ♗c5 6 c3 ♕e7 7 d4 ♗b6 8 0-0 d6 9 ♗d5 ♗b7 10 a4 ♘f6 11 axb5 axb5 12 ♖xa8+ ♗xa8 13 ♕b3 ♘xd5 14 exd5 ♘a7 15 ♘a3 0-0 16 dxe5 dxe5 17 ♖e1 f6 18 ♘xb5 ♕c5 19 ♘xa7 ♗xd5 20 ♕c2 ♕a5 21 b4 ♕xa7 22 ♘h4 ♕b7 23 c4 ♕c6 24 c5 ♗a7 25 ♗e3 ♕b7 26 c6 ♕xb4 27 ♖b1 ♕xh4 28 ♗xa7 ♕e4 29 ♕xe4 ♗xe4 30 ♖b7 ♗xc6 31 ♖xc7 ♖d8 32 f3 ♖d1+ 33 ♔f2 ♖d2+ 34 ♔g3 ♗d7 35 ♗e3 ♖e2 36 ♗c5 ♗e8 37 h4 f5 38 ♔h3 f4 39 ♖e7 ♗g6 40 ♗d4 ♗f5+ 41 g4 ♗e4 42 ♖xe5 ♗xf3 43 ♖xe2 ♗xe2 44 ♗e5 f3 45 ♔g3 ♔f7 46 ♔f2 ♔g6 47 h5+ ♔f7 48 g5 g6 49 h6 **½-½** L/N6051

**1864-★AS-7** vii 64
**Schallopp, E.– Anderssen, A.**
Berlin
1 e4 e5 2 ♘f3 ♘c6 3 ♗b5 ♘f6 4 0-0 ♘xe4 5 d4 ♗e7 6 ♕e2 ♘d6 7 ♗xc6 bxc6 8 dxe5 ♘b7 9 ♗e3 0-0 10 ♖d1 ♕e8 11 ♘c3 d5 12 ♘d4 ♘c5 13 f4 ♘e6 14 ♘f5 ♗b4 15 ♕g4 ♔h8 16 ♘e2 ♖g8 17 ♕h4 ♘c5 18 ♘fg3 ♘e4 19 ♘xe4 dxe4 20 ♘g3 ♗e7 21 ♕h5 f5 22 exf6 ♗xf6 23 ♕xe8 ♖xe8 24 c3 ♖b8 25 ♖d2 a5 26 ♖e1 ♗a6 27 ♗a7 ♖a8 28 ♗d4 ♗d3 29 ♗xf6 gxf6 30 f5 c5 31 b3 c4 32 bxc4 ♖ab8 33 ♔f2 ♖e5 34 ♔e3 a4 35 ♔f4 a3 36 ♘xe4 ♗xc4 37 ♖ed1 ♖e7 38 ♘xf6 ♖b2 39 ♘e4 ♗xa2 40 f6 ♖e8 41 ♖d8 ♖b8 42 ♖xe8+ ♖xe8 43 ♖a1 ♗d5 44 ♘d2 ♖a8 45 g4 a2 46 h4 ♔g8 47 g5 ♔f7 48 ♔e5 ♗e6 49 c4 ♖a5+ 50 ♔d4 ♔g6 51 ♘f3 ♔f5 52 ♘e5 c5+ **0-1** L/N6051-1865

**1864-★AS-8** vii 64
**Schallopp, E.– Anderssen, A.**
Berlin [Anderssen & Neumann]
1 e4 e5 2 ♘f3 ♘c6 3 ♗c4 ♗c5 4 b4 ♗xb4 5 c3 ♗a5 6 d4 exd4 7 0-0 dxc3 8 ♕b3 ♕f6 9 e5 ♕g6 10 ♘xc3 ♗xc3 11 ♕xc3 ♘ge7 12 ♘g5 [◻ 12 ♗a3] 12 ... ♘d8 13 ♖e1 b6 14 f4 ♗b7 15 ♗a3 c5 16 ♖ad1 ♗c6 17 ♕h3 ♘e6 18 ♘xe6 fxe6 19 ♗e2 0-0 20 ♗d3 ♘f5 21 ♖e3 ♕h6 22 ♗xf5 ♖xf5 23 ♕xh6 gxh6 24 ♗c1 h5 25 ♖g3+ ♔f7 26 h4 h6 27 ♔f2 b5 28 ♗e3 c4 29 ♖d4 ♗d5 30 ♗d2 ♖c8 31 ♖a3 ♖c7 32 ♖a5 ♖b7 33 ♗b4 ♔g6 34 a3 ♖f7 35 g3 ♔f5 36 ♖d1 ♖g7 37 ♗c5 ♖g8 38 ♖xa7 ♖xa7 39 ♗xa7 ♖c8 40 ♗d4 c3 41 ♖c1 c2 42 ♗e3 ♖c3 43 ♖a1 ♔g4 44 ♔e2 ♗f3+ 45 ♔d2 ♖xe3 46 ♔xe3 ♔xg3 47 ♖g1+ ♔h2 48 ♖c1 ♗d1 49 ♔d4 ♔g3 50 ♔c5 ♔xh4 51 f5 ♔g5! 52 f6 ♔g6 53 ♔d6 ♔f7 **0-1** L/N6051-1865

**1864-★AS-9** vii 64
**Schallopp, E.– Anderssen, A.**
Berlin
1 e4 e5 2 f4 exf4 3 ♗c4 d5 4 ♗xd5 c6 5 ♗b3 ♕h4+ 6 ♔f1 g5 7 d4 ♗g7 8 ♘c3 ♘e7 9 ♘f3 ♕h5 10 h4 h6 11 ♘e2 ♗g4 12 ♔f2 ♕g6 13 ♕d3 ♘d7 14 c4 0-0-0 15 ♕c2 ♗xd4+ 16 ♘fxd4 ♘c5 17 ♘f5 ♘xf5 18 ♗xf4 ♘d3+ 19 ♔g1 gxf4 20 exf5 ♗xf5 21 h5 ♕g4 22 ♘c3 f3 23 ♖h2 ♕d4+ 24 ♔f1 ♖hg8 25 ♖d1 ♖de8 **0-1** L/N6051

**1864-★AS-10** vii 64
**Schallopp, E.+ Anderssen, A.**
Berlin [Anderssen & Neumann]
1 e4 e5 2 ♘f3 ♘c6 3 ♗b5 ♘f6 4 d3 ♗c5 [◻ 4 ... d6] 5 c3 0-0 6 ♗xc6 bxc6 7 ♘xe5 d5 8 0-0 ♗a6 9 ♖e1 dxe4 10 d4 ♕e8 11 ♗g5 ♗e7 12 ♘d2 c5 13 ♗xf6 gxf6 14 ♘g4 f5 15 ♘h6+ ♔h8 16 ♘xf5 ♗f6 17 ♘xe4 ♕e6 18 ♘eg3 ♕b6 19 ♕h5 cxd4 20 cxd4 ♕xb2 21 ♘e4

21 ... ♗xd4 22 ♖ab1 ♗xf2+ 23 ♘xf2 ♖ae8 24 ♖ed1 ♕f6 25 ♘g4 ♕g6 26 ♕xg6 hxg6 27 ♘g3 f5 28 ♘f2 f4 29 ♘ge4 ♗e2 30 ♖d7 f3 31 g3 ♖b8 32 ♖xb8 ♖xb8 33 h4 ♖b1+ 34 ♔h2 ♔g8 35 ♘f6+ ♔f8 36 ♘2e4 **1-0** L/N6051

**1864-★AS-11**
**Schmidt, E. von+ Anderssen, A.**
Breslau
1 e4 e5 2 ♘f3 ♘c6 3 ♗b5 ♘f6 4 d4 exd4 5 e5 ♘e4 6 0-0 ♗e7 7 ♖e1 ♘c5 8 ♘xd4 ♘xd4 9 ♕xd4 0-0 10 ♗c4 b5 11 ♗xb5 d5 12 exd6

**100** Schmidt, E. von M1647. BL

♗xd6 13 ♗e3 ♗b7 14 ♘c3 ♔h8 15 ♖ad1 ♘e6 16 ♕d2 f5 17 f4 ♕h4 18 g3 ♕h5 19 ♗c4 ♘g5 20 fxg5 f4 21 ♗d4 ♕xg5 22 ♘e4 ♕g4 23 ♘xd6 fxg3 24 ♘xb7 ♖f2 25 ♗xg7+ ♕xg7 26 ♕d4 ♖f6 27 ♘d8 **1-0** L/N6047-1864

**1864-★AZ-1** 30 iv 64
**Zukertort, J.H.–Anderssen, A.**
Breslau [Anderssen & Zukertort]
1 e4 e5 2 ♘f3 ♘c6 3 ♗b5 ♘f6 4 0-0 ♗e7 5 ♘c3 d6 6 d4 ♗d7 7 d5 ♘b8 8 ♕d3 0-0 9 ♗xd7 ♘bxd7 10 ♗e3 ♘h5 11 ♘d2 g6 12 ♘e2 [◻ 12 ♗h6, 13 f4] 12 ... f5 13 f4 ♘g7 14 ♖f3? [◻ 14 fxe5 ♘xe5 15 ♕b3 b6 16 ♗d4 ♗f6 17 ♘f4] 14 ... exf4 15 ♖xf4 ♘e5 16 ♕b3 g5 17 ♖f2 f4 18 ♗d4 ♗f6 19 h3 ♔h8 20 c4 c5 21 ♗c3 b6 22 ♕c2 ♕e8 23 b3 ♕g6 24 ♘f3 ♖ae8 25 ♔h1 g4 26 ♘xe5 dxe5 27 ♖g1 ♘h5 28 ♕d3 ♕h6 29 g3 f3 30 ♗d2? [◻ 30 ♖h2] 30 ... ♗g5 31 ♗xg5 ♕xg5 32 ♘c3 ♕h6 33 ♘d1 ♖g8 34 ♕e3 ♖g5 35 ♔h2 [◻ 35 ♖h2] 35 ... ♘f4 36 h4 ♖h5 37 ♖h1 ♖f8 38 ♘c3? ♖xh4+ 39 gxh4 g3+ **0-1** L/N6051-1867

**1864-★AZ-2** 1 v 64
**Zukertort, J.H.+Anderssen, A.**
Breslau
1 e4 e5 2 ♘f3 ♘c6 3 ♗b5 ♗c5 4 c3 ♕e7 5 0-0 f6 6 d4 ♗b6 7 ♔h1 ♘d8 8 ♘h4 g6 9 f4 exd4 10 cxd4 ♘h6 11 f5! g5 12 ♘f3 ♘hf7 13 e5 0-0 14 ♗c4 ♔h8 15 exf6 ♕xf6 16 ♗d2 d6 17 ♗c3 ♗xf5 18 d5 ♘e5 19 ♘xe5 dxe5 20 ♗d3 ♕g6 21 ♕f3 ♘e6 22 ♗xe5+ ♔g8 23 ♗xf5 ♖xf5 24 ♕xf5 ♘c5 25 ♘c3 ♘d3 26 ♕xg6+ hxg6 27 ♗g3 ♖e8 28 ♖f6 ♔g7 29 ♖af1 ♘xb2 30 ♖e6 ♖c8 31 ♖ff6 ♗d4 32 ♖xg6+ ♔f7 33 ♘e4 **1-0** L/N6051-1867

**1864-★AZ-3** 29 x 64

**Zukertort,J.H.=Anderssen, A.**

Breslau [Anderssen & Zukertort]

1 e4 e5 2 ♘f3 ♘c6 3 ♗c4 ♗c5 4 c3 ♘f6 5 d4 exd4 6 cxd4 ♗b4+ 7 ♗d2 ♗xd2+ [7 ... ♘xe4 8 ♗xb4 ♘xb4 9 ♗xf7+ ♔xf7 10 ♕b3+ d5 11 ♘e5+] 8 ♘bxd2 d5 9 exd5 ♘xd5 10 0-0 [□ 10 ♕b3!] 10 ... 0-0 11 ♘e4 h6 12 ♘e5 ♗e6 13 a3 [□ 13 ♖e1] 13 ... ♘f4 14 ♘xc6 bxc6 15 ♗xe6 fxe6 16 g3 ♕d5 17 f3 ♘h3+ 18 ♔g2 ♘g5 19 ♕d3 c5 20 ♘xc5 [20 ♘xg5 ♕xg5 21 dxc5 ♕xc5 22 ♖ac1±] 20 ... e5 21 ♕b3 ♕xb3 22 ♘xb3 ♖ab8! 23 ♘d2 ♖xb2 24 ♖ad1 e4 25 f4 ♘f3 26 ♖f2 e3 27 ♖xf3 ♖e8 28 ♔h3! ♖xd2 [28 ... e2 29 ♖e1 ♖xd2 30 ♔g2 ♖xd4 31 ♔f2 ♖de4 32 ♖c3 ♖8e7 33 ♖c6, 34 ♖a6] 29 ♖xe3 ♖xe3 30 ♖xd2 ♖xa3 31 ♖c2 ♖d3 32 ♖xc7 ♖xd4 33 ♖xa7 ♖d2 34 f5 ♖f2 35 g4 h5 36 ♔g3 ♖f1 37 h3 ♔h7 38 ♔h4 ♖f3 39 ♔xh5 ♖xh3+ 40 ♔g5 ♖f3 41 ♖f7 ♖a3 42 f6 ♖a5+ 43 ♔h4 ♔g6 44 ♖xg7+ ♔xf6 45 ♖g8 ♖a1 ½-½

L/N6051-1867

**1864-★AZ-4** 11 xi 64

**Zukertort,J.H.–Anderssen, A.**

Breslau [Anderssen & Zukertort]

1 e4 e5 2 ♘f3 ♘c6 3 ♗c4 ♗c5 4 b4 ♗xb4 5 c3 ♗a5 6 0-0? [□ 6 d4] 6 ... ♘f6! 7 d4 [□ 7 ♗a3] 7 ... 0-0 8 ♗g5 d6 9 d5 ♘e7 10 ♗xf6 gxf6 11 ♘h4 ♘g6 12 ♘xg6? hxg6! 13 f4 ♗b6+ 14 ♔h1 ♔g7 15 f5! ♖h8 16 ♕g4 ♗d7 17 ♖f3 ♕e7 18 ♘d2 ♖h6 19 ♖h3 ♖ah8 20 ♖xh6 ♖xh6 21 ♖f1 ♗e3 22 ♘f3 ♕f8 23 ♖e1 ♗f2 24 ♖e2? [□ 24 ♖f1] 24 ... ♗c5 25 ♖e1 ♕h8 26 ♖f1 ♔f8 27 h3 gxf5 28 exf5 ♕h7 29 ♗d3 c6 30 c4 b5 31 dxc6 ♗xc6 32 cxb5 ♗b7 33 ♖c1! ♗b6 34 ♔h2 ♔e7 35 ♗c2 ♕h8 36 ♗e4 d5 37 ♗xd5! ♗xd5 38 ♕b4+ ♔d7 [38 ... ♔e8 39 ♖c8+ ♗d8 40 ♕d6] 39 ♖d1 ♕a8 40 ♕d2? [□ 40 ♕c4 ♔d6 41 ♕b4+ ♔d7 (41 ... ♔c7 42 ♕e7+ ♔b8 43 ♕f8+ ♔b7 44 ♕xh6+–; 42 ... ♔c8 43 ♖c1+–) 42 ♕c4=] 40 ... ♖h8 41 ♕xd5+ ♕xd5 42 ♖xd5+ ♔e7 43 ♘d2 ♖c8 44 a4 ♖c2 45 ♘b3 e4 46 ♘d4 ♖a2 47 ♘c6+ ♔e8 48 a5 ♗c7+ [48 ... ♗xa5 49 ♘xa5 ♖xa5 50 ♔g3=] 49 ♔g1 e3 50 ♖d1 [50 ♔f1 e2+ 51 ♔f2 ♗g3+ 52 ♔f3! ♔f8!–+] 50 ... e2 51 ♖b1 ♗g3 [52 b6 axb6 53 axb6 ♖d2 (53 ... e1♕+ 54 ♖xe1 ♗xe1 55 b7 ♗g3 56 b8♕+ ♗xb8 57 ♘xb8=) 54 ♖e1 ♗xe1 55 b7 ♖b2! 56 b8♕+ ♖xb8 57 ♘xb8 ♗g3–+] 0-1

L/N6051-1867

**1864-★AZ-5** xi 64

**Zukertort,J.H.+Anderssen, A.**

Breslau [Anderssen & Zukertort]

1 e4 e5 2 ♘f3 ♘c6 3 ♗b5 ♘f6 4 0-0 ♗e7 5 d4 exd4 6 e5 ♘e4 7 ♖e1 ♘c5 8 ♘xd4 ♘xd4 9 ♕xd4 0-0 10 ♘c3 a6 11 ♗c4 b5 12 ♗d5 c6 13 ♗f3 ♘e6 14 ♕d3 f5 15 exf6 ♗xf6 16 ♘e4 d5 17 ♘xf6+ ♕xf6 18 c3 ♖a7! 19 ♗e3 ♖af7 20 ♖ad1! ♘g5 21 ♗h5 g6 22 ♗d4 ♕f4? [□ 22 ... ♕f5] 23 ♗xg6! ♖g7 [23 ... hxg6 24 ♕xg6+–; 23 ... ♖d7 24 ♗xh7+ ♖xh7 25 ♕g6+–] 24 ♗xg7 ♕xf2+ 25 ♔h1 ♔xg7 26 ♖f1 ♕c5 27 ♖xf8 ♕xf8 28 ♗h5 ♘e4 29 ♕d4+ ♔h6 30 ♗f3 ♘g5? [□ 30 ... ♗f5] 31 ♕h4+ ♔g6 32 ♗h5+ ♔f6 [32 ... ♔h6 33 ♗f7+ ♔g7 34 ♕xg5+–] 33 ♖f1+ ♗f5 34 ♗g4 1-0

L/N6051-1867

**1864-★AZ-6** xi 64

**Zukertort,J.H.+Anderssen, A.**

Breslau

1 e4 e5 2 ♘f3 ♘c6 3 ♗b5 ♗c5 4 c3 ♘f6 5 0-0 ♘xe4 6 ♕e2 ♘xf2 7 ♖xf2 ♗xf2+ 8 ♔xf2 f6 9 ♕c4 ♘e7 10 ♗a4 c6 11 ♗b3 d5 12 ♕e2 0-0 13 d4 ♔h8 14 dxe5 fxe5 15 ♕xe5 ♗g4 16 ♗g5 ♗xf3 17 ♗xe7 ♗g4+ 18 ♗xf8 ♕xf8+ 19 ♔g1 ♖e8 20 ♕g3 ♕c5+ 21 ♔h1 d4 22 ♘d2 h5 23 cxd4 ♕xd4 24 ♘f3 ♕xb2 25 ♖e1 ♖f8 26 ♘e5 ♗f5 27 ♕g5 1-0

L/N6051-1867

**1864-★AZ-7** xi 64

**Zukertort,J.H.–Anderssen, A.**

Breslau

1 e4 e5 2 ♘f3 ♘c6 3 ♗b5 ♘f6 4 0-0 ♗e7 5 d4 exd4 6 e5 ♘e4 7 ♖e1 ♘c5 8 ♘xd4 ♘xd4 9 ♕xd4 0-0 10 ♘c3 a6 11 ♗c4 b5 12 ♗d5 c6 13 ♗f3 ♘e6 14 ♕d3 f5 15 exf6 ♗xf6 16 ♘e4 d5 17 ♘xf6+ ♕xf6 18 c3 ♗d7 19 ♗e3 ♖ae8 20 ♗d4 ♕h4 21 ♗e5 ♘g5 22 ♗g3 ♕h6 23 ♖e3 ♖xe3 24 ♕xe3 ♘xf3+ 25 gxf3 ♕xe3 26 fxe3 ♖xf3 27 ♖e1 ♗h3 0-1

L/N6051-1867

**1864-★AZ-8** xi 64

**Zukertort,J.H.–Anderssen, A.**

Breslau

1 e4 e5 2 ♘f3 ♘c6 3 ♗b5 ♗c5 4 c3 ♘f6 5 0-0 ♘xe4 6 ♕e2 ♘xf2 7 ♖xf2 ♗xf2+ 8 ♔xf2 f6 9 d4 0-0 10 ♗xc6 dxc6 11 dxe5 fxe5 12 ♕xe5 ♗g4 13 ♘bd2 ♕d7 14 b3 ♖ae8 15 ♕d4 ♕e7 16 ♕c4+ ♔h8 17 ♗b2 ♕e3+ 18 ♔f1 ♗xf3 19 ♘xf3 ♖xf3+ 20 gxf3 ♕xf3+ 21 ♔g1 ♖e2 22 ♕xe2 ♕xe2 0-1

L/N6051-1867

**1864-★BF-1**

**Blackburne,J.H.& Kling, J.+Falkbeer,E.K.& Zytogorski,A.**

London [Blackburne]

1 e4 e5 2 ♘f3 ♘c6 3 ♗b5 a6 4 ♗a4 ♘f6 5 0-0 ♘xe4 6 d4 ♗e7 7 ♖e1 d5 8 ♘xe5 ♗d7 9 ♗xc6 bxc6 10 ♘d2 ♘xd2 11 ♗xd2 0-0 12 ♕e2 ♗d6 13 f4 c5 14 ♕f3 cxd4 [□ 14 ... c6] 15 ♕xd5 ♗e6 16 ♕e4 [16 ♕xd4 ♗xe5–+] 16 ... ♗c5 17 ♘d3 ♗d5 [□ 17 ... ♗b6] 18 ♕f5 g6? 19 ♕h3 ♗b6 20 f5 ♕f6 21 ♖e5 c6? [□ 21 ... ♗b7] 22 ♖f1 g5 23 ♕g4 h6 24 h4 ♕g7 25 f6 ♕g6 26 ♗xg5!+– ♔h7 27 h5 ♕g8 28 ♖xd5 cxd5 29 ♕f5+ ♔h8 30 ♗xh6 ♕h7 31 ♗xf8 ♖xf8 32 ♕xd5 1-0

L/N3036

**1864-★BP-1**

**Beuthner, R.–Paulsen, L.**

Leipzig

1 e4 e5 2 ♘f3 ♘c6 3 ♗c4 ♗c5 4 c3 ♘f6 5 d4 exd4 6 cxd4 ♗b4+ 7 ♗d2 ♗xd2+ 8 ♘bxd2 d5 9 exd5 ♘xd5 10 0-0 0-0 11 ♘b3 ♗f5 12 a3 ♕d6 13 ♖e1 ♘f4 14 ♘h4 ♗e6 15 ♗xe6 fxe6 16 ♕d2 ♕d5 17 ♕c3 ♕h5 18 ♘f3 ♘xg2 19 ♔xg2 ♕g4+ 20 ♔h1 ♖xf3 21 ♖e3 ♖xf2 22 ♖g1 ♕h4 23 ♖g2 ♖af8 24 ♖eg3 ♖f1+ 25 ♖g1 ♕e4+ 26 ♖3g2 ♖8f2 27 ♕g3 ♖xg1+ 28 ♔xg1 ♕e1# 0-1

L/N6047-1864

**1864-★BS-1**

**Blackburne,J.H.+ Steinkühler,A.**

Manchester [Blackburne]

1 e4 e5 2 ♘f3 ♘c6 3 ♗c4 ♗c5 4 b4 ♗xb4 5 c3 ♗c5 6 0-0 d6 7 d4 exd4 8 cxd4 ♗b6 9 ♘c3 ♘a5 10 ♘g5 ♘xc4 11 ♕a4+ c6 12 ♕xc4 ♘h6? [□ 12 ... ♕c7] 13 ♔h1 0-0 14 f4 ♔h8 15 f5 f6 16 ♘e6 ♗xe6 17 fxe6 ♘g8 18 ♖f3 ♘e7 19 ♖h3 d5 20 ♕e2 g6 21 ♗h6 ♖e8 22 ♖f1 ♗xd4 23 ♕d2 ♗xc3 24 ♗g7+ 1-0

L/N3036

**1864-★CM-1 ●○⬠** v 64

**Morphy,P.C.+Capdevielle, P.**

1 e4 e5 2 ♘f3 ♘c6 3 ♗c4 ♗c5 4 b4 ♗xb4 5 c3 ♗c5 6 0-0 ♘f6 7 d4 exd4 8 cxd4 ♗b4 9 e5 ♘e4 10 ♗d5 ♗c3 11 ♗xe4 ♗xa1 12 ♗g5 f6 13 exf6 gxf6 14 ♗xc6 dxc6 15 ♖e1+ ♔f7 16 ♘e5+ ♔g7 17 ♗h6+ ♔xh6 18 ♘f7+ ♔g7 19 ♘xd8 ♖xd8 20 ♕h5 ♖d7 21 ♘d2 ♖f7 22 ♖xa1 ♗e6 23 ♖e1 ♗d5 24 ♖e3 ♔h8 25 ♘e4 ♖g7 26 ♘xf6 ♖xg2+ 27 ♔f1 ♖g7 28 ♖e8+ ♖xe8 29

♕xe8+ ♗g8 30 h4 h6 31 ♕f8 h5 32 ♘xg8 ♔h7 33 ♘f6+ ♔h6 34 ♘e8 ♔g6 35 ♕f6+ ♔h7 36 ♕xg7# **1-0** +13

**1864-★CP-1 ●○⌂** 8 v 64
**Paulsen, L.= Cordel, O.**
Berlin [Anderssen & Neumann]
1 e4 e5 2 ♘f3 ♘c6 3 ♗b5 ♘f6 4 0-0 ♘xe4 5 d4 ♗e7 6 ♕e2 ♘d6 7 ♗xc6 bxc6! 8 dxe5 ♘f5 9 ♕e4 [□ 9 g4] 9 ... d5 10 exd6 ♕xd6 11 ♘c3 ♕e6 12 ♕d3 [□ 12 ♖e1] 12 ... 0-0 13 ♗f4 ♖d8 14 ♕e4 ♕xe4 15 ♘xe4 ♘d6 16 ♘g3 ♗f6 17 c3 ♖b8 18 ♖ab1 ♗e6 19 b3 ♗xc3 20 ♖bc1 ♗a5 21 ♘d4 ♗d5 22 ♘xc6 ♗xc6 23 ♖xc6 ♖d7 24 ♖fc1 ♖bd8 **½-½** L/N6051

**1864-★DM-1 ●○⌂** 16 ii 64
**Morphy, P.C.+Dominguez, P.**
Habana [Maróczy]
1 e4 e5 2 ♘f3 ♘c6 3 ♗c4 ♘f6 4 d4 exd4 5 0-0 ♗c5 6 e5 ♘e4 [□ 6 ... d5! 7 exf6 dxc4 8 ♖e1+ ♗e6 (8 ... ♔f8 9 ♗g5 gxf6 10 ♗h6+) 9 ♘g5 ♕d5 10 ♘c3 ♕f5 11 ♘ce4 ♗b6 12 ♘g3 (12 fxg7 ♖g8 13 g4 ♕g6 14 ♘xe6 fxe6 15 ♗g5! ♖xg7 16 ♕f3) 12 ... ♕g6! 13 ♘xe6 fxe6 14 ♖xe6+ ♔d7 15 ♘h5] 7 ♗d5 f5 8 exf6 ♘xf6 9 ♗g5! [9 ♖e1+] 9 ... ♗e7 10 ♗xf6 ♗xf6 [10 ... gxf6 11 ♘g5! ♘e5 12 ♕h5+ ♘g6 13 ♗f7+ ♔f8 14 ♕h6#] 11 ♖e1+ ♘e7 12 ♘e5 ♗xe5 13 ♕h5+ g6 14 ♕xe5 ♖f8 15 ♘d2 c6 [□ 15 ... d6 16 ♕xd4 c6 17 ♗e6 ♗xe6 18 ♖xe6 d5 19 ♖ae1 ♖f7 20 ♘f3] 16 ♘c4 d6 17 ♘xd6+ ♔d7 18 ♗e6+ ♔c7 19 ♘xc8+ ♕d6 20 ♕xd6# **1-0** L/N3203

**1864-★DS-1**
**De Vere, C.– Steinitz, W.**
London [Bachmann]
1 e4 e5 2 ♘f3 ♘c6 3 ♗c4 ♗c5 4 c3 ♘f6 5 0-0 ♘xe4?! 6 d4 exd4 7 cxd4 ♗e7 8 d5 ♘d6 9 dxc6 ♘xc4 10 ♕d4 bxc6 11 ♕xg7 [□ 11 ♕xc4] 11 ... ♖f8 12 ♖e1 d5 13 ♗h6 ♗e6 14 ♘g5 [□ 14 ♘d4] 14 ... ♗xg5 15 ♗xg5 [□ 15 ♕xf8+] 15 ... ♕d6 16 f4 ♕c5+ 17 ♔h1 ♘e3 18 b3 [□ 18 ♘a3] 18 ... ♕c2 19 ♗h6 0-0-0 20 ♘a3 ♕d3! [20 ... ♕f2] 21 ♕g3 d4 22 ♗xf8 ♖xf8 23 ♘b1 ♗d5 24 a4 ♘xg2 25 ♔g1 ♘xe1 26 ♕xe1 ♖g8+ **0-1** L/N3131

**1864-★GM-1**
**Morphy, P.C.– Golmayo, C.**
Habana [Maróczy]
⟨♘b1⟩ 1 e4 e5 2 f4 exf4 3 ♘f3 g5 4 ♗c4 ♗g7 5 0-0 d6 6 c3 h6 7 ♕b3 ♕d7? [□ 7 ... ♘c6] 8 d4 ♘c6 9 ♕c2 ♘ge7 10 h4 g4 11 ♘h2 [11 ♘e1 f3 12 gxf3 g3∓] 11 ... g3 12 ♘f3 ♕g4 13 h5 ♕xh5 14 ♗xf4 ♘xd4 15 ♕d1 ♘xf3+ 16 ♖xf3 ♕h2+ 17 ♔f1 ♕h1+ 18 ♔e2 ♕xg2+ 19 ♔e1 ♗g4 **0-1** L/N3203

**1864-★GM-2 ●○⌂** 18 ii 64
**Morphy, P.C.+ Golmayo, C.**
Habana [Maróczy]
1 e4 e5 2 ♘f3 ♘c6 3 ♗c4 ♗c5 4 b4 ♗xb4 5 c3 ♗c5 6 0-0 d6 7 d4 exd4 8 cxd4 ♗b6 9 ♘c3 ♘f6? 10 e5 dxe5 11 ♗a3 ♗xd4 12 ♕b3 ♗e6 13 ♗xe6 fxe6 14 ♕xe6+ ♘e7 15 ♘xd4 exd4 16 ♖fe1 ♕d7 17 ♕xe7+ ♕xe7 18 ♖xe7+ ♔d8 19 ♖d1 b6 20 ♖xd4+ ♔c8 21 ♘b5! ♔b8 [21 ... c5 22 ♖c7+ ♔b8 23 ♖d6 ♖c8 24 ♖e7! ♖e8 25 ♖xe8+ ♘xe8 26 ♖d8+ ♔b7 28 ♖xe8+-] 22 ♖xc7 ♖e8 23 g3 a6 24 ♗d6 ♘e4 [24 ... axb5 25 ♖xg7+ ♔c8 26 ♖c7+ ♔b8 27 ♖xh7+ ♔c8 28 ♖c7+ ♔b8 29 ♖f7++-] 25 ♖xe4 ♖xe4 26 ♖e7+ ♔c8 27 ♖xe4 axb5 28 ♖e8+ ♔b7 29 ♖xa8 **1-0** L/N3203

**1864-★GN-1** xi 64
**Göhle, A.+ Neumann, G.R.**
Berlin [Anderssen & Neumann]
1 e4 e5 2 ♘f3 ♘c6 3 ♗c4 ♗c5 4 b4 ♗xb4 5 c3 ♗c5 6 0-0 d6 7 d4 exd4 8 cxd4 ♗b6 9 ♘c3 ♘a5 10 ♗d3 ♘e7 11 ♕c2 ♗g4 12 d5 ♘g6 13 e5 ♗xf3 14 gxf3 dxe5 [□ 14 ... ♘xe5 15 ♖fe1 0-0 16 ♗xh7+ ♔h8 17 ♗e4 f5] 15 f4 ♘xf4 16 ♗xf4 exf4 17 ♕a4+ c6 18 ♖ae1+ ♔f8 19 ♕b4+ ♔g8 20 ♕xf4 cxd5 21 ♘b5 ♕d7 22 ♖e2 a6 23 ♖fe1 ♗c5 [25 ... ♘c6 26 ♗f5 ♕d8 25 ♘d6 ♕f8 (25 ... g6 26 ♗xg6) 26 ♘xf7±] 24 ♘c7 ♖c8 25 ♖e8+ ♖xe8 26 ♖xe8+ ♗f8 27 ♗f5 ♕c6 28 ♗e6 ♕xe8 29 ♘xe8 fxe6 30 ♕c7 ♘c4 31 ♕d7 h5 32 ♕xe6+ ♔h7 33 ♕f7 ♔h6 34 h4 **1-0** L/N6051

**1864-★GN-2** xi 64
**Neumann, G.R.+ Göhle, A.**
Berlin [Anderssen & Neumann]
1 e4 e5 2 ♘f3 ♘c6 3 ♗c4 ♗c5 4 b4 ♗xb4 5 c3 ♗c5 6 0-0 d6 7 d4 exd4 8 cxd4 ♗b6 9 d5 ♘a5 10 ♗b2 f6 11 ♗d3 c5 12 ♘c3 ♗d7 13 ♘h4 ♘e7 14 ♕h5+ ♔f8 15 ♘e2 ♕e8 16 ♕f3 ♖c8 17 e5 dxe5 18 ♗xe5 ♘xd5 19 ♗d6+ ♘e7 20 ♘f4 ♖c6 21 ♗xe7+ ♔xe7! 22 ♖fe1+ ♗e6 23 ♗f5 ♘c4 24 ♗xe6 ♘e5 25 ♘f5+ ♔f8 26 ♖xe5 fxe5 27 ♘d6 **1-0** L/N6051

**1864-★GN-3** vii 64
**Neumann, G.R. & Treskow, E.+ Göhle, A. & Schallopp, E.**
Berlin [Anderssen & Neumann]
1 e4 e5 2 ♘f3 ♘c6 3 ♗b5 ♘f6 4 0-0 ♘xe4 5 d4 ♗e7 6 ♕e2 ♘d6 7 ♗xc6 bxc6! 8 dxe5 ♘b7 9 ♗e3 0-0 10 ♘c3 [□ 10 ♖d1] 10 ... d5 11 ♖ad1 ♕e8 12 ♘d4 c5 [□ 12 ... ♘c5; 12 ... ♔h8] 13 ♘db5 d4 14 ♘xc7 ♕c6 15 ♘3d5 ♗d8 16 ♕f3! ♔h8 17 ♘xa8 dxe3 18 ♕xe3! ♗e6 19 c4 ♕c8 [19 ... ♘a5 (19 ... ♗a5 20 b4) 20 b3] 20 f4 ♗g4 [□ 20 ... g6] 21 ♖d2 ♗a5? 22 ♖df2 f5? 23 exf6 gxf6 24 ♕e7 ♕xa8 25 ♘xf6 ♗f5 **1-0** L/N6051

**1864-★GN-4** vii 64
**Göhle, A. & Schallopp, E.+ Neumann, G.R.**
Berlin [Anderssen & Neumann]
1 e4 e5 2 ♘f3 ♘c6 3 ♗b5 ♘f6 4 d3 d6 5 ♗xc6+ bxc6 6 h3 ♗e7 7 0-0 0-0 8 ♘c3 c5 9 ♘e2 ♖b8 10 ♘g3 ♘e8 11 c3 f5 12 ♘xf5 ♗xf5 13 exf5 ♖xf5 14 ♘h2 d5 15 ♕a4! ♖b6 [15 ... ♕c8 16 ♕c6 d4 17 g4±; □ 15 ... ♖a8] 16 ♕xa7 h5 17 ♕a4 d4 18 c4 ♖e6 19 f3! ♗h4 20 ♗d2 ♗g3 21 ♗e1 ♗f4 22 ♔h1 [△ 22 ... ♕d6 23 g3] 22 ... h4 23 ♘g4 ♖h5 24 ♕c2 ♘d6 25 a4 ♘f5 26 a5 ♖a6! 27 ♕a4 ♖h8 [27 ... ♘g3+? 28 ♗xg3 hxg3 29 ♕b5 ♕a8! 30 ♕xc5] 28 ♕b5 ♕d6 29 b4 cxb4 30 ♗xb4 ♕e6 [30 ... ♕g6 31 ♖fd1] 31 ♖fb1 ♔h7 32 ♕b7 ♖c8 33 ♗c5 ♘g3+ 34 ♔g1 ♗d2 35 ♗b6 ♖aa8 36 ♗xc7 **1-0** L/N6051

**1864-★GN-5** 3 iii 64
**Neumann, G.R.+ Guretsky-Cornitz, B. v.**
Berlin [Anderssen & Neumann]
1 e4 e5 2 f4 d5 3 exd5 e4 4 ♗b5+ c6 5 dxc6 ♘xc6 6 ♗xc6+ bxc6 7 d4 ♘f6 8 ♘e2 ♗g4 9 c3 ♗d6 10 0-0 0-0 11 h3 ♗h5 12 g4 ♗xg4 13 hxg4 ♘xg4 14 ♕e1 f5 15 ♔g2 ♖f6 16 ♖h1 ♖g6 17 ♔f1 e3 18 ♕h4 ♕c7 19 ♕xh7+ ♔f7 20 ♕h5 ♗xf4 21 ♘a3 ♗g3 [21 ... ♘h2+] 22 ♘c4 ♖e8 23 b3 ♖e4 24 ♗a3 ♘h2+ 25 ♖xh2 ♗xh2 26 ♔e1 ♗g3+ 27 ♔d1 ♖h4 28 ♕f3 ♖h2 29 ♔c2 ♖f2 30 ♕h5 ♗f4 31 ♔d3 ♔f6 32 ♕h4+ ♗g5 33 ♕h1 f4 34 ♘d6 **1-0** L/N6051-1866

**1864-★GP-1 ●○⌂** 8 v 64
**Paulsen, L.– Göhle, A.**
Berlin [Anderssen & Neumann]
1 e4 e5 2 f4 ♗c5 3 ♘f3 d6 4 c3 ♗g4 5 ♗e2 ♘c6 6 d3 ♗b6? 7 ♘a3 ♕e7 8 ♘c4 ♘f6 9 ♘xb6 axb6 10 0-0 ♗xf3 11 ♗xf3 h6 12 d4 ♘h7 13 fxe5 dxe5 14 d5 ♘b8 15 ♗e3 ♘d7 16 ♗e2 0-0 17 ♗d3 ♖ad8 18 ♕e2 ♘c5 19 ♗c2 ♖d6 20 ♖f5 ♖g6 21 ♖af1 ♘d7 22 ♗b3 ♘hf6 23 ♗c1 [□ 23 ♕d3] 23 ... ♘e8 24 ♖xf7? ♖xf7 25 ♖xf7 ♕xf7 26 d6 ♖e6 27 ♕g4 ♘c5 28 ♗xe6 ♕xe6 29 ♕xe6+ ♘xe6 30 dxc7 ♘8xc7 31 ♔f2 ♘e8 32 b4 ♘d6 33 ♔f3 ♘c4 34 a4 ♔f7 35 h4 ♘c7 36 g4 ♘e8 37 g5 ♔g6 38 ♔e2 ♘ed6 39 ♔d3 ♔h5 40 b5

♔g6 41 gxh6 gxh6 42 ♗e3 ♘xe3 43 ♔xe3 ♔h5 44 ♔d3 ♔xh4 45 c4 ♔g3 46 c5 bxc5 47 a5 ♘xb5 48 ♔c4 ♘d6+ 49 ♔xc5 ♘c8 50 ♔d5 ♔f4 51 ♔e6 ♘a7 52 ♔d7 ♘c6 53 a6 bxa6 54 ♔xc6 h5 55 ♔b6 h4 56 ♔xa6 h3 **0-1** L/N6051

### 1864-★GP-2 — 8 v 64

**Guretsky-Cornitz,B.v.+ Paulsen, L.**

Berlin [Anderssen & Neumann]

1 e4 e5 2 ♘f3 ♘c6 3 ♗c4 ♗c5 4 b4 ♗xb4 5 c3 ♗a5 6 d4 exd4 7 0-0 d6 8 cxd4 ♗b6 9 ♘c3 ♘a5! 10 ♘g5 [□ 10 ♗d3] 10 ... ♘h6! 11 ♗e3 0-0 12 ♗e2 f5 13 f4 fxe4 14 ♘cxe4 ♘f5 15 ♕d3 d5 16 ♘d2 ♘c4 [□ 16 ... ♖e8] 17 ♘xc4 dxc4 18 ♕e4! h6 19 ♗xc4+ ♔h8 20 ♘f3 [20 ♘f7+ ♖xf7 21 ♗xf7 ♘xe3] 20 ... ♖e8 21 ♘e5 ♗xd4 [□ 21 ... ♖xe5 22 fxe5 ♘xe3 23 ♕xe3 (23 ♗d3 ♘f5 24 ♖xf5 ♕xd4+) 23 ... ♗xd4 24 ♖f8+ ♕xf8 25 ♕xd4 ♗e6] 22 ♖ae1 ♗xe5 23 fxe5 ♘d6 24 ♕g6 ♘xc4 25 ♗xh6 **1-0** L/N6051

### 1864-★HK-1 — xi 64

**Kolisch,I.F.von+ Hirschfeld,P.**

Paris

1 e4 e5 2 ♘f3 ♘c6 3 ♗c4 ♗c5 4 b4 ♗xb4 5 c3 ♗c5 6 0-0 d6 7 d4 exd4 8 cxd4 ♗b6 9 ♘c3 ♗g4 10 ♕a4 ♗d7 11 ♕b3 ♘a5 12 ♗xf7+ ♔f8 13 ♕c2 ♔xf7 14 e5 h6 15 d5 ♗g4 16 e6+ ♗xe6 17 dxe6+ ♔xe6 18 ♕g6+ ♕f6 19 ♖e1+ ♔d7 20 ♕g4+ ♔d8 21 ♘d5 ♕f7 22 ♗g5+ hxg5 23 ♘xg5 ♕h5 24 ♘e6+ ♔d7 25 ♘f8+ ♔c6 26 ♘b4+ ♔c5 27 ♘d7+ ♔b5 28 a4# **1-0** M954-1865

### 1864-★HK-2 — xi 64

**Hirschfeld,P.-Kolisch,I.F. von**

Paris

1 e4 e5 2 ♘f3 ♘c6 3 ♗c4 ♘f6 4 ♘g5 d5 5 exd5 ♘a5 6 ♗b5+ c6 7 dxc6 bxc6 8 ♗e2 h6 9 ♘f3 e4 10 ♘e5 ♕d4 11 f4 ♗c5 12 ♖f1 ♗d6 13 c3 ♕b6 14 b4 ♘b7 15 ♕a4 ♘d8 16 ♘a3 ♗e6 17 ♘ac4 ♗xc4 18 ♗xc4 0-0 19 d4 exd3 20 ♘xd3 ♖e8+ 21 ♔d1 ♘e4 22 ♔c2 ♕c7 23 g3 a5 24 bxa5 ♖xa5 25 ♕b3 ♘b7 26 ♖b1 ♘ec5 27 ♘xc5 ♘bxc5 28 ♕b6 ♕d7 29 ♕xa5 ♕f5+ 30 ♔d1 ♕xb1 31 ♕a7 ♖d8 32 ♕xf7+ ♔h8 33 ♔e2 ♕e4+ 34 ♔f2 ♘d3+ 35 ♗xd3 ♗c5+ 36 ♗e3 ♗xe3+ **0-1** L/N6047-1865

### 1864-★HK-3 — xi 64

**Hirschfeld,P.+Kolisch,I.F. von**

Paris

1 e4 e5 2 ♘f3 ♘c6 3 ♗c4 ♘f6 4 ♘g5 d5 5 exd5 ♘a5 6 ♗b5+ c6 7 dxc6 bxc6 8 ♗e2 h6 9 ♘f3 e4 10 ♘e5 ♕d4 11 f4 ♗c5 12 ♖f1 ♕d6 13 c3 ♘b7 14 ♕a4 ♘d8 15 b4 ♗b6 16 ♘a3 ♗e6 17 ♘ac4 ♗xc4 18 ♗xc4 0-0 19 ♗a3 ♘d5 20 b5 c5 21 g3 ♔h7 22 0-0-0 f5 23 ♕b3 ♘f6 24 d4 ♕c7 25 ♗e6 g6 26 g4 ♘xe6 27 ♕xe6 fxg4 28 f5 g5 29 dxc5 ♖ae8 30 ♖d7+ ♘xd7 31 ♕g6+ ♔h8 32 ♕xh6+ ♔g8 33 ♕xg5+ ♔h7 34 ♕h5+ ♔g7 35 ♕xg4+ ♔f6 36 ♕g6+ ♔xe5 37 ♕g7+ ♖f6 **1-0** L/N6047-1865

### 1864-★HN-1 — ix 64

**Neumann, G.R.+Henoch**

Berlin [Anderssen & Neumann]

⟨♘b1⟩ 1 e4 e5 2 f4 exf4 3 ♘f3 g5 4 ♗c4 ♗g7 5 d4 g4 [□ 5 ... d6] 6 0-0 gxf3 7 ♕xf3 ♗xd4+ 8 ♔h1 ♗e5 9 ♗xf7+ ♔f8 [9 ... ♔xf7 10 ♕h5+ ♔e6 11 ♕f5+ ♔d6 12 ♗xf4 ♗xf4 13 ♕d5+ ♔e7 14 ♖xf4 ♕e8 15 ♖af1+-] 10 ♗xf4 ♗xf4 11 ♗xg8 ♔xg8 12 ♕xf4

12 ... ♕e7 13 ♕g4+ ♕g7 14 ♕h5 ♕g6 [14 ... h6 15 ♕d5+ ♔h7 16 ♖f7] 15 ♕d5+ ♕e6 [15 ... ♔g7 16 ♕e5+ ♔g8 (16 ... ♔h6 17 ♕xh8 △ 18 ♖f6) 17 ♕e7] 16 ♕g5+ ♕g6 17 ♕e7 **1-0** L/N6051-1865

### 1864-★HP-1 — 8 v 64

**Helmersen, von-Paulsen, L.**

Berlin [Anderssen & Neumann]

1 e4 e5 2 ♘f3 d6 3 d4 f5 4 ♘c3 fxe4 5 ♘xe4 d5 6 ♘g3 e4 7 ♘e5 ♘f6 8 ♗g5 ♗d6 9 f3 0-0 10 ♗e2 ♕e8 11 f4 c5 12 c3 cxd4 13 ♗xf6 [□ 13 cxd4 ♗b4+ 14 ♔f2] 13 ... gxf6! 14 ♗h5 ♕e7 15 ♘g4 ♗xf4 16 ♕xd4 ♗e6 17 ♖f1 ♘c6 18 ♕f2 ♗g5 19 ♘f5 ♗xf5 20 ♕xf5 ♘e5 21 ♘xe5 fxe5 22 ♕g4 ♔h8 23 g3 ♗h6 24 b4 a5 25 ♖d1? axb4 26 ♖xf8+ ♖xf8 27 ♖xd5 bxc3 28 ♕xe4 ♕f6!

29 ♕xe5 [29 ♕e2 c2-+] 29 ... ♕xe5+ 30 ♖xe5 c2 **0-1** L/N6051

### 1864-★KM-1

**Maczuski,L.+Kolisch,I.F. von**

Paris

1 e4 e5 2 ♘f3 ♘c6 3 d4 exd4 4 ♘xd4 ♕h4 5 ♘c3 ♗b4 6 ♕d3 ♘f6 7 ♘xc6 dxc6 8 ♗d2 ♗xc3 9 ♗xc3 ♘xe4 10 ♕d4 ♕e7 11 0-0-0 ♕g5+ 12 f4 ♕xf4+ 13 ♗d2 ♕g4 14 ♕d8+

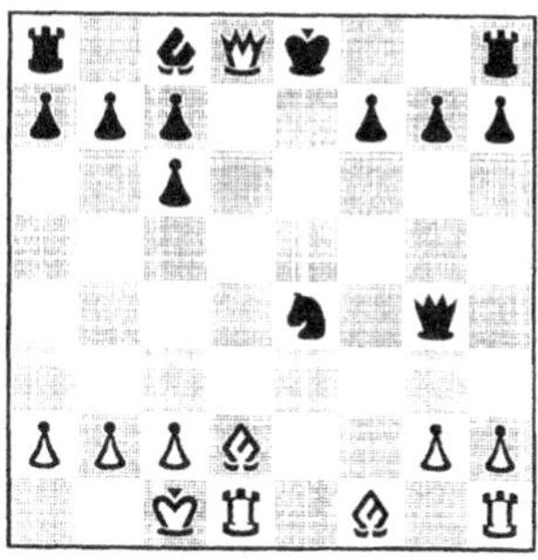

14 ... ♔xd8 15 ♗g5+ ♔e8 16 ♖d8# **1-0** L/N6047-1864

### 1864-★KN-1 — 6 ix 64

**Neumann, G.R.+Kähler**

Berlin [Anderssen & Neumann]

1 e4 e5 2 ♘f3 ♘c6 3 ♗c4 ♗e7 4 d4 d6 5 d5 ♘b8 [△ 6 ... f5] 6 ♗d3 ♘f6 7 0-0 ♗g4 8 c4 0-0 9 ♘c3 ♘bd7 10 ♗e3± b6 11 h3 ♗xf3 12 ♕xf3 ♘c5 13 ♗c2 a5 14 ♕e2 ♕c8 15 f4 exf4 16 ♗xf4 ♘e8 17 e5 dxe5 18 ♗xe5 f5? 19 ♗xg7 ♘xg7 20 ♕xe7 ♖f7 21 ♕g5 ♔h8 22 ♖ae1 ♕d7 23 ♖e5 ♖af8 24 ♖fe1 ♕d6 25 ♘b5 ♕g6 26 ♕xg6 hxg6 27 ♖e7 ♘h5? 28 ♘xc7 **1-0** L/N6051-1865

### 1864-★KN-2 — ii 64

**Neumann, G.R.+Knorre, V.**

Berlin [Anderssen & Neumann]

1 e4 e5 2 ♘f3 ♘c6 3 ♗c4 ♗c5 4 b4 ♗xb4 5 c3 ♗c5 6 0-0 d6 7 d4 exd4 8 cxd4 ♗b6 9 ♘c3 ♗g4 10 ♗b5 ♔f8 11 ♗xc6 bxc6 12 e5 c5 13 ♗a3 cxd4 14 ♘e4 f5 15 exd6

cxd6 16 ♘xd6 ♘ge7 17 ♖e1 ♖b8 18 ♕b3 ♗h5 19 ♕e6 **1-0** L/N6051

**1864-★KN-3** xiii 64
**Knorre, V.+ Neumann, G.R.**
Berlin [Anderssen & Neumann]
1 e4 e5 2 ♘f3 ♘c6 3 ♗b5 ♘f6 4 d3 ♗d6 [□ 4 ... d6] 5 ♗g5 h6 6 ♗h4 a6 7 ♗xc6 dxc6 8 0-0 g5 9 ♗g3 ♗g4 10 ♘bd2 h5? [□ 10 ... ♕e7, 11 ... 0-0-0] 11 ♕e1 ♗xf3 12 ♘xf3 ♘d7 13 d4 f6 14 dxe5 fxe5 15 ♕c3 ♕f6 16 h4 g4 17 ♘g5 0-0-0 18 ♖ad1 ♖de8 19 f4 ♕e7 20 fxe5 ♘xe5 [△ 21 ... ♘f3+] 21 ♔h1 ♖hg8 22 ♖f5 [△ 23 ♗xe5 ♗xe5 24 ♖xe5 ♕xe5 25 ♖d8++-] 22 ... ♔b8 [□ 22 ... ♖g7; 22 ... ♘g6 23 e5] 23 ♗xe5 ♗xe5 24 ♖xe5 ♕xe5 25 ♖d8+ ♔a7 26 ♕xe5 ♖xe5 27 ♖xg8 **1-0** L/N6051

**1864-★KP-1 ●○** 8 v 64
**Kähler+ Paulsen, L.**
Berlin [Anderssen & Neumann]
1 e4 e5 2 ♘f3 ♘c6 3 ♗c4 ♗c5 4 c3 ♘f6 5 0-0 ♘xe4 6 ♗d5 ♘f6 7 ♗xc6 dxc6 8 ♘xe5 0-0 9 d4 ♗d6 10 ♕c2 c5 11 ♗g5 cxd4 [□ 11 ... h6] 12 cxd4 c5 13 ♖d1! cxd4 [13 ... h6 14 dxc5] 14 ♖xd4 ♕b6 15 ♖h4 ♕c7 16 ♘c3 ♗xe5 17 ♗xf6 g6? [□ 17 ... h6] 18 ♘d5 ♗f5 19 ♕xc7 **1-0** L/N6051

**1864-★KP-2 ●○** 8 v 64
**Knorre, V.+ Paulsen, L.**
Berlin [Anderssen & Neumann]
1 e4 e5 2 ♘f3 ♘c6 3 ♗b5 a6 4 ♗a4 ♘f6 5 0-0 ♗e7 6 ♖e1 d6 7 ♗xc6+ bxc6 8 ♘c3 0-0 9 d4 exd4 10 ♘xd4 ♕d7 [□ 10 ... ♗d7 Paulsen] 11 ♘f5 ♗d8 12 ♕e2 ♔h8 [△ 13 ... ♘xe4] 13 ♘g3 ♗b7 14 b3 ♘g8 15 e5 ♘e7 16 ♘ce4 ♘g6 17 f4 f5 18 ♘f2 dxe5 19 fxe5 ♘xe5 20 ♗b2 ♘g6 21 ♖ad1 ♕f7 22 ♘h5 ♗f6 23 ♘xf6 gxf6 24 ♕e6 c5 25 ♖d7 ♖ae8 26 ♕xf6+ ♕xf6 27 ♗xf6+ ♖xf6 28 ♖xe8+ ♘f8 29 ♖xc7 ♗d5 30 ♖xc5 ♗g8 31 ♘d3 ♔g7 32 ♖c7+ ♔h8 33 ♖cc8 ♔g7 34 ♘f4 ♖f7 35 ♘h5+ **1-0** L/N6051

**1864-★LP-1 ●○** 8 v 64
**Paulsen, L.= Lichtenstein, A.**
Berlin [Anderssen & Neumann]
1 e4 e6 2 d4 d5 3 ♘c3 ♗b4! 4 exd5 exd5 5 ♘f3 h6? 6 ♗d3 ♘f6 7 0-0 0-0 8 ♘e2 ♗d6 9 ♘g3 ♗e6 10 ♘e5 c5 11 c3 ♕c7 12 f4 ♘c6 13 ♘xc6 bxc6 14 dxc5 ♗xc5+ 15 ♔h1 ♗g4 16 ♕c2 ♖fe8 17 ♗d2 ♖e7 18 ♖ae1 ♖ae8 19 ♖xe7 ♖xe7 20 ♗c1 ♗e3 21 h3 ♗c8 22 ♖f3 ♗xc1 23 ♕xc1 c5 24 ♔h2 c4 25 ♗b1 ♘e4 26 ♕c2 f5 27 ♘e2 g6 28 ♘d4 ♘g5 29 ♖f1 ♘e4

**1864-★LP-2 ●○** 8 v 64
**Paulsen, L.= Lindner**
Berlin [Anderssen & Neumann]
1 e4 b6 2 d4 ♗b7 3 ♘c3 e6 4 ♗d3 ♘f6 5 ♘ge2 c5 6 ♗e3 cxd4 7 ♘xd4 ♗b4 8 ♗g5 h6 9 ♗xf6 ♕xf6 10 ♘b5 ♘a6 [□ 10 ... 0-0 △ 11 ♘c7? ♗xc3+] 11 0-0 0-0 12 ♕h5 d6 13 f4 ♗xc3 14 bxc3 ♕e7 15 e5 dxe5 16 fxe5 ♘c5 17 ♘d6 ♕g5! 18 ♕e2 ♗c6 19 ♖f2 ♘b7 20 ♘c4 ♖ad8 21 ♘d2 ♘c5 22 ♘f3 ♕h5 23 ♖af1 f5 24 exf6 ♖xf6 25 ♕e1 [△ 26 ♘d4] 25 ... ♖xd3 **½-½** L/N6051

**1864-★LP-3**
**Paulsen, L.+Lemke& Seifert**
1 e4 e5 2 ♘f3 ♘c6 3 ♗c4 ♗c5 4 b4 ♗xb4 5 c3 ♗a5 6 d4 exd4 7 0-0 d6 8 cxd4 ♗b6 9 ♘c3 ♘a5 10 ♗d3 ♘e7 11 ♘d5 ♘xd5 12 exd5 0-0 13 ♘g5 h6 14 ♕h5 ♗xd4 15 ♖ab1 c6 16 ♘f3 ♕f6 17 ♗g5 ♗xf2+ 18 ♖xf2 ♕c3 19 ♗c2 ♘c4 20 ♖c1 ♕a3 21 ♗xh6 gxh6 22 ♕xh6 f5 23 ♖e1 ♘e5 24 ♘g5 ♖f7 25 ♖xe5 **1-0** L/N6047-1864

**1864-★LP-4**
**Lepge, C.− Paulsen, L.**
Leipzig [Minckwitz & von Schmidt]
1 e4 e5 2 ♘f3 ♘c6 3 ♗b5 ♘f6 4 0-0 ♗e7 5 ♘c3 ♘d4 6 ♗c4 d6 7 h3 ♗e6 8 ♗b3 0-0 9 d3 ♘xb3 10 axb3 ♘d7 11 d4 exd4 12 ♘xd4 c5 13 ♘de2 a6 14 ♘g3 ♘b6 15 f4 ♗h4 16 ♕f3 ♗xg3 17 ♕xg3 f5 18 ♗e3 fxe4 19 ♖ad1 ♖f5 20 ♘xe4 ♗d5 21 ♘c3 ♕f8 22 ♖d2 ♗c6 23 ♕f2 ♖e8 24 ♖fd1 ♖f6 25 f5? ♖xf5 26 ♕g3 d5 27 ♘a4 ♗xa4 28 bxa4 ♘c4 **0-1** L/N6047-1864

**1864-★LZ-1 ●** 31 viii 64
**Zukertort, J.H.+Lehmann, F.& Waldstein, L.**
Posen [Anderssen & Neumann]
1 e4 c6 2 d4 d5 3 e5 f6 4 f4 e6 5 ♘f3 c5 6 c3 ♘c6 7 ♗e3 cxd4 8 cxd4 ♗b4+ 9 ♘c3 ♗d7 10 ♗d3 ♘ge7 11 a3 ♗xc3+ 12 bxc3 fxe5 [□ 12 ... f5] 13 fxe5 0-0 14 ♕c2 ♘f5 15 ♗g5 ♕a5 16 0-0 ♖ac8 17 ♗d2 ♘cxd4? 18 ♘xd4 ♕b6 [18 ... ♘xd4 19 ♗xh7+ ♔h8 20 ♖xf8+ ♖xf8 21 cxd4] 19 ♗xf5 exf5 20 ♗e3 f4 21 ♗f2 ♕h6 22 ♖ae1 f3 23 ♗e3 ♕h4 24 ♘xf3 ♖xf3 25 gxf3 d4 26 ♕a2+! ♔h8 27 ♗xd4 ♗h3 28 ♖f2 ♖f8 29 ♕d2 ♖f5 30 e6 ♖g5+ 31 ♔h1 ♕h5 32 e7 ♗d7 33 ♕xg5! **1-0** L/N6051-1867

**1864-★LZ-2 ●○** 21 v 64
**Zukertort, J.H.+ Löwinsohn**
Posen [Anderssen & Zukertort]
1 e4 e5 2 ♘f3 ♘c6 3 ♗c4 ♗c5 4 0-0 ♘h6? 5 c3 ♕f6 6 d4 exd4 7 e5 ♕g6 8 cxd4 ♗e7 9 ♘c3 0-0 10 ♗d3 ♕h5 11 ♗xh7+! ♔h8 [11 ... ♔xh7 12 ♘g5+ ♕g6 13 ♕d3+ ♘f5 (13 ... f5 14 exf6+ ♔xf6 15 ♘d5#) 14 f3, 15 g4+-] 12 ♗c2 f6 13 ♕d3 ♘g8 14 ♘e4 ♘b4 15 ♕c3 ♘d5 [□ 15 ... ♘xc2] 16 ♕b3 c6 17 ♘g3 ♕f7 18 ♕d3 g5 19 exf6 ♗xf6 20 ♗xg5 ♘b4 21 ♕e4 ♘xc2 22 ♕xc2 d6 23 ♖ae1 ♗e6 24 ♖e4! ♔g7 25 ♖h4! ♕g6 26 ♘h5+ ♔f7 27 ♕d2 [□ 27 ♕xg6+ ♔xg6 28 ♘f4+ ♔f7 (28 ... ♔f5 29 g4+ ♔e4 30 ♖e1+ ♔xf3 31 ♖e3#) 29 ♖h7+ ♗g7 30 ♖xg7+ ♔xg7 31 ♘xe6++-] 27 ... ♔e8 28 ♖e1 ♔d7 29 ♖xe6! **1-0** L/N6051-1868

**1864-★MM-1**
**Morphy, P.C.+ Medina, A.**
Habana [Maróczy]
⟨♘b1⟩ 1 e4 e6 2 f4 d5 3 e5 ♗c5 4 d4 ♗b6 5 ♗e3 ♘e7 6 ♘f3 ♘f5 7 ♗f2 ♕e7 8 c3 c5 9 g4 ♘h6 10 ♗h4 ♕c7 11 h3 ♘c6 12 ♗e2 cxd4 13 cxd4 ♗a5+ 14 ♔f2 ♗d7 15 a3 ♕c8 [15 ... ♕b8] 16 b4 ♗d8 17 ♗g3 ♗b6 [□ 17 ... 0-0 △ f6] 18 ♖c1 ♕d8 19 ♔g2 f6 20 ♗h4 ♕e7 [□ 20 ... ♘f7] 21 ♖hf1 ♕f7 22 ♔h2 ♘g8 [□ 22 ... 0-0] 23 ♕d2 ♘ge7 24 g5 f5 25 g6 ♘xg6 [□ 25 ... hxg6] 26 ♘g5 ♕g8 27 ♗h5 ♔f8 28 ♖xc6! bxc6 29 b5 c5 30 dxc5 ♗xc5 31 ♖c1 ♗e7 32 ♖c7 ♗e8 33 ♗xg6 hxg6 34 ♖xe7 ♖xh4 35 ♕b4 ♖xh3+ 36 ♘xh3 **1-0** L/N3203

**1864-★MM-2** 9 v 64
**Morphy, P.C.− Maurian, C.A.**
New Orleans
⟨♘b1⟩ 1 e4 e5 2 ♘f3 ♘c6 3 ♗c4 ♗c5 4 b4 ♗xb4 5 c3 ♗c5 6 0-0 d6 7 d4 exd4 8 cxd4 ♗b6 9 ♗b2 ♗g4 10 ♗b5 ♔f8 11 ♗xc6 bxc6 12 h3 h5 13 ♕d3 ♗xf3 14 ♕xf3 ♖h6 15 a4 a5 16 ♖ac1 ♘e7 17 ♕e3 f5 18 ♕g5 fxe4 19 ♖fe1 ♘d5 20 ♕f5+ ♘f6 21 ♖xe4 ♕d7 22 ♖e6 ♕f7 23 d5 ♘xd5 24 ♗xg7+ ♔xg7 25 ♕xf7+ ♔xf7 26 ♖xh6 ♘f6 27 g4 hxg4 28 hxg4 ♘xg4 29 ♖h7+ ♔g6 30 ♖h3 ♗xf2+ **0-1** +13

**1864-★MS-1 ●○** 16 ii 46
**Morphy, P.C.+ Sicre, F.**
Habana [Maróczy]
1 e4 e5 2 ♘f3 d6 3 d4 exd4 4 ♗c4 h6? 5 c3 c6 6 0-0 dxc3 7 ♕b3 ♕c7 8 ♘xc3 g5 9 ♗e3 ♗g7 10 ♖ac1! ♗xc3 11 ♕xc3 ♖h7 12 e5 ♘d7 13 ♗d3 ♘f8 14 exd6 ♕d8 [14 ... ♕xd6 15 ♗c5, 16 ♗xf8, 17 ♗xh7+-]

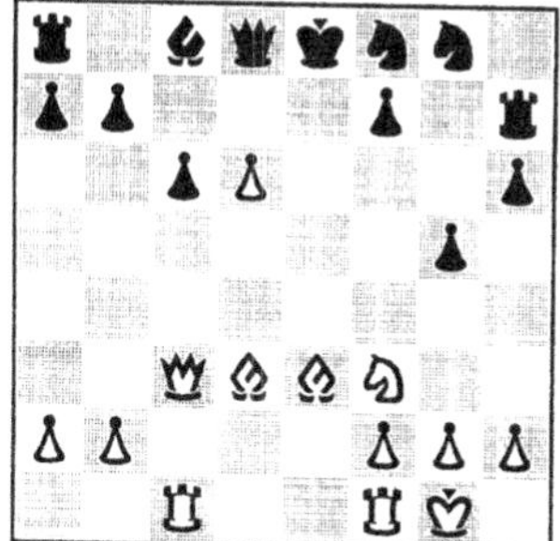

15 ♖fe1 ♗e6 16 ♘e5 ♘f6 17 ♗xh7 ♘8xh7 18 ♗c5 ♘d7 19 ♘g4 b6 20 ♕g7 ♘hf8 21 ♗d4 [△ 22 ♗f6 ♘xf6 23 ♘xf6+−; 22 ♗f6 ♔c8 23 ♖xe6+, 24 ♕e7#] **1-0** L/N3203

**1864-★MN-1** xi 64
**Mayet, K.− Neumann, G.R.**
Berlin [Anderssen & Neumann]

1 e4 e5 2 f4 exf4 3 ♗c4 f5 4 ♕h5+ g6 5 ♕e2 fxe4 6 ♕xe4+ ♕e7 7 ♘c3 c6 8 ♗xg8 ♖xg8 9 d3 g5 10 h4 h6 11 hxg5 hxg5 12 ♗d2 d5 13 ♕e2 ♗g4 14 ♘f3 ♘d7 15 0-0-0 ♕xe2 16 ♘xe2 0-0-0 17 ♖de1 ♗d6 18 ♘ed4 ♗xf3 19 gxf3 ♘e5 20 ♖ef1 ♖h8 21 ♔d1 ♔d7 22 ♖hg1 ♖hg8 23 ♖g2 c5 24 ♘b5 a6 25 ♘xd6 ♔xd6 26 ♔e2 ♖de8 27 ♔f2 ♔e6 28 ♖fg1 ♔f5 29 ♗a5 [□ 29 ♖h1 g4] 29 ... ♖e6 30 ♗d2 ♖h6 **0-1** L/N6051-1865

**1864-★MP-1** v 64
**Paulsen, L.+ Mayet, K.**
Berlin [Anderssen & Neumann]

1 e4 e5 2 ♘f3 ♘c6 3 d4 exd4 4 ♘xd4 ♗c5 5 ♗e3 ♕f6 6 c3 a6? 7 ♗c4 ♕g6 8 0-0 ♘e5 [8 ... ♕xe4? 9 ♗xf7+ ♔xf7 10 ♕h5+] 9 ♗d3 d6 10 f3 ♗d7 11 b4 ♗b6 12 ♘a3 ♘e7 13 ♘ac2 c5 14 ♘f5 ♘7c6 [14 ... ♘xd3; 14 ... c4 15 ♘xe7] 15 bxc5 dxc5 16 ♖b1 ♘xd3 17 ♕xd3 0-0-0 18 ♘d6+ ♔c7 19 ♖xb6!

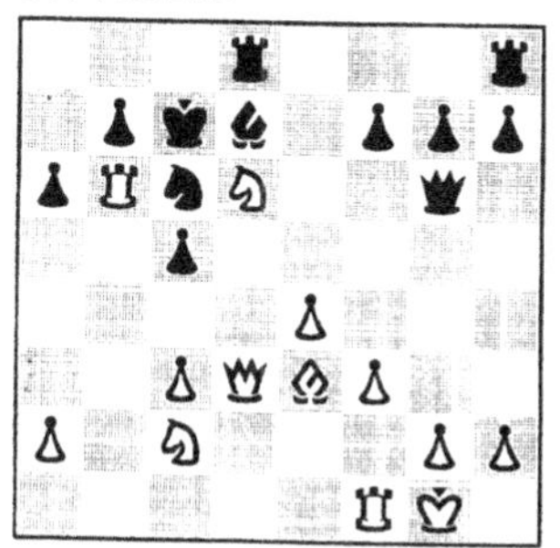

19 ... ♗c8 [19 ... ♕xd6 20 ♖xb7+; 19 ... ♔xb6 20 ♖b1+] 20 ♖xc6+ bxc6 21 ♗f4 ♖xd6 22 ♖d1 ♖hd8 23 ♘e3 ♕f6 24 ♗g3 ♕g6 [△ 25 ... ♕xg3] 25 ♕e2 ♔b7? 26 ♖b1+ ♔c7 [26 ... ♔a7; 26 ... ♔a8 27 ♕b2+−] 27 ♘c4 f5 28 ♘xd6 ♖xd6 29 exf5 ♗xf5 30 ♕e7+ ♗d7 31 ♗xd6+ **1-0** L/N6051-1865

**1864-★NP-1** 1 v 64
**Neumann, G.R.= Paulsen, L.**
Berlin [Anderssen & Neumann]

1 e4 e5 2 ♘f3 ♘c6 3 ♗b5 ♘f6 4 0-0 ♗e7 5 ♘c3 ♘d4 6 ♘xd4 exd4 7 e5 dxc3 8 exf6 ♗xf6 [8 ... cxb2 9 ♗xb2 ♗xf6 10 ♖e1+ ♔f8 11 ♗a3+ ♔g8 12 ♖b1±] 9 ♖e1+ ♗e7 10 dxc3 0-0 11 ♗f4 d5 12 ♕f3 ♗d6 13 ♖ad1 c6 14 ♗d3 ♗e6 15 ♕h5 g6 16 ♕h6 ♗xf4 17 ♕xf4 ♕d7 18 ♕f6 ♖ae8 19 h3 ♕d8 20 ♕xd8 ♖xd8 21 f4 ♖de8 22 g4 f5 23 g5 ♗d7 24 ♔f2 ♔f7 25 h4 ♖xe1 26 ♖xe1 h5 **½-½** L/N6051

**1864-★NP-2** 8 ix 64
**Posse, L.− Neumann, G.R.**
Berlin [Anderssen & Neumann]

1 e4 e5 2 ♘f3 ♘c6 3 ♗c4 ♗c5 4 0-0 ♘f6 5 d4 ♗xd4 6 ♘xd4 ♘xd4 7 f4 d6 8 fxe5 dxe5 9 ♗g5 ♗e6! 10 ♗xf6 gxf6 11 ♗xe6 ♘xe6 12 ♕xd8+ ♖xd8 13 ♖xf6 ♖d1+ 14 ♖f1 ♖xf1+ 15 ♔xf1 ♘d4 [□ 15 ... f5] 16 ♘a3 f5 17 c3 ♘c6 18 exf5 ♖f8 19 ♖d1 [19 g4 ♖g8! 20 h3 h5] 19 ... ♖xf5+ 20 ♔g1 a6 21 ♘c2 ♖f7 22 ♖f1 ♖xf1+ 23 ♔xf1 ♔e7 24 ♔f2 ♔e6 25 g4 ♘d8 26 ♔f3 ♘f7 27 h4 ♘d6 28 ♘e3 c6 29 g5 ♘f5 30 h5? [□ 30 ♘g2] 30 ... ♘xe3 31 ♔xe3 ♔f5 32 g6 hxg6 33 h6 ♔f6 34 h7 ♔g7 35 ♔e4 ♔xh7 36 ♔xe5 ♔h6 **0-1** L/N6051-1865

**1864-★NR-1** x 64
**Neumann, G.R.+ Rivière, J.A.de**
Berlin [Anderssen & Neumann]

1 e4 e5 2 f4 exf4 3 ♗c4 ♘f6 4 ♘c3 d5 5 ♗xd5 ♗b4 6 ♘f3 0-0 7 0-0 c6 [7 ... ♗xc3 8 dxc3!] 8 ♗b3 ♗g4 9 d3 ♘h5 [10 ... ♗xf3 11 ♕xf3 ♕d4+ 12 ♔h1 ♗xc3 13 bxc3 ♕xc3 14 ♗xf4±] 10 d4 g5 11 e5 ♘a6 12 ♘e4 ♗e7 13 c3 ♔h8? 14 ♗xf7 ♖xf7 15 ♘fxg5 ♕d7 [15 ... ♗xd1 16 ♘xf7+±] 16 e6 ♗xe6 17 ♕xh5 ♗xg5 18 ♘xg5 ♖f5 19 ♗xf4 ♗c4 20 ♗e5+ ♔g8 21 ♖xf5 ♕xf5 22 ♕h6 ♕g6! 23 ♕h4 ♖f8 24 ♘e4 ♗d3 25 ♘f6+ ♔f7 26 ♖e1 ♘c7 27 ♗d6+− ♘e6 28 ♗xf8 ♘xf8 29 ♘g4 ♔g8 30 ♘h6+ ♔h8 31 ♖e8 ♔g7! 32 ♖e7+ ♔h8 33 ♕f4 **1-0** L/N6051

**1864-★NR-2** x 64
**Rivière, J.A.de− Neumann, G.R.**
Berlin [Anderssen & Neumann]

1 e4 e5 2 ♘f3 ♘c6 3 c3 ♘f6 [□ 3 ... f5; 3 ... d5?!] 4 ♗c4 [□ 4 d4] 4 ... ♘xe4 5 0-0 d5 6 ♗b5 ♗d6 7 d3 ♘f6 8 ♘xe5 ♗xe5 9 ♖e1? [□ 9 ♗xc6+] 9 ... 0-0 10 ♗xc6 ♗xh2+ 11 ♔xh2 bxc6 12 ♗f4 ♖b8 13 ♘d2 ♖xb2 14 ♕c1 ♖b6 15 ♘b3 c5 16 ♘xc5 ♘g4+ 17 ♔g1 ♕h4 18 ♗g3 ♕h5 19 f3 ♖h6 20 fxg4 ♕h1+ 21 ♔f2 ♖f6+ 22 ♗f4 [22 ♔e3 ♕xg2 23 ♖g1 d4+−+] 22 ... ♕h2 23 ♖e3 ♖xf4+ 24 ♖f3 ♖xf3+ 25 ♔xf3 f5 26 g5 f4 27 ♕g1 ♗g4+ 28 ♔f2 [28 ♔xg4 ♕g3+−+] 28 ... ♕g3+ 29 ♔f1 f3 **0-1** L/N6051

**1864-★NR-3** x 64
**Rivière, J.A.de+ Neumann, G.R.**
Berlin [Anderssen & Neumann]

1 e4 e5 2 ♘f3 ♘c6 3 ♗c4 ♗c5 4 b4 ♗xb4 5 c3 ♗c5 6 0-0 d6 7 d4 exd4 8 cxd4 ♗b6 9 ♘c3 ♘a5! 10 ♗d3 ♘e7 11 ♘a4 [11 e5 d5] 11 ... 0-0 12 ♘xb6 axb6 13 ♗b2 ♘g6 14 ♖c1 c5 15 ♘d2 [15 d5 f6∓] 15 ... f6 [□ 15 ... f5] 16 f4 f5 17 ♕c2 ♕h4 [17 ... ♕e7] 18 g3 ♕g4 19 e5 dxe5 20 dxe5 ♗e6 21 ♘c4 ♘xc4 22 ♗xc4 ♖fe8 23 ♗xe6+ ♖xe6 24 ♕c4 ♘f8 25 ♖cd1 ♕g6 26 ♖d6 ♕f7 27 ♖fd1 ♖xd6 28 ♕xf7+ ♔xf7 29 ♖xd6

29 ... ♖a6 [□ 29 ... ♖xa2] 30 a3 b5 31 ♖d5 ♖c6 32 ♔f2 ♔e7 33 ♔e3 ♘d7 34 ♗c1 ♘b6 35 ♖d3 ♔e6 36 ♖d8 ♘d5+ 37 ♔d3 b4 38 ♔c4 ♘c7 39 a4 ♔e7 40 ♖g8 ♘e8 41 ♗e3 ♔f7 [41 ... b6 42 a5 (42 ♔b5 b3 43 ♗c1 ♖h6 44 ♔c4! ♖xh2 45 ♔xb3 ♖g2−+) 42 ... bxa5 43 ♗xc5+ ♖xc5+ 44 ♔xc5 b3−+] 42 ♖h8 h6 43 ♔b3 ♔e7 44 a5 ♖c8 45 h3 ♔d7 46 g4 fxg4 47 hxg4 ♔c6 48 f5 ♖d8? 49 f6 ♖d3+ 50 ♔c2 ♖c3+ [50 ... ♖xe3 51 f7+−] 51 ♔d2 ♘xf6 52 exf6 gxf6 53 ♖xh6 ♔b5 54 ♖xf6 ♔xa5 55 g5 c4 56 ♖f5+ ♔a4 57 ♖d5 ♖a3 58 g6 c3+ 59 ♔e2 [59 ♔d3? c2+] 59 ... ♔b3 60 ♖d8 ♖a6 61 g7 ♖g6 62 g8♕+ ♖xg8 63 ♖xg8 ♔c2 64

♖g1 b3 65 ♖c1+ ♔b2 66 ♔d3 c2 67 ♔d2 ♔a2 68 ♗d4 **1-0** L/N6051

**1864-★NR-4** x 64
**Rivière,J.A.de−Neumann, G.R.**
Berlin [Anderssen & Neumann]
1 e4 e5 2 ♘f3 ♘c6 3 c3 ♘f6 4 ♗c4 ♘xe4 5 0-0 d5 6 ♗b5 ♗d6 7 d3 ♘f6 8 ♘xe5 ♗xe5 9 ♗xc6+ bxc6 10 ♖e1 0-0 11 ♖xe5 ♘g4∓ 12 ♖e2 ♕d6 13 g3 ♕g6 14 f3 ♘f6 15 d4 ♖b8 16 b3 ♗f5 17 ♗e3 ♖fe8 18 ♘d2 ♗c2 19 ♕e1 ♗d3 20 ♖g2 ♖e7 21 ♕f2 ♖be8 22 ♖e1 ♕h6 [□ 22 ... ♘h5 23 ♘f1 f5 24 ♕d2 ♗a6] 23 ♘f1 ♕g6 24 ♕d2 h5 25 h4 ♗a6 26 c4? dxc4 27 ♕a5 ♘d5! 28 ♕xa6 ♘xe3 29 ♘xe3 ♖xe3 30 ♖f1 [30 ♖xe3 ♖xe3 31 ♕xc4 ♕b1+ 32 ♔h2 ♖xf3∓] 30 ... c3 31 g4 hxg4 32 ♖xg4 ♕d3 33 ♕xd3 ♖xd3 34 ♖e4 ♖xe4 35 fxe4 c2 **0-1** L/N6051

**1864-★NR-5** xii 64
**Neumann, G.R.+Rocholl**
Berlin [Anderssen & Neumann]
⟨♘b1⟩ 1 e4 e5 2 ♘f3 ♘c6 3 ♗c4 ♗c5 4 c3 ♘f6 5 0-0 ♘xe4 [5 ... 0-0? 6 d4 exd4 7 cxd4±] 6 d4 exd4 7 cxd4 ♗e7 8 d5 ♘b8 9 ♖e1 f5 10 d6 ♗xd6 11 ♕d5 ♕f6 12 ♗g5 ♕g6 13 ♖xe4+ fxe4 14 ♖e1 ♘c6 [14 ... c6 15 ♖xe4+ ♔f8 16 ♕d4 h6 17 ♖f4+ ♗xf4 18 ♕xf4+ ♔e8 19 ♕e5+−] 15 ♖xe4+ ♗e7 16 ♘h4 ♕d6 [16 ... ♕h5 17 g4+−] 17 ♕f7+ ♔d8 18 ♖xe7 ♘xe7 19 ♘f5 ♕d1+ 20 ♗f1 **1-0** L/N6051-1865

**1864-★NS-1** 27 viii 64
**Schallopp,E.−Neumann, G.R.**
Berlin [Anderssen & Neumann]
1 c4 f5 2 ♘c3 ♘f6 3 d4 e6 4 a3 ♗e7 5 ♗f4 0-0 6 e3 d6 7 ♘f3 ♘h5 8 ♗g3 f4 9 exf4 ♘xf4 10 ♗xf4 ♖xf4 11 ♕d2 ♕f8 12 ♗d3 ♘c6 13 ♘e2 ♖f7 14 0-0-0 ♗d7 15 h4 d5 16 ♘g5 ♗xg5 17 hxg5 g6 18 f4 ♘e7 19 ♖h2 ♖c8 20 ♖dh1 c5 21 ♕c2 [△ 22 ♗xg6 ♘xg6 23 ♕xg6+] 21 ... ♘f5 22 ♗xf5 [□ 22 g4] 22 ... exf5 23 ♔b1 cxd4 24 ♘xd4 ♖xc4 25 ♕d3 ♕c5 26 ♘f3 ♗b5 27 ♕d2 ♖c7∓ 28 ♘e5 ♖c2 29 ♕e1 ♗e2 30 ♘xg6 ♖xb2+ [□ 30 ... hxg6 31 ♖h8+ ♔f7 32 ♖1h7+ ♔e6 33 ♖xc7 ♕xc7 34 ♖e8+ ♔ 35 ♖xe2] 31 ♔xb2 ♕d4+ 32 ♔b3 ♕d3+ 33 ♔b2! ♖c2+ 34 ♔b1 ♕b3+ 35 ♔a1 ♕b2# **0-1** L/N6051-8166

**1864-★NS-2** x 64
**Schallopp,E.−Neumann, G.R.**
Berlin [Anderssen & Neumann]
1 e4 e5 2 ♘f3 ♘c6 3 ♗b5 ♘f6 4 d3 d6 5 ♗xc6+ bxc6 6 h3 ♗e7 7 0-0 0-0 8 ♘c3 c5 [□ 8 ... ♘e8] 9 ♘e2 ♘h5 10 ♘g3 ♘xg3 11 fxg3 f5 12 exf5 ♗xf5 13 g4 ♗g6 14 ♕e1 [□ 14 b3] 14 ... c4 15 dxc4 ♗xc2 16 b3 ♗d3 17 ♖f2 e4 18 ♕e3? ♗f6 19 ♗b2 ♗xb2 20 ♖xb2 ♕f6 21 ♘d4 c5 **0-1** L/N6051-1865

**1864-★NW-1** xii 64
**Neumann,G.R.+Weiss, E.von**
Berlin [Anderssen & Neumann]
⟨♘b1⟩ 1 e4 e5 2 ♘f3 ♘c6 3 d4 exd4 4 ♗c4 ♗b4+ 5 c3 dxc3 6 0-0 cxb2 7 ♗xb2 ♘f6? 8 ♘g5 0-0 9 e5 ♘e8 10 ♕h5 h6 11 ♘xf7 ♖xf7 12 ♗xf7+ ♔f8 13 ♕f3 ♘f6 14 exf6 ♔xf7 15 fxg7+ ♔g8 16 ♕d5++− ♔h7 17 ♕f7 **1-0** L/N6051-1865

**1864-★NZ-1** 18 iv 64
**Neumann,G.R.+Zukertort, J.H.**
Breslau [Anderssen & Neumann]
1 e4 c5 2 ♘f3 e6 3 d4 [□ 3 ♘c3] 3 ... cxd4 4 ♘xd4 ♘f6 5 ♘c3 ♘c6 6 ♗e3 d5 7 exd5 exd5 8 ♗e2 ♗d6 9 0-0 0-0 10 ♗g5 ♗e6 11 ♖e1 ♔h8! 12 ♘xe6 fxe6 13 ♗g4 ♘xg4! 14 ♕xg4 [14 ♗xd8 ♗xh2+ 15 ♔h1 ♘xf2+ 16 ♔xh2 ♘xd1∓] 14 ... ♕b6 15 ♖f1 ♖ae8 16 ♖ae1 ♘e5 17 ♕h3 ♖f5 18 ♗h4 ♖ef8 19 ♘d1 ♘c4 20 ♕d3 ♗c5 21 ♗g3 ♘xb2 22 ♘xb2 ♕xb2 23 ♖xe6 ♕xa2 24 ♖e2 ♕c4! 25 ♕xc4 dxc4 26 h3 b5 27 ♔h2 ♗d4 28 f3 h6 29 ♗d6 ♖8f7 30 ♖d1 ♖d5 31 ♗g3 ♖fd7 32 ♖e6 a5 33 ♖a6 b4 34 ♖c6 c3 35 ♖c8+ ♔h7 36 ♖a8 b3 **0-1** L/N6051-1867

**1864-★NZ-2** 21 iv 64
**Neumann,G.R.+Zukertort, J.H.**
Breslau [Anderssen & Neumann]
1 e4 e5 2 ♘f3 ♘c6 3 ♗c4 ♗c5 4 b4 ♗xb4 5 c3 ♗c5 6 0-0 d6 7 d4 exd4 8 cxd4 ♗b6 9 ♘c3 ♘a5 10 ♗d3 ♘e7 11 e5 0-0 12 ♗g5 ♕d7 13 ♘e4 ♘g6 14 h3! dxe5 15 dxe5 ♘c6 16 ♘f6+ gxf6 17 ♗xf6 h6 18 ♘g5 [△ 19 ♕h5] **1-0** L/N6051-1867

**1864-★PS-1 ●o⬠** 8 v 64
**Schallopp, E.− Paulsen, L.**
Berlin [Anderssen & Neumann]
1 f4 e5 2 e4 exf4 3 ♘f3 g5 4 ♗c4 g4 5 0-0 gxf3 6 ♕xf3 ♕f6 7 e5 ♕xe5 8 d3 ♗h6 9 ♘c3 ♘e7 10 ♗d2 ♘bc6 11 ♖ae1 ♕f5 12 ♘d5 ♔d8 13 ♗c3 ♖e8 14 ♗f6 d6 15 ♗b5 ♗e6 16 ♗xc6 bxc6 17 ♗xe7+ ♖xe7 18 ♘xe7 ♕c5+ 19 d4 ♕xd4+ 20 ♔h1 ♔xe7 21 ♕xc6 ♖c8 22 c3 ♕b6 23 ♕e4 ♖g8 24 ♕xh7 ♖g6 25 ♖e2 ♕c5 [□ 25 ... ♕b5] 26 ♕h8 ♔d7 27 ♕a8 ♕c6 28 ♕xc6+! ♔xc6 29 b3 ♔d7 30 c4 ♗f5 31 ♖fe1 ♖e6 32 ♔g1 ♗g4 33 ♖e4 ♗f5 34 ♖4e2 ♗d3 35 ♖xe6 fxe6 36 ♔f2 e5 37 g3 fxg3+ 38 hxg3 e4 39 ♖h1 ♗d2 **0-1** L/N6051

**1864-★PS-2**
**Schmidt, E. von− Paulsen, L.**
Leipzig [Löwenthal]
1 e4 e5 2 ♘f3 ♘c6 3 ♗b5 ♘f6 4 d4 exd4 5 e5 ♘e4 6 0-0 ♗e7 7 ♘xd4 0-0 8 ♘f5 d5 9 ♘xe7+ ♘xe7 10 f3 ♘c5 11 ♗e3 ♘e6 12 f4 ♘f5 13 ♗d2 c6 14 ♗d3 ♕b6+ 15 ♔h1 ♘c5 16 g4 [16 ♗e2 ♘e4] 16 ... ♘xd3 17 cxd3 ♘e3 18 ♗xe3 ♕xe3 19 ♘c3 f6 20 exf6 ♖xf6 21 f5 h5 22 ♖e1? [□ 22 ♕f3] 22 ... ♕g5 23 ♖e8+ ♔h7 24 ♕b3 ♕xg4 25 ♖g1 ♕f3+ 26 ♖g2 ♗xf5 27 ♖e2 ♗h3 28 ♘e4 ♕f1+ 29 ♖g1 ♕xg1+ 30 ♔xg1 ♖f1# **0-1** M324

**1864-★PS-3**
**Saalbach, A.− Paulsen, L.**
Leipzig [Lange]
1 e4 e5 2 ♘f3 ♘c6 3 d4 exd4 4 ♘xd4 ♗c5 5 ♗e3 ♕f6 6 c3 ♘ge7 7 ♗e2 d5 8 exd5 [□ 8 ♗f3] 8 ... ♘xd5 9 0-0 ♘xe3 10 fxe3 ♕h6 11 ♗b5 ♕xe3+ 12 ♔h1 0-0 13 ♘xc6 bxc6 14 ♗xc6 ♖ab8 15 b3 ♖b6 16 ♗f3 [16 ♕f3 ♕h6 17 ♗d5 ♖f6 18 ♕d3 ♖xf1+ 19 ♕xf1 ♗d6 20 h3 ♗a6 21 ♕e1 ♕f4 22 g3 ♕f5∓] 16 ... ♖h6 17 ♕d2 ♕e5 18 g3 ♗a6 19 ♕e1 ♕f6 **0-1** L/N6047-1864

**1864-★PS-4**
**Paulsen, L.+Schmidt, E. von**
Leipzig [Lange]
1 e4 e5 2 ♘f3 ♘c6 3 d4 exd4 4 ♘xd4 ♗c5 5 ♗e3 ♕f6 6 c3 ♘ge7 7 ♗e2 d5 8 ♗f3 dxe4 9 ♗xe4 ♘xd4 10 cxd4 ♗b4+ [□ 10 ... ♗d6] 11 ♘c3 0-0 12 0-0 ♗d6 13 ♕d2 ♘f5 14 ♖ad1 ♕h4 15 g3 ♕h5 16 ♗g2 ♖e8 17 ♗f4 c6 18 ♘e4 ♗xf4 19 ♕xf4 ♗e6 20 ♘g5 ♘h6 21 ♘xe6 ♖xe6 22 d5 cxd5 23 ♖xd5 ♕e2 24 ♕d4 ♖ae8 25 ♖d7 ♖a6 26 ♗d5 b5 27 ♗b3 ♖e7 28 ♖d8+ ♖e8 29 ♕d7 ♔f8 30 ♖d1 ♖xd8 31 ♕xd8+ ♕e8 32 ♕g5 ♖f6 33 ♕c5+ ♔g8 34 ♕c7 **1-0** L/N6047-1864

**1864-★PS-5**
**Paulsen, L.+Schmidt, E. von**
Leipzig
1 e4 c5 2 ♘c3 e6 3 ♘f3 ♘c6 4 g3 d5 5 d3 ♘f6 6 ♗g5 ♗e7 7 ♗g2 0-0 8 0-0 h6 9 ♗d2 ♘h7 10 ♕e2 d4 11 ♘d1 e5 12 ♘e1 f5 13 f4 fxe4 14 dxe4 ♗e6 15 b3 ♕d7 16 ♘f2 ♖ae8 17 ♘f3 exf4 18 gxf4 a6 19 a4 ♘f6 20 f5 ♗f7 21 e5 ♗d8 22 e6 ♗h5 23 ♕c4 ♕d5 24 ♕d3 ♘g4 25 ♘xg4

♗xg4 26 ♘h4 ♕d6 27 ♗f4 ♕e7 28 ♘g6 ♕f6 29 ♘xf8 ♗xf5 30 ♕c4 ♔xf8 31 ♗d6+ ♗e7 32 ♖xf5 ♕xf5 33 ♖f1 ♕xf1+ 34 ♕xf1+ **1-0**

L/N6047-1864

**1864-★PS-6**
**Paulsen, L.+ Schmidt, E. von**
Leipzig [Löwenthal]

1 e4 e5 2 ♘f3 ♘c6 3 d4 exd4 4 ♘xd4 ♗c5 5 ♗e3 ♕f6 6 c3 ♘ge7 7 ♗e2 d5 8 ♗f3 [◻ 8 ♘d2] 8 ... ♘xd4 9 cxd4 ♗b4+ 10 ♘c3 dxe4 11 ♗xe4 0-0 12 0-0 ♗d6 13 ♕d2 ♘f5 14 ♖ad1 ♕h4 15 g3 ♕h5 16 ♗g2 ♖e8 17 ♗f4 c6 18 ♘e4 ♗xf4 19 ♕xf4 ♗e6 20 ♘g5 [20 g4 ♕h6] 20 ... ♘h6 21 ♘xe6 ♖xe6 22 d5 cxd5 23 ♖xd5 ♕e2 24 ♕d4 ♖ae8 25 ♖d7 ♖a6 26 ♗d5! b5 27 ♗b3 ♖e7 28 ♖d8+ ♖e8 29 ♕d7 ♔f8 30 ♖d1 ♖xd8 31 ♕xd8+ ♕e8 32 ♕g5 ♖f6 33 ♕c5+ ♔g8 34 ♕c7 **1-0**

M324-1864

**1968-★PS-7**
**Paulsen, L.– Schmidt, E. von**
Leipzig [Lange]

1 e4 c5 2 ♘f3 e6 3 ♘c3 ♘c6 [◻ 3 ... a6] 4 ♘b5 [◻ 4 d4 cxd4 5 ♘xd4 a6! 6 g3 d5 7 exd5 exd5 8 ♗g2] 4 ... ♘d4 [◻ 4 ... a6] 5 ♘xd4 cxd4 6 ♘e2 a6 7 ♗c4 b5 8 ♗b3 ♗c5 [8 ... d3 9 cxd3 d5! 10 exd5! exd5 11 d4±] 9 d3 ♘e7 10 0-0 ♗b7 11 ♘g3 d5 12 f4 [◻ 12 ♕g4 0-0 13 ♗g5 △ 14 ♗f6] 12 ... dxe4 13 ♘xe4 ♗a7 14 ♔h1 0-0 15 ♕h5 ♘f5 16 ♘g5 h6 17 ♘xe6

[17 ♘xf7 ♖xf7 18 ♗xe6 ♕f6 19 ♗xf7+ ♕xf7 20 ♕xf7+ ♔xf7 21 ♗d2 ♘e3∓] 17 ... fxe6 18 ♗xe6+ ♔h8 19 ♗xf5 ♕d5 20 ♕g4 ♕xf5 21 ♕xf5 ♖xf5 22 ♗d2 ♖af8 23 ♖ae1 ♗c5 [23 ... ♗b8 24 ♗b4] 24 ♔g1 ♗d6 25 g3 [25 g4 ♗xf4 26 gxf5 ♗xd2, 27 ... ♗e3+] 25 ... h5 26 ♖e6 ♖5f6 27 ♖fe1 h4 28 c4 hxg3 29 hxg3 ♖xe6 30 ♖xe6 ♖f6 31 ♖xf6 gxf6 32 b4 f5 33 ♔f2 ♔g7 34 a3 ♔f7 35 ♗c1 ♗e7 36 ♗b2 ♗f6 37 c5 ♗d5 38 ♗c1 ♗b3 39 ♗d2 ♔g6 40 ♗e1 ♔h5 41 ♔e2 ♔g4 42 ♗f2 ♗d5 43 ♗e1 ♔h3 44 ♔f2 ♗b3 45 ♔f3 ♗c2 46 c6 ♗d8 47 ♔e2 ♔g2 48 ♗f2 ♗xd3+ 49 ♔xd3 ♔xf2 50 g4 fxg4 51 f5 g3 52 f6 g2 53 f7 ♗e7 54 c7 g1♕ 55 c8♕ ♕d1+ 56 ♔e4 ♕f3+ 57 ♔e5 d3 58 ♕e8 ♕f6+ 59 ♔e4 d2 60 ♕d7 ♕f3+ 61 ♔e5 d1♕ 62 ♕xe7 ♕1d5# **0-1**

L/N6047-1864

**1864-★PS-8**
**Schmidt, E. von– Paulsen, L.**
Leipzig

1 e3 d5 2 d4 ♘f6 3 c4 e6 4 ♘c3 ♗e7 5 ♘f3 0-0 6 ♗d3 b6 7 ♗d2 ♗b7 8 0-0 ♘bd7 9 ♕e2 c5 10 ♖fd1 ♘e4 11 cxd5 exd5 12 ♖ac1 f5 13 a4 ♘df6 14 ♗b1 ♕e8 15 ♘e5 ♘xd2 16 ♖xd2 ♘e4 17 ♖dc2 ♘xc3 18 ♖xc3 ♗d6 19 ♘d3 cxd4 20 ♖3c2 ♕xa4 21 exd4 ♖ae8 22 ♕f3 ♕xd4 23 ♗a2 ♔h8 24 ♖d1 ♕e4 25 ♕h3 ♖e6 26 g3 d4 27 f3 ♕xf3 28 ♘f2 ♖h6 **0-1**

L/N6047-1864

**1864-★PS-9**
**Paulsen, L.+ Schmorl, A.**
Leipzig [Lange]

1 e4 e6 2 d4 d5 3 ♘c3 dxe4 4 ♘xe4 ♘f6 5 ♘xf6+ ♕xf6 6 ♗d3 ♗d7 7 c3 ♗c6 8 ♕g4 h5 9 ♕g3 ♗d6 10 f4 h4 11 ♕g4 h3 12 ♘xh3 ♖h4 13 ♕g3 ♘d7 14 0-0 0-0-0 15 ♘g5 ♖dh8 16 h3 ♘f8 17 ♗d2 ♘g6 [◻ 17 ... g6; 18 ... ♕g7; ... f5] 18 ♘xf7 ♕xf7 19 ♕xg6 ♕xg6 20 ♗xg6 ♖8h6 21 f5 ♖h8 22 fxe6 ♗xg2 23 ♔xg2 ♖xh3 24 ♗f4 ♗xf4 25 ♖xf4 ♖h2+ 26 ♔f3 ♖8h3+ 27 ♔e4 ♖e2+ 28 ♔d5 c6+ 29 ♔d6 ♖h8 30 e7 **1-0**

L/N6047-1864

**1864-★PS-10**
**Schmorl, A.= Paulsen, L.**
Leipzig

1 e4 e5 2 ♘f3 ♘c6 3 ♗c4 ♗c5 4 c3 ♘f6 5 d3 d6 6 ♗g5 ♘e7 7 ♗xf6 gxf6 8 d4 exd4 9 ♘xd4 0-0 10 ♘d2 ♗xd4 11 cxd4 ♘c6 12 d5 ♘e5 13 ♕h5 ♘xc4 14 ♘xc4 ♕e7 15 f3 f5 16 0-0 ♕f6 17 ♖ae1 ♖e8 18 e5 dxe5 19 f4 e4 20 ♘e5 ♖e7 21 ♖e3 h6 22 ♖c1 a5 23 ♖cc3 ♖a6 24 ♖g3+ ♔h7 25 h4 ♖d6 26 ♖g5 ♖xd5 27 ♖cg3 ♖d8 28 ♘c4 ♖ee8 29 ♔h2 ♖g8 30 ♘e5 ♗e6 31 b3 c5 32 ♕e2 ♖c8 33 ♔h3 ♖cd8 34 ♔h2 ♖c8 35 ♔h3 hxg5 36 hxg5 ♕h8 37 ♔h2 ♔g7+ 38 ♖h3 f6 39 gxf6+ ♔xf6 40 ♖xh8 ♖xh8+ 41 ♔g1 ♖hg8 42 ♕h5 ♗d5 43 ♕h6+ ♔e7 44 ♕h7+ ♔f6 ½-½

L/N6047-1864

**1864-★PS-11**
**Schurig, R.– Paulsen, L.**
Leipzig [Lange]

1 e4 e5 2 f4 exf4 3 ♘f3 g5 4 h4 g4 5 ♘e5 ♗g7 6 ♘xg4 d5 7 ♘f2 ♘e7 8 d3 0-0 9 c3 f5 10 e5! ♗xe5 11 d4 ♗g7! [11 ... ♗d6 12 ♕f3±] 12 ♗xf4 ♘g6 13 ♗g5 ♕d6 14 ♘d3 ♕g3+ 15 ♔d2 h6 16 ♕h5 ♔h7 17 ♗e2 f4 18 ♗f3 ♗f5 19 ♘a3 ♘d7 20 ♖ae1 c5 21 ♖e2 cxd4 22 cxd4 ♘f6 23 ♗xf6 ♖xf6 24 ♘b5 ♖af8 25 ♘c3 ♖c6 26 ♘b4 ♖c4 27 ♘c2 ♗xd4 28 ♘xd4 ♖xd4+ 29 ♔c1 ♖d3 30 ♖he1 ♖e3 31 ♖xe3 [31 ♘xd5 ♕xe1+ 32 ♖xe1 ♖xe1+ 33 ♔d2 ♖e5∓] 31 ... fxe3 32 ♖xe3 d4 33 ♘e4 ♕c7+ 34 ♔d1 dxe3 **0-1**

L/N6047-1864

**1864-★PS-12**
**Schurig, R.– Paulsen, L.**
Leipzig

1 d4 e6 2 ♗f4 ♘f6 3 e3 d5 4 ♗d3 ♗d6 5 ♘e2 0-0 6 ♘d2 c5 7 c3 ♘c6 8 ♘f3 cxd4 9 exd4 ♗xf4 10 ♘xf4 ♕d6 11 ♘e2 e5 12 dxe5 ♘xe5 13 ♘xe5 ♕xe5 14 ♕c2 ♗d7 15 0-0-0 b5 16 ♔b1 a5 17 f3 b4 18 ♘d4 bxc3 19 ♕xc3 ♖fc8 20 ♕a3 ♔h8 21 ♘b5 ♗xb5 22 ♗xb5 d4 23 ♕d3 ♖ab8 24 a4 ♖d8 25 g3 ♕d6 26 ♖he1 ♕b4 27 ♖e2 ♘d5 28 ♖ed2 ♘b6 29 ♕f5 ♘xa4 30 ♗xa4 ♕xa4 31 ♖c1 ♕b4 32 ♕d3 h6 33 ♖c4 ♕b7 34 f4 ♕h1+ 35 ♔a2 ♖b4 36 ♖xb4 axb4 37 ♔b3 ♕d5+ 38 ♕c4 ♕f3+ 39 ♕d3 ♕b7 40 ♕c4 ♕a7 41 ♕d3 ♖e8 42 ♕c4 d3 43 ♖xd3 ♖a8 44 ♕c6 ♕a2+ 45 ♔c2 ♖b8 46 ♕c7 b3+ 47 ♔c3 ♕a8 48 ♕xf7 ♕a5+ 49 ♔d4 ♖d8+ 50 ♔e4 ♕b4+ **0-1**

L/N6047-1864

**1864-★PS-13**
**Schurig, R.– Paulsen, L.**
[Lange]

1 e4 e5 2 ♘f3 ♘c6 3 ♗c4 ♗c5 4 c3 ♘f6 5 d4 exd4 6 cxd4 ♗b4+ 7 ♗d2 ♗xd2+ 8 ♘bxd2 d5 9 exd5 ♘xd5 10 0-0 0-0 11 ♖e1 ♘f4 12 ♘e5 ♘xd4 13 ♘xf7 ♖xf7 14 ♘f3 ♗e6! 15 ♖xe6 ♘dxe6 16 ♕b3 ♕f6! 17 g3 ♘h3+ 18 ♔g2 ♘hg5 19 ♘xg5 ♘xg5 20 f4 ♘e4 21 ♕xb7 ♖e8 22 ♖e1 ♘d6 23 ♖xe8+ ♘xe8 24 ♗xf7+ ♔xf7 25 a3 ♕b6 26 ♕d5+ ♕e6 27 ♕d3 ♘f6 28 ♕c3 ♕e4+ 29 ♔h3 ♘d5 30 ♕d2 ♘e3 31 ♕e2 ♕e6+ 32 g4 h5 33 f5 hxg4+ **0-1**

L/N6047-1864

**1864-★PS-14**
**Schurig, R.– Paulsen, L.**
[Lange]

1 e4 e5 2 f4 exf4 3 ♗c4 ♕h4+ 4 ♔f1 d6 5 ♕f3 ♘c6 6 g3 ♗h3+ 7 ♔f2 ♕f6 8 c3 fxg3+ 9 hxg3 ♗g4 10 ♕xf6 ♘xf6 11 d3 ♘e5 12 ♘a3 ♘xc4 13 ♘xc4 0-0-0 14 a4 d5 15 ♘e5 ♗e6 16 ♘gf3 dxe4 17 ♘g5 exd3 18 ♗e3 ♖d5 19 ♘gxf7 ♘g4+ 20 ♘xg4 ♗xf7 21 ♔e1 ♗e6 22 ♘f2

♖e5 23 ♘d1 [23 ♔d2 ♖xe3 24 ♔xe3 ♗c5+] 23 ... ♗f5 24 b4 c5 25 ♔d2 cxb4 26 ♖h4 bxc3+ 27 ♘xc3 ♗c5 28 ♖c4 b6 29 ♘b5 ♖xe3 30 ♘d6+ ♔b8 31 ♘xf5 ♖f3 32 ♘xg7 ♗e3+ 33 ♔c3 ♗g5 34 ♘h5 d2+ 35 ♔c2 ♖e8 36 ♖d1 ♖a3 37 ♘f4 ♖a2+ 38 ♔b3 ♖e1 39 ♔xa2 ♖xd1 40 ♖d4 ♗f6 **0-1** L/N6047-1864

### 1864-★PW-1
**Paulsen, L.+Windberg**

Leipzig [Löwenthal]

1 e4 e5 2 ♘f3 ♘c6 3 ♗c4 ♗e7 4 d4 d6 5 0-0 ♘f6 6 d5 ♘b8 7 ♗d3 0-0 8 ♘e1 ♗g4 9 ♕d2 h6 10 h3 ♗h5 11 f4 exf4 12 ♕xf4 ♘bd7 13 ♘f3 ♗xf3 14 ♕xf3 ♘e5 15 ♕e2 ♘h7 16 ♘d2 c6 17 ♘c4 ♘xd3 18 ♕xd3 cxd5 19 exd5 b5 20 ♘e3 ♕b6 21 ♔h1 ♗g5 22 ♘f5 ♗xc1 23 ♖axc1 ♕d8 24 ♖ce1 ♔h8 25 ♘e7 ♘f6?? [□ 25 ... ♕d7] 26 ♖xf6 gxf6 27 ♕e3 ♔g7 28 ♘f5+ [28 ... ♔g6 29 ♕xh6+ ♔xf5 30 g4#] **1-0** M324

### 1864-★ST-1 viii 64
**Steinitz, W.+Thorold, E.**

London [Löwenthal]

1 e4 e5 2 f4 exf4 3 ♘f3 g5 4 h4 g4 5 ♘e5 ♘f6 6 ♗c4 d5 7 exd5 ♗d6 8 d4 ♘h5 9 ♘c3 ♕e7 10 ♗b5+ ♔f8! [10 ... ♘d7+−; 10 ... ♗d7+−; 10 ... c6?!; 10 ... ♔d8!] 11 0-0 ♗xe5 12 dxe5 ♕xe5 [□ 12 ... ♕c5+ 13 ♔h2! ♕e7 14 ♗xf4 (14 ♖xf4?; 14 ♔g1=) 14 ... ♕xh4+ 15 ♔g1 g3 16 ♗h6+ ♔g8 17 ♖f3 ♕h2+ 18 ♔f1 ♕h1+ 19 ♔e2 ♕xd1+ (19 ... ♕xg2+ 20 ♔d3 ♗g4?? 21 ♖xf7+−) 20 ♖xd1 ♗g4∓] 13 ♘e2 c6 14 ♘xf4!! cxb5 15 ♘xh5 ♕xh5 16 ♕d4 ♔g8 [16 ... ♖g8 17 ♕c5+ ♔g7 18 ♕c3++−] 17 ♗g5 h6 18 ♗f6 ♖h7 19 ♖ae1 ♗d7 20 ♖e5 ♕g6 21 h5 ♕xc2 22 ♕xg4+ ♔f8 23 ♗e7+ ♔e8 24 ♕g8# **1-0** L/N6124

### 1864-★S♀-1 ii 64
**Steinitz, W.+♀**

London [Löwenthal]

⟨♘b1⟩ 1 e4 e5 2 ♘f3 ♘c6 3 ♗c4 ♗c5 4 b4 ♗xb4 5 c3 ♗c5 6 0-0 d6 7 h3 ♘f6 8 d4 exd4 9 cxd4 ♗b6 10 e5! dxe5 11 ♗a3 ♘xd4 12 ♘xe5 ♘e6 13 ♕a4+ ♗d7 14 ♕b3 c5 15 ♖ad1 ♕e7 [15 ... 0-0? 16 ♘xf7] 16 ♖fe1 0-0 17 ♘xd7 ♘xd7 18 ♗xe6 fxe6 19 ♖xe6 ♕f7 20 ♖xd7 ♕xf2+ 21 ♔h2 c4? 22 ♕d1 ♖f5 23 ♖ee7 ♖g5 24 ♕d5+!+− ♔h8 [24 ... ♖xd5 25 ♖xg7++−] 25 ♕xg5 ♕g1+ 26 ♔g3 ♕f2+ 27 ♔g4 ♕xg2+ 28 ♔f5 ♕f3+ 29 ♕f4 ♕h5+ 30 ♔e6 ♕g6+ 31 ♔e5 ♕h5+ 32 ♕f5 ♕e2+ 33 ♔d6 ♕d2+ 34 ♔e6 ♕e2+ 35 ♔f7 ♕xa2 36 ♗d6 c3+ 37 ♖e6 ♗d4 38 ♔e7 c2 39 ♖d8+ ♖xd8 40 ♔xd8 ♗b6+ 41 ♔e7 h6 42 ♖xh6+ gxh6 43 ♗e5+ ♔g8 44 ♕g6# **1-0** M324

### 1864-★S♀-2
**Steinitz, W.+♀**

Manchester♀

1 e4 e5 2 ♘f3 ♘c6 3 ♗c4 ♗c5 4 b4 ♗xb4 5 c3 ♗a5 6 0-0 ♘f6 7 ♗a3 ♗b6 8 d4 exd4 9 ♕b3 d5 10 exd5 ♘a5 11 ♖e1+ ♗e6 12 dxe6 ♘xb3 **1-0** L/N6047

### 1864-★S♀-3
**♀−Steinitz, W.**

London

1 e4 e5 2 ♘f3 ♘c6 3 ♗c4 ♗c5 4 b4 ♗xb4 5 c3 ♗c5 6 d4 exd4 7 0-0 d6 8 cxd4 ♗b6 9 ♘c3 ♗g4 10 ♗b5 ♔f8 11 ♗xc6 bxc6 12 ♗a3 ♗xf3 13 gxf3 ♕g5+ 14 ♔h1 ♘e7 15 ♘e2 ♘g6 16 ♖g1 ♕f6 17 ♕d3 ♔g8 18 ♗c1 h6 19 f4 ♔h7 20 f5 ♘e7 21 ♗b2 d5 22 f3 ♖ad8 23 ♘f4 ♖hg8 24 ♘h5 ♕h4 25 f6 ♕xh5 26 fxe7 ♖d7 27 exd5+ g6 28 ♖ae1 ♖e8 29 ♖e5 ♕h4 30 ♖f5 ♕xe7 31 dxc6 ♖dd8 32 ♗a3 ♕e6 33 ♖f4 f5 34 ♖h4 h5 35 ♗b2 ♖d5 36 ♕c2 ♕e2 37 ♕b3 ♕b5 38 ♕c3 ♖e2 39 f4 ♖xd4 40 ♕f3 ♕d5 **0-1** L/N6047-1865

### 1864-★WZ-1 ○● 21 v 64
**Waldstein, L.−Zukertort, J.H.**

Posen [Anderssen & Zukertort]

1 e4 e5 2 f4 exf4 3 ♘f3 g5 4 h4 g4 5 ♘e5 ♘f6 6 ♘xg4 ♘xg4 [□ 6 ... ♘xe4] 7 ♕xg4 d5 8 ♕xf4 ♗d6 9 ♕e3 [9 e5 ♕e7 10 d4 c5→] 9 ... dxe4 10 ♕xe4+ ♗e6 11 d4 ♘d7 12 ♗c4 ♗g3+ 13 ♔d1 ♘f6 14 ♕e3 ♕d6 15 ♘c3 ♘g4 16 ♕e2 ♘f2+ 17 ♔d2 ♕xd4+ 18 ♗d3 0-0-0! 19 ♖f1 ♗g4 20 ♕e7 [20 ♕e1 ♗f4+ 21 ♕e3 ♕xe3#] 20 ... ♖he8 21 ♕xf7 ♕e3# **0-1** L/N6051-1868

### 1864-★Z♀-1 iv 64
**Zukertort, J.H.+♀**

Breslau [Anderssen & Neumann]

1 e4 e5 2 ♘f3 d6 3 d4 f5 4 ♘c3! fxe4 5 ♘xe4 d5 6 ♘xe5 dxe4 7 ♕h5+ g6 8 ♘xg6 ♘f6 9 ♕e5+ ♔f7 10 ♘xh8+ [□ 10 ♗c4+] 10 ... ♔g8 11 ♗g5 ♗g7 12 ♘f7 ♔xf7 13 ♗c4+ ♔f8 14 0-0-0 ♘c6 15 ♗xf6 ♗xf6 16 ♕xe4 ♔g7 17 ♗d3 ♕g8 18 c3 ♗d7 19 ♔b1 ♖e8 20 ♕f4 ♗d8 21 ♖he1 ♖f8 22 ♕g3+ ♔h8 23 ♕xg8+ ♖xg8 24 ♗e4 b6 25 d5! ♘e7 26 d6! cxd6 27 ♖xd6 ♗f5 28 ♗xf5 ♘xf5 29 ♖de6! ♖f8 [29 ... ♖xg2 30 ♖e8++−] 30 ♖e8 ♔g7 31 g4 ♘h6 32 ♖xf8 ♔xf8 33 h3 ♘f7 34 f4 ♗h4 35 ♖e6 ♗g3 36 f5 ♘g5 37 ♖e3 ♗f4 38 ♖d3 ♘f7 39 ♔c2 a5 40 ♔b3 ♘d6 41 ♖d4 [□ 41 ♖d5] 41 ... ♗e5 42 ♖d5 ♗f4 43 ♔a4 h6 44 b4 axb4 45 ♔xb4 ♔e7 46 a4 ♗g3 47 a5 bxa5+ 48 ♔xa5 ♗f2 49 ♔b4 ♔d7 50 c4 ♔c6 51 f6 ♗e1+ 52 ♔b3 ♗h4 53 ♖h5 ♗xf6 54 ♖xh6 ♗g5 55 ♖h5 ♗e3 56 g5 ♘f5 57 g6 ♘g7 58 ♖h7 ♗d4 59 h4 ♔d7 60 h5 ♔e6 61 h6 ♘h5 62 g7 ♔f7 63 ♖h8 ♘xg7 64 hxg7 ♗xg7 65 ♖d8 [□ 65 ♖h7 ♔g6 66 ♖xg7+ ♔xg7 67 ♔b4 ♔f6 68 ♔c5+−] 65 ... ♔e7 66 ♖d1 ♗e5 67 c5 ♗c7 68 ♔a4 ♗g3 69 ♔b5 ♗c7 70 ♔c6 ♗g3 71 ♔b7 **1-0** L/N6051-1867

## DUBLIN 1865

### 1865-BAC-1 27 ix 65
**Cordner, E.J.−MacDonnell, G.A.**

[Steen]

1 e4 e5 2 ♗c4 ♗c5 3 ♘f3 ♘c6 4 c3 ♘f6 5 d3 [5 d4] 5 ... d6 6 h3 [□ 6 d4] 6 ... ♗e6 7 ♗b3 ♕d7 8 ♗e3 ♗b6 9 ♗a4 ♕e7 10 ♕e2 0-0 11 ♗xc6 bxc6 12 ♘bd2 ♖ab8 13 b3 h6 14 ♗xb6? cxb6 15 a4 ♘h7 16 d4 exd4 17 ♘xd4 ♗d7 18 ♘4f3 ♖be8 19 0-0 f5 20 ♖ae1 fxe4 21 ♕xe4 ♕xe4 22 ♘xe4 ♖xf3! 23 gxf3 ♗xh3 24 ♘xd6 ♖d8 25 ♖e8+ ♖xe8 26 ♘xe8 ♗xf1 27 ♔xf1 ♘g5 28 ♔g2 ♔f7 29 ♘d6+ ♔e6 30 ♘e8 g6 31 ♘c7+ ♔d6 32 ♘a6 c5 33 b4 ♘e6 34 b5 ♘f4+ 35 ♔f1 ♘d3 36 ♘b8 ♘e5 37 ♔g2 ♘c4 38 ♘c6 a6 39 ♘e7 ♔xe7 40 bxa6 b5 41 a7 ♘b6 **0-1** M1584

**183** Steinitz, W. M1647.BL

### 1865-BAC-2
**Steinitz, W.+ Cordner, E.J.**

[Staunton]

1 e4 e5 2 f4 d5 3 exd5 exf4 [□3 ... e4] 4 ♘f3 ♕xd5 5 ♘c3 ♕e6+ 6 ♔f2 ♗d6? 7 ♗b5+ ♔f8 8 ♖e1 ♗e5 9 ♖xe5 ♕b6+ 10 d4 ♘d7 11 ♘d5 ♕d6 [11 ... ♕xb5 12 ♘xc7 △ 13 ♖e8#+-] 12 ♗xd7 ♗xd7 13 ♗xf4 ♗e6 14 ♕d2 ♘f6 15 ♘xf6 gxf6 16 ♖xe6 ♕xe6 17 ♖e1 ♕f5 18 g4 ♕g6 19 ♗h6+ ♔g8 20 ♘h4 ♕xg4 21 ♖g1 **1-0** M954

### 1865-BAC-3
**Cronhelm, E.− Cordner, E.J.**

[Löwenthal]

1 e4 e5 2 ♘f3 ♘c6 3 ♗c4 h6 4 d3 ♗c5 5 c3 ♘f6 6 h3 0-0 7 ♗e3 ♗b6 8 ♘h4 ♔h8 [□8 ... ♘xe4 9 ♘g6 (9 ♗xb6 ♕xh4 10 dxe4 ♕xe4+∓) 9 ... ♗xe3 10 fxe3 ♕f6∓] 9 ♘f5 ♗xe3 10 ♘xe3 d6 11 ♘d2 ♘a5 12 0-0 c6 13 f4 ♕b6 14 ♕e2 ♕xb2 15 ♖ab1 ♕xc3 16 ♖fc1 ♕d4 [□16 ... ♕a3] 17 ♘f3 ♕c5 18 ♗xf7 ♕a3 19 ♘c2 ♕c5+ 20 ♘e3 ♕a3 21 fxe5 dxe5 22 ♘xe5 ♔h7 23 ♖f1 ♕d6 24 ♖xf6 gxf6 [24 ... ♕xf6 25 ♗g6+ ♔g8 26 d4 ♗e6 27 ♖f1 ♕e7 28 ♘f5±] 25 ♕h5 fxe5 26 ♖f1 ♗d7 27 g4 ♗e8 28 g5 ♗xf7 29 ♖xf7+ ♖xf7 30 ♕xf7+ ♔h8 31 g6 ♕xg6+ 32 ♕xg6 ♖g8 33 ♕xg8+ ♔xg8 34 ♘g4 c5 35 ♘xe5= b6 36 ♔f2 ♔g7 37 ♔e3 ♔f6 38 ♘g4+ [□38 ♔f4] 38 ... ♔g5 39 e5? ♘c6 40 ♔e4 ♘d4 41 ♔d5? [□41 ♘e3 h5 (41 ... ♔h4 42 ♘f5+-; 41 ... ♘e6 42 ♘g2=) 42 h4+ ♔xh4 43 ♘f5+=] 41 ... h5 42 ♘f6 h4 43 ♔e4 ♔g6 44 ♘d5 ♔f7 45 ♘f4 ♘e6 **0-1** M324

### 1865-BAC-4
**MacDonnell, G.A.+ Cronhelm, E.**

[Staunton]

1 e4 e6 2 d4 d5 3 exd5 exd5 4 ♗d3 ♗d6 5 ♘f3 ♗e6 6 0-0 ♘f6 7 ♗e3 ♘bd7 8 ♘c3 c6 9 ♘e2 ♕c7 10 h3 h5 [□10 ... h6] 11 ♘g5 0-0-0 12 c4 dxc4 13 ♘xe6 fxe6 14 ♗xc4 ♘d5 15 ♗g5 ♖df8 16 ♘c3 ♘7b6 17 ♗b3 ♘xc3 18 bxc3 ♘d5 19 c4 ♘f4 20 c5 ♗e7 21 ♗xf4 ♕xf4 22 ♗xe6+ ♔c7 23 ♕b3 ♖d8 24 ♖ab1 ♖b8 25 ♕c3 ♔d8 26 ♕a5+ ♕c7 27 ♕xa7 ♖e8 28 ♖b6 ♗xc5 29 dxc5 ♖xe6 30 ♕a4 ♕e7 31 ♕d1+ ♔c7 32 ♕xh5 ♖e5 [□32 ... ♖b] 33 ♕g4 ♕xc5 34 ♖fb1 ♕e7 35 ♕g3 ♔c8 36 ♔h2 ♕c7 37 f4 ♖f5 38 ♖6b4 ♕f7 39 ♕e3 ♕d7 40 ♖d4 ♖d5 41 ♕e4 ♖d3 42 ♕e8+ ♔c7 43 ♕b6+ ♔d6 44 ♖xb8 **1-0** M954

### 1865-BAC-5
**Bolt, W.− MacDonnell, G.A.**

[Boden]

1 e4 e5 2 ♘f3 ♘f6 3 ♘xe5 d6 4 ♘f3 ♘xe4 5 d4 d5 6 ♗d3 ♗e7 7 0-0 ♘c6 8 c3? 0-0 9 ♘e5 ♘xe5 10 dxe5 f6? [□10 ... ♗f5] 11 ♗xe4 dxe4 12 exf6 ♕xd1 13 ♖xd1 ♗xf6 14 ♘d2 ♖d8 [□14 ... ♗f5] 15 ♖e1 ♗f5 16 ♘f1 ♖d6 17 ♗e3 ♖e8 18 ♖ad1 ♖ed8 19 ♖xd6 ♖xd6 20 h3 ♗e5 21 ♗c1 [21 ♗xa7?] 21 ... ♗f6 22 ♗f4 ♖b6 23 ♖e2 c5 24 ♘g3 ♗g6 25 ♗c1 ♖d6 26 ♗f4 ♖d1+ 27 ♔h2 ♖b1 28 ♖d2 h5 29 ♘e2 ♗f7 30 a3 g5 31 ♗d6 b6 32 ♗b8 a6 33 g3 ♗e7 34 ♗c7 b5 35 ♗d8 ♗xd8 36 ♖xd8+ ♔g7 37 ♖d2 ♗c4 38 ♔g2 ♔f6 39 h4 gxh4 40 gxh4 ♗xe2 41 ♖xe2 ♔f5 42 f3 exf3+ 43 ♔xf3 c4 44 ♖g2 ♔f6 45 ♔f4 ♖f1+ 46 ♔g3 [□46 ♔e4] 46 ... ♔f5 47 ♖e2 [□47 ♖d2] 47 ... ♖g1+ 48 ♔f3 ♖h1 49 ♔g3 ♖d1 50 ♖f2+ ♔e4 51 ♖f4+ ♔e3 52 ♖f3+ ♔d2 53 ♖f6 ♖b1 54 ♖xa6 ♖xb2 55 ♔f4 ♔xc3 56 ♔g5 ♖d2 57 ♔xh5 ♖d5+ 58 ♔g6 ♖c5 59 h5 ♔b3 60 h6 c3 61 h7 ♖c8 62 ♖a7 c2 63 ♖g7 c1♕ 64 ♖g8 **0-1** M392

### 1865-BAC-6
**MacDonnell, G.A.=Steinitz, W.**

[Löwenthal]

1 e4 e5 2 ♘f3 ♘c6 3 ♗b5 ♘f6 4 0-0 ♘xe4 [4 ... ♗e7 5 d4 ♘xd4 6 ♘xd4 exd4 7 e5 ♘d5 8 ♕xd4±] 5 d4 [5 ♖e1 (5 ♕e2 ♘f6=) 5 ... ♘d6 (5 ... ♘f6=) 6 ♘xe5 ♘xe5 7 ♖xe5+ ♗e7 8 ♗a4 0-0 9 ♗b3 ♗f6 10 ♖e1 ♘f5 11 c3 d5 12 d4 g6=] 5 ... ♗e7 [5 ... d5 6 ♘xe5 ♗d7 Jaenisch] 6 d5 ♘d6 7 dxc6 ♘xb5 8 cxd7+ ♗xd7 9 ♘xe5 ♗e6 10 ♘d3 0-0 11 ♗e3 ♗c4 12 ♕f3 ♗f6 13 ♘d2 ♗xd3 14 cxd3 ♕xd3 15 ♕xb7 ♗xb2 16 ♖ab1 ♖ab8 17 ♕a6 ♗d4

18 ♗xd4 ♕xd4 19 ♖xb5 ♖xb5 20 ♕xb5 ♕xd2 21 ♕a6 ♕d4 22 ♖b1 g6 23 h3 ♖e8 24 ♕b5 ♖e6 25 ♕b8+ ♔g7 26 ♕xc7 ♖e2 27 ♕g3 ♖xa2 28 ♖b7 ♕f6 29 ♕e3 **½-½** L/N6124

### 1865-BAC-7
**Steinitz, W.+MacDonnell, G.A.**

[Löwenthal]

1 e4 e5 2 ♘f3 d6 3 ♗c4 [3 d4] 3 ... ♗e7 4 c3 ♘f6 5 d3 0-0 6 0-0 ♗g4 7 h3 ♗xf3 8 ♕xf3 c6 9 ♗b3 ♘bd7 10 ♕e2 ♘c5 11 ♗c2 ♘e6 12 g3 ♕c7 13 f4± ♖fe8 14 ♘d2 ♖ad8 15 ♘f3 ♔h8 16 f5 ♘f8 17 g4 h6 18 g5 hxg5 19 ♘xg5 ♔g8 20 ♔h1 ♘6h7 21 ♘f3 ♖d7 [□21 ... ♗f6] 22 ♖g1 ♗d8 23 ♗h6 f6 24 ♖g2 d5 25 ♖ag1 ♖ee7 26 exd5 cxd5 [□26 ... b5] 27 ♗a4 ♖d6 28 ♖xg7+ ♖xg7 29 ♖xg7+ ♕xg7 30 ♗xg7 ♔xg7 31 ♕g2+ ♔h8 32 ♘d2 ♗b6 33 ♗e8 ♗e3 34 ♘f1 ♗f4 35 ♗f7 ♘g5 36 ♗h5 [36 ♗xd5 ♖d7 38 h4 ♖h7 39 ♕g4 ♘d7 40 ♔g2 ♖g7] 36 ... ♖d7 37 ♗g4 e4 38 ♕f2 ♗b8 39 ♕d4 ♗e5 40 ♕xa7 exd3 41 ♔g2 d4 42 c4 ♔g7 43 ♕a3 ♘e4 44 ♕xd3 ♘c5 45 ♕f3 ♗d6 46 ♘g3 d3 47 ♘h5+ ♔f7 48 b4 ♘a6 49 c5 ♗e5 50 c6 **1-0** L/N6124

### 1865-BAC-8
**Steinitz, W.+ Bolt, W.**

[Löwenthal]

1 e4 e5 2 ♘c3 ♘c6 3 ♗c4 ♗b4? [□3 ... ♘f6] 4 ♘f3 d6 5 0-0 ♘f6 6 d3 0-0 7 ♗g5 ♗xc3? 8 bxc3 h6 9 ♗h4 ♕e7 10 ♕d2 ♗e6 11 ♗b3 ♖ad8 12 ♖ae1 [△13 d4] 12 ... ♔h7 13 d4 ♗c8 [□13 ... ♗g4] 14 ♕e3 a6 15 ♘d2 g5 16 ♗g3 ♘g4 17 ♕d3 h5 18 f3 ♘h6 19 h3 f6 20 ♘c4 ♕g7 21 ♘e3 ♔h8 22 ♗f2 ♘e7 23 ♕d2 ♘g6 24 ♘d5 ♘f4 [□24 ... c6, 25 ... ♘f4] 25 ♘xf4 gxf4 26 ♔h2 c6 27 ♗h4 ♘g8 28 g3

28 ... fxg3+ 29 ♗xg3 ♘e7 30 f4 ♘g6 31 f5 ♘e7 32 ♖g1 ♕h7 33 ♗h4 b5 34 dxe5 dxe5 35 ♕xd8! [35 ... ♖xd8 36 ♗xf6+ ♕g7 37 ♖xg7+-] **1-0** L/N6124

## BERLIN 1865

### 1865-BRL-1
3 iii 65

**Neumann, G.R.+ Knorre, V.**

[Anderssen & Neumann]

1 e4 e5 2 ♘f3 ♘c6 3 ♗c4 ♗c5 4 b4

♗xb4 5 c3 ♗c5 6 0-0 d6 7 d4 exd4 8 cxd4 ♗b6 9 ♘c3 ♘a5 10 ♗d3 ♘e7 11 ♗b2 0-0 12 ♘e2 ♘g6 13 ♘g3 ♗d7 14 ♕d2 a6 15 ♖ac1 ♗b5 16 ♘f5 f6 [16 ... ♗xd3 17 d5 ♗xf1 18 ♕h6] 17 d5 ♘e5 18 ♘xe5 fxe5 [◻ 18 ... dxe5] 19 ♔h1 ♗xd3 20 ♕xd3 ♕e8 [20 ... g5 21 f4; 20 ... ♕f6 21 f4 ♖ae8 22 fxe5 dxe5 23 ♗a3 ♖f7 24 ♘e7++-] 21 f4 g6 22 ♘h6+ ♔g7 23 fxe5 ♖xf1+ 24 ♖xf1 ♕b5 25 ♖f7+ **1-0** L/N6051

**1865-BRL-2** 7 iii 65

**Neumann, G.R.+Schulten, W.**

[Anderssen & Neumann]

1 e4 e5 2 ♘f3 ♘c6 3 ♗c4 ♗c5 4 b4 ♗xb4 5 c3 ♗c5 6 0-0 d6 7 d4 exd4 8 cxd4 ♗b6 9 d5 ♘a5 10 ♗b2 f6 11 ♗d3 ♗g4 12 ♘c3 ♘e7 13 ♘e2 ♘g6 [13 ... ♗xf3 14 gxf3 ♘g6 (14 ... ♕d7 15 ♘f4) 15 f4 0-0 16 f5 ♘e5 17 ♘f4±] 14 ♘fd4 0-0 15 f3 ♗d7 16 ♔h1 c5 17 ♘e6 ♗xe6 18 dxe6 ♕e7 19 f4 ♘c6 20 ♗c4 ♘d8 21 ♘c3 ♔h8 22 ♕h5 ♕e8 23 ♖ad1 ♗c7 24 ♖d3 h6 25 ♗b5 ♘c6 26 ♘d5 ♗d8 27 ♖g3 ♔h7 [27 ... ♘ge7 28 ♕xe8 ♖xe8 29 ♘xf6] 28 ♕g4 a6 [28 ... ♖g8 29 ♗d3+-] 29 ♗xc6 bxc6 30 e7 ♗xe7 31 ♘xe7 **1-0** L/N6051

**1865-BRL-3** 10 iii 65

**Schulten, W.−Neumann, G.R.**

[Anderssen & Neumann]

1 e4 e5 2 f4 exf4 3 ♗c4 f5 4 ♕e2 ♕h4+ 5 ♔f1 [◻ 5 ♔d1] 5 ... fxe4 6 ♕xe4+ ♗e7 7 ♘f3 ♕h5 8 ♘c3 ♘f6 9 ♕xf4 d5 10 ♕xc7 ♘c6 11 ♗b5 ♗d7 12 ♗xc6 bxc6 13 ♕e5 0-0 14 ♕xh5 [14 ♕xe7 ♖ae8 15 ♕d6 ♗g4 16 ♕g3 ♘e4-+] 14 ... ♘xh5 15 d4 ♗g4 16 ♔e2 ♖ae8 17 ♖f1 ♗f6+ 18 ♔d3 ♗f5+ 19 ♔d2 ♘f4 20 g3 ♘e6 21 ♘e2 c5 22 c3 cxd4 23 ♘exd4 ♘xd4 24 cxd4 ♗h3 25 ♖e1 ♗e7 26 ♖e3 ♗b4+ **0-1** L/N6051

**1865-BRL-4** 4 iv 65

**Neumann, G.R.+Schallopp, E.**

[Anderssen & Neumann]

1 e4 e5 2 ♘f3 ♘c6 3 ♗b5 ♘f6 4 0-0 ♘xe4 5 d4 ♗e7 6 ♕e2 ♘d6 7 ♗xc6 bxc6! 8 dxe5 ♘b7 9 ♗e3 0-0 10 ♖d1 ♕e8 11 ♘c3 ♘d8 12 ♘d4 f5 13 f4 d5 14 ♘f3 ♕g6 15 ♘a4 ♘e6 16 b3 ♕g4 17 ♕d2 g5 18 h3 ♕h5 19 ♔f2 g4 20 ♘d4 [△ 20 ... gxh3 21 g3] 20 ... ♘g5?! 21 fxg5 f4 22 ♗xf4 ♗xg5 23 g3 ♕xh3 24 ♖h1 [24 ♖g1 ♕h2+ 25 ♖g2 ♗xf4 26 gxf4 ♖xf4+ 27 ♔e3 ♖e4+-+] 24 ... ♗xf4 25 gxf4 g3+ 26 ♔g1 ♕g4 27 ♖f1 ♗f5 28 ♘c5 h5 29 ♕e2 **1-0** L/N6051

**1865-BRL-5** 15 iv 65

**Knorre, V.+Lichtenhein, A.**

[Anderssen & Neumann]

1 e4 e6 2 d4 d5 3 exd5 exd5 4 ♘f3 ♘f6 5 ♗d3 ♗d6 6 0-0 0-0 7 c4 c5 8 ♘c3 dxc4 9 ♗xc4 cxd4 10 ♘xd4 h6 11 ♘db5 ♗c7 12 ♕c2 a6 13 ♘xc7 ♕xc7 14 ♗b3 ♘c6 15 ♘e2 ♗d7? 16 ♗xh6 ♘g4 17 ♗f4 ♕a5 18 ♗d2 ♕h5 19 h3 ♘f6 20 ♘g3 ♕h4 21 ♗c3 ♖ac8 22 ♖ad1 ♖fd8 23 ♕g6 ♗e6 24 ♘f5 ♗xf5 25 ♕xf5 ♘e7 26 ♕f3 ♕e4 27 ♖xd8+ ♖xd8 28 ♕xe4 ♘xe4 29 ♖e1 ♘xc3 30 ♖xe7 ♘b5 [30 ... ♘d5+-] 31 ♖xf7 ♔h8 32 ♖xb7 ♖d2 33 ♖b6 ♖d6 34 ♖b8+ ♔h7 35 ♗c4 ♘c7 36 ♖b7 ♖c6 37 ♗d3+ ♔h6 38 ♖a7 ♔g5 39 b4 ♔f6 40 ♔h2 ♔e5 41 ♗xa6 ♖xa6 42 ♖xc7 ♖xa2 43 ♖xg7 ♖xf2 44 b5 ♖b2 45 h4 ♔f6 46 ♖g5 **1-0** L/N6051

**1865-BRL-6**

**Knorre, V.+Schallopp, E.**

[Knorre]

1 e4 e5 2 ♘f3 ♘c6 3 ♗c4 ♗c5 4 b4 ♗xb4 5 c3 ♗a5 6 d4 exd4 7 0-0 ♗b6 8 cxd4 d6 9 d5 ♘a5 10 ♗b2 ♘e7 11 ♗d3 0-0 12 ♘c3 ♘g6 13 ♘e2 c5 14 ♕d2 a6 15 ♘g3 f6 16 ♘f5 ♗xf5 17 exf5 ♘e7 18 ♘h4 ♘xd5? 19 ♗c4 ♘xc4 20 ♕xd5+ ♖f7 21 ♕xc4 d5 22 ♕d3 ♕d7 23 ♖ae1 c4 24 ♕h3 d4 25 ♖e4 c3

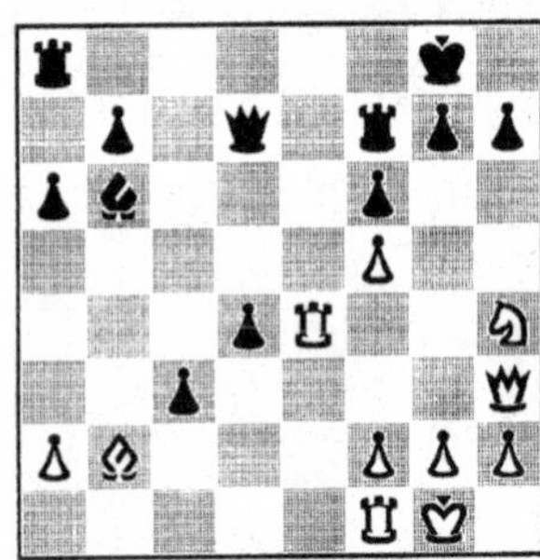

26 ♘g6 h6 [26 ... cxb2 27 ♕xh7++-; 26 ... hxg6 27 ♖h4 ♖ff8 (27 ... ♔f8 28 ♗a3+ ♖e7 29 ♖h8+ ♔f7 30 fxg6+ ♔xg6 31 ♕h5#) 28 ♖h8+ ♔f7 29 fxg6+ ♔e7 30 ♗a3+ ♔d8 31 ♖xf8+ ♔c7 32 ♖f7+-] 27 ♗a3 ♖e8 28 ♖e6 [△ 29 ♖xb6; 29 ♖fe1] 28 ... ♖c8 29 ♖xb6 d3 30 ♖d6 ♕a4 31 ♕xd3 ♕xa3 32 ♖d8+ ♖f8 33 ♕d5+ ♔h7 34 ♘xf8+ **1-0** L/N6051

## ELBERFELD 1865

**1865-ELB-1** 27 viii 65

**Neumann, G.R.+Pinedo, J.**

[Anderssen & Neumann]

1 e4 c5 2 ♗c4 e6 3 ♘c3 d6 4 d3 ♘e7 5 ♗g5 h6 6 ♗h4 [◻ 6 ♗xe7] 6 ... g5 7 ♗g3 a6 8 a4 ♘g6 9 ♘ge2 ♘c6 10 f4 ♗e7 11 0-0 h5 12 f5 ♘ge5 13 ♗xe5 ♘xe5 14 ♘g3 g4 15 ♘ge2 ♗f6 16 ♗b3 ♘c6 17 fxe6 fxe6 18 ♘f4 ♘d4 19 ♗c4 ♖h6 20 ♖b1 [△ 21 ♘ce2] 20 ... ♗e5 21 ♘ce2 ♕g5 22 ♘xd4 ♗xd4+ 23 ♔h1 ♗e3 24 ♘e2 ♗d7 25 ♗b3 ♗c6 26 c4 h4 27 a5 ♔e7 28 ♗a4 h3 29 g3 b5 30 axb6 ♗b7 31 ♘f4 ♕e5 [△ 31 ... ♗xe4+ 32 dxe4 ♕xe4+-+] 32 ♕xg4 ♖g8 33 ♕f3! ♗xf4 34 ♕xf4 ♕h5 35 b4 e5 36 ♕f5 ♕xf5 37 ♖xf5 ♔e6 38 bxc5 dxc5 39 ♖bf1 **1-0** L/N6051

**1865-ELB-2** viii 65

**Knorre, V.=Höing, C.**

[Anderssen & Neumann]

1 e4 e5 2 ♘f3 ♘f6 3 ♘xe5 d6 4 ♘f3 ♘xe4 5 d4 ♗g4 6 ♗d3 d5 7 0-0 ♗d6 8 c4 c6 9 ♘bd2 [◻ 9 ♖e1] 9 ... f5? [◻ 9 ... ♘xd2] 10 cxd5 cxd5 11 ♕a4+ ♕d7 12 ♗b5 ♘c6 13 ♘e5 ♗xe5 14 dxe5 ♘xd2 15 ♗xd2 0-0 16 ♗b4 ♖fc8 17 ♖ac1 [◻ 17 ♗d6, 17 ... a6 18 ♗d3] 17 ... a6 18 ♗xc6 bxc6= 19 f3 ♗h5 20 ♗d6 ♗e8 21 ♕f4 ♕e6 22 g4 ♗d7 **½-½** L/N6051

## LEIPZIG 1865
## Augustea

**1865-LPZ-1** i 65

**von Gottschall, R.−Minckwitz, J.**

[Minckwitz & von Schmidt]

1 e4 e5 2 ♗c4 ♗c5 3 c3 ♘f6 4 ♕e2 0-0 5 b4 ♗b6 6 a4 a5 7 ♘f3 d5 8 exd5 e4 9 ♘e5 ♕d6 10 d4 exd3 11 ♘xd3 [◻ 11 ♗xd3, 12 ♗f4] 11 ... ♖e8 12 ♗e3 ♘g4 13 ♔d2 ♘xe3 14 fxe3 ♗xe3+ 15 ♔c2 ♗f5 16 g4 ♗g6 17 h4 ♘d7 18 ♕f1 axb4 19 cxb4 ♕xb4 20 ♗b5 ♘c5 21 ♖a3 ♗d4 **0-1** L/N6047

**1865-LPZ-2** 22 i 85

**Minckwitz, J.=Lange, M.**

[Minckwitz & von Schmidt]

1 e4 e5 2 ♘f3 ♘c6 3 ♗b5 ♘f6 4 0-0 ♗e7 5 d4 exd4 6 e5 ♘e4 7 ♘xd4 ♘xd4 8 ♕xd4 ♘c5 9 f4 ♘e6 [9 ... 0-0] 10 ♕d1! c6 11 ♗d3 d5 12 ♘c3 ♘c5 [◻ 12 ... ♗c5+, ♕h4] 13 f5 ♘xd3 14 ♕xd3 f6 15 e6 ♗c5+ 16 ♔h1 0-0!? 17 ♗d2 [◻ 17 ♕h3, ♖f4] 17 ...

b6 18 ♖ae1 a5 19 ♕g3 ♖a7 20 ♘e2 ♗a6 21 ♖f3 ♗xe2 22 ♖xe2 ♕e7 23 h4 [◻ 23 ♕h4 ♗d6 (23 ... g5 24 fxg6 hxg6 25 ♖h3 ♕h7 26 ♕g4 ♕g7 27 ♗h6 f5 28 ♗xg7+-) 24 ♖h3 h6 25 ♖ee3 ♖c8 26 ♖ef3 ♕f8! 27 ♕g4 ♔h8! 28 ♖h4 ♗e5! 29 ♖fh3 ♖cc7! 30 ♕g6 ♕g8 31 ♗xh6 gxh6 32 ♖xh6+ ♖h7 33 ♖xh7+ ♖xh7 34 ♖xh7+ ♕xh7 35 ♕xh7+ ♔xh7 36 e7+-] 23 ... ♕e8 24 ♕g4 ♗d6 25 h5 ♔h8 26 ♖h3 c5 27 ♕f3 d4 28 ♕d5 ♗b8 [△ 29 ... ♕b5] 29 ♕e4 a4 30 g4 ♗e5 31 ♗f4 ♗xf4 32 ♕xf4 ♕c6+ 33 ♔g1 ♕b5 34 ♔f2 [△ g5] 34 ... h6 35 c3 dxc3! 36 ♖xc3 ♖d8 37 ♖ce3 ♕c6 38 e7 ♖e8 39 ♕c4 ♕d6 40 ♕f7 ♖aa8 41 ♖e4 b5 42 ♔f3 c4 43 ♕e6 [◻ 43 ♕g6 ~ 44 g5 hxg5 (44 ... fxg5 44 f6) 45 h6] 43 ... ♕xe6 44 ♖xe6 a3 45 ♔e4 axb2 46 ♖xb2 c3 47 ♖xb5 ♖xa2 48 ♖c5 ♖a4+ 49 ♔f3 [49 ♔d5=] 49 ... ♖a3 50 ♖e3 ♔g8 51 ♖cxc3 ♖xc3 52 ♖xc3 ♔f7 53 ♖e3 ♖xe7 54 ♖xe7+ ♔xe7 55 ♔e4 ♔d6 56 ♔d4 ♔c6 ½-½

L/N6047

**1865-LPZ-3** 1 ii 65
**Schmidt, E. von= Pici**
[Minckwitz & von Schmidt]

1 e3 e6 2 c4 c5 3 d4 cxd4 4 exd4 d5 5 ♗d3 ♘f6 6 ♘c3 h6 [◻ 6 ... ♗e7] 7 ♘f3 ♗e7 8 0-0 ♘c6 9 ♗e3 a6 10 ♘e5 dxc4 11 ♗xc4 ♘xe5 12 dxe5 ♕xd1 13 ♖axd1 ♘g4 14 ♗d4 h5 15 ♘e4 ♘h6 [◻ 15 ... b5] 16 ♗b6 ♗d7 17 ♘d6+ ♗xd6! 18 exd6 ♖c8 19 ♗c7 ♘f5 20 ♗d3 ♘e7 21 ♗e4 ♘c6 22 ♖fe1 g6 23 ♖e3 f5 24 ♗f3 g5 25 g3 ♔f7 26 ♖b3 b5 27 ♖a3 e5 28 ♗d5+ ♔e8 29 ♖xa6 ♘b4 30 ♖a8 ♖xa8 31 ♗xa8 ♔f7 32 ♗b7 ♔e6 33 a3 ♘c6 34 ♔f1 ♘d4 35 f4 ♘c2 36 ♗d5+ ♔f6 37 fxe5+ ♔xe5 38 ♔f2 f4 39 ♗a5 [◻ 39 ♗c6] 39 ... fxg3+ 40 hxg3 b4 41 ♗g2 h4 42 ♖d5+ ♔f6 43 ♖c5 h3 44 ♗h1 ♖c8 45 ♖xc8 ♗xc8 46 axb4 ♘d4 47 ♗b6 ♘b5 48 ♗d8+ ♔f5 49 ♗e7 ♗d7 50 ♔e3 g4 51 ♔d3 ♔e6 ½-½

L/N6047

**1865-LPZ-4** ii 65
**Minckwitz,J.=Schmidt,E. von**
[Minckwitz & von Schmidt]

1 e4 e5 2 ♘f3 ♘c6 3 ♗b5 a6 4 ♗a4 ♘f6 5 0-0 ♘xe4 6 ♕e2 ♘c5 7 ♗xc6 dxc6 8 d4 ♘e6 9 dxe5 ♗c5! 10 ♘c3 0-0 11 ♘e4 ♘d4 12 ♘xd4 ♕xd4 13 ♘xc5 ♕xc5 14 ♔h1 ♗f5= 15 c3 ♖ae8 16 f4 f6 17 ♗e3 ♕e7 18 ♗d4 b6 19 b4 [19 ♕xa6?] 19 ... ♗c8 20 ♖fe1 fxe5 21 ♗xe5 [21 fxe5 ♖f6] 21 ... ♖xf4 22 ♗xf4 ♕xe2 23 ♖xe2 ♖xe2 24 ♗xc7 ♗e6 25 ♗xb6 ♗d5 26 ♖g1 ♖xa2 27 ♗d4 ♔f7 28 h4 ½-½

L/N6047

**1865-LPZ-5** ii 65
**Schmidt,E.von+Lange, M.**
[Minckwitz & von Schmidt]

1 e4 e5 2 ♘f3 ♘c6 3 ♗b5 ♘f6 4 0-0 ♗e7 5 d3 d6 6 h3 ♗d7 7 c3 h6 8 ♗e3 0-0 9 ♘bd2 a6 10 ♗a4 b5 11 ♗b3 ♔h8 [11 ... ♘a5 12 ♗c2] 12 d4 ♘h7 13 ♘h2 exd4 [13 ... f5 14 f4] 14 cxd4 ♗f6 15 ♗d5 ♖b8 16 ♗xc6 ♗xc6 17 f4 ♗b7! 18 e5 ♗e7 19 ♘df3 f5 [19 ... f6 20 ♘h4] 20 ♕e2 ♕e8 21 ♖ac1 ♖c8 22 g4 ♕f7 23 b3 ♖g8 24 ♖f2 g5 25 fxg5! f4! 26 ♗d2 hxg5 27 ♗a5 c5 28 dxc5 ♖xc5 29 ♗c3 [29 ♖xc5 dxc5 30 e6±] 29 ... ♕g7 30 exd6 ♖xc3 31 ♖xc3 ♗xd6 32 ♖c2 ♗b8 33 ♖f1 ♘f6 34 ♖fc1 ♖e8 35 ♕d1 ♗a7+ 36 ♔g2 ♘d5 37 ♘f1 ♖e3 [◻ 37 ... ♗e3]

38 ♖c8+ ♔h7 39 ♕c2+ ♔h6 40 ♖c6+ ♗xc6 41 ♕xc6+ ♔h7 42 ♘xe3 ♗xe3 43 ♖c2 ♘b6 44 ♕c7 ♘d5 45 ♘xg5+ ♔g6 46 ♕xg7+ ♔xg7 **1-0**

L/N6047

**1865-LPZ-6** ii 65
**Minckwitz, J.+ Schurig, R.**
[Minckwitz & von Schmidt]

1 e4 e5 2 ♘f3 ♘c6 3 ♗c4 ♘f6 4 ♘g5 d5 5 exd5 ♘a5 6 ♗b5+ c6 7 dxc6 bxc6 8 ♗e2 ♗c5 9 c3 ♘b7! 10 0-0 0-0 11 b4 ♗b6 12 ♘a3 h6 13 ♘f3 ♖e8 14 ♘c4 ♗c7 15 ♘e3 ♗e6 16 ♗b2 ♘d6 17 d4 e4 18 ♘e1 ♘f5 19 ♘1c2 ♕d6 20 g3 ♖ad8 21 ♘xf5 ♗xf5 22 ♘e3 ♗h3 23 ♖e1 ♘h7 24 ♗f1 ♘g5 25 ♗xh3 ♘xh3+ 26 ♔g2 ♘g5 27 ♘f5 ♕d7 28 ♕g4 ♔h7 29 h4 g6 30 ♘xh6 ♘e6! 31 ♗c1 f5 32 ♕e2 [◻ 32 ♘xf5 gxf5 33 ♕xf5+ ♔g8 34 ♖xe4±] 32 ... f4 33 gxf4 ♗xf4 34 ♘g4 ♕f7 35 ♗e3! ♖d5 36 ♖h1 ♖h5 37 ♖h3 ♕f5 38 ♖ah1 ♔g7 39 ♘e5 ♖eh8 [◻ 39 ... ♗xe5 40 dxe5 ♕xe5] 40 ♕g4 ♕f6 41 ♘xc6 ♖f5 [◻ 41 ... ♖f8] 42 ♘e5 ♗xe3 43 fxe3 ♖f8 44 ♖g1 ♘g5 45 hxg5 ♖xg5 46 ♕xg5 ♕xg5+ 47 ♖g3 ♕h5 48 ♖xg6+ ♔h7 49 ♖h1 ♖f2+ 50 ♔xf2 ♕xh1 51 ♖g1 ♕h3 52 c4 ♕c8 [52 ... ♕h4+ 53 ♔e2±] 53 ♖g4 ♕f8+ 54 ♔g3 ♕xb4 55 ♖xe4 ♕e1+ 56 ♔f4 ♕h4+ 57 ♔f5 ♕h5+ 58 ♔f6 ♕h6+ 59 ♔e7 ♕g7+ 60 ♘f7 ♕g3 61 ♖e5 ♕f3 62 d5 ♕f1 63 ♖h5+ ♔g7 64 ♖g5+ ♔h7 65 ♔f8 **1-0**

L/N6047

**1865-LPZ-7** ii 65
**Schmidt,E.von+von Gottschall,R.**
[Minckwitz & von Schmidt]

1 d4 d5 2 c4 e6 3 ♘c3 ♘f6 4 e3 ♗e7 [◻ 4 ... c5] 5 ♘f3 ♘c6 6 a3 a5 7 ♗d3 0-0 8 0-0 b6 9 ♕e2 ♗b7 10 cxd5 exd5 11 ♗d2 ♖e8 12 ♖ac1 ♘a7 13 ♘e5 c5 14 f4 ♗d6 15 ♔h1 cxd4 16 exd4± h6 17 g4 ♘d7 18 ♗b1 ♘xe5 19 fxe5 ♗xe5 20 dxe5 d4+ 21 ♘e4 ♖xe5 22 ♗f4 ♖e7 [◻ 22 ... d3 23 ♗xd3 ♕xd3=] 23 ♔g1 ♕d7 24 ♖c7 ♕e6 25 ♖xe7 ♕xe7 26 ♕d3 ♕e6 27 ♘d6 ♕xg4+ 28 ♗g3 ♗d5 29 ♕h7+ ♔f8 30 ♖e1 f6 **1-0**

L/N6047

**1865-LPZ-8**
**Gottschall,R.+Schmidt,E. von**
[Minckwitz & von Schmidt]

1 e4 e5 2 f4 exf4 3 ♘f3 g5 4 ♗c4 ♗g7 5 d4 d6 6 c3 g4 7 ♗xf4 gxf3 8 ♕xf3 ♗e6! 9 d5! [9 ♗xe6?] 9 ... ♗d7 [◻ 9 ... ♗c8] 10 0-0 ♕e7 [◻ 10 ... ♕f6] 11 ♘d2 ♘h6 12 ♖ae1 0-0 13 ♕g3 ♔h8 14 e5 dxe5 15 ♗xe5 ♕c5+ 16 ♔h1 ♖g8 17 ♕h4 ♗xe5 18 ♖xe5 ♘g4 19 ♖xf7 ♖g7

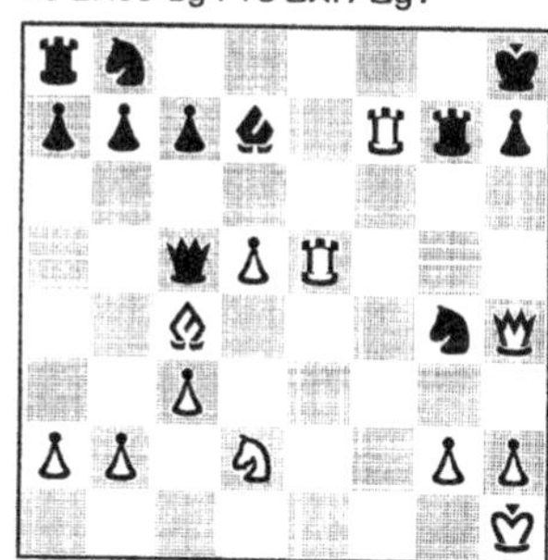

20 ♘e4 ♖xf7 [20 ... ♕xc4 21 ♖f8+ ♖g8 22 ♖e7+-] 21 ♘xc5 ♘xe5 22 ♕d8+ ♔g7 23 ♕g5+ ♔f8 24 ♕xe5 **1-0**

L/N6047

**1865-LPZ-9**
**Schmidt,E.von+ Minckwitz,J.**
[Minckwitz & von Schmidt]

1 d4 e6 2 e4 d5 3 exd5 exd5 4 ♘f3 ♘f6 5 ♗d3 ♗d6 [5 ... c5] 6 0-0 0-0 7 c4 dxc4 8 ♗xc4 ♘c6 9 ♘c3 ♗g4 10 ♗e3 ♕d7 11 h3 ♗h5 12 d5 ♗xf3 [12 ... ♘e5 13 ♗e2] 13 ♕xf3 ♘e5 14 ♕e2 ♖fe8 15 ♗b5 c6 16 dxc6 bxc6 17 ♗a4 ♕c7 18 ♖ac1 ♗c5 19 ♘b5± cxb5 20 ♖xc5 ♕e7 21

♗xb5 ♖ed8 22 ♖fc1 ♘d5 23 ♗d4 ♘g6 24 ♕xe7 ♘gxe7 25 ♗e5 a6 26 ♗c4 **1-0** L/N6047

## DE VERE⚔STEINITZ London

[1865-⚔DS]

| | | | | | | | | | | | | | |
|---|---|---|---|---|---|---|---|---|---|---|---|---|---|
| C. De Vere | 0 | 1 | 1 | 1 | 0 | 1 | 1 | 0 | ½ | ½ | 1 | 1 | 8 |
| W. Steinitz | 1 | 0 | 0 | 0 | 1 | 0 | 0 | 1 | ½ | ½ | 0 | 0 | 4 |

### 1865-⚔DS-1

**De Vere, C.– Steinitz, W.**

[Löwenthal]

⟨Δf7⟩ 1 e4 ♘c6 2 d4 e5 3 dxe5 ♘xe5 4 f4 ♘f7 5 ♗c4 ♘gh6 6 ♘f3 ♗c5 7 ♘c3 0-0 8 ♕d3 [8 ♘g5?!] 8 ... c6∞ 9 ♗d2 [□ 9 ♗e3] 9 ... d5 10 ♗b3 b5 11 0-0-0 [□ 11 exd5] 11 ... a5 12 a4 b4 13 ♘xd5 cxd5 14 ♗xd5 ♗a6 15 ♕b3 ♖b8 16 ♘g5 ♕e7 17 f5 ♔h8 18 ♘e6 ♖fe8 19 ♕g3 ♖g8 20 h4 ♗d6 21 ♕b3 ♗e5 22 ♘g5 ♖gf8 23 g4 ♗c8 24 ♘f3 [□ 24 ♖dg1, ♘f3] 24 ... ♘xg4 25 ♗xf7 ♘f2 26 ♘xe5 ♕xe5 27 ♖hf1 ♘xd1 28 ♗f4 ♕xe4 29 ♗xb8 ♘e3 30 ♖e1 ♗xf5!→ 31 ♗h5 [31 ♖xe3 ♕h1+→; 31 ♕d3 ♕c6→] 31 ... ♖xb8 32 ♖xe3 ♕h1+ 33 ♗d1 ♖d8 34 c4 ♕xh4 35 ♖e2 ♕f4+ 36 ♕e3 ♕xc4+ 37 ♗c2 ♗xc2 **0-1** L/N6124-1866

### 1865-⚔DS-2

**De Vere, C.+ Steinitz, W.**

[Löwenthal]

⟨Δf7⟩ 1 e4 e6 2 d4 d5 3 e5 c5 4 ♘f3 cxd4 5 ♘xd4 ♘c6 6 ♘xc6 bxc6 7 ♗d3 ♘e7 8 ♗g5 ♕b6 9 b3 [9 ♗xe7 ♗xe7 10 ♕h5+ ♔d8 11 ♘d2 (11 b3? ♕d4) 11 ... ♕xb2 12 0-0 c5; 9 ... ♕xb2?! 10 ♗xf8 ♖xf8 (10 ... ♕xe5+ 11 ♗e2 ♕xa1 12 ♗b4±; 10 ... ♕xa1 11 ♗xg7 ♖g8 12 ♕h5+−) 11 ♘d2 ♕xe5+ 12 ♗e2 ♗a6 13 ♖b1] 9 ... ♗d7 10 0-0 0-0-0 11 ♘c3 h6 12 ♘a4! ♕c7 13 ♗e3 ♘f5 14 ♗xf5 exf5 15 ♕d4 ♔b8 16 f4 ♗c8 17 ♘c5± ♔a8 18 a4 ♗e7 [□ 18 ... ♗xc5 Δ=] 19 b4 ♖he8 20 b5 ♕b6 21 bxc6 ♗xc5 22 ♕xc5 ♕xc5 23 ♗xc5 ♗a6 24 ♖fd1 ♖c8 25 ♖xd5 ♖xc6 26 ♖d6! ♗b7 [26 ... ♖xc5+−] 27 ♖xc6 ♗xc6 28 ♗d6 ♔b7 29 h4 ♖g8 30 ♔f2 g5 31 fxg5 hxg5 32 h5 ♖h8 33 ♖h1 ♗xa4 34 h6 ♗xc2 35 e6 f4 36 ♗e5 ♖h7 37 ♗g7 a5 38 e7 ♗g6 39 ♖d1 **1-0** L/N6124-1866

### 1865-⚔DS-3

**De Vere, C.+ Steinitz, W.**

[Lowenthal]

⟨Δf7⟩ 1 e4 e6 2 d4 d5 3 exd5 exd5 4 ♗d3 ♘f6 5 ♗g5 ♗e7 [□ 5 ... ♗d6] 6 ♘c3 ♗g4 7 f3 ♗h5 8 ♕e2 0-0 9 0-0-0 c6 10 ♘h3 ♗b4 11 ♘f4 ♖e8 12 ♗xf6 ♕xf6 13 ♘xh5 ♕h6+ 14 ♕d2 ♕xh5 15 h4 ♘d7 16 ♕g5! ♕xg5+ [□ 16 ... ♕f7] 17 hxg5 ♘f8 18 ♘e2 ♖e3 19 a3 ♗d6 20 f4 ♖ae8 21 ♔d2 b6 22 ♖df1 ♖3e7 23 f5 ♖f7 24 g4 ♗e7 25 g6 hxg6 26 fxg6 ♗g5+ 27 ♔d1 ♖f6 28 ♖f5 ♖xf5 29 gxf5 ♘d7 30 b4 ♘f6 31 ♖g1 ♗h6 32 a4 ♔f8 33 ♖g2 ♔e7 34 ♘g1 ♔d6 35 ♘f3 ♗f4 36 ♘g5 ♗xg5 37 ♖xg5 c5 38 dxc5+ bxc5 39 bxc5+ ♔xc5 40 ♖g2 ♔b4 41 ♔d2! ♔xa4 42 ♖g1 ♖e7 43 ♔c3 ♖c7+ 44 ♔d4 ♔a3 45 ♖a1+ ♔b2 46 ♖a6!+− ♔c1 47 ♖xf6 gxf6 48 ♔xd5 a5 49 ♔e6 ♖c8 50 ♗b5 ♔xc2 51 ♔d7 **1-0** L/N6124

### 1865-⚔DS-4

**De Vere, C.+ Steinitz, W.**

[Löwenthal]

⟨Δf7⟩ 1 d4 ♘f6 2 ♘c3 e6 3 e4 ♗b4 4 ♗g5 h6 5 ♗xf6 ♕xf6 6 e5 ♕f7 7 ♗d3 0-0 8 ♘f3 ♘c6 9 0-0 ♗e7 10 ♘e4 b6 11 c3 ♗b7 12 ♗c2 ♗d8 13 ♕d3 g6 14 ♖ae1 ♔g7 15 ♘g3 ♘e7 16 ♘h5+ ♔h8 17 ♘f6 ♘f5 18 g4 ♗xf6 19 gxf5 [19 exf6 ♘d6 20 ♘h4±; 19 ... ♖g8! 20 gxf5 gxf5+ 21 ♔h1 ♕h5 22 ♗d1 ♖g4 23 ♖g1 ♖ag8] 19 ... gxf5! 20 exf6 ♖g8+ 21 ♔h1 ♕h5 22 ♗d1 ♖g4 23 ♖g1 ♖ag8 24 c4 ♗e4 25 ♕e3 ♖8g5 [Δ 26 ... ♕xh2+ 27 ♔xh2 ♖h5+ 28 ♘h4 ♖gxh4+ 29 ♔g3 f4+ 30 ♕xf4 ♖h3+ 31 ♔g4 ♖5h4#]

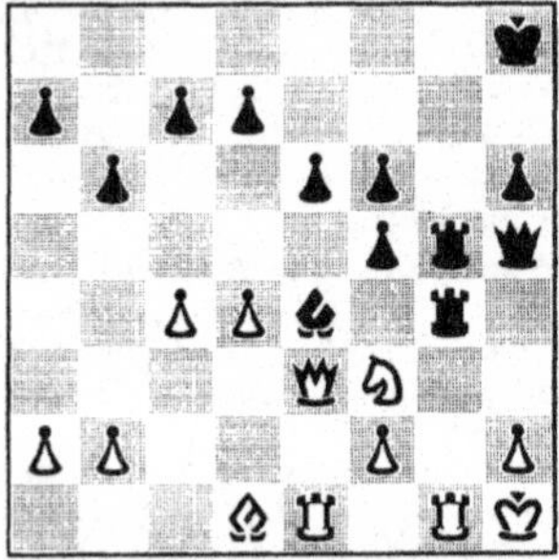

26 ♕xe4!! fxe4 27 ♘xg5 ♖xg1+ 28 ♖xg1 ♕g6 29 f7 ♕f6 30 ♗h5 hxg5 31 ♖xg5 ♕xg5 32 f8♕+ ♔h7 33 ♕f7+ ♔h6 34 ♗d1 ♕d2 35 ♕h5+ ♔g7 36 ♕g4+ ♔f8 37 ♔g2 ♕xd4 38 h4 ♕xc4 39 h5 ♕xa2 40 ♕f4+ ♔g8 41 ♕g5+ ♔f7 42 ♕g6+ ♔e7 43 ♕g7+ **1-0** L/N6124

### 1865-⚔DS-5

**De Vere, C.– Steinitz, W.**

[Löwenthal]

⟨Δf7⟩ 1 e4 b6 2 d4 ♗b7 3 ♗d3 ♘c6 4 d5 ♘e5 5 f4 ♘xd3+ 6 ♕xd3 g6 7 ♗e3 ♗g7 8 ♗d4 ♘f6 9 ♘c3 0-0 10 ♗xf6 [□ 10 ♘ge2] 10 ... ♗xf6 11 e5 ♗g7 12 ♘ge2 d6 13 e6 c6 14 0-0 cxd5 15 ♘xd5 ♗xb2 16 ♖ab1 ♗g7 17 ♘g3 ♗xd5 18 ♕xd5 ♕c7 19 c4 ♖ac8 20 ♖bc1 ♕c5+!→ 21 ♔h1 ♕xd5 22 cxd5 ♖xc1 23 ♖xc1 ♖xf4 24 ♖c8+ ♗f8 25 h3 ♖d4 26 ♖a8 ♖xd5 27 ♖xa7 ♖e5 28 ♖a6 ♖xe6 29 ♖xb6 ♖e1+ 30 ♔h2 ♗g7 31 ♖b3 ♗e5 32 h4 ♖a1 33 a3 d5 34 ♔h3 h6 **0-1** L/N6124

### 1865-⚔DS-6

**De Vere, C.+ Steinitz, W.**

⟨Δf7⟩ 1 e4 b6 2 d4 ♗b7 3 ♗d3 ♘c6 4 ♘f3 e6 5 0-0 ♘ge7 6 ♗g5 h6 7 ♗e3 g6 8 c3 ♗g7 9 ♘h4 0-0 10 e5 g5 11 ♘f3 ♘f5 12 ♘bd2 g4 13 ♘e1 ♕h4 14 ♗e4 d5 15 ♗xf5 ♖xf5 16 f4 ♗a6 [16 ... ♖h5? 17 h3 gxh3 18 ♗f2+−] 17 g3 ♕d8 18 ♖f2 h5 19 ♘g2 ♘e7 20 ♘h4 ♖f7 21 h3 ♘f5 22 ♘xf5 exf5 23 h4 ♗f8 24 ♕c2 ♕d7 25 a4 c5 26 ♖e1 ♕c6 27 ♘f1 ♗c8 28 ♖d2 ♗e6 29 ♗f2 c4 30 b3 cxb3 31 ♕xb3 ♖c8 32 ♖c1 ♕c4 33 ♕d1 [33 ♕xc4?] 33 ... ♗a3 34 ♘e3 ♕a6 35 ♖cc2 ♖d7 [35 ... ♕xa4? 36 c4 ♖fc7 37 cxd5 ♖xc2 38 ♖xc2 ♖xc2 39 ♕xc2 ♕xc2 40 ♘xc2+−] 36 ♕a1 ♗f8 37 ♕a2 ♕b7 38 ♕b3 ♖dc7 39 ♖d1 ♕c6 40 ♖dc1 ♕b7 41 ♕b5 ♔f7 [41 ... ♗a3? 42 ♖a1 ♖xc3 43 ♖xc3 ♖xc3 44 ♕e8++] 42 ♕d3 ♔g6 43 ♗e1 ♕c6 44 ♕b5 ♗a3 45 ♖a1 ♕xb5 46 axb5 ♗e7 47 ♖ca2 ♖a8 48 ♔g2 ♖d7 49 ♗f2 ♔f7 50 c4?! [□ 50 ♖a6 ♖b7 51 c4±] 50 ... dxc4 51 d5 ♗xd5+ 52 ♘xd5 ♖xd5 53 ♖xa7 ♖xa7 54 ♖xa7 ♖xb5 55 ♖c7 ♖b4! [55 ... ♖b2? 56 ♔f1 b5 57 ♗c5+−] 56 ♖c6 ♖b2!→ 57 ♔f1 [57 ♖xc4? ♗c5] 57 ... b5 58 e6+ ♔g6 59 ♗d4 ♖d2 60 ♗e5 ♖d8 61 ♔e2 ♖a8 62 ♖c7 ♗f6 63 ♖b7 ♖a2+ 64 ♔d1 ♗xe5 65 fxe5 ♖a6 66 e7 ♖e6?? 67 ♖b6 ♔f7 68 ♖xe6 **1-0** L/N6124

### 1865-⚔DS-7

**De Vere, C.+ Steinitz, W.**

[Löwenthal]

⟨Δf7⟩ 1 e4 b6 2 d4 ♗b7 3 ♗d3 ♘c6 4 ♘f3 e6 5 0-0 ♘h6 6 ♘c3 ♘f7 7 ♗f4 ♗e7 8 ♗g3 0-0 9 a3 ♖c8 10 d5 exd5 [□ 10 ... ♘b8] 11 exd5 ♘b8 12 ♘b5 ♘a6 13 ♘xa7 ♖a8 14 ♘b5 ♗f6 15 c3 ♔h8 16 ♗c2 ♕e7 17 b4 d6 18 ♕d3 g6 19 ♖ae1 ♕d7 20 c4 ♘b8 21 ♖e6 ♘d8 22 ♖xf6 ♖xf6 23 ♕c3 ♔g7 24 ♗h4 ♕f7 25 ♘g5 ♕f8 26 ♘xc7+− ♔g8 [26 ... ♖a7 27 ♘ce6+] 27 ♘xa8 ♗xa8 28 ♘xh7 **1-0** L/N6124

### 1865-⚔DS-8

**De Vere, C.– Steinitz, W.**

[Löwenthal]

⟨Δf7⟩ 1 e4 d6 2 d4 ♘f6 3 ♘c3 ♘c6 4 ♗g5 e6 5 ♘f3 h6 6 ♗xf6 ♕xf6 7 ♗d3 ♗d7 8 a3?! ♘xd4 9 ♘xd4

♕xd4 10 ♕h5+ ♔d8 11 0-0 ♗e7 12 ♖ad1 c6 13 ♕e2 ♔c7 14 ♗c4 ♕c5 15 ♖d2 ♖ad8 16 b4 ♕e5∓ 17 ♕e3 g5 18 ♗e2 ♔b8 19 ♖b1 h5 20 b5 c5 21 b6 a6 22 a4 [22 ♗xa6 bxa6 23 ♕e2 ♗c8 24 b7 ♗xb7 25 ♕xa6 ♖d7] 22 ... ♗c6 23 ♗c4 h4 24 h3 g4! 25 ♕d3 d5 26 exd5 exd5 27 ♖e2 ♕g5 28 ♗xd5 ♗xd5 29 ♘xd5 ♖xd5 30 ♕e4 ♗d8 31 hxg4 ♖d4 32 ♕e6 ♖xg4 33 ♕d6+ ♔a8 34 f3 ♖d4 **0-1** L/N6124

## 1865-⚔DS-9
**De Vere, C.= Steinitz, W.**

[Löwenthal]

⟨♙f7⟩ 1 e4 d6 2 d4 ♘f6 3 ♘c3 ♘c6 4 ♗g5 e6 5 ♘f3 h6 6 ♗h4 g5 7 ♗g3 ♗g7 8 ♗b5 0-0 9 0-0 ♘h7 10 h3 ♔h8 11 ♗xc6 bxc6 12 e5 ♕e7 13 ♘e4 ♖d8 14 ♕e2 a5 15 ♕e3 ♘f8 16 ♕a3 c5 17 exd6 cxd6 18 dxc5 dxc5 19 ♘e5 ♖d5 20 ♘d3 ♗a6 21 ♖fe1 ♗xd3 22 cxd3 ♕b7 23 ♖ab1 ♕b4 24 ♖e3 ♘d7 25 ♘d6 ♕xa3 26 bxa3 e5 27 ♘c4 a4 28 ♘b6 ♖b8 29 ♘xd5 ♖xb1+ 30 ♔h2 ♖d1 [30 ... ♖b2] 31 ♘e7 ♖d2 32 ♘g6+ ♔h7 33 ♘xe5 ♘xe5 34 ♗xe5 ♖xa2 35 ♗xg7 ♔xg7 36 ♖e5 ♖xa3 37 ♖xc5 ♖xd3 38 ♖c6 a3= 39 ♖a6 h5 40 g3 ♔f7 41 ♔g2 ♔e7 42 h4 gxh4 43 gxh4 ♔f7 44 f3 ♖d2+ 45 ♔g3 a2 46 ♔f4 ♖g2 47 ♔f5 ♖b2 48 ♖a7+ ♔f8 49 f4 ♖g2 50 ♔f6 ♔g8 51 f5 ♔h8 52 ♖a8+ ♔h7 53 ♖a7+ ♔h8 54 ♔e6 ♔g8 55 f6 ♖e2+ 56 ♔f5 ♖g2 **½-½** L/N6124

## 1865-⚔DS-10
**De Vere, C.= Steinitz, W.**

[Löwenthal]

⟨♙f7⟩ 1 e4 d6 2 d4 ♘f6 3 ♘c3 ♘c6 [3 ... b5!?] 4 d5 ♘e5 5 f4 ♘f7 6 ♘f3 e5 7 dxe6 ♗xe6 8 f5± ♗d7 9 ♗c4 ♕e7 10 0-0 0-0-0 11 ♗g5 c6 12 ♕d4 b6 13 a4± ♔b8 14 ♗xf7 [14 a5] 14 ... ♕xf7 15 a5 b5 16 e5 dxe5 17 ♘xe5 ♕e7 18 ♗e3 ♗e8 19 ♕f4 ♕c7 20 ♖fe1 ♗d6 21 ♗f2 ♗h5 22 ♕e3 ♗xe5 23 ♕xe5 ♕xe5 24 ♖xe5+- ♘g4 **½-½** L/N6124

## 1865-⚔DS-11
**De Vere, C.+ Steinitz, W.**

[Löwenthal]

⟨♙f7⟩ 1 e4 d6 2 d4 ♘f6 3 ♘c3 e6 [□ 3 ... e5 4 dxe5 (4 d5 c6) 4 ... dxe5=] 4 ♗d3 ♘c6 5 ♘f3 ♗e7 6 ♘e2 0-0 7 c3 ♕e8 8 ♘g3 e5 9 d5 ♘d8 10 h3 ♘f7 11 ♗e3 ♘h8 12 ♕b3 ♘g6 13 0-0-0 a5 14 ♘f5 ♗d8 [□ 14 ... a4] 15 g4 ♘e7 16 ♖dg1 ♔h8 17 ♘g5 g6? 18 ♘h6 ♘fg8 19 ♗b5! c6 [19 ... ♗d7 20 ♗xd7 ♕xd7 21 ♘hf7+ ♔g7 22 ♘xd8+-] 20 dxc6 bxc6 21 ♘hf7+ ♔g7 22 ♘xd6 ♕d7 23 ♘xc8 ♕xc8 24 ♘e6+ ♔f7 25 ♘xd8+ ♔e8 26 ♘e6 **1-0** L/N6124

## 1865-⚔DS-12
**De Vere, C.+ Steinitz, W.**

[Löwenthal]

⟨♙f7⟩ 1 e4 d6 2 d4 ♘f6 3 ♘c3 e6 4 ♘f3 ♘c6 5 ♗b5 a6 6 ♗xc6+ bxc6 7 0-0 ♗e7 8 ♕d3 0-0 9 ♘e2 a5 10 ♘g3 ♗a6 11 c4 d5 12 b3 c5 13 exd5 [13 ♘g5!?] 13 ... exd5 14 ♕e3 dxc4 15 ♘f5! ♖f7 16 ♖e1 ♘d5 17 ♕e6 ♗f6 18 ♘e5 ♗xe5 19 ♖xe5 ♘b4

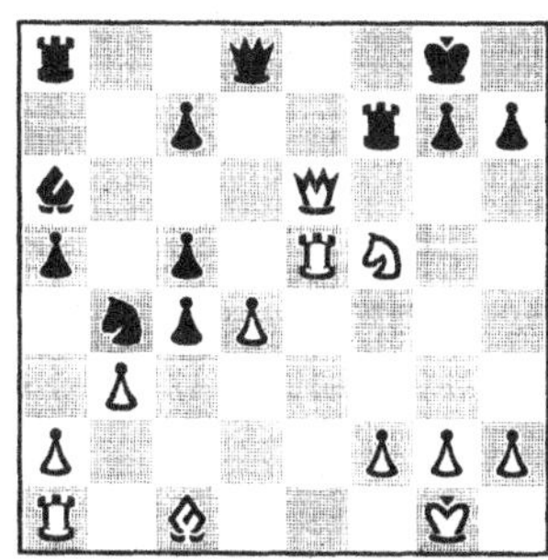

20 ♘h6+ gxh6 21 ♗xh6 ♕f6 22 ♖g5+ ♕xg5 23 ♗xg5 ...? **1-0** L/N6124

## 1865-★AG-1
**Anderssen, A.+ Guretsky-Cornitz, B.v.**

1 e4 e5 2 ♘f3 ♘f6 3 ♘xe5 d6 4 ♘f3 ♘xe4 5 d4 d5 6 ♗d3 ♘c6 7 0-0 ♗e7 8 c4 ♗e6 9 cxd5 ♗xd5 10 ♘c3 f5 11 ♕e2 ♘xc3 12 bxc3 0-0 13 ♖b1 ♕d7 14 ♗c4 ♔h8 15 ♗xd5 ♕xd5 16 ♖xb7 ♗d6 17 ♖b5 ♕f7 18 ♘g5 ♕g6 19 f4 ♖ae8 20 ♕c4 ♘d8 21 ♘f3 a6 22 ♖b1 ♖e4 23 ♕xa6 ♘e6 24 ♘e5 ♕h5 25 ♗a3 ♖xf4 26 ♗xd6 cxd6 27 ♕xd6 **1-0** L/N6051-1865

## 1865-★AG-2
**Guretsky-Cornitz, B.v.+ Anderssen, A.**

[Anderssen & Neumann]

1 e4 e5 2 ♘c3 ♗c5 3 f4 d6 4 ♘f3 ♘f6 5 ♗c4 0-0 6 d3 ♘c6 7 f5 ♖e8 8 ♗g5 a6 9 ♘d5 b5 10 ♗b3 ♘a5 11 ♘xf6+ gxf6 12 ♗h6 ♘xb3 13 ♘h4 [13 ♘xe5 ♗xf5] 13 ... ♔h8 14 ♕h5 ♕e7 [14 ... ♘xa1 15 ♕xf7 ♖g8 16 ♘g6+ hxg6 17 fxg6 ♕d7 18 ♗g7+ ♖xg7 19 ♕f8+ ♖g8 20 ♕h6+] 15 axb3 ♖g8 16 ♖f1 d5 17 ♖f3 dxe4 18 ♖h3 exd3? [□ 18 ... ♗b7 19 ♗f8 ♖axf8 20 ♕xh7+ ♔xh7 21 ♘f3+ ♔g7 22 ♖g3+=] 19 ♗f8 d2+ 20 ♔e2 ♗xf5 21 ♘xf5 **1-0** L/N6051-1865

## 1865-★AG-3
**Guretsky-Cornitz, B.v.- Anderssen, A.**

[Anderssen & Neumann]

1 e4 e5 2 ♘c3 ♗c5 3 f4 d6 4 ♘f3 ♘f6 5 d4 exd4 6 ♘xd4 0-0 7 ♗e3 ♖e8 8 ♗d3 ♘g4 9 ♗g1 c6 [□ 9 ... f5] 10 ♕f3 ♕b6 11 ♘ce2 ♕xb2 12 ♖d1 ♕xa2 13 h3 ♘f6 14 g4 ♕a5+ 15 ♔f1 ♕d8 16 g5 ♘fd7 17 ♘f5 ♗xg1 18 ♖xg1 ♘f8

19 ♘h6+ gxh6 20 gxh6+ ♘g6 21 f5 ♕h4 22 ♘f4 ♕xh6 23 ♗c4 d5 24 fxg6 fxg6 [24 ... dxc4 25 gxf7+ ♔xf7 26 ♘g6+ ♔e6 (26 ... ♔g8 27 ♘e7+ ♔h8 28 ♕c3+) 27 ♕f5#] 25 exd5 ♖f8 26 dxc6+ ♔h8 27 cxb7 ♗xb7 28 ♕c3+ [28 ♕xb7 ♕xf4+ 29 ♔g2 ♘c6 30 ♕xc6 ♖ac8] 28 ... ♕g7 29 ♕xg7+ ♔xg7 30 ♖d4 ♘c6 31 ♖d7+ ♔h8 32 ♗f7 ♗a6+ **0-1** L/N6051-1865

## 1865-★AK-1
**Anderssen, A.+ Knorre, V.**

[Anderssen & Neumann]

1 e4 e5 2 f4 exf4 3 ♘f3 g5 4 h4 g4 5 ♘e5 ♗g7 6 ♘xg4 d5 7 ♘f2 dxe4 8 ♘xe4 ♕e7 9 ♕e2 ♘c6 10 c3 ♘h6 11 ♘g5 ♗g4 12 ♕xe7+ ♘xe7 13 ♗c4 0-0 14 0-0 ♘hf5 15 ♖xf4 h5 16 d4 ♘g6 17 ♖f1 ♘gxh4 18 ♗f4 ♗h6 [18 ... ♘xd4 19 cxd4 ♗xd4+ 20 ♔h1 ♗xb2 21 ♘d2 ♗xa1 22 ♖xa1±] 19 ♘xf7 ♗xf4 20 ♘g5+ ♔h8 21 ♖xf4 ♘e3 22 ♖xf8+ ♖xf8 23 ♘d2 ♘hxg2 24 ♗b3 ♘f4 25 ♘de4 ♘e2+ 26 ♔h2 ♖f4 27 ♖e1 ♔g7?

28 ♖xe2 ♖xe4 29 ♘xe4 ♗xe2 30 ♘c5 ♘c4 31 ♘e6+ ♔f6 32 ♘f4 ♗f1

33 ♔g1 ♔f5 34 ♔xf1 ♘d2+ 35 ♔f2 ♘xb3? 36 ♘xh5 ♘c1 37 ♘g3+ ♔e6 38 ♔e3 ♘xa2 39 ♔d3 b5 40 ♔c2 **1-0** L/N6051-1865

### 1865-★AK-2
**Anderssen, A.+Knorre, V.**
[Anderssen & Neumann]

1 e4 e5 2 ♘f3 ♘c6 3 ♗c4 ♗c5 4 b4 ♗xb4 5 c3 ♗c5 6 0-0 d6 7 d4 exd4 8 cxd4 ♗b6 9 d5 ♘a5 10 ♗b2 ♘e7 11 ♗d3 0-0 12 ♘c3 ♘g6 13 ♘e2 c5 14 ♘g3 f6 15 ♕d2 ♗d7 16 ♔h1 ♖c8 17 ♘f5 ♗c7 [◻ 17 ... ♗xf5 18 exf5 ♘e5 19 ♘xe5 dxe5 20 ♖ac1 ♔h8 (20 ... ♕xd5 21 ♗c4) 21 ♗e4 ♘c6 22 f4 ♘d4] 18 g4 b5 19 ♖g1 ♘e5 20 ♘xe5 fxe5 21 f4 ♘b7 22 fxe5 dxe5 23 ♖af1 c4 24 ♗c2 ♗a5 25 ♕d1 c3 26 ♗c1 ♗b6 27 ♖g2 g6 28 ♖f3 ♔h8 [28 ... gxf5 29 gxf5+ ♔f7 30 ♖h3 ♕c7 31 d6 ♕xd6 32 ♕h5+ ♔e7 33 ♗g5+ ♖f6 34 ♕xh7+ ♔e8 35 ♗xf6+−] 29 ♖h3 gxf5 30 gxf5 ♕e7 31 d6 ♘xd6 [31 ... ♕xd6 32 ♕h5 ♕e7 33 ♗g5 ♕f7 34 ♗f6+] 32 ♗g5 ♕f7 33 ♕xd6 ♗d4 34 ♖xh7+ **1-0** L/N6051-1865

### 1865-★AK-3
**Knorre, V.−Anderssen, A.**

1 e4 e5 2 ♘f3 ♘c6 3 ♗c4 ♗c5 4 b4 ♗xb4 5 c3 ♗c5 6 0-0 d6 7 d4 exd4 8 cxd4 ♗b6 9 d5 ♘a5 10 ♗b2 ♘e7 11 ♗d3 0-0 12 ♘c3 ♘g6 13 ♘e2 c5 14 ♘g3 a6 15 ♕d2 f6 16 ♖ac1 ♗d7 17 ♔h1 ♗b5 18 ♘e1 ♘e5 19 ♗xe5 fxe5 20 f4 ♗xd3 21 ♕xd3 c4 22 ♕e2? ♖xf4 23 ♖xf4 exf4 24 ♘f5 ♕f6 25 ♕f1 g6 26 ♘g3 ♗e3 27 ♖c2 ♕d4 28 ♘f3 ♕d3 **0-1** L/N6051-1865

### 1865-★AK-4
**Knorre, V.+Anderssen, A.**

1 e4 e5 2 ♘f3 ♘c6 3 ♗c4 ♗c5 4 b4 ♗xb4 5 c3 ♗c5 6 0-0 d6 7 d4 exd4 8 cxd4 ♗b6 9 ♘c3 ♘a5 10 ♗d3 ♘e7 11 ♗b2 0-0 12 d5 ♘g6 13 ♘e2 c5 14 ♖c1 ♗d7 15 ♘e1 a6 16 ♕d2 f6 17 ♔h1 ♗c7 18 f4 b5 19 ♘f3 b4 20 f5 ♘e5 21 ♗xe5 fxe5 22 ♘g5 ♗b6 23 ♖f3 b3 24 ♖cf1 bxa2 25 ♘e6 ♗xe6 26 dxe6 c4 27 ♕xa2 ♕c7 28 ♖c1 ♖fc8 29 ♗xc4 ♗d4 30 e7+ ♘xc4 31 ♘xd4 exd4 32 ♖xc4 ♔h8 33 e8♕+ **1-0** L/N6051-1865

### 1865-★AK-5
**Knorre, V.−Anderssen, A.**
[Anderssen & Neumann]

1 e4 e5 2 ♘f3 ♘c6 3 ♗c4 ♗c5 4 b4 ♗xb4 5 c3 ♗c5 6 0-0 d6 7 d4 exd4 8 cxd4 ♗b6 9 ♘c3 ♘ge7 [◻ 9 ... ♘a5] 10 ♘g5 d5 11 ♘xd5 [◻ 11 exd5] 11 ... ♗xd4 12 ♘xe7 ♕xe7 [12 ... ♗xa1 13 ♗xf7+ ♔xe7 (13 ... ♔f8 14 ♗a3+−) 14 ♗a3+ ♔f6 15 ♕f3+ ♔xg5 (15 ... ♔e5 16 ♕g3+ ♔f6 17 ♕f4+ ♗f5 18 ♕xf5#; 16 ... ♔d4 17 ♖d1#) 16 h4+ ~ 17 ♕h5#] 13 ♗xf7+ ♔f8 14 ♕a4 ♘b4 15 ♖b1 c5 16 ♗e3 ♗d7 17 ♕b3 ♘c6 18 ♕xb7 ♖d8 [18 ... ♖b8 19 ♕xb8+ ♘xb8 20 ♖xb8+ ♗e8 21 ♖xe8+ ♕xe8 22 ♗xe8+−] 19 ♗d5 ♘e5 20 ♔h1 h6 21 ♗xd4 [◻ 21 f4 hxg5 (21 ... ♗xe3 22 exf5+ ♔e8 23 ♗f7+ ♔f8 24 ♗g6+ ♔g8 25 ♕b3++−) 22 fxe5+ ♔e8 23 ♗f7+ ♔f8 (23 ... ♕xf7 24 ♖xf7 ♔xf7 25 ♕d5+ ♔e8 26 ♗xg5 ♖c8 27 e6 ♗c6 28 ♕xc6++−; 25 ... ♔g6 26 e6 ♗xe3 27 ♕f5+ ♔h6 28 exd7 ♗d4 29 ♖b3 g6 30 ♖h3+ ♔g7 31 ♖xh8) 24 ♗xd4 cxd4 25 e6 ♗c8 26 ♗g6++−; 21 ... ♘f3 22 ♘xf3 ♗xe3 23 ♘e5 ♕d6 (23 ... ♕e8 24 ♗f7+−) 24 ♘c4+−] 21 ... hxg5 22 f4

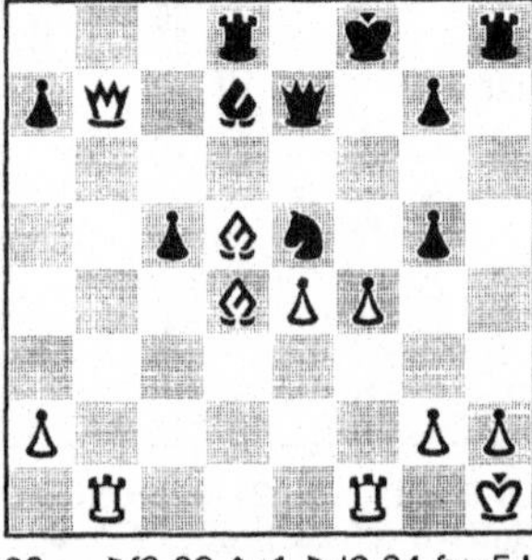

22 ... ♘f3 23 ♗g1 ♘d2 24 fxg5+ ♘xf1 25 ♖xf1+ ♔e8 26 g6 ♕d6 27 ♗f7+ ♔e7 28 ♕xa7 ♖a8 29 ♕xc5 ♖xh2+ **0-1** L/N6051-1865

### 1865-★AM-1 iv65
**Anderssen, A.−Mayet, K.**
Berlin [Anderssen & Neumann]

1 e4 e5 2 ♘f3 ♘c6 3 ♗c4 ♗c5 4 b4 ♗xb4 5 c3 ♗c5 6 0-0 d6 7 d4 exd4 8 cxd4 ♗b6 9 d5 ♘b8 10 ♗b2 ♘f6 11 ♘c3 [11 e5 dxe5 12 ♗a3] 11 ... ♗g4 12 ♗d3 ♘bd7 13 ♘e2 0-0 14 ♕d2 ♖e8 15 ♕f4 ♗xf3 16 gxf3 ♘e5 17 ♖ad1 ♘h5 18 ♕f5 ♕h4 19 ♔h1 g6 20 ♖g1 ♗xf2 21 ♖g4 ♘xg4 22 ♕xg4 c5 23 ♕g2 a6 24 ♗c1 f6 25 f4 b5 26 ♖f1 c4! 27 ♗c2 ♗c5 28 ♗d2 ♘g7! 29 ♖f3 ♖e7 30 ♗c3 ♖f8 31 a3 ♖a7 32 ♘d4 ♗xd4 33 ♗xd4 ♖e7 34 ♗f2 ♕h6 35 ♗e3 ♘h5 36 e5 fxe5 37 fxe5 ♘f4 38 ♕d2 dxe5 39 ♗c5 ♖ef7 40 ♗xf8 ♕xf8 41 ♖g3 ♕d6 42 ♗e4 ♔g7 43 h4 ♘h5 **0-1** L/N6051

### 1865-★AM-2 iv65
**Anderssen, A.+Mayet, K.**
[Anderssen & Neumann]

1 e4 e5 2 ♘f3 ♘c6 3 ♗c4 ♗c5 4 b4 ♗xb4 5 c3 ♗c5 6 0-0 d6 7 d4 exd4 8 cxd4 ♗b6 9 d5 ♘b8? 10 ♗b2 ♘f6 11 e5 dxe5 12 ♘xe5 0-0 13 ♘c3 ♘bd7 14 ♘f3 ♖e8 15 ♘e2 ♗c5 16 ♘g3 a6 17 ♕c2 b5 18 ♗d3 ♗d6 19 ♘e4 ♘xd5 20 ♘xd6 cxd6 21 ♗xh7+ ♔f8 22 ♖fe1 ♖xe1+ 23 ♖xe1 ♗b7 24 ♕f5 ♘5f6 25 ♘g5 ♗d5 26 ♕h3 ♕a5 27 ♗c3 b4 28 ♗f5 ♔g8 29 ♗xf6 ♘xf6

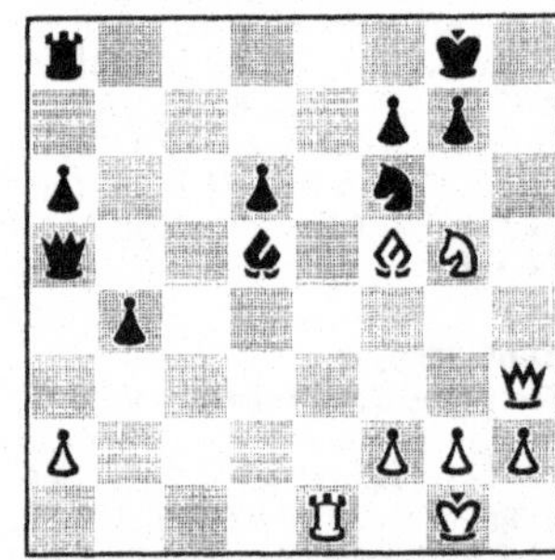

30 ♘h7! ♘e8 31 ♘f8 ♘f6 32 ♘d7 ♗e6 33 ♖xe6 **1-0** L/N6051

### 1865-★AM-3 iv65
**Anderssen, A.+Mayet, K.**
Berlin [Anderssen & Neumann]

1 e4 e5 2 ♘f3 ♘c6 3 ♗c4 ♗c5 4 b4 ♗xb4 5 c3 ♗c5 6 0-0 d6 7 d4 exd4 8 cxd4 ♗b6 9 d5 ♘b8? 10 ♗b2 ♘f6 11 ♘c3 0-0 12 ♘d4 ♘bd7 13 f4 ♘c5 14 ♕f3 ♖e8 15 ♖ae1 ♗g4 16 ♕g3 ♘e6 17 ♘b5 ♘xd4 18 ♘xd4 ♗d7 19 ♔h1 ♗xd4 20 ♗xd4 c5 21 dxc6 ♗xc6 22 ♗d3 d5 23 e5 ♘e4 24 ♕g4 ♕d7 25 f5 ♔h8 26 ♖e3 f6 27 e6 ♕e7 28 ♗xe4 dxe4 29 ♖h3 h6 30 ♕g6 ♖f8 31 ♖f4 **1-0** L/N6051

### 1865-★AM-4 iv65
**Anderssen, A.+Mayet, K.**
Berlin [Anderssen & Neumann]

1 e4 e5 2 ♘f3 ♘c6 3 ♗c4 ♗c5 4 b4 ♗xb4 5 c3 ♗c5 6 0-0 d6 7 d4 exd4 8 cxd4 ♗b6 9 d5 ♘b8? 10 ♗b2 f6 11 e5 dxe5 12 ♘xe5 ♘e7 13 ♕h5+ g6 14 ♘xg6 ♘xg6 15 ♖e1+

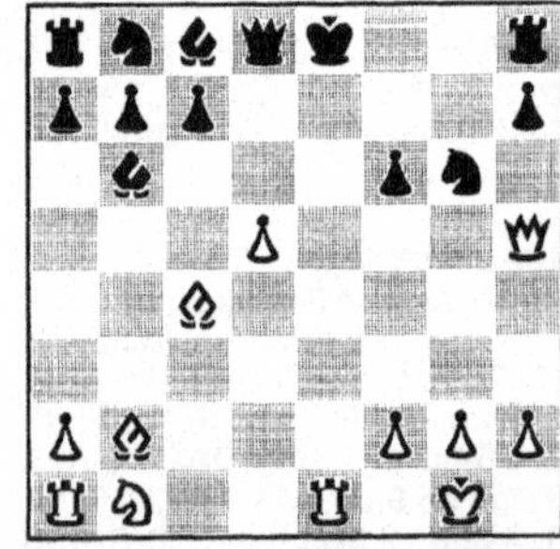

15 ... ♔f7 [15 ... ♔d7 (15 ... ♔f8 16 ♕h6+ ♔f7 17 d6+) 16 ♕f5+ ♔d6 17 ♖e6+ ♗xe6 18 ♕xe6+ ♔c5 19 ♗a3+ ♔xc4 20 ♘d2+ ♔b5 (20 ... ♔d3 21 ♕e4+ ♔xd2 22 ♗b4#) 21 ♕e2+ ♔a5 22 ♘b3+ ♔a4 23 ♕c+ ♔a3 24 ♘d2] 16 d6+ ♔g7 17 ♖e7+ ♕xe7

18 dxe7 ♖e8 19 ♘c3 ♖xe7 20 ♘d5 ♖e5 21 ♗xe5 fxe5 22 ♘e7 ♘d7 23 ♖d1 ♘f6 24 ♘f5+ ♗xf5 25 ♕xf5 ♖f8 26 g4 ♔h8 27 ♖d8 ♔g7 28 g5 ♘e8 29 ♖xe8 **1-0** L/N6051

**1865-★AM-5** iv 65
**Mayet, K.− Anderssen, A.**
Berlin [Anderssen & Neumann]
1 e4 e5 2 f4 exf4 3 ♗c4 d5 4 exd5 ♕h4+ 5 ♔f1 ♗d6 6 d4 ♘e7 7 ♘c3 ♗f5 8 ♘f3 ♕h5 9 ♘b5 g5 10 ♕e1 ♘d7 11 ♘xd6+ cxd6 12 ♕b4 g4 13 ♘e1 f3 14 ♕xd6 [□ 14 ♗f4] 14 ... ♖c8 15 ♗b3 fxg2+ 16 ♘xg2 g3 17 ♕xg3 [17 ♗e3 ♕f3+ 18 ♔g1 ♗e4 19 ♕xg3 ♖g8−+] 17 ... ♖g8 18 ♕f2 ♖xg2 19 ♕xg2 [19 ♔xg2 ♗h3+−+] 19 ... ♗h3 20 ♕xh3 ♕xh3+ 21 ♔f2 ♘f6 22 ♗f4 ♘e4+ 23 ♔e2 ♘xd5 24 ♗g3 ♕g2+ **0-1** L/N6051

**1865-★AM-6** iv 65
**Mayet, K.= Anderssen, A.**
Berlin [Anderssen & Neumann]
1 e4 e5 2 f4 exf4 3 ♗c4 d5 4 exd5 ♕h4+ 5 ♔f1 ♗d6 6 ♘f3 ♕h5 7 ♘c3 ♗f5 8 ♔f2 ♘e7 9 ♖e1 g5 10 ♘b5 ♘d7 11 d4 g4 12 ♘xd6+ cxd6 13 ♕e2 0-0-0 14 ♕xe7 gxf3 15 ♗xf4 ♕g4 16 g3 ♘b6 17 ♗f1 ♘xd5 18 h3 ♕g6 19 ♕h4 h6 20 ♔xf3 ♘f6 21 ♖e3 ♗e4+ 22 ♔f2 ♘d5 23 ♖a3 f5? 24 ♖xa7 ♔b8 25 ♖a5 ♕g7 26 c3 ♕c7 27 ♖a3 ♖de8 28 ♖c1 ♖e6 29 c4 ♕b6 30 cxd5 ♕xb2+ 31 ♗e2 ♗xd5 32 ♖e3 ♖he8 33 ♗xd6+ ♔a7 34 ♖a3+ ♕xa3 35 ♗xa3 ♖xe2+ 36 ♔f1 ♖h2 37 g4 f4 **½-½** L/N6051

**1865-★AM-7** iv 65
**Mayet, K.− Anderssen, A.**
Berlin [Anderssen & Neumann]
1 e4 e5 2 ♘f3 ♘c6 3 ♗b5 ♘f6 4 d3 ♗c5 5 c3 0-0 6 ♗xc6 bxc6 7 ♘xe5 d5 8 ♘xc6 ♕e8 9 ♘d4 dxe4 10 ♗e3 ♗a6 11 dxe4 ♘xe4 12 ♘d2 ♖b8 13 ♕c2 f5 14 0-0-0 ♘xd2 15 ♗xd2 ♕f7 16 ♔b1 ♗c4 17 b4 a5 18 ♘c6

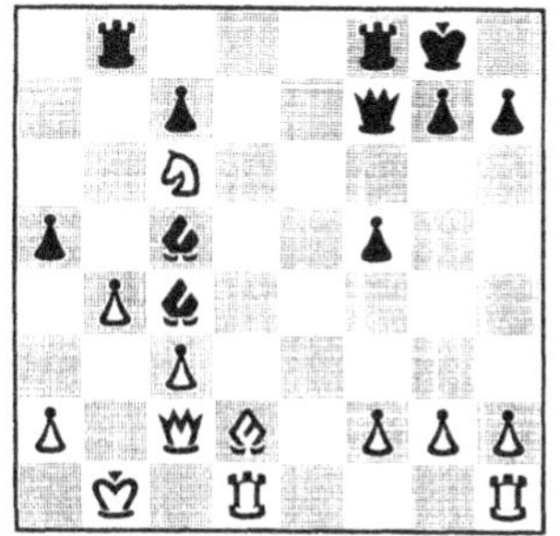

18 ... axb4 19 ♘xb8 b3! 20 axb3 ♗xb3 21 ♕b2 ♖xb8 22 ♔c1 ♖a8 23 ♗g5? [□ 23 ♗e3] 23 ... ♖a2 24 ♖d8+ ♗f8 25 ♗e7 ♖xb2 26 ♗xf8 ♖c2+ 27 ♔b1 h6 **0-1** L/N6051

**1865-★AM-8**
**Mayet, K.+ Anderssen, A.**
[Anderssen & Neumann]
1 e4 e5 2 f4 exf4 3 ♗c4 d5 4 exd5 ♗d6 5 ♘f3 ♘e7 6 0-0 ♘d7 7 ♘c3 ♘f6 8 a3? h6 [□ 8 ... 0-0, 9 ... ♘g6] 9 d4 g5 10 ♘e5 a6 11 g3 ♗h3 12 ♖f2 ♗xe5 13 dxe5 ♘g4 14 gxf4 ♘xf2 15 ♔xf2 gxf4 16 ♕h5 ♗f5 17 ♗xf4 ♗g6 18 ♕f3 ♘f5 19 ♗g3 ♕d7 20 ♖e1 0-0-0 21 ♗xa6! bxa6 22 e6 ♕e8 23 d6 **1-0** L/N6051-1865

**1865-★AM-9**
**Mieses, S.+ Anderssen, A.**
1 e4 e5 2 ♘f3 ♘c6 3 ♗b5 ♘f6 4 0-0 ♘xe4 5 d4 ♗e7 6 d5 ♘d6 7 ♗a4 e4 8 ♖e1 exf3 9 dxc6 0-0 10 ♕xf3 dxc6 11 ♘c3 ♘f5 12 ♗f4 ♗d6 13 ♖ad1 ♕f6 14 ♘e4 ♕g6 15 ♘xd6 cxd6 16 ♔h1 d5 17 h3 ♘d6 18 c3 ♘e4 19 ♗c2 f5 20 ♔h2 ♕f6 21 ♕h5 ♗d7 22 ♗xe4 fxe4 23 ♗e5 ♕f5 24 ♕xf5 ♖xf5 25 ♗g3 ♖af8 26 c4 g5 27 ♗d6 ♖8f6 28 ♗c5 b6 29 ♗e3 ♖h6 30 b4 ♗e6 31 cxd5 cxd5 32 ♖c1 ♖hf6 33 ♖c7 ♖f7 34 ♖c6 ♗d7 35 ♖d6 h5 36 ♖c1 ♔h7 37 ♖c7 ♗e8 38 ♖c8 ♖d7 39 ♖xd7+ ♗xd7 40 ♖c7 ♖f7 41 ♖xa7 b5 42 ♗d4 ♗e8 43 ♖a8 ♖e7 44 ♖d8 ♗c6 45 ♔g3 ♖e6 46 h4 g4 47 ♔f4 ♖e8 48 ♖d6 ♖f8+ 49 ♔g5 ♖g8+ 50 ♔f5 ♖f8+ 51 ♗f6 g3 52 fxg3 e3 53 ♖xc6 d4 54 ♖e6 **1-0** L/N6047

**1865-★AN-1** iv 65
**Anderssen, A.+ Neumann, G.R.**
Berlin
1 e4 e5 2 ♘f3 ♘c6 3 ♗c4 ♗c5 4 b4 ♗xb4 5 c3 ♗a5 6 d4 exd4 7 0-0 ♗b6 8 cxd4 d6 9 d5 ♘a5 10 ♗b2 ♘e7 11 ♗d3 0-0 12 ♘c3 ♘g6 13 ♘e2 c5 14 ♕d2 f6 15 ♔h1 ♗d7 16 ♘e1 a6 17 f4 ♗b5 18 ♖c1 ♖c8 19 f5 ♘e5 20 ♘f4 ♕d7 21 ♗xe5 fxe5 22 ♘e6 ♖f7 23 ♖f3 c4 24 ♗e2 ♗d8 25 ♖g3 c3 26 ♖gxc3 ♖xc3 27 ♖xc3 ♗xe2 28 ♕xe2 b5 29 ♖h3 ♘b7 30 ♕h5 g6 31 ♕h6 ♘c5 32 ♖f3 gxf5 33 ♖g3+ ♔h8 34 ♘f8 **1-0** L/N6051

**1865-★AN-2** iv 65
**Neumann, G.R.+ Anderssen, A.**
Berlin [Neumann]
1 e4 e5 2 ♘f3 ♘c6 3 ♗b5 ♘ge7 4 0-0? ♘g6 5 d4 ♗d6 6 dxe5 ♘cxe5 7 ♘xe5 ♗xe5 8 f4 c6 9 ♗c4 ♕b6+? 10 ♔h1 ♗xb2 11 ♗xb2 ♕xb2 12 ♘d2 ♕d4

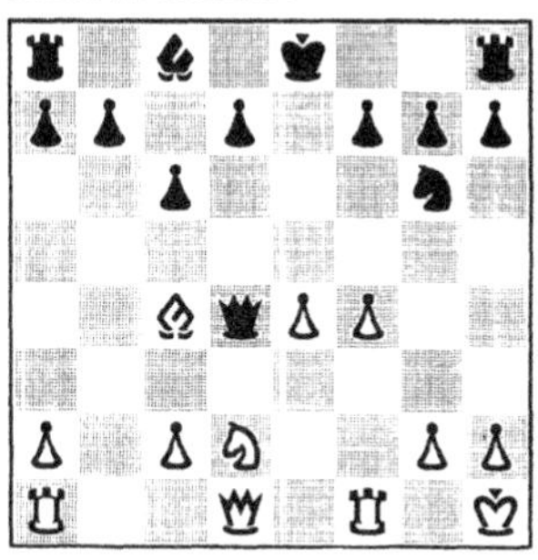

13 c3! ♕xc3 14 e5 [14 ♖c1 ♕d4 15 ♘f3 ♕f6 (15 ... ♕b6 16 ♘g5) 16 e5 ♕xf4 (16 ... ♕e7 17 f5) 17 ♕d6±] 14 ... ♕d4 15 ♕e2 b5 16 ♘e4 bxc4 17 ♖ad1± ♕b6 18 ♘d6+ ♔d8 [18 ... ♔f8 19 f5±] 19 f5 ♘e7 20 f6 gxf6 21 exf6 ♘g6 22 ♘xf7+ ♔c7 23 ♘xh8 ♘xh8 24 ♕e5+ ♔b7 [24 ... ♔d8+−] 25 ♖b1 ♘g6 26 ♕d6 c3 27 f7 c2 28 ♖xb6+ axb6 29 a3 ♖a4 30 f8♕ ♘xf8 31 ♕xf8 ♖c4 32 ♖c1 ♖d4 33 ♕f1 **1-0** L/N3164

**1865-★AN-3** iv 65
**Neumann, G.R.+ Anderssen, A.**
Berlin
1 e4 e5 2 ♘f3 ♘c6 3 ♗b5 ♘ge7 4 d4 exd4 5 0-0 d5 6 ♖e1 ♗g4 7 ♗xc6+ bxc6 8 ♕xd4 ♗xf3 9 gxf3 ♕d6 10 exd5 cxd5 11 ♘c3 c6 12 ♗f4 ♕g6+ 13 ♔h1 ♕f6 14 ♕a4 ♖d8 15 ♖ad1 g5 16 ♗e5 ♕xf3+ 17 ♔g1 ♖g8 18 ♖e3 ♕f5 19 ♗c7 ♖d7 20 ♕xc6 ♕g4+ 21 ♔h1 ♕f3+ 22 ♖xf3 ♘xc6 23 ♘xd5 ♗e7 24 ♖fd3 ♔f8 25 ♘xe7 ♖xd3 26 ♖xd3 ♔xe7 27 b4 ♖c8 28 ♗d6+ ♔e6 29 ♗c5 ♘e5 30 ♖d6+ ♔f5 31 ♖a6 ♔e4 32 ♖xa7 h5 33 ♔g2 f5 34 ♖e7 ♖d8 35 f3+ ♔f4 36 ♗e3+ ♔xe3 37 ♖xe5+ ♔f4 38 ♖e2 g4 39 fxg4 hxg4 40 a4 ♖d4 41 c3 ♖c4 42 ♖b2 ♔e3 43 a5 f4 44 a6 ♖xc3 45 b5 **1-0** L/N6051

**1865-★AN-4**
**Anderssen, A.+ Neumann, G.R.**
1 e4 e5 2 ♘f3 ♘c6 3 ♗c4 ♗c5 4 b4 ♗xb4 5 c3 ♗c5 6 0-0 d6 7 d4 exd4 8 cxd4 ♗b6 9 d5 ♘a5 10 ♗b2 ♘e7 11 ♗d3 0-0 12 ♘c3 ♘g6 13 ♘e2 c5 14 ♔h1 ♗c7 15 ♘e1 f6 16 f4 a6 17 ♘f3 b5 18 h4 ♗g4 19 f5 ♘e5 20 ♘f4 ♗xf3? 21 gxf3 ♖f7 22 ♘e6 ♕e7 23 ♖g1 ♗b6 24 ♗xe5 dxe5 25 ♖g4 c4 26 ♗c2 ♕d6 27 ♕d2 ♔h8 28 ♖f1 b4 29 h5 c3 30 ♕g2 ♘c4 31 ♖xg7 ♘e3 32 ♖xf7 ♘xg2 33 ♔xg2 ♖g8+ 34 ♔h3 ♗d8

35 h6 a5 36 ♖f2 ♕a6 37 ♖g7 ♖e8? 38 ♗a4 **1-0** L/N6051-1865

**1865-★AN-5**
**Anderssen,A.+Neumann, G.R.**

1 e4 e5 2 ♘f3 ♘c6 3 ♗c4 ♗c5 4 b4 ♗xb4 5 c3 ♗c5 6 0-0 d6 7 d4 exd4 8 cxd4 ♗b6 9 d5 ♘a5 10 ♗b2 ♘e7 11 ♗d3 0-0 12 ♘c3 ♘g6 13 ♘e2 c5 14 ♔h1 ♗d7 15 ♘e1 ♖c8 16 f4 c4 17 ♗c2 f6 18 ♗c3 ♗c7 19 ♘d4 b5 20 ♘e6 ♗xe6 21 dxe6 a6 22 ♕h5 ♘c6 23 ♖f3 ♘ce7 24 f5 ♘e5 25 ♖h3 h6 26 ♖g3 ♔h7 27 ♘f3 ♕e8 28 ♕h3 ♗b6 29 ♖f1 ♘xf3 30 ♖fxf3 ♘g8 31 ♖g6 ♗c5 32 ♗d2 ♕e7 33 ♕h4 ♖fe8 34 ♖h3 ♕f8 35 g4 ♗d4 36 e5 ♗xe5 37 g5

37 ... fxg5 38 f6 ♔h8 39 ♖xg7 ♕xg7 40 fxg7+ **1-0**
L/N6051-1865

**1865-★AN-6**
**Anderssen,A.−Neumann, G.R.**
[Anderssen & Neumann]

1 e4 e5 2 ♘f3 ♘c6 3 ♗b5 ♘f6 4 d3 d6 5 ♗xc6+ bxc6 6 h3 ♗e7 7 ♘c3 0-0 8 0-0 c5 9 ♘e2 ♘h5 10 g4 ♘f6 11 ♘g3 h5 12 ♘h2 hxg4 13 hxg4 ♘h7 14 ♔g2 g6 15 ♖h1 [◻ 15 ♗h6 ♖e8 16 f4] 15 ... f5 16 gxf5 gxf5 17 ♕h5 ♕e8 18 ♕h6 ♖f6 19 ♕h3 f4 20 ♘g4 ♕g6 21 ♘xf6+? ♘xf6 22 ♕h8+ ♔f7 23 ♗d2 [23 ♖h6 ♗h3+-+] 23 ... fxg3 24 fxg3 ♗b7 25 ♕h6 ♖g8 26 ♕xg6+ ♖xg6 27 ♖hf1 c4 28 a4 ♔e6 29 a5 d5 30 a6 ♗c6 31 exd5+ ♗xd5+ 32 ♔h2 ♖g8 33 ♖a5 ♖h8+ 34 ♔g1 ♘g4 35 ♖xd5 ♔xd5 36 dxc4+ ♔xc4 37 b3+ ♔b5 38 c4+ ♔xa6 39 b4 ♖d8 40 ♖a1+ ♔b7 41 ♗e1 ♖d4 **0-1**
L/N6051-1865

**1865-★AN-7**
**Anderssen,A.−Neumann, G.R.**
[Anderssen & Neumann]

1 e4 e5 2 f4 exf4 3 ♘f3 g5 4 ♗c4 ♗g7 5 d4 d6 6 h4 h6 7 ♕d3 ♘c6 8 hxg5 hxg5 9 ♖xh8 ♗xh8 10 e5 ♗g7 11 ♕h7 ♔f8 12 ♘c3 ♘h6 13 ♗d3 ♘b4 14 ♗e4 d5 15 ♗d3 g4 16 ♘g1 ♕h4+ 17 ♔f1 ♘xd3 18 ♕xd3 f3 19 gxf3 g3 20 ♗e3 [20 ♘xd5 ♗h3+ 21 ♔e2 ♖d8] 20 ... ♕h1 21 ♕e2 ♗h3+ 22 ♔e1 ♘f5 23 ♔d2 c5 24 ♘xd5 cxd4 25 ♗g5 ♖e8 26 ♗f6 ♗h6+ 27 ♔d3 ♘e3 28 ♔xd4 ♘xd5 29 ♔xd5 ♗e6+ 30 ♔d4 ♖c8 31 b3 ♕h5 32 c4 b5 33 c5 b4 34 a3 ♖b8 35 ♕a6 [△ 36 ♕d6+] 35 ... ♕h2 36 ♕e2 [36 ♕d6+ ♔g8 37 ♕xb8+ ♔h7 38 ♕h8+ ♔g6 39 ♕g8+ ♔h5 40 ♖d1 ♕b2+ 41 ♔d3 ♕c3+ 42 ♔e2 ♕e3+ 43 ♔f1 ♕f1‡] 36 ... bxa3 37 c6 ♖b4+ 38 ♔c5 ♖xb3 39 ♖d1 ♔g8 40 ♖d8+ ♗f8+ **0-1**
L/N6051-1865

**1865-★AN-8**
**Anderssen,A.−Neumann, G.R.**

1 e4 e5 2 f4 exf4 3 ♘f3 g5 4 ♗c4 ♗g7 5 d4 d6 6 h4 h6 7 ♕d3 ♘c6 8 hxg5 hxg5 9 ♖xh8 ♗xh8 10 e5 ♗g7 11 ♘c3 g4 12 ♕h7 ♔f8 13 ♘h4 ♘h6 14 g3

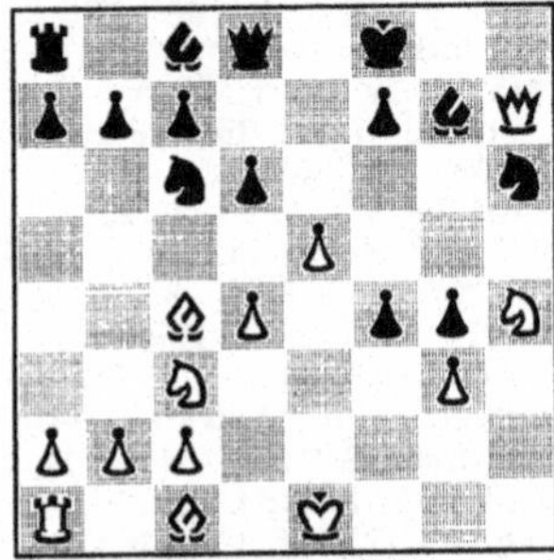

14 ... ♕xh4! 15 gxh4 ♗f5 16 ♕xg7+ ♔xg7 17 ♗xf4 dxe5 18 dxe5 ♗xc2 19 ♔d2 ♗g6 20 h5 ♖d8+ 21 ♔e2 ♗f5 22 ♖f1 ♘d4+ 23 ♔f2 ♘e6 24 ♗xh6+ ♔xh6 25 ♔g3 ♔g5 26 ♗d5 c6 27 ♗e4 ♘g7 28 h6 ♘h5+ 29 ♔h2 ♖d2+ 30 ♔g1 ♘g3 31 ♗xf5 ♘xf1 32 ♘e4+ ♔xh6 33 ♘xd2 ♘xd2 34 ♗xg4 ♘c4 35 e6 fxe6 36 ♗xe6 ♘xb2 37 ♔f2 ♔g6 38 ♔e3 ♔f6 39 ♗b3 ♔e5 40 ♗g8 b5 41 ♗f7 c5 42 ♗g8 a5 43 ♗f7 c4 44 ♔d2 ♔d4 45 ♔c2 ♘d3 46 ♗e8 b4 47 ♗f7 ♘c5 48 ♗g8 a4 49 ♗f7 b3+ 50 axb3 axb3+ 51 ♔b2 c3+ **0-1** L/N6051-1865

**1865-★AN-9**
**Anderssen,A.+Neumann, G.R.**

1 e4 e5 2 ♘f3 ♘c6 3 ♗c4 ♗c5 4 b4 ♗xb4 5 c3 ♗c5 6 0-0 d6 7 d4 exd4 8 cxd4 ♗b6 9 d5 ♘a5 10 ♗b2 ♘e7 11 ♗d3 0-0 12 ♘c3 ♘g6 13 ♘e2 c5 14 ♔h1 f6 15 ♘e1 ♗d7 16 f4 ♖c8 17 f5 ♘e5 18 ♘f4 c4 19 ♗e2 c3 20 ♗c1 c2 21 ♕d2 ♘ac4 22 ♗xc4 ♘xc4 23 ♕e2 ♗d4 24 ♘xc2 ♗xa1 25 ♘xa1 ♘e5 26 ♘b3 ♖c4 27 ♘e6 ♗xe6 28 dxe6 ♕c7 29 ♗a3 b5 30 ♕d2 ♖d8 31 ♘d4 ♕b6 32 ♘f3 ♘xf3? 33 gxf3 ♖d4 34 ♕g2 ♖a4 35 ♖g1 ♕c7 **1-0**
L/N6051-1865

**1865-★AN-10**
**Anderssen,A.−Neumann, G.R.**

1 e4 e5 2 f4 exf4 3 ♘f3 g5 4 ♗c4 ♗g7 5 d4 d6 6 h4 h6 7 ♘c3 ♘c6 8 hxg5 hxg5 9 ♖xh8 ♗xh8 10 ♕d3 ♘b4 11 ♗xf7+ ♔xf7 12 ♕c4+ ♗e6 13 d5 ♗d7 14 ♕xb4 g4 15 ♘g1 ♕h4+ 16 ♔f1 f3 17 ♗e3 ♕g3 18 gxf3 gxf3 19 ♖d1 ♕g2+ 20 ♔e1 ♗e5 21 ♗f2 ♗g3 22 ♗xg3 ♕xg1+ 23 ♔d2 ♕xg3 24 ♔c1 ♕f4+ 25 ♔b1 f2 26 ♕c4 ♘f6 **0-1**
L/N6051-1865

**1865-★AN-11**
**Anderssen,A.+Neumann, G.R.**
[Anderssen & Neumann]

1 e4 e5 2 f4 exf4 3 ♘f3 g5 4 ♗c4 ♗g7 5 d4 d6 6 h4 h6 7 ♘c3 ♘c6 8 ♘e2 ♕e7 9 ♕d3 ♗d7 10 c3 0-0-0 11 b4 f5 12 exf5 ♖f8 13 ♗e6 d5 14 ♗xd7+ ♔xd7 15 a4 ♕f6 16 hxg5 hxg5 17 ♖xh8 ♗xh8 18 g4 fxg3? [◻ 18 ... ♘h6 19 ♘h2 ♗f7, 20 ... ♘d6] 19 ♘xg3 ♕e7+ 20 ♔f2 ♗f6 21 b5 ♘d8 22 ♗a3 ♕g7 23 ♗xf8 ♕xf8 24 ♘e5+ **1-0** L/N6051-1865

**1865-★AN-12**
**Anderssen,A.−Neumann, G.R.**

1 e4 e5 2 f4 exf4 3 ♘f3 g5 4 ♗c4 ♗g7 5 d4 d6 6 h4 h6 7 ♕d3 ♘c6 8 hxg5 hxg5 9 ♖xh8 ♗xh8 10 e5 ♗g7 11 ♘c3 g4 12 ♕h7 ♔f8 13 ♕h5 ♕e8 14 ♗xf4 gxf3 15 0-0-0 dxe5 16 dxe5 ♗e6 17 ♗d3 fxg2 18 ♕h2 ♗g4 19 ♖e1 ♕e6 20 ♕xg2 ♘xe5 21 ♔b1 c6 22 ♗h7 f5 23 ♘d1 ♗xd1 24 ♗xg8 ♕xg8 25 ♖xd1 ♕e6 26 ♖g1 ♘g4 27 ♕g3 ♖d8 28 ♖e1 ♗e5 29 ♕h4 ♕d6 30 ♗c1 ♖d7 31 b3 ♕d4 **0-1**
L/N6051-1865

**1865-★AN-13**
**Anderssen,A.−Neumann, G.R.**

1 e4 e5 2 f4 d5 3 exd5 e4 4 ♗b5+ c6 5 dxc6 bxc6 6 ♗c4 ♘f6 7 d4 ♗d6 8 ♘e2 0-0 9 0-0 ♘bd7 10 a4 a5 11 ♗a2 c5 12 d5 c4 13 ♗xc4 ♗c5+ 14 ♔h1 ♘b6 15 ♗a2 ♘bxd5 16 ♘bc3 ♘xc3 17 ♘xc3 ♗b7 18 ♕e2 ♕b6 19 ♘d1 ♖ad8 20 ♘e3 ♗a6 21 c4 ♖d3 22 ♖e1 ♖fd8 23 g4 g6 24 ♘f1 e3 25 ♘xe3 ♗xe3 26 ♗xe3 ♗b7+ 27 ♔g1 ♕c6 28 ♔f1

♖xe3 **0-1** L/N6051-1865

**1865-★AN-14**
**Neumann, G.R.+ Anderssen, A.**
1 e4 e5 2 ♘f3 ♘c6 3 ♗c4 ♗c5 4 b4 ♗xb4 5 c3 ♗a5 6 d4 exd4 7 0-0 dxc3 8 ♕b3 ♕f6 9 e5 ♕g6 10 ♘xc3 ♗xc3 11 ♕xc3 ♘d8 12 ♗a3 ♘h6 13 ♖fe1 b6 14 ♗d5 ♗b7 15 e6 **1-0** L/N6051-1865

**1865-★AN-15**
**Neumann, G.R.+ Anderssen, A.**
1 e4 e5 2 ♘f3 ♘c6 3 ♗b5 ♘ge7 4 0-0 ♘g6 5 d4 ♗d6 6 dxe5 ♘cxe5 7 ♘xe5 ♗xe5 8 f4 c6 9 ♗c4 ♗c7 10 ♕h5 0-0 11 f5 ♘e5 12 ♗g5 ♕e8 13 f6 d5 14 fxg7 dxc4 15 ♗h6 ♘g6 16 ♕g5 f6? 17 gxf8♕+ ♕xf8 18 ♖xf6 ♕e8 19 ♖f8+ ♕xf8 20 ♗xf8 ♔xf8 21 ♘d2 ♗e6? 22 ♕f6+ ♗f7 23 ♖f1 **1-0** L/N6051-1865

**1865-★AN-16**
**Neumann, G.R.+ Anderssen, A.**
1 e4 e5 2 f4 exf4 3 ♘f3 g5 4 ♗c4 g4 5 0-0 gxf3 6 ♕xf3 ♕e7 7 ♕xf4 ♘h6 8 ♘c3 c6 9 d4 d6 10 ♗d2 ♖g8 11 ♖ae1 ♗h3 12 ♖f2 ♘d7 13 ♖e3 ♗e6 14 ♘d5 cxd5 15 exd5 0-0-0 16 dxe6 fxe6 17 ♗xe6 ♖g7 18 ♗b4 ♕g5 19 ♗xd6 ♗xd6 20 ♖c3+ ♔b8 21 ♕xd6+ ♔a8 22 ♗xd7 a6 23 ♖c8+ ♖xc8 24 ♗xc8 ♕c1+ 25 ♖f1 ♕e3+ 26 ♔h1 ♕e2 27 ♖g1 ♕xc2 28 ♕f8 ♕c7 29 ♗d7+ **1-0** L/N6051-1865

**1865-★AN-17**
**Neumann, G.R.– Anderssen, A.**
1 e4 e5 2 ♘f3 ♘c6 3 ♗b5 ♘f6 4 0-0 ♘xe4 5 d4 ♗e7 6 ♕e2 ♘d6 7 ♗xc6 bxc6 8 dxe5 ♘b7 9 ♗e3 0-0 10 ♖d1 ♕e8 11 ♘c3 ♘d8 12 ♘d4 f5 13 f4 ♕g6 14 ♘f3 ♘e6 15 ♕f2 h6 16 ♘a4 a5 17 c4 d6 18 ♖ac1 c5 19 ♘c3 ♖f7 20 ♘d5 ♗f8 21 ♖d2 ♖b8 22 b3 a4 23 bxa4 ♕h5 24 ♘c3 ♖b4 25 ♘e2 g5 26 a5 ♗a6 27 ♖dc2 gxf4 28 ♗xf4 d5 **0-1** L/N6051-1865

**1865-★AN-18**
**Neumann, G.R.– Anderssen, A.**
1 e4 e5 2 ♘f3 ♘c6 3 ♗c4 ♗c5 4 b4 ♗xb4 5 c3 ♗c5 6 0-0 d6 7 d4 exd4 8 cxd4 ♗b6 9 d5 ♘a5 10 ♗b2 ♘e7 11 ♗d3 0-0 12 ♘c3 ♘g6 13 ♘e2 c5 14 ♕d2 f6 15 ♘e1 ♗d7 16 ♔h1 a6 17 f4 ♗b5 18 f5 ♘e5 19 ♗xe5 fxe5 20 ♖f3 ♖c8 21 ♖h3 c4 22 ♗c2 c3 23 ♘xc3 ♘c4 24 ♕e2 ♕c7 25 ♘xb5 axb5 26 ♗d3 ♕c5 27 ♘c2 ♘b2 28 ♖c1 ♘xd3 29 ♖xd3 ♖c7 30 ♖g3 ♕f2 31 ♕d3 ♖fc8 **0-1** L/N6051-1865

**1865-★AN-19**
**Neumann, G.R.+ Anderssen, A.**
[Anderssen & Neumann]
1 e4 e5 2 ♘f3 ♘c6 3 ♗b5 ♘f6 4 0-0 ♘xe4 5 d4 ♗e7 6 ♕e2 ♘d6 7 ♗xc6 bxc6 8 dxe5 ♘b7 9 ♗e3 0-0 10 ♖d1 ♕e8 11 ♘c3 d5 12 ♘d4 ♘c5 13 f4 ♘e6 14 ♘f3 f5 15 ♕f2 g5 16 g3 gxf4 17 gxf4 ♔h8 18 ♔h1 ♗b7 19 b4 ♕h5 20 ♖d4 ♘xd4 21 ♗xd4 h6 22 ♖b1? ♖g8 23 ♘e2 ♖g4 24 ♘g3 ♕g6 25 e6+ ♗f6 26 ♕e3 ♔h7 27 ♘e5 ♗xe5 28 ♕xe5 ♖c8 29 ♘xf5 ♗a6 30 ♖e1 ♕h5 31 ♘e3 ♕xe5 32 ♗xe5 ♖h4 33 ♖g1 **1-0** L/N6051-1865

**1865-★AN-20**
**Neumann, G.R.– Anderssen, A.**
Berlin [Anderssen & Neumann]
1 e4 e5 2 ♘f3 ♘c6 3 ♗b5 d6 4 ♗xc6+ bxc6 5 d4 exd4 6 ♘xd4 c5 7 ♘f3 g6 8 0-0 ♗g7 9 ♘c3 ♘e7 10 e5 0-0 11 ♗g5 f6 12 exf6 ♗xf6 13 ♗xf6 ♖xf6 14 ♖e1 ♗b7 15 ♘g5 ♕d7 16 ♘ce4 ♖f5 17 ♕d3 ♖af8 18 ♖ad1 ♘d5 19 ♕h3? ♘f4 20 ♕b3+ ♗d5 21 c4

21 ... ♖xg5! 22 ♘xg5 ♕g4 23 ♕g3 [23 g3 ♕xg5 24 cxd5 ♘h3+→] 23 ... ♕xd1 24 ♖xd1 ♘e2+ 25 ♔h1 ♘xg3+ 26 fxg3 ♗xc4 27 b3 ♗d5 28 ♘h3 ♗e4 29 ♖e1 d5 30 ♔g1 ♖f6 31 ♖c1 ♖c6 32 ♘g5 ♗d3 33 ♔f2 c4 34 ♔e3 cxb3 **0-1** L/N6051-1865

**1865-★AN-21**
**Neumann, G.R.– Anderssen, A.**
[Anderssen & Neumann]
1 e4 e5 2 ♘f3 ♘c6 3 ♗c4 ♗c5 4 b4 ♗xb4 5 c3 ♗c5 6 0-0 d6 7 d4 exd4 8 cxd4 ♗b6 9 ♘c3 ♘a5 10 ♗d3 ♘e7 11 ♗b2 0-0 12 ♘e2 ♘g6 13 ♘g3 ♗d7 14 ♕d2 a6 15 ♖ac1 ♗b5 16 ♘f5? ♗xd3 17 ♕xd3 ♘c6 18 ♔h1 d5 19 e5 ♕d7 20 g4 ♘d8 21 ♘g1 ♘e6 22 ♘e2 c5 23 f4 cxd4 24 ♗a3 ♖fc8 25 ♘d6 ♖xc1 26 ♗xc1 f6 27 ♕b3 ♕c6 28 ♗a3 fxe5 29 ♖c1 ♗c5 30 fxe5 ♘xe5 31 ♘xb7 ♖b8 32 ♕g3 ♖xb7 33 ♕xe5 d3 34 ♗xc5 d4+ 35 ♔g1 dxe2 36 ♕xe2 ♘f4 37 ♕f1 ♖b2 **0-1** L/N6051-1865

**1865-★AN-22**
**Neumann, G.R.= Anderssen, A.**
1 e4 e5 2 ♘f3 ♘c6 3 ♗c4 ♗c5 4 b4 ♗xb4 5 c3 ♗c5 6 0-0 d6 7 d4 exd4 8 cxd4 ♗b6 9 d5 ♘a5 10 ♗b2 ♘e7 11 ♗d3 0-0 12 ♘c3 ♘g6 13 ♘e2 c5 14 ♕d2 ♗d7 15 ♘g3 f6! 16 h4 ♗c7 17 h5 ♘h8 18 h6 g6 19 ♖ac1 b5 20 ♘h4 ♘b7 21 ♕e3 ♖c8 22 ♗e2 ♗b6 23 ♘h5 ♕e7 24 ♕g3 c4 25 ♖fe1 ♘c5 26 ♘f5 ♗xf5 27 exf5 ♘e4 28 ♗g4 ♘xg3 29 ♖xe7 ♘xh5 30 ♗xh5 ♖f7 31 ♖xf7 ♔xf7 32 ♗g4 ♖d8 33 ♖e1 b4 34 fxg6+ ♔xg6 35 ♖e7 ♘f7 36 ♗h5+ ♔xh5 37 ♖xf7 c3 38 ♗c1 ♗d4 39 ♖g7 ♖e8 40 ♔f1 c2 41 ♖g3 ♗c3 42 ♖h3+ ♔g6 43 ♖g3+ ♔f7 44 ♖e3 ♖xe3 45 fxe3 ♔g6? 46 e4 f5 47 exf5+ ♔xf5 48 ♔e2 **½-½** L/N6051-1865

**1865-★AN-23**
**Neumann, G.R.+ Anderssen, A.**
1 e4 e5 2 ♘f3 ♘c6 3 ♗b5 ♘ge7 4 d4! exd4 5 0-0 d5? 6 ♖e1 ♗g4 7 ♕xd4 ♗xf3 8 gxf3 dxe4 9 ♕xe4 ♕d6 10 ♗xc6+ ♕xc6 11 ♕xc6+ bxc6 12 ♗e3 f6 13 ♘c3 ♔f7 14 ♖ad1 ♘d5 15 ♘xd5 cxd5 16 ♖xd5 ♗d6 17 c4 ♖he8 18 c5 ♗e5 19 ♖d7+ ♔g6 20 ♔h1 ♖ab8 21 b3 ♔f5 22 ♖xg7 h5 23 c6 ♖b4 24 ♗d2 ♖h4 25 f4 ♖d8 26 fxe5 ♖xd2 27 e6 ♖xf2 28 ♖g2 ♖xg2 29 ♔xg2 ♖g4+ 30 ♔h3 ♖g8 31 b4 ♖e8 32 e7 ♔f4 33 b5 ♔f3 34 a4 f5 35 a5 f4 36 b6 ♔f2 37 ♖e4 axb6 38 axb6 cxb6 39 c7 f3 40 ♖e6 ♔g1 41 ♖g6+ ♔f1 42 ♖xb6 f2 43 ♔h4 ♔g1 44 ♖b1+ f1♕ 45 ♖xf1+ ♔xf1 46 ♔xh5 **1-0** L/N6051-1865

**1865-★AN-24**
**Neumann, G.R.– Anderssen, A.**
1 e4 e5 2 ♘f3 ♘c6 3 ♗b5 ♘ge7 4 0-0? d6 5 d4 ♗d7 6 ♘c3 ♘g6 7 ♗e3 ♗e7 8 ♘e2? 0-0 9 d5 ♘b8 10 ♗d3 ♗f6 11 ♘g3 ♘f4 12 ♗xf4 exf4 13 ♘e2 g5 14 ♘e1 ♗c8 15 ♖b1 ♘d7 16 c4 ♘e5 17 f3 c5 18 b3 ♔h8 19 g4 ♖g8 20 ♗c2 h5 21 h3

♕f8 22 ♘d3 ♕h6 23 ♘xe5 ♗xe5 24 ♔g2 ♗d7 25 b4 ♖g7 26 bxc5 dxc5 27 ♖h1 b6 28 ♗a4 ♗c8 29 ♗c6 ♖b8 30 ♕a4 a6 31 ♕b3 ♖h7 32 a4 ♕g6 33 a5 bxa5 34 ♕xb8 ♗xb8 35 ♖xb8 ♕f6 36 ♖xc8+ ♔g7 37 ♖b8 a4 38 ♗xa4 hxg4 39 ♗c2 gxf3+ 40 ♔xf3 g4+ 41 ♔xg4 ♕e5 42 ♖bb1 ♕h5+ 43 ♔xf4 ♕xe2 44 ♖hg1+ ♔f8 45 ♖b8+ ♔e7 46 ♖b7+ ♔d6 **0-1**

L/N6051-1865

**1865-★AN-25**
**Neumann, G.R.– Anderssen, A.**

1 e4 e5 2 f4 exf4 3 ♘f3 g5 4 ♗c4 g4 5 0-0 gxf3 6 ♕xf3 ♕e7 7 d3 b5 8 ♗b3 b4 9 ♕xf4 ♘c6 10 ♕xc7 ♗g7 11 ♗xf7+ ♕xf7 12 ♖xf7 ♗e5 13 ♕xe5+ ♘xe5 14 ♖f1 ♘e7 15 ♗f4 d6 16 ♘d2 ♗e6 17 a3 ♘7c6 18 axb4 ♘xb4 19 ♗xe5 dxe5 20 ♖a5 ♘c6 21 ♖c5 ♔d7 22 ♖f6 ♖ac8 23 ♘f3 ♔d6 24 ♖c3 ♘d4 25 ♘xd4 exd4 26 ♖a3 ♔e7 27 ♖f2 ♖c7 28 c3 ♖d8 29 ♖d2 ♖b7 30 ♖a4 dxc3 31 bxc3 ♗b3 32 ♖a3 ♖c8 33 c4 ♖d8 34 ♔f2? ♗xc4 35 ♔e3 ♗e6 36 d4 ♖b3+ 37 ♖d3 ♖xa3 38 ♖xa3 ♖a8 39 d5 ♗c8 40 ♔d4 a5 41 e5 a4 42 h3 ♗d7 43 g4 ♖a5 44 ♔c4 ♗e8 45 ♔d4 ♗f7 **0-1** L/N6051-1865

**1865-★AN-26**
**Neumann, G.R.= Anderssen, A.**

1 e4 e5 2 ♘f3 ♘c6 3 ♗c4 ♗c5 4 b4 ♗xb4 5 c3 ♗c5 6 0-0 d6 7 d4 exd4 8 cxd4 ♗b6 9 d5 ♘a5 10 ♗b2 ♘e7 11 ♗d3 0-0 12 ♘c3 ♘g6 13 ♘e2 c5 14 ♕d2 f6 15 ♔h1 ♗c7 16 ♘e1 ♗d7 17 f4 b5 18 ♘f3 b4 19 ♖ac1 ♗b6 20 f5 ♘e5 21 ♗xe5 dxe5 22 ♘h4 ♖c8 23 ♗a6 ♖b8 24 ♖f3 ♗a4 25 ♖h3 b3 26 ♘c3 ♗e8 27 ♕e2 c4 28 ♗xc4 ♘xc4 29 ♕xc4 b2 30 ♖b1 ♗d4 31 ♕e2 ♕c8 32 ♕c2 ♗xc3 33 ♖xc3 ♗a4 34 ♕d2 ♕a6 35 ♘f3 ♖b4 36 d6 h6 37 d7 ♖bb8 38 ♖xb2 ♖xb2 39 ♕xb2 ♗xd7 40 h3 ♔h7 41 ♔h2 ♗c6 42 ♕b4 ♖c8 43 ♕c4 ♕xc4 44 ♖xc4 g6 45 g4 h5 46 ♔g3 hxg4 47 hxg4 gxf5 48 exf5 ♔g7 49 g5 ♗d7 50 ♖xc8 ♗xc8 51 ♔g4 fxg5 52 ♘xg5 ♗b7 53 ♘e6+ ♔f6 54 ♘c5 ♗c6 55 a3 a5 56 ♘b3 ♗d7 57 ♘xa5 ♗xf5+ 58 ♔f3 **½-½**

L/N6051-1865

**1865-★AN-27**
**Neumann, G.R.– Anderssen, A.**

[Anderssen & Neumann]

1 e4 e5 2 ♘f3 ♘c6 3 ♗b5 ♘f6 4 0-0 ♘xe4 5 d4 ♗e7 6 ♕e2 ♘d6 7 ♗xc6 bxc6 8 dxe5 ♘b7 9 ♗e3 0-0 10 ♖d1 ♕e8 11 ♘c3 ♘d8 12 ♘d4 f5 13 f4 ♕g6 14 ♘f3 ♘e6 15 ♕f2 h6 16 ♘a4 a5 17 c4 d6 18 c5 dxc5 19 ♖ac1 ♗a6 20 ♖d7 ♖f7 21 b3? c4 22 bxc4 ♗a3 23 ♖dd1 ♗xc1 24 ♖xc1 ♖d8 25 ♘c5 ♘xc5 26 ♗xc5 ♗c8 27 ♘d4 ♔h7 28 ♖e1 ♗e6 29 ♘xc6 ♖d3 30 ♘d4 ♖d7 31 h3 ♖d8 32 ♘c6 ♖d2 33 ♘xd8 ♖xf2 34 ♔xf2 ♗xc4 35 e6 ♗d5 36 g3 ♕h5 37 ♖e3 ♕d1 38 e7 ♗c4 39 g4 g5 **0-1** L/N6051-1865

**1865-★AN-28**
**Neumann, G.R.= Anderssen, A.**

1 e4 e5 2 ♘f3 ♘c6 3 ♗c4 ♗c5 4 b4 ♗xb4 5 c3 ♗c5 6 0-0 d6 7 d4 exd4 8 cxd4 ♗b6 9 d5 ♘a5 10 ♗b2 ♘e7 11 ♗d3 0-0 12 ♘c3 ♘g6 13 ♘e2 c5 14 ♖c1 ♗d7 15 ♔h1 f6 16 ♘e1 a6 17 f4 ♗b5 18 ♖f3 ♖c8 19 ♖h3 c4 20 ♗b1 c3 21 ♖hxc3 ♗xe2 22 ♕xe2 ♖xc3 23 ♗xc3 ♘xf4 24 ♕g4 ♘e3 25 ♖d1 ♘c4 26 ♕f3 ♕b6 27 ♘d3 ♘e5 28 ♗xe5 fxe5 29 ♘xf4 ♖xf4 30 ♕h3 h6 31 g3 ♖f2 32 ♖f1 ♖xf1+ 33 ♕xf1 ♕b2 34 ♕d1 ♕f2 35 a4 b5 36 axb5 axb5 37 ♗d3 b4 38 ♗e2 b3 39 ♕f1 b2 40 ♕xf2 b1♕+ 41 ♕f1 ♕xe4+ 42 ♕f3 ♕d4 43 ♔g2 ♕d2 44 ♔h3 ♕d4 45 ♕g4 **½-½**

L/N6051

**1865-★AP-1 ○●○** viii 65
**Arnold, E.– Paulsen, L.**
Elberfeld [Anderssen & Neumann]

1 e4 e5 2 ♘f3 ♘c6 3 ♗b5 a6 4 ♗a4 ♘f6 5 d4 exd4 6 0-0 ♗e7 7 e5 [□ 7 ♖e1] 7 ... ♘e4 8 ♘xd4 ♘xd4 9 ♕xd4 ♘c5 10 ♘c3 0-0 11 f4 ♘xa4 12 ♕xa4 f6 13 ♕c4+ ♔h8 14 b3 [□ 14 ♗e3] 14 ... fxe5 15 fxe5 b5 16 ♖xf8+ ♕xf8 17 ♕e2 ♗c5+ 18 ♗e3 ♗b7 19 ♖f1 ♕e7 20 ♗xc5 ♕xc5+ 21 ♕f2 ♕xf2+ 22 ♖xf2 ♔g8 23 ♖d2 ♖d8 24 ♘d5 ♗xd5 25 ♖xd5 ♔f7 26 ♖c5 c6 27 c4 ♔e6 28 cxb5 axb5 29 a4 ♖a8 30 axb5 ♖a5 31 b4 ♖xb5 32 ♖c4 ♔xe5 33 ♔f2 ♖b6 34 ♔e3 d5 35 ♖h4 h6 36 ♔d3 ♖a6 37 ♔c3 ♖a3+ 38 ♔b2 ♖e3 39 g3 ♖e4 40 ♖h5+ ♔f6 **0-1**

L/N6051

**1865-★AP-2 ○●○** viii 65
**Asbeck, F.= Paulsen, L.**
Elberfeld [Anderssen & Neumann]

1 e4 e5 2 ♗c4 ♘f6 3 d3 c6 4 h3? d5 5 exd5 cxd5 6 ♗b3 ♘c6 7 ♘e2 h6? 8 0-0 ♗d6 9 f4 e4 10 ♗e3 0-0 11 ♘bc3 d4

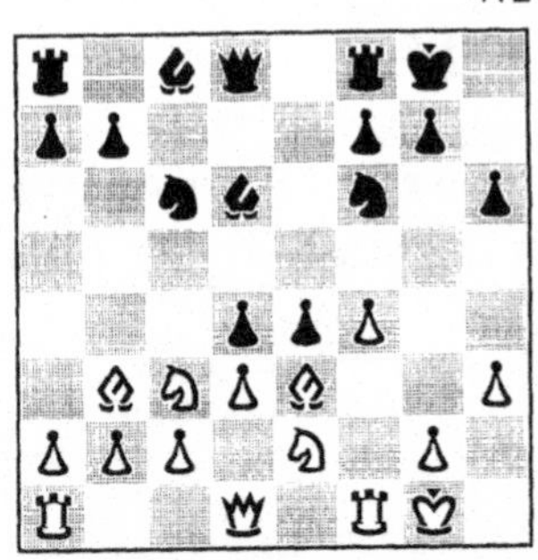

12 dxe4 dxc3 13 e5 cxb2 14 ♖b1 ♖e8 15 ♖f3 ♗c7 16 ♕xd8 ♗xd8 17 exf6 ♗xf6 18 c3 ♗f5 19 ♖xb2 ♖ad8 20 ♗c2 ♗xc2 21 ♖xc2 ♖d3 22 ♔f2 ♗d8 23 ♘d4 **½-½**

L/N6051

**1865-★AS-1** iv 65
**Anderssen, A.+ Schallopp, E.**
Berlin [Anderssen & Neumann]

1 e4 e5 2 f4 exf4 3 ♘f3 g5 4 h4 g4 5 ♘e5 ♗g7 6 ♘xg4 d5 7 ♘f2 dxe4 8 ♘xe4 ♘f6 9 ♘bc3 0-0 10 d3 ♖e8 11 ♗e2 ♘d5 12 ♘xd5 ♕xd5 13 ♗xf4 f5? 14 ♘c3 ♕xg2 [±] 15 ♔d2 ♘c6 16 ♖g1 ♕f2 17 ♘d5 ♘d4 18 ♖xg7+ ♔xg7 19 ♕g1+ ♕xg1 20 ♖xg1+ ♔h8 21 ♗h5 **1-0** L/N6051

**1865-★AS-2** iv 65
**Schulten, J.W.–Anderssen, A.**
Berlin [Anderssen & Neumann]

1 e4 e5 2 f4 exf4 3 ♗c4 d5 4 exd5 ♕h4+ 5 ♔f1 ♗d6 6 ♗b3 ♘e7 7 c4 0-0 8 d4 b6 9 ♘c3 ♗a6 10 ♘f3 ♕h5 11 ♘e2 [□ 11 ♔f2] 11 ... ♘g6 12 ♗d2 ♘d7 13 ♕c1 ♘f6 14 ♔g1 ♘xd5 15 ♘g3 fxg3 16 hxg3 ♕g4 17 cxd5 ♗xg3 18 ♕c3 ♖ae8 19 ♘g5 ♗f2+ 20 ♔h2 ♖e3 21 ♕xe3 ♗xe3 22 ♗xe3 ♘f4 **0-1** L/N6051

**1865-★AS-3** viii 65
**Avery, T.– Staunton, H.**
Birmingham

1 f4 c5 2 e4 ♘c6 3 ♘f3 d6 4 c4 e5 5 fxe5 ♘xe5 6 ♘c3 ♗g4 7 ♗e2 ♗xf3 8 ♗xf3 ♘d3+ 9 ♔e2 ♘f4+ 10 ♔f2 ♘d3+ 11 ♔e2 ♘e5 12 d3 ♘f6 13 ♔f2 ♗e7 14 ♗f4 ♘fd7 15 ♖f1 ♗f6 16 ♔g1 0-0 17 ♘d5 ♘xf3+ 18 ♕xf3 ♗xb2 19 ♖ab1 ♗d4+ 20 ♗e3 ♘e5 21 ♕g3 ♗xe3+ 22 ♕xe3 b6 23 ♕g3 ♔h8 24 ♖f5 ♕d7 25 ♖bf1 ♘g6 26 h4 ♖ae8 27 h5 ♘e5 28 h6 ♖g8 29 hxg7+ ♖xg7 30 ♖g5 ♖eg8 31 ♖ff5 [31 ♘f6 ♕d8] 31 ... ♕d8 [31 ... ♕a4 32 ♘f6 (32 ♖xg7 ♖xg7 33 ♖g5 ♕d1+ 34 ♔h2 ♘f3+ 35 gxf3 ♕d2+∓) 32 ... ♕d1+ 33 ♔h2 ♘g4+ 34 ♖xg4 (34 ♘xg4?) 34 ... ♖xg4 35 ♘xg4 ♖xg4 36 ♕f3 ♕xf3 37 gxf3=] 32 ♘f6 ♖xg5 33 ♖xg5 ♖xg5

34 ♕xg5 ♘g4+ 35 ♘xh7 ♕xg5 36 ♘xg5 ♘e5 37 ♔f2 f6 **0-1** M954

### 1865-★AZ-1 v 65
**Anderssen,A.+Zukertort, J.H.**

Breslau [Anderssen & Zukertort]

1 e4 e5 2 f4 exf4 3 ♘f3 g5 4 h4 g4 5 ♘e5 h5 6 ♗c4 ♖h7 7 d4 d6 8 ♘d3 f3 9 gxf3 ♗e7 10 ♗e3 ♗xh4+ 11 ♔d2 ♗g5 12 f4 ♗h6 13 ♘c3 ♘f6 14 ♕g1 ♘c6 15 b4 b6 16 d5 ♘e7 17 ♖e1 ♗b7 18 f5 ♗g7 19 ♗g5 ♕d7 20 ♕d4 c5 21 bxc5 bxc5 22 ♕f2 ♔f8 23 ♘f4 ♘eg8 24 e5 dxe5 25 ♖xe5 ♕d6 26 ♖he1 a6

27 ♘g6+! fxg6 28 fxg6 ♖h6 29 ♕f4! ♕d8 30 ♗d3 ♖c8 31 d6 ♖c6 32 ♖e7 ♖xg6 33 ♖e8+ ♕xe8 34 ♖xe8+ ♔xe8 35 ♗xg6+ ♔d7 36 ♗f5+ ♔d8 37 ♘e4 **1-0** L/N6051-1868

### 1865-★AZ-2 22 vi 65
**Anderssen,A.+Zukertort, J.H.**

Breslau [Anderssen & Neumann]

1 e4 e5 2 f4 exf4 3 ♘f3 g5 4 ♗c4 g4 5 0-0 ♕e7? 6 ♘c3 gxf3 7 d4 d6 8 ♘d5 ♕d7 9 ♕xf3 ♘c6 10 ♕xf4 ♘d8 11 ♕g3! c6?

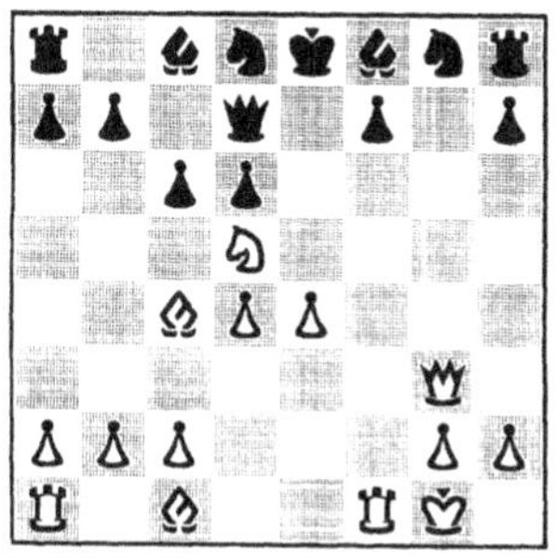

12 ♕xg8! ♖xg8 13 ♘f6+ ♔e7 14 ♘xg8+ ♔e8 15 ♘f6+ ♔e7 16 ♘xd7 ♗xd7 17 ♗g5+ **1-0** L/N6051-1867

### 1865-★AZ-3 v 65
**Anderssen,A.+Zukertort, J.H.**

Breslau

1 e4 e5 2 f4 exf4 3 ♘f3 g5 4 h4 g4 5 ♘e5 h5 6 ♗c4 ♖h7 7 d4 d6 8 ♘d3 f3 9 gxf3 ♗e7 10 ♗e3 ♗xh4+ 11 ♔d2 ♗g5 12 f4 ♗h6 13 ♘c3 ♘f6 14 ♕g1 ♘c6 15 b4 b6 16 d5 ♘e7 17 ♖e1 ♗b7 18 f5 ♗g7 19 ♗g5 ♕d7 20 ♕d4 c5 21 bxc5 bxc5 22 ♕f2 a6 23 e5 dxe5 24 ♘xe5 ♕d6 25 ♘d3 ♗h6 26 ♗xh6 ♖xh6 27 ♖xe7+ ♔xe7 28 ♕e3+ ♔d7 29 ♘xc5+ ♔c7 30 ♘xb7 ♔xb7 31 ♖b1+ ♔c7 32 ♗xa6 ♕xa6 33 ♕e7+ ♔c8 34 ♕f8+ ♔d7 35 ♕xf7+ ♔d8 36 ♕f8+ ♘e8 37 ♖e1 **1-0** L/N3034

### 1865-★AZ-4 vi 65
**Anderssen,A.−Zukertort, J.H.**

Breslau [Anderssen & Zukertort]

1 e4 e5 2 f4 exf4 3 ♘f3 g5 4 ♗c4 g4! 5 0-0 gxf3 6 ♕xf3 ♕e7 7 d4 [7 ♕xf4 d6] 7 ... ♘c6 8 ♘c3 [8 ♕xf4 ♗h6 9 ♕xc7 ♗xc1 10 ♗xf7+ ♕xf7 11 ♖xf7 ♔xf7 12 ♘c3 ♕e3+ 13 ♔h1 ♗xd4] 8 ... ♘xd4 9 ♕d3 ♘e6 10 ♘d5 ♕c5+ 11 ♔h1 c6? [□ 11 ... b5] 12 b4 ♕d6 13 e5 ♕xe5 14 ♗xf4 ♘xf4 15 ♘xf4 ♔d8 16 ♗xf7 ♔c7 17 ♖ae1 ♕g5 [□ ♕g7] 18 ♖e8 ♘h6 19 ♕d4!? ♗g7 [19 ... ♘xf7 20 ♘e6+ dxe6 21 ♖xf7+ ♔b8 22 ♖xc8+ ♔xc8 23 ♕d7+] 20 ♕d2 ♖xe8 21 ♘d5+ [□ 21 ♘e6+ ♖xe6 22 ♕xg5 ♘xf7 23 ♕xg7] 21 ... ♕xd5 22 ♗xd5 cxd5 23 ♕g5 ♗f8 24 ♕xd5 ♖e6 25 ♕c4+ ♖c6 26 ♕f4+ ♗d6 27 ♕xh6 ♗xb4 28 ♕xh7 b6 29 ♖f4 ♗c5 30 h4 ♗b7 31 ♖f7 ♖d6 32 h5 ♖d2 33 ♖g7 ♖f8 34 ♔h2 ♖ff2 35 ♕g8 ♖xc2 36 h6 ♖xg2+ 37 ♔h3 ♖c3+ **0-1** L/N6051-1868

### 1865-★AZ-5 vi 65
**Anderssen,A.+Zukertort, J.H.**

Breslau [Anderssen & Zukertort]

1 e4 e5 2 f4 exf4 3 ♘f3 g5 4 ♗c4 g4 5 0-0 gxf3 6 ♕xf3 ♕f6 7 e5 ♕xe5 8 d3 ♗h6 9 ♘c3 ♘e7 10 ♗d2 ♘bc6 11 ♖ae1 ♕f5! 12 ♘d5 ♔d8 13 ♗c3 ♖e8 14 ♘f6 ♖f8 15 g4 ♕g6 16 h4 d6? [□ 16 ... d5] 17 g5 ♗g7 18 ♕xf4 h6 19 ♕h2 a6 20 d4 hxg5? [□ 20 ... b5 21 ♗b3 b4] 21 d5 gxh4+ 22 ♔h1 ♘b8? [□ 22 ... ♕g3 23 ♕xg3 hxg3 24 dxc6 bxc6]

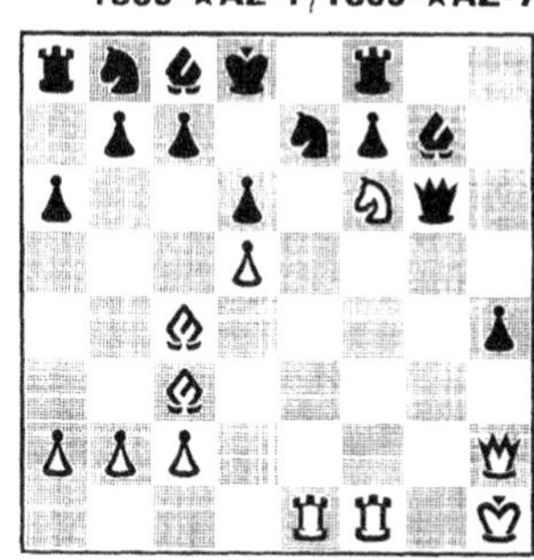

23 ♕xd6+! ♗d7 24 ♕xe7+ **1-0** L/N6051-1868

### 1865-★AZ-6 viii 65
**Anderssen,A.+Zukertort, J.H.**

Breslau [Anderssen & Zukertort]

1 e4 e5 2 ♘f3 ♘c6 3 d4 exd4 4 ♗c4 ♗c5 5 0-0 d6! 6 c3 ♗g4! 7 b4 [7 ♕b3 ♗xf3 8 ♗xf7+ ♔f8 9 ♗xg8 ♖xg8 10 gxf3 g5∓] 7 ... ♗b6 8 ♗b2 ♕f6! 9 ♕e2 h5 [□ 9 ... d3] 10 ♘xd4 [10 cxd4 ♗xf3 11 ♗xf3 ♘xd4] 10 ... ♘xd4 11 ♗xg4 hxg4 12 cxd4 ♕h4 13 h3 gxh3 14 g3 ♕xe4! [△ 15 ... h2#] 15 f3 ♕e3+ 16 ♔h1 0-0-0 17 ♘d2! d5 [17 ... ♗xd4 18 ♘c4] 18 ♘b3 ♘e7 [□ 18 ... ♘f6] 19 ♗c1! ♕e6 20 ♗f4! f6! 21 ♖e1 ♕f7 22 g4 g5 23 ♗h2 f5 24 a4 c6 25 a5 ♗c7 26 ♗xc7 ♔xc7 27 b5 fxg4 28 b6+ ♔b8 29 bxa7+ ♔xa7? [□ 29 ... ♔a8] 30 fxg4 ♘g6 31 ♖f1 ♘f4 32 ♘c5 ♖de8 33 ♕b3 ♕c7 34 ♕b6+ ♕xb6 35 axb6+ **1-0** L/N6051-1867

### 1865-★AZ-7 6 i 65
**Zukertort, J.H.= Anderssen, A.**

Breslau [Anderssen & Zukertort]

1 e4 e5 2 ♘f3 ♘c6 3 ♗c4 ♗c5 4 b4 ♗xb4 5 c3 ♗a5 6 d4 exd4 7 0-0 dxc3? 8 ♕b3 ♕f6 9 e5 ♕g6 10 ♘xc3 ♗xc3 11 ♕xc3 ♘h6 12 ♗a3? [□ 12 ♘g5, 13 ♗d3] 12 ... b6 13 e6 fxe6 14 ♗xe6 ♗a6 15 ♖fe1 0-0-0 16 ♕xc6 ♗b7 17 ♕c3 [17 ♗xd7+?!] 17 ... dxe6 18 ♖ec1 ♖d7 19 ♗d6 ♔b8 20 ♗g3 ♘f7 21 a4 h5 22 h4? [□ 22 a5 h4 23 ♗xc7+ ♔a8 24 axb6; 22 ... ♗xf3 23 ♕xf3 ♕g4 24 ♕c6] 22 ... e5 23 a5 ♕e4 24 axb6 axb6 25 ♖e1 ♕c6 26 ♕a3 ♕d6 27 ♕a7+ ♔c8 28 ♖ad1 ♕xd1 29 ♖xd1 ♖xd1+ 30 ♔h2 ♖d5 31 ♕a4 b5 32 ♕c2 ♘d6 33 ♕g6 ♖e8 34 ♕xh5 b4 35 ♘xe5 b3 36 ♕e2 ♖b5 37 ♕b2 ♘f5 38 ♗f4 ♖e6 39 ♘d3 ♖e4 40 ♕c1! c5! 41 f3 ♖e2 42 ♕c4! [42 ♘xc5 b2] 42 ... ♘d4! 43 ♕g8+ ♔d7 44 ♕xg7+ ♔c6 45 ♕c7+ ♔d5 46 ♘xc5! b2 47 ♘a4! ♖c2 [47 ... b1♕ 48 ♘c3+ ♔e6 49 ♘xb1 ♖xb1 50 ♕d6+] 48 ♕f7+ ♔c6 [48

... ♘e6 49 ♕d7+ ♔c4 50 ♕xe6+] 49 ♕c7+ ♔d5 50 ♕f7+ ½-½ L/N6051-1867

**1865-★AZ-8** i 65
**Zukertort, J.H.– Anderssen, A.**
Breslau
1 e4 e5 2 f4 exf4 3 ♘f3 g5 4 ♗c4 g4 5 ♘e5 ♕h4+ 6 ♔f1 f3 7 d4 ♘f6 8 ♘c3 ♘c6 9 ♗xf7+ ♔d8 10 ♗b3 ♘xe5 11 dxe5 fxg2+ 12 ♔xg2 ♕h3+ 13 ♔f2 ♗c5+ 14 ♔e1 ♕h4+ 15 ♔d2 ♘h5 16 ♖f1 ♕xh2+ 17 ♕e2 ♘g3 **0-1** L/N6051-1867

**1865-★AZ-9** i 65
**Zukertort, J.H.+ Anderssen, A.**
Breslau [Anderssen & Neumann]
1 e4 e5 2 ♘f3 ♘c6 3 ♗b5 ♘ge7 4 c3 d6 5 d4 ♗d7 6 0-0 ♘g6 7 ♘g5! h6 8 ♘xf7! ♔xf7 9 ♗c4+ ♔e7 [9 ... d5 10 exd5 ♘b8 (10 ... ♘a5 11 ♗d3 b6 12 ♕h5 ♕f6 13 dxe5) 11 ♕h5 ♗d6 12 ♗d3 ♕f6 13 dxe5 ♗xe5 14 f4!+–] 10 ♕h5 ♕e8 [10 ... ♗e8 11 ♗g5+ hxg5 12 ♕xg5+ ♔d7 13 ♕f5+ ♔e7 14 ♕e6#] 11 ♕g5+ hxg5 12 ♗xg5# **1-0** L/N6051-1867

**1865-★AZ-10** i 65
**Zukertort, J.H.+ Anderssen, A.**
Breslau
1 e4 e5 2 ♘f3 ♘c6 3 ♗c4 ♗c5 4 b4 ♗xb4 5 c3 ♗c5 6 d4 exd4 7 0-0 d6 8 cxd4 ♗b6 9 d5 ♘a5 10 ♗b2 ♘e7 11 ♗d3 0-0 12 ♘c3 ♘g6 13 ♘e2 c5 14 ♕d2 f6 15 ♔h1 ♗c7 16 ♖ac1 ♖b8 17 ♘g3 ♖f7 18 ♘f5 ♗xf5 19 exf5 ♘e5 20 ♗xe5 dxe5 21 ♗e4 ♕d6 22 g4 h6 23 ♖g1 b5 24 ♖g3 c4 25 ♖cg1 ♗b6 26 g5 fxg5 27 ♘xg5 hxg5 28 ♖xg5 ♕h6 29 ♖xg7+ ♕xg7 30 ♖xg7+ ♖xg7 31 f6 ♖f7 32 ♕g5+ ♔f8 33 ♕h6+ ♔g8 34 ♗f5 ♖e8 35 ♗e6 **1-0** L/N3034

**1865-★AZ-11** v 65
**Zukertort, J.H.+ Anderssen, A.**
Breslau [Anderssen & Zukertort]
1 e4 e5 2 f4 exf4 3 ♘f3 g5 4 h4 g4 5 ♘e5 h5 6 ♗c4 ♖h7 7 d4 d6 8 ♘d3 f3 9 gxf3 ♗e7 10 ♗e3! ♗xh4+ 11 ♔d2 ♗g5 12 f4 ♗h6 13 ♘c3 [13 ♖xh5 ♘f6] 13 ... ♘f6 14 ♕g1 ♘c6 15 b4 b6 [□ 15 ... g3 16 ♕xg3 ♘g4, 17 ... ♖g7] 16 d5 ♘e7 17 ♖e1 ♗b7 18 f5 ♗g7 19 ♗g5 ♕d7

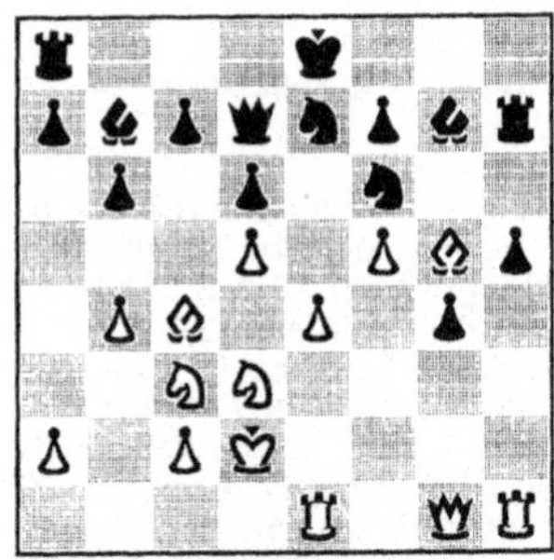

20 ♕d4! [20 e5 ♕xf5 21 ♗xf6 ♗h6+ 22 ♔d1 ♕f3+ 23 ♘e2 ♗xd5–+] 20 ... c5 21 bxc5 bxc5 22 ♕f2 a6 23 e5 dxe5 24 ♘xe5 ♕d6 25 ♘d3 ♗h6 26 ♗xh6 ♖xh6 27 ♖xe7+? [□ 27 ♕xc5] 27 ... ♔xe7! 28 ♕e3+ ♔d7 29 ♘xc5+ [29 ♕xh6?? ♘e4+] 29 ... ♔c7 30 ♘xb7 ♔xb7 31 ♖b1+ ♔c7 32 ♗xa6 ♕xa6 33 ♕e7+ ♔c8 [33 ... ♔d7 34 ♘b5+ ♔c8 35 ♕e8++–] 34 ♕f8+ ♔d7 35 ♕xf7+ ♔d8 36 ♕f8+ ♘e8? [□ 36 ... ♔d7] 37 ♖e1 **1-0** L/N6051-1868

**1865-★AZ-12** v 65
**Zukertort, J.H.+ Anderssen, A.**
Breslau
1 e4 e5 2 ♘f3 ♘c6 3 ♗c4 ♗c5 4 b4 ♗xb4 5 c3 ♗c5 6 d4 exd4 7 0-0 d6 8 cxd4 ♗b6 9 d5 ♘a5 10 ♗b2 ♘e7 11 ♗d3 0-0 12 ♘c3 ♘g6 13 ♘e2 c5 14 ♕d2 f6 15 ♔h1 ♗c7 16 ♖ac1 ♖b8 17 ♘g3 ♖f7 18 ♘f5 ♗xf5 19 exf5 ♘e5 20 ♘xe5 dxe5 21 ♗e4 ♕d6 22 ♖c3 b5 23 ♕e2 c4 24 ♖h3 h6 25 f4 b4 26 ♖ff3 c3 27 ♗c1 ♘b7 28 fxe5 fxe5 29 ♖fg3 ♔f8 30 ♖g6 ♖f6 31 ♗xh6 ♖xg6 32 fxg6 gxh6 33 ♕f3+ ♔e7 34 ♕f7+ ♔d8 35 g7 **1-0** L/N3034

**1865-★AZ-13** 15 vi 65
**Zukertort, J.H.+ Anderssen, A.**
Breslau
1 e4 e5 2 f4 exf4 3 ♘f3 g5 4 ♗c4 g4 5 0-0 ♕e7 6 ♘c3 ♕c5+ 7 d4 ♕xc4 8 ♘e5 ♕e6 9 ♘d5 ♔d8 10 ♘xf4 ♕e8 11 ♘d5 f6 12 ♘xg4 ♗g7 13 ♘gxf6 ♘xf6 14 ♗g5 ♕g6 15 ♗h4 ♕xe4 16 ♕h5 ♖f8 17 ♖ae1 ♕xd4+ 18 ♔h1 c6 19 ♖xf6 cxd5 20 ♖xf8+ ♔c7 21 ♗g3+ d6 22 ♗f2 ♕c4 23 ♖xc8+ ♔xc8 24 ♕e8+ ♔c7 25 ♖e7+ **1-0** L/N6051-1867

**1865-★AZ-14** 17 vi 65
**Zukertort, J.H.+ Anderssen, A.**
Breslau
1 e4 e5 2 f4 exf4 3 ♘f3 g5 4 ♗c4 g4 5 0-0 ♕e7 6 ♘c3 gxf3 7 d4 d6 8 ♘d5 ♕d8 9 ♕xf3 ♘c6 10 ♕xf4 ♗e6 11 ♘xc7+ ♕xc7 12 ♗xe6 ♗h6 13 ♗xf7+ ♔f8 14 ♕h4 ♗xc1 15 ♖axc1 ♘d8 16 ♗h5+ ♔g7 17 ♕g5# **1-0** L/N6051-1867

**1865-★AZ-15** 18 vi 65
**Zukertort, J.H.= Anderssen, A.**
Breslau [Anderssen & Zukertort]
1 e4 e5 2 f4 exf4 3 ♘f3 g5 4 ♗c4 g4 5 0-0 ♕e7? 6 ♘c3! gxf3 7 d4 d6 8 ♘d5 ♕d7 9 ♕xf3 ♘c6 10 ♕xf4 ♘d8 11 e5 c6 12 ♘f6+ ♘xf6 13 ♕xf6 ♖g8 14 exd6 ♗xd6 15 ♗g5 [△ 16 ♖ae1+ ♘e6 17 ♗xe6 fxe6 18 ♖xe6+] 15 ... ♕e7! 16 ♗xf7+ ♘xf7 17 ♖ae1 ♘xg5 [17 ... ♘e5 18 ♖xe5] 18 ♖xe7+ ♗xe7 19 ♖e1! ♗e6 20 ♖xe6 ♘xe6 21 ♕xe6 ♖g6 22 ♕h3 ♖g7 23 ♕b3 0-0-0 24 ♕e6+ ♖d7 25 a4 ♗d8 26 b4 ♗c7 27 c4 ♔b8 28 ♕e3 ♖de7 29 ♕c3 h5 30 b5 cxb5 31 axb5 ♗f4 32 g3 ♖e3 33 ♕b4! ♖e8 34 c5 h4 35 d5! ♗e3+ 36 ♔g2 hxg3 37 hxg3 ♖f7 38 ♕c3 ♖f2+ 39 ♔h3 ♖f1 40 c6 ♖h1+ 41 ♔g2 ♖g1+ 42 ♔h3 ♗f2 43 ♕f6! ♖xg3+ [43 ... ♗xg3 44 ♕g7+–] 44 ♔h2 ♖gg8 45 ♕d6+ [45 ♕xf2?? ♖h8+–+] 45 ... ♔a8 46 cxb7+ ♔xb7 47 ♕c6+ ♔b8 48 ♕d6+ ½-½ L/N6051-1867

**1865-★AZ-16** vi 65
**Zukertort, J.H.+ Anderssen, A.**
Breslau [Anderssen & Zukertort]
1 e4 e5 2 f4 exf4 3 ♘f3 g5 4 ♗c4 g4 5 0-0 ♕e7? 6 ♘c3! ♕c5+ 7 d4 ♕xc4 8 ♘e5 ♕e6 9 ♘d5! ♘a6 10 ♘xf4 ♕d6 11 ♘d5 f6

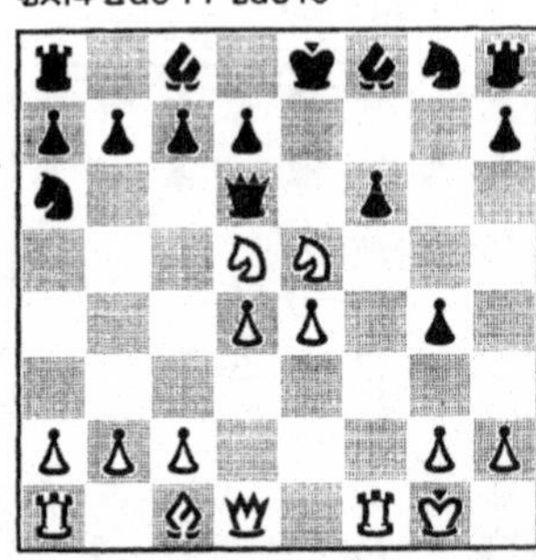

12 ♕xg4! fxe5 13 ♕h5+ ♕g6 [13 ... ♔d8 14 ♖xf8+ ♕xf8 15 ♗g5+ ♘e7 16 ♘xe7 ♕xe7 17 ♗xe7+ ♔xe7 18 ♕xe5++–] 14 ♕xe5+ ♘e7 [14 ... ♕e6 15 ♕xh8 c6 16 ♘f6+ ♘xf6 17 ♖xf6 ♕e7 18 ♗h6] 15

♖xf8+ ♔xf8 16 ♕xe7+ ♔g8 17 ♘f6+ ♕xf6 18 ♕xf6 h5 19 ♗h6 **1-0** L/N6051-1867

**1865-★AZ-17** vi 65
**Zukertort, J.H.+ Anderssen, A.**
Breslau
1 e4 c5 2 ♘f3 e6 3 d4 cxd4 4 ♘xd4 ♘f6 5 ♘c3 ♗b4 6 ♗d3 ♘c6 7 ♗e3 d5 8 exd5 ♘xd5 9 0-0 ♘xc3 10 bxc3 ♗xc3 11 ♘xc6 bxc6 12 ♖b1 0-0 13 ♖b3 ♗a5 14 ♗c5 ♖e8 15 ♗xh7+ ♔xh7 16 ♖h3+ ♔g8 17 ♕h5 f5 18 ♖d1 ♗d7 19 ♕h7+ ♔f7 20 ♖g3 ♗c3 21 ♕g6+ ♔g8 22 ♖xc3 f4 23 ♖h3 ♖e7 24 ♕h7+ ♔f7 25 ♕h5+ ♔g8 26 ♗xe7 ♕xe7 27 ♕h8+ ♔f7 28 ♕xa8 **1-0** L/N6051-1868

**1865-★AZ-18** vi 65
**Zukertort, J.H.+ Anderssen, A.**
Breslau
1 e4 e5 2 f4 exf4 3 ♘f3 g5 4 ♗c4 g4 5 0-0 gxf3 6 ♕xf3 ♕f6 7 e5 ♕xe5 8 d3 ♗h6 9 ♘c3 ♘e7 10 ♗d2 c6 11 ♖ae1 ♕c5+ 12 ♔h1 d5 13 ♗xd5 cxd5 14 ♘xd5 ♗e6 15 ♘f6+ ♔d8 16 ♕xb7 ♘ec6 17 ♖xf4 ♗c8 18 ♖d4+ ♘xd4 19 ♗a5+ ♕xa5 20 ♕e7# **1-0** L/N3034

**1865-★AZ-19** vi 65
**Zukertort, J.H.+ Anderssen, A.**
Breslau
1 e4 e5 2 f4 exf4 3 ♘f3 g5 4 ♗c4 g4 5 0-0 gxf3 6 ♕xf3 ♕f6 7 e5 ♕xe5 8 d3 ♗h6 9 ♘c3 ♘e7 10 ♗d2 c6 11 ♖ae1 ♕c5+ 12 ♔h1 d5 13 ♕h5 ♕d6 14 ♗xd5 cxd5 15 ♘xd5 ♘c6 16 ♗c3 ♗d7 17 ♖xe7+ ♘xe7 18 ♖e1 ♗f8 19 ♗b4 ♕g6 20 ♕e5 ♗c6 21 ♗xe7 ♗xd5 22 ♗f6+ ♗e6 23 ♕b5# **1-0** L/N3034

**1865-★AZ-20** vii 65
**Zukertort, J.H.= Anderssen, A.**
Breslau [Anderssen & Zukertort]
1 e4 e5 2 ♘f3 ♘c6 3 d4 exd4 4 ♘xd4 ♗c5 5 ♗e3 ♕f6 6 c3 ♘ge7 7 ♗e2 d6 [7 ... d5 8 ♗f3] 8 0-0 h5 9 f4 ♕g6 10 ♕d3 h4 11 ♗f3 f5 12 e5 dxe5 13 ♘xc6 e4 14 ♘xe7 ♗xe7 15 ♕c2 exf3 16 ♖xf3 ♗d7 17 ♘d2 0-0-0 18 ♘c4 ♗c6 19 ♖f2? [□ 19 ♘e5] 19 ... ♗e4 20 ♕a4 a6 21 b4 h3 22 ♘e5 ♕e6 23 g3 ♗d6 24 ♗d4 ♗xe5 25 ♗xe5 ♖d3! 26 ♕a5! b6 27 ♕xa6+ ♔b8 28 a4 ♕g6! [△ 29 ... ♖xg3+] 29 ♔f1 ♖e3! 30 ♖d1! ♗g2+ 31 ♔g1 [31 ♖xg2 hxg2+ 32 ♔xg2 (32 ♔g1 ♕h6; 32 ♔f2 ♖xe5 33 fxe5 f4 34 gxf4 ♕c2+ 35 ♔e2 g1♕+ 36 ♖xg1 ♖xh2+) 32 ... ♖xh2+ 33 ♔xh2 ♕g3+ -+] 31 ... ♗b7 32 ♗xc7+ ♔xc7 [32 ... ♔c8 33 ♕xb6+-] 33 ♖d7+ ♔xd7 34 ♕xb7+ ♔e8 [34 ... ♔e6 35 ♕xb6+ ♔f7 36 ♕xe3+-] 35 ♕c8+ ♔f7 36 ♕xh8 ♕g4 37 ♕h7 ♖e1+ 38 ♖f1 ♖xf1+ 39 ♔xf1 ♕d1+ 40 ♔f2 ♕d2+ **½-½** L/N6051-1867

**1865-★AZ-21** vii 65
**Zukertort, J.H.+ Anderssen, A.**
1 e4 c5 2 ♘f3 e6 3 d4 cxd4 4 ♘xd4 ♘f6 5 ♘c3 ♗b4 6 ♗d3 ♘c6 7 ♗e3 d5 8 ♘xc6 bxc6 9 e5 ♘d7 10 f4 0-0 11 0-0 f5 12 exf6 ♕xf6 13 ♔h1 c5 14 f5 ♗xc3 15 fxe6 ♕xe6 16 bxc3 ♕xe3 17 ♕h5 ♖xf1+ 18 ♖xf1 ♘f6 19 ♗xh7+ ♔f8 20 ♕xd5 ♕e2 21 ♕g8+ ♔e7 22 ♕xg7+ ♔d8 23 ♕xf6+ ♕e7 24 ♖d1+ ♗d7 25 ♕f3 ♖c8 26 ♗f5 ♖c7 27 ♕a8+ ♖c8 28 ♕xa7 ♖c7 29 ♕b8+ ♖c8 30 ♕b6+ **1-0** L/N6051-1868

**1865-★AZ-22** xi 65
**Zukertort, J.H.+ Anderssen, A.**
Breslau [Anderssen & Zuckertort]
1 e4 e5 2 ♘f3 ♘c6 3 d4 exd4 4 ♗c4 ♗c5 5 c3 ♘f6 6 e5 d5 7 ♗b5 ♘e4 8 cxd4 ♗b4+ [□ 8 ... ♗b6] 9 ♗d2 ♗xd2+ 10 ♘bxd2 0-0 11 0-0 f5 12 ♖c1 ♗d7 [12 ... ♘e7] 13 ♘b3 ♗e8 14 ♘c5 ♕c8 15 ♕b3 ♘e7 16 ♗d3! ♘xc5 17 ♖xc5 c6 18 ♗b1 b6 19 ♖c3 f4 20 ♖e1 ♕g4 21 e6 ♖f6 22 ♕b4 ♖xe6 23 ♖xe6 ♕xe6 24 ♗xh7+ ♔f8 25 ♖c1 ♖d8 26 ♖e1 ♕d6 27 ♕d2 ♕f6 [27 ... g6 28 ♖e5 ♔g7 29 ♕xf4 ♗f7 (29 ... ♔xh7 30 ♕h4+, 31 ♖xe7) 30 ♘g5±] 28 ♗b1 c5 29 h4 [△ 30 ♘g5 ♔g8 31 ♖e6+-] 29 ... ♖d6 30 dxc5 bxc5 31 ♘g5 ♔g8 32 ♕e2 ♖d7 33 ♕g4 ♖b7 34 ♗f5! ♗f7 35 ♗e6 ♗xe6 36 ♖xe6 ♕f8 37 ♕h5 ♕f5 38 ♖e5! ♕g6 39 ♖xd5! ♖b8 40 ♕xg6 ♘xg6 41 ♖xc5 **1-0** L/N6051-1867

**1865-★AZ-23** xi 65
**Zukertort, J.H.= Anderssen, A.**
Breslau [Anderssen & Zukertort]
1 e3 f5 2 d4 e6 3 c4 ♘f6 4 f4 c5 5 d5 ♕c7 6 ♘f3 ♗e7 7 ♗e2 0-0 8 0-0 b6 9 ♘c3 a6 10 b3 ♗b7 11 ♗b2 b5 12 dxe6 dxe6 13 cxb5 ♘g4 14 ♕c1 ♗f6 15 h3 ♘h6 16 ♗c4 ♖e8 17 ♕c2 ♘d7 18 ♖ad1 ♗e4 19 ♘xe4 fxe4 20 ♕xe4!? ♗xb2 21 ♗xe6+ ♔h8? [□ 21 ... ♔f8] 22 ♖xd7! ♕xd7 23 ♘g5! g6 24 ♗xd7 ♖xe4 25 ♘xe4 axb5 26 ♗xb5 ♖xa2 27 ♘xc5 ♘f5 28 ♘d3 [28 ♖e1 ♘xe3 29 ♖xe3 ♗d4; 28 e4 ♗d4+ 29 ♔h2 ♘e3] 28 ... ♘xe3 29 ♖f2 ♖a1+ 30 ♔h2 ♗d4 31 ♘e5! ♖b1 32 ♖d2 ♘f5 33 g4 ♗g1+ 34 ♔g2 ♘h4+ 35 ♔g3 ♖xb3+ 36 ♔xh4 ♖xb5 37 ♖d8+ ♔g7 38 ♖d7+ ♔f6 39 ♖f7+ [39 ♖xh7?? ♗f2#] 39 ... ♔e6 40 ♖xh7 ♗e3! 41 ♔g3 [41 ♘xg6?? ♗f2#] 41 ... g5 42 ♘g6 ♔f6 43 f5 ♗c5 44 h4 ♖b3+ 45 ♔g2 ♗d6 46 ♖d7 ♗b8 47 ♖d4?? [□ 47 h5 ♖g3+ 48 ♔f2 ♖xg4 49 h6 ♔xf5 50 h7 ♗e5 51 ♘xe5 ♖h4 52 ♘f3 ♖h6 53 ♖f7+ ♔g6 54 ♘e5+ ♔h5+-; 47 ... ♖b2+ 48 ♔f3 ♖h2 49 ♖d8 ♗e5! 50 ♘xe5 ♔xe5 51 ♖e8+ ♔f6 52 ♖e6+ ♔f7 53 ♖g6+-] 47 ... ♖g3+ 48 ♔f1 gxh4 49 ♘xh4 ♔g5 50 ♘g6 ♖xg4 51 ♖xg4+ ♔xg4 **½-½** L/N6051-1868

**1865-★AZ-24** xi 65
**Zukertort, J.H.– Anderssen, A.**
Breslau
1 e4 e5 2 ♘f3 ♘c6 3 ♗b5 ♘f6 4 d3 d6 5 ♗xc6+ bxc6 6 h3 g6 7 ♘c3 ♗g7 8 ♘e2 0-0 9 0-0 ♘h5 10 g4 ♕f6 11 ♔g2 ♘f4+ 12 ♗xf4 exf4 13 ♘ed4 c5 14 ♘b3 g5 15 c3 h5 16 ♘fd2 ♕h6 17 f3 f6 18 ♘a5 ♔f7 19 ♖b1 ♗e6 20 c4 ♖h8 21 ♖h1 ♖h7 22 b4 ♖ah8 23 bxc5 dxc5 24 ♕g1 ♗f8 25 ♘b7 ♗c8 26 ♘xc5 hxg4 27 fxg4

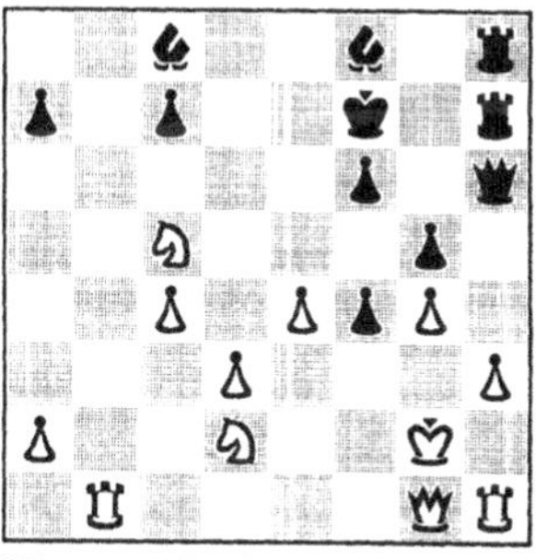

27 ... ♕xh3+ 28 ♖xh3 ♖xh3 29 ♕d4 ♖h2+ 30 ♔f1 ♗xg4 **0-1** L/N6051-1867

**1865-★BC-1** 11 ii 65
**Bergell, R. & Knorre, V. & Raaz, O.=Cordel, O. & Neumann, G.R.**
Berlin [Anderssen & Neumann]
1 e4 e5 2 ♘f3 ♘c6 3 d4 exd4 4 ♘xd4 ♕h4 5 ♕d3 ♘f6 6 ♘b5 [6 ♘d2 ♘xd4 7 ♕xd4 d5 8 ♕e5+ ♔d8 9 exd5 ♗d6∓] 6 ... ♔d8 7 ♘d2 ♗c5 8 g3 ♕g4 9 ♗g2 d6 10 c3 ♖e8 11 f3 ♕h5 12 ♘c4 ♗e6 13 ♘d4 ♗xd4∓ 14 cxd4 ♗xc4 15 ♕xc4 d5 16 ♕c5 dxe4 17 fxe4 ♕xc5 18 dxc5 ♘xe4 19 0-0 f6 20 ♗e3 ♘xg3? 21 ♖ad1+ ♔c8 22 ♗h3+ ♔b8 23 ♖fe1 ♘h5 24 ♗g4 g6 25 ♗xh5 gxh5 26 ♗f4 ♖xe1+ 27 ♖xe1 b6 28 cxb6 axb6 29 ♖e8+ ♔b7 30 ♖xa8 ♔xa8 31 ♗xc7 ♔b7 32 ♗d6 ♘d4 33 ♗e7 f5

34 ♗f6 ♘e6 35 ♔f2 ♘f4 36 ♔f3 ♘g6 37 h4 ♔c6 38 ♔e3 ♔d5 39 b3 b5 ½-½ L/N6051

### 1865-★BC-2 25 ii 65

**Cordel,O.& Knorre,V.– Bergell,R& Neumann,G.R.**

Berlin [Anderssen & Neumann]

1 e4 e5 2 ♘f3 ♘c6 3 ♗c4 ♗c5 4 0-0 d6 5 c3 ♘f6 6 d4 exd4 7 cxd4 ♗b6 8 ♘c3 0-0 9 d5 ♘e5 10 ♘xe5 dxe5 11 ♗g5 ♕d6 12 h3 ♗d7 13 ♔h1 h6 14 ♗h4 g5 15 ♗g3 ♔h7 16 ♗e2 ♖ae8 17 ♕c2 a6? 18 f4 gxf4 19 ♖xf4 ♘g8 20 ♖af1 [□ 21 ♖f3, 22 ♖af1] 20 ... f5 [20 ... exf4 21 e5+ ♔g6 22 ♗d3 fxg3 23 ♖xf7+ ♖xf7 24 ♗xg6+ ♔g7 25 ♗xf7 ♔xf7 26 ♕h7+ ♔f8 27 e6 ♗xe6 28 dxe6 ♖xe6 30 ♘e4±] 21 ♖4f3 f4 22 ♗h2 ♘e7 23 g4 ♘g6 24 ♗d3 ♔g7! 25 ♖e1 ♘h4 26 ♖ff1 f3 **0-1** L/N6051

### 1865-★BC-3 4 iii 65

**Bergell,R.& Neumann, G.R.+Cordel,O.& Knorre,V.**

Berlin

1 e4 e5 2 ♘f3 ♘c6 3 ♗c4 ♗c5 4 b4 ♗xb4 5 c3 ♗a5 6 d4 exd4 7 0-0 dxc3 8 ♕b3 ♕f6 9 e5 ♕g6 10 ♘xc3 ♗xc3 11 ♕xc3 b6 12 ♘g5 ♘h6 [□ 12 ... ♘d8] 13 e6 fxe6 14 ♘xe6 dxe6 15 ♗d3 **1-0** L/N6051

### 1865-★BC-4 1 iv 65

**Bergell,R.& Guretsky-Cornitz,B.v.& Knorre,V.=Cordel,O.& Neumann,G.R.**

Berlin [Anderssen & Neumann]

1 e4 e5 2 ♘f3 ♘c6 3 ♗c4 ♗c5 4 b4 ♗xb4 5 c3 ♗a5 6 d4 exd4 7 0-0 ♗b6 8 cxd4 d6 9 ♘c3 ♘a5 10 ♗d3 ♘e7 11 ♗b2 0-0 12 ♘e2 f5 13 ♕c2 d5 14 exf5 [□ 14 exd5] 14 ... ♗xf5 15 ♗a3 ♘ac6 16 ♗xf5 ♖xf5 17 ♗xe7 ♘xe7 18 ♘g3 ♖f6 19 ♖ae1 ♘g6 20 ♘g5 ♕d7 21 ♘h5 ♖f5∓ 22 f4 ♘xf4 23 h4 ♖xg5 24 ♘xf4 ♗xd4+ 25 ♔h2 ♖g4 [□ 25 ... ♖f5] 26 g3 ♖f8 27 ♕d1 c5 28 ♕b3 ♖f5? 29 ♘xd5 c4 [29 ... ♖xd5 30 ♕xd5++–] 30 ♘e7+ ♔f8 31 ♕a3 ♖xf1 32 ♖xf1+ ♔e8 33 ♘g6 ♗g1+ ½-½ L/N6051

### 1865-★BC-7

**Neumann,G.R.& Bergell, R.+Cordel,O.& Knorre,V.**

Berlin [Anderssen & Neumann]

1 e4 e5 2 ♘f3 ♘c6 3 ♗c4 ♗c5 4 b4 ♗xb4 5 c3 ♗c5 6 0-0 d6 7 d4 exd4 8 cxd4 ♗b6 9 ♘c3 ♘a5 10 ♗d3 ♘e7 11 ♗b2 0-0 12 d5 c5 [□ 12 ... ♘g6] 13 ♘e2 [□ 13 e5] 13 ... ♘g6 14 ♘e1 ♗c7 15 f4 c4 16 ♗c2 b5 17 f5 ♘e5 18 ♗xe5 dxe5 19 f6 gxf6 20 ♘g3 ♗b6+ 21 ♔h1 ♗e3 22 ♖b1 ♖b8 23 ♘f5? ♗xf5 24 ♖xf5 ♔h8! 25 ♕h5 [△ 26 ♖f3 ♗g5 27 ♖h3 h6 28 ♘f3±] 25 ... ♖g8 26 ♕xf7 ♖g6 27 ♖h5 ♖g7 28 ♕e6 ♕b6 29 ♕h3 ♗f2 30 ♘f3 ♕e3 31 ♕f5 ♕e2 [31 ... ♖f8 32 ♘xe5±] 32 ♖xh7+ ♖xh7 33 ♕xf6+ ½-½ L/N6051

### 1865-★BC-6 17 vi 65

**Bergell, R. & Rivière, J.A. de & Neumann, G.R.– Cordel, O. & Göhle, A. & Knorre, V.**

Berlin [Minckwitz & von Schmidt]

1 e4 e5 2 ♘f3 ♘c6 3 ♗c4 ♗c5 4 b4 ♗xb4 5 c3 ♗a5 6 d4 exd4 7 0-0 ♗b6 8 cxd4 d6 9 ♗b2 ♘a5 10 ♗d3 ♘e7 11 ♘c3 0-0 12 ♘e2 d5! 13 ♘g3 dxe4 14 ♘xe4 ♘d5 15 ♗a3 ♖e8 16 ♘eg5 f5 17 ♕c2 ♕f6 [□ 17 ... h6 18 ♘h3 ♕f6] 18 ♖ae1 ♗d7 19 ♖e5 ♘f4 20 ♗c4+ ♘xc4 21 ♕xc4+ ♔h8 22 ♘f7+ ♔g8 23 ♘d6+ ♗e6 24 ♘xe8 ♕xe5 25 ♕b4 c5 26 dxc5 ♕xc5 27 ♕b2? [□ 27 ♕xf4 ♕xa3 28 ♘xg7 ♕xa2 29 ♘h5 ♗f7] 27 ... ♕c3 28 ♘d6? [□ 28 ♕xc3] 28 ... ♘h3+ 29 gxh3 ♕xf3 **0-1** L/N6047

### 1865-★BC-7

**Neumann, G.R. & Bergell, R.+ Cordel, O. & Knorre, V.**

Berlin

1 e4 e5 2 ♘f3 ♘c6 3 ♗c4 ♗c5 4 b4 ♗xb4 5 c3 ♗a5 6 d4 exd4 7 0-0 dxc3 8 ♕b3 ♕f6 9 e5 ♕g6 10 ♘xc3 ♗xc3 11 ♕xc3 b6 12 ♘g5 ♘h6 13 e6 fxe6 14 ♘xe6 dxe6 15 ♗d3 **1-0** M954-1865

### 1865-★BK-1 28 i 65

**Bergell,R.& Cordel,C.& Raaz,O.=Knorre,V.& Neumann,G.R.**

Berlin [Anderssen & Neumann]

1 e4 e5 2 ♘f3 ♘c6 3 ♗b5 ♘f6 4 0-0 ♗e7 5 ♘c3 d6 6 ♗xc6+ bxc6 7 d4 exd4 8 ♘xd4 ♗d7 9 f4 0-0 10 ♕d3 ♖b8 11 h3 [□ 11 ♔h1; 11 b3] 11 ... d5 12 e5 ♘e8 13 f5 c5 14 ♘de2 d4 15 ♘d5 ♗b5 16 ♕e4 ♗xe2 17 ♘xe7+ ♕xe7 18 ♕xe2 c4 19 f6 ♕c5 20 ♔h1 ♖b6 21 ♗g5 ♖e6 22 ♖ae1 gxf6 23 ♗h6? [□ 23 ♗xf6] 23 ... fxe5 24 ♗xf8 ♔xf8 25 ♕h5 ♘f6 26 ♕h6+ ♔e7 27 ♖f5 ♕d6 28 ♕g5 e4 29 ♖xf6 ♖xf6 30 ♖xe4+ ♔f8 31 ♔g1 d3 32 ♕d2 ½-½ L/N6051

### 1865-★BK-2 25 ii 65

**Knorre,V.& Neumann, G.R.+Cordel,O.& Bergell, R.**

Berlin [Anderssen & Neumann]

1 e4 e5 2 ♘f3 ♘f6 3 ♘xe5 d6 4 ♘f3 ♘xe4 5 d4 d5 6 ♗d3 ♗e7 7 0-0 0-0 8 c4 c6 9 ♘c3 ♗f5? 10 ♕c2 ♗f6 11 ♘xe4 dxe4 12 ♗xe4 ♗xe4 13 ♕xe4 ♘d7 14 ♗e3 ♖e8 15 ♕c2 ♘f8 16 ♖ad1 ♖c8 17 ♖d2 ♖e7 18 ♖fd1 ♖d7 19 ♘e5 ♗xe5 20 dxe5 ♕e7 21 ♖xd7 ♘xd7 22 ♕f5 ♖c7 23 f4 c5 24 ♕d3 ♘f8 25 ♕d6 b6 26 f5 ♖d7 27 ♕xe7 ♖xe7 28 ♖d5 [□ 28 ♖d8] 28 ... h6 29 ♖d8 ♖d7 [29 ... ♖xe5 30 ♗f4 ♖xf5 31 ♗d6+–] 30 ♖e8 ♖d3 31 ♔f2 ♖d7 32 e6 fxe6 33 fxe6 ♖d6 34 e7 **1-0** L/N6051

### 1865-★BK-3 13 v 65

**Knorre,V.& Neumann, G.R.+Bergell,R.& Cordel, O.**

Berlin [Minckwitz]

1 e4 e5 2 ♘f3 ♘c6 3 ♗c4 ♗c5 4 b4 ♗xb4 5 c3 ♗c5 6 0-0 d6 7 d4 exd4 8 cxd4 ♗b6 9 d5 ♘a5 10 ♗b2 ♘e7 11 ♗d3 0-0 12 ♘c3 ♘g6 13 ♘e2 c5 14 ♕d2 f6 15 ♔h1 a6 16 ♘e1 ♗d7 17 f4 ♗b5 18 ♖f3 ♘c4 19 ♗xc4 ♗xc4 20 ♖g3 ♗xe2 21 ♕xe2 ♘xf4 22 ♖g4 ♘g6 23 ♘d3 ♕e7 24 ♖h3 ♘e5 25 ♕h4 g5? [□ 25 ... g6, 26 ... ♕g7; 26 ... ♖f7] 26 ♕g3 ♔h8 27 ♖f1 ♖ae8 28 ♘f2 c4 29 ♘g4 ♘xg4 30 ♕xg4 ♕xe4 31 ♕d7 ♕e7 32 ♖xf6 ♔g8 [33 ♖g6++–] **1-0** L/N6047-68

### 1865-★BK-4

**Knorre,V.& Neumann, G.R.=Bergell,R.& Cordel,O.**

Berlin [Minckwitz & von Schmidt]

1 e4 e5 2 ♘f3 ♘f6 3 ♘xe5 d6 4 ♘f3 ♘xe4 5 d4 d5 6 ♗d3 ♗e7 7 0-0 ♘d6 8 ♘c3 ♗e6 9 ♘e2 0-0 10 ♖e1 ♗f5 11 ♗xf5 ♘xf5 12 ♕d3 ♘d6 13 b3 ♘d7 14 c4 ♘f6 15 ♘f4 ♘de8 16 ♗d2 c6 17 ♖e2 ♘c7 18 ♖ae1 ♗d6 19 c5 ♗xf4 20 ♗xf4 ♘e6 21 ♗d6 ♘e4 22 ♗xf8 ♘f4 23 ♗e7 ♘xd3 24 ♗xd8 ♘xe1 25 ♗h4 ♘xf3+ 26 gxf3 ♘c3 27 ♖e7 b6 28 ♔g2 ½-½ L/N6047

### 1865-★BS-1 ●○

**Steinitz, W.+ Barry, G.R.**

Dublin [Anderssen & Neumann]

1 e4 e5 2 ♘c3 ♗c5 3 f4 ♗xg1? [□ 2 ... d6] 4 ♖xg1 d6 5 d4 exd4 6 ♕xd4 ♘f6 7 ♗e3 [□ 7 e5] 7 ... 0-0 8 h3 ♘c6 9 ♕d2 ♖e8 10 g4 ♘xe4 11 ♘xe4 ♖xe4 12 0-0-0 ♕e7 13 ♗f2 ♕f6 14 f5 ♖a4 15 ♔b1 b5 16 ♗d3 ♖b8 17 g5 ♕e7 18 f6 ♕e6 19 b3 ♖a3 20 ♖de1 ♘e5 21 ♗c5! ♖a6 22 ♕f4 g6 23 ♕h4 ♕xh3 24 ♕d4 ♗f5 25 ♖h1 ♕g4 26 ♗xf5 ♕xd4 27 ♗xd4 ♘f3 [27 ... gxf5 28 ♗xe5 dxe5 29 ♖h6 △ 30 ♖eh1]

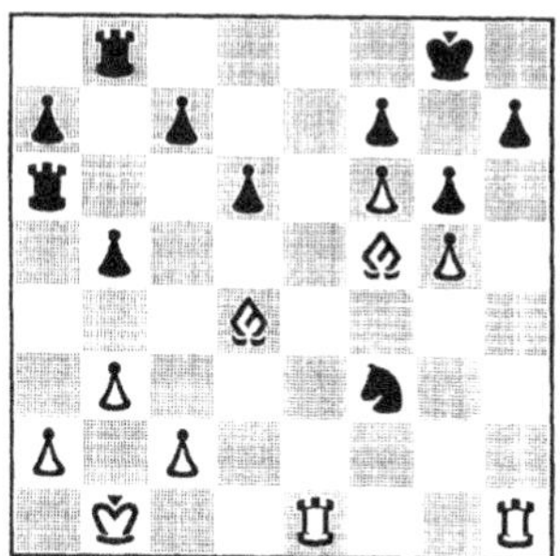

28 ♗xg6 ♘xe1 [28 ... hxg6 29 ♖e3 ♘xg5 30 ♖g3] 29 ♗xh7+ ♔f8 30 ♗f5 **1-0** L/N6051-1866

**1865-★CK-1** 4 ii 65
**Knorre,V.& Neumann, G.R.+Cordel,O.& Raaz,O.**
Berlin [Anderssen & Neumann]
1 e4 e6 2 d4 d5 3 exd5 exd5 4 ♘f3 ♘f6 5 ♗d3 ♗d6 6 0-0 h6 [□6 ... 0-0] 7 ♖e1+ ♗e6 8 ♗f5 ♕d7 9 ♕e2 ♔e7 [9 ... 0-0 10 ♗xe6 fxe6 11 ♕xe6+ ♕xe6 12 ♖xe6 ♘e4 13 ♘c3 ♔f7 14 ♖xe4 dxe4 15 ♘xe4±] 10 ♘c3 c6 11 ♗xe6 fxe6 12 ♘e5 ♗xe5 13 dxe5 ♘e8 14 ♕g4 ♔d8 15 ♘e4 ♘a6 16 c4 ♔c7 17 cxd5 cxd5 18 ♘d6 ♖d8 19 ♗e3 ♔b8 20 a4 ♘xd6 21 exd6 ♖he8 22 ♕d4 b6 23 ♗f4 ♘c5 24 a5 ♘b3 25 ♕c3

25 ... ♘xa5 [25 ... ♘xa1 26 ♕c7+ ♔a8 27 axb6 ♕xc7 28 bxc7 ♖d7 29 ♖xa1 ♔b7! 30 ♖a3∞] 26 ♕c7+ ♔a8 27 b4 ♘c6 28 ♖ec1 ♕xc7 29 dxc7 ♖c8 30 ♖xc6 e5 31 ♗g3! ♔b7 32 b5 ♖e7 33 ♖e1 **1-0** L/N6051

**1865-★CK-2** 23 vii 65
**Cordel,O.& Göhle,A.+ Knorre,V.& Neumann,G.R.**
Berlin [Minckwitz & von Schmidt]
1 e4 c5 2 ♘f3 ♘c6 3 d4 cxd4 4 ♘xd4 ♘f6 5 ♘c3 d6? 6 f4 ♕b6 7 ♗b5 ♗d7 8 ♗xc6 ♗xc6 9 ♘xc6 bxc6 10 ♕d3 g6 11 ♗e3 ♕c7 12 0-0 ♗g7 13 ♖f3 0-0 14 ♖af1 [□14 ♖d1; 14 ♖e1] 14 ... ♘g4 15 ♗d2 f5 16 ♔h1 e6 17 ♕c4 ♖ae8 18 exf5 gxf5 19 ♘b5 ♕d7 20 ♘d4 c5 21 ♘b5 ♖b8 22 ♖b3 a6 23 ♘c3 ♗d4 24 ♘d1 ♖b5 25 ♖e1 d5 26 ♕e2 ♖e8 27 ♖g3 [□27 h3 ♘h6] 27 ... ♗g7 28 h3 ♘f6

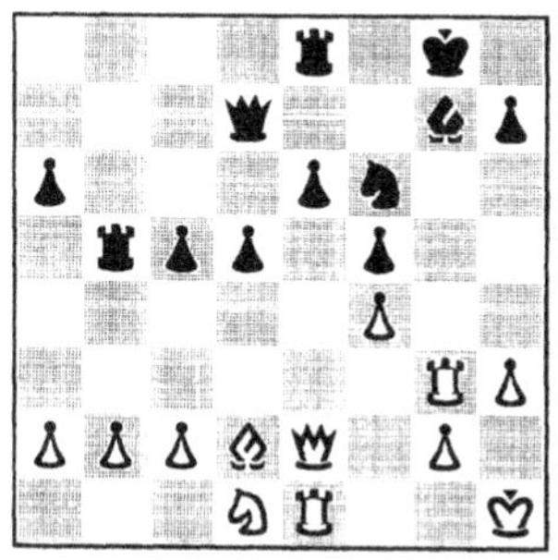

29 c4 ♘e4 30 ♖d3 ♖b6 31 b3 ♗d4 32 ♕f3 dxc4 33 bxc4 ♖b1 34 ♗e3 ♖d8 35 ♖g1 ♕a4? 36 g4 ♔h8 37 gxf5 exf5 **1-0** L/N6047

**1865-★DS-1**
**Steinitz, W.+ Duffy**
London [Bachmann]
1 e4 e5 2 ♘f3 ♘c6 3 ♗c4 ♗c5 4 b4 ♗xb4 5 c3 ♗c5 6 0-0 d6 7 d4 exd4 8 cxd4 ♗b6 9 d5 ♘a5 10 e5 ♗d7 11 ♗d3 ♘e7 12 ♘c3 0-0 13 ♗g5 ♕e8? [□13 ... dxe5 14 ♘xe5 f6 15 ♘xd7 ♕xd7] 14 ♘e4 ♘g6 [□14 ... dxe5 15 ♘f6+ gxf6 16 ♗xf6 ♘xd5 17 ♗xh7+ ♔xh7 18 ♕xd5 ♗c6 19 ♕d3+ e4 20 ♘g5+ ♔g6] 15 ♘f6+ gxf6 16 ♗xf6 dxe5 17 ♕d2 ♘f4 18 ♕xf4!? [□18 ♘xe5] 18 ... exf4 19 ♘g5 ♕e4 20 ♗xe4 ♖fe8 21 ♗xh7+ ♔f8 22 ♗d3 a6 23 ♘h7+ ♔g8 24 ♗c3 ♖e7 25 ♘f6+ ♔f8 26 ♗b4 **1-0** L/N3131

**1865-★EN-1**
**Neumann, G.R.+ Erner**
[Anderssen & Neumann]
⟨♘b1⟩ 1 e4 e5 2 ♘f3 d6 3 d4 ♗g4 4 dxe5 ♗xf3 5 ♕xf3 dxe5 6 ♗c4 ♕f6 7 ♕b3 b6 8 0-0 ♗c5 9 ♗e3 ♘d7 10 ♖ad1 ♕e7 11 ♗xf7+ ♔f8 12 ♗xg8 ♖xg8 13 ♗xc5 ♘xc5 14 ♕d5 ♖e8 15 f4 g6 16 b4 ♘a4? [□16 ... ♘a6] 17 ♕c6 **1-0** L/N6051-1865

**1865-★GN-1** 10 xi 65
**Göhle, A.− Neumann, G.R.**
Berlin [Anderssen & Neumann]
1 e4 e5 2 ♘f3 ♘c6 3 ♗c4 ♗c5 4 b4 ♗xb4 5 c3 ♗c5 6 ♕b3 ♕e7 7 0-0 ♘f6 8 d4 exd4 9 cxd4 ♗xd4 10 ♘c3 ♗xc3 11 ♕xc3 0-0 12 e5 ♘e4 13 ♕c2 ♘c5 14 ♗g5 ♕e8 15 ♖fe1 ♘e6 16 ♗f6 d5 17 ♗xd5 ♘b4 18 ♕e4 ♘xd5 19 ♕xd5 gxf6 20 exf6 ♔h8 21 ♘g5 ♖g8 22 ♘xh7 ♘f4 23 ♕f3 ♕c6 24 ♖e4 ♖xg2+ 25 ♔h1 ♗f5 26 ♖xf4 ♕xf3 27 ♖xf3 ♗e4 28 ♖e3 ♗c6 29 f3 ♖g6 **0-1** L/N6051

**1865-★GS-2**
**G?− Steinitz, W.**
London [Bachmann]
1 e4 e5 2 f4 exf4 3 ♗c4 d5 4 ♗xd5 ♕h4+ 5 ♔f1 ♘e7 6 ♘c3 g5 7 ♘f3 ♕h5 8 h4? [□8 d4] 8 ... h6 9 ♔g1 g4 10 ♘d4 f3 11 gxf3 [□11 ♘b3] 11 ... gxf3 12 ♕xf3 [12 ♘xf3 ♗g4 13 ♔f2 ♘bc6] 12 ... ♖g8+ 13 ♔f1 ♗g4 14 ♕f6? ♘d7 15 ♕f4 ♘xd5 16 ♘xd5 ♗c5! 17 ♘xc7+ ♔d8 18 ♘xa8 ♗h3+ 19 ♔e1 [19 ♖xh3 ♕d1+ 20 ♔f2 ♗xd4+−+] 19 ... ♗d6 20 ♕xd6 ♕xh4+ 21 ♔e2 ♕xe4+ 22 ♔f2 ♖g2+ 23 ♔f1 ♖e2+ 24 ♖xh3 ♕g2# **0-1** L/N3131

**1865-★KN-1** 31 i 65
**Knorre,V.& Redlich,I.− Neumann, G.R.**
Berlin [Anderssen & Neumann]
1 e4 e5 2 ♘f3 ♘c6 3 ♗c4 ♗c5 4 b4 ♗xb4 5 c3 ♗c5 6 0-0 d6 7 d4 exd4 8 cxd4 ♗b6 9 ♘c3 ♘a5 10 ♗d3 ♘e7 11 ♕c2 ♗g4 12 ♘e2 ♗xf3 13 gxf3 0-0 14 ♗b2 ♘ac6 15 a3 ♕d7 16 ♔h1 ♕h3 17 ♘g1 ♕h4 18 d5 ♘e5 19 ♖ad1 ♘7g6 20 ♗c1 ♖ac8 21 ♗e2 ♗xf2 22 ♗g5 ♕xg5 23 ♖xf2 ♘f4 24 ♗f1 [△25 ♘h3] 24 ... ♕h4 25 ♗g2 c5 26 ♖fd2 c4 27 ♘e2 ♘xg2 28 ♔xg2 c3 29 ♖d4 [29 ♘xc3 ♘xf3 30 ♔xf3 ♕h3+∓] 29 ... ♖c5 30 ♖b1 b5 31 ♖b3 ♖fc8 32 ♖d1 a5 33 ♘d4 ♖c4 34 ♖xb5 ♖xd4 35 ♖xd4 ♘xf3 36 ♔xf3 [36 ♕xc3 ♕xh2+ 37 ♔f1 ♕h3+−+] 36 ... ♕h3+ 37 ♔e2 [37 ♔f4 f6 38 e5 g5+ 36 ♔e4 f5#] 37 ... ♖g2+ **0-1** L/N6051

**1865-★KN-2** 17 ii 65
**Neumann,G.R.−Knorre,V. & Redlich,N.**
Berlin [Anderssen & Neumann]
1 e4 e5 2 f4 exf4 3 ♗c4 f5 4 ♕e2 ♕h4+ 5 ♔d1 fxe4 6 ♘c3 ♔d8 7 ♘xe4 c6 8 g3? ♕e7 9 ♗xg8 ♖xg8 10 gxf4 d5 11 ♘g5 ♗f5 12 ♕e5? ♕f6 13 d4 ♘d7 14 ♕xf6+ gxf6 15 ♘5f3 ♗e4 16 ♔e2 ♖g2+ 17 ♔e3 ♔c7 18 ♘e1 ♖e8 [19 ♘h3 ♗xc2+ 20 ♔f3 ♗e4+ 21 ♔e3 ♖g6−+; 19 ♘gf3 ♗f5+ 20 ♘e5 ♖g6−+; 19 ♘d3 ♖xc2 20 ♘f3 ♗f5+−+; 19 c3 ♘e5 20 ♘xg2 ♘g4+ 21 ♔d2 ♗xg2 22 h3 ♘e3 23 ♔d3 ♘f1 24 ♗d2 ♗e4+ 25 ♔e2 ♘g3+−+]

**0-1** L/N6051

**1865-★KN-3** 29 iii 65
**Neumann, G.R.+ Knorre, V.**
Berlin [Anderssen & Neumann]

1 e4 e5 2 ♘f3 ♘c6 3 ♗b5 ♘f6 4 0-0 ♗e7 5 ♘c3 d6 6 d4 ♗d7 7 d5 ♘b8 8 ♕e2 0-0 9 ♗xd7 ♘bxd7 10 ♘d1 ♘c5 11 ♘d2 ♘e8 12 f4 exf4 13 ♖xf4 ♗g5 14 ♖f3 ♕e7 15 b4 ♘d7 [15 ... ♗xd2 16 bxc5 ♗xc1 17 ♖xc1 dxc5±] 16 ♘e3 ♕e5? 17 ♖b1 ♘ef6 18 ♗b2 ♕e8 19 ♖g3 ♗f4 20 ♖xg7+ ♔h8 [20 ... ♔xg7 21 ♕g4+ ♔h8 22 ♕xf4] 21 ♘g4 ♗e5 22 ♗xe5 ♔xg7 23 ♕e3 dxe5 24 ♕h6+ ♔h8 25 ♘xf6 ♘xf6 26 ♕xf6+ ♔g8 27 ♖b3 **1-0**
L/N6051

**1865-★KN-4** 2 iv 65
**Knorre, V.– Neumann, G.R.**
Berlin [Anderssen & Neumann]

1 e4 e5 2 ♘f3 ♘c6 3 ♗c4 ♗c5 4 b4 ♗xb4 5 c3 ♗c5 6 0-0 d6 7 d4 exd4 8 cxd4 ♗b6 9 ♘c3 ♘a5 10 ♗d3 ♘e7 11 ♗b2 0-0 12 ♘e2 f5 13 ♕c2 d5 14 exd5 ♘xd5 15 ♗a3 ♖f6 16 ♘e5 ♗e6 17 ♖ad1 ♕e8 18 ♖fe1 c6 19 ♘f3 [△ ♘g5, ♘xe6] 19 ... h6 20 ♘g3 g6 21 h4 ♘f4 [△ 22 h5 ♘xd3] 22 ♕c3 ♗d8 23 ♗c2 [□ 23 ♗b1] 23 ... ♘d5 24 ♕d3 b5 25 ♘e5 a6 26 ♕d2 h5 27 ♗d3 ♖a7 28 ♘e2 ♖g7 29 ♖c1 ♗c8 30 ♗xb5 axb5 31 ♘c4 ♖e6 32 ♘xa5 ♖a7! 33 ♖xe6 ♗xe6 34 ♘xc6 ♖xa3 35 ♕e2 ♖c3 **0-1**
L/N6051

**1865-★KN-5** 24 x 65
**Knorre,V. & Weiss,E.von– Neumann,G.R.**
Berlin [Anderssen & Neumann]

1 e4 e5 2 ♘f3 ♘c6 3 ♗c4 ♗c5 4 b4 ♗xb4 5 c3 ♗c5 6 0-0 d6 7 d4 exd4 8 cxd4 ♗b6 9 d5 ♘a5 10 ♗b2 ♘e7 11 ♗d3 0-0 12 ♘c3 ♘g6 13 ♘e2 c5 14 ♘g3 a6 15 ♔h1 f6 16 ♘g1 c4 17 ♗c2 ♗c5 18 f4 b5 19 f5 ♘e5 20 ♘1e2 b4 21 ♘f4 c3 22 ♗c1 ♘ac4 23 ♘e6 ♗xe6 24 fxe6 ♘e3 25 ♗xe3 ♗xe3 26 ♘f5 ♕b6 27 ♖b1 a5 28 a3 [△ 29 axb4 axb4 30 ♘xe3 ♕xe3 31 ♖xb4±] 28 ... ♗d2 29 ♕e2 g6 30 ♘h4 ♕c5 31 a4 ♖ac8 32 ♘f3 ♘c4 33 ♗b3 ♘e3 34 ♘xd2 cxd2 35 ♖g1 ♕c3 36 ♕f3 [△ 37 g4] 36 ... ♔g7 37 g4 ♘xd5 **0-1** L/N6051

**1865-★KN-6** 26 xii 65
**Neumann, G.R.– Knorre, V.**
Berlin [Minckwitz]

1 e4 e5 2 ♘f3 ♘c6 3 ♗b5 ♘f6 4 0-0 ♘xe4 5 ♖e1 [□ 5 d4 ♗e7 6 ♕e2±] 5 ... ♘d6 6 ♘xe5 ♘xe5 7 ♖xe5+ ♗e7 8 ♗a4 0-0 9 ♗b3 ♗f6 10 ♖e1 ♘f5∓ 11 ♘c3 d6 12 ♘d5 g6 13 ♘xf6+ ♕xf6 14 c3 ♘h4 15 d4 ♗e6 16 ♗c2 ♖ae8 [△ 17 ... ♗d5, 18 ... ♖xe1+ 19 ♕xe1 ♘f3+ 20 gxf3 ♕xf3−+] 17 ♗h6? ♗d5 18 ♗xf8 ♕g5 **0-1**
L/N6047-169

**1865-★KP-1 ●o⬠** viii 65
**Paulsen, L.= Keller, A.**
Elberfeld

1 e4 e6 2 d4 d5 3 ♘c3 ♘c6 4 ♘f3 ♗b4 5 exd5 exd5 6 ♗d3 ♘f6 7 0-0 0-0 8 ♘e2 ♗d6 9 c3 ♘e7 10 ♘g3 ♘g6 11 ♗g5? h6 12 ♗e3 ♖e8 13 ♘f5 ♗xf5 14 ♗xf5 ♘e7 15 ♗c2 ♘e4 16 ♕d3 ♘g6 17 ♖ae1 c6 18 ♘d2 ♕h4 19 g3 ♕d8 20 f4 f5 21 ♘f3 b6 22 ♘e5 ♘e7 23 ♗c1 ♖f8 24 g4 ♕c8 25 gxf5 ♕xf5 26 ♕f3 ♘g6 27 ♖xe4 dxe4 28 ♗xe4 ♘xe5 29 dxe5 ♗c5+ **½-½** L/N6051

**1865-★KP-2 ●o⬠** viii 65
**Paulsen,L.ΦKotzh,F.& Schnitzler,G.**
Elberfeld

1 e4 e5 2 ♘f3 ♘c6 3 ♗c4 ♗c5 4 b4 ♗xb4 5 c3 ♗c5 6 0-0 d6 7 d4 exd4 8 cxd4 ♗b6 9 d5 ♘a5 10 ♗b2 ♘e7 11 ♗d3 0-0 12 ♘c3 ♘g6 13 ♘e2 c5 14 ♖c1 f6 15 ♔h1 ♗d7 16 ♕d2 ♖c8 17 ♘g3 a6 18 ♘e1 ♗c7 19 f4 ♗b5 20 ♘h5 ♕d7 21 ♗c3 ♗xd3 22 ♘xd3 ♘c4 23 ♕e2 b5 24 f5 ♘ge5 25 ♘df4 ♔f7 26 ♘e6 ♖g8 27 ♖f4 ♗d8 28 ♖cf1 ♗e7 29 ♖h4 L/N6051

**1865-★KP-3**
**Kachler– Paulsen, L.**
[Löwenthal]

1 e4 e5 2 ♘f3 ♘c6 3 ♗c4 ♗c5 4 b4 ♗xb4 5 c3 ♗a5 6 d4 exd4 7 0-0 ♗b6 8 cxd4 d6 9 ♘g5 ♘h6 10 ♘f3 ♗g4 11 ♗xh6 gxh6 12 ♕b3 ♘a5 13 ♕a4+ ♗d7 14 ♗b5 c6 15 ♗e2 c5 16 ♕d1 cxd4 17 ♘xd4 ♕f6 18 e5 dxe5 19 ♘b5 0-0-0 20 ♘d2 ♖hg8 21 a4 ♗c6 22 ♗g4+? [□ 22 g3] 22 ... ♔b8 23 ♗h3 ♖xg2+ 24 ♗xg2 ♖g6 **0-1** M324-1865

**1865-★KP-4**
**Paulsen, L.+ Knorre, V.**
Leipzig [Löwenthal]

1 e4 e5 2 ♘f3 ♘c6 3 ♗c4 ♗e7 4 d4 exd4 [□ 4 ... d6 5 c3 (5 d5 ♘b8 6 ♗d3 ♗g4 7 0-0 ♘f6 8 c4 c6 9 ♘c3 ♘a6=) 5 ... ♘f6 6 ♕c2 0-0 7 ♗e2 ♗g4 8 ♗e3±] 5 0-0 ♘f6 6 ♖e1 0-0 7 e5 ♘e8 8 ♘xd4 d5 9 ♘xc6 bxc6 10 ♗d3 g6 11 ♘d2 ♘g7 12 ♘f3 f6 13 ♘d4! fxe5 [13 ... c5 14 ♘c6 ♕d7 15 ♗b5±; 13 ... ♗d7 14 e6 c5 15 exd7 cxd4 16 ♗b5±] 14 ♘xc6 ♕d6 15 ♘xe5 ♗h4? [□ 15 ... ♗f6] 16 g3 ♗f6 17 ♗f4 g5 18 ♘f7 ♕b6 19 ♘xg5 ♗xg5 20 ♗xg5 ♕xf2+ 21 ♔h1 ♗h3 [□ 21 ... ♗b7 22 ♕d2 d4+ 23 ♗e4 ♕xd2 24 ♗xd2 ♗xe4+ 25 ♖xe4 ♖f2 26 ♖d1 c5 27 ♔g1 ♖af8] 22 ♗f1 ♗xf1 23 ♖xf1 ♕c5 24 ♗f4 ♖ae8 25 ♕d2 ♘e6 26 ♗h6 ♖xf1+ 27 ♖xf1 ♕c4 28 ♕e1 ♘f8 29 ♖xf8+ **1-0** M324-1865

**1865-★MN-1** i 65
**Mayet, K.– Neumann, G.R.**
Berlin [Anderssen & Neumann]

1 e4 e5 2 f4 exf4 3 ♗c4 f5 4 d3 [□ 4 ♕e2] 4 ... ♕h4+ 5 ♔f1 fxe4 6 dxe4 ♗c5 7 ♕f3 ♘h6 8 ♗xf4 [□ 8 g3 ♕e7 9 gxf4! ♘c6 10 ♘e2 d6∓] 8 ... ♖f8 9 g3 ♕g4 10 ♔g2 g5 11 ♕xg4 ♘xg4 12 ♗xg5 ♖f2+ 13 ♔h3 d5 14 ♗xd5 ♘e3+ 15 ♔h4 ♘d7 16 b4 ♘g2+ 17 ♔h5 ♗f8 18 ♘h3 ♘f6+ 19 ♗xf6 ♖xf6 20 ♘f4 ♘xf4+ 21 gxf4 ♖h6+ 22 ♔g5 ♖g6+ 23 ♔h5 ♗g4+ 24 ♔h4 ♗f3 25 ♖g1 ♖xg1 26 ♘d2 ♗e7+ 27 ♔h3 ♗g4# **0-1**
L/N6051

**1865-★MN-2** i 65
**Neumann, G.R.+ Mayet, K.**
Berlin [Anderssen & Neumann]

1 e4 e5 2 ♘f3 ♘c6 3 ♗c4 ♗c5 4 b4 ♗xb4 5 c3 ♗d6 6 d4 [6 0-0 ♘a5] 6 ... ♕e7 7 0-0 f6 8 a4 [8 ♘h4 g6 9 f4 exf4 10 ♗xf4 ♗xf4 11 ♖xf4 d6∓] 8 ... b6 9 ♘a3 [△ 10 ♘b5, 11 ♘xd6+] 9 ... ♗xa3 10 ♗xa3 d6 11 dxe5 ♘xe5 12 ♗xg8 **1-0** L/N6051

**1865-★MN-3** iii 65
**Mayet, K.– Neumann, G.R.**
Berlin [Anderssen & Neumann]

1 e4 e5 2 ♘f3 ♘c6 3 ♗b5 a6 4 ♗a4 ♘f6 5 d3 ♗c5 6 0-0 b5 7 ♗b3 d6 8 a4 b4 9 ♗g5? [□ 9 a5, 10 c3] 9 ... h6 10 ♗h4 g5 11 ♗g3 ♗g4 12 ♘bd2 ♕d7 13 h3 ♗h5 14 ♗d5 ♖g8 15 ♕e1 g4 16 hxg4 ♖xg4 17 d4? [□ 17 ♔h1]

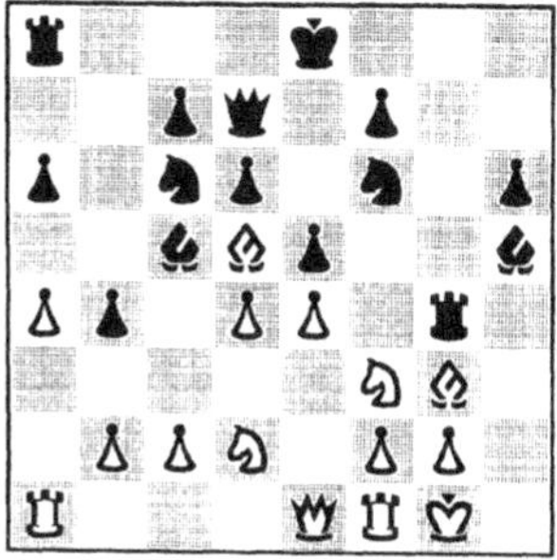

17 ... ♘xd4 18 ♗xa8 ♘xf3+ 19 ♘xf3 ♖xg3 20 ♔h2 ♖xg2+ 21 ♔xg2 ♗xf3+ 22 ♔h2! ♕g4 **0-1** L/N6051-1866

**1865-★MN-4** iii 65
**Neumann, G.R.+ Minckwitz, J.**
Berlin [Minckwitz & von Schmidt]
1 e4 e5 2 ♘f3 ♘c6 3 ♗c4 ♗c5 4 b4 ♗xb4 5 c3 ♗c5 6 0-0 d6 7 d4 exd4 8 cxd4 ♗b6 9 d5 ♘a5 10 ♗b2 f6 [□ 10 ... ♘e7] 11 ♗d3 ♘e7 12 ♘c3 0-0 13 ♘e2 ♘g6 14 ♔h1 c5 15 ♘e1 c4 16 ♗c2 ♗c7 17 f4 b5 18 f5 ♘e5 19 ♘f4 [Δ ♗xe5, ♘g6, ♕h5] 19 ... ♕e8 20 ♘e6 ♗xe6 21 dxe6 ♘ac6 22 ♕e2 ♗b6 23 ♖ad1 ♗c5 24 g4 a5 25 ♘g2 a4 [25 ... b4 26 ♗xe5] 26 ♘f4 a3 [□ 26 ... b4; 26 ... ♘b4] 27 ♗xe5 ♘xe5 28 ♘d5 ♖a7 29 ♖b1 ♖b7? 30 ♕g2 [□ 30 e7 ♖f7 31 ♗a4 ♕b8 32 ♗xb5 ♖xb5 33 ♖xb5 ♕xb5 34 ♘c7+-] 30 ... h6 31 ♗d1 [Δ 32 h4, 33 g5] 31 ... g5 32 h4 ♔g7 33 ♕g3 ♕a8 34 ♖e1 ♕a5 35 ♖e2 ♖h8 36 ♖h2 ♕d8? [□ 36 ... ♖bb8]

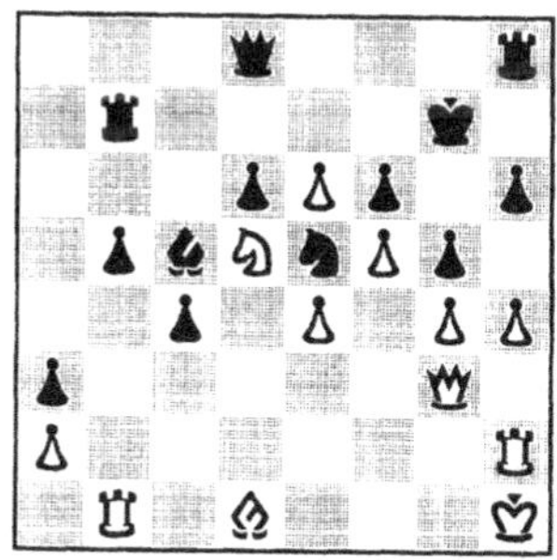

37 ♗e2 b4? 38 ♕xa3 ♖a7 [38 ... bxa3 39 ♖xb7+ ♔g8! 40 e7 ♕e8 41 ♘xf6+ ♔f7 42 ♘xe8±; □ 38 ... c3 39 ♕xc3 bxc3 40 ♖xb7+ ♔f8! 41 e7+ ♕xe7 42 ♘xe7 c2!] 39 ♕h3 ♖xa2 40 hxg5 hxg5 41 e7! ♖xh3 42 exd8♕ ♖xh2+ 43 ♔xh2 ♖xe2+ 44 ♔h3 **1-0** L/N6047

**1865-★MN-5** iii 65
**Minckwitz, J.=Neumann, G.R.**
Berlin [Minckwitz & von Schmidt]
1 e4 e5 2 ♘f3 ♘c6 3 ♗b5 ♘f6 4 0-0 ♘xe4 5 ♖e1 ♘f6 6 ♘xe5 ♗e7 7 d4 0-0 8 ♘c3 ♖e8 9 ♗e3 ♗b4 10 ♗g5 ♗xc3 11 bxc3 a6 12 ♗d3 d5 13 f4 ♕d6 14 ♕f3 ♘e7 15 ♕f2 [Δ ♕h4] 15 ... ♗f5 16 g4 ♗xd3 17 cxd3 ♘d7 18 f5 f6 19 ♘xd7 ♕xd7 20 ♗d2 ♘c6 21 ♕g3 ♖ad8 22 ♗f4 ♖xe1+ 23 ♖xe1 ♖e8 24 ♖xe8+? ♕xe8 [Δ 25 ... ♕e2] 25 ♔f1 h5 26 h3 hxg4 27 hxg4 ♕e7 28 ♗xc7 ♕a3 29 ♕e1 ♕xa2 30 ♗f4 ♕c2 31 ♕e8+ ♔h7 32 ♕g6+ ♔g8 **½-½** L/N6047

**1865-★MN-6**
**Mayet, K.– Neumann, G.R.**
1 e4 e5 2 f4 exf4 3 ♗c4 f5 4 d3 ♕h4+ 5 ♔f1 fxe4 6 dxe4 ♗c5 7 ♕f3 ♘h6 8 ♗xf4 ♖f8 9 g3 ♕g4 10 ♔g2 g5 11 ♕xg4 ♘xg4 12 ♗xg5 ♖f2+ 13 ♔h3 d5 14 ♗xd5 ♘e3+ 15 ♔h4 ♘d7 16 b4 ♘g2+ 17 ♔h5 ♗f8 18 ♘h3 ♘f6+ 19 ♗xf6 ♖xf6 20 ♘f4 ♘xf4+ 21 gxf4 ♖h6+ 22 ♔g5 ♖g6+ 23 ♔h5 ♗g4+ 24 ♔h4 ♗f3 25 ♖g1 ♖xg1 **0-1** M954-1865

**1865-★MP-1**
**Mayet, K.– Paulsen, L.**
[Löwenthal]
1 e4 e5 2 f4 exf4 3 ♗c4 ♕h4+ 4 ♔f1 d6 5 ♘f3 ♕h6 6 d4 ♘f6 7 ♘c3 c6 8 h4 ♘h5 9 ♘e2 ♗e7 10 g3 ♕g6! 11 ♘xf4 ♘xg3+ 12 ♔g2 ♕g4 13 ♘h2 ♕xd1 14 ♖xd1 ♘xe4 15 ♖e1 f5 16 ♗e6 ♘a6 17 ♘f3 ♗xe6 18 ♘xe6 ♔d7 19 ♘eg5 ♗xg5 20 ♗xg5 h6 21 ♗f4 g5 22 ♗h2 ♖ag8 23 h5 ♘c7 **0-1** L/N6124-1865

**1865-★M?-1**
**?– Morphy, P.C.**
⟨♘b8⟩ 1 e4 e5 2 ♗c4 ♗c5 3 ♘f3 d6 4 b4 ♗xb4 5 c3 ♗c5 6 ♕b3 ♕f6 7 0-0 ♘h6 8 d4 ♗b6 9 dxe5 ♕g6 10 ♘g5 0-0 11 e6 fxe6 12 ♗xe6+ ♔h8 13 ♗xc8 ♖axc8 14 ♕e6 ♕h5 15 ♘f3 ♘g4 16 h3 ♘xf2 17 ♖xf2 ♖ce8 18 ♕d5 ♕xd5 19 exd5 ♖e2 20 ♔h2 ♗xf2 21 ♘bd2 ♗e3 22 ♘c4 ♗xc1 23 ♖xc1 ♖xf3 **0-1** +13

**1865-★NP-1**
**Neumann, G.R.– Paulsen, L.**
1 e4 e5 2 ♘f3 ♘c6 3 ♗c4 ♗c5 4 b4 ♗xb4 5 c3 ♗a5 6 d4 exd4 7 0-0 d6 8 cxd4 ♗b6 9 ♘c3 ♘a5 10 ♗d3 ♘e7 11 d5 0-0 12 ♗b2 f6 13 ♕d2 ♘g6 14 ♔h1 ♗d7 15 ♘e1 ♘e5 16 f4 ♘ec4 17 ♕e2 ♘xb2 18 ♕xb2 c5 19 f5 c4 20 ♗b1 ♗d4 21 ♘f3 ♗e5 22 ♘xe5 fxe5 23 ♖f3 b5 24 ♗c2 ♖b8 25 a3 ♘b7 26 a4 bxa4 27 ♕a3 ♘c5 28 ♖3f1 ♕g5 29 ♖fe1 ♕h4 30 ♕a2 ♖b4 31 ♖ab1 a5 32 g3 ♕g5 33 ♕a3 ♖fb8 ...? **0-1** L/N6124-1865

**1865-★NP-2**
**Paulsen, L.+ Neumann, G.R.**
1 e4 e5 2 ♘f3 ♘c6 3 d4 exd4 4 ♘xd4 ♗c5 5 ♗e3 ♘xd4 6 ♗xd4 ♗xd4 7 ♕xd4 ♕f6 8 e5 ♕b6 9 ♕xb6 axb6 10 ♘c3 ♖a5 11 f4 f6 12 0-0-0 fxe5 13 b4 ♖a8 14 fxe5 ♘h6 15 ♗c4 ♘f5 16 ♘d5 ♔d8 17 ♖hf1 g6 18 g4 ♘e7 19 ♘xe7 ♔xe7 20 ♖f7+ ♔e8 21 e6 dxe6 22 ♖xc7 **1-0** L/N6124-1865

**1865-★NP-3**
**Paulsen, L.+ Neumann, G.R.**
1 e4 e5 2 ♘f3 ♘c6 3 ♗c4 ♗c5 4 0-0 ♘f6 5 d3 d6 6 ♗g5 h6 7 ♗h4 g5 8 ♗g3 ♗g4 9 ♘bd2 ♘d4 10 c3 ♘xf3+ 11 ♘xf3 ♗b6 12 ♖e1 ♘d7 13 d4 f6 14 h3 ♗h5 15 ♗e6 ♕e7 16 ♗xd7+ ♕xd7 17 ♘xe5 ♗xd1 18 ♘xd7 ♔xd7 19 ♖axd1 ♖ae8 20 b4 a5 21 b5 c6 22 bxc6+ ♔xc6 23 ♖b1 ♗d8 24 d5+ ♔c7 25 f3 **1-0** L/N6124-1865

**1865-★NR-1** v 65
**Neumann, G.R.+Rivière, J.A.de**
Berlin [Anderssen & Neumann]
1 e4 e5 2 f4 exf4 3 ♗c4 ♘f6 4 ♘c3 ♗b4 5 ♘f3 d6 6 0-0 ♗g4 7 e5 dxe5 [7 ... ♗xf3 8 ♕xf3 dxe5 9 ♕xb7±] 8 ♗xf7+ ♔f8 9 ♗b3 ♗c5+ 10 ♔h1 ♘c6 11 d3 ♘d4 12 ♘xd4 ♗xd4 13 ♕e1 g5 14 ♘e4 ♘d7 15 ♕b4+ ♔g7 16 ♘xg5 ♗c5 [16 ... ♕xg5 14 ♗xf4±] 17 ♕c4 ♖f8 18 ♘f3 ♗d6 19 ♗d2 ♖f6 20 ♗c3 ♕e8 21 ♖ae1 ♕h5 22 d4 ♖e8? 23 dxe5 ♗xe5 24 ♘xe5 ♘xe5 25 ♖xe5 **1-0** L/N6051

**1865-★NR-2** vi 65
**Neumann, G.R.= Rivière, J.A. de**
Berlin [Anderssen & Neumann]
1 e4 e5 2 f4 exf4 3 ♘f3 g5 4 ♗c4 ♗g7 5 d4 h6 6 h4 d6 7 ♕d3 ♘d7 [7 ... ♘c6] 8 hxg5 hxg5 9 ♖xh8 ♗xh8 10 e5 ♘f8 11 ♘c3 dxe5 [□ 11 ... g4] 12 dxe5 ♕xd3 13 cxd3 ♗e6 14 ♘xg5 ♗xe5 15 ♘xe6 fxe6 16 ♗d2 0-0-0 17 0-0-0 ♘f6 18 ♖e1 ♘g4 19 ♖e4 ♖d4 20 ♖xd4 ♗xd4 21 ♗xf4 ♗e3+ 22 ♗xe3 ♘xe3 23 g3 ♘xc4 24 dxc4 **½-½** L/N6051

### 1865-★NR-3 vi 65
**Neumann,G.R.+Rivière, J.A.de**

Berlin [Anderssen & Neumann]

1 e4 e5 2 ♘f3 ♘c6 3 ♗c4 ♗c5 4 b4 ♗xb4 5 c3 ♗c5 6 0-0 d6 7 d4 exd4 8 cxd4 ♗b6 9 d5 ♘a5 10 ♗b2 ♘e7 11 ♗d3 0-0 12 ♘c3 f5 13 ♘g5 h6 14 ♘e6 ♗xe6 15 dxe6 f4 [15 ... fxe4 16 ♘xe4 d5 17 ♕g4 d4 18 f4 ♘f5 19 ♗a3 ♘e3 20 ♕g6±] 16 ♘d5 ♘ac6 17 ♕g4 [17 ♕h5 ♕e8] 17 ... ♘e5 18 ♗xe5 dxe5 19 ♖fd1 ♗d4 20 ♖ac1 c6 [20 ... ♘xd5 21 exd5 ♕xd5 22 ♕g6 ♖fe8 23 ♕h7+ ♔f8 24 ♕h8+ ♔e7 25 ♕xg7+-] 21 ♘xe7+ ♕xe7 22 ♗c4 ♔h7 23 ♖d3 a5 24 a4 ♖f6

25 ♖xd4! exd4 [25 ... ♖g6 26 ♖d7+-] 26 e5 ♕a3 [26 ... ♖f8 (26 ... ♖g6 27 ♗d3 ♕e8 28 h4+-) 27 ♗d3+ g6 (27 ... ♔g8 28 ♕g6; 27 ... ♔h8 28 ♕g6) 28 ♕xg6+ ♔h8 29 ♕xh6+ ♔g8 30 ♗c4 ♖fd8 31 ♖d1 d3! 32 ♕xf4+-] 27 ♖d1 ♖g6! 28 ♕f5 [28 ♗d3 ♕xd3-+] 28 ... ♖f8 29 ♕e4 ♕xa4 30 ♖xd4 ♕a1+ 31 ♗f1 ♖e8 32 ♖d6 [□ 32 e7] 32 ... ♖e7 33 ♕f5 f3 34 g3 ♕c1 35 h4 h5 36 ♖d8 ♖xe6 [36 ... a4 37 ♕xh5+ ♖h6! 38 ♕f5+-] 37 ♕f8 ♖xg3+ 38 fxg3 ♖xe5 39 ♕g8+ ♔g6 40 ♖d6+ **1-0** L/N6051-1866

### 1865-★NR-4 vi 65
**Rivière,J.A.de=Neumann, G.R.**

Berlin [Anderssen & Neumann]

1 e4 e5 2 ♘f3 ♘c6 3 ♗c4 ♗c5 4 c3 ♘f6 5 0-0 ♘xe4! 6 b4 ♗b6 [6 ... ♘xf2] 7 a4 a6 8 a5 ♗a7 [8 ... ♘xf2 9 ♖xf2 ♗xf2+ 10 ♔xf2 d5] 9 ♗d5 ♘f6 10 ♗xc6 dxc6 11 ♘xe5 0-0 12 d4 ♘e4 13 ♕f3 f5 14 ♘d2 ♗e6 15 ♘xe4 ♗d5 16 ♗g5 fxe4 17 ♕e3 ♕e8 18 ♗f4 [18 c4 ♕xe5 19 dxe5! ♗xe3 20 ♗xe3 ♗xc4] 18 ... ♖d8 19 ♖ad1 ♕e6 20 ♖fe1 ♔h8 21 ♕g3 ♖de8 22 ♖c1 ♕f5 23 ♗e3 c5 24 bxc5 ♗xc5 25 dxc5 ♖xe5 26 ♗d4 ♖e7 27 c4 ♗c6 28 f3 ♖ef7 29 fxe4 ♗xe4 30 ♕e5 ♕xe5 31 ♗xe5 **½-½** L/N6051

### 1865-★NR-5
**Neumann,G.R.+Rivière, J.A.de**

Berlin [Anderssen & Neumann]

1 e4 e5 2 ♘f3 ♘c6 3 ♗c4 ♗c5 4 b4 ♗xb4 5 c3 ♗c5 6 0-0 d6 7 d4 exd4 8 cxd4 ♗b6 9 ♘c3 ♘a5 10 ♗d3 ♘e7 11 ♗b2 0-0 12 ♘e2 ♘g6 13 ♕c2 ♘c6! 14 a3 ♗g4 15 ♔h1 ♗xf3 16 gxf3 ♕f6∓ 17 f4 ♘xd4 18 ♕c4 c5 19 ♖g1 ♘xf4 20 ♘xf4 ♕xf4 21 ♖g3 ♖ae8 22 ♖f1 ♖e6 23 ♗c1 ♕h4 24 ♗g5 ♕h5 25 f4 ♗d8 26 f5 ♗xg5∓ 27 fxe6 fxe6 28 ♖fg1 ♖f2 29 ♖3g2 b5 30 ♕c3 ♖xg2 31 ♖xg2 ♕d1+ 32 ♖g1 ♕f3+ 33 ♖g2 ♗e3 34 ♕e1 c4 35 ♗e2 [35 ♗b1 c3] 35 ... ♘xe2 36 ♕xe2 ♕xe4 37 ♕c2 ♕xc2 38 ♖xc2 ♗c5 39 a4 a6 40 ♔g2 d5 **0-1** L/N6051-1866

### 1865-★NR-6 v 65
**Neumann, G.R.–Rivière, J.A. de**

Berlin [Anderssen & Neumann]

1 e4 e5 2 ♘f3 ♘c6 3 ♗c4 ♗c5 4 b4 ♗xb4 5 c3 ♗c5 6 0-0 d6 7 d4 exd4 8 cxd4 ♗b6 9 d5 ♘a5 10 ♗b2 ♘e7 11 ♗d3 0-0 12 ♘c3 ♘g6 13 ♘e2 c5 14 ♔h1 ♗d7 15 ♘e1 a6 16 f4 c4 17 ♗c2 f6 18 ♗c3 ♗c7 19 ♘d4 b5 20 ♘e6 ♗xe6 21 dxe6 ♘c6 22 f5 ♘ge5 23 ♕h5 ♕e8 24 ♕h4 ♗b6 25 ♖d1 ♖d8 26 g4 ♗e3 27 ♕g3 ♗h6 28 h4 g5 29 ♗d2 gxh4 30 ♕xh4 ♗xd2 31 ♖xd2 ♔h8 32 ♖h2 ♕e7 33 ♘g2 ♖g8 34 ♘e3

34 ... ♖df8 35 ♗d1 ♘b4 36 a3 ♘bd3 37 ♘d5 ♕g7 38 ♕h5 ♘c6 39 g5 fxg5 40 f6? [□ 40 e7 ♘xe7! 41 f6 ♕g6 42 ♘xe7 ♕xe4+ 43 ♗f3+-] 40 ... ♕g6 41 ♕xg6 ♖xg6 42 e7 ♘xe7 43 ♘xe7 ♖gxf6 44 ♖xf6 ♖xf6 45 ♘f5 d5 46 ♗f3 ♘c5? 47 ♖d2 ♘d3 48 ♔g2 a5 49 ♔g3 b4 50 axb4 axb4 51 ♘e3 dxe4 52 ♗xe4 ♖e6 **0-1** L/N6051

### 1865-★NR-7
**Rivière,J.A.de–Neumann, G.R.**

Berlin [Anderssen & Neumann]

1 e4 e5 2 ♘c3 ♘c6 3 f4 exf4 4 ♗c4 ♕h4+ 5 ♔f1 ♗c5 6 g3 [□ 6 ♕e1] 6 ... hxg3 7 ♔g2 gxh2 8 ♖xh2 ♕g5+ 9 ♔h1 ♕xg1+ 10 ♕xg1 ♗xg1 11 ♔xg1 ♘e5 12 ♗e2 d6 13 d4 ♘g4 [□ 13 ... ♘g6] 14 ♖g2 h5 15 ♘d5 ♔d8 16 ♗f4 ♘e7 17 c4 ♘g6 18 ♗g3 ♗e6 19 c5

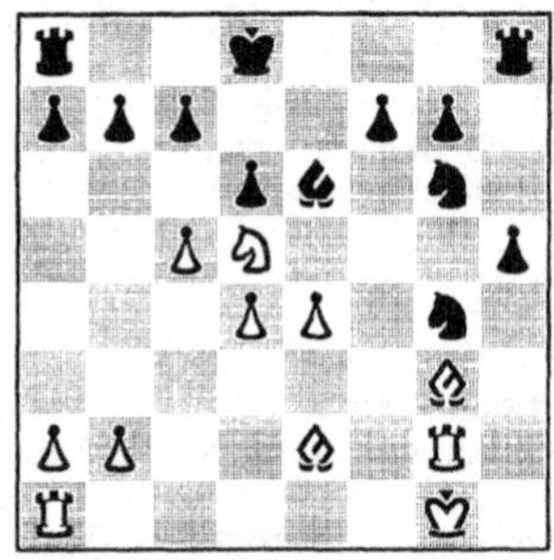

19 ... ♗xd5 20 exd5 dxc5 21 dxc5 ♖e8 22 ♗b5 ♖e4 23 ♖f1 ♘f6 [23 ... ♘e3 24 ♖xf7 ♘xg2 25 ♗xc7+ ♔c8 26 d6 ♖e7 27 dxe7+-] 24 d6 c6 [□ 24 ... cxd6] 25 ♗d3 ♖g4 26 ♗f5 ♖g5 27 ♗xg6 fxg6 28 ♗h4 ♖xg2+ 29 ♔xg2 ♔d7 30 ♗xf6 gxf6 31 ♖xf6 ♖g8 32 ♖f7+ ♔c8 33 ♖c7+ ♔b8 34 b4 g5 35 ♔g3 a6 36 ♖h7 h4+ 37 ♔g4 ♔c8 38 ♖c7+ ♔b8 39 a4 ♖h8 [39 ... ♖g6] 40 ♖e7 h3 41 ♖e1 h2 42 ♖h1 ♖h4+ 43 ♔xg5 ♖xb4 44 ♖xh2 ♖c4 45 ♖h8+ ♔a7 46 d7 ♖xc5+ 47 ♔f6 ♖d5 48 d8♕ ♖xd8 49 ♖xd8 **0-1** L/N6051-1866

### 1865-★NR-8
**Rivière,J.A.de+Neumann, G.R.**

Berlin [Anderssen & Neumann]

1 e4 c5 2 ♘c3 e6 3 ♗c4 ♘c6 4 d3 ♘f6 5 ♗g5 ♗e7 6 ♗xf6 ♗xf6 7 ♘ge2 a6 8 a4 ♖b8 [Δ 9 ... b5] 9 0-0 ♘d4 10 f4 b5 11 axb5 axb5 12 ♗a2 b4 13 ♘a4 ♘xe2+ 14 ♕xe2 0-0 15 ♔h1 ♗e7 16 f5 d5 [□ 16 ... d6] 17 fxe6 fxe6 18 exd5 ♖xf1+ 19 ♖xf1 ♖a8 20 ♗b3 ♗d7 [□ 20 ... exd5 21 ♗xd5+ ♕xd5 22 ♕xe7 ♗b7] 21 ♘xc5 ♗xc5 22 dxe6 ♗xe6 23 ♕xe6+ ♔h8 24 ♗d5 ♖b8 25 ♗e4 ♕g8 26 ♕xg8+ ♔xg8 27 c3 ♗e7 28 d4 ♗f6 29 ♖a1 h6 30 ♖a8 ♖xa8 31 ♗xa8 ♔f8 32 ♔g1 ♔e7 33 ♔f2 ♔e6 34 ♔e2 ♗g5 35 ♔d3 ♗c1 36 ♔c2 ♗f4 37 g3 ♗d6 38 c4 ♗e7 39 ♔d3 ♗f6 40 b3 ♔d6 41 c5+ ♔c7 42 ♔c4 ♔b8 43 ♗e4 h5 44 d5 ♗c3 45 d6 **1-0** L/N6051-1866

**1865-★NR-9** i 65
**Neumann, G.R.+Ruhland**
Berlin [Anderssen & Neumann]
1 e4 e5 2 ♘f3 ♘c6 3 ♗c4 ♗c5 4 b4 ♗xb4 5 c3 ♗a5 6 d4 exd4 7 0-0 dxc3 [▭ 7 ... ♗b6] 8 ♕b3 ♕e7 [▭ 8 ... ♕f6] 9 ♘xc3 ♗xc3 10 ♕xc3 ♘f6 [▭ 10 ... f6] 11 ♖e1 0-0 12 e5 ♘e8 13 ♗a3 d6 14 exd6 ♕f6 15 ♕xf6 ♘xf6 16 dxc7 ♖e8 17 ♘g5 ♗e6 18 ♘xe6 fxe6 19 ♖xe6 ♔h8 20 ♖ae1 ♖ec8 21 ♗d6 ♘e8 22 ♖xe8+ ♖xe8 23 ♖xe8+ ♖xe8 24 ♗e6 **1-0**
L/N6051

**1865-★NR-10**
**Rivière, J.A.de+Neumann, G.R.**
1 e4 e5 2 ♘f3 ♘c6 3 ♗c4 ♗c5 4 b4 ♗xb4 5 c3 ♗c5 6 0-0 d6 7 d4 exd4 8 cxd4 ♗b6 9 ♘c3 ♘a5 10 ♗d3 ♘e7 11 ♘a4 0-0 12 ♘xb6 axb6 13 ♗b2 ♘g6 14 ♖c1 c5 15 ♘d2 f6 16 f4 f5 17 ♕c2 ♕h4 18 g3 ♕g4 19 e5 dxe5 20 dxe5 ♗e6 21 ♘c4 ♘xc4 22 ♗xc4 ♖fe8 23 ♗xe6+ ♖xe6 24 ♕c4 ♘f8 25 ♖cd1 ♕g6 26 ♖d6 ♕f7 27 ♖fd1 ♖xd6 28 ♕xf7+ ♔xf7 29 ♖xd6 ♖a6 30 a3 b5 31 ♖d5 ♖c6 32 ♔f2 ♔e7 33 ♔e3 ♘d7 34 ♗c1 ♘b6 35 ♖d3 ♔e6 36 ♖d8 ♘d5+ 37 ♔d3 b4 38 ♔c4 ♘c7 39 a4 ♔e7 40 ♖g8 ♘e8 41 ♗e3 ♔f7 42 ♖h8 h6 43 a5 ♖c8 44 ♔b3 ♔e7 45 h3 ♔d7 46 g4 fxg4 47 hxg4 ♔c6 48 f5 ♖d8 49 f6 ♖d3+ 50 ♔c2 ♖c3+ 51 ♔d2

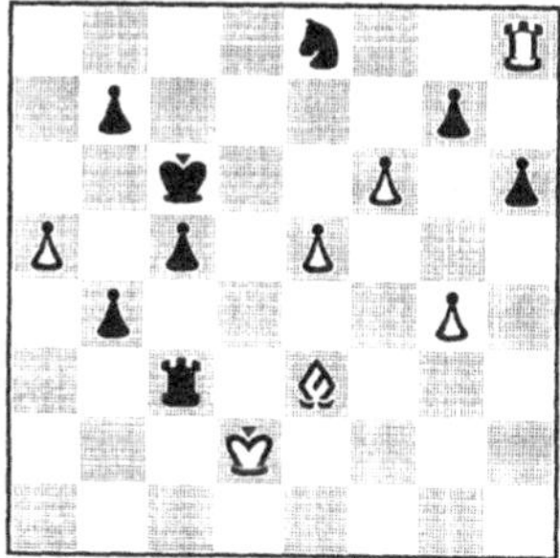

51 ... ♘xf6 52 exf6 gxf6 53 ♖xh6 ♔b5 54 ♖xf6 ♔xa5 55 g5 c4 56 ♖f5+ ♔a4 57 ♖d5 ♖a3 58 g6 c3+ 59 ♔e2 ♔b3 60 ♖d8 ♖a6 61 g7 ♖g6 62 g8♕+ ♖xg8 63 ♖xg8 ♔c2 64 ♖g1 b3 65 ♖c1+ ♔b2 66 ♔d3 c2 67 ♔d2 ♔a2 68 ♗d4 **1-0**
L/N6124-1865

**1865-★NR-11**
**Rivière, J.A.de–Neumann, G.R.**
1 e4 e5 2 ♘f3 ♘c6 3 c3 ♘f6 4 ♗c4 ♘xe4 5 0-0 d5 6 ♗b5 ♗d6 7 d3 ♘f6 8 ♘xe5 ♗xe5 9 ♖e1 0-0 10 ♗xc6 ♗xh2+ 11 ♔xh2 bxc6 12 ♗f4 ♖b8 13 ♘d2 ♖xb2 14 ♕c1 ♖b6 15 ♘b3 c5 16 ♘xc5 ♘g4+ 17 ♔g1 ♕h4 18 ♗g3 ♕h5 19 f3 ♖h6 20 fxg4 ♕h1+ 21 ♔f2 ♖f6+ 22 ♗f4 ♕h2 23 ♖e3 ♖xf4+ 24 ♖f3 ♖xf3+ 25 ♔xf3 f5 26 g5 f4 27 ♕g1 ♗g4+ 28 ♔f2 ♕g3+ 29 ♔f1 f3 ...? **0-1**
M954-1865

**1865-★NS-1** iv 65
**Neumann, G.R.+Schulten, W.**
Berlin [Anderssen & Neumann]
1 e4 e5 2 ♘f3 ♘c6 3 ♗b5 ♗c5? 4 c3 ♘ge7 5 0-0 0-0 6 d4 cxd4 7 cxd4 ♗b6 8 d5 ♘b8 9 d6 ♘g6 [▭ 9 ... cxd6 10 ♗f4 ♗c7 11 ♘c3 a6 12 ♗c4 b5 13 ♗b3 ♗b7 14 ♗xd6 ♗xd6 15 ♕xd6 h6? 16 ♖ad1 ♘c8 17 ♕f4 ♘b6 18 ♘e5 ♕f6? 19 ♕xf6 gxf6 20 ♘g4 ♔g7 21 ♘xf6 ♗c6 22 e5 a5 23 ♖d3 ♖h8 24 ♘cd5 ♘c4 25 ♗xc4 bxc4 26 ♖g3+ ♔f8 27 ♘b6 ♖a7 28 ♖d1 ♗b5 29 ♖d4 ♖c7 30 ♖dg4+– Morphy - Schulten] 10 e5 ♘c6 11 ♖e1 ♖e8 12 ♗g5 f6 13 ♗c4+ ♔h8 14 exf6 ♖xe1+ 15 ♕xe1 gxf6 [▭ 15 ... ♕f8] 16 ♕e8+ **1-0**
L/N6051

**1865-★PP-1** viii 65
**Pinedo, J.–Paulsen, L.**
Barmen [Anderssen & Neumann]
1 e4 e5 2 ♘f3 ♘c6 3 ♗c4 ♗c5 4 c3 ♘f6 5 0-0 0-0? 6 d3 [▭ 6 d4] 6 ... d6 7 b4 ♗b6 8 a4 a6 9 ♕c2 ♗e6 10 ♘bd2 ♘h5 11 ♗b2 ♕f6 12 ♗xe6 fxe6 13 ♘c4 ♗a7 14 ♘e3 ♘f4 15 ♔h1? ♘xg2 16 ♘xg2 ♕xf3 17 ♕d1 ♕xd1 18 ♖axd1 ♖xf2 19 ♗c1 ♖af8 20 ♖xf2 ♖xf2 21 ♘e3 ♘e7 22 ♘g4 ♖a2 23 ♗g5 ♘g6 24 a5 ♖e2 25 h3 h6 26 ♗d2 ♘f4 **0-1**
L/N6051-1866

**1865-★PS-1 ●○** viii 65
**Paulsen, L.=Schlieper, A.**
Elberfeld
1 e4 e5 2 f4 exf4 3 ♘f3 g5 4 ♗c4 ♗g7 5 d4 d6 6 c3 ♘c6 7 0-0 h6 8 ♘a3 ♘ge7 9 b4 ♘g6 10 ♘c2 ♘ce7 11 a4 ♗e6 12 ♕d3 0-0 13 ♗d2 c6 14 ♘a3 d5 15 ♗a2 dxe4 16 ♕xe4 ♗f5 17 ♕e2 ♘d5 18 ♘c4 ♖e8 19 ♕f2 ♕c7 20 ♗b1 ♗xb1 21 ♖axb1 ♖e6 22 ♖be1 ♖ae8 23 ♖xe6 ♖xe6 24 ♖e1 **½-½**
L/N6051

**1865-★PW-1 ●○** viii 65
**Paulsen, L.+Witthaus, C.**
Elberfeld [Anderssen & Neumann]
1 e4 c5 2 ♘c3 ♘c6 3 ♘f3 e6 4 d4 cxd4 5 ♘xd4 ♘f6 6 ♘db5 d6 7 ♗f4 e5 8 ♗e3 ♗e6 9 ♘d5 ♖c8 10 ♘xf6+ gxf6 11 ♘c3 f5 12 exf5 ♗xf5 13 ♗b5 ♗e6 14 ♕h5 a6 15 ♗xc6+ ♖xc6 16 0-0 ♖c4 17 ♗g5 ♗e7 18 ♗xe7 ♕xe7 19 f4! e4 20 f5 ♗d7 21 ♘d5 ♕e5 22 ♘e3 ♖c5 23 c3 ♖b5 24 ♘g4 ♕c5+ 25 ♔h1 ♗xf5 26 ♘f6+ ♔e7 27 ♕h4 ♔e6 28 ♘xe4 ♗xe4 29 ♕xe4+ ♕e5 30 ♕g4+ f5 31 ♕g5 ♕f6 32 ♕f4 ♖d8 33 ♖ad1 ♖e5 34 ♖d3 ♖e4 35 ♕d2 d5 36 ♖h3 f4 37 ♖xh7 ♕e5 38 ♕d3 ♖f8 39 ♕h3+ ♕f5 40 ♕h6+ ♖f6 41 ♕g7 ♖f7 42 ♖h6+ ♔d7 43 ♕h8 ♕e5 44 ♕a8 ♔c7 45 ♕a7 ♖a4? 46 ♕b6+ ♔b8 47 ♖e6 ♕h8 48 ♖fe1 **1-0**
L/N6051

**1865-★PW-2**
**Paulsen, L.+Wilberg**
[Löwenthal]
1 e4 e6 2 d4 ♘e7? 3 ♗d3 d5 4 ♘c3 a6 5 ♘f3 ♘bc6 6 0-0 h6 7 ♗e3 ♘b4 8 ♗e2 dxe4 9 ♘xe4 ♘f5 10 ♕d2 ♘d5 11 c4 ♗b4 12 ♕d3 ♘dxe3 13 fxe3 ♗e7 14 ♖ae1 0-0 15 ♗d1 b6 16 ♗c2 ♗d6 17 ♘xd6 ♕xd6 18 e4 ♘xd4 19 ♕xd4 ♗b7 20 ♕e3 e5 21 ♘h4 ♗c8 22 ♘f5 ♗xf5 23 exf5 f6 24 ♗e4 ♖ad8 25 ♗d5+ ♔h7 26 ♕g3 c6 27 ♗e6 ♕c5+ 28 ♔h1 ♖d2 29 ♖e4 ♖fd8 30 ♖h4 ♕e7 31 h3 ♖xb2 32 ♖xh6+ [△ #] **1-0**
M324-1865

**1865-★ST-1 ●○**
**Steinitz, W.+Twigg**
Dublin [Anderssen & Neumann]
1 e4 e6 2 d4 d5 3 ♘c3 ♗b4 4 exd5 ♗xc3+ 5 bxc3 exd5 6 ♘f3 ♘f6 7 ♗d3 0-0 8 0-0 ♗g4 9 h3 ♗h5 10 ♗e3 ♘e4 11 c4 f5 12 cxd5 ♘c3 13 ♕e1 ♗xf3 14 ♕xc3 ♗xd5 15 ♕d2 ♕f6? 16 c4 ♗e4 17 ♗xe4 fxe4 18 f3 exf3 19 ♖xf3 ♕d6 20 ♖xf8+ ♔xf8 21 ♖f1+ ♔g8 22 ♕f2 ♘d7 23 ♕f7+ ♔h8 24 c5 ♕c6 25 d5 ♕b5 26 c6 ♘f6 27 ♖xf6 [27 ... gxf6 28 ♕xf6+ ♔g8 29 ♕e6+ ♔g7 30 ♗h6+ ♔h8 31 ♕f6+ ♔g8 32 ♕g7#] **1-0**
L/N6051-1866

**1865-★SZ-1**
**Schmidt, E.von–Zukertort, J.H.**
Breslau [Anderssen & Zukertort]
1 e4 e5 2 f4 exf4 3 ♗e2 d5! 4 e5 [4 exd5 ♕h4+ 5 ♔f1 ♗d6 6 ♘f3 ♕h6 7 ♘c3 ♗f5 8 d4 ♘d7 9 ♕e1 0-0-0∓] 4 ... f6 5 exf6 [5 d4 fxe5 6 dxe5 ♕h4+] 5 ... ♘xf6 6 d4 ♗d6 7 ♘c3 0-0 8 ♘f3 c6 9 0-0 ♘bd7 10 ♕d3 ♕e8 11 ♗d2 ♘e4 12 ♖ae1 ♘df6 13 ♘h4 g5 14 ♘f3 ♗f5 15 ♘xe4! ♘xe4 [15 ... dxe4? 16 ♕b3+ ♗e6 17 ♗c4!] 16 ♗d1 [16 ♕b3 g4] 16 ... ♕f7 17 ♕e2 ♖ae8 18 ♘e5 ♗xe5 19 dxe5 ♖xe5 20 ♗c3 ♖e6 21 ♕d3! ♘xc3 [21 ... ♘g3? 22 ♕d4] 22 ♕xc3 ♖fe8 23 ♕d2 ♖xe1 24 ♖xe1 ♖xe1+ 25 ♕xe1 ♕e6 26 ♕xe6+ ♗xe6 27 h3 d4 28 a3 ♔g7 29 ♔f2 ♔f6 30 ♔f3 ♔e5 31 ♔f2 a5 32 a4 c5 33 b3 ♗d5 34 ♗e2 ♗e4 35 ♗d1 ♔d5 36 g4 c4 37 ♔e2 c3 38 ♔e1

♔c5 39 ♔e2 ♔b4 40 ♔e1 d3 41 cxd3 ♗xd3 42 ♔f2 c2 **0-1**
L/N6051-1869

### 1865-★S?-1 viii 65
**Staunton, H.+?**
Birmingham [Staunton]

1 e4 e5 2 ♘f3 ♘c6 3 ♗c4 ♗c5 4 b4 ♗xb4 5 c3 ♗c5 6 d4 exd4 7 0-0 d6 8 cxd4 ♗b6 9 ♘c3 ♗g4 10 ♗b5! [10 ♕a4] 10 ... ♗d7 11 e5 a6? [11 ... ♘ge7] 12 ♗xc6 bxc6 13 ♗g5 ♘e7 14 exd6 cxd6 15 ♖e1 ♗e6 16 d5 cxd5 17 ♘xd5 ♖a7 18 ♕a4+ ♔f8 19 ♘xe7 ♖xe7 20 ♗xe7+ [20 ♕f4! f6 21 ♗xf6 gxf6 22 ♕xf6+ ♔g8 23 ♖xe6+-; 20 ♖ad1!+-] 20 ... ♔xe7 21 ♖ab1 a5 22 ♕b5 [△ 23 ♕g5+; ◻ 22 ♕c6] 22 ... ♗c5 23 ♘e5 ♗xf2+ 24 ♔xf2 dxe5 25 ♕c5+ ♔f6 26 ♕xe5+ ♔g6 27 ♕g3++- ♕g5? 28 ♕xg5+ ♔xg5 29 ♖b5+ ♔g6 30 ♖xa5 ♖c8 31 h3 h6 32 ♖e2 ♔f6 33 a4 g5 34 ♖a7 ♔f5 35 a5 h5 36 ♖b2 ♔g6 37 a6 ♗d5 38 ♖d2 ♗e6 39 ♖b7 ♖a8 40 a7 f5 41 ♖d6 ♔f6 42 ♖a6 ...? **1-0**
M954

### 1865-★Z?-1 vi 65
**Zukertort, J.H.+?**
Breslau [Anderssen & Zukertort]

1 e4 e5 2 ♘f3 ♘c6 3 ♗c4 ♗c5 4 b4 ♗xb4 5 c3 ♗c5 6 d4 exd4 7 0-0 d6 8 cxd4 ♗b6 9 d5 ♘a5 10 ♗b2 ♘e7 11 ♗d3 0-0 12 ♘c3 ♘g6 13 ♘e2 c5 14 ♕d2 f6 15 ♔h1 ♗c7 16 ♖ac1 ♗d7? 17 ♘g3 a6 18 ♘f5 ♗xf5 19 exf5 ♘e7? 20 g4 b5 [20 ... ♘xd5 21 ♗c4 ♘xc4 22 ♕xd5+ ♔h8 23 ♕xc4] 21 g5 ♘c4 [21 ... ♘xd5 22 ♗e4] 22 ♗xc4! bxc4 23 gxf6 ♘xf5 24 ♕g5 g6 25 ♕xf5 gxf5 26 ♖g1+ ♔f7! 27 ♖g7+ ♔e8 28 ♖e1+ ♕e7 29 ♖exe7+ ♔d8 30 ♖d7+ ♔c8! 31 ♖xc7+ ♔b8 32 ♖b7+ ♔c8 33 ♖gc7+ ♔d8 34 ♘g5 ♖xf6! 35 ♗xf6+ ♕e8 36 ♘e6 **1-0**
L/N6051-1870

## LONDON 1 1866

### 1866-LON1-1 vi 66
**De Vere, C.+ Bird, H.E.**
[Löwenthal & Medley]

1 e4 e5 2 ♘f3 ♘c6 3 ♗b5 ♘d4 4 ♘xd4 exd4 5 0-0 ♗c5 6 d3 ♘e7 7 ♕h5 ♗b6 8 ♗g5 0-0 9 ♗c4 ♕e8 10 f4 ♔h8 11 e5 d6 12 ♗xe7 [◻ 12 ♘d2] 12 ... ♕xe7 13 ♘d2 ♗e6 14 exd6 cxd6 15 ♖ae1 d5? 16 ♗xd5 ♕c5 17 ♖e5 ♗xd5 [17 ... g6 18 ♕f3] 18 ♖xd5 ♕xc2 19 ♘f3 ♕xd3 20 f5 ♕e2 21 ♖e1 d3+ 22 ♔h1 ♕f2 [22 ... ♕c2 23 f6 gxf6 24 ♕h6 ♖g8 25 ♕xf6+ ♖g7 26 ♖g5 △#] 23 f6 gxf6 24 ♕h6 ♖g8 25 ♕xf6+ ♖g7 26 g3 [26 ♖g5? ♗d4-+] 26 ... ♖g8 27 ♖xd3 ♗a5 28 ♖ed1 ♖e8 29 b4 ♕b6 30 ♕xb6 ♗xb6 31 ♖d7 f6 32 a4 ♖ee7 33 ♖7d6 ♖gf7 34 ♘h4 f5 35 ♖6d5 ♖f8 36 ♘xf5 ♖e4 37 a5 ♗c7 38 ♖d7 ♖c4 39 ♘e3 ♖c6 40 ♘d5 ♗d6 41 b5 ♖c2 42 ♖xd6 ♖ff2 43 ♘f4 **1-0** L/N5193

### 1866-LON1-4 vi 66
**MacDonnell, G.A.–De Vere, C.**

1 e4 e5 2 ♘f3 ♘c6 3 d4 exd4 4 ♗c4 ♗c5 5 c3 ♘f6 6 e5 d5 7 ♗b5 ♘e4 8 cxd4 ♗b6 9 0-0 0-0 10 ♗xc6 bxc6 11 ♘c3 f5 12 exf6? ♕xf6 13 ♘xe4 dxe4 14 ♘e5 ♖d8 15 ♕b3+? ♗e6 16 ♗g5 ♗xb3 17 ♗xf6 gxf6 18 ♘xc6 ♗d5 19 ♘xd8 ♗xd4 **0-1** L/N6124

### 1866-LON1-5 vi 66
**De Vere, C.+MacDonnell, G.A.**
[Löwenthal & Medley]

1 e4 e5 2 ♘f3 d6 3 d4 exd4 4 ♕xd4 ♗e6 [◻ 4 ... ♗d7] 5 ♘c3 a6 6 ♗e3 ♘c6 7 ♕d2 ♘f6 8 ♗e2 ♗e7 9 0-0 0-0 10 ♖ad1 b5 11 a3 ♘e5 12 ♘g5 c5?! [12 ... ♘fg4] 13 f4 ♘c4 14 ♕c1 ♘xe3 15 ♕xe3 ♕c7 16 ♘xe6 fxe6 17 e5! dxe5 18 fxe5 ♘d7 19 ♖xf8+ ♖xf8 20 ♕h3! ♕xe5 [◻ 20 ... ♘b6; 20 ... ♘xe5? 21 ♕xe6++- △ ♘d5] 21 ♖xd7 ♗d6 22 ♖xd6 ♕xd6 23 ♕e3 b4 24 axb4 cxb4 25 ♘d1 a5 26 b3 ♖f5 27 ♘f2 ♖e5 28 ♘e4 ♕e7 29 ♗d3 ♕c7 30 h3 h6 31 ♕g3 ♕b6+ 32 ♔h2 ♕d4 33 ♘f6+ ♔f8 34 ♘d7+ **1-0** L/N5193

### 1866-LON1-6 vi 66
**MacDonnell, G.A.–De Vere, C.**
[Löwenthal & Medley]

1 e4 e6 2 d4 d5 3 exd5 exd5 4 ♗d3 ♘c6 5 ♗e3 ♗e6 6 ♘f3 ♘f6 7 ♘c3 ♗d6 8 0-0 0-0 9 h3?! ♕d7 10 ♘g5 ♗f5 11 ♗xf5 ♕xf5 12 g4? ♕d7 13 f4?

13 ... ♖ae8! 14 ♕d2 [14 ♕f3? h6; 14 ♕d3? ♘b4; 14 ♗f2 ♗xf4; 14 ♗d2 ♘xd4; ◻ 14 ♗c1∓] 14 ... ♘xg4! 15 hxg4 ♕xg4+ 16 ♔f2 ♖xe3 17 ♕xe3 ♗xf4 18 ♕h3 [18 ♕f3? ♕h4+-+] 18 ... ♕xg5 19 ♘e2 ♖e8 20 c3 ♗e3+ 21 ♔e1 ♗xd4 22 ♖d1 [22 cxd4 ♘xd4 23 ♖f2 ♕g1+-+] 22 ... ♗e3 23 ♖f5 ♕g6 24 ♖dxd5 ♗b6 25 ♕f3 ♕g1+ 26 ♕f1 ♕e3 27 ♔d1 ♘e7 28 ♘d4 [28 ♖fe5 ♘xd5 29 ♖xe3 ♘xe3+-+] 28 ... ♘xd5 29 ♖xd5 ♕e4 30 ♖f5 ♗xd4 31 cxd4 ♕b1+ **0-1** L/N5193

### 1866-LON1-7 vi 66
**Minchin, J.I.+ Bird, H.E.**
[Löwenthal & Medley]

1 e4 e5 2 ♗c4 ♘f6 3 ♘f3 ♘xe4 4 ♘c3 ♘f6 [◻ 4 ... ♘xc3, ... f6∓] 5 ♘xe5 d5 6 ♕e2 ♗e6 7 ♗b3 c6 8 d4 h6? 9 0-0 [◻ 9 ♘g6] 9 ... ♗e7 10 f4 g6 11 ♗d2 [◻ 11 ♘xg6] 11 ... ♕d6 12 ♖ae1 ♖g8 13 ♔h1 ♘bd7 14 g4 ♘f8 15 f5 ♗c8 16 ♗f4 gxf5 17 ♘b5! cxb5 18 ♘g6 ♕e6 19 ♕xb5+ ♗d7 20 ♕xb7 fxg6 21 ♕xa8+ ♔f7 22 ♖xe6 ♘xe6 23 ♕xa7 ♗b5 24 ♖e1 ♖e8 25 ♗e5 fxg4 26 ♗xf6 ♔xf6 27 ♖xe6+ **1-0** L/N5193

### 1866-LON1-8 vi 66
**Bird, H.E.–Minchin, J.I.**
[Löwenthal & Medley]

1 e4 e5 2 ♘f3 ♘c6 3 ♗b5 a6 4 ♗a4 ♘f6 5 d4 exd4 6 e5 ♘e4 7 0-0 ♗e7 8 c3 dxc3 9 ♖e1? cxb2 10 ♗xb2 ♘c5 11 ♗c2 0-0 12 ♘c3 d6 13 ♘d5 ♗g4 14 ♘xe7+ ♕xe7 15 ♕d5? [15 exd6 △ 15 ... ♕xd6 16 ♗xh7+] 15 ... ♘b4 16 ♕d4 ♘xc2 17 ♕xg4 ♕e6! 18 ♕h4 ♘xe1 19 ♖xe1 ♘d3 20 ♖e4 ♘xb2 21 ♖g4 ♕f5 22 h3 dxe5 23 ♕g3 g6 24 ♘g5 ♖ad8 25 ♕h4 h5 26 ♘e4 ♖d1+ 27 ♔h2 hxg4 28 ♘g5 ♕f4+ **0-1** L/N5193

### 1866-LON1-9 vi 66
**Minchin, J.I.– Bird, H.E.**
[Löwenthal & Medley]

1 e4 e5 2 ♗c4 ♘c6 3 ♘f3 ♗c5 4 0-0 ♘f6 5 d3 0-0 6 ♘c3 d6 7 h3 ♗e6 8 ♗b3 ♕d7 9 ♘e2 ♘h5 10 ♔h2 ♖ae8 11 ♘g3 [◻ 11 g4 △ 11 ... ♗xg4?] 11 ... ♘xg3 12 fxg3 ♗xb3 13 axb3 f5 14 exf5 ♖xf5 15 ♖a4 ♖ef8 16 ♖g4 d5 17 c3 ♗e7 18 ♗g5 h5 19 ♗xe7 ♕xe7 20 ♖h4 e4 21 ♘d2? [21 dxe4± dxe4 22 ♘d2 ♖xf1 (22 ... e3 23 ♕e1 ♖f2 24 ♘c4 e2 25 ♕d5+ ♖8f7 26 ♖e4+-) 23 ♘xf1 e3 24 ♕d5+ ♖f7 25 ♘xe3 ♕xe3 26 ♖e4+-] 21 ... exd3 22 ♖xh5 ♖xf1 23 ♘xf1 ♕e2 **0-1** L/N5193

### 1866-LON1-10 vi 66
**Bird, H.E.– Minchin, J.I.**
[Löwenthal & Medley]

1 e4 e5 2 ♘f3 ♘c6 3 ♗b5 a6 4 ♗a4 ♘f6 5 0-0 ♗e7 6 d4 exd4 7 e5 ♘e4 8 ♗b3 0-0 9 ♘xd4 ♘xd4 10 ♕xd4 ♘c5 11 ♘c3 ♘xb3 12 axb3 d6 13

♘e4 dxe5 14 ♕xe5 ♖e8 15 ♖e1 ♗d7 16 ♗d2 ♗c6 17 ♗c3 ♗f8 18 ♕f4 ♕d5 19 f3 ♖e6 20 ♖ad1 ♕h5 21 ♘g5 ♗d6 22 ♘xe6? [22 ♗e5; 22 ♕~?] 22 ... ♗xf4 23 ♘xf4 ♕g5 24 ♘d5 f6 [24 ... ♗xd5 25 ♖e5] 25 h4 ♕h5 26 ♘e7+ ♔f7 27 ♘xc6 bxc6 28 ♖d7+ ♔f8 29 ♖ee7 ♕c5+ 30 ♗d4 ♕xe7 31 ♖xe7 ♔xe7 32 ♔f2 ♔d6 33 b4 ♖e8 34 c4 ♔e6 35 g4 g6 36 f4 h5 37 g5 fxg5 38 fxg5 ♔f5 **0-1** L/N5193

**1866-LON1-11** vi 66
**Minchin, J.I.– De Vere, C.**
[Löwenthal & Medley]

1 e4 e5 2 ♘f3 ♘c6 3 ♗c4 ♗c5 4 b4 ♗b6 5 a4 a6 6 0-0 d6 7 a5 ♗a7 8 c3 ♘f6 9 d3 h6 10 ♗e3 0-0 11 ♕b3 ♘e7 12 ♘bd2 c6 13 ♕c2 d5 14 ♗a2 ♘g6 15 ♖ae1 ♖e8 [15 ... d4!-+] 16 ♗b1? dxe4? [16 ... d4] 17 dxe4 ♕d7 18 ♗xa7 ♖xa7 19 ♘c4 ♕g4 20 ♘e3 [20 ♖d1] 20 ... ♕h5 21 ♘f5 ♘f4 22 ♘g3 ♕g6 23 ♘h4 ♕g4 24 ♘hf5 ♗xf5 25 exf5 h5 26 f3 ♕g5 27 ♔h1 h4 28 ♘e4 ♘xe4 29 ♖xe4 ♕xf5 30 ♕f2 ♖aa8 31 ♕xh4 ♘g6 32 ♕f2 ♕f6 33 g3 ♖ad8 34 ♖fe1 ♔f8 35 h4 [□ 35 f4] 35 ... ♕d6 36 h5 ♘h8 37 ♕e3 ♕d2 38 ♕c5+ ♕d6 39 ♕xd6+? ♖xd6 40 f4 f6 41 ♗a2?! ♖d3 42 fxe5 ♖xe5 43 ♖xe5 fxe5 44 ♗e6 ♖xc3 45 ♖xe5 ♖xg3 46 ♗d7 ♖d3 47 ♖e8+ [□ 47 ♗c8 ♘f7 48 ♖f5 ♔e7 49 ♗xb7 ♘d6 50 ♗xa6 ♖d1+ 51 ♖f1±] 47 ... ♔f7 48 ♗xc6 bxc6 49 ♖xh8 ♖b3 50 ♖a8 ♖xb4 51 ♖xa6 ♖b5 52 ♖a7+ [□ 52 ♖xc6] 52 ... ♔e6 53 a6 ♖xh5+ 54 ♔g2 ♖a5 55 ♖a8 ♔d6 56 a7 ♔c5 57 ♔f3 ♔b6 58 ♖b8+ ♔xa7 59 ♖b3 ♖b5 **0-1** L/N5193

**124** De Vere, C.V. DLC . DL

**1866-LON1-12** vi 66
**De Vere, C.+ Minchin, J.I.**
[Löwenthal & Medley]

1 e4 e5 2 d4 exd4 3 ♘f3 ♘c6 4 ♗c4 ♗c5 5 c3 ♘f6 6 e5 d5 7 ♗b5 ♘e4 8 cxd4 ♗b6 9 0-0 0-0 10 ♗xc6 bxc6 11 ♗e3 f6 12 ♕c2 ♗b7 13 ♘c3 f5 14 ♖ad1 ♕e7 15 h3 f4 16 ♗c1 ♘g5 [□ 16 ... ♘xc3, ... c5] 17 ♘xg5 ♕xg5 18 ♘e2 ♗a6 [□ 18 ... ♕h4 (Δ ... f3) 19 f3] 19 ♖fe1 ♗a5

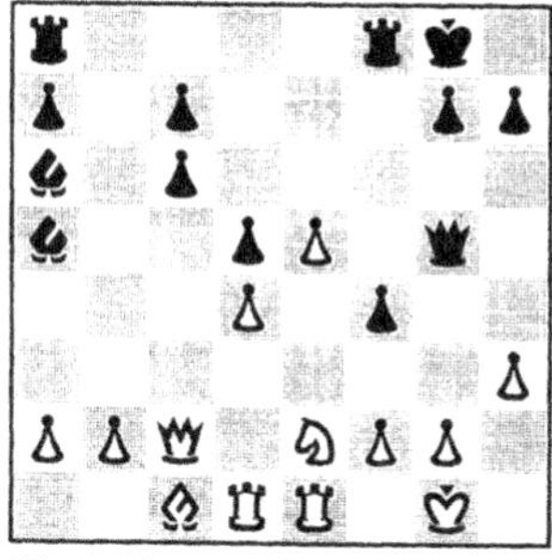

20 ♕xc6! ♗xe1 21 ♖xe1 ♗xe2 22 ♕xd5+ ♔h8 23 ♖xe2 ♕h5 24 f3 ♖ad8 25 ♕e4 ♕h4 [□ 25 ... ♕f5] 26 e6 ♖de8 27 e7 ♖f7 28 ♕c6 ♖fxe7 29 ♕xe8+ ♖xe8 30 ♖xe8# **1-0** L/N5193

**1866-LON1-13** vi 66
**Minchin, J.I.– De Vere, C.**
[Löwenthal & Medley]

1 e4 e5 2 f4 ♗c5 3 ♘f3 d6 4 c3 ♗g4 5 ♗e2 ♗xf3 6 ♗xf3 ♘c6 7 b4 ♗b6 8 b5 ♘ce7 9 d4 exd4 10 cxd4 d5 11 e5 ♘f5 12 ♗b2 ♕e7 13 ♕d3 ♘gh6 14 g4? ♕h4+ 15 ♔d1 ♘xg4 16 ♗xg4 ♕xg4+ 17 ♔c1 ♕xf4+ 18 ♘d2 ♗xd4 19 ♖b1 ♗e3 20 ♗c3 ♗xd2+ 21 ♗xd2 ♕e4 **0-1** L/N5193

**1866-LON1-14** vi 66
**Minchin,J.I.–Macdonnell, G.A.**
[Löwenthal & Medley]

1 e4 e5 2 f4 ♗c5 3 ♘f3 d6 4 c3 ♗g4 5 ♗e2 ♗xf3 6 ♗xf3 ♘f6 7 d4 exd4 8 cxd4 ♗b4+ [□ 8 ... ♗b6] 9 ♘c3 [□ 9 ♔f1±] 9 ... 0-0 10 0-0 [□ 10 e5] 10 ... ♘c6 11 ♗e3 ♗xc3 12 bxc3 ♕e7 13 e5 dxe5 14 fxe5 ♘d7 15 ♗xc6? [15 ♗e4] 15 ... bxc6 16 ♕f3 c5 17 ♕g3 cxd4 18 cxd4 f6 19 exf6 ♘xf6 20 ♗g5 ♕d7 21 ♕h4 ♘g4 22 ♖xf8+ ♖xf8 23 ♖d1 h6 24 ♗c1 ♕f5 25 ♕e1 ♘f2 26 ♗a3 ♖f6 27 ♖d2 ♘h3+ 28 gxh3 ♕f3 29 ♖g2 ♕xa3 30 ♕e8+ ♖f8 31 ♕e6+ ♔h8 32 ♖f2 ♕c1+ 33 ♔g2 ♖xf2+ 34 ♔xf2 ♕f4+ 35 ♔g2 ♕xd4 36 ♕c8+ ♔h7 37 ♕f5+ [□ 37 ♕xc7] 37 ... g6 38 ♕e6 h5 39 h4? ♕g4+ 40 ♕xg4 hxg4 41 ♔g3 ♔h6 42 ♔xg4 c5 43 ♔f4 ♔h5 **0-1** L/N5193

**1866-LON1-15** vi 66
**MacDonnell, G.A.= Minchin, J.I.**
[Löwenthal & Medley]

1 e4 e5 2 ♘f3 ♘c6 3 ♗b5 ♘f6 4 0-0 ♘xe4 5 d4 ♘d6 6 ♗xc6 dxc6 [□ 6 ... bxc6] 7 dxe5 ♘e4 8 ♕xd8+ ♔xd8 9 ♖e1 ♘c5 10 ♘g5 ♗e6 11 ♘c3 h6 12 ♘xe6+ ♘xe6 13 ♘e4 ♗b4 14 c3 ♗a5 15 ♗e3 ♗b6 16 ♘g3 g6 17 ♗xb6 cxb6 18 ♖e4 [□ 18 ♘e4] 18 ... ♔e7 19 f4?! [□ 19 ♖ae1 Δ f4; Δ 19 ... f5? 20 exf6+; Δ 19 ... g5 20 ♘f5+] 19 ... f5 20 exf6+ ♔xf6 21 ♖f1 ♘c5 22 ♖e5 ♖he8 23 ♖fe1 ♖xe5 24 ♖xe5 ♖d8 25 ♖e1 ♖d2 26 b4 [□ 26 ♖e2] 26 ... ♘d3 27 ♘e4+ ♔f5 28 ♘xd2 ♘xe1 29 ♔f2 ♘d3+ 30 ♔f3 h5 [30 ... ♘xf4 31 g4+ ♔e5 32 ♘c4+ ♔d5 33 ♘xb6+ (33 ♘e3+=) 33 ... axb6 34 ♔xf4 ♔c4 35 ♔e5? (35 g5=) 35 ... ♔xc3-+] 31 g3 b5 32 ♘b3 ♘b2 33 ♘a5 [□ 33 ♘c5] 33 ... ♘d1 34 ♘xb7 ♘xc3 35 ♘a5 ♘xa2 36 ♘xc6 a6 37 h3 ♔e6 38 ♘d4+ ♔d5 39 ♘c2 ♘c3 40 g4 ♔e6 41 ♘e1 ♘d5 42 ♘d3 hxg4+ 43 hxg4 ♔f7 44 g5 ♔e6 45 ♔e4 [45 ♘c5+=] 45 ... ♘c3+ 46 ♔d4 ♘a4 47 ♘c5+ ♔f5 [47 ... ♘xc5? 48 bxc5+-] 48 ♘xa6 ♔xf4 49 ♘c7 ♔xg5 50 ♘xb5 ♔f4 51 ♘c7 g5 52 ♘e6+ ♔f5 53 ♘xg5 ♔xg5 **½-½** L/N5193

**1866-LON1-16** vi 66
**MacDonnell, G.A.+ Minchin, J.I.**
[Lowenthal & Medley]

1 e4 e5 2 ♘f3 ♘c6 3 ♗b5 a6 4 ♗a4 ♘f6 5 0-0 ♗e7 6 d4 0-0? 7 d5 ♘b8 8 ♖e1 d6 9 h3 h6 10 c4 ♘h7 11 ♗c2 f5 12 exf5 ♗xf5 13 ♘c3 ♘d7 14 ♗e3 ♘g5 15 ♗xg5 ♗xg5 16 ♗xf5 ♖xf5 17 ♘e4 ♗h4 [□ 17 ... ♗e7] 18 b4 ♕e7 19 a4 ♖af8 20 a5 ♖f4 21 ♖a3 ♘f6 22 ♘ed2 ♕f7? 23 g3 ♕g6 24 ♔h2 ♘h5 25 ♖g1 ♕f5 26 ♘xh4 ♖xf2+ 27 ♖g2 ♖xg2+ 28 ♘xg2 ♕f2 29 ♘e4 **1-0** L/N5193

**1866-LON1-17** vi 66
**Minchin, J.I.– MacDonnell, G.A.**
[Löwenthal & Medley]

1 a3 e5 2 c4 f5 3 ♘c3 ♘f6 4 e3 ♗e7 5 d4 e4 6 ♗e2 0-0 7 ♘h3 c6 8 0-0 ♔h8 9 b3 d5 10 f3 ♗d6 11 f4 ♗e6 12 ♔h1 ♘bd7 13 ♖g1 ♘g4 14 ♕e1 h6 15 ♘f2 [□ 15 ♘d1, ♘df2; ♘hf2] 15 ... g5 16 h3 ♘xf2+ 17 ♕xf2 g4 18 hxg4 fxg4 19 g3 ♔g7 20 ♗b2 ♘f6 21 ♔g2 ♗f5 22 ♖h1 ♗e7 23 ♖h2 a5 24 ♖ah1 ♖h8 25 ♕f1 ♔g6 26 ♕d1 h5 27 ♘b1 ♕d7 28 ♘d2 ♖h7 29 ♘f1 ♖ah8 30 ♕e1 ♕d8 31 c5

♘d7 32 ♗c3 b6 33 b4 a×b4 34 a×b4 b5 35 ♕c1 [□ 35 ♕d1] 35 ... h4 36 g×h4 ♗×h4 37 ♗e1 ♗×e1 38 ♕×e1 [□ 38 ♖×h7, 39 ♖×h7] 38 ... ♖×h2+ 39 ♘×h2 [□ 39 ♖×h2] 39 ... ♘f6

40 ♖g1? [40 ♘×g4? ♗×g4? 41 ♕g3 ♖×h1 42 ♗×g4 ♖a1 (42 ... ♖h2+ 43 ♔×h2; 42 ... ♖h8? 43 ♗h5+, #) 43 ♗e6+=; 40 ... ♘×g4 41 ♕g3 ♖×h1 42 ♗×g4 ♕h4-+] 40 ... ♖×h2+ 41 ♔×h2 ♕h8+ 42 ♔g2 ♕h3+ 43 ♔f2 ♕h2+ 44 ♖g2 [□ 44 ♔f1 ♕h3+ 45 ♖g2 ♕×e3-+; 45 ♔f2 ♘h5 46 ♖h1 (46 ♔f1 ♕h4+-+) 46 ... ♕g3+, ... ♕×e3-+] **0-1**

L/N5193

**1866-LON1-18** vi 66
**Minchin, J.I.+Trelawny, J.**
[Löwenthal & Medley]

1 e4 e6 2 d4 c5 3 d5 g6 4 ♘f3 ♗g7 5 ♗e2 ♘f6 6 ♘c3 ♕a5 7 0-0 a6 8 d×e6 [8 d6] 8 ... d×e6 9 ♕d6 ♘bd7 10 ♗g5 ♗f8 11 ♕f4 ♘h5 12 ♕h4 h6 13 ♗d2 ♕c7 14 e5?! ♘×e5 15 ♘×e5 ♕×e5 16 ♕a4+ ♗d7 17 ♗b5 ♖d8 [17 ... 0-0-0] 18 ♗×d7+ ♖×d7 19 ♖fe1 ♕d4 20 ♕b3 c4 [20 ... ♕×d2] 21 ♕a4 ♕b6 [21 ... ♕×d2? 22 ♖ad1 b5 23 ♕×a6, 24 ♖×d7, 25 ♖d1+-] 22 ♗e3 ♕c6 23 ♕×c6 b×c6 24 ♘e4 f5 25 ♘c3 ♔f7 26 ♘a4 ♗b4 27 c3 ♗e7 28 ♗c5 ♘f4 29 ♗×e7 ♖×e7 30 ♖ad1 ♘d3 31 ♖e2 ♖d7 32 ♘b6 ♖d5!? 33 ♘×c4 ♘f4 34 ♖ed2 ♖hd8 35 g3 ♖×d2 36 ♖×d2 ♖×d2 37 ♘×d2 ♘d3 38 ♘c4 ♔f6 [□ 38 ... e5, ... ♔f6] 39 ♔f1 e5 40 ♔e2 ♘c5 41 f3 f4 42 ♘d6 f×g3 43 h×g3 ♘a4 44 ♘e4+ ♔e7 45 b3 ♘b6 46 c4 ♘d7 47 a4 a5 48 ♔d3 ♔e6 49 ♔c3 c5 50 ♔d3 h5 51 ♔e3 ♔e7 52 f4 ♔e6 53 ♔f3 ♔f5 54 ♘d6+ ♔e6 55 ♘b7 ♔f5 56 f×e5 ♘×e5+ 57 ♔g2 ♘d3 58 ♘×a5 ♘c1 59 ♘c6 ♘×b3 60 a5 ♘d4 61 ♘×d4+ c×d4 62 a6 **1-0**

L/N5193

## LONDON 2 1866

**1866-LON2-1** vi 66
**De Vere, C.=Steinitz, W.**
[Löwenthal & Medley]

1 e4 e5 2 ♘f3 ♘c6 3 ♗b5 ♘f6 4 0-0 ♘×e4 5 ♖e1 ♘d6 6 ♗×c6 d×c6 7 ♘×e5 ♗e7 8 d3 0-0 9 ♘c3 ♘f5 10 ♘f3 ♗e6 11 ♗f4 ♗d6 12 ♕d2 ♕f6?! 13 ♗×d6 [13 ♘e4 ♕×b2 14 ♘×d6 ♘×d6 15 ♗×d6 c×d6 16 ♖fb1 ♕f6∓; 13 d4 ♘×d4 14 ♗g5 (14 ♘×d4?) 14 ... ♘×f3+ 15 g×f3 ♕g6-+] 13 ... c×d6 14 ♕f4 d5 15 g4 ♘h6 [□ 15 ... ♕g6] 16 ♕×f6 g×f6 17 h3 ♖fe8 18 ♘e2 [□ 18 ♘h4 △ f4] 18 ... ♗d7 19 ♘f4 ♔f8 20 ♔f1 ♘g8 21 ♘h5 ♖e6 22 ♘d4 ♖d6 23 f4 c5 24 ♘f3± a5 25 ♖ad1?! a4 26 f5 a3 27 b3 ♘e7 28 c4 ♘c6 29 ♘f4 ♘b4 30 ♖d2 d×c4 31 b×c4 ♗c6 32 ♔f2 ♖ad8 33 ♖ed1 ♗a4 34 ♖c1 ♘×d3+ 35 ♘×d3 ♖×d3 36 ♖×d3 ♖×d3 37 ♔e2 ♖d6 38 ♖c3 ♗d1+ [38 ... ♖a6] 39 ♔f2 ♗×f3 40 ♔×f3 ♖d4 41 ♖×a3 ♖×c4 42 ♖b3 ♖a4 43 ♖×b7 ♖×a2 44 ♖c7 ♖c2 45 ♔e4 ♔g7 46 ♔d5 ♖c3 47 ♖×c5 ♖×h3 48 ♔e4 h5 49 g×h5 ♖×h5 50 ♖c6 **½-½**

L/N5193

**1866-LON2-2** vi 66
**Steinitz, W.+De Vere, C.**
[Löwenthal & Medley]

1 e4 e6 2 d4 d5 3 ♘c3 ♗b4 4 e×d5 e×d5 5 ♘f3 ♘f6 6 ♗d3 ♘c6 7 0-0 0-0 8 ♘e2 ♘e7 9 ♘e5 ♘g6 [□ 9 ... ♗f5] 10 f4 ♘e4 11 c3 ♗a5 12 ♗×e4 d×e4 13 ♘g3 [□ 13 ♕c2] 13 ... ♘×e5 14 f×e5 ♗b6 15 ♗e3 [15 ♘×e4 ♕d5] 15 ... f5 16 e×f6 ♖×f6 17 ♕h5 g6 18 ♕h6 ♗f5 19 ♗g5 ♕f8 20 ♕h4 ♖e6

21 ♖×f5 g×f5 22 ♖f1 e3 23 ♖×f5 ♕d6 24 ♗f6 **1-0**

L/N5193

**1866-LON2-3** vi 66
**De Vere, C.=Steinitz, W.**
[Löwenthal & Medley]

1 e4 e5 2 ♘f3 ♘c6 3 ♗b5 ♘f6 4 0-0 ♗e7 5 ♘c3 d6 6 d4 e×d4 7 ♘×d4 ♗d7 8 ♘×c6 ♕e2 ♕g6 26 ♔g1 [△ ♘e4] 26 ... ♔f8 27 ♘d1 ♕d6 [△ ... ♕c5+; ... d4, ... c5] 28 ♘f2 ♘×f2 29 ♔×f2 ♕c5+ 30 ♕e3 d4 31 ♕e5 ♕×e5 32 f×e5 ♔e7 33 ♔f3 c5 34 a4 ♗f5 35 g4 ♗g6 36 h4 c4 37 ♗×c4 ♗×c2 38 b3 c5 39 ♗d5 ♗d1+ 40 ♔f4 ♗c2 41 g5 ♗g6 42 ♗e4 ♗×e4 43 ♔×e4 ♔d7 44 b4 c×b4 45 ♔×d4 ♔e6 46 ♔c4 ♔×e5 47 ♔×b4 ♔d6 48 ♔b5 ♔c7 49 ♔a6 ♔c6 50 ♔a7 [50 h5 g6 (50 ... ♔c7? 51 ♔a7 ♔c6 52 ♔b8 ♔c5 53 ♔c7+-) 51 h6 ♔c5 52 ♔a7 b5 53 a×b5 ♔×b5 54 ♔b7 ♔c5 55 ♔c7 ♔d5 56 ♔d7 ♔e5 57 ♔e7 ♔d5 58 ♔f7 ♔d6 59 ♔g7 ♔e7 60 ♔×h7 ♔f7=] 50 ... b5
**½-½**

L/N5193

**1866-LON2-4** vi 66
**Steinitz, W.+De Vere, C.**
[Löwenthal & Medley]

1 e4 g6 2 d4 ♗g7 3 ♘f3 b6 4 ♗d3 e6 5 ♘c3 ♗b7 6 ♗e3 d6 7 ♕d2 ♘d7 8 0-0-0 ♘e7 9 h4 h5 [□ 9 ... c5] 10 ♘g5 e5 11 ♗c4 0-0 12 g4 e×d4 13 ♗×d4 ♗×d4 14 ♕×d4 ♘e5 15 ♗e2 h×g4 16 h5 ♘d5 17 e×d5 ♕×g5+ 18 ♔b1 ♖ae8?! 19 ♖dg1 c5 20 ♕a4 ♕f5 21 ♕×a7 ♗×d5 22 ♘×d5 ♘c6 23 ♕a4 ♕×d5 24 h×g6 ♖e4 [24 ... ♖×e2? 25 g×f7++-] 25 g×f7+ ♔×f7 26 ♕a6 ♘b4 27 ♕a7+ ♔e6 28 ♗b5 [□ 28 ♖h7] 28 ... ♖f7 29 ♖h6+ ♔e5 30 ♖h5+ ♔e6 31 ♖×d5 ♖×a7 32 ♖d2 c4 33 ♖gd1 d5 34 a3 ♖a5? 35 a×b4 ♖×b5 36 c3 ♔e5 37 ♔a2 ♔f4 38 ♖d4 ♔f3 39 ♔a3
**1-0**

L/N5193

**1866-LON2-5** vi 66
**Thorold, E.−MacDonnell, G.A.**
[Löwenthal & Medley]

1 e4 e5 2 f4 ♗c5 3 ♘f3 d6 4 c3 ♗g4 5 ♗e2 ♗×f3 6 ♗×f3 ♘c6 7 b4 ♗b6 8 b5 ♘ce7 9 d4 e×d4 10 c×d4 a6 11 b×a6 ♖×a6 12 0-0 ♘c6 13 ♗e3 ♕a8 14 ♖f2 ♕a7 15 ♖d2 ♖a4 16 ♘c3 ♖×d4 17 ♔h1 ♖×d2 18 ♗×d2 ♘ge7 19 ♘b5 ♕b8 20 ♕b3 0-0 [□ 20 ... ♕d8] 21 ♗c3 [□ 21 ♘×d6] 21 ... ♕c8 [□ 21 ... ♕d8] 22 ♘×d6 ♕e6 23 ♘c4 ♗d4 24 f5 ♕f6 25 ♖c1 ♗×c3 26 ♕×c3 ♕×c3 27 ♖×c3 ♖d8 28 g4 b5 29 ♘e3 b4 30 ♖c1 ♖d3 31 ♖e1 ♖a3-+ 32 ♖e2 ♘d4 33 f6 g×f6 34 ♘c2 ♘×c2 35 ♖×c2 ♖×f3 36 ♖×c7 ♘g6 37 ♖c4 ♘f4 38 ♔g1 ♖c3
**0-1**

L/N5193

### 1866-LON2-6 vi 66
**Thorold,E.–MacDonnell, G.A.**

[Löwenthal & Medley]

1 e4 e5 2 ♘c3 ♘f6 3 f4 d5 4 fxe5 ♘xe4 5 ♘f3 ♗g4 6 d3 ♘xc3 7 bxc3 d4 8 h3 ♗xf3 9 ♕xf3 ♘c6 10 ♗f4 dxc3 11 ♖b1?! ♘b4 12 ♕d1 [□ 12 ♖xb4] 12 ... ♕d4 13 ♗h2 ♕e3+ 14 ♗e2 ♗e7 15 g3 0-0 16 ♔f1 f6 17 e6 ♕xe6 18 ♔g2 ♕d5+ 19 ♗f3 ♕xa2 20 ♖xb4 ♗xb4 21 ♗xb7 ♖ab8 22 ♗f3 ♗d6 23 d4 ♖fe8 24 ♕d3 ♕b2 25 ♗e4 a5 26 ♗xh7+ ♔h8 27 ♗g6 ♖e7 28 ♖f1 [□ 28 ♕f5 ♕b7+? (28 ... ♕b5–+) 29 ♔f2 ♖e2+ 30 ♔xe2 ♕g2+ 31 ♔e3 ♕xh1–+; 31 ... ♖e8+ 32 ♗xe8 ♕xh1 33 ♗g6+–] 28 ... ♕b5 29 ♖f5 ♖e2+ 30 ♔f1 ♕xd3 31 ♖h5+ ♔g8 32 ♗xd3 g6 [32 ... ♖xh2? 33 ♗c4, 34 ♖h8+] 33 ♗c4+ ♔g7 34 ♔xe2 gxh5 35 h4 a4 36 ♔d3 c5 37 ♗g1 cxd4 38 ♗xd4 ♗xg3 39 ♗xc3 ♗xh4 **0-1** L/N5193

### 1866-LON2-7 vi 66
**Mann, H.–Mocatta, A.**

[Löwenthal & Medley]

1 e4 e5 2 ♘f3 ♘c6 3 ♗b5 a6 4 ♗a4 ♘f6 5 ♕e2 b5 6 ♗b3 ♗e7 7 c3 d6 8 h3 ♗e6 9 ♗c2 0-0 10 0-0 h6 11 d3 ♕c8 12 ♘h2 ♖b8 13 f4 exf4 14 ♗xf4 ♘e5 15 ♗xe5 dxe5 16 ♘d2 b4 17 ♘df3 bxc3 18 bxc3 ♗c5+ 19 d4 exd4 20 cxd4 ♗a7 21 ♕d3 c5 22 ♗b1 [□ 22 e5] 22 ... cxd4 23 ♘d2 ♕c3 24 e5 ♕xd3 25 ♗xd3 ♘d5 26 ♗xa6? ♘b4 27 ♗c4 ♘c2 28 ♖ac1 ♘e3 29 ♖f3 ♗xc4 30 ♘xc4 ♖fc8 31 ♘xe3 ♖xc1+ 32 ♘ef1 d3+ 33 ♔h1 d2 **0-1** L/N5193

### 1866-LON2-8 vi 66
**Lyttleyton, G.W.– Chinnery, W.M.**

[Löwenthal & Medley]

1 e4 e5 2 ♘f3 ♘c6 3 ♗b5 a6 4 ♗a4 ♘f6 5 ♘c3 d6 6 h3 ♗e7 7 0-0 0-0 8 d3 h6 9 ♗e3 ♘h7 10 ♗b3 ♗e6 11 ♗xe6 fxe6 12 ♘h2 ♕e8 13 ♕g4 ♖f6 14 f4 ♖g6 15 ♕e2 exf4 16 ♖xf4 ♗g5 17 ♖f3 ♘e5 18 ♖3f1 ♕e7 19 ♗xg5 ♘xg5 20 ♔h1 ♘d7 21 ♖f4 c6 22 ♖af1 e5 23 ♖f5 ♘f6 24 h4 ♘e6 25 ♕f2 ♘f4 26 g3 ♘6h5 27 g4 ♘h3 28 ♕f3? [28 ♕e3 ♘5f4 29 ♖f3 ♕xh4 30 ♖h5 ♕xh5 31 gxh5 ♖g1+ 32 ♕xg1+–] 28 ... ♘5f4 29 h5 ♖g5 30 ♖xg5 ♕xg5 31 ♕g3 ♔h7 32 ♘f3 ♕e7 33 ♘h4 ♖g8 34 ♘g6 ♕g5 35 ♘e2 ♘xe2 36 ♕xh3 ♘f4 37 ♘xf4 exf4 38 ♖f3 g6 39 hxg6+ ♖xg6 40 ♔h2 h5 41 ♖f1 ♖h6 42 ♔g1 hxg4 43 ♕g2 ♕c5+ 44 ♕f2 ♕xf2+ 45 ♖xf2 f3 46 ♖f1 ♔g6 47 ♔f2 ♔g5 48 ♔e3 ♖h2 49 ♖f2 ♖xf2 50 ♔xf2 ♔f4 **0-1** L/N5193

### 1866-LON2-9 vi 66
**Lyttelton, G.W.– Chinnery, W.M.**

[Löwenthal & Medley]

1 e4 e5 2 ♘f3 ♘f6 3 ♘c3 ♘c6 4 ♗c4 ♗c5 5 0-0 d6 6 h3 0-0 7 d3 ♘e7 8 ♗g5 c6 9 ♗xf6 gxf6 10 ♕d2 [□ 10 ♘h4] 10 ... ♘g6 11 d4 exd4 12 ♘xd4 ♘e5 13 ♗b3 [□ 13 ♗e2] 13 ... ♗xh3 14 f4 [14 gxh3? ♗xd4 △ 15 ♕xd4 ♘f3+] 14 ... ♔h8? [14 ... ♗~] 15 fxe5? [15 gxh3] 15 ... ♖g8 16 ♖f2 dxe5 17 ♕h6 ♗xg2 18 ♖xg2 [18 ♔h2 ♕xd4?+–; 18 ... ♖g6∓] 18 ... ♕xd4+ 19 ♔h2 ♖xg2+ 20 ♔xg2 ♕f2+ 21 ♔h3 ♖g8 22 ♘e2 ♕g2+ 23 ♔h4 ♕g4# **0-1** L/N5193

### 1866-LON2-10 vi 66
**Mongredien,A.Jnr.– Trelawny,J.**

[Löwenthal & Medley]

⟨Δf7⟩ 1 e4 ... 2 d4 e6 3 ♗e3 ♗b4+ 4 c3 ♗e7 5 ♗d3 ♘c6 6 ♘d2 ♘f6 7 e5 ♘d5 8 ♕h5+ ♔f8 9 ♘gf3 ♔g8 10 h4 ♘xe3 11 fxe3 ♕f8 12 ♘g5 g6 13 ♕g4 h5 14 ♕g3 ♗xg5 15 ♕xg5 ♕h6 16 ♕f6 [□ 16 ♕xg6++–] 16 ... ♕xe3+ 17 ♗e2 ♕g3+ 18 ♕f2 [□ 18 ♔d1] 18 ... ♕xf2+ 19 ♔xf2 d5 20 ♖af1 ♗d7 21 ♔e1 ♔g7 22 ♖f6 ♖af8 23 ♖hf1 ♘e7 24 c4 c6 25 b4 [□ 25 g4] 25 ... ♘f5 26 ♖xf8 ♖xf8 27 ♖f4 ♘e3 28 ♖xf8 ♔xf8 29 ♗d3 ♘xg2+ 30 ♔f2 ♘xh4 31 ♔g3 g5 32 ♗e2 ♘f5+ 33 ♔f2 g4 **0-1** L/N5193

### 1866-LON2-11 vi 66
**MacDonnell,G.A.–Steinitz, W.**

[Löwenthal & Medley]

1 e4 e5 2 ♘f3 d6 3 d4 exd4 4 ♗c4 ♘f6 5 0-0 ♗e7 6 ♗g5 c5 7 c3 [□ 7 e5] 7 ... dxc3 8 ♘xc3 0-0 9 ♕e2 ♘c6 10 h3 ♗e6 11 ♗d3 a6 12 ♖ad1 ♕c7 13 ♗xf6 ♗xf6 14 ♘d5 ♕d8 15 ♗b1 ♗d4 16 g4?

16 ... h5! 17 ♘xd4 ♘xd4 18 ♖xd4 cxd4 19 ♕d3 hxg4 20 e5 ♕h4 21 ♘e7+ ♔h8 22 exd6 gxh3 23 f4 ♗c4! 24 ♕f3 ♗xf1 25 ♔xf1 h2 26 ♗e4 ♖ad8 27 ♘f5 h1♕+ 28 ♕xh1 ♕xh1+ 29 ♗xh1 d3 30 ♗xb7 g6 31 ♗xa6 gxf5 32 ♗xd3 ♖xd6 33 ♗c4 ♖d2 **0-1** L/N5193

### 1866-LON2-12 vi 66
**Steinitz,W.+MacDonnell, G.A.**

[Löwenthal & Medley]

1 e4 e5 2 f4 d5 3 exd5 e4 4 ♘c3 ♘f6 5 d3 ♗b4 6 dxe4 ♘xe4 7 ♕d4 ♗xc3+ 8 bxc3 0-0 9 ♘f3 ♖e8 10 ♗e2 ♘f6 [□ 10 ... c5 11 dxc6 ♕xd4, ... ♘c3] 11 c4 ♗g4 12 ♕d3 c6 13 0-0 cxd5 14 cxd5 ♘xd5 15 h3 ♗d7 [□ 15 ... ♕b6+, 16 ... ♘b4] 16 ♕xd5 ♖xe2 17 ♘e5 ♕f6 [□ 17 ... ♕b6+] 18 ♕d3 ♖xe5 [18 ... ♕b6+ 19 ♔h1 ♗b5 20 c4±] 19 fxe5 ♕xe5 20 ♗a3 ♕c7

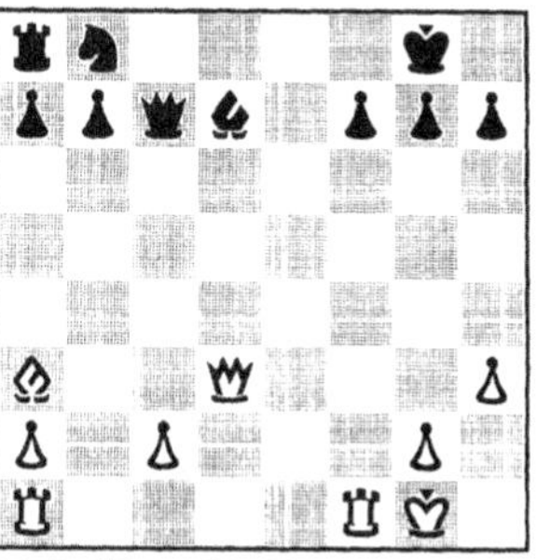

21 ♖xf7! ♕b6+ 22 ♔h1 ♔xf7 23 ♖f1+ ♕f6 24 ♕d5+ ♔g6 25 ♖xf6+ gxf6 26 ♕g8+ ♔f5 27 ♗d6 **1-0** L/N5193

### 1866-LON2-13 vi 66
**Chinnery,W.M.=Mocatta, A.**

[Löwenthal & Medley]

1 e4 e5 2 ♘f3 ♘c6 3 ♗b5 a6 4 ♗a4 ♘f6 5 d4 exd4 6 e5 ♘e4 7 0-0 ♗e7 8 ♗xc6 dxc6 9 ♘xd4 0-0 10 ♗e3 c5 11 ♘e2 ♕xd1 12 ♖xd1 b6 13 f3 ♘g5 14 ♘bc3 c6 15 f4 [□ 16 ♗xg5 △ ♖d6] 15 ... ♘e6 16 f5 ♘d4 17 ♗xd4 cxd4 18 ♘xd4 ♗c5 19 ♔h1 [19 g4!?] 19 ... ♗xd4 20 ♖xd4 ♗xf5 21 ♖d6 ♖fe8 22 ♖xc6 ♖xe5 23 ♖xb6 ♗xc2 24 h3 h6 **½-½** L/N5193

### 1866-LON2-14 vi 66
**Green, S.J.+Minchin, J.I.**

[Löwenthal & Medley]

1 e4 e5 2 ♗c4 ♗c5 3 ♘f3 d6 4 d3 ♘f6 5 h3 ♘c6 6 ♘c3 ♘e7 7 0-0 ♘g6 8 ♘h2 ♗e6 9 ♗xe6 fxe6 10 ♗e3 ♗b6 11 ♘a4 0-0 12 ♘xb6 axb6 13 f4 exf4 14 ♗xf4 ♘h5 15 ♗e3 ♘hf4 16 ♗xf4 ♘xf4 17 a3 ♖a5 18 ♘f3 ♖h5 19 ♔h2 e5 20 ♘g1 ♖g5 21 g3 ♘h5 22 g4 [□ 22 ♘e2] 22 ... ♘f4 23 ♔g3 h5 24 c3 [24 ♘f3 ♖g6 25 g5 h4+] 24 ... ♕f6 25 ♘f3 ♖g6 26 ♘h4 ♖g5 27 ♕f3 hxg4 28 hxg4

♕h6 29 ♕h1 ♖xg4+? [29 ... ♘e2+ 30 ♔h3 ♖f4 31 ♖xf4 ♘xf4+ 32 ♔g3 ♘e2+ 33 ♔h3∓; 33 ♔f3∓] 30 ♔xg4 ♕h5+ 31 ♔g3 ♕g5+ 32 ♔f3 ♘h5+ 33 ♘f5 ♕f4+ [33 ... ♖xf5++] 34 ♔e2 **1-0** L/N5193

**1866-LON2-15** vi 66
**Mongredien, A. Jnr.+ Green, V.**
[Löwenthal & Medley]

⟨Δf7⟩ 1 e4 ... 2 d4 d6 3 f4 c5 4 dxc5 [□ 4 d5] 4 ... ♕a5+ 5 ♘c3 ♕xc5 6 ♗d3 ♘f6 7 ♘f3 ♘c6 8 ♕e2 ♗g4 9 ♗b5 e6 10 ♗e3 ♕h5 11 0-0-0 ♗e7 12 ♗xc6+ bxc6 13 ♖hf1 0-0 14 h3 ♗xf3 15 ♖xf3 ♖ab8 [□ 15 ... ♕a5] 16 f5 exf5 17 exf5 ♕f7 18 ♕a6 d5 19 ♕xc6 ♖fc8 20 ♕e6 ♖xc3?! 21 ♕xf7+ ♔xf7 22 bxc3 ♘e4 23 ♖d3 ♗a3+ 24 ♔d1 ♖b2 25 ♗xa7 ♖xa2 26 ♖xd5 ♗b2 27 ♖d7+ ♔e8 28 ♖xg7 ♘xc3+ 29 ♖xc3 ♗xc3 30 ♖xh7 ♖a1+ 31 ♔e2 ♖e1+ 32 ♔d3 ♗f6 33 ♗c5 ♖e5 34 ♗d4 ♖xf5 35 ♗xf6 ♖xf6 36 g4 **1-0** L/N5193

**1866-LON2-16** vi 66
**Mocatta, A.– Steinitz, W.**
[Löwenthal & Medley]

⟨Δf7⟩ 1 e4 d6 2 d4 ♘f6 3 ♗d3 [□ 3 ♘c3] 3 ... ♘c6 4 c3 e5 5 ♘f3 ♗g4 6 ♗e3 ♕d7 7 ♘bd2 ♗e7 8 ♕b3 exd4 9 cxd4 ♘d8 10 0-0 c6 11 ♖ac1 ♗e6 12 d5 ♗f7 [12 ... cxd5? 13 ♗b5, 14 ♘d4] 13 ♗c4 0-0 14 ♘g5 a6 15 ♘xf7 ♘xf7 16 f4 [□ 16 dxc6, 17 ♗e6] 16 ... b5 17 ♗e2 cxd5 18 exd5 ♗d8 19 ♗f3 ♖e8 20 ♗d4 ♗a5 21 ♕d1 ♕f5 22 ♗xf6 ♕xf6 23 ♖c2 ♕xf4 24 ♔h1 ♕d4 25 ♘b3 ♕xd1 26 ♗xd1 ♗b6 27 ♖c6 ♗e3 28 ♗g4? [28 ♗c2] 28 ... ♘e5 29 h3 ♘xc6 30 dxc6 ♗b6 31 ♘c1 ♖e3 32 ♖d1 ♖ae8 33 ♘d3 ♖8e4 34 a3 ♖d4 35 ♘f2 ♖xd1+ 36 ♘xd1 ♖e1+ 37 ♔h2 g6 38 ♘c3 ♖c1 39 ♔g3 ♔f8 40 ♗f3 ♔e8 41 ♔f4 ♔d8 42 ♗e4 ♗d4 43 ♘e2 ♖f1+ 44 ♔g5 ♗xb2 45 ♔h6 ♖f7 46 ♗d5 ♖e7 47 ♗f3 ♗xa3 48 g4 ♖e3 49 ♘d4 ♗b2 **0-1** L/N5193

**1866-LON2-17** vi 66
**Mocatta, A.= Steinitz, W.**
[Löwenthal & Medley]

⟨Δf7⟩ 1 e4 e6 2 d4 ♘c6 3 ♘f3 b6 4 ♗d3 ♗b7 5 c4 ♘h6 6 ♘c3 [□ 6 ♗xh6] 6 ... ♘f7 7 0-0 g6 8 ♗e3 ♗g7 9 ♕d2 0-0 10 e5 ♖c8 11 ♘e4 ♘e7 12 ♘fg5 ♘xg5 13 ♗xg5 ♗xe4 14 ♗xe4 ♕e8 15 g4 c5 16 ♖ac1 cxd4 17 ♕xd4 ♘c6 18 ♗xc6 ♖xc6 19 ♗f6 ♗xf6 20 exf6 e5 [□ 20 ... ♖c5 Δ ... e5] 21 ♕d5+ ♔h8 22 g5 ♖c5 23 ♕e4 ♕e6 24 b4 ♖c7 25 ♖c3 ♖fc8 26 ♖fc1 ♔g8 27 a3 a6 28 a4 ♔f8 29 ♔f1 a5 30 b5 ♔e8 31 h4 ♔f8 32 ♔e2 ♔e8 33 ♔d2 ♕f5 34 ♕xf5 gxf5 35 ♔d3 ♔f7 36 ♖d1 d5 37 ♖dc1 d4 38 ♖3c2 ♖c5 39 f4 e4+ 40 ♔xd4 ♖d8+ 41 ♔e3 ♖d3+ 42 ♔e2 ♖h3 43 ♖cd2 ♖h2+ 44 ♔e3 ♖h3+ **½-½** L/N5193

**1866-LON2-18** vi 66
**Mocatta, A.– Steinitz, W.**
[Löwenthal & Medley]

⟨Δf7⟩ 1 e4 e6 2 d4 d5 3 ♕h5+ g6 4 ♕e5 ♘f6 5 ♗g5 ♗e7 6 exd5 [6 ♗b5+] 6 ... 0-0 7 dxe6 ♘g4 [7 ... ♘c6] 8 ♗xe7 ♕xe7 9 ♕e2 ♘xf2 10 ♘f3 ♘xh1 11 d5 ♘a6 12 ♘c3 c6 13 dxc6 bxc6 14 0-0-0 ♘c5 15 ♕e3 ♗xe6 16 ♗c4 ♖ae8 17 ♗xe6+ ♘xe6 18 ♖xh1

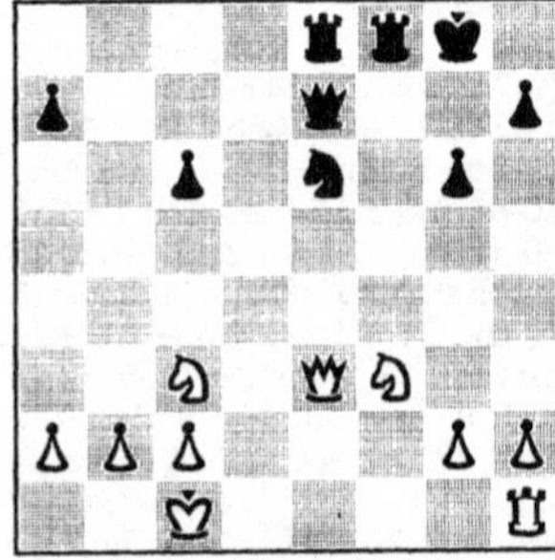

18 ... ♘f4! 19 ♕f2 ♘xg2 20 ♕xg2 ♕e3+ 21 ♘d2 ♖f2 22 ♕xf2 ♕xf2 23 ♘ce4 ♕g2 24 ♘f6+ ♔h8 25 ♖f1 ♖f8 26 b3 ♕g5 **0-1** L/N5193

**1866-LON2-19** vi 66
**Green, S.J.– Steinitz, W.**
[Löwenthal & Medley]

⟨Δf7⟩ 1 e4 ... 2 d4 e6 3 ♗d3 c5 4 c3 g6 5 e5 ♘c6 6 ♘f3 d6 7 ♗b5?! [7 exd6] 7 ... d5 8 h4 cxd4 9 cxd4 ♕a5+ 10 ♘c3 ♗b4 11 ♗xc6+ bxc6 12 ♗d2 ♗a6 13 ♘g5 ♔d7? 14 ♘f7 ♘e7 15 ♘xh8 ♖xh8 16 a3 ♗xc3 17 ♗xc3 ♕b5 18 a4 [□ 18 g4; □ 18 ♕c2; □ 18 ♕d2] 18 ... ♕c4 19 a5?! ♕b5 20 ♖a4 c5 21 dxc5 ♘c6 22 ♖h3? ♔c8 23 ♖f3? d4 24 ♗xd4 ♖d8 25 ♖e3 ♘xd4 26 ♖xd4 ♕f1+ **0-1** L/N5193

**1866-LON2-20** vi 66
**Green, S.J.– Steinitz, W.**
Löwenthal & Medley]

⟨Δf7⟩ 1 e4 ... 2 d4 ♘c6 3 d5 ♘e5 4 f4 ♘f7 5 e5 ♘gh6 6 c4 g6 7 ♘f3 ♗g7 8 c5 c6 9 ♘c3 0-0 10 ♗c4 cxd5 11 ♕xd5 e6 12 ♕e4 ♕c7 13 ♗e3 ♘f5 14 ♗f2 ♖b8 15 b4? d5 16 cxd6 [□ 16 ♗xd5] 16 ... ♘7xd6 17 exd6 ♗xc3+ 18 ♔e2 ♘xd6 19 ♗xe6+ ♗xe6 20 ♕xe6+ ♔h8 21 ♗e3 ♖be8 22 ♕d5 ♗xa1 23 ♖xa1 ♖xe3+ 24 ♔xe3 ♕c3+ 25 ♔f2 ♕b2+ 26 ♔g3 ♘f5+ 27 ♔h3 ♕xa1 28 ♕xb7 ♕xa2 29 ♘g5 ♘g7 30 ♕e4 h6 31 ♘f3 ♕e6+ **0-1** L/N5193

## ANDERSSEN✕STEINITZ

London

[1866-✕AS]

| | | | | | | | | | | | | | | | |
|---|---|---|---|---|---|---|---|---|---|---|---|---|---|---|---|
| A. Anderssen | 1 | 0 | 0 | 0 | 0 | 1 | 1 | 1 | 1 | 0 | 0 | 0 | 0 | 0 | 5 |
| W. Steinitz | 0 | 1 | 1 | 1 | 1 | 0 | 0 | 0 | 0 | 1 | 1 | 1 | 1 | 1 | 9 |

**1866-✕AS-1** 18 vii 66
**Anderssen, A.+ Steinitz, W.**
[Anderssen & Neumann]

1 e4 e5 2 ♘f3 ♘c6 3 ♗c4 ♗c5 4 b4 ♗xb4 5 c3 ♗c5 6 d4 exd4 7 0-0 d6 8 cxd4 ♗b6 9 d5 ♘a5 10 ♗b2 ♘e7! 11 ♗d3 0-0 12 ♘c3 c6 [□ 12 ... c5] 13 ♘e2 f5 14 ♖c1 fxe4 15 ♗xe4 ♗f5 16 ♗xf5 ♖xf5 17 dxc6 bxc6 [□ 17 ... ♘axc6] 18 ♘ed4 ♖f6 19 ♘xc6 ♘exc6 20 ♗xf6 ♕xf6 21 ♖xc6 ♘xc6 22 ♕d5+ ♕f7 23 ♕xc6 ♖d8 24 a4 d5 25 ♖d1 d4 26 ♖d3 ♕f5 27 ♕c4+ ♔h8 28 h3 ♖c8 29 ♕b3 h6 30 g4 ♕f6 31 ♕d5 ♖c3 32 ♘e5 ♖c5 33 ♕a8+ ♔h7 34 ♕e4+ ♔g8 35 ♘g6 ♖c3 [35 ... ♕d8 36 ♘e7+ ♔h8 37 ♖f3±] 36 ♕e8+ **1-0** L/N6051

**1866-✕AS-2**
**Steinitz, W.+ Anderssen, A.**
[Anderssen & Neumann]

1 e4 e5 2 f4 exf4 3 ♘f3 g5 4 ♗c4 g4 5 ♘e5 ♕h4+ 6 ♔f1 ♘h6 7 d4 d6 [□ 7 ... f3] 8 ♘d3 f3 9 g3 ♕h3+? [□ 9 ... ♕e7] 10 ♔e1 ♕h5 11 ♘c3 c6 12 ♗d2 ♕g6 13 ♘f4 ♕f6 14 ♗e3 ♘d7 15 ♔f2 ♘g8 [□ 15 ... ♘b6] 16 e5 ♕e7 17 e6 fxe6 18 ♘xe6 ♘df6 19 ♗f4 ♗xe6 20 ♗xe6 ♔d8 21 ♖e1 ♕g7 22 d5 c5 23 ♘b5 ♘e8 24 ♕d2 ♘gf6 25 ♕a5+ b6 26 ♕a4 [Δ 27 ♘xd6, 28 ♕c6±] 26 ... ♕b7 27 ♗g5 ♗e7 28 ♗f7 ♕d7 29 ♗xe8 ♖xe8 30 ♖e6± a6 31 ♖ae1 ♕xb5 32 ♕xb5 axb5 33 ♗xf6 ♖a7 34 ♖xd6+ ♖d7 35 ♖de6 ♗xf6 36 ♖xe8+ ♔c7 37 ♖8e6 ♗xb2 38 ♖e7 ♗d4+ 39 ♔f1 ♖xe7 40 ♖xe7+ ♔d6 41 ♖xh7 ♔xd5 42 ♖h4 ♔c4 43 ♖xg4 ♔c3 44 h4 ♔xc2 45 h5 ♗e3 46 ♖f4 c4 47 h6 ♗xf4 48 gxf4 c3 49 h7 ♔b1 50 h8♕ c2 51 ♕h7 ♔b2 52 ♕g7+ ♔xa2 53 ♕c3 **1-0** L/N6051

**1866-✕AS-3** 21 vii 66
**Anderssen, A.– Steinitz, W.**
[Anderssen & Neumann]

1 e4 e5 2 ♘f3 ♘c6 3 ♗c4 ♗c5 4 b4 ♗xb4 5 c3 ♗c5 6 d4 exd4 7 0-0 d3? [□ 7 ... d6] 8 ♕xd3 [8 ♘g5 ♘h6 9 ♘xf7 ♘xf7 10 ♗xf7+ ♔xf7 11 ♕h5+ g6 12

♕xc5 d6 13 ♕d5+ ♗e6 14 ♕d3±] 8 ... d6 9 ♗g5 ♘ge7 10 ♘bd2 h6 11 ♗h4 0-0 12 ♘b3 ♗b6 13 h3 ♗e6 14 ♖ad1 ♕d7 15 ♗d5 ♘g6 16 ♗g3 ♖ae8 17 c4 ♗xd5 18 exd5 ♘ce5 19 ♘xe5 ♘xe5 20 ♕c3 ♘g6 21 c5 dxc5 22 ♘xc5 ♕f5 23 ♘xb7 ♖e2 24 d6 cxd6 25 ♘xd6 ♕e6 26 a4 ♗d8

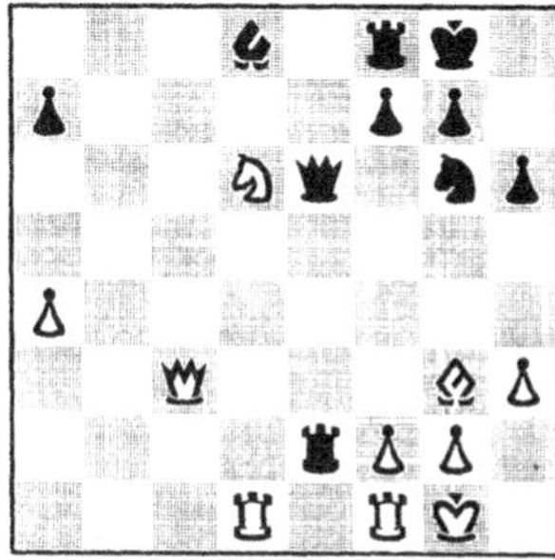

27 ♕c5? [◻ 27 ♖fe1] 27 ... f5 28 ♕xa7 f4 29 ♗h2 ♘h4 30 ♕b7 ♕g6 31 ♖d4? ♗b6 32 ♖dd1 [32 ♖xf4 ♖xf2→] 32 ... ♖e6 33 a5 ♗c5 34 a6 ♖e7 35 ♕d5+ ♔h8 36 a7 ♗xa7 37 ♖fe1 ♖xe1+ 38 ♖xe1 ♔h7 39 ♕e4 ♖f6 40 ♘b5 ♖e6 41 ♕xg6+ ♖xg6 42 ♘xa7 ♖xg2+ 43 ♔h1 ♖xh2+ 44 ♔xh2 ♘f3+ 45 ♔g2 ♘xe1+ 46 ♔f1 ♘d3 47 ♘c6 ♔g6 48 ♔e2 ♘c5 49 ♔f3 ♘e6 50 ♘e5+ ♔f5 51 ♘d3 [◻ 51 ♘c4] 51 ... g6 52 ♘e1 ♘d4+ 53 ♔g2 ♔e4 54 ♔f1 f3 55 ♔g1 g5 56 ♔h2 h5 57 ♔g3 ♘f5+ 58 ♔h2 g4 59 hxg4 hxg4 60 ♔g1 ♔d4 61 ♘c2+ ♔d3 62 ♘a3 [◻ 62 ♘b4+] 62 ... g3 63 ♘b5 g2 **0-1** L/N6051

## 1866-✕AS-4 23 vii 66
**Steinitz, W.+ Anderssen, A.**
[Anderssen & Neumann]

1 e4 e5 2 f4 exf4 3 ♘f3 g5 4 ♗c4 g4 5 ♘e5 ♕h4+ 6 ♔f1 ♘h6 7 d4 d6 8 ♘d3 f3 9 g3 ♕e7 10 ♘f2 [◻ 10 ♘c3] 10 ... ♗e6 11 ♘a3 ♗xc4+ 12 ♘xc4 ♕e6 13 d5 ♕g6 14 h3 ♘d7 15 ♗xh6 ♗xh6 16 hxg4 b5 17 ♘a3 ♘e5 18 ♘xb5 ♖b8 19 ♘d4 ♗e3 20 ♘xf3 ♕f6 21 ♔g2 ♗xf2 [◻ 21 ... ♖xb2] 22 ♘xe5 ♗xg3! 23 ♘d3 ♗h4 24 ♕e2 ♕e7 25 ♖af1 ♗g5 26 ♖f5 f6 27 ♖hf1 0-0 28 b3 ♖be8 29 ♖e1 ♔h8 30 ♘f2 ♗h4 31 ♖h5 ♗xf2 32 ♕xf2 ♖g8 33 ♕f5 ♖g7 34 ♖h6 ♖eg8 35 ♖eh1 ♖xg4+ 36 ♔f3 ♖g3+ 37 ♔e2 ♖3g7 38 ♖xf6 ♖g2+ 39 ♔d3 ♖8g3+? 40 ♔c4 ♖e3 41 ♖f8+ ♖g8 42 ♖xg8+ ♔xg8 43 ♖g1+ **1-0** L/N6051

## 1866-✕AS-5 25 vii 66
**Anderssen, A.– Steinitz, W.**
[Anderssen & Neumann]

1 e4 e5 2 ♘f3 ♘c6 3 ♗c4 ♗c5 4 b4 ♗xb4 5 c3 ♗c5 6 d4 exd4 7 0-0 d6 8 cxd4 ♗b6 9 d5 ♘a5 10 ♗b2 ♘e7 11 ♗d3 0-0 12 ♘c3 c6 13 ♕d2 [13 ♘e2] 13 ... f5 14 ♖ae1 fxe4 15 ♘xe4 ♘xd5 16 ♘eg5 h6 17 ♘e6 ♗xe6 18 ♖xe6 ♕d7∓ 19 ♖g6 ♘f4 20 ♖xg7+ ♕xg7 21 ♗xg7 ♔xg7 22 ♘h4 [◻ 22 ♗b1] 22 ... ♘xd3 23 ♕xd3 ♖f6 24 ♘f5+ ♔f8 25 ♕h3 ♖e8 26 ♕g4 ♖ee6 27 ♕g7+ ♔e8 28 g4 d5 29 ♔g2 ♘c4 30 ♕xb7 ♖e2 31 ♕g7 ♖fe6 32 h4 d4? 33 ♕g8+ ♔d7 34 ♕f7+ ♔c8 35 ♘g7 ♘e3+ 36 ♔g1? [36 ♔f3+–] 36 ... ♖e4 37 f3 d3 38 fxe4 ♘xg4+ 39 ♖f2 ♗xf2+ 40 ♔h1 ♖e1+ 41 ♔g2 ♖g1+ 42 ♔f3 ♘e5+ 43 ♔xf2 ♘xf7 44 ♔xg1 d2 **0-1** L/N6051

## 1866-✕AS-6 27 vii 66
**Steinitz, W.– Anderssen, A.**
[Anderssen & Neumann]

1 e4 c5 2 g3 ♘c6 3 ♗g2 e5! 4 ♘e2 ♘f6 5 ♘bc3 d6 6 0-0 ♗e7 7 f4 h5 8 h3 ♗d7 9 ♘d5 ♕c8 10 ♘xf6+ ♗xf6 11 f5 ♘e7 12 c4 ♕d8 13 ♘c3 ♗c6 14 d3 ♕d7 15 a3 a5 16 b3 b5 17 ♗e3 b4 18 axb4 cxb4 19 ♘a4 ♗xa4 20 ♖xa4 ♘c6 21 ♕d2 ♗d8 22 d4 ♗b6 23 d5 ♕a7 24 ♗xb6 ♕xb6+ 25 ♔h1 ♘d8∓ 26 ♕g5 ♔f8 27 f6 g6 28 h4 ♘b7 29 ♗h3 ♖d8 30 ♖a2 ♔e8 31 ♖d1 ♖a8 32 ♕d2 ♘c5 33 ♕e3 ♔d8 34 ♗e6 ♕b7 35 ♔g1 a4 36 bxa4 b3 37 ♖aa1 b2 38 ♖ab1 ♖xa4 39 ♗h3 ♔c7 40 ♗f1 ♖ha8 41 ♖d2 ♖b4 42 ♔h2 ♖a1 43 ♖dd1 ♖b3 44 ♕h6 ♖xb1 45 ♖xb1 ♕b4 46 ♕f8 ♕d2+ 47 ♗g2 ♕d3 48 ♕xf7+ ♘d7 49 c5 ♕xg3+ 50 ♔g1 ♖c3 51 cxd6+ ♔b6 52 ♖xb2+ ♔c5 53 ♖b1 ♖c2 54 ♖b5+ ♔c4 **0-1** L/N6051

## 1866-✕AS-7 28 vii 66
**Anderssen, A.+ Steinitz, W.**
[Anderssen & Neumann]

1 e4 e5 2 ♘f3 ♘c6 3 ♗c4 ♗c5 4 b4 ♗xb4 5 c3 ♗c5 6 0-0 d6 7 d4 exd4 8 cxd4 ♗b6 9 d5 ♘a5 10 ♗b2 ♘e7 11 ♗d3 ♘g6 12 ♘c3 0-0 13 ♕d2 ♗d7 14 ♘e2 c5 15 ♘g3 ♗c7? [15 ... f6] 16 ♗xg7

16 ... f6 [16 ... ♔xg7? 18 ♘h5+ ♔h8! 19 ♕h6 ♖g8 20 ♘g5+–] 17 ♗xf8 ♕xf8 18 ♘f5 b5 19 ♖ac1 ♘b7 20 ♔h1 a5 21 g4 ♖e8 22 g5 c4 23 gxf6 ♕xf6 24 ♘g5 ♘e5 25 ♗b1 ♘c5 26 ♖g1 ♔h8 27 ♕c3 ♗xf5 28 exf5 b4 29 ♕g3 ♗d8 30 ♘xh7 ♕f7 [30 ... ♔xh7 31 ♕h3+ ♕h6 32 f6+ ♘d3 33 ♖g7+ ♔h8 33 ♕xh6#] 31 f6 ♕xd5+ 32 ♖g2 ♖g8 33 ♘g5 ♗xf6 34 ♘f7+ **1-0** L/N6051

## 1866-✕AS-8 30 vii 66
**Steinitz, W.– Anderssen, A.**
[Anderssen & Neumann]

1 e4 e5 2 f4 exf4 3 ♘f3 g5 4 ♗c4 g4 5 ♘e5 ♕h4+ 6 ♔f1 ♘h6 7 d4 d6 8 ♘d3 f3 9 g3 ♕e7 10 ♘c3 [10 ♘f2] 10 ... ♗e6 11 d5 ♗c8 12 e5 dxe5 13 ♘xe5 ♕xe5 14 ♗f4 ♕g7 15 ♘b5 ♗d6! 16 ♕e1+ [16 ♗xd6 cxd6∓] 16 ... ♔d8 17 ♗xd6 cxd6 18 ♕b4 ♘f5 19 ♗d3 ♘a6 20 ♕a3 ♘c5 21 ♗xf5 ♕h6! 22 ♗d3 [22 ♗xc8 ♕d2–+] 22 ... ♖e8 23 h4 ♕d2 24 ♖g1 ♖e2 **0-1** L/N6051

## 1866-✕AS-9 1 viii 66
**Anderssen, A.+ Steinitz, W.**
[Anderssen & Neumann]

1 e4 e5 2 ♘f3 ♘c6 3 ♗c4 ♗c5 4 b4 ♗xb4 5 c3 ♗c5 6 0-0 d6 7 d4 exd4 8 cxd4 ♗b6 9 d5 ♘a5 10 ♗d3 ♘e7 11 ♗b2 0-0 12 ♘c3 ♘g6 13 ♘e2 c5 14 ♕d2 ♗c7 15 ♖ac1 ♖b8 16 ♘g3 f6 17 ♘f5 b5 18 ♔h1 b4 19 ♖g1 [△ 20 g4] 19 ... ♗xf5 20 exf5 ♘e5 21 ♗xe5 fxe5 22 ♘g5 ♕d7 23 ♘e6± ♖fc8 24 g4 b3 25 g5 bxa2 26 g6 ♘b3 27 gxh7+ ♔h8 28 ♕g5 [△ 29 f6] 28 ... ♗d8 29 ♘xd8 ♘xc1 [29 ... ♖xd8 30 f6 ♖b7 31 fxg7+ ♕xg7 32 ♕xd8+] 30 f6 ♖c7 31 f7 ♕xf7 32 ♘xf7+ ♖xf7 33 ♖xc1 ♖xf2 34 ♕e7 ♖bf8 35 ♕xa7 ♖8f7 36 ♕b8+ ♖f8 37 ♕xd6 e4 38 ♗xe4 c4 39 ♕b4 c3 40 ♖g1 ♖8f7 41 ♕xc3 ♖7f6 42 d6 **1-0** L/N6051

## 1866-✕AS-10 3 viii 66
**Steinitz, W.+ Anderssen, A.**
[Anderssen & Neumann]

1 e4 e5 2 f4 exf4 3 ♘f3 g5 4 ♗c4 g4 5 ♘e5 ♕h4+ 6 ♔f1 ♘h6 7 d4 d6? 8 ♘d3 f3 9 g3 ♕e7 10 ♘c3 ♗e6 11 ♗b3 ♗g7 12 ♗e3 ♗xb3 13 axb3 c6 14 ♕d2 ♘g8 15 e5 d5 16 ♗g5 ♕e6 17 ♘a4 ♘a6 [◻ 17 ... h6] 18 ♘ac5 ♘xc5 19 ♘xc5 ♕g6 20 ♘xb7 ♘h6 21 ♘d6+ ♔d7 22 h3 f6 23 exf6 ♗f8 [23 ... ♗xf6 24 ♗xh6 ♔xd6 25 ♕b4+±] 24 ♘b7 ♘f5 25 ♗f4 gxh3 26 ♔f2 ♕xf6 27 ♗e5 ♕g6 28 ♖xh3! ♗h6 29 ♘c5+ ♔e8 30 ♖xh6 ♘xh6 31 ♗xh8 ♔f7 32 ♗e5 ♕h5 33 ♕f4+ ♔g8 34 ♖h1 ♘g4+ [34 ... ♕xh1 35 ♕g5+ ♔f8 36 ♕g7+ ♔e8 37

♕d7+ ♔f8 38 ♘e6+ ♔g8 39 ♕g7#] 35 ♔g1 **1-0** L/N6051

**1866-⚔AS-11** 4 viii 66
**Anderssen, A.– Steinitz, W.**
[Anderssen & Neumann]

1 e4 e5 2 ♘f3 ♘c6 3 ♗c4 ♗c5 4 b4 ♗xb4 5 c3 ♗c5 6 0-0 d6 7 d4 exd4 8 cxd4 ♗b6 9 d5 ♘a5 10 ♗b2 ♘e7 11 ♗d3 0-0 12 ♘c3 c6 13 ♕d2 cxd5 14 ♘xd5 ♘g6 15 ♘xb6 ♕xb6 16 ♖ab1 ♕d8 17 ♘d4 [□ 17 ♗c3] 17 ... ♘e5 18 ♗a1 ♘xd3 19 ♕xd3 ♘c6 20 ♘b5 [□ 20 ♘xc6 bxc6 21 ♕c3±] 20 ... ♕e7 21 ♘xd6 ♖d8 22 ♕g3 f6 23 ♖bd1 ♗e6 24 ♖fe1? ♗xa2 25 ♘f5 ♕f8

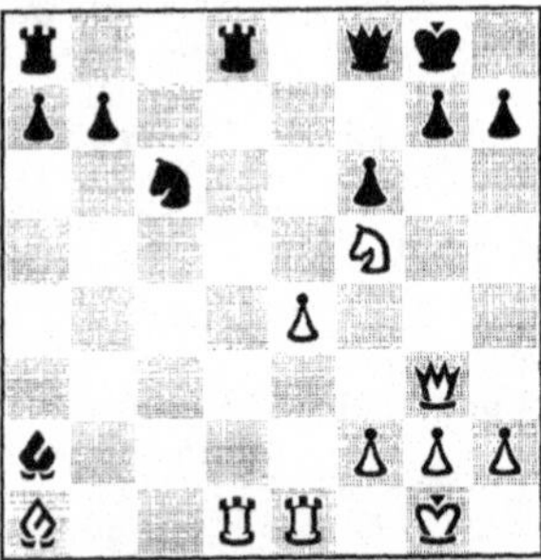

26 ♘d6 [□ 26 ♖d6] 26 ... ♖d7 27 ♖d2 ♖ad8 28 ♖ed1 ♗e6 29 h4 a5 30 ♗c3 a4 31 ♖d3 a3 32 h5 h6 33 ♖3d2 a2 34 ♗b2 ♘e5 35 ♗a3 ♖xd6 36 ♗xd6 ♖xd6 37 ♖xd6 ♕xd6 38 ♖c1 ♕d4 39 ♕a3 ♘g4 40 ♖f1 ♘xf2 41 ♔h2 ♘g4+ 42 ♔h1 ♕e5 43 g3 ♕xe4+ **0-1** L/N6051

**1866-⚔AS-12** 6 viii 66
**Steinitz, W.+ Anderssen, A.**
[Anderssen & Neumann]

1 e4 c5 2 g3 ♘c6 3 ♗g2 e5! 4 ♘e2 d6 5 0-0 ♘f6 6 c3 ♕c7 7 d4 ♗d7 8 ♘a3 a6 9 ♘c2 ♕c8 10 ♘e3 ♗e7 11 ♘d5 ♗d8 12 dxc5 dxc5 13 ♗g5 ♘xd5 14 ♗xd8 ♘xc3 [□ 14 ... ♘e3 Löwenthal] 15 ♘xc3 ♕xd8 16 ♕d6 ♕e7 17 ♕c7 0-0 18 ♘d5 ♕d8 19 ♕xb7 ♖b8 20 ♕xa6 ♖xb2 21 ♕c4 ♕a5 22 ♖fc1 ♖a8 23 ♕xc5 ♕xc5 24 ♖xc5 ♘d4 25 ♖c7 ♗e6 26 a4 h6 27 h3 ♖a5 28 ♖a3 ♔h8 29 ♖a1= ♔h7 30 ♖a3 h5 31 ♖a1 ♔h6 32 ♘c3? ♖c2 33 ♖e1 ♖xa4 34 ♘xa4 ♖xc7 35 ♘b6 ♖c2 36 ♘d5 ♖d2 37 ♘e3 g6 38 ♖a1 ♗a2 39 ♗f1 f6 40 ♘c4 ♗xc4 41 ♗xc4 h4 42 g4 ♘f3+ 43 ♔g2 ♘g5 44 ♗d5 ♖d3 45 ♖a6 ♘xh3 46 ♖xf6 ♔g5 47 ♖d6 ♘f4+ 48 ♔h2 ♖d2 49 ♔g1 h3 50 ♖a6 ♔h4 51 ♗c4 ♖d4 52 ♗b5 ♔xg4 53 ♖a3 ♔h4 54 ♖a8 g5 55 ♖e8 ♖d1+ 56 ♔h2 ♖d2 57 ♔g1 h2+ 58 ♔xh2 ♖xf2+ 59 ♔h1 g4 60 ♖xe5 g3 61 ♖e8 ♖h2+ **0-1** L/N6051

**1866-⚔AS-13** 8 viii 66
**Anderssen, A.– Steinitz, W.**
[Anderssen & Neumann]

1 e4 e5 2 ♘f3 ♘c6 3 ♗b5 ♘f6 4 d3 d6 5 ♗xc6+ bxc6 6 h3 g6 7 ♘c3 ♗g7 8 0-0 0-0 9 ♗g5 h6 10 ♗e3 c5 11 ♖b1 ♘e8 12 b4 cxb4 13 ♖xb4 c5 14 ♖a4 ♗d7 15 ♖a3 f5 16 ♕b1 ♔h8 17 ♕b7? a5 18 ♖b1 a4 19 ♕d5 ♕c8 20 ♖b6 ♖a7 21 ♔h2 f4 22 ♗d2 g5 23 ♕c4 ♕d8 24 ♖b1 ♘f6 25 ♔g1 ♘h7 26 ♔f1 h5 27 ♘g1 g4 28 hxg4 hxg4 29 f3 ♕h4 30 ♘d1 ♘g5 31 ♗e1 ♕h2 32 d4 gxf3 33 gxf3 ♘h3∓ 34 ♗f2 ♘xg1 35 dxc5 ♕h3+ 36 ♔e1 ♘xf3+ 37 ♖xf3 ♕xf3 38 ♘c3 dxc5 39 ♗xc5 ♖c7 40 ♘d5 ♖xc5 41 ♕xc5 ♕xe4+ 42 ♔f2 ♖c8 **0-1** L/N6051

**1866-⚔AS-14** 10 viii 66
**Steinitz, W.+ Anderssen, A.**
[Anderssen & Neumann]

1 e4 e5 2 f4 ♗c5 3 ♘f3 d6 4 ♗c4 ♘f6 5 d3 0-0 6 ♕e2 ♗g4 7 fxe5 [7 h3? ♘h5 8 hxg4 ♘g3∓] 7 ... dxe5 8 ♗e3 ♘bd7 9 ♘bd2 c6 10 ♗b3 b5 11 0-0 ♕b6 12 ♗xc5 ♘xc5 13 ♔h1 ♖ae8 14 ♕f2 a5? 15 a4 h6 16 ♘h4 bxa4 17 ♗xa4 ♗e6 18 b3 ♘g4 19 ♕g1 ♕b4 20 ♘hf3 ♗d7 21 ♘c4 ♘xa4 22 ♖xa4 ♕c3 23 h3 ♘f6 24 ♖c1 ♘h5 25 ♕e1 ♕xe1+ 26 ♖xe1 f6 27 ♖xa5 ♖e6 28 d4 ♖b8 29 dxe5 ♗e8 30 ♘d4 ♖e7 31 ♖c5 ♖c7 32 ♘d6 fxe5 33 ♘xe8 ♖xe8 34 ♖xc6 ♖ec8 35 ♖xc7 ♖xc7 36 ♘f3 ♖xc2 37 ♘xe5 ♖c3 38 b4 ♖b3 39 ♘c6 ♘f4 40 e5 ♘d3 41 ♖a1 ♘xb4 42 ♖a8+ ♔h7 43 ♖b8 ♘xc6 44 ♖xb3 ♘xe5 45 ♖b6 ♘g6 46 ♔h2 ♘e5 47 ♔g3 ♘d7 48 ♖d6 ♘f6 49 ♔f4 ♘g8 50 g4 ♘e7 51 h4 ♘g6+ 52 ♔g3 ♘e7 53 ♖e6 ♘g6 54 h5 ♘f8 55 ♖e7 ♔g8 56 ♔f4 ♘h7 57 ♔f5 ♔f8 58 ♖a7 ♔g8 59 ♖c7 ♘g5 60 ♔g6 ♘e6 61 ♖c8+ ♘f8+ 62 ♔f5 ♔f7 63 ♖a8 ♔g8 64 ♔e5 ♔f7 65 ♖a7+ ♔g8 66 ♔d6 ♘h7 67 ♔e6 ♘f6 68 ♔f5 ♔h7 69 ♖e7 ♘d5 70 ♖e6 ♘c7 71 ♖e5 ♘a6 72 ♔e6 ♘b4 73 ♔f7 ♘d3 74 ♖e8 ♘f4 75 ♔f8 ♘d5 76 ♖e5 ♘f4 77 ♔f7 ♘h3 78 ♖e3 ♘g5+? [78 ... ♘f4=] 79 ♔f8 ♔h8 80 ♖e7 ♘h7+ 81 ♔f7 ♘f6 82 ♔g6 ♘g8 83 ♖xg7 ♘f6 84 ♖a7 ♘g8 85 ♖h7# **1-0** L/N6051

**BIRD⚔STEINITZ** London
**[1866-⚔BS]**

H.E. Bird

0 ½ 0 1 ½ 0 1 0 0 1 1 ½ 0 ½ ½ 1 Φ ?

W. Steinitz

1 ½ 1 0 ½ 1 0 1 1 0 0 ½ 1 ½ ½ 0 Φ ?

**1866-⚔BS-1**
**Steinitz, W.+ Bird, H.E.**
[Boden]

1 e4 e5 2 ♘c3 ♘c6 3 f4 ♘f6 4 fxe5 ♘xe5 5 d4 ♘g6 6 e5+– ♘g8 7 ♘f3 ♗b4 8 ♗d3 d5 9 0-0 ♗e6 10 ♘g5 ♘8e7 11 ♘xe6 fxe6 12 ♕g4 ♕d7 13 ♗g5 0-0-0 14 ♖f7 ♖de8 15 ♘e2 ♕c6 16 c3 ♗a5 17 a4 [△ 18 ♗b5 ♕~ 19 ♗xe8; 18 b4 ♗b6 19 a5] 17 ... ♕b6 18 b4 ♗xb4 19 cxb4 ♘xe5 20 a5! ♕xb4 21 ♕xe6+ ♘d7 22 ♖b1 ♕a3 23 ♗f5 **1-0** M392

**1866-⚔BS-2**
**Bird, H.E.= Steinitz, W.**

1 e4 e5 2 ♘f3 ♘c6 3 ♗b5 ♘f6 4 d4 exd4 5 e5 ♘e4 6 0-0 ♗e7 7 c3 dxc3 8 ♘xc3 ♘xc3 9 bxc3 0-0 10 ♕c2 d6 11 ♗f4 ♘xe5 12 ♘xe5 dxe5 13 ♖ad1 ♗d6 14 ♗xe5 ♗g4 15 ♖d4 ♗h5 16 ♗d3 ♗g6 17 ♗xg6 hxg6 18 ♕d2 ♕e7 19 ♗xd6 cxd6 20 ♖e1 ♕c7 21 ♖xd6 ♖ad8 22 ♖xd8 ♖xd8 23 ♕g5 ♖c8 24 ♖d1 **½-½** M392

**1866-⚔BS-3**
**Steinitz, W.+ Bird, H.E.**

1 e4 e6 2 d4 d5 3 ♘c3 dxe4 4 ♘xe4 f5 5 ♘c3 ♘f6 6 ♘f3 ♗d6 7 ♗c4 0-0 8 0-0 c6 9 ♖e1 ♘d5 10 ♘g5 ♖f6 11 ♕h5 h6 12 ♘f3 ♗d7 13 ♘e5 ♗e8 14 ♕f3 ♘d7 15 ♗b3 ♔h7 16 ♗d2 g5 17 ♘e2 ♘f8 18 c4 ♘e7 19 ♘g3 ♗c7 20 ♗c3 h5 21 ♘e4 ♗xe5 22 ♘xg5+ ♔g7 23 ♖xe5 ♘eg6 24 ♖ee1 ♔h6 25 ♘h3 f4 26 d5 ♘h4 27 ♕e4 ♖f5 28 dxe6 ♘h7 29 e7 ♕d7 30 ♖ad1 ♕c7 31 ♕e6+ ♗g6 32 ♖d7 **1-0** M392

**1866-⚔BS-4**
**Bird, H.E.+ Steinitz, W.**
[Boden]

1 e4 e5 2 ♘f3 ♘c6 3 ♗b5 ♘f6 4 0-0 ♘xe4 5 ♖e1 ♘d6 6 ♗xc6 dxc6 7 d4 e4 8 ♘c3 f5?! 9 ♘e5 ♗e6 10 d5 cxd5 11 ♘xd5 ♘f7!? 12 ♘f4! ♕f6 13 ♘f3 ♗e7 14 ♘h5 ♕g6 15 ♘d4! ♗d7 16 ♘f4 ♕d6 17 c4 0-0-0 18 ♘d5 ♖he8 19 ♕b3 ♘e5 20 ♗f4 g5?? 21 c5 ♕a6 22 ♗xe5 ♗a4 23 ♘xc7! ♗xb3 24 ♘xa6 ♗c4 25 ♘c7 ♖g8 26 ♘xf5 ♗f8 27 ♘d6+ **1-0** M392

**1866-⚔BS-5**
**Steinitz, W.= Bird, H.E.**
[Boden]

1 e4 e6 2 d4 d5 3 ♘c3 dxe4 4 ♘xe4 ♘c6 5 ♘f3 f5 6 ♘c3 ♘f6 7 ♗c4 ♗b4 8 0-0 ♗xc3 9 bxc3 0-0 10 ♘e5? ♘a5 [□ 10 ... ♘xe5 11 dxe5 ♘d5∓] 11 ♗b3 b6 12 ♖e1 ♘xb3 13 axb3 ♗b7 14 ♘d3 ♘e4 15 ♗b2 ♕h4 16 f3 ♘g5∓ 17 ♕e2 ♖f6 18 ♕f2

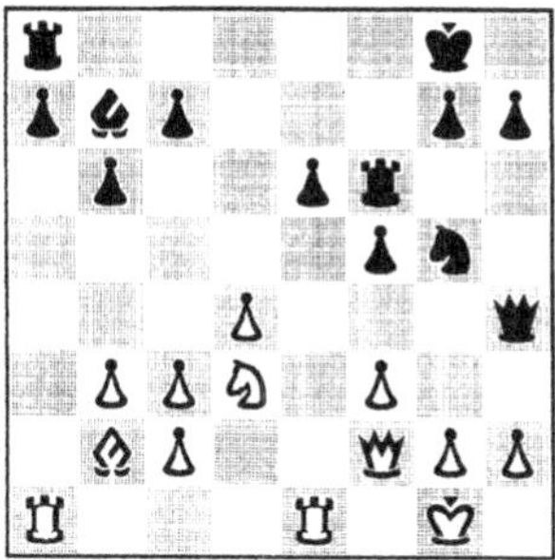

18 ... ♖g6 [□ 18 ... ♘h3+ 19 gxh3 ♖g6+ 20 ♔f1 (20 ♔h1 ♕xf2 21 ♘xf2 ♗xf3#) 20 ... ♕xh3+ 21 ♔e2 ♖g2→ Barnes] 19 ♕xh4 ♘xf3+ 20 ♔f2 ♘xh4 21 ♘f4 ♘xg2 22 ♘xg6 ♘xe1 23 ♖xe1 hxg6 24 ♖xe6 ♔f7∓ 25 ♖e2 ♗e4 26 ♗c1 ♖h8 27 ♔g3 ♔e6 28 c4 c6 29 h4 a5 30 ♗f4 ♔d7 31 c3 ♖a8 32 ♗e5 a4 33 bxa4 ♗d3 34 ♖e3 ♗xc4 35 ♗xg7 ♖xa4 36 ♔f4 ♖a1 37 ♗h6 ♖g1 38 ♗g5 ♖g4+ 39 ♔e5 ♗d5 40 ♖e1 ♖e4+ 41 ♖xe4 ♗xe4 42 ♔f6 f4 43 ♗xf4 ½-½ M392

**1866-⚔BS-6**
**Bird, H.E.– Steinitz, W.**
[Boden]

1 f4 e5 2 fxe5 d6 3 exd6 ♗xd6 4 ♘f3 ♘f6 5 d4 ♘c6 6 ♗g5 ♗g4 7 e3 ♕d7 8 ♗xf6 gxf6 9 ♗b5 0-0-0 10 d5?? [□ 10 ♘c3] 10 ... ♕e7 11 ♗xc6 [□ 11 ♕e2 (11 dxc6?? ♗b4+ △ 12 ... ♖xd1)] 11 ... ♕xe3+ 12 ♕e2 ♕c1+ 13 ♕d1 ♖de8+ 14 ♗xe8 ♖xe8+ 15 ♔f2 ♕e3+ 16 ♔f1 ♗xf3 17 gxf3 ♗c5 18 ♔g2 ♖g8+ **0-1** M392

**1866-⚔BS-7**
**Steinitz, W.– Bird, H.E.**
[Boden]

1 e4 e6 2 d4 d5 3 ♘c3 dxe4 4 ♘xe4 f5 5 ♘g5 ♗e7 6 ♘1h3 ♘c6 7 ♗b5 ♘f6 8 0-0 0-0 9 ♗xc6 bxc6 10 ♘f4 ♕d6 11 c4 c5 12 dxc5 ♕c6 13 b4 ♘g4 14 ♘f3 ♗f6 15 ♖b1 g5 16 ♘d3 [□ 16 ♘h5] 16 ... e5 17 ♘xg5 f4 18 b5 ♕e8 19 ♘e4 ♗f5 20 f3 ♘xh2 21 ♔xh2 ♕h5+ 22 ♔g1 ♖ad8 [22 ... ♗h4] 23 ♕e2 ♗h4 24 g4? fxg3 25 ♗b2 ♗xe4 26 ♕xe4 ♗g5 27 ♕e2 ♗e3+ 28 ♘f2 ♕h2# **0-1** M392

**1866-⚔BS-8**
**Bird, H.E.– Steinitz, W.**
[Boden]

1 e4 e5 2 ♘f3 ♘c6 3 ♗b5 ♘f6 4 d4 exd4 5 0-0 ♗e7 6 e5 ♘e4 7 ♖e1 ♘c5 8 ♘xd4 ♘xd4 9 ♕xd4 0-0 10 ♘c3 ♔h8 11 ♗e3 ♘e6 12 ♕e4 f5 13 exf6 ♗xf6 14 ♗d3 g6 15 ♖ad1 [□ 15 ♗h6] 15 ... c6 16 ♕b4 d5 17 ♗e2 ♗e7 18 ♕b3 ♘c5 19 ♗d4+ ♔g8 20 ♗xc5 ♗xc5 21 ♗f3 ♕b6 22 ♕xb6 axb6 23 a3 ♗f5 24 ♖ad2 b5 25 g4 ♗d7 26 ♔g2 ♖f7 27 ♖d3 ♖af8 28 ♖e2 ♔g7 29 b4 ♗d6 30 h3 ♔h6 31 ♖d2 ♗f4 32 ♖d1 ♔g7 33 ♘e2 ♗c7 34 ♘g3 h5 35 ♖1d2 hxg4 36 ♗xg4 ♗xg4 37 hxg4 ♔h6 38 ♖e2 ♔g5 39 f3 ♖h8 40 ♘f1 ♖fh7 41 ♖de3 ♖h1 42 ♖e8 ♖8h6 43 ♖f8 ♗d6 44 ♖f7 ♖h7 45 ♖xh7 ♖xh7 46 ♖e8? ♖e7 47 ♖xe7 ♗xe7 48 ♘e3 ♗f6 49 ♘d1 ♔f4 50 ♔f2 ♗d4+ 51 ♔e2 b6 52 c3 ♗f6 53 ♔f2 c5 54 ♘e3 d4 55 ♘d5+ ♔e5 56 ♘xf6 dxc3 57 ♔e3 ♔xf6 58 f4 c4 59 ♔e2 ♔e6 60 ♔d1 ♔d5 61 ♔c2 ♔e4 62 f5 gxf5 63 gxf5 ♔xf5 64 ♔xc3 ♔e4 65 a4 bxa4 66 ♔xc4 b5+ **0-1** M392

**1866-⚔BS-9**
**Steinitz, W.+ Bird, H.E.**
[Boden]

1 e4 e6 2 d4 d5 3 ♘c3 dxe4 4 ♘xe4 ♘c6 5 ♘f3 ♘f6 6 ♘xf6+ ♕xf6 7 ♗g5 ♕f5 [□ 7 ... ♕g6] 8 ♗d3 ♕g4?? 9 h3 ♕xg2 10 ♖h2 ♕xh2 11 ♘xh2 ♘xd4 12 ♗b5+ **1-0** M392

**1866-⚔BS-10**
**Bird, H.E.+ Steinitz, W.**

1 e4 e5 2 ♘f3 d6 3 d4 exd4 4 ♕xd4 ♘c6 5 ♗b5 ♗d7 6 ♗xc6 ♗xc6 7 ♘c3 ♘f6 8 ♗g5 ♗e7 9 0-0-0 0-0 10 h3 ♖e8 11 ♖he1 h6 12 ♗h4 ♘d7 13 ♗xe7 ♕xe7 14 ♘h2 ♘c5 15 f3 f5 16 ♘d5 ♕f7 17 e5 ♘e6 18 ♕c4 ♘f8 19 f4 ♖ad8 20 ♘f3 ♘g6 21 e6 ♖xe6 22 ♖xe6 ♗xd5 23 ♕xd5 ♘xf4 24 ♕xb7 ♘xe6 25 ♕xa7 ♘c5 26 b4 ♘e4 27 ♔b2 ♖e8 28 ♖d3 ♖e7 29 ♕a8+ ♔h7 30 ♕d5 ♕f6+ 31 c3 ♘f2 32 ♖d2 ♘e4 33 ♖c2 g6 34 a4 c5 35 b5 c4 36 ♘d4 ♘c5 37 a5 ♕f8 38 ♕xd6 ♘d3+ 39 ♔a2 ♘c1+ 40 ♔b1 ♘d3 41 ♖e2 **1-0** M392

**1866-⚔BS-11**
**Steinitz, W.– Bird, H.E.**
[Boden]

1 e4 e6 2 d4 d5 3 ♘c3 ♘f6 4 ♗g5 ♗e7 5 e5 ♘fd7 6 ♗xe7 ♕xe7 7 f4 a6 8 ♘f3 c5 9 dxc5 ♘xc5 10 ♕d2 b5 11 a3 ♗b7 12 ♘d4 ♘c6 13 ♗e2 ♕h4+ 14 g3 ♕e7 15 ♗f3 ♖c8 16 0-0 0-0 17 ♖ae1 ♖fd8 18 f5?? ♘xd4 19 ♕xd4 exf5 20 ♕b4 g6 21 ♖e2 d4 22 ♘d1 ♗xf3 23 ♖xf3 ♕b7 24 ♖f1 ♘e4 25 ♕b3 ♖e8 26 ♕f3 ♖xe5 27 ♘f2 ♖ce8 28 ♖fe1 ♕e7 29 ♕g2 ♖e6 30 ♘d3 ♕b7 [30 ... ♘c5] 31 ♘f4 ♖6e7 32 ♘d3 h5 33 ♖d1 ♕b6 34 ♖de1 ♔g7 35 h3 ♕d6 36 g4 ♔h7 37 b4 h4 38 ♘c1 ♘g3 39 ♖xe7 ♖xe7 40 ♕f2 ♖xe1+ 41 ♕xe1 ♕c6 42 gxf5 gxf5 43 ♘b3 ♕d5 44 ♘c5 ♕h1+ 45 ♔f2 ♘e4+ 46 ♔e2 ♕g2+ 47 ♔d1 ♕f3+ 48 ♔c1 ♕xa3+ 49 ♔d1 ♕xh3 50 ♘xe4 ♕g4+ 51 ♔c1 fxe4 52 ♕f2 ♕g5+ 53 ♔b1 f5 54 ♕xd4 h3! 55 ♕a7+ ♔h6 56 ♕xa6+ ♕g6 57 ♕c8 ♔h5 58 ♕c3 ♕g1+ 59 ♔b2 h2 60 ♕h8+ ♔g4 61 ♕g7+ ♔f3 62 ♕c3+ ♕e3 63 ♕h8 ♔g2 **0-1** M392

**1866-⚔BS-12**
**Bird, H.E.= Steinitz, W.**
[Staunton]

1 e4 e5 2 ♘f3 ♘c6 3 ♗b5 ♘f6 4 d4 exd4 5 e5 ♘e4 6 0-0 a6 7 ♗a4 ♘c5 8 c3 ♘xa4 9 ♕xa4 b5 10 ♕c2 dxc3 11 ♘xc3 ♗e7 12 ♘d5 ♗b7 13 ♗d2 h6 14 ♖fe1 0-0 15 ♕f5= f6 16 ♗xh6! fxe5 [16 ... gxh6?? 17 ♕g6+ ♔h8 18 ♕xh6+ ♔g8 19 ♕g6+ ♔h8 20 ♖e4+-] 17 ♕g6 ♖f7∞

18 ♖e4 ♕f8 19 ♗g5 ♖xf3! 20 gxf3 ♗xg5 21 ♕xg5 ♖e8 22 ♖ae1 ♖e6 23 ♘xc7 ♖h6 [23 ... ♘d4? 24 ♘xe6 ♘xf3+ 25 ♔f1 ♘xg5 26 ♘xf8 ♘xe4 27 ♘xd7+-] 24 ♖g4 ♔h7 25 ♘e8 ♘d4 26 ♕xg7+ ♕xg7 27 ♖xg7+ ♔h8 28 ♖g3 ♘xf3+ 29 ♖xf3 ♗xf3 30 ♖xe5 ♖g6+ 31 ♔f1 ♖c6 32 ♔e1 ♖c2 33 ♖e3 ♗g4 34 f3 ♗e6 35 ♖e2 ♖xe2+ 36 ♔xe2 ♗xa2 37 b4 ♗d5 38 f4 ♗c6 39 ♔e3 ♔g8 40 ♔d4 ♔f7 41 ♘c7 ♗b7 42 ♔c5 ♔f6 43 ♔b6 ♗f3 44 ♔xa6 ♔f5 45 ♔xb5 ♗c6+ 46 ♔c5 ♔xf4 47 b5 ♔g4 48 b6 ♔h3 49 ♘d5 ♔xh2 50 ♘b4 ♗a8 51 ♔d6 ♔g3 52 ♔xd7 ♔f4 53 ♔c7

♔e5 54 ♔d7 ♔d4 55 ♔c7 ♔c5 56 ♘d3+ ½-½ M954

**1866-✕BS-13**
**Steinitz, W.+ Bird, H.E.**
[Boden]
1 e4 e6 2 d4 d5 3 ♘c3 ♘f6 4 ♗g5 ♗e7 5 exd5 exd5 6 ♗d3 ♗g4 7 f3 ♗e6 8 ♘ge2 c5 9 dxc5 ♗xc5 10 ♕d2 ♘bd7?! 11 ♗b5 ♗e7 12 0-0-0 0-0 13 ♗xd7 ♘xd7 14 ♗xe7 ♕xe7 15 ♘f4! ♘b6 16 ♖he1 ♖fd8 17 ♕e3! ♘c4 18 ♘fxd5 ♕f8 19 ♕f4 ♗xd5 20 ♘xd5 ♖xd5 21 ♖xd5 ♕b4 22 ♖e4 ♕xb2+ 23 ♔d1 ♕b1+ 24 ♔e2 ♕xc2+ 25 ♔e1 b5 26 ♖d7 ♖f8 27 ♖xf7 ♕b1+ 28 ♔f2 ♕xa2+ 29 ♔g3 ♕a3 30 ♖xf8+ ♕xf8 31 ♕g5 ♕d6+ 32 ♔h3 ♕d7+ 33 g4 h6 34 ♕g6 ♘d6 35 ♖d4 ♕b7 36 ♕xd6 ♕xf3+ 37 ♕g3 ♕f6 38 ♕d3 a5 39 ♖d8+ ♔f7 40 ♕d5+ **1-0** M392

**1866-✕BS-14**
**Bird, H.E.= Steinitz, W.**
[Boden]
1 e4 e5 2 ♘f3 ♘c6 3 ♗b5 ♘f6 4 d4 ♘xd4 5 ♘xd4 exd4 6 e5 c6 7 0-0 cxb5 8 ♗g5 ♗e7 9 exf6 ♗xf6 10 ♖e1+ ♔f8 11 ♗xf6 ♕xf6 12 ♕e2± [□ 12 c3] 12 ... g6 13 ♘d2 d6 14 ♕xb5 a6 15 ♕d5 ♗f5 16 ♘e4 ♗xe4 17 ♖xe4 ♔g7 18 g3 ♖ac8!= 19 ♖f4 ♕e6 20 ♕xb7 ♖xc2 21 ♖d1 ♕xa2 22 b3 ♖f8 23 ♕d5 **½-½** M392

**1866-✕BS-15**
**Steinitz, W.= Bird, H.E.**
[Staunton]
1 e4 e6 2 d4 d5 3 ♘c3 ♘f6 4 ♗g5 ♗e7 5 exd5 exd5 6 ♗d3 0-0 7 ♘f3 ♗g4 8 0-0 ♘c6 9 ♘e2 ♘e4 10 ♗e3 f5 11 c3 ♔h8 [□ 11 ... g5] 12 ♘f4 ♕d6 13 h3 g5 14 ♘xd5 ♗xf3 15 gxf3 ♕xd5 16 fxe4 fxe4 17 ♗e2 ♗d6 [□ 17 ... ♖f3-+] 18 ♗g4 ♕f7 19 ♕e2 [19 ♗xg5? ♖g8] 19 ... ♕g6 20 ♖ae1 ♕g8 21 c4 ♕g7 22 ♖d1! ♖ae8 23 c5 ♗f4 24 d5 ♗xe3 25 dxc6 ♗xc5 26 cxb7 ♕e5! 27 ♕c4 [△ 28 ♕c3] 27 ... h5!= 28 ♗c8! [28 ♗xh5? ♕g3+ 29 ♔h1 ♕xh3+-+] 28 ... ♕g3+ 29 ♔h1 ♕f3+ 30 ♔h2 ♕f4+ [30 ... ♗d6+?? 31 ♖xd6 ♕f4+ 32 ♔g1+-] 31 ♔h1 ♕f3+ 32 ♔h2 ♕f4+ **½-½** M954

**1866-✕BS-16**
**Bird, H.E.+ Steinitz, W.**
[Boden]
1 e4 e5 2 ♘f3 ♘c6 3 ♗b5 ♘f6 4 d4 exd4 5 e5 ♘e4 6 0-0 a6 7 ♗a4 ♗e7 8 c3 dxc3 9 bxc3?! 0-0 10 ♕d5 ♘c5 11 ♗c2 b6 12 ♗e3 ♗b7 13 ♗xc5 ♗xc5 14 e6? dxe6 15 ♗xh7+?? ♔xh7 16 ♕h5+ ♔g8 17 ♘g5 ♖e8?? [□ 17 ... ♕d3-+] 18 ♕xf7+ ♔h8 19 ♕h5+ ♔g8 20 ♕h7+ ♔f8 21 ♕h8+ ♔e7 22 ♕xg7+ [22 ... ♔d6 23 ♖d1++-] **1-0** M392

**1866-✕BS-17**
**Steinitz, W.Φ Bird, H.E.**
[Boden]
1 e4 e6 2 d4 g6 3 ♘f3 ♘c6? 4 d5 ♘ce7 5 dxe6 dxe6 6 ♕xd8+ ♔xd8 7 ♘c3 ♘c6 8 ♗f4 f6 9 0-0-0+ ♗d7 10 ♗b5 h5 11 e5 f5 12 ♖d2 ♔e8 13 ♖hd1 ♖h7 14 ♘g5 ♗h6 15 ♗xc6 bxc6 16 ♘a4+- M392

## HIRSCHFELD✕URUSOV
[1866-✕HU]

| | | | | | | |
|---|---|---|---|---|---|---|
| P. Hirschfeld | 0 | ½ | ½ | 0 | 1 | 2 |
| S.S. Urusov | 1 | ½ | ½ | 1 | 0 | 3 |

**1866-✕HU-1** 14 iii 66
**Hirschfeld, P.– Urusov, S.S.**
[Anderssen & Neumann]
1 e4 e5 2 ♘f3 ♘c6 3 ♗c4 ♗c5 4 b4 ♗xb4 5 c3 ♗c5 6 0-0 ♕e7? 7 d4 ♗b6 8 ♔h1 [□ 8 dxe5 ♘xe5 9 ♘xe5 ♕xe5 10 ♕b3 ♕e7 11 e5] 8 ... d6 9 dxe5 dxe5 10 ♘g5 ♘h6 11 f4 ♗g4 12 ♗xf7+ [□ 12 ♕a4 0-0 13 f5] 12 ... ♕xf7 13 ♘xf7 ♗xd1 14 ♘xh6 ♗c2 15 ♘g4 0-0 16 ♘a3 ♗d3 17 ♖e1 exf4 18 h3 h5 19 ♘h2 ♗f2 20 ♖d1 ♗e2 21 ♖d2 ♖ad8 22 ♘c4? ♗xc4 **0-1** L/N6051

**1866-✕HU-2** 14 iii 66
**Urusov, S.S.= Hirschfeld, P.**
[Anderssen & Neumann]
1 e4 e5 2 ♘f3 ♘c6 3 d4 exd4 4 ♘xd4 ♗c5 5 ♗e3 [5 c3 ♕e7∓] 5 ... ♕f6 6 c3 d6 [□ 6 ... ♘ge7 7 ♗e2 d5] 7 f4 ♘ge7 8 ♗d3 0-0 9 ♗c2 ♗b6 10 0-0 ♕h6 11 ♘d2 f5 12 ♘xf5 ♗xe3+ [□ 12 ... ♘xf5] 13 ♘xe3 ♖xf4 14 ♗b3+ ♔h8 15 ♕e2 ♖xf1+ 16 ♖xf1 ♗e6 17 ♘d5 ♗xd5 18 exd5 ♘e5 19 ♘f3 ♘7g6 20 ♘d4 ♘f4 21 ♕e4 ♖f8 22 ♘f5± ♕g5 23 ♖xf4 g6 24 h4 ♕f6 25 ♗c2 gxf5 26 ♖xf5 ♕xf5 27 ♕xf5 ♖xf5 28 ♗xf5 ♘c4 29 b3 ♘e3 30 ♗e6 ♔g7 31 c4 ♔f6 32 g4 h6 33 ♔f2 ♘c2 34 ♗f5 ♘d4 35 ♗d3 a6 36 ♔e3 c5 37 ♔f4 b5 38 ♔e3? b4 39 ♔f4 ♔g7 40 g5 h5 41 ♔e3 a5 42 ♔f4 ♔f7 43 g6+ ♔f6 44 g7 ♔xg7 45 ♔g5 ♘f3+ 46 ♔xh5 ♔f6 **½-½**

**1866-✕HU-3** 18 iii 66
**Hirschfeld, P.= Urusov, S.S.**
[Anderssen & Neumann]
1 e4 e5 2 ♘f3 ♘c6 3 ♗b5 a6 4 ♗a4 ♘f6 5 d4 exd4 6 0-0 ♗e7 7 ♖e1 0-0 8 e5 [8 ♘xd4 ♘xd4 9 ♕xd4 c5, 10 ... b5∓] 8 ... ♘e8 9 ♘xd4 ♘xd4 10 ♕xd4 c5 11 ♕e4 ♘c7 12 c4 d5 13 cxd5 ♕xd5 14 ♘c3 ♕xe4 15 ♘xe4 b5 16 ♗c2 ♖d8 17 ♗e3 ♘e6 18 ♖ad1 ♗b7 19 f4 [□ 19 ♘d6] 19 ... ♘d4 20 ♗xd4 cxd4 21 ♘f2 ♖ac8 22 ♗f5 ♖c5 23 ♖c1 ♖c4 24 ♗d3 ♗d5!? 25 ♗xc4 bxc4 26 ♖ed1 d3 27 b3 ♗a3 28 ♖xc4 [28 ♖b1 c3-+] 28 ... ♗xc4 29 bxc4 d2 30 ♔f1 ♖d4 31 g3 ♗b4 32 ♔e2 ♖xc4 33 ♔d3 ♖c1 34 ♔e2 ♖c4 35 ♘h3 ♔f8 36 ♘g5 ♔e7 37 ♘f3 f6 38 exf6+ gxf6 39 ♘xd2 ♖c2 40 a4 ♖a2 41 ♔d3 ♖xa4 42 ♖e1+ ♔f7 43 ♖e2 ♖a2 44 ♘c4 ♖xe2 **½-½**

**1866-✕HU-4** 18 iii 66
**Urusov, S.S.+ Hirschfeld, P.**
[Anderssen & Neumann]
1 e4 c5 2 ♘f3 e6 3 d4 cxd4 4 ♘xd4 ♘f6 5 ♗d3 ♗c5 6 ♗e3? ♕b6 7 ♘b5 ♗xe3 8 fxe3 a6 [□ 8 ... ♕xe3+] 9 ♘d4 ♘c6 10 ♘d2 ♘xd4 11 ♘c4 ♕c5 12 exd4 ♕xd4 13 ♘d2 ♕xb2 14 c3 ♕b6 15 ♘c4 ♕c7 16 e5 ♘d5 17 ♘d6+ ♔e7 18 c4 ♘b4 19 ♗e4 f6 20 exf6+! gxf6 21 ♕g4

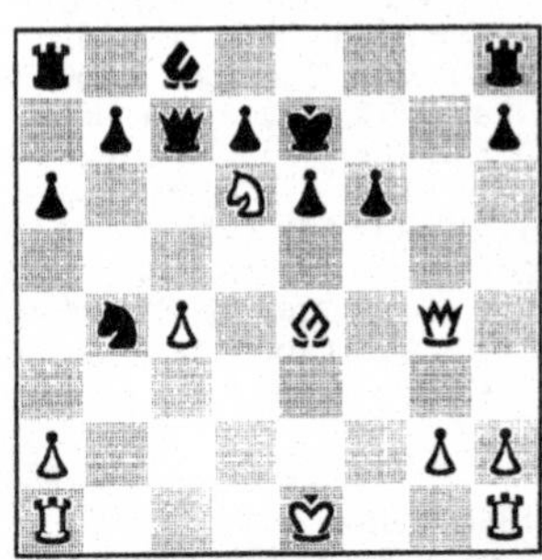

21 ... ♘c2+ [21 ... ♕xd6 (21 ... ♔xd6 22 ♕f4+) 22 ♕g7+] 22 ♗xc2 ♕a5+ 23 ♔e2 ♕e5+ 24 ♘e4 f5 25 ♕g5+ ♔f7 26 ♖ad1 d5 27 cxd5 exd5 28 ♖xd5 ♕xd5 29 ♗b3 **1-0** L/N6051

**1866-✕HU-5** 18 iii 66
**Hirschfeld, P.+ Urusov, S.S.**
[Anderssen & Neumann]
1 e4 e5 2 ♘c3 ♘f6 3 f4 d5 4 d3 dxe4 5 fxe5 ♘g4 6 d4 e3 7 ♘h3 ♘c6 8 ♘e2 ♗f5 9 c3 ♘cxe5 10 ♘g3 ♘f2 11 ♘xf2 exf2+ 12 ♔xf2 ♘g4+ 13 ♔g1 ♕f6 14 h3 ♘h6 15 ♗xh6 gxh6 16 ♘xf5 ♕xf5 **1-0** L/N6051

## MACKENZIE✕REICHHELM
[1866-✕MR]

| | | | | | | | |
|---|---|---|---|---|---|---|---|
| G.H. Mackenzie | ½ | 1 | 1 | 1 | 1 | 1 | 5½ |
| G.C. Reichhelm | ½ | 0 | 0 | 0 | 0 | 0 | ½ |

**1866-✕MR-1** 15 & 16 iii 66
**Mackenzie,G.H.= Reichhelm,G.C.**

[Romeyn]

1 e4 e5 2 ♘f3 ♘c6 3 ♗b5 a6 4 ♗a4 ♘f6 5 0-0 ♗e7 6 ♘c3 b5 7 ♗b3 0-0 8 d3 h6 9 ♘d5 d6 10 h3 ♘a5! 11 ♘xe7+ ♕xe7 12 ♘h2 ♘xb3 13 axb3 ♘h7 14 f4 f5 15 fxe5 dxe5 16 exf5 ♗xf5 17 ♗e3 ♕e6 18 ♕d2 ♘f6 19 ♖ae1 e4 20 ♗c5 ♖f7 21 b4 ♕d7 22 ♕f2 ♗h7 23 d4 ♖e8 24 ♕g3 ♕e6 25 ♘f3 ♘d7 26 ♘e5 ♘xe5 27 dxe5 ♕xe5 28 ♕xe5 ♖xe5 29 ♖xf7 ♔xf7 30 ♗d4 ♖d5 31 c3 h5 32 ♖e3 ♗f5 33 ♖g3 g6 34 ♖e3 ♖d8 35 ♖e1 ♖a8 36 ♖a1 ♔e6 37 ♔f2 ♔d5 38 ♔e3 ♔c4 39 ♖a3 ♗d7 40 b3+ ♔d5 41 ♖a2 ♗f5 42 ♔f4 ♖f8 43 ♔e3 ♗c8 44 ♖d2 ♔e6 45 ♔xe4 ♖f1 46 ♖e2 ♗b7+ 47 ♔d3+ ♔d7 48 g3 ♖f3+ 49 ♖e3 ♖xe3+ 50 ♗xe3 ♗g2 51 h4 ♔e6 52 ♗f4 c6 53 ♔d4 ♗d5 **½-½**

M628

**1866-✕MR-2** 16 iii 66
**Reichhelm,G.C.– Mackenzie,G.H.**

[Warner]

1 e4 e5 2 ♘f3 ♘c6 3 ♗c4 ♗c5 4 b4 ♗xb4 5 c3 ♗c5 6 0-0 d6 7 d4 exd4 8 cxd4 ♗b6 9 ♗b2 ♘a5 10 ♗d3 ♘e7 11 ♘g5? [□ 11 ♘c3] 11 ... h6 12 ♕h5 ♘g6 [□ 12 ... 0-0] 13 ♘xf7! ♔xf7 14 e5 ♕g5 15 ♕f3+ ♔e8 16 exd6 cxd6 17 ♘c3 [□ 17 ♗c1±] 17 ... ♘e7 18 ♘e4 ♕d5 19 ♖fe1 [△ 20 ♘f6++-] 19 ... ♔d8 20 ♗a3 ♗c7 21 ♖ac1 ♘ac6 22 ♗c4 ♕f5 23 ♕g3 ♕g6 [23 ... d5 24 ♕xg7 ♖f8 25 ♗xd5] 24 ♕xg6 ♘xg6 25 ♗xd6 ♗xd6 26 ♘xd6 ♖f8 27 ♘f7+ ♔c7 28 d5 ♖xf7 29 d6+ ♔xd6 30 ♗xf7 ♘ge5 31 ♗b3 ♗f5 [□ 31 ... ♗d7] 32 ♖cd1+ ♔c7 33 ♖d5 ♖e8 34 f4 [□ 34 ♔f1 ♖e7 35 f4 ♘d3 36 ♖d1; 34 ♔f1 g5 35 ♗a4 ♖e6 36 ♗xc6] 34 ... ♘f3+ 35 gxf3 ♖xe1+ 36 ♔f2 ♖h1 37 ♔g2 ♗e6 38 ♔xh1 ♗xd5 39 ♗xd5 ♔d6 40 ♗f7 ♘d8 41 ♗g8 ♘e6 42 ♔g2 ♘xf4+ 43 ♔g3 ♔e5 44 ♔g4 b5 45 ♗f7 a5 46 ♗e8 b4 47 ♗a4 ♘d5 48 ♔h5 ♔f6 49 ♗b3 ♘c3 50 ♔g4 a4 51 ♗c2 b3 52 ♗xb3 axb3 53 axb3 ♘d5 54 ♔h5 ♔f5 55 h3 ♘f4+ **0-1** M628

**1866-✕MR-3** 16 iii 66
**Mackenzie,G.H.+ Reichhelm,G.C.**

[Warner]

1 e4 e5 2 ♘f3 ♘c6 3 ♗b5 ♘f6 4 0-0 ♘xe4 5 d4 ♘xd4? 6 ♘xd4 exd4 7 ♖e1 f5 8 f3 ♗d6? 9 fxe4 ♗xh2+ 10 ♔xh2 ♕h4+ 11 ♔g1 0-0 12 ♗c4+ d5 13 ♗xd5+ ♔h8 14 e5 c6 15 ♗b3 f4 16 ♕e2 ♗g4 17 ♕f2 ♕h5 18 ♘d2 f3 19 ♖f1 ♖f5 20 ♘xf3 ♖af8 21 ♕g3 ♗xf3 22 ♖xf3 h6 23 e6! ♖xf3 24 gxf3 ♖xf3 25 ♕g2 ♖f6 26 ♗f4 ♖xf4 27 e7 d3 28 ♕g3 d2 29 ♕xf4 d1♕+ 30 ♖xd1 ♕xd1+ 31 ♔f2 **1-0** M628

**1866-✕MR-4** 17 iii 66
**Reichhelm,G.C.– Mackenzie,G.H.**

[Warner]

1 e4 e5 2 ♘f3 ♘c6 3 ♗b5 a6 4 ♗a4 ♘f6 5 d4 exd4 6 0-0 ♗e7 7 e5 ♘e4 8 ♘xd4 ♘xd4 9 ♕xd4 ♘c5 10 ♘c3 ♘xa4 11 ♕xa4 0-0 12 ♗e3 d5 13 ♖ad1 c6 14 f4 [□ 14 ♘e4] 14 ... f6 15 ♕b3 ♔h8 16 ♗d4 [□ 16 exf6, 17 ♘e4] 16 ... ♗g4 17 ♖d2 fxe5 18 ♗xe5 ♗c5+ 19 ♔h1 [□ 19 ♗d4] 19 ... ♕e7 20 ♖e1 ♖xf4 21 ♖de2 ♖f5 22 ♗xg7+ ♕xg7 23 ♖e8+ ♖xe8 24 ♖xe8+ ♖f8 25 ♖e1 ♕e5 **0-1**

M628

**1866-✕MR-5** 19 iii 66
**Mackenzie,G.H.+ Reichhelm,G.C.**

[Warner]

1 e4 e5 2 ♘f3 ♘c6 3 ♗b5 ♘f6 4 0-0 ♘xe4 5 d4 ♗e7 6 ♕e2 d5 7 ♘xe5 ♗d7 8 ♘xd7 ♕xd7 9 f3 ♘f6 [□ 9 ... ♘d6] 10 ♖e1 ♔f8 11 ♗xc6 bxc6 12 ♗e3 c5!? 13 ♕f2 cxd4 [□ 13 ... c4] 14 ♗xd4 ♕c6 15 ♘c3 ♘d7? 16 ♗xg7+ ♔xg7 17 ♖xe7 ♖he8 18 ♕d4+ ♘f6 19 ♖ae1 ♖xe7 20 ♖xe7 ♕d6 [□ 20 ... ♖e8] 21 ♖e5 c5 22 ♕f4 ♖d8 23 ♕g5+ ♔h8 24 ♖f5 c4 25 ♕xf6+ ♕xf6 26 ♖xf6 **1-0** M628

**1866-✕MR-6** 20 iii 66
**Reichhelm,G.C.– Mackenzie,G.H.**

[Romeyn]

1 e4 e5 2 ♘f3 ♘c6 3 ♗c4 ♗c5 4 b4 ♗xb4 5 c3 ♗c5 6 0-0 d6 7 d4 exd4 8 cxd4 ♗b6 9 ♗b2 ♘a5 10 ♗d3 ♘e7 11 ♘g5 h6 12 ♕h5 0-0 13 e5 ♗f5 14 ♗xf5 ♘xf5 15 ♘f3 ♕d7 16 ♘bd2 d5 17 g4 g6 18 e6?

18 ... gxh5 19 exd7 hxg4 20 ♘e5 ♗xd4 21 ♗xd4 ♘xd4 22 ♘xg4 ♔g7 23 ♔h1 ♖ad8 24 ♖g1 ♘e2 25 ♖g2 ♘f4 26 ♖g3 ♘g6 27 f4! ♘xf4 28 ♖f1 ♘g6 29 ♘f6 ♘c6 30 h4 ♔h8 31 ♖fg1 h5 32 ♖g5 ♘ce5 33 ♖xh5+ ♔g7 34 ♘e8+ ♖fxe8 35 dxe8♕ ♖xe8 36 ♖f5 ♖h8 37 h5 f6 38 ♖xe5 fxe5 39 ♖xg6+ ♔f7 40 ♖g5 ♔f6 41 ♘f3 e4 42 ♖g6+ ♔e7 43 ♘d4 ♖xh5+ 44 ♔g2 a6 45 ♔g3 ♔f7 46 ♖g4 ♔f6 47 ♘b3 b6 48 ♖g8 ♖g5+ 49 ♖xg5 ♔xg5 **0-1**

M628

**1866-★AG-1** iv 66
**Guretsky–Cornitz,B.v.= Anderssen,A.**
Berlin

1 e4 e5 2 ♘f3 ♘c6 3 ♗c4 ♗c5 4 0-0 ♘f6 5 d3 d6 6 c3 ♗b6 7 ♗g5 h6 8 ♗h4 ♕e7 9 ♘bd2 ♗g4 10 b4 g5 11 ♗g3 h5 12 h4 gxh4 13 ♗xh4 0-0-0 14 a4 a5 15 ♕b3 ♖df8 16 ♗d5 ♖hg8 17 ♗xc6 bxc6 18 bxa5 ♗xa5 19 ♕c4 ♔d7 20 d4 ♗xf3 21 ♘xf3 ♕e6 22 d5 ♕g4 23 ♘xe5+ dxe5 24 ♕xc6+ ♔c8 **½-½**

L/N6047-1868

**1866-★AK-1**
**Knorre, V.+ Anderssen, A.**
Berlin

1 e4 e5 2 ♘f3 ♘c6 3 ♗c4 ♗c5 4 c3 ♘f6 5 d4 exd4 6 e5 d5 7 ♗b5 ♘e4 8 cxd4 ♗b4+ 9 ♗d2 ♗xd2+ 10 ♘bxd2 0-0 11 0-0 f5 12 ♖c1 ♘e7 13 ♘xe4 fxe4 14 ♘e1 ♘g6 15 g3 ♗h3 16 ♘g2 ♗xg2 17 ♔xg2 ♕g5 18 ♔h1 ♖f3 19 ♖xc7 ♖af8 20 e6 ♖xf2 21 ♖xf2 ♖xf2 22 ♖c8+ ♘f8 23 ♕e1 ♕f5 24 ♕e3 ♖xb2 25 e7 ♕xc8 26 e8♕ ♕c2 27 ♕e2 ♕xe2 28 ♗xe2 ♖xe2 29 ♕b5 ♖e1+ 30 ♔g2 ♘e6 31 ♕d7 **1-0**

L/N6047-1869

**1866-★AM-1** 31 iii 66
**Anderssen,A.+Minckwitz, J.**
Berlin

1 e4 e5 2 f4 ♗c5 3 ♘f3 d6 4 ♗c4 ♘f6 5 d3 ♗g4 6 h3 ♗xf3 7 ♕xf3 0-0 8 ♘c3 c6 9 f5 ♘bd7 10 g4 ♘b6 11 ♗d3 a5 12 a4 ♗b4 13 ♗d2 d5 14 g5 ♘fd7 15 h4 ♘c5 16 f6 ♘xb3 17 cxb3 ♕d6 18 ♖d1 ♖ad8 19 fxg7 ♔xg7 20 ♔e2 ♕e6 21 h5 d4 22 ♘b1 ♗xd2 23 ♘xd2 f5 23 ♕g2 f4 25 ♘f3 ♘c8 26 g6 h6 27 ♖hg1 ♕f6 28 ♖df1 ♘d6 29 ♕h3 ♖de8 30 ♘h4 ♖e7 31 ♔f3 b6 32 ♖c1 c5 33 b4 axb4 34 a5 ♖b8 35 axb6 c4 36 ♖xc4 ♖xb6 34 ♖gc1 ♕g5 38 ♖c7 ♕xh5+ 39 ♔f2 ♕g5 40 ♔f1 ♖a6 41 ♕e6 ♖a7 42 ♕xd6 ♕xh4 43 ♕xe5+ ♕f6! 44 ♕xf6+ ♔xf6 45 ♖1c6+ ♔g7 46 ♖xe7+ ♖xe7 47 ♖d6 ♖b7 48 ♔f2 ♖b5 49 ♔f3 **1-0**

L/N6047

### 1866-★AM-2 — 31 iii 66
**Anderssen,A.−Minckwitz, J.**

Berlin

1 e4 c5 2 ♘f3 e6 3 ♘c3 a6 4 d4 cxd4 5 ♘xd4 ♘c6 6 ♗e3 ♘f6 7 ♗d3 d5 8 exd5 exd5 9 0-0 ♗d6 10 h3 0-0 11 ♕d2 ♗e6 12 ♖ae1 ♖e8 13 ♘xc6 bxc6 14 ♗g5 h6 15 ♗h4 ♗e7 16 ♕e2 ♕b6 17 ♕f3 ♕c7 18 g4 ♘h7 19 ♗g3 ♕d7 20 ♕g2 f5 21 f3 fxg4 22 fxg4 h5 23 ♘a4 hxg4 24 hxg4 ♘g5 25 ♗f2 ♖ab8 26 ♗d4 ♖b4 27 ♘b6 ♕a7 28 ♖xe6 ♖xd4 29 ♖xc6 ♗c5 30 ♖xc5 ♕xb6 31 ♕e2 ♖de4 32 ♗xe4 ♕xc5+ 33 ♔h1 ♖xe4 **0-1** L/N6047

### 1866-★AM-3 — 31 iii 66
**Minckwitz,J.+Anderssen, A.**

Berlin

1 e4 e5 2 ♘f3 ♘c6 3 ♗b5 ♘f6 4 0-0 ♘xe4 5 ♕e2 ♘d6 6 ♗xc6 dxc6 7 ♕xe5+ ♗e7 8 ♖e1 ♗e6 9 ♘d4 0-0 10 ♘xe6 fxe6 11 ♕xe6+ ♖f7 12 d3 ♘f5 13 ♗e3 ♗d6 14 ♘d2 ♕h4 15 ♘f3 ♕h5 16 ♕e4 ♖f6 17 ♗f4 ♘h4 18 ♗g3 ♘xf3+ 19 gxf3 ♖h6 20 f4 ♖f8 21 ♕e3 ♖hf6 22 ♖f1 ♗xf4 23 ♗xf4 ♖xf4 24 ♕g2 ♖h4 25 ♖g3 ♕h6 26 ♖g4 ♖h5 27 c3 ♕f6 28 d4 h6 29 ♖g6 ♕f7 30 ♕g4 ♖f5 31 ♕g2 ♔h8 32 a3 a5 33 ♖g3 a4 34 f3 ♖f6 35 ♕c2 ♖e8 36 ♕d2 ♖fe6 37 ♖g2 g5 38 ♖gf2 ♖e3 39 ♔g2 h5 40 ♕d1 h4 41 ♕d2 ♕f4 42 ♕d1 h3+ 43 ♔xh3 g4+ 44 ♔g2 gxf3+ 45 ♖xf3 ♖g8+ 46 ♔h1 ♕e4? 47 ♕d2 ♖f8 48 ♕xe3 ♕xe3 49 ♖xf8+ ♔h7 50 ♖8f3 ♕e4 51 ♖1f2 ♕e1+ 52 ♔g2 ♕e4 53 h4 b6 54 ♔h3 ♕e6+ 55 ♖f5 c5 56 d5 ♕e3+ 57 ♔g4 ♕e4+ 58 ♔h5 ♕e8+ 59 ♖f7+ ♔g8 60 ♔h6 ♕e3+ 61 ♖2f4 **1-0** L/N6047

### 1866-★AM-4 — 31 iii 66
**Minckwitz,J.+Anderssen, A.**

Berlin

1 e4 e5 2 ♘f3 ♘c6 3 ♗c4 ♗c5 4 c3 ♘f6 5 d4 exd4 6 cxd4 ♗b4+ 7 ♗d2 ♗xd2+ 8 ♘bxd2 d5 9 exd5 ♘xd5 10 0-0 0-0 11 ♘e4 h6 12 ♘e5 ♘ce7 13 ♖e1 ♗e6 14 ♖c1 ♘f4 15 ♗xe6 fxe6 16 g3 ♘fd5 17 ♕g4 ♖f5 18 ♘c5 ♘f6 19 ♕e2 ♕d5 20 ♘ed3 ♖f8 21 ♕xe6+ ♖f7 22 ♘e5 ♖xf2 23 ♕xf7+ ♕xf7 24 ♘xf7 **1-0** L/N6047

### 1866-★AM-5 — 1 iv 66
**Minckwitz,J.−Anderssen, A.**

Berlin [Bachmann]

1 e4 e5 2 ♘f3 ♘c6 3 ♗c4 ♗c5 4 c3 ♘f6 5 d4 exd4 6 cxd4 ♗b4+ 7 ♗d2 ♗xd2+ 8 ♘bxd2 d5 9 exd5 ♘xd5 10 0-0 0-0 11 ♘e4 h6 12 ♖c1 [□ 12 ♘e5; 12 ♕d2] 12 ... ♗g4 13 h3? [□ 13 ♔h1] 13 ... ♗xf3 14 ♕xf3 ♘xd4 15 ♕d1 ♘f4 16 ♕d2 ♘xh3+! 17 ♔h2 ♖e8 18 ♔xh3 ♖xe4 19 g4 ♕f6 **0-1** L/N3033

### 1866-★AN-1 — 7 xii 66
**Neumann, G.R.+Ahnert**

Berlin [Anderssen & Neumann]

1 e4 e5 2 f4 exf4 3 ♗c4 ♕h4+ 4 ♔f1 ♗c5 5 d4 ♗b6 6 ♘f3 ♕e7 7 ♗xf4 ♕xe4 8 ♗xf7+ ♔d8? 9 ♗g5+ ♘f6 10 ♘c3 ♕e7 11 ♘e5 ♖f8 12 ♘d5 ♘xd5 [12 ... ♕d6 13 ♕e2 △ 14 ♘c4] 13 ♗xe7+ ♔xe7 14 ♕h5 ♗xd4 [14 ... d6 15 ♕g5+ ♘f6 16 ♕xg7 dxe5 17 ♗h5+−] 15 ♕g5+ [15 ♕h4+?] 15 ... ♔d6? **1-0** L/N6051

### 1866-★AN-2 — iii 66
**Anderssen,A.−Neumann, G.R.**

Berlin [Neumann]

1 e4 e5 2 f4 exf4 3 ♘f3 g5 4 ♗c4 ♗g7 5 d4 d6 6 h4 h6 7 c3 ♘c6 8 ♘a3 g4 9 ♘g1 ♘f6 10 ♗d3 d5 11 e5 ♘h5 12 ♘e2 f3 13 gxf3 gxf3 14 ♘f4 ♘g3! 15 ♖h2 ♗g4 16 ♔f2 ♘e4+ 17 ♗xe4 dxe4 18 ♕e1 ♗f5 19 ♘h5?−+ [□ 19 ♘c4] 19 ... ♗xe5! 20 dxe5 ♘xe5 21 ♔g1 ♖g8+ 22 ♔h1 f2! 23 ♘f6+ ♕xf6 24 ♕xf2 e3 ...? **0-1** L/N6020-1869

### 1866-★AN-3 — iv 66
**Anderssen,A.−Neumann, G.R.**

Berlin [Neumann]

1 e4 e5 2 f4 exf4 3 ♘f3 g5 4 h4 g4 5 ♘e5 ♗g7! 6 ♘xg4 d5 7 ♘f2 [7 exd5? ♕e7+ 8 ♔f2 ♗d4+ 9 ♔f3 h5 10 ♘f2 ♗g4+ 11 ♘xg4 hxg4+ 12 ♔xg4 ♘f6+ 13 ♔h3 ♖xh4+ 14 ♔xh4 ♘e4+−+] 7 ... dxe4 8 ♘xe4 ♕e7 9 ♕e2 ♘c6 10 c3 ♘h6 11 ♘f2 ♕xe2+ 12 ♗xe2 ♘f5 13 ♘a3 [13 0-0 0-0 14 ♗b5 f6] 13 ... ♘g3 14 ♖h2 0-0 15 ♗f3 ♖e8+ 16 ♔d1 ♗f5 17 ♘c2 ♖ad8 18 d4 ♗xd4 19 cxd4 ♘xd4 [20 ♘xd4 ♖xd4+ 21 ♗d2 ♘f1] **0-1** L/N6020-1869

### 1866-★AN-4 — iv 66
**Anderssen,A.+Neumann, G.R.**

Berlin [Neumann]

1 e4 e5 2 f4 exf4 3 ♘f3 g5 4 ♗c4 ♗g7 5 d4 d6 6 h4 h6 7 ♘c3 ♘c6 8 ♘e2 ♕e7 9 ♕d3 ♗d7 10 ♗d2 0-0-0 11 ♗c3 ♖e8 12 d5 ♘e5 13 ♘xe5 dxe5 14 0-0-0 ♘f6 15 a3 ♘g4 16 ♗b4 ♕f6 17 ♗c5 b6 18 ♗a6+ ♔b8?+− [18 ... ♔d8] 19 d6! c6 [19 ... cxd6? 20 ♗xd6+ ♔a8 21 ♕d5+−] 20 ♕b3 ♗e6 [□ 20 ... ♕d8] 21 ♕b4 ♕d8 22 d7 ♖eg8 [22 ... ♗xd7 23 ♖xd7 ♕xd7 24 ♖d1 ♕e6 25 ♗xb6+−] 23 ♗e7 **1-0** L/N6020-1868

### 1866-★AN-5 — iv 66
**Anderssen,A.+Neumann, G.R.**

Berlin [Anderssen, & Neumann]

1 e4 e5 2 ♘f3 ♘c6 3 ♗c4 ♗c5 4 b4 ♗xb4 5 c3 ♗c5 6 0-0 d6 7 d4 exd4 8 cxd4 ♗b6 9 d5 ♘a5 10 ♗b2 f6 11 ♗d3 ♘e7 12 ♘c3 ♘g6 13 ♘e2 0-0 14 ♕d2 c5 15 ♖ac1 ♗d7 16 ♘g3 c4 17 ♗b1 ♗c5 18 ♗c3 b6 19 ♔h1 ♘b7 20 ♘d4 ♗xd4 21 ♗xd4 a5 22 f4 b5 23 f5 ♘e5 24 ♘h5 b4 25 ♘f4 c3 26 ♕e2 ♕e7 27 ♘e6 ♖fc8 28 ♖f4 ♘d8 29 ♖h4 ♗e8 30 ♖h3 a4 31 ♗c2 ♖ab8 32 ♕d1 ♘c4

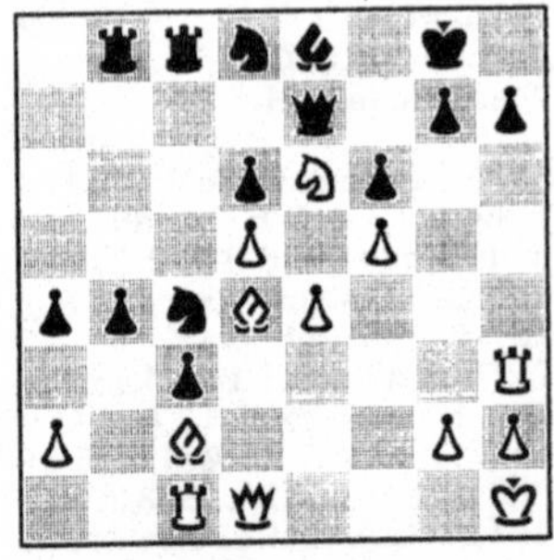

33 ♗xa4! ♘b2 34 ♕g4 ♘xa4 35 ♕h4 g5 36 ♕h6 ♘xe6 37 ♗xf6 ♕xf6 38 ♕xf6 ♘f8 39 ♕xg5+ ♘g6 40 fxg6 ♗xg6 41 ♖h6 ♖c7 42 ♖xg6+ hxg6 43 ♕xg6+ ♖g7 44 ♕xd6 **1-0** L/N6047

### 1866-★AN-6 — iv 66
**Anderssen,A.−Neumann, G.R.**

Berlin [Anderssen & Neumann]

1 e4 e5 2 f4 exf4 3 ♘f3 g5 4 ♗c4 ♗g7 5 d4 d6 6 h4 h6 7 ♘c3 ♘c6 8 ♘e2 ♕e7 9 ♕d3 ♗d7 10 ♗d2 0-0-0 11 ♗c3 ♘f6 12 d5 ♘e5 13 ♘xe5 dxe5 14 a3 ♘g4 15 ♗b4 ♕f6 16 ♗c5 b6 17 ♗a6+ ♔b8 18 ♕b3 ♗f8 19 ♘g1 ♗e7 20 a4 ♕d6 21 c3 f5 22 exf5 ♗xf5 23 ♗c4 ♗e4 24 a5 ♗xd5 25 axb6 cxb6 26 ♕a4 ♕c7? 27 ♗xd5 ♖xd5 28 b4 ♖hd8 29 c4 ♖d2 30 c5 e4 31 cxb6 ♖xe2+ 32 ♔f1! ♕c4 33 ♕xa7+ ♔c8 34 b7+ ♔d7 35 b8♕+ ♔e8 36 ♕a4+ ♔f7 37 ♕bb5 ♖f2+ 38 ♔e1 ♖f1# **0-1** L/N6051

**1866-★AN-7** iv66
**Neumann, G.R.+ Anderssen, A.**
Berlin [Neumann]
1 e4 e5 2 ♘f3 ♘c6 3 ♗b5 ♘f6 4 d3 ♗c5 5 c3 0-0 6 0-0 [6 ♗xc6 bxc6 7 ♘xe5 d5!∞] 6 ... d6 7 d4 ♗b6 8 ♗g5 h6 9 ♗h4 g5 10 ♘xg5! hxg5 11 ♗xg5 ♔g7 12 ♗xc6 bxc6 13 a4! a5 14 f4 exd4 15 cxd4 ♕d7 16 f5 ♕e7 17 ♘c3 ♖g8 18 ♔h1 ♕f8 19 h4! ♖xg5 20 hxg5 ♘xe4 21 ♘xe4 ♕xe4 22 ♕h5 ♕xd4 23 ♖ae1 **1-0** L/N6020-1869

**1866-★AN-8** ii66
**Neumann, G.R.= Anderssen, A.**
Berlin [Anderssen & Neumann]
1 c4 e6 2 d4 f5 3 ♘c3 ♘f6 4 a3 a5 5 ♘f3 ♗e7 6 ♗f4 d6 7 e3 0-0 8 ♗d3 ♘h5 9 ♗g3 ♘d7 10 h3 ♘xg3 11 fxg3 ♘f6 12 g4!? fxg4 13 hxg4 h6 14 g5 ♘g4 15 gxh6 ♘xh6 16 ♕c2 [□16 ♕e2] 16 ... ♗g5 17 ♔e2 e5 18 ♘e4 ♗g4 19 dxe5 dxe5 20 c5 ♕e7 21 ♖ag1 ♖ad8 22 ♘f2 ♗e6 23 ♗h7+ [□ 23 ♖h5] 23 ... ♔h8 24 ♘xe5 ♗f5 25 ♗xf5 ♕xe5 26 ♗e4

26 ... ♗xe3 27 ♘g4 ♕g3 28 ♗f3 ♖d2+ 29 ♕xd2 ♗xd2 30 ♔xd2 ♕f4+ 31 ♔c2 ♖d8 32 ♔b1 ♔g8 33 ♘xh6+ gxh6 34 ♖d1 ♖xd1+ 35 ♖xd1 b5 36 cxb6 cxb6 37 ♖d5 ♔f7 38 ♖b5 ♕e3 39 ♔a2 ♔e7 40 ♖d5 **½-½** L/N6051

**1866-★AN-9**
**Anderssen,A.–Neumann, G.R.**
1 e4 e5 2 f4 exf4 3 ♘f3 g5 4 ♗c4 ♗g7 5 d4 d6 6 h4 h6 7 c3 ♘c6 8 ♘a3 g4 9 ♘g1 ♘f6 10 ♗xf4 ♘xe4 11 ♕c2 d5 12 ♘b5 0-0 13 0-0-0 ♗f5 14 ♗d3 ♖c8 15 ♘f3 a6 16 ♘a3 ♗h7 17 ♘e5 ♘xe5 18 dxe5 f5 19 ♘c4 ♕e7 20 ♘e3 c6 21 ♔b1 b5 22 g3 h5 23 e6 ♕xe6 24 c4 bxc4 25 ♘xc4 ♖b8 26 ♗xb8 ♖xb8 27 ♖de1 ♕f6 28 ♖h2 dxc4 29 ♗xc4+ ♔h8 30 ♗b3 f4 31 ♖xe4 fxg3 32 ♖he2 g2 **0-1** L/N6051-1866

**1866-★AN-10**
**Anderssen,A.–Neumann, G.R.**
1 e4 e5 2 ♘f3 ♘c6 3 ♗c4 ♗c5 4 b4 ♗b6 5 0-0 d6 6 a4 a6 7 a5 ♗a7 8 b5 axb5 9 ♗xb5 ♗d7 10 c3 ♘f6 11 d4 exd4 12 cxd4 0-0 13 ♘c3 ♗g4 14 ♗e3 ♘e7 15 ♗d3 ♘g6 16 ♘e2 d5 17 e5 ♘e4 18 h3 ♗xf3 19 gxf3 ♘g5 20 ♗xg5 ♕xg5+ 21 ♔h2 ♗xd4 22 ♘xd4 ♕xe5+ 23 ♔h1 ♕xd4 24 ♖a4 ♕e5 25 ♖g1 ♕e6 26 ♕f1 c5 27 f4 f5 28 ♗e2 ♖f7 29 ♗f3 ♘h4 30 ♗h5 ♕e7 31 ♕c1 c4 32 ♖a3 d4 33 ♖a4 b5 34 ♖a2 d3 **0-1** L/N6051-1866

**1866-★AN-11**
**Anderssen,A.+Neumann, G.R.**
[Anderssen & Neumann]
1 e4 e5 2 ♘f3 ♘c6 3 ♗c4 ♘f6? 4 ♘g5 d5 5 cxd5 ♘a5 6 ♗b5+ c6 7 dxc6 bxc6 8 ♗e2 h6 9 ♘f3 e4 10 ♘e5 ♕c7 [□ 10 ... ♕d4] 11 f4 ♗d6 12 d4 exd3 13 ♘xd3 0-0 14 0-0 ♖e8 15 ♘c3 ♗f5 16 b3 ♖ad8 17 ♗d2 ♘b7 18 h3 ♘c5 19 ♖f3 ♘fe4 20 ♘xe4 ♗xe4 21 ♖f1 ♘xd3 22 cxd3 ♗xd3 23 ♗xd3 ♗c5+ 24 ♔h1 ♖xd3 25 ♕c2 ♕d6 26 ♖ae1 ♖d8 27 ♗a5 ♕d5 28 ♔h2 ♗b6 29 ♖e5 ♕d7 30 ♗xb6 axb6 31 ♖f2 f6 32 ♕c4+ ♖d5 33 ♖e3 ♔h8 34 ♖fe2 ♖d4 35 ♕c2 ♔g8 36 ♖e7 **1-0** L/N6051-1866

**1866-★AN-12**
**Anderssen,A.–Neumann, G.R.**
[Anderssen & Neumann]
1 e4 e5 2 f4 exf4 3 ♘f3 g5 4 h4 g4 5 ♘e5 ♗g7 6 ♘xg4 d5 7 ♘f2 dxe4 8 ♘xe4 ♕e7 9 ♕e2 ♘c6 10 c3 ♘h6 11 ♘f2 ♕xe2+! 12 ♗xe2 ♘f5 13 0-0 0-0! 14 ♗b5 [14 d4 ♘g3] 14 ... f3! 15 gxf3 ♘xh4 16 ♘e4 ♗f5 [△ 17 ... ♘xf3+] 17 d3 ♘e5 18 f4 ♘ef3+ 19 ♔f2 c6 20 ♗c4 b5 21 ♗b3 ♖ad8 22 ♗c2 ♖fe8 23 ♗e3 ♘h2 24 ♖g1 ♘g4+ 25 ♔e2 ♘g6 26 ♘bd2 ♗c8 [△ 27 ... ♘xe3 28 ♔xe3 f5] 27 ♗b3 ♘xe3 28 ♔xe3 ♗h6 29 ♔f2 ♔g7 30 a4 ♗xf4 31 axb5 f5 32 ♖xa7+ ♖d7 33 ♖ga1 fxe4 34 bxc6 e3+ 35 ♔f3 ♖de7 36 ♘e4 h5 37 ♖xe7+ ♖xe7 38 ♖a8 ♗g4+ 39 ♔g2 ♘h4+ **0-1** L/N6051-1866

**1866-★AN-13**
**Anderssen,A.+Neumann, G.R.**
[Anderssen & Neumann]
1 e4 e5 2 ♘f3 ♘c6 3 ♗c4 ♗c5 4 b4 ♗b6 5 0-0 ♘f6 6 b5 ♘a5 7 ♘xe5 d6 [7 ... 0-0 8 ♗xf7+ ♖xf7 9 ♘xf7 ♔xf7 10 e5 ♘e8 11 ♗a3 ♔g8 12 ♕f3 d6 13 ♖e1±] 8 ♘xf7 ♕e7 9 ♘xh8 ♘xc4 10 d4 ♗d7 11 ♕d3 ♗xb5 12 ♘c3 ♗a6 13 a4 0-0-0 14 ♘b5 ♘a5 15 e5 dxe5 16 ♕h3+ ♔b8 17 ♗a3 ♕e8 18 dxe5 ♘d5 19 ♕h4 ♕xh8? [□ 19 ... c5] 20 c4 g5 21 ♕e4 ♗xb5 22 axb5 ♘c3 23 ♕c2 ♕xe5 24 c5 ♘e2+ 25 ♔h1 ♘d4 26 ♕c3 ♘ab3 27 ♖ae1 ♕d5 28 cxb6 axb6 29 ♗e7 ♖c8 30 f4 ♘xb5 31 ♕h3 gxf4 32 ♖xf4 c5 33 ♕g3 ♔a7 34 ♖a4+ ♘a5 35 ♖ea1 ♖g8 36 ♕f2 [△ 37 ♗xc5] 36 ... ♖c8 37 ♕e1 ♖c6 38 ♖d1 ♘d4 39 ♗xc5 bxc5 40 ♖xd4 **1-0** L/N6051-1866

**1866-★AN-14**
**Anderssen,A.–Neumann, G.R.**
[Anderssen & Neumann]
1 e4 e5 2 ♘f3 ♘c6 3 ♗c4 ♘f6? 4 ♘g5 d5 5 exd5 ♘a5 6 ♗b5+ c6 7 dxc6 bxc6 8 ♗e2 h6 9 ♘f3 e4 10 ♘e5 ♕c7 11 d4 [□ 11 f4] 11 ... exd3 12 ♘xd3 ♗d6 13 h3 0-0 14 ♘d2 ♖e8 15 0-0 ♗f5 16 ♘f3 ♖ad8 17 ♗d2 ♘c4 18 ♗c3 ♘d5 19 ♘d4 ♗g6 20 ♗f3 ♘xc3 21 bxc3 ♘e5 22 ♖b1 ♘xd3 23 cxd3 c5 24 ♘b5 ♕a5 25 ♗c6 ♖e6 26 ♖e1 ♗e5 27 ♕b3 c4 28 dxc4 ♗xb1 29 ♕xb1 a6 30 ♗d5 axb5 31 ♗xe6 ♗xc3 32 ♖e2 fxe6 33 cxb5 e5 34 ♕b3+ ♔h8 35 ♖c2 ♗d4 36 ♔h2 ♖f8 37 a4 ♕e1 38 ♕a3 ♖g8 39 ♕a2 e4 40 ♖e2 ♕f1 41 a5 ♖f8 **0-1** L/N6051-1866

**1866-★AN-15**
**Anderssen,A.–Neumann, G.R.**
[Anderssen & Neumann]
1 e4 e5 2 f4 exf4 3 ♘f3 g5 4 ♗c4 g4 5 0-0 gxf3 6 ♕xf3 ♕f6 7 e5 ♕xe5 8 d3 ♗h6 9 ♗d2 ♘e7 10 ♘c3 ♘bc6 11 ♖ae1 ♕f5 12 g4 ♖g8 13 h3 ♘d4 14 ♕f2 ♘e6 15 d4 c6 16 ♗d3 ♕f6 17 ♘e4 ♕g7 [17 ... ♕xd4 18 ♕xd4 ♘xd4 19 ♘d6+ ♔f8 20 ♗xf4] 18 ♘d6+ ♔d8 19 c4 b6 20 ♗c3 ♕f8 21 ♗b4 ♗g7 22 ♖e4 ♘g5 23 ♔h1 ♘xe4 24 ♗xe4 ♗h6 25 ♖e1 ♔c7 26 ♗xh7 ♗g5 27 ♗xg8 ♕xg8 28 ♘e4 c5 29 ♗d2 ♗b7 30 d5 ♘xd5 [30 ... d6 31 ♘xg5 ♕xg5 32 ♗xf4 ♕f6 33 g5+–] 31 cxd5 ♗xd5 32 ♗xf4+ ♔c6! 33 ♔h2 ♗xf4+ 34 ♕xf4 ♕g6 35 ♕f6+ ♕xf6 36 ♘xf6 ♗xa2 37 h4 ♗e6 38 h5 ♖h8 39 ♔g3 d5 40 ♔f4 ♔d6 41 ♔g5 a5 42 h6 d4 43 h7 ♔e7 44 ♖f1 d3 45 ♔h6 ♔f8 46 g5 c4 47 ♘e4 ♔e7! 48 ♔g7 ♖xh7+ 49 ♔xh7 b5 50 ♖e1 b4 51 g6 fxg6 52 ♘c5 ♔d6 53 ♘xe6 d2 54 ♖d1 ♔xe6 55 ♖xd2 ♔e5 56 ♔xg6 ♔e4 57 ♔f6 a4 58 ♔e6 b3 59 ♖h2 a3 60 bxa3 c3 61 ♖h4+

♔d3 62 ♔d5 b2 63 ♖h3+ ♔d2 64 ♔d4 c2 65 ♖h2+ ♔d1 66 ♖h1+ ♔e2 67 ♖h2+ ♔f3 68 ♖xc2 b1♕ 69 ♔c3 ♔e4 70 ♖b2 ♕d3+ 71 ♔b4 ♕d4+ 72 ♔b3 ♔d3 73 a4? ♕c4+ 74 ♔a3 ♔c3 75 ♖b5 ♔c2 76 ♖b2+ ♔c1 77 ♖b5 ♕c3+ 78 ♔a2 ♔c2 79 ♖b8 ♕c4+ 80 ♔a3 ♕c5+ 81 ♔a2 ♕d5+ **0-1** L/N6051-1866

### 1866-★AN-16
**Anderssen,A.+Neumann, G.R.**

1 e4 e5 2 ♘f3 ♘c6 3 ♗c4 ♗c5 4 b4 ♗xb4 5 c3 ♗c5 6 0-0 d6 7 d4 exd4 8 cxd4 ♗b6 9 d5 ♘a5 10 ♗b2 f6 11 ♗d3 ♘e7 12 ♘c3 ♘g6 13 ♘e2 c5 14 ♔h1 ♗d7 15 ♖c1 a6 16 ♘g3 ♖c8 17 ♘f5 ♗xf5 18 exf5 ♘e5 19 ♘xe5 dxe5 20 f4 exf4 21 ♖xf4 ♔f8 22 ♗e2 ♕d6 23 ♖e4 ♗c7 24 g3 ♖d8 25 ♗f3 ♖e8 26 ♖e6 ♖xe6 27 dxe6 ♔e7 28 ♕a4 ♕d3 29 ♕g4 ♔f8 30 ♖d1 **1-0** L/N6051-1866

### 1866-★AN-17
**Neumann, G.R.+ Anderssen, A.**

[Anderssen & Neumann]

1 e4 e5 2 ♘f3 ♘c6 3 ♗c4 ♗c5 4 b4 ♗xb4 5 c3 ♗c5 6 0-0 d6 7 d4 exd4 8 cxd4 ♗b6 9 d5 ♘a5 10 ♗b2 ♘e7 11 ♗d3 0-0 12 ♘c3 f6 13 ♘e2 c5 14 ♘f4 ♗d7 15 ♖c1 ♖c8 16 ♕d2 a6 17 ♕c3 ♘g6 18 ♘xg6 hxg6 19 ♘h4 ♗e8 20 ♔h1 c4? 21 ♗b1 ♗c5 22 f4 b5 23 f5 g5 24 ♘g6 ♔f7 25 ♕h3 ♖g8 26 ♕h5 b4 27 ♖cd1 c3 28 ♗c1 ♕c7 29 ♗xg5 **1-0** L/N6051-1866

### 1866-★AN-18
**Neumann, G.R.– Anderssen, A.**

1 d4 f5 2 e4 fxe4 3 ♘c3 ♘f6 4 ♗g5 c6 5 ♗xf6 exf6 6 ♘xe4 d5 7 ♘g3 ♗d6 8 ♗d3 0-0 9 ♘1e2 ♗e6 10 0-0 f5 11 f4 ♘d7 12 ♔h1 g6 13 ♘g1 ♘f6 14 ♘3e2 ♘e4 15 ♘f3 ♖c8 16 b3 ♖c7 17 c4 ♖g7 18 ♕c2 h6 19 g3 g5 20 ♘e5 ♕e8 21 ♖ae1 gxf4 22 ♘xf4 ♗xe5 23 dxe5 ♖g5 24 ♗xe4 dxe4 25 ♖d1 ♗f7 26 ♕c3 ♗h5 27 ♖d6 ♗f3+ 28 ♔g1 ♖g4 29 ♖xh6 ♕e7 30 c5 ♖xf4 31 ♕c4+ ♔g7 **0-1** L/N6051-1866

### 1866-★AN-19
**Neumann, G.R.+ Anderssen, A.**

1 e4 e5 2 ♘f3 ♘c6 3 ♗c4 ♗c5 4 b4 ♗xb4 5 c3 ♗c5 6 0-0 d6 7 d4 exd4 8 cxd4 ♗b6 9 d5 ♘a5 10 ♗b2 ♘e7 11 ♗d3 0-0 12 ♘c3 ♘g6 13 ♘e2 c5 14 ♔h1 f6 15 ♖c1 ♗d7 16 ♘g3 ♖f7 17 ♘f5 ♗xf5 18 exf5 ♘e5 19 ♘xe5 dxe5 20 ♗e4 ♕d6 21 f4 exf4 22 ♕g4 ♗c7 23 ♗f3 b5 24 ♖fe1 ♘c4! 25 ♖e6 ♕d7 26 ♗xf6 ♖af8 27 ♗a1 ♘e3 28 ♕h3 ♖xf5 29 ♗e4 c4 30 ♗d4 g6 31 ♕h6 ♗e5 32 ♗xe5 ♖xe5 33 ♖xe5 b4 34 ♖e6 **1-0** L/N6051-1866

### 1866-★AN-20
**Neumann, G.R.– Anderssen, A.**

1 e4 e5 2 ♘f3 ♘c6 3 d4 exd4 4 ♗c4 ♗c5 5 ♗g5 ♘ge7 6 c3 dxc3 7 ♘xc3 h6 8 ♗h4 0-0 9 0-0 d6 10 ♖e1 ♗g4 11 ♘d5 ♕d7 12 b4 ♘xd5 13 bxc5 ♘f4 14 ♗g3 ♘h5 15 cxd6 ♘xg3 16 hxg3 cxd6 17 ♕d2 ♗e6 18 ♗xe6 fxe6 19 ♖ad1 ♖ad8 20 e5 d5 21 g4 ♕f7 22 g5 ♕h5 23 gxh6 gxh6 24 ♕e3 ♖d7 25 ♘d4 ♘xd4 26 ♖xd4 ♖g7 27 ♖f4 ♖xf4 28 ♕xf4 ♕g4 29 ♕xg4 ♖xg4 30 ♖b1 b6 31 ♖c1 ♖c4 32 ♖xc4 dxc4 33 ♔f1 b5 **0-1** L/N6051-1866

### 1866-★AN-21
**Neumann, G.R.= Anderssen, A.**

1 e4 e5 2 ♘f3 ♘c6 3 ♗c4 ♗c5 4 0-0 ♘f6 5 c3 ♘xe4! 6 ♗d5 ♘xf2 7 ♖xf2 ♗xf2+ 8 ♔xf2 ♘e7 9 ♗b3 e4 10 ♘e5 d5 11 d4 0-0 12 ♔g1 f6 13 ♘g4 c6 14 ♘f2 ♔h8 15 c4 ♗e6 16 cxd5 ♗xd5 17 ♗xd5 cxd5 18 ♘c3 ♕b6 19 ♘a4 ♕c6 20 ♗f4 ♘g6 21 ♖c1 ♕e6 22 ♘c5 ♕e7 23 ♘h3 ♖ac8 24 ♘a4 f5 25 ♘c3 ♕d7 26 ♕h5 ♖c6 27 ♘g5 h6 28 ♘h3 b5 29 ♘e2 ♘xf4 30 ♘hxf4 ♖xc1+ 31 ♘xc1 ♖f6 32 ♘ce2 g5 33 ♘g6+ ♔g7 34 ♘e5 ♕c8 35 h4 g4 36 ♔h2 b4 37 ♘f4 ♕d8 38 ♔g3 ♔h7 39 ♘e6 ♕d6 40 ♘f4 ♕d8 41 ♘f7 ♕d7 **½-½** L/N6051-1866

### 1866-★AN-22
**Neumann, G.R.+ Anderssen, A.**

1 e4 e5 2 ♘f3 ♘c6 3 ♗c4 ♗c5 4 c3 ♘f6 5 0-0 ♘xe4 6 ♗d5 ♘xf2 7 ♖xf2 ♗xf2+ 8 ♔xf2 ♘e7 9 ♗b3 e4 10 ♘e1 d5 11 d3 ♗f5 12 dxe4 dxe4 13 ♕xd8+ ♖xd8 14 ♘d2 ♗g6 15 ♘c2 f5 16 g3 ♗f7 17 ♘d4 c6 18 ♘f1 h6 19 h4 g6 20 ♗f4 ♘d5 21 ♗xd5 ♖xd5 22 ♘e3 ♖d7 23 h5 g5 24 ♗e5 0-0 25 ♘dxf5 ♖d2+ 26 ♔g1 ♔h7 27 g4 ♖xb2 28 c4 ♖d2 29 ♖f1 ♗g8 30 ♗g7 ♖xf5 31 ♘xf5 ♗xc4 32 ♖e1 ♗d5 33 ♗xh6 ♖xa2 34 ♗xg5 b5 35 ♗f6 ♗e6 36 ♖xe4 ♗xf5 37 gxf5 ♔h6 38 ♗e7 ♔xh5 39 ♖h4# **1-0** L/N6051-1866

### 1866-★AN-23
**Neumann, G.R.– Anderssen, A.**

1 d4 f5 2 e4 fxe4 3 ♘c3 ♘f6 4 ♗g5 c6 5 ♗xf6 exf6 6 ♘xe4 d5 7 ♘g3 ♗d6 8 ♗d3 0-0 9 ♕h5 g6 10 ♕h6 ♖f7 11 ♘1e2 ♘d7 12 h4 ♘f8 13 f4 ♕e7 14 ♔d2 ♗g4 15 ♖ae1 ♖e8 16 f5 ♗xg3 17 ♘xg3 ♕b4+ 18 c3 ♕xb2+ 19 ♗c2 ♖fe7 20 ♖xe7 ♖xe7 21 h5 ♗xf5 22 ♘xf5 gxf5 23 g4 ♖e4 24 ♖f1 ♖xg4 25 ♕e3 c5 26 ♖g1 ♖xg1 27 ♕xg1+ ♔f7 28 dxc5 ♘e6 29 c6 d4 30 cxb7 dxc3+ 31 ♔d3 ♘f4+ 32 ♔c4 ♕xb7 33 ♗b3 ♕c7+ 34 ♔b4+ ♘e6 35 h6 ♕b6+ 36 ♕xb6 axb6 37 ♔xc3 f4 38 ♗c2 ♘g5 39 ♗f5 ♔e7 40 ♔d4 ♔d6 41 ♗c2 ♔e6 42 ♗d3 f5 43 ♗c4+ ♔d6 44 ♗g8 f3 45 ♗c4 f4 46 ♗f1 f2 47 ♔d3 ♔e5 48 ♔e2 ♘e4 49 ♗g2 ♔f5 50 a3

50 ... f3+ 51 ♗xf3 f1♕+ 52 ♔xf1 ♘d2+ 53 ♔f2 ♘xf3 54 ♔xf3 ♔g5 **0-1** L/N6051-1866

### 1866-★AN-24
**Neumann, G.R.+ Anderssen, A.**

1 e4 e5 2 f4 exf4 3 ♘f3 g5 4 ♗c4 g4 5 0-0 gxf3 6 ♕xf3 ♕f6 7 e5 ♕xe5 8 d3 ♗h6 9 ♗d2 ♘e7 10 ♘c3 ♘bc6 11 ♖ae1 ♕f5 12 ♘d5 ♔d8 13 ♗c3 ♖e8 14 g4 ♕g6 15 h4 ♘xd5 16 ♖xe8+ ♔xe8 17 ♗xd5 ♘e7 18 ♖e1 ♔d8 19 ♕e2 ♗f8 20 g5 ♕b6+ 21 ♔h1 ♕e3 22 ♕g2 ♕g3 23 ♗xf7 ♕xg2+ 24 ♔xg2 d6 25 ♗f6 ♗f5 26 h5 ♔d7 27 ♔f3 ♘c6 28 ♔xf4 ♗h3 29 ♖e3 ♘e5 30 ♗g8 ♗e6 31 ♗xh7 ♗e7 32 ♗g7 ♘f7

33 ♖xe6 ♔xe6 34 ♗f5+ ♔d5 35 ♗e4+ ♔c5 36 d4+ ♔b6 37 g6 ♗f8 38 ♗xf8 ♖xf8 39 gxf7 ♖xf7+ 40 ♗f5 c6 41 h6 ♔c7 42 h7 ♖f8 43 ♔g5 ♔d8 44 ♗e6 ♖h8 45 ♗g8 ♔e7 46 ♔g6 ♔f8 47 c4 ♖xg8+ 48 hxg8♕+ ♔xg8 49 ♔f6 **1-0** L/N6051

**1866-★AN-25**
**Neumann, G.R.– Anderssen, A.**

1 e4 e5 2 ♘f3 ♘c6 3 ♗b5 ♘f6 4 0-0 ♘xe4 5 ♖e1 ♘d6 6 ♘xe5 ♗e7 7 ♗f1 ♘xe5 8 ♖xe5 0-0 9 d4 ♗f6 10 ♖e1 ♘f5 11 d5 d6 12 ♘c3 ♗xc3 13 bxc3 ♕f6 14 ♕f3 ♗d7 15 ♖b1 b6 16 c4 ♖fe8 17 ♖d1 ♕g6 18 ♗f4 ♖e7 19 ♔h1 ♖ae8 20 ♗d3 ♘h4 21 ♕g3 ♕h5 22 f3 ♘g6 23 ♗d2 ♗f5 24 ♖e1 ♗xd3 25 cxd3 ♕f5 26 ♖e4 ♕d7 27 ♖be1 ♖xe4 28 ♖xe4 ♖xe4 29 fxe4 ♕a4 30 h4 ♕xa2 31 ♗c3 ♕e2 32 ♔h2 a5 33 c5 bxc5 34 ♗xa5 ♘e5 35 ♗xc7 h5 36 ♗xd6 ♘g4+ 37 ♔h3 ♕f1 38 ♕f4 ♕xd3+ 39 ♕f3 ♕b1 40 ♕f4 ♕xe4 41 ♕xe4 ♘f2+ 42 ♔h2 ♘xe4 43 ♗f4 f5 44 ♔g1 ♔f7 45 ♔f1 c4 46 ♔e1 ♘f6 47 d6 ♔e6 48 ♔d1 ♘e4 49 ♔c2 ♘xd6 50 ♔c3 ♔d5 51 ♗xd6 ♔xd6 52 ♔xc4 ♔e5 53 ♔d3 ♔f4 54 ♔d4 ♔g4 55 ♔e5 f4 56 ♔e4 g6 57 ♔e5 ♔g3 **0-1** L/N6051-1866

**1866-★AN-26**
**Neumann, G.R.+ Anderssen, A.**

1 e4 e5 2 ♘c3 ♗c5 3 f4 d6 4 ♘f3 ♘f6 5 ♗c4 0-0 6 d3 ♗g4 7 h3 ♗xf3 8 ♕xf3 c6 9 f5 d5 10 exd5 b5 11 ♗b3 b4 12 ♘e4 ♘xe4 13 dxe4 ♕b6 14 f6 ♖d8 15 fxg7 ♖d7! 16 ♗h6 ♕c7 17 0-0-0 a5 18 ♖hf1 a4 19 ♗c4 ♗d4 20 d6 ♕b7 21 ♖xd4 exd4 22 e5 **1-0** L/N6051-1866

**1866-★AP-1 ○●** 26x66
**Asbeck,J.& Asbeck,E.& Trappenburg,W.=Paulsen, L.**

Barmen [Anderssen & Neumann]

1 e4 e5 2 ♗c4 ♘f6 3 ♘f3 ♘xe4 4 d3 [□ 4 ♘c3] 4 ... ♘f6 5 ♘xe5 d5 6 ♕e2 ♗e7 7 ♗b3 0-0 8 0-0 c5 9 c3 ♘c6 10 ♗f4 ♘xe5 11 ♗xe5 ♗e6 12 h3 ♘d7 13 d4 c4 14 ♗c2 ♖e8 15 ♕f3 ♘xe5 16 dxe5 ♕b6 17 b3 d4 18 ♗e4 ♖ad8 19 ♘d2 cxb3 20 ♘xb3 dxc3 21 ♕xc3 f5 22 ♗f3 ♗b4 23 ♕e3 ♕xe3 24 fxe3 ♗xb3? 25 axb3 ♗c5 26 ♗xb7 ♖xe5 27 ♗a6 f4 28 ♗c4+ ♔h8 29 ♔h1 fxe3 30 ♖ae1 h6 31 g4 ♖d2 32 ♖e2 ♖e4 33 ♖fe1 ♖f4 34 ♔g2 ♖f2+ 35 ♖xf2 ♖xf2+ 36 ♔h1 g5 37 ♖e2 ♖f4 38 ♔g2 a5 39 ♗e6 ♔g7 40 ♗d5 ♔f6 41 ♗g8 ♔e5 42 ♗h7 ♔d5 43 ♗g6 ♔d4 44 ♖c2 ½-½ L/N6051

**1866-★AP-2 ●○** 26/27x66
**Paulsen,L.+Asbeck.E.& Asbeck,J.& Halbach,W.& Rave,C.**

Barmen [Anderssen Neumann]

1 e4 e5 2 ♘f3 ♘c6 3 ♗c4 ♗c5 4 b4 ♗xb4 5 c3 ♗c5 6 0-0 d6 7 d4 exd4 8 cxd4 ♗b6 9 d5 ♘e5 [□ 9 ... ♘a5] 10 ♘xe5 dxe5 11 ♗b2 [□ 11 ♗a3 ♗d4 12 ♘d2 ♗xa1 13 ♕xa1] 11 ... ♕g5 12 ♔h1 ♘f6 13 ♘d2 ♘g4 14 ♘f3 ♕h5 15 ♕c2 0-0 16 h3 ♔h8 [□ 16 ... f6] 17 ♔g1 f5 18 exf5 ♖xf5 19 hxg4 ♕xg4 20 ♗e2 ♕g3 21 ♘d4 exd4 22 ♕xf5 ♕xg2+ 23 ♔xg2 ♗xf5 24 ♖ad1 ♖d8 25 ♗xd4 ♗xd4 26 ♖xd4 ♖e8 27 ♗f3 **1-0** L/N6051

**1866-★AP-3 ○●** 27x66
**Asbeck, J.& Böckmann, C.& Döpper, F. & Witthaus, C.– Paulsen, L.**

Barmen [Anderssen & Neumann]

1 e4 e5 2 ♘f3 ♘c6 3 ♗c4 ♗c5 4 b4 ♗xb4 5 c3 ♗c5 6 0-0 d6 7 d4 exd4 8 cxd4 ♗b6 9 ♗b2 ♘a5 10 d5 ♘e7 11 ♗d3 0-0 12 ♘bd2 ♘g6 13 ♕c2 ♘f4 14 ♕c3 f6 15 ♖fe1 ♘xd3 16 ♕xd3 c5 17 ♔h1 ♗c7 18 ♘h4 b5 19 f4 [19 ♕xb5 ♖b8→] 19 ... c4 20 ♕c3 ♘b7 21 ♗a3 a5 22 ♕g3 ♗b6 23 f5 b4 24 ♗c1 ♗d4 25 ♖b1 c3 26 ♘df3 c2 27 ♗h6 ♖f7 28 ♖b3 ♗c3 29 ♗d2 a4 30 ♖xb4 ♗xb4 31 ♗xb4 ♕b6 32 a3 ♘c5 33 ♗xc5 [33 ♘d4 c1♕ 34 ♖xc1 ♘xe4→] 33 ... ♕xc5 34 ♖c1 ♖b8 35 ♕e1 ♖fb7 36 ♘d2 ♕c3 37 ♘hf3 ♖b1? 38 h3? [□ 38 ♘xb1] 38 ... ♖xc1 39 ♕xc1 ♕b2 40 ♕xb2 ♖xb2 **0-1** L/N6051

**1866-★AS-1**
**Schallopp, E.– Anderssen, A.**

1 e4 e5 2 ♘f3 ♘c6 3 ♗b5 ♘f6 4 0-0 ♘xe4 5 d4 ♗e7 6 ♕e2 ♘d6 7 ♗xc6 bxc6 8 dxe5 ♘b7 9 ♗e3 0-0 10 ♖d1 f5 11 ♘d4 ♕e8 12 f4 ♘d8 13 ♘c3 ♕g6 14 ♖ab1 ♔h8 15 b4 ♗b7 16 ♘a4 d6 17 ♘f3 ♘e6 18 c4 a5 19 bxa5 ♖xa5 20 ♖xb7 ♖xa4 21 ♖db1 d5 22 cxd5 cxd5 23 ♕d2 ♖e4 24 ♖b8 h6 25 ♖xf8+ ♗xf8 26 ♖b8 ♔h7 27 ♘d4 ♗c5 28 ♘xe6 ♗xe3+ 29 ♕xe3 ♕xe6 30 ♕g3 ♕a6 31 ♖b2 ♕a7+ 32 ♔h1 ♕d4 **0-1** L/N6051-1866

**1866-★AZ-1** xii 66
**Anderssen,A.–Zukertort, J.H.**

Breslau [Anderssen/Zukertort]

1 e4 e5 2 f4 exf4 3 ♘f3 g5 4 h4 g4 5 ♘e5 ♗g7 6 d4 ♘f6 7 ♘c3 d6 8 ♘d3 0-0 9 ♘xf4 ♘xe4 10 ♘h5 ♖e8 11 ♗e2 ♘c6 12 ♘xg7 ♔xg7 13 ♘xe4 ♖xe4 14 ♕d3 ♕e8 15 c3 ♗d7 16 ♖f1? [□ 16 ♔d1] 16 ... ♘xd4 17 ♖f2 [17 cxd4 ♗b5] 17 ... ♗b5 18 c4 ♗xc4 **0-1** L/N6051-1869

**1866-★AZ-2** xii 66
**Anderssen,A.–Zukertort, J.H.**

Breslau [Anderssen & Zukertort]

1 e4 e5 2 f4 exf4 3 ♘f3 g5 4 h4 g4 5 ♘e5 ♗g7! 6 ♘xg4 d5 7 ♘f2 dxe4 8 ♘xe4 ♕e7 9 ♕e2 ♘c6 10 c3 ♘h6 11 ♘f2 ♘f5! 12 ♕xe7+! ♔xe7 13 d4 ♘g3 14 ♖h2 ♖e8 15 ♗b5! ♔f8+ 16 ♔d1 ♘h5 17 ♘d2 ♗f5 18 ♘f3 ♖ad8 [Δ 19 ... bxd4 20 cxd4 ♘xd4 21 ♘xd4 ♖xd4+] 19 ♗xc6 bxc6 20 b3 [□ 20 b4] 20 ... ♔g8 [20 ... c5 21 ♗a3] 21 ♗a3 ♖e3 22 ♔d2 ♘g3 23 ♖e1 ♖de8 24 ♔d1 ♖e2! [Δ 25 ... ♗c2+ 26 ♔c1 ♖xe1+ 27 ♘xe1 ♖xe1+ 28 ♔xc2 ♖e2+ 29 ♔~ ♖xf2] 25 ♘h3 ♗c2+ 26 ♔c1 ♖xe1+ 27 ♘xe1 ♖xe1+ 28 ♔xc2 ♖e2+ 29 ♔d3 f3! 30 d5 cxd5 31 ♗c5 ♘f1! **0-1** L/N6051-1868

**1866-★AZ-3** xii 66
**Zukertort, J.H.= Anderssen, A.**

Breslau [Anderssen & Zukertort]

1 e4 e5 2 ♘f3 ♘c6 3 ♗c4 ♗c5 4 b4 ♗xb4 5 c3 ♗c5 6 d4 exd4 7 0-0 d6 8 cxd4 ♗b6 9 d5 ♘a5 10 ♗b2 ♘e7 11 ♗d3 0-0 12 ♘c3 ♘g6 13 ♘e2 c5 14 ♕d2 f6 15 ♔h1 ♗c7 16 ♖ac1 ♖b8 17 ♘fg1 b5 18 f4 c4 19 ♗b1 b4 20 ♗d4 c3 21 ♕d1 ♗b6 22 ♘f3 ♗a6 23 f5 ♗xe2 24 ♕xe2 ♘e5 25 ♗xe5 dxe5 26 ♘h4 ♘b7 27 ♖f3 a5 28 ♖h3 ♕e8 29 ♕g4 ♖f7 30 ♘g6 h6 31 ♖f1 ♖c8 32 ♗c2 ♗d4 33 ♖ff3 ♘c5 34 ♖h5 a4 35 ♖fh3 b3

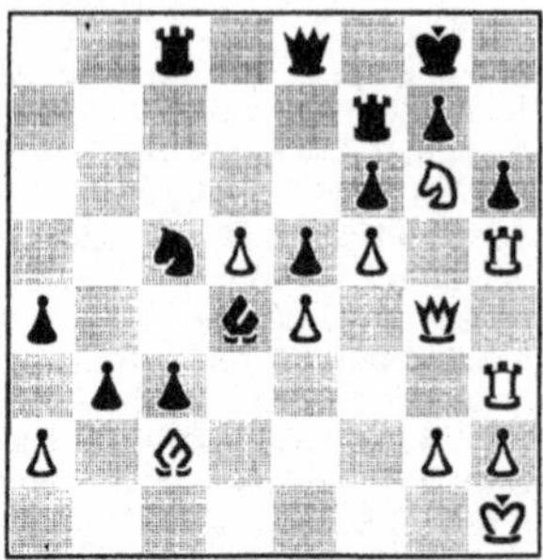

36 ♘e7+! ♔f8! [36 ... ♕xe7 37 ♖xh6+-; 36 ... ♖xe7 37 ♖xh6 ♖ec7 38 ♖h8+ ♕f7 39 ♕xg7+! ♔xg7 40 ♖3h7#; 36 ... ♔h7 37 ♕g6++-] 37 ♘g6+ ♔g8 38 ♘e7+ ♔f8 39 ♘g6+ ♔g8 40 ♘e7+ ♔h8 41 ♘g6+ ♔h7 42 ♘xe5 ♗e3 [42 ... bxc2; 42 ... ♕xe5 43 ♖xh6++-] 43 ♘xf7! [43 ♖xh6+ ♗xh6 44 ♖xh6+ ♔g8!] 43 ... ♕xf7 [43 ... bxc2 44 ♖xh6+ ♗xh6 45 ♖xh6+ ♔g8 46 ♖h8+ ♔xf7 47 ♕g6+ ♕e7 48 ♖xe8+ ♖xe8 49 ♕xg7+ ♔d8 50 ♕xf6+; 51 ♕xc3+-] 44 ♖xe3 ♘d3!! [44 ... bxc2 45 ♖xc3 ♘d3 46 ♕g6+ ♕xg6 47 fxg6+ ♔xg6 48 ♖xc8 ♔xh5 49 ♖xc2+-] 45 ♕e2 [45 ♗xd3 c2; 45 ♖xd3 bxc2] 45 ... ♕xh5! 46 ♕xd3 [46 ♕xh5 bxc2-+] 46 ... bxc2 47 ♕xc2 ♕h4 48 h3 ♕f4 49 ♖xc3 ♖xc3 50 ♕xc3 ♕xe4 ½-½

L/N6051-1870

**1866-★AZ-4** xii 66

**Zukertort, J.H.– Anderssen, A.**

Breslau [Minckwitz & von Schmidt]

1 e4 e5 2 ♘f3 ♘c6 3 ♗c4 ♗c5 4 b4 ♗xb4 5 c3 ♗c5 6 d4 exd4 7 0-0 d6 8 cxd4 ♗b6 9 d5 ♘a5 10 ♗b2 ♘e7 11 ♘c3 0-0 12 ♗d3 ♘g6 13 ♘e2 c5 14 ♕d2 f6 15 ♖ac1 ♗c7 16 ♔h1 a6 17 ♘fg1 b5 18 f4 ♗b6 19 ♘gf3 ♕e8 20 ♗c3! b4 21 ♗a1 ♗d7 22 f5 ♘e5 23 ♘f4 ♖f7 24 ♘e6 ♘xd3 25 ♕xd3 c4! 26 ♕e2 c3 27 g4 ♗b5 28 ♕g2 ♗xf1 29 ♖xf1 ♘c4 30 ♕h3 ♘e3! 31 g5! ♘xf1 32 g6 h6 33 gxf7+ ♕xf7 34 ♕xf1 ♕h5 35 h3! ♖c8 36 ♔g2 c2 37 ♗b2 ♔h7! 38 ♗c1 ♖c3 39 ♘f4 ♕e8 40 ♘e6 ♗e3! 41 ♗xe3 ♖xe3 42 ♕c1 ♖e2+ 43 ♔g3

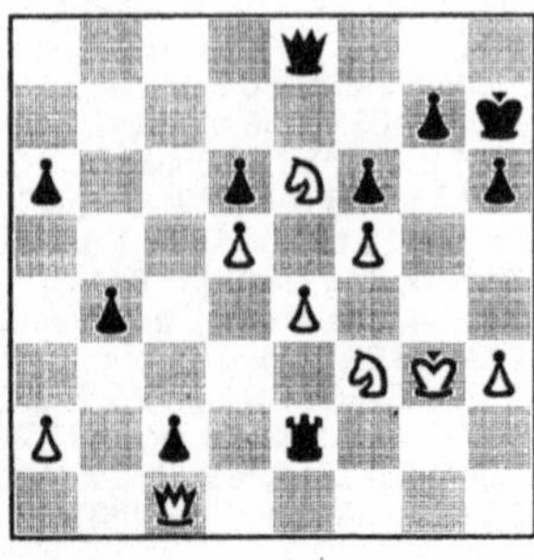

43 ... h5!! 44 ♘fd4 h4+ 45 ♔xh4 ♖g2 46 ♘xc2 ♕h8 47 ♘f4 ♔g8+ 48 ♘h5 ♖g5 49 ♕d1 ♕h6 50 ♕f3 ♖g1 51 ♕f4 ♕g5+ 52 ♕xg5 fxg5# **0-1**

L/N6047-1867

**1866-★A?-1** iv 66

**Anderssen, A.+?**

Berlin

1 e4 e5 2 ♘f3 ♘c6 3 ♗c4 ♗c5 4 b4 ♗xb4 5 c3 ♗c5 6 d4 exd4 7 0-0 d6 8 cxd4 ♗b6 9 d5 ♘a5 10 ♗b2 ♘e7 11 ♗d3 0-0 12 ♘c3 ♘g6 13 ♘e2 f6 14 ♕d2 c5 15 ♖ac1 ♗c7 16 ♘g3 ♖b8 17 ♔h1 b5 18 ♘f5 b4 19 ♖g1 ♘e5 20 ♘xe5 fxe5 21 g4 g6 22 ♘h6+ ♔h8 23 f4 ♕e7 24 g5 ♗d7 25 f5 ♗e8 26 f6 ♕d8 27 ♖g4 ♗b5 28 ♗xb5 ♖xb5 29 ♕e2 c4 30 ♖f1 ♕d7 31 ♖h4 c3 32 ♗c1 b3 33 axb3 ♘xb3 34 f7 ♘xc1 35 ♖xc1 ♖c5 36 ♖g4 ♗d8 37 ♖g3 ♗e7 38 h4 ♖fc8 39 h5 ♔g7 40 ♕h2 ♕a4 41 ♕h4 ♖xd5 42 hxg6 ♖d1+ 43 ♔h2 ♖d2+ 44 ♔h3 ♔xg6 45 ♘f5 ♗f8 46 ♖f1 ♕d7 47 ♖g4 c2 48 ♕xh7+ ♔xh7 49 g6+ ♔h8 50 ♖h4+ ♗h6 51 ♖xh6# **1-0**

L/N3034

**1866-★BC-1**

**Bergell, R. & Göhle, A.– Cordel, O. & Neumann, G.R.**

Berlin [Minckwitz & von Schmidt]

1 e4 e5 2 ♘f3 ♘c6 3 ♗c4 ♗c5 4 b4 ♗xb4 5 c3 ♗c5 6 0-0 d6 7 d4 exd4 8 cxd4 ♗b6 9 ♘c3 ♘a5 10 ♗d3 [10 e5] 10 ... ♘e7 11 e5 d5 12 ♗a3 ♘ac6 13 ♘g5 [◻ 13 ♖c1] 13 ... ♗f5 14 e6 ♗xe6 15 ♗xe7 ♕xe7 [◻ 15 ... ♘xe7] 16 ♘xe6 fxe6 17 ♘xd5 ♕f7 18 ♘xb6 axb6 19 d5? [19 ♗c4 0-0! 20 ♕g4 ♖ae8 21 ♖ae1 ♘d8 22 d5±] 19 ... exd5 20 ♖e1+ ♘e7 21 ♕e2 ♖d8 22 ♖ac1 ♖d7 23 ♕e5 0-0 24 f4 ♘c6 25 ♕e6 ♕xe6 26 ♖xe6 ♖xf4 27 ♗b5 ♖f6 28 ♗xc6 bxc6 29 ♖exc6 ♖xc6 30 ♖xc6 d4 **0-1**

L/N6047-66

**1866-★BN-1** xiii 66

**Beer, von– Neumann, G.R.**

Jicin [Anderssen & Neumann]

1 e4 e5 2 ♘f3 ♘c6 3 d4 exd4 4 ♘xd4 ♗c5 5 ♗e3 ♕f6 6 c3 ♘ge7 7 ♗b5 0-0 8 ♗xc6 dxc6 9 0-0 ♗b6 10 ♖e1 ♕g6 11 ♕f3 f5 12 e5 f4 13 ♗xf4? ♘d5∓ 14 ♘a3 [14 ♘e2 ♗g4; 14 ♖e4 ♗g4] 14 ... ♖xf4 15 ♕e2 ♗g4 16 ♕d2 ♖af8 17 ♘c4 ♗xd4 18 cxd4 ♗f3 19 g3 ♖h4 [△ 20 ... ♖xh2 21 ♔xh2 ♕h5+ 22 ♔g1 ♕h1#] **0-1**

L/N6051

**1866-★DF-1** vi 66

**Forster & Medley, G.W. & Ranken, C.E. & Steinitz, W.= De Vere, C. & Hewitt, J. & Kennedy, H.A. & Löwenthal, J.J.**

London [Löwenthal & Medley]

1 e4 e5 2 f4 d5 3 exd5 e4 4 ♘c3 ♘f6 5 ♕e2 ♗e7 6 ♘xe4 ♘xd5 7 d3 0-0 8 ♗d2 f5 9 ♘c3 ♗h4+ 10 ♔d1 ♘c6 11 g3 ♗f6 12 ♗g2 ♘db4 13 ♘f3 ♖e8 14 ♕f2 ♘d4 15 ♖c1 [15 a3? ♘dxc2] 15 ... ♗e6 16 ♘xd4 ♗xd4 17 ♕f3 c6 18 ♖e1 ♕d6 [◻ 18 ... ♗xc3] 19 a3 ♘d5 [◻ 19 ... ♗xc3] 20 ♖xe6 ♕xe6 21 ♘xd5 cxd5 22 c3 ♗f6 23 ♕xd5 ♖ad8 24 ♕xe6+ ♖xe6 25 d4 b5 **½-½**

L/N5193

**1866-★DS-1** vii 66

**De Vere, C. & Ranken, C.E.– Staunton, H.**

London [Staunton]

1 e4 e5 2 ♘f3 ♘c6 3 ♗c4 ♘f6 4 ♘g5 d5 5 exd5 ♘a5 6 ♗b5+ [6 d3!] 6 ... c6 [6 ... ♗d7] 7 dxc6 bxc6 8 ♗e2 [8 ♕f3? ♕b6 9 ♗a4 ♗g4 10 ♕g3 h6 11 ♘f3 0-0 12 ♘c3 e4 13 ♘e5 ♗d6 14 h3 ♗f5-+; 8 ♕f3? cxb5!? 9 ♕xa8 ♗c5 10 ♕f3 ♗b7 11 ♕g3 0-0 12 d3 (12 0-0 h6 13 ♘f3 ♘e4 14 ♕xe5 ♖e8) 12 ... e4] 8 ... h6 9 ♘f3 e4 10 ♘g1 [10 ♘e5 ♕d4 11 ♘g4 ♗xg4 12 ♗xg4 ♘c4 (12 ... e3) 13 c3 ♕b6 14 b3 ♘e5∓] 10 ... ♗c5 [△ 11 ... ♕b6] 11 ♔f1 0-0 12 c3 ♗b6 13 d4 exd3 14 ♕xd3 ♕e7 15 ♗f4 ♖d8 16 ♕c2 ♘e4 17 ♗g3 ♗f5 18 ♕c1 ♖d7 19 ♘f3 ♖e8 20 ♕e1 ♘c4 21 b3 [21 ♗xc4 ♘xg3+ 22 hxg3 ♕xe1+ 23 ♘xe1 ♖d1 24 ♗e2 ♗d3-+] 21 ... ♘b2+ 22 ♘d4 ♗xd4 23 cxd4 ♖xd4 24 f3 ♘d3 ... **0-1**

M954-1866

**1866-★GN-1** 20 ii 66

**Göhle, A.– Neumann, G.R.**

1 e4 e5 2 f4 exf4 3 ♗c4 f5 4 ♕e2 fxe4 5 ♕h5+ g6 6 ♕e5+ ♕e7 7 ♕xh8 ♘f6 8 b3 d5 9 ♗e2 c5 10 ♗b2 d4 11 c3 d3 12 c4 ♘bd7 13 ♗d1 e3 14 dxe3 ♕xe3+ 15 ♔f1 ♘e4 16 ♘h3 d2 17 ♗e2 f3 18 gxf3 ♘df6 **0-1**

L/N6051

**1866-★GN-2** 8 xi 66

**Göhle, A.– Neumann, G.R.**

Berlin [Anderssen & Neumann]

1 e4 e5 2 f4 exf4 3 ♘f3 g5 4 ♗c4 ♗g7 5 d4 d6 6 0-0 ♘c6 7 c3 h6 8 g3 g4 9 ♘h4? f3 10 ♘xf3 gxf3 11 ♕xf3 ♘f6 12 ♘d2 [12 e5 dxe5 13 dxe5 ♘xe5 14 ♕e2 ♕e7 15 ♖e1 ♘f3+] 12 ... ♕e7 13 e5 dxe5 14 ♘e4 ♘xe4 15 ♗x7+ ♔d8 16 ♕xe4 ♗h3 17 ♕g6 [17 ♖f2 exd4] 17 ... ♗xf1 18 ♕xg7 ♖f8 19 ♗xh6 ♖xf7 20 ♕g4 ♗e2 21 ♕xe2 ♕f6 22 ♕d2 ♔c8 23 ♗g5 ♕f5 24 dxe5 b6 25 ♗f6 ♘xe5 26 ♕d8+ ♔b7 27 ♕d5+ c6 **0-1**

L/N6051

### 1866-★GN-3 8 xi 66
**Neumann,G.R.+Göring, C.T.**
Berlin [Anderssen & Neumann]

1 e4 c5 2 ♗c4 e6 3 ♘c3 ♘c6 4 d3 a6 5 a4 ♘b4 6 ♗d2 d5 7 ♗b3 ♗e7 8 ♘ge2 ♘f6 9 ♘g3 dxe4 10 dxe4 ♕c7 11 ♗c4 ♘c6 12 0-0 ♘ce5 13 ♗f4 ♗d7 14 ♕e2 0-0 [□ 14 ... ♗d6] 15 ♗xe5 ♕xe5 16 f4 ♕c7 17 ♖ae1 ♗c6 18 e5 ♘d5 19 f5 ♔h8 20 f6 gxf6 21 ♘xd5 exd5 22 exf6 ♗xf6 [22 ... ♗d6 23 ♗d3 c4 24 ♗xh7+-] 23 ♖xf6 dxc4 24 ♕h5 ♖ad8 25 ♘f5 **1-0** L/N6051

### 1866-★HK-1 vi 66
**Hampton,T.I.& Medley, G.W.& Steinitz,W.= Kennedy,H.A.& Löwenthal, J.J.& Ranken,C.E.**
London [Löwenthal & Medley]

1 e4 e5 2 f4 ♗c5 3 ♘f3 d6 4 ♗c4 ♘f6 5 d3 ♘c6 6 c3 ♗b6 7 ♕e2 ♗g4 8 ♘a3?! [□ 8 h3] 8 ... exf4 9 ♗xf4 ♘h5 10 ♗d2 ♘e5 11 0-0-0 ♕f6 12 ♖hf1 ♗xf3 13 gxf3 ♘f4 14 ♗xf4 ♕xf4+ 15 ♔b1 0-0-0 16 ♗b3 ♖he8 17 d4 ♘g6 18 ♕g2 ♔b8 19 ♕g3 ♖e7 20 ♘c2 c6 21 ♘b4 ♗c7 22 ♘d3 ♕h6 23 ♖de1 ♖de8 24 ♗c2 f6 [△ ... d5] 25 ♖e2 d5 26 ♕g2 ♘h4 27 ♕h1 ♕h5 28 ♘c1 ♘g6 29 ♖ee1! ♕xh2 30 ♕xh2 ♗xh2 31 ♖h1 ♗f4 32 ♖xh7 ♗h6 33 ♘e2 ♘h4 34 ♖f1 ♘f5 35 ♗d3 ♘d6 36 ♘g3 dxe4 37 fxe4 ♘xe4 38 ♘xe4 ♖xe4 39 ♗xe4 ♖xe4 40 ♖f2 ♔c8?! [40 ... ♖e8] 41 ♔c2 ♔d8 42 ♔d3 ♖e8 43 ♖e2 ♖f8 44 ♔e4 ♔e7 45 ♔f5+ ♔f7 46 ♖e6 ♗g5 47 d5! cxd5 48 ♖d6 ♔e7 49 ♖xd5 ♗h6 50 c4 ♖c8 51 c5 a5 52 b3 ♖c7 53 ♖h8 ♗e3 54 c6 ♖xc6 55 ♖xa5 ♔f7 56 ♖b8 ♖c7 57 ♖b5 b6 58 a4 ♖e7 59 b4 g6+ 60 ♔g4 f5+ 61 ♔f3 ♖e6 62 a5 bxa5 63 ♖xa5 ♗d4

64 b5 ♖e3+ 65 ♔g2 f4 66 ♖a6 [△ #] 66 ... ♖g3+ 67 ♔h2 ♔g7 68 b6 ♗g1+ 69 ♔h1 f3 70 b7 ♗d4 71 ♖g8+ ♔h7 72 ♖h8+ ♗xh8 73 b8♕ ♖h3+ 74 ♕h2 ♖xh2+ 75 ♔xh2 ♗e5+ 76 ♔h3 g5 77 ♖a3 f2 78 ♔g2 ½-½ L/N5193

### 1866-★HN-1 7 xii 66
**Neumann, G.R.+Hirtler**
Berlin [Anderssen & Neumann]

1 e4 e5 2 ♘f3 ♘c6 3 ♗c4 ♗c5 4 b4 ♗xb4 5 c3 ♗c5 6 0-0 d6 7 d4 exd4 8 cxd4 ♗b6 9 d5 ♘ce7 10 e5 ♗g4 11 ♕a4+ ♔f8 [11 ... ♕d7 12 ♗b5 c6 13 e6 fxe6 14 ♕xg4 Anderssen-Hamel] 12 ♘bd2 dxe5 [12 ... ♗xf3 13 ♘xf3 dxe5 14 ♗a3 e4 (14 ... f6 15 ♖ad1, 16 d6+-) 15 ♘g5 e3 16 d6+-] 13 ♘xe5 ♗d4 14 ♘xg4 ♗xa1 15 ♗a3 h5 16 ♖xa1 hxg4 17 ♖e1 a6 18 ♗b3 b6 [△ 19 ... c5] 19 ♕f4 ♖h6 [□ 19 ... f6 20 ♘e4, 21 ♘g5; 21 d6] 20 d6 ♖f6 21 dxe7+ ♘xe7 22 ♕e4 c5 23 ♗b2 ♖f5 24 ♘c4 [△ 25 ♘xb6] 24 ... b5 25 ♘d6 c4 26 ♘xf5 ♘xf5 27 ♕xf5 cxb3 28 ♕h7 f6 29 ♗a3+ ♔f7 30 axb3 **1-0** L/N6051

### 1866-★KK-1
**Königsbeck & Neumann, G.R.–Knorre,V.& Weiss,E. von**
Berlin [Minckwitz & von Schmidt]

1 e4 e5 2 ♘f3 ♘c6 3 ♗b5 ♘f6 4 0-0 ♘xe4 5 d4 ♗e7 6 ♕e2 ♘d6 7 ♗xc6 bxc6 8 dxe5 ♘b7 9 ♗e3 0-0 10 ♖d1 ♕e8 11 ♘c3 ♘d8 12 ♘d4 f5 13 f4 ♕g6 14 ♘a4 d5 15 ♘f3 ♘e6 16 c4? ♗a6 17 b3 ♕g4 18 ♕d2 ♖ad8 19 ♕a5 ♗c8 20 exd5 cxd5 21 ♘c3 [21 ♖xd5 ♗b7∓] 21 ... d4 22 h3 ♕g6 23 ♘xd4 ♗b7 24 g4 [24 ♖d2 ♘xd4 25 ♗xd4 ♖xd4] 24 ... ♘xd4 25 ♖xd4 fxg4 26 h4 ♖xd4 27 ♗xd4 ♕c2 28 ♘d5 ♗xh4 29 ♕c3 ♕e2 **0-1** L/N6047-66

### 1866-★KN-1 iv 66
**Neumann, G.R.–Knorre, V.**
Berlin

1 e4 e5 2 f4 exf4 3 ♗c4 f5 4 ♕e2 ♕h4+ 5 ♔d1 fxe4 6 ♘c3 ♘f6 7 ♘xe4 ♗e7 8 ♘f3 ♕h6 9 ♖e1 ♘c6 10 d4 d5 11 ♘xf6+ ♕xf6 12 ♗xd5 ♗d7 13 ♗xf4 0-0-0 14 ♗g5 ♕d6 15 ♗xc6 [□ 15 ♗xe7 ♘xe7 16 ♗xb7+ ♔xb7 17 ♕xe7±] 15 ... ♗xg5 16 ♗xd7+ ♖xd7 17 ♘xg5 ♕xd4+ 18 ♔c1 ♕f4+ 19 ♕e3? [□ 19 ♔b1 ♕xg5∓] 19 ... ♖e8 **0-1** L/N6047-67

### 1866-★KZ-1 28 i 66
**Zukertort, J.H.+Knorre, V.**
Breslau [Anderssen & Neumann]

1 e4 e5 2 ♘f3 ♘c6 3 ♗b5 ♘f6 4 0-0 ♘xe4 5 d4 ♗e7 6 ♕e2 ♘d6 7 ♗xc6 bxc6! 8 dxe5 ♘b7 9 c4 0-0 10 ♗e3 [□ 10 ♘c3] 10 ... f5! 11 exf6 ♗xf6 12 c5 ♕e8 [△ 13 ... ♘xc5] 13 ♘c3 ♗xc3 14 ♕c4+ ♔h8 [14 ... d5 15 cxd6+ ♔h8 16 d7! ♗xd7 17 ♕xc3] 15 ♕xc3 d5 16 ♖fe1 ♖xf3 17 gxf3 ♗h3 18 ♔h1 ♕f7 19 ♗d4 ♘d8? [19 ... ♘a5 20 ♖g1 ♖g8 21 ♖xg7 ♖xg7 22 ♖g1] 20 ♗xg7+ ♕xg7 21 ♖e8# **1-0** L/N6051-1870

### 1866-★KZ-2 31 i 66
**Zukertort, J.H.+Knorre, V.**
Breslau [Anderssen & Zukertort]

1 e4 e5 2 ♘f3 ♘c6 3 ♗c4 ♗c5 4 b4 ♗xb4 5 c3 ♗c5 6 0-0 d6 7 d4 exd4 8 cxd4 ♗b6 9 d5 ♘a5 10 ♗b2 ♘e7 11 ♗d3 0-0 12 ♘c3 ♘g6 13 ♘e2 c5 14 ♕d2 f6 15 ♔h1 ♗c7 16 ♖ac1 a6 17 ♘g3 ♗d7 18 ♘f5 b5 19 g4 b4 20 ♖g1! b3? 21 a3 ♗b5 22 g5 ♗xd3 23 ♕xd3 ♘e5?

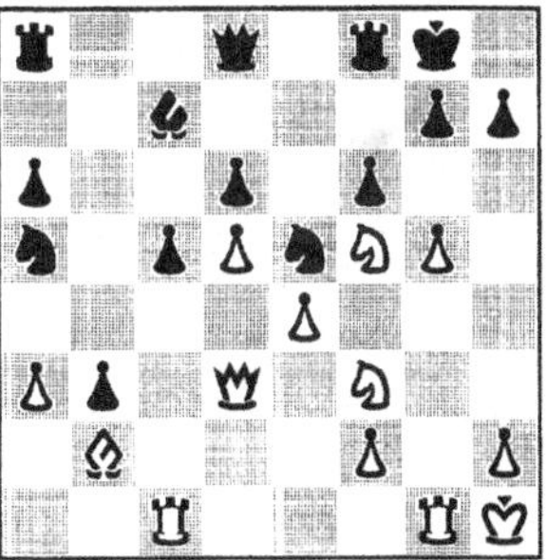

24 gxf6! ♖xf6 [24 ... ♘xd3 25 ♘h6+ ♔h8 26 fxg7#] 25 ♖xg7+ ♔f8 26 ♘xe5 ♖xf5 27 ♘d7+ ♔e8 28 exf5 **1-0** L/N6051-1870

### 1866-★KZ-3 i 66
**Knorre, V.+Zukertort, J.H.**
Breslau [Minckwitz & von Schmidt]

1 e4 e5 2 ♘f3 ♘c6 3 ♗b5 a6 4 ♗a4 ♘f6 5 0-0 ♗e7 6 c3 0-0 7 d4 exd4 8 ♗xc6 bxc6 9 e5 ♘e4 10 cxd4 d5 11 ♘c3 f5 12 ♘e2 c5 13 ♘e1 c6 14 f3 ♘g5 15 ♗e3 cxd4 16 ♘xd4 ♕e8 17 ♕c1 c5 18 ♗xg5 ♗xg5 19 ♕xg5 cxd4 20 ♕f4 ♖b8 21 ♕xd4 ♗e6 22 ♘d3 ♕e7 23 b4 ♔h8 24 a3 ♖fd8 25 ♖fc1 ♗c8 26 ♖c5 ♖b5 27 ♖ac1 ♖xc5 28 ♖xc5 ♕a7 29 ♔h1 [△ 30 ♖xc8] 29 ... h6 30 ♘f4 g5 31 e6+ ♕g7 32 e7 ♖e8 33 ♘g6+ ♔h7 34 ♘f8+ ♔h8 35 ♖xd5 ♕xd4 36 ♖xd4 ♔g7 37 ♖d8 ♖xe7 38 ♔g1 ♗b7 39 ♘e6+ ♖xe6 40 ♖d7+ ♔g6 41 ♖xb7 f4 42 a4 ♖c6 43 h3 ♔f5 44 a5 ♔e5 45 ♖b6 ♔d5 46 b5 [46 ... ♖xb6=] 46 ... axb5 47 ♖xb5+ ♔c4 48 ♖b6 ♔c5 49 ♖xc6+ ♔xc6 50 h4 ♔b5 51 ♔h2 ♔xa5 52 ♔h3 **1-0** L/N6047-1867

### 1866-★KZ-4 i 66
**Knorre, V.+Zukertort, J.H.**
Breslau [Minckwitz & von Schmidt]

1 e4 e5 2 ♘f3 ♘c6 3 ♗b5 a6 4 ♗a4 ♘f6 5 0-0 ♗e7 6 c3 0-0 7 d4 exd4

8 ♗xc6 bxc6 9 e5 ♘e4 10 cxd4 d5 11 ♘c3 f5 12 ♘e2 c5 13 ♘e1 cxd4 14 ♘xd4 ♕e8 15 ♕b3 c6 16 f3 ♗c5 17 ♘c2 ♕xe5 18 ♗e3 ♘d2 19 ♗xd2 ♗xd4+ 20 ♘xd4 ♕xd4+ 21 ♗e3 ♕e5 22 ♗c5 ♖b8 23 ♕a3 ♖f6 24 ♖ae1? ♕xb2 25 ♖e8+ ♔f7 26 ♕e3 [26 ♖xc8; 26 ♕xb2] 26 ... ♖e6 27 ♖e7+ ♖xe7 28 ♕xe7+ ♔g6 29 ♕e8+ ♔h6 30 ♗e3+ g5 31 ♕f8+ ♔g6 32 ♕d6+ ♔h5 33 g4+ fxg4 34 ♕e7 ♔g6 35 fxg4 **1-0**
L/N6047-1867

**1866-★KZ-5** i66
**Knorre, V.+Zukertort, J.H.**
Breslau [Minckwitz & von Schmidt]
1 e4 e5 2 ♘f3 ♘c6 3 ♗c4 ♗c5 4 b4 ♗xb4 5 c3 ♗c5 6 0-0 d6 7 d4 exd4 8 cxd4 ♗b6 9 d5 ♘a5 10 ♗b2 ♘e7 11 ♗d3 0-0 12 ♘c3 ♘g6 13 ♘e2 c5 14 ♕d2 ♗d7 15 ♔h1 ♗c7 16 ♘g3 f6 17 ♖ac1 b5 18 ♘f5 b4 19 ♖g1 b3 20 g4 bxa2 21 g5 ♘b3 22 ♕e3 ♗xf5 23 exf5 ♖e8 24 ♗e4 ♘xc1? [□ 24 ... ♕e7] 25 fxg6 ♕e7 26 gxh7+ ♔h8 27 gxf6 ♕xe4 28 fxg7+ ♔xh7 29 g8♕+ **1-0** L/N6047-1867

**1866-★KZ-6** i66
**Knorre, V.+Zukertort, J.H.**
Breslau [Minckwitz & von Schmidt]
1 e4 e5 2 ♘f3 ♘c6 3 ♗b5 ♘f6 4 0-0 ♘xe4 5 d4 ♗e7 6 ♕e2 [□ 6 dxe5! a6] 6 ... ♘d6 7 ♗xc6 bxc6 8 dxe5 ♘b7 9 c4 0-0 10 ♗e3 d5 11 ♘c3 ♗e6 12 ♖ad1 ♗b4 13 cxd5 cxd5 14 ♘g5 h6 [□ 14 ... c6; 14 ... ♗xc3] 15 ♘xe6 fxe6 16 ♕g4 ♕e7 17 ♗xh6 ♗xc3 18 bxc3 ♖f5 19 f4 ♘c5 20 ♖xd5 exd5 21 ♕xf5 gxh6 22 ♕g6+ ♔f8 [22 ... ♕g7 23 ♕c6] 23 ♕xh6+ ♔g8 24 f5 ♕xe5 25 f6 ♘e6 26 f7# **1-0** L/N6047-1867

**1866-★KZ-7** i66
**Knorre, V.–Zukertort, J.H.**
Breslau [Minckwitz & von Schmidt]
1 e4 e5 2 ♘f3 ♘c6 3 ♗b5 ♘f6 4 0-0 ♘xe4 5 d4 ♗e7 6 ♕e2 f5 7 ♗xc6 bxc6 8 ♘xe5 0-0 9 ♕c4+ d5 10 ♕xc6 ♖b8 11 c4 ♘f6 12 ♘c3 ♖b6 13 ♕a4 ♖a6 14 ♕d1 dxc4 15 ♕f3 ♕xd4 16 ♘c6 ♕d6 17 ♘d5 ♗d8 18 ♘xd8 [□ 18 ♘cb4] 18 ... ♕xd5 19 ♕xd5+ ♘xd5 20 ♗g5 h6 21 ♖ad1 ♖d6 **0-1** L/N6047-1867

**1866-★KZ-8** i66
**Knorre, V.–Zukertort, J.H.**
Breslau [Minckwitz & von Schmidt]
1 e4 e5 2 ♘f3 ♘c6 3 ♗b5 ♘f6 4 0-0 ♘xe4 5 d4 ♗e7 6 ♕e2 ♘d6 7 ♗xc6 bxc6 8 dxe5 ♘b7 9 c4 0-0 10 ♗e3 ♘c5 11 ♘c3 f5 12 ♖ad1 ♘e6 13 ♕c2 ♕e8 14 ♘e2 a5 15 ♘ed4 ♘xd4 16 ♘xd4 [□ 16 ♗xd4] 16 ... f4 17 ♗c1 c5 18 ♘f3 ♖a6 19 g3 ♗b7 20 ♘e1 ♕h5 21 f3 ♖g6 22 g4 ♗h4 23 ♘g2?

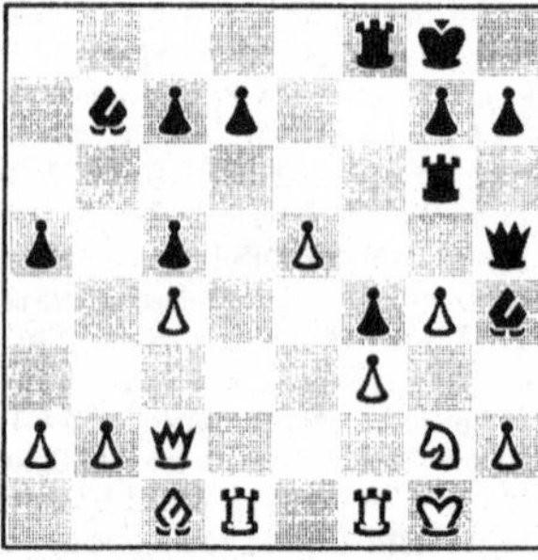

23 ... ♖xg4 24 fxg4 ♕xg4 25 h3 ♕xh3 26 ♖xf4 ♗g3 27 ♖xf8+ ♔xf8 28 ♗e3 ♔g8 29 ♖d2 ♕h2+ 30 ♔f1 ♕h1+ 31 ♗g1 ♗h2 32 ♘e1 ♕xg1+ 33 ♔e2 ♗g3 34 ♖d1 ♕f2+ 35 ♔d3 ♕d4+ 36 ♔e2 ♕xe5+ 37 ♔f1 ♕f4+ 38 ♔e2 ♗e4 **0-1**
L/N6047-1867

**1866-★KZ-9** i66
**Zukertort, J.H.–Knorre, V.**
Breslau [Minckwitz & von Schmidt]
1 e4 e5 2 ♘f3 ♘c6 3 ♗c4 ♗c5 4 b4 ♗xb4 5 c3 ♗c5 6 0-0 d6 7 d4 exd4 8 cxd4 ♗b6 9 d5 ♘a5 10 ♗b2 ♘e7 11 ♗d3 0-0 12 ♘c3 ♘g6 13 ♘e2 c5 14 ♕d2 a6 15 ♔h1 ♗d7 16 ♘g3 f6 17 ♖ac1 ♗c7 18 ♘g1 b5 19 f4 b4 20 ♘1e2 ♖e8 21 f5 ♘e5 22 ♘f4 [□ 22 ♗xe5 fxe5 23 ♘h5, 24 g4] 22 ... ♘xd3 23 ♕xd3 c4 24 ♕f3 c3 25 ♗a1 ♘c4 26 ♕g4 ♗b6 27 ♘gh5 ♕e7 28 ♖f3 ♘e5 29 ♕h4 ♘xf3 30 gxf3 ♖ac8 31 ♘e6 [□ 31 ♖c2] 31 ... ♗xe6 32 dxe6 ♗e3 33 ♖c2 ♗d2 34 ♔g2 ♔h8 35 ♖xd2 cxd2 36 ♘xf6 ♕xf6 37 ♗xf6 d1♕ 38 ♗xg7+ ♔g8 [38 ... ♔xg7?=] 39 ♕g3 ♖c2+ 40 ♔h3 ♕f1+ 41 ♔h4 ♖g2 **0-1**
L/N6047-1867

**1866-★KZ-10** i66
**Zukertort, J.H.+Knorre, V.**
Breslau [Minckwitz & von Schmidt]
1 e4 e5 2 ♘f3 ♘c6 3 ♗c4 ♗c5 4 b4 ♗xb4 5 c3 ♗c5 6 0-0 d6 7 d4 exd4 8 cxd4 ♗b6 9 d5 ♘a5 10 ♗b2 ♘e7 11 ♗d3 0-0 12 ♘c3 ♘g6 13 ♘e2 c5 14 ♕d2 a6 15 ♔h1 ♗d7 16 ♘g3 f6 17 ♘g1 ♗c7 18 f4 b5 19 ♘1e2 b4 20 ♖ac1 ♗b6 21 e5 f5 22 e6 ♗b5 23 ♗xf5 ♘e7 24 ♗e4 ♘c4 25 ♖xc4± ♗xc4 26 f5 ♖a7 27 ♘h5 ♘xf5 28 ♖xf5 ♖xf5 29 ♗xf5 ♗xe2 30 ♕xe2 ♕f8 31 ♕e4 ♔h8 32 ♘xg7 ♖xg7 33 e7 ♕e8 34 ♕h4 ♔g8 35 ♗xg7 ♔xg7 36 ♕g5+ ♔f7 37 ♗e6# **1-0** L/N6047-1867

**1866-★KZ-11** i66
**Zukertort, J.H.–Knorre, V.**
Breslau [Minckwitz & von Schmidt]
1 e4 e5 2 ♘f3 ♘c6 3 ♗c4 ♗c5 4 b4 ♗xb4 5 c3 ♗c5 6 0-0 d6 7 d4 exd4 8 cxd4 ♗b6 9 d5 ♘a5 10 ♗b2 ♘e7 11 ♗d3 0-0 12 ♘c3 ♘g6 13 ♘e2 c5 14 ♕d2 a6 15 ♔h1 ♗d7 16 ♘g3 f6 17 ♘f5 ♗xf5 18 exf5 ♘e5 19 ♘xe5 dxe5 20 ♖ac1 ♕d6 21 f4 ♖ad8 22 fxe5 ♕xd5 23 ♕xa5 ♗xa5 24 ♗c4 ♕xc4 25 ♖xc4 fxe5 26 ♖xc5 ♖xf5 27 ♖fc1 ♗d2 28 ♖d1 ♖df8 29 g3 ♗e3 30 ♖xe5 ♖f1+ 31 ♖xf1 ♖xf1+ 32 ♔g2 ♖f2+ 33 ♔h3 ♖xb2 34 ♖xe3 ♖xa2 35 ♖e8+ ♔f7 36 ♖b8 ♖b2
**0-1** L/N6047-1867

**1866-★KZ-12** i66
**Zukertort, J.H.–Knorre, V.**
Breslau [Minckwitz & von Schmidt]
1 e4 e5 2 ♘f3 ♘c6 3 ♗b5 ♘f6 4 d3 d6 5 ♗xc6+ bxc6 6 h3 c5 [6 ... h6, 7 ... g6, 8 ... ♗g7] 7 ♘c3 h6 8 ♘e2 g6 9 ♘g3 ♗g7 10 0-0 0-0 11 ♗e3 ♖b8 12 ♕c1 ♔h7 13 ♘d2 ♘g8 14 c3 f5 15 f4 g5! 16 exf5 gxf4 17 ♗xf4 exf4 18 ♖xf4 ♗e5 19 ♖f3 ♕h4 20 ♘df1 ♗b7 21 ♘e4 ♗xe4 22 dxe4 ♕xe4 23 ♘d2 ♕e2 24 ♕c2 ♘f6 25 ♖af1 ♖g8 26 ♖1f2 ♕e1+ 27 ♖f1 ♕h4 28 b3 ♖g3 29 ♘c4 ♖xf3 30 ♖xf3 ♕e1+ 31 ♖f1 ♗h2+ 32 ♔xh2 ♕xf1 **0-1** L/N6047-1867

**1866-★KZ-13** i66
**Zukertort, J.H.+Knorre, V.**
Breslau [Minckwitz & von Schmidt]
1 e4 e5 2 ♘f3 ♘c6 3 ♗c4 ♗c5 4 b4 ♗xb4 5 c3 ♗c5 6 0-0 d6 7 d4 exd4 8 cxd4 ♗b6 9 d5 ♘a5 10 ♗b2 ♘e7 11 ♗d3 0-0 12 ♘c3 ♘g6 13 ♘e2 c5 14 ♕d2 a6 15 ♘g3 f6 16 ♘f5 ♗xf5 [16 ... ♖f7] 17 exf5 ♘e5 18 ♘xe5 dxe5 19 ♖ac1 ♔h8 20 ♗e4 ♘c6 21 ♕d1 ♘d4 22 ♖c3 ♕d6 [□ 22 ... ♕d7, ♖f7] 23 ♖h3 ♗d8 24 ♕h5 h6 25 ♗c1 **1-0** L/N6047-1867

**1866-★MM-1**
**Morphy, P.C.+Maurian, C.A.**
New Orleans [Maróczy]
⟨♘b1⟩ 1 e4 e5 2 ♘f3 ♘c6 3 ♗c4 ♘f6 4 d4 exd4 5 0-0 ♘xe4 6 ♗d5 ♘c5 7 ♘g5 ♘e6 8 ♖e1 ♗e7 9 ♕h5 ♘xg5 [□ 9 ... ♗xg5] 10 ♗xg5 0-0 11 ♖xe7 ♘xe7 12 ♖e1 g6? [□ 12 ... c6! 13 ♗xe7 (13 ♗b3 d5 14 ♗xe7 ♖e8 15 ♗b4 ♖xe1+ 16 ♗xe1 ♕e7) 13 ... ♕a5 14 ♖e5 cxd5 15 ♗xf8 d6! 16 ♗xd6 (16 ♖e8 ♗e6) 16 ... ♗e6] 13 ♕f3 c6 14 ♗xe7 ♕a5 15 ♖e5 ♕d2 [15 ... cxd5 16 ♗xf8 d6 19 ♕f6+–] 16 h3 d6 17 ♗g5 dxe5 [17 ... ♕b4 18 ♕f6, 19 ♗h6+–] 18 ♗xd2 cxd5 19 ♕f6 **1-0** L/N3203

**1866-★MM-2**
**Morphy, P.C.+Maurian, C.A.**
New Orleans [Maróczy]
⟨♘b1⟩ 1 e4 e5 2 f4 d5 3 exd5 ♕xd5 4 ♘f3 ♗g4 5 ♗e2 ♗xf3 6 ♗xf3 e4 7 ♕e2 ♘f6 [□ 7 ... f5] 8 d3 ♕b5 9 c4 ♕b4+ 10 ♗d2 ♕xb2 11 0-0 ♘c6 12 ♗xe4 ♘xe4 13 ♕xe4+ ♗e7 14 ♗e3 ♕f6 15 d4 0-0 16 d5 ♖fe8 [□ 16 ... ♖ae8] 17 dxc6 ♗c5 18 cxb7! ♖ad8 19 ♕xe8+ ♖xe8 20 ♗xc5 ♕c6 [20 ... ♕a6 21 ♖ab1 ♖b8 22 ♖fd1 h6!] 21 ♗xa7 ♕xb7 22 ♗f2 f5 23 a4 ♖e2 24 a5 ♖e6 25 ♖ab1 ♕c8 26 ♖b5 g6 27 ♖e5 ♖a6 28 ♖fe1 ♖a8 29 ♗d4 ♕a6 30 ♖e7 ♕xc4 31 ♖d7 ♔f8 [□ 31 ... c5] 32 h3 **1-0** L/N3203

**1866-★MM-3**
**Morphy, P.C.+Maurian, C.A.**
New Orleans [Maróczy]
⟨♘b1⟩ 1 b3 e5 2 ♗b2 ♘c6 3 e3 d5 4 g3 f5 5 ♘h3 ♘f6 6 ♗b5? [□ 6 ♗g2] 6 ... ♗d6 7 f4 ♕e7 8 0-0 0-0 9 c4 a6 10 ♗xc6 bxc6 11 fxe5 ♗xe5 12 d4 ♗d6 13 c5 ♕xe3+ 14 ♔g2 ♗e7 15 ♖e1 ♘g4 16 ♗c1 ♕c3 17 ♗d2 ♕xd4 18 ♖xe7 ♕xc5 19 ♕e2 d4 20 b4 ♕d5+ 21 ♔g1 d3 22 ♗c3! ♖f7 [22 ... dxe2 23 ♖xg7+ ♔h8 24 ♖xg4++−] 23 ♖e8+ ♖f8 24 ♕e7 ♕f7 25 ♘g5! ♕xe7 26 ♖xe7 ♘f6 27 ♖ae1 a5 28 ♖xc7 ♖e8 29 ♖d1 axb4 30 ♗xf6 gxf6 31 ♘xh7 ♖e6 32 ♖xd3 ♗a6 33 ♖3d7 ♗c4 34 a4! [34 ♖g7+? ♔ 35 ♘f8 ♖e1+ 36 ♔f2! ♖e2+ 37 ♔g1=] 34 ... bxa3 35 ♖g7+ ♔h8 36 ♘f8 **1-0** L/N3203

**1866-★MM-4** 9 v 66
**Morphy, P.C.=Maurian, C.A.**
New Orleans [Maróczy]
⟨♘b1⟩ 1 e4 e5 2 ♘f3 ♘c6 3 ♗c4 ♗c5 4 b4 ♗xb4 5 c3 ♗c5 6 0-0 d6 7 d4 exd4 8 cxd4 ♗b6 9 ♗b2 ♗g4 10 ♗b5 ♔f8 [10 ... a6!] 11 ♗xc6 bxc6 12 h3 h5! 13 ♕d3 [13 hxg4 hxg4 14 ♘h2 ♕h4] 13 ... ♗xf3 14 ♕xf3 ♖h6 15 a4 a5 16 ♖ac1 ♘e7 17 ♕e3 f5 18 ♕g5 fxe4 19 ♖fe1 ♘d5 [19 ... d5 20 ♗a3!] 20 ♕f5+ ♘f6 21 ♖xe4 ♕d7 22 ♖e6 ♕f7 23 d5 ♘xd5 [□ 23 ... cxd5, ♘e4; ♖e8] 24 ♗xg7+ ♔xg7 25 ♕xf7+ ♔xf7 26 ♖xh6 ♘f6 27 g4 hxg4 28 hxg4 ♘xg4 29 ♖h7+ ♔g6 30 ♖h3 ♗xf2+ 31 ♔g2 ♗c5 32 ♖g3 ♔f5 33 ♖f1+ ♔g5? [□ 33 ... ♘f2; 33 ... ♗f2] 34 ♖f7 ♖g8 35 ♔f3 ♔g6 36 ♖f4 ♔h5 37 ♖h3+ ♔g6 38 ♖xg4+ ♔f7 39 ♖h7+ ♔f8 40 ♖f4+ ♔e8 41 ♖xc7 [41 ♖e4+ ♔d8 42 ♖ee7 ♗b6] 41 ... ♔d8 **½-½** L/N3203

**1866-★MM-5**
**Morphy, P.C.+Maurian, C.A.**
New Orleans [Maróczy]
⟨♘b1⟩ 1 e4 e6 2 d4 d5 3 ♘h3 dxe4 4 ♗c4 ♘f6 5 0-0 b6 6 f3 e3 [□ 6 ... ♗b7; 6 ... exf3 7 ♕xf3 ♕xd4+ 8 ♗e3 ♕e4] 7 ♗xe3 ♗e7 8 ♕e2 0-0 9 ♖ad1 ♘d5 10 ♗c1 ♘c6 11 c3 ♗d6 [□ 11 ... ♗f6] 12 ♗d3 f5 13 ♗b5 ♘ce7 14 c4 ♘b4 [□ 14 ... ♘f6] 15 a3 c6 [15 ... a6 16 axb4 axb5 17 c5] 16 ♗a4 b5 17 c5 ♗c7 [□ 17 ... ♗b8 △ ♘bd5, a6, ♗a7] 18 ♗b3 ♘bd5 19 ♗g5 ♕e8 20 ♗xe7 ♕xe7 21 ♗xd5 cxd5 22 ♕xb5 e5? [□ 22 ... ♖b8! 23 ♕e2 a5] 23 ♕c6 ♗e6 24 dxe5 ♖ac8 [24 ... ♗xe5 25 ♖fe1 ♗f7 26 ♖xd5 ♗d4+ 27 ♔f1 ♗xd5 28 ♕xd5+, 29 ♕xd4±] 25 ♘g5 ♕xg5 26 ♕xe6+ ♔h8 27 f4 ♕g4 28 ♖f3 ♗b6! 29 b4 [29 cxb6 ♖c2∓] 29 ... ♗xc5+ 30 bxc5 ♖xc5 31 ♕d6 ♖fc8 32 ♖xd5 ♖c1+ 33 ♖d1 h6 34 h3 ♕h4 35 ♖xc1 ♖xc1+ 36 ♔h2 ♕e1 37 ♕f8+ ♔h7 38 ♕xf5+ ♔g8 39 ♖d3 ♕g1+ 40 ♔g3 ♕e1+ 41 ♔g4 ♕e2+ 42 ♔h4 ♕f2+ 43 g3 ♕b6 44 ♖d6 ♕c7 45 ♖d7 **1-0** L/N3203

**1866-★MM-6**
**Morphy, P.C.+Maurian, C.A.**
New Orleans [Maróczy]
⟨♘b1⟩ 1 e4 e5 2 ♘f3 ♘c6 3 ♗c4 ♗c5 4 b4 ♗xb4 5 c3 ♗c5 6 0-0 d6 7 d4 exd4 8 cxd4 ♗b6 9 d5 ♘a5 10 e5 ♘xc4 11 ♕a4+ ♕d7 [□ 11 ... ♗d7 12 ♕xc4 ♘e7 13 e6 fxe6 14 dxe6 ♗c6 15 ♗g5 ♗xf3 16 gxf3 d5∓] 12 ♕xc4 ♘e7 13 ♖e1 dxe5? [□ 13 ... 0-0] 14 ♘xe5 ♕xd5 15 ♕a4+ [15 ♕xd5 ♘xd5 16 ♘g6+ ♗e6 17 ♘xh8 ♔f8] 15 ... ♗d7 16 ♘xd7 ♕xd7 17 ♖xe7+ [17 ♕h4 0-0 18 ♕xe7 ♖ae8!] 17 ... ♔xe7 18 ♗a3+ ♔e8 [□ 18 ... c5 19 ♖e1+ ♔d8 20 ♖d1 ♕xd1+ 21 ♕xd1 ♔c7, ♖ad8] 19 ♖e1+ ♗e3 20 ♕b3! ♔d8 [20 ... c6 21 ♖xe3+; 22 ♖d3] 21 ♕xb7 ♖c8 [21 ... ♗xf2+ (21 ... ♕c8 22 ♖d1+; 21 ... ♕d2 22 ♗b4 ♕xf2+ 23 ♔h1 ♖c8 24 ♕d5+ ♔e8 25 ♕e4+ ♔d7 26 ♖d1+) 22 ♔xf2 ♕d2+ 23 ♖e2 ♕d4+ (23 ... ♕f4+ 24 ♔e1) 24 ♖e3 ♕f4+ 25 ♔e2 ♕g4+ 26 ♔e1+−] 22 fxe3 ♕d3 [□ 22 ... c6 23 ♕b3 ♕e6] 23 ♗b4 f5 24 ♖e2! ♖e8 [24 ... ♕xe2 25 ♕d5++−] 25 ♖d2 ♖xe3 26 ♖xd3+ ♖xd3 27 ♗e7+ ♔d7 28 ♕b5+ **1-0** L/N3203

**1866-★MM-7**
**Morphy, P.C.+Maurian, C.A.**
New Orleans [Maróczy]
⟨♘b1⟩ 1 e4 e5 2 ♘f3 ♘c6 3 ♗c4 ♗c5 4 b4 ♗xb4 5 c3 ♗a5 6 0-0 ♘f6 7 ♘g5 0-0 8 ♕b3 ♕e7 9 ♗a3 d6 10 d4 ♗b6 [□ 10 ... h6] 11 f4 ♘a5 12 ♕a4 ♘xc4 13 ♕xc4 h6 14 ♘f3 ♘g4 15 fxe5 ♘xe5 16 ♕e2 ♗g4 17 ♔h1 ♘xf3 18 gxf3 ♗d7 [18 ... ♗h5] 19 ♖g1 ♖fe8 20 ♖g3 ♕h4 21 ♖ag1 g5 22 ♗c1 f6 23 ♕d3 ♖e7 [□ 23 ... ♔h8] 24 c4 ♔h8 25 ♕c3 ♖xe4 26 c5 dxc5 27 dxc5 ♖f8 28 fxe4 ♕xe4+ 29 ♖1g2 ♗c6 30 cxb6 ♕f5 31 h3 ♕f1+ 32 ♔h2 ♗xg2 33 ♖xg2 cxb6 34 ♕c2 ♔g7 35 ♖f2 ♕b5 36 ♗b2 ♕c6 37 ♕d3 ♕c5 38 ♕d7+ ♔g6 [38 ... ♖f7 39 ♗xf6+ ♔g6 40 ♕d3++−] 39 ♗d4 ♕c6 40 ♕f5+ ♔g7 41 ♗e5 b5 42 h4 ♖f7 43 h5 ♔f8 44 ♗xf6 ♕c7+ 45 ♔h3 ♕c4 46 ♖c2 ♕h4+ 47 ♔g2 **1-0** L/N3203

**1866-★MM-8**
**Morphy, P.C.+Maurian, C.A.**
New Orleans [Maróczy]
⟨♘b1⟩ 1 e4 e5 2 f4 exf4 3 ♘f3 g5 4 ♗c4 g4 5 d4 gxf3 6 ♕xf3 ♘c6? [□ 6 ... d5!] 7 ♗xf7+ ♔xf7 8 ♕h5+ ♔e7 9 ♗xf4 ♘f6 10 ♗g5 ♗g7 11 e5 ♕e8 12 ♕h4 ♕g6 13 0-0 d5 14 exf6+ ♔f7 15 fxg7+ ♔xg7 16 ♖f6 ♗f5 17 ♖xg6+ hxg6 18 ♗f6+ **1-0** L/N3203

**1866-★MM-9** 7 xi 66
**Morphy, P.C.−Maurian, C.A.**
New Orleans [Maróczy]
⟨♘b1⟩ 1 e4 e5 2 ♘f3 ♘c6 3 ♗c4 ♗c5 4 b4 ♗xb4 5 c3 ♗c5 6 0-0 d6 7 d4 exd4 8 cxd4 ♗b6 9 ♗b2 ♘a5 10 ♗d3 ♘e7 11 ♘g5 0-0 12 f4 f6 13 ♘f3 c5 14 ♔h1 cxd4 15 f5 d5! 16 ♘h4 ♘c4 17 ♗xc4 dxc4 18 ♖f3 ♕d6∓ 19 ♖g3 ♗d7 20 ♗c1 d3 21 ♗h6 ♖f7 22 ♕h5 ♗f2 23 ♖g4 d2 24 ♖d1 c3 25 ♖f4 c2 26 ♖xf2 cxd1♕+ 27 ♕xd1

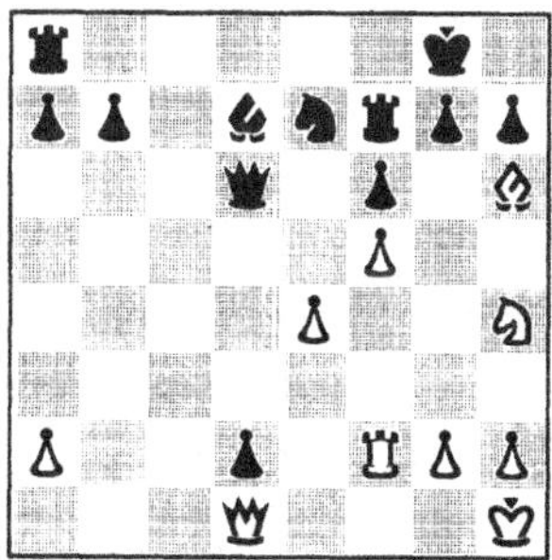

27 ... ♗a4! 28 ♕xd2 ♕xd2 29 ♗xd2 ♖d8 30 ♘f3 ♘c6 31 h4 ♖fd7 32 ♗f4 ♘d4 33 ♘xd4 ♖xd4 34 ♖e2 ♗c6 **0-1** L/N3203

**1866-★MM-10** xi 66
**Morphy, P.C.+Maurian, C.A.**
New Orleans [Maróczy]
⟨♘b1⟩ 1 e4 e5 2 ♘f3 ♘c6 3 ♗c4 ♗c5 4 b4 ♗xb4 5 c3 ♗c5 6 0-0 d6 7 d4 exd4 8 cxd4 ♗b6 9 d5 ♘a5 10 e5 ♘xc4 11 ♕a4+ ♗d7 12 ♕xc4 ♘e7 13 ♖e1 0-0 14 ♗g5 ♖e8 15 e6 ♗c8 [□ 15 ... fxe6, 16 ... ♗c6] 16 exf7+ ♔xf7 17 ♕f4+ ♔g8 18

♕h4 ♔f8 19 ♕xh7 ♕d7 20 ♗xe7+ ♖xe7 21 ♘g5 ♗xf2+ 22 ♔h1 ♖xe1+ 23 ♖xe1 ♗xe1 24 ♕h8+ ♔e7 25 ♕xg7+ ♔d8 [25 ... ♔e8 26 ♕g8+ ♔e7 27 ♕f7+ ♔d8 28 ♘e6+] 26 ♘e6+ ♕xe6 27 dxe6 ♗xe6 [27 ... c6 28 ♕f8+ ♔c7 29 e7+−] 28 ♕f8+ ♔d7 29 ♕xa8 **1-0** L/N3203

**1866-★MM-11** xi 66
**Morphy, P.C.+Maurian, C.A.**
New Orleans [Maróczy]
⟨♘b1⟩ 1 e4 e5 2 ♘f3 ♘c6 3 ♗c4 ♗c5 4 b4 ♗xb4 5 c3 ♗c5 6 0-0 d6 7 d4 exd4 8 cxd4 ♗b6 9 d5 ♘a5 10 e5 ♘xc4 11 ♕a4+ ♗d7 12 ♕xc4 ♘e7 13 e6 fxe6 14 dxe6 ♗c6 15 ♗g5 h6 [□15 ... 0-0, ♖e8] 16 ♕h4 ♗xf3 17 gxf3 d5 18 f4 ♗d4 19 ♖ad1 c5 20 f5 ♕d6 [20 ... ♘xf5 21 ♕h5+ +−] 21 ♖fe1 g6 22 ♖xd4 cxd4 23 f6 ♘f5 24 ♕h3 ♖c8 25 f7+ ♔f8 26 ♗f6 ♕f4 [26 ... ♘g7 27 ♕g4 g5 28 ♕xd4 ♘f5 29 ♕d3 ♘g7 30 ♕g6] 27 ♗xh8 ♖c3 28 ♕xf5 **1-0** L/N3203

**1866-★MM-12** 9 xii 66
**Morphy, P.C.−Maurian, C.A.**
New Orleans [Maróczy]
⟨♘b1⟩ 1 e4 e5 2 ♘f3 ♘c6 3 ♗c4 ♗c5 4 d4 ♗xd4? [□4 ... exd4] 5 c3 ♗b6 6 ♘g5 ♘h6 7 ♕h5 ♕f6 8 0-0 0-0 9 ♔h1 ♕g6 10 ♕e2 d6 11 h3 ♔h8 12 g4 f6 13 ♘f3 ♘xg4! 14 hxg4 ♗xg4 15 ♕d3 ♗xf3+ 16 ♕xf3 f5 17 ♖g1 fxe4 18 ♕xf8+ ♖xf8 19 ♖xg6 hxg6 20 ♗g5 ♖xf2 21 ♖g1 ♖f3 [□21 ... ♘a5! 22 ♗e6 ♖f6!] 22 ♖g4 ♖h3+ 23 ♔g2 ♖h5 [24 ♗f7! e3 (24 ... ♔h7 25 ♗h4) 25 ♗xg6 e2 26 ♗h4 ♖h6 27 ♗d3∞] **0-1** L/N3203

**1866-★MM-13**
**Morphy, P.C.+Maurian, C.A.**
New Orleans [Maróczy]
⟨♘b1⟩ 1 e4 e5 2 ♘f3 ♘c6 3 ♗c4 ♗c5 4 b4 ♗xb4 5 c3 ♗a5 6 0-0 ♘f6 7 d4 0-0 8 ♕c2 exd4 [□8 ... d6!] 9 cxd4 d5 10 exd5 ♘e7 11 ♗a3 ♗f5 12 ♕a4 ♗b6 13 ♖fe1 ♘e4 14 ♗xe7 ♕xe7 15 ♗d3 ♖ae8 16 ♕c2 ♕b4? [16 ... ♗g6!, f6] 17 ♗xe4 ♗xe4 18 ♖xe4 f5 19 a3 ♕a5 20 ♖xe8 ♖xe8 21 ♕xf5 ♗xd4 22 ♖b1 ♖e2 23 ♕c8+ ♔f7 24 ♕g4 ♖b2 25 ♕e6+ ♔f8 26 ♖xb2 ♗xb2 27 ♘g5 **1-0** L/N3203

**1866-★MM-14** 30 xii 66
**Morphy, P.C.−Maurian, C.A.**
New Orleans [Maróczy]
⟨♘b1⟩ 1 e4 e5 2 ♘f3 ♘c6 3 ♗c4 ♗c5 4 0-0 ♘f6 5 b4 ♗xb4 6 c3 ♗e7! [7 ... ♗a5?] 7 ♘g5 0-0 8 d4 d5 9 exd5 ♘xd5 10 ♕h5 ♗xg5 11 ♗xg5 ♘f4 12 ♕h4 ♕d7 13 dxe5 ♘g6 14 e6 ♕d6! 15 exf7+ ♔h8 16 ♕g3 ♕xg3 17 fxg3 ♘a5 18 ♗d5 c6 19 c4 cxd5 20 cxd5 ♘c4 21 ♖ae1 ♘d6 22 ♗e7 ♘xe7 23 ♖xe7 ♗f5 24 h3 ♖ad8 **0-1** L/N3203

**1866-★MM-15**
**Morphy, P.C.+McConnell, J.**
[Maróczy]
⟨♘b1⟩ 1 e4 e5 2 ♘f3 ♘c6 3 ♗c4 ♗c5 4 b4 ♗xb4 5 c3 ♗c5 6 0-0 d6 7 d4 exd4 8 cxd4 ♗b6 9 d5 ♘e5 [□9 ... ♘a5] 10 ♘xe5 dxe5 11 ♗b2 ♕e7 12 ♕b3 ♘f6 13 ♔h1 ♘g4 14 ♕g3 ♕c5 15 ♗b3 ♘xf2+? [□15 ... ♕xf2! 16 ♖xf2 ♘xf2+ 17 ♕xf2 (17 ♔g1 ♘xe4+, 18 ♘xg3+−+) 17 ... ♗xf2 18 ♗xe5 f6−+] 16 ♖xf2 ♕xf2 17 ♕xe5+ ♔d8 18 ♕xg7 ♖e8 19 ♗f6+ ♔d7 20 ♕xf7+ ♔d6 21 e5+ ♖xe5 22 ♕f8+ **1-0** L/N3203

**1866-★MM-16** 11 xi 66
**Morphy, P.C.+Maurian, C.A.**
New Orleans
⟨♘b1⟩ 1 e4 e5 2 ♘f3 ♘c6 3 ♗c4 ♗c5 4 b4 ♗xb4 5 c3 ♗c5 6 0-0 d6 7 d4 exd4 8 cxd4 ♗b6 9 d5 ♘a5 10 e5 ♘xc4 11 ♕a4+ ♗d7 12 ♕xc4 ♗f5 13 ♖e1 ♘e7 14 ♗g5 dxe5 15 ♗xe7 ♕xe7 16 ♖xe5 ♕xe5 17 ♘xe5 0-0 18 g4 ♖ae8 19 ♖e1 ♗c8 20 ♔g2 f5 21 g5 f4 22 ♘f3 ♖d8 23 d6+ ♔h8 24 ♘e5 f3+ 25 ♔g3 **1-0** L/N3203

**1866-★MN-1** 13 xi 66
**Mayet, K.−Neumann, G.R.**
Berlin [Anderssen & Neumann]
1 e4 e5 2 f4 d5 3 exd5 e4 4 ♗b5+ c6 5 dxc6 bxc6 6 ♗a4 ♘f6 7 d4 ♗d6 8 c4 0-0 9 ♘c3 e3 10 ♕f3 ♖e8 11 h3 ♗xf4 12 ♕xf4 ♘h5 13 ♕f3 ♕h4+ 14 ♔d1 ♕xd4+ 15 ♔c2 ♘f4 16 g4 ♘a6 17 ♔b1 ♘b4 18 ♕d1 ♕xc4 19 ♗xe3 ♗f5+ 20 gxf5 ♖xe3 21 ♗b3 ♕c5 22 ♕g4 ♖e1+ 23 ♗d1 ♖xd1+ 24 ♕xd1 ♕xf5+ 25 ♔c1 ♘fd3+ 26 ♔d2 ♕f4+ 27 ♔e2 ♕f2# **0-1** L/N6051

**1866-★MN-2** 16 xi 66
**Mayet, K.−Neumann, G.R.**
Berlin [Anderssen & Neumann]
1 e4 e5 2 f4 exf4 3 ♗c4 f5 4 ♗xg8? ♖xg8 5 ♕h5+ g6 6 ♕xh7 ♖g7 7 ♕h8 fxe4 8 ♘e2 f3 9 0-0 ♖f7 10 gxf3 exf3 11 ♘g3 d5 12 d4 [12 ♖e1+ ♔d7] 12 ... ♘c6 13 ♗h6 ♕f6 14 ♕xf6 ♖xf6 15 ♗xf8 ♔xf8 16 c3 ♗h3 17 ♖f2 ♔g7 18 ♘d2 ♖af8 19 ♖e1 ♖8f7 20 ♖e3 ♗g4

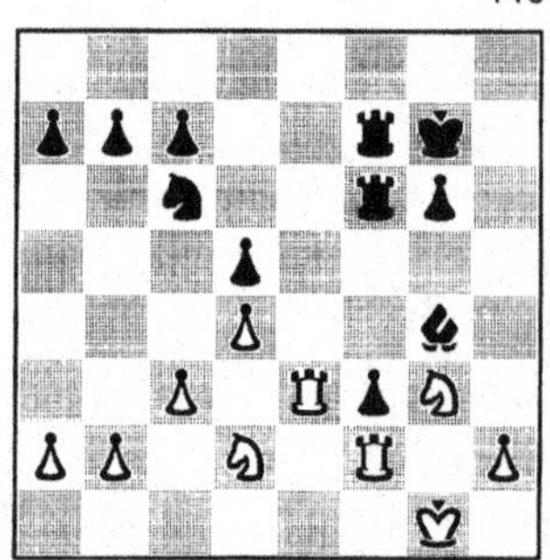

21 h4 [□21 h3] 21 ... ♘d8 [△ ♘e6, ♘f4, ♘h3] 22 ♖e5 ♘e6 23 ♖xd5? ♘f4 24 ♖g5 ♘h3+ 25 ♔f1 ♘xg5 26 hxg5 ♖e6 27 d5 ♖e5 28 c4 ♖xg5 29 ♔e1 ♖f4 30 ♔d1 ♖e5 31 b4 b5 **0-1** L/N6051

**1866-★MN-3** 16 xi 66
**Mayet, K.=Neumann, G.R.**
Berlin [Anderssen & Neumann]
1 e4 e5 2 f4 d5 3 exd5 e4 4 ♗b5+ c6 5 dxc6 bxc6 6 ♗a4 [□6 ♗c4 ♗c5 7 ♗xf7+] 6 ... ♗c5 7 ♘e2 [7 ♕h5 ♕b6⇆; 7 ♘c3 ♗xg1 8 ♖xg1 ♕h4+ 9 g3 ♕xh2 10 ♘e2 ♗g4] 7 ... ♕h4+ 8 g3 [8 ♘g3 ♕xf4 9 d4 e3] 8 ... ♕h3 9 d4 exd3 10 ♕xd3 ♕g2 11 ♖f1 ♗h3 12 ♘ec3 [12 ♕f3 ♕h1+ 13 ♔d2 ♗g4] 12 ... ♕xf1+ [□12 ... ♕xh2] 13 ♕xf1 ♗xf1 14 ♔xf1 ♘e7 15 ♘e4 ♘d7 16 ♘bd2 0-0 17 ♘b3 ♗b6 18 c4 ♖ad8 19 c5 ♗c7 20 ♗d2 ♘b8 21 ♗e1 h6 22 ♗f2 ♖fe8 23 ♖ae1 ♘d5 24 a3 f5 25 ♘ed2 ♖xe1+ 26 ♔xe1 ♖e8+ 27 ♔f1 ♘e3+ 28 ♔g1 ♘d1 29 ♘d4 ♘xf2 [29 ... ♘xb2 30 ♗c2] 30 ♔xf2 ♖d8 31 ♘2f3 ♖f8 32 b4 a5 [32 ... ♖f6 33 ♗b3+, 34 ♘e6] 33 ♘xc6 ♘xc6 34 ♗xc6 axb4 35 axb4 ♖b8 36 b5 ♗a5 37 ♔e3 ♖d8 38 ♘e5 ♗b4 39 ♘d7 ♖xd7= 40 ♗xd7 ♗xc5+ 41 ♔f3 g6 42 h3 ♔f7 43 g4 ♔f6 **½-½** L/N6051

**1866-★MN-4** 16 xi 66
**Mayet, K.−Neumann, G.R.**
Berlin [Anderssen & Neumann]
1 e4 e5 2 f4 exf4 3 ♗c4 f5 4 ♕e2 ♕h4+ 5 ♔d1 fxe4 6 ♕xe4+ ♗e7 7 ♘f3 ♕h5 8 ♖e1 ♘c6 9 ♗xg8 ♖xg8 10 ♘c3 d6 11 ♘d5 ♗f5 12 ♕c4 ♗xc2+ 13 ♕xc2 [13 ♔xc2 ♕xd5 14 ♕xd5 ♘b4+∞] 13 ... ♕xd5 14 ♕xh7 0-0-0 15 b3 ♗f6 16 ♖b1 g5 17 ♕e4 ♕xe4 18 ♖xe4 g4 19 ♘e1 [19 ♖xf4 gxf3 20 ♖xf6 fxg2] 19 ... ♗e5 20 ♗b2 ♗xb2 21 ♖xb2 ♖df8 22 d3 d5 23 ♖ee2 ♘d4 24 ♖f2 ♘f5 25 ♔c1 ♘e3 26 d4 g3 27 hxg3 fxg3 28 ♖fe2 ♘f5 29 ♘f3 ♘d6 30 ♔d1 ♘e4 31 ♖bc2 ♘f2+ 32 ♔e1 ♔d8 [32 ... ♖xf3 33 gxf3 g2 34 ♖e8+] 33 ♖e3 ♘g4 34 ♖ec3 c6 35 ♖e2 ♘h2 36 ♘d2

♔d7 37 ♖ee3 ♖e8 38 ♔e2 ♔d6 39 b4 b6 40 a4 ♖gf8 41 ♖xe8 ♖xe8+ 42 ♖e3 ♖xe3+ 43 ♔xe3 ♘g4+ 44 ♔f4 ♘f2 45 b5 ♘d3+ 46 ♔xg3 c5 47 ♔g4 c4−+ 48 ♔f5 c3 49 ♘b3 c2 50 g4 c1♕ 51 ♘xc1 ♘xc1 52 g5 ♘b3 53 ♔f6 ♘xd4 54 g6 ♘e6 55 ♔f5 d4 56 ♔e4 ♔e7 **0-1** L/N6051

**1866-★MN-5** 16 xi 66
**Neumann, G.R.+Mayet, K.**
Berlin [Anderssen & Neumann]

1 e4 e5 2 ♘f3 ♘c6 3 ♗c4 ♗c5 4 b4 ♗xb4 5 c3 ♗c5 6 0-0 h6 7 d4 exd4 8 cxd4 ♗b6 9 ♘c3 ♘ge7 10 d5 ♘a5 11 ♗d3 d6 12 ♘e2 c5 13 ♗b2 0-0 14 ♘g3 g6 15 ♕d2 ♔h7 16 ♗f6 ♕d7 17 ♖fe1 ♘g8 18 e5 c4 [18 ... ♘xf6 19 exf6 ♗d8 20 ♘f5 gxf5 (20 ... ♗xf6 21 ♕xh6+ ♔g8 22 ♘g5 ♖d8 23 ♕h7+ ♔f8 24 ♘h6) 21 ♘h4 ♗xf6 (21 ... ♕a4 22 ♘xf5) 22 ♗xf5+ ♕xf5 23 ♘xf5 ♗xf5 24 ♕xa5 ♗xa1 25 ♖xa1] 19 ♘g5+ hxg5 20 ♗f5 ♕xf5 [20 ... ♕a4 21 ♕xg5 ♘h6 (21 ... ♘xf6 22 exf6 ♗d8 23 ♕h5+ ♔g8 24 ♗xg6) 22 ♖e4 △ 23 ♕xh6+ ♔xh6 24 ♖h4#] 21 ♘xf5 ♘xf6 22 exf6 ♗xf5 23 ♕xg5 ♖h8 24 ♖e7 ♔g8 25 ♖ae1 ♖f8 26 g4 ♗d3 27 h4 c3 28 h5 ♘c4 [28 ... ♖h7 29 hxg6 ♗xg6 30 ♖xf7 ♖hxf7 31 ♕xg6+ ♔h8 32 ♔g2 ♖h7 33 ♖h1 ♖f7 34 ♖xh7+ ♖xh7 35 ♕e8#] 29 hxg6 [29 ... ♗xg6 30 ♕xg6+ fxg6 31 ♖g7#] **1-0** L/N6051

**1866-★MN-6** 16 xi 66
**Neumann, G.R.+Mayet, K.**
Berlin [Anderssen & Neumann]

1 e4 e5 2 ♘f3 ♘c6 3 ♗c4 ♗c5 4 b4 ♗xb4 5 c3 ♗c5 6 0-0 h6 7 d4 exd4 8 cxd4 ♗b6 9 ♘c3 ♘ge7 10 d5 ♘a5 11 ♗d3 d6 12 ♘e2 f5 13 ♘g3 0-0 14 ♘h4 ♘xd5 15 ♘hxf5 ♘b4 16 ♗b1 ♕f6 17 ♕d2 ♕xa1 18 ♕xb4 c5 19 ♕b5 ♗xf5 20 ♘xf5 ♕c3 21 ♗b2 ♕c4 22 ♕d7 ♖f7 [22 ... ♕f7 23 ♘xh6+ gxh6 24 ♕g4+ ♔h7 25 e5+ ♔h8 26 e6+ ♕f6 27 ♕g6] 23 ♕xd6 ♖d8 24 ♕g6 ♖dd7 25 ♘xg7 ♖xg7 26 ♗xg7 [26 ♕e8+ ♔h7 27 e5+ ♖d3 28 ♖d1 ♖xg2+ 29 ♔h1 (29 ♔xg2 ♕g4+ 30 ♔f1 ♕xd1+ 31 ♔g2 ♕g4+ 32 ♔f1 c4−+) 29 ... ♖g1+ 30 ♖xg1! ♕e4+ 31 f3! ♕xf3+=] 26 ... ♕f7 27 ♕xf7+ ♖xf7 28 ♗xh6 **1-0** L/N6051

**1866-★MN-7** 16 xi 66
**Neumann, G.R.+Mayet, K.**
Berlin [Anderssen & Neumann]

1 e4 e5 2 f4 exf4 3 ♗c4 ♕h4+ 4 ♔f1 g5 5 ♘c3 ♘e7 [□ 5 ... ♗g7] 6 g3 fxg3 7 ♔g2 gxh2 8 ♖xh2 ♕f4 9 d4 ♕f6 10 ♘f3 d6 [10 ... ♗h6 11 ♘e5±] 11 ♘xg5 ♖g8 12 ♕h5 ♗e6 13 ♗xe6 ♕xe6 14 ♔h1 ♕f6 15 ♗e3 h6 16 e5 dxe5 17 ♘ge4 ♕f5 [17 ... ♕c6 18 ♖f1, 19 ♖hf2±; 17 ... ♕g6 18 ♕xe5±] 18 ♕xf5 ♘xf5 19 ♘f6+ ♔d8 20 ♘xg8 ♘xe3 21 dxe5 ♘g4 22 ♖d2+ ♔e8 23 ♖e1 ♘d7 24 ♘f6+ ♘gxf6 25 exf6+ ♔d8 26 ♖ed1 ♗d6 27 ♘e4 **1-0** L/N6051

**1866-★MN-8** 21 xii 66
**Mayet, K.−Neumann, G.R.**
Berlin [Anderssen & Neumann]

1 e4 e5 2 ♘f3 ♘c6 3 ♗c4 ♗c5 4 0-0 ♘f6 5 d3 d6 6 ♘c3 ♗g4 7 h3 ♗h5 8 g4 ♘xg4 9 hxg4 ♗xg4 10 ♔g2 [10 ♗e3 ♖f8; 10 ♗b5 0-0 11 ♗xc6 bxc6 12 ♔g2 f5 13 ♕d2 (13 ♕e1 fxe4 14 ♘h2 ♗f3+ 15 ♔g1 exd3) 13 ... fxe4 14 ♘h2 ♗f3+ 15 ♔g1 e3 16 fxe3 ♕g5+ 17 ♔f2 ♕h4+] 10 ... ♘d4 11 ♗xf7+ ♔xf7 12 ♘xe5+ dxe5 13 ♕xg4 h5 14 ♕d1 ♕h4 15 f4 ♖af8 16 ♘d5 ♔e8 17 ♘xc7+ [□ 17 ♖h1] 17 ... ♔d8 18 ♘d5 ♖h6 19 f5 ♘xc2 20 ♕xc2 ♖g6+ 21 fxg6 ♕g4+ 22 ♔h2 ♖xf1 **0-1** L/N6051

**1866-★MS-1**
**Minchin, J.I.−Steinitz, W.**
London [Anderssen & Neumann]

1 e4 e5 2 ♘f3 ♘c6 3 ♗c4 ♗c5 4 b4 ♗xb4 5 c3 ♗c5 6 d4 exd4 7 cxd4 ♗b4+ [□ 7 ... ♗b6] 8 ♔f1 ♕e7 9 e5 f6 10 exf6 [□ 10 a3 ♗a5 11 ♖a2] 10 ... ♘xf6 11 ♗g5 b6 12 a3 ♗d6 13 ♖a2 ♕f8 14 ♖e2+ ♗e7 15 ♘c3 ♗b7 16 ♘e5 0-0-0 [□ 16 ... ♘xe5] 17 ♘f7 d5 18 ♘xd8 ♕xd8 19 ♗xf6 ♗xf6 20 ♗xd5 ♗xd4 21 ♖d2 [21 ♗xc6 ♗xc6 22 ♖d2 ♕g5 23 ♖xd4 ♕xg2+ 24 ♔e2 ♖e8+ 25 ♔d2 ♕xf2+−+ Lowenthal] 21 ... ♗xc3 22 ♗e6+ ♔b8 23 ♖xd8+ ♖xd8 24 ♕a4? [□ 24 ♕g4] 24 ... ♖d4 25 ♕c2 ♗a6+ 26 ♔g1 ♖d2 27 ♕c1 ♘d4 28 ♗g4 ♘e2+ 29 ♗xe2 ♗xe2 30 h4 ♖d1+ 31 ♔h2 ♖xc1 32 ♖xc1 ♗f6 **0-1** L/N6051-1866

**1866-★MS-2**
**Murphy−Steinitz, W.**
London?

⟨♙f7⟩ 1 e4 ♘c6 2 d4 e5 3 dxe5 ♘xe5 4 f4 ♘f7 5 ♗c4 ♘gh6 6 ♘f3 [□ 6 ♕d4] 6 ... ♗c5 7 ♕d5?! ♕e7 8 ♘c3 c6 9 ♕d3 d5 10 ♗b3 ♗f5 11 ♗xd5! cxd5 12 ♕b5+ ♗d7 13 ♕xb7 0-0 14 ♕xd5 ♗e6 15 ♕d1 ♗c4! 16 b3 ♖ad8 17 ♗d2 ♗a6 18 e5 ♘xe5!! 19 fxe5 ♕xe5+ 20 ♘e2 [20 ♘xe5 ♗f2#] 20 ... ♖xf3 21 gxf3 ♗xe2 22 f4 [22 ♕xe2 ♕xa1+, 23 ... ♖e8+] 22 ... ♕e4 **0-1** L/N6124-1867

**1866-★N?-1** 30 xi 66
**?−Neumann, G.R.**
Berlin [Anderssen & Neumann]

1 e4 e5 2 f4 exf4 3 ♗c4 f5 4 d3 ♕h4+ 5 ♔f1 fxe4 6 dxe4 ♗c5 7 ♕f3 ♘h6 8 ♗xf4 ♖f8 9 g3 ♕e7 10 ♔g2 g5 11 ♕h5+ ♘f7 12 ♗xf7+ ♖xf7 13 ♗xg5 ♕xe4+ 14 ♘f3 ♕e2+ 15 ♔h3 d5+ 16 ♔h4 ♕e4+ 17 ♗f4 h6 18 ♘bd2 **0-1** L/N6051

**1866-★RS-1**
**Robey, J.+Steinitz, W.**
London [Löwenthal]

1 e4 e5 2 ♘f3 ♘c6 3 ♗c4 ♗c5 4 b4 ♗xb4 5 c3 ♗c5 6 0-0 d6 7 d4 exd4 8 cxd4 ♗b6 9 ♘c3 ♘a5 10 e5 dxe5 11 ♗xf7+ ♔f8 [11 ... ♔xf7 ♘xe5+±] 12 ♗a3+ ♘e7 13 ♘xe5 ♕xd4 14 ♕h5 ♕xc3 15 ♖ad1 c5 16 ♖d3! [16 ♗b3! (△ 17 ♕f7#) 16 ... g6 (16 ... ♘g6 17 ♘xg6+ hxg6 18 ♕xh8+, 19 ♖fe1+−) 17 ♕h6+ ♔e8 18 ♗f7#] 16 ... ♕xd3 [16 ... ♕c2 17 ♗b3] 17 ♘xd3 g6 18 ♕f3 ♔g7 19 ♗b2+ ♔h6 **1-0** L/N6124

**1866-★RS-2**
**Ranken, C.E. & Wayte, W.−Staunton, H.**
London [Staunton]

1 e4 e5 2 ♘f3 ♘c6 3 d4 exd4 4 ♗c4 ♗c5 5 ♘g5 ♘h6 6 ♘xf7 ♘xf7 7 ♗xf7+ ♔xf7 8 ♕h5+ g6 9 ♕d5+ ♔g7 10 ♕xc5 ♖e8 [10 ... d5] 11 0-0 [11 ♗g5] 11 ... ♖xe4 12 b4 b6 13 ♕c4 ♗b7 14 f4 d5 15 ♕b3 ♕d6 16 b5 ♘a5 17 ♕d3 [□ 17 ♕f3] 17 ... ♘c4 18 ♘a3 ♘e3 19 ♖f3 [19 ♗xe3 dxe3∓] 19 ... ♖ae8 20 c3? [20 ♗b2] 20 ... ♘c4 21 ♘xc4 dxc4 22 ♕xc4 d3 23 ♕xd3 ♖e1+ 24 ♔f2 ♗xf3 **0-1** M954-1866

**1866-★RS-3**
**Ranken, C.E. & Wayte, W.+Staunton, H.**
London [Staunton]

1 e4 e5 2 ♘f3 ♘c6 3 d4 exd4 4 ♗c4 ♗c5 5 c3 d3 6 b4 ♗b6 7 b5 ♘ce7? [7 ... ♘a5; 7 ... ♕d7!? 8 0-0 ♘d8 9 a4] 8 ♕b3 f6 9 0-0 d6 10 ♗f4? [10 h3] 10 ... ♗g4 11 ♗f7+ ♔f8 12 ♘bd2 ♘g6 13 ♗xg8 ♖xg8 14 ♗g3 ♕e7 15 c4 ♗xf3 16 gxf3 ♗d4∓ 17 ♖ae1 ♗e5 18 ♕xd3 h5 19 ♔h1 ♗f4 20 ♕d5 ♗xd2 21 ♕xd2 ♕e6 22 ♖g1! ♔f7 23 ♗f4 a6?? [23 ... ♘h4 24 ♖g3 g5 25 ♗e3 g4∓] 24 b6! cxb6 25 ♖b1 ♖ad8 26 ♖xb6 ♖d7 27 ♖xd6 ♖gd8? 28 ♖xe6 ♖xd2 29 ♗xd2 ♔xe6 30 ♗a5 ♖d3 31 ♖xg6 ...? **1-0** M954-1866

**1866-★S?-1**
**Steinitz, W.+?**
London [Staunton]

⟨♘b1⟩ 1 e4 e5 2 ♘f3 d6 3 ♗c4 ♗g4 4 c3 ♗xf3 5 gxf3 ♕f6 6 d4 ♘d7 7 0-0 0-0-0 8 ♗d3 ♘h6 9 ♗e2 ♔b8 10 a4 ♕g6+ 11 ♔h1 f5 12 ♖g1 ♕f7 13 a5 exd4 14 cxd4 f4 15 ♗d2 ♕f6 16 a6 b6 17 ♕a4 d5 18 e5 ♕e6 19 ♗xf4 ♗e7 20 ♖ac1 c5 21 ♗d3 cxd4 22 ♖xg7 ♘c5 23

♖xe7! ♘xa4 24 ♖xe6 ♘xb2 25 ♖e7 ♘xd3 26 ♖b7+ ♔a8 27 ♖cc7 ♘c5 [27 ... ♘xf4 28 ♖xa7+ ♔b8 29 ♖cb7+ ♔c8 30 ♖a8#] 28 e6 ♘xa6 [28 ... ♘xb7 29 axb7+ ♔b8 30 ♖d7#] 29 ♖xa7+ ♔b8 30 ♖cb7+ ♔c8 31 ♖b8+ ♘xb8 32 ♖c7# **1-0** M954

**1866-★S?-2**
**Steinitz, W.+?**

[Anderssen & Neumann]

⟨♘g1⟩ 1 d4 d5 2 c4 c6 3 ♘c3 f6 4 ♗f4 ♘d7? 5 cxd5 cxd5 6 ♘xd5 e5 7 dxe5 fxe5 8 ♗g3 ♕a5+ 9 ♘c3 ♗b4 10 ♕c2 ♘gf6 11 ♖c1 0-0 12 e3 ♘b6? 13 ♕b3+ ♔h8 14 ♗xe5 ♘e4 5 f3 ♘c5 16 ♕d1 ♗f5 17 e4 ♖ad8 18 ♕c2 ♗g6 19 f4 ♘e6 20 ♗e2 ♗c5 21 h4 ♗e3 22 h5 ♗d2+ 23 ♕xd2 ♖xd2 24 hxg6 ♖d7 [⌓ 24 ... ♖xe2+ 25 ♔xe2 ♘xf4+] 25 ♗g4 ♖e7 26 ♗xe6 ♖xe6 27 ♖xh7+ ♔g8 28 ♖xg7+ ♔h8 29 ♖h7+ ♔g8 30 ♖h8# **1-0** L/N6051-1866

# LONDON (ENG) [1849-LON]

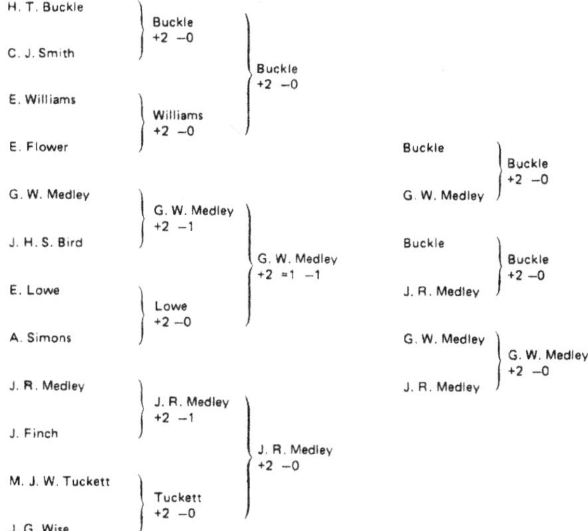


1 Buckle
2 Medley, G. W.
3 Medley, J. R.

## LONDON (ENG) 27 v- 15 vii 1851 [1851-LON1]

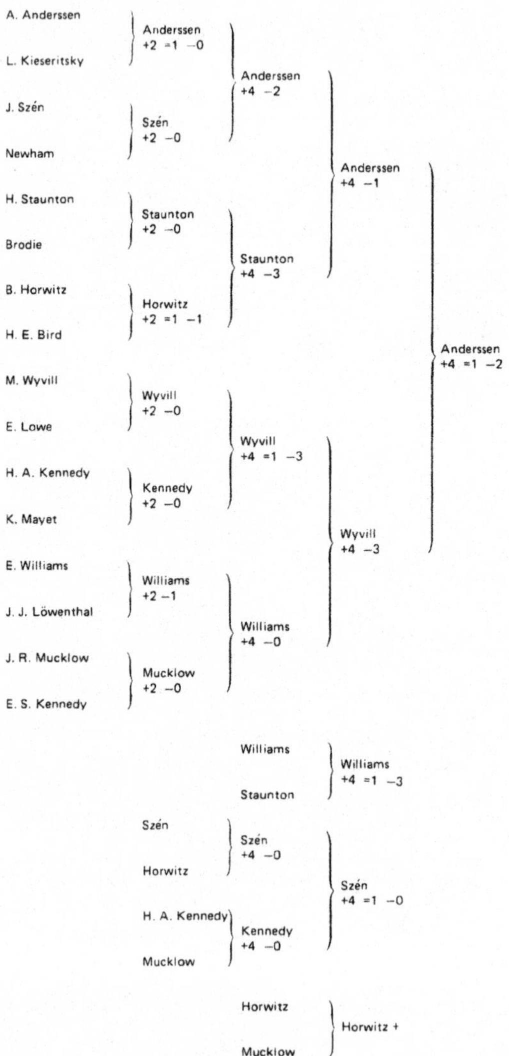


1 Anderssen
2 Wyvill
3 Williams
4 Staunton
5 Szén
6 Kennedy, H. A.
7 Horwitz
8 Mucklow

## LONDON (ENG) 3 vi- ? 1851 [1851-LON2]

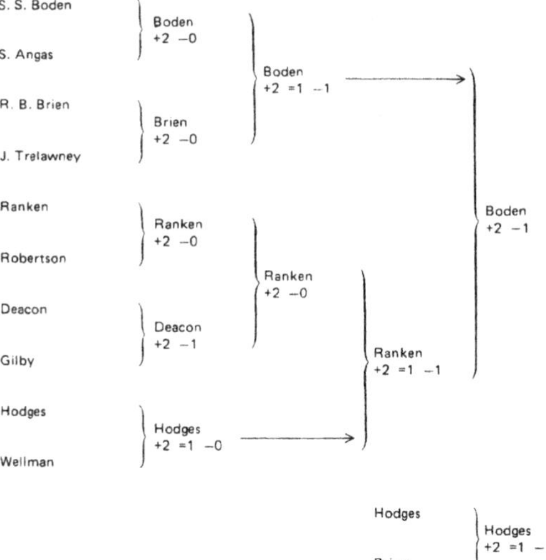


1 Boden
2 Ranken
3 Hodges
4 Brien

## MANCHESTER (ENG) 5 viii- ? viii 1857 [1857-MNC]

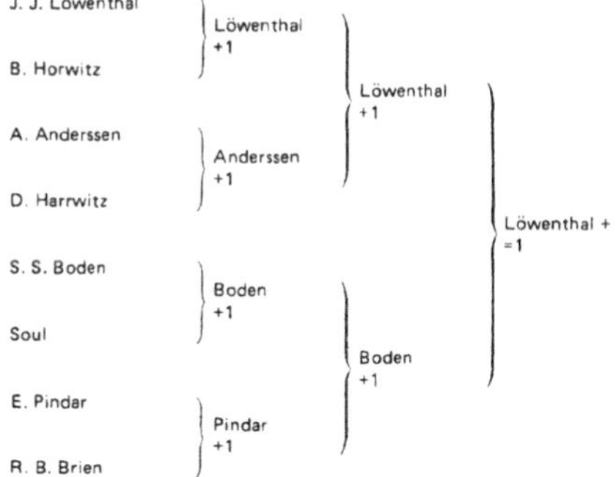


1 Löwenthal
2 Boden

## NEW YORK (USA) 1st American Chess Congress 6 x- 10 xi 1857 [1857-NYC1]

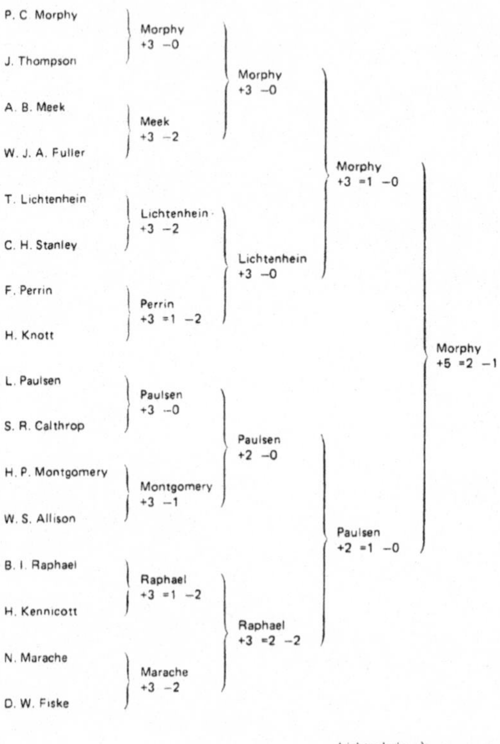


Lichtenhein
Raphael
Lichtenhein +3 –0

1 Morphy
2 Paulsen
3 Lichtenhein
4 Raphael

# NEW YORK (USA) 12 x- 7 xi 1857 [1857-NYC2]

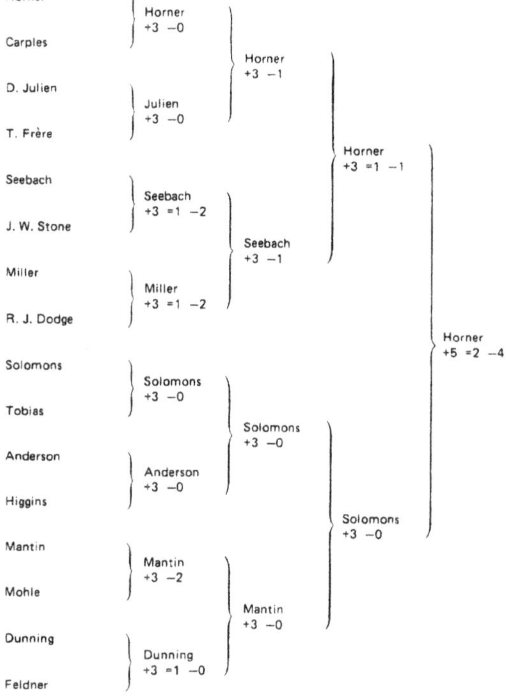


Seebach
Mantin
Seebach
+3 –0

1 Horner
2 Solomons
3 Seebach
4 Mantin

## BIRMINGHAM (ENG) 24 viii–23 ix 1858 [1858-BIR]

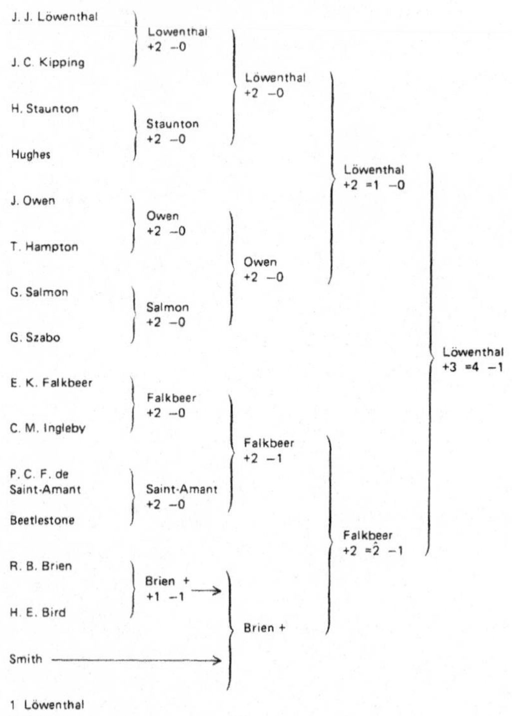


1 Löwenthal
2 Falkbeer

## CAMBRIDGE (ENG) 28 viii– 1 ix 1860 [1860-CMB]

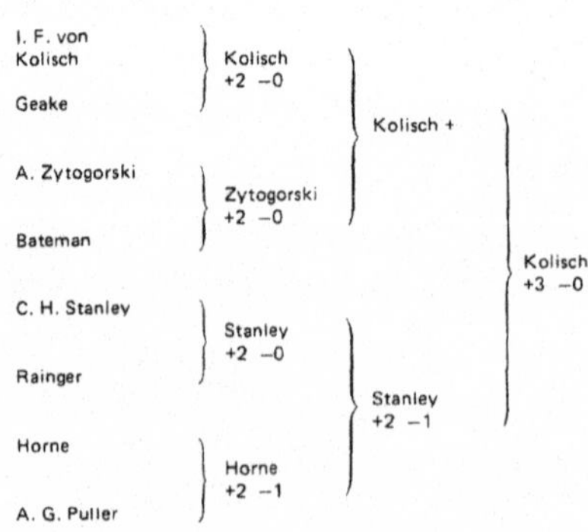


1 Kolisch
2 Stanley

## BRISTOL (ENG) 10 ix- 21 ix 1861 [1861-BRI]

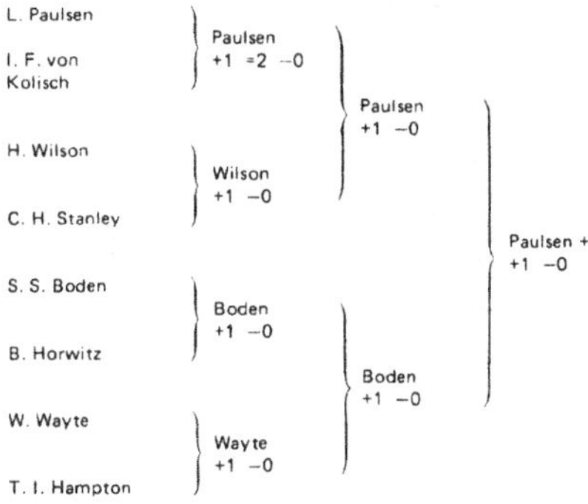


1 Paulsen
2 Boden

## MANCHESTER (ENG) i- iv 1861 [1861-MNC]

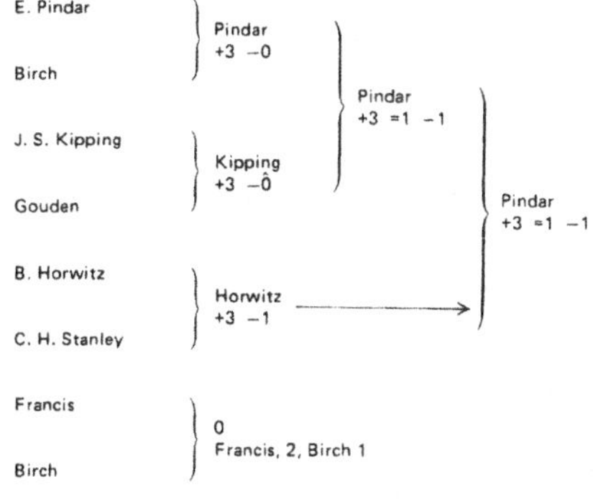


1 Pindar

## DÜSSELDORF (GER) **[1862-DUS]**

| | | 1 | 2 | 3 | 4 | 5 | 6 | 7 | 8 | Total |
|---|---|---|---|---|---|---|---|---|---|---|
| 1 | M. Lange | x | | | 1 | 1 | 1 | 1 | 1 | +5 =0 –0 |
| 2 | F. A. Hipp | | x | 1̂ | | | 0 | 1 | 1̂ | +3̂ =0 –1 |
| 3 | W. Paulsen | | 0̂ | x | 1 | | 1 | | 1̂ | +3̂ =0 –1̇ |
| 4 | G. Schultz | 0 | | 0 | x | 1 | 0 | 1 | 1̂ | +3̂ =0 –3 |
| 5 | von Hanneken | 0 | | | 0 | x | 1 | ½ | ½ | +1 =2 –2 |
| 6 | O. Wülfing | 0 | 1 | 0 | 1 | 0 | x | | | +2 =0 –3 |
| 7 | R. Lichtenscheidt | 0 | 0 | | 0 | ½ | | x | 1 | +1 =1 –3 |
| 8 | J. Kohtz | 0 | 0̂ | 0̂ | 0̇ | ½ | | 0 | x | +0̇ =1 –5̂ |

## LONDON (ENG) 16 vi– 31 vii 1862 **[1862-LON1]**

| | | 1 | 2 | 3 | 4 | 5 | 6 | 7 | 8 | 9 | 10 | 11 | 12 | 13 | 14 | Total |
|---|---|---|---|---|---|---|---|---|---|---|---|---|---|---|---|---|
| 1 | A. Anderssen | x | 1 | 0 | 1 | 1 | 1 | 1 | 1 | 1 | + | 1 | ½1 | 1 | 1 | +12 =0 –1 |
| 2 | L. Paulsen | 0 | x | 1 | 0 | 1 | 1 | ½1 | 1 | ½1 | + | + | 1 | 1 | 1 | +11 =0 –2 |
| 3 | J. Owen | 1 | 0 | x | ½+ | 0 | ½1 | 1 | 1 | 0 | + | + | ½½1 | ½½1 | 1 | +10 =0 –3 |
| 4 | S. Dubois | 0 | 1 | ½0 | x | 0 | 0 | 1 | 1 | ½+ | + | + | ½1 | 1 | + | +9 =0 –4 |
| 5 | G. A. MacDonnell | 0 | 0 | 1 | + | x | 1 | 0 | 0 | 1 | + | 1 | 1 | 1 | 1 | +9 =0 –4 |
| 6 | W. Steinitz | 0 | 0 | ½0 | 1 | 0 | x | 1 | 1 | 0 | + | + | 1 | ½½1 | 1 | +8 =0 –5 |
| 7 | T. W. Barnes | 0 | ½0 | 0 | 0 | 1 | 0 | x | ½1 | 1 | 0 | ½1 | 1 | 1 | 1 | +7 =0 –6 |
| 8 | J. W. Hannah | 0 | 0 | 0 | 0 | 1 | 0 | ½0 | x | 1 | + | + | 1 | 1 | + | +7 =0 –6 |
| 9 | J. H. Blackburne | 0 | ½0 | 1 | ½0 | 0 | 1 | 0 | 0 | x | + | 0 | ½½0 | 1 | 0 | +4 =0 –9 |
| 10 | J. J. Löwenthal | 0 | 0 | 0 | 0 | 0 | 0 | 1 | 0 | 0 | x | 0 | 1 | 1 | + | +4 =0 –9 |
| 11 | F. H. Deacon | 0 | 0 | 0 | 0 | 0 | 0 | ½0 | 0 | 1 | + | x | 0 | 1 | 0 | +3 =0 –10 |
| 12 | A. Mongredien | 0 | 0 | ½½0 | ½0 | 0 | 0 | 0 | 0 | ½½+ | 0 | 1 | x | 0 | 1 | +3 =0 –10 |
| 13 | V. Green | 0 | 0 | ½½0 | 0 | 0 | ½½0 | 0 | 0 | 0 | 0 | 0 | 1 | x | 1 | +2 =0 –11 |
| 14 | J. Robey | 0 | 0 | 0 | 0 | 0 | 0 | 0 | 0 | 1 | 0 | 1 | 0 | 0 | x | +2 =0 –11 |

# LONDON (ENG) [1862-LON2]

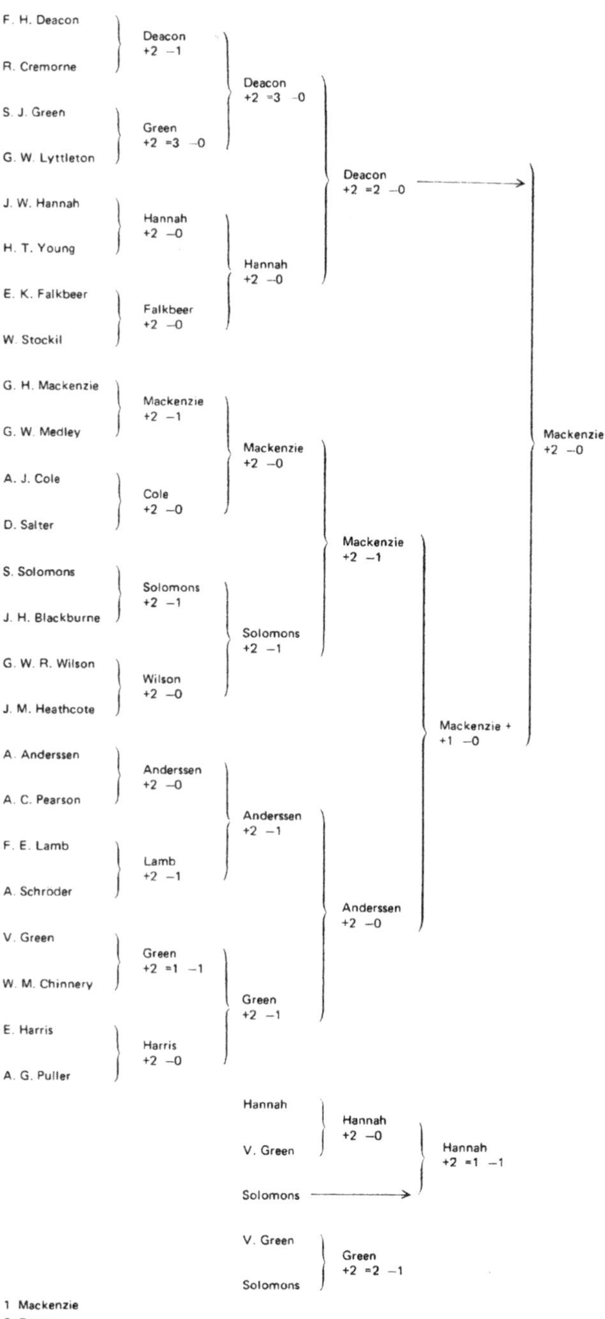


1 Mackenzie
2 Deacon
3 Anderssen
4 Hannah
5 Green, V.
6 Solomons

## DÜSSELDORF (GER) 30 viii- 3 ix 1863 [1863-DUS]

M. Lange
G. Schultz } Lange +1 −0

C. Hengstenberg
C. Möhringer } Hengstenberg +1 −0

Lange, Hengstenberg } Lange +1 −0

W. Paulsen
C. Schultz } Paulsen +1 −0

P. Schwengers
V. Knorre } Schwengers +1 −0

Paulsen, Schwengers } Paulsen +1 −0

C. Höing
von der Busch } Höing +1 −0

M. Rossy
R. Lichtenscheidt } Rossy +1 =1 −0

Höing, Rossy } Höing +1 −0

| | | 1 | 2 | 3 | Total |
|---|---|---|---|---|---|
| 1 | Lange | x | ½ | 1 | 1½ |
| 2 | Paulsen | ½ | x | 1 | 1½ |
| 3 | Höing | 0 | 0 | x | 0 |

Lange
Paulsen } Lange +1 =1 −0

1 Lange
2 Paulsen
3 Höing

## DÜSSELDORF (GER) 28 viii- 31 viii 1864 [1864-DUS]

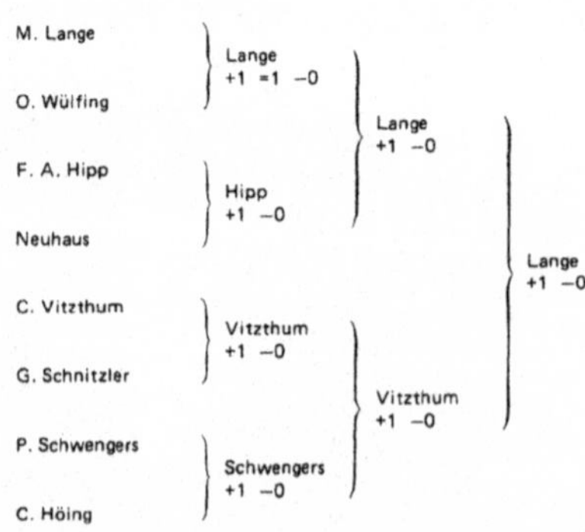


1 Lange
2 Vitzthum

## DUBLIN (IRL) 26 ix– 25 x 1865 [1865-BAC]

| | 1 | 2 | 3 | 4 | 5 | Total |
|---|---|---|---|---|---|---|
| 1 W. Steinitz | x | ½1 | 1 | 1 | 1 | +4 –0 |
| 2 G. A. MacDonnell | ½0 | x | 1 | 1 | 1 | +3 –1 |
| 3 W. Bolt | 0 | 0 | x | 1 | 1 | +2 –2 |
| 4 E. Cordner | 0 | 0 | 0 | x | 1 | +1 –3 |
| 5 E. Cronhelm | 0 | 0 | 0 | 0 | x | +0 –4 |

## ELBERFELD (GER) [1865-ELB]

| | 1 | 2 | 3 | 4 | Total |
|---|---|---|---|---|---|
| 1 G. R. Neumann | x | 1 | 1 | 1 | +3 –0 |
| 2 C. Höing | 0 | x | ½½ | 1 | +2 –2 |
| 3 V. Knorre | 0 | ½½ | x | 1 | +2 –2 |
| 4 J. Pinedo | 0 | 0 | 0 | x | +0 –3 |

## LONDON (ENG) [1866-LON1]

| | 1 | 2 | 3 | 4 | 5 | Match results |
|---|---|---|---|---|---|---|
| 1 C. De Vere | x | 111 | 111 | 111 | +++ | +4 –0 |
| 2 G. A. MacDonnell | 000 | x | 111½ | | +++ | +2 –1 |
| 3 J. I. Minchin | 000 | 000½ | x | 1110 | 111 | +2 –2 |
| 4 H. E. Bird | 000 | | 0001 | x | +++ | +1 –2 |
| 5 J. Trelawney | 000 | 000 | 000 | 000 | x | +0 –4 |

## LONDON (ENG) 20 vi- ? vii 1866 [1866-LON2]

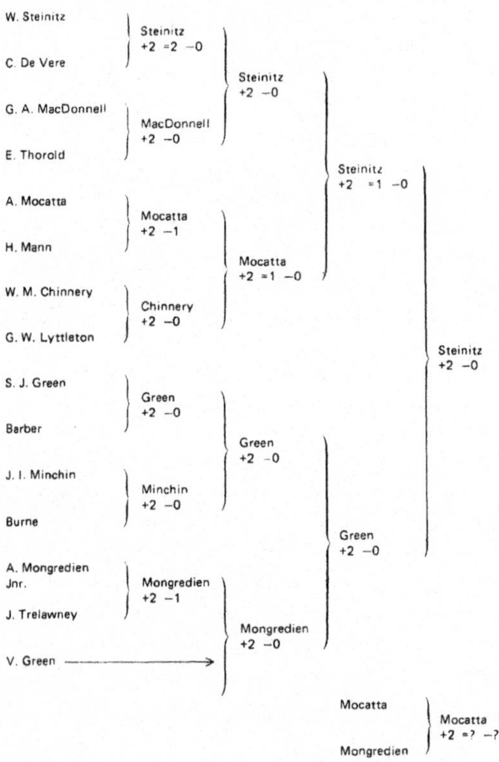


1 Steinitz
2 Green, S. J.
3 Mocatta
4 Mongredien

## BIBLIOGRAPHY


**Bibliotheca van der Linde-Niemeijeriana**

L/N 398 *Games of Greco*, ed. Professor Hoffmann, London, 1900

739 *The Chess Player's Handbook*, Staunton, London, 1847

875 *Chess Praxis*, Staunton, London, 1889

3030 *Bezoek van Prof A. Anderssen aan Amsterdam*, Timme, Amsterdam, 1861

3031 *Prof A. Anderssen uit Breslau in Nederland*, Wijk bij Duurstede, 1861

3033 *Prof Adolph Anderssen*, Bachmann, Ansbach, 1914

3034 *Adolf Anderssen, der Altmeister deutscher Schachspielkunst,* Gottschall Leipzig, 1912

3036 *Mr Blackburne's Games at Chess*, Graham, London, 1899

3043 *My Chess Career*, Capablanca, London, 1923

3087 *Paul Morphy, the Chess Champion*, Edge, London, 1859

3131 *Schachmeister Steinitz*, 4 vols., Bachmann, Ansbach, 1910–21

3145 *Chess Studies*, Walker, London, 1844

3151 *Morphy's Games of Chess and Frère's Problem Tournament*, Frère, New York, 1859

3161 *Morphy's Games of Chess*, Löwenthal, London, 1909

3164 *A. Anderssen's Schachpartien 1864/5*, Neumann, Berlin, 1866

3202 *Mesterjátszmák*, Halász, Budapest, 1908

3203 *Paul Morphy*, Maróczy, Leipzig, 1909

3371 *The Games of the Match of Chess Played by the London and Edinburgh Chess Clubs 1824–8*, Lewis, London, 1828

3303 *Világversenyek élén I rész Az 1900–1903*, Maróczy, Budapest, 1943

5178 *Schaakpartijen gespeeld in 1851*, Wijk bij Duurstede, 1852

5184 *The Book of the First American Chess Congress*, Fiske, New York, 1859

5186 *Der Schachcongress zu London. . .*, Suhle, Berlin, 1864

5187 *Jahrbuch des westdeutschen Schachbundes*, Lange, Leipzig, 1862

5188 *The Chess Congress of 1862*, Löwenthal, London, 1864

5192 *Jahrbuch des westdeutschen Schachbundes*, Lange, Leipzig, 1863

5193 *The Transactions of the British Chess Association 1866/7*, Löwenthal and Medley, London, 1868

5197 *Internationaler Schachcongress zu Baden-Baden*, Baden-Baden, 1870

6013 *Le Palamède*

6014 *La Régence*

6016 *La nouvelle Régence*

6018 *Le Sphinx*

6020 *La Stratégie*

6046 *Deutsche Schachzeitung*

6047 *Schachzeitung*

6051 *Neue Berliner Schachzeitung*

6122 *The British Miscellany and Chess Player's Chronicle*

6123 *The Chess Player's Chronicle*

6124 *The Chess Player's Magazine*

6125 *The Chess Player's Quarterly Chronicle*

6126 *The Chess Player's Chronicle*

6127 *The Chess Player*

6128 *The British Chess Review*

6131 *The Westminster Papers*
6135 *The British Chess Magazine*
6137 *The City of London Chess Magazine*
6138 *The Chess Monthly*
6308 *Shakhmatnyy listok* 1859–63
6309 *Shakhmatnyy listok* 1876–79
6384 *The New Zealand Chessplayer*
6395 *The American Chess Journal*
6396 *Brentano's Monthly*

**H. J. R. Murray collection, Bodleian Library, Oxford**

M 58 *Scientific American Supplement*, New York
212 *New York Clipper*
268 *New Orleans Sunday Delta*, New Orleans
291 *Sunday Dispatch*, Cincinnati
427 *Daily Gazette*, Cincinnati
582 *L'Illustration*, Paris
628 *Journal*, Kingston, New York
658 *Frank Leslie's New York Journal*, New York
713 *Land & Water*
730 *New York Ledger*
749 *Bell's Life in London*, London
954 *Illustrated London News*
960 *Illustrated Sporting and Dramatic News*, London
979 *Illustrated News of the World*, London
980 *Illustrated News of the World*
985 *Frank Leslie's Illustrated Newspaper*, New York
1109 *New York Saturday Press*, New York
1285 *California Spirit of the Times*, San Francisco
1431 *Sunday Times*, London
1481 *Times-Democrat*
1584 *Northern Whig*, Belfast
1647 *Illustrierte Zeitung*, Leipzig

**Additional items**

+1 MS H. J. Murray 64, Bodleian Oxford, "Collection of European Games"
+3 Report of the annual meeting of the Chess Association held at Manchester, 1857
+4 Report of the annual meeting of the British Chess Association held at Cambridge in August 1860
+6 Thirty-one games at chess, comprising the whole number of games played in a match between Mr Eugene Rousseau of New Orleans and Mr C. H. Stanley, secretary of the New York chess club, Stanley 1845(?)
+9 *Westdeutsche Zeitung*
+13 *Paul Morphy, the Pride and Sorrow of Chess*, Lawson, New York
+14 Murray MS 61, Bodleian Oxford

# OPENING INDEX

# ENDING INDEX

♘ v ♖



♖ v ♖

♖+♖ v ♖+♖



♕ v ♕



♕ v ♘/♗/♖



♙ v ♘/♗/♖/♕

# PLAYERS' INDEX

□=Boden, S.S. 1858-★BM-19
□+Boden, S.S. 1858-★BM-20
■=Boden, S.S. 1858-★BM-22
□+Boden, S.S. 1858-★BM-23
□+Boden, S.S. 1858-★BM-24
■-Boden, S.S. 1858-★BM-25
□=Boden, S.S. 1859-★BM-8
□+Bonaparte, Prince A. 1859-★MN-1
□+Bornemann 1858-★BM-26
□+Bottin, A. 1858-★BM-27
□+Bousserolles, A. 1859-★BM-10
□+Braunschweig, C. ○ 1858-★BM-28
□+Broughton, W.R. 1859-★BM-2
□+Broughton, W.R. 1859-★BM-3
□+Bryan, T.J. 1859-★BM-4
□+Budzinski, J. 1859-★BM-1
□+Capdevielle, P. 1864-★CM-1
□+Carpentier, C. le 1849-★CM-1
□+Carr, G.S. 1858-★CM-1
□+Catlley, H.G. 1859-★CM-3
□+Chamouillet, M. ○ 1858-★CM-2
□-Cheney, G.N. 1859-★CM-1
□+Conway, M.D. 1859-★CM-2
□+Cremorne, R. 1859-★CM-4
□+Cunningham 1859-★CM-5
□+Delannoy, A. 1859-★DM-3
■+Devinck, A. 1858-★DM-1
■+Devinck, A. 1858-★DM-2
■=Devinck, A. 1859-★DM-2
□+Dominguez, P. 1864-★DM-1
■=Ehrmann, A. 1859-★EM-1
■+Elkin, L. 1857-★EM-1
□+Freeman, J. 1858-★FM-1
□+Golmayo, C. 1864-★GM-2
□=Greenaway, F.E. 1859-★GM-1
□=Guibert 1858-★GM-1
■+Hammond, G. 1857-★HM-1
□+Hammond, G. 1857-★HM-2
□+Hammond, G. ○ 1859-★HM-1
□+Hampton, H. 1858-★HM-1
■-Harrwitz, D. 1858-★HM-1
□+Hart 1854-★HM-1
□=Hay, A. 1859-★HM-2
□=Janssens, F.G. 1859-★JM-3
□+Jones, J.P. 1859-★JM-4
■-Journoud, P. ○ 1858-★JM-1
■+Journoud, P. 1858-★JM-2
□+Journoud, P. 1858-★JM-3
□+Journoud, P. 1859-★JM-1
□+Julien, D. 1857-★JM-1
□+Julien, D. 1857-★JM-2
□+Julien, D. 1857-★JM-3
□+Julien, D. 1859-★JM-2
□+Kennedy, H.A. 1859-★KM-2
□+Kennicott, H. 1857-★KM-1
■+Kennicott, H. 1857-★KM-2
■+Kipping, J.S. 1858-★KM-1
□+Kipping, J.S. 1858-★KM-2
□-Kipping, J.S. 1858-★KM-3
□+Knight, T. 1856-★KM-1
□+Knott, H. 1859-★KM-1
□+Laroche 1859-★LM-1
■+Laroche 1859-★LM-6
□=Le Carp ○ 1855-★LM-1
□=Lequesne, E. 1858-★LM-1
□+Lewis, S. 1859-★LM-5
□=Lichtenheim, T. 1859-★LM-4
□+Lichtenhein, T. 1857-★LM-1
□+Lichtenhein, T. 1857-★LM-2
□-Lichtenhein, T. 1859-★LM-2
□-Lichtenhein, T. 1859-★LM-3
□+Lichtenhein, T. 1859-★LM-7
□+Lichtenhein, T. 1859-★LM-8
□+Lichtenhein, T. 1859-★LM-13
□+Löwenthal, J.J. 1850-★LM-1
□+Löwenthal, J.J. 1850-★LM-2
□=○Löwenthal, J.J. ○ 1858-★GL-1
□-Löwenthal, J.J. 1858-★LM-2
□+Löwenthal, J.J. 1858-★LM-3
■=○Löwenthal, J.J. ○ 1858-★LM-4
□=Löwenthal, J.J. 1859-★LM-9
■=Löwenthal, J.J. 1859-★LM-10
■-Löwenthal, J.J. 1859-★LM-11
□+Löwenthal, J.J. 1859-★LM-12
□+Lyttleton, G.W. 1858-★LM-5
■+Marache, N. 1857-★MM-5
■+Marache, N. 1857-★MM-7
□+Marache, N. 1859-★MM-1
□+Maude, P. 1859-★MM-7
□-Maurian, C.A. 1854-★MM-2
□ΦMaurian, C.A. 1854-★MM-3
□-Maurian, C.A. 1854-★MM-4
□+Maurian, C.A. 1854-★MM-5
■+Maurian, C.A. 1854-★MM-6
■-Maurian, C.A. 1854-★MM-7
■+Maurian, C.A. 1854-★MM-8
■-Maurian, C.A. 1854-★MM-9
■+Maurian, C.A. 1854-★MM-10
■-Maurian, C.A. 1854-★MM-11
□+Maurian, C.A. 1854-★MM-12
□=Maurian, C.A. 1854-★MM-13
□+Maurian, C.A. 1854-★MM-14
□-Maurian, C.A. 1855-★MM-1
□-Maurian, C.A. 1855-★MM-2
■-Maurian, C.A. 1856-★MM-1
□+Maurian, C.A. 1857-★MM-6
□-Maurian, C.A. 1858-★MM-1
□-Maurian, C.A. 1858-★MM-2
■+Maurian, C.A. 1858-★MM-3
□+Maurian, C.A. 1858-★MM-4
□+Maurian, C.A. 1858-★MM-5
□-Maurian, C.A. 1858-★MM-6
□-Maurian, C.A. 1861-★MM-1
□-Maurian, C.A. 1864-★MM-2
□+Maurian, C.A. 1866-★MM-1
□+Maurian, C.A. 1866-★MM-2
□+Maurian, C.A. 1866-★MM-3
□=Maurian, C.A. 1866-★MM-4
□+Maurian, C.A. 1866-★MM-5
□+Maurian, C.A. 1866-★MM-6
□+Maurian, C.A. 1866-★MM-7
□+Maurian, C.A. 1866-★MM-8
□-Maurian, C.A. 1866-★MM-9
□+Maurian, C.A.

■=Staunton, H. 1851-⚔SW-12
□+Staunton, H. 1851-⚔SW-13
Williams, P.W.
■-Lewis, W. 1819̂-★LW-1
Wills, W.R.
■-Morphy, P.C. 1858-★MW-1
Wilson
■-Steinitz, W. 1862-★SW-1
■-Steinitz, W. 1862-★SW-2
Wilson, D.
■-Bourdonnais, L.C.M. de la 1837̂-★BW-1
Wilson, G.W.R.
■+Heathcote, J.H. 1862-LON2-9
■+Heathcote, J.H. 1862-LON2-10
■+Solomons, S. 1862-LON2-36
□-Solomons, S. 1862-LON2-37
■-Solomons, S. 1862-LON2-38
Wilson, H.
□-Paulsen, L. 1861-BRI-7
□+Stanley, C.H. 1861-BRI-4
■-Lewis, W. 1819-⚔LW-1̂
■-Lewis, W. 1819-⚔LW-2̂
■-Lewis, W. 1819̂-★LW-2
■-Lewis, W. 1819̂-★LW-3
Wilson, J.
■-Atwood, G. 179̂?-★AW-1
■-Atwood, G. 179̂?-★AW-2
■-Atwood, G. 179̂?-★AW-3
□○Atwood, G. 1795-★AW-1
□+Atwood, G. 1795-★AW-2
□○Atwood, G. 1795-★AW-3
□+Atwood, G. 1795-★AW-4
■-Atwood, G. 1795-★AW-5
■○Atwood, G. 1795-★AW-6
□○Atwood, G. 1796-★AW-1
□-Atwood, G. 1796-★AW-2
■-Atwood, G. 1796-★AW-3
■-Atwood, G. 1797-★AW-1
■-Atwood, G. 1798-★AW-1
□-Atwood, G. 1798-★AW-2
■-Atwood, G. 1798-★AW-3
■-Philidor, F.A.D. 1789-★PW-1
■-Philidor, F.A.D. 1789-★PW-2
■=Philidor, F.A.D. 1795-★PW-1
Windberg
■-Paulsen, L. 1864-★PW-1
Wise, J.G.
■-Tuckett, M.J.W. 1849-LON-13
□-Tuckett, M.J.W. 1849-LON-14
Witthaus, C.
■-Paulsen, L. 1865-★PW-1
Wood, J.
□=Lewis, W. 1815-★LW-1
□-Samuda, A. 1810-★SW-1
Wormald, R.B.
■-Kolisch, I.F. von 1861-★KW-1
■-Campbell 1859-⚔CW-1̂
■+Campbell 1859-⚔CW-2̂
■=Campbell 1859-⚔CW-4̂
■-Campbell 1859-⚔CW-6̂
□+Campbell 1859-⚔CW-8̂
■-Campbell 1859-⚔CW-21
Worral, T.H.
■-Kolisch, I.F. von 1860-★KW-1
■-Kolisch, I.F. von 1860-★KW-2
■-Kolisch, I.F.von 1860-★KW-3
■-Morphy, P.C. 1858-★MW-2
■-Morphy, P.C. 1858-★MW-3
■-Morphy, P.C. 1858-★MW-4
■-Morphy, P.C. 1858-★MW-5
■-Morphy, P.C. 1858-★MW-6
■-Morphy, P.C. 1859-★MW-4
□-Saint-Amant, P.C.F. de 1845̂-★SW-3
■-Staunton 1858̂-★SW-9
■=Staunton, H. 1858̂-★SW-1
■-Staunton, H. 1858̂-★SW-2
■=Staunton, H. 1858̂-★SW-3
■-Staunton, H. 1858̂-★SW-4
■-Staunton, H. 1858̂-★SW-5
■+Staunton, H. 1858̂-★SW-6
■+Staunton, H. 1858̂-★SW-7
■-Staunton, H. 1858̂-★SW-8
■-Staunton, H. 1858̂-★SW-9
■-Staunton, H. 1858̂-★SW-10
■-Staunton, H. 1858̂-★SW-11
■+Staunton, H. 1858̂-★SW-12
■+Staunton, H. 1858̂-★SW-13
■=Staunton, H. 1858̂-★SW-14
■+Staunton, H. 1859̂-★SW-1
■-Staunton, H. 1860-★SW-1
■+Staunton, H. 1860-★SW-2
■-Staunton, H. 1860-★SW-3
■-Staunton, H. 1860-★SW-4
■+Staunton, H. 1860-★SW-5
■-Staunton, H. 1856̂-⚔SW-1̂
■-Staunton, H. 1856̂-⚔SW-2̂
■+Staunton, H. 1856̂-⚔SW-3̂
■-Staunton, H. 1856̂-⚔SW-4̂
■-Staunton, H. 1856̂-⚔SW-5̂
■+Staunton, H. 1856̂-⚔SW-7̂
■-Staunton, H. 1856̂-⚔SW-12̂
■+Staunton, H. 1856̂-⚔SW-13̂
■-Staunton, H. 1856̂-⚔SW-14̂
■+Staunton, H. 1856̂-⚔SW-15̂
■-Staunton, H. 1856̂-⚔SW-16̂
■-Staunton, H. 1856̂-⚔SW-17̂
Worrell
□+Macdonnell, A. 1829-★MW-2
□-Macdonnell, A. 183?̂-★MW-14
Wülfing, O.
□-Hanneken, von 1862-DUS-12
■+Hipp, F.A. 1862-DUS-11
□+Kohtz, J. 1862-DUS-9
□-Lange, M. 1862-DUS-6
□=Lange, M. 1864-DUS-1
■-Lange, M. 1864-DUS-2
■-Paulsen, W. 1862-DUS-4
□+Schultz, G. 1862-DUS-10
Wyvill, M.
■-Anderssen, A. 1851-LON1-66
□=Anderssen, A. 1851-LON1-67
■+Anderssen, A. 1851-LON1-68
□-Anderssen, A. 1851-LON1-69
■-Anderssen, A. 1851-LON1-70
□+Anderssen, A. 1851-LON1-71
■-Anderssen, A. 1851-LON1-72
□+Kennedy, H.A. 1851-LON1-34
■-Kennedy, H.A. 1851-LON1-35
□-Kennedy, H.A. 1851-LON1-36
□=Kennedy, H.A. 1851-LON1-38
■-Kennedy, H.A. 1851-LON1-39
□+Kennedy, H.A. 1851-LON1-40
■+Kennedy, H.A. 1851-LON1-41
■+Lowe, E. 1851-LON1-12
□+Lowe, E. 1851-LON1-13
■-Williams, E. 1851-LON1-51
□-Williams, E. 1851-LON1-52
■-Williams, E. 1851-LON1-53
□+Williams, E. 1851-LON1-54
■+Williams, E. 1851-LON1-55
□+Williams, E. 1851-LON1-56
■+Williams, E. 1851-LON1-57
■-Bourdonnais, L.C.M. de la 183?̂-★BW-1
□=Staunton, H. 1854̂-★SW-1
■+Staunton, H. 1854̂-★SW-2
■-Staunton, H. 1854̂-★SW-3
□=○Rivière, J.A. de○

CPSIA information can be obtained
at www.ICGtesting.com
Printed in the USA
BVOW03s0133150917
494973BV00001B/16/P